RUSSIA
NORWAY
SWEDEN
FINLAND
ESTONIA
LATVIA
LITHUANIA
GREAT BRITAIN
DENMARK
POLAND
BELARUS
NETH.
GERMANY
BELGIUM
LUX.
CZECH
UKRAINE
SLOVAKIA
LIECH.
AUST.
HUNGARY
MOLD.
FRANCE
SW.
SLO.
CRO.
BO. HER.
YUGO.
ITALY
BULGARIA
ALB.
MACE.
GREECE
SPAIN
GEORGIA
ARM.
AZER.
TURKEY
KAZAKHSTAN
MONGOLIA
UZBEKISTAN
KYRGYZSTAN
TURKMENISTAN
TAJIKISTAN
N. KOREA
S. KOREA
JAPAN
CHINA
MALTA
TUNISIA
SYRIA
CYPRUS
LEB.
ISRAEL
IRAQ
JORDAN
IRAN
AFGHAN-ISTAN
MOROCCO
ALGERIA
LIBYA
EGYPT
KUWAIT
SAUDI ARABIA
BAHRAIN
UNITED ARAB EMIR.
OMAN
NEPAL
BHUTAN
BANGLADESH
INDIA
MYANMAR (BURMA)
VIETNAM
LAOS
TAIWAN
PACIFIC OCEAN
MALI
NIGER
CHAD
SUDAN
YEMEN
ERITREA
THAILAND
CAMBODIA
PHILIPPINES
BURKINA FASO
BENIN
NIGERIA
IVORY COAST
DJIBOUTI
ETHIOPIA
SRI LANKA
CENTRAL AFRICAN REP.
GHANA
TOGO
CAMEROON
SOMALIA
UGANDA
BRUNEI
MALAYSIA
EQUATORIAL GUINEA
GABON
RWANDA
KENYA
DEM. REP. OF THE CONGO
REP. OF THE CONGO
SEYCHELLES
INDIAN OCEAN
INDONESIA
TANZANIA
BURUNDI
CABINDA (ANGOLA)
PAPUA NEW GUINEA
COMOROS
MALAWI
ANGOLA
ZAMBIA
MOZAMBIQUE
NAMIBIA
ZIMBABWE
MAURITIUS
MADAGASCAR
BOTSWANA
REUNION (FRANCE)
AUSTRALIA
SWAZILAND
SOUTH AFRICA
LESOTHO
ARCTICA

COMPREHENSIVE VOLUME

WORLD HISTORY

3RD EDITION

WILLIAM J. DUIKER
THE PENNSYLVANIA STATE UNIVERSITY

JACKSON J. SPIELVOGEL
THE PENNSYLVANIA STATE UNIVERSITY

Australia • Canada • Mexico • Singapore • Spain • United Kingdom • United States

History Publisher: Clark Baxter
Senior Development Editor: Sharon Adams Poore
Assistant Editor: Cherie Hackelberg
Editorial Assistant: Jennifer Ellis
Marketing Manager: Diane McOscar
Marketing Assistant: Kristin Anderson
Print Buyer: Barbara Britton
Permissions Editor: Bob Kauser
Production Service: Dovetail Publishing Services
Text Designer: Diane Beasley
Photo Researcher: Image Quest
Copy Editors: Pat Lewis and Brian Jones
Maps: Mapquest.com
Compositor: New England Typographic Service
Cover Designer: Diane Beasley
Cover Image: *Arrival of the Portuguese in Japan*, Kano School. Namba Byobu. Giraudon/Art Resource, NY
Cover Printer: Von Hoffmann Press
Printer: Von Hoffmann Press
Photo credits begin on page 1029

Printed in the United States of America
1 2 3 4 5 6 7 04 03 02 01 00

Wadsworth/Thomson Learning
10 Davis Drive
Belmont, CA 94002-3098
USA

For more information about our products, contact us:
Thomson Learning Academic Resource Center
1-800-423-0563
http://www.wadsworth.com

International Headquarters
Thomson Learning
International Division
290 Harbor Drive, 2nd Floor
Stamford, CT 06902-7477
USA

UK/Europe/Middle East/South Africa
Thomson Learning
Berkshire House
168-173 High Holborn
London WC1V 7AA
United Kingdom

Asia
Thomson Learning
60 Albert Street, #15-01
Albert Complex
Singapore 189969

Canada
Nelson Thomson Learning
1120 Birchmount Road
Toronto, Ontario M1K 5G4
Canada

Library of Congress Cataloging-in-Publication Data

Duiker, William J., 1932–
World history / William J. Duiker, Jackson J. Spielvogel. — 3rd ed.
p. cm.
"Comprehensive volume"
Includes bibliographical references and index.
ISBN 0-534-57168-9
1. World history. I. Spielvogel, Jackson J., 1939– II. Title.
D20.D92 2001
909 — dc21 00-040860

About the Authors

WILLIAM J. DUIKER is liberal arts professor emeritus of East Asian studies at The Pennsylvania State University. A former U.S. diplomat with service in Taiwan, South Vietnam, and Washington, D.C., he received his doctorate in Far Eastern history from Georgetown University in 1968, where his dissertation dealt with the Chinese educator and reformer Cai Yuanpei. At Penn State, he has written widely on the history of Vietnam and modern China, including the widely acclaimed *The Communist Road to Power in Vietnam* (revised edition, Westview Press, 1996), which was selected for a Choice Outstanding Academic Book Award in 1982–1983 and 1996–1997. Other recent books are *China and Vietnam: The Roots of Conflict* (Berkeley, 1987) and *Sacred War: Nationalism and Revolution in a Divided Vietnam* (McGraw-Hill, 1995). His biography of the revolutionary Ho Chi Minh will be published by Hyperion Press in the fall of 2000. While his research specialization is in the field of nationalism and Asian revolutions, his intellectual interests are considerably more diverse. He has traveled widely and has taught courses on the History of Communism and non-Western civilizations at Penn State, where he was awarded a Faculty Scholar Medal for Outstanding Achievement in the spring of 1996.

JACKSON J. SPIELVOGEL is associate professor emeritus of history at The Pennsylvania State University. He received his Ph.D. from The Ohio State University, where he specialized in Reformation history under Harold J. Grimm. His articles and reviews have appeared in such journals as *Moreana*, *Journal of General Education*, *Catholic Historical Review*, *Archiv für Reformationsgeschichte*, and *American Historical Review*. He has also contributed chapters or articles to *The Social History of the Reformation*, *The Holy Roman Empire: A Dictionary Handbook*, *Simon Wiesenthal Center Annual of Holocaust Studies*, and *Utopian Studies*. His work has been supported by fellowships from the Fullbright Foundation and the Foundation for Reformation Research. At Penn State, he helped inaugurate the Western civilization courses as well as a popular course on Nazi Germany. His book *Hitler and Nazi Germany* was published in 1987 (fourth edition, 2001). He is the author of *Western Civilization*, published in 1991 (fourth edition, 2000). Professor Spielvogel has won five major university-wide teaching awards. During the year 1988–1989, he held the Penn State Teaching Fellowship, the university's most prestigious teaching award. In 1996, he won the Dean Arthur Ray Warnock Award for Outstanding Faculty Member, and in 1997, he became the first recipient of the Schreyer Institute's Student Choice Award for innovative and inspiring teaching.

To Yvonne,
for adding sparkle to this book,
and to my life
W.J.D.

To Diane,
whose love and support made it all possible
J.J.S.

BRIEF CONTENTS

Detailed Contents

PART II New Patterns of Civilization 166

CHAPTER 6 The New World 168

CHAPTER 7 The World of Islam 192

CHAPTER 8 Early Civilizations in Africa 216

CHAPTER 9 The Expansion of Civilization in Southern Asia 240

CHAPTER 10

From the Tang to the Mongols: The Flowering of Traditional China 266

CHAPTER 11

The East Asian Rimlands: Early Japan, Korea, and Vietnam 294

CHAPTER 12

The Making of Europe and the World of the Byzantine Empire, 500–1300 318

CHAPTER 13

Crisis and Rebirth: Europe in the Fourteenth and Fifteenth Centuries 356

PART IV MODERN PATTERNS OF WORLD HISTORY (1800–1945) 586

CHAPTER 24

The Beginning of the Twentieth-Century Crisis: War and Revolution 716

CHAPTER 25

Nationalism, Revolution, and Dictatorship: Africa, Asia, and Latin America from 1919 to 1939 746

CHAPTER 26

The Crisis Deepens: World War II 772

Reflection: Modern Patterns of World History (1800–1945) 806

PART V Toward a Global Civilization? The World Since 1945 812

Document Credits

CHAPTER 1

THE CODE OF HAMMURABI 12

From Pritchard, James B., ed., *Ancient Near Eastern Texts: Relating to the Old Testament*, 3rd Edition with Supplement. Copyright © 1969 by Princeton University Press. Reprinted by permission of Princeton University Press.

THE GREAT FLOOD 15

From *The Epic of Gilgamesh*, translated by N K Sanders (Penguin Classics, revised edition 1964), copyright © N K Sanders, 1960, 1964. Reproduced by permission of Penguin Books, Ltd.

THE SIGNIFICANCE OF THE NILE RIVER AND THE PHARAOH 16

Hymn to the Nile: From Pritchard, James B., ed., *Ancient Near Eastern Texts: Relating to the Old Testament*, 3rd Edition with Supplement. Copyright © 1969 by Princeton University Press. Reprinted by permission of Princeton University Press. Hymn to the Pharaoh: Reprinted from *The Literature of the Ancient Egyptians*, Adolf Erman, copyright (1927) by E. P. Dutton. Reprinted by permission of the publisher, Methuen and Co.

AKHENATON'S HYMN TO ATON 21

From Pritchard, James B., ed., *Ancient Near Eastern Texts: Relating to the Old Testament*, 3rd Edition with Supplement. Copyright © 1969 by Princeton University Press. Reprinted by permission of Princeton University Press.

THE COVENANT AND THE LAW: THE BOOK OF EXODUS 28

Reprinted from the Holy Bible, New International Version.

THE HEBREW PROPHETS: MICAH ISAIAH AND AMOS 29

Reprinted from the Holy Bible, New International Version.

THE ASSYRIAN MILITARY MACHINE 30

King Sennacherib Describes a Battle with the Elamites in 691: Reprinted with permission of the publisher from *The Might That Was Assyria*, by H. W. Saggs. Copyright © 1984 by Sidgwick & Jackson Limited. King Sennacherib Describes His Siege of Jerusalem and King Ashurbanipal Describes His Treatment: From Pritchard, James B., ed., *Ancient Near Eastern Texts: Relating to the Old Testament*, 3rd Edition with Supplement. Copyright © 1969 by Princeton University Press. Reprinted by permission of Princeton University Press.

CHAPTER 2

THE DUTIES OF A KING 44

Excerpt from *Sources of Indian Tradition*, by William Theodore de Bary. Copyright © 1988 by Columbia University Press, New York. Reprinted with permission of the publisher.

SOCIAL CLASSES IN ANCIENT INDIA 46

Excerpt from *Sources of Indian Tradition*, by William Theodore de Bary. Copyright © 1988 Columbia University Press, New York. Reprinted with permission of the publisher.

THE POSITION OF WOMEN IN ANCIENT INDIA 48

Excerpt from *Sources of Indian Tradition*, by William Theodore de Bary. Copyright © 1988 Columbia University Press, New York. Reprinted with permission of the publisher.

THE HENPECKED MONK 49

From *The Wonder That Was India*, in A. L. Basham (London: Sidgwick & Jackson, 1954), pp. 459–460.

HOW TO ACHIEVE ENLIGHTENMENT 53

From *The Teachings of the Compassionate Buddha*, E. A. Burtt, ed. Copyright 1955 by Mentor. Used by permission of the E. A. Burtt Estate.

THE VOICES OF SILENCE 54

"Sumangalamata" (*A woman well set free! How free I am*). Translated from Pali by Uma Chakravarti and Kumkum Roy. Reprinted by permission of The Feminist Press at the City University of New York, from *Women Writing in India: 600 B.C. to the Present*, Volume One, edited by Susie Tharu and K. Lalita. Compilation copyright by Susie Tharu and K. Lalita. "Akkamahadevi" (*It was like a stream*), 12th century. Translated from Kannada by A. K. Ramanujan. English translation copyright 1991 by A. K. Ramanujan. Reprinted by permission of The Feminist Press at the City University of New York, from *Women Writing in India: 600 B.C. to the Present*, Volume One, edited by Susie Tharu and K. Lalita. Compilation copyright by Susie Tharu and K. Lalita. "Venmanipputi" (*What she said to her girlfriend*), translated by A. K. Ramanujan from *The Interior Landscape*. Edited by A. K. Ramanujan (London: Peter Owen, 1967). Reprinted with permission of the publisher.

BITS OF WISDOM FROM ANCIENT INDIA 58

From William Buck, *Mahabharata*. Introduced by B. A. Van Nooten. Illustrations by Shirley Triest. Copyright © 1973 The Regents of the University of California. Used with permission.

THE MONKEY-KING IN SRI LANKA 60

From William Buck, *Ramayana*. Illustrated by Shirley Triest. Introduction by B. A. Van Nooten, pp. 235–236. Copyright © 1976 The Regents of the University of California. Used with permission.

CHAPTER 3

A TREATISE ON THE YELLOW RIVER AND ITS CANALS 67

Excerpt from *Records of the Grand Historian of China*, by Burton Watson, trans., Copyright © 1961 Columbia University Press, New York. Reprinted with permission of the publisher.

LIFE IN THE FIELDS 69

Reprinted from *Ancient China in Transition*, by Cho-yun Hsu, with the permission of the publishers, Stanford University Press. © 1965 by the Board of Trustees of the Leland Stanford Junior University.

ENVIRONMENTAL CONCERNS IN ANCIENT CHINA 71

Excerpt from D. C. Lau, *Mencius* (Harmondsworth: Penguin, 1970), pp. 51–52.

THE WAY OF THE GREAT LEARNING 73

Excerpt from *Sources of Chinese Tradition*, by William Theodore De Bary. Copyright © 1960 by Columbia University Press, New York. Reprinted with permission of the publisher.

Continues on page 1019

Chronologies

Maps

PREFACE

For several million years after primates first appeared on the surface of the earth, human beings lived in small communities, seeking to survive by hunting, fishing, and foraging in a frequently hostile environment. Then suddenly, in the space of a few thousand years, there was an abrupt change of direction as human beings in a few widely scattered areas of the globe began to master the art of cultivating food crops. As food production increased, the population in those areas rose correspondingly, and people began to congregate in larger communities. Governments were formed to provide protection and other needed services to the local population. Cities appeared and became the focal point of cultural and religious development. Historians refer to this process as the beginnings of civilization.

For generations, historians in Europe and the United States have pointed to the rise of such civilizations as marking the origins of the modern world. Courses on Western civilization conventionally begin with a chapter or two on the emergence of advanced societies in Egypt and Mesopotamia and then proceed to ancient Greece and the Roman Empire. From Greece and Rome, the road leads directly to the rise of modern civilization in the West.

There is nothing inherently wrong with this approach. Important aspects of our world today can indeed be traced back to these early civilizations, and all human beings the world over owe a considerable debt to their achievements. But all too often this interpretation has been used to imply that the course of civilization has been linear in nature, leading directly from the emergence of agricultural societies in ancient Mesopotamia to the rise of advanced industrial societies in Europe and North America. Until recently, most courses on world history taught in the United States routinely focused almost exclusively on the rise of the West, with only a passing glance at other parts of the world, such as Africa, India, and East Asia. The contributions made by those societies to the culture and technology of our own time were often passed over in silence.

Several reasons have been advanced to justify this approach. Some have argued that students simply are not interested in what is unfamiliar to them. Others have said that it is more important that young minds understand the roots of their own heritage than that of peoples elsewhere in the world. In many cases, however, the motivation for this Eurocentric approach has been the belief that since the time of Socrates and Aristotle Western civilization has been the sole driving force in the evolution of human society.

Such an interpretation, however, represents a serious distortion of the process. During most of the course of human history, the most advanced civilizations have been not in the West, but in East Asia or the Middle East. A relatively brief period of European dominance culminated with the era of imperialism in the late nineteenth century, when the political, military, and economic power of the advanced nations of the West spanned the globe. During recent generations, however, that dominance has gradually eroded, partly as the result of changes taking place within Western societies and partly because new centers of development are emerging elsewhere on the globe—notably in East Asia, where the growing economic strength of Japan and many of its neighbors has led to the now familiar prediction that the twenty-first century will be known as the Pacific Century.

World history, then, is not simply a chronicle of the rise of the West to global dominance, nor is it a celebration of the superiority of the civilization of Europe and the United States over other parts of the world. The history of the world has been a complex process in which many branches of the human community have taken an active part, and the dominance of any one area of the world has been a temporary rather than a permanent phenomenon. It will be our purpose in this book to present a balanced picture of this story, with all respect for the richness and diversity of the tapestry of the human experience. Due attention must be paid to the rise of the West, of course, since that has been the most dominant aspect of world history in recent centuries. But the contributions made by other peoples must be given adequate consideration as well, not only in the period prior to 1500 when the major centers of civilization were located in Asia, but also in our own day, where a multipolar picture of development is clearly beginning to emerge.

Anyone who wishes to teach or write about world history must decide whether to present the topic as an integrated whole or as a collection of different cultures. The world that we live in today, of course, is in many respects an interdependent one in terms of economics as well as culture and communications, a reality that is often expressed by the phrase "global village." The convergence of peoples across the surface of the earth into an integrated world system began in early times and intensified after the rise of capitalism in the early modern era. In growing recognition of this trend, historians trained in global history, as well as instructors in the growing number of world history courses, have now begun to speak and write of a "global approach" that turns attention away from the study of individual civilizations and focuses instead on the "big picture" or, as the world historian Fernand Braudel termed it, interpreting world history as a river with no banks.

On the whole, this development is to be welcomed as a means of bringing the common elements of the evolution of human society to our attention. But there is a risk involved in this approach. For the vast majority of their time on earth, human beings have lived in partial or virtually total isolation from each other. Differences in climate, location, and geographical features have created human societies very different from each other in culture and historical experience. Only in relatively recent times—the commonly accepted date has long been the beginning of the age of European exploration at the end of the fifteenth century, but some would now push it back to the era of the Mongol empire or even further—have cultural interchanges begun to create a common "world system," in which events taking place in one part of the world are rapidly transmitted throughout the globe, often with momentous consequences. In recent generations, of course, the process of global interdependence has been proceeding even more rapidly. Nevertheless, even now the process is by no means complete, as ethnic and regional differences continue to exist and to shape the course of world history. The tenacity of these differences and sensitivities is reflected not only in the rise of internecine conflicts in such divergent areas as Africa, India, and Eastern Europe, but also in the emergence in recent years of such regional organizations as the Organization of African Unity, the Association for the Southeast Asian Nations, and the European Economic Community. Political leaders in various parts of the world speak routinely of "Arab unity," the "African road to socialism," and the "Confucian path to economic development."

The second problem is a practical one. College students today are all too often not well informed about the distinctive character of civilizations such as China and India and, without sufficient exposure to the historical evolution of such societies, will assume all too readily that the peoples in these countries have had historical experiences similar to ours and will respond to various stimuli in a similar fashion to those living in Western Europe or the United States. If it is a mistake to ignore those forces that link us together, it is equally a mistake to underestimate those factors that continue to divide us and to differentiate us into a world of diverse peoples.

Our response to this challenge has been to adopt a global approach to world history while at the same time attempting to do justice to the distinctive character and development of individual civilizations and regions of the world. The presentation of individual cultures will be especially important in Parts I and II, which cover a time when it is generally agreed that the process of global integration was not yet far advanced. Later chapters will begin to adopt a more comparative and thematic approach, in deference to the greater number of connections that have been established among the world's peoples since the fifteenth and sixteenth centuries. Part V will consist of a series of chapters that will center on individual regions of the world while at the same time focusing on common problems related to the Cold War and the rise of global problems such as overproduction and environmental pollution. Moreover, sections entitled "Reflection" at the close of the five major parts of the book will attempt to link events together in a broad comparative and global framework.

We have sought balance in another way as well. Many textbooks tend to simplify the content of history courses by emphasizing an intellectual or political perspective or, most recently, a social perspective, often at the expense of sufficient details in a chronological framework. This approach is confusing to students whose high school social studies programs have often neglected a systematic study of world history. We have attempted to write a well-balanced work in which political, economic, social, religious, intellectual, cultural, and military history have been integrated into a chronologically ordered synthesis.

To enliven the past and let readers see for themselves the materials that historians use to create their pictures of the past, we have included primary sources (boxed documents) in each chapter that are keyed to the discussion in the text. The documents include examples of the religious, artistic, intellectual, social, economic, and political aspects of life in different societies and reveal in a vivid fashion what civilization meant to the individual men and women who shaped it by their actions.

Each chapter has a lengthy introduction and conclusion to help maintain the continuity of the narrative and to provide a synthesis of important themes. Time lines at the end of each chapter enable students to see the major developments of an era at a glance, while the more detailed chronologies reinforce the events discussed in the text. An annotated bibliography at the end of each chapter reviews the most recent literature on each period and also gives references to some of the older, "classic" works in each field. Extensive maps and illustrations serve to deepen the reader's understanding of the text. To facilitate comprehension of cultural movements, illustrations of artistic works discussed in the text are placed next to the discussions. New to the third edition are chapter outlines and focus questions at the beginning of each chapter, which will help students with an overview and guide them to the main subjects of each chapter. Also new to the third edition are a glossary of important terms and a pronunciation guide.

After reexamining the entire book and analyzing the comments and reviews of many colleagues who have found the book to be a useful instrument for introducing their students to world history, we have also made a number of other changes for the third edition. In the first place, it is now noticeably shorter than its predecessors. Textbooks on world history have a natural tendency to increase in length as a result of updates and the incorporation of new historical evidence from the world of scholarship. In this third edition, we have tried to delete excess words while retaining all essential material as well as the narrative thrust of previous editions. We hope that our readers will agree that the result is a more manageable and yet superior product.

Second, we have sought to strengthen the global framework of the book, but not at the expense of reducing the attention assigned to individual regions of the world. The essays entitled "Reflection" that appear at the end of each of the five parts have been lengthened slightly in order to provide us with more opportunity to draw comparisons and contrasts across geographical, cultural, and chronological lines. Each Reflection section now contains two boxed essays, each highlighted with an illustration, to single out issues of particular importance to that period of history. Moreover, additional comparative material has also been added to each chapter to help students be aware of similar developments globally. We hope that these techniques will assist instructors who wish to encourage their students to adopt a comparative approach to their understanding of the human experience.

Third, this new edition contains additional information on the role of women in world history. In conformity with our own convictions, as well as what we believe to be recent practice in the field, we have tried where possible to introduce such material at the appropriate point in the text, rather than to set aside separate sections devoted exclusively to women's issues. New material on women include: women in ancient India, women in ancient China, Aristotle's view of women, women in the work of Homer, women in early Christianity, women in pre-Columbian societies, women in Muslim society, women in Indian history during the Gupta era, women in the Ming era, women in Germanic society, women in the Renaissance, women in early socialism, the movement for women's rights, Soviet women, and women in the postwar Western world. Coverage of notable women in history, including Marie Curie, Berthe Morisot, Margaret Thatcher and Betty Friedan has been added. Several new boxed documents have also been added to introduce more women's voices to the historical record.

Finally, almost all of the chapters in the book have been updated to take account of new scholarship, as well as to bring our treatment of contemporary events up to the present, as we begin to enter a new millennium. A number of new illustrations, boxed documents, and maps have been added, and the bibliographies have been revised to take account of newly published material. The chronologies and maps have been fine-tuned, as well, to help the reader locate in time and space the multitude of individuals and place names that appear in the book.

Changes to the New Edition by Chapter

Chapter 1 New material on early humans; new material on Hatshepsut in New Kingdom Egypt; thorough revision of material on ancient Israel based on the most recent research.

Chapter 2 Minor changes have been made to the section on Harappan civilizations to conform to recent evidence appearing in scholarly literature. Specifically, it is now believed that, unlike other ancient civilizations in the Middle East, the political system on Harappa was decentralized and lacked a theoretical base. The section on the *Arthasastra* has been shortened, while continuing to present the essentials of Kautilya's famous work. New material has been introduced on the role of women in ancient India.

Chapter 3 New material on the role of women in ancient China, in addition to new illustrations.

Chapter 4 New material on women in the work of Homer; new material on Aristotle's view of women; new material on Sparta; revision of material on philosophy in the Hellenistic Era.

Chapter 5 Revision of material on Roman conquest of Italy, decline and fall of the Roman Republic, the Age of Augustus, and Roman law; revision and reorganization of material of Christianity and the Late Roman Empire; new material on women in early Christianity.

Chapter 6 New evidence raises serious questions about the date of arrival of the first human beings in the Americas, as well as suggesting the possibility that some early settlers may have come from Africa. Additional material on the role of women in pre-Columbian societies in the Americas is introduced. There is a brief reference to the recent controversy over the possibility of cannibalistic practices among the Anasazi peoples in North America.

Chapter 7 A new boxed document containing an excerpt from the Koran illustrates the traditional attitude toward the role of women in Muslim society. New material on women's role in rug-weaving is introduced.

Chapter 8 The chapter has been reorganized to focus on the importance of Islam in changing social patterns in early African history.

Chapter 9 New material is introduced to illustrate the role of women in Indian history during the Gupta era.

Chapter 10 Material on the early Ming dynasty (1369–1644) has been moved to a later chapter. The Ming era is now covered primarily in chapter 17. New material on marriage practices and the tradition of footbinding has been added.

Chapter 12 New material on the Vikings and on women in Germanic society; revision of material on fiefholding and manorialism.

Chapter 13 New material on the Black Death, the Hundred Years' War, Machiavelli, Catherine of Siena, Christine de Pizan, and women in the Renaissance; revision of material on education in the Renaissance.

Chapter 14 The psychological impact of early colonial expansion on Europeans is introduced. The section on political systems in Southeast Asia has been shortened, while the essential points continue to be stressed.

Chapter 15 Revision of material on the Protestant Reformation; new material on the Catholic Reformation; England in the seventeenth century, the Thirty Years' War and the military revolution, and Artemisia Gentileschi.

Chapter 17 Material on the early Ming dynasty, previously contained in chapter 10, is now covered here.

Chapter 18 Revision of material on the Scientific Revolution in medicine; revision on the path to Enlightenment.

Chapter 19 New map on the Columbian Exchange; revision of material on the wars of the eighteenth century, the American Revolution, and Enlightened Absolutism; new material on Napoleon.

Chapter 20 New material on European efforts to limit the spread of industrialization to the nonindustrialized world; new material on women in early socialism; revision of material on nationalistic revolts in Latin America, nation building in Latin America, and the national state in Europe.

Chapter 21 Revision of material on the Social Structure of Mass Society; new material on the movement for women's rights, the New Woman at the end of the nineteenth century, the United States as a world power, Marie Curie, and Berthe Morisot.

Chapter 22 The section on colonial philosophy and policy has been streamlined. Material related to the first stages of resistance to colonialism—previously in chapter 25 is now covered here.

Chapter 24 Revision of material on peace treaties at the end of World War I; new material on the social repercussions of the Great Depression and social changes in the Russian Revolution; both new and revised material on the cultural and intellectual trends between World War I and World War II, including a new box on the work of Hermann Hesse.

Chapter 25 Material on the first stages of nationalism has been moved to chapter 22. A reference to recent criticism of Kemal Ataturk's role in the modernization of Turkey is introduced.

Chapter 26 New material on Soviet women, the rise of militarism in Japan, the New Order in Asia, and the home front in Japan.

Chapter 28 Updated to take into account changes in Russia and Eastern Europe in the last three years.

Chapter 29 Updated to include new material on developments in the Western European states, Latin America, Canada, and the United States; revision of material on Great Britain, including a new document on Margaret Thatcher; reorganization and revision of material on Society and Culture in the Western world; new material on women in the postwar Western world; Betty Friedan; new section on Transformation in Women's Lives.

Chapter 30 Updated to include references to recent elections in Nigeria, as well as the evolving political situation in South Africa. Several new illustrations illustrate social conditions in sub-Saharan Africa.

Chapter 31 References to the rise of Vajpayee to the prime ministership, and to the overthrow of Sharif in Pakistan, have been added. The section on Indonesia has been reorganized, and there is a brief discussion of the results of the financial crisis of 1997.

Chapter 32 Updated to include references to the new Obuchi administration in Japan.

Because courses in world history at American and Canadian colleges and universities follow different chronological divisions, a one-volume comprehensive edition and a two-volume edition of this text are being made available to fit the needs of instructors. Teaching and learning ancillaries include:

Instructor's Manual with Testbank Prepared by Charles F. Ames, Jr., Salem State College. Contains Chapter Outlines, Class Lecture/Discussion Topics, Thought/Discussion Questions for Primary Sources (Boxed Documents), Possible Student Projects, and Examination Questions (Essay, Identification, and Multiple Choice).

ExamView® Create, deliver, and customize tests and study guides (both print and online) in minutes with this easy-to-use assessment and tutorial system. *ExamView®* offers both a Quick Test Wizard and an Online Test Wizard that guide you step-by-step through the process of creating tests, while its unique "WYSIWYG" capability allows you to see the test you are creating on the screen exactly as it will print or display online. You can build tests of up to 250 questions using up to 12 question types. Using *ExamView®*'s complete word processing capabilities, you can enter an unlimited number of new questions or edit existing questions.

Map Acetates and Commentary for World History, 2001 Edition Includes more than 100 four-color map images from the text and other sources. Map commentary for each map is prepared by James Harrison, Siena College. Three-hole punched and shrinkwrapped.

History Video Library Includes Film For Humanities (these are available to qualified adoptions), CNN videos, and Grade Improvement: Taking Charge of Your Learning.

2001 World HistoryLink–Available on a multi-platform CD-ROM. With its easy-to-use interface, you can use our existing presentations (which consist of map images from the text and other sources) or customize your own presentation by importing your lecture or other material you choose.

Sights and Sounds of History Short, focused video clips, photos, artwork, animations, music, and dramatic readings are used to bring life to historical topics and events which are most difficult for students to appreciate from a textbook alone. For example, students will experience the grandeur of Versailles and the defeat felt by a German soldier at Stalingrad. The video segments, each averaging 4 minutes long, make excellent lecture launchers. Available on Laserdisk or VHS video.

Study Guide Prepared by Dianna Rhyan Kardulias, Columbus State Community College. Contains Chapter Outlines, Terms and Persons to Know, Mapwork, Datework, Primary Sourcework, Artwork, Identifying Important Concepts Behind the Conclusion, and new Multiple Choice questions and Web Resources. Available in two volumes.

Map Exercise Workbook Prepared by Cynthia Kosso, Northern Arizona University. Has been thoroughly revised and improved. Contains over 20 maps and exercises, which ask students to identify important cities and countries. Also includes critical thinking questions for each unit. Available in two volumes.

World History MapTutor This new mapping CD-ROM allows students to learn by manipulating maps through "locate and label" exercises, animations, and critical thinking exercises.

Migrations in Modern World History 1500–2000 CD-ROM An interactive multimedia curriculum on CD-ROM by Patrick Manning and the World History Center. Includes over 400 primary source documents; analytical questions to help the student develop his/her own interpretations of history; timelines; and additional suggested resources, including books, films, and web sites.

Document Exercise Workbooks Prepared by Donna Van Raaphorst, Cuyahoga Community College. Contains a collection of exercises based around primary source documents pertaining to world history.

Journey of Civilizations CD ROM for Windows This CD takes students on 18 interactive journeys through history. Enhanced with QuickTime movies, animations, sound clips, maps, and more, the journeys allow students engage in history as active participants rather than as readers of past events.

Magellan World History Atlas
Available to bundle with any history text; contains 44 historical four-color maps.

Internet Guide for History, Third Edition Prepared by John Soares. Provides newly revised and up-to-date Internet exercises by topic. Available at

http://history.wadsworth.com.

Kishlansky, Sources in World History, Second Edition
This reader is a collection of documents designed to supplement any world history text. Available in two volumes.

Web Tutor™ There are two volumes to correspond with Volumes I and II of the main text. This content-rich, Web-based teaching and learning tool helps students succeed by taking the course beyond classroom boundaries to an anywhere, anytime environment. *Web Tutor™* offers real-time access to a full array of study tools, including flashcards (with audio), practice quizzes, online tutorials, and Web links. Available in two volumes.

InfoTrac® College Edition An online university that lets students explore and use full-length articles from more than 900 periodicals for four months. When students log on with their personal ID, they will immediately see how easy it is to search. Students can print out the articles, which date back as far as four years.

Historic Times: The Wadsworth History Resource Center

http://history.wadsworth.com/

Features a career section, forum, and links to museums, historical documents, and other fascinating sites. From the Resource Center you can access the book-specific web site, which contains the following: chapter by chapter tutorial quizzing, *InfoTrac®* activities, Internet activities, and hyperlinks for the student, and an online instructor's manual and downloadable PowerPoint files for the Instructor.

ACKNOWLEDGMENTS

Both authors gratefully acknowledge that without the generosity of many others, this project could not have been completed. William Duiker would like to thank Kumkum Chatterjee and On-cho Ng for their helpful comments about unfamiliar issues related to the history of India and premodern China. His longtime colleague Cyril Griffith, now deceased, was a cherished friend and a constant source of information about modern Africa. Art Goldschmidt has been of invaluable assistance in reading several chapters of the manuscript, as well as in unraveling many of the mysteries of Middle Eastern civilization. Finally, he remains profoundly grateful to his wife, Yvonne V. Duiker, Ph.D. She has not only given her usual measure of love and support when this appeared to be an insuperable task, but she has also contributed her own time and expertise to enrich the sections on art and literature, thereby adding life and sparkle to this, as well as the earlier editions of the book. To her, and to his daughters Laura and Claire, he will be forever thankful for bringing joy to his life.

Jackson Spielvogel would like to thank Art Goldschmidt, David Redles, and Christine Colin for their time and ideas and, above all, his family for their support. The gifts of love, laughter, and patience from his daughters, Jennifer and Kathryn, his sons, Eric and Christian, and his daughter-in-law, Liz, were invaluable. Diane, his wife and best friend, provided him with editorial assistance, wise counsel, and the loving support that made a project of this magnitude possible.

Thanks to Wadsworth's comprehensive review process, many historians were asked to evaluate our manuscript. We are grateful to the following for the innumerable suggestions that have greatly improved our work:

Charles F. Ames, Jr.
Salem State College
Nancy Anderson
Loyola University
Gloria M. Aronson
Normandale College
Charlotte Beahan
Murray State University
Doris Bergen
University of Vermont
Martin Berger
Youngstown State University
Deborah Biffton
University of Wisconsin-LaCrosse
Charmarie Blaisdell
Northeastern University
Patricia J. Bradley
Auburn University at Montgomery
Dewey Browder
Austin Peay State University
Antonio Calabria
University of Texas at San Antonio
Alice-Catherine Carls
University of Tennessee-Martin
Yuan Ling Chao
Middle Tennessee State University
Mark W. Chavalas
University of Wisconsin
Hugh Clark
Ursinus College
Joan Coffey
Sam Houston State University
John Davis
Radford University
Ross Dunn
San Diego State University
Lane Earn
University of Wisconsin-Oshkosh
Edward L. Farmer
University of Minnesota
William W. Farris
University of Tennessee
Ronald Fritze
Lamar University
Joe Fuhrmann
Murray State University
Robert Gerlich
Loyola University
Marc J. Gilbert
North Georgia College
William J. Gilmore-Lehne
Richard Stockton College of New Jersey
Richard M. Golden
University of North Texas
Joseph M. Gowaskie
Rider College
Jonathan Grant
Florida State University
Don Gustafson
Augsburg College
Deanna Haney
Lansing Community College
Ed Haynes
Winthrop College
Linda Kerr
University of Alberta at Edmonton
Zoltan Kramar
Central Washington University
Craig A. Lockard
University of Wisconsin-Green Bay
George Longenecker
Norwich University
Robert Luczak
Vincennes University
Patrick Manning
Northeastern University
Dolores Nason McBroome
Humboldt State University
John McDonald
Northern Essex Community College
Andrea McElderry
University of Louisville
Jeff McEwen
Chattanooga State Technical Community College
John A. Mears
Southern Methodist University
Marc A. Meyer
Berry College

Stephen S. Michot
Mississippi County Community College
John Ashby Morton
Benedict College
William H. Mulligan
Murray State University
Henry A. Myers
James Madison University
Marian P. Nelson
University of Nebraska at Omaha
Sandy Norman
Florida Atlantic University
Patrick M. O'Neill
Broome Community College
Norman G. Raiford
Greenville Technical College
Jane Rausch
University of Massachusetts-Amherst
Dianna K. Rhyan
Columbus State Community College
Merle Rife
Indiana University of Pennsylvania
Patrice C. Ross
Columbus State Community College
John Rossi
LaSalle University
Eric C. Rust
Baylor University
Keith Sandiford
University of Manitoba
Elizabeth Sarkinnen
Mt. Hood Community College
Bill Schell
Murray State University
Robert M. Seltzer
Hunter College
David Shriver
Cuyahoga Community College
Amos E. Simpson
University of Southwestern Louisiana
Wendy Singer
Kenyon College
Marvin Slind
Washington State University
Paul Smith
Washington State University
John Snetsinger
California Polytechnic State University
George Stow
LaSalle University
Patrick Tabor
Chemeketa Community College
Tom Taylor
Seattle University
John G. Tuthill
University of Guam
Joanne Van Horn
Fairmont State College
Pat Weber
University of Texas-El Paso
Douglas L. Wheeler
University of New Hampshire
David L. White
Appalachian State University
Elmira B. Wicker
Southern University-Baton Rouge
Glee Wilson
Kent State University
Harry Zee
Cumberland County College

The authors are truly grateful to the people who have helped us to produce this book. We especially want to thank Clark Baxter, whose faith in our ability to do this project was inspiring, and Sharon Adams Poore for her development work. Hal Humphrey, Production Services Coordinator at Wadsworth, was both patient and thoughtful as he guided us through the process of revision for the third edition of our book. Cherie Hackelberg thoughtfully guided the preparation of outstanding teaching and learning ancillaries. Pat Lewis and Brian Jones were outstanding copy editors. Sarah Evertson provided valuable assistance in obtaining permissions for the illustrations. We are grateful to the staff of New England Typographic Service for providing their array of typesetting and page layout abilities. Jon Peck, of Dovetail Publishing Services, was as cooperative and cheerful as he was competent in matters of production management.

A Note to Students about Languages and the Dating of Time

One of the most difficult challenges in studying world history is coming to grips with the multitude of names, words, and phrases in unfamiliar languages. Unfortunately, this problem has no easy solution. We have tried to alleviate the difficulty, where possible, by providing an English-language translation of foreign words or phrases, a glossary, and a pronunciation guide. The issue is especially complicated in the case of Chinese, since two separate systems are commonly used to transliterate the spoken Chinese language into the Roman alphabet. The Wade-Giles system, invented in the nineteenth century, was the most frequently used until recent years, when the pinyin system was adopted by the People's Republic of China as its own official form of transliteration. We have opted to use the latter, since it appears to be gaining acceptance in the United States, but the initial use of a Chinese word is accompanied by its Wade-Giles equivalent in parentheses for the benefit of those who may encounter the term in their outside reading.

In our examination of world history, we need also to be aware of the dating of time. In recording the past, historians try to determine the exact time when events occurred. World War II in Europe, for example, began on September 1, 1939, when Adolf Hitler sent German troops into Poland, and ended on May 7, 1945, when Germany surrendered. By using dates, historians can place events in order and try to determine the development of patterns over periods of time.

If someone asked you when you were born, you would reply with a number, such as 1981. In the United States, we would all accept that number without question, because it is part of the dating system followed in the Western world (Europe and the Western Hemisphere). In this system, events are dated by counting backward or forward from the birth of Christ (assumed to be the year 1). An event that took place 400 years before the birth of Christ would most commonly be dated 400 B.C. (before Christ). Dates after the birth of Christ are labeled as A.D. These letters stand for the Latin words *anno domini*, which mean "in the year of the Lord" (or the year of the birth of Christ). Thus an event that took place 250 years after the birth of Christ is written A.D. 250, or in the year of the Lord 250. It can also be written as 250, just as you would not give your birth year as A.D.1981, but simply 1981.

Some historians now prefer to use the abbreviations B.C.E. ("before the common era") and C.E. ("common era") instead of B.C. and A.D. This is especially true of world historians who prefer to use symbols that are not so Western or Christian oriented. The dates, of course, remain the same. Thus, 1950 B.C.E. and 1950 B.C. would be the same year, as would A.D. 40 and 40 C.E. In keeping with the current usage by many world historians, this book will use the terms B.C.E. and C.E.

Historians also make use of other terms to refer to time. A decade is 10 years; a century is 100 years; and a millennium is 1,000 years. The phrase fourth century B.C.E. refers to the fourth period of 100 years counting backward from 1, the assumed date of the birth of Christ. Since the first century B.C.E. would be the years 100 B.C.E. to 1 B.C.E., the fourth century B.C.E. would be the years 400 B.C.E. to 301 B.C.E. We could say, then, that an event in 350 B.C.E. took place in the fourth century B.C.E.

The phrase fourth century C.E. refers to the fourth period of 100 years after the birth of Christ. Since the first period of 100 years would be the years 1 to 100, the fourth period or fourth century would be the years 301 to 400. We could say, then, for example, that an event in 350 took place in the fourth century. Likewise, the first millennium B.C.E. refers to the years 1000 B.C.E. to 1 B.C.E.; the second millennium C.E. refers to the years 1001 to 2000.

The dating of events can also vary from people to people. Most people in the Western world use the Western calendar, also known as the Gregorian calendar after Pope Gregory XIII who refined it in 1582. The Hebrew calendar, on the other hand, uses a different system in which the year one is the equivalent of the Western year 3760 B.C.E., considered by Jews to be the date of the creation of the world. Thus, the Western year 2000 will be the year 5760 on the Jewish calendar. The Islamic calendar begins year 1 on the day Muhammad fled Mecca, which is the year 622 on the Western calendar.

THEMES FOR UNDERSTANDING WORLD HISTORY

In examining the past, historians often organize their material on the basis of themes that enable them to ask and try to answer basic questions about the past. The following ten themes are especially important.

1. *Political systems*. The study of politics seeks to answer certain basic questions that historians have about the structure of a society: How were people governed? What was the relationship between the ruler and the ruled? What people or groups of people (the political elites) held political power? What actions did people take to change their form of government? Historians also examine the causes and results of wars in order to understand the impact of war on human development.

2. *The role of ideas*. Ideas have great power to move people to action. For example, in the twentieth century, the idea of nationalism, which is based on a belief in loyalty to one's nation, helped produce two great conflicts—World War I and World War II. Together these wars cost the lives of more than fifty million people. The spread of ideas from one society to another has also played an important role in world history. From the earliest times, trade has especially served to bring different civilizations into contact with one another, and the transmission of religious and cultural ideas soon followed.

3. *Economics and history*. A society depends for its existence on certain basic needs. How did it grow its food? How did it make its goods? How did it provide the services people needed? How did individual people and governments use their limited resources? Did they spend more money on hospitals or military forces? By answering these questions, historians examine the different economic systems that have played a role in history.

4. *Social life and gender issues*. From a study of social life, we learn about the different social classes that make up a society. But we also examine how people dressed and found shelter, how and what they ate, and what they did for fun. The nature of family life and how knowledge was passed from one generation to another through education are also part of the social life of a society. So, too, are gender issues: What different roles did men and women play in their societies? How and why were those roles different?

5. *The importance of culture*. We cannot understand a society without looking at its culture, or the common ideas, beliefs, and patterns of behavior that are passed on from one generation to another. Culture includes both high culture and popular culture. High culture consists of the writings of a society's thinkers and the works of its artists. A society's popular culture is the world of ideas and experiences of ordinary people. Today the media have embraced the term *popular culture* to describe the most current trends and fashionable styles.

6. *Religion in history*. Throughout history, people have sought to find a deeper meaning to human life. How have the world's great religions, such as Hinduism, Buddhism, Judaism, Christianity, and Islam, influenced people's lives? How have these religions spread to create new patterns of culture?

7. *The role of individuals*. In discussing the role of politics, ideas, economics, social life, cultural developments, and religion, we have dealt with groups of people and forces that often seem beyond the control of any one person. But mentioning the names of Cleopatra, Queen Elizabeth I, Napoleon, and Hitler reminds us of the role of individuals in history. Decisive actions by powerful individuals have indeed played a crucial role in the course of history.

8. *The impact of science and technology*. For thousands of years, people around the world have made scientific discoveries and technological innovations that have changed our world. From the creation of stone tools that made farming easier to the advanced computers that guide our airplanes, science and technology have altered how humans have related to their world.

9. *The environment and history*. Throughout history, peoples and societies have been affected by the physical world in which they live. Climatic changes alone have been an important factor in human history. Peoples and societies, in turn, have also made an impact on their world. Human activities have affected the physical environment and even endangered the very existence of entire societies and species.

10. *The migration of peoples*. One characteristic of world history is an almost constant migration of peoples. Vast numbers of peoples abandoned their homelands and sought to live elsewhere. Sometimes the migration was peaceful. More often than not, however, the migration meant invasion and violent conflict.

PART

1

THE FIRST CIVILIZATIONS AND THE RISE OF EMPIRES (PREHISTORY TO 500 C.E.)

For hundreds of thousands of years, human beings lived in small communities, seeking to survive by hunting, fishing, and foraging in an often hostile environment. Then, in the space of a few thousand years, there was an abrupt change of direction, as human beings in a few widely scattered areas of the globe began to master the art of cultivating food crops. As food production increased, the population in such areas grew, and people began to congregate in larger communities. Cities appeared and became centers of cultural and religious development. Historians refer to these changes as the beginnings of civilization.

The first civilizations that emerged in Mesopotamia, Egypt, India, and China all shared a number of basic characteristics. Each developed in a river valley that was able to provide the agricultural resources needed to maintain a large population. In each civilization a part of the population lived in cities, which became the focal points for political, economic, social, cultural, and religious development. All of these early civilizations established some kind of government bureaucracy to meet the administrative demands of the growing population and organized armies for protection and to gain land and power. A new social structure based on economic power arose. While kings and an upper class of priests, political leaders, and warriors dominated, there also existed a large group of free people (farmers, artisans, craftspeople) and, at the very bottom stratum, a class of slaves. Abundant agricultural yields in these regions created opportunities for economic specialization as a surplus of goods enabled artisans and craftspeople to create new products.

The new urban civilizations were also characterized by significant religious and cultural developments. The gods were often deemed critical to a community's success, and professional priestly classes regulated relations with the gods. Rulers, priests, merchants, and artisans used writing to keep records and even create new kinds of literary expression. New forms of artistic activity, including monumental architectural structures, occupied a prominent place in the new urban environments.

By and large the early river valley civilizations developed independently, with each grounded in local developments ultimately related to new agricultural practices. Still, contacts between them were already under way and in some cases were affected by new ideas and technology. This trade was often carried out by nomadic peoples from beyond the frontiers of settled states. Though not as organized, these nomadic peoples also began to play a major role in the human experience.

From the beginnings of the first civilizations around 3000 B.C.E., there was an ongoing movement toward the creation of larger territorial states with more sophisticated systems of control. This process reached a high point in the first millennium B.C.E. Between 1000 and 500 B.C.E., the Assyrians and Persians amassed empires that encompassed either large areas or all of the ancient Middle East. The conquests of Alexander the Great in the fourth century B.C.E. created an even larger, if short-lived, empire that soon divided into four kingdoms. Later, the western portion of these kingdoms as well as the Mediterranean world and much of western Europe fell subject to the mighty empire of the Romans. At the same time, much of India became part of the Mauryan empire. Finally, in the last few centuries B.C.E., the Qin and Han dynasties of China created a unified Chinese state.

CHAPTER

I

THE FIRST CIVILIZATIONS: THE PEOPLES OF WESTERN ASIA AND EGYPT

CHAPTER OUTLINE

- THE FIRST HUMANS
- THE EMERGENCE OF CIVILIZATION
- CIVILIZATION IN MESOPOTAMIA
- EGYPTIAN CIVILIZATION: "THE GIFT OF THE NILE"
- NEW CENTERS OF CIVILIZATION
- THE RISE OF NEW EMPIRES
- CONCLUSION

FOCUS QUESTIONS

- In what areas of the world did systematic agriculture develop during the Neolithic Age, and how did this development affect the lives of men and women?
- What are the characteristics of civilization, and what are some explanations for why early civilizations emerged?
- What effects did geography have on the civilizations that arose in Mesopotamia and Egypt?
- What role did religion play in the early civilizations of western Asia and Egypt, and how did Judaism and Zoroastrianism differ from the other religions of the region?
- What methods and institutions did the Assyrians and Persians use to amass and maintain their respective empires?

In 1849, a daring young Englishman made a hazardous journey into the deserts and swamps of southern Iraq. Braving high winds and temperatures that reached 120 degrees Fahrenheit, William Loftus led a small expedition southward along the banks of the Euphrates River in search of the roots of civilization. As he said, "From our childhood we have been led to regard this place as the cradle of the human race."

Guided by native Arabs into the southernmost reaches of Iraq, Loftus and his small band of explorers were soon overwhelmed by what they saw. He wrote, "I know of nothing more exciting or impressive than the first sight of one of these great piles, looming in solitary grandeur from the surrounding plains and marshes." One of these piles, known to the natives as the mound of Warka, contained the ruins of Uruk, one of the first cities in the world and part of the world's first civilization.

Southern Iraq, known to ancient peoples as Mesopotamia, was one of the four areas in the world where civilization began. In the fertile valleys of the Tigris and Euphrates, the Nile, the Indus, and the Yellow rivers, in Mesopotamia, Egypt, India, and China, respectively, intensive agriculture became capable of supporting large groups of people. In these regions civilization was born. The first civilizations emerged in western Asia (now known as the Middle East) and Egypt, where people developed organized societies and created the ideas and institutions that we associate with civilization.

Before considering the early civilizations of western Asia and Egypt, however, we must briefly examine humankind's prehistory and observe how human beings made the shift from hunting and gathering to agricultural communities and, ultimately, to cities and civilization.

THE FIRST HUMANS

Historians rely mostly on documents to create their pictures of the past, but no written records exist for the prehistory of humankind. In their absence, the story of early humanity depends on archaeological and, more recently, biological information, which anthropologists and archaeologists use to formulate theories about our early past.

Although science has given us more precise methods for examining prehistory, much of our understanding of early humans still relies on considerable conjecture. Given the rate of new discoveries, the following account of the current theory of early human life might well be changed in a few years. As the great British archaeologist Louis Leakey reminded us years ago, "Theories on prehistory and early man constantly change as new evidence comes to light."

The earliest humanlike creatures—known as hominids—lived in Africa some three to four million years ago. Known as Australopithecines, they flourished in eastern and southern Africa and were the first hominids to make simple stone tools. The oldest known stone tool—a knife blade that is probably 2.6 million years old—was found in Africa.

A second stage in early human development occurred around 1.5 million years ago with the emergence of *Homo erectus* ("upright human being"). *Homo erectus* made use of larger and more varied tools and was the first hominid to leave Africa and move into both Europe and Asia.

Around 250,000 years ago, a third—and crucial—stage in human development began with the emergence of *Homo sapiens* ("wise human being"). By 100,000 B.C.E., two groups of *Homo sapiens* had developed. One type was the Neanderthal, whose remains were first found in the Neander valley in Germany. Neanderthal remains have since been found in both Europe and the Middle East and have been dated to between 100,000 and 30,000 B.C.E. Neanderthals relied on a variety of stone tools and were the first early people to bury their dead. (Some scientists maintain that burial of the dead indicates a belief in an afterlife.) Neanderthals in Europe made clothes from the skins of animals that they had killed for food.

The first anatomically modern humans, known as *Homo sapiens sapiens* ("wise, wise human being"), appeared in Africa between 200,000 and 150,000 years ago. Recent evidence indicates that they began to spread outside Africa around 100,000 years ago. Map 1.1 on p. 4 shows probable dates for different movements, although many of these dates are still controversial. By 30,000 B.C.E., *Homo sapiens sapiens* had replaced the Neanderthals, who had largely become extinct.

The movement of the first modern humans was rarely deliberate. Groups of people advanced beyond their old hunting grounds at a rate of only two to three miles per generation. This was enough, however, to populate the world in some tens of thousands of years. Some scholars have suggested that such advanced human creatures may have emerged independently in different parts of the world, rather than in Africa alone, but the latest genetic evidence strongly supports the out-of-Africa theory as the most likely explanation of human origin. In any case, by 10,000 B.C.E., members of the *Homo sapiens sapiens* species could be found throughout the world. By that time, it was the only human species left. All humans today, be they Europeans, Australian Aborigines, or Africans, belong to the same subspecies of human being.

The Hunter-Gatherers of the Old Stone Age

One of the basic distinguishing features of the human species is the ability to make tools. The earliest tools were made of stone, and the term *Paleolithic* (Greek for "old stone") *Age* is used to designate this early period of human history (c. 2,500,000–10,000 B.C.E.).

For hundreds of thousands of years, humans relied on hunting and gathering for their daily food. Paleolithic peoples had a close relationship with the world around them, and over a period of time, they came to know which animals to hunt and which plants to eat. They did not know how to grow crops or raise animals, however. They

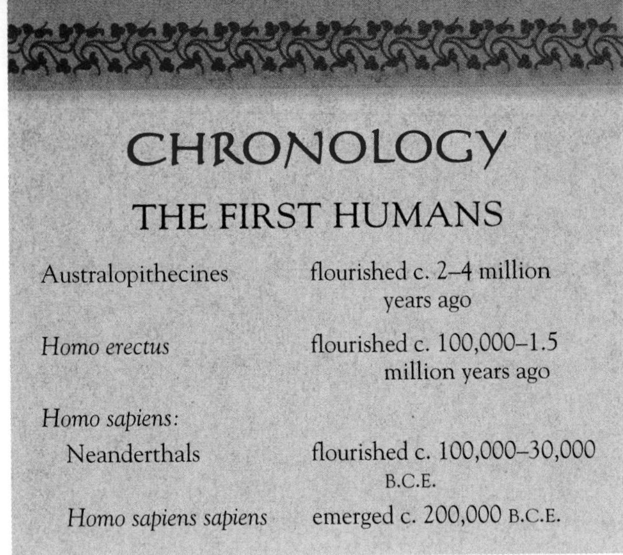

CHRONOLOGY

THE FIRST HUMANS

Australopithecines	flourished c. 2–4 million years ago
Homo erectus	flourished c. 100,000–1.5 million years ago
Homo sapiens:	
Neanderthals	flourished c. 100,000–30,000 B.C.E.
Homo sapiens sapiens	emerged c. 200,000 B.C.E.

gathered wild nuts, berries, fruits, and a variety of wild grains and green plants. Around the world, they hunted and consumed various animals, including buffalo, horses, bison, wild goats, and reindeer. In coastal areas, fish provided a rich source of food.

The hunting of animals and the gathering of wild plants no doubt led to certain patterns of living. Archaeologists and anthropologists have speculated that Paleolithic people lived in small bands of twenty or thirty people. They were nomadic (they moved from place to place) since they had no choice but to follow animal migrations and vegetation cycles. Hunting depended on careful observation of animal behavior patterns and required a group effort to have any real degree of success. Over the years, tools became more refined and more useful. The invention of the spear, and later the bow and arrow, made hunting considerably easier. Harpoons and fishhooks made of bone increased the catch of fish.

Both men and women were responsible for finding food—the chief work of Paleolithic people. Since women bore and raised the children, they generally stayed close to the camps, but they played an important role in acquiring food by gathering berries, nuts, and grains. Men hunted for wild animals, an activity that took them far from camp. Because both men and women played important roles in providing for the band's survival, scientists have argued that a rough equality existed between men and women. Indeed, some speculate that both men and women made the decisions that governed the activities of the Paleolithic band.

These groups of Paleolithic peoples, especially those who lived in cold climates, found shelter in caves. Over time, they created new types of shelter as well. Perhaps the most common was a simple structure of wood poles or sticks covered with animal hides. Where wood was scarce, Paleolithic hunter-gatherers might use the bones of mammoths for the framework and cover it with animal hides. The systematic use of fire, which archaeologists believe began around 500,000 years ago, made it possible for the caves and human-made structures to have a source of light and heat. Fire also enabled early humans to cook their food, making it better tasting, longer lasting, and, in the case of some plants, such as wild grain, easier to chew and digest.

MAP 1.1 The Spread of *Homo sapiens sapiens*

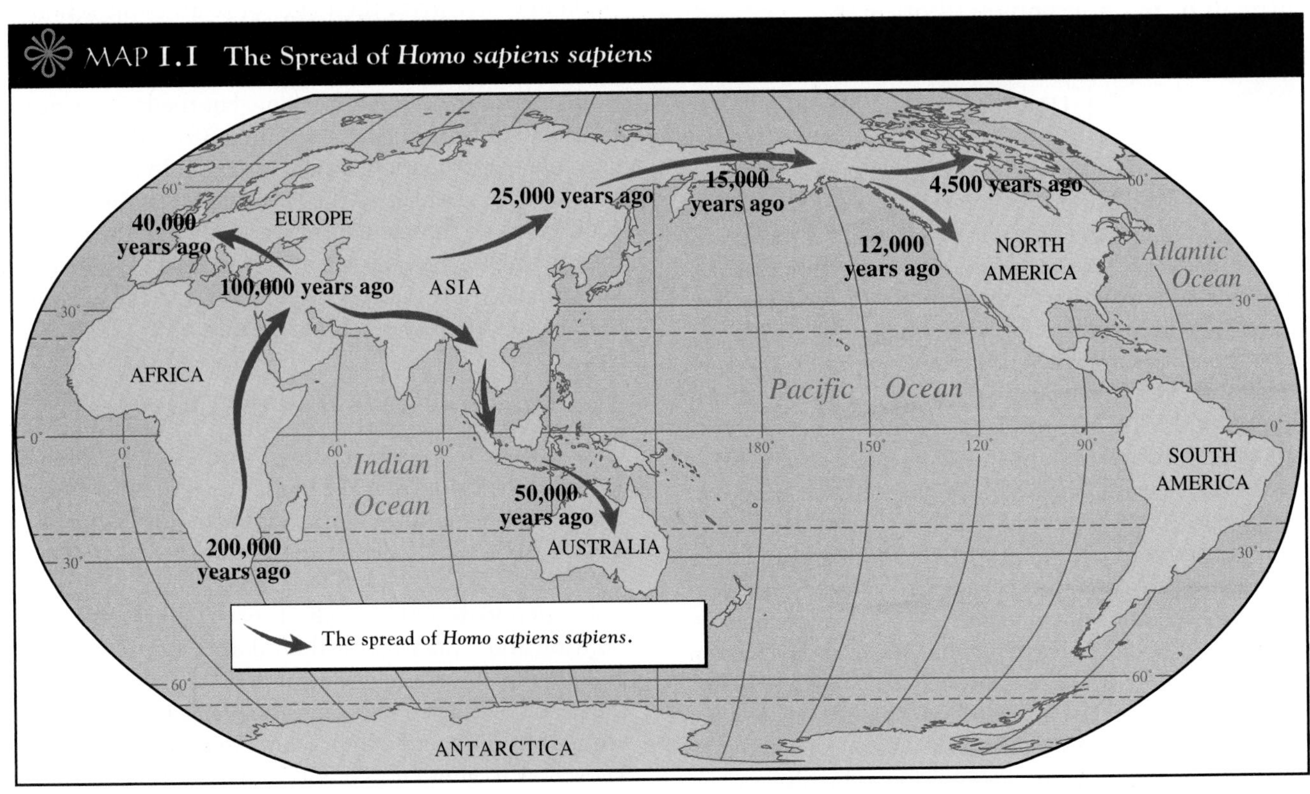

The making of tools and the use of fire—two important technological innovations of Paleolithic peoples—remind us how crucial the ability to adapt was to human survival. Changing physical conditions during periodic ice ages posed a considerable threat to human existence. Paleolithic peoples used their technological innovations—such as the ability to make tools and use fire—to change their physical environment. By working together, they found a way to survive. And by passing on their common practices, skills, and material products to their children, they ensured that later generations, too, could survive in a harsh environment.

But Paleolithic peoples did more than just survive. The cave paintings of large animals found in southwestern France and northern Spain bear witness to the cultural activity of Paleolithic peoples. A cave discovered in southern France in 1994 contains more than three hundred paintings of lions, oxen, owls, panthers, and other animals. Most of these are animals that Paleolithic people did not hunt, which suggests that the paintings were created for religious or even decorative purposes.

The Agricultural Revolution, c. 10,000–4000 B.C.E.

The end of the last ice age around 10,000 B.C.E. was followed by what is called the Neolithic Revolution; that is, the revolution that occurred in the New Stone Age (the word *Neolithic* is Greek for "new stone"). The name New Stone Age is misleading, however. Although Neolithic peoples made a new type of polished stone axes, this was not the major change that occurred after 10,000 B.C.E.

The real change was the shift from hunting animals and gathering plants for sustenance to producing food by systematic agriculture. The planting of grains and vegetables provided a regular supply of food while the taming of animals, such as sheep, goats, cattle, and pigs, added a steady source of meat, milk, and fibers such as wool for clothing. Larger animals could also be used as beasts of burden. The growing of crops and the taming of food-producing animals created a new relationship between humans and nature. Historians like to speak of this as an agricultural revolution. Revolutionary change is dramatic and requires great effort, but the ability to acquire food on a regular basis gave humans greater control over their environment. It also enabled them to give up their nomadic ways of life and begin to live in settled communities.

The shift to food producing from hunting and gathering was not as sudden as was once believed, however. The Mesolithic period ("Middle Stone Age," c. 10,000–7000 B.C.E.) saw a gradual transition from a food-gathering and hunting economy to a food-producing one and witnessed a gradual domestication of animals as well. Likewise, the movement toward the use of plants and their seeds as an important source of nourishment was also not sudden. Evidence seems to support the possibility that the Paleolithic hunters and gatherers had already grown crops to supplement their traditional sources of food. Moreover, throughout the Neolithic period, hunting and gathering as well as nomadic herding remained ways of life for many people around the world.

Systematic agriculture developed independently in different areas of the world between 8000 and 5000 B.C.E. Inhabitants of the Middle East began cultivating wheat and barley and domesticating pigs, cattle, goats, and sheep by 8000 B.C.E. From the Middle East, farming spread into the Balkans region of Europe by 6500 B.C.E. By 4000 B.C.E., it was well established in the south of France, central Europe, and the coastal regions of the Mediterranean. The cultivation of wheat and barley also spread from western Asia into the Nile valley of Egypt by 6000 B.C.E. and soon spread up the Nile to other areas of Africa, especially the Sudan and Ethiopia. In the woodlands and tropical forests of central Africa, a separate agricultural system emerged based on the cultivation of tubers or root crops such as yams and tree crops such as bananas. The cultivation of wheat and barley also eventually moved eastward into the highlands of northwestern and central India, between 7000 and 5000 B.C.E. By 5000 B.C.E., rice was being cultivated in southeastern Asia, from where it spread into southern China. In northern China, the cultivation of millet and the domestication of pigs and dogs seem well established by 6000 B.C.E. In the Western Hemisphere, Mesoamericans (inhabitants of present-day Mexico and Central America) domesticated beans, squash, and maize (or corn) as well as dogs and fowl between 7000 and 5000 B.C.E.

The growing of crops on a regular basis made possible the support of larger populations and gave rise to more-permanent settlements, which historians refer to as Neolithic farming villages or towns. Although Neolithic villages appeared in Europe, India, Egypt, China, and Mesoamerica,

PALEOLITHIC CAVE PAINTING. Cave paintings of large animals provide good examples of the cultural creativity of Paleolithic peoples. This scene is part of a large underground chamber found accidentally in 1940 at Lascaux, France, by some boys looking for their dog. This work is dated around 14,000 B.C.E.

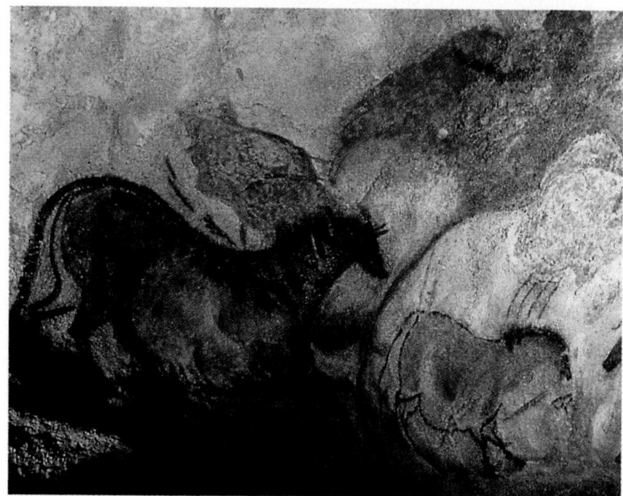

the oldest and most extensive ones were located in the Middle East. Jericho, in Palestine near the Dead Sea, was in existence by 8000 B.C.E. and covered several acres by 7000 B.C.E. It had a wall several feet thick that enclosed houses made of sun-dried mud bricks. Çatal Hüyük, located in modern Turkey, was an even larger community. Its walls enclosed thirty-two acres, and its population probably reached six thousand inhabitants during its high point from 6700 to 5700 B.C.E. People lived in simple mudbrick houses that were built so close to one another that there were few streets. To get to their homes, people had to walk along the rooftops and then enter the house through a hole in the roof.

Archaeologists have discovered twelve cultivated products in Çatal Hüyük, including fruits, nuts, and three kinds of wheat. People grew their own food and stored it in storerooms in their homes. Domesticated animals, especially cattle, yielded meat, milk, and hides. Hunting scenes on the walls would indicate that the people of Çatal Hüyük hunted as well, but unlike earlier hunter-gatherers, they no longer relied on hunting to survive. Food surpluses also made it possible for people to do things other than farming. Some people became artisans and made weapons and jewelry that were traded with neighboring peoples, thus connecting the inhabitants of Çatal Hüyük to the wider world around them.

Religious shrines housing figures of gods and goddesses have been found at Çatal Hüyük, as have a number of female statuettes. Molded with noticeably large breasts and buttocks, these "earth mothers" perhaps symbolically represented the fertility of both "our mother" earth and human mothers. Both the shrines and the statues point to the growing role of religion in the lives of these Neolithic peoples.

The Neolithic agricultural revolution had far-reaching consequences. Once people settled in villages or towns, they built houses for protection and other structures for the storage of goods. As organized communities stored food and accumulated material goods, they began to engage in trade. In the Middle East, for example, the new communities exchanged such objects as shells, flint, and semiprecious stones. People also began to specialize in certain crafts, and a division of labor developed. Pottery was made from clay and baked in fire to make it hard. The pots were used for cooking and to store grains. Woven baskets were also used for storage. Stone tools became refined as flint blades were used to make sickles and hoes for use in the fields. In the course of the Neolithic Age, many of the food plants still in use today came to be cultivated. Moreover, vegetable fibers from such plants as flax and cotton were used to make thread that was woven into cloth.

The change to systematic agriculture in the Neolithic Age also had consequences for the relationship between men and women. Men assumed the primary responsibility for working in the fields and herding animals, jobs that kept them away from the home. Women remained behind, caring for the children and weaving cloth, making cheese from milk, and performing other tasks that required considerable labor in one place. In time, as work outside the

MAP I.2 The Development of Agriculture

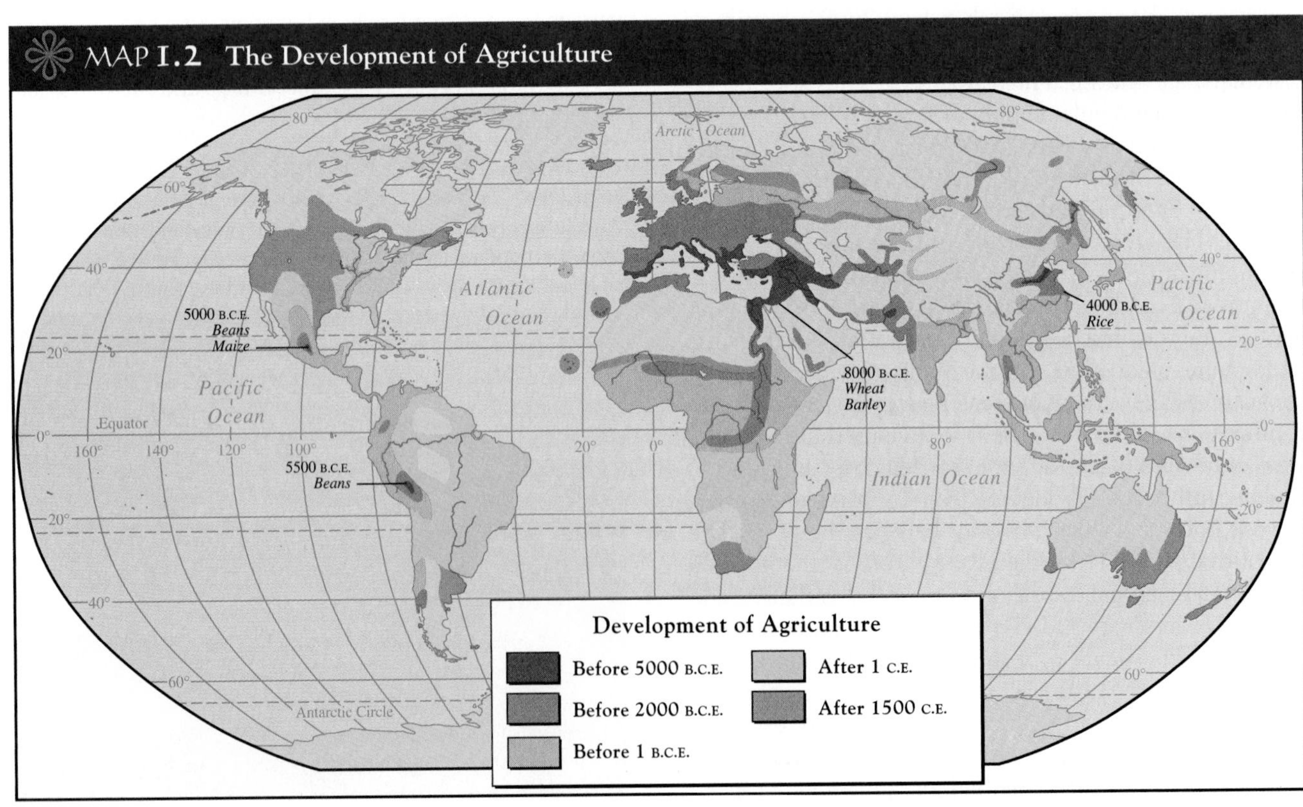

STATUES FROM AIN GHAZAL. These life-size statues made of plaster and bitumen date from 6500 B.C.E. and were discovered in 1984 in Ain Ghazal, an archaeological site near Amman, Jordan. They are among the oldest statues ever found of the human figure. Archaeologists are studying the statues to try to understand their purpose and meaning.

home was increasingly perceived as more important than work done in the home, men came to play the more dominant role in human society, a basic pattern that would persist until our own times.

Other patterns set in the Neolithic Age also proved to be enduring elements of human history. Fixed dwellings, domesticated animals, regular farming, a division of labor, men holding power—all of these are part of the human story. For all of our scientific and technological progress, human survival still depends on the growing and storing of food, an accomplishment of people in the Neolithic Age. The Neolithic Revolution was truly a turning point in human history.

Between 4000 and 3000 B.C.E., significant technical developments began to transform the Neolithic towns. The invention of writing enabled records to be kept, while the use of metals marked a new level of human control over the environment and its resources. Already before 4000 B.C.E., artisans had discovered that metal-bearing rocks could be heated to liquefy the metal, which could then be cast in molds to produce tools and weapons that were more useful than stone instruments. Although copper was the first metal to be used for producing tools, after 4000 B.C.E., metalworkers in western Asia discovered that a combination of copper and tin created bronze, a harder and more durable metal than copper. Its widespread use has led historians to speak of a Bronze Age from around 3000 to 1200 B.C.E., after which bronze was increasingly replaced by iron.

The Emergence of Civilization

At first, Neolithic settlements were hardly more than villages, but as their inhabitants mastered the art of farming, the villages gradually began to give rise to more sophisticated and complex human societies. As wealth increased, these societies began to develop armies and to build walled cities. By the beginning of the Bronze Age, the concentration of larger numbers of people in river valleys was leading to a whole new pattern for human life—the more complex form of existence that we call civilization.

The first civilizations emerged in Mesopotamia, Egypt, India, and China; in each case, the civilization developed in a river valley that was able to provide the agricultural resources needed to maintain a large population. Although agricultural practices varied considerably from civilization to civilization, each one exhibited certain basic characteristics:

1. *An urban revolution*. Cities became the focal points for political, economic, social, cultural, and religious development. The cities that emerged were much larger than the Neolithic towns that preceded them, and the new configurations in turn gave rise to significant changes in political, military, social, and economic structures.
2. *New political and military structures*. An organized bureaucracy arose to meet the administrative needs of the growing population, and armies were created to provide protection and gain land and power.
3. *A new social structure based on economic power*. Kings and an upper class of priests, political leaders, and warriors dominated, but a large group of free common people (farmers, artisans, and craftspeople) also existed, as did a class of slaves, who were socially at the very bottom.
4. *The development of more complexity in a material sense*. Abundant agricultural yields created opportunities for economic specialization as a surplus of goods enabled some people to work in occupations other than farming. The demand of ruling elites for luxury items encouraged artisans and craftspeople to create new products. As urban populations exported finished goods in exchange for raw materials from neighboring populations, organized trade grew substantially.
5. *A distinct religious structure*. The gods were deemed crucial to the community's success, and professional priestly classes, as stewards of the gods' property, regulated relations with the gods.
6. *The development of writing*. Kings, priests, merchants, and artisans used writing to keep records and even to create new kinds of literary expression.
7. *New forms of significant artistic and intellectual activity*. Monumental architectural structures, usually religious, occupied a prominent place in the urban environments, and smaller examples of individual creativity also proliferated.

Why early civilizations developed remains difficult to explain. Since civilizations developed independently in India, China, Mesopotamia, and Egypt, can general causes be identified that would explain why all of these civilizations emerged? A number of possible explanations of the beginning of civilization have been suggested. A theory of challenge and response maintains that challenges forced human beings to make efforts that resulted in the rise of civilization. Some scholars have adhered to a material explanation. Material forces, such as the growth of food surpluses, made possible the specialization of labor and development of large communities with bureaucratic organization. But some areas were not naturally conducive to agriculture. Abundant food could only be produced with a massive human effort to carefully manage the water, an effort that created the need for organization and bureaucratic control and led to civilized cities. Some historians have argued that nonmaterial forces, primarily religious, provided the sense of unity and purpose that made such organized activities possible. Finally, some scholars doubt that we are capable of ever discovering the actual causes of early civilization.

Civilization in Mesopotamia

The Greeks spoke of the valley between the Tigris and Euphrates rivers as Mesopotamia, the land "between the rivers." The region receives little rain, but the soil of the plain of southern Mesopotamia was enlarged and enriched over the years by layers of silt deposited by the two rivers. In late spring, the Tigris and Euphrates overflow their banks and deposit their fertile silt, but since this flooding depends on the melting of snows in the upland mountains where the rivers begin, it is irregular and sometimes catastrophic. In such circumstances, farming could be accomplished only with human intervention in the form of irrigation and drainage ditches. A complex system was required to control the flow of the rivers and produce the crops. Large-scale irrigation made possible the expansion of agriculture in this region, and the abundant food provided the material base for the emergence of civilization in Mesopotamia.

The City-States of Ancient Mesopotamia

The creators of the first Mesopotamian civilization were the Sumerians, a people whose origins remain unclear. By 3000 B.C.E., they had established a number of independent cities in southern Mesopotamia, including Eridu, Ur, Uruk, Umma, and Lagash. As the cities expanded in size, they came to exercise political and economic control over the surrounding countryside, forming city-states. These city-states were the basic units of Sumerian civilization.

Sumerian cities were surrounded by walls. Uruk, for example, occupied an area of approximately a thousand acres encircled by a wall six miles long with defense towers located every thirty to thirty-five feet along the wall. City dwellings, built of sun-dried bricks, included both the small flats of peasants and the larger dwellings of the civic and priestly officials. Although Mesopotamia had little stone or wood for building purposes, it did have plenty of mud. Mudbricks, easily shaped by hand, were left to bake in the hot sun until they were hard enough to use for building. People in Mesopotamia were remarkably inventive with mudbricks, inventing the arch and the dome and constructing some of the largest brick buildings in the world. Mudbricks are still used in rural areas of the Middle East today.

The most prominent building in a Sumerian city was the temple, which was dedicated to the chief god or goddess of the city and often built atop a massive stepped tower called a ziggurat. The Sumerians believed that gods and goddesses owned the cities, and much wealth was used to build temples as well as elaborate houses for the priests and priestesses who served the gods. Priests and priestesses, who supervised the temples and their property, had much power. The temples owned much of the city land and livestock and served not only as the physical center of the city, but also as its economic and political center.

In fact, historians believe that in the early stages of the city-states, priests and priestesses played an important role in ruling. The Sumerians believed that the gods ruled the cities, making the state a theocracy (government by a divine authority). Eventually, however, ruling power passed into the hands of worldly figures known as kings.

Sumerians viewed kingship as divine in origin—kings, they believed, derived their power from the gods and were the agents of the gods. As one person said in a petition to his king: "You in your judgement, you are the son of Anu [god of the sky]; Your commands, like the word of a god, cannot be reversed, Your words, like rain pouring down from heaven, are without number."[1] Regardless of their origins, kings had power—they led armies, initiated legislation, supervised the building of public works, provided courts, and organized workers for the irrigation projects upon which Mesopotamian agriculture depended. The army, the government bureaucracy, and the priests and priestesses all aided the kings in their rule. Befitting their power, Sumerian kings lived in large palaces with their wives and children.

The economy of the Sumerian city-states was primarily agricultural, but commerce and industry became important as well. The people of Mesopotamia produced woolen textiles, pottery, and the metalwork for which they were especially well known. Foreign trade, which was primarily a royal monopoly, could be extensive. Royal officials imported luxury items, such as copper and tin, aromatic woods, and fruit trees, in exchange for dried fish, wool, barley, wheat, and the metal goods produced by Mesopotamian metalworkers. Traders traveled by land to the eastern Mediterranean in the west and by sea to India in the east.

MAP 1.3 Ancient Mesopotamia

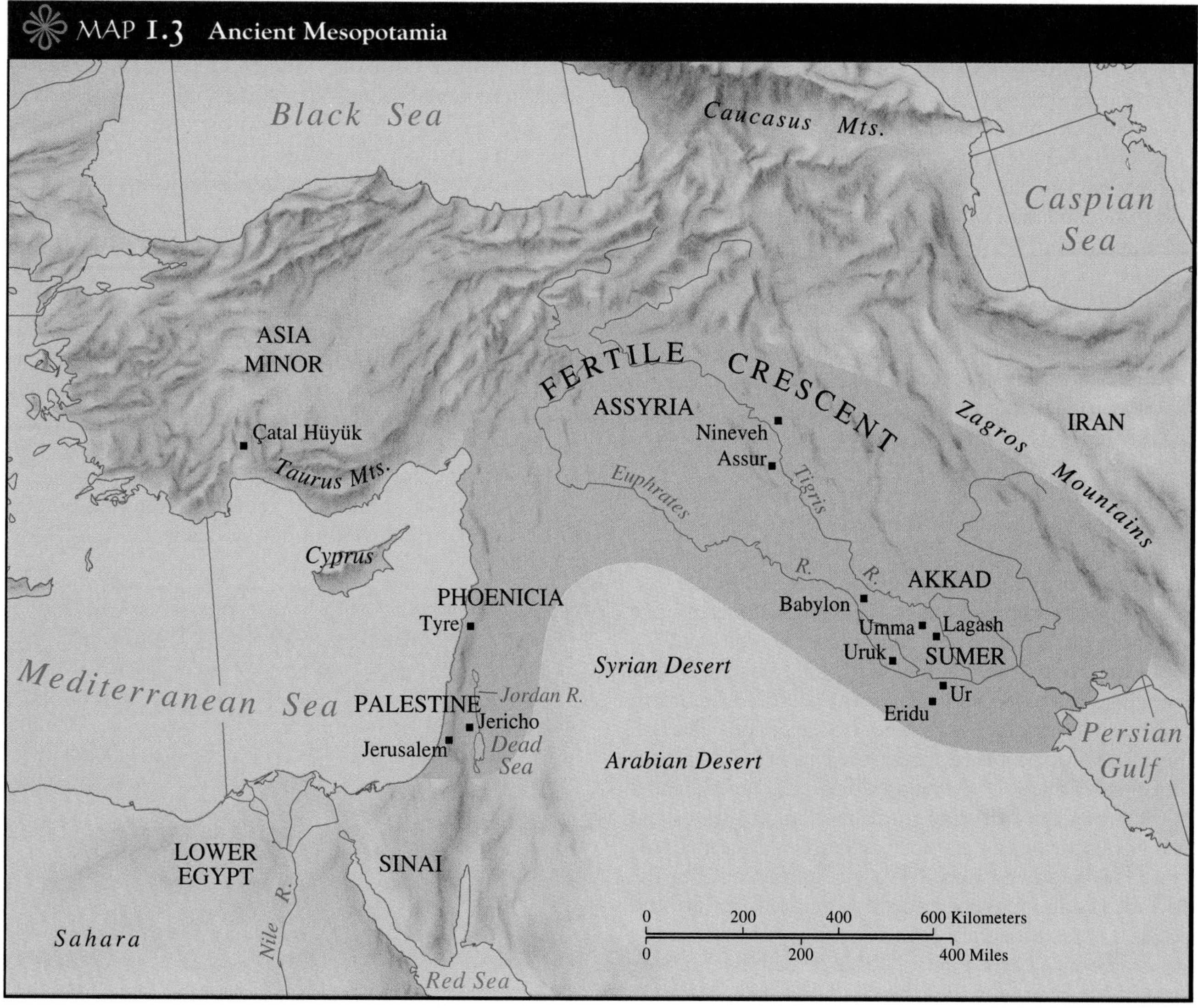

THE "ROYAL STANDARD" OF UR. This series of panels is from the "Royal Standard" of Ur, a box dating from c. 2700 B.C.E. and discovered in a stone tomb from the royal cemetery of the Sumerian city-state of Ur. These scenes from the box depict the activities of the king and his court after a military victory. In the top panel, the king and his court drink wine while at the right a musician plays a bull-headed harp. The middle panel shows bulls, rams, and fish being brought to the banquet hall. The bottom panel shows booty from the king's victory.

The invention of the wheel around 3000 B.C.E. led to carts with wheels that made the transport of goods easier.

Sumerian city-states contained three major social groups: nobles, commoners, and slaves. Nobles included royal and priestly officials and their families. Commoners included the nobles' subjects who worked for the palace and temple estates and other free citizens who worked as farmers, merchants, fishers, scribes, and craftspeople. Probably 90 percent or more of the population were farmers. They could exchange their crops for the goods of the artisans in free town markets. Slaves belonged to palace officials, who used them mostly in building projects; temple officials, who used mostly female slaves to weave cloth and grind grain; and rich landowners, who used them for farming and domestic work.

Empires in Ancient Mesopotamia

As the number of Sumerian city-states grew and the states expanded, new conflicts arose as city-state fought city-state for control of land and water. The fortunes of various city-states rose and fell over the centuries. The constant wars, with their burning and sacking of cities, left many Sumerians in deep despair, as is evident in the words of this Sumerian poem from the city of Ur: "Ur is destroyed, bitter is its lament. The country's blood now fills its holes like hot bronze in a mold. Bodies dissolve like fat in the sun. Our temple is destroyed, the gods have abandoned us, like migrating birds. Smoke lies on our city like a shroud."

Located in the flat land of Mesopotamia, the Sumerian city-states were also open to invasion. To the north of the Sumerian city-states were the Akkadians. We call them a Semitic people because of the type of language they spoke (see Table 1.1). Around 2340 B.C.E., Sargon, leader of the Akkadians, overran the Sumerian city-states and established an empire that included most of Mesopotamia as well as lands westward to the Mediterranean. But the Akkadian empire eventually disintegrated, and its end by 2100 B.C.E. brought a return to the system of warring city-states until Ur-Nammu of Ur succeeded in reunifying most of Mesopotamia. But this final flowering of Sumerian culture collapsed with the coming of the Amorites. Under Hammurabi, the Amorites or Old Babylonians, a large group of Semitic-speaking seminomads, created a new empire.

Hammurabi (1792–1750 B.C.E.) employed a well-disciplined army of foot soldiers who carried axes, spears, and copper or bronze daggers. He learned to divide his opponents and subdue them one by one. Using such methods, he gained control of Sumer and Akkad and reunified Mesopotamia almost to the old borders established by Sargon of Akkad. After his conquests, he called himself "the sun of Babylon, the king who has made the four quarters of the world subservient," and established a new capital at Babylon, north of Akkad.

Hammurabi, the man of war, was also a man of peace. He followed in the footsteps of previous conquerors by assimilating Mesopotamian culture with the result that Sumerian ways continued to exist despite the end of the Sumerians as a political entity. A collection of his letters, found by archaeologists, reveals that he took a strong interest in state affairs. He built temples, defensive walls, and irrigation canals; encouraged trade; and brought an economic revival. After his death, however, a series of weak kings were unable to keep Hammurabi's empire united, and it finally fell to new invaders.

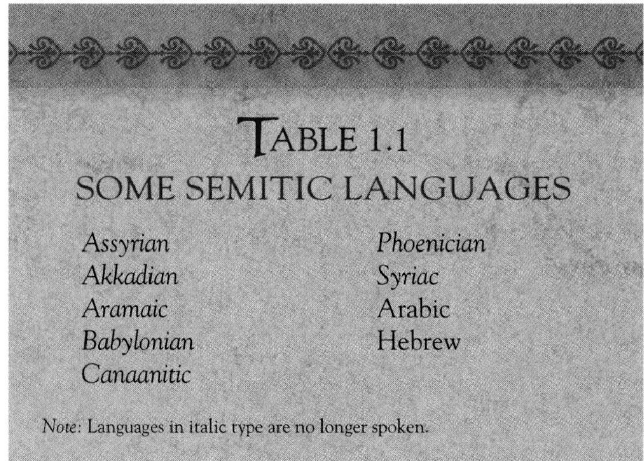

TABLE 1.1
SOME SEMITIC LANGUAGES

Assyrian	*Phoenician*
Akkadian	*Syriac*
Aramaic	Arabic
Babylonian	Hebrew
Canaanitic	

Note: Languages in italic type are no longer spoken.

CHRONOLOGY

CHIEF EVENTS IN MESOPOTAMIAN HISTORY

Early development of Sumerian city-states	c. 3000–2350 B.C.E.
The Akkadian empire	c. 2340–2100 B.C.E.
The dynasty of Ur-Nammu	c. 2113–2000 B.C.E.
Hammurabi's reign	c. 1792–1750 B.C.E.

STELE OF HAMMURABI (CODE OF HAMMURABI, KING OF BABYLONIA). Although the Sumerians compiled earlier law codes, Hammurabi's code was the most famous in early Mesopotamian history. The code recognized three social classes in Babylonia (nobles, free commoners, and slaves) and included laws dealing with marriage and divorce, job performance, punishments for crimes, and even sexual relations. The upper section of the stele depicts Hammurabi standing in front of the seated sun god Shamash (who was also the god of justice), who orders the king to record the law. The lower section contains the actual code.

THE CODE OF HAMMURABI

Hammurabi is best remembered for his law code, a collection of 282 laws (see the box on p. 12). For centuries, laws had regulated people's relationships with one another in the lands of Mesopotamia, but only fragments of these earlier codes survive. Hammurabi's collection provides considerable insight into almost every aspect of everyday life there and provides us a priceless glimpse of the values of this early society.

The Code of Hammurabi reveals a society with a system of strict justice. Penalties for criminal offenses were severe and varied according to the social class of the victim. A crime against a member of the upper class (a noble) by a member of the lower class (a commoner) was punished more severely than the same offense against a member of the lower class. Moreover, the principle of retaliation ("an eye for an eye, a tooth for a tooth") was fundamental to this system of justice. It was applied in cases where members of the upper class committed crimes against their social equals. For crimes against members of the lower classes, a money payment was made instead.

Hammurabi's code took seriously the responsibilities of public officials. The governor of an area and city officials were expected to catch burglars. If they failed to do so, officials in the district where the crime was committed had to replace the lost property. If murderers were not found, the officials had to pay a fine to the relatives of the victim. Soldiers were likewise expected to fulfill their duties and responsibilities for the order and maintenance of the state. If a soldier hired a substitute to fight for him, he was put to death, and the substitute was given control of his estate.

The law code also furthered the proper performance of work with what virtually amounted to consumer protection laws. Builders were held responsible for the buildings they constructed. If a house collapsed and caused the death of the owner, the builder was put to death. If the collapse caused the death of the son of the owner, the son of the builder was put to death. If goods were destroyed by the collapse, they had to be replaced and the house itself reconstructed at the builder's expense.

The number of laws in Hammurabi's code dedicated to land tenure and commerce reveals the importance of agriculture and trade in the Mesopotamian economy. Numerous laws dealt with questions of landholding, such as the establishment of conditions for renting farmland and the division of produce between tenants and their landlords. Laws concerning land use and irrigation were especially strict, an indication of the danger of declining crop yields if the lands were used incompetently. Commercial activity was also carefully regulated. Rates of interest on loans were watched closely. If the lender raised his rate of interest after a loan was made, he lost the entire amount of the loan. The Code of Hammurabi even specified the precise wages of laborers and artisans, such as brick makers and jewelers.

The largest category of laws in the Code of Hammurabi focused on marriage and the family. Parents arranged marriages for their children. After marriage, the parties involved signed a marriage contract; without it, no one

THE CODE OF HAMMURABI

Although there were earlier Mesopotamian law codes, Hammurabi's is the most complete. The law code emphasizes the principle of retribution ("an eye for an eye") and punishments that vary according to social status. Punishments could be severe. Marriage and family affairs also play a large role in the code. The following examples illustrate these concerns.

25. If fire broke out in a free man's house and a free man, who went to extinguish it, cast his eye on the goods of the owner of the house and has appropriated the goods of the owner of the house, that free man shall be thrown into that fire.

129. If the wife of a free man has been caught while lying with another man, they shall bind them and throw them into the water. If the husband of the woman wishes to spare his wife, then the king in turn may spare his subject.

131. If a free man's wife was accused by her husband, but she was not caught while lying with another man, she shall make affirmation by god and return to her house.

196. If a free man has destroyed the eye of a member of the aristocracy, they shall destroy his eye.

198. If he has destroyed the eye of a commoner or broken the bone of a commoner, he shall pay one mina of silver.

199. If he has destroyed the eye of a free man's slave or broken the bone of a free man's slave, he shall pay one-half his value.

209. If a free man struck another free man's daughter and has caused her to have a miscarriage, he shall pay ten shekels of silver for her fetus.

210. If that woman has died, they shall put his daughter to death.

211. If by a blow he has caused a commoner's daughter to have a miscarriage, he shall pay five shekels of silver.

212. If that woman has died, he shall pay one-half mina of silver.

213. If he struck a free man's female slave and has caused her to have a miscarriage, he shall pay two shekels of silver.

214. If that female slave has died, he shall pay one-third mina of silver.

was considered legally married. While the husband provided a bridal payment, the woman's parents were responsible for a dowry to the new husband.

As in many patriarchal societies, women possessed far fewer privileges and rights in the married relationship than men. A woman's place was in the home, and failure to fulfill her expected duties was grounds for divorce. If she was not able to bear children, her husband could divorce her, but he did have to return the dowry to her family. If a wife tried to leave home to engage in business, thus neglecting her house, her husband could divorce her and did not have to repay the dowry. Furthermore, a wife who was a "gadabout, ... neglecting her house [and] humiliating her husband" could be drowned. We do know that in practice not all women remained at home. Some worked in business and were especially prominent in the running of taverns.

Women were guaranteed some rights, however. If a woman was divorced without good reason, she received the dowry back. A woman could seek divorce and get her dowry back if her husband was unable to show that she had done anything wrong. In theory, a wife was guaranteed use of her husband's legal property in the event of his death. The mother could also decide which of her sons would receive an inheritance.

Sexual relations were strictly regulated as well. Husbands, but not wives, were permitted sexual activity outside marriage. A wife caught committing adultery was pitched into the river, although her husband could ask the king to pardon her. Incest was strictly forbidden. If a father had incestuous relations with his daughter, he would be banished. Incest between a son and mother resulted in both being burned.

Fathers ruled their children as well as their wives. Obedience was duly expected: "If a son has struck his father, they shall cut off his hand." If a son committed a serious enough offense, his father could disinherit him, although fathers were not permitted to disinherit their sons arbitrarily.

The Culture of Mesopotamia

A spiritual worldview was of fundamental importance to Mesopotamian culture. To the peoples of Mesopotamia, the gods were living realities who affected all aspects of life. It was crucial, therefore, that the correct hierarchies be observed. Leaders could prepare armies for war, but success really depended on a favorable relationship with the gods. This helps to explain the importance of the priestly class and is the reason why even the kings took great care to dedicate offerings and monuments to the gods.

THE IMPORTANCE OF RELIGION

The Mesopotamians viewed their city-states as earthly copies of a divine model and order. Each city-state was sacred because it was linked to a god or goddess. Hence, Nippur, the earliest center of Sumerian religion, was dedicated to Enlil, the god of wind. Moreover, located at the heart of each city-state was a temple complex. Occupying several acres, this sacred area consisted of a ziggurat with a temple at the top dedicated to the god or goddess who owned the city.

The temple complex was the true center of the community. The main god or goddess dwelt there symbolically in the form of a statue, and the ceremony of dedication included a ritual that linked the statue to the god or goddess and thus supposedly harnessed the power of the deity for the city's benefit. Considerable wealth was poured into the construction of temples as well as other buildings used for the residences of the priests and priestesses who served the gods. Although the gods literally owned the city, the temple complex used only part of the land and rented out the remainder. Essentially, the temples dominated individual and commercial life, an indication of the close relationship between Mesopotamian religion and culture.

The physical environment had an obvious impact on the Mesopotamian view of the universe. Ferocious floods, heavy downpours, scorching winds, and oppressive humidity were all part of the Mesopotamian climate. These conditions and the resulting famines easily convinced Mesopotamians that this world was controlled by supernatural forces and that the days of human beings "are numbered; whatever he may do, he is but wind," as *The Epic of Gilgamesh* put it. In the presence of nature, Mesopotamians could easily feel helpless, as this poem relates:

> *The rampant flood which no man can oppose,*
> *Which shakes the heavens and causes earth to tremble,*
> *In an appalling blanket folds mother and child,*
> *Beats down the canebrake's full luxuriant greenery,*
> *And drowns the harvest in its time of ripeness.*[2]

The Mesopotamians discerned cosmic rhythms in the universe and accepted its order, but perceived that it was not completely safe because of the presence of willful, powerful cosmic powers that they identified with gods and goddesses.

With its numerous gods and goddesses animating all aspects of the universe, Mesopotamian religion was polytheistic in nature. The four most important deities were An, god of the sky and hence the most important force in the universe; Enlil, god of wind; Enki, god of the earth, rivers, wells, and canals as well as inventions and crafts; and Ninhursaga, a goddess associated with soil, mountains, and vegetation, who came to be worshiped as a mother goddess, a "mother of all children," who manifested her power by giving birth to kings and conferring the royal insignia upon them.

Human beings' relationship with the gods was based on subservience since, according to Sumerian myth, human beings were created to do the manual labor the gods were unwilling to do for themselves. Moreover, humans were insecure because they could never be sure of the gods' actions. But humans did attempt to relieve their anxiety by discovering the intentions of the gods through divination.

Divination took a variety of forms. A common form, at least for kings and priests who could afford it, involved killing animals, such as sheep or goats, and examining their livers or other organs. Supposedly, features seen in the organs of the sacrificed animals foretold events to come. Thus, one handbook states that if the animal organ has shape *x*, then the outcome of the military campaign will be *y*. Private individuals relied on cheaper divinatory techniques. These included interpreting patterns of smoke from burning incense or the pattern formed when oil was poured into water. The Mesopotamian arts of divination arose out of the desire to discover the purposes of the gods. If people could decipher the signs that foretold events, the events would be predictable and humans could act wisely.

THE CULTIVATION OF NEW ARTS AND SCIENCES

The realization of writing's great potential was another aspect of Mesopotamian culture. The oldest Mesopotamian texts date to around 3000 B.C.E. and were written by the Sumerians, who used a cuneiform ("wedge-shaped") system of writing. Using a reed stylus, they made wedge-shaped impressions on clay tablets, which were then baked or dried in the sun. Once dried, these tablets were virtually indestructible, and the several hundred thousand that have been found so far have provided a valuable source of information for modern scholars. Sumerian writing evolved from pictures of concrete objects to simplified and stylized signs, leading eventually to a phonetic system that made possible the written expression of abstract ideas.

Mesopotamian peoples used writing primarily for record keeping, but another category of cuneiform inscriptions includes the large body of basic texts produced for teaching purposes. Schools for scribes were in operation by 2500 B.C.E. Such schools were necessary because considerable time was needed to master the cuneiform system of writing. The primary goal of scribal education was to produce professionally trained scribes for careers in the temples and palaces, the military, and government service. Pupils were male and primarily from wealthy families. Gradually, the schools became important centers for culture because Mesopotamian literature was used for instructional purposes.

Writing was important because it enabled a society to keep records and maintain knowledge of previous practices and events. Writing also made it possible for people to communicate ideas in new ways, which is especially evident in Mesopotamian literary works. The most famous piece of Mesopotamian literature is *The Epic of Gilgamesh*, an epic poem that records the exploits of a legendary king of Uruk. Gilgamesh, wise, strong, and perfect in body, part man and part god, befriends a hairy beast named Enkidu.

Pictographic sign c. 3100 B.C.E.	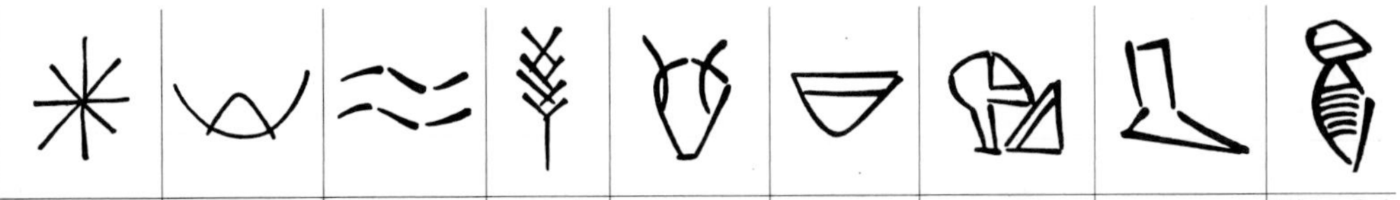								
Interpretation	star	?sun over horizon	?stream	ear of barley	bull's head	bowl	head + bowl	lower leg	?shrouded body
Cuneiform sign c. 2400 B.C.E.	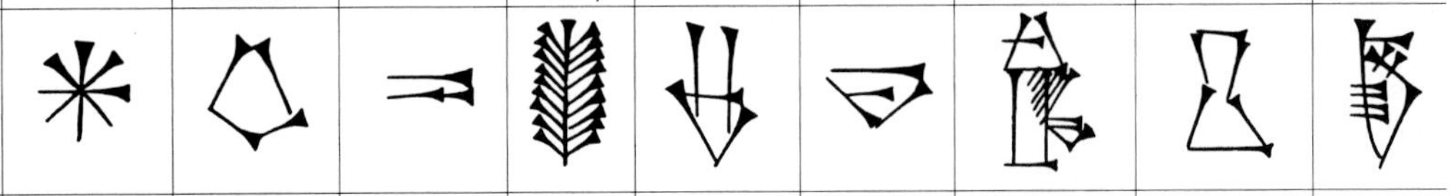								
Cuneiform sign c. 700 B.C.E. (turned through 90°)									
Phonetic value*	dingir, an	u_4, ud	a	še	gu_4	nig_2, ninda	ku_2	du, gin, gub	lu_2
Meaning	god, sky	day, sun	water, seed, son	barley	ox	food, bread	to eat	to walk, to stand	man

*Some signs have more than one phonetic value, and some sounds are represented by more than one sign. U_4 means the fourth sign with the phonetic value u.

THE DEVELOPMENT OF CUNEIFORM. Pictured here is the cone of Uruinimgina, an example of early cuneiform script from an early Sumerian dynasty. The inscription announces reductions in taxes. The table above shows the development of writing from pictographic signs to the evolution of cuneiform script.

Together they set off in pursuit of heroic deeds. When Enkidu dies, Gilgamesh experiences the pain of mortality and begins a search for the secret of immortality. But his efforts fail (see the box on p. 15). Gilgamesh remains mortal. The desire for immortality, one of humankind's great searches, ends in complete frustration. "Everlasting life," as this Mesopotamian epic makes clear, is only for the gods.

Peoples in Mesopotamia also made outstanding achievements in mathematics and astronomy. In math, the Sumerians devised a number system based on 60, using combinations of 6 and 10 for practical solutions. Geometry was used to measure fields and erect buildings. In astronomy, the Sumerians made use of units of 60 and charted the heavenly constellations. Their calendar was based on twelve lunar months and was brought into harmony with the solar year by adding an extra month from time to time.

Egyptian Civilization: "The Gift of the Nile"

Although contemporaneous with Mesopotamia, civilization in Egypt evolved along somewhat different lines. Of central importance to the development of Egyptian civilization was the Nile River. That the Egyptian people recognized its significance is apparent in this Hymn to the Nile (also see the box on p. 16): "The bringer of food, rich in provisions, creator of all good, lord of majesty, sweet of fragrance. . . . He who . . . fills the magazines, makes the granaries wide, and gives things to the poor. He who makes every beloved tree to grow. . . ."[3] Egypt, like Mesopotamia, India, and China, was a river valley civilization.

The Nile is a unique river, beginning in the heart of Africa and coursing northward for thousands of miles. It is the longest river in the world. The Nile was responsible for creating an area several miles wide on both banks of

THE GREAT FLOOD

The great epic poem of Mesopotamian literature, The Epic of Gilgamesh, *includes an account by Utnapishtim (a Mesopotamian version of the later biblical Noah), who had built a ship and survived the flood unleashed by the gods to destroy humankind. In this selection, Utnapishtim recounts his story to Gilgamesh, telling how the god Ea advised him to build a boat and how he came to land the boat at the end of the flood.*

THE EPIC OF GILGAMESH

In those days the world teemed, the people multiplied, the world bellowed like a wild bull, and the great god was aroused by the clamor. Enlil heard the clamor and he said to the gods in council, "The uproar of mankind is intolerable and sleep is no longer possible by reason of the babel." So the gods agreed to exterminate mankind. Enlil did this, but Ea [Sumerian Enki, god of the waters] because of his oath warned me in a dream.... "tear down your house and build a boat, abandon possessions and look for life, despise worldly goods and save your soul alive. Tear down your house, I say, and build a boat.... then take up into the boat the seed of all living creatures...." [Utnapishtim did as he was told and then the destruction came.]

For six days and six nights the winds blew, torrent and tempest and flood overwhelmed the world, tempest and flood raged together like warring hosts. When the seventh day dawned the storm from the south subsided, the sea grew calm, the flood was stilled; I looked at the face of the world and there was silence, all mankind was turned to clay. The surface of the sea stretched as flat as a rooftop; I opened a hatch and the light fell on my face. Then I bowed low, I sat down and I wept, the tears streamed down my face, for on every side was the waste of water. I looked for land in vain, but fourteen leagues distant there appeared a mountain, and there the boat grounded; on the mountain of Nisir the boat held fast, she held fast and did not budge.... When the seventh day dawned I loosed a dove and let her go. She flew away, but finding no resting place she returned. Then I loosed a swallow, and she flew away but finding no resting place she returned. I loosed a raven, she saw that the waters had retreated, she ate, she flew around, she cawed, and she did not come back. Then I threw everything open to the four winds, I made a sacrifice and poured out a libation on the mountaintop.

the river that was fertile and capable of producing abundant harvests. The "miracle" of the Nile was its annual flooding. The river rose in the summer from rains in central Africa, crested in Egypt in September and October, and left a deposit of silt that created an area of rich soil. The Egyptians called this fertile land the "Black Land," because it was dark in color from the silt and the lush crops that grew on it. Beyond these narrow strips of fertile fields lay the deserts (the "Red Land").

Unlike the floods of Mesopotamia's rivers, the flooding of the Nile was gradual and usually predictable, and the river itself was seen as life enhancing, not life threatening. Although a system of organized irrigation was still necessary, the small villages along the Nile could create such systems without the massive state intervention that was required in Mesopotamia. Egyptian civilization, consequently, tended to remain more rural, with many small population centers congregated along a narrow band on both sides of the Nile. About one hundred miles before it empties into the Mediterranean, the river splits into two major branches, forming the delta, a triangular-shaped territory called Lower Egypt to distinguish it from Upper Egypt, the land upstream to the south. Egypt's important cities developed at the tip of the delta. Even today, most of Egypt's people are crowded along the banks of the Nile River.

The surpluses of food that Egyptian farmers grew in the fertile Nile valley made Egypt prosperous. But the Nile also served as a unifying factor in Egyptian history. In ancient times, the Nile was the fastest way to travel through the land, making both transportation and communication easier. Winds from the north pushed sailboats south, and the current of the Nile carried them north. Often when they headed downstream (or north), people used long poles or paddles to propel their boats forward.

Unlike Mesopotamia, which was subject to constant invasion, Egypt was blessed by natural barriers that fostered isolation, protected it from invasion, and gave it a sense of security. These barriers included the deserts to the west and east, the cataracts (rapids) on the southern part of the Nile, which made defense relatively easy, and the Mediterranean Sea to the north. These barriers, however, did not prevent the development of trade. Indeed, there is evidence of very early trade between Egypt and Mesopotamia itself.

In essence, Egyptian geography and topography played important roles in the early history of the country. The regularity of the Nile floods and the relative isolation of the Egyptians created a sense of security that was accompanied by a feeling of changelessness. Egyptian civilization was characterized by a remarkable degree of continuity over thousands of years. It was certainly no accident that Egyptians believed in cyclical rather than linear progress. Just as the sun passed through its daily cycle and the Nile its annual overflow, Egyptian kings reaffirmed the basic, unchanging principles of justice at the beginning of each new cycle of rule.

THE SIGNIFICANCE OF THE NILE RIVER AND THE PHARAOH

Two of the most important sources of life for the ancient Egyptians were the Nile River and the pharaoh. Egyptians perceived that the Nile River made possible the abundant food that was a major source of their well-being. This Hymn to the Nile, *probably from the nineteenth and twentieth dynasties in the New Kingdom, expresses the gratitude Egyptians felt for the Nile.*

HYMN TO THE NILE

Hail to you, O Nile, that issues from the earth and comes to keep Egypt alive! . . .
He that waters the meadows which Re created, in order to keep every kid alive.
He that makes to drink the desert and the place distant from water: that is his dew coming down from heaven. . . .
The lord of fishes, he who makes the marsh-birds to go upstream. . . .
He who makes barley and brings emmer into being, that he may make the temples festive.
If he is sluggish, then nostrils are stopped up, and everybody is poor. . . .
When he rises, then the land is in jubilation, then every belly is in joy, every backbone takes on laughter, and every tooth is exposed.
The bringer of good, rich in provisions, creator of all good, lord of majesty, sweet of fragrance. . . .
He who makes every beloved tree to grow, without lack of them.

The Egyptian king, or pharaoh, was viewed as a god and the absolute ruler of Egypt. His significance and the gratitude of the Egyptian people for his existence are evident in this hymn from the reign of Sesotris III (c. 1880–1840 B.C.E.*).*

HYMN TO THE PHARAOH

He has come unto us that he may carry away Upper Egypt; the double diadem [crown of Upper and Lower Egypt] has rested on his head.
He has come unto us and has united the Two Lands; he has mingled the reed with the bee [symbols of Lower and Upper Egypt].
He has come unto us and has brought the Black Land under his sway; he has apportioned to himself the Red Land.
He has come unto us and has taken the Two Lands under his protection; he has given peace to the Two Riverbanks.
He has come unto us and has made Egypt to live; he has banished its suffering.
He has come unto us and has made the people to live; he has caused the throat of the subjects to breathe. . . .
He has come unto us and has done battle for his boundaries; he has delivered them that were robbed.

The Old and Middle Kingdoms

The basic framework for the study of Egyptian history was provided by Manetho, an Egyptian priest and historian who lived in the early third century B.C.E. He divided Egyptian history into thirty-one dynasties of kings. Based on Manetho and other king lists, modern historians have divided Egyptian history into three major periods, known as the Old Kingdom, the Middle Kingdom, and the New Kingdom. These were periods of long-term stability characterized by strong monarchical authority, competent bureaucracy, freedom from invasion, much construction of temples and pyramids, and considerable intellectual and cultural activity. But between the periods of stability were times of political chaos known as the Intermediate periods, which were characterized by weak political structures and rivalry for leadership, invasions, a decline in building activity, and a restructuring of society.

According to the Egyptians' own tradition, their land consisted initially of numerous populated areas ruled by tribal chieftains. Around 3100 B.C.E., the first Egyptian royal dynasty, under a king called Menes, united both Upper and Lower Egypt into a single kingdom. Henceforth, the king would be called "King of Upper and King of Lower Egypt," and the royal crown would be a double diadem, signifying the unification of all Egypt. Just as the Nile served to unite Upper and Lower Egypt physically, kingship served to unite the two areas politically.

The Old Kingdom encompassed the third through sixth dynasties of Egyptian kings, lasting from around 2700 to 2200 B.C.E. It was an age of prosperity and splendor, made visible in the construction of the greatest and largest pyramids in Egypt's history. The capital of the Old Kingdom was located at Memphis, south of the delta.

Kingship was a divine institution in ancient Egypt and formed part of a universal cosmic scheme (see the box above): "What is the king of Upper and Lower Egypt? He is a god by whose dealings one lives, the father and mother of all men, alone by himself, without an equal."[4] In obeying their king, subjects helped to maintain the cosmic order. A breakdown in royal power could only mean that citizens were offending divinity and weakening the universal structure. Among the various titles of Egyptian kings, that of pharaoh (originally meaning "great house" or "palace") eventually came to be the most common.

MAP 1.4 Ancient Egypt

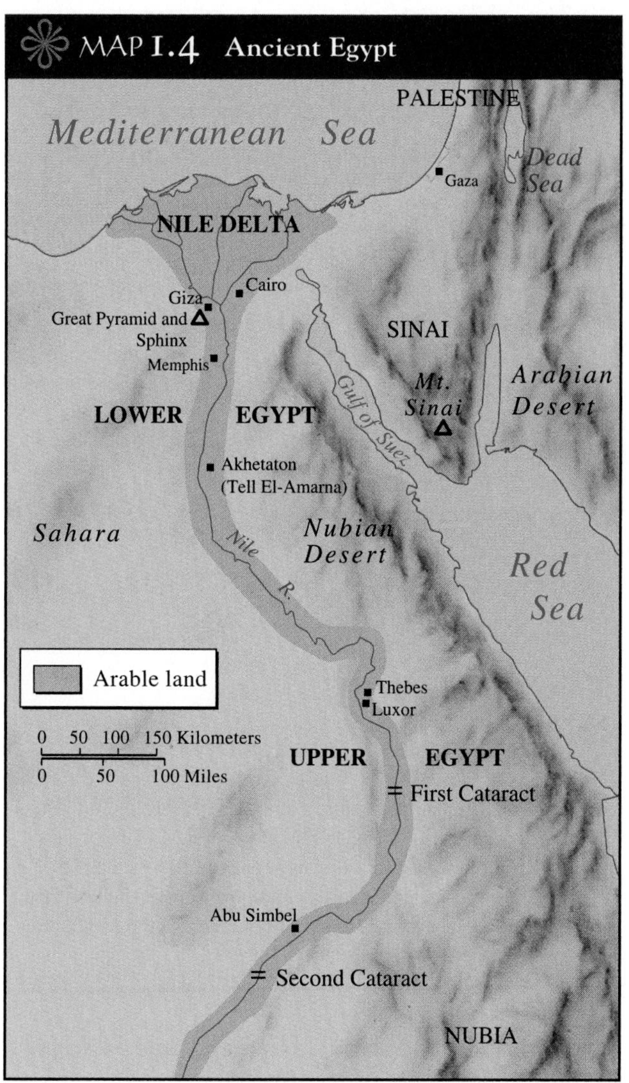

Although they possessed absolute power, Egyptian kings were not supposed to rule arbitrarily, but according to set principles. The chief principle was called *Ma'at*, a spiritual precept that conveyed the ideas of truth and justice but especially right order and harmony. To ancient Egyptians, this fundamental order and harmony had existed throughout the universe since the beginning of time. Pharaohs were the divine instruments who maintained it and were themselves subject to it.

Although theoretically absolute in their power, in practice Egyptian kings did not rule alone. Initially, members of the king's family performed administrative tasks, but by the fourth dynasty a bureaucracy with regular procedures had developed. Especially important was the office of vizier, "steward of the whole land." Directly responsible to the king, the vizier was in charge of the bureaucracy with its numerous departments, such as police, justice, river transport, and public works. Agriculture and the treasury were the two most important departments. Agriculture was, of course, the backbone of Egyptian prosperity, and the treasury collected the taxes that were paid in kind. A careful assessment of land and tenants was undertaken to provide the tax base. For administrative purposes, Egypt was divided into provinces or nomes, as they were later called by the Greeks—twenty-two in Upper and twenty in Lower Egypt. A governor, called by the Greeks a nomarch, was head of each nome and was responsible to the king and vizier. Nomarchs, however, tended to build up large holdings of land and power within their nomes, creating a potential rivalry with the pharaohs.

Despite the theory of divine order, the Old Kingdom eventually collapsed, ushering in a period of chaos. Finally, a new royal dynasty managed to pacify all Egypt and inaugurated the Middle Kingdom, a new period of stability lasting from c. 2050 to 1652 B.C.E. Egyptians later portrayed the Middle Kingdom as a golden age, a clear indication of its stability. Several factors contributed to its vitality. The nome structure was reorganized. The boundaries of each nome were now settled precisely, and the obligations of the nomes to the state were clearly delineated. Nomarchs were confirmed as hereditary officeholders but with the understanding that their duties must be performed faithfully. These included the collection of taxes for the state and the recruitment of labor forces for royal projects, such as stone quarrying.

The Middle Kingdom was characterized by a new concern of the pharaohs for the people. In the Old Kingdom, the pharaoh had been viewed as an inaccessible god-king. Now he was portrayed as the shepherd of his people with the responsibility to build public works and provide for the public welfare. As one pharaoh expressed it: "He [a particular god] created me as one who should do that which he had done, and to carry out that which he commanded should be done. He appointed me herdsman of this land, for he knew who would keep it in order for him."[5]

Society and Economy in Ancient Egypt

Egyptian society had a simple structure in the Old and Middle Kingdoms; basically, it was organized along hierarchical lines with the god-king at the top. The king was surrounded by an upper class of nobles and priests who participated in the elaborate rituals of life that surrounded the pharaoh. This ruling class ran the government and managed its own landed estates, which provided much of its wealth.

Below the upper classes were merchants and artisans. Within Egypt, merchants engaged in an active trade up and down the Nile as well as in town and village markets. Some merchants also engaged in international trade; they were sent by the king to Crete and Syria, where they obtained wood and other products. Expeditions traveled into Nubia for ivory and down the Red Sea to Punt for incense and spices. Egyptian artisans exhibited unusually high standards of artisanship and physical beauty while producing an incredible variety of goods: stone dishes; beautifully painted boxes made of clay; wooden furniture; gold, silver, and copper tools and containers; paper and rope made of papyrus; and linen clothes.

CHRONOLOGY

THE EGYPTIANS

Early Dynastic Period (Dynasties 1–2)	c. 3100–2700 B.C.E.
Old Kingdom (Dynasties 3–6)	c. 2700–2200 B.C.E.
First Intermediate Period (Dynasties 7–10)	c. 2200–2050 B.C.E.
Middle Kingdom (Dynasties 11–12)	c. 2050–1652 B.C.E.
Second Intermediate Period (Dynasties 13–17)	c. 1652–1567 B.C.E.
New Kingdom (Dynasties 18–20)	c. 1567–1085 B.C.E.
Post-Empire (Dynasties 21–31)	c. 1085–30 B.C.E.

PAIR STATUE OF KING MENKAURE AND HIS QUEEN. The period designated as the Old Kingdom began approximately four centuries after Egypt's unification (c. 3100 B.C.E.) and lasted until approximately 2200 B.C.E. The kings of Egypt (eventually called "pharaohs") were regarded as gods, divine instruments who maintained the fundamental order and harmony of the universe and wielded absolute power. This statue depicts King Menkaure and his queen (fourth dynasty).

By far the largest number of people in Egypt simply worked the land. In theory, the king owned all the land but granted out portions of it to his subjects. Large sections were in the possession of nobles and the temple complexes. Moreover, although free farmers who owned their own land had once existed, by the end of the Old Kingdom, this group had disappeared. Most of the lower classes were serfs, or common people bound to the land, who cultivated the estates. They paid taxes in the form of crops to the king, nobles, and priests, lived in small villages or towns, and provided military service and forced labor for building projects.

The Culture of Egypt

Egypt produced a culture that dazzled and awed its later conquerors. The Egyptians' technical achievements, especially visible in the construction of the pyramids, demonstrated a measure of skill unequaled in the world at that time. To the Egyptians, all of these achievements were part of a cosmic order suffused with the presence of the divine.

SPIRITUAL LIFE IN EGYPTIAN SOCIETY

The Egyptians had no word for religion, because it was an inseparable element of the entire world order to which Egyptian society belonged. The Egyptians possessed a remarkable number of gods associated with heavenly bodies and natural forces. Two groups, sun gods and land gods, came to have special prominence, hardly unusual in view of the importance of the sun, the river, and the fertile land along its banks to Egypt's well-being. The sun was the source of life and hence worthy of worship. A sun cult developed, and the sun god took on different forms and names, depending on his specific function. He was worshiped as Atum in human form and as Re, who had a human body but the head of a falcon. The pharaoh took the title of "Son of Re," since he was regarded as the earthly embodiment of Re. Eventually, Re became associated with Amon, an air god of Thebes, as Amon-Re.

River and land deities included Osiris and Isis with their child Horus, who was related to the Nile and to the sun as well. Osiris became especially important as a symbol of resurrection or rebirth. A famous Egyptian myth told of the struggle between Osiris, who brought civilization to Egypt, and his evil brother Seth, who killed him, cut his body into fourteen parts, and tossed them into the Nile River. Osiris's faithful wife Isis found the pieces and, with help from other gods, restored Osiris to life. As a symbol of resurrection and judge of the dead, Osiris took on an important role for the Egyptians. By identifying with Osiris, one could hope to gain new life just as Osiris had done. The dead, embalmed and mummified, were placed in tombs (in the case of kings, in pyramidal tombs), given the name of Osiris, and, by a process of magical identification, became Osiris. Like Osiris, they could then be reborn. The flood of the Nile and the new life it brought to Egypt were symbolized by Isis gathering all of Osiris's parts together and were celebrated each spring in the festival of the new land.

Later Egyptian spiritual practice began to emphasize morality by stressing Osiris's role as judge of the dead. The dead were asked to give an account of their earthly deeds to show whether they deserved a reward. Other means were also employed to gain immortality. Magical incantations, preserved in the *Book of the Dead,* were used to ensure a favorable journey to a happy afterlife. Specific instructions explained what to do when confronted by the judge of the dead. These instructions had two aspects. The negative confession gave a detailed list of what one had not done:

What is said on reaching the Broad-Hall of the Two Justices [the place of the next-world judgment], absolving X [the name and title of the deceased] of every sin which he had committed. . . .

I have not committed evil against men.
I have not mistreated cattle.
I have not blasphemed a god. . . .
I have not done violence to a poor man.
I have not done that which the gods abominate.
I have not defamed a slave to his superior.
I have not made anyone sick.
I have not made anyone weep.
I have not killed. . . .
I have not caused anyone suffering. . . .
I have not had sexual relations with a boy.
I have not defiled myself. . . .[6]

Later the suppliant made a speech listing his good actions: "I have done that which men said and that with which gods are content. . . . I have given bread to the hungry, water to the thirsty, clothing to the naked, and a ferry-boat to him who was marooned. I have provided divine offerings for the gods and mortuary offerings for the dead."[7]

At first the Osiris cult was reserved for the very wealthy, who could afford to take expensive measures to preserve the body after death. During the Middle Kingdom, however, the cult became "democratized"—extended to all Egyptians who aspired to an afterlife.

THE PYRAMIDS

One of the great achievements of Egyptian civilization, the building of pyramids, occurred in the time of the Old Kingdom. Pyramids were not built in isolation but as part of a larger complex dedicated to the dead—in effect, a city of the dead. The area included a large pyramid for the king's burial, smaller pyramids for his family, and mastabas, rectangular structures with flat roofs, as tombs for the pharaoh's noble officials. The tombs were well prepared for their residents. The rooms were furnished and stocked with numerous supplies, including chairs, boats, chests, weapons, games, dishes, and a variety of foods. The Egyptians believed that human beings had two bodies, a physical one and a spiritual one, which they called the *ka.* If the physical body was properly preserved (hence mummification) and the tomb furnished with all the various objects of regular life, the *ka* could return and continue its life despite the death of the physical body. A pyramid was not only the king's tomb; it was also an important symbol of royal power. It could be seen for miles away as a visible reminder of the glory and might of the ruler who was a living god on earth.

The largest and most magnificent of all the pyramids was built under King Khufu. Constructed at Giza around 2540 B.C.E., this famous Great Pyramid covers thirteen

THE PYRAMIDS AT GIZA. The three pyramids at Giza, across the Nile River from Cairo, are the most famous in Egypt. Pyramids served as tombs for both the king and his immediate family. At the rear is the largest of the three pyramids—the Great Pyramid of Khufu. In the foreground is the smaller pyramid of Menkaure, standing behind the even smaller pyramids for the pharaoh's wives.

acres, measures 756 feet at each side of its base, and stands 481 feet high. Its four sides are almost precisely oriented to the four points of the compass. The interior included a grand gallery to the burial chamber, which was built of granite with a lidless sarcophagus for the pharaoh's body. The Great Pyramid still stands as a visible symbol of the power of Egyptian kings and the spiritual conviction that underlay Egyptian society. No pyramid built later ever matched its size or splendor.

ART AND WRITING

Commissioned by kings or nobles for use in temples and tombs, Egyptian art was largely functional. Wall paintings and statues of gods and kings in temples served a strictly spiritual purpose. They were an integral part of the performance of ritual, which was thought necessary to preserve the cosmic order and hence the well-being of Egypt. Likewise, the mural scenes and sculptured figures found in the tombs had a specific function: they were supposed to assist the journey of the deceased into the afterworld.

Egyptian art was also formulaic. Artists and sculptors were expected to observe a strict canon of proportions that determined both form and presentation. This canon gave Egyptian art a distinctive appearance for thousands of years. Especially characteristic was the convention of combining the profile, semiprofile, and frontal views of the human body in relief work and painting in order to represent each part of the body accurately. The result was an art that was highly stylized yet still allowed distinctive features to be displayed.

Writing emerged in Egypt during the first two dynasties. The Greeks later labeled Egyptian writing hieroglyphics, meaning "priest-carvings" or "sacred writings." Hieroglyphs were sacred characters used as picture signs that depicted objects and had a sacred value at the same time. Although hieroglyphs were later simplified into two scripts for writing purposes, they never developed into an alphabet. Egyptian hieroglyphs were initially carved in stone, but later the two simplified scripts were written on papyrus, a paper made from the papyrus reed that grew along the Nile. Most of the ancient Egyptian literature that has come down to us was written on papyrus rolls and wooden tablets.

Chaos and a New Order: The New Kingdom

The Middle Kingdom came to an end in the midst of another period of instability. An incursion into the delta region by a people known as the Hyksos initiated this second age of chaos. The Hyksos were part of a larger group of peoples who spoke Semitic languages and originally lived in the Arabian peninsula. Some of these Semitic-speaking peoples had moved into northern Mesopotamia as well as Syria and Palestine. The Hyksos infiltrated Egypt in the seventeenth century B.C.E. and came to dominate much of the country. However, the presence of the Hyksos was not entirely negative for Egypt. They introduced Egypt to Bronze Age technology by teaching the Egyptians how to make bronze for use in new agricultural tools and weapons. More significantly, the Hyksos introduced new aspects of warfare to Egypt, including the horse-drawn war chariot, a heavier sword, and the compound bow. Eventually, a new line of pharaohs—the eighteenth dynasty—made use of the new weapons to throw off Hyksos domination, reunite Egypt, establish the New Kingdom (c. 1567–1085 B.C.E.), and launch the Egyptians along a new militaristic and imperialistic path. During the period of the New Kingdom, Egypt became the most powerful state in the Middle East. The Egyptians occupied Palestine and Syria but permitted the local native princes to continue to rule under Egyptian control. Egyptian armies also moved westward into Libya. The achievements of the empire were made visible in the construction of magnificent new buildings and temples, especially the temple centers at Karnak and Luxor.

The eighteenth dynasty was not without its own troubles, however. Amenhotep IV (c. 1364–1347 B.C.E.) introduced the worship of Aton, god of the sun disk, as the chief god (see the box on p. 21) and pursued his worship with great enthusiasm. Changing his own name to Akhenaton ("It is well with Aton"), the pharaoh closed the temples of other gods and especially endeavored to lessen the power of Amon-Re and his priesthood at Thebes. Akhenaton strove to reduce their influence by replacing Thebes as the capital of Egypt with Akhetaton ("dedicated to Aton"), a new city located near modern Tell el-Amarna, two hundred miles north of Thebes.

Akhenaton's attempt at religious change proved to be a failure. It was too much to ask Egyptians to give up their traditional ways and beliefs, especially since they saw the destruction of the old gods as subversive of the very cosmic order upon which Egypt's survival and continuing prosperity depended. Moreover, the priests at Thebes were unalterably opposed to the changes, which had diminished their influence and power. At the same time, Akhenaton's preoccupation with religion caused him to ignore foreign affairs and led to the loss of both Syria and Palestine. Akhenaton's changes were soon undone after his death by those who influenced his successor, the boy-pharaoh Tutankhamon (1347–1338 B.C.E.). Tutankhamon returned the government to Thebes and restored the old gods. The Aton experiment had failed to take hold, and the eighteenth dynasty itself came to an end in 1333.

The nineteenth dynasty managed to restore Egyptian power one more time. Under Rameses II (c. 1279–1213 B.C.E.), the Egyptians regained control of Palestine but were unable to reestablish the borders of their earlier

AKHENATON'S HYMN TO ATON

Amenhotep IV, more commonly known as Akhenaton, created a religious upheaval in Egypt by introducing the worship of Aton, god of the sun disk, as the sole god. Akhenaton's attitude to Aton is seen in this hymn. Some authorities have noted a similarity in spirit and wording to the 104th Psalm of the Old Testament.

HYMN TO ATON

Your rays suckle every meadow.
When you rise, they live, they grow for you.
You make the seasons in order to rear all that you have made,
The winter to cool them,
And the heat that they may taste you.
You have made the distant sky in order to rise therein,
In order to see all that you do make.
While you were alone,
Rising in your form as the living Aton,
Appearing, shining, withdrawing or approaching,
You made millions of forms of yourself alone.
Cities, towns, fields, road, and river—
Every eye beholds you over against them,
For you are the Aton of the day over the earth. . . .
The world came into being by your hand,
According as you have made them.
When you have risen they live,
When you set they die.
You are lifetime your own self,
For one lives only through you.
Eyes are fixed on beauty until you set.
All work is laid aside when you set in the west.
But when you rise again,
Everything is made to flourish for the king, . . .
Since you did found the earth
And raise them up for your son,
Who came forth from your body:
the King of Upper and Lower Egypt, . . .
Akh-en-Aton, . . . and the Chief Wife of the King . . .
Nefert-iti, living and youthful forever and ever.

empire. New invasions in the thirteenth century by the "Sea Peoples," as Egyptians called them, destroyed Egyptian power in Palestine and drove the Egyptians back within their old frontiers. The days of Egyptian empire were ended, and the New Kingdom itself expired with the end of the twentieth dynasty in 1085. For the next thousand years, despite periodical revivals of strength, Egypt was dominated by Libyans, Nubians, Persians, and finally Macedonians, after the conquest of Alexander the Great (see Chapter 4). In the first century B.C.E., Egypt became a province in Rome's mighty empire. Egypt continued, however, to influence its conquerors through the richness of its heritage and the awesome magnificence of its physical remains.

Daily Life in Ancient Egypt: Family and Marriage

Ancient Egyptians had a very positive attitude toward daily life on earth and followed the advice of the wisdom literature, which suggested that people marry young and establish a home and family. Monogamy was the general rule, although a husband was allowed to keep additional wives if his first wife was childless. Pharaohs, of course, were entitled to harems. The queen was acknowledged, however, as the Great Wife, with a status higher than that of the other wives. The husband was master in the house, but wives were very much respected and in charge of the household and education of the children. From a book of wise sayings (which the Egyptians called "instructions") came this advice:

> If you are a man of standing, you should found your household and love your wife at home as is fitting. Fill her belly; clothe her back. Ointment is the prescription for her body. Make her heart glad as long as you live. She is a profitable field for her lord. You should not contend with her at law, and keep her far from gaining control. . . . Let her heart be soothed through what may accrue to you; it means keeping her long in your house.[8]

Women's property and inheritance remained in their hands, even in marriage. Although most careers and public offices were closed to women, some did operate businesses. Peasant women worked long hours in the fields and at numerous domestic tasks. Upper-class women could function as priestesses, and a few queens even became pharaohs in their own right. Most famous was Hatshepsut in the New Kingdom. She initially served as regent for her stepson Thutmosis III but then assumed the throne for herself and remained in power until her death.

Hatshepsut's reign was a properous one, as is especially evident in her building activity. She is most famous for the temple dedicated to herself at Deir el Bahri, on the west bank of the Nile at Thebes. As pharaoh, Hatshepsut sent out military expeditions, encouraged mining, fostered agriculture, and sent a trading expedition up the Nile. Because pharaohs were almost always male, Hatshepsut's official statues show her clothed and bearded like a king. She was addressed as "His Majesty." That Hatshepsut was aware of her unusual position is evident from an inscription she had

STATUE OF HATSHEPSUT. Wife of Thutmosis II, Hatshepsut served as regent for her stepson Thutmosis III after her husband's death. In 1473 B.C.E., however, she proclaimed herself pharaoh. This red granite statue shows her as a woman, although most official statues portrayed her dressed and bearded like a king.

placed on one of her temples. It read: "Now my heart turns to and fro, in thinking what will the people say, they who shall see my monument in after years, and shall speak of what I have done."

Little is known about marital arrangements and ceremonies, although it does appear that marriages were arranged by parents. The primary concerns were family and property, and clearly the chief purpose of marriage was to produce children, especially sons. From the New Kingdom came this piece of wisdom: "Take to yourself a wife while you are [still] a youth, that she may produce a son for you."[9] Only sons could carry on the family name. Daughters were not slighted, however. Numerous tomb paintings show the close and affectionate relationship parents had with both sons and daughters. Although marriages were arranged, some of the surviving love poems from ancient Egypt suggest that some marriages included an element of romance. Here is the lament of a lovesick boy for his "sister" (lovers referred to each other as "brother" and "sister"):

Seven days to yesterday I have not seen the sister, and a sickness has invaded me;
My body has become heavy,
And I am forgetful of my own self.
If the chief physicians come to me,
My heart is not content with their remedies. . . .
What will revive me is to say to me: "Here she is!"
Her name is what will lift me up. . . .
My health is her coming in from outside:
When I see her, then I am well.[10]

Marriages could and did end in divorce, which was allowed, apparently with compensation for the wife. Adultery, however, was strictly prohibited, with stiff punishments—especially for women, who could have their noses cut off or be burned at the stake.

New Centers of Civilization

Our story of civilization so far has been dominated by Mesopotamia and Egypt. But significant developments were also taking place on the fringes of these civilizations. Farming had spread into the Balkan peninsula of Europe by 6500 B.C.E., and by 4000 B.C.E., it was well established in southern France, central Europe, and the coastal regions of the Mediterranean. Although migrating farmers from the Middle East may have brought some farming techniques into Europe, historians now believe that the Neolithic peoples of Europe domesticated animals and began to farm largely on their own.

One outstanding feature of late Neolithic Europe was the building of megalithic structures. Megalith is Greek for "large stone." Radiocarbon dating, a technique that allows scientists to determine the ages of objects, shows that the first megalithic structures were built around 4000 B.C.E., more than a thousand years before the great pyramids were built in Egypt. Between 3200 and 1500 B.C.E., standing stones that were placed in circles or lined up in rows were erected throughout the British Isles and northwestern France. Other megalithic constructions have been found as far north as Scandinavia and as far south as the islands of Corsica, Sardinia, and Malta. Some archaeologists have demonstrated that the stone circles were used as observatories to detect not only such simple astronomical phenomena as midwinter and midsummer sunrises, but also such sophisticated phenomena as the major and minor standstills of the moon.

The Impact of the Indo-Europeans

In large part, both the details of construction and the purpose of the megalithic structures of Europe remain a mystery. Also puzzling is the role of the Indo-European

STONEHENGE. By far the most famous megalithic construction, Stonehenge in England, consists of a series of concentric rings of standing stones. Its construction sometime between 2100 and 1900 B.C.E. was no small accomplishment. The eighty bluestones used at Stonehenge weighed four tons each and were transported to the site from their original source, 135 miles away. Like other megalithic structures, Stonehenge indicates a remarkable awareness of astronomy on the part of its builders, as well as an elaborate coordination of workers.

peoples. The term Indo-European refers to people who used a language derived from a single parent tongue. Indo-European languages include Greek, Latin, Persian, Sanskrit, and the Germanic and Slavic languages (see Table 1.2). It has been suggested that the original Indo-European-speaking peoples were based somewhere in the steppe region north of the Black Sea or in southwestern Asia, in modern Iran or Afghanistan. Although there had been earlier migrations, around 2000 B.C.E. the original Indo-European-speaking peoples began major nomadic movements into Europe (including present-day Italy and Greece), India, and western Asia. One group of Indo-Europeans who moved into Asia Minor and Anatolia (modern Turkey) around 1750 B.C.E. coalesced with the native peoples to form the Hittite kingdom, with its capital at Hattusha (Bogazköy in modern Turkey).

Between 1600 and 1200 B.C.E., the Hittites created their own empire in western Asia and even threatened the power of the Egyptians. The Hittites were the first of the Indo-European peoples to make use of iron, enabling them to construct weapons that were stronger and cheaper to make because of the widespread availability of iron ore. But around 1200 B.C.E., new waves of invading Indo-European peoples destroyed the Hittite empire. The destruction of the Hittite kingdom and the weakening of Egypt around 1200 B.C.E. temporarily left no dominant powers in western Asia, allowing a patchwork of petty kingdoms and city-states to emerge, especially in the area of Syria and Palestine. The Phoenicians were one of these peoples.

TABLE 1.2
SOME INDO-EUROPEAN LANGUAGES

Subfamily	Languages
Indo-Iranian	*Sanskrit*, Persian
Balto-Slavic	Russian, Serbo-Croatian, Czech, Polish, Lithuanian
Hellenic	Greek
Italic	*Latin*, Romance languages (French, Italian, Spanish, Portuguese, Romanian)
Celtic	Irish, Gaelic
Germanic	Swedish, Danish, Norwegian, German, Dutch, English

Note: Languages in italic type are no longer spoken.

The Phoenicians

A Semitic-speaking people, the Phoenicians lived in the area of Palestine along the Mediterranean coast on a narrow band of land 120 miles long. Their newfound political independence after the demise of Hittite and Egyptian power helped the Phoenicians expand the trade that was already the foundation of their prosperity. The chief cities of Phoenicia—Byblos, Tyre, and Sidon—were ports on the eastern Mediterranean, but they also served as distribution centers for the lands to the east in Mesopotamia. The Phoenicians themselves produced a number of goods for foreign markets, including purple dye, glass, wine, and lumber from the famous cedars of Lebanon. In addition, the Phoenicians improved their ships and became great international sea traders. They charted new routes, not only in the Mediterranean, but also in the Atlantic Ocean, where they reached Britain and sailed south along the west coast of Africa. The Phoenicians established a number of colonies in the western Mediterranean, including settlements in southern Spain, Sicily, and Sardinia. Carthage, the Phoenicians' most famous colony, was located on the north coast of Africa.

Culturally, the Phoenicians are best known as transmitters. Instead of using pictographs or signs to represent whole words and syllables (as the Mesopotamians and Egyptians did), the Phoenicians simplified their writing by using twenty-two different signs to represent the sounds of their speech. These twenty-two characters or letters could be used to spell out all the words in the Phoenician language. Although the Phoenicians were not the only people to invent an alphabet, theirs would have special significance because it was eventually passed on to the Greeks. From the Greek alphabet was derived the Roman alphabet that we still use today (see Table 1.3). The Phoenicians achieved much while independent, but they ultimately fell subject to the Assyrians and Persians.

The Hebrews: The "Children of Israel"

To the south of the Phoenicians lived another group of Semitic-speaking people known as the Hebrews. Although they were a minor factor in the politics of the region, their religion—known as Judaism—influenced both Christianity and Islam and flourished as a world religion. The Hebrews had a tradition concerning their origins and history that was eventually written down as part of the Hebrew Bible, known to Christians as the Old Testament. Describing them as a nomadic people, the Hebrews' own tradition states that they were descendants of the patriarch Abraham, who had migrated from Mesopotamia to the land of Palestine, where the Hebrews became identified as the "Children of Israel." Moreover, according to tradition, a drought in Palestine caused many Hebrews to migrate to Egypt, where they lived peacefully until they were enslaved by pharaohs who used them as laborers on their numerous building projects. The Hebrews remained in bondage until Moses led his people out of Egypt in the well-known "exodus," which some historians have argued would have occurred in the first half of the thirteenth century B.C.E. According to the biblical account, the Hebrews then wandered for many years in the desert, until they entered Palestine. Organized into twelve tribes, the Hebrews became embroiled in conflict with the Philistines, a people who had settled in the coastal area of Palestine but were beginning to move into the inland areas.

Many scholars today doubt that the early books of the Hebrew Bible reflect the true history of the early Israelites. They argue that the early books of the Bible, written centuries after the events described, preserve only what the Israelites came to believe about themselves and that recent archaeological evidence often contradicts the details of the biblical account. Some of these scholars have even argued that the Israelites were not nomadic invaders but indigenous peoples in the Palestinian hill country. What is generally agreed, however, is that between 1200 and 1000 B.C.E., the Israelites emerged as a distinct group of people, possibly organized into tribes or a league of tribes, who established a united kingdom known as Israel.

THE UNITED KINGDOM

The first king of the Israelites was Saul (c. 1020–1000 B.C.E.), who initially achieved some success in the ongoing struggle with the Philistines. But after his death in a disastrous battle with this enemy, a brief period of anarchy ensued, until one of Saul's lieutenants, David (c. 1000–970 B.C.E.), reunited the Israelites, defeated the Philistines, and established control over all of Palestine. Among David's conquests was the city of Jerusalem, which he made into the capital of a united kingdom. David centralized Israel's orga-nization and accelerated the integration of the Israelites into a settled community based on farming and urban life.

David's son Solomon (c. 970–930 B.C.E.) did even more to strengthen royal power. He expanded the political and military establishments and was especially active in extending the trading activities of the Israelites. Solomon is known for his building projects, of which the most famous was the Temple in the city of Jerusalem. The Israelites viewed the Temple as the symbolic center of their religion and hence of the kingdom of Israel itself. The Temple now housed the Ark of the Covenant, the holy chest containing the sacred relics of the Hebrew religion and, symbolically, the throne of the invisible God of Israel. Under Solomon, ancient Israel was at the height of its power, but his efforts to extend royal power throughout his kingdom led to dissatisfaction among some of his subjects.

THE DIVIDED KINGDOM

After Solomon's death, tensions between the northern and southern tribes within Israel led to the establishment of two separate kingdoms—a kingdom of Israel, composed of the ten northern tribes, with its capital eventually at Samaria, and a southern kingdom of Judah, consisting of two tribes, with its capital at Jerusalem. By the end of the ninth century, the independence of the kingdom of Israel was increasingly threatened by the rising power of the Assyrians. In 722 B.C.E., the Assyrians destroyed Samaria,

TABLE 1.3
THE PHOENICIAN, GREEK, AND ROMAN ALPHABETS

PHOENICIAN			GREEK			ROMAN	
Phoenician	*Phoenician Name*	*Modern Symbol*	*Early Greek*	*Classical Greek*	*Greek Name*	*Early Latin*	*Classical Latin*
𐤀	’aleph	’	Α	Α	alpha	A	A
𐤁	beth	b	Β	Β	beta		B
𐤂	gimel	g	Γ	Γ	gamma		C
𐤃	daleth	d	Δ	Δ	delta	D	D
𐤄	he	h	Ε	Ε	epsilon	E	E
𐤅	waw	w	Ϝ		digamma	F	F
							G
𐤆	zayin	z	Ι	Ζ	zeta		
𐤇	heth	h	Η	Η	eta	H	H
𐤈	teth	t	⊗	Θ	theta		
𐤉	yod	y	Ι	Ι	iota	I	I
𐤊	kaph	k	Κ	Κ	kappa	K	K
𐤋	lamed	l	Λ	Λ	lambda		L
𐤌	mem	m	Μ	Μ	mu	M	M
𐤍	nun	n	Ν	Ν	nu	N	N
𐤎	samek	s			xi		
𐤏	ayin	‘	Ο	Ο	omnicron	O	O
𐤐	pe	p	Π	Π	pi		P
𐤑	sade	s	Ϻ		saw		
𐤒	qoph	o	Ϙ		qoppa		Q
𐤓	rěs	r	Ρ	Ρ	rho		R
𐤔	ˇsin	sh/s	Σ	Σ	sigma	S	S
𐤕	taw	t	Χ		tau		T
				Υ	upsilon	V	V
				Χ	chi		X
							Y
				Ω	omega		Z

SOURCE: Andrew Robinson, *The Story of Writing* (London, 1995), p. 170.

overran the kingdom of Israel, and deported many Hebrews to other parts of the Assyrian Empire. These dispersed Hebrews (the "ten lost tribes") merged with neighboring peoples and gradually lost their identity.

The southern kingdom of Judah was also forced to pay tribute to Assyria but managed to retain its independence as Assyrian power declined. However, a new enemy appeared on the horizon. The Chaldeans brought the final destruction of Assyria, conquered the kingdom of Judah, and completely destroyed Jerusalem in 586 B.C.E. Many upper-class people from Judah were deported to Babylonia; the memory of their exile is still evoked in the stirring words of Psalm 137:

> *By the rivers of Babylon, we sat and wept when we remembered Zion. . . .*
> *How can we sing the songs of the Lord while in a foreign land?*
> *If I forget you, O Jerusalem, may my right hand forget its skill.*
> *May my tongue cling to the roof of my mouth if I do not remember you,*
> *if I do not consider Jerusalem my highest joy.*[11]

But the Babylonian captivity of the people of Judah did not last. A new set of conquerors, the Persians, destroyed the Chaldean kingdom and allowed the people of Judah to return to Jerusalem and rebuild their city and Temple. The revived kingdom of Judah remained under Persian control until the conquests of Alexander the Great in the fourth century B.C.E. The people of Judah survived, eventually becoming known as the Jews and giving their name to Judaism, the religion of Yahweh, the Jewish God.

THE KING OF ISRAEL PAYS TRIBUTE TO THE KING OF ASSYRIA. By the end of the ninth century B.C.E., the kingdom of Israel had been forced to pay tribute to the Assyrian Empire. The Assyrians overran the kingdom in 722 B.C.E. and destroyed the capital city of Samaria. In this scene from a black obelisk, Jehu, king of Israel, is shown paying tribute to the king of Assyria.

THE SPIRITUAL DIMENSIONS OF ISRAEL

The spiritual perspective of the Israelites evolved over a period of time. Early Israelites probably worshiped many gods, including nature spirits dwelling in trees and rocks. For some Israelites, Yahweh was the chief god of Israel, but many, including kings of Israel and Judah, worshiped other gods as well. It was among the Babylonian exiles that Yahweh—the God of Israel—came to be seen as the only God. After the return of these exiles to Judah, their point of view eventually became dominant, which resulted in pure monotheism, or the belief that there is only one God for all peoples, as the major tenet of Judaism.

According to the Jewish conception, there is but one God, whom the Jews called Yahweh. God is the creator of the world and everything in it. Indeed, Yahweh means "he causes to be." To the Jews, the gods of all other peoples were simply idols. The Jewish God ruled the world; he was subject to nothing. All peoples were his servants, whether they knew it or not. This God was also transcendent. He

MAP 1.5 Palestine in the First Millennium B.C.E.

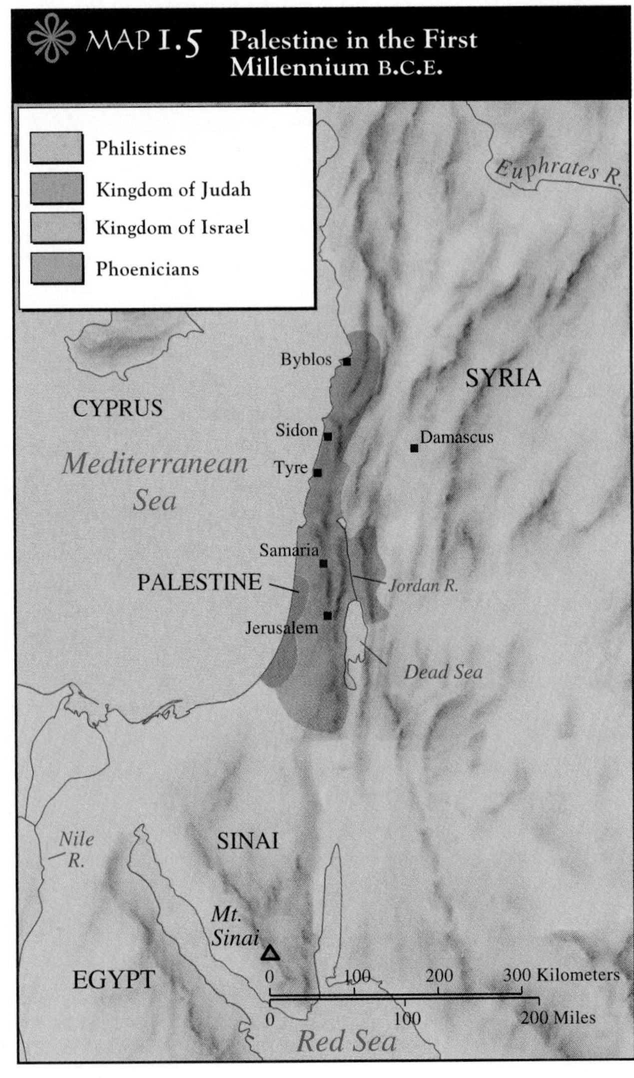

CHRONOLOGY

THE ISRAELITES

Israelites	
Saul—First king	c. 1020–1000 B.C.E.
King David	c. 1000–970 B.C.E.
King Solomon	c. 970–930 B.C.E.
Northern kingdom of Israel destroyed by Assyria	722 B.C.E.
Fall of southern kingdom of Judah to Chaldeans; destruction of Jerusalem	586 B.C.E.
Return of exiles to Jerusalem	538 B.C.E.

had created nature but was not in nature. The stars, moon, rivers, wind, and other natural phenomena were not divinities or suffused with divinity, as other peoples of the ancient Near East believed, but God's handiwork. All of God's creations could be admired for their awesome beauty but not worshiped as God.

Nevertheless, this omnipotent creator of the universe was not removed from the life he had created but was a just and good God who expected goodness from his people. If they did not obey his will, they would be punished. But he was also a God of mercy and love: "The Lord is gracious and compassionate, slow to anger and rich in love. The Lord is good to all; he has compassion on all he has made."[12] Despite the powerful dimensions of God as creator and sustainer of the universe, the Jewish message also emphasized that each person could have a personal relationship with this powerful being. As the psalmist sang: "My help comes from the Lord, the Maker of heaven and earth. He will not let your foot slip—he who watches over you will not slumber."[13]

Three aspects of the Jewish religious tradition had special significance: the covenant, the law, and the prophets. The Israelites believed that during the exodus from Egypt, when Moses supposedly led his people out of bondage and into the promised land, a special event occurred that determined the Jewish experience for all time. According to tradition, God entered into a covenant or contract with the tribes of Israel, who believed that Yahweh had spoken to them through Moses (see the box on p. 28). The Israelites promised to obey Yahweh and follow his law. In return, Yahweh promised to take special care of his chosen people, "a peculiar treasure unto me above all people."

This covenant between Yahweh and his chosen people could be fulfilled, however, only through obedience to the law of God. Law became a crucial element of the Jewish world and had a number of different dimensions. In some instances, the law set forth specific requirements, such as payments for offenses. Most important, since the major characteristic of God was his goodness, ethical concerns stood at the center of the law. Sometimes these took the form of specific standards of moral behavior: "You shall not murder. You shall not commit adultery. You shall not steal."[14] But these concerns were also expressed in decrees that regulated the economic, social, and political life of the community since God's laws of morality applied to all areas of life. These laws made no class distinctions and emphasized the protection of the poor, widows, orphans, and slaves.

The prophets were "holy men" who supposedly had special communion with God and felt called upon to serve as his voice to his people. In the ninth century B.C.E., the prophets were particularly vociferous about the tendency of the Israelites to accept other gods, chiefly the fertility and earth gods of other peoples in Palestine. The prophets warned of the terrible retribution that God would exact from the Israelites if they did not keep the covenant to remain faithful to him alone and just in their dealings with one another (see the box on p. 29).

The golden age of prophecy began in the mid-eighth century and continued during the time when the people of Israel and Judah were threatened by Assyrian and Chaldean conquerors. The "men of God" went through the land warning the Israelites that they had failed to keep God's commandments and would be punished for breaking the covenant: "I will punish you for all your iniquities." Amos prophesied the fall of the northern kingdom of Israel to Assyria; twenty years later, Isaiah said the kingdom of Judah too would fall.

Out of the words of the prophets came new concepts that enriched the Jewish tradition, including a notion of universalism and a yearning for social justice. Although their religious practices gave Jews a sense of separateness from other peoples, the prophets transcended this by embracing a concern for all humanity. All nations would someday come to the God of Israel: "all the earth shall worship thee." A universal community of all people under God would someday be established by Israel's efforts. This vision encompassed the elimination of war and the establishment of peace for all the nations of the world. In the words of the prophet Isaiah: "He will judge between the nations and will settle disputes for many people. They will beat their swords into plowshares and their spears into pruning hooks. Nation will not take up sword against nation, nor will they train for war anymore."[15]

The prophets also cried out against social injustice. They condemned the rich for causing the poor to suffer, denounced luxuries as worthless, and threatened Israel with prophecies of dire punishments for these sins. God's command was to live justly, share with one's neighbors, care for the poor and the unfortunate, and act with compassion. When God's command was not followed, the social fabric of the community was threatened. These proclamations

THE COVENANT AND THE LAW: THE BOOK OF EXODUS

According to the biblical account, it was during the exodus from Egypt that the Israelites supposedly made their covenant with Yahweh. They agreed to obey their God and follow his law. In return, Yahweh promised to take special care of his chosen people. This selection from the book of Exodus describes the making of the covenant and God's commandments to the Hebrews.

EXODUS 19: 1–8

In the third month after the Israelites left Egypt—on the very day—they came to the Desert of Sinai. After they set out from Rephidim, they entered the desert of Sinai, and Israel camped there in the desert in front of the mountain. Then Moses went up to God, and the Lord called to him from the mountain, and said, "This is what you are to say to the house of Jacob and what you are to tell the people of Israel: 'You yourselves have seen what I did to Egypt, and how I carried you on eagles' wings and brought you to myself. Now if you obey me fully and keep my covenant, then out of all nations you will be my treasured possession. Although the whole earth is mine, you will be for me a kingdom of priests and a holy nation.' These are the words you are to speak to the Israelites." So Moses went back and summoned the elders of the people and set before them all the words the Lord had commanded him to speak. The people all responded together, "We will do everything the Lord has said." So Moses brought their answer back to the Lord.

EXODUS 20: 1–3, 7–17

And God spoke all these words, "I am the Lord your God, who brought you out of Egypt, out of the land of slavery. You shall have no other gods before me. . . . You shall not misuse the name of the Lord your God, for the Lord will not hold anyone guiltless who misuses his name. Remember the Sabbath day by keeping it holy. Six days you shall labor and do all your work, but the seventh day is a Sabbath to the Lord your God. On it you shall not do any work, neither you, nor your son or daughter, nor your manservant or maidservant, nor your animals, nor the alien within your gates. For in six days the Lord made the heavens and the earth, the sea, and all that is in them, but he rested on the seventh day. Therefore the Lord blessed the Sabbath day and made it holy. Honor your father and your mother, so that you may live long in the land the Lord your God is giving you. You shall not murder. You shall not commit adultery. You shall not steal. You shall not give false testimony against your neighbor. You shall not covet your neighbor's house. You shall not covet your neighbor's wife, or his manservant or maidservant, his ox or donkey, or anything that belongs to your neighbor."

of Israel's prophets spawned universal ideals of social justice, even if they have never been perfectly realized.

Although the Jewish prophets ultimately developed a sense of universalism, the demands of the Jewish religion (the need to obey their God) eventually encouraged a separation between the Jews and their non-Jewish neighbors. Unlike most other peoples of the Middle East, Jews could not simply be amalgamated into a community by accepting the gods of their conquerors and their neighbors. To remain faithful to the demands of their God, they might even have to refuse loyalty to political leaders.

The Rise of New Empires

An independent Israelite state could exist only because there was a power vacuum in western Asia after the destruction of the Hittite kingdom and the weakening of the Egyptian empire. But this condition did not last; new empires soon arose that came to dominate vast stretches of the ancient world.

The Assyrian Empire

The first of these empires was formed in Assyria, located on the upper Tigris River, an area that brought it into both cultural and political contact with Mesopotamia. The Assyrians were a Semitic-speaking people who exploited the use of iron weapons to establish an empire by 700 B.C.E. that included Mesopotamia, parts of the Iranian plateau, sections of Asia Minor, Syria, Palestine, and Egypt down to Thebes. Ashurbanipal (669–626 B.C.E.) was one of the strongest Assyrian rulers, but during his reign it was already becoming apparent that the Assyrian Empire was greatly overextended. Internal strife intensified as powerful Assyrian nobles gained control of vast territories and waged their own private military campaigns. Moreover, subject peoples, such as the Babylonians, greatly resented Assyrian rule and rebelled against it. Soon after Ashurbanipal's reign, the Assyrian Empire began to disintegrate rapidly. The capital city of Nineveh fell to a coalition of Chaldeans and Medes in 612 B.C.E., and in 605 B.C.E., the rest of the empire was finally divided between the coalition powers.

At its height, the Assyrian Empire was ruled by kings whose power was considered absolute. Under their lead-

THE HEBREW PROPHETS: MICAH, ISAIAH, AND AMOS

The Hebrew prophets warned the Israelites that they must obey God's commandments or face being punished for breaking their covenant with God. These selections from the prophets Micah, Isaiah, and Amos make clear that God's punishment would fall upon the Israelites for their sins. Even the Assyrians, as Isaiah indicated, would be used as God's instrument to punish them.

MICAH 6:9–16

Listen! The Lord is calling to the city—and to fear your name is wisdom—"Heed the rod and the One who appointed it. Am I still to forget, O wicked house, your ill-gotten treasures . . . ? Shall I acquit a man with dishonest scales, with a bag of false weights? Her rich men are violent; her people are liars and their tongues speak deceitfully. Therefore, I have begun to destroy you, to ruin you because of your sins. You will eat but not be satisfied; your stomach will still be empty. You will store up but save nothing, because what you save I will give to the sword. You will plant but not harvest; you will press olives but not use the oil on yourselves, you will crush grapes but not drink the wine. . . . Therefore I will give you over to ruin and your people to derision; you will bear the scorn of the nations."

ISAIAH 10: 1–6

Woe to those who make unjust laws, to those who issue oppressive decrees, to deprive the poor of their rights and withhold justice from the oppressed of my people, making widows their prey and robbing the fatherless. What will you do on the day of reckoning, when disaster comes from afar? To whom will you run for help? Where will you leave your riches? Nothing will remain but to cringe among the captives or fall among the slain. Yet for all this, his anger is not turned away, his hand is still upraised. "Woe to the Assyrian, the rod of my anger, in whose hand is the club of my wrath! I send him against a godless nation, I dispatch him against a people who anger me, to seize loot and snatch plunder, and to trample them down like mud in the streets."

AMOS 3: 1–2

Hear this word the Lord has spoken against you, O people of Israel—against the whole family I brought up out of Egypt: "You only have I chosen of all the families of the earth; therefore I will punish you for all your sins."

ership, the Assyrian Empire came to be well organized. By eliminating governorships held by nobles on a hereditary basis and instituting a new hierarchy of local officials directly responsible to the king, the Assyrian kings gained greater control over the resources of the empire. The Assyrians also developed an efficient system of communication to administer their empire more effectively. A network of posting stages was established throughout the empire that used relays of horses (mules or donkeys in mountainous terrain) to carry messages. The system was so effective that a provincial governor anywhere in the empire (except Egypt) could send a question and receive an answer from the king in his palace within a week.

The ability of the Assyrians to conquer and maintain an empire was due to a combination of factors. Over many years of practice, the Assyrians developed effective military leaders and fighters. They were able to enlist and deploy troops numbering in the hundreds of thousands, although most campaigns were not on such a large scale. In 845 B.C.E., an Assyrian army of 120,000 men crossed the Euphrates on a campaign. Size alone was not decisive, however. The Assyrian army was extremely well organized and disciplined. It included a standing army of infantrymen as its core, accompanied by cavalry and horse-drawn war chariots that were used as mobile platforms for shooting arrows. Moreover, the Assyrians had the advantage of having the first large armies equipped with iron weapons. The Hittites had been the first to develop iron metallurgy, but iron came to be used extensively only after new methods for hardening it became common after 1000 B.C.E.

Another factor in the army's success was its ability to use different kinds of military tactics (see the box on p. 30). The Assyrian army was capable of waging guerrilla warfare in the mountains and set battles on open ground as well as laying siege to cities. The Assyrians were especially renowned for their siege warfare. They would hammer a city's walls with heavy, wheeled siege towers and armored battering rams, while sappers dug tunnels to undermine the walls' foundations and cause them to collapse. The besieging Assyrian armies learned to cut off supplies so effectively that if a city did not fall to them, the inhabitants could be starved into submission.

A final factor in the effectiveness of the Assyrian military machine was its ability to create a climate of terror as an instrument of warfare. The Assyrians became famous for their terror tactics, although some historians believe that their policies were no worse than those of other conquerors. As a matter of regular policy, the Assyrians laid waste the land in which they were fighting, smashing dams, looting and destroying towns, setting crops on fire, and cutting down trees, particularly fruit trees. The Assyrians were especially known for committing atrocities on

THE ASSYRIAN MILITARY MACHINE

The Assyrians achieved a reputation for possessing a mighty military machine. They were able to use a variety of military tactics and were successful whether they were waging guerrilla warfare, fighting set battles, or laying siege to cities. In these three selections, Assyrian kings boast of their military conquests.

KING SENNACHERIB (704–681 B.C.E.) Describes a Battle with the Elamites in 691

At the command of the god Ashur, the great Lord, I rushed upon the enemy like the approach of a hurricane. . . . I put them to rout and turned them back. I transfixed the troops of the enemy with javelins and arrows. . . . I cut their throats like sheep. . . . My prancing steeds, trained to harness, plunged into their welling blood as into a river; the wheels of my battle chariot were bespattered with blood and filth. I filled the plain with the corpses of their warriors like herbage. . . . As to the sheikhs of the Chaldeans, panic from my onslaught overwhelmed them like a demon. They abandoned their tents and fled for their lives, crushing the corpses of their troops as they went. . . . In their terror they passed scalding urine and voided their excrement into their chariots.

KING SENNACHERIB Describes His Siege of Jerusalem in 701

As to Hezekiah, the Jew, he did not submit to my yoke, I laid siege to 46 of his strong cities, walled forts, and the countless small villages in their vicinity, and conquered them by means of well-stamped earth-ramps, and battering-rams brought thus near to the walls combined with the attack by foot soldiers, using mines, breeches, as well as sapper work. I drove out of them 200,150 people, young and old, male and female, horses, mules, donkeys, camels, big and small cattle beyond counting, and considered them booty. Himself I made a prisoner in Jerusalem, his royal residence, like a bird in a cage. I surrounded him with earthwork in order to molest those who were leaving his city's gate.

KING ASHURBANIPAL (669–626 B.C.E.) Describes His Treatment of Conquered Babylon

I tore out the tongues of those whose slanderous mouths had uttered blasphemies against my god Ashur and had plotted against me, his god-fearing prince; I defeated them completely. The others, I smashed alive with the very same statues of protective deities with which they had smashed my own grandfather Sennacherib—now finally as a belated burial sacrifice for his soul. I fed their corpses, cut into small pieces, to dogs, pigs, . . . vultures, the birds of the sky, and also to the fish of the ocean. After I had performed this and thus made quiet again the hearts of the great gods, my lords, I removed the corpses of those whom the pestilence had felled, whose leftovers after the dogs and pigs had fed on them were obstructing the streets, filling the places of Babylon, and of those who had lost their lives through the terrible famine.

their captives. King Ashurnasirpal recorded this account of his treatment of prisoners:

> 3000 of their combat troops I felled with weapons. . . . Many of the captives taken from them I burned in a fire. Many I took alive; from some of these I cut off their hands to the wrist, from others I cut off their noses, ears and fingers; I put out the eyes of many of the soldiers. . . . I burned their young men and women to death.

After conquering another city, the same king wrote: "I fixed up a pile of corpses in front of the city's gate. I flayed the nobles, as many as had rebelled, and spread their skins out on the piles. . . . I flayed many within my land and spread their skins out on the walls."[16] It should be noted that this policy of extreme cruelty to prisoners was not used against all enemies but was primarily reserved for those who were already part of the empire and then rebelled against Assyrian rule.

ASSYRIAN SOCIETY AND CULTURE

Unlike the Hebrews, the Assyrians were not fearful of mixing with other peoples. In fact, Assyrian deportation policies created a polyglot society in which ethnic differences were not very important. What gave identity to the Assyrians themselves was their language, although even that was akin to the language of their southern neighbors in Babylonia, who also spoke a Semitic language. Religion was also a cohesive force. Assyria was literally "the land of Ashur," a reference to its chief god. The king, as the human representative of the god Ashur, provided a final unifying focus.

Agriculture formed the principal basis of Assyrian life. Assyria was a land of farming villages with relatively few significant cities, especially in comparison to Mesopotamia. Unlike Mesopotamia, where farming required the minute organization of large numbers of people to control irrigation, Assyrian farms received sufficient moisture from regular rainfall.

Trade was second to agriculture in economic importance. For internal trade, metals—such as gold, silver, copper, and bronze—were used as a medium of exchange. Various agricultural products also served as a form of payment or exchange. Because of their geographical location, the Assyrians served as intermediaries and participated in an international trade in which they imported timber, wine, and precious metals and stones while exporting textiles produced in palaces, temples, and private workshops.

The culture of the Assyrian Empire was essentially hybrid in nature. The Assyrians assimilated much of Mesopotamian civilization and saw themselves as guardians of Sumerian and Babylonian culture. Ashurbanipal, for example, established a large library at Nineveh that included the available works of Mesopotamian history. Assyrian kings also tried to maintain old traditions when they rebuilt damaged temples by constructing the new buildings on the original foundations, not in new locations. Assyrian religion reflected this assimilation of other cultures as well. Although the Assyrians had their own national god (Ashur) as their chief deity, virtually all of their remaining gods and goddesses were Mesopotamian.

Among the best-known objects of Assyrian art are the relief sculptures found in the royal palaces in three of the Assyrian capital cities, Nimrud, Nineveh, and Khorsabad. These reliefs, which were begun in the ninth century and reached their high point in the reign of Ashurbanipal in the seventh century, depicted two different kinds of subject matter: ritual or ceremonial scenes revolving around the person of the king and scenes of hunting and war. The latter show realistic action scenes of the king and his warriors engaged in battle or hunting animals, especially lions. These pictures depict a strongly masculine world where discipline, brute force, and toughness are the enduring values—indeed, the very values of the Assyrian military monarchy.

The Persian Empire

The Chaldeans, a Semitic-speaking people, had gained ascendancy in Babylonia by the seventh century and came to form the chief resistance to Assyrian control of Mesopotamia. After the collapse of the Assyrian Empire, the Chaldeans, under their king Nebuchadnezzar II (605–562 B.C.E.), restored Babylonia to its position as the leading state in western Asia. Nebuchadnezzar rebuilt Babylon as the center of his empire, giving it a reputation as one of the great cities of the ancient world. But the splendor of Chaldean Babylonia proved to be short-lived when Babylon fell to the Persians in 539 B.C.E.

The Persians were an Indo-European-speaking people who lived in southwestern Iran and fell subject to the ethnically related Medes. Primarily nomadic, the Persians were organized into tribes or clans led by petty kings assisted by a group of warriors who formed a class of nobles. At the beginning of the seventh century, the Achaemenid dynasty, based in Persis, in southern Iran, managed to unify the Persians. One of the dynasty's members, Cyrus (559–530 B.C.E.), created a powerful Persian state that rearranged the political map of western Asia. In 550 B.C.E., he extended Persian control over the Medes, making Media the first Persian satrapy or province. Three years later, Cyrus defeated the prosperous Lydian kingdom in western Asia Minor, and Lydia became another Persian satrapy. Cyrus's forces then went on to conquer the Greek city-states that had been established on the Ionian coast. Cyrus then turned eastward, subduing the eastern part of the Iranian plateau, Sogdia, and even western India. His eastern frontiers secured, Cyrus entered Mesopotamia in 539 and captured Babylon. His treatment of Babylonia showed remarkable restraint and wisdom. Babylonia was made into a Persian province under a Persian satrap, but many government officials were kept in their positions. Cyrus took the title "King of All, Great King, Mighty King, King of Babylon, King of the Land of Sumer and Akkad, King of the Four Rims (of the Earth), the Son of Cambyses the Great King, King of Anshan"[17] and insisted that he stood in the ancient, unbroken line of Babylonian kings. By appealing to the vanity of the Babylonians, he won their loyalty. Cyrus also issued an edict permitting the Hebrews, who had been brought to Babylon in the sixth century B.C.E., to return to Jerusalem with their sacred temple objects and to rebuild their Temple as well.

To his contemporaries, Cyrus the Great was deserving of his epithet. The Greek historian Herodotus recounted that the Persians viewed him as a "father," a ruler who was "gentle, and procured them all manner of goods."[18] Certainly, Cyrus must have been an unusual ruler for his time,

KING ASHURBANIPAL'S LION HUNT. This relief, sculptured on alabaster as a decoration for the northern palace in Nineveh, depicts King Ashurbanipal engaged in a lion hunt. The relief sculpture, one of the best-known forms of Assyrian art, ironically reached its high point under Ashurbanipal at the same time that the Assyrian Empire began to disintegrate.

a man who demonstrated considerable wisdom and compassion in the conquest and organization of his empire. Cyrus attempted—successfully—to obtain the favor of the priesthoods in his conquered lands by restoring temples and permitting a wide degree of religious toleration. He won approval by using not only Persians, but also native peoples as government officials in their own states. Unlike the Assyrian rulers of an earlier empire, he had a reputation for mercy. Medes, Babylonians, and Hebrews all accepted him as their legitimate ruler. Indeed, the Hebrews regarded him as the anointed one of God: "I am the Lord who says of Cyrus, 'He is my shepherd and will accomplish all that I please'; he will say of Jerusalem, 'Let it be rebuilt'; and of the Temple, 'Let its foundations be laid.' This is what the Lord says to his anointed, to Cyrus, whose right hand I take hold of to subdue nations before him."[19] Cyrus had a genuine respect for ancient civilizations—in building his palaces, he made use of Assyrian, Babylonian, Egyptian, and Lydian practices. Indeed, Cyrus had a sense that he was creating a "world empire" that included peoples who had ancient and venerable traditions and institutions.

Cyrus's successors extended the territory of the Persian Empire. His son Cambyses (530–522 B.C.E.) undertook a successful invasion of Egypt and made it into a satrapy with Memphis as its capital. Darius (521–486 B.C.E.) added a new Persian province in western India that extended to the Indus River and moved into Europe proper, conquering Thrace and making the Macedonian king a vassal. A revolt of the Ionian Greek cities in 499 B.C.E. resulted in temporary freedom for these communities in western Asia Minor. Aid from the Greek mainland, most notably from Athens, encouraged the Ionians to invade Lydia and burn Sardis, center of the Lydian satrap. This event led to Darius's involvement with the mainland Greeks. After reestablishing control of the Ionian Greek cities, Darius undertook an invasion of the Greek mainland, which culminated in the famous Athenian victory in the Battle of Marathon, in 490 B.C.E. (see Chapter 4).

GOVERNING THE EMPIRE

By the reign of Darius, the Persians had created the largest empire the world had yet seen. It not only included all the old centers of power in Egypt and western Asia, but also extended into Thrace and Asia Minor in the west and into India in the east. For administrative purposes, the empire

MAP 1.6 The Assyrian and Persian Empires

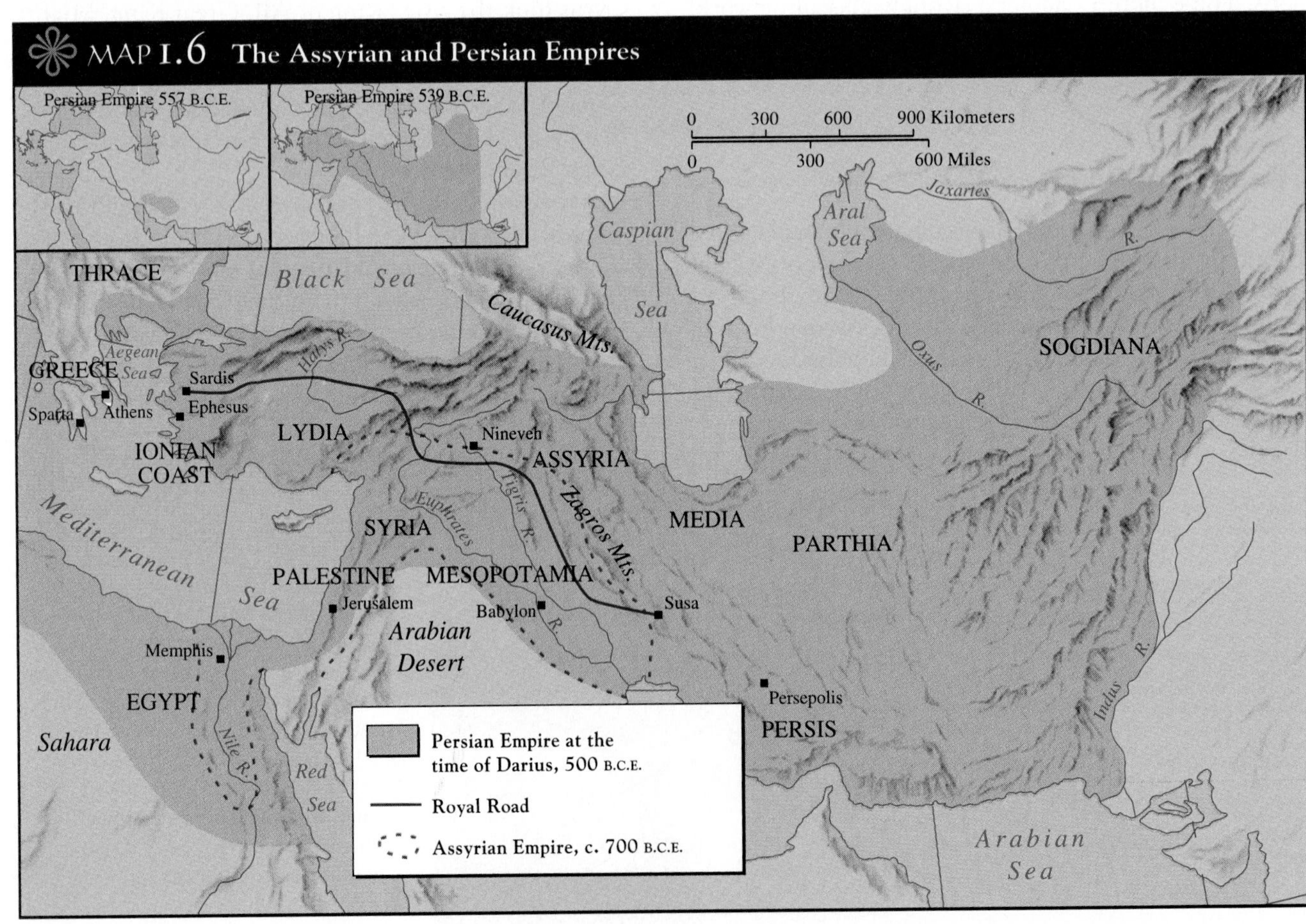

CHRONOLOGY

THE EMPIRES

The Assyrians	
Height of power	700 B.C.E.
Ashurbanipal	669–626 B.C.E.
Fall of Nineveh	612 B.C.E.
Assyrian Empire destroyed	605 B.C.E.
The Persians	
Unification under Achaemenid dynasty	600s B.C.E.
Persian control over Medes	550 B.C.E.
Conquests of Cyrus the Great	559–530 B.C.E.
Cambyses and conquest of Egypt	530–522 B.C.E.
Reign of Darius	521–486 B.C.E.

had been divided into approximately twenty provinces called satrapies. Each province was ruled by a governor or satrap, literally a "protector of the kingdom." Although Darius had not introduced the system of satrapies, he did see that it was organized more rationally. He created a sensible system for calculating the tribute that each satrapy owed to the central government and gave satraps specific civil and military duties. They collected tributes, were responsible for justice and security, raised military levies for the royal army, and normally commanded the military forces within their satrapies. In terms of real power, the satraps were miniature kings with courts imitative of the Great King's.

From the time of Darius on, satraps were men of Persian descent. The major satrapies were given to princes of the royal family, and their position became essentially hereditary. The minor satrapies were placed in the hands of Persian nobles. Their offices, too, tended to pass from father to son. The hereditary nature of the governors' offices made it necessary to provide some checks to their power. Consequently, royal officials at the satrapal courts acted as spies for the Great King.

An efficient system of communication was crucial to sustaining the Persian Empire. Well-maintained roads facilitated the rapid transit of military and government personnel. One in particular, the so-called Royal Road, stretched from Sardis, the center of Lydia in Asia Minor, to Susa, the chief capital of the Persian Empire. Like the Assyrians, the Persians established staging posts equipped with fresh horses for the king's messengers.

In this vast administrative system, the Persian king occupied an exalted position. Although not considered to be a god in the manner of an Egyptian pharaoh, he was nevertheless the elect one or regent of the Persian god Ahuramazda (see the next section). All subjects were the king's servants, and he was the source of all justice, possessing the power of life and death over everyone. Persian kings were largely secluded and not easily accessible. They resided in a series of splendid palaces. Darius in particular was a palace builder on a grand scale. His description of the construction of a palace in the chief Persian capital of Susa demonstrated what a truly international empire Persia was:

> This is the . . . palace which at Susa I built. From afar its ornamentation was brought. . . . The cedar timber was brought from a mountain named Lebanon; the Assyrians brought it to Babylon, and from Babylon the Carians and Ionians brought it to Susa. Teakwood was brought from Gandara and from Carmania. The gold which was used here was brought from Sardis and from Bactria. The stone—lapis lazuli and carnelian—was brought from Sogdiana. . . . The silver and copper were brought from Egypt. The ornamentation with which the wall was adorned was brought from Ionia. The ivory was brought from Ethiopia, from India, and from Arachosia. The stone pillars were brought from . . . Elam. The artisans who dressed the stone were Ionians and Sardians. The goldsmiths who wrought the gold were Medes and Egyptians. . . . Those who worked the baked brick (with figures) were Babylonians. The men who adorned the wall were Medes and Egyptians. At Susa here a splendid work was ordered; very splendid did it turn out.[20]

But Darius was unhappy with Susa. He did not really consider it his homeland, and it was oppressively hot in the summer months. He built another residence at Persepolis, a new capital located to the east of the old one and at a higher elevation.

The policies of Darius also tended to widen the gap between the king and his subjects. As the Great King himself said of all his subjects: "What was said to them by me, night and day it was done."[21] Over a period of time, the Great Kings in their greed came to hoard immense quantities of gold and silver in the various treasuries located in the capital cities. Both their hoarding of wealth and their later overtaxation of their subjects are considered crucial factors in the ultimate weakening of the Persian Empire.

In its heyday, however, the empire stood supreme, and much of its power depended on the military. By the time of Darius, the Persian monarchs had created a standing army of professional soldiers. This army was truly international in character, composed of contingents from the various peoples who made up the empire. At its core was a cavalry force of 10,000 and an elite infantry force of 10,000 Medes and Persians known as the Immortals because they were never allowed to fall below 10,000 in number. When one was killed, he was immediately replaced. The Persians made effective use of their cavalry, especially for operating behind enemy lines and breaking up lines of communication.

PERSIAN RELIGION

Of all the Persians' cultural contributions, the most original was their religion. The popular religion of the Iranians before the advent of Zoroastrianism in the sixth century focused on the worship of the powers of nature, such as the sun, moon, fire, and winds. Mithras was an especially popular god of light and war who came to be viewed as a sun god. The people worshiped and sacrificed to these powers of nature with the aid of priests, known as Magi.

Zoroaster was a semilegendary figure who, according to Persian tradition, was born in 660 B.C.E. After a period of wandering and solitude, he experienced revelations that caused him to be revered as a prophet of the "true religion." It is difficult to know what Zoroaster's original teachings were since the sacred book of Zoroastrianism, the Zend Avesta, was not written down until the third century C.E. Scholars believe, however, that the earliest section of the Zend Avesta, known as the Yasna, consisting of seventeen hymns or gathas, contains the actual writings of Zoroaster. This enables us to piece together his message.

ARCHERS OF THE PERSIAN GUARD. One of the main pillars supporting the Persian Empire was the military. This frieze, composed of enamel brick, depicts members of the famous infantry force known as the Immortals, so called because their number was never allowed to drop below 10,000. Those killed would be replaced immediately. They carry the standard lance and bow and arrow of the infantry.

Zoroaster did not introduce a new god but taught that Ahuramazda, who had long been one of the Iranians' deities, was the only god and that his religion was the only perfect one. Ahuramazda (the "Wise Lord") was the supreme deity who brought all things into being:

This I ask of You, O Ahuramazda; answer me well:
Who at the Creation was the first father of Justice?—
Who assigned their path to the sun and the stars?—
Who decreed the waxing and waning of the moon, if it was not You?— . . .
Who has fixed the earth below, and the heaven above with its clouds that it might not be moved?—
Who has appointed the waters and the green things upon the earth?—
Who has harnessed to the wind and the clouds their steeds?— . . .
Thus do I strive to recognize in You, O Wise One,
Together with the Holy Spirit, the Creator of all things.[22]

According to Zoroaster, Ahuramazda also possessed abstract qualities or states that all humans should aspire to, such as Good Thought, Right, and Piety. Although Ahuramazda was supreme, he was not unopposed. Right is opposed by the Lie, Truth by Falsehood, Life by Death. At the beginning of the world, the good spirit of Ahuramazda was opposed by the evil spirit (in later Zoroastrianism, the evil spirit is identified with Ahriman). Although it appears that Zoroaster saw it as simply natural that where there is good, there will be evil, later followers had a tendency to make these abstractions concrete and overemphasize the reality of an evil spirit. Humans also played a role in this cosmic struggle between good and evil. Ahuramazda, the creator, gave all humans free will and the power to choose between right and wrong. The good person chooses the right way of Ahuramazda. Zoroaster taught that there would be an end to the struggle between good and evil. Ahuramazda would eventually triumph, and at the last judgment at the end of the world, the final separation of good and evil would occur. Zoroaster also provided for individual judgment. Each soul faced a final evaluation of its actions. If a person had performed good deeds, he or she would achieve paradise, the "House of Song" or the "Kingdom of Good Thought"; if evil deeds, then the soul would be thrown into an abyss, the "House of Worst Thought," where it would experience future ages of darkness, torment, and misery.

The spread of Zoroastrianism was due to its acceptance by the Great Kings of Persia. The inscriptions of Darius make clear that he believed Ahuramazda was the only god. Although Darius himself may have been a monotheist, as the kings and Magi, or priests of Persia, propagated Zoroaster's teachings on Ahuramazda, dramatic changes occurred. Zoroastrianism lost its monotheistic emphasis, and the old nature worship resurfaced. Hence, Persian religion returned to polytheism, with Ahuramazda becoming only the chief of a number of gods of light. Mithras, the sun god, became a helper of Ahuramazda and later, in Roman times, the source of another religion. Persian kings were also very tolerant of other religions, and gods and goddesses of those religions tended to make their way into the Persian pantheon. Moreover, as frequently happens to the ideas of founders of religions, Zoroaster's teachings acquired concrete forms that he had never originally intended. The struggle between good and evil was taken beyond the abstractions of Zoroaster into a strong ethical dualism. The spirit of evil became an actual being, who had to be warded off by the use of spells and incantations. Descriptions of the last judgment came to be filled with minute physical details. Some historians believe that Zoroastrianism, with its emphasis on good and evil, a final judgment, and individual judgment of souls, had an impact on Christianity, a religion that eventually surpassed it in significance.

CONCLUSION

The peoples of Mesopotamia and Egypt, like the peoples of India and China, built the first civilizations. They developed cities and struggled with the problems of organized states. They developed writing to keep records and created literature. They constructed monumental architecture to please their gods, symbolize their power, and preserve their culture for all time. They developed new political, military, social, and religious structures to deal with the basic problems of human existence and organization. These first literate civilizations left detailed records that allow us to view how they grappled with three of the fundamental problems that humans have pondered: the nature of human relationships, the nature of the universe, and the role of divine forces in that cosmos. Although other peoples would provide different answers from those of the Mesopotamians and Egyptians, they posed the questions, gave answers, and wrote them down. Human memory begins with the creation of civilizations.

By the middle of the second millennium B.C.E., much of the creative impulse of the Mesopotamian and Egyptian civilizations was beginning to wane. Around 1200 B.C.E., the decline of the Hittites and Egyptians had created a power vacuum that allowed a number of small states to emerge and flourish temporarily. All of them were eventually overshadowed by the rise of the great empires of the Assyrians and Persians. The Assyrian Empire had been the first to unite almost all of the ancient Middle East. Even larger, however, was the empire of the Great Kings of Persia. Although it owed much to the administrative organization created by the Assyrians, the Persian Empire had its own peculiar strengths. Persian rule was tolerant as well as efficient. Conquered peoples were allowed to keep their own religions, customs, and methods of doing business. The many years of peace that the Persian Empire brought to the Middle East facilitated trade and the general well-being of its peoples. It is no wonder that many peoples expressed their gratitude for being subjects of the Great Kings of Persia. Among these peoples were the Hebrews, who created no empire but nevertheless left an important spiritual legacy. The evolution of Hebrew monotheism created in Judaism one of the world's greatest religions; moreover, Judaism influenced the development of both Christianity and Islam.

The Persians had also extended their empire to the Indus River, which brought them into contact with another river valley civilization that had developed independently of the civilizations in the Middle East and Egypt. It is to India that we must now turn.

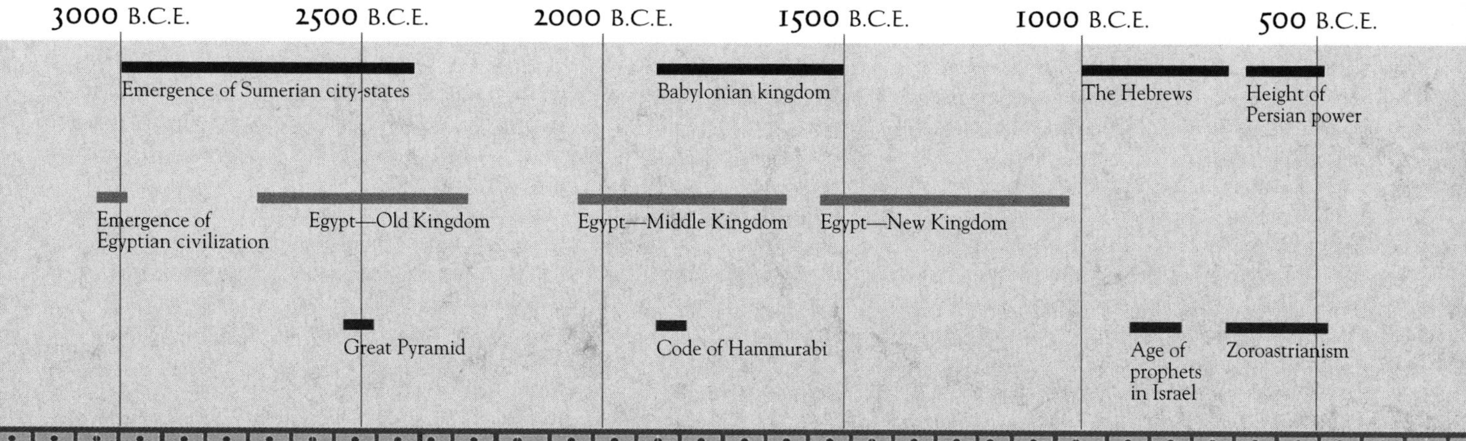

Chapter Notes

1. Quoted in Amélie Kuhrt, *The Ancient Near East, c. 3000–330* B.C. (London, 1995), Vol. 1, p. 68.
2. Quoted in Thorkild Jacobsen, "Mesopotamia," in Henri Frankfort et al., Before Philosophy (Baltimore, 1949), p. 139.
3. James B. Pritchard, Ancient Near Eastern Texts, 3d ed. (Princeton, N.J., 1969), p. 372.
4. Quoted in Milton Covensky, The Ancient Near Eastern Tradition (New York, 1966), p. 51.
5. Quoted in B. G. Trigger, B. J. Kemp, D. O'Connor, and A. B. Lloyd, Ancient Egypt: A Social History (Cambridge, 1983), p. 74.
6. Pritchard, Ancient Near Eastern Texts, p. 34.
7. Ibid., p. 36.
8. Ibid., p. 413.
9. Ibid., p. 420.
10. Quoted in John A. Wilson, The Culture of Ancient Egypt (Chicago, 1956), p. 264.
11. Psalms 137: 1, 4–6.
12. Psalms 145: 8–9.
13. Psalms 121: 2–3.
14. Exodus 20: 13–15.
15. Isaiah 2: 4.
16. Quoted in H. W. F. Saggs, The Might That Was Assyria (London, 1984), pp. 261–62.
17. Quoted in J. M. Cook, The Persian Empire (New York, 1983), p. 32.
18. Herodotus, The Persian Wars, trans. George Rawlinson (New York, 1942), p. 257.
19. Isaiah, 44: 28; 45: 1.
20. Quoted in A. T. Olmstead, History of the Persian Empire (Chicago, 1948), p. 168.
21. Quoted in Cook, The Persian Empire, p. 76.
22. Yasna 44: 3–4, 7, as quoted in A. C. Bouquet, Sacred Books of the World (Harmondsworth, 1954), pp. 111–12.

Suggested Readings

For a beautifully illustrated introduction to the ancient world, see *Past Worlds: The Times Atlas of Archaeology* (Maplewood, N.J., 1988), written by an international group of scholars. The following works are of considerable value in examining the prehistory of humankind: R. Leakey, *The Making of Mankind* (London, 1981); P. Mellars and C. Stringer, *The Human Revolution* (Edinburgh, 1989); and D. O. Henry, *From Foraging to Agriculture* (Philadelphia, 1989).

A fascinating introduction to the world of ancient Near Eastern studies can be found in W. D. Jones, *Venus and Sothis: How the Ancient Near East Was Rediscovered* (Chicago, 1982). A very competent general survey primarily of the political history of Mesopotamia and Egypt is W. W. Hallo and W. K. Simpson, *The Ancient Near East: A History* (New York, 1971). Also valuable are A. B. Knapp, *The History and Culture of Ancient Western Asia and Egypt* (Chicago, 1987); and W. von Soden, *The Ancient Orient: An Introduction to the Study of the Ancient Near East* (Grand Rapids, Mich., 1994). For a detailed survey, see A. Kuhrt, *The Ancient Near East, c. 3000–330* B.C., 2 vols. (London, 1996). H. W. F. Saggs, *Babylonians* (Norman, Okla., 1995) provides an overview of the people of ancient Mesopotamia. On the economic and social history of the ancient Near East, see D. C. Snell, *Life in the Ancient Near East* (New Haven, Conn., 1997). The fundamental collection of translated documents from the ancient Near East is J. B. Pritchard, *Ancient Near Eastern Texts*, 3d ed. with Supplement (Princeton, N.J., 1969).

General works on ancient Mesopotamia include J. N. Postgate, *Early Mesopotamia: Society and Economy at the Dawn of History* (London, 1992); A. L. Oppenheim, *Ancient Mesopotamia*, 2d ed. (Chicago, 1977); and S. Lloyd, *The Archaeology of Mesopotamia*, rev. ed. (London, 1984). A beautifully illustrated survey can be found in M. Roaf, *Cultural Atlas of Mesopotamia and the Ancient Near East* (New York, 1996). The world of the Sumerians has been well described in S. N. Kramer, *The Sumerians* (Chicago, 1963) and *History Begins at Sumer* (New York, 1959). See also the recent summary of the historical and archaeological evidence by H. Crawford, *Sumer and the Sumerians* (Cambridge, 1991). The fundamental work on the spiritual perspective of ancient Mesopotamia is T. Jacobsen, *The Treasures of Darkness: A History of Mesopotamian Religion* (New Haven, Conn., 1976).

For a good introduction to ancient Egypt, see the beautifully illustrated works by J. Baines and J. Málek, *The Cultural Atlas of the World: Ancient Egypt* (Alexandria, Va., 1991); and D. P. Silverman, ed., *Ancient Egypt* (New York, 1997). Other general surveys include N. Grant, *The Egyptians* (New York, 1996); and N. Grimal, *A History of Ancient Egypt*, trans. Ian Shaw (Oxford, 1992). Egyptian religion is covered in S. Morenz, *Egyptian Religion* (London, 1973). The importance of the afterlife in Egyptian civilization is examined in A. Spencer, *Death in Ancient Egypt* (Harmondsworth, 1982). On culture in general, see J. A. Wilson, *The Culture of Ancient Egypt* (Chicago, 1956). The leading authority on the pyramids is I. E. S. Edwards, *The Pyramids of Egypt*, rev. ed. (Harmondsworth, 1976). Daily life in ancient Egypt can be examined in E. Strouhal, *Life of the Ancient Egyptians* (Norman, Okla., 1992). An important new study on women is G. Robins, *Women in Ancient Egypt* (Cambridge, Mass., 1993).

On the Sea Peoples, see the standard work by N. Sanders, *The Sea Peoples: Warriors of the Ancient Mediterranean* (London, 1978). A good introductory survey on the Hittites can be found in O. R. Gurney, *The Hittites*, 2d ed. (Harmondsworth, 1981).

For a good account of Phoenician domestic history and overseas expansion, see D. Harden, *The Phoenicians*, rev. ed. (Harmondsworth, 1980). See also M. E. Aubet, *The Phoenicians and the West: Politics, Colonies and Trade* (Cambridge, 1993). There is an enormous literature on ancient Israel. Two good studies on the archaeological aspects are Y. Aharoni, *The Archaeology of the Land of Israel* (Philadelphia, 1982); and A. Ben-Tor, ed., *The Archaeology of Ancient Israel* (New Haven, 1992). For historical narratives, see especially J. Bright, *A History of Israel*, 3d ed. (Philadelphia, 1981), a fundamental study; the survey by M. Grant, *The History of Ancient Israel* (New York, 1984); and H. Shanks, *Ancient Israel: A Short History from Abraham to the Roman Destruction of the Temple* (Englewood Cliffs, N.J., 1988). For general studies on the religion of the Hebrews, see R. Albertz, *A History of Israelite Religion in the Old Testament Period* (Louisville, Ky., 1994); and W. J. Doorly, *The Religion of Israel* (New York, 1997).

A recent detailed account of Assyrian political, economic, social, military, and cultural history is H. W. F. Saggs, *The Might That Was Assyria* (London, 1984). On one aspect of Assyrian culture, see R. D. Barnett, *Assyrian Sculpture* (Toronto, 1975). The Chaldean empire can be examined in H. W. F. Saggs, *Babylonians* (Norman, Okla., 1995).

The classic work on the Persian Empire is A. T. Olmstead, *History of the Persian Empire* (Chicago, 1948), but a recent work by J. M. Cook, *The Persian Empire* (New York, 1983), provides new material and fresh interpretations on the Persians. Also of value is J. Curtis, *Ancient Persia* (Cambridge, Mass., 1990). On the history of Zoroastrianism, see especially R. C. Zaehner, *The Dawn and Twilight of Zoroastrianism* (London, 1961). Also helpful is M. Boyce, *Zoroastrians: Their Religious Beliefs and Practices* (London, 1979).

For additional reading, go to InfoTrac College Edition, your online research library at http://web1.infotrac-college.com

Enter the search term "Neolithic" using Keywords.

Enter the search term "Mesopotamia" using Keywords.

Enter the search terms "Sumer or Sumerian" using Keywords.

Enter the search term "antiquities" using the Subject Guide.

Enter the search terms "Egypt history" using the Subject Guide.

CHAPTER

2

ANCIENT INDIA

CHAPTER OUTLINE

- BACKGROUND TO THE EMERGENCE OF CIVILIZATION IN INDIA
- HARAPPAN CIVILIZATION: A FASCINATING ENIGMA
- THE ARRIVAL OF THE ARYANS
- ESCAPING THE WHEEL OF LIFE: THE RELIGIOUS WORLD OF ANCIENT INDIA
- THE RULE OF THE FISHES: INDIA AFTER THE MAURYAS
- THE EXUBERANT WORLD OF INDIAN CULTURE
- CONCLUSION

FOCUS QUESTIONS

- What were the chief features of Harappan civilization, and in what ways was it similar to the civilizations that arose in Egypt and Mesopotamia?
- What effects did the Aryans have on Indian civilization?
- What roles did the caste system and the family play in Indian society?
- What are the main tenets of Hinduism and Buddhism, and how did each religion influence Indian civilization?
- Why was India unable to maintain a unified empire in the first millennium B.C.E., and how was the Mauryan Empire temporarily able to overcome the tendencies toward disunity?

Arjuna was despondent as he prepared for battle. In the opposing army were many of his friends and colleagues, some of whom he had known since childhood. In despair he turned for advice to Krishna, his chariot driver, who, unknown to Arjuna, was in actuality an incarnation of the Indian deity Vishnu. "Do not despair of your duty," Krishna advised his friend.

To be born is certain death,
to the dead, birth is certain.
It is not right that you should sorrow
for what cannot be avoided. . . .

If you do not fight this just battle
you will fail in your own law
and in your honor,
and you will incur sin.

Krishna's advice to Arjuna is contained in the Bhagavadgita, one of India's most sacred classical writings, and reflects one of the key tenets in Indian philosophy—the belief in reincarnation, or rebirth of the soul. It also points up the importance of doing one's duty without regard for the consequences. Arjuna was a warrior, and according to Aryan tribal tradition, he was obliged to follow the code of his class. "There is more joy in doing one's own duty badly," advised Krishna, "than in doing another man's duty well."

In advising Arjuna to fulfill his obligation as a warrior, the author of the Bhagavadgita, writing around the second century B.C.E. about a battle that took place almost a thousand years earlier, was by implication urging all readers to adhere to their own responsibility as members of one of India's major classes. Henceforth, this hierarchical vision of a society divided into groups, each with clearly distinct roles, would become a defining characteristic of Indian history.

The Bhagavadgita is part of a larger work that deals with the early history of the Aryan peoples who entered India from beyond the mountains north of the Khyber Pass between 1500 and 1000 B.C.E. When the Aryans arrived, India had already had a thriving civilization for almost two thousand years. The Indus valley civilization, although not as well known today as the civilizations of Mesopotamia and Egypt, was just as old; and its political, social, and cultural achievements were equally impressive. That civilization, known to historians by the names of its two major cities, Harappa and Mohenjo-Daro, emerged in the late fourth millennium B.C.E, flourished for over one thousand years, and then came to an abrupt end about 1500 B.C.E. It was soon replaced by a new society dominated by the Aryan peoples. The new civilization that emerged represented a rich mixture of the two cultures—Harappan and Aryan—and evolved over the next three thousand years into what we know today as India.

Thus, India was and still is a land of diversity. This diversity is evident in its languages and cultures as well as in its physical characteristics. India possesses a bewildering array of languages, few of which are mutually intelligible. It has a deserved reputation, along with the Middle East, as a cradle of religion. Two of the world's major religions, Hinduism and Buddhism, originated in India; and a number of others, including Sikhism and Islam (the latter of which entered the South Asian subcontinent in the ninth or tenth century C.E.), continue to flourish there.

Although today this beautiful mosaic of peoples and cultures has been broken up into a number of separate independent states, the region still possesses a coherent history that, despite its internal diversity, is recognizably Indian. It is to the origins and early development of that culture that we now turn.

Background to the Emergence of Civilization in India

In its size and diversity, India seems more like a continent than a single country. That diversity begins with the geographical environment. The Indian subcontinent, shaped like a spade hanging from the southern ridge of Asia, is composed of a number of core regions. In the far north are the Himalayan and Karakoram mountain ranges, home to the highest mountains in the world. Directly to the south of the Himalayas and the Karakoram range is the rich valley of the Ganges, India's "holy river" and one of the core regions of Indian culture. To the west is the Indus River valley. Today the latter is a relatively arid plateau that forms the backbone of the modern state of Pakistan, but in ancient times it enjoyed a more balanced climate and served as the cradle of Indian civilization.

South of India's two major river valleys lies the Deccan, a region of hills and an upland plateau that extends from the Ganges valley to the southern tip of the Indian subcontinent. The interior of the plateau is relatively hilly and dry, but the eastern and western coasts are occupied by lush plains, which are historically among the most densely populated regions of India. Off the southeastern coast is the island known today as Sri Lanka. Although Sri Lanka is now a separate country quite distinct politically and culturally from India, the island's history is intimately linked with that of its larger neighbor.

In this vast region live a rich mixture of peoples: Dravidians, probably descended from the Indus River culture that flourished at the dawn of Indian civilization, over four thousand years ago; Aryans, descended from the pastoral peoples who flooded southward from Central Asia in the second millennium B.C.E; and hill peoples, who may have lived in the region prior to the rise of organized societies and thus may have been the earliest inhabitants of all.

Harappan Civilization: A Fascinating Enigma

In the 1920s, archaeologists discovered the existence of agricultural settlements dating back well over six thousand years in the lower reaches of the Indus River valley in modern Pakistan. Those small mudbrick villages eventually gave rise to the sophisticated human communities that historians call Harappan civilization. Although today the area is relatively arid, during the third and fourth millennia B.C.E, it evidently received much more abundant rainfall, and the valleys of the Indus River and its tributaries supported a thriving civilization that extended a distance of several hundred miles, from the Himalayas to the

MAP 2.1 Ancient Harappan Civilization

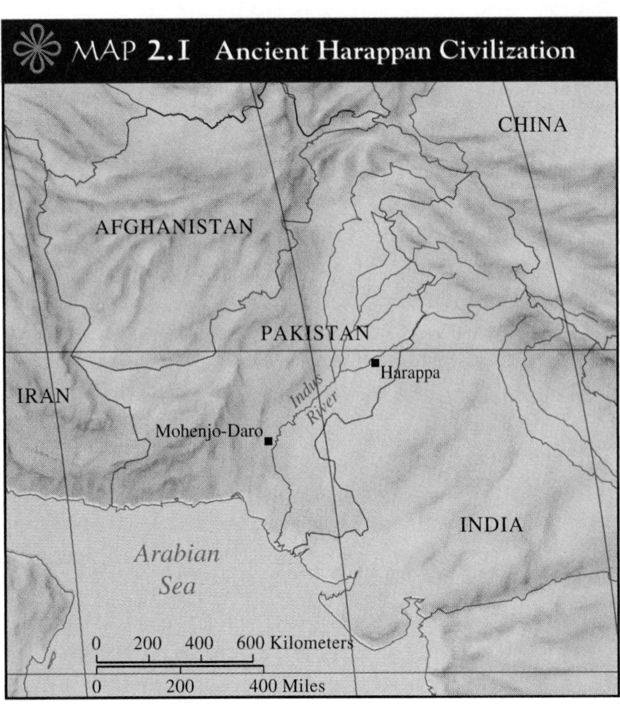

coast of the Indian Ocean. More than seventy sites have been unearthed since the area was first discovered in the 1850s, but the main sites are at the two major cities, Harappa, in the Punjab, and Mohenjo-Daro, nearly four hundred miles to the south near the mouth of the Indus River.

The origin of the Harappans is still debated, but some scholars have suggested on the basis of ethnographic and linguistic analysis that the language and physical characteristics of the Harappans were similar to those of the Dravidian peoples who live in the Deccan Plateau today. If that is so, Harappa is not simply a dead civilization, whose culture and peoples have disappeared into the sands of history, but a part of the living culture of the Indian subcontinent.

Political and Social Structures

In several respects, Harappan civilization closely resembled the cultures of Mesopotamia and the Nile valley. Like them, it probably began in tiny farming villages scattered throughout the river valley, some dating back to as early as 6500 or 7000 B.C.E. These villages thrived and grew until eventually they could support a privileged ruling elite living in walled cities of considerable magnitude and affluence. The center of power was the city of Harappa, which was surrounded by a brick wall over forty feet thick at its base and more than three and one-half miles in circumference. The city was laid out on an essentially rectangular grid, with some streets as wide as thirty feet. Most buildings were constructed of kiln-dried mudbricks and were square in shape, reflecting the grid pattern. At its height, the city may have had as many as 35,000 inhabitants.

Both Harappa and Mohenjo-Daro were divided into large walled neighborhoods, with narrow lanes separating the rows of houses. Houses varied in size, with some as high as three stories, but all followed the same general plan based on a square courtyard surrounded by rooms. Bathrooms featured an advanced drainage system, which carried wastewater out to drains located under the streets and thence to sewage pits beyond the city walls. But the cities also had the equivalent of the modern slum. At Harappa, tiny dwellings for workers have been found near metal furnaces and the open areas used for pounding grain.

Unfortunately, Harappan writing has not yet been deciphered, so historians know relatively little about the organization of the Harappan state. However, recent archaeological evidence suggests that, unlike its contemporaries in Egypt and Sumer, Harappa was not a centralized monarchy with a theocratic base, but a collection of over 1,500 towns and cities loosely connected by ties of trade and alliance. There was no royal precinct or imposing burial monuments, and there are few surviving stone or terra-cotta images that might represent kings, priests, or military commanders. What was once thought to represent a royal residence at Mohenjo-Daro is now considered to be

MAP 2.2 The City of Mohenjo-Daro

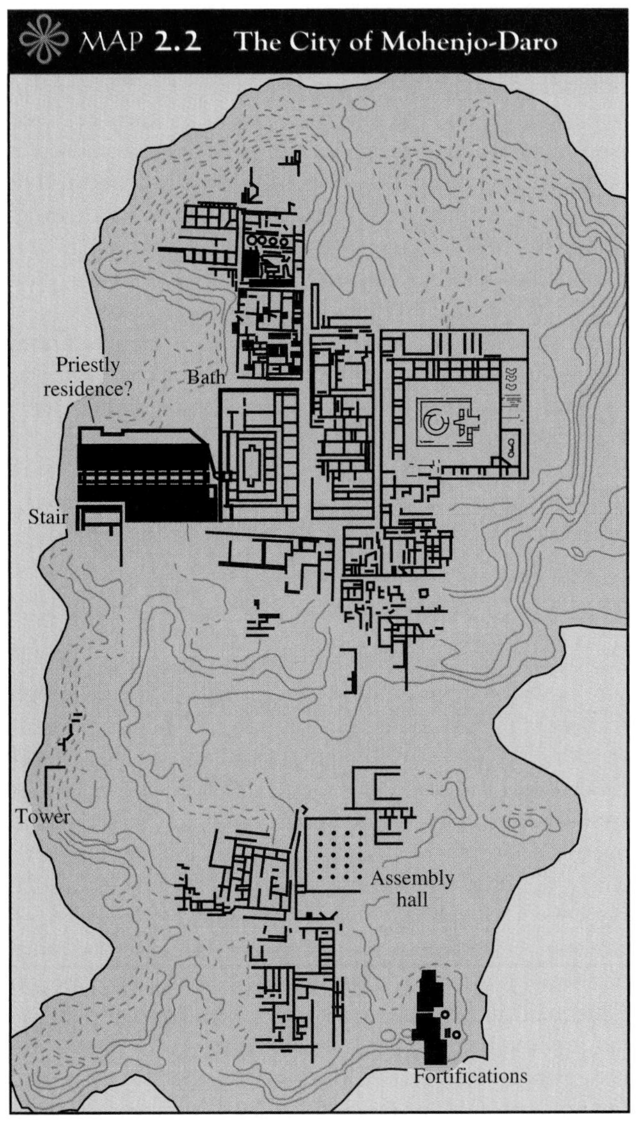

a Buddhist stupa built at the site centuries later. There are clear signs, however, that religious belief had advanced beyond the stage of spirit worship to belief in a single god or goddess of fertility. Presumably, priests at court prayed to this deity to maintain the fertility of the soil and guarantee the annual harvest. At Mohenjo-Daro archaeologists have found an oblong bathing pool, surrounded by a cloister, that was apparently used for purification ceremonies like the tank in a modern Hindu temple.

As in Mesopotamia and Egypt, the Harappan economy was based primarily on agriculture. Wheat, barley, and peas were apparently the primary crops. The presence of cotton seeds at various sites suggests that the Harappan peoples may have been the first to master the cultivation of this useful crop and possibly introduced it to other societies in the region. But Harappa also developed an extensive trading network that extended to Sumer and other civilizations to the west. Textiles and foodstuffs were apparently imported from Sumer in exchange for metals such as copper, lumber, precious stones, and various types of luxury goods. Much of this trade was conducted by ship via the Persian Gulf, although some undoubtedly went by land.

Harappan Culture

Archaeological remains indicate that the Indus valley peoples possessed a culture as sophisticated as that of the Sumerians to the west. Although Harappan architecture was purely functional and shows little artistic sensitivity, the aesthetic quality of some of the pottery and sculpture is superb. Harappan painted pottery, wheel-turned and kiln-fired, rivals equivalent work produced elsewhere. Sculpture, however, represents the Harappans' highest artistic achievement. Some artifacts possess a wonderful vitality of expression. Fired clay seals show a deft touch in

THE CITY OF THE DEAD. Mohenjo-Daro was one of the two major cities of the ancient Indus River civilization. In addition to rows on rows of residential housing, it had a ceremonial center, with a royal palace and a sacred bath that was probably used by the priests as a means of achieving ritual purity. The bath is shown in the center of the photograph here, with the remnants of a Buddhist stupa, constructed centuries later, on the right.

HARAPPAN SEALS. The Harappan peoples, like their contemporaries in Mesopotamia, developed a writing system to record their spoken language. Unfortunately, it has not yet been deciphered. Most extant examples of Harappan writing are found on fired clay seals depicting human figures and animals. These seals have been found in houses and were probably used to identify the owners of goods for sale. Other seals may have been used as amulets or have had other religious significance. Several depict religious figures or ritualistic scenes of sacrifice.

carving animals such as elephants, tigers, rhinoceros, and antelope, and figures made of copper or terra-cotta show a lively sensitivity and a sense of grace and movement that is almost modern.

Unfortunately, the only surviving examples of Harappan writing are the pictographic symbols inscribed on the clay seals. The script contained more than four hundred characters, but most are too stylized to be identified by their shape, and scholars have thus far been unable to decipher them. There are no apparent links with Mesopotamian scripts. Until the script is deciphered, much about the Harappan civilization must remain, as one historian termed it, a fascinating enigma.

The Arrival of the Aryans

One of the great mysteries of Harappan civilization is how it came to an end. Archaeologists working at Mohenjo-Daro have discovered signs of first a gradual decay and then a sudden destruction of the city and its inhabitants, sometime around 1500 B.C.E. Many of the surviving skeletons have been found in postures of running or hiding, reminiscent of the ruins of the Roman city of Pompeii, destroyed by the eruption of Mount Vesuvius in 79 C.E.

These tantalizing signs of flight before a sudden catastrophe have led some scholars to surmise that the city of Mohenjo-Daro (the name was applied by archaeologists and means "city of the dead") and perhaps the remnants of Harappan civilization were destroyed by the Aryans, nomadic peoples from the north, who arrived in the subcontinent around the middle of the second millennium B.C.E. Although the Aryans were almost certainly not as sophisticated culturally as the Harappans, like many nomadic peoples, they excelled at the art of war. As in Mesopotamia and the Nile valley, most contacts between pastoral and agricultural peoples proved to be unstable and ended in armed conflict. Nevertheless, it is doubtful that the Aryan invaders were directly responsible for the final destruction of Mohenjo-Daro. More likely, Harappan civilization had already fallen on hard times, perhaps as a result of climatic change in the Indus valley. Archaeologists have found clear signs of social decay, including evidence of trash in the streets, neglect of public services, and overcrowding in urban neighborhoods. Mohenjo-Daro itself may have been destroyed by an epidemic or by natural phenomena such as floods, an earthquake, or a shift in the course of the Indus River. If that was the case, the Aryans conquered a people whose moment of greatness had already passed.

The Early Aryans

Historians know relatively little about the origins and culture of the Aryans before they entered India, although they were part of the extensive group of Indo-European-speaking peoples who inhabited vast areas in what is now Siberia and the steppes of Central Asia. Whereas other Indo-European-speaking peoples moved westward and eventually settled in Europe, the Aryans moved south across the Hindu Kush into the plains of northern India. Between 1500 and 1000 B.C.E., they gradually advanced eastward from the Indus valley, across the fertile plain of the Ganges, and later southward into the Deccan Plateau until they had eventually extended their political mastery over the entire subcontinent and its Dravidian inhabitants. Nevertheless, the Dravidians survived to remain a prominent element in traditional Indian civilization and play a key role in the creation of modern Indian society.

After they settled in India, the Aryans gradually adapted to the geographical realities of their new homeland and abandoned the pastoral life for agricultural pursuits. They were assisted by the introduction of iron, which probably came from the Middle East, where it had first been introduced by the Hittites (see Chapter 1) about 1500 B.C.E. The invention of the iron plow, along with the development of irrigation, allowed the Aryans and their indigenous subjects to clear the dense jungle growth along the Ganges River and transform the Ganges valley into one of the richest agricultural regions in all of South Asia. The Aryans also developed their first writing system and were thus able to transcribe the legends that previously had been passed down from generation to generation by memory. Most of what is known about the early Aryans is based on oral traditions passed on in the Rigveda, an ancient work that was written down after the Aryans arrived in India (the Rigveda is one of several Vedas, or collections of sacred instructions and rituals).

As in other Indo-European societies, each of the various groups of Aryans were led by a tribal chieftain, called a *raja* ("prince"). The chief was assisted by a council of elders composed of other leading members of the tribe, and like them, he was normally a member of the warrior class, called the *kshatriya*. The chief derived his power from his ability to protect his tribe from rival groups, an ability that was crucial in the warring kingdoms and shifting tribal alliances that were typical of early Aryan society. Though the *rajas* claimed to be representatives of the gods, they were not gods themselves.

As Aryan society grew in size and complexity, the chieftains began to be transformed into kings, usually called *maharajas* ("great princes"). Nevertheless, the tradition that the ruler did not possess absolute authority remained strong. Like all human beings, the ruler was required to follow the *dharma*, a set of laws that set behavioral standards for all individuals and classes in Indian society (see the box on p. 44).

While warring groups squabbled for precedence in India, powerful new empires were rising to the west. First came the Persian Empire of Cyrus and Darius. Then came the Greeks. After two centuries of sporadic rivalry and warfare, the Greeks achieved a brief period of regional dominance in the late fourth century B.C.E. with the rise of Macedonia under Alexander the Great. Alexander had heard of the riches of India, and in 330 B.C.E., after conquering Persia, he launched an invasion of the east (see Chapter 4). In 326 his armies arrived in the plains of northwestern India. They departed almost as suddenly as they had come, leaving in their wake Greek administrators and a veneer of cultural influence that would affect the area for generations to come.

The Mauryan Empire

The Alexandrian conquest was only a brief interlude in the history of the Indian subcontinent, but it played a formative role, for on the heels of Alexander's departure came the rise of the first dynasty to control much of the region. The founder of the new state, who took the royal title Chandragupta Maurya (324–301 B.C.E.), drove out the Greek occupation forces after the departure of Alexander and solidified his control over the northern Indian plain. He established the capital of his new Mauryan Empire at Pataliputra (modern Patna) in the Ganges valley (see the map on p. 54). Little is known of his origins, although some sources say he had originally fought on the side of the invading Greek forces but then angered Alexander with his outspoken advice. Other sources say he may have been the illegitimate son of an Indian king, whom he overthrew to form his own dynasty.

Little, too, is known of Chandragupta Maurya's empire. Most accounts of his reign rely on a work (no longer existing) by Megasthenes, a Greek ambassador to the Mauryan court at Pataliputra in about 302 B.C.E. Chandragupta Maurya was apparently advised by a brilliant court official named Kautilya, whose name has been attached to a treatise on politics called the *Arthasastra*. The work actually dates from a later time, but it may well reflect Kautilya's ideas.

Although the author of the *Arthasastra* follows Aryan tradition in stating that the happiness of the king lies in the happiness of his subjects, the treatise also asserts that when the sacred law of the *dharma* and practical politics collide, the latter must take precedence:

> Whenever there is disagreement between history and sacred law or between evidence and sacred law, then the matter should be settled in accordance with sacred law. But whenever sacred law is in conflict with rational law, then reason shall be held authoritative.[1]

The *Arthasastra* also emphasizes ends rather than means, achieved results rather than the methods employed. For this reason, it has often been compared to the famous political treatise of the Italian Renaissance, Machiavelli's *The Prince*, written over a thousand years later.

NAKED DANCER. Relatively little remains to indicate the creative talents of the Harappan peoples. This five-inch bronze figure of a young dancer in repose is one of the few surviving metal sculptures from Mohenjo-Daro. The detail and grace of her stance reflect the skill of the artist who molded her four thousand years ago.

THE DUTIES OF A KING

Kautilya, India's earliest known political philosopher, was an adviser to the Mauryan rulers. The Arthasastra, *though written down at a later date, very likely reflects his ideas. This passage sets forth some of the necessary characteristics of a king, including efficiency, diligence, energy, compassion, and concern for the security and welfare of the state.*

THE ARTHASASTRA

Only if a king is himself energetically active do his officers follow him energetically. If he is sluggish, they too remain sluggish. And, besides, they eat up his works. He is thereby easily overpowered by his enemies. Therefore, he should ever dedicate himself energetically to activity. . . .

A king should attend to all urgent business; he should not put it off. For what has been thus put off becomes either difficult or altogether impossible to accomplish.

The vow of the king is energetic activity; his sacrifice is constituted of the discharge of his own administrative duties; his sacrificial fee [to the officiating priests] is his impartiality of attitude toward all; his sacrificial consecration is his anointment as king.

In the happiness of the subjects lies the happiness of the king; in their welfare, his own welfare. The welfare of the king does not lie in the fulfillment of what is dear to him; whatever is dear to the subjects constitutes his welfare.

Therefore, ever energetic, a king should act up to the precepts of the science of material gain. Energetic activity is the source of material gain; its opposite, of downfall.

In the absence of energetic activity, the loss of what has already been obtained and of what still remains to be obtained is certain. The fruit of one's works is achieved through energetic activity—one obtains abundance of material prosperity.

At least as described in the *Arthasastra*, Chandragupta Maurya's government was highly centralized and even despotic: "It is power and power alone which, only when exercised by the king with impartiality, and in proportion to guilt, over his son or his enemy, maintains both this world and the next."[2] The king possessed a large army and a secret police responsible to his orders (according to the Greek ambassador Megasthenes, Chandragupta Maurya was chronically fearful of assassination, a not unrealistic concern for someone who had allegedly come to power by violence). Reportedly, all food was tasted in his presence, and he made a practice of never sleeping twice in the same bed in his sumptuous palace. To guard against corruption, a board of censors was empowered to investigate cases of possible malfeasance and incompetence within the bureaucracy.

The ruler's authority beyond the confines of the capital may often have been limited, however. The empire was divided into provinces that were ruled by governors. At first, most of these governors were appointed by and reported to the ruler, but later the position became hereditary. The provinces themselves were divided into districts, each under a chief magistrate appointed by the governor. At the base of the government pyramid was the village, where the vast majority of the Indian people lived. The village was governed by a council of elders; membership in the council was normally hereditary and was shared by the wealthiest families in the village.

Caste and Class: Social Structures in Ancient India

When the Aryans arrived in India, they already possessed a strong class system based on a ruling warrior class. They apparently held the indigenous peoples in some contempt and assigned them to a lower position in society. The result was a set of social institutions and class divisions that have persisted with only minor changes down to the present day.

THE CASTE SYSTEM

At the base of the social system that emerged from the clash of cultures was the concept of the superiority of the invading peoples over their conquered subjects. In a sense, it became an issue of color, because the Aryan invaders, a primarily light-skinned people, were contemptuous of their subjects, who were dark. Light skin came to imply high status, whereas dark skin suggested the opposite.

The concept of color, however, was only the physical manifestation of a division that took place in Indian society on the basis of economic functions. Indian classes (called *varna*, literally, "color," and commonly known as "castes" in English) did not simply reflect an informal division of labor. Instead, they were a set of rigid social classifications that determined not only one's occupation, but also one's status in society and one's hope for ultimate salvation (see Escaping the Wheel of Life later in this chapter). There were five major castes in Indian society in ancient times. At the top were two castes, collectively viewed as the aristocracy, which clearly represented the ruling elites in Aryan society prior to their arrival in India: the priests and the warriors.

The priestly caste, known as the *brahmins*, was usually considered to be at the top of the social scale. Descended from a class of seers who had advised the ruler on religious matters in Aryan tribal society (*brahmin* meant "one possessed of *Brahman*," a term for the supreme god in the Hindu religion), they were eventually transformed into an official class after their religious role declined in importance. The Greek ambassador Megasthenes described this caste as follows:

> From the time of their conception in the womb they are under the care and guardianship of learned men who go to the mother and . . . give her prudent hints and counsels, and the women who listen to them most willingly are thought to be the most fortunate in their offspring. After their birth the children are in the care of one person after another, and as they advance in years their masters are men of superior accomplishments. The philosophers reside in a grove in front of the city within a moderate-sized enclosure. They live in a simple style and lie on pallets of straw and [deer] skins. They abstain from animal food and sexual pleasures, and occupy their time in listening to serious discourse and in imparting knowledge to willing ears.[3]

The second caste was the *kshatriya*, or the warriors. Although often listed below the *brahmins* in social status, many *kshatriyas* were probably descended from the ruling warrior class in Aryan society prior to the conquest of India and thus may have originally ranked socially above the *brahmins*, although they were ranked lower in religious terms. Like the *brahmins*, the *kshatriyas* were originally identified with a single occupation—that of fighting—but as the character of Aryan society changed, they often switched to other forms of employment. At the same time, new conquering families from other castes were sometimes tacitly accepted into the ranks of the warriors.

The third-ranked caste in Indian society was the *vaisya* (literally, "commoner"). The *vaisyas* were usually viewed in economic terms as the merchant caste. Some historians have speculated that the *vaisyas* were originally guardians of the tribal herds, but that after settling in India many moved into commercial pursuits. The Greek observer Megasthenes noted that members of this caste "alone are permitted to hunt and keep cattle and to sell beasts of burden or to let them out on hire. In return for clearing the land of wild beasts and birds which infest sown fields, they receive an allowance of corn from the king. They lead a wandering life and dwell in tents."[4] Although this caste was ranked below the first two in social status, it shared with them the privilege of being considered "twice-born," a term referring to a ceremony at puberty whereby young males were initiated into adulthood and introduced into Indian society. After the ceremony, male members of the top three castes were allowed to wear the "sacred thread" for the remainder of their lives.

Below the three "twice-born" castes were the *sudras*, who represented the great bulk of the Indian population. The *sudras* were not considered fully Aryan, and the term probably originally referred to the conquered Dravidian population. Most *sudras* were peasants or artisans or worked at other forms of manual labor. They had only limited rights in society (see the box on p. 46).

At the lowest level of Indian society, and in fact not even considered a legitimate part of the caste system itself, were the untouchables (also known as outcastes, or *pariahs*). The untouchables probably originated as a slave class consisting of prisoners of war, criminals, tribal minorities, and other groups considered outside Indian society. Even after slavery was outlawed, the untouchables were given menial and degrading tasks that other Indians would not accept, such as collecting trash, handling dead bodies, or serving as butchers or tanners (i.e., handling dead meat). According to the estimate of one historian, they may have comprised somewhat more than 5 percent of the total population of India in antiquity.

The life of the untouchables was extremely demeaning. They were not considered human, and their very presence was considered polluting to members of the other *varna*. No Indian would touch or eat food handled or prepared by an untouchable. Untouchables lived in special ghettos and were required to tap two sticks together to announce their presence when they traveled outside their quarters, so that others could avoid them.

Technically, the caste divisions were absolute. Individuals supposedly were born, lived, and died in the same caste. In practice, some upward or downward mobility probably took place in early times, and as time went on, there was undoubtedly some flexibility in economic functions. But throughout most of Indian history caste taboos remained strict. Members were generally not permitted to marry outside their caste (although, in practice, men were occasionally allowed to marry below their caste, but not above it). At first, attitudes toward the handling of food were relatively loose, but eventually that taboo grew stronger, and social mores dictated that sharing meals and marrying outside one's caste were unacceptable.

The people of ancient India did not belong to a particular caste as individuals, but as part of a larger kin group commonly referred to as the *jati*, a system of large extended families that originated in ancient India and still exists in somewhat changed form today. Although the origins of the *jati* system are unknown, the *jati* eventually became identified with a specific caste living in a specific area and carrying out a specific function in society. Each caste was divided into thousands of separate *jatis*, each with its own separate economic function.

Caste was thus the basic social organization into which traditional Indian society was divided. Each *jati* was itself composed of hundreds if not thousands of individual nuclear families and was governed by its own council of elders. Membership in this ruling council was usually hereditary and was based on the wealth or social status of particular families within the community.

In theory, each *jati* was assigned a particular form of economic activity. Obviously, though, not all families in a given caste could take part in the same vocation, and as time went on, members of a single *jati* commonly engaged in several different lines of work. Sometimes an entire *jati* would have to move its location in order to continue a particular form of activity. In other cases, a *jati* would adopt an entirely new occupation in order to remain in a certain

SOCIAL CLASSES IN ANCIENT INDIA

The Law of Manu *is a set of behavioral norms allegedly prescribed by India's mythical founding ruler Manu. The treatise was probably written in the first or second century* B.C.E. *The following excerpt describes the various social classes in India and their prescribed duties.*

THE *LAW OF MANU*

For the sake of the preservation of this entire creation, the Exceedingly Resplendent One [the Creator of the Universe] assigned separate duties to the classes which had sprung from his mouth, arms, thighs, and feet.

Teaching, studying, performing sacrificial rites, so too making others perform sacrificial rites, and giving away and receiving gifts—these he assigned to the [brahmins].

Protection of the people, giving away of wealth, performance of sacrificial rites, study, and nonattachment to sensual pleasures—these are, in short, the duties of a kshatriya.

Tending of cattle, giving away of wealth, performance of sacrificial rites, study, trade and commerce, usury, and agriculture—these are the occupations of a vaisya.

The Lord has prescribed only one occupation [karma] for a sudra, namely, service without malice of even these other three classes.

Of created beings, those which are animate are the best; of the animate, those which subsist by means of their intellect; of the intelligent, men are the best; and of men, the [brahmins] are traditionally declared to be the best.

The code of conduct—prescribed by scriptures and ordained by sacred tradition—constitutes the highest dharma; hence a twice-born person, conscious of his own Self [seeking spiritual salvation], should be always scrupulous in respect of it.

area. Such changes in habitat or occupation introduced the possibility of movement up or down the social scale. In this way, an entire *jati* could sometimes engage in upward mobility, even though it was not possible for individuals, who were tied to their caste identity for life, to do so.

The caste system may sound highly constricting, but there were persuasive social and economic reasons why it survived for so many centuries. In the first place, it provided an identity for individuals in a highly hierarchical society. Although an individual might rank lower on the social scale than members of other castes, it was always possible to find others ranked at a lower level. Caste was also a means for new groups, such as mountain tribal people, to achieve a recognizable place in the broader community. Perhaps equally important, caste was a primitive form of welfare system. Each *jati* was obliged to provide for any of its members who were poor or destitute. Caste also provided an element of stability in a society that, all too often, was in a state of political anarchy.

DAILY LIFE IN ANCIENT INDIA

Beyond these rigid social stratifications was the Indian family. Not only was life centered around the family, but the family, not the individual, was the most basic unit in society. The ideal was an extended family, with three generations living under the same roof. It was essentially patriarchal, except along the Malabar coast, near the southwestern tip of the subcontinent, where a matriarchal form of social organization prevailed down to modern times. In the rest of India, the oldest male traditionally possessed legal authority over the entire family unit.

The family was linked together in a religious sense by a series of commemorative rites to ancestral members. This ritual originated in the Vedic era and consisted of family ceremonies to honor the departed and to link the living and the dead. The male family head was responsible for leading the ritual. At his death, his eldest son had the duty of conducting the funeral rites.

The importance of the father and the son in family ritual underlined the importance of males in Indian society. Male superiority was expressed in a variety of ways. Women could not serve as priests (although, in practice, some were accepted as seers), nor were they normally permitted to study the Vedas. In general, males had a monopoly on education, since the primary goal of learning to read was to carry on family rituals. In high-class families, young men, after having been initiated into the sacred thread, began Vedic studies with a *guru* (teacher). Some then went on to higher studies in one of the major cities. The goal of such an education might be either professional or religious. Such young men were not supposed to marry until after twelve years of study.

In general, only males could inherit property, except in a few cases where there were no sons. According to law, a woman was always considered a minor. Divorce was prohibited, although it sometimes took place. According to the *Arthasastra,* a wife who had been deserted by her husband could seek a divorce. Polygamy was fairly rare and apparently occurred mainly among the higher classes, but husbands were permitted to take a second wife if the first was barren. Producing children was an important aspect of marriage, both because they provided security for their parents in old age and because they were a physical proof of male potency. Child marriage was common for young girls, whether because of the desire for children or because daughters represented an economic liability to their parents. But perhaps the most graphic symbol of women's subjection to men was the ritual of *sati* (often written *suttee*), which required the wife to throw herself on her dead husband's funeral pyre. The Greek visitor Megasthenes reported "that he had heard from some persons of wives burning themselves along with their deceased husbands and doing so gladly; and that those women who refused to burn themselves were held in disgrace." All in all, it was undoubtedly a difficult existence. According to the *Law of Manu*, an early treatise on social organization and behavior in ancient India, probably written in the first or second century B.C.E., women were subordinated to men, first to their father, then to their husband, and finally to their sons:

She should do nothing independently
even in her own house.
In childhood subject to her father,
in youth to her husband,
and when her husband is dead to her sons,
she should never enjoy independence. . . .

She should always be cheerful,
and skillful in her domestic duties,
with her household vessels well cleansed,
and her hand tight on the purse strings. . . .

In season and out of season
her lord, who wed her with sacred rites,
ever gives happiness to his wife,
both here and in the other world.

Though he be uncouth and prone to pleasure,
though he have no good points at all,
the virtuous wife should ever
worship her lord as a god.[5]

At the root of female subordination to the male was the practical fact that, as in most agricultural societies, men did most of the work in the fields. Females were viewed as having little utility outside the home and indeed were considered an economic burden, since parents were obliged to provide a dowry to acquire a husband for a daughter. Female children also appeared to offer little advantage in maintaining the family unit, since they joined the families of their husbands after the wedding ceremony.

Despite all of these indications of female subjection to the male, there are numerous signs that in some ways, women often played an influential role in Indian society, and the Hindu code of behavior stressed that they should be treated with respect (see the box on p. 48). Indians appeared to be fascinated by female sexuality, and tradition held that women often used their sexual powers to achieve domination over men. The author of the Mahabharata, a vast epic of early Indian society, complained that "the fire has never too many logs, the ocean never too many rivers, death never too many living souls, and fair-eyed woman never too many men." Despite the legal and social constraints, women often played an important role within the family unit, and many were admired and honored for their talents. It is probably significant that paintings and sculpture from ancient and medieval India frequently show women in a role equal to that of men, and the tradition of the henpecked husband is as prevalent in India as in many Western societies (see the box on p. 49).

Homosexuality was not unknown in India. It was condemned in the law books, however, and generally ignored by literature, which devoted its attention entirely to erotic heterosexuality. The *Kamasutra*, a textbook on sexual practices and techniques dating from the second century C.E. or slightly thereafter, mentions homosexuality briefly and with no apparent enthusiasm.

The Economy

The Aryan conquest did not drastically change the economic character of Indian society. Not only did most Aryans take up farming, but it is likely that agriculture expanded rapidly under Aryan rule with the invention of the iron plow and the spread of northern Indian culture into the Deccan Plateau. One consequence of this process was to shift the focus of Indian culture from the Indus valley further eastward to the Ganges River valley, which even today is one of the most densely populated regions on earth. The flatter areas in the Deccan Plateau and in the coastal plains were also turned into cropland.

For most Indian farmers, life was harsh indeed. Among the most fortunate were those who owned their own land, although they were, of course, required to pay taxes to the state. Many others were sharecroppers or landless laborers. They were subject to the vicissitudes of the market and often paid exorbitant rents to their landlord. Concentration of land in large holdings was limited by the tradition of dividing property among all the sons, but large estates worked by hired laborers or rented out to sharecroppers were not uncommon, particularly in areas where local *rajas* derived much of their wealth from their property.

Another problem for Indian farmers was the unpredictability of the climate. India is in the monsoon zone. The monsoon is a seasonal wind pattern in southern Asia that blows from the southwest during the summer months and from the northeast during the winter. The southwest monsoon is commonly marked by heavy rains. When the rains were late, thousands starved, particularly in the drier areas, which were especially dependent on rainfall. Strong governments attempted to deal with such problems by building state-operated granaries and maintaining the irrigation works, but strong governments were rare and famine was probably all too common. The staple crops in the north were wheat, barley, and millet, with wet rice common in the fertile river valleys. In the south, grain and vegetables were supplemented by various tropical products, cotton, and spices such as pepper, ginger, cinnamon, and saffron.

By no means were all Indians farmers. As time passed, India became one of the most advanced trading and manufacturing civilizations in the ancient world. After the rise

THE POSITION OF WOMEN IN ANCIENT INDIA

The ambivalence toward women in ancient India is apparent in this passage from the Law of Manu, *which states that men should respect women. At the same time, it also makes clear that women's place is in the home. Legal and religious texts delineated the prescribed conduct of women from birth to death, with precise formulae for healing, safe birth, how to love a man, even the ritual for celebrating a baby's first tooth.*

THE *LAW OF MANU*

Women must be honored and adorned by their father, brothers, husbands, and brothers-in-law who desire great good fortune.

Where women, verily, are honored, there the gods rejoice; where, however, they are not honored, there all sacred rites prove fruitless.

Where the female relations live in grief—that family soon perishes completely; where, however, they do not suffer from any grievance—that family always prospers. . . .

Her father protects her in childhood, her husband protects her in youth, her sons protect her in old age—a woman does not deserve independence.

The father who does not give away his daughter in marriage at the proper time is censurable; censurable is the husband who does not approach his wife in due season; and after the husband is dead, the son, verily, is censurable, who does not protect his mother.

Even against the slightest provocations should women be particularly guarded; for unguarded they would bring grief to both the families.

Regarding this as the highest dharma of all four classes, husbands, though weak, must strive to protect their wives.

His own offspring, character, family, self, and dharma does one protect when he protects his wife scrupulously. . . .

The husband should engage his wife in the collection and expenditure of his wealth, in cleanliness, in dharma, in cooking food for the family, and in looking after the necessities of the household. . . .

Women destined to bear children, enjoying great good fortune, deserving of worship, the resplendent lights of homes on the one hand and divinities of good luck who reside in the houses on the other—between these there is no difference whatsoever.

of the Mauryas, India's role in regional trade began to expand, and the subcontinent became a major transit point in a vast commercial network that extended from the rim of the Pacific to the Middle East and the Mediterranean Sea. This regional trade went both by sea and by camel caravan. Maritime trade across the Indian Ocean may have begun as early as the fifth century B.C.E. It extended eastward as far as Southeast Asia and China and southward as far as the straits between Africa and the island of Madagascar. Westward went spices, perfumes, jewels, textiles, precious stones and ivory, and wild animals. In return, India received gold, tin, lead, and wine.

India's expanding role as a manufacturing and commercial hub of the ancient world was undoubtedly a spur to the growth of the state. Under Chandragupta Maurya, the central government became actively involved in commercial and manufacturing activities. It owned mines and vast crown lands and undoubtedly earned massive profits from its role in regional commerce. Separate government departments were established for trade, agriculture, mining, and the manufacture of weapons, and the movement of private goods was vigorously taxed. Nevertheless, a significant private sector also flourished; it was dominated by great caste guilds, which monopolized key sectors of the economy. A money economy probably came into operation during the second century B.C.E., when copper and gold coins were introduced from the Middle East. This in turn led to the development of banking. But village trade continued to be conducted by means of cowry shells (a highly polished shell used as a medium of exchange throughout much of Africa and Asia) or barter throughout the ancient period.

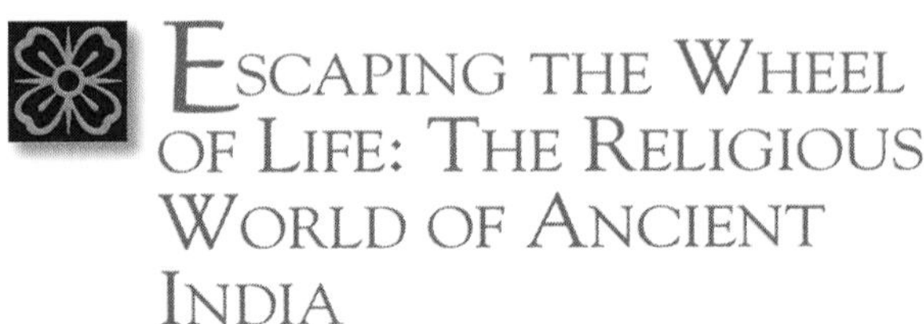

Escaping the Wheel of Life: The Religious World of Ancient India

Like Indian politics and society, Indian religion is a blend of Aryan and Dravidian culture. The clash and subsequent intermingling of those two civilizations gave rise to an extraordinarily complex set of religious beliefs and practices, filled with diversity and contrast. Out of this cultural mix came two of the world's great religions, Buddhism and Hinduism, and several smaller ones, including Jainism and Sikhism.

Hinduism

Evidence about the earliest religious beliefs of the Aryan peoples comes primarily from sacred texts such as the Vedas, a set of four collections of hymns and religious ceremonies transmitted by memory through the centuries by Aryan priests. Many of these religious ideas were probably common to all of the Indo-European peoples before their separation into different groups at least four thousand years

THE HENPECKED MONK

Women were often portrayed in traditional Indian literature as seductresses, luring innocent males from following their higher spiritual nature. This passage is from the Sutrakrtanga, *one of the sacred books of the Jain religion. While the object of concern is technically not that familiar figure of ridicule, the henpecked husband, the passage indicates the concern that many men in ancient India felt when exposed to the wiles of their female contemporaries.*

THE SUTRAKRTANGA

A celibate monk shouldn't fall in love,
and though he hankers after pleasure he should hold himself in check,
for these are the pleasures
which some monks enjoy.

If a monk breaks his vows,
and falls for a woman,
she upbraids him and raises her foot to him,
and kicks him on the head.

"Monk, if you won't live with me
as husband and wife,
I'll pull out my hair and become a nun,
for you shall not live without me!"

But when she has him in her clutches
it's all housework and errands!

"Fetch a knife to cut this gourd!"
"Get me some fresh fruit!"

"We want wood to boil the greens,
and for a fire in the evening!"
"Now paint my feet!"
"Come and massage my back!". . .

"Bring me the chair with the twine seat,
and my wooden-soled slippers to go out walking!"
So pregnant women boss their husbands,
just as though they were household slaves.

When a child is born, the reward of their labors,
she makes the father hold the baby.
And sometimes the fathers of sons
stagger under their burdens like camels.

They get up at night, as though they were nurses,
to lull the howling child to sleep,
and, though they are shamefaced about it,
scrub dirty garments, just like washermen. . . .

So, monks, resist the wiles of women;
avoid their friendship and company.
The little pleasure you get from them
will only lead you into trouble!

ago. Early Aryan beliefs were based on the common concept of a pantheon of gods and goddesses representing great forces of nature similar to the immortals of Greek mythology. The Aryan ancestor of the Greek father-god Zeus, for example, may have been the deity known in early Aryan tradition as Dyaus (see Chapter 4).

The parent god Dyaus was a somewhat distant figure, however, who was eventually overshadowed by other, more functional gods possessing more familiar human traits. For a while, the primary Aryan god was the great warrior god Indra. Indra summoned the Aryan tribal peoples to war and was represented in nature by thunder. Later, Indra declined in importance and was replaced by Varuna, lord of justice, who eventually evolved into the modern deity Vishnu. Other gods and goddesses represented various forces of nature or the needs of human beings, such as fire, fertility, wealth, and so forth.

The concept of sacrifice was a key element in Aryan religious belief in Vedic times. As in many other ancient cultures, the practice may have begun as human sacrifice, but later animals were used as substitutes, although human sacrifice was practiced in some isolated communities down to modern times. The priestly class, or *brahmins*, played a key role in these ceremonies.

Another element of Aryan religious belief in ancient times was the ideal of asceticism. By the sixth century B.C.E., self-sacrifice or even self-mutilation had begun to replace sacrifice as a means of placating or communicating with the gods. Apparently, the original motive for asceticism was to achieve magical powers, but later, in the Upanishads (a set of commentaries on the Vedas compiled in the sixth century B.C.E.), it was seen as a means of spiritual meditation that would enable the practitioner to reach beyond material reality to a world of truth and bliss beyond earthly joy and sorrow:

> Those who practice penance and faith in the forest, the tranquil ones, the knowers of truth, living the life of wandering mendicancy—they depart, freed from passion, through the door of the sun, to where dwells, verily . . . the imperishable Soul.[6]

It is possible that another motive was to permit those with strong religious convictions to communicate directly with metaphysical reality without having to rely on the priestly class at court.

Asceticism, of course, has been practiced in other religions, including Christianity and Islam, but it seems particularly identified with Hinduism, the religion that

FEMALE EARTH SPIRIT. This 2,200-year-old earth spirit, a sandstone gatepost from the Buddhist stupa at Bharhut, illustrates how earlier Indian representations of the fertility goddess were incorporated into Buddhist art. Women were revered as powerful fertility symbols and considered dangerous when menstruating or after having given birth. Voluptuous and idealized, these earth spirits could allegedly cause a tree to blossom if they merely touched a branch with their arm or wrapped a leg around its trunk. Graceful and sensuous, this female spirit seems to be breathing and moving out of the stone.

emerged from early Indian religious tradition. Eventually, asceticism evolved into the modern practice of body training that we know as *yoga* (union), which is accepted today as a meaningful element of Hindu religious practice.

Eventually, as Indians began to speculate about the nature of the cosmic order, they came to believe in the existence of a single monistic force in the universe, a form of ultimate reality called *Brahman*. Today the early form of Hinduism is sometimes called Brahmanism. In the Upanishads, the concept began to emerge as an important element of Indian religious belief. It was the duty of the individual self—called the *Atman*—to achieve an understanding of this ultimate reality so that after death the self would merge in spiritual form with *Brahman*. Sometimes *Brahman* was described in more concrete terms as a creator god—eventually known as Vishnu—but more often in terms of a shadowy ultimate reality. According to one of the Upanishads,

> In the beginning, my dear, this world was just being, one only, without a second. Some people, no doubt, say: "In the beginning, verily, this world was just nonbeing, one only, without a second; from that nonbeing, being was produced." But how, indeed, my dear, could it be so? said he. How could being be produced from nonbeing?
>
> On the contrary, my dear, in the beginning this world was being alone, one only, without a second. Being thought to itself: "May I be many, may I procreate." It produced fire. That fire thought to itself: "May I be many, may I procreate." It produced water. Therefore, whenever a person grieves or perspires, then it is from fire [heat] alone that water is produced. That water thought to itself: "May I be many; may I procreate." It produced food. Therefore, whenever it rains, then there is abundant food; it is from water alone that food for eating is produced. . . . That divinity (Being) thought to itself: "Well, having entered into these three divinities [fire, water, and food] by means of this living self, let me develop names and forms.[7]

REINCARNATION

Another new concept also probably began to appear around the time the Upanishads were written—the idea of reincarnation. This is the idea that the individual soul is reborn in a different form after death and progresses through several existences on the wheel of life until it reaches its final destination in a union with the Great World Soul, known as *Brahman*. Because life is harsh, this final release is the objective of all living souls.

A key element in this process is the idea of *karma*—that one's rebirth in a next life is determined by one's *karma* (actions) in this life. Hinduism places all living species on a vast scale of existence, including the four classes and the untouchables in human society. The current status of an individual soul, then, is not simply a cosmic accident, but the inevitable result of actions that that soul has committed in a past existence.

At the top of the scale are the *brahmins* (the priestly caste), who by definition are closest to ultimate release from the law of reincarnation. The *brahmins* are followed in descending order by the other castes in human society and the world of the beasts. Within the animal kingdom, an especially high position is reserved for the cow, which even today is revered by Hindus as a sacred beast. Some have speculated that the unique role played by the cow in Hinduism derives from the value of cattle in Aryan pastoral society. But others have pointed out that cattle were a source of both money and food and suggest that the cow's sacred position may have descended from the concept of the sacred bull in Dravidian culture.

The concept of *karma* is governed by the *dharma*, or the Law. A law regulating human behavior, the *dharma* imposes different requirements on different individuals depending on their status in society. Those high on the social scale, such as *brahmins* and *kshatriyas*, are held to a more strict form of behavior than are *sudras*. The *brahmin*, for example, is expected to abstain from eating meat, because that would entail the killing of another living being, thus interrupting its *karma*.

How the concept of reincarnation originated is not known, although it was apparently not unusual for early peoples to believe that the individual soul would be reborn in a different form in a later life. In any case, in India the concept may have had practical causes as well as consequences. In the first place, it tended to provide religious sanction for the rigid class divisions that had begun to emerge in Indian society after the Aryan conquest, and it provided moral and political justification for the privileges of those on the higher end of the scale.

At the same time, the concept of reincarnation provided certain compensations for those lower on the ladder of life. For example, it gave hope to the poor that if they behaved properly in this life, they might improve their condition in the next. It also provided a means for unassimilated groups such as tribal peoples to find a place in Indian society while at the same time permitting them to maintain their distinctive way of life.

The ultimate goal of achieving "good" *karma*, as we have seen, was to escape the cycle of existence. To the sophisticated, the nature of that release was a spiritual union of the individual soul with the Great World Soul, *Brahman*, described in the Upanishads as a form of dreamless sleep, free from earthly desires. Such a concept, however, was undoubtedly too ethereal for the average Indian, who needed a more concrete form of heavenly salvation, a place of beauty and bliss after a life of disease and privation.

It was probably for this reason that the Hindu religion—in some ways so otherworldly and ascetic—came to be peopled with a multitude of very human gods and goddesses. It has been estimated that the Hindu pantheon contains more than 33,000 deities. Only a small number are primary ones, however, notably the so-called trinity of gods: Brahman the Creator, Vishnu the Preserver, and Siva (originally the Vedic god Rudra) the Destroyer. Although Brahman (sometimes in his concrete form called Brahma) is considered to be the highest god, Vishnu and Siva take

DANCING SIVA. The Hindu deity Siva is often presented in the form of a bronze statue, performing his cosmic dance in which he simultaneously creates and destroys the universe. While his upper right hand creates the cosmos, his upper left hand reduces it in flames, and the lower two hands offer eternal blessing. Siva's dancing statues present to his followers the visual message of his power and compassion.

precedence in the devotional exercises of many Hindus, who can be roughly divided into Vishnuites and Saivites. In addition to the trinity of gods, all of whom have wives with readily identifiable roles and personalities, there are countless minor deities, each again with his or her own specific function, such as bringing good fortune, arranging a good marriage, or guaranteeing a son in childbirth.

The rich variety and earthy character of many Hindu deities are repugnant to many Christians and Muslims, to whom God is an all-seeing and transcendent deity. Many Hindus, however, regard the multitude of gods as simply different manifestations of one ultimate reality. The various deities also provide a useful means for ordinary Indians to personify their religious feelings. Even though some individuals among the early Aryans attempted to communicate with the gods through sacrifice or asceticism, most Indians undoubtedly sought to satisfy their own individual religious needs through devotion, which they expressed through ritual ceremonies and offerings at a Hindu temple. Such offerings were not only a way to seek salvation, but also a means of satisfying all the aspirations of daily life.

Over the centuries, then, Hinduism changed radically from its origins in Aryan tribal society and became a religion of the vast majority of the Indian people. Concern with a transcendental union between the individual soul and the Great World Soul contrasted with practical desires for material wealth and happiness; ascetic self-denial contrasted with an earthy emphasis on the pleasures and values of sexual union between marriage partners. All of these became aspects of Hinduism, the religion of 70 percent of the Indian people.

Buddhism: The Middle Path

In the sixth century B.C.E, a new doctrine appeared in northern India that soon began to rival Hinduism's popularity throughout the subcontinent. This new doctrine was called Buddhism. The historical founder of Buddhism, Siddhartha Gautama, was a native of a small principality in the foothills of the Himalaya Mountains in what is today southern Nepal. He was born in the mid-sixth century B.C.E, the son of a ruling *kshatriya* family. According to tradition, the young Siddhartha was raised in affluent surroundings and trained, like many other members of his class, in the martial arts. On reaching maturity, he married and began to raise a family. However, at the age of twenty-nine he suddenly discovered the pain of illness, the sorrow of death, and the degradation caused by old age in the lives of ordinary people and exclaimed: "Would that sickness, age, and death might be forever bound!" From that time on, he decided to dedicate his life to determining the cause and seeking the cure for human suffering.

To find the answers to these questions, Siddhartha abandoned his home and family and traveled widely. At first he tried to follow the model of the ascetics, but he eventually decided that self-mortification did not lead to a greater understanding of life and abandoned the practice. Then one day after a lengthy period of meditation under a tree, he finally achieved enlightenment as to the meaning of life and spent the remainder of his life preaching it. His conclusions, as embodied in his teachings, became the philosophy (or, as some would have it, the religion) of Buddhism. According to legend, the Devil (the Indian term is *Mara*) attempted desperately to tempt him with political power and the company of beautiful girls. But Siddhartha Gautama resisted:

> *Pleasure is brief as a flash of lightning*
> *Or like an autumn shower, only for a moment. . . .*
> *Why should I then covet the pleasures you speak of?*
> *I see your bodies are full of all impurity:*
> *Birth and death, sickness and age are yours.*
> *I seek the highest prize, hard to attain by men—*
> *The true and constant wisdom of the wise.*[8]

How much the modern doctrine of Buddhism resembles the original teachings of Siddhartha Gautama is open to debate, since much time has elapsed since his death and original texts relating his ideas are lacking. Nor is it certain that Siddhartha Gautama even intended to found a new religion or doctrine. In some respects, his ideas could be viewed as a reformist form of Hinduism, much as Martin Luther saw Protestantism as a reformation of Christianity. Siddhartha accepted much of the belief system of Hinduism, if not all of its practices. For example, he accepted the concept of reincarnation and the role of *karma* as a means of influencing the movement of individual souls up and down in the scale of life. He followed Hinduism in praising nonviolence and borrowed the idea of living a life of simplicity and chastity from the ascetics. Moreover, his vision of metaphysical reality—commonly known as Nirvana—is closer to the Hindu concept of *Brahman* than it is to the Christian concept of heavenly salvation. Nirvana, which involves an extinction of selfhood and a final reunion with the Great World Soul, is sometimes likened to a dreamless sleep or to a kind of "blowing out" (as of a candle). Buddhists occasionally remark that someone who asks for a description does not understand the concept.

At the same time, the new doctrine differed from existing Hindu practices in a number of key ways. In the first place, Siddhartha denied the existence of an individual soul. To him, the Hindu concept of *Atman*—the individual soul—meant that the soul was subject to rebirth and thus did not achieve a complete liberation from the cares of this world. In fact, Siddhartha denied the ultimate reality of the material world in its entirety and taught that humans' physical surroundings are an illusion to be transcended. Siddhartha's idea of achieving Nirvana was based on his conviction that the pain, poverty, and sorrow that afflict human beings are caused essentially by their attachment to the things of this world. Once worldly cares are abandoned, pain and sorrow can be forgotten. With this knowledge comes *bodhi*, or wisdom (thus, the term Buddhism and the familiar name of Gautama Buddha, or Gautama the Wise, for Siddhartha Gautama).

Achieving this understanding is a key step on the road to Nirvana, which, as in Hinduism, is a form of release from the wheel of life. According to tradition, Siddhartha transmitted this message in a sermon to his disciples in a deer park at Sarnath, not far from the modern city of Benares (also known as Varanasi). Like so many messages, it is deceptively simple and is enclosed in four noble truths: life is suffering; suffering is caused by desire; the way to end suffering is to end desire; and the way to end desire is to avoid the extremes of a life of vulgar materialism and a life of self-torture and to follow the "Middle Path." This Middle Path, which is also known as the Eightfold Way, calls for right knowledge, right purpose, right speech, right conduct, right occupation, right effort, right awareness, and right meditation (see the box on p. 53).

HOW TO ACHIEVE ENLIGHTENMENT

One of the most famous passages in Buddhist literature is the sermon at Sarnath, which Siddhartha Gautama delivered to his followers in a deer park outside the holy city of Varanasi (Benares), in the Ganges River valley. Here he set forth the key ideas that would define Buddhist beliefs for centuries to come.

THE SERMON AT BENARES

Thus have I heard: at one time the Lord dwelt at Benares at Isipatana in the Deer Park. There the Lord addressed the five monks:—

"These two extremes, monks, are not to be practiced by one who has gone forth from the world. What are the two? That conjoined with the passions and luxury, low, vulgar, common, ignoble, and useless; and that conjoined with self-torture, painful, ignoble, and useless. Avoiding these two extremes the Tathagata has gained the enlightenment of the Middle Path, which produces insight and knowledge and tends to calm, to higher knowledge, enlightenment, Nirvana.

"And what, monks, is the Middle Path, of which the Tathagata has gained enlightenment, which produces insight and knowledge, and tends to calm, to higher knowledge, enlightenment, Nirvana? This is the noble Eightfold Way: namely, right view, right intention, right speech, right action, right livelihood, right effort, right mindfulness, right concentration. This, monks, is the Middle Path, of which the Tathagata has gained enlightenment, which produces insight and knowledge, and tends to calm, to higher knowledge, enlightenment, Nirvana.

1. "Now this, monks, is the noble truth of pain: birth is painful, old age is painful, sickness is painful, death is painful, sorrow, lamentation, dejection, and despair are painful. Contact with unpleasant things is painful, not getting what one wishes is painful. In short the five groups of graspings are painful.
2. Now this, monks, is the noble truth of the cause of pain: the craving, which tends to rebirth, combined with pleasure and lust, finding pleasure here and there; namely, the craving for passion, the craving for existence, the craving for nonexistence.
3. Now this, monks, is the noble truth of the cessation of pain, the cessation without a remainder of craving, the abandonment, forsaking, release, nonattachment.
4. Now this, monks, is the noble truth of the way that leads to the cessation of pain: this is the noble Eightfold Way; namely, right view, right intention, right speech, right action, right livelihood, right effort, right mindfulness, right concentration.

"And when, monks, in these four noble truths my due knowledge and insight with its three sections and twelve divisions was well purified, then monks . . . I had attained the highest complete enlightenment. This I recognized. Knowledge arose in me, insight arose that the release of my mind is unshakable; this is my last existence; now there is no rebirth."

Buddhism also differed from Hinduism in its relative egalitarianism. Although Siddhartha accepted the idea of reincarnation (and thereby the idea that human beings differ as a result of *karma* accumulated in a previous existence), he rejected the Hindu division of humanity into rigidly defined castes based on previous reincarnations and taught that all human beings could aspire to Nirvana as a result of their behavior in this life—a message that likely helped Buddhism win support among people at the lower end of the social scale.

In addition, Buddhism was much simpler than Hinduism. Siddhartha rejected the panoply of gods that had become identified with Hinduism and forbade his followers to worship his person or his image after his death. In fact, many Buddhists view Buddhism as a philosophy rather than a religion.

After Siddhartha Gautama's death in 480 B.C.E., dedicated disciples carried his message the length and breadth of India. Buddhist monasteries were established throughout the subcontinent, and temples and stupas (stone towers housing relics of the Buddha) sprang up throughout the countryside.

Women were permitted to join the monastic order but only in an inferior position. As Siddhartha had explained, "Women are soon angered . . . women are full of passion . . . women are stupid . . . That is the reason . . . why women have no place in public assemblies . . . and do not earn their living by any profession." Still, the position of women tended to be better in Buddhist societies than it was elsewhere in ancient India (see the box on p. 54).

During the next centuries, Buddhism began to compete actively with Hindu beliefs, as well as with another new faith known as Jainism. Jainism was founded by Mahavira, a contemporary of Siddhartha Gautama. Resembling Buddhism in its rejection of the reality of the material world, Jainism was more extreme in practice. Where Siddhartha Gautama called for the "middle way" between passion and luxury and pain and self-torture, Mahavira preached a doctrine of extreme simplicity to his followers, who kept no possessions and relied on begging for a living. Some even

THE VOICES OF SILENCE

Most of what is known about the lives of women in ancient India comes from the Vedas, or from other texts written by men. Classical Sanskrit was the exclusive property of upper-caste males for use in religious and court functions. There are a few examples of women's writings, however, that date from this period. In the first poem quoted below, a Buddhist nun living in the sixth century B.C.E. *reflects on her sense of spiritual salvation and physical release from the drudgery of daily life. The remaining two poems were produced several hundred years later in southern India by anonymous female authors at a time when strict Hindu traditions had not yet been established in the area. Poetry and song were an essential part of daily life, as women sang while working in the fields, drawing water at the well, or reflecting on the hardships of their daily lives. The second poem quoted below breathes the sensuous joy of sex, while the third expresses the simultaneous grief and pride of a mother as she sends her only son off to war.*

"A WOMAN WELL SET FREE! HOW FREE I AM"

A woman well set free! How free I am,
How wonderfully free, from kitchen drudgery.
Free from the harsh grip of hunger,
And from empty cooking pots,
Free too of that unscrupulous man,
The weaver of sunshades.
Calm now, and serene I am,
All lust and hatred purged.
To the shade of the spreading trees I go
And contemplate my happiness.

Translated by Uma Chakravarti and Kumkum Roy

"WHAT SHE SAID TO HER GIRLFRIEND"

What she said to her girlfriend:
On beaches washed by seas
older than the earth,
in the groves filled with bird-cries,
on the banks shaded by a punnai
clustered with flowers,
when we made love
my eyes saw him
and my ears heard him;

my arms grow beautiful
in the coupling
and grow lean
as they come away.
What shall I make of this?

Translated by A. K. Ramanujan

"HER PURPOSE IS FRIGHTENING, HER SPIRIT CRUEL"

Her purpose is frightening, her spirit cruel.
That she comes from an ancient house is fitting, surely.
In the battle the day before yesterday,
her father attacked an elephant and died there on the field.
In the battle yesterday,
her husband faced a row of troops and fell.
And today,
she hears the battle drum,
and, eager beyond reason, gives him a spear in his hand,
wraps a white garment around him,
smears his dry tuft with oil,
and, having nothing but her one son,
"Go!" she says, sending him to battle.

Translated by George L. Hart III

rejected clothing and wandered through the world naked. Perhaps because of its insistence on a life of poverty, Jainism failed to attract enough adherents to become a major doctrine and never received official support. According to tradition, however, Chandragupta Maurya accepted Mahavira's doctrine after abdicating the throne and fasted to death in a Jain monastery.

ASOKA, A BUDDHIST MONARCH

Buddhism received an important boost when Asoka, the grandson of Chandragupta Maurya, converted to Buddhism sometime in the third century B.C.E. Asoka (269–232 B.C.E) is generally considered to be the greatest ruler in the history of India. Reportedly, Asoka began his reign conquering, pillaging, and killing, but after his conversion to Buddhism, he began to regret his bloodthirsty past and attempted to rule benevolently.

Asoka directed that banyan trees and shelters be placed along the road to provide shade and rest for weary travelers. He sent Buddhist missionaries throughout India and ordered the erection of stone pillars with official edicts and Buddhist inscriptions to instruct people in the proper way. According to tradition, his son converted the island of Sri Lanka to Buddhism, and the peoples there accepted a tributary relationship with the Mauryan Empire.

The Rule of the Fishes: India After the Mauryas

After Asoka's death in 232 B.C.E., the Mauryan Empire began to decline. In 183 B.C.E., the last Mauryan ruler was overthrown by one of his military commanders, and India slipped back into disunity. A number of new kingdoms, some of them perhaps influenced by the memory of the Alexandrian conquests, arose along the fringes of the subcontinent in Bactria, known today as Afghanistan. In the first century C.E., Indo-European-speaking peoples fleeing from the nomadic Xiongnu warriors in Central Asia seized power in the area and proclaimed the new Kushan Kingdom (see Chapter 3). For the next two centuries, the Kushanas extended their political sway over northern India as far as the central Ganges valley, while other kingdoms scuffled for predominance elsewhere on the subcontinent. India would not see unity again for another five hundred years.

Several reasons for India's failure to maintain a unified empire have been proposed. Some historians suggest that a decline in regional trade during the first millennium C.E. may have contributed to the growth of small land-based kingdoms, which drew their primary income from agriculture. The tenacity of the Aryan tradition with its emphasis on tribal rivalries may also have contributed. Although the Mauryan rulers tried to impose a more centralized organization, clan loyalties once again came to the fore after the collapse of the Mauryan dynasty. Furthermore, the behavior of the ruling class was characterized by what Indians call the "rule of the fishes," which glorified warfare as the natural activity of the king and the aristocracy. The *Arthasastra,* which set forth a model of a centralized Indian state, assumed that war was the "sport of kings."

MAP 2.3 The Empire of Asoka

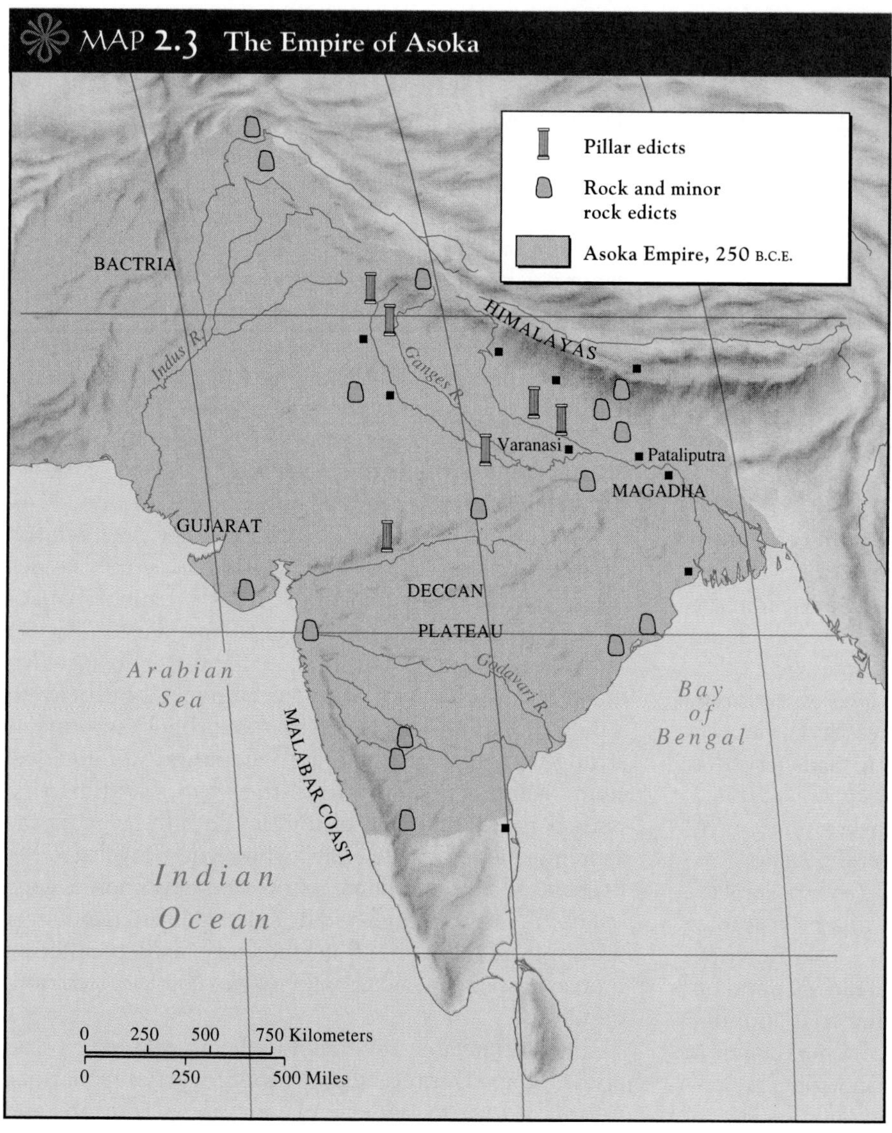

CHRONOLOGY

ANCIENT INDIA

Harappan civilization	c. 3000–1500 B.C.E.
Arrival of the Aryans	c. 1500 B.C.E.
Life of Gautama Buddha	c. 560–480 B.C.E.
Invasion of India by Alexander the Great	326 B.C.E.
Mauryan dynasty founded	324 B.C.E.
Reign of Chandragupta Maurya	324–301 B.C.E.
Reign of Asoka	269–232 B.C.E.
Collapse of Mauryan dynasty	183 B.C.E.
Rise of Kushan Kingdom	c. first century C.E.

THE EXUBERANT WORLD OF INDIAN CULTURE

Few cultures in the world are as rich and varied as that of India. Most societies excel in some forms of artistic and literary achievement and not in others, but India has produced great works in almost all fields of cultural endeavor—art and sculpture, science, architecture, literature, and music.

Literature

The earliest known Indian literature consists of the four Vedas, which were passed down orally from generation to generation until they were finally written down after the Aryan conquest of India. The Rigveda dates from the second millennium B.C.E. and consists of over a thousand hymns that were used at religious ceremonies. The other three Vedas were written considerably later and contain instructions for performing ritual sacrifices and other ceremonies. The Brahmanas and the Upanishads served as commentaries on the Vedas.

The language of the Vedas was Sanskrit, one of the Indo-European family of languages. After the Aryan conquest of India, Sanskrit gradually declined as a spoken language and was replaced in northern India by a simpler tongue known as Prakrit. Nevertheless, Sanskrit continued to be used as the language of the bureaucracy and literary expression for many centuries after that and, like Latin in medieval Europe, served as a common language of communication (*lingua franca*) between various regions of India. In the south, a variety of Dravidian languages continued to be spoken.

As early as the fifth century B.C.E., Indian grammarians had already codified Sanskrit in order to preserve the authenticity of the Vedas for the spiritual edification of future generations. A famous grammar written by the scholar Panini in the fourth century B.C.E. set forth four thousand grammatical rules prescribing the correct usage of the spoken and written language. This achievement is particularly impressive in that Europe did not have a science of linguistics until the nineteenth century, when it was developed partly as a result of the discovery of the works of Panini and later Indian linguists.

After the development of a writing system some time in the first millennium B.C.E., India's holy literature was probably inscribed on palm leaves stitched together into a book somewhat similar to the bamboo strips used during the same period in China. Also written for the first time were India's great historical epics, the Mahabharata and the Ramayana. Both of these epics may have originally been recited at religious ceremonies, but they are essentially historical writings that recount the martial exploits of great Aryan rulers and warriors.

The Mahabharata, consisting of more than 90,000 stanzas, was probably written about 100 B.C.E. and describes in great detail a war between cousins for control of the kingdom about 1000 B.C.E. Interwoven in the narrative are many fantastic legends of the Hindu gods. Above all, the Mahabharata is a tale of moral confrontations and an elucidation of the ethical precepts of the *dharma*. The most famous section of the book is the so-called Bhagavadgita, a sermon by the legendary Indian figure Krishna on the eve of a major battle. In this sermon, mentioned at the beginning of this chapter, Krishna sets forth one of the key ethical maxims of Indian society: in taking action, one must be indifferent to success or failure and consider only the moral rightness of the act itself (see the box on p. 58).

The Ramayana, written at about the same time, is much shorter than the Mahabharata. It is an account of a semi-legendary ruler named Rama who, as the result of a palace intrigue, is banished from the kingdom and forced to live as a hermit in the forest. Later, he fights the demon-king of Sri Lanka (Ceylon), who has kidnapped his beloved wife, Sita. Like the Mahabharata, the Ramayana is strongly imbued with religious and moral significance. Rama himself is portrayed as the ideal Aryan hero, a perfect ruler and an ideal son, while Sita projects the supreme duty of female chastity and wifely loyalty to her husband. The Ramayana is a story of the triumph of good over evil, duty over self-indulgence, and generosity over selfishness. It combines filial and erotic love, conflicts of human passion, character analysis, and poetic descriptions of nature.

The Ramayana also has all the ingredients of an enthralling adventure: giants, wondrous flying chariots, invincible arrows and swords, and magic potions and mantras. One of the real heroes of the story is the monkey-

ASOKA'S PILLAR. Stone pillars like this polished sandstone column, which is thirty-two feet high, were erected during the reign of Emperor Asoka in the third century B.C.E. Commemorating events in the life of the Buddha announcing official edicts, or marking routes to the holy sites, they were placed on major trunk roads throughout the Indian subcontinent. The massive size of these pillars, some of which weighed up to fifty tons, underscores the engineering skills of the peoples of ancient India.

king Hanuman, who flies from India to Sri Lanka to set the great battle in motion. Although the theme is a serious one, there are many humorous moments, such as Hanuman's nocturnal visit to King Ravana's palace (see the box on p. 60). It is no wonder that the Ramayana became a popular favorite among Indians of all age groups and the source of folktales and dramas that have been recited in Indian villages up to the present day.

Architecture and Sculpture

After literature, the greatest achievements of early Indian civilization were in architecture and sculpture. Some of the earliest examples of Indian architecture stem from the time of Emperor Asoka, when Buddhism became the religion of the state. Until the time of the Mauryas, Aryan buildings had been constructed of wood. With the rise of the empire, stone began to be used, as artisans arrived in India seeking employment after the destruction of the Persian Empire by Alexander. Many of these stone carvers accepted the patronage of Emperor Asoka, who used them to spread Buddhist ideas throughout the subcontinent.

THE LIONS OF SARNATH. Their beauty and Buddhist symbolism make the Lions of Sarnath the most famous of the capitals topping Asoka's pillars. Sarnath, located just north of the city of Varanasi, was the holy site where Siddhartha Gautama first preached, and these roaring lions echo the proclamation of Buddhist teachings to the four corners of the world. The wheel not only represents Buddha's law but also proclaims Asoka's imperial legitimacy as the enlightened Indian ruler.

BITS OF WISDOM FROM ANCIENT INDIA

The Mahabharata, the great epic of the early Aryan peoples, includes both moral exhortations for the ruling class and bits of simple wisdom that still touch us today. In this passage, a voice personifying the dharma, *or code of behavior, tests the hero's worthiness to become king by posing riddles about the meaning of life. The questions are eternal ones that still have relevance in our own time. The use of riddles as a means of testing mental skills was common to many early societies, including ancient Greece and China.*

THE MAHABHARATA

"What is swifter than the wind?"
"The mind is swifter than the wind."
"What is more numerous than the blades of grass in a meadow?"
"Our thoughts number more than that."
"What is the best of all things that are praised?"
"Skill."
"What is the most valuable possession?"
"Knowledge."
"What is not thought of until it departs?"
"Health."
"What is the best happiness?"
"Contentment."
"What covers all the world?"
"Darkness."
"What keeps a thing from discovering itself?"
"That is also darkness."
"What enemy cannot be overcome?"
"That is anger."
"What is honesty?"
"That is to look and to see every living creature as yourself, bearing your own will to live, and your own fear of death."
"How may peace be false?"
"When it is tyranny."

There were three main types of religious structure: the pillar, the stupa, and the rock chamber. During Asoka's reign, many stone columns were erected alongside roads to commemorate the events in the Buddha's life and mark pilgrim routes to holy places. Weighing up to fifty tons each and rising as high as thirty feet, these polished sandstone pillars were topped with a carved capital, usually depicting lions uttering the Buddha's message. Ten remain standing today.

A stupa was originally meant to house a relic of the Buddha, such as a lock of his hair or a branch of the famous Bodhi tree, and was constructed in the form of a burial mound (the pyramids in Egypt also derived from burial mounds). Eventually, the stupa became a place for devo-

SANCHI GATE AND STUPA. First constructed during the reign of Emperor Asoka, in the third century B.C.E., the stupa at Sanchi was enlarged over time, eventually becoming the greatest Buddhist monument in the entire Indian subcontinent. Originally intended to house a relic of the Buddha, the stupa became a holy place for devotion and a familiar form of Buddhist architecture. Sanchi's four elaborately carved stone gates, each over forty feet high, display exciting statues of Buddhist symbolism, including both animals and human figures.

A BUDDHIST PRAYER HALL. Carved out of solid rock cliffs during the Mauryan dynasty, these rock chambers served as small meditation halls for traveling Buddhist monks. By the first century C.E., they had evolved into elaborate temples, the greatest being this example at Karli. Measuring over 120 feet in length and 45 feet high, with pillars, an altar, and a vault, it is reminiscent of the Roman basilica in the West.

tion and the most familiar form of Buddhist architecture. It rose to considerable heights and was surmounted with a spire, possibly representing the stages of existence en route to Nirvana. According to legend, Asoka ordered the construction of 84,000 stupas throughout India to promote the Buddha's message. A few survive today, including the famous stupa at Sanchi, begun under Asoka and completed two centuries later.

The final form of early Indian architecture is the rock chamber carved out of a cliff on the side of a mountain. Asoka began the construction of these chambers to provide rooms to house monks or wandering ascetics and to serve as halls for religious ceremonies. The chambers were rectangular in form, with pillars, an altar, and a vault, reminiscent of the Roman basilica in the West. The three most famous chambers of this period are at Bhaja, Karli, and Ajanta; the latter contains twenty-nine rooms.

All three forms of architecture were embellished with decorations. Consisting of detailed reliefs and free-standing statues of deities, other human figures, and animals, these decorations are permeated with a sense of nature and the vitality of life. Many reflect an amalgamation of popular and sacred themes, of Buddhist, Vedic, and pre-Aryan religious motifs, such as male and female earth spirits. Until the second century C.E., Siddhartha Gautama was represented only through symbols, such as the wheel of life, the Bodhi tree, and the footprint, perhaps because artists felt that it was impossible to render a visual impression of the Buddha in the state of Nirvana. After the spread of Mahayana Buddhism in the second century, when the Buddha was portrayed as a god, his image began to appear in stone.

By this time, India had established its own unique religious art. The art is permeated by sensuousness and exuberance and is often overtly sexual. These scenes are meant to express otherworldly delights, not the pleasures of this world. The sensuous paradise that adorned the religious art of ancient India represented salvation and fulfillment for the ordinary Indian.

Science

Our knowledge of Indian science is limited by the paucity of written sources, but it is evident that ancient Indians had amassed an impressive amount of scientific knowledge in a number of areas. Especially notable was their work in astronomy, where they charted the movements of the heavenly bodies and recognized the spherical nature of the planet at an early date. Their ideas of physics were similar to those of the Greeks; matter was divided into the five elements of earth, air, fire, water, and ether. Many of their technological achievements are impressive, notably the quality of their textiles and the massive stone pillars erected during the reign of Asoka. The pillars weighed up to fifty tons each and were transported many miles to their final destination.

THE MONKEY-KING IN SRI LANKA

In the famous classic the Ramayana, Rama is assisted in his effort to free his wife from Ravana, the king of Sri Lanka, by the monkey-king Hanuman. In this passage, Hanuman unexpectedly intrudes into the royal harem.

THE RAMAYANA

That was the entrance to Ravana's bedroom. Hanuman ducked under the left corner of the draw-curtain and stood just inside with his back to the wall, looking out at a huge floor lit by flaming lamps of gold and covered with sleeping women so tumbled together that Hanuman could not tell where one lady left off and the next began.

There was hardly space to step anywhere. Those were the countless wives of the Demon King asleep in disarray, lying all over each other, women beautiful and bright as flashes of lightning now locked fast in Sleep's embrace. Hanuman thought, "When even the form of a heavenly star is less than enough, virtue's divine reward for a good life must be to receive such fair shapes and lovely limbs as these!"

Once arriving in that room of women, it would be harder for any man to remember who he was or where he stood or why, than to fly across the sea in the first place. And though Hanuman was not a man, still when he looked at each one he thought no other woman could be fairer, and when he saw the next sleeper she was in turn the best and most beautiful as he looked at her. Truly, among those magnificent women the rays of the one's beauty showed off the charms of another; they slept deeply after an evening of drinking and dancing and playing music. Their fragrant hair was loosened and their bracelets scattered; their beauty marks of sandal paste were smudged and their colored robes unclasped and their waist-chains ran loosely straying to the side; their hazy garlands were disbanded and their pearls had gone and their earrings were lost.

Even the bedroom lamps looked openly out at all those women while they had the chance, as Ravana slept. Hanuman picked his way among the love-skilled Queens of Lanka who were draped over the floor and looked at their faces. They smiled or frowned or sighed in their sleep; their pillows were others' arms and legs and laps; they pulled each other's robes and wrapped themselves in them. With their eyes lashed shut in sleep they were desirable as closed flowers; when they touched each other they smiled and drew closer, believing they pressed Ravana with their breasts. Even asleep the dancers moved enticingly; the girl musicians slept embracing drums and hugging lutes like their long-absent lovers.

The golden lamps on the walls watched over them unblinking, and in their light the gold and jewels of those Queens made a river of lights and colors and shimmering waves of gold and silver. Their pearl necklaces were white water-birds asleep between their breasts, rising and falling; their strings of turquoise were families of blue teal and their hips were the waves and the riverbanks; their faces of golden or white or deep blue skin were the lotuses; when they stirred sleepily, the small bells sewn on their silken clothes were the ripples moving with little sounds; and the bruises and scratches of love on their tender breasts were signs of where the lion and tiger had come to drink.

CONCLUSION

While the peoples of North Africa and the Middle East were actively building the first civilizations, a similar process was getting under way in the Indus River valley. Much has been learned about the nature of the Indus valley civilization in recent years, but without written records there are inherent limits to our understanding. How did the Harappan people deal with those fundamental human problems that were mentioned at the close of the previous chapter? The answers remain tantalizingly elusive.

As often happened elsewhere, however, the collapse of Harappan civilization did not lead to the total disappearance of its culture. The new society that eventually emerged throughout the subcontinent after the coming of the Aryans was clearly the product of an amalgam of two highly distinctive cultures, Aryan and Dravidian, each of which made a significant contribution to the politics, the social institutions, and the creative impulse of ancient Indian civilization.

With the rise of the Mauryan dynasty in the fourth century B.C.E., the distinctive features of a great civilization begin to be clearly visible. It was extensive in its scope, embracing the entire Indian subcontinent and eventually, in the form of Buddhism and Hinduism, spreading to China and Southeast Asia. But the underlying ethnic, linguistic, and cultural diversity of the Indian people posed a constant challenge to the unity of the state. After the collapse of the Mauryas, the subcontinent would not come under a single authority again for several hundred years.

In the meantime, another great experiment was taking place far to the northeast, across the Himalaya Mountains. Like many other civilizations of antiquity, the first Chinese state was concentrated on a major river system. And like them, too, its political and cultural achievements eventually spread far beyond their original habitat. In the next chapter, we turn to the civilization of ancient China.

THE IDEAL BUDDHIST COUPLE. Although originally the Aryans, a pastoral people, espoused a patriarchal religion peopled with male deities preoccupied with conquest and war, after their arrival in India they gradually incorporated female fertility spirits inherited from the local agrarian societies into their pantheon. This stylized couple, who welcome the faithful to the Buddhist rock temple at Karli, symbolize the essence of human life, at harmony with both the temporal and spiritual worlds. This sculpture dates from the first century C.E.

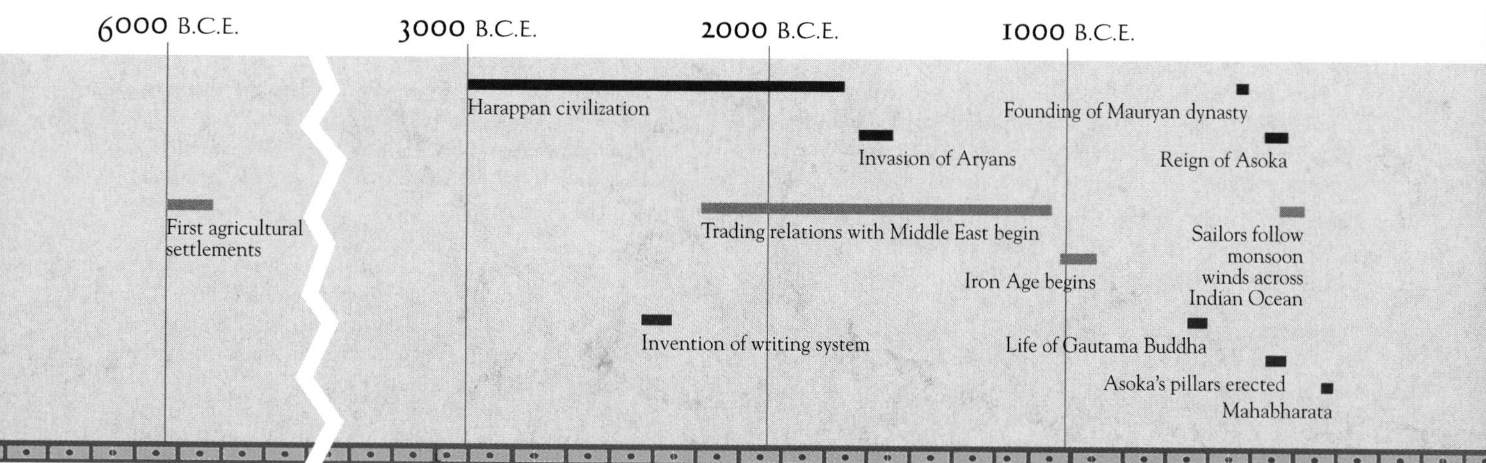

Chapter Notes

1. Quoted in Richard Lannoy, *The Speaking Tree: A Study of Indian Culture and Society* (London, 1971), p. 318.
2. The quotation is from ibid., p. 319. Note also that the *Law of Manu* says that "punishment alone governs all created beings. . . . The whole world is kept in order by punishment, for a guiltless man is hard to find."
3. Strabo's *Geography*, Book 15, quoted in Michael Edwardes, *A History of India: From the Earliest Times to the Present Day* (London, 1961), p. 55.
4. Ibid., p. 54.
5. From the *Law of Manu*, quoted in A. L. Basham, *The Wonder That Was India* (London, 1961), pp. 180–81.
6. *Mundaka Upanishad*, 1:2, quoted in William Theodore de Bary, et al., eds., *Sources of Indian Tradition* (New York, 1966), pp. 28–29.
7. *Chandogya Upanishad*, 6:1–3, 12–14 and *passim*, in ibid., pp. 33–35.
8. Quoted in Ananda K. Coomaraswamy, *Buddha and the Gospel of Buddhism* (New York, 1964), p. 34.

Suggested Readings

For easy reference to the history and archaeology of India, see the colorful and schematic *Past Worlds: The Times Atlas of Archaeology* (Maplewood, N.J., 1988). Several standard histories of India are available today, all of which provide a good overview of the ancient period. One of the most readable and reliable is S. Wolpert, *New History of India*, 3d ed. (New York, 1989). V. A. Smith's edition of *The Oxford History of India*, 4th ed. (Oxford, 1981), although somewhat out of date, contains a wealth of information on various aspects of early Indian history. For a discussion of the Mauryan period directed to the lay reader, see M. Edwardes, *A History of India* (London, 1961). Also of note is H. H. Dodwell, ed., *The Cambridge History of India*, 6 vols. (Cambridge, 1922–1953).

By far the most informative and readable narrative on the history of India in premodern times is still A. L. Basham, *The Wonder That Was India* (London, 1961), which contains informative sections on prehistory, economy, language, art and literature, society, and everyday life. Also useful is A. L. Basham, ed., *A Cultural History of India* (Oxford, 1975). For a stimulating analysis of Indian culture and society in general, consult R. Lannoy, *The Speaking Tree* (London, 1971). R. Thapar, *Interpreting Early India* (Delhi, 1992), provides a view by an Indian historian.

Because of the relatively recent nature of archaeological exploration in South Asia, evidence for the Harappan period is not as voluminous as for areas such as Mesopotamia and the Nile valley. Some of the best work has been written by scholars who actually worked at the sites. For a recent account, see J. M. Kenoyer, *Ancient Cities of the Indus Valley Civilization* (Karachi, Pakistan, 1998). A somewhat more extensive study is A. and B. Allchin, *The Birth of Indian Civilization, India and Pakistan before 500* B.C. (Harmondsworth, 1968). For a detailed and well-illustrated analysis, see G. L. Possehlt, ed., *Harappan Civilization: A Contemporary Perspective* (Warminster, 1982). Commercial relations between Harappa and its neighbors are treated in S. Ratnagar, *Encounters: The Westerly Trade of the Harappan Civilization* (Oxford, 1981). See also *The Cultural Heritage of India*, vol. 1, *The Early Phase* (Calcutta, 1958) and J. Marshall's classic *Mohenjo-Daro and the Indus Civilization*, 3 vols. (London, 1931).

On the Mauryan period, see D. D. Kosambi, *The Culture and Civilization of Ancient India* (London, 1965) and R. Thapar, *Asoka and the Decline of the Mauryas* (Oxford, 1961).

There are a number of good books on the introduction of Buddhism into Indian society. Buddha's ideals are presented in A. K. Coomaraswamy, *Buddha and the Gospel of Buddhism* (London, 1916; revised, New York, 1964) and E. Conze, *Buddhism: Its Essence and Development* (Oxford, 1951). Also see H. Nakamura and M. B. Dasgupta, *Indian Buddhism: A Survey with Bibliographical Notes* (New Delhi, 1987). H. Akira, *A History of Indian Buddhism: From Sakyamuni to Early Mahayana* (Hawaii, 1990) provides a detailed analysis of early activities by Siddhartha Gautama and his followers. The intimate relationship between Buddhism and commerce is discussed in Liu Hsin-ju, *Ancient India and Ancient China: Trades and Religious Exchanges* (Oxford, 1988).

Hinduism, its origins and development, is the subject of S. Radhakrishnan, *The Hindu View of Life* (Oxford, 1926) and B. Walker, *Hindu World*, 2 vols. (London, 1969). For a more general treatment, see S. N. Dasgupta, *A History of Indian Philosophy*, 5 vols. (Cambridge, 1922–1955) and S. Radhakrishnan, *Indian Philosophy*, revised ed., 2 vols. (London, 1958).

There are a number of excellent surveys of Indian art, including the comprehensive S. L. Huntington, *The Art of Ancient India: Buddhist, Hindu, Jain* (New York, 1985) and the concise *Indian Art* (London, 1976) by R. Craven. See also V. Dehejia's *Devi: The Great Goddess* (Washington, D.C., 1999) and *Indian Art* (London, 1997).

Few general surveys of Indian literature exist, perhaps because of the magnitude and diversity of India's literature. A good textbook for college students is E. C. Dimock, *The Literatures of India: An Introduction* (Chicago, 1974), which traces Indian literary achievement from the epics to the modern Hindi film.

Many editions of Sanskrit literature are available in English translation. Many are available in the multivolume *Harvard Oriental Series*. For a one-volume annotated anthology of selections from the Indian classics, consult S. N. Hay, ed., *Sources of Indian Tradition*, 2 vols. (New York, 1988), or J. B. Alphonso-Karkala, *An*

Anthology of Indian Literature, 2d revised ed. (New Delhi, 1987), put out by the Indian Council for Cultural Relations.

The Mahabharata and Ramayana have been rewritten for 2,500 years. Fortunately, the vibrant versions, retold by William Buck and condensed to 400 pages each, reproduce the spirit of the originals and enthrall today's imagination. See W. Buck, *Mahabharata* (Berkeley, 1973) and *Ramayana* (Berkeley, 1976). For the role played by women writers in ancient India, see S. Tharu and K. Lalita, eds., *Women Writing in India: 600 B.C. to the Present*, vol. 1 (New York, 1991).

For additional reading, go to InfoTrac College Edition, your online research library at http://web1.infotrac-college.com

Enter the search term "Vedas" using Keywords.

Enter the search term "Hinduism" using the Subject Guide.

Enter the search term "Buddhism" using the Subject Guide.

Enter the search terms "India history" using Keywords.

Enter the search terms "Upanishad or Rigveda or Mahabharata" using Keywords.

CHAPTER

3

CHINA IN ANTIQUITY

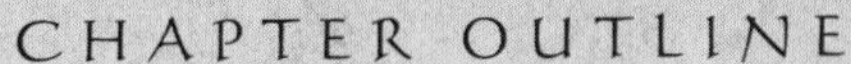

CHAPTER OUTLINE

- THE LAND AND PEOPLE OF CHINA
- THE DAWN OF CHINESE CIVILIZATION: THE SHANG DYNASTY
- THE ZHOU DYNASTY
- THE RISE OF THE CHINESE EMPIRE: THE QIN AND THE HAN
- DAILY LIFE IN ANCIENT CHINA
- THE WORLD OF CULTURE
- CONCLUSION

FOCUS QUESTIONS

- How did geography influence the civilization that arose in China?
- What concepts of kingship and political and governmental institutions characterized each of the major dynasties of early China—the Shang, the Zhou, the Qin, and the Han?
- What were the major tenets of Confucianism, Legalism, and Daoism, and what role did each play in Chinese civilization?
- What were the key aspects of social and economic life in early China?
- What role did nomadic peoples play in early Chinese history?

The Master said: "If the government seeks to rule by decree, and to maintain order by the use of punishment, the people will seek to evade punishment and have no sense of shame. But if government leads by virtue and governs through the rules of propriety, the people will feel shame and seek to correct their mistakes."

That statement is from the *Analects*, a collection of remarks by the Chinese philosopher Confucius that were gathered together by his disciples and published after his death in the fifth century B.C.E. Confucius lived at a time when Chinese society was in a state of growing disarray. The political principles that had governed society since the founding of the Zhou dynasty six centuries earlier were widely ignored, and squabbling principalities scuffled for primacy as the power of the Zhou court steadily declined. The common people groaned under the weight of an oppressive manorial system that left them at the mercy of their feudal lords.

In the midst of this confusion, Confucius traveled the length of the kingdom observing events and seeking employment as a political counselor. In the process he attracted a number of disciples, to whom he proposed a set of ideas that in later years served as the guiding principles for the Chinese empire. Some of his ideas are strikingly modern in their thrust. Among them is the revolutionary proposition that government depends on the will of the people.

The civilization that produced Confucius had originated more than fifteen hundred years earlier along the two great river systems of East Asia, the Yellow and the Yangtze. This vibrant new civilization, which we know today as ancient China, expanded gradually over its neighboring areas. By the third century B.C.E., it had emerged as a great empire, as well as the dominant cultural and political force in the entire region.

Like Sumer, Harappa, and Egypt, the civilization of ancient China began as a collection of autonomous villages cultivating food crops along a major river system. Improvements in agricultural techniques led to a food surplus and the growth of an urban civilization characterized by more complex political and social institutions, as well as new forms of artistic and intellectual creativity.

Like its counterparts elsewhere, ancient China faced the challenge posed by the appearance of pastoral peoples on its borders. Unlike Harappa, Sumer, and Egypt, however, ancient China was able to avoid destruction at the hands of the invaders, and many of its institutions and cultural values survived intact down to the beginning of the twentieth century. For that reason, Chinese civilization is sometimes described as the oldest continuous civilization on earth.

The Land and People of China

According to Chinese legend, Chinese society was founded by a series of rulers who brought the first rudiments of civilization to the region nearly five thousand years ago. The first was Fu Xi (Fu Hsi), the ox-tamer, who "knotted cords for hunting and fishing," domesticated animals, and introduced the beginnings of family life. The second was Shen Nong (Shen Nung), the divine farmer, who "bent wood for plows and hewed wood for plowshares." He taught the people the techniques of agriculture. Last came Huang Di (Huang Ti), the Yellow Emperor, who "strung a piece of wood for the bow, and whittled little sticks of wood for the arrows." Legend credits Huang Di with creating the Chinese system of writing, as well as with inventing the bow and arrow.[1] Modern historians, of course, do not accept the literal accuracy of such legends but view them instead as part of the process whereby early peoples attempt to make sense of the world and their role in it. Nevertheless, such re-creations of a mythical past often contain an element of truth. Although there is no clear evidence that the "three sovereigns" actually existed, their achievements do symbolize some of the defining characteristics of Chinese civilization: the interaction between nomadic and agricultural peoples, the importance of the family as the basic unit of Chinese life, and the development of a unique system of writing.

Human communities have existed in China for several hundred thousand years. Sometime around the eighth millennium B.C.E., the early peoples living along the riverbanks of northern China began to master the cultivation of crops. A number of these early agricultural settlements were in the neighborhood of the Yellow River, where they gave birth to two Neolithic societies known to archaeologists as the Yangshao and the Longshan cultures (sometimes identified in terms of their pottery as the painted and black pottery cultures). Similar agricultural settlements have been found in the Yangtze valley in central China and along the coast to the south. These settlements were based on the cultivation of rice rather than dry crops such as millet, barley, and wheat, but these settlements are as old as those in the north. Thus, agriculture, and perhaps other elements of early civilization, may have developed spontaneously in several areas of China rather than radiating outward from one central nuclear region.

At first, these simple Neolithic settlements were hardly more than villages, but as the inhabitants mastered the rudiments of agriculture, the little communities gradually gave rise to more sophisticated and complex societies. In a pattern that we have already seen else where, civilization gradually spread from these nuclear settlements in the valleys of the Yellow and Yangtze rivers to other lowland areas of eastern and central China. The two great river valleys, then, can be considered the core regions in the development of Chinese civilization.

Although these densely cultivated valleys were among the great food-producing areas of the ancient world, China is not just a land of fertile fields. In fact, only 12 percent of the total land area is arable, compared with 23 percent in the United States. Much of the remainder consists of mountains and deserts that ring the country on its northern and western frontiers.

This often arid and forbidding landscape is a dominant feature of Chinese life and has played a significant role in Chinese history. The geographical barriers served to isolate the Chinese people from advanced agrarian societies in other parts of Asia. The frontier regions in the Gobi Desert, Central Asia, and the Tibetan plateau were sparsely inhabited by peoples of Mongolian, Indo-European, or Turkish extraction. Most were pastoral societies, and as was the case in the other river valley civilizations, their contacts with the Chinese were often characterized by mutual distrust and conflict. Although fewer in number than the Chinese, many of these peoples possessed impressive skills in war and were sometimes aggressive in seeking wealth or territory in the settled regions south of the Gobi Desert. Over the next two thousand years, the northern frontier became one of the great fault lines of conflict in Asia, as Chinese armies attempted to protect precious farmlands from marauding peoples from beyond the frontier. When China was unified and blessed with capable rulers, it could usually keep the nomadic intruders at bay and even bring them under a loose form of Chinese administration. But in times of internal weakness, China was vulnerable to attack from the north, and on several occasions, nomadic peoples succeeded in overthrowing native Chinese rulers and setting up their own dynastic regimes.

From other directions, China normally had little to fear. To the east lay the China Sea, a lair for pirates and the source of powerful typhoons that occasionally ravaged the Chinese coast, but otherwise rarely a source of concern. South of the Yangtze River was a hilly region inhabited by a mixture of peoples of varied language and ethnic stock who lived by farming, fishing, or food gathering. They were gradually absorbed in the inexorable expansion of Chinese civilization.

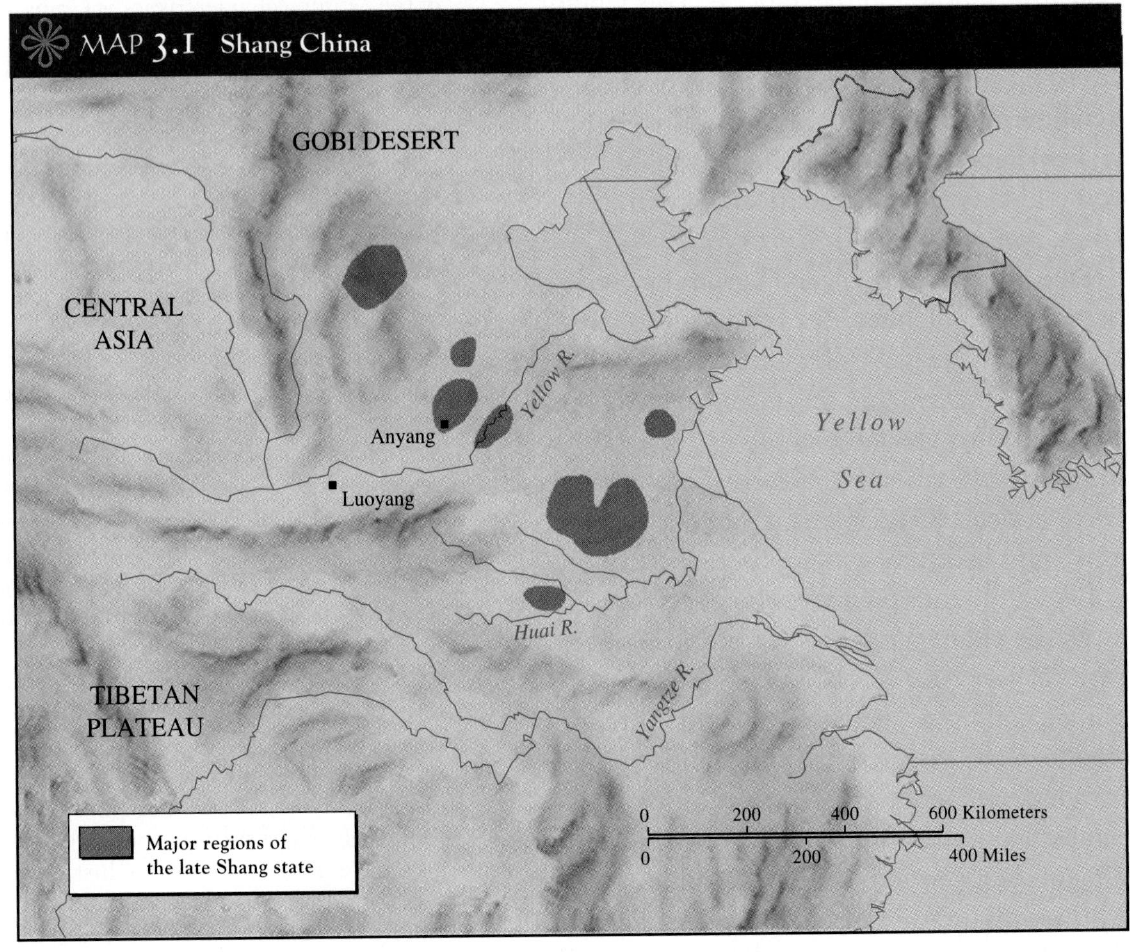

A TREATISE ON THE YELLOW RIVER AND ITS CANALS

Sima Qian (Szu-ma Ch'ien) was a famous historian of the Han dynasty who lived during the second and first centuries B.C.E. *In his most famous work, entitled* Historical Records, *he describes the public works projects undertaken during the Xia dynasty to convert the dangerous waters of the Yellow River to human use. Although the identification of irrigation with Yu may be apocryphal, China later became one of the foremost hydraulic societies in the ancient world.*

SIMA QIAN, *HISTORICAL RECORDS*

The documents on the Hsia dynasty tell us that Emperor Yu spent thirteen years controlling and bringing an end to the floods, and during that period, though he passed by the very gate of his own house, he did not take the time to enter. On land he traveled in a cart and on water in a boat; he rode a sledge to cross the mud and wore cleated shoes in climbing the mountains. In this way he marked out the nine provinces, led the rivers along the bases of the mountains, decided what tribute was appropriate for each region in accordance with the quality of its soil, opened up the nine roads, built embankments around the nine marshes, and made a survey of the nine mountains.

Of all the rivers, the Yellow River caused the greatest damage to China by overflowing its banks and inundating the land, and therefore he turned all his attention to controlling it. Thus he led the Yellow River in a course from Chi-shih past Lung-men and south to the northern side of Mount Hua; from there eastward along the foot of Ti-chu Mountain, past the Meng Ford and the confluence of the Lo River to Ta-p'ei. At this point Emperor Yu decided that, since the river was descending from high ground and the flow of the water was rapid and fierce, it would be difficult to guide it over level ground without danger of frequent disastrous breakthroughs. He therefore divided the flow into two channels, leading it along the higher ground to the north, past the Chiang River and so to Ta-lu. There he spread it out to form the Nine Rivers, brought it together again to make the Backward-Flowing River [i.e., tidal river], and thence led it into the Gulf of Pohai. When he had thus opened up the rivers of the nine provinces and fixed the outlets of the nine marshes, peace and order were brought to the lands of the Hsia, and his achievements continued to benefit the Three Dynasties which followed.

THE DAWN OF CHINESE CIVILIZATION: THE SHANG DYNASTY

Historians of China have traditionally dated the beginning of Chinese civilization to the founding of the Xia (Hsia) dynasty more than four thousand years ago. Although the precise date for the rise of the Xia is in dispute, legend maintains that the founder was a ruler named Yu, who is also credited with introducing irrigation and draining the floodwaters that periodically threatened to inundate the northern China plain (see the box above). The Xia dynasty, in turn, was replaced by a second dynasty, the Shang, around the sixteenth century B.C.E. The Shang capital at Anyang, just north of the Yellow River in north-central China, has been excavated by archaeologists. Among the finds were thousands of so-called oracle bones, ox and chicken bones or turtle shells that were used by Shang rulers for divination and to communicate with the gods. The inscriptions on these oracle bones are the earliest known form of Chinese writing and provide much of our information about the beginnings of civilization in China. They describe a culture gradually emerging from the Neolithic to the early Bronze Age.

Political Organization

China under the Shang dynasty was a predominantly agricultural society ruled by an aristocratic class whose major occupation was war. One ancient chronicler complained that "the big affairs of state consist of sacrifice and soldiery."[2] Combat was carried on by means of two-horse chariots. The appearance of chariots in China in the mid-second millennium B.C.E. coincides roughly with similar developments elsewhere, leading some historians to suggest that the Shang ruling class may originally have invaded China from elsewhere in Asia. But items found in Shang burial mounds are similar to Longshan pottery, implying that the Shang ruling elites were linear descendants of the indigenous Neolithic peoples in the area. If that was the case, the Shang may have acquired their knowledge of horse-drawn chariots through contact with the peoples of neighboring regions.

Some recent support for that assumption has come from evidence unearthed in the sandy wastes of Xinjiang, China's far-northwestern province. There archaeologists have discovered corpses dating back as early as the second millennium B.C.E. with physical characteristics that are clearly European. They are also clothed in textiles similar to those worn at the time in Europe, suggesting that they may have been members of an Indo-European migration

SHELL AND BONE WRITING. The earliest known form of writing in China dates back to the early Shang dynasty and was inscribed on shells or animal bones. Questions for the gods were scratched on bones, which cracked after being exposed to fire. The cracks were then interpreted by sorcerers. The questions often expressed practical concerns: Will it rain? Will the king be victorious in battle? Will he recover from his illness? Originally composed of pictographs and ideographs 4,000 years ago, Chinese writing has evolved into an elaborate system of stylized symbols still in use today.

from areas much further to the west. If that is the case, it is not improbable that they were familiar with advances in chariot making that occurred a few hundred years earlier in southern Russia and Kazakstan. By about 2000 B.C.E. spoked wheels were being deposited at grave sites in Ukraine and also in the Gobi Desert, just north of the great bend of the Yellow River. It is thus not unlikely that the new technology became available to the founders of the Shang dynasty and may have aided their rise to power in northern China.

The Shang king ruled with the assistance of a central bureaucracy in the capital city. His realm was divided into a number of territories governed by aristocratic chieftains, but the king appointed these chieftains and could apparently depose them at will. He was also responsible for the defense of the realm and controlled large armies that often fought on the fringes of the kingdom. The transcendent importance of the ruler was graphically displayed in the ritual sacrifices undertaken at his death, when hundreds of his retainers were buried with him in the royal tomb.

As the inscriptions on the oracle bones make clear, the Chinese ruling elite believed in the existence of supernatural forces and thought that they could communicate with those forces to obtain divine intervention on matters of this world. In fact, the purpose of the oracle bones was to communicate with the gods (see the illustration at left). This evidence also suggests that the king was already being viewed as an intermediary between Heaven and earth. In fact, an early Chinese character for king (王) consists of three horizontal lines connected by a single vertical line; the middle horizontal line represents the king's place between human society and the divine forces in nature.

The early Chinese also had a clear sense of life in the hereafter. Though some of the human sacrifices discovered in the royal tombs were presumably intended to propitiate the gods, others were meant to accompany the king or members of his family on the journey to the next world. From this conviction would come the concept of the veneration of ancestors (commonly known in the West as "ancestor worship") and the practice, which continues to the present day in many Chinese communities, of burning replicas of physical objects to accompany the departed on their journey to the next world.

Social Structures

In the Neolithic period, the farm village was apparently the basic social unit of China, at least in the core region of the Yellow River valley. Villages were organized by clans rather than by nuclear family units, and all residents probably took the common clan name of the entire village. In some cases, a village may have included more than one clan. At Banpo (Pan P'o), an archaeological site near modern Xian that dates back at least eight thousand years, the houses in the village are separated by a ditch, which some scholars think may have served as a divider between two clans. The individual dwellings at Banpo housed nuclear families, but a larger building in the village was apparently used as a clan meeting hall. The tribal origins of Chinese society may help to explain the continued importance of the joint family in traditional China, as well as the relatively small number of family names in Chinese society. Even today there are only about four hundred commonly used family names in a society of more than one billion people.

By Shang times, the classes were becoming increasingly differentiated. It is likely that some poorer peasants did not own their farms but were obliged to work the land of the chieftain and other elite families in the village (see the box on p. 69). The aristocrats not only made war and served as officials (indeed, the first Chinese character for official originally meant warrior), but they were also the primary landowners. In addition to the aristocratic elite and the peasants, there were also a small number of merchants and artisans, as well as slaves, probably consisting primarily of criminals or prisoners taken in battle.

LIFE IN THE FIELDS

The following passage is from the Book of Songs, a famous classic that was written sometime during the early Zhou dynasty. This excerpt describes the calendar of peasant life on an estate in ancient China and indicates the various types of service that peasants provided for their lord.

THE BOOK OF SONGS

In the seventh month the Fire Star passes the meridian;
In the ninth month clothes are given out.
In the days of [our] first month, the wind blows cold;
In the days of [our] second, the air is cold.
Without coats, without garments of hair,
How could we get to the end of the year?
In the days of [our] third month we take our plows in hand;
In the days of [our] fourth we make our way to the fields.
Along with wives and children,
We eat in those south-lying acres.
The surveyor of the fields comes and is glad.

In the seventh month the Fire Star passes the meridian;
In the ninth month clothes are given out.
With the spring days the warmth begins,
And the oriole utters its song.
The young women take their deep baskets
And go along the small paths,
Looking for the tender [leaves of the] mulberry trees
As the spring days lengthen out,
They gather in crowds the white southern wood.
The girl's heart is wounded with sadness,
For she will soon be going with one of the young lords.

. . .
In the eighth month spinning is begun;
We make dark fabrics and yellow,
"With our red dye so bright,
We make robes for our young lords."

In the ninth month we prepare the stockyard,
And in the tenth we bring in the harvest.
The millets, the early and the late,
Together with paddy and hemp, beans and wheat.
. . .
Now we go up to work in the manor.
"In the day you gather the thatch-reeds;
In the evening twist them into rope;
Go quickly on to the roofs;
Soon you are to sow the grain."

In the days of [our] second month we cut the ice with tingling blows;
In the days of [our] third month [it is] stored in the icehouse.
In the days of [our] fourth month, very early,
A lamb with scallions is offered in sacrifice.
In the ninth month are shrewd frosts;
In the tenth month the stockyard is cleared.
With twin pitchers we hold the feast,
Killed for it is a young lamb.
Up we go into the lord's hall,
Raise the cup of buffalo horn;
"Long life for our lord; may he live forever and ever!"

The Shang are perhaps best known for their mastery of the art of bronze casting. Utensils, weapons, and ritual objects made of bronze have been found in royal tombs in urban centers throughout the area known to be under Shang influence (see Metalwork and Sculpture later in this chapter). It is also clear that the Shang had achieved a fairly sophisticated writing system; the oracle bones provide concrete evidence of the existence of a system of ideographs and pictographs that is the direct precursor of the written language used in China today.

THE ZHOU DYNASTY

In the eleventh century B.C.E., the Shang dynasty was overthrown by an aggressive young state located somewhat to the west of Anyang, the Shang capital, and near the great bend of the Yellow River as it begins to flow directly eastward to the sea. The new dynasty, which called itself the Zhou (Chou), survived for about eight hundred years and was thus the longest-lived dynasty in the history of China. According to tradition, the last of the Shang rulers was a tyrant who oppressed the people (Chinese sources assert that he was a degenerate who built "ponds of wine" and ordered the composing of lustful music that "ruined the morale of the nation"), leading the ruler of the principality of Zhou to revolt and establish a new dynasty.[3]

The Zhou located their capital in their home territory, near the present-day city of Xian. Later they established a second capital city at modern Luoyang, farther to the east, to administer new territories captured from the Shang. This established a pattern of eastern and western capitals that would endure off and on in China for nearly two thousand years.

SHANG AND ZHOU BRONZES. From the eighteenth to the twelfth centuries B.C.E., the most significant artistic contribution of the Shang dynasty was its bronze ritual vessels. Used initially as food containers in ceremonial rites for ancestral devotion by the emperors, these magnificent objects were the product of an advanced technology unmatched by any contemporary civilization. The Zhou dynasty continued the tradition, as illustrated here by the ninth-century bell with four tigers. Note the stylized face of a dragon. This mysterious animal-mask design, known as a Taotie, is characteristic of both Shang and Zhou bronze objects. Sought by museums everywhere, these bronzes are considered one of the art wonders of the world.

Political Structures

The Zhou dynasty (1045–221 B.C.E.) adopted the political system of its predecessors with some changes. The Shang practice of dividing the kingdom into a number of territories governed by officials appointed by the king was continued under the Zhou. At the apex of the government hierarchy was the Zhou king, who was served by a bureaucracy of growing size and complexity. It now included several ministries responsible for rites, education, law, and public works. Beyond the capital, the Zhou kingdom was divided into a number of principalities, governed by members of the hereditary aristocracy, who were appointed by the king and were at least theoretically subordinated to his authority.

But the Zhou kings also introduced some innovations. According to the *Rites of Zhou*, one of the oldest surviving documents on statecraft, the Zhou dynasty ruled China because it possessed the "mandate of Heaven." According to this concept, Heaven (viewed as an impersonal law of nature rather than as an anthropomorphic deity) maintained order in the universe through the Zhou king, who thus ruled as a representative of Heaven, but not as a divine being. The king, who was selected to rule because of his talent and virtue, was then responsible for governing the people with compassion and efficiency. It was his duty to propitiate the gods in order to protect the people from natural calamities or a bad harvest. But if the king failed to rule effectively, theoretically at least he could be overthrown and replaced by a new ruler. As noted earlier, this idea was used to justify the Zhou conquest of the Shang. Eventually, the concept of the heavenly mandate would become a cardinal principle of Chinese statecraft.[4] Each founder of a new dynasty would routinely assert that he had earned the mandate of Heaven, and who could disprove it except by overthrowing the king? As a pragmatic Chinese proverb put it: "He who wins is the king; he who loses is the rebel."

By the sixth century B.C.E., the Zhou dynasty began to decline. As the power of the central government disintegrated, bitter internal rivalries arose among the various principalities, where the governing officials had succeeded in making their positions hereditary at the expense of the king. As the power of these officials grew, they began to regulate the local economy and seek reliable sources of revenue for their expanding armies, such as a uniform tax system and government monopolies on key commodities such as salt and iron.

Economy and Society

During the Zhou dynasty, the essential characteristics of Chinese economic and social institutions began to take shape. The Zhou continued the pattern of land ownership that had existed under the Shang: the peasants worked on lands owned by their lord but also had land of their own that they cultivated for their own use. The practice was called the "well field system," since the Chinese character for well (井) resembles a simplified picture of the division of the farmland into nine separate segments. Each peasant family tilled an outer plot for its own use and then joined with other families to work the inner one for the hereditary lord (see the box on p. 69). How widely this system was used is unclear, but it represented an ideal described by Confucian scholars of a later day. As the following poem indicates, life for the average farmer was a difficult one. The "big rat" is probably a reference to the high taxes imposed on the peasants by the government or lord.

Big rat, big rat
Do not eat my millet!
Three years I have served you,
But you will not care for me.

ENVIRONMENTAL CONCERNS IN ANCIENT CHINA

Even in antiquity, China possessed a large population that often stretched the limits of the productive potential of the land. In the following excerpt, the late Zhou philosopher Mencius appeals to his sovereign to adopt policies that will conserve precious resources and foster the well-being of his subjects. Clearly, Mencius was concerned that environmental needs were being neglected. Unfortunately, his advice has not always been followed, as environmental degradation remains a problem in China today. The destruction of the forests, for example, has deprived China of much of its wood resources, and the present government has launched an extensive program to plant trees.

THE BOOK OF MENCIUS

If you do not interfere with the busy season in the fields, then there will be more grain than the people can eat; if you do not allow nets with too fine a mesh to be used in large ponds, then there will be more fish and turtles than they can eat; if hatchets and axes are permitted in the forests on the hills only in the proper seasons, then there will be more timber than they can use. When the people have more grain, more fish and turtles than they can eat, and more timber than they can use, then in the support of their parents when alive and in the mourning of them when dead, they will be able to have no regrets over anything left undone. This is the first step along the Kingly way.

If the mulberry is planted in every homestead of five mu of land, then those who are fifty can wear silk; if chickens, pigs, and dogs do not miss their breeding season, then those who are seventy can eat meat; if each lot of a hundred mu is not deprived of labor during the busy seasons, then families with several mouths to feed will not go hungry. Exercise due care over the education provided by the village schools, and discipline the people by teaching them the duties proper to sons and younger brothers, and those whose heads have turned gray will not be carrying loads on the roads. When those who are seventy wear silk and eat meat and the masses are neither cold nor hungry, it is impossible for their prince not to be a true King.

Now when food meant for human beings is so plentiful as to be thrown to dogs and pigs, you fail to realize that it is time for garnering, and when men drop dead from starvation by the wayside, you fail to realize that it is time for distribution. When people die, you simply say, "It is none of my doing. It is the fault of the harvest." In what way is that different from killing a man by running him through, while saying all the time, "It is none of my doing. It is the fault of the weapon." Stop putting the blame on the harvest and the people of the whole Empire will come to you.

I am going to leave you
And go to that happy land;
Happy land, happy land,
Where I will find my place.[5]

Trade and manufacturing were carried out by merchants and artisans, who lived in walled towns under the direct control of the local lord. Merchants did not operate independently but were considered the property of the local lord and on occasion could even be bought and sold like chattels. A class of slaves performed a variety of menial tasks and perhaps worked on local irrigation projects. Most of them were probably prisoners of war captured during conflicts with the neighboring principalities. Scholars do not know how extensive slavery was in ancient times, but slaves probably did not comprise a large proportion of the total population.

The period of the later Zhou, from the sixth to the third century B.C.E., was an era of significant economic growth and technological innovation, especially in agriculture. During that time, large-scale water control projects were undertaken to regulate the flow of rivers and distribute water evenly to the fields, as well as to construct canals to facilitate the transport of goods from one region to another (see the box on p. 67). Perhaps the most impressive technological achievement of the period was the construction of the massive water control project on the Min River, a tributary of the Yangtze. This system of canals and spillways, which was put into operation by the state of Qin a few years prior to the end of the Zhou dynasty, diverted excess water from the river into the local irrigation network and watered an area populated by as many as five million people. The system is still in use today, over two thousand years later.

Food production was also stimulated by a number of advances in farm technology. By the mid-sixth century B.C.E., the introduction of iron had led to the development of iron plowshares, which permitted deep plowing for the first time. Other innovations dating from the later Zhou were the use of natural fertilizer, the collar harness, and the technique of leaving land fallow to preserve or replenish nutrients in the soil (see the box above).

The advances in agriculture, which enabled the population of China to rise as high as 20 million people during the late Zhou era, were also undoubtedly a major factor in the growth of commerce and manufacturing. During the later Zhou, economic wealth began to replace noble birth as the prime source of power and influence. Utensils made of iron became more common, and trade developed in a variety of useful commodities, such as cloth, salt, and various manufactured goods.

One of the most important items of trade in ancient China was silk. There is evidence of silkworm raising as early as the Neolithic period. Remains of silk material have been found on Shang bronzes, and a large number of fragments have been recovered in tombs dating from the mid-Zhou era. Silk cloth was used not only for clothing and quilts, but also to wrap the body of the dead prior to burial. Fragments have been found throughout Central Asia and as far away as Athens, suggesting that the famous "Silk Road" was in operation as early as the fifth century B.C.E. (for a discussion of the Silk Road, see Chapter 10).

With the development of trade and manufacturing, China began to move toward a money economy. The first form of money may have been seashells (the Chinese character for goods or property contains the ideographic symbol for "shell"), but by the Zhou dynasty pieces of iron shaped like a knife or round coins with a hole in the middle so they could be carried in strings of a thousand were being used. Most ordinary Chinese, however, simply used a system of barter. Even taxes and rents, as well as the salaries of government officials, were normally paid in grain.

The Hundred Schools of Ancient Philosophy

In China, as in other great river valley societies, the birth of civilization was accompanied by the emergence of an organized effort to comprehend the nature of the cosmos and the role of human beings within it. Speculation over such questions began in the very early stages of civilization and culminated at the end of the Zhou era in the "hundred schools" of ancient philosophy, a wide-ranging debate over the nature of human beings, society, and the universe.

The first hint of religious belief in ancient China comes from relics found in royal tombs of Neolithic times. By then, the Chinese had already developed a religious sense beyond the primitive belief in the existence of spirits in nature. The Shang had already begun to believe in the existence of one transcendent god, known as Shang Di, who presided over all the forces of nature. As time went on, the Chinese concept of religion began to evolve from a vaguely anthropomorphic god to a somewhat more impersonal symbol of universal order known as Heaven (*Tian*, or *T'ien*). There was also much speculation among Chinese intellectuals about the nature of the cosmic order. One of the earliest ideas was that the universe was divided into two primary forces of good and evil, light and dark, male and female, called the *yang* and the *yin*, represented symbolically by the sun (*yang*) and the moon (*yin*). According to this theory, life was a dynamic process of interaction between the forces of *yang* and *yin*. Early Chinese could attempt only to understand the process and perhaps to have some minimal effect on its operation. They could not hope to reverse it. It is sometimes asserted that this belief has contributed to the heavy element of fatalism in Chinese popular wisdom. The Chinese have traditionally believed that bad times will be followed by good times, and vice versa.

The belief that there was some mysterious "law of nature" that could be interpreted by human beings led to various attempts to predict the future, such as the Shang oracle bones and other methods of divination. Philosophers invented various ways to interpret the will of nature, while shamans, playing a role similar to the *brahmins* in India, were employed at court to assist the emperor in his policy deliberations until at least the fifth century C.E. One of the most famous manuals used for this purpose was the *Yi Jing (I Ching)*, known in English as the *Book of Changes*.

CONFUCIANISM

Such efforts to divine the mysterious purposes of Heaven notwithstanding, Chinese thinking about metaphysical reality also contained a strain of pragmatism, which is readily apparent in the ideas of the great philosopher Confucius. Confucius (the Latin form of his honorific title Kung Fuci, or K'ung Fu-tzu, meaning Master Kung) was born in the state of Lu (in the modern province of Shandong) in 551 B.C.E. After reaching maturity, he apparently hoped to find employment as a political adviser in one of the principalities into which China was divided at that time, but he had little success in finding a patron. Nevertheless, he made an indelible mark on history as an independent (and somewhat disgruntled) political and social philosopher.

In conversations with his disciples contained in the *Analects*, Confucius often adopted a detached and almost skeptical view of Heaven. "You are unable to serve man," he commented on one occasion, "how then can you hope to serve the spirits? While you do not know life, how can you know about death?" In many instances, he appeared to advise his followers to revere the deities and the ancestral spirits but to keep them at a distance. Confucius believed it was useless to speculate too much about metaphysical questions. Better by far to assume that there was a rational order to the universe and then concentrate one's attention on ordering the affairs of this world.[6]

Confucius's interest in philosophy, then, was essentially political and ethical. The universe was constructed in such a way that if human beings could act harmoniously in accordance with its purposes, their own affairs would prosper. Much of his concern was with human behavior. The key to proper behavior was to behave in accordance with the *Dao* (Way). Confucius assumed that all human beings had their own *Dao*, depending on their individual role in life, and it was their duty to follow it. Even the ruler had

THE WAY OF THE GREAT LEARNING

Unfortunately, few texts exist today that were written by Confucius himself. Most were written or edited by his disciples. The following text, entitled The Great Learning, *was probably written two centuries after Confucius's death, but it illustrates his view that good government begins with the cultivation of individual morality and proper human relationships at the basic level. This conviction that "to bring peace to the world, cultivate your own person" continued to win general approval down to modern times.*

THE GREAT LEARNING

The Way of the Great Learning consists in clearly exemplifying illustrious virtue, in loving the people, and in resting in the highest good.

Only when one knows where one is to rest can one have a fixed purpose. Only with a fixed purpose can one achieve calmness of mind. Only with calmness of mind can one attain serene repose. Only in serene repose can one carry on careful deliberation. Only through careful deliberation can one have achievement. Things have their roots and branches; affairs have their beginning and end. He who knows what comes first and what comes last comes himself near the Way.

The ancients who wished clearly to exemplify illustrious virtue throughout the world would first set up good government in their states. Wishing to govern well their states, they would first regulate their families. Wishing to regulate their families, they would first cultivate their persons. Wishing to cultivate their persons, they would first rectify their minds. Wishing to rectify their minds, they would first seek sincerity in their thoughts. Wishing for sincerity in their thoughts, they would first extend their knowledge. The extension of knowledge lay in the investigation of things. For only when things are investigated is knowledge extended; only when knowledge is extended are thoughts sincere; only when thoughts are sincere are minds rectified; only when minds are rectified are our persons cultivated; only when our persons are cultivated are our families regulated; only when families are regulated are states well governed; and only when states are well governed is there peace in the world.

From the emperor down to the common people, all, without exception, must consider cultivation of the individual character as the root. If the root is in disorder, it is impossible for the branches to be in order. To treat the important as unimportant and to treat the unimportant as important—this should never be. This is called knowing the root; this is called the perfection of knowledge.

his own *Dao*, and he ignored it at his peril, for to do so could mean the loss of the mandate of Heaven. The idea of the *Dao* is reminiscent of the concept of *dharma* in ancient India and played a similar role in governing the affairs of society.

Two elements in the Confucian interpretation of the *Dao* are particularly worthy of mention. The first is the concept of duty. It was the responsibility of all individuals to subordinate their own interests and aspirations to the broader need of the family and the community. Confucius assumed that if each individual worked hard to fulfill his or her assigned destiny, the affairs of society as a whole would surely prosper as well. In this respect, it was important for the ruler to set a good example. If he followed his "kingly way," the beneficial effects would radiate throughout society (see the box above).

The second key element is the idea of humanity, sometimes translated as "human heartedness." This concept involves a sense of compassion and empathy for others. It is similar in some ways to Christian concepts, but with a subtle twist. Where Christian teachings call on human beings to "behave toward others as you would have them behave toward you," the Confucian maxim is put in a different way: "Do not do unto others what you would not wish done to yourself." To many Chinese, this attitude symbolizes an element of tolerance in the Chinese character that has not always been practiced in other societies.[7]

Confucius may have considered himself a failure because he never attained the position he wanted, but many of his contemporaries found his ideas appealing, and in the generations after his death, his message spread widely throughout China. Confucius was an outspoken critic of his times and lamented the disappearance of what he regarded as the Golden Age of the early Zhou.

In fact, however, Confucius was not just another disgruntled Chinese conservative mourning the passing of the good old days, but a revolutionary thinker, many of whose key ideas looked forward rather than backward. Perhaps his most striking political idea was that the government should be open to all men of superior quality, and not limited to those of noble birth. As one of his disciples reports in the *Analects*: "The Master said, by nature, men are nearly alike; by practice, they get to be wide apart."[8] Confucius undoubtedly had himself in mind as one of those "superior" men, but the rapacity of the hereditary lords must have added strength to his convictions.

The concept of rule by merit was, of course, not an unfamiliar idea in the China of his day; the *Rites of Zhou* had clearly stated that the king himself deserved to rule because of his talent and virtue, rather than as the result of noble birth. In practice, however, aristocratic privilege must often have opened the doors to political influence, and many of Confucius's contemporaries must have regarded his appeal for government by talent as both exciting and dangerous. Confucius did not explicitly question the right of the hereditary aristocracy to play a leading role in the political process, nor did his ideas have much effect in his lifetime. Still, they introduced a new concept that was later implemented in the form of a bureaucracy selected through a civil service examination (see the section on Confucianism and the State later in this chapter).

Confucius's ideas, passed on to later generations through the *Analects* as well as through other writings allegedly written by Confucius, had a strong impact on Chinese political thinkers of the late Zhou period, a time when the existing system was in disarray and open to serious question. But as with most great thinkers, Confucius's ideas were sufficiently ambiguous to be interpreted in very contradictory ways. Some, like the philosopher Mencius (370–290 B.C.E.), stressed the humanistic side of Confucian ideas, arguing that human beings were by nature good and thus could be taught their civic responsibilities by example. He also stressed that the ruler had a duty to govern with compassion:

> It was because Chieh and Chou lost the people that they lost the empire, and it was because they lost the hearts of the people that they lost the people. Here is the way to win the empire: win the people and you win the empire. Here is the way to win the people: win their hearts and you win the people. Here is the way to win their hearts: give them and share with them what they like, and do not do to them what they do not like. The people turn to a human ruler as water flows downward or beasts take to wilderness.[9]

Here is a prescription for political behavior that could win wide support in our own day. Other thinkers, however, rejected Mencius's rosy view of human nature and argued for a different approach.

LEGALISM

One school of thought that became quite popular during the "hundred schools" era in ancient China was the philosophy of Legalism. Taking issue with the view of Mencius and other disciples of Confucius that human nature was essentially good, the Legalists argued that human beings were by nature evil and would follow the correct path only if coerced by harsh laws and stiff punishments. These thinkers were referred to as the "School of Law," because they rejected the Confucian view that government by "superior men" could solve society's problems and argued instead for a system of impersonal laws.

The Legalists disagreed with the Confucian belief that the universe has a moral core. They therefore believed that only firm action by the state could bring about social order. Fear of harsh punishment, more than the promise of material reward, could best motivate the common people to serve the interests of the ruler. Because human nature was essentially corrupt, officials could not be trusted to carry out their duties in a fair and evenhanded manner, and only a strong ruler could create an orderly society. All human actions should be subordinated to the effort to create a strong and prosperous state subject to his will.

DAOISM

One of the most popular alternatives to Confucianism was the philosophy of Daoism (frequently spelled Taoism). According to Chinese tradition, the Daoist school was founded by a contemporary of Confucius popularly known as Lao Tzu (Lao Zi), or the Old Master. Many modern scholars, however, are skeptical that Lao Tzu actually existed.

Obtaining a clear understanding of the original concepts of Daoism is difficult because its primary document, a short treatise known as the *Dao De Jing* (sometimes translated as *The Way of the Tao*), is an enigmatic book whose interpretation has baffled scholars for centuries. The opening line, for example, explains less what the *Dao* is than what it is not: "The Tao [Way] that can be told of is not the eternal Tao. The name that can be named is not the eternal name."[10]

Nevertheless, the basic concepts of Daoism are not especially difficult to understand. Like Confucianism, Daoism does not anguish over the underlying meaning of the cosmos. Rather, it attempts to set forth proper forms of behavior for human beings here on earth. In most other respects, however, Daoism presents a view of life and its ultimate meaning that is almost diametrically opposed to that of Confucianism. Where Confucian doctrine asserts that it is the duty of human beings to work hard to improve life here on earth, Daoists contend that the true way to interpret the will of Heaven is not action, but inaction (*wu wei*). The best way to act in harmony with the universal order is to act spontaneously and let nature take its course (see the box on p. 75).

Such a message could be very appealing to those who were uncomfortable with the somewhat rigid flavor of the Confucian work ethic and preferred a more individualistic approach. This image would eventually find graphic expression in Chinese landscape painting, which in its classical form would depict naturalistic scenes of mountains, water, and clouds and underscore the fragility and smallness of individual human beings.

Daoism achieved considerable popularity in the waning years of the Zhou dynasty. It was especially popular among intellectuals, who may have found it appealing as

THE DAOIST ANSWER TO CONFUCIANISM

The Dao De Jing *(The Way of the Dao) is the great classic of philosophical Daoism (Taoism). Traditionally attributed to the legendary Chinese philosopher Lao Tzu (Old Master), it was probably written sometime during the era of Confucius. This opening passage illustrates two of the key ideas that characterize Daoist belief: it is impossible to define the nature of the universe, and "inaction" (not Confucian "action") is the key to ordering the affairs of human beings.*

THE WAY OF THE DAO

The Tao that can be told of is not the eternal Tao;
The name that can be named is not the eternal name.
The Nameless is the origin of Heaven and Earth;
The Named is the mother of all things.

Therefore let there always be nonbeing, so we may see their subtlety.
And let there always be being, so we may see their outcome.
The two are the same,
But after they are produced, they have different names.
They both may be called deep and profound.
Deeper and more profound,
The door of all subtleties!
When the people of the world all know beauty as beauty,
There arises the recognition of ugliness.
When they all know the good as good,
There arises the recognition of evil.
Therefore:
Being and nonbeing produce each other;
Difficult and easy complete each other;
Long and short contrast each other;
High and low distinguish each other;
Sound and voice harmonize each other;
Front and behind accompany each other.

Therefore the sage manages affairs without action
And spreads doctrines without words.
All things arise, and he does not turn away from them.
He produces them but does not take possession of them.
He acts but does not rely on his own ability.
He accomplishes his task but does not claim credit for it.
It is precisely because he does not claim credit that his accomplishment remains with him.

an escapist antidote in a world characterized by growing disorder.

POPULAR BELIEFS

Daoism also played a second role as a somewhat loose framework for popular spiritualistic and animistic beliefs among the common people. Popular Daoism was less a philosophy than a religion; it comprised a variety of rituals and forms of behavior that were regarded as a means of achieving heavenly salvation or even a state of immortality on earth. Daoist sorcerers practiced various types of mind- or body-training exercises in the hope of achieving power, sexual prowess, and long life. It was primarily this form of Daoism that survived into a later age.

The philosophical forms of Confucianism and Daoism did not provide much meaning to the mass of the population, for whom philosophical debate over the ultimate meaning of life was not as important as the daily struggle for survival. For most Chinese, Heaven was not a vague impersonal law of nature, as it was for many Confucian and Daoist intellectuals, but a terrain peopled with innumerable gods and spirits of nature, both good and evil, who existed in trees, mountains, and streams as well as in heavenly bodies. As human beings mastered the techniques of farming, they called on divine intervention to guarantee a good harvest. Other gods were responsible for the safety of fishers, transportation workers, or prospective mothers.

Another aspect of popular religion was the belief that the spirits of deceased human beings lived in the atmosphere for a time before ascending to Heaven or descending to Hell. During that period, surviving family members had to care for the spirits through proper ritual, or they would become evil spirits and haunt the survivors.

Thus, in ancient China, human beings were offered a variety of interpretations of the nature of the universe. Confucianism satisfied the need for a rational doctrine of nation building and social organization at a time when the existing political and social structure was beginning to disintegrate. Philosophical Daoism provided an alternative to Confucianism and a framework for a set of diverse animistic beliefs at the popular level. But neither could satisfy the deeper emotional needs that sometimes inspire the human spirit. Neither could effectively provide solace in a time of sorrow or the hope of a better life in the hereafter. Something else would be needed to fill the gap.

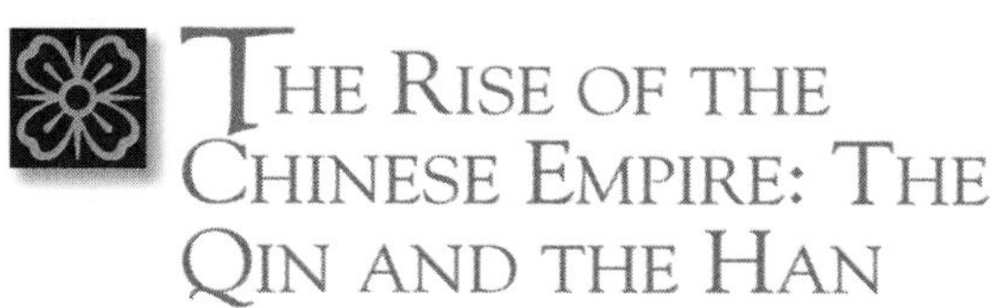

THE RISE OF THE CHINESE EMPIRE: THE QIN AND THE HAN

During the last two centuries of the Zhou dynasty (the fourth and third centuries B.C.E.), the authority of the king became increasingly nominal, and several of the small

THE ART OF WAR

With the possible exception of the nineteenth-century German military strategist Karl von Clausewitz, there is probably no more famous or respected writer on the art of war than the ancient Chinese thinker Sun Tzu. Yet surprisingly little is known about him. Recently discovered evidence suggests that he lived sometime in the fifth century B.C.E., *during the chronic conflict of the Period of Warring States, and that he was an early member of an illustrious family of military strategists who advised Zhou rulers for more than two hundred years. But despite the mystery surrounding his life, there is no doubt of his influence on later generations of military planners. Among his most avid followers in our century have been the revolutionary leaders Mao Zedong and Ho Chi Minh, as well as the Japanese military strategists who planned the attacks on Port Arthur and Pearl Harbor.*

The following brief excerpt from his classic The Art of War *provides a glimmer into the nature of his advice, still so timely today.*

SELECTIONS FROM SUN TZU

Sun Tzu said:

"In general, the method for employing the military is this: . . . Attaining one hundred victories in one hundred battles is not the pinnacle of excellence. Subjugating the enemy's army without fighting is the true pinnacle of excellence. . . .

"Thus the highest realization of warfare is to attack the enemy's plans; next is to attack their alliances; next to attack their army; and the lowest is to attack their fortified cities.

"This tactic of attacking fortified cities is adopted only when unavoidable. Preparing large movable protective shields, armored assault wagons, and other equipment and devices will require three months. Building earthworks will require another three months to complete. If the general cannot overcome his impatience but instead launches an assault wherein his men swarm over the walls like ants, he will kill one-third of his officers and troops, and the city will still not be taken. This is the disaster that results from attacking [fortified cities].

"Thus one who excels at employing the military subjugates other people's armies without engaging in battle, captures other people's fortified cities without attacking them, and destroys others people's states without prolonged fighting. He must fight under Heaven with the paramount aim of 'preservation.' . . .

"In general, the strategy of employing the military is this: If your strength is ten times theirs, surround them; if five, then attack them; if double, then divide your forces. If you are equal in strength to the enemy, you can engage him. If fewer, you can circumvent him. If outmatched, you can avoid him. . . .

"Thus there are five factors from which victory can be known:

"*One who knows when he can fight, and when he cannot fight, will be victorious.*

"*One who recognizes how to employ large and small numbers will be victorious.*

"*One whose upper and lower ranks have the same desires will be victorious.*

"*One who, fully prepared, awaits the unprepared will be victorious.*

"*One whose general is capable and not interfered with by the ruler will be victorious.*

"These five are the Way (Tao) to know victory. . . .

"Thus it is said that one who knows the enemy and knows himself will not be endangered in a hundred engagements. One who does not know the enemy but knows himself will sometimes be victorious, sometimes meet with defeat. One who knows neither the enemy nor himself will invariably be defeated in every engagement."

principalities into which the Zhou kingdom had been divided began to evolve into powerful states that presented a potential challenge to the Zhou ruler himself. Chief among these were Qu (Ch'u) in the central Yangtze valley, Wu in the Yangtze delta, and Yue (Yueh) along the southeastern coast. At first, their mutual rivalries were in check, but by the late fifth century B.C.E., competition intensified into civil war, giving birth to the "Period of the Warring States" (see the box above). Powerful principalities vied with each other for preeminence and largely ignored the now purely titular authority of the Zhou court. New forms of warfare also emerged with the invention of iron weapons and the introduction of the foot soldier. Cavalry, too, made its first appearance, armed with the powerful crossbow.

Eventually, the relatively young state of Qin, located in the original homeland of the Zhou, became a key player in these conflicts. Benefiting from a strong defensive position in the mountains to the west of the great bend of the Yellow River, as well as from their control of the rich Sichuan plains, the Qin gradually subdued their main rivals through conquest or diplomatic maneuvering. In 221 B.C.E., the Qin ruler declared the establishment of a new dynasty, the first truly unified government in Chinese history.

The Qin Dynasty (221–206 B.C.E.)

One of the primary reasons for the triumph of the Qin was probably the character of the Qin ruler, known to history as Qin Shi Huangdi (Ch'in Shih Huang Ti), or the

First Emperor of Qin. A man of forceful personality and immense ambition, Qin Shi Huangdi had ascended to the throne of Qin in 246 B.C.E. at the age of thirteen. Described by the famous Han dynasty historian Sima Qian as having "the chest of a bird of prey, the voice of a jackal, and the heart of a tiger," the new king of Qin found the Legalist views of his adviser Li Su (Li Ssu) only too appealing. In 221 B.C.E., Qin Shi Huangdi defeated the last of Qin's rivals and founded a new dynasty with himself as emperor.

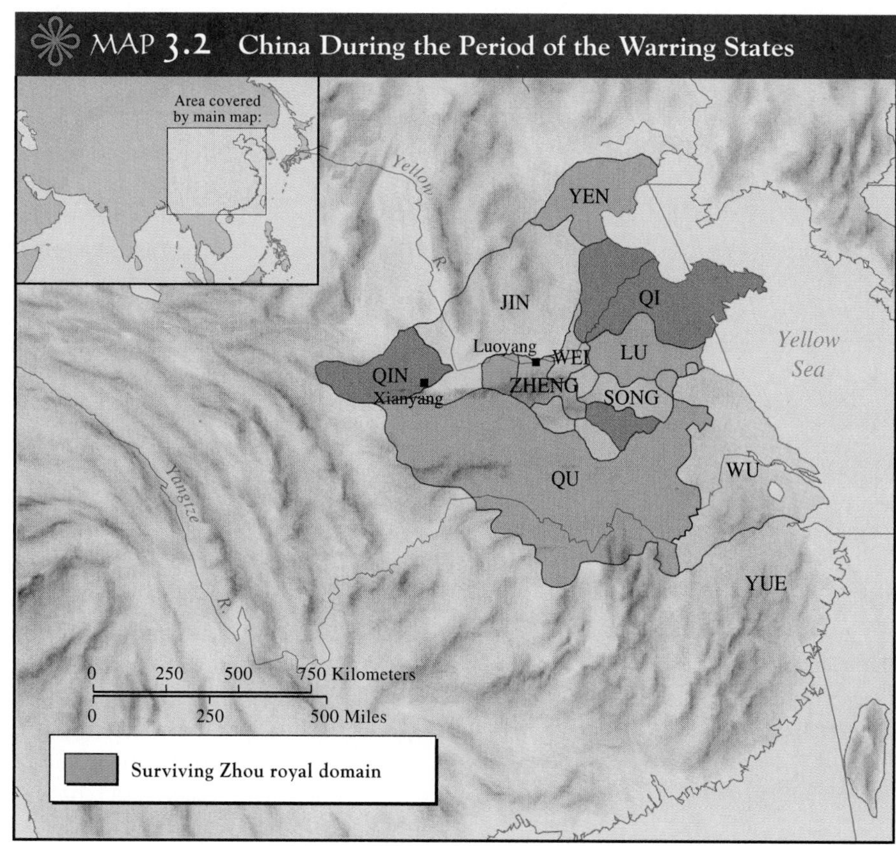

The Qin dynasty transformed Chinese politics. Philosophical doctrines that had proliferated during the late Zhou period were prohibited, and Legalism was adopted as the official ideology. Those who opposed the policies of the new regime were punished and sometimes executed, while books presenting ideas contrary to the official orthodoxy were publicly put to the torch, perhaps the first example of book burning in history (see the box on p. 79).

Legalistic theory gave birth to a number of fundamental administrative and political developments, some of which would survive the Qin and serve as a model for future dynasties. In the first place, unlike the Zhou the Qin was a highly centralized state. The central bureaucracy was divided into three primary ministries: a civil authority, a military authority, and a censorate, whose inspectors surveyed the efficiency of officials throughout the system. This would later become standard administrative procedure for future Chinese dynasties.

Below the central government were two levels of administration: provinces and counties. Unlike the Zhou system, officials at these levels did not inherit their positions but were appointed by the court and were subject to dismissal at the emperor's whim. Apparently, some form of merit system was used, although there is no evidence that selection was based on performance in an examination. The civil servants may have been chosen on the recommendation of other government officials. A penal code provided for harsh punishments for all wrongdoers. Officials were watched by the censors, who reported directly to the throne. Those guilty of malfeasance in office were executed.

Qin Shi Huangdi, who had a passion for centralization, unified the system of weights and measures, standardized the monetary system and the written forms of Chinese characters, and ordered the construction of a system of roads extending throughout the entire empire. He also attempted to eliminate the remaining powers of the landed aristocrats and divided their estates among the peasants, who were now taxed directly by the state. He thus eliminated potential rivals and secured tax revenues for the central government. Members of the aristocratic clans were required to live in the capital city at Xianyang (Hsienyang), just north of modern Xian, so that the court could monitor their activities. Such a system may not have been advantageous to the peasants in all respects, however, since the central government could now collect taxes more effectively and mobilize the peasants for military service and for various public works projects.

The Qin dynasty was equally unsympathetic to the merchants, whom it viewed as parasites. Private commercial activities were severely restricted and heavily taxed; and many of the more vital forms of commerce and manufacturing, such as mining, wine making, and the distribution of salt, were placed under a government monopoly.

Qin Shi Huangdi was equally aggressive in foreign affairs. His armies continued the gradual advance to the south that had taken place during the final years of the Zhou dynasty, extending the border of China to the edge of the Red River in modern Vietnam. To supply the Qin armies operating in the area, a canal was dug that provided

QIN SHI HUANGDI. Qin Shi Huangdi, the First Emperor of Qin, who reigned from 221 to 210 B.C.E., was one of the most influential figures in the history of China. Although considered ruthless by many historians, he created the first unified Chinese state, ordered the construction of a system of roads throughout the country, standardized the Chinese currency and written language, and brought together the scattered defensive battlements into what we now know as the Great Wall.

direct inland navigation from the Yangtze River in central China to what is now the modern city of Guangzhou (Canton) in the south.

BEYOND THE FRONTIER: THE NOMADIC PEOPLES AND THE GREAT WALL OF CHINA

The main area of concern for the Qin emperor, however, was in the north, where a nomadic people, known to the Chinese as the Xiongnu (Hsiung-nu) and possibly related to the Huns (see Chapter 5), had become increasingly active in the area of the Gobi Desert. The area north of the Yellow River had been sparsely inhabited since prehistoric times. At that time, the climate of North China was somewhat milder and moister than it is today, and parts of the region were heavily forested. The local population probably lived by hunting and fishing, practicing limited forms of agriculture, or herding animals such as cattle or sheep.

As the climate gradually became drier, such peoples were forced to rely increasingly on animal husbandry as a means of livelihood. Their response was to master the art of riding on horseback and adopt the nomadic life. Organized loosely into tribes consisting of a number of kinship groups, they ranged far and wide in search of pasture for their herds of cattle, goats, or sheep. As they moved seasonally from one pasture to another, they often traveled several hundred miles carrying their goods and their circular felt tents, called *yurts*.

But the new way of life presented its own challenges. Increased food production led to a growing population, which in times of drought outstripped the available resources. Rival tribes then competed for the best pastures. After they mastered the art of fighting on horseback sometime during the middle of the first millennium B.C.E., territorial warfare became commonplace throughout the entire frontier region from the Pacific Ocean to Central Asia.

By the end of the Zhou dynasty in the third century B.C.E., the nomadic Xiongnu posed a serious threat to the security of China's northern frontier, and a number of Chinese principalities in the area began to build walls and fortifications to keep them out. But warriors on horseback possessed significant advantages over the infantry of the Chinese.

Qin Shi Huangdi's answer to the problem was to strengthen the walls to keep the marauders out. In Sima Qian's words:

> [The] First Emperor of the Ch'in dispatched Meng T'ien to lead a force of a hundred thousand men north to attack the barbarians. He seized control of all the lands south of the Yellow River and established border defenses along the river, constructing forty-four walled district cities overlooking the river and manning them with convict laborers transported to the border for garrison duty. Thus he utilized the natural mountain barriers to establish the border defenses, scooping out the valleys and constructing ramparts and building installations at other points where they were needed. The whole line of defenses stretched over ten thousand *li* [a *li* is one-third of a mile] from Lin-t'ao to Liao-tung and even extended across the Yellow River and through Yang-shan and Pei-chia.[11]

Today, of course, we know Qin Shi Huangdi's project as the Great Wall, which extends nearly four thousand miles from the sandy wastes of Central Asia to the sea. It is constructed of massive granite blocks and is wide enough on top to provide a roadway for horse-drawn chariots. Although the wall that appears in most photographs today was built 1,500 years after the Qin, during the Ming dynasty, some of the walls built by the Qin remain stand-

MEMORANDUM ON THE BURNING OF BOOKS

Li Su, the author of the following passage, was a chief minister of the First Emperor of Qin. An exponent of Legalism, Li Su hoped to eliminate all rival theories on government. His recommendation to the emperor on the subject was recorded by the Han dynasty historian Sima Qian. The emperor approved the proposal and ordered all books contrary to the spirit of Legalist ideology to be destroyed on pain of death. Fortunately, some texts were preserved by being hidden, or even memorized by their owners, and were thus available to later generations. For centuries afterward, the First Emperor of Qin and his minister were singled out for criticism because of their intolerance and their effort to control the very minds of their subjects. Totalitarianism, it seems, is not exclusively a modern concept.

SIMA QIAN, *HISTORICAL RECORDS*

In earlier times the empire disintegrated and fell into disorder, and no one was capable of unifying it. Thereupon the various feudal lords rose to power. In their discourses they all praised the past in order to disparage the present and embellished empty words to confuse the truth. Everyone cherished his own favorite school of learning and criticized what had been instituted by the authorities. But at present Your Majesty possesses a unified empire, has regulated the distinctions of black and white, and has firmly established for yourself a position of sole supremacy. And yet these independent schools, joining with each other, criticize the codes of laws and instructions. Hearing of the promulgation of a decree, they criticize it, each from the standpoint of his own school. At home they disapprove of it in their hearts; going out they criticize it in the thoroughfare. They seek a reputation by discrediting their sovereign; they appear superior by expressing contrary views, and they lead the lowly multitude in the spreading of slander. If such license is not prohibited, the sovereign power will decline above and partisan factions will form below. It would be well to prohibit this.

Your servant suggests that all books in the imperial archives, save the memoirs of Ch'in, be burned. All persons in the empire, except members of the Academy of Learned Scholars, in possession of the *Book of Odes*, the *Book of History*, and discourses of the hundred philosophers should take them to the local governors and have them indiscriminately burned. Those who dare to talk to each other about the *Book of Odes* and the *Book of History* should be executed and their bodies exposed in the marketplace. Anyone referring to the past to criticize the present should, together with all members of his family, be put to death. Officials who fail to report cases that have come under their attention are equally guilty. After thirty days from the time of issuing the decree, those who have not destroyed their books are to be branded and sent to build the Great Wall. Books not to be destroyed will be those on medicine and pharmacy, divination by the tortoise and milfoil, and agriculture and arboriculture. People wishing to pursue learning should take the officials as their teachers.

ing. Their construction was a massive project that required the efforts of thousands of laborers, many of whom met their deaths there and, according to legend, are now buried within the wall.

THE FALL OF THE QIN

The Legalist system put in place by the First Emperor of Qin was designed to achieve maximum efficiency as well as total security for the state. It did neither. Qin Shi Huangdi was apparently aware of the dangers of factions within the imperial family and established a class of eunuchs (males whose testicles have been removed) who served as personal attendants for himself and female members of the royal family. The original idea may have been to restrict the influence of male courtiers, and the eunuch system later became a standard feature of the Chinese imperial system. But as confidential advisers to the royal family, eunuchs were clearly in a position of influence. The rivalry between the "inner" imperial court and the "outer" court of bureaucratic officials led to tensions that persisted until the end of the imperial system.

By ruthlessly gathering control over the empire into his own hands, Qin Shi Huangdi had hoped to establish a rule that, in the words of Sima Qian, "would be enjoyed by his sons for ten thousand generations." In fact, his centralizing zeal alienated many key groups. Landed aristocrats and Confucian intellectuals, as well as the common people, groaned under the censorship of thought and speech, harsh taxes, and forced labor projects. "He killed men," recounted the historian, "as though he thought he could never finish, he punished men as though he were afraid he would never get around to them all, and the whole world revolted against him."[12] Shortly after the emperor died in 210 B.C.E., the dynasty quickly descended into factional rivalry, and four years later it was overthrown.

The disappearance of the Qin brought an end to an experiment in absolute rule that later Chinese historians would view as a betrayal of humanistic Confucian principles. But in another sense, the Qin system was a

THE GREAT WALL. The section of the Great Wall that is often visited by tourists today is not the work of the First Emperor of Qin but was built at the order of a Ming ruler many centuries later. The original walls were often composed of loose stone, dirt, or piled rubble and posed little obstacle to invading nomads from the north. The section illustrated here is located north of the city of Dunhuang in Central Asia.

response—though somewhat extreme—to the problems of administering a large and increasingly complex society. Although later rulers would denounce Legalism and enthrone Confucianism as the new state orthodoxy, in practice they would make use of a number of the key tenets of Legalism to administer the empire and control the behavior of their subjects.

The Glorious Han Dynasty (202 B.C.E.–221 C.E.)

The fall of the Qin was followed by a brief period of civil strife as aspiring successors competed for hegemony. Out of this strife emerged one of the greatest and most durable dynasties in Chinese history—the Han. The Han dynasty would later become so closely identified with the advance of Chinese civilization that even today the Chinese sometimes refer to themselves as "people of Han" and to their language as the "language of Han."

The founder of the Han dynasty was Liu Bang (Liu Pang), a commoner of peasant origin who would be known

MAP 3.3 The Han Empire

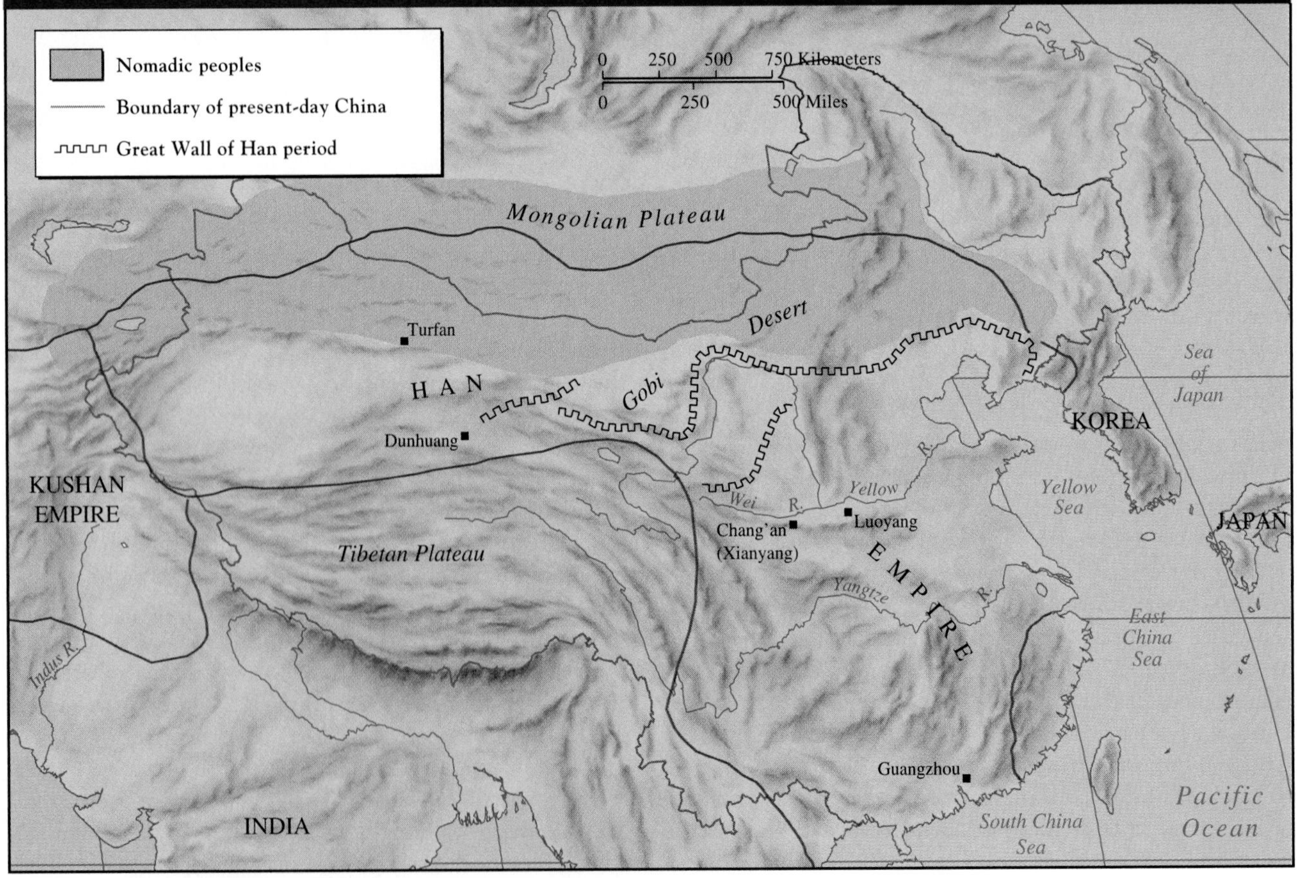

historically by his title of Han Gaozu (Han Kao Tsu, or Exalted Emperor of Han). Under his strong rule and that of his successors, the new dynasty quickly moved to consolidate its control over the empire and promote the welfare of its subjects. Efficient and benevolent, at least by the standards of the time, Gaozu maintained the centralized political institutions of the Qin but abandoned their harsh Legalistic approach to law enforcement. Han rulers also reversed the effort by the First Emperor of Qin to enforce a single ideology and discovered in Confucian principles a useful foundation for the creation of a new state philosophy. Under the Han, Confucianism began to take on the character of an official ideology.

CHRONOLOGY

ANCIENT CHINA

Xia (Hsia) dynasty	?–1570? B.C.E
Shang dynasty	1570?–1045? B.C.E
Zhou (Chou) dynasty	1045?–221 B.C.E
Life of Confucius	551–479 B.C.E
Period of the Warring States	403–221 B.C.E
Life of Mencius	370–290 B.C.E
Qin (Ch'in) dynasty	221–206 B.C.E
Life of the First Emperor of Qin	259–210 B.C.E
Formation of Han dynasty	202 B.C.E
Wang Mang interregnum	9–23 C.E.
Collapse of Han dynasty	221 C.E.

CONFUCIANISM AND THE STATE

The integration of Confucian doctrine with Legalist practice, creating a system generally known as State Confucianism, did not take long to accomplish. Although the founding Han ruler declared his intention to discard the harsh methods adopted by the Qin, he and his successors found it convenient to retain many of the institutions introduced by the First Emperor of Qin. For example, they borrowed the tripartite division of the central government into civilian and military authorities and a censorate. The government was headed by a Grand Council including representatives from all three segments of government. The Han also retained the system of local government, dividing the empire into provinces and districts.

Finally, and perhaps most important, the Han continued the Qin system of selecting government officials on the basis of merit rather than birth. Shortly after founding the new dynasty, Emperor Gaozu decreed that local officials would be asked to recommend promising candidates for public service. Thirty years later, in 165 B.C.E., the first known civil service examination was administered to candidates for positions in the bureaucracy. Shortly after that, an academy was established to train candidates. Nevertheless, the first candidates were almost all from aristocratic or other wealthy families, and the Han bureaucracy itself was still dominated by the traditional hereditary elite. Still, the principle of selecting officials on the basis of talent had been established and would eventually become standard practice.

Under the Han dynasty, the population increased rapidly—by some estimates rising from about 20 million to over 60 million at the height of the dynasty—creating a growing need for a large and efficient bureaucracy to maintain the state in proper working order. Unfortunately, the Han were unable to resolve all of the problems left over from the past. Factionalism at court remained a serious problem and undermined the efficiency of the central government. Equally important, despite their efforts, the Han rulers were never able to restrain the great aristocratic families, who continued to play a dominant role in political and economic affairs. The failure to curb the power of the wealthy clans eventually became a major factor in the final collapse of the dynasty.

SOCIETY AND ECONOMY IN THE HAN EMPIRE

Han rulers also retained some of the economic and social policies of their predecessors. In particular, they saw that a free peasantry paying taxes directly to the state would both limit the wealth and power of the great noble families and increase the state's revenues. The Han had difficulty preventing the recurrence of the economic inequities that had characterized the last years of the Zhou, however. The land taxes were relatively light, but the peasants also faced a number of other exactions, including military service and forced labor of up to one month annually. Although the use of iron tools brought new lands under the plow and food production increased steadily, the trebling of the population under the Han eventually reduced the average size of the individual farm plot to about one acre per capita, barely enough for survival. As time went on, many poor peasants were forced to sell their land and become tenant farmers, paying rents ranging up to half of the annual harvest. Thus, land once again came to be concentrated in the hands of the powerful landed clans, which often owned thousands of acres worked by tenants and mustered their own military forces to bully free farmers into becoming tenants.

Although such economic problems contributed to the eventual downfall of the dynasty, in general the Han era was one of unparalleled productivity and prosperity. The

OUTPOST OF EMPIRE. Located at the junction of two rivers passing through the sandy wastes of the Turfan Depression, in modern Xinjiang Province, the town of Jiaohe was one of the first outposts established by the Han Dynasty as it expanded westward into Central Asia in the first century C.E. Previously inhabited by the Indo-European-speaking Tocharian peoples, eventually Jiaohe would become a prominent stopping point on the Silk Road before being overrun by the Mongols in the thirteenth century. The town was located on top of the plateau to the left. On the right side of the photograph are storage bins used today to dry grapes.

MAP 3.4 Trade Routes of the Ancient World

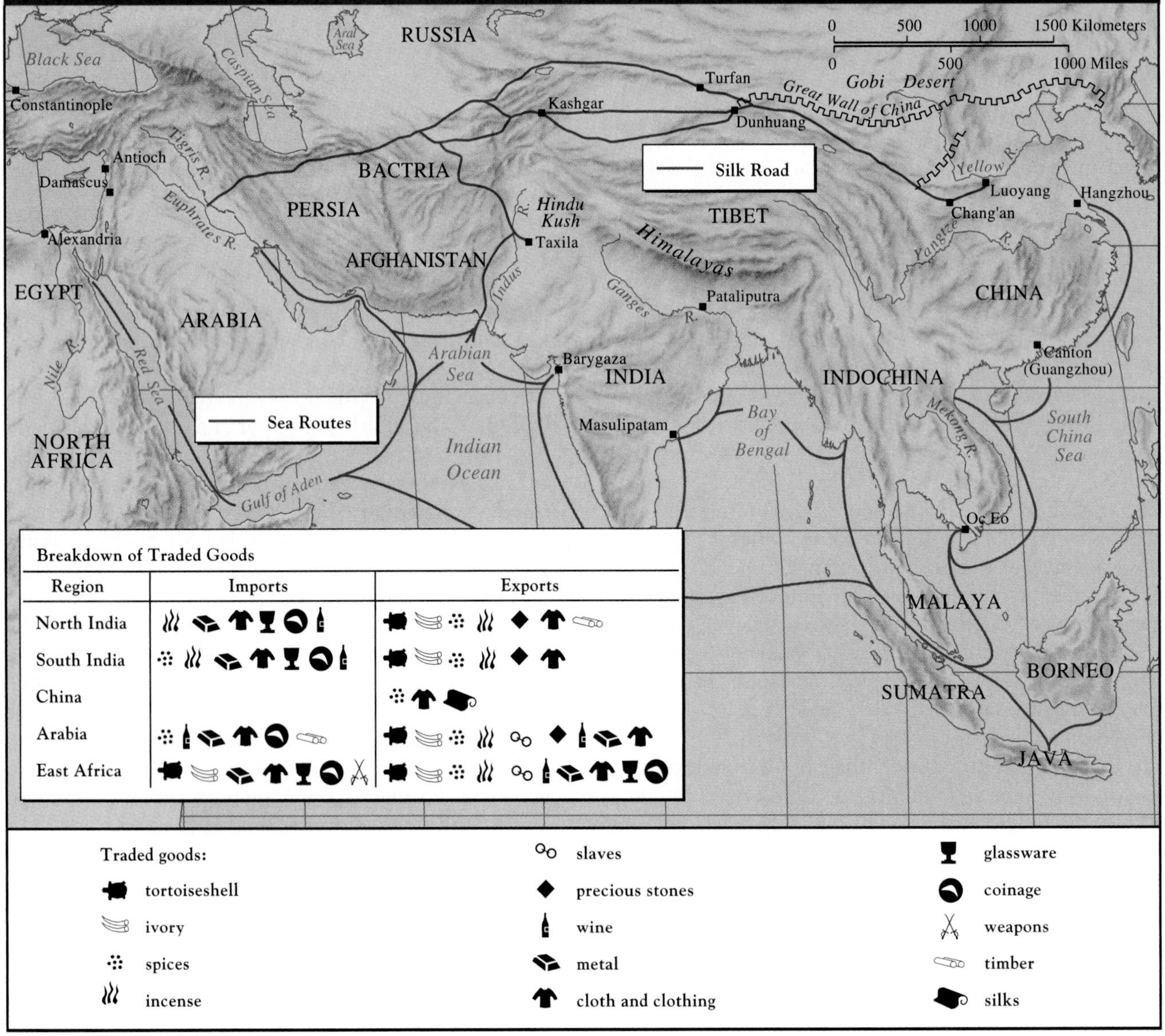

0 500 1000 1500 Kilometers
0 500 1000 Miles
RUSSIA
Aral Sea
Black Sea
Caspian Sea
Constantinople
Antioch
Damascus
Alexandria
Tigris R.
Euphrates R.
BACTRIA
PERSIA
AFGHANISTAN
Hindu Kush
Taxila
Kashgar
Turfan
Dunhuang
Gobi Desert
Great Wall of China
Silk Road
TIBET
Himalayas
Yellow R.
Luoyang
Chang'an
Hangzhou
Yangtze R.
CHINA
EGYPT
ARABIA
Nile R.
Red Sea
Indus R.
Ganges R.
Pataliputra
Arabian Sea
Barygaza
INDIA
Masulipatam
Bay of Bengal
INDOCHINA
Mekong R.
Canton (Guangzhou)
South China Sea
Sea Routes
NORTH AFRICA
Gulf of Aden
Indian Ocean
Oc Eo
MALAYA
SUMATRA
BORNEO
JAVA

Breakdown of Traded Goods

Region	Imports	Exports
North India	incense, metal, cloth and clothing, glassware, coinage, wine	tortoiseshell, ivory, spices, incense, precious stones, cloth and clothing, timber
South India	spices, incense, metal, cloth and clothing, glassware, coinage, wine	tortoiseshell, ivory, spices, incense, precious stones, cloth and clothing
China		spices, cloth and clothing, silks
Arabia	spices, wine, metal, cloth and clothing, coinage, timber	tortoiseshell, ivory, spices, incense, slaves, precious stones, wine, metal, cloth and clothing
East Africa	tortoiseshell, ivory, metal, cloth and clothing, glassware, coinage, weapons	tortoiseshell, ivory, spices, incense, slaves, wine, metal, cloth and clothing, glassware, coinage

Traded goods:
tortoiseshell
ivory
spices
incense
slaves
precious stones
wine
metal
cloth and clothing
glassware
coinage
weapons
timber
silks

period was marked by a major expansion of trade, both domestic and foreign. This was not necessarily due to official encouragement. In fact, the Han were as suspicious of private merchants as their predecessors had been and levied stiff taxes on trade in an effort to limit commercial activities. Merchants were also subject to severe social constraints. They were disqualified from seeking office, restricted in their place of residence, and viewed in general as parasites providing little true value to Chinese society.

The state itself directed much trade and manufacturing; it manufactured weapons, for example, and operated shipyards, granaries, and mines. The government also moved cautiously into foreign trade, mostly with neighboring areas in Central and Southeast Asia, although trade relations were established with countries as far away as India and the Mediterranean. Some of this long-distance trade was carried by sea through southern ports like Quangzhou, but more was transported by overland caravans on the Silk Road (see Chapter 10) and other routes that led westward into Central Asia. Some of the trade was organized in the form of tribute missions, with neighboring countries providing local specialties like tropical products and precious stones in return for Chinese silks, glazed pottery (an early form of porcelain), and various manufactured products. China often gave more than it received to ensure that neighboring monarchs would accept China's benevolent protection and not harbor its enemies.

New technology contributed to the economic prosperity of the Han era. Significant progress was achieved in such areas as textile manufacturing, water mills, and iron casting; the latter led to the invention of steel a few centuries later. Paper was invented under the Han, while the invention of the rudder and fore-and-aft rigging permitted ships to sail into the wind for the first time. Thus equipped, Chinese merchant ships carrying heavy cargoes could sail throughout the islands of Southeast Asia and into the Indian Ocean.

Finally, the Han emperors continued the process of territorial expansion and consolidation that had begun under the Zhou and the Qin. Han rulers, notably Han Wudi (Han Wu Ti, or Martial Emperor of Han), successfully completed the assimilation into the empire of the regions south of the Yangtze River, including the Red River delta in what is today northern Vietnam. Han armies also marched westward as far as the Caspian Sea, pacifying nomadic tribal peoples and extending China's boundary far into Central Asia. The Han continued to have problems with the Xiongnu beyond the Great Wall to the north. Nomadic raids on Chinese territory continued intermittently to the end of the dynasty, once reaching almost to the gates of the capital city, now located at Chang'an (Ch'ang An, or Eternal Peace), on the site of modern Xian.

JADE BURIAL SUIT. During the Han dynasty, members of the imperial family were buried in jade body suits such as this one, which dates from the second century B.C.E. It is composed of jade squares that were sewn together with gold thread. Extremely expensive to produce, they were eventually banned by the court as too extravagant.

THE DECLINE AND FALL OF THE HAN

In 9 C.E., the reformist official Wang Mang, who was troubled by the plight of the peasants, seized power from the Han court and declared the foundation of a new Xin (New) dynasty. In the years prior to his seizure of power, the empire had begun to fall into decay. As frivolous or depraved rulers amused themselves with the pleasures of court life, the power and influence of the central government began to wane, and the great noble families filled the vacuum, amassing vast landed estates and transforming free farmers into tenants. Wang Mang tried to confiscate the great estates, restore the ancient well field system, and abolish slavery. In so doing, however, he alienated powerful interests, who conspired to overthrow him. In 23 C.E., beset by administrative chaos and a collapse of the frontier defenses, Wang Mang was killed in a coup d'etat.

For a time, strong leadership revived some of the glory of the early Han. The court did attempt to reduce land taxes and carry out land resettlement programs. The growing popularity of nutritious crops like rice, wheat, and soybeans, along with the introduction of new crops such as alfalfa and grapes, helped to boost food production. But the monopoly of land and power by the great landed families continued. Weak rulers were isolated within their imperial chambers and dominated by eunuchs and other powerful figures at court. Official corruption and the concentration of land in the hands of the wealthy led to widespread peasant unrest. The population of the empire, which had been estimated at about 60 million in China's first census in the year 2 C.E., had shrunk to less than 20 million two hundred years later. In the early third century C.E., the dynasty was finally brought to an end when power was seized by Cao Cao (Ts'ao Ts'ao), a general well known to millions of later Chinese as one of the main characters in the famous Chinese epic *The Romance of the Three Kingdoms*. But Cao Cao was unable to consolidate his power, and China entered a period of almost constant anarchy and internal division, compounded by invasions of northern tribal peoples. The next great dynasty did not arise until the beginning of the seventh century, four hundred years later.

FLOODED RICE FIELDS. Rice is a very labor-intensive crop, which requires many workers to plant the seedlings and organize the distribution of water. Initially, the fields are flooded to facilitate the rooting of the rice seedlings and to add nutrients to the soil. Fish breeding in the flooded fields help keep mosquitoes and other insects in check. As the plants mature, the fields are drained, and the plants complete their four-month growing cycle in dry soil.

Daily Life in Ancient China

Few social institutions have been as closely identified with China as the family. As in most agricultural civilizations, the family served as the basic economic and social unit in society. In traditional China, however, it took on an almost sacred quality as a microcosm of the entire social order.

In Neolithic times, the farm village, organized around the clan, was the basic social unit in China, at least in the core region of the Yellow River valley. Even then, however, the smaller family unit was becoming more important, at least among the nobility, who attached considerable significance to the ritual veneration of their immediate ancestors.

During the Zhou dynasty, the family took on increasing importance, in part because of the need for cooperation in agriculture. The cultivation of rice, which had become the primary crop along the Yangtze River and in the provinces to the south, is highly labor-intensive. The seedlings must be planted in several inches of water in a nursery bed and then transferred individually to the paddy beds, which must be irrigated constantly. During the harvest, the stalks must be cut and the kernels carefully separated from the stalks and husks. As a result, children—and the labor they supplied—were considered essential to the survival of the family, not only during their youthful years but also later, when sons were expected to provide for their parents. Loyalty to family members came to be considered even more important than loyalty to the broader community or the state. Confucius commented that it is the mark of a civilized society that a son should protect his father even if the latter has committed a crime against the community.

At the crux of the concept of family was the idea of filial piety, which called on all members of the family to subordinate their needs and desires to the patriarchal head of the family. More broadly, it created a hierarchical system in which every family member had his or her place. All Chinese learned the "five relationships" that were the key to a proper social order. The son was subordinate to the father, the wife to her husband, the younger brother to the older brother, and all were subject to their king. The final relationship was the proper one between friend and friend. Only if all members of the family and the community as a whole behaved in a properly filial manner would society function effectively.

A stable family system based on obedient and hardworking members can serve as a bulwark for an efficient government, but putting loyalty to the family and the clan over loyalty to the state can also present a threat to a centralizing monarch. For that reason, the Qin dynasty attempted to destroy the clan system in China and assert the primacy of the state. Legalists even imposed heavy taxes on any family with more than two adult sons in order to break down the family concept. The Qin reportedly also originated the practice of organizing several family units into larger groups of five and ten families that would exercise mutual control and surveillance. Later dynasties continued the practice under the name of the *Bao-jia* (*Pao-chia*) system.

But the efforts of the Qin to eradicate or at least reduce the importance of the family system ran against tradition and the dynamics of the Chinese economy, and under the Han the family revived and increased in importance. Under the Han, with official encouragement, the family system began to take on the character that it would possess until our own day. The family was not only the basic economic unit; it was also the basic social unit for education, religious observances, and training in ethical principles.

We know much more about the lifestyle of the elites than that of the common people in ancient China. The first houses were probably constructed of wooden planks, but later Chinese mastered the art of building in tile and brick. By the first millennium B.C.E., most public buildings and the houses of the wealthy were probably constructed in this manner. By Han times, most Chinese probably lived in simple houses of mud, wooden planks, or brick with thatch or occasionally tile roofs. But in some areas, especially the loess (pronounced "less," a type of soil common in North China) regions of North China, cave dwelling remained common down to modern times. The most famous cave dweller of modern times was Mao Zedong, who lived in a cave in Yan'an during his long struggle against Chiang Kai-shek.

Chinese houses usually had little furniture; most people squatted or sat with their legs spread out on the packed mud floor. Chairs were apparently not introduced until the sixth or seventh centuries C.E. Clothing was simple, consisting of cotton trousers and shirts in the summer and wool or burlap in the winter.

The staple foods were millet in the north and rice in the south. Other common foods were wheat, barley, mustard greens, and bamboo shoots. In early times, such foods were often consumed in the form of porridge, but by the Zhou dynasty, stir-frying in a wok was becoming common. Where possible, the Chinese family would vary its diet of grain foods with vegetables, fruit (including pears, peaches, apricots, and plums), and fish or meat; but for most, such additions to the daily plate of rice, millet, or soybeans were a rare luxury.

Alcohol in the form of ale was drunk at least by the higher classes and by the early Zhou era had already begun to inspire official concern. According to the *Book of History*, "King Wen admonished . . . the young nobles . . . that they should not ordinarily use spirits; and throughout all the states he required that they should be drunk only on occasion of sacrifices, and that then virtue should preside so that there might be no drunkenness."[13]

Most Chinese, then as now, lived in the countryside. But as time went on, cities began to play a larger role in Chinese society. The first towns were little more than forts for the local aristocracy; they were small in size and limited in population. By the Zhou era, however, larger towns, usually located on the major trade routes, began to combine administrative and economic functions, serving as regional markets or manufacturing centers. Such cities were usually surrounded by a wall and a moat, and a raised platform might be built within the walls to provide a place for ritual ceremonies and housing for the ruler's family.

By the Han, the major city in China was Chang'an, the imperial capital. The city covered a total area of nearly forty square kilometers and was enclosed by a twelve-foot earthen wall surrounded by a moat. Twelve gates provided entry into the city, and eight major avenues ran east-west or north-south. Each avenue was forty-five meters wide; a center strip in each avenue was reserved for the emperor, whose palace and gardens occupied nearly half the southern and central part of the city.

The Humble Estate: Women in Ancient China

Female subservience was a key element in the social system of ancient China. As in many traditional societies, the male was considered of transcendent importance because of his role as food procurer or, in the case of farming communities, food producer. In ancient China, men worked in the fields and women raised children and served in the home. The Chinese written language graphically demonstrates how ancient Chinese society regarded the sexes. The character for man (**男**) combines the symbols for strength and a rice field, whereas the character for woman (**女**) represents a person in a posture of deference and respect. The character for peace (**安**) is a woman under a roof. A wife is symbolized by a woman with a broom.

Confucian thought, while not denigrating the importance of women as mothers and homemakers, accepted the dual roles of men and women in Chinese society. Men governed society. They carried on family ritual through the veneration of ancestors. They were the warriors, scholars, and ministers. Their dominant role was firmly enshrined in the legal system. Men were permitted to have more than one wife and to divorce a spouse who did not produce a male child. Women were denied the right to own property, and there was no dowry system in ancient China that would have provided the wife with a degree of financial security from her husband and his family. As the third-century C.E. woman poet Fu Xuan lamented:

How sad it is to be a woman
Nothing on earth is held so cheap.
No one is glad when a girl is born.
By her the family sets no store.
No one cries when she leaves her home
Sudden as clouds when the rain stops.[14]

Not surprisingly, women were taught to accept their secondary role in life. Ban Zhao, a prominent female historian of the Han dynasty, whose own career was an exception to the rule, described that role as follows:

> To be humble, yielding, respectful and reverential; to put herself after others . . . these qualities are those exemplifying woman's low and humble estate. To retire late and rise early; not to shirk exertion from dawn to dark . . . this is called being diligent. To behave properly and decorously in serving her husband; to be serene and self-possessed, shunning jests and laughter . . . this is called being worthy of continuing the husband's lineage. If a woman possess the above-mentioned three qualities, then her reputation shall be excellent.[15]

Some women did become a force in politics, especially at court, where wives of the ruler or other female members of the royal family were often influential in palace intrigues. Such activities were frowned on, however, as the following passage from the *Book of Songs* attests:

A clever man builds a city,
A clever woman lays one low;
With all her qualifications, that clever woman
Is but an ill-omened bird.
A woman with a long tongue
Is a flight of steps leading to calamity;
For disorder does not come from heaven,
But is brought about by women.
Among those who cannot be trained or taught
Are women and eunuchs.[16]

HAN POTTERY HOUSE. During the Han dynasty, the Chinese people thought that even in heaven one could still be surrounded by one's earthly possessions, such as family, servants, and house. Since such material goods could not accompany one directly into the afterworld, pottery models such as the one shown here were made and then placed in tombs with the dead.

The World of Culture

Modern knowledge about artistic achievements in ancient civilizations is limited because often little has survived the ravages of time. Fortunately, many ancient civilizations, such as Egypt and Mesopotamia, were located in relatively arid areas where many artifacts were preserved, even over thousands of years. In more humid regions, such as China and Southeast Asia, the cultural residue left by the civilizations of antiquity has been adversely affected by climate.

As a result, relatively little remains of the cultural achievements of the prehistoric Chinese aside from Neolithic pottery and the relics found at the site of the Shang dynasty capital at Anyang. In recent years, a rich trove from the time of the Qin Empire has been unearthed near the tomb of Qin Shi Huangdi near Xian in central China and at Han tombs nearby. But little remains of the literature of ancient China and almost none of the painting, architecture, and music.

Metalwork and Sculpture

Discoveries at archaeological sites indicate that ancient China was a society rich in cultural achievement. The pottery found at Neolithic sites such as Banpo, Longshan, and Yangshao exhibits a freshness and vitality of form and design, while the ornaments, such as rings and beads, show a strong aesthetic sense.

The pace of Chinese cultural development began to quicken during the Shang dynasty, which ruled in northern China from the eighteenth to the twelfth century B.C.E. At that time, objects cast in bronze, which are among the most extraordinary and admired creations of Chinese art, began to appear. A variety of bronze vessels were produced for use in preparing and serving food and drink in the ancestral rites. Later vessels were used for decoration or for dining at court.

Shang bronzes, with their highly sophisticated and intricate relief work, are technically unequaled and are considered one of the highest cultural achievements of antiquity. Many Shang bronzes were decorated with a *taotie* (t'ao-t'ieh) mask with two large globular eyes, nostrils, fangs, and sometimes claws and horns. It is normally presented as the silhouette of two dragons face to face, so that each forms half the mask. Although fierce in appearance, the *taotie* represented a guardian force against evil spirits.

The method of casting used was one reason for the extraordinary quality of Shang bronze work. Bronze workers in most ancient civilizations used the lost-wax method, where a model was first made in wax. After a clay mold had been formed around it, the model was heated so that the wax would disappear, and the empty space was filled with molten metal. In China, clay molds composed of several sections were tightly fit together prior to the introduction of the liquid bronze. This technique, which had evolved from ceramic techniques used during the Neolithic period, enabled the artisans to apply the design directly to the mold and thus contributed to the clarity of line and rich surface decoration of the Shang bronzes.

Bronze casting became a large-scale business, and more than ten thousand vessels of an incredible variety of form and design survive today. The art of bronze working continued into the Zhou and the Han dynasties, but the quality and originality declined. The Shang bronzes remain the pinnacle of creative art in ancient China.

One reason for the decline of bronze casting in China was the rise in popularity of iron. Iron making developed in China around the ninth or eighth century B.C.E., much later than in the Middle East, where it had been mastered almost a millennium earlier. Once familiar with the process, however, the Chinese quickly moved to the forefront. Iron workers in Europe and the Middle East, lacking the technology to achieve the high temperatures necessary to melt iron ore for casting, were forced to work with wrought iron, a cumbersome and expensive process. By the fourth century B.C.E., the Chinese had invented the technique of the blast furnace, powered by a person operating a bellows. They were therefore able to manufacture cast-iron ritual vessels and agricultural tools centuries before an equivalent technology appeared in the West.

Another reason for the deterioration of the bronze-casting tradition was the development of lacquerware and ceramics. Lacquer, obtained from a resinous substance

A BRONZE HORSE. This horse from a second-century C.E. Han tomb is a beautiful example of Chinese bronze sculpture. Caught in a pose of suspended animation, it suggests the divine power that the Chinese of this time attributed to horses.

deposited on trees by the *lac* insect, had been produced since Neolithic times, and by the Han it had become a popular method of applying a hard coating to objects made of wood or fabric. Pottery, too, had existed since early times, but technological advances during the Han led to the production of a high-quality form of pottery covered with a brown or gray-green glaze, the latter known popularly as celadon. During the Han, both lacquerware and pottery replaced bronze in popularity and value.

In 1974, in a remarkable discovery, farmers digging a well about thirty-five miles east of Xian unearthed a number of terra-cotta figures in an underground pit about one mile east of the burial mound of the First Emperor of Qin. Chinese archaeologists sent to work at the site discovered a vast terra-cotta army that they believed was a re-creation of Qin Shi Huangdi's imperial guard, which was to accompany the emperor on his journey to the next world.

One of the astounding features of the terra-cotta army is its size. The army is enclosed in four pits that were originally encased in a wooden framework, which has since disintegrated. More than a thousand figures have already been unearthed in the first pit, along with horses, wooden chariots, and seven thousand bronze weapons. Archaeologists estimate that there are more than six thousand figures in that pit alone.

QIN SHI HUANGDI'S TOMB. The First Emperor of Qin ordered the construction of an elaborate mausoleum, an underground palace complex protected by an army of terra-cotta soldiers and horses to accompany him on his journey to the afterlife. This massive formation of 6,000 life-sized armed soldiers, discovered accidentally by farmers in 1974, reflects the grandeur and power that was Qin Shi Huangdi's.

Equally impressive is the quality of the work. Slightly larger than life-size, the figures were molded of finely textured clay, then fired and painted. The detail on the uniforms is realistic and sophisticated, but the most striking feature is the individuality of the facial features of the soldiers. Apparently, ten different head shapes were used and were then modeled further by hand to reflect the variety of ethnic groups and personality types in the army.

The discovery of the terra-cotta army also shows that the Chinese had come a long way from the human sacrifices that had taken place at the death of Shang sovereigns more than a thousand years earlier. But the project must have been ruinously expensive and is additional evidence of the burden the Qin ruler imposed on his subjects. One historian has estimated that one-third of the national income in Qin and Han times may have been spent on preparations for the ruler's afterlife. The emperor's mausoleum has not yet been unearthed, but it is enclosed in a mound seventy-six meters in height and is surrounded by a rectangular wall six kilometers in circumference. According to the Han historian Sima Qian, the ceiling is a replica of the heavens, while the floor contains a relief model of the entire Qin kingdom, with rivers flowing in mercury. According to tradition, traps were set within the mausoleum to prevent intruders, and the workers putting in the final touches were buried alive in the tomb with its secrets.

Qin Shi Huangdi's ambitious effort to provide for his immortality became a pattern for his successors during the Han dynasty, although apparently on a somewhat more modest scale. In 1990, Chinese workers discovered a similar underground army for a Han emperor of the second century B.C.E. Like the imperial guard of the First Qin Emperor, the underground soldiers were buried in parallel pits and possessed their own weapons and individual facial features. But they were smaller—only one-third the height of the average human adult—and were armed with wooden weapons and were dressed in silk clothing, now decayed. A burial pit nearby indicates that as many as ten thousand workers, probably slaves or prisoners, died in the process of building the emperor's mausoleum, which took an estimated ten years to construct.

Language and Literature

Precisely when writing developed in China cannot be determined, but certainly by Shang times, as the oracle bones demonstrate, the Chinese had developed a simple but functional script. Like many other languages of antiquity, it was primarily ideographic and pictographic in form. Symbols, usually called "characters," were created to represent an idea or to form a picture of the object to be represented. For example, the Chinese characters for mountain (山), the sun (日), and the moon (月) were meant to represent the objects themselves. Other characters, such as "big" (大) (a man with his arms outstretched), represent an idea. The word "east" (東) symbolizes the sun coming up behind the trees.

Each character, of course, would be given a sound by the speaker when pronounced. In other cultures, this process led to the abandonment of the system of ideographs and the adoption of a written language based on phonetic symbols. The Chinese language, however, has never entirely abandoned its original ideographical format, although the phonetic element has developed into a significant part of the individual character. In that sense, the Chinese written language is virtually unique in the world today.

One reason the language retained its ideographic quality may have been the aesthetic quality of the written characters. By the time of the Han dynasty, if not earlier, the written language came to be seen as an art form as well as a means of communication, and calligraphy

TOMB SOLDIER (QIN SHI HUANGDI'S TOMB). This is one of the 6,000 soldiers guarding the underground palace complex of Emperor Qin Shi Huangdi's tomb. Incredibly, each soldier has individualized facial features and expressions. Originally, they carried real weapons, and their uniforms were painted in brilliant colors. They are a most majestic and foreboding sight.

became one of the most prized forms of painting in China.

More importantly, if the written language had developed in the direction of a phonetic alphabet, it could no longer have served as the written system for all the peoples of an expanding civilization. Although the vast majority spoke a tongue derived from a parent Sinitic language (a system distinguished by its tonal nature, a characteristic that gives Chinese its lilting quality even today), the languages spoken in various regions of the country differed from each other in pronunciation and to a lesser degree in vocabulary and syntax; for the most part, they were (and are today) mutually unintelligible.

The Chinese answer to this problem was to give all the spoken languages the same writing system. Although any character might be pronounced differently in different regions of China, that character would be written the same way (after the standardization undertaken under the Qin) no matter where it was written. This system of written characters could be read by educated Chinese from one end of the country to the other. It became the language of the bureaucracy and the vehicle for the transmission of Chinese culture to all Chinese from the Great Wall to the southern border and even beyond. The written language, however, was not identical with the spoken. Written Chinese evolved a totally separate vocabulary and grammatical structure from the spoken tongues. As a result, those who used it required special training.

The earliest extant form of Chinese literature dates from the Zhou dynasty. It was written on silk or strips of bamboo and consisted primarily of historical records such as the *Rites of Zhou*, philosophical treatises such as the *Analects* and *The Way of the Dao*, and poetry, as recorded in the *Book of Songs* and the *Song of the South* (see the box on p. 90). In later years, when Confucian principles had been elevated to a state ideology, the key works identified with the Confucian School were integrated into a set of so-called Confucian Classics. These works became required reading for generations of Chinese schoolchildren and introduced them to the forms of behavior that would be required of them as adults.

Under the Han dynasty, although poetry and philosophical essays continued to be popular, historical writing became the primary form of literary creativity. Historians such as Sima Qian and Ban Gu (the dynasty's official historian and the older brother of the female historian Ban Zhao) wrote works that became models for later dynastic histories. These historical works combined political and social history with biographies of key figures. Like so much literary work in China, their primary purpose was moral and political—to explain the underlying reasons for the rise and fall of individual human beings and dynasties.

Music

From early times in China, music was viewed not just as an aesthetic pleasure, but as a means of achieving political order and refining the human character. In fact, music may have originated as a means of accompanying sacred ritual at the royal court. According to the *Historical Records*, a history written during the Han dynasty: "When our sage-kings of the past instituted rites and music, their objective was far from making people indulge in the . . . amusements of singing and dancing. . . . Music is produced to purify the heart, and rites introduced to rectify the behavior."[17] Eventually, however, music began to be appreciated for its own sake as well as for singing and dancing, especially among the common people.

A wide variety of musical instruments were used, including flutes, various stringed instruments, bells and chimes, drums, and gourds. Bells cast in bronze were first used as musical instruments in the Shang period; they were hung in rows and then struck with a wooden mallet. The finest were produced during the mid-Zhou era and are

LOVE SPURNED IN ANCIENT CHINA

The Book of Songs is an anthology of about three hundred poems written during the early Zhou dynasty. According to tradition, they were selected by Confucius from a much larger collection. In later years, many were given political interpretations. The poem reprinted here, however, expresses a very human cry of love spurned.

THE BOOK OF SONGS: THE ODES

You seemed a guileless youth enough,
Offering for silk your woven stuff;
But silk was not required by you;
I was the silk you had in view.
With you I crossed the ford, and while
We wandered on for many a mile
I said, "I do not wish delay,
But friends must fix our wedding-day. . . .
Oh, do not let my words give pain,
But with the autumn come again."

And then I used to watch and wait
To see you passing through the gate;
And sometimes, when I watched in vain,
My tears would flow like falling rain;
But when I saw my darling boy,
I laughed and cried aloud for joy.
The fortune-tellers, you declared,
Had all pronounced us duly paired;
"Then bring a carriage," I replied,
"And I'll away to be your bride."

The mulberry tree upon the ground,
Now sheds its yellow leaves around.
Three years have slipped away from me
Since first I shared your poverty;
And now again, alas the day!
Back through the ford I take my way.

My heart is still unchanged, but you
Have uttered words now proved untrue;
And you have left me to deplore
A love that can be mine no more.

For three long years I was your wife,
And led in truth a toilsome life;
Early to rise and late to bed,
Each day alike passed o'er my head.
I honestly fulfilled my part,
And you—well, you have broke my heart.
The truth my brothers will not know,
So all the more their gibes will flow.
I grieve in silence and repine
That such a wretched fate is mine.

Ah, hand in hand to face old age!—
Instead, I turn a bitter page.
O for the riverbanks of yore;
O for the much-loved marshy shore;
The hours of girlhood, with my hair
Ungathered, as we lingered there.
The words we spoke, that seemed so true,
I little thought that I should rue;
I little thought the vows we swore
Would some day bind us two no more.

considered to be among the best examples of early bronze work in China.

By the late Zhou era, bells had begun to give way as the instrument of choice to strings and wind instruments, while the purpose of music shifted from ceremony to entertainment. This led conservative critics to rail against the onset of an age of debauchery.

Ancient historians stressed the relationship between music and court life, but it is highly probable that music, singing, and dancing were equally popular among the common people. The *Book of History,* purporting to describe conditions in the late third millennium B.C.E., suggests that ballads emanating from the popular culture were welcomed at court. Nevertheless, court music and popular music differed in several respects. Among other things, popular music was more likely to be motivated by the desire for pleasure than for the purpose of law and order and moral uplift. Those differences continued to be reflected in the evolution of music in China down to modern times.

CONCLUSION

Of the great classical civilizations discussed in Part I of this book, China was the last to come into full flower. By the time the Shang began to emerge as an organized state, the societies in Mesopotamia and the Nile valley had already reached an advanced level of civilization.

Unfortunately, not enough is known about the early stages of these civilizations to allow us to determine why some developed earlier than others, but one likely reason for China's late arrival was that it was virtually isolated from other emerging centers of culture elsewhere in the world and thus was compelled to develop essentially on its own. Only at the end of the first millennium B.C.E. did the Han dynasty come into regular contact with other civilizations in South Asia, the Middle East, and the Mediterranean.

Once embarked on its own path toward the creation of a complex society, however, China achieved results that were in all respects the equal of its counterparts elsewhere. During the glory years of the Han dynasty, China extended the boundaries of its empire far into the sands of Central Asia and southward along the coast of the South China Sea into what is now Vietnam. The doctrine of State Confucianism provided an effective ideology for the state, and Chinese culture appeared unrivaled. In many respects, its scientific and technological achievements were unsurpassed.

One reason for China's striking success undoubtedly was that, unlike its contemporary civilizations, it long was able to fend off the danger from nomadic peoples (along the northern frontier). By the end of the second century B.C.E., however, the Xiongnu were looming ominously, and tribal warriors began to nip at the borders of the empire. While the dynasty was strong, the problem was manageable, but when internal difficulties began to corrode the unity of the state, China became increasingly vulnerable to the threat from the north and entered its own time of troubles.

During the glory years of the Han, another great civilization was beginning to take form on the northern shores of the Mediterranean Sea. Unlike China and the other ancient societies discussed thus far, this new civilization in Europe was based as much on trade as on agriculture. Yet the political and cultural achievements of ancient Greece were the equal of any of the great human experiments that had preceded it and soon began to exert a significant impact on the rest of the ancient world.

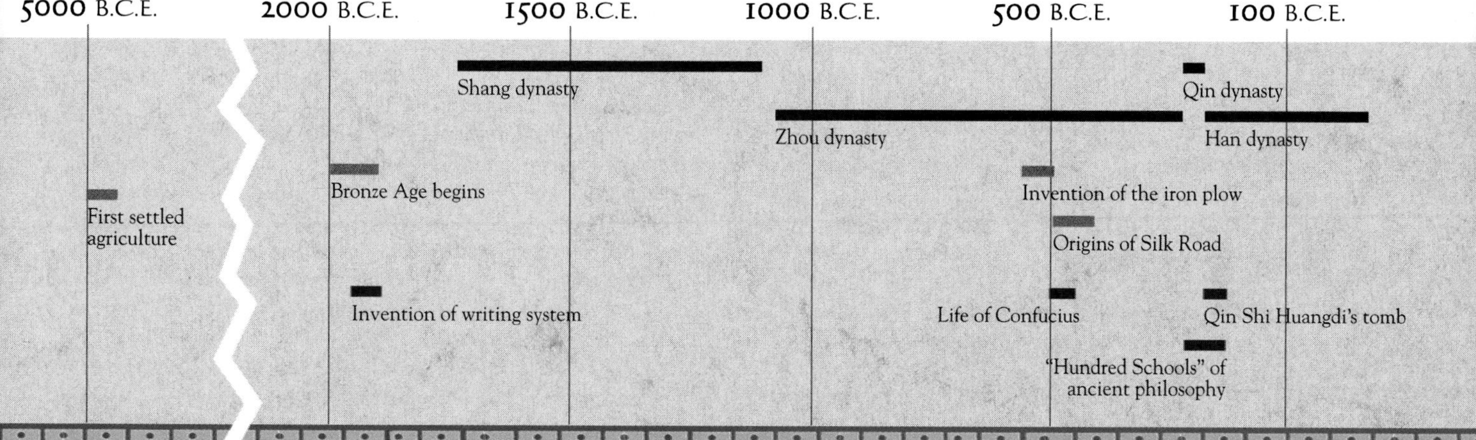

Chapter Notes

1. *Book of Changes*, quoted in Chang Chi-yun, *Chinese History of Fifty Centuries*, vol. 1, *Ancient Times* (Taipei, 1962), pp. 15, 31, and 65.
2. Ibid., p. 381.
3. Quoted in E. N. Anderson, *The Food of China* (New Haven, Conn., 1988), p. 21.
4. According to Chinese tradition, the *Rites of Zhou* was written by the duke of Zhou himself near the time of the founding of the Zhou dynasty. However, modern historians believe that it was written much later, perhaps as late as the fourth century B.C.E.
5. From *The Book of Songs*, quoted in Sebastian de Grazia, ed., *Masters of Chinese Political Thought: From the Beginnings to the Han Dynasty* (New York, 1973), pp. 40–41.
6. *Confucian Analects* (Lun Yu), ed. James Legge (Taipei, 1963), 11:11 and 6:20.

7. Ibid., 15:23.
8. Ibid., 17:2.
9. *Book of Mencius (Meng Zi)*, 4 A:9, quoted in William Theodore de Bary et al., eds., *Sources of Chinese Tradition*, (New York, 1960), p. 107.
10. Quoted in de Bary, *Sources of Chinese Tradition*, p. 53.
11. Burton Watson, *Records of the Grand Historian of China* (New York, 1961), vol. 2, pp. 155, 160.
12. Ibid., pp. 32, 53.
13. Clae Waltham, *Shu Ching: Book of History* (Chicago, 1971), p. 154.
14. Arthur Waley, ed., *Chinese Poems* (London, 1983), p. xx.
15. Lloyd E. Eastman, *Family, Fields, and Ancestors: Constancy and Change in China's Social and Economic History, 1550–1949* (New York, 1988), p. 19.
16. Quoted in Herbert A. Giles, *A History of Chinese Literature* (New York, 1923), p. 19.
17. Chang Chi-yun, *Chinese History of Fifty Centuries*, p. 183.

Suggested Readings

There are several general histories of China that provide a useful overview of the period of antiquity. Perhaps the best known is the classic *East Asia: Tradition and Transformation* (Boston, 1973), by J. K. Fairbank, E. O. Reischauer, and A. M. Craig. Also of use are C. Schirokauer, *A Brief History of Chinese and Japanese Civilizations*, 2d ed. (San Diego, 1989); and M. Elvin, *The Pattern of the Chinese Past* (Stanford, Calif., 1973), which presents a provocative interpretation of key issues in Chinese history. Political and social maps of China can be found in A. Herrmann, *An Historical Atlas of China* (Chicago, 1966).

The period of the Neolithic era and the Shang dynasty has received increasing attention in recent years. For an impressively documented and annotated overview, see Kwang-chih Chang, *Shang Civilization* (New Haven, Conn., 1980) and *Studies in Shang Archaeology* (New Haven, Conn., 1982). D. Keightley, *The Origins of Chinese Civilization* (Berkeley, 1983) presents a number of interesting articles on selected aspects of the period. An older but still interesting work is H. Maspero, *China in Antiquity* (Amherst, Mass., 1988), a translation of his *La Chine Antique*.

The Zhou and Qin dynasties have also received considerable attention. The former is exhaustively analyzed in Cho-yun Hsu and J. M. Linduff, *Western Zhou Civilization* (New Haven, Conn., 1988) and Li Xueqin, *Eastern Zhou and Qin Civilizations* (New Haven, Conn., 1985). The latter is a translation of an original work by a mainland Chinese scholar and is especially interesting for its treatment of the development of the silk industry and the money economy in ancient China. Also of interest is the study of Qin Shi Huangdi by A. Cotterell, *The First Emperor of China* (New York, 1981). On bronze casting, see E. L. Shaughnessy, *Sources of Eastern Zhou History* (Berkeley, 1991). Also of value for its treatment of the formation of social classes is Cho-yun Hsu, *Ancient China in Transition* (Stanford, Calif., 1965).

There are a number of useful books on the Han dynasty. Zhongshu Wang, *Han Civilization* (New Haven, Conn., 1982) presents new evidence from the mainland on recent excavations from Han tombs and the old imperial capital of Chang'an. M. Loewe, *Everyday Life in Early Imperial China during the Han Period, 202 BC–220 AD* (London, 1968) contains useful material on religious beliefs and the development of social classes during the Han. Also, see the lavishly illustrated *The Han Civilization of China* (Oxford, 1982) by M. P. Serstevens. For a firsthand view, see B. Watson, *Records of the Grand Historian of China* (New York, 1961), a translation of key passages from Sima Qian's history of the period. For the historian's life, consult *Ssu-ma Ch'ien: Grand Historian of China* (New York, 1958).

The philosophy of ancient China has attracted considerable attention from Western scholars. Some standard works include A. Waley, *Three Ways of Thought in Ancient China* (New York, 1939); H. G. Creel, *Chinese Thought: From Confucius to Mao Tse-Tung* (Chicago, 1953); Feng Yu-lan, *A Short History of Chinese Philosophy* (New York, 1960); and F. Mote, *Intellectual Foundations of China*, 2d ed. (New York, 1989). On Confucius, see Liu Wu-chi, *A Short History of Confucian Philosophy* (Middlesex, 1955); and H. G. Creel, *Confucius: The Man and the Myth* (London, 1951). The latter is a sympathetic treatment that emphasizes the humanistic side of Confucian philosophy. S. de Grazia, ed., *Masters of Chinese Political Thought: From the Beginnings to the Han Dynasty* (New York, 1973) includes passages from the ancient philosophers that deal with the political realm.

For works on general culture and science, consult the illustrated work by R. Temple, *The Genius of China: 3000 Years of Science, Discovery, and Invention* (New York, 1986); and J. Needham, *Science in Traditional China: A Comparative Perspective* (Boston, 1981). See also E. N. Anderson, *The Food of China* (New Haven, Conn., 1988).

The most comprehensive collection of original writings is W. T. de Bary and Irene Bloom, *Sources of Chinese Tradition*, 2d ed. (New York, 1999), which includes excerpts from most of the ancient texts. The complete translations of the Confucian Classics are in J. Legge, *The Chinese Classics*, 5 vols. (Hong Kong, 1960), with critical and exegetical notes. For a modernized edition of the *Book of History*, see C. Waltham, *Shu Ching: Book of History* (Chicago, 1971). For an annotated version of Lao Tzu, see Wing-Tsit Chan, *The Way of Lao Tzu* (Indianapolis, 1963).

For an introduction to classical Chinese literature, consult the three standard anthologies: Liu Wu-Chi, *An Introduction to Chinese Literature* (New York, 1961); V. H. Mair, ed., *The Columbia Anthology of Traditional Chinese Literature* (New York, 1994); and S. Owen, ed., *An Anthology of Chinese Literature: Beginnings to 1911* (New York, 1996). For a comprehensive introduction to Chinese art, consult M. Sullivan, *The Arts of China*, 4th ed. (Berkeley, 1999), with good illustrations in color. Also, see M. Tregear, *Chinese Art*, revised (London, 1997) and, by the same author, *Art Treasures in China* (New York, 1994).

For additional reading, go to InfoTrac College Edition, your online research library at http://web1.infotrac-college.com

Enter the search terms "Confucius or Confucian" using Keywords.

Enter the search terms "Taoism or Daoism" using the Subject Guide.

Enter the search terms "Han dynasty" using Keywords.

Enter the search terms "China history" using Keywords.

CHAPTER 4

THE CIVILIZATION OF THE GREEKS

CHAPTER OUTLINE

FOCUS QUESTIONS

- What was the *polis*, or city-state, and how did the city-states of Athens and Sparta differ?
- What effects did the Persian Wars and the Great Peloponnesian War have on Greek civilization?
- How was Alexander the Great able to amass his empire, and what was his legacy?
- How did the political, economic, and social institutions of the Hellenistic world differ from those of Classical Greece?
- In what ways did the schools of philosophy and major religions of the Hellenistic period differ from those of the classical period, and what do those differences suggest about society in the two periods?

During the era of civil war in China known as the "Period of the Warring States," a civil war also erupted on the northern shores of the Mediterranean Sea. In 431 B.C.E., two very different Greek city-states—Athens and Sparta—fought for domination of the Greek world. The people of Athens felt secure behind their walls and in the first winter of the war held a public funeral to honor those who had died in battle. On the day of the ceremony, the citizens of Athens joined in a procession, with the relatives of the dead wailing for their loved ones. As was the custom in Athens, one leading citizen was asked to address the crowd, and on this day it was Pericles who spoke to the people. He talked about the greatness of Athens and reminded the Athenians of the strength of their political system: "Our constitution," he said, "is called a democracy because power is in the hands not of a minority but of the whole people. When it is a question of settling private disputes, everyone is equal before the law. . . . Just as our political life is free and open, so is our day-to-day life in our relations with each other. . . . Here each individual is interested not only in his own affairs but in the affairs of the state as well."

In this famous funeral oration, Pericles gave voice to the ideals of democracy and the importance of the individual, ideals that were quite different from those of ancient China, in which the individual was subordinated to a larger order based on obedience to an exalted emperor. The Greeks asked some basic questions about human life: What is the nature of the universe? What is the purpose of human existence? What is our relationship to divine forces? What constitutes a community? What constitutes a state? What is true education? What are the true sources of law? What is truth itself and how do we realize it? The Greeks not only gave answers to these questions; they proceeded to create a system of logical, analytical thought in order to examine them. Their answers and their system of rational thought laid the intellectual foundation for Western civilization's understanding of the human condition.

The story of ancient Greek civilization is a remarkable one that begins with the first arrival of the Greeks around 1900 B.C.E. By the eighth century B.C.E., the characteristic institution of ancient Greek life, the *polis* or city-state, had emerged. Greek civilization flourished and reached its height in the classical era of the fifth century B.C.E., which has come to be closely identified with the achievements of Athenian democracy. But the inability of the Greek city-states to end their fratricidal warfare eventually left them vulnerable to the Macedonian king Philip II and helped to bring an end to the Greek world of independent city-states.

Although the Greek city-states were never the same after their defeat by the Macedonian monarch, this defeat did not bring an end to the influence of the Greeks. Philip's son Alexander led the Macedonians and Greeks on a spectacular conquest of the Persian Empire and opened the door to the spread of Greek culture throughout the Middle East. We use the term *Hellenistic* to designate this new period of Greek history.

EARLY GREECE

Geography played an important role in the evolution of Greek history. Compared to the landmasses of Mesopotamia and Egypt, Greece occupied a small area. It was a mountainous peninsula that encompassed only 45,000 square miles of territory, about the size of the state of Louisiana. The mountains and the sea played especially significant roles in the development of Greek history. Much of Greece consists of small plains and river valleys surrounded by mountain ranges 8,000–10,000 feet high. The mountainous terrain had the effect of isolating Greeks from one another. Consequently, Greek communities tended to follow their own separate paths and develop their own way of life. Over a period of time, these communities became so fiercely attached to their independence that they were unwilling to join into larger units of organization and only too willing to fight one another to gain advantage. No doubt the small size of these independent Greek communities fostered participation in political affairs and unique cultural expressions, but the rivalry among these communities also led to the internecine warfare that ultimately devastated Greek society.

The sea also influenced the evolution of Greek society. Greece had a long seacoast, dotted by bays and inlets that provided numerous harbors. The Greeks also inhabited a number of islands to the west, south, and particularly the east of the Greek mainland. It is no accident that the Greeks became seafarers who sailed out into the Aegean and the Mediterranean Seas first to make contact with the outside world and later to establish colonies that would spread Greek civilization throughout the Mediterranean world.

Greek topography helped to determine the major territories into which Greece was ultimately divided. South of the Gulf of Corinth was the Peloponnesus, virtually an island as seen on a map. Consisting mostly of hills, mountains, and small valleys, the Peloponnesus was the location of Sparta, as well as the site of Olympia, where the famous athletic games were held. Northeast of the Peloponnesus was the Attic peninsula (or Attica), the home of Athens, hemmed in by mountains to the north and west and surrounded by the sea to the south and east. Northwest of Attica was Boeotia in central Greece, with its chief city of Thebes. To the north of Boeotia was Thessaly, which contained the largest plains and became a great producer of grain and horses. To the north of Thessaly lay Macedonia, which was not of much importance in Greek history until 338 B.C.E., when the Macedonian king Philip II conquered the Greeks.

Minoan Crete

The earliest civilization in the Aegean region emerged on Crete. By 2800 B.C.E., a Bronze Age civilization that used metals, especially bronze, in the construction of weapons had been established on the large island of Crete, southeast of the Greek mainland. The civilization of Minoan Crete was first discovered by the English archaeologist Arthur Evans, who named it Minoan after Minos, the legendary king of Crete. Evans's excavations on Crete at the beginning of the twentieth century led to the discovery of an enormous palace complex at Knossus near modern Heracleion. The remains revealed a rich and prosperous culture with Knossus as the probable center of a far-ranging "sea empire," probably largely commercial in nature. Because Evans found few military fortifications for the defense of Knossus itself, he assumed that Minoan Crete had a strong navy. We do know from archaeological remains that the people of Minoan Crete were accustomed to sea travel and had made contact with the more advanced civilization of Egypt. Egyptian products have been found in Crete and Cretan products in Egypt. Minoan Cretans also made contact and exerted influence on the Greek-speaking inhabitants of the Greek mainland.

The Minoan civilization reached its height between 2000 and 1450 B.C.E. The palace at Knossus, the royal seat of the kings, demonstrates the obvious prosperity and power of this civilization. It was an elaborate structure built around a central courtyard and included numerous private living rooms for the royal family and workshops for making decorated vases, small sculptures such as ivory figurines, and jewelry. Even bathrooms, with elaborate drains, formed part of the complex. The rooms were decorated with frescoes in bright colors showing sporting events and naturalistic scenes that have led some to assume that the Cretans had a great love of nature. Storerooms in the palace held enormous jars of oil, wine, and grain, presumably paid as taxes in kind to the king. A large bureaucracy that kept detailed records of the payments apparently assisted the kings.

The centers of Minoan civilization on Crete suffered a sudden and catastrophic collapse around 1450 B.C.E. The cause of this destruction has been vigorously debated. Some historians believe that a tsunami triggered by a powerful volcanic eruption on the island of Thera was responsible for the devastation. Most historians, however, maintain

THE MINOAN SPORT OF BULL LEAPING. Minoan bull games were held on festival days in the great palaces on the island of Crete. As seen in this fresco from the east wing of the palace at Knossus, women and men acrobats (the man in red) somersaulted over the back of the bull. Another person waited behind the bull to catch the leapers.

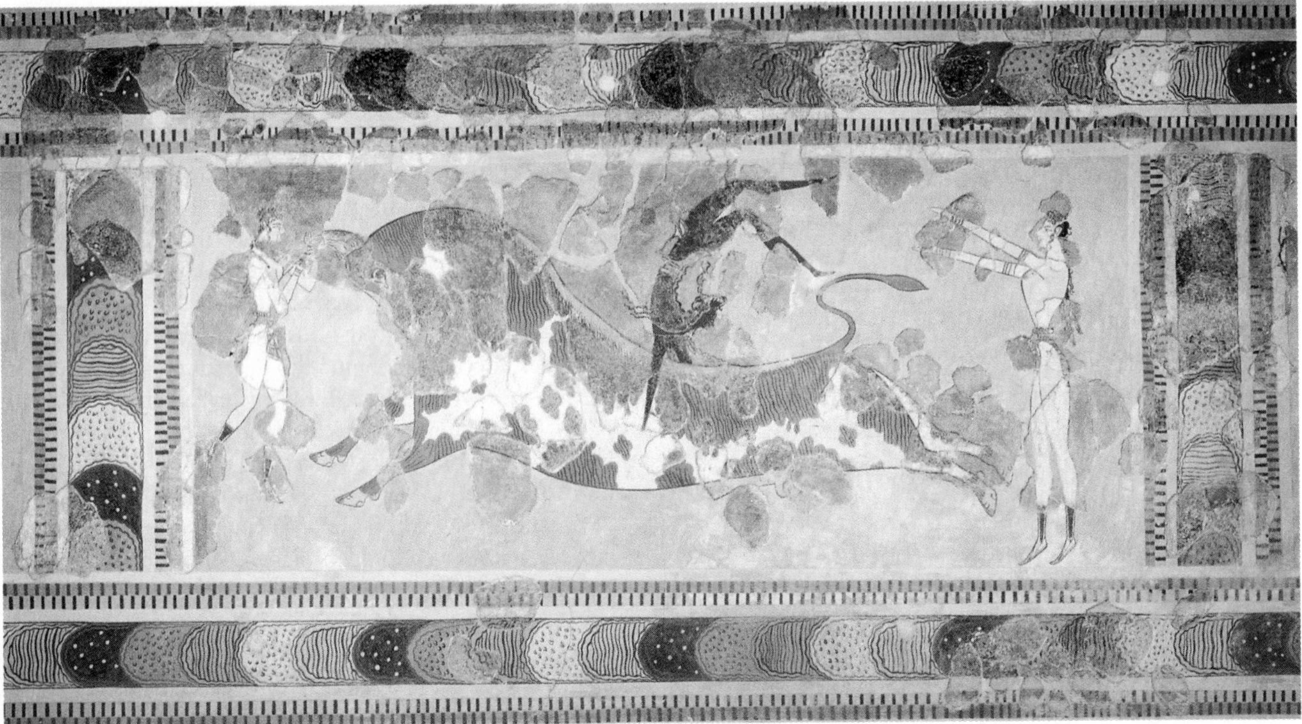

that the destruction was the result of invasion and pillage by mainland Greeks known as the Mycenaeans.

The Mycenaean Greeks

The term *Mycenaean* is derived from Mycenae, a remarkable fortified site first excavated by the amateur German archaeologist Heinrich Schliemann. Mycenae was one center in a Mycenaean Greek civilization that flourished between 1600 and 1100 B.C.E. The Mycenaean Greeks were part of the Indo-European family of peoples (see Chapter 1), who spread from their original location into southern and western Europe, India, and Iran. One group entered the territory of Greece from the north around 1900 B.C.E. and, over a period of time, managed to gain control of the Greek mainland and develop a civilization.

Mycenaean civilization, which reached its high point between 1400 and 1200 B.C.E., consisted of a number of powerful monarchies based in fortified palace complexes, which were built on hills and surrounded by gigantic stone walls, such as those found at Mycenae, Tiryns, Pylos, Thebes, and Orchomenos. These various centers of power probably formed a loose confederacy of independent states, with Mycenae the strongest. Next in importance to the kings in these states were the army commanders, the priests, and the bureaucrats, who kept careful records. The free citizenry included peasants, soldiers, and artisans, with the lowest rung of the social ladder consisting of serfs and slaves.

The Mycenaeans were, above all, a warrior people who prided themselves on their heroic deeds in battle. Archaeological evidence indicates that the Mycenaean monarchies also developed an extensive commercial network. Mycenaean pottery has been found throughout the Mediterranean basin, in Syria and Egypt to the east and Sicily and southern Italy to the west. But some scholars also believe that the Mycenaeans, led by Mycenae itself, spread outward militarily, conquering Crete and making it part of the Mycenaean world. The most famous of all their supposed military adventures has come down to us in the epic poetry of Homer (see Homer later in this chapter). Did the Mycenaean Greeks, led by Agamemnon, king of Mycenae, sack the city of Troy on the northwestern coast of Asia Minor around 1250 B.C.E.? Since the excavations of Heinrich Schliemann, begun in 1870, scholars have debated this question. Many do believe in the basic authenticity of the Homeric legend, even if the details have become shrouded in mystery.

By the late thirteenth century, Mycenaean Greece was showing signs of serious trouble. Modern scholars have proposed a number of theories to explain the collapse of Mycenaean civilization. According to the Greeks' own legend, their mainland was invaded from the north by another Greek-speaking people who were less civilized than the Mycenaeans. Called the Dorians, these invaders supposedly destroyed the old centers of Mycenaean power and ultimately established themselves in the Peloponnesus. But there is little archaeological evidence to support the idea of massive Dorian invasions. Other historians argue that internal conflict among the Mycenaean kings and major earthquakes were more important factors in the Mycenaean decline. What is certain is that by 1100 B.C.E., Mycenaean civilization had collapsed.

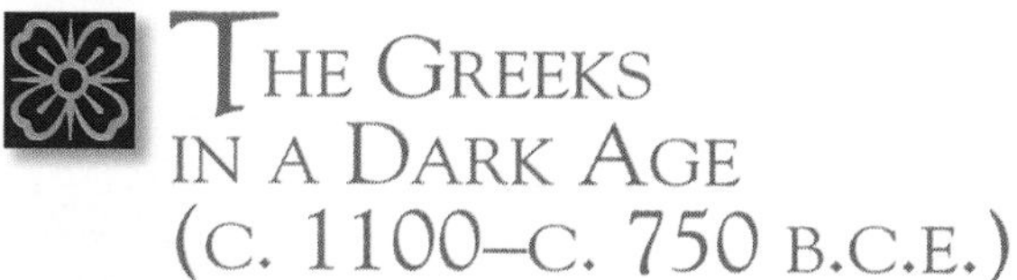

The Greeks in a Dark Age (c. 1100–c. 750 B.C.E.)

After the collapse of Mycenaean civilization, Greece entered a difficult era of declining population and falling food production. Moreover, we have few records to help us reconstruct what happened in this period. Because of the difficult conditions and our lack of knowledge about the period, historians refer to it as a Dark Age. Not until 850 B.C.E. did farming revive. At the same time, some new developments were forming the basis for a revived Greece.

During the Dark Age, large numbers of Greeks left the mainland and migrated across the Aegean Sea to various islands, and especially to the southwestern shore of Asia Minor, a strip of territory that came to be called Ionia. Based on their dialect, the Greeks who resided there were called Ionians. Two other major groups of Greeks settled in established parts of Greece. The Aeolian Greeks who were located in northern and central Greece colonized the large island of Lesbos and the adjacent territory of the mainland. The Dorians established themselves in southwestern Greece, especially in the Peloponnesus, as well as on some of the south Aegean islands, including Crete.

Other important activities occurred in this Dark Age as well. There was a revival of some trade and some economic activity besides agriculture. Iron replaced bronze in the construction of weapons, making them affordable for more people. And at some point in the eighth century B.C.E., the Greeks adopted the Phoenician alphabet to give themselves a new system of writing. Near the very end of this so-called Dark Age appeared the work of Homer, who has come to be viewed as one of the truly great poets of all time.

Homer

The origins of the *Iliad* and the *Odyssey*, the first great epics of early Greece, are to be found in the oral tradition of reciting poems recounting the deeds of heroes of the Mycenaean age. It is generally assumed that early in the eighth century B.C.E., Homer made use of these oral traditions to compose the *Iliad*, his epic of the Trojan War. The war was caused by an act of Paris, a prince of Troy. By kidnapping Helen, wife of the king of the Greek state of Sparta, he outraged all the Greeks. Under the leadership of the Spartan king's brother, Agamemnon of Mycenae,

THE SLAYING OF HECTOR. This scene from a late-fifth-century B.C.E. Athenian vase depicts the final battle between Achilles and the Trojan hero Hector. Achilles is shown lunging forward with his spear to deliver the final, deadly blow to the Trojan prince, a scene taken from Homer's *Iliad*. The *Iliad* is Homer's masterpiece and was important to later Greeks as a means of teaching the aristocratic values of courage and honor.

the Greeks attacked Troy. Ten years later, the Greeks finally won and sacked the city.

But the *Iliad* is not so much the story of the war itself as it is the tale of the Greek hero Achilles and how the "wrath of Achilles" led to disaster. As is true of all great literature, the *Iliad* abounds in universal lessons. Underlying them all is the clear message, as one commentator has observed, that "men will still come and go like the generations of leaves in the forest; that he will still be weak, and the gods strong and incalculable; that the quality of a man matters more than his achievement; that violence and recklessness will still lead to disaster, and that this will fall on the innocent as well as on the guilty." [1]

Although the *Odyssey* has long been considered Homer's other masterpiece, some scholars believe that it was composed later than the *Iliad* and was probably not the work of Homer. The *Odyssey* is an epic romance that recounts the journeys of one of the Greek heroes, Odysseus, after the fall of Troy and his ultimate return to his wife. But there is a larger vision here as well: the testing of the heroic stature of Odysseus until, by both cunning and patience, he prevails. In the course of this testing, the underlying moral message is "that virtue is a better policy than vice."[2]

Although the *Iliad* and the *Odyssey* supposedly deal with the heroes of the Mycenaean age of the thirteenth century B.C.E., many scholars believe that they really describe the social conditions of the Dark Age. According to the Homeric view, Greece was a society based on agriculture in which a landed warrior-aristocracy controlled much wealth and exercised considerable power. There is no doubt that Homer's society was divided along class lines with the warrior-aristocrats as the dominant group. Homer's world reflects the values of aristocratic heroes.

This, of course, explains the importance of Homer to later generations of Greeks. Homer did not so much record history: he made it. The Greeks regarded the *Iliad* and the *Odyssey* as authentic history and as the works of one poet, Homer. These masterpieces gave the Greeks an ideal past with a legendary age of heroes and came to be used as standard texts for the education of generations of Greek males. As one Athenian stated, "My father was anxious to see me develop into a good man . . . and as a means to this end he compelled me to memorize all of Homer."[3] The values Homer inculcated were essentially the aristocratic values of courage and honor (see the box on p. 99). It was important to strive for the excellence befitting a hero, which the Greeks called *arete*. In the warrior-aristocratic world of Homer, *arete* is won in struggle or contest. In his willingness to fight, the hero protects his family and friends, preserves and expands his own honor and that of his family, and earns his reputation. In the Homeric world, aristocratic women, too, were expected to pursue excellence. Penelope, for example, the wife of Odysseus, the hero of the *Odyssey*, remains faithful to her husband and displays great courage and in-telligence in preserving their household during her husband's long absence. Upon his return, Odysseus praises her for her excellence: "Madame, there is not a man in the wide world who could find fault with you. For your fame has reached heaven itself, like that of some perfect king, ruling a populous and mighty state with the fear of god in his heart, and upholding the right."[4]

To a later generation of Greeks, these heroic values formed the core of aristocratic virtue, a fact that explains the tremendous popularity of Homer as an educational tool. Homer gave to the Greeks a single universally accepted model of heroism, honor, and nobility. But in time, as a new world of city-states emerged in Greece, new values of cooperation and community also transformed what the Greeks learned from Homer.

HOMER'S IDEAL OF EXCELLENCE

The Iliad *and the* Odyssey, *which the Greeks believed were both written by Homer, were used as basic texts for the education of Greeks for hundreds of years during antiquity. This passage from the* Iliad, *describing the encounter between Hector, prince of Troy, and his wife Andromache, illustrates the Greek ideal of gaining honor through combat. At the end of the passage, Homer also reveals what became the Greek attitude toward women: they are supposed to spin and weave and take care of their households and children.*

HOMER, *ILIAD*

Hector looked at his son and smiled, but said nothing. Andromache, bursting into tears, went up to him and put her hand in his. "Hector," she said, "you are possessed. This bravery of yours will be your end. You do not think of your little boy or your unhappy wife, whom you will make a widow soon. Some day the Achaeans [Greeks] are bound to kill you in a massed attack. And when I lose you I might as well be dead. . . . I have no father, no mother, now. . . . I had seven brothers too at home. In one day all of them went down to Hades' House. The great Achilles of the swift feet killed them all. . . .

"So you, Hector, are father and mother and brother to me, as well as my beloved husband. Have pity on me now; stay here on the tower; and do not make your boy an orphan and your wife a widow. . . ."

"All that, my dear," said the great Hector of the glittering helmet, "is surely my concern. But if I hid myself like a coward and refused to fight, I could never face the Trojans and the Trojan ladies in their trailing gowns. Besides, it would go against the grain, for I have trained myself always, like a good soldier, to take my place in the front line and win glory for my father and myself. . . ."

As he finished, glorious Hector held out his arms to take his boy. But the child shrank back with a cry to the bosom of his girdled nurse, alarmed by his father's appearance. He was frightened by the bronze of the helmet and the horsehair plume that he saw nodding grimly down at him. His father and his lady mother had to laugh. But noble Hector quickly took his helmet off and put the dazzling thing on the ground. Then he kissed his son, dandled him in his arms, and prayed to Zeus and the other gods: "Zeus, and you other gods, grant that this boy of mine may be, like me, preeminent in Troy; as strong and brave as I; a mighty king of Ilium. May people say, when he comes back from battle, 'Here is a better man than his father.' Let him bring home the bloodstained armor of the enemy he has killed, and make his mother happy."

Hector handed the boy to his wife, who took him to her fragrant breast. She was smiling through her tears, and when her husband saw this he was moved. He stroked her with his hand and said, "My dear, I beg you not to be too much distressed. No one is going to send me down to Hades before my proper time. But Fate is a thing that no man born of woman, coward or hero, can escape. Go home now, and attend to your own work, the loom and the spindle, and see that the maidservants get on with theirs. War is men's business; and this war is the business of every man in Ilium, myself above all."

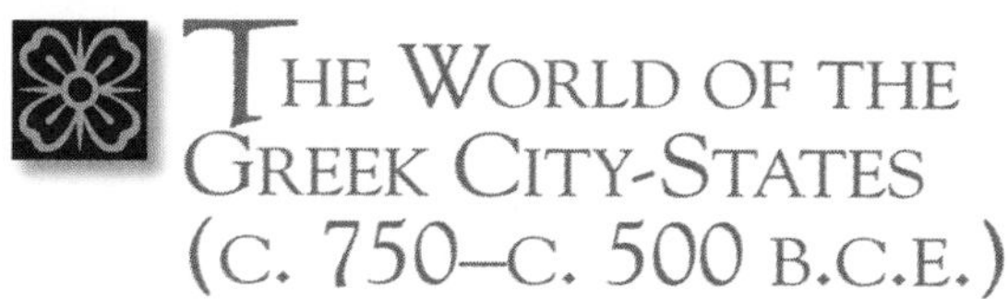

The World of the Greek City-States (c. 750–c. 500 B.C.E.)

In the eighth century B.C.E., Greek civilization burst forth with new energies. Two major developments stand out in this era: the evolution of the *polis* as the central institution in Greek life and the Greeks' colonization of the Mediterranean and Black Seas.

The *Polis*

By the eighth century B.C.E., the Greek *polis* (plural, *poleis*) had emerged as a truly unique and fundamental institution in Greek society. In the most basic sense, a *polis* could be defined as a small but autonomous political unit in which all major political, social, and religious activities were carried out at one central location.

In a physical sense, the *polis* encompassed a town or city or even a village and its surrounding countryside. But the town or city or village served as the focus or central point where the citizens of the *polis* could assemble for political, social, and religious activities. In some *poleis*, this central meeting point was a hill, like the Acropolis at Athens, which could serve as a place of refuge during an attack and later in some sites came to be the religious center on which temples and public monuments were erected. Below the acropolis would be an *agora*, an open space that served both as a place where citizens could assemble and as a market. Citizens resided in town and country alike, but the town remained the center of political activity.

Poleis could vary greatly in size, from a few square miles to a few hundred square miles. The larger ones were the product of consolidation. The territory of Attica, for example, had once had twelve *poleis* but eventually became a single *polis* (Athens) through a process of amalgamation. Athens grew to have a population of more than 300,000 by the fifth century B.C.E., with an adult male citizen body of about 43,000. Most *poleis* were considerably smaller than Athens, however.

Although our word *politics* is derived from the Greek term *polis*, the *polis* itself was much more than just a political institution. It was, above all, a community of citizens in which all political, economic, social, cultural, and religious activities were focused. As a community, the *polis* consisted of citizens with political rights (adult males), citizens with no political rights (women and children), and noncitizens (slaves and resident aliens). All citizens of a *polis* possessed fundamental rights, but these rights were coupled with responsibilities. The Greek philosopher Aristotle argued that the citizen did not just belong to himself: "we must rather regard every citizen as belonging to the state." However, the loyalty that citizens had to their city-states also had a negative side. City-states distrusted one another, and the division of Greece into fiercely patriotic independent units helped bring about its ruin.

The development of the *polis* was paralleled by the emergence of a new military system. Greek fighting had previously been dominated by aristocratic cavalrymen, who reveled in individual duels with enemy soldiers. But by the end of the eighth century and beginning of the seventh century B.C.E., the hoplite infantry formation—the phalanx—came into being. Hoplites were heavily armed infantrymen, who wore bronze or leather helmets, breastplates, and greaves (shin guards). Each carried a round shield, a short sword, and a thrusting spear about nine feet long. Hoplites advanced into battle as a unit, forming a phalanx (a rectangular formation) in tight order, usually eight ranks deep. As long as the hoplites kept their order, were not outflanked, and did not break, they either secured victory or, at the very least, suffered no harm. The phalanx was easily routed, however, if it broke its order. The safety of the phalanx depended, above all, on the soli-

THE HOPLITE FORCES. The Greek hoplites were infantrymen equipped with large round shields and long thrusting spears. In battle they advanced in tight phalanx formation and were dangerous opponents as long as this formation remained unbroken. This vase painting of the seventh century B.C.E. shows two groups of hoplite warriors engaged in battle. The piper on the left is leading another line of soldiers preparing to enter the fray.

darity and discipline of its members. As one seventh-century B.C.E. poet noted, a good hoplite was "a short man firmly placed upon his legs, with a courageous heart, not to be uprooted from the spot where he plants his legs."[5]

The hoplite force had political as well as military repercussions. The aristocratic cavalry was now outdated. Since each hoplite provided his own armor, men of property, both aristocrats and small farmers, made up the new phalanx. Those who could become hoplites and fight for the state could also challenge aristocratic control.

Colonization and the Rise of Tyrants

Between 750 and 550 B.C.E., the Greek people left their homeland in large numbers to settle in distant lands. Poverty and land hunger created by the growing gulf between rich and poor, overpopulation, and the development of trade were all factors that led to the establishment of colonies. Each colony was founded as a *polis* and was usually independent of the mother *polis* (hence the word *metropolis*) that had established it. Invariably, the colony saw itself as an independent entity whose links to the mother city were not political but were based on sharing common social, economic, and especially religious practices.

In the western Mediterranean, new Greek settlements were established along the coastline of southern Italy, southern France, eastern Spain, and northern Africa west of Egypt. To the north, the Greeks set up colonies in Thrace, where they sought good agricultural lands to grow grains. Greeks also settled along the shores of the Black Sea and secured the approaches to it with cities on the Hellespont and Bosphorus, most notably Byzantium, site of the later Constantinople (Istanbul). By establishing these settlements, the Greeks spread their culture throughout the Mediterranean basin. Colonization also led to increased trade and industry. The Greeks sent their pottery, wine, and olive oil to the colonies; in return, they received grains and

MAP 4.1 Classical Greece

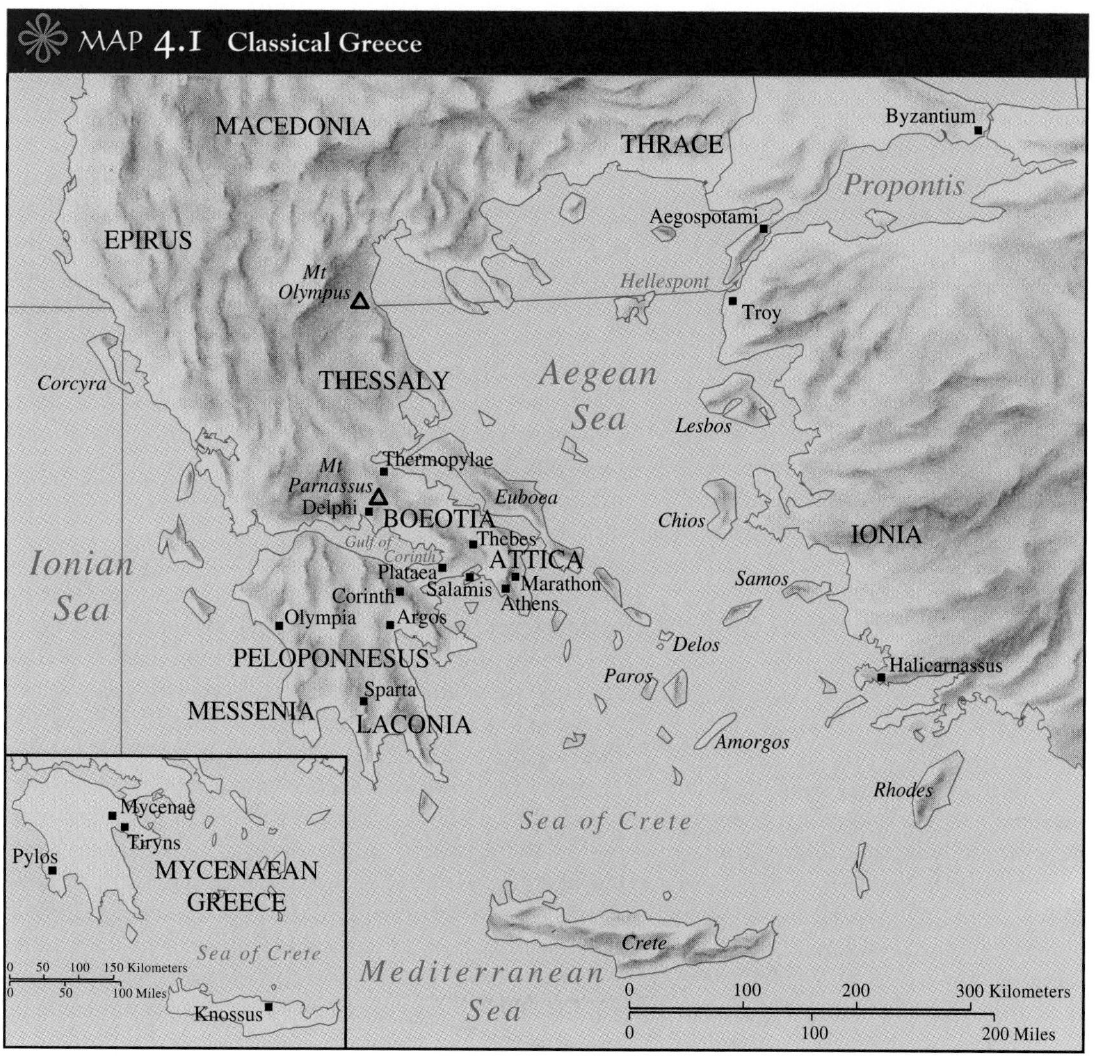

metals from the west and fish, timber, wheat, metals, and slaves from the Black Sea region. In many *poleis*, the expansion of trade and industry created a new group of rich men who desired political privileges commensurate with their wealth but found such privileges impossible to gain because of the power of the ruling aristocrats.

The aspirations of the newly rising industrial and commercial groups opened the door to the rise of tyrants in the seventh and sixth centuries B.C.E. They were not necessarily oppressive or wicked as our word *tyrant* connotes. Greek tyrants were rulers who came to power in an unconstitutional way; a tyrant was not subject to the law. Many tyrants were actually aristocrats who opposed the control of the ruling aristocratic faction in their cities. The support for the tyrants, however, came from the new rich who made their money in trade and industry as well as from poor peasants who were becoming increasingly indebted to landholding aristocrats. Both groups were opposed to the domination of political power by aristocratic oligarchies.

Tyrants usually achieved power by a local coup d'etat and maintained it by using mercenary soldiers. Once in power, they promoted public works projects, such as the construction of new marketplaces, temples, and walls, that not only glorified the city but also enhanced their own popularity. Tyrants also favored the interests of merchants and traders. Despite these achievements, however, tyranny was largely extinguished by the end of the sixth century B.C.E. Its very nature as a system outside the law seemed contradictory to the ideal of law in a Greek community. Although tyranny did not last, it played a significant role in the evolution of Greek history by ending the rule of narrow aristocratic oligarchies. Once the tyrants were eliminated, the door was opened to the participation of new and more people in governing the affairs of the community. Although this trend culminated in the development of democracy in some communities, in other states expanded oligarchies of one kind or another managed to remain in power. Greek states exhibited considerable variety in their governmental structures; this can perhaps best be seen by examining the two most famous and most powerful Greek city-states, Sparta and Athens.

Sparta

Located in the southwestern Peloponnesus, in an area known as Laconia, the Spartans had originally occupied four small villages that eventually became unified into a single *polis*. This unification made Sparta a strong community in Laconia and enabled the Spartans to conquer the Laconians and subject them to serfdom. Known as Helots (the name is derived from a Greek word for "capture"), these conquered Laconians were bound to the land and forced to work on farms and as household servants for the Spartans.

When the land in Laconia proved unable to maintain the growing number of Spartan citizens, the Spartans looked for land nearby and, beginning around 730 B.C.E., undertook the conquest of neighboring Messenia despite its larger size and population. Messenia possessed a large, fertile plain ideal for growing grain. After its conquest, which was not completed until the seventh century B.C.E., the Messenians were reduced to serfdom and made to work for the Spartans. To ensure control over their conquered Laconian and Messenian Helots, the Spartans made a conscious decision to create a military state.

Sometime between 800 and 600 B.C.E., the Spartans instituted a series of reforms that are associated with the name of the lawgiver Lycurgus (see the box on p. 103). Although historians are not sure that Lycurgus ever existed, there is no doubt about the result of the reforms that were made: Sparta was transformed into a perpetual military camp.

The lives of Spartans were now rigidly organized and tightly controlled (thus, our word *spartan*, meaning "highly self-disciplined"). At birth each child was examined by state officials who decided whether he or she was fit to live. Those judged unfit were exposed to die. Boys were taken from their mothers at the age of seven and put under control of the state. They lived in quasi-military barracks, where they were subjected to harsh discipline to make them tough and given an education that stressed military training and obedience to authority. At twenty, Spartan males were enrolled in the army for regular military service. Although allowed to marry, they continued to live in the barracks and ate all their meals in public dining halls with their fellow soldiers. Meals were simple; the famous Spartan black broth consisted of a piece of pork boiled in blood, salt, and vinegar, causing a visitor who ate in a public mess to remark that he now understood why Spartans were not afraid to die. At thirty, Spartan males were recognized as mature and allowed to vote in the assembly and live at home, but they remained in military service until the age of sixty.

While their husbands remained in military barracks until age thirty, Spartan women lived at home. Because of this separation, Spartan women had greater freedom of movement and greater power in the household than was common for women elsewhere in Greece. Spartan women were encouraged to exercise and remain fit to bear and raise healthy children. Like the men, Spartan women engaged in athletic exercises in the nude. At solemn feasts, the young women marched naked in processions, and in the presence of the young men, they sang songs about those who had showed special gallantry or cowardice on the battlefield. Many Spartan women upheld the strict Spartan values, expecting their husbands and sons to be brave in war. The story is told that as a Spartan mother was burying her son, an old woman came up to her and said, "You poor woman, what a misfortune." "No," replied the mother, "because I bore him so that

THE LYCURGAN REFORMS

In order to maintain their control over the conquered Messenians, the Spartans instituted the reforms that created their military state. In this account of the supposed lawgiver Lycurgus, the Greek historian Plutarch discusses the effect of these reforms on the treatment and education of boys.

PLUTARCH, *LYCURGUS*

Lycurgus was of another mind; he would not have masters bought out of the market for his young Spartans, . . . nor was it lawful, indeed, for the father himself to breed up the children after his own fancy; but as soon as they were seven years old they were to be enrolled in certain companies and classes, where they all lived under the same order and discipline, doing their exercises and taking their play together. Of these, he who showed the most conduct and courage was made captain; they had their eyes always upon him, obeyed his orders, and underwent patiently whatsoever punishment he inflicted; so that the whole course of their education was one continued exercise of a ready and perfect obedience. The old men, too, were spectators of their performances, and often raised quarrels and disputes among them, to have a good opportunity of finding out their different characters, and of seeing which would be valiant, which a coward, when they should come to more dangerous encounters. Reading and writing they gave them, just enough to serve their turn; their chief care was to make them good subjects, and to teach them to endure pain and conquer in battle. To this end, as they grew in years, their discipline was proportionately increased; their heads were close-clipped, they were accustomed to go barefoot, and for the most part to play naked.

After they were twelve years old, they were no longer allowed to wear any undergarments; they had one coat to serve them a year; their bodies were hard and dry, with but little acquaintance of baths and unguents; these human indulgences they were allowed only on some few particular days in the year. They lodged together in little bands upon beds made of the rushes which grew by the banks of the river Eurotas, which they were to break off with their hands with a knife; if it were winter, they mingled some thistledown with their rushes, which it was thought had the property of giving warmth. By the time they were come to this age there was not any of the more hopeful boys who had not a lover to bear him company. The old men, too, had an eye upon them, coming often to the grounds to hear and see them contend either in wit or strength with one another, and this as seriously . . . as if they were their fathers, their tutors, or their magistrates; so that there scarcely was any time or place without someone present to put them in mind of their duty, and punish them if they had neglected it.

[Spartan boys were also encouraged to steal their food.] They stole, too, all other meat they could lay their hands on, looking out and watching all opportunities, when people were asleep or more careless than usual. If they were caught, they were not only punished with whipping, but hunger, too, being reduced to their ordinary allowance, which was but very slender, and so contrived on purpose, that they might set about to help themselves, and be forced to exercise their energy and address. This was the principal design of their hard fare.

he might die for Sparta and that is what has happened, as I wished."[6]

The so-called Lycurgan reforms also reorganized the Spartan government, creating an oligarchy. Two kings from different families were primarily responsible for military affairs and served as the leaders of the Spartan army on its campaigns. Moreover, the kings served as the supreme priests within the state religion and had some role in foreign policy.

The two kings shared power with a body called the *gerousia*, a council of elders. It consisted of twenty-eight citizens over the age of sixty, who were elected for life, and the two kings. The primary task of the *gerousia* was to prepare proposals that would be presented to the *apella*, an assembly of all male citizens. The assembly did not debate but only voted on the proposals put before it by the *gerousia;* rarely did the assembly reject these proposals. The assembly also elected the *gerousia* and another body known as the *ephors*, a group of five men who were responsible for supervising the education of youth and the conduct of all citizens.

To make their new military state secure, the Spartans deliberately turned their backs on the outside world. Foreigners, who might bring in new ideas, were discouraged from visiting Sparta. Furthermore, except for military reasons, Spartans were not allowed to travel abroad, where they might pick up new ideas that might be dangerous to the stability of the state. Likewise, Spartan citizens were discouraged from studying philosophy, literature, or the arts—subjects that might encourage new thoughts. The art of war was the Spartan ideal, and all other arts were frowned upon.

In the sixth century, Sparta used its military might and the fear it inspired to gain greater control of the Peloponnesus by organizing an alliance of almost all the Peloponnesian states. Sparta's strength enabled it to dominate this Peloponnesian League and determine its policies. By 500 B.C.E., the Spartans had organized a powerful military state that maintained order and stability in the Peloponnesus. Raised from early childhood to believe that total loyalty to the Spartan state was the basic reason for existence, the Spartans viewed their strength as justification for their militaristic ideals and regimented society.

Athens

By 700 B.C.E., Athens had established a unified *polis* on the peninsula of Attica. Although early Athens had been ruled by a monarchy, by the seventh century B.C.E., it had fallen under the control of its aristocrats. They possessed the best land and controlled political and religious life by means of a council of nobles, assisted by a board of nine officials called archons. Although there was an assembly of full citizens, it possessed few powers.

Near the end of the seventh century B.C.E., Athens was experiencing political and social discontent stemming from the development of rival factions within the aristocracy and serious economic problems. Increasing numbers of Athenian farmers found themselves sold into slavery when they were unable to repay the loans they had borrowed from their aristocratic neighbors, pledging themselves as collateral. Repeatedly, revolutionary cries for cancellation of debts and a redistribution of land were heard.

The ruling Athenian aristocrats responded to this crisis by choosing Solon, a reform-minded aristocrat, as sole archon in 594 B.C.E. and giving him full power to make changes. Solon's reforms dealt with both the economic and political problems. He canceled all current land debts, outlawed new loans based on humans as collateral, and freed people who had fallen into slavery for debts. He refused, however, to carry out the redistribution of the land and hence failed to deal with the basic cause of the economic crisis. This failure, however, was overshadowed by the commercial and industrial prosperity that Athens began to experience in the following decades.

Like his economic reforms, Solon's political measures were also a compromise. Though by no means eliminating the power of the aristocracy, they opened the door to the participation of new people, especially the nonaristocratic wealthy, in the government. But Solon's reforms, though popular, did not truly solve Athens's problems. Aristocratic factions continued to vie for power, and the poorer peasants resented Solon's failure to institute land redistribution. Internal strife finally led to the very institution Solon had hoped to avoid—tyranny. Pisistratus, an aristocrat, seized power in 560 B.C.E. Pursuing a foreign policy that aided Athenian trade, Pisistratus remained popular with the mercantile and industrial classes. But the Athenians rebelled against his son and ended the tyranny in 510 B.C.E. Although the aristocrats attempted to reestablish an aristocratic oligarchy, Cleisthenes, another aristocratic reformer, opposed this plan and, with the backing of the Athenian people, gained the upper hand in 508 B.C.E.

Cleisthenes created a new council of 500, chosen by lot by the ten tribes in which all citizens had been enrolled. The new council of 500 was responsible for the administration of both foreign and financial affairs and prepared the business that would be handled by the assembly. This assembly of all male citizens had final authority in the passing of laws after free and open debate; thus, Cleisthenes' reforms had reinforced the central role of the assembly of citizens in the Athenian political system.

The reforms of Cleisthenes created the foundations for Athenian democracy. More changes would come in the fifth century, when the Athenians themselves would begin to use the word *democracy* to describe their system (our word *democracy* comes from the Greek words *demos* [people] and *kratia* [power]). By 500 B.C.E., Athens was more united than it had been and was on the verge of playing a more important role in Greek affairs.

THE HIGH POINT OF GREEK CIVILIZATION: CLASSICAL GREECE

Classical Greece is the name given to the period of Greek history from around 500 B.C.E. to the conquest of Greece by the Macedonian king Philip II in 338 B.C.E. It was a period of brilliant achievement, much of it associated with the flowering of democracy in Athens under the leadership of Pericles. Many of the lasting contributions of the Greeks occurred during this period. The age began with a mighty confrontation between the Greek states and the mammoth Persian Empire.

The Challenge of Persia

As Greek civilization grew and expanded throughout the Mediterranean, it was inevitable that it would come into contact with the Persian Empire to the east. The Ionian Greek cities in western Asia Minor had already fallen subject to the Persian Empire by the mid-sixth century B.C.E. An unsuccessful revolt by the Ionian cities in 499 B.C.E.—assisted by the Athenian navy—led the Persian ruler Darius to seek revenge by attacking the mainland Greeks in 490 B.C.E. The Persians landed an army on the plain of Marathon, only twenty-six miles from Athens. The Athenians and their allies were clearly outnumbered, but led by Miltiades, one of the Athenian leaders who insisted on attacking, the Greek hoplites charged across the plain of Marathon and crushed the Persian forces. Although a minor defeat to the Persians, the Battle of Marathon was of great importance to the Athenians, who had proved that the Persians could be beaten.

Xerxes, the new Persian monarch after the death of Darius in 486 B.C.E., vowed revenge and renewed the inva-

THE GREEK TRIREME. The trireme became the standard warship of ancient Greece. Highly maneuverable, fast, and outfitted with metal prows, Greek triremes were especially effective at ramming enemy ships. The strenuous work of the oarsmen aboard a trireme is shown in the relief dating from the fourth century B.C.E. The photo shows the *Olympias*, a trireme reconstructed by the Greek navy.

sion of Greece. In preparation for the attack, some of the Greek states formed a defensive league under Spartan leadership, while the Athenians pursued a new military policy by developing a navy. By the time of the Persian invasion in 480 B.C.E., the Athenians had produced a fleet of about 200 vessels.

Xerxes led a massive invasion force into Greece: close to 150,000 troops, almost 700 naval ships, and hundreds of supply ships to keep the large army fed. The Greeks decided to fight a delaying action at the pass of Thermopylae along the main road into central Greece, probably to give the Greek fleet of 300 ships the chance to fight the Persian fleet. The Greeks knew that the Persian army was dependent on the fleet for supplies. A Greek force numbering close to 9,000, under the leadership of the Spartan king, Leonidas, and his contingent of 300 Spartans, held off the Persian army for two days. The Spartan troops were especially brave. When told that Persian arrows would darken the sky in battle, one Spartan warrior supposedly responded, "That is good news. We will fight in the shade!" Unfortunately for the Greeks, a traitor told the Persians how to use a mountain path to outflank the Greek force. King Leonidas and the 300 Spartans fought to the last man.

The Athenians, now threatened by the onslaught of the Persian forces, abandoned their city. While the Persians sacked and burned Athens, the Greek fleet remained offshore near the island of Salamis and challenged the Persian navy to fight. Although the Greeks were outnumbered, they managed to outmaneuver the Persian fleet and utterly defeated it. A few months later, early in 479 B.C.E., the Greeks formed the largest Greek army seen up to that time and decisively defeated the Persian army at Plataea, northwest of Attica. The Greeks had won the war and were now free to pursue their own destiny.

The Growth of an Athenian Empire in the Age of Pericles

After the defeat of the Persians, Athens stepped in to provide new leadership against the Persians by forming a confederation called the Delian League. Organized in the winter of 478–477 B.C.E., the Delian League was dominated by the Athenians from the beginning. Its main headquarters was on the island of Delos, but its chief officials, including the treasurers and commanders of the fleet, were Athenian. Under the leadership of the Athenians, the Delian League pursued the attack against the Persian Empire. Virtually all of the Greek states in the Aegean were liberated from Persian control. Arguing that the

CHRONOLOGY

THE PERSIAN WARS

Rebellion of Greek cities in Asia Minor	499–494 B.C.E.
Battle of Marathon	490 B.C.E.
Xerxes invades Greece	480–479 B.C.E.
Battles of Thermopylae and Salamis	480 B.C.E.
Battle of Plataea	479 B.C.E.

Persian threat was now over, some members of the Delian League wished to withdraw. But the Athenians forced them to remain in the league and to pay tribute. In 454 B.C.E., the Athenians moved the treasury of the league from the island of Delos to Athens. By controlling the Delian League, Athens had created an empire.

At home, Athenians favored the new imperial policy, especially after 461 B.C.E., when a political faction, led by a young aristocrat named Pericles, triumphed. Under Pericles, who was a dominant figure in Athenian politics until 429 B.C.E., Athens embarked on a policy of expanding democracy at home and its new empire abroad. This period of Athenian and Greek history, which historians have subsequently labeled the age of Pericles, witnessed the height of Athenian power and the culmination of its brilliance as a civilization.

In the age of Pericles, the Athenians became deeply attached to their democratic system. The will of the people was embodied in the assembly, which consisted of all male citizens over eighteen years of age. In the 440s, that was probably a group of about 43,000. Not all attended, however, and the number present at the meetings, which were held every ten days on a hillside east of the Acropolis, seldom reached 6,000. The assembly passed all laws and made final decisions on war and foreign policy. Pericles expanded the Athenians' involvement in their democracy (see the box on p. 107) by making lower-class citizens eligible for public offices formerly closed to them and introducing state pay for officeholders, including those who served on the large Athenian juries. Poor citizens could now afford to participate in public affairs.

A large body of city magistrates, usually chosen by lot without regard to class, handled routine administrative tasks. The overall directors of policy, a board of ten officials known as generals, were elected by public vote and were usually wealthy aristocrats, even though the people were free to select otherwise. The generals could be reelected, enabling individual leaders to play an important political role. Pericles, for example, was elected to the generalship thirty times between 461 and 429 B.C.E. The Athenians, however, had also devised the practice of ostracism to protect themselves against overly ambitious politicians. Members of the assembly could write on a broken pottery fragment (*ostrakon*) the name of the person they most disliked or considered most harmful to the *polis*. A person who received a majority (if at least 6,000 votes were cast) was exiled for ten years.

Under Pericles, Athens became the leading center of Greek culture. The Persians had destroyed much of the city during the Persian Wars, but Pericles used the treasury money of the Delian League to set in motion a massive rebuilding program. New temples and statues soon made visible the greatness of Athens. Art, architecture, and philosophy flourished, and Pericles broadly boasted that Athens had become the "school of Greece." But the achievements of Athens alarmed the other Greek states, especially Sparta, and soon all Greece was confronted with a new war.

The Great Peloponnesian War and the Decline of the Greek States

During the forty years after the defeat of the Persians, the Greek world came to be divided into two major camps: Sparta and its supporters and the Athenian maritime empire. In his classic *History of the Peloponnesian War*, the great Greek historian Thucydides pointed out that the fundamental, long-range cause of the Peloponnesian War was the fear that the growing Athenian empire aroused in Sparta and its allies. Then, too, Athens and Sparta had created two very different kinds of societies, and neither state was able to tolerate the other's system. A series of disputes finally led to the outbreak of war in 431 B.C.E.

At the beginning of the war, both sides believed they had winning strategies. The Athenians planned to remain behind the protective walls of Athens while the overseas empire and the navy would keep them supplied. Pericles knew perfectly well that the Spartans and their allies could beat the Athenians in pitched battles, which, of course, formed the focus of the Spartan strategy. The Spartans and their allies invaded Attica and ravaged the fields and orchards, hoping that the Athenians would send out their army to fight beyond the walls. But Pericles was convinced that Athens was secure behind its walls and retaliated by sending out naval excursions to ravage the seacoast of the Peloponnesus. In the second year of the war, however, plague devastated the crowded city of Athens and wiped out possibly one-third of the Athenian population. Pericles himself died the following year (429 B.C.E.), a severe loss to Athens. Despite the losses from the plague, the Athenians fought on in a struggle that witnessed numerous instances of futile destruction. War weariness finally led to a truce in 421 B.C.E., but it proved to be short-lived.

ATHENIAN DEMOCRACY: THE FUNERAL ORATION OF PERICLES

In his History of the Peloponnesian War, *the Greek historian Thucydides presented his reconstruction of the eulogy given by Pericles in the winter of 431–430* B.C.E. *to honor the Athenians killed in the first campaigns of the Great Peloponnesian War. It is a magnificent, idealized description of Athenian democracy at its height.*

THUCYDIDES, *HISTORY OF THE PELOPONNESIAN WAR*

Our constitution is called a democracy because power is in the hands not of a minority but of the whole people. When it is a question of settling private disputes, everyone is equal before the law; when it is a question of putting one person before another in positions of public responsibility, what counts is not membership of a particular class, but the actual ability which the man possesses. No one, so long as he has it in him to be of service to the state, is kept in political obscurity because of poverty. And, just as our political life is free and open, so is our day-to-day life in our relations with each other. We do not get into a state with our next-door neighbor if he enjoys himself in his own way, nor do we give him the kind of black looks which, though they do no real harm, still do hurt people's feelings. We are free and tolerant in our private lives; but in public affairs we keep to the law. This is because it commands our deep respect.

We give our obedience to those whom we put in positions of authority, and we obey the laws themselves, especially those which are for the protection of the oppressed, and those unwritten laws which it is an acknowledged shame to break. . . . Here each individual is interested not only in his own affairs but in the affairs of the state as well: even those who are mostly occupied with their own business are extremely well-informed on general politics—this is a peculiarity of ours: we do not say that a man who takes no interest in politics is a man who minds his own business; we say that he has no business here at all. We Athenians, in our own persons, take our decisions on policy or submit them to proper discussions: for we do not think that there is an incompatibility between words and deeds; the worst thing is to rush into action before the consequences have been properly debated. . . . Taking everything together then, I declare that our city is an education to Greece, and I declare that in my opinion each single one of our citizens, in all the manifold aspects of life, is able to show himself the rightful lord and owner of his own person, and do this, moreover, with exceptional grace and exceptional versatility. And to show that this is no empty boasting for the present occasion, but real tangible fact, you have only to consider the power which our city possesses and which has been won by those very qualities which I have mentioned.

The Athenians initiated a second phase of the war in 415 B.C.E., when they decided to invade the island of Sicily, believing that its conquest would give them a strong source of support to carry on a lengthy war. But the "great expedition" of the Athenians suffered a massive defeat outside the city of Syracuse. All of the Athenians were killed or sold into slavery. Despite this disaster, the Athenians refused to give up, but raised new armies and sent out new fleets. The final crushing blow came, however, in 405 B.C.E., when the Athenian fleet was destroyed at Aegospotami on the Hellespont. Athens was besieged and surrendered in 404 B.C.E. Its walls were torn down, the navy disbanded, and the Athenian empire destroyed. The great war was finally over.

The Great Peloponnesian War weakened the major Greek states and certainly destroyed any possibility of cooperation among the Greek states. The next seventy years of Greek history are a sorry tale of efforts by Sparta, Athens, and Thebes, a new Greek power, to dominate Greek affairs. In continuing their petty wars, the Greek states remained oblivious to the growing power of Macedonia to their north and demonstrated convincingly that the genius of the Greeks did not lie in politics. Culture, however, was quite a different story.

The Culture of Classical Greece

Classical Greece saw a period of remarkable intellectual and cultural growth throughout the Greek world. Historians agree, however, that Periclean Athens was the most important center of classical Greek culture. Indeed, the eighteenth-century French philosopher and writer Voltaire listed the Athens of Pericles as one of four happy ages "when the arts were brought to perfection and which, marking an era of the greatness of the human mind, are an example to posterity."[7]

THE WRITING OF HISTORY

History as we know it, as the systematic analysis of past events, was a Greek creation. Herodotus (c. 484–c. 425 B.C.E.), an Ionian Greek from Asia Minor, was the author of the *History of the Persian Wars*, a work commonly regarded as the first real history in Western civilization.

CHRONOLOGY

THE GREAT PELOPONNESIAN WAR

Invasion of Attica	431 B.C.E.
Athenian invasion of Sicily	415–413 B.C.E.
Battle of Aegospotami	405 B.C.E.
Surrender of Athens	404 B.C.E.

The Greek word *historia* (from which we derive our word *history*) means "research" or "investigation," and it is in the opening line of Herodotus's *History* that we find the first recorded use of the word:

> Here are presented the researches (*historiae*) carried out by Herodotus of Halicarnassus. The purpose is to prevent the traces of human events from being erased by time, and to preserve the fame of the important and remarkable achievements produced by both Greeks and non-Greeks; among the matters covered is, in particular, the cause of the hostilities between Greeks and non-Greeks.[8]

The central theme of Herodotus's work is the conflict between the Greeks and the Persians, which he viewed as a struggle between Greek freedom and oriental despotism. His account demonstrates a remarkable range of interests, including geography, politics, social structures, economics, religion, and even psychology. Herodotus traveled extensively for his information and was dependent for his sources on what we today would call oral history. Although he was a master storyteller and sometimes included considerable fanciful material, Herodotus was also capable of exhibiting a critical attitude toward the materials he used. Regardless of its weaknesses, Herodotus's *History* is an important source of information on the Persians and certainly our chief source for the Persian Wars themselves.

Thucydides (c. 460–c. 400 B.C.E.) was, by far, the better historian; in fact, historians consider him the greatest historian of the ancient world. Thucydides was an Athenian and a participant in the Peloponnesian War. He had been elected a general, but a defeat in battle led the fickle Athenian assembly to send him into exile, which gave him the opportunity to write his *History of the Peloponnesian War*.

Unlike Herodotus, Thucydides was not concerned with underlying divine forces or gods as explanatory causal factors in history. He saw war and politics in purely rational terms, as the activities of human beings. He examined the long-range and immediate causes of the Peloponnesian War in a clear, methodical, objective fashion, placing much emphasis on accuracy and the precision of his facts. As he stated:

> And with regard to my factual reporting of the events of the war I have made it a principle not to write down the first story that came my way, and not even to be guided by my own general impressions; either I was present myself at the events which I have described or else I heard of them from eyewitnesses whose reports I have checked with as much thoroughness as possible.[9]

Thucydides also provided remarkable insight into the human condition. He believed that human nature was a constant. He was not so naive as to believe in an exact repetition of events but felt that political situations recur in similar fashion and that the study of history is therefore of great value in understanding the present.

GREEK DRAMA

Drama as we know it in Western culture was created by the Greeks. Plays were presented in outdoor theaters as part of a religious festival. The form of Greek plays remained rather stable. Three male actors who wore masks acted all the parts. A chorus (also male) spoke the important lines that explained what was going on. Action was very limited, because the emphasis was on the story and its meaning.

The first Greek dramas were tragedies, plays based on the suffering of a hero and usually ending in disaster. Aeschylus (525–456 B.C.E.) is the first tragedian whose plays are known to us. Although he wrote ninety tragedies, only seven have survived. As was customary in Greek tragedy, his plots are simple, and the characters are primarily embodiments of a single passion. The entire drama focuses on a single tragic event and its meaning. At the festival known as the City Dionysia, Greek tragedies were supposed to be presented in a trilogy (a set of three plays) built around a common theme. The only complete trilogy we possess, called the *Oresteia*, was written by Aeschylus. The theme of this trilogy is derived from Homer. Agamemnon, the king of Mycenae, returns a hero from the defeat of Troy. His wife Clytemnestra revenges the sacrificial death of her daughter Iphigenia by murdering Agamemnon, who had been responsible for Iphigenia's death. In the second play of the trilogy, Agamemnon's son Orestes avenges his father by killing his mother. Orestes is now pursued by the avenging furies, who torment him for killing his mother. Evil acts breed evil acts and suffering is one's lot, suggests Aeschylus. But Orestes is put on trial and acquitted by Athena, the patron goddess of Athens. Personal vendetta has been eliminated and law has prevailed. Reason has triumphed over the forces of evil.

Another great Athenian playwright was Sophocles (c. 496–406 B.C.E.), whose most famous play was *Oedipus the King*. In this play, the oracle of Apollo foretells how a man (Oedipus) will kill his own father and marry his mother. Despite all attempts at prevention, the tragic events occur. Although it appears that Oedipus suffered the fate determined by the gods, Oedipus also accepts that he himself as a free man must bear responsibility for his actions: "It was Apollo, friends, Apollo, that brought this bitter bitterness, my sorrows to completion. But the hand that struck me was none but my own."[10]

The third outstanding Athenian tragedian, Euripides (c. 485–406 B.C.E.), moved beyond his predecessors in creating more realistic characters. His plots also became more complex, with a greater interest in real-life situations. Perhaps the greatest of all his plays was *The Bacchae*, which dealt with the introduction of the hysterical rites associated with Dionysus, god of wine. Euripides is often seen as a skeptic, who questioned traditional moral and religious values. Euripides was also critical of the traditional view that war was glorious. He portrayed war as brutal and barbaric and expressed deep compassion for the women and children who suffered from it.

Greek tragedies dealt with universal themes still relevant to our day. They probed such problems as the nature of good and evil, the conflict between spiritual values and the demands of the state or family, the rights of the individual, the nature of divine forces, and the nature of human beings. Over and over again, the tragic lesson was repeated: humans were free and yet could operate only within limitations imposed by the gods. The real task was to cultivate the balance and moderation that led to awareness of one's true position. But the pride in human accomplishment and independence is real. As the chorus chants in Sophocles' *Antigone*: "Is there anything more wonderful on earth, our marvelous planet, than the miracle of man?"[11]

Greek comedy developed later than tragedy. We first see comedies organized at the festival of Dionysus in Athens in 488–487 B.C.E. The plays of Aristophanes (c. 450–c. 385 B.C.E.), who used both grotesque masks and obscene jokes to entertain the Athenian audience, are examples of Old Comedy. But comedy in Athens was also more clearly political than tragedy. It was used to attack or savagely satirize both politicians and intellectuals. In *The Clouds*, for example, Aristophanes characterized the philosopher Socrates as the operator of a thought factory where people could learn deceitful ways of handling other people. Later plays gave up the element of personal attack and featured contemporary issues. Of special importance to Aristophanes was his opposition to the Peloponnesian War. *Lysistrata*, performed in 411 B.C.E., at a time when Athens was in serious danger of losing the war, had a comic but effective message against the war (see the box on p. 110).

THE ARTS: THE CLASSICAL IDEAL

The artistic standards established by the Greeks of the classical period have largely dominated the arts of the Western world. Classical Greek art did not aim at experimentation for experiment's sake, but was concerned with expressing eternally true ideals. Its subject matter was basically the human being, but presented harmoniously as an object of great beauty. The classic style, based on the ideals of reason, moderation, symmetry, balance, and harmony in all things, was meant to civilize the emotions.

In architecture the most important form was the temple dedicated to a god or goddess. Because Greek religious ceremonies were held at altars in the open air, temples were not used to enclose the faithful, as modern churches are. At the center of Greek temples were walled rooms that housed the statues of deities and treasuries in which gifts to the gods and goddesses were safeguarded. These central rooms were surrounded by a screen of columns that made Greek temples open structures rather than closed ones. The columns were originally made of wood but changed to limestone in the seventh century and to marble in the fifth century B.C.E. The most significant formal element in Greek temples was the shape and size of the columns in combination with the features above and below the column. The Doric order, which evolved first in the Dorian Peloponnesus, consisted of thick, fluted columns with simple capitals resting directly on a platform without a base. Above the capitals was a fairly complex entablature. The Greeks considered the Doric order grave, dignified, and masculine. The Ionic style was first developed in western Asia Minor and consisted of slender columns with a more elaborate base and volute or spiral-shaped capitals. The Greeks characterized the Ionic order as slender, elegant, and feminine in principle. Corinthian columns, with their more detailed capitals modeled after acanthus leaves, came later, near the end of the fifth century B.C.E.

Some of the finest examples of Greek classical architecture were built in fifth-century Athens. The most famous building, regarded as the greatest example of the classical Greek temple, was the Parthenon, built between 447 and 432 B.C.E. The master builders Ictinus and Callicrates directed the construction of this temple consecrated to Athena, the patron goddess of Athens. The Parthenon, an expression of Athenian enthusiasm, was also dedicated to the glory of Athens and the Athenians. The Parthenon typifies the principles of classical architecture: the search for calmness, clarity, and freedom from superfluous detail. The individual parts of the temple were constructed in accordance with certain mathematical ratios also found in natural phenomena. The architects' concern with these laws of proportion is paralleled by the attempt of Greek philosophers to understand the general laws underlying nature.

Greek sculpture also developed a classical style that differed significantly from the artificial stiffness of the figures of an earlier period. Statues of the male nude, the favorite subject of Greek sculptors, now exhibited more relaxed

ATHENIAN COMEDY: SEX AS AN ANTIWAR INSTRUMENT

Greek comedy became a regular feature of the dramatic presentations at the festival of Dionysus in Athens beginning in 488–487 B.C.E. Aristophanes used his comedies to present political messages, especially to express his antiwar sentiments. The plot of Lysistrata *centers on a sex strike by wives in order to get their husbands to end the Peloponnesian War. In this scene from the play, Lysistrata (whose name means "she who dissolves the armies") has the women swear a special oath. The oath involves a bowl of wine offered as a libation to the gods.*

ARISTOPHANES, *LYSISTRATA*

LYSISTRATA: Lampito: all of you women: come, touch the bowl, and repeat after me: I WILL HAVE NOTHING TO DO WITH MY HUSBAND OR MY LOVER
KALONIKE: I will have nothing to do with my husband or my lover
LYSISTRATA: THOUGH HE COME TO ME IN PITIABLE CONDITION
KALONIKE: Though he come to me in pitiable condition (Oh, Lysistrata! This is killing me!)
LYSISTRATA: I WILL STAY IN MY HOUSE UNTOUCHABLE
KALONIKE: I will stay in my house untouchable
LYSISTRATA: IN MY THINNEST SAFFRON SILK
KALONIKE: In my thinnest saffron silk
LYSISTRATA: AND MAKE HIM LONG FOR ME.
KALONIKE: And make him long for me.
LYSISTRATA: I WILL NOT GIVE MYSELF
KALONIKE: I will not give myself
LYSISTRATA: AND IF HE CONSTRAINS ME
KALONIKE: And if he constrains me
LYSISTRATA: I WILL BE AS COLD AS ICE AND NEVER MOVE
KALONIKE: I will be as cold as ice and never move
LYSISTRATA: I WILL NOT LIFT MY SLIPPERS TOWARD THE CEILING
KALONIKE: I will not lift my slippers toward the ceiling
LYSISTRATA: OR CROUCH ON ALL FOURS LIKE THE LIONESS IN THE CARVING
KALONIKE: Or crouch on all fours like the lioness in the carving
LYSISTRATA: AND IF I KEEP THIS OATH LET ME DRINK FROM THIS BOWL
KALONIKE: And if I keep this oath let me drink from this bowl
LYSISTRATA: IF NOT, LET MY OWN BOWL BE FILLED WITH WATER.
KALONIKE: If not, let my own bowl be filled with water.
LYSISTRATA: You have all sworn?
MYRRHINE: We have.

attitudes; their faces were self-assured, their bodies flexible and smooth-muscled. Although the figures possessed natural features that made them lifelike, Greek sculptors sought to achieve not realism but a standard of ideal beauty. Polyclitus, a fifth-century sculptor, authored a treatise (now lost) on a canon of proportions that he illustrated in a work known as the *Doryphoros*. His theory maintained that the use of ideal proportions, based on mathematical ratios found in nature, could produce an ideal human form, beautiful in its perfected and refined features. This search for ideal beauty was the dominant feature of the classical standard in sculpture.

THE GREEK LOVE OF WISDOM

Philosophy is a Greek word that originally meant "love of wisdom." Early Greek philosophers were concerned with the development of critical or rational thought about the nature of the universe and the place of divine forces and souls in it. Many Greeks, however, were simply not interested in such speculations. The Sophists were a group of philosophical teachers in the fifth century B.C.E. who rejected such speculation as foolish; they argued that understanding the universe was beyond the reach of the human mind. It was more important for individuals to improve themselves, so the only worthwhile object of study was human behavior. The Sophists were wandering scholars who sold their services as professional teachers to the young men of Greece, especially those of Athens. The Sophists stressed the importance of rhetoric (the art of persuasive oratory) in winning debates and swaying an audience, a skill that was especially valuable in democratic Athens. The Sophists tended to be skeptics who questioned the traditional values of their societies. To the Sophists, there was no absolute right or wrong. What was right for one individual might be wrong for another. True wisdom consisted of being able to perceive and pursue one's own good. Because of these ideas, many people viewed the Sophists as harmful to society and especially dangerous to the values of young people.

In classical Greece, Athens became the foremost intellectual and artistic center. Its reputation is perhaps strongest of all in philosophy. After all, Socrates, Plato, and Aristotle raised basic questions that have been debated for two thousand years; these are still largely the same philosophical questions we wrestle with today.

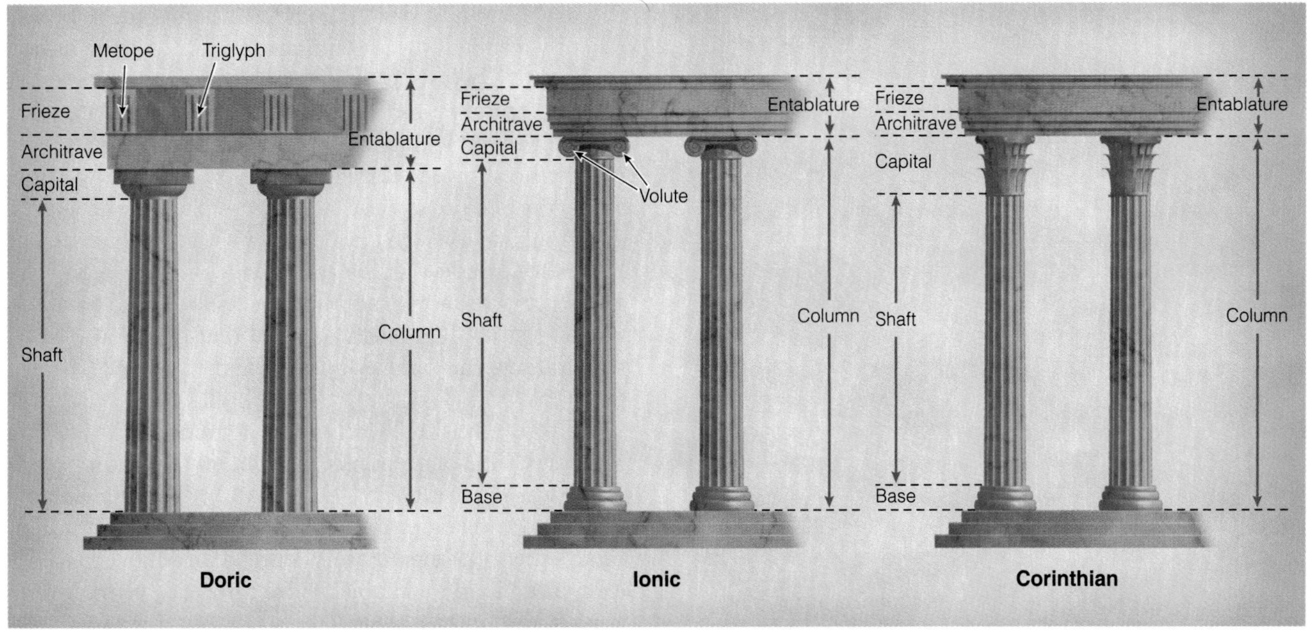

DORIC, IONIC, AND CORINTHIAN ORDERS. The illustration depicts the Doric, Ionic, and Corinthian orders of columns. The size and shape of a column constituted one of the most important aspects of Greek temple architecture. The Doric order, with plain capitals and no base, developed first in the Dorian Peloponnesus and was rather simple in comparison to the slender Ionic column, which had an elaborate base and spiral-shaped capitals, and the Corinthian column, which featured leaf-shaped capitals.

Socrates (469–399 B.C.E.) left no writings, but we know about him from his pupils, especially his most famous one, Plato. By occupation, Socrates was a stonemason, but his true love was philosophy. He taught a number of pupils, but not for pay, because he believed that the goal of education was only to improve the individual. He made use of a teaching method that is still known by his name. The "Socratic method" utilizes a question-and-answer technique to lead pupils to see things for themselves by using their own reason. Socrates believed that all real knowledge is within each person; only critical examination was needed to call it forth. This was the real task of philosophy since "the unexamined life is not worth living."

Socrates' questioned authority, and this soon led him into trouble. Athens had had a tradition of free thought and inquiry, but its defeat in the Peloponnesian War had created an environment intolerant of open debate and soul-searching. Socrates was accused and convicted of corrupting the youth of Athens by his teaching. An Athenian jury sentenced him to death.

One of Socrates' disciples was Plato (c. 429–347 B.C.E.), considered by many the greatest philosopher of Western civilization. Unlike his master Socrates, who wrote nothing, Plato wrote a great deal. He was fascinated with the question of reality: How do we know what is real? According to Plato, a higher world of eternal, unchanging Ideas or Forms has always existed. To know these Forms is to know truth. These ideal Forms constitute reality and can only be apprehended by a trained mind—which, of course, is the goal of philosophy. The objects that we perceive with our senses are simply reflections of the ideal Forms. Hence, they are shadows whereas reality is found in the Forms themselves.

THE PARTHENON. The arts in classical Greece were designed to express the eternal ideals of reason, moderation, symmetry, balance, and harmony. In architecture, the most important form was the temple, and the classical example of this kind of architecture is the Parthenon, built between 447 and 432 B.C.E. The Parthenon, located on the Acropolis, was dedicated to Athena, the patron goddess of Athens, but it also served as a shining example of the power and wealth of the Athenian empire.

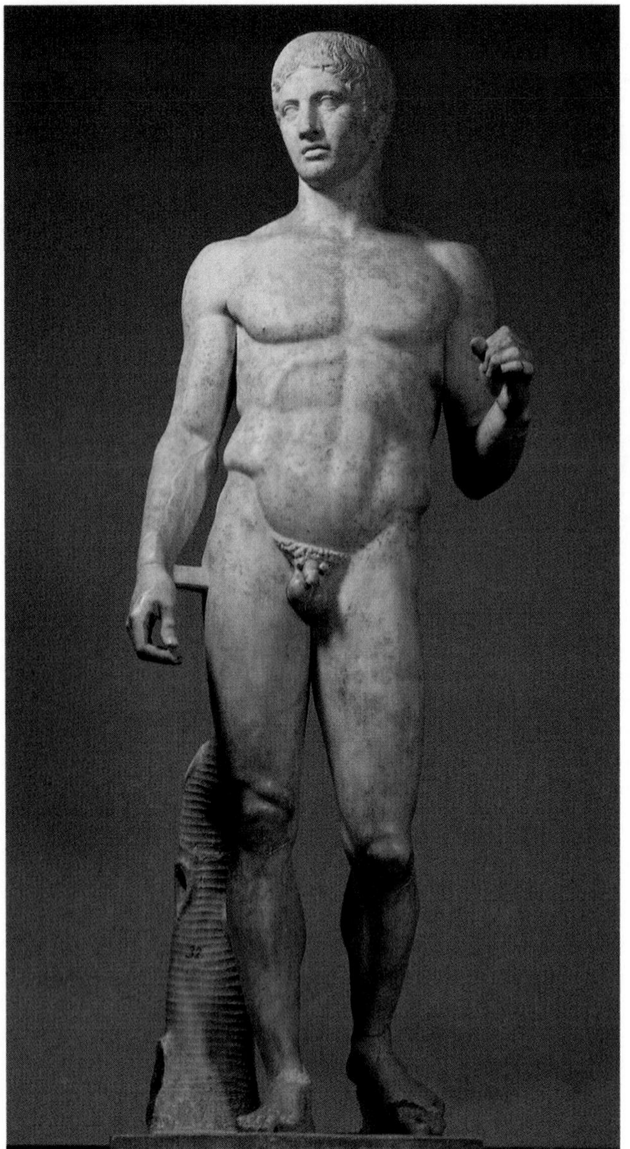

DORYPHOROS. This statue, known as the *Doryphoros*, or spear-carrier, is by the fifth-century B.C.E. sculptor Polyclitus, who believed it illustrated the ideal proportions of the human figure. Classical Greek sculpture moved away from the stiffness of earlier figures but retained the young male nude as the favorite subject matter. The statues became more lifelike, with relaxed poses and flexible, smooth-muscled bodies. The aim of sculpture, however, was not simply realism, but rather the expression of ideal beauty.

Plato's ideas of government were set out in his dialogue entitled *The Republic*. Based on his experience in Athens, Plato had come to distrust the workings of democracy. It was obvious to him that individuals could not attain an ethical life unless they lived in a just and rational state. Plato's search for the just state led him to construct an ideal state in *The Republic* in which the population was divided into three basic groups. At the top was an upper class, a ruling elite, the famous philosopher-kings: "Unless either philosophers become kings in their countries or those who are now called kings and rulers come to be sufficiently inspired with a genuine desire for wisdom; unless, that is to say, political power and philosophy meet together . . . there can be no rest from troubles . . . for states, nor yet, as I believe, for all mankind."[12] The second group were those who showed courage; they would be the warriors who protected the society. All the rest made up the masses, essentially people driven, not by wisdom or courage, but by desire. They would be the producers of society—the artisans, tradespeople, and farmers. Contrary to common Greek custom, Plato also believed that men and women should have the same education and equal access to all positions.

Plato established a school at Athens known as the Academy. One of his pupils, who studied there for twenty years, was Aristotle (384–322 B.C.E.), who later became a tutor to Alexander the Great. Aristotle did not accept Plato's theory of ideal Forms. Instead he believed that by examining individual objects, we can perceive their form and arrive at universal principles; but that these principles do not exist as a separate higher world of reality beyond material things, but are a part of things themselves. Aristotle's interests, then, lay in analyzing and classifying things based on thorough research and investigation. His interests were wide-ranging, and he wrote treatises on an enormous number of subjects: ethics, logic, politics, poetry, astronomy, geology, biology, and physics.

Like Plato, Aristotle wished for an effective form of government that would rationally direct human affairs. Unlike Plato, he did not seek an ideal state based on the embodiment of an ideal Form of justice, but tried to find the best form of government by a rational examination of existing governments. For his *Politics*, Aristotle examined the constitutions of 158 states and arrived at general categories for organizing governments. He identified three good forms of government: monarchy, aristocracy, and constitutional government. But based on his examination, he warned that monarchy can easily turn into tyranny, aristocracy into oligarchy, and constitutional government into radical democracy or anarchy. He favored constitutional government as the best form for most people.

Aristotle's philosophical and political ideas played an enormous role in the development of Western thought during the Middle Ages (see Chapter 12). So, too, did his ideas on women. Aristotle believed that marriage was meant to provide mutual comfort between man and woman and contributed to the overall happiness of a community: "The community needs both male and female excellences or it can only be half-blessed." Nevertheless, Aristotle maintained that women were biologically inferior to men: "A woman is, as it were, an infertile male. She is female in fact on account of a kind of inadequacy." Therefore, according the Aristotle, women must be subordinated to men, not only in the community but also in marriage: "The association between husband and wife is clearly an aristocracy. The man rules by virtue of merit, and in the sphere that is his by right; but he hands over to his wife such matters as are suitable for her."[13]

Greek Religion

Greek religion was intricately connected to every aspect of daily life; it was both social and practical. Public festivals, which originated from religious practices, served specific functions: boys were prepared to be warriors, girls to be mothers. Since religion was related to every aspect of life, citizens had to have a proper attitude toward the gods. Religion was a civic cult necessary for the well-being of the state. Temples dedicated to a god or goddess were the major buildings in Greek cities.

The poetry of Homer gave an account of the gods that provided Greek religion with a definite structure. Over a period of time, all Greeks came to accept a common Olympian religion. There were twelve chief gods who supposedly lived on Mount Olympus, the highest mountain in Greece. Among the twelve were Zeus, the chief deity and father of the gods; Athena, goddess of wisdom and crafts; Apollo, god of the sun and poetry; Aphrodite, goddess of love; and Poseidon, brother of Zeus and god of the seas and earthquakes.

The twelve Olympian gods were common to all Greeks, who thus shared a basic polytheistic religion. Each *polis* usually singled out one of the twelve Olympians as a guardian deity of the community. Athena was the patron goddess of Athens, for example. But each *polis* also had its own local deities who remained important to the community as a whole, and each family had patron gods as well.

Greek religion did not have a body of doctrine, nor did it focus on morality. It gave little or no hope of life after death for most people. The spirits of most people, regardless of what they had done in life, went to a gloomy underworld ruled by the god Hades. Because the Greeks wanted the gods to look favorably upon their activities, ritual assumed enormous proportions in Greek religion. Prayers were often combined with gifts to the gods based on the principle "I give so that you [the gods] will give [in return]." Ritual also meant sacrifices, whether of animals or agricultural products. Animal victims were burned on an altar in front of a temple or a small altar in front of a home.

Festivals also developed as a way to honor the gods and goddesses. Some of these (the Panhellenic celebrations) came to have international significance and were held at special locations, such as those dedicated to the worship of Zeus at Olympia or to Apollo at Delphi. Numerous events were held in honor of the gods at the great festivals, including athletic competitions to which all Greeks were invited. The first such games were held at the Olympic festival in 776 B.C.E. and were then held every four years thereafter to honor Zeus. Initially, the Olympic contests consisted of footraces and wrestling, but later boxing, javelin throwing, and various other contests were added.

As another practical side of Greek religion, Greeks wanted to know the will of the gods. To do so, they made use of the oracle, a sacred shrine dedicated to a god or goddess who revealed the future. The most famous was the oracle of Apollo at Delphi, located on the side of Mount Parnassus, overlooking the Gulf of Corinth. At Delphi, a priestess listened to questions while in a state of ecstasy that was believed to be induced by Apollo. Her responses were interpreted by the priests and given in verse form to the person asking questions. Representatives of states and individuals traveled to Delphi to consult the oracle of Apollo. States might inquire whether they should undertake a military expedition; individuals might raise such questions as "Heracleidas asks the god whether he will have offspring from the wife he has now." Responses were often enigmatic and at times even politically motivated. Croesus, the king of Lydia in Asia Minor who was known for his incredible wealth, sent messengers to the oracle at Delphi, asking "whether he shall go to war with the Persians." The oracle replied that if Croesus attacked the Persians, he would destroy a mighty empire. Overjoyed to hear these words, Croesus made war on the Persians but was crushed by his enemy. A mighty empire—that of Croesus—was destroyed.

Daily Life in Classical Athens

The Greek city-state was, above all, a male community: only adult male citizens took part in public life. In Athens, this meant the exclusion of women, slaves, and foreign residents, or roughly 85 percent of the total population in Attica. There were probably 150,000 citizens in Athens, of whom about 43,000 were adult males who exercised political power. Resident foreigners, who numbered about 35,000, received the protection of the laws but were also subject to some of the responsibilities of citizens, namely, military service and the funding of festivals. The remaining social group, the slaves, numbered around 100,000.

Slavery was a common institution in the ancient world. Economic needs dictated the desirability of owning at least one slave, although the very poor in Athens did not own any. The really wealthy might own large numbers, but those who did usually employed them in industry. Most often, slaves in Athens performed domestic tasks, such as being cooks and maids, or worked in the fields. Few peasants could afford more than one or two. Other slaves worked as unskilled and skilled laborers. Those slaves who worked in public construction were paid the same as citizens.

The Athenian economy was largely agricultural but highly diversified as well. Agriculture consisted of growing grains, vegetables, and fruit trees for local consumption; raising vines and olive trees for wine and olive oil, which were exportable products; and grazing sheep and goats for wool and milk products. Given the size of the population in Attica and the lack of abundant fertile land,

Athens had to import between 50 and 80 percent of its grain, a staple in the Athenian diet. Trade was thus highly important to the Athenian economy. The building of the port at Piraeus and the Long Walls (a series of defensive walls four and one-half miles long connecting Athens and Piraeus) created the physical conditions that made Athens the leading trade center in the fifth-century Greek world.

Artisans were more important to the Athenian economy than their relatively small numbers might suggest. In particular, Athens was the chief producer of high-quality painted pottery in the fifth century. Other crafts had moved beyond the small workshops into the factory through the use of slave labor. The shield factory of Lysias, for example, employed 120 slaves. Public works projects also provided considerable livelihood for Athenians. The building program of Pericles, financed from the Delian League treasury, made possible the hiring of both skilled and unskilled labor.

WOMEN IN THE LOOM ROOM. In Athens, women were considered to be citizens and could participate in religious cults and festivals, but they had no rights and were barred from any political activity. Women were thought to belong in the house, caring for the children and the needs of the household. A principal activity of Greek women was the making of clothes. This vase shows two women working on a warp-weighted loom.

The Athenian lifestyle was basically simple. Athenian houses were furnished with necessities bought from artisans, such as beds, couches, tables, chests, pottery, stools, baskets, and cooking utensils. Wives and slaves made clothes and blankets at home. The Athenian diet was rather plain and relied on such basic foods as barley, wheat, millet, lentils, grapes, figs, olives, almonds, bread made at home, vegetables, eggs, fish, cheese, and chicken. Olive oil was widely used, not only for eating, but for lighting lamps and rubbing on the body after washing and exercise. Although country houses kept animals, they were used for reasons other than their flesh: oxen for plowing, sheep for wool, and goats for milk and cheese.

The family was an important institution in ancient Athens. It was composed of husband, wife, and children (a nuclear family), although other dependent relatives and slaves were regarded as part of the family economic unit. The family's primary social function was to produce new citizens. Strict laws of the fifth century had stipulated that a citizen must be the offspring of a legally acknowledged marriage between two Athenian citizens whose parents were also citizens.

Women who were citizens could participate in most religious cults and festivals but were otherwise excluded from public life. They could not own property beyond personal items and always had a male guardian. The function of the Athenian woman as wife was very clear. Her foremost obligation was to bear children, especially male children who would preserve the family line. The marriage formula that Athenians used put it succinctly: "I give this woman for the procreation of legitimate children." Secondly, a wife was to take care of her family and her house, either doing the household work herself or supervising the slaves who did the actual work (see the box on p. 115).

Women were kept under strict control. Since they were married at fourteen or fifteen, they were taught about their responsibilities at an early age. Although many managed to learn to read and play musical instruments, they were often cut off from any formal education. And women were expected to remain at home out of sight unless they attended funerals or festivals. If they left the house, they were to be accompanied. A woman working alone in public was either poverty-stricken or not a citizen.

Male homosexuality was also a prominent feature of Athenian life. The Greek homosexual ideal was a relationship between a mature man and a young male. It is most likely that this was an aristocratic ideal and not one practiced by the common people. While the relationship was frequently physical, the Greeks also viewed it as educational. The older male (the "lover") won the love of his "beloved" by his value as a teacher and by the devotion he demonstrated in training his charge. In a sense, this love relationship was seen as a way of initiating young males into the male world of political and military dominance.

HOUSEHOLD MANAGEMENT AND THE ROLE OF THE ATHENIAN WIFE

In fifth-century Athens, a woman's place was in the home. She had two major responsibilities: the bearing and raising of children and the management of the household. In his dialogue on estate management, Xenophon relates the advice of an Attican gentleman on how to train a wife.

XENOPHON, *OECONOMICUS*

[Ischomachus addresses his new wife] For it seems to me, dear, that the gods with great discernment have coupled together male and female, as they are called, chiefly in order that they may form a perfect partnership in mutual service. For, in the first place, that the various species of living creatures may not fail, they are joined in wedlock for the production of children. Secondly, offspring to support them in old age is provided by this union, to human beings, at any rate. Thirdly, human beings live not in the open air, like beasts, but obviously need shelter. Nevertheless, those who mean to win stores to fill the covered place, have need of someone to work at the open-air occupations; since plowing, sowing, planting, and grazing are all such open-air employments; and these supply the needful food. . . . For he made the man's body and mind more capable of enduring cold and heat, and journeys and campaigns; and therefore imposed on him the outdoor tasks. To the woman, since he has made her body less capable of such endurance, I take it that God has assigned the indoor tasks. And knowing that he had created in the woman and had imposed on her the nourishment of the infants, he meted out to her a larger portion of affection for newborn babes than to the man. . . . Now since we know, dear, what duties have been assigned to each of us by God, we must endeavor, each of us, to do the duties allotted to us as well as possible. . . .

Your duty will be to remain indoors and send out those servants whose work is outside, and superintend those who are to work indoors, and to receive the incomings, and distribute so much of them as must be spent, and watch over so much as is to be kept in store, and take care that the sum laid by for a year be not spent in a month. And when wool is brought to you, you must see that cloaks are made for those that want them. You must see too that the dry corn is in good condition for making food. One of the duties that fall to you, however, will perhaps seem rather thankless: you will have to see that any servant who is ill is cared for.

The Greeks did not feel that the coexistence of homosexual and heterosexual predilections created any special problems for individuals or their society.

The Rise of Macedonia and the Conquests of Alexander

While the Greek city-states were continuing to fight each other, to their north a new and ultimately powerful kingdom was emerging in its own right. Its people, the Macedonians, were viewed as barbarians by their southern neighbors, the Greeks. The Macedonians were mostly rural folk, organized in tribes, not city-states, and not until the end of the fifth century B.C.E. did Macedonia emerge as an important kingdom. When Philip II (359–336 B.C.E.) came to the throne, he built an efficient army and turned Macedonia into the chief power of the Greek world. He was soon drawn into the internecine conflicts of the Greeks.

The Greeks had mixed reactions to Philip's growing strength. Some viewed Philip as a savior who would rescue the Greeks from themselves by uniting them. Many Athenians, however, especially the orator Demosthenes, portrayed Philip as ruthless, deceitful, treacherous, and barbaric and called upon the Athenians to undertake a struggle against him. Demosthenes' repeated calls for action, combined with Philip's rapid expansion, finally spurred Athens into action. Allied with a number of other Greek states, Athens fought the Macedonians at the Battle of Chaeronea, near Thebes, in 338 B.C.E. The Macedonian army crushed the Greeks, and Philip was now free to consolidate his control over the Greek peninsula. The Greek states were joined together in an alliance that we call the Corinthian League because they met at Corinth. All members took an oath of loyalty: "I swear by Zeus, Earth, Sun, Poseidon, Athena, Ares, and all the gods and goddesses. I will abide by the peace, and I will not break the agreements with Philip the Macedonian, nor will I take up arms with hostile intent against any one of those who abide by the oaths either by land or by sea."[14] Although Philip allowed the Greek city-states autonomy in domestic affairs, he retained the general direction of their foreign affairs. Many Greeks still objected to being subject to the less civilized master from the north, but Philip insisted that the Greek states end their bitter rivalries and cooperate with him in a war against Persia. Before Philip could undertake his invasion of Asia, however, he was assassinated, leaving the task to his son Alexander.

Alexander the Great

Alexander was only twenty when he became king of Macedonia. The illustrious conqueror was, in many ways, prepared for kingship by his father, who had taken Alexander along on military campaigns and, indeed, had given him control of the cavalry at the important battle of Chaeronea. After his father's assassination, Alexander moved quickly to assert his authority, securing the Macedonian frontiers and smothering a rebellion in Greece. He then turned to his father's dream, the invasion of the Persian Empire.

There is no doubt that Alexander was taking a chance in attacking the Persian Empire, which was still a strong state. Alexander's fleet was inferior to that of the Persians, and his finances were shaky at best. In the spring of 334 B.C.E., Alexander entered Asia Minor with an army of 37,000 men. About half were Macedonians, the rest being Greeks and other allies. The cavalry, which would play an important role as a striking force, numbered about 5,000. Architects, engineers, historians, and scientists accompanied the army, a clear indication of Alexander's grand vision and positive expectations at the beginning of his campaign.

CHRONOLOGY

THE RISE OF MACEDONIA AND THE CONQUESTS OF ALEXANDER

Reign of Philip II	359–336 B.C.E.
Battle of Chaeronea; Philip II conquers Greece	338 B.C.E.
Reign of Alexander the Great	336–323 B.C.E.
Alexander invades Asia; Battle of Granicus River	334 B.C.E.
Battle of Issus	333 B.C.E.
Battle of Gaugamela	331 B.C.E.
Fall of Persepolis, the Persian capital	330 B.C.E.
Alexander enters India	327 B.C.E.
Death of Alexander	323 B.C.E.

BUST OF ALEXANDER THE GREAT. This bust of Alexander the Great is a Roman copy of the head of a statue, possibly by Lysippus. Although he aspired to be another Achilles, the tragic hero of Homer's *Iliad,* Alexander also sought more divine honors. He claimed to be descended from Heracles, a Greek hero worshiped as a god, and as pharaoh of Egypt, he gained recognition as a living deity.

His first confrontation with the Persians, at a battle at the Granicus River in 334 B.C.E., almost cost him his life but resulted in a major victory. By the spring of 333 B.C.E., the entire western half of Asia Minor was in Alexander's hands, and the Ionian Greek cities of western Asia Minor had been "liberated" from the Persian oppressor. Meanwhile, the Persian king, Darius III, mobilized his forces to stop Alexander's army. Although the Persian troops outnumbered Alexander's, the Battle of Issus was fought on a narrow field that canceled the advantage of superior numbers and resulted in another Macedonian success. After his victory at Issus in 333 B.C.E., Alexander turned south, and by the winter of 332, Syria, Palestine, and Egypt were under his domination. He took the traditional title of pharaoh of Egypt and founded the first of a series of cities named after him (Alexandria) as the Greek administrative capital of Egypt. It became (and remains today) one of Egypt's and the Mediterranean world's most important cities.

In 331 B.C.E., Alexander renewed his offensive, moved into the territory of the ancient Mesopotamian kingdoms, and fought the decisive battle with the Persians at Gaugamela, not far from Babylon. After his victory, Alexander entered Babylon and then proceeded to the Persian capitals at Susa and Persepolis, where he acquired the Persian treasuries and took possession of vast quantities of gold and silver (see the box on p. 117). By 330, Alexander was again on the march, pursuing Darius. After Darius was killed by one of his own men, Alexander took the title and office of the Great King of the Persians. But he was not content to rest with the spoils of the Persian Empire. Over the next three years, he moved east and northeast, as far as modern Pakistan. By the summer of 327 B.C.E., he had entered India. But two more years of fighting in an exotic and difficult ter-

THE DESTRUCTION OF THE PERSIAN PALACE AT PERSEPOLIS

After Alexander's decisive victory at Gaugamela, he moved into Persia, where he captured the chief Persian cities. At Persepolis, he burned the Persian grand palace to the ground. The ancient historians Arrian and Diodorus of Sicily gave different explanations for this act: one argues that it was a deliberate act of revenge for the Persian invasion of Greece in the fifth century; the other, that the burning resulted from a wild drinking party. Modern historians do not agree on which version is more plausible. Arrian was a Greek-speaking Roman senator of the second century C.E. *Diodorus of Sicily lived in the first century* B.C.E.

DIODORUS OF SICILY, *LIBRARY OF HISTORY*

Alexander held games in honor of his victories. He performed costly sacrifices to the gods and entertained his friends bountifully. While they were feasting and the drinking was far advanced, as they began to be drunken a madness took possession of the minds of the intoxicated guests. At this point one of the women present, Thaïs by name and Attic by origin, said that for Alexander it would be the finest of all his feats in Asia if he joined them in a triumphal procession, set fire to the palaces, and permitted women's hands in a minute to extinguish the famed accomplishments of the Persians. This was said to men who were still young and giddy with wine, and so, as would be expected someone shouted out to form the procession and light torches, and urged all to take vengeance for the destruction of the Greek temples. Others took up the cry and said that this was a deed worthy of Alexander alone. When the king had caught fire at their words, all leaped up from their couches and passed the word along to form a victory procession in honor of Dionysus [god of wine and religious ecstasy].

Promptly many torches were gathered. Female musicians were present at the banquet, so the king led them all out for the procession to the sound of voices and flutes and pipes, Thaïs the courtesan leading the whole performance. She was the first, after the king, to hurl her blazing torch into the palace. As the others all did the same, immediately the entire palace area was consumed, so great was the conflagration. It was most remarkable that the impious act of Xerxes, king of the Persians, against the acropolis at Athens should have been repaid in kind after many years by one woman, a citizen of the land which had suffered it, and in sport.

ARRIAN, *THE LIFE OF ALEXANDER THE GREAT*

Thence he marched to Persepolis with such rapidity that the garrison had no time to plunder the city's treasure before his arrival. He also captured the treasure of Cyrus the First at Pasargadae. . . . He burnt the palace of the Persian kings, though this act was against the advice of Parmenio, who urged him to spare it for various reasons, chiefly because it was hardly wise to destroy what was now his own property, and because the Asians would, in his opinion, be less willing to support him if he seemed bent merely upon passing through their country as a conqueror rather than upon ruling it securely as a king. Alexander's answer was that he wished to punish the Persians for their invasion of Greece; his present act was retribution for the destruction of Athens, the burning of the temples, and all the other crimes they had committed against the Greeks.

rain exhausted his troops, who mutinied and refused to go on. Reluctantly, Alexander turned back, leading his men across the arid lands of southern Iran. Conditions in the desert were appalling; the blazing sun and lack of water led to thousands of deaths before Alexander and his remaining troops reached Babylon. Alexander planned still more campaigns, but in June 323 B.C.E., weakened from wounds, fever, and probably excessive alcohol consumption, he died at the young age of thirty-two.

THE LEGACY OF ALEXANDER

Alexander is one of the most puzzling great figures in history. Historians relying on the same sources give vastly different pictures of him. Some portray him as an idealistic visionary and others as a ruthless Machiavellian. How did Alexander the Great view himself? We know that he sought to imitate Achilles, the warrior-hero of Homer's *Iliad*. Alexander kept a copy of the *Iliad*—and a dagger—under his pillow. He also claimed to be descended from Heracles, the Greek hero who came to be worshiped as a god. No doubt, Alexander aspired to divine honors; as pharaoh of Egypt, he became a living god according to Egyptian tradition and at one point even sent instructions to the Greek cities to "vote him a god."

Regardless of his ideals, motives, or views about himself, one fact stands out: Alexander truly created a new age, the Hellenistic era. The word *Hellenistic* is derived from a Greek word meaning "to imitate Greeks." It is an

MAP 4.2 The Conquests of Alexander the Great

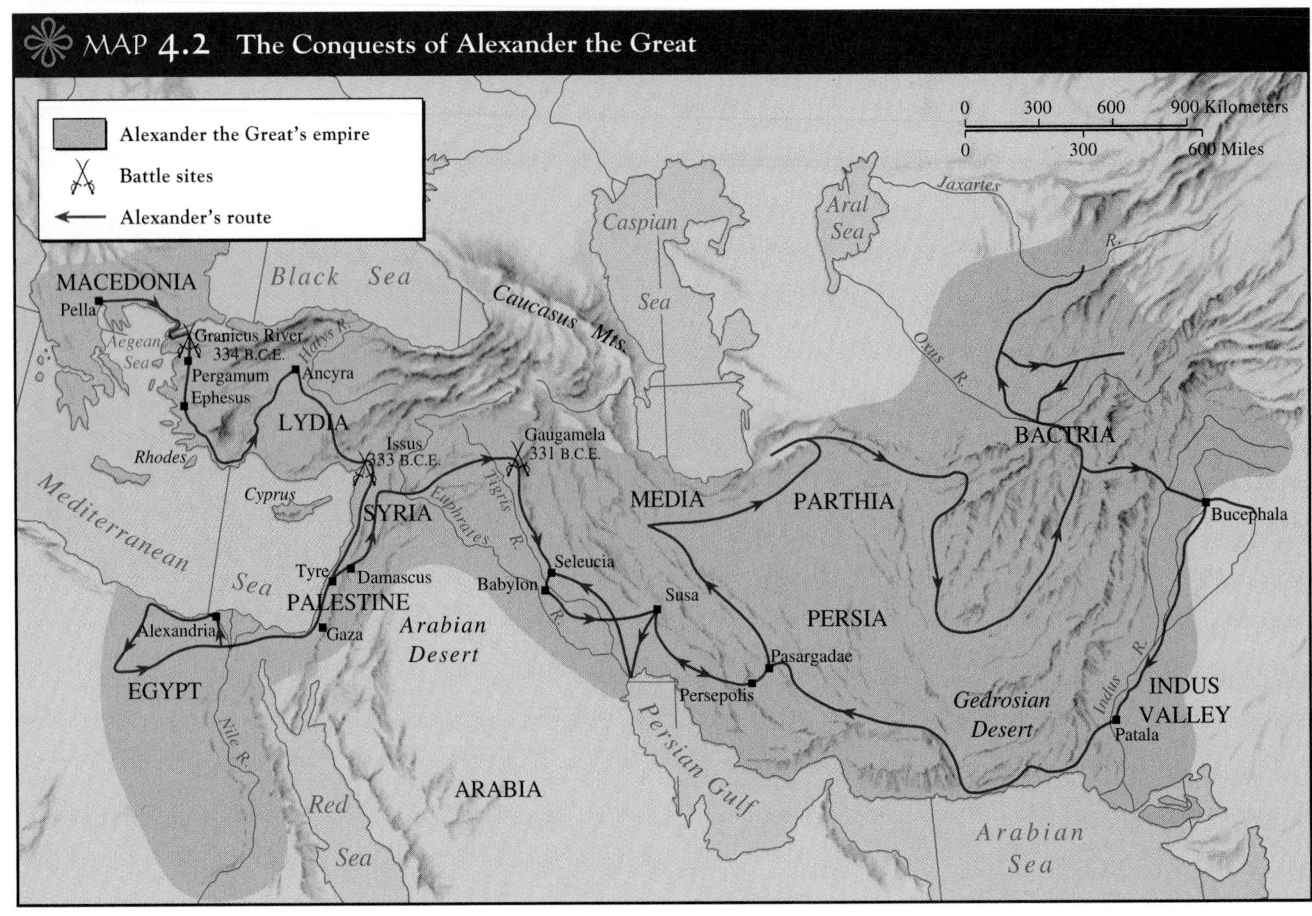

appropriate way, then, to describe an age that saw the extension of the Greek language and ideas to the non-Greek world of the Middle East. Alexander's destruction of the Persian monarchy created opportunities for Greek engineers, intellectuals, merchants, soldiers, and administrators. Those who followed Alexander and his successors participated in a new political unity based on the principle of monarchy. His successors used force to establish military monarchies that dominated the Hellenistic world after his death. Autocratic power became a regular feature of those Hellenistic monarchies and was part of Alexander's political legacy to the Hellenistic world. His vision of empire no doubt inspired the Romans, who were, of course, the real heirs of Alexander's legacy.

But Alexander also left a cultural legacy. As a result of his conquests, Greek language, art, architecture, and literature spread throughout the Middle East. The urban centers of the Hellenistic age, many founded by Alexander and his successors, became springboards for the diffusion of Greek culture. While the Greeks spread their culture in the east, they were also inevitably influenced by eastern ways. Thus, Alexander's legacy created one of the basic characteristics of the Hellenistic world: the clash and fusion of different cultures.

The World of the Hellenistic Kingdoms

The united empire that Alexander created by his conquests disintegrated soon after his death. All too soon, the most important Macedonian generals were engaged in a struggle for power. By 300 B.C.E., any hope of unity was dead, and eventually four Hellenistic kingdoms emerged as the successors to Alexander: Macedonia under the Antigonid dynasty, Syria and the east under the Seleucids, the Attalid kingdom of Pergamum in western Asia Minor, and Egypt under the Ptolemies. All were eventually conquered by the Romans.

The Hellenistic monarchies created a semblance of stability for several centuries, even though Hellenistic kings refused to accept the new status quo and periodically engaged in wars to alter it. At the same time, an underlying strain always existed between the new Greco-Macedonian ruling class and the native populations. Together these factors created a certain degree of tension that was never truly ended until the vibrant Roman state to the west stepped in and imposed a new order.

Although Alexander the Great apparently had planned to fuse Greeks and easterners—he used Persians as admin-

MAP 4.3 The World of the Hellenistic Monarchs

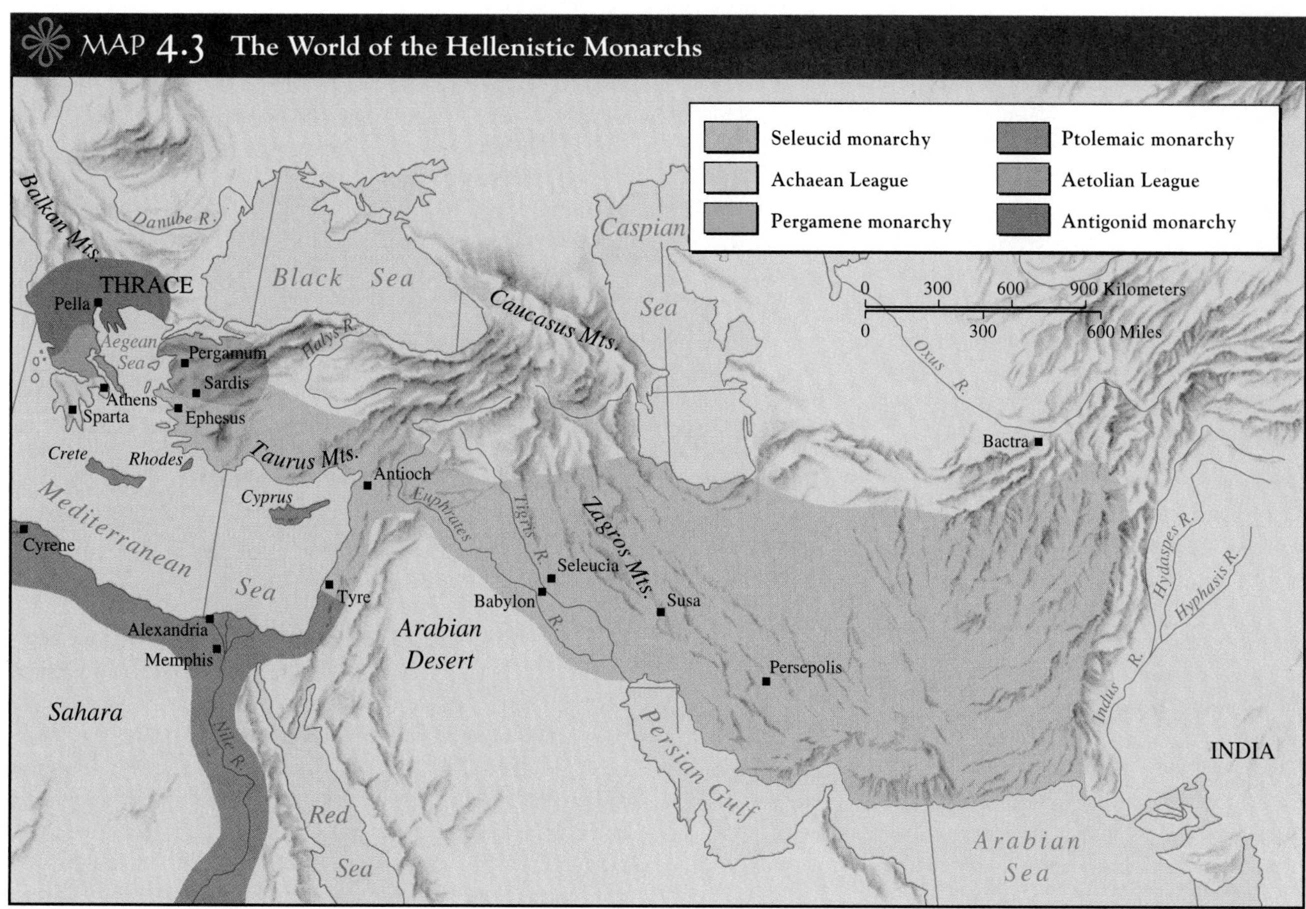

istrators, encouraged his soldiers to marry easterners, and did so himself—Hellenistic monarchs relied primarily on Greeks and Macedonians to form the new ruling class. It has been estimated that in the Seleucid kingdom, for example, only 2.5 percent of the people in authority were non-Greek, and most of them were commanders of local military units. Those who did advance to important administrative posts had learned Greek (all government business was transacted in Greek) and had become hellenized in a cultural sense. The policy of excluding non-Greeks from leadership positions, it should be added, was not due to the incompetence of the natives, but to the determination of the Greek ruling class to maintain its privileged position. It was the Greco-Macedonian ruling class that provided the only unity in the Hellenistic world.

Since the hellenizing process was largely an urban phenomenon, the creation of new Greek cities is an especially important topic. In his conquests, Alexander had founded a series of new cities and military settlements, and Hellenistic kings did likewise. The new population centers varied considerably in size and importance. Military settlements were meant to maintain order and might consist of only a few hundred men strongly dependent on the king. But there were also new independent cities with thousands of inhabitants. Alexandria in Egypt was the largest city in the Mediterranean region by the first century B.C.E.

Hellenistic rulers encouraged this massive spread of Greek colonists to the Middle East because of their intrinsic value to the new monarchies. Greeks (and Macedonians) provided not only a recruiting ground for the army, but also a pool of civilian administrators and workers who would contribute to economic development. Even architects, engineers, dramatists, and actors were in demand in the new Greek cities. Many Greeks and Macedonians were quick to see the advantages of moving to the new urban centers and gladly sought their fortunes in the Middle East. The Greek cities of the Hellenistic era were the chief agents in the spread of Greek culture in the Middle East—as far, in fact, as modern Afghanistan and India.

Economic and Social Trends

Agriculture was still of primary importance to both the native populations and the new Greek cities of the Hellenistic world. The Greek cities continued their old agrarian patterns. A well-defined citizen body owned land and worked it with the assistance of slaves. But their farms were isolated units in a vast area of land ultimately owned by

A NEW AUTONOMY FOR WOMEN

Upper-class women in Hellenistic society enjoyed noticeable gains, and even in the lives of ordinary women, a new assertiveness came to the fore despite the continuing domination of society by men. The first selection is taken from the letter of a wife to her husband, complaining about his failure to return home. In the second selection, a father complains that his daughter has abandoned him, contrary to an Egyptian law providing that children who have been properly raised should support their parents.

LETTER FROM ISIAS TO HEPHAISTION, 168 B.C.E.

If you are well and other things are going right, it would accord with the prayer that I make continually to the gods. I myself and the child and all the household are in good health and think of you always. When I received your letter from Horos, in which you announce that you are in detention in the Serapeum at Memphis, for the news that you are well I straightway thanked the gods, but about your not coming home, when all the others who had been secluded there have come, I am ill-pleased, because after having piloted myself and your child through such bad times and been driven to every extremity owing to the price of wheat, I thought that now at least, with you at home, I should enjoy some respite, whereas you have not even thought of coming home nor given any regard to our circumstances, remembering how I was in want of everything while you were still here, not to mention this long lapse of time and these critical days, during which you have sent us nothing. As, moreover, Horos who delivered the letter has brought news of your having been released from detention, I am thoroughly ill-pleased. Notwithstanding, as your mother also is annoyed, for her sake as well as for mine please return to the city, if nothing more pressing holds you back. You will do me a favor by taking care of your bodily health. Farewell.

LETTER FROM KTESIKLES TO KING PTOLEMY, 220 B.C.E.

I am wronged by Dionysios and by Nike my daughter. For though I raised her, my own daughter, and educated her and brought her to maturity, when I was stricken with bodily ill-health and was losing my eyesight, she was not minded to furnish me with any of the necessities of life. When I sought to obtain justice from her in Alexandria, she begged my pardon, and in the eighteenth year she swore me a written royal oath to give me each month twenty drachmas, which she was to earn by her own bodily labor. . . . But now corrupted by Dionysios, who is a comic actor, she does not do for me anything of what was in the written oath, despising my weakness and ill-health. I beg you, therefore, O king, not to allow me to be wronged by my daughter and by Dionysios the actor who corrupted her, but to order Diophanes the strategus [a provincial administrator] to summon them and hear us out; and if I am speaking the truth, let Diophanes deal with her corrupter as seems good to him and compel my daughter Nike to do justice to me. If this is done I shall no longer be wronged but by fleeing to you, O king, I shall obtain justice.

the king or assigned to large estate owners and worked by native peasants dwelling in villages. Overall, then, neither agricultural patterns nor methods of production underwent significant changes.

Commerce experienced considerable expansion in the Hellenistic era. Indeed, trading contacts linked much of the Hellenistic world together. The decline in the number of political barriers encouraged more commercial traffic. Although Hellenistic monarchs still fought wars, the conquests of Alexander and the policies of his successors made possible greater trade between east and west. An incredible variety of products were traded: gold and silver from Spain; salt from Asia Minor; timber from Macedonia; ebony, gems, ivory, and spices from India; frankincense (used on altars) from Arabia; slaves from Thrace, Syria, and Asia Minor; fine wines from Syria and western Asia Minor; olive oil from Athens; and numerous exquisite foodstuffs, such as the famous prunes of Damascus. The greatest trade, however, was in the basic staple of life—grain.

One of the more noticeable features of social life in the Hellenistic world was the emergence of new opportunities for women—at least, for upper-class women—especially in the economic area. Documents show increasing numbers of women involved in managing slaves, selling property, and making loans. Even then, legal contracts in which women were involved had to include their official male guardians, although in numerous instances these men no longer played an important function but were only listed to satisfy legal requirements. Only in Sparta were women free to control their own economic affairs. Many Spartan women were noticeably wealthy; females owned 40 percent of Spartan land.

Spartan women, however, were an exception, especially on the Greek mainland. Women in Athens, for example, still remained highly restricted and supervised. Although a few philosophers welcomed female participation in men's affairs, many philosophers rejected equality between men and women and asserted that the traditional roles of wives and mothers were most satisfying for women.

But the opinions of philosophers did not prevent upper-class women from making gains in areas other than the economic sphere (see the box on p. 120). New possibilities for females arose when women in some areas of the Hellenistic world were allowed to pursue education in the traditional fields of literature, music, and even athletics. Education, then, provided new opportunities for women: female poets appeared in the third century, and there are instances of women involved in both scholarly and artistic activities.

The creation of the Hellenistic monarchies, which represented a considerable departure from the world of the city-state, also gave new scope to the role played by the monarchs' wives, the Hellenistic queens. In Macedonia, a pattern of alliances between mothers and sons provided openings for women to take an active role in politics, especially in political intrigue. In Egypt, opportunities for royal women were even greater because the Ptolemaic rulers reverted to an Egyptian custom of kings marrying their own sisters. Of the first eight Ptolemaic rulers, four wed their sisters. Ptolemy II and his sister-wife Arsinoë II were both worshiped as gods in their lifetimes. Arsinoë played an energetic role in government and was involved in the expansion of the Egyptian navy. She was also the first Egyptian queen whose portrait appeared on coins with her husband. Hellenistic queens also showed an intense interest in culture. They wrote poems, collected art, and corresponded with intellectuals.

Culture in the Hellenistic World

Although the Hellenistic kingdoms encompassed vast territories and many diverse peoples, the Greeks provided a sense of unity as a result of the diffusion of Greek culture throughout the Hellenistic world. The Hellenistic era was a period of considerable cultural accomplishment in many areas—literature, art, science, and philosophy. Although these achievements occurred throughout the Hellenistic world, certain centers, especially the great Hellenistic cities of Alexandria and Pergamum, stood out. In both cities, cultural developments were encouraged by the rulers themselves. Rich Hellenistic kings had considerable resources with which to patronize culture.

New Directions in Literature and Art

The Hellenistic age produced an enormous quantity of literature, most of which has not survived. Hellenistic monarchs, who held literary talent in high esteem, subsidized writers on a grand scale. The Ptolemaic rulers of Egypt were particularly lavish. The combination of their largesse and a famous library with over 500,000 scrolls drew a host of scholars and authors to Alexandria, including a circle of poets. Theocritus (c. 315–250 B.C.E.), originally a native of the island of Sicily, wrote "little poems" or idylls dealing with erotic subjects, lovers' complaints, and, above all, pastoral themes expressing his love of nature and his appreciation of nature's beauties. In writing short poems, Theocritus was following the advice of Greek literary scholars who argued that Homer could never be superseded and urged writers to stick to well-composed, short poems instead.

In the Hellenistic era, Athens remained the theatrical center of the Greek world. While little remained of tragedy, a New Comedy developed, which completely

PORTRAIT OF QUEEN ARSINOË II. Arsinoë II, sister and wife of King Ptolemy II, played an active role in Egyptian political affairs. This statue from around 270–240 B.C.E. shows the queen in the traditional style of a pharaoh.

OLD MARKET WOMAN. Greek architects and sculptors were highly valued throughout the Hellenistic world, as kings undertook projects to beautify the cities of their kingdoms. Unlike the sculptors of the classical period, Hellenistic sculptors no longer tried to capture ideal beauty in their sculptures but moved toward a more emotional and realistic art. This statue of an old market woman is typical of this new trend in art.

rejected political themes and sought only to entertain and amuse. The Athenian playwright Menander (c. 342–291 B.C.E.) was perhaps the best representative of New Comedy. Plots were simple: typically, a hero falls in love with a not-really-so-bad prostitute, who turns out eventually to be the long-lost daughter of a rich neighbor. The hero marries her and they live happily ever after.

The Hellenistic period saw a great outpouring of historical and biographical literature. The chief historian of the Hellenistic age was Polybius (c. 203–c. 120 B.C.E.), a Greek who lived for some years in Rome. He is regarded by many historians as second only to Thucydides among Greek historians. His major work consisted of forty books narrating the history of the "inhabited Mediterranean world" from 221 to 146 B.C.E. Only the first five books are extant, although long extracts from the rest of the books survive. His history focuses on the growth of Rome from a city-state to a vast empire. It is apparent that Polybius understood the significance of the Romans' achievement. He followed Thucydides in seeking rational motives for historical events. He also approached his sources critically and used firsthand accounts.

In addition to being patrons of literary talent, the Hellenistic monarchs were eager to spend their money to beautify and adorn the cities within their states. The founding of new cities and the rebuilding of old ones provided numerous opportunities for Greek architects and sculptors. Hellenistic architects laid out their new cities on the rectilinear grid model first used by Hippodamus of Miletus in the fifth century B.C.E. The buildings of the Greek homeland—gymnasia, baths, theaters, and, of course, temples—lined the streets of these cities.

Both Hellenistic kings and rich citizens patronized sculptors. Thousands of statues, many paid for by the people honored, were erected in towns and cities all over the Hellenistic world. Hellenistic sculptors traveled throughout this world, attracted by the material rewards offered by wealthy patrons. As a result, although distinct styles developed in Alexandria, Rhodes, and Pergamum, Hellenistic sculpture was characterized by a considerable degree of uniformity. While maintaining the technical skill of the classical period, Hellenistic sculptors moved away from the idealism of fifth-century classicism to a more emotional and realistic art, seen in numerous statues of old women, drunks, and little children at play.

A Golden Age of Science

The Hellenistic era witnessed a more conscious separation of science from philosophy. In classical Greece, what we would call the physical and life sciences had been divisions of philosophical inquiry. Nevertheless, by the time of Aristotle, the Greeks had already established an important principle of scientific investigation, empirical research or systematic observation as the basis for generalization. In the Hellenistic age, the sciences tended to be studied in their own right. While Athens remained the philosophical center, Alexandria and Pergamum, the two leading cultural centers of the Hellenistic world, played a significant role in the development of Hellenistic science.

By far the most famous scientist of the period, Archimedes (287–212 B.C.E.) of Syracuse, came from the western Mediterranean region. Archimedes was especially important for his work on the geometry of spheres and cylinders, for establishing the value of the mathematical constant pi, and for creating the science of hydrostatics. Archimedes was also a practical inventor. He may have devised the so-called Archimedean screw used to pump water out of mines and to lift irrigation water, as well as a compound pulley for transporting heavy weights. During the Roman siege of his native city of Syracuse, he constructed a number of devices to thwart the attackers. According to Plutarch's account, the Romans became so frightened "that if they did but see a little rope or a

THE STOIC IDEAL OF HARMONY WITH GOD

The Stoic Cleanthes (331–232 B.C.E.) succeeded Zeno as head of this school of philosophy. One historian of Hellenistic civilization has called this work by Cleanthes the greatest religious hymn in Greece. Certainly, it demonstrates that Stoicism, unlike Epicureanism, did have an underlying spiritual foundation. This poem has been compared to the great psalms of the Hebrews.

CLEANTHES, *HYMN TO ZEUS*

Nothing occurs on the earth apart from you, O God, nor in the heavenly regions nor on the sea, except what bad men do in their folly; but you know how to make the odd even, and to harmonize what is dissonant; to you the alien is akin.
And so you have wrought together into one all things that are good and bad,
So that there arises one eternal logos [rationale] of all things,
Which all bad mortals shun and ignore,
Unhappy wretches, ever seeking the possession of good things
They neither see nor hear the universal law of God,
By obeying which they might enjoy a happy life.

piece of wood from the wall, instantly crying out, that there it was again, Archimedes was about to let fly some engine at them, they turned their backs and fled."[15] Archimedes' accomplishments inspired a wealth of semilegendary stories. Supposedly, he discovered specific gravity by observing the water he displaced in his bath and became so excited by his realization that he jumped out of the water and ran home naked, shouting, "Eureka" ("I have found it"). He is said to have emphasized the importance of levers by proclaiming to the king of Syracuse: "Give me a lever and a place to stand and I will move the earth." The king was so impressed that he encouraged Archimedes to lower his sights and build defensive weapons instead.

Philosophy: New Schools of Thought

While Alexandria and Pergamum became the renowned cultural centers of the Hellenistic world, Athens remained the prime center for philosophy. After Alexander the Great, the home of Socrates, Plato, and Aristotle continued to attract the most illustrious philosophers from the Greek world, who chose to establish their schools there. New schools of philosophical thought—the Epicureans and Stoics—reinforced Athens's reputation as a philosophical center.

Epicurus (341–270 B.C.E.), the founder of Epicureanism, established a school in Athens near the end of the fourth century B.C.E. Epicurus believed that human beings were free to follow self-interest as a basic motivating force. Happiness was the goal of life, and the means to achieve it was the pursuit of pleasure, the only true good. But the pursuit of pleasure was not meant in a physical, hedonistic sense (which is what our word *epicurean* has come to mean). Pleasure was not satisfying one's desire in an active, gluttonous fashion, but freedom from emotional turmoil, freedom from worry, the freedom that came from a mind at rest. To achieve this kind of pleasure, one had to free oneself from public activity: "We must release ourselves from the prison of affairs and politics." But this was not a renunciation of all social life, for to Epicurus, a life could only be complete when it was centered on the basic ideal of friendship. Epicurus's own life in Athens was an embodiment of his teachings. He and his friends created their own private community where they could pursue their ideal of true happiness.

Another school of thought was Stoicism, which became the most popular philosophy of the Hellenistic world and later flourished in the Roman Empire as well. It was the product of a teacher named Zeno (335–263 B.C.E.), who came to Athens and began to teach in a public colonnade known as the Painted Portico (the *Stoa Poikile*—hence Stoicism). Like Epicureanism, Stoicism was concerned with how individuals find happiness. But Stoics took a radically different approach to the problem. To them, happiness, the supreme good, could be found only by living in harmony with the will of God, by which people gained inner peace (see the box above). Life's problems could not disturb these people, and they could bear whatever life offered (hence our word *stoic*). Unlike Epicureans, Stoics did not believe in the need to separate oneself from the world and politics. Public service was regarded as noble, and the real Stoic was a good citizen and could even be a good government official. In fact, the Roman emperor Marcus Aurelius was a noted Stoic philosopher.

Epicureanism and especially Stoicism appealed to large numbers of people in the Hellenistic world. Both of these philosophies focused primarily on the problem of human happiness. Their popularity would suggest a fundamental change in the character of the Greek lifestyle. In the classical Greek world, the happiness of individuals and the meaning of life were closely associated with the life of the *polis:* one found fulfillment within the community. In the Hellenistic kingdoms, although the *polis* continued to exist, the sense that one could find satisfaction and fulfillment through life in the *polis* had weakened. Not only

THE CULT OF ISIS. The cult of Isis was one of the most popular mystery religions in the Hellenistic world. This fresco from Herculaneum in Italy depicts a religious ceremony in front of the temple of Isis. At the top, a priest holds a golden vessel, while below him another priest leads the worshipers with a staff. A third priest fans the flames at the altar.

did individuals seek new philosophies that offered personal happiness, but in the cosmopolitan world of the Hellenistic states, a new openness to thoughts of universality could also emerge. For some people, Stoicism embodied this larger sense of community. The appeal of new philosophies in the Hellenistic era can also be explained by the apparent decline in certain aspects of traditional religion, which we can see by examining the status of Hellenistic religion.

Religion in the Hellenistic World

When the Greeks spread throughout the Hellenistic kingdoms, they took their gods with them. Although the construction of temples may have been less important than in classical times, there were still many demonstrations of a lively religious faith. But over a period of time, there was a noticeable decline in the vitality of the traditional Greek Olympian religion. Much of Greek religion had always revolved around ritual, but the civic cults based on the traditional gods no longer seemed sufficient to satisfy people's emotional needs.

The decline in traditional Greek religion left Greeks receptive to the numerous religious cults of the eastern world. The Greeks were always tolerant of other religious institutions. Hence, in the Hellenistic cities of the Middle East, the traditional civic cults of their own gods and foreign cults existed side by side. Alexandria had cults of the traditional Greek gods, Egyptian deities, such as Isis and Horus, the Babylonian Astarte, and the Syrian Atargatis. The eastern religions that appealed most to Greeks, however, were the mystery religions. What was the source of their attraction?

The normal forms of religious worship in Hellenistic communities had lost some of their appeal. The practices of traditional, ritualized Greek religion in the civic cults seemed increasingly meaningless. For many people, the search for personal meaning remained unfulfilled, and they sought alternatives. Among educated Greeks, the philosophies of Epicureanism and especially Stoicism offered help. Another source of solace came in the form of mystery religions.

Mystery cults, with their secret initiations and promises of individual salvation, were not new to the Greek world. But the Greeks of the Hellenistic era were also strongly influenced by eastern mystery cults, such as those of Egypt, which offered a distinct advantage over the Greek mystery religions. The latter had usually been connected to specific locations (such as Eleusis), which meant that a would-be initiate had to undertake a pilgrimage in order to participate in the rites. In contrast, the eastern mystery religions were readily available since temples to their gods and goddesses were located throughout the Greek cities of the east. All of the mystery religions were based on the same fundamental premises. Individuals could pursue a path to salvation and achieve eternal life by being initiated into a union with a savior god or goddess who had died and risen again.

The Egyptian cult of Isis was one of the most popular of the mystery religions. The cult of Isis was very ancient but became truly universal in Hellenistic times. Isis was the goddess of women, marriage, and children; as one of her hymns states: "I am she whom women call goddess. I ordained that women should be loved by men: I brought wife and husband together, and invented the marriage contract. I ordained that women should bear children."[16] Isis was also portrayed as the giver of civilization, who had brought laws and letters to all humankind. The cult of Isis offered a precious commodity to its initiates—the promise of eternal life. In many ways, the cult of Isis and the other mystery religions of the Hellenistic era helped to pave the way for the coming and the success of Christianity.

Conclusion

Unlike the great centralized empires of the Persians and the Chinese, ancient Greece consisted of a large number of small, independent city-states, most of which had populations of only a few thousand. Despite the small size of their city-states, these ancient Greeks created a civilization that was the fountainhead of Western culture. Socrates, Plato, and Aristotle established the foundations of Western philosophy. Western literary forms are largely derived from Greek poetry and drama. Greek notions of harmony, proportion, and beauty have remained the touchstones for all subsequent Western art. A rational method of inquiry, so important to modern science, was conceived in ancient Greece. Many political terms are Greek in origin, and so too are concepts of the rights and duties of citizenship, especially as they were conceived in Athens, the first great democracy the world had seen. Especially during their classical period, the Greeks raised and debated the fundamental questions about the purpose of human existence, the structure of human society, and the nature of the universe that have concerned thinkers ever since.

All of these achievements came from a group of small city-states in ancient Greece. And yet there remains an element of tragedy about Greek civilization. For all of their brilliant accomplishments, the Greeks were unable to rise above the divisions and rivalries that caused them to fight each other and undermine their own civilization. Of course, their cultural contributions have outlived their political struggles. And the Hellenistic era, which emerged after the Greek city-states had lost their independence, made possible the spread of Greek ideas to larger areas.

The Hellenistic period was a vibrant one. New cities arose and flourished. New philosophical ideas captured the minds of many. Significant achievements were made in art, literature, and science. Greek culture spread throughout the Middle East and made an impact wherever it was carried. But serious problems remained. Hellenistic kings continued to engage in inconclusive wars. Much of the formal culture was the special preserve of the Greek conquerors, whose attitude of superiority kept them largely separated from the native masses of the Hellenistic kingdoms. Although the Hellenistic world achieved a degree of political stability, by the late third century B.C.E. signs of decline were beginning to multiply. Some of the more farsighted perhaps realized the danger the growing power of Rome presented to the Hellenistic world. The Romans would ultimately inherit Alexander's empire and Greek culture, and we must now turn to them and try to understand what made them such successful conquerors.

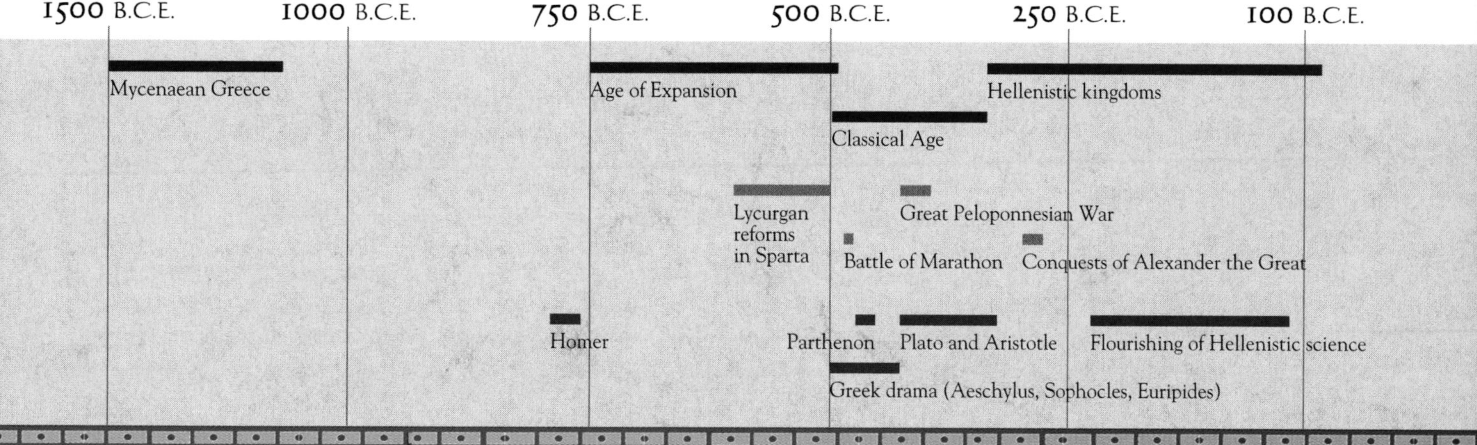

Chapter Notes

1. H. D. F. Kitto, *The Greeks* (Harmondsworth, 1951), p. 64.
2. Homer, *Odyssey*, trans. E. V. Rieu (Harmondsworth, 1946), p. 337.
3. Xenophon, *Symposium*, trans. O. J. Todd (Harmondsworth, 1946), III, 5.
4. Homer, *Odyssey*, trans. E. V. Rieu (Harmondsworth, 1959), pp. 290–91.
5. Quoted in Thomas R. Martin, *Ancient Greece* (New Haven, Conn., 1996), p. 62.
6. These words from Plutarch are quoted in E. Fantham, H. P. Foley, N. B. Kampen, S. B. Pomeroy, and H. A. Shapiro, *Women in the Classical World* (New York, 1994), p. 64.
7. Voltaire, *The Age of Louis XIV*, trans. Martyn Pollack (London, 1926), p. 1.
8. Herodotus, *The Persian Wars*, trans. Robin Waterfield (New York, 1998), p. 3.
9. Thucydides, *The Peloponnesian War*, trans. Rex Warner (Harmondsworth, 1954), p. 24.
10. Sophocles, *Oedipus the King*, trans. David Grene (Chicago, 1959), pp. 68–69.

11. Sophocles, *Antigone*, trans. Don Taylor (London, 1986), p. 146.
12. Plato, *The Republic*, trans. F. M. Cornford (New York, 1945), pp. 178–79.
13. Quotations from Aristotle are in Sue Blundell, *Women in Ancient Greece* (London, 1995), pp. 106, 186.
14. Quoted in Sarah B. Pomeroy, Stanley M. Burstein, Walter Donlan, Jennifer Tolbert Roberts, *Ancient Greece: A Political, Social, and Cultural History* (Oxford, 1999), p. 390.
15. Plutarch, *Life of Marcellus*, trans. John Dryden (New York, n.d.), p. 378.
16. Quoted in W. W. Tarn, *Hellenistic Civilization* (London, 1930), p. 324.

Suggested Readings

A standard one-volume reference work for Greek history is J. B. Bury and R. Meiggs, *A History of Greece to the Death of Alexander the Great*, 4th ed. (New York, 1975). Other good general introductions to Greek history include *The Oxford History of the Classical World*, ed. J. Boardman, J. Griffin, and O. Murray (Oxford, 1986), pp. 19–314; T. R. Martin, *Ancient Greece* (New Haven, Conn., 1996); P. Cartledge, *The Cambridge Illustrated History of Ancient Greece* (Cambridge, 1998); and W. Donlan, S. B. Pomeroy, J. T. Roberts, and S. M. Burstein, *Ancient Greece: A Political, Social, and Cultural History* (New York, 1998). For a general survey of economic and social aspects, see M. M. Austin and P. Vidal-Naquet, *Economic and Social History of Ancient Greece: An Introduction* (Berkeley, 1978).

Early Greek history is examined in O. Murray, *Early Greece*, 2d ed. (Cambridge, Mass., 1993), and J. L. Fitton, *The Discovery of the Greek Bronze Age* (Cambridge, 1995). For a good introduction to Homer and the Homeric problem, see J. Griffin, *Homer* (Oxford, 1980).

A good general work on the Greek age of expansion is A. M. Snodgrass, *Archaic Greece* (London, 1980). Economic and social history of the period is covered in C. Starr, *The Economic and Social Growth of Early Greece, 800–500* B.C. (Oxford, 1977). On colonization, see J. Boardman, *The Greeks Overseas*, rev. ed. (Baltimore, 1980). On tyranny, see J. F. McGlew, *Tyranny and Political Culture in Ancient Greece* (Ithaca, N.Y., 1993). On Sparta, see W. Forrest, *A History of Sparta, 950–121* B.C., 2d ed. (London, 1980). On early Athens, see the still valuable A. Jones, *Athenian Democracy* (London, 1957), and R. Osborne, *Demos* (Oxford, 1985). The Persian Wars are examined in A. Burn, *Persia and the Greeks: The Defense of the West*, rev. ed. (Stanford, Calif., 1984).

A general history of classical Greece can be found in S. Hornblower, *The Greek World, 479–323* B.C. (London, 1983). Important works on Athens include C. W. Fornara and L. J. Samons II, *Athens from Cleisthenes to Pericles* (Berkeley, 1991); D. Stockton, *The Classical Athenian Democracy* (Oxford, 1990); and D. Kagan, *Pericles of Athens and the Birth of Democracy* (New York, 1991). On the development of the Athenian Empire, see M. F. Mc-Gregor, *The Athenians and Their Empire* (Vancouver, 1987). The best way to examine the Great Peloponnesian War is to read the work of Thucydides, *History of the Peloponnesian War*, trans. R. Warner (Harmondsworth, 1954).

For a comprehensive history of Greek art, see M. Robertson, *A History of Greek Art*, 2 vols. (Cambridge, 1975). A good brief study is J. Boardman, *Greek Art* (London, 1985). On sculpture, see A. Stewart, *Greek Sculpture: An Exploration* (New Haven, Conn., 1990). A basic survey of architecture is H. W. Lawrence, *Greek Architecture*, rev. ed. (Harmondsworth, 1983). On Greek drama, see the general work by J. De Romilly, *A Short History of Greek Literature* (Chicago, 1985). On Greek philosophy, a detailed study is available in W. K. C. Guthrie, *A History of Greek Philosophy*, 6 vols. (Cambridge, 1962–1981). On Greek religion, see J. N. Bremmer, *Greek Religion* (Oxford, 1994).

On the family and women, see S. C. Humphreys, *The Family, Women and Death* (London, 1983); S. B. Pomeroy, *Goddesses, Whores, Wives, and Slaves* (New York, 1975); E. Fantham, H. P. Foley, N. B. Kampen, S. B. Pomeroy, and H. A. Shapiro, *Women in the Classical World* (New York, 1994); and S. Blundell, *Women in Ancient Greece* (Cambridge, Mass., 1995). On homosexuality, see E. Cantarella, *Bisexuality in the Ancient World* (New Haven, Conn., 1992).

The best general survey of the Hellenistic era is F. W. Walbank, *The Hellenistic World* (London, 1981). For a good introduction to the early history of Macedonia, see E. N. Borza, *In the Shadow of Olympus: The Emergence of Macedon* (Princeton, N.J., 1990). Philip of Macedon is covered well in N. Hammond and G. Griffith, *A History of Macedonia*, vol. 2, *550–336* B.C. (Oxford, 1979). There are considerable differences of opinion on Alexander the Great. The best biographies include R. L. Fox, *Alexander the Great* (London, 1973); J. R. Hamilton, *Alexander the Great* (London, 1973); and P. Green, *Alexander of Macedon* (Berkeley, Calif., 1991).

The various Hellenistic monarchies can be examined in N. G. L. Hammond and F. W. Walbank, *A History of Macedonia*, vol. 3, *336–167* B.C. (Oxford, 1988); S. Sherwin-White and A. Kuhrt, *From Samarkand to Sardis: A New Approach to the Seleucid Empire* (Berkeley and Los Angeles, 1993); and N. Lewis, *Greeks in Ptolemaic Egypt* (Oxford, 1986). On economic and social trends, see the classic and still indispensable M. I. Rostovtzeff, *Social and Economic History of the Hellenistic World*, 3 vols., 2d ed. (Oxford, 1953). Hellenistic women are examined in two works by S. B. Pomeroy, *Goddesses, Whores, Wives, and Slaves* (New York, 1975), pp. 120–48, and *Women in Hellenistic Egypt* (New York, 1984).

For a general introduction to Hellenistic culture, see J. Onians, *Art and Thought in the Hellenistic Age* (London, 1979). The best general survey of Hellenistic philosophy is A. A. Long, *Hellenistic Philosophy: Stoics, Epicureans, Skeptics*, 2d ed. (London, 1986). A superb work on Hellenistic science is G. E. R. Lloyd, *Greek Science After Aristotle* (London, 1973). On one facet of Hellenistic religion, see R. E. Witt, *Isis in the Graeco-Roman World* (London, 1971). On the entry of Rome into the Hellenistic world, see the basic work by E. S. Gruen, *The Hellenistic World and the Coming of Rome*, 2 vols. (Berkeley, 1984).

InfoTrac College Edition

For additional reading, go to InfoTrac College Edition, your online research library at http://web1.infotrac-college.com

Enter the search terms "Greece history" using Keywords.

Enter the search terms "Peloponnesian War" using Keywords.

Enter the search terms "Greek mythology" using the Subject Guide.

Enter the search terms "Plato or Aristotle or Socrates" using Keywords.

Enter the search terms "Alexander the Great" using Keywords.

CHAPTER 5

THE WORLD OF THE ROMANS

CHAPTER OUTLINE

FOCUS QUESTIONS

- What policies and institutions help to explain the Romans' success in conquering and then ruling their empire?
- What problems did Rome face during the last century of the Republic, and how were they ultimately resolved?
- What were the chief features of the Roman Empire at its height in the second century C.E., and what happened to bring it near collapse in the next century?
- What characteristics of Christianity enabled it to grow and ultimately to triumph?
- In what ways were the Roman Empire and the Han Chinese Empire similar, and in what ways were they different?

Although the Assyrians, Persians, and Indians under the Mauryan dynasty had created empires, they were neither as large nor as well controlled as the Han Chinese and Roman Empires that flourished at the beginning of the first millennium C.E. These two were the most extensive empires the world had yet seen (the Han Empire, as we saw in Chapter 3, extended from Central Asia to the Pacific Ocean; the Roman Empire encompassed the lands around the Mediterranean as well as parts of the Middle East and western and central Europe). Although there was little contact between them, the Han Empire and the Roman

Empire had some remarkable similarities: their empires lasted for centuries; they had remarkable success in establishing centralized control over their empires; and throughout their empires they maintained their law and political institutions, their technical skills, and their languages. But there were also important differences between the Han and Roman Empires, which will become evident as we examine the world of the Romans in this chapter.

Roman history is basically the remarkable story of how a group of Latin-speaking people who established a small community on a plain called Latium in central Italy went on to conquer all of Italy and then the entire Mediterranean world. Why were the Romans able to do this? Scholars do not really know all the answers, but the Romans had their own explanation. Early Roman history is filled with legendary stories that tell of the heroes who made Rome great. One of the best known is the story of Horatius at the bridge. Threatened by attack from the neighboring Etruscans, Roman farmers abandoned their fields and moved into the city, where they would be protected by the walls. One weak point in the Roman defenses, however, was a wooden bridge over the Tiber River. Horatius was on guard at the bridge when a sudden assault by the Etruscans caused many Roman troops to throw down their weapons and flee. Horatius urged them to make a stand at the bridge behind him while he held the Etruscans back. Astonished at the sight of a single defender, the confused Etruscans threw their spears at Horatius, who caught them on his shield and barred the way. By the time the Etruscans had regrouped and were about to overwhelm the lone defender, the Roman soldiers brought down the bridge. When Horatius heard the bridge crash into the river behind him, he dove fully armed into the water and swam safely to the other side through a hail of arrows. Rome had been saved by the courageous act of a Roman who knew his duty and was determined to carry it out. Courage, duty, determination—these qualities would also serve the many Romans who believed that it was their divine mission to rule nations and peoples. As one Roman writer proclaimed: "By heaven's will my Rome shall be capital of the world."

The Emergence of Rome

Italy is a peninsula extending about 750 miles from north to south. It is not very wide, however, averaging about 120 miles across. The Apennines traverse the peninsula from north to south, forming a ridge down the middle that divides west from east. Nevertheless, Italy has some fairly large fertile plains ideal for farming. Most important were the Po valley in the north, probably the most fertile agricultural area; the plain of Latium, on which Rome was located; and Campania to the south of Latium. To the east of the Italian peninsula is the Adriatic Sea and to the west the Tyrrhenian Sea with the nearby large islands of Corsica and Sardinia. Sicily lies just west of the toe of the boot-shaped Italian peninsula.

Geography had an impact on Roman history. Although the Apennines bisected Italy, they were less rugged than the mountain ranges of Greece and did not divide the peninsula into many small isolated communities. Italy also possessed considerably more productive agricultural land than Greece, enabling it to support a large population. Rome's location was favorable from a geographical point of view. Located eighteen miles inland on the Tiber River, Rome had access to the sea and yet was far enough inland to be safe from pirates. Built on the famous seven hills, it was easily defended. Situated where the Tiber could be readily forded, Rome became a natural crossing point for north-south traffic in western Italy. All in all, Rome had a good central location in Italy from which to expand.

Moreover, the Italian peninsula juts into the Mediterranean, making it an important crossroads between the western and eastern Mediterranean. Once Rome had unified Italy, involvement in Mediterranean affairs was natural. And after the Romans had conquered their Mediterranean empire, governing it was made considerably easier by Italy's central location.

Early Rome

According to Roman legend, Rome was founded by the twin brothers Romulus and Remus in 753 B.C.E., and archaeologists have found that by the eighth century B.C.E. there was a settlement consisting of huts on the tops of Rome's hills. The early Romans, basically a pastoral people, spoke Latin, which, like Greek, belongs to the Indo-European family of languages (see the table in Chapter 1). The Roman historical tradition also maintained that early

ETRUSCAN MARRIED COUPLE. This sculpture, dating from 550 B.C.E., depicts a wealthy Etruscan married couple reclining on a couch. The Etruscans greatly influenced the early development of Rome and had an impact on Roman religion, sporting events, and military institutions.

Rome (753–509 B.C.E.) had been under the control of seven kings and that two of the last three had been Etruscans, a people who were located north of Rome in Etruria. Some historians believe that the king list may have some historical accuracy. What is certain is that Rome did fall under the influence of the Etruscans for about a hundred years during the period of the kings. The Etruscans found Rome a pastoral community but left it a city.

By the beginning of the sixth century B.C.E., under Etruscan influence, Rome began to emerge as an actual city. The Etruscans were responsible for an outstanding building program. They constructed the first roadbed of the chief street through Rome—the Sacred Way—before 575 B.C.E. and oversaw the development of temples, markets, shops, streets, and houses. By 509 B.C.E., the date when the monarchy supposedly was overthrown and a republican form of government established, a new Rome had emerged, essentially a result of the fusion of Etruscan and native Roman elements.

The Roman Republic

The transition from monarchy to a republican government was not easy. Rome felt threatened by enemies from every direction and, in the process of meeting these threats, embarked on a military course that led to the conquest of the entire Italian peninsula.

The Roman Conquest of Italy

At the beginning of the Republic, Rome was surrounded by enemies, including the Etruscans to the north and the Sabines, Volscians, and Aequi to the east and south. The Latin communities on the plain of Latium posed an even more immediate threat. If we are to believe Livy, one of the chief ancient sources for the history of the early Roman Republic, Rome was engaged in almost continuous warfare with the Volscians, Sabines, Aequi, and others for the next hundred years.

In his account of these years, the historian Livy provided a detailed narrative of Roman efforts. Many of Livy's stories were legendary in character and indeed were modeled after events in Greek history. But Livy, writing in the first century B.C.E., used such stories to teach Romans the moral values and virtues that had made Rome great. These included tenacity, duty, courage, and especially discipline (see the box on p. 131). Indeed, Livy recounted stories of military leaders who executed their own sons for leaving their place in battle, a serious offense, since the success of the hoplite infantry depended on maintaining a precise order. These stories had little basis in fact, but like the story of George Washington and the cherry tree in American history, they provided mythical images to reinforce Roman patriotism.

By 340 B.C.E., Rome had crushed the Latin states in Latium. During the next fifty years, the Romans waged a fierce struggle with the Samnites, a hill people from the central Apennines, some of whom had settled in Campania, south of Rome. Rome was again victorious. The conquest of the Samnites gave Rome considerable control over a large part of Italy and also brought it into direct contact with the Greek communities. The Greeks had arrived on the Italian peninsula in large numbers during the age of Greek colonization (750–550 B.C.E.; see Chapter 4). Initially, the Greeks settled in southern Italy and then crept around the coast and up the peninsula. They also occupied the eastern two-thirds of Sicily. The Greeks had much influence on Rome. They cultivated the olive and the vine, and provided artistic and cultural models through their sculpture, architecture, and literature. Soon after their conquest of the Samnites, the Romans were involved in hostilities with some of these Greek cities and by 267 B.C.E. had completed their conquest of southern Italy. After crushing the remaining Etruscan states to the north in 264 B.C.E., Rome had conquered all of Italy except the extreme north.

To rule Italy, the Romans devised the Roman Confederation. Under this system, Rome allowed some peoples—especially the Latins—to have full Roman citizenship. Most of the remaining communities were made allies. They remained free to run their own local affairs but were required to provide soldiers for Rome. Moreover, the Romans made it clear that loyal allies could improve their status and even have hope of becoming Roman citizens.

CINCINNATUS SAVES ROME: A ROMAN MORALITY TALE

There is perhaps no better account of how the virtues of duty and simplicity enabled good Roman citizens to prevail during the travails of the fifth century B.C.E. *than Livy's account of Cincinnatus. He was chosen dictator, supposedly in 457* B.C.E., *to defend Rome against the attacks of the Aequi. The position of dictator was a temporary expedient used only in emergencies; the consuls would resign and a leader with unlimited power would be appointed for a limited period (usually six months). In this account, Cincinnatus did his duty, defeated the Aequi, and returned to his simple farm in just fifteen days.*

LIVY, *THE EARLY HISTORY OF ROME*

The city was thrown into a state of turmoil, and the general alarm was as great as if Rome herself were surrounded. Nautius was sent for, but it was quickly decided that he was not the man to inspire full confidence; the situation evidently called for a dictator, and, with no dissentient voice, Lucius Quinctius Cincinnatus was named for the post.

Now I would solicit the particular attention of those numerous people who imagine that money is everything in this world, and that rank and ability are inseparable from wealth: let them observe that Cincinnatus, the one man in whom Rome reposed all her hope of survival, was at that moment working a little three-acre farm ... west of the Tiber, just opposite the spot where the shipyards are today. A mission from the city found him at work on his land—digging a ditch, maybe, or plowing. Greetings were exchanged, and he was asked—with a prayer for divine blessing on himself and his country—to put on his toga and hear the Senate's instructions. This naturally surprised him, and, asking if all were well, he told his wife Racilia to run to their cottage and fetch his toga. The toga was brought, and wiping the grimy sweat from his hands and face he put it on; at once the envoys from the city saluted him, with congratulations, as Dictator, invited him to enter Rome, and informed him of the terrible danger of Municius's army. A state vessel was waiting for him on the river, and on the city bank he was welcomed by his three sons who had come to meet him, then by other kinsmen and friends, and finally by nearly the whole body of senators. Closely attended by all these people and preceded by his lictors he was then escorted to his residence through streets lined with great crowds of common folk who, be it said, were by no means so pleased to see the new Dictator, as they thought his power excessive and dreaded the way in which he was likely to use it.

[Cincinnatus proceeds to raise an army, march out, and defeat the Aequi.]

In Rome the Senate was convened by Quintus Fabius the City Prefect, and a decree was passed inviting Cincinnatus to enter in triumph with his troops. The chariot he rode in was preceded by the enemy commanders and the military standards, and followed by his army loaded with its spoils. . . . Cincinnatus finally resigned after holding office for fifteen days, having originally accepted it for a period of six months.

Thus, the Romans had found a way to give conquered peoples a stake in Rome's success.

The Romans' conquest of Italy can hardly be said to be the result of a direct policy of expansion. Much of it was opportunistic. The Romans did not hesitate to act once they felt their security threatened. And surrounded by potential enemies, Rome in a sense never felt secure. Yet once embarked on a course of expansion, the Romans pursued consistent policies that help to explain their success. The Romans were superb diplomats who excelled at making the correct diplomatic decisions. While firm and even cruel when necessary—rebellions were crushed without mercy—they were also shrewd in extending their citizenship and allowing autonomy in domestic affairs. In addition, the Romans were not only good soldiers, but persistent ones. The loss of an army or a fleet did not cause them to quit, but spurred them on to build new armies and new fleets. Finally, the Romans had a practical sense of strategy. As they conquered, they settled Romans and Latins in new communities outside Latium. By 264 B.C.E., the Romans had established colonies—fortified towns—at all strategic locations. By building roads to these settlements and connecting them, the Romans assured themselves of an impressive military and communications network that enabled them to rule effectively and efficiently. By insisting upon military service from its allies in the Roman confederation, Rome essentially mobilized the entire military might of all Italy for its wars.

The Roman State

In law and politics, as in conquest, the Romans took a practical approach. They did not concern themselves with the construction of an ideal government, but instead fashioned political institutions in response to problems as they arose.

The chief executive officers of the Roman Republic were the consuls and praetors. Two consuls, chosen annually, administered the government and led the Roman army into battle. They possessed *imperium,* or "the right to command." In 366 B.C.E., a new office, that of the praetor, was created. The praetor also possessed *imperium* and could govern Rome when the consuls were away from the city and could also lead armies. The praetor's primary function, however, was the execution of justice. He was in

MAP 5.1 Ancient Italy and the City of Rome

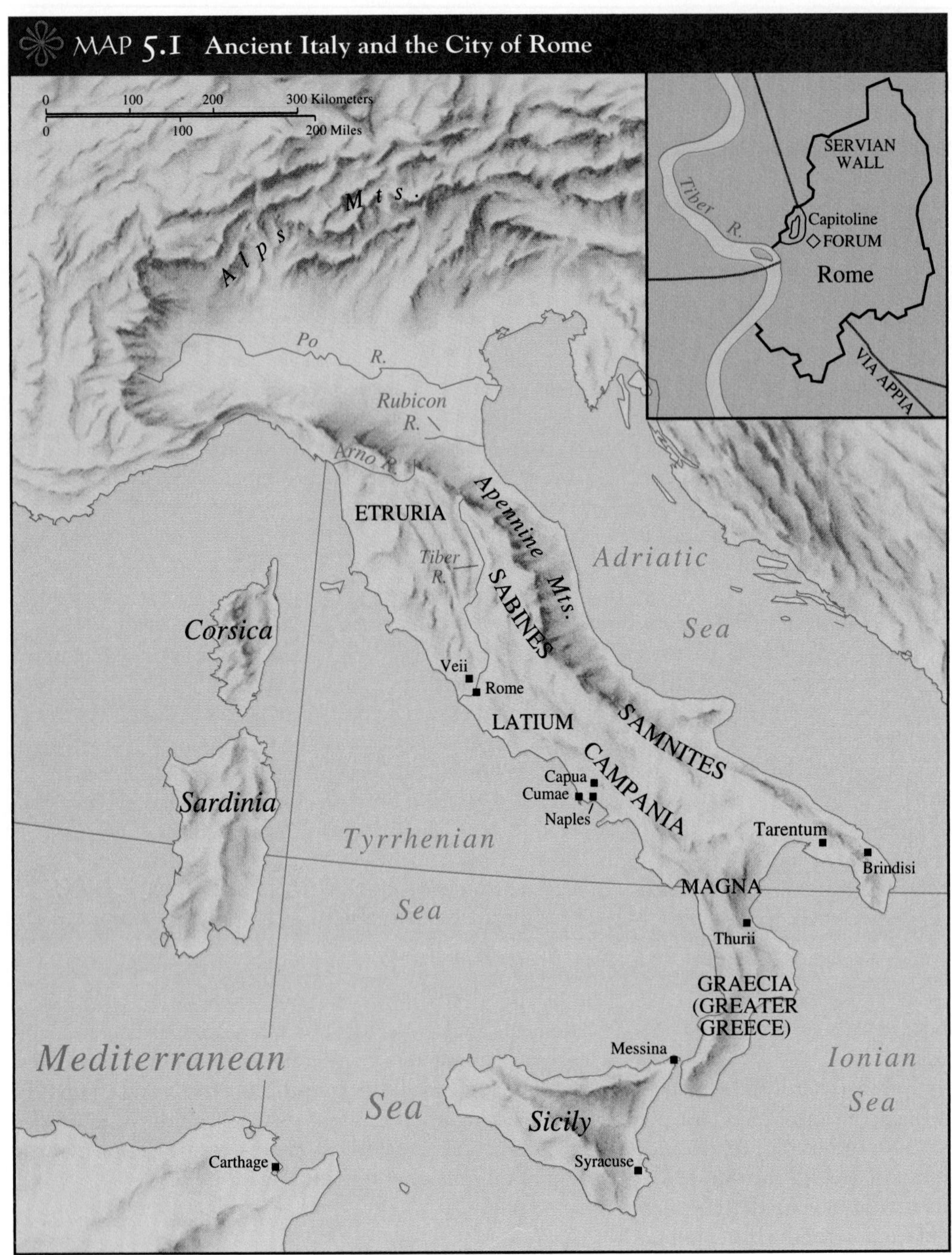

charge of the civil law as it applied to Roman citizens. In 242 B.C.E., reflecting Rome's growth, another praetor was added to judge cases in which one or both people were noncitizens. The Roman state also had a number of administrative officials who handled specialized duties, such as the administration of financial affairs and supervision of the public games of Rome.

The Roman senate came to hold an especially important position in the Roman Republic. The senate or council of elders was a select group of about 300 men who served for life. The senate could only advise the magistrates, but this advice of the senate was not taken lightly, and by the third century B.C.E. had virtually the force of law. No doubt the prestige of the senate's members furthered this development.

The Roman Republic possessed a number of popular assemblies. By far the most important was the centuriate assembly, essentially the Roman army functioning in its political role. Organized by classes based on wealth, it was structured in such a way that the wealthiest citizens always had a majority. The centuriate assembly elected the chief magistrates and passed laws. Another assembly, the council of the plebs, came into being in 471 B.C.E. as a result of the struggle of the orders.

The Roman Republic, then, witnessed the interplay of three major elements. Two consuls and later other elected officials served as magistrates and ran the state. An assembly of adult males (the centuriate assembly), controlled by the wealthiest citizens, elected these officials, while the Senate, a small group of large landowners, advised them. The Roman state, then was an aristocratic republic controlled by a relatively small group of privileged people.

THE STRUGGLE OF THE ORDERS: SOCIAL DIVISIONS IN THE ROMAN REPUBLIC

The most noticeable element in the social organization of early Rome was the division between two groups—the patricians and the plebeians. The patrician class in Rome consisted of those families who were descended from the original senators appointed during the period of the kings. Their initial emergence was probably due to their wealth as great landowners. Thus, patricians constituted an aristocratic governing class. Only they could be consuls, other magistrates, and senators. Through their patronage of large numbers of dependent clients, they controlled the centuriate assembly and many other facets of Roman life. The plebeians constituted the considerably larger group of "independent, unprivileged, poorer and vulnerable men" as well as nonpatrician large landowners, less wealthy landholders, artisans, merchants, and small farmers. Although they were citizens, they did not possess the same rights as the patricians. Both patricians and plebeians could vote, but only the patricians could be elected to governmental offices. Both had the right to make legal contracts and marriages, but intermarriage between patricians and plebeians was forbidden. At the beginning of the fifth century B.C.E., the plebeians began a struggle to seek both political and social equality with the patricians.

The struggle between the patricians and plebeians dragged on for hundreds of years but led to success for the plebeians. A popular assembly for plebeians only, called the council of the plebs, was created in 471 B.C.E., while new officials, known as tribunes of the plebs, were given the power to protect plebeians. A new law allowed marriages between patricians and plebeians, and in the fourth century B.C.E., plebeians were permitted to become consuls. Finally, in 287 B.C.E., the council of the plebs received the right to pass laws for all Romans.

The struggle between the orders, then, had a significant impact on the development of the Roman constitution. Plebeians could now hold the highest offices of state, they could intermarry with the patricians, and they could pass laws binding on the entire Roman community. Theoretically, by 287 B.C.E., all Roman citizens were equal under the law, and all could strive for political office. But in reality, as a result of the right of intermarriage, a select number of patrician and plebeian families formed a new senatorial aristocracy that came to dominate the political offices. The Roman Republic had not become a democracy.

THE ROMAN CONQUEST OF THE MEDITERRANEAN (264–133 B.C.E.)

After their conquest of the Italian peninsula, the Romans found themselves face-to-face with a formidable Mediterranean power—Carthage. Founded around 800 B.C.E. by Phoenicians from Tyre, Carthage in North Africa was located in a favorable position for commanding Mediterranean trade routes and had become an important commercial center. It had become politically and militarily strong as well. By the third century B.C.E., the Carthaginian empire included the coast of northern Africa, southern Spain, Sardinia, Corsica, and western Sicily. With its monopoly of western Mediterranean trade, Carthage

A ROMAN LEGIONARY. The Roman legionaries, with their legendary courage and tenacity, made possible the creation of the Roman Empire. This picture shows a bronze figure of a Roman legionary in full dress at the time of the height of the empire in the second century C.E. The soldier's cuirass is constructed of overlapping metal bands.

was the largest and richest state in the area. The presence of Carthaginians in Sicily made the Romans apprehensive about Carthaginian encroachment on the Italian coast. In 264 B.C.E., mutual suspicions drove the two powers into a lengthy struggle for control of the western Mediterranean.

The Punic Wars

The First Punic War (the Latin word for Phoenician was *punicus*) began in 264 B.C.E. when the Romans decided to intervene in a struggle between two Sicilian cities and sent an army to Sicily. The Carthaginians, who considered Sicily within their own sphere of influence, considered this just cause for war. In going to war, both sides determined on the conquest of Sicily. The Romans—a land power—realized that they could not win the war without a navy and promptly developed a substantial naval fleet. After a long struggle in which both sides lost battles in North Africa and Sicily, a Roman fleet defeated the Carthaginian navy off Sicily, and the war quickly came to an end. In 241 B.C.E., Carthage gave up all rights to Sicily and had to pay an indemnity to Rome. Sicily became the first Roman province.

Carthage vowed revenge and added new lands in Spain to compensate for the loss of Sicily. When the Romans encouraged one of Carthage's Spanish allies to revolt against Carthage, Hannibal, the greatest of the Carthaginian generals, struck back, beginning the Second Punic War (218–201 B.C.E.).

This time the Carthaginian strategy aimed at bringing the war home to the Romans and defeating them in their own backyard. Hannibal crossed the Alps with an army of 30,000–40,000 men and 6,000 horses and elephants and inflicted a series of defeats on the Romans. At Cannae in 216 B.C.E., the Romans lost an army of almost 40,000 men. Rome seemed on the brink of disaster but refused to give up, raised yet another army, and gradually recovered. Although Hannibal remained free to roam in Italy, he had neither the men nor the equipment to lay siege to the major cities, including Rome itself. The Romans began to reconquer some of the Italian cities that had rebelled against Roman rule after Hannibal's successes. More important, the Romans pursued a strategy aimed at undermining the Carthaginian empire in Spain. By 206 B.C.E., the Romans had pushed the Carthaginians out of Spain.

The Romans then took the war directly to Carthage, forcing the Carthaginians to recall Hannibal from Italy. At the Battle of Zama in 202 B.C.E., the Romans decisively defeated Hannibal's forces, and the war was over. By the

MAP 5.2 Roman Conquests in the Mediterranean

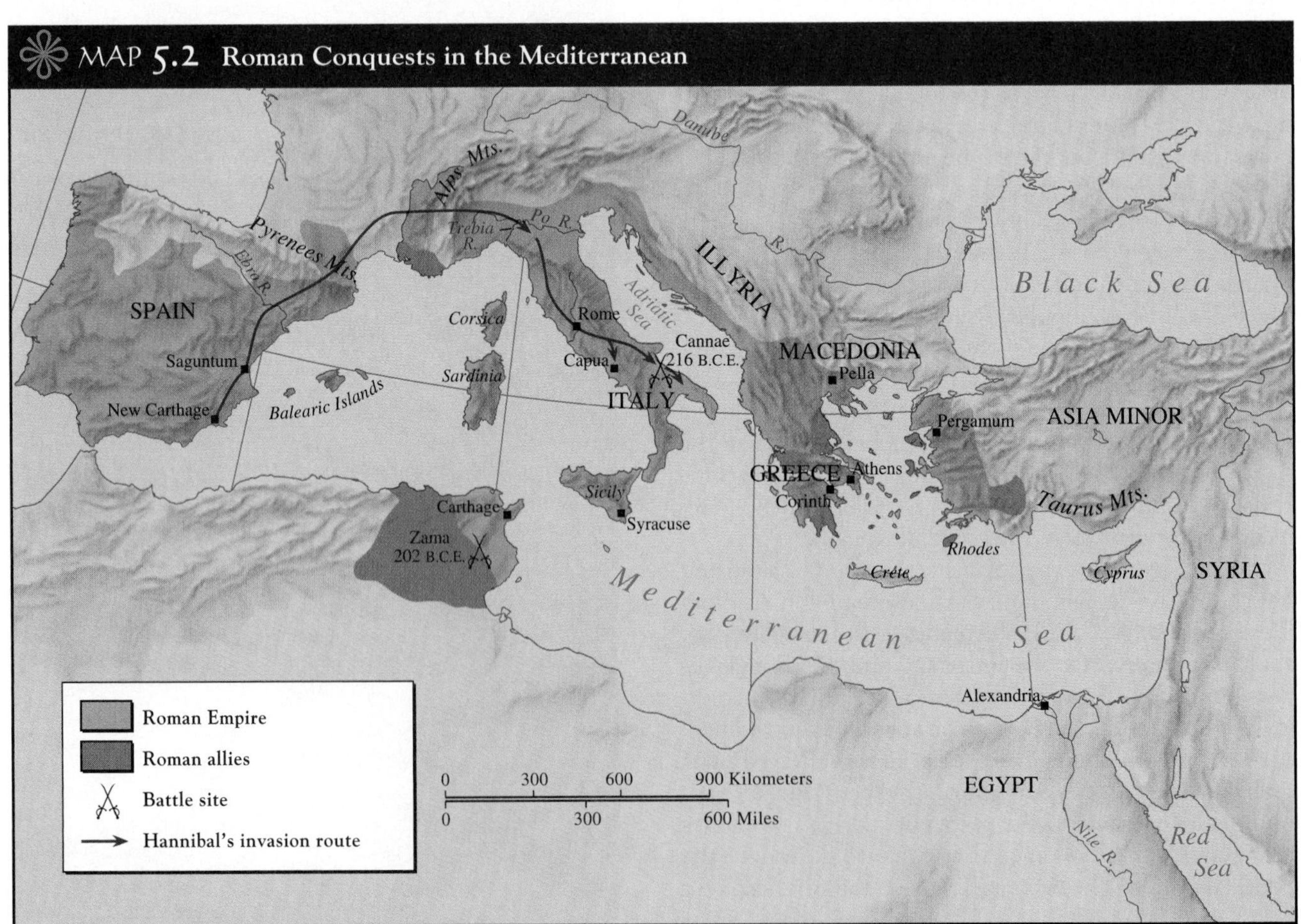

THE DESTRUCTION OF CARTHAGE

The Romans used a technical breach of Carthage's peace treaty with Rome to undertake a third and final war with Carthage (149–146 B.C.E.). Although Carthage posed no real threat to Rome's security, the Romans still remembered the traumatic experiences of the Second Punic War, when Hannibal had ravaged much of their homeland. The hard-liners gained the upper hand in the senate and called for the complete destruction of Carthage. The city was razed, the survivors sold into slavery, and the land turned into a province. In this passage, the historian Appian of Alexandria describes the final destruction of Carthage by the Romans under the command of Scipio Aemilianus.

APPIAN, ROMAN *HISTORY*

Then came new scenes of horror. The fire spread and carried everything down, and the soldiers did not wait to destroy the buildings little by little, but pulled them all down together. So the crashing grew louder, and many fell with the stones into the midst dead. Others were seen still living, especially old men, women, and young children who had hidden in the inmost nooks of the houses, some of them wounded, some more or less burned, and uttering horrible cries. Still others, thrust out and falling from such a height with the stones, timbers, and fire, were torn asunder into all kinds of horrible shapes, crushed and mangled. Nor was this the end of their miseries, for the street cleaners, who were removing the rubbish with axes, mattocks, and boat hooks, and making the roads passable, tossed with these instruments the dead and the living together into holes in the ground, sweeping them along like sticks and stones or turning them over with their iron tools, and man was used for filling up a ditch. Some were thrown in head foremost, while their legs, sticking out of the ground, writhed a long time. Others fell with their feet downward and their heads above ground. Horses ran over them, crushing their faces and skulls, not purposely on the part of the riders, but in their headlong haste. Nor did the street cleaners either do these things on purpose; but the press of war, the glory of approaching victory, the rush of the soldiery, the confused noise of heralds and trumpeters all round, the tribunes and centurions changing guard and marching the cohorts hither and thither—all together made everybody frantic and heedless of the spectacle before their eyes.

Six days and nights were consumed in this kind of turmoil, the soldiers being changed so that they might not be worn out with toil, slaughter, want of sleep, and these horrid sights. . . .

Scipio, beholding this city, which had flourished 700 years from its foundation and had ruled over so many lands, islands, and seas, as rich in arms and fleets, elephants, and money as the mightiest empires, but far surpassing them in hardihood and high spirit . . . now come to its end in total destruction—Scipio, beholding this spectacle, is said to have shed tears and publicly lamented the fortune of the enemy. After meditating by himself a long time and reflecting on the inevitable fall of cities, nations, and empires, as well as of individuals, upon the fate of Troy, that once proud city, upon the fate of the Assyrian, the Median, and afterwards of the great Persian empire, and, most recently of all, of the splendid empire of Macedon, either voluntarily or otherwise the words of the poet [Homer, *Iliad*] escaped his lips:

The day shall come in which our sacred Troy
And Priam, and the people over whom
Spear-bearing Priam rules, shall perish all.

Being asked by Polybius in familiar conversation (for Polybius had been his tutor) what he meant by using these words, Polybius says that he did not hesitate frankly to name his own country, for whose fate he feared when he considered the mutability of human affairs. And Polybius wrote this down just as he heard it.

peace treaty signed in 201 B.C.E., Carthage lost Spain, agreed to pay an indemnity, and promised not to go to war without Rome's permission. Spain was made into another Roman province. Rome had become the dominant power in the western Mediterranean.

Fifty years later, the Romans fought their third and final struggle with Carthage. The Carthaginians had technically broken their peace treaty with Rome by going to war against one of Rome's North African allies who had been encroaching on Carthage's home territory. The Romans used this opportunity to carry out the complete destruction of Carthage in 146 B.C.E., a policy advocated by a number of Romans, especially the conservative politician Cato, who ended every speech he made to the senate with the words, "And I think Carthage must be destroyed" (see the box above). The territory of Carthage became a Roman province called Africa.

The Eastern Mediterranean

During the Punic Wars, Rome had become acutely aware of the Hellenistic states of the eastern Mediterranean when the king of Macedonia made an alliance with Hannibal after the Roman defeat at Cannae. But Rome was preoccupied with the Carthaginians, and it was not until after the defeat of Carthage that Rome became involved in the world of Hellenistic politics as an advocate of the freedom of the Greek states. This support of the Greeks brought the Romans into conflict with both Macedonia and the kingdom of the Seleucids. Roman military

CHRONOLOGY

THE ROMAN CONQUEST OF ITALY AND THE MEDITERRANEAN

Rome crushes Latin revolt	340 B.C.E.
Creation of the Roman confederation	338 B.C.E.
Samnite Wars	343–290 B.C.E.
The First Punic War	264–241 B.C.E.
The Second Punic War	218–201 B.C.E.
Battle of Cannae	216 B.C.E.
Rome completes seizure of Spain	206 B.C.E.
Battle of Zama	202 B.C.E.
The Third Punic War	149–146 B.C.E.
Macedonia made a Roman province	148 B.C.E.
Destruction of Carthage	146 B.C.E.
Kingdom of Pergamum deeded to Rome	133 B.C.E.

victories and diplomatic negotiations rearranged the territorial boundaries of the Hellenistic kingdoms and brought the Greek states their freedom in 196 B.C.E. For fifty years, Rome tried to be a power broker in the affairs of the Greeks without assuming direct control of their lands. When these efforts failed, the Romans changed their policy.

In 148 B.C.E., Macedonia was made a Roman province, and when some of the Greek states rose in revolt against Rome's restrictive policies, Rome acted decisively. The city of Corinth, leader of the revolt, was destroyed in 146 B.C.E. to teach the Greeks a lesson, and Greece was placed under the control of the Roman governor of Macedonia. Thirteen years later, in 133 B.C.E., the king of Pergamum deeded his kingdom to Rome, giving Rome its first province in Asia. Rome was now master of the Mediterranean Sea.

The Nature of Roman Imperialism

Rome's empire was built in three stages: the conquest of Italy, the conflict with Carthage and expansion into the western Mediterranean, and the involvement with and domination of the Hellenistic kingdoms in the eastern Mediterranean. The Romans did not possess a master plan for the creation of an empire. Much of their expansion was opportunistic; once involved in a situation that threatened their security, the Romans did not hesitate to act. And the more they expanded, the more threats to their security appeared on the horizon, involving them in yet more conflicts. Indeed, the Romans liked to portray themselves as declaring war only for defensive reasons or to protect allies. That is only part of the story, however. It is likely, as some historians have recently suggested, that at some point a group of Roman aristocratic leaders emerged who favored expansion both for the glory it offered and for the economic benefits it provided. Certainly, by the second century B.C.E., aristocratic senators perceived new opportunities for lucrative foreign commands, enormous spoils of war, and an abundant supply of slave labor for their growing landed estates. By that same time, the destruction of Corinth and Carthage indicate Roman imperialism had become more arrogant and brutal as well. Rome's foreign success also had enormous repercussions for the internal development of the Roman Republic.

THE DECLINE AND FALL OF THE ROMAN REPUBLIC (133–31 B.C.E.)

By the mid-second century B.C.E., Roman domination of the Mediterranean Sea was well established. Yet the process of creating an empire had weakened and threatened the internal stability of Rome. This led to a series of crises that plagued Rome for the next hundred years.

Growing Inequality and Unrest

By the second century B.C.E., the senate had become the effective governing body of the Roman state. It comprised some 300 men, drawn primarily from the landed aristocracy; they remained senators for life and held the chief magistracies of the Republic. During the wars of the third and second centuries, the senate came to exercise enormous power. It directed the wars and took control of both foreign and domestic policy, including financial affairs.

Moreover, the magistracies and senate were increasingly controlled by a relatively select circle of wealthy and powerful families—both patrician and plebeian—called the *nobiles* ("nobles"). In the hundred years from 233 to 133 B.C.E., 80 percent of the consuls came from twenty-six families; moreover, 50 percent came from only ten families. Hence, the *nobiles* constituted a governing oligarchy that managed, through its landed wealth, system of patronage, and intimidation, to maintain its hold over the magistracies and senate and thus guide the destiny of Rome while running the state in its own interests.

Of course, these aristocrats formed only a tiny minority of the Roman people. The backbone of the Roman state and army had traditionally been the small farmers. But over a period of time many small farmers had found themselves unable to compete with large, wealthy landowners and had lost their lands. By taking over state-owned land and buying out small peasant owners, these landed aristocrats had developed large estates called *latifundia* that used slave labor. Thus, the rise of *latifundia* contributed to a decline in the number of small farmers. Since the latter group traditionally provided the foundation of the Roman army, the number of men available for military service declined. Moreover, many of these small farmers drifted to the cities, especially Rome, forming a large class of landless poor.

Some aristocrats tried to remedy this growing economic and social crisis. Two brothers, Tiberius and Gaius Gracchus, came to believe that the underlying cause of Rome's problems was the decline of the small farmer. To help the landless poor, they bypassed the senate by having the council of the plebs pass land-reform bills that called for the government to reclaim public land held by large landowners and distribute it to landless Romans. Many senators, themselves large landowners whose estates included large areas of public land, were furious. A group of senators took the law into their own hands and killed Tiberius in 133 B.C.E. Twelve years later, his brother Gaius suffered the same fate. The attempts of the Gracchus brothers to bring reforms had opened the door to more instability and further violence. Changes in the Roman army soon brought even worse problems.

A New Role for the Roman Army

In the closing years of the second century B.C.E., a Roman general named Marius began to recruit his armies in a new way. The Roman army had traditionally been a conscript army of small farmers who were landholders. Marius recruited volunteers from both the urban and rural poor who possessed no property. These volunteers swore an oath of loyalty to the general, not the senate, thus inaugurating a professional-type army that might no longer be subject to the state. Moreover, to recruit these men, a general would promise them land, forcing generals to play politics in order to get legislation passed that would provide the land for their veterans. Marius left a powerful legacy. He had created a new system of military recruitment that placed much power in the hands of the individual generals.

Lucius Cornelius Sulla was the next general to take advantage of the new military system. The senate had given him command of a war in Asia Minor, but when the council of the plebs tried to transfer command of this war to Marius, a civil war broke out. Sulla won and seized Rome itself in 82 B.C.E., conducting a reign of terror to wipe out all opposition. Then Sulla restored power to the hands of the senate and eliminated most of the powers of the popular assemblies. Sulla hoped that he had created a firm foundation for the traditional Republic governed by a powerful senate, but his real legacy was quite different from what he had intended. His example of using an army to seize power would prove most attractive to ambitious men.

The Collapse of the Republic

For the next fifty years, Roman history would be characterized by two important features: the jostling for power by a number of powerful individuals and the civil wars generated by their conflicts. Three powerful individuals came to hold enormous military and political power—Crassus, Pompey, and Julius Caesar. Crassus, who was known as the richest man in Rome, had successfully put down a major slave rebellion. Pompey had returned from a successful military command in Spain in 71 B.C.E. and been hailed as a military hero. Julius Caesar also had a military command in Spain. In 60 B.C.E., Caesar joined with Crassus and Pompey to form a coalition that historians called the First Triumvirate.

The combined wealth and power of these three men was enormous, enabling them to dominate the political scene and achieve their basic aims: Pompey received lands for his veterans and a command in Spain; Crassus was given a command in Syria; and Caesar was granted a special military command in Gaul (modern France). When Crassus was killed in battle in 53 B.C.E., his death left two powerful men with armies in direct competition. During his time in Gaul, Caesar had conquered all of Gaul and gained fame, wealth, and military experience as well as an army of seasoned veterans who were loyal to him. When leading senators fastened on Pompey as the least harmful to their cause and voted for Caesar to lay down his command and return as a private citizen to Rome, Caesar refused. He chose to keep his army and moved into Italy by illegally crossing the Rubicon, the river that formed the southern boundary of his province. ("Crossing the Rubicon" is a phrase used today to mean doing something after which there is no turning back.) Caesar marched on Rome, thus guaranteeing a civil war between his forces and those of Pompey and his allies. The defeat of Pompey's forces left Caesar in complete control of the Roman government.

Caesar was officially made dictator in 47 B.C.E., and in 44 B.C.E. he was made dictator for life. Realizing the need for reforms, he gave land to the poor and increased the size of the senate to 900 members. By filling it with many of his supporters and increasing the membership, he effectively weakened the power of the senate. He granted citizenship to a number of people in the provinces who had helped him. He also reformed the calendar by introducing the Egyptian solar year of 365 days (with later changes in 1582, it became the basis of our own calendar). Caesar planned much more in the way of building projects and military adventures in the east, but in 44 B.C.E., a group of leading senators assassinated him (see the box on p. 139).

Within a few years after Caesar's death, two men had divided the Roman world between them—Octavian, Caesar's heir and grandnephew, taking the west and Antony, Caesar's ally and assistant, the east. But the empire of the Romans, large as it was, was still too small for two

CHRONOLOGY

THE DECLINE AND FALL OF THE REPUBLIC

Reforms of Tiberius Gracchus	133 B.C.E.
Reforms of Gaius Gracchus	123–121 B.C.E.
Marius: Consecutive consulships	104–100 B.C.E.
Sulla as dictator	82–79 B.C.E.
First Triumvirate (Caesar, Pompey, Crassus)	60 B.C.E.
Caesar as dictator	47–44 B.C.E.
Octavian defeats Antony at Actium	31 B.C.E.

CAESAR. Conqueror of Gaul and member of the First Triumvirate, Julius Caesar is perhaps the best-known figure of the late Republic. Caesar became dictator of Rome in 47 B.C.E. and, after his victories in the civil war, was made dictator for life. Some members of the senate who resented his power assassinated him in 44 B.C.E. Pictured is a marble copy of the bust of Caesar.

masters, and Octavian and Antony eventually came into conflict. Antony allied himself with the Egyptian queen Cleopatra VII, with whom, like Caesar before him, he fell deeply in love. Octavian began a propaganda campaign, accusing Antony of catering to Cleopatra and giving away Roman territory to this "whore of the east." Finally, at the Battle of Actium in Greece in 31 B.C.E., Octavian's forces smashed the army and navy of Antony and Cleopatra. Both fled to Egypt, where, according to the account of the Roman historian Florus, they committed suicide a year later:

> Antony was the first to commit suicide, by the sword. Cleopatra threw herself at Octavian's feet, and tried her best to attract his gaze: in vain, for his self-control was impervious to her beauty. It was not her life she was after, for that had already been granted, but a portion of her kingdom. When she realized this was hopeless and that she had been earmarked to feature in Octavian's triumph in Rome, she took advantage of her guard's carelessness to get herself into the mausoleum, as the royal tomb is called. Once there, she put on the royal robes which she was accustomed to wear, and lay down in a richly perfumed coffin beside her Antony. Then she applied poisonous snakes to her veins and slipped into death as though into a sleep.[1]

Octavian, at the age of thirty-two, stood supreme over the Roman world. The civil wars were ended. And so was the Republic.

THE AGE OF AUGUSTUS (31 B.C.E.–14 C.E.)

In 27 B.C.E., Octavian proclaimed the "restoration of the Republic." He understood that only traditional republican forms would satisfy the senatorial aristocracy. At the same time, Octavian was aware that the Republic could not be fully restored. Although he gave some power to the senate, in fact, Octavian became the first Roman emperor. In 27 B.C.E., the senate awarded him the title of Augustus—"the revered one"—a fitting title in view of his power, previously reserved for gods. Augustus proved to be highly popular. No doubt, people were glad the civil wars had ended. At the same time, his continuing control of the army was the chief source of Augustus's power. The senate gave Augustus the title of *imperator,* or commander-in-chief. *Imperator* is Latin for our word *emperor.*

Augustus maintained a standing army of twenty-eight legions or about 150,000 men (a legion was a military unit of about 5,000 troops). Only Roman citizens could be legionaries, while subject peoples could serve as auxiliary forces, which numbered around 130,000 under Augustus. Augustus was also responsible for setting up a praetorian guard of roughly 9,000 men who had the important task of guarding the person of the emperor. Eventually, the praetorian guard would play a weighty role in making and deposing emperors.

THE ASSASSINATION OF JULIUS CAESAR

When it quickly became apparent that Julius Caesar had no intention of restoring the Republic as they conceived it, about sixty senators, many of them his friends or pardoned enemies, formed a conspiracy to assassinate the dictator. It was led by Gaius Cassius and Marcus Brutus, who naively imagined that this act would restore the traditional Republic. The conspirators set the Ides of March (March 15), 44 B.C.E. *as the date for the assassination. Caesar was in the midst of preparations for a campaign in the eastern part of the empire. Although informed that there was a plot against his life, he chose to disregard the warning. This account of Caesar's death is taken from his biography by the Greek writer Plutarch.*

PLUTARCH, *LIFE OF CAESAR*

Fate, however, is to all appearance more unavoidable than unexpected. For many strange prodigies and apparitions are said to have been observed shortly before this event. . . . One finds it also related by many that a soothsayer bade him [Caesar] prepare for some great danger on the Ides of March. When this day was come, Caesar, as he went to the senate, met this soothsayer, and said to him by way of raillery, "The Ides of March are come," who answered him calmly, "Yes, they are come, but they are not past. . . ."

All these things might happen by chance. But the place which was destined for the scene of this murder, in which the senate met that day, was the same in which Pompey's statue stood, and was one of the edifices which Pompey had raised and dedicated with his theater to the use of the public, plainly showing that there was something of a supernatural influence which guided the action and ordered it to that particular place. Cassius, just before the act, is said to have looked toward Pompey's statue, and silently implored his assistance. . . . When Caesar entered, the senate stood up to show their respect to him, and of Brutus's confederates, some came about his chair and stood behind it, others met him, pretending to add their petitions to those of Tillius Cimber, in behalf of his brother, who was in exile; and they followed him with their joint applications till he came to his seat. When he was sat down, he refused to comply with their requests, and upon their urging him further began to reproach them severely for their importunities, when Tillius, laying hold of his robe with both his hands, pulled it down from his neck, which was the signal for the assault. Casca gave him the first cut in the neck, which was not mortal nor dangerous, as coming from one who at the beginning of such a bold action was probably very much disturbed; Caesar immediately turned about, and laid his hand upon the dagger and kept hold of it. And both of them at the same time cried out, he that received the blow, in Latin, "Vile Casca, what does this mean?" and he that gave it, in Greek to his brother, "Brother, help!" Upon this first onset, those who were not privy to the design were astonished, and their horror and amazement at what they saw were so great that they dared not fly nor assist Caesar, nor so much as speak a word. But those who came prepared for the business enclosed him on every side, with their naked daggers in their hands. Which way soever he turned he met with blows, and saw their swords leveled at his face and eyes, and was encompassed like a wild beast in the toils on every side. For it had been agreed they should each of them make a thrust at him, and flesh themselves with his blood: for which reason Brutus also gave him one stab in the groin. Some say that he fought and resisted all the rest, shifting his body to avoid the blows, and calling out for help, but that when he saw Brutus's sword drawn, he covered his face with his robe and submitted, letting himself fall, whether it were by chance or that he was pushed in that direction by his murderers, at the foot of the pedestal on which Pompey's statue stood, and which was thus wetted with his blood. So that Pompey himself seemed to have presided, as it were, over the revenge done upon his adversary, who lay here at his feet, and breathed out his soul through his multitude of wounds, for they say he received three-and-twenty. And the conspirators themselves were many of them wounded by each other, whilst they all leveled their blows at the same person.

While claiming to have restored the Republic, Augustus inaugurated a new system for governing the provinces. Under the Republic, the senate had appointed the governors of the provinces. Now, certain provinces were given to the emperor, who assigned deputies known as legates to govern them. The senate continued to name the governors of the remaining provinces, but the authority of Augustus enabled him to overrule the senatorial governors and establish a uniform imperial policy.

Augustus also stabilized the frontiers of the Roman Empire. He conquered the central and maritime Alps and then expanded Roman control of the Balkan peninsula up to the Danube River. His attempt to conquer Germany failed when three Roman legions were massacred in 9 C.E. by a coalition of German tribes. His defeats in Germany taught Augustus that Rome's power was not unlimited and also devastated him; for months he would beat his head on a door, shouting "Varus [the defeated Roman general in Germany], give me back my legions!"

Augustan Society

Roman society in the Early Empire was characterized by a system of social stratification, inherited from the Republic, in which Roman citizens were divided into three basic classes: the senatorial, equestrian, and lower classes.

AUGUSTUS. Octavian, Caesar's adopted son, emerged victorious from the civil conflict that rocked the Republic after Caesar's assassination. Augustus operated through a number of legal formalities to ensure that control of the Roman state rested firmly in his hands. This marble statue from Prima Porta depicts the *princeps* Augustus.

Although each class had its own functions and opportunities, the system was not completely rigid. There were possibilities for mobility from one group to another.

Augustus had accepted the senatorial order as a ruling class for the empire. Senators filled the chief magistracies of the Roman government, held the most important military posts, and governed the provinces. One needed to possess property worth 1,000,000 sesterces (an unskilled laborer in Rome received 3 sesterces a day; a Roman legionary, 900 sesterces a year in pay) to belong to the senatorial order. The equestrian order was expanded under Augustus and given a share of power in the new imperial state. The equestrian order was open to all Roman citizens of good standing who possessed property valued at 400,000 sesterces. They, too, could now hold military and governmental offices, but the positions open to them were less important than those of the senatorial order.

Those citizens not of the senatorial or equestrian orders belonged to the lower classes, who obviously constituted the overwhelming majority of the free citizens. The diminution of the power of the Roman assemblies ended whatever political power they may have possessed earlier in the Republic. Many of these people were provided with free grain and public spectacles to keep them from creating disturbances. Nevertheless, by gaining wealth and serving as lower officers in the Roman legions, it was sometimes possible for them to advance to the equestrian order.

The Augustan Age was a lengthy one. Augustus died in 14 C.E. after dominating the Roman world for forty-five years. He had created a new order while placating those who yearned for the old by restoring and maintaining traditional values, a fitting combination for a leader whose favorite maxim was "make haste slowly." By the time of his death, his new order was so well established that few agitated for an alternative. Indeed, as the Roman historian Tacitus pointed out, "Actium had been won before the younger men were born. Even most of the older generation had come into a world of civil wars. Practically no one had ever seen truly Republican government. . . . Political equality was a thing of the past; all eyes watched for imperial commands."[2] The Republic was now only a memory and, given its last century of warfare, an unpleasant one at that. The new order was here to stay.

THE EARLY EMPIRE (14–180)

There was no serious opposition to Augustus's choice of his stepson Tiberius as his successor. By his actions, Augustus established the Julio-Claudian dynasty; the next four successors of Augustus were related either to his own family or that of his wife, Livia.

Several major tendencies emerged during the reigns of the Julio-Claudians (14–68 C.E.). In general, more and more of the responsibilities that Augustus had given to the senate tended to be taken over by the emperors, who also instituted an imperial bureaucracy, staffed by talented freedmen, to run the government on a daily basis. As the Julio-Claudian successors of Augustus acted more openly as real rulers rather than as "first citizens of the state," the opportunity for arbitrary and corrupt acts also increased. Nero (54–68) freely eliminated people he wanted out of the way, including his own mother, whom he had murdered. Without troops, the senators proved unable to oppose these excesses. However, Nero's extravagances did provoke a revolt of the Roman legions. Abandoned by his guards, Nero chose to commit suicide by stabbing himself in the throat after uttering his final words, "What an artist the world is losing in me." A new civil war erupted in 69, known as the year of the four emperors. The significance of the year 69 was summed up precisely by Tacitus when he stated that "a well-hidden secret of the principate had been revealed: it was possible, it seemed, for an emperor to be chosen outside Rome."[3]

The Five "Good Emperors" (96–180)

At the beginning of the second century, however, a series of five so-called good emperors created a period of peace and prosperity that lasted for almost a hundred years. These rulers treated the ruling classes with respect, cooperated with the senate, ended arbitrary executions, maintained peace throughout the empire, and supported domestic policies generally beneficial to the empire. Though absolute monarchs, they were known for their tolerance and diplomacy. By adopting capable men as their successors, the first four good emperors reduced the chances of succession problems.

Under the five good emperors, the powers of the emperor continued to be extended at the expense of the senate. Increasingly, imperial officials appointed and directed by the emperor took over the running of the government. The good emperors also extended the scope of imperial administration to include areas previously untouched by the imperial government. Trajan (98–117) implemented the establishment of an alimentary program that provided state funds to assist poor parents in raising and educating their children.

The good emperors were widely praised by their subjects for their extensive building programs. Trajan and Hadrian (117–138) were especially active in constructing public works—aqueducts, bridges, roads, and harbor facilities—throughout the provinces and in Rome. Trajan built a new forum in Rome to provide a setting for his celebrated

MAP 5.3 The Roman Empire from 14 to 117

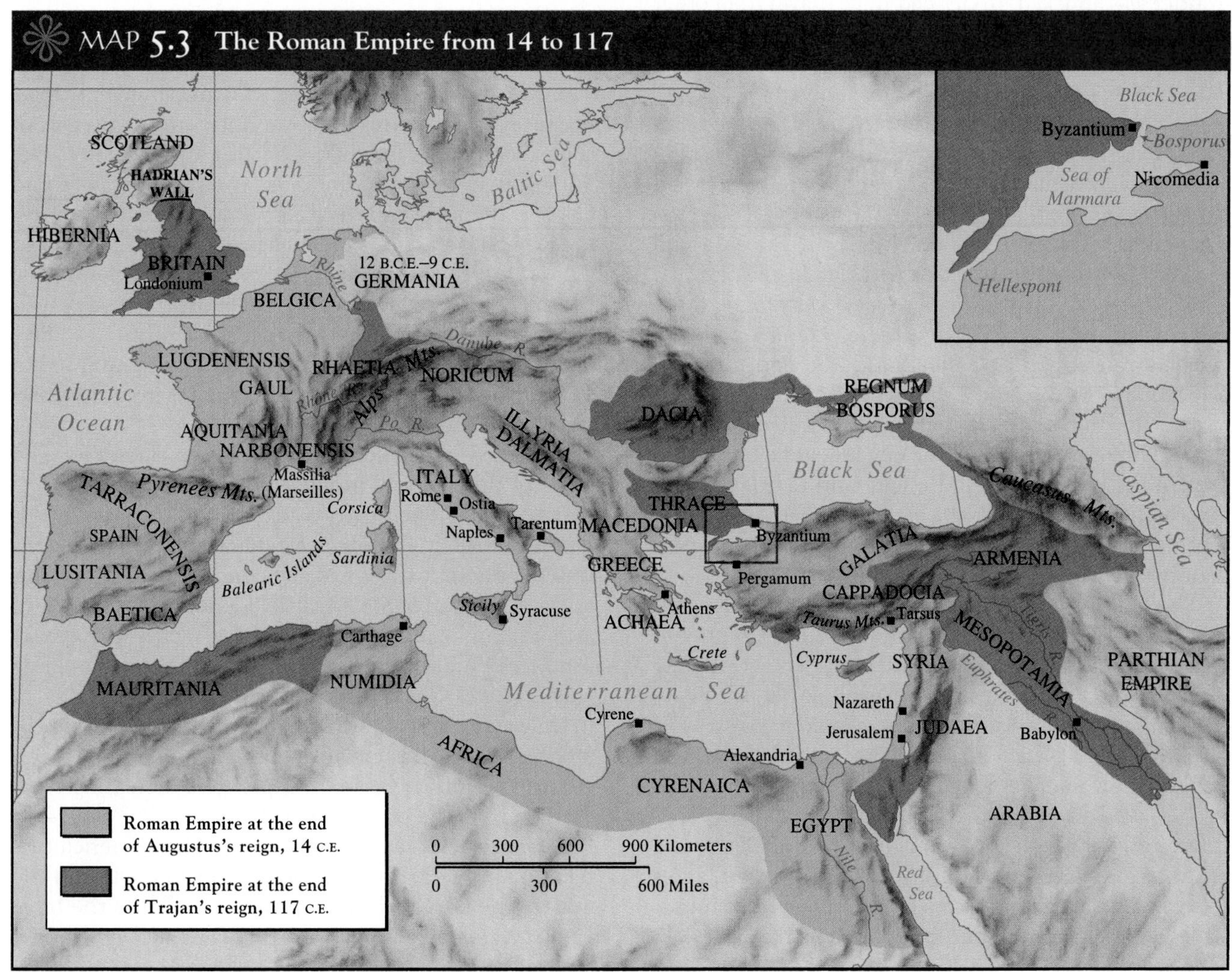

victory column. Hadrian's Pantheon, a temple of "all the gods," is one of the grandest ancient buildings surviving in Rome.

The Roman Empire at Its Height: Frontiers and the Provinces

Although Trajan broke with Augustus's policy of defensive imperialism by extending Roman rule into Dacia (modern Romania), Mesopotamia, and the Sinai peninsula, his conquests represent the high-water mark of Roman expansion. His successors recognized that the empire was overextended and pursued a policy of retrenchment. Hadrian withdrew Roman forces from much of Mesopotamia. Although he retained Dacia and Arabia, he went on the defensive in his frontier policy by reinforcing the fortifications along a line connecting the Rhine and Danube Rivers and building a defensive wall eighty miles long across northern Britain to keep the Scots out of Roman Britain. By the end of the second century, the vulnerability of the empire had become apparent. Frontiers were stabilized, and the Roman forces were established in permanent bases behind the frontiers. But when one frontier was attacked, troops had to be drawn from other frontiers, leaving them vulnerable to attack. The empire lacked a real strategic reserve, and in the next century its weakness would be ever more apparent.

At its height in the second century, the Roman Empire was one of the greatest states the world had seen. It covered about three and a half million square miles and had a population, like that of Han China, that has been estimated at more than 50 million. While the emperors and the imperial administration provided a degree of unity, considerable leeway was given to local customs, and the privileges of Roman citizenship were extended to many people throughout the empire. In 212, the emperor Caracalla completed the process by giving Roman citizenship to every free inhabitant of the empire. Latin was the language of the western part of the empire, while Greek was used in the east. Although Roman culture spread to all parts of the empire, there were limits to romanization since local languages persisted and many of the empire's residents spoke neither Latin nor Greek.

The administration and cultural life of the Roman Empire depended greatly upon cities and towns. A provincial governor's staff was not large, so local city officials were expected to act as Roman agents in carrying out many government functions, especially those related to taxes. Most towns and cities were not large by modern standards. The largest was Rome, but there were also some large cities in the east: Alexandria in Egypt numbered over 300,000 inhabitants, Ephesus in Asia Minor had 200,000, and Antioch in Syria had around 150,000. In the west, cities were usually small, with only a few thousand inhabitants. Cities were important in the spread of Roman culture, law, and the Latin language. They were also uniform in physical appearance, with similar temples, markets, amphitheaters, and other public buildings.

Magistrates and town councillors chosen from the ranks of the wealthy upper classes directed municipal administration. These municipal offices were unsalaried but were nevertheless desired by wealthy citizens because they received prestige and power at the local level as well as Roman citizenship. Roman municipal policy effectively tied the upper classes to Roman rule and ensured that these classes would retain control over the rest of the population.

The process of romanization in the provinces was reflected in significant changes in the governing classes of the empire. In the course of the first century, there was a noticeable decline in the number of senators from Italian families. By the end of the second century, Italian senators made up less than 50 percent of the total. Increasingly, the Roman senate was being recruited from wealthy provincial equestrian families. The provinces also provided many of the legionaries for the Roman army and, beginning with Trajan, supplied many of the emperors.

Prosperity in the Early Empire

The Early Empire was a period of considerable prosperity. Internal peace resulted in unprecedented levels of trade. Merchants from all over the empire came to the chief Italian ports of Puteoli on the Bay of Naples and Ostia at the mouth of the Tiber. Trade extended beyond the Roman boundaries and included even silk goods from China. But the patterns of trade were somewhat unbalanced. The importation of large quantities of grain to feed the populace of Rome and an incredible quantity of luxury items for the wealthy upper classes in the west led to a steady drainage of gold and silver coins from Italy and the west to the eastern part of the empire.

Increased trade helped to stimulate manufacturing. The cities of the east still produced the items made in Hellenistic times. The first two centuries of the empire also witnessed the high point of industrial development in Italy. Some industries became concentrated in certain areas, such as bronze work in Capua and pottery in Arretium in Etruria. Other industries, such as brick making, were pursued in rural areas as by-products of large landed estates. Much industrial production remained small in scale and was done by individual artisans, usually freedmen or slaves. In the course of the first century, Italian centers of industry began to experience increasing competition from the provinces.

Despite the extensive trade and commerce, agriculture remained the chief occupation of most people and the underlying basis of Roman prosperity. While the large landed estates called *latifundia* still dominated agriculture,

THE SHIPPING OF GRAIN. Trade was an important ingredient in the prosperity of the Early Empire. This tomb painting from Ostia, the port of Rome at the mouth of the Tiber, shows workers loading grain onto the *Isis Giminiana*, a small merchant ship, for shipment upriver to Rome. The captain of the ship stands by the rudder. Next to him is Abascantus, the ship's owner.

especially in southern and central Italy, small peasant farms persisted, particularly in Etruria and the Po valley. Although large estates concentrating on sheep and cattle raising used slaves, the lands of some *latifundia* were worked by free tenant farmers who paid rent in labor, produce, or sometimes cash.

In considering the prosperity of the Roman world, it is important to remember the enormous gulf between rich and poor. The development of towns and cities, so important to the creation of any civilization, is based in large degree upon the agricultural surpluses of the countryside. In ancient times, the margin of surplus produced by each farmer was relatively small. Therefore, the upper classes and urban populations had to be supported by the labor of a large number of agricultural producers who never found it easy to produce much more than they needed for themselves. In lean years, when there were no surpluses, the townspeople often took what they wanted, leaving little for the peasants.

Culture and Society in the Roman World

One of the most noticeable characteristics of Roman culture and society is the impact of the Greeks. Greek ambassadors, merchants, and artists traveled to Rome and spread Greek thought and practices. After their conquest of the Hellenistic kingdoms, Roman military commanders shipped Greek manuscripts and artworks back to Rome. Multitudes of educated Greek slaves labored in Roman households. Rich Romans hired Greek tutors and sent their sons to Athens to study. As the Roman poet Horace said, "captive Greece took captive her rude conqueror." Greek thought captivated Roman minds, and the Romans became willing transmitters of Greek culture—not, however, without some resistance from Romans who had nothing but contempt for Greek politics and feared that Greek notions would put an end to the old Roman values. Even those who favored Greek culture blamed the Greeks for Rome's new vices, including luxury and homosexual practices.

Roman Literature

The Latin literature that first emerged in the third century B.C.E. was strongly influenced by Greek models, and it was not until the last century of the Republic that the Romans began to produce a new poetry in which Latin poets were able to use various Greek forms to express their own feelings about people, social and political life, and love. The finest example of this can be seen in the work of Catullus (c. 87–54 B.C.E.), the "best lyric poet" Rome produced and one of the greatest in world literature.

Catullus became a master at adapting and refining Greek forms of poetry to express his emotions. He wrote a variety of poems on, among other things, political figures, social customs, the use of language, the death of his brother, and the travails of love. Catullus became infatuated with Clodia, the promiscuous sister of a tribune and wife of a provincial governor, and addressed a number of poems to her (he called her Lesbia), describing his passionate love and hatred for her (Clodia had many other lovers besides Catullus):

You used to say that you wished to know only Catullus,
Lesbia, and wouldn't take even Jove before me!
I didn't regard you just as my mistress then: I cherished you
as a father does his sons or his daughters' husbands.
Now that I know you, I burn for you even more fiercely,
though I regard you as almost utterly worthless.
How can that be, you ask? It's because such cruelty forces
lust to assume the shrunken place of affection.[4]

The ability of Catullus to express in simple fashion his intense feelings and curiosity about himself and his world had a noticeable impact on later Latin poets.

The development of Roman prose was greatly aided by the practice of oratory. Romans had great respect for oratory because the ability to persuade people in public debate meant success in politics. Oratory was brought to perfection in a literary fashion by Cicero (106–43 B.C.E.), the best exemplar of the literary and intellectual interests of the senatorial elite of the late Republic and, indeed, the greatest prose writer of that period. For Cicero, oratory was not simply skillful speaking. An orator was a statesman,

ROMAN THEATER: REHEARSAL OF A GREEK PLAY. This mosaic found at Pompeii shows Roman actors preparing to present a Greek play. The seated figure is the chorus master, who observes two actors dancing to the music of a pipe.

a man who achieved his highest goal by pursuing an active life in public affairs.

The high point of Latin literature was reached in the age of Augustus. The literary accomplishments of the Augustan age were such that the period has been called the golden age of Latin literature. The most distinguished poet of the Augustan age was Virgil (70–19 B.C.E.). The son of a small landholder in northern Italy, he welcomed the rule of Augustus and wrote his greatest work in his honor. Virgil's masterpiece was *The Aeneid,* an epic poem clearly meant to rival the work of Homer. The connection between Troy and Rome is made in the poem when Aeneas, a hero of Troy, survives the destruction of Troy and eventually settles in Latium; hence, Roman civilization is linked to Greek history. The character of Aeneas is portrayed as the ideal Roman—his virtues are duty, piety, and faithfulness. Virgil's overall purpose was to show that Aeneas had fulfilled his mission to establish the Romans in Italy and thereby start Rome on its divine mission to rule the world.

> *Let others fashion from bronze more lifelike, breathing images—*
> *For so they shall—and evoke living faces from marble;*
> *Others excel as orators, others track with their instruments*
> *The planets circling in heaven and predict when stars will appear.*
> *But, Romans, never forget that government is your medium!*
> *Be this your art:—to practice men in the habit of peace,*
> *Generosity to the conquered, and firmness against aggressors.*[5]

As Virgil expressed it, ruling was Rome's gift.

Another prominent Augustan poet was Horace (65–8 B.C.E.), a friend of Virgil. He was a very sophisticated writer whose overriding concern was to point out to his contemporaries the "follies and vices of his age." In his *Satires*, a medley of poems on a variety of subjects, Horace is revealed as a detached observer of human weaknesses. He directed his attacks against movements, not living people, and took on such subjects as sexual immorality, greed, and job dissatisfaction ("How does it happen, Maecenas, that no man alone is content with his lot?"[6]). Horace mostly laughs at the weaknesses of humankind and calls for forbearance: "Supposing my friend has got liquored and wetted my couch, . . . is he for such a lapse to be deemed less dear as a friend, or because when hungry he snatched up before me a chicken from my side of the dish?"[7]

Ovid (43 B.C.E.–18 C.E.) was the last of the great poets of the golden age. He belonged to a youthful, privileged social group in Rome that liked to ridicule old Roman values. In keeping with the spirit of this group, Ovid wrote a series of frivolous love poems known as the *Amores*. Intended to entertain and shock, they achieved their goal. Another of Ovid's works was *The Art of Love*. This was essentially a takeoff on didactic poems. Whereas authors of earlier didactic poems had written guides to farming, hunting, or some such subject, Ovid's work was a handbook on the seduction of women (see the box on p. 145).

The most famous Latin prose work of the golden age was written by the historian Livy (59 B.C.E.–17 C.E.). Livy's masterpiece was the *History of Rome,* which covered the period from the foundation of the city to 9 B.C.E. Only 35 of the original 142 books have survived, although we do possess brief summaries of the whole work from other authors. Livy perceived history in terms of moral lessons. He stated in the preface that

> The study of history is the best medicine for a sick mind; for in history you have a record of the infinite variety of human experience plainly set out for all to see; and in that record you can find for yourself and your country both examples and warnings: fine things to take as models, base things, rotten through and through, to avoid.[8]

For Livy, human character was the determining factor in history.

Livy's history celebrated Rome's greatness. He included scene upon scene that not only revealed the character of the chief figures but also demonstrated the virtues that had made Rome great. Of course, he had serious weaknesses as a historian. He was not always concerned about the factual accuracy of his myriad stories and was not overly critical of his sources. But he did tell a good story, and his work became the standard history of Rome for a long time.

In the history of Latin literature, the century and a half after Augustus is often labeled the "silver age" to indicate that the literary efforts of the period, while good, were not equal to the high standards of the Augustan "golden age." The popularity of rhetorical training encouraged the use of clever and ornate literary expressions at the expense of original and meaningful content. A good example of this trend can be found in the works of Seneca.

Educated in Rome, Seneca (c. 4 B.C.E.–65 C.E.) became strongly attached to the philosophy of Stoicism. In letters written to a young friend, he expressed the basic tenets

OVID AND THE ART OF LOVE

Ovid has been called the last great poet of the Augustan golden age of literature. One of his most famous works was The Art of Love, *a guidebook on the seduction of women. Unfortunately for Ovid, the work appeared at a time when Augustus was anxious to improve the morals of the Roman upper class. Augustus considered the poem offensive, and Ovid soon found himself in exile.*

OVID, *THE ART OF LOVE*

Now I'll teach you how to captivate and hold the woman of your choice. This is the most important part of all my lessons. Lovers of every land, lend an attentive ear to my discourse; let goodwill warm your hearts, for I am going to fulfill the promises I made you.

First of all, be quite sure that there isn't a woman who cannot be won, and make up your mind that you will win her. Only you must prepare the ground. Sooner would the birds cease their song in the springtime, or the grasshopper be silent in the summer . . . than a woman resist the tender wooing of a youthful lover. . . .

Now the first thing you have to do is to get on good terms with the fair one's maid. She can make things easy for you. Find out whether she is fully in her mistress's confidence, and if she knows all about her secret dissipations. Leave no stone unturned to win her over. Once you have her on your side, the rest is easy. . . .

In the first place, it's best to send her a letter, just to pave the way. In it you should tell her how you dote on her; pay her pretty compliments and say all the nice things lovers always say. . . . Even the gods are moved by the voice of entreaty. And promise, promise, promise. Promises will cost you nothing. Everyone's a millionaire where promises are concerned. . . .

If she refuses your letter and sends it back unread, don't give up; hope for the best and try again. . . .

Don't let your hair stick up in tufts on your head; see that your hair and your beard are decently trimmed. See also that your nails are clean and nicely filed; don't have any hair growing out of your nostrils; take care that your breath is sweet, and don't go about reeking like a billy goat. All other toilet refinements leave to the women or to perverts. . . .

When you find yourself at a feast where the wine is flowing freely, and where a woman shares the same couch with you, pray to that god whose mysteries are celebrated during the night, that the wine may not overcloud your brain. 'Tis then you may easily hold converse with your mistress in hidden words whereof she will easily divine the meaning. . . .

By subtle flatteries you may be able to steal into her heart, even as the river insensibly overflows the banks which fringe it. Never cease to sing the praises of her face, her hair, her taper fingers and her dainty foot. . . .

Tears, too, are a mighty useful resource in the matter of love. They would melt a diamond. Make a point, therefore, of letting your mistress see your face all wet with tears. Howbeit, if you can't manage to squeeze out any tears—and they won't always flow just when you want them to—put your finger in your eyes.

of Stoicism: living according to nature, accepting events dispassionately as part of the divine plan, and a universal love for all humanity. Thus, "the first thing philosophy promises us is the feeling of fellowship, of belonging to mankind and being members of a community. . . . Philosophy calls for simple living, not for doing penance, and the simple way of life need not be a crude one."[9] Viewed in retrospect, Seneca displays some glaring inconsistencies. While preaching the virtues of simplicity, he amassed a fortune and was ruthless at times in protecting it. His letters show humanity, benevolence, and fortitude, but his sentiments are often undermined by an attempt to be clever with words.

The greatest historian of the silver age was Tacitus (c. 56–120). His main works included the *Annals* and *Histories,* which presented a narrative account of Roman history from the reign of Tiberius through the assassination of Domitian (14–96). Tacitus believed that history had a moral purpose: "It seems to me a historian's foremost duty is to ensure that merit is recorded, and to confront evil deeds and words with the fear of posterity's denunciations."[10] As a member of the senatorial class, Tacitus was disgusted with the abuses of power perpetrated by the emperors and determined that the "evil deeds" of wicked men would not be forgotten. His work *Germania* is especially important as a source of information about the early Germans. But it too is colored by Tacitus's attempt to show the Germans as noble savages in comparison to the decadent Romans.

Art

The Romans were also dependent on the Greeks for artistic inspiration. During the third and second centuries B.C.E., they adopted many features of the Hellenistic style of art. The Romans developed a taste for Greek statues, which they placed not only in public buildings, but in their private houses. Once demand outstripped the supply of original works, reproductions of Greek statues became fashionable. The Romans' own portrait sculpture was characterized by an intense realism that included even unpleasant physical details. Wall paintings and frescoes in the houses of the rich realistically depicted

INTERIOR OF THE COLOSSEUM OF ROME. The Colosseum was a large amphitheater constructed under the emperor Vespasian and his son Titus. The amphitheaters in which the gladiatorial contests were held varied in size throughout the empire. The Roman emperors understood that gladiatorial shows and other forms of entertainment helped to divert the poor and destitute from any political unrest.

landscapes, portraits, and scenes from mythological stories.

The Romans excelled in architecture, a highly practical art. Although they continued to utilize Greek styles and made use of colonnades, rectangular structures, and post and lintel construction, the Romans were also innovative. They made considerable use of curvilinear forms: the arch, vault, and dome. The Romans were also the first people in antiquity to use concrete on a massive scale. By combining concrete and curvilinear forms, they were able to construct massive buildings—public baths, such as those of Caracalla, and amphitheaters, the most famous of which was the Colosseum in Rome, capable of seating 50,000 spectators. These large buildings were made possible by Roman engineering skills. These same skills were put to use in constructing roads (the Romans built a network of 50,000 miles of roads throughout their empire), aqueducts (in Rome, almost a dozen aqueducts kept a population of one million supplied with water), and bridges.

Roman Law

One of Rome's chief gifts to the Mediterranean world of its day and to later generations was its system of law. The Twelve Tables of 450 B.C.E. was Rome's first code of laws, but it was a product of a simple farming society and proved inadequate for later Roman needs. Nevertheless, from the Twelve Tables the Romans developed a system of civil law that applied only to Roman citizens. As Rome expanded, Romans became involved in problems between Romans and non-Romans as well as between two non-Romans. The Romans found that although some of their rules of civil law could be used in these cases, special rules were often needed. These rules gave rise to a body of law known as the law of nations, defined by the Romans as "that part of the law which we apply both to ourselves and to foreigners." Under the influence of Stoicism (see Chapter 4), the Romans came to identify their law of nations with natural law, or universal law based on reason. This enabled them to establish standards of justice that applied to all people.

These standards of justice included principles that we would immediately recognize. A person was regarded as innocent until proven otherwise. People accused of wrongdoing were allowed to defend themselves before a judge. A judge, in turn, was expected to weigh evidence carefully before arriving at a decision. These principles lived on long after the fall of the Roman Empire.

The Roman Family

At the heart of the Roman social structure stood the family, headed by the *paterfamilias*—the dominant male. The household also included the wife, sons with their wives and children, unmarried daughters, and slaves. A family was virtually a small state within the state, and the power of the *paterfamilias* was parallel to that of the state magistrates over the citizens. Like the Greeks, Roman males believed that the weakness of the female sex necessitated male guardians (see the box on p. 147). The *paterfamilias* exercised that authority; upon his death, sons or nearest male relatives assumed the role of guardians. By the late Republic, however, although the rights of male guardians remained legally in effect, upper-class women found numerous ways to circumvent the power of their guardians.

Fathers arranged the marriages of their daughters, although there are instances of mothers and daughters having influence on the choice. In the Republic, women married "with legal control" passing from father to husband. By the mid-first century B.C.E., the dominant practice had changed to "without legal control," which meant that married daughters officially remained within the father's legal power. Since the fathers of most married women were dead, not being in the "legal control" of a husband entailed independent property rights that forceful women could translate into considerable power within the household and outside it. Traditionally, Roman marriages were intended to be for life, but divorce was introduced in the third century B.C.E. and became relatively easy to obtain since either party could initiate it and no one needed to prove the breakdown of the marriage. Divorce became especially prevalent in the first century B.C.E.—a period of political turmoil—when marriages were used to cement political alliances.

Some parents in upper-class families provided education for their daughters. Some girls had private tutors and others may have gone to primary schools. But, at the

CATO THE ELDER ON WOMEN

During the Second Punic War, the Romans enacted the Oppian Law, which limited the amount of gold women could possess and restricted their dress and use of carriages. In 195 B.C.E.*, an attempt to repeal the law was made, and women demonstrated in the streets on behalf of this effort. According to the Roman historian Livy, the conservative Roman official Cato the Elder spoke against repeal and against the women favoring it. Although the words are probably not Cato's own, they do reflect a traditional male Roman attitude toward women.*

LIVY, *THE HISTORY OF ROME*

"If each of us, citizens, had determined to assert his rights and dignity as a husband with respect to his own spouse, we should have less trouble with the sex as a whole; as it is, our liberty, destroyed at home by female violence, even here in the Forum is crushed and trodden underfoot, and because we have not kept them individually under control, we dread them collectively. . . . But from no class is there not the greatest danger if you permit them meetings and gatherings and secret consultations. . . .

"Our ancestors permitted no women to conduct even personal business without a guardian to intervene in her behalf; they wished them to be under the control of fathers, brothers, husbands; we (Heaven help us!) allow them now even to interfere in public affairs, yes, and to visit the Forum and our informal and formal sessions. What else are they doing now on the streets and at the corners except urging the bill of the tribunes and voting for the repeal of the law? Give loose rein to their uncontrollable nature and to this untamed creature and expect that they will themselves set bounds to their license; unless you act, this is the least of the things enjoined upon women by custom or law and to which they submit with a feeling of injustice. It is complete liberty or, rather, if we wish to speak the truth, complete license that they desire.

"If they win in this, what will they not attempt? Review all the laws with which your forefathers restrained their license and made them subject to their husbands; even with all these bonds you can scarcely control them. What of this? If you suffer them to seize these bonds one by one and wrench themselves free and finally to be placed on a parity with their husbands, do you think that you will be able to endure them? The moment they begin to be your equals, they will be your superiors. . . .

"Now they publicly address other women's husbands, and, what is more serious, they beg for a law and votes, and from sundry men they get what they ask. In matters affecting yourself, your property, your children, you, Sir, can be importuned; once the law has ceased to set a limit to your wife's expenditures you will never set it yourself. Do not think, citizens, that the situation which existed before the law was passed will ever return."

age when boys were entering secondary schools, girls were pushed into marriage. The legal minimum age for marriage was twelve, although fourteen was a more common age in practice. Although some Roman doctors warned that pregnancy could be dangerous for young girls, early marriages persisted due to the desire to benefit from the dowries as soon as possible and the reality of early mortality. A good example is Tullia, Cicero's beloved daughter. She was married at sixteen, widowed at twenty-two, remarried one year later, divorced at twenty-eight, remarried at twenty-nine, and divorced at thirty-three. She died at thirty-four, not unusual for females in Roman society.

By the second century C.E., significant changes were occurring in the Roman family. The foundations of the authority of the *paterfamilias* over his family, which had already begun to weaken in the late Republic, were further undermined. The *paterfamilias* no longer had absolute authority over his children; he could no longer sell them into slavery or have them put to death. Moreover, the husband's absolute authority over his wife also disappeared, a trend that had begun in the late Republic. In the Early Empire, the idea of male guardianship continued to weaken significantly, and by the late second century,

A ROMAN LADY. Roman women, especially those of the upper class, developed comparatively more freedom than women in classical Athens despite the persistent male belief that women required guardianship. This mural decoration was found in the remains of a villa destroyed by the eruption of Mount Vesuvius.

THE ROMAN FEAR OF SLAVES

The lowest stratum of the Roman population consisted of slaves. They were used extensively in households, at the court, as artisans in industrial enterprises, as business managers, and in numerous other ways. Although some historians have argued that slaves were treated more humanely during the Early Empire, these selections by the Roman historian Tacitus and the Roman statesman Pliny indicate that slaves still rebelled against their masters because of mistreatment. Many masters continued to live in fear of their slaves as witnessed by the saying, "As many enemies as you have slaves."

TACITUS, *THE ANNALS OF IMPERIAL ROME*

Soon afterwards the City Prefect, Lucius Pedanius Secundus, was murdered by one of his slaves [61 C.E.]. Either Pedanius had refused to free the murderer after agreeing to a price, or the slave, in a homosexual infatuation, found competition from his master intolerable. After the murder, ancient custom required that every slave residing under the same roof must be executed. But a crowd gathered, eager to save so many innocent lives; and rioting began. The senate-house was besieged. Inside, there was feeling against excessive severity, but the majority opposed any change. Among the latter was Gaius Cassius Longinus, who when his turn came spoke as follows. . . .

"An ex-consul has been deliberately murdered by a slave in his own home. None of his fellow-slaves prevented or betrayed the murderer, though the senatorial decree threatening the whole household with execution still stands. Exempt them from the penalty if you like. But then, if the City Prefect was not important enough to be immune; who will be? Who will have enough slaves to protect him if Pedanius's four hundred were too few? Who can rely on his household's help if even fear for their own lives does not make them shield us?"

[The sentence of death was carried out.]

PLINY THE YOUNGER TO ACILIUS

This horrible affair demands more publicity than a letter—Larcius Macedo, a senator and ex-praetor, has fallen a victim to his own slaves. Admittedly he was a cruel and overbearing master, too ready to forget that his father had been a slave, or perhaps too keenly conscious of it. He was taking a bath in his house at Formiae when suddenly he found himself surrounded; one slave seized him by the throat while the others struck his face and hit him in the chest and stomach and—shocking to say—in his private parts. When they thought he was dead they threw him onto the hot pavement, to make sure he was not still alive. Whether unconscious or feigning to be so, he lay there motionless, thus making them believe that he was quite dead. Only then was he carried out, as if he had fainted with the heat, and received by his slaves who had remained faithful, while his concubines ran up, screaming frantically. Roused by their cries and revived by the cooler air he opened his eyes and made some movement to show that he was alive, it being now safe to do so. The guilty slaves fled, but most of them have been arrested and a search is being made for the others. Macedo was brought back to life with difficulty, but only for a few days; at least he died with the satisfaction of having revenged himself, for he lived to see the same punishment meted out as for murder. There you see the dangers, outrages, and insults to which we are exposed. No master can feel safe because he is kind and considerate; for it is their brutality, not their reasoning capacity, which leads slaves to murder masters.

though guardianships had not been abolished, they had become a formality.

Upper-class Roman women in the Early Empire had considerable freedom and independence. They had acquired the right to own, inherit, and dispose of property. Wives were not segregated from males in the home but were appreciated as enjoyable company and were at the center of household social life. Upper-class women could attend the races, the theater, and events in the amphitheater, although in the latter two places they were forced to sit in separate female sections. Moreover, ladies of rank were still accompanied by maids and companions when they went out. Some women operated businesses, such as shipping firms. Women could not participate in politics, but the Early Empire saw a number of important women who influenced politics through their husbands, including Livia, the wife of Augustus, Agrippina, the mother of Nero, and Plotina, the wife of Trajan.

Slaves and Their Masters

Although slavery was a common institution throughout the ancient world, no people possessed more slaves or relied so much on slave labor as the Romans eventually did. Before the third century B.C.E., a small Roman farmer might possess one or two slaves who would help farm his few acres and perform domestic chores. These slaves would most likely be from Italy and be regarded as part of the family household. Only the very rich would have large numbers of slaves.

The Roman conquest of the Mediterranean brought a drastic change in the use of slaves. Large numbers of foreign slaves were brought back to Italy. During the Republic, Rome's wars were the chief source of slaves, followed by piracy; the children of slaves also became slaves. While some Roman generals brought back slaves to be sold to benefit the public treasury, ambitious generals of the first century, such as Pompey and Caesar, made personal fortunes by treating slaves captured by their armies as their own private property.

The Romans used slaves in many ways. The rich, of course, owned the most and the best. In the late Republic, it became a badge of prestige to be attended by many slaves. Greeks were in much demand as household slaves, where they served as tutors, musicians, doctors, and artists. Many slaves of all nationalities were used as menial household workers, such as cooks, valets, waiters, cleaners, and gardeners. Roman businessmen would employ slaves as shop assistants or artisans. Slaves were also used as farm laborers; in fact, huge gangs of slaves worked the large landed estates under pitiful conditions. Cato the Elder argued that it was cheaper to work slaves to death and then replace them than to treat them favorably. In addition, the roads, aqueducts, and public buildings were constructed by contractors using slave labor. The total number of slaves is difficult to judge—estimates range from two to four free men to every slave.

It is also difficult to generalize about the treatment of Roman slaves. There are numerous instances of humane treatment by masters and situations where slaves even protected their owners from danger out of gratitude and esteem. But there are also examples of slaves murdering their owners, causing some Romans to live in unspoken fear of their slaves (see the box on p. 148). Slaves were also subject to severe punishments, torture, abuse, and hard labor that drove some to run away or even revolt against their owners. The Romans had stringent laws against aiding a runaway slave. The murder of a master by a slave might mean the execution of all the other household slaves. Near the end of the second century B.C.E., large-scale slave revolts occurred in Sicily, where enormous gangs of slaves were subjected to horrible working conditions on large landed estates. Slaves were branded, beaten, fed inadequately, worked in chains, and housed at night in underground prisons. It took three years (from 135 to 132 B.C.E.) to crush a revolt of 70,000 slaves, and the great revolt on Sicily (104–101 B.C.E.) involved most of the island and took a Roman army of 17,000 men to suppress it. The most famous revolt on the Italian peninsula occurred in 73 B.C.E. Led by a Thracian gladiator named Spartacus, the revolt broke out in southern Italy and involved 70,000 slaves. Spartacus managed to defeat several Roman armies before he was finally trapped and killed in southern Italy in 71 B.C.E. Six thousand of his followers were crucified, the traditional form of execution for slaves.

Imperial Rome

At the center of the colossal Roman Empire was the ancient city of Rome. Truly a capital city, Rome had the largest population of any city in the empire. It is estimated that its population was close to one million by the time of Augustus. Only Chang'an, the imperial capital of the Han Chinese Empire, had a comparable population during this time. For anyone with ambitions, Rome was the place to be. A magnet to many people, Rome was extremely cosmopolitan. Nationalities from all over the empire resided there, with entire sections inhabited by specific groups, such as Greeks and Syrians.

Rome was, no doubt, an overcrowded and noisy city. Because of the congestion, cart and wagon traffic was banned from the streets during the day. The noise from the resulting vehicular movement at night often made sleep difficult. Evening pedestrian travel was dangerous. Although Augustus had organized a police force, lone travelers might be assaulted, robbed, or soaked by filth thrown out of the upper-story windows of Rome's massive apartment buildings.

An enormous gulf existed between rich and poor in the city of Rome. While the rich had comfortable villas, the poor lived in apartment blocks called *insulae*, which might be six stories high. Constructed of concrete, they were often poorly built and not infrequently collapsed. The use

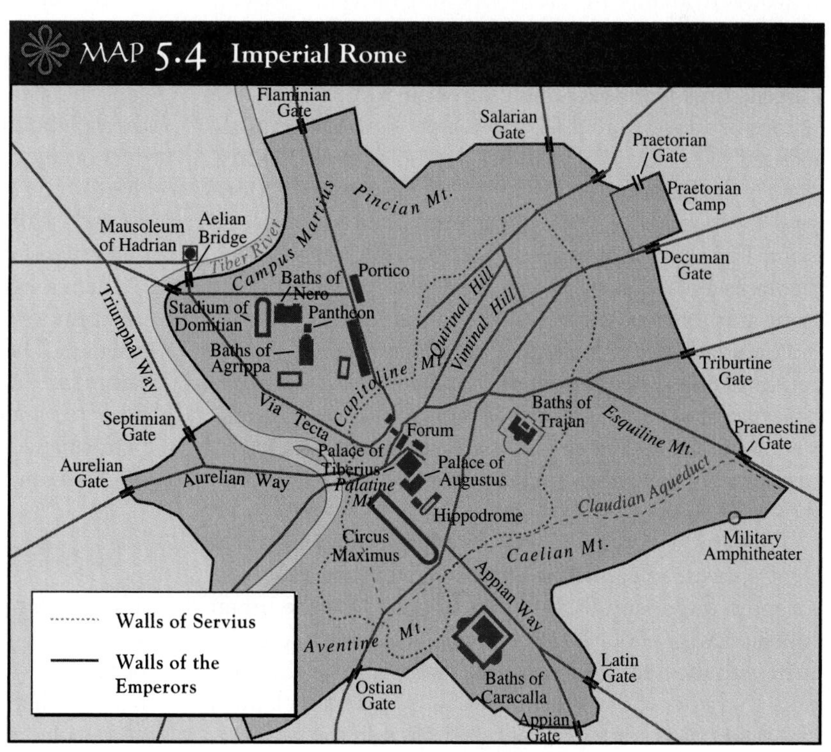

MAP 5.4 Imperial Rome

THE PUBLIC BATHS OF THE ROMAN EMPIRE

The public baths in Rome and other cities played an important role in urban life. Introduced to Rome in the second century B.C.E. *as a result of Greek influence, the number of public baths grew at a rapid pace in the Early Empire as the emperors contributed funds for their construction. The public baths were especially noisy near the end of the afternoon when Romans stopped in after work to use the baths before dinner. The following description is by Lucian, a traveling lecturer who lived in the second century and wrote satirical dialogues in Greek. This selection is taken from* Hippias, or the Bath.

LUCIAN, *HIPPIAS, OR THE BATH*

The building suits the magnitude of the site, accords well with the accepted idea of such an establishment, and shows regard for the principles of lighting. The entrance is high, with a flight of broad steps of which the tread is greater than the pitch, to make them easy to ascend. On entering, one is received into a public hall of good size, with ample accommodations for servants and attendants. On the left are the lounging rooms, also of just the right sort for a bath, attractive, brightly lighted retreats. Then, besides them, a hall, larger than need be for the purposes of a bath, but necessary for the reception of richer persons. Next, capacious locker rooms to undress in, on each side, with a very high and brilliantly lighted hall between them, in which are three swimming pools of cold water; it is finished in Laconian marble, and has two statues of white marble in the ancient style. . . .

On leaving this hall, you come into another which is slightly warmed instead of meeting you at once with fierce heat; it is oblong, and has an apse on each side. Next to it, on the right, is a very bright hall, nicely fitted up for massage. . . . Then near this is another hall, the most beautiful in the world, in which one can stand or sit with comfort, linger without danger, and stroll about with profit. It also is refulgent with Phrygian marble clear to the roof. Next comes the hot corridor, faced with Numidian marble. The hall beyond it is very beautiful, full of abundant light and aglow with color like that of purple hangings. It contains three hot tubs.

When you have bathed, you need not go back through the same rooms, but can go directly to the cold room through a slightly warmed chamber. Everywhere there is copious illumination and full indoor daylight. . . . Why should I go on to tell you of the exercising floor and of the cloak rooms?. . . Moreover, it is beautiful with all other marks of thoughtfulness—with two toilets, many exits, and two devices for telling time, a water clock that makes a bellowing sound and a sundial.

of wooden beams in the floors and movable stoves, torches, candles, and lamps within the rooms for heat and light made the danger of fire a constant companion. Once started, fires were extremely difficult to put out. The famous conflagration of 64 C.E., which Nero was unjustly accused of starting, devastated a good part of the city. Besides the hazards of collapse and fire, living conditions were also poor. High rents forced entire families into one room. The absence of plumbing, central heating, and open fireplaces made life so uncomfortable that poorer Romans spent most of their time outdoors in the streets.

Fortunately for these people, Rome boasted public buildings unequaled anywhere in the empire. Its temples, fora, markets, baths, theaters, triumphal arches, governmental buildings, and amphitheaters gave parts of the city an appearance of grandeur and magnificence (see the box above).

Though the center of a great empire, Rome was also a great parasite. Beginning with Augustus, the emperors accepted responsibility for providing food for the urban populace, with about 200,000 people receiving free grain. Even with the free grain, conditions were grim for the poor. Early in the second century C.E., a Roman doctor claimed that rickets was common among children in the city.

In addition to food, entertainment was provided on a grand scale for the inhabitants of Rome. The poet Juvenal said of the Roman masses: "But nowadays, with no vote to sell, their motto is 'Couldn't care less.' Time was when their plebiscite elected generals, heads of state, commanders of legions: but now they've pulled in their horns, there's only two things that concern them: Bread and Circuses."[11] Public spectacles were provided by the emperor and other state officials as part of the great festivals—most of them religious in origin—celebrated by the state. Over one hundred days a year were given over to these public holidays. The festivals included three major types of entertainment. At the Circus Maximus, horse and chariot races attracted hundreds of thousands, while dramatic and other performances were held in theaters. But the most famous of all the public spectacles were the gladiatorial shows.

The Gladiatorial Shows

The gladiatorial shows were an integral part of Roman society. They took place in amphitheaters, with the first permanent one having been constructed at Rome in 29 B.C.E. Perhaps the most famous was the Flavian amphitheater, called the Colosseum, constructed at Rome to seat

50,000 spectators. Amphitheaters were not limited to the city of Rome but were constructed throughout the empire. They varied greatly in size, with capacities ranging from a few thousand to tens of thousands. Considerable resources and ingenuity went into building them, especially in the arrangements for moving wild beasts efficiently into the arena. In most cities and towns, amphitheaters came to be the biggest buildings, rivaled only by the circuses for races and the public baths. Where a society invests its money gives an idea of its priorities. Since the amphitheater was the primary location for the gladiatorial games, it is fair to say that public slaughter was an important part of Roman culture.

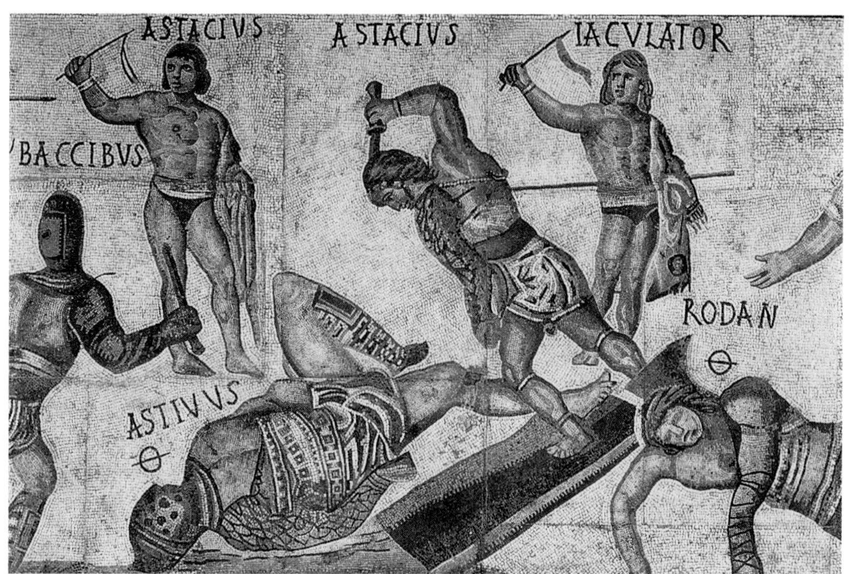

THE GLADIATORIAL GAMES. Although some gladiators were free men enticed by the possibility of rewards, most were condemned criminals, slaves, or prisoners of war who were trained in special schools. A great gladiator could win his freedom through the games. This mosaic, from the fourth century C.E., depicts different aspects of gladiatorial fighting and clearly shows the bloody nature of the gladiatorial games.

Gladiatorial games were held from dawn to dusk. Contests to the death between trained fighters formed the central focus of these games. Most gladiators were slaves or condemned criminals, although some free men lured by the hope of popularity and patronage by wealthy fans participated voluntarily. They were trained for combat in special gladiatorial schools.

Gladiatorial games included other forms of entertainment as well. Criminals of all ages and both sexes were sent into the arena without weapons to face certain death from wild animals who would tear them to pieces. Numerous kinds of animal contests were also staged: wild beasts against each other, such as bears against buffalo; staged hunts with men shooting safely from behind iron bars; and gladiators in the arena with bulls, tigers, and lions. Reportedly, five thousand beasts were killed in one day of games when the Emperor Titus inaugurated the Colosseum in 80 C.E. Enormous resources were invested in the capture and shipment of wild animals for slaughter, while whole species were hunted to extinction in parts of the empire.

These bloodthirsty spectacles were highly popular with the Roman people. The Roman historian Tacitus said, "Few indeed are to be found who talk of any other subjects in their homes, and whenever we enter a classroom, what else is the conversation of the youths."[12] But the gladiatorial games served a purpose beyond mere entertainment. To the Romans, the gladiatorial games, as well as the other forms of public entertainment, fulfilled both a political and a social need. Certainly, the games served to divert the idle masses from any political unrest. It was said of the Emperor Trajan that he understood that although the distribution of grain and money satisfied the individual, spectacles were necessary for the "contentment of the masses."

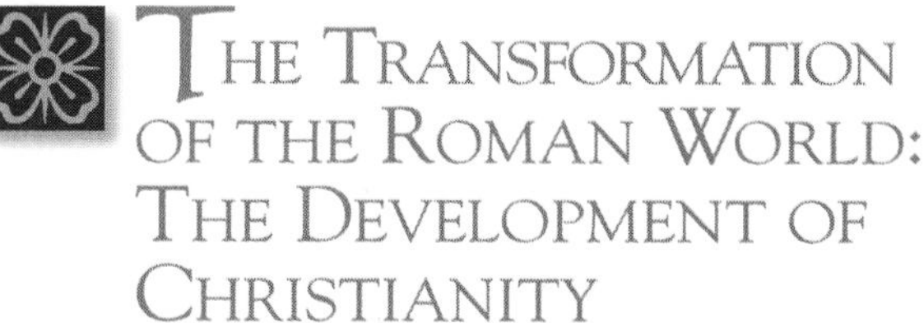

The Transformation of the Roman World: The Development of Christianity

The rise of Christianity marks a fundamental break with the dominant values of the Greco-Roman world. Christian views of God, human beings, and the world were quite different from those of the Greeks and Romans. Nevertheless, Christianity also had much in common with its contemporary religions. Consequently, to understand the rise of Christianity, we must first examine both the religious environment of the Roman world and the Jewish background from which Christianity emerged.

The Religious World of the Romans

Augustus had taken a number of steps to revive the Roman state religion, which had declined during the turmoil of the late Republic. The official state religion focused on the worship of a pantheon of Greco-Roman gods and goddesses, including Juno, the patron goddess of women, Minerva, the goddess of artisans, Mars, the god of war, and Jupiter Optimus Maximus (best and greatest), who became the patron deity of Rome and assumed a central place in the religious life of the city. The Romans believed that observance of proper ritual by state priests brought the Romans into a proper relationship with the gods and guaranteed security, peace, and prosperity. No doubt, the Roman success in creating an empire was a visible confirmation of divine favor. As Cicero, the first-century politician and writer, claimed: "We have overcome all the nations of the world, because we have realized that the world is directed and governed by the gods."[13]

The polytheistic Romans were extremely tolerant of other religions. The Romans allowed the worship of native gods and goddesses throughout their provinces and even adopted some of the local gods. In addition, the imperial cult of Roma and Augustus was developed to bolster support for the emperors. After Augustus, any dead emperors deified by the Roman senate were added to the official imperial cult.

In addition to the formal, official religion, the Romans had cults of household and countryside spirits whose worship appealed especially to the common people. Here, too, proper ritual was important, and it was the responsibility of the *paterfamilias* as head of the family to ensure proper fulfillment of religious obligations. Although these cults gave the Romans a more immediate sense of spiritual contact than they found in the official religion, these cults, too, failed to satisfy many people.

The desire for a more emotional spiritual experience led many people to the mystery religions of the Hellenistic east, which flooded into the western Roman world during the Early Empire. The mystery religions offered secret teachings that supposedly brought special benefits. They promised their followers advantages unavailable through Roman religion: an entry into a higher world of reality and the promise of a future life superior to the present one. They also featured elaborate rituals with deep emotional appeal. By participating in their ceremonies and performing their rites, an adherent could achieve communion with spiritual beings and undergo purification that opened the door to life after death.

The Jewish Background

In Hellenistic times, the Jewish people had been granted considerable independence by their Seleucid rulers (see Chapter 4). Roman involvement with the Jews began in 63 B.C.E., and by 6 C.E., Judaea (which embraced the lands of the old Hebrew kingdom of Judah) had been made a province and placed under the direction of a Roman procurator. But unrest continued, augmented by divisions among the Jews themselves. The Sadducees favored cooperation with the Romans. The Pharisees, although they wanted Judaea to be free from Roman control, did not advocate violent means to achieve this goal. The Essenes, as revealed in the Dead Sea Scrolls, a collection of documents first discovered in 1947, constituted a Jewish sect that lived in a religious community near the Dead Sea. They, like most other Jews, awaited a Messiah who would save Israel from oppression, usher in the kingdom of God, and establish a true paradise on earth. A fourth group, the Zealots, were militant extremists who advocated the violent overthrow of Roman rule. A Jewish revolt in 66 C.E. was crushed by the Romans four years later. The Jewish Temple in Jerusalem was destroyed, and Roman power once more stood supreme in Judaea.

The Rise of Christianity

It was in the midst of the confusion and conflict in Judaea that Jesus of Nazareth (c. 6 B.C.E.–29 C.E.) began his public preaching. Jesus—a Palestinian Jew—grew up in Galilee, an important center of the militant Zealots. Jesus' message was basically simple. He reassured his fellow Jews that he did not plan to undermine their traditional religion: "Do not think that I have come to abolish the Law or the Prophets; I have not come to abolish them but to fulfill them."[14] According to Jesus, what was important was not strict adherence to the letter of the law and attention to rules and prohibitions, but the transformation of the inner person: "So in everything, do to others what you would have them do to you, for this sums up the Law and the Prophets."[15] God's command was simple—to love God and one another: "Love the Lord your God with all your heart and with all your soul and with all your mind and with all your strength. The second is this: Love your neighbor as yourself."[16] In the Sermon on the Mount (see the box on p. 153), Jesus presented the ethical concepts—humility, charity, and brotherly love—that would form the basis for the value system of medieval Western civilization.

Although some people welcomed Jesus as the Messiah who would save Israel from oppression and establish God's kingdom on earth, Jesus spoke of a heavenly kingdom, not an earthly one: "My kingdom is not of this world."[17] Consequently, he disappointed the radicals. On the other hand, conservative religious leaders believed Jesus was undermining respect for traditional Jewish religion. To the Roman authorities of Palestine and their local allies, the Nazarene was a potential revolutionary who might transform Jewish expectations of a messianic kingdom into a revolt against Rome. Therefore, Jesus found himself denounced on many sides and was given over to the Roman authorities. The procurator Pontius Pilate ordered his crucifixion. But that did not solve the problem. A few loyal followers of Jesus spread the story that Jesus had overcome death, had been resurrected, and had then ascended into heaven. The belief in Jesus' resurrection became an important tenet of Christian doctrine. Jesus was now hailed as the "anointed one" (*Christos* in Greek) or the Messiah who would return and usher in the kingdom of God on earth.

Christianity began, then, as a religious movement within Judaism and was viewed that way by Roman authorities for many decades. Although tradition holds that one of Jesus' disciples, Peter, founded the Christian church at Rome, the most important figure in early Christianity after Jesus was Paul of Tarsus (c. 5–c. 67). Paul

CHRISTIAN IDEALS: THE SERMON ON THE MOUNT

Christianity was simply one of many religions competing for attention in the Roman Empire during the first and second centuries. The rise of Christianity marked a fundamental break with the value system of the upper-class elites who dominated the world of classical antiquity. As these excerpts from the Sermon on the Mount in the Gospel of Saint Matthew illustrate, Christians emphasized humility, charity, brotherly love, and a belief in the inner being and a spiritual kingdom superior to this material world. These values and principles were not those of classical Greco-Roman civilization as exemplified in the words and deeds of its leaders.

THE GOSPEL ACCORDING TO SAINT MATTHEW

Now when he saw the crowds, he went up on a mountainside and sat down. His disciples came to him, and he began to teach them, saying:

Blessed are the poor in spirit: for theirs is the kingdom of heaven.
Blessed are those who mourn: for they will be comforted.
Blessed are the meek: for they will inherit the earth.
Blessed are those who hunger and thirst for righteousness: for they will be filled.
Blessed are the merciful: for they will be shown mercy.
Blessed are the pure in heart: for they will see God.
Blessed are the peacemakers: for they will be called sons of God.
Blessed are those who are persecuted because of righteousness: for theirs is the kingdom of heaven. . . .

You have heard that it was said, "Eye for eye, and tooth for tooth." But I tell you, Do not resist an evil person. If someone strikes you on the right cheek, turn to him the other also. . . .

You have heard that it was said, "Love your neighbor, and hate your enemy." But I tell you, Love your enemies and pray for those who persecute you. . . .

Do not store up for yourselves treasures on earth, where moth and rust destroy, and where thieves break in and steal. But store up for yourselves treasures in heaven, where moth and rust do not destroy, and where thieves do not break in and steal. For where your treasure is, there your heart will be also. . . .

No one can serve two masters. Either he will hate the one and love the other, or he will be devoted to the one and despise the other. You cannot serve both God and Money.

Therefore I tell you, do not worry about your life, what you will eat or drink; or about your body, what you will wear. Is not life more important than food, and the body more important than clothes? Look at the birds of the air; they do not sow or reap or store away in barns, and yet your heavenly Father feeds them. Are you not much more valuable than they? . . . So do not worry, saying, What shall we eat? or What shall we drink? or What shall we wear? For the pagans run after all these things, and your heavenly Father knows that you need them. But seek first his kingdom and his righteousness, and all these things will be given to you as well.

reached out to non-Jews and transformed Christianity from a Jewish sect into a world religion.

Called the "second founder of Christianity," Paul was a Jewish Roman citizen who had been strongly influenced by Hellenistic Greek culture. He believed that the message of Jesus should be preached not only to Jews but to Gentiles (non-Jews) as well. Paul was responsible for founding Christian communities throughout Asia Minor and along the shores of the Aegean.

Paul provided a universal foundation for the spread of Jesus' ideas. He taught that Jesus was, in effect, a savior-god, the son of God, who had come to earth to save all humans, who were basically sinners as a result of Adam's original sin of disobedience against God. By his death, Jesus had atoned for the sins of all humans and made possible a new beginning for all men and women, with the potential for individual salvation. By accepting Jesus as their savior, they too could be saved.

At first, Christianity spread slowly. Although it was disseminated mostly by the preaching of convinced Christians, written materials also appeared. Among them were a series of letters or epistles written by Paul outlining Christian beliefs for different Christian communities. Some of Jesus' disciples may also have preserved some of the sayings of the master in writing and would have passed on personal memories that became the basis of the written gospels—the "good news" concerning Jesus—which were written down between 50 and 150 and which attempted to give a record of Jesus' life and teachings and formed the core of the New Testament. Although Jerusalem was the first center of Christianity, its destruction by the Romans in 70 C.E. dispersed the Christians and left individual Christian churches with considerable independence. By 100, Christian churches had been established in most of the major cities of the east and in some places in the western part of the empire. Many early Christians came from the ranks of Hellenized Jews and the Greek-speaking populations of the east. But in the second and third centuries, an increasing number of followers came from Latin-speaking people. A Latin translation of the Greek New Testament that appeared soon after 200 aided this process.

JESUS AND HIS APOSTLES. Pictured is a fourth-century C.E. fresco from a Roman catacomb depicting Jesus and his apostles. Catacombs were underground cemeteries where early Christians buried their dead. Christian tradition holds that in times of imperial repression, Christians withdrew to the catacombs to pray and even hide.

Although some of the fundamental values of Christianity differed markedly from those of the Greco-Roman world, the Romans initially did not pay much attention to the Christians, whom they regarded at first as simply another sect of Judaism. The structure of the Roman Empire itself aided the growth of Christianity. Christian missionaries, including some of Jesus' original twelve disciples or apostles, used Roman roads to travel throughout the empire spreading their "good news."

As time passed, however, the Roman attitude toward Christianity began to change. The Romans were tolerant of other religions except when they threatened public order or public morals. Many Romans came to view Christians as harmful to the order of the Roman state. Since Christians held their meetings in secret and seemed to be connected to Christian groups in other areas, the government could view them as potentially dangerous to the state.

Some Romans felt that Christians were overly exclusive and hence harmful to the community and public order. The refusal of Christians to recognize other gods meant that they abstained from public festivals that honored these divinities. Finally, Christians refused to participate in the worship of the state gods and imperial cult. Since the Romans regarded these as important to the state, the Christians' refusal undermined the security of the state and hence constituted an act of treason, punishable by death. But to the Christians, who believed that there was only one real god, the worship of state gods and the emperors was idolatry and would endanger their own salvation.

Nevertheless, Roman persecution of Christians in the first and second centuries was only sporadic and local, never systematic. Persecution began during the reign of Nero. After the fire that destroyed much of Rome, the emperor used the Christians as scapegoats, accusing them of arson and hatred of the human race and subjecting them to cruel deaths in Rome. In the second century, Christians were largely ignored as harmless. By the end of the reigns of the five good emperors, Christians still represented a small minority, but one of considerable strength.

The Triumph of Christianity

The Romans' sporadic persecution of Christians in the first and second centuries had done nothing to stop the growth of Christianity. It had, in fact, served to strengthen Christianity as an institution in the second and third centuries by causing it to shed the loose structure of the first century and move toward a more centralized organization of its various church communities. Crucial to this change was the emerging role of the bishops, who began to assume more control over church communities. The Christian church was creating a well-defined hierarchical structure in which the bishops and clergy were salaried officers separate from the laity, or regular church members.

Christianity grew slowly in the first century, took root in the second, and by the third had spread widely. Why was Christianity able to attract so many followers? Certainly, the Christian message had much to offer the Roman world. The promise of salvation, made possible by Jesus' death and resurrection, made a resounding impact on a world full of suffering and injustice. Christianity seemed to imbue life with a meaning and purpose beyond the simple material things of everyday reality. Secondly, Christianity was not entirely unfamiliar. It could be viewed as simply another eastern mystery religion, offering immortality as the result of the sacrificial death of a savior-god. At the same time, it offered advantages that the other mystery religions lacked. Jesus had been a human figure, not a mythological one. Moreover, Christianity had universal appeal. Unlike some mystery religions, it was not restricted to men, nor did it require a painful or expensive initiation rite, as other mystery religions did. Initiation was accomplished simply by baptism—a purification by water—through which one entered into a personal relationship with Jesus. In addition, Christianity gave new meaning to life and offered what the Roman state religions could not—a personal relationship with God and connection to higher worlds.

Finally, Christianity fulfilled the human need to belong. Christians formed communities bound to one another in which people could express their love by helping each other and offering assistance to the poor, sick, widows, and orphans. Christianity satisfied the need to belong in a way that the huge, impersonal, and remote Roman Empire could never do.

Christianity proved attractive to all classes. The promise of eternal life was for all—rich, poor, aristocrats, slaves, men, and women. As Paul stated in his Epistle to the Colossians: "And [you] have put on the new self, which is being renewed in knowledge in the image of its Creator. Here there is no Greek nor Jew, circumcised or uncircumcised, barbarian, Scythian, slave or free, but Christ is all, and is in all."[18] Although it did not call for revolution or social upheaval, Christianity emphasized a sense of spiritual equality for all people.

Many women, in fact, found that Christianity offered them new roles and new forms of companionship with other women. Christian women fostered the new religion in their homes and preached their convictions to other people in their towns and villages. Many also died for their faith, and their deaths gave rise to a literature known as the Apocryphal Gospels, in which women were honored for creating new role models as virgins and widows dedicated to their faith, who defied fathers and their traditional gender roles to pursue their new lives.

As the Christian church became more organized, some emperors in the third century responded with more systematic persecutions, but their schemes failed to work. The last great persecution was at the beginning of the fourth century, but by that time Christianity had become too strong to be eradicated by force.

In the fourth century, Christianity prospered as never before after the Emperor Constantine (306–337) became the first Christian emperor. Although he was not baptized until the end of his life, in 313 Constantine issued the famous Edict of Milan, officially tolerating the existence of Christianity. Under Theodosius "the Great" (378–395), it was made the official religion of the Roman Empire. Christianity had triumphed.

The Decline and Fall of the Roman Empire

In the course of the third century, the Roman Empire came near to collapse. Military monarchy under the Severan rulers (193–235), which restored order after a series of civil wars, was followed by military anarchy. For a period of almost fifty years, from 235 to 284, the Roman Empire was mired in the chaos of continual civil war. The imperial throne was occupied by anyone who had the military strength to seize it. In these almost fifty years, there were twenty-two emperors, only two of whom did not meet a violent death. At the same time, the empire was beset by a series of invasions, no doubt exacerbated by the civil wars. In the east, the Sassanid Persians made inroads into Roman territory. Germanic tribes also poured into the empire. The Goths overran the Balkans and moved into Greece and Asia Minor. The Franks advanced into Gaul and Spain. Not until the reign of Aurelian (270–275) were most of the boundaries restored.

Invasions, civil wars, and plague came close to causing an economic collapse of the Roman Empire in the third century. The population declined drastically, possibly by as much as one-third. There was a noticeable decline in trade and small industry. The labor shortage created by the plague affected both military recruiting and the economy. Farm production deteriorated significantly. Fields were ravaged by Germanic tribes, but even more often by the defending Roman armies. Provincial governors seemed powerless to stop these depredations, and some even joined in the extortion. The monetary system began to show signs of collapse as a result of debased coinage and the beginnings of serious inflation.

Armies were needed more than ever, but financial strains made it difficult to pay and enlist the necessary soldiers. Whereas in the second century the Roman army had been recruited among the inhabitants of frontier provinces, by the mid-third century, the state had to rely on hiring Germans to fight under Roman commanders. These soldiers had no understanding of Roman traditions and no real attachment to either the empire or the emperors.

The Reforms of Diocletian and Constantine

At the end of the third and beginning of the fourth centuries, the Roman Empire gained a new lease on life through the efforts of two strong emperors, Diocletian and Constantine, who restored order and stability. The Roman Empire was virtually transformed into a new state: the so-called Late Empire, which included a new governmental structure, a rigid economic and social system, and a new state religion—Christianity.

Believing that the empire had grown too large for a single ruler, Diocletian (284–305) divided it into four administrative units. Despite the appearance of four-man rule, however, Diocletian's military seniority enabled him to claim a higher status and hold the ultimate authority. Constantine (306–337) continued and even expanded the autocratic policies of Diocletian. Both rulers greatly strengthened and enlarged the administrative bureaucracies of the Roman Empire. Henceforth, civil and military bureaucracies were sharply separated. Each contained a hierarchy of officials who exercised control at the various levels. The emperor presided over both hierarchies of officials and served as the only link between them. New titles of nobility—such as *illustres* ("illustrious ones") and *illustrissimi* ("the most illustrious ones")—were instituted to dignify the holders of positions in the civil and military bureaucracies.

Additional military reforms were also inaugurated. The army was enlarged to 500,000 men, including German units. Mobile units were established that could be quickly moved to support frontier troops where the borders were threatened.

Constantine's biggest project was the construction of a new capital city in the east on the site of the Greek city of Byzantium on the shores of the Bosporus. Eventually renamed Constantinople (modern Istanbul), it was developed for defensive reasons: it had an excellent strategic location. Calling it his "New Rome," Constantine endowed the city with a forum, large palaces, and a vast amphitheater.

The political and military reforms of Diocletian and Constantine greatly enlarged two institutions—the army and civil service—that drained most of the public funds. Though more revenues were needed to pay for the army and bureaucracy, the population was not growing, so the tax base could not be expanded. Diocletian and Constantine devised new economic and social policies to deal with these financial burdens, but like their political policies, these measures were all based on coercion and loss of individual freedom. To fight inflation, Diocletian resorted to issuing a price edict in 301 that established maximum wages and prices for the entire empire, but despite severe penalties, it was unenforceable and failed to work.

Coercion also came to form the underlying basis for numerous occupations in the Late Roman Empire. In order to ensure the tax base and keep the empire going despite the shortage of labor, the emperors issued edicts that forced people to remain in their designated vocations. Hence, basic jobs, such as bakers and shippers, became hereditary. Free tenant farmers continued to decline and soon found themselves bound to the land by large landowners who

MAP 5.5 Divisions of the Restored Roman Empire

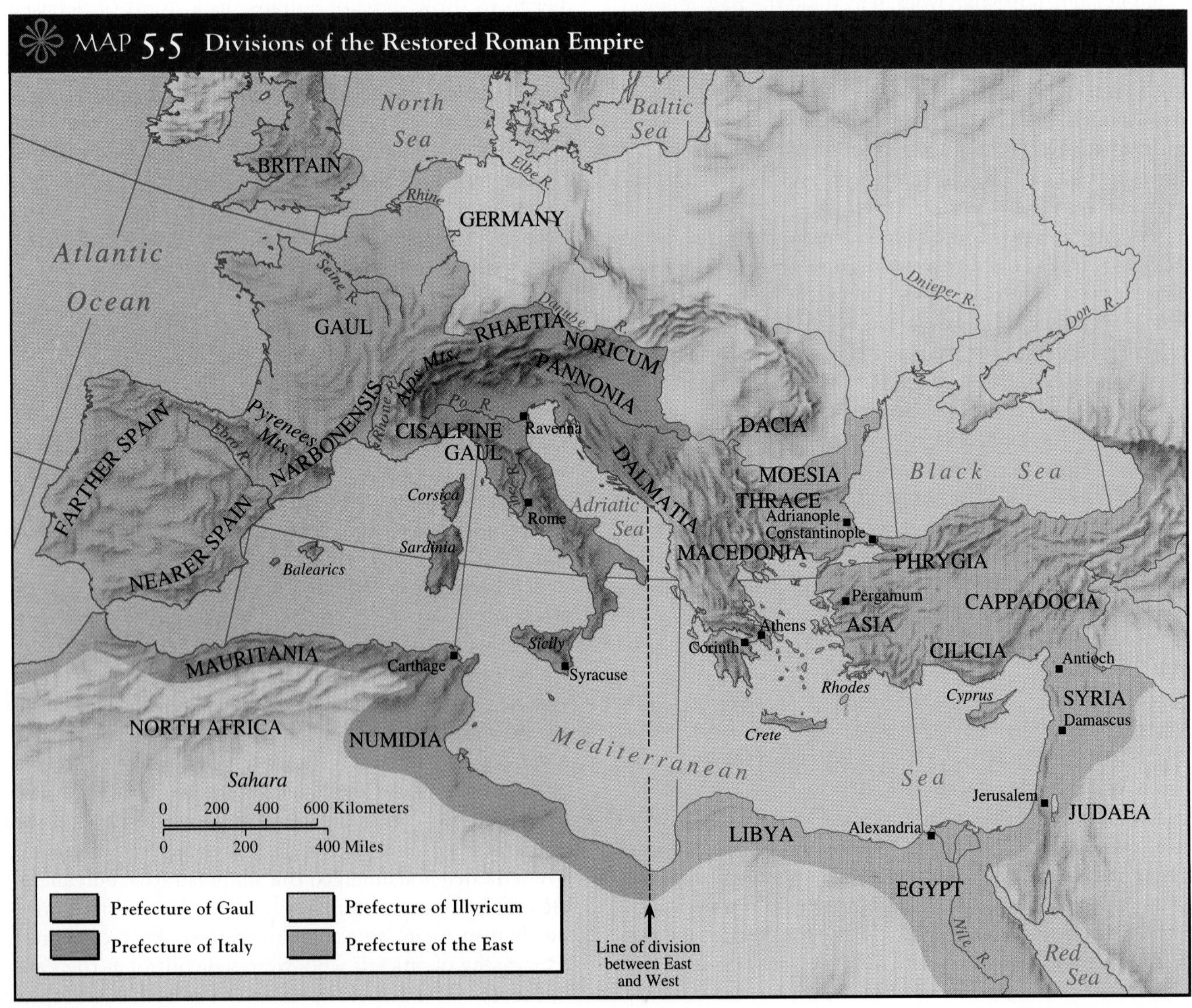

took advantage of depressed agricultural conditions to enlarge their landed estates.

In general, the economic and social policies of Diocletian and Constantine were based on an unprecedented degree of control and coercion. Though temporarily successful, such authoritarian policies in the long run stifled the very vitality the Late Empire needed to revive its sagging fortunes.

The Fall of the Western Roman Empire

The restored empire of Diocletian and Constantine limped along for more than a century. After Constantine, the empire continued to divide into western and eastern parts. The west came under increasing pressure from the invading Germanic tribes. The major breakthrough into the Roman Empire came in the second half of the fourth century. Ferocious warriors from Asia, known as Huns (who may have been related to the Xiongnu, the invaders of the Han Chinese Empire), moved into eastern Europe and put pressure on the Germanic Visigoths, who in turn moved south and west, crossed the Danube into Roman territory, and settled down as Roman allies. But the Visigoths soon revolted, and the Roman attempt to stop them at Adrianople in 378 led to a crushing defeat.

Increasing numbers of Germans now crossed the frontiers. In 410, the Visigoths sacked Rome. Vandals poured into southern Spain and Africa, Visigoths into Spain and Gaul. The Vandals crossed into Italy from North Africa and sacked Rome in 455. Twenty-one years later, the western emperor Romulus Augustulus (475–476) was deposed, and a series of Germanic kingdoms replaced the Roman Empire in the west while an Eastern Roman Empire continued with its center at Constantinople.

The end of the Roman Empire has given rise to numerous theories that attempt to provide a single, all-encompassing reason for the "decline and fall of the Roman Empire." These include the following: Christianity's emphasis on a spiritual kingdom undermined Roman military virtues and patriotism; traditional Roman values declined as non-Italians gained prominence in the empire; lead poisoning through leaden water pipes and cups caused a mental decline; plague decimated the population; Rome failed to advance technologically because of slavery; and Rome was unable to achieve a workable political system. There may be an element of truth in each of these theories, but each of them has also been challenged. History is an intricate web of relationships, causes, and effects. No single explanation will ever suffice to explain historical events. One thing is clear. Weakened by a shortage of manpower, the Roman army in the west was simply not able to fend off the hordes of people invading Italy and Gaul. In contrast, the Eastern Roman Empire, which would survive for another thousand years, remained largely free from invasion.

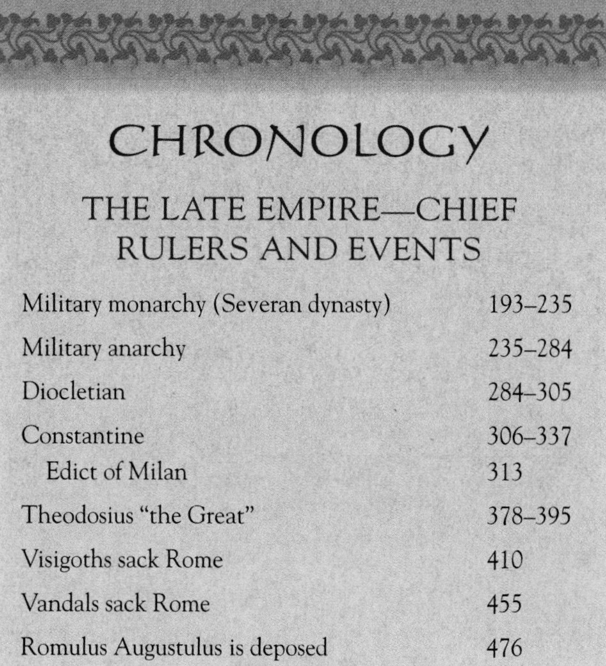

CHRONOLOGY

THE LATE EMPIRE—CHIEF RULERS AND EVENTS

Military monarchy (Severan dynasty)	193–235
Military anarchy	235–284
Diocletian	284–305
Constantine	306–337
Edict of Milan	313
Theodosius "the Great"	378–395
Visigoths sack Rome	410
Vandals sack Rome	455
Romulus Augustulus is deposed	476

CONCLUSION

Between 509 and 264 B.C.E., the Latin-speaking community of Rome expanded and brought about the union of almost all of Italy under its control. Even more dramatically, between 264 and 133 B.C.E., Rome expanded to the west and east and became master of the Mediterranean Sea and its surrounding territories, creating one of the largest empires in antiquity. Rome's republican institutions proved inadequate for the task of ruling an empire, however, and after a series of bloody civil wars, Octavian created a new order that would rule the empire in an orderly fashion. His successors established a Roman imperial state.

Like the Han Chinese Empire, however, the Roman Empire was eventually faced with serious problems. Both empires suffered from overexpansion, and both fortified their long borders with walls, forts, and military garrisons to guard against invasions of nomadic peoples. Both empires were eventually overcome by these peoples: the Han dynasty was weakened by the incursions of the Xiongnu, and the western Roman Empire eventually collapsed in the face of invasions by the Germanic peoples. Nevertheless, a significant difference between these two contemporary empires remained. Although the Han dynasty collapsed, the Chinese imperial tradition as well as the class structure and set of values that sustained it continued, and the Chinese Empire, under new dynasties, continued well into the twentieth century as a single political entity.

The Roman Empire, on the other hand, collapsed and lived on only as an idea, although Roman achievements were bequeathed to the future. The Romance languages of today (French, Italian, Spanish, Portuguese, and Romanian) are based on Latin. Western practices of impartial justice and trial by jury owe much to Roman law. As great builders, the Romans left monuments to their skills throughout Europe, some of which, such as aqueducts and roads, are still in use today. Aspects of Roman administrative practices survived in the Western world for centuries. The Romans also preserved the intellectual heritage of the Greco-Roman world of antiquity. Nevertheless, while many aspects of the Roman world would continue, the heirs of Rome created new civilizations—European, Islamic, and Byzantine—that would carry on yet another stage in the development of human society.

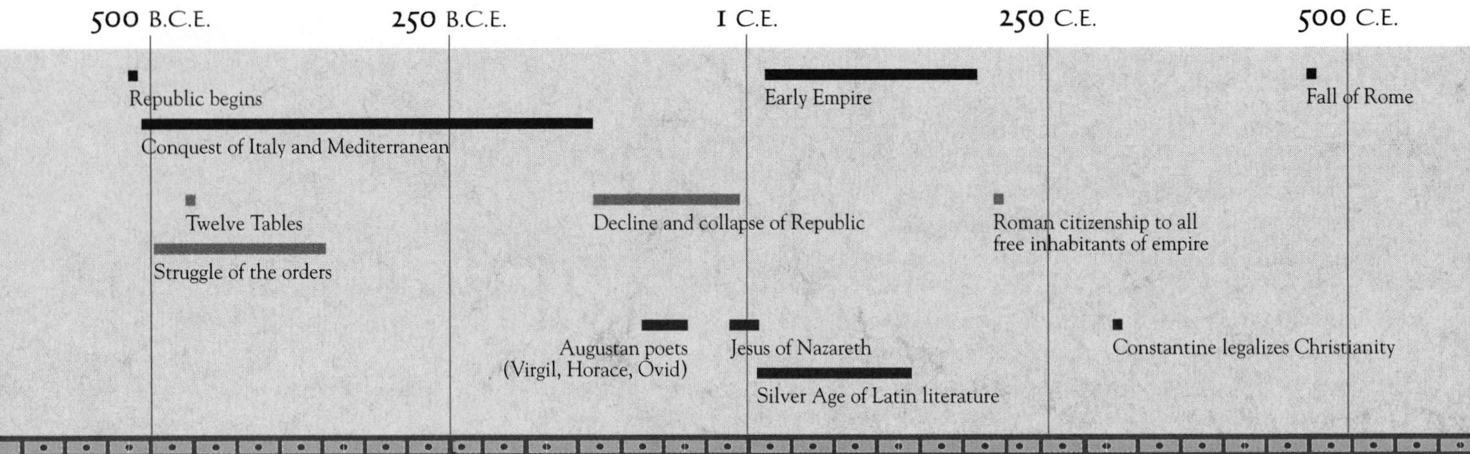

Chapter Notes

1. Florus, *Epitome of Roman History*, trans. E. S. Forster (Cambridge, Mass., 1961), IV, ii, 149–51.
2. Tacitus, *The Annals of Imperial Rome*, trans. Michael Grant (Harmondsworth, 1956), p. 31.
3. Tacitus, *The Histories*, trans. Kenneth Wellesley (Harmondsworth, 1964), p. 23.
4. *The Poems of Catullus*, trans. Charles Martin (Baltimore, 1990), p. 109.
5. Virgil, *The Aeneid*, trans. C. Day Lewis (Garden City, N.Y., 1952), p. 154.
6. Horace, *Satires*, in *The Complete Works of Horace*, trans. Lord Dunsany and Michael Oakley (London, 1961), 1.1, p. 139.
7. Ibid., 1.3, p. 151.
8. Livy, *The Early History of Rome*, trans. Aubrey de Selincourt (Harmondsworth, 1960), p. 18.
9. Seneca, *Letters from a Stoic*, trans. Robin Campbell (Harmondsworth, 1969), Letter 5.
10. Tacitus, *The Annals of Imperial Rome*, p. 147.
11. Juvenal, *The Sixteen Satires*, trans. Peter Green (Harmondsworth, 1967), Satire 10, p. 207.
12. Tacitus, *A Dialogue on Oratory*, in *The Complete Works of Tacitus*, trans. Alfred Church and William Brodribb (New York, 1942), 29, p. 758.
13. Quoted in Chester Starr, *Past and Future in Ancient History* (Lanham, Md., 1987), pp. 38–39.
14. Matthew 5: 17.
15. Matthew 7: 12.
16. Mark 12: 30–31.
17. John 18: 36.
18. Colossians 3: 10–11.

Suggested Readings

For a general account of Roman history, see J. Boardman, J. Griffin, and O. Murray, eds., *The Oxford History of the Roman World* (Oxford, 1991). A brief but excellent guide to recent trends in scholarship can be found in C. Starr, *Past and Future in Ancient History* (Lanham, Md., 1987), pp. 33–57. A standard one-volume reference on the Roman Republic is M. Cary and H. H. Scullard, *A History of Rome Down to the Reign of Constantine*, 3d ed. (New York, 1975).

Good surveys of the Roman Republic include M. H. Crawford, *The Roman Republic*, 2d ed. (Cambridge, Mass., 1993); H. H. Scullard, *History of the Roman World, 753–146 B.C.*, 4th ed. (London, 1978); M. Le Glay, J.-L. Voisin, and Y. Le Bohec, *A History of Rome*, trans. A. Nevill (Oxford, 1996); and A. Kamm, *The Romans* (London, 1995). For a beautifully illustrated survey, see J. F. Drinkwater and A. Drummond, *The World of the Romans* (New

York, 1993). The history of early Rome is well covered in T. J. Cornell, *The Beginnings of Rome: Italy and Rome from the Bronze Age to the Punic Wars (c. 1000–264 B.C.)* (London, 1995).

Aspects of the Roman political structure can be studied in R. E. Mitchell, *Patricians and Plebeians: The Origin of the Roman State* (Ithaca, N.Y., 1990). Changes in Rome's economic life can be examined in A. H. M. Jones, *The Roman Economy* (Oxford, 1974). On the Roman social structure, see G. Alfoeldy, *The Social History of Rome* (London, 1985).

Accounts of Rome's expansion in the Mediterranean world are provided by J.-M. David, *The Roman Conquest of Italy*, trans. A. Nevill (Oxford, 1996), and R. M. Errington, *The Dawn of Empire: Rome's Rise to World Power* (Ithaca, N.Y., 1971). Especially important works on Roman expansion and imperialism include W. V. Harris, *War and Imperialism in Republican Rome* (Oxford, 1979), and E. Badian, *Roman Imperialism in the Late Republic* (Oxford, 1968).

An excellent account of basic problems in the late Republic can be found in M. Beard and M. H. Crawford, *Rome in the Late Republic* (London, 1984). The classic work on the fall of the Republic is R. Syme, *The Roman Revolution* (Oxford, 1960). Also valuable is D. Shotter, *The Fall of the Roman Republic* (London, 1994).

Good surveys of the Early Roman Empire include P. Garnsey and R. Saller, *The Roman Empire: Economy, Society and Culture* (London, 1987); C. Wells, *The Roman Empire*, 2d ed. (London, 1992); and J. Wacher, *The Roman Empire* (London, 1987). A fundamental work on Roman government and the role of the emperor is F. Millar, *The Emperor in the Roman World* (London, 1977).

The Roman army is examined in G. Webster, *The Roman Imperial Army of the First and Second Centuries A.D.*, 2d ed. (London, 1979), and J. B. Campbell, *The Emperor and the Roman Army* (Oxford, 1984). On the provinces and Roman foreign policy, see E. N. Luttwak, *The Grand Strategy of the Roman Empire from the First Century A.D. to the Third* (Baltimore, 1976), and B. Isaac, *The Limits of Empire: The Roman Empire in the East* (Oxford, 1990).

A good survey of Roman literature can be found in R. M. Ogilvie, *Roman Literature and Society* (Harmondsworth, 1980). On Roman art and architecture, see R. Ling, *Roman Painting* (New York, 1991); D. E. Kleiner, *Roman Sculpture* (New Haven, Conn., 1992); and M. Wheeler, *Roman Art and Architecture* (London, 1964). General studies of daily life in Rome include F. Dupont, *Daily Life in Ancient Rome* (Oxford, 1994), and J. P. V. D. Balsdon, *Life and Leisure in Ancient Rome* (London, 1969). On the city of Rome, see O. F. Robinson, *Ancient Rome: City Planning and Administration* (New York, 1992). On the Roman family, see S. Dixon, *The Roman Family* (Baltimore, 1992). Roman women are examined in S. Pomeroy, *Goddesses, Whores, Wives, and Slaves: Women in Classical Antiquity* (New York, 1976), pp. 149–226, and R. Baumann, *Women and Politics in Ancient Rome* (New York, 1995). On slavery, see K. R. Bradley, *Slavery and Rebellion in the Roman World* (Bloomington, Ind., 1989). On the gladiators, see T. Wiedemann, *Emperors and Gladiators* (New York, 1992).

For a general introduction to early Christianity, see J. Court and K. Court, *The New Testament World* (Cambridge, 1990). Useful works on early Christianity include W. A. Meeks, *The First Urban Christians* (New Haven, Conn., 1983); W. H. C. Frend, *The Rise of Christianity* (Philadelphia, 1984); and R. MacMullen, *Christianizing the Roman Empire* (New Haven, Conn., 1984). On Christian women, see D. M. Scholer, ed., *Women in Early Christianity* (New York, 1993), and R. Kraemer, *Her Share of the Blessings: Women's Religion Among the Pagans, Jews and Christians in the Graeco-Roman World* (Oxford, 1995).

The classic work on the "decline and fall" of the Roman Empire is Edward Gibbon, *Decline and Fall of the Roman Empire*, J. B. Bury edition (London, 1909–14). An excellent survey is P. Brown, *The World of Late Antiquity* (London, 1971). Also valuable are A. Cameron, *The Later Roman Empire* (Cambridge, Mass., 1993), and R. MacMullen, *Corruption and the Decline of Rome* (New Haven, Conn., 1988). On the fourth century, see T. D. Barnes, *The New Empire of Diocletian and Constantine* (Cambridge, Mass., 1982), and M. Grant, *Constantine the Great: The Man and His Times* (New York, 1993). Recent studies analyzing the aristocratic circles, the barbarian invasions, and the military problem include E. A. Thompson, *Romans and Barbarians* (Madison, Wis., 1982), and A. Ferrill, *The Fall of the Roman Empire: The Military Explanation* (London, 1986).

For additional reading, go to InfoTrac College Edition, your online research library at http://web1.infotrac-college.com

Enter the search terms "Rome history" using Keywords.

Enter the search terms "Roman republic" using Keywords.

Enter the search terms "Julius and Caesar" using Keywords.

Enter the search terms "Roman empire" using Keywords.

Enter the search terms "Roman law" using the Subject Guide.

REFLECTION

THE FIRST CIVILIZATIONS AND THE RISE OF EMPIRES

In Part I of this book, we have focused our attention on the emergence of the first civilizations during the ancient era. As we have seen, each civilization developed somewhat independently of the others, and we have therefore treated them as distinct entities, each with its own pattern of development. But clearly, these civilizations encountered a number of similar experiences, and contacts between the civilizations and with other nearby peoples sometimes played a significant role in their development. Let us now retrace our steps and evaluate the process in a comparative perspective. How and why did these first civilizations arise? What role did cross-cultural contacts play in their development? What was the nature of the relationship between these permanent settlements and nonagricultural peoples living elsewhere in the world, and how did each influence the other? Finally, what brought about the demise of these early civilizations, and what legacy did they leave for their successors in the region?

How and why the first civilizations arose has long been a matter of debate. In his classic work entitled *The Study of History*, historian Arnold Toynbee explained the origins of social change through the concept of challenge and response. Challenges, posed either by the environment or by actions taken by other peoples, compel human beings to make efforts that sometimes result in technological innovations that help to overcome the challenge. The world historian William McNeill carries the idea further, suggesting that encounters with other societies, especially stronger ones, are the primary factor provoking innovation and thus "the principal drive wheel of historic change."

Such theories are undoubtedly helpful to historians as general explanations for the process of social change, but we need to be more specific if we wish to find an explanation for the rise of the first civilizations. Why did some societies transform themselves into civilizations, while others did not? What factors determined how they responded? The evidence from the examples discussed here suggests that an important stimulus behind the rise of all of these early civilizations was the development of settled agriculture, which unleashed a series of changes in the organization of human communities that culminated in the rise of large ancient empires.

The exact time and place that crops were first cultivated successfully is uncertain. Many prehistorians believe that farming may have emerged independently in several different areas of the world when small human communities, driven by increasing population and a decline in available food resources, began to plant seeds in the ground in an effort to guarantee their survival. The first farmers, who may have lived as long as 10,000 years ago, undoubtedly used simple techniques and still relied primarily on other forms of food production, such as hunting, foraging, or pastoralism. The real breakthrough took place when farmers began to cultivate crops along the flood plains of river systems. The advantage was that crops grown in such areas were not as dependent on rainfall and therefore produced a more reliable harvest. An additional benefit was that the sediment carried by the river waters deposited nutrients in the soil, thus enabling the farmer to cultivate a single plot of ground for many years without moving to a new location. Thus, the first truly sedentary (that is, nonmigratory) societies were born. As time went on, such communities gradually learned how to direct the flow of water to enhance the productive capacity of the land, while the introduction of the iron plow eventually led to the cultivation of heavy soils not previously susceptible to agriculture.

The spread of this river valley agriculture in various parts of Asia and Africa was the decisive factor in the rise of the first civilizations. The increase in food production in these regions led to a significant growth in population, while efforts to control the flow of water to maximize the irrigation of cultivated areas and to protect the local inhabitants from hostile forces outside the community provoked the first steps toward cooperative activities on a large scale. The need to oversee the entire process brought about the emergence of an elite that was eventually transformed into a government.

As we have seen, the first clear steps in the rise of the first civilizations took place in the fourth and third millennia B.C.E. in Mesopotamia, northern Africa, India, and China. How the first governments took shape in these areas is not certain, but anthropologists studying the evolution of human communities in various parts of the world have discovered that one common stage in the process is the emergence of what are called "big men" within a single village or a collection of villages. By means of their military prowess, dominant personalities, or political acumen, these people gradually emerge as the leaders of that community. In time, the "big men" begin to assume formal symbols of authority and to pass on that authority to others within their own family. As the communities continue to grow in size and material wealth, the "big men" assume hereditary status, and their allies and family members are transformed into a hereditary monarchy.

The appearance of these sedentary societies has a major impact on the social organizations, religious beliefs, and way of life of the peoples living within their boundaries. With the increase in population and the development of centralized authority came the emergence of cities. While some of these urban centers were identified with a particular economic function, such as proximity to gold or iron deposits or a strategic location on a major trade route, others served primarily as administrative centers or the site of temples for the official cult or other ritual observances. Within these cities, new forms of livelihood appeared to satisfy the growing need for social services and consumer goods. Some people became artisans or merchants, while others became warriors, scholars, or priests. In some cases, the physical divisions within the first cities reflected the strict hierarchical character of the society as a whole, with a royal palace surrounded by an imposing wall and separate from the remainder of the urban population. In other instances, as in the Indus River Valley, the cities lacked a royal precinct and the ostentatious palaces that marked their contemporaries elsewhere. While the layout of many ancient cities followed the natural contours of the land or were built on ancient transportation routes, others, such as was the case in China and India, were sometimes laid out on a grid pattern that was almost modern in its composition.

The quality of housing in the new cities varied according to location and the status of the owner. In general,

RULERS AND GODS

All of the world's earliest civilizations believed that there was a close relationship between rulers and gods. In Egypt, pharaohs were considered gods whose role was to maintain the order and harmony of the universe in their own kingdom. In the words of an Egyptian hymn, "What is the king of Upper and Lower Egypt? He is a god by whose dealings one lives, the father and mother of all men, alone by himself, without an equal." In Mesopotamia, India, and China, rulers were thought to rule with divine assistance. Kings were often seen as rulers who derived their power from the gods and who were the agents or representatives of the gods. As one person said in a petition to his king, "You in your judgment, you are the son of Anu [god of the sky in ancient Mesopotamia]; your commands, like the word of a god, cannot be reversed; your words, like rain pouring down from heaven, are without number." In ancient India, rulers claimed to be representatives of the gods because they were descended from Manu, the first man who had been made a king by Brahman, the chief god. Many Romans certainly believed that their success in creating an empire was a visible sign of divine favor. As the Roman statesman Cicero stated, "We have overcome all the nations of the world, because we have realized that the world is directed and governed by the gods."

Their supposed connection to the gods also caused rulers to seek divine aid in the affairs of the world. This led to the art of divination, or an organized method to discover the intentions of the gods. In Mesopotamian and Roman society, one form of divination involved the examination of the livers of sacrificed animals; features seen in the livers were interpreted to foretell events to come. Another form of divination for Mesopotamian and Roman rulers was based on a careful observation of natural phenomena; the flights of birds or the movements of planetary bodies in the skies, for example, could also be interpreted to determine the will of the gods. The Chinese used oracle bones to receive advice from supernatural forces that were beyond the power of human beings. Questions to the gods were scratched on turtle shells or animal bones, which were then exposed to fire. Shamans then interpreted the meaning of the resulting cracks on the surface of the shells or bones as messages from supernatural forces. The Greeks divined the will of the gods by use of the oracle, a sacred shrine dedicated to a god or goddess who revealed the future in response to a question.

Underlying all of these divinatory practices was a belief in a supernatural universe, that is, a world in which divine forces were in charge and in which humans were dependent for their own well-being on those divine forces. It was not until the Scientific Revolution of the modern world that many people began to believe in a natural world that was not governed by spiritual forces.

VISHNU. Brahma the Creator, Siva the Destroyer, and Vishnu the Preserver are the three chief Hindu gods of India. Vishnu is known as the Preserver because he mediates between Brahma and Siva and is thus responsible for maintaining the stability of the universe.

THE USE OF METALS

Sometime around 6000 B.C.E., people in western Asia discovered the use of metals. They soon realized the advantage in using metal rather than stone to make both tools and weapons. Metal could be shaped more exactly, allowing artisans to make more refined tools and weapons with sharp edges and more precise shapes. Copper, silver, and gold, which were commonly found in their elemental form, were the first metals to be used. These were relatively soft and could be more easily pounded into different shapes. But an important step was taken when people discovered that a rock that contained metal could be heated to liquefy the metal (a process called smelting). The liquid metal could then be poured into molds of clay or stone to make precisely shaped tools and weapons.

Copper was the first metal to be used in making tools. The first known copper smelting furnace, dated to 3800 B.C.E., was found in the Sinai. At about the same time, however, artisans in Southeast Asia discovered that tin could be added to copper to make bronze. By 3000 B.C.E., artisans in West Asia were also making bronze. Bronze has a lower melting point that makes it easier to cast, but it is also a harder metal than copper and corrodes less. By 1400 B.C.E., the Chinese were making bronze decorative objects as well as battle-axes and helmets. The widespread use of bronze has led historians to speak of a Bronze Age from around 3000 to 1200 B.C.E., although this is a somewhat misleading term, since many people continued to use stone tools and weapons even after bronze became available.

But there were limitations in the use of bronze. Tin was not as available as copper, which made bronze tools and weapons expensive. After 1200 B.C.E., bronze was increasingly replaced by iron, which was probably first used around 1500 B.C.E. in western Asia, where the Hittites made use of it to develop new weapons. Between 1500 and 600 B.C.E., iron making spread across Europe, North Africa, and Asia. Bronze continued to be used, but mostly for jewelry and other domestic purposes. Iron was used to make tools and weapons with sharper edges. Because wrought-iron weapons were cheaper than bronze ones, larger numbers of warriors could be armed, and wars could be fought on a larger scale.

Iron was handled differently than bronze: it was heated until it could be beaten into a desired shape. Each hammering produced increased strength for the metal. This wrought iron, as it was called, was typical of iron manufacturing in the West until the late Middle Ages. In China, however, the use of heat-resistant clay in the walls of their blast furnaces raised temperatures to 1,537 degrees Celsius, enabling artisans already in the fourth century B.C.E. to liquefy iron so that it too could be cast in a mold. Europeans would not develop such blast furnaces until the fifteenth century C.E.

BRONZE AXE HEAD. This axe head was made around 2000 B.C.E. by pouring liquid metal into an axe-shaped mold of clay or stone. Artisans would then polish the surface of the axe to produce a sharp cutting edge.

however, the urban population probably lived better than their less affluent contemporaries in the countryside. Many houses had plumbing facilities, sophisticated heating systems, and a variety of utensils and luxury articles made of wood, glass, metal, or ceramics. The expansion of trade permitted many urban residents to partake of a varied diet and clothing to fit the changing seasons.

Although the emergence of the first civilizations led to the appearance of major cities, the vast majority of the population were undoubtedly peasants or slaves working on the lands of the wealthy. In general, rural peoples were less affected by the change than were their urban counterparts. Most continued to live in simple mud-and-thatch huts and lacked the amenities that were increasingly available to the more affluent residents inside the city walls. Peasants in most societies still faced severe legal restrictions on their freedom of action and movement, and slavery was still commonly practiced in virtually all ancient societies.

Within these civilizations, the nature of social organization and relationship also began to change. As the concept of private property spread, people were less likely to live in large kinship groups, and the concept of the nuclear family became increasingly prevalent. Gender roles increasingly came to be differentiated, with men working in the fields or at various specialized occupations and women remaining in the home. Wives were less likely to be viewed as partners and more often as under the control of their husbands.

With the increase in the availability of food, people were now living longer. At the same time, increasingly crowded conditions in the emerging cities led to a higher incidence of disease. Some reached epidemic proportions and wiped out a high percentage of the population. As the danger of illness increased, families began having larger numbers of children to protect themselves in their old age. As a result of these countervailing trends, it is estimated that the overall population of the world may have increased by about four times between the rise of the Sumerian population in about 3500 B.C.E. and the end of the second millennium B.C.E.

These new civilizations were also the scene of significant religious and cultural developments. All of them gave birth to new religions as a means of explaining the functioning of the forces of nature. In place of a belief in a multitude of deities representing the forces of nature, new religious systems based on the existence of a single transcendent god who presided over a rational universal order began to appear. The approval of gods was deemed critical to a community's chances of success, and a professional class of priests emerged to govern relations with the divine world. Temples were built as places for worship or sacrifice, and painting and sculpture were invented as ritualistic means of portraying the deities or other forces in the natural world.

Writing was an important development in the evolution of these new civilizations. In China and Egypt, priests used writing to communicate with the gods. In Mesopotamia and the Indus River civilization, merchants relied on writing to maintain their accounts. Eventually all of these civilizations used writing as a primary means of communication as well as of creative expression.

The development of writing undoubtedly provided a major impetus to the emergence of sophisticated philosophical ideas concerning the relationship between the individual and society and the nature of the universe. Many historians have remarked on the possible significance of the fact that many of the major religious and philosophical systems of the ancient world emerged within a relatively limited period of two or three centuries in the middle of the first millennium B.C.E. By the end of the era, competition among the advocates of such systems had already become intense and sometimes led to conflict.

At first, the authority of these new civilizations was probably restricted to the area immediately adjacent to the river valleys where they had originated, and they had relatively little contact with peoples in the surrounding regions. But there is growing evidence that a pattern of regional trade had begun to develop in the Middle East, and probably in southern and eastern Asia as well, at a very early date. As the population increased, the volume of trade undoubtedly rose with it, and the new civilizations began to move outward to acquire new lands and access to needed resources. As they expanded, they began to encounter peoples along the periphery of their growing empires.

Not much evidence has survived to chronicle the nature of these first encounters, but it is likely that the results varied widely according to time and place. In some cases, the growing civilizations found it relatively easy to absorb isolated communities of agricultural or food-gathering peoples whom they encountered. Such was the case in southern China and in the southern part of the South Asian peninsula. But in other instances, notably among the nomadic or seminomadic peoples in Central and Northeast Asia, the problem was more complicated and often resulted in bitter and extended conflict.

To the sedentary societies, the peoples living along the frontier appeared hostile and warlike, motivated solely by desire for plunder and lacking in the basic attributes of civilization. Over the centuries, historians generally accepted that assessment. For many recent observers, however, the issue is not that clear-cut. For one thing, many pastoral societies, far from being primitive in character and isolated from the emerging centers of civilization, were as advanced in their own way as were the river valley societies that had sprung up in Eurasia and North Africa. While not possessing the supposed accoutrements of civilization such as a writing system, a complex bureaucracy, and clearly defined economic roles, such "frontier societies" were as well adapted to their own environmental circumstances as were their sedentary counterparts. Often people living on the periphery of civilizations were residing in areas of marginal economic utility and were forced to seek their livelihood through a mixture of farming, hunting, and animal husbandry. Agriculture may have been practiced in parts of Central Asia by the seventh millennium B.C.E., but when the climate throughout the region grew increasingly dry about 5,000 years ago, many of these communities were forced to adapt to changing circumstances by migrating to new areas, or by the domestication of animals, such as the horse. Some, like the Hyksos, the Israelites, and the Indo-European peoples, began to live by a combination of farming and herding. Others, like the Scythians and the Xiongnu, took up the purely nomadic life. Because of their wandering existence, such communities had not generally adopted the concept of statehood and operated as a fluid mixture of semiautonomous tribes, each under its own chieftain.

Contacts between these nomadic or seminomadic peoples and settled civilizations probably developed gradually over an extended period of time. Often the relationship, at least at the outset, was mutually beneficial, as each needed goods produced by the other. Nomadic peoples in Central Asia also served as an important conduit for goods and ideas between sedentary civilizations transporting goods over long distances as early as 3000 B.C.E. At first, the trade was carried by donkeys, but later the camel became the preferred means of transportation. Overland trade throughout Southwest Asia was already well established by the third and second millennia B.C.E. As we have seen, the silk route between China and the Mediterranean became an important avenue of long-distance commerce during the first millennium B.C.E.

Eventually, for reasons that are not always clear, the relationship between the settled peoples and the nomadic peoples became increasingly characterized by conflict. In some cases, the expanding sedentary empires attempted to drive the nomadic peoples off their land or to deprive them of access to trade with settled populations. In other cases, the increasing desiccation of the land may have deprived such peripheral peoples of their livelihood and forced them into desperate measures to find new means of survival. Sometimes the conflict may simply have been a consequence of the increasing aggressiveness of the nomadic peoples, as better techniques of warfare, such as the ability to fight on horseback, gave them new advantages over their rivals. Taking advantage of their military superiority, nomadic peoples often raided settled areas, terrorized the inhabitants, and pillaged their belongings.

Where conflict occurred, the governments of the sedentary civilizations used a variety of techniques to resolve the problem, including negotiations, conquest, or alliance with other pastoral peoples to isolate their primary tormentors. We have seen all of these techniques at work in China, where the Qin and the Han tried a combination of the carrot and the stick to pacify the frontier and bring these unruly peoples under control. The Romans did not hesitate to ally with one Germanic tribe to ward off another.

As it turned out, few of these techniques had any lasting effect. The relationship along the frontier was inherently unstable and in the end was disastrous for the settled empires, all of whom were eventually destroyed or seriously weakened as the result of invasion from beyond the frontier. The first to experience such a fate was the Harappan civilization in the Indus River valley, which may have been brought down at least in part as a result of the intrusion by Indo-European Aryan peoples along the northern frontier. Several hundred years later, the peoples of Mesopotamia fell at the hands of the Assyrians, who were in turn conquered by the Indo-European-speaking Persians. The empire of the pharaohs was conquered by the Hyksos, while the Roman Empire was brought to its knees as the result of constant pressure from the Germanic tribes to the north. Although the empire of the Han was not overthrown by the Xiongnu, pressure along the northern frontier contributed to the weakening of the dynasty, and after its collapse in the early third century B.C.E., the entire northern part of the country was overrun by peoples from beyond the Great Wall.

The nomadic peoples along the frontier understandably sparked fear among peoples in settled areas of the ancient world, but in broad historical terms, these nomadic peoples played an important role in the development of the first civilizations and the later evolution of humankind. Not only were they the crucial link in the growing trade relationship between the Mediterranean, the Middle East, and far-off China, but they were also the means of introducing new technology to sedentary societies. The Assyrians probably introduced the knowledge of iron to the settled peoples of Mesopotamia, while the Hyksos played a similar role for Egypt. Acquaintance with prolific new crops such as wheat and rice may have passed from one society to another by caravan. The pastoral peoples were the first to domesticate the horse and the camel, both destined ultimately to become a useful form of transportation for settled societies, and probably introduced the chariot to several sedentary civilizations throughout the Eurasian supercontinent. Although their unruly behavior undoubtedly posed a serious threat to settled societies, the nomadic peoples were a vital factor in the creation of the first global civilization in the Old World.

The increasing evidence that nomadic peoples outside the bounds of settled civilization played an important role in spreading technological advances throughout the inhabited world has brought about a significant change in the way historians view the classical empires. Until recently, national pride tended to reinforce the view that each of these civilizations evolved essentially on its own. In the last few years, however, there is a growing recognition that "cultural diffusion," as these exchanges of technology and ideas are labeled, played a major role in the emergence of the classical civilizations.

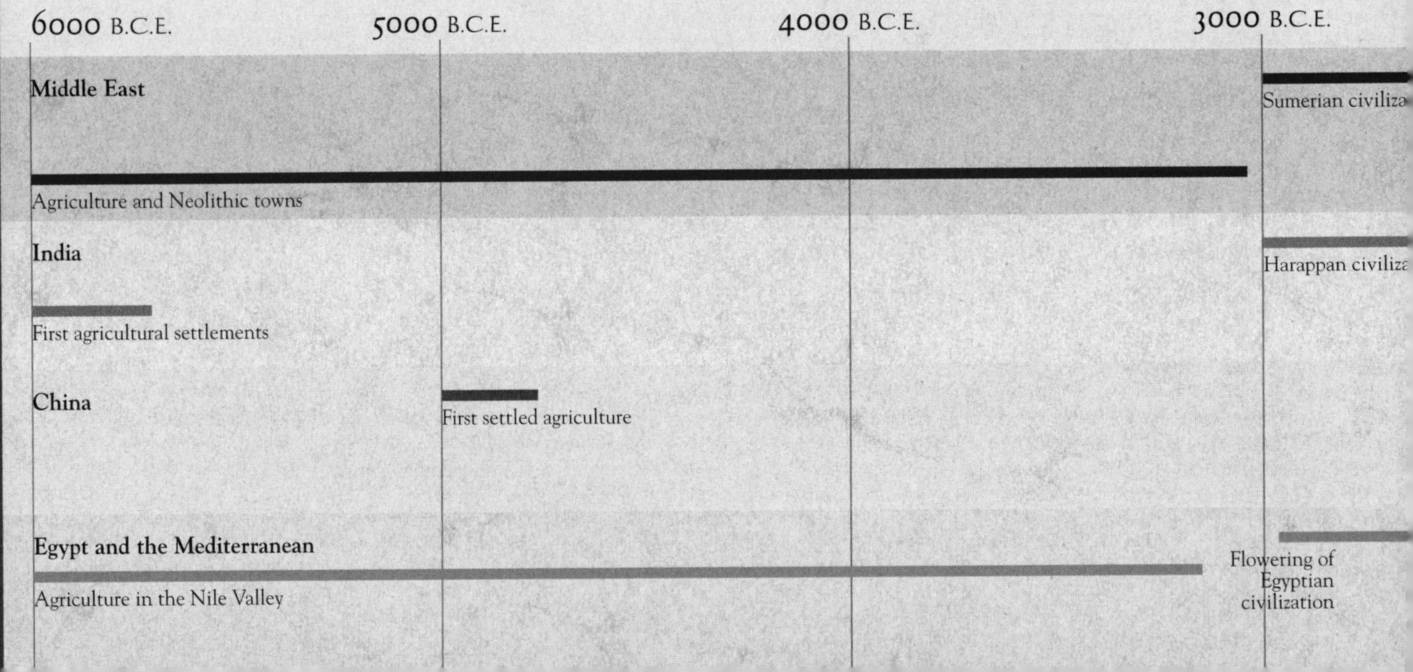

6000 B.C.E. | 5000 B.C.E. | 4000 B.C.E. | 3000 B.C.E.

Middle East

Agriculture and Neolithic towns

Sumerian civiliza

India

First agricultural settlements

Harappan civiliza

China

First settled agriculture

Egypt and the Mediterranean

Agriculture in the Nile Valley

Flowering of Egyptian civilization

At the same time, it is also increasingly evident that these early civilizations were brought to their knees not just by nomadic invasions, but by their own weaknesses, which made them increasingly vulnerable to attacks along the frontier. In the Roman Empire, bloated bureaucracies as well as excessive taxation to support them, an inability to achieve a workable political system, evident in frequent military struggles over succession to the throne, the decline of Roman military virtues and a reliance on noncitizen mercenaries, and population decline in part caused by plague all played a role in undermining Rome's ability to protect itself. In China, growing internal strains within the Han society more than depredations along the frontier caused the collapse of the Han empire.

Another possible factor in the decline and collapse of the first civilizations was the role of the environment. Although proof is still lacking, much evidence suggests that ecological changes caused severe difficulties for peoples in the ancient world. Floods or drought may have brought an end to the Harappan empire, while the infestation of salt water may have leached the nutrients from the soils of the Fertile Crescent. Imperial Rome may have suffered food shortages as a result of the desiccation of the wheat fields of northern Africa, while the flooding of mines in Spain may have brought about a shortage of silver and the debased coinage of the empire.

The fall of the ancient empires, of course, did not mark the end of civilization. Although the immediate consequences of the fall of Rome and the Han dynasty were a precipitous drop in world trade and a general decline of prosperity throughout the known world, new societies eventually rose on the ashes of the ancient empires. Although many were different in key respects from those they replaced, they still carried the legacy of their predecessors. In the meantime, the forces that had been unleashed in the civilizations of antiquity sent out strands of influence that were laying the basis for new societies elsewhere in the world: south of the Sahara in western and eastern Africa, where new societies were beginning to take shape; beyond the Alps in central Europe, where the Germanic peoples were in the process of forming a new society; in southeastern Asia, where the influence of India and China was beginning to help shape new societies among the trading and agricultural societies in the region; and across the Sea of Japan in the Japanese islands, where native rulers would import Chinese ideas to form a new civilization uniquely their own. In the meantime, new civilizations were on the verge of creation in the New World, across the oceans in the continents of North and South America. Isolated from contact with the Old World since their migration across the Bering Strait at the end of the Ice Age, the peoples of America were beginning to form civilizations of their own. It is to this new stage of human development, marked by a broadening of global contacts, that we will turn in Part II of this book.

SUGGESTED READINGS

For a beautifully illustrated introduction to the ancient world, see *Past Worlds: The Times Atlas of Archaeology* (Maplewood, N.J., 1988), written by an international group of scholars. A global view of important turning points in world history can be found in M. K. Matossian, *Shaping World History: Breakthroughs in Ecology, Technology, Science, and Politics* (Armonk, N.Y., 1997). For a general introduction to prehistory, see B. M. Fagan, *People of the Earth: An Introduction to World Prehistory*, 8th ed. (New York, 1995), and C. Gamble, *Timewalkers: The Prehistory of Global Colonization* (Cambridge, Mass., 1994). On the importance of the shift to agriculture, see A. W. Johnson and T. Earle, *The Evolution of Human Societies: From Foraging Group to Agrarian State* (Stanford, 1987), and R. S. McNeish, *Origins of Agriculture and Settled Life* (Norman, Okla., 1992). A global perspective on the emergence of civilization can be found in G. Burenhult, *Old World Civilizations: The Rise of Cities and States* (New York, 1994). On the use of metals, see R. Raymond, *Out of the Fiery Furnace: The Impact of Metals on the History of Mankind* (University Park, Pa., 1986).

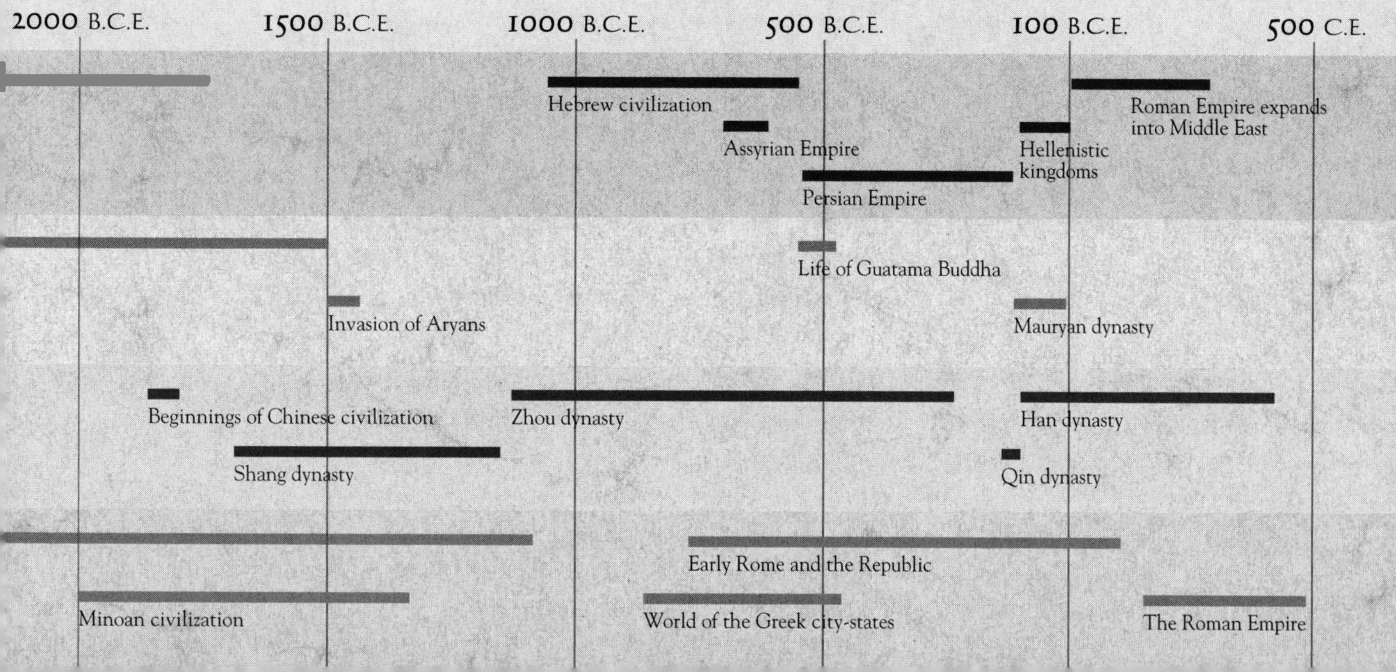

PART

II

NEW PATTERNS OF CIVILIZATION

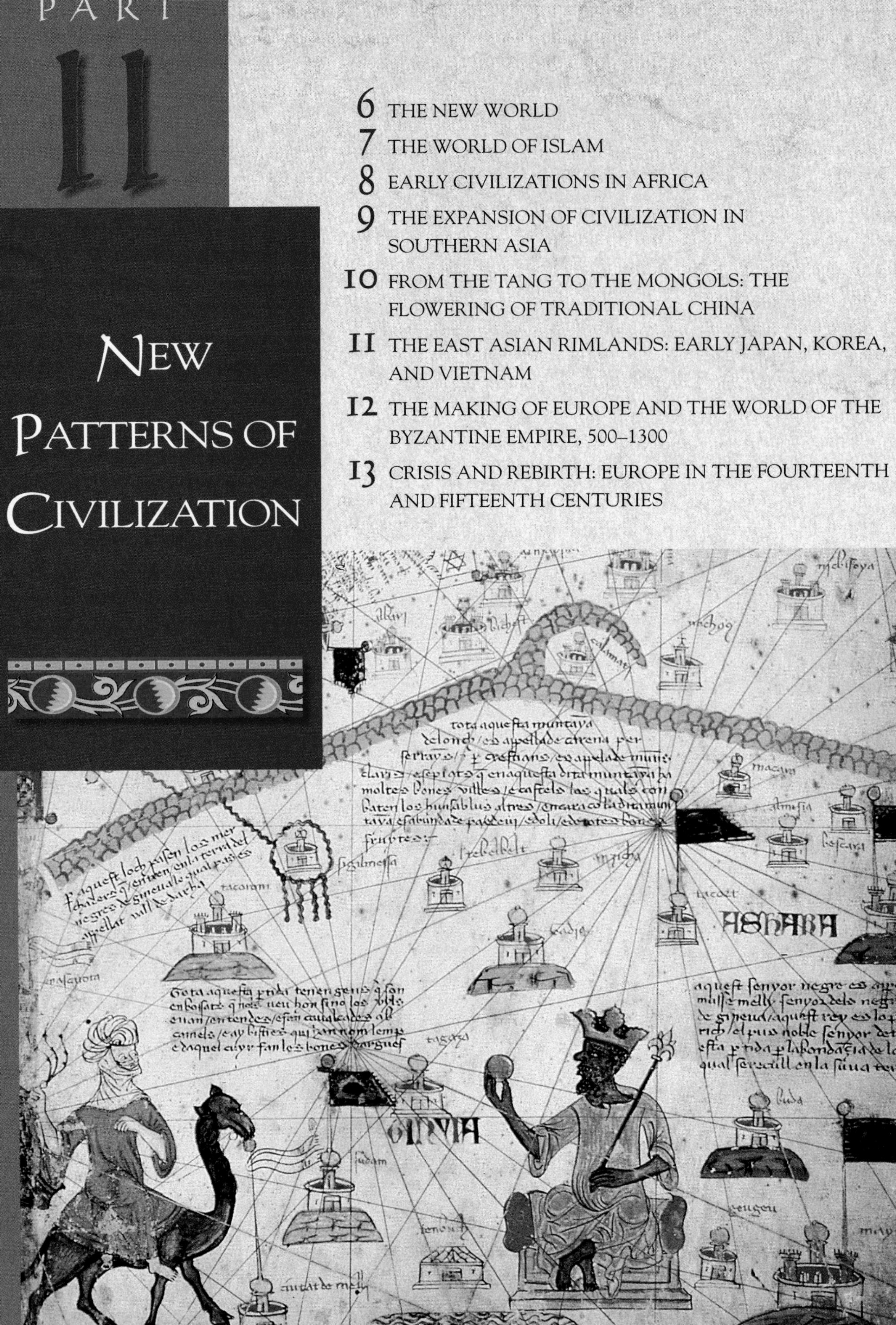

By the beginning of the first millennium C.E., the great states of the ancient world were mostly in a state of decline; some were even at the point of collapse. On the ruins of these ancient empires, new patterns of civilization began to take shape between 400 and 1500 C.E. In some cases, these new societies were built on the political and cultural foundations of their predecessors. The Tang dynasty in China and the Guptas in India both looked back to the ancient period to provide an ideological model for their own time. The Byzantine Empire carried on parts of the classical Greek tradition while also adopting the powerful creed of Christianity from the Roman Empire. In other cases, new states incorporated some elements of the former classical civilizations while embarking on markedly different directions, as in the new European civilization of the Middle Ages and the Arabic states in the Middle East.

In the meantime, complex societies were also beginning to appear in a number of other parts of the world—in Japan, in Southeast Asia, in sub-Saharan Africa, and across the Atlantic in the Americas. Except for the latter, which was developing in isolation, all of these civilizations were influenced to a greater or lesser degree by older or more powerful empires in the region, and all were increasingly linked by commercial and cultural contacts into the first "global civilization." At the same time, each was able to combine borrowed ideas with indigenous characteristics.

Like their classical predecessors, most of these new states obtained much of their wealth from agriculture. India, China, and medieval Europe were all predominantly agricultural societies. But what is most striking about the period is the growing importance of trade as a factor in national and global development. It was during the first millennium C.E. that the great trade routes of the traditional world—the Silk Road from China to the Middle East and then on to the Mediterranean, the caravan trade route across the Sahara, and the commercial network that stretched across the Indian Ocean—all reached their maturity.

The expansion of regional and global trade also led to the spread of ideas. It was commerce that brought Buddhism to China and Southeast Asia and Islam to sub-Saharan Africa and the Indonesian archipelago. At first the impact was felt primarily in the cities, but eventually it began to spread to the countryside. Kings and princes became converts to the new faiths and provided funds and other forms of patronage for their support.

The spread of religious and cultural ideas sometimes led to conflict. The popularity of Buddhism led eventually to its suppression in China. Tensions between the Islamic and Christian worlds were particularly strong and culminated in the Crusades and the Christian reconquest of Spain and Portugal. But often the assimilation of new religions and cultural ideas took place through a peaceful process, as with the spread of Islam into various areas of sub-Saharan and East Africa. Christianity, aided by the zeal of its missionary monks, was an active agent in converting new peoples in central and eastern Europe and transforming their cultures.

CHAPTER

6

THE NEW WORLD

CHAPTER OUTLINE

- THE FIRST AMERICANS
- EARLY CIVILIZATIONS IN CENTRAL AMERICA
- THE FIRST CIVILIZATIONS IN SOUTH AMERICA
- STATELESS SOCIETIES IN THE NEW WORLD
- CONCLUSION

FOCUS QUESTIONS

- Who were the first Americans, and when and how did they arrive?
- What were the main characteristics of the civilizations of the Maya, the Aztecs, and the Inca?
- What role did religion play in the civilizations of the New World?
- In what ways were the civilizations of the New World similar to the early civilizations of the Old World, and in what ways were they different?
- What were the main characteristics of the stateless societies in the Americas, and how did they differ from the civilizations that arose in Central America and the Andes?

In August 1519, five hundred Spanish soldiers of fortune left their anchorage near the modern city of Veracruz and began the long trek from the coast across the dusty plateau of Mexico to the capital of the Aztecs. At their head was Hernán Cortés, a Spanish conquistador who had just burned their ship to ensure that his followers would not launch a mutiny and sail back to Europe. In Tenochtitlán, the Aztec capital located in what is now Mexico City, Emperor Moctezuma received the news of the foreigners' presence and awaited their arrival with anticipation. According to Aztec legend, one of their ancestors, the godlike Quetzalcoatl, had left the area hundreds of years earlier, vowing to return one day to reclaim his heritage. Could this stranger with his band of men be Quetzalcoatl or his representative? When Cortés and his forces, now accompanied by a crowd of people they had encountered en route, reached the vicinity of Moctezuma's capital, the two men met face to face. With this encounter, the last barrier between the Old World and the previously unknown civilizations in the Western Hemisphere had been bridged, and a new era dawned.

The Aztecs were only the latest in a series of sophisticated societies that had sprung up at various locations in North and South America since human beings first crossed the Bering Strait several millennia earlier. Most of these early peoples, today often referred to as Amerindians, lived by hunting and fishing or by food gathering. But by the second and first millennia B.C.E., the first organized societies began to take root in Central and South America. One key area of development was on the plateau of central Mexico. Another was in the lowland regions along the Gulf of Mexico and extending into modern Guatemala. A third was in the central Andes Mountains, adjacent to the Pacific coast of South America. Others were just beginning to emerge in the river valleys and great plains of North America.

For the next two millennia, these societies developed in apparently total isolation from their counterparts elsewhere in the world. This lack of contact with other human beings deprived them of access to technological and cultural developments taking place in Africa, Asia, and Europe. They did not know of the wheel, for example, and their written languages were rudimentary compared to equivalents in complex civilizations in other parts of the globe. But in other respects, their cultural achievements were the equal of those realized elsewhere. When the first European explorers arrived in the New World at the turn of the sixteenth century, they described much that they observed in glowing terms.

Unfortunately for their own needs, one technological development that the peoples of America lacked was the knowledge of firearms. In a few short years, tiny bands of Spanish conquistadors were able to conquer the magnificent civilizations that we know today as the Aztecs, the Maya, and the Inca and turn them into ruins. Still, enough archaeological evidence remains to enable us to appreciate their impressive achievements.

The First Americans

When the first human beings arrived in the New World has long been a matter of dispute. In the first centuries following the voyages of Christopher Columbus, speculation centered on the possibility that the first settlers to reach the American continents had crossed the Atlantic Ocean. Were they the lost tribes of Israel? Were they Phoenician seafarers from Carthage? Or were they refugees from the legendary lost continent of Atlantis? In all cases, the assumption was that they were relatively recent arrivals.

By the mid-nineteenth century, under the influence of the new Darwinist concept of evolution, a new theory developed. It proposed that the peopling of America had taken place much earlier as a result of the migration of small communities across the Bering Strait. Recent evidence, including numerous physical similarities between some early Americans and contemporary peoples living in northeastern Asia, has confirmed this hypothesis. The debate on when the migrations began continues, however. Archaeologist Louis Leakey, one of the pioneers in the search for the origins of humankind in Africa, suggested that the first hominids may have arrived in America as long as 100,000 years ago. Others estimate that the first Americans were members of *Homo sapiens sapiens* who crossed from Asia by foot between 10,000 and 15,000 years ago in pursuit of herds of bison and caribou that moved into the area in search of grazing land at the end of the Ice Age. Recently obtained genetic evidence, however, suggests the possibility of an earlier date, perhaps as early as 29,000 years ago. Other recent discoveries indicate that some early settlers may have originally come from Africa, rather than from eastern Asia. Clearly, the question has not yet been definitively answered.

In any case, it is now generally accepted that human beings were living in the New World at least 15,000 years ago. They gradually spread throughout the North American continent and had penetrated almost to the southern tip of South America by about 10,000 B.C.E. These first Americans were hunters and food gatherers, who lived in small nomadic communities close to the source of their food supply. Although it is not known when agriculture was first practiced, beans and squash seeds have been found at sites that date back at least 8,000 years. The cultivation of maize, and perhaps other crops as well, appears to have been under way as early as 5000 B.C.E. in the

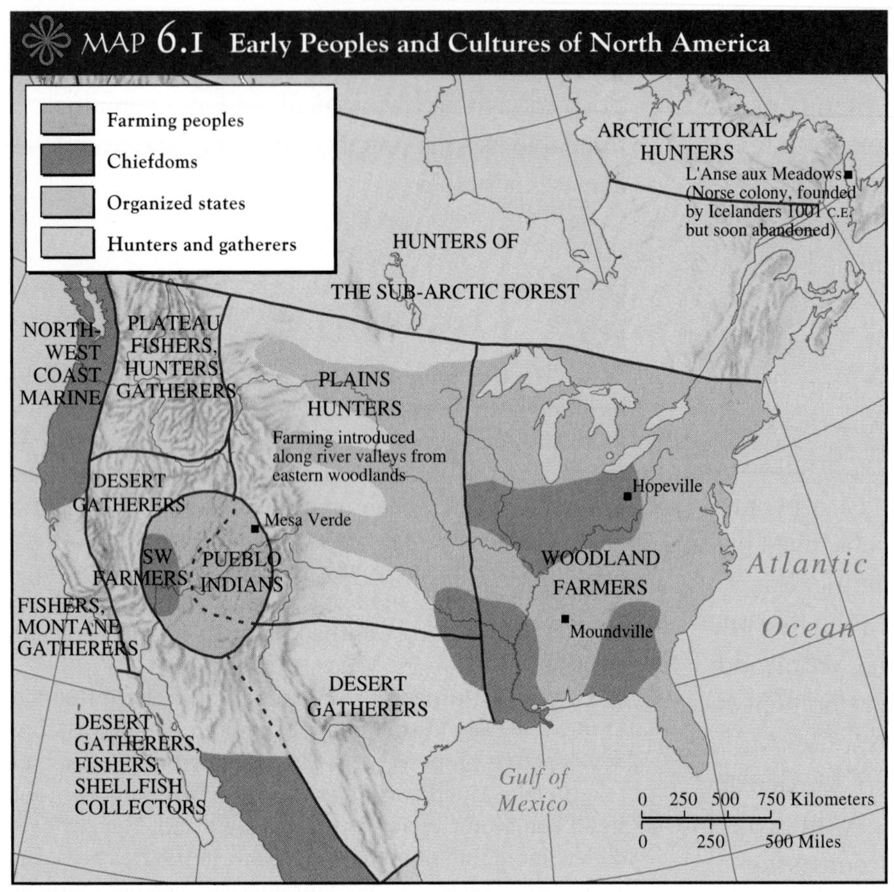

MAP 6.1 Early Peoples and Cultures of North America

Tehuacan valley in the southern portion of the central plateau of Mexico. A similar process may have been underway in the lowland regions near the modern city of Veracruz and in the Yucatán peninsula further to the east. There, in the region that archaeologists call Mesoamerica, the first civilizations in the New World began to appear.

Early Civilizations in Central America

The first signs of civilization in Mesoamerica appeared in the first millennium B.C.E., with the emergence of what is called Olmec culture in the hot and swampy lowlands along the coast of the Gulf of Mexico south of Veracruz. Olmec civilization was characterized by intensive agriculture along the muddy riverbanks in the area and by the carving of stone ornaments, tools, and monuments at sites such as San Lorenzo and La Venta. The site at La Venta includes a ceremonial precinct with a thirty-foot-high earthen pyramid, the largest of its date in all Mesoamerica. The Olmec peoples organized a widespread trading network, carried on religious rituals, and devised an as yet undeciphered system of hieroglyphics that is similar in some respects to later Mayan writing (see Mayan Hieroglyphs later in this chapter) and may be the ancestor of the first true writing systems in the New World.

Olmec society apparently consisted of several classes, including a class of skilled artisans who produced a series of massive stone heads, some of which are more than ten feet high. The Olmec peoples supported themselves primarily by cultivating crops, such as corn and beans, but also engaged in fishing and hunting. The Olmec apparently played a ceremonial game on a stone ball court, a ritual that would later be widely practiced throughout the region (see The Mysterious Maya later in this chapter).

Eventually, Olmec civilization began to decline and apparently collapsed around the fourth century B.C.E. During its heyday, however, it extended from Mexico City to El Salvador and perhaps to the shores of the Pacific Ocean.

In the meantime, parallel developments were occurring at Monte Alban, on a hillside overlooking the modern city of Oaxaca, in central Mexico. Around the middle of the first millennium B.C.E., the Zapotec peoples created an extensive civilization that flourished for several hundred years in the highlands. Like the Olmec sites, Monte Alban contains a number of temples and pyramids, but they are located in much more awesome surroundings on a massive stone terrace atop a 1,200-foot-high mountain overlooking the Oaxaca valley. The majority of the population, estimated at about 20,000, dwelled on terraces cut into the sides of the mountain.

Teotihuacán: America's First Metropolis

The first major metropolis in Mesoamerica was the city of Teotihuacán, capital of an early kingdom about thirty miles northeast of Mexico City that arose sometime around the third century B.C.E. and flourished for nearly a millennium until it collapsed under mysterious circumstances about 800 C.E. Along the main thoroughfare were temples and palaces, all dominated by a massive Pyramid of the Sun, under which archaeologists have discovered the remains of sacrificial victims, probably put to death during the dedication of the structure. In the vicinity are the remains of a large market, where goods from distant regions as well as agricultural produce grown by farmers in the vicinity were exchanged. The products traded included cacao, rubber, feathers, and various types of vegetables and meat. Pulque, a liquor extracted from the agave plant, was used in religious ceremonies. An obsidian mine nearby may explain the location of the city; obsidian is a volcanic glass that was prized in Mesoamerica for use in tools, mirrors, and the blades of sacrificial knives.

Most of the city consisted of one-story stucco apartment compounds; some were as large as 35,000 square feet, sufficient to house more than a hundred people. Each apartment was divided into several rooms, while the compounds were covered by flat roofs made of wooden beams, poles, and stucco. The compounds were separated by wide streets laid out on a rectangular grid and were entered through narrow alleys.

Living within the fertile Valley of Mexico, an upland plateau surrounded by magnificent snowcapped mountains, the inhabitants of Teotihuacán probably obtained the bulk of their wealth from agriculture. At that time, the valley floor was filled with swampy lakes containing the water runoff from the surrounding mountains. The combination of fertile soil and adequate water combined to make the valley one of the richest farming areas in Mesoamerica.

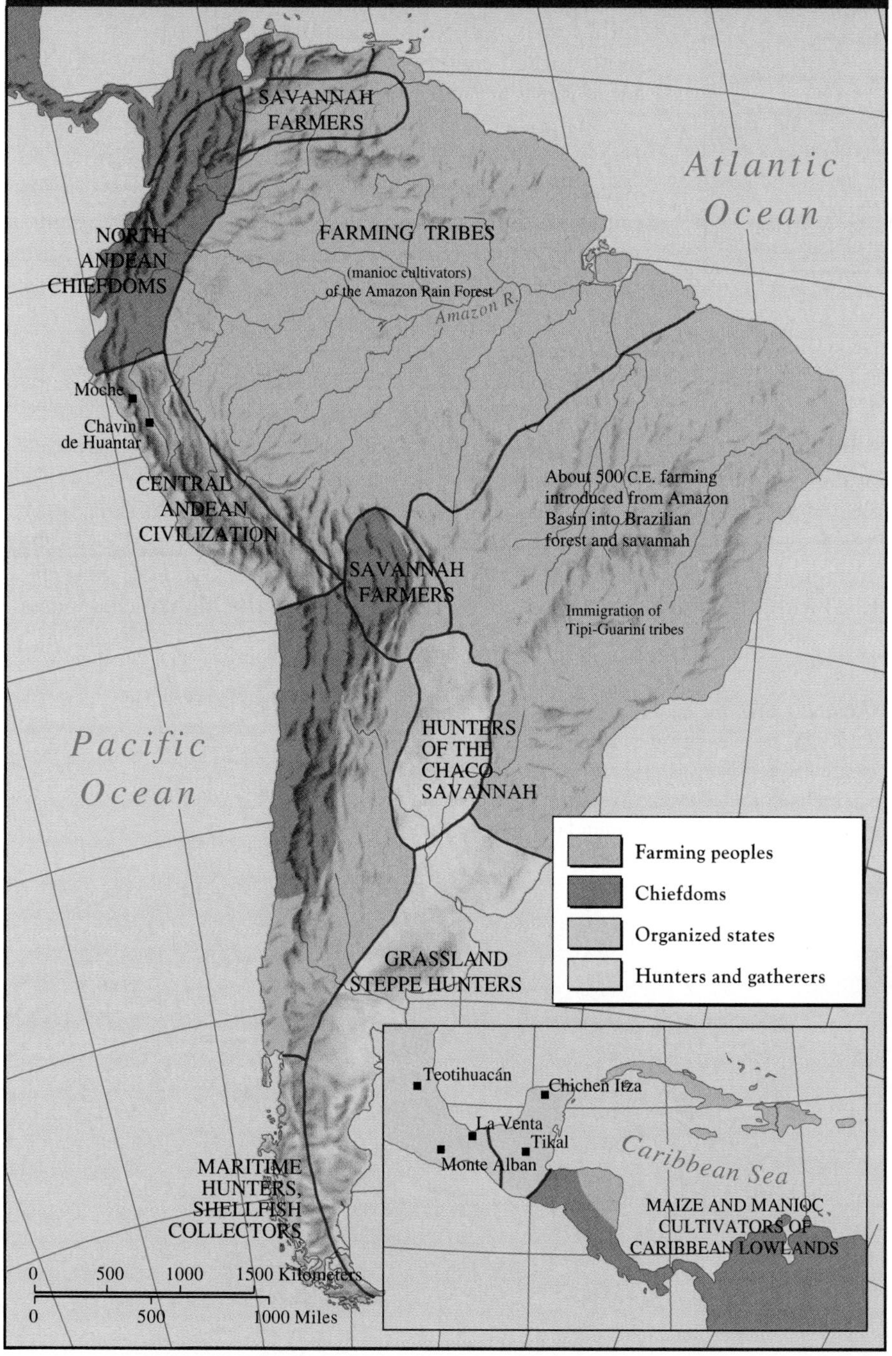

Sometime during the eighth century, for unknown reasons the wealth and power of the city began to decline, and eventually its ruling class departed, with the priests carrying stone images of local deities on their backs. The next two centuries were a time of troubles throughout the region, as feuding principalities fought over limited farmland. The problem was compounded in later centuries when peoples from surrounding areas, attracted by the rich farmlands, migrated into the Valley of Mexico and began to compete for territory with small city-states already established there. As the local population expanded, farmers began to engage in more intensive agriculture. They drained the lakes to build *chinampas*, swampy islands crisscrossed by canals that provided water for their crops and easy transportation to local markets for their excess produce.

MAP 6.2 Early Peoples and Cultures of Central and Latin America

The Mysterious Maya

Far to the east of the Valley of Mexico, another major civilization had taken form in the Yucatán peninsula. This was the civilization of the Maya, which was older and equally as sophisticated as the society at Teotihuacán.

Like the Aztecs and the inhabitants of Teotihuacán, the Maya trace their origins to the parent Olmec civilization in the lowlands along the Gulf of Mexico. It is not known when human beings first inhabited the Yucatán peninsula, but peoples contemporaneous with the Olmecs were already cultivating such crops as corn,

MAP 6.3 The Heartland of Mesoamerica

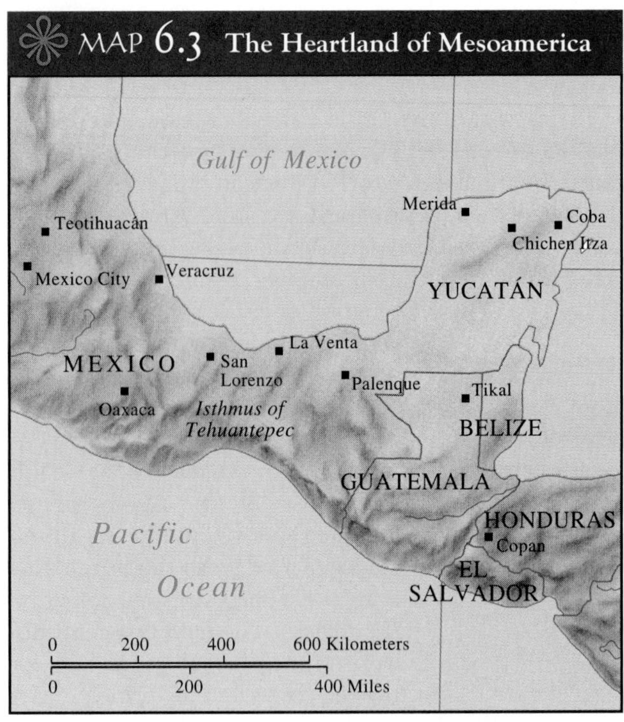

yams, and manioc in the area during the first millennium B.C.E. As the population increased, an early civilization began to emerge along the Pacific coast directly to the south of the peninsula and in the highlands of modern Guatemala. Contacts were already established with the Olmec to the west.

Since the area was a source for cacao trees and obsidian, the inhabitants soon developed relations with other early civilizations in the region. Cacao trees were the source of chocolate, which was used as a beverage by the upper classes, while cocoa beans, the fruit of the cacao tree, were used as currency in markets throughout the region.

As the population in the area increased, the inhabitants began to migrate into the central Yucatán peninsula to the north. The overcrowding forced farmers in the lowland areas to shift from slash-and-burn cultivation to swamp agriculture of the type practiced in the lake region of the Valley of Mexico. By the middle of the first millennium C.E., the entire area was honeycombed with a patchwork of small city-states competing with each other for land and resources. The most important of such city-states were probably Tikal and Copan, but it is doubtful that any was sufficiently powerful to dominate the entire area. The largest urban centers such as Tikal may have had 100,000 inhabitants at their height.

The power of the rulers of the city-states was certainly impressive. One of the monarchs at Copan—known to scholars as "18 rabbit" from the hieroglyphs composing his name—ordered the construction of a grand palace requiring more than 30,000 person-days of labor. Around the ruler was a class of aristocrats whose wealth was probably based on the ownership of land farmed by their poorer relatives. Eventually, many of the aristocrats became priests or scribes at the royal court or adopted honored professions as sculptors or painters. As the society's wealth grew, so did the need for artisans and traders, who began to form a small middle class.

The majority of the population on the peninsula, however (estimated at roughly three million at the height of Mayan power), were farmers. They lived on their *chinampa* plots or on terraced hills in the highlands. Houses

THE PYRAMID OF THE SUN, TEOTIHUACÁN. The first major metropolis in Central America was Teotihuacán, which was inhabited by as many as 150,000 people during its zenith sometime after 400 C.E. Covering an area of at least eight square miles, in size and sophistication it rivaled its contemporary, the city of Rome. The ceremonial center of Teotihuacán, which contained more than five thousand structures, was laid out in a north-south and an east-west axis; it was dominated by the Pyramid of the Sun, rising in four tiers to a height of over two hundred feet.

THE CREATION OF THE WORLD: A MAYAN VIEW

Popul Vuh, a sacred work of the ancient Maya, is an account of Mayan history and religious beliefs. No written version in the original Mayan script is extant, but shortly after the Spanish conquest, it was written down in Quiche (the spoken language of the Maya), using the Latin script, apparently from memory. This version was later translated into Spanish. The following excerpt from the opening lines of Popul Vuh recounts the Mayan myth of the creation.

POPUL VUH: THE SACRED BOOK OF THE MAYA

This is the account of how all was in suspense, all calm, in silence; all motionless, still, and the expanse of the sky was empty.

This is the first account, the first narrative. There was neither man, nor animal, birds, fishes, crabs, trees, stones, caves, ravines, grasses, nor forests; there was only the sky.

The surface of the earth had not appeared. There was only the calm sea and the great expanse of the sky.

There was nothing brought together, nothing which could make a noise, nor anything which might move, or tremble, or could make noise in the sky.

There was nothing standing; only the calm water, the placid sea, alone and tranquil. Nothing existed.

There was only immobility and silence in the darkness, in the night. Only the Creator, the Maker, Tepeu, Gucumatz, the Forefathers, were in the water surrounded with light. They were hidden under green and blue feathers, and were therefore called Gucumatz. By nature they were great sages and great thinkers. In this manner the sky existed and also the Heart of Heaven, which is the name of God and thus He is called.

Then came the word. Tepeu and Gucumatz came together in the darkness, in the night, and Tepeu and Gucumatz talked together. They talked then, discussing and deliberating; they agreed, they united their words and their thoughts.

Then while they meditated, it became clear to them that when dawn would break, man must appear. Then they planned the creation, and the growth of the trees and the thickets and the birth of life and the creation of man. Thus it was arranged in the darkness and in the night by the Heart of Heaven who is called Huracan.

The first is called Caculha Huracan. The second is Chipi-Caculha. The third is Raxa-Caculha. And these three are the Heart of Heaven.

So it was that they made perfect the work, when they did it after thinking and meditating upon it.

were built of adobe and thatch and probably resembled the houses of the majority of the population in the area today. There was a fairly clear-cut division of labor along gender lines. The men were responsible for fighting and hunting, and the women for homemaking and the preparation of cornmeal, the staple food of much of the population.

Some noble women seem to have played important roles in both political and religious life. In the seventh century C.E., for example, Pacal became king of Palenque, one of the most powerful of the Mayan city-states, through the royal line of his mother and grandmother, thereby breaking the patrilineal descent twice. His mother ruled Palenque for three years and was the power behind the throne for her son's first twenty-five years of rule. Pacal legitimized his kingship by transforming his mother into a divine representation of the "first mother" goddess.

Mayan religion was polytheistic. Although the names were different, Mayan gods shared many of the characteristics of deities of nearby cultures. The supreme god was named Itzamna (Lizard House). Deities were ranked in order of importance, and some, like the jaguar god of night, were evil rather than good. Some scholars believe that many of the nature deities may have been viewed as manifestations of one supreme godhead (see the box above). As at Teotihuacán, human sacrifice (normally by decapitation) was practiced to propitiate the heavenly forces. Scenes from paintings and rock carvings depict a society preoccupied with war and the seizure of captives for sacrifice.

Physically, the Mayan cities were built around a ceremonial core dominated by a central pyramid surmounted by a shrine to the gods. Nearby were other temples, palaces, and a sacred ball court. The ball court was a rectangular space surrounded by vertical walls with metal rings through which the contestants attempted to drive a hard rubber ball. Although the rules of the game are only imperfectly understood, it apparently had religious significance, and the vanquished players were sacrificed in ceremonies held after the close of the game. Similar courts have been found at sites throughout Mesoamerica.

MAYAN HIEROGLYPHS

In some ways, Mayan culture was more advanced than the later Aztec civilization in the Valley of Mexico. In particular, the Mayan writing system was much more sophisticated than the relatively primitive system used by the

A SAMPLE OF MAYAN WRITING

The Maya were the only Mesoamerican people to devise a complete written language. Like the Sumerian and Egyptian scripts, the Mayan system was composed of a mixture of ideographs and phonetic symbols, which were written in double columns to be read from left to right and top to bottom. The language was rudimentary in many ways. It had few adjectives or adverbs, and the numbering system comprised only three symbols: a shell for zero, a dot for one, and a bar for five.

During the classical era from 300 to 900 C.E., the Maya used the script to record dynastic statistics with deliberate precision, listing the date of the ruler's birth, his accession to power, and his marriage and death, while highlighting victories in battle, the capture of prisoners, and ritual ceremonies. The symbols were carved on stone panels, stelae, and funerary urns or were painted with a brush on folding screen books made of bark paper; only four of these books from the late period remain extant today.

A sample of Mayan hieroglyphs is shown below.

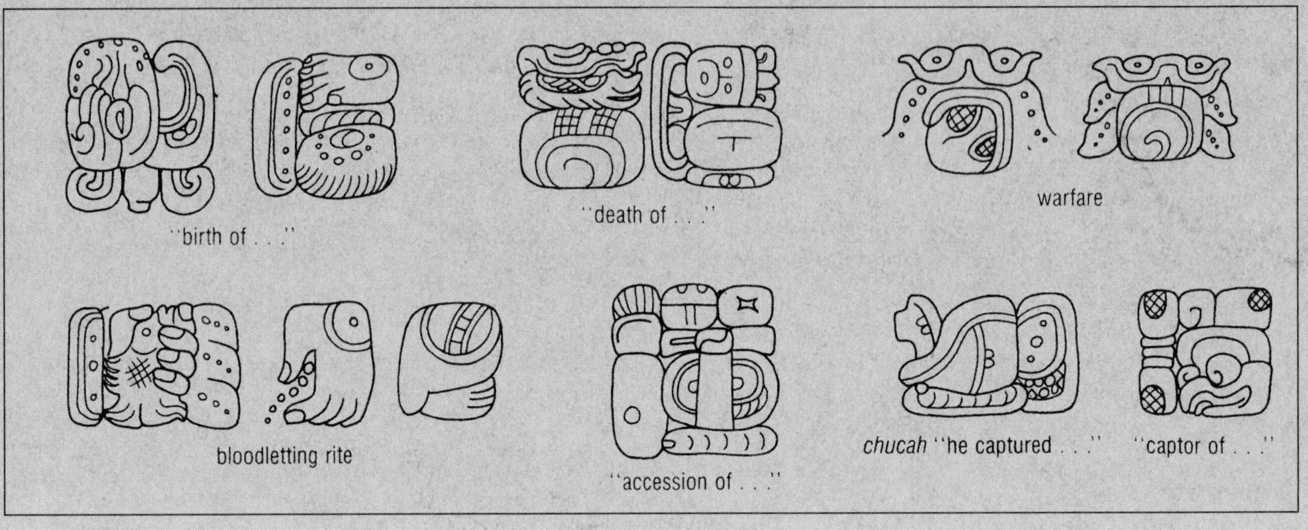

Aztecs (see the box above). Unfortunately, when the Spanish conquered the remains of Mayan civilization, they made no attempt to decipher the language with the assistance of natives familiar with the script. The Spanish Bishop Diego de Landa, otherwise an astute and sympathetic observer of Mayan culture, remarked: "We found a large number of books in these characters and, as they contained nothing in which there were not to be seen superstition and lies of the devil, we burned them all, which they regretted to an amazing degree, and which caused them much affliction."[1]

The Mayan hieroglyphs remained undeciphered until scholars discovered that many passages contained symbols that recorded dates in the Mayan calendar. This cal-

PREPARING FOR SACRIFICE. This copy of a wall painting from the 800 C.E. Mayan temple at Bonampak shows a ruler accepting a human sacrifice, which was offered to appease the anger of the deities. The Maya went on raids for victims and then sacrificed them in elaborate rites with ornate costumes and dancing. Here nobles wearing the pelts and the headdress of jaguars, the symbol of power and rank, preside over the ceremonial preparation of the victim.

A BALL COURT. Throughout Mesoamerica a dangerous game was played on ball courts such as this one. A large ball of solid rubber was propelled from the hip at such tremendous speed that players had to wear extensive padding. More than an athletic contest, the game had religious significance. The court is thought to have represented the cosmos and the ball the sun, and the losers were sacrificed to the gods in postgame ceremonies.

endar, which measures time back to a particular date in August 3114 B.C.E., required a sophisticated understanding of astronomical events and mathematics to compile. Starting with these known symbols as a foundation, modern scholars have gradually deciphered the script. Like the scripts of the Sumerians and ancient Egyptians, the Mayan hieroglyphs were both ideographic and phonetic in nature and, in fact, were becoming more phonetic as time passed.

One of the most important repositories of Mayan hieroglyphs is at Palenque, an archaeological site deep in the jungles in the neck of the Mexican peninsula, considerably to the west of the Yucatán. In a chamber located under the Temple of Inscriptions, archaeologists discovered a royal tomb and a massive limestone slab covered with hieroglyphs. By deciphering the message on the slab, archaeologists for the first time identified a historical figure in Mayan history. He was a ruler named Pacal, known from his glyph as "the shield"; Pacal ordered the construction of the Temple of Inscriptions in the mid-seventh century, and it was his body that was buried in the tomb.

As befits their intense interest in the passage of time, the Maya also had a sophisticated knowledge of astronomy and kept voluminous records of the movements of the heavenly bodies. There were practical reasons for their concern. The arrival of the planet Venus in the evening sky, for example, was a traditional time to prepare for war. The Temple of Inscriptions was oriented so that an

THE TEMPLE OF THE INSCRIPTIONS. King Pacal and his eldest son helped to create the "golden age" of Mayan civilization with their innovative architecture and the detailed carvings of glyphs on the many limestone monuments at Palenque. Pacal was apparently obsessed with the need to legitimize his royal status, since his claim to the throne descended not from his father's line, but from that of his mother and grandmother. The Temple of the Inscriptions was built at Pacal's order in 675 C.E. to serve as his mausoleum after his death. His body was placed at the foot of a staircase leading down into the crypt. Adorning the many carved walls of the temple are additional glyphs that attempt to portray his mother as the "first mother" goddess of Palenque and thus confirm his own divine provenance as her offspring. The Temple is considered to be one of the most important monuments in Mesoamerica.

observer could stand on the platform at the spring equinox and watch the setting of the sun.

THE MYSTERY OF MAYAN DECLINE

Sometime in the eighth or ninth century, the classical Mayan civilization in the central Yucatán peninsula began to decline. At Copan, for example, it ended abruptly in 822 C.E., when work on various stone sculptures ordered by the ruler suddenly ceased. The end of Palenque, a rival state to the west, soon followed. Whether the decline was caused by overuse of the land, invasion, internal revolt, or a natural disaster such as a volcanic eruption is a question that has puzzled archaeologists for decades. Recent evidence supports the theory that overcultivation of the land due to a growing population gradually reduced crop yields. Another theory is that a long drought, which lasted for almost two centuries in the ninth and tenth centuries C.E., may have played a major role. Certainly, the period was characterized by an increase in internecine war among the states and the rise of powerful nobles.

Whatever the case, cities like Tikal and Palenque were abandoned to the jungles, though newer urban centers in the northern part of the peninsula, like Uxmal and Chichen Itza, survived and continued to prosper. According to local history, this latter area was taken over by peoples known as the Toltecs, led by a man known as Kukulcan ("feathered serpent"), who migrated to the peninsula from Tula in central Mexico sometime in the tenth century. Some scholars believe this flight was associated with the legend of the departure of Quetzalcoatl, the feathered serpent who promised that he would someday return to reclaim his homeland.

The Toltecs apparently controlled the upper peninsula from their capital at Chichen Itza for several centuries, and then they too declined. When the Spaniards arrived, the area was divided into a number of small principalities, and the cities such as Uxmal and Chichen Itza had been abandoned.

The Aztecs

Among the groups moving into the Valley of Mexico after the fall of Teotihuacán were the Mexica (pronounced Mesheeca). No one knows their origins, although folk legend held that their original homeland was an island in a lake called Aztlan. From that legendary homeland comes the name *Aztec,* by which they are known to the modern world. Sometime during the early twelfth century, the Aztecs left their original habitat and, carrying an image of their patron deity Huitzilopochtli, began a lengthy migration that climaxed with their arrival in the Valley of Mexico sometime late in the century.

Less sophisticated than many of their neighbors, the Aztecs at first were forced to seek alliances with stronger city-states. They were excellent warriors, however, and (like Sparta in ancient Greece and the state of Qin in Zhou dynasty China) had become the leading city-state in the lake region by the early fifteenth century. Establishing their capital at Tenochtitlán, on an island in the middle of Lake Texcoco, they set out to bring the entire region under their domination.

For the remainder of the fifteenth century, the Aztecs consolidated their control over much of what is modern Mexico, from the Atlantic to the Pacific Ocean and as far south as the Guatemalan border. The new kingdom was not a centralized state but a collection of semiautonomous territories. To provide a unifying focus for the kingdom, the Aztecs promoted their patron god Huitzilopochtli as the guiding deity of the entire population, which now numbered several million.

POLITICS AND SOCIETY

Like all great empires in ancient times, the Aztec state was authoritarian in nature. Power was vested in the monarch, whose authority had both a divine and a secular character. The Aztec ruler claimed descent from the gods and served as an intermediary between the material and the metaphysical worlds. Unlike many of his counterparts in the Old World, however, the monarch did not obtain his position by a rigid law of succession. On the death of the ruler, his successor was selected from within the royal family by a small group of senior officials, who were also members of the family and were therefore eligible for the position. Once placed on the throne, the Aztec ruler was advised by a small council of lords, headed by a prime minister who served as the chief executive of the government, and a bureaucracy. Beyond the capital, the power of the central government was limited. Rulers of territories subject to the Aztecs were allowed considerable autonomy in return for paying tribute, in the form of goods or captives, to the central government. The most important government officials in the provinces were the tax collectors, who collected the tribute. They used the threat of military action against those who failed to carry out their tribute obligations and therefore understandably were not popular with the taxpayers. According to Bernal Díaz, a Spaniard who accompanied Hernán Cortés on his expedition to Tenochtitlán in 1519,

> All these towns complained about Montezuma [Moctezuma, the Aztec ruler at the time of the Cortés expedition] and his tax collectors, speaking in private so that the Mexican ambassadors should not hear them, however. They said these officials robbed them of all they possessed, and that if their wives and daughters were pretty they would violate them in front of their fathers and husbands and carry them away. They also said that the Mexicans [that is, the representatives from the capital] made the men work like slaves, compelling them to carry pine trunks and stone and firewood and maize overland and in canoes, and to perform other tasks, such as planting maize fields, and that they took away the people's lands as well for the service of their idols.[2]

Positions in the government bureaucracy were the exclusive privilege of the hereditary nobility, all of whom traced their lineage to the founding family of the Aztec clan. Male children in noble families were sent to temple schools, where they were exposed to a harsh regimen consisting of manual labor, military training, and the memorization of information about Aztec society and religion. On reaching adulthood, they would select a career in the military service, the government bureaucracy, or the priesthood. As a reward for their services, senior officials received large estates from the government, and they alone had the right to hire communal labor.

The remainder of the population consisted of commoners, indentured workers, and slaves. Most indentured workers were landless laborers who contracted to work on the nobles' estates, while slaves served in the households of the wealthy. Slavery was not an inherited status, and the children of slaves were considered to be free citizens. Commoners might sell themselves into slavery when in debt and then later purchase their freedom.

The vast majority of the population were commoners. All commoners were members of large kinship groups called *calpullis*. Each *calpulli*, often consisting of as many as a thousand members, was headed by an elected chief, who ran its day-to-day affairs and served as an intermediary with the central government. Each *calpulli* was responsible for providing taxes (usually in the form of goods) and conscript labor to the state.

MAP 6.4 The Valley of Mexico Under Aztec Rule

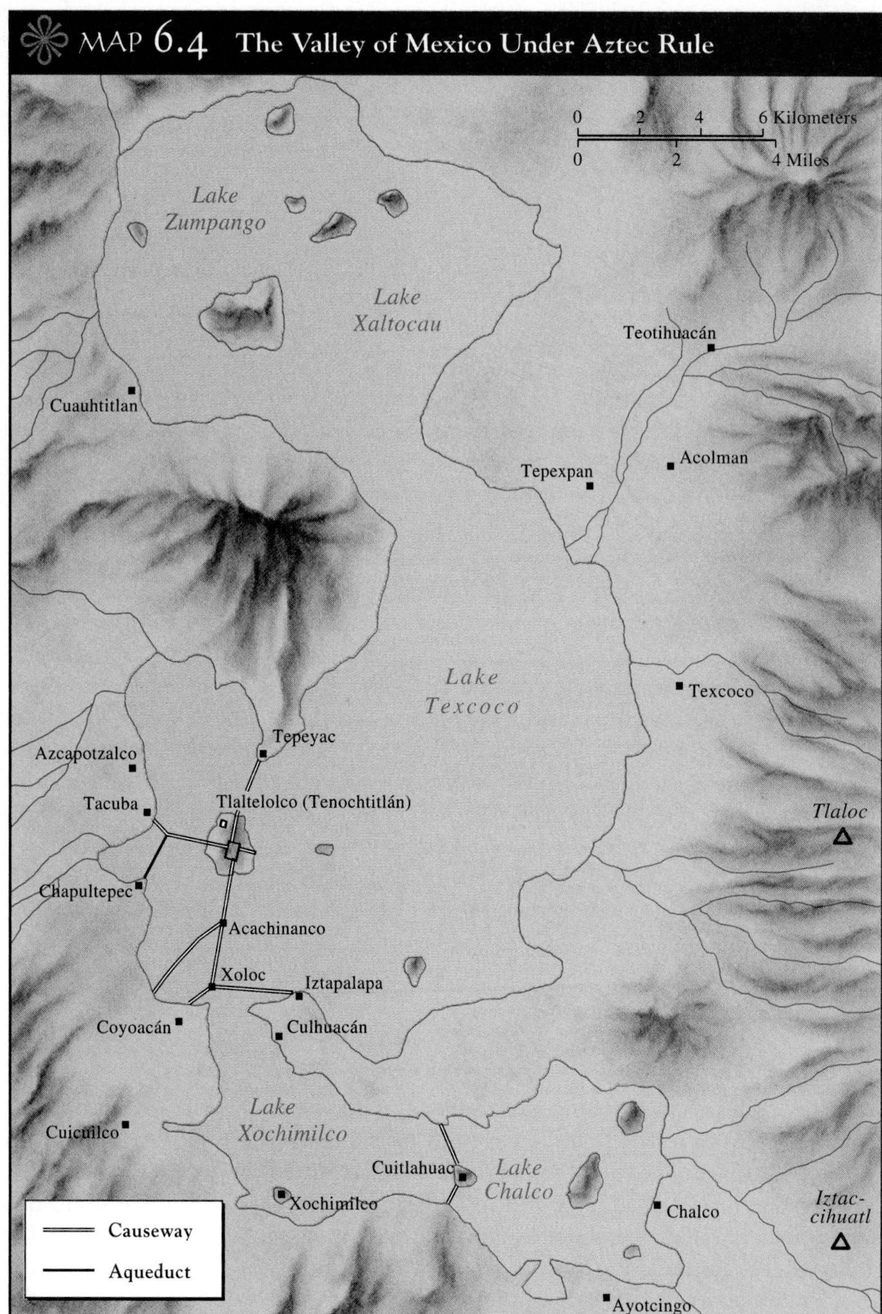

Each *calpulli* maintained its own temples and schools and administered the land held by the community. Farmland within the *calpulli* was held in common and could not be sold, although it could be inherited within the family. Within the cities, each *calpulli* occupied a separate neighborhood, where its members often performed a particular function, such as metalworking, stonecutting, weaving, carpentry, or commerce. Apparently, a large proportion of the population engaged in some form of trade, at least in the densely populated Valley of Mexico, where an estimated half of the people lived in an urban environment. Many farmers brought their goods to the markets via the canals and sold them directly to retailers (see the box on p. 178).

The *calpulli* compounds themselves were divided into smaller family units. Individual families lived in small flat-roofed dwellings containing one or two rooms. Each house was separate from its neighbors and had direct access to the surrounding streets and canals. The houses of farmers living on the *chinampas* were set on raised dirt platforms built above the surrounding fields to prevent flooding.

Gender roles within the family were rigidly stratified. Male children were trained for war and were expected to

MARKETS AND MERCHANDISE IN AZTEC MEXICO

One of our most valuable descriptions of Aztec civilization is The Conquest of New Spain, *written by Bernal Díaz, a Spaniard who accompanied Hernán Cortés on his expedition to Mexico in 1519. In the following passage, Díaz describes the great market at Tenochtitlán.*

BERNAL DÍAZ, *THE CONQUEST OF NEW SPAIN*

Let us begin with the dealers in gold, silver, and precious stones, feathers, cloaks, and embroidered goods, and male and female slaves who are also sold there. They bring as many slaves to be sold in that market as the Portuguese bring Negroes from Guinea. Some are brought there attached to long poles by means of collars round their necks to prevent them from escaping, but others are left loose. Next there were those who sold coarser cloth, and cotton goods and fabrics made of twisted thread, and there were chocolate merchants with their chocolate. In this way you could see every kind of merchandise to be found anywhere in New Spain, laid out in the same way as goods are laid out in my own district of Medina del Campo, a center for fairs, where each line of stalls has its own particular sort. So it was in this great market. There were those who sold sisal cloth and ropes and the sandals they wear on their feet, which are made from the same plant. All these were kept in one part of the market, in the place assigned to them, and in another part were skins of tigers and lions, otters, jackals, and deer, badgers, mountain cats, and other wild animals, some tanned and some untanned, and other classes of merchandise.

There were sellers of kidney beans and sage and other vegetables and herbs in another place, and in yet another they were selling fowls, and birds with great dewlaps, also rabbits, hares, deer, young ducks, little dogs, and other such creatures. Then there were the fruiterers; and the women who sold cooked food, flour and honey cake, and tripe, had their part of the market. Then came pottery of all kinds, from big water jars to little jugs, displayed in its own place, also honey, honey paste, and other sweets like nougat. Elsewhere they sold timber too, boards, cradles, beams, blocks, and benches, all in a quarter of their own.

Then there were the sellers of pitch pine for torches, and other things of that kind, and I must also mention, with all apologies, that they sold many canoe loads of human excrement, which they kept in the creeks near the market. This was for the manufacture of salt and the curing of skins, which they say cannot be done without it. I know that many gentlemen will laugh at this, but I assure them it is true. I may add that on all the roads they have shelters made of reeds or straw or grass so that they can retire when they wish to do so, and purge their bowels unseen by passersby, and also in order that their excrement shall not be lost.

serve in the army on reaching adulthood. Women were expected to work in the home, weave textiles, and raise children, although like their brothers they were permitted to enter the priesthood. According to Bernal Díaz, a female deity presided over the rites of marriage. As in most traditional societies, chastity and obedience were desirable female characteristics. Although women in Aztec society enjoyed more legal rights than women in some traditional Old World civilizations, they were still not equal to men. Women were permitted to own and inherit property and to enter into contracts. Marriage was usually monogamous, although noble families sometimes practiced polygyny (the state or practice of having more than one wife at a time). Wedding partners were normally selected from within the lineage group but not the immediate family. As in most societies at the time, parents usually selected their child's spouse, often for purposes of political or social advancement.

Classes in Aztec society were rigidly stratified. Commoners were not permitted to enter the nobility, although some occasionally rose to senior positions in the army or the priesthood as the result of exemplary service. As in medieval Europe, such occupations often provided a route of upward mobility for ambitious commoners. A woman of noble standing would sometimes marry a commoner, because the children of such a union would inherit her higher status, while she could be expected to be treated better by her husband's family, who would be proud of the marriage relationship.

LAND OF THE FEATHERED SERPENT: AZTEC RELIGION AND CULTURE

The Aztecs, like their contemporaries throughout Mesoamerica, lived in an environment populated by a multitude of gods. Scholars have identified more than a hundred deities in the Aztec pantheon; some of them were nature spirits, like the rain god Tlaloc, and some were patron deities, like the symbol of the Aztecs themselves, Huitzilopochtli. A supreme deity, called Ometeotl, represented the all-powerful and omnipresent forces of the heavens, but he was rather remote, and

QUETZALCOATL. Quetzalcoatl was one of the favorite deities of the Central American peoples. His visage of a plumed serpent, as shown here, was prominent in the royal capital of Teotihuacán. According to legend, Quetzalcoatl, the leader of the Toltecs, was tricked into drunkenness and humiliated by a rival god. In disgrace he left his homeland but promised to return. In 1519, the Aztec monarch Moctezuma welcomed Hernán Cortés, the leader of the Spanish expedition, believing he was a representative of Quetzalcoatl.

other gods, notably the feathered serpent Quetzalcoatl, had a more direct impact on the lives of the people. Representing the forces of creation, virtue, and learning and culture, Quetzalcoatl bears a distinct similarity to Siva in Hindu belief. According to Aztec tradition, this godlike being had left his homeland in the Valley of Mexico in the tenth century, promising to return in triumph (see The Mystery of Mayan Decline earlier in this chapter).

Aztec cosmology was based on a belief in the existence of two worlds, the material and the divine. The earth was the material world and took the form of a flat disc surrounded by water on all sides. The divine world, which consisted of both heaven and hell, was the abode of the gods. Human beings could aspire to a form of heavenly salvation but first had to pass through a transitional stage, somewhat like Christian purgatory, before reaching their final destination, where the soul was finally freed from the body. To prepare for the final day of judgment, as well as to help them engage in proper behavior through life, all citizens underwent religious training at temple schools during adolescence and took part in various rituals throughout their lives. The most devout were encouraged to study for the priesthood. Once accepted, they served at temples ranging from local branches at the *calpulli* level to the highest shrines in the ceremonial precinct at Tenochtitlán.

Aztec religion contained a distinct element of fatalism that was inherent in their creation myth, which described an unceasing struggle between the forces of good and evil throughout the universe. This struggle led to the creation and destruction of four worlds, or suns. The world was now living in the time of the fifth sun. But that world, too, was destined to end with the destruction of this earth and all that is within it:

Even jade is shattered,
Even gold is crushed,
Even quetzal plumes are torn . . .
One does not live forever on this earth:
We endure only for an instant![3]

In an effort to postpone the day of reckoning, the Aztecs practiced human sacrifice. The Aztecs believed

AZTEC RELIGION THROUGH SPANISH EYES

Although early Spanish visitors were impressed with many aspects of Aztec culture, they were revolted by its religious beliefs and practices. The following passage from Father Diego Duran's History of the Indies of New Spain *describes the ritual of human sacrifice that was a central part of Aztec religion. The Aztecs believed that only the gift of human hearts would appease their god Huitzilopochtli and prevent him from bringing disaster to their civilization.*

DIEGO DURAN, *HISTORY OF THE INDIES OF NEW SPAIN*

When the day of the feast arrived, [Moctezuma] and Tlacaelel blackened their bodies with soot and applied it in such a way that it caught the light. . . . They placed crowns of fine feathers, adorned with gold and precious stones, upon their heads, and on each arm they wore a sheath of gold reaching from the elbow to the shoulder. On their feet were richly worked jaguar skin sandals, inlaid with gold and gems. . . .

The king and Tlacaelel now appeared before the assembly and went to stand upon the stone which was the likeness and image of the sun. The five priests of sacrifice followed them. They were to hold down the feet, hands, and heads of the victims, and they were painted all over with red ocher, even their loincloths and tunics. Upon their heads they wore paper crowns surmounted by little shields which hung to the middle of their foreheads, also painted in ocher. On the top of their heads they wore long stiff feathers which had been tied to their hair and which stood straight up. On their feet were very common, worthless sandals. . . .

The five priests entered and claimed the prisoner who stood first in the line at the skull rack. Each prisoner they took to the place where the king stood and, when they had forced him to stand upon the stone which was the figure and likeness of the sun, they threw him upon his back. One took him by the right arm, another by the left, one by his left foot, another by his right, while the fifth priest tied his neck with a cord and held him down so that he could not move.

The king lifted the knife on high and made a gash in his breast. Having opened it he extracted the heart and raised it high with his hand as an offering to the sun. When the heart had cooled he tossed it into the circular depression, taking some of the blood in his hand and sprinkling it in the direction of the sun. In this way the sacrificers killed four, one by one; then Tlacaelel came and killed another four in his turn. And so, four by four, the prisoners were slain, till every last man that had been brought from the Mixteca had perished.

that by appeasing the sun god Huitzilopochtli with sacrifices, they could delay the final destruction of their world. Victims were prepared for the ceremony through elaborate rituals and then brought to the holy shrine, where their hearts were ripped out of their chests and presented to the gods as a holy offering. It was an honor to be chosen for sacrifice, and captives in particular were often used as sacrificial victims, since they represented valor, the trait the Aztecs prized most. One of the few descriptions we have of the ceremonies comes from the pen of Father Diego Duran, a Dominican friar who lived in Mexico during the mid-sixteenth century and left a description of the civilization of the Aztecs (see the box above).

Like the art of the Olmecs, most Aztec architecture, art, and sculpture had religious significance. At the center of the capital city of Tenochtitlán was the sacred precinct, dominated by the massive pyramid dedicated to Huitzilopochtli and the rain god Tlaloc. According to Bernal Díaz, at its base the pyramid was equal to the plots of six large European town houses and tapered from there to the top, which was surmounted by a platform containing shrines to the gods and an altar for performing human sacrifices (see the box on p. 181). The entire pyramid was covered with brightly colored paintings and sculptures.

Although little Aztec painting survives, it was evidently of high quality. Bernal Díaz compared the best work with that of Michelangelo. Artisans worked with stone and with soft metals such as gold and silver, which they cast with the lost-wax technique. They did not have the knowledge of making implements in bronze or iron, however. Stoneworking consisted primarily of representations of the gods and bas-reliefs depicting religious ceremonies. Among the most famous is the massive disc called the Stone of the Sun, carved for use at the central pyramid at Tenochtitlán.

The Aztecs had devised a form of writing based on hieroglyphs that represented an object or a concept. The symbols had no phonetic significance and did not constitute a writing system as such but could give the sense of a message and were probably used by civilian or religious officials as notes or memoranda for their orations. Although many of the notes simply recorded dates in the complex calendar that had evolved since Olmec times, others provide insight into the daily lives of the Aztec peoples. A trained class of scribes carefully painted the notes

A DESCRIPTION OF TENOCHTITLÁN

The Aztec capital of Tenochtitlán was built on an island in the Lake of Mexico. After the Spanish conquest, the lake was drained, and the area became the foundation of the modern capital of Mexico, Mexico City. Here Díaz describes the city as he viewed it from the top of the Temple of the Sun. The Spaniards razed the temple and built a cathedral in its place.

BERNAL DÍAZ, *THE CONQUEST OF NEW SPAIN*

When we arrived near the great temple and before we had climbed a single step, the great Moctezuma sent six *papas* [priests] and two chieftains down from the top, where he was making his sacrifices, to escort our Captain; and as he climbed the steps, of which there were one hundred and fourteen, they tried to take him by the arms to help him up in the same way as they helped Moctezuma, thinking he might be tired, but he would not let them near him.

The top of the *cue* [pyramid] formed an open square on which stood something like a platform, and it was here that the great stones stood on which they placed the poor Indians for sacrifice. Here also was a massive image like a dragon, and other hideous figures, and a great deal of blood that had been spilled that day. Emerging in the company of two *papas* from the shrine which housed his accursed images, Moctezuma made a deep bow to us all and said: "My lord Malinche, you must be tired after climbing this great *cue* of ours." And Cortés replied that none of us was ever exhausted by anything. Then Moctezuma took him by the hand, and told him to look at his great city and all the other cities standing in the water, and the many others on the land round the lake; and he said that if Cortés had not had a good view of the great marketplace he could see it better from where he now was. So we stood there looking, because that huge accursed *cue* stood so high that it dominated everything. We saw the three causeways that led into Mexico: the causeway of Iztapalapa by which we had entered four days before, and that of Tacuba along which we were afterwards to flee on the night of our great defeat, when the new prince Cuitlahuac drove us out of the city (as I shall tell in due course), and that of Tepeaqualla. We saw the freshwater which came from Chapultepec to supply the city, and the bridges that were constructed at intervals on the causeways so that the water could flow in and out from one part of the lake to another. We saw a great number of canoes, some coming with provisions and others returning with cargo and merchandise; and we saw too that one could not pass from one house to another of that great city and the other cities that were built on the water except over wooden drawbridges or by canoe. We saw *cues* and shrines in these cities that looked like gleaming white towers and castles: a marvelous sight. All the houses had flat roofs, and on the causeways were other small towers and shrines built like fortresses.

Having examined and considered all that we had seen, we turned back to the great market and the swarm of people buying and selling. The mere murmur of their voices talking was loud enough to be heard more than three miles away. Some of our soldiers who had been in many parts of the world, in Constantinople, in Rome, and all over Italy, said that they had never seen a market so well laid out, so large, so orderly, and so full of people.

THE STONE OF THE FIFTH SUN. This basaltic disc, which weighs twenty-six tons, recorded the Aztec view of the cosmos. It portrays the perpetual struggle between forces of good and evil in the universe; in the center is an intimidating image of the sun god clutching human hearts with his talons. Having previously traversed the creation and destruction of four worlds, the Aztecs believed they were living in the world of the fifth and final sun—hence this stone carving that was found in the central pyramid at Tenochtitlán.

MOCTEZUMA'S GREETING TO HERNÁN CORTÉS

As his small party arrived in the Aztec capital of Tenochtitlán, Cortés was greeted by King Moctezuma, who was under the impression that Cortés was the representative of Quetzalcoatl, the Aztec deity who had departed centuries earlier with a promise that he would one day return. In this letter to Queen Isabella of Spain, Cortés describes the welcoming ceremony and King Moctezuma's opening address. As Moctezuma would soon discover, he had been deceived as to his visitor's identity and intentions.

HERNÁN CORTÉS, *LETTER FROM MEXICO*

Close to the city there is a wooden bridge ten paces wide across a breach in the causeway to allow the water to flow, as it rises and falls. . . .

After we had crossed this bridge, Moctezuma came to greet us and with him some two hundred lords, all barefoot and dressed in a different costume, but also very rich in their way and more so than the others. They came in two columns, pressed very close to the walls of the street, which is very wide and beautiful and so straight that you can see from one end to the other. It is two-thirds of a league long and has on both sides very good and big houses, both dwellings and temples.

[After an exchange of gifts, Moctezuma then] addressed me in the following way:

"For a long time we have known from the writings of our ancestors that neither I, nor any of those who dwell in this land, are natives of it, but foreigners who came from very distant parts; and likewise we know that a chieftain, of whom they were all vassals, brought our people to this region. And he returned to his native land and after many years came again, by which time all those who had remained were married to native women and had built villages and raised children. And when he wished to lead them away again they would not go nor even admit him as their chief; and so he departed. And we have always held that those who descended from him would come and conquer this land and take us as their vassals. So because of the place from which you claim to come, namely, from where the sun rises, and the things you tell us of the great lord or king who sent you here, we believe and are certain that he is our natural lord, especially as you say that he has known of us for some time. So be assured that we shall obey you and hold you as our lord in place of that great sovereign of whom you speak; . . . I know full well of all that has happened to you from Puntunchan to here, and I also know how those of Cempoal and Tascalteca have told you much evil of me; believe only what you see with your eyes, for those are my enemies, and some were my vassals, and have rebelled against me at your coming and said those things to gain favor with you. I also know that they have told you the walls of my houses are made of gold, and that the floor mats in my rooms and other things in my household are likewise of gold, and that I was, and claimed to be, a god; and many other things besides. The houses as you see are of stone and lime and clay."

Then he raised his clothes and showed me his body, saying, as he grasped his arms and trunk with his hands, "See that I am of flesh and blood like you and all other men, and I am mortal and substantial. See how they have lied to you? It is true that I have some pieces of gold left to me by my ancestors; anything I might have shall be given to you whenever you ask. Now I shall go to other houses where I live, but here you shall be provided with all that you and your people require, and you shall receive no hurt, for you are in your own land and your own house."

on paper made from the inner bark of fig trees. Unfortunately, many of these notes were destroyed by the Spaniards as part of their effort to eradicate all aspects of Aztec religion and culture.

THE DESTRUCTION OF AZTEC CIVILIZATION

For a century, the Aztec kingdom dominated much of central Mexico from the Atlantic to the Pacific coast, and its influence penetrated as far south as present-day Guatemala. Most local officials had accepted the sovereignty of the king in Tenochtitlán, but in Tlaxcallan to the east, the authorities were restive under Aztec rule.

In 1519, a Spanish expedition under the command of Hernán Cortés landed at Veracruz, on the Gulf of Mexico (see Chapter 14). Marching to Tenochtitlán at the head of a small contingent of troops, Cortés received a friendly welcome from the Aztec monarch Moctezuma Xocoyotzin (often called Montezuma), who initially believed his visitor was a representative of Quetzalcoatl, the godlike "feathered serpent" who had departed from his homeland centuries before (see the box above). But tensions soon erupted between the Spaniards and the Aztecs, provoked in part by demands by Cortés that the Aztecs denounce their native beliefs and accept Christianity. When the Spanish took Moctezuma hostage and began to destroy Aztec religious shrines, the local population revolted and drove the invaders from the city. Receiving assistance from the state of Tlaxcallan, Cortés managed to fight his way back into the city. Meanwhile the Aztecs were beginning to suffer the first effects of the diseases brought by the Europeans, which would eventually wipe out the majority of the local population. In a battle that to many Aztecs must have seemed to symbolize the dying of the legendary fifth sun, the Aztecs were finally vanquished. Within months, their magnificent city and its temples, believed by the conquerors to be the work of Satan, had been destroyed.

The First Civilizations in South America

South America is a vast continent, characterized by extremes in climate and geography. The north is dominated by the vast Amazon River, which flows through dense tropical jungles carrying a larger flow of water than any other river system in the world. Further to the south, the jungles are replaced by prairies and steppes stretching westward to the Andes Mountains, which extend the entire length of the continent, from the Isthmus of Panama to the Strait of Magellan far to the south. Along the Pacific coast, on the western slopes of the mountains, are some of the driest desert regions in the world.

South America has been inhabited by human beings for at least 12,000 years. Wall paintings recently discovered at the "cavern of the painted rock" in the Amazon region suggest that Stone Age peoples were living in the area at least 11,000 years ago. Evidence of human settlement dating back to 9500 B.C.E. has been found on the Tierra del Fuego, at the southern tip of the continent. Early peoples were hunters and food gatherers, but there are indications that irrigated farming was practiced in the northern fringe of the Andes Mountains as early as 2000 B.C.E. Other farming communities of similar age have been discovered in the Amazon River valley and on the western slopes of the Andes Mountains, where evidence of terraced agriculture dates back about four thousand years.

By the sixth millennium B.C.E., more complex societies had emerged in the central Andes Mountains, in the region of modern Peru, Bolivia, and Ecuador. Archaeologists have discovered the remains of ceremonial precincts, complete with temples, ancestral tombs, and pyramids, similar to those of Mesoamerica. This early Andes civilization reached its height during the first millennium B.C.E. with the emergence of the Chavin style, named for a site near the modern city of Chavin de Huantar, in the central mountains of modern Peru. The ceremonial precinct at the Chavin site contained an impressive stone temple complete with interior galleries, a stone-block ceiling, and a system of underground canals that probably channeled water into the temple complex for ritualistic purposes. The structure was surrounded by stone figures depicting various deities and two pyramids, possibly dedicated to the sun and the moon.

Early in the first millennium C.E., another advanced civilization appeared, at Moche, in northern Peru, in the valley of the Moche River, which flows from the foothills of the Andes Mountains into the Pacific Ocean. Artifacts found at Moche, especially the metalwork and stone and ceramic figures, exhibit a high quality of artisanship. They were imitated at river valley sites throughout the surrounding area, which suggests that the authority of the Moche rulers may have extended as far as four hundred miles along the coast. The artifacts also indicate that the people at Moche, like those in Central America, were preoccupied with warfare. Paintings and pottery as well as other artifacts in stone, metal, and ceramics frequently portray warriors, prisoners, and sacrificial victims. The Moche were also fascinated by the heavens, and much of their art consisted of celestial symbols and astronomical constellations.

The Moche River valley is extremely arid, receiving less than an inch of rain annually. The peoples in the area compensated by building a sophisticated irrigation

MAP 6.5 The Inca Empire About 1500 C.E.

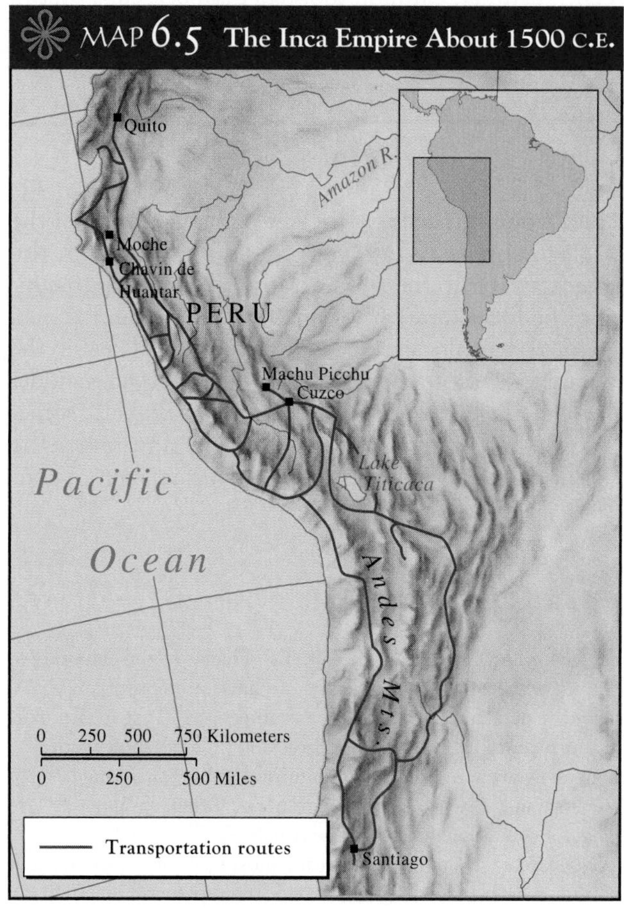

system to carry water from the river to the parched fields. At its zenith, Moche culture was spectacular. By the eighth century C.E., however, the civilization was in a state of collapse, the irrigation canals had been abandoned, and the remaining population suffered from severe malnutrition.

What had happened to bring Moche culture to this untimely end? Archaeologists speculate that environmental changes, perhaps brought on by changes in the water temperature known as El Niño, led to major flooding of coastal regions and the advance of sand dunes into the irrigated fields.

Three hundred years later, a new power, the kingdom of Chimor, with its capital at Chanchan, at the mouth of the Moche River, emerged in the area. Built almost entirely of adobe, Chanchan housed an estimated 30,000 residents in an area of over twelve square miles and included a number of palace compounds surrounded by walls nearly thirty feet high. One compound contained an intricate labyrinth that wound its way progressively inward until it ended in a central chamber, probably occupied by the ruler. Like the Moche before them, the people of Chimor relied on irrigation to funnel the water from the river into their fields. An elaborate system of canals brought the water through hundreds of miles of hilly terrain to the fields near the coast. Nevertheless, by the fifteenth century, Chimor, too, had disappeared, a victim of floods and a series of earthquakes that destroyed the intricate irrigation system that had been the basis of its survival.

CHRONOLOGY

EARLY AMERICA

Arrival of human beings in America	At least 15,000 years ago
First organized societies in the Andes	c. 6000 B.C.E.
Agriculture first practiced	c. 5000 B.C.E.
Rise of Olmec culture	First millennium B.C.E.
Origins of Mayan civilization	First millennium C.E.
Teotihuacán civilization	c. 300 B.C.E.–800 C.E.
Moche civilization	c. 150 C.E.–800 C.E.
Decline of the Maya	c. ninth century
Civilization of Chimor	c. 1100–1450
Migration of Mexica to Valley of Mexico	Late twelfth century
Kingdom of the Aztecs	Fifteenth century
Inca take over central Andes	Fifteenth century
Arrival of Hernán Cortés in Mexico	1519
Pizarro's conquest of the Inca	1532

The Inca

The Chimor kingdom was eventually succeeded in the late fifteenth century by an invading force from the mountains far to the south. In the late fourteenth century, the Incas were only a small community in the area of Cuzco, a city located at an altitude of 10,000 feet in the mountains of southern Peru. In the 1440s, however, under the leadership of their powerful ruler Pachakuti (sometimes called Pachacutec, or "he who transforms the world"), the Inca peoples launched a campaign of con-

FANTASTIC CREATURE POT. Thanks to the elaborate pottery of the Moche valley artists, we have an impressive visual record of the daily lives of the Peruvian peoples living in the sixth to ninth centuries C.E. Many of these colorful pots show scenes from everyday activities, such as hunting, fishing, weaving, cooking, and playing musical instruments. Others display religious ceremonies and sacrifice rituals. As illustrated in the fanged face of this fantastic creature, most probably a jaguar, these potters often blended the natural with the supernatural, which expressed the Moche worldview.

quest that eventually brought the entire region under their authority. Under Pachakuti and his immediate successors, Topa Inca and Huayna Inca (the word *Inca* means "ruler"), the boundaries of the kingdom were extended as far as Ecuador, central Chile, and the edge of the Amazon basin.

THE WORLD OF THE FOUR QUARTERS: INCA POLITICS AND SOCIETY

Pachakuti created a highly centralized state. With a stunning concern for mathematical precision, he divided his empire, called Tahuantinsuyu or "the world of the four quarters," into provinces and districts. Each province contained about 10,000 residents (at least in theory) and was ruled by a governor related to the royal family. Excess inhabitants were transferred to other locations. The capital of Cuzco was divided into four quarters, or residential areas, and the social status and economic functions of the residents of each quarter were rigidly defined.

The state was built on forced labor. Often entire communities of workers were moved from one part of the country to another to open virgin lands or engage in massive construction projects. Under Pachakuti the capital of Cuzco was transformed from a city of mud and thatch into an imposing metropolis of stone. The walls built of close-fitting stones without the use of mortar were a wonder to early European visitors. The most impressive structure in the city was a temple dedicated to the sun. According to a Spanish observer, "all four walls of the temple were covered from top to bottom with plates and slabs of gold."[4] Equally impressive are the ruins of the abandoned city of Machu Picchu, built on a lofty hilltop far above the Urubamba River.

Another major construction project was a system of 24,800 miles of highways and roads that extended from the border of modern Colombia to a point south of modern Santiago, Chile. Two major roadways extended in a north-south direction, one through the Andes Mountains and the other along the coast, with connecting routes between them. Rest houses and storage depots were placed along the roads. Suspension bridges made of braided fiber and fastened to stone abutments on opposite banks were built over ravines and waterways. Use of the highways was restricted to official and military purposes. Trained runners carried messages rapidly from one way station to another, enabling information to travel up to 140 miles in a single day.

In rural areas, the population lived mainly by farming. In the mountains, the most common form was terraced agriculture, watered by irrigation systems that carried precise amounts of water into the fields, which were planted with maize, potatoes, and other crops. The plots were tilled by collective labor regulated by the state. Like other aspects of Inca society, marriage was strictly regulated, and men and women were required to select a marriage partner from within the immediate tribal group. For women, there was one escape from a life of domestic servitude. Fortunate maidens were selected to serve as "chosen virgins" in temples throughout the country (see the box on p. 186). Noblewomen were eligible to compete for service in the Temple of the Sun at Cuzco, while commoners might hope to serve in temples in the provincial capitals. Punishment for breaking the vow of chastity was harsh, and few evidently took the risk.

MACHU PICCHU. Situated in the Andes in modern Peru, Machu Picchu reflects the glory of Inca civilization. To farm such rugged terrain, the Incas constructed terraces and stone aqueducts. To span vast ravines, they built suspension bridges made of braided fiber and fastened them to stone abutments on the opposite banks. The most revered of the many temples and stone altars at Machu Picchu was the thronelike "hitching post of the sun" at the left, so called because of its close proximity to the sun god.

VIRGINS WITH RED CHEEKS

A letter from a Peruvian chief to King Philip III of Spain written four hundred years ago gives us a firsthand account of the nature of traditional Incan society. The purpose of author Huaman Poma was both to justify the history and culture of the Incan peoples and to record their sufferings under Spanish domination. In his letter, Poma describes Incan daily life from birth to death, in minute detail. He explains the different tasks assigned to men and women, beginning with their early education. Whereas boys were taught to watch the flocks and trap animals, girls were taught to dye, spin and weave cloth, as well as to perform other domestic chores. Most interesting, perhaps, was the emphasis that the Inca placed on virginity, as is witnessed in the document below. The Incan tradition of temple virgins is reminiscent of similar practices in ancient Rome, where young girls from noble families were chosen as priestesses to tend the sacred fire in the Temple of Vesta for thirty years. If one lost her virginity, she was condemned to be buried alive in an underground chamber.

HUAMAN POMA, *LETTER TO A KING*

During the time of the Incas certain women, who were called *accla* or "the chosen," were destined for lifelong virginity. Mostly they were confined in houses and they belonged to one of two main categories, namely sacred virgins and common virgins.

The so-called "virgins with red cheeks" entered upon their duties at the age of twenty and were dedicated to the service of the Sun, the Moon, and the Day-Star. In their whole life they were never allowed to speak to a man.

The virgins of the Inca's own shrine of Huanacauri were known for their beauty as well as their chastity. The other principal shrines had similar girls in attendance. At the less important shrines there were the older virgins who occupied themselves with spinning and weaving the silklike clothes worn by their idols. There was a still lower class of virgins, over forty years of age and no longer very beautiful, who performed unimportant religious duties and worked in the fields or as ordinary seamstresses.

Daughters of noble families who had grown into old maids were adept at making girdles, headbands, string bags, and similar articles in the intervals of their pious observances.

Girls who had musical talent were selected to sing or play the flute and drum at Court, weddings and other ceremonies, and all the innumerable festivals of the Inca year.

There was yet another class of *accla* or "chosen," only some of whom kept their virginity and others not. These were the Inca's beautiful attendants and concubines, who were drawn from noble families and lived in his palaces. They made clothing for him out of material finer than taffeta or silk. They also prepared a maize spirit of extraordinary richness, which was matured for an entire month, and they cooked delicious dishes for the Inca. They also lay with him, but never with any other man.

INCA CULTURE

Like many other civilizations in pre-Columbian Latin America, the Inca state was built on war. Soldiers for the 200,000-man Inca army, the largest and best armed in the region, were raised by universal male conscription. Military units were moved rapidly along the highway system and were housed in the rest houses located along the roadside. Since the Inca had no wheeled vehicles, supplies were carried on the backs of llamas. Once an area was placed under Incan authority, the local inhabitants were instructed in the Quechua language, which became the *lingua franca* of the state, and were introduced to the state religion. The Inca had no writing system but kept records using a system of knotted strings called *quipu* (see the box on p. 187).

As in the case of the Aztecs and the Maya, the lack of a fully developed writing system did not prevent the Inca from realizing a high level of cultural achievement. Most

THE *QUIPU*. Not having a writing system, the Inca tallied the various data of their kingdom on strands of knotted yarn. Highly skilled and esteemed, official secretaries recorded population census data, crop and household inventories, government inspector reports, crime investigations, taxes, legal decisions and contracts, and all the official statistics of the realm by an intricate system of tying knots on a circular grouping of strings of yarn. One Peruvian chronicler boasted 400 years ago that these dextrous officials recorded their facts "with such skill that the knots in their cords had the clarity of written letters."[5]

AN INCAN AIDE-MÉMOIRE

The Inca did not possess a written script. To record events and other aspects of their lives that they wished to remember, they used an ingenious system of knotted strings, called quipu. *This description of the process comes from the* Royal Commentaries of the Incas, *an account of Inca civilization and history written by Garcilaso de la Vega. Garcilaso, who was of mixed Inca and Spanish blood, was born shortly before the Spanish conquest of the Incan capital of Cuzco.*

GARCILASO DE LA VEGA, ROYAL COMMENTARIES OF THE INCAS

These men recorded on their knots all the tribute brought annually to the Inca, specifying everything by kind, species, and quality. They recorded the number of men who went to the wars, how many died in them, and how many were born and died every year, month by month. In short they may be said to have recorded on their knots everything that could be counted, even mentioning battles and fights, all the embassies that had come to visit the Inca, and all the speeches and arguments the king had uttered. But the purpose of the embassies or the contents of the speeches, or any other descriptive matter could not be recorded on the knots, consisting as it did of continuous spoken or written prose, which cannot be expressed by means of knots, since these can give only numbers and not words. To supply this want they used signs that indicated historical events or facts or the existence of any embassy, speech, or discussion in time of peace or war. Such speeches were preserved by the *quipucamayus* by memory in a summarized form of a few words: they were committed to memory and taught by tradition to their successors and descendants from father to son. This was especially practiced in the villages or provinces where the event in question had occurred: there naturally such traditions were preserved better than elsewhere, because the natives would treasure them. Another method too was used for keeping alive in the memory of the people their deeds and the embassies they sent to the Inca and the replies he gave them. The *amautas* who were their philosophers and sages took the trouble to turn them into stories, no longer than fables, suitable for telling to children, young people, and the rustics of the countryside: they were thus passed from hand to hand and age to age, and preserved in the memories of all. Their stories were also recounted in the form of fables of an allegorical nature, some of which we have mentioned, while others will be referred to later. Similarly the *harauicus*, who were their poets, wrote short, compressed poems, embracing a history, or an embassy, or the king's reply. In short, everything that could not be recorded on the knots was included in these poems, which were sung at their triumphs and on the occasion of their greater festivals, and recited to the young Incas when they were armed knights. Thus they remembered their history.

of what survives was recorded by the Spanish and consists of entertainment for the elites. The Inca had a highly developed tradition of court theater, including both tragic and comic works. There was also some poetry, composed in blank verse and often accompanied by music played on reed instruments.

THE CONQUEST OF THE INCA

The Inca empire was still in existence when the first Spanish expeditions arrived in the central Andes. The leader of the Spanish invaders, Francisco Pizarro, was accompanied by only a few hundred companions, but like Hernán Cortés he possessed steel weapons, gunpowder, and horses, none of which were familiar to his hosts. In the meantime, internal factionalism, combined with the onset of contagious diseases spread unknowingly by the Europeans, had weakened the ruling elite, and the empire fell rapidly to the Spanish forces in 1532. The last Inca ruler was tried by the Spaniards and executed. Pre-Columbian South America's greatest age was over.

STATELESS SOCIETIES IN THE NEW WORLD

Beyond Central America and the high ridges of the Andes Mountains, on the Great Plains of North America, along the Amazon River in South America, and on the islands of the Caribbean Sea, other communities of Amerindians were also beginning to master the art of agriculture and to build organized societies.

Although human beings had occupied much of the continent of North America during the early phase of human settlement in the New World, the switch to farming as a means of survival did not occur until the third millennium B.C.E. at the earliest, and not until much later in most areas of the continent. Until that time, most Amerindian communities lived by hunting, fishing, or foraging. As the supply of large animals began to diminish, they turned to smaller game and to fishing and foraging for wild plants, fruits, and nuts.

It was probably during the third millennium B.C.E. that peoples in selected parts of North America began to cultivate indigenous plants for food in a systematic way. As wild game and food became scarce, some communities began to place more emphasis on cultivating crops. This shift first occurred in the Mississippi River valley from Ohio, Indiana, and Illinois down to the Gulf of Mexico. Among the most commonly cultivated crops were maize, squash, beans, and various types of grasses.

As the population in the area increased, people began to congregate in villages, and sedentary communities began to develop in the alluvial lowlands, where the soil could be cultivated for many years at a time because of the nutrients deposited by the river water. Village councils were established to adjudicate disputes, and in a few cases several villages banded together under the authority of a local chieftain. Urban centers began to appear, some of them inhabited by as many as 10,000 people or more. At the same time, regional trade increased. The people of the Hopewell culture in Ohio ranged from the shores of Lake Superior to the Appalachian Mountains and the Gulf of Mexico in search of metals, shells, obsidian, and manufactured items to support their economic needs and religious beliefs.

At the site of Cahokia, near the modern city of East St. Louis, Illinois, archaeologists found a burial mound more than ninety-eight feet high with a base larger than that of the Great Pyramid in Egypt. A hundred smaller mounds were also found in the vicinity. The town itself, which covered almost 300 acres and was surrounded by a wooden stockade, was apparently the administrative capital of much of the surrounding territory until its decline in the thirteenth century C.E. Cahokia carried on extensive trade with other communities throughout the region, and there are some signs of regular contacts with the civilizations in Mesoamerica, such as the presence of ball courts in the Central American style. But wars were not uncommon, leading the Iroquois, who inhabited much of the modern states of Pennsylvania and New York as well as parts of southern Canada, to create a tribal alliance called the League of Iroquois.

West of the Mississippi River basin, most Amerindian peoples lived by hunting or food gathering. During the first millennium C.E., knowledge of agriculture gradually spread up the rivers to the Great Plains, and farming was practiced as far west as southwestern Colorado, where the Anasazi peoples (Navajo for "alien ancient ones") established an extensive agricultural community in an area extending from northern New Mexico and Arizona to southwestern Colorado and parts of southern Utah. Although they apparently never discovered the wheel or used beasts of burden, the Anasazi created a system of roads that facilitated an extensive exchange of technology, products, and ideas throughout the region. By the ninth century, they had mastered the art of irrigation, which allowed them to expand their productive efforts to squash and beans, and had established an important urban center at Chaco Canyon, in southern New Mexico, where they built a walled city with dozens of three-story adobe houses with timbered roofs. Community religious functions were carried out in two large circular chambers called kivas. Clothing was made from hides or cotton cloth. At its height, Pueblo Bonito contained several hundred compounds housing several thousand residents. Another urban community was eventually established along a cliff face at Mesa Verde, in southwestern Colorado.

Sometime during the late twelfth and thirteenth centuries, however, these settlements were suddenly abandoned, as the inhabitants migrated southward. Their descendants, the Zuni and the Hopi, now occupy pueblos in central Arizona and New Mexico. For years, archaeologists surmised that a severe drought was the root cause of the migration, but in recent years new evidence has raised doubts that decreasing rainfall, by itself, was a sufficient explanation. An increase in internecine warfare, perhaps brought about by climatic changes, may also have played a role in the decision to relocate. Some archaeologists point to evidence that cannibalism was practiced at Pueblo Bonito and suggest that migrants from the south may have arrived in the area, provoking bitter rivalries within Anasazi society. In any event, with increasing aridity and the importation of the horse by the Spanish in the sixteenth century (a native version of the horse had died out thousands of years earlier), hunting revived, and mounted nomads like the Apache and the Navajo came to dominate much of the Southwest.

East of the Andes Mountains in South America, other Amerindian societies were beginning to make the transition to agriculture. Perhaps the most prominent were the Arawak, a people living along the Orinoco River in modern Venezuela. Having begun to cultivate manioc (a tuber used today in the manufacture of tapioca) along the banks of the river, they gradually migrated down to the coast and then proceeded to move eastward along the northern coast of the continent. Some occupied the islands of the Caribbean Sea. In their new island habitat, they lived by a mixture of fishing, hunting, and cultivating maize, beans, manioc, and squash, as well as other crops such as peanuts, peppers, and pineapples. As the population increased, a pattern of political organization above the village level appeared, along with recognizable social classes headed by a chieftain whose authority included control over the economy. The Arawak practiced human sacrifice, and some urban centers contained ball courts, suggesting the possibility of contacts with Mesoamerica.

In most such societies, where clear-cut class stratifications had not as yet taken place, the roles of men and women were considered to be of equal status. Men were responsible for hunting, warfare, and dealing with out-

CLIFF PALACE AT MESA VERDE. Mesa Verde is one of the best-developed sites of the Anasazi peoples in southwestern North America. At one time they were farmers who tilled the soil atop the mesas, but eventually they were forced to build their settlements in more protected locations. At Cliff Palace, shown here, adobe houses were hidden on the perpendicular face of the mesa. Access was achieved only by a perilous descent via indented finger- and toeholds on the rock face.

siders, while women were accountable for the crops, the distribution of food, maintaining the household, and bearing and raising the children. Their roles were complementary and were often viewed as a divine division of labor. In such cases, Indian women in the stateless societies of North America held a position of greater respect than their counterparts in the river valley civilizations of the Old World.

CONCLUSION

The first human beings did not arrive in the New World until quite late in the prehistorical period. For the next several millennia, their descendants were forced to respond to the challenges of the environment in total isolation from other parts of the world. Nevertheless, around 5000 B.C.E., farming settlements began to appear in river valleys and upland areas in both Central and South America. Not long afterward—at least in historical time—organized communities located along the coast of the Gulf of Mexico and the western slopes of the central Andes Mountains embarked on the long march toward civilization.

What is perhaps most striking about these developments is how closely the process in the New World paralleled that in the Old. Although the civilizations in Central and South America were less advanced in terms of technology (the lack of iron and the wheel, for example, and the absence of a sophisticated writing system), in many other respects the states in Central America and the Andes were the equal of those that we will discuss in later chapters. One need only point to the awed comments of early Spanish visitors, who said that the cities of the Aztecs were the equal of Seville and the other great metropolitan centers of Spain.

What was most repugnant to those early European visitors were the religious beliefs and practices of the civilizations that they encountered. They were repelled, of course, by the worship of strange idols, but even more by the human sacrifices on a massive scale. Before rushing to judgment, however, we should remember that similar practices had been carried out in many societies of the Old World, including the ancient civilizations of Egypt, India, and China. The Spaniards were perhaps most surprised to discover that civilizations that in other respects had achieved such a high degree of culture also practiced human sacrifice.

In recent years, some scholars have speculated that the peoples in the Americas were more peaceful than their counterparts in the Old World. The bulk of the evidence, however, suggests that the Amerindian peoples were every bit as addicted to warfare as were those of the ancient empires of Africa and Asia. Yet in both hemispheres it appears that the first civilizations formed by the human species were brought to an end as much by environmental changes as by war. In the next chapter, we shall return to the Old World, where new civilizations were in the process of replacing the ancient empires.

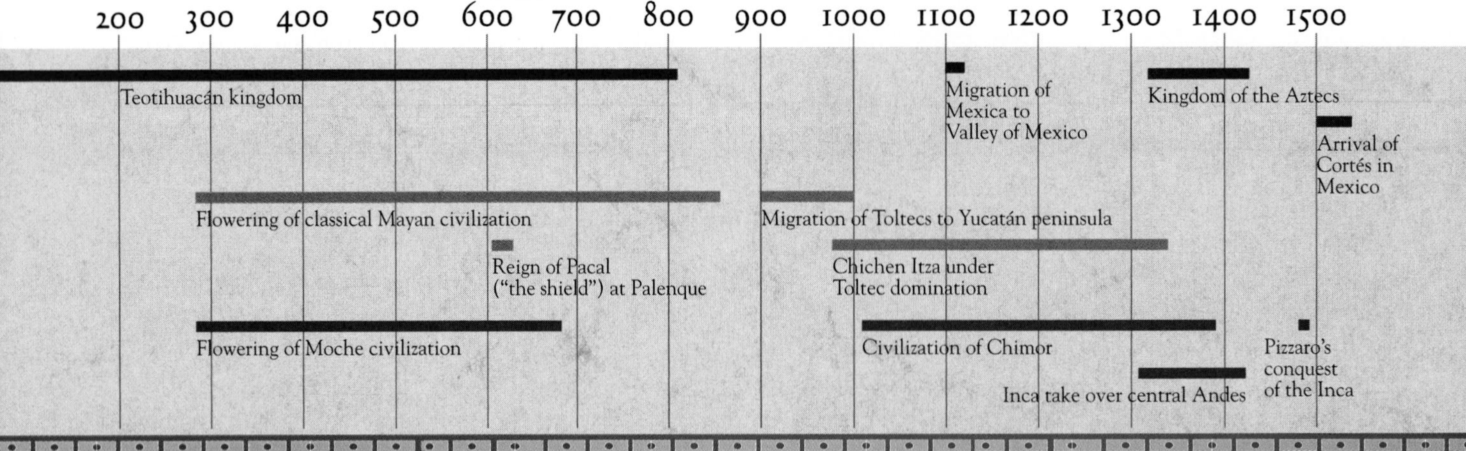

Chapter Notes

1. Quoted in Sylvanus Morley and George W. Brainerd, *The Ancient Maya* (Stanford, Calif., 1983), p. 513.
2. Bernal Díaz, *The Conquest of New Spain* (Harmondsworth, 1975), p. 210.
3. Michael Coe, Dean Snow, and Elizabeth Benson, *Atlas of Ancient America* (New York, 1988), p. 149.
4. Garcilaso de la Vega, El Inca, *Royal Commentaries of the Incas and General History of Peru,* Part I, trans. Harold V. Livermore (Austin, Tex., 1966), p. 180.
5. Quote from Huaman Poma, *Letter to a King* (New York, 1978), p. 101.

Suggested Readings

For a profusely illustrated and informative overview of the early civilizations of the Americas, see M. Coe, D. Snow, and E. Benson, *Atlas of Ancient America* (New York, 1988). The first arrival of human beings in the New World is discussed in J. D. Jennings, ed., *Ancient Native Americans* (San Francisco, 1978), and B. Fagan, *The Great Journey: The Peopling of Ancient America* (London, 1987).

For an early classical work on Mayan civilization, see S. G. Morley and G. W. Brainerd, *The Ancient Maya* (Stanford, Calif., 1983). N. Hammond, *Ancient Maya Civilization* (New Brunswick, N.J., 1982) provides a general survey for the nonspecialist. See also M. D. Coe, *The Maya* (London, 1993). For a richly illustrated general survey, see G. E. Stuart and G. S. Stuart, *The Mysterious Maya* (Washington, D.C., 1977).

For a recent overview of Aztec civilization in Mexico, see B. Fagan, *The Aztecs* (New York, 1984). S. D. Gillespie, *The Aztec Kings: The Construction of Rulership in Mexican History* (Tucson, 1989) is an imaginative effort to uncover the symbolic meaning in Aztec traditions. On the Olmecs and the Zapotecs, see E. P. Benson, *The Olmec and Their Neighbors* (Washington, D.C., 1981); M. D. Coe and R. A. Diehl, *In the Land of the Olmec* (Austin, Tex., 1980); and R. E. Blanton, *Monte Alban: Settlement Patterns at the Ancient Zapotec Capital* (New York, 1978).

Much of our information about the lives of the peoples of ancient Central America comes from Spanish writers who visited or lived in the area during the sixteenth and seventeenth centuries. For the original Spanish conquest of Mexico, see H. Cortés, *Letters from Mexico* (New Haven, Conn., 1986), and B. Díaz, *The Conquest of New Spain* (Harmondsworth, 1975). See also Fray D. Duran, *The Aztecs: The History of the Indies of New Spain* (New York, 1964).

On the Inca and their predecessors, see R. W. Keatinge, ed., *Peruvian Prehistory: An Overview of Pre-Inca and Inca Society* (Cambridge, 1988); G. Bankes, *Peru Before Pizarro* (Oxford, 1977); and E. P. Lanning, *Peru Before the Incas* (Englewood Cliffs, N.J., 1967). The arrival of the Spanish is chronicled in C. Howard, *Pizarro and the Conquest of Peru* (New York, 1967). For an extended account of Inca civilization, see G. de la Vega, El Inca, *Royal Commentaries of the Incas and General History of Peru* (Austin, Tex., 1966).

On the art and culture of the ancient Americas, see E. Pasztory, *Aztec Art* (New York, 1983); E. Henning and J. Raney, *Monuments of the Inca* (Boston, 1982); and L. Schele and M. E. Miller, *The Blood of Kings: A New Interpretation of Maya Art* (Austin, Tex., 1986). Writing systems are discussed in D. H. Kelley, *Deciphering the Maya Script* (Austin, Tex., 1976), and J. E. S. Thompson, *Maya Hieroglyphic Writing: An Introduction* (Norman, Okla., 1971).

For recent studies on social issues, see Linda Schele and David Freidel, *A Forest of Kings: The Untold Story of the Ancient Maya* (New York, 1990); Rudolph van Zantwijk, *The Aztec Arrangement: The Social History of Pre-Spanish Mexico* (Norman, Okla., 1985); and Nancy Shoemaker, *Negotiators of Change: Historical Perspectives on Native American Women* (New York, 1995).

For additional reading, go to InfoTrac College Edition, your online research library at http://web1.infotrac-college.com

Enter the search terms "Inca or Incan" using Keywords.

Enter the search term "Aztec" using Keywords.

Enter the search terms "Maya or Mayan" using Keywords.

Enter the search terms "Machu Picchu" using Keywords.

Enter the search terms "Latin America history" using Keywords.

CHAPTER

7

THE WORLD OF ISLAM

CHAPTER OUTLINE

- THE RISE OF ISLAM
- THE TEACHINGS OF MUHAMMAD
- THE ARAB EMPIRE AND ITS SUCCESSORS
- ISLAMIC CIVILIZATION
- CONCLUSION

FOCUS QUESTIONS

- What are the main tenets of Islam, and how does it compare with Judaism and Christianity?
- Why did the Arabs undergo such a rapid expansion in the seventh and eighth centuries, and why were they so successful in amassing an empire?
- What were the basic political structures of the Arab empire under the Umayyads and the Abbasids?
- How did the Seljuk Turks, the Crusades, and the Mongols affect Islamic civilization?
- What were the main features of Islamic society and culture?

In the year 570, in the Arabian city of Mecca, there was born a child named Muhammad whose life changed the course of world history. The son of a merchant, Muhammad grew to maturity in a time of transition. Old empires that had once ruled the entire Middle East were only a distant memory. The region was now divided into many separate states, and the people adhered to many different faiths.

Within a few decades of Muhammad's death, the Middle East was united once again. The initial triumph was primarily political and military. Arab armies marched westward across North Africa and eastward into Mesopotamia and Persia, imposing their authority and creating a new empire that stretched from the Iberian peninsula to the Indus valley. But Arab rule also brought with it a new religion and a new culture—that of Islam.

Islamic beliefs and culture exerted a powerful influence in all areas occupied by Arab armies. Initially, Arab beliefs and customs, as reflected through the prism of Muhammad's teachings, transformed the societies and cultures of the peoples living within the new empire. But eventually the distinctive political and cultural forces that had long characterized the region began to reassert themselves. Factional struggles led to the decline and then the destruction of the Arab empire. Invading forces from Central Asia established their control over the great mercantile cities of the region, while Christian crusaders attacked the empire from the west. New states formed in Spain, North Africa, and Persia and began to put their own stamp on the cultures of the region. Like the empires that had preceded it, the Arab empire, with its capital at Baghdad, became a thing of the past.

Still, the Arab conquest left a powerful legacy that survived the decline of Arab political power. The ideological and emotional appeal of Islam remained strong throughout the Middle East and even extended into areas not occupied by Arab armies, such as the Indian subcontinent, Southeast Asia, and sub-Saharan Africa. At the same time, the political unification of the entire region, although temporary, provided an environment conducive to the revival and expansion of long-distance trade and the exchange of culture and ideas that had taken place before the collapse of the classical empires at the beginning of the first millennium C.E. Although the vision of regional political and cultural unity that had inspired Muhammad and his followers was never realized, Islam remained a powerful force that provided a measure of religious and cultural unity for the region.

The Rise of Islam

The Arabs were a Semitic-speaking people of southwestern Asia with a long history. They were mentioned in Greek sources of the fifth century B.C.E. and even earlier in the Old Testament. The Greek historian Herodotus had applied the name *Arab* to the entire peninsula, calling it Arabia. In 106 B.C.E., the Romans extended their authority to the Arabian peninsula, transforming it into a province of their growing empire.

During Roman times, the region was inhabited primarily by the Bedouin Arabs, nomadic peoples who came originally from the northern part of the peninsula. Bedouin society was organized on a tribal basis. The ruling member of the tribe was called the *sheikh* and was selected from one of the leading families by a council of elders called the *majlis*. The *sheikh* ruled the tribe with the consent of the council. Each tribe was autonomous but felt a general sense of allegiance to the larger unity of all the clans in the region. In early times, the Bedouins had supported themselves primarily by sheepherding or by raiding passing caravans, but after the domestication of the camel during the first millennium B.C.E., the Bedouins began to participate in the caravan trade themselves and became major carriers of goods between the Persian Gulf and the Mediterranean Sea.

The Arabs of pre-Islamic times were polytheistic, with a supreme god known as Allah presiding over a community of spirits. It was a communal faith, involving all members of the tribe, and had no priesthood. The supreme deity was symbolized by a sacred stone. Each tribe possessed its own stone, but all worshiped a massive black meteorite, which was located in a central shrine called the *Ka'aba* in the commercial city of Mecca.

THE KA'ABA IN MECCA. The Ka'aba, a massive black meteorite in the Arabian city of Mecca, is the sacred stone of the Islamic faith. Wherever Muslims pray, they are instructed to face Mecca; each thus becomes a spoke of the Ka'aba, the holy center of the wheel of Islam. If they are able to do so, all Muslims are encouraged to visit the Ka'aba at least once in their lifetime. Called the *hajj*, this pilgrimage to Mecca represents the ultimate in spiritual fulfillment.

In the fifth and sixth centuries C.E., the economic importance of the Arabian peninsula began to increase. As a result of the political disorder in Mesopotamia—a consequence of the constant wars between the Byzantine and Persian Empires—and in Egypt, the trade routes that ran directly across the peninsula or down the Red Sea became increasingly risky, and a third route, which passed from the Mediterranean through Mecca to Yemen and then by ship across the Indian Ocean, became more popular. The communities in that part of the peninsula benefited from the change. As a consequence, relations between the Bedouins of the desert and the increasingly wealthy merchants of the towns began to become strained.

Into this intense world stepped Muhammad (also known as Mohammed), a man whose spiritual visions unified the Arab world with a speed no one would have suspected possible. Born in Mecca to a merchant family and orphaned at the age of six, Muhammad (570–632) grew up to become a caravan manager and eventually married a rich widow, Khadija, who was also his employer. For several years he lived in Mecca as a merchant but was apparently troubled by the growing gap between the Bedouin values of honesty and generosity (he himself was a member of the local Hashemite clan of the Quraishi tribe) and the acquisitive behavior of the affluent commercial elites in the city. Deeply concerned, he began to visit the nearby hills to meditate in isolation.

On one of these occasions, he experienced visions and heard a voice that he was convinced was inspired by Allah. According to tradition, the message was conveyed by the angel Gabriel, who commanded Muhammad to preach the revelations that he would be given.

Muhammad was acquainted with Jewish and Christian beliefs and came to believe that while Allah had already revealed himself in part through Moses and Jesus—and thus through the Hebraic and Christian traditions—the final revelations were now being given to him. Out of his revelations, which were eventually dictated to scribes, came the Koran or Qur'an, the holy scriptures of Islam (meaning "submission to the will of Allah"). The Koran contained the guidelines by which followers of Allah, known as Muslims (i.e., those who practice Islam), were to live. Like the Christians and the Jews, Muslims (also known as Moslems) were a "People of the Book."

After returning home, Muhammad set out to comply with Gabriel's command by preaching to the residents of Mecca about his revelations. At first, many were convinced that he was mad or a charlatan. Others were undoubtedly concerned that his vigorous attacks on traditional beliefs and the corrupt society around him could severely shake the social and political order. After three years of proselytizing, he had only thirty followers.

Discouraged by the systematic persecution of his followers, which was undertaken with a brutality reminiscent of the cruelties suffered by early Christians, as well as the failure of the Meccans to accept his message, in 622 Muhammad and some of his closest supporters (mostly from his own Hashemite clan) left the city and retreated north to the rival city of Yathrib, later renamed Medina, or "city of the Prophet." That flight, known in history as the Hegira (*Hijrah*), marks the first date of the official calendar of Islam. At Medina Muhammad failed in his original purpose—to convert the Jewish community in Medina to his beliefs. But he was successful in win-

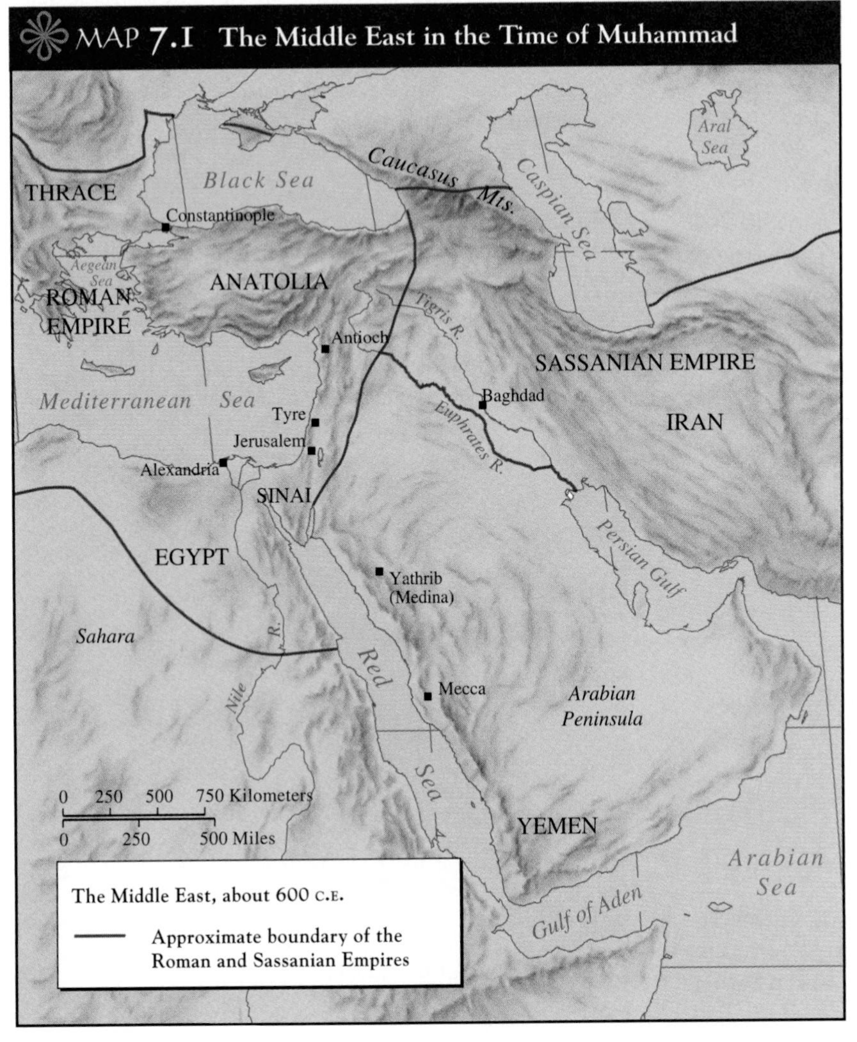

MUHAMMAD AND THE SACRED STONE. In pre-Islamic times, the Arabs were polytheistic, with a supreme deity symbolized by a sacred stone. Although each tribe possessed its own stone, all worshiped the black meteorite stone at a shrine in Mecca called the Ka'aba. In 630 Muhammad proclaimed the Ka'aba to be the sacred shrine of Islam. In this fourteenth-century miniature, we see Muhammad restoring the black stone to its rightful place in the wall of the Ka'aba.

ning support from many residents of the city as well as from Bedouins in the surrounding countryside. From this mixture, he formed the first Muslim community (the *umma*). Returning to his birthplace at the head of a considerable military force, Muhammad conquered Mecca and converted the townspeople to the new faith. In 630 he made a symbolic visit to the Ka'aba, where he declared it a sacred shrine of Islam and ordered the destruction of the idols of the traditional faith. Two years later, Muhammad died, just as Islam was beginning to spread throughout the peninsula.

The Teachings of Muhammad

Like Christianity and Judaism, Islam is monotheistic. Allah is the all-powerful being who created the universe and everything in it. Islam is also concerned with salvation and offers the hope of an afterlife. Those who hope to achieve it must subject themselves to the will of Allah. Unlike Christianity, Islam makes no claim to the divinity of its founder. Muhammad, like Jesus, Moses, and other figures of the Old Testament, was a prophet, but he was also a man like other men. Because human beings rejected his earlier messengers, Allah sent his final revelation through Muhammad.

At the heart of Islam is the Koran (meaning "recitation"), with its basic message that there is no God but Allah and Muhammad is his Prophet (see the box on p. 196). Consisting of 114 *suras* (chapters) that were drawn together into an integrated whole by a committee established after Muhammad's death, the Koran is not only the sacred book of Islam, but an ethical guidebook and a code of law and political theory combined.

Islam was a direct and simple faith, emphasizing the need to obey the will of Allah. This meant following a basic ethical code that consisted of what are popularly termed the "five pillars" of Islam: belief in Allah and Muhammad as his Prophet; standard prayer five times a day and public prayer on Friday at midday to worship Allah; observation of the holy month of Ramadan including fasting from dawn to sunset; making a pilgrimage, if possible, to Mecca in one's lifetime (see the box on p. 197); and giving alms (called the *zakat*) to the poor and unfortunate. The faithful who observed the law were guaranteed a place in an eternal paradise with the sensuous delights so obviously lacking in the midst of the Arabian desert.

Islam was not just a set of religious beliefs, but a way of life as well. After the death of Muhammad, Muslim scholars, known as the *ulama*, drew up a law code, called the *Shari'ah*, to provide believers with a set of prescriptions to regulate their daily lives. Much of the *Shari'ah* was drawn from the Koran or from the *Hadith*, a collection of the sayings of the Prophet that was used to supplement the revelations contained in the holy scriptures.

Believers were subject to strict behavioral requirements. In addition to the "five pillars," Muslims were forbidden to gamble, to eat pork, to drink alcoholic beverages, and to engage in dishonest behavior. Sexual mores were also strict. Contacts between unmarried men and women were discouraged, and ideally marriages were to be arranged by the parents. In accordance with Bedouin custom, polygyny was permitted, but Muhammad attempted to limit the practice by restricting males to four wives.

THE KORAN AND THE SPREAD OF THE MUSLIM FAITH

The Koran is the sacred book of Islam, holding a place comparable to that of the Bible in Christianity. In this selection from Chapter 47, it is apparent that Islam encourages the spreading of the faith, known to Muslims as Jihad. A garden of paradise quite unlike the arid desert homeland of the Arab warriors awaited all believers who died for Allah.

THE KORAN: CHAPTER 47, "MUHAMMAD, REVEALED AT MEDINA"

Allah will bring to nothing the deeds of those who disbelieve and debar others from His path. As for the faithful who do good works and believe in what is revealed to Muhammad—which is the truth from their Lord—He will forgive them their sins and ennoble their state.

This, because the unbelievers follow falsehood, while the faithful follow the truth from their Lord. Thus Allah coins their sayings for mankind.

When you meet the unbelievers in the battlefield strike off their heads and, when you have laid them low, bind your captives firmly. Then grant them their freedom or take ransom from them, until War shall lay down her armour.

Thus shall you so. Had Allah willed, He could Himself have punished them; but He has ordained it thus that He might test you, the one by the other.

As for those who are slain in the cause of Allah, He will not allow their works to perish. He will vouchsafe them guidance and ennoble their state; He will admit them to the Paradise He has made known to them.

Believers, if you help Allah, Allah will help you and make you strong. But the unbelievers shall be consigned to perdition. He will bring their deeds to nothing. Because they have opposed His revelations, He will frustrate their works.

Have they never journeyed through the land and seen what was the end of those who have gone before them? Allah destroyed them utterly. A similar fate awaits the unbelievers, because Allah is the protector of the faithful; because the unbelievers have no protector.

Allah will admit those who embrace the true faith and do good works to gardens watered by running streams. The unbelievers take their fill of pleasure and eat as the beasts eat: but Hell shall be their home. . . .

This is the Paradise which the righteous have been promised. There shall flow in it rivers of unpolluted water, and rivers of milk forever fresh; rivers of delectable wine and rivers of clearest honey. They shall eat therein of every fruit and receive forgiveness from their Lord. Is this like the lot of those who shall abide in Hell forever and drink scalding water which will tear their bowels? . . .

Know that there is no god but Allah. Implore Him to forgive your sins and to forgive the true believers, men and women. Allah knows your busy haunts and resting places.

THE QUIET SPIRIT OF A MOSQUE. For Muslims, the mosque is a revered oasis for worship, reflection, and the reading of the Koran. The practicing Muslim is required to pray to Allah five times a day. While women normally pray at home, men are expected to visit a mosque. If a mosque is not available, they may pray wherever they are at the time of the muezzin's call. At that time, each Muslim stops whatever he is doing and kneels down, facing Mecca, on his portable prayer rug. Above all, the mosque is a place for quiet devotion, a refuge from the bustle of daily life. The artwork in a mosque should reflect motifs from the Koran. In this illustration, two of the faithful pray in a mosque under iron lamps on plush layers of carpets decorated with Koranic symbols.

A PILGRIMAGE TO MECCA

The pilgrimage to Mecca, one of the "five pillars of Islam," is the duty of every Muslim. Ibn Jubayr, a twelfth-century Spanish Muslim, left a description of his trip in his journal. The work is famous for its vivid and abundant detail. In this almost lyrical passage, Ibn Jubayr tells of reaching his final destination, the Ka'aba at Mecca, containing the Black Stone. The Qarmata were an extremist religious sect in ninth- and tenth-century Mesopotamia.

IBN JUBAYR, *TRAVELS*

The blessed Black Stone is encased in the corner [of the Ka'aba] facing east. The depth to which it penetrates it is not known, but it is said to extend two cubits into the wall. Its breadth is two-thirds of a span, its length one span and a finger joint. It has four pieces, joined together, and it is said that it was the Qarmata—may God curse them—who broke it. Its edges have been braced with a sheet of silver whose white shines brightly against the black sheen and polished brilliance of the Stone, presenting the observer a striking spectacle which will hold his gaze. The Stone, when kissed, has a softness and moistness which so enchants the mouth that he who puts his lips to it would wish them never to be removed. This is one of the special favors of Divine Providence, and it is enough that the Prophet—may God bless and preserve him—declare it to be a covenant of God on earth. May God profit us by the kissing and touching of it. By His favor may all who yearn fervently for it be brought to it. In the sound piece of the stone, to the right of him who presents himself to kiss it, is a small white spot that shines and appears like a mole on the blessed surface. Concerning this white mole, there is a tradition that he who looks upon it clears his vision, and when kissing it one should direct one's lips as closely as one can to the place of the mole.

The Arab Empire and Its Successors

The death of Muhammad presented his followers with a dilemma. Although Muhammad had not claimed divine qualities, Muslims saw no separation between political and religious authority. Submission to the will of Allah meant submission to his Prophet Muhammad. According to the Koran, "Whoso obeyeth the messenger obeyeth Allah."[1] Muhammad's charismatic authority and political skills had been at the heart of his success. But he never named a successor, and although he had several daughters, he left no sons. In a male-oriented society, who would lead the community of the faithful?

Shortly after Muhammad's death, a number of his closest followers selected Abu Bakr, a wealthy merchant from Medina who was Muhammad's father-in-law and one of his first supporters, as caliph (*khalifa*, literally "successor"). The caliph was the temporal leader of the Islamic community and was also considered, in general terms, to be a religious leader, or *imam*. Under Abu Bakr's prudent leadership, the movement succeeded in suppressing factional tendencies among some of the Bedouin tribes in the peninsula and began to direct its attention to wider fields. Muhammad had used the Arabic tribal custom of the *razzia* or raid in the struggle against his enemies. Now his successors turned to the same custom to expand the authority of the movement (see the box on p. 196). The Koran called this activity "striving in the way of the Lord," or *jihad*. Although sometimes translated as "holy war," the *jihad* grew out of the Arabic tradition of tribal raids, which were permitted as a way to channel the warlike energies of the Bedouin tribes.

Once the Arabs had become unified under Muhammad's successor, they began to conduct a *jihad* on a larger scale, directing outward against neighboring peoples the energy they had formerly directed against each other. The Byzantine and the Persian Empires were the first to feel the strength of the newly united Arabs, now aroused to a peak of zeal by their common faith. At Yarmuk in 636, the Muslims defeated the Byzantine army. Four years later, they took possession of the Byzantine province of Syria. To the east, the Arabs defeated a Persian force in 637 and then went on to conquer the entire empire of the Sassanids by 650. In the meantime, Egypt and other areas of North Africa were also brought under Arab authority (see Chapter 8).

What explains this rapid expansion of the Arabs after the rise of Islam in the early seventh century? Historians have proposed various explanations ranging from a prolonged drought on the Arabian peninsula to the desire of Islam's leaders to channel the energies of their new converts. Another hypothesis is that the expansion was deliberately planned by the ruling elites in Mecca to extend their trade routes and bring surplus-producing regions under their control. Whatever the case, Islam's ability to unify the Bedouin peoples certainly played a role. Although the Arab triumph was made substantially easier by the ongoing conflict between the Byzantine and Persian Empires, which had weakened both powers, the strength of the Bedouin armies should not be overlooked. Led by a series of brilliant generals, the Arabs put together a large, highly motivated army, whose valor was enhanced by the belief that Muslim warriors who died in battle were guaranteed a place in paradise.

Once the armies had prevailed, Arab administration of the conquered areas was relatively tolerant. Sometimes, due to a shortage of trained Arab administrators, government was left to local officials. Conversion to Islam was voluntary in accordance with the maxim in the Koran that "there shall be no compulsion in religion."[2] Those who chose not to convert were required only to submit to Muslim rule and pay a head tax in return for exemption from military service, which was required of all Muslim males. Under such conditions, the local populations often welcomed Arab rule as preferable to Byzantine rule or that of the Sassanid dynasty in Persia. Furthermore, the simple and direct character of the new religion, as well as its egalitarian qualities (all people were viewed as equal in the eyes of Allah), were undoubtedly attractive to peoples throughout the region.

Succession Problems and the Rise of the Umayyads

The main challenge to the growing empire came from within. Some of Muhammad's followers had not agreed with the selection of Abu Bakr as the first caliph and promoted the candidacy of Muhammad Ali, Muhammad's cousin and son-in-law, as an alternative. Ali's claim was ignored by other leaders, however, and after Abu Bakr's death, the office was passed to Umar, another of Muhammad's followers. In 656, Umar's successor Uthman was assassinated, and Ali was finally selected for the position. But Ali's rivals were convinced that he had been implicated in the death of his predecessor, and a factional struggle broke out within the Muslim leadership. In 661 Ali himself was assassinated, and Mu'awiyah, the governor of Syria and one of Ali's chief rivals, replaced him in office. Mu'awiyah thereupon made the caliphate hereditary in his own family, called the Umayyads, who were a branch of the Quraishi clan. The new caliphate, with its capital at Damascus, remained in power for nearly a century.

The factional struggle within Islam did not bring an end to Arab expansion. At the beginning of the eighth century, new attacks were launched at both the western and the eastern end of the Mediterranean world. Arab armies advanced across North Africa and conquered the Berbers, a primarily pastoral people living along the Mediterranean coast and in the mountains in the interior. Then, around 710 Arab forces, supplemented by Berber allies under their commander Tariq, crossed the Strait of Gibraltar and occupied southern Spain. The Visigothic kingdom, already weakened by internecine warfare, quickly collapsed, and by 725 most of the Iberian peninsula had become a Muslim state with its center in Andalusia. Seven years later, an Arab force, making a foray into southern France, was defeated by the army of Charles Martel between Tours and Poitiers. Some historians think that internal exhaustion would have forced the invaders to retreat even without their defeat at the hands of the Franks. In any event, the Battle of Tours (or Poitiers) would be the high-water mark of Arab expansion in Europe.

In the meantime, in 717 another Muslim force had launched an attack on Constantinople with the hope of destroying the Byzantine Empire. But the Byzantines' use of Greek fire, an incendiary mixture of unknown composition, destroyed the Muslim fleet, thus saving the empire and indirectly Christian Europe, since the fall of Constantinople would have opened the door to an Arab invasion of eastern Europe. The Byzantine Empire and Islam now established an uneasy frontier in southern Asia Minor.

Arab power also extended to the east, consolidating Islamic rule in Mesopotamia and Persia and northward into Central Asia. But factional disputes continued to plague the empire. Many Muslims of non-Arab extraction resented the favoritism shown by local administrators to Arabs. In some cases, resentment led to revolt, as in Iraq, where Ali's second son, Hussein, disputed the legitimacy of the Umayyads and incited his supporters—to be known in the future as Shi'ites (from the Arabic phrase *shi'at Ali*, or "partisans of Ali")—to rise up against Umayyad rule in 680. Hussein's forces were defeated, but a schism between Shi'ite and Sunnite (usually translated as "orthodox") Muslims had been created that continues to the present.

Umayyad rule, always (in historian Arthur Goldschmidt's words) "more political than pious," created resentment, not only in Mesopotamia, but also in North Africa, where Berber resistance continued, especially in the mountainous areas south of the coastal plains. The Umayyads contributed to their own demise by their decadent behavior. One caliph allegedly swam in a pool of wine and then imbibed enough of the contents to lower the wine level significantly. Finally, in 750 a revolt led by Abu al-Abbas, a descendant of Muhammad's uncle, led to the overthrow of the Umayyads and the establishment of the Abbasid dynasty (750–1258) in what is now Iraq.

The Abbasids

The Abbasid caliphs brought political, economic, and cultural change to the world of Islam. While stressing religious orthodoxy, they tried to break down the distinctions between Arab and non-Arab Muslims. All Muslims were now allowed to hold both civil and military offices. This change helped to open Islamic culture to the influences of the occupied civilizations. Many Arabs now began to intermarry with the peoples they had conquered. In many parts of the Islamic world, notably North Africa and the eastern Mediterranean, most Muslim converts began to consider themselves Arabs. In 762, the Abbasids built a new capital city at Baghdad, on the Tigris River far to the east of the Umayyad capital at Damascus. The new capital was strategically positioned to take advantage of river traffic to the Persian Gulf and also lay astride the caravan route from the Mediterranean to Central Asia. The move eastward allowed Persian influence to come to the fore, encouraging a new cultural orientation. Under the Abbasids, judges, merchants, and government officials, rather than warriors, were viewed as the ideal citizens.

The new Abbasid caliphate experienced a period of splendid rule well into the ninth century. Best known of the caliphs of the time was Harun al-Rashid (786–809), or Harun "the upright," whose reign is often described as the golden age of the Abbasid caliphate. His son al-Ma'mun (813–833) was a patron of learning who founded an astronomical observatory and established a foundation for undertaking translations of classical Greek works. This was also a period of growing economic prosperity. The Arabs had conquered many of the richest provinces of the Roman Empire and now controlled the routes to the east. Baghdad became the center of an enormous commercial market that extended into Europe, Central Asia, and Africa, greatly adding to the wealth of the Islamic world and promoting an exchange of culture, ideas, and technology from one end of the known world to the other. Paper was introduced from China and eventually passed on to North Africa and Europe. Crops from India and Southeast Asia such as rice, sugar, sorghum, and cotton moved toward the west, while glass, wine, and indigo dye were introduced into China.

Under the Abbasids, the caliphs became more regal. More kings than spiritual leaders, described by such august phrases as the "caliph of God," they ruled by autocratic means hardly distinguishable from the kings and emperors in neighboring civilizations. A thirteenth-century Chinese author, who compiled a world geography based on accounts by Chinese travelers, left the following description of one of the later caliphs:

> The king wears a turban of silk brocade and foreign cotton stuff (buckram). On each new moon and full moon he puts on an eight-sided flat-topped headdress of pure gold, set with the most precious jewels in the world. His robe is of silk brocade and is bound around him with a jade girdle. On his feet he wears golden shoes. . . . The king's throne is set with pearls and precious stones, and the steps of the throne are covered with pure gold.[3]

As the caliph took on more of the trappings of a hereditary autocrat, the bureaucracy assisting him in administering the growing empire grew more complex as well. The caliph was advised by a council (called a *diwan*) headed by a prime minister, known as a *vizier* (*wazir*). The caliph did not attend meetings of the *diwan* in the normal manner, but sat behind a screen and then communicated his divine will to the *vizier*. Some historians have ascribed the change in the caliphate to Persian influence,

MAP 7.2 The Expansion of Islam

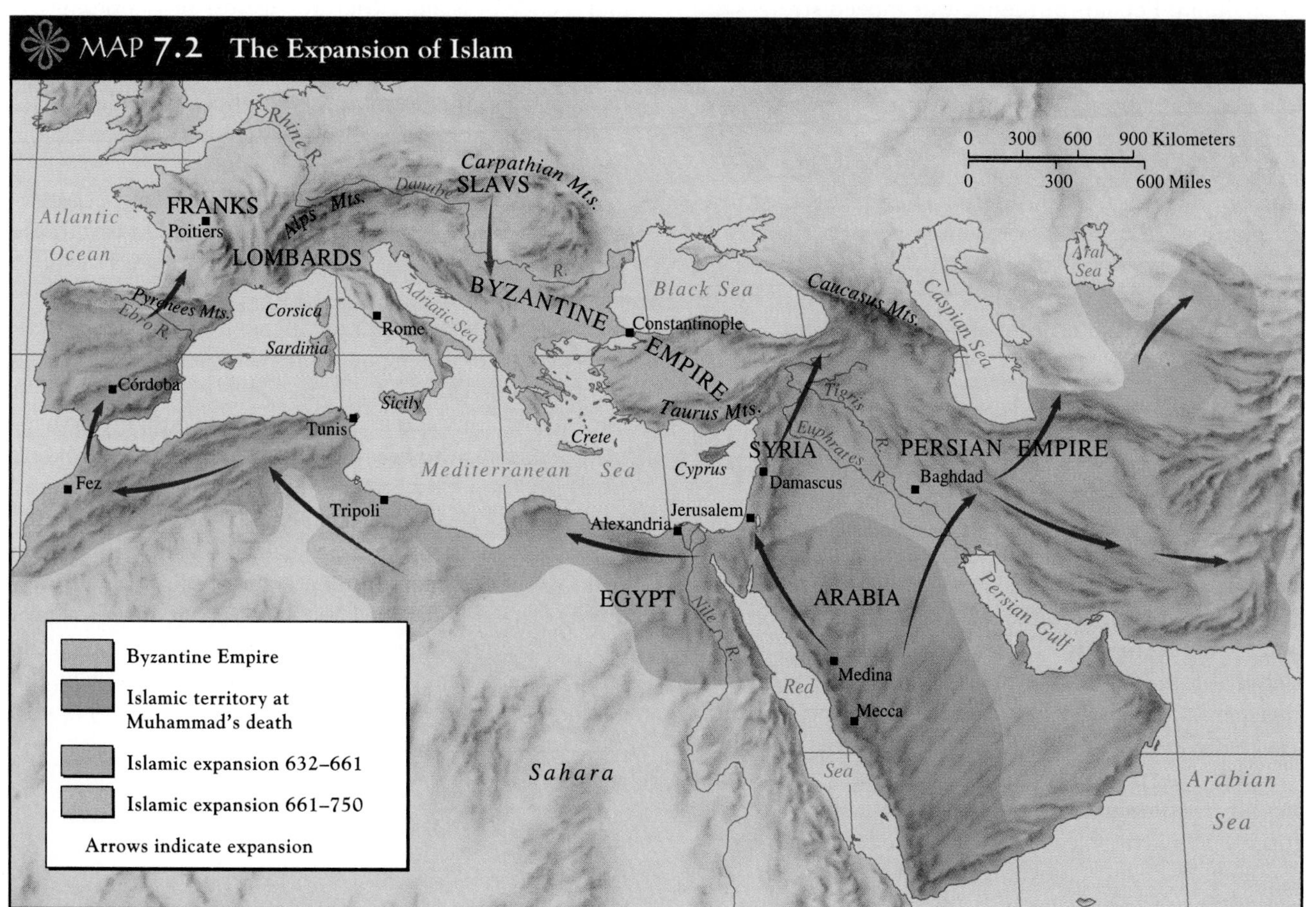

MAP 7.3 The Abbasid Caliphate at the Height of Its Power

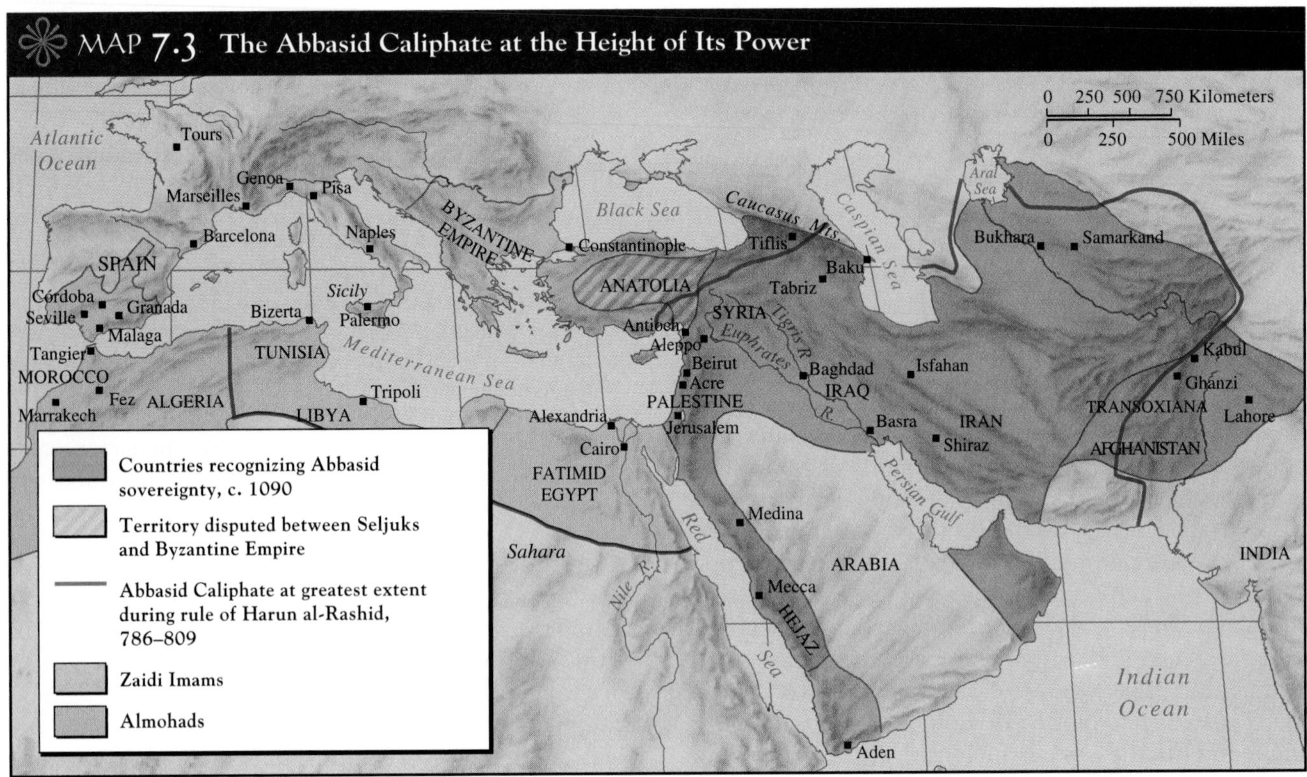

which permeated the empire after the capital was moved to Baghdad. Persian influence was indeed strong (the mother of the caliph al-Ma'mun, for example, was a Persian), but more likely, the increase in pomp and circumstance was a natural consequence of the growing power and prosperity of the empire.

However, an element of instability lurked below the aura of prosperity. Disputes over the succession to the caliphate were common. At Harun's death, the rivalry between his two sons Amin and al-Ma'mun led to civil war and the destruction of Baghdad. As described by the tenth-century Muslim historian al-Mas'udi,

> Mansions were destroyed, most remarkable monuments obliterated; prices soared. . . . Brother turned his sword against brother, son against father, as some fought for Amin, others for Ma'mun. Houses and palaces fueled the flames; property was put to the sack.[4]

Vast wealth also contributed to financial corruption. By awarding important positions to court favorites, the Abbasid caliphs began to undermine the foundations of their own power and eventually became mere figureheads. Under Harun al-Rashid, members of his Hashemite clan received large pensions from the state treasury, and his wife Zubaida reportedly spent vast sums while shopping on a pilgrimage to Mecca. One powerful family, the Barmakids, amassed vast wealth and power until Harun al-Rashid eliminated the entire clan in a fit of jealousy (see the box on p. 201).

The life of luxury enjoyed by the caliph and other political and economic elites in Baghdad seemingly undermined the stern fiber of Arab society as well as the strict moral code of Islam. Strictures against sexual promiscuity were widely ignored, and caliphs were rumored to maintain thousands of concubines in their harems. Divorce was common, homosexuality was widely practiced, and alcohol was consumed in public despite Islamic law's prohibition against imbibing spirits.

The process of disintegration was accelerated by changes that were taking place within the armed forces and the bureaucracy of the empire. Given the shortage of qualified Arabs for key positions in the army and the administration, the caliphate began to recruit officials from among the non-Arab peoples in the empire, such as Persians and Turks from Central Asia. These people gradually became a dominant force in the army and administration. Eventually, provincial rulers began to break away from central control and establish their own independent dynasties. Spain had already established its own caliphate when a prince of the Umayyad dynasty had escaped execution and fled there in 750. Morocco became independent, and in 973 a new Shi'ite dynasty under the Fatimids was established in Egypt with its capital at Cairo. With increasing disarray in the empire, the Islamic world was held together only by the common commitment to the Koran and the use of Arabic as the prevailing means of communication.

The Seljuk Turks

In the eleventh century, the Abbasid caliphate faced an even more serious threat in the form of the Seljuk Turks.

THE MURDER OF JA'FAR AL-BARMAKI

The historian al-Mas'udi is our best source for inside information about the reign of the caliph Harun al-Rashid. In this excerpt, Harun begins to suspect his favorite courtier, the handsome Ja'far of the powerful Barmakid family, of breaking his word. The story illustrates the intense jealousies and personal rivalries that affected court life in the Abbasid era. Some historians suspect that Harun's love for Ja'far was sexual.

AL-MAS'UDI, *THE MEADOWS OF GOLD*: THE FALL OF THE BARMAKIDS

'Yahya, the son of Khalid ibn Barmak, his two sons Ja'far and Fadl, and other members of this family were at the height of their power, which was without limit, and unassailable in their high offices. The days of their rule, it is said, were like a perpetual wedding feast, filled with unending happiness and joy. It was during this time that Harun al-Rashid said to Ja'far:

"Ja'far, there is no one in the world dearer or closer to me than yourself and no one whose conversation is sweeter or more desirable than yours. Now my sister Abbasa holds in my heart a place not inferior to that which I have given you. I have considered the feelings that each of you inspire in me and I have realized that I cannot easily dispense either with you or with my sister. . . . I know of only one way to procure myself this double pleasure and to enjoy henceforth the sweetness of both your companies. . . . I wish to have you marry Abbasa and to give you the right, by this marriage, to pass your evenings with her, to see her, to be near her, whenever I am with you both. But your privileges will end there."

[Ja'far accepted these conditions, and after the marriage took place, considered himself bound by his word and did not assert his conjugal rights. Abbasa, however, was secretly fond of Ja'far and determined to win his love. When her advances were spurned, she enlisted the help of Ja'far's mother in a secret plot to have a child by her husband. One day Ja'far's mother went to her son and said:]

"My child, I have been told of a young slave girl who . . . is lettered and learned, gracious and charming, her beauty is beyond compare. . . . I resolved to buy her for you and the matter is almost settled with her owner."

[Ja'far was delighted, and ... his mother agreed that on a given night she would present him with the pretty slave. Then she told Abbasa of her plan. When the time came, she dressed as a slave girl and went to the house of Ja'far's mother.] That night Ja'far, his head still turning from wine, left the Caliph's palace to come to the tryst. . . . Abbasa, on going in to her husband, found a man sufficiently drunk not to know her face or figure. Once the marriage had been consummated and her husband's lust satisfied, Abbasa asked:

"What do you think of the ruses of the daughters of kings?"

"Whom do you mean?" he asked, convinced that he was talking to some Byzantine slave girl.

"Of myself!" she answered. "I, your mistress, Abbasa, daughter of Mahdi!"

Ja'far rose in horror, his drunkenness suddenly gone, and returned to his senses. At once he went to his mother and said to her:

"You have sold me cheap and placed me on the edge of an abyss. See what the outcome of my predicament will be!"

[Abbasa became pregnant, and in due course gave birth to a son, whom she later sent to Mecca in the care of two servants to keep Harun al-Rashid from learning of his identity. But the caliph's wife Zubaida found out about the affair and informed her husband. In revenge, Harun ordered his courtier Ja'far to be assassinated. Then, out of remorse, he executed the assassin.]

The Seljuk Turks were a nomadic people from Central Asia who had converted to Islam and flourished as military mercenaries for the Abbasid caliphate, where they were known for their ability as mounted archers. Moving gradually into Iran and Armenia as the Abbasids weakened, the Seljuk Turks grew in number until by the eleventh century they were able to occupy the eastern provinces of the Abbasid empire. In 1055, a Turkish leader captured Baghdad and assumed command of the empire with the title of sultan (the term means "holder of power"). While the Abbasid caliph remained the chief representative of Sunni religious authority, the real military and political power of the state was in the hands of the Seljuk Turks. The latter did not establish their headquarters in Baghdad, which now entered a period of decline.

By the last quarter of the eleventh century, the Seljuks were exerting military pressure on Egypt and the Byzantine Empire. In 1071, when the Byzantines foolishly challenged the Turks, their army was routed at Manzikert, near Lake Van in eastern Turkey, and the victors took over most of the Anatolian peninsula. In dire straits, the Byzantine Empire turned to the west for help, setting in motion the papal pleas that led to the crusades.

In Europe, and undoubtedly within the Muslim world itself, the arrival of the Turks was regarded as a disaster. The Turks were viewed as barbarians who destroyed civilizations and oppressed populations. In fact, in many respects Turkish rule in the Middle East was probably beneficial. Converted to Islam, the Turkish rulers temporarily brought an end to the fraternal squabbles between Sunni and Shi'ite Muslims, while supporting the Sunnites. They put their energies into revitalizing Islamic law and institutions and provided much-needed political stability to the empire, which helped to restore its former

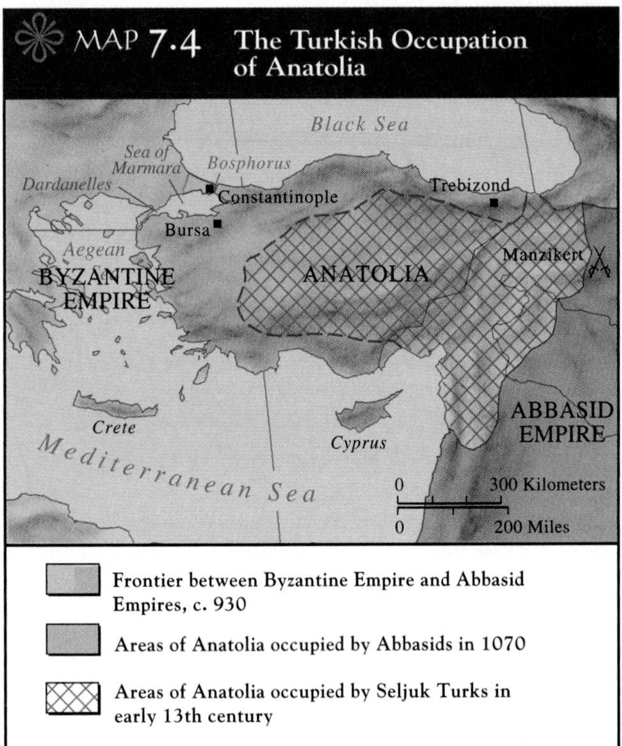

CHRONOLOGY

ISLAM: THE FIRST MILLENNIUM

Life of Muhammad	570–632
Flight to Medina	622
Conquest of Mecca	630
Fall of Cairo	640
Defeat of Persians	650
Election of Ali to caliphate	656
Muslim entry into Spain	c. 710
Abbasid caliphate	750–1258
Construction of city of Baghdad	762
Reign of Harun al-Rashid	786–809
Founding of Fatimid dynasty in Egypt	973
Capture of Baghdad by Seljuk Turks	1055
Seizure of Anatolia by Seljuk Turks	1071
First crusade	1096
Saladin destroys Fatimid kingdom	1169
Fourth crusade	1204
Mongols seize Baghdad	1258
Ottoman Turks capture Constantinople	1453

prosperity. In one respect, however, their policies may have been detrimental to the later development of Islam. Adopting a narrow interpretation of the Koran and the *Shari'ah*, they encouraged a rigid approach to sacred doctrine that would make it more difficult for the faithful to respond effectively to social changes taking place within Islamic society.

The Crusades

Just before the end of the eleventh century, the Byzantine emperor Alexius I desperately called for assistance from other Christian states in Europe to protect his empire against the invading Seljuk Turks. As part of his appeal, he said that the Muslims were desecrating Christian shrines in the Holy Land and also molesting Christian pilgrims en route to the shrines. In actuality, the Muslims had never threatened the shrines or cut off Christian access to them. But tension between Christendom and the world of Islam was on the rise, and the Byzantine emperor's appeal received a ready response in Europe. Beginning in 1096 and continuing into the thirteenth century, a series of crusades brought the Holy Land and adjacent areas on the Mediterranean coast from Antioch to the Sinai peninsula under Christian rule (see Chapter 12).

At first, Muslim rulers in the area were taken aback by the invading crusaders, whose armored cavalry presented a new challenge to local warriors, and their response was ineffectual. The Seljuk Turks by that time were preoccupied with events taking place further to the east and took no action themselves. But in 1169, Sunni Muslims under the leadership of Saladin (Salah al-Din), vizier to the last Fatimid caliph, brought an end to the Fatimid dynasty. Proclaiming himself sultan, Saladin succeeded in establishing his control over both Egypt and Syria, thereby confronting the Christian states in the area with united Muslim power on two fronts. In 1187 Saladin's army invaded the kingdom of Jerusalem and destroyed the Christian forces concentrated there. Further operations reduced Christian occupation in the area to a handful of fortresses along the northern coast. Unlike the Christians, however, Saladin did not permit a massacre of the civilian population and even tolerated the continuation of Christian religious services in conquered territories.

The Christians returned for another try a few years after the fall of Jerusalem, but the campaign succeeded only in securing some of the coastal cities. Although the Christians would retain a toehold on the coast for much of the thirteenth century (Acre, their last stronghold, fell to the Muslims in 1291), they were no longer a significant force in Middle Eastern affairs. In retrospect, the crusades had only minimal importance in the history of the Middle East and may even have served to unite the forces of Islam against the foreign invaders (see the box on p. 203). Far more important in their impact

THE CRUSADES IN MUSLIM EYES

Usamah, an early-twelfth-century Muslim warrior and gentleman, had close associations with the crusaders. When he was ninety years old, he wrote his memoirs including many entertaining observations on the crusaders, or "Franks" as he called them. Here Usamah is astounded at the Franks' rudeness to Muslims and at their assumption of cultural superiority.

USAMAH, *BOOK OF REFLECTIONS*

1. Everyone who is a fresh emigrant from the Frankish lands is ruder in character than those who have become acclimatized and have held long association with the Moslems. Here is an illustration of their rude character.

   Whenever I visited Jerusalem I always entered the Aqsa Mosque, beside which stood a small mosque which the Franks had converted into a church. When I used to enter the Aqsa Mosque, which was occupied by the Templars [an order of crusading knights], who were my friends, the Templars would evacuate the little adjoining mosque so that I might pray in it. One day I entered this mosque, repeated the first formula, "Allah is great," and stood up in the act of praying, upon which one of the Franks rushed on me, got hold of me, and turned my face eastward, saying, "This is the way thou shouldst pray!" A group of Templars hastened to him, seized him, and repelled him from me. I resumed my prayer. The same man, while the others were otherwise busy, rushed once more on me and turned my face eastward, saying, "This is the way thou shouldst pray!" The Templars again came in to him and expelled him. They apologized to me, saying, "This is a stranger who has only recently arrived from the land of the Franks, and he has never before seen anyone praying except eastward." Thereupon I said to myself, "I have had enough prayer." So I went out, and have ever been surprised at the conduct of this devil of a man, at the change in the color of his face, his trembling, and his sentiment at the sight of one praying toward the *qiblah*.
2. In the army of King Fulk, son of Fulk, was a Frankish reverend knight who had just arrived from their land in order to make the holy pilgrimage and then return home. He was of my intimate fellowship and kept such constant company with me that he began to call me "my brother." Between us were mutual bonds of amity and friendship. When he resolved to return by sea to his homeland, he said to me:

   "My brother, I am leaving for my country and I want thee to send with me thy son (my son, who was then fourteen years old, was at that time in my company) to our country, where he can see the knights and learn wisdom and chivalry. When he returns, he will be like a wise man."

   Thus there fell upon my ears words which would never come out of the head of a sensible man; for even if my son were to be taken captive, his captivity could not bring him a worse misfortune than carrying him into the lands of the Franks.

were the Mongols, a pastoral people who swept out of the Gobi Desert in the early thirteenth century to seize control over much of the known world (see Chapter 12). Beginning with the advances of Genghis Khan in northern China, Mongol armies later spread across Central Asia, and in 1258, under the leadership of Hulegu, brother of the more famous Khubilai Khan, they seized Persia and Mesopotamia, bringing an end to the caliphate at Baghdad.

The Mongols

Unlike the Seljuk Turks, the Mongols were not Muslims, and they found it difficult to adapt to the settled conditions that they found in the major cities in the Middle East. Their treatment of the local population in conquered territories was brutal (according to one historian, after conquering a city, they wiped out not only entire families but also their household pets) and destructive to the economy. Cities were razed to the ground, and dams and other irrigation works were destroyed, reducing prosperous agricultural societies to the point of mass starvation. The Mongols advanced as far as the Red Sea, but their attempt to seize Egypt failed, in part because of the effective resistance posed by the Mamluks (a Turkish military class originally composed of slaves; sometimes written as Mamelukes), who had recently overthrown the administration set up by Saladin and seized power for themselves.

Eventually, the Mongol rulers in the Middle East began to take on the coloration of the peoples that they had conquered. Mongol elites converted to Islam, Persian influence became predominant at court, and the cities began to be rebuilt. By the fourteenth century, the Mongol empire began to split into separate kingdoms and then to disintegrate. In the meantime, however, the old Islamic empire originally established by the Arabs in the seventh and eighth centuries had come to an end. The new center of Islamic civilization was in Cairo, now about to promote a renaissance in Muslim culture under the sponsorship of the Mamluks.

To the north, another new force began to appear on the horizon with the rise of the Ottoman Turks on the Anatolian peninsula. In 1453, Sultan Mehmet II seized Constantinople and brought an end to the decrepit Byzantine Empire. Then the Ottomans began to turn their attention to the rest of the Middle East (see Chapter 16).

ISLAMIC CIVILIZATION

To be a Muslim is not simply to worship Allah but also to live according to his law as revealed in the Koran, which is viewed as fundamental and immutable doctrine, not to be revised by human beings.

As Allah has decreed, so must human beings behave. Therefore, Islamic doctrine must be consulted to determine questions of politics, economic behavior, civil and criminal law, and social ethics. In Islamic society there is no rigid demarcation between church and state, between the sacred and the secular.

A TANGIER SPICE MARKET. For centuries, the spices of the East have passed through southwestern Asia and North Africa on their way to Europe. Some came by caravan across the Arabian peninsula, while others were carried on ships across the Indian Ocean and up the Red Sea to the Mediterranean. Even today, the markets of the region boast a colorful and pungent display of spices, such as the one shown here in a shop in Tangier, on the coast of Morocco.

The Wealth of Araby: Trade and Cities in the Middle East

As we have noted, overall this era was probably one of the most prosperous periods in the history of the Middle East. Trade in particular flourished, not only within the Islamic world, but also with China (now in a period of efflorescence during the era of the Tang and the Song dynasties—see Chapter 10), with the Byzantine Empire, and with the trading societies in Southeast Asia (see Chapter 9). Trade goods were carried both by ship and by the "fleets of the desert," the camel caravans that traversed the arid land from Morocco in the far west to the countries beyond the Caspian Sea. From the Sahara came gold and slaves; from China, silk and porcelain; from East Africa, gold, ivory, and rhinoceros horn; and from the lands of South Asia, sandalwood, cotton, wheat, sugar, and spices. Within the empire, Egypt contributed grain; Iraq, linens, dates, and precious stones; Spain, leather goods, olives, and wine; and western India, various textile goods. The exchange of goods was facilitated by the development of banking and the use of currency and letters of credit.

Under these conditions, urban areas flourished. While the Abbasids were in power, Baghdad was probably the greatest city in the empire, but after the rise of the Fatimids in Egypt, the focus of trade shifted to Cairo, described by the traveler Leo Africanus as "one of the greatest and most famous cities in all the whole world, filled with stately and admirable palaces and colleges, and most sumptuous temples."[5] Other great commercial cities included Basra at the head of the Persian Gulf, Aden at the southern tip of the Arabian peninsula, Damascus in modern Syria, and Marrakech in Morocco. Within the cities the inhabitants were generally segregated by religion, with Jews and Christians living in separate neighborhoods. But all were equally subject to the most common threats to urban life—fire, flood, and disease.

The most impressive urban buildings were usually the palace for the caliph or the local governor and the great mosque. Houses were often constructed of stone or brick around a timber frame. The larger houses were often built around an interior courtyard, where the residents could retreat from the dust, noise, and heat of the city streets. Sometimes domestic animals such as goats or sheep would be stabled there. The houses of the wealthy were often multistoried, with balconies and windows covered with latticework to provide privacy for those inside. The poor in both urban and rural areas lived in simpler houses composed of clay or unfired bricks. The Bedouins lived in tents that could be dismantled and moved according to their needs.

Eating habits varied in accordance with economic standing and religious preference. Muslims did not eat pork, but those who could afford it often served other meats such as mutton, lamb, poultry, or fish. Fruit, spices, and vari-

A CONSUMER'S GUIDE TO THE IDEAL SLAVE

Slavery was widely practiced in the Middle East under the Abbasid caliphate. In this excerpt from a much longer passage, Kai Ka'us, an eleventh-century Persian, instructs his son on what to look for when buying a slave. Clearly, different slaves would serve different purposes, and the ideal qualities would vary according to the individual case. What is striking is that the slaves were evaluated not as human beings but as pieces of merchandise.

A FATHER'S INSTRUCTIONS TO HIS SON

Now let me describe to the best of my ability what is essential in the purchasing of slaves, both white and black, and what their good and bad points are, so that they may be known to you. Understand then that there are three essentials in the buying of slaves; first is the recognition of their good and bad qualities, whether external or internal, by means of physiognomy; second is the awareness of diseases, whether latent or apparent, by their symptoms; third is the knowledge of the various classes and the defects and merits of each.

With regard to the first requirement, that of physiognomy, it consists of close observation when buying slaves. . . . Whoever it may be that inspects the slave must first look at the face, which is always open to view, whereas the body can only be seen as occasion offers. Then look at eyes and eyebrows, followed by nose, lips and teeth, and lastly at the hair. The reason for this is that God placed the beauty of human beings in eyes and eyebrows, delicacy in the nose, sweetness in the lips and teeth, and freshness in the skin. . . .

The learned say that one must know the indications and signs by which to buy the slaves suited for particular duties. The slave that you buy for your private service and conviviality should be of middle proportions, neither tall nor short, fat nor lean, pale nor florid, thickset nor slender, curly-haired nor with hair overstraight. When you see a slave soft-fleshed, fine-skinned, with regular bones and wine-colored hair, black eyelashes, dark eyes, . . . slender waisted, round-chinned, red-lipped, with white regular teeth, and all his members such as I have described, such a slave will be decorative and companionable, loyal, of delicate character, and dignified.

The mark of the slave suited for arms bearing is that his hair is thick, his body tall and erect, his build powerful, his flesh hard, his bones thick, his skin coarse and his limbs straight, the joints being firm. . . . Shoulders must be broad, the chest deep, the neck thick, and the head round; also for preference he should be bald. . . . Any slave who possesses these qualities will be a champion in single combat, brave and successful.

The mark of the slave suited for employment in the women's apartments is that he should be dark-skinned and sour-visaged and have withered limbs, scanty hair, a shrill voice, little [slender] feet, thick lips, a flat nose, stubby fingers, a bowed figure, and a thin neck. A slave with these qualities will be suitable for service in the women's quarters. He must not have a white skin nor a fair complexion. . . . His eyes, further, should not be languorous or moist; a man having such qualities is either overfond of women or prone to act as a go-between.

ous sweets were delicacies. The poor were generally forced to survive on boiled millet or peas with an occasional lump of meat or fat. Bread—white or whole meal—could be found on tables throughout the region except in the deserts, where boiled grain was the staple food.

Islamic Society

In some ways, Arab society was probably one of the most egalitarian of its time. Both the principles of Islam, which held that all were equal in the eyes of Allah, and the importance of trade to the prosperity of the state probably contributed to this egalitarianism. Although there was a fairly well defined upper class, consisting of the ruling families, senior officials, tribal elites, and the wealthiest merchants, there was no hereditary nobility as in many contemporary societies, and the merchants enjoyed a degree of respect that they did not receive in Europe, China, or India.

Though the Arab empire was more urbanized than most other societies at the time, the bulk of the population continued to live in the countryside and supported themselves by farming or herding animals. During the early stages, most of the farmland was owned by independent peasants, but later some concentration of land in the hands of wealthy owners began to take place. In river valleys like the Tigris and Euphrates and the Nile, the majority of the farmers probably continued to be independent peasants.

Not all benefited from the high degree of social mobility in the Islamic world, however. Slavery was widespread (see the box above). Since a Muslim could not be enslaved, the supply came from sub-Saharan Africa or from non-Islamic populations elsewhere in Asia. Most were employed in the army (which was sometimes a road to power, as in the case of the Mamluks) or as domestic servants, where they were sometimes permitted to purchase their freedom. The slaves who worked the large estates

DRAW THEIR VEILS OVER THEIR BOSOMS

In the early Islamic era, many upper-class women greeted men on the street, entertained their husband's friends at home, went on pilgrimages to Mecca, and even accompanied their husbands to battle. Such women were obviously neither veiled nor secluded. Eventually, however, Muhammad specified that his own wives, who (according to the Koran) were "not like any other women," should be modestly attired and should be addressed by men from behind a curtain. Over the centuries, Muslim theologians, fearful that female sexuality could threaten the established order, interpreted Muhammad's "modest attire" and his reference to curtains to mean segregated seclusion and body concealment for all Muslim women. In fact, one strict scholar in fourteenth-century Cairo went so far as to prescribe that ideally a women should be allowed to leave her home only three times in her life: when entering her husband's home after marriage, after the death of parents, and after her own death.

In traditional Islamic societies, veiling and seclusion were more prevalent among urban women than among their rural counterparts. The latter, who worked in the fields and rarely saw people outside their extended family, were less restricted. In this excerpt from the Koran, women are instructed to "guard their modesty" and "draw veils over their bosoms." Nowhere in the Koran, however, does it stipulate that women should be sequestered or covered from head to toe.

THE KORAN: CHAPTER 24

And say to the believing women
That they should lower
Their gaze and guard
Their modesty: that they
Should not display their
Beauty and ornaments except
What [must ordinarily] appear
Thereof: that they should
Draw their veils over
Their bosoms and not display
Their beauty except
To their husbands, their fathers,
Their husbands' fathers, their sons,
Their husbands' sons,
Their brothers or their brothers' sons,
Or their sisters' sons,
Or their women, or the slaves
Whom their right hands
Possess, or male servants
Free of physical needs,
Or small children who
Have no sense of the shame
Of sex; and that they
Should not strike their feet
In order to draw attention
To their hidden ornaments.

probably experienced the worst living conditions and rose in revolt on several occasions.

The Islamic principle of human equality also fell short in the treatment of women. Although the Koran instructed men to treat women with respect, and women did have the right to own and inherit property, in general the male was dominant in Muslim society. Polygyny was permitted, and the right of divorce was in practice restricted to the husband, although some schools of legal thought permitted women to stipulate that their husband could have only one wife or to seek a separation in certain specific circumstances. Adultery and homosexuality were stringently forbidden (although such prohibitions were frequently ignored in practice), and Islamic custom required that women be cloistered in their homes (thus the tradition of the harem) and prohibited from social contacts with males outside their own family. The custom of requiring women to cover virtually all parts of their body when appearing in public was common in urban areas and continues to be practiced in many Islamic societies today. It should be noted, however, that these customs owed more to traditional Arab practice than to Koranic law (see the box above), and that the position of women under Islam was probably better than it had been in former times, when they were often treated like slaves.

The Culture of Islam

From the beginning of their empire, Muslim Arabs had demonstrated a willingness to absorb the culture of their conquered peoples. The Arabs were truly heirs to many elements of the remaining Greco-Roman culture of the Roman Empire. Just as readily, they assimilated Byzantine and Persian culture. In the eighth and ninth centuries, numerous Greek, Syrian, and Persian scientific and philosophical works were translated into Arabic. As the chief language in the southern Mediterranean and the Middle East, Arabic became a truly international language. Later, Persian and Turkish also came to be important in administration and culture.

The spread of Islam led to the emergence of a new culture throughout the entire Arab empire. This was true in all fields of endeavor, from literature to art and architecture. But pre-Islamic traditions were not extinguished and they fre-

LOVE FOR A CAMEL

Early Arabic poetry focused on simple pleasures, such as wine, women, song, and the faithful camel. This excerpt is from a longer work by the sixth-century Arab poet Tarafah. Tarafah was one of a group of seven poets called the "suspended ones." Their poems, having won a prize in an annual competition, were suspended on a wall for all to read.

THE ODE OF TARAFAH

Ah, but when grief assails me, straightway I ride it off
mounted on my swift, lean-flanked camel, night and day racing, . . .
Her long neck is very erect when she lifts it up, calling to
mind the rudder of a Tigris-bound vessel. Her skull is
most like an anvil, the junction of its two halves meeting
together as it might be on the edge of a file.
Her cheek is smooth as Syrian parchment, her split lip
a tanned hide of Yemen, its slit not bent crooked;
her eyes are a pair of mirrors, sheltering in the caves of
her brow-bones, the rock of a pool's hollow, . . .
I am at her with the whip, and my she-camel quickens pace
what time the mirage of the burning stone-tract shimmers;
elegantly she steps, as a slave-girl at a party will sway,
showing her master skirts of a trailing white gown.
I am not one that skulks fearfully among the hilltops, but
when the folk seek my succor I gladly give it; if you look
for me in the circle of the folk you'll find me there, and if
you hunt me in the taverns there you'll catch me.
Come to me when you will, I'll pour you a flowing cup, and
if you don't need it, well, do without and good luck to you!
Whenever the tribe is assembled you'll come upon me at the
summit of the noble House, the oft-frequented; my boon-
companions are white as stars, and a singing-wench
comes to us in her striped gown or her saffron robe, wide
the opening of her collar, delicate her skin to my compan-
ions' fingers, tender her nakedness.
When we say, "Let's hear from you," she advances to us
chanting fluently, her glance languid, in effortless song.

quently combined with Muslim motifs to produce creative works of a high degree of imagination and originality.

PHILOSOPHY AND SCIENCE

During the centuries following the rise of the Arab empire, it was the Islamic world that was most responsible for preserving and spreading the scientific and philosophical achievements of ancient civilizations. At a time when ancient Greek philosophy was largely unknown in Europe, key works by Aristotle, Plato, and other Greek philosophers were translated into Arabic and stored in a "House of Wisdom" in Baghdad, where they were read and studied by Muslim scholars. Through the writings of the Spanish Muslim philosopher Ibn Rushd (known in the West as Averroës), the contents of many of these works eventually became known in Europe and influenced Christian thought. Texts on mathematics and linguistics were brought from India. The process was undoubtedly stimulated by the introduction of paper manufacturing from China in the eighth century. By the end of the century, the first paper factories had been established in Baghdad, and booksellers and libraries soon followed. The first paper mill in Europe appeared in the Pyrenees Mountains in Spain in the twelfth century.

Although Islamic scholars are justly praised for preserving much of classical knowledge for the West, they also made considerable advances of their own. Nowhere is this more evident than in mathematics and the natural sciences. Islamic scholars adopted and passed on the numerical system of India, including the use of the zero, and a ninth-century Iranian mathematician created the mathematical discipline of algebra (*al-jebr*). In astronomy, Muslims set up an observatory at Baghdad to study the position of the stars. They were aware that the earth was round and in the ninth century produced a world map based on the tradition of the Greco-Roman astronomer Ptolemy.

Muslim scholars also made many new discoveries in optics and chemistry and, with the assistance of texts on anatomy by the ancient Greek physician Galen (c. 180–200 C.E.), developed medicine as a distinctive field of scientific inquiry. Especially well known was Ibn Sina (980–1037). Known as Avicenna in the West, he compiled a medical encyclopedia that, among other things, emphasized the contagious nature of certain diseases and showed how they could be spread by contaminated water supplies. After its translation into Latin, Avicenna's work became a basic medical textbook for medieval European university students.

ISLAMIC LITERATURE

Islam brought major changes to the culture of the Middle East, not least to literature. Muslims regarded the Koran as their greatest literary work, but pre-Islamic traditions continued to influence writers throughout the region.

An established tradition of Arabic poetry already existed prior to Muhammad. It extolled Bedouin tribal life, courage in battle, hunting, sports, and respect for the animals of the desert, especially the camel (see the box above). Because the Arabic language did not possess a written script until the fourth century C.E., poetry was

BE THANKFUL FOR SMALL FAVORS

The Rose Garden, *an entertaining collection of moral anecdotes and maxims, was written in the thirteenth century by Sadi, considered by many to be Persia's greatest author. Here, in his usual mixture of prose and poetry, Sadi advises his readers to be content with what they have.*

SADI, *THE ROSE GARDEN*: STORY 7

A padshah was in the same boat with a Persian slave who had never before been at sea and experienced the inconvenience of a vessel. He began to cry and to tremble to such a degree that he could not be pacified by kindness, so that at last the king became displeased as the matter could not be remedied. In that boat there happened to be a philosopher, who said: "With thy permission I shall quiet him." The padshah replied: "It will be a great favor." The philosopher ordered the slave to be thrown into the water so that he swallowed some of it, whereon he was caught and pulled by his hair to the boat, to the stern of which he clung with both his hands. Then he sat down in a corner and became quiet. This appeared strange to the king who knew not what wisdom there was in the proceeding and asked for it. The philosopher replied: "Before he had tasted the calamity of being drowned, he knew not the safety of the boat; thus also a man does not appreciate the value of immunity from a misfortune until it has befallen him."

O thou full man, barley-bread pleases thee not.
She is my sweetheart who appears ugly to thee.
To the houris of paradise purgatory seems hell.
Ask the denizens of hell. To them purgatory is paradise.
There is a difference between him whose friend is in his arms
And him whose eyes of expectation are upon the door.

originally passed on by memory. Later, in the eighth and ninth centuries, it was compiled in anthologies.

Pre-Muslim Persia also boasted a long literary tradition, most of it oral and written down in later centuries in the Arabic alphabet. The Persian poetic tradition remained strong under Islam. Rabe'a of Qozdar, Persia's first known woman poet, lived in the second half of the tenth century. Describing the suffering love brings, she wrote: "Beset with impatience I did not know/That the more one seeks to pull away, the tighter becomes the rope."[6]

To Western observers, the most famous works of Middle Eastern literature are undoubtedly the *Rubaiyat* of Omar Khayyam and *The Tales from 1001 Nights* (also called *The Arabian Nights*). Paradoxically, these two works are not as popular with Middle Eastern readers. Both, in fact, were freely translated into Western languages for nineteenth-century European readers, who found themes of wine, women, and hedonistic pleasure more acceptable when set in a quaint foreign disguise.

Unfortunately, very little is known of the life or the poetry of the twelfth-century poet Omar Khayyam. Skeptical, reserved, and slightly contemptuous of his peers, he combined poetry with scientific works on mathematics and astronomy and a revision of the calendar that was more accurate than the Gregorian version devised in Europe hundreds of years later. Omar Khayyam did not write down his poems, but composed them orally over wine with friends at a neighborhood tavern. They were recorded later by friends or scribes. Many poems attributed to him were actually written long after his death. Among them is the well-known couplet translated into English in the nineteenth century: "Here with a loaf of bread beneath the bough, a flask of wine, a book of verse, and thou."

Omar Khayyam's poetry is simple and down to earth. Key themes are the impermanence of life, the impossibility of knowing God, and disbelief in an afterlife. Ironically, recent translations of his work appeal to modern attitudes of skepticism and minimalist simplicity that may make him even more popular in the West:

In youth I studied for a little while;
Later I boasted of my mastery.
Yet this was all the lesson that I learned:
We come from dust, and with the wind are gone.

Of all the travelers on this endless road
No one returns to tell us where it leads,
There's little in this world but greed and need;
Leave nothing here, for you will not return. . . .

Since no one can be certain of tomorrow,
It's better not to fill the heart with care.
Drink wine by moonlight, darling, for the moon
Will shine long after this, and find us not.[7]

Like Omar Khayyam's verse, *The Arabian Nights* was loosely translated into European languages and adapted to Western tastes. A composite of folktales, fables, and romances of Indian and indigenous origin, the stories interweave the natural with the supernatural. The earliest stories were told orally and were later transcribed, with many later additions, in Arabic and Persian versions. The famous story of Aladdin and the Magic Lamp, for example, was an eighteenth-century addition. Nevertheless, *The Arabian Nights* has entertained readers for centuries, allowing them to enter a land of wish fulfillment through extraordinary plots, sensuality, comic and tragic situations, and a cast of unforgettable characters.

Sadi (1210–1292), considered the Persian Shakespeare, remains to this day the favorite author in Iran. His *Rose Garden* is a collection of entertaining stories written in prose sprinkled with verse (see the box above). He is also

THE PASSIONS OF A SUFI MYSTIC

Sufism was an unorthodox form of Islam that flourished in many parts of the Muslim world. It preached the importance of a highly personal relationship between Allah and the individual believer. Sufi orders began to assume considerable influence by the thirteenth century, perhaps because of the disintegration of the Abbasid empire and the heightened instability throughout the Islamic world. Sufi missionaries played a major role in efforts to spread Islam to India and Central Asia. In this poem, the thirteenth-century Persian poet Rumi describes the mystical relationship achieved by means of passionate music and dance.

RUMI, CALL TO THE DANCE

Come!
But don't join us without music.
We have a celebration here.
Rise and beat the drums.

We are Mansur who said "I am God!"

We are in ecstasy—
Drunk, but not from wine made of grapes.

Whatever your thoughts are about us,
We are far, far from them.

This is the night of the same
When we whirl to ecstasy.
There is light now,
There is light, there is light.

This is true love,
Which means farewell to the mind.
There is farewell today, farewell.

Tonight each flaming heart is a friend of music.
Longing for your lips,
My heart pours out of my mouth.

Hush!
You are made of feeling and thought and passion;
The rest is nothing but flesh and bone.
We are the soul of the world,
Not heavy or sagging like the body.
We are the spirit's treasure,
Not bound to this earth, to time or space.

How can they talk to us of prayer rugs and piety?
We are the hunter and the hunted,
Autumn and spring,
Night and day,
Visible and hidden.
Love is our mother.
We were born of Love.

renowned for his sonnetlike love poems, which set a model for generations to come. Sadi was a master of the pithy maxim:

A cat is a lion in catching mice
But a mouse in combat with a tiger.

He has found eternal happiness who lived a good life,
Because, after his end, good repute will keep his name alive.

When thou fightest with anyone, consider
Whether thou wilt have to flee from him or he from thee.[8]

Such maxims are typical of the Middle East, where the proverb, a one-line witty observation on the vagaries of life, has long been popular. Proverbs are not only a distinctive feature of Middle Eastern verse, especially Persian, but are also a part of daily life—a scholar recently recovered over four thousand in one Lebanese village! The following are some typical examples:

Trust in God, but tie up your camel. (Persian)
The world has not promised anything to anybody. (Moroccan)
An old cat will not learn how to dance. (Moroccan)
Lower your voice and strengthen your argument. (Lebanese)
He who has money can eat sherbet in Hell. (Lebanese)
What is brought by the wind will be carried away by the wind. (Persian)
You can't pick up two melons with one hand. (Persian)

Some Arabic and Persian literature reflected the deep spiritual and ethical concerns of the Koran. Many writers, however, carried Islamic thought in novel directions. The thirteenth-century poet Rumi, for example, embraced Sufism, a form of religious belief that called for a mystical relationship between Allah and human beings (the term *Sufism* stems from the Arabic word for wool, referring to the rough wool garments that its adherents wore). Converted to Sufism by a wandering dervish (dervishes, from the word for "poor" in Persian, sought to achieve a mystical union with Allah through violent dancing and chanting in an ecstatic trance), Rumi abandoned orthodox Islam to embrace God directly through ecstatic love. Realizing that love transcends intellect, he sought to reach God through a trance attained by the whirling dance of the dervish, set to mesmerizing music. As he twirled, the poet extemporized some of the most passionate lyrical verse ever conceived. His faith and art remain an important force in Islamic society today (see the box above).

The Islamic world also made a major contribution to historical writing, another discipline that was stimulated by the introduction of paper manufacturing. The first great

Islamic historian was al-Mas'udi. Born in Baghdad in 896, he wrote about both the Muslim and the non-Muslim world, traveling widely in the process. His *Meadows of Gold* is the source of much of our knowledge about the golden age of the Abbasid caliphate. Translations of his work reveal a wide-ranging mind and a keen intellect, combined with a human touch that practitioners of the art in our century might find reason to emulate (see the box on p. 201). Equaling al-Mas'udi in talent and reputation was the fourteenth-century historian Ibn Khaldun. Combining scholarship with government service, Ibn Khaldun was one of the first historians to attempt a philosophy of history.

ISLAMIC ART AND ARCHITECTURE

The art of Islam is a blend of Arab, Turkish, and Persian traditions. Although local influences can be discerned in Egypt, Anatolia, Spain, and other areas and the Mongols introduced an East Asian accent in the thirteenth century, for a long time Islamic art remained remarkably coherent over a wide area. First and foremost, the Arabs, with their new religion and their writing system, served as a unifying force. Fascinated by the mathematics and astronomy they inherited from the Romans or the Babylonians, they developed a sense of rhythm and abstraction that found expression in their use of repetitive geometric ornamentation. The Turks brought abstraction in figurative and nonfigurative designs, and the Persians added their lyrical poetical mysticism. Much Islamic painting, for example, consists of illustrations of Persian texts.

The ultimate expression of Islamic art is to be found in the magnificent architectural monuments beginning in the late seventh century. The first great example is the Dome of the Rock, which was built in 691 to proclaim the spiritual and political legitimacy of the new religion to the ancient world. Set in the sacred heart of Jerusalem on Muhammad's holy rock and touching both the Western Wall of the Jews and the oldest Christian church, the Dome of the Rock remains one of the most revered Islamic monuments. Constructed on Byzantine lines with an octagonal shape and marble columns and ornamentation, the interior reflects Persian motifs with mosaics of precious stones. Although rebuilt several times and incorporating influences from both East and West, this first monument to Islam represents the birth of a new art.

At first, desert Arabs, whether nomads or conquering armies, prayed in an open court, shaded along the *kibla*

THE TEMPLE MOUNT AT JERUSALEM. The Temple Mount is one of the most sacred sites in the city of Jerusalem. Originally it was the site of a temple built during the reign of Solomon, king of the Jews, about 1000 B.C.E. The Western Wall of the temple is shown in the foreground. Beyond the Wall is the Dome of the Rock complex, built on the place from which Muslims believe that Muhammad ascended to heaven.

AN ENTRANCE PORTAL. This entrance gate to an Iranian mosque displays the variety and delicacy of the geometrical decorations that often accompanied Islamic architecture. The brilliant blue-and-white mosaic tile shown here eventually evolved into polychromy by the fifteenth century. Note the veiled women in the foreground.

THE MOSQUE AT CÓRDOBA. Perhaps the most impressive of all Islamic religious structures is the Mosque of Córdoba, in southern Spain, which was built between the eighth and tenth centuries. Shown here is the interior of the mosque, showing some of the columns that give the entire structure such an effect of mass as well as lightness.

(the wall facing the holy city of Mecca) by a thatched roof supported by rows of palm trunks. There was also a ditch where the faithful could wash off the dust of the desert prior to prayer. As Islam became better established, enormous mosques were constructed, but they were still modeled on the open court, which would be surrounded on all four sides with pillars supporting a wooden roof over the prayer area facing the *kibla* wall. The largest mosque ever built, the Great Mosque of Samarra (848–852), covered ten acres and contained 464 pillars in aisles surrounding the court. Set in the *kibla* wall was a niche, or *mihrab*, containing a decorated panel pointing to Mecca and representing Allah. Remains of the massive thirty-foot-high outer wall still stand, but the most famous section of the Samarra mosque was its ninety-foot-tall minaret, the tower accompanying a mosque from which the *muezzin* calls the faithful to prayer five times a day.

No discussion of mosques would be complete without mentioning the famous ninth-century mosque at Córdoba in southern Spain, which is still in remarkable condition. Its 514 columns supporting double horseshoe arches transform this architectural wonder into a unique forest of trees pointing upward, contributing to a light and airy effect. The unparalleled sumptuousness and elegance make the Córdoba mosque one of the wonders of world art, let alone Islamic art.

Since the Muslim religion combines spiritual and political power in one, palaces also reflected the glory of Islam. Beginning in the eighth century with the spectacular castles of Syria, the rulers constructed large domiciles reminiscent of Roman design, with protective walls,

THE ALHAMBRA IN GRANADA. Islamic civilization reached its zenith with the fourteenth-century fairy-tale castle of Alhambra in southern Spain. Perched on a hill high above the city of Granada and framed by snowcapped mountains, the Alhambra is widely considered the most perfect expression of Islamic art. Renowned for its lacelike plaster decorations and imaginative use of reflecting pools and fountains, the Alhambra stands as an exquisite gem of Islam.

gates, and baths. Constructed of brick, they unfortunately no longer exist. With a central courtyard surrounded by two-story arcades and massive gate-towers, they resembled a fortress as much as a palace. Characteristic of such "desert palaces" was the gallery over the entrance gate, with holes through which boiling oil could be poured down on the heads of attacking forces. This architectural feature was exported by the crusaders and was later incorporated repeatedly into medieval European castles.

The ultimate in Islamic palaces, however, is the fourteenth-century Alhambra in Spain. The extensive succession of courtyards, rooms, gardens, and fountains created a fairy-tale castle perched high above the city of Granada. Every inch of surface is decorated in intricate floral and semiabstract patterns; much of the decoration is done in carved plasterwork so fine that it resembles lace. The Lion Court in the center of the harem is world renowned for its lion fountain and surrounding arcade with elegant columns and carvings.

One of the most significant contributions of Islamic art is the knotted woolen rug. Originating in the pre-Muslim era, rugs were initially used to insulate stone palaces against the cold as well as to warm the shepherd's tent. Eventually they were applied to religious purposes, since every practicing Muslim is required to pray five times a day on clean ground. Small rugs served as prayer mats for individual use, while larger and more elaborate ones were given by rulers as rewards for political favors. Bedouins in the Arabian desert covered their sandy floors with rugs to create a cozy environment in their tents.

THE KORAN AS SCULPTURED DESIGN. Muslim sculptors and artists, reflecting the official view that any visual representation of the prophet Muhammad was blasphemous, turned to geometric patterns, as well as to flowers and animals, as a means of fulfilling their creative urge. The predominant motif, however, was the reproduction of Koranic verse in the Arabic script. Calligraphy, which was almost as important in the Middle East as it was in traditional China, used the Arabic script to decorate all of the Islamic arts, from painting to pottery, to tile and iron work, and to wall decorations such as this carved plaster panel in a courtyard of the Alhambra palace in Spain. Since a recitation from the Koran was an important component of the daily devotional activities for all practicing Muslims, elaborate scriptural panels such as this one perfectly blended the spiritual and the artistic realms.

In villages throughout the Middle East, the art of rug weaving has been passed down from mother to daughter over the centuries. Small girls as young as four years old took part in the process by helping to spin and prepare the wool shorn from the family sheep. By the age of six, girls would begin their first rug, and before adolescence their slender fingers would be producing fine carpets. Skilled artisanship represented an extra enticement to prospective bridegrooms, while rugs often became an important part of a woman's dowry to her future husband. After the wedding, the wife would continue to make rugs for home use, as well as for sale to augment the family income. Eventually, rugs began to be manufactured in workshops by professional artisans, who reproduced the designs from detailed painted diagrams.

Most decorations on the rugs, as well as on all forms of Islamic art, consisted of Arabic script and natural plant and figurative motifs. Repeated continuously in naturalistic or semiabstract geometrical patterns called arabesques, these decorations completely covered the surface and left no area undecorated. This dense decor was also evident in brick, mosaic, and stucco ornamentation and culminated in the magnificent tile work of later centuries.

No representation of the Prophet Muhammad ever adorned a mosque, in painting or in any other art form. Although no passage of the Koran forbids representational painting, the *Hadith*, an early collection of the Prophet's sayings, warned against any attempt to imitate God through artistic creation or idolatry. From the time of the Dome of the Rock, no figurative representations appear in Islamic religious art.

Human beings and animals could still be represented in secular art, but relatively little survives from the early centuries aside from a very few wall paintings from the royal palaces. Although the Persians used calligraphy and art to decorate their books, the Arabs had no pictorial tradition of their own and only began to develop the art of book illustration in the late twelfth century to illustrate translations of Greek scientific works.

In the thirteenth century, a Mongol dynasty established at Tabriz, west of the Caspian Sea, offered the Middle East its first direct contact with the art of East Asia. Mongol painting, done in the Chinese manner with a full brush and expressing animated movement and intensity (see Chapter 10), freed Islamic painters from traditional confines and enabled them to experiment with new techniques.

Chinese art also influenced Islamic art with its sense of space. A new sense of perspective pervaded Islamic painting, leading to some of the great paintings of the Herat School under the fifteenth-century autocrat Tamerlane. Artists working in the Herat style often depicted mounted warriors battling on a richly detailed background of trees and birds. These paintings served as the classical model for later Islamic painting, which culminated in the glorious artistic tradition of sixteenth-century Iran, Turkey, and India (see Chapter 16).

A MIDDLE EAST CARPET BAZAAR. Treasured by museums and wealthy patrons throughout the world, handwoven Middle Eastern carpets are both colorful and durable and reflect the grandeur of Islamic civilization. The best carpets, made of wool, silk, or cotton, are extremely time-consuming to manufacture. Some have as many as 650 knots per square inch, requiring a considerable amount of time to complete and thus raising the cost of the finished product. A small five-foot-square carpet, for example, could take a single weaver more than a year to complete. Today, among the best carpets are those manufactured in Turkey. Shown here is a rug market in Istanbul.

CONCLUSION

From ancient times, the Middle East has been the site of great empires. In the seventh century, a new force blossomed in the Arabian peninsula and spread rapidly throughout the Middle East. In the eyes of some European writers during the Middle Ages, the Arab empire was a malevolent force that posed a serious threat to the security of Christianity. Indian rajas undoubtedly also felt threatened. The image is not entirely inaccurate, for within half a century after the death of the Prophet, Arab armies overran Christian states in North Africa and the Iberian peninsula, while Turkish Muslims moved eastward onto the fringes of the Indian subcontinent.

But although the teachings of Muhammad brought war and conquest to much of the known world, they also brought hope to millions and a sense of political and economic stability to peoples throughout the region. For many, the arrival of Islam was a welcome event. Islam brought a code of law and a written language to societies that had previously not possessed them. Finally, by creating a revitalized trade network stretching from West Africa to East Asia, it established a vehicle for the exchange of technology and ideas that brought untold wealth to thousands and a better life to millions.

Like other empires in the region, the Arab empire did not last. It fell victim to a combination of internal and external pressures, and by the end of the thirteenth century, it was no more than a memory. But it left a powerful legacy in Islam, which remains one of the great religions of the world. In succeeding centuries, Islam began to penetrate into new areas beyond the fringes of the Sahara and across the Indian Ocean into the islands of the Indonesian archipelago. The next chapters will explore this development.

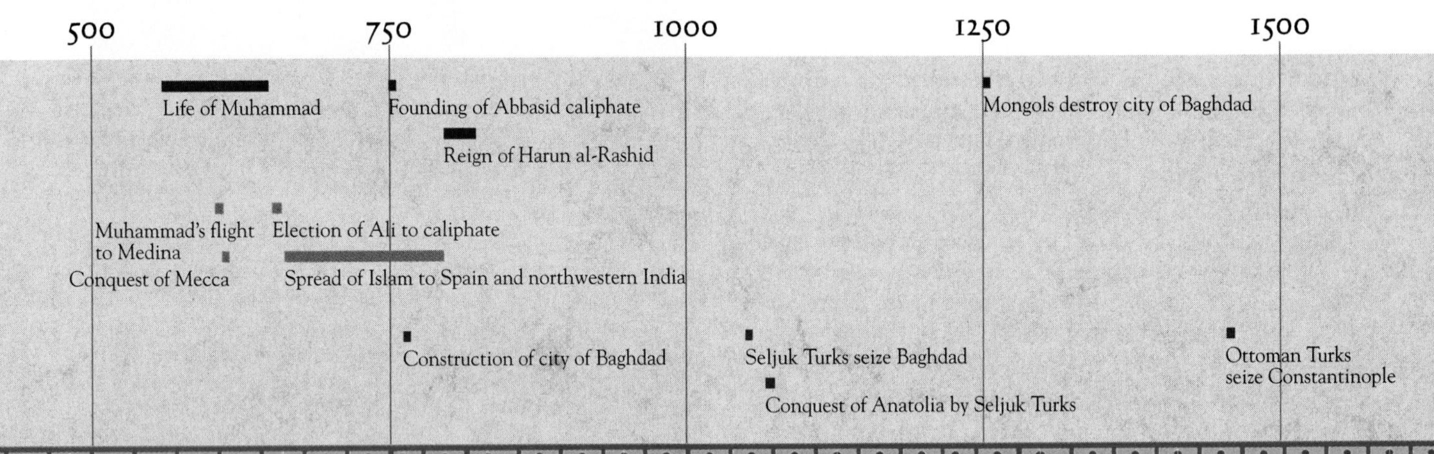

Chapter Notes

1. Mohammed Marmaduke Pickthall, trans., *The Meaning of the Glorious Koran* (New York, 1953), p. 89.
2. Quoted in Thomas W. Lippman, *Understanding Islam: An Introduction to the Moslem World* (New York, 1982), p. 118.
3. Friedrich Hirth and W. W. Rockhill, trans., *Chau Ju-kua: His Work on the Chinese and Arab Trade in the Twelfth and Thirteenth Centuries, Entitled Chu-fan-chi* (New York, 1966), p. 115.
4. Mas'udi, *The Meadows of Gold: The Abbasids*, ed. Paul Lunde and Caroline Stone (London, 1989), p. 151.
5. Leo Africanus, *The History and Description of Africa and of the Notable Things Therein Contained* (New York, n.d.), pp. 820–21.
6. Ehsan Yarshater, ed., *Persian Literature* (Albany, N.Y., 1988), pp. 125–26.
7. Ibid., pp. 154–59.
8. E. Rehatsek, trans., *The Gulistan or Rose Garden of Sa'di* (New York, 1964), pp. 65, 67, 71.

Suggested Readings

Standard works on the Arab empire and the rise of Islam include B. Lewis, *The Arabs in History* (New York, 1961), and T. Lippman, *Understanding Islam: An Introduction to the Moslem World* (New York, 1982). More up-to-date is G. E. Perry, *The Middle East: Fourteen Islamic Centuries*, 2d ed. (Englewood Cliffs, N.J., 1992). A more detailed treatment can be found in P. M. Holt et al., eds., *The Cambridge History of Islam*, two vols. (Cambridge, 1970), and J. L. Esposito, ed. *The Oxford History of Islam* (New York, 1999). For a popularized history, see A. Nutting, *The Arabs: A Narrative History from Mohammed to the Present* (New York, 1964). For an overview with rich illustrations, see *People and Places of the Past* (National Geographic Society, 1983). For anthropological background, see

D. Bates and A. Rassam, *Peoples and Cultures of the Middle East* (Englewood Cliffs, N.J., 1983). On women, see S. Botman et al., *Women in the Middle East* (London, 1987), and N. Keddie et al., eds., *Women in Middle Eastern History: Shifting Boundaries in Sex and Gender* (New Haven, Conn., 1991).

On Islam, see F. Denny, *An Introduction to Islam* (New York, 1985), and J. Esposito, *Islam: the Straight Path* (New York, 1988). Among the various translations of the Koran, two of the best for the introductory student are N. J. Dawood, trans., *The Koran* (Harmondsworth, 1990), and M. M. Pickthall, trans., *The Meaning of the Glorious Koran* (New York, 1953). See also R. W. Bulliet, *Conversion to Islam in the Medieval Period: An Essay in Quantitative History* (Cambridge, 1979).

Specialized works on various historical periods are numerous. For a view of the crusades from an Arab perspective, see A. Maalouf, *The Crusades Through Arab Eyes* (London, 1984). On the Mamluks, see R. Irwin, *The Middle East in the Middle Ages: The Early Mamluk Sultanate, 1250–1382* (Carbondale, Ill., 1986).

On the economy, see E. Ashtor, *A Social and Economic History of the Near East in the Middle Ages* (Berkeley, 1976); K. N. Chaudhuri, *Asia Before Europe: Economy and Civilization of the Indian Ocean from the Rise of Islam to 1750* (Cambridge, 1990); and C. Issawi, *The Middle East Economy: Decline and Recovery* (Princeton, N.J., 1995). On the crucial role of the camel in Middle Eastern society, see the interesting study by R. W. Bulliet, *The Camel and the Wheel* (Cambridge, 1975). On the role of women during this period, see F. Hussain, *Muslim Women* (New York, 1984).

For the best introduction to Islamic literature, consult J. Kritzeck, ed., *Anthology of Islamic Literature* (New York, 1964), with its concise commentaries and introduction. An excellent introduction to Persian literature can be found in E. Yarshater, *Persian Literature* (Albany, N.Y., 1988). Of particular interest are the chapters on Omar Khayyam, by L. P. Elwell-Sutton, and on Rumi, by T. S. Halman. A stimulating analysis of Persian poetry is found in A. Schimmel, *A Two-Colored Brocade: The Imagery of Persian Poetry* (Chapel Hill, N.C., 1992). For the student, H. Haddawy, trans., *The Arabian Nights* (New York, 1990) is the best version. It presents 271 "nights" in a clear and colorful style.

For the best introduction to Islamic art, consult the concise yet comprehensive work by D. T. Rice, *Islamic Art*, rev. ed. (London, 1975). Also see J. Bloom and S. Blair, *Islamic Arts* (London, 1997). For carpets, a beautifully illustrated source is E. Sakhai's *The Story of Carpets* (London, 1991).

InfoTrac College Edition

For additional reading, go to InfoTrac College Edition, your online research library at http://web1.infotrac-college.com

Enter the search term "Islam" using the Subject Guide.

Enter the search terms "caliph or caliphate" using Keywords.

Enter the search term "Koran" using Keywords.

Enter the search term "Crusades" using Keywords.

Enter the search terms "Sufi or Sufism or Rumi" using Keywords.

CHAPTER

8

EARLY CIVILIZATIONS IN AFRICA

CHAPTER OUTLINE

- THE LAND
- THE EMERGENCE OF CIVILIZATION
- THE COMING OF ISLAM
- STATES AND STATELESS SOCIETIES IN SOUTHERN AFRICA
- AFRICAN SOCIETY
- AFRICAN CULTURE
- CONCLUSION

FOCUS QUESTIONS

- What were the main developments in African history before the coming of Islam, and what contacts did early African civilizations and societies have with civilizations outside Africa?
- What effects did the coming of Islam and the Arabs have on African religion, society, political structures, trade, and culture?
- What were the main characteristics of the West African states of Ghana and Mali?
- What roles did lineage groups, women, and slavery play in African society?
- What are some of the characteristics of African sculpture and carvings, music, and architecture, and what purpose did these forms of creative expression serve in African society?

In 1871, the German explorer Karl Mauch began to search southern Africa's central plateau for the colossal stone ruins of a legendary lost civilization. In late August, he found what he had been looking for. According to his diary: "Presently I stood before it and beheld a wall of a height of about 20 feet of granite bricks. Very close by there was a place where a kind of footpath led over rubble into the interior. Following this path I stumbled over masses of rubble and parts of walls and dense thickets. I stopped in front of a towerlike structure. Altogether it rose to a height of about 30 feet." Mauch was convinced that "a civilized nation must once have lived here." Like many other nineteenth-century Europeans, however, Mauch was equally convinced that the Africans who had lived there could never have built such splendid structures like the ones he had found at Great Zimbabwe. To Mauch and other archaeologists, Great Zimbabwe must have been the work of "a northern race closely akin to the Phoenician and Egyptian." It was not until the twentieth century that Europeans could overcome their prejudices and finally admit that Africans south of Egypt had also developed advanced civilizations with spectacular achievements.

The continent of Africa has played a central role in the long evolution of humankind. It was in Africa that the first hominids appeared more than three million years ago. It was probably in Africa that the immediate ancestors of modern human beings—*Homo sapiens*—emerged for the first time. Both the cultivation of crops and the domestication of animals may have occurred first in Africa. Certainly, one of the first states appeared in Africa, in the Nile valley in the northeastern corner of the continent, in the form of the kingdom of the pharaohs. Recent evidence suggests that Egyptian civilization was significantly influenced by cultural developments taking place to the south, in Nubia in modern Sudan.

After the decline of the Egyptian empire during the first millennium B.C.E., the focus of social change began to shift from the lower Nile valley to other areas of the continent: to West Africa, where a series of major trading states began to take part in the caravan trade with the Mediterranean through the vast wastes of the Sahara; to the region of the upper Nile River, where the states of Kush and Axum dominated trade for several centuries; and to the eastern coast from the Horn of Africa to the straits between the continent and the island of Madagascar, where African peoples began to play an active role in the commercial traffic in the Indian Ocean. In the meantime, a gradual movement of agricultural peoples brought Iron Age farming to the central portion of the continent, leading eventually to the creation of several states in the Zaire River basin and the plateau region south of the Zambezi River. When European seafarers began to round the Cape of Good Hope at the end of the fifteenth century C.E., Western historians would herald their voyages as the beginning of an Age of Discovery. That label was a misnomer, however, for the peoples of Africa had played a significant role in the changing human experience since ancient times.

The Land

After Asia, Africa is the largest of the continents. It stretches nearly five thousand miles from the Cape of Good Hope in the south to the Mediterranean in the north and extends a similar distance from Cape Verde on the west coast to the Horn of Africa on the Indian Ocean. Africa is as diverse as it is vast. The northern fringe, on the coast washed by the Mediterranean Sea, is mountainous through much of its length. South of the mountains lies the greatest desert on earth, the Sahara, which stretches from the Atlantic to the Indian Ocean. To the east is the Nile River, heart of the ancient Egyptian civilization. Beyond that lies the Red Sea, separating Africa from Asia.

The Sahara acts as a great divide separating the northern coast from the rest of the continent. Africa south of the Sahara is itself divided among a number of major regions. In the west is the so-called hump of Africa, which juts like a massive shoulder into the Atlantic Ocean. Here the Sahara gradually gives way to grasslands in the interior and then to tropical jungles along the coast. This region, which is dominated by the Niger River, is rich in natural resources and was the home of many ancient civilizations.

Far to the east bordering the Indian Ocean is a very different terrain of snowcapped mountains, upland plateaus, and lakes. Much of this region is grassland populated by wild beasts, which have given it the modern designation of Safari Country. Here, in the East African Rift valley in the lake district of modern Kenya, early hominids began their long trek to civilization several million years ago.

Further to the south lies the Congo basin, with its jungles watered by the mighty Zaire (formerly Congo) River. The jungles of equatorial Africa then fade gradually into the hills, plateaus, and deserts of the south. This rich land contains some of the most valuable mineral resources known today.

The Emergence of Civilization

It is not certain when agriculture was first practiced on the continent of Africa. Until recently, historians assumed that crops were first cultivated in the lower Nile valley (the northern part near the Mediterranean) about seven or eight thousand years ago, when wheat and barley were introduced, possibly from the Middle East. Eventually, as Chapter 1 explained, this area gave rise to the civilization of ancient Egypt.

Kush

Recent evidence suggests that this hypothesis may need some revision. South of Egypt, near the junction of the White and the Blue Nile, is an area known historically as Nubia. Some archaeologists suggest that agriculture may have appeared first in Nubia rather than in the lower Nile valley. Stone Age farmers from Nubia may have begun to cultivate local crops such as sorghum and millet along the banks of the upper Nile (the southern part near the river's source) as early as the eleventh millennium B.C.E.

Recent archaeological finds also imply that the first true African kingdom may have been located in Nubia rather than in Egypt. A drawing on an incense burner dated at about 3100 B.C.E. or earlier depicts a seated ruler with the falcon motif later adopted by the pharaohs of Egypt. Some scholars suggest that the Nubian concept of kingship may have spread to the north, past the cataracts along the Nile, where it eventually gave birth to the better known civilization of Egypt.

Whatever the truth of such conjectures, it is clear that contacts between the upper and lower Nile had been established by the late third millennium B.C.E., when Egyptian merchants traveled to Nubia to obtain ivory, ebony, frankincense, and leopard skins. A few centuries later Nubia had become an Egyptian tributary. At the end of the second millennium B.C.E., Nubia profited from the disintegration of the Egyptian New Kingdom to become the independent state of Kush. Egyptian influence continued, however, as Kushite culture borrowed extensively from Egypt, including religious beliefs, the practice of interring kings in pyramids, and hieroglyphics.

Although its economy was probably founded primarily on agriculture and animal husbandry, Kush developed into a major trading state that endured for hundreds of years. Its commercial activities were stimulated by the discovery of iron ore in a floodplain near the river at Meroë. Strategically located at the point where a land route across the desert to the north intersected the Nile River, Meroë eventually became the capital of the state. In addition to iron products, Kush supplied goods from Central and East Africa, notably ivory, gold, ebony, and slaves, to the Roman Empire, as well as to Arabia and India. At first goods were transported by donkey caravans to the point where the river north was navigable. By the last centuries of the first millennium B.C.E., however, the donkeys were being replaced by camels, newly introduced from the Arabian peninsula.

Little is known about Kushite society, but it seems likely that it was predominantly urban. At first foreign trade was probably a monopoly of the state, but the extensive luxury goods in the numerous private tombs in the vicinity indicate that at one time material prosperity was relatively widespread. This suggests that commercial activities were being conducted by a substantial merchant class.

MAP 8.1 Ancient Africa

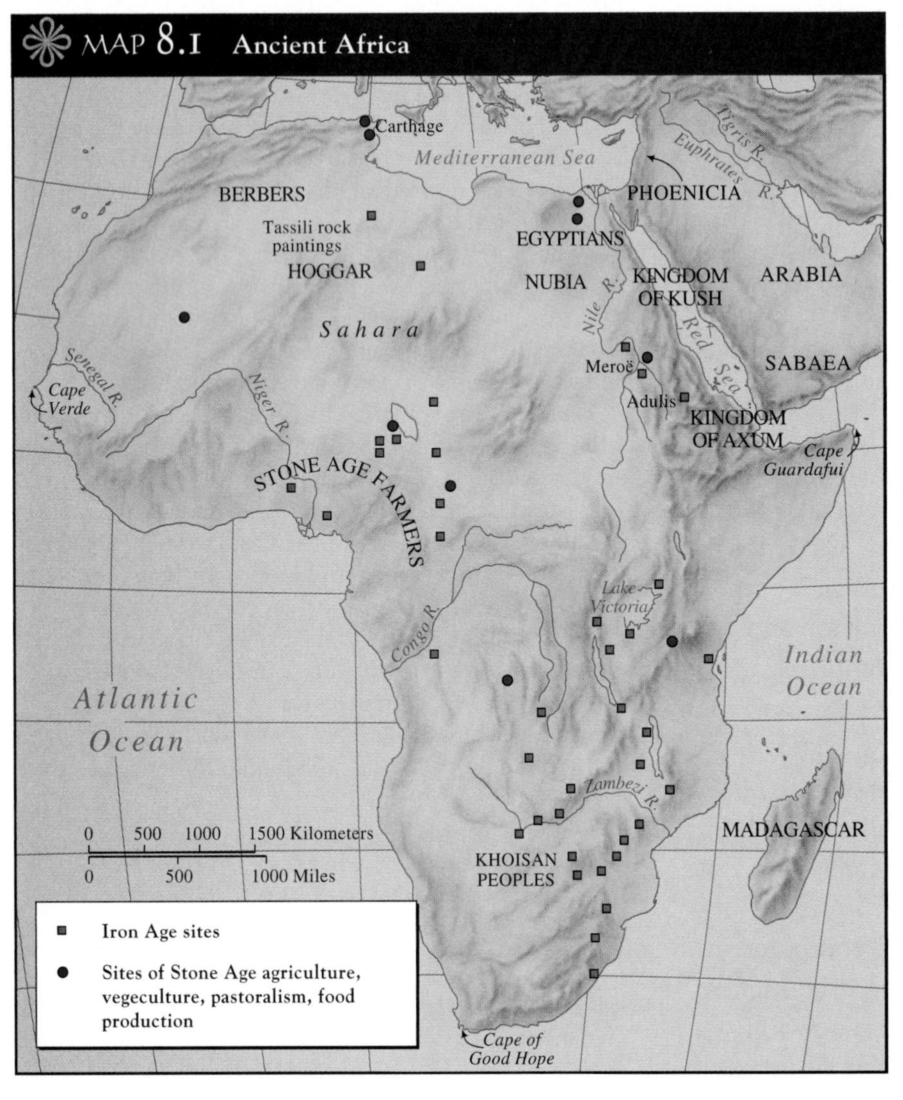

Axum, Son of Saba

In the first millennium C.E., Kush declined and was eventually conquered by Axum, a new power located in the highlands of modern Ethiopia. Axum had been founded during the first millennium B.C.E. as a colony of the kingdom of Saba (popularly known as Sheba) across the Red Sea on the southern tip of the Arabian peninsula. During antiquity, Saba was a major trading state, serving as a transit point for goods carried from South Asia into the lands surrounding the Mediterranean. Biblical sources credited the "queen of Sheba" with vast wealth and resources. In fact, much of that wealth had originated much further to the east and passed through Saba en route to the countries adjacent to the Mediterranean.

When Saba declined, perhaps because of the desiccation of the Arabian Desert, Axum broke away and survived for centuries as an independent state. Like Saba, Axum owed much of its prosperity to its location on the commercial trade route between India and the Mediterranean, and Greek ships from the Ptolemaic kingdom in Egypt stopped regularly at the port of Adulis on the Red Sea. Axum exported ivory, frankincense, myrrh, and slaves, while its primary imports were textiles, metal goods, wine, and olive oil. For a time, Axum competed for control of the ivory trade with the neighboring state of Kush, and hunters from Axum armed with imported iron weapons scoured the entire region for elephants. Probably as a result of this competition, in the fourth century C.E., the Axumite ruler, claiming he had been provoked, launched an invasion of Kush and conquered it (see the box on p. 220).

Perhaps the most distinctive feature of Axumite civilization was its religion. Originally, the rulers of Axum (who claimed descent from King Solomon through the visit of the queen of Sheba to Israel in biblical times) followed the religion of their predecessors in Saba. But in the fourth century C.E., Axumite rulers adopted Christianity from the Egyptians. This commitment to the Egyptian form of Christianity (often called Coptic, from the local language of the day) was retained even after the collapse of Axum and the expansion of Islam through the area in later centuries. Later, Axum (now renamed Ethiopia) would be identified by Europeans as the "hermit kingdom" and the home of Prester John, a legendary Christian king of East Africa.

THE PYRAMIDS AT MEROË. The kingdom of Kush borrowed much of its culture from the Egyptian empire to the north, while placing its own imprint on all imports. Kushite rulers, for example, modeled their political institutions after those of the pharaohs, but governmental authority was somewhat more decentralized, and monarchical power was apparently limited by the influence of priests and the local aristocracy. The pyramids at Meroë, on the banks of the Nile River, are another example. Younger, smaller, unpointed at the top, and more standardized in size and shape than their famous counterparts at Giza, they remain a dramatic reminder of the glory of ancient Kush.

THE CONQUEST OF KUSH

One of the few written descriptions of life along the Nile River in ancient times comes from this inscription, which was included in the Periplus, *a Greek account probably written in the first century* C.E. *Here an Axumite king describes his campaign against Meroë, Axum's neighbor to the west in the upper Nile valley.*

AN AXUMITE KING PROCLAIMS HIS VICTORY

With the help of the Lord of Heaven, who in heaven and earth conquers all, Ezana son of Ella Amica, a member of [the group] Halen, king of Axum and of Hemer [Himyar] and of Raydan and of Sab'a and of Salhen and of Tsyamo and of Bega and of Kasu, king of kings . . . never conquered by an enemy . . . by the power of the Lord of the Earth and fought at the Takazi, by the Ford of Kemalke . . . I burnt their towns, those with stone houses and those with straw huts, and [my troops] pillaged their corn and bronze and iron and copper; they destroyed the effigies in their houses [temples], and also their stores of corn and cotton, and threw them into the river Seda. . . . And I reached the Kasu, whom I fought and made captive at the confluence of the rivers Seda and Takazi; and the next day I sent my troops . . . on a campaign up the Seda to the towns of stone and of straw; the names of the towns of stone are Alwa and Daro. . . . Then I sent troops . . . down the Seda to the four straw villages of the Noba and the king. The stone towns of the Kasu which the Noba took [were] Tabito, Pertoti; and they [my troops] went as far as the Red Noba.

THE STELE AT AXUM. Axum was a prosperous trading state by the third century C.E., selling ivory, glass crystal, brass, copper, and frankincense and myrrh. The latter were resins, used in burials and as medicines by the peoples of Egypt and the eastern Roman Empire. In the fourth century, the Axumite rulers erected stelae, or slender columns, to mark the location of the royal tombs. Shown here is the tallest of the still-standing Axum stelae, in present-day Ethiopia. Note the differences between these pillars and those constructed in India during the reign of Emperor Asoka.

The Sahara and Its Environs

Kush and Axum were part of the ancient trading network originally established by the Egyptians and were affected in various ways by the cross-cultural contacts that took place throughout that region. Elsewhere in Africa, somewhat different patterns prevailed; they varied from area to area depending on the geography and climate.

At one time, when the world's climate was much colder than it is today, Central Africa may have been one of the few areas that was habitable for the first hominids. Later, from 8000 to 4000 B.C.E., a warm, humid climate prevailed in the Sahara, creating lakes and ponds, as well as vast grasslands (known as savannahs) replete with game. Rock paintings found in what are today some of the most uninhabitable parts of the region are a clear indication that the environment was much different several thousand years ago.

By 7000 B.C.E., the peoples of the Sahara were herding animals—first sheep and goats and later cattle. During the sixth and fifth millennia B.C.E., the climate became more arid, however, and the desertification of the Sahara began. From the rock paintings, which for the most part date from the fourth and third millennia B.C.E., we know that by that time the herds were being supplemented by fishing and limited cultivation of crops such as millet, sorghum, and a drought-resistant form of dry rice. After 3000 B.C.E., as the desiccation of the Sahara proceeded and the lakes dried up, farming began to spread into the savannahs on the southern fringes of the desert and eventually into the tropical forest areas to the south, where crops were no longer limited to drought-resistant cereals but could include tropical fruits and tubers.

Historians do not know when goods first began to be exchanged across the Sahara in a north-south direction, but certainly during the first millennium B.C.E. the commercial center of Carthage on the Mediterranean had become a focal point of the trans-Saharan trade. The Berbers, a pastoral people of North Africa, served as intermediaries, carrying food products and manufactured goods from Carthage across the desert and exchanging them for salt, gold and copper, skins, various agricultural products, and perhaps slaves.

This trade initiated a process of cultural exchange that would exert a significant impact on the peoples of tropical Africa. Among other things it may have spread the knowledge of ironworking south of the desert. Although historians once believed that ironworking knowledge reached sub-Saharan Africa from Meroë in the upper Nile valley in the first centuries C.E., recent finds suggest that the peoples along the Niger River were smelting iron as early as the middle of the first millennium B.C.E. Some scholars believe that the technique developed independently there, but others believe that it was introduced by the Berbers, who had learned it from the Carthaginians.

MAP 8.2 Ancient Ethiopia and Nubia

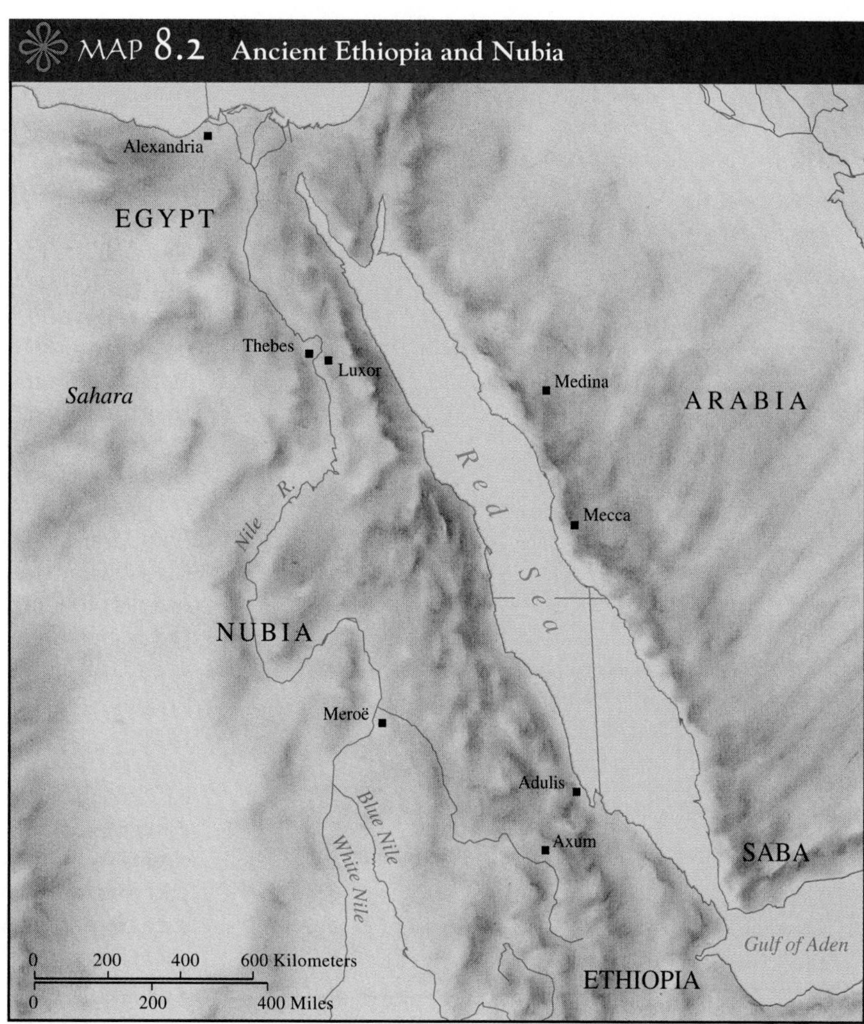

Whatever the case, the Nok culture in northern Nigeria eventually became one of the most active ironworking societies in Africa. Excavations have unearthed numerous terra-cotta and iron figures, as well as stone and iron farm implements, dating back as far as 500 B.C.E. The remains of smelting furnaces confirm that the iron was produced locally.

Early in the first millennium C.E., the introduction of the camel provided a major stimulus to the trans-Saharan trade. With its ability to store considerable amounts of food and water in its hump, the camel was far better equipped to handle the arduous conditions of the desert than the oxen, which had been used previously. The camel caravans of the Berbers became known as the "fleets of the desert."

East Africa

South of Axum, along the shores of the Indian Ocean and in the inland plateau that stretches from the mountains of Ethiopia through the lake district of Central Africa, lived a mixture of peoples, some living by hunting and food gathering and others following pastoral pursuits.

Beginning in the first millennium B.C.E., new peoples began to migrate into East Africa from the west. Farming peoples speaking dialects of the Bantu family of languages began to move from the region of the Niger River into East Africa and the Zaire River basin. They were probably responsible for introducing the widespread cultivation of crops and knowledge of ironworking to much of East Africa, although there are signs of some limited iron smelting in the area before their arrival.

The Bantu settled in rural communities based on subsistence farming. The primary crops were millet and sorghum, along with yams, melons, and beans. The land was often tilled with both iron and stone tools, and the former were usually manufactured in a local smelter. Some people kept domestic animals such as cattle, sheep, goats, or chickens or supplemented their diets by hunting and food gathering. Because the population was still small and an ample supply of cultivable land was available, most settlements were relatively small; each village formed a self-sufficient political and economic entity.

As early as the era of the New Kingdom in the second millennium B.C.E., Egyptian ships had plied the waters off the East African coast in search of gold, ivory, palm oil, and perhaps slaves. By the first century C.E., the region was an established part of a trading network that included the Mediterranean and the Red Seas. In that century, a Greek seafarer from Alexandria wrote an

CHRONOLOGY

EARLY AFRICA

Origins of agriculture in Africa	c. 7000 B.C.E.
Desiccation of the Sahara	Begins c. 5000 B.C.E.
Kingship appears in the Nile valley	c. 3100 B.C.E.
Kingdom of Kush in Nubia	c. 500 B.C.E.
Iron Age begins	c. sixth century B.C.E.
Beginnings of trans-Sahara trade	c. first millennium B.C.E.
Rise of Axum	First century C.E.
Conquest of Kush by Axum	Fourth century C.E.
Arrival of Bantus in East Africa	Early centuries C.E.
Arrival of Malays on island of Madagascar	Second century C.E.
Origins of Ghana	Fifth century C.E.
Arab takeover of lower Nile valley	641 C.E.
Development of Swahili culture	c. first millennium C.E.
Spread of Islam across North Africa	Seventh century C.E.
Spread of Islam in Horn of Africa	Ninth century C.E.
Decline of Ghana	Twelfth century C.E.
Establishment of Zagwe dynasty in Ethiopia	c. 1150
Rise of Mali	c. 1250
Kingdom of Zimbabwe	c. 1300–c. 1450
Portuguese ships explore West African coast	Mid-fifteenth century

account of his travels down the coast from Cape Guardafui at the tip of the Horn of Africa to the Strait of Madagascar thousands of miles to the south. Called the *Periplus*, this work provides generally accurate descriptions of the peoples and settlements along the African coast and the trade goods they supplied.

According to the *Periplus*, the port of Rhapta (possibly modern Dar es Salaam) was a commercial metropolis, exporting ivory, rhinoceros horn, and tortoiseshell and importing glass, wine, grain, and metal goods such as weapons and tools. The identity of the peoples taking part in this trade is not clear, but it seems likely that the area was already inhabited by a mixture of local peoples and immigrants from the Arabian peninsula. According to the *Periplus*, the area around Rhapta was under the control of an Arabian kingdom. Out of this mixture would eventually emerge an African-Arabian "Swahili" culture (see East Africa: The Land of Zanj later in this chapter) that continues to exist in coastal areas today. Beyond Rhapta was "unexplored ocean." Some contemporary observers believed that the Indian and Atlantic Oceans were connected. Others were convinced that the Indian Ocean was an enclosed sea and that the continent of Africa could not be circumnavigated (see the box on p. 223).

Trade across the Indian Ocean and down the coast of East Africa, facilitated by the monsoon winds, would gradually become one of the most lucrative sources of commercial profit in the ancient and medieval worlds. Although the origins of the trade remain shrouded in mystery, traders eventually came by sea from as far away as the mainland of Southeast Asia. Early in the first millennium C.E., Malay peoples bringing cinnamon to the Middle East began to cross the Indian Ocean directly and landed on the southeastern coast of Africa. Eventually, a Malay settlement was established on the island of Madagascar, where the population is still of mixed Malay-African origin. Historians suspect that Malay immigrants were responsible for introducing such Southeast Asian foods as the banana and the yam to the African peoples. With its high yield and ability to grow in uncultivated rain forest, the banana often became the preferred crop of the Bantu peoples.

Southern Africa

South of the East African plateau and the Congo basin is a vast land of hills, grasslands, and arid desert stretching almost to the Cape of Good Hope at the tip of the continent. As Bantu-speaking farmers spread southward during the final centuries of the first millennium B.C.E., they began to encounter Stone Age peoples in the area who still lived primarily by hunting and foraging. These peoples, many of whom apparently belonged to the Khoisan family of languages (Khoisan languages are distinguished by their numerous "clicking" sounds), were lighter in skin color and generally shorter than the Bantu speakers who were beginning to arrive from the north.

Available evidence suggests that early relations between these two peoples were relatively harmonious. Intermarriage between members of the two groups was apparently not unusual, and many of the Khoisan-speaking peoples were gradually absorbed into what became a dominantly Bantu-speaking pastoral and agricultural society that spread throughout much of southern Africa during the first millennium C.E.

BEYOND THE PILLARS OF HERCULES

The first suggestion that seafarers could pass from the Atlantic to the Indian Ocean around the southern tip of Africa came from the Greek historian Herodotus. In the following passage from his History of the Persian Wars, *Herodotus describes a voyage by Phoenician sailors that was recounted to him during his visit to Egypt. The reference to the position of the sun reflects a phenomenon that could only have occurred if the Phoenicians were sailing south of the equator.*

HERODOTUS, *HISTORY OF THE PERSIAN WARS*

Africa proves to be completely surrounded by water except for as much of it as borders on Asia. Of all men of whom we have any knowledge, the Egyptian king Necho was the first to establish this fact. After he had ceased from trying to dig the canal that extends from the Nile to the Arabian Gulf, he dispatched some Phoenicians in ships with orders to sail back into our northern sea by passing through the Pillars of Hercules and so to return to Egypt.

Accordingly these Phoenicians set out and from the Red Sea sailed into the southern ocean. Whenever autumn came, they went ashore wherever in Africa they chanced to be on their voyage, to sow grain in the earth and await the harvest. On reaping the new grain they put again to sea. In this wise, after two years had elapsed, they rounded the Pillars of Hercules and in the third year reached Egypt.

Now, they told a tale that I personally do not believe (though others may, if they choose), how they had the sun on their right hand as they sailed along the African coast.

THE COMING OF ISLAM

As we saw in the previous chapter, the rise of Islam during the first half of the seventh century C.E. had ramifications far beyond the Arabian peninsula. Arab armies swept across North Africa, incorporating it into the Arab empire and isolating the Christian state of Axum to the south. Although East Africa and West Africa south of the Sahara were not conquered by the Arab forces, Islam eventually penetrated these areas as well.

African Religious Beliefs Before Islam

When Islam arrived, most African societies already had well-developed systems of religious beliefs. Like other aspects of African life, early African religious beliefs varied from place to place, but certain characteristics appear to have been shared by most African societies. One of these common features was a belief in a single creator god. The supreme god of the Bantu, for example, was a pantheistic force from whom all things came. Sometimes, the creator god was accompanied by a whole pantheon of lesser deities. The Ashanti people of Ghana in West Africa believed in a supreme being called Nyame, whose sons were lesser gods. Each son served a different purpose: one was the rainmaker, another the compassionate, and a third was responsible for the sunshine. This heavenly hierarchy paralleled earthly arrangements: worship of Nyame was the exclusive preserve of the king through his priests; lesser officials and the common people worshiped Nyame's sons, who might intercede with their father on behalf of ordinary Africans.

Many African religions also shared a belief in a form of afterlife. Human existence was believed to consist of two stages: the first stage was life on earth (*sasa*); the second stage was eternal existence (*zamani*), during which the soul floated in the atmosphere through eternity. Belief in an afterlife was closely connected to the importance of ancestors and the lineage, or clan, in African society. Each lineage group could trace itself back to a founding ancestor or group of ancestors. These ancestral souls would not be extinguished as long as the lineage group continued to perform rituals in their name. The rituals could also benefit the lineage group on earth, for the ancestral souls, being closer to the gods, had the power to influence, for good or evil, the lives of their descendants.

Such beliefs were challenged but not always replaced by the arrival of Islam. In some ways, the tenets of Islam were in conflict with traditional African beliefs and customs. Although the concept of a single transcendent deity presented no problems in many African societies, Islam's rejection of spirit worship and a priestly class ran counter to the beliefs of many Africans and was often ignored in practice. Similarly, as various Muslim travelers observed, Islam's insistence on the separation of the sexes contrasted with the relatively informal relationships that prevailed in many African societies and was probably slow to take root. In the long run, imported ideas were synthesized with native beliefs to create a unique brand of Africanized Islam.

The Arabs in North Africa

In 641, Arab forces advanced into Egypt, seized the delta of the Nile River, and brought two centuries of Byzantine rule to an end. To guard against attacks from the Byzantine fleet, the Arabs eventually built a new capital at Cairo, inland from the previous Byzantine capital of

Alexandria, and began to consolidate their control over the entire region.

The Arab conquerors were probably welcomed by many, if not the majority, of the local inhabitants. Although Egypt had been a thriving commercial center under the Byzantines, the average Egyptian had not shared in this prosperity. Tax rates were generally high, and Christians were subjected to periodic persecution by the Byzantines, who viewed the local Coptic faith and other sects in the area as heresies. Although the new rulers continued to obtain much of their revenue from taxing the local farming population, tax rates were generally lower than they had been under the corrupt Byzantine government, and conversion to Islam brought exemption from taxation. During the next generations, many Egyptians converted to the Muslim faith, but Islam did not move into the upper Nile valley until several hundred years later. As Islam spread southward, it was adopted by many lowland peoples, but it had less success in the mountains of Ethiopia, where Coptic Christianity continued to win adherents (see the next section).

In the meantime, Arab rule was gradually being extended westward along the Mediterranean coast. When the Romans conquered Carthage in 146 B.C.E., they had called their new province Africa, thus introducing a name that would eventually be applied to the entire continent. After the fall of the Roman Empire, much of the area had reverted to the control of local Berber chieftains, but the Byzantines captured Carthage in the mid-sixth century C.E. In 690, the city was seized by the Arabs, who then began to extend their control over the entire area, which they called Al Maghrib (the west).

At first, the local Berber peoples resisted their new conquerors. The Berbers were tough fighters, and for several generations, Arab rule was limited to the towns and lowland coastal areas. But Arab persistence eventually paid off, and by the early eighth century, the entire North African coast as far west as the Strait of Gibraltar was under Arab rule. The Arabs were now poised to cross the strait and expand into southern Europe and to push south beyond the fringes of the Sahara.

The Kingdom of Ethiopia: A Christian Island in a Muslim Sea

By the end of the sixth century C.E., the kingdom of Axum, long a dominant force in the trade network through the Red Sea, was in a state of decline. Both overexploitation of farmland and a shift in trade routes away from the Red Sea to the Arabian peninsula and Persian Gulf contributed to this decline. By the beginning of the ninth century, the capital had been moved further into the mountainous interior, and Axum was gradually transformed from a maritime power into an isolated agricultural society.

The rise of Islam on the Arabian peninsula hastened this process, as the Arab world increasingly began to serve as the focus of the regional trade passing through the area. By the eighth century, a number of Muslim trading states had been established on the African coast of the Red Sea, a development that contributed to the transformation of Axum into a landlocked society with primarily agricultural interests. At first relations between Christian Axum and its Muslim neighbors were relatively peaceful, as the larger and more powerful Axumite kingdom attempted with some success to compel the coastal Islamic states to accept a tributary relationship. Axum's role in the local commercial network temporarily revived, and the area became a prime source for ivory, resins like frankincense and myrrh, and slaves. Slaves came primarily from the south, where Axum had been attempting to subjugate restive tribal peoples living in the Amharic plateau beyond its southern border.

Beginning in the twelfth century, however, relations between Axum and its neighbors deteriorated, as the Muslim states along the coast began to move inland to gain control over the growing trade in slaves and ivory. Axum responded with force and at first had some success in reasserting its hegemony over the area. But in the early fourteenth century, the Muslim state of Adal, located at the juncture of the Indian Ocean and the Red Sea, launched a new attack on the Christian kingdom.

Axum also underwent significant internal change during this period. The Zagwe dynasty, which seized control of the country in the mid-twelfth century, centralized the government and extended the Christian faith throughout the kingdom, now known as Ethiopia. Military commanders or civilian officials who had personal or kinship ties with the royal court established vast landed estates to maintain security and facilitate the collection of taxes from the local population. In the meantime, Christian missionaries established monasteries and churches to propagate the faith in outlying areas. Close relations were reestablished with leaders of the Coptic church in Egypt and with Christian officials in the Holy Land. This process was continued by the Solomonids, who succeeded the Zagwe dynasty in 1270. But by the early fifteenth century, the state had become more deeply involved in an expanding conflict with Muslim Adal to the east, a conflict that lasted for over a century and gradually took on the characteristics of a holy war.

East Africa: The Land of Zanj

The rise of Islam also had a lasting impact on the coast of East Africa, which the Greeks had called Azania and the Arabs called Zanj. During the seventh and eighth centuries, peoples from the Arabian peninsula and the Persian Gulf began to settle at ports along the coast and on the small islands offshore. Then, according to legend, in the middle of the tenth century, a Persian from Shiraz, a city in southern Iran, sailed to the area with his six sons. As his small fleet stopped along the coast, each son disembarked on one of the coastal islands and founded a small community; these settlements later grew into the commercial centers of Mombasa, Pemba, Zanzibar (literally, "the coast of Zanj"), and Kilwa.

Although the legend underestimates the degree to which the area had already become a major participant in local commerce as well as the role of the local inhabitants in the process, it does reflect the importance of Arab and Persian immigrants in the formation of a string of trading ports stretching from Mogadishu (today the capital of Somalia) in the north to Kilwa (south of present-day Dar es Salaam) in the south. Kilwa became especially important as it was near the southern limit for a ship hoping to complete the round-trip journey in a single season. Goods such as ivory, gold, and rhinoceros horn were exported across the Indian Ocean to countries as far away as China, while imports included iron goods, glassware, Indian textiles, and Chinese porcelain. Merchants in these cities often amassed considerable profit, as evidenced by their lavish stone palaces, some of which still stand in the modern cities of Mombasa and Zanzibar. Though now in ruins, Kilwa was one of the most magnificent cities of its day. The fourteenth-century Arab traveler Ibn Battuta described it as "amongst the most beautiful of cities and most elegantly built. All of it is of wood, and the ceilings of its houses are of *al-dis* [reeds]."[1]

Most of the coastal states were self-governing, although sometimes several towns were grouped together under a single dominant authority. Government revenue came primarily from taxes imposed on commerce. Some trade went on between these coastal city-states and the peoples of the interior, who provided gold and iron, ivory, and various agricultural goods and animal products in return for textiles, manufactured articles, and weapons (see the box on p. 226). Relations apparently varied, and the coastal merchants sometimes resorted to force to obtain goods from the inland peoples. A Portuguese visitor recounted that "the men thereof [of Mombasa] are oft-times at war and but seldom at peace with those of the mainland, and they carry on trade with them, bringing thence great store of honey, wax, and ivory."[2]

By the twelfth and thirteenth centuries, a mixed African-Arabian culture, eventually known as Swahili (from the Arabic *sahel* meaning "coast"; thus, "peoples of the coast"), began to emerge throughout the coastal area. Intermarriage between the immigrants and the local population was common, although a distinct Arab community, made up primarily of merchants, persisted in many areas. The members of the ruling class were often of mixed heritage but usually traced their genealogy to Arab or Persian ancestors. By this time, too, many members of the ruling class had converted to Islam. Middle Eastern urban architectural styles and other aspects of Arab culture were implanted within a society still predominantly African. Arabic words and phrases were combined with Bantu grammatical structures to form a mixed language, also known as Swahili; it is the national language of the countries of Kenya and Tanzania today.

The States of West Africa

During the eighth century, merchants from the Maghrib began to carry Muslim beliefs to the savannah areas south of the Sahara. At first, conversion took place on an individual basis rather than through official encouragement. The first rulers to convert to Islam were the royal

A LOST CITY IN AFRICA. Gedi was founded in the early fourteenth century and abandoned three hundred years later. Its romantic ruins suggest the grandeur of the Swahili civilization that once flourished along the eastern coast of Africa. Located sixty miles north of Mombasa, in present-day Kenya, Gedi once contained several thousand residents but was eventually abandoned after it was attacked by nomadic peoples from the north. Today the ruins of the town, surrounded by a nine-foot wall, seem dwarfed by towering baobab trees populated only by chattering monkeys. Shown here is the entrance to the palace, which probably served as the residence of the chief official in the town. Neighboring houses, constructed of coral stone, contain sumptuous rooms, with separate women's quarters and enclosed lavatories with urinal channels and double-sink washing benches.

THE COAST OF ZANJ

From early times, the people living on the coast of East Africa took an active part in trade along the coast and across the Indian Ocean. The process began with the arrival of Arab traders early in the first millennium C.E. *According to local legends, Arab merchants often married the daughters of the local chieftains and then received title to coastal territories as part of their wife's dowry. This description of the area was written by the Arab traveler al-Mas'udi, who visited the "land of Zanj" in 916.*

AL-MAS'UDI IN EAST AFRICA

The land of Zanj produces wild leopard skins. The people wear them as clothes, or export them to Muslim countries. They are the largest leopard skins and the most beautiful for making saddles. . . . They also export tortoise shell for making combs, for which ivory is likewise used. . . . The Zanj are settled in that area, which stretches as far as Sofala, which is the furthest limit of the land and the end of the voyages made from Oman and Siraf on the sea of Zanj. . . . The Zanj use the ox as a beast of burden, for they have no horses, mules or camels in their land. . . . There are many wild elephants in this land but no tame ones. The Zanj do not use them for war or anything else, but only hunt and kill them for their ivory. It is from this country that come tusks weighing fifty pounds and more. They usually go to Oman, and from there are sent to China and India. This is the chief trade route. . . .

The Zanj have an elegant language and men who preach in it. One of their holy men will often gather a crowd and exhort his hearers to please God in their lives and to be obedient to him. He explains the punishments that follow upon disobedience, and reminds them of their ancestors and kings of old. These people have no religious law: their kings rule by custom and by political expediency.

The Zanj eat bananas, which are as common among them as they are in India; but their staple food is millet and a plant called kalari which is pulled out of the earth like truffles. They also eat honey and meat. They have many islands where the coconut grows: its nuts are used as fruit by all the Zanj peoples. One of these islands, which is one or two days' sail from the coast, has a Muslim population and a royal family. This is the island of Kanbulu [thought to be modern Pemba].

family of Gao at the end of the tenth century. By the end of the fifteenth century, much of the population in the grasslands south of the Sahara had accepted Islam.

The expansion of Islam into West Africa had a major impact on the political system. By introducing Arabic as the first written language in the region and Muslim law codes and administrative practices from the Middle East, Islam provided local rulers with the tools to increase their authority and the efficiency of their governments. Moreover, as Islam gradually spread throughout the region, a common religion united previously diverse peoples into a more coherent community.

When Islam arrived in the grasslands south of the Sahara, the region was beginning to undergo significant political and social change. A number of major trading states were in the process of creation, and they eventually transformed the Sahara into one of the leading avenues of world trade, crisscrossed by caravan routes leading to destinations as far away as the Atlantic Ocean, the Mediterranean, and the Red Sea.

GHANA

The first of these great commercial states was Ghana, which emerged in the fifth century C.E. in the upper Niger valley, a grassland region between the Sahara and the tropical forests along the West African coast (the modern state of Ghana, which takes its name from the trading society under discussion here, is located in the forest region to the south). The majority of the people in the area were Iron Age farmers living in villages under the authority of a local chieftain. Gradually, these local communities were united to form the kingdom of Ghana.

Although the people of the region had traditionally lived from agriculture, a primary reason for Ghana's growing importance was gold. The heartland of the state was located near one of the richest gold-producing areas in all of Africa. Ghanaian merchants transported the gold to Morocco, whence it was distributed throughout the known world. This trade began in ancient times, as the Greek historian Herodotus relates:

> The Carthaginians also tell us that they trade with a race of men who live in a part of Libya beyond the Pillars of Heracles [the Strait of Gibraltar]. On reaching this country, they unload their goods, arrange them tidily along the beach, and then, returning to their boats, raise a smoke. Seeing the smoke, the natives come down to the beach, place on the ground a certain quantity of gold in exchange for the goods, and go off again to a distance. The Carthaginians then come ashore and take a look at the gold; and if they think it represents a fair price for their wares, they collect it and go away; if, on the other hand, it seems too little, they go back aboard and wait, and the natives come and add to the gold until they are satisfied. There is perfect honesty on both sides; the Carthaginians never touch the gold until it equals in value what they have offered for sale, and the natives never touch the goods until the gold has been taken away.[3]

THE GREAT GATE AT MARRAKECH. The Moroccan city of Marrakech, founded in the ninth century C.E., was a major northern terminus of the trans-Saharan trade and one of the chief commercial centers in premodern Africa. Widely praised by such famous travelers as Ibn Battuta, the city was an architectural marvel in that all its major public buildings were constructed in red sandstone. Shown here is the Great Gate to the city, through which camel caravans passed en route to and from the vast desert. In the Berber language, Marrakech means "pass without making a noise," a reference to the need for caravan traders to be aware of the danger of thieves in the vicinity.

Later, Ghana became known to Arab-speaking peoples in North Africa as "the land of gold." Actually, the name was misleading, for the gold did not come from Ghana, but from a neighboring people, who sold it to merchants from Ghana.

Eventually, other exports from Ghana found their way to the bazaars of the Mediterranean coast and beyond—ivory, ostrich feathers, hides, leather goods, and ultimately slaves. The origins of the slave trade in the area probably go back to the first millennium B.C.E., when Berber tribesmen seized African villagers in the regions south of the Sahara and sold them for profit to buyers in Europe and the Middle East. In return, Ghana imported metal goods (especially weapons), textiles, horses, and salt.

Much of the trade across the desert was still conducted by the nomadic Berbers, but Ghanaian merchants played an active role as intermediaries, trading tropical products such as bananas, kola nuts, and palm oil from the forest states of Guinea along the Atlantic coast to the south. By the eighth and ninth centuries, much of this trade was conducted by Muslim merchants, who purchased the goods from local traders (using iron and copper cash or cowrie shells from Southeast Asia as the primary means of exchange) and then sold them to Berbers, who carried them across the desert. The merchants who carried on this trade often became quite wealthy and lived in splendor in cities like Saleh, the capital of Ghana. So did the king, of course, who taxed the merchants as well as the farmers and the producers.

Like other West African kings, the king of Ghana ruled by divine right and was assisted by a hereditary aristocracy composed of the leading members of the prominent clans, who also served as district chiefs responsible for main-

MAP 8.3 Trans-Saharan Trade Routes

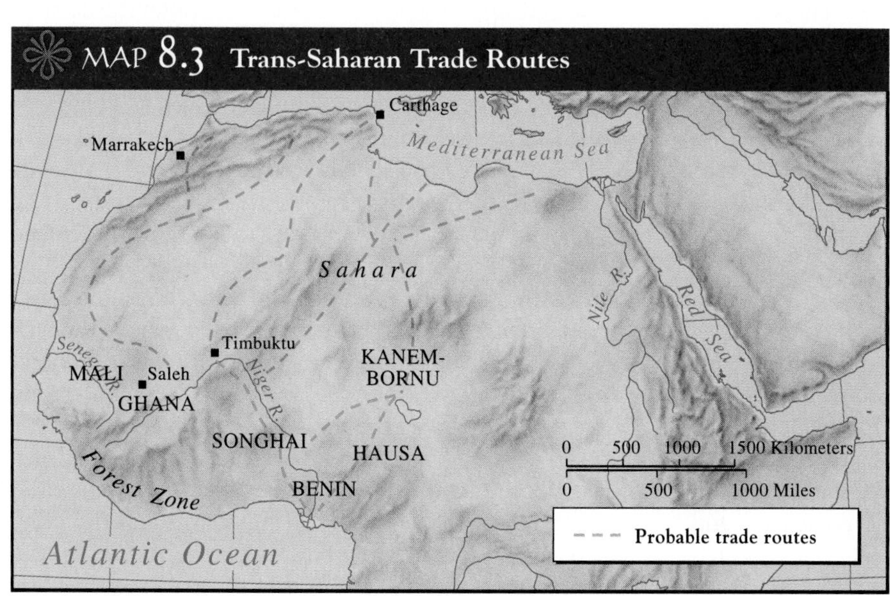

MAP 8.4 The Emergence of States in Africa

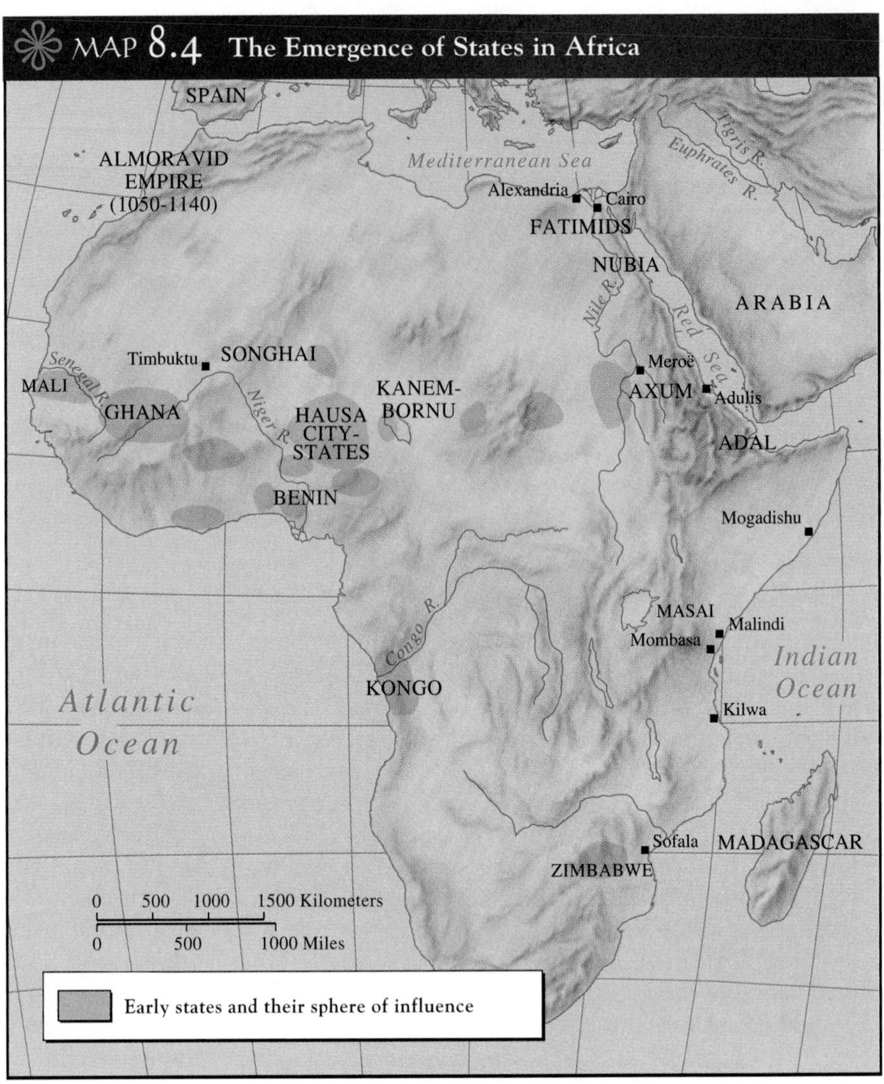

taining law and order and collecting taxes. The king was responsible for maintaining the security of his kingdom, serving as an intermediary with local deities, and functioning as the chief law officer to adjudicate disputes. The kings of Ghana did not convert to Islam themselves, although they welcomed Muslim merchants and apparently did not discourage their subjects from adopting the new faith (see the box on p. 229).

MALI

The state of Ghana flourished for several hundred years, but by the twelfth century, weakened by ruinous wars with Berber tribesmen, it had begun to decline, and it collapsed at the end of the century. In its place rose a number of new trading societies, including large territorial states like Mali and Songhai in the west, Kanem-Bornu in the east, and small commercial city-states like the Hausa states, located in what is today northern Nigeria.

The greatest of the states that emerged after the destruction of Ghana was Mali. Extending from the Atlantic coast inland as far as the famous trading metropolis of Timbuktu and Gao, a modern city on the Niger River, Mali built its wealth and power on the gold trade. But the heartland of Mali was situated considerably to the south of the old state of Ghana in the savannah region, where sufficient moisture enabled farmers to grow such crops as sorghum, millet, and even rice. The farmers lived in villages ruled by a local chieftain (called a *mansa*), who served as both religious and administrative leader and was responsible for forwarding tax revenues from the village to higher levels of government.

The primary wealth of the country was accumulated in the cities. Here lived the merchants, who were primarily of local origin, although many were now practicing Muslims. Commercial activities were taxed, but apparently were so lucrative that both the merchants and the kings prospered. One of the most powerful kings of Mali, known as Mansa Musa (1312–1337), was so wealthy that when

A DESCRIPTION OF A GHANAIAN CAPITAL

After its first appearance in West Africa in the decades following the death of the Prophet, Islam competed with native African religions for followers. Eventually, several local rulers converted to the Muslim faith. This passage by the Arab geographer al-Bakri shows how both religions flourished side by side in the state of Ghana during the eleventh century.

AL-BAKRI'S DESCRIPTION OF GHANA

The king's residence comprises a palace and conical huts, the whole surrounded by a fence like a wall. Around the royal town are huts and groves of thorn trees where live the magicians who control their religious rites. These groves, where they keep their idols and bury their kings, are protected by guards who permit no one to enter or find out what goes on in them.

None of those who belong to the imperial religion may wear tailored garments except the king himself and the heir-presumptive, his sister's son. The rest of the people wear wrappers of cotton, silk or brocade according to their means. Most of the men shave their beards and the women their heads. The king adorns himself with female ornaments around the neck and arms. On his head he wears gold-embroidered caps covered with turbans of finest cotton. He gives audience to the people for the redressing of grievances in a hut around which are placed 10 horses covered in golden cloth. Behind him stand 10 slaves carrying shields and swords mounted with gold. On his right are the sons of vassal kings, their heads plaited with gold and wearing costly garments. On the ground around him are seated his ministers, whilst the governor of the city sits before him. On guard at the door are dogs of fine pedigree, wearing collars adorned with gold and silver. The royal audience is announced by the beating of a drum, called daba, made out of a long piece of hollowed-out wood. When the people have gathered, his coreligionists draw near upon their knees sprinkling dust upon their heads as a sign of respect, whilst the Muslims clap hands as their form of greeting.

he embarked on a pilgrimage to Mecca in the early fourteenth century, his spending splurge in Egypt depressed the price of gold there for a dozen years.

Mansa Musa's primary contribution to his people was probably not economic prosperity, but the Muslim faith. Early rulers of Mali apparently adhered to traditional African faiths, assuming the role of *mansa* for their subjects, but later rulers converted to Islam. Mansa Musa strongly encouraged the building of mosques and the study of the Koran in his kingdom and imported scholars and books to introduce his subjects to the message of Allah. One visitor from Europe, writing in the late fifteenth century, reported that in Timbuktu "are a great store of doctors, judges, priests, and other learned men, that are bountifully maintained at the king's cost and charges. And hither are brought divers manuscripts of written books out of Barbary [North Africa] which are sold for more money than any other merchandise."[4]

MANSA MUSA. Mansa Musa (1312–1337), king of the West African state of Mali, was one of the richest and most powerful rulers of his day. During his famous pilgrimage to Mecca, he arrived in Cairo with a hundred camels laden with gold and gave away so much gold that its value depreciated there for several years. His fame spread to Europe as well, evidenced by this Spanish map of 1375, which depicts Mansa Musa seated on his throne in Mali, holding an impressive gold nugget.

THE CITY OF TIMBUKTU. The city of Timbuktu sat astride one of the major trade routes that passed through the Sahara between the kingdoms of West Africa and the Mediterranean Sea. Caravans transported food and various manufactured articles southward in exchange for salt, gold, copper, skins, agricultural goods, and slaves. Salt was at such a high premium in Timbuktu that a young Moroccan wrote in 1513 that one camel's load, brought 500 miles by caravan, sold for 80 gold ducats, while a horse sold for only 40 ducats. Timbuktu became a prosperous city as well as a great center of Islamic scholarship. By 1550, it had three universities connected to its principal mosques and 180 Koranic schools.

States and Stateless Societies in Southern Africa

In the southern half of the African continent, from the great basin of the Zaire River to the Cape of Good Hope, states formed somewhat more slowly than in the north. Until the eleventh century C.E., most of the peoples in this region lived in what are sometimes called "stateless societies," characterized by autonomous villages organized by clans and ruled by a local chieftain or clan head. Beginning in the eleventh century, in some parts of southern Africa, these independent villages gradually began to consolidate. Out of these groupings came the first states.

One area where this process occurred was the Zaire River valley, where the combination of fertile land and nearby deposits of copper and iron enabled the inhabitants to enjoy an agricultural surplus and engage in regional commerce. Two new states in particular underwent this transition. Sometime during the fourteenth century, the kingdom of Luba was founded in the center of the continent, in a rich agricultural and fishing area near the shores of Lake Kisale. Luba had a relatively centralized government, in which the king appointed provincial governors, who were responsible for collecting tribute from the village chiefs. At about the same time, the kingdom of Kongo was formed just south of the mouth of the Zaire River on the Atlantic coast.

These new states were primarily agricultural, although both had a thriving manufacturing sector and took an active part in the growing exchange of goods throughout the region. As time passed, both began to expand southward to absorb the mixed farming and pastoral peoples in the area of modern Angola. In the drier grassland area to the south, other small communities continued to support themselves by herding, hunting, or food gathering. We know little about these peoples, however, since they possessed no writing system and had few visitors. A Portuguese sailor who encountered them in the late sixteenth century left the following description:

> These people are herdsmen and cultivators. . . . Their main crop is millet, which they grind between two stones or in wooden mortars to make flour. . . . Their wealth consists mainly in their huge number of dehorned cows. . . . They live together in small villages, in houses made of reed mats, which do not keep out the rain.[5]

Zimbabwe

Further to the east, the situation was somewhat different. In the grassland regions immediately to the south of the Zambezi River, a mixed economy involving farming, cattle herding, and commercial pursuits had begun to develop during the early centuries of the first millennium C.E. Characteristically, villages in this area were constructed inside walled enclosures to protect the animals at night. The most famous of these communities was Zimbabwe, located on the plateau of the same name between the Zambezi and Limpopo Rivers. From the twelfth to the middle of the fifteenth century, Zimbabwe was the most powerful and prosperous state in the region and played a major role in the gold trade with the Swahili trading communities on the eastern coast.

The ruins of Zimbabwe's capital, known as Great Zimbabwe (the term *Zimbabwe* means "sacred house" in the Bantu language), provide a vivid illustration of the kingdom's power and influence. Strategically situated between substantial gold reserves to the west and a small river leading to the coast, Great Zimbabwe was well placed to benefit from the expansion of trade between the coast and the interior. The town sits on a hill overlooking the river and is surrounded by stone walls, which enclosed an area large enough to hold over 10,000 residents. The houses of the wealthy were built of cement on stone foundations, while those of the common people were of dried mud with thatched roofs. In the valley below is the royal palace surrounded by a stone wall thirty feet high. Artifacts found at the site include household implements and ornaments made of gold and copper, as well as jewelry and even porcelain imported from China.

Most of the royal wealth probably came from two sources: the ownership of cattle and the king's ability to levy heavy taxes on the gold that passed through the kingdom en route to the coast. By the middle of the fifteenth century, however, the city was apparently abandoned, possibly because of environmental damage caused by overgrazing. With the decline of Zimbabwe, the focus of economic power began to shift northward to the valley of the Zambezi River.

South of the Limpopo River, pastoralism and hunting continued to be the primary means of livelihood. As we saw earlier, some of these peoples had been absorbed by the Iron Age farming communities that spread southward from Central Africa during the first millennium C.E. Others remained independent in isolated villages or small kingdoms, although they often carried on active trade with the growing states to their north.

One such people were the San, called Bushmen by later Europeans. A hunting and foraging people who spoke a Khoisan language, the San lived in small family communities of twenty to twenty-five members throughout southern Africa from Namibia in the west to the Drakensberg Mountains near the southeastern coast. Scholars have learned about the early life of the San by interviewing their modern descendants and by studying rock paintings found in caves throughout the area. These multicolored paintings, which predate the coming of the Europeans, were drawn with a brush made of small feathers fastened to a reed. They depict various aspects of the San's lifestyle, including their hunting techniques and religious rituals.

When the Europeans arrived in the area, they regarded the San as troublesome pests who raided their cattle. One nineteenth-century European missionary dismissed the San contemptuously, saying: "He has no religion, no laws, no government, no recognized authority, no patrimony, no fixed abode."[6] Over time, as the Europeans constantly encroached on their hunting grounds, the San found it virtually impossible to maintain their way of life. Only a few survive today, most of them in the Kalahari Desert in Botswana.

African Society

Drawing generalizations about social organization, cultural development, and daily life in traditional Africa is difficult because of the diversity of the continent and the absence of written languages in much of the area. Historians must therefore rely on accounts of the occasional visitor, such as al-Mas'udi and the famous fourteenth-century chronicler Ibn Battuta. Such travelers, however, tended to come into contact mostly with the wealthy and the powerful, leaving us to speculate about what life was like for ordinary Africans during this early period.

Urban Life

African towns often began as fortified walled villages and gradually evolved into larger communities serving several purposes. Here, of course, were the center of government and the teeming markets filled with goods from distant regions. Here also were artisans skilled in metal- or woodworking, pottery making, and other crafts. Unlike the rural areas, where

GREAT ZIMBABWE. Situated on an important trade route and a center for cattle and agriculture, Great Zimbabwe was originally settled by pastoral peoples during the first millennium B.C.E. Later it became the capital of a prosperous state. Its thirty-foot walls were the first in Africa to be constructed without the use of mortar. The section of the walled palace shown here indicate why Great Zimbabwe is generally regarded as the most impressive archaeological site in southern Africa.

a village was usually composed of a single lineage group or clan, the towns drew their residents from several clans, although individual clans usually lived in their own compounds and were governed by their own clan heads.

In the states of West Africa, the focal point of the major towns was the royal precinct. The relationship between the ruler and the merchant class differed from the situation in most Asian societies, where the royal family and the aristocracy were largely isolated from the remainder of the population. In Africa, the chasm between the king and the common people was not so great. Often the ruler would hold an audience to allow people to voice their complaints or to welcome visitors from foreign countries.

This is not to say that the king was not elevated above all others in status. In wealthier states, the walls of the audience chamber would be covered with sheets of beaten silver and gold, and the king would be surrounded by hundreds of armed soldiers and some of his trusted advisers. Nevertheless, the symbiotic relationship between the ruler and merchant class served to reduce the gap between the king and his subjects. The relationship was mutually beneficial, since the merchants received honors and favors from the palace, while the king's coffers were filled with taxes paid by the merchants. Certainly, it was to the benefit of the king to maintain law and order in his domain so that the merchants could ply their trade. As Ibn Battuta observed, among the good qualities of the peoples of West Africa was the prevalence of peace in the region. "The traveler is not afraid in it," he remarked, "nor is he who lives there in fear of the thief or of the robber by violence."[7]

Village Life

The vast majority of Africans lived in small rural villages. Their identities were established by their membership in a nuclear family and a lineage group. At the basic level was the nuclear family composed of parents and preadult children; sometimes it included an elderly grandparent and other family dependents as well. They lived in small round huts constructed of packed mud and topped with a conical thatch roof. In most African societies, these nuclear family units would in turn be combined into larger kinship communities known as households or lineage groups.

The lineage group was similar in many respects to the clan in China or the caste system in India in that it was normally based on kinship ties, although sometimes outsiders such as friends or other dependents may have been admitted to membership. Throughout the precolonial era, lineages served, in the words of one historian, as the "basic building blocks" of African society. The authority of the leading members of the lineage group was substantial. As in China, the elders had considerable power over the economic functions of the other people in the group, which provided mutual support for all members.

A village would usually be composed of a single lineage group, although some communities may have consisted of several unrelated families. At the head of the village was the familiar "big man," who was often assisted by a council of representatives of the various households in the community. Often the "big man" was believed to possess supernatural powers, and as the village grew in size and power, he might eventually be transformed into a local chieftain or monarch.

The Role of Women

Although generalizations are risky, women were usually subordinate to men in Africa, as in most early societies. In some cases, they were valued for the work they could do or for their role in increasing the size of the lineage group. Polygyny was not uncommon, particularly in Muslim societies. Women often worked in the fields while the men of the village tended the cattle or went on hunting expeditions. In some communities, the women specialized in commercial activities. In one area in southern Africa, young girls were sent into the mines to extract gold because of their smaller physiques.

But there were some key differences between the role of women in Africa and elsewhere. In many African societies, lineage was matrilinear rather than patrilinear. In the words of Ibn Battuta, "a man does not pass on inheritance except to the sons of his sister to the exclusion of his own sons." He said he had never encountered this custom before except among the unbelievers of the Malabar coast in India. Women were often permitted to inherit property, and the husband was often expected to move into his wife's house.

Relations between the sexes were also sometimes more relaxed than in China or India, with none of the taboos characteristic of those societies. Again, in the words of Ibn Battuta, himself a Muslim:

> With regard to their women, they are not modest in the presence of men, they do not veil themselves in spite of their perseverance in the prayers. . . . The women there have friends and companions amongst men outside the prohibited degrees of marriage [i.e., other than brothers, fathers, etc.]. Likewise for the men, there are companions from amongst women outside the prohibited degrees. One of them would enter his house to find his wife with her companion and would not disapprove of that conduct.

When Ibn Battuta asked an African acquaintance about these customs, the latter responded: "Women's companionship with men in our country is honorable and takes place in a good way: there is no suspicion about it. They are not like the women in your country." Ibn Battuta noted his astonishment at such a "thoughtless" answer and did not accept further invitations to visit his friend's house.[8]

Such informal attitudes toward the relationship between the sexes were not found everywhere in Africa and were probably curtailed as many Africans converted to Islam (see the box on p. 233). But it is a testimony to

WOMEN AND ISLAM IN NORTH AFRICA

In Muslim societies in North Africa, as elsewhere, women were required to cover their bodies to avoid giving temptations to men, but Islam's puritanical insistence on the separation of the sexes contrasted with the relatively informal relationships that prevailed in many African societies. In this excerpt from The History and Description of Africa, *Leo Africanus describes the customs along the Mediterranean coast of Africa. A resident of Spain of Muslim parentage who was captured by Christian corsairs in 1518 and later served under Pope Leo X, Leo Africanus undertook many visits to Africa.*

LEO AFRICANUS, *THE HISTORY AND DESCRIPTION OF AFRICA*

Their women (according to the guise of that country) go very gorgeously attired: they wear linen gowns dyed black, with exceeding wide sleeves, over which sometimes they cast a mantle of the same color or of blue, the corners of which mantle are very artificially fastened about their shoulders with a fine silver clasp. Likewise they have rings hanging at their ears, which for the most part are made of silver; they wear many rings also upon their fingers. Moreover they usually wear about their thighs and ankles certain scarfs and rings, after the fashion of the Africans. They cover their faces with certain masks having only two holes for the eyes to peep out at. If any man chance to meet with them, they presently hide their faces, passing by him with silence, except it be some of their allies or kinsfolks; for unto them they always discover their faces, neither is there any use of the said mask so long as they be in presence. These Arabians when they travel any journey (as they oftentimes do) they set their women upon certain saddles made handsomely of wicker for the same purpose, and fastened to their camel backs, neither be they anything too wide, but fit only for a woman to sit in. When they go to the wars each man carries his wife with him, to the end that she may cheer up her good man, and give him encouragement. Their damsels which are unmarried do usually paint their faces, breasts, arms, hands, and fingers with a kind of counterfeit color: which is accounted a most decent custom among them.

the tenacity of traditional customs that the relatively puritanical views about the role of women in society brought by Muslims from the Middle East made little impression even among Muslim families in West Africa.

Slavery

African slavery is often associated with the period after 1500. Indeed, the slave trade did reach enormous proportions in the seventeenth and eighteenth centuries, when European slave ships transported millions of unfortunate victims abroad to Europe or the Americas (see Chapter 14).

Slavery did not originate with the coming of the Europeans, however. It had been practiced in Africa since ancient times and probably originated with prisoners of war who were forced into perpetual servitude. Slavery was common in ancient Egypt and became especially prevalent during the New Kingdom, when slaving expeditions brought back thousands of captives from the upper Nile to be used in labor gangs, for tribute, and even as human sacrifices.

Slavery persisted during the early period of state building, in the first and early second millennia C.E. Berber tribes may have regularly raided agricultural communities south of the Sahara for captives who were transported northward and eventually sold throughout the Mediterranean. Some were enrolled as soldiers, while others, often women, were used as domestic servants in the homes of the well-to-do. The use of captives for forced labor or for sale was apparently also common in African societies further to the south and along the eastern coast.

Certainly, life was difficult for the average slave. The least fortunate were probably those who worked on plantations owned by the royal family or other wealthy landowners. Those pressed into service as soldiers were sometimes more fortunate, since in Muslim societies in the Middle East, they might at some point win their freedom. Many slaves were employed in the royal household or as domestic servants in private homes. In general, they probably had the most tolerable existence. Although they normally were not permitted to purchase their freedom, their living conditions were often decent and sometimes were practically indistinguishable from those of the free individuals in the household. In some societies in North Africa, slaves reportedly made up as much as 75 percent of the entire population. Elsewhere, the percentage was much lower, in some cases less than 10 percent.

AFRICAN CULTURE

In early Africa, as in much of the rest of the world at the time, creative expression, whether in the form of painting, literature, or music, was above all a means of serving religion. Though to the uninitiated a wooden mask or the bronze and iron statuary of southern Nigeria is simply a work of art, to the artist it was often a means of expressing religious convictions. Some African historians reject the use of the term *art* to describe such artifacts because they were produced for religious rather than aesthetic purposes.

NOK POTTERY HEAD. The Nok peoples of the Niger River are the oldest known culture in West Africa to have created sculpture. This is a typical terra-cotta head from the Nok culture, dating from 500 B.C.E. to 200 C.E. Discovered accidentally in the twentieth century by tin miners, these heads exhibit perforated eyes set in triangles or circles, stylized eyebrows, open thick lips, broad noses with wide perforated nostrils, and large ears. Although the function of these statutes is not known for certain, they likely were connected with religious rituals or ancestor devotion.

Painting and Sculpture

The earliest extant art forms in Africa are rock paintings. The most famous examples are in the Tassili Mountains in the central Sahara, where the earliest paintings may date back as far as c. 5000 B.C.E., though the majority are a millennium or so younger. Some of the later paintings depict the two-horse chariots used to transport goods prior to the introduction of the camel. Rock paintings are also found elsewhere in the continent, including the Nile valley and in eastern and southern Africa. Those of the San peoples of southern Africa are especially interesting for their illustrations of ritual ceremonies in which village shamans induce rain, propitiate the spirits, or cure illnesses.

More familiar, perhaps, are African wood carvings and sculpture. Wood-carvers throughout the continent produced remarkable masks (actually headpieces) and statuary. The carvings often represent gods, spirits, or ancestral figures and were believed to embody the spiritual powers of the subject in symbolic form. Terra-cotta and metal figurines served a similar purpose. For example, the impressive figures found near the city of Nok in northern Nigeria are believed to have had religious significance. Dating from the first millennium B.C.E., they include human figures and heads in terra-cotta, as well as in iron and stone.

In the thirteenth and fourteenth centuries C.E., metalworkers at Ife in what is now southern Nigeria produced handsome bronze and iron statues using the lost-wax method, in which melted wax is replaced in a mold by molten metal. The Ife sculptures, in turn, may have influenced artists in Benin, in West Africa, who produced equally impressive works in bronze during the same period. The Benin sculptures include bronze heads, relief plaques depicting life at court, ornaments, and figures of various types of animals.

Westerners once regarded African wood carvings and metal sculpture as a form of "primitive art," but the label is not appropriate. The metal sculpture of Benin, for example, is highly sophisticated, and some of the best works are considered masterpieces. Such artistic works were often created by artisans in the employ of the royal court.

Music

Like sculpture and wood carving, African music and dance often served a religious function. With their characteristic heavy rhythmic beat, dances were a means of communicating with the spirits, and the frenzied movements that are often identified with African dance were intended to represent the spirits acting through humans.

African music during the traditional period varied to some degree from one society to another. A wide variety of instruments were used, including drums and other percussion instruments, xylophones, bells, horns and flutes, and stringed instruments like the fiddle, harp, and zither. Still, the music throughout the continent had sufficient common characteristics to justify a few generalizations. In the first place, a strong rhythmic pattern was an important feature of most African music, although the desired effect was achieved through a wide variety of means, including gourds, pots, bells, sticks beaten together, and hand clapping as well as drums.

Another important feature of African music was the integration of voice and instrument into a total musical experience. Musical instruments and the human voice were often woven together to tell a story, and instruments, such as the famous "talking drum," were often used to represent the voice. Choral music and individual voices were frequently used in a pattern of repetition and variation, sometimes known as the "call and response" technique. Through this technique, the audience participated in the music by uttering a single phrase over and over as a choral response to the changing call sung by the soloist. Sometimes instrumental music achieved a similar result.

AFRICAN METALWORK, BENIN. By 1500 the West African state of Benin had expanded into an extensive and powerful empire with a highly developed official court art, especially in metalwork. Rulers were commemorated with bronze, brass, and copper sculpture, such as the stunning head of a queen mother shown here. These pieces were intended as ancestral memorial portraits and were placed on the altar of the deceased ruler by his successor. The queen mother, who claimed a revered position in Benin culture, would have ordered several such artistic renderings. The delicate attention to detail and the graceful sense of movement of this head attest to the technical excellence and sophistication of Benin bronze casting.

Much music was produced in the context of social rituals, such as weddings and funerals, religious ceremonies, and official inaugurations. It could also serve an educational purpose by passing on to the young people information about the history and social traditions of the community. In the absence of written languages in sub-Saharan Africa (except for the Arabic script, used in Muslim societies in East and West Africa), music served as the primary means of transmitting folk legends and religious traditions from generation to generation. Storytelling, which was usually undertaken by a priestly class or a specialized class of storytellers, served a similar function.

Architecture

No aspect of African artistic creativity is more varied than architecture. From the pyramids along the Nile to the ruins of Great Zimbabwe south of the Zambezi River, from the Moorish palaces at Zanzibar to the turreted mud mosques of West Africa, African architecture shows a striking diversity of approach and technique that is unmatched in other areas of creative endeavor.

The earliest surviving architectural form found in Africa, of course, is the pyramid (see Chapter 1). The Kushite kingdom at Meroë apparently adopted the pyramidal form from Egypt during the last centuries of the first millennium B.C.E. Although used for the same purpose as their earlier counterparts at Giza, the pyramids at Meroë were distinctive in style; they were much smaller and were topped with a flat platform rather than rising to a point. Remains of temples with massive carved pillars at Meroë also reflect Egyptian influence.

Further to the south, the kingdom of Axum was developing its own architectural traditions. Most distinctive were the carved stone pillars, known as stelae, that were used to mark the tombs of dead kings. Some stood as high as a hundred feet. The advent of Christianity eventually had an impact on Axumite architecture. During the Zagwe dynasty in the twelfth and thirteenth centuries C.E., churches carved out of solid rock were constructed throughout the country. Stylistically, they combined indigenous techniques inherited from the pre-Christian period with elements borrowed from Christian churches in the Holy Land.

A COPTIC CHURCH IN ETHIOPIA. In 1200 C.E., Christian monks in Ethiopia began to construct a remarkable series of eleven churches carved out of solid volcanic rock. After a forty-foot trench was formed by removing the bedrock, the central block of stone was hewed into the shape of a Greek cross; then it was hollowed out and decorated. These churches, which are still in use today, testify to the fervor of Ethiopian Christianity.

A CHINESE VIEW OF AFRICA

This passage from Chau Ju-kua's thirteenth-century treatise on geography describes various aspects of life along the eastern coast of Africa in what is now Somalia, including the urban architecture. The author was an inspector of foreign trade in the city of Quanzhou (sometimes called Zayton) on the southern coast of China. His account was compiled from reports of seafarers. Note the varied uses that the local people make of a whale carcass.

CHAU JU-KUA ON EAST AFRICA

The inhabitants of the Chung-li country [the Somali coast] go bareheaded and barefooted; they wrap themselves in cotton stuffs, but they dare not wear jackets, for the wearing of jackets and turbans is a privilege reserved to the ministers and the king's courtiers. The king lives in a brick house covered with glazed tiles, but the people live in huts made of palm leaves and covered with grass-thatched roofs. Their daily food consists of baked flour cakes, sheep's and camel's milk. There are great numbers of cattle, sheep, and camels....

There are many sorcerers among them who are able to change themselves into birds, beasts, or aquatic animals, and by these means keep the ignorant people in a state of terror. If some of them in trading with some foreign ship have a quarrel, the sorcerers pronounce a charm over the ship so that it can neither go forward nor backward, and they only release the ship when it has settled the dispute. The government has formally forbidden this practice.

When one of the inhabitants dies, and they are about to bury him in his coffin, his kinsfolk from near and far come to condole. Each person, flourishing a sword in his hand, goes in and asks the mourners the cause of the person's death. If he was killed by the hand of man, each one says, we will revenge him on the murderer with these swords. Should the mourners reply that he was not killed by any one, but that he came to his end by the will of Heaven, they throw away their swords and break into violent wailing.

Every year there are driven on the coast a great many dead fish measuring two hundred feet in length and twenty feet through the body. The people do not eat the flesh of these fish, but they cut out their brains, marrow, and eyes, from which they get oil. They mix this oil with lime to caulk their boats, and use it also in lamps. The poor people use the ribs of these fish to make rafters, the backbones for door leaves, and they cut off vertebrae to make mortars with.

In West Africa, buildings constructed in stone were apparently a rarity until the emergence of states during the first millennium C.E. At that time, the royal palace, as well as other buildings of civic importance, were often built of stone or cement, while the houses of the majority of the population continued to be constructed of dried mud. On his visit to the state of Guinea on the West African coast, the sixteenth-century traveler Leo Africanus noted that the houses of the ruler and other elites were built of chalk with roofs of straw. Even then, however, well into the state-building period, mosques were often built of mud.

Along the east coast, the architecture of the elite tended to reflect Middle Eastern styles. In the coastal towns and islands from Mogadishu to Kilwa, the houses of the wealthy were built of stone and reflected Moorish influence. As elsewhere, the common people lived in huts of mud, thatch, or palm leaves (see the box above). Mosques were built of stone.

The most famous stone buildings in sub-Saharan Africa are those at Great Zimbabwe. Constructed of carefully cut stones that were set in place without mortar, the great wall and the public buildings at Great Zimbabwe are an impressive monument to the architectural creativity of the peoples of the region.

Literature

Literature in the sense of written works did not exist in sub-Saharan Africa during the early traditional period, except in regions where Islam had brought the Arabic script from the Middle East. But African societies compensated for the absence of a written language with a rich tradition of oral lore. The bard, or professional storyteller, was an ancient African institution by which history was transmitted orally from generation to generation. In many

THE MOSQUE AT JENNE, MALI. With the opening of the gold fields south of Mali, in present-day Ghana, Jenne became an important trading center for gold. Shown here is its distinctive fourteenth-century mosque made of unbaked clay without reinforcements. The projecting timbers offer easy access for repairing the mud exterior, as was regularly required.

A WEST AFRICAN ORAL TRADITION

In this passage from the West African Epic of Son-Jara, *Son-Jara's sister, Sugulun Kulunkan, offers to seduce his enemy Sumamuru in order to obtain the Manden secret, or magic spell, needed to control the Kingdom of Mali. Sumamuru divulges his all-powerful secret and is rebuked by his mother; both son and mother then disown one another with the trenchant symbols of the slashed breast and cut cloth. After each line of the verse, the bard's assistant would shout the endorsement "true," perhaps the distant origin of today's African American practice of approving each line of religious oratory with "Amen."*

THE EPIC OF SON-JARA

Son-Jara's flesh-and-blood sister, Sugulun Kulunkan,
She said, "O Magan Son-Jara,
"One person cannot fight this war.
"Let me go seek Sumamuru.
"Were I then to reach him,
"To you I will deliver him,
"So that the folk of the Manden be yours,
"And all the Mandenland you shield."
Sugulun Kulunkan arose,
And went up to the gates of Sumamuru's fortress:
. . .
"Come open the gates, Susu Mountain Sumamuru!
"Come make me your bed companion!"
Sumamuru came to the gates:
"What manner of person are you?"
"It is I Sugulun Kulunkan!"
"Well, now, Sugulun Kulunkan,
"If you have come to trap me,
"To turn me over to some person,
"Know that none can ever vanquish me.
"I have found the Manden secret,
"And made the Manden sacrifice,
"And in five score millet stalks placed it,
"And buried them here in the earth.
"'Tis I who found the Manden secret,
"And made the Manden sacrifice,
"And in a red piebald bull did place it,
"And buried it here in the earth.
"Know that none can vanquish me.
"'Tis I who found the Manden secret
"And made a sacrifice to it,
"And in a pure white cock did place it.
"Were you to kill it,
"And uproot some barren groundnut plants,
"And strip them of their leaves,
"And spread them round the fortress,
"And uproot more barren peanut plants,
"And fling them into the fortress,
"Only then can I be vanquished."
His mother sprang forward at that:
"Heh! Susu Mountain Sumamuru!
"Never tell all to a woman,
"To a one-night woman!
"The woman is not safe, Sumamuru."
Sumamuru sprang towards his mother,
And came and seized his mother,
And slashed off her breast with a knife, magasi!
She went and got the old menstrual cloth.
"Ah! Sumamuru!" she swore.
"If your birth was ever a fact,
"I have cut your old menstrual cloth!"

West African societies, bards were highly esteemed and served as counselors to kings as well as protectors of local tradition. Bards were revered for their oratory and singing skills, phenomenal memory, and astute interpretation of history. As one African scholar wrote, the death of a bard was equivalent to the burning of a library.

Bards served several necessary functions in society. They were chroniclers of history, preservers of social customs and proper conduct, and entertainers who possessed a monopoly over the playing of several musical instruments, which accompanied their narratives. Because of their unique position above normal society, bards often played the role of mediator between hostile families or clans in a community. They were also credited with possessing occult powers and could read divinations and give blessings and curses. Traditionally, bards also served as advisers to the king, sometimes inciting him to action (such as going to battle) through the passion of their poetry. When captured by the enemy, bards were often treated with respect and released or compelled to serve the victor with their art.

One of the most famous West African epics is *Son-Jara* (also known as *Sunjata* or *Sundiata*). Passed down orally by bards for more than seven hundred years, it relates the heroic exploits of Son-Jara, the founder and ruler (1230–1255) of Mali's empire. Although Mansa Musa is famous throughout the world because of his flamboyant pilgrimage to Mecca in the fourteenth century, Son-Jara is more celebrated in West Africa because of the dynamic and unbroken oral traditions of the West African peoples (see the box above).

In addition to the bards, women too were appreciated for their storytelling talents, as well as for their role as purveyors of the moral values and religious beliefs of African societies. In societies that lacked a written tradition, women represented the societal glue that held the community together. Through the recitation of fables, proverbs, poems, and songs, mothers conditioned the communal bonding and moral fiber of succeeding generations in a way that was rarely encountered in the patriarchal societies of Europe, eastern and southern Asia, and the Middle East. Such activities were not only vital aspects of education in traditional Africa; they also offered a welcome respite from the drudgery of everyday life as well as a spark to develop the imagination and artistic awareness of the young. Renowned for its many proverbs, Africa also offers the following: "A good story is like a garden carried in the pocket."

CONCLUSION

Thanks to the dedicated work of a generation of archaeologists, anthropologists, and historians, we now have a much better understanding of the evolution of human societies in Africa than we did a few decades ago. Intensive efforts by archaeologists have demonstrated beyond reasonable doubt that the first hominids lived there. Recent evidence suggests that farming may have been practiced in Africa more than 12,000 years ago, while the concept of kingship may have originated not in Sumer or in Egypt, but in the upper Nile valley as long ago as the fourth millennium B.C.E.

Less is known about more recent African history, partly because of the paucity of written records. Still, historians have established that the first civilizations had begun to take shape in sub-Saharan Africa by the first millennium C.E., while the continent as a whole was an active participant in emerging regional and global trade with the Mediterranean world and across the Indian Ocean.

Thus, the peoples of Africa were not as isolated from the main currents of human history as was once assumed. Although the state-building process in sub-Saharan Africa was still in its early stages compared with the ancient civilizations of India, China, and Mesopotamia, in many respects these new states were as impressive and sophisticated as their counterparts elsewhere in the world.

In the fifteenth century, a new factor was added to the equation. Urged on by the tireless efforts of Prince Henry the Navigator, Portuguese fleets began to probe southward along the coast of West Africa. At first their sponsors were in search of gold and slaves, but at the end of the century, Vasco da Gama's voyage around the Cape of Good Hope signaled Portugal's determination to dominate the commerce of the Indian Ocean in the future. The new situation posed a challenge to the peoples of Africa, whose nascent states and technology would be severely tested by the rapacious demands of the Europeans (see Chapter 14).

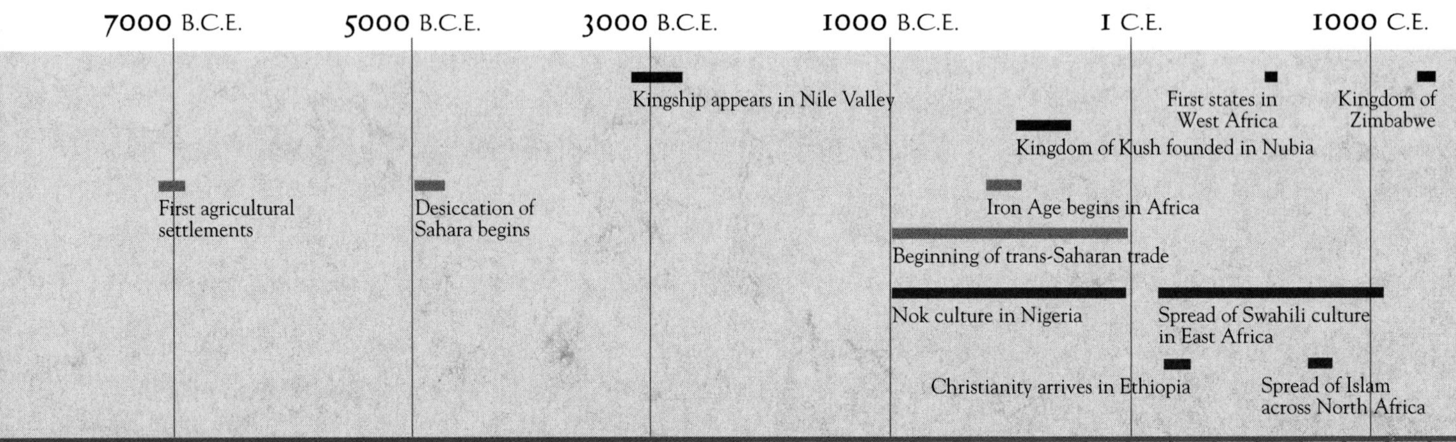

CHAPTER NOTES

1. Said Hamdun and Noel King, eds., *Ibn Battuta in Africa* (London, 1975), p. 19.
2. *The Book of Duarte Barbosa* (Nedeln, Liechtenstein, 1967), p. 28.
3. Herodotus, *The Histories*, trans. Aubrey de Sélincourt (Baltimore, 1964), p. 307.
4. Margaret Shinnie, *Ancient African Kingdoms* (London, 1965), p. 60.
5. C. R. Boxer, ed., *The Tragic History of the Sea, 1589–1622* (Cambridge, 1959), pp. 121–22, quoted in Kevin Shillington, *History of Africa* (New York, 1989), p. 155.
6. Quoted in Brian Fagan, *New Treasures of the Past: Fresh Finds That Deepen Our Understanding of the Archaeology of Man* (Leicester, 1987), p. 154.
7. Hamdun and King, *Ibn Battuta in Africa*, p. 47.
8. Ibid., pp. 28–30.

Suggested Readings

In few areas of world history is scholarship advancing as rapidly as in African history. New information is constantly forcing archaeologists and historians to revise their assumptions about the early history of the continent. Standard texts therefore quickly become out-of-date as their conclusions are supplanted by new evidence.

Still, there are several worthwhile general surveys that provide a useful overview of the early period of African history. The dean of African historians, and certainly one of the most readable, is B. Davidson. For a sympathetic portrayal of the African people, see his *African History* (New York, 1968) and *Lost Cities in Africa,* rev. ed. (Boston, 1970). Other respected accounts are R. Oliver and J. D. Fage, *A Short History of Africa* (Middlesex, 1986); J. M. Harris, *Africans and Their History* (New York, 1972); and V. B. Khapoya, *The African Experience: An Introduction* (Englewood Cliffs, N.J., 1994). A more detailed interpretation, by four respected historians, is P. Curtin et al., *African History* (Boston, 1978). For a readable treatment embodying recent scholarly evidence, see K. Shillington, *History of Africa* (New York, 1989). R. O. Collins, ed., *Problems in African History: The Precolonial Centuries* (New York, 1993) provides a useful collection of scholarly articles on key issues in precolonial Africa.

Specialized studies are beginning to appear with frequency on many areas of the continent. For a popular account of recent archaeological finds, see B. Fagan, *New Treasures of the Past: Fresh Finds That Deepen Our Understanding of the Archaeology of Man* (Leicester, 1987). For a more detailed treatment of the early period, see the early volumes in *The Cambridge History of Africa* (Cambridge, 1976–1986). See also R. Oliver, ed., *The Dawn of African History* (New York, 1968), and R. Oliver and B. Fagan, *Africa in the Iron Age* (Cambridge, 1975). J. D. Clarke and S. A. Brandt, eds., *From Hunters to Farmers* (Berkeley, Calif., 1984), takes an economic approach. Also see D. A. Welsby, *The Kingdom of Kush: The Napataean Meroitic Empire* (London, British Museum Press, 1996), and J. Middleton, *Swahili: An African Mercantile Civilization* (New Haven, 1992). For a fascinating account of trans-Saharan trade, see E. W. Bovill, *The Golden Trade of the Moors: West African Kingdoms in the Fourteenth Century,* 2d ed. (Princeton, N.J., 1995). On the cultural background, see R. Olaniyan, ed., *African History and Culture* (Lagos, 1982), and J. Vansina, *Paths in the Rainforest: Toward a History of Political Tradition in Equatorial Africa* (Madison, Wis., 1990). Although there exist many editions of *The Epic of Son-Jara,* based on recitations of different bards, the most conclusive edition is by F.-D. Sisòkò, translated and thoroughly annotated by J. W. Johnson (Bloomington, Ind., 1992).

On East Africa, see D. Nurse and T. Spear, *The Swahili: Reconstituting the History and Language of an African Society, 800–1500* (Philadelphia, 1985). The maritime story is recounted with documents in G. S. P. Freeman-Grenville, *The East African Coast: Select Documents from the First to the Earlier Nineteenth Century* (Oxford, 1962). For the larger picture, see K. N. Chaudhuri, *Trade and Civilization in the Indian Ocean: An Economic History from the Rise of Islam to 1750* (Cambridge, 1985). On the early history of Ethiopia, see the classic work by S. H. Sellassie, *Ancient and Medieval Ethiopian History* (1972), and J. D. Fage and R. Oliver, eds., *The Cambridge History of Africa,* vol. 4 (Cambridge, 1977–1985).

For useful general surveys of southern Africa, see N. Parsons, *A New History of Southern Africa* (New York, 1983), and K. Shillington, *A History of Southern Africa* (Essex, 1987), a profusely illustrated account. For an excellent introduction to the art of precolonial Africa, consult O. Egonwa, *African Art* (Benin City, Nigeria, 1994), and the beautifully illustrated T. Phillips, ed., *Africa: The Art of a Continent* (Munich, 1995).

InfoTrac College Edition

For additional reading, go to InfoTrac College Edition, your online research library at http://web1.infotrac-college.com

Enter the search term "Africa" using the Subject Guide.

Enter the search terms "slave trade" using Keywords.

Enter the search term "Bantu" using Keywords.

Enter the search terms "Africa history" using Keywords.

CHAPTER

9

THE EXPANSION OF CIVILIZATION IN SOUTHERN ASIA

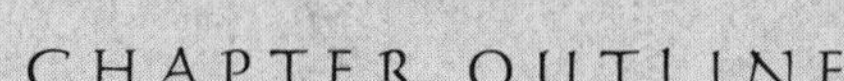

CHAPTER OUTLINE

FOCUS QUESTIONS

- How did Buddhism change in the centuries after Siddhartha Gautama's death, and why did it ultimately decline in popularity in India?
- What impact did Muslim rule have on Indian society?
- What are some of the most important cultural achievements of Indian civilization in the era between the Mauryas and the Mughals?
- What were the main characteristics of Southeast Asian social and economic life, culture, and religion before 1500 C.E.?
- How did Indian civilization influence the civilizations that arose in Southeast Asia?

As the traveler wandered through the length and breadth of the land, he carefully recorded his impressions of the people, from the king down to his most insignificant subject. Their dress, he remarked, was quite different from that of his own country. People wore loose-fitting clothing gathered at the armpits. Most garments were white and were fashioned of cotton, wool, or silk. The robes of the women fell to the ground and completely covered their shoulders. In some areas, the common people wore garments made of leaves or bark or even went naked.

The visitor was especially impressed with the people's personal cleanliness. All wash themselves before eating, he said, and when they completed their meal, they cleaned their teeth with a willow stick and washed their hands and mouths. After relieving themselves, they washed their bodies and used perfume of sandalwood or turmeric.

The visitor was Xuan Zang (Hsuan Tsang), a Buddhist monk from China who traveled to India in the seventh century C.E. to search for holy scriptures to take back to his own country for translation into Chinese. Because little of the literature of the Indian people from that period survives, Xuan Zang's observations are a valuable resource for our knowledge of the daily lives of the people and show us that the *dhoti* and the *sari*, common forms of Indian dress today, have a long history on the subcontinent.

India from the Mauryas to the Mughals

The India Xuan Zang visited was no longer the unified land it had been under the Mauryan dynasty. The overthrow of the Mauryas in the early second century B.C.E. had been followed by several hundred years of disunity, when the subcontinent was divided into a number of separate kingdoms and principalities. The dominant force in the north was the Kushan state, established by Indo-European-speaking peoples who had been driven out of Central Asia by the Xiongnu. The Kushans penetrated into the mountains north of the Indus River, where they eventually formed a kingdom with its capital at Bactria, not far from modern Kabul. Over the next two centuries, the Kushans expanded their supremacy along the Indus River and into the central Ganges valley. Then the dynasty began to weaken, and it collapsed sometime in the third century C.E. After the disintegration of the Kushan state, northern India remained divided until the rise of the Gupta dynasty in the early fourth century. The Guptas revived the ancient tradition of the Mauryas for nearly two hundred years, until they too were overthrown in about 500 C.E.

Meanwhile, to the south, a number of kingdoms arose among the Dravidian peoples of the Deccan Plateau, which had been only partly under Mauryan rule. The most famous of these kingdoms was Cola (sometimes spelled "Chola") on the southeastern coast. Cola developed into a major trading power and sent merchant fleets eastward across the Bay of Bengal, where they introduced Indian culture as well as Indian goods to the peoples of Southeast Asia. In the fourth century C.E., Cola was overthrown by the Pallavas, who ruled from their capital at Kanchipuram (known today as Kanchi), just southwest of modern Madras, for the next four hundred years.

Beginning in the eleventh century, much of northern India fell under the rule of Turkic-speaking peoples who penetrated into the subcontinent from the northwest. Eventually, Turkic dynasties were set up in many areas and introduced the peoples of India to Islamic religion and civilization. These dynasties were able to survive attacks by the forces of Tamerlane (Timur the Lame), but by the end of the fifteenth century, they were coming under severe pressure from the Mughals, a powerful new force from the mountains.

The Kushan Kingdom: Linchpin of the Silk Road

The Kushan kingdom, with its power base beyond the Khyber Pass in modern Afghanistan, became the dominant political force in northern India in the centuries immediately after the fall of the Mauryas. Sitting astride the main trade routes across the northern half of the subcontinent, the Kushans thrived on the commerce that passed through the area. The bulk of that trade was between the Roman Empire and China and was transported along the route known as the Silk Road, one segment of which passed through the mountains northwest of India (see Chapter 10). From there, goods were shipped to Rome through the Persian Gulf or the Red Sea.

Trade between India and Europe had begun even before the rise of the Roman Empire, but it expanded rapidly in the first century C.E., when sailors mastered the pattern of the monsoon winds in the Indian Ocean (from the southwest in the summer and the northeast in the winter). Commerce between the Mediterranean and the Indian Ocean, as described in the *Periplus*, a first-century C.E. account by a Greek participant, was extensive and often profitable, and it resulted in the establishment of several small Roman settlements along the Indian coast. Rome imported ivory, indigo, textiles, precious stones, and pepper from India and silk from China. The Romans sometimes paid cash for these goods but also exported silver, wine, perfume, slaves, and glass and cloth from Egypt. Overall, Rome appears to have imported much more than it sold to the Far East, leading Emperor Tiberius to grumble that "the ladies and their baubles are transferring our money to foreigners."

The emergence of the Kushan kingdom as a major commercial power was due not only to its role as an intermediary in the Rome-China trade, but also to the rising popularity of Buddhism. Sometime during the second century C.E. (the precise dates of his reign are unknown), Kanishka, the greatest of the Kushan monarchs, began to patronize Buddhism. Under Kanishka and his successors, an intimate and mutually beneficial relationship was established between Buddhist monasteries and the local merchant community in thriving urban centers like Taxila and

THE GOOD LIFE IN MEDIEVAL INDIA

Much of what we know about life in medieval India comes from the accounts of Chinese missionaries who visited the subcontinent in search of documents recording the teachings of the Buddha. Here the Buddhist monk Fa Xian, who spent several years there in the fifth century C.E.*, reports on conditions in the kingdom of Mathura (Mo-tu-lo), a vassal state in western India that was part of the Gupta Empire. Although he could not have been pleased that the Gupta monarchs had adopted the Hindu faith, he found that the people were contented and prosperous except for the outcastes, whom he called Chandalas.*

FA XIAN, *THE TRAVELS OF FA XIAN*

Going southeast from this somewhat less than 80 *joyanas*, we passed very many temples one after another, with some myriad of priests in them. Having passed these places, we arrived at a certain country. This country is called Mo-tu-lo. Once more we followed the Pu-na river. On the sides of the river, both right and left, are twenty *sangharamas*, with perhaps 3,000 priests. The law of Buddha is progressing and flourishing. Beyond the deserts are the countries of western India. The kings of these countries are all firm believers in the law of Buddha. They remove their caps of state when they make offerings to the priests. The members of the royal household and the chief ministers personally direct the food giving; when the distribution of food is over, they spread a carpet on the ground opposite the chief seat (the president's seat) and sit down before it. They dare not sit on couches in the presence of the priests. The rules relating to the almsgiving of kings have been handed down from the time of Buddha till now. Southward from this is the so-called middle country (Madhyadesa). The climate of this country is warm and equable, without frost or snow. The people are very well off, without poll tax or official restrictions. Only those who till the royal lands return a portion of profit of the land. If they desire to go, they go; if they like to stop, they stop. The kings govern without corporal punishment; criminals are fined, according to circumstances, lightly or heavily. Even in cases of repeated rebellion they only cut off the right hand. The king's personal attendants, who guard him on the right and left, have fixed salaries. Throughout the country the people kill no living thing nor drink wine, nor do they eat garlic or onions, with the exception of Chandalas only. The Chandalas are named "evil men" and dwell apart from others; if they enter a town or market, they sound a piece of wood in order to separate themselves; then men, knowing who they are, avoid coming in contact with them. In this country they do not keep swine nor fowls, and do not deal in cattle; they have no shambles or wine shops in their marketplaces. In selling they use cowrie shells. The Chandalas only hunt and sell flesh.

Varanasi. Merchants were eager to build stupas and donate money to monasteries in return for social prestige and the implied promise of a better life in this world or the hereafter.

For their part, the wealthy monasteries ceased to be simple communities where monks could find a refuge from the material cares of the world; instead they became major consumers of luxury goods provided by their affluent patrons. Monasteries and their inhabitants became increasingly involved in the economic life of society, and Buddhist architecture began to be richly decorated with precious stones and glass purchased from local merchants or imported from abroad. The process was highly reminiscent of the changes that occurred in the church in medieval Europe.

The Gupta Dynasty

The Kushan kingdom came to an end under uncertain conditions sometime in the third century C.E. In 320, a new state was established in the central Ganges valley by a local raja named Chandragupta (no relation to Chandragupta Maurya, the founder of the Mauryan dynasty). Chandragupta located his capital at Pataliputra, the site of the now decaying palace of the Mauryas. Under his successor Samudragupta, the territory under Gupta rule was extended into surrounding areas, and eventually the new kingdom became the dominant political force throughout northern India. It also established a loose suzerainty over the Dravidian state of Pallava to the south, thus becoming the greatest state in the subcontinent since the decline of the Mauryan Empire. Under a succession of powerful, efficient, and highly cultured monarchs, notably Samudragupta and Chandragupta II, India enjoyed a new "classical age" of civilization.

The Gupta era was a time of prosperity and thriving commerce with China, Southeast Asia, and the Mediterranean. Great cities, notable for their temples and Buddhist monasteries as well as for their economic prosperity, rose along the main trade routes throughout the subcontinent. The religious trade also prospered, as pilgrims from across India and as far away as China came to visit the major religious centers (see the box above).

As in the Mauryan Empire, much of the trade in the Gupta Empire was managed or regulated by the government. The Guptas owned mines and vast crown lands and earned massive profits from their commercial dealings. But there was also a large private sector, dominated by great caste guilds that monopolized key sectors of the economy. A money economy had probably been in operation since the second century B.C.E., when copper and gold coins had been introduced from the Middle East. This in turn led to the development of banking. Nevertheless, there are indications that the circulation of coins was limited. The Chinese missionary Xuan Zang, who visited India early in the seventh century, remarked that most commercial transactions were conducted by barter.[1]

But the good fortunes of the Guptas proved to be relatively short-lived. Beginning in the late fifth century C.E., incursions by nomadic warriors from the northwest gradually reduced the power of the empire. Soon northern India was once more divided into myriad small kingdoms engaged in seemingly constant conflict.

Buddhism at Bay

The Chinese pilgrims who traveled to India during the Gupta era found a Buddhism that had changed in a number of ways in the centuries since the time of Siddhartha Gautama. They also found a doctrine that was beginning to decline in popularity in the face of a resurgent Hinduism.

The transformation in Buddhism had come about in part because the earliest written sources were transcribed two centuries after Siddhartha's death and in part because his message was reinterpreted as it became part of the everyday life of the people. Abstract concepts of a Nirvana that cannot be described began to be replaced, at least in the popular mind, with more concrete visions of heavenly salvation, and Siddhartha was increasingly regarded as a divinity rather than as a sage. The Buddha's teachings that all four classes were equal gave way to the familiar Hindu conviction that some people, by reason of previous reincarnations, were closer to Nirvana than others.

These developments led to a split in the movement. Purists emphasized what they insisted were the original teachings of the Buddha (describing themselves as the school of Theravada, or "the teachings of the elders"). Followers of Theravada considered Buddhism a way of life, not a salvationist creed. Theravada stressed the importance of strict adherence to personal behavior and the quest for understanding as a means of release from the wheel of life.

In the meantime, another interpretation of Buddhist doctrine was emerging in the northwest. Here Buddhist believers, perhaps hoping to compete with other salvationist faiths circulating in the region, began to promote the view that Nirvana could be achieved through devotion and not just through painstaking attention to one's behavior. According to advocates of this school, eventually to be known as Mahayana ("greater vehicle"), Theravada teachings were too demanding or strict for ordinary people to follow and therefore favored the wealthy, who were more apt to have the time and resources to spend weeks or months away from their everyday occupations. Mahayana Buddhists referred to their rivals as Hinayana, or "lesser vehicle," because in Theravada fewer would reach enlightenment. Mahayana thus attempted to provide hope for the masses in their efforts to reach Nirvana, but to the followers of Theravada, it did so at the expense of an insistence on proper behavior.

MAP 9.1 The Gupta Empire

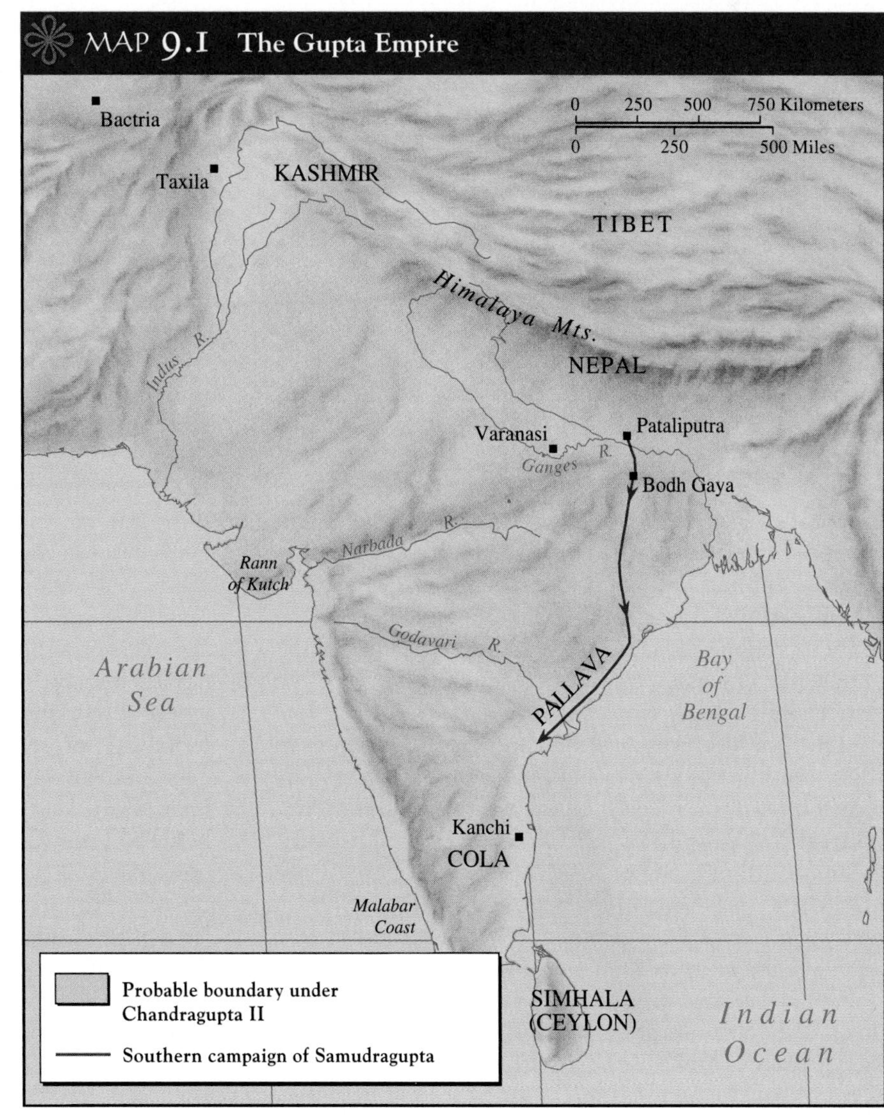

MAMALLAPURAM OCEAN TEMPLE. The eighth-century remnants of one of the earliest freestanding Hindu temples grace the shore at Mamallapuram, south of Madras. It stands as a visual confirmation of the rising influence of the Hindu faith in southern India during the era of the Colas and the Pallavas. The temple was constructed of granite blocks and was originally covered with ornate carvings, but centuries of wind and sea have softened its surfaces. It would be difficult to conceive of a more romantic temple than this, especially at dawn with the sun and the ocean intensifying its mystery.

CHRONOLOGY

MEDIEVAL INDIA

Kushan Kingdom	c. 150 B.C.E.–c. 200 C.E.
Gupta dynasty	320–600s
Chandragupta I	320–c. 330
Samudragupta	c. 330–375
Chandragupta II	375–415
Arrival of Fa Xian in India	c. 406
First Buddhist temples at Ellora	Seventh century
Travels of Xuan Zang in India	630–643
Conquest of Sind by Arab armies	c. 711
Mahmud of Ghazni	997–1030
Mongol invasion of northern India	1221
Delhi sultanate at peak	1220
Invasion of Tamerlane	1398

To advocates of the Mahayana school, salvation could also come from the intercession of a bodhisattva ("he who possesses the essence of Buddhahood"). According to Mahayana beliefs, some individuals who had achieved bodhi and were thus eligible to enter the state of Nirvana after death chose instead, because of their great compassion, to remain on earth in spirit form to help all human beings achieve release from the life cycle. Followers of Theravada, who believed the concept of bodhisattva applied only to Siddhartha Gautama himself, denounced such ideas as "the teaching of demons." But to their proponents, such ideas extended the hope of salvation to the masses. Mahayana Buddhists revered the saintly individuals who, according to tradition, had become bodhisattvas at death, and erected temples in their honor, where the local population could pray and render offerings. The most famous bodhisattva was Avalokitesvara, a mythic figure whose name in Sanskrit means "Lord of Compassion." Perhaps because of the identification of Avalokitesvara with the concept of mercy, in China he was gradually transformed into a female figure known as Guan Yin (Kuan Yin).

A final distinguishing characteristic of Mahayana Buddhism was its reinterpretation of Buddhism as a religion rather than as a philosophy. Although Mahayana had philosophical aspects, its adherents increasingly regarded the Buddha as a divine figure, and an elaborate Buddhist cosmology developed. Nirvana was not a form of extinction, but a true heaven with many rest stations along the way for the faithful.

Under Kushan rule, Mahayana achieved considerable popularity in northern India and for a while even made inroads in such Theravada strongholds as the island of Sri Lanka. But in the end, neither Mahayana nor Theravada was able to retain its popularity in Indian society. By the seventh century C.E., Theravada had declined rapidly on the subcontinent, although it retained its foothold in Sri Lanka and across the Bay of Bengal in Southeast Asia, where it remained an influential force to modern times. Mahayana prospered in the northwest for centuries, but eventually it was supplanted by a revived Hinduism and later by a new arrival, Islam. But Mahayana too would find better fortunes abroad, as it was carried over the Silk Road or by sea to China and then to Korea and Japan (see Chapters 10 and 11). In all three countries, Buddhism has coexisted with Confucian doctrine and indigenous beliefs to the present.

Why was Buddhism unable to retain its popularity in its native India, although it became a major force elsewhere in Asia? Some have speculated that in denying the

THE EDUCATION OF A BRAHMIN

Although the seventh-century Chinese traveler Xuan Zang was a Buddhist, he faithfully recorded his impressions of the Hindu religion in his memoirs. Here he describes the education of a brahmin, *the highest class in Indian society.*

XUAN ZANG, *RECORDS OF WESTERN COUNTRIES*

The Brahmans study the four *Veda Sastras*. The first is called *Shau* [longevity]; it relates to the preservation of life and the regulation of the natural condition. The second is called *Sse* [sacrifice]; it relates to the [rules of] sacrifice and prayer. The third is called *Ping* [peace or regulation]; it relates to decorum, casting of lots, military affairs, and army regulations. The fourth is called *Shue* [secret mysteries]; it relates to various branches of science, incantations, medicine.

The teachers [of these works] must themselves have closely studied the deep and secret principles they contain, and penetrated to their remotest meaning. They then explain their general sense, and guide their pupils in understanding the words that are difficult. They urge them on and skillfully conduct them. They add luster to their poor knowledge, and stimulate the desponding. If they find that their pupils are satisfied with their acquirements, and so wish to escape to attend to their worldly duties, then they use means to keep them in their power. When they have finished their education, and have attained thirty years of age, then their character is formed and their knowledge ripe. When they have secured an occupation they first of all thank their master for his attention. There are some, deeply versed in antiquity, who devote themselves to elegant studies, and live apart from the world, and retain the simplicity of their character. These rise above mundane presents, and are as insensible to renown as to the contempt of the world. Their name having spread afar, the rulers appreciate them highly, but are unable to draw them to the court. The chief of the country honors them on account of their [mental] gifts, and the people exalt their fame and render them universal homage. . . . They search for wisdom, relying on their own resources. Although they are possessed of large wealth, yet they will wander here and there to seek their subsistence. There are others who, whilst attaching value to letters, will yet without shame consume their fortunes in wandering about for pleasure, neglecting their duties. They squander their substance in costly food and clothing. Having no virtuous principle, and no desire to study, they are brought to disgrace, and their infamy is widely circulated.

existence of the soul, Buddhism ran counter to traditional Hindu belief. Perhaps, too, one of Buddhism's strengths was also a weakness. In rejecting the class divisions that defined the Indian way of life, Buddhism appealed to those very groups who lacked an accepted place in Hindu society, such as the untouchables. But at the same time, it represented a threat to those with a higher status. Moreover, by emphasizing the responsibility of each person to seek an individual path to Nirvana, Buddhism undermined the strong social bonds of the Indian caste system.

Perhaps a final factor in the decline of Buddhism was the revival of Hinduism. In its early development, Hinduism had been highly elitist. Not only was observance of court ritual a monopoly of the *brahmin* class (see the box above), but the major route to individual salvation, asceticism, was hardly realistic for the average Indian. However, in the centuries after the fall of the Mauryas, a growing emphasis on devotion *(bhakti)* as a means of religious observance brought the possibility of improving one's *karma* by means of ritual acts within the reach of Indians of all classes. It seems likely that Hindu devotionalism rose precisely to combat the inroads of Buddhism and reduce the latter's appeal among the Indian population. The Chinese Buddhist missionary Fa Xian, who visited India in the mid-Gupta era, reported that mutual hostility between the Buddhists and the *brahmins* was quite strong:

> Leaving the southern gate of the capital city, on the east side of the road is a place where Buddha once dwelt. Whilst here he bit (a piece from) the willow stick and fixed it in the earth; immediately it grew up seven feet high, neither more or less. The unbelievers and Brahmans, filled with jealousy, cut it down and scattered the leaves far and wide, but yet it always sprung up again in the same place as before.[2]

For a while, Buddhism was probably able to stave off the Hindu challenge by its own salvationist creed of Mahayana, which also emphasized the role of devotion, but the days of Buddhism as a dominant faith in the subcontinent were numbered.

Islam on the March

While India was still suffering from the disarray left by the collapse of the Gupta Empire, a new and dynamic force in the form of Islam was arising in the Arabian peninsula to the west. As we have seen, during the seventh and eighth centuries, Arab armies carried the new faith westward to the Iberian peninsula and eastward across the arid

MAP 9.2 India at the Death of Mahmud of Ghazni

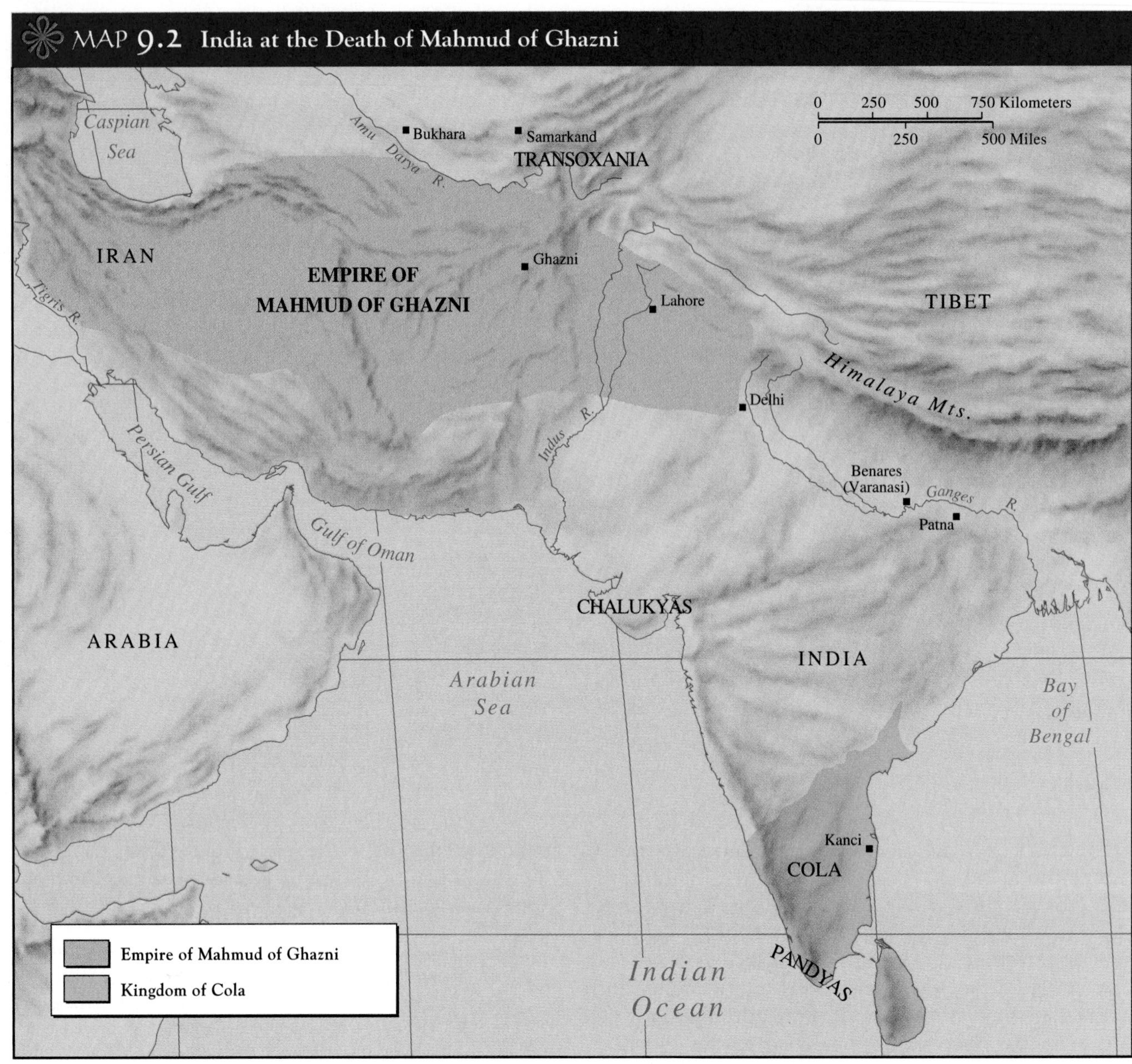

wastelands of Persia and into the rugged mountains of the Hindu Kush. Islam first reached India through the Arabs in the eighth century, but a second onslaught in the tenth and eleventh centuries by Turkic-speaking converts had a more lasting effect.

Although Arab merchants had been active along the Indian coasts for centuries, Arab armies did not reach India until the early eighth century. When Indian pirates attacked Arab shipping near the delta of the Indus River, the Muslim ruler in Iraq demanded an apology from the ruler of Sind, a Hindu state in the Indus valley. When the latter refused, Muslim forces conquered lower Sind in 711 and then moved northward into the Punjab, bringing Arab rule into the frontier regions of the subcontinent for the first time.

For the next three centuries, Islam made no further advances into India. But a second phase began at the end of the tenth century with the rise of the state of Ghazni, located in the area of the old Kushan kingdom in present-day Afghanistan. The new kingdom was founded in 962, when Turkic-speaking slaves seized power from the Samanids, a Persian dynasty. When the founder of the new state died in 997, his son, Mahmud of Ghazni (997–1030), succeeded him. Brilliant and ambitious, Mahmud used his patrimony as a base of operations for sporadic forays against neighboring Hindu kingdoms to the southeast. Before his death in 1030, he was able to extend his rule throughout the upper Indus valley and as far south as the Indian Ocean. In wealth and cultural brilliance, his court at Ghazni rivaled that of the Abbasid dynasty in neighboring Baghdad. But his achievements had a dark side. Describing Mahmud's conquests in northwestern India, the contemporary historian al-Biruni wrote:

> Mahmud utterly ruined the prosperity of the country, and performed wonderful exploits by which the Hindus became like atoms scattered in all directions, and like a tale of old in the mouth of the people. Their scattered remains cherish, of course, the most inveterate aversion towards all Muslims. This is the reason, too, why Hindu sciences have retired far away from those parts of the country conquered by us, and have fled to places which our hand cannot yet reach, to Kashmir, Benares, and other places.[3]

Resistance against the advances of Mahmud and his successors into northern India was led by the Rajputs, aristocratic Hindu clans who were probably descended from tribal groups that had penetrated into northwestern India from Central Asia in earlier centuries. The Rajputs possessed a strong military tradition and fought bravely, but their military tactics, based on infantry supported by elephants, were no match for the fearsome cavalry of the invaders, whose ability to strike with lightning speed contrasted sharply with the slow-footed forces of their adversaries. Moreover, the incessant squabbling among the Rajput leaders put them at a disadvantage against the single-minded intensity and religious fervor of Mahmud's armies. Although the power of Ghazni declined after his death, a successor state in the area resumed the advance in the late twelfth century, and by 1200 Muslim power, in the form of a new Delhi sultanate, had been extended over the entire plain of northern India.

South of the Ganges River valley, Muslim influence spread more slowly and in fact had little immediate impact. Muslim armies launched occasional forays into the Deccan Plateau, but at first they had little success, even though the area was divided among a number of warring kingdoms, including the Colas along the eastern coast and the Pandyas far to the south.

One reason the Delhi sultanate failed to take advantage of the disarray of its rivals was the threat posed by the Mongols on the northwestern frontier (see Chapter 10). Mongol armies unleashed by the great tribal warrior Genghis Khan occupied Baghdad and destroyed the Abbasid caliphate in the 1250s, while other forces occupied the Punjab around Lahore, from which they threatened Delhi on several occasions. For the next half-century, the attention of the sultanate was focused on the Mongols. That threat finally declined in the early fourteenth century with the gradual breakup of the Mongol Empire, and a new Islamic state emerged in the form of a new Tughluq dynasty (1320–1413), which extended its power into the Deccan Plateau. In praise of his sovereign, the Tughluq monarch Ala-ud-din, the poet Amir Khusrau exclaimed:

> *Happy be Hindustan, with its splendor of religion,*
> *Where Islamic law enjoys perfect honor and dignity;*
> *In learning Delhi now rivals Bukhara;*
> *Islam has been made manifest by the rulers.*
> *From Ghazni to the very shore of the ocean*
> *You see Islam in its glory.*[4]

Such happiness was not destined to endure, however. During the latter half of the fourteenth century, the Tughluq dynasty gradually fell into decline. In 1398, a new military force crossed the Indus River from the northwest, raided the capital of Delhi, and then withdrew. According to some contemporary historians, as many as 100,000 Hindu prisoners were massacred before the gates of the city. Such was India's first encounter with Tamerlane.

Tamerlane (b. 1330s), also known as Timur-i-lang (Timur the Lame), was the ruler of a Mongol khanate based in Samarkand to the north of the Pamir Mountains. His kingdom had been founded on the ruins of the Mongol Empire, which had begun to disintegrate as a result of succession struggles in the thirteenth century.

MAP 9.3 The Empire of Tamerlane

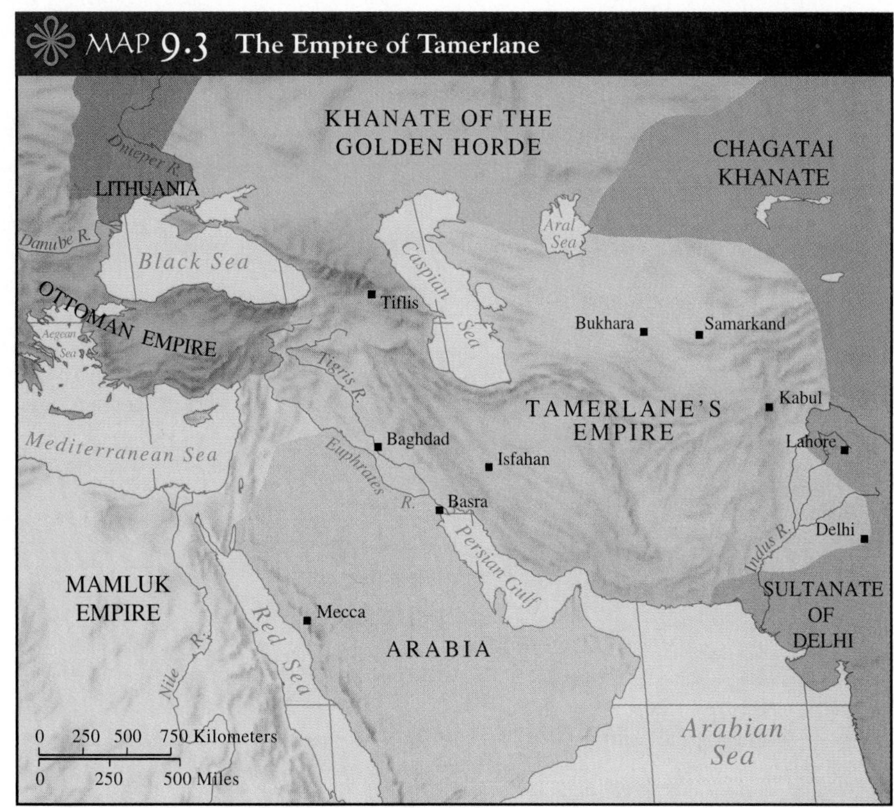

Tamerlane, the son of a local aristocrat, seized power in Samarkand in 1369 and immediately launched a program of conquest. During the 1380s, he brought the entire region east of the Caspian Sea under his authority and then conquered Baghdad and occupied Mesopotamia. After his brief foray into northern India, he turned to the west and raided the Anatolian peninsula. Defeating the army of the Ottoman Turks, he advanced almost as far as the Bosporus before withdrawing. "The last of the great nomadic conquerors," as one recent historian described him, died in 1405 in the midst of a final military campaign.

The passing of Tamerlane removed a major menace from the diverse states of the Indian subcontinent. But the respite from external challenge was not a long one. By the end of the fifteenth century, two new challenges had appeared from beyond the horizon: the Mughals, a newly emerging nomadic power beyond the Khyber Pass in the north, and the Portuguese traders, who arrived by sea from the eastern coast of Africa in search of gold and spices. Both, in their different ways, would exert a major impact on the later course of Indian civilization.

ISLAM AND INDIAN SOCIETY

Like their counterparts in other areas that came under Islamic rule, many Muslim rulers in India were quite tolerant of other faiths and used peaceful means, if any, to encourage nonbelievers to convert to Islam. Even the more enlightened, however, could be fierce when their religious zeal was aroused. One ruler, on being informed that a Hindu fair had been held near Delhi, ordered the promoters of the event to be put to death. Hindu temples were razed, and mosques were erected in their place. Eventually, however, most Muslim rulers realized that not all Hindus could be converted and recognized the necessity of accepting what to them was an alien and repugnant

SAMARKAND, GEM OF AN EMPIRE. The city of Samarkand has a long history. First settled during the first millennium B.C.E. as a caravan stop on the Silk Road, it was later occupied by Alexander the Great, the Abbasids, and the Mongols, before becoming the capital of Tamerlane's expanding empire. Tamerlane expended great sums in creating a city worthy of his own imperial ambitions. Shown here is the great square, known as the Registan. Site of a mosque, a library, and a Muslim university, all built in the exuberant Persian style, Samarkand was the jumping-off point for trade with China far to the east.

THE ISLAMIC CONQUEST OF INDIA

One consequence of the Muslim conquest of northern India was the imposition of many Islamic customs on Hindu society. In this excerpt, the fourteenth-century Muslim historian Zia-ud-din Barani describes the attempt of one Muslim ruler, Ala-ud-din, to forbid the use of alcohol and gambling, two practices expressly forbidden in Muslim society. Ala-ud-din had seized power in Delhi from a rival in 1294.

A MUSLIM RULER SUPPRESSES HINDU PRACTICES

Thirdly, he forbade wine, beer, and intoxicating drugs to be used or sold; dicing, too, was prohibited. Vintners and beer sellers were turned out of the city, and the heavy taxes which had been levied from them were abolished. All the china and glass vessels of the Sultan's banqueting room were broken and thrown outside the gate of Badaun, where they formed a mound. Jars and casks of wine were emptied out there till they made mire as if it were the season of the rains. The Sultan himself entirely gave up wine parties. Self-respecting people at once followed his example; but the ne'er-do-wells went on making wine and spirits and hid the leather bottles in loads of hay or firewood and by various such tricks smuggled it into the city. Inspectors and gatekeepers and spies diligently sought to seize the contraband and the smugglers; and when seized the wine was given to the elephants, and the importers and sellers and drinkers flogged and given short terms of imprisonment. So many were they, however, that holes had to be dug for their incarceration outside the great thoroughfare of the Badaun gate, and many of the wine bibbers died from the rigor of their confinement and others were taken out half-dead and were long in recovering their health. The terror of these holes deterred many from drinking. Those who could not give it up had to journey ten or twelve leagues to get a drink, for at half that distance, four or five leagues from Delhi, wine could not be publicly sold or drunk. The prevention of drinking proving very difficult, the Sultan enacted that people might distill and drink privately in their own homes, if drinking parties were not held and the liquor not sold. After the prohibition of drinking, conspiracies diminished.

religion. While Hindu religious practices were generally tolerated, non-Muslims were compelled to pay a tax to the state. Some Hindus likely converted to Islam to avoid paying the tax, but were then expected to make the traditional charitable contribution required of Muslims in all Islamic societies.

Over time, millions of Hindus did turn to the Muslim faith. Some were individuals or groups in the employ of the Muslim ruling class, such as government officials, artisans, or merchants catering to the needs of the court. But many others were probably peasants from the *sudra* class or even untouchables who found in the egalitarian message of Islam a way of removing the stigma of low-class status in the Hindu social hierarchy.

Seldom have two major religions been so strikingly different. Where Hinduism tolerated a belief in the existence of several deities (although admittedly they were all considered by some to be manifestations of one supreme god), Islam was uncompromisingly monotheistic. Where Hinduism was hierarchical, Islam was egalitarian. Where Hinduism featured a priestly class to serve as an intermediary with the ultimate force of the universe, Islam permitted no one to come between believers and their god. Such differences contributed to the mutual hostility that developed between the adherents of the two faiths in the Indian subcontinent, but more mundane issues, such as the Muslim habit of eating beef and the idolatry and sexual frankness in Hindu art, were probably a greater source of antagonism at the popular level (see the box above).

In other cases, the two peoples borrowed from each other. Some Muslim rulers found the Indian idea of divine kingship appealing. In their turn, Hindu rajas learned by bitter experience the superiority of cavalry mounted on horses instead of elephants, the primary assault weapon in early India. Some upper-class Hindu males were attracted to the Muslim tradition of *purdah* and began to keep their women in seclusion (termed locally "behind the curtain") from everyday society. Hindu sources claimed that one reason for adopting the custom was to protect Hindu women from the roving eyes of foreigners. But it is likely that many Indian families adopted the practice for reasons of prestige or because they were convinced that *purdah* was a practical means of protecting female virtue. Adult Indian women had already begun to cover their heads with a scarf during the Gupta era.

All in all, Muslim rule probably did not have a significant impact on the lives of most Indian women. *Purdah* was practiced more commonly among high castes than among the lower castes. Though it was probably of little consolation, sexual relations in poor and low-caste families were relatively egalitarian, as men and women worked together on press gangs or in the fields. Muslim customs apparently had little effect on the Hindu tradition of *sati* (see the box on p. 250). In fact, in many respects Muslim women had more rights than their Hindu counterparts. They had more property rights than Hindu women and were legally permitted to divorce under certain conditions and to remarry after the death of their husband. The

THE PRACTICE OF *SATI*

One of the most distinctive aspects of medieval Indian society was the Hindu custom of sati, *whereby a widow was immolated on the funeral pyre of her husband during his cremation. In so doing, she was not only honoring her dead husband, but also declaring her allegiance to deeply-held community beliefs in the sanctity of the marriage vow. Here the Portuguese adventurer Duarte Barbosa describes such a practice in the southern state of Narsyngua.*

DUARTE BARBOSA, ON *SATI*

In this kingdom of Narsyngua . . . the women are bound by very ancient custom, when their husbands die, to burn themselves alive with their corpses, which are also burnt. This they do to honor the husband. If such a woman is poor and of low estate, when her husband dies she goes with him to the burning ground, "where there is a great pit" in which a pile of wood burns. When the husband's body has been laid therein and begins to burn she throws herself of her own free will into the midst of the said fire, where both their bodies are reduced to ashes. But if she is a woman of high rank, rich, and with distinguished kindred, whether she be a young maid or an old woman, when her husband dies she accompanies the aforesaid corpse of her husband to the aforesaid burning ground, bewailing him; and there they dig a round pit, very wide and deep, which they fill with wood . . . and, when they have kindled it, they lay the man's body therein, and it is burnt while she weeps greatly. Wishing to do all honor to her husband she then causes all his kindred and her own to be called together, that they may come to feast and honor her thereby. . . . Thereafter she attires herself very richly with all the jewels she possesses, and then distributes to her sons, relatives, and friends all the property that remains. Thus arrayed she mounts on a horse . . . that she may be the better seen of all the people. Mounted on this horse they lead her through the whole city with great rejoicings, until they come back to the very spot where the husband has been burnt, where, they cast a great quantity of wood into the pit itself and on its edge they make a great fire. When it has burnt up somewhat they erect a wooden scaffold with four or five steps where they take her up just as she is. When she is on the top she turns herself round thereon three times, worshipping towards the direction of sunrise, and, this done, she calls her sons, kindred, and friends, and to each she gives a jewel, whereof she has many with her, and in the same way every piece of her clothing until nothing is left except a small piece of cloth with which she is clothed from the waist down. Then she tells the men who are with her on the scaffold to consider what they owe to their wives who, being free to act, yet burn themselves alive for the love of them, and the women she tells to see how much they owe to their husbands, to such a degree as to go with them even to death. Then . . . they place in her hands a pitcher full of oil, and she puts it on her head, and with it she again turns round thrice on the scaffold and again worships towards the rising sun. Then she casts the pitcher of oil into the fire and throws herself after it with as much goodwill as if she were throwing herself on a little cotton, from which she could receive no hurt. The kinsfolk all take part at once and cast into the fire many pitchers of oil and butter which they hold ready for this purpose, and much wood on this, and therewith bursts out such a flame that no more can be seen.

primary role for Indian women in general, however, was to produce children. Sons were preferred over daughters, not only because they alone could conduct ancestral rights, but also because a daughter was a financial liability. Not only did she require a costly dowry in marriage, but after the wedding she would eventually transfer her labor assets to her husband's family. Still, women shared with men a position in the Indian religious pantheon. The cult of the mother-goddess, which had originated in the Harappan era, revived during the Gupta era stronger than ever. The Hindu female deity, known as Devi, was celebrated by both men and women as the source of cosmic power, bestower of wishes, and symbol of fertility.

Overall, the Muslims continued to view themselves as foreign conquerors and generally maintained a strict separation between the Muslim ruling class and the mass of the Hindu population. Although a few Hindus rose to important positions in the local bureaucracy, in general high posts in the central government and the provinces were reserved for Muslims. Only with the founding of the Mughal dynasty was a serious effort undertaken to reconcile the differences.

One result of this effort was the religion of the Sikhs. Founded by the guru Nanak in the early sixteenth century in the Punjab, Sikhism attempted to integrate the best of the two faiths in a single religion. Sikhism (the term means "disciple") originated in the devotionalist movement in Hinduism, which taught that God was the single true reality. All else is illusion. But Nanak rejected the Hindu tradition of asceticism and mortification of the flesh and, like Muhammad, taught his disciples to participate in the world. Sikhism achieved considerable popularity in northwestern India, where Islam and Hinduism confronted each other directly, and eventually evolved into a militant faith that fiercely protected its adherents against its two larger rivals. In the end, Sikhism did not

UNTOUCHABLES IN SOUTH INDIA

Some of the best descriptions of Indian society in the late medieval era came from European merchants and missionaries. The following passage was written by the Portuguese traveler Duarte Barbosa and describes an untouchable caste on the southwestern coast of India in the early sixteenth century. The Nayres mentioned in this excerpt were a higher caste in the region.

DUARTE BARBOSA, *FROM THE LAND OF MALABAR*

And there is yet another caste of Heathen lower than these whom they call Poleas, who among all the rest are held to be accursed and excommunicate; they dwell in the fields and open campaigns [plots] in secret lurking places, whither folk of good caste never go save by mischance, and live in huts very strait and mean. They are tillers of rice with buffaloes and oxen. They never speak to the Nayres save from afar off, shouting so that they may hear them, and when they go along the roads they utter loud cries, that they may be let past, and whosoever hears them leaves the road, and stands in the wood till they have passed by; and if anyone, whether man or woman, touches them his kinsfolk slay him forthwith, and in vengeance therefore they slay Poleas until they weary without suffering any punishment. In certain months of the year they do their utmost to touch some Nayre woman by night as secretly as they can, and this only for the sake of doing evil. They go by in order to get into the houses of the Nayres to touch women, and during these months the women guard themselves carefully, and if they touch any woman, even though none have seen it, and there may be no witnesses, yet she declares it at once, crying out, and she will stay no longer in her house that her caste may not be destroyed; in general she flees to the house of some other low caste folk, and hides herself, that her kinsfolk may not slay her; and that thence she may help herself and be sold to foreigners, which is ofttimes done. And the manner of touching is this, even though no words are exchanged, they throw something at her, a stone or a stick, and if it touches her she is touched and ruined. These people are also great sorcerers and thieves; they are a very evil race.

reconcile Hinduism and Islam but provided an alternative to both.

One complication for both Muslims and Hindus as they tried to come to terms with the existence of a mixed society was the problem of caste. Could non-Hindus form castes, and if so, how were these castes related to the Hindu castes? Where did the Turkic-speaking elites who made up the ruling class in many of the Islamic states fit into the equation?

The problem was resolved in a pragmatic manner that probably followed an earlier tradition of assimilating non-Hindu tribal groups into the system. Members of the Turkic ruling groups formed social groups that were roughly equivalent to the Hindu *brahmin* or *kshatriya* caste. During the Delhi sultanate in the north, members of the local Rajput nobility who converted to Islam were occasionally permitted to join such caste groupings. Ordinary Indians who converted to Islam also formed Muslim castes, although at a lower level on the social scale. Many who did so were probably artisans who converted en masse to obtain the privileges that conversion could bring.

In most of India, then, Muslim rule did not substantially disrupt the caste system. One perceptive European visitor in the early sixteenth century reported that in Malabar, along the southwestern coast, there were separate castes for fishing, pottery making, weaving, carpentry and metalworking, salt mining, sorcery, and labor on the plantations. There were separate castes for doing the laundry, one for the elite and the other for the common people (see the box above).

Economy and Daily Life

India's landed and commercial elites lived in the cities, often in conditions of considerable opulence. The rulers, of course, possessed the most wealth. One maharaja of a relatively small state in southern India, for example, had over 100,000 soldiers in his pay along with 900 elephants and 20,000 horses. Another maintained a thousand high-caste women to serve as sweepers of his palace. Each carried a broom and a brass basin containing a mixture of cow dung and water, and followed him from one house to another, plastering the path where he was to tread. Most urban dwellers, of course, did not live in such style. Xuan Zang, the Chinese Buddhist missionary who visited India in the early seventh century, left us a description of ordinary homes in urban areas:

> Their houses are surrounded by low walls, and form the suburbs. The earth being soft and muddy, the walls of the towns are mostly built of brick or tiles. The towers on the walls are constructed of wood or bamboo; the houses have balconies and belvederes, which are made of wood, with a coating of lime or mortar, and covered with tiles. The different buildings have the same form as those in China; rushes, or dry branches, or tiles, or boards are used for covering them. The walls are covered with lime and mud, mixed with cow's dung for purity. At different seasons they scatter flowers about. Such are some of their different customs.[5]

The majority of India's population (estimated at slightly more than 100 million in the first millennium C.E.), however, lived on the land. Most were peasants who tilled small plots of land with a wooden plow pulled by oxen and paid a percentage of the harvest to their landlord. The landlord, in turn, forwarded part of the payment to the local ruler. In effect, the landlord functioned as a tax collector for the king, who retained ultimate ownership of all farmland in his domain. At best, most peasants lived at the subsistence level. At worst, they were forced into debt and fell victim to moneylenders who charged exorbitant rates of interest.

In the north and in the upland regions of the Deccan Plateau, the primary grain crops were wheat and barley. In the Ganges valley and the southern coastal plains, the main crop was rice. Vegetables were grown everywhere, and southern India produced many spices, fruits, sugarcane, and cotton. The cotton plant apparently originated in the Indus River valley and spread from there. Although some cotton was cultivated in Spain and North Africa by the eighth and ninth centuries, India remained the primary producer of cotton goods. Spices such as cinnamon, pepper, ginger, sandalwood, cardamom, and cumin were also major export products.

Agriculture, of course, was not the only source of wealth in India. Since ancient times, the subcontinent had served as a major entrepôt for trade between the Middle East and the Pacific basin, as well as the source of other goods shipped throughout the known world. Although civil strife and piracy, heavy taxation of the business community by local rulers to finance their fratricidal wars, and increased customs duties between principalities may have contributed to a decline in internal trade, the level of foreign trade remained high, particularly in the Dravidian kingdoms in the south and along the northwestern coast, which were located along the traditional trade routes to the Middle East and the Mediterranean Sea. Much of this foreign trade was carried on by wealthy Hindu castes with close ties to the royal courts. But there were other participants as well, including such non-Hindu minorities as the Muslims, the Parsis, and the Jain community. The Parsis, expatriates from Persia who practiced the Zoroastrian religion, dominated banking and the textile industry in the cities bordering the Rann of Kutch. Later they would become a dominant economic force in the modern city of Bombay. The Jains became prominent in trade and manufacturing even though their faith emphasized simplicity and the rejection of materialism.

According to early European travelers, merchants often lived quite well. One Portuguese observer described the "Moorish" population in Bengal as follows:

> They have girdles of cloth, and over them silk scarves; they carry in their girdles daggers garnished with silver and gold, according to the rank of the person who carries them; on their fingers many rings set with rich jewels, and cotton turbans on their heads. They are luxurious, eat well and spend freely, and have many other extravagances as well. They bathe often in great tanks which they have in their houses. Everyone has three or four wives or as many as he can maintain. They keep them carefully shut up, and treat them very well, giving them great store of gold, silver and apparel of fine silk.[6]

Outside these relatively small, specialized trading communities, most manufacturing and commerce were in the hands of petty traders and artisans, who generally were limited to local markets. This failure to build on the promise of antiquity has led some historians to ask why India failed to produce an expansion of commerce and growth of cities

ROCK PAINTINGS AT SIGIRIYA, SRI LANKA. Closely linked to Indian art and culture are these surviving paintings at the sixth-century rock fortress at Sigiriya, on the island of Sri Lanka. Portraits of serving girls from the king's harem were painted high up along the cliff wall. Many were destroyed by Buddhist monks when they reclaimed the area after the king's sudden death. Thankfully, a few of these graceful, languid maidens were left unharmed to captivate viewers over the centuries.

ROCK TEMPLE AT ELLORA. An estimated 3 million cubic feet of stone were excavated out of solid rock to build the massive eighth-century Kailasantha Rock Temple at Ellora. Renowned for its elaborate sculptures dedicated to the legends of the Hindu deities, Ellora is one of India's greatest architectural sites.

similar to the developments that began in Europe during the High Middle Ages or even in China during the Song dynasty (see Chapter 10). Some have pointed to the traditionally low status of artisans and merchants in Indian society, symbolized by the comment in the *Arthasastra* that merchants were "thieves that are not called by the name of thief."[7] Yet commercial activities were frowned upon in many areas in Europe throughout the Middle Ages, a fact that did not prevent the emergence of capitalist societies throughout much of the West.

Another factor may have been the monopoly on foreign trade held by the government in many areas of India. More important, perhaps, was the impact of the caste system, which reduced the ability of entrepreneurs to expand their activities and have dealings with other members of the commercial and manufacturing community. Successful artisans, for example, normally could not set up as merchants to market their products, nor could merchants compete for buyers outside their normal area of operations. The complex interlocking relationships among the various castes in a given region were a powerful factor inhibiting the development of a thriving commercial sector in medieval India.

The Wonder of Indian Culture

The era between the Mauryas and the Mughals in India was a period of cultural evolution, as Indian writers and artists built on the literary and artistic achievements of their predecessors. This is not to say, however, that Indian culture rested on its ancient laurels. To the contrary, it was an era of tremendous innovation in all fields of creative endeavor.

ART AND ARCHITECTURE

At the end of antiquity, the primary forms of religious architecture were the Buddhist cave temples and monasteries. The next millennium witnessed the evolution of religious architecture from underground cavity to monumental structure.

The twenty-eight caves of Ajanta in the Deccan Plateau are one of India's greatest artistic achievements. They are as impressive for their sculpture and painting as for their architecture. Except for a few examples from the second century B.C.E., most of the caves were carved out of solid rock over an incredibly short period of eighteen years, from 460 to 478 C.E. In contrast to the early unadorned temple halls, these temples were exuberantly decorated with ornate pillars, friezes, beamed ceilings, and statues of the Buddha and bodhisattvas. Several caves served as monasteries, which by then had been transformed from simple holes in the wall to large complexes with living apartments, halls, and shrines to the Buddha.

All of the inner surfaces of the caves, including the ceilings, sculptures, walls, door frames, and pillars, were painted in vivid colors. Perhaps best known are the wall paintings, which illustrate the various lives and incarnations of the Buddha. These paintings are in an admirable state of preservation, making it possible to reconstruct the customs, dress, house interiors, and physical characteristics of the peoples of fifth-century India.

Near Ajanta are the equally famous rock temples at Ellora. These temples, carved out of a mountain of solid rock, were originally built by Buddhists during the eighth century C.E. Later, they were taken over by Hindus and at one time were used by followers of Jainism. Though the complex consists of several temples, the most famous is the Hindu temple of Kailasantha, dedicated to Siva. The floor of the temple is similar in size to the Parthenon in Greece, but the building is three stories high and required the excavation of an estimated three million cubic feet of stone. Unlike earlier temples, which were constructed in the form of caves, the Kailasantha temple was open to the sky (although many of the freestanding shrines are covered with roofs), and the walls are festooned with some of India's finest sculptures. The overall impression is one of wonder and massive grandeur.

Among the most impressive rock carvings in southern India are the cave temples at Mamallapuram (also known as Mahabalipuram), south of the modern city of Madras. The sculpture, called the Descent of the Ganges River, depicts the role played by Siva in intercepting the heavenly waters of the Ganges and allowing them to fall gently on the earth. Mamallapuram also boasts an eighth-century shore temple, which is considered to be one of the earliest surviving freestanding structures in the subcontinent.

From the eighth century until the time of the Mughals, Indian architects built a multitude of magnificent Hindu

DESCENT OF THE GANGES RIVER. One of India's most outstanding sculptures is found at Mamallapuram, an eighth-century site on the eastern coast south of Madras. This open relief, known as the Descent of the Ganges River, is about twenty feet high and eighty feet long. It portrays Siva's effort to deflect the waters of the heavenly River Ganges on his head to spare the earth from destruction. Although it presents a rich panorama of gods, animals, and men, the gentle elephant in particular delights one and all.

temples, now constructed exclusively above ground. Each temple consisted of a central shrine surmounted by a sizable tower, a hall for worshipers, a vestibule, and a porch, all set in a rectangular courtyard that might also contain other minor shrines. Temples became progressively more ornate until the eleventh century, when the sculpture began to dominate the structure itself. The towers became higher and the temple complexes more intricate, some becoming virtual walled compounds set one within the other and resembling a town in themselves.

Among the best examples of temple art are those in the eastern state of Orissa. The Sun Temple at Konarak, standing at the edge of the sea and covered with intricate carvings, is generally considered the masterpiece of its genre. Although now in ruins, the Sun Temple still boasts some of India's most memorable sculptures. Especially renowned are the twelve pairs of carved wheels; each is ten feet high and represents one of the twelve signs of the zodiac.

The greatest example of medieval Hindu temple art, however, is probably Khajuraho. Of the original eighty temples, dating from the tenth century, twenty remain standing today. All of the towers are buttressed at various levels on the sides, giving the whole a sense of unity and creating a vertical movement similar to Mount Kailasa in the Himalayas, sacred to Hindus. Everywhere the viewer is entertained by voluptuous temple dancers bringing life to the massive structures. One is removing a thorn from her foot, another is applying eye makeup, and yet another is wringing out her hair.

In the Deccan Plateau, a different style prevailed. The southern temple style was marked by massive oblong stone towers, some as much as two hundred feet high. The towers were often covered with a profusion of sculpted figures and were visible for miles. The walls surrounding the temple complex were also surmounted with impressive gate towers, known as *gopuras*.

LITERATURE

During this period, Indian authors produced a prodigious number of written works, both religious and secular. Indian religious poetry was written in both Sanskrit and the languages of southern India. As Hinduism was transformed from a contemplative to a more devotional religion, its poetry became more ardent and erotic and prompted a sense of divine ecstasy. Much of the religious verse extolled the lives and heroic acts of Siva, Vishnu, Rama, and Krishna by repeating the same themes over and over, which is also a characteristic of Indian art. In the eighth century, a tradition of poet-saints inspired by intense mystical devotion to a deity emerged in southern India. Many were women who sought to escape the drudgery of domestic toil through an imagined sexual union with the god-lover. Such was the case for the twelfth-century mystic whose poem here expresses her sensuous joy in the physical-mystical union with her god:

It was like a stream
running into the dry bed
of a lake,
like rain pouring on plants
parched to sticks.
It was like this world's pleasure
and the way to the other,
both walking towards me.
Seeing the feet of the master,
O lord white as jasmine
I was made worthwhile.[8]

The great secular literature of traditional India was also written in Sanskrit in the form of poetry, drama, and prose. Some of the best medieval Indian poetry is found in single-stanza poems, which create an entire emotional scene in just four lines. Witness this poem by the poet Amaru:

We'll see what comes of it, I thought,
and I hardened my heart against her.
What, won't the villain speak to me? she
thought, flying into a rage.
And there we stood, sedulously refusing to look one
another in the face,
Until at last I managed an unconvincing laugh,
and her tears robbed me of my resolution.[9]

One of India's most famous authors was Kalidasa, who lived during the Gupta dynasty. Although little is known of him, including his dates, he probably wrote for the court of Chandragupta II (375–415 C.E.). Even today Kalidasa's hundred-verse poem, *The Cloud Messenger,* remains one of the most popular Sanskrit poems (see the box on p. 256).

In addition to being a poet, Kalidasa was also a great dramatist. He wrote three plays, all dramatic romances that blend the erotic with the heroic and the comic. *Shakuntala,* perhaps the best-known play in all Indian literature, tells the story of a king who, while out hunting, falls in love with the maiden Shakuntala. He asks her to marry him and offers her a ring of betrothal but is suddenly recalled to his kingdom on urgent business. Shakuntala, who is pregnant, goes to him, but the king has been cursed by a hermit and no longer recognizes her. With the help of the gods, the king eventually does recall their love and is reunited with Shakuntala and their son.

Each of Kalidasa's plays is propelled by the magic powers of a goddess, and each ends in affirmation and unity. Another interesting aspect of Kalidasa's plays is that they combine several languages as well as poetry and prose. The language and form of the characters' speeches correspond to their position in the social hierarchy. Thus, the king speaks in Sanskrit poetry, while the other characters in the play use prose in three different vernaculars of everyday life.

Kalidasa was one of the greatest Indian dramatists, but he was by no means the only one. Sanskrit plays typically contained one to ten acts. They were performed in theaters in the palaces or in court temples by troupes of actors of both sexes who were trained and supported by the royal family. The plots were usually taken from Indian legends of gods and kings. No scenery or props were used, but costumes and makeup were elaborate. The theaters had to be small because much of the drama was conveyed through intricate gestures and dance conventions. There were many different positions for various parts of the body, including one hundred for the hands alone.

Like poetry, prose developed in India from the Vedic period. The use of prose was well established by the sixth and seventh centuries C.E. This is truly astonishing considering that the novel did not appear until the tenth century in Japan and until the seventeenth century in Europe.

One of the greatest masters of Sanskrit prose was Dandin, who lived during the seventh century. In *The Ten Princes,* he created a fantastic and exciting world that fuses history and fiction. His keen powers of observation, details of low life, and humor give his writing considerable vitality.

MUSIC

Another area of Indian creativity that developed during this era was music. Ancient Indian music had come from the chanting of the Vedic hymns and thus inevitably had a strong metaphysical and spiritual flavor. The actual physical vibrations of music *(nada)* were considered to be related to the spiritual world. An off-key or sloppy rendition of a sacred text could upset the harmony and balance of the entire universe.

SCULPTURAL DECORATIONS AT KHAJURAHO. This Hindu temple, one of the greatest in India, is literally covered with the statues of temple dancers, who bring life to its massive architecture. Frozen in stone, they mesmerize the viewer. Many represent the ideal couple or divine lovers, who symbolize the union of the worshipers with the deity, thus blending physical and spiritual beauty.

In form, Indian classical music is based on a scale, called a *raga.* There are dozens, if not hundreds, of separate scales, which are grouped into separate categories depending on the time of day during which they are to be performed. The performers use a stringed instrument called a *sitar* and various types of wind instruments and drums. The performers select a basic *raga* and then are free to improvise the melodic structure and rhythm. A good performer never performs a particular *raga* the same way twice. As with jazz music in the West, the audience is concerned not so much with faithful reproduction, but with the performer's creativity.

AN INDIAN LOVE POEM

Kalidasa, who lived during the Gupta period, was India's greatest dramatist and poet. This is a brief excerpt from The Cloud Messenger, *one of the most popular and beautiful poems in the Sanskrit language. It describes the anguish of a young Indian who has been sent into exile and misses his wife. In the poem he watches clouds drifting northward and describes to them the route to his home in the Himalaya Mountains.*

KALIDASA, THE CLOUD MESSENGER

Stay for a while over the thickets, haunted by the girls of the hill-folk, then press on with faster pace, having shed your load of water,
and you'll see the Narmada river, scattered in torrents, by the rugged rocks at the foot of the Vindhyas,
looking like the plastered pattern of stripes on the flank of an elephant.

Note by the banks the flowers of the nipa trees, greenish brown, with their stamens half developed,
and the plantains, displaying their new buds.
Smell the most fragrant earth of the burnt-out woodlands,
and as you release your raindrops the deer will show you the way.

. . . where the wind from the Sipra river prolongs the shrill melodious cry of the cranes,
fragrant at early dawn from the scent of the opening lotus,
and, like a lover, with flattering requests,
dispels the morning languor of women, and refreshes their limbs.

Your body will grow fat with the smoke of incense from open windows where women dress their hair.
You will be greeted by palace peacocks, dancing to welcome you, their friend.
If your heart is weary from travel you may pass the night above mansions fragrant with flowers,
whose pavements are marked with red dye from the feet of lovely women.

. . . where yaksas dwell with lovely women in white mansions, whose crystal terraces reflect the stars like flowers.
They drink the wine of love distilled from magic trees,
while drums beat softly, deeper than your thunder.

I see your body in the sinuous creeper, your gaze in the startled eyes of deer,
your cheek in the moon, your hair in the plumage of peacocks,
and in the tiny ripples of the river I see your sidelong glances,
but alas, my dearest, nowhere do I find your whole likeness!

THE GOLDEN REGION: EARLY SOUTHEAST ASIA

Between China and India lies the region that today is called Southeast Asia. It has two major components: a mainland region extending southward from the Chinese border down to the tip of the Malay peninsula and an extensive archipelago, most of which is part of present-day Indonesia and the Philippines. Travel between the islands and regions to the west, north, and east was not difficult, so Southeast Asia has historically served as a vast land bridge for the movement of peoples between China, the Indian subcontinent, and the more than 25,000 islands of the South Pacific.

Mainland Southeast Asia consists of several north-south mountain ranges, separated by river valleys that run in a southerly or southeasterly direction. During the first millennium C.E., two groups of migrants—the Thai from southwestern China and the Burmans from the Tibetan highlands—came down these valleys in search of new homelands, as earlier peoples had done before them. Once in Southeast Asia, most of these migrants settled in the fertile deltas of the rivers—the Irrawaddy and the Salween in Burma, the Chao Phraya in Thailand, and the Red River and the Mekong in Vietnam—or in lowland areas in the islands to the south.

Although the river valleys facilitated north-south travel on the Southeast Asian mainland, movement between east and west was relatively difficult. The mountains are densely forested and often infested with malaria-carrying mosquitoes. Consequently, the lowland peoples in the river valleys were often isolated from each other and had only limited contacts with the upland peoples in the mountains. These geographical barriers may help explain why Southeast Asia is one of the few regions in Asia that was never unified under a single government.

Given Southeast Asia's location between China and India, it is not surprising that both civilizations influenced developments in the region. In 111 B.C.E. Vietnam was conquered by the Han dynasty and remained under Chinese control for more than a millennium; it will be discussed in Chapter 11. The Indian states never exerted much political control over Southeast Asia, but their influ-

THE KINGDOM OF ANGKOR

Angkor (known to the Chinese as Chon-la) was the greatest kingdom of its time in Southeast Asia. This passage, probably written in the thirteenth century by the Chinese port official Chau Ju-kua, includes a brief description of the capital city, Angkor Thom, which is still one of the great archaeological sites of the region. Angkor was already in decline when Chau Ju-kua described the kingdom, and the capital was abandoned soon afterward, in 1432.

CHAU JU-KUA, *RECORDS OF FOREIGN NATIONS*

The officials and the common people dwell in houses with sides of bamboo matting and thatched with reeds. Only the king resides in a palace of hewn stone. It has a granite lotus pond of extraordinary beauty with golden bridges, some three hundred odd feet long. The palace buildings are solidly built and richly ornamented. The throne on which the king sits is made of gharu wood and the seven precious substances; the dais is jewelled, with supports of veined wood [ebony?]; the screen [behind the throne] is of ivory.

When all the ministers of state have audience, they first make three full prostrations at the foot of the throne; they then kneel and remain thus, with hands crossed on their breasts, in a circle round the king, and discuss the affairs of state. When they have finished, they make another prostration and retire. . . .

[The people] are devout Buddhists. There are serving [in the temples] some three hundred foreign women; they dance and offer food to the Buddha. They are called *a-nan* or slave dancing girls.

As to their customs, lewdness is not considered criminal; theft is punished by cutting off a hand and a foot and by branding on the chest.

The incantations of the Buddhist and Taoist priests [of this country] have magical powers. Among the former those who wear yellow robes may marry, while those who dress in red lead ascetic lives in temples. The Taoists clothe themselves with leaves; they have a deity called P'o-to-li which they worship with great devotion.

[The people of this country] hold the right hand to be clean, the left unclean, so when they wish to mix their rice with any kind of meat broth, they use the right hand to do so and also to eat with.

The soil is rich and loamy; the fields have no bounds. Each one takes as much as he can cultivate. Rice and cereals are cheap; for every tael of lead one can buy two bushels of rice.

The native products comprise elephants' tusks, the *chan* and *su* [varieties of gharu wood], good yellow wax, kingfisher's feathers, . . . resin, foreign oils, ginger peel, gold-colored incense, . . . raw silk and cotton fabrics.

The foreign traders offer in exchange for these gold, silver, porcelainware, sugar, preserves, and vinegar.

ence was pervasive nevertheless. By the first centuries C.E., Indian merchants were sailing to Southeast Asia; they were soon followed by Buddhist and Hindu missionaries. Indian influence can be seen in many aspects of Southeast Asian culture—from political institutions to religion, architecture, language, and literature.

Paddy Fields and Spices: The States of Southeast Asia

The traditional states of Southeast Asia can be generally divided between agricultural societies and trading societies. The distinction between farming and trade was a product of the environment. The agricultural societies—notably, Vietnam, Angkor in what is now Cambodia, and the Burman state of Pagan—were situated in rich river deltas that were conducive to the development of a wet rice economy. Although all produced some goods for regional markets, none was tempted to turn to commerce as the prime source of national income. In fact, none was situated astride the main trade routes that crisscrossed the region.

The kingdom of Angkor, which took shape in the ninth century, was the most powerful state to emerge in mainland Southeast Asia before the sixteenth century (see the box above). The remains of its capital city Angkor Thom give a sense of the magnificence of Angkor civilization. The city formed a square two miles on each side. Its massive stone walls were several feet thick and were surrounded by a moat. Four main gates led into the city, which at its height had a substantial population. By the fourteenth century, however, Angkor had begun to decline, and in 1432 Angkor Thom was destroyed by the Thai, who had migrated into the region from southwestern China in the thirteenth century.

The islands of the Indonesian archipelago gave rise to two of the region's most notable trading societies—Srivijaya and Majapahit. Both were based in large part on spices. As the wealth of the Arab empire in the Middle East and then of western Europe increased, so did the demand for the products of East Asia. Merchant fleets from India and the Arabian peninsula sailed to the Indonesian islands to buy cloves, pepper, nutmeg, cinnamon, precious woods, and other exotic products coveted by the

CHRONOLOGY

EARLY SOUTHEAST ASIA

Chinese conquest of Vietnam	111 B.C.E.
Arrival of Burman peoples	c. seventh century
Formation of Srivijaya	c. 670
Construction of Borobudur	c. eighth century
Creation of Angkor kingdom	c. ninth century
Thai migrations into Southeast Asia	c. thirteenth century
Rise of Majapahit empire	1292
Fall of Angkor kingdom	1432

MAP 9.4 Southeast Asia in the Thirteenth Century

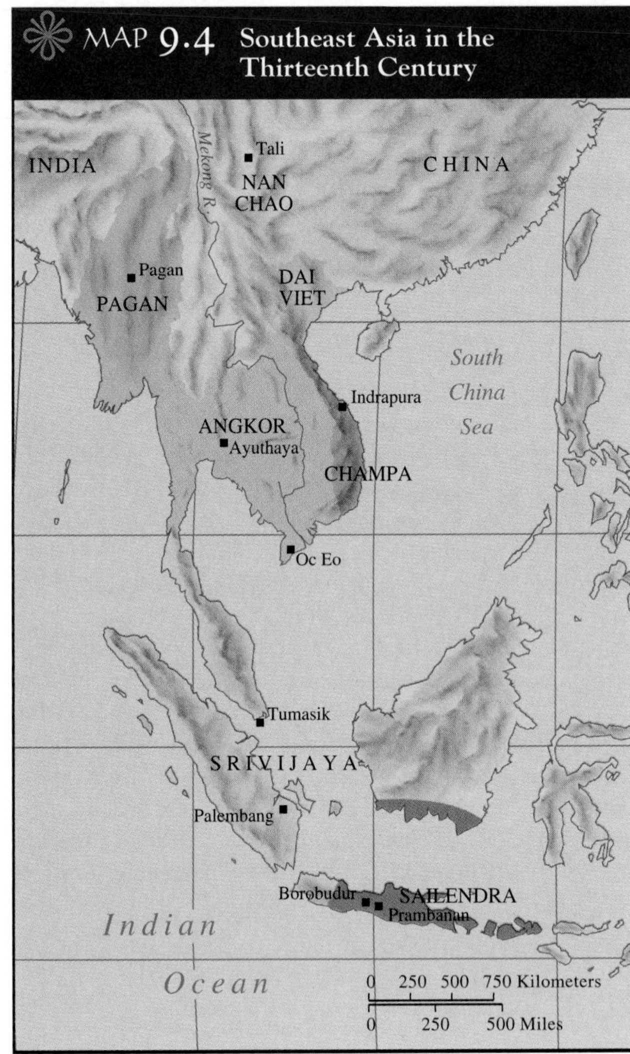

wealthy. In the eighth century, Srivijaya, located along the eastern coast of Sumatra, became a powerful commercial state that dominated the trade route passing through the Strait of Malacca, at that time the most convenient route from East Asia into the Indian Ocean. The rulers of Srivijaya had helped to bring the route to prominence by controlling the pirates who had previously plagued shipping in the strait. Another inducement was Srivijaya's capital at Palembang, a deepwater port where sailors could wait out the change in the monsoon season before making their return voyage. In 1025, however, Cola, one of the Dravidian kingdoms of southern India and a commercial rival of Srivijaya, inflicted a devastating defeat on the island kingdom. Although Srivijaya survived, it was unable to regain its former dominance, in part because the main trade route had shifted to the east, through the Strait of Sunda and directly out into the Indian Ocean. In the late thirteenth century, this shift in trade patterns led to the founding of a new kingdom of Majapahit on the island of Java. In the mid-fourteenth century, Majapahit succeeded in uniting most of the archipelago and perhaps even part of the Southeast Asian mainland under its rule.

Indian influence was evident in all of these societies to various degrees. Based on models from the Dravidian kingdoms of southern India, Southeast Asian kings were believed to possess special godlike qualities that set them apart from ordinary people. In some societies such as Angkor, the most prominent royal advisers constituted a *brahmin* class on the Indian model. In Pagan and Angkor, some division of the population into separate classes based on occupation and ethnic background seems to have occurred, although these divisions do not seem to have developed the rigidity of Indian castes.

India also supplied Southeast Asians with a writing system. The societies of the region had no written scripts for their spoken languages before the arrival of the Indian merchants and missionaries. Indian phonetic symbols were borrowed and used to re-cord the spoken language. Initially, Southeast Asian literature was written in the Indian Sanskrit but eventually came to be written in the local languages. Southeast Asian authors borrowed popular Indian themes, such as stories from the Buddhist scriptures and tales from the Ramayana.

A popular form of entertainment among the common people, the *wayang kulit,* or shadow play, may have come originally from India or possibly China, but it became a distinctive art form in Java and other islands of the Indonesian archipelago. In a shadow play, flat leather puppets were manipulated behind an illuminated screen while the narrator recited tales from the Indian classics. The plays were often ac-companied by gamelan, a type of music performed by an orchestra composed primarily of percus-

ANGKOR WAT. The Khmer rulers of Angkor constructed a number of remarkable temples and palaces. Devised as either Hindu or Buddhist shrines, the temples also reflected the power and sanctity of the king. This twelfth-century temple known as Angkor Wat is renowned both for its spectacular architecture and for the thousands of fine bas-reliefs relating Hindu legends and Khmer history. Most memorable are the heavenly dancing maidens and the royal processions with elephants and soldiers.

sion instruments such as gongs and drums that apparently originated in Java.

Daily Life

Because of the diversity of ethnic backgrounds, religions, and cultures, making generalizations about daily life in Southeast Asia during the early historical period is difficult. Nevertheless, it appears that Southeast Asian societies did not always apply the social distinctions that were sometimes imported from India. For example, although the local population, as elsewhere, was divided according to a variety of economic functions, the dividing lines between classes were not as rigid and imbued with religious significance as they were in the Indian subcontinent.

Still, traditional societies in Southeast Asia had some clearly hierarchical characteristics. At the top of the social ladder were the hereditary aristocrats, who monopolized both political power and economic wealth and enjoyed a borrowed aura of charisma by virtue of their proximity to the ruler. Most aristocrats lived in the major cities, which were the main source of power, wealth, and foreign influence. Beyond the major cities lived the mass of the population, composed of farmers, fishers, artisans, and merchants. In most Southeast Asian societies, the vast majority were probably rice farmers, living at a bare level of subsistence and paying heavy rents or taxes to a landlord or a local ruler.

The average Southeast Asian peasant was not actively engaged in commerce except as a consumer of various necessities. But accounts by foreign visitors indicate that in the Malay world some were involved in growing or mining products for export, such as tropical food products, precious woods, tin, and precious gems. Most of the regional trade was carried on by local merchants, who purchased products from local growers and then transported them to the major port cities. During the early state-building era, roads were few and relatively primitive, so most of the trade was transported by small boats down rivers to the major ports along the coast. There the goods were loaded onto larger ships for delivery outside the region. Growers of export goods in areas near the coast were thus indirectly involved in the regional trade network but received few economic benefits from the relationship.

As we might expect from an area of such ethnic and cultural diversity, social structures differed significantly from country to country. In the Indianized states on the mainland, the tradition of a hereditary tribal aristocracy was probably accentuated by the Hindu practice of dividing the population into separate classes, called *varna* in imitation of the Indian model. In Angkor and Pagan, for example, the divisions were based on occupation or ethnic background. Some people were considered free subjects of the king, although there may have been legal restrictions against changing occupations. Others, however, may have been indentured to an employer. Each community was under a chieftain, who in turn was subordinated to a higher official responsible for passing on the tax revenues of each group to the central government.

In the kingdoms in the Malay peninsula and the Indonesian archipelago, social relations were generally less formal. Most of the people in the region, whether farmers, fishers, or artisans, lived in small *kampongs* (the Malay word for "village") in wooden houses built on stilts to avoid flooding during the monsoon season. Some of the farmers were probably sharecroppers who paid a part of their harvest to a landlord, who was often a member of the aristocracy. But in other areas the tradition of free farming was strong. In some cases, some of the poorer land belonged to the village as a collective unit and was assigned for use by the neediest families.

The women of Southeast Asia during this era have been described as the most fortunate in the world. Although most women worked side by side with men in the fields, as in Africa they often played an active role

MOUNT AGUNG IN BALI. In Southeast Asia as in many other cultures, mountains are considered to be the abode of the gods. This was notably the case on the island of Bali, where beautiful Mount Agung is still viewed by Hindus as the local equivalent of sacred Mt. Meru in India. In Balinese cosmology, the sea is the home of evil spirits, while humans occupy the profane world in between. An active volcano, Mount Agung erupted in 1964, killing thousands of islanders in a cloud of volcanic ash.

in trading activities. This not only led to a higher literacy rate among women than among their male counterparts, but it also allowed them more financial independence than their counterparts in China and India, a fact that was noticed by the Chinese traveler Zhou Daguan at the end of the thirteenth century: "In Cambodia it is the women who take charge of trade. For this reason a Chinese arriving in the country loses no time in getting himself a mate, for he will find her commercial instincts a great asset."[10]

Although, as elsewhere, warfare was normally part of the male domain, women sometimes played a role as bodyguards as well. According to the Zhou Daguan, women were used to protect the royal family in Angkor, as well as in kingdoms located on the islands of Java and Sumatra. While there is no evidence that such female units ever engaged in battle, they did give rise to wondrous tales of amazon warriors in the writings of foreign travelers such as the fourteenth-century Muslim adventurer Ibn Battuta.

One reason for the enhanced status of women in traditional Southeast Asia is that the nuclear family was more common than the joint family system prevalent in China and the Indian subcontinent. Throughout the region, wealth in marriage was passed from the male to the female, in contrast to the dowry system applied in China and India. In most societies, virginity was usually not a valued commodity in brokering a marriage, and divorce proceedings could be initiated by either party. Still, most marriages were monogamous, and marital fidelity was taken seriously.

The relative availability of cultivable land in the region may help explain the absence of joint families. Joint families under patriarchal leadership tend to be found in areas where land is scarce and individual families must work together to conserve resources and maximize income. With the exception of a few crowded river valleys, few areas in Southeast Asia had a high population density per acre of cultivable land. Throughout most of the area, water was plentiful, and the land was relatively fertile. In parts of Indonesia, it was possible to survive by living off the produce of wild fruit trees—bananas, coconuts, mangoes, and a variety of other tropical fruits.

World of the Spirits: Religious Belief

Indian religions also had a profound effect on Southeast Asia. Traditional religious beliefs in the region took the familiar form of spirit worship and animism that we have seen in other cultures. Southeast Asians believed that spirits dwelled in the mountains, rivers, streams, and other sacred places in their environment. Mountains were probably particularly sacred, since they were considered to be the abode of ancestral spirits, the place to which the souls of all the departed would retire after death.

When Hindu and Buddhist ideas began to penetrate the area early in the first millennium C.E., they exerted a strong appeal among local elites. Not only did the new doctrines offer a more convincing explanation of the nature of the cosmos, but they also provided local rulers with a means of enhancing their prestige and power and conferred an aura of legitimacy on their relations with their subjects. In the Javanese kingdoms and in Angkor, Hindu gods like Vishnu and Siva provided a new and more sophisticated veneer for existing beliefs in nature deities and ancestral spirits. In Angkor, the king's duties included performing sacred rituals on the mountain in the capital city; in time the ritual became a state cult uniting Hindu gods with local nature deities and ancestral spirits in a complex pantheon.

This state cult, financed by the royal court, eventually led to the construction of temples throughout the country. Many of these temples housed thousands of priests and retainers and amassed great wealth, including vast estates farmed by local peasants. It has been estimated that there were as many as 300,000 priests in Angkor at the height of its power. This vast wealth, which was often exempt from taxes, may be one explanation for the gradual decline of Angkor in the thirteenth and fourteenth centuries.

Initially, the spread of Hindu and Buddhist doctrines was essentially an elite phenomenon. Although the common people participated in the state cult and helped construct the temples, they did not give up their traditional beliefs in local deities and ancestral spirits. A major transformation began in the eleventh century, however, when Theravada Buddhism began to penetrate the kingdom of Pagan in mainland Southeast Asia from the island of Sri Lanka. From Pagan, it spread rapidly to other areas in Southeast Asia and eventually became the religion of the masses throughout the mainland west of the Annamite Mountains.

Theravada's appeal to the peoples of Southeast Asia is reminiscent of the original attraction of Buddhist thought centuries earlier on the Indian subcontinent. By teaching that individuals could seek *Nirvana* through their own actions rather than through the intercession of the ruler or a priest, Theravada was more accessible to the masses than were the state cults promoted by the rulers. During the next centuries, Theravada gradually undermined the influence of state-supported religions and became the dominant faith in several mainland societies, including Burma, Thailand, Laos, and Cambodia. In the process, however, it was gradually appropriated by local rulers, who portrayed themselves as "immanent Buddhas," higher than ordinary mortals on the scale of human existence.

Theravada did not penetrate far into the Malay peninsula or the Indonesian island chain, perhaps because it

THE BAYON AT ANGKOR. Whereas Angkor Wat was dedicated to Hindu mythology, the Bayon Temple was a Buddhist structure. In addition to its extraordinary bas-reliefs, which illuminate the everyday life of thirteenth-century Cambodia, the Bayon is known for its huge heads of the Bodhisattva of Mercy. These 172 giant heads, looking in all four cardinal directions for souls to save, are reputedly modeled after the monarch Jayavarman, whose conversion from Hinduism to Buddhism as an adult contributed to the mixture of architectural styles in the temple. The faces are mesmerizing with their haunting smiles, reflecting the mystery of enlightenment.

entered Southeast Asia through Burma further to the north. But the Malay world found its own popular alternative to state religions when Islam began to enter the area in the thirteenth and fourteenth centuries. Because Islam's expansion into Southeast Asia took place for the most part after 1500, its emergence as a major force in the region will be discussed in a later chapter.

Not surprisingly, Indian influence extended to the Buddhist and Hindu temples of Southeast Asia. Temple architecture reflecting Gupta or southern Indian styles began to appear in Southeast Asia during the first centuries C.E. Most famous is the Buddhist temple at Borobudur, in central Java. Begun in the late eighth century at the behest of a king of Sailendra (an agricultural kingdom based in eastern Java), Borobudur is a massive stupa with nine terraces. Sculpted on the sides of each terrace are bas-reliefs depicting the nine stages in the life of Siddhartha Gautama, from childhood to his final release from the chain of human existence. Surmounted by hollow bell-like towers containing representations of the Buddha and capped by a single stupa, the entire structure dominates the landscape for miles around.

Second only to Borobudur in technical excellence and even more massive in size are the ruins of the old capital city of Angkor Thom. The temple of Angkor Wat is the most famous and arguably the most beautiful of all the existing structures at Angkor Thom. Built on the model of the legendary Mount Meru (the home of the gods in Hindu tradition), it combines Indian architectural techniques with native inspiration in a structure of impressive delicacy and grace.

With its over six hundred years of existence, Angkor Thom serves as a bridge between the Hindu and Buddhist architectural styles. The last of its great temples, known as the Bayon, followed the earlier Hindu model but was topped with sculpted towers containing four-sided representations of a bodhisattva, searching, it is said, for souls to save. Shortly after the Bayon was built, Theravada Buddhist societies in Burma and Thailand began to create a new Buddhist architecture based on the concept of a massive stupa surmounted by a spire. Most famous, perhaps, is the Shwedagon Pagoda in Rangoon, Burma, which is covered with gold leaf contributed by devout Buddhists from around the country.

THE TEMPLE OF BOROBUDUR. The colossal pyramid temple at Borobudur, on the island of Java, is one of the greatest Buddhist monuments. Constructed in the eighth century, it depicts the path to spiritual enlightenment in stone. The reliefs along the lowest walls depict the world of desire, while the higher levels represent the world of the spirit, culminating at the summit with the empty and closed stupa, signifying the state of Nirvana. Shortly after it was built, Borobudur was abandoned, as a new ruler switched his allegiance to Hinduism and ordered the erection of the Hindu temple of Prambanan nearby. Buried for a thousand years under volcanic ash and jungle, Borobudur was rediscovered in the nineteenth century and recently restored to its former splendor.

FOLLOWERS OF THE BUDDHA AT BOROBUDUR. Although the primary purpose of the stone carvings on the walls of the temple at Borobudur was to transmit the life of the Buddha, to modern viewers they are an important source of information about life in early Southeast Asia. Intricate bas-relief sculptures decorating the lower levels of the temple reveal the customs and costumes of eighth-century Java. Here followers of Siddhartha Gautama seek enlightenment under the Bodhi tree.

CONCLUSION

During the more than 1,500 years from the fall of the Mauryas to the rise of the Mughals, Indian civilization faced a number of severe challenges. One challenge was primarily external in nature and took the form of a continuous threat from beyond the mountains in the northwest. A second was generated by internal causes and stemmed from the tradition of factionalism and internal rivalry that had marked relations within the aristocracy since the Aryan invasion in the second millennium B.C.E. (see Chapter 2). Despite the abortive efforts of the Guptas, that tradition continued almost without interruption down to the founding of the Mughal Empire in the sixteenth century.

The third challenge was primarily cultural and appeared in the religious divisions between Hindus and Buddhists, and later between Hindus and Muslims, that took place throughout much of this period. It is a measure of the strength and resilience of Hindu tradition that it was able to surmount the challenge of Buddhism and by the late first millennium C.E. had managed to reassert its dominant position in Indian society. But that triumph was short-lived. One result of the foreign conquest of northern India was the introduction of Islam into the region. As we shall see later, the new religion was about to become a serious rival to traditional beliefs among the Indian people.

During the same period that Indian civilization faced these challenges at home, it was having a profound impact on the emerging states of Southeast Asia. Situated at the crossroads between two oceans and two great civilizations, Southeast Asia has long served as a bridge linking peoples and cultures, and as complex societies began to develop in the area, it is not surprising that they were strongly influenced by the older civilizations of neighboring China and India. At the same time, the Southeast Asian peoples put their own unique stamp on the ideas that they adopted and eventually rejected those that were inappropriate to local conditions.

The result was a region characterized by an almost unparalleled cultural richness and diversity, reflecting influences from as far away as the Middle East, yet preserving indigenous elements that were deeply rooted in the local culture. Unfortunately, that very diversity posed potential problems for the peoples of Southeast Asia as they faced a new challenge from beyond the horizon. We shall deal with that challenge when we return to the region in a later chapter. In the meantime, we must turn our attention to the other major civilization that spread its shadow over the societies of southern Asia—that of China.

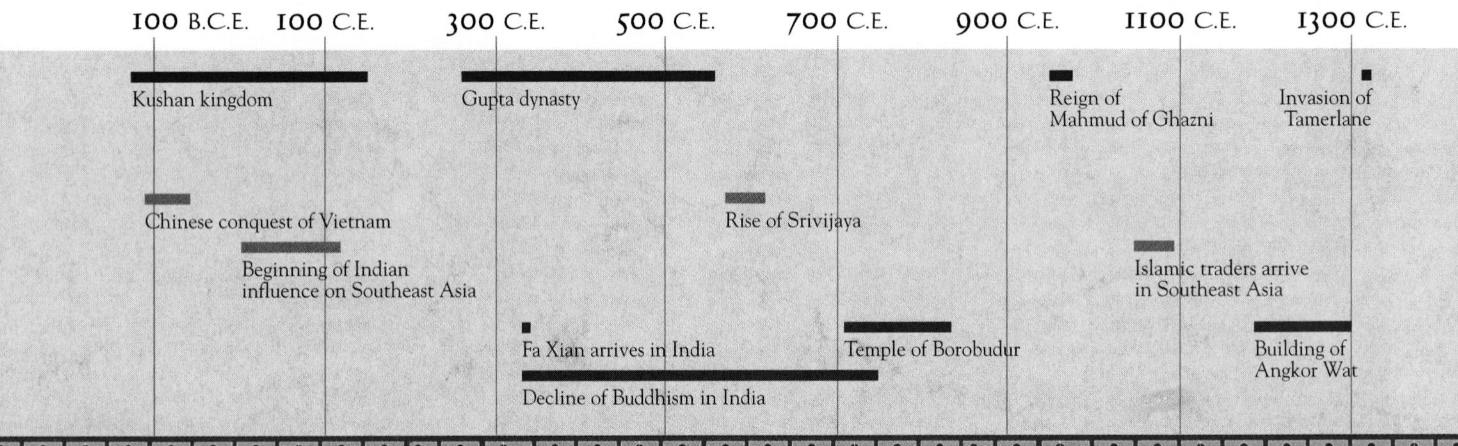

Chapter Notes

1. Hiuen Tsiang, *Si-Yu-Ki: Buddhist Records of the Western World,* trans. Samuel Beal (London, n.d.), pp. 89–90.
2. Fo-Kwo-Ki (Travels of Fa Xian), in ibid., Chapter 20, xliii.
3. E. C. Sachau, *Alberoni's India* (London, 1914), 1:22, quoted in S. M. Ikram, *Muslim Civilization in India* (New York, 1964), pp. 31–32.
4. Ibid., p. 68.
5. Hieun Tsiang, *Si-Yu-Ki,* pp. 73–74.
6. Duarte Barbosa, *The Book of Duarte Barbosa* (Nedeln, Lichtenstein, 1967), pp. 147–48.
7. Quoted in Richard Lannoy, *The Speaking Tree: A Study of Indian Culture and Society* (London, 1971), p. 232.
8. S. Tharu and K. Lalita, *Women Writing in India,* vol. I (New York, 1991), p. 77.
9. Cited in A. L. Basham, *The Wonder That Was India* (London, 1954), p. 426.
10. S. Hughes and B. Hughes, *Women in World History,* vol. I (Armonk, N.Y., 1995), p. 217.

Suggested Readings

The period from the decline of the Mauryas to the rise of the Mughals in India is not especially rich in terms of materials in English. Still, a number of the standard texts on Indian history contain useful sections on the period. Particularly good are A. L. Basham, *The Wonder That Was India* (London, 1954), and S. Wolpert, *New History of India* (New York, 1989).

A number of studies of Indian society and culture deal with this period. See, for example, R. Lannoy, *The Speaking Tree* (Oxford, 1971) for a sophisticated interpretation of Indian culture during the medieval period. On Buddhism, see H. Nakamura, *Indian Buddhism: A Survey with Bibliographical Notes* (Delhi, 1987), and H. Akira, *A History of Indian Buddhism from Sakyamuni to Early Mahayana* (Hawaii, 1990). For an interesting treatment of the Buddhist influence on commercial activities that is reminiscent of the role of Christianity in Europe, see L. Xinru, *Ancient India and Ancient China: Trade and Religious Changes* A.D. *1–600* (Delhi, 1988).

For a discussion of women's issues, see S. Hughes and B. Hughes, *Women in World History,* vol. I (Armonk, N.Y., 1995); S. Tharu and K. Lalita, *Women Writing in India,* vol. I (New York, 1991); and V. Dehejia, *Devi: The Great Goddess* (Washington, D.C., 1999).

The most up-to-date treatment of the Indian economy and, in particular, the regional trade throughout the Indian Ocean is K. N. Chaudhuri, *Trade and Civilization in the Indian Ocean: An Economic History from the Rise of Islam to 1750* (Cambridge, 1985), a groundbreaking comparative study. See also his more recent and massive *Asia Before Europe: Economy and Civilization of the Indian Ocean from the Rise of Islam to 1750* (Cambridge, 1990), which owes a considerable debt to F. Braudel's classical work on the Mediterranean Sea.

The Islamic period in Indian history is treated in S. M. Ikram, *Muslim Civilization in India* (New York, 1964), and C. E. Bosworth, *The Later Ghaznavids: Splendour and Decay* (New York, 1977). On the career of Tamerlane, see B. F. Manz, *The Rise and Rule of Tamerlane* (Cambridge, 1989).

For Indian art during the medieval period, see S. Huntington, *The Art of Ancient India: Buddhist, Hindu and Jain* (New York, 1985), and V. Dehejia, *Indian Art* (London, 1997).

For a brief introduction to Indian literature, see A. L. Basham, *A Cultural History of India* (Oxford, 1975). See also E. C. Dimock, *The Literature of India: An Introduction* (Chicago, 1974), and A. K. Warder, *Indian Kavya Literature*, 5 vols. (Delhi, 1972–1988). For Kalidasa, consult B. S. Miller, ed., *Theater of Memory: The Plays of Kalidasa* (New York, 1984).

The early history of Southeast Asia is not as well documented as that of China or India. Except for Vietnam, where histories written in Chinese appeared shortly after the Chinese conquest, written materials on societies in the region are relatively sparse. Historians have therefore been compelled to rely on stone inscriptions and the accounts of travelers and historians from other countries. Still, a number of us m are now dated in the light of recent information but still provide a useful overview. The most detailed is D. G. E. Hall, *A History of South-east Asia* (New York, 1966). See also J. F. Cady, *Southeast Asia: Its Historical Development* (New York, 1964). For a more recent account, see D. R. SarDesai, *Southeast Asia: Past and Present* (Boulder, Colo., 1989). For a useful survey of the ethnographic background, see R. Provencher, *Mainland Southeast Asia: An Anthropological Perspective* (Pacific Palisades, Calif., 1975). R. Burling, *Hill Farms and Padi Fields: Life in Mainland Southeast Asia* (Englewood Cliffs, N.J., 1965) provides a short discussion of the dynamic forces that have shaped the mainland societies in the region. See also P. Wheatley, *The Golden Khersonese: Studies in the Historical Geography of the Malay Peninsula Before* A.D. *1500* (Kuala Lumpur, 1961).

Working with limited resources, modern scholars are bringing out some fascinating interpretations of the early history of the region. An extensive analysis of the "Indianized" states of mainland Southeast Asia is available in G. Coedes, *The Making of Southeast Asia* (Berkeley, Calif., 1966). More recently, some scholars have tended to emphasize the role of indigenous forces in the evolution of the region. See, for example, O. W. Wolters, *Early Indonesian Commerce: A Study of the Origins of Sri Vijaya* (Ithaca, N.Y., 1967), and *The Fall of Srivijaya in Malay History* (Ithaca, N.Y., 1970).

The role of commerce has recently been highlighted as a key aspect in the development of the region. For two fascinating accounts, see K. R. Hall, *Maritime Trade and State Development in Early Southeast Asia* (Honolulu, 1985), and A. Reid, *Southeast Asia in the Era of Commerce, 1450–1680: The Lands Below the Winds* (New Haven, Conn., 1989). The latter is also quite useful on the role of women.

The nature of kingship has attracted attention from scholars in recent years. K. R. Hall and J. K. Whitmore, eds., *Explorations in Early Southeast Asian History: The Origins of Southeast Asian Statecraft* (Ann Arbor, Mich., 1976), and L. Gesick, ed., *Centers, Symbols, and Hierarchies: Essays on the Classical States of Southeast Asia* (New Haven, Conn., 1983) provide interesting essays on the subject. See also L. Castles and A. Reid, eds., *Pre-Colonial State Systems in Southeast Asia* (Kuala Lumpur, 1975).

For additional reading, go to InfoTrac College Edition, your online research library at http://web1.infotrac-college.com

Enter the search terms "India history" using Keywords.

Enter the search term "Hinduism" using the Subject Guide.

Enter the search term "Buddhism" using the Subject Guide.

Enter the search term "Tamerlane" using Keywords.

CHAPTER 10

FROM THE TANG TO THE MONGOLS: THE FLOWERING OF TRADITIONAL CHINA

CHAPTER OUTLINE

- CHINA AFTER THE HAN
- CHINA REUNIFIED: THE SUI, THE TANG, AND THE SONG
- EXPLOSION IN CENTRAL ASIA: THE MONGOL EMPIRE
- IN SEARCH OF THE WAY
- THE APOGEE OF CHINESE CULTURE
- CONCLUSION

FOCUS QUESTIONS

- How did Chinese historians traditionally view Chinese history, and has this view of China's past been challenged in any ways?
- What major changes in political structures and social and economic life occurred during the Sui, Tang, and Song dynasties?
- Why were the Mongols able to amass an empire, and what were the main characteristics of their rule in China?
- What roles did Buddhism, Daoism, and Neo-Confucianism play in Chinese intellectual life in the period between the Sui dynasty and the Ming?
- What were the main achievements in Chinese literature and art in the period between the Tang dynasty and the Ming, and what technological innovations and intellectual developments contributed to these achievements?

On his first visit to the city, the traveler was mightily impressed. Its streets were so straight and wide that he could see through the city from one end to the other. Along the wide boulevards were beautiful palaces and inns in great profusion. The city was laid out in squares "like a chessboard," and within each square were spacious courts and gardens. Truly, said the visitor, this must be one of the largest and wealthiest cities on earth—a city so splendid that "it is impossible to give a description that should do it justice."[1]

The visitor was Marco Polo, and the city was Khanbaliq (later known as Beijing), capital of the Yuan dynasty (1279–1368) and one of the great commercial centers of the Chinese Empire. Marco Polo was an Italian merchant who had traveled to China in the late thirteenth century and then served as an official at the court of Khubilai Khan. His diary, published after his return to Italy almost twenty years later, astonished readers with tales of this magnificent but unknown civilization far to the east.

When Marco Polo arrived, China was ruled by the Mongols, a nomadic people from Central Asia who had overthrown the Song (Sung) dynasty and assumed control of the Chinese Empire. The Yuan dynasty, as the Mongol rulers were called, was only one of a succession of dynasties to rule China after the collapse of the Han dynasty in the third century C.E. The end of the Han had led to a period of internal division and civil war that lasted nearly four hundred years and was aggravated by the threat posed by nomadic peoples from the north. This time of troubles ended in the early seventh century C.E., however, when the dynamic Tang dynasty led China to some of its finest achievements.

To this point, Chinese history appeared to be following a pattern similar to that of India. There, as we have seen, the passing of the Mauryan dynasty in the second century B.C.E. unleashed a period of internal division that lasted for several hundred years. Although the Guptas were able to revive the magnificence of India's first golden age, their glorious era soon flickered and died, and it was not until the rise of the Mughal Empire in the early sixteenth century that unity returned to the subcontinent.

But China did not recapitulate the Indian experience. The Tang dynasty collapsed in 907, but after a brief interregnum, China was reunified under the Song, who ruled most of China for nearly three hundred years. The Song in turn were overthrown by the Mongols in the late thirteenth century, and they in turn gave way to a powerful new native dynasty, the Ming, in 1368. Dynasty followed dynasty, with periods of extraordinary cultural achievement alternating with periods of internal disorder, but in general Chinese society continued to build on the political and cultural foundations of the Zhou and the Han.

Chinese historians, viewing this vast process as it evolved over time, began to hypothesize that Chinese history was cyclical in nature, driven by the dynamic interplay of the forces of good and evil, *yang* and *yin*, growth and decay. Beyond the forces of conflict and change lay the essential continuity of Chinese history, based on the timeless principles established by Confucius and other thinkers during the Zhou dynasty in antiquity. If India often appeared to be a politically and culturally diverse entity, only sporadically knit together by ambitious rulers, China, at least in the eyes of its historians, was a coherent civilization struggling to relive the glories of its ancient golden age while contending against the divisive forces of *yin* and *yang* operating throughout the cosmos. In actuality, this picture of a succession of dynasties each seeking to replicate the glories of China's golden age under the early Zhou dynasty disguises the reality that under the surface Chinese society was undergoing significant changes and bore scant resemblance to the kingdom that had been founded by the house of Zhou more than twenty centuries earlier.

China After the Han

After the collapse of the Han dynasty at the beginning of the third century C.E., China fell into an extended period of division and civil war. Taking advantage of the absence of organized government in China, nomadic forces from the Gobi Desert penetrated south of the Great Wall and established their own rule over northern China. In the Yangtze valley and further to the south, native Chinese rule was maintained, but constant civil war and instability led later historians to refer to the period as the "era of the six dynasties."

The decline and fall of the Han Empire had a marked effect on the Chinese psyche. The Confucian principles that emphasized hard work, the subordination of the individual to community interests, and belief in the essentially rational order of the universe came under severe challenge, and many Chinese began to turn to more messianic creeds that emphasized the supernatural or the promise of earthly or heavenly salvation. Intellectuals began to reject the stuffy moralism and complacency of State Confucianism and sought emotional satisfaction in hedonistic pursuits or philosophical Daoism (see the box on p. 269).

Eccentric behavior and a preference for philosophical Daoism became a common response to a corrupt age. A group of writers known as the "seven sages of the bamboo forest" exemplified the period. Among the best known was the poet Liu Ling, whose odd behavior is described in this oft-quoted passage:

> Liu Ling was an inveterate drinker and indulged himself to the full. Sometimes he stripped off his clothes and sat in his room stark naked. Some men saw him and rebuked him. Liu Ling said, "Heaven and earth are my dwelling, and my house is my trousers. Why are you all coming into my trousers?"[2]

But neither popular beliefs in the supernatural nor philosophical Daoism could satisfy deeper emotional needs or provide solace in time of sorrow or the hope of a better life in the hereafter. Instead, Buddhism filled that gap.

Buddhism was brought to China in the first or second century C.E., probably by missionaries and merchants traveling over the Silk Road. The concept of rebirth was probably unfamiliar to most Chinese, and the intellectual hairsplitting that often accompanied discussion of Buddha's message in India was somewhat too esoteric for the Chinese taste. Still, in the difficult years surrounding the decline of the Han dynasty, Buddhist ideas, especially those of the Mahayana school, began to find adherents among intellectuals and ordinary people alike. As Buddhism increased in popularity, it was frequently attacked by supporters of Confucianism and Daoism for its foreign origins. Some even claimed that Gautama Buddha had been a disciple of Lao Tzu. But such sniping did not halt the progress of Buddhism, and eventually the new faith was assimilated into Chinese culture, assisted by the efforts of such tireless advocates as the missionaries Fa Xian and Xuan Zang and the support of ruling elites in both northern and southern China (see The Rise and Decline of Buddhism and Daoism later in this chapter).

THE BUDDHIST PILGRIM XUAN ZANG. Although the first recorded Buddhist pilgrimage from China across Central Asia to India was that of Fa Xian in 399 C.E., the seventh century was the golden age of these religious pilgrimages. The most famous was that of Xuan Zang, whose sixteen-year journey was recorded by a disciple: "Alone and abandoned he traversed the sandy waste . . . following the heaps of bones and horse-dung." Here Xuan Zang holds a fly whisk in his left hand to drive away demons, while in his right he brandishes the khakkhara, a symbol of the Buddhist monk. With sacred texts on his back and a hat against the desert sun, Xuan Zang proceeds on his pilgrimage protected by the image of the Lord Buddha.

China Reunified: The Sui, the Tang, and the Song

After nearly four centuries of internal division, China was unified once again in 581 when Yang Jian (Yang Chien), a member of a respected aristocratic family in northern China, founded a new dynasty, known as the Sui (581–618 C.E.). Yang Jian (who is also known by his reign title of Sui Wendi, or Sui Wen Ti) established his capital at the historic metropolis of Chang'an and began to extend his authority throughout the heartland of China.

Like his predecessors, the new emperor sought to create a unifying ideology for the state to enhance its efficiency. But where Liu Bang, the founder of the Han dynasty, had adopted Confucianism as the official doctrine to hold the empire together, Yang Jian turned to Daoism and Buddhism. He founded monasteries for both doctrines in the capital and appointed Buddhist monks to key positions as political advisers.

A DAOIST CRITIQUE OF CONFUCIANISM

This document is a biting Daoist attack on the type of pompous and hypocritical Confucian "gentleman" who feigned high moral principles while secretly engaging in corrupt and licentious behavior. It was written during the chaotic period following the collapse of the Han dynasty, in the third century C.E.

THE BIOGRAPHY OF A GREAT MAN

What the world calls a gentleman [chun-tzu] is someone who is solely concerned with moral law [fa], and cultivates exclusively the rules of propriety [li]. His hand holds the emblem of jade [authority]; his foot follows the straight line of the rule. He likes to think that his actions set a permanent example; he likes to think that his words are everlasting models. In his youth, he has a reputation in the villages of his locality; in his later years, he is well known in the neighboring districts. Upward, he aspires to the dignity of the Three Dukes; downward, he does not disdain the post of governor of the nine provinces.

Have you ever seen the lice that inhabit a pair of trousers? They jump into the depths of the seams, hiding themselves in the cotton wadding, and believe they have a pleasant place to live. Walking, they do not risk going beyond the edge of the seam; moving, they are careful not to emerge from the trouser leg; and they think they have kept to the rules of etiquette. But when the trousers are ironed, the flames invade the hills, the fire spreads, the villages are set on fire and the towns burned down; then the lice that inhabit the trousers cannot escape.

What difference is there between the gentleman who lives within a narrow world and the lice that inhabit trouser legs?

Yang Jian was a builder as well as a conqueror, ordering the construction of a new canal from the capital to the confluence of the Wei and the Yellow Rivers nearly one hundred miles to the east. His son, the emperor Sui Yangdi (Sui Yang Ti), continued the process, and the 1,400-mile-long Grand Canal, linking the two great rivers of China, the Yellow and the Yangtze, was completed during his reign. The new canal facilitated the shipment of grain and other commodities from the rice-rich southern provinces to the densely populated north. The canal also served other purposes, such as speeding communications between the two regions and permitting the rapid dispatch of troops to troubled provinces. Sui Yangdi also used the canal as an imperial highway for inspecting his empire. One imperial procession from the capital to the central Yangtze region was described as follows:

> The emperor caused to be built dragon boats, . . . red battle cruisers, multi-decked transports, lesser vessels of bamboo slats. Boatmen hired from all the waterways . . . pulled the vessels by ropes of green silk on the imperial progress to Chiang-tu [Yangzhou]. The Emperor rode in the dragon boat, and civil and military officials of the fifth grade and above rode in the multi-decked transports; those of the ninth grade and above were given the vessels of yellow bamboo. The boats followed one another poop to prow for more than 200 leagues [about 65 miles]. The prefectures and counties through which they passed were ordered to prepare to offer provisions. Those who made bountiful arrangements were given an additional office or title; those who fell short were given punishments up to the death penalty.[3]

Despite such efforts to project the majesty of the imperial personage, the Sui dynasty came to an end immediately after Sui Yangdi's death. The Sui emperor was a tyrannical ruler, and his expensive military campaigns aroused widespread unrest. After his return from a failed campaign against Korea in 618, the emperor was murdered in his palace. One of his generals, Li Yuan, took advantage of the instability that ensued and declared the foundation of a new dynasty, known as the Tang (T'ang). Building on the successes of its predecessor, the Tang lasted for three hundred years, until 907.

Li Yuan ruled for a brief period and then was elbowed aside by his son, Li Shimin (Li Shih-min), who assumed the reign title Tang Taizong (T'ang T'ai-tsung). Under his vigorous leadership, the Tang launched a program of internal renewal and external expansion that would make it one of the greatest dynasties in the long history of China. Under the Tang, the northwest was pacified and given the name of Xinjiang, or "new region." A long conflict with Tibet led for the first time to the extension of Chinese control over the vast and desolate plateau north of the Himalaya Mountains. The southern provinces below the Yangtze were fully assimilated into the Chinese Empire, and the imperial court established commercial and diplomatic relations with the states of Southeast Asia. With reason, China now claimed to be the foremost power in East Asia, and the emperor demanded fealty and tribute from all his fellow rulers beyond the frontier. Korea accepted tribute status and attempted to adopt the Chinese model, and the Japanese dispatched official missions to China to learn more about its customs and institutions (see Chapter 11).

Finally, the Tang dynasty witnessed a flowering of Chinese culture. Many modern observers feel that the era represents the apogee of Chinese creativity in poetry and sculpture. One reason for this explosion of culture was the influence of Buddhism, which affected art, literature, and philosophy, as well as religion and politics. Monasteries

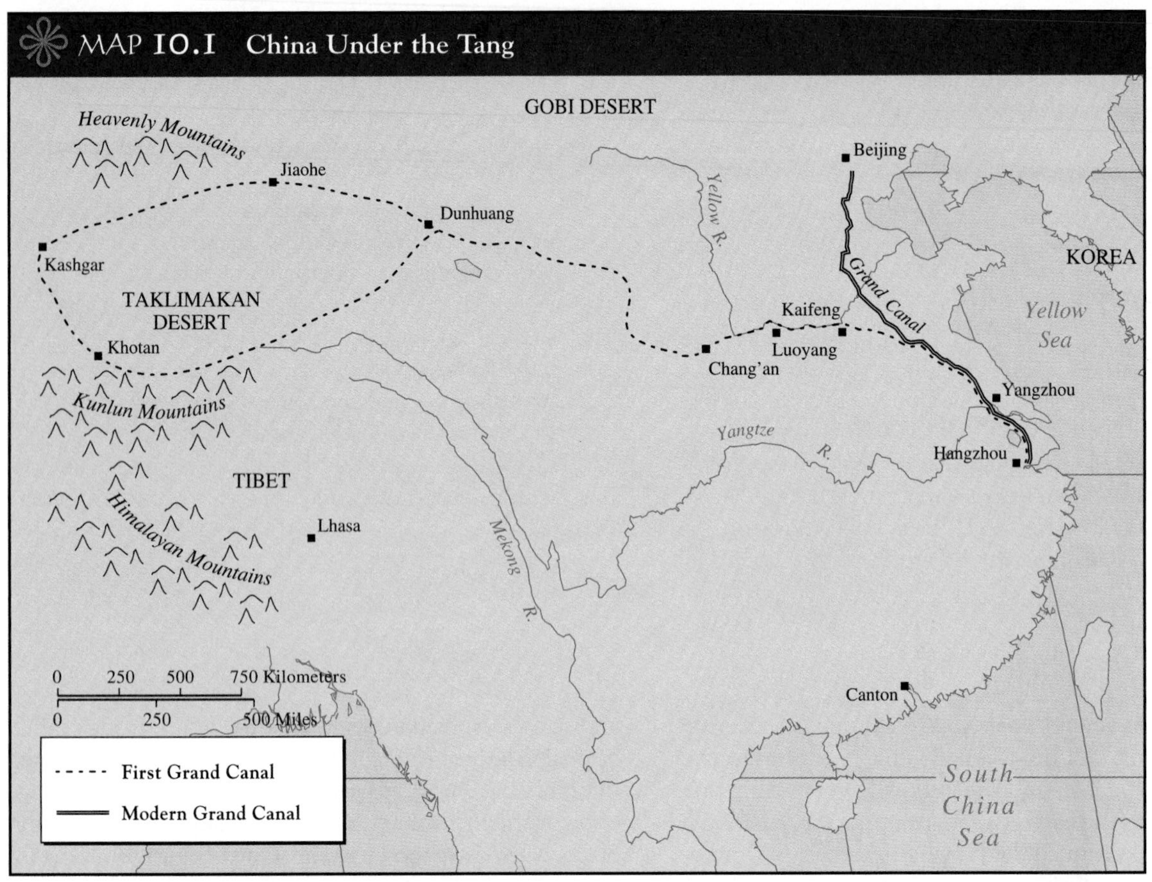

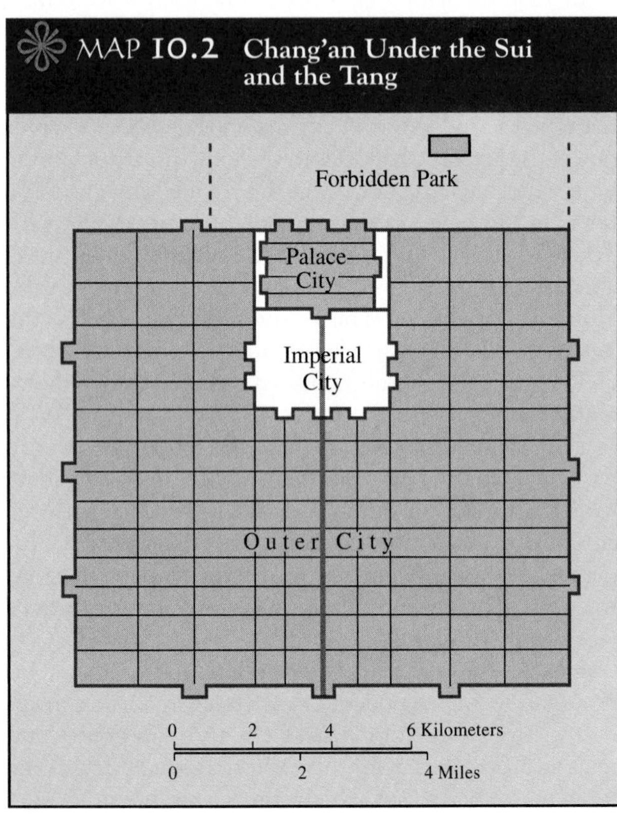

sprang up throughout China, and (as under the Sui) Buddhist monks served as advisers at the Tang imperial court. The city of Chang'an, now restored to the glory it had known as the capital of the Han dynasty, once again became the seat of the empire. It was possibly the greatest city in the world of its time, with an estimated population of nearly two million. The city was filled with temples and palaces, and its markets teemed with goods from all over the known world (see the box on p. 271).

But the Tang, like the Han, sowed the seeds of their own destruction. Tang rulers could not prevent the rise of internal forces that would ultimately weaken the dynasty and bring it to an end. Two ubiquitous problems were court intrigues and official corruption. Xuanzong (Hsuan Tsung, who reigned from 712 to 756), one of the great Tang emperors and a renowned patron of the arts, was dominated in later life by one of his favorite concubines, the beautiful Yang Guifei (Yang Kuei-fei). One of her protégés launched a rebellion in 755 and briefly seized power in the capital of Chang'an. The revolt was eventually suppressed, and Yang Guifei, who is viewed as one of the great villains of Chinese history, was put to death. But the Tang never fully recovered from the catastrophe. The loss of power by the central government led to increased influence by great landed families inside China and chronic instability along

THE GOOD LIFE IN THE HIGH TANG

At the height of the Tang dynasty, China was at the apex of its power and magnificence. Here the Tang poet Du Fu describes a gala festival in the capital of Chang'an (Ch'ang-an) attended by the favored elite. The author's distaste for the spectacle of arrogance and waste is expressed in muted sarcasm.

DU FU, A POEM

Third day of the third month
The very air seems new
In Ch'ang-an along the water
Many beautiful girls . . .
Firm, plump contours,
Flesh and bone proportioned.
Dresses of gauze brocade
Mirror the end of spring
Peacocks crimped in thread of gold
Unicorns in silver. . . .
Some are kin to the imperial favorite
Among them the Lady of Kuo and the Lady of Ch'in [Qin].
Camel-humps of purple meat
Brought in shining pans
The white meat of raw fish
Served on crystal platters
Don't tempt the sated palate.
All that is cut with fancy and
Prepared with care—left untouched.
Eunuchs, reins a-flying
Disturb no dust
Bring the "eight chef d'oeuvres"
From the palace kitchens.
Music of strings and pipes . . .
Accompanying the feasting
Moving the many guests
All of rank and importance.
Last comes a horseman
See him haughtily
Dismount near the screen
And step on the flowery carpet. . . .
The chancellor is so powerful
His mere touch will scorch
Watch you don't come near
Lest you displease him.

the northern and western frontiers, where local military commanders ruled virtually without central government interference. It was an eerie repetition of the final decades of the Han.

The end finally came in the early tenth century, when border troubles with northern nomadic peoples increased, leading to the final collapse of the dynasty in 907. The Tang had followed the classic strategy of "using a barbarian to oppose a barbarian" by allying with a new nomadic people called the Uighurs (a Turkic-speaking people whose descendants continue to live throughout Central Asia) against their old rivals. But yet another nomadic people called the Kirghiz defeated the Uighurs and then turned on the Tang government in its moment of weakness and overthrew it.

For two generations, China slipped once again into chaos. This time, the period of foreign invasion and division was much shorter. In 960 a new dynasty, known as the Song (960–1279), rose to power. From the start, however, the Song (Sung) rulers encountered more problems than their predecessors. Although the founding emperor Song Taizu (Sung T'ai-tsu) was able to co-opt many of the powerful military commanders whose rivalry had brought the Tang dynasty to an end, he was unable to reconquer the northwestern part of the country from the nomadic Khitan peoples. The emperor therefore established his capital further to the east, at Kaifeng, where the Grand Canal intersected the Yellow River. Later, when pressures from the nomads in the north increased, the court was forced to move the capital even further south, to Hangzhou (Hangchow), on the coast just south of the Yangtze River delta; the emperors who ruled from Hangzhou are known as the southern Song. The Song also lost control over Tibet. Despite its political and military weaknesses, the dynasty nevertheless ruled during a period of economic expansion, prosperity, and cultural achievement and is therefore considered among the more successful Chinese dynasties.

Yet the Song dynasty was never able to surmount the external challenge from the north, and that failure eventually brought about the end of the dynasty. During its final decades, the Song rulers were forced to pay tribute to the Jurchen peoples from Manchuria. In the early thirteenth century, the Song, ignoring precedent and the fate of the Tang, formed an alliance with the Mongols, a new and obscure nomadic people from the Gobi Desert. As under the Tang, the decision proved to be a disaster. Within a few years, the Mongols had become a much more serious threat to China than the Jurchen. After defeating the Jurchen, the Mongols turned their attention to the Song, advancing on Song territory from both the north and the west. By this time, the Song empire had been weakened by internal factionalism and a loss of tax revenue to wealthy families. After a series of river battles and sieges marked by the use of catapults and gunpowder, the Song were defeated, and the conquerors announced the creation of a new Yuan (Mongol) dynasty. Ironically, the Mongols had first learned about gunpowder from the Chinese (see Explosion in Central Asia: The Mongol Empire later in this chapter).

Political Structures: The Triumph of Confucianism

During the nearly seven hundred years from the Sui to the end of the Song, a mature political system based on principles originally established during the Qin and Han dynasties gradually emerged in China. After the Tang dynasty's brief flirtation with Buddhism, State Confucianism became the ideological cement that held the system together. The development of this system took several centuries, and it did not reach its height until the period of the Song dynasty.

EQUAL OPPORTUNITY IN CHINA: THE CIVIL SERVICE EXAMINATION

At the apex of the government hierarchy was a Grand Council, assisted by a secretariat and a chancellery; it included representatives from all three authorities—civil, military, and censorate. Under the Grand Council was a Department of State Affairs composed of six ministries responsible for justice, military affairs, personnel, public works, revenue, and rites (ritual). This department was in effect the equivalent of a modern cabinet.

The Tang dynasty revived the practice of selecting bureaucrats through civil service examinations but was unable to curb the influence of the great aristocratic clans. The Song were more successful at limiting aristocratic control over the bureaucracy, in part because the power of the nobility had been irreparably weakened during the final years of the Tang dynasty and did not recover during the interregnum that followed its collapse.

One way of strengthening the power of the central administration was to make the civil service examination system into the primary route to an official career. To reduce the power of the noble families, relatives of individuals serving in the imperial court, as well as eunuchs, were prohibited from taking the examinations. But if the Song rulers' objective was to make the bureaucracy more subservient to the court, they may have been disappointed. The rising professionalism of the bureaucracy provided it with an esprit de corps and an influence that sometimes enabled it to resist the whims of individual emperors.

Under the Song, the examination system attained the form that it would retain in later centuries. In general, three levels of examinations were administered. The first was a qualifying examination given annually at the provincial capital. Candidates who succeeded in this first stage were considered qualified but normally were not given positions in the bureaucracy except at the local level. Many stopped at this level and accepted positions as vil-

CHRONOLOGY

MEDIEVAL CHINA

Arrival of Buddhism in China	c. first century C.E.
Fall of the Han dynasty	220 C.E.
Sui dynasty	581–618
Tang dynasty	618–907
Li Bo and Du Fu	700s
Emperor Xuanzong	712–756
Song dynasty	960–1279
Wang Anshi	1021–1086
Southern Song dynasty	1127–1279
Mongol conquest of China	1279
Reign of Khubilai Khan	1260–1294
Fall of the Yuan dynasty	1368
Ming dynasty	1369–1644

THE GRAND CANAL. Built over centuries, the Grand Canal is one of the wonders of China and a crucial conduit for carrying goods between northern and southern China. After the Song dynasty, when the region south of the Yangtze River became the heartland of the empire, the canal was used to carry rice and other agricultural products to the food-starved northern provinces. Many of the towns and cities located along the canal became famous for their wealth and cultural achievements. Among the most renowned was Suzhou, a center for silk manufacture, which is sometimes described as the "Venice of China" because of its many canals. Shown here is a classical example of a humpback bridge, crossing an arm of the canal in downtown Suzhou.

lage teachers to train other candidates. Candidates who wished to go on could take a second examination given at the provincial capital every three years. Successful candidates could apply for an official position. Some went on to take the final examination, which was given in the imperial capital, including a session at the imperial palace, once every three years. Those who passed were eligible for high positions in the central bureaucracy or for appointments as district magistrates.

During the early Tang the examinations included questions on Buddhist and Daoist as well as Confucian texts, but by Song times examinations were based entirely on the Confucian classics. Candidates were expected to memorize passages and to be able to define the moral lessons they contained. The system guaranteed that successful candidates—and therefore officials—would have received a full dose of Confucian political and social ethics. Whether they followed those ethics, of course, was another matter. Many students complained about the rigors of memorization and the irrelevance of the process. Others brought crib notes into the examination hall (one enterprising candidate concealed an entire Confucian text in the lining of his cloak). One famous Tang scholar complained that if Mencius and other Confucian worthies had lived in his own day, they would have refused to sit for the examinations.

The Song authorities ignored such criticisms, but they did open the system to more people by allowing all males except criminals or members of certain restricted occupations to take the examinations. To provide potential candidates with schooling, training academies were set up at the provincial and district level. Without such academies, only individuals fortunate enough to receive training in the classics in family-run schools would have had the expertise to pass the examinations. Such policies represented a considerable improvement over earlier times, when most candidates came from the ranks of the elite. According to one historian, more than half of the successful candidates during the mid-Song period came from families that had not previously had a successful candidate for at least three generations. In time, the majority of candidates came from the landed gentry, nonaristocratic landowners who controlled much of the wealth in the countryside. Because the gentry prized education and became the primary upholders of the Confucian tradition, they were often called the scholar-gentry.

But certain aspects of the system still prevented it from truly providing equal opportunity to all. In the first place, only males were eligible. Then again, the Song did not attempt to establish a system of universal elementary education. In practice, only those who had been given a basic education in the classics at home were able to enter the state-run academies and compete for a position in the bureaucracy. The poor had little chance.

Despite such weaknesses, the civil service examination system was an impressive achievement for its day and probably provided a more efficient government and more opportunity for upward mobility than were found in any other civilization of its time. Most Western governments, for example, only began to recruit officials on the basis of merit in the nineteenth century. Furthermore, by regulating the content of the examinations, the system helped provide China with a cultural uniformity lacking in empires elsewhere in Asia.

Nor could the system guarantee an honest, efficient bureaucracy. Official arrogance, bureaucratic infighting, corruption, and legalistic interpretations of government regulations were as prevalent in medieval China as in bureaucracies the world over. Another problem was that officials were expected to use their positions to help their relatives. As we observed earlier, even Confucius held that filial duty transcends loyalty to the community. What is nepotism in Western eyes was simply proper behavior in China. Chinese rulers attempted to circumvent this problem by assigning officials outside their home region, but this policy met with only limited success.

The court also attempted to curb official misbehavior through the censorate. These specially trained officials were assigned to investigate possible cases of official wrongdoing and report directly to the court. The censorate was supposed to be independent of outside pressures to ensure that its members would feel free to report wrongdoing wherever it occurred. In practice, censors who displeased high court officials were often removed or even subjected to more serious forms of punishment, which reduced the effectiveness of the system.

LOCAL GOVERNMENT

The Song dynasty maintained the local government institutions that it had inherited from its predecessors. At the base of the government pyramid was the district (or county), governed by a magistrate. The magistrate, assisted by his staff, was responsible for maintaining law and order and collecting taxes within his jurisdiction. A district could exceed 100,000 people. Below the district was the basic unit of Chinese government, the village. Because villages were so numerous in China, the central government did not appoint an official at that level and allowed the villages to administer themselves. Village government was normally in the hands of a village council of elders, usually assisted by a village chief. The council, usually made up of the heads of influential families in the village, maintained the local irrigation and transportation network, adjudicated local disputes, organized and maintained a militia, and assisted in collecting taxes and delivering them to the district magistrate.

As a rule, most Chinese had little involvement with government matters. When they had to deal with the government, they almost always turned to their village officials. Although the district magistrate was empowered to settle local civil disputes, most villagers preferred to resolve the problem among themselves. It was expected that the magistrate and his staff would supplement their income by charging for such services, a practice that reduced the costs of the central government but also provided an opportunity for bribes, a problem that plagued the Chinese bureaucracy down to modern times.

Economy and Society

During the long period between the Sui and the Song, the Chinese economy, like the government, grew considerably in size and complexity. China was still an agricultural society, but major changes were taking place within the economy and the social structure. The urban sector of the economy was becoming increasingly important, new social classes were beginning to appear, and the economic focus of the empire was beginning to shift from the Yellow River valley in the north to the Yangtze River valley in the center—a process that was encouraged both by the expansion of cultivation in the Yangtze delta and by the control exerted over the north by nomadic peoples during the Song.

The economic revival began shortly after the rise of the Tang. During the long period of internal division, land had become concentrated in the hands of aristocratic families, while most peasants were reduced to serfdom or slavery. The early Tang tried to reduce the power of the landed nobility and maximize tax revenue by adopting the ancient "equal field" system, in which land was allocated to farmers for life in return for an annual tax payment and three weeks of conscript labor.

At first the new system was vigorously enforced and led to increased rural prosperity and government revenue. But eventually the rich and the politically influential learned to manipulate the system for their own benefit and accumulated huge tracts of land. The growing population, caused by a rise in food production and the extended period of social stability, also put steady pressure on the system. Finally, the government abandoned the effort to equalize landholdings and returned the land to private hands, while attempting to prevent inequalities through the tax system. The failure to resolve the land problem contributed to the decline and fall of the Tang dynasty in the early tenth century.

The Song tried to resolve the land problem by returning to the successful programs of the early Tang and reducing the power of the wealthy landed aristocrats. During the late eleventh century, the reformist official Wang Anshi (Wang An-shih) attempted to limit the size of landholdings through progressive land taxes and provided cheap credit to poor peasants to help them avoid bankruptcy. His reforms met with some success, but other developments probably contributed more to the general agricultural prosperity under the Song. These included the opening of new lands in the Yangtze River valley, improvements in irrigation techniques such as the chain pump (a circular chain of square pallets on a treadmill that enabled farmers to lift considerable amounts of water or mud to a higher level), and the introduction of a new strain of quick-growing rice from Southeast Asia, which permitted farmers in warmer regions to plant and harvest two crops each year.

Major changes also took place in the Chinese urban economy, which witnessed a significant increase in trade and manufacturing. This process began under the Tang dynasty, but it was not entirely a product of deliberate state policy. In fact, early Tang rulers shared some of the traditional prejudice against commercial activities that had been prevalent under the Han and enacted a number of regulations that restricted trade. As under the Han, the state maintained monopolies over key commodities such as salt.

Despite the restrictive policies of the state, the urban sector grew steadily larger and more complex, helped by several new technological developments. During the Tang, the Chinese mastered the art of manufacturing steel by mixing cast iron and wrought iron. The blast furnace was heated to a high temperature by burning coal, which had been used as a fuel in China from about the fourth century C.E. The resulting product was used in the manufacture of swords, sickles, and even suits of armor. By the eleventh century, more than 35,000 tons of steel were being produced annually. The introduction of cotton offered new opportunities in textile manufacturing. Gunpowder was invented by the Chinese during the Tang dynasty and used primarily for explosives and a primitive form of flamethrower; it reached the West via the Arabs in the twelfth century.

OCEAN TRADE AND THE SILK ROAD

By the late Tang and the Song, the nature of trade was also changing. In the past, most long-distance trade had been undertaken by state monopoly. By the time of the Song, private commerce was being actively encouraged, and many merchants engaged in shipping as well as in wholesale and retail trade. Guilds began to appear, along with a new money economy. Paper currency began to be used in the eighth and ninth centuries. Credit (at first called "flying money") also made its first appearance during the Tang. With the increased circulation of paper money, banking began to develop, as merchants found that strings of copper coins were too cumbersome for their increasingly complex operations. Unfortunately, early issues of paper currency were not backed by metal coinage and led to price inflation. Equally useful, if more prosaic, was the invention of the abacus, an early form of calculator that simplified the calculations needed for commercial transactions.

Long-distance trade, both overland and by sea, expanded under the Tang and the Song. Trade with countries and peoples to the west had been carried on for centuries (see Chapter 3), but it had declined dramatically between the fourth and the sixth century C.E. as a result of the collapse of the Han and the Roman Empire. It began to revive with the rise of the Tang and the simultaneous unification of much of the Middle East under the Arabs. During the Tang era, the Silk Road revived and then reached its zenith. Much of the trade was carried by the Turkic-speaking Uighurs. During the Tang, Uighur caravans of two-humped Bactrian camels (a hardy variety native to Iran and regions to the northeast) carried goods back and forth between China and the countries of South Asia and the Middle East.

In actuality, the Silk Road was composed of a number of separate routes. The first to be used, probably because of the jade found in the mountains south of Khotan, ran along the southern rim of the Taklimakan Desert via Kashgar and thence through the Pamir Mountains into Bactria. The first Buddhist missionaries traveled this route from India to China. Eventually, however, this area began to dry up, and traders were forced to seek other routes. From a climatic standpoint, the best route for the Silk Road was to the north of the Tian Shan (Heavenly Mountains), where moisture-laden northwesterly winds created pastures where animals could graze. But the area was frequently infested by bandits who preyed on unwary travelers. Most caravans therefore followed the southern route, which passed along the northern fringes of the Taklimakan Desert to Kashgar and down into northwestern India. Travelers avoided the direct route through the desert (in the Uighur language, the name means "go in, and you won't come out") and trudged from oasis to oasis along the southern slopes of the Tian Shan. The oases were created by the water runoff from winter snows in the mountains, which then dried up in the searing heat of the desert.

The Silk Road was so hazardous that shipping goods by sea became increasingly popular. China had long been engaged in sea trade with other countries in the region, but most of the commerce was originally in the hands of Korean, Japanese, or Southeast Asian merchants. Chinese maritime trade, however, was stimulated by the invention of the compass and technical improvements in shipbuilding such as the widespread use of the sternpost rudder and the lug sail (which enabled ships to sail close to the wind). If Marco Polo's observations can be believed, by the thirteenth century Chinese junks had multiple sails and weighed up to two thousand tons, much larger than contemporary ships in the West. The Chinese governor of Canton in the early twelfth century remarked:

> According to the government regulations concerning seagoing ships, the larger ones can carry several hundred men, and the smaller ones may have more than a hundred men on board. . . . The ship's pilots are acquainted with the configuration of the coasts; at night they steer by the stars, and in the daytime by the Sun. In dark weather they look at the south-pointing needle. They also use a line a hundred feet long with a hook at the end, which they let down to take samples of mud from the seabottom; by its appearance and smell they can determine their whereabouts.[4]

A wide variety of goods passed through Chinese ports. The Chinese exported tea, silk, and porcelain to the countries beyond the South China Sea, receiving exotic woods, precious stones, and various tropical goods in exchange. Seaports on the southern China coast exported sweet oranges, lemons, and peaches in return for grapes, walnuts, and pomegranates. Along the Silk Road to China came raw hides, furs, and horses. Chinese aristocrats, their appetite for material consumption stimulated by the affluence of Chinese society during much of the Tang and the Song periods, were fascinated by the exotic goods and the flora and the fauna of the desert and the tropical lands of the South Seas. The city of Chang'an became the eastern terminus of the Silk Road and perhaps the wealthiest city in the world during the Tang era. The major port of exit in southern China was Canton, where an estimated 100,000 merchants lived. Their activities were controlled by an imperial commissioner sent from the capital.

Some of this trade was a product of the tribute system, which the Chinese rulers used as an element of their foreign policy. The Chinese viewed the outside world as they viewed their own society—in a hierarchical manner.

A TANG HORSE. During the Tang dynasty, trade between China, India, and the Middle East along the famous Silk Road increased rapidly and introduced new Central Asian motifs to Chinese culture. Ceramic representations of the sturdy Central Asian horse and the two-humped Bactrian camel were often produced as decorative objects in the homes of the wealthy, or as tomb figures. Preserved for us today, these ceramic studies of horses and camels, as well as of officials, court ladies, and servants, painted in brilliant gold, green, and blue lead glazes, are among the more impressive examples of Tang cultural achievement.

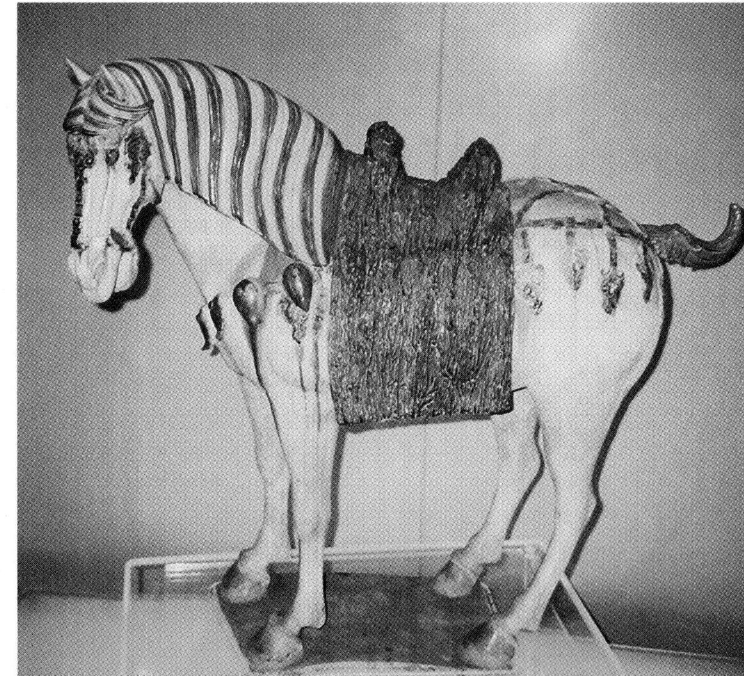

THE HEAVENLY MOUNTAINS. Of the three possible routes over the Silk Road between China and Central Asia, the most satisfactory, from an ecological point of view, was along the northern slopes of the Heavenly Mountains, where moist northwesterly winds and runoff from the snowy peaks of the mountains provided lush grasses for the camels to feed on and water for parched and weary merchants. Unfortunately, this region, shown above, also harbored nomadic peoples who preyed on merchant caravans for their livelihood.

Rulers of smaller countries along the periphery were viewed as "younger brothers" of the Chinese emperor and owed fealty to him. Foreign rulers who accepted the relationship were required to pay tribute and to promise not to harbor enemies of the Chinese Empire. But the foreign rulers also benefited from the relationship. Not only did it confer legitimacy upon them, but they often received magnificent gifts from their "elder brother" as a reward for good behavior. Merchants from their countries also gained access to the vast Chinese market.

DAILY LIFE IN TRADITIONAL CHINA

These political and economic changes affected Chinese society during the Tang and Song era. For one thing, it became much more complex. Whereas previously China had been almost exclusively rural, with a small urban class of merchants, artisans, and workers almost entirely dependent on the state, the cities had now grown into an important, if statistically still insignificant, part of the population. Urban life, too, had changed. Cities were no longer primarily administrative centers dominated by officials and their families, but now included a much broader mix of officials, merchants, artisans, touts, and entertainers.

In the countryside, equally significant changes were taking place, as the relatively rigid demarcation between the landed aristocracy and the mass of the rural population gave way to a more complex mixture of landed gentry, free peasants, sharecroppers, and landless laborers. Perhaps the most significant development was the rise of the landed gentry as the most influential force in Chinese society. The gentry class controlled much of the wealth in the rural areas and produced the majority of the candidates for the bureaucracy.

By virtue of their possession of land and specialized knowledge of the Confucian classics, the gentry had replaced the aristocracy as the political and economic elite of Chinese society. Unlike the aristocracy, however, the gentry did not form an exclusive class separated by the accident of birth from the remainder of the population. Upward and downward mobility between the scholar-gentry class and the remainder of the population was not uncommon and may have been a key factor in the stability and longevity of the system. A position in the bureaucracy opened the doors to wealth and prestige for the individual and his family, but it was no guarantee of success, and the fortunes of individual families might experience a rapid rise and fall. The soaring ambitions and arrogance of China's landed gentry are vividly described in the following wish list set in poetry by a young bridegroom of the Tang dynasty:

Chinese slaves to take charge of treasury and barn,
Foreign slaves to take care of my cattle and sheep.
Strong-legged slaves to run by saddle and stirrup when I ride,
Powerful slaves to till the fields with might and main,
Handsome slaves to play the harp and hand the wine;
Slim-waisted slaves to sing me songs, and dance;
Dwarfs to hold the candle by my dining-couch.[5]

For affluent Chinese in this era, life offered many more pleasures than had been available to their ancestors. There were new forms of entertainment, such as playing cards and chess (brought from India, although an early form had been invented in China during the Zhou dynasty); new forms of transportation, such as the paddle-wheel boat and horseback riding (made possible by the introduction of the stirrup); better means of communication (block printing was first invented in the eighth century C.E.); and new tastes for the palate introduced from lands beyond the frontier. Tea had been introduced from the Burmese frontier by monks as early as the Han dynasty, and brandy and other concentrated spirits produced by the distillation of alcohol were invented in the seventh century.

The vast majority of the Chinese people still lived off the land in villages ranging in size from a few dozen residents to several thousand. The life of the peasants was bounded by their village. Although many communities were connected to the outside world by roads or rivers, the average Chinese rarely left the confines of their native village except for an occasional visit to a nearby market town. This isolation was psychological as well as physical, for most Chinese identified with their immediate environment and had difficulty envisioning themselves living beyond the bamboo hedges or mud walls that marked the limit of their horizon.

An even more basic unit than the village in the lives of most Chinese, of course, was the family. The ideal was the joint family—with at least three generations under one roof. Because of the heavy labor requirements of rice farming, the tradition of the joint family was especially prevalent in the south. When a son married, he was expected to bring his new wife back to live in his parents' home (see

SPRING FESTIVAL ON THE RIVER. Besides being an artistic masterpiece, this Chinese scroll, known as *Spring Festival on the River,* is one of the most remarkable social documents of early twelfth-century China. Nearly thirty-three feet in length, it records with encyclopedic detail various aspects of Chinese society, from the imperial court down to the lowliest peasants, as they prepare for the spring festival. The viewer is expected to unfold the scroll slowly from right to left and linger on each segment as the scroll follows the path along the Yellow River to the Song capital of Kaifeng, then the most sophisticated city in the world.

THE SAINTLY MISS WU

The idea that a wife should sacrifice her wants to the needs of her husband and family was deeply embedded in traditional Chinese society. Widows in particular had few rights, and their remarriage was strongly condemned. In this account from a story by Hung Mai, a twelfth-century writer, the widowed Miss Wu wins the respect of the entire community by faithfully serving her mother-in-law.

HUNG MAI, *A SONG FAMILY SAGA*

Miss Wu served her mother-in-law very filially. Her mother-in-law had an eye ailment and felt sorry for her daughter-in-law's solitary and poverty-stricken situation, so suggested that they call in a son-in-law for her and thereby get an adoptive heir. Miss Wu announced in tears, "A woman does not serve two husbands. I will support you. Don't talk this way." Her mother-in-law, seeing that she was determined, did not press her. Miss Wu did spinning, washing, sewing, cooking, and cleaning for her neighbors, earning perhaps a hundred cash a day, all of which she gave to her mother-in-law to cover the cost of firewood and food. If she was given any meat, she would wrap it up to take home. . . .

Once when her mother-in-law was cooking rice, a neighbor called to her, and to avoid overcooking the rice she dumped it into a pan. Owing to her bad eyes, however, she mistakenly put it in the dirty chamber pot. When Miss Wu returned and saw it, she did not say a word. She went to a neighbor to borrow some cooked rice for her mother-in-law and took the dirty rice and washed it to eat herself.

One day in the daytime neighbors saw [Miss Wu] ascending into the sky amid colored clouds. Startled, they told her mother-in-law, who said, "Don't be foolish. She just came back from pounding rice for someone, and is lying down on the bed. Go and look." They went to the room and peeked in and saw her sound asleep. Amazed, they left.

When Miss Wu woke up, her mother-in-law told her what happened, and she said, "I just dreamed of two young boys in blue clothes holding documents and riding on the clouds. They grabbed my clothes and said the Emperor of Heaven had summoned me. They took me to the gate of heaven and I was brought in to see the emperor, who was seated beside a balustrade. He said 'Although you are just a lowly ignorant village woman, you are able to serve your old mother-in-law sincerely and work hard. You really deserve respect.' He gave me a cup of aromatic wine and a string of cash, saying, 'I will supply you. From now on you will not need to work for others.' I bowed to thank him and came back, accompanied by the two boys. Then I woke up."

There was in fact a thousand cash on the bed, and the room was filled with a fragrance. They then realized that the neighbors' vision had been a spirit journey. From this point on even more people asked her to work for them, and she never refused. But the money that had been given to her she kept for her mother-in-law's use. Whatever they used promptly reappeared, so the thousand cash was never exhausted. The mother-in-law also regained her sight in both eyes.

the box above). Often the parents added a new wing to the house for the new family. If a woman married, she went to live with her husband; women who did not marry remained in the home where they grew up.

Chinese village architecture reflected these traditions. Most family dwellings were simple, consisting of one or at most two rooms. They were usually constructed of dried mud, stone, or brick, depending on available materials and the prosperity of the family. Roofs were of thatch or tile, and the floors were usually of packed dirt. Large houses were often built in a square around an inner courtyard, thus guaranteeing privacy from the outside world.

Within the family unit, the eldest male theoretically ruled as an autocrat. He was responsible for presiding over ancestral rites at an altar, usually in the main room of the house. He had traditional legal rights over his wife, and if she did not provide him with a male heir, he was permitted to take a second wife. She, on the other hand, had no recourse to divorce. As the old saying went, "Marry a chicken, follow the chicken; marry a dog, follow the dog." Wealthy Chinese might keep concubines, who lived in a separate room in the house and sometimes competed with the legal wife for precedence.

In accordance with Confucian tradition, children were expected, above all, to obey their parents, who not only determined their children's careers but normally selected their marriage partners. Filial piety was viewed as an absolute moral good, above virtually all other moral obligations. Even today duty to one's parents is considered important in traditional Chinese families, and the tombstones of deceased Chinese are often decorated with tile paintings depicting the filial acts that they performed during their lifetime.

The tradition of male superiority continued from ancient times into the medieval era, especially under the southern Song when it was reinforced by Neo-Confucianism. Female children were considered to be less desirable than males, because they could not undertake heavy work in the fields or carry on the family traditions. Poor families often sold their daughters to wealthy villagers to serve as concubines, and female infanticide was not uncommon in times of famine to ensure there would be food for the remainder of the family. Concubines had few legal rights, and female domestic servants even fewer.

During the Song era, two new practices emerged that changed the equation for women seeking to obtain a successful marriage contract. First, a new form of dowry appeared. Whereas previously the prospective husband offered the bride's family a bride price, now the reverse became the norm, with the bride's parents paying the groom's family a dowry. With the prosperity that characterized Chinese society during much of the Song era, affluent parents sought to buy a satisfactory husband for their daughter, preferably one with a higher social standing and good prospects for an official career.

A second source of marital bait during the Song period was the promise of a bride with tiny bound feet. The process of foot binding, carried out on girls aged five to thirteen, was excruciatingly painful, since it bent and compressed the foot to half its normal size by imprisoning it in restrictive bandages. But the procedure was often performed by ambitious mothers intent on assuring their daughters the best possible prospects for marriage. The zealous mother also wanted her daughter to possess a competitive edge in dealing with the other wives and concubines of her future husband. Bound feet represented submissiveness and self-discipline, two required attributes for the ideal Confucian wife.

Throughout northern China, foot binding became a common practice for women of all social classes. It was less common in southern China, where the cultivation of wet rice could not be carried out with bandaged feet; there it tended to be limited to the scholar-gentry class. Still, most Chinese women with bound feet contributed to the labor force to supplement the family income. Although foot binding was eventually prohibited, the practice lasted into the twentieth century, particularly in rural villages.

As in most traditional societies, there were exceptions to the low status of women in Chinese society. Women had substantial property rights and retained control over their dowries even after divorce or the death of the husband. Wives were frequently an influential force within the home, often handling the accounts and taking primary responsibility for raising the children. Some were active in politics. The outstanding example was Wu Zhao (625?–706?), popularly known as Empress Wu. Selected by Emperor Tang Taizong as a concubine, after his death she rose to a position of supreme power at court. At first she was content to rule through her sons, but in 690 she declared herself empress of China. To bolster her claim of legitimacy, she cited a Buddhist sutra to the effect that a woman would rule the world seven hundred years after the death of Gautama Buddha. For her presumption, she has been vilified by later Chinese historians, but she was actually a quite capable ruler. She was responsible for giving meaning to the civil service examination system and was the first to select graduates of the examinations for the highest positions in government. During her last years, she reportedly fell under the influence of courtiers and was deposed in 705, at the age of eighty.

Explosion in Central Asia: The Mongol Empire

The Mongols, who succeeded the Song as the rulers of China in the late thirteenth century, rose to power in Asia with stunning rapidity. When Genghis Khan (also known as Chinggis Khan), the founder of Mongol greatness, was born, the Mongols were a relatively obscure pastoral people in the region of modern Outer Mongolia. Like most of the nomadic peoples in the region, they were organized loosely into clans and tribes and even lacked a common name for themselves. Rivalry among the various tribes over pasture, livestock, and booty was intense and increased at the end of the twelfth century as a result of a growing population and the consequent overgrazing of pastures.

This challenge was met by the great Mongol chieftain Genghis Khan. Born sometime during the 1160s, Genghis Khan (his original name was Temuchin, or Temujin) was the son of one of the more impoverished nobles of his tribe. When Temuchin was still a child, his father was murdered by a rival, and the young boy was temporarily forced to seek refuge in the wilderness. Nevertheless, through his prowess and the power of his personality he gradually unified the Mongol tribes. In 1206 he was elected Genghis Khan (universal ruler) at a massive tribal meeting. From that time on, he devoted himself to military pursuits. Mongol nomads were now forced to pay taxes and were subject to military conscription. "Man's highest joy," Genghis Khan reportedly remarked, "is in victory: to conquer one's enemies, to pursue them, to deprive them of their possessions, to make their beloved weep, to ride on their horses, and to embrace their wives and daughters."[6]

The army that Genghis Khan unleashed on the world was not exceptionally large—totaling less than 130,000 in 1227, at a time when the total Mongol population numbered between one and two million. But their mastery of military tactics set the Mongols apart from their rivals. Their tireless flying columns of mounted warriors surrounded their enemies and harassed them like cattle, luring them into pursuit, then ambushing them with flank attacks. John Plano Carpini, a contemporary Franciscan friar, described their tactics:

> As soon as they discover the enemy they charge and each one unleashes three or four arrows. If they see that they can't break him, they retreat in order to entice the enemy to pursue, thus luring him into an ambush prepared in advance. . . . Their military stratagems are numerous. At the moment of

A LETTER TO THE POPE

In 1243 Pope Innocent IV dispatched the Franciscan friar John Plano Carpini to the Mongol headquarters at Karakorum to appeal to the great khan to cease his attacks on Christians. After a considerable wait, Carpini was given the following reply, which could not have pleased the pope. The letter was discovered recently in the Vatican archives.

A LETTER FROM KUYUK KHAN TO POPE INNOCENT IV

By the power of the Eternal Heaven, We are the all-embracing Khan of all the Great Nations. It is our command:

This is a decree, sent to the great Pope that he may know and pay heed.

After holding counsel with the monarchs under your suzerainty, you have sent us an offer of subordination, which we have accepted from the hands of your envoy.

If you should act up to your word, then you, the great Pope, should come in person with the monarchs to pay us homage and we should thereupon instruct you concerning the commands of the Yasak.

Furthermore, you have said it would be well for us to become Christians. You write to me in person about this matter, and have addressed to me a request. This, your request, we cannot understand.

Furthermore, you have written me these words: "You have attacked all the territories of the Magyars and other Christians, at which I am astonished. Tell me, what was their crime?" These, your words, we likewise cannot understand. Jenghiz Khan and Ogatai Khakan revealed the commands of Heaven. But those whom you name would not believe the commands of Heaven. Those of whom you speak showed themselves highly presumptuous and slew our envoys. Therefore, in accordance with the commands of the Eternal Heaven the inhabitants of the aforesaid countries have been slain and annihilated. If not by the command of Heaven, how can anyone slay or conquer out of his own strength?

And when you say: "I am a Christian. I pray to God. I arraign and despise others," how do you know who is pleasing to God and to whom He allots His grace? How can you know it, that you speak such words?

Thanks to the power of the Eternal Heaven, all lands have been given to us from sunrise to sunset. How could anyone act other than in accordance with the commands of Heaven? Now your own upright heart must tell you: "We will become subject to you, and will place our powers at your disposal." You in person, at the head of the monarchs, all of you, without exception, must come to tender us service and pay us homage, then only will we recognize your submission. But if you do not obey the commands of Heaven, and run counter to our orders, we shall know that you are our foe.

That is what we have to tell you. If you fail to act in accordance therewith, how can we foresee what will happen to you? Heaven alone knows.

> an enemy cavalry attack, they place prisoners and foreign auxiliaries in the forefront of their own position, while positioning the bulk of their own troops on the right and left wings to envelop the adversary, thus giving the enemy the impression that they are more numerous than in reality. If the adversary defends himself well, they open their ranks to let him pass through in flight, after which they launch in pursuit and kill as many as possible.[7]

In the years after the election of Temuchin as universal ruler, the Mongols defeated tribal groups to their west and then turned their attention to the seminomadic non-Chinese kingdoms in northern China. There they discovered that their adversaries were armed with a weapon called a fire-lance, an early form of flamethrower. Gunpowder had been invented in China during the late Tang period, and by the early thirteenth century a type of fire-lance had been developed that could spew out a combination of flame and projectiles that could travel as far as thirty or forty yards and inflict considerable damage on the enemy. By the end of the thirteenth century, the fire-lance had evolved into the much more effective handgun and cannon. These inventions came too late to save China from the Mongols, however, and were transmitted to Europe by the early fourteenth century by foreigners employed by the Mongol rulers of China.

While some Mongol armies were engaged in the conquest of northern China, others traveled farther afield and advanced as far as central Europe (see the box above). Only the death of the Great Khan may have prevented an all-out Mongol attack on western Europe. In 1231 they attacked Persia and then defeated the Abbasids at Baghdad in 1258 (see Chapter 7). Mongol forces attacked the Song from the west in the 1260s and finally defeated the remnants of the Song navy in 1279.

By then, the Mongol Empire was quite different from what it had been under its founder. Prior to the conquests of Genghis Khan, the Mongols had been purely nomadic. They spent their winters in the southern plains, where they found suitable pastures for their cattle, and traveled north in the summer to wooded areas where the water was sufficient. They lived in round tents covered with felt (called yurts) that were easily transported. For food, the Mongols depended on milk and meat from their herds and game from hunting.

To administer the new empire, Genghis Khan set up a capital city at Karakorum, in present-day Outer Mongolia, but prohibited his fellow Mongols from practicing sedentary occupations or living in cities. But under his successors, Mongol aristocrats began to enter administrative positions, while commoners took up sedentary occupations as farmers or merchants. As one khan remarked, quoting his Chinese adviser, "Although you inherited the Chinese Empire on horseback, you cannot rule it from that position."[8]

The territorial nature of the empire also changed. Following tribal custom, at the death of the ruling khan, the territory was distributed among his heirs. Genghis Khan's empire was thus divided into several separate khanates, each under the autonomous rule of one of his sons by his principal wife. One of his sons was awarded the khanate of Chaghadai in Central Asia with its capital at Samarkand; another ruled Persia from the conquered city of Baghdad; a third took charge of the khanate of Kipchak (commonly known as the Golden Horde). But it was one of his grandsons, named Khubilai Khan (1260–1294), who completed the conquest of the Song and established a new Chinese dynasty, called the Yuan (from a phrase in the *Book of Changes* referring to the "original creative force" of the universe). Khubilai moved the capital of China northward to Khanbaliq (the city of the Khan), which was located on a major trunk route from the Great Wall to the plains of northern China. Later the city would be known by the Chinese name Beijing, or Peking (Northern Capital).

Mongol Rule in China

At first China's new rulers exhibited impressive vitality. After a failed attempt to administer their conquest as they had ruled their own tribal society (some advisers reportedly even suggested that the plowed fields be transformed into pasture), Mongol rulers adapted to the Chinese political system and made use of local talents in the bureaucracy, although the highest positions were usually reserved for Mongols. The tripartite division of the administration into civilian, military, and censorate was retained, as were the six ministries. Eventually, even the civil service system was revived, as was the state cult of Confucius, although Khubilai Khan himself was a Buddhist. Some

MAP 10.3 Asia Under the Mongols

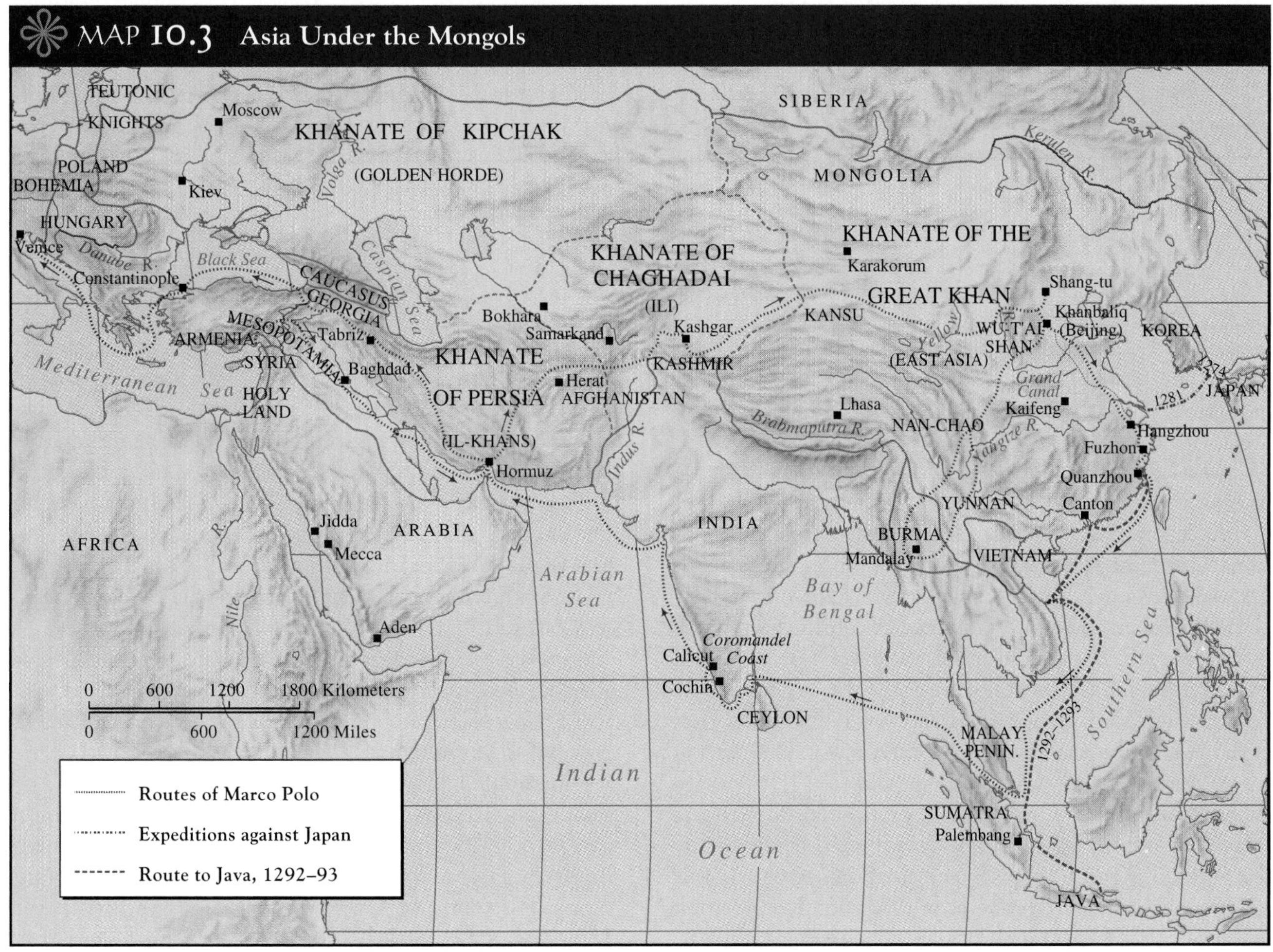

HOW KHUBILAI KHAN CHOOSES HIS CONSORTS

All Chinese emperors had a number of concubines in addition to their formal wives. Although this practice helped ensure that there would be one or more potential heirs to the throne, it also often led to disputes over the succession. In this passage, the Italian adventurer Marco Polo describes how the great Mongol ruler Khubilai Khan selected members of his harem. Since all of the official wives had large numbers of courtiers in their entourage, rivalry within the imperial court was not uncommon. Although some historians doubt that Marco Polo was ever in China, his account is generally viewed as a reliable description of thirteenth-century China.

MARCO POLO, *THE TRAVELS OF MARCO POLO*

The personal appearance of the great Khan, lord of lords, whose name is Kublai, is such as I shall now tell you. He is of a good stature, neither tall nor short, but of a middle height. He has a becoming amount of flesh, and is very shapely in all his limbs. His complexion is white and red, the eyes black and fine, the nose well formed and well set on. He has four wives, whom he retains permanently as his legitimate consorts. . . .

When the emperor desires the society of one of these four consorts, he will sometimes send for the lady to his apartment and sometimes visit her at her own. He has also a great number of concubines, and I will tell you how he obtains them.

You must know that there is a tribe of Tartars called Kungurat, who are noted for their beauty. The great Khan sends his commissioners to the province to select four or five hundred, or whatever number may be ordered, of the most beautiful young women, according to the scale of beauty enjoined upon them. . . . The commissioners on arriving assemble all the girls of the province, in the presence of appraisers appointed for the purpose. These carefully survey the points of each girl in succession, as for example her hair, her complexion, eyebrows, mouth, lips, and the proportion of all her limbs. . . . And whatever standard the great Khan may have fixed for those that are to be brought to him, . . . the commissioners select the required number from those who have attained that standard, and bring them to him. And when they reach his presence he has them appraised anew by other parties, and has a selection made of thirty or forty of those, who then get the highest valuation. Now every year a hundred of the most beautiful maidens of this tribe are sent to the great Khan, who commits them to the charge of certain elderly ladies dwelling in his palace. And these old ladies make the girls sleep with them, in order to ascertain if they have sweet breath and do not snore, and are sound in all their limbs. Then such of them as are of approved beauty, and are good and sound in all respects, are appointed to attend on the emperor by turns. Thus six of these damsels take their turn for three days and nights, and wait on him when he is in his chamber and when he is in his bed, to serve him in any way, and to be entirely at his orders. At the end of the three days and nights they are relieved by another six. And so throughout the year, there are reliefs of maidens by six and six, changing every three days and nights.

leading Mongols followed their ruler in converting to Buddhism, but most commoners retained their traditional religion. In general, the Mongols remained apart as a separate class with their own laws.

The Mongols' greatest achievement may have been the prosperity they fostered. At home, they continued the relatively tolerant economic policies of the southern Song, and by bringing the entire Eurasian landmass under a single rule, they encouraged long-distance trade, particularly along the Silk Road, now dominated by Muslim merchants from Central Asia. To promote trade, the Grand Canal was extended from the Yellow River to the capital. Adjacent to the canal, a paved highway was constructed that extended all the way from the Song capital of Hangzhou to its Mongol counterpart at Khanbaliq.

The capital was a magnificent city. According to the Italian merchant Marco Polo, who resided there during the reign of Khubilai Khan (see the box above), it was twenty-four miles in diameter and surrounded by thick walls of earth penetrated by twelve massive gates. He described the old Song capital of Hangzhou as a noble city where "so many pleasures may be found that one fancies himself to be in Paradise."

But the Yuan eventually fell victim to the same fate that had afflicted other powerful dynasties in China. Excessive spending on foreign campaigns, inadequate tax revenues, factionalism and corruption at court and in the bureaucracy, and growing internal instability, brought about in part by a famine in central China in the 1340s, all contributed to the dynasty's demise. Khubilai Khan's successors lacked his administrative genius, and by the middle of the fourteenth century, the Yuan dynasty in China, like the Mongol khanates elsewhere in Central Asia, had begun to decline rapidly.

The immediate instrument of Mongol defeat was Zhu Yuanzhang (Chu Yuan-chang), the son of a poor peasant in the lower Yangtze valley. After losing most of his family in the famine of the 1340s, Zhu became an itinerant monk and then the leader of a band of bandits. In the 1360s, unrest spread throughout the country, and after

BUDDHIST SHRINE STATUE. The oasis settlement of Jiaohe, located at the confluence of two rivers on a plateau in Chinese Central Asia, had been a stopping point on the Silk Road since the first millennium B.C.E. During the Tang dynasty, when Buddhist merchants carried goods and ideas eastward from India to the Chinese capital at Chang'an, the town's inhabitants were primarily Buddhist. Shown here are the remnants of a Buddhist shrine, with an image of the Buddha set in a niche along the central wall of the building. Like all other structures in the town, the shrine was constructed of sun-dried brick. Eventually the community was occupied by Uighurs, who brought the Muslim faith. Jiaohe was abandoned after the Mongols swept through the area in the thirteenth century, but later a new settlement arose in the nearby Turfan depression, the lowest point in China.

defeating a number of rivals, Zhu Yuanzhang put an end to the disintegrating Yuan regime and declared the foundation of a new Ming (Bright) dynasty (1369–1644).

In Search of the Way

By the time of the Sui and the Tang dynasties, Buddhism and Daoism had emerged as major rivals of Confucianism as the ruling ideology of the state. But in the eighth and ninth centuries, during the last half of the Tang dynasty, Confucianism revived and once again became dominant at court, a position it would retain to the end of the dynastic period in the early twentieth century. Buddhist and Daoist beliefs, however, remained popular at the local level.

The Rise and Decline of Buddhism and Daoism

As noted earlier, Buddhism arrived in China with merchants from India and found its first adherents among the merchant community and intellectuals intrigued by the new ideas. During the chaotic centuries following the collapse of the Han dynasty, Buddhism and Daoism appealed to those who were searching for more emotional and spiritual satisfaction than Confucianism could provide. Both faiths reached beyond the common people and found support among the ruling classes as well. There was even a small Christian church in the capital of Chang'an, introduced to China by Syrian merchants in the sixth century C.E.

As Buddhism attracted more followers, it began to take on Chinese characteristics and divided into a number of separate sects. Some, like the *Chan* (Zen in Japanese) sect, called for mind training and a strict regimen as a means of seeking enlightenment, a technique that reflected Daoist ideas and appealed to many intellectuals (see the box on p. 284). Others, like the Pure Land sect, stressed the role of devotion, an approach that was more appealing to ordinary Chinese, who lacked the time and inclination for strict monastic discipline. Still others were mystical sects, like Tantrism, which emphasized the importance of magical symbols and ritual in seeking a preferred way to enlightenment. Some Buddhist sects, like their Daoist counterparts, had political overtones. The White Lotus sect, founded in 1133, often adopted the form of a rebel movement, seeking political reform or the overthrow of a dynasty and forecasting a new era when a "savior Buddha" would come to earth to herald the advent of a new age. Most believers, however, assimilated Buddhism into their daily lives, where it joined Confucian ideology and spirit worship as an element in the highly eclectic and tolerant Chinese worldview.

The burgeoning popularity of Buddhism continued into the early years of the Tang dynasty. Early Tang rulers lent their support to the Buddhist monasteries that had been established throughout the country. Buddhist scriptures were regularly included in the civil service examinations, and Buddhist and Daoist advisers replaced shamans and Confucian scholar-officials as advisers at court. But ultimately, Buddhism and Daoism lost favor at court and were increasingly subjected to official persecution. Part of the reason was xenophobia. Envious Daoists and Confucianists made a point of criticizing the foreign origins of Buddhist doctrines, which one prominent Confucian scholar characterized as nothing but "silly relics." To deflect such criticism, Buddhists attempted to make the doctrine more Chinese, equating the Indian concept of *dharma* (law) with the Chinese concept of *Dao* (the Way). Emperor Tang Taizong ordered the Buddhist monk Xuan Zang to translate Lao Zi's classic *The Way of the Dao* into Sanskrit, reportedly to show visitors from India that China had its own equivalent to the Buddhist scriptures. But another reason for this change of heart may have been financial. The great Buddhist monasteries had accumulated thousands of acres of land and serfs that were exempt from

THE WAY OF THE GREAT BUDDHA

According to Buddhists, it is impossible to describe the state of nirvana, which is sometimes depicted as an extinction of self. Yet Buddhist scholars found it difficult to avoid trying to interpret the term for their followers. The following passage by the Chinese monk Shen-Hui, one of the leading exponents of Chan Buddhism, dates from the eighth century and attempts to describe the means by which an individual may hope to seek enlightenment. There are clear similarities with philosophical Daoism.

SHEN-HUI, *ELUCIDATING THE DOCTRINE*

"Absence of thought" is the doctrine.
"Absence of action" is the foundation.
True Emptiness is the substance.
And all wonderful things and beings are the function.
True Thusness is without thought; it cannot be known through conception and thought.
The True State is noncreated—can it be seen in matter and mind?
There is no thought except that of True Thusness.
There is no creation except that of the True State.
Abiding without abiding, forever abiding in Nirvana.
Acting without acting, immediately crossing to the Other Shore.
Thusness does not move, but its motion and functions are inexhaustible.
In every instant of thought, there is no seeking; the seeking itself is no thought.
Perfect wisdom is not achieved, and yet the Five Eyes all become pure and the Three Bodies are understood.
Great Enlightenment has no knowledge, and yet the Six Supernatural Powers of the Buddha are utilized and the Four Wisdoms of the Buddha are made great.
Thus we know that calmness is at the same time no calmness, wisdom at the same time no wisdom, and action at the same time no action.
The nature is equivalent to the void and the substance is identical with the Realm of Law.
In this way, the Six Perfections are completed.
None of the ways to arrive at Nirvana is wanting.
Thus we know that the ego and the dharmas are empty in reality and being and nonbeing are both obliterated.
The mind is originally without activity; the Way is always without thought.
No thought, no reflection, no seeking, no attainment;
No this, no that, no coming, no going.
With such reality one understands the True Insight [into previous and future mortal conditions and present mortal suffering].
With such a mind one penetrates the Eight Emancipations [through the eight stages of mental concentration].
By merits one accomplishes the Ten Powers of the Buddha.

paying taxes to the state. Such wealth contributed to the corruption of the monks and other Buddhist officials, and this corruption in turn aroused popular resentment and official disapproval. As the state attempted to eliminate the great landholdings of the aristocracy, the large monasteries also attracted its attention. During the later Tang, countless temples and monasteries were destroyed, and over 100,000 monks were compelled to leave the monasteries and return to secular life.

Yet there were probably deeper political and ideological reasons for the growing antagonism between Buddhism and the state. By preaching the illusory nature of the material world, Buddhism was denying the very essence of Confucian teachings—the necessity for filial piety and hard work. By encouraging young Chinese to abandon their rice fields and seek refuge and wisdom in the monasteries, Buddhism was undermining the foundation stones of Chinese society—the family unit and the work ethic. In the last analysis, Buddhism was incompatible with the activist element in Chinese society, an orientation that was most effectively expressed by State Confucianism (see the box on p. 285). In the competition with Confucianism for support by the state, Buddhism, like Daoism, was almost certain to lose, at least in the more this-worldly, secure, and prosperous milieu of late Tang and Song China. The two doctrines continued to win converts at the local level, but official support ceased. In the meantime, Buddhism was under attack in Central Asia as well. In the eighth century, the Uighur kingdom adopted Manichaeanism, an offshoot of the ancient Zoroastrian religion with some influence from Christianity. Manichaeanism spread rapidly throughout the area and may have been a reason for the European belief that a Christian king (the legendary Prester John) ruled somewhere in Asia. By the tenth century, Islam was beginning to move east along the Silk Road, posing a severe threat to both Manichaean and Buddhist centers in the area.

Neo-Confucianism: The Investigation of Things

Into the vacuum left by the decline of Buddhism and Daoism stepped a revived Confucianism. But it was a Confucianism that had been significantly altered by its competition with Buddhist and Daoist teachings. Challenged by Buddhist and Daoist ideas about the nature of the universe, Confucian thinkers began to flesh out the spare metaphysical structure of classical Confucian doctrine

A CONFUCIAN WEDDING CEREMONY

During the twelfth century, the philosopher Zhu Xi attempted to reinvigorate Confucian teachings in a contemporary setting that would be more accessible in its appeal to a broad audience. His goal was militantly Confucian, to combat both popular Buddhist doctrines and the superstitious practices of the common people. With his new moral code, Zhu Xi hoped to point Chinese society back on the Confucian track, with its emphasis on proper behavior. He therefore set forth the proper rituals required to carry out the special days that marked the lives of all Chinese: entry into adolescence, marriage, and funeral and ancestral rites. In the excerpt below he prescribes the proper protocol for the Confucian wedding ceremony.

4. WELCOMING IN PERSON

On the day before the wedding, the bride's family sends people to lay out the dowry furnishings in the groom's chamber. At dawn the groom's family sets places in the chamber. Meanwhile, the bride's family sets up places outside. As the sun goes down, the groom puts on full attire. After the presiding man makes a report at the offering hall, he pledges the groom and orders him to go to fetch the bride. The groom goes out and mounts his horse. When he gets to the bride's home he waits at his place. The presiding man of the bride's family makes a report at the offering hall, after which he pledges the bride and instructs her. Then he goes out to greet the groom. When the groom enters, he presents a goose. The duenna takes the girl out to climb into the conveyance. The groom mounts his horse and leads the way for the bridal vehicle. When they arrive at his house he leads the bride in and they take their seats. After the eating and drinking are done, the groom leaves the chamber. On reentering, he takes off his clothes and the candles are removed.

5. THE BRIDE IS PRESENTED TO HER PARENTS-IN-LAW

The next day, having risen at dawn, the bride meets her parents-in-law, who entertain her. Then the bride is presented to the elders. If she is the wife of the eldest son, she serves food to her parents-in-law. Then the parents-in-law feast the bride.

6. PRESENTATION AT THE FAMILY SHRINE

On the third day the presiding man takes the bride to be presented at the offering hall.

7. THE GROOM IS PRESENTED TO THE WIFE'S PARENTS

The day after that the groom goes to see his wife's parents. Afterward he is presented to his wife's relatives. The bride's family entertains the groom, as in ordinary etiquette.

with a set of sophisticated theories about the nature of the cosmos and humans' place in it. Although the origins of this effort can be traced to the early Tang period, it reached fruition during the intellectually prolific Song dynasty, when it became the dominant ideology of the state.

The fundamental purpose of Neo-Confucianism, as the new doctrine was called, was to unite the metaphysical speculations of Buddhism and Daoism with the pragmatic Confucian approach to society. In response to Buddhism and Daoism, Neo-Confucianism maintained that the world is real, not illusory, and that fulfillment comes from participation, not withdrawal.

The primary contributor to this intellectual effort was the philosopher Zhu Xi (Chu Hsi). Raised during the southern Song era, Zhu Xi accepted the division of the world into a material world and a transcendent world (called by Neo-Confucianists the Supreme Ultimate, or *Tai Ji*). The latter was roughly equivalent to the *Dao,* or Way, in classical Confucian philosophy. To Zhu Xi, this Supreme Ultimate was a set of abstract principles governed by the law of *yin-yang* and the five elements.

Human beings served as a link between the two halves of this bifurcated universe. Although human beings live in the material world, each individual has an identity that is linked with the Supreme Ultimate, and the goal of individual action is to transcend the material world in a Buddhist sense to achieve an essential identity with the Supreme Ultimate. According to Zhu Xi and his followers, the means of transcending the material world is self-cultivation, which is achieved by the "investigation of things."

During the remainder of the Song dynasty and into the early years of the Ming, Zhu Xi's ideas became the central core of Confucian ideology and a favorite source of questions for the civil service examinations. But during the mid-Ming era, his ideas came under attack from a Confucian scholar named Wang Yangming. Wang and his supporters disagreed with Zhu Xi's focus on learning through an investigation of the outside world and asserted that the correct way to transcend the material world was through an understanding of self. According to this "School of Mind," the mind and the universe were a single unit. Knowledge was thus intuitive rather than empirical and was obtained through internal self-searching rather than through an investigation of the outside world. Wang Yangming's ideas attracted many followers during the Ming dynasty, and the school briefly rivaled that of Zhu Xi in popularity among Confucian scholars. Nevertheless, it never won official acceptance, probably because it was too much like Buddhism in denying the importance of a life of participation and social action.

Neo-Confucianism remained the state doctrine until the end of the dynastic system in the twentieth century. Some historians have asked whether the doctrine can help to explain why China failed to experience scientific and industrial revolutions of the sort that occurred in the West. In particular, it has been suggested that Neo-Confucianism tended to encourage an emphasis on the elucidation of moral principles rather than the expansion of scientific knowledge. Though the Chinese excelled in practical technology, inventing gunpowder, the compass, printing and paper, and cast iron, among other things, they had less interest in scientific theory. Their relative backwardness in mathematics is a good example. Chinese scholars had no knowledge of the principles of geometry and lagged behind other advanced civilizations in astronomy, physics, and optics. Until the Mongol era, they had no knowledge of Arabic numerals and lacked the concept of zero. Even after that time, they continued to use a cumbersome numbering system based on Chinese characters.

Furthermore, in China intellectual affairs continued to be dominated by the scholar-gentry, the chief upholders of Neo-Confucianism, who not only had little interest in the natural sciences or economic change, but legitimately viewed them as a threat to their own dominant status within Chinese society. The commercial middle-class, who lacked social status and an independent position in society, had little say in intellectual matters. In contrast, in the West an urban middle-class emerged that was a source not only of wealth, but also of social prestige, political power, and intellectual ideas. The impetus for the intellectual revolution in the West came from the members of the commercial bourgeoisie, who were interested in the conquest of nature and the development of technology. In China, however, the scholar-gentry continued to focus on the sources of human behavior and a correct understanding of the relationship between humankind and the universe. The result was an intellectual environment that valued continuity over change and tradition over innovation.

The Apogee of Chinese Culture

The period between the Tang and the Ming dynasties was in many ways the great age of achievement in Chinese literature and art. Enriched by Buddhist and Daoist images and themes, Chinese poetry and painting reached the pinnacle of their creativity. Porcelain emerged as the highest form of Chinese ceramics, and sculpture flourished under the influence of styles imported from India and Central Asia.

Literature

The development of Chinese literature was stimulated by two technological innovations: the invention of paper during the Han dynasty and the invention of woodblock printing during the Tang. At first, paper was used for clothing, wrapping material, toilet paper, and even for armor, but by the first century B.C.E. it was being used for writing as well.

In the seventh century C.E., the Chinese developed the technique of carving an entire page of text into a wooden block, inking it, and then pressing it onto a sheet of paper. Ordinarily, a text was printed on a long sheet of paper like a scroll. Then the paper was folded and stitched together to form a book. The earliest printed book known today is a Buddhist text published in 868 C.E.; it is more than sixteen feet long. Although the Chinese eventually developed movable type as well, block printing continued to be used until relatively modern times because of the large number of characters needed to produce a lengthy text.

MAKING PAPER. One of China's most important contributions to the world was the invention of paper during the Han dynasty. Although the first known use of paper for writing dates back to the first century B.C.E., paper was also used for clothing, wrapping materials, military armor, and toilet paper. It was even suggested to a prince in 93 B.C.E. that he use a paper handkerchief. Pounded fibers of hemp and linen were placed on a flat meshed surface and soaked in a large vat. After it dried, the residue was peeled away as a sheet of paper, seen piled at the right in this eighteenth-century painting.

TWO TANG POETS

Li Bo was one of the great poets of the Tang dynasty. The first selection is probably the best-known poem in China and has been memorized by schoolchildren for centuries. The second poem, entitled "Drinking Alone in Moonlight," reflects the poet's carefree attitude toward life.

Du Fu, Li Bo's prime competitor as the greatest poet of the Tang dynasty, was often the more reflective of the two. In the final piece here, the poet has returned to his home in the capital after a rebellion against the dynasty has left the city in ruins.

LI BO, *QUIET NIGHT THOUGHTS*

Beside my bed the bright moonbeams bound
Almost as if there were frost on the ground.
Raising up, I gaze at the Mountain moon;
Lying back, I think of my old hometown.

LI BO, *DRINKING ALONE IN MOONLIGHT*

Among the flowers, with a jug of wine,
I drink all alone—no one to share.
Raising my cup, I welcome the moon.
And my shadow joins us, making a threesome.
Alas! the moon won't take part in the drinking,
And my shadow just does whatever I do.
But I'm friends for a while with the moon and my shadow,
And we caper in revels well suited to spring.
As I sing the moon seems to sway back and forth;
As I dance my shadow goes flopping about.
As long as I'm sober we'll enjoy one another,
And when I get drunk, we'll go our own ways:
Forever committed to carefree play,
We'll all meet again in the Milky Way!

DU FU, *SPRING PROSPECT*

The capital is taken. The hills and streams are left,
And with spring in the city the grass and trees grown dense.
Mourning the times, the flowers trickle their tears;
Saddened with parting, the birds make my heart flutter.
The army beacons have flamed for three months;
A letter from home would be worth ten thousand in gold.
My white hairs I have anxiously scratched ever shorter;
But such disarray! Even hairpins will do no good!

Even with printing, books remained too expensive for most Chinese, but they did help to popularize all forms of literary writing among the educated elite.

During the post-Han era, historical writing and essays continued to be favorite forms of literary activity. Each dynasty produced an official dynastic history of its predecessor to elucidate sober maxims about the qualities of good and evil in human nature, and local gazetteers added to the general knowledge about the various regions. Encyclopedias brought together in a single location information and documents about all aspects of Chinese life.

But it was in poetry, above all, that Chinese of the Tang to the Ming dynasties most effectively expressed their literary talents. Chinese poems celebrated the beauty of nature, the changes of the seasons, the joys of friendship and drink, sadness at the brevity of life, and old age and parting. Given the frequency of imperial banishment and the requirement that officials serve away from their home district, it is little wonder that separation was an important theme. Love poems existed, but were neither as intense as Western verse nor as sensual as Indian poetry.

The nature of the Chinese language imposed certain characteristics on Chinese poetry, the first being compactness. The most popular forms were four-line and eight-line poems, with five or seven words in each line. Because Chinese grammar does not rely on case or gender and makes no distinction between verb tenses, five-character Chinese poems were not only brief but often cryptic and ambiguous. As an illustration, compare the following poem by Du Fu in Chinese with its English translation:

Moonlit Night	月夜
The moon tonight in Fu-chou	今夜鄜州月
She watches alone from her chamber,	閨中只獨看
While faraway I think lovingly on daughters and sons,	遙憐小兒女
Who do not yet know how to remember Ch'ang-an.	未解憶長安
In scented fog, her cloudlike hairdo moist,	香霧雲鬟濕
In its clear beams, her jade-white arms are cold.	清輝玉臂寒
When shall we lean in the empty window,	何時倚虛幌
Moonlit together, its light drying traces of tears.[9]	雙照淚痕乾

Two Tang poets, Li Bo (Li Po, sometimes known as Li Bai or Li Taibo) and Du Fu (Tu Fu), symbolized the genius of the era as well as the two most popular styles. Li Bo was a free spirit. His writing often centered on nature and shifted easily between moods of revelry and melancholy. Two of his best-known poems are "Resolution on Waking with a Hangover on a Spring Morning" and "Drinking Alone in Moonlight." (see the box above).

Where Li Bo was a carefree Daoist, Du Fu was a sober Confucian. His poems often dealt with historical issues or ethical themes, befitting a scholar-official living during the chaotic times of the late Tang era. Many of his works reflect a concern with social injustice and the plight of the unfortunate rarely to be found in the writings of his contemporaries (see the box on p. 287). Neither the poetry nor the prose of the great writers of the Tang and Song dynasties was written for, or penetrated to, the bulk of the Chinese population. The millions of Chinese peasants and artisans living in rural villages and market towns acquired their knowledge of Chinese history, Confucian moralisms, and even Buddhist scripture from stories, plays, and songs passed down by storytellers, wandering minstrels, and itinerant monks in a rich oral tradition.

By the Song dynasty, China had 60 million people, one million in Hangzhou alone. With the growth of cities came an increased demand for popular entertainment. Although the Tang dynasty had imposed a curfew on urban residents, the Song did not. The city gates and bridges were closed at dark, but food stalls and entertainment continued through the night. On fairgrounds throughout the year, one could find comedians, musicians, boxers, fencers, wrestlers, acrobats, puppets and marionettes, shadow plays, and especially storytellers. Many of these arts had come from India centuries before and now became the favorite forms of amusement of the Chinese people.

During the Yuan dynasty, new forms of literary creativity including popular theater and the novel began to appear. The two most famous novels were the *Romance of the Three Kingdoms* and *Tale of the Marshes*. The former had been told orally for centuries, appearing in written form during the Song as a scriptbook for storytellers. It was first printed in 1321 but was not published for mass consumption until 1522. Each new edition was altered in some way, making the final edition a composite effort of generations of the Chinese imagination. The plot recounts the power struggle that took place among competing groups after the fall of the Han dynasty. Packed with court intrigues, descriptions of peasant life, and gripping battles, the *Romance of the Three Kingdoms* stands as a magnificent epic, China's counterpart to the Mahabharata.

Tale of the Marshes is an often violent tale of bandit heroes, who at the end of the northern Song banded together to oppose government taxes and official oppression. They rob from those in power to share with the poor. *Tale of the Marshes* is the first prose fiction that describes the daily ordeal of ordinary Chinese people in their own language. Unlike the picaresque novel in the West, *Tale of the Marshes* does not limit itself to the exploits of one hero, offering instead 108 different story lines. This multitude of plots is a natural outgrowth of the tradition of the professional storyteller, who attempts to keep the audience's attention by recounting as many adventures as the market will bear. The frightening description of a tiger's attack on one of the bandits is typical of the author's exciting style (see the box on p. 289).

Art

Although painting flourished in China under the Han and reached a level of artistic excellence under the Tang, little remains from those periods. The painting of the Song and the Yuan, however, is considered the apogee of painting in traditional China.

Like literature, Chinese painting found part of its inspiration in Buddhist and Daoist sources. Some of the best surviving examples of the Tang period are the Buddhist

LONGMEN CAVES BUDDHIST SCULPTURE. The Silk Road, which stretched through Central Asia from the Middle East to China, was an avenue for ideas as well as trade. Over the centuries, Christian, Buddhist, and Muslim teachings came to China across the sandy wastes of the Taklimakan Basin. In the seventh century, the Tang emperor Gaozong commissioned this massive temple carving as part of the large complex of cave art devoted to Buddha at Longmen in central China. Bold and grandiose in their construction, these statues reflect the glory that was the Tang dynasty.

A BATTLE TO THE DEATH

Tale of the Marshes is one of China's earliest novels. It is a swashbuckling tale of epic proportions that recounts the life of a group of bandits living on the margin of Chinese society. In its realistic description, this account of a battle with a tiger is stunningly modern.

TALE OF THE MARSHES

Seeing it thus, Wu Sung cried "Ah-ya," then rolled down from the green rock. Cudgel in hand, he slipped away alongside the rock. The big beast was both hungry and thirsty. Barely touching the ground with its paws, it sprang upward with its whole body and then swooped down from midair. Wu Sung was so startled that the wine he had drunk turned into cold sweat. In a moment Wu Sung saw the tiger was about to pounce on him and he quickly dodged behind the beast's back. It was most difficult for the beast to find anyone from that position, so planting its front paws on the ground and raising its legs at the waist, it lifted itself up. Wu Sung again dodged and slid to one side. When the tiger saw that it had failed this time, it gave out a big roar like a thunderbolt from the mid sky, shaking the mountain ridge. Then it made a scissors-cut, its iron cudgel–like tail standing upside down, but Wu Sung again slipped aside. Ordinarily, the big beast seized its prey either with one swoop, one lift, or one scissors-cut. Failing to grab him by these three means, it lost half of its spirited temper. After a second failure with a scissors-cut, it roared once more and moved around in another circle. When Wu Sung saw the beast turn back, he lifted his cudgel with both hands and brought it down from midair with one swift and mighty blow. There was a loud sound and a tree fell, its twigs and leaves streaming down all over his face. Opening his eyes, he gazed fixedly. In his excitement, he had missed the big beast but struck instead an old withered tree. The cudgel had broken in two, and one half of it he now held in his hand.

Its temper now thoroughly aroused, the big beast bellowed and again turned round with a forward thrust. Wu Sung made another leap, retreating ten steps. The creature had barely managed to place its forepaws in front of Wu Sung when, throwing away his broken cudgel, he clutched the tiger's mottled neck with a cracking sound and pushing it down, held it tightly. The animal attempted to struggle, but Wu Sung grabbed it with all his might and never relaxed his grip for a moment. With his foot he kicked the beast over its face and eyes. The tiger started roaring again and dug up with its paws two heaps of yellow mud beneath its body, forming an earthen pit. Wu Sung pressed the beast's mouth straight down the yellow mud pit. It became helpless and impotent. With his left hand grasping tightly the beast's mottled neck, Wu Sung freed his right hand and lifting up his fist—the size of an iron hammer—kept pommeling it with all his strength. After it had been struck fifty to seventy times, fresh blood began to gush out from its eyes, mouth, nose, and ears. Wu Sung, using all his superhuman strength and inborn prowess, in a short while pounded the tiger into a heap as it lay there like an embroidered cloth bag.

wall paintings in the caves at Dunhuang, in Central Asia. These paintings were commissioned by Buddhist merchants who stopped at Dunhuang and, while awaiting permission to enter China, wished to give thanks for surviving the rigors of the Silk Road. The entrances to the caves were filled with stones after the tenth century, when Muslim zealots began to destroy Buddhist images throughout Central Asia, and have only recently been uncovered. Like the few surviving Tang scroll paintings, these wall paintings display a love of color and refinement that are reminiscent of styles in India and Iran.

Daoism ultimately had a greater influence than Buddhism on Chinese painting. From early times, Chinese artists removed themselves to the mountains to write and paint and find the *Dao*, or Way, in nature. In the fifth century, one Chinese painter, who was too old to travel, began to paint mountain scenes from memory and announced that depicting nature could function as a substitute for contemplating nature itself. Painting, he said, could be the means of realizing the *Dao*. This explains in part the emphasis on nature in traditional Chinese painting. The word *landscape* in Chinese means "mountain-water," and the Daoist search for balance between earth and water, hard and soft, *yang* and *yin*, is at play in the tradition of Chinese painting. To enhance the effect, poems were added to the paintings, underscoring the fusion of poetry and painting in Chinese art. Many artists were proficient in both media, the poem inspiring the painting and vice versa.

To represent the totality of nature, Chinese artists attempted to reveal the quintessential forms of the landscape. Rather than depicting the actual realistic shape of a specific mountain, they tried to portray the idea of "mountain." Empty spaces were left in the paintings because in the Daoist vision, one cannot know the whole truth. Daoist influence was also evident in the tendency to portray human beings as insignificant in the midst of nature. In contrast to the focus on the human body and personality in Western art, Chinese art presented people as tiny figures fishing in a small boat, meditating on a cliff, or wandering up a hillside trail, coexisting with but not dominating nature.

The Chinese displayed their paintings on long scrolls of silk or paper that were attached to a wooden cylindrical bar at the bottom. Varying in length from three to twenty feet, the paintings were unfolded slowly, so that the eye could enjoy each segment, one after the other, beginning at the bottom with water or a village and moving upward into the hills to the mountain peaks and the sky.

A MOUNTAIN SCENE. As a means of reproducing the totality of nature, Chinese artists often attempted to visualize physical reality. In this famous eleventh-century painting by Fan K'uan, the mountain seems to take on an existence all its own, independent of the interpretation of the artist. Daoist influence is evident here in that human beings play an insignificant role in the grand scheme of nature. The two tiny figures driving mules, a bridge, and a half-hidden temple are eclipsed by the mountain.

By the tenth century, Chinese painters began to eliminate color from their paintings, preferring the challenge of capturing the distilled essence of the landscape in washes of black ink on white silk. Borrowing from calligraphy, now a sophisticated and revered art, they emphasized the brush stroke and created black-and-white landscapes characterized by a gravity of mood and dominated by overpowering mountains.

Other artists turned toward more expressionist and experimental painting. These so-called literati artists were scholars and administrators, highly educated and adept in music, poetry, and painting. Being scholars first and artists second, however, they believed that the purpose of painting was not representation but expression. No longer did painters wish to evoke the feeling of wandering in nature. Instead they tried to reveal to the viewer their own mind and feelings. Like many Western painters in the nineteenth and twentieth centuries, many of these artists were misunderstood by the public and painted only for themselves and one another. They even developed a style of pointillism. Witness the incredibly "modern" painting of the Tang poet Li Bo, created by the thirteenth-century artist Liang Kai. With just a few bold black strokes, he managed to convey the whole man, standing calmly but poised, with inner intensity.

Second only to painting in creativity was the field of ceramics, notably, the manufacture of porcelain. Made of fine clay baked at unusually high temperatures in a kiln, porcelain was first produced during the period after the fall of the Han and became popular during the Tang era. During the Song, porcelain came into its own. Most renowned perhaps are the celadons, in a delicate gray-green, but Song artists also excelled in other colors and techniques. As in painting, Song delicacy and grace contrasted with the bold and often crude styles popular under the Tang. The translucent character of Chinese porcelain represented the final product of a technique that did not reach Europe until the eighteenth century. During the Yuan and the Ming, new styles appeared. Most notable is the cobalt blue and white porcelain usually identified with the Ming dynasty, which actually originated during the Yuan. The Ming also produced a multicolored porcelain—often in green, yellow, and red—covered with exotic designs.

CONCLUSION

Traditionally, Chinese historians believed that Chinese history tended to be cyclical in nature. The pattern of history was marked by the rise and fall of great dynasties, interspersed with periods of internal division and foreign invasion. Underlying the waxing and waning of dynasties was the essential continuity of Chinese civilization.

This view of the dynamic forces of Chinese history was long accepted as valid by historians in China and in the West and led many to assert that Chinese history was unique and could not be placed within a European or universal framework. Whereas Western history was linear, leading steadily away from the past, China's always returned to its moorings and was rooted in the values and institutions of antiquity.

In recent years, however, this traditional view of a changeless China has come under increasing challenge from historians who see patterns of change that made the China of 1400 a very different place from the country that had existed at the rise of the Tang dynasty in the seventh century C.E. To such scholars, China had passed through its own version of the "middle ages" and was on the verge of beginning a linear evolution into a posttraditional society.

As we have seen, China at the beginning of the Ming had advanced in many ways since the end of the great Han dynasty over a thousand years earlier. The industrial and commercial sector had grown considerably in size, complexity, and technological capacity, while in the countryside the concentration of political and economic power in the hands of the aristocracy had been replaced by a more stable and equitable mixture of landed gentry, freehold farmers, and sharecroppers. In addition, Chinese society had achieved a level of stability and social tranquillity that not only surpassed conditions during the final years of the Han, but was the envy of observers from other lands, near and far. The civil service provided an avenue of upward mobility that was virtually unknown elsewhere in the world, while the state tolerated a diversity of beliefs that responded to the emotional needs and preferences of the Chinese people. In many respects, China's achievements were unsurpassed throughout the world and marked a major advance beyond the world of antiquity.

Yet there were also some key similarities between the China of the Ming and the China of late antiquity. Ming China was still a predominantly agrarian society, with wealth based primarily on the ownership of land. Commercial activities flourished but remained under a high level of government regulation and by no means represented a major proportion of the national income. China also remained a relatively centralized empire based on an official ideology that stressed the virtue of hard work, social conformity, and hierarchy. In foreign affairs, the long frontier struggle with the nomadic peoples along the northern and western frontiers continued unabated.

Thus, the significant change that China experienced during its medieval era can probably be best described as change within continuity, an evolutionary working out of trends that had first become visible during the Han dynasty or even earlier. The result was a civilization that was the envy of its neighbors and of the world. It also influenced other states in the region, including Japan, Korea, and Vietnam. It is to these societies along the Chinese rimlands that we now turn.

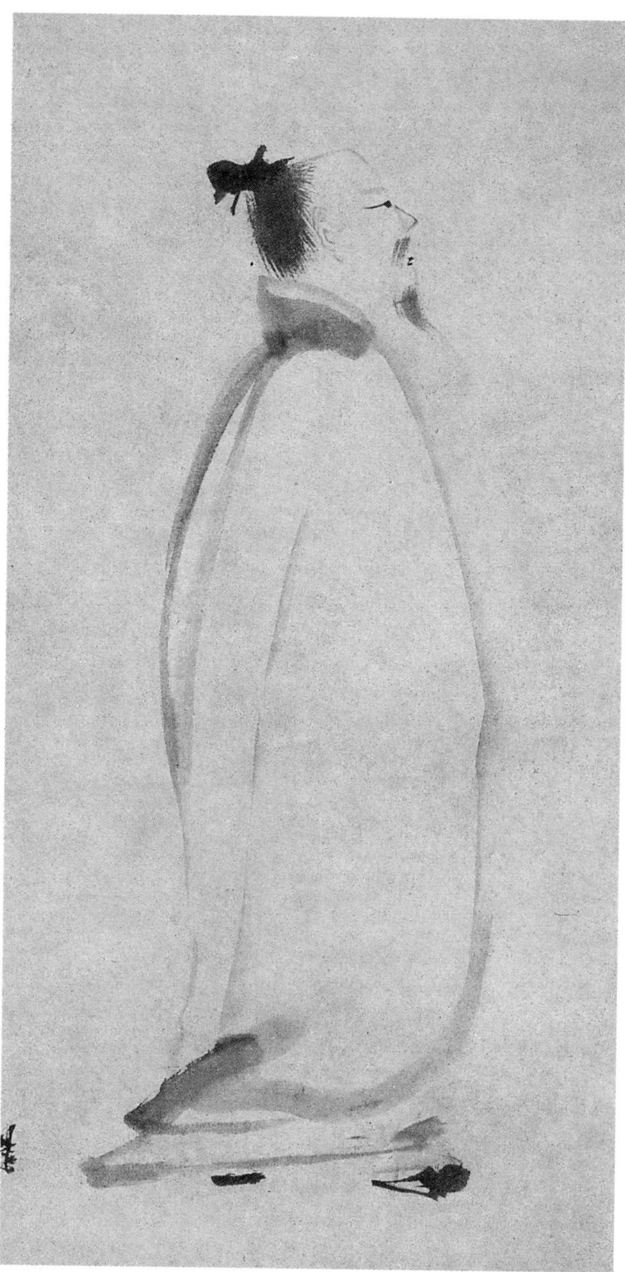

LI BO CHANTING A POEM. Li Bo, one of the most celebrated Tang poets, wrote about the changing seasons, the joys of friendship and drink, and his sadness at the brevity of life, old age, and parting. The legend of his death undoubtedly added to his reputation. Reportedly, he drowned while reaching out in a drunken stupor to embrace the reflection of the moon in the water. Here he is portrayed by the thirteenth-century painter Liang Kai, who gave up a promising career as an official to retreat to a Buddhist monastery near Hangzhou.

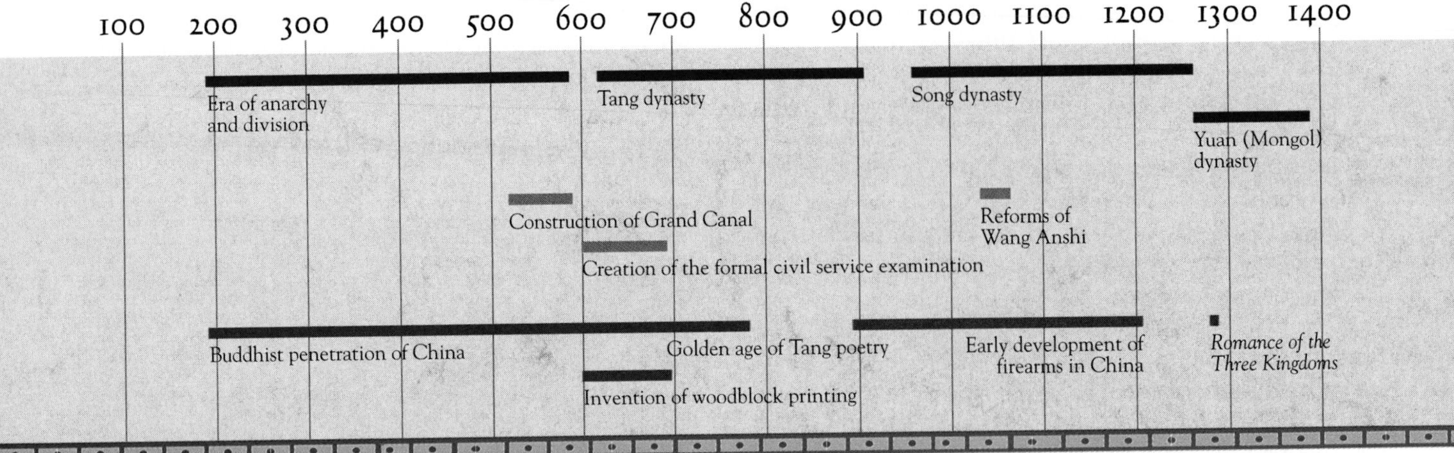

Chapter Notes

1. The Travels of Marco Polo (New York, n.d.), p. 119.
2. Quoted in Arthur F. Wright, Buddhism in Chinese History (Stanford, Calif., 1959), p. 30.
3. Quoted in Arthur F. Wright, The Sui Dynasty (New York, 1978), p. 180.
4. Chu-yu, P'ing chow Table Talks, quoted in Robert Temple, The Genius of China: 3,000 Years of Science, Discovery, and Invention (New York, 1986), p. 150.
5. Quoted in Edward H. Schafer, The Golden Peaches of Samerkand: A Study of T'ang Exotics (Berkeley, Calif., 1963), p. 43.
6. Quoted in John K. Fairbank, Edwin O. Reischauer, and Albert M. Craig, East Asia: Tradition and Transformation (Boston, 1973), p. 164.
7. John Plano Carpini, quoted in Rene Grousset, L'Empire des Steppes (Paris, 1939), p. 285.
8. A. M. Khazanov, Nomads and the Outside World (Cambridge, 1983), p. 241.
9. Steve Owen, The Great Age of Chinese Poetry: The High T'ang (New Haven, Conn., 1981), p. 200.

Suggested Readings

A number of general histories of China provide a good overview of this period. See, for example, C. O. Hucker, *China's Imperial Past: An Introduction to Chinese History and Culture* (Stanford, Calif., 1975), and C. Schirokauer, *A Brief History of Chinese and Japanese Civilizations*, rev. ed. (San Diego, Calif., 1989). For an interpretative treatment, see M. Elvin, *The Pattern of the Chinese Past* (Stanford, Calif., 1973). A global perspective is presented in S. A. M. Adshead, *China in World History* (New York, 1988).

A vast body of material is available on almost all periods of early Chinese history. For the post-Han period, see A. E. Dien, ed., *State and Society in Early Medieval China* (Stanford, Calif., 1990); E. Balazs, *Chinese Civilization and Bureaucracy: Variations on a Theme* (New Haven, Conn., 1964); and D. Twitchett and M. Loewe, *Cambridge History of China*, vol. 3, *Medieval China* (Cambridge, 1986).

For a readable treatment of the brief but tempestuous Sui dynasty, see A. F. Wright, *The Sui Dynasty* (New York, 1978). For a popularized treatment of one of China's most controversial female figures, see C. P. Fitzgerald, *The Empress Wu* (London, 1968).

The Song dynasty has been studied in considerable detail by Chinese historians. For a new and exciting interpretation, see J. T. C. Liu, *China Turning Inward: Intellectual Changes in the Early Twelfth Century* (Cambridge, Mass., 1988). Song problems with the northern frontier are chronicled in Tao Jing-shen, *Two Sons of Heaven: Studies in Sung-Liao Relations* (Tucson, Ariz., 1988).

There are a number of recent studies on the Mongol period in Chinese history. See, for example, W. A. Langlois, *China Under Mongol Rule* (Princeton, N.J., 1981), and J. W. Dardess, *Conquerors and Confucians: Aspects of Political Change in Late Yuan China* (New York, 1973). M. Rossabi, *Khubilai Khan: His Life and Times* (Berkeley, Calif., 1988) is a recent biography of the dynasty's greatest emperor, while M. Rossabi, ed., *China Among Equals: The Middle Kingdom and Its Neighbors* (Berkeley, Calif., 1983) deals with foreign affairs. For the rise of the Mongols, see M. Prawdin, *The Mongol Empire: Its Rise and Legacy* (New York, 1966). A more analytic account of the dynamics of nomadic society is A. M. Khazanov, *Nomads and the Outside World* (Cambridge, 1983). For a provocative new interpretation of Chinese relations with nomadic peoples, see T. J. Barfield, *The Perilous Frontier: Nomadic Empires and China* (Cambridge, 1989).

For an introduction to women's issues during this period, consult P. B. Ebrey, *The Inner Quarters: Marriage and the Lives of Chinese Women in the Sung Period* (Berkeley Calif., 1993); *Chu Hsi's Family Rituals* (Princeton, N.J., 1991); and "Women, Marriage, and the Family in Chinese History," in P. S. Ropp, *Heritage of China: Contemporary Perspectives on Chinese Civilization* (Berkeley, Calif., 1990). For an overview of Chinese foot binding, see C. F. Blake, "Foot-Binding in Neo-Confucian China and the Appropriation of Female Labor," *Signs* 19 (Spring, 1994).

On Central Asia, two popular accounts are J. Myrdal, *The Silk Road* (New York, 1979), and N. Marty, *The Silk Road* (Methuen, Mass., 1987). A more interpretive approach is found in S. A. M. Adshead, *Central Asia in World History* (New York, 1993).

The period from the fall of the Han to the early Ming was an important period in Chinese intellectual history. For developments in Confucianism, see Fung Yu-lan, *A Short History of Chinese Philosophy*, ed. D. Bodde (New York, 1948), and Carsun Chang, *The Development of Neo-Confucian Thought*, 2 vols. (New Haven, Conn., 1963). For a more scholarly study, see W. T. de Bary, *Self and Society in Ming Thought* (New York, 1970). A classic survey of the role of Buddhism in Chinese society is A. F. Wright, *Buddhism in Chinese History* (Stanford, Calif., 1959). See also E. O. Reischauer, *Ennin's Diary: The Record of a Pilgrimage to China in Search of the Law* (New York, 1955).

The classic work on Chinese literature is Liu Wu-Chi, *An Introduction to Chinese Literature* (Bloomington, Ind., 1966). Also consult the more recent and scholarly S. Owen, *An Anthology of Chinese Literature: Beginnings to 1911* (New York, 1996), and V. Mair, *The Columbia Anthology of Traditional Chinese Literature* (New York, 1994). For poetry see Liu Wu-Chi and I. Yucheng Lo, *Sunflower Splendor: Three Thousand Years of Chinese Poetry* (Bloomington, Ind., 1975), and S. Owen, *The Great Age of Chinese Poetry: The High T'ang* (New Haven, Conn., 1981), the latter presenting poems in both Chinese and English.

For a comprehensive introduction to Chinese art, see the classic M. Sullivan, *The Arts of China*, 4th ed. (Berkeley, Calif., 1999); M. Tregear, *Chinese Art*, rev ed. (London, 1997); and C. Clunas, *Art in China* (Oxford, 1997). The standard introduction to Chinese painting can be found in J. Cahill, *Chinese Painting* (New York, 1985), and Yang Xin, J. Cahill, et al., *Three Thousand Years of Chinese Painting* (New Haven, Conn., 1997).

For additional reading, go to InfoTrac College Edition, your online research library at http://web1.infotrac-college.com

Enter the search terms "Tang Dynasty or Song Dynasty" using Keywords.

Enter the search terms "China history" using Keywords.

Enter the search terms "China and Buddhism" using Keywords.

Enter the search term "Mongol" using Keywords.

Enter the search terms "Taoism or Daoism" using the Subject Guide.

CHAPTER

11

THE EAST ASIAN RIMLANDS: EARLY JAPAN, KOREA, AND VIETNAM

CHAPTER OUTLINE

- JAPAN: LAND OF THE RISING SUN
- KOREA
- VIETNAM: THE SMALLER DRAGON
- CONCLUSION

FOCUS QUESTIONS

- How did Chinese civilization influence the civilizations that arose in Japan, Korea, and Vietnam?
- What centralizing and decentralizing forces were at work in Japan before 1500, and how did they influence the political and governmental structures that arose?
- What were the main characteristics of economic and social life in early Japan?
- What were the most important cultural achievements of early Japan, and how do they illustrate the Japanese ability to blend indigenous and imported elements?
- What were the main developments in Korean and Vietnamese history before 1500?

These people, the exasperated official complained, are like birds and beasts. "They wear their hair tied up and go barefoot, while for clothing they simply cut a hole in a piece of cloth for their head or they fasten their garments on the left side [in barbarian style]." Their women are untrustworthy "and promiscuously wander about." In some areas, "men and women go naked without shame" and are little better than bugs.[1]

The speaker was Xue Tong, a Chinese administrator stationed in northern Vietnam at the end of the Han dynasty. His comments vividly reflected the frustration of Chinese bureaucrats faced with what they regarded as the uncivilized behavior of the untutored peoples living along the frontiers of the Chinese Empire. To Xue Tong and other upright Confucian officials like him, it was hopeless to try to civilize these people.

Such comments should not surprise us. During ancient times, China was the most technologically advanced society in East Asia. To the north and west were nomadic pastoral peoples whose military exploits were often impressive but whose political and cultural attainments were still limited, at least by comparison with the great river valley civilizations of the day. In inland areas south of the Yangtze River were scattered clumps of rice farmers and hill peoples, most of whom had not yet entered the era of state building and certainly had little knowledge of the niceties of Confucian ethics.

But Xue Tong and officials like him were being a little too hasty in their judgments. Along the fringes of Chinese civilization were a number of other agricultural societies that were beginning to follow a pattern of development similar to that of China, although somewhat later in time. One of these was in the islands of Japan, where an organized agricultural society was beginning to take shape just about the time Xue Tong was complaining about the barbarian peoples in the south. These developments may have been hastened by events on the Korean peninsula, where an advanced Neolithic society had begun to develop a few centuries earlier. Even in the Red River valley, where Xue Tong viewed the local inhabitants with such disdain, a relatively advanced civilization had been in existence for several hundred years before the area was conquered by the Han dynasty in the second century B.C.E.

All of these early agricultural societies were eventually influenced to some degree by their great neighbor China. Vietnam remained under Chinese rule for a thousand years. Korea retained its separate existence but was for long a tributary state of China and in many ways followed the cultural example of its larger patron. Only Japan retained both its political independence and its cultural uniqueness. Yet even the Japanese were strongly influenced by the glittering culture of their powerful neighbor, and today many Japanese institutions and customs still bear the imprint of several centuries of borrowing from the Middle Kingdom. In this chapter, we will take a closer look at these emerging societies along the Chinese rimlands and consider how their cultural achievements reflected or contrasted with those of the Chinese Empire.

Japan: Land of the Rising Sun

The geographical environment helps to explain some of the historical differences between Chinese and Japanese society. Whereas China is a continental civilization, Japan is an island country. It consists of four main islands: Hokkaido in the north, the main island of Honshu in the center, and the two smaller islands of Kyushu and Shikoku in the southwest. Its total land area is about 146,000 square miles (378,000 square kilometers), about the size of the state of Montana. Japan's main islands are at approximately the same latitude as the eastern seaboard of the United States.

Like the eastern United States, Japan is blessed with a temperate climate. It is slightly warmer on the east coast, which is washed by the Pacific Current that sweeps up from the south. The east coast also has a number of natural harbors that provide protection from the winds and high waves of the Pacific Ocean. As a consequence, in recent times the majority of the Japanese people have tended to live along the east coast, especially in the flat plains surrounding the cities of Tokyo, Osaka, and Kyoto. In these favorable environmental conditions, Japanese farmers have been able to harvest two crops of rice annually since early times.

By no means, however, is Japan an agricultural paradise. Like China, much of the country is mountainous, with only about 20 percent of the total land area susceptible to cultivation. These mountains are volcanic in origin, since the Japanese islands are located at the juncture of the Asian and Pacific tectonic plates. This location is both an advantage and a disadvantage. Volcanic soils are extremely fertile, which helps to explain the exceptionally high productivity of Japanese farmers. At the same time, the area is prone to earthquakes, such as the famous earthquake of 1923, which destroyed almost the entire city of Tokyo.

The fact that Japan is an island country has had a significant impact on Japanese history. As we have seen, the continental character of Chinese civilization, with its constant threat of invasion from the north, had a number of consequences for Chinese history. One effect was to make the Chinese more sensitive to the preservation of their culture from destruction at the hands of non-Chinese

THE EASTERN EXPEDITION OF EMPEROR JIMMU

Japanese myths maintained that the Japanese nation could be traced to the sun goddess Amaterasu, who was the ancestor of the founder of the Japanese imperial family, the Emperor Jimmu. This passage from the Nihon Shoki (The Chronicles of Japan) *describes the campaign in which the "devine warrior" Jimmu occupied the central plains of Japan, symbolizing the founding of the Japanese nation. Legend dates this migration to about 660* B.C.E., *but modern historians believe that it took place much later (perhaps as late as the fourth century* C.E.) *and that the account of the "divine warrior" may represent an effort by Japanese chroniclers to find a local equivalent to the Sage Kings of prehistoric China.*

THE CHRONICLES OF JAPAN

Emperor Jimmu was forty-five years of age when he addressed the assemblage of his brothers and children: "Long ago, this central land of the Reed Plains was bequeathed to our imperial ancestors by the heavenly deities, Takamimusubi-no-Kami and Amaterasu Omikami. . . . However, the remote regions still do not enjoy the benefit of our imperial rule, with each town having its own master and each village its own chief. Each of them sets up his own boundaries and contends for supremacy against other masters and chiefs."

"I have heard from an old deity knowledgeable in the affairs of the land and sea that in the east there is a beautiful land encircled by blue mountains. This must be the land from which our great task of spreading our benevolent rule can begin, for it is indeed the center of the universe. . . . Let us go there, and make it our capital. . . ."

In the winter of that year . . . the Emperor personally led imperial princes and a naval force to embark on his eastern expedition. . . .

When Nagasunehiko heard of the expedition, he said: "The children of the heavenly deities are coming to rob me of my country." He immediately mobilized his troops and intercepted Jimmu's troops at the hill of Kusaka and engaged in a battle. . . . The imperial forces were unable to advance. Concerned with the reversal, the Emperor formulated a new divine plan and said to himself: "I am the descendant of the Sun Goddess, and it is against the way of heaven to face the sun in attacking my enemy. Therefore our forces must retreat to make a show of weakness. After making sacrifice to the deities of heaven and earth, we shall march with the sun on our backs. We shall trample down our enemies with the might of the sun. In this way, without staining our swords with blood, our enemies can be conquered." . . . So, he ordered the troops to retreat to the port of Kusaka and regroup there. . . .

[After withdrawing to Kusaka, the imperial forces sailed southward, landed at a port in the present-day Kita peninsula, and again advanced north toward Yamato.]

The precipitous mountains provided such effective barriers that the imperial forces were not able to advance into the interior, and there was no path they could tread. Then one night Amaterasu Omikami appeared to the Emperor in a dream: "I will send you the Yatagarasu, let it guide you through the land." The following day, indeed, the Yatagarasu appeared flying down from the great expanse of the sky. The Emperor said: "The coming of this bird signifies the fulfillment of my auspicious dream. How wonderful it is! Our imperial ancestor, Amaterasu Omikami, desires to help us in the founding of our empire."

invaders. Proud of their own considerable cultural achievements and their dominant position throughout the region, the Chinese have traditionally been reluctant to dilute the purity of their culture with foreign innovations. Culture more than race is a determinant of the Chinese sense of identity.

By contrast, the island character of Japan probably had the effect of strengthening the Japanese sense of ethnic and cultural distinctiveness. Although the Japanese view of themselves as the most ethnically homogeneous people in East Asia may not be entirely accurate (the modern Japanese probably represent a mix of peoples, much as do their neighbors on the continent), their sense of racial and cultural homogeneity has enabled them to import ideas from abroad without worrying that the borrowings will destroy the uniqueness of their own culture.

A Gift from the Gods: Prehistoric Japan

According to an ancient legend recorded in historical chronicles written in the eighth century C.E., the islands of Japan were formed as a result of the marriage of the god Izanagi and the goddess Izanami. After giving birth to Japan, Izanami gave birth to a sun goddess whose name was Amaterasu. A descendant of Amaterasu later descended to earth and became the founder of the Japanese nation. This Japanese creation myth is reminiscent of similar beliefs in other ancient societies, which often saw themselves as the product of a union of deities. What is interesting about the Japanese version is that it has survived into modern times as an explanation for the uniqueness of the Japanese people and the divinity of the Japanese emperor, who is still believed by some Japanese to be a direct descendant of the sun goddess Amaterasu (see the box above).

Modern scholars have a more prosaic explanation for the origins of Japanese civilization. According to archaeological evidence, the Japanese islands have been occupied by human beings for at least 100,000 years. The earliest known Neolithic inhabitants, known as the Jomon people from the so-called cord pattern of their pottery, lived in the islands as much as 10,000 years ago. They lived

SIXTH-CENTURY WAREHOUSE. During the sixth century C.E. an organized society was just beginning to form in the central valley around the modern cities of Kyoto and Osaka. Shown here is a twentieth-century model of a warehouse, located in downtown Osaka. On this site, one of Japan's early rulers ordered the construction of sixteen such structures to hold grain and perhaps other foodstuffs. Each warehouse measured nine by ten meters and was supported by several massive wooden posts.

by hunting, fishing, and food gathering and probably had not mastered the techniques of agriculture.

Agriculture probably first appeared in Japan sometime during the first millennium B.C.E., although some archaeologists believe that the Jomon people had already learned how to cultivate some food crops considerably earlier than that. About 400 B.C.E. rice cultivation was introduced, probably by immigrants from the mainland by way of the Korean peninsula. Until recently, historians believed that these immigrants drove out the existing inhabitants of the area and gave rise to the emerging Yayoi culture (from the site near Tokyo where pottery from the period was found). It is now thought, however, that Yayoi culture was a product of a mixture between the Jomon people and the new arrivals, enriched by imports such as wet-rice agriculture, which had been brought by the immigrants from the mainland. In any event, it seems clear that the Yayoi peoples were the ancestors of the vast majority of present-day Japanese.

At first the Yayoi lived primarily on the southern island of Kyushu, but eventually they moved northward onto the main island of Honshu, conquering, assimilating, or driving out the previous inhabitants of the area, some of whose descendants, known as the Ainu, still live in the northern islands. Finally, in the first centuries C.E., the Yayoi settled in the Yamato plain in the vicinity of the modern cities of Osaka and Kyoto. Japanese legend recounts the story of a "divine warrior" (in Japanese, Jimmu) who led his people eastward from the island of Kyushu to establish a kingdom in the Yamato plain (see the box on p. 296).

In central Honshu, the Yayoi set up a tribal society based on a number of clans, called *uji*. Each *uji* was ruled by a hereditary chieftain, who provided protection to the local population in return for a proportion of the annual harvest. The population itself was divided between a small aristocratic class and the majority of the population, composed of rice farmers, artisans, and other household servants of the aristocrats. Yayoi society was highly decentralized, although eventually the chieftain of the dominant clan in the Yamato region, who claimed to be descended from the sun goddess Amaterasu, achieved a kind of titular primacy. There is no evidence, however, of a central ruler equivalent in power to the Chinese rulers of the Shang and the Zhou eras.

The Rise of the Japanese State

Although the Japanese had been aware of China for centuries, they paid relatively little attention to their more advanced neighbor until the early seventh century. Then the rise of the centralized and expansionistic Tang dynasty presented a new challenge. The Tang began to meddle in the affairs of the Korean peninsula, conquering the southwestern coast and arousing anxiety in Japan. Yamato rulers attempted to deal with the potential threat posed by the Chinese in two ways. First, they sought alliances with the remaining Korean states. Second, they attempted to centralize their authority so that they could mount a more effective resistance in the event of a Chinese invasion. The key figure in this effort was Shotoku Taishi (572–622), a leading aristocrat in one of the dominant clans in the Yamato region. Prince Shotoku sent missions

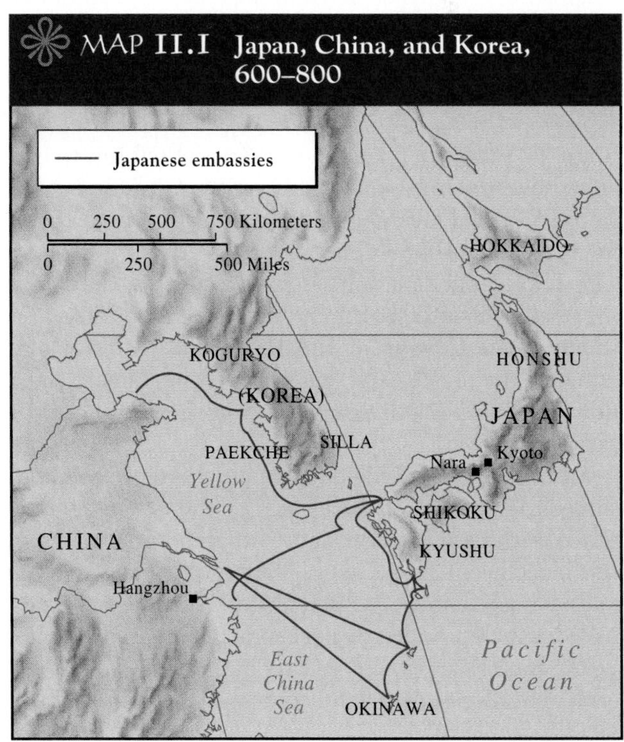

THE SEVENTEEN-ARTICLE CONSTITUTION

The following excerpt from the Nihon Shoki (The Chronicles of Japan) *is a passage from the seventeen-article constitution promulgated in 604 C.E. Although the opening section reflects Chinese influence in its emphasis on social harmony, there is also a strong focus on obedience and hierarchy. The constitution was put into practice during the reign of the famous Prince Shotoku.*

THE CHRONICLES OF JAPAN

Summer, 4th month, 3rd day [12th year of Empress Suiko, 604 C.E.]. The Crown Prince personally drafted and promulgated a constitution consisting of seventeen articles, which are as follows:

I. Harmony is to be cherished, and opposition for opposition's sake must be avoided as a matter of principle. Men are often influenced by partisan feelings, except a few sagacious ones. Hence there are some who disobey their lords and fathers, or who dispute with their neighboring villages. If those above are harmonious and those below are cordial, their discussion will be guided by a spirit of conciliation, and reason shall naturally prevail. There will be nothing that cannot be accomplished.

II. With all our heart, revere the three treasures. The three treasures, consisting of Buddha, the Doctrine, and the Monastic Order, are the final refuge of the four generated beings, and are the supreme objects of worship in all countries. Can any man in any age ever fail to respect these teachings? Few men are utterly devoid of goodness, and men can be taught to follow the teachings. Unless they take refuge in the three treasures, there is no way of rectifying their misdeeds.

III. When an imperial command is given, obey it with reverence. The sovereign is likened to heaven, and his subjects are likened to earth. With heaven providing the cover and earth supporting it, the four seasons proceed in orderly fashion, giving sustenance to all that which is in nature. If earth attempts to overtake the functions of heaven, it destroys everything. . . . If there is no reverence shown to the imperial command, ruin will automatically result. . . .

VII. Every man must be given his clearly delineated responsibility. If a wise man is entrusted with office, the sound of praise arises. If a wicked man holds office, disturbances become frequent. . . . In all things, great or small, find the right man, and the country will be well governed. . . . In this manner, the state will be lasting and its sacerdotal functions will be free from danger.

to the Tang capital of Chang'an to learn about the political institutions already in use in the relatively centralized Tang kingdom.

EMULATING THE CHINESE MODEL

Shotoku Taishi then launched a series of reforms to create a new system based roughly on the Chinese model. In the so-called seventeen-article constitution, he called for the creation of a centralized government under a supreme ruler and a merit system for selecting and ranking public officials (see the box above). His objective was to limit the powers of the hereditary nobility and enhance the prestige and authority of the Yamato ruler, now emerging as a divine figure and the symbol of the Japanese nation.

After Shotoku Taishi's death in 622, his successors continued to introduce reforms based on the Chinese model to make the government more efficient. In a series of so-called Taika ("great change") reforms that began in the mid-seventh century, a Grand Council of State was established, which presided over a cabinet of eight ministries. To the traditional six ministries of Tang China were added ministers representing the central secretariat and the imperial household. The territory of Japan was divided into administrative districts on the Chinese pattern. The rural village, composed ideally of fifty households, was the basic unit of government. The village chief was responsible for "the maintenance of the household registers, the assigning of the sowing of crops and the cultivation of mulberry trees, the prevention of offenses, and the requisitioning of taxes and forced labor." A law code was introduced, and a new tax system was established; now all farmland technically belonged to the state, so taxes were paid directly to the central government rather than through the local nobility, as had previously been the case.

As a result of their new acquaintance with China, the Japanese also developed a strong interest in Buddhism. Some of the first Japanese to travel to China during this period were Buddhist pilgrims hoping to learn more about the exciting new doctrine and bring back scriptures. Buddhism became quite popular among the aristocrats, who endowed wealthy monasteries that became active in Japanese politics. At first the new faith did not penetrate to the masses, but eventually popular sects such as the Pure Land Sect, an import from China, won many adherents among the common people.

CHRONOLOGY

THE FORMATION OF THE JAPANESE STATE

Shotoku Taishi	572–622
Era of Taika reforms	Mid-seventh century
Nara period	710–784
Heian (Kyoto) period	794–1185
Murasaki Shikibu	978–1016?
Minamoto Yoritomo	1142–1199
Kamakura shogunate	1185–1333
Mongol invasions	Late thirteenth century
Ashikaga period	1333–1600
Onin War	1462–1477

THE NARA AND HEIAN PERIODS

At first the effort to build a new state modeled roughly after the Tang state was successful. After Shotoku Taishi's death in 622, political influence fell into the hands of the powerful Fujiwara clan, which managed to marry into the ruling family and continue the reforms Shotoku had begun. In 710, a new capital, laid out on a grid similar to the great Tang city of Chang'an, was established at Nara, on the eastern edge of the Yamato plain. The Yamato ruler began to use the title "son of Heaven" in the Chinese fashion. In deference to the allegedly divine character of the ruling family, the mandate remained in perpetuity in the imperial house rather than being bestowed on an individual who was selected by Heaven because of his talent and virtue, as was the case in China.

MAP 11.2 Early Japan

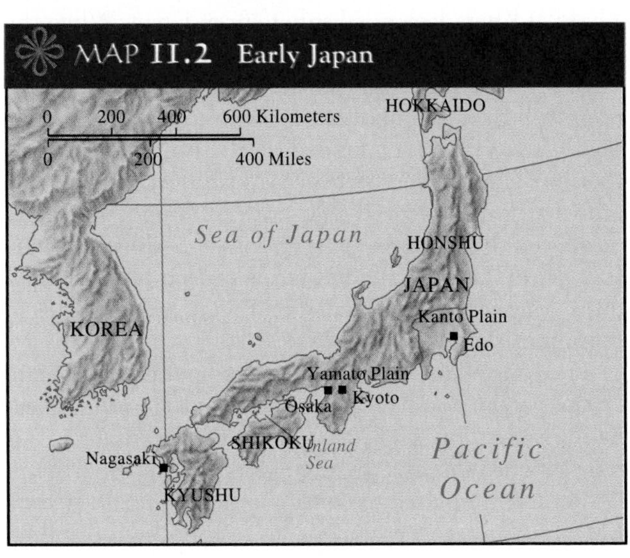

Had these reforms succeeded, Japan might have followed the Chinese pattern and developed a centralized bureaucratic government. But as time passed, the central government proved unable to curb the power of the aristocracy. Unlike in Tang China, the civil service examinations in Japan were not open to all but were restricted to individuals of noble birth. Leading officials were awarded large tracts of land, and they and other powerful families were able to keep the taxes from the lands for themselves. Increasingly starved for revenue, the central government steadily lost power and influence.

In 794, the emperor moved the capital to his family's original power base at nearby Heian, on the site of present-day Kyoto. The new capital was laid out in the now familiar Chang'an checkerboard pattern, but on a larger scale than at Nara. Now increasingly self-confident, the rulers ceased to emulate the Tang and sent no more missions to Chang'an. At Heian, the emperor—as the royal line descended from the sun goddess was now styled—continued to rule in name, but actual power was in the hands of the Fujiwara clan, which had managed through intermarriage to link its fortunes closely with the imperial family. A senior member of the clan began to serve as regent (in practice, the chief executive of the government) for the emperor.

In fact, what was happening was a return to the decentralization that had existed prior to Shotoku Taishi. The central government's attempts to impose taxes directly on the rice lands failed, and rural areas came under the control of powerful families whose wealth was based on the ownership of tax-exempt farmland (called *shoen*). To avoid paying taxes, peasants would often surrender their lands to a local aristocrat, who then would allow the peasants to cultivate the lands in return for the payment of rent. To obtain protection from government officials, these local aristocrats in turn might grant title of their lands to a more powerful aristocrat with influence at court. In return, these individuals would receive inheritable rights to a portion of the income from the estate.

With the decline of central power at Heian, local aristocrats tended to take justice into their own hands and increasingly used military force to protect their interests. A new class of military retainers called the samurai emerged whose purpose was to protect the security and property of their patron. They frequently drew their leaders from disappointed aristocratic office seekers, who thus began to occupy a prestigious position in local society, where they often served an administrative as well as a military function. The samurai lived a life of simplicity and self-sacrifice and were expected to maintain an intense and unquestioning loyalty to their lord. Bonds of loyalty were also quite strong among members of the samurai class, and homosexuality was common. Like the knights of medieval Europe, the samurai fought on horseback (although a samurai carried a sword and a bow and arrows

JAPAN'S WARRIOR CLASS

The samurai was the Japanese equivalent of the medieval European knight. Like the knight, he was expected to adhere to a strict moral code. Although this passage comes from a document dating only to the seventeenth century, it shows the importance of hierarchy and duty in a society influenced by the doctrine of Confucius. Note the similarity with Krishna's discourse on the duties of an Indian warrior in Chapter 2.

THE WAY OF THE SAMURAI

The master once said: . . . Generation after generation men have taken their livelihood from tilling the soil, or devised and manufactured tools, or produced profit from mutual trade, so that peoples' needs were satisfied. Thus the occupations of farmer, artisan, and merchant necessarily grew up as complementary to one another. However, the samurai eats food without growing it, uses utensils without manufacturing them, and profits without buying or selling. . . . The samurai is one who does not cultivate, does not manufacture, and does not engage in trade, but it cannot be that he has no function at all as a samurai. . . .

If one deeply fixes his attention on what I have said and examines closely one's own function, it will become clear what the business of the samurai is. The business of the samurai consists in reflecting on his own station in life, in discharging loyal service to his master if he has one, in deepening his fidelity in associations with friends, and, with due consideration of his own position, in devoting himself to duty above all. . . . The samurai dispenses with the business of the farmer, artisan, and merchant and confines himself to practicing this Way; should there be someone in the three classes of the common people who transgresses against these moral principles, the samurai summarily punishes him and thus upholds proper moral principles in the land. . . . Outwardly he stands in physical readiness for any call to service, and inwardly he strives to fulfill the Way of the lord and subject, friend and friend, father and son, older and younger brother, and husband and wife. Within his heart he keeps to the ways of peace, but without he keeps his weapons ready for use. The three classes of the common people make him their teacher and respect him. By following his teachings, they are enabled to understand what is fundamental and what is secondary.

Herein lies the Way of the samurai, the means by which he earns his clothing, food, and shelter; and by which his heart is put at ease, and he is enabled to pay back at length his obligation to his lord and the kindness of his parents. Were there no such duty, it would be as though one were to steal the kindness of one's parents, greedily devour the income of one's master, and make one's whole life a career of robbery and brigandage. This would be very grievous.

rather than lance and shield) and were supposed to live by a strict warrior code, known in Japan as *Bushido*, or "way of the warrior" (see the box above). As time went on, they became a major force and almost a pseudo-government in much of the Japanese countryside.

THE KAMAKURA SHOGUNATE AND AFTER

By the end of the twelfth century, as rivalries among noble families led to almost constant civil war, once again centralizing forces asserted themselves. This time the instrument was a powerful noble from a warrior clan named Minamoto Yoritomo (1142–1199), who defeated several rivals and set up his power base on the Kamakura peninsula, south of the modern city of Tokyo. To strengthen the state, he created a more centralized government (the *bakufu*, or "tent government") under a powerful military leader, known as the shogun (general). The shogun attempted to increase the powers of the central government while reducing rival aristocratic clans to vassal status. This "shogunate system," in which the emperor was the titular authority while the shogun exercised actual power, served as the political system in Japan until the last half of the nineteenth century.

At first the system worked effectively, and it was fortunate that it did, because during the next century Japan faced the most serious challenge it had confronted yet. The Mongols, who had destroyed the Song dynasty in China, were now attempting to assert their hegemony throughout all of Asia (see Chapter 10). In 1266 Emperor Khubilai Khan demanded tribute from Japan. When the Japanese refused, he invaded with an army of over 30,000 troops. Bad weather and difficult conditions forced a retreat, but the Mongols tried again in 1281. An army nearly 150,000 strong landed on the northern coast of Kyushu. The Japanese were able to contain them for two months, until virtually the entire Mongol fleet was destroyed by a massive typhoon—a "divine wind" (*kamikaze*). Japan would not face a foreign invader again until American forces landed on the Japanese islands in the summer of 1945.

The resistance to the Mongols had put a heavy strain on the system, however, and in 1333 the Kamakura shogunate was overthrown by a coalition of powerful clans. A new shogun, supplied by the Ashikaga family, arose in Kyoto and attempted to continue the shogunate system. But the Ashikaga were unable to restore the centralized power of their predecessors. With the central government

SAMURAI. During the Kamakura period, painters began to depict the adventures of the new warrior class. Here is an imposing mounted samurai warrior, the Japanese equivalent of the medieval knight in fief-holding Europe. Like his European counterpart, the samurai was supposed to live by a strict moral code and was expected to maintain an unquestioning loyalty to his liege lord. Above all, a samurai's life was one of simplicity and self-sacrifice.

reduced to a shell, the power of the local landed aristocracy increased to an unprecedented degree. Heads of great noble families, now called daimyo (great names), controlled vast landed estates that owed no taxes to the government or to the court in Kyoto. As clan rivalries continued, the daimyo relied increasingly on the samurai for protection, and political power came into the hands of a loose coalition of noble families.

By the end of the fifteenth century, Japan was again close to anarchy. A disastrous civil conflict known as the Onin War (1467–1477) led to the virtual destruction of the capital city of Kyoto and the disintegration of the shogunate. With the disappearance of any central authority, powerful aristocrats in rural areas now seized total control over large territories and ruled as independent great lords. Territorial rivalries and claims of precedence led to almost constant warfare in this period of "warring states," as it is called (in obvious parallel with a similar era during the Zhou dynasty in China). The trend back toward central authority did not begin until the last quarter of the sixteenth century.

Economic and Social Structures

From the time the Yayoi culture was first established on the Japanese islands, Japan was a predominantly agrarian society. Although Japan lacked the spacious valleys and

THE BURNING OF THE PALACE. The Kamakura era is represented in this thirteenth-century action-packed scene from the *Scroll of the Heiji Period,* which depicts the burning of a retired emperor's palace in the middle of the night. Servants and ladies of the court flee in vain from the massive flames. Confusion and violence reign. The determined faces of the warriors only add to the ferocity of the attack.

deltas of the river valley societies, its inhabitants were able to take advantage of their limited amount of tillable land and plentiful rainfall to create a society based on the cultivation of wet rice.

As in China, commerce was slow to develop in Japan. During ancient times, each *uji* had a local artisan class, composed of weavers, carpenters, and ironworkers, but trade was essentially local and was regulated by the local clan leaders. With the rise of the Yamato state, a money economy gradually began to develop, although most trade was still conducted through barter until the twelfth century, when metal coins introduced from China became more popular.

Trade and manufacturing began to develop more rapidly during the Kamakura period, with the appearance of trimonthly markets in the larger towns and the emergence of such industries as paper, iron casting, and porcelain. Foreign trade, mainly with Korea and China, began during the eleventh century. Japan exported raw materials, paintings, swords, and other manufactured items in return for silk, porcelain, books, and copper cash. Some Japanese traders were so aggressive in pressing their interests that authorities in China and Korea attempted to limit the number of Japanese commercial missions that could visit each year. Such restrictions were often ignored, however, and encouraged some Japanese traders to turn to piracy.

Significantly, manufacturing and commerce developed rapidly during the more decentralized period of the Ashikaga shogunate and the era of the "warring states," perhaps because of the rapid growth in the wealth and autonomy of local daimyo families. Market towns, now operating on a full money economy, began to appear, and local manufacturers formed guilds to protect their mutual interests. Sometimes local peasants would sell products made in their homes, such as clothing made of silk or hemp, household items, or food products, at the markets. In general, however, trade and manufacturing remained under the control of the local daimyo, who would often provide tax breaks to local guilds in return for other benefits. Although Japan remained a primarily agricultural society, it was on the verge of a major advance in manufacturing.

DAILY LIFE

One of the first descriptions of the life of the Japanese people comes from a Chinese dynastic history from the third century C.E. It describes lords and peasants living in an agricultural society that was based on the cultivation of wet rice. Laws had been enacted to punish offenders, local trade was conducted in markets, and government granaries stored the grain that was paid as taxes (see the box on p. 303).

SCENE OF URBAN LIFE. Although traditional Japan was largely an agricultural society, trade and manufacturing began to develop during the Kamakura period, sparked by the rapid growth of local daimyo families and market towns. Intraregional trade was transported by horse-drawn carts or by boats on rivers or along the coast. Portrayed here is a detail from a thirteenth-century scroll depicting the bustle and general confusion of the city of Edo (now Tokyo).

LIFE IN THE LAND OF WA

Some of the earliest descriptions of Japan come from Chinese sources. The following passage from the History of the Wei Dynasty *was written in the late third century* C.E. *The term* Wa *is a derogatory word meaning "dwarf" and was frequently used in China to refer to the Japanese people. The author of this passage, while remarking on the strange habits of the Japanese, writes without condescension.*

HISTORY OF THE WEI DYNASTY

The people of Wa make their abode in the mountainous islands located in the middle of the ocean to the southeast of the Taifang prefecture. . . .

All men, old or young, are covered by tattoos. Japanese fishers revel in diving to catch fish and shell-fish. Tattoos are said to drive away large fish and water predators. They are considered an ornament. . . . Men allow their hair to cover both of their ears and wear head-bands. They wear loincloths wrapped around their bodies and seldom use stitches. Women gather their hair at the ends and tie it in a knot and then pin it to the top of their heads. They make their clothes in one piece, and cut an opening in the center for their heads. They plant wet-field rice, China-grass [a type of nettle], and mulberry trees. They raise cocoons and reel the silk off the cocoons. They produce clothing made of China-grass, of coarse silk, and of cotton. In their land, there are no cows, horses, tigers, leopards, sheep, or swan. They fight with halberds, shields, and wooden bows. . . . Their arrows are made of bamboo, and iron and bone points make up the arrowhead.

People . . . live long, some reaching one hundred years of age, and others to eighty or ninety years. Normally men of high echelon have four or five wives, and the plebeians may have two or three. When the law is violated, the light offender loses his wife and children by confiscation, and the grave offender has his household and kin exterminated. There are class distinctions within the nobility and the base, and some are vassals of others. There are mansions and granaries erected for the purpose of collecting taxes. . . .

When plebeians meet the high-echelon men on the road, they withdraw to the grassy area (side of the road) hesitantly. When they speak or are spoken to, they either crouch or kneel with both hands on the ground to show their respect. When responding they say "aye," which corresponds to our affirmative "yes."

Life for the common people probably changed very little over the next several hundred years. Most were peasants, who worked on land owned by their lord or, in some cases, by the state or by Buddhist monasteries. By no means, however, were all peasants equal either economically or socially. Although in ancient times all land was owned by the state and peasants working the land were taxed at an equal rate depending on the nature of the crop, after the Yamato era variations began to develop. At the top were local officials who were often well-to-do peasants. They were responsible for organizing collective labor services and collecting tax grain from the peasants and in turn were exempt from such obligations themselves.

The mass of the peasants were under the authority of these local officials. In general, peasants were free to dispose of their harvest as they saw fit after paying their tax quota, but in practical terms their freedom was limited. Those who were unable to pay the tax sank to the level of *genin*, or landless laborers, who could be bought and sold by their proprietors like slaves along with the land on which they worked. Some fled to escape such a fate and attempted to survive by clearing plots of land in the mountains or by becoming bandits.

In addition to the *genin*, the bottom of the social scale was occupied by the *eta*, a class of hereditary slaves who were responsible for what were considered degrading occupations, such as curing leather and burying the dead. The origins of the *eta* are not entirely clear, but they probably were descendants of prisoners of war, criminals, or mountain dwellers who were not related to the dominant Yamato peoples. As we shall see, the *eta* are still a distinctive part of Japanese society, and although their full legal rights are guaranteed under the current constitution, discrimination against them is not uncommon.

Daily life for ordinary people in early Japan resembled that of their counterparts throughout much of Asia. The vast majority lived in small villages, several of which normally made up a single *shoen*. Housing was simple. Most lived in small two-room houses of timber, mud, or thatch, with dirt floors covered by straw or woven mats (the origin, perhaps, of the well-known *tatami*, or woven-mat floor, of more modern times). Their diet consisted of rice (if some was left after the payment of the grain tax), wild grasses, millet, roots, and some fish and birds. Life must have been difficult at best; as one eighth-century poet lamented:

Here I lie on straw
Spread on bare earth,
With my parents at my pillow,
My wife and children at my feet,
All huddled in grief and tears.
No fire sends up smoke
At the cooking place,
And in the cauldron
A spider spins its web.[2]

Evidence about the relations between men and women in early Japan presents a mixed picture. The Chinese dynastic history reports that "in their meetings and daily living, there is no distinction between . . . men and women." It notes that a woman "adept in the ways of shamanism" had briefly ruled Japan in the third century C.E. But it also remarks that polygyny was common, with nobles normally having four to five wives, and commoners two or three.[3] An eighth-century law code guaranteed the inheritance rights of women, and wives abandoned by their husbands were permitted to obtain a divorce and remarry. A husband could divorce his wife if she did not produce a male child, committed adultery, disobeyed her parents-in-law, talked too much, engaged in theft, was jealous, or had a serious illness.[4]

When Buddhism was introduced, women were initially relegated to a subordinate position in the new faith. Although they were permitted to take up monastic life—many widows entered a monastery at the death of their husbands—they were not permitted to visit Buddhist holy places, nor were they even (in the accepted wisdom) equal with men in the afterlife. One Buddhist commentary from the late thirteenth century said that a woman could not attain enlightenment because "her sin is grievous, and so she is not allowed to enter the lofty palace of the great Brahma, nor to look upon the clouds which hover over his ministers and people."[5] Other Buddhist scholars were more egalitarian: "Learning the Law of Buddha and achieving release from illusion have nothing to do with whether one happens to be a man or a woman."[6] Such views ultimately prevailed, and women were eventually allowed to participate fully in Buddhist activities in medieval Japan.

Although women did not possess the full legal and social rights of their male counterparts, they played an active role at various levels of Japanese society. Aristocratic women were prominent at court, and some, such as the author Lady Murasaki, became renowned for their artistic or literary talents. Though few commoners could aspire to such prominence, women often appear in the scroll paintings of the period along with men, doing the spring planting, threshing and hulling the rice, and acting as carriers, peddlers, salespersons, and entertainers.

In Search of the Pure Land: Religion in Early Japan

In Japan, as elsewhere, religious belief began with the worship of nature spirits. Early Japanese worshiped spirits, called *kami*, who resided in trees, rivers and streams, and mountains. They also believed in ancestral spirits present in the atmosphere. In Japan, these beliefs eventually evolved into a kind of state religion called Shinto (the Sacred Way or the Way of the Gods) that is still practiced today. Shinto still serves as an ideological and emotional force that knits the Japanese into a single people and nation.

Shinto does not have a complex metaphysical superstructure or an elaborate moral code. It does require certain ritual acts, usually undertaken at a shrine, and a process of purification, which may have originated in primitive concerns about death, childbirth, illness, and menstruation. This traditional concern about physical purity may help to explain the strong Japanese concern for personal cleanliness and the practice of denying women entrance to the holy places.

Another feature of Shinto is its stress on the beauty of nature and the importance of nature itself in Japanese life. Shinto shrines are usually located in places of exceptional beauty and are often dedicated to a nearby physical feature. As time passed, such primitive beliefs contributed to the characteristic Japanese love of nature. In this sense, early Shinto beliefs have been incorporated into the lives of all Japanese.

In time, Shinto evolved into a state doctrine that was linked with belief in the divinity of the emperor and the sacredness of the Japanese nation. A national shrine was established at Ise, north of the early capital of Nara, where the emperor annually paid tribute to the sun goddess. But although Shinto had evolved well beyond its primitive origins, like its counterparts elsewhere it could not satisfy all the religious and emotional needs of the Japanese people. For those needs, the Japanese turned to Buddhism.

As we have seen, Buddhism was introduced into Japan from China during the sixth century C.E. and had begun to spread beyond the court to the general population by the eighth century. As in China, most Japanese saw no contradiction between worshiping both the Buddha and their local nature gods, many of whom were considered to be later manifestations of the Buddha. Most of the Buddhist sects that had achieved popularity in China were established in Japan, and many of them attracted powerful patrons at court. Great monasteries were established that competed in wealth and influence with the noble families that had traditionally ruled the country.

Perhaps the two most influential Buddhist sects were the Pure Land (Jodo) sect and Zen (in Chinese, Chan or Ch'an). The Pure Land sect, which taught that devotion alone could lead to enlightenment and release, was very popular among the common people, for whom monastic life was one of the few routes to upward mobility. Among the aristocracy, the most influential school was Zen, which exerted a significant impact on Japanese life and culture during the era of the warring states. In its emphasis on austerity, self-discipline, and communion with nature, Zen complemented many traditional beliefs in Japanese society and became an important component of the samurai warrior's code.

In Zen teachings, there were various ways to achieve enlightenment (*satori* in Japanese). Some stressed that it could be achieved suddenly. One monk, for example, reportedly achieved *satori* by listening to the sound of a bamboo striking against roof tiles, another by carefully watching the opening of peach blossoms in the spring. But other practitioners, sometimes called adepts, said that enlightenment could come only through studying the scriptures and arduous self-discipline (known as *zazen*, or "seated Zen"). Seated Zen involved a lengthy process of meditation that cleansed the mind of extraneous thoughts so that it could concentrate on the essential.

Sources of Traditional Japanese Culture

Nowhere is the Japanese genius for blending indigenous and imported elements into an effective whole better demonstrated than in culture. In such widely diverse fields as art, architecture, sculpture, and literature, the Japanese from early times showed an impressive capacity to borrow selectively from abroad without destroying essential native elements.

Growing contact with China during the period of the rise of the Yamato state stimulated Japanese artists. Missions sent to China and Korea during the seventh and eighth centuries returned with examples of Tang literature, sculpture, and painting, all of which influenced the Japanese.

LITERATURE

Borrowing from Chinese models was somewhat complicated for Japanese authors, however. The early Japanese had no writing system for recording their own spoken language and initially adopted the Chinese written language for writing. But resourceful Japanese soon began to adapt the Chinese written characters so that they could be used for recording the Japanese language. In some cases, Chinese characters were given Japanese pronunciations. But Chinese characters ordinarily could not be used to record Japanese words, which normally contain more than one syllable. Sometimes the Japanese simply used Chinese characters as phonetic symbols that were combined to form Japanese words. Later they simplified the characters into phonetic symbols that were used alongside Chinese characters. This hybrid system continues to be used today.

At first, many educated Japanese preferred to write in Chinese, and a court literature—consisting of essays, poetry, and official histories—appeared in the classical Chinese language. But the native Japanese spoken language never totally disappeared among the educated classes and eventually became the instrument of a unique literature. With the lessening of Chinese political and cultural influence in the tenth century, Japanese verse resurfaced. Between the tenth and the fifteenth centuries, twenty imperial anthologies of poetry were compiled. Initially, they were written primarily by courtiers, but with the fall of the Heian court and the rise of the warrior and merchant classes, all literate segments of society began to produce poetry.

Japanese poetry is unique. It expresses its themes in a simple form, a characteristic stemming from traditional Japanese aesthetics, Zen religion, and the language itself. The aim of the Japanese poet was to create a mood, perhaps the melancholic effect of gently falling cherry blossoms or leaves. With a few specific references, the poet suggested a whole world, just as Zen Buddhism sought enlightenment from a sudden perception. Poets often alluded to earlier poems by repeating their images with small changes, a technique that was viewed not as plagiarism, but as an elaboration on the meaning of the earlier poem. The following poems in English translation illustrate this technique; the first poem is by Fujiwara no Michimune; the second is by Lady Sagami.

The under leaves
In the autumn wind
Must have become cold:
In the moor of little lespedezas
The quail are crying.

The under leaves of the lespedeza
When the dew is gathering
Must be cold:
In the autumn moor
The young deer are crying.[7]

By the fourteenth century, the technique of the "linked verse" had become the most popular form of Japanese poetry. Known as haiku, it is composed of seventeen syllables divided into lines of five, seven, and five syllables. The poems usually focused on images from nature and the mutability of life. Often the poetry was written by several individuals alternately composing verses and linking them together into long sequences of hundreds and even thousands of lines (see the box on p. 306).

Poetry served a unique function at the Heian court, where it was the initial means of communication between lovers. By custom, aristocratic women were isolated from all contact with men outside their immediate family and spent their days hidden behind screens. Some amused themselves by writing poetry. When courtship began, poetic exchanges were the only means a woman had to attract her prospective lover, who would be enticed solely by her poetic art.

During the Heian period, male courtiers wrote in Chinese, believing that Chinese civilization was superior and worthy of emulation. Like the Chinese, they viewed prose fiction as "vulgar gossip." Consequently, from the ninth to the twelfth century, Japanese women were the most prolific writers of prose fiction in Japanese. Excluded from school, they learned to read and write at home and wrote diaries, stories, and novels to pass the time. Some of the most talented women were invited to court as authors in residence.

From this tradition of female prose appeared one of the world's truly great novels, *The Tale of Genji*, written by the

A SAMPLE OF LINKED VERSE

One of the distinctive features of medieval Japanese literature was the technique of "linked verse." In a manner similar to haiku poetry today, such poems, known as renga, *were written by groups of individuals who would join together to compose the poem, verse by verse. The following example, by three famous poets named Sogi, Shohaku, and Socho, is one of the most famous of the period.*

THE THREE POETS AT MINASE

Snow clinging to slope, Sogi
On mist-enshrouded mountains
At eveningtime.
In the distance flows Shohaku
Through plum-scented villages.
Willows cluster Socho
In the river breeze
As spring appears.
The sound of a boat being poled Sogi
In the clearness at dawn
Still the moon lingers Shohaku
As fog o'er-spreads
The night.
A frost-covered meadow; Socho
Autumn has drawn to a close.
Against the wishes Sogi
Of droning insects
The grasses wither.

diarist and court author Murasaki Shikibu around the year 1000. The novel traces the life and loves of the courtier Genji as he strives to remain in favor with those in power while at the same time pursuing his cult of love and beauty (see the box on p. 307). The essential element in the story line, however, is the artistic refinement and sensitivity of the characters. The most important aspect of their lives is the style with which they write letters and poetry, sing songs, dance, or play the flute or the zither.

After the refined and gentle sadness of the era of Genji, Japanese fiction entered the increasingly pessimistic world of the warring states of Kamakura (1185–1333). Typically, the novels of this period focus on a solitary figure, who is aloof from the refinements of the court and faces battle and possibly death. Understandably, a new genre, that of the heroic war tale, developed out of the new warrior class. Such works described the military exploits of warriors, coupled with an overwhelming sense of sadness and loneliness.

During this period, the famous classical Japanese drama known as *No* also originated. *No* developed out of a variety of entertainment forms, such as dancing and juggling, that were part of the native tradition or had been imported from China and other regions of Asia. The plots were normally based on stories from Japanese history or legend. Eventually, *No* evolved into a highly stylized drama in which the performers wore masks and danced to the accompaniment of instrumental music. Like much of Japanese culture, *No* was restrained, graceful, and refined.

ART AND ARCHITECTURE

In art and architecture, as in literature, the Japanese pursued their interest in beauty, simplicity, and nature. To some degree, Japanese artists and architects were influenced by Chinese forms. As they became familiar with Chinese architecture, Japanese rulers and aristocrats tried to emulate the splendor of Tang civilization and began constructing their palaces and temples in Chinese style.

During the Heian period (794–1185), the search for beauty was reflected in various art forms, such as narrative hand scrolls, screens, sliding door panels, fans, and lacquer decoration. As in the case of literature, nature themes dominated, such as seashore scenes, a spring rain, moon and mist, or flowering wisteria and cherry blossoms. All were intended to evoke an emotional response on the part of the viewer. Japanese painting suggested the frail beauty of nature by presenting it on a smaller scale. The majestic mountain in a Chinese painting became a more intimate Japanese landscape with rolling hills and a rice field. Faces were rarely shown, and human drama was indicated by a woman lying prostrate or hiding her face in her sleeve. Tension was shown by two people talking at a great distance or with their backs to one another.

During the Kamakura period (1185–1333), the hand scroll with its physical realism and action-packed paintings of the new warrior class achieved great popularity. Reflecting these chaotic times, the art of portraiture flourished, and a scroll would include a full gallery of warriors and holy men in starkly realistic detail, including such unflattering features as stubble, worry lines on a forehead, and crooked teeth. Japanese sculptors also produced naturalistic wooden statues of generals, nobles, and saints. By far the most distinctive, however, were the fierce heavenly "guardian kings," who still intimidate the viewer today. In contrast to the refined atmosphere of the Fujiwara court, the Kamakura era was a warrior's world.

THE SEDUCTION OF THE AKASHI LADY

The Tale of Genji, Japan's most famous novel, is a panoramic portrayal of court life in tenth-century Japan. In this excerpt, the courtier Genji has just seduced a lady at court and now feels misgivings at having betrayed his child bride. A koto is a Japanese string instrument similar to a zither.

THE TALE OF GENJI

A curtain string brushed against a koto, to tell him that she had been passing a quiet evening at her music.

"And will you not play for me on the koto of which I have heard so much?"

"Would there were someone with whom I might share my thoughts
And so dispel some part of these sad dreams."
"You speak to one for whom the night has no end.
How can she tell the dreaming from the waking?"

The almost inaudible whisper reminded him strongly of the Rokujo lady.

This lady had not been prepared for an incursion and could not cope with it. She fled to an inner room. How she could have contrived to bar it he could not tell, but it was very firmly barred indeed. Though he did not exactly force his way through, it is not to be imagined that he left matters as they were. Delicate, slender—she was almost too beautiful. Pleasure was mingled with pity at the thought that he was imposing himself upon her. She was even more pleasing than reports from afar had had her. The autumn night, usually so long, was over in a trice. Not wishing to be seen, he hurried out, leaving affectionate assurances behind.

Genji called in secret from time to time. The two houses being some distance apart, he feared being seen by fishers, who were known to relish a good rumor, and sometimes several days would elapse between his visits. . . .

Genji dreaded having Murasaki [his bride] learn of the affair. He still loved her more than anyone, and he did not want her to make even joking reference to it. She was a quiet, docile lady, but she had more than once been unhappy with him. Why, for the sake of brief pleasure, had he caused her pain? He wished it were all his to do over again. The sight of the Akashi lady only brought new longing for the other lady.

He got off a more earnest and affectionate letter than usual, at the end of which he said: "I am in anguish at the thought that, because of foolish occurrences for which I have been responsible but have had little heart, I might appear in a guise distasteful to you. There has been a strange, fleeting encounter. That I should volunteer this story will make you see, I hope, how little I wish to have secrets from you. Let the gods be my judges.

"It was but the fisherman's brush with the salty sea pine.
Followed by a tide of tears of longing."

Her reply was gentle and unreproachful, and at the end of it she said: "That you should have deigned to tell me a dreamlike story which you could not keep to yourself calls to mind numbers of earlier instances.

"Naive of me, perhaps; yet we did make our vows.
And now see the waves that wash the Mountain of Waiting!"

It was the one note of reproach in a quiet, undemanding letter. He found it hard to put down, and for some nights he stayed away from the house in the hills.

Zen Buddhism, an import from China in the thirteenth century, also influenced Japanese aesthetics. With its emphasis on immediate enlightenment without recourse to intellectual analysis and elaborate ritual, Zen reinforced the Japanese predilection for simplicity and self-discipline. During this era, Zen philosophy found expression in the Japanese garden, the tea ceremony, the art of flower arranging, pottery and ceramics, and miniature plant display (the famous *bonsai*, literally "pot scenery").

Landscape served as an important means of expression in both Japanese art and architecture. Japanese gardens were initially modeled on Chinese examples. Early court texts during the Heian period emphasized the importance of including a stream or pond when creating a garden. The landscape surrounding the fourteenth-century Golden Pavilion in Kyoto displays a harmony of garden, water, and architecture that makes it one of the treasures of the world. Because of the shortage of water in the city, later gardens concentrated on rock composition, using white pebbles to represent water.

Like the Japanese garden, the tea ceremony represents the fusion of Zen and aesthetics. Developed in the fifteenth century, it was practiced in a simple room devoid of external ornament except for a *tatami* floor, sliding doors, and an alcove with a writing desk and asymmetrical shelves. The participants could therefore focus completely on the activity of pouring and drinking tea. "Tea and Zen have the same flavor," goes the Japanese saying. Considered the ultimate symbol of spiritual

GUARDIAN KINGS. Larger than life and intimidating in its presence, this thirteenth-century wooden statue departs from the refined atmosphere of the Heian court and pulsates with the masculine energy of the Kamakura period. Placed strategically at the entrance to Buddhist shrines, guardian kings such as this one protected the temple and the faithful.

A SEATED BUDDHA. Buddhist statuary originated in India and China, and evolved as a popular art form in Japan from the seventh century on. Characteristic of these statues are the *mudras,* or hand and body positions by which the Buddha communicated with his followers. Here, his connected fingers indicate meditation. Whereas earlier Japanese sculptors worked in bronze, the depletion of metal reserves eventually necessitated the use of wood. This remarkable eleventh-century gilded wood carving, over ten feet in height, is composed of fifty-three pieces of cypress and exudes a feeling of stability and calm, expressing the Buddha's deep spirituality.

deliverance, the tea ceremony had great aesthetic value and moral significance in traditional times as well as today.

Japan and the Chinese Model

Few societies in Asia have historically been as isolated as Japan. Cut off from the mainland by 120 miles of frequently turbulent ocean, the Japanese had only minimal contact with the outside world during most of their early development.

Whether this isolation was ultimately beneficial to Japanese society cannot be determined. The lack of knowledge of developments taking place elsewhere probably delayed the process of change in Japan. On the other hand, the Japanese were spared the destructive invasions that afflicted other ancient civilizations. Certainly, once the Japanese became acquainted with Chinese culture at the height of the Tang era, they were quick to take advantage of the opportunity. In the space of a few decades, the young state adopted many aspects of Chinese society and culture and thereby introduced major changes into Japanese life.

Nevertheless, Japanese political institutions failed to follow all aspects of the Chinese pattern. Despite Prince Shotoku's effort to make effective use of the imperial traditions of Tang China, the decentralizing forces inside

THE GOLDEN PAVILION IN KYOTO. The landscape surrounding the Golden Pavilion displays a harmony of garden, water, and architecture that makes it one of the treasures of the world. Constructed in the fourteenth century as a retreat for the shoguns to withdraw from their administrative chores, the pavilion is named for the gold foil that covered its exterior. Completely destroyed by an arsonist in 1950 as a protest against the commercialism of modern Buddhism, it was rebuilt and reopened in 1987.

Japanese society remained dominant throughout the period under discussion in this chapter. Adoption of the Confucian civil service examination did not lead to a breakdown of Japanese social divisions; instead, the examination was administered in a manner that preserved and strengthened them. Although Buddhist and Daoist doctrines made a significant contribution to Japanese religious practices, Shinto beliefs continued to play a major role in shaping the Japanese worldview.

Why Japan did not follow the Chinese road to centralized authority has been the subject of some debate among historians. Some argue that the answer lies in differing cultural traditions, while others suggest that Chinese institutions and values were introduced too rapidly to be assimilated effectively by Japanese society. One factor may have been the absence of a foreign threat (except for the Mongols) in Japan. A recent view holds that diseases (such as smallpox and measles) imported inadvertently from China led to a marked decline in the population of the islands, reducing the food output and preventing the population from coalescing in more compact urban centers.

In any event, Japan was not the only society in Asia to assimilate ideas from abroad while at the same time preserving customs and institutions inherited from the past. Across the Sea of Japan to the west and several thousand miles to the south, other Asian peoples were embarked on a similar journey. We now turn to their experience.

KOREA

No society in East Asia was more strongly influenced by the Chinese model than was that of Korea. Slightly larger than the state of Minnesota, the Korean peninsula was probably first settled by Altaic-speaking fishing and hunting peoples from neighboring Manchuria during the Neolithic Age. Because the area is relatively mountainous (only about one-fifth of the peninsula is adaptable to cultivation), farming was apparently not practiced until about 2000 B.C.E. The other aspect of Korea's geography that has profoundly affected its history is its proximity to both China and Japan.

In 109 B.C.E., the northern part of the peninsula came under direct Chinese rule. During the next several generations, the area was ruled by the Han dynasty, which divided the territory into provinces and introduced Chinese institutions. With the decline of the Han in the third century C.E., power gradually shifted to local tribal leaders, who drove out the Chinese administrators but continued to absorb Chinese cultural influence. Eventually, three separate kingdoms emerged on the peninsula: Koguryo in the north, Paekche in the southwest, and Silla in the southeast. The Japanese, who had recently established their own state on the Yamato plain, maintained a small colony on the southern coast.

The Three Kingdoms

From the fourth to the seventh centuries, the three kingdoms were bitter rivals for influence and territory on the peninsula. At the same time, all began to absorb Chinese political and cultural institutions. Chinese influence was most notable in Koguryo, where Buddhism was introduced in the late fourth century C.E., and the first Confucian academy on the peninsula was established in the capital at Pyongyang. All three kingdoms also appear to have accepted a tributary relationship with one or another of the squabbling states that emerged in China after the fall of the Han. The kingdom of Silla, less exposed than its two rivals to Chinese influence, was at first the weakest of the three, but eventually its greater internal cohesion—perhaps a consequence of the tenacity of its tribal traditions—enabled it to become the dominant power on

RYOANJI TEMPLE GARDEN IN KYOTO. As the result of a water shortage in the fifteenth century, Japanese landscape designers began to make increasing use of rocks and pebbles to represent water. In the Ryoanji Temple in the hills west of Kyoto, seventeen rocks surrounded by wavy raked pebbles are arranged in five groups to suggest mountains emerging from the sea. Here we experience the quintessential Japanese aesthetic expression of allusion, simplicity, restraint, and tranquillity.

the peninsula. Then the rulers of Silla forced the Chinese to withdraw from all but the area adjacent to the Yalu River. To pacify the haughty Chinese, Silla accepted tributary status under the Tang dynasty. The remaining Japanese colonies in the south were eliminated.

With the country unified for the first time, the rulers of Silla attempted to use Chinese political institutions and ideology to forge a centralized state. Buddhism, now rising in popularity, became the state religion, and Korean monks followed the paths of their Japanese counterparts on journeys to the Middle Kingdom. Chinese architecture and art became dominant in the capital at Kyongju and other urban centers, and the written Chinese language became the official means of communication at court. But powerful aristocratic families, long dominant in the southeastern part of the peninsula, were still influential at court. They were able to prevent the adoption of the Tang civil service examination system and resisted the distribution of manorial lands to the poor. The failure to adopt the Chinese model was fatal. Squabbling among noble families steadily increased, and after the assassination of the king of Silla in 780, the country sank into civil war.

Unification

In the early tenth century, a new dynasty called Koryo (the root of the modern word for Korea) arose in the north. The new kingdom adopted Chinese political institutions in an effort to strengthen its power and unify its territory. The civil service examination system was introduced in 958, but as in Japan, the bureaucracy continued to be dominated by influential aristocratic families.

The Koryo dynasty remained in power for four hundred years, protected from invasion by the absence of a strong dynasty in neighboring China. Under the Koryo, industry and commerce slowly began to develop, but as in China, agriculture was the prime source of wealth. In theory, all land was the property of the king, but in actuality noble families controlled their holdings. The lands were worked by peasants who were subject to burdens similar to those of European serfs. At the bottom of society was a class of "base people" (*chonmin*), composed of slaves, artisans, and other specialized workers.

KOREAN ROYAL CROWN. The Silla dynasty was renowned for the high quality of its gold, jewelry, crowns, and sword sheaths. Shown here is a jewel-inlaid royal crown of the fifth century C.E. that was excavated from a royal tomb in eastern Korea. Although much Silla artwork reflects Chinese influence, royal crowns located in Silla tombs often contain antler-like motifs, reflecting the animistic traditions of Korea's pre-Chinese past. The comma-shaped jewels symbolize the King's Heaven-sanctioned authority on earth.

PULGUKSA BELL TOWER. Among the greatest architectural achievements on the Korean peninsula is the Pulguksa (Monastery of the Land of Buddha), built near the ancient capital of Silla in the eighth century C.E. Shown here is the Bell Tower, located in the midst of beautiful parklands on the monastery grounds. Young Korean couples often come to this monastery after their weddings to be photographed in the stunning surroundings.

From a cultural point of view, the Koryo era was one of high achievement. Buddhist monasteries, run by sects introduced from China like the Pure Land and Zen (Chan), controlled vast territories, while their monks served as royal advisers at court. At first Buddhist themes dominated in Korean art and sculpture, and the entire Tripitaka (the "three baskets" of the Buddhist canon) was printed by wooden blocks (see the box on p. 312). Eventually, however, with the appearance of landscape painting and porcelain, Confucian themes began to predominate.

Under the Mongols

Like its predecessor in Silla, the kingdom of Koryo was unable to overcome the power of the nobility and the absence of a reliable tax base. In the thirteenth century, the Mongols seized the northern part of the country and assimilated it into the Yuan empire. The weakened kingdom of Koryo became a tributary of the great khan in Khanbaliq (see Chapter 10).

The era of Mongol rule was one of profound suffering for the Korean people, especially the thousands of peasants and artisans who were compelled to perform corvée labor to help build the ships in preparation for Khubilai Khan's invasion of Japan. On the positive side, the Mongols introduced many new ideas and technology from China and further afield. The Koryo dynasty had managed to survive, but only by accepting Mongol authority, and when the power of the Mongols declined, the kingdom declined with it. With the rise to power of the Ming in China, Koryo collapsed, and power was seized by the military commander Yi Song-gye, who declared the founding of the new Yi dynasty in 1392. Once again, the Korean people were in charge of their own destiny.

THE FLOWER GARDEN SCRIPTURE

By the eighth century, Buddhism had come to Korea from China, and like their counterparts in Christian Europe, Korean monks could accumulate merit toward salvation by copying the scriptures. In this passage, the eighth-century Master Yongi of Hwangyong monastery has volunteered to copy a scripture as a way of expressing gratitude for the love of his parents and assisting others in following the Buddhist eightfold path to wisdom. Note the careful attention to ritual as the process is brought to realization. This scripture, which was discovered in 1979, consisted of two scrolls of thirty white papers joined together, with characters in black ink. Each scroll was fourteen meters long.

AN EIGHTH-CENTURY BUDDHIST SCRIPTURE

The scripture is made as follows: First scented water is sprinkled around the roots of a paperbark mulberry tree to quicken its growth; the bark is then peeled and pounded to make paper with a clean surface. The copyists, the artisans who make the centerpiece of the scroll, and the painters who draw the images of buddhas and bodhisattvas all receive the bodhisattva ordination and observe abstinence. After relieving themselves, sleeping, eating, or drinking, they take a bath in scented water before returning to the work. Copyists are adorned with new pure garments, loose trousers, a coarse crown, and a deva crown. Two azure-clad boys sprinkle water on their heads and . . . azure-clad boys and musicians perform music. The processions to the copying site are headed by one who sprinkles scented water on their path, another who scatters flowers, a dharma master who carries a censer, and another dharma master who chants Buddhist verses. Each of the copyists carries incense and flowers and invokes the name of the Buddha as he progresses.

Upon reaching the site, all take refuge in the Three Jewels (the Buddha, the Dharma, and the Order), make three bows, and offer the *Flower Garland Scripture* and others to buddhas and bodhisattvas. Then they sit down and copy the scripture, make the centerpiece of the scroll, and paint the buddhas and bodhisattvas. Thus, azure-clad boys and musicians cleanse everything before a piece of relic is placed in the center.

Now I make a vow that the copied scripture will not break till the end of the future—even when a major chiliocosm is destroyed by the three calamities, this scripture shall be intact as the void. If all living beings rely on this scripture, they shall witness the Buddha, listen to his dharma, worship the relic, aspire to enlightenment without backsliding, cultivate the vows of the Universally Worthy Bodhisattva, and achieve Buddhahood.

VIETNAM: THE SMALLER DRAGON

While the Korean people were attempting to establish their own identity in the shadow of the powerful Chinese empire, the peoples of Vietnam, on China's southern frontier, were trying to do the same. The Vietnamese began to practice irrigated agriculture in the flooded regions of the Red River delta at an early date and entered the Bronze Age sometime during the second millennium B.C.E. By about 200 B.C.E., a young state had begun to form in the area but immediately encountered the expanding power of the Qin empire (see Chapter 3). The Vietnamese were not easy to subdue, however (see the box on p. 313), and the collapse of the Qin dynasty temporarily enabled them to preserve their independence. Nevertheless, a century later, they were absorbed into the Han empire.

At first, the Han were satisfied to rule the delta as an autonomous region under the administration of the local landed aristocracy. But Chinese taxes were oppressive, and in 39 C.E. a revolt led by the Trung Sisters (widows of local nobles who had been executed by the Chinese) briefly brought Han rule to an end. The Chinese soon suppressed the rebellion, however, and began to rule the area directly through officials dispatched from China. In time, however, these foreign officials began to intermarry with the local nobility and form a Sino-Vietnamese ruling class who, though trained in Chinese culture, began to identify with the cause of Vietnamese autonomy.

For nearly a thousand years, the Vietnamese were exposed to the art, architecture, literature, philosophy, and even the written language of China, as the Chinese attempted to integrate the area culturally as well as politically and administratively into their empire. To all intents and purposes, the Red River delta, then known to the Chinese as the "pacified South" (Annam), became a part of China.

The Rise of Great Viet

Despite the Chinese efforts to assimilate Vietnam, the Vietnamese sense of ethnic and cultural identity proved inextinguishable, and in the tenth century the Vietnamese took advantage of the collapse of the Tang dynasty in China to overthrow Chinese rule.

The new Vietnamese state, which called itself Dai Viet (Great Viet), became a dynamic new force on the South-

THE CHINESE CONQUEST OF VIETNAM

In the third century B.C.E., *the armies of the Chinese state of Qin [Ch'in] invaded the Red River delta to launch an attack on the small Vietnamese state located there. As this passage by a Chinese historian shows, the Vietnamese were not easy to conquer, and the new state soon declared its independence from the Qin. It was a lesson that was too often forgotten by would-be conquerors in later centuries.*

THE HUAI NAN TZU

Ch'in Shih Huang Ti was interested in the rhinoceros horn, the elephant tusks, the kingfisher plumes, and the pearls of the land of Yueh [Viet]; he therefore sent Commissioner T'u Sui at the head of five hundred thousand men divided into five armies. . . . For three years the sword and the crossbow were in constant readiness. Superintendent Lu was sent; there was no means of assuring the transport of supplies, so he employed soldiers to dig a canal for sending grain, thereby making it possible to wage war on the people of Yueh. The lord of Western Ou, I Hsu Sung, was killed; consequently, the Yueh people entered the wilderness and lived there with the animals; none consented to be a slave of Ch'in; choosing from among themselves men of valor, they made them their leaders and attacked the Ch'in by night, inflicting on them a great defeat and killing Commissioner T'u Sui; the dead and wounded were many. After this, the emperor deported convicts to hold the garrisons against the Yueh people.

The Yueh people fled into the depths of the mountains and forests, and it was not possible to fight them. The soldiers were kept in garrisons to watch over abandoned territories. This went on for a long time, and the soldiers grew weary. Then the Yueh came out and attacked; the Ch'in soldiers suffered a great defeat. Subsequently, convicts were sent to hold the garrisons against the Yueh.

east Asian mainland. As the population of the Red River delta expanded, Dai Viet soon came into conflict with Champa, its neighbor to the south. Located along the central coast of modern Vietnam, Champa was a trading society based on Indian cultural traditions. Over the next several centuries, the two states fought on numerous occasions, until by the end of the fifteenth century Dai Viet had conquered Champa. The Vietnamese then resumed their march southward, establishing agricultural settlements in the newly conquered territory. By the seventeenth century, the Vietnamese had reached the Gulf of Siam.

The Vietnamese faced an even more serious challenge from the north. The Song dynasty in China, beset with its own problems on the northern frontier, eventually accepted the Dai Viet ruler's offer of tribute status, but later dynasties attempted to reintegrate the Red River delta into the Chinese empire. The first effort was made in the late thirteenth century by the Mongols, who attempted on two occasions to conquer the Vietnamese. After a series of bloody battles, during which the Vietnamese displayed an impressive capacity for guerrilla warfare, the invaders were driven out. A little over a century later, the Ming dynasty tried again, and for twenty years Vietnam was once more under Chinese rule. In 1428, the Vietnamese evicted the Chinese again, but the experience had contributed to the strong sense of Vietnamese identity.

THE CHINESE LEGACY

Despite their stubborn resistance to Chinese rule, after the restoration of independence in the tenth century, Vietnamese rulers quickly discovered the convenience of the Confucian model in administering a river valley society and therefore attempted to follow Chinese practice in forming their own state. The ruler styled himself an emperor like his counterpart to the north (although he prudently termed himself a king in his direct dealings with the Chinese court), adopted Chinese court rituals, claimed the Mandate of Heaven, and arrogated to himself the same authority and privileges in his dealings with his subjects. But unlike a Chinese emperor, who had no particular symbolic role as defender of the Chinese people or Chinese culture, a Vietnamese monarch was viewed, above all, as the symbol and defender of Vietnamese independence.

Like their Chinese counterparts, Vietnamese rulers fought to preserve their authority from the challenges of powerful aristocratic families and turned to the Chinese bureaucratic model, including civil service examinations, as a means of doing so. Under the pressure of strong monarchs, the concept of merit eventually took hold, and the power of the landed aristocracy was weakened if not entirely broken. The Vietnamese adopted much of the Chinese administrative structure, including the six ministries, the censorate, and the various levels of provincial and local administration.

Another aspect of the Chinese legacy was the spread of Buddhist, Daoist, and Confucian ideas, which supplemented the Viets' traditional belief in nature spirits. Buddhist precepts became popular among the local population, who integrated the new faith into their existing belief system by founding Buddhist temples dedicated to the local village deity in the hope of guaranteeing an abundant harvest. Upper-class Vietnamese educated in the Confucian classics tended to follow the

CHRONOLOGY

EARLY KOREA AND VIETNAM

Chinese conquest of Korea and Vietnam	First century B.C.E.
Trung Sisters' Revolt	39 C.E.
Foundation of Champa	192
Era of Three Kingdoms in Korea	Fourth–seventh centuries C.E.
Restoration of Vietnamese independence	939
Mongol invasion of Korea and Vietnam	1257–1285
Foundation of Yi dynasty in Korea	1392
Vietnamese conquest of Champa	1471

more agnostic Confucian doctrine, but some joined Buddhist monasteries. Daoism also flourished at all levels of society and, as in China, provided a structure for animistic beliefs and practices that still predominated at the village level.

During the early period of independence, Vietnamese culture also borrowed liberally from its larger neighbor. Educated Vietnamese tried their hand at Chinese poetry, wrote dynastic histories in the Chinese style, and followed Chinese models in sculpture, architecture, and porcelain. Many of the notable buildings of the medieval period, such as the Temple of Literature and the famous One-Pillar Pagoda in Hanoi, are classic examples of Chinese architecture.

But there were signs that Vietnamese creativity would eventually transcend the bounds of Chinese cultural norms. Although most classical writing was undertaken in literary Chinese, the only form of literary expression deemed suitable by Confucian conservatives, an adaptation of Chinese written characters, called *Chu Nom* (southern characters), was devised to provide a written system for spoken Vietnamese. In use by the early ninth century, it eventually began to be used for the composition of essays and poetry in the Vietnamese language. Such pioneering efforts would lead in later centuries to the emergence of a vigorous national literature totally independent of Chinese forms.

Society and Family Life

Vietnamese social institutions and customs were also strongly influenced by those of China. As in China, the introduction of a Confucian system and the adoption of

THE TEMPLE OF LITERATURE, HANOI. When the Vietnamese regained their independence from China in the tenth century C.E., they retained Chinese institutions that they deemed beneficial. A prime example was the establishment of the Temple of Literature, Vietnam's first university, in 1076. Here the sons of mandarins were educated in the Confucian classics in preparation for an official career. Beginning in the fifteenth century, those receiving doctorates had stelae erected to identify their achievements. Shown here is the central hall of the temple, where advanced students took the metropolitan examinations for the doctorate.

THE ONE-PILLAR PAGODA, HANOI. This eleventh-century pagoda was built at the order of a Vietnamese monarch who had dreamed that the Buddhist goddess of mercy, while seated on a lotus, had promised him a son. Shortly after the dream, the emperor fathered a son. In gratitude he constructed this distinctive pagoda on one pillar, resembling a lotus blossom, the Buddhist symbol of purity, rising out of the mud.

civil service examinations undermined the role of the old landed aristocrats and led eventually to their replacement by the scholar-gentry class. Also as in China, the examinations were open to most males, regardless of family background, which opened the door to a degree of social mobility unknown in most of the Indianized states elsewhere in the region. Candidates for the bureaucracy read many of the same Confucian classics and absorbed the same ethical principles as their counterparts in China. At the same time, they were also exposed to the classic works of Vietnamese history, which strengthened their sense that Vietnam was a distinct culture similar to, but separate from, that of China.

The vast majority of the Vietnamese people, however, were peasants. Most were small landholders or sharecroppers, who rented their plots from wealthier farmers, but large estates were rare due to the systematic efforts of the central government to prevent the rise of a powerful local landed elite.

Family life in Vietnam was similar in many respects to that in China. The Confucian concept of family took hold during the period of Chinese rule, along with the related concepts of filial piety and gender inequality. Perhaps the most striking difference between family traditions in China and Vietnam was that Vietnamese women possessed more rights both in practice and by law. Since ancient times wives had been permitted to own property and initiate divorce proceedings. One consequence of Chinese rule was a growing emphasis on male dominance, but the tradition of women's rights was never totally extinguished and was legally recognized in a law code promulgated in 1460.

Moreover, Vietnam had a strong historical tradition associating heroic women with the defense of the homeland. The Trung Sisters were the first but by no means the only example. In the following passage, a Vietnamese historian of the eighteenth century recounts their story:

> The imperial court was far away; local officials were greedy and oppressive. At that time the country of one hundred sons was the country of the women of Lord To. The ladies [the Trung Sisters] used the female arts against their irreconcilable foe; skirts and hairpins sang of patriotic righteousness, uttered a solemn oath at the inner door of the ladies' quarters, expelled the governor, and seized the capital. . . . Were they not grand heroines? . . . Our two ladies brought forward an army of all the people, and, establishing a royal court that settled affairs in the territories of the sixty-five strongholds, shook their skirts over the Hundred Yueh [the Vietnamese people].[8]

CONCLUSION

There are some tantalizing similarities among the three countries we have examined in this chapter. All borrowed liberally from the Chinese model. At the same time, all adapted Chinese institutions and values to the conditions prevailing in their own societies. Though all expressed admiration and respect for China's achievement, all sought to keep Chinese power at a distance.

As an island nation, Japan was the most successful of the three in protecting its political sovereignty and its cultural identity. Both Korea and Vietnam were compelled on various occasions to defend their independence by force of arms. That experience may have shaped their strong sense of national distinctiveness, which we shall discuss further in a later chapter.

The appeal of Chinese institutions can undoubtedly be explained by the fact that Japan, Korea, and Vietnam were all agrarian societies, much like their larger neighbor. But it is undoubtedly significant that the aspect of Chinese political culture that was least amenable to adoption abroad was the civil service examination system. The Confucian concept of meritocracy ran directly counter to the strong aristocratic tradition that flourished in all three societies during their early stage of development. Even when the system was adopted, it was put to quite different uses. Only in Vietnam did the concept of merit eventually triumph over that of birth, as strong rulers of Dai Viet attempted to initiate the Chinese model as a means of creating a centralized system of government.

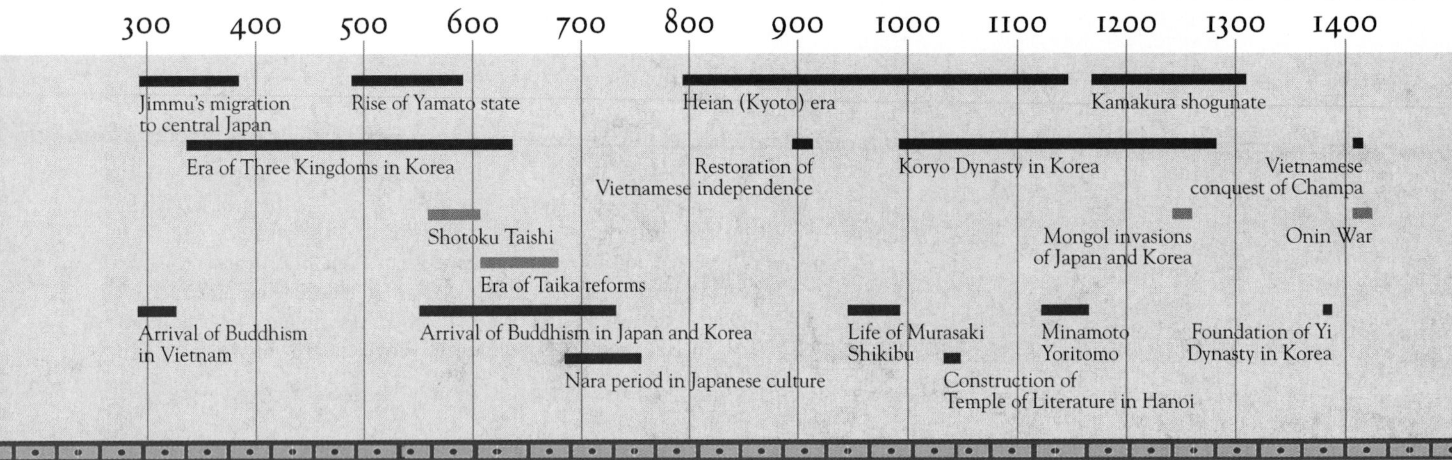

Chapter Notes

1. Keith W. Taylor, *The Birth of Vietnam* (Berkeley, Calif., 1983), p. 75.
2. Quoted in David John Lu, *Sources of Japanese History*, vol. 1 (New York, 1974), p. 7.
3. From "The History of Wei," quoted in ibid., p. 10.
4. From "The Law of Households," quoted in ibid., p. 32.
5. From "On the Salvation of Women," quoted in ibid., p. 127.
6. Quoted in Barbara Ruch, "The other side of culture in medieval Japan," in Kozo Yamamura, ed., *The Cambridge History of Japan*, vol. 3, *Medieval Japan* (Cambridge, 1990), p. 506.
7. From Donald Keene, *Anthology of Japanese Literature* (New York, 1955), p. 24.
8. Quoted in Taylor, *The Birth of Vietnam*, pp. 336–37.

Suggested Readings

Some of the standard treatments of the rise of Japanese civilization appear in textbooks dealing with the early history of East Asia. Two of the best are J. K. Fairbank, E. O. Reischauer, and A. M. Craig, *East Asia: Tradition and Transformation* (Boston, 1973), and C. Schirokauer, *A Brief History of Chinese and Japanese Civilizations* (San Diego, Calif., 1989). A number of historical works deal specifically with early Japan. G. Sansom, *A History of Japan to 1334* (Stanford, Calif., 1958) is now somewhat out of date but is still informative and very well written. For the latest scholarship on the early period, see the first three volumes of *The Cambridge History of Japan*, ed. J. W. Hall, M. B. Jansen, M. Kanai, and D. Twitchett (Cambridge, 1988).

The best available collections of documents on the early history of Japan are D. J. Lu, ed., *Sources of Japanese History*, vol. 1 (New York, 1974), and Ryusaku Tsunoda et al., eds., *Sources of Japanese Tradition*, vol. 1 (New York, 1958). For some stunning illustrations with a brief text, see *Peoples and Places of the Past: The National Geographic Illustrated Cultural Atlas of the Ancient World* (Rockville, Md., 1983).

For specialized books on the early historical period, see R. J. Pearson, ed., *Windows on the Japanese Past: Studies in Archaeology and Prehistory* (Ann Arbor, Mich., 1986). J. W. Hall, *Government and Local Power in Japan, 500–1700* (Princeton, 1966) provides a detailed analysis of the development of Japanese political institutions. The relationship between disease and state building is analyzed in W. W. Farris, *Population, Disease, and Land in Early Japan, 645–900* (Cambridge, 1985). The Kamakura period is covered in J. P. Mass, ed., *Court and Bakufu in Japan: Essays in Kamakura History* (New Haven, 1982). See also H. P. Varley, *The Onin War* (New York, 1977). For Japanese Buddhism, see W. T. de Bary, ed., *The Buddhist Tradition in India, China, and Japan* (New York, 1972).

A concise and provocative introduction to women's issues during this period in Japan, as well as in other parts of the world, can be found in S. S. Hughes and B. Hughes, *Women in World History* (Armonk, N.Y., 1995). For a tenth-century account of daily life for women at the Japanese court, see I. Morris, trans. and ed., *The Pillow Book of Sei Shonagon* (New York, 1991). For the changes that took place from matrilocal and matrilineal marriages to a patriarchal society, consult H. Tonomura, "Black Hair and Red Trousers: Gendering the Flesh in Medieval Japan," in *American Historical Review* 99 (1994).

The best introduction to Japanese literature for college students is still the concise and insightful D. Keene, *Japanese Literature: An Introduction for Western Readers* (London, 1953). The most comprehensive anthology is D. Keene, *Anthology of Japanese Literature* (New York, 1955), while the best history of Japanese literature, also by D. Keene, is *Seeds in the Heart: Japanese Literature from Earlier Times to the Late Sixteenth Century* (New York, 1993).

For the text of *The Tale of Genji*, see A. Waley's translation (New York, 1935) and a more recent one by E. Seidensticker (Tokyo, 1977). The best translation for college students is the latter's abridged Vintage Classics edition of 1990, which captures the spirit of the original in 360 pages. Of the many works on the novel, a most accessible and stimulating presentation is I. Morris, *The World of the Shining Prince: Court Life in Ancient Japan* (New York, 1964).

For the most comprehensive and accessible introduction to Japanese art, consult P. Mason, *History of Japanese Art* (New York, 1993). Also see the concise J. Stanley-Baker, *Japanese Art* (London, 1984). For a stimulating text with magnificent illustrations, see D. and V. Elisseeff, *Art of Japan* (New York, 1985). See also J. E. Kidder, Jr., *The Art of Japan* (London, 1985) for an insightful text accompanied by beautiful photographs.

For an informative and readable history of Korea that emphasizes the early period, see W. E. Henthorn, *A History of Korea* (New York, 1971). P. H. Lee, ed., *Sourcebook of Korean Civilization*, vol. 1 (New York, 1993) is a rich collection of documents dating from the period prior to the sixteenth century.

Vietnam often receives little attention in general studies of Southeast Asia because it was part of the Chinese empire for much of the traditional period. For a detailed investigation of the origins of Vietnamese civilization, see K. W. Taylor, *The Birth of Vietnam* (Berkeley, Calif., 1983). T. Hodgkin, *Vietnam: The Revolutionary Path* (New York, 1981) provides an overall survey of Vietnamese history to modern times. See also J. Buttinger, *The Smaller Dragon: A Political History of Vietnam* (New York, 1966).

For additional reading, go to InfoTrac College Edition, your online research library at http://web1.infotrac-college.com

Enter the search terms "Asia history" using Keywords.

Enter the search terms "Japan history" using Keywords.

Enter the search term "Shinto" using Keywords.

Enter the search terms "Korea history" using Keywords.

Enter the search terms "Zen Buddhism" using Keywords.

CHAPTER

12

THE MAKING OF EUROPE AND THE WORLD OF THE BYZANTINE EMPIRE, 500–1300

CHAPTER OUTLINE

FOCUS QUESTIONS

- What contributions did the Romans, the Christian church, and the Germanic peoples make to the new civilization that emerged in Europe after the collapse of the Western Roman Empire?
- What roles did aristocrats and peasants play in medieval European civilization, and how did their lifestyles differ?
- What were the main aspects of the economic, intellectual, cultural, and spiritual revivals that took place in Europe during the High Middle Ages?
- What were the main characteristics of the Byzantine Empire, and how did it differ from the kingdoms that emerged in western Europe?
- What were the main reasons for the Crusades, and what did they accomplish?

In 800, Charlemagne, the king of the Franks, journeyed to Rome to help Pope Leo III, head of the Catholic church, who was barely clinging to power in the face of rebellious Romans. On Christmas Day, Charlemagne and his family, attended by Romans, Franks, and even visitors from the Byzantine Empire, crowded into St. Peter's Basilica to hear mass. Quite unexpectedly, according to a Frankish writer, "as the king rose from praying before the tomb of the blessed apostle Peter, Pope Leo placed a golden crown on his head." In keeping with ancient tradition, the people in the church shouted, "Long life and victory to Charles Augustus, crowned by God the great and peace-loving Emperor of the

Romans." Seemingly, the Roman Empire in the West had been reborn, and Charles had become the first Roman emperor since 476. But this "Roman emperor" was actually a German king, and he had been crowned by the head of the western Christian church. In truth, the coronation of Charlemagne was a sign not of the rebirth of the Roman Empire, but of the emergence of a new European civilization that came into being in western Europe after the collapse of the Western Roman Empire.

This new civilization—European civilization—was formed by the coming together of three major elements: the legacy of the Romans, the Christian church, and the Germanic peoples who moved in and settled the Western Roman Empire. The Germans were another prominent example of the almost constant migration of nomadic peoples during this period. By 800, the contours of a new European civilization were beginning to emerge in western Europe. Increasingly, Europe would become the focus and center of Western civilization. European civilization developed during a period that historians call the Middle Ages, or the medieval period, which lasted from about 500 to 1500. To the historians who first used the title, the Middle Ages were a middle period between the ancient and modern worlds.

At the same time that medieval European civilization was emerging in the west, the eastern part of the old Roman Empire, increasingly Greek in culture, continued to survive as the Byzantine Empire. While serving as a buffer between Europe and the peoples to the east, the Byzantine or Eastern Roman Empire also preserved the intellectual and legal accomplishments of the Greeks and Romans.

The Transformation of the Roman World

The Germanic peoples were an important component of the new European civilization. Already by the third century C.E., they had begun to move into the lands of the Roman Empire. As imperial authority vanished in the fifth century, a number of German kings set up new states. By 500, the Western Roman Empire had been replaced politically by a series of states ruled by German kings.

The New Germanic Kingdoms

The fusion of Romans and Germans took different forms in the various Germanic kingdoms. Both the kingdom of the Ostrogoths in Italy and the kingdom of the Visigoths in Spain maintained the Roman structure of government for the larger native populations, while a Germanic warrior caste came to dominate. Over a period of time, Germans and natives began to fuse. In Britain, however, when the Roman armies abandoned Britain at the beginning of the fifth century, the Angles and Saxons, Germanic tribes from Denmark and northern Germany, moved in and settled there. Eventually, these peoples succeeded in carving out small kingdoms throughout the island.

THE KINGDOM OF THE FRANKS

Only one of the German states on the European continent proved long-lasting—the kingdom of the Franks. The establishment of a Frankish kingdom was the work of Clovis (c. 482–511), a member of the Merovingian dynasty who became a Catholic Christian around 500. He was not the first German king to convert to Christianity, but the others had joined the Arian sect of Christianity, a group who believed that Jesus had been human and thus not truly God. The Christian church in Rome, which had become known as the Roman Catholic church, regarded the Arians as heretics, or people who believed in teachings different from the official church doctrine. To Catholics, Jesus was human, but of the "same substance" as God and therefore also truly God. Clovis found that his conversion to Catholic Christianity gained him the support of the Roman Catholic church, which was only too eager to obtain the friendship of a major Germanic ruler who was a Catholic Christian.

By 510, Clovis had established a powerful new Frankish kingdom stretching from the Pyrenees in the west to German lands in the east (modern France and western Germany). After Clovis's death, however, his sons divided his newly created kingdom, as was the Frankish custom. During the sixth and seventh centuries, the once united Frankish kingdom came to be divided into three major areas: Neustria, in northern Gaul; Austrasia, consisting of the ancient Frankish lands on both sides of the Rhine; and the former kingdom of Burgundy.

THE SOCIETY OF THE GERMANIC PEOPLES

As Germans and Romans intermarried and began to create a new society, some of the social customs of the Germanic peoples came to play an important role. The crucial

THE BAPTISM OF CLOVIS. The conversion of Clovis to Catholic Christianity was an important factor in gaining papal support for his Frankish kingdom. In this illustration from a medieval manuscript, bishops and nobles look on while Clovis is baptized. One of the nobles holds a crown while a dove, symbol of the Holy Spirit, descends from heaven, bringing sacred oil for the ceremony.

social bond among the Germanic peoples was the family, especially the extended family of husbands, wives, children, brothers, sisters, cousins, and grandparents. In addition to working the land together and passing it down to future generations, the extended family also provided protection, which was sorely needed in the violent atmosphere of Merovingian times.

The Frankish family structure was quite simple. Males were dominant and made all the important decisions. A woman obeyed her father until she married and then fell under the legal domination of her husband. For most women in the new Germanic kingdoms, their legal status reflected the material conditions of their lives. Archaeological evidence suggests that most women had life expectancies of only thirty or forty years, while about 10 to 15 percent of women died in their childbearing years, no doubt due to complications associated with childbirth. For most women, life consisted of domestic labor: providing food and clothing for the household, caring for the children, and assisting with numerous farming chores. Of all the labors of women, the most important was childbearing, because it was a crucial element in providing for the maintenance of the family and its properties.

The German conception of family affected the way Germanic law treated crime and punishment. In the Roman system, as in our own, a crime such as murder was considered an offense against society or the state and was handled by a court that heard evidence and arrived at a decision. Germanic law was personal. An injury by one person against another could lead to a blood feud in which the family of the injured party took revenge on the family of the wrongdoer. Feuds could lead to savage acts of revenge, such as hacking off hands or feet, gouging out eyes, or slicing off ears and noses. Because this system could easily get out of control, an alternative system arose that made use of a fine called *wergeld,* which was paid by a wrongdoer to the family of the person he had injured or killed. *Wergeld,* which means "money for a man," was the value of a person in monetary terms. That value varied considerably according to social status. An offense against a nobleman, for example, cost considerably more than one against a freeperson or a slave.

Germanic law provided two common means of determining guilt: compurgation and the ordeal. Compurgation involved the swearing of an oath by the accused person, backed up by a group of twelve or twenty-five "oath helpers," who would also swear that the accused was telling the truth. The ordeal was based on the idea of divine intervention; divine forces (whether pagan or Christian) would not allow an innocent person to be harmed (see the box on p. 321).

The Role of the Christian Church

By the end of the fourth century, Christianity had become the predominant religion of the Roman Empire. As the official Roman state disintegrated, the Christian church played an increasingly important role in the emergence and growth of the new European civilization.

THE ORGANIZATION OF THE CHURCH

By the fourth century, the Christian church had developed a system of government. The Christian community in each city was headed by a bishop, whose area of jurisdiction was known as a bishopric, or diocese; the bishoprics of each Roman province were joined together under the direction of an archbishop. The bishops of four

GERMANIC CUSTOMARY LAW: THE ORDEAL

In Germanic customary law, the ordeal was used as a means by which accused persons might clear themselves. Although the ordeal took different forms, all involved a physical trial of some sort, such as holding a red-hot iron. It was believed that God would protect the innocent and allow them to come through the ordeal unharmed. This sixth-century account by Gregory of Tours describes an ordeal by hot water.

GREGORY OF TOURS, AN ORDEAL OF HOT WATER (c. 580)

An Arian presbyter disputing with a deacon of our religion made venomous assertions against the Son of God and the Holy Ghost, as is the habit of that sect [the Arians]. But when the deacon had discoursed a long time concerning the reasonableness of our faith and the heretic, blinded by the fog of unbelief, continued to reject the truth, . . . the former said: "Why weary ourselves with long discussions? Let acts approve the truth; let a kettle be heated over the fire and someone's ring be thrown into the boiling water. Let him who shall take it from the heated liquid be approved as a follower of the truth, and afterward let the other party be converted to the knowledge of the truth. And do you also understand, O heretic, that this our party will fulfill the conditions with the aid of the Holy Ghost; you shalt confess that there is no discordance, no dissimilarity in the Holy Trinity." The heretic consented to the proposition and they separated after appointing the next morning for the trial. But the fervor of faith in which the deacon had first made this suggestion began to cool through the instigation of the enemy. Rising with the dawn he bathed his arm in oil and smeared it with ointment. But nevertheless he made the round of the sacred places and called in prayer on the Lord. . . . About the third hour they met in the marketplace. The people came together to see the show. A fire was lighted, the kettle was placed upon it, and when it grew very hot the ring was thrown into the boiling water. The deacon invited the heretic to take it out of the water first. But he promptly refused, saying, "You who did propose this trial are the one to take it out." The deacon all of a tremble bared his arm. And when the heretic presbyter saw it besmeared with ointment he cried out: "With magic arts you have thought to protect yourself, that you have made use of these salves, but what you have done will not avail." While they were thus quarreling there came up a deacon from Ravenna named Iacinthus and inquired what the trouble was about. When he learned the truth he drew his arm out from under his robe at once and plunged his right hand into the kettle. Now the ring that had been thrown in was a little thing and very light so that it was thrown about by the water as chaff would be blown about by the wind; and searching for it a long time he found it after about an hour. Meanwhile the flame beneath the kettle blazed up mightily so that the greater heat might make it difficult for the ring to be followed by the hand; but the deacon extracted it at length and suffered no harm, protesting rather that at the bottom the kettle was cold while at the top it was just pleasantly warm. When the heretic beheld this he was greatly confused and audaciously thrust his hand into the kettle saying, "My faith will aid me." As soon as his hand had been thrust in all the flesh was boiled off the bones clear up to the elbow. And so the dispute ended.

great cities—Rome, Jerusalem, Alexandria, and Antioch—held positions of special power in church affairs because the churches in these cities all asserted that they had been founded by the original apostles sent out by Jesus. Soon, however, one of them—the bishop of Rome—claimed even more, that he was the leader of the western Christian church. According to church tradition, Jesus had given the keys to the kingdom of heaven to Peter, who was considered the chief apostle and the first bishop of Rome. Subsequent bishops of Rome were considered Peter's successors and came to be known as popes (from the Latin word *papa,* meaning father) of the Catholic church.

Although western Christians came to accept the bishop of Rome as head of the church in the fourth and fifth centuries, there was certainly no unanimity on the extent of the powers the pope possessed as a result of his position. Nevertheless, in the sixth century, a strong pope, Gregory I, known as Gregory the Great, strengthened the power of the papacy and the Roman Catholic church. As pope, Gregory I (590–604) assumed direction of Rome and its surrounding territories, thus giving the papacy a source of political power in a territorial unit that eventually came to be known as the Papal States. Gregory also extended papal authority over the Christian church in the west and was especially active in converting the pagan peoples of Germanic Europe. His primary instrument was the monastic movement.

THE MONKS AND THEIR MISSIONS

A monk (Latin *monachus,* meaning "someone who lives alone") was one who sought to live a life divorced from the world, cut off from ordinary human society, in order to pursue an ideal of godliness, or total dedication to the will of God. At first, Christian monasticism was based on the

MAP 12.1 The New Kingdoms of the Old Western Empire

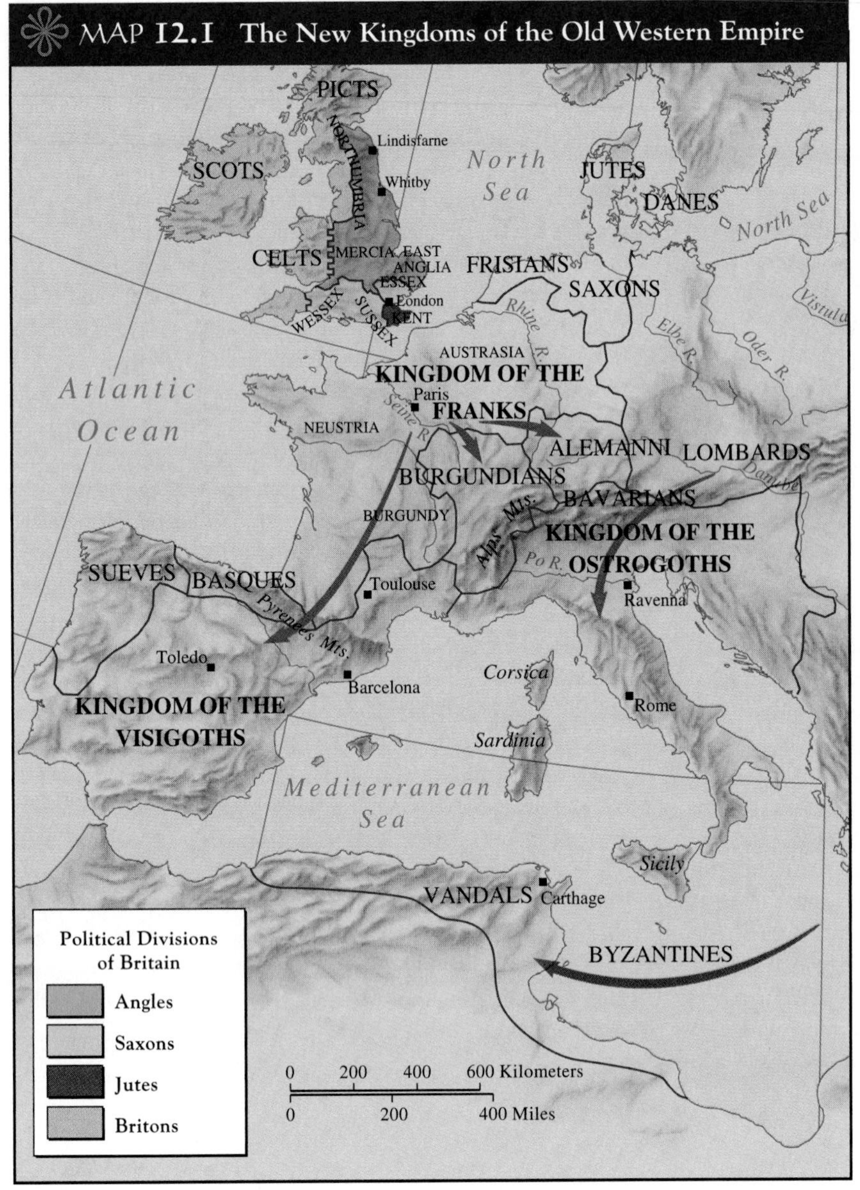

model of the solitary hermit who gives up all civilized society to pursue a spiritual life. Saint Simeon the Stylite, for example, lived for thirty years in a basket atop a pillar more than sixty feet high.

These early monks, however, soon found themselves unable to live in solitude. Their feats of holiness attracted followers on a wide scale, and as the monastic ideal spread, a new form of monasticism based on living together in a community soon became the dominant form. Monastic communities came to be seen as the ideal Christian society that could provide a moral example to the wider society around them.

Saint Benedict (c. 480–c. 543), who founded a monastic house for which he wrote a set of rules, established the basic form of monastic life in the western Christian church. The Benedictine rule came to be used by other monastic groups and was crucial to the growth of monasticism in the western Christian world.

Benedict's rule divided each day into a series of activities with primary emphasis on prayer and manual labor. All monks were required to perform physical work of some kind for several hours a day because idleness was "the enemy of the soul." At the very heart of community practice was prayer, the proper "Work of God." While this included private meditation and reading, all monks in the monastery gathered together seven times during the day for common prayer and chanting of psalms. A Benedictine life was a communal one. Monks ate, worked, slept, and worshiped together.

Each Benedictine monastery was strictly ruled by an abbot, or "father" of the monastery, who had complete authority over his fellow monks. Unquestioning obedience to the will of the abbot was expected of each monk. Each Benedictine monastery held lands that enabled it to be a self-sustaining community, isolated from and independent of the world surrounding it. Within the monastery, however, monks were to fulfill their vow of poverty: "Let all things be common to all, as it is written, lest anyone should say that anything is his own."[1] The first monks were men, but women (called nuns) also began to withdraw from the world to dedicate themselves to God.

Monasticism played an indispensable role in early medieval civilization. Monks became the new heroes of Christian civilization, and their dedication to God became the highest ideal of Christian life. They were the social workers of their communities: monks provided schools for the young, hospitality for travelers, and hospitals for the sick. Monks also copied Latin works and passed on the legacy of the ancient world to the new European civilization. Monasteries became centers of learning wherever they were located. Moreover, the monks were important in spreading Christianity to the entire European world. English and Irish monks were particularly enthusiastic missionaries, who undertook the conversion of pagan peoples, especially in Germany.

Women, too, played an important role in the monastic missionary movement and the conversion of the Germanic kingdoms. Many of the abbesses (an abbess was the head

THE ACHIEVEMENTS OF CHARLEMAGNE

Einhard, the biographer of Charlemagne, was born in the valley of the Main River in Germany about 775. Raised and educated in the monastery of Fulda, an important center of learning, he arrived at the court of Charlemagne in 791 or 792. Although he did not achieve high office under Charlemagne, he served as private secretary to Louis the Pious, Charlemagne's son and successor. In this selection, Einhard discusses some of Charlemagne's accomplishments.

EINHARD, *LIFE OF CHARLEMAGNE*

Such are the wars, most skillfully planned and successfully fought, which this most powerful king waged during the forty-seven years of his reign. He so largely increased the Frank kingdom, which was already great and strong when he received it at his father's hands, that more than double its former territory was added to it. . . . He subdued all the wild and barbarous tribes dwelling in Germany between the Rhine and the Vistula, the Ocean and the Danube, all of which speak very much the same language, but differ widely from one another in customs and dress. . . .

He added to the glory of his reign by gaining the good will of several kings and nations; so close, indeed, was the alliance that he contracted with Alfonso, King of Galicia and Asturias, that the latter, when sending letters or ambassadors to Charles, invariably styled himself his man. . . . The Emperors of Constantinople [the Byzantine emperors] sought friendship and alliance with Charles by several embassies; and even when the Greeks [the Byzantines] suspected him of designing to take the empire from them, because of his assumption of the title Emperor, they made a close alliance with him, that he might have no cause of offense. In fact, the power of the Franks was always viewed with a jealous eye, whence the Greek proverb, "Have the Frank for your friend, but not for your neighbor."

This King, who showed himself so great in extending his empire and subduing foreign nations, and was constantly occupied with plans to that end, undertook also very many works calculated to adorn and benefit his kingdom, and brought several of them to completion. Among these, the most deserving of mention are the basilica of the Holy Mother of God at Aix-la-Chapelle [Aachen], built in the most admirable manner, and a bridge over the Rhine River at Mainz, half a mile long, the breadth of the river at this point. . . . Above all, sacred buildings were the object of his care throughout his whole kingdom; and whenever he found them falling to ruin from age, he commanded the priests and fathers who had charge of them to repair them, and made sure by commissioners that his instructions were obeyed. . . . Thus did Charles defend and increase as well as beautify his kingdom. . . .

He cherished with the greatest fervor and devotion the principles of the Christian religion, which had been instilled into him from infancy. Hence it was that he built the beautiful church at Aix-la-Chapelle, which he adorned with gold and silver and lamps, and with rails and doors of solid brass. He had the columns and marbles for this structure brought from Rome and Ravenna, for he could not find such as were suitable elsewhere. He was a constant worshiper at this church as long as his health permitted, going morning and evening, even after nightfall, besides attending mass. . . .

He was very forward in caring for the poor, so much so that he not only made a point of giving in his own country and his own kingdom, but when he discovered that there were Christians living in poverty in Syria, Egypt, and Africa, at Jerusalem, Alexandria, and Carthage, he had compassion on their wants, and used to send money over the seas to them. . . . He sent great and countless gifts to the popes, and throughout his whole reign the wish that he had nearest at heart was to reestablish the ancient authority of the city of Rome under his care and by his influence, and to defend and protect the Church of St. Peter, and to beautify and enrich it out of his own store above all other churches.

of a monastery or convent for nuns) belonged to royal houses, especially in Anglo-Saxon England. In the kingdom of Northumbria, for example, Saint Hilda founded the monastery of Whitby in 657. As abbess, she was responsible for giving learning an important role in the life of the monastery. Five future bishops were educated under her direction.

Charlemagne and the World of the Carolingians

During the seventh and eighth centuries, within the Frankish kingdom of western Europe, the mayors of the palace of Neustria and Austrasia had expanded their power at the expense of the Merovingian dynasty. One of these mayors, Pepin, finally took the logical step of deposing the decadent Merovingians and assuming the kingship of the Frankish state for himself and his family. Upon his death in 768, his son came to the throne of the Frankish kingdom.

This new king was the dynamic and powerful ruler known to history as Charles the Great or Charlemagne (from the Latin *Carolus magnus*). Charlemagne was a determined and decisive man, highly intelligent and inquisitive. A fierce warrior, he was also a strong statesman (see the box above). Unable to read and write, he was nevertheless a wise patron of learning. He greatly expanded the territory of the Carolingian Empire during his lengthy rule from 768 to 814.

In the tradition of the Germanic kings, Charlemagne was a determined warrior who undertook fifty-four military campaigns, which took him to many areas of Europe. His most successful campaigns were in Germany, especially against the Saxons located between the Elbe River and the North Sea. At its height, Charlemagne's empire covered much of western and central Europe; not until the time of Napoleon in the nineteenth and Hitler in the twentieth century would an empire its size be seen again in Europe.

Charlemagne continued the efforts of his father in organizing the Carolingian kingdom. To administer the empire, Charlemagne depended on both his household staff and the counts who were his chief representatives in local areas. The counts were members of the nobility that had already existed under the Merovingians. They had come to control government functions in their own lands and thus acted as judges, military leaders, and agents of the king. As an important check on the power of the counts, Charlemagne established the *missi dominici* ("messengers of the lord king"), two men, one lay lord and one church official, who were sent out to local districts to ensure that the counts were executing the king's wishes.

CHARLEMAGNE AS EMPEROR

As Charlemagne's power grew, so too did his prestige as the most powerful Christian ruler; one monk even wrote that he ruled the "kingdom of Europe." In 800, Charlemagne acquired a new title—emperor of the Romans. Charlemagne welcomed the new title; after all, as an emperor, he was now on a level of equality with the Byzantine emperor (see The Byzantine Empire and the Crusades later in this chapter). Moreover, the coronation also meant that the papacy now had a defender of great stature.

Charlemagne's coronation as Roman emperor demonstrated the strength, even after three hundred years, of the concept of an enduring Roman Empire. More importantly, it symbolized the fusion of those Roman, Christian, and Germanic elements that constituted the foundation of European civilization. A Germanic king had been crowned emperor of the Romans by the spiritual leader of western Christendom. A new civilization had emerged.

MAP 12.2 The Carolingian Empire

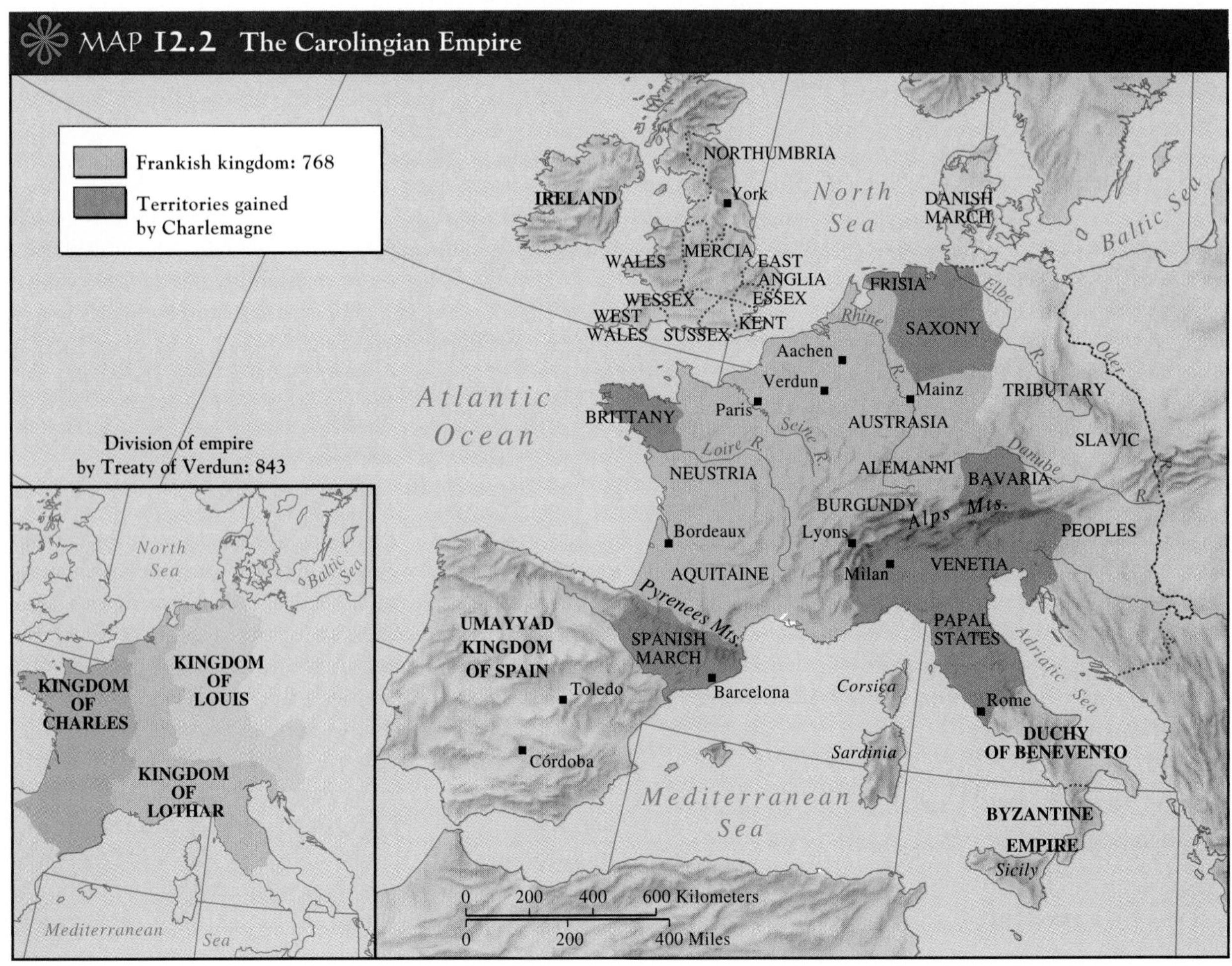

AN INTELLECTUAL RENEWAL

Charlemagne had a strong desire to revive learning in his kingdom, an attitude that stemmed from his own intellectual curiosity as well as the need to provide educated clergy for the church and literate officials for the government. His efforts led to a revival of learning and culture that some historians have labeled a Carolingian Renaissance or "rebirth" of learning.

For the most part, the revival of classical studies and the efforts to preserve Latin culture took place in the monasteries, many of which had been established by Irish and English missionaries in the seventh and eighth centuries. By the ninth century, the "work" required of Benedictine monks was the copying of manuscripts. Monasteries established *scriptoria,* or writing rooms, where monks copied not only the works of early Christianity, such as the Bible, but also the works of Latin classical authors. The copying of manuscripts in Carolingian monastic *scriptoria* was a crucial factor in the preservation of the ancient legacy. About eight thousand manuscripts survive from Carolingian times. Virtually 90 percent of the ancient Roman works that we have today exist because they were copied by Carolingian monks.

The World of Lords and Vassals

The Carolingian Empire began to disintegrate soon after Charlemagne's death in 814, and less than thirty years later, in 843, it was divided among his grandsons into three major sections. The division did not lead to peace, however, for the rulers and their heirs engaged in almost incessant struggles—squabbles that allowed powerful aristocrats to acquire even more power in their own local territories at the expense of the rulers. In the meantime, invasions in different parts of the old Carolingian world added to the process of disintegration.

Invasions of the Ninth and Tenth Centuries

In the ninth and tenth centuries, western Europe was beset by several waves of invasions. Muslims raided the southern coast of Europe and sent raiding parties into southern France. The Magyars, a people from western Asia, moved into central Europe at the end of the ninth century and settled on the plains of Hungary; from there they made raids into western Europe. After suffering a crushing defeat at the Battle of Lechfeld in Germany in 955, the Magyars converted to Christianity and settled down to create the kingdom of Hungary.

By far, the most far-reaching attacks of the time came from the Northmen or Norsemen of Scandinavia, also known to us as the Vikings. The Vikings were a Germanic people based in Scandinavia. Their great love of adventure and their search for booty and new avenues of trade may have led them to invade other areas of Europe.

Two features of Viking society help to explain the Vikings' success. First of all, they were warriors. Second, they were superb shipbuilders and sailors. Their ships were the best of the period. Long and narrow with beautifully carved arched prows, the Viking dragon ships carried about fifty men. Their shallow draft enabled the Vikings to sail up European rivers and attack places at some distance

THE CORONATION OF CHARLEMAGNE. After rebellion in 799 forced Pope Leo III to seek refuge at Charlemagne's court, Charlemagne went to Rome to settle the affair. There, on Christmas Day 800, he was crowned emperor of the Romans by the pope. This manuscript illustration shows Leo III placing a crown on Charlemagne's head.

THE VIKINGS ATTACK ENGLAND. This illustration from an eleventh-century English manuscript depicts a band of armed Vikings invading England. Two ships have already reached the shore, and a few Vikings are shown walking down a long gangplank onto English soil.

inland. In the ninth century, Vikings sacked villages and towns, destroyed churches, and easily defeated small local armies. Viking attacks frightened people and led many a clergyman to plead with them to change their behavior and appease God's anger, as is revealed in this sermon in 1014 by an English archbishop:

> Things have not gone well now for a long time at home or abroad, but there has been devastation and persecution in every district again and again, and the English have been for a long time now completely defeated and too greatly disheartened through God's anger; and the pirates [Vikings] so strong with God's consent that often in battle one puts to flight ten, and sometimes less, sometimes more, all because of our sins. . . . We pay them continually and they humiliate us daily; they ravage and they burn, plunder, and rob and carry on board; and lo, what else is there in all these events except God's anger clear and visible over this people?[2]

Early Viking raids were largely limited to the summer, but by the mid-ninth century, the Norsemen had begun to build settlements and spend the winter in different areas of Europe. By 850, Norsemen from Norway had settled in Ireland, while the Danes occupied northeastern England by 878. Beginning in 911, the ruler of the western Frankish lands gave one band of Vikings land at the mouth of the Seine river in the section of France that came to be known as Normandy. This policy of settling the Vikings and converting them to Christianity was a deliberate one; by their conversion to Christianity, the Vikings were soon made a part of European civilization.

The Development of Fief-holding

The disintegration of all central authority in the Carolingian world and the invasions by Muslims, Magyars, and Vikings led to the emergence of a new type of relationship between free individuals. When governments ceased to be able to defend their subjects, it became important to find some powerful lord who could offer protection in exchange for service. The contract sworn between a lord and his subordinate (known as a vassal) is the basis of a form of social organization that later generations of historians viewed as an organized system of government, which they called feudalism. But feudalism was never a system, and many historians today prefer to avoid using the term.

With the breakdown of royal governments, powerful nobles took control of large areas of land. They needed men to fight for them, so the practice arose of giving grants of land to vassals who in return would fight for their lord. The Frankish army had originally consisted of foot soldiers dressed in coats of mail and armed with swords. But in the eighth century, when larger horses and the stirrup were introduced, a military change began to occur. Earlier, horsemen had been throwers of spears. Now they wore armored coats of mail (the larger horse could carry the weight) and wielded long lances that enabled them to act as battering rams (the stirrups kept them on their horses). For almost five hundred years, warfare in Europe would be dominated by heavily armored cavalry, or knights as they came to be called. The knights came to have the greatest social prestige and formed the backbone of the European aristocracy.

Of course, a horse, armor, and weapons were expensive to purchase and maintain, and learning to wield these instruments skillfully from a horse took much time and practice. Consequently, lords who wanted men to fight for them had to grant each vassal a piece of land that provided for the support of the vassal and his family. In return for the land, the vassal provided his lord with one major service, his fighting skills. Each needed the other. In the society of the Early Middle Ages (the period between 400 and 1000), where there was little trade and wealth was based primarily on land, land became the most important gift a lord could give to a vassal in return for military service.

The relationship between lord and vassal was made official by a public ceremony. To become a vassal, a man performed an act of homage to his lord, as described in this passage from a medieval treatise on feudal practice:

> The man should put his hands together as a sign of humility, and place them between the two hands of his lord as a token that he vows everything to him and promises faith to him; and the lord should receive him and promise to keep faith with him. Then the man should say: "Sir, I enter your homage and faith and become your man by mouth and hands [i.e., by taking the oath and placing his hands between those of the lord], and I swear and promise to keep faith and loyalty to you against all others, and to guard your rights with all my strength.[3]

Loyalty to one's lord was the chief virtue.

By the ninth century, the land granted to a vassal in return for military service had come to be known as a fief. In time, many vassals who held such grants of land came to exercise rights of jurisdiction or political and legal authority within their fiefs. As the Carolingian world disintegrated politically under the impact of internal dissension and invasions, an increasing number of powerful lords arose. Instead of a single government, many people were now responsible for keeping order.

Fief-holding also became increasingly complicated with the development of subinfeudation. The vassals of a king, who were themselves great lords, might also have vassals, who would owe them military service in return for a grant of land from their estates. Those vassals, in turn, might likewise have vassals, who at this low level would be simple knights with barely enough land to provide their equipment. The lord-vassal relationship, then, bound together both greater and lesser landowners. At all levels, the lord-vassal relationship was always an honorable relationship between free men and did not imply any sense of servitude.

Fief-holding came to be characterized by a set of practices—known as the feudal contract—that determined the relationship between a lord and his vassal. The major obligation of a vassal to his lord was to perform military service, usually about forty days a year. A vassal was also required to appear at his lord's court when summoned to give advice. He might also be asked to sit in judgment in a legal case because the important vassals of a lord were peers and only they could judge each other. Finally, vassals were also responsible for aids, or financial payments to the lord on a number of occasions, including the knighting of the lord's eldest son, the marriage of his eldest daughter, and the ransom of the lord's person in the event he was captured.

In turn, a lord had responsibilities toward his vassal. His major obligation was to protect his vassal, either by defending him militarily or by taking his side in a court of law if necessary. The lord was also responsible for the maintenance of the vassal, usually by granting him a fief.

The Nobility of the Middle Ages

In the High Middle Ages (the period between 1000 and 1300), European society, like that of Japan during the same period, was dominated by men whose chief concern was warfare. Like the Japanese samurai, many nobles loved war. As one nobleman wrote in a poem:

> *And well I like to hear the call of "Help" and see the*
> *wounded fall,*
> *Loudly for mercy praying,*
> *And see the dead, both great and small,*
> *Pierced by sharp spearheads one and all.*[4]

The men of war were the lords and vassals of medieval society.

The lords were the kings, dukes, counts, barons, and viscounts (and even bishops and archbishops), who held extensive lands and considerable political power. They formed an aristocracy or nobility that consisted of people who held real political, economic, and social power. As warriors united by the institution of knighthood, the great lords and ordinary knights came to form a common group, albeit a group with social divisions based on extremes of wealth and landholdings.

Medieval theory maintained that the warlike qualities of the nobility were justified by their role as defenders of society, and the growth of the European nobility in the High Middle Ages was made visible by an increasing number of castles scattered across the landscape. Although castle architecture varied considerably, castles did possess two common features: they were permanent residences for the noble family, its retainers, and servants, and they were defensible fortifications. For defensive purposes, castles were surrounded by open areas and large stone walls. At the heart of the castle was the keep, a large, multistoried building that housed kitchens, stables, storerooms, a great hall for visitors, dining, and administrative business, and numerous rooms for sleeping and living. The growing wealth of the High Middle Ages made it possible for the European nobility to build more elaborate castles, with thicker walls and better furnished and decorated interiors. As castles became more elaborate and securely built, they proved to be more easily defended and harder to seize by force.

THE WAY OF THE WARRIOR

At the age of seven or eight, the sons of the nobility were sent either to a clerical school to pursue a religious career or to another nobleman's castle, where they prepared for the life of a noble. Their chief lessons were military; they learned how to joust, hunt, ride, and handle weapons properly. Occasionally, aristocrats' sons might also learn the basic fundamentals of reading and writing. After his apprenticeship in knighthood, at about the age of twenty-one, a young man formally entered the adult world in a

THE TOURNAMENT. The tournament arose as a socially acceptable alternative to the private warfare that plagued the nobility. This illustration from *The Book of Tourneys*, by King René of Anjou, shows opposing teams behind ropes. At the top center, red-robed judges prepare to signal the men waiting below to cut the cords, at which point the two sides will begin their mock battle. Female supporters of the two sides look on.

ceremony of "knighting." A sponsor girded a sword on the young candidate and struck him on the cheek or neck with an open hand (or later touched him three times on the shoulder with the blade of a sword), possibly signifying the passing of the sponsor's military valor to the new knight.

In the eleventh and twelfth centuries, under the influence of the church, an ideal of civilized behavior called chivalry gradually evolved among the nobility. Chivalry represented a code of ethics that knights were supposed to uphold. In addition to defending the church and the defenseless, knights were expected to treat captives as honored guests instead of putting them in dungeons. Chivalry also implied that knights should fight only for glory, but this account of a group of English knights by a medieval writer reveals another motive for battle: "The whole city was plundered to the last farthing, and then they proceeded to rob all the churches throughout the city, . . . and seizing gold and silver, cloth of all colors, women's ornaments, gold rings, goblets, and precious stones . . . they all returned to their own lords rich men."[5] Apparently, not all the ideals of chivalry were taken seriously.

After his formal initiation into the world of warriors, a young man returned home to find himself once again subject to his parents' authority. Young men were discouraged from marrying until their fathers died, at which time they could marry and become lords of the castle. Trained to be warriors, but with no adult responsibilities, young knights had little to do but fight. In the twelfth century, tournaments began to appear as an alternative to the socially destructive fighting that the church was increasingly trying to curb. Initially, tournaments consisted of the "melee," in which warriors on horseback fought with blunted weapons in free-for-all combat. By the late twelfth century, the melee was preceded by the joust or individual combat between two knights. Gradually, the joust became the main part of the tournament. Knights saw tournaments as an excellent way to train for war. As one knight explained: "A knight cannot distinguish himself in that

[war] if he has not trained for it in tourneys. He must have seen his blood flow, heard his teeth crack under fist blows, felt his opponent's weight bear down upon him as he lay on the ground and, after being twenty times unhorsed, have risen twenty times to fight."[6]

ARISTOCRATIC WOMEN

Although women could legally hold property, most women remained under the control of men—of their fathers until they married and their husbands after they married. Nevertheless, aristocratic women had many opportunities for playing important roles. Because the lord was often away at war or court, the lady of the castle had to manage the estate. A household could include large numbers of officials and servants, so this was no small responsibility. Maintaining the financial accounts alone took considerable financial knowledge. The lady of the castle was also responsible on a regular basis for overseeing the food supply and maintaining all the other supplies needed for the smooth operation of the household.

Although women were expected to be subservient to their husbands, there were many strong women who advised and sometimes even dominated their husbands. Perhaps the most famous was Eleanor of Aquitaine (c. 1122–1204), heiress to the duchy of Aquitaine in southwestern France. Married to King Louis VII of France (1137–1180), Eleanor accompanied her husband on a crusade, but her alleged affair with her uncle during the crusade led Louis to have their marriage annulled. Eleanor then married Henry, duke of Normandy and count of Anjou, who became King Henry II of England (1154–1189). She took an active role in politics, even assisting her sons in rebelling against Henry in 1173–1174. Imprisoned for her activities, after Henry's death she again assumed an active political life, providing both military and political support for her sons.

THE GROWTH OF EUROPEAN KINGDOMS

The domination of society by the nobility reached its apex in the High Middle Ages. During the same period, however, kings began the process of extending their power in more effective ways. Out of these growing monarchies would eventually come the European states that dominated much of later European and world history.

Kings possessed some sources of power that other lords did not. Usually, kings had greater opportunities to increase their lands through war and marriage alliances and then could use their new acquisitions to reward their followers and bind powerful nobles to them. In the High Middle Ages, kings found new ways to extend their powers. The growth of cities, the revival of commerce, and the emergence of a money economy—all of which we will examine in the next sections—enabled monarchs to hire soldiers and officials and to rely less on their vassals.

England in the High Middle Ages

In 1066, an army of heavily armed knights under William of Normandy landed on the coast of England and soundly defeated King Harold and the Anglo-Saxon foot soldiers at the Battle of Hastings on October 14. William (1066–1087) was crowned king of England at Christmastime in London and then began the process of combining Anglo-Saxon and Norman institutions to create a new England. Many of the Norman knights were given parcels of land that they held as fiefs from the new English king. William made all nobles swear an oath of loyalty to him as sole ruler of England and insisted that all people owed loyalty to the king.

The Norman ruling class spoke French, but as the Norman-French and the Anglo-Saxon nobility intermarried, Anglo-Saxon and French gradually merged to form a new English language. The Normans also took over existing Anglo-Saxon institutions, such as the office of sheriff. William took a census and more fully developed the system of taxation and royal courts begun by the Anglo-Saxon kings of the tenth and eleventh centuries. All in all, William of Normandy created a strong, centralized monarchy.

The Norman conquest of England had other repercussions as well. Because the new king of England was still the duke of Normandy, he was both a king (of England) and at the same time a vassal to a king (of France), but a vassal who was now far more powerful than his lord. This connection with France kept England heavily involved in European affairs throughout the High Middle Ages.

In the twelfth century, the power of the English monarchy was greatly enlarged during the reign of Henry II (1154–1189), the founder of the Plantagenet dynasty. The new king was particularly successful in strengthening the power of the royal courts. Henry expanded the number of criminal cases tried in the king's court and also devised ways of taking property cases from local courts to the royal courts. Henry's goals were clear: expanding the power of the royal courts expanded the king's power and, of course, brought revenues into his coffers. Moreover, because the royal courts were now found throughout England, a body of common law (law that was common to the whole kingdom) began to replace the different law codes that often varied from place to place.

Henry was less successful at imposing royal control over the church and became involved in a famous struggle between church and state in medieval England. Henry claimed the right to punish clergymen in church courts, but Thomas à Becket, archbishop of Canterbury, the highest ranking English cleric, claimed that only church courts could try clerics. Attempts at compromise failed, and

MURDER IN THE CATHEDRAL

The most famous church-state controversy in medieval England arose between Henry II and Thomas à Becket, archbishop of Canterbury, the highest ranking English cleric.

This excerpt is from a letter by John of Salisbury, who served as secretaty to Theobald, archbishop of Canterbury, and his successor, Thomas à Becket. John was present at the murder of the archbishop in 1170.

JOHN OF SALISBURY TO JOHN OF CANTERBURY, BISHOP OF POITIERS

The martyr [Becket] stood in the cathedral, before Christ's altar, as we have said, ready to suffer; the hour of slaughter was at hand. When he heard that he was sought—heard the knights who had come for him shouting in the throng of clerks and monks "Where is the archbishop?"—he turned to meet them on the steps which he had almost climbed, and said with steady countenance: "Here am I! What do you want?" One of the knight-assassins flung at him in fury: "That you die now! That you should live longer is impossible." No martyr seems ever to have been more steadfast in his agony than he . . . and thus, steadfast in speech as in spirit, he replied: "And I am prepared to die for my God, to preserve justice and my church's liberty. If you seek my head, I forbid you on behalf of God almighty and on pain of anathema to do any hurt to any other man, monk, clerk or layman, of high or low degree. Do not involve them in the punishment, for they have not been involved in the cause: on my head not on theirs be it if any of them have supported the Church in its troubles. I embrace death readily, so long as peace and liberty for the Church follow from the shedding of my blood. . . ." He spoke, and saw that the assassins had drawn their swords; and bowed his head like one in prayer. His last words were "To God and St. Mary and the saints who protect and defend this church, and to the blessed Denis, I commend myself and the Church's cause." No one could dwell on what followed without deep sorrow and choking tears. A son's affection forbids me to describe each blow the savage assassins struck, spurning all fear of God, forgetful of all fealty and any human feeling. They defiled the cathedral and the holy season [Christmas] with a bishop's blood and with slaughter; but that was not enough. They sliced off the crown of his head, which had been specially dedicated to God by anointing with holy chrism—a fearful thing even to describe; then they used their evil swords, when he was dead, to spill his brain and cruelly scattered it, mixed with blood and bones, over the pavement. . . . Through all the agony the martyr's spirit was unconquered, his steadfastness marvelous to observe; he spoke not a word, uttered no cry, let slip no groan, raised no arm nor garment to protect himself from an assailant, but bent his head, which he had laid bare to their swords with wonderful courage, till all might be fulfilled. Motionless he held it, and when at last he fell his body lay straight; and he moved neither hand nor foot.

the angry king publicly expressed the desire to be rid of Becket: "Who will free me of this priest?" he screamed. Four knights took the challenge, went to Canterbury, and murdered the archbishop in the cathedral (see the box above). Faced with public outrage, Henry was forced to allow the right of appeal from English church courts to the papal court.

Many English nobles came to resent the ongoing growth of the king's power and rose in rebellion during the reign of Henry's son, King John (1199–1216). At Runnymeade in 1215, John was forced to put his seal on the Magna Carta (the Great Charter) of feudal liberties. Magna Carta was, above all, a feudal document. Feudal custom had always recognized that the relationship between king and vassals was based on mutual rights and obligations. Magna Carta gave written recognition to that fact and was used in later years to strengthen the idea that the monarch's power was limited, not absolute.

During the reign of Edward I (1272–1307), an institution of great importance in the development of representative government—the English Parliament—emerged. Originally, the word *parliament* was applied to meetings of the king's Great Council, in which the greater barons and chief prelates of the church met with the king's judges and principal advisers to deal with judicial affairs. But in his need for money, Edward I in 1295 invited two knights from every county and two residents from each town to meet with the Great Council to consent to new taxes. This was the first Parliament.

The English Parliament, then, came to be composed of two knights from every county and two burgesses from every borough, as well as the barons and ecclesiastical lords. Eventually, barons and church lords formed the House of Lords; knights and burgesses, the House of Commons. The Parliaments of Edward I granted taxes, discussed politics, passed laws, and handled judicial business. Although not as yet the important body it would eventually become, the English Parliament had clearly emerged as an institution by the end of the thirteenth century. The law of the realm was beginning to be determined not by the king alone, but by the king in consultation with representatives of various groups that constituted the community.

The Growth of the French Kingdom

In 843, the Carolingian Empire had been divided into three major sections. The west Frankish lands formed the core of the eventual kingdom of France. In 987, after the death of the last Carolingian king, the west Frankish nobles chose Hugh Capet as the new king, thus establishing the Capetian dynasty of French kings. Although they carried the title of kings, the Capetians had little real power. They controlled as the royal domain (the lands of the king) only the lands around Paris known as the Ile-de-France. As kings of France, the Capetians were formally the overlords of the great lords of France, such as the dukes of Normandy, Brittany, Burgundy, and Aquitaine. In reality, however, many of the dukes were considerably more powerful than the Capetian kings. All in all, it would take the Capetian dynasty hundreds of years to create a truly centralized monarchical authority in France.

The reign of King Philip II Augustus (1180–1223) was an important turning point. Philip II waged war against the Plantagenet rulers of England, who also ruled the French territories of Normandy, Maine, Anjou, and Aquitaine, and was successful in gaining control of most of these territories. Through these conquests, Philip II quadrupled the income of the French monarchy and greatly enlarged its power. To administer justice and collect royal revenues in his new territories, Philip appointed new royal officials, thus inaugurating a French royal bureaucracy in the thirteenth century.

Capetian rulers after Philip II continued to add lands to the royal domain. Although Philip had used military force, other kings used both purchase and marriage to achieve the same end. Philip IV the Fair (1285–1314) was especially effective in strengthening the French monarchy. The machinery of government became even more specialized. French kings going back to the early Capetians had possessed a household staff for running their affairs. Over time, however, this household staff was enlarged and divided into three groups to form three major branches of government: a council for advice, a chamber of accounts for finances, and a *parlement* or royal court. By the beginning of the fourteenth century, the

MAP 12.3 Europe in the High Middle Ages

CHRONOLOGY

THE EUROPEAN KINGDOMS

England	
Norman Conquest	1066
William the Conqueror	1066–1087
Henry II, founder of Plantagenet dynasty	1154–1189
John	1199–1216
Magna Carta	1215
Edward I	1272–1307
First Parliament	1295
France	
Philip II Augustus	1180–1223
Philip IV	1285–1314
First Estates-General	1302
Germany and the Empire	
Otto I	936–973
Henry IV	1056–1106
Frederick I Barbarossa	1152–1190
Northern Italian cities defeat Frederick	1176
Frederick II	1212–1250
The Eastern World	
Mongol conquest of Russia	1230s
Alexander Nevsky, prince of of Novgorod	c. 1220–1263

Capetians had laid the firm foundations for a royal bureaucracy.

Philip IV also brought a French parliament into being by asking representatives of the three estates—or classes—the clergy (first estate), the nobles (second estate), and the townspeople (third estate) to meet with him. They did so in 1302, inaugurating the Estates-General, the first French parliament, although it had little real power. By the end of the thirteenth century, France was the largest, wealthiest, and best-governed monarchical state in Europe.

The Lands of the Holy Roman Empire

In the tenth century, the powerful dukes of the Saxons became kings of the eastern Frankish kingdom (or Germany, as it came to be called). The best known of the Saxon kings of Germany was Otto I (936–973), who intervened in Italian politics and for his efforts was crowned emperor of the Romans by the pope in 962, reviving a title that had not been used since the time of Charlemagne. Otto's creation of a new "Roman Empire" in the hands of the eastern Franks (or Germans, as they came to be called) added a tremendous burden to the king of Germany, who now took on the onerous task of ruling Italy as well.

In the eleventh century, German kings created a strong monarchy and a powerful empire by leading armies into Italy. To strengthen their power, they relied on their ability to control the church and select bishops, whom they could then use as royal administrators. But the struggle between church and state during the reign of Henry IV (1056–1106) weakened the king's ability to use church officials in this way (see Reform of the Papacy later in this chapter). The German kings also tried to bolster their power by using their position as emperors to exploit the resources of Italy. But this strategy tended to backfire; many a German king lost armies in Italy in pursuit of a dream of empire, and no German dynasty demonstrates this better than the Hohenstaufens.

The two most famous members of the Hohenstaufen dynasty, Frederick I (1152–1190) and Frederick II (1212–1250), tried to create a new kind of empire. Previous German kings had focused on building a strong German kingdom, but Frederick I planned to get his chief revenues from Italy as the center of a "holy empire," as he called it (hence the name Holy Roman Empire). But his attempt to conquer northern Italy ran into severe problems. The pope opposed him, fearful that the emperor wanted to include Rome and the Papal States as part of his empire. The cities of northern Italy, which had become used to their freedom, were also not willing to be Frederick's subjects. An alliance of these northern Italian cities, with the support of the pope, defeated the emperor's forces in 1176.

The main goal of Frederick II was the establishment of a strong centralized state in Italy dominated by the kingdom in Sicily he had inherited from his mother. Frederick's major task was to gain control of northern Italy. In attempting to conquer Italy, however, he became involved in a deadly struggle with the popes, who feared that a single ruler of northern and southern Italy would mean the end of papal power in central Italy. The northern Italian cities were also unwilling to give up their freedom. Frederick waged a bitter struggle in northern Italy, winning many battles but ultimately losing the war.

The struggle between popes and emperors had dire consequences for the Holy Roman Empire. While they were fighting in Italy, the German emperors left Germany in the hands of powerful German lords who ignored the emperor and created their own independent kingdoms. This ensured that the German monarchy would remain weak and incapable of maintaining a centralized monarchical state; thus, the German Holy Roman emperor had no real power over either Germany or Italy. Unlike France and England, neither Germany nor Italy created a unified national monarchy in the Middle Ages. Both Germany and Italy consisted of many small, independent states, and both had to wait until the nineteenth century to form united states.

The Slavic Peoples of Central and Eastern Europe

East of the Carolingian Empire lay a spacious plain through which a number of Asiatic nomads, such as the Huns, Bulgars, Avars, and Magyars, had pushed their way westward. Eastern Europe was ravaged by these successive waves of invaders, who found it relatively easy to create large empires that, in turn, were overthrown by the next invaders. Over time, the invaders themselves were largely assimilated with the native Slavic peoples of the area.

The Slavic peoples were originally a single people in central Europe, but they gradually divided into three major groups: the western, southern, and eastern Slavs. The western Slavs eventually formed the Polish and Bohemian kingdoms. German Christian missionaries converted both the Czechs in Bohemia and the Slavs in Poland by the tenth century. The non-Slavic kingdom of Hungary, which emerged after the Magyars settled down after their defeat in 955, was also converted to Christianity by German missionaries. The Poles, Czechs, and Hungarians all accepted Catholic or western Christianity and became closely tied to the Roman Catholic church and its Latin culture.

The southern and eastern Slavic populations largely took a different path because of their proximity to the Byzantine Empire. The Slavic peoples of Moravia were converted to the Orthodox Christianity of the Byzantine Empire by two Byzantine missionary brothers, Cyril and Methodius, who began their activities in 863. They created a Slavonic (Cyrillic) alphabet, translated the Bible into Slavonic, and developed Slavonic church services. Although the southern Slavic peoples accepted Christianity, a split eventually developed between the Croats, who accepted the Roman Catholic church, and the Serbs, who remained loyal to Orthodox Christianity.

Much of the Balkan peninsula was conquered by the Bulgars, who were originally an Asiatic people but were eventually absorbed by the larger native southern Slavic population. Together, they formed a largely Slavic Bulgarian kingdom that embraced the church services developed earlier by Cyril and Methodius. The acceptance of Eastern Orthodoxy by the southern Slavic peoples, the Serbs and Bulgarians, meant that their cultural life was linked to the Byzantine state.

The eastern Slavic peoples, from whom the modern Russians and Ukrainians are descended, had settled in the territory of present-day Ukraine and European Russia. There, beginning in the late eighth century, they began to encounter Swedish Vikings who moved down the extensive network of rivers into the lands of the eastern Slavs in search of booty and new trade routes (see the box on p. 334). These Vikings built trading settlements and eventually came to dominate the native peoples who called them "the Rus," from which the name Russia is derived.

THE DEVELOPMENT OF RUSSIA

A Viking leader named Oleg (c. 873–913) settled in Kiev at the beginning of the tenth century and created the Rus state known as the principality of Kiev. His successors extended their control over the eastern Slavs and expanded the territory of Kiev until it included all the lands between the Baltic and Black Seas and the Danube and Volga Rivers. By marrying Slavic wives, the Viking ruling class was gradually assimilated into the Slavic population.

The growth of the principality of Kiev attracted religious missionaries, especially from the Byzantine Empire.

MAP 12.4 The World of the Slavs

A MUSLIM'S DESCRIPTION OF THE RUS

Despite the difficulties that travel presented, early medieval civilization did witness some contact among the various cultures. This might occur through trade, diplomacy, or the conquest and migration of peoples. This document is a description of the Swedish Rus, who eventually merged with the native Slavic peoples to form the principality of Kiev, commonly regarded as the first Russian state. It was written by Ibn Fadlan, a Muslim diplomat sent from Baghdad in 921 to a settlement on the Volga River. His comments on the filthiness of the Rus reflect the Muslim preoccupation with cleanliness.

IBN FADLAN, DESCRIPTION OF THE RUS

I saw the Rus folk when they arrived on their trading mission and settled at the river Atul (Volga). Never had I seen people of more perfect physique. They are tall as date palms, and reddish in color. They wear neither coat nor kaftan, but each man carried a cape which covers one half of his body, leaving one hand free. No one is ever parted from his axe, sword, and knife. Their swords are Frankish in design, broad, flat, and fluted. Each man has a number of trees, figures, and the like from the fingernails to the neck. Each woman carried on her bosom a container made of iron, silver, copper, or gold—its size and substance depending on her man's wealth.

They [the Rus] are the filthiest of God's creatures. They do not wash after discharging their natural functions, neither do they wash their hands after meals. They are as lousy as donkeys. They arrive from their distant lands and lay their ships alongside the banks of the Atul, which is a great river, and there they build big houses on its shores. Ten or twenty of them may live together in one house, and each of them has a couch of his own where he sits and diverts himself with the pretty slave girls whom he had brought along for sale. He will make love with one of them while a comrade looks on; sometimes they indulge in a communal orgy, and, if a customer should turn up to buy a girl, the Rus man will not let her go till he has finished with her.

They wash their hands and faces every day in incredibly filthy water. Every morning the girl brings her master a large bowl of water in which he washes his hands and face and hair, then blows his nose into it and spits into it. When he has finished the girl takes the bowl to his neighbor—who repeats the performance. Thus the bowl goes the rounds of the entire household. . . .

If one of the Rus folk falls sick they put him in a tent by himself and leave bread and water for him. They do not visit him, however, or speak to him, especially if he is a serf. Should he recover he rejoins the others; if he dies they burn him. But if he happens to be a serf they leave him for the dogs and vultures to devour. If they catch a robber they hang him to a tree until he is torn to shreds by wind and weather.

One Rus ruler, Vladimir (c. 980–1015), married the Byzantine emperor's sister and officially accepted Christianity for himself and his people in 987. From the end of the tenth century, Byzantine Christianity became the model for Russian religious life.

The Kievan Rus state prospered and reached its high point in the first half of the eleventh century. Kievan society was dominated by a noble class of landowners known as the boyars, while Kievan merchants carried on a regular trade with Scandinavia to the north and the Islamic and Byzantine worlds to the south. But civil wars and new invasions by Asiatic nomads caused the principality of Kiev to collapse, and the sack of Kiev by north Russian princes in 1169 brought an end to the first Russian state. That state had remained closely tied to the Byzantine Empire, not to the new Europe. Its Christianity had been Orthodox Christianity, not the Catholicism of Europe. In the thirteenth century, the Mongols conquered Russia and cut it off even more from Europe.

The Mongols had exploded on the scene in the thirteenth century, moving east into China, where they created a new ruling Mongol dynasty, and west into the Middle East and central Europe. Although they conquered Russia, they were not numerous enough to occupy all of its vast lands. Instead, they required the Russian princes to pay tribute to them. One Russian prince soon emerged as more powerful than the others. Alexander Nevsky (c. 1220–1263), prince of Novgorod, defeated a German invading army in northwestern Russia in 1242. His cooperation with the Mongols won him their favor. The khan, leader of the western part of the Mongol empire, rewarded Alexander Nevsky with the title of grand-prince, enabling his descendants to become the princes of Moscow and eventually leaders of all Russia.

THE WORLD OF THE PEASANTS

In the Early Middle Ages, Europe had a relatively small population, but in the High Middle Ages, the population increased dramatically. The number of people in Europe almost doubled between 1000 and 1300, rising from 38 million to 74 million. Why this dramatic increase in population? For one thing, conditions in Europe were more settled and peaceful after the invasions of the Early

Middle Ages had stopped. Then, too, agricultural production also expanded dramatically after 1000. Whether this new productivity was a cause or effect of the population increase is uncertain, but without such a significant rise in food supplies, the growth in population could never have been sustained.

The New Agriculture

During the High Middle Ages, Europeans began to farm in new ways. Although an improvement in climate produced better growing conditions, another important factor in increasing the output of food was the expansion of cultivated or arable land, accomplished primarily by clearing forested areas for cultivation. Eager for land, peasants of the eleventh and twelfth centuries cut down trees and drained swamps. By the thirteenth century, the total acreage available for farming in Europe was greater than the amount tilled at any time before or since.

Technological changes also furthered the development of farming. The Middle Ages witnessed an explosion of labor-saving devices, many of which were made from iron, which was mined in different areas of Europe. Iron was in demand to make swords and armor, but it was also used to make scythes, axes, and hoes for use on farms, as well as saws, hammers, and nails for building purposes. Iron was crucial in making the *carruca,* a heavy, wheeled plow with an iron plowshare, which could turn over the heavy clay soil north of the Alps and allow for its drainage.

Because of the *carruca*'s weight, six or eight oxen were needed to pull it, but oxen were slow. Two new inventions for the horse made it possible to plow even faster. A new horse collar, which appeared in the tenth century, distributed the weight around the shoulders and chest, rather than the throat, and could be used to hitch up a series of horses, enabling them to pull the new heavy plow faster and cultivate more land. The use of the horseshoe, an iron shoe nailed to the horse's hooves, made it easier for horses to pull the heavy plow through the rocky and heavy clay soil of northern Europe.

The use of the heavy, wheeled plow also led to the growth of agricultural villages, where people had to work together. Because iron was expensive, a heavy, wheeled plow had to be purchased by the entire community. Likewise an individual family could not afford a team of animals, so villagers shared their beasts. Moreover, the size and weight of the plow made it necessary to plow the land in long strips to minimize the amount of turning that would have to be done.

Besides using horsepower, the High Middle Ages harnessed the power of water and wind to do jobs formerly done by human or animal power. Located along streams, mills powered by water were used to grind grains and produce flour. Where rivers were not available or not easily dammed, Europeans developed windmills to harness the power of the wind. By the end of the twelfth century, they were beginning to dot the European landscape. Like the watermill, the windmill was first used for grinding grains. The watermill and windmill were the most important devices for harnessing power before the invention of the steam engine in the eighteenth century. Their spread had revolutionary consequences in enabling Europeans to produce more food.

The shift from a two-field to a three-field system also contributed to the increase in food production. In the Early Middle Ages, farmers commonly planted one field while allowing another of equal size to lie fallow to regain its fertility. Now estates were divided into three parts. One field was planted in the fall with winter grains, such as rye and wheat, while spring grains, such as oats or barley, and vegetables, such as peas, beans, or lentils, were planted in the second field. The third was allowed to lie fallow. By rotating the fields, only one-third rather than one-half of the land lay fallow at any time. The rotation of crops also kept the soil from being exhausted so quickly, and more crops could now be grown.

The Manorial System

The landholding class of nobles and knights comprised a military elite whose ability to function as warriors depended on having the leisure time to pursue the arts of war. Landed estates, located on the fiefs given to a vassal by his lord and worked by a dependent peasant class, provided the economic sustenance that made this way of life possible. A manor or villa was simply an agricultural estate operated by a lord and worked by peasants. While a large class of free peasants continued to exist, increasing numbers of free peasants became serfs—peasants bound to the land and required to provide labor services, pay rents, and be subject to the lord's jurisdiction. By the ninth century, probably 60 percent of the population of western Europe had become serfs.

Labor services consisted of working the lord's demesne, the land retained by the lord, which might consist of one-third to one-half of the cultivated lands scattered throughout the manor. The rest would be used by the peasants for themselves. Building barns and digging ditches were also part of the labor services. Serfs usually worked about three days a week for their lord.

The serfs paid rents by giving the lord a share of every product they raised. Moreover, serfs paid the lord for the use of the manor's common pasturelands, streams, ponds, and surrounding woodlands. For example, if a serf fished in the pond or stream on a manor, he turned over part of the catch to his lord. Peasants were also obliged to pay a tithe (a tenth of their produce) to their local village church.

Lords possessed a variety of legal rights over their serfs as a result of their unfree status. Serfs were legally bound to the lord's lands and could not leave without his

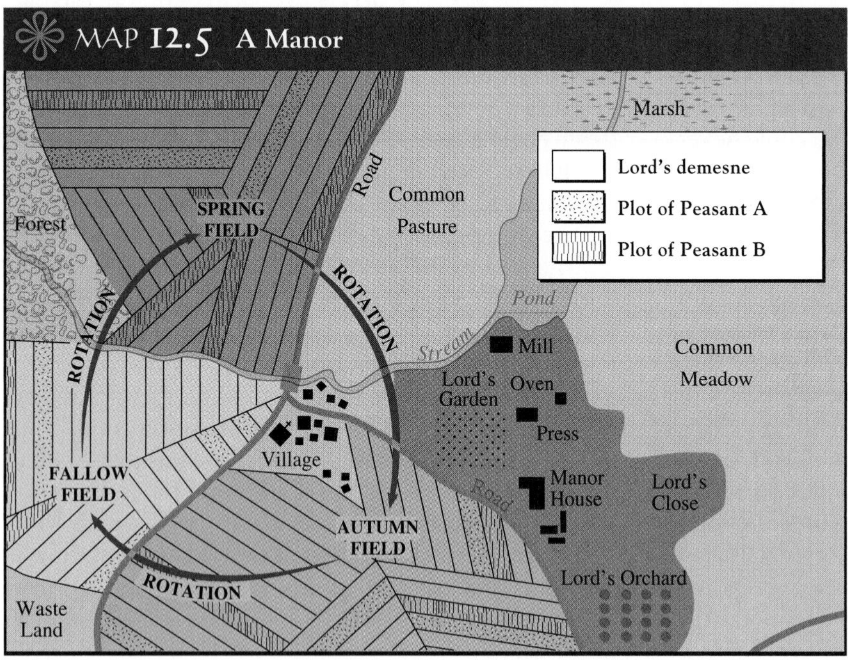

permission. Although free to marry, serfs could not marry anyone outside their manor without the lord's approval. Moreover, lords sometimes exercised public rights or political authority on their lands, which gave them the right to try peasants in their own courts. In fact, the manorial court provided the only law that most peasants knew. Peasants also had to pay the lord for certain services; for example, they might be required to bring their grain to the lord's mill and pay a fee to have it ground into flour.

As the growing towns and cities needed more food, food prices tended to rise in the thirteenth century. This led lords to try to grow more food for profit. One way to do so was to lease their demesne land to their serfs. Labor services were then transformed into money payments or fixed rents, thereby converting many unfree serfs into free peasants. Although many peasants still remained economically dependent on their lords, they were no longer legally tied to the land. Lords, in turn, became collectors of rents, rather than operators of a manor with both political and legal privileges. The political and legal powers formerly exercised by lords were increasingly reclaimed by the monarchical states.

Daily Life of the Peasantry

Peasant activities were largely determined by the seasons of the year. Each season brought a new round of tasks appropriate for the time, although some periods were considerably more hectic than others, especially harvest time in August and September. A new cycle began in October, when the peasants prepared the ground for planting winter crops. In February and March, the land was plowed for spring crops—oats, barley, peas, beans, and lentils. Early summer was a comparatively relaxed time, although there was still weeding and sheepshearing to be done. In every season, the serfs worked not only their own land, but also the lord's demesne. They also tended the small gardens next to their dwellings where they grew the vegetables that made up part of their diet.

The lifestyle of the peasants was quite simple. Their cottages consisted of wood frames covered by sticks with the space between them filled with straw and rubble and then plastered over with clay. Roofs were simply thatched. The houses of poorer peasants consisted of a single room, but

PEASANTS IN THE MANORIAL SYSTEM. In the manorial system, peasants were required to provide labor services for their lord. This thirteenth-century illustration shows a group of English peasants harvesting grain. Overseeing their work is a bailiff, or manager, who supervised the work of the peasants.

others had at least two rooms—a main room for cooking, eating, and other activities and another room for sleeping. There was little privacy in a medieval peasant household.

Peasant women occupied both an important and a difficult position in manorial society. They were expected to carry and bear their children and at the same time fulfill their obligation to labor in the fields. Their ability to manage the household might determine whether a peasant family would starve or survive in difficult times.

Though simple, a peasant's daily diet was adequate when food was available. The staple of the peasant diet, and the medieval diet in general, was bread. While women made the dough for the bread, the loaves were usually baked in community ovens, which were owned by the lord of the manor. Peasant bread was highly nutritious because it contained not only wheat and rye, but also barley, millet, and oats, giving it a dark appearance and a very heavy, hard texture. Bread was supplemented by numerous vegetables from the household gardens, cheese from cow's or goat's milk, nuts and berries from woodlands, and fruits, such as apples, pears, and cherries. Chickens provided eggs and sometimes meat.

Grains were important not only for bread, but also for making ale. In northern European countries, ale was the most common drink of the poor. If records are accurate, enormous quantities of ale were consumed. A monastery in the twelfth century records a daily allotment to the monks of three gallons a day. Peasants in the field undoubtedly consumed even more. This high consumption of alcohol might help to explain the large number of accidental deaths recorded in medieval court records.

The New World of Trade and Cities

Medieval Europe was overwhelmingly an agrarian society, with most people living in small villages. In the eleventh and twelfth centuries, however, new elements were introduced that began to transform the economic foundation of European civilization: a revival of trade, the emergence of specialized craftspeople and artisans, and the growth and development of towns. These changes were made possible by the new agricultural practices and subsequent increase in food production, which freed part of the European population from producing their own food. Merchants and craftspeople could now buy their necessities.

The Revival of Trade

The revival of trade was a gradual process. During the chaotic conditions of the Early Middle Ages, large-scale trade had declined in western Europe except for Byzantine contacts with Italy and the Jewish traders who moved back and forth between the Muslim and Christian worlds. By the end of the tenth century, however, people with both the skills and the products for commercial activity were emerging in Europe. Cities in Italy took the lead in this revival of trade. By the end of the eighth century, for example, Venice had emerged as a town with close trading ties to the Byzantine Empire. It developed a mercantile fleet and by the end of the tenth century had become the chief western trading center for Byzantine and Islamic commerce.

While the northern Italian cities were busy trading in the Mediterranean, the towns of Flanders were doing likewise in northern Europe. Flanders, the area along the coast of present-day Belgium and northern France, was known for its much desired, high-quality woolen cloth. Flanders's location made it an ideal center for the traders of northern Europe. Merchants from England, Scandinavia, France, and Germany converged there to trade their goods for woolen cloth. Flanders prospered in the eleventh and twelfth centuries, and such Flemish towns as Bruges and Ghent became centers for the trade and manufacture of woolen cloth.

By the twelfth century, it was almost inevitable that a regular exchange of goods would develop between Flanders and Italy, the two major centers of northern and southern European trade, respectively. To encourage this trade, the counts of Champagne in northern France instituted an annual series of six fairs in the chief towns of their territory. Northern merchants brought the furs, woolen cloth, tin, hemp, and honey of northern Europe to the fairs of Champagne and exchanged those goods for the cloth and swords of northern Italy and the silks, sugar, and spices of the East.

As trade increased, both gold and silver came to be in demand at fairs and trading markets of all kinds. Slowly, a money economy began to emerge. New trading companies as well as banking firms were set up to manage the exchange and sale of goods. All of these new practices were part of the rise of commercial capitalism, an economic system in which people invested in trade and goods in order to make profits.

The Growth of Cities

The revival of trade led to a revival of cities. Merchants needed places where they could live and build warehouses to store their goods. To meet the needs of merchants, cities were usually located near sources of protection (such as castles) and alongside rivers or roads that provided favorable routes of transportation.

Towns had greatly declined in the Early Middle Ages, especially in Europe north of the Alps. Old Roman cities continued to exist but had dwindled in size and population. With the revival of trade, merchants began to settle in these old cities, followed by craftspeople or artisans, people who on manors or elsewhere had developed skills and now saw an opportunity to ply their trade and make goods that could be sold by the merchants. In the course of the eleventh and twelfth centuries, the old Roman cities came alive with new populations and growth.

Beginning in the late tenth century, many new cities or towns were also founded, particularly in northern Europe. Usually, a group of merchants established a settlement near some fortified stronghold, such as a castle or monastery. The original meaning of the English *borough* or *burgh* and the German *burg* as a fortress or walled enclosure is still evident in the names of many cities, such as Edinburgh and Nuremberg. Castles were particularly favored because they were generally located along major routes of transportation or at the intersection of two trade routes; the lords of the castle also offered protection. If the settlement prospered and expanded, new walls were built to protect it.

Most towns were closely tied to their surrounding territories because they depended on the countryside for their food supplies. In addition, they were often part of the territory belonging to a lord and were subject to his jurisdiction. Although lords wanted to treat towns and townspeople as they would their vassals and serfs, cities had totally different needs and a different perspective. Townspeople needed mobility to trade. Consequently, these townspeople (the merchants and artisans came to be called burghers or bourgeoisie from the word *burgus*, a Latinized version of the German *burg*, meaning a walled enclosure) constituted a revolutionary group who needed their own unique laws to meet their requirements. Since the townspeople were profiting from the growth of trade and the sale of their products, they were willing to pay for the right to make their own laws and govern themselves. In many instances, lords and kings saw that they could also make money and were willing to sell to the townspeople the liberties they were beginning to demand.

SHOPS IN A MEDIEVAL TOWN. Most urban residents were merchants involved in trade and artisans who manufactured a wide variety of products. Master craftsmen had their workshops in the ground-level rooms of their houses. In this illustration, two well-dressed burghers are touring the shopping district of a French town. Tailors, furriers, a barber, and a grocer (from left to right) are visible at work in their shops.

By 1100, townspeople were obtaining charters of liberties from their territorial lords that granted them the privileges they wanted, including the right to bequeath goods and sell property, freedom from any military obligation to the lord, written urban law that guaranteed their freedom, and the right to become a free person after residing a year and a day in the town. The last provision made it possible for a runaway serf who could avoid capture to become a free person in a city. Almost all new urban communities gained these elementary liberties, but only some towns obtained the right to govern themselves by choosing their own officials and administering their own courts of law.

Over time, medieval cities developed their own governments for running the affairs of the community. Only males who had been born in the city or had lived there for some time could be citizens. In many cities, these citizens elected members of a city council who served as judges and city officials and passed laws. Elections were carefully rigged to ensure that only members of the wealthiest and most powerful families, who came to be called the patricians, were elected.

City governments kept close watch over the activities of their communities. To care for the welfare of the community, a government might regulate air and water pollution; provide water barrels and delegate responsibility to people in every section of the town to fight fires, which were an ever present danger; construct warehouses to store grain in the event of food shortages; and set the standards for the weights and measures used in local goods and industries.

Urban crime was not a major problem in medieval cities because the relatively small size of the communities made it difficult for criminals to operate openly. But medieval urban governments did hire guards to patrol the streets at night, to break up fights and prevent robberies. People caught committing criminal acts were quickly tried for their offenses. Serious crimes, such as murder, were punished by execution, usually by hanging. Lesser crimes were punished by fines, flogging, or branding.

Medieval cities remained relatively small in comparison to either ancient or modern cities. A large trading city would number about 5,000 inhabitants. By 1200, London was the largest city in England, with 30,000 people. Otherwise, north of the Alps, only a few great urban centers of commerce, such as Bruges and Ghent, had a population

THE MEDIEVAL CITY

Environmental pollution is not new to the twentieth century. Medieval cities and towns had their own problems with filthy living conditions. This excerpt is taken from an order sent by the king of England to the town of Boutham. It demands rectification of the town's pitiful physical conditions. There is little evidence to indicate that the king's order changed the situation dramatically.

THE KING'S COMMAND TO BOUTHAM

To the bailiffs of the abbot of St. Mary's, York, at Boutham. Whereas it is sufficiently evident that the pavement of the said town of Boutham is so very greatly broke up that all and singular passing and going through that town sustain immoderate damages and grievances, and in addition the air is so corrupted and infected by the pigsties situated in the king's highways and in the lanes of that town and by the swine feeding and frequently wandering about in the streets and lanes and by dung and dunghills and many other foul things placed in the streets and lanes, that great repugnance overtakes the king's ministers staying in that town and also others there dwelling and passing through, the advantage of more wholesome air is impeded, the state of men is grievously injured, and other unbearable inconveniences and many other injuries are known to proceed from such corruption, to the nuisance of the king's ministers aforesaid and of others there dwelling and passing through, and to the peril of their lives . . . the king, being unwilling longer to tolerate such great and unbearable defects there, orders the bailiffs to cause the pavement to be suitably repaired within their liberty before All Saints next, and to cause the pigsties, aforesaid streets and lanes to be cleansed from all dung and dunghills, and to cause proclamation to be made throughout their bailiwick forbidding any one, under pain of grievous forfeiture, to cause or permit their swine to feed or wander outside his house in the king's streets or the lanes aforesaid.

close to 40,000. Italian cities tended to be larger, with Venice, Florence, Genoa, Milan, and Naples numbering almost 100,000. Even the largest European city, however, seemed small alongside the Byzantine capital of Constantinople or the Arab cities of Damascus, Baghdad, and Cairo. For a long time to come, Europe remained a rural society, but in the long run, the growth of trade and the rise of towns laid the foundations for the eventual transformation of Europe from a rural agricultural society to an urban, industrial one.

DAILY LIFE IN THE MEDIEVAL CITY

Medieval towns were surrounded by stone walls that were expensive to build, so the space within was precious and tightly filled. This gave medieval cities their characteristic appearance of narrow, winding streets with houses crowded against each other and the second and third stories of the dwellings built out over the streets. Because dwellings were constructed mostly of wood before the fourteenth century and candles and wood fires were used for light and heat, the danger of fire was great. Medieval cities burned rapidly once a fire started.

Most of the people who lived in cities were merchants involved in trade and artisans engaged in manufacturing of some kind. Generally, merchants and artisans had their own sections within a city. The merchant area included warehouses, inns, and taverns. Artisan sections were usually divided along craft lines; each craft had its own street where its activity was pursued.

The physical environment of medieval cities was not pleasant. They were often dirty and rife with smells from animal and human waste deposited in backyard privies or on the streets (see the box above). Air pollution was also a fact of life, not only from the ubiquitous wood fires, but also from a cheaper fuel, coal, used industrially by lime burners, brewers, and dyers, as well as poor people who could not afford to purchase wood. Cities were also unable to stop water pollution, especially from the tanning and animal-slaughtering industries. Butchers dumped blood and all remaining waste products from their butchered animals into the river, while tanners unloaded tannic acid, dried blood, fat, hair, and the other waste products of their operations.

Because of the pollution, cities did not use the rivers for drinking water but relied instead on wells. Some cities repaired the aqueducts left over from Roman times and even constructed new ones. Private and public baths also existed in medieval towns. Paris, for example, had thirty-two public baths for men and women. City laws did not allow lepers and people with "bad reputations" to use them, but such measures did not prevent the public baths from being known for permissiveness due to public nudity. One contemporary commented on what occurred in public bathhouses: "Shameful things. Men make a point of staying all night in the public baths and women at the break of day come in and through 'ignorance' find themselves in the men's rooms."[7] Authorities came under increasing pressure to close the baths down, and the great plague of the fourteenth century sealed their fate.

There were considerably more men than women in medieval cities. Women, in addition to supervising the household, purchasing food and preparing meals, raising the children, and managing the family finances, were also often expected to help their husbands in their trades. Some women also developed their own trades to earn extra money. When some master craftspeople died, their widows even carried on their trades. Some women in medieval towns were thus able to lead lives of considerable independence.

Industry in Medieval Cities

The revival of trade enabled cities and towns to become important centers for manufacturing a wide range of goods, such as cloth, metalwork, shoes, and leather goods. A host of crafts were carried on in houses along the narrow streets of the medieval cities. From the twelfth century on, artisans began to organize themselves into guilds, which came to play a leading role in the economic life of the cities.

By the thirteenth century, virtually every group of craftspeople, such as tanners, carpenters, and bakers, had their own guild, while specialized groups of merchants, such as dealers in silk, spices, wool, or banking, had their separate guilds as well. Craft guilds directed almost every aspect of the production process. They established standards for the articles produced, specified the actual methods of production to be used, and even fixed the price at which the finished goods could be sold. Guilds also determined the number of men who could enter a specific trade and the procedure they must follow to do so.

A person who wanted to learn a trade first became an apprentice to a master craftsperson, usually at around the age of ten. Apprentices were not paid but did receive room and board from their masters. After five to seven years of service, in which they learned their craft, apprentices became journeymen (or journeywomen, although most were male), who then worked for wages for other masters. Journeymen aspired to become masters as well. To do so, they were expected to produce a "masterpiece," a finished piece in their craft that allowed the master craftspeople of the guild to judge whether the journeymen were qualified to become masters and join the guild.

Christianity and Medieval Civilization

Christianity was an integral part of the fabric of European society and the consciousness of Europe. Papal directives affected the actions of kings and princes alike, while Christian teachings and practices touched the lives of all Europeans.

The Papal Monarchy

Since the fifth century, the popes of the Catholic church had reigned supreme over the affairs of the church. They had also come to exercise control over the territories in central Italy that came to be known as the Papal States; this role kept the popes involved in political matters, often at the expense of their spiritual obligations. At the same time, the church became increasingly entangled in the evolving feudal relationships. High officials of the church, such as bishops and abbots, came to hold their offices as fiefs from nobles. As vassals, they were obliged to carry out the usual duties, including military service. Of course, lords assumed the right to choose their vassals and thus came to appoint bishops and abbots. Because lords often chose their vassals from other noble families for political reasons, these bishops and abbots were often worldly figures who cared little about their spiritual responsibilities.

REFORM OF THE PAPACY

By the eleventh century, church leaders realized the need to free the church from the interference of lords in the appointment of church officials. This issue of lay investiture, or the practice by which secular rulers both chose and invested their nominees to church offices with the symbols of their office, was dramatically taken up by the greatest of the reform popes of the eleventh century, Gregory VII (1073–1085).

Elected pope in 1073, Gregory was convinced that he had been chosen by God to reform the church. In pursuit of those aims, Gregory claimed that he—the pope—was truly God's "vicar on earth" and that the pope's authority extended over all of Christendom, including rulers. Gregory sought nothing less than the elimination of lay investiture. Only in this way could the church regain its freedom, by which Gregory meant the right of the church to appoint clergy and run its own affairs. If rulers did not accept these "divine" commands, then they could be deposed by the pope acting in his capacity as the vicar of Christ.

Gregory VII soon found himself in conflict with the king of Germany over these claims. King Henry IV (1056–1106) of Germany was just as determined as the pope. For many years, German kings had appointed high-ranking clerics, especially bishops, as their vassals in order to use them as administrators. Without them, the king could not hope to maintain his own power vis-à-vis the powerful German nobles. In 1075, Pope Gregory issued a decree forbidding high-ranking clerics from receiving their investiture from lay leaders: "We decree that no one of the clergy shall receive the investiture with a bishopric or abbey or church from the hand of an emperor or king or of any layperson."[8] Henry had no intention of obeying a decree that challenged the very heart of his administration.

The struggle between Henry IV and Gregory VII, which is known as the Investiture Controversy, was one of the great conflicts between church and state in the High Middle Ages. It dragged on until 1122, when a new German king and a new pope reached a compromise called the Concordat of Worms. Under this agreement, a bishop in Germany was first elected by church officials. After election, the nominee paid homage to the king as his feudal lord, who then invested him with the symbols of temporal office. A representative of the pope then invested the new bishop with the symbols of his spiritual office.

THE CHURCH SUPREME

The popes of the twelfth century did not abandon the reform ideals of Pope Gregory VII, but they were less dogmatic and more inclined to consolidate their power and build a strong administrative system. During the papacy of Pope Innocent III (1198–1216), the Catholic church reached the height of its political, intellectual, and secular power. At the beginning of his pontificate, in a letter to a priest, the pope made a clear statement of his views on papal supremacy:

> As God, the creator of the universe, set two great lights in the firmament of heaven, the greater light to rule the day, and the lesser light to rule the night, so He set two great dignities in the firmament of the universal church, . . . the greater to rule the day, that is, souls, and the lesser to rule the night, that is, bodies. These dignities are the papal authority and the royal power. And just as the moon gets her light from the sun, and is inferior to the sun . . . so the royal power gets the splendor of its dignity from the papal authority.[9]

Innocent III's actions were those of a man who believed that he, as pope, was the supreme judge of European affairs. He forced King Philip Augustus of France to take back his wife and queen after Philip had tried to have the marriage annulled. The pope also compelled King John of England to accept the papal choice for the position of archbishop of Canterbury. To achieve his political ends, Innocent did not hesitate to use the spiritual weapons at his command, especially the interdict, which forbade priests to dispense the sacraments of the church in the hope that the people, deprived of the comforts of religion, would exert pressure against their ruler. Pope Innocent's interdict was so effective that it caused Philip to restore his wife to her rightful place as queen of France.

New Religious Orders and New Spiritual Ideals

In the second half of the eleventh century and the first half of the twelfth century, a wave of religious enthusiasm seized Europe, leading to a spectacular growth in the number of monasteries and the emergence of new monastic orders. Most important was the Cistercian order, founded in 1098 by a group of monks dissatisfied with the lack of strict discipline at their own Benedictine monastery. Cistercian monasticism spread rapidly from southern France into the rest of Europe.

A GROUP OF NUNS. Although still viewed by the medieval church as inferior to men, women were as susceptible to the spiritual fervor of the twelfth century as men, and female monasticism grew accordingly. This miniature shows a group of Flemish nuns listening to the preaching of an abbot, Gilles li Muisis. The nun wearing a white robe at the far left is a novice.

The Cistercians were strict. They ate a simple diet and possessed only a single robe apiece. All decorations were eliminated from their churches and monastic buildings. More time for prayer and manual labor was provided by shortening the number of hours spent at religious services. The Cistercians played a major role in developing a new, activist spiritual model for twelfth-century Europe. A Benedictine monk often spent hours in prayer to honor god. The Cistercian ideal had a different emphasis: "Arise, soldier of Christ, arise! Get up off the ground and return to the battle from which you have fled! Fight more boldly after your flight, and triumph in glory!"[10] These were the words of Saint Bernard of Clairvaux (1090–1153), who more than any other person embodied the new spiritual ideal of Cistercian monasticism (see the box on p. 342).

Women were also active participants in the spiritual movements of the age. The number of women joining religious houses grew perceptibly with the rise of the new orders of the twelfth century. In the High Middle Ages, most nuns were from the ranks of the landed aristocracy. Convents were convenient for families unable or unwilling to find husbands for their daughters and for aristocratic women who did not wish to marry. Female intellectuals found them a haven for their activities. Most of the learned women of the Middle Ages, especially in Germany, were nuns. One of the most distinguished was Hildegard of Bingen (1098–1179), who became abbess of a convent in western Germany.

Hildegard shared in the religious enthusiasm of the twelfth century. Soon after becoming abbess, she began to

A MIRACLE OF SAINT BERNARD

Saint Bernard of Clairvaux has been called "the most widely respected holy man of the twelfth century." He was an outstanding preacher, wholly dedicated to the service of God. His reputation reportedly influenced many young men to join the Cistercian order. He also inspired a myriad of stories dealing with his miracles.

A MIRACLE OF ST. BERNARD

A certain monk, departing from his monastery . . . , threw off his habit, and returned to the world at the persuasion of the Devil. And he took a certain parish living; for he was a priest. Because sin is punished with sin, the deserter from his Order lapsed into the vice of lechery. He took a concubine to live with him, as in fact is done by many, and by her he had children.

But as God is merciful and does not wish anyone to perish, it happened that many years after, the blessed abbot [St. Bernard] was passing through the village in which this same monk was living, and went to stay at his house. The renegade monk recognized him, and received him very reverently, and waited on him devoutly . . . but as yet the abbot did not recognize him.

On the morrow, the holy man said Matins and prepared to be off. But as he could not speak to the priest, since he had got up and gone to the church for Matins, he said to the priest's son "Go, give this message to your master." Now the boy had been born dumb. He obeyed the command and feeling in himself the power of him who had given it, he ran to his father and uttered the words of the Holy Father clearly and exactly. His father, on hearing his son's voice for the first time, wept for joy, and made him repeat the same words . . . and he asked what the abbot had done to him. "He did nothing to me," said the boy, "except to say 'Go and say this to your father.'"

At so evident a miracle the priest repented, and hastened after the holy man and fell at his feet saying "My Lord and Father, I was your monk so-and-so, and at such-and-such a time I ran away from your monastery. I ask your Paternity to allow me to return with you to the monastery, for in your coming God has visited my heart." The saint replied unto him, "Wait for me here, and I will come back quickly when I have done my business, and I will take you with me." But the priest, fearing death (which he had not done before), answered, "Lord, I am afraid of dying before then." But the saint replied, "Know this for certain, that if you die in this condition, and in this resolve, you will find yourself a monk before God."

The saint [eventually] returned and heard that the priest had recently died and been buried. He ordered the tomb to be opened. And when they asked him what he wanted to do, he said, "I want to see if he is lying as a monk or a clerk in his tomb." "As a clerk," they said; "we buried him in his secular habit." But when they had dug up the earth, they found that he was not in the clothes in which they had buried him; but he appeared in all points, tonsure and habit, as a monk. And they all praised God.

write down an account of the mystical visions she had had for years. "A great flash of light from heaven pierced my brain and . . . in that instant my mind was imbued with the meaning of the sacred books," she wrote in a description typical of the world's mystical literature. Eventually, she produced three books based on her visions. Hildegard gained considerable renown as a mystic and prophet, and popes, emperors, kings, dukes, bishops, abbots, and abbesses eagerly sought her advice.

In the thirteenth century, two new religious orders emerged that had a profound impact on the lives of ordinary people: the Franciscan and Dominican friars. The friars were particularly active in the cities, where, by their example, they strove to provide a more personal religious experience. Like their founder, Saint Francis of Assisi (1182–1226), the Franciscans lived among the people, preaching repentance and aiding the poor. Their calls for a return to the simplicity and poverty of the early church, reinforced by their own example, were especially effective and made them very popular.

Dominicans arose out of the desire of a Spanish priest, Dominic de Guzmán (1170–1221), to defend church teachings from heresy. The spiritual revival of the High Middle Ages had also led to the emergence of heretical movements, which became especially widespread in southern France. Unlike Francis, Dominic was an intellectual, who was appalled by the growth of heresy within the church. He believed that a new religious order of men who lived lives of poverty but were learned and capable of preaching effectively would best be able to attack heresy. The Dominicans became especially well known for their roles as the inquisitors of the papal Inquisition.

The Holy Office, as the papal Inquisition was formally called, was a court that had been established by the church to find and try heretics. Gradually, the Holy Office developed a regular procedure to deal with heretics. If an accused heretic confessed, he or she was forced to perform public penance and was subjected to punishment, such as flogging. The heretic's property was then confiscated and divided between the secular authorities and the church. Beginning in 1252, those who did not confess voluntarily were tortured. Those who refused to confess and were still considered guilty were turned over to the state for execution. So also were relapsed heretics—those who confessed, did penance, and then reverted to heresy again. To the Christians of the thirteenth century, who believed that there was only one path to salvation, heresy was a crime against God and against humanity. In their minds, force should be used to save souls from damnation.

Popular Religion in the High Middle Ages

We have witnessed the actions of popes, bishops, and monks. But what of ordinary clergy and laypeople? What were their religious hopes and fears? What were their spiritual aspirations?

The sacraments of the Catholic church ensured that the church was an integral part of people's lives, from birth to death. There were (and still are) seven sacraments, administered only by the clergy. Sacraments, such as baptism and the eucharist, were viewed as outward symbols of an inward grace and were considered imperative for a Christian's salvation. Therefore, the clergy were seen to have a key role in the attainment of salvation.

Other church practices were also important to ordinary people. Saints were seen as men and women who, through their holiness, had achieved a special position in heaven, enabling them to act as intercessors before the throne of God. The saints' ability to protect poor souls enabled them to take on great importance at the popular level. Jesus' apostles were, of course, recognized throughout Europe as saints, but there were also numerous local saints that were of special significance to a single area. New cults rapidly developed, especially in the intense religious atmosphere of the eleventh and twelfth centuries. The English, for example, introduced Saint Nicholas, the patron saint of children, who is known today as Santa Claus.

In the High Middle Ages, the foremost position among the saints was occupied by the Virgin Mary, the mother of Jesus. Mary was viewed as the most important mediator with her son Jesus, the judge of all sinners. Moreover, from the eleventh century on, a fascination with Mary as Jesus' human mother became more evident. A sign of Mary's importance was the growing number of churches all over Europe that were dedicated to her in the twelfth and thirteenth centuries.

Emphasis on the role of the saints was closely tied to the use of relics, which also increased noticeably in the High Middle Ages. Relics were usually the bones of saints or objects intimately connected to saints that were considered worthy of veneration by the faithful. A twelfth-century English monk began his description of the abbey's relics by saying that "There is kept there a thing more precious than gold, . . . the right arm of St. Oswald. . . . This we have seen with our own eyes and have kissed, and have handled with our own hands. . . . There are kept here also part of his ribs and of the soil on which he fell."[11] The monk went on to list additional relics possessed by the abbey, including two pieces of Jesus' swaddling clothes, pieces of Jesus' manger, and part of the five loaves of bread with which Jesus fed five thousand people. Because the holiness of the saint was considered to be inherent in his relics, these objects were believed to be capable of healing people or producing other miracles.

The Cultural World of the High Middle Ages

The High Middle Ages was a time of extraordinary intellectual and artistic vitality. It witnessed the birth of universities, a quickening of theological thought, a rebirth of interest in ancient culture, new developments in literature, and a building spree that left Europe bedecked with churches and cathedrals.

The Rise of Universities

The university as we know it—with faculty, students, and degrees—was a product of the High Middle Ages. The word *university* is derived from the Latin word *universitas,* meaning a corporation or guild, and referred to either a corporation of teachers or a corporation of students. Medieval universities were educational guilds or corporations that produced educated and trained individuals.

The first European university appeared in Bologna, Italy, where a great teacher named Irnerius (1088–1125), who taught Roman law, attracted students from all over Europe. Most of them were laymen, usually older individuals who served as administrators for kings and princes and were eager to learn more about law so they could apply it in their own jobs. To protect themselves, students at Bologna formed a guild or *universitas,* which was recognized by Emperor Frederick Barbarossa and given a charter in 1158. Although the faculty also organized themselves as a group, the guild of students at Bologna was far more influential. It obtained a promise of freedom for students from local authorities, regulated the price of books and lodging, and determined the curriculum, fees, and standards for their masters. Teachers were fined if they missed a class or began their lectures late.

The first university in northern Europe was the University of Paris. In the second half of the twelfth century, a number of students and masters left Paris and started their own university at Oxford, England. In the Late Middle Ages, kings, popes, and princes competed to found new universities, and by the end of the Middle Ages, Europe had eighty universities, most of them located in England, France, Italy, and Germany.

Students at a medieval university began their studies with the traditional liberal arts curriculum, which consisted of grammar, rhetoric, logic, arithmetic, geometry, music,

A UNIVERSITY CLASSROOM. This illustration shows a university classroom in fourteenth-century Germany. As was customary in medieval classrooms, the master is reading from a text. The students obviously vary considerably in age and in their attentiveness to the lecturer.

and astronomy. Teaching was done through lectures. (The word *lecture* is derived from the Latin and means "to read.") Before the development of the printing press in the fifteenth century, books were prohibitively expensive—few students could afford them—so teachers read from a basic text (such as a collection of law if the subject was law) and then added their explanations. No exams were given after a series of lectures, but when a student applied for a degree, he (women did not attend universities in the Middle Ages) was given a comprehensive oral examination by a committee of teachers. The exam was taken after a four- or six-year period of study. The first degree a student could earn was an A.B., the *artium baccalaureus,* or bachelor of arts; later, he might receive an A.M., *artium magister,* or master of arts. All degrees were licenses to teach, although most students receiving them did not become teachers.

After completing the liberal arts curriculum, a student could go on to study law, medicine, or theology. The latter was the most highly regarded subject of the medieval university. The study of law, medicine, or theology could take a decade or more. A student who passed his final oral examinations was granted a doctor's degree, which officially enabled him to teach his subject. Students who received degrees from medieval universities could pursue other careers besides teaching that would be much more lucrative. A law degree was necessary for those who wished to serve as advisers to kings and princes. The growing administrative bureaucracies of popes and kings also demanded a supply of educated clerks, who could keep records and draw up official documents. Universities provided the teachers, administrators, lawyers, and doctors for medieval society.

The Development of Scholasticism

The importance of Christianity in medieval society made it certain that theology would play a central role in the European intellectual world. Theology, the formal study of religion, was "queen of the sciences" in the new universities.

Beginning in the eleventh century, the effort to apply reason or logical analysis to the church's basic doctrines had a significant impact on the study of theology. The word *scholasticism* refers to the philosophical and theological system of the medieval schools. A primary preoccupation of scholasticism was the attempt to reconcile faith and reason—to demonstrate that what was accepted on faith was in harmony with what could be learned by reason. Scholasticism had its beginnings in the theological world of the eleventh and twelfth centuries but reached its high point in the brilliant synthesis of Thomas Aquinas in the thirteenth century.

The overriding task of scholasticism in the thirteenth century was to harmonize Christian revelation with the work of Aristotle. In the twelfth century, due largely to the work of Muslim and Jewish scholars, western Europe was introduced to a large number of Greek scientific and philosophical works and, above all, to the works of Aristotle. The great influx of Aristotle's works into the West in the High Middle Ages threw many theologians into consternation. Aristotle was so highly regarded that he was called "the philosopher," yet he had arrived at his conclusions by rational thought—not revelation—and some of his doctrines, such as the mortality of the individual soul, contradicted the teachings of the church. The most famous attempt to reconcile Aristotle and the doctrines of Christianity was made by Saint Thomas Aquinas.

Thomas Aquinas (1225–1274) studied theology at Cologne and Paris and taught at both Naples and Paris. It was at the latter that he finished his famous *Summa Theologica* (*A Summa of Theology*—a summa was a compendium of knowledge that attempted to bring together all the received learning of the preceding centuries on a given subject into a single whole). Aquinas's masterpiece was organized according to the dialectical method of the scholastics. Aquinas first posed a question, cited sources that offered opposing opinions on the question, and then resolved them by arriving at his own conclusions. In this fashion, he raised and discussed some six hundred articles.

Aquinas's reputation is based on his masterful attempt to reconcile faith and reason. He took it for granted that there were truths derived by reason and truths derived by faith. He was certain, however, that the two truths could not be in conflict with each other. The natural mind, unaided by faith, could arrive at truths concerning the physical universe. Without the help of God's grace, however, unaided reason alone could not grasp spiritual truths, such as the Trinity or the Incarnation.

Vernacular Literature

Latin was the universal language of medieval civilization. Used in the church and schools, it enabled learned men to communicate anywhere in Europe. But in the twelfth century much new literature was being written in the vernacular (the language used in a particular region, such as Spanish, French, English, or German). A new market for vernacular literature appeared in the twelfth century when educated laypeople at courts and in the cities sought fresh avenues of entertainment.

Perhaps the most popular vernacular literature of the twelfth century was troubadour poetry, which was chiefly the product of nobles and knights. This poetry told of the love of a knight for a lady, who inspires him to become a braver knight and a better poet. A good example is found in the laments of the noble Jaufré Rudel, who cherished a dream lady from afar whom he would always love, but feared he would never meet:

> *Most sad, most joyous shall I go away,*
> *Let me have seen her for a single day,*
> *My love afar,*
> *I shall not see her, for her land and mine*
> *Are sundered, and the ways are hard to find,*
> *So many ways, and I shall lose my way,*
> *So wills it God.*[12]

Though it originated in southern France, troubadour poetry also spread to northern France, Italy, and Germany.

Romanesque Architecture: "A White Mantle of Churches"

The eleventh and twelfth centuries witnessed an explosion of building, both private and public. The construction of castles and churches absorbed most of the surplus resources of medieval society and at the same time reflected its basic preoccupations, God and warfare. The churches were by far the most conspicuous of the public buildings. As a chronicler of the eleventh century commented,

> As the year 1003 approached, people all over the world, but especially in Italy and France, began to rebuild their churches. Although most of them were well built and in little need of alterations, Christian nations were rivaling each other to have the most beautiful edifices. One might say the world was shaking herself, throwing off her old garments, and robing herself with a white mantle of churches. Then nearly all the cathedrals, the monasteries dedicated to different saints, and even the small village chapels were reconstructed more beautifully by the faithful.[13]

BARREL VAULTING. The eleventh and twelfth centuries witnessed an enormous amount of church construction. Utilizing the basilica shape, master builders replaced flat wooden roofs with long, round stone vaults, known as barrel vaults. As this illustration of a Romanesque church in Vienne, France, indicates, the barrel vault limited the size of a church and left little room for windows.

Hundreds of new cathedrals and abbey and pilgrimage churches, as well as thousands of parish churches in rural villages, were built in the eleventh and twelfth centuries. The building spree was a direct reflection of a revived religious culture and the increased wealth of the period produced by agriculture, trade, and the growth of cities.

The cathedrals of the eleventh and twelfth centuries were built in the Romanesque style, a truly international style. The construction of churches required the services of professional master builders, whose employment throughout Europe guaranteed an international uniformity in basic features.

Romanesque churches were normally built in the basilica shape used in the construction of churches in the Late Roman Empire. Basilicas were simply rectangular buildings with flat wooden roofs. While using this basic plan, Romanesque builders made a significant innovation by replacing the flat wooden roof with a long, curved stone vault, called a barrel vault or a cross vault where two barrel vaults intersected. The latter was used when a transept was added to create a church plan in the shape of a cross. Although barrel and cross vaults were difficult to build, they were considered aesthetically more pleasing and technically more proficient than flat roofs and were also less apt to catch fire.

Because stone roofs were extremely heavy, Romanesque churches required massive pillars and walls to hold them up. This left little space for windows, and the churches were correspondingly dark on the inside. Their massive walls and pillars gave Romanesque churches a sense of solidity and almost the impression of a fortress.

The Gothic Cathedral

Begun in the twelfth century and brought to perfection in the thirteenth, the Gothic cathedral remains one of the greatest artistic triumphs of the High Middle Ages. Soaring skyward, almost as if to reach heaven, it was a fitting symbol for medieval people's preoccupation with God.

Two fundamental innovations of the twelfth century made Gothic cathedrals possible. The combination of ribbed vaults and pointed arches replaced the barrel vault of Romanesque churches and enabled builders to make Gothic churches higher than their Romanesque counterparts. The use of pointed arches and ribbed vaults created an impression of upward movement, a sense of weightless upward thrust that implied the energy of God. Another technical innovation, the flying buttress, basically a heavy arched pier of stone built onto the outside of the wall, made it possible to distribute the weight of the church's vaulted ceilings outward and down and thus eliminate the heavy walls used in Romanesque churches to hold the weight of the massive barrel vaults. Thus, Gothic cathedrals could be built with thin walls that were filled with magnificent stained-glass windows, which created a play of light inside that varied with the sun at different times of the day. This preoccupation with colored light in Gothic cathedrals was not accidental but was executed by people who believed that natural light was a symbol of the divine light of God.

THE GOTHIC CATHEDRAL. The Gothic cathedral was one of the great artistic triumphs of the High Middle Ages. Seen here is the cathedral of Notre Dame in Paris. Begun in 1163, it was not completed until the beginning of the fourteenth century.

The first fully Gothic church was the abbey church of Saint-Denis near Paris, inspired by its famous abbot Suger (1122–1151) and built between 1140 and 1150. Although the Gothic style was a product of northern France, by the mid-thirteenth century, French Gothic architecture had spread to England, Spain, Germany—virtually all of Europe. By the mid-thirteenth century, French Gothic architecture was displayed most brilliantly in cathedrals in Paris (Notre Dame), Reims, Amiens, and Chartres.

A Gothic cathedral was the work of an entire community. All classes contributed to its construction. Money was raised from wealthy townspeople, who had profited from the new trade and industries, as well as from kings and nobles. Master masons, who were both architects and engineers, designed the cathedrals. They drew up the plans and supervised the work of construction. Stonemasons and other craftspeople were paid a daily wage and provided the skilled labor to build the cathedrals. A Gothic cathedral symbolized the chief preoccupation of a medieval Christian community, its dedication to a spiritual ideal. As we have observed before, the largest buildings of an era reflect the values of its society. The Gothic cathedral with its towers soaring toward heaven gave witness to an age when a spiritual impulse still underlay most of existence.

The Byzantine Empire and the Crusades

In the fourth century, a noticeable separation between the western and eastern parts of the Roman Empire began to develop. In the course of the fifth century, the Germanic tribes moved into the western part of the empire and established their states, while the Roman Empire in the east, centered on Constantinople, continued to exist.

MAP 12.6 The Byzantine Empire in the Time of Justinian

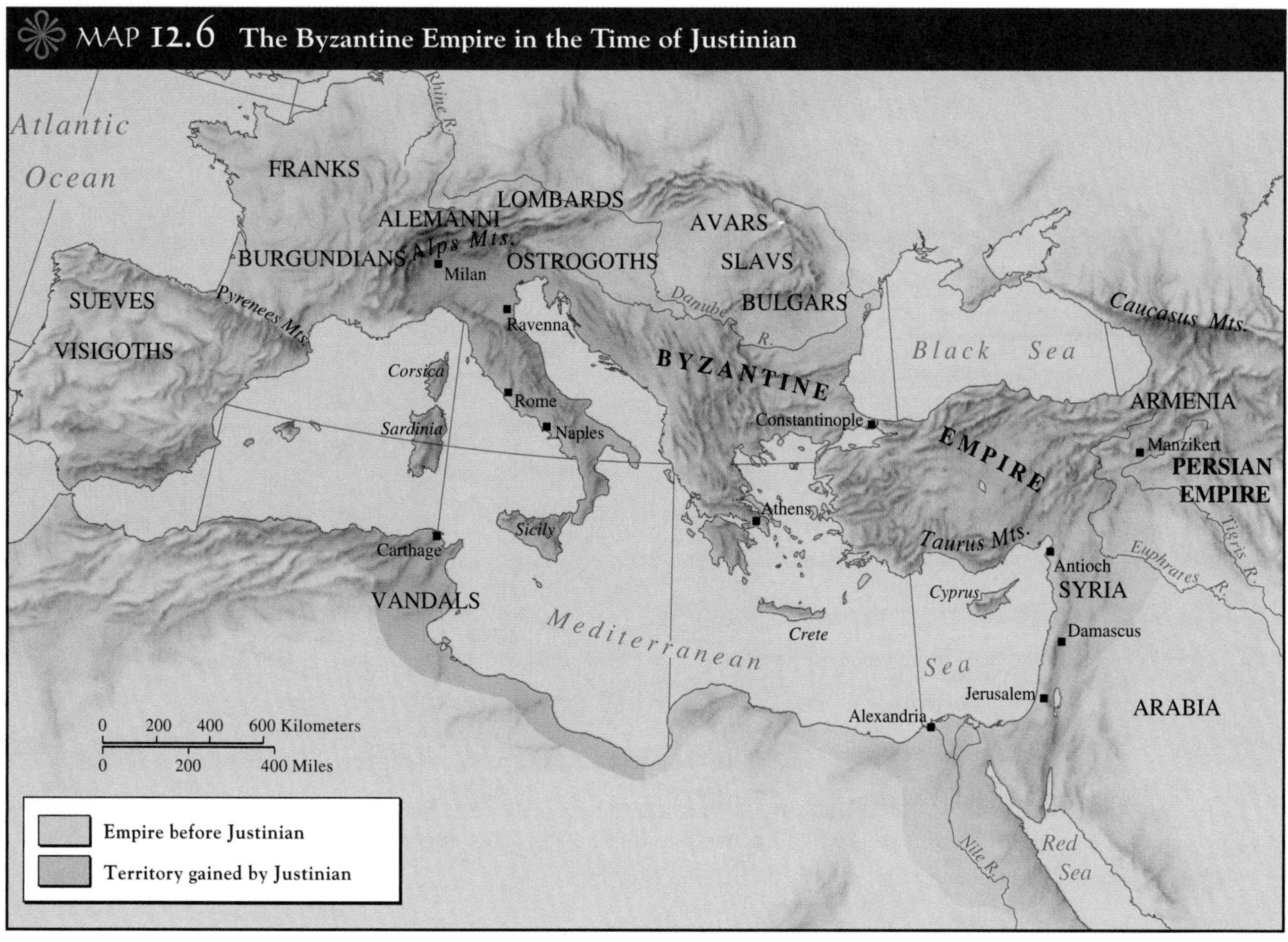

The Reign of Justinian (527–565)

When he became emperor of the Eastern Roman Empire, Justinian was determined to reestablish the Roman Empire in the entire Mediterranean world. His army, commanded by Belisarius, probably the best general of the late Roman world, sailed to North Africa and quickly destroyed the Vandals in two major battles. From North Africa Belisarius led his forces onto the Italian peninsula and defeated the Ostrogoths. By 552, Justinian appeared to have achieved his goals. He had restored the Roman Empire in the Mediterranean. His empire included Italy, part of Spain, North Africa, Asia Minor, Palestine, and Syria. But the reconquest of the western empire proved fleeting. Only three years after Justinian's death, the Lombards conquered much of Italy. Although the eastern empire maintained the fiction of Italy as a province, its forces were limited to southern and central Italy, Sicily, and some coastal areas.

Justinian's most important contribution was his codification of Roman law. The eastern empire had inherited a vast quantity of legal materials connected to the development of Roman law, which Justinian wished to simplify. The result was the *Corpus Iuris Civilis* (*The Body of Civil Law*), a codification of Roman law that remained the basis of imperial law in the Eastern Roman Empire until its end in 1453. More importantly, however, because it was written in Latin (it was, in fact, the last product of eastern Roman culture to be written in Latin, which was soon replaced by Greek), it was also eventually used in the west and, in fact, became the basis of the legal systems of all of continental Europe.

From Eastern Roman to Byzantine Empire

Justinian's accomplishments had been spectacular, but he left the Eastern Roman Empire with serious problems: too much territory to protect far from Constantinople, an empty treasury, a decline in population after a plague, and renewed threats to its frontiers. In the first half of the seventh century, the empire was attacked by the Persians to the east and the Slavs to the north. The empire survived, only to face a new series of threats.

The most serious challenge to the Eastern Roman Empire came from the rise of Islam, which unified the Arab tribes and created a powerful new force that swept through the east (see Chapter 8). The defeat of an eastern Roman army at Yarmuk in 636 meant the loss of the

THE EMPEROR JUSTINIAN SURROUNDED BY HIS COURT. The church of San Vitale at Ravenna contains some of the finest examples of sixth-century Byzantine mosaics. This mosaic depicts the Byzantine emperor Justinian and his court dressed in their elaborate court robes.

provinces of Syria and Palestine. Problems arose along the northern frontier as well, especially in the Balkans, where the Bulgars had arrived earlier, in the sixth century. In 679, the Bulgars defeated the eastern Roman forces and took possession of the lower Danube valley, creating a strong Bulgarian kingdom.

By the beginning of the eighth century, the Eastern Roman Empire was greatly diminished in size. Consisting only of the eastern Balkans and Asia Minor, it was no longer an eastern Mediterranean state. The external challenges had important internal repercussions as well. By the eighth century, the Eastern Roman Empire had been transformed into what historians call the Byzantine Empire, a civilization with its own unique character that would last until 1453.

The Byzantine Empire was both a Greek and a Christian state. Increasingly, Latin fell into disuse as Greek became both the common and the official language of the empire. The Byzantine Empire was also a Christian state. The empire was built on a faith in Jesus that was shared in a profound way by almost all of its citizens. An enormous amount of artistic talent was poured into the construction of churches, church ceremonies, and church decoration. Spiritual principles deeply permeated Byzantine art.

The emperor occupied a crucial position in the Byzantine state. Portrayed as chosen by God, the emperor was crowned in sacred ceremonies, and his subjects were expected to prostrate themselves in his presence. His power was considered absolute and was limited in practice only by deposition or assassination. Since the emperor appointed the head of the church (known as the patriarch), he also exercised control over both church and state. The Byzantines believed that God had commanded their state to preserve the true Christian faith. Emperor, clergy, and state officials were all bound together in service to this ideal. It can be said that spiritual values truly held the Byzantine state together.

LIFE IN CONSTANTINOPLE

After riots destroyed much of Constantinople in 532, Emperor Justinian rebuilt the city and gave it the appearance it would keep for almost a thousand years. With a population estimated in the hundreds of thousands, Constantinople was the largest city in Europe during the Middle Ages. But even Constantinople could not compare to the Chinese capital city of Chang'an under the Tang dynasty; it numbered almost two million inhabitants.

Until the twelfth century, Constantinople was Europe's greatest commercial center, the chief marketplace where western and eastern products were exchanged. Highly desired in Europe were the products of the east: silk from China, spices from Southeast Asia and India, jewelry and ivory from India (the latter used by Byzantine craftspeople for church items), wheat and furs from southern Russia, and flax and honey from the Balkans. Many of these eastern goods were then shipped to the Mediterranean area and northern Europe. Some imported raw materials were used in Constantinople for local industries. During Justinian's reign, two Christian monks smuggled silkworms from China to begin a Byzantine silk industry. The state controlled the production of silk cloth, and the workshops themselves were housed in Constantinople's royal palace complex. European demand for silk cloth made it the city's most lucrative product.

Before Justinian's program of rebuilding in the sixth century, Emperor Theodosius II (408–450) in the mid-fifth century had erected an enormous defensive wall to protect the city on its land side. The city was dominated by an immense palace complex, hundreds of churches, and a huge arena known as the Hippodrome. No residential district was particularly fashionable; palaces, tenements, and slums ranged alongside one another. Justinian added many new buildings. His public works projects included roads, bridges, walls, public baths, law courts, and colossal underground reservoirs to hold the city's water supply. He also built hospitals, schools, monasteries, and churches. The latter were his special passion, and in Constantinople alone he built or rebuilt thirty-four of them. His greatest achievement was the famous Hagia Sophia—the Church of the Holy Wisdom—completed in 537. The center of Hagia Sophia consisted of four large piers crowned by an enormous dome, which seemed to be floating in space. In part, this impression was created by ringing the base of the dome with forty-two windows, which allowed an incredible play of light within the cathedral. Light served to remind the worshipers of God. As invisible light illuminates darkness, so too, it was believed, invisible spirit illuminates the world.

The Hippodrome was a huge amphitheater, constructed of brick covered by marble, holding between 40,000 and 60,000 spectators. Although gladiator fights were held there, the main events were the chariot races; twenty-four would usually be presented in one day. The citizens of Constantinople were passionate fans of chariot racing. Successful charioteers were acclaimed as heroes and honored with public statues.

New Heights and New Problems

By 750, the Byzantine Empire consisted only of Asia Minor, some lands in the Balkans, and the southern coast of Italy. But Byzantium recovered and not only endured, but even expanded through the efforts of a new dynasty of Byzantine emperors known as the Macedonians, who ruled from 867 to 1081. This line of emperors managed to beat off the empire's external enemies and switch to the offensive. The empire was expanded to include Bulgaria in the Balkans, the islands of Crete and Cyprus, and Syria. By 1025, the Byzantine Empire was the largest it had been since the beginning of the seventh century.

The Macedonian emperors also fostered a burst of economic prosperity by expanding trade relations with western Europe, especially by selling silks and metalwork. Thanks to this prosperity, the city of Constantinople flourished. Foreign visitors continued to be astounded by its size, wealth, and physical surroundings. To western Europeans, it was the stuff of legends and fables (see the box on p. 350).

Although the Macedonians had restored much of the power of the Byzantine Empire in the tenth and eleventh centuries, their incompetent successors reversed most of the gains as struggles for power between ambitious military leaders and aristocratic families led to political and social disorder in the late eleventh century. The Byzantine Empire had also been troubled by the growing split

INTERIOR VIEW OF HAGIA SOPHIA. Pictured here is the interior of the Church of the Holy Wisdom, constructed under Justinian by Anthemius of Tralles and Isidore of Milan. The pulpits and the great plaques bearing inscriptions from the Koran were introduced when the Turks converted this church into a mosque, in the fifteenth century.

A WESTERN VIEW OF THE BYZANTINE EMPIRE

Bishop Liudprand of Cremona undertook diplomatic missions to Constantinople on behalf of two western kings, Berengar of Italy and Otto I of Germany. This selection is taken from his description of his mission to the Byzantine emperor Constantine VII in 949 as an envoy for Berengar, king of Italy from 950 until his overthrow by Otto I of Germany in 964. Liudprand had mixed feelings about Byzantium: admiration, yet also envy and hostility because of its superior wealth.

LIUDPRAND OF CREMONA, *ANTAPODOSIS*

Next to the imperial residence at Constantinople there is a palace of remarkable size and beauty which the Greeks call Magnavra . . . the name being equivalent to "Fresh breeze." In order to receive some Spanish envoys, who had recently arrived, as well as myself . . . , Constantine gave orders that this palace should be got ready. . . .

Before the emperor's seat stood a tree, made of bronze gilded over, whose branches were filled with birds, also made of gilded bronze, which uttered different cries, each according to its varying species. The throne itself was so marvelously fashioned that at one moment it seemed a low structure, and at another it rose high into the air. It was of immense size and was guarded by lions, made either of bronze or of wood covered over with gold, who beat the ground with their tails and gave a dreadful roar with open mouth and quivering tongue. Leaning upon the shoulders of two eunuchs I was brought into the emperor's presence. At my approach the lions began to roar and the birds to cry out, each according to its kind; but I was neither terrified nor surprised, for I had previously made enquiry about all these things from people who were well acquainted with them. So after I had three times made obeisance to the emperor with my face upon the ground, I lifted my head, and behold! The man whom just before I had seen sitting on a moderately elevated seat had now changed his raiment and was sitting on the level of the ceiling. How it was done I could not imagine, unless perhaps he was lifted up by some such sort of device as we use for raising the timbers of a wine press. On that occasion he did not address me personally, . . . but by the intermediary of a secretary he enquired about Berengar's doings and asked after his health. I made a fitting reply and then, at a nod from the interpreter, left his presence and retired to my lodging.

It would give me some pleasure also to record here what I did then for Berengar. . . . The Spanish envoys . . . had brought handsome gifts from their masters to the emperor Constantine. I for my part had brought nothing from Berengar except a letter and that was full of lies. I was very greatly disturbed and shamed at this and began to consider anxiously what I had better do. In my doubt and perplexity it finally occurred to me that I might offer the gifts, which on my account I had brought for the emperor, as coming from Berengar, and trick out my humble present with fine words. I therefore presented him with nine excellent cuirasses, seven excellent shields with gilded bosses, two silver gilt cauldrons, some swords, spears, and spits, and what was more precious to the emperor than anything, four carzimasia; that being the Greek name for young eunuchs who have had both their testicles and their penis removed. This operation is performed by traders at Verdun, who take the boys into Spain and make a huge profit.

between the Catholic church of the west and the Eastern Orthodox church of the Byzantine Empire. The Eastern Orthodox church was unwilling to accept the pope's claim that he was the sole head of the church. In 1054, Pope Leo IX and Patriarch Michael Cerularius, head of the Byzantine church, formally excommunicated each other, initiating a schism between the two great branches of Christianity that has not been completely healed to this day.

The Byzantine Empire faced threats from abroad as well. The greatest challenge came from the advance of the Seljuk Turks (see Chapter 8) who had moved into Asia Minor—the heartland of the empire and its main source of food and labor. In 1071, a Turkish army disastrously defeated the Byzantine forces under Emperor Romanus IV Diogenes at Manzikert. Lacking the resources to undertake new campaigns against the Turks, the new emperor, Alexius I Comnenus (1081–1118), turned to Europe for military assistance. It was the positive response of Europeans to the emperor's request that led to the Crusades. The Byzantine Empire lived to regret it.

The Crusades

The Crusades were based on the idea of a holy war against the infidels or unbelievers. The wrath of Christians was directed against the Muslims, and at the end of the eleventh century, Christian Europe found itself with a glorious opportunity to attack them. The immediate impetus for the Crusades came when the Byzantine emperor Alexius I asked Pope Urban II for help against the Seljuk Turks, who were Muslims. The pope saw a golden opportunity to provide papal leadership for a great cause: to rally the warriors of Europe for the liberation of Jerusalem and the Holy Land from the infidel. At the Council of Clermont in southern France near the end of 1095, Urban II challenged Christians to take up their weapons and join in a holy war to recover the Holy Land. The pope promised remission of sins: "All who die by the way, whether by land or by sea, or in battle against the pagans, shall have immediate remission of sins. This I grant them through the power of God with which I am invested."[14] The enthusiastic crowd cried out in response: "It is the will of God, it is the will of God."

The warriors of western Europe, particularly France, formed the first crusading armies. The knights who made up this first crusading host were motivated by religious fervor, but there were other attractions as well. Some sought adventure and welcomed a legitimate opportunity to pursue their favorite pastime—fighting. Others saw an opportunity to gain territory, riches, and possibly a title. From the perspective of the pope and European monarchs, the Crusades offered the potential of freeing Europe of contentious young nobles who disturbed the peace and wasted lives fighting each other. Then, too, merchants in many Italian cities sought new trading opportunities in Muslim lands.

Three organized crusading bands of noble warriors, most of them French, made their way to the east. The crusading army probably numbered several thousand cavalry and as many as 10,000 infantry. After the capture of Antioch in 1098, much of the crusading host proceeded down the Palestinian coast, evading the well-defended coastal cities, and reached Jerusalem in June 1099. After a five-week siege, the Holy City was taken amidst a horrible massacre of the inhabitants—men, women, and children.

After further conquest of Palestinian lands, the crusaders ignored the wishes of the Byzantine emperor (who foolishly believed the crusaders were working on his

CHRONOLOGY

THE CRUSADES

Urban's call for a crusade at Clermont	1095
First Crusade	1096–1099
Fall of Edessa	1144
Second Crusade	1147–1149
Saladin's conquest of Jerusalem	1187
Third Crusade	1189–1192
Fourth Crusade—sack of Constantinople	1204
Latin Empire of Constantinople	1204–1261
Children's Crusade	1212

MAP 12.7 The Early Crusades

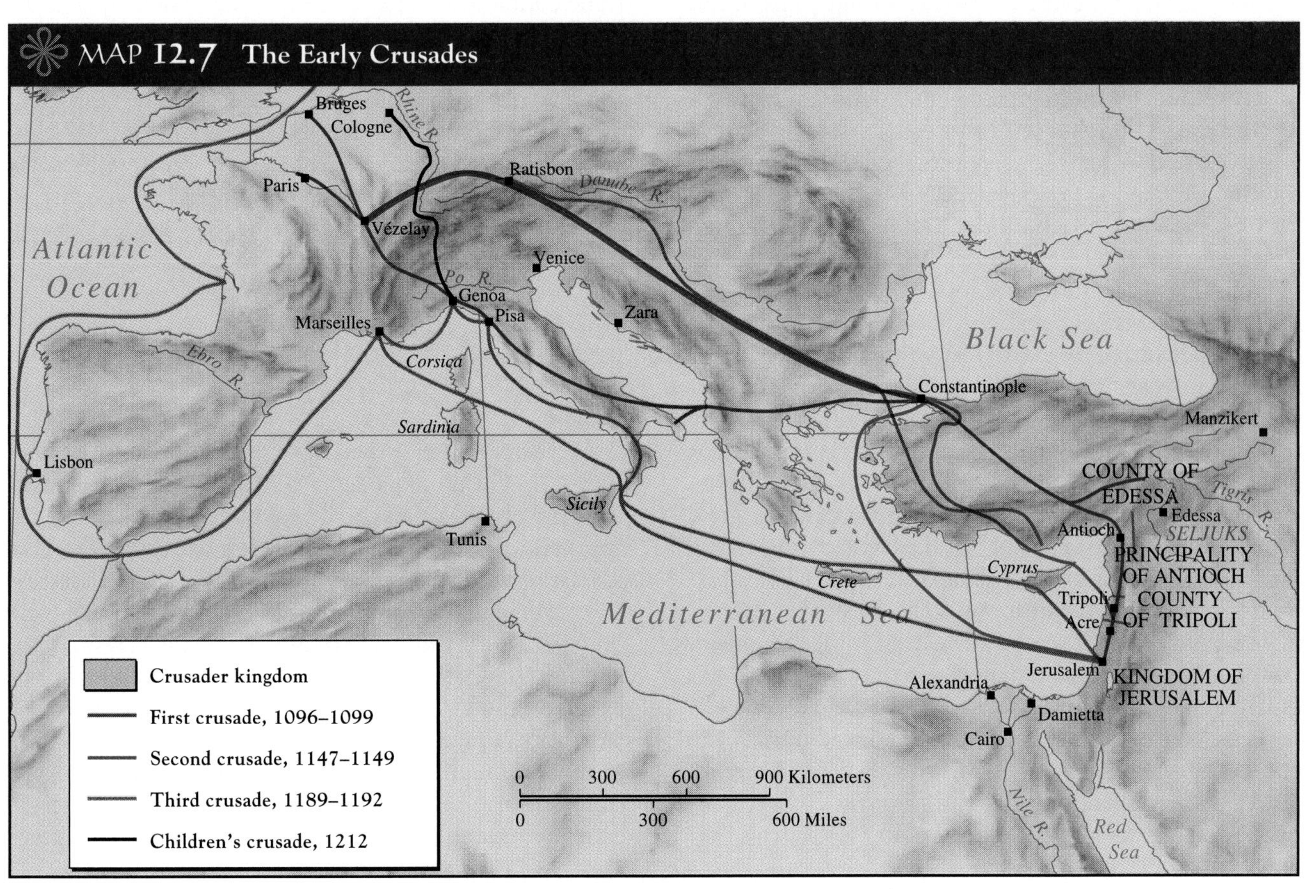

behalf) and organized four Latin crusader states. Because the crusader states were surrounded by Muslims, they grew increasingly dependent on the Italian commercial cities for supplies from Europe. Some Italian cities, such as Genoa, Pisa, and, above all, Venice, grew rich and powerful in the process.

But it was not easy for the crusader states to maintain themselves in the east. Already by the 1120s, the Muslims had begun to strike back. In 1144, Edessa became the first of the four Latin states to be recaptured. Its fall led to renewed calls for another Crusade, especially from the monastic firebrand Saint Bernard of Clairvaux. He exclaimed: "Now, on account of our sins, the enemies of the cross have begun to show their faces. . . . What are you doing, you servants of the cross? Will you throw to the dogs that which is most holy? Will you cast pearls before swine?"[15] Bernard aimed his message at knights and even managed to enlist two powerful rulers, King Louis VII of France (1137–1180) and Emperor Conrad III of Germany (1138–1152). Their Second Crusade, however, proved to be a total failure.

The Third Crusade was a reaction to the fall of the Holy City of Jerusalem in 1187 to the Muslim forces under Saladin. Now all of Christendom was ablaze with calls for a new Crusade. Three major monarchs agreed to lead their forces in person: Emperor Frederick Barbarossa of Germany (1152–1190), Richard I the Lionhearted of England (1189–1199), and Philip II Augustus of France (1180–1223). Some of the crusaders finally arrived in the east by 1189 only to encounter problems. Frederick Barbarossa drowned while swimming in a local river, and his army quickly disintegrated. The English and French arrived by sea and met with success against the coastal cities, where they had the support of their fleets, but when they moved inland, they failed miserably. Eventually, after Philip went home, Richard the Lionhearted negotiated a settlement whereby Saladin agreed to allow Christian pilgrims free access to Jerusalem.

After the death of Saladin in 1193, Pope Innocent III initiated a Fourth Crusade. On its way to the east, the crusading army became involved in a dispute over the succession to the Byzantine throne. The Venetian leaders of the Fourth Crusade saw an opportunity to neutralize their greatest commercial competitor: the Byzantine Empire. Diverted to Constantinople, the crusaders sacked the great capital city of Byzantium in 1204 and created a new Latin Empire of Constantinople. Not until 1261 did a Byzantine army recapture Constantinople. The Byzantine Empire had been saved, but it was no longer a great Mediterranean power. The restored empire now comprised only the city of Constantinople and its surrounding lands as well as some lands in Asia Minor. Though reduced in size, the empire limped along for another 190 years, until its weakened condition finally enabled the Ottoman Turks to conquer it in 1453.

Despite the failures, the crusading ideal was not yet completely lost. In Germany in 1212, a youth known as Nicholas of Cologne announced that God had inspired him to lead a "children's crusade" to the Holy Land. Thousands of young people joined Nicholas and made their way down the Rhine and across the Alps to Italy, where the pope told them to go home. Most tried to do so. At about the same time, a group of about 20,000 French children made their way to Marseilles, where two shipowners agreed to transport them to the Holy Land. Seven ships packed with hymn-singing youths soon left the port. Two of the ships perished in a storm near Sardinia; the other five sailed to North Africa, where the children were sold into slavery. The next Crusades of adult warriors were hardly more successful.

All in all, the Crusades had little impact on the Islamic world; after all, the crusaders failed to accomplish their primary goal of holding the Holy Land for the Christian west. Whether the Crusades had much effect on European civilization is widely debated. Did the Crusades help to stabilize European society by removing large numbers of young warriors who would have fought each other in Europe? Some historians think so and believe that western monarchs established their control more easily as a result. There is no doubt that the Italian seaports, especially Genoa, Pisa, and Venice, benefited economically from the Crusades, but even without the Crusades, Italian merchants would have pursued new trade contacts with the eastern world. The Crusades did have unfortunate side effects that would afflict European society for generations. The first widespread attacks on the Jews occurred during the Crusades. Some Christians argued that to undertake holy wars against infidel Muslims while the "murderers of Christ" ran free at home was unthinkable. The massacre of Jews became a regular feature of medieval European life (see the box on p. 353).

CONCLUSION

After the collapse of the Han dynasty in the third century C.E., China experienced nearly four centuries of internal chaos, until the Tang dynasty in the seventh century C.E. attempted to follow the pattern of the Han dynasty and restore the power of the Chinese empire. The fall of the Roman Empire in the fifth century brought a quite different result as three new civilizations emerged out of the collapse of Roman power in the Mediterranean. A new world of Islam emerged in the east; it occupied large parts of the old Roman Empire, preserved much of Greek culture, and created its own flourishing civilization. The eastern part of the old Roman Empire, increasingly Greek in culture, continued

TREATMENT OF THE JEWS

The development of new religious sensibilities in the High Middle Ages also had a negative side, turning Christians against their supposed enemies. Although the Crusades provide the most obvious example, Christians also turned on the Jews as the "murderers of Christ." As a result, Jews suffered increased persecution. These two documents show different sides of the picture. The first is a chronicler's account of a completely unfounded charge levied against the Jews—that they were guilty of the ritual murder of Christian children to obtain Christian blood for the Passover service. This charge led to the murder of many Jews. The second document, taken from a list of regulations issued by the city of Avignon, France, illustrates the contempt Christian society held for the Jews.

THE JEWS AND THE RITUAL MURDER OF CHRISTIAN CHILDREN

[The eight-year-old boy] Harold, who is buried in the Church of St. Peter the Apostle, at Gloucester . . . is said to have been carried away secretly by Jews, in the opinion of many, on Feb. 21, and by them hidden till March 16. On that night, on the sixth of the preceding feast, the Jews of all England coming together as if to circumcise a certain boy, pretend deceitfully that they are about to celebrate the feast [Passover] appointed by law in such case, and deceiving the citizens of Gloucester with that fraud, they tortured the lad placed before them with immense tortures. It is true no Christian was present, or saw or heard the deed, nor have we found that anything was betrayed by any Jew. But a little while after when the whole convent of monks of Gloucester and almost all the citizens of that city, and innumerable persons coming to the spectacle, saw the wounds of the dead body, scars of fire, the thorns fixed on his head, and liquid wax poured into the eyes and face, and touched it with the diligent examination of their hands, those tortures were believed or guessed to have been inflicted on him in that manner. It was clear that they had made him a glorious martyr to Christ, being slain without sin, and having bound his feet with his own girdle, threw him into the river Severn.

THE REGULATIONS OF AVIGNON, 1243

Likewise, we declare that Jews or whores shall not dare to touch with their hands either bread or fruit put out for sale, and that if they should do this they must buy what they have touched.

to survive as the Christian Byzantine Empire. At the same time, a new Christian European civilization was establishing its roots in the West. By the eleventh and twelfth centuries, these three heirs of Rome began their own conflict for control of the lands of the eastern Mediterranean.

The coronation of Charlemagne (who was a descendant of a Germanic tribe converted to Christianity) as Roman emperor in 800 symbolized the fusion of the three chief components of the new European civilization: the German tribes, the Roman legacy, and the Christian church. In the long run, the creation of Charlemagne's empire fostered the idea of a distinct European identity. The lands north of the Alps now became the political center of Europe.

With the disintegration of the Carolingian Empire, new forms of political institutions began to develop in Europe. Power came into the hands of many different lords, who came to constitute a powerful group of nobles that dominated the political, economic, and social life of Europe. But quietly and surely, within this world of castles and private power, kings gradually began to extend their public power. Though they could not know it then, their actions laid the foundations for the European kingdoms that in one form or another have dominated the European political scene ever since.

European civilization began to flourish in the High Middle Ages. The revival of trade, the expansion of towns and cities, and the development of a money economy did not mean the end of a predominantly rural European society, but they did open the door to new ways to make a living and new opportunities for people to expand and enrich their lives. At the same time, the High Middle Ages also gave birth to an intellectual and spiritual revival that transformed European society.

While a new Christian civilization arose in Europe, the Byzantine Empire created its own unique Christian civilization in the eastern Mediterranean. While Europe struggled in the Early Middle Ages, the Byzantine world continued to prosper and flourish. The Crusades to Palestine, however, ostensibly for religious motives, eventually had the result of weakening the Christian power that had initiated the whole process: the Byzantine Empire.

Growth and optimism had characterized the new European civilization of the High Middle Ages, but underneath the calm exterior lay seeds of discontent and change. In the fourteenth and fifteenth centuries, Europe would experience both a real time of troubles and a dramatic revival, while Constantinople and the remnants of the Byzantine Empire would finally fall to the world of Islam.

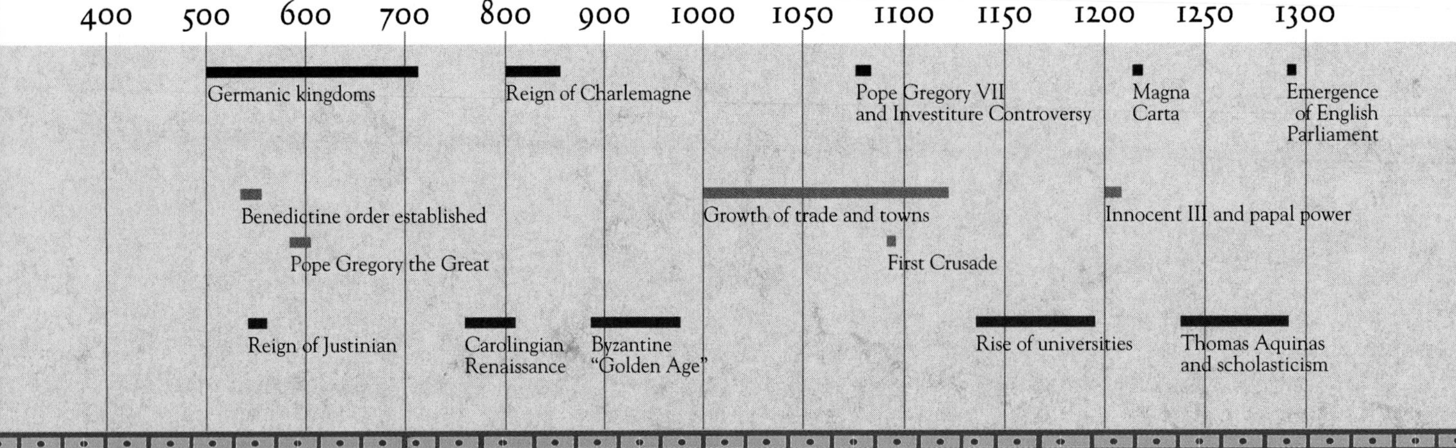

Chapter Notes

1. Norman F. Cantor, ed., *The Medieval World: 300–1300* (New York, 1963), p. 104.
2. Quoted in Simon Keynes, "The Vikings in England, c. 790–1016," in Peter Sawyer, ed., *The Oxford Illustrated History of the Vikings* (Oxford, 1997), p. 81.
3. Quoted in Oliver Thatcher and Edgar McNeal, eds., *A Source Book for Medieval History* (New York, 1905), p. 363.
4. Quoted in Marvin Perry, Joseph Peden, and Theodore Von Laue, *Sources of the Western Tradition*, vol. 1 (Boston, 1987), p. 218.
5. Quoted in Joseph and Frances Gies, *Life in a Medieval Castle* (New York, 1974), p. 175.
6. Quoted in Robert Delort, *Life in the Middle Ages*, trans. Robert Allen (New York, 1972), p. 218.
7. Quoted in Jean Gimpel, *The Medieval Machine* (Harmondsworth, 1977), p. 92.
8. Ernest F. Henderson, ed., *Select Historical Documents of the Middle Ages* (London, 1892), p. 365.
9. Thatcher and McNeal, *A Source Book for Medieval History*, p. 208.
10. Quoted in R. H. C. Davis, *A History of Medieval Europe from Constantine to Saint Louis*, 2d ed. (London and New York, 1988), p. 252.
11. Quoted in Rosalind Brooke and Christopher Brooke, *Popular Religion in the Middle Ages* (London, 1984), p. 19.
12. Helen Waddell, *The Wandering Scholars* (New York, 1961), p. 222.
13. Quoted in John W. Baldwin, *The Scholastic Culture of the Middle Ages, 1000–1300* (Lexington, Mass., 1971), p. 15.
14. Thatcher and McNeal, *A Source Book for Medieval History*, p. 517.
15. Quoted in Hans E. Mayer, *The Crusades*, trans. John Gillingham (New York, 1972), pp. 99–100.

Suggested Readings

Good general histories of the entire medieval period can be found in B. Tierney and S. Painter, *Western Europe in the Middle Ages, 300–1475* (New York, 1983); E. Peters, *Europe and the Middle Ages*, 2d ed. (Englewood Cliffs, N.J., 1989); and D. Nicholas, *The Evolution of the Medieval World: Society, Government, and Thought in Europe, 312–1500* (London, 1993). For a good general survey of the social history of the Middle Ages, see C. B. Bouchard, *Life and Society in the West: Antiquity and the Middle Ages* (San Diego, 1988). A brief history of the Early Middle Ages can be found in R. Collin, *Early Medieval Europe, 300–1000* (New York, 1991).

Surveys of Carolingian Europe include P. Riche, *The Carolingians, A Family Who Forged Europe* (Philadelphia, 1993), and R. McKitterick, *The Frankish Kingdoms Under the Carolingians, 751–987* (London, 1983). On Charlemagne, see H. R. Loyn and J. Percival, *The Reign of Charlemagne* (New York, 1976).

Two introductory works on feudalism are J. R. Strayer, *Feudalism* (Princeton, N.J., 1985), and the classic work by M. Bloch, *Feudal Society* (London, 1961). For an important revisionist view, see S. Reynolds, *Fiefs and Vassals* (Oxford, 1994). Works on the function and activities of the nobility in the High Middle Ages include S. Reynolds, *Kingdoms and Communities in Western Europe, 900–1300* (Oxford, 1984); R. W. Barber, *The Knight and Chivalry* (Rochester, N.Y., 1995); and G. Duby, *The Chivalrous Society* (Berkeley, Calif., 1977). G. Duby discusses the theory of medieval social order in *The Three Orders* (Chicago, 1980).

There are numerous works on the various feudal principalities. On England, see F. Barlow, *The Feudal Kingdom of England, 1042–1216*, 3d ed. (New York, 1972). On Germany, see H. Fuhrmann, *Germany in the High Middle Ages, c. 1050–1250* (Cambridge, 1986), an excellent account, and B. Arnold, *Princes and Territories in Medieval Germany* (Cambridge, 1991). On France, see J. Dunbabib, *France in the Making, 843–1180* (Oxford, 1985). On Italy, see D. J. Herlihy, *Cities and Society in Medieval Italy* (London, 1980). On eastern Europe, see N. Davies, *God's Playground: A History of Poland*, vol. 1 (Oxford, 1981), and C. J. Halperin, *Russia and the Golden Horde: The Mongol Impact on Medieval Russian History* (Bloomington, Ind., 1987).

On economic conditions in the Middle Ages, see N. J. G. Pounds, *An Economic History of Medieval Europe* (New York, 1974), and R. S. Lopez, *The Commercial Revolution of the Middle Ages, 950–1350* (Englewood Cliffs, N.J., 1971). Urban history is covered in D. Nicholas, *The Growth of the Medieval City: From Late Antiquity to the Early Fourteenth Century* (New York, 1997). A good short introduction to medieval society is C. Brooke, *The Structure of Medieval Society* (London, 1971). On women in general, see L. Bitel, "Women in Early Medieval Northern Europe," in R. Bridenthal, S. M. Stuard, and M. E. Wiesner, *Becoming Visible*, 3d ed. (New York, 1998), and D. Herlihy, *Opera Muliebria: Women and Work in Medieval Europe* (New York, 1990). On peasant life, see R. Fossier, *Peasant Life in the Medieval West* (New York, 1988).

For a general survey of church life, see R. W. Southern, *Western Society and the Church in the Middle Ages*, rev. ed. (New York, 1990). On the papacy in the High Middle Ages, see C. Morris, *The Papal Monarchy* (Oxford, 1989), and I. S. Robinson, *The Papacy* (Cambridge, 1990). The papacy of Innocent III is covered in J. E. Sayers, *Innocent III, Leader of Europe, 1198–1216* (New York, 1994). Good works on monasticism include B. Bolton, *The Medieval Reformation* (London, 1983); C. H. Lawrence, *Medieval Monasticism* (London, 1984), a good general account; and H. Leyser, *Hermits and the New Monasticism* (London, 1984). For a good introduction to popular religion in the eleventh and twelfth centuries, see R. Brooke and C. N. L. Brooke, *Popular Religion in the Middle Ages* (London, 1984). On the Inquisition, see B. Hamilton, *The Medieval Inquisition* (New York, 1981).

The development of universities is covered in S. Ferruolo, *The Origin of the University* (Stanford, 1985), and the brief, older work by C. H. Haskins, *The Rise of Universities* (Ithaca, N.Y., 1957). Various aspects of the intellectual and literary developments of the High Middle Ages are examined in J. W. Baldwin, *The Scholastic Culture of the Middle Ages, 1000–1300* (Lexington, Mass., 1971); T. O'Meara, *Thomas Aquinas Theologian* (Notre Dame, Ind., 1997); and H. Waddell, *The Wandering Scholars* (New York, 1961). A good introduction to Romanesque style is A. Petzold, *Romanesque Art* (New York, 1995). On the Gothic movement, see M. Camille, *Gothic Art: Glorious Visions* (New York, 1996), and C. Wilson, *The Gothic Cathedral* (London, 1990).

Brief but good introductions to Byzantine history can be found in H. W. Haussig, *A History of Byzantine Civilization* (New York, 1971), and C. Mango, *Byzantium: The Empire of New Rome* (London, 1980). The best single political history is G. Ostrogorsky, *A History of the Byzantine State*, 2d ed. (New Brunswick, N.J., 1968). For a comprehensive survey of the Byzantine Empire, see W. Treadgold, *A History of the Byzantine State and Society* (Stanford, 1997). On Justinian, see J. Moorhead, *Justinian* (London, 1995). The zenith of Byzantine civilization is examined in R. Jenkins, *Byzantium: The Imperial Centuries, 610–1071* (New York, 1969).

Two good general surveys on the crusades are H. E. Mayer, *The Crusades* (London, 1970), and J. Riley-Smith, *The Crusades: A Short History* (New Haven, Conn., 1987). Other works of value are J. Riley-Smith, ed., *The Oxford Illustrated History of the Crusades* (New York, 1995), and R. C. Smail, *Crusading Warfare, 1097–1193*, 2d ed. (New York, 1995).

For additional reading, go to InfoTrac College Edition, your online research library at http://web1.infotrac-college.com

Enter the search term "Charlemagne" using the Keywords.

Enter the search term "Byzantium" using the Subject Guide.

Enter the search terms "early Christianity" using the Keywords.

Enter the search term "feudalism" and also the search term "feudal" using the Subject Guide.

Enter the search terms "Cities and Towns, Medieval" using the Subject Guide.

CHAPTER

13

Crisis and Rebirth: Europe in the Fourteenth and Fifteenth Centuries

CHAPTER OUTLINE

- A TIME OF TROUBLES: BLACK DEATH AND SOCIAL CRISIS
- POLITICAL INSTABILITY AND POLITICAL RENEWAL
- THE DECLINE OF THE CHURCH
- MEANING AND CHARACTERISTICS OF THE ITALIAN RENAISSANCE
- THE MAKING OF RENAISSANCE SOCIETY
- THE INTELLECTUAL RENAISSANCE IN ITALY
- THE ARTISTIC RENAISSANCE
- CONCLUSION

FOCUS QUESTIONS

- What problems did Europe face during the fourteenth century, and what impact did they have on European economic and social life?
- What were the "new monarchies" of the late fifteenth century, and how did their political structures differ from those found in eastern Europe and Italy?
- How and why did the moral prestige of the papacy decline after the thirteenth century?
- What were the main features of the Renaissance, and how did it differ from the Middle Ages?
- What were the chief characteristics of Renaissance art, and how did it differ in Italy and northern Europe?

As a result of their conquests in the thirteenth and fourteenth centuries, the Mongols created a vast empire, stretching from Russia in the west to China in the east. Mongol rule brought stability to the Eurasian trade routes; increased trade brought prosperity but also facilitated the spread of flea-infested rats that brought bubonic plague to both East Asia and Europe. In the mid-fourteenth century, one of the most destructive natural disasters in history erupted—the Black Death. A contemporary observer named Henry Knighton, a canon of Saint Mary-of-the-Meadow Abbey in Leicester, England, was simply overwhelmed by the magnitude of the catastrophe. Knighton began his account of the great plague with these words: "In this year [1348] and in the following one there was a general mortality of people throughout the whole world." Few were left untouched; even in isolated monasteries, the plague struck: "At Montpellier, there remained out of a hundred and forty friars only seven." Knighton was also stunned by the economic and social consequences of the Black Death. Prices dropped: "And the price of everything was cheap, because of the fear of death; there were very few who took any care for their wealth, or for anything else." Laborers became scarce, and their wages increased: "In the following autumn, one could not hire a reaper at a lower wage than eight pence with food, or a mower at less than twelve pence with food. Because of this, much grain rotted in the fields for lack of harvesting." So many people died that some towns were deserted and some villages disappeared altogether: "Many small villages and hamlets were completely deserted; there was not one house left in them, but all those who had lived in them were dead." To some people, the end of the world seemed at hand.

Plague was not the only disaster in the fourteenth century, however. Signs of disintegration were everywhere: famine, economic depression, war, social upheaval, a rise in crime and violence, and a decline in the power of the Catholic church. Periods of disintegration, however, are often fertile grounds for change and new developments. Although the disintegrative patterns of the fourteenth century continued into the fifteenth, at the same time elements of recovery made the fifteenth century a period of significant political, economic, artistic, and intellectual change. The humanists or intellectuals of the age called their period (from the mid-fourteenth to the mid-sixteenth century) an age of rebirth, believing that they had restored arts and letters to new glory after they had been "neglected" or "dead" for centuries. The humanists' view of their age as a rebirth of the classical civilizations of the Greeks and Romans ultimately led historians to use the word *Renaissance* to identify this period.

A Time of Troubles: Black Death and Social Crisis

At the beginning of the fourteenth century, there were noticeable changes in weather patterns as Europe entered a period that has been called a "little Ice Age." Shortened growing seasons and disastrous weather conditions, including heavy storms and constant rain, led to widespread famine and hunger. The great famine of 1315–1317 in northern Europe began an all-too-familiar pattern, as evident in this scene described by a contemporary chronicler:

> We saw a larger number of both sexes, not only from nearby places but from as much as five leagues away, barefooted and maybe even, except for women, in a completely nude state, together with their priests coming in procession at the Church of the Holy Martyrs, their bones bulging out, devoutly carrying bodies of saints and other relics to be adorned, hoping to get relief.[1]

Some historians have pointed out that famine could have led to chronic malnutrition, which in turn contributed to increased infant mortality, lower birthrates, and higher susceptibility to disease because malnourished people are less able to resist infection. This, they argue, helps to explain the high mortality of the great plague known as the Black Death.

The Black Death

The Black Death of the mid-fourteenth century was the most devastating natural disaster in European history, ravaging Europe's population and causing economic, social, political, and cultural upheaval. Contemporary chroniclers lamented how parents abandoned their children; one related the words: "Oh father, why have you abandoned me? . . . Mother, where have you gone?"[2] People were horrified by an evil force they could not understand and by the subsequent breakdown of all normal human relations.

Bubonic plague, which was the most common and most important form of plague in the diffusion of the Black Death, was spread by black rats infested with fleas who were host to the deadly bacterium *Yersinia pestis*. Symptoms of bubonic plague include high fever, aching joints, swelling of the lymph nodes, and dark blotches caused by bleeding beneath the skin. Bubonic plague was actually the least toxic form of plague but nevertheless killed 50 to 60 percent of its victims. In pneumonic plague, the bacterial infection spread to the lungs, resulting in severe coughing, bloody sputum, and the relatively easy spread of the bacillus from human to human by coughing.

The Black Death was all the more horrible because it was the first major epidemic disease to strike Europe since the seventh century, an absence that helps explain medieval Europe's remarkable population growth. This great plague originated in Asia. After disappearing from Europe and the Middle East in the Middle Ages, bubonic plague continued to haunt areas of southwestern China, especially isolated rural territories. The arrival of Mongol troops in this area in the mid-thirteenth century became the means for the spread of the plague, as flea-infested rats carrying bubonic plague spread with the movement of the Mongols into central and northwestern China and Central Asia. From there, trading caravans brought the plague to Caffa, on the Black Sea, in 1346.

The plague reached Europe in October of 1347 when Genoese merchants brought it from Caffa to the island of Sicily, off the coast of southern Italy. It quickly spread to southern Italy and southern France by the end of 1347. Usually, the diffusion of the Black Death followed commercial trade routes. In 1348, the plague spread through Spain, France, and the Low Countries and into Germany. By the end of that year, it had moved to England, ravaging it in 1349. By the end of 1349, the plague had reached northern Europe and Scandinavia. Eastern Europe and Russia were affected by 1351, although mortality rates were never as high in eastern Europe as they were in western and central Europe.

Overall, mortality figures for the Black Death were incredibly high. Italy was especially hard hit. Its crowded cities suffered losses of 50 to 60 percent. In northern France, farming villages suffered mortality rates of 30 percent, while cities such as Rouen were more severely affected and experienced losses of 30 to 40 percent. In England and Germany, entire villages simply disappeared from history. In Germany, of approximately 170,000 inhabited locations, only 130,000 were left by the end of the fourteenth century.

It has been estimated that the European population declined by 25 to 50 percent between 1347 and 1351. If we accept the recent scholarly assessment of a European population of 75 million in the early fourteenth century, this means a death toll in four years of 19 to 38 million

MAP 13.1 Spread of the Black Death

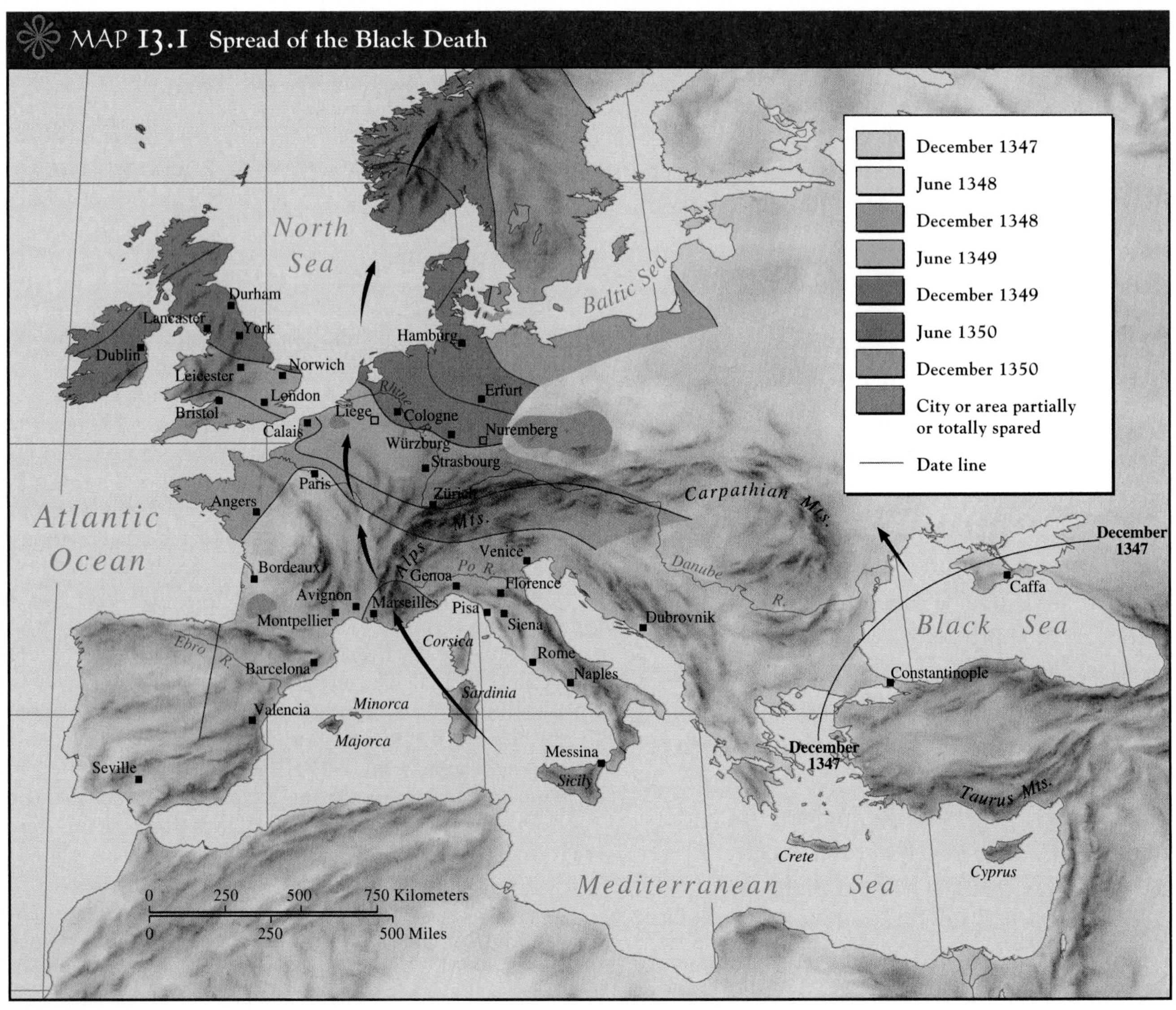

people. And the plague did not end in 1351. There were major outbreaks again in 1361–1362 and 1369 and then regular recurrences during the remainder of the fourteenth and all of the fifteenth century. The European population did not start to recover until the end of the fifteenth century; not until the mid-sixteenth century did Europe begin to regain its thirteenth-century population levels.

The attempt of contemporaries to explain the Black Death and mitigate its harshness led to extreme sorts of behavior. To many, the plague had either been sent by God as a punishment for humans' sins or caused by the evil one, the devil. Some—the flagellants—resorted to extreme measures to gain God's forgiveness. Groups of flagellants, both men and women, wandered from town to town, flogging each other with whips to win the forgiveness of a God who they felt had sent the plague to punish humans for their sinful ways. One contemporary chronicler described their activities:

> The penitents went about, coming first out of Germany. They were men who did public penance and scourged themselves with whips of hard knotted leather with little iron spikes. Some made themselves bleed very badly between the shoulder blades, and some foolish women had cloths ready to catch the blood and smear it on their eyes, saying it was miraculous blood. While they were doing penance, they sang very mournful songs about the nativity and the passion of Our Lord. The object of this penance was to put a stop to the mortality, for in that time . . . at least a third of all the people in the world died.[3]

The flagellants attracted attention and created mass hysteria wherever they went. The Catholic church, however, became alarmed when flagellant groups began to kill Jews and attack the clergy who opposed them. Pope Clement VI condemned the flagellants in October 1349 and urged the public authorities to crush them. By the end of 1350, most of the flagellant movements had been destroyed.

An outbreak of virulent anti-Semitism also accompanied the Black Death. Jews were accused of causing the plague by poisoning town wells. Although Jews were persecuted in Spain, the worst pogroms against this minority were carried out in Germany, where more than sixty major Jewish communities were exterminated by 1351 (see the box on p. 360). Many Jews fled eastward to Russia and especially to Poland, where the king offered them protection. Eastern Europe became home to large Jewish communities.

Economic Dislocation and Social Upheaval

The death of so many people in the fourteenth century also had severe economic consequences. Trade declined, and some industries suffered greatly. Florence's woolen industry, one of the giants, had produced 70,000 to 80,000 pieces of cloth in 1338; in 1378, it was yielding only 24,000 pieces.

Both peasants and noble landlords were also affected. A shortage of workers caused a dramatic rise in the price of labor, while the decline in the number of people lowered the demand for food, resulting in falling prices. Landlords were now paying more for labor at the same time that their rents or income was declining. Concurrently, the decline in the number of peasants after the Black Death made it easier for some to convert their labor services to rent, thus freeing them from serfdom. But there were limits to how much the peasants could advance. They faced the same economic hurdles as the lords, while the latter also attempted to impose wage restrictions and reinstate old forms of labor service. New governmental taxes also hurt. Peasant complaints became widespread and soon gave rise to rural revolts.

In 1358, a peasant revolt known as the *Jacquerie* broke out in northern France. The outburst of peasant anger led to savage confrontations. Castles were burned and nobles murdered (see the box on p. 361). Such atrocities did not go unanswered, however. The *Jacquerie* soon failed

MASS BURIAL OF PLAGUE VICTIMS. The Black Death had spread to northern Europe by the end of 1348. Shown here is a mass burial of victims of the plague in Tournai, located in modern Belgium. As is evident in the illustration, at this stage of the plague, there was still time to make coffins for the victims' burial. Later, as the plague intensified, the dead were thrown into open pits.

A MEDIEVAL HOLOCAUST: THE CREMATION OF THE STRASBOURG JEWS

In their attempt to explain the widespread horrors of the Black Death, medieval Christian communities looked for scapegoats. As at the time of the Crusades, the Jews were accused of poisoning wells and hence spreading the plague. This selection by a contemporary chronicler, written in 1349, gives an account of how Christians in the town of Strasbourg in the Holy Roman Empire dealt with their Jewish community. It is apparent that financial gain was also an important factor in killing the Jews.

JACOB VON KÖNIGSHOFEN, "THE CREMATION OF THE STRASBOURG JEWS"

In the year 1349 there occurred the greatest epidemic that ever happened. Death went from one end of the earth to the other. . . . And from what this epidemic came, all wise teachers and physicians could only say that it was God's will. . . . This epidemic also came to Strasbourg in the summer of the above-mentioned year, and it is estimated that about sixteen thousand people died.

In the matter of this plague the Jews throughout the world were reviled and accused in all lands of having caused it through the poison which they are said to have put into the water and the wells—that is what they were accused of—and for this reason the Jews were burnt all the way from the Mediterranean into Germany. . . .

[The account then goes on to discuss the situation of the Jews in the city of Strasbourg.]

On Saturday . . . they burnt the Jews on a wooden platform in their cemetery. There were about two thousand people of them. Those who wanted to baptize themselves were spared. [Some say that about a thousand accepted baptism.] Many small children were taken out of the fire and baptized against the will of their fathers and mothers. And everything that was owed to the Jews was canceled, and the Jews had to surrender all pledges and notes that they had taken for debts. The council, however, took the cash that the Jews possessed and divided it among the workingmen proportionately. The money was indeed the thing that killed the Jews. If they had been poor and if the feudal lords had not been in debt to them, they would not have been burnt. . . .

Thus were the Jews burnt at Strasbourg, and in the same year in all the cities of the Rhine, whether Free Cities or Imperial Cities or cities belonging to the lords. In some towns they burnt the Jews after a trial; in others, without a trial. In some cities the Jews themselves set fire to their houses and cremated themselves.

It was decided in Strasbourg that no Jew should enter the city for a hundred years, but before twenty years had passed, the council and magistrates agreed that they ought to admit the Jews again into the city for twenty years. And so the Jews came back again to Strasbourg in the year 1368 after the birth of our Lord.

PEASANT REBELLION. The fourteenth century witnessed a number of revolts of the peasantry against noble landowners. Although the revolts were initially successful, they were soon crushed. This illustration shows nobles massacring the rebels in the French *Jacquerie*.

as the privileged classes closed ranks, savagely massacred the rebels, and ended the revolt.

The English Peasants' Revolt of 1381 was the most prominent of all. It was not a revolt caused by desperation but was a product of rising expectations. After the Black Death, the English peasants had enjoyed improved conditions, with greater freedom and higher wages or lower rents. Aristocratic landlords had fought back with legislation to depress wages and an attempt to reimpose old feudal dues. The most immediate cause of the revolt, however, was the monarchy's attempt to raise revenues by imposing a poll tax, or a flat charge on each adult member of the population. Peasants in eastern England, the wealthiest part of the country, refused to pay the tax and expelled the collectors forcibly from their villages.

This action produced a widespread rebellion of both peasants and townspeople led by a well-to-do peasant called Wat Tyler and a preacher named John Ball. The revolt was initially successful as the rebels burned down the manor houses of aristocrats, lawyers, and government officials and murdered several important officials, including the archbishop of Canterbury. After the peasants

A REVOLT OF FRENCH PEASANTS

In 1358, French peasants rose up in a revolt known as the Jacquerie. The relationship between aristocrats and peasants had degenerated as a result of the social upheavals and privations caused by the Black Death and the Hundred Years' War. This excerpt from the chronicle of an aristocrat paints a horrifying picture of the barbarities that occurred during the revolt.

JEAN FROISSART, *CHRONICLES*

Not long after the King of Navarre had been set free, there were very strange and terrible happenings in several parts of the kingdom of France. . . . They began when some of the men from the country towns came together in the Beauvais region. They had no leaders and at first they numbered scarcely a hundred. One of them got up and said that the nobility of France, knights and squires, were disgracing and betraying the realm, and that it would be a good thing if they were all destroyed. At this they all shouted: "He's right! He's right! Shame on any man who saves the gentry from being wiped out!"

They banded together and went off, without further deliberation and unarmed except for pikes and knives, to the house of a knight who lived nearby. They broke in and killed the knight, with his lady and his children, big and small, and set fire to the house. Next they went to another castle and did much worse; for, having seized the knight and bound him securely to a post, several of them violated his wife and daughter before his eyes. Then they killed the wife, who was pregnant, and the daughter and all the other children, and finally put the knight to death with great cruelty and burned and razed the castle.

They did similar things in a number of castles and big houses, and their ranks swelled until there were a good six thousand of them. Wherever they went their numbers grew, for all the men of the same sort joined them. The knights and squires fled before them with their families. They took their wives and daughters many miles away to put them in safety, leaving their houses open with their possessions inside. And those evil men, who had come together without leaders or arms, pillaged and burned everything and violated and killed all the ladies and girls without mercy, like mad dogs. Their barbarous acts were worse than anything that ever took place between Christians and Saracens. Never did men commit such vile deeds. They were such that no living creature ought to see, or even imagine or think of, and the men who committed the most were admired and had the highest places among them. I could never bring myself to write down the horrible and shameful things which they did to the ladies. But, among other brutal excesses, they killed a knight, put him on a spit, and turned him at the fire and roasted him before the lady and her children. After about a dozen of them had violated the lady, they tried to force her and the children to eat the knight's flesh before putting them cruelly to death.

marched on London, the young king Richard II (1377–1399) promised to accept the rebels' demands if they would return to their homes. They accepted the king's word and began to disperse, but the king reneged and with the assistance of the aristocrats brutally crushed the rebels. The poll tax was eliminated, however.

Although the peasant revolts sometimes resulted in short-term gains for the participants, the uprisings were relatively easily crushed and their gains quickly lost. Accustomed to ruling, the established classes easily combined and crushed dissent when faced with social uprising. Nevertheless, the revolts of the fourteenth century had introduced a new element to European life; henceforth social unrest would be a characteristic of European history.

FAMILY LIFE AND GENDER ROLES IN LATE MEDIEVAL CITIES

The effects of plague were also felt in other areas of medieval urban life. The basic unit of the late medieval urban environment was the nuclear family of husband, wife, and children. Especially in wealthier families, there might also be servants, apprentices, and other relatives, including widowed mothers and the husband's illegitimate children.

Before the Black Death, late marriages were common for urban couples. It was not unusual for husbands to be in their late thirties or forties and wives in their early twenties. The expense of setting up a household probably necessitated the delay in marriage. But the situation changed dramatically after the plague, as the survivors found new economic opportunities and were reluctant to postpone living after experiencing so much death. The economic difficulties of the fourteenth century also tended to strengthen the development of gender roles and to set new limits on employment opportunities for women. Based on the authority of Aristotle, Thomas Aquinas and other thirteenth-century scholastic theologians had advanced the belief that according to the natural order, men were active and domineering while women were passive and submissive. As more and more lawyers, doctors, and priests, who had been trained in universities where these notions were taught, entered society, these ideas of the different natures of men and women became widely accepted.

Increasingly, women were expected to forgo any active functions in society and remain subject to direction from males. A fourteenth-century Parisian provost commented on glass cutters that "no master's widow who keeps working at his craft after her husband's death may take on apprentices, for the men of the craft do not believe that a woman can master it well enough to teach a child to master it, for the craft is a very delicate one."[4] Although this statement suggests that some women were in fact running businesses, it also reveals that they were viewed as incapable of undertaking all of men's activities. Based on this view of gender, Europeans created a division of labor roles between men and women that persisted until the Industrial Revolution of the eighteenth and nineteenth centuries.

Economic Recovery

After the severe economic reversals and social upheavals of the second half of the fourteenth century, the European economy gradually recovered during the fifteenth century as manufacturing and trade increased in volume. Before the plague, Italian merchants were already carrying on a flourishing commerce throughout the Mediterranean and had also expanded their lines of trade north along the Atlantic seaboard. The great galleys of the Venetian Flanders Fleet maintained a direct sea route from Venice to England and the Netherlands, where Italian merchants came into contact with the increasingly powerful Hanseatic League of merchants. Hard hit by the plague, the Italians lost their commercial preeminence in the second half of the fourteenth century, while the Hanseatic League continued to prosper.

As early as the thirteenth century, a number of north German coastal towns had formed a commercial and military league known as the Hansa or Hanseatic League to protect themselves from marauding pirates and competition from Scandinavian merchants. By 1500, more than eighty cities belonged to the league, which established settlements and commercial bases in northern Europe and England. For almost two hundred years, the Hansa had a monopoly on northern European trade in timber, fish, grain, metals, honey, and wines. Its southern outlet in Flanders, the city of Bruges, became the economic crossroads of Europe in the fourteenth century because it served as the meeting place between Hanseatic merchants and the Flanders Fleet of Venice. In the fifteenth century, however, Bruges, as its harbor began to silt up, slowly began to decline, paralleling the decline of the Hanseatic League itself as it proved increasingly unable to compete with the developing larger territorial states.

Overall, trade recovered dramatically from the economic contraction of the fourteenth century. The Italians and especially the Venetians continued to maintain a wealthy commercial empire. Not until the sixteenth century, when the overseas discoveries gave new importance to the states facing the Atlantic, did the small Italian city-states begin to suffer from the competitive advantages of the ever growing and more powerful national territorial states.

The economic depression of the fourteenth century also affected patterns of manufacturing. The woolen industries of Flanders and the northern Italian cities had been particularly devastated. By the beginning of the fifteenth century, however, the Florentine woolen industry was experiencing a recovery. At the same time, the Italian cities began to develop and expand luxury industries, especially lace and silk, glassware, and handworked items in metal and precious stones.

Other new industries, especially printing, mining, and metallurgy, began to rival the textile industry in importance in the fifteenth century. New machinery and techniques for digging deeper mines and for separating metals from ore and purifying them were put into operation. When rulers began to transfer their titles to underground mineral rights to financiers as collateral for loans, these entrepreneurs quickly developed large mining operations to produce copper, iron, and silver. Especially valuable were the rich mineral deposits in central Europe, Hungary, the Tyrol, Bohemia, and Saxony. Expanding iron production and new skills in metalworking, in turn, contributed to the development of firearms that were more effective than the crude weapons used in the fourteenth century.

The city of Florence regained its preeminence in banking in the fifteenth century, primarily due to the Medici family. In its best days (in the fifteenth century), the House of Medici was the greatest banking house in Europe, with branches in Venice, Milan, Rome, Avignon, Bruges, London, and Lyons. Moreover, the family had controlling interests in industrial enterprises for wool, silk, and the mining of alum, which was used in dyeing textiles. Despite its great success in the early and middle part of the fifteenth century, the Medici bank declined suddenly at the end of the century due to poor management and a series of bad loans, especially uncollectible loans to rulers. In 1494, when the French expelled the Medici from Florence and confiscated their property, the Medicean financial edifice collapsed.

Political Instability and Political Renewal

Famine, plague, economic turmoil, social upheaval, and violence were not the only problems of the fourteenth century. War and political instability must also be added to the list. Of all the struggles that ensued in the fourteenth century, the Hundred Years' War was the most violent.

CHRONOLOGY

THE HUNDRED YEARS' WAR

Outbreak of hostilities	1337
Battle of Crécy	1346
Henry V renews the war	1415
Battle of Agincourt	1415
French recovery under Joan of Arc	1429–1431
End of the war	1453

The Hundred Years' War

In the thirteenth century, the English king, Henry III, still held one small possession in France known as the duchy of Gascony. As duke of Gascony, the English king pledged loyalty as a vassal to the French king, but when King Philip VI of France (1328–1350) seized Gascony in 1337, the duke of Gascony—King Edward III of England (1327–1377)—declared war on Philip. The attack on Gascony was a convenient excuse; Edward III had already laid claim to the throne of France after the senior branch of the Capetian dynasty had become extinct in 1328.

The Hundred Years' War began in a burst of knightly enthusiasm. Trained to be warriors, knights viewed the clash of battle as the ultimate opportunity to demonstrate their fighting abilities. The Hundred Years' War proved to be an important watershed, however, because peasant foot soldiers, not knights, decided the chief battles of the war. The French army of 1337 with its heavily armed noble cavalry resembled its twelfth- and thirteenth-century forebears. Considering themselves a fighting elite, the noble cavalry looked with contempt upon the foot soldiers and crossbowmen, whom they regarded as social inferiors. The English army, however, had evolved differently and made use of paid foot soldiers. Armed with pikes, many of these foot soldiers had also adopted the longbow, invented by the Welsh. The longbow had greater striking power, longer range, and more rapid speed of fire than the crossbow. Although the English also used heavily armed cavalry, they relied even more on their large numbers of foot soldiers.

Edward III's early campaigns in France were indecisive and achieved little. In 1346, Edward was forced to fight at Crécy, just south of Flanders. The larger French army followed no battle plan but simply attacked the English lines in a disorderly fashion. The arrows of the English archers decimated the French cavalry. As the chronicler Froissart described it, "[with their longbows] the English continued to shoot into the thickest part of the crowd, wasting none of their arrows. They impaled or wounded horses and riders, who fell to the ground in great distress, unable to get up again without the help of several men."[5] It was a stunning victory for the English.

The Battle of Crécy was not decisive, however. The English simply did not possess the resources to subjugate all of France, and hostilities continued intermittently for another fifty years until a twenty-year truce was negotiated in 1396, seemingly bringing an end to this protracted series of struggles. In 1415, however, the English king, Henry V (1413–1422), renewed the war. At the Battle of Agincourt (1415), the heavily armored French knights attempted to attack across a field turned to mud by heavy rain; the result was a disastrous French defeat and the death of 1,500 French nobles. Henry went on to forge an alliance with the duke of Burgundy, making the English masters of northern France.

The seemingly hopeless French cause fell into the hands of the dauphin Charles, the heir to the throne, who governed the southern two-thirds of France. Charles's cause seemed doomed until a French peasant woman quite unexpectedly saved the timid prince. Born in 1412, the daughter of well-to-do peasants, Joan of Arc was a deeply religious person who experienced visions and came to believe that her favorite saints had commanded her to free France. In February 1429, Joan made her way to the dauphin's court, where her sincerity and simplicity persuaded Charles to allow her to accompany a French army to Orléans. Apparently inspired by the faith of the peasant woman who called herself "the Maid," the French armies found new confidence in themselves and liberated Orléans. Within a few weeks, the entire Loire valley had been freed of the English. Joan had brought the war to a decisive turning point.

But she did not live to see the war concluded. Captured by the Burgundian allies of the English in 1430, Joan was turned over first to the English and then to the Inquisition to face charges of witchcraft (see the box on p. 364). In the fifteenth century, spiritual visions were thought to be inspired either by God or the devil. Joan was condemned to death as a heretic and burned at the stake in 1431. To the end, as the flames rose up around her, she declared "that her voices came from God and had not deceived her." Twenty-five years later, a new ecclesiastical court exonerated her of these charges, and five centuries later, in 1920, she was made a saint of the Roman Catholic church.

Joan of Arc's accomplishments proved decisive. Although the war dragged on for another two decades, defeats of English armies in Normandy and Aquitaine led to French victory by 1453. Important to the French success was the use of the cannon, a new weapon made possible by the invention of gunpowder. The Chinese had

THE TRIAL OF JOAN OF ARC

Feared by the English and Burgundians, Joan of Arc was put on trial on charges of witchcraft and heresy after her capture. She was condemned for heresy and burned at the stake on May 30, 1431. This excerpt is taken from the records of Joan's trial, which presented a dramatic confrontation between the judges, trained in the complexities of legal questioning, and a nineteen-year-old woman who relied only on the "voices" of saints who gave her advice. In this selection, Joan describes what these voices told her to do.

THE TRIAL OF JOAN OF ARC

Afterward, she declared that at the age of thirteen she had a voice from God to help her and guide her. And the first time she was much afraid. And this voice came towards noon, in summer, in her father's garden. . . . She heard the voice on her right, in the direction of the church; and she seldom heard it without a light. This light came from the same side as the voice, and generally there was a great light. . . .

Asked what instruction this voice gave her for the salvation of her soul: she said it taught her to be good and to go to church often. . . . She said that the voice told her to come, and she could no longer stay where she was; and the voice told her again that she should raise the siege of the city of Orléans. She said moreover that the voice told her that she, Joan, should go to Robert de Baudricourt, in the town of Vaucouleurs of which he was captain, and he would provide an escort for her. And the said Joan answered that she was a poor maid, knowing nothing of riding or fighting. She said she went to an uncle of hers, and told him she wanted to stay with him for some time; and she stayed there about eight days. And she told her uncle she must go to the said town of Vaucouleurs, and so her uncle took her.

Then she said that when she reached Vaucouleurs she easily recognized Robert de Baudricourt, although she had never seen him before; and she knew him through her voice, for the voice had told her it was he. . . . The said Robert twice refused to hear her and repulsed her; the third time he listened to her and gave her an escort. And the voice had told her that it would be so.

invented gunpowder in the eleventh century and devised a simple cannon by the thirteenth century. The Mongols greatly improved this technology, developing more accurate cannons and cannonballs; both spread to the Middle East by the thirteenth century and to Europe by the fourteenth. The use of gunpowder eventually brought drastic changes to European warfare by making castles, city walls, and armored knights obsolete.

The "New Monarchies"

By the fourteenth century, the feudal order had begun to break down. With money from taxes, kings could now hire professional soldiers, who tended to be more reliable than feudal knights anyway. No longer needed as warriors, some nobles banded together, looking for new opportunities to advance their power and wealth at the expense of their monarchs. Others went to the royal courts, offering to serve the kings.

Fourteenth-century kings had their own problems, however. Many dynasties in Europe were unable to produce male heirs, while the founders of new dynasties had to fight for their positions as groups of nobles, trying to gain advantages for themselves, supported opposing candidates. Rulers found themselves with financial problems as well. Hiring professional soldiers left monarchs always short on cash, adding yet another element of uncertainty and confusion to fourteenth-century politics.

In the second half of the fifteenth century, however, recovery set in as attempts were made to reestablish the centralized power of monarchical governments. To characterize the results, some historians have spoken of the "new monarchies," especially those of France, England, and Spain at the end of the fifteenth century. There were, of course, variations from area to area in the degree to which monarchs were successful in extending their political authority. Unlike in western Europe, in central and eastern Europe, rulers were often weak and unable to impose their authority.

WESTERN EUROPE

The Hundred Years' War left France prostrate. Depopulation, desolate farmlands, ruined commerce, and independent and unruly nobles made it difficult for the kings to assert their authority. But the war had also developed a strong degree of French national feeling toward a common enemy, which the kings could use to reestablish monarchical power. The process of developing a French territorial state was greatly advanced by King Louis XI (1461–1483), known as the Spider because of his wily and devious ways. Louis strengthened the use of the *taille*—an annual direct tax usually on land or property—as a permanent tax imposed by royal authority, giving him a sound, regular source of income. Louis also repressed the French nobility and brought the provinces of Anjou, Maine, Bar, and Provence under royal control. Many historians believe that Louis created a base for the later development of a strong French monarchy.

The Hundred Years' War had also strongly affected the other protagonist in that conflict—the English. The cost

JOAN OF ARC. Pictured here in a suit of armor, Joan of Arc is holding aloft a banner that shows Jesus and two angels. This portrait dates from the late fifteenth century; there are no portraits of Joan made from life.

of the war in its final years and the losses in manpower strained the English economy. Moreover, with the end of the war, England experienced even greater domestic turmoil as a civil war erupted and aristocratic factions fought over the monarchy until 1485, when Henry Tudor established a new dynasty.

As the first Tudor king, Henry VII (1485–1509) worked to reduce internal dissension and establish a strong monarchical government. Henry eliminated the private wars of the nobility by abolishing their private armies. The new king was particularly successful in obtaining sufficient income from the traditional financial resources of the English monarch, such as crown lands, judicial fees and fines, and customs duties. By using diplomacy to avoid wars, which are always expensive, the king avoided having to call Parliament on any regular basis to grant him funds. By not overburdening the landed gentry and middle class with taxes, Henry won their favor, and they provided much support for his monarchy. Henry's policies enabled him to leave England with a stable and prosperous government and an enhanced status for the monarchy itself.

Spain, too, experienced the growth of a strong national monarchy by the end of the fifteenth century, a development that might have seemed unlikely at the beginning of the century. During the Middle Ages, several independent Christian kingdoms had emerged in the course of the long reconquest of the Iberian peninsula from the Muslims. Aragon and Castile were the strongest Spanish kingdoms; in the west was the independent monarchy of Portugal; in the north the small kingdom of Navarre; and in the south the Muslim kingdom of Granada. Few people at the beginning of the fifteenth century could have predicted the national unification of Spain.

A major step in that direction was taken with the marriage of Isabella of Castile (1474–1504) and Ferdinand of Aragon (1479–1516) in 1469. This marriage was a dynastic union of two rulers, not a political union. Both kingdoms maintained their own parliaments (Cortes), courts, laws, coinage, speech, customs, and political organs. Nevertheless, the two rulers worked to strengthen royal control of government, especially in Castile. The royal council, which was supposed to supervise local administration and oversee the implementation of government policies, was stripped of aristocrats and filled primarily with middle-class lawyers. Trained in the principles of Roman law, these officials operated on the belief that the monarchy embodied the power of the state.

The towns were also enlisted in the policy of state building. Medieval town organizations known as *hermandades* ("brotherhoods"), which had been organized to maintain law and order, were revived. Ferdinand and Isabella transformed them into a kind of national militia whose primary goal was to stop the wealthy landed aristocrats from disturbing the peace. The *hermandades* were disbanded by 1498 when the royal administration became strong enough to deal with lawlessness.

Ferdinand and Isabella reorganized the military forces of Spain, seeking to replace the undisciplined feudal levies they had inherited with a more professional royal army. The development of a strong infantry force as the heart of the new Spanish army made it the best in Europe by the sixteenth century, and Spain emerged as an important power in European affairs.

Recognizing the importance of controlling the Catholic church with its vast power and wealth, Ferdinand and Isabella secured from the pope the right to select the most important church officials in Spain, virtually making the clergy an instrument for the extension of royal power. Ferdinand and Isabella also pursued a policy of strict religious uniformity. Spain possessed two large religious minorities, the Jews and Muslims, both of whom had generally been tolerated in medieval Spain. Increased persecution in the fourteenth century, however, led the majority of Spanish Jews to convert to Christianity. But complaints that these Jewish converts were not always faithful to Christianity prompted Ferdinand and Isabella to ask the pope to introduce the Inquisition into Spain in 1478. Under royal control, the Inquisition worked with cruel efficiency

MAP 13.2 Europe in the Fifteenth Century

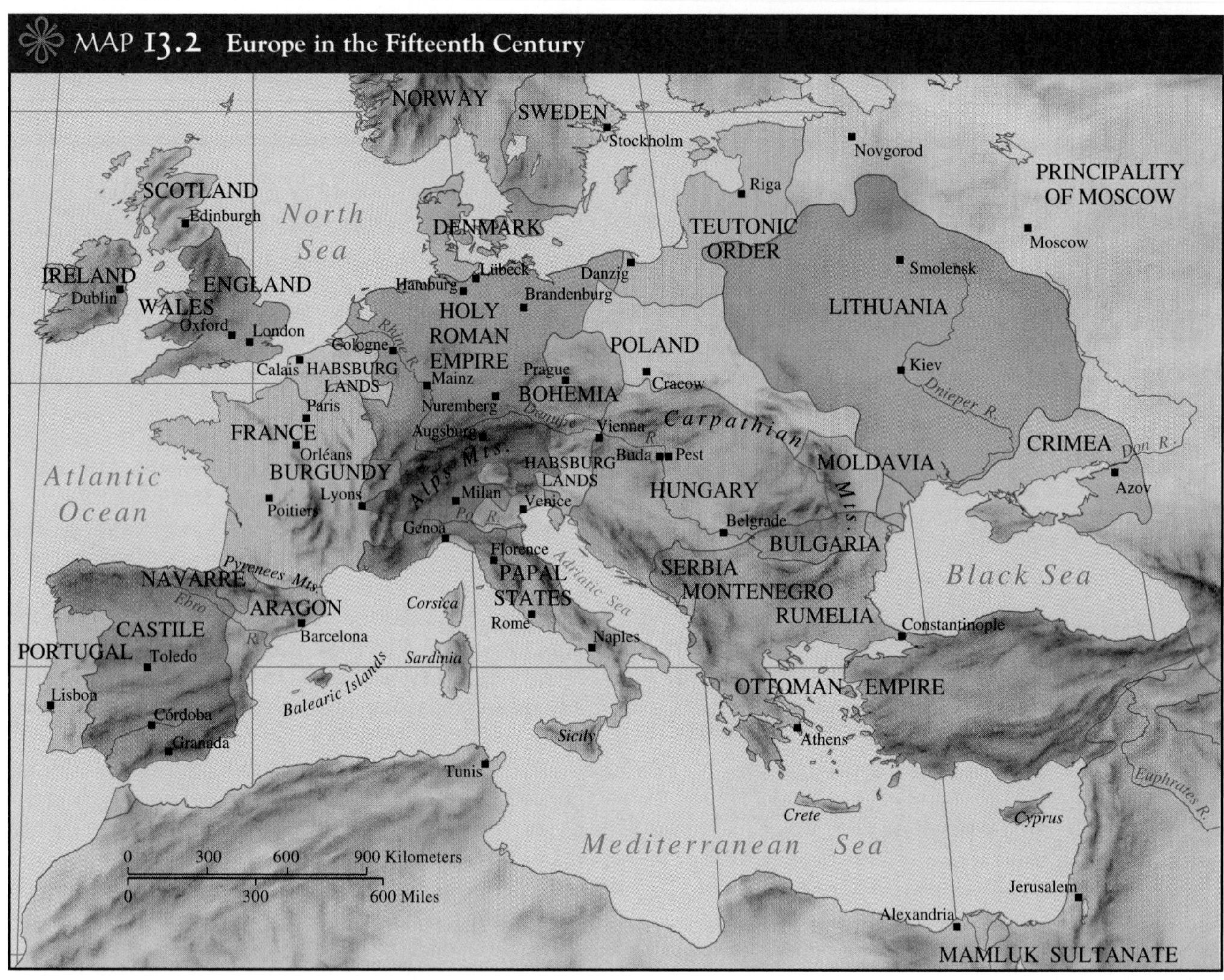

to guarantee the orthodoxy of the converts but had no authority over practicing Jews. Consequently, in 1492, flush with the success of the conquest of Muslim Granada, Ferdinand and Isabella took the drastic step of expelling all professed Jews from Spain. It is estimated that 150,000 out of possibly 200,000 Jews fled. Muslims, too, were then "encouraged" to convert to Christianity, and in 1502, Isabella issued a decree expelling all professed Muslims from her kingdom. To a very large degree, the "Most Catholic" monarchs had achieved their goal of absolute religious orthodoxy as a basic ingredient of the Spanish state. To be Spanish was to be Catholic, a policy of uniformity enforced by the Inquisition.

CENTRAL EUROPE: THE HOLY ROMAN EMPIRE

Unlike France, England, and Spain, the Holy Roman Empire failed to develop a strong monarchical authority. The failure of the Hohenstaufens in the thirteenth century ended any chance of centralized monarchical authority, and Germany became a land of hundreds of virtually independent states. These varied in size and power and included princely states, such as the duchies of Bavaria and Saxony; free imperial city-states, such as Nuremberg; modest territories of petty imperial knights; and ecclesiastical states in which a high church official, such as a bishop, archbishop, or abbot, served in a dual capacity as an administrative official of the Catholic church and a secular lord over the territories of his ecclesiastical state. Although all of the rulers of these various states had some obligations to the German king and Holy Roman emperor, increasingly they acted independently of the German ruler. After 1438, the position of Holy Roman emperor was in the hands of the Habsburg dynasty. Having gradually acquired a number of possessions along the Danube, known collectively as Austria, the house of Habsburg had become one of the wealthiest landholders in the empire and by the mid-fifteenth century began to play an important role in European affairs. Much of the Habsburg success in the fifteenth century was due not to military prowess, but to a well-executed policy of dynastic marriages. So successful were the Habsburgs in matrimonial arrangements that at the beginning of the sixteenth century, one of their members, Charles, succeeded in inheriting the traditional lands of the Habsburg, Burgundian, and Spanish monarchical lines, making him the leading monarch of his age (see Chapter 15).

EASTERN EUROPE

In eastern Europe, rulers struggled to achieve the centralization of their territorial states but faced serious obstacles to that goal. Although the population was mostly Slavic, there were islands of other ethnic groups who caused untold difficulties. Religious differences also troubled the area, as Roman Catholics, Greek Orthodox Christians, and pagans confronted each other.

Much of Polish history revolved around a bitter struggle between the crown and the landed nobility, until the end of the fifteenth century when the Polish monarchy's preoccupation with problems in Bohemia and Hungary as well as war with the Russians and Turks enabled the aristocrats to reestablish their power. Through their control of the *Sejm*, or national diet, the magnates reduced the peasantry to serfdom by 1511 and established the right to elect their kings. The Polish kings proved unable to establish a strong royal authority.

Since the conversion of Hungary to Roman Catholicism by German missionaries, its history had been closely tied to that of central and western Europe. The church became a large and prosperous institution. Wealthy bishops, along with great territorial lords, became powerful, independent political figures. For a brief while, however, Hungary developed into an important European state, the dominant power in eastern Europe. King Matthias Corvinus (1458–1490) broke the power of the wealthy lords and created a well-organized central administration. After his death, Hungary returned to weak rule, however, and the work of Corvinus was largely undone.

Since the thirteenth century, Russia had been under the domination of the Mongols. Gradually, the princes of Moscow rose to prominence by using their close relationship to the Mongol khans to increase their wealth and expand their possessions. During the reign of the great prince Ivan III (1462–1505), a new Russian state was born. Ivan III annexed other Russian principalities and took advantage of dissension among the Mongols to throw off their yoke by 1480.

CHRONOLOGY

THE EUROPEAN STATES

France	
Louis XI the Spider	1461–1483
England	
Henry VII	1485–1509
Spain	
Isabella of Castile	1474–1504
Ferdinand of Aragon	1479–1516
Marriage of Ferdinand and Isabella	1469
Introduction of the Inquisition	1478
Expulsion of the Jews	1492
Expulsion of the Muslims	1502
Eastern Europe	
Hungary: Matthias Corvinus	1458–1490
Russia: Ivan III	1462–1505
Fall of Constantinople and Byzantine Empire	1453

The Ottoman Turks and the End of the Byzantine Empire

Eastern Europe was increasingly threatened by the steadily advancing Ottoman Turks. The Byzantine Empire had served as a buffer between the Muslim Middle East and the Latin West for centuries, but it was severely weakened by the sack of Constantinople in 1204 and its occupation by the west. Although the Paleologus dynasty (1260–1453) had tried to reestablish Byzantine power in the Balkans after the overthrow of the Latin Empire, the threat from the Turks finally doomed the long-lasting empire.

Beginning in northeastern Asia Minor in the thirteenth century, the Ottoman Turks spread rapidly, seizing the lands of the Seljuk Turks and the Byzantine Empire (see Chapter 16). In 1345, they bypassed Constantinople and moved into the Balkans, which they conquered by the end of the century. Finally, in 1453, the great city of Constantinople fell to the Turks after a siege of several months. After consolidating their power, the Turks prepared to exert renewed pressure on the west, both in the Mediterranean and up the Danube valley toward Vienna. By the end of the fifteenth century, they were threatening Hungary, Austria, Bohemia, and Poland.

The Italian States

As we have seen, by the end of the fifteenth century, many European rulers had begun to rebuild their governments by restraining turbulent nobles, curbing violence, and establishing internal order. But like the Holy Roman

Empire, Italy failed to develop a centralized monarchical state. Papal opposition to the Hohenstaufens in the thirteenth century had virtually guaranteed that. Moreover, the kingdom of Naples in the south was dominated by the French house of Anjou (Sicily was ruled by the Spanish house of Aragon), while the papacy remained in shaky control of much of central Italy as rulers of the Papal States. Lack of centralized authority had enabled numerous city-states in northern and central Italy to remain independent of any political authority. Three of them—Milan, Venice, and Florence—managed to become fairly well centralized territorial states.

Milan, located at the crossroads of the main trade routes from Italian coastal cities to the Alpine passes, was one of the richest city-states in Italy. In the fourteenth century, members of the Visconti family established themselves as dukes of Milan and extended their power over all of Lombardy. After the death of the last Visconti ruler of Milan in 1447, Francesco Sforza, one of the leading *condottieri* (a *condottiere* was a leader of a mercenary band) of the time, turned on his Milanese employers, conquered the city, and became its new duke. Both the Visconti and the Sforza rulers worked to create the institutions of a strongly centralized territorial state. They were especially successful in devising systems of taxation that generated enormous revenues for the government.

The second major northern Italian state was the maritime republic of Venice, which had grown rich from commercial activity throughout the eastern Mediterranean and

CHRONOLOGY

THE ITALIAN STATES

Duchy of Milan	
Visconti establish themselves as rulers of Milan	1322
Sforzas	1450–1494
Florence	
Cosimo de' Medici	1434–1464
Beginning of Italian Wars—French invasion of Italy	1494
Sack of Rome	1527

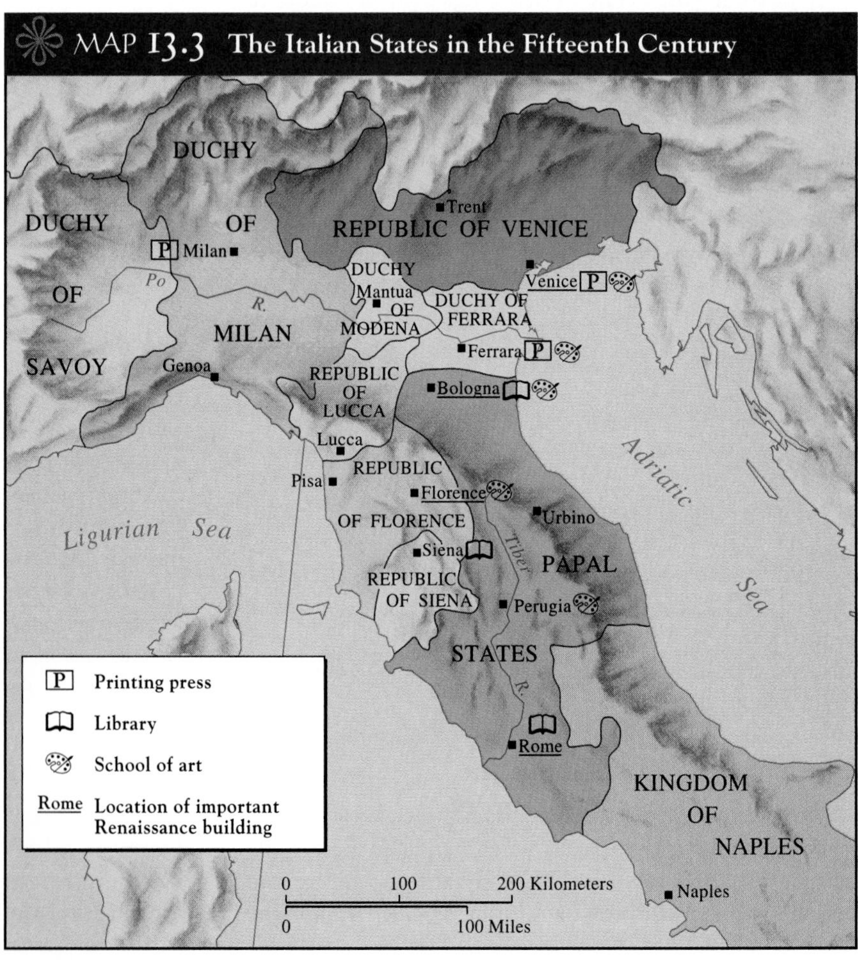

PIERO DELLA FRANCESCA, *DUKE AND DUCHESS OF URBINO.* Federigo da Montefeltro and his wife, Battista Sforza, ruled the small central Italian principality of Urbino. These profile portraits by Piero della Francesca gave a realistic rendering of the two figures. Visible in the background are the hills and valleys of Urbino.

into northern Europe. Venice remained an extremely stable political entity governed by a small oligarchy of merchant-aristocrats who had become extremely wealthy through their trading activities. Venetian government was respected by contemporaries for its stability. Venice's commercial empire brought in enormous revenues and gave it the status of an international power. At the end of the fourteenth century, Venice embarked upon the conquest of a territorial state in northern Italy to protect its food supply and its overland trade routes.

The republic of Florence dominated the region of Tuscany. In the course of the fourteenth century, a small but wealthy merchant oligarchy took control of the Florentine government, led the Florentines in a series of successful wars against their neighbors, and established Florence as a major territorial state in north-central Italy. In 1434, Cosimo de' Medici (1434–1464) assumed control of the ruling oligarchy. Although the wealthy Medici family maintained republican forms of government for appearance's sake, they ran the government from behind the scenes. Through their lavish patronage and careful courting of political allies, the Medici were successful in dominating the city at a time when Florence was the cultural center of Italy.

A number of independent city-states under the control of powerful ruling families also became brilliant centers of culture in the fifteenth century. Perhaps the most famous was Urbino, ruled by the Montefeltro dynasty. Federigo da Montefeltro, who ruled Urbino from 1444 to 1482, received a classical education. He had also learned the skills of fighting, since the Montefeltro family compensated for the poverty of Urbino by hiring themselves out as *condottieri*. Federigo was not only a good ruler, but a rather unusual *condottiere* by fifteenth-century standards. Although not a brilliant general, he was reliable and honest. At the same time, Duke Federigo was one of the greatest patrons of Renaissance culture. Under his direction, Urbino became a well-known cultural and intellectual center. Though despotic, he was also benevolent. It was said that he could walk safely through the streets of Urbino, unaccompanied by a bodyguard, a feat few Italian rulers dared to emulate.

A noticeable feature of these smaller Italian courts was the important role played by women. The most famous of the Italian ruling women was Isabella d'Este (1474–1539), daughter of the duke of Ferrara, who married Francesco Gonzaga, marquis of Mantua. Their court was another important center of art and learning in the Renaissance. Educated at the brilliant court of Ferrara, Isabella was known for her intelligence and political wisdom. Called the "first lady of the world," she attracted artists and intellectuals to the Mantuan court and was

THE LETTERS OF ISABELLA D'ESTE

Many Italian and European rulers at the beginning of the sixteenth century saw Isabella d'Este as an important political figure. In these excerpts from her letters, Isabella reveals her political skills and her fierce determination. After her husband was taken prisoner by the Venetians in 1509, she refused to accept the condition for his release—namely, that her son Federico would be kept as a hostage by the Venetians or the Holy Roman emperor. She wrote to both the emperor and her husband, refusing to agree to their demands.

LETTER OF ISABELLA D'ESTE TO THE IMPERIAL ENVOY

As to the demand for our dearest first-born son Federico, besides being a cruel and almost inhuman thing for anyone who knows the meaning of a mother's love, there are many reasons which render it difficult and impossible. Although we are quite sure that his person would be well cared for and protected by His Majesty [the Holy Roman emperor], how could we wish him to run the risk of this long and difficult journey, considering the child's tender and delicate age? And you must know what comfort and solace, in his father's present unhappy condition, we find in the presence of this dear son, the hope and joy of all our people and subjects. To deprive us of him, would be to deprive us of life itself, and of all we count good and precious. If you take Federico away you might as well take away our life and state. . . . Once for all, we will suffer any loss rather than part from our son, and this you may take to be our deliberate and unchanging resolution.

LETTER OF ISABELLA D'ESTE TO HER HUSBAND [WHO HAD ORDERED HER TO SEND THE BOY TO VENICE]

If in this matter Your Excellency were to despise me and deprive me of your love and grace, I would rather endure such harsh treatment, I would rather lose our State, than deprive us of our children. I am hoping that in time your own prudence and kindness will make you understand that I have acted more lovingly toward you than you have to yourself.

Have patience! You can be sure that I think continuously of your liberation and when the time comes I will not fail you, as I have not relaxed my efforts. As witness I cite the Pope, the Emperor, the King of France, and all the other reigning heads and potentates of Christendom. Yes, and the infidels as well [she had written to the Turkish sultan for help]. If it were *really* the only means of setting you free, I would not only send Federico but all the other children as well. I will do everything imaginable. Someday I hope I can make you understand. . . .

Pardon me if this letter is badly written and worse composed, but I do not know if I am dead or alive.

Isabella, who desires the
best for Your Excellency,
written with her own hand

[Isabella's husband was not pleased with her response. His angry reaction was: "That whore of a wife is the cause of it all. Send me into battle alone, do what you like with me. I have lost in one blow my state, my honor, and my freedom. If she does not obey, I'll cut her vocal cords."]

responsible for amassing one of the finest libraries in all of Italy. Her numerous letters to friends, family, princes, and artists all over Europe disclose her political acumen as well as a good sense of humor (see the box above). Both before and after the death of her husband Francesco, she effectively ruled Mantua and was well known as a clever negotiator.

The growth of powerful monarchical states led to trouble for the Italians and brought an end to the independence of the Italian states. Attracted by the riches of Italy, the French king Charles VIII (1483–1498) led an army of 30,000 men into Italy and occupied the kingdom of Naples. Other Italian states turned for help to the Spanish, who gladly complied. For the next thirty years, the French and Spanish competed to dominate Italy, which was only a pawn for the two great powers, a convenient arena for fighting battles. The terrible sack of Rome in 1527 by the armies of the Spanish king Charles I brought a temporary end to the Italian wars. Thereafter, the Spaniards dominated Italy.

Machiavelli and the New Statecraft

No one gave better expression to the Italians' preoccupation with political power than Niccolò Machiavelli (1469–1527). Although he ably served as a diplomat for Florence, he was eventually forced into exile. Embittered by this and compelled by the great love of his life—politics—he wrote *The Prince*, one of the most influential works on political power in the Western world.

Machiavelli's major concerns in *The Prince* were the acquisition, maintenance, and expansion of political power as the means to restore and maintain order in his time. In the Middle Ages, many political theorists stressed the ethical side of a prince's activity—how a ruler ought to behave based on Christian moral principles. Machiavelli bluntly contradicted this approach:

> But my hope is to write a book that will be useful, at least to those who read it intelligently, and so I thought it sensible to go straight to a discussion of how things are in real life and not waste time with a discussion of an imaginary world . . . for the gap between how people actually behave and how they ought to behave is so great that anyone who ignores everyday reality in order to live up to an ideal will soon discover he had been taught how to destroy himself, not how to preserve himself.[6]

Machiavelli considered his approach far more realistic than that of his medieval forebears.

In Machiavelli's view, a prince's attitude toward power must be based on an understanding of human nature, which he perceived as basically self-centered. He said, "For of men one can, in general, say this: They are ungrateful, fickle, deceptive and deceiving, avoiders of danger, eager to gain." Political activity, therefore, could not be restricted by moral considerations. The prince acts on behalf of the state, and for the sake of the state, he must be willing to let his conscience sleep. As Machiavelli put it:

> You need to understand this: A ruler, and particularly a ruler who is new to power, cannot conform to all those rules that men who are thought good are expected to respect, for he is often obliged, in order to hold on to power, to break his word, to be uncharitable, inhumane, and irreligious. So he must be mentally prepared to act as circumstances and changes in fortune require. As I have said, he should do what is right if he can; but he must be prepared to do wrong if necessary.[7]

In Cesare Borgia, the son of Pope Alexander VI, who used ruthless measures to achieve his goal of carving out a new state in central Italy, Machiavelli found a good example of the new Italian ruler. As he said, "So anyone who decides that the policy to follow when one has newly acquired power is to destroy one's enemies, to secure some allies, to win wars, whether by force or by fraud, to make oneself both loved and feared by one's subjects, . . . cannot hope to find, in the recent past, a better model to imitate than Cesare Borgia."[8] Machiavelli was among the first to abandon morality as the basis for the analysis of political activity.

THE DECLINE OF THE CHURCH

The papacy of the Roman Catholic church reached the height of its power in the thirteenth century. Theories of papal supremacy included a doctrine of "fullness of power" as the spiritual head of Christendom and claims to universal temporal authority over all secular rulers. But the growing secular monarchies of Europe presented a challenge to papal claims of temporal supremacy, which led the papacy into a conflict with these territorial states that it was unable to win. Papal defeat, in turn, led to other crises that brought into question and undermined not only the pope's temporal authority over all Christendom, but his spiritual authority as well.

Boniface VIII and the Conflict with the State

The struggle between the papacy and the secular monarchies began during the pontificate of Pope Boniface VIII (1294–1303). One major issue appeared to be at stake between the pope and King Philip IV (1285–1314) of France. Looking for a source of new revenues, Philip asserted the right to tax the clergy of France. Boniface VIII claimed that the clergy of any state could not pay taxes to their secular ruler without the pope's consent. Underlying this issue, however, was a basic conflict between the claims of the papacy to universal authority over both church and state, which necessitated complete control over the clergy, and the claims of the monarchs that all subjects, including the clergy, were under the jurisdiction of the crown and subject to the king's authority on matters of taxation and justice. In short, the fundamental issue was the universal sovereignty of the papacy versus the royal sovereignty of the monarchs.

Boniface VIII asserted his position in a series of papal bulls or letters, the most important of which was *Unam Sanctam*, issued in 1302. It was the strongest statement ever made by a pope on the supremacy of the spiritual authority over the temporal authority (see the box on p. 372). When it became apparent that the pope had decided to act on his principles by excommunicating Philip IV of France, the latter sent a small contingent of French soldiers to capture Boniface and bring him back to France for trial. The pope was captured in Anagni, although Italian nobles from the surrounding countryside soon rescued him. Boniface died shortly thereafter from the shock of this experience, however. Philip's strong-arm tactics had produced a clear victory for the national monarchy over the papacy since no later pope dared renew the extravagant claims of Boniface VIII. To ensure his position and avoid any future papal threat, Philip IV brought enough pressure on the college of cardinals to achieve the election of a Frenchman, Clement V (1305–1314), as pope. Using the excuse of turbulence in the city of Rome, the new pope took up residence in Avignon, on the east bank of the Rhone River. Although Avignon was located in the Holy Roman Empire and was not a French possession, it lay just across the river from the territories of King Philip IV and was French in culture.

BONIFACE VIII'S DEFENSE OF PAPAL SUPREMACY

One of the more remarkable documents of the fourteenth century was the exaggerated statement of papal supremacy issued by Pope Boniface VIII in 1302 in the heat of his conflict with the French king Philip IV. Ironically, this strongest statement ever made of papal supremacy was issued at a time when the rising power of the secular monarchies made it increasingly difficult for the premises to be accepted. Not long after issuing it, Boniface was taken prisoner by the French. Although freed by his fellow Italians, the humiliation of his defeat brought his death a short time later.

POPE BONIFACE VIII, *UNAM SANCTAM*

We are compelled, our faith urging us, to believe and to hold—and we do firmly believe and simply confess—that there is one holy catholic and apostolic church, outside of which there is neither salvation nor remission of sins. . . . In this church there is one Lord, one faith, and one baptism. . . . Therefore, of this one and only church there is one body and one head . . . Christ, namely, and the vicar of Christ, St. Peter, and the successor of Peter. For the Lord himself said to Peter, feed my sheep. . . .

We are told by the word of the gospel that in this His fold there are two swords—a spiritual, namely, and a temporal. . . . Both swords, the spiritual and the material, therefore, are in the power of the church; the one, indeed, to be wielded for the church, the other by the church; the one by the hand of the priest, the other by the hand of kings and knights, but at the will and sufferance of the priest. One sword, moreover, ought to be under the other, and the temporal authority to be subjected to the spiritual. . . .

Therefore if the earthly power err it shall be judged by the spiritual power; but if the lesser spiritual power err, by the greater. But if the greatest, it can be judged by God alone, not by man, the apostle bearing witness. A spiritual man judges all things, but he himself is judged by no one. This authority, moreover, even though it is given to man and exercised through man, is not human but rather divine, being given by divine lips to Peter and founded on a rock for him and his successors through Christ himself whom he has confessed; the Lord himself saying to Peter: "Whatsoever thou shalt bind, etc." Whoever, therefore, resists this power thus ordained by God, resists the ordination of God. . . .

Indeed, we declare, announce, and define that it is altogether necessary to salvation for every human creature to be subject to the Roman pontiff.

The Papacy at Avignon (1305–1378)

The residency of the popes in Avignon for almost three-quarters of the fourteenth century led to a decline in papal prestige and a growing antipapal sentiment. The city of Rome was the traditional capital of the church. The pope was the bishop of Rome, and his position was based on being the successor to the apostle Peter, the first bishop of Rome. It was unseemly that the head of the Catholic church should reside in Avignon instead of Rome. In the 1330s, the popes began to construct a stately palace in Avignon, a clear indication that they intended to stay for some time.

Other factors also led to a decline in papal prestige during the Avignonese residency. Many contemporaries believed that the popes at Avignon were captives of the French king. Although questionable, since Avignon did not belong to the French monarchy, it was easy to believe in view of Avignon's proximity to French lands. Moreover, during the seventy-three years of the Avignonese papacy, of the 134 new cardinals created by the popes, 113 of them were French. At the same time, the popes attempted to find new sources of revenue to compensate for their loss of revenue from the Papal States and began to impose new taxes on the clergy. Furthermore, the splendor in which the pope and cardinals were living in Avignon led to a highly vocal criticism of both clergy and papacy. Avignon had become a powerful symbol of abuses within the church, and many people began to call for the pope's return to Rome. One of the most prominent calls came from Catherine of Siena (c. 1347–1380), whose saintly demeanor and claims of visions from God led the city of Florence to send her on a mission to Pope Gregory XI in Avignon. She told the pope: "Because God has given you authority and because you have accepted it, you ought to use your virtue and power; if you do not wish to use it, it might be better for you to resign what you have accepted; it would give more honor to God and health to your soul."[9]

The Great Schism

Catherine of Siena's admonition seemed to be heeded in 1377, when at long last Pope Gregory XI, perceiving the disastrous decline in papal prestige, returned to Rome. He died soon afterward, however, in the spring of 1378. When the college of cardinals met in conclave to elect a new pope, the citizens of Rome, fearful that the French majority would choose another Frenchman who would return the papacy to Avignon, threatened that the cardinals would not leave Rome alive unless a Roman or Italian was elected pope. Wisely, the terrified cardinals duly elected the Italian archbishop of Bari as Pope Urban VI (1378–1389). Five months later, a group of dissenting cardinals—the French ones—declared Urban's election null and void and chose one of their number, a Frenchman, who took the title of Clement VII and promptly returned to Avignon. Since Urban remained in Rome, there were now two popes, initiating what has been called the Great Schism of the church. Europe became divided in its loyalties: France, Spain, Scotland, and southern Italy supported Clement, while England, Germany, Scandinavia, and most of Italy supported Urban. These divisions generally followed political lines. Since the French supported the Avignonese, so did their allies; their enemies, particularly England and its allies, supported the Roman pope. The need for political support caused both popes to subordinate their policies to the policies of these states.

The Great Schism badly damaged the faith of Christian believers. The pope was widely believed to be the true leader of Christendom and, as Boniface VIII had pointed out, held the keys to the kingdom of heaven. Since both lines of popes denounced the other as the Antichrist, such a spectacle could not help but undermine the institution that had become the very foundation of the church. The Great Schism introduced uncertainty into the daily lives of ordinary Christians.

As dissatisfaction with the papacy grew, so also did the calls for a revolutionary approach to solving the church's institutional problems. Final authority in spiritual matters must reside not with the popes, reformers claimed, but with a general church council representing all members. The Great Schism led large numbers of serious churchmen to take up the theory of conciliarism in the belief that only a general council of the church could end the schism and bring reform to the church in its "head and members."

Leadership in convening a council eventually passed to the Holy Roman emperor Sigismund, and as a result of his efforts, an ecumenical church council met at Constance from 1414 to 1418. It had three major objectives: to end the schism, to eradicate heresy, and to reform the church in "head and members." The ending of the schism proved to be the Council of Constance's easiest task. After the competing popes either resigned or were deposed, a new conclave elected a Roman cardinal, a member of a prominent Roman family, as Pope Martin V (1417–1431). The council was much less successful in dealing with the problems of heresy and reform.

The Problems of Heresy and Reform

The crisis in the Catholic church led to renewed calls for reform. A group of Czech reformers led by the chancellor of the university of Prague, John Hus (1374–1415), called for an end to the worldliness and corruption of the clergy and attacked the excessive power of the papacy within the Catholic church. Hus's objections fell on receptive ears because there was already widespread criticism of the Catholic church as one of the largest landowners in Bohemia. Moreover, many clergymen were German, and the native Czechs' strong resentment of the Germans who dominated Bohemia also contributed to Hus's movement.

The Council of Constance attempted to deal with the growing problem of heresy by summoning John Hus to the council. Granted a safe conduct by Emperor Sigismund, Hus went in the hope of receiving a free hearing for his ideas. Instead he was arrested, condemned as a heretic, and burned at the stake in 1415. This action turned the unrest in Bohemia into revolutionary upheaval, and the resulting Hussite wars wracked the Holy Roman Empire until a truce was arranged in 1436.

The reform of the church in "head and members" was even less successful than the attempt to eradicate heresy. The Council of Constance passed two startling reform decrees. One boldly stated that a general council of the church received its authority from God; hence, every Christian, including the pope, was subject to its authority. The other decree provided for the regular holding of general councils in order to maintain an ongoing reform of the church. Decrees alone, however, proved insufficient to reform the church. Councils could issue decrees, but popes had to execute them, and popes would not cooperate with councils that diminished their absolute authority. Beginning already in 1417, successive popes worked

CHRONOLOGY

THE DECLINE OF THE CHURCH

Pope Boniface VIII	1294–1303
Unam Sanctam	1302
The papacy at Avignon	1305–1378
Pope Gregory XI returns to Rome	1377
The Great Schism begins	1378
Pope Urban VI	1378–1389
Council of Constance	1414–1418
End of the Great Schism	1417
The Renaissance papacy	
Sixtus IV	1471–1484
Alexander VI	1492–1503
Julius II	1503–1513
Leo X	1513–1521

A RENAISSANCE POPE: SIXTUS IV. The Renaissance popes allowed secular concerns to overshadow their spiritual duties. They became concerned with territorial expansion, finances, and Renaissance culture. Pope Sixtus IV built the Sistine Chapel and later had it decorated by some of the leading artists of his day. This fresco by Melozzo da Forlì shows the pope on his throne receiving the humanist Platina (kneeling), who was keeper of the Vatican Library.

steadfastly for the next thirty years to defeat the conciliar movement.

By the mid-fifteenth century, the popes had reasserted their supremacy over the Catholic church. No longer, however, did they have any possibility of asserting supremacy over temporal governments as the medieval papacy had. The papal monarchy had been maintained, although it had lost much moral prestige. In the fifteenth and early sixteenth centuries, the Renaissance popes contributed to an even further decline in the moral leadership of the papacy.

The Renaissance Papacy

The phrase *Renaissance papacy* refers to the line of popes from the end of the Great Schism (1417) to the beginnings of the Reformation in the early sixteenth century. The primary concern of the papacy is governing the Catholic church as its spiritual leader. But as heads of the church, popes had temporal preoccupations as well, and the story of the Renaissance papacy is really an account of how the latter came to overshadow the pope's spiritual functions.

The manner in which Renaissance popes pursued their interests in the Papal States and Italian politics, especially their use of intrigue, deceit, and open bloodshed, seemed shocking. Of all the Renaissance popes, Julius II (1503–1513) was most involved in war and politics. The fiery "warrior-pope" personally led armies against his enemies, much to the disgust of pious Christians who viewed the pope as a spiritual leader. As one intellectual wrote at the beginning of the sixteenth century: "How, O bishop standing in the room of the Apostles, dare you teach the people the things that pertain to war?"

To further their territorial aims in the Papal States, the popes needed loyal servants. Because they were not hereditary monarchs, popes could not build dynasties over several generations and came to rely on the practice of nepotism to promote their families' interests. Pope Sixtus IV (1471–1484), for example, made five of his nephews (the word *nepotism* is, in fact, derived from *nepos*, meaning nephew) cardinals and gave them an abundance of church offices to build up their finances. The infamous Borgia pope, Alexander VI (1492–1503), known for his debauchery and sensuality, raised one son, one nephew, and the brother of one mistress to the cardinalate. Alexander scandalized the church by encouraging his son Cesare to carve a territorial state out of the territories of the Papal States in central Italy.

The Renaissance popes were great patrons of Renaissance culture, and their efforts made Rome a cultural leader at the beginning of the sixteenth century. For the warrior-pope Julius II, the patronage of Renaissance culture was mostly a matter of policy as he endeavored to add to the splendor of his pontificate by tearing down the old basilica of Saint Peter and beginning construction of what was to be the greatest building in Christendom, Saint Peter's Basilica. Julius's successor, Leo X (1513–1521), was also a patron of Renaissance culture, not as a matter of policy, but as a deeply involved participant. A member of the Medici family, he was made a cardinal at the age of thirteen and acquired a refined taste in art, manners, and social life among the Florentine elite. He became pope at the age of thirty-seven, supposedly remarking to the Venetian ambassador, "Let us enjoy the papacy, since God has given it to us." Raphael was commissioned to do paintings, and the construction of St. Peter's was accelerated as Rome became the literary and artistic center of the Renaissance.

Meaning and Characteristics of the Italian Renaissance

The word *Renaissance* means "rebirth." A number of people who lived in Italy between c. 1350 and c. 1550 believed that they had witnessed a rebirth of antiquity or

Greco-Roman civilization, which marked a new age. To them, the approximately thousand years between the end of the Roman Empire and their own era was a middle period (hence the "Middle Ages"), characterized by darkness because of its lack of classical culture. Historians of the nineteenth century later used similar terminology to describe this period in Italy. The Swiss historian and art critic Jacob Burckhardt created the modern concept of the Renaissance in his celebrated work *The Civilization of the Renaissance in Italy*, published in 1860. He portrayed Italy in the fourteenth and fifteenth centuries as the birthplace of the modern world and saw the revival of antiquity, the "perfecting of the individual," and secularism ("worldliness of the Italians") as its distinguishing features. No doubt, Burckhardt exaggerated the individuality and secularism of the Renaissance and failed to recognize the depths of its religious sentiment. Nevertheless, he established the framework for all modern interpretations of the Renaissance. Although contemporary scholars do not believe that the Renaissance represents a sudden or dramatic cultural break with the Middle Ages (as Burckhardt argued)—there was after all much continuity between the two periods in economic, political, and social life—the Renaissance can still be viewed as a distinct period of European history, which manifested itself first in Italy and then spread to the rest of Europe. What, then, are the characteristics of the Italian Renaissance?

Renaissance Italy was largely the product of an urban society. The city-states became the centers of Italian political, economic, and social life. Within this new urban society, a secular spirit emerged as increasing wealth created new possibilities for the enjoyment of worldly things.

Above all, the Renaissance was an age of recovery from the "calamitous fourteenth century." Italy and Europe began a slow process of recuperation from the effects of the Black Death, political disorder, and economic recession. Recovery was accompanied by rebirth, specifically, a rebirth of classical antiquity. Increasingly aware of their own historical past, Italian intellectuals became intensely interested in the Greco-Roman culture that had informed the ancient Mediterranean world. This revival of classical antiquity affected activities as diverse as politics and art and led to new attempts to see human beings in a new light.

Though not entirely new, a revived emphasis on individual ability became characteristic of the Italian Renaissance. As the fifteenth-century Florentine architect Leon Battista Alberti expressed it, "Men can do all things if they will."[10] A high regard for human dignity and worth and a realization of individual potentiality created a new social ideal of the well-rounded personality or universal person (*l'uomo universale*) who was capable of achievements in many areas of life.

These general features of the Italian Renaissance were not characteristic of all Italians, but were primarily the preserve of the wealthy upper classes who constituted a small percentage of the total population. The Italian Renaissance was an elitist, not a mass, movement, although indirectly it did have some impact on ordinary people, especially in the cities, where so many of the intellectual and artistic accomplishments of the period were most apparent.

The Making of Renaissance Society

The Renaissance inherited a tripartite division of society from the Middle Ages. Society was fundamentally divided into three estates: the clergy, whose preeminence was grounded in the belief that people should be guided to spiritual ends; the nobility, whose privileges rested on the principle that the nobles provided security and justice for society; and the third estate, which consisted of the peasants and inhabitants of the towns and cities. This social order experienced certain adaptations in the Renaissance, which we can see by examining the second and third estates (the clergy will be examined in Chapter 15).

The Social Classes: The Nobility

Throughout much of Europe, the landholding nobles were faced with declining real incomes during the greater part of the fourteenth and fifteenth centuries. But many members of the old nobility survived, while new blood infused their ranks. A reconstruction of the aristocracy was well under way by 1500. As a result of this reconstruction, the nobles, old and new, who constituted between 2 and 3 percent of the population in most countries, managed to dominate society as they had done in the Middle Ages, holding important political posts and serving as advisers to the king.

By 1500, certain ideals came to be expected of the noble or aristocrat. These were best expressed in *The Book of the Courtier*, by the Italian Baldassare Castiglione (1478–1529). First published in 1528, Castiglione's work soon became popular throughout Europe, and it remained a fundamental handbook for European aristocrats well into the twentieth century.

In *The Book of the Courtier*, Castiglione described the three basic attributes of the perfect courtier. First, nobles should possess fundamental native endowments, such as impeccable character, grace, talents, and noble birth. The perfect courtier must also cultivate certain achievements. Primarily, he should participate in military and bodily exercises because the principal profession of a courtier was arms. For a medieval knight, military skill had been the only requirement, but this was not true of the Renaissance courtier, who must seek a classical education and adorn his life with the arts by playing a musical instrument, drawing, and painting. In Castiglione's hands, the Renaissance ideal of the well-developed personality became a social ideal of the aristocracy. Finally, the aristocrat was expected to follow a certain standard of conduct. Nobles were expected to make good impressions; while being modest, they should not hide their accomplishments, but show them off with grace.

But what was the purpose of these courtly standards? Castiglione said:

> Therefore, I think that the aim of the perfect Courtier, which we have not spoken of up to now, is so to win for himself, by means of the accomplishments ascribed to him by these gentlemen, the favor and mind of the prince whom he serves that he may be able to tell him, and always will tell him, the truth about everything he needs to know, without fear or risk of displeasing him; and that when he sees the mind of his prince inclined to a wrong action, he may dare to oppose him . . . so as to dissuade him of every evil intent and bring him to the path of virtue.[11]

The aim of the perfect noble, then, was to serve his prince in an effective and honest way. Nobles would adhere to Castiglione's principles for hundreds of years while they continued to dominate European life socially and politically.

The Social Classes: The Third Estate of Peasants and Townspeople

Traditionally, peasants made up the overwhelming mass of the third estate and indeed continued to constitute as much as 85 to 90 percent of the total European population, except in the highly urbanized areas of northern Italy and Flanders. The most noticeable trend produced by the economic crisis of the fourteenth century was the decline of the manorial system and the continuing elimination of serfdom. The contraction of the peasantry after the Black Death simply accelerated the process of converting servile labor dues into rents paid in money. By the end of the fifteenth century, serfdom was declining, especially in western Europe, and more and more peasants were becoming legally free.

The remainder of the third estate centered around the people of the towns and cities, originally the merchants and artisans who formed the so-called middle class. The town or city of the fifteenth century actually possessed a multitude of inhabitants widely separated socially and economically.

At the top of urban society were the patricians, whose wealth from capitalistic enterprises in trade, industry, and banking enabled them to dominate their urban communities economically, socially, and politically. Below them were the petty burghers, the shopkeepers, artisans, guildmasters, and guildsmen, who were largely concerned with providing goods and services for local consumption. Below these two groups were the propertyless workers earning pitiful wages and the unemployed, who lived squalid and miserable lives. These people constituted as much as 30 or 40 percent of the urban population. Everywhere in Europe in the late fourteenth and fifteenth centuries, urban poverty had increased dramatically. One rich merchant of Florence wrote:

> Those that are lazy and indolent in a way that does harm to the city, and who can offer no just reason for their condition, should either be forced to work or expelled from the Commune. The city would thus rid itself of that most harmful part of the poorest class. . . . If the lowest order of society earn enough food to keep them going from day to day, then they have enough.[12]

But even this large group was not at the bottom of the social scale; beneath them stood a significantly large group of slaves, especially in the cities of Italy.

WEDDING BANQUET. Parents arranged marriages in Renaissance Italy to strengthen business or family ties. A legally binding marriage contract was considered a necessary part of the marital arrangements. So, too, was a wedding feast. This painting by Botticelli shows the wedding banquet in Florence that celebrated the marriage of Nastagio degli Onesti and the daughter of Paulo Traversaro.

Family and Marriage in Renaissance Italy

The family bond was a source of great security in the dangerous urban world of Renaissance Italy. To maintain the family, careful attention was given to marriages, which were arranged by parents, often to strengthen business or family ties. Details were worked out well in advance, sometimes when children were only two or three, and reinforced by a legally binding marriage contract (see the box on p. 377). The important aspect of the contract was the size of the dowry, a sum of money presented by the wife's family to the husband upon marriage. He would control this money thereafter. The

MARRIAGE NEGOTIATIONS

Marriages were so important in maintaining families in Renaissance Italy that much energy was put into arranging them. Parents made the choices for their children, most often for considerations that had little to do with the modern notion of love. This selection is taken from the letters of a Florentine matron of the illustrious Strozzi family to her son Filippo in Naples. The family's considerations were complicated by the fact that the son was in exile.

ALESSANDRA STROZZI TO HER SON FILIPPO IN NAPLES

[April 20, 1464] Concerning the matter of a wife [for Filippo], it appears to me that if Francesco di Messer Tanagli wishes to give his daughter, that it would be a fine marriage. . . . Now I will speak with Marco [Parenti, Alessandra's son-in-law], to see if there are other prospects that would be better, and if there are none, then we will learn if he wishes to give her [in marriage]. . . . Francesco Tanagli has a good reputation, and he has held office, not the highest, but still he has been in office. You may ask: "Why should he give her to someone in exile?" There are three reasons. First, there aren't many young men of good family who have both virtue and property. Secondly, she has only a small dowry, 1,000 florins, which is the dowry of an artisan [although not a small sum, either—senior officials in the government bureaucracy earned 300 florins a year]. . . . Third, I believe that he will give her away, because he has a large family and he will need help to settle them. . . .

[July 26, 1465] Francesco is a good friend of Marco and he trusts him. On S. Jacopo's day, he spoke to him discreetly and persuasively, saying that for several months he had heard that we were interested in the girl and . . . that when we had made up our minds, she will come to us willingly. [He said that] you were a worthy man, and that his family had always made good marriages, but that he had only a small dowry to give her, and so he would prefer to send her outside of Florence to someone of worth, rather than to give her to someone here, from among those who were available, with little money. . . . We have information that she is affable and competent. She is responsible for a large family (there are twelve children, six boys and six girls), and the mother is always pregnant and isn't very competent. . . .

[August 31, 1465] I have recently received some very favorable information [about the Tanagli girl] from two individuals. . . . They are in agreement that whoever gets her will be content. . . . Concerning her beauty, they told me what I had already seen, that she is attractive and well-proportioned. Her face is long, but I couldn't look directly into her face, since she appeared to be aware that I was examining her . . . and so she turned away from me like the wind. . . . She reads quite well . . . and she can dance and sing. . . .

So yesterday I sent for Marco and told him what I had learned. And we talked about the matter for a while, and decided that he should say something to the father and give him a little hope, but not so much that we couldn't withdraw, and find out from him the amount of the dowry. . . . May God help us to choose what will contribute to our tranquility and to the consolation of us all. . . .

[September 13, 1465] Marco came to me and said that he had met with Francesco Tanagli, who had spoken very coldly, so that I understand that he had changed his mind. [Filippo Strozzi eventually married Fiametta di Donato Adimari in 1466.]

dowry could involve large sums of money and was expected of all families.

The father-husband was the center of the Italian family. He gave it his name, was responsible for it in all legal matters, managed all finances (his wife had no share in his wealth), and made the crucial decisions that determined his children's lives. A father's authority over his children was absolute until he died or formally freed his children. In Renaissance Italy, children did not become adults on reaching a certain age; instead adulthood came only when the father went before a judge and formally emancipated them. The age of emancipation varied from early teens to late twenties.

The wife managed the household, a position that gave women a certain degree of autonomy in their daily lives. Most wives, however, also knew that their primary function was to bear children. Upper-class wives were frequently pregnant; Alessandra Strozzi of Florence, for example, who had been married at the age of sixteen, bore eight children in ten years. Poor women did not conceive at the same rate since they nursed their own babies. Wealthy women gave their infants out to wet nurses, which enabled them to become pregnant more quickly after the birth of a child.

For women in the Renaissance, childbirth was a fearful occasion. Not only was it painful, but it could be deadly; possibly as many as 10 percent of mothers died in childbirth. In his memoirs, the Florence merchant Gregorio Dati recalled that three of his four wives died in childbirth. His third wife, after bearing eleven children in fifteen years, "died in childbirth after lengthy suffering, which she bore with remarkable strength and patience."[13] Nor did the tragedies end with childbirth. Surviving mothers often faced the death of their children as well. In Florence in the fifteenth century, for example, almost 50 percent of the children born to merchant families died before the age of twenty. Given these mortality rates, many upper-class families sought to have as many children as possible in order to ensure a surviving male heir to the family fortune. This concern is evident in the Florentine humanist Leon Battista Alberti's treatise *On the Family,* when one of the characters remarks, "How many families do we see today in decadence and ruin! . . . Of all these families not only the magnificence and greatness but the very men, not only the men but the very names are shrunk away and gone. Their memory . . . is wiped out and obliterated."[14]

The Intellectual Renaissance in Italy

Individualism and secularism—two characteristics of the Italian Renaissance—were most noticeable in the intellectual and artistic realms. Italian culture had matured by the fourteenth century. During the fifteenth and sixteenth centuries, Italy was the cultural leader of Europe. This new Italian culture was primarily the product of a relatively wealthy, urban lay society. The most important literary movement associated with the Renaissance was humanism.

Italian Renaissance Humanism

Renaissance humanism was an intellectual movement based on the study of the classics, or the literary works of Greece and Rome. Humanists studied the liberal arts—grammar, rhetoric, poetry, moral philosophy or ethics, and history—all based on the study of ancient Greek and Roman authors. These subjects are what we call the humanities.

Petrarch (1304–1374) has often been called the father of Italian Renaissance humanism. He did more than any other individual in the fourteenth century to foster the development of Renaissance humanism. He was the first intellectual to characterize the Middle Ages as a period of darkness, promoting the mistaken belief that medieval culture was ignorant of classical antiquity. Petrarch's interest in the classics led him on a passionate search for forgotten Latin manuscripts and set in motion a ransacking of monastic libraries throughout Europe. In his preoccupation with the classics and their secular content, Petrarch doubted at times whether he was sufficiently attentive to spiritual ideals. His qualms, however, did not prevent him from inaugurating the humanist emphasis on pure classical Latin, making it fashionable for humanists to use Cicero as a model for prose and Virgil for poetry. As Petrarch said, "Christ is my God; Cicero is the prince of the language." Humanists would always have a tendency to emphasize style, often at the expense of content.

In Florence, the humanist movement took a new direction at the beginning of the fifteenth century. Fourteenth-century humanists such as Petrarch had glorified intellectual activity pursued in a life of solitude and had rejected a life of action in the community and family. In the busy civic world of Florence, intellectuals began to take a new view of their role as intellectuals, a trend that intensified when the city's liberty was threatened at the beginning of the fifteenth century by the Milanese tyrant Giangaleazzo Visconti. Cicero, the classical Roman statesman and intellectual, became their model. Leonardo Bruni (1370–1444), a humanist, Florentine patriot, and chancellor of the city, wrote a biography of Cicero entitled *New Cicero,* in which he waxed enthusiastically about the fusion of political action and literary creation in Cicero's life. Cicero's literary and political activities were simply two sides of the same coin, the work of a Roman citizen on behalf of his state. From Bruni's time on, Cicero served as the inspiration for the Renaissance ideal that one must live an active life for one's state, and everything, including riches, must be considered good if it increases one's power of action. An active civic life does not distract from but actually stimulates the highest intellectual energies. An individual only "grows to maturity—both intellectually and morally—through participation" in the life of the state.

Civic humanism emerged in Florence but soon spread to other Italian cities and beyond. It reflected the values of the urban society of the Italian Renaissance. Civic humanism intensified the involvement of humanist intellectuals in government and guaranteed that the rhetorical discipline they praised would be put to the service of the state. It is no accident that humanists served the state as chancellors, councillors, and advisers. Rhetoricians had become diplomats.

Also evident in the humanism of the first half of the fifteenth century was a growing interest in classical Greek civilization. One of the first Italian humanists to gain a thorough knowledge of Greek was Leonardo Bruni, who became an enthusiastic pupil of the Byzantine scholar Manuel Chrysoloras, who taught in Florence from 1396 to 1400. Humanists eagerly perused the works of Plato as well as Greek poets, dramatists, historians, and orators, such as Thucydides, Euripides, and Sophocles, all of whom had been neglected by the scholastics of the High Middle Ages.

Humanism and Philosophy

The second half of the fifteenth century saw a dramatic upsurge of interest in the works of Plato. Cosimo de' Medici, the de facto ruler of Florence, encouraged this development by commissioning a translation of Plato's dialogues by Marsilio Ficino (1433–1499), who dedicated his life to the translation of Plato and the exposition of the Platonic philosophy known as Neoplatonism.

In two major works, Marsilio Ficino undertook the synthesis of Christianity and Platonism into a single system. His Neoplatonism was based on two primary ideas, the Neoplatonic hierarchy of substances and a theory of spiritual love. The former postulated a hierarchy of substances, or great chain of being, from the lowest form of physical matter (plants) to the purest spirit (God), in which humans occupied a central or middle position. They were the link between the material world (through the body) and the spiritual world (through the soul), and their highest duty was to apprehend higher things and ascend toward that union with God that was the true end of human existence. Ficino's theory of spiritual or Platonic love maintained that just as all people are bound together in their common humanity by love, so too are all parts of the universe held together by bonds of sympathetic love.

Renaissance Hermeticism was another product of the Florentine intellectual environment of the late fifteenth century. Upon the request of Cosimo de' Medici, Marsilio Ficino translated into Latin a Greek manuscript entitled *Corpus Hermeticum*. This work contained two kinds of writings. One type stressed the occult sciences with emphasis on astrology, alchemy, and magic. The other focused on theological and philosophical beliefs and speculations. For Renaissance intellectuals, the Hermetic revival offered a new view of humankind. They believed that human beings had been created as divine beings endowed with divine creative power, but had freely chosen to enter the material world (nature). They could recover their divinity, however, through a regenerative experience or purification of the soul. Thus regenerated, they became true sages or magi, as the Renaissance called them, who had knowledge of God and of truth. In regaining their original divinity, they reacquired an intimate knowledge of nature and the ability to employ its powers for beneficial purposes. Serious Renaissance magi believed in humans' ability to control nature and became involved in the practice of magic as a means of organizing and controlling experience.

In Italy, the most prominent magi in the late fifteenth century were Ficino and his friend and pupil Giovanni Pico della Mirandola (1463–1494). Pico produced one of the most famous writings of the Renaissance, the *Oration on the Dignity of Man*. Pico combed diligently through the writings of many philosophers of different backgrounds for the common "nuggets of universal truth" that he believed were all part of God's revelation to humanity. In the *Oration* (see the box on p. 380), Pico offered a ringing statement of unlimited human potential: "To him it is granted to have whatever he chooses, to be whatever he wills."[15] Like Ficino, Pico took an avid interest in Hermetic magic, accepting it as the "science of the Divine," which "embraces the deepest contemplation of the most secret things, and at last the knowledge of all nature."[16]

Education in the Renaissance

The humanist movement had a profound effect on education. Renaissance humanists believed that human beings could be dramatically changed by education, and as a result, they wrote treatises on education and opened schools based on their ideas. At the core of humanist schools were the "liberal studies." Humanists believed that the "liberal studies" (what we call the liberal arts) were the key to true freedom, enabling individuals to reach their full potential. According to one humanist, "we call those studies liberal which are worthy of a free man; those studies by which we attain and practice virtue and wisdom; that education which calls forth, trains, and develops those highest gifts of body and mind which ennoble men."[17] What, then, were the "liberal studies"? According to the humanists, they included history, moral philosophy, and eloquence (or rhetoric), letters (grammar and logic), poetry, mathematics, astronomy, and music. In short, the purpose of a liberal education—and thus the purpose of the study of the liberal arts—was to produce individuals who followed a path of virtue and wisdom and possessed the rhetorical skills by which they could persuade others to take it. Following the Greek precept of a sound mind in a sound body, humanist educators also stressed physical education. Pupils were taught the skills of javelin throwing, archery, and dancing and encouraged to run, wrestle, hunt, and swim.

The purpose of these humanist schools was to educate an elite, the ruling classes of their communities. Largely absent from such schools were females. The few female students who did attend humanist schools studied the classics and were encouraged to know some history and to ride, dance, sing, play the lute, and appreciate poetry. But they were told not to learn mathematics and rhetoric. Religion and morals were thought to "hold the first place in the education of Christian ladies," helping to prepare them for their roles as mothers and wives.

Humanist educators thought that humanist education was a practical preparation for life. Its aim was not the creation of a great scholar but a complete citizen. As one humanist said, "Not everyone is obliged to excel in philosophy, medicine, or the law, nor are all equally favored by nature; but all are destined to live in society and to practice virtue."[18] Humanist schools provided the model for the basic education of the European ruling classes until the twentieth century.

The Development of Vernacular Literature

The humanist emphasis on classical Latin led to its widespread use in the fifteenth and sixteenth centuries,

PICO DELLA MIRANDOLA AND THE DIGNITY OF MAN

Giovanni Pico della Mirandola was one of the foremost intellects of the Italian Renaissance. Pico boasted that he had studied all schools of philosophy, which he tried to demonstrate by drawing up nine hundred theses for public disputation at the age of twenty-four. As a preface to his theses, he wrote his famous oration, On the Dignity of Man, *in which he proclaimed the unlimited potentiality of human beings.*

PICO DELLA MIRANDOLA, *ORATION ON THE DIGNITY OF MAN*

At last the best of artisans [God] ordained that that creature to whom He had been able to give nothing proper to himself should have joint possession of whatever had been peculiar to each of the different kinds of being. He therefore took man as a creature of indeterminate nature, and assigning him a place in the middle of the world, addressed him thus: "Neither a fixed abode nor a form that is yours alone nor any function peculiar to yourself have we given you, Adam, to the end that according to your longing and according to your judgment you may have and possess what abode, what form, and what functions you yourself shall desire. The nature of all other beings is limited and constrained within the bounds of laws prescribed by Us. You, constrained by no limits, in accordance with your own free will, in whose hand We have placed you, shall ordain yourself the limits of your nature. We have set you at the world's center that you may from there more easily observe whatever is in the world. We have made you neither of heaven nor of earth, neither mortal nor immortal, so that with freedom of choice and with honor, as though the maker and molder of yourself, you may fashion yourself in whatever shape you shall prefer. You shall have the power to degenerate into the lower forms of life, which are brutish. You shall have the power, out of your soul's judgment, to be reborn into the higher forms, which are divine."

O supreme generosity of God the Father, O highest and most marvelous felicity of man! To him it is granted to have whatever he chooses, to be whatever he wills. Beasts as soon as they are born bring with them from their mother's womb all they will ever possess. Spiritual beings, either from the beginning or soon thereafter, become what they are to be forever and ever. On man when he came into life the Father conferred the seeds of all kinds and the germs of every way of life. Whatever seeds each man cultivates will grow to maturity and bear in him their own fruit. If they be vegetative, he will be like a plant. If sensitive, he will become brutish. If rational, he will grow into a heavenly being. If intellectual, he will be an angel and the son of God.

especially among scholars, lawyers, and theologians. However, some writers used the vernacular (the language spoken in their own regions, such as Italian, French, or German) to write their works. In the fourteenth and fifteenth centuries, the works of Dante and Christine de Pizan helped make vernacular languages more popular. By the late fifteenth and early sixteenth centuries, vernacular languages became broad enough in scope to create national literary forms that could compete with and eventually replace Latin.

Dante (1265–1321) came from an old Florentine noble family that had fallen on hard times. His masterpiece in the Italian vernacular was *The Divine Comedy*, written between 1313 and 1321. Cast in a typical medieval framework, *The Divine Comedy* is basically the story of the soul's progression to salvation, a fundamental medieval preoccupation. The lengthy poem was divided into three major sections corresponding to the realms of the afterworld: hell, purgatory, and heaven or paradise. In "Inferno," Dante is led on an imaginary journey through hell by his guide, the classical author Virgil (see the box on p. 381). Symbolically, "Inferno" reflects despair, while "Purgatory," the second stage of his journey, reflects hope. In "Paradise," Dante is eventually guided by Saint Bernard, a symbol of mystical contemplation. The saint turns Dante over to the Virgin Mary because grace is necessary to achieve the final step of entering the presence of God, where one beholds "The love that moves the sun and the other stars."[19] Allegorically, "Paradise" reflects perfection or salvation.

One of the extraordinary vernacular writers of the age was Christine de Pizan (c. 1364–1430). Because of her father's position at the court of Charles V of France, she received a good education. When her husband died when she was only twenty-five (they had been married for ten years), she was left with little income and the need to support her three small children and her mother. Christine took the unusual step of becoming a writer in order to earn her living. Her poems were soon in demand, and by 1400 she had achieved financial security.

Christine de Pizan is best known, however, for her French prose works written in defense of women. In *The Book of the City of Ladies*, written in 1404, she de-

DANTE'S VISION OF HELL

The *Divine Comedy* of Dante Alighieri is regarded as one of the greatest literary works of all time. Many consider it the supreme summary of medieval European thought. It combines allegory with a remarkable amount of contemporary history. Indeed, forty-three of the seventy-nine people consigned to hell in the "Inferno" were Florentines. This excerpt is taken from Canto XVIII of the "Inferno," in which Dante and Virgil visit the eighth circle of hell, which is divided into ten trenches containing those who had committed malicious frauds upon their fellow human beings.

DANTE, "INFERNO," *THE DIVINE COMEDY*

We had already come to where the walk
crosses the second bank, from which it lifts
another arch, spanning from rock to rock.

Here we heard people whine in the next chasm,
and knock and thump themselves with open palms,
and blubber through their snouts as if in a spasm.

Steaming from that pit, a vapor rose
over the banks, crusting them with a slime
that sickened my eyes and hammered at my nose.

That chasm sinks so deep we could not sight
its bottom anywhere until we climbed
along the rock arch to its greatest height.

Once there, I peered down; and I saw long lines
of people in a river of excrement
that seemed the overflow of the world's latrines.

I saw among the felons of that pit
one wraith who might or might not have been tonsured—
one could not tell, he was so smeared with shit.

He bellowed: "You there, why do you stare at me
more than at all the others in this stew?"
And I to him: "Because if memory

serves me, I knew you when your hair was dry.
You are Alessio Interminelli da Lucca.
That's why I pick you from this filthy fry."

And he then, beating himself on his clown's head:
"Down to this have the flatteries I sold
the living sunk me here among the dead."

And my Guide prompted then: "Lean forward a bit
and look beyond him, there—do you see that one
scratching herself with dungy nails, the strumpet

who fidgets to her feet, then to a crouch?
It is the whore Thäis who told her lover
when he sent to ask her, 'Do you thank me much?'

'Much? Nay, past all believing!' And with this
Let us turn from the sight of this abyss."

nounced the many male writers who had argued that women by their very nature were prone to evil, unable to learn, and easily swayed, as a result of which they needed to be controlled by men. With the help of Reason, Righteousness, and Justice, who appear to her in a vision, Christine refutes these antifeminist attacks. Women, she argues, are not evil by nature, and they, too, could learn as well as men if they could attend the same schools: "Should I also tell you whether a woman's nature is clever and quick enough to learn speculative sciences as well as to discover them, and likewise the manual arts. I assure you that women are equally well-suited and skilled to carry them out and to put them to sophisticated use once they have learned them."[20] Much of the book includes a detailed discussion of women from the past and present who have distinguished themselves as leaders, warriors, wives, mothers, and martyrs for their religious faith. She ends by encouraging women to defend themselves against the attacks of men who are unable to understand them.

The Impact of Printing

The period of the Renaissance witnessed the development of printing, one of the most important technological innovations of civilization. The art of printing made an immediate impact on European intellectual life and thought. Printing from hand-carved wooden blocks had been present in the West since the twelfth century and in China even before that. What was new in the fifteenth century in Europe was multiple printing with movable metal type. The development of printing from movable type was a gradual process that culminated sometime between 1445 and 1450; Johannes Gutenberg

THE VISION OF CHRISTINE DE PIZAN. Christine de Pizan is one of the extraordinary vernacular writers of the late fourteenth and early fifteenth centuries. She is pictured here in a cover illustration from her book, *The Book of the City of Ladies*. Reason, Righteousness, and Justice are shown appearing to Christine in a dream.

of Mainz played an important role in bringing the process to completion. Gutenberg's Bible, completed in 1455 or 1456, was the first real book produced from movable type.

The new printing spread rapidly throughout Europe in the last half of the fifteenth century. Printing presses were established throughout the Holy Roman Empire in the 1460s and within ten years had spread to Italy, France, the Low Countries, Spain, and eastern Europe. Especially well known as a printing center was Venice, home by 1500 to almost one hundred printers, who among them had produced almost two million volumes.

By 1500, there were more than a thousand printers in Europe, who collectively had published almost 40,000 titles (between eight and ten million copies). Probably 50 percent of these books were religious in character—Bibles and biblical commentaries, books of devotion, and sermons. Next in importance were the Latin and Greek classics, medieval grammars, legal handbooks, works on philosophy, and an ever growing number of popular romances.

Printing became one of the largest industries in Europe, and its effects were soon felt in many areas of European life. Although some humanists condemned printing because they believed that it vulgarized learning, the printing of books actually encouraged the development of scholarly research and the desire to attain knowledge. Moreover, printing facilitated cooperation among scholars and helped produce standardized and definitive texts. Printing also stimulated the rise of an ever expanding lay reading public, a development that had an enormous impact on European society. Indeed, the new religious ideas of the Reformation would never have spread as rapidly as they did in the sixteenth century without the printing press.

The Artistic Renaissance

Leonardo da Vinci, one of the great Italian Renaissance artists, once explained: "Hence the painter will produce pictures of small merit if he takes for his standard the pictures of others, but if he will study from natural objects he will bear good fruit . . . those who take for their standard anyone but nature . . . weary themselves in vain."[21] Renaissance artists considered the imitation of nature to be their primary goal. Their search for naturalism became an end in itself: to persuade onlookers of the reality of the object or event they were portraying. At the same time, the new artistic standards reflected a new attitude of mind as well, one in which human beings became the focus of attention, the "center and measure of all things," as one artist proclaimed.

The frescoes by Masaccio (1401–1428) in the Brancacci Chapel have long been regarded as the first masterpieces of Early Renaissance art. With his use of monumental figures, the demonstration of a more realistic relationship between figures and landscape, and the visual representation of the laws of perspective, a new realistic style of painting was born. Onlookers become aware of a world of reality that appears to be a continuation of their own.

This new or Renaissance style was absorbed and modified by other Florentine painters in the fifteenth century. Especially important was the development of an experimental trend that took two directions. One emphasized the mathematical side of painting, the working out of the laws of perspective and the organization of outdoor space and light by geometry and perspective. The other aspect of the experimental trend involved the investigation of movement and anatomical structure.

MASACCIO, *TRIBUTE MONEY*. With the frescoes of Masaccio, regarded by many as the first great works of Early Renaissance art, a new realistic style of painting was born. *Tribute Money* was one of a series of frescoes that Masaccio painted in the Brancacci Chapel in the church of Santa Maria del Carmine in Florence. In illustrating a story from the Bible, Masaccio used a rational system of perspective to create a realistic relationship between the figures and their background.

Indeed, the realistic portrayal of the human nude became one of the foremost preoccupations of Italian Renaissance art. The fifteenth century, then, was a period of experimentation and technical mastery. By the end of the century, Italian painters had created a new artistic environment. Many artists had mastered the new techniques for a scientific observation of the world around them and were now ready to move into individualistic forms of creative expression. This marked the shift to the High Renaissance.

The High Renaissance was dominated by the work of three artistic giants, Leonardo da Vinci (1452–1519), Raphael (1483–1520), and Michelangelo (1475–1564). Leonardo represents a transitional figure in the shift to High Renaissance principles. He carried on the fifteenth-century experimental tradition by studying everything and even dissecting human bodies in order to better see how nature worked. But Leonardo stressed the need to advance beyond such realism and initiated the High Renaissance's preoccupation with the idealization of nature, or the attempt to generalize from realistic portrayal to an ideal form. Leonardo's *Last Supper* is a brilliant summary of fifteenth-century trends in its organization of space and use of perspective to depict subjects three-dimensionally in a two-dimensional medium. But it is also more. The figure of Philip is idealized, and there are profound psychological dimensions to the work. The words of Jesus that "one of you shall betray me" are experienced directly as each of the apostles reveals his personality and his relationship to the Savior. In one of his notebooks, Leonardo wrote that the highest and most difficult aim of painting is to depict "the intention of man's soul." Through gestures and movement, Leonardo hoped to reveal a person's inner life.

Raphael blossomed as a painter at an early age; at twenty-five, he was already regarded as one of Italy's best painters. Raphael was acclaimed for his numerous Madonnas, in which he attempted to achieve an ideal of beauty far surpassing human standards. He is well-known for his frescoes in the Vatican Palace; his *School of Athens* reveals a world of balance, harmony, and order—basically, the underlying principles of the art of the classical world of Greece and Rome.

Michelangelo, an accomplished painter, sculptor, and architect, was another giant of the High Renaissance. Fiercely driven by his desire to create, he worked with great passion and energy on a remarkable number of projects. Michelangelo was influenced by Neoplatonism,

LEONARDO DA VINCI, *THE LAST SUPPER*. Leonardo da Vinci was the impetus behind the High Renaissance concern for the idealization of nature, moving from a realistic portrayal of the human figure to an idealized form. Evident in Leonardo's *Last Supper* is his effort to depict a person's character and inner nature through gesture and movement. Unfortunately, Leonardo used an experimental technique in this fresco, which soon led to its physical deterioration.

RAPHAEL, *SCHOOL OF ATHENS*. Raphael arrived in Rome in 1508 and began to paint a series of frescoes commissioned by Pope Julius II for the papal apartments at the Vatican. In *School of Athens*, painted about 1510–1511, Raphael created an imaginary gathering of ancient philosophers. In the center stand Plato and Aristotle. At the left is Pythagoras, showing his system of proportions on a slate. At the right is Ptolemy, holding a celestial globe.

MICHELANGELO, *CREATION OF ADAM.* In 1508, Pope Julius II recalled Michelangelo to Rome and commissioned him to decorate the ceiling of the Sistine Chapel. This colossal project was not completed until 1512. Michelangelo attempted to tell the story of the Fall of Man by depicting nine scenes from the biblical book of Genesis. In this scene, the well-proportioned figure of Adam, meant by Michelangelo to be a reflection of divine beauty, awaits the divine spark.

especially evident in his figures on the ceiling of the Sistine Chapel. These muscular figures reveal an ideal type of human being with perfect proportions. In good Neoplatonic fashion, their beauty is meant to be a reflection of divine beauty; the more beautiful the body, the more God-like the figure.

The Northern Artistic Renaissance

In trying to provide an exact portrayal of their world, the artists of the north (especially the Low Countries) and Italy took different approaches. In Italy, the human form became the primary vehicle of expression as Italian artists sought to master the technical skills that allowed them to portray humans in realistic settings. The large wall spaces of Italian churches had given rise to the art of fresco painting, but in the north, the prevalence of Gothic cathedrals with their stained glass windows resulted in more emphasis on illuminated manuscripts and wooden panel painting for altarpieces. The space available in these works was limited, and great care was required to depict each object, leading northern painters to become masters at rendering details.

The most influential northern school of art in the fifteenth century was centered in Flanders. Jan van Eyck (1380?–1441) was among the first to use oil paint, a medium that enabled the artist to use a varied range of colors and make changes to create fine details. In his *Giovanni Arnolfini and His Bride*, van Eyck's attention to detail is staggering: precise portraits, a glittering chandelier, a mirror reflecting the objects in the room, and the effects of light filtering through the window. Although each detail was rendered as observed, it is evident that van Eyck's comprehension of perspective was still uncertain. His work is truly indicative of northern Renaissance painters, who, in their effort to imitate nature, did so not by mastery of the laws of perspective and proportion, but by empirical observation of visual reality and the accurate portrayal of details. Moreover, northern painters placed great emphasis on the emotional intensity of religious feeling. Michelangelo summarized the difference between northern and Italian Renaissance painting in these words:

> In Flanders, they paint, before all things, to render exactly and deceptively the outward appearance of things. The painters choose, by preference, subjects provoking transports of piety, like the figures of saints or of prophets. But most of the time they paint what are called landscapes with plenty of figures. Though the eye is agreeably impressed, these pictures have neither choice of values nor grandeur. In short, this art is without power and without distinction; it aims at rendering minutely many things at the same time, of which a single one would have sufficed to call forth a man's whole application.[22]

JAN VAN EYCK, *GIOVANNI ARNOLFINI AND HIS BRIDE*. Northern painters took great care in depicting each object and became masters at rendering details. This emphasis on a realistic portrayal is clearly evident in this oil painting, supposedly a portrait of Giovanni Arnolfini, an Italian merchant who had settled in Bruges, and his wife, Giovanna Cenami.

ALBRECHT DÜRER, *ADORATION OF THE MAGI*. By the end of the fifteenth century, northern artists began studying in Italy and adopting many of the techniques used by Italian painters. As is evident in this painting, which was the central panel for an altarpiece done for Frederick the Wise in 1504, Albrecht Dürer masterfully incorporated the laws of perspective and the ideals of proportion into his works. At the same time, he did not abandon the preoccupation with detail typical of northern artists.

By the end of the fifteenth century, however, artists from the north began to study in Italy and were visually influenced by what artists were doing there.

One northern artist of this later period who was greatly affected by the Italians was Albrecht Dürer (1471–1528), from Nuremberg. Dürer made two trips to Italy and absorbed most of what the Italians could teach, as is evident in his mastery of the laws of perspective and Renaissance theories of proportion. He wrote detailed treatises on both subjects. At the same time, as in his famous *Adoration of the Magi*, Dürer did not reject the use of minute details characteristic of northern artists. He did try, however, to integrate those details more harmoniously into his works and, like the Italian artists of the High Renaissance, tried to achieve a standard of ideal beauty by a careful examination of the human form.

CONCLUSION

In the High Middle Ages, European civilization developed many of its fundamental features. Territorial states, parliaments, capitalist trade and industry, banks, cities, and vernacular literatures were all products of that fertile period. During the same time, the Catholic church under the direction of the papacy reached its apogee. Fourteenth-century European society, however, was challenged by an overwhelming number of disintegrative forces. Devastating plague, decline in trade and industry, bank failures, peasant revolts pitting lower classes against the upper classes, seemingly constant warfare, aristocratic factional conflict that undermined political stability, the absence of the popes from Rome, and even the spectacle of two popes condemning each other as the Antichrist all seemed to overpower Europeans in this "calamitous century." Not surprisingly, much of the art of the period depicted the Four Horsemen of the Apocalypse described in the New

Testament book of Revelation: Death, Famine, Pestilence, and War. No doubt, to some people it appeared that the last days of the world were at hand.

The new European society, however, proved remarkably resilient. Periods of disintegration are usually paralleled by the emergence of new ideas and new practices. The Renaissance was a period of transition that witnessed a continuation of the economic, political, and social trends that had begun in the High Middle Ages. It was also a new age in which intellectuals and artists proclaimed a new vision of humankind and raised fundamental questions about the value and importance of the individual.

Europeans were also engaging in new adventures in the age of the Renaissance. The discovery of new trade routes to the East and the "accidental" discovery of the Americas encouraged Europeans to venture outside the medieval world in which they had been enclosed for virtually a thousand years. For much of that period, Europeans had been unable to match the achievements and splendors of civilizations in the Middle East and China. Europeans had, however, borrowed many of the tools, including gunpowder and firearms, that they would now use to move out into the world and impose their power on much of it. A new era of world history was beginning to dawn, and it is to that story that we must now turn.

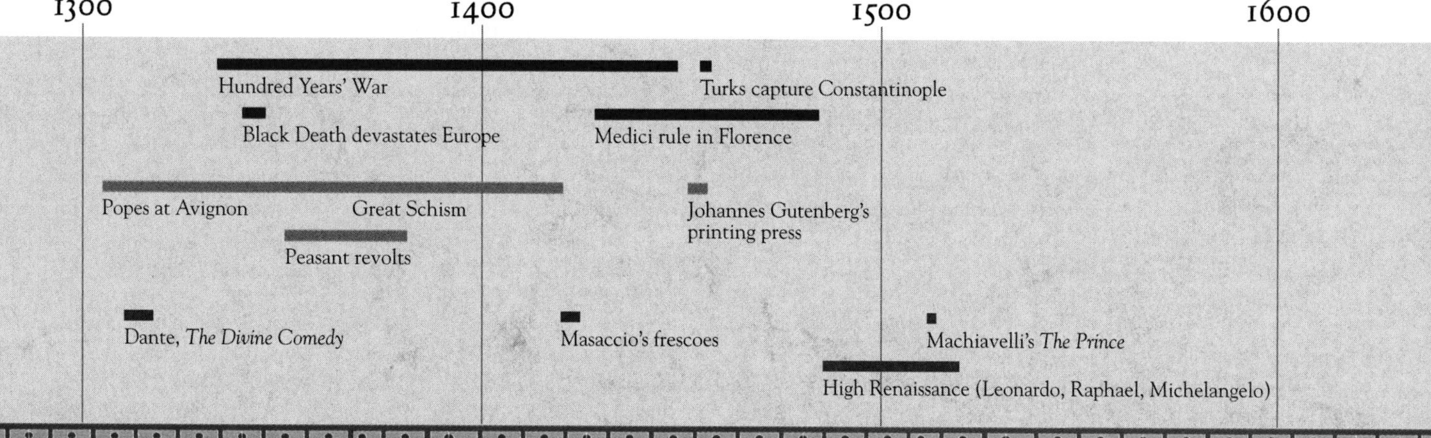

Chapter Notes

1. Quoted in H. S. Lucas, "The Great European Famine of 1315, 1316, and 1317," *Speculum* 5 (1930): 359.
2. Quoted in David Herlihy, *The Black Death and the Transformation of the West*, ed. Samuel K. Cohn, Jr. (Cambridge, Mass., 1997), p. 9.
3. Jean Froissart, *Chronicles*, ed. and trans. Geoffrey Brereton (Harmondsworth, 1968), p. 111.
4. Quoted in Susan Stuard, "Dominion of Gender: Women's Fortunes in the High Middle Ages," in Renate Bridenthal, Claudia Koonz, and Susan Stuard, eds., *Becoming Visible: Women in European History*, 2d ed. (Boston, 1987), p. 169.
5. Froissart, *Chronicles*, p. 89.
6. Niccolò Machiavelli, *The Prince*, trans. David Wootton (Indianapolis, 1995), p. 48.
7. Ibid., p. 55.
8. Ibid., p. 27.
9. Quoted in Robert Coogan, *Babylon on the Rhone: A Translation of Letters by Dante, Petrarch, and Catherine of Siena* (Washington, D.C., 1983), p. 115.
10. Quoted in Jacob Burckhardt, *The Civilization of the Renaissance in Italy*, trans. S. G. C. Middlemore (London, 1960), p. 81.
11. Baldassare Castiglione, *The Book of the Courtier*, trans. Charles S. Singleton (Garden City, N.Y., 1959), pp. 288–89.
12. Quoted in De Lamar Jensen, *Renaissance Europe* (Lexington, Mass., 1981), p. 94.
13. Gene Brucker, ed., *Two Memoirs of Renaissance Florence* (New York, 1967), p. 132.
14. Quoted in Margaret L. King, *Women of the Renaissance* (Chicago, 1991), p. 3.
15. Giovanni Pico della Mirandola, *Oration on the Dignity of Man*, in E. Cassirer, P. O. Kristeller, J. H. Randall, Jr., eds., *The Renaissance Philosophy of Man* (Chicago, 1948), p. 225.
16. Ibid., pp. 247–49.
17. W. H. Woodward, *Vittorino da Feltre and Other Humanist Educators* (Cambridge, 1897), p. 102.
18. Quoted in Iris Origo, "The Education of Renaissance Man," in *The Light of the Past* (New York, 1959), p. 136.

19. Dante Alighieri, *The Divine Comedy*, trans. Dorothy Sayers (New York, 1962), "Paradise," Canto XXXIII, line 145.
20. Christine de Pizan, *The Book of the City of Ladies*, trans. E. Jeffrey Richards (New York, 1982), pp. 83–84.
21. Quoted in Elizabeth G. Holt, ed., *A Documentary History of Art* (Garden City, N.Y., 1957), 1:286.
22. Quoted in Johan Huizinga, *The Waning of the Middle Ages* (Garden City, N.Y., 1956), p. 265.

Suggested Readings

For a general introduction to the fourteenth and fifteenth centuries, see D. P. Waley, *Later Medieval Europe*, 2d ed. (London, 1985), and G. Holmes, *Europe: Hierarchy and Revolt, 1320–1450* (New York, 1975).

On the Black Death, see P. Ziegler, *The Black Death* (New York, 1969), and D. Herlihy, *The Black Death and the Transformation of the West*, ed. S. K. Cohn, Jr. (Cambridge, Mass., 1997). On the peasant and urban revolts of the fourteenth century, see M. Mollat and P. Wolff, *The Popular Revolutions of the Late Middle Ages* (Winchester, Mass., 1973). Brief but basic works on economic matters are H. A. Miskimin, *The Economy of Early Renaissance Europe, 1300–1460* (New York, 1975), and *The Economy of Later Renaissance Europe, 1460–1600* (New York, 1978).

Recent accounts of the Hundred Years' War include A. Curry, *The Hundred Years' War* (New York, 1993), and R. H. Neillands, *The Hundred Years' War* (New York, 1990). On Joan of Arc, see M. Warner, *Joan of Arc: The Image of Female Heroism* (New York, 1981). On the political history of the fourteenth and fifteenth centuries, see B. Guenée, *States and Rulers in Later Medieval Europe*, trans. J. Vale (Oxford, 1985). Works on individual countries and their rulers include P. M. Kendall, *Louis XI: The Universal Spider* (New York, 1971); J. R. Lander, *Crown and Nobility, 1450–1509* (London, 1976); F. R. H. Du Boulay, *Germany in the Later Middle Ages* (London, 1983); and J. N. Hillgarth, *The Spanish Kingdoms, 1250–1516*, vol. 2, *Castilian Hegemony, 1410–1516* (New York, 1978). Some good works on eastern Europe include P. W. Knoll, *The Rise of the Polish Monarchy* (Chicago, 1972), and C. A. Macartney, *Hungary: A Short History* (Edinburgh, 1962). On the fall of Constantinople, see the classic work by S. Runciman, *The Fall of Constantinople, 1453* (Cambridge, 1965).

The best overall study of the Italian states is L. Martines, *Power and Imagination: City-States in Renaissance Italy* (New York, 1979), although D. Hay and J. Law, *Italy in the Age of the Renaissance* (London, 1989) is also a good, up-to-date survey. The best introduction to Renaissance Florence is G. A. Brucker, *Renaissance Florence*, rev. ed. (New York, 1983). On the Medici period, see J. R. Hale, *Florence and the Medici: The Pattern of Control* (London, 1977). A popular biography of Isabella d'Este is G. Marek, *The Bed and the Throne* (New York, 1976). On the *condottieri*, see M. Mallett, *Mercenaries and Their Masters: Warfare in Renaissance Italy* (Totowa, N.J., 1974). Machiavelli's life can be examined in Q. Skinner, *Machiavelli* (Oxford, 1981).

A good general study of the church in the fourteenth century is F. P. Oakley, *The Western Church in the Later Middle Ages* (Ithaca, N.Y., 1980). On the Avignonese papacy, see Y. Renouard, *The Avignon Papacy, 1305–1403* (London, 1970). Aspects of the Renaissance papacy can be examined in E. Lee, *Sixtus IV and Men of Letters* (Rome, 1978); M. Mallet, *The Borgias* (New York, 1969); and P. Partner, *Renaissance Rome, 1500–1559: A Portrait of a Society* (Berkeley, Calif., 1976).

The classic study of the Italian Renaissance is J. Burckhardt, *The Civilization of the Renaissance in Italy* (London, 1960), first published in 1860. General works on the Renaissance in Europe include D. L. Jensen, *Renaissance Europe*, 2d ed. (Lexington, Mass., 1991); P. Burke, *The European Renaissance: Centres and Peripheries* (Oxford, 1998); E. Breisach, *Renaissance Europe, 1300–1517* (New York, 1973); J. Hale, *The Civilization of Europe in the Renaissance* (New York, 1994); and the classic work by M. P. Gilmore, *The World of Humanism, 1453–1517* (New York, 1962). For a good summary of recent literature on the Renaissance, see P. Burke, *The Renaissance* (New York, 1997). For beautifully illustrated introductions to the Renaissance, see G. Holmes, *Renaissance* (New York, 1996), and M. Aston, ed., *The Panorama of the Renaissance* (New York, 1996).

Numerous facets of social life in the Renaissance are examined in J. R. Hale, *Renaissance Europe: The Individual and Society* (London, 1971); B. Pullan, *Rich and Poor in Renaissance Venice* (Cambridge, Mass., 1971); and G. Ruggiero, *The Boundaries of Eros: Sex Crime and Sexuality in Renaissance Venice* (Oxford, 1985). On family and marriage, see D. Herlihy, *The Family in Renaissance Italy* (St. Louis, 1974); the valuable C. Klapisch-Zuber, *Women, Family, and Ritual in Renaissance Italy* (Chicago, 1985); and the well-told story by G. Brucker, *Giovanni and Lusanna: Love and Marriage in Renaissance Florence* (Berkeley, Calif., 1986). Women are examined in M. L. King, *Women of the Renaissance* (Chicago, 1991).

Brief introductions to Renaissance humanism can be found in D. Kelley, *Renaissance Humanism* (Boston, 1991), and C. G. Nauert, Jr., *Humanism and the Culture of Renaissance Europe* (Cambridge, 1995). The fundamental work on fifteenth-century civic humanism is H. Baron, *The Crisis of the Early Italian Renaissance*, 2d ed. (Princeton, N.J., 1966). The impact of printing is exhaustively examined in E. Eisenstein, *The Printing Press as an Agent of Change*, 2 vols. (New York, 1978). The best work on Christine de Pizan is by C. C. Willard, *Christine de Pizan: Her Life and Works* (New York, 1984). Good surveys of Renaissance art include R. Turner, *Renaissance Florence: The Invention of a New Art* (New York, 1997); F. Hartt, *History of Italian Renaissance Art*, 4th ed. (Englewood Cliffs, N.J., 1994); and L. Murray, *The High Renaissance* (New York, 1967). Also of value is B. Cole, *The Renaissance Artist at Work from Pisano to Titian* (London, 1983).

For additional reading, go to InfoTrac College Edition, your online research library at http://web1.infotrac-college.com

Enter the search terms "Middle Ages" using the Subject Guide.

Enter the search terms "Black Death" using Keywords.

Enter the search terms "Medieval England" using Keywords.

Enter the search term "Renaissance" using the Subject Guide.

Enter the search term "Machiavelli" using Keywords.

REFLECTION

NEW PATTERNS OF CIVILIZATION

In Part II of this book, we examined the period that followed the collapse of the civilizations of antiquity down to the end of the fifteenth century, a date that marks the beginning of the European Age of Exploration and the inauguration of a new stage of world history. During this period of over one thousand years, a number of significant forces were at work in human society. The concept of civilization gradually spread from such heartland regions as the Middle East, the Mediterranean basin, the South Asian subcontinent, and China into new areas of the world—to sub-Saharan Africa, to central and western Europe, to Southeast Asia, and even to the islands of Japan, off the eastern edge of the Eurasian landmass. Across the oceans, unique but advanced civilizations began to take shape in the Americas. In the meantime, the vast migration of peoples continued, leading not only to bitter conflict but also to increased interchange of technology as well as ideas. The end result was the transformation of separate and distinct cultures and civilizations into an increasingly complex and vast world system embracing not only technology and trade, but also ideas and religious beliefs. Although this world system did not by any means extend to all the peoples and societies in the world—the Amerindian civilizations in the New World were almost certainly totally isolated from it, as were peoples living in stateless societies in various parts of Africa and Asia—its network of goods and ideas extended from the Atlantic to the Pacific and created (in a phrase often used today) an interdependent world, in which the economic livelihood, the physical well-being, and even the religious beliefs of one people were linked to the fate of other peoples often living thousands of miles away.

What explains this explosion in human activity? Certainly one answer is the advance in technology. Better technology, in the form of improved irrigation methods, the introduction of new crops, and the increased use of the iron plow, led to a substantial rise in food production, thus creating wealth that could be used for the purchase of other goods. Improved technology also contributed to advances in ship construction and navigational techniques. Other factors were the mastery of monsoon patterns in the Indian Ocean and the domestication of the camel in North Africa and the Middle East. The wealth brought about by increased trade undoubtedly helped to stimulate the demand for new luxury goods and other commodities, many of which could only be imported from foreign countries. During the first millennium C.E., the great trade routes of the traditional world—the Silk Road from China to the Middle East and then on to the Mediterranean, the caravan trade across the Sahara, and the maritime network that stretched across the Indian Ocean—all reached their maturity.

As had been the case during antiquity, the Middle East was the heart of this activity. During the first centuries of the first millennium C.E., trade passing through the region declined as a result of the collapse of the Han dynasty and the Roman Empire, but it began to revive in the sixth century and then spurted forward with the rise of the Tang in China and the gradual revival of societies in the Mediterranean. The Arab Empire, which took shape after the death of Muhammad in the early seventh century, provided the key link in the revived trade routes through the region. Muslim traders—both Arab and Berber—opened contacts with West African societies south of the Sahara, while their ships followed the monsoon winds eastward as far as the Spice Islands in Southeast Asia. Nomads from Central Asia carried goods back and forth along the Silk Road between the Middle East and China. For the next several hundred years, the great cities of the Middle East—Mecca, Damascus, and Baghdad—became among the wealthiest in the known world. The great Chinese city of Chang'an lay at the eastern extremity of the Silk Road as it snaked eastward across Central Asia.

Islam's contributions to the human experience during this period were cultural and technological as well as economic. Muslim philosophers preserved the works of the ancient Greeks for posterity, Muslim scientists and mathematicians made new discoveries about the nature of the universe and the human body, and Arab cartographers and historians mapped the known world and speculated about the fundamental forces in human society. The mosques in Córdoba and Cairo were built with techniques unknown to the architects and engineers of medieval Europe.

But the Middle East was not the only or necessarily even the primary contributor to world trade and civilization during this period. While the Arab Empire became the linchpin of trade between the Mediterranean and eastern and southern Asia, a new center of primary importance in world trade was emerging in East Asia, focused on China. China had been a major participant in regional trade during the Han dynasty, when its silks were already being transported to Rome via Central Asia, but its role had declined after the fall of the Han. Now, with the rise of the great Tang and Song dynasties, China reemerged as a major commercial power in East Asia, trading by sea with Southeast Asia and Japan and by land with the nomadic peoples of Central Asia. In general, overland trade was carried on by non-Chinese peoples in Central Asia, but the Chinese themselves became directly involved in the maritime trade with the countries in the South Seas.

By now, China was not only a regional economic power, but a global one as well. The Silk Road through Turkestan became one of the most important trade routes of the era, and during the Ming dynasty, Chinese fleets briefly sailed across the Indian Ocean as far as the Red Sea and the eastern coast of Africa.

Like the Middle East, China was also a prime source of new technology. From China came paper, printing, and

TRADE AND CIVILIZATION

Traditionally, historians have viewed the great civilizations that arose in the classical era as essentially autonomous entities, each representing the product of its own local environment. In Part I, we sought to qualify that assumption by pointing out that even in antiquity, the great river valley civilizations had already begun to learn from each other. While each civilization was unique and distinctive, they had all been influenced in various ways by developments taking place beyond their frontiers.

Between 500 and 1500, the level of interdependence among human societies began to intensify, as three major trade routes—the Indian Ocean, the Silk Road, and the trans-Saharan caravan route—began to create the framework for a single world trade system. New technology, new crops, and new ideas crossed from one end of the known world to the other. Contacts occurred in the realm of technology as in that of ideas, including inventions such as paper, the compass, and gunpowder; crops such as sugar, cotton, and spices; and great religious systems such as Buddhism, Hinduism, Christianity, and Islam. One interesting aspect of this process was the close relationship between missionary activities and trade. Buddhist merchants first brought the teachings of Siddhartha Gautama to China, and Muslim traders carried the words of the prophet Muhammad to Southeast Asia and sub-Saharan Africa. At the same time, Christian missionaries may have brought the first accurate knowledge of silk manufacturing from China to the Mediterranean.

What were the major causes of the rapid expansion of trade during this period? One key factor was the introduction of new technology in the field of transportation. The development of the compass, improved techniques in mapmaking and shipbuilding, and greater knowledge of wind patterns all contributed to the expansion of maritime trade far from familiar shores. Caravan trade, once carried by wheeled chariots or on the backs of oxen, now used the camel as the preferred beast of burden through the parched deserts of Africa and the Middle East. With its ability to store considerable amounts of food and water in its hump, the camel was well equipped to handle the arduous conditions of the desert and soon became the standard means by which nomads carried goods from oasis to oasis on the long trek to their eventual destination.

Another factor in the expansion of commerce during this period was the appearance of several multinational empires that created zones of stability and affluence in key areas from North Africa eastward toward the Pacific. Central to the process was the emergence of the empire of the Abbasids in the Middle East, which created, in the words of the historian K. N. Chaudhuri, "an enormously powerful zone of economic consumption" throughout the region. To the east was China, which reached a zenith of prosperity during the Tang and Song dynasties; to the west was Europe, slowly emerging from the collapse of the Roman Empire. In the thirteenth century, the Mongol invasions brought this era to an end but then created a new era of peace and stability that lasted for over a century and fostered long-distance trade throughout the known world.

The global impact of the expansion in international commerce was enormous. Although humans still had only a limited awareness of their fellow creatures (Europeans, after all, still knew almost nothing about Chinese civilization), the stage was set for a more dramatic period of expansion in the near future.

ARAB MERCHANTS IN A CARAVAN. By land or by sea, Arab trade routes extended over half the globe. The world of Islam and the camel, both portrayed in this thirteenth-century miniature, were essential components of Muslim commercial ventures.

FEUDAL ORDERS AROUND THE WORLD

When we use the word *feudalism*, we usually think of European knights on horseback clad in iron coats and armed with sword and lance. However, between 800 and 1500, a form of social organization that a later generation of historians called feudalism developed in different parts of the world. By the term *feudalism*, these historians meant a decentralized political order in which local lords owed loyalty and provided military service to a king or more powerful lord. In Europe, a feudal order based on lords and vassals arose between 800 and 900 and flourished for the next four hundred years.

In Japan, a feudal order much like that found in Europe developed between 800 and 1500. By the end of the ninth century, powerful nobles in the countryside, while owing a loose loyalty to the Japanese emperor, began to exercise political and legal power in their own extensive lands. In order to protect their property and security, these nobles retained samurai, or warriors who owed loyalty to the nobles and provided military service for them. Like knights in Europe, the samurai followed a warrior code and fought on horseback, clad in iron. However, they carried a sword and bow and arrow rather than a sword and lance.

In some respects, the political relationships among the Indian states beginning in the fifth century took on the character of the feudal system that emerged in Europe in the Middle Ages. Like medieval European lords, local Indian rajas were technically vassals of the king, but unlike in European feudalism, the relationship was not a contractual one. Still, the Indian model became highly complex, with "inner" and "outer" vassals, depending on their physical or political proximity to the king, and "greater" or "lesser" vassals, depending on their power and influence. As in Europe, the vassals themselves often had vassals. The one constant factor was the perennial state of rivalry and civil strife that characterized the vassals' relationships and plagued the lives of ordinary Indians.

A KNIGHT'S EQUIPMENT. Pictured here is a charging European knight with his equipment. The introduction of the high saddle, stirrups, and larger horses allowed horsemen to wear heavier armor and to wield long lances. Compare the equipment of the European knight to that of the samurai warrior on page 301.

In the Valley of Mexico, the Aztecs developed a political system between 1300 and 1500 that bore some similarities to the Japanese, Indian, and European feudal orders. Although the Aztec king was a powerful, authoritarian ruler, the local rulers of lands outside the capital city were allowed considerable freedom. However, they did pay tribute to the king and also provided him with military forces. Unlike the knights and samurai of Europe and Japan, however, Aztec warriors were armed with sharp knives made of stone and spears of wood fitted with razor-sharp blades cut from stone.

the compass as well as gunpowder. The double-hulled Chinese junks that entered the Indian Ocean during the Ming dynasty were slow and cumbersome but extremely seaworthy and capable of carrying substantial quantities of goods over long distances. Among China's other contributions were porcelain, chess, the mechanical clock, and the iron stirrup. Many such inventions arrived in Europe by way of India or the Middle East, and therefore their Chinese origins were unknown in the West.

Increasing trade on a regional or global basis also led to the exchange of ideas. Buddhism was brought to China by merchants, and Islam first arrived in sub-Saharan Africa and the Indonesian archipelago in the same manner. In their new environments, these religions initially had an impact mainly on other merchant groups and in the cities, but in some cases they gradually gained favor in the countryside. Sometimes this was the result of support from kings or princes, who viewed conversion to the new faith as politically or economically advantageous. Not all religions, of course, succeeded in transplanting themselves. Although a small community of Christians established roots in Central Asia and China, their religion was never able to make the transition to a mass faith.

Merchants were not the only way religious and cultural ideas spread, however. Sometimes migration, conquest, or relatively peaceful processes played a part. The case of the Bantu-speaking peoples in Central Africa is apparently an example of peaceful expansion; while Islam sometimes followed the path of Arab warriors, although they apparently rarely imposed their religion by force on the local population. In some instances, as with the Mongols, the conquerors made no effort to convert others to their own religions. Christian monks, motivated by missionary fervor, converted many of the peoples of central and eastern Europe. Roman Catholic monks brought Latin Christianity to the Germanic and western Slavic peoples, while monks from the Byzantine Empire largely converted the southern and eastern Slavic populations to Eastern Orthodox Christianity.

How precisely did the exchange of ideas and beliefs work during this period? According to Jerry Bentley, author of *Old World Encounters: Cross-Cultural Contacts and Exchanges in Pre-Modern Times*, the process was quite complex and varied considerably, depending on the time and place. When conversion to a different religion did occur, it usually took place over a protracted period of time and was undertaken primarily for practical reasons. Those who attempted to promote conversions often used incentives or various forms of punishment for noncompliance, such as exemption from taxation for Muslims. One way to facilitate conversions was to use the syncretic technique—to relate or identify new beliefs and rituals to familiar ones, as Buddhists did by adopting Daoist concepts in China.

Attempts at conversion did not always work. Sometimes new religions were resisted fiercely, as the Christians in the Balkans and Spain resisted Islam. On the other hand, conversion to Christianity was resisted in the Middle East during the Crusades and in Central Asia during the Mongol era. In general, Islam and Buddhism were the most successful. Islam spread quite quickly and readily throughout the Middle East and Central Asia as well as in much of North Africa, while Buddhism took root in China, Japan, and Southeast Asia.

Why were conversion efforts successful in some areas but not in others? In the case of Islam, successful conversion was often the result of strong state sponsorship, as well as a variety of incentives such as exemption from the poll tax and access to various means of livelihood. Islam also undoubtedly benefited from its egalitarian character and its association with material rewards. This was apparently the case in Africa as well as in much of Central Asia. The success of Buddhism in China and Southeast Asia can be partly ascribed to state support, but also to its salvationist message in societies that did not possess any other form of universal world religion. In general, it seems clear that conversion was easier and much more likely to succeed in societies that did not already possess a world religion. Where such religions already existed, as in India and much of Europe, conversion to Islam was less likely. Followers of Gautama Buddha had the same experience in India.

In any event, as Bentley points out, conversion usually was an extended process, even when it did occur. Although the conversion to Islam in much of the Middle East was relatively rapid, it took much longer among the Berbers. Buddhism took several hundred years to spread beyond the urban community in China and among the Mongol tribal peoples.

Even when conversion did take place, key elements of the core doctrine were often changed to adapt to new circumstances. Buddhism in China took on a strong local character, as did Islam in Southeast Asia, where it was forced to coexist with existing spirit beliefs. The practice of Christianity was much different in the Byzantine Empire than it was in areas controlled by the pope in Rome. In the end, religion took on much of the color of local society.

The same can be said about the transfer of political and social institutions from one society to another. Throughout this period, ruling elites in societies along the periphery of the major empires borrowed liberally from the political and social systems of their more powerful neighbors as a means of strengthening their own power and status. Confucian ideology, Muslim law, and the Indian god-king concept were also useful in hastening the state-building process. Similarly, the influence of patriarchal values emanating from China, India, and the Middle East gradually took root in the small societies in Southeast Asia and sub-Saharan Africa. Still, impact was always limited by local conditions. In Japan, Korea, and Vietnam, Confucian values were significantly altered to fit the local environment, as were Indian values after crossing the Bay of Bengal to the rising states of Southeast Asia. In Africa, Muslim travelers were sometimes scandalized by the degree of freedom possessed by women in states that had already accepted the word of the Koran.

Another characteristic of the period between 500 and 1500 C.E. was the almost constant migration of nomadic and seminomadic peoples. Dynamic forces in the Gobi Desert, Central Asia, the Arabian peninsula, and Central Africa provoked vast numbers of peoples to abandon their homelands and seek their livelihood elsewhere. Sometimes the migration was peaceful, as was apparently the case with the Bantu-speaking peoples in Central Africa. More often than not, however, migration produced violent conflict and sometimes invasion and subjugation. Peoples had been moving since the earliest times, as human communities shifted their habitat in search of grazing lands, herds, or fertile lands for agriculture, and migration continued to be a major factor in this period. As had been the case during antiquity, the most active source of migration was Central Asia. From here, Turkic-speaking peoples spilled over the Hindu Kush into northern India, southwest into Persia, and farther west into the Balkans in southeastern Europe. Later, Central Asia gave birth to an even more fearsome force in the form of the Mongols. Mongol expansion began with the unification of Mongol tribes in the Gobi Desert by Genghis Khan and culminated in the advance of Mongolian armies to the gates of central Europe and the conquest of China in the thirteenth century. Wherever they went, they left a train of enormous destruction and loss of life. Contemporaries recount that entire cities were laid waste, and their populations massacred and irrigation networks destroyed. Inadvertently, the Mongols were also the source of a new wave of epidemics that swept through much of Europe and the Middle East in the fourteenth century. The spread of the plague—known at the time as the Black Death—took much of the population of Europe to an early grave.

But there was another side to the era of nomadic expansion. Often, as historian Thomas J. Barfield has noted, the nomadic peoples had a symbiotic relationship with the sedentary societies, propping up governments like the Tang dynasty in China in order to protect their source of income. Once nomadic warriors completed their conquests, they settled down to become administrators. Often the results were constructive. The spread of Islam across the Middle East and North Africa not only introduced millions of people to a dynamic new faith but brought a measure of political stability and economic prosperity to the area that it had not possessed since the fall of the Persian Empire. German migrations and Viking incursions contributed to the creation of dynamic new societies in Europe, while Turkish invasions led to the rise of states in the Anatolian Peninsula and North India.

Even the invasions of the Mongols—the "scourge of God" as Europeans of the thirteenth and fourteenth centuries called them—had constructive as well as destructive consequences. After their initial conquests, for a brief period of three generations, the Mongols provided an avenue for trade throughout the most extensive empire (known as the Pax Mongolica) the world had yet seen. When the pope dispatched envoys to the imperial court in Mongolia in the mid-thirteenth century, it was the first time Europeans had traveled the entire distance by land to East Asia.

What had caused this vast movement of peoples? Probably a number of factors were involved, but perhaps the major ones were ecological—changes in the climate or the exhaustion of the land by population pressure. Exhaustion of the land may have driven the Bantu peoples from their original habitat in the Niger River valley and forced the Aztecs and related Amerindian communities into the Valley of Mexico. Other peoples, such as the Thai and the Burmese, may have been forced to move into Southeast Asia because they in turn had been displaced by new arrivals in their own territories.

The Mongols were the last, and arguably the greatest, of the nomadic peoples who came thundering out of the steppes of Central Asia, pillaging and conquering the territories of their adversaries all the way to the shores of the South Pacific and the plains of eastern Europe. What caused this extraordinary burst of energy, and why were the Mongols so much more successful than their predecessors? Historians are divided. Some have suggested that drought and overpopulation may have depleted the available pasture on the steppes. Others have cited the ambition and genius of Genghis Khan, who was able to arouse a sense of personal loyalty unusual in a society where commitments were ordinarily tribal in nature. Still others point to his reliance on the organizational unit known as the *ordos*, described by the historian S. A. M. Adshead as "a system of restructuring tribes into decimal units whose top

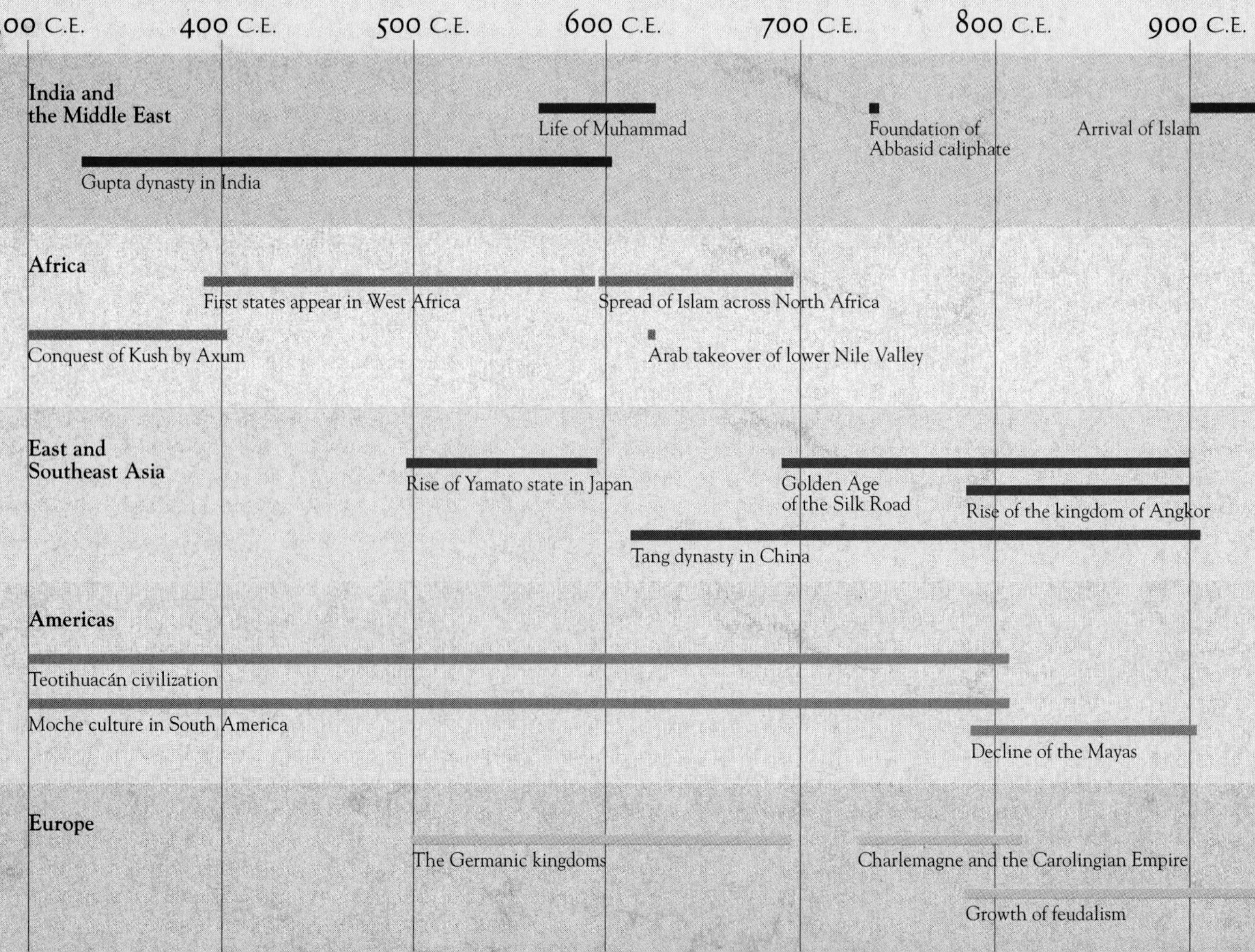

level of leadership was organized on bureaucratic lines." Although the *ordos* system had been used by other nomadic peoples before them, the Mongols applied it to create disciplined military units that were especially effective against the mobile tactics of their rivals on the steppes and devastating against the relatively immobile armies of the sedentary states in their path. Once organized, the Mongols used their superior horsemanship and blitzkrieg tactics effectively, while taking advantage of divisions within the enemy ranks and borrowing more advanced military technology. Once in power, however, the Mongols' underlying weaknesses eventually proved fatal. Unlike some of their predecessors, the Mongols had difficulty making the transition from the nomadic life of the steppes to the sedentary life of conquered peoples. Still, although the Mongol era was a relatively brief interlude in the long sweep of human history, it was rich in consequences.

The approximately thousand-year period following the destruction of the ancient empires brought about enormous changes in human society. During the era of Mongol expansion there was widespread death and suffering throughout the known world. At the same time, by the early fifteenth century the world had witnessed a significant expansion in the technological and material capacity of human societies and in the depth of contact among them. The era of widespread peace brought about as the result of the Mongol conquests also inaugurated what one scholar has described as the "idea of the unified conceptualization of the globe," creating a "basic information circuit" that spread commodities, ideas, and inventions from one end of the Eurasian supercontinent to the other. The way was prepared for a new stage of world history.

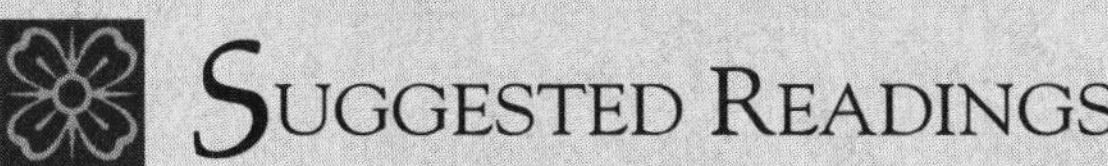

SUGGESTED READINGS

The importance of international trade in this period is discussed in P. D. Curtin, *Cross-Cultural Trade in World History* (Cambridge, 1984); Janet L. Abu-Lughod, *Before European Hegemony, the World System A.D. 1250–1350* (New York, 1989); M. Adas, ed., *Islamic and European Expansion: The Forging of a Global Order* (Philadelphia, 1993); and J. D. Tracy, *The Political Economy of Merchant Empires: State Power and World Trade, 1350–1750* (New York, 1991). For an informative study on the exchange of ideas and beliefs, see J. H. Bentley, *Old World Encounters: Cross-Cultural Contacts and Exchanges in Pre-Modern Times* (New York, 1993). The migration of nomadic peoples is examined in S. A. M. Adshead, *Central Asia in World History* (New York, 1993), and T. S. Barfield, *The Perilous Frontier: Nomadic Empires and China* (Cambridge, Mass., 1989).

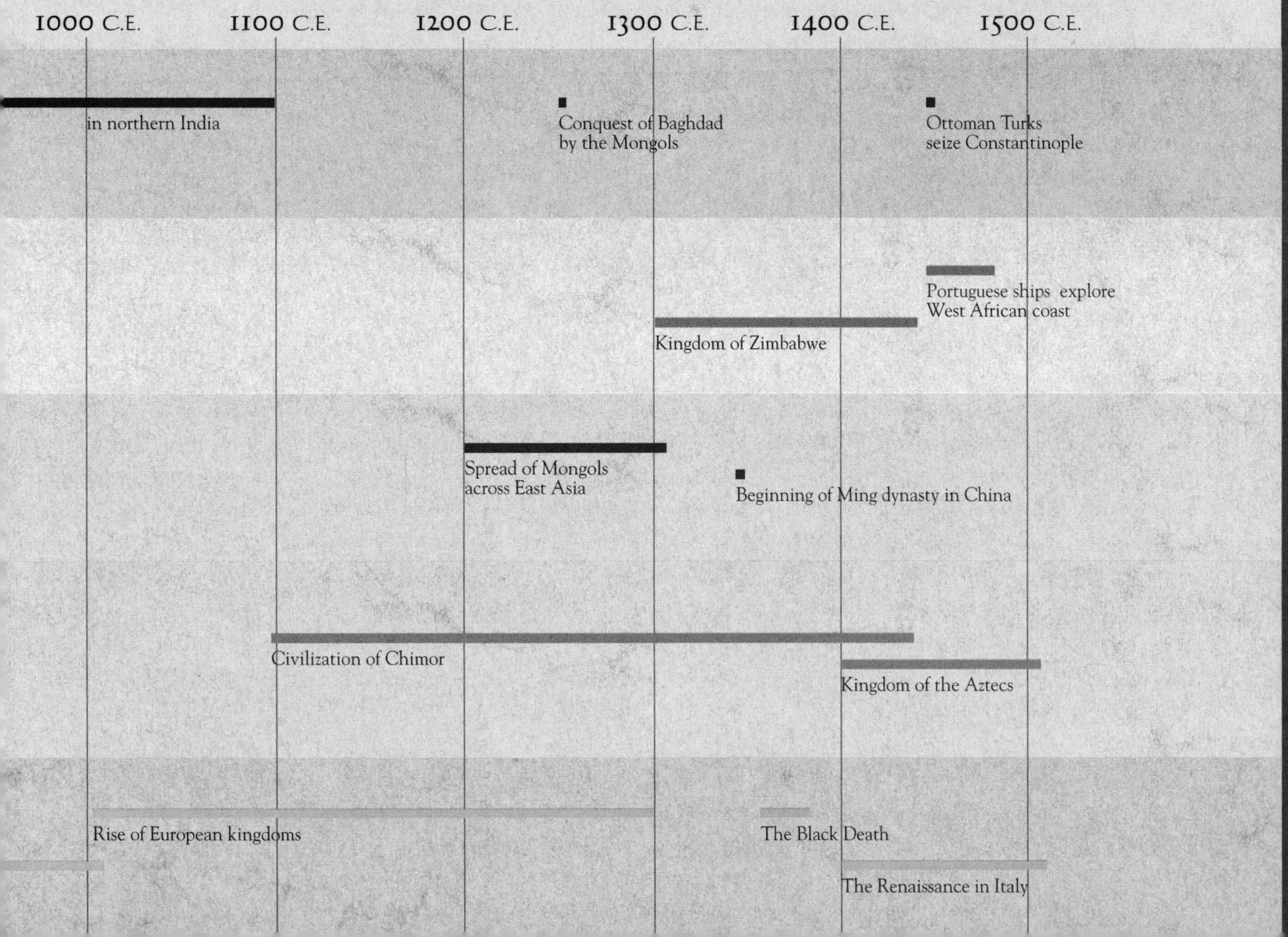

1000 C.E. 1100 C.E. 1200 C.E. 1300 C.E. 1400 C.E. 1500 C.E.

in northern India

Conquest of Baghdad by the Mongols

Ottoman Turks seize Constantinople

Portuguese ships explore West African coast

Kingdom of Zimbabwe

Spread of Mongols across East Asia

Beginning of Ming dynasty in China

Civilization of Chimor

Kingdom of the Aztecs

Rise of European kingdoms

The Black Death

The Renaissance in Italy

PART III

THE EMERGENCE OF NEW WORLD PATTERNS (1500–1800)

Beginning in the late fifteenth century, a new force entered the world scene in the form of a revived Europe. The period of history known as the early modern era (1500–1800) was marked in Europe by an explosion of scientific knowledge and the appearance of a new secular ideology that emphasized the power of human beings to dominate nature and improve their material surroundings. After the breakdown of Christian unity in the Reformation era, Europeans engaged in a vigorous period of state building that resulted in the creation of independent monarchies in western and central Europe, which formed the basis for a new European state system.

The rise of early modern Europe had an immediate as well as a long-term impact on the rest of the world. The first stage began with the discovery of the Americas by Christopher Columbus in 1492 and the equally important voyages of Vasco da Gama and Ferdinand Magellan into the Indian and Pacific Oceans. These voyages and those that followed—collectively known as the Age of Discovery or Age of Exploration—not only injected European sea power into new areas of the world, but also vastly extended the maritime trade network, until for the first time it literally encircled the globe. Some historians have labeled this period the beginning of an era of European dominance.

Significant as it was, however, the emergence of Europe as a major player on the world stage was by no means the only important feature of this period. An excessive emphasis on the expanding European civilization tends to overlook the fact that other areas of the world were realizing impressive achievements of their own. Two great new Islamic empires, the Ottomans in Turkey and the Safavids in Persia, arose in the Middle East, while a third—the Mughals—unified the Indian subcontinent for the first time in nearly two thousand years. The religion of Islam was now firmly established in Africa south of the Sahara, and as far east as the Indonesian archipelago.

Another area of the world where the level of achievement was little affected by the European revival was East Asia. Portuguese merchants reached the coast of China in the early sixteenth century and landed on the islands of Japan a generation later. Merchants and missionaries from various European countries were active in both countries by the end of the century. But the ruling authorities in China and Japan, like their counterparts in the mainland states in Southeast Asia, became increasingly wary of the impact of Europeans activities on their own societies, and by the eighteenth century the Western presence in the region had markedly declined.

The first thrust of European expansion, then, significantly changed the shape of the world, but it did not firmly establish European dominance. China remained, in the eyes of many, the most advanced and sophisticated civilization on the face of the earth, and its achievements were imitated by its neighbors and admired by philosophers in far-off Europe. The era of Muslim dominance over the seas had come to an end, but Islam was still a force to be reckoned with. The bulk of Africa remained essentially outside the purview of European influence.

CHAPTER

14

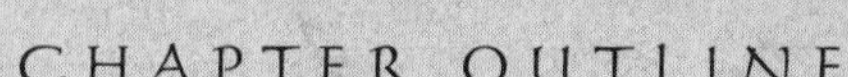

NEW ENCOUNTERS: THE CREATION OF A WORLD MARKET

CHAPTER OUTLINE

- AN AGE OF EXPLORATION AND EXPANSION
- AFRICA IN AN ERA OF TRANSITION
- SOUTHEAST ASIA IN THE ERA OF THE SPICE TRADE
- CONCLUSION

FOCUS QUESTIONS

- Why did Europeans begin to embark on voyages of discovery and expansion at the end of the fifteenth century?
- How did Portugal and Spain acquire their overseas empires, and how did their empires differ?
- How and why did the Europeans expand into Africa, and what were the main consequences of their presence there?
- What were the main features of the African slave trade, and what effects did it have on Africa?
- What were the main characteristics of Southeast Asian civilization, and how was it affected by the coming of Islam and the Europeans?

When a local official asked the Portuguese explorer Vasco da Gama why he had come all the way to India from his homeland in Europe, the latter replied simply, "Christians and spices." Da Gama might have been more accurate if he had reversed the order of his objectives. As it turned out, God was probably much less important than gold and glory to Europeans like himself who participated in the Age of Exploration that was already under way. Still, da Gama's comments at Calicut were an accurate forecast of the future, for his voyage inaugurated an extended period of European expansion into Asia, led by merchant adventurers and missionaries, that lasted for several hundred years and had effects that are still felt today. Eventually, it resulted in a Western takeover of existing trade routes in the Indian Ocean and the establishment of colonies throughout Asia, Africa, and

Latin America. So complete did Western dominance seem that some historians assumed that the peoples of the non-Western world were mere passive recipients in this process, absorbing and assimilating the advanced knowledge of the West and offering nothing in return. Historians writing about the period after 1500 often talked metaphorically about the "impact of the West" and the "response" of non-Western peoples.

That image of impact and response, however, is not an entirely accurate description of what took place between the end of the fifteenth and the end of the eighteenth century. Although European rule was firmly established in Latin America and the island regions of Southeast Asia, traditional governments and institutions elsewhere remained largely intact and, in some areas, notably South Asia and the Middle East, displayed considerable vitality. Moreover, although da Gama and his contemporaries are deservedly famous for their contribution to a new era of maritime commerce that circled the globe, they were not alone in extending the world trade network and transporting goods and ideas from one end of the earth to the other. Islam, too, was on the march, blazing new trails into Southeast Asia and across the Sahara to the civilizations that flourished along the banks of the Niger River. In this chapter we shall turn our attention to the stunning expansion in the scope and volume of commercial and cultural contacts that took place in the generations preceding and following da Gama's historic voyage to India, as well as to the factors that brought about this expansion.

An Age of Exploration and Expansion

The voyage of Vasco da Gama has customarily been seen as a crucial step in the opening of trade routes to the East. In the sense that the voyage was a harbinger of future European participation in the spice trade, this view undoubtedly has merit. In fact, however, as has been pointed out in earlier chapters, the Indian Ocean had been a busy thoroughfare for centuries. The spice trade had been carried on by sea in the region since the days of the legendary Queen of Sheba, and Chinese junks had sailed to the area in search of cloves and nutmeg since the Tang dynasty. Then, during the early fifteenth century, Chinese fleets sailed into the Indian Ocean and all the way to the coast of East Africa in search of trade and alliances (see Chapter 17).

Islam and the Spice Trade

By the fourteenth century, a growing percentage of the spice trade was being transported in Muslim ships sailing from ports in India or the Middle East. Muslims, either Arabs or Indian converts, had taken part in the Indian Ocean trade for centuries, and by the thirteenth century, Islam had established a presence in seaports on the islands of Sumatra and Java and was gradually moving inland. In 1292 the Venetian traveler Marco Polo observed that Muslims were engaging in missionary activity in northern Sumatra: "This kingdom is so much frequented by the Saracen merchants that they have converted the natives to the Law of Mahomet—I mean the townspeople only, for the hill people live for all the world like beasts, and eat human flesh, as well as other kinds of flesh, clean or unclean."[1]

But the major impact of Islam came in the early fifteenth century with the rise of the new sultanate at Malacca, whose founder was a Muslim convert. With its strategic location astride the strait of the same name, Malacca "is a city that was made for commerce; . . . the trade and commerce between the different nations for a thousand leagues on every hand must come to Malacca,"[2] said a sixteenth-century Portuguese visitor. Within a few years, Malacca had surpassed the old Hindu state of Majapahit on the island of Java and become the leading power in the region.

Unfortunately for the Muslim traders who had come to Southeast Asia for the spice trade, others would also covet that trade. Although China's interest in the area would soon come to an end, the arrival of Vasco da Gama's fleet was a sure sign that others would soon follow. Southeast Asia was on the verge of a new era in which outside forces would compete aggressively to exploit the region's vast riches.

A New Player Enters the Game

For almost a millennium, Catholic Europe had been confined to one area. Its one major attempt to expand beyond those frontiers, the Crusades, had largely failed. Of course, Europe had never completely lost contact with the outside world: the goods of Asia and Africa made their way into medieval castles; the works of Muslim philosophers were read in medieval universities; and the Vikings in the

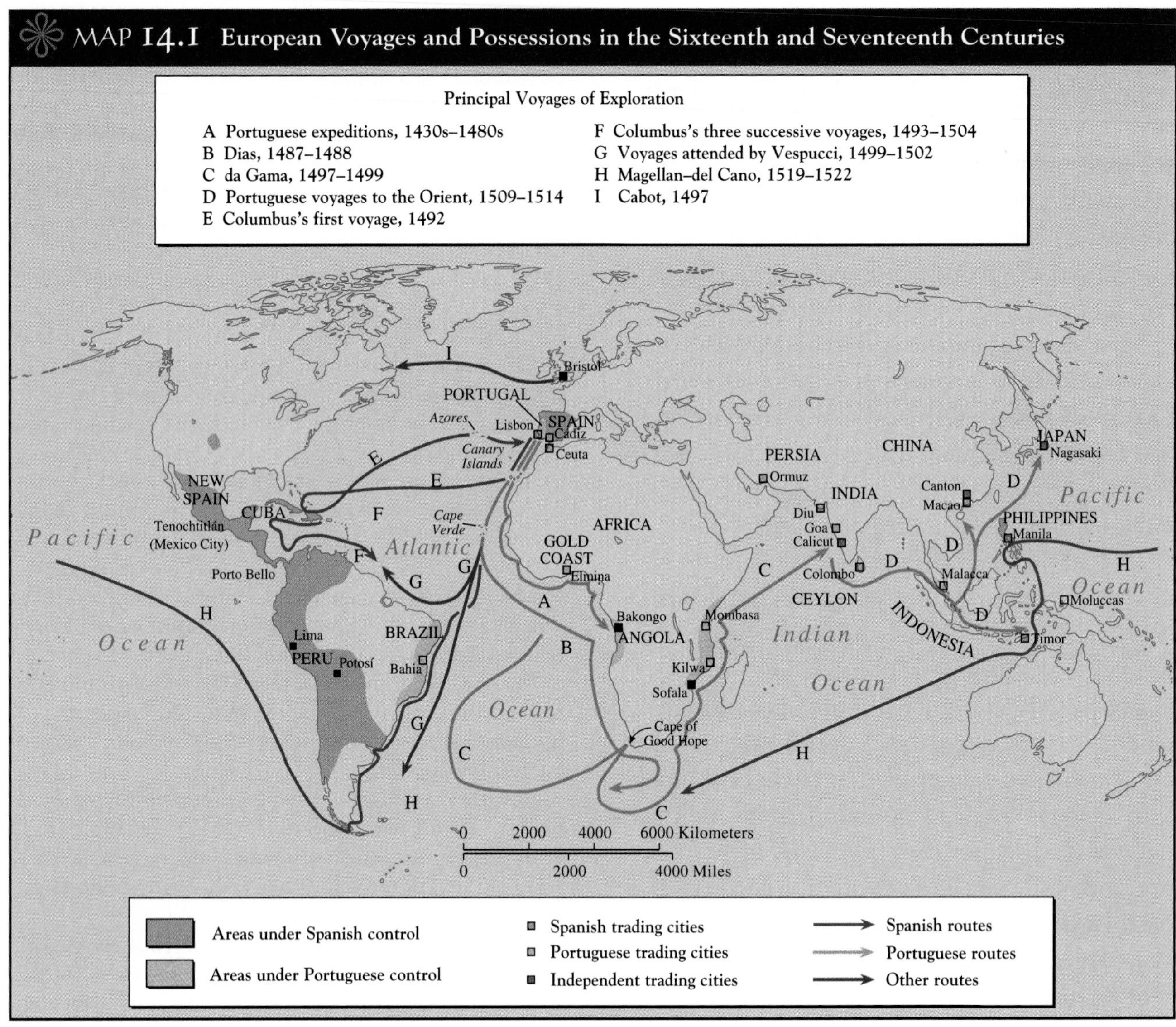

MAP 14.1 European Voyages and Possessions in the Sixteenth and Seventeenth Centuries

ninth and tenth centuries had even made their way to the eastern fringes of North America. Nevertheless, Europe's contacts with non-European civilizations remained limited until the end of the fifteenth century, when Europeans embarked on a remarkable series of overseas journeys. What caused European seafarers to undertake such dangerous voyages to the ends of the earth?

Europeans had long been attracted to the east. In the Middle Ages, myths and legends of an exotic land of great riches and magic were widespread. Although Muslim control of Central Asia cut Europe off from the countries further east, the Mongol conquests in the thirteenth century had reopened the doors. The most famous medieval travelers to the East were the Polos of Venice. In 1271, Nicolò and Maffeo, merchants from Venice, accompanied by Nicolò's son Marco, undertook the lengthy journey to the court of the great Mongol ruler Khubilai Khan (see Chapter 10). As one of the great Khan's ambassadors, Marco traveled to Japan as well and did not return to Italy until 1295. An account of his experiences, the *Travels*, proved to be the most informative of all the descriptions of Asia by medieval European travelers. Others, like the Franciscan friar John Plano Carpini, had preceded the Polos, but in the fourteenth century the conquests of the Ottoman Turks and then the breakup of the Mongol Empire reduced Western traffic to the east. With the closing of the overland routes, a number of people in Europe became interested in the possibility of reaching Asia by sea. Christopher Columbus had a copy of Marco Polo's *Travels* in his possession when he began to envision his epoch-making voyage across the Atlantic Ocean.

An economic motive thus looms large in Renaissance European expansion. The rise of capitalism in Europe was undoubtedly a powerful spur to the process. Merchants, adventurers, and government officials had high hopes of finding precious metals and expanding the areas of trade, especially for the spices of the East. The latter continued to be transported to Europe via Arab intermediaries but were outrageously expensive. Adventurous Europeans did not hesitate to express their desire to share in the wealth. As one Spanish conquistador explained, he and his kind went to the New World to "serve God and His Majesty, to give light to those who were in darkness, and to grow rich, as all men desire to do."[3]

This statement expresses another major reason for the overseas voyages—religious zeal. A crusading mentality was particularly strong in Portugal and Spain, where the Muslims had largely been driven out in the Middle Ages. Contemporaries of Prince Henry the Navigator of Portugal (see the next section) said that he was motivated by "his great desire to make increase in the faith of our Lord Jesus Christ and to bring him all the souls that should be saved." The naval academy established by the prince to promote overseas exploration was subsidized in part by a militantly anti-Muslim Christian brotherhood. Although most scholars believe that the religious motive was secondary to economic considerations, it would be foolish to overlook the genuine desire on the part of both explorers and conquistadors, let alone missionaries, to convert the heathen to Christianity. Hernán Cortés, the conqueror of Mexico, asked his Spanish rulers if it was not their duty to ensure that the native Mexicans "are introduced into and instructed in the holy Catholic faith."[4] Spiritual and secular affairs were closely intertwined in the sixteenth century. No doubt, grandeur and glory as well as plain intellectual curiosity and a spirit of adventure also played some role in European expansion.

If "God, glory, and gold" were the primary motives, what made the voyages possible? First of all, the expansion of Europe was a state enterprise, tied to the growth of centralized monarchies during the Renaissance. By the second half of the fifteenth century, European monarchies had increased both their authority and their resources and were in a position to turn their energies beyond their borders. That meant the invasion of Italy for France, but for Portugal, a state not strong enough to pursue power in Europe, it meant going abroad. The Spanish scene was more complex, since the Spanish monarchy was strong enough by the sixteenth century to pursue power on both the continent and beyond.

At the same time, by the end of the fifteenth century, European states had a level of knowledge and technology that enabled them to achieve a regular series of voyages beyond Europe. Although the highly schematic and symbolic medieval maps were of little help to sailors, the *portolani*, or detailed charts made by medieval navigators and mathematicians in the thirteenth and fourteenth centuries, were more useful. With details on coastal contours, distances between ports, and compass readings, they proved of great value for voyages in European waters. But because the *portolani* were drawn on a flat scale and took no account of the curvature of the earth, they were of little use for longer overseas voyages. Only when seafarers began to venture beyond the coasts of Europe did they begin to accumulate information about the actual shape of the earth. By the end of the fifteenth century, cartography had developed to the point that Europeans possessed fairly accurate maps of the known world.

In addition, Europeans had developed remarkably seaworthy ships as well as new navigational techniques.

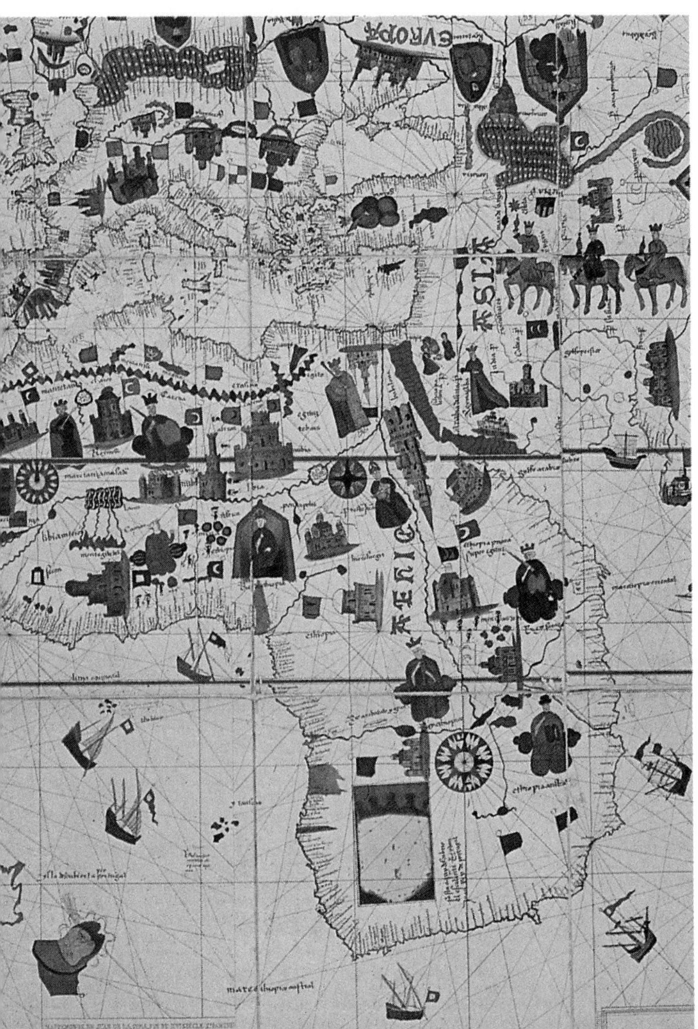

A SIXTEENTH-CENTURY MAP OF AFRICA. Advances in mapmaking also contributed to the European Age of Exploration. Here a section of a world map by the early-sixteenth-century Spanish cartographer Juan de la Cosa shows the continent of Africa. Note the drawing of the legendary Prester John, mentioned in Chapter 8, at the right, and the Portuguese caravels with their lateen sails in the South Atlantic Ocean.

European shipmakers had mastered the use of the sternpost rudder (an import from China) and had learned how to combine the use of lateen sails with a square rig. With these innovations, they could construct ships mobile enough to sail against the wind and engage in naval warfare and also large enough to mount heavy cannon and carry a substantial amount of goods over long distances. Previously, sailors had used a quadrant and their knowledge of the position of the polestar to ascertain their latitude. Below the equator, however, this technique was useless. Only with the assistance of new navigational aids such as the compass and the astrolabe (an astronomical instrument used to measure the altitude of the sun and the stars above the horizon) were they able to explore the high seas with confidence.

A final spur to exploration was the growing knowledge of the wind patterns in the Atlantic Ocean (see Map 14.4, on p. 420). The first European fleets sailing southward along the coast of West Africa had found their efforts to return hindered by the strong winds that blew steadily from the north along the coast. By the late fifteenth century, however, sailors had learned to tack out into the ocean, where they were able to catch westerly winds in the vicinity of the Azores islands that brought them back to the coast of western Europe. Christopher Columbus used this technique in his voyages to the Americas, and others relied on their new knowledge of the winds to round the continent of Africa in search of the Spice Islands.

MALINDI, GATEWAY TO ASIA. The seaport of Malindi, located on the eastern coast of present-day Kenya, was Vasco da Gama's jumping-off point for his historic voyage to India. It was here that he located a navigator willing to guide his fleet eastward across the Indian Ocean. A few years later, the Portuguese erected this monument to mark the spot of his departure. Inspecting the site in this photograph are students from a high school in Mombasa, Kenya's primary port city, about fifty miles to the south. A few yards from this monument is the first church erected by the Portuguese on the eastern coast of Africa.

The Development of a Portuguese Maritime Empire

Portugal took the lead in exploration when it began exploring the coast of Africa under the sponsorship of Prince Henry the Navigator (1394–1460). Prince Henry's motives were a blend of seeking a Christian kingdom as an ally against the Muslims, acquiring new trade opportunities for Portugal, and extending Christianity. In 1419, he founded a school for navigators on the southwestern coast of Portugal. Shortly thereafter, Portuguese fleets began probing southward along the western coast of Africa in search of gold, which had for centuries been carried northward from south of the Atlas Mountains in central Morocco. In 1441, Portuguese ships reached the Senegal River, just north of Cape Verde, and brought home a cargo of black Africans, most of whom were sold as slaves to wealthy buyers elsewhere in Europe. Within a few years, an estimated thousand slaves were shipped annually from the area back to Lisbon. Inadvertently, the Portuguese had found a way to circumvent the traditional trans-Saharan slave route from central Africa to the Mediterranean.

Continuing southward, in 1471 the Portuguese discovered a new source of gold along the southern coast of the hump of West Africa (an area that would henceforth be known to Europeans as the Gold Coast). A few years later, they established contact with the state of Bakongo, near the mouth of the Zaire (Congo) River in Central Africa, and with the inland state of Benin, north of the Gold Coast. To facilitate trade in gold, ivory, and slaves (some of the latter were brought back to Lisbon and others were bartered to local merchants for gold), the Portuguese leased land from local rulers and built stone forts along the coast.

Hearing reports of a route to India around the southern tip of Africa, Portuguese sea captains continued their probing. In 1487, Bartolomeu Dias took advantage of westerly winds in the South Atlantic to round the Cape of Good Hope, but he feared a mutiny from his crew and returned home without continuing onward. Ten years later, a fleet under the command of Vasco da Gama rounded the cape and stopped at several ports controlled by Muslim merchants along the coast of East Africa, including Sofala, Kilwa, and Mombasa. Then, having located a Muslim navigator who was familiar with seafaring in the region, da Gama's fleet crossed the Arabian Sea and arrived off the port of Calicut on the southwestern coast of India, on May 18, 1498. The Portuguese crown had sponsored da Gama's voyage with the clear objective of destroying the Muslim monopoly over the spice trade, a monopoly that had been intensified by the Ottoman conquest of Constantinople in 1453 (see Chapter 16). Calicut was a major entrepôt on the long route from the Spice Islands to the Mediterranean Sea, but the ill-informed Europeans believed it was the source of the spices themselves. They had also heard there was a Chris-

THE PORTUGUESE CONQUEST OF MALACCA

In 1511, a Portuguese fleet led by Afonso de Albuquerque attacked the Muslim sultanate at Malacca, on the west coast of the Malay peninsula. Occupation of the port gave the Portuguese control over the strategic Strait of Malacca and the route to the Spice Islands. In this passage, Albuquerque tells his men the reasons for the attack. Note that he sees control of Malacca as a way to reduce the power of the Muslim world. The relevance of economic wealth to military power continues to underlie conflicts among nations today. The Pacific War in the 1940s, for example, began as a result of a conflict over control of the rich resources of Southeast Asia.

THE COMMENTARIES OF THE GREAT AFONSO DE ALBUQUERQUE, SECOND VICEROY OF INDIA

Although there be many reasons which I could allege in favor of our taking this city and building a fortress therein to maintain possession of it, two only will I mention to you, on this occasion. . . .

The first is the great service which we shall perform to Our Lord in casting the Moors out of this country. . . . If we can only achieve the task before us, it will result in the Moors resigning India altogether to our rule, for the greater part of them—or perhaps all of them—live upon the trade of this country and are become great and rich, and lords of extensive treasures. . . . For when we were committing ourselves to the business of cruising in the Straits (of the Red Sea), where the King of Portugal had often ordered me to go (for it was there that His Highness considered we could cut down the commerce which the Moors of Cairo, of Mecca, and of Judah, carry on with these parts), Our Lord for his service thought right to lead us hither, for when Malacca is taken the places on the Straits must be shut up, and they will never more be able to introduce their spiceries into those places.

And the other reason is the additional service which we shall render to the King D. Manuel in taking this city, because it is the headquarters of all the spiceries and drugs which the Moors carry every year hence to the Straits without our being able to prevent them from so doing; but if we deprive them of this their ancient market there, there does not remain for them a single port, nor a single situation, so commodious in the whole of these parts, where they can carry on their trade in these things. . . . I hold it as very certain that if we take this trade of Malacca away out of their hands, Cairo and Mecca are entirely ruined, and to Venice will no spiceries be conveyed except that which her merchants go and buy in Portugal.

tian community in the area, supposedly established by the apostle Thomas in the first century C.E.

On arriving in Calicut, da Gama announced to his surprised hosts that he had arrived in search of "Christians and spices." He did not find the first, but he did find the second. Although he lost two ships en route, da Gama's remaining vessels returned to Europe with their holds filled with ginger and cinnamon, a cargo that earned the investors a profit of several thousand percent.

During the next years, the Portuguese set out to gain control of the spice trade. In 1510, Admiral Afonso de Albuquerque established his headquarters at Goa, on the western coast of India south of present-day Bombay. From there the Portuguese raided Arab shippers, provoking the following comment from an Arab source: "[The Portuguese] took about seven vessels, killing those on board and making some prisoner. This was their first action, may God curse them."[5] In 1511, Albuquerque attacked Malacca itself.

For Albuquerque, control of Malacca would serve two purposes. It could help to destroy the Arab spice trade network by blocking passage through the Strait of Malacca, and it could also provide the Portuguese with a way station en route to the Spice Islands and other points east (see the box above). After a short but bloody battle, the Portuguese seized the city and put the local Arab population to the sword. They then proceeded to erect the normal accoutrements of the day—a fort, a factory (a common term at the time for a warehouse), and a church.

From Malacca, the Portuguese launched expeditions further east, to China and the Moluccas, then known as the Spice Islands. There they signed a treaty with a local sultan for the purchase and export of cloves to the European market. Within a few years, they had managed to seize control of the spice trade from Muslim traders and had garnered substantial profits for the Portuguese monarchy.

Why were the Portuguese so successful? Basically, their success was a matter of guns and seamanship. The first Portuguese fleet to arrive in Indian waters was relatively modest in size. It consisted of three ships and twenty guns, a force sufficient for self-defense and intimidation, but not for serious military operations. Sixteenth-century Portuguese fleets were more heavily armed and were capable of inflicting severe defeats if necessary on local naval and land forces. The Portuguese by no means possessed a monopoly on the use of firearms and explosives, but they used the manueverability of their light ships to maintain their distance while bombarding the enemy with their powerful cannon. Such tactics gave them a military superiority over lightly armed rivals that they were able to exploit until the arrival of other European forces several decades later.

THE CARAVEL, WORKHORSE OF THE AGE OF EXPLORATION. Prior to the fifteenth century, most European ships were either small craft with lateen sails used in the Mediterranean or slow, unwieldy square-rigged vessels operating in the North Atlantic. By the sixteenth century, European naval architects began to build ships that combined the maneuverability and speed offered by lateen sails with the carrying capacity and seaworthiness of the square-riggers. For a century, caravels were the feared "sea-raiders" of the oceans. Shown here is a representation of Christopher Columbus's flagship *Santa Maria,* which combined lateen with square sails and took part in the first Spanish voyage across the Atlantic Ocean.

Voyages to the "New World"

While the Portuguese were seeking access to the spice trade of the Indies by sailing eastward through the Indian Ocean, the Spanish attempted to reach the same destination by sailing westward across the Atlantic. Although the Spanish came to overseas discovery and exploration later than the Portuguese, their greater resources enabled them to establish a far grander overseas empire.

An important figure in the history of Spanish exploration was an Italian from Genoa, Christopher Columbus (1451–1506). Knowledgeable Europeans were aware that the world was round but had little understanding of its circumference or the extent of the continent of Asia. Convinced that the circumference of the earth was smaller than contemporaries believed and that Asia was larger, Columbus felt that Asia could be reached by sailing west instead of east around Africa. After being rejected by the Portuguese, he persuaded Queen Isabella of Spain to finance his exploratory expedition, which reached the Americas in October 1492 and explored the coastline of Cuba and the northern shores of the neighboring island of Hispaniola. Columbus believed that he had reached Asia and in three subsequent voyages (1493, 1498, and 1502) sought in vain to find a route through the outer islands to the Asian mainland. In his four voyages, Columbus reached all the major islands of the Caribbean and Honduras in Central America, which he called the Indies.

Although Columbus clung to his belief until his death, other explorers soon realized that he had discovered a new frontier altogether. State-sponsored explorers joined the race to the New World. A Venetian seafarer, John Cabot, explored the New England coastline of the Americas under a license from King Henry VII of England. The continent of South America was discovered accidentally by the Portuguese sea captain Pedro Cabral in 1500. Amerigo Vespucci, a Florentine, accompanied several voyages and wrote a series of letters describing the geography of the New World. The publication of these letters led to the use of the name "America" (after Amerigo) for the new lands.

The newly discovered territories were called the New World, although they possessed flourishing civilizations populated by millions of people when the Europeans arrived. The Americas were, of course, new to the Europeans, who quickly saw opportunities for conquest and exploitation. The Spanish, in particular, were interested because in 1494 the Treaty of Tordesillas had divided the newly discovered world into separate Portuguese and Spanish spheres of influence. Hereafter the route east around the Cape of Good Hope was to be reserved for the Portuguese, while the route across the Atlantic (except for the eastern hump of South America) was assigned to Spain. The Spanish conquistadors were a hardy lot of mostly upper-class individuals motivated by a typical sixteenth-century blend of glory, greed, and religious crusading zeal. Although sanctioned by the Castilian crown, these groups were financed and outfitted privately, not by the government.

Their superior weapons, organizational skills, and determination brought the conquistadors incredible success. Beginning in 1519 with a small band of men, Hernán Cortés took three years to overthrow the mighty Aztec empire in central Mexico, led by the chieftain Moctezuma (see Chapter 6). Between 1531 and 1550, the Spanish gained control of northern Mexico. Between 1531 and 1536, another expedition led by a hardened and somewhat corrupt soldier, Francisco Pizarro (1470–1541), took control of the Inca empire high in the Peruvian Andes. The

Spanish conquests were undoubtedly facilitated by the previous arrival of European diseases, which had decimated the local population. Although it took another three decades before the western part of Latin America was brought under Spanish control (the Portuguese took over Brazil), already by 1535, the Spanish had created a system of colonial administration that made the New World an extension of the old—at least in European eyes.

THE ADMINISTRATION OF THE SPANISH EMPIRE IN THE NEW WORLD

Spanish policy toward the Indians of the New World was a combination of confusion, misguided paternalism, and cruel exploitation. Confusion arose over the nature of the Indians. Unsure whether these strange creatures were "full men" or not, Spanish doctors of law debated how to fit them into currently existing European legal patterns. While the conquistadors made decisions based on expediency and their own interests, Queen Isabella declared the Indians (literally, "Indios") to be subjects of Castile and instituted the *encomienda* system, which permitted the conquering Spaniards to collect tribute from the natives and use them as laborers. In return, the holders of an *encomienda* were supposed to protect the Indians and supervise their spiritual and material needs. In practice, this meant that the settlers were free to implement the system as they pleased. Three thousand miles from Spain, Spanish settlers largely ignored their government and brutally used the Indians to pursue their own economic interests. Indians were put to work on sugar plantations and in the lucrative gold and silver mines. Forced labor, starvation, and especially disease took a fearful toll of Indian lives. With little or no natural resistance to European diseases, the Indians of America were ravaged by smallpox, measles, and typhus. These "killers" came

MAP 14.2 European Possessions in the West Indies

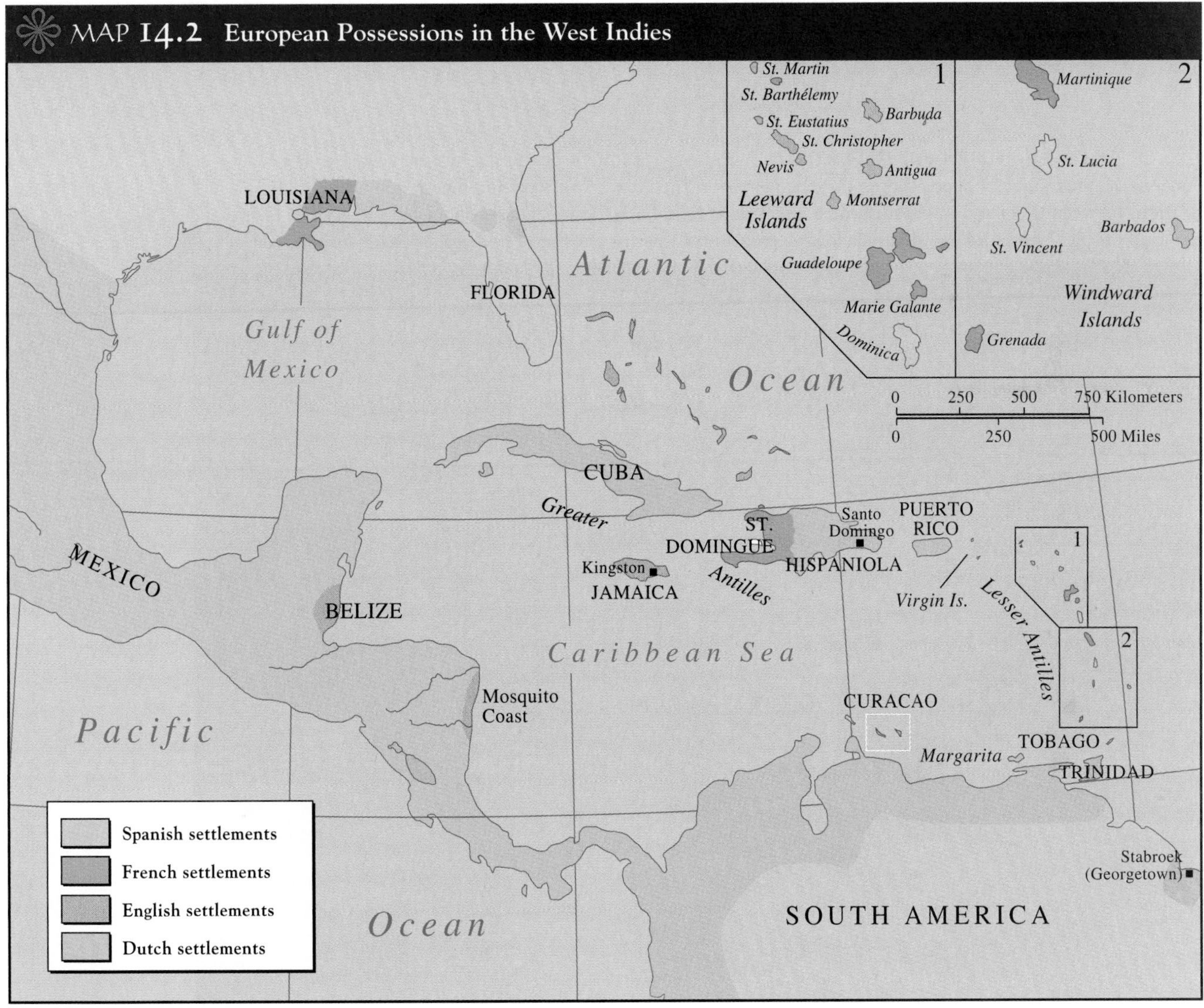

with the explorers and the conquistadors. Although scholarly estimates of native populations vary drastically, a reasonable guess is that at least half of the natives died of European diseases. On Hispaniola alone, out of an initial population of 100,000 natives when Columbus arrived in 1493, only 300 Indians survived by 1570. In 1542, largely in response to the publications of Bartolomé de Las Casas, a Dominican monk who championed the Indians (see the box on p. 407), the government abolished the *encomienda* system and provided more protection for the natives.

A board of trade known as the *Casa de Contratactión* supervised all economic matters related to the New World, but the chief organ of colonial administration was the Council of the Indies. The council nominated colonial viceroys, oversaw their activities, and kept an eye on ecclesiastical affairs in the colonies. Spanish possessions in the New World were initially divided between New Spain (Mexico, Central America, and the Caribbean islands), with its center in Mexico City, and Peru (western South America), with its capital at Lima. Each area was governed by a viceroy who served as the king's chief civil and military officer and was aided by advisory groups called *audiencias*, which also functioned as supreme judicial bodies.

By papal agreement, the Catholic monarchs of Spain were given extensive rights over ecclesiastical affairs in the New World. They could nominate church officials, build churches, collect fees, and supervise the various religious orders that conducted missionary activities. Catholic monks had remarkable success converting and baptizing hundreds of thousands of Indians in the early years of the conquest. Soon after the missionaries came the establishment of dioceses, parishes, schools, and hospitals—all the trappings of a European society.

The Impact of European Expansion

The arrival of the Europeans had an enormous impact on both the conquerors and the conquered. The native American civilizations, which (as we discussed in Chapter 6) had their own unique qualities and a degree of sophistication rarely appreciated by the conquerors, were virtually destroyed, while the native populations were ravaged by diseases inadvertently introduced by the Euro-

COLUMBUS LANDS IN THE NEW WORLD. In the log that he wrote during his first voyage to the Americas, Christopher Columbus noted that the peoples of the New World were intelligent and friendly, and relations between them and the Spanish were amicable at first. Later, however, the conquistadors began to mistreat the local people. Here is a somewhat imaginative painting of the first encounter from a European perspective.

LAS CASAS AND THE SPANISH TREATMENT OF THE AMERICAN NATIVES

Bartolomé de Las Casas (1474–1566) was a Dominican monk who participated in the conquest of Cuba and received land and Indians in return for his efforts. But in 1514 he underwent a radical transformation that led him to believe that the Indians had been cruelly mistreated by his fellow Spaniards. He spent the remaining years of his life (he lived to the age of ninety-two) fighting for the Indians. This section is taken from his most influential work, Brevísima Relación de la Destrucción de las Indias, *known to English readers as* The Tears of the Indians. *This work was largely responsible for the legend of the Spanish as inherently "cruel and murderous fanatics." Many scholars today feel that Las Casas may have exaggerated his account to shock his contemporaries into action.*

BARTOLOMÉ DE LAS CASAS, *THE TEARS OF THE INDIANS*

There is nothing more detestable or more cruel than the tyranny which the Spaniards use toward the Indians for the getting of pearl. Surely the infernal torments cannot much exceed the anguish that they endure, by reason of that way of cruelty; for they put them under water some four or five ells deep, where they are forced without any liberty of respiration, to gather up the shells wherein the Pearls are; sometimes they come up again with nets full of shells to take breath, but if they stay any while to rest themselves, immediately comes a hangman row'd in a little boat, who as soon as he hath well beaten them, drags them again to their labor. Their food is nothing but filth, and the very same that contains the Pearl, with small portion of that bread which that Country affords; in the first whereof there is little nourishment; and as for the latter, it is made with great difficulty, besides that they have not enough of that neither for sustenance; they lie upon the ground in fetters, lest they should run away; and many times they are drown'd in this labor, and are never seen again till they swim upon the top of the waves; oftentimes they also are devoured by certain sea monsters, that are frequent in those seas. Consider whether this hard usage of the poor creatures be consistent with the precepts which God commands concerning charity to our neighbor, by those that cast them so undeservedly into the dangers of a cruel death, causing them to perish without any remorse or pity, or allowing them the benefit of the Sacraments, or the knowledge of Religion; it being impossible for them to live any time under the water; and this death is so much the more painful, by reason that by the coarctation of the breast, while the lungs strive to do their office, the vital parts are so afflicted that they die vomiting the blood out of their mouths. Their hair also, which is by nature black, is hereby changed and made of the same color with that of the sea Wolves; their bodies are also so besprinkled with the froth of the sea, that they appear rather like monsters than men.

peans. Ancient social and political structures were ripped up and replaced by European institutions, religion, language, and culture (see the box on p. 408).

How does one evaluate the psychological impact of colonization on the colonizers? The relatively easy European success in dominating native peoples undoubtedly reinforced the conviction of Europeans in the inherent superiority of their civilization. The Scientific Revolution of the eighteenth century, to be followed by the era of imperialism a century later, then served to strengthen the Eurocentric perspective that has long pervaded Western civilization in its relationship with the rest of the world.

European expansion also affected the conquerors in the economic arena. Wherever they went in the Americas, Europeans sought gold and silver. One Aztec observer commented that the Spanish conquerors "longed and lusted for gold. Their bodies swelled with greed, and their hunger was ravenous; they hungered like pigs for that gold."[6] Rich silver deposits were found and exploited in Mexico and southern Peru (modern Bolivia). When the mines at Potosí in Peru were opened in 1545, the value of precious metals imported into Europe quadrupled. It has been estimated that between 1503 and 1650, sixteen million kilograms of silver and 185,000 kilograms of gold entered the port of Seville, helping to create a price revolution that affected the Spanish economy.

But gold and silver were only two of the products sent to Europe from the New World. Into Seville flowed sugar, dyes, cotton, vanilla, and hides from livestock raised on the South American pampas. New agricultural products native to the Americas such as potatoes, coffee, corn, manioc, and tobacco were also imported. Because of its trading posts in Asia, Portugal soon challenged the Italian states as the chief entry point of the eastern trade in spices, jewels, silk, carpets, ivory, leather, and perfumes, although the Venetians clung tenaciously to a portion of the spice trade until they lost out to the Dutch in the seventeenth century. Economic historians believe that the increase in the volume and area of European trade and the rise in fluid capital due to this expansion were crucial factors in producing a new era of commercial capitalism that

AN AZTEC'S LAMENT

In a previous chapter, we observed the Spanish conquest of Mexico from the point of view of the invaders. Here we present an Aztec account. Aztec memoirs of the battle were collected by the Spanish a few years after the seizure of Tenochtitlán and were later translated from the original Nahuatl language into Spanish or other European languages. In this passage, an Aztec observer describes the enormous sense of sorrow he felt at the tragedy that had befallen his compatriots. Note that the writer concludes that the defeat was ordained by the "Giver of Life" because of his displeasure with the Aztec people.

FLOWERS AND SONGS OF SORROW

Nothing but flowers and songs of sorrow
are left in Mexico and Tlatelolco,
where once we saw warriors and wise men.

We know it is true
that we must perish,
for we are mortal men.
You, the Giver of Life,
you have ordained it.

We wander here and there
in our desolate poverty.
We are mortal men.
We have seen bloodshed and pain
where once we saw beauty and valor.

We are crushed to the ground;
we lie in ruins.
There is nothing but grief and suffering
in Mexico and Tlatelolco,
where once we saw beauty and valor.

Have you grown weary of your servants?
Are you angry with your servants,
O Giver of Life?

represented the first step toward the world economy that has characterized the modern era.

European expansion, which was in part a product of European rivalries, also deepened those rivalries and increased the tensions among European states. Bitter conflicts arose over the cargoes coming from the New World and Asia. Although the Spanish and Portuguese were first in the competition, by the end of the sixteenth century, new competitors were entering the scene and beginning to challenge the dominance of the Iberian powers. The first to arrive were the English and the Dutch.

Why did Europeans risk their lives to explore new lands far from friendly shores? For some, expansion abroad brought hopes for land, riches, and social advancement. One Spaniard commented in 1572 that many "poor young men" left Spain for Mexico, where they might hope to acquire landed estates and call themselves "gentlemen." Although some wives accompanied their husbands abroad, many ordinary European women found new opportunities for marriage in the New World because of the lack of white women. In the violence-prone world of early Spanish America, a number of women also found themselves rich after their husbands were killed unexpectedly. In one area of Central America, women owned about 25 percent of the landed estates by 1700.

New Rivals Enter the Scene

Portugal's efforts to dominate the trade of the Indian Ocean were never totally successful. The Portuguese lacked both the numbers and the wealth to overcome local resistance and colonize the Asian regions. Moreover, their massive investments in ships and laborers for their empire (hundreds of ships and hundreds of thousands of workers in ship-

HAVANA, SPAIN'S LIFELINE TO THE NEW WORLD. After the conquest of Mexico by Hernán Cortés, trade between Spain and its new possession flourished. Spanish navigators soon discovered that the city of Havana, the capital of present-day Cuba, was an ideal stopping-point for fleets en route to and from the New World, and a city sprang up along the banks of its protected harbor. To protect the population from the ravages of enemy fleets—notably the English—Spanish authorities erected a number of fortifications on both shores of the bay that borders the city. Shown here is the Castle of the Royal Force, erected in 1559 and the first stone castle built in the New World. A previous wooden fort had been set aflame by pirates.

yards and overseas bases) proved very costly. Only half of the ships involved in the India trade survived for a second journey. Disease, shipwreck, and battles took a heavy toll of life. The empire was simply too large and Portugal too small to maintain it, and by the end of the century, the Portuguese were being severely challenged by rivals.

The Spanish had established themselves in Asia in the early 1520s, when Ferdinand Magellan, seeking a western route to the Spice Islands across the Pacific Ocean, had landed on the island of Cebu in the Philippine Islands. Although Magellan and some forty of his crew were killed in a skirmish with the local population, one of the two remaining ships, now under the command of the Spanish navigator Sebastian del Cano, sailed on to Tidor, in the Moluccas, and thence around the world via the Cape of Good Hope. In the words of a contemporary historian, they arrived in Cádiz "with precious cargo and fifteen men surviving out of a fleet of five sail."[7]

As it turned out, the Spanish could not follow up on Magellan's accomplishment, and in 1529 they sold their rights in Tidor to the Portuguese. But Magellan's voyage was not a total loss. In the absence of concerted resistance from the local population, the Spanish managed to consolidate their control over the Philippines, which eventually became a major Spanish base in the carrying trade across the Pacific. Spanish galleons carried silk and other luxury goods to Acapulco in exchange for silver from the mines of Mexico.

The primary threat to the Portuguese toehold in Southeast Asia, however, came from the English and the Dutch both of whom were now strongly influenced by mercantilist theory (see Chapter 15). In 1591, the first English expedition to the Indies through the Indian Ocean arrived in London with a cargo of pepper. Nine years later, a private joint-stock company, the East India Company, was founded to provide a stable source of capital for future voyages. In 1608, an English fleet landed at Surat, on the northwestern coast of India. Eventually, a commercial treaty was signed, and a permanent English representative was assigned to the Mughal imperial court. Trade with Southeast Asia soon followed.

CHRONOLOGY

SPANISH ACTIVITIES IN THE AMERICAS

Christopher Columbus's first voyage to the Americas	1492
Last voyages of Columbus	1502–1504
Spanish conquest of Mexico	1519–1522
Francisco Pizarro's conquest of the Incas	1531–1536

The Dutch were quick to follow suit. Dutch sailors had managed to obtain Portuguese maps of the Indian coast, and the first Dutch fleet arrived in India in 1595. In 1602, the Dutch East India Company was established under government sponsorship and soon was actively competing with the English and the Portuguese in the region.

The Dutch and the English also began to make inroads on Spanish and Portuguese possessions in the Americas. War and steady pressure from their Dutch and English rivals eroded Portuguese trade in both the west and east, although Portugal continued to profit from its large colonial empire in Brazil. A formal administration system had been instituted in Brazil in 1549, and Portuguese migrants had established massive plantations there to produce sugar for export to the Old World. The Spanish also maintained an enormous South American empire, but Spain's importance as a commercial power declined rapidly in the seventeenth century because of a drop in the output of the silver mines, the poverty of the Spanish monarchy, and the stifling hand of the Spanish aristocracy as well as the pressure of its English rival.

SEAT OF ARGENTINE INDEPENDENCE. The Argentine city of Buenos Aires was founded in 1536 by the Spanish explorer Pedro de Mendoza. In 1580 a town council was erected on the city's main square, the Plaza de Mayo. In 1751 it was replaced with a new building, shown below. It was here that Argentine patriots planned their struggle for independence from Spain in 1810.

The Dutch formed their own Dutch West India Company in 1621 to compete with Spanish and Portuguese interests in the Americas. But although it made some inroads in Portuguese Brazil and the Caribbean, the company's profits were never large enough to compensate for the expenditures. Dutch settlements were also established on the North American continent. The mainland colony of New Netherlands stretched from the mouth of the Hudson River as far north as Albany, New York. Present-day names such as Staten Island, Harlem, and the Catskills remind us that it was the Dutch who initially settled the Hudson River valley.

In the second half of the seventeenth century, however, rivalry and years of warfare with the English and the French (who had also become active in North America) brought the decline of the Dutch commercial empire in the New World. In 1664, the English seized the colony of New Netherlands and renamed it New York, while the Dutch West India Company soon went bankrupt. In 1663, Canada became the property of the French crown and was administered like a French province. But the French failed to provide adequate men or money, allowing their continental wars to take precedence over the conquest of the North American continent. By the early eighteenth century, the French began to cede some of their American possessions to their English rival.

The English meanwhile had proceeded to create a colonial empire in the New World along the Atlantic seaboard of North America. The failure of the Virginia Company made it evident that colonizing American lands was not necessarily conducive to quick profits. But the desire to escape from religious oppression combined with economic interests did make successful colonization possible, as the Massachusetts Bay Company demonstrated. The Massachusetts colony had only 4,000 settlers in its early years, but by 1660 their number had swelled to 40,000. Although the English had established control over most of the eastern seaboard by the end of the seventeenth century, the North American colonies still remained of minor significance to the English economy.

Africa in an Era of Transition

Although the primary objective of the Portuguese in rounding the Cape of Good Hope was to find a sea route to the Spice Islands, they soon discovered that profits were to be made en route, along the eastern coast of Africa. In the early sixteenth century, a Portuguese fleet commanded by Francisco de Almeida seized a number of East African port cities, including Kilwa, Sofala, and Mombasa, and built forts along the coast in an effort to control the trade in the area. Above all, the Portuguese wanted to monopolize the trade in gold, which was mined by Bantu workers in the hills along the upper Zambezi River and then shipped to Sofala on the coast (see Chapter 8). For centuries, the gold trade had been monopolized by local Shona peoples at Zimbabwe. In the fifteenth century, it had come under the control of a Shona dynasty known as the Mwene Metapa (known to Europeans as Monomotapa). The Mwene Metapa had originally controlled the region south of the Zambezi River and may have been the builders of the impressive city known today as Great Zimbabwe, but sometime in the fifteenth century, they moved northeastward to the valley of the Zambezi. Here they encountered the arriving Portuguese, who had begun to move inland to gain access to the lucrative gold trade and had established ports at Tete and Sena on the Zambezi River. The Portuguese opened treaty relations with the Mwene Metapa, and Jesuit priests were eventually posted to the court in 1561. At first the Mwene Metapa found the Europeans useful as an ally against local rivals, but by the end of the

PASSAGE TO THE UNKNOWN. During its historic first voyage around the world in the early sixteenth century, Ferdinand Magellan's fleet passed through this passage near the southern tip of South America. Now known as the Strait of Magellan, this narrow body of water between the mainland and the nearby island of Tierra del Fuego remains to sailors one of the most terrifying in the world, with 100-mile-per-hour winds gusting regularly through this passage between the Pacific and the Atlantic Oceans.

sixteenth century, the Portuguese had transformed the kingdom of the Mwene Metapa into a protectorate and forced the local ruler to grant title to large tracts of land to Portuguese officials and private individuals living in the area. Eventually, those lands would be integrated into the colony of Mozambique. The Portuguese, however, lacked the personnel, the capital, and the expertise to dominate the trade in the area. In the late seventeenth century, a vassal of the Mwene Metapa succeeded in driving the Portuguese from the plateau; his descendants maintained control of the area for the next two hundred years.

North of the Zambezi River, Bantu peoples were coming under pressure not only from the Portuguese, but also from pastoralists migrating southward from the southern Sudan. The latter were frequently aggressive and began to occupy the rift valley and parts of the lake district that had previously been controlled by Bantu farmers. In some cases, the conflict between farmers and pastoralists was fairly clear-cut. In Rwanda and Burundi, immediately west of Lake Victoria, farming Hutu peoples (Bantu speakers) defended their hilltop communities against roving Tutsi pastoralists occupying the surrounding lowlands.

The first Europeans to settle in southern Africa were the Dutch. After an unsuccessful attempt to seize the Portuguese settlement on the island of Mozambique off the East African coast, in 1652 the Dutch set up a way station at the Cape of Good Hope to serve as a base for Dutch fleets en route to the East Indies. At first, the new settlement was meant simply to provide food and other provisions to Dutch ships, but eventually it developed into a permanent colony. Dutch farmers, known as Boers and speaking a Dutch dialect that evolved into Afrikaans, began to settle in the sparsely occupied areas outside the city of Capetown. The temperate climate and the absence of tropical diseases made the territory near the cape almost the only land south of the Sahara that the Europeans had found suitable for habitation.

West Africa had been penetrated from across the Sahara since ancient times, and contact undoubtedly increased after the establishment of Muslim control over the Mediterranean coastal regions. Muslim traders crossed the desert carrying Islamic values, political culture, and legal traditions along with their goods. The early stage of state formation had culminated with the kingdom of Mali, symbolized by the renowned Mansa Musa, whose pilgrimage to Mecca in the fourteenth century had left an indelible impression on observers.

After Mali's decline, it was succeeded in the east by the kingdom of Songhai. Under King Askia Mohammed (1493–1528), the leader of a pro-Islamic faction who had seized power from members of the original founding family, the state increasingly relied on Islamic institutions and ideology to strengthen national unity and centralize authority (see the box on p. 412). Askia Mohammed himself embarked on a pilgrimage to Mecca and was recognized by the caliph of Cairo as the Muslim ruler of the Niger River valley. On his return from Mecca, he tried to revive Timbuktu as a major center of Islamic learning but had little success in converting his subjects. He did preside over a significant increase in trans-Saharan trade, which provided a steady source of income to Songhai and other kingdoms in the region. Despite the efforts of Askia Mohammed and his successors, centrifugal forces within Songhai eventually led to its breakup after his death.

The period of Songhai's decline was also a time of increased contact with Europeans. The English, the French, and the Dutch all became active in the West African trade in the mid-sixteenth century. The Dutch, in particular, encroached on the Portuguese spheres of influence. During the mid-seventeenth century, the Dutch seized a number of Portuguese forts along the West African coast, while at the same time taking over the bulk of the Portuguese trade across the Indian Ocean.

The Slave Trade

The European exploration of the African coastline had little apparent significance for most peoples living in the interior of the continent, except for a few who engaged in direct or indirect trade with the foreigners. But for peoples living on or near the coast, the impact was often great indeed. As the trade in slaves increased during the

FORT JESUS AT MOMBASA. Mombasa, a port city on the eastern coast of Africa, was a jumping-off point for the Portuguese as they explored the lands bordering on the Indian Ocean. Erected in the early sixteenth century atop a bluff overlooking the harbor, Fort Jesus remained an imposing symbol of European power until 1698, when the Portuguese were expelled by the Arabs. Castles built in this style are situated along the sea routes to the Spice Islands, but the European presence has now departed.

KING OF SONGHAI

The Epic of Askia Mohammed is an oral history passed down through generations of West Africans. It relates the heroic deeds of the famous monarch who led the kingdom of Songhai to the zenith of its power in the early sixteenth century. In the epic, the young hero, called Mamar Kassaye, becomes chieftain by killing his evil uncle Si (Sonni Ali Ber, who ruled Songhai from 1463 to 1492). Once in power, Mamar consolidated the expanding Songhai kingdom and ruled it until his death in 1528. He was revered for his piety, his patronage of scholarship at Timbuktu, and his celebrated pilgrimage to Mecca. The following passage describes his assumption of power and the means he used to convert his subjects to Islam.

THE EPIC OF ASKIA MOHAMMED

His father gave him a white stallion, really white, really, really, really, really, really, really, really white like, like percale.
He gave him all the things necessary.
He gave him two lances.
He gave him a saber, which he wore.
He gave him a shield.
He bid him good-bye.
...
The horse gallops swiftly, swiftly, swiftly, swiftly, swiftly, swiftly he is approaching.
He comes into view suddenly, leaning forward on his mount.
Until, until, until, until, until, until, until he touches the prayer skin of his uncle, then he reins his horse there.
...
As he approaches the prayer skin of his uncle,
He reins his horse.
He unslung his lance, and pierced his uncle with it until the lance touched the prayer skin.
Until the spear went all the way to the prayer skin.
...
They took away the body, and Mamar came to sit down on the prayer skin of his uncle.
They prayed.
They took away the body to bury it.
That is how Mamar took the chieftaincy.
...
He ruled then, he ruled, he ruled, he ruled, he converted.
Throughout Mamar's reign, what he did was to convert people.
Any village that he hears is trying to resist,
That is not going to submit,
He gets up and destroys the village.
If the village accepts, he makes them pray.
If they resist, he conquers the village, he burns the village.
Mamar made them convert, Mamar made them convert, Mamar made them convert.
Until, until, until, until, until, until he got up and said he would go to Mecca.
...
They build a mosque before his arrival.
When he arrives, he and his people,
He teaches the villagers prayers from the Koran.
He makes them pray.
They—they learn how to pray.
After that, in the morning, he continues on.
Every village that follows his orders, that accepts his wishes,
He conquers them, he moves on.
Every village that refuses his demand,
He conquers it, he burns it, he moves on.
Until the day—Mamar did that until, until, until, until the day he arrived at the Red Sea.

sixteenth through the eighteenth centuries, thousands, and then millions, were removed from their homes and forcibly exported to plantations in the New World.

Traffic in slaves had existed for centuries before the arrival of Portuguese fleets along African shores. West African states like the kingdoms of Mali and Songhai routinely used slaves (mostly captured in battles with neighboring rivals) as agricultural laborers. In East Africa and the upper Nile valley, slavery had been practiced since ancient times and continued at a fairly steady level during the fifteenth century, with the major trade routes snaking across the Sahara and up the Nile River. The primary market for African slaves was the Middle East, where most were used as domestic servants. Slavery also existed in many European countries, where a few slaves from Africa or war captives from the regions north of the Black Sea were used for domestic purposes or as agricultural workers in the lands adjacent to the Mediterranean.

At first, the Portuguese simply replaced European slaves with African ones. During the last half of the fifteenth century, about a thousand slaves were taken to Portugal each year; the vast majority were apparently destined to serve as domestic servants for affluent families throughout Europe. But the discovery of the New World in the 1490s and the subsequent planting of sugarcane in South America and the islands of the Caribbean changed the situation. Cane sugar was native to Indonesia and had first been introduced to Europeans from the Middle East during the Crusades. By the fifteenth century, it was grown (often by slaves from Africa or the region of the Black Sea) in modest amounts on Cyprus, Sicily, and southern regions of the Iberian peninsula. In 1490, the

Portuguese established sugar plantations worked by African laborers at São Tomé, an island in the Bay of Biafra off the central coast of Africa. Demand increased as sugar gradually replaced honey as a sweetener, especially in northern Europe.

But the primary impetus to the sugar industry came from the colonization of the Americas. During the sixteenth century, plantations were established along the eastern coast of Brazil and on several islands in the Caribbean. Because the cultivation of cane sugar is an arduous process demanding both skill and large quantities of labor, the new plantations required more workers than could be provided by the small and inexperienced American Indian population in the New World, many of whom had in any case died of diseases imported from the Old World. Since the climate and soil of much of West Africa were not especially conducive to the cultivation of sugar, African slaves began to be shipped to Brazil and the Caribbean to work on the plantations. The first were sent from Portugal, but in 1518 a Spanish ship carried the first boatload of African slaves directly from Africa to the New World.

During the next two centuries, the trade in slaves increased by massive proportions. An estimated 275,000 enslaved Africans were exported to other countries during the sixteenth century, with 2,000 going annually to the Americas alone. During the next century, the total climbed to over a million and jumped to six million in the eighteenth century, when the trade spread from West and Central Africa to East Africa. Even during the nineteenth century, when Great Britain and a number of other European countries attempted to end the slave trade, nearly two million were exported. It has been estimated that altogether as many as ten million African slaves were transported to the Americas between the early sixteenth and the late nineteenth century. As many as two million were exported to other areas during the same period.

One reason for these astonishing numbers, of course, was the tragically high death rate. Though figures on the number of slaves who died on the journey are almost entirely speculative, a high proportion undoubtedly died on the voyage before arriving at their destination. According to one source, mortality rates among crew

MAP 14.3 The Slave Trade

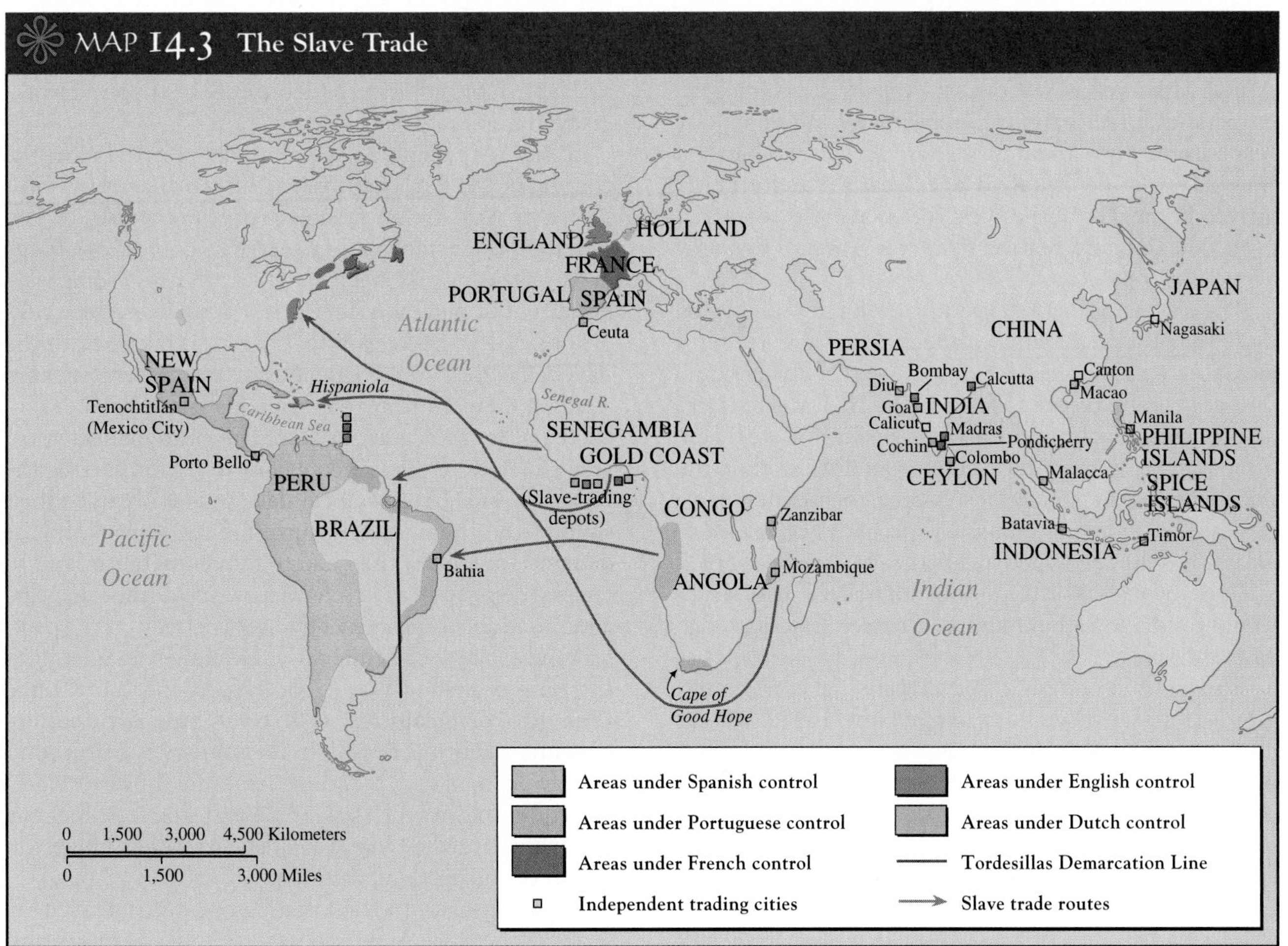

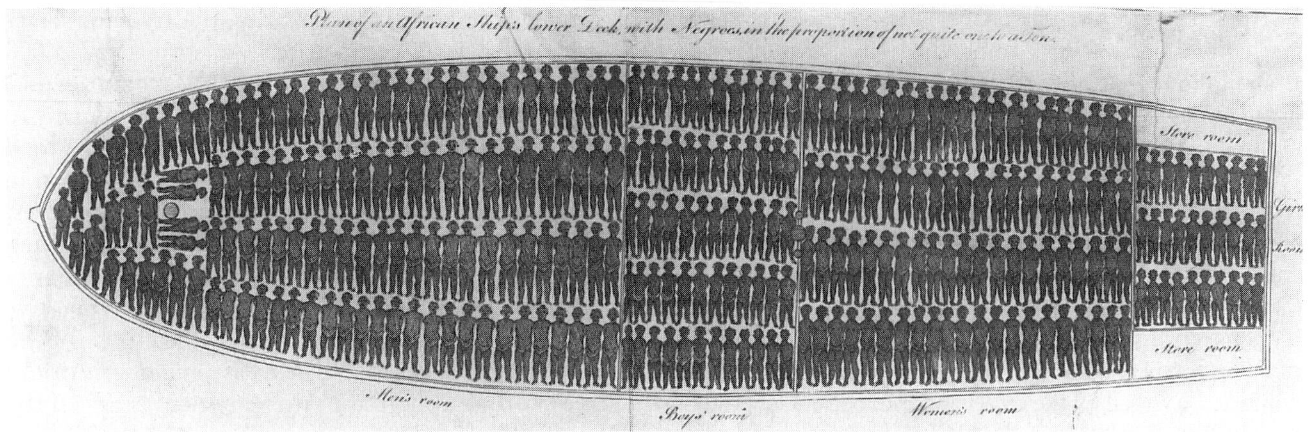

A SLAVE SHIP. Beginning in the sixteenth century, European traders began to ship native Africans to the Americas to be used as slave labor on the plantations. During the first shipments, up to one-third of the human cargo died of disease. Later merchants became more efficient and reduced losses to about 10 percent. As this sketch shows, the victims were still crammed together in an inhumane manner.

members were as high as one in four. Later, mortality rates among slaves were apparently reduced to an average of about 10 percent per voyage, still a figure of epidemic proportions. Mortality rates for Europeans in the West Indies were ten to twenty times higher on average than in Europe, and a European arriving in the West Indies had a life expectancy of five to ten years (in Africa, where yellow fever was prevalent, the average life expectancy for an arriving European was only about one year). Ironically, African slaves fared somewhat better if they survived the brutal voyage. Death rates for newly arrived Europeans in the West Indies averaged over 125 per 1,000 annually, but the figure for Africans was only about 30 per 1,000.

The reason for these staggering death rates was clearly more than maltreatment, although that was certainly a factor. As we have seen, the transmission of diseases from one continent to another brought high death rates among those lacking immunity. African slaves were somewhat less susceptible to European diseases than the American Indian populations. Indeed, they seem to have possessed a degree of immunity, perhaps because their ancestors had developed antibodies to "white people's diseases" owing to the trans-Saharan trade. The Africans would not have had immunity to native American diseases, however.

The mortality rates, of course, were higher for immigrants than for those born in the New World, who as children gradually developed at least a partial immunity to many of the more fatal diseases. Death rates for native-born slaves tended to be significantly lower than for recent arrivals, which raises the question of why the slave population did not begin to rise after the initial impact of settlement had worn off. The answer appears to be a matter of economics. In the first place, only half as many women were enslaved as men, birthrates for women living in slavery were low, and infant mortality was high. In the second place, as long as the price of slaves was low, many slave owners in the West Indies apparently believed that purchasing a new slave was less expensive than raising a child from birth to working age at adolescence. After the price of slaves began to rise during the eighteenth century, plantation owners started to devote more efforts to replenishing the supply of workers by natural means.

Slaves were obtained by traditional means. Before the coming of the Europeans in the fifteenth century, most slaves in Africa were prisoners or war captives or had inherited their status. Many served as domestic servants or as wageless workers for the local ruler, and some were permitted to purchase their freedom under certain conditions. When Europeans first began to take part in the slave trade, they would normally purchase slaves from local African merchants at the infamous "slave markets" in exchange for gold, guns, or other European manufactured goods such as textiles or copper or iron utensils (see the box on p. 415). At first, local slave traders obtained their supply from immediately surrounding regions, but as demand increased, they had to move further inland to locate their victims. In a few cases, local rulers became concerned about the impact of the slave trade on the political and social well-being of their societies. In a letter to the king of Portugal in 1526, King Affonso of Congo (Bakongo) complained that "so great, Sire, is the corruption and licentiousness that our country is being completely depopulated."[8] As a general rule, however, local monarchs viewed the slave trade as a source of income, and many launched forays against defenseless villages in search of unsuspecting victims.

Historians once thought that Europeans controlled the terms of the slave trade and were able to obtain victims at bargain prices. Recently, however, it has become clear

A SLAVE MARKET IN AFRICA

Traffic in slaves had been carried on in Africa since the kingdom of the pharaohs in ancient Egypt. But the slave trade increased dramatically after the arrival of European ships off the coast of West Africa. The following passage by a Dutch observer describes a slave market in Africa and the conditions on the ships that carried the slaves to the New World. Note the difference in tone between this account and the far more critical views expressed in Chapter 22.

SLAVERY IN AFRICA: A FIRSTHAND REPORT

Not a few in our country fondly imagine that parents here sell their children, men their wives, and one brother the other. But those who think so deceive themselves, for this never happens on any other account but that of necessity, or some great crime; most of the slaves that are offered to us are prisoners of war, who are sold by the victors as their booty.

When these slaves come to Fida, they are put in prison all together; and when we treat concerning buying them, they are brought out into a large plain. There, by our surgeons, whose province it is, they are thoroughly examined, even to the smallest member, and that naked too, both men and women, without the least distinction or modesty. Those that are approved as good are set on one side; and the lame or faulty are set by as invalids. . . .

The invalids and the maimed being thrown out, . . . the remainder are numbered, and it is entered who delivered them. In the meanwhile, a burning iron, with the arms or name of the companies, lies in the fire, with which ours are marked on the breast. This is done that we may distinguish them from the slaves of the English, French, or others (which are also marked with their mark), and to prevent the Negroes exchanging them for worse, at which they have a good hand.

I doubt not but this trade seems very barbarous to you, but since it is followed by mere necessity, it must go on; but we take all possible care that they are not burned too hard, especially the women, who are more tender than the men.

When we have agreed with the owners of the slaves, they are returned to their prison. There from that time forward they are kept at our charge, costing us two pence a day a slave; which serves to subsist them, like our criminals, on bread and water. To save charges, we send them on board our ships at the very first opportunity, before which their masters strip them of all they have on their backs so that they come aboard stark naked, women as well as men. In this condition they are obliged to continue, if the master of the ship is not so charitable (which he commonly is) as to bestow something on them to cover their nakedness.

You would really wonder to see how these slaves live on board, for though their number sometimes amounts to six or seven hundred, yet by the careful management of our masters of ships, they are so regulated that it seems incredible. And in this particular our nation exceeds all other Europeans, for the French, Portuguese and English slave ships are always foul and stinking; on the contrary, ours are for the most part clean and neat.

The slaves are fed three times a day with indifferent good victuals, and much better than they eat in their own country. Their lodging place is divided into two parts, one of which is appointed for the men, the other for the women, each sex being kept apart. Here they lie as close together as it is possible for them to be crowded.

We are sometimes sufficiently plagued with a parcel of slaves which come from a far inland country who very innocently persuade one another that we buy them only to fatten and afterward eat them as a delicacy. When we are so unhappy as to be pestered with many of this sort, they resolve and agree together (and bring over the rest to their party) to run away from the ship, kill the Europeans, and set the vessel ashore, by which means they design to free themselves from being our food.

I have twice met with this misfortune; and the first time proved very unlucky to me, I not in the least suspecting it, but the uproar was quashed by the master of the ship and myself by causing the abettor to be shot through the head, after which all was quiet.

that African intermediaries—whether private merchants, local elites, or trading state monopolies—were very active in the process and were often able to dictate the price, volume, and availability of slaves to European purchasers. The majority of the slaves sold to European buyers were males; females, who were in great demand in Africa and on the trans-Saharan trade, tended to be reserved for those markets. The slave merchants were often paid in various types of imported goods, including East Asian textiles (highly desired for their bright colors and durability), furniture, and other manufactured products. Until the end of the seventeenth century, the Portuguese preferred gold to slaves and would sometimes pay for the gold by selling slaves to African kingdoms that were short of labor. In fact, not until the beginning of the eighteenth century did slaves surpass gold and ivory as the continent's leading exports.

The effects of the slave trade varied from area to area. It might be assumed that, apart from the tragic effects on the lives of individual victims and their families, the practice would have led to the depopulation of vast areas of the continent. This did occur in some areas, notably in modern Angola, south of the Zaire River basin, and in

CHRONOLOGY

THE PENETRATION OF AFRICA

Life of Prince Henry the Navigator	1394–1460
Portuguese ships reach the Senegal River	1441
Bartolomeo Dias sails around the tip of Africa	1487
First Portuguese sugar plantation at São Tomé	1490
First boatload of slaves to the Americas	1518
Dutch way station established at Cape of Good Hope	1652
Ashanti kingdom established in West Africa	1680
Portuguese expelled from Mombasa	1728

thinly populated areas in East Africa, but it was less true in West Africa. There high birthrates were often able to counterbalance the loss of able-bodied adults, and the introduction of new crops from the New World, such as maize, peanuts, and manioc, led to an increase in food production that made it possible to support a larger population. One of the many cruel ironies of history is that while the institution of slavery was a tragedy for many, it benefited others.

Still, there is no denying the reality that from a moral point of view, the slave trade represented a tragic loss for millions of Africans, not only for the individual victims, but also for their families. One of the more poignant aspects of the trade is that as many as 20 percent of those sold to European slavers were children, a statistic that may be partly explained by the fact that many European countries had enacted regulations that permitted more children than adults to be transported aboard the ships.

Political and Social Structures in a Changing Continent

Of course, the Western economic penetration of Africa had other dislocating effects. As in other parts of the non-Western world, the importation of inexpensive manufactured goods from Europe undermined the foundations of local cottage industry and impoverished countless families. Both the demand for slaves and the introduction of firearms intensified political instability and civil strife. At the same time, the impact of the Europeans should not be exaggerated. Only in a few isolated areas, such as South Africa and Mozambique, were anything like permanent European settlements established. Elsewhere, at the insistence of African rulers and merchants, European influence generally did not penetrate beyond the coastal regions.

Nevertheless, inland areas were often affected by events taking place elsewhere. In the western Sahara, for example, the diversion of trade routes toward the coast led to the irreparable weakening of the old Songhai trading empire and its eventual conquest by a vigorous new Moroccan dynasty in the late sixteenth century. Morocco had long hoped to expand its influence into the Sahara in order to seize control over the commerce in gold and salt, and in 1590 Moroccan forces defeated Songhai's army at Gao, on the Niger River, and then occupied the great caravan center of Timbuktu. Even after the departure of the invaders, Songhai was beyond recovery, and the next two centuries were marked by civil disorder among tribal groups and intense competition between Muslims in the cities and towns and adherents of traditional African religions in rural areas.

European influence had a more direct impact along the coast of West Africa, especially in the vicinity of European forts and factories such as Dakar and Sierra Leone, but no European colonies were established there before 1800. Most of the numerous African states in the area from Cape Verde to the delta of the Niger River were sufficiently strong to resist Western encroachments, and they often allied with each other to force European purchasers to respect their monopoly on trading operations. Some, like the powerful Ashanti kingdom, established in 1680 on the Gold Coast, profited substantially from the rise in seaborne commerce. Some states, particularly along the so-called Slave Coast, in what is now Dahomey and Togo, or in the densely populated Niger River delta, took an active part in the slave trade. The demands of slavery and the temptations of economic profit, however, also contributed to the increase in conflict among the states in the area.

This was especially true in the region of the Zaire River, where Portuguese activities eventually led to the splintering of the Congo Empire and two centuries of rivalry and internal strife among the successor states in the area. A similar pattern developed in East Africa, where Portuguese activities led to the decline and eventual collapse of the Mwene Metapa. Northward along the coast, in present-day Kenya and Tanzania, African rulers, assisted by Arab forces from Oman and Muscat in the Arabian peninsula, expelled the Portuguese from Mombasa in 1728. Swahili culture now regained some of the dynamism it had possessed before the arrival of Vasco da Gama and his successors. But with much shipping now diverted southward to the route around the Cape of Good Hope, the commerce of the area never completely recovered and was increasingly dependent on the export of slaves and ivory obtained through contacts with African states in the interior.

Southeast Asia in the Era of the Spice Trade

In Southeast Asia, the encounter with the West that began with the arrival of Portuguese fleets in the Indian Ocean at the end of the fifteenth century eventually resulted in the breakdown of traditional societies and the advent of colonial rule. In general, however, the process was a gradual one. By 1700, although the Dutch retained their hold on the islands, Europeans had generally abandoned the Southeast Asian mainland. As we will see in a later chapter, though, the mainland's reprieve was only temporary.

CHRONOLOGY

THE SPICE TRADE

Vasco da Gama lands at Calicut in southwestern India	1498
Portuguese seize Malacca	1511
Portuguese ships land in southern China	1514
Magellan's voyage around the world	1519–1522
East India Company established	1600
Vereenigde Oost-Indische Compagnie (VOC) established	1602
English arrive at Surat in northwestern India	1608
Dutch fort established at Batavia	1619
Dutch seize Malacca from the Portuguese	1641
Burmese sack of Ayuthaya	1767
British seize Malacca from the Dutch	1795

The Arrival of the West

As we have seen, the Spanish soon followed the Portuguese into Southeast Asia. By the seventeenth century, the Dutch, English, and French had begun to join the scramble for rights to the lucrative spice trade.

Within a short time, the Dutch, through the aggressive and well-financed Dutch East India Company (Vereenigde Oost-Indische Compagnie, or VOC, which possessed ten times the capital of the English East India Company), had not only succeeded in elbowing their rivals out of the spice trade but had also begun to consolidate their political and military control over the area. On the island of Java, where they established a fort at Batavia (today's Jakarta) in 1619, the Dutch found that it was necessary to bring the inland regions under their control to protect their position. Rather than establishing a formal colony, however, they tried to rule as much as possible through the local landed aristocracy. On Java and the neighboring island of Sumatra, the VOC established pepper plantations, which soon became the source of massive profits for Dutch merchants in Amsterdam. Elsewhere they attempted to monopolize the clove trade by limiting cultivation of the crop to one island. By the end of the eighteenth century, the Dutch had succeeded in bringing almost the entire Indonesian archipelago under their control.

The arrival of the Europeans had somewhat less impact on mainland Southeast Asia, where cohesive monarchies in Burma, Thailand, and Vietnam resisted foreign encroachment. In addition, the coveted spices did not thrive on the mainland, so the Europeans' efforts there were far less determined than in the islands. In the sixteenth century, the Portuguese established limited trade relations with several mainland states, including the Thai kingdom at Ayuthaya, Burma, Vietnam, and the remnants of the old Angkor kingdom in Cambodia. By the early seventeenth century, other nations had followed and had begun to compete actively for trade and missionary privileges. As was the case elsewhere, the Europeans soon became involved in local factional disputes as a means of obtaining political and economic advantages. In Burma, the English and the French supported rival groups in the internal struggles of the monarchy until a new dynasty emerged and threw the foreigners out. A similar process took place at Ayuthaya, where the French were forced to evacuate the area in the late seventeenth century.

In Vietnam, the arrival of Western merchants and missionaries coincided with a period of internal conflict among ruling groups in the country. After their arrival in the mid-seventeenth century, the European powers characteristically began to intervene in local politics, with the Portuguese and the Dutch supporting rival factions. By the end of the century, when it became clear that economic opportunities were limited, most European states abandoned their factories (trading stations) in the area. French missionaries attempted to remain, but their efforts were hampered by the local authorities, who viewed the Catholic insistence that converts give their primary loyalty to the pope as a threat to the legal status and prestige of the Vietnamese emperor (see the box on p. 419).

State and Society in Precolonial Southeast Asia

Between 1500 and 1800, Southeast Asia experienced the last flowering of traditional culture before the advent of European colonial rule in the nineteenth century. Although the coming of the Europeans had an immediate and direct impact in some areas, notably the Philippines and parts of the Malay world, in most areas Western influence was still relatively limited. Europeans occasionally dabbled in local politics and modified regional trade patterns, but they generally were not a decisive factor in the evolution of local political or social systems.

Nevertheless, Southeast Asian societies were changing in several subtle ways—in their trade patterns, their means of livelihood, and their religious beliefs. In some ways, these changes accentuated the differences between individual states in the region. Yet beneath these differences was an underlying commonality of life for most people. Despite the diversity of cultures and religious beliefs in the area, in most respects, Southeast Asians were closer to

THE THAI CAPITAL AT AYUTHAYA. The Thai peoples arrived in Southeast Asia in the thirteenth century, after being driven out of southern China by the Mongols. They then destroyed the Angkor Empire and set up their capital at Ayuthaya, which was one of the finest cities in Asia from the fifteenth to the eighteenth century. After a Burmese invasion in 1767, most of Ayuthaya's inhabitants were killed, and all official Thai records were destroyed. Here the remains of some Buddhist stupas, erected in a ceremonial precinct in the center of the city, are a visual confirmation of the influence of Theravada Buddhism on Thai society.

AN EXCHANGE OF ROYAL CORRESPONDENCE

In 1681, King Louis XIV of France wrote a letter to the "king of Tonkin" (the Trinh family head, then acting as viceroy to the Vietnamese ruler) requesting permission for Christian missionaries to proselytize in Vietnam. The latter politely declined the request on the grounds that such activity was prohibited by ancient custom. In fact, Christian missionaries had been active in Vietnam for years, and their intervention in local politics had aroused the anger of the court in Hanoi.

A LETTER TO THE KING OF TONKIN FROM LOUIS XIV

Most high, most excellent, most mighty, and most magnanimous Prince, our very dear and good friend, may it please God to increase your greatness with a happy end!

We hear from our subjects who were in your Realm what protection you accorded them. We appreciate this all the more since we have for you all the esteem that one can have for a prince as illustrious through his military valor as he is commendable for the justice which he exercises in his Realm. We have even been informed that you have not been satisfied to extend this general protection to our subjects but, in particular, that you gave effective proofs of it to Messrs. Deydier and de Bourges. We would have wished that they might have been able to recognize all the favors they received from you by having presents worthy of you offered you; but since the war which we have had for several years, in which all of Europe had banded together against us, prevented our vessels from going to the Indies, at the present time, when we are at peace after having gained many victories and expanded our Realm through the conquest of several important places, we have immediately given orders to the Royal Company to establish itself in your kingdom as soon as possible, and have commanded Messrs. Deydier and de Bourges to remain with you in order to maintain a good relationship between our subjects and yours, also to warn us on occasions that might present themselves when we might be able to give you proofs of our esteem and of our wish to concur with your satisfaction as well as with your best interests.

By way of initial proof, we have given orders to have brought to you some presents which we believe might be agreeable to you. But the one thing in the world which we desire most, both for you and for your Realm, would be to obtain for your subjects who have already embraced the law of the only true God of heaven and earth, the freedom to profess it, since this law is the highest, the noblest, the most sacred, and especially the most suitable to have kings reign absolutely over the people.

We are even quite convinced that, if you knew the truths and the maxims which it teaches, you would give first of all to your subjects the glorious example of embracing it. We wish you this incomparable blessing together with a long and happy reign, and we pray God that it may please Him to augment your greatness with the happiest of endings.

Written at Saint-Germain-en-Laye, the 10th day of January, 1681,

Your very dear and good friend,
Louis

ANSWER FROM THE KING OF TONKIN TO LOUIS XIV

The King of Tonkin sends to the King of France a letter to express to him his best sentiments, saying that he was happy to learn that fidelity is a durable good of man and that justice is the most important of things. Consequently practicing of fidelity and justice cannot but yield good results. Indeed, though France and our Kingdom differ as to mountains, rivers, and boundaries, if fidelity and justice reign among our villages, our conduct will express all of our good feelings and contain precious gifts. Your communication, which comes from a country which is a thousand leagues away, and which proceeds from the heart as a testimony of your sincerity, merits repeated consideration and infinite praise. Politeness toward strangers is nothing unusual in our country. There is not a stranger who is not well received by us. How then could we refuse a man from France, which is the most celebrated among the kingdoms of the world and which for love of us wishes to frequent us and bring us merchandise? These feelings of fidelity and justice are truly worthy to be applauded. As regards your wish that we should cooperate in propagating your religion, we do not dare to permit it, for there is an ancient custom, introduced by edicts, which formally forbids it. Now, edicts are promulgated only to be carried out faithfully; without fidelity nothing is stable. How could we disdain a well-established custom to satisfy a private friendship? . . .

We beg you to understand well that this is our communication concerning our mutual acquaintance. This then is my letter. We send you herewith a modest gift, which we offer you with a glad heart.

This letter was written at the beginning of winter and on a beautiful day.

each other than they were to peoples outside the region. For the most part, the states and peoples of Southeast Asia were still in control of their own destiny.

RELIGION AND KINGSHIP

During the early modern era, both Buddhism and Islam became well established in Southeast Asia, and Christianity began to attract some converts, especially in the Philippines. Buddhism became dominant on the mainland, at least in lowland areas, from Burma to Vietnam. At first, Muslim influence was felt mainly on the Malay peninsula and along the northern coast of Java and Sumatra, where urban merchants encountered their Muslim counterparts from foreign lands on a regular basis. At the same time, traditional religious beliefs continued to survive, especially in the inland villages, where the local populations either ignored the new doctrines or integrated them into their traditional forms of spirit worship. Buddhists in rural Burma and Thailand, for example, might also believe in nature spirits. On Java and Sumatra, where Islam was slow to penetrate into the interior, the result was a division between devout Muslims in the cities and the still essentially animist peasants in the rural villages that persists to this day in Indonesian society.

Both Buddhism and Islam brought other changes in their train—temple education for Buddhists and schools for Islamic scholars and new religious and moral restrictions on human behavior such as refraining from eating pork and drinking wine for Muslims (though some foreign Muslims complained that the latter was not always followed). Because Islam discouraged the traditional tattooing of the body, Muslim converts turned to the technique of decorating textiles called *batik*.

Buddhism and Islam also helped to shape Southeast Asian political institutions. As the political systems began to mature, they evolved into four main types: Buddhist kings, Javanese kings, Islamic sultans, and Vietnamese emperors (for the case of Vietnam, which was strongly influenced by China, see Chapter 11). In each case, institutions and concepts imported from abroad were adapted to local circumstances.

The Buddhist style of kingship took shape between the eleventh and the fifteenth century, as Theravada Buddhism spread throughout the area. It became the pre-

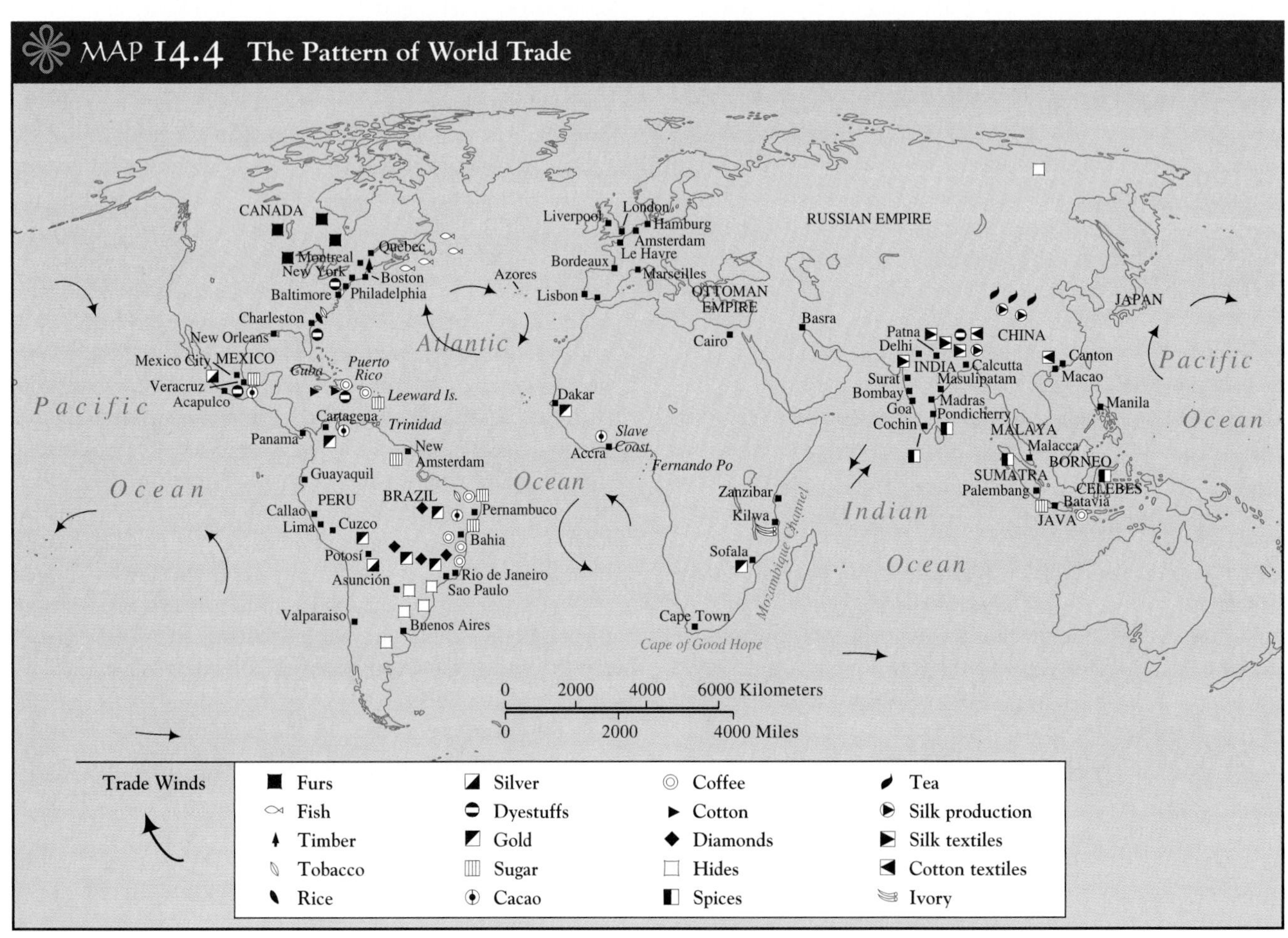

MAP 14.4 The Pattern of World Trade

THE TIMELY END OF SULTAN ZAINAL-'ABIDIN

Acheh, on the northern tip of the island of Sumatra, was one of the first areas in Southeast Asia to be converted to Islam. This passage from the History of Acheh *describes the cruel habits of Sultan Zainal-'Abidin, who ruled in the early seventeenth century. Note the understated way in which the author describes his deposition.*

HISTORY OF ACHEH

Then Sultan Seri'Alam was deposed and Sultan Zainal was installed.

The former had occupied the throne for one year before passing away. He passed away in the year 995 (A.H.) [1617 C.E.]. . . .

After the kingdom of Acheh Dar as-Salam and all its subject territories had been handed over to Sultan Zainal-'Abidin, he would always go out on to the arena and would have rutting elephants as well as ones which were not rutting charge each other, and as a result several people were gored to death by them, and the Bunga Setangkai palace was rammed and then collapsed in ruins together with its annexes. . . . He would order men to beat each other and to duel with staves and shields, and would order Achehnese champion fencers to compete with Indian ones, so that several of the Achehnese and Indian fencers were killed and some were wounded. . . .

If the Sultan were holding audience in a certain place all the chiefs were instructed to sit in homage in the hot sun or in the rain without distinction between the good or the evil. . . .

When the chiefs noticed these habits of the Sultan, and observed that they were growing worse day by day, they said to each other, "What should we do about our lord, for if his oppression of us is like this while he is still young, what will it be like when he is older? According to us, if he continues to be ruler everything will certainly fall in ruins about our ears." Then Sharif al-Muluk Maharaja Lela said, "If that is how it is, it would be best for us to depose our lord the Sultan."

After the chiefs had reached agreement on this matter, one evening the Sultan summoned persons to recite texts in praise of God, and the chiefs were summoned along with them. On that occasion they were reciting texts in the Friday annex. The Sultan was then put on an elephant and was taken to Makota 'Alam. When he arrived at Makota 'Alam . . . [where he was put to death] . . . the Sultan had occupied the throne for two years when he passed away. He passed away in the year 997 (A.H.) [1619 C.E.]. In that same year Sultan 'Ala ad-Din Ri'ayat Shah Marhum Sayyid al-Mukkamil was installed.

dominant form of political system in the Buddhist states of mainland Southeast Asia—Burma, Ayuthaya, Laos, and Cambodia. Perhaps the dominant feature of the Buddhist model was the godlike character of the monarch. The king, by virtue of his karma, was considered to be innately superior to other human beings and, in fact, served as a link between human society and the cosmos. Court rituals stressed the sacred character of the monarch, and even the palace was modeled after the symbolic design of the Hindu universe. In its center was an architectural rendering of sacred Mount Meru, the legendary home of the gods.

The Javanese model was a blend of Buddhist and Islamic political traditions. Like their Buddhist counterparts, Javanese monarchs possessed a sacred quality and maintained the balance between the sacred and the material world, but as Islam penetrated the Indonesian islands in the fifteenth and sixteenth centuries, the monarchs began to lose their semidivine quality.

The Islamic model was found mainly on the Malay peninsula and in the small coastal states of the Indonesian archipelago. In this pattern, the head of state was a sultan, who was viewed as a mortal, although he still possessed some magical qualities. The sultan served as a defender of the faith and staffed his bureaucracy mainly with aristocrats, but he also frequently relied on the Muslim community of scholars—the *ulama*—and was expected, at least in theory, to rule according to the *Shari'ah* (see the box above).

ECONOMY AND SOCIETY

During the early period of European penetration, the economy of virtually all Southeast Asian societies continued to be based on agriculture, as it had been for thousands of years. Still, by the sixteenth century, commerce was beginning to affect the daily lives of many Southeast Asians, especially in the cities that were beginning to proliferate along the coasts or on navigable rivers. In part, this was because agriculture itself was becoming more commercialized to a limited degree, as cash crops like sugar and spices replaced subsistence farming in rice or other cereals in some areas.

Regional and interregional trade were already expanding before the coming of the Europeans. The central geographical location of Southeast Asia enabled it to become a focal point in an interregional trading network. The spices, of course, were the mainstay of the interregional trade, but Southeast Asia exchanged other products as

BRINGING LUMBER TO JAVA. Long before the Europeans arrived, a brisk trade was taking place throughout the Indonesian islands and the South China Sea. Many of the goods that were transported through the area were carried on sturdy boats—called pinisi—that were manned by the Bugi, a trading people who lived mainly in the eastern islands. This trade continues today, as these cargo ships in the harbor of Jakarta attest. The Bugi were also widely feared as pirates.

well. The region exported tin (mined in Malaya since the tenth century), copper, gold, tropical fruits and other agricultural products, cloth, gems, and luxury goods in exchange for manufactured goods, ceramics including Chinese porcelain, and high-quality textiles such as silk from China. Although Southeast Asia on balance was an importer of manufactured goods, the region produced some high-quality goods of its own. The ceramics of Vietnam and Thailand, though not made with the high-firing techniques used in China, were still of good quality. The Portuguese traveler Duarte Barbosa observed that the Javanese were skilled cabinetmakers, weapons manufacturers, shipbuilders, and locksmiths. The royal courts were both the main producers and the primary consumers of luxury goods, most of which were produced by highly skilled slaves in the employ of the court.

In general, Southeast Asians probably enjoyed a somewhat higher living standard than most of their contemporaries elsewhere in Asia. Although most of the population was poor by modern Western standards, starvation and even widespread hunger were probably fairly rare. Several factors help explain this relative prosperity. In the first place, most of Southeast Asia has been blessed by a salubrious climate. The uniformly high temperatures and the abundant rainfall enable as many as two or even three crops to be grown each year. Second, although the soil in some areas is poor, the alluvial deltas on the mainland are fertile, and the volcanoes of Indonesia periodically spew forth rich volcanic ash that renews the mineral resources of the soil of Sumatra and Java. Finally, with some exceptions, most of Southeast Asia was relatively thinly populated. According to one estimate, the population of the entire region in 1600 was about 20 million, or about 5.5 persons per square kilometer, well below levels elsewhere in Asia. Only in a few areas such as the Red River delta in northern Vietnam was overpopulation a serious problem.

Social institutions tended to be fairly homogeneous throughout Southeast Asia. Compared with China and India, there was little social stratification, and the nuclear family predominated. In general, women fared better in Southeast Asia than anywhere else in Asia. Although they were usually restricted to specialized work, such as making ceramics, weaving, or transplanting the rice seedlings into the main paddy fields, and rarely possessed legal rights equal to those of men, they enjoyed a comparatively high degree of freedom and status in most societies in the region and, as we saw in Chapter 9, were sometimes involved in commerce. Daughters often had the same inheritance rights as sons, and family property was held jointly between husband and wife. Wives were often permitted to divorce their husbands, and monogamy was the rule rather than the exception. In some cases, the family of the groom provided the dowry in marriage, and married couples often went to live in the wife's village.

FLEETS OF THE FOREST. The peoples of Nias, a small island off the western coast of Sumatra, had long been isolated from other societies in the region, until the arrival of Dutch traders in the seventeenth century. Although Christian missionaries converted much of the population to the Christian faith two hundred years later, much of their Stone Age way of life has survived. In this hilltop village located in the center of the island, however, the houses in the background strongly resemble the hulls of the sturdy Dutch galleons that once anchored offshore.

CONCLUSION

At the end of the fifteenth century, Europeans burst upon the world scene. Beginning with the seemingly modest ventures of the Portuguese ships that sailed southward along the West African coast in the mid-fifteenth century, the process accelerated with the epoch-making voyages of Christopher Columbus to the Americas and Vasco da Gama to the Indian Ocean in the 1490s. Soon a number of other European states had entered the scene, and by the end of the eighteenth century, they had created a global trade network dominated by Western ships and Western power.

In less than three hundred years, the European Age of Exploration changed the shape of the world. In some areas, such as the Americas and the Spice Islands, it led to the destruction of indigenous civilizations and the establishment of European colonies. In others, as in Africa, South Asia, and mainland Southeast Asia, it left native regimes intact but had a strong impact on local societies and regional trade patterns.

At the time, many European observers viewed the process in a favorable light. It not only expanded world trade and introduced new crops and discoveries between the Old and the New Worlds (a process sometimes called the "Columbian Exchange" that will be discussed in the Reflection at the end of Part III), but it also introduced "heathen peoples" to the message of Jesus Christ. Some modern historians have been much more critical, concluding that European activities during the sixteenth and seventeenth centuries had already created a "tributary mode of production" based on European profits from unequal terms of trade that foreshadowed the highly exploitative relationship characteristic of the later colonial period. Some recent scholars have questioned that contention, however, and argue that although Western commercial operations had a significant impact on global trade patterns, they did not—at least before the eighteenth century—freeze out non-European participants. Muslim merchants, for example, were long able to evade European efforts to eliminate them from the spice trade, and the trans-Saharan caravan trade was relatively unaffected by European merchant shipping along the West African coast. In some cases, the European presence may even have encouraged new economic activity, as in the Indian subcontinent (see Chapter 16). If there was an "age of Western dominance," then, it did not take shape before the end of the period under consideration here.

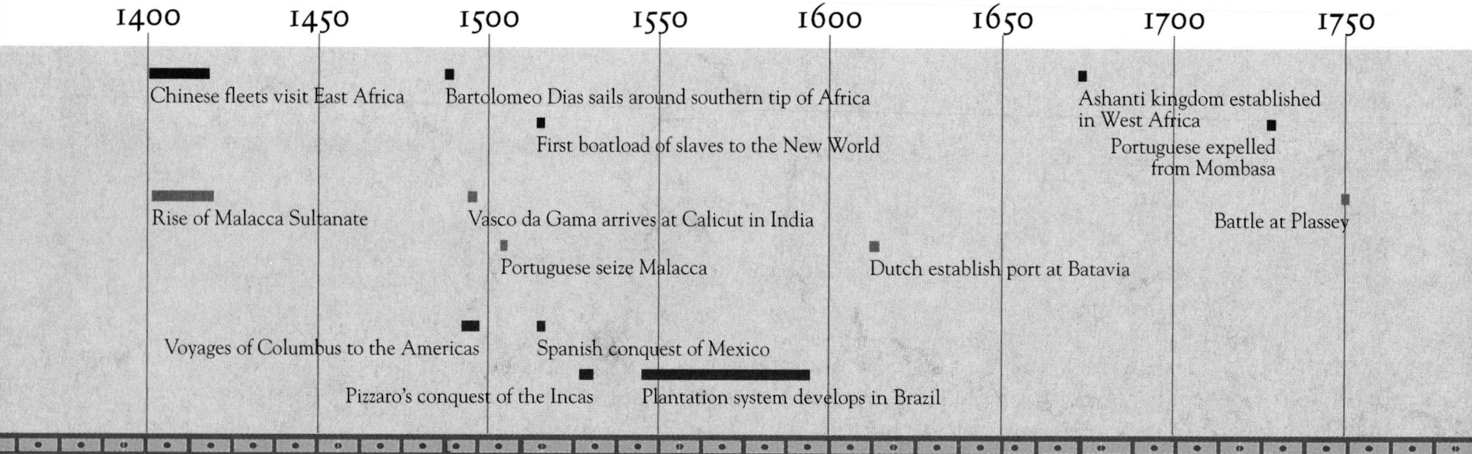

Chapter Notes

1. Harry J. Benda and John A. Larkin, eds., *The World of Southeast Asia: Selected Historical Readings* (New York, 1967), p. 13.
2. J. H. Parry, *The European Reconnaissance: Selected Documents* (New York, 1968), p. 113, quoting from Armando Cortesao, *The Summa Oriental of Tome Pires* (London, 1944), 2:283–87.
3. Quoted in J. H. Parry, *The Age of Reconnaissance: Discovery, Exploration and Settlement, 1450 to 1650* (New York, 1963), p. 33.
4. Quoted in Richard B. Reed, "The Expansion of Europe," in Richard DeMolen, ed., *The Meaning of the Renaissance and Reformation* (Boston, 1974), p. 308.
5. K. N. Chaudhuri, *Trade and Civilization in the Indian Ocean: An Economic History from the Rise of Islam to 1750* (Cambridge, 1985), p. 65.
6. Miguel Leon-Portilla, ed., *The Broken Spears: The Aztec Account of the Conquest of Mexico* (Boston, 1969), p. 51.
7. Quoted in Parry, *The Age of Reconnaissance*, pp. 176–77.
8. Quoted in Basil Davidson, *Africa in History: Themes and Outlines* (London, 1968), p. 137.

Suggested Readings

Classic works on the period of European expansion include J. H. Parry, *The Age of Reconnaissance: Discovery, Exploration and Settlement, 1450 to 1650* (New York, 1963); B. Penrose, *Travel and Discovery in the Renaissance, 1420–1620* (New York, 1962); and the brief work by J. H. Parry, *The Establishment of European Hegemony, 1415–1715* (New York, 1961). Also, see K. M. Panikkar, *Asia and Western Dominance* (London, 1959), and H. Furber, *Rival Empires of Trade in the Orient, 1600–1800* (Minneapolis, 1976). For a more critical interpretation, see E. Wolf, *Europe and the People Without History* (Berkeley, Calif., 1982), and A. G. Frank, *World Accumulation, 1492–1789* (New York, 1978).

On the technological aspects, see C. M. Cipolla, *Guns, Sails, and Empires: Technological Innovation and the Early Phases of European Expansion, 1400–1700* (New York, 1965); F. Fernandez-Armesto, ed., *The Times Atlas of World Exploration* (New York, 1991); R. C. Smith, *Vanguard of Empire: Ships of Exploration in the Age of Columbus* (Oxford, 1993); and D. Boorstin, *The Discoverers* (New York, 1983). For an overview on the impact of European expansion in the Indian Ocean, see K. N. Chaudhuri, *Trade and Civilization in the Indian Ocean: An Economic History from the Rise of Islam to 1750* (Cambridge, 1985). For a series of stimulating essays reflecting recent scholarship, see J. D. Tracy, *The Rise of Merchant Empires: Long-Distance Trade in the Early Modern World, 1350–1750* (Cambridge, 1990).

On European expansion in the Americas, see S. E. Morison, *The European Discovery of America: The Southern Voyages,* A.D. *1492–1616* (New York, 1974). On Columbus, see the brief biography by J. S. Collis, *Christopher Columbus* (London, 1976). For a fundamental work on Spanish colonization, see J. H. Parry, *The Spanish Seaborne Empire* (New York, 1966). The standard work on the conquistadors is F. A. Kirkpatrick, *The Spanish Conquistadores* (Cleveland, 1968). See also the richly illustrated H. Innes, *The Conquistadors* (New York, 1969). The human effects of the interaction of New and Old World cultures are examined thoughtfully in A. W. Crosby, *The Columbia Exchange: Biological and Cultural Consequences of 1492* (Westport, Conn., 1972).

On Portuguese expansion, the fundamental work is C. R. Boxer, *The Portuguese Seaborne Empire, 1415–1825* (New York, 1969). For a more recent interpretation, see W. B. Diffie and G. D. Winius, *Foundations of the Portuguese Empire, 1415–1580* (Minneapolis, 1979). On the Dutch, see J. I. Israel, *Dutch Primacy in World Trade, 1585–1740* (Oxford, 1989). The effects of European trade in Southeast Asia are discussed in A. Reid, *Southeast Asia in the Age of Commerce, 1450–1680* (New Haven, Conn., 1989).

On the African slave trade, the standard work is P. Curtin, *The African Slave Trade: A Census* (Madison, Wis., 1969). For more recent treatments, see H. S. Klein, *The Middle Passage: Comparative Studies in the Atlantic Slave Trade* (Princeton, N.J., 1978); P. Lovejoy, *Transformations in Slavery: A History of Slavery in Africa* (1983); and P. Manning, *Slavery and African Life* (1990). Also, see C. Palmer, *Human Cargoes: The British Slave Trade to Spanish America, 1700–1739* (Urbana, Ill., 1981), and K. F. Kiple, *The Caribbean Slave: A Biological History* (Cambridge, 1984).

For a brief introduction to women's experiences during the Age of Exploration and global trade, see S. Hughes and B. Hughes, *Women in World History*, vol. 2 (Armonk, N.Y., 1997). For a more theoretical discussion of violence and gender in the early modern period, consult R. Trexler, *Sex and Conquest: Gendered Violence, Political Order and the European Conquest of the Americas* (Ithaca, N.Y., 1995). The native American female experience with the European encounter is presented in R. Gutierrez, *When Jesus Came the Corn Mothers Went Away: Marriage, Sexuality and Power in New Mexico, 1500–1846* (Stanford, Calif., 1991), and K. Anderson, *Chain Her by One Foot: The Subjugation of Women in Seventeenth Century New France* (London, 1991).

For additional reading, go to InfoTrac College Edition, your online research library at http://web1.infotrac-college.com

Enter the search terms "Vasco da Gama" using Keywords.

Enter the search terms "Christopher Columbus" using the Subject Guide.

Enter the search term "mercantilism" using the Subject Guide.

Enter the search terms "Africa history" using Keywords.

CHAPTER 15

RELIGIOUS REFORM AND STATE BUILDING IN EUROPE

CHAPTER OUTLINE

- THE PROTESTANT REFORMATION
- THE CATHOLIC REFORMATION
- EUROPE IN CRISIS: WAR, REVOLUTION, AND SOCIAL DISINTEGRATION, 1560–1650
- RESPONSE TO CRISIS: THE PRACTICE OF ABSOLUTISM
- LIMITED MONARCHY: ENGLAND AND THE EMERGENCE OF CONSTITUTIONAL MONARCHY
- THE WORLD OF EUROPEAN CULTURE
- CONCLUSION

FOCUS QUESTIONS

- What were Martin Luther's main disagreements with the Roman Catholic church, and why did the movement he started spread so quickly across Europe?
- What were the main tenets of Lutheranism, Zwinglianism, Calvinism, and Anabaptism, and how did they differ from each other and from Catholicism?
- Why is the period between 1560 and 1650 in Europe called an age of crisis, and how did the turmoil contribute to the artistic and intellectual developments of the period?
- What was absolutism, and what were the main characteristics of the absolute monarchies that emerged in France, Prussia, Austria, and Russia?
- What were the main issues in the struggle between king and Parliament in seventeenth-century England, and how were they resolved?

On April 18, 1520, a lowly monk stood before the emperor and princes of Germany in the city of Worms. He had been called before this august gathering to answer charges of heresy, charges that could threaten his very life. The monk was confronted with a pile of his books and asked if he wished to defend them all or reject a part. Courageously, Martin Luther defended them all and asked to be shown where any part was in error on the basis of "Scripture and plain reason." The emperor was outraged by Luther's response and made his own position clear the next day: "Not only I, but you of this noble German nation, would be forever disgraced if by our negligence not only heresy but the very suspicion of heresy were to survive. After having heard yesterday the obstinate defense of Luther, I regret that I have so long delayed in proceeding against him and his false teaching. I will have no more to do with him." Luther's appearance at Worms set the stage for a serious challenge to the authority of the Catholic church. It was by no means the first in the church's fifteen-hundred-year history, but its consequences were more far-reaching than anyone at Worms in 1520 could have imagined. The unity of Christendom was shattered by the Protestant Reformation initiated by Martin Luther.

Although the Protestant and Catholic Reformations of the sixteenth century made religion a central focus of people's lives, by the middle of the sixteenth century this renewal of religious passion had been accomplished at a great cost—the breakup of the religious unity of medieval Europe. This religious division (Catholics versus Protestants) was instrumental in beginning a series of wars that dominated much of European history from 1560 to 1650 and, in turn, exacerbated the economic and social crises that were besetting Europe. Wars, revolutions and constitutional crises, economic depression, social disintegration, the witchcraft craze, and demographic crisis all afflicted Europe.

One of the responses to these crises was a search for order and harmony. The most general trend was an extension of monarchical power as a stabilizing force. This development, which historians have called absolutism or absolute monarchy, was most evident in France during the flamboyant reign of Louis XIV. But other states, such as England, responded differently to domestic crisis, and another very different system emerged in which monarchs were limited by the power of their representative assemblies. Whether absolutist or limited monarchies, European states also developed larger military forces and economies to support larger governmental bureaucracies and more wars. In the process, European states gained the resources to move out into the global stage in a dramatic fashion.

The Protestant Reformation

Beginning in the Late Middle Ages, there seemed to be an increasing number of calls for the reform of the Catholic church, whether it be to end the corruption in the clergy or to reduce the excessive power of the papacy. The church had managed to crush these early efforts at reform, but at the beginning of the sixteenth century it came to face an even more menacing reform movement. The Protestant Reformation had its beginnings in a typical medieval question: What must I do to be saved? Martin Luther, a deeply religious man, found an answer that did not fit within the traditional teachings of the late-medieval church. Ultimately he split with that church, destroying the religious unity of western Christendom. That other people were concerned with the same question is evident in the rapid spread of the Reformation.

Prelude to Reformation

Martin Luther's reform movement was not the first in sixteenth-century Europe. During the second half of the fifteenth century, the new classical learning that was part of Italian Renaissance humanism spread to northern Europe and spawned a movement called Christian or Northern Renaissance humanism, whose major goal was the reform of Christendom.

The Christian humanists believed in the ability of human beings to reason and improve themselves. They thought that if people would read the classics, and especially the basic works of Christianity, they would become more pious. This inner piety, or inward religious feeling, would bring about a reform of the church and society. For this reason, Christian humanists supported schools, brought out new editions of the classics, and prepared new editions of the Bible and writings of early Christianity. In the preface to his edition of the Greek New Testament, the famous humanist Erasmus wrote:

> Indeed, I disagree very much with those who are unwilling that Holy Scripture, translated into the vulgar tongue, be read by the uneducated, as if Christ taught such intricate doctrines that they could scarcely be understood by very few theologians, or as if the strength of the Christian religion consisted in men's ignorance of it . . . I would that even the lowliest women read the Gospels and the Pauline Epistles. And I would that they were translated into all languages so that they could be read and understood not only by Scots and Irish but also by Turks and Saracens. . . . Would that, as a result, the farmer sing some portion of them at the plow, the weaver hum some parts of them to the movement of his shuttle, the traveler lighten the weariness of the journey with stories of this kind![1]

This belief in the power of education would remain an important characteristic of European civilization. Like later intellectuals, Christian humanists believed that to change society they must first change the human beings who compose it.

The most influential of all the Christian humanists was Erasmus (1466–1536). After withdrawing from a monastery, he wandered to France, England, Italy, Germany, and Switzerland, conversing everywhere in the classical Latin that might be called his mother tongue. *The Handbook of the Christian Knight*, published in 1503, reflected his preoccupation with religion. He called his conception of religion "the philosophy of Christ," by which he meant that Christianity should be a guiding philosophy for the direction of daily life rather than the system of dogmatic beliefs and practices that the medieval church seemed to stress. In other words, he emphasized inner piety and ethics while de-emphasizing the external forms of religion (such as the sacraments, pilgrimages, fasts, veneration of saints, and relics).

To reform the church, Erasmus wanted to spread the philosophy of Christ, provide education in the works of Christianity, and criticize the abuses in the church. In his work *The Praise of Folly*, written in 1509, Erasmus humorously criticized aspects of his society that he believed were most in need of reform. He was especially harsh on the abuses in the church and singled out the monks for special treatment. Monks, he said, "insist that everything be done in precise detail. . . . Just so many knots must be on each shoe and the shoelace must be of only one color, . . . and they can sleep only the specified number of hours per day." Because of this attention to detail, he continued, "they think that they are superior to all people" and will be rewarded in heaven.

Erasmus's reform program, however, did not achieve its goal. Undoubtedly, his work helped to prepare the way for the Reformation; as contemporaries proclaimed, "Erasmus laid the egg that Luther hatched." Yet Erasmus eventually disapproved of Luther and the Protestant reformers. He had no intention of destroying the unity of the medieval Christian church; instead, his whole program was based on reform within the church.

Church and Religion on the Eve of the Reformation

Corruption in the Catholic church was another factor that encouraged people to want reform. No doubt, the failure of the Renaissance popes to provide spiritual leadership had affected the spiritual life of all Christendom. The preoccupation of the papal court with finances had an especially strong impact on the clergy. So, too, did the economic changes of the fourteenth and fifteenth centuries. The highest positions of the clergy were increasingly held by either nobles or wealthy members of the bourgeoisie. At the same time, to increase their revenues, high church officials (such as bishops, archbishops, and cardinals) took over more than one church office. This practice of pluralism (the holding of many church offices) led, in turn, to the problem of absenteeism. Church officeholders ignored their duties and paid underlings to run their offices who were often little interested in performing their duties. No wonder that so many people complained in the fifteenth century about the ignorance and failure of parish priests.

While the leaders of the church were failing to meet their responsibilities, ordinary people were clamoring for meaningful religious expression and certainty of salvation. As a result, for some the process of salvation became almost mechanical. Collections of relics grew as more and more people sought certainty of salvation through their veneration. Frederick the Wise, elector of Saxony and Luther's prince, had amassed over 5,000 relics to which were attached indulgences that could reduce one's time in purgatory by 1,443 years (an indulgence is a remission of the penalties due to sin). Other people sought certainty of salvation in the popular mystical movement known as the Modern Devotion. The Modern Devotion downplayed religious dogma and stressed the need to follow the teachings of Christ. Thomas à Kempis, author of *The Imitation of Christ,* wrote that "Truly, at the day of judgment we shall not be examined by what we have read, but what we have done; not how well we have spoken, but how religiously we have lived."

What is striking about the revival of religious piety in the fifteenth century—whether expressed through such external forces as the veneration of relics and the buying of indulgences or the mystical path—was its adherence to the orthodox beliefs and practices of the Catholic church. The agitation for certainty of salvation and spiritual peace was done within the framework of the "holy mother Church." But disillusionment grew as the devout experienced the clergy's inability to live up to their expectations. The deepening of religious life, especially in the second half of the fifteenth century, found little echo among the worldly-wise clergy, and it is this divergence that helps to explain the tremendous and immediate impact of Luther's ideas.

Martin Luther and the Reformation in Germany

Martin Luther was born in Germany on November 10, 1483. His father wanted him to become a lawyer, so Luther enrolled at the University of Erfurt. In 1505, after becoming a master in the liberal arts, the young Martin began to study law. But Luther was not content with the study of law and all along had shown religious inclinations. In the summer of 1505, en route back to Erfurt after a brief visit home, he was caught in a ferocious thunderstorm and vowed that if he were spared, he would become a monk. He then entered the monastic order of the Augustinian Hermits in Erfurt. Later, he studied theology at the University of Wittenberg, where he received his doctorate in 1512 and then became a professor in the theological

LUTHER AND THE NINETY-FIVE THESES

To most historians, the publication of Luther's Ninety-Five Theses marks the beginning of the Reformation. To Luther, they were simply a response to what he considered to be the blatant abuses committed by sellers of indulgences. Although written in Latin, the theses were soon translated into German and disseminated widely across Germany. They made an immense impression on Germans already dissatisfied with the ecclesiastical and financial policies of the papacy.

MARTIN LUTHER, SELECTIONS FROM THE NINETY-FIVE THESES

5. The Pope has neither the will nor the power to remit any penalties beyond those he has imposed either at his own discretion or by canon law.
20. Therefore the Pope, by his plenary remission of all penalties, does not mean "all" in the absolute sense, but only those imposed by himself.
21. Hence those preachers of Indulgences are wrong when they say that a man is absolved and saved from every penalty by the Pope's Indulgences.
27. It is mere human talk to preach that the soul flies out [of purgatory] immediately [when] the money clinks in the collection box.
28. It is certainly possible that when the money clinks in the collection box greed and avarice can increase; but the intercession of the Church depends on the will of God alone.
50. Christians should be taught that, if the Pope knew the exactions of the preachers of Indulgences, he would rather have the basilica of St. Peter reduced to ashes than built with the skin, flesh, and bones of his sheep [the indulgences that so distressed Luther were being sold to raise money for the construction of the new St. Peter's Basilica in Rome].
81. This wanton preaching of pardons makes it difficult even for learned men to redeem respect due to the Pope from the slanders or at least the shrewd questionings of the laity.
82. For example: "Why does not the Pope empty purgatory for the sake of most holy love and the supreme need of souls? This would be the most righteous of reasons, if he can redeem innumerable souls for sordid money with which to build a basilica, the most trivial of reasons."
86. Again: "Since the Pope's wealth is larger than that of the crassest Crassi of our time, why does he not build this one basilica of St. Peter with his own money, rather than with that of the faithful poor?"
90. To suppress these most conscientious questionings of the laity by authority only, instead of refuting them by reason, is to expose the Church and the Pope to the ridicule of their enemies, and to make Christian people unhappy.
94. Christians should be exhorted to seek earnestly to follow Christ, their Head, through penalties, deaths, and hells.
95. And let them thus be more confident of entering heaven through many tribulations rather than through a false assurance of peace.

faculty, lecturing on the Bible. Probably sometime between 1513 and 1516, through his study of the Bible, he arrived at an answer to a problem—the assurance of salvation—that had disturbed him since his entry into the monastery.

Catholic doctrine had emphasized that both faith and good works were required of a Christian to achieve personal salvation. In Luther's eyes, human beings, weak and powerless in the sight of an almighty God, could never do enough good works to merit salvation. Through his study of the Bible, Luther rediscovered another way of viewing this problem. To Luther, humans are not saved through their good works, but through faith in the promises of God, made possible by the sacrifice of Christ on the cross. The doctrine of salvation or justification by grace through faith alone became the primary doctrine of the Protestant Reformation. Because Luther had arrived at this doctrine from his study of the Bible, the Bible became for him, as it would be for all other Protestants, the chief guide to religious truth. Justification by faith and the Bible as the sole authority in religious affairs were the twin pillars of the Protestant Reformation.

Luther did not see himself as a rebel, but he was greatly upset by the widespread selling of indulgences. Especially offensive in his eyes was the monk Johann Tetzel, who hawked indulgences with the slogan: "As soon as the coin in the coffer [money box] rings, the soul from purgatory springs." Luther believed that people were simply harming their chances for salvation by buying these pieces of paper. Greatly angered, he issued his Ninety-Five Theses, which were a stunning indictment of the abuses in the sale of indulgences (see the box above). Luther did not intend any break with the church over the issue of indulgences, but he did want the pope to stop their sale. But the Renaissance pope Leo X did not take the issue seriously and is reported to have said that Luther was simply "some drunken German who will amend his ways when he sobers up." Thousands of copies of the Ninety-Five Theses were printed and quickly spread to all parts of Germany.

Under pressure from the church and his followers, Luther began to move toward a more definite break with the Catholic church. He called on the German princes to overthrow the papacy in Germany and establish a

WOODCUT: LUTHER VERSUS THE POPE. In the 1520s, after Luther's return to Wittenberg, his teachings began to spread rapidly, ending ultimately in a reform movement supported by state authorities. Pamphlets containing picturesque woodcuts were important in the spread of Luther's ideas. In the woodcut shown here, the crucified Jesus attends Luther's service on the left, while on the right the pope is at a table selling indulgences.

reformed German church. He attacked the system of sacraments as the means by which the pope and church had destroyed the real meaning of the Gospel for one thousand years. He kept only two sacraments, baptism and the Lord's Supper, and called for the clergy to marry. Through all these calls for change, Luther expounded more and more on his new doctrine of salvation. It is faith alone, he said, not good works, which justifies and brings salvation through Christ.

Unable to accept Luther's forcefully worded dissent from traditional Catholic teachings, the church excommunicated him in January 1521. He was also summoned to appear before the imperial diet or Reichstag of the Holy Roman Empire, convened by the newly elected emperor Charles V (1519–1556). Expected to recant the heretical doctrines he had espoused, Luther refused and made the famous reply that became the battle cry of the Reformation:

> Since then Your Majesty and your lordships desire a simple reply, I will answer without horns and without teeth. Unless I am convicted by Scripture and plain reason—I do not accept the authority of popes and councils, for they have contradicted each other—my conscience is captive to the Word of God. I cannot and I will not recant anything, for to go against conscience is neither right nor safe. Here I stand; I cannot do otherwise. God help me. Amen.[2]

The young emperor Charles was outraged at Luther's audacity and gave his opinion that "a single friar who goes counter to all Christianity for a thousand years must be wrong." By the Edict of Worms, Martin Luther was made an outlaw within the empire. His works were to be burned and Luther himself captured and delivered to the emperor.

Between 1521 and 1525, Luther's religious movement became a revolution. Luther was able to gain the support of his prince, the elector of Saxony, as well as other German rulers among the three hundred–odd states that made up the Holy Roman Empire. These rulers were instrumental in instituting new state-dominated churches in their territories. The Lutheran churches in Germany (and later in Scandinavia) quickly became territorial or state churches in which the state supervised and disciplined church members. As part of the development of these state-dominated churches, Luther also instituted new religious services to replace the mass. These featured a worship service consisting of a German liturgy that focused on Bible reading, preaching of the word of God, and song. Following his own denunciation of clerical celibacy, Luther married a former nun, Katherina von Bora, in 1525. His union provided a model of married and family life for the new Protestant minister.

A series of crises in the mid-1520s made it apparent, however, that spreading the word of God was not as easy as Luther had originally envisioned, the usual plight of most reformers. Luther experienced dissent within his own ranks in Wittenberg as well as defection from many Christian humanists who feared that Luther's movement threatened the unity of Christendom. The Peasants' War constituted Luther's greatest challenge, however. In June 1524, peasants in Germany rose in revolt against their lords and looked to Luther for support. But Luther, who knew how much his reformation of the church depended on the full support of the German princes and magistrates, supported the rulers. To Luther, God had ordained the state and its rulers and given them the authority to maintain the peace and order necessary for the spread of the Gospel. It was the duty of princes to suppress all revolts. By May 1525, the German princes had ruthlessly suppressed the peasant hordes. By this time, Luther found himself ever more dependent on state authorities for the growth and maintenance of his reformed church.

Politics and Religion in the German Reformation

From its very beginning, the fate of Luther's movement had been closely tied to political affairs. In 1519, Charles I, king of Spain and the grandson of the Emperor Maximilian, had been elected Holy Roman emperor as

CHARLES V. Charles V sought to maintain religious unity throughout his vast empire by keeping all his subjects within the bounds of the Catholic church. Due to his conflict with Francis I as well as difficulties with the Turks, the papacy, and the German princes, Charles was never able to check the spread of Lutheranism. This is a portrait of Charles V by the Venetian painter Titian.

Charles V (1519–1556). Charles V ruled over an immense empire, consisting of Spain and its overseas possessions, the traditional Austrian Habsburg lands, Bohemia, Hungary, the Low Countries, and the kingdom of Naples in southern Italy. Politically, Charles wanted to maintain his dynasty's control over his enormous empire; religiously, he hoped to preserve the unity of his empire in the Catholic faith. Despite his strengths, Charles spent a lifetime in futile pursuit of his goals. Four major problems—the French, the papacy, the Turks, and Germany's internal situation—kept him preoccupied and cost him both his dream and his health. At the same time, these four factors contributed to the survival of Lutheranism by giving the Lutherans time to organize before having to face the concerted onslaught of the Catholic forces.

Between 1521 and 1544, Charles fought a series of wars with his chief rival, the French king Francis I (1515–1547). At the same time, Charles faced opposition from Pope Clement VII (1523–1534), who, guided by political considerations, joined the side of Francis I. The advance of the Ottoman Turks (see Chapter 16) into the eastern part of Charles's empire forced the emperor to divert forces there as well.

Finally, the internal political situation in the Holy Roman Empire was also not in Charles's favor. Germany was a land of several hundred territorial states: princely states, ecclesiastical principalities, and free imperial cities. Although all owed loyalty to the emperor, Germany's development in the Middle Ages had enabled these states to become quite independent of imperial authority. They had no desire to have a strong emperor. By the time Charles V was able to bring military forces to Germany—in 1546—Lutheranism had become well established and the Lutheran princes well organized. Unable to impose his will on Germany, Charles was forced to negotiate a truce. An end to religious warfare in Germany came in 1555 with the Peace of Augsburg, which marks an important turning point in the history of the Reformation. The division of Christianity was formally acknowledged when Lutheranism was granted the same legal rights as Catholicism. Moreover, the peace settlement accepted the right of each German ruler to determine the religion of his subjects.

The Peace of Augsburg was a victory for the German princes. The independence of the numerous German territorial states guaranteed the weakness of the Holy Roman Empire and the continued decentralization of Germany. Charles's hope for a united empire had been completely dashed. At the same time, what had at first been merely feared was now confirmed: the ideal of medieval Christian unity was irretrievably lost. The rapid proliferation of new Protestant groups served to underscore the new reality.

The Spread of the Protestant Reformation

Switzerland was home to two major Reformation movements, Zwinglianism and Calvinism. Ulrich Zwingli (1484–1531) was ordained a priest in 1506 and accepted an appointment as a cathedral priest in the Great Minster of Zürich in 1518. Zwingli's preaching of the Gospel caused such unrest that in 1523 the city council held a public disputation or debate in the town hall. Zwingli's party was accorded the victory, and the council declared that "Mayor, Council and Great Council of Zürich, in order to do away with disturbance and discord, have upon due deliberation and consultation decided and resolved that Master Zwingli should continue as heretofore to proclaim the Gospel and

A REFORMATION DEBATE: THE MARBURG COLLOQUY

Debates played a crucial role in the Reformation period. They were a primary instrument in introducing the Reformation into innumerable cities as well as a means of resolving differences among like-minded Protestant groups. This selection contains an excerpt from Luther's and Zwingli's vivacious and often brutal debate over the sacrament of the Lord's Supper at Marburg in 1529. The two protagonists failed to reach agreement.

THE MARBURG COLLOQUY, 1529

THE HESSIAN CHANCELLOR FEIGE: My gracious prince and lord [Landgrave Philip of Hesse] has summoned you for the express and urgent purpose of settling the dispute over the sacrament of the Lord's Supper. . . . And let everyone on both sides present his arguments in a spirit of moderation, as becomes such matters. . . . Now then, Doctor Luther, you may proceed.

LUTHER: Noble prince, gracious lord! Undoubtedly the colloquy is well intentioned. . . . Although I have no intention of changing my mind, which is firmly made up, I will nevertheless present the grounds of my belief and show where the others are in error. . . . Your basic contentions are these: In the last analysis you wish to prove that a body cannot be in two places at once, and you produce arguments about the unlimited body which are based on natural reason. I do not question how Christ can be God and man and how the two natures can be joined. For God is more powerful than all our ideas, and we must submit to his word.

Prove that Christ's body is not there where the Scripture says, "This is my body!" Rational proofs I will not listen to. . . . God is beyond all mathematics and the words of God are to be revered and carried out in awe. It is God who commands, "Take, eat, this is my body." I request, therefore, valid scriptural proof to the contrary.

Luther writes on the table in chalk, "This is my body," and covers the words with a velvet cloth.

OECOLAMPADIUS [leader of the reform movement in Basel and a Zwinglian partisan]: The sixth chapter of John clarifies the other scriptural passages. Christ is not speaking there about a local presence. "The flesh is of no avail," he says [John 6:63]. It is not my intention to employ rational, or geometrical, arguments—neither am I denying the power of God—but as long as I have the complete faith I will speak from that. For Christ is risen; he sits at the right hand of God; and so he cannot be present in the bread. Our view is neither new nor sacrilegious, but is based on faith and Scripture. . . .

ZWINGLI: I insist that the words of the Lord's Supper must be figurative. This is ever apparent, and even required by the article of faith: "taken up into heaven, seated at the right hand of the Father." Otherwise, it would be absurd to look for him in the Lord's Supper at the same time that Christ is telling us that he is in heaven. One and the same body cannot possibly be in different places. . . .

LUTHER: I call upon you as before: your basic contentions are shaky. Give way, and give glory to God!

ZWINGLI: And we call upon you to give glory to God and to quit begging the question! The issue at stake is this: Where is the proof of your position? I am willing to consider your words carefully—no harm meant! You're trying to outwit me. I stand by this passage in the sixth chapter of John, verse 63 and shall not be shaken from it. You'll have to sing another tune.

LUTHER: You're being obnoxious.

ZWINGLI *(excitedly)*: Don't you believe that Christ was attempting in John 6 to help those who did not understand?

LUTHER: You're trying to dominate things! You insist on passing judgment! Leave that to someone else! . . . It is your point that must be proved, not mine. But let us stop this sort of thing. It serves no purpose.

ZWINGLI: It certainly does! It is for you to prove that the passage in John 6 speaks of a physical repast.

LUTHER: You express yourself poorly and make about as much progress as a cane standing in a corner. You're going nowhere.

ZWINGLI: No, no, no! This is the passage that will break your neck!

LUTHER: Don't be so sure of yourself. Necks don't break this way. You're in Hesse, not Switzerland. . . .

the pure sacred Scriptures."[3] Over the next two years, evangelical reforms were promulgated in Zürich by a city council strongly influenced by Zwingli. Relics and images were abolished; all paintings and decorations were removed from the churches and replaced by whitewashed walls. The mass was replaced by a new liturgy consisting of Scripture reading, prayer, and sermons. Monasticism, pilgrimages, the veneration of saints, clerical celibacy, and the pope's authority were all abolished as remnants of papal Christianity.

As his movement began to spread to other cities in Switzerland, Zwingli sought an alliance with Martin Luther and the German reformers. Although both the German and the Swiss reformers realized the need for unity to defend against the opposition of the Catholic authorities, they were unable to agree on the interpretation of the Lord's Supper (see the box above). Zwingli believed that the scriptural words "This is my Body, This is my blood" should be taken figuratively, not literally, and refused to accept Luther's insistence on the real presence of the body and blood of Christ "in, with, and under the bread and wine." In October 1531, war erupted between the Swiss Protestant and Catholic states. Zürich's army was routed, and Zwingli was found wounded on the battlefield. His enemies killed him, cut up his body, and burned the pieces, scattering the ashes. The leadership of Swiss Protestantism now passed to John Calvin (1509–1564), the systematic theologian and organizer of the Protestant movement.

John Calvin was educated in his native France, but after his conversion to Protestantism, he was forced to flee France for the safety of Switzerland. In 1536, he published the first edition of the *Institutes of the Christian Religion*, a masterful synthesis of Protestant thought and a work that immediately secured his reputation as one of the new leaders of Protestantism.

On most important doctrines, Calvin stood very close to Luther. He adhered to the doctrine of justification by faith alone to explain how humans achieved salvation. But Calvin also placed much emphasis on the absolute sovereignty of God or the "power, grace, and glory of God." Thus, "God asserts his possession of omnipotence, and claims our acknowledgment of this attribute; not such as is imagined by sophists, vain, idle, and almost asleep, but vigilant, efficacious, operative and engaged in continual action."[4]

One of the ideas derived from his emphasis on the absolute sovereignty of God—predestination—gave a unique cast to Calvin's teachings. This "eternal decree," as Calvin called it, meant that God had predestined some people to be saved (the elect) and others to be damned (the reprobate). According to Calvin, "He has once for all determined, both whom he would admit to salvation, and whom he would condemn to destruction."[5] Although Calvin stressed that there could be no absolute certainty of salvation, his followers did not always make this distinction. The practical psychological effect of predestination was to give later Calvinists an unshakable conviction that they were doing God's work on earth. Thus, Calvinism became a dynamic and activist faith. It is no accident that Calvinism became the militant international form of Protestantism.

In 1536, Calvin began working to reform the city of Geneva. He created a church government that used both clergy and laymen in the service of the church. The Consistory, a special body for enforcing moral discipline, was set up as a court to oversee the moral life and doctrinal purity of Genevans. The Consistory had the right to punish people who deviated from the church's teachings and moral principles. Indeed, citizens in Geneva were punished for such varied "crimes" as dancing, singing obscene songs, drunkenness, swearing, and playing cards.

Calvin's success in Geneva enabled the city to become a vibrant center of Protestantism. John Knox, the Calvinist reformer of Scotland, called Geneva "the most perfect school of Christ on earth." Following Calvin's lead, missionaries trained in Geneva were sent to all parts of Europe. Calvinism became established in France, the Netherlands, Scotland, and central and eastern Europe. By the mid-sixteenth century, Calvinism had replaced Lutheranism as the militant international form of Protestantism, while Calvin's Geneva stood as the fortress of the Reformation.

While Calvin was forging his militant brand of Protestantism in Switzerland, the English Reformation had been initiated by an act of state. King Henry VIII (1509–1547) had a strong desire to divorce his first wife, Catherine of Aragon, who had failed to produce a male heir. Normally, church authorities might have been willing to grant the king an annulment of his marriage, but Pope Clement VII was dependent on the Holy Roman emperor Charles V, who happened to be the nephew of Queen Catherine.

JOHN CALVIN. After a conversion experience, John Calvin abandoned his life as a humanist and became a reformer. In 1536, Calvin began working to reform the city of Geneva, where he remained until his death in 1564. This sixteenth-century portrait of Calvin pictures him near the end of his life.

CHRONOLOGY

KEY EVENTS OF THE REFORMATION ERA

Luther's Ninety-Five Theses	1517
Excommunication of Luther	1521
Beginning of Zwingli's reformation in Switzerland	1523
Peasants' War in Germany	1524–1525
Act of Supremacy in England	1534
Pontificate of Paul III	1534–1549
John Calvin's *Institutes of the Christian Religion*	1536
Jesuits recognized as a religious order	1540
Council of Trent	1545–1563
Peace of Augsburg	1555

Impatient with the pope's inaction, Henry sought to obtain an annulment of his marriage in England's own ecclesiastical courts. As archbishop of Canterbury and head of the highest ecclesiastical court in England, Thomas Cranmer held official hearings on the king's case and ruled in May 1533 that the king's marriage to Catherine was "null and absolutely void."

In 1534, upon Henry's request, Parliament moved to finalize the break of the Church of England with Rome. An Act of Supremacy of 1534 declared that the king was "taken, accepted, and reputed the only supreme head on earth of the Church of England," a position that gave him control of doctrine, clerical appointments, and church discipline. Using his new powers, Henry dissolved the monasteries. About four hundred religious houses were closed in 1536, and their land and possessions confiscated by the king. Many were sold to nobles, gentry, and some merchants. The king not only received a great boost to his treasury, but also created a group of supporters who now had a stake in the new Tudor order.

Although Henry VIII had broken with the papacy, little change occurred in matters of doctrine, theology, and ceremony. Some of his supporters, such as Archbishop Thomas Cranmer, wished to have a religious reformation as well as an administrative one, but Henry was unyielding. He died in 1547 and was succeeded by his son, the underage and sickly Edward VI (1547–1553). During Edward's reign, Archbishop Cranmer and others inclined toward Protestant doctrines were able to move the Church of England (or Anglican church) in more of a Protestant direction. New acts of Parliament instituted the right of the clergy to marry and the creation of a revised Protestant liturgy that was elaborated in a new prayer book and liturgical guide known as the Book of Common Prayer. These rapid changes in doctrine and liturgy aroused much opposition and prepared the way for the reaction that occurred when Mary, Henry's first daughter by Catherine of Aragon, came to the throne.

There was no doubt that Mary (1553–1558) was a Catholic who intended to return England to Roman Catholicism. But her restoration of Catholicism aroused much opposition. There was widespread antipathy to Mary's unfortunate marriage to Philip II, the son of Charles V and future king of Spain. Philip was strongly disliked in England, and Mary's foreign policy based on alliance with Spain aroused further hostility. The burning of over three hundred Protestant heretics roused further ire against "bloody Mary." As a result of her policies, Mary managed to achieve the opposite of what she had intended: England was more Protestant by the end of her reign than it had been at the beginning.

Although many reformers were ready to allow the state to play an important, if not dominant, role in church affairs, some people rejected this kind of magisterial reformation and favored a far more radical reform movement. Collectively called the Anabaptists, these radicals actually formed a large variety of different groups, who nevertheless shared some common characteristics. Anabaptism was especially attractive to those peasants, weavers, miners, and artisans who had been adversely affected by the economic changes of the age.

Anabaptists everywhere shared some common ideas. To them, the true Christian church was a voluntary association of believers who had undergone spiritual rebirth and had then been baptized into the church. Anabaptists advocated adult rather than infant baptism. They also took literally a return to the practices and spirit of early Christianity. Adhering to the accounts of early Christian communities in the New Testament, they followed a strict sort of democracy in which all believers were considered equal. Each church chose its own minister, who might be any member of the community because all Christians were considered priests (though women were often excluded). Those chosen as ministers led the services, which were very simple and contained nothing not found in the early church. Anabaptists rejected theological speculation in favor of simple Christian living according to what they believed was the pure word of God. The Lord's Supper was interpreted as a remembrance, a meal of fellowship celebrated in the evening in private houses according to Christ's example. Finally, unlike the Catholics and other Protestants, most Anabaptists believed in the complete separation of church and state. Not only was government to be excluded from the realm of religion, but it was not even supposed to exercise political jurisdiction over real Christians. Anabaptists refused to hold political office or bear arms because many took literally the commandment "Thou shall not kill," although

A PROTESTANT WOMAN

In the initial zeal of the Protestant Reformation, women were frequently allowed to play unusual roles. Catherine Zell of Germany (c. 1497–1562) first preached beside her husband in 1527. After the death of her two children, she devoted the rest of her life to helping her husband and their Anabaptist faith. This selection is taken from one of her letters to a young Lutheran minister who had criticized her activities.

CATHERINE ZELL TO LUDWIG RABUS OF MEMMINGEN

I, Catherine Zell, wife of the late lamented Mathew Zell, who served in Strasbourg, where I was born and reared and still live, wish you peace and enhancement in God's grace. . . .

From my earliest years I turned to the Lord, who taught and guided me, and I have at all times, in accordance with my understanding and His grace, embraced the interests of His church and earnestly sought Jesus. Even in youth this brought me the regard and affection of clergymen and others much concerned with the church, which is why the pious Mathew Zell wanted me as a companion in marriage; and I, in turn, to serve the glory of Christ, gave devotion and help to my husband, both in his ministry and in keeping his house. . . . Ever since I was ten years old I have been a student and a sort of church mother, much given to attending sermons. I have loved and frequented the company of learned men, and I conversed much with them, not about dancing, masquerades, and worldly pleasures but about the kingdom of God. . . .

Consider the poor Anabaptists, who are so furiously and ferociously persecuted. Must the authorities everywhere be incited against them, as the hunter drives his dog against wild animals? Against those who acknowledge Christ the Lord in very much the same way we do and over which we broke with the papacy? Just because they cannot agree with us on lesser things, is this any reason to persecute them and in them Christ, in whom they fervently believe and have often professed in misery, in prison, and under the torments of fire and water?

Governments may punish criminals, but they should not force and govern belief, which is a matter for the heart and conscience not for temporal authorities. . . . When the authorities pursue one, they soon bring forth tears, and towns and villages are emptied.

some Anabaptist groups did become quite violent. Their political beliefs as much as their religious beliefs caused the Anabaptists to be regarded as dangerous radicals who threatened the very fabric of sixteenth-century society. Indeed, the chief thing Protestants and Catholics could agree on was the need to persecute Anabaptists.

The Social Impact of the Protestant Reformation

Christianity was such an integral part of European life that it was inevitable that the Reformation would have an impact on the family and popular religious practices.

THE FAMILY

For centuries, Catholicism had praised the family and sanctified its existence by making marriage a sacrament. But the Catholic church's high regard for abstinence from sex as the surest way to holiness made the celibate state of the clergy preferable to marriage. Nevertheless, since not all men could remain chaste, marriage offered the best means to control sexual intercourse and give it a purpose, the procreation of children. To some extent, this attitude persisted among the Protestant reformers; Luther, for example, argued that sex in marriage allowed one to "make use of this sex in order to avoid sin," and Calvin advised that every man should "abstain from marriage only so long as he is fit to observe celibacy." If "his power to tame lust fails him," then he must marry.

But the Reformation did bring some change to the conception of the family. Both Catholic and Protestant clergy preached sermons emphasizing a more positive side to family relationships. The Protestants were especially important in developing this new view of the family. Because Protestantism had eliminated any idea of special holiness for celibacy, abolishing both monasticism and a celibate clergy, the family could be placed at the center of human life, and a new stress on "mutual love between man and wife" could be extolled. But were doctrine and reality the same? For more radical religious groups, at times they were (see the box above). One Anabaptist wrote to his wife before his execution: "My faithful helper, my loyal friend. I praise God that he gave you to me, you who have sustained me in all my trial."[6] But more often reality reflected the traditional roles of husband as the ruler and wife as the obedient servant whose chief duty was to please her husband. Luther stated it clearly:

> The rule remains with the husband, and the wife is compelled to obey him by God's command. He rules the home and the state, wages war, defends his possessions, tills the soil, builds, plants, etc. The woman on the other hand is like a nail driven into the wall . . . so the wife should stay at home and look after the affairs of the household, as one who has been deprived of the ability of administering those affairs that

> are outside and that concern the state. She does not go beyond her most personal duties.[7]

Obedience to her husband was not a wife's only role; her other important duty was to bear children. To Calvin and Luther, this function of women was part of the divine plan. God punishes women for the sins of Eve by the burdens of procreation and feeding and nurturing their children. Although Protestantism sanctified this role of woman as mother and wife, viewing it as a holy vocation, it also left few alternatives for women. Because monasticism had been destroyed, that career avenue was no longer available; for most Protestant women, family life was their only destiny. At the same time, by emphasizing the father as "ruler" and hence the center of household religion, Protestantism even removed the woman from her traditional role as controller of religion in the home. Overall, the Protestant Reformation did not noticeably transform women's subordinate place in society.

RELIGIOUS PRACTICES AND POPULAR CULTURE

The attacks of Protestant reformers on the Catholic church led to radical changes in religious practices. The Protestant Reformation abolished or severely curtailed such customary practices as indulgences, the veneration of relics and saints, pilgrimages, monasticism, and clerical celibacy. The elimination of saints put an end to the numerous celebrations of religious holy days and changed a community's sense of time. Thus, in Protestant communities, religious ceremonies and imagery, such as processions and statues, tended to be replaced with individual private prayer, family worship, and collective prayer and worship at the same time each week on Sunday.

In addition to abolishing saints' days and religious carnivals, some Protestant reformers even tried to eliminate customary forms of entertainment. English Puritans (as English Calvinists were called), for example, attempted to ban drinking in taverns, dramatic performances, and dancing. Dutch Calvinists denounced the tradition of giving small presents to children on the feast of Saint Nicholas, near Christmas. Many of these Protestant attacks on popular culture were unsuccessful, however. The importance of taverns in English social life made it impossible to eradicate them, while celebrating at Christmastime persisted in the Dutch Netherlands.

THE CATHOLIC REFORMATION

By the mid-sixteenth century, Lutheranism had become established in Germany and Scandinavia and Calvinism in Switzerland, France, the Netherlands, and eastern Europe. In England, the split from Rome had resulted in the creation of a national church. The situation in Europe did not look particularly favorable to the Roman Catholic church. But even at the beginning of the sixteenth century, constructive, positive forces were at work for reform within the Catholic church, and by the mid-sixteenth century, these forces had given the Catholic church new strength. There were three chief pillars of the Catholic Reformation: the development of the Jesuits, the emergence of a reformed and revived papacy, and the Council of Trent.

The Society of Jesus, known as the Jesuits, was founded by a Spanish nobleman, Ignatius of Loyola (1491–1556). Loyola gathered together a small group of individuals who were recognized as a religious order by a papal bull in 1540.

IGNATIUS LOYOLA. The Jesuits became the most important new religious order of the Catholic Reformation. Shown here in a sixteenth-century painting by an unknown artist is Ignatius Loyola, founder of the Society of Jesus. Loyola is seen kneeling before Pope Paul III, who officially recognized the Jesuits in 1540.

The new order was grounded on the principles of absolute obedience to the papacy, a strict hierarchical order for the society, the use of education to achieve its goals, and a dedication to engage in "conflict for God." Jesuit organization came to resemble the structure of a military command. Executive leadership was put in the hands of a general, who nominated all important positions in the order and was to be revered as its absolute head. Loyola served as the first general of the order until his death in 1556. A special vow of absolute obedience to the pope made the Jesuits an important instrument for papal policy. Jesuit missionaries proved singularly successful in restoring Catholicism to parts of Germany and eastern Europe.

Another prominent Jesuit activity was the propagation of the Catholic faith among non-Christians. Francis Xavier (1506–1552), one of the original members of the Society of Jesus, carried the message of Catholicism to the East, ministering to India and Japan before dying of fever. Although conversion efforts in Japan proved short-lived, Jesuit activity in China, especially that of the Italian Matteo Ricci, was more long lasting.

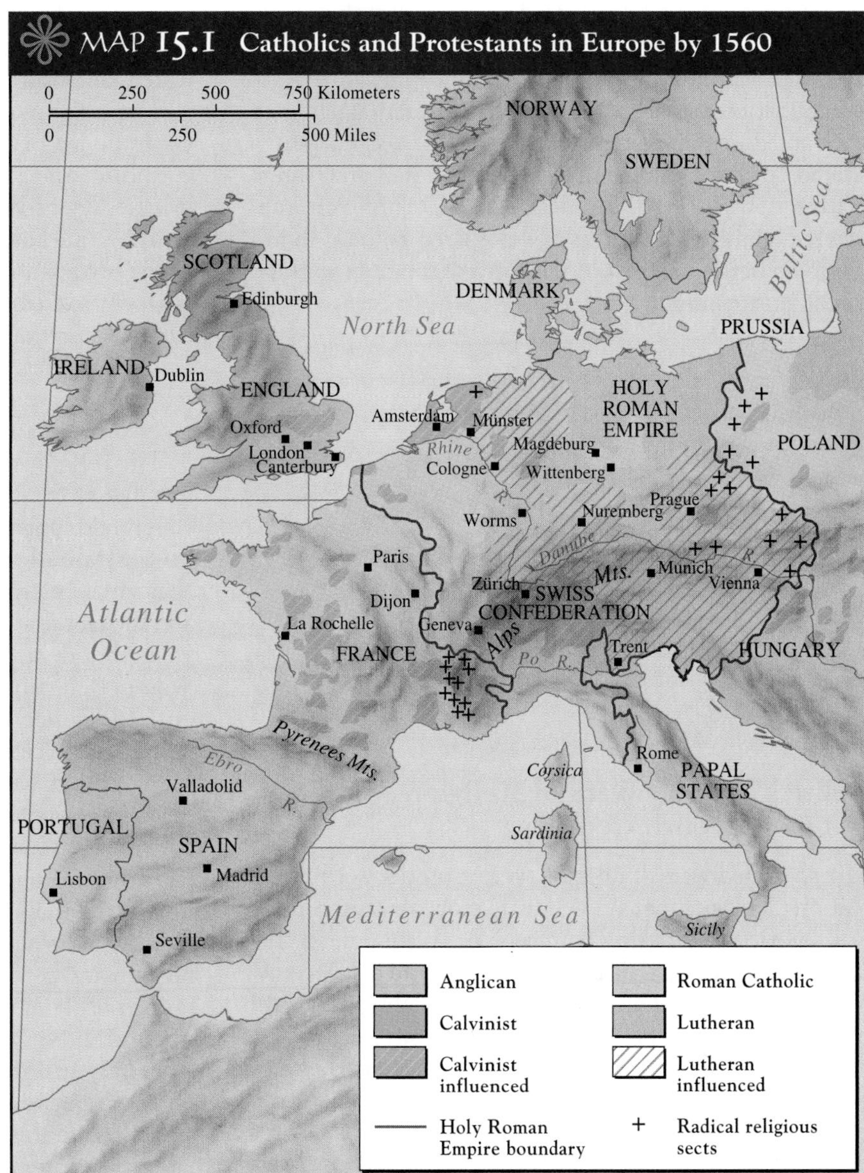

A reformed papacy was another important factor in the development of the Catholic Reformation. The involvement of the Renaissance papacy in dubious finances and Italian political and military affairs had created numerous sources of corruption. It took the jolt of the Protestant Reformation to bring about serious reform. The pontificate of Pope Paul III (1534–1549) proved to be a turning point. He perceived the need for change and expressed it decisively. Advocates of reform were made cardinals. In 1535, Paul took the audacious step of appointing a Reform Commission to ascertain the church's ills. The commission's report in 1537 blamed the church's problems on the corrupt policies of popes and cardinals. It was also Paul III who formally recognized the Jesuits and initiated the Council of Trent, the third major pillar of the Catholic Reformation.

In March 1545, a group of cardinals, archbishops, bishops, abbots, and theologians met in the city of Trent, on the border between Germany and Italy, and initiated the Council of Trent, which met intermittently from 1545 to 1563 in three major sessions. Moderate Catholic reformers hoped that compromises would be made in formulating doctrinal definitions that would encourage Protestants to return to the church. Conservatives, however, favored an uncompromising restatement of Catholic doctrines in strict opposition to Protestant positions. The latter group won. The final doctrinal decrees of the Council of Trent reaffirmed traditional Catholic teachings in opposition to Protestant beliefs. Scripture and tradition were affirmed as equal authorities in religious matters; only the church could interpret Scripture. Both faith and good works were declared necessary for salvation. The seven sacraments, the Catholic doctrine of transubstantiation, and clerical celibacy were all upheld. Belief in purgatory and in the efficacy of indulgences was strengthened, although hawking of indulgences was prohibited.

After the Council of Trent, the Roman Catholic church possessed a clear body of doctrine and a unified church under the acknowledged supremacy of the popes who had triumphed over bishops and councils. The Roman Catholic church had become one Christian denomination among many, with an organizational framework and doctrinal pattern that would not be significantly altered until Vatican Council II four hundred years later. With a new spirit of confidence, the Catholic church entered a militant phase, as well prepared as the Calvinists to do battle for the Lord. An era of religious warfare was about to unfold.

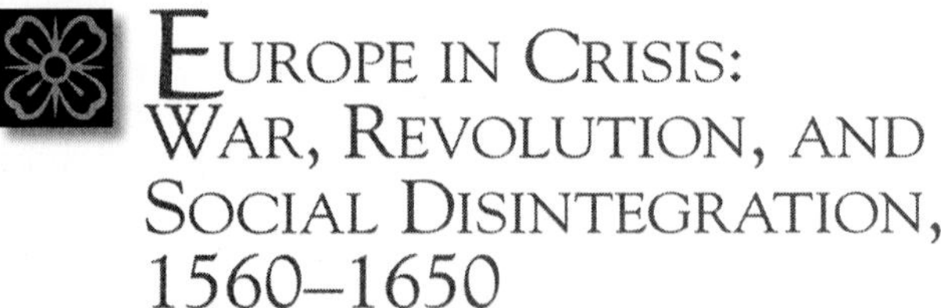

Europe in Crisis: War, Revolution, and Social Disintegration, 1560–1650

Between 1560 and 1650, Europe experienced religious wars, revolutions and constitutional crises, economic and social disintegration, and a witchcraft craze. It was truly an age of crisis.

Politics and the Wars of Religion in the Sixteenth Century

The so-called wars of religion were a product of Reformation ideologies that allowed little room for compromise or toleration of differing opinions. By the middle of the sixteenth century, Calvinism and Catholicism had become highly militant religions dedicated to spreading the word of God as they interpreted it. While their struggle for the minds and hearts of Europeans was at the heart of the religious wars of the sixteenth century, economic, social, and political forces also played an important role in these conflicts. Of the sixteenth-century religious wars, none was more momentous nor shattering than the French civil wars known as the French Wars of Religion.

THE FRENCH WARS OF RELIGION (1562–1598)

Religion was at the heart of the French civil wars of the sixteenth century. The growth of Calvinism had led to persecution by the French kings, but the latter did little to stop the spread of Calvinism. Huguenots (as the French Calvinists were called) came from all layers of society: artisans and shopkeepers hurt by rising prices and a rigid guild system, merchants and lawyers in provincial towns whose local privileges were tenuous, and members of the nobility. Possibly 40 to 50 percent of the French nobility became Huguenots, including the house of Bourbon, which stood next to the Valois in the royal line of succession and ruled the southern French kingdom of Navarre. The conversion of so many nobles made the Huguenots a potentially dangerous political threat to monarchical power. Although the Calvinists constituted only about 7 percent of the population, they were a dedicated, determined, and well-organized minority.

The Calvinist minority was greatly outnumbered by the Catholic majority. The Valois monarchy was staunchly Catholic, and its control of the Catholic church gave it little incentive to look favorably upon Protestantism. At the same time, an extreme Catholic party—known as the ultra-Catholics—favored strict opposition to the Huguenots. Possessing the loyalty of Paris and large sections of northern and northwestern France, the ultra-Catholics could recruit and pay for large armies and received support abroad from the papacy and Jesuits, who favored their noncompromising Catholic position.

The religious issue was not the only factor that contributed to the French civil wars. Towns and provinces, which had long resisted the growing power of monarchical centralization, were only too willing to join a revolt against the monarchy. This was also true of the nobility, and the fact that so many of them were Calvinists created an important base of opposition to the crown. The French Wars of Religion, then, constituted a major constitutional crisis for France and temporarily halted the development of the French centralized territorial state. The claim of the ruling dynasty to a person's loyalties was temporarily superseded by loyalty to one's religious belief. For thirty years, battles raged in France between Catholic and Calvinist parties, who obviously considered the unity of France less important than religious truth. But there also emerged in France a group of *politiques* who placed politics before religion and believed that no religious truth was worth the ravages of civil war. The *politiques* ultimately prevailed, but not until both sides were exhausted by bloodshed.

Finally, in 1589, Henry of Navarre, the political leader of the Huguenots and a member of the Bourbon dynasty, succeeded to the throne as Henry IV (1589–1610). Realizing, however, that he would never be accepted by Catholic France, Henry took the logical way out and converted to Catholicism. With his coronation in 1594, the wars of religion finally came to an end. The Edict of Nantes in 1598 solved the religious problem by acknowledging Catholicism as the official religion of France while guaranteeing the Huguenots the right to worship and to enjoy all political privileges, including the holding of public offices.

PHILIP II AND THE CAUSE OF MILITANT CATHOLICISM

The greatest advocate of militant Catholicism in the second half of the sixteenth century was King Philip II of Spain (1556–1598), the son and heir of Charles V. Philip's reign ushered in an age of Spanish greatness, both politically and culturally. His first major goal was to consolidate and secure the lands he had inherited from his father. These included Spain, the Netherlands, and possessions in Italy and the New World. To strengthen his control, Philip insisted on a strict conformity to Catholicism and a strong, monarchical authority. Achieving the latter was not easy, because each of the states and territories of his empire had its own structure of government. Even in Spain, there was no really deep sense of nationhood. Philip did manage, however, to expand royal power by making the monarchy less dependent on the landed aristocrats.

The Catholic faith was crucial to both Philip II and the Spanish people. During the Late Middle Ages, Catholic kingdoms in Spain had gradually reconquered most of the land from the Muslims and expelled the Spanish Jews. Driven by this heritage of crusading fervor, it was not difficult for Spain to see itself as a nation of people chosen by God to save Catholic Christianity from the Protestant heretics. Philip II, the "Most Catholic King," became the champion of Catholicism throughout Europe, a role that led to spectacular victories and equally spectacular defeats for the Spanish king. Spain's leadership of a Holy League against Turkish encroachments in the Mediterranean resulted in a stunning victory over the Turkish fleet in the Battle of Lepanto in 1571. But Philip's attempt to crush the revolt in the Netherlands and his tortured policy with the English Queen Elizabeth led to his greatest misfortunes.

One of the richest parts of Philip's empire, the Spanish Netherlands was of great importance to the "Most Catholic King." Philip's attempt to strengthen his control in the Netherlands, which consisted of seventeen provinces (modern Netherlands, Belgium, and Luxembourg), soon led to a revolt. The nobles, who stood to lose the most politically if their jealously guarded privileges and freedoms were weakened, strongly opposed Philip's efforts. Resentment against Philip was also aroused by the collection of taxes when the residents of the Netherlands realized that these revenues were being used for Spanish interests. Finally, religion became a major catalyst for rebellion when Philip attempted to crush Calvinism. Violence erupted in 1566, when Calvinists—especially nobles—began to destroy statues and stained glass windows in Catholic churches. Philip responded by sending 10,000 veteran Spanish and Italian troops to crush the rebellion.

But the revolt became organized, especially in the northern provinces, where the Dutch, under the leadership of William of Nassau, the prince of Orange, offered growing resistance. The struggle dragged on for decades until 1609, when a twelve-year truce ended the war, virtually recognizing the independence of the northern provinces. These seven northern provinces, which began to call themselves the United Provinces of the Netherlands in 1581, became the core of the modern Dutch state. The new state was officially recognized by the Peace of Westphalia in 1648. The seventeenth century has often been called the "golden age" of the Dutch Republic as the United Provinces held center stage as one of Europe's great powers. Like France and England, the United Provinces was an Atlantic power, underlining the importance of the shift of political and economic power in the seventeenth century from the Mediterranean Sea to the countries on the Atlantic seaboard.

At the beginning of the seventeenth century, Spain possessed the most populous empire in the world, controlling almost all of South America and a number of settlements in Asia and Africa. To most Europeans, Spain still seemed the greatest power of the age, but the reality was quite different. The treasury was empty; Philip II went bankrupt in 1596 from excessive expenditures on war, while his successor did the same in 1607 by spending a fortune on his court. The armed forces were out-of-date, and the government was inefficient. Spain continued to play the role of a great power, but appearances were deceiving.

THE ENGLAND OF ELIZABETH

When Elizabeth Tudor, the younger daughter of Henry VIII, ascended the throne in 1558, the population of England numbered fewer than four million people. During her reign, England rose to prominence as the relatively small island kingdom, became the leader of the Protestant nations of Europe, and laid the foundations for a world empire.

Intelligent, cautious, and self-confident, Elizabeth moved quickly to solve the difficult religious problem she inherited from her half sister, Queen Mary Tudor. Elizabeth's religious policy was based on moderation and compromise. The Catholic laws of Mary's reign were repealed, and a new Act of Supremacy designated Elizabeth "the only supreme governor" of both church and state. The church service used during the reign of Edward VI was revised to make it more acceptable to Catholics. The Church of England under Elizabeth was basically Protestant, but it was a moderate Protestantism that kept most people satisfied in the second half of the sixteenth century.

Caution, moderation, and expediency also dictated Elizabeth's foreign policy. Fearful of other countries' motives, Elizabeth realized that war could be disastrous for her island kingdom and her own rule. While encouraging English piracy and providing clandestine aid to French Huguenots and Dutch Calvinists to weaken France and Spain, she pretended complete aloofness and avoided alliances that would force her into war with any major power. Gradually, however, Elizabeth was drawn into conflict with Spain. After resisting for years the idea of invading England as too impractical, Philip II of Spain was finally persuaded to do so by advisers who assured him that the people of England would rise against their queen when the Spaniards arrived. Moreover, Philip was easily convinced that the revolt in the Netherlands would never be crushed as long as England provided support for it. In any case, a successful invasion of England would mean the overthrow of heresy and the return of England to Catholicism. Accordingly, Philip ordered preparations for an armada to spearhead the invasion of England.

The Spanish Armada proved to be a disaster. The Spanish fleet that finally set sail had neither the ships nor the troops that Philip had planned to send. Battered by a number of encounters with the English, the Spanish fleet sailed back to Spain by a northerly route around Scotland and Ireland, where it was further pounded by storms. Although the English and Spanish would continue their war for another sixteen years, the defeat of the armada guaranteed for the time being that England would remain a Protestant country. Although Spain made up for its losses within a year and a half, the defeat was a psychological blow to the Spaniards.

Economic and Social Crises: The Witchcraft Craze

The period of European history from 1560 to 1650 witnessed severe economic and social crises as well as political upheaval. The inflation-fueled prosperity of the sixteenth century showed signs of slackening by the beginning of the seventeenth century. Economic contraction began to be evident in some parts of Europe by the 1620s. In the 1630s and 1640s, as imports of silver from the Americas declined, economic recession intensified, especially in the Mediterranean area. Italy, the industrial and financial center of Europe in the age of the Renaissance, was now becoming an economic backwater. Spain's economy was also encountering serious problems by the decade of the 1640s.

Population trends of the sixteenth and seventeenth centuries also reveal Europe's worsening conditions. The sixteenth century was a period of expanding population, possibly related to a warmer climate and increased food supplies. It has been estimated that the population of Europe increased from 60 million in 1500 to 85 million by 1600, the first major recovery of the European population since the devastation of the Black Death in the mid-fourteenth century. However, records also indicate a leveling off of the population by 1620 and even a decline by 1650, especially in central and southern Europe. Europe's longtime adversaries—war, famine, and plague—continued to affect population levels. Another "little ice

THE PERSECUTION OF WITCHES. Hysteria over witchcraft affected the daily lives of many Europeans in the sixteenth and seventeenth centuries. This picture by Frans Francken the Young, painted in 1607, shows a number of activities commonly attributed to witches. In the center, several witches are casting spells with their magic books and instruments, while at the top, a witch on a post prepares to fly off on her broomstick.

age" after the middle of the sixteenth century, when average temperatures fell, affected harvests and gave rise to famines. These economic problems created social tensions that manifested themselves in various ways, including the witchcraft craze.

Hysteria over witchcraft affected the lives of many Europeans in the sixteenth and seventeenth centuries. Witchcraft trials were prevalent in England, Scotland, Switzerland, Germany, some parts of France and the Low Countries, and even New England in America.

Witchcraft was not a new phenomenon in the sixteenth and seventeenth centuries. Although its practice had been part of traditional village culture for centuries, the medieval church made witchcraft both sinister and dangerous by connecting witches to the activities of the devil, thereby transforming witchcraft into a heresy that had to be extirpated. By the thirteenth century, after the creation of the Inquisition, people were being accused of a variety of witchcraft practices and, following the biblical injunction "Thou shalt not suffer a witch to live," were turned over to secular authorities for burning at the stake or hanging (in England).

What distinguished witchcraft in the sixteenth and seventeenth centuries from these previous developments was the high level of hysteria at which neighbors accused neighbors of witchcraft, leading to widespread trials of witches. Perhaps more than 100,000 people were prosecuted throughout Europe on charges of witchcraft. As more and more people were brought to trial, the fear of witches as well as the fear of being accused of witchcraft escalated to frightening proportions. Although larger cities were affected first, the trials also spread to smaller towns and rural areas as the hysteria persisted well into the seventeenth century (see the box on p. 442).

Although even city officeholders were not immune to persecution, women of the lower classes were more likely to be accused of witchcraft. Indeed, where lists are given, those mentioned most often are milkmaids, peasant women, and servant girls. In the witchcraft trials of the sixteenth and seventeenth centuries, more than 75 percent of those accused were women, most of them single or widowed and many over fifty years old. Moreover, almost all victims belonged to the lower classes, the poor and propertyless.

The accused witches usually confessed to a number of practices, most often after intense torture. Many said that they had sworn allegiance to the devil and attended sabbats or nocturnal gatherings where they feasted, danced, and even copulated with the devil in sexual orgies. More common, however, were admissions of using evil incantations and special ointments and powders to wreak havoc on neighbors by killing their livestock, injuring their children, or raising storms to destroy their crops.

A number of contributing factors have been suggested to explain why the witchcraft craze became so widespread in the sixteenth and seventeenth centuries. Religious uncertainties clearly played some part. Many witchcraft trials occurred in areas where Protestantism had been recently victorious or in regions, such as southwestern Germany, where Protestant-Catholic controversies still raged. As religious passions became inflamed, accusations of being in league with the devil became common on both sides. Recently, however, historians have emphasized the importance of social conditions, especially the problems of a society in turmoil, in explaining the witchcraft hysteria. At a time when the old communal values that stressed working together for the good of the community were disintegrating, property owners became more fearful of the growing numbers of poor among them and transformed them psychologically into agents of the devil. Old women were particularly susceptible to suspicion. Many of them, no longer the recipients of the local charity found in traditional society, may even have tried to survive by selling herbs, potions, or secret remedies for healing. When problems arose, and there were many in this crisis-laden period, these same women were the most likely scapegoats.

That women should be the chief victims of witchcraft trials was hardly accidental. Nicholas Rémy, a witchcraft judge in France in the 1590s, found it "not unreasonable that this scum of humanity, i.e., witches, should be drawn chiefly from the feminine sex." To another judge, it came as no surprise that witches would confess to sexual experiences with satan: "The devil uses them so, because he knows that women love carnal pleasures, and he means to bind them to his allegiance by such agreeable provocations."[8] Of course, witch hunters were not the only ones to hold such low estimates of women. Most theologians, lawyers, and philosophers in early modern Europe maintained a belief in the natural inferiority of women, making it plausible to them that women would be more susceptible to witchcraft.

By the mid-seventeenth century, the witchcraft hysteria began to subside. The destruction of the religious wars had at least forced people to accept a grudging toleration that allowed religious passions to subside. Moreover, as governments began to stabilize after the period of crisis, fewer magistrates were willing to accept the unsettling and divisive conditions generated by the trials of witches. Finally, by the end of the seventeenth century and the beginning of the eighteenth, more and more people were questioning their old attitudes toward religion altogether and found it especially contrary to reason to believe in a world haunted by evil spirits.

Seventeenth-Century Crises: Revolution and War

Although many Europeans responded to the upheavals of the second half of the sixteenth century with a desire for peace and order, the first fifty years of the seventeenth century continued to be a period of crisis. A series of rebellions and civil wars stemming from the discontent of both nobles and commoners rocked the domestic stability of

A WITCHCRAFT TRIAL IN FRANCE

Persecutions for witchcraft reached their high point in the sixteenth and seventeenth centuries, when tens of thousands of people were brought to trial. In this excerpt from the minutes of a trial in France in 1652, we can see why the accused witch stood little chance of exonerating herself.

THE TRIAL OF SUZANNE GAUDRY

28 May, 1652. . . . Interrogation of Suzanne Gaudry, prisoner at the court of Rieux. . . . During interrogations on May 28 and May 29, the prisoner confessed to a number of activities involving the devil.]

Deliberation of the Court—June 3, 1652

The undersigned advocates of the Court have seen these interrogations and answers. They say that the aforementioned Suzanne Gaudry confesses that she is a witch, that she had given herself to the devil, that she had renounced God, Lent, and baptism, that she has been marked on the shoulder, that she has cohabited with the devil and that she has been to the dances, confessing only to have cast a spell upon and caused to die a beast of Philippe Cornié. . . .

Third Interrogation, June 27

This prisoner being led into the chamber, she was examined to know if things were not as she had said and confessed at the beginning of her imprisonment.

—Answers no, and that what she has said was done so by force.

Pressed to say the truth, that otherwise she would be subjected to torture, having pointed out to her that her aunt was burned for this same subject.

—Answers that she is not a witch. . . .

She was placed in the hands of the officer in charge of torture, throwing herself on her knees, struggling to cry, uttering several exclamations, without being able, nevertheless, to shed a tear. Saying at every moment that she is not a witch.

The Torture

On this same day, being at the place of torture.

This prisoner, before being strapped down, was admonished to maintain herself in her first confessions and to renounce her lover.

—Says that she denies everything she has said, and that she has no lover. Feeling herself being strapped down, says that she is not a witch, while struggling to cry . . . and upon being asked why she confessed to being one, said that she was forced to say it.

Told that she was not forced, that on the contrary she declared herself to be a witch without any threat.

—Says that she confessed it and that she is not a witch, and being a little stretched [on the rack] screams ceaselessly that she is not a witch.

Asked if she did not confess that she had been a witch for twenty-six years.

—Says that she said it, that she retracts it, crying that she is not a witch.

Asked if she did not make Philippe Cornié's horse die, as she confessed.

—Answers no, crying Jesus-Maria, that she is not a witch.

The mark having been probed by the officer, in the presence of Doctor Bouchain, it was adjudged by the aforesaid doctor and officer truly to be the mark of the devil.

Being more tightly stretched upon the torture rack, urged to maintain her confessions.

—Said that it was true that she is a witch and that she would maintain what she had said.

Asked how long she has been in subjugation to the devil.

—Answers that it was twenty years ago that the devil appeared to her, being in her lodgings in the form of a man dressed in a little cowhide and black breeches. . . .

Verdict

July 9, 1652. In the light of the interrogations, answers, and investigations made into the charge against Suzanne Gaudry, . . . seeing by her own confessions that she is said to have made a pact with the devil, received the mark from him, . . . and that following this, she had renounced God, Lent, and baptism and had let herself be known carnally by him, in which she received satisfaction. Also, seeing that she is said to have been a part of nocturnal carols and dances.

For expiation of which the advice of the undersigned is that the office of Rieux can legitimately condemn the aforesaid Suzanne Gaudry to death, tying her to a gallows, and strangling her to death, then burning her body and burying it here in the environs of the woods.

many European governments. To strengthen their power, monarchs attempted to extend their authority at the expense of traditional powerful elements who resisted their rulers' efforts. At the same time, to pay for armies to fight their battles, governments increased taxes and created such hardships that common people also rose in opposition. By far the most famous and wide-ranging struggle was the civil war and rebellion in England, commonly known as the English Revolution (see Limited Monarchy: England and the Emergence of Constitutional Monarchy later in this chapter). A devastating war that affected much of Europe also added to the sense of crisis.

CHRONOLOGY

EUROPE IN CRISIS, 1560–1650: KEY EVENTS

Reign of Philip II	1556–1598
The French Wars of Religion	1562–1598
Outbreak of revolt in the Netherlands	1566
The Spanish Armada	1588
Edict of Nantes	1598
Twelve-year truce (Spain and the Netherlands)	1609
The Thirty Years' War	1618–1648
Peace of Westphalia	1648
Independence of the United Provinces	1648

THE THIRTY YEARS' WAR (1618–1648)

Religion, especially the struggle between a militant Catholicism and a militant Calvinism, certainly played an important role in the outbreak of the Thirty Years' War, often called the "last of the religious wars." As the war progressed, however, it became increasingly clear that secular, dynastic-nationalist considerations were far more important.

The Thirty Years' War began in 1618 in the Germanic lands of the Holy Roman Empire as a struggle between Catholic forces, led by the Habsburg Holy Roman emperors, and Protestant—primarily Calvinist—nobles in Bohemia who rebelled against Habsburg authority. What began as a struggle over religious issues soon became a wider conflict perpetuated by political considerations as both minor and major European powers—Denmark, Sweden, France, and Spain—entered the war. The rivalry between the Bourbon dynasty of France and the Habsburg dynasties of Spain and the Holy Roman Empire for European leadership was an especially important factor. Nevertheless, most of the battles were fought on German soil, with devastating results for the German people.

The war in Germany was officially ended by the Peace of Westphalia in 1648. What were the results of this "basically meaningless conflict," as one historian has called it? The Peace of Westphalia ensured that all German states, including the Calvinist ones, were free to determine their own religion. The major combatants gained new territories, and one of them, France, emerged as the dominant nation in Europe. The more than three hundred states that made up the Holy Roman Empire were virtually recognized as independent, since each received the power to conduct its own foreign policy; this brought an end to the Holy Roman Empire as a political entity and ensured German disunity for another two hundred years. The Peace of Westphalia made it clear that religion and politics were now separate worlds. Political motives became the guiding forces in public affairs as religion was in the process of becoming primarily a matter of personal conviction and individual choice.

Germany suffered the most from the Thirty Years' War. Some areas of the country were completely devastated. Many people in Germany would have agreed with this comment by Otto von Guericke, a councillor in the city of Magdeburg, which was sacked ten times:

> Then there was nothing but beating and burning, plundering, torture, and murder. Most especially was every one of the enemy bent on securing much booty.... In this frenzied rage, the great and splendid city ... was now ... given over to the flames, and thousands of innocent men, women and children, in the midst of a horrible din of heartrending shrieks and cries, were tortured and put to death in so cruel and shameful a manner that no words would suffice to describe.... Thus in a single day this noble and famous city, the pride of the whole country, went up in fire and smoke.[9]

The Thirty Years' War was undoubtedly the most destructive conflict Europeans had yet experienced.

By the end of the Thirty Years' War, it was apparent that a number of important innovations had occurred in European warfare. These military changes included an increased use of firearms and cannons, greater flexibility and mobility in tactics, and better disciplined and trained armies. These innovations necessitated standing armies, based partly on conscription, which grew ever larger and more expensive as the seventeenth century progressed. Such armies could only be maintained by levying heavier taxes, making war an economic burden and an ever more important part of the early modern European state. To some historians, the creation of large bureaucracies to supervise the military resources of the state was the real reason for the rise of royal absolutism in the seventeenth century.

RESPONSE TO CRISIS: THE PRACTICE OF ABSOLUTISM

Many people responded to the crises of the seventeenth century by searching for order and harmony. An increase in monarchical power became an obvious means of achieving stability. The result was what historians have called absolutism or absolute monarchy. Absolute monarchy or absolutism meant that the sovereign power or ultimate authority in the state rested in the hands of a king or queen who claimed to rule by divine right—the idea that rulers received their power from God and were responsible to no one (including parliaments) except God. But what did sovereignty mean? Late-sixteenth-century political theorists believed that sovereign power consisted of the authority to make laws, tax, administer justice, control the state's administrative system, and determine foreign policy. These powers made a ruler sovereign.

The Practice of Absolutism: France Under Louis XIV

France during the reign of Louis XIV (1643–1715) has traditionally been regarded as the best example of the practice of absolute monarchy in the seventeenth century. French culture, language, and manners reached into all levels of European society. French diplomacy and wars overwhelmed the political affairs of western and central Europe. The court of Louis XIV seemed to be imitated everywhere in Europe. Of course, the stability of Louis's reign was magnified by the instability that had preceded it.

The fifty years of French history before Louis were a period of struggle by royal and ministerial governments to avoid the breakdown of the state. The situation was especially complicated by the fact that in both 1610 and 1643, when Louis XIII and Louis XIV, respectively, succeeded to the throne, they were only boys, leaving the government dependent on royal ministers. Two especially competent ministers played crucial roles in maintaining monarchical authority.

Cardinal Richelieu, Louis XIII's chief minister from 1624 to 1642, initiated policies that eventually strengthened the power of the monarchy. By eliminating the political and military rights of the Huguenots while preserving their religious ones, Richelieu transformed the Huguenots into more reliable subjects. Richelieu acted more cau-

MAP 15.2 Europe in the Seventeenth Century

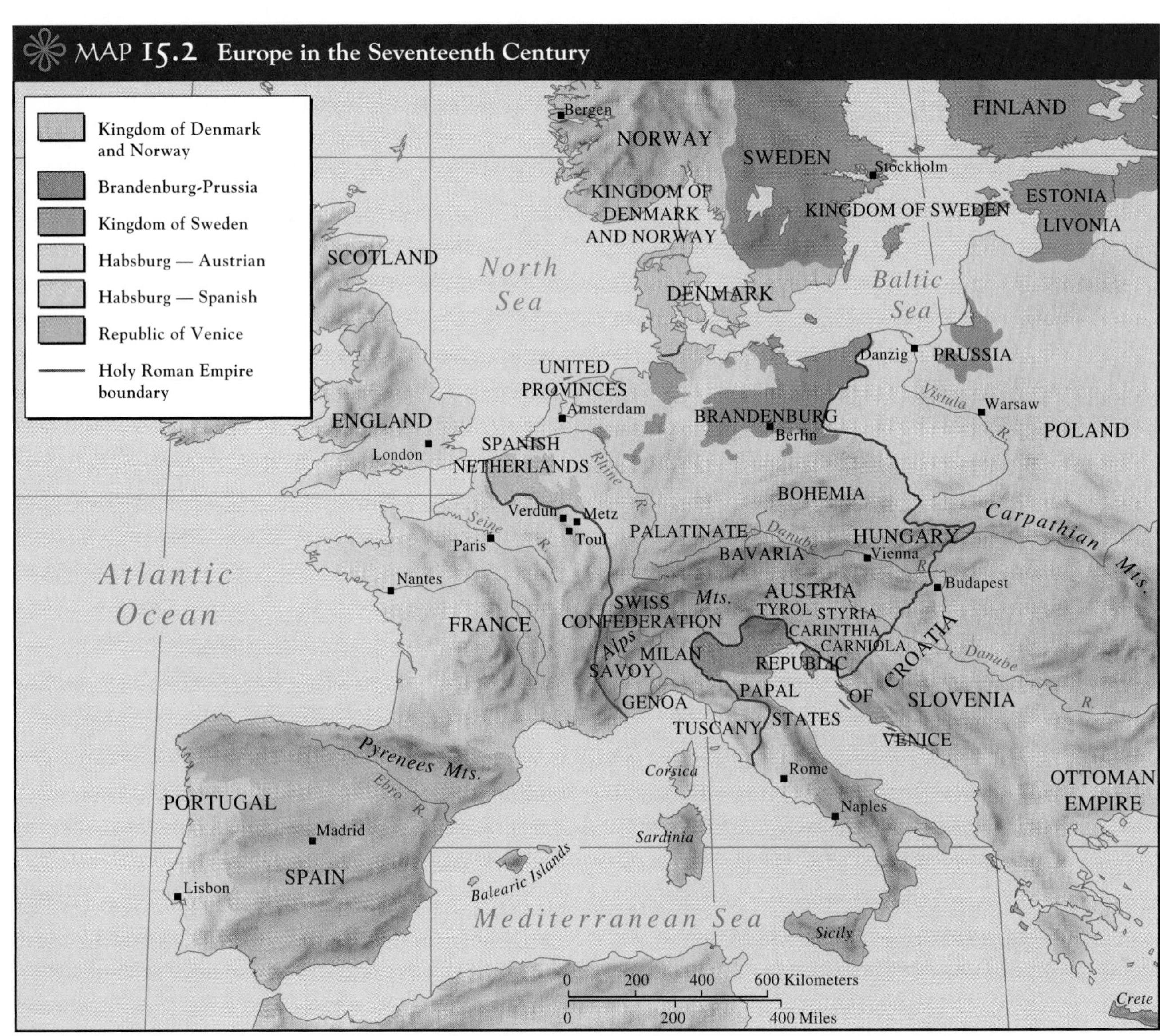

tiously in "humbling the pride of the great men," the important French nobility. He understood the influential role played by the nobles in the French state. The dangerous ones were those who asserted their territorial independence when they were excluded from participating in the central government. Proceeding slowly but determinedly, Richelieu developed an efficient network of spies to uncover noble plots and then crushed the conspiracies and executed the conspirators.

When Louis XIV succeeded to the throne in 1643 at the age of four, Cardinal Mazarin, the trained successor of Cardinal Richelieu, came to dominate the government. The most important event during Mazarin's rule was the Fronde, a revolt led primarily by nobles who wished to curb the centralized administrative power being built up at the expense of the provincial nobility. The Fronde was crushed by 1652, and with its end, a vast number of French people concluded that the best hope for stability in France lay in the crown. When Mazarin died in 1661, the greatest of the seventeenth-century monarchs, Louis XIV, took over supreme power. The day after Cardinal Mazarin's death, the new king, at the age of twenty-three, expressed his determination to be a real king and the sole ruler of France:

> Up to this moment I have been pleased to entrust the government of my affairs to the late Cardinal. It is now time that I govern them myself. You [secretaries and ministers of state] will assist me with your counsels when I ask for them. I request and order you to seal no orders except by my command, . . . I order you not to sign anything, not even a passport . . . without my command; to render account to me personally each day and to favor no one.[10]

Louis proved willing to pay the price of being a strong ruler.

LOUIS XIV. Louis XIV was determined to be the sole ruler of France. Louis eliminated the threat of the high nobility by removing them from the royal council and replacing them with relatively new aristocrats, whom he could dominate. This portrait by Hyacinth Rigaud captures the king's sense of royal dignity and grandeur.

Although Louis may have believed in the theory of absolute monarchy and consciously fostered the myth of himself as the Sun King, the source of light for all of his people, historians are quick to point out that the realities fell far short of the aspirations. Despite the centralizing efforts of Cardinals Richelieu and Mazarin, France in the seventeenth century still possessed a bewildering system of overlapping authorities. Provinces had their own regional courts, their own local Estates, and their own sets of laws. Members of the high nobility with their huge estates and clients among the lesser nobility still exercised much authority. Both towns and provinces possessed privileges and powers seemingly from time immemorial that they would not easily relinquish.

One of the keys to Louis's power was that he was able to restructure the central policy-making machinery of government because it was part of his own court and household. The royal court located at Versailles was an elaborate structure that served three purposes simultaneously: it was the personal household of the king, the location of central governmental machinery, and the place where powerful subjects came to find favors and offices for themselves and their clients, as well as the main arena where rival aristocratic factions jostled for power. The greatest danger to Louis's personal rule came from the very high nobles and princes of the blood (the royal princes), who considered it their natural function to assert the policy-making role of royal ministers. Louis eliminated this threat by removing them from the royal council, the chief administrative body of the king and overseer of the central machinery of government, and enticing them to his court, where he could keep them preoccupied with court life and out of politics. Instead of the high nobility and royal princes, Louis relied for his ministers on nobles who came from relatively new aristocratic families. His ministers were expected to be subservient; said Louis, "I had no intention of sharing my authority with them."

PALACE OF VERSAILLES. Louis XIV spent untold sums of money in the construction of a new royal residence at Versailles. The enormous palace of Versailles also housed the members of the king's government and served as home for thousands of French nobles. As the largest royal residence in Europe, Versailles impressed foreigners and became a source of envy for other rulers.

Louis's domination of his ministers and secretaries gave him control of the central policy-making machinery of government and thus authority over the traditional areas of monarchical power: the formulation of foreign policy, the making of war and peace, the assertion of the secular power of the crown against any religious authority, and the ability to levy taxes to fulfill these functions. However, Louis had considerably less success with the internal administration of the kingdom. The traditional groups and institutions of French society—the nobles, officials, town councils, guilds, and representative Estates in some provinces—were simply too powerful for the king to have direct control over the lives of his subjects. As a result, the control of the central government over the provinces and the people was carried out largely by carefully bribing the important people to ensure that the king's policies were executed.

The maintenance of religious harmony had long been considered an area of monarchical power. The desire to keep it led Louis to pursue an anti-Protestant policy, aimed at converting the Huguenots to Catholicism. In October 1685, Louis revoked the Edict of Nantes and ordered the destruction of Huguenot churches and the closing of their schools. Although they were forbidden to leave France, an estimated 200,000 Huguenots left for shelter in England, the United Provinces, and the German states.

The cost of building palaces, maintaining his court, and pursuing his wars made finances a crucial issue for Louis XIV. He was most fortunate in having the services of Jean-Baptiste Colbert (1619–1683) as controller-general of finances. Colbert sought to increase the wealth and power of France by general adherence to mercantilism, a name historians use to identify a set of economic principles that dominated economic thought in the seventeenth century. According to the mercantilists, the prosperity of a nation depended on a plentiful supply of bullion, or gold and silver. For this reason, it was desirable to achieve a favorable balance of trade, in which exported goods were of greater value than those imported, promoting an influx of gold and silver payments that would increase the quantity of bullion. To encourage exports, governments should stimulate and protect export industries and trade by granting trade monopolies, encouraging investment in new industries through subsidies, and improving transportation systems by building roads, bridges, and canals. By imposing high tariffs on foreign goods, they could be kept out of the country and prevented from competing with the products of domestic industries. Colonies were also deemed valuable as sources of raw materials and markets for finished goods. As a system of economic principles, mercantilism focused on the role of the state, believing that state intervention in some aspects of the economy was desirable for the sake of the national good.

Colbert was an avid practitioner of mercantilism. To decrease imports and increase exports, he founded new luxury industries and granted special privileges, including tax exemptions, loans, and subsidies to those who established new industries. To improve communications and the transportation of goods internally, he built roads and canals. To decrease imports directly, Colbert raised tariffs on foreign manufactured goods and created a merchant marine to carry French goods.

The increase in royal power that Louis pursued led the king to develop a professional army numbering 100,000 men in peacetime and 400,000 in time of war. Louis made war an almost incessant activity of his reign. To achieve the prestige and military glory befitting a Sun King, and also, to ensure the domination of his Bourbon dynasty over European affairs, Louis waged four wars between 1667 and 1713. His ambitions roused much of Europe to form coalitions aimed at preventing a Bourbon hegemony that would mean the certain destruction of the European balance of power. Although Louis added some territory to France's northeastern frontier and established a member of his own Bourbon dynasty on the throne of Spain, he also left France impoverished and surrounded by enemies.

Absolutism in Central and Eastern Europe

During the seventeenth century, a development of great importance for the modern Western world took place in central and eastern Europe, the appearance of three new powers: Prussia, Austria, and Russia.

The Peace of Westphalia, which officially ended the Thirty Years' War in 1648, left each of the three hundred or more German states comprising the Holy Roman Empire virtually autonomous and sovereign. Properly speaking, there was no German state, but rather over three hundred "Germanies." Of these states, two emerged in the seventeenth and eighteenth centuries as great European powers.

The development of Brandenburg as a state was largely the story of the Hohenzollern dynasty. By the seventeenth century, the dominions of the house of Hohenzollern, now called Brandenburg-Prussia, consisted of three disconnected masses in western, central, and eastern Germany. Frederick William the Great Elector (1640–1688) laid the foundation for the Prussian state. Realizing that Brandenburg-Prussia was a small, open territory with no natural frontiers for defense, Frederick William built a competent and efficient standing army. By 1678, he possessed a force of 40,000 men, making the Prussian army the fourth largest in Europe. To sustain the army and his own power, Frederick William established the General War Commissariat to levy taxes for the army and oversee its growth and training. The Commissariat soon evolved into an agency for civil government as well. Directly responsible to the elector, the new bureaucratic machine became his chief instrument for governing the state. Many of its officials were members of the Prussian landed aristocracy, the Junkers, who also served as officers in the all-important army.

Frederick William the Great Elector established the foundations for the Prussian state. In 1701, his son Frederick officially gained the title of king. Elector Frederick III was transformed into King Frederick I, and Brandenburg-Prussia became simply Prussia. In the eighteenth century, Prussia emerged as a great power on the European stage.

The Austrian Habsburgs had long played a significant role in European politics as Holy Roman emperors. By the end of the Thirty Years' War, the Habsburg hopes of creating an empire in Germany had been dashed. In the seventeenth century, the house of Austria made a difficult transition; the German empire was lost, but a new empire was created in eastern and southeastern Europe.

The nucleus of the new Austrian Empire remained the traditional Austrian hereditary possessions: Lower and Upper Austria, Carinthia, Carniola, Styria, and Tyrol. To these had been added the kingdom of Bohemia and parts of northwestern Hungary. After the defeat of the Turks in 1687 (see Chapter 18), Austria took control of all of Hungary, Transylvania, Croatia, and Slovenia, thus establishing an Austrian Empire in southeastern Europe. By the beginning of the eighteenth century, the house of Austria had acquired a new empire of considerable size.

The Austrian monarchy, however, never became a highly centralized, absolutist state, primarily because it contained so many different national groups. The Austrian Empire remained a collection of territories held together by a personal union. The Habsburg emperor was archduke of Austria, king of Bohemia, and king of Hungary. Each of these areas, however, had its own laws, Estates-General, and political life. There was no common sentiment to tie the regions together; only the ideal of service to the house of Habsburg, whether as military officers or government bureaucrats, provided a common bond that linked the landed aristocracies throughout the empire. Nevertheless, by the beginning of the eighteenth century, Austria was a populous empire in central Europe of great potential military strength.

FROM MUSCOVY TO RUSSIA

A new Russian state had emerged in the fifteenth century under the leadership of the principality of Muscovy and its grand dukes. In the sixteenth century, Ivan IV the Terrible (1533–1584), who was the first ruler to take the title of tsar (the Russian word for *Caesar*), expanded the territories of Russia eastward, after finding westward expansion blocked by the powerful Swedish and Polish states. Ivan also extended the autocracy of the tsar by crushing the power of the Russian nobility known as the boyars. Ivan's dynasty came to an end in 1598 and was followed by a resurgence of aristocratic power in a period of anarchy known as the Time of Troubles. It did not end until the Zemsky Sobor or national assembly chose Michael Romanov as the new tsar, establishing a dynasty that lasted until 1917.

In the seventeenth century, Muscovite society was highly stratified. At the top was the tsar, who claimed to be a divinely ordained autocratic ruler. Russian society was dominated by an upper class of landed aristocrats who, in the course of the seventeenth century, managed to bind their peasants to the land. An abundance of land and a shortage of peasants made serfdom desirable to the landowners, who sustained a highly oppressive system. Townspeople were also controlled. Many merchants were not allowed to move from their cities without government permission or to sell their businesses to anyone outside their class. In the seventeenth century, merchant and peasant revolts as well as a schism in the Russian Orthodox church created very unsettled conditions. In the midst of these political and religious upheavals, seventeenth-century Muscovy was experiencing more frequent contacts with the West while Western ideas also began to penetrate a few Russian circles. At the end of the seventeenth century, Peter the Great noticeably accelerated this westernizing process.

Peter the Great (1689–1725) was an unusual character. A strong, towering man at six feet, nine inches tall, Peter was coarse in his tastes and rude in his behavior. He enjoyed a low kind of humor—belching contests and crude jokes—and vicious punishments including floggings, impalings, and roastings (see the box on p. 449). Peter obtained a firsthand view of the West when he made a trip there in 1697–1698 and returned to Russia with a firm determination to westernize Russia. Perhaps too much has been made of Peter's desire to westernize a "backward country." Peter's policy was largely technical. He admired Western technology and gadgets and wanted to transplant them to Russia. Only this kind of modernization could give him the army and navy he needed to make Russia a great power.

As could be expected, one of his first priorities was the reorganization of the army and the creation of a navy. Employing both Russians and Europeans as officers, he conscripted peasants for twenty-five-year stints of service to build a standing army of 210,000 men. Peter has also been given credit for forming the first Russian navy.

To impose the rule of the central government more effectively throughout the land, Peter divided Russia into eight provinces and later, in 1719, into fifty. Although he hoped to create a "police state," by which he meant a well-ordered community governed in accordance with law, few of his bureaucrats shared his concept of honest service and duty to the state. Peter hoped for a sense of civic duty, but his own forceful personality created an atmosphere of fear that prevented it. He wrote to one administrator: "According to these orders act, act, act. I won't write more, but you will pay with your head if you interpret orders again."[11] Peter wanted his administrators to be slaves and freemen at the same time, and it did not occur to him that the task was impossible.

To satisfy his insatiable need of money for an army and navy that absorbed as much as four-fifths of the state revenue, Peter adopted Western mercantilistic policies to stimulate economic growth. He tried to increase exports and develop new industries while exploiting domestic resources like the iron mines in the Urals. But his military needs were endless, and he came to rely on the old expedient of simply raising taxes, placing additional burdens on hapless peasants, whose position in Peter's Russia grew ever more oppressed.

Peter also sought to gain state control of the Russian Orthodox church. In 1721, he abolished the position of patriarch and created a body called the Holy Synod to make decisions for the church. At its head stood a procurator, a layman who represented the interests of the tsar and assured Peter of effective domination of the church.

Already after his first trip to the West in 1697–1698, Peter had begun to introduce Western customs, practices, and manners into Russia. He ordered the preparation of the first Russian book of etiquette to teach Western manners. Among other things, it pointed out that it was not polite to spit on the floor or scratch oneself at dinner. Since westerners did not wear beards or the traditional long-skirted coat, Russian beards had to be shaved and coats shortened, a reform Peter personally enforced at court by shaving off his nobles' beards and cutting their coats at the knees with his own hands. Outside the court, the edicts were enforced by barbers and tailors planted at town gates with orders to cut the beards and cloaks of those who entered or left. One group of Russians benefited greatly from Peter's cultural reforms—women. Having watched women mixing freely with men in Western courts, Peter shattered the seclusion of upper-class Russian women and demanded that they remove the traditional veils that covered their faces. Peter also encouraged gatherings in which both sexes could mix for conversation and dancing, which Peter had learned in the West. The tsar also now insisted that women could marry of their own free will.

PETER THE GREAT. Peter the Great wished to westernize Russia, especially in the realm of technical skills. His foremost goal was the creation of a strong army and navy in order to make Russia a great power. A Dutch artist painted this portrait of the armored tsar during his visit to the West in 1697.

The object of Peter's domestic reforms was to make Russia into a great state and military power. His primary goal

PETER THE GREAT DEALS WITH A REBELLION

During his first visit to the West, in 1697–1698, Peter received word that the Streltsy, an elite military unit stationed in Moscow, had revolted against his authority. Peter hurried home and crushed the revolt in a very savage fashion. This selection is taken from an Austrian account of how Peter dealt with the rebels.

PETER AND THE STRELTSY

How sharp was the pain, how great the indignation, to which the tsar's Majesty was mightily moved, when he knew of the rebellion of the Streltsy, betraying openly a mind panting for vengeance! He was still tarrying at Vienna, quite full of the desire of setting out for Italy; but, fervid as was his curiosity of rambling abroad, it was, nevertheless, speedily extinguished on the announcement of the troubles that had broken out in the bowels of his realm. Going immediately to Lefort . . . , he thus indignantly broke out: "Tell me, Francis, how I can reach Moscow by the shortest way, in a brief space, so that I may wreak vengeance on this great perfidy of my people, with punishments worthy of their abominable crime. Not one of them shall escape with impunity. Around my royal city, which, with their impious efforts, they planned to destroy, I will have gibbets and gallows set upon the walls and ramparts, and each and every one of them will I put to a direful death." Nor did he long delay the plan for his justly excited wrath; he took the quick post, as his ambassador suggested, and in four weeks' time he had got over about three hundred miles without accident, and arrived the 4th of September, 1698—a monarch for the well disposed, but an avenger for the wicked.

His first anxiety after his arrival was about the rebellion—in what it consisted, what the insurgents meant, who dared to instigate such a crime. And as nobody could answer accurately upon all points, and some pleaded their own ignorance, others the obstinacy of the Streltsy, he began to have suspicions of everybody's loyalty. . . . No day, holy or profane, were the inquisitors idle; every day was deemed fit and lawful for torturing. There were as many scourges as there were accused, and every inquisitor was a butcher. . . . The whole month of October was spent in lacerating the backs of culprits with the knout and with flames; no day were those that were left alive exempt from scourging or scorching; or else they were broken upon the wheel, or driven to the gibbet, or slain with the ax. . . .

To prove to all people how holy and inviolable are those walls of the city which the Streltsy rashly meditated scaling in a sudden assault, beams were run out from all the embrasures in the walls near the gates, in each of which two rebels were hanged. This day beheld about two hundred and fifty die that death. There are few cities fortified with as many palisades as Moscow has given gibbets to her guardian Streltsy.

was to "open a window to the west," meaning an ice-free port easily accessible to Europe. This could only be achieved on the Baltic, but at that time the Baltic coast was controlled by Sweden, the most important power in northern Europe. A long and hard-fought war with Sweden, then ruled by Charles XII, a brilliant military leader, enabled Peter to acquire the lands he sought. Already in 1703, in these northern lands on the Baltic, Peter had begun the construction of a new city, St. Petersburg, his window on the west and a symbol that Russia was looking westward to Europe. Built on marshland, St. Petersburg cost the lives of thousands of peasants during its construction. Nevertheless, the city was finished during Peter's lifetime and remained the Russian capital until 1917.

Peter modernized and westernized Russia to the extent that it became a great military power, and by his death in 1725, it was an important member of the European state system. But his policies were also detrimental to Russia. Westernization was a bit of a sham, since Western culture reached only the upper classes, while the real object of the reforms, the creation of a strong military, only added more burdens to the masses of the Russian people. Moreover, the forceful way in which Peter the Great brought westernization led many Russians to distrust Europe and Western civilization.

LIMITED MONARCHY: ENGLAND AND THE EMERGENCE OF CONSTITUTIONAL MONARCHY

One of the most prominent examples of resistance to absolute monarchy came in seventeenth-century England where king and Parliament struggled to determine the roles each should play in governing England. But the struggle over this political issue was complicated by a deep and profound religious controversy. With the victory of Parliament, the foundation for constitutional monarchy was laid by the end of the seventeenth century.

Revolution and Civil War

With the death of Queen Elizabeth I in 1603, the Tudor dynasty became extinct, and the Stuart line of rulers was inaugurated with the accession to the throne of Elizabeth's cousin, King James VI of Scotland, who became James I (1603–1625) of England. Although used to royal power as king of Scotland, James understood little about the laws, institutions, and customs of the English. He espoused the divine right of kings, the belief that kings receive their power directly from God and are responsible to no one except God. This viewpoint alienated Parliament, which had grown accustomed under the Tudors to act on the premise that monarch and Parliament together ruled England as a "balanced polity." Then, too, the Puritans—those Protestants within the Anglican church who, inspired by Calvinist theology, wished to eliminate any trace of popery from the Church of England—were alienated by the king's strong defense of the Anglican church. Many of England's lesser landed nobility, the gentry, had become Puritans, and these Puritan gentry not only formed an important and substantial part of the House of Commons, the lower house of Parliament, but also held important positions locally as justices of the peace and sheriffs. It was not wise to alienate them.

The conflict that had begun during the reign of James came to a head during the reign of his son Charles I (1625–1649). Charles believed as strongly in divine-right monarchy as his father had, and from the first stormy session of Parliament, it became apparent that the constitutional issues between this king and Parliament would not be easily resolved. In 1628, Parliament passed a Petition of Right that the king was supposed to accept before being granted any taxes. This petition prohibited taxes without Parliament's consent, arbitrary imprisonment, the quartering of soldiers in private houses, and the declaration of martial law in peacetime. Although he initially accepted it, Charles later reneged on the agreement because of its limitations on royal power.

Religious differences also added to the hostility between Charles I and Parliament. The king's attempt to impose more ritual on the Anglican church struck the Puritans as a return to Catholic "popery." Charles's efforts to force them to conform to his religious policies infuriated the Puritans, thousands of whom went to the "howling wildernesses" of America.

Grievances mounted until England finally slipped into a civil war (1642–1648) that was won by the parliamentary forces. Most important to Parliament's success was the creation of the New Model Army by Oliver Cromwell, the only real military genius of the war. The New Model Army was composed primarily of more extreme Puritans known as the Independents, who, in typical Calvinist fashion, believed they were doing battle for God. As Cromwell wrote in one of his military reports, "Sir, this is none other

EXECUTION OF CHARLES I. When Charles I attempted to arrest radical members of Parliament, a civil war erupted that eventually led to the rise of Oliver Cromwell and the execution of the king. This contemporary painting of the execution of Charles I shows a woman fainting at the bottom while the executioner holds the king's head aloft at the top. At the top left is a portrait of Charles I.

but the hand of God; and to Him alone belongs the glory." We might give some credit to Cromwell as well, because his soldiers were well disciplined and trained in the new military tactics developed in the course of the Thirty Years' War.

Between 1648 and 1660, England faced a trying situation. After the execution of Charles I on January 30, 1649, Parliament abolished the monarchy and the House of Lords and proclaimed England a republic or Commonwealth. But Cromwell and his army, unable to work effectively with Parliament, dispersed it by force and established a military dictatorship. Unable to find a constitutional basis for a working government, Cromwell had resorted to military force to maintain the rule of the Independents, ironically using even more arbitrary policies than those of Charles I.

Oliver Cromwell died in 1658. After floundering for eighteen months, the military establishment decided that arbitrary rule by the army was no longer feasible and reestablished the monarchy in the person of Charles II (1660–1685), the son of Charles I. The restoration of the Stuart monarchy ended England's time of troubles, but it would not be long before England would experience yet another constitutional crisis.

CHRONOLOGY

ABSOLUTE AND LIMITED MONARCHY

France	
Louis XIII	1610–1643
Cardinal Richelieu as chief minister	1624–1642
Ministry of Cardinal Mazarin	1642–1661
Louis XIV	1643–1715
Revocation of Edict of Nantes	1685
Brandenburg-Prussia	
Frederick William the Great Elector	1640–1688
Elector Frederick III (King Frederick I)	1688–1713
Russia	
Ivan IV the Terrible	1533–1584
Time of Troubles	1598–1613
Peter the Great	1689–1725
First trip to the West	1697–1698
Construction of St. Petersburg begins	1703
England	
Civil wars	1642–1648
Commonwealth	1649–1653
Charles II	1660–1685
Declaration of Indulgence	1672
Test Act	1673
James II	1685–1688
Declaration of Indulgence	1687
Glorious Revolution	1688
Bill of Rights	1689

Restoration and a Glorious Revolution

The restoration of the monarchy did not mean that the work of the English Revolution was undone. Parliament kept much of the power it had won: arbitrary courts were still abolished; Parliament's role in government was acknowledged; and the necessity for its consent to taxation was accepted. Yet Charles II continued to push his own ideas, some of which were clearly out of step with many of the English people.

Charles was sympathetic to and perhaps even inclined toward Catholicism. Moreover, Charles's brother James, heir to the throne, did not hide the fact that he was a Catholic. Parliament's suspicions were therefore aroused in 1672 when Charles took the audacious step of issuing a Declaration of Indulgence that suspended the laws that Parliament had passed against Catholics and Puritans after the restoration of the monarchy. Parliament would have none of it and induced the king to suspend the declaration. Propelled by a strong anti-Catholic sentiment, Parliament then passed a Test Act in 1673, specifying that only Anglicans could hold military and civil offices.

The accession of James II (1685–1688) to the crown virtually guaranteed a new constitutional crisis for England. An open and devout Catholic, his attempt to further Catholic interests made religion once more a primary cause of conflict between king and Parliament. In 1687, James issued a Declaration of Indulgence, which suspended all laws excluding Catholics and Puritans from office. Parliamentary outcries against James's policies stopped short of rebellion because members knew that he was an old man and his successors were his Protestant daughters Mary and Anne, born to his first wife. But on June 10, 1688, a son was born to James's second wife, also a Catholic. Suddenly, the specter of a Catholic hereditary monarchy loomed large. A group of prominent English noblemen invited the Dutch chief executive, William of Orange, husband of James's daughter Mary, to invade England. William and Mary raised an army and invaded England, while James, his wife, and their infant son fled to France. With almost no bloodshed, England had undergone a "Glorious Revolution," not over the issue of whether there would be a monarchy, but rather over who would be the monarch.

THE BILL OF RIGHTS

In 1688, the English experienced yet another revolution, a rather bloodless one in which the Stuart king James II was replaced by Mary, James's daughter, and her husband, William of Orange. After William and Mary had assumed power, Parliament passed a Bill of Rights that specified the rights of Parliament and laid the foundation for a constitutional monarchy.

THE BILL OF RIGHTS

Whereas the said late King James II having abdicated the government, and the throne being thereby vacant, his Highness the prince of Orange (whom it hath pleased Almighty God to make the glorious instrument of delivering this kingdom from popery and arbitrary power) did (by the device of the lords spiritual and temporal, and diverse principal persons of the Commons) cause letters to be written to the lords spiritual and temporal, being Protestants, and other letters to the several counties, cities, universities, boroughs, and Cinque Ports, for the choosing of such persons to represent them, as were of right to be sent to parliament, to meet and sit at Westminster upon the two and twentieth day of January, in this year 1689, in order to such an establishment as that their religion, laws, and liberties might not again be in danger of being subverted; upon which letters elections have been accordingly made.

And thereupon the said lords spiritual and temporal and Commons, pursuant to their respective letters and elections, being now assembled in a full and free representation of this nation, taking into their most serious consideration the best means for attaining the ends aforesaid, do in the first place (as their ancestors in like case have usually done), for the vindication and assertion of their ancient rights and liberties, declare:

1. That the pretended power of suspending laws, or the execution of laws, by regal authority, without consent of parliament is illegal.
2. That the pretended power of dispensing with the laws, or the execution of law by regal authority, as it hath been assumed and exercised of late, is illegal.
3. That the commission for erecting the late court of commissioners for ecclesiastical causes, and all other commissions and courts of like nature, are illegal and pernicious.
4. That levying money for or to the use of the crown by pretense of prerogative, without grant of parliament, for longer time or in other manner than the same is or shall be granted, is illegal.
5. That it is the right of the subjects to petition the king, and all commitments and prosecutions for such petitioning are illegal.
6. That the raising or keeping a standing army within the kingdom in time of peace, unless it be with consent of parliament, is against law.
7. That the subjects which are Protestants may have arms for their defense suitable to their conditions, and as allowed by law.
8. That election of members of parliament ought to be free.
9. That the freedom of speech, and debates or proceedings in parliament, ought not to be impeached or questioned in any court or place out of parliament.
10. That excessive bail ought not to be required, nor excessive fines imposed, nor cruel and unusual punishments inflicted.
11. That jurors ought to be duly impaneled and returned, and jurors which pass upon men in trials for high treason ought to be freeholders.
12. That all grants and promises of fines and forfeitures of particular persons before conviction are illegal and void.
13. And that for redress of all grievances, and for the amending, strengthening, and preserving of the laws, parliament ought to be held frequently.

The events of late 1688 constituted only the initial stage of the Glorious Revolution. In January 1689, Parliament offered the throne to William and Mary, who accepted it along with the provisions of a Bill of Rights (see the box above). The Bill of Rights affirmed Parliament's right to make laws and levy taxes and made it impossible for kings to oppose or do without Parliament by stipulating that standing armies could be raised only with the consent of Parliament. The rights of citizens to petition the sovereign, keep arms, have a jury trial, and not be subject to excessive bail were also confirmed. The Bill of Rights helped to fashion a system of government based on the rule of law and a freely elected Parliament, thus laying the foundation for a constitutional monarchy.

The Bill of Rights did not settle the religious questions that had played such a large role in England's troubles in the seventeenth century. The Toleration Act of 1689 granted Puritan Dissenters the right of free public worship (Catholics were still excluded). Although the Toleration Act did not mean complete religious freedom and equality, it marked a departure in English history because few people would ever again be persecuted for religious reasons.

Many historians have viewed the Glorious Revolution as the end of the seventeenth-century struggle between king and Parliament. By deposing one king and establishing another, Parliament had destroyed the divine-right theory of kingship (William was, after all, king by grace of

Parliament, not God) and confirmed its right to participate in the government. Parliament did not have complete control of the government, but it now had an unquestioned right to participate in affairs of state. Over the next century, it would gradually prove to be the real authority in the English system of constitutional monarchy.

Responses to Revolution

The English revolutions of the seventeenth century prompted very different responses from two English political thinkers—Thomas Hobbes and John Locke. Thomas Hobbes (1588–1679), who lived during the English civil wars, was alarmed by the revolutionary upheavals in his contemporary England. Hobbes's name has since been associated with the state's claim to absolute authority over its subjects, which he elaborated in his major treatise on political thought, *Leviathan*, published in 1651.

Hobbes claimed that in the state of nature, before society was organized, human life was "solitary, poor, nasty, brutish, and short." Humans were guided not by reason and moral ideals, but by animalistic instincts and a ruthless struggle for self-preservation. To save themselves from destroying each other, people contracted to form a commonwealth, which Hobbes called "that great Leviathan (or rather, to speak more reverently, that mortal god) to which we owe our peace and defense." This commonwealth placed its collective power into the hands of a sovereign authority, preferably a single ruler, who served as executor, legislator, and judge. This absolute ruler possessed unlimited power. Subjects may not rebel; if they do, they must be suppressed.

John Locke (1632–1704), who wrote a political work called *Two Treatises of Government*, viewed the exercise of political power quite differently from Hobbes and argued against the absolute rule of one man. Like Hobbes, Locke began with the state of nature before human existence became organized socially. But, unlike Hobbes, Locke believed humans lived then in a state of equality and freedom rather than a state of war. In this state of nature, humans had certain inalienable natural rights—to life, liberty, and property. Like Hobbes, Locke did not believe all was well in the state of nature. People found it difficult to protect these natural rights, so they mutually agreed to establish a government to ensure the protection of their rights. This agreement established mutual obligations: government would protect the people's rights while the people would act reasonably toward government. But if a government broke this agreement—if a monarch, for example, failed to live up to his obligation to protect the natural rights or claimed absolute authority and made laws without the consent of the community—the people might form a new government. For Locke, however, the community of people meant primarily the landholding aristocracy, who were represented in Parliament, not the landless masses. Locke was hardly an advocate of political democracy, but his ideas proved important to both Americans and French in the eighteenth century and were used to support demands for constitutional government, the rule of law, and the protection of rights.

The World of European Culture

In the sixteenth and seventeenth centuries, European art and literature passed through a number of stylistic stages. These changes were closely linked to the religious, political, and intellectual developments of the period.

Art

The artistic Renaissance came to an end when a new movement called Mannerism emerged in Italy in the decades of the 1520s and 1530s. The age of the Reformation had brought a revival of religious values accompanied by much political turmoil. Especially in Italy, the worldly enthusiasm of the Renaissance gave way to anxiety, uncertainty, suffering, and a yearning for spiritual experience. Mannerism reflected this environment in its deliberate attempt to break down the High Renaissance principles of balance, harmony, and moderation. Italian Mannerist painters deliberately distorted the rules of proportion by portraying elongated figures that conveyed a sense of suffering and a strong emotional atmosphere filled with anxiety and confusion.

Mannerism spread from Italy to other parts of Europe and perhaps reached its apogee in the work of El Greco (1541–1614). Doménikos Theotocópoulos (called "the Greek"—El Greco) was from Crete, but after studying in Venice and Rome, in the 1570s he moved to Spain, where he became a church painter in Toledo. El Greco's elongated and contorted figures, portrayed in unusual shades of yellow and green against an eerie background of turbulent grays, reflect well the artist's desire to create a world of intense emotions.

Mannerism was eventually replaced by a new movement—the Baroque—that dominated the artistic world for another century and a half. The Baroque began in Italy in the last quarter of the sixteenth century and spread to the rest of Europe. Baroque artists sought to harmonize the classical traditions of Renaissance art with the intense religious feelings fostered by the revival of religion in the Reformation. Although Protestants were also influenced, it was the Catholic reform movement that most wholeheartedly adopted the Baroque, as is evident at Catholic courts, especially those of the Habsburgs in Madrid, Prague, Vienna, and Brussels. Eventually, the Baroque style spread to all of Europe and Latin America.

In large part, Baroque art and architecture reflected the search for power that was characteristic of much of the seventeenth century. Baroque churches and palaces featured richly ornamented facades, sweeping staircases, and an overall splendor that were meant to impress people. Kings and princes wanted other kings and princes as well as their subjects to be in awe of their power.

Baroque painting was known for its use of dramatic effects to heighten emotional intensity, especially evident in the works of Peter Paul Rubens (1577–1640), a prolific artist and an important figure in the spread of the Baroque from Italy to other parts of Europe. In his artistic masterpieces, bodies in violent motion, heavily fleshed nudes, a dramatic use of light and shadow, and rich sensuous pigments converge to show intense emotions. The restless forms and constant movement blend together into a dynamic unity.

Perhaps the greatest figure of the Baroque was the Italian architect and sculptor Gian Lorenzo Bernini

EL GRECO, *LAOCÖON*. Mannerism reached one of its highest expressions in the work of El Greco. Born in Crete, trained in Venice and Rome, and settling finally in Spain, El Greco worked as a church painter in Toledo. Pictured here is his version of the *Laocöon,* a famous piece of Hellenistic sculpture that had been discovered in Rome in 1506. The elongated, contorted bodies project a world of suffering while the somber background scene of the city of Toledo adds a sense of terror and doom.

PETER PAUL RUBENS, *THE LANDING OF MARIE DE' MEDICI AT MARSEILLES.* Peter Paul Rubens played a key role in spreading the Baroque style from Italy to other parts of Europe. In *The Landing of Marie de' Medici at Marseilles*, Rubens made a dramatic use of light and color, bodies in motion, and luxurious nudes to heighten the emotional intensity of the scene. This was one of a cycle of twenty-one paintings dedicated to the queen mother of France.

ARTEMISIA GENTILESCHI, *JUDITH BEHEADING HOLOFERNES.* Artemisia Gentileschi painted a series of pictures portraying scenes from the lives of courageous Old Testament women. In this painting, a determined Judith, armed with her victim's sword, struggles to saw off the head of Holofernes. Gentileschi realistically and dramatically shows the bloody nature of Judith's act.

(1598–1680), who completed Saint Peter's Basilica and designed the vast colonnade enclosing the piazza in front of it. Action, exuberance, profusion, and dramatic effects mark Bernini's work in the interior of Saint Peter's, where his *Throne of St. Peter* hovers in midair. Above the chair, rays of heavenly light drive a mass of clouds and angels toward the spectator.

Less well known than the male artists who dominated the seventeenth-century art world in Italy but prominent in her own right was Artemisia Gentileschi (1593–1653). Born in Rome, she studied painting under her father's direction. In 1616, she moved to Florence and began a successful career as a painter. At the age of twenty-three, she became the first woman to be elected to the Florentine Academy of Design. Although she was known internationally in her day as a portrait painter, her fame now rests on a series of pictures of heroines from the Old Testament, including Judith, Esther, and Bathsheba. Most famous is her *Judith Beheading Holofernes*, a dramatic rendering of the biblical scene in which Judith slays the Assyrian general Holofernes in order to save her besieged town from the Assyrian army.

In the second half of the seventeenth century, France replaced Italy as the cultural leader of Europe. Rejecting the Baroque style as overly showy and passionate, the French remained committed to the classical values of the High Renaissance. French late classicism, with its emphasis on clarity, simplicity, balance, and harmony of design was, however, a rather "frigid" version of the High Renaissance style. Its triumph reflected the shift in seventeenth-century French society from chaos to order. While French classicism rejected the emotionalism and high drama of the Baroque, the latter's conception of grandeur was still evident in the portrayal of noble subjects, especially those from classical antiquity. The paintings of Nicholas Poussin (1594–1665) exemplified these principles.

NICHOLAS POUSSIN, *LANDSCAPE WITH THE BURIAL OF PHOCIAN.* France became the new cultural leader of Europe in the second half of the seventeenth century. French classicism upheld the values of High Renaissance style, but in a more static version. In Nicholas Poussin's work, we see the emphasis of French classicism on the use of scenes from classical sources and the creation of a sense of grandeur and noble strength in both human figures and landscape.

A Golden Age of Literature: England and Spain

Periods of crisis often produce great writing, and this period, which was characterized by a golden age of theater, was no exception. In both England and Spain, writing for the stage reached new heights between 1580 and 1640. The golden age of English literature is often called the Elizabethan Era because much of the English cultural flowering of the late sixteenth and early seventeenth centuries occurred during her reign. Elizabethan literature exhibits the exuberance and pride associated with English exploits under Queen Elizabeth (see the box on p. 457). Of all the forms of Elizabethan literature, none expressed the energy and intellectual versatility of the era better than drama. Of all the dramatists, none is more famous than William Shakespeare (1564–1614).

Shakespeare was the son of a prosperous glover from Stratford-upon-Avon. When he appeared in London in 1592, Elizabethans were already addicted to the stage. By 1576, two professional theaters run by actors' companies were in existence. Elizabethan theater became a tremendously successful business. Soon at least four to six theaters were open six afternoons a week in or near London. They ranged from the Globe, which was a circular unroofed structure holding 3,000, to the Blackfriars, which was roofed and held only 500. In the former, an admission charge of one or two pennies enabled even the lower classes to attend, while the higher prices in the latter ensured an audience of the well-to-do. Elizabethan audiences varied greatly, putting pressure on playwrights to write works that pleased nobles, lawyers, merchants, and even vagabonds.

William Shakespeare was a "complete man of the theater." Although best known for writing plays, he was also an actor and shareholder in the chief company of the time, the Lord Chamberlains' Company, which played in theaters as diverse as the Globe and the Blackfriars. Shakespeare has long been recognized as a universal genius. A master of the English language, he was instrumental in transforming a language that was still in a period of transition. His technical proficiency, however, was matched by an incredible insight into human psychology. Whether in his tragedies or comedies, Shakespeare exhibited a remarkable understanding of the human condition.

The theater was one of the most creative forms of expression during Spain's golden century. The first professional theaters established in Seville and Madrid in the 1570s were run by actors' companies as in England. Soon, every large town had a public playhouse, including Mexico City in the New World. Touring companies brought the latest Spanish plays to all parts of the Spanish empire. Beginning in the 1580s, the agenda for playwrights was set by Lope de Vega (1562–1635). Like Shakespeare, he was from a middle-class background. He was an incredibly prolific writer; almost 500 of his 1,500 plays survive. They have been characterized as witty, charming, action-packed, and realistic. Lope de Vega made no apologies for the fact that he wrote his plays to please his audiences. In a treatise on drama written in 1609, he stated that the foremost duty of the playwright was to satisfy public demand. He remarked that if anyone thought he had written his plays for fame, "undeceive him and tell him that I wrote them for money."

WILLIAM SHAKESPEARE: IN PRAISE OF ENGLAND

William Shakespeare is one of the most famous playwrights in the Western world. He was a universal genius, outclassing all others in his psychological insights, depth of characterization, imaginative skills, and versatility. His historical plays reflected the patriotic enthusiasm of the English in the Elizabethan Era, as this excerpt from Richard II *illustrates.*

WILLIAM SHAKESPEARE, *RICHARD II*

This royal throne of kings, this sceptered isle,
This earth of majesty, this seat of Mars,
This other Eden, demi-Paradise,
This fortress built by Nature for herself
Against infection and the hand of war,
This happy breed of men, this little world,
This precious stone set in the silver sea,
Which serves it in the office of a wall
Or as a moat defensive to a house
Against the envy of less happier lands—
This blessed plot, this earth, this realm, this England,
This nurse, this teeming womb of royal kings,
Feared by their breed and famous by their birth,
Renowned for their deeds as far from home,
For Christian service and true chivalry,
As is the sepulcher in stubborn Jewry [the Holy Sepulcher in Jerusalem]
Of the world's ransom, blessed Mary's Son—
This land of such dear souls, this dear dear land,
Dear for her reputation through the world,
Is now leased out, I die pronouncing it,
Like a tenement or pelting farm.
England, bound in with the triumphant sea,
Whose rocky shore beats back the envious siege
Of watery Neptune, is now bound in with shame,
With inky blots and rotten parchment bonds.
That England, that was wont to conquer others,
Hath made a shameful conquest of itself.
Ah, would the scandal vanish with my life,
How happy then were my ensuing death!

One of the crowning achievements of the golden age of Spanish literature was the work of Miguel de Cervantes (1547–1616), whose *Don Quixote* has been acclaimed as one of the greatest literary works of all time. In the two main figures of his famous work, Cervantes presented the dual nature of the Spanish character. The knight Don Quixote from La Mancha is the visionary who is so involved in his lofty ideals that he is oblivious to the hard realities around him. To him, for example, windmills appear as four-armed giants. In contrast, the knight's fat and earthy squire, Sancho Panza, is the realist who cannot get his master to see the realities in front of him. But after adventures that took them to all parts of Spain, each came to see the value of the other's perspective. We are left with Cervantes's conviction that both visionary dreams and the hard work of reality are necessary to the human condition.

CONCLUSION

In Chapter 14, we observed how the movement of Europeans outside of Europe began to change the shape of world history. But what had made this development possible? After all, the religious division of Europe had led to almost a hundred years of religious warfare complicated by serious political, economic, and social issues—the worst series of wars and civil wars since the collapse of the Western Roman Empire—before Europeans finally admitted that they would have to tolerate different ways to worship God.

At the same time, the concept of a united Christendom, held as an ideal since the Middle Ages, had been irrevocably destroyed by the religious wars, enabling a system of nation-states to emerge in which power politics took on increasing significance. The growth of political thought focusing on the secular origins of state power reflected the changes that were going on in seventeenth-century society. Within those states slowly emerged some of the machinery that made possible a growing centralization of power. In those states called absolutist, strong monarchs with the assistance of their aristocracies took the lead in providing the leadership for greater centralization. In all the major European states, a growing concern for power led to larger armies, stronger economies, and more powerful governments. From a global point of view, the political and economic power of Europeans was beginning to slowly outstrip that of other peoples.

And yet, despite the spread of European states to the rest of the world, where they began to dominate global trade markets, Europeans had not yet achieved their goal of diminishing the power of Islam, a goal that had first begun during the Crusades. In fact, as we shall see in the next chapter, in the midst of European expansion and exploration, three new and powerful Muslim empires were taking shape in the Middle East and South Asia.

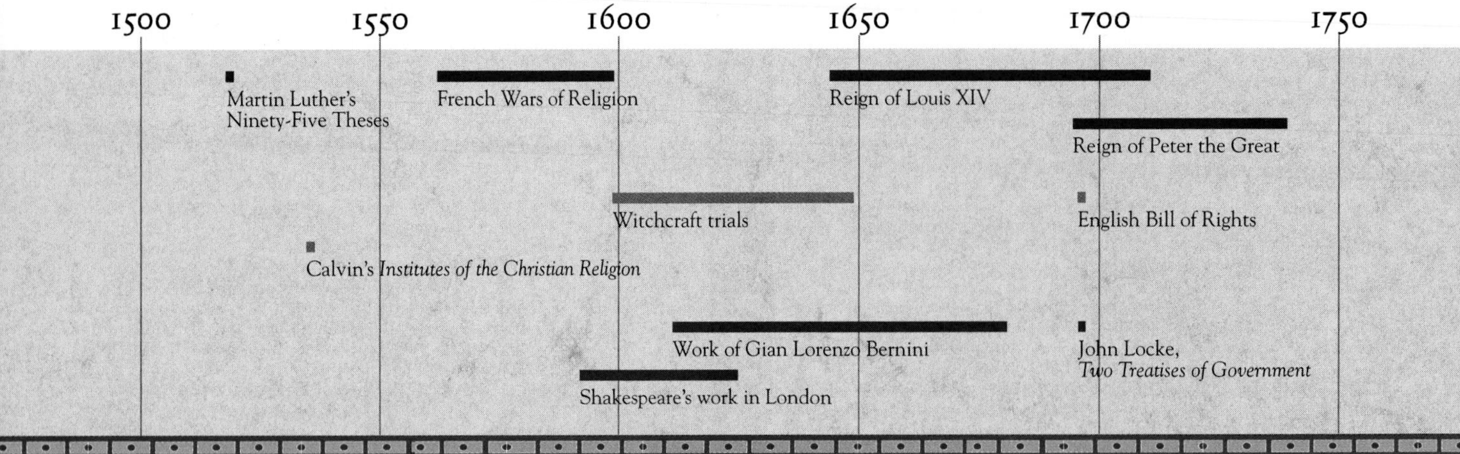

Chapter Notes

1. Erasmus, *The Paraclesis*, in John Olin, ed., *Christian Humanism and the Reformation: Selected Writings of Erasmus*, 3d ed. (New York, 1987), p. 101.
2. Quoted in Roland Bainton, *Here I Stand: A Life of Martin Luther* (New York, 1950), p. 144.
3. Quoted in De Lamar Jensen, *Reformation Europe* (Lexington, Mass., 1981), p. 83.
4. John Calvin, *Institutes of the Christian Religion*, trans. John Allen (Philadelphia, 1936), 1:220.
5. Ibid., 1:228; 2:181.
6. Quoted in Roland Bainton, *Women of the Reformation in Germany and Italy* (Boston, 1971), p. 154.
7. Quoted in Bonnie S. Anderson and Judith P. Zinsser, *A History of Their Own: Women in Europe from Prehistory to the Present* (New York, 1988), 1:259.
8. Quoted in Joseph Klaits, *Servants of Satan: The Age of the Witch Hunts* (Bloomington, Ind., 1985), p. 68.
9. Quoted in James Harvey Robinson, *Readings in European History* (Boston, 1934), 2:211–12.
10. Quoted in John B. Wolf, *Louis XIV* (New York, 1968), p. 134.
11. Quoted in B. H. Sumner, *Peter the Great and the Emergence of Russia* (New York, 1962), p. 122.

Suggested Readings

Basic surveys of the Reformation period include H. J. Grimm, *The Reformation Era, 1500–1650*, 2d ed. (New York, 1973); D. L. Jensen, *Reformation Europe*, 2d ed. (Lexington, Mass., 1990); G. R. Elton, *Reformation Europe, 1517–1559* (Cleveland, 1963); C. Lindberg, *The European Reformations* (Cambridge, Mass., 1996); and E. Cameron, *The European Reformation* (New York, 1991). Also see the interesting and useful book by S. Ozment, *Protestants: The Birth of a Revolution* (New York, 1992). The best general biography of Erasmus is still R. Bainton, *Erasmus of Christendom* (New York, 1969), although the shorter works by J. K. Sowards, *Desiderius Erasmus* (Boston, 1975), and J. McConica, *Erasmus* (Oxford, 1991) are also good.

The classic account of Martin Luther's life is R. Bainton, *Here I Stand: A Life of Martin Luther* (New York and Nashville, 1950). More recent works include J. M. Kittelson, *Luther the Reformer: The Story of the Man and His Career* (Minneapolis, Minn., 1986), and H. A. Oberman, *Luther: Man Between God and the Devil* (New York, 1992). The best account of Ulrich Zwingli is G. R. Potter, *Zwingli* (Cambridge, 1976), although W. P. Stephens, *Zwingli* (Oxford, 1994) is an important study of Zwingli's ideas. The most comprehensive account of the various groups and individuals who are called Anabaptist is G. H. Williams, *The Radical Reformation*, 2d ed. (Kirksville, Mo., 1992). Two worthwhile surveys of the English Reformation are A. G. Dickens, *The English Reformation*, 2d ed. (New York, 1989), and G. R. Elton, *Reform and Reformation: England, 1509–1558* (Cambridge, Mass., 1977). On John Calvin, see A. McGrath, *A Life of John Calvin: A Study in the Shaping of Western Culture* (Cambridge, Mass., 1990), and W. J. Bouwsma, *John Calvin* (New York, 1988).

On the impact of the Reformation on the family, see J. F. Harrington, *Reordering Marriage and Society in Reformation Germany* (New York, 1995). M. E. Wiesner's *Working Women in Renaissance Germany* (New Brunswick, N.J., 1986) covers primarily the sixteenth century. A good introduction to the Catholic Reformation can be found in M. R. O'Connell, *The Counter Reformation, 1559–1610* (New York, 1974).

General works on the sixteenth and seventeenth centuries include C. Wilson, *The Transformation of Europe, 1558–1648* (Berkeley, 1976); D. H. Pennington, *Europe in the Seventeenth Century*, 2d ed. (London and New York, 1989); R. S. Dunn, *The Age of Reli-*

gious Wars, 1559–1715, 2d ed. (New York, 1979); and R. Bonney, *The European Dynastic States 1494–1660* (Oxford, 1991).

For good introductions to the French Wars of Religion, see M. P. Holt, *The French Wars of Religion, 1562–1629* (New York, 1995), and R. J. Knecht, *The French Wars of Religion, 1559–1598*, 2d ed. (New York, 1996). The best biographies of Philip II are P. Pierson, *Philip II of Spain* (London, 1975), and G. Parker, *Philip II*, 3d ed. (Chicago, 1995). Elizabeth's reign can be examined in C. Haigh, *Elizabeth I*, 2d ed. (New York, 1998). On the Thirty Years' War, see G. Parker, *The Thirty Years War*, 2d ed. (London, 1997), and R. G. Asch, *The Thirty Years War: The Holy Roman Empire and Europe, 1618–1648* (New York, 1997). A good general work on the period of the English Revolution is M. A. Kishlansky, *A Monarchy Transformed* (London, 1996). On Oliver Cromwell, see R. Howell, Jr., *Cromwell* (Boston, 1977), and P. Gaunt, *Oliver Cromwell* (Cambridge, Mass., 1996).

The story of the witchcraft craze can be examined in two works, J. B. Russell, *A History of Witchcraft* (London, 1980), and B. P. Levack, *The Witch-Hunt in Early Modern Europe* (London, 1987).

For brief accounts of seventeenth-century French history, see R. Briggs, *Early Modern France, 1560–1715* (Oxford, 1977), and J. B. Collins, *The State in Early Modern France* (Cambridge, 1995). A solid and very readable biography of Louis XIV is J. B. Wolf, *Louis XIV* (New York, 1968). For a brief study, see P. R. Campbell, *Louis XIV, 1661–1715* (London, 1993). A now classic work on life in Louis XIV's France is W. H. Lewis, *The Splendid Century* (Garden City, N.Y., 1953). Well-presented summaries of revisionist views on Louis's monarchical power are R. Mettam, *Power and Faction in Louis XIV's France* (Oxford, 1988), and W. Beik, *Absolutism and Society in Seventeenth-Century France* (Cambridge, 1985). On the creation of an Austrian state, see R. J. W. Evans, *The Making of the Habsburg Monarchy, 1550–1700* (Oxford, 1979), and C. Ingrao, *The Habsburg Monarchy, 1618–1815* (Cambridge, 1994). The older work by F. L. Carsten, *The Origins of Prussia* (Oxford, 1954), remains an outstanding study of early Prussian history. Works on Peter the Great include M. S. Anderson, *Peter the Great*, 2d ed. (New York, 1995); L. Hughes, *Russia in the Age of Peter the Great* (New Haven, Conn., 1998); and the massive popular biography by R. K. Massie, *Peter the Great* (New York, 1980). On England, see J. P. Kenyon, *Stuart England* (London, 1978). A more specialized study is W. A. Speck, *The Revolution of 1688* (Oxford, 1988).

For a brief, readable guide to Mannerism, see L. Murray, *The Late Renaissance and Mannerism* (New York, 1967). For a general survey of Baroque culture, see J. S. Held, *Seventeenth and Eighteenth Century Art: Baroque Painting, Sculpture, Architecture* (New York, 1971). On French classicism, see A. Merot, *French Painting in the Seventeenth Century* (New Haven, Conn., 1995). On the Spanish golden century of literature, see R. O. Jones, *The Golden Age: Prose and Poetry*, which is volume 2 of *The Literary History of Spain* (London, 1971). The literature on Shakespeare is enormous. For a biography, see A. L. Rowse, *The Life of Shakespeare* (New York, 1963).

For additional reading, go to InfoTrac College Edition, your online research library at http://web1.infotrac-college.com

Enter the search term "Reformation" using the Subject Guide.

Enter the search term "Counter-Reformation" using the Subject Guide.

Enter the search terms "Martin and Luther not King" using Keywords.

Enter the search terms "Thirty Years' War" using Keywords.

Enter the search terms "Louis XIV" using Keywords.

CHAPTER

16

THE MUSLIM EMPIRES

CHAPTER OUTLINE

- THE OTTOMAN EMPIRE
- THE SAFAVIDS
- THE GRANDEUR OF THE MUGHALS
- CONCLUSION

FOCUS QUESTIONS

- Why are the Ottoman, Safavid, and Mughal Empires sometimes called "gunpowder empires," and how accurate is that characterization?
- How did each of the great Muslim empires—Ottoman, Safavid, and Mughal—come into existence, and why did they ultimately decline?
- What were the main characteristics of each of the Muslim empires, and in what ways were they similar?
- What contact did each of the Muslim empires have with Europeans, and how was each empire affected by that contact?
- What role did women play in each of the Muslim empires?

One of the European states' primary objectives in seeking a route to the Spice Islands was to lessen the political and economic power of Islam by reducing the Muslims' strong position in the global trade network. As we saw in Chapter 14, Portuguese fleets, followed by those of the Spanish, the English, and the Dutch, had some success in wresting control over the spice trade from Muslim shippers, although the latter were never totally driven out of the business. By the eighteenth century, the Indian Ocean had ceased to be an Arab preserve and had become, in some respects, a European lake.

Thus, the European dream of controlling global trade markets had become a reality. But in the broader scheme of things, the goal of crippling the power of Islam was not entirely realized, for Europe's success had not been achieved by the collapse of its great Muslim rival. To the contrary, the Muslim world, which appeared to have entered a period of decline with the collapse of the Abbasid caliphate during the era of the Mongols, managed to revive in the shadow of Europe's Age of Exploration, a period that also saw the rise of three great Muslim empires. Known as the Ottomans, the Safavids, and the Mughals, these three powerful Muslim states dominated the Middle East and the South Asia subcontinent and brought stability to a region that had been in turmoil for centuries.

This stability lasted for about two hundred years. By the end of the eighteenth century, much of India and the Middle East had come under severe European pressure and had returned to a state of anarchy, and the Ottoman Empire had entered a period of gradual decline. But that decline was due more to internal factors than to the challenge posed by a resurgent Europe.

The Ottoman Empire

The Ottoman Turks were among the various Turkic-speaking peoples who had spread westward from Central Asia in the ninth to the eleventh centuries C.E. The first to dominate were the Seljuk Turks, who initially attempted to revive the declining Abbasid caliphate in Baghdad. Later they established themselves in the Anatolian peninsula at the expense of the Byzantine Empire. Turks served as warriors or administrators, while the peasants who tilled the farmland were mainly Greek.

In the late thirteenth century, a new group of Turks under the tribal leader Osman (1280–1326) began to

MAP 16.1 The Ottoman Empire

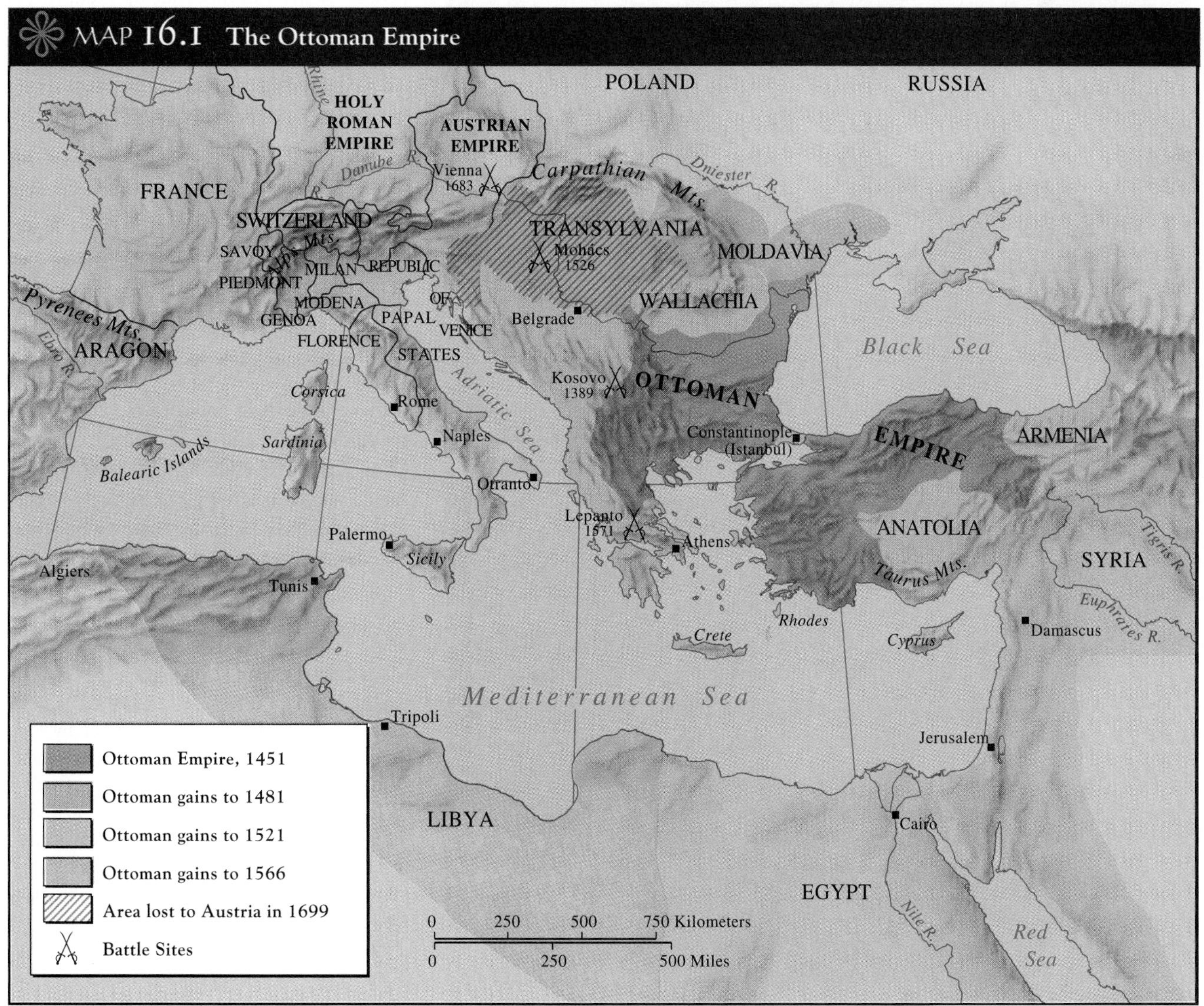

consolidate their power in the northwestern corner of the Anatolian peninsula. That land had been given to them by the Seljuk rulers as a reward for helping to drive out the Mongols in the late thirteenth century. At first, the Osman Turks were relatively peaceful and engaged in pastoral pursuits, but as the Seljuk empire began to disintegrate in the early fourteenth century, they began to expand and founded the Osmanli (later to be known as Ottoman) dynasty.

A key advantage for the Ottomans was their location in the northwestern corner of the peninsula. From there they were able to expand westward and eventually control the Bosporus and the Dardanelles, between the Mediterranean and the Black Seas. The Byzantine Empire, of course, had controlled the area for centuries, serving as a buffer between the Muslim Middle East and the Latin West. The Byzantines, however, had been severely weakened by the sack of Constantinople in the Fourth Crusade (of 1204) and the Western occupation of much of the empire for the next half century. In 1345, Ottoman forces under their leader Orkhan I (1326–1360) crossed the Bosporus for the first time to support a usurper against the Byzantine emperor in Constantinople. Setting up their first European base at Gallipoli at the Mediterranean entrance to the Dardanelles, Turkish forces expanded gradually into the Balkans and allied with fractious Serbian and Bulgar forces against the Byzantines. In these unstable conditions, the Ottomans gradually established permanent settlements throughout the area, where Turkish beys (provincial governors in the Ottoman Empire; from the Turkish *beg*, "knight") drove out the previous landlords and collected taxes from the local Slavic peasants. The Ottoman leader now began to claim the title of sultan or sovereign of his domain.

In 1360, Orkhan was succeeded by his son Murad I, who consolidated Ottoman power in the Balkans, set up a capital at Edirne (today Adrianople), and gradually reduced the Byzantine emperor to a vassal. Murad did not initially attempt to conquer Constantinople, because his forces were composed mostly of the traditional Turkish cavalry and lacked the ability to breach the strong walls of the city. Instead, he began to build up a strong military administration based on the recruitment of Christians into an elite guard. Called Janissaries (from the Turkish *Yeni Cheri*, "new troops"), they were recruited from the local Christian population in the Balkans and then converted to Islam and trained as foot soldiers or administrators. One of the major advantages of the Janissaries was that they were directly subordinated to the sultanate and therefore owed their loyalty to the person of the sul-

THE TURKISH CONQUEST OF CONSTANTINOPLE. Mehmet II put a stranglehold on the Byzantine capital of Constantinople with a surprise attack by Turkish ships, which were dragged overland and placed in the water behind the enemy's defense lines. In addition, the Turks made use of massive cannons that could launch stone balls weighing up to 1,200 pounds each. The heavy bombardment of the city walls presaged the beginning of a new era of warfare in Europe. Notice the fanciful Gothic interpretation of the city in this contemporary French miniature of the siege of Constantinople.

CHRONOLOGY

THE OTTOMAN EMPIRE

Reign of Osman I	1280–1326
Ottoman Turks first cross the Bosporus	1345
Murad I consolidates Turkish power in the Balkans	1360
Ottomans defeat Serbian Army at Kosovo	1389
Tamerlane defeats Ottoman army at Ankara	1402
Rule of Mehmet II (the Conqueror)	1451–1481
Turkish conquest of Constantinople	1453
Turks defeat Mamluks in Syria and seize Cairo	1516–1517
Reign of Suleyman I (the Magnificent)	1520–1566
Defeat of Hungarians at Battle of Mohács	1526
Defeat of Turks at Vienna	1529
Battle of Lepanto	1571
Sinan era in Ottoman architecture	Sixteenth century

tan. Other military forces were organized by the beys and were thus loyal to their local tribal leaders.

The Janissary corps also represented a response to changes in warfare. As the knowledge of firearms spread in the late fourteenth century, the Turks began to master the new technology, including siege cannons and muskets. The traditional nomadic cavalry charge was now outmoded and was superseded by infantry forces armed with muskets. Thus, the Janissaries provided a well-armed infantry who served both as an elite guard to protect the palace and as a means of extending Turkish control in the Balkans. With his new forces, Murad defeated the Serbs at the famous Battle of Kosovo in 1389 and ended Serbian hegemony in the area.

Under Murad's successor Bayazid I (1389–1402), the Ottomans advanced northward, annexed Bulgaria, and slaughtered the flower of French cavalry at a major battle on the Danube. A defeat at the hands of the Mongol warrior Tamerlane (see Chapter 9) in 1402 proved to be only a temporary setback. When Mehmet II (1451–1481) succeeded to the throne, he was determined to capture Constantinople. Already in control of the Dardanelles, he ordered the construction of a major fortress on the Bosporus just north of the city, which put the Turks in a position to strangle the Byzantines.

The last Byzantine emperor desperately called for help from the Europeans, but only the Genoese came to his defense. With 80,000 troops ranged against only 7,000 defenders, Mehmet laid siege to Constantinople in 1453. In their attack on the city, the Turks made use of massive cannons with twenty-six-foot barrels that could launch stone balls weighing up to 1,200 pounds each. The Byzantines stretched heavy chains across the Golden Horn the inlet that forms the city's harbor, to prevent a naval attack from the north and prepared to make their final stand behind the thirteen-mile-long wall along the western edge of the city. But Mehmet's forces seized the tip of the peninsula north of the Golden Horn and then dragged their ships overland across the peninsula from the Bosporus and put them into the water behind the chains. Finally, the walls were breached; the Byzantine emperor died in the final battle (see the box on p. 464). Mehmet II, standing before the palace of the emperor, paused to reflect on the passing nature of human glory. But it was not long before he and the Ottomans were again on the march.

Expansion of the Empire

With their new capital at Constantinople, renamed Istanbul, the Ottoman Turks were now a dominant force in the Balkans and the Anatolian peninsula. At the end of the fifteenth century, they began to advance to the east against the Shi'ite kingdom of the Safavids in Persia (see The Safavids later in this chapter), which had been promoting rebellion among the Anatolian tribal population and disrupting Turkish trade through the Middle East. After defeating the Safavids at a major battle in 1514, Emperor Selim I (1512–1520) consolidated Turkish control over Mesopotamia and then turned his attention to the Mamluks in Egypt, who had failed to support the Ottomans in their struggle against the Safavids. The Mamluks were defeated in Syria in 1516; Cairo fell a year later. Now controlling several of the holy cities of Islam, including Jerusalem, Mecca, and Medina, Selim declared himself to be the new caliph, or successor to Muhammad. During the next few years, Turkish armies and fleets advanced westward along the African coast, occupying Tripoli, Tunis, and Algeria and eventually penetrating almost to the Strait of Gibraltar. In their advance, the invaders had taken advantage of the progressive disintegration of the Nasrid dynasty in Morocco, which had been in decline for decades and had lost its last foothold on the European continent when Granada fell to the rising power of Spain in 1492.

The impact of Turkish rule on the peoples of North Africa was relatively light. Like their predecessors, the Turks were Muslims, and they preferred where possible to administer their conquered regions through local rulers. Central government direction was achieved through appointed *pashas* who collected taxes (and then paid a

THE FALL OF CONSTANTINOPLE

Few events in the history of the Ottoman Empire are more dramatic than the conquest of Constantinople in 1453. In this excerpt, the conquest is described by Kritovoulos, a Greek who later served in the Ottoman administration. Although the author did not witness the conquest itself, he was apparently well informed about the event and provides us with a vivid description.

KRITOVOULOS, *LIFE OF MEHMED THE CONQUEROR*

So saying, he [the Sultan] led them himself. And they, with a shout on the run and with a fearsome yell, went on ahead of the Sultan, pressing on up to the palisade. After a long and bitter struggle they hurled back the Romans [Byzantines] from there and climbed by force up the palisade. They dashed some of their foe down into the ditch between the great wall and the palisade, which was deep and hard to get out of, and they killed them there. The rest they drove back to the gate.

He had opened this gate in the great wall, so as to go easily over to the palisade. Now there was a great struggle there and great slaughter among those stationed there, for they were attacked by the heavy infantry and not a few others in irregular formation, who had been attracted from many points by the shouting. There the Emperor Constantine [Constantine XIII Paleologus], with all who were with him, fell in gallant combat.

The heavy infantry were already streaming through the little gate into the City, and others had rushed in through the breach in the great wall. Then all the rest of the army, with a rush and a roar, poured in brilliantly and scattered all over the City. And the Sultan stood before the great wall, where the standard also was and the ensigns, and watched the proceedings. The day was already breaking. . . .

The soldiers fell on them [the citizens] with anger and great wrath. For one thing, they were actuated by the hardships of the siege. For another, some foolish people had hurled taunts and curses at them from the battlements all through the siege. Now, in general they killed so as to frighten all the City, and to terrorize and enslave all by the slaughter.

When they had had enough of murder, and the City was reduced to slavery, some of the troops turned to the mansions of the mighty, by bands and companies and divisions, for plunder and spoil. Others went to the robbing of churches, and others dispersed to the simple homes of the common people, stealing, robbing, plundering, killing, insulting, taking and enslaving men, women, and children, old and young, priests, monks—in short, every age and class. . . .

They say that many of the maidens, even at the mere unaccustomed sight and sound of these men, were terror-stricken and came near losing their very lives. And there were also honorable old men who were dragged by their white hair, and some of them beaten unmercifully. And well-born and beautiful young boys were carried off. . . .

After this the Sultan entered the City and looked about to see its great size, its situation, its grandeur and beauty, its teeming population, its loveliness, and the costliness of its churches and public buildings and of the private houses and community houses and those of the officials. . . . When he saw what a large number had been killed, and the ruin of the buildings, and the wholesale ruin and destruction of the City, he was filled with compassion and repented not a little at the destruction and plundering. Tears fell from his eyes as he groaned deeply and passionately: "What a city we have given over to plunder and destruction."

Thus he suffered in spirit. And indeed this was a great blow to us, in this one City, a disaster the like of which had occurred in no one of the great renowned cities of history, whether one speaks of the size of the captured City or of the bitterness and harshness of the deed. And no less did it astound all others than it did those who went through it and suffered, through the unreasonable and unusual character of the event and through the overwhelming and unheard-of horror of it.

As for the great City of Constantine, raised to a great height of glory and dominion and wealth in its own times, overshadowing to an infinite degree all the cities around it, renowned for its glory, wealth, authority, power, and greatness, and all its other qualities, it thus came to its end.

fixed percentage as tribute to the central government), maintained law and order, and were directly responsible to Istanbul. The Turks ruled from coastal cities like Algiers, Tripoli, and Tunis and made no attempt to control the interior beyond maintaining the trade routes through the Sahara to the trading centers along the Niger River. Meanwhile local pirates along the Barbary Coast competed with their Christian rivals in raiding the shipping that passed through the Mediterranean.

By the seventeenth century, the links between the imperial court in Istanbul and its appointed representatives in the Turkish regencies in North Africa had begun to decline. Some of the *pashas* were dethroned by local elites while others, such as the bey of Tunis, became hereditary rulers. Even Egypt, whose agricultural wealth and control over the route to the Red Sea made it the most important country in the area to the Turks, gradually became autonomous under a new official class of Janissaries. Many of them became wealthy landowners by exploiting their official function to collect tax revenues far in excess of what they had to remit to Istanbul. In the early eighteenth century, the Mamluks returned to power,

A PORTRAIT OF SULEYMAN THE MAGNIFICENT

Suleyman the Magnificent was perhaps the greatest of all Ottoman sultans. Like King Louis XIV of France and Emperor Kangxi of China, he presided over his domain at the peak of its military and cultural achievement. This description of him was written by Ghislain de Busbecq, the Habsburg ambassador to Constantinople. Busbecq observed Suleyman at firsthand and, as this excerpt indicates, was highly impressed by the Turkish ruler.

GHISLAIN DE BUSBECQ, *THE TURKISH LETTERS*

The Sultan was seated on a rather low sofa, no more than a foot from the ground and spread with many costly coverlets and cushions embroidered with exquisite work. Near him were his bow and arrows. His expression, as I have said, is anything but smiling, and has a sternness which, though sad, is full of majesty. On our arrival we were introduced into his presence by his chamberlains, who held our arms—a practice which has always been observed since a Croatian sought an interview and murdered the Sultan Amurath in a revenge for the slaughter of his master, Marcus the Despot of Serbia. After going through the pretense of kissing his hand, we were led to the wall facing him backwards, so as not to turn our backs or any part of them toward him. He then listened to the recital of my message, but, as it did not correspond with his expectations (for the demands of my imperial master [the Habsburg emperor Ferdinand I] were full of dignity and independence, and, therefore, far from acceptable to one who thought that his slightest wishes ought to be obeyed) he assumed an expression of disdain, and merely answered "Giusel, Giusel," that is, "Well, Well." We were then dismissed to our lodging....

You will probably wish me to describe the impression which Suleyman made upon me. He is beginning to feel the weight of years, but his dignity of demeanor and his general physical appearance are worthy of the ruler of so vast an empire. He has always been frugal and temperate, and was so even in his youth, when he might have erred without incurring blame in the eyes of the Turks. Even in his earlier years he did not indulge in wine or in those unnatural vices to which the Turks are often addicted. Even his bitterest critics can find nothing more serious to allege against him than his undue submission to his wife and its result in his somewhat precipitate action in putting Mustapha [his firstborn son, by another wife] to death, which is generally imputed to her employment of love potions and incantations. It is generally agreed that, ever since he promoted her to the rank of his lawful wife, he has possessed no concubines, although there is no law to prevent his doing so. He is a strict guardian of his religion and its ceremonies, being not less desirous of upholding his faith than of extending his dominions. For his age—he has almost reached his sixtieth year—he enjoys quite good health, though his bad complexion may be due to some hidden malady; and indeed it is generally believed that he has an incurable ulcer or gangrene on his leg. This defect of complexion he remedies by painting his face with a coating of red powder, when he wishes departing ambassadors to take with them a strong impression of his good health; for he fancies that it contributes to inspire greater fear in foreign potentates if they think that he is well and strong. I noticed a clear indication of this practice on the present occasion; for his appearance when he received me in the final audience was very different from that which he presented when he gave me an interview on my arrival.

although the Turkish government managed to retain some control by means of a viceroy appointed from Istanbul.

TURKISH EXPANSION IN EUROPE

After their conquest of Constantinople in 1453, the Ottoman Turks tried to complete their conquest of the Balkans, where they had been established since the fourteenth century. Although they were successful in taking the Romanian territory of Wallachia in 1476, the resistance of the Hungarians initially kept the Turks from advancing up the Danube valley. From 1480 to 1520, internal problems and the need to consolidate their eastern frontiers kept the Turks from any further attacks on Europe.

Suleyman I the Magnificent (1520–1566), the greatest of the Ottoman sultans (see the box above), however, brought the Turks back to Europe's attention. Advancing up the Danube, the Turks seized Belgrade in 1521 and won a major victory over the Hungarians at the Battle of Mohács on the Danube in 1526. Subsequently, the Turks overran most of Hungary, moved into Austria, and advanced as far as Vienna, where they were finally repulsed in 1529. At the same time, the Turks extended their power into the western Mediterranean and threatened to turn it into a Turkish lake until a large Turkish fleet was destroyed by the Spanish at Lepanto in 1571. Despite the defeat, the Turks continued to hold nominal suzerainty over the southern shores of the Mediterranean.

Although Europeans frequently called for new Christian crusades against the "infidel" Turks, by the beginning of the seventeenth century the Ottoman Empire was being treated like any other European power by European rulers seeking alliances and trade concessions. During the first half of the seventeenth century, the Ottoman Empire was a "sleeping giant." Involved in domestic bloodletting and heavily threatened by a challenge from Persia, the Ottomans were content with the status quo in eastern Europe. But under a new line of grand vezirs in the second half of the seventeenth century, the Ottoman Empire again took the offensive. By mid-1683, the Ottomans had marched through the Hungarian plain and laid siege to Vienna. Repulsed by a mixed army of Austrians, Poles, Bavarians, and Saxons, the Turks retreated and were pushed out of Hungary by a new European coalition. Although they retained the core of their empire, the Ottoman Turks would never again be a threat to Europe. Although the Turkish empire held together for the rest of the seventeenth and the eighteenth centuries, it would be faced with new challenges from the ever growing Austrian Empire in southeastern Europe and the new Russian giant to the north.

The Nature of Turkish Rule

Like other Muslim empires in Persia and India, the Ottoman political system was the result of the evolution of tribal institutions into a sedentary empire. The three states are often called "gunpowder empires" because to a considerable extent they owed their success to their mastery of the technology of firearms. At the apex of the Ottoman system was the sultan, who was the supreme authority in both a political and a military sense. The origins of this system can be traced back to the bey, who was only a tribal leader, a first among equals, who could claim loyalty from his chiefs so long as he could provide booty and grazing lands for his subordinates. Disputes were settled by tribal law, while Muslim laws were secondary. Tribal leaders collected taxes—or booty—from areas under their control and sent one-fifth on to the bey. Both administrative and military power were centralized under the bey, and the capital was wherever the bey and his administration happened to be.

But the rise of empire brought about changes and an adaptation to Byzantine traditions of rule. The status and prestige of the sultan now increased relative to the subordinate tribal leaders, and the position took on the trappings of imperial rule. Court rituals were inherited from the Byzantines and Persians, and a centralized administrative system was adopted that increasingly isolated the sultan in his palace. The position of the sultan was hereditary, with a son, although not necessarily the eldest, always succeeding the father. This practice led to chronic succession struggles upon the death of individual sultans, and the losers were often executed (strangled with a silk bowstring) or later imprisoned. Heirs to the throne were assigned as provincial governors to provide them with experience.

The heart of the sultan's power was in the Topkapi (meaning "cannon gate") Palace in the center of Istanbul. Topkapi was constructed in 1459 by Mehmet II and served as an administrative center as well as the private residence of the sultan and his family. Eventually, it had a staff of 20,000 employees. The private domain of the sultan was called the harem (sacred place). Here he resided with his concubines. Normally, a sultan did not marry but chose several concubines as his favorites; they were accorded this status after they gave birth to sons. When a son became a sultan, his mother became known as the queen mother and served as adviser to the throne. This tradition, initiated by the influential wife of Suleyman the Magnificent, often resulted in considerable authority for the queen mother in the affairs of state.

Members of the harem, like the Janissaries, were often of slave origins and formed an elite element in Ottoman society. Since the enslavement of Muslims was forbidden, slaves were taken among non-Islamic peoples. Some concubines were prisoners selected for the position, while others were purchased or offered to the sultan as a gift. They were then trained and educated like the Janissaries in a system called *devshirme* (collection). The *devshirme* had originated in the practice of requiring local clan leaders to

MEHMET II, CONQUEROR OF CONSTANTINOPLE. Identified with the seizure of Constantinople from the Byzantine Empire in 1453, Mehmet II was one of the most illustrious Ottoman sultans. This Turkish miniature portrays Mehmet II with his handkerchief, a symbol of the supreme power of the Ottoman ruler. He is also smelling a rose, representing his cultural interests, especially as patron of the arts.

provide prisoners to the sultan as part of their tax obligation. Talented males were given special training for eventual placement in military or administrative positions, while their female counterparts were trained for service in the harem, with instruction in reading, the Koran, sewing and embroidery, and musical performance. They were ranked according to their status, and some were permitted to leave the harem to marry officials. If they were later divorced, they were sometimes allowed to return to the harem.

Unique to the Ottoman Empire from the fifteenth century onward was the exclusive use of slaves to reproduce its royal heirs. Contrary to myth, few of the women of the imperial harem were used for sexual purposes, as the majority were relatives of the sultan's extended family, comprised of sisters, daughters, widowed mothers, and in-laws, with their own personal slaves and entourage. Contemporary European observers compared the atmosphere in the Topkapi harem to a Christian nunnery, with its hierarchical organization, enforced chastity, and the rule of silence.

Because of their proximity to the sultan, the women of the harem often wielded so much political power that the era has been called "the sultanate of women." Queen mothers administered the imperial household and engaged in diplomatic relations with other countries, while controlling the marital alliances of their daughters with senior civilian and military officials or members of other royal families in the region. One princess was married seven separate times from the age of two after her previous husbands died either in battle or by execution.

The sultan ruled through an imperial council that met four days a week and was chaired by the chief minister known as the grand vezir (*wazir,* sometimes known in English as vizier). The sultan often attended behind a screen, whence he could privately indicate his desires to the grand vezir. The latter presided over the imperial bureaucracy. Like the palace guard, the bureaucrats were not an exclusive group, but were chosen at least partly by merit from a palace school for training officials. Most officials were Muslims by birth, but some talented Janissaries became senior members of the bureaucracy, and almost all the later grand vezirs came from the *devshirme* system.

Local administration during the imperial period was a product of Turkish tribal tradition and was similar in some respects to fief holding in Europe. The empire was divided into provinces and districts governed by officials who, like their tribal predecessors, combined both civil and military functions. They were assisted by bureaucrats trained in the palace school in Istanbul. Senior officials were assigned land in fief by the sultan and were then responsible for collecting taxes and supplying armies to the empire. These lands were then farmed out to the local cavalry elite called the *sipahis*, who exacted a tax from all peasants in their fiefdoms for their salary. These local officials were not hereditary aristocrats, but sons often inherited their father's landholdings, and the vast majority were descendants of the tribal beys who had served as a tribal elite during the preimperial period.

Religion and Society in the Ottoman World

Like most Turkic-speaking peoples in the Anatolian peninsula and throughout the Middle East, the Ottoman ruling elites were Sunni Muslims. Ottoman sultans had claimed the title of caliph (defender of the faith) since the early sixteenth century and thus theoretically were responsible for guiding the flock and maintaining Islamic law, the *Shari'ah*. In practice, the sultan assigned these duties to a supreme religious authority, who administered the law and maintained a system of schools for educating Muslims.

Islamic law and customs were applied to all Muslims in the empire. Like their rulers, most Turkic-speaking people were Sunni Muslims, but some communities were attracted to Sufism (see Chapter 7) or other heterodox doctrines. The government tolerated such activities so long as their practitioners remained loyal to the empire, but in the early sixteenth century unrest among these groups—some of whom converted to the Shi'ite version of Islamic doctrine—outraged the conservative *ulama* and eventually led to the war against the Safavids (see The Safavids later in this chapter).

Non-Muslims—mostly Orthodox Christians (Greeks and Slavs), Jews, and Armenian Christians—formed a significant minority within the empire, which treated them with relative tolerance. Non-Muslims were compelled to pay a head tax (because of their exemption from military service), but they were permitted to practice their religion or convert to Islam, although Muslims were prohibited from adopting another faith. Most of the population in European areas of the empire remained Christian, but in some places, such as the territory now called Bosnia, substantial numbers converted to Islam.

Each religious group within the empire was organized as an administrative unit called a *millet* (nation or community). Each group, including the Muslims themselves, had its own patriarch or grand rabbi who dealt as an intermediary with the government and administered the community according to its own laws. The leaders of the individual nations were responsible to the sultan and his officials for the behavior of the subjects under their care and collected taxes for transmission to the government. Each nation established its own system of justice, set its own educational policies, and provided welfare for the needy.

Technically, women in the Ottoman Empire were subject to the same restrictions that afflicted their counterparts in other Muslim societies, but their position was ameliorated to some degree by various factors. In the first place, non-Muslims were subject to the laws and customs of their own religions; thus, Orthodox Christian, Jewish, and Armenian Christian women were spared some of the

A TURKISH DISCOURSE ON COFFEE

Coffee was first introduced to Turkey from the Arabian peninsula in the mid-sixteenth century and allegedly came to Europe during the Turkish seige of Vienna in 1527. The following account was written by Katib Chelebi, a seventeenth-century Turkish author who, among other things, compiled an extensive encyclopedia and bibliography. Here, in The Balance of Truth, *he describes how coffee entered the empire and the problems it caused for public morality. Chelebi died in Istanbul in 1657, reportedly while drinking a cup of coffee.*

KATIB CHELEBI, *THE BALANCE OF TRUTH*

It [coffee] originated in Yemen and has spread, like tobacco, over the world. Certain sheikhs, who lived with their dervishes in the mountains of Yemen, used to crush and eat the berries . . . of a certain tree. Some would roast them and drink their water. Coffee is a cold dry food, suited to the ascetic life and sedative of lust. . . .

It came to Asia Minor by sea, about 1543, and met with a hostile reception, fetwas [decrees] being delivered against it. For they said, Apart from its being roasted, the fact that it is drunk in gatherings, passed from hand to hand, is suggestive of loose living. It is related of Abul-Suud Efendi that he had holes bored in the ships that brought it, plunging their cargoes of coffee into the sea. But these strictures and prohibitions availed nothing. . . . One coffeehouse was opened after another, and men would gather together, with great eagerness and enthusiasm, to drink. Drug addicts in particular, finding it a life-giving thing, which increased their pleasure, were willing to die for a cup.

Storytellers and musicians diverted the people from their employments, and working for one's living fell into disfavor. Moreover the people, from prince to beggar, amused themselves with knifing one another. Toward the end of 1633, the late Ghazi Gultan Murad, becoming aware of the situation, promulgated an edict, out of regard and compassion for the people, to this effect: Coffeehouses throughout the Guarded Domains shall be dismantled and not opened hereafter. Since then, the coffeehouses of the capital have been as desolate as the heart of the ignorant. . . . But in cities and towns outside Istanbul, they are opened just as before. As has been said above, such things do not admit of a perpetual ban.

restrictions applied to their Muslim sisters. In the second place, Islamic laws as applied in the Ottoman Empire defined the legal position of women comparatively tolerantly. Women were permitted to own and inherit property, including their dowries. They could not be forced into marriage and in certain cases were permitted to seek a divorce. As we have seen, women often exercised considerable influence in the palace and in a few instances even served as senior officials, such as governors of provinces. The relatively tolerant attitude toward women in Ottoman-held territories has been ascribed by some to Turkish tribal traditions, which took a more egalitarian view of sex roles than did the sedentary societies of the region.

The Ottomans in Decline

The Ottoman Empire reached its zenith under Suleyman the Magnificent, often known as Suleyman Kanuni, or "the lawgiver," who launched the conquest of Hungary. But Suleyman also sowed the seeds of the Ottomans' eventual decline. He executed his two most able sons on suspicion of factionalism and was succeeded by Selim II (the Sot, or "the drunken sultan"), the only surviving son.

By the seventeenth century, signs of internal rot had begun to appear, although the first loss of imperial territory did not occur until 1699, at the Battle of Carlowitz. Apparently, a number of factors were involved. In the first place, the administrative system inherited from the tribal period began to break down. Although the *devshirme* system of training officials continued to function, *devshirme* graduates were now permitted to marry and inherit property and to enroll their sons in the palace corps. Thus, they were gradually transformed from a meritocratic administrative elite into a privileged and often degenerate hereditary caste. Local administrators were corrupted and taxes rose as the central bureaucracy lost its links with rural areas. The imperial treasury was depleted by constant wars, and transport and communications were neglected. In addition, the empire was increasingly beset by economic difficulties, caused by the diversion of trade routes away from the eastern Mediterranean and the price inflation brought about by the influx of cheap American silver.

Another sign of change within the empire was the increasing degree of material affluence and the impact of Western ideas and customs. Sophisticated officials and merchants began to mimic the habits and lifestyles of their European counterparts, dressing in the European fashion, purchasing Western furniture and art objects, and ignoring Muslim strictures against the consumption of alcohol and sexual activities outside marriage. During the sixteenth and early seventeenth centuries, coffee and tobacco were introduced into polite Ottoman society, and cafés for the consumption of both began to appear in the major cities (see the box above). One sultan in the early seventeenth century issued a decree prohibiting the consumption of both coffee and tobacco, arguing (correctly, no doubt) that many cafés were nests of antigovernment intrigue. He even began to wander incognito through the streets of Istanbul at night. Any of his subjects detected in immoral or illegal acts were summarily executed and their bodies left on the streets as an example to others.

There were also signs of a decline in competence within the ruling family. Whereas the first sultans reigned twenty-seven years on average, later ones averaged only thirteen years. The throne now went to the oldest surviving male, while his rivals were kept secluded in a latticed cage and thus had no governmental experience if they succeeded to rule. Later sultans also became less involved in government, and more power flowed to the office of the grand vezir (called the *Sublime Porte*) or to eunuchs and members of the harem. Palace intrigue increased as a result.

Ottoman Art

The Ottoman sultans were enthusiastic patrons of the arts and maintained large ateliers of artisans and artists, primarily at the Topkapi Palace in Istanbul but also in other important cities of the vast empire. The period from Mehmet II in the fifteenth century to the early eighteenth century witnessed the flourishing of pottery, rugs, silk and other textiles, jewelry, arms and armor, and calligraphy. All adorned the palaces of the new rulers, testifying to their opulence and exquisite taste. The artists came from all parts of the realm and beyond. Besides Turks, there were Persians, Greeks, Armenians, Hungarians, and Italians, all vying for the esteem and generous rewards of the sultans and fearing that losing favor might mean losing their heads! In the second half of the sixteenth century, Istanbul alone listed over 150 craft guilds, ample proof of the artistic activity of the era.

By far the greatest contribution of the Ottoman Empire to world art was its architecture, especially the magnificent mosques of the last half of the sixteenth century. Traditionally, prayer halls in mosques were subdivided by numerous pillars that supported small individual domes, creating a private forestlike atmosphere. The Turks, however, modeled their new mosques on the open floor plan of the Byzantine church of Santa Sophia (completed in 537), which had been turned into a mosque by Mehmet II, and began to push the pillars toward the outer wall to create a prayer hall with an uninterrupted central area under one large dome. With this plan, large numbers of believers could worship in unison in accordance with Muslim preference. By the mid-sixteenth century, the greatest of all Ottoman architects, Sinan, began erecting the first of his eighty-one mosques with an uncluttered prayer area. Each was topped by an imposing dome, and often, as at Edirne, the entire building was framed with four towering narrow minarets. By emphasizing its vertical lines, the minarets camouflaged the massive stone bulk of the structure and gave it a feeling of incredible lightness. These four graceful minarets would find new expression sixty years later in India's white marble Taj Mahal (see Mughal Culture later in this chapter).

The lightness of the exterior was reinforced in the mosque's interior by the soaring height of the dome and the numerous windows. Added to this were delicate plasterwork and tile decoration that transformed the mosque into a monumental oasis of spirituality, opulence, and power. Sinan's masterpieces, such as the Suleymaniye and the Blue Mosque of Istanbul, were always part of a large socioreligious compound that included a library, school, hospital, mausolea, and even bazaars, all of equally magnificent construction.

Earlier, the thirteenth-century Seljuk Turks of Anatolia had created beautiful tile decorations with two-color mosaics. Now Ottoman artists invented a new glazed tile art with painted flowers and geometrical designs in brilliant blue, green, yellow, and their own secret "tomato red." Entire walls, both interior and exterior, were covered with the painted tiles, which adorned palaces as well as mosques. Produced at Iznik (the old Nicaea), the distinctive tiles and pottery were in great demand; the city's ateliers boasted more than three hundred artisans in the late sixteenth century.

The sixteenth century also witnessed the flourishing of textiles and rugs. The Byzantine emperor Justinian had introduced the cultivation of silkworms to the West in the sixth century, and the silk industry resurfaced under the Ottomans. Its capital was at Bursa, where factories produced silks for wall hangings, soft covers, and especially court costumes. Perhaps even more famous than Turkish silk are the rugs. But whereas silks were produced under the patronage of the sultans, rugs were a peasant industry. Each village boasted its own distinctive design and color scheme for the rugs it produced. Common to all the rugs, however, was the use of the knot from the Gordes region—hence the term "Gordian knot."

THE SAFAVIDS

After the collapse of the empire of Tamerlane in the early fifteenth century, the area extending from Persia into Central Asia lapsed into anarchy. The Uzbeks, Turkic-speaking peoples from Central Asia, were the chief political and military force in the area. From their capital at Bokhara, they maintained a semblance of control over the highly fluid tribal alignments until the emergence of the Safavid dynasty in Persia at the beginning of the sixteenth century.

The Safavid dynasty was founded by Shah Ismail, the descendant of a sheikh called Safi al-Din (thus the name Safavid), who traced his origins to Ali, the fourth imam of the Muslim faith. In the early fourteenth century, Safi had been the leader of a community of Turkic-speaking tribespeople in Azerbaijan, near the Caspian Sea. Safi's community was only one of many Sufi mystical religious groups throughout the area. In time the doctrine spread among nomadic groups throughout the Middle East and was transformed into the more activist Shi'i heresy. Its adherents were known as "red heads" because of their distinctive red cap with twelve folds, meant to symbolize allegiance to the twelve imams of the Shi'i faith.

In 1501, Ismail's forces seized much of Iran and Iraq, and he called himself the shah of a new Persian state. Baghdad was subdued in 1508 and the Uzbeks in Bokhara shortly thereafter. Ismail (1487–1524) now sent Shi'ite preachers into Anatolia to proselytize and promote rebellion among Turkish tribal peoples in the Ottoman Empire. In retaliation, the Ottoman sultan Selim I advanced against the Safavids in Iran and won a major battle near Tabriz in 1514. But Selim could not maintain control of the area, and Ismail regained Tabriz a few years later.

The Ottomans returned to the attack in the 1580s and forced the new Safavid shah, Abbas I (1587–1629), to sign a punitive peace in which much territory was lost. The capital was subsequently moved from Tabriz in the northwest to Isfahan in the south. Still, it was under Shah Abbas that the Safavids reached the zenith of their glory. He established a system similar to the Janissaries in Turkey to train administrators to replace the traditional warrior elite. He also used the period of peace to strengthen his army, now armed with modern weapons, and in the early seventeenth century he attempted to regain the lost territories. Although he had some initial success, war resumed in the 1620s, and a lasting peace was not achieved until 1638.

Abbas the Great had managed to strengthen the dynasty significantly, and for a time after his death in 1629, it remained stable and vigorous. But succession conflicts plagued the dynasty. Partly as a result, the power of the more militant Shi'ites began to increase at court and in Safavid society at large. The intellectual freedom that had characterized the empire at its height was cur-

THE BLUE MOSQUE, ISTANBUL. The magnificent mosques built under the patronage of Suleyman the Magnificent are a great legacy of the Ottoman Empire and a fitting supplement to Santa Sophia (Hagia Sophia) Cathedral, built by the Byzantine emperor Justinian in the sixth century C.E. Towering under a central dome, they seem to defy gravity, and, like European Gothic cathedrals, convey to the viewer a sense of weightlessness. The Blue Mosque, so called for the blue tiles in its interior, is one of the most impressive and graceful in Istanbul. A far cry from the seventh-century desert mosques constructed of palm trunks, the Ottoman mosques stand as one of the architectural wonders of the world.

CHRONOLOGY

THE SAFAVIDS

Ismail seizes Iran and Iraq and becomes shah of Persia	1501
Ismail conquers Baghdad and defeats Uzbeks	1508
Reign of Shah Abbas I	1587–1629
Truce achieved between Ottomans and Safavids	1638
Collapse of Safavid empire	1723

tailed under the pressure of religious orthodoxy, and Iranian women, who had enjoyed considerable freedom and influence during the early empire, were forced to withdraw into seclusion and to the veil. Meanwhile, attempts to suppress the religious beliefs of minorities led to increased popular unrest. In the early eighteenth century, Afghan warriors took advantage of local revolts to seize the capital of Isfahan, forcing the remnants of the Safavid ruling family to retreat to Azerbaijan, their original homeland. The Ottomans seized territories along the western border. Eventually, order was restored by the military adventurer Nadir Shah Afshar, who launched an extended series of campaigns that restored the country's borders and even occupied the Mughal capital of Delhi (see Twilight of the Mughals later in this chapter). After his death, the Zand dynasty ruled until the end of the eighteenth century.

Safavid Politics and Society

Like the Ottoman Empire, Iran under the Safavids was a mixed society. The Safavids had come to power with the support of nomadic Turkic-speaking tribal groups, and leading elements from those groups retained considerable influence within the empire. But the majority of the population were Iranian; most of them were farmers or townspeople, with attitudes inherited from the relatively sophisticated and urbanized culture of pre-Safavid Iran. Faced with the problem of integrating unruly Turkic-speaking tribal peoples with the sedentary Persian-speaking population of the urban areas, the Safavids used the Shi'ite faith as a unifying force (see the box on p. 472). The shah himself acquired an almost divine

MAP 16.2 The Ottoman and Safavid Empires, c. 1683

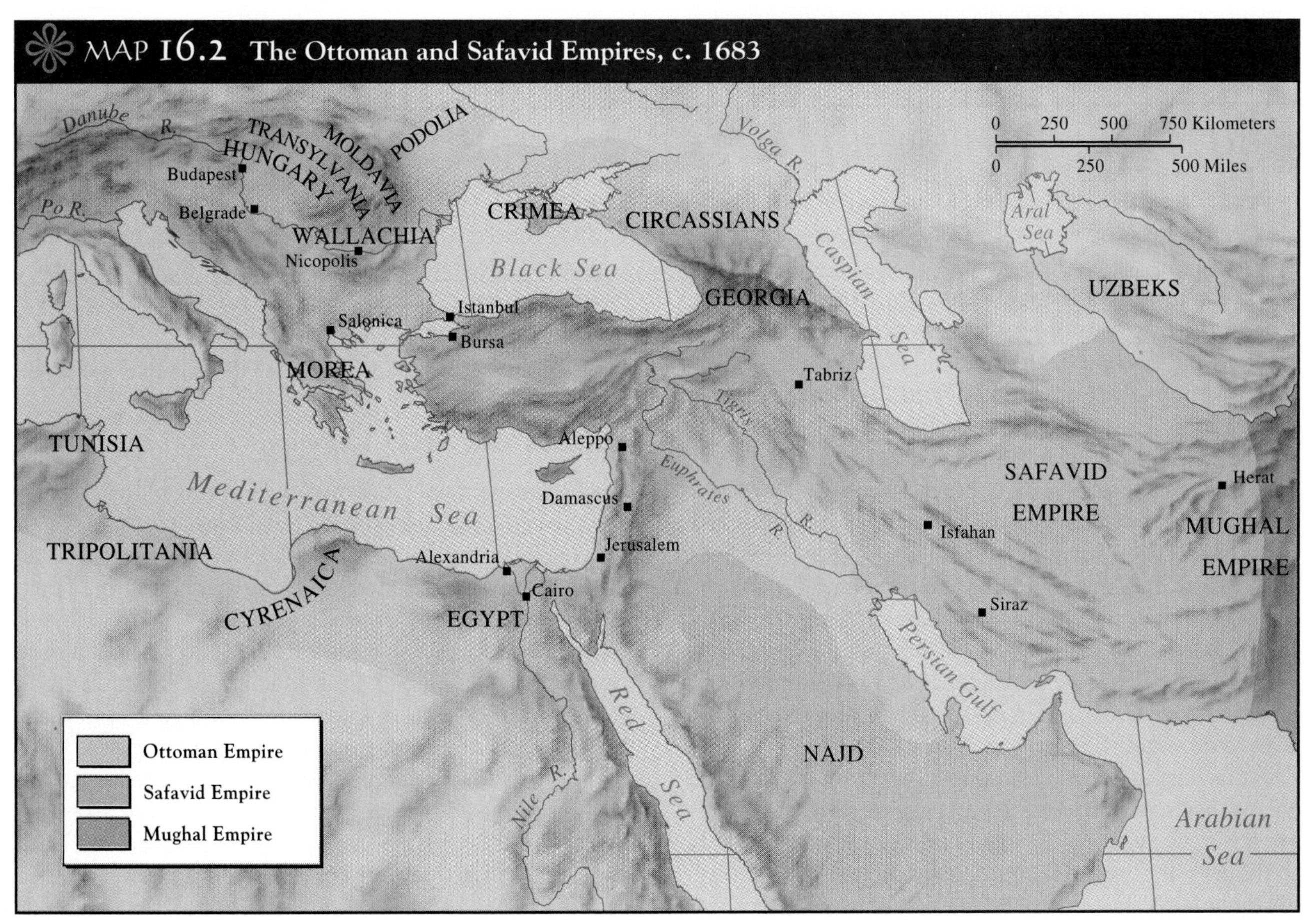

THE RELIGIOUS ZEAL OF SHAH ABBAS THE GREAT

Shah Abbas I, probably the greatest of the Safavid rulers, expanded the borders of his empire into areas of the southern Caucasus inhabited by Christians and other non-Muslim peoples. After Persian control was assured, he instructed that the local population be urged to convert to Islam for their own protection and the glory of God. In this passage, his biographer, the Persian historian Eskander Beg Monshi, recounts the story of that effort.

THE CONVERSION OF A NUMBER OF CHRISTIANS TO ISLAM

This year the Shah decreed that those Armenians and other Christians who had been settled in [the southern Caucasus] and had been given agricultural land there, should be invited to become Muslims. Life in this world is fraught with vicissitudes, and the Shah was concerned lest, in a period when the authority of the central government was weak, these Christians, . . . might be subjected to attack by the neighboring Lor tribes (who are naturally given to causing injury and mischief), and their women and children carried off into captivity. In the areas in which these Christian groups resided, it was the Shah's purpose that the places of worship which they had built should become mosques, and the muezzin's call should be heard in them, so that these Christians might assume the guise of Muslims, and their future status accordingly be assured. . . .

Some of the Christians, guided by God's grace, embraced Islam voluntarily; others found it difficult to abandon their Christian faith and felt revulsion at the idea. They were encouraged by their monks and priests to remain steadfast in their faith. After a little pressure had been applied to the monks and priests, however, they desisted, and these Christians saw no alternative but to embrace Islam, though they did so with reluctance. The women and children embraced Islam with great enthusiasm, vying with one another in their eagerness to abandon their Christian faith and declare their belief in the unity of God. Some five thousand people embraced Islam. As each group made the Muslim declaration of faith, it received instruction in the Koran and the principles of the religious law of Islam, and all bibles and other Christian devotional material were collected and taken away from the priests.

In the same way, all the Armenian Christians who had been moved to [the area] were also forcibly converted to Islam. . . . Most people embraced Islam with sincerity, but some felt an aversion to making the Muslim profession of faith. True knowledge lies with God! May God reward the Shah for his action with long life and prosperity!

quality and claimed to be the spiritual leader of all Islam. Shi'ism was declared the state religion.

Although there was a landed aristocracy, aristocratic power and influence were firmly controlled by strong-minded shahs, who confiscated aristocratic estates when possible and brought them under the control of the crown. Appointment to senior positions in the bureaucracy was by merit rather than birth. To avoid encouraging competition between Turkish and non-Turkish elements, Shah Abbas I hired a number of foreigners from neighboring countries for positions in his government.

The Safavid shahs took a direct interest in the economy and actively engaged in commercial and manufacturing activities, although there was also a large and affluent urban bourgeoisie. Like the Ottoman sultan, one shah regularly traveled the city streets incognito to check on the honesty of his subjects. When he discovered that a baker and butcher were overcharging for their products, he had the baker cooked in his own oven and the butcher roasted on a spit.

At its height, Safavid Iran was a worthy successor of the great Persian empires of the past, although it was probably not as wealthy as its Mughal and Ottoman neighbors to the east and west. Hemmed in by the sea power of the Europeans to the south and by the land power of the Ottomans to the west, the early Safavids had no navy and were forced to divert overland trade with Europe through southern Russia to avoid an Ottoman blockade. In the early seventeenth century, the situation improved when Iranian forces, in cooperation with the English, seized the island of Hormuz from Portugal and established a new seaport on the southern coast at Bandar Abbas. As a consequence, commercial ties with Europe began to increase.

Safavid Art and Literature

Persia witnessed an extraordinary flowering of the arts during the reign of Shah Abbas I. His new capital of Isfahan was a grandiose planned city with wide visual perspectives and a sense of order almost unique in the region. Shah Abbas ordered his architects to position his palaces, mosques, and bazaars around the Maydan-i-Shah, a massive rectangular polo ground. Much of the original city is still in good condition and remains the gem of modern Iran. The immense mosques are richly decorated with elaborate blue tiles. The palaces are delicate structures with unusual slender wooden columns. These architectural wonders of Isfahan epitomize the grandeur, delicacy, and color that defined the Safavid golden age. To adorn the splendid buildings, Safavid artisans created

THE ROYAL ACADEMY OF ISFAHAN. Along with institutions such as libraries and hospitals, theological schools were often included in the mosque compound. One of the most sumptuous was the Royal Academy of Isfahan, built by the shah of Iran in the early eighteenth century. This view shows the large courtyard surrounded by arcades of student rooms, reminiscent of the arrangement of monks' cells in European cloisters.

imaginative metalwork, tile decorations, and original and delicate glass vessels. The ceramics of the period, imitating Chinese prototypes of celadon or blue-and-white Ming design, largely ignored traditional Persian designs.

The greatest area of productivity, however, was in textiles. Silk weaving based on new techniques became a national industry. The silks depicted birds, animals, and flowers in a brilliant mass of color with silver and gold threads. Above all, carpet weaving flourished, stimulated by the great demand for Persian carpets in the West. Still highly prized all over the world, these seventeenth-century carpets reflect the grandeur and artistry of the Safavid dynasty.

The long tradition of Persian painting continued in the Safavid era, but changed from paintings to line drawings and from landscape scenes to portraits, mostly of young ladies, boys, lovers, or dervishes. Although some Persian artists studied in Rome, Safavid art was little influenced by the West. Riza-i-Abassi, the most famous artist of this period, created exquisite works on simple naturalistic subjects, such as an ox plowing, hunters, or lovers. Soft colors, delicacy, and flowing movement were the dominant characteristics of the painting of this era.

TWO LOVERS. Safavid painting continued Persian tradition but shifted from landscapes to portraits, mostly of young ladies, boys, lovers, or dervishes. This delicate painting of a couple embracing was produced in the early seventeenth century by Riza-i-Abassi, the most famous artist of Isfahan. It conveys passion with refined elegance.

THE GRANDEUR OF THE MUGHALS

In retrospect, the period from the sixteenth to the eighteenth century can be viewed both as a high point of traditional culture in India and as the first stage of perhaps its greatest challenge. The era began with the creation of one of the subcontinent's greatest empires—that of the Mughals. Mughal rulers, although foreigners and Muslims like many of their immediate predecessors, nevertheless brought India to a peak of political power and cultural achievement. For the first time since the Mauryan dynasty, the entire subcontinent was united under a single government, with a common culture that inspired admiration and envy throughout the entire region.

The Mughal Empire reached its peak in the sixteenth century under the famed Emperor Akbar and maintained its vitality under a series of strong rulers for another century. Then the dynasty began to weaken, a process that was hastened by the increasingly insistent challenge of the foreigners arriving by sea. The Portuguese, who first arrived in 1498, were little more than an irritant. Two centuries later, however, Europeans began to seize control of regional trade routes and to meddle in the internal politics of the subcontinent. By the end of the eighteenth century, nothing remained of the empire but a shell.

But some historians see the seeds of decay less in the challenge from abroad than in internal weakness—in the very nature of the dynasty itself, which was always more a heterogeneous collection of semiautonomous political forces than a centralized empire in the style of neighboring China. At its height, the dynasty was fully capable of fending off the demands of the Europeans. But after two centuries of expansion and consolidation, it began to lose its vitality, and by the end of the eighteenth century, it had lapsed into a mere shadow of its former self. Into the vacuum left by its final decrepitude stepped the British, who used a combination of firepower and guile to consolidate their power over the subcontinent.

The Mughal Dynasty: A "Gunpowder Empire"?

When the Portuguese fleet led by Vasco da Gama arrived at the port of Calicut in the spring of 1498, the Indian subcontinent was still divided into a number of Hindu and Muslim kingdoms. But it was on the verge of a new era of unity that would be brought about by a foreign dynasty called the Mughals. Like so many recent rulers of northern India, the founders of the Mughal Empire were not natives of India, but came from the mountainous region north of the Ganges River. The founder of the dynasty, known to history as Babur (1483–1530), had an illustrious pedigree. His father was descended from the great Asian conqueror Tamerlane, his mother from the Mongol conqueror Genghis Khan.

Babur had inherited a fragment of Tamerlane's empire in an upland valley of the Syr Darya River. Driven south by the rising power of the Uzbeks and then the Safavid dynasty in Persia, Babur and his warriors seized Kabul in 1504 and, thirteen years later, crossed the Khyber Pass to India.

Following a pattern that we have seen before, Babur began his rise to power by offering to help an ailing dynasty against its opponents. Although his own forces were far smaller than those of his adversaries, he possessed advanced weapons, including artillery, and used them to great effect. His use of mobile cavalry was particularly successful against the massed forces, supplemented by mounted elephants, of his enemy. In 1526, with only 12,000 troops against an enemy force nearly ten times that size, Babur captured Delhi and established his power in the plains of northern India (see the box on p. 475). Over the next several years, he continued his conquests in northern India, until his early death in 1530 at the age of forty-seven.

Babur's success was due in part to his vigor and his charismatic personality, which earned him the undying loyalty of his followers. His son and successor Humayun (1530–1556) was, in the words of one British historian, "intelligent but lazy." Whether or not this is a fair characterization, Humayun clearly lacked the will to consolidate his father's conquests and the personality to inspire personal loyalty among his subjects. In 1540 he was forced to flee to Persia, where he lived in exile for sixteen years. Finally, with the aid of the Safavid shah of Persia, he returned to India and reconquered Delhi in 1555, but died the following year in a household accident, reportedly from injuries suffered from a fall after smoking a pipeful of opium.

Humayun was succeeded by his son Akbar (1556–1605). Born while his father was living in exile, Akbar was only fourteen when he mounted the throne. Illiterate but highly intelligent and industrious, Akbar set out to extend his domain, then limited to Punjab and the upper Ganges River valley. "A monarch," he remarked, "should be ever intent on conquest, otherwise his neighbors rise in arms against him. The army should be exercised in warfare, lest from want of training they become self-indulgent."[1] By the end of his life, he had brought Mughal rule to most of the subcontinent, from the Himalaya Mountains to the Godavari River in central India and from Kashmir to the mouths of the Brahmaputra and the Ganges. In so doing, Akbar had created the greatest Indian empire since the Mauryan dynasty nearly two thousand years before. Some historians believe Akbar's success was due to the use of heavy artillery, which enabled his armies to besiege and subdue the traditional stone fortresses of his rivals. This "gunpowder empire" thesis has been challenged by the historian Douglas Streusand, who argues that the Mughals used the "carrot and the stick" to extend their authority, relying not just on heavy artillery, but also on other forms of siege warfare and

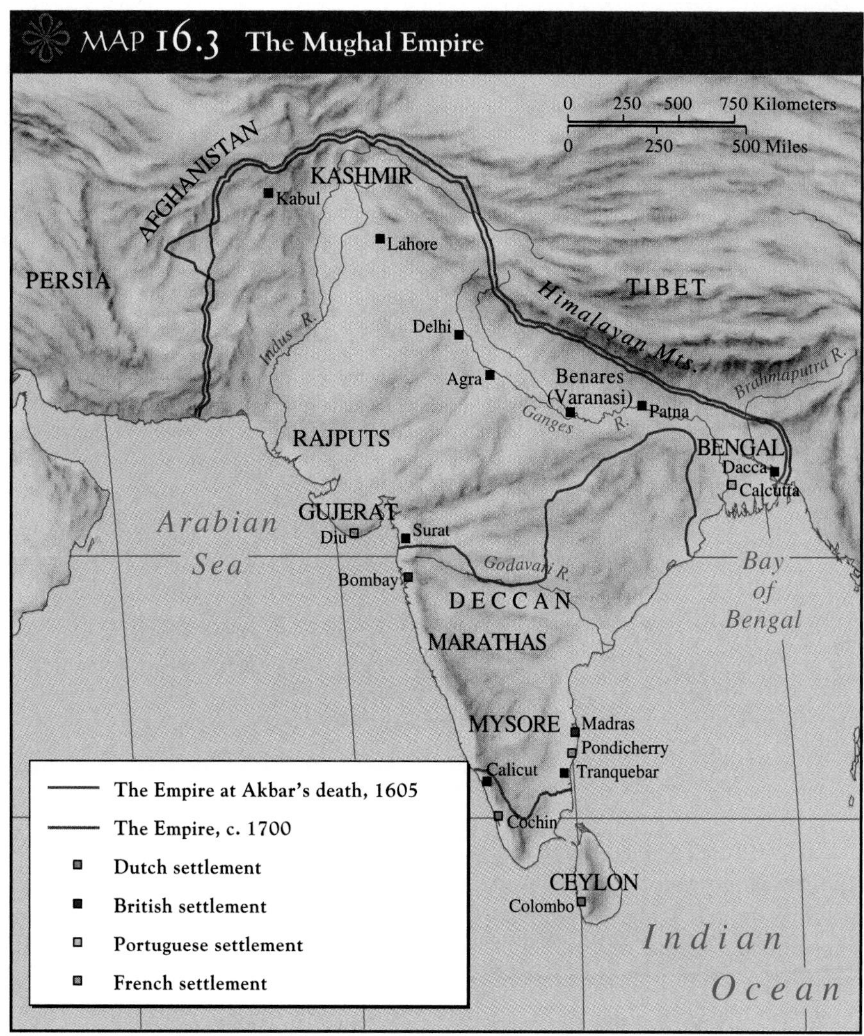

MAP 16.3 The Mughal Empire

the offer of negotiations. Whatever the case, the end result was an empire that appeared highly centralized from the outside, but was actually a collection of semiautonomous principalities ruled by provincial elites and linked together by the overarching majesty of the Mughal emperor.

Akbar and Indo-Muslim Civilization

Although Akbar was probably the greatest of the conquering Mughal monarchs, like his famous predecessor Asoka, he is best known for the humane character of his rule. Above all, he accepted the diversity of Indian society and took steps to reconcile his Muslim and Hindu subjects.

Though raised an orthodox Muslim, Akbar had been exposed to other beliefs during his childhood and had little patience with the pedantic views of Muslim scholars at court. As emperor, he displayed a keen interest in other religions, not only tolerating Hindu practices in his own domains, but also welcoming the expression of Christian views by his Jesuit advisers. Akbar put his policy of religious tolerance into practice by taking a Hindu princess as one of his wives, and the success of this marriage may well have had an effect on his religious convictions. He patronized classical Indian arts and architecture and abolished many of the restrictions faced by Hindus in a Muslim-dominated society.

During his later years, Akbar became steadily more hostile to Islam. To the dismay of many Muslims at court, he sponsored a new form of worship called the "Divine Faith" (*Din-i-Ilahi*), which combined characteristics of several religions with a central belief in the infallibility of all decisions reached by the emperor. Some historians have maintained that Akbar totally abandoned Islam and adopted a Persian model of imperial divinity. But others have pointed out that the emperor was claiming only divine guidance, not divine status, and suggest that the new ideology was designed to cement the loyalty of officials to the person of the monarch. Whatever the case, the new faith aroused deep hostility in Muslim circles and rapidly vanished after his death.

Akbar also extended his innovations to the empire's administration. Although the upper ranks of the govern-

THE MUGHAL CONQUEST OF NORTHERN INDIA

Babur, the founder of the great Mughal dynasty, began his career by allying with one Indian prince against another and then turned on his ally to put himself in power, a tactic that had been used by the Ottomans and the Mongols before him. In this excerpt from his memoirs, Babur describes his triumph over the powerful army of his Indian enemy, the Sultan Ibrâhim.

BABUR, *MEMOIRS*

They made one or two very poor charges on our right and left divisions. My troops making use of their bows, plied them with arrows, and drove them in upon their center. The troops on the right and the left of their center, being huddled together in one place, such confusion ensued, that the enemy, while totally unable to advance, found also no road by which they could flee. The sun had mounted spear-high when the onset of battle began, and the combat lasted till midday, when the enemy were completely broken and routed, and my friends victorious and exulting. By the grace and mercy of Almighty God, this arduous undertaking was rendered easy for me, and this mighty army, in the space of half a day, laid in the dust. Five or six thousand men were discovered lying slain, in one spot, near Ibrâhim. We reckoned that the number lying slain, in different parts of this field of battle, amounted to fifteen or sixteen thousand men. On reaching Agra, we found, from the accounts of the natives of Hindustân, that forty or fifty thousand men had fallen in this field. After routing the enemy, we continued the pursuit, slaughtering, and making them prisoners. . . .

It was now afternoon prayers when Tahir Taberi, the younger brother of Khalîfeh, having found Ibrâhim lying dead amidst a number of slain, cut off his head, and brought it in. . . .

In consideration of my confidence in Divine aid, the Most High God did not suffer the distress and hardships that I had undergone to be thrown away, but defeated my formidable enemy, and made me the conqueror of the noble country of Hindustân. This success I do not ascribe to my own strength, nor did this good fortune flow from my own efforts, but from the fountain of the favor and mercy of God.

ment continued to be dominated by nonnative Muslims, a substantial proportion of lower-ranking officials were Hindus, and a few Hindus were appointed to positions of importance. At first, most officials were paid salaries, but later they were ordinarily assigned sections of agricultural land for their temporary use; they kept a portion of the taxes paid by the local peasants in lieu of a salary. These local officials, known as *zamindars*, were expected to forward the rest of the taxes from the lands under their control to the central government. *Zamindars* often recruited a number of military and civilian retainers and accumulated considerable power in their localities.

The same tolerance that marked Akbar's attitude toward religion and administration extended to the Mughal legal system. While Muslims were subject to the Islamic codes (the *Shari'ah*), Hindu law (the *Dharmashastra*) applied to areas settled by Hindus, who after 1579 were no longer required to pay the hated *jizya*, or poll tax on non-Muslims. Punishments for crime were relatively mild, at least by the standards of the day, and justice was administered in a relatively impartial and efficient manner.

Overall, Akbar's reign was a time of peace and prosperity. Although all Indian peasants were required to pay about one-third of their annual harvest to the state through the *zamindars*, the system was applied fairly, and when drought struck in the 1590s, the taxes were reduced or even suspended altogether. Thanks to a long period of relative peace and political stability, commerce and manufacturing flourished. Foreign trade, in particular, thrived as Indian goods, notably textiles, tropical food products, spices, and precious stones, were exported in exchange for gold and silver. Tariffs on imports were low. Much of the foreign commerce was handled by Arab traders, since the Indians, like their Mughal rulers, did not care for travel by sea. Internal trade, however, was dominated by large merchant castes, who also were active in banking and handicrafts.

Twilight of the Mughals

Akbar died in 1605 and was succeeded by his son Jahangir (1605–1628). During the early years of his reign, Jahangir continued to strengthen central control over the vast empire. Eventually, however, his grip began to weaken (according to his memoirs, he "only wanted a bottle of wine and a piece of meat to make merry"), and the court fell under the influence of one of his wives, the Persian-born Nur Jahan. The empress took advantage of her position to enrich her own family and arranged for her niece Mumtaz Mahal to marry her husband's third son and ultimate successor Shah Jahan. When Shah Jahan succeeded to the throne in 1628, he quickly demonstrated the single-minded quality of his grandfather (albeit in a much more brutal manner), ordering the assassination of all of his rivals in order to secure his position.

During a reign of three decades, Shah Jahan maintained the system established by his predecessors while expanding the boundaries of the empire by successful campaigns in the Deccan Plateau and against Samarkand, north of the Hindu Kush. But Shah Jahan's rule was marred by his failure to deal with the growing domestic problems.

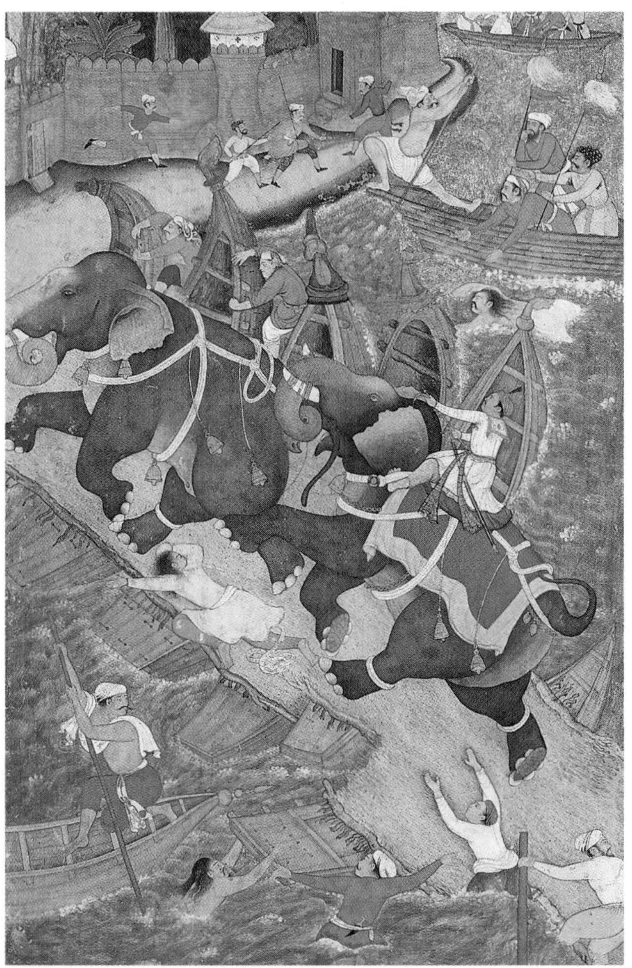

AKBAR RESTRAINS AN ELEPHANT. Akbar was probably the greatest of the conquering Mughal monarchs. In this contemporary Indian miniature, the young Akbar is seen mounted on a fierce elephant, leading an attack. The pontoon bridge is sinking under the heavy weight, while on the shore, before the towers of the royal palace at the Red Fort of Agra, his chief minister is begging Akbar to cease his reckless behavior.

He had inherited a nearly empty treasury because of Empress Nur Jahan's penchant for luxury and ambitious charity projects. Though the majority of his subjects lived in grinding poverty, Shah Jahan's frequent military campaigns and expensive building projects put a heavy strain on the imperial finances and compelled him to raise taxes. At the same time, the government did little to improve rural conditions. In a country where transport was primitive (it often took three months to travel the 600 miles between Patna, in the middle of the Ganges River valley, and Delhi) and drought conditions frequent, the dynasty made few efforts to increase agricultural efficiency or to improve the roads or the irrigation network. A Dutch merchant in Gujarat described conditions during a famine in the mid-seventeenth century:

> As the famine increased, men abandoned towns and villages and wandered helplessly. It was easy to recognize their condition: eyes sunk deep in head, lips pale and covered with slime, the skin hard, with the bones showing through, the belly nothing but a pouch hanging down empty, knuckles and kneecaps showing prominently. One would cry and howl for hunger, while another lay stretched on the ground dying in misery; wherever you went, you saw nothing but corpses.[2]

In 1648, Shah Jahan moved his capital from Agra to Delhi and built the famous Red Fort in his new capital city (see the box on p. 478). But he is best known for the Taj Mahal in Agra, widely considered to be the most beautiful building in India, if not in the entire world. The story is a romantic one—that the Taj was built by the emperor in memory of his wife Mumtaz Mahal, who had died giving birth to her thirteenth child at the age of thirty-nine. But the story has a less attractive side: the expense of the building, which employed 20,000 masons over twenty years, forced the government to raise agricultural taxes, further impoverishing many Indian peasants.

Succession struggles returned to haunt the dynasty in the mid-1650s when Shah Jahan's illness led to a struggle for power between his sons Dara Shikoh and Aurangzeb. Dara Shikoh was described by his contemporaries as progressive

AN ELEPHANT FIGHT FOR THE KING'S ENTERTAINMENT

François Bernier was a well-traveled Frenchman who visited India during the mid-seventeenth century. In this excerpt from his account of the visit, he describes a festival held just outside the Red Fort at Delhi for the amusement of the emperor. Bernier's sympathy is obviously with the elephants. The account is indicative of the wealth and majesty of the Mughal Empire at its height.

FRANÇOIS BERNIER, *TRAVELS IN THE MOGUL EMPIRE*

The festivals generally conclude with an amusement unknown in Europe—a combat between two elephants; which takes place in the presence of all the people on the sandy space near the river: the King, the principal ladies of the court, and the *Omrahs* viewing the spectacle from different apartments in the fortress.

A wall of earth is raised three or four feet wide and five or six high. The two ponderous beasts meet one another face to face, on opposite sides of the wall, each having a couple of riders, that the place of the man who sits on the shoulders, for the purpose of guiding the elephant with a large iron hook, may immediately be supplied if he should be thrown down. The riders animate the elephants either by soothing words, or by chiding them as cowards, and urge them on with their heels, until the poor creatures approach the wall and are brought to the attack. The shock is tremendous, and it appears surprising that they ever survive the dreadful wounds and blows inflicted with their teeth, their heads, and their trunks. There are frequent pauses during the fight; it is suspended and renewed; and the mud wall being at length thrown down, the stronger or more courageous elephant passes on and attacks his opponent, and, putting him to flight, pursues and fastens upon him with so much obstinacy, that the animals can be separated only by means of *cherkys*, or fireworks, which are made to explode between them; for they are naturally timid, and have a particular dread of fire, which is the reason why elephants have been used with so very little advantage in armies since the use of firearms. The boldest come from Ceylon, but none are employed in war which have not been regularly trained, and accustomed for years to the discharge of muskets close to their heads, and the bursting of crackers between their legs.

The fight of these noble creatures is attended with much cruelty. It frequently happens that some of the riders are trodden underfoot, and killed on the spot, the elephant having always cunning enough to feel the importance of dismounting the rider of his adversary, whom he therefore endeavors to strike down with his trunk. So imminent is the danger considered, that on the day of combat the unhappy men take the same formal leave of their wives and children as if condemned to death. They are somewhat consoled by the reflection that if their lives should be preserved, and the King be pleased with their conduct, not only will their pay be augmented, but a sack of *Peyssas* (equal to fifty francs) will be presented to them the moment they alight from the elephant. . . . The mischief with which this amusement is attended does not always terminate with the death of the rider: it often happens that some of the spectators are knocked down and trampled upon by the elephants, or by the crowd; for the rush is terrible when, to avoid the infuriated combatants, men and horses in confusion take to flight. The second time I witnessed this exhibition I owed my safety entirely to the goodness of my horse and the exertions of my two servants.

and humane, although possessed of a violent temper and a strong sense of mysticism. But he apparently lacked political acumen and was outmaneuvered by Aurangzeb (1658–1707), who had Dara Shikoh put to death and then imprisoned his father in the fort at Agra.

Aurangzeb is one of the most controversial individuals in the history of India. A man of high principle, he attempted to eliminate many of what he considered to be India's social evils, prohibiting the immolation of widows on their husband's funeral pyre (*sati*), the castration of eunuchs, and the exaction of illegal taxes. With less success, he tried to forbid gambling, drinking, and prostitution. But Aurangzeb, a devout and somewhat doctrinaire Muslim, also adopted a number of measures that reversed the policies of religious tolerance established by his predecessors. The building of new Hindu temples was prohibited and the Hindu poll tax was restored. Forced conversions to Islam were resumed and non-Muslims were driven from the court. Aurangzeb's heavy-handed religious policies led to considerable domestic unrest and to a revival of Hindu fervor during the last years of his reign. A number of revolts also broke out against imperial authority.

During the eighteenth century, Mughal power was threatened from both within and without. Fueled by the growing power and autonomy of the local gentry and merchants, rebellious groups in provinces throughout the empire, from the Deccan to the Punjab, began to reassert local authority and reduce the power of the Mughal emperor to that of a "tinsel sovereign." Increasingly divided, India was vulnerable to attack from abroad. In 1739, Delhi was sacked by the Persians, who left it in ashes and carried off its splendid Peacock Throne (see The Safavids earlier in this chapter).

CHRONOLOGY

THE MUGHAL ERA

Arrival of Vasco da Gama at Calicut	1498
Babur seizes Delhi	1526
Death of Babur	1530
Humayun recovers throne in Delhi	1555
Death of Humayun and accession of Akbar	1556
First Jesuit Mission to Agra	1580
Death of Akbar and accession of Jahangir	1605
Arrival of English at Surat	1608
Reign of Emperor Shah Jahan	1628–1657
Foundation of English fort at Madras	1639
Aurangzeb succeeds to the throne	1658
Bombay ceded to England	1661
Death of Aurangzeb	1707
French capture Madras	1746
Battle of Plassey	1757

A number of obvious reasons for the virtual collapse of the Mughal Empire can be identified, including the draining of the imperial treasury and the decline in competence of the Mughal rulers. But it should also be noted that even at its height under Akbar, the empire was a loosely knit collection of heterogeneous principalities held together by the authority of the throne, which tried to combine Persian concepts of kingship with the Indian tradition of decentralized power. Decline set in when centrifugal forces gradually began to predominate over centripetal ones.

Ironically, one element in this process was the very success of the system, which led to the rapid expansion of wealth and autonomous power at the local level. As local elites increased their wealth and influence, they became less willing to accept the authority and financial demands from Delhi. The reassertion of Muslim orthodoxy under Aurangzeb and his successors simply exacerbated the problem. This process was hastened by the growing European military and economic presence along the periphery of the empire.

The Impact of Western Power in India

As we have seen, the first to arrive were the Portuguese. Although they established a virtual monopoly over regional trade in the Indian Ocean, they did not aggressively seek to penetrate the interior of the subcontinent. The situation changed at the end of the sixteenth century, when the English and the Dutch entered the scene. Soon both powers were in active competition with Portugal, and with each other, for trading privileges in the region (see the box on p. 480).

Penetration of the new market was not easy. When the first English fleet arrived at Surat (a thriving port along the northwestern coast of India) in 1608, their request for trading privileges was rejected by Emperor Jahangir, at the suggestion of the Portuguese advisers already in residence at the imperial court. Needing lightweight Indian cloth to trade for spices in the East Indies, the English persisted, and in 1616 they were finally permitted to install their own ambassador at the imperial court in Agra. Three years later the first English factory was established at Surat.

During the next several decades, the English presence in India steadily increased while Mughal power gradually waned. By mid-century additional English factories had been established at Fort William (now the great city of Calcutta) on the River Hoogly near the Bay of Bengal and at Madras on the southeastern coast. From there English ships carried Indian-made cotton goods to the East Indies, where they were bartered for spices, which were shipped back to England. Tensions between local

THE CHINESE NETS AT COCHIN. Cochin, one of the port cities visited by Vasco da Gama during his first visit to India in 1498, had long been a major stopover on the trade routes across the Indian Ocean. Nearly a century previously, it had been visited by Chinese fleets en route to Africa. These voyages, to be discussed in the next chapter, left their own legacy, as Indian fishers learned from Chinese sailors how to place large nets in the water of the harbor to catch fish. After the arrival of the Portuguese, much of the local population was converted to Christianity. Shown here are the "Chinese nets" of Cochin, which are still in use. A few yards away is the first Christian church erected in India. An old synagogue, which perhaps dates back to the pre-European era, is located a mile away.

THE USES OF THE COCONUT

The Portuguese traveler Duarte Barbosa was one of the most astute observers of the lands that he visited as an official of the Portuguese crown in the early sixteenth century. Here, in a section devoted to the lands of Malabar, on the southwestern coast of India, he writes of the many uses that the local population made of the coconut palm. Many peoples of Asia still use the coconut in similar ways in our own day.

DUARTE BARBOSA, *THE BOOK OF DUARTE BARBOSA*

This land, or rather the whole land of Malabar, is covered along the strand with palm trees as high as lofty cypresses, the trunk whereof is extremely clean and smooth, and on the top a crown of branches among which grows a great fruit which they call *cocos,* it is a fruit of which they make great profit, and whereof they load many cargoes yearly. They bear their fruit every year without fail, never either more or less. All the folk of Malabar have these palms, and by their means they are free from any dearth, even though other food be lacking, for they produce ten or twelve things all very needful for the service of man, by which they help and profit themselves greatly, and everything is produced in every month of the year.

In the first place they produce these cocos, a very sweet and grateful fruit when green; from them is drawn milk like that of almonds, and each one when green, has within it a pint of a fresh and pleasant water, better than that from a spring. When they are dry this same water thickens within them into a white fruit as large as an apple which also is very sweet and dainty. The coco itself after being dried is eaten, and from it they get much oil by pressing it, as we do. And from the shell which they have close to the kernel is made charcoal for the goldsmiths, who work with no other kind. And from the outer husk which throws out certain threads, they make all the cord which they use, a great article of trade in many parts. And from the sap of the tree itself they extract a *must,* from which they make wine, or properly speaking a strong water, and that in such abundance that many shops are laden with it, for export. From this same *must* they make very good vinegar, and also a sugar of extreme sweetness which is much sought after in India. From the leaf of the tree they make many things, in accordance with the size of the branch. They thatch the houses with them, for as I have said above, no house is roofed with tiles, save the temples or the palaces; all others are thatched with palm leaves. From the same tree they get timber for their houses and firewood as well, and all this in such abundance that ships take in cargoes thereof for export.

Other palm trees there are of a lower kind whence they get the leaves on which the Heathen write; it serves as paper. There are other very slender palms the trunks of which are of extreme height and smoothness; these bear a fruit as large as walnuts which they call Areca, which they eat with betel. Among them it is held in high esteem. It is very ugly and disagreeable in taste.

authorities and the English over the payment of taxes led to a short war in 1686. The English were briefly expelled, but after differences were patched up, Aurangzeb permitted them to return.

English success in India attracted rivals, including the Dutch and the French. The Dutch abandoned their interests to concentrate on the spice trade in the middle of the seventeenth century, but the French were more persistent and established factories of their own. For a brief period, under the ambitious empire builder Joseph François Dupleix, the French competed successfully with the British. But the military genius of Sir Robert Clive, an aggressive British administrator and empire builder who eventually became the chief representative of the East India Company in the subcontinent, and the refusal of the French government to provide financial support for Dupleix's efforts eventually left the French with only their fort at Pondicherry and a handful of small territories on the southeastern coast.

In the meantime, Clive began to consolidate British control in Bengal, where the local ruler had attacked Fort William and imprisoned the local British population in the infamous "Black Hole of Calcutta" (an underground prison for holding the prisoners, many of whom died in captivity). In 1757, a small British force numbering about 3,000 defeated a Mughal-led army over ten times that size in the Battle of Plassey. As part of the spoils of victory, the British East India Company exacted from the now-decrepit Mughal court the authority to collect taxes from extensive lands in the area surrounding Calcutta. Less than ten years later, British forces seized the reigning Mughal emperor in a skirmish at Buxar, and the British began to consolidate their economic and administrative control over Indian territory through the surrogate power of the now powerless Mughal court.

To officials of the East India Company, the expansion of their authority into the interior of the subcontinent probably seemed like a simple commercial decision, a move designed to seek guaranteed revenues to pay for the increasingly expensive military operations in India. To historians, it marks a major step in the gradual transfer of all of the Indian subcontinent to the British East India Company and later, in 1858, to the British crown. The process was more haphazard than deliberate. Under a new governor general, Warren Hastings, the British attempted to consolidate areas under their control and defeat such rivals as the rising Hindu Marathas, who exploited the decline of the Mughals to expand their own empire in Maharashtra.

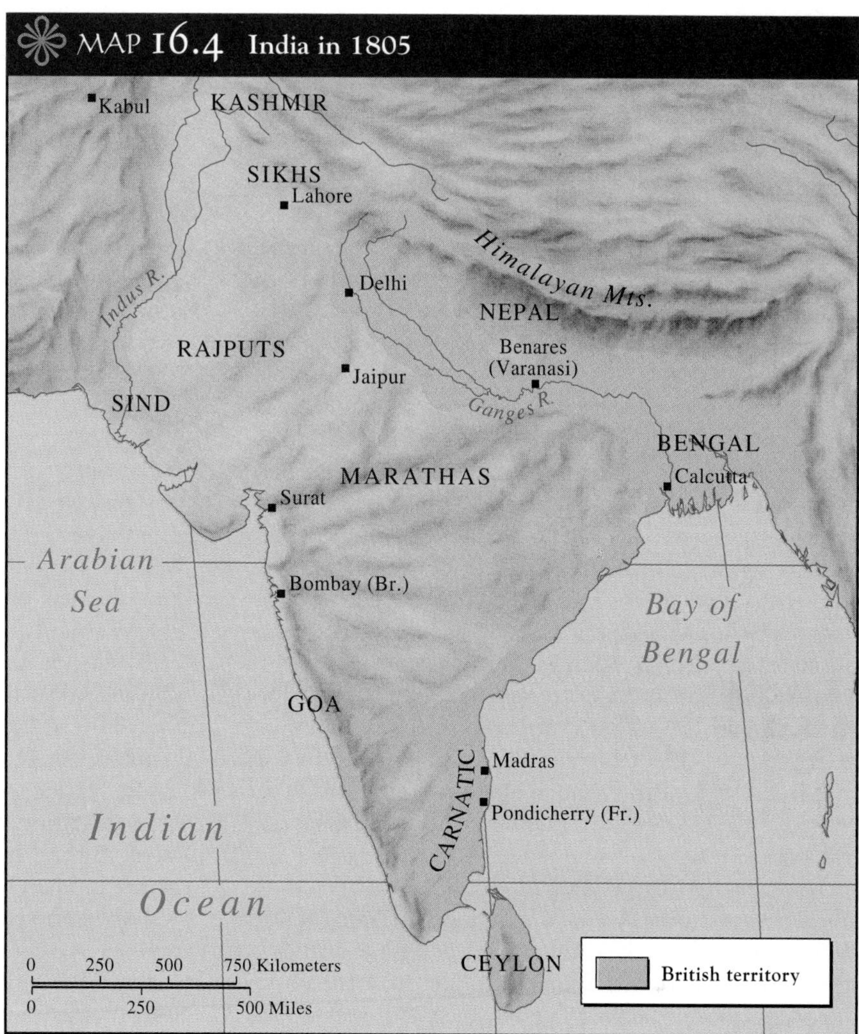

The company's takeover of vast landholdings, notably in the eastern Indian states of Orissa and Bengal, may have been a windfall for enterprising British officials, but it was a disaster for the Indian economy. In the first place, it resulted in the transfer of capital from the local Indian aristocracy to company officials, most of whom sent their profits back to Britain. Second, it hastened the destruction of once healthy local industries, because British goods such as machine-made textiles were imported duty-free into India to compete against local products. Finally, British expansion hurt the peasants. As the British took over the administration of the land tax, they also applied British law, which allowed the lands of those unable to pay the tax to be confiscated. In the 1770s, a series of massive famines led to the death of an estimated one-third of the population in the areas under company administration. The British government attempted to resolve the problem by assigning tax lands to the local revenue collectors (*zamindars*) in the hope of transforming them into English-style rural gentry, but many collectors themselves fell into bankruptcy and sold their lands to absentee bankers while the now landless peasants remained in abject poverty. It was hardly an auspicious beginning to "civilized" British rule.

As a result of such problems, Britain's rise to power in India did not go unchallenged. Astute Indian commanders avoided pitched battles with the well-armed British troops but harassed and ambushed them in the manner of guerrillas in our time. Said Haidar Ali, one of Britain's primary rivals for control in southern India:

> You will in time understand my mode of warfare. Shall I risk my cavalry which cost a thousand rupees each horse, against your cannon ball which cost two pice? No! I will march your troops until their legs swell to the size of their bodies. You shall not have a blade of grass, nor a drop of water. I will hear of you every time your drum beats, but you shall not know where I am once a month. I will give your army battle, but it must be when I please, and not when you choose.[3]

Unfortunately for India, not all its commanders were as astute as Haidar Ali. In the last years of the eighteenth century, when the East India Company's authority came into the capable hands of Lord Cornwallis and his successor, Lord Mornington, the future marquess of Wellesley, the stage was set for the final consolidation of British rule over the subcontinent.

Society and Culture Under the Mughals

The Mughals were the last of the great traditional Indian dynasties. Like so many of their predecessors since the fall of the Guptas nearly a thousand years before, the Mughals were Muslims. But to their credit, the best Mughal rulers did not simply impose Islamic institutions and beliefs on a predominantly Hindu population, but combined Muslim with Hindu and even Persian concepts and cultural values in a unique social and cultural synthesis that still today seems to epitomize the greatness of Indian civilization.

DAILY LIFE

Whether Mughal rule had much effect on the lives of ordinary Indians seems somewhat problematic. The treatment of women is a good example. Women had traditionally played an active role in Mongol tribal society—many actually fought on the battlefield alongside the men—and Babur and his successors often relied on the women in their families for political advice. Women from aristocratic families were often awarded honorific titles, received salaries, and were permitted to own land and engage in business. Women at court sometimes received an education, and Emperor Akbar reportedly established a girls' school at Fatehpur Sikri to provide teachers for his own daughters. Aristocratic women often expressed their creative talents by writing poetry, painting, or playing music. Women of all castes were adept at spinning thread, either for their own use or to sell to weavers to augment the family income. Weaving was carried out in home production units by all the members of the subcaste weaving families. They sold simple cloth to local villages and fine cottons, silks, and wool to the Mughal court. By Akbar's rule, in fact, the textile manufacturing was of such high quality and so well established that India sold cloth to much of the world: Arabia, the coast of East Africa, Egypt, Southeast Asia, and especially Europe.

To a certain degree, these Mughal attitudes toward women may have had an impact on Indian society. Women were allowed to inherit land, and some even possessed *zamindar* rights. Women from mercantile castes sometimes took an active role in business activities. At the same time, however, as Muslims, the Mughals subjected women to certain restrictions under Islamic law. On the whole, these Mughal practices coincided with and even accentuated existing tendencies in Indian society. The Muslim practice of isolating women and preventing them from associating with men outside the home (*purdah*) was adopted by many upper-class Hindus as a means of enhancing their status or protecting their women from unwelcome advances by Muslims in positions of authority. In other ways, Hindu practices continued unabated. The custom of *sati* continued to be practiced despite efforts by the Mughals to abolish it, and child marriage (most women were betrothed before the age of ten) remained common. Women were still instructed to obey their husbands without question and to remain chaste.

For their part, Hindus sometimes attempted to defend themselves and their religious practices against the efforts of some Mughal monarchs to impose the Islamic religion and Islamic mores on the indigenous population. In some cases, despite official prohibitions Hindu men forcibly married Muslim women and then converted them to the native faith, while converts to Islam normally lost all of their inheritance rights within the Indian family. Government orders to destroy Hindu temples were often ignored by local officials, sometimes as the result of bribery or intimidation. Sometimes Indian practices had an influence on the Mughal elites, as many Mughal chieftains married Indian women and adopted Indian forms of dress.

Long-term stability led to increasing commercialization and the spread of wealth to new groups within Indian society. The Mughal era saw the emergence of an affluent landed gentry and a prosperous merchant class. Members of prestigious castes from the pre-Mughal period reaped many of the benefits of the increasing wealth, but some of these changes transcended caste boundaries and led to the emergence of new groups who achieved status and wealth on the basis of economic achievement rather than traditional kinship ties. During the late eighteenth century, this economic prosperity was shaken by the decline of the Mughal Empire

THE PALACE OF THE WINDS AT JAIPUR. Built by the maharaja of Jaipur in 1799, this imposing building, part of a palace complex, is today actually only a facade. Behind the intricate pink sandstone window screens, the women of the palace were able to observe city life while at the same time remaining invisible to prying eyes. The palace, like most of the buildings in the city of Jaipur, was constructed of sandstone, a product of the nearby desert of Rajasthan.

and the increasing European presence. But many prominent Indians reacted by establishing commercial relationships with the foreigners. For a time, that relationship often worked to the Indians' benefit. Later, as we shall see, they would have cause to regret the arrangement.

MUGHAL CULTURE

The era of the Mughals was one of synthesis in culture as well as in politics and religion. The Mughals combined Islamic themes with Persian and indigenous motifs to produce a unique style that enriched and embellished Indian art and culture. The Mughal emperors were zealous patrons of the arts and enticed painters, poets, and artisans from as far away as the Mediterranean. Apparently, the generosity of the Mughals made it difficult to refuse a trip to India. It was said that they would reward a poet with his weight in gold.

Undoubtedly, the Mughals' most visible achievement was in architecture. Here they integrated Persian and Indian styles in a new and sometimes breathtakingly beautiful form best symbolized by the Taj Mahal, built by the emperor Shah Jahan in the mid-seventeenth century. Although the human and economic cost of the Taj tarnishes the romantic legend of its construction, there is no denying the beauty of the building. It had evolved from a style that originated several decades earlier with the tomb of Humayun, which was built by his widow in Agra in 1565 during the reign of Akbar.

Humayun's mausoleum had combined Persian and Islamic motifs in a square building finished in red sandstone and topped with a dome. The style was repeated in a number of other buildings erected throughout the empire, but the Taj brought the style to perfection. Working with a model created by his Persian architect, Shah Jahan raised the dome and replaced the red sandstone with brilliant white marble. The entire exterior and interior surface is decorated with cut-stone geometrical patterns, delicate black stone tracery, or intricate inlay of colored precious stones in floral and Koranic arabesques. The technique of creating dazzling floral mosaics of lapis lazuli, malachite, carnelian, turquoise, and mother of pearl may have been introduced by Italian artists at the Mughal court. Shah Jahan had intended to erect a similar building in black marble across the river for his own remains, but the plans were abandoned after he was deposed by his son Aurangzeb. Shah Jahan spent his last years imprisoned in a room in the Red Fort at Agra; from his windows, he could see the beautiful memorial to his beloved wife.

The Taj was by no means the only magnificent building erected during the Mughal era. Akbar, who, in the words of a contemporary, "dresses the work of his mind and heart in the garment of stone and clay," was the first of the great Mughal builders. His first palace at Agra, the Red Fort, was begun in 1565. A few years later, he ordered the construction of a new palace at Fatehpur Sikri, twenty-six miles west of Agra. The new palace was built in honor of a Sufi mystic who had correctly forecast the birth of a son to the emperor. In gratitude, Akbar decided to build a new capital city and palace on the site of the mystic's home in the village of Sikri. Over a period of fifteen years, from 1571 to 1586, a magnificent new city in red sandstone was constructed. Unfortunately, it was soon discovered that water resources in the area were inadequate, and shortly before completion the city was abandoned and now stands almost untouched, although it is a popular destination for tourists and pilgrims.

The other major artistic achievement of the Mughal period was painting. Painting had never been one of the great attainments of Indian culture due in part to a technological difficulty. Paper was not introduced to India from Persia until the latter part of the fourteenth century, so traditionally painting had been done on palm leaves, which had severely hampered artistic creativity. By the fifteenth century, Indian painting had made the transition from palm leaf to paper, and the new medium eventually stimulated a burst of creativity, particularly in the genre of miniatures, or book illustrations.

THE TAJ MAHAL. The Taj Mahal was completed in 1653 by Emperor Shah Jahan as a tomb to glorify his beloved wife's memory. Raised on a marble platform above the Jumna River, the Taj is dramatically framed by contrasting twin red sandstone mosques, magnificent gardens, and a long reflecting pool that mirrors and magnifies its beauty. The effect is one of monumental size, near blinding brilliance, and delicate lightness.

FATEHPUR SIKRI. In gratitude to a Sufi mystic who had correctly forecast the birth of his son, Akbar chose the mystic's village of Sikri as the site for his new palace and capital city. Completed at great speed in 1586, the splendid city, which was built of red sandstone and measured two miles long and one mile wide, was soon abandoned because of an inadequate water supply. Its elaborate palaces, mosque, reflecting pools and courtyards, harems, and impressive Gate of Victory all symbolize the elegance and greatness of Akbar's reign.

As in so many other areas of endeavor, painting in Mughal India resulted from the blending of two cultures. While living in exile, Emperor Humayun had learned to admire Persian miniatures. On his return to India in 1555, he invited two Persian masters to live in his palace and introduce the technique to his adopted land. His successor, Akbar, appreciated the new style and popularized it with his patronage. He established a state workshop at Fatehpur Sikri for two hundred artists, mostly Hindus, who worked under the guidance of the Persian masters to create the Mughal school of painting.

The "Akbar style" combined Persian with Indian motifs, such as the use of extended space and the portrayal of physical human action, characteristics not usually seen in Persian art. Akbar also apparently encouraged the imitation of European art forms, including the portrayal of Christian subjects, the use of perspective, lifelike portraits, and the shading of colors in the Renaissance style. The depiction of the human figure in Mughal painting outraged orthodox Muslims at court, but Akbar argued that the painter, "in sketching anything that has life . . . must come to feel that he cannot bestow individuality upon his work, and is thus forced to think of God, the Giver of Life, and will thus increase in knowledge."[4]

Painting during Akbar's reign followed the trend toward realism and historical narrative that had originated in the Ottoman Empire. For example, Akbar had the illustrated *Book of Akbar* made to record his military exploits and court activities. Many of these paintings of Akbar's life portray him in action in his real world. After his death, his son and grandson continued the patronage of the arts.

The development of Indian literature was held back by the absence of printing, which was not introduced until the end of the Mughal era. Literary works were inscribed by calligraphers, and one historian has estimated that the library of Agra contained more than 24,000 volumes. Poetry, in particular, flourished under the Mughals, who established poet laureates at court. Poems were written in the Persian style and in the Persian language. In fact, Persian became the official language of the court until the sack of Delhi in 1739. At the time, the Indians' anger at their conquerors led them to adopt Urdu as the new language for the court and for poetry. By that time, Indian verse on the Persian model had already lost its original vitality and simplicity and had become more artificial in the manner of court literature everywhere.

Another aspect of the long Mughal reign was a Hindu revival of devotional literature, much of it dedicated to Krishna and Rama. The retelling of the Ramayana in the vernacular, beginning in the southern Tamil languages in the eleventh century and spreading slowly northward, culminated in the sixteenth-century Hindi version by the great poet Tulsidas (1532–1623). His *Ramcaritmanas* presents the devotional story with a deified Rama and Sita. Tulsidas's genius was in combining the conflicting cults of Vishnu and Siva into a unified and overwhelming love for the divine, which he expressed in some of the most moving of all Indian poetry. The *Ramcaritmanas* has eclipsed its 2,000-year-old Sanskrit ancestor in popularity and even became the basis of an Indian television series in the late 1980s.

CONCLUSION

The three empires that we have discussed in this chapter exhibit a number of striking similarities. First of all, they were, of course, Muslim in their religious affiliation, although the Safavids were Shi'ite rather than Sunni in persuasion, a distinction that often led to mutual tensions and conflict. More importantly, perhaps, they were all nomadic in origin, and the political and social institutions that they adopted carried the imprint of their preimperial past. Once they achieved imperial power, however, all three ruling dynasties displayed an impressive capacity to administer a large empire and brought a degree of stability to peoples who had all too often lived in conditions of internal division and war.

Another similarity is that the mastery of the techniques of modern warfare, including the use of firearms, played a central role in all three empires' ability to overcome their rivals and rise to regional hegemony. Some scholars have therefore labeled them "gunpowder empires" in the belief that technical prowess in the art of warfare was a key element in their success. Although that is undoubtedly true, we should not forget that other factors, such as dynamic leadership, political acumen, and the possession of an ardent following motivated by religious zeal, were equally if not more important in their drive to power and ability to retain it. Weapons by themselves do not an empire make.

The rise of these powerful Muslim states coincided with the opening period of European expansion at the end of the fifteenth and the beginning of the sixteenth century. The military and political talents of these empires helped to protect much of the Muslim world from the resurgent forces of Christianity. To the contrary, the Ottoman Turks carried their empire into the heart of Christian Europe and briefly reached the gates of the great city of Vienna. By the end of the eighteenth century, however, the Safavid dynasty had collapsed, and the powerful Mughal Empire was in a state of virtual collapse. Only the Ottoman Empire was still a functioning enterprise. Yet it too had lost much of its early expansionistic vigor and was showing signs of internal decay.

The reasons for the decline of these empires have inspired considerable debate among historians. One factor was undoubtedly the expansion of European power into the Indian Ocean and the Middle East. But internal causes were probably more important in the long run. All three empires experienced growing factionalism within the ruling elite, incompetence within the palace, and the emergence of divisive forces in the empire at large—factors that have marked the passing of traditional empires since early times. Climatic change (the region was reportedly hotter and drier after the beginning of the seventeenth century) may have been a hidden reason. Paradoxically, one of the greatest strengths of these empires—their mastery of gunpowder—may have simultaneously been a serious weakness in that it allowed them to develop a complacent sense of security. With little incentive to turn their attention to new developments in science and technology, they were increasingly vulnerable to attack by the advanced nations of the West. The weakening of the "gunpowder empires" created a political vacuum into which the dynamic and competitive forces of European capitalism were quick to enter.

The gunpowder empires, however, were not the only states in the Old World that were able to resist the first outward thrust of European expansion. Further to the east, the mature civilizations in China and Japan successfully faced a similar challenge from Western merchants and missionaries. Unlike their counterparts in South Asia and the Middle East, as the nineteenth century dawned, they continued to thrive.

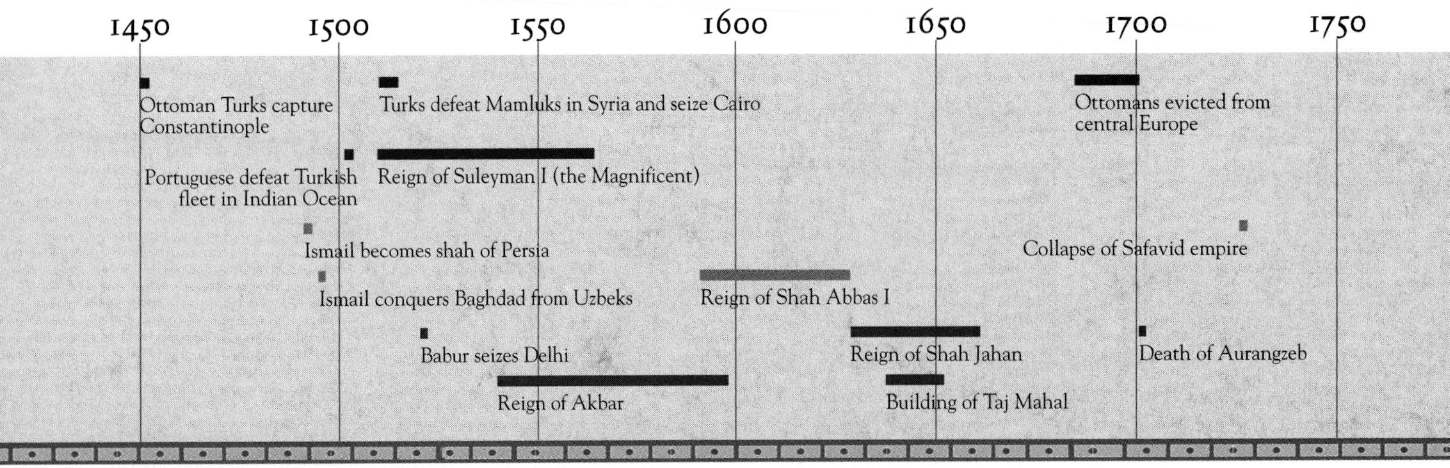

Chapter Notes

1. Vincent A. Smith, *The Oxford History of India* (Oxford, 1967), p. 341.
2. Quoted in Michael Edwardes, *A History of India: From the Earliest Times to the Present Day* (London, 1961), p. 188.
3. Quoted in Edwardes, *A History of India*, p. 220.
4. Quoted in Roy C. Craven, *Indian Art: A Concise History* (New York, 1976), p. 205.

Suggested Readings

The most complete general survey of the Ottoman Empire is S. J. Shaw, *History of the Ottoman Empire and Modern Turkey* (Cambridge, 1976). Volume 2 of the two-volume set deals with the period up to the beginning of the nineteenth century. Shaw is difficult reading but informative on administrative matters. A more readable albeit less definitive account is Lord Kinross, *The Ottoman Centuries: The Rise and Fall of the Ottoman Empire* (New York, 1977), which is larded with human-interest stories. Also of interest is B. Lewis, *Istanbul and the Civilization of the Ottoman Empire* (Norman, Okla., 1963), written by a veteran Arabist.

For a dramatic account of the conquest of Constantinople in 1453, see S. Runciman, *The Fall of Constantinople, 1453* (Cambridge, 1965). The life of Mehmet II is chronicled in F. Babinger, *Mehmed the Conqueror and His Time*, trans. R. Manheim (Princeton, N.J., 1979). On Suleyman the Magnificent, see R. Merriman, *Suleiman the Magnificent, 1520–1566* (Cambridge, 1944). On the Safavids, see R. M. Savory, *Iran Under the Safavids* (Cambridge, 1980), and E. B. Monshi, *History of Shah Abbas the Great*, 2 vols. (Boulder, Colo., 1978).

For a concise introduction to Ottoman art, consult D. T. Rice, *Islamic Art* (London, 1975), and E. J. Grube, *The World of Islam* (New York, 1967). For Ottoman architecture, see G. Michell, ed., *Architecture of the Islamic World* (London, 1978). For an interesting discussion of the minor military arts of the Ottomans, see Z. Zygulski, Jr., *Ottoman Art in the Service of the Empire* (New York, 1992).

For an overview of the Mughal era, see such standard works as S. Wolpert, *New History of India* (New York, 1989), and the more detailed V. A. Smith, *The Oxford History of India* (Oxford, 1967). A more dramatic account for the general reader is W. Hansen, *The Peacock Throne: The Drama of Mogul India* (New York, 1972).

There are a number of specialized works on various aspects of the period. For a treatment of the Mughal era in the context of Islamic rule in India, see S. M. Ikram, *Muslim Civilization in India* (New York, 1964). The concept of "gunpowder empires" is persuasively analyzed in D. E. Streusand, *The Formation of the Mughal Empire* (Delhi, 1989). Economic issues predominate in much of the recent scholarship. For example, S. Subrahmanyan, *The Political Economy of Commerce: Southern India, 1500–1650* (Cambridge, 1990) focuses on the interaction between internal and external trade in southern India during the early stages of the period. For a persuasive view of the relationship between economic changes and the extension of British rule, see C. A. Bayly, *Indian Society and the Making of the British Empire* (Cambridge, 1988). Finally, K. N. Chaudhuri, *Trade and Civilization in the Indian Ocean: An Economic History from the Rise of Islam to 1750* (Cambridge, 1985) views Indian commerce in the perspective of the regional trade network throughout the Indian Ocean.

Personal accounts of the period are numerous, although most are by European visitors. For some examples, see R. C. Temple, ed., *The Travels of Peter Mundy, in Europe and Asia, 1608–1667* (Cambridge, 1907–1936); J. B. Tavernier, *Travels in India* (London, 1925); T. Roe, *The Embassy of Sir Thomas Roe, 1615–1619* (London, 1926); and F. Bernier, *Travels in the Mogul Empire, A.D. 1656–1668* (London, 1968). For an inside look, see J. Leyden and W. Erskine, trans., *Memoirs of Zehir-ed-Din Muhammad Babur* (London, 1921). Excerpts from this and other works cited here can be found in M. Edwardes, *A History of India: From the Earliest Times to the Present Day* (London,

1961); J. Kritzeck, *Anthology of Islamic Literature* (New York, 1964); and J. H. Parry, ed., *The European Reconnaissance: Selected Documents* (New York, 1968).

Standard works on Mughal art and culture include A. L. Basham, *A Cultural History of India* (Oxford, 1975); E. C. Dimock, *The Literature of India: An Introduction* (Chicago, 1974); and R. C. Craven, *Indian Art: A Concise History* (New York, 1976).

For treatments of all three Muslim empires in a comparative context, see J. J. Kissling et al., *The Last Great Muslim Empires* (Princeton, N.J., 1996), and M. G. S. Hodgson, *Rethinking World History: Essays on Europe, Islam, and World History* (Cambridge, 1993).

For an introduction to the women of the Ottoman Empire and those of the Mughal Empire, see S. Hughes and B. Hughes, *Women in World History*, vol. 2 (Armonk, N.Y., 1997). For a more detailed presentation of women in the imperial harem, consult L. P. Peirce, "Beyond Harem Walls: Ottoman Royal Women and the Exercise of Power," in *Gendered Domains: Rethinking Public and Private in Women's History*, ed. D. O. Helly and S. M. Reverby (Cornell, 1992), and L. P. Peirce, *The Imperial Harem: Women and Sovereignty in the Ottoman Empire* (Oxford, 1993). The fascinating story of the royal woman who played an important role behind the scenes is found in E. B. Findly, *Nur Jahan: Empress of Mughal India* (Oxford, 1993).

For additional reading, go to InfoTrac College Edition, your online research library at http://web1.infotrac-college.com

Enter the search term "Islam" using the Subject Guide.

Enter the search terms "Ottoman Empire" using Keywords.

Enter the search term "Safavid" using Keywords.

Enter the search term "Mughal" using Keywords.

CHAPTER

17

THE EAST ASIAN WORLD

CHAPTER OUTLINE

- CHINA AT ITS APEX
- TOKUGAWA JAPAN
- KOREA: THE HERMIT KINGDOM
- CONCLUSION

FOCUS QUESTIONS

- Why were the Manchus so successful at establishing a foreign dynasty in China, and what were the main characteristics of their rule?
- How did the economy and society of China change during the Ming and Qing eras, and to what degree did these changes seem to be leading toward an industrial revolution on the Western model?
- How did China and Japan respond to the coming of the Europeans, and what impact did the Europeans have on these East Asian civilizations in the sixteenth through eighteenth centuries?
- How did the unification of Japan come about, and how did the Tokugawa rulers maintain that unity?
- How did the economy and society of Japan change during the Tokugawa era, and how did Japanese culture reflect those changes?

In December 1717, the emperor Kangxi returned from a hunting trip north of the Great Wall and began to suffer from dizzy spells. Conscious of his approaching date with mortality—he was now nearly seventy years of age—the emperor called together his sons and leading government officials in the imperial palace and issued the following edict:

> *The rulers of the past all took reverence for Heaven's laws and reverence for their ancestors as the fundamental way in ruling the country. To be sincere in reverence for Heaven and ancestors entails the following: Be kind to men from afar and keep the able ones near, nourish the people, think of the profit of all as being the real profit and the mind of the whole country as being the real mind, be considerate to officials and act as the father to the people, protect the state before danger comes and govern well before there is any disturbance, be always diligent and always careful, and maintain the balance between leniency and strictness, between principle and expediency, so that long-range plans can be made for the country: That's all there is to it.*[1]

As a primer for political leadership, the emperor's edict reflects the genius of Confucian philosophy at its best and has a timeless quality that applies to our age as well as to the Golden Age of the Qing dynasty.

Kangxi reigned during one of the most glorious eras in the long history of China. Under the Ming (1369–1644) and the early Qing (1644–1911) dynasties, the empire expanded its borders to a degree not seen since the Han and the Tang. Chinese culture was the envy of its neighbors and earned the admiration of many European visitors, including Jesuit priests and Enlightenment philosophes.

On the surface, China appeared to be an unchanging society patterned after the Confucian vision of a "Golden Age" in the remote past. This indeed was the image presented by China's rulers, who referred constantly to tradition as a model for imperial institutions and cultural values. In actuality, however, China was changing—and rather rapidly. Although few observers could have been aware of it at the time, Confucian precepts were increasingly irrelevant in a society that was becoming ever more complex.

A similar process was under way in neighboring Japan. A vigorous new shogunate called the Tokugawa rose to power in the early seventeenth century and managed to revitalize the traditional system in a somewhat more centralized form that enabled it to survive for another two hundred fifty years. But major structural changes were taking place in Japanese society, and by the nineteenth century, tensions were growing as the gap between theory and reality widened.

One of the many factors involved in the quickening pace of change in both countries was contact with the West, which began with the arrival of Portuguese ships in Chinese and Japanese ports in the first half of the sixteenth century. The Ming and the Tokugawa initially opened their doors to European trade and missionary activity. Later, however, Chinese and Japanese rulers became concerned at the corrosive effects of Western ideas and practices and attempted to protect their traditional societies from external intrusion. But neither could forever resist the importunities of Western trading nations, nor could they arrest the pace of change taking place within. When the doors to the West were finally reopened in the mid-nineteenth century, both societies were ripe for radical change.

China at Its Apex

In 1514, a Portuguese fleet dropped anchor off the coast of China, just south of the Pearl River estuary and present-day Hong Kong. It was the first direct contact between the Chinese Empire and the West since the arrival of Marco Polo two centuries earlier, and it opened an era that would eventually change the face of China and, indeed, all of Asia.

From the Ming to the Qing

The magnificence of China had originally been reported to Europe by the Venetian adventurer Marco Polo, who visited Beijing during the reign of Khubilai Khan, the great Mongol ruler. By the time the Portuguese fleet arrived off the coast of China, of course, the Mongol Empire had long since disappeared. It had gradually weakened after the death of Khubilai Khan and was finally overthrown in 1368 by a massive peasant rebellion under the leadership of Zhu Yuanzhang, who had declared himself the founding emperor of a new Ming (Bright) dynasty and assumed the reign title of Ming Hongwu (Ming Hung Wu, or Ming Martial Emperor). The Ming inaugurated a new era of greatness in Chinese history. Under a series of strong rulers, China extended its rule into Mongolia and Central Asia. The Ming even briefly reconquered Vietnam, which, after a thousand years of Chinese rule, had reclaimed its independence following the collapse of the Tang dynasty in the tenth century. Along the northern frontier, the Emperor Yongle (Yung Lo; 1402–1424) strengthened the Great Wall and pacified the nomadic tribespeople who had troubled China in previous centuries. A tributary relationship was established with the Yi dynasty in Korea.

The internal achievements of the Ming were equally impressive. When they replaced the Mongols in the fourteenth century, the Ming turned to traditional Confucian institutions as a means of ruling their vast empire. These included the six ministries at the apex of the bureaucracy, the use of the civil service examinations to select members of the bureaucracy, and the division of the empire into provinces, districts, and counties. As before, Chinese villages were relatively autonomous, and local councils

❀ **THE GREAT WALL OF CHINA** Although the Great Wall is popularly believed to be over 2,000 years old, in actuality the part of the wall that is most frequently visited by tourists was a reconstruction undertaken during the early Ming Dynasty as a means of protection against invasion from the north. Part of that wall, which was built to protect the imperial capital of Beijing, appears here.

of elders continued to be responsible for adjudicating disputes, initiating local construction and irrigation projects, mustering a militia, and assessing and collecting taxes.

The society that was governed by this vast hierarchy of officials was a far cry from the predominantly agrarian society that had been ruled by the Han and the Tang. In the burgeoning cities near the coast and along the rich Yangtze River valley, factories and workshops were vastly increasing the variety and output of their manufactured goods. The population had doubled, and new crops had been introduced, greatly expanding the agricultural economy of the empire.

In 1405, in a splendid display of Chinese maritime might, Yongle sent a fleet of Chinese trading ships under the eunuch admiral Zhenghe (Cheng Ho) through the Strait of Malacca and out into the Indian Ocean; there they traveled as far west as the east coast of Africa, stopping on the way at ports in South Asia. The size of the fleet was impressive: it included nearly 28,000 sailors on sixty-two ships, some of them junks larger by far than any other oceangoing vessels the world had yet seen. China seemed about to become a direct participant in the vast trade network that extended as far west as the Atlantic Ocean, thus culminating the process of opening China to the wider world that had begun with the Tang dynasty.

Why the expeditions were undertaken has been a matter of some debate. Some historians assume that economic profit was the main reason. Others point to Yongle's native curiosity and note that the voyage—and the six others that followed it—returned not only with goods, but also with a plethora of information about the outside world as well as with some items unknown in China (the emperor was especially intrigued by the giraffes and placed them in the imperial zoo, where they were identified by soothsayers with the coming of good government). Others speculate that the emperor was seeking to ascertain the truth of rumors that his immediate predecessor, Emperor Jianwen or Chien Wen (1398–1402), had escaped to Southeast Asia to live in exile.

Whatever the case, the voyages resulted in massive profits for their sponsors, including individuals connected with the admiral Zhenghe at court. This aroused resentment among conservatives within the bureaucracy, some of whom viewed commercial activities with a characteristic measure of Confucian disdain. One commented that an end to the voyages would provide the Chinese people with a respite "so that they can devote themselves to husbandry [agriculture] and schooling."

Shortly after Yongle's death, the voyages were discontinued, never to be revived. An early European visitor reported that "no one sails the sea from north to south; it is prohibited by the king, in order that the country may not become known."[2] The decision had long-term consequences and in the eyes of many modern historians marks a turning inward of the Chinese state, away from commerce and toward a more traditional emphasis on agriculture, away from the exotic lands to the south and toward the heartland of the country in the Yellow River valley.

Ironically, the move toward the Yellow River had been initiated by Yongle himself, when he had decided to move the Ming capital from Nanjing, in central China (where the ships were built and the voyages launched), back to Beijing (where official eyes were firmly focused on the threat from beyond the Great Wall to the north). As a means of reducing that threat, Yongle ordered the resettlement of thousands of families from the rich Yangtze valley. The emperor had presumably not intended to set forces in motion that would divert the country from its growing contacts with the external world. After all, he had been the driving force behind Zhenghe's voyages. But the end result was a shift in the balance of power from central China (where it had been since the southern Song dynasty) back to northern China, where it had originated and would remain for the rest of the Ming era. China would not look outward again for over four centuries.

FIRST CONTACTS WITH THE WEST

Despite the Ming's retreat from active participation in the maritime trade, when the Portuguese arrived in 1514, China was in command of a vast empire that stretched from the steppes of Central Asia to the China Sea, from the Gobi Desert to the tropical rain forests of Southeast Asia. From the lofty perspective of the imperial throne in Beijing, the Europeans could only have seemed like an unusually exotic form of barbarian to be placed within the familiar framework of the tributary system, the hierarchical arrangement in which rulers of all other countries were regarded as "younger brothers" of the Son of Heaven. Indeed, the bellicose and uncultured behavior of the Portuguese so outraged Chinese officials that they expelled the Europeans, but after further negotiations the Portuguese were permitted to occupy the tiny territory of Macao, a foothold they would retain until the end of the twentieth century.

Initially, the arrival of the Europeans did not have much impact on Chinese society. Direct trade between Europe and China was limited, and Portuguese ships became involved in the regional trade network, carrying silk to Japan in return for Japanese silver. Eventually, the Spanish also began to participate, using the Philippines as an anchor in the galleon trade between China and the great silver mines in the Americas.

More influential than trade, perhaps, were the ideas introduced by Christian missionaries. Among the most active and the most effective were highly educated Jesuits, who were familiar with European philosophical and scientific developments. Recognizing the Chinese pride in their own culture, the Jesuits attempted to draw parallels between Christian and Confucian concepts (for example, they identified the Western concept of God with the Chinese character for Heaven) and to show the similarities between Christian morality and Confucian ethics. European inventions such as the clock, the prism, and various astronomical and musical instruments impressed Chinese officials, hitherto deeply imbued with a sense of the superiority of Chinese civilization, and helped Western ideas win acceptance at court. An elderly Chinese scholar expressed his wonder at the miracle of eyeglasses:

> *White glass from across the Western Seas*
> *Is imported through Macao:*
> *Fashioned into lenses big as coins,*
> *They encompass the eyes in a double frame.*
> *I put them on—it suddenly becomes clear;*
> *I can see the very tips of things!*
> *And read fine print by the dim-lit window*
> *Just like in my youth.*[3]

For their part, the missionaries were much impressed with many aspects of Chinese civilization, and reports of their experiences heightened European curiosity about this great society on the other side of the world (see the box on p. 492).

THE MING BROUGHT TO EARTH

During the late sixteenth century, however, the Ming began to decline as a series of weak rulers led to an era of corruption, concentration of land ownership, and ultimately peasant rebellions and tribal unrest along the northern frontier. The inflow of vast amounts of foreign

MAP 17.1 China and Its Enemies During the Late Ming Era

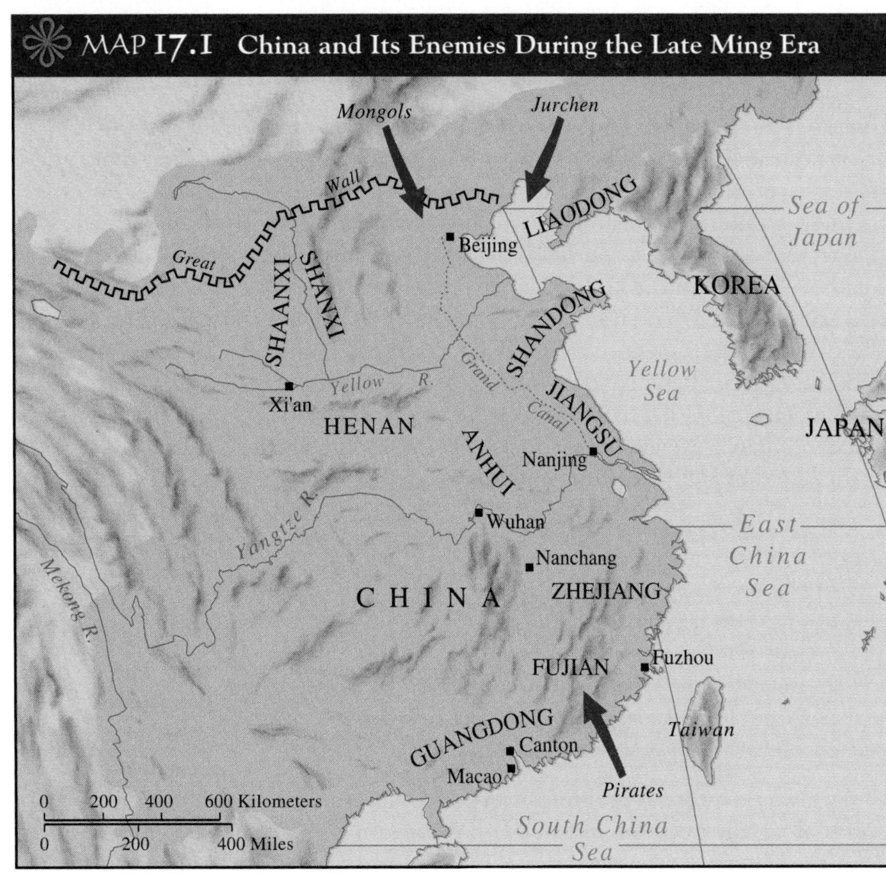

THE ART OF PRINTING

Europeans obtained much of their early information about China from the Jesuits who served at the Ming court in the sixteenth and seventeenth centuries. Clerics such as the Italian Matteo Ricci (1552–1610) found much to admire in Chinese civilization. Here Ricci expresses a keen interest in Chinese printing methods, which at that time were well in advance of the techniques used in the West.

MATTEO RICCI, *THE DIARY OF MATTHEW RICCI*

The art of printing was practiced in China at a date somewhat earlier than that assigned to the beginning of printing in Europe, which was about 1405. It is quite certain that the Chinese knew the art of printing at least five centuries ago, and some of them assert that printing was known to their people before the beginning of the Christian era, about 50 B.C. Their method of printing differs widely from that employed in Europe, and our method would be quite impracticable for them because of the exceedingly large number of Chinese characters and symbols. . . .

Their method of making printed books is quite ingenious. The text is written in ink, with a brush made of very fine hair, on a sheet of paper which is inverted and pasted on a wooden tablet. When the paper has become thoroughly dry, its surface is scraped off quickly and with great skill, until nothing but a fine tissue bearing the characters remains on the wooden tablet. Then, with a steel graver, the workman cuts away the surface following the outlines of the characters until these alone stand out in low relief. From such a block a skilled printer can make copies with incredible speed, turning out as many as fifteen hundred copies in a single day. . . . This scheme of engraving wooden blocks is well adapted for the large and complex nature of the Chinese characters, but I do not think it would lend itself very aptly to our European type, which could hardly be engraved upon wood because of its small dimensions.

Their method of printing has one decided advantage, namely, that once these tablets are made, they can be preserved and used for making changes in the text as often as one wishes. Additions and subtractions can also be made as the tablets can be readily patched. . . . We have derived great benefit from this method of Chinese printing, as we employ the domestic help in our homes to strike off copies of the books on religious and scientific subjects which we translate into Chinese from the languages in which they were written originally. In truth, the whole method is so simple that one is tempted to try it for himself after once having watched the process. The simplicity of Chinese printing is what accounts for the exceedingly large numbers of books in circulation here and the ridiculously low prices at which they are sold.

silver led to an alarming increase in inflation. Then the arrival of the English and the Dutch disrupted the silver trade; silver imports plummeted, severely straining the Chinese economy by raising the value of the metal relative to that of copper. Crop yields declined due to harsh weather—linked to the "Little Ice Age" of the early seventeenth century—and the resulting scarcity reduced the ability of the government to provide food in times of imminent starvation. High taxes, provoked in part by increased official corruption, led to peasant unrest and worker violence in urban areas. A folk song of the period, addressed to the "Lord of Heaven," complained,

> *Old skymaster,*
> *You're getting on, your ears are deaf, your eyes are gone.*
> *Can't see people, can't hear words.*
> *Glory for those who kill and burn;*
> *For those who fast and read the scriptures,*
> *Starvation.*
> *Fall down, old master sky, how can you be so high?*
> *How can you be so high? Come down to earth.*[4]

As always, internal problems were accompanied by unrest along the northern frontier. Following long precedent, the Ming had attempted to pacify the frontier tribes by forging alliances with them, arranging marriages between them and the local aristocracy, and granting trade privileges. One of the alliances was with the Manchus (also known as the Jurchen), the descendants of peoples who had briefly established a kingdom in northern China during the early thirteenth century. The Manchus, a mixed agricultural and hunting people, lived northeast of the Great Wall in the area known today as Manchuria.

At first the Manchus were satisfied with consolidating their territory and made little effort to extend their rule south of the Great Wall. But during the first decades of the seventeenth century, the problems of the Ming dynasty began to come to a head. A major epidemic devastated the population in many areas of the country. The suffering brought on by the epidemic helped spark a vast peasant revolt led by Li Zicheng (Li Tzu-ch'eng, 1604–1651). Li was a postal worker in central China who had been dismissed from his job as part of a cost-saving measure by the imperial court, now increasingly preoccupied by tribal attacks along the frontier. In the 1630s, Li managed to extend the revolt throughout the country and finally occupied the capital of Beijing in 1644. The last Ming emperor committed suicide by hanging himself from a tree in the palace gardens.

But Li was unable to hold his conquest. The overthrow of the Ming dynasty presented a great temptation to the Manchus. With the assistance of many military commanders who had deserted from the Ming, they conquered Beijing on their own. Li Zicheng's army disintegrated, and the Manchus declared the creation of a new dynasty with the reign title of the Qing (Ch'ing, or Pure). Once again, China was under foreign rule.

The Greatness of the Qing

The accession of the Manchus to power in Beijing was not universally applauded. Their ruthless policies and insensitivity to Chinese customs soon provoked resistance. Some Ming loyalists fled to Southeast Asia, but others continued their resistance to the new rulers from inside the country. To make it easier to identify the rebels, the government ordered all Chinese to adopt Manchu dress and hairstyles. All Chinese males were to shave their foreheads and braid their hair into a queue; those who refused were to be executed. As a popular saying put it, "lose your hair or lose your head."[5]

But the Manchus eventually proved to be more adept at adapting to Chinese conditions than their predecessors, the Mongols. Unlike the latter, who had tried to impose their own methods of ruling, the Manchus adopted the Chinese political system (although, as we shall see, they retained their distinct position within it) and were gradually accepted by most Chinese as the legitimate rulers of the country.

Like all of China's great dynasties, the Qing was blessed with a series of strong early rulers who pacified the country, rectified many of the most obvious social and economic inequities, and restored peace and prosperity. For the Ming dynasty, these strong emperors had been Hongwu and Yongle; under the Qing, they would be Kangxi (K'ang Hsi) and Qianlong (Ch'ien Lung). The two Qing monarchs ruled China for well over a century, from the middle of the seventeenth century to the end of the eighteenth, and were responsible for much of the greatness of Manchu China.

Kangxi (1661–1722) was arguably the greatest ruler in Chinese history. Ascending to the throne at the age of seven, he was blessed with diligence, political astuteness, and a strong character and began to take charge of Qing administration while still in his adolescence. During the six decades of his reign, Kangxi not only stabilized imperial rule by pacifying the restive peoples along the northern and western frontiers, but he also managed to make the dynasty acceptable to the general population. As an active patron of arts and letters, he cultivated the support of scholars through a number of major projects.

During Kangxi's reign, the activities of the Western missionaries, Dominicans and Franciscans as well as Jesuits, reached their height. The emperor was quite tolerant of the Christians, and several Jesuit missionaries became influential at court. Several hundred court officials converted to Christianity, as did an estimated 300,000 ordinary Chinese.

CHRONOLOGY

CHINA DURING THE EARLY MODERN ERA

Rise of Ming Dynasty	1369
Voyages of Zhenghe	1405–1433
Portuguese arrive in southern China	1514
Matteo Ricci arrives in China	1601
Li Zicheng occupies Beijing	1644
Manchus seize China	1644
Reign of Kangxi	1661–1722
Treaty of Nerchinsk	1689
First English trading post at Canton	1699
Reign of Qianlong	1736–1795
Lord Macartney's mission to China	1793
White Lotus Rebellion	1796–1804

But ultimately the Christian effort was undermined by squabbling among the Western religious orders over the Jesuit policy of accommodating local beliefs and practices in order to facilitate conversion. The Jesuits had acquiesced to the emperor's insistence that traditional Confucian rituals such as ancestor worship were civil ceremonies and thus could be undertaken by Christian converts. Jealous Dominicans and Franciscans complained to the pope, who issued an edict ordering all missionaries and converts to conform to the official orthodoxy set forth in Europe. At first Kangxi attempted to resolve the problem by appealing directly to the Vatican, but the pope was uncompromising. After Kangxi's death, his successor began to suppress Christian activities throughout China.

Kangxi's achievements were carried on by his successors, Yongzheng (Yung Cheng, 1722–1736) and Qianlong (1736–1795). Like Kangxi, Qianlong was known for his diligence, tolerance, and intellectual curiosity, and he too combined vigorous military action against the unruly tribes along the frontier with active efforts to promote economic prosperity, administrative efficiency, and scholarship and artistic excellence. The result was continued growth for the Manchu Empire throughout much of the eighteenth century.

QING POLITICS

Certainly, one reason for the success of the Manchus was their ability to adapt to their new environment. They retained the Ming political system with relatively few changes. They also tried to establish their legitimacy as

A CONFUCIAN SIXTEEN COMMANDMENTS

Although the Qing dynasty was of foreign origin, its rulers found Confucian maxims convenient for maintaining the social order. In 1670, the great emperor Kangxi issued the Sacred Edict to popularize Confucian values among the common people. The edict was read publicly at periodic intervals in every village in the country and set the standard for behavior throughout the empire. Note the similarities and differences with the Japanese decree on p. 509 later in this chapter.

KANGXI'S SACRED EDICT

1. Esteem most highly filial piety and brotherly submission, in order to give due importance to the social relations.
2. Behave with generosity toward your kindred, in order to illustrate harmony and benignity.
3. Cultivate peace and concord in your neighborhoods, in order to prevent quarrels and litigations.
4. Recognize the importance of husbandry and the culture of the mulberry tree, in order to ensure a sufficiency of clothing and food.
5. Show that you prize moderation and economy, in order to prevent the lavish waste of your means.
6. Give weight to colleges and schools, in order to make correct the practice of the scholar.
7. Extirpate strange principles, in order to exalt the correct doctrine.
8. Lecture on the laws, in order to warn the ignorant and obstinate.
9. Elucidate propriety and yielding courtesy, in order to make manners and customs good.
10. Labor diligently at your proper callings, in order to stabilize the will of the people.
11. Instruct sons and younger brothers, in order to prevent them from doing what is wrong.
12. Put a stop to false accusations, in order to preserve the honest and good.
13. Warn against sheltering deserters, in order to avoid being involved in their punishment.
14. Fully remit your taxes, in order to avoid being pressed for payment.
15. Unite in hundreds and tithing, in order to put an end to thefts and robbery.
16. Remove enmity and anger, in order to show the importance due to the person and life.

China's rightful rulers by stressing their devotion to the principles of Confucianism. Emperor Kangxi ostentatiously studied the sacred Confucian classics and issued a "Sacred Edict" that proclaimed to the entire empire the importance of the moral values established by the master (see the box above).

Still, the Manchus, like the Mongols, were ethnically, linguistically, and culturally distinct from their subject population. The Qing attempted to cope with this reality by adopting a two-pronged strategy. On the one hand, the Manchus, representing less than 2 percent of the entire population, were legally defined as distinct from everyone else in China. The Manchu nobles retained their aristocratic privileges, while their economic base was protected by extensive landholdings and revenues provided from the state treasury. Other Manchus were assigned farmland and organized into military units, called banners, which were stationed as separate units in various strategic positions throughout China. These "bannermen" were the primary fighting force of the empire. Ethnic Chinese were prohibited from settling in Manchuria and were still compelled to wear their hair in a queue as a sign of submission to the ruling dynasty.

But while the Qing attempted to protect their distinct identity within an alien society, they also recognized the need to bring ethnic Chinese into the top ranks of imperial administration. Their solution was to create a system, known as dyarchy, in which all important administrative positions were shared equally by Chinese and Manchus. Of the six members of the grand secretariat, three were Manchu and three were Chinese. Each of the six ministries had an equal number of Chinese and Manchu members, and Manchus and Chinese also shared responsibilities at the provincial level. Below the provinces, Chinese were dominant. Although the system did not work perfectly, the Manchus' willingness to share power did win over the allegiance of many Chinese. Meanwhile, the Manchus themselves, despite official efforts to preserve their separate language and culture, were increasingly assimilated into Chinese civilization.

The new rulers also tinkered with the civil service examination system. In an effort to make it more equitable, quotas were established for each major ethnic group and each province to prevent the positions from being monopolized by candidates from certain provinces in central China that had traditionally produced large numbers of officials. In practice, however, the examination system probably became less equitable during the Manchu era, because increasingly positions were assigned to candidates who had purchased their degree rather than competing through the system. Moreover, positions were becoming harder to obtain because their number did not rise fast enough to match the unprecedented increase in population under Qing rule.

CHINA ON THE EVE OF THE WESTERN ONSLAUGHT

In some ways, China was at the height of its power and glory in the mid-eighteenth century. But it was also under Qianlong that the first signs of the internal decay of the Manchu dynasty began to appear. The clues were familiar ones. Qing military campaigns along the frontier were expensive and placed heavy demands on the imperial treasury. As the emperor aged, he became less astute in selecting his subordinates and fell under the influence of corrupt elements at court, including the notorious Manchu official Heshen (Ho Shen). Funds officially destined for military or other official use were increasingly siphoned off to Heshen or his favorites, arousing resentment among military and civilian officials.

Corruption at the center led inevitably to unrest in rural areas, where higher taxes, bureaucratic venality, and rising pressure on the land because of the growing population had produced economic hardship. The heart of the unrest was in central China, where discontented peasants who had recently been settled on infertile land launched a revolt known as the White Lotus Rebellion (1796–1804). The revolt was eventually suppressed but at great expense.

Unfortunately for China, the decline of the Qing dynasty occurred just as China's modest relationship with the West was about to give way to a new era of military confrontation and increased pressure for trade. The first problems came in the north, where Russian traders seeking skins and furs began to penetrate the region between Siberian Russia and Manchuria. Earlier the Ming dynasty had attempted to deal with the Russians by the traditional method of placing them in a tributary relationship and playing them off against other non-Chinese groups in the area. But the tsar refused to play by Chinese rules. His envoys to Beijing ignored the tribute system and refused to perform the kowtow (the ritual of prostration and knocking the head on the ground performed by foreign emissaries before the emperor), the classical symbol of fealty demanded of all foreign ambassadors to the Chinese court.

MAP 17.2 The Qing Empire in the Eighteenth Century

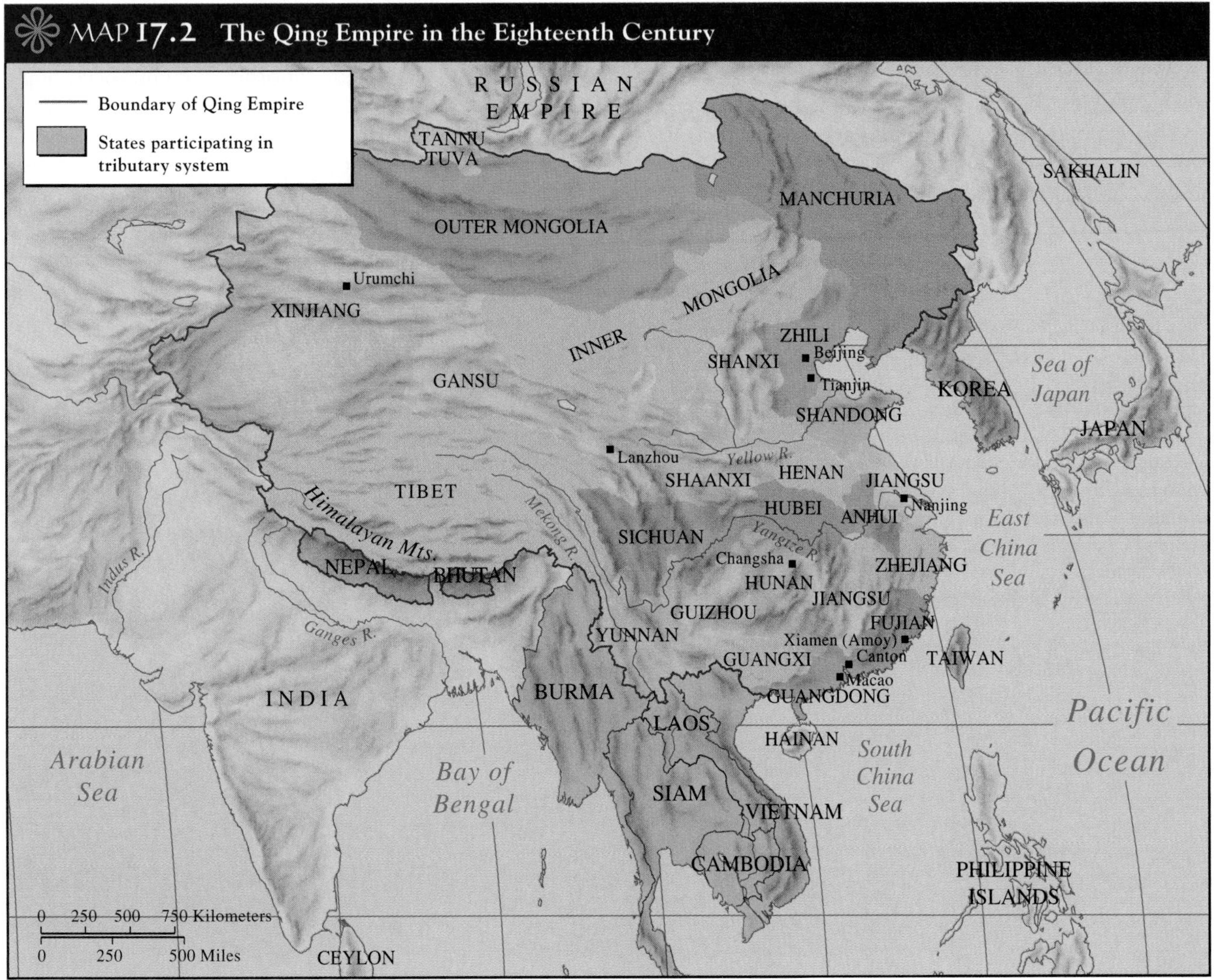

Formal diplomatic relations were finally established in 1689, when the Treaty of Nerchinsk (negotiated with the aid of Jesuit missionaries resident at the Qing court) settled the boundary dispute and provided for regular trade between the two countries. Through such arrangements, the Manchus were able not only to pacify the northern frontier but also to extend their rule over Xinjiang and Tibet to the west and southwest. In the meantime, tributary relations were established with such neighboring countries as Korea, Burma, Vietnam, and Ayuthaya.

Dealing with the foreigners who arrived by sea was more difficult. By the end of the seventeenth century, the English had replaced the Portuguese as the dominant force in European trade. Operating through the East India Company, which served as both a trading unit and the administrator of English territories in Asia, the English established their first trading post at Canton in 1699. Over the next decades, trade with China, notably the export of tea and silk to England, increased rapidly. To limit contact between Chinese and Europeans, the Qing licensed Chinese trading firms at Canton to be the exclusive conduit for trade with the West. Eventually, the Qing confined the Europeans to a small island just outside the city walls and permitted them to reside there only from October through March.

For a while, the British tolerated this system, which brought considerable profit to the East India Company and its shareholders. But by the end of the eighteenth century, the British had begun to demand access to other cities along the Chinese coast and that the country be opened to British manufactured goods. The British government and traders alike were restive at the uneven balance of trade between the two countries, which forced the British to ship vast amounts of silver bullion to China in exchange for its silks, porcelains, and teas. In 1793, a mission under Lord Macartney visited Beijing to press for liberalization of trade restrictions. A compromise was reached on the kowtow (Macartney was permitted to bend on one knee as was the British custom), but Qianlong expressed no interest in British manufactured products (see the box on p. 497). An exasperated Macartney compared the Chinese Empire to "an old, crazy, first-rate man-of-war" that had once awed its neighbors "merely by her bulk and appearance" but was now destined under incompetent leadership to be "dashed to pieces on the shore."[6] With his contemptuous dismissal of the British request, the emperor had inadvertently sowed the seeds for a century of humiliation.

Changing China

During the late Ming and Qing periods, China remained a predominantly agricultural society; nearly 85 percent of the population were farmers. But although most Chinese still lived in rural villages, the economy was undergoing a number of changes that have led some historians to suggest that China, under other circumstances, might have undergone an industrial revolution as in the West. In this view, the arrival of Western imperialism in the nineteenth century not only failed to stimulate economic change but may actually have hindered it.

EMPEROR QIANLONG MEETS LORD MACARTNEY. In 1793, Lord Macartney was dispatched to China to press for the liberalization of trade restrictions. Although he offered gifts of Western scientific instruments and texts, the Chinese, who believed their nation had been the cultural center of the world for the last two thousand years, were not impressed. Lord Macartney won little Chinese sympathy for his refusal to kowtow to the emperor. Here the two prepare to meet.

THE TRIBUTE SYSTEM IN ACTION

In 1793, the British emissary Lord Macartney visited the Qing Empire to request the opening of formal diplomatic and trading relations between his country and China. Emperor Qianlong's reply, addressed to King George III of Britain, illustrates how the imperial court in Beijing viewed the world. King George could not have been pleased. The document provides a good example of the complacency with which the Celestial Empire viewed the world beyond its borders.

A DECREE OF EMPEROR QIANLONG

An Imperial Edict to the King of England: You, O King, are so inclined toward our civilization that you have sent a special envoy across the seas to bring to our Court your memorial of congratulations on the occasion of my birthday and to present your native products as an expression of your thoughtfulness. On perusing your memorial, so simply worded and sincerely conceived, I am impressed by your genuine respectfulness and friendliness and greatly pleased.

As to the request made in your memorial, O King, to send one of your nationals to stay at the Celestial Court to take care of your country's trade with China, this is not in harmony with the state system of our dynasty and will definitely not be permitted. Traditionally people of the European nations who wished to render some service under the Celestial Court have been permitted to come to the capital. But after their arrival they are obliged to wear Chinese court costumes, are placed in a certain residence, and are never allowed to return to their own countries. This is the established rule of the Celestial Dynasty with which presumably you, O King, are familiar. Now you, O King, wish to send one of your nationals to live in the capital, but he is not like the Europeans who come to Peking as Chinese employees, live there, and never return home again, nor can he be allowed to go and come and maintain any correspondence. This is indeed a useless undertaking.

Moreover the territory under the control of the Celestial Court is very large and wide. There are well-established regulations governing tributary envoys from the outer states to Peking, giving them provisions (of food and traveling expenses) by our post-houses and limiting their going and coming. There has never been a precedent for letting them do whatever they like. Now if you, O King, wish to have a representative in Peking, his language will be unintelligible and his dress different from the regulations; there is no place to accommodate him. . . .

The Celestial Court has pacified and possessed the territory within the four seas. Its sole aim is to do its utmost to achieve good government and to manage political affairs, attaching no value to strange jewels and precious objects. The various articles presented by you, O King, this time are accepted by my special order to the office in charge of such functions in consideration of the offerings having come from a long distance with sincere good wishes. As a matter of fact, the virtue and prestige of the Celestial Dynasty having spread far and wide, the kings of the myriad nations come by land and sea with all sorts of precious things. Consequently there is nothing we lack, as your principal envoy and others have themselves observed. We have never set much store on strange or ingenious objects, nor do we need any more of your country's manufactures. . . .

THE POPULATION EXPLOSION

In the first place, the center of gravity was continuing to shift steadily from the north to the south. In the early centuries of Chinese civilization, the bulk of the population had been located along the Yellow River. Smaller settlements were located along the Yangtze and in the mountainous regions of the south, but the administrative and economic center of gravity was clearly in the north. By the Song period, however, that emphasis had already begun to shift drastically as a result of climatic changes, deforestation, and continuing pressure from nomads in the Gobi Desert. By the late Ming and early Qing, the economic breadbasket of China, if not the administrative headquarters, was located along the Yangtze River or in the mountains to the south. One concrete indication of this shift occurred during the Ming dynasty, when Emperor Yongle ordered the renovation of the Grand Canal to facilitate the shipment of rice from the Yangtze delta to the food-starved north.

Moreover, the population was beginning to increase rapidly. For centuries, China's population had remained within a range of 50 to 100 million, rising in times of peace and prosperity and falling in periods of foreign invasion and internal anarchy. During the late Ming and the early Qing, however, the population increased from an estimated 70 to 80 million in 1390 to over 300 million at the end of the eighteenth century. There were probably several reasons for this population increase: the relatively long period of peace and stability under the early Qing; the introduction of new crops from the Americas, including peanuts, sweet potatoes, and maize; and the planting of a new species of faster-growing rice from Southeast Asia.

Of course, this population increase meant much greater population pressure on the land, smaller farms, and a razor-thin margin of safety in case of climatic disaster. The imperial court attempted to deal with the problem through a variety of means, most notably by preventing the concentration of land in the hands of wealthy landowners. Nevertheless, by the eighteenth century, almost all the land that could be irrigated was already under cultivation, and the problems of rural hunger and landlessness became increasingly serious.

SEEDS OF INDUSTRIALIZATION

Another change that took place during the early modern period in China was the steady growth of manufacturing and commerce. Taking advantage of the long era of peace and prosperity, merchants and manufacturers began to expand their operations beyond their immediate provinces. Commercial networks began to operate on a regional and sometimes even a national basis, as trade in silk, metal and wood products, porcelain, cotton goods, and cash crops like cotton and tobacco developed rapidly. Foreign trade also expanded, as Chinese merchants set up extensive contacts with countries in Southeast Asia.

Although this rise in industrial and commercial activity resembles the changes occurring in Western Europe, China and western Europe differed in several key ways. In the first place, the bourgeoisie in China were not as independent as their European counterparts. In China, trade and manufacturing remained under the firm control of the state. In addition, political and social prejudices against commercial activity remained strong. Reflecting an ancient preference for agriculture over manufacturing and trade, the state levied heavy taxes on manufacturing and commerce while attempting to keep agricultural taxes low.

One of the consequences of these differences was a growing technological gap between China and Europe. The Chinese reaction to European clock-making techniques provides an example. In the early seventeenth century, the Jesuit Matteo Ricci introduced advanced European clocks driven by weights or springs. The emperor was fascinated and found the clocks more reliable than Chinese methods of keeping time. Over the next decades, European timepieces became a popular novelty at court, but the Chinese expressed little curiosity about the technology involved, provoking one European to remark that playthings like cuckoo clocks "will be received here with much greater interest than scientific instruments or *objets d'art*."[7]

Daily Life in Qing China

Despite the changes in the economy, daily life in China under the Ming and early Qing dynasties continued to follow traditional patterns. As in earlier periods, Chinese society was organized around the family. As in earlier times, the ideal family unit in Qing China was the joint family, in which as many as three or even four generations lived under the same roof. When sons married, they brought their wives to live with them in the family homestead. Prosperous families would add a separate section to the house to accommodate the new family unit. Unmarried daughters would also remain in the house. Aging parents and grandparents remained under the same roof until they died and were cared for by younger members of the household. This ideal did not always correspond to reality, however, since many families did not possess sufficient land to support a large household. One historian has estimated that only about 40 percent of Chinese families actually lived in joint families.

The family continued to be important in early Qing China for much the same reasons as in earlier times. As a labor-intensive society based primarily on the cultivation of rice, the Chinese needed large families not only to help with the harvest, but also to provide security for the parents when they were too old to work in the fields. Sons were particularly prized, not only because they had strong backs, but also because they would raise their own families under the parental roof. With few opportunities for employment outside the family, sons had little choice but to remain with their parents and help on the land. Within the family, the oldest male was king, and his wishes theoretically had to be obeyed by all family members. These values were reiterated in Emperor Kangxi's Sacred Edict, which listed filial piety and loyalty to the family as its first two maxims (see the box on p. 494).

For many Chinese, the effects of these values were most apparent in the choice of a marriage partner. Marriages were normally arranged for the benefit of the family, often by a go-between, and the groom and bride were usually not consulted. Frequently, they did not meet until the marriage ceremony. Under such conditions, love was clearly a secondary consideration. In fact, it was often viewed as detrimental, since it inevitably distracted the attention of the husband and wife from their primary responsibility to the larger family unit.

Although this emphasis on filial piety might seem to represent a blatant disregard for individual rights, the obligations were not all on the side of the children. The father was expected to provide support for his wife and children and, like the ruler, was supposed to treat those in his care with respect and compassion. All too often, however, the male head of the family was able to exact his privileges without performing his responsibilities in return.

Beyond the joint family was the clan. Sometimes called a lineage, a clan was an extended kinship unit consisting of dozens or even hundreds of joint and nuclear families linked together by a clan council of elders and a variety of other common social and religious functions. The clan served a number of useful purposes. Some clans possessed lands that could be rented out to poorer families, or richer families within the clan might provide land for the poor. Since there was no general state-supported educational system, sons of poor families might be invited to study in a school established in the home of a more prosperous relative. If the young man succeeded in becoming an official, he would be expected to provide favors and prestige for the clan as a whole.

Like joint families, clans were not universal, and millions of Chinese had none. The clans apparently originated in the great landed families of the Tang period and managed to survive despite periodic efforts by the imperial court to weaken and destroy them. In many cases, clan solidarity was weakened by intralineage conflicts or differing levels of status and economic achievement. Nevertheless, in the early modern period, they were still an influential force at the local level and were particularly prevalent in the south.

THE ROLE OF WOMEN

In traditional China, the role of women had always been inferior to that of men. A sixteenth-century Spanish visitor to South China observed that Chinese women were "very secluded and virtuous, and it was a very rare thing for us to see a woman in the cities and large towns, unless it was an old crone." Women were more visible, he said, in rural areas, where they frequently could be seen working in the fields.[8]

The concept of female inferiority had deep roots in Chinese history. This view was embodied in the belief that only a male would carry on sacred family rituals and that only males had the talent to govern others. Only males could aspire to a career in government or scholarship. Within the family system, the wife was clearly subordinated to the husband. Legally, she could not divorce her husband or inherit property. The husband, however, could divorce his wife if she did not produce male heirs, or he could take a second wife as well as a concubine for his pleasure. A widow suffered especially, because she had to either raise her children on a single income or fight off her former husband's greedy relatives, who would coerce her to remarry since, according to the law, they would then inherit all of her previous property and her original dowry.

Female children were less desirable because of their limited physical strength and because their parents would be required to pay a dowry to the parents of their future husband. Female children normally did not receive an education, and in times of scarcity when food was in short supply, daughters might even be put to death.

Though women were clearly inferior to men in theory, this was not always the case in practice. Capable women often compensated for their legal inferiority by playing a strong role within the family. Women were often in charge of educating the children and handled the family budget. Some privileged women also received training in the Confucian classics, although their schooling was generally for a shorter time and less rigorous than that of their male counterparts. A few produced significant works of art and poetry.

All in all, however, life for women in traditional China was undoubtedly difficult. In Chinese novels, women were treated as scullery maids or love objects. They were frequently under the domination of both their husband and their mother-in-law, and in some cases the bullying was so brutal that suicide appeared to be the only way out.

Cultural Developments

During the late Ming and the early Qing dynasties, traditional culture in China reached new heights of achievement. With the rise of a wealthy urban class, the demand for art, porcelain, textiles, and literature was at a premium.

THE RISE OF THE CHINESE NOVEL

During the Ming dynasty, a new form of literature arose that eventually evolved into the modern Chinese novel. Although considered less respectable than poetry and nonfiction prose, these groundbreaking works (often written anonymously or under pseudonyms) were enormously popular, especially among well-to-do urban dwellers.

Written in a colloquial style, the new fiction was characterized by a realism that resulted in vivid portraits of Chinese society. Many of the stories sympathized with society's downtrodden, often helpless maidens, and dealt with such crucial issues as love, money, marriage, and power. Adding to the realism were sexually explicit passages that depicted the private side of Chinese life. Readers delighted in sensuous tales that, no matter how pornographic, always professed a moral lesson; the villains were punished and the virtuous rewarded. During the more puritanical Qing era, a number of the more erotic works were censored or banned and found refuge in Japan, where several have recently been rediscovered by scholars.

Gold Vase Plum, known in English translation as *The Golden Lotus*, presents a cutting exposé of the decadent aspects of late Ming society. Considered by many the first realistic social novel—preceding its European counterparts by two centuries—*The Golden Lotus* depicts the depraved life of a wealthy landlord who cruelly manipulates those around him for sex, money, and power. In a rare exception in Chinese fiction, the villain is not punished for his evil ways; justice is served instead by the misfortunes that befall his descendants.

Even today *The Dream of the Red Chamber* is generally considered to be China's most distinguished popular novel (see the box on p. 500). Published in 1791, 150 years after *The Golden Lotus*, it tells of the tragic love between two young people caught in the financial and moral disintegration of a powerful Chinese clan. The hero and the heroine, both sensitive and spoiled, represent the inevitable decline of the Chia family and come to an equally inevitable tragic end, she in death and he in an unhappy marriage to another.

THE ART OF USING CHOPSTICKS

This passage from The Dream of the Red Chamber *is characteristic of the historical detail of the novel. It describes a country cousin's visit to the elegant mansion of her city relatives and the comic scene that she provokes by her naïveté. Such writing brings to life the wealth and luxury of the Qing dynasty and shows that Europeans were not the only people who had trouble with chopsticks.*

THE DREAM OF THE RED CHAMBER

As soon as Old Dame Liu was seated, she picked up the chopsticks, which were uncannily heavy and hard to manage. It was because Phoenix and Mandarin Duck had previously plotted to give her a pair of old-fashioned, angular-shaped ivory chopsticks gilded with gold. Looking at them, Old Dame Liu remarked: "These forklike things are even heavier than our iron prongs. How can one hold them up?" Everyone laughed. By this time a woman servant had brought in a tiny food box and, as she stood there, another maid came forward to lift the lid. Inside were two bowls of food. Li Huan took one bowl and placed it on the Matriarch's table as Phoenix picked up a bowl of pigeon eggs to place it on Old Dame Liu's table.

Just as the Matriarch had finished saying, "Please eat," Old Dame Liu rose from her seat and said aloud:

Old Liu, Old Liu, her appetite as big as a cow!
She eats like an old sow without lifting her head.

Having said her piece, with her cheeks puffed out she looked straight ahead without uttering another word. At first, all those present were astonished, but upon a moment's reflection, all burst out laughing at the same time. Unable to restrain herself, River Cloud (Matriarch's grandniece) spluttered out a mouthful of tea; Black Jade was choked with laughter and leaning on the table, could only cry and groan, "Ai-ya!" Madame Wang also laughed, then pointed her finger at Phoenix, but could not utter one word. . . . Only Phoenix and Mandarin Duck controlled themselves and kept urging Old Dame Liu to eat.

Old Dame Liu lifted up the chopsticks but they were hardly manageable. Looking at the bowl in front of her, she remarked: "Well, well, even your hens are smarter than ours! They lay such tiny delicate eggs, very dainty indeed. Let me try one!" All the people had just stopped laughing but they burst out again upon hearing these words. The Matriarch laughed so much that tears dropped down; she just couldn't stop them, and Amber (Matriarch's maidservant) had to pound her back to relieve her.

Old Dame Liu was still exclaiming about how tiny and dainty the eggs were when Phoenix said jocularly to her: "They cost an ounce of silver apiece. You had better hurry up and taste one before they get cold." Old Dame Liu then stretched out her chopsticks to seize the eggs with both ends, but how could she pick them up? After having chased them all over the bowl, she finally captured one with no little effort and was about to crane her neck to eat it when lo! it slipped off and fell on the floor. She was going to pick it up herself when a woman servant got it and took it out. Old Dame Liu sighed: "An ounce of silver! How it disappears without even making a noise!"

THE ART OF THE MING AND THE QING

During the Ming and the early Qing, China produced its last outpouring of traditional artistic brilliance. Although most of the creative work was modeled on past examples, the art of this period is impressive for its technical perfection and breathtaking quantity.

In architecture, the most outstanding example is the Imperial City in Beijing. Building on the remnants of the palace of the Yuan dynasty, the third Ming emperor ordered renovations when he returned the capital to Beijing in 1421. Succeeding emperors continued to add to the palace, but the basic design has not changed since the Ming era. Surrounded by six and one-half miles of walls, the immense enclosed compound is divided into a maze of private apartments and offices and an imposing ceremonial quadrangle with a series of stately halls for imperial audiences and banquets. The grandiose scale, richly carved marble, spacious gardens, and graceful upturned roofs also contribute to the splendor of the "Forbidden City."

The decorative arts flourished in this period, especially the intricately carved lacquerware and the boldly shaped and colored cloisonné, a type of enamelwork in which colored areas are attached to a piece by metal bands. Silk production reached its zenith, and the best-quality silks were highly prized in Europe, where chinoiserie, as Chinese art of all kinds was called, was in vogue. Perhaps the most famous of all the achievements of the Ming era was the blue-and-white porcelain, which is still prized by collectors throughout the world. One variety caused a sensation in Holland and led to the manufacture of blue-and-white porcelain at the Dutch porcelain factory at Delft.

During the Qing dynasty, artists produced great quantities of paintings, mostly for home consumption. The wealthy city of Yangzhou on the Grand Canal emerged as an active artistic center. Inside the Forbidden City in Beijing, court painters worked alongside Jesuit artists and experimented with Western techniques. European art, however, did not greatly influence Chinese painting at this

THE TEMPLE OF HEAVEN. This temple, located in the capital Beijing, is one of the most important historical structures in China. Built in 1420 at the order of the Ming emperor Yongle, it served as the location for the emperor's annual ceremony appealing to Heaven for a good harvest. Yongle's temple burned to the ground in 1889 but was immediately rebuilt according to the original design.

THE IMPERIAL CITY IN BEIJING. During the fifteenth century, the Ming dynasty erected an immense Imperial City on the remnants of the palace of Khubilai Khan in Beijing. Surrounded by six and one-half miles of walls, the enclosed compound is divided into a maze of private apartments and offices; it also includes an imposing ceremonial quadrangle with stately halls for imperial audiences and banquets. Because it was off-limits to commoners, the compound was known as the "Forbidden City."

WORLD-CLASS CHINA WARE. Ming porcelain was noted throughout the world for its delicate blue-and-white floral decorations. The blue coloring was produced with cobalt that had originally been brought from the Middle East along the Silk Road and was known in China as "Mohammadan blue." In the early seventeenth century, the first Ming ware arrived in Holland, where it was called "kraak" because it had been loaded on two Portuguese carracks seized by the Dutch fleet. It took Dutch artisans over a century to learn how to produce a porcelain as fine as the examples brought from China.

time; some dismissed it as mere "craftsmanship." Scholarly painters and the literati totally rejected foreign techniques and became obsessed with traditional Chinese styles. As a result, Qing painting became progressively more repetitive and stale. Ironically, the Qing dynasty thus represents the apogee of traditional Chinese art and the beginning of its decline.

TOKUGAWA JAPAN

At the end of the fifteenth century, the traditional Japanese system was at a point of near anarchy. With the decline in the authority of the Ashikaga shogunate at Kyoto, clan rivalries had exploded into an era of "warring states" similar to the period of the same name in Zhou dynasty China. Even at the local level, power was frequently diffuse. The typical daimyo (great lord) domain had often become little more than a coalition of fief holders held together by a loose allegiance to the manor lord. Prince Shotoku's dream of a united Japan appeared to be only a distant memory (see Chapter 11). In actuality, Japan was on the verge of an extended era of national unification and peace under the rule of its greatest shogunate—the Tokugawa.

The Three Great Unifiers

The process began in the mid-sixteenth century with the emergence of three very powerful political figures, Oda Nobunaga (1568–1582), Toyotomi Hideyoshi (1582–1598), and Tokugawa Ieyasu (1598–1616). In 1568, Oda Nobunaga, the son of a samurai and a military commander under the Ashikaga shogunate, seized the imperial capital of Kyoto and placed the reigning shogun under his domination. During the next few years, the brutal and ambitious Nobunaga attempted to consolidate his rule throughout the central plains by defeating his rivals and suppressing the power of the Buddhist estates, but he was killed by one of his generals in 1582 before the process was complete. He was succeeded by Toyotomi Hideyoshi, a farmer's son who had worked his way up within the ranks to become a military commander. Originally lacking a family name of his own, he eventually adopted the name Toyotomi ("abundant provider") to embellish his reputation for improving the material standards of his domain. Hideyoshi located his capital at Osaka, where he built a castle to accommodate his headquarters, and gradually extended his power outward to the southern islands of Shikoku and Kyushu. By 1590, he had persuaded most of the daimyo on the Japanese islands to accept his authority and created a national currency. Then he invaded Korea in an abortive effort to export his rule to the Asian mainland.

Despite their efforts, however, neither Nobunaga nor Hideyoshi was able to eliminate the power of the local daimyo. Both were compelled to form alliances with some daimyo in order to destroy other more powerful rivals. At the conclusion of his conquests in 1590, Toyotomi Hideyoshi could claim to be the supreme proprietor of all registered lands in areas under his authority. But he then reassigned those lands as fiefs to the local daimyo, who declared their allegiance to him. The daimyo in turn began to pacify the countryside, carrying out extensive "sword hunts" to disarm the population and attracting samurai to their service. The Japanese tradition of decentralized rule had not been overcome.

After Hideyoshi's death in 1598, Tokugawa Ieyasu, the powerful daimyo of Edo (modern Tokyo), moved to fill the vacuum. Neither Hideyoshi nor Oda Nobunaga had claimed the title of shogun, but Ieyasu named himself shogun in 1603, initiating the most powerful and longlasting of all Japanese shogunates. The Tokugawa rulers completed the restoration of central authority begun by Nobunaga and Hideyoshi and remained in power until 1868, when a war dismantled the entire system. As a contemporary phrased it, "Oda pounds the national rice cake, Hideyoshi kneads it, and in the end Ieyasu sits down and eats it."[9]

Opening to the West

The unification of Japan took place almost simultaneously with the coming of the Europeans. Portuguese traders sailing in a Chinese junk that may have been blown off course by a typhoon had landed on the islands in 1543. Within a few years, Portuguese ships were stopping at Japanese ports on a regular basis to take part in the regional trade between Japan, China, and Southeast Asia. The first Jesuit missionary, Francis Xavier, arrived in 1549.

Initially, the visitors were welcomed. The curious Japanese (the Japanese were "very desirous of knowledge," said Francis Xavier) were fascinated by tobacco, clocks, spectacles, and other European goods, and local daimyo were interested in purchasing all types of European weapons and armaments (see the box on p. 504). Oda Nobunaga and Toyotomi Hideyoshi found the new firearms helpful in defeating their enemies and unifying the islands. The effect on Japanese military architecture was particularly striking, as local lords began to erect castles on the European model. Many of these castles, such as Hideyoshi's castle at Osaka, still exist today.

The missionaries also had some success. Though confused by misleading translations of sacred concepts in both cultures (Francis Xavier was notoriously poor at learning foreign languages), they converted a number of local daimyo, some of whom may have been motivated in part by the desire for commercial profits. By the end of the sixteenth century, thousands of Japanese in the southernmost islands of Kyushu and Shikoku had become Christians. One converted daimyo ceded the superb natural harbor of the modern city of Nagasaki to the Society of Jesus, which proceeded to use the new settlement for both missionary and trading purposes. But papal claims to the loyalty of all Japanese Christians and the European habit of intervening in local politics soon began to arouse suspicion in official circles. Missionaries added to the problem by deliberately destroying local idols and shrines and turning some temples into Christian schools or churches.

Inevitably, the local authorities reacted. In 1587, Toyotomi Hideyoshi issued an edict prohibiting further Christian activities within his domains. Japan, he declared, was "the land of the Gods" and the destruction of shrines by the foreigners was "something unheard of in previous ages." To "corrupt and stir up the lower classes" to commit such sacrileges, he declared, was "outrageous."[10] Those responsible (the Jesuits) were ordered to leave the country within twenty days. Hideyoshi was careful to distinguish

THE SIEGE OF OSAKA CASTLE. After the death of Toyotomi Hideyoshi in 1598, titular authority in Japan passed on to his infant son Hideyori, whose supporters located their headquarters at Osaka Castle in central Japan. In 1615, the powerful warlord Tokugawa Ieyasu seized the castle as shown here, and scattered Hideyori's supporters. The family's control over Japan lasted nearly 250 years.

A PRESENT FOR LORD TOKITAKA

The Portuguese introduced firearms to Japan in the sixteenth century, and Japanese warriors were quick to explore the possibilities of these new weapons. In this passage, the daimyo of a small island off the southern tip of Japan receives an explanation of how to use the new weapons and is fascinated by the results. Note how Lord Tokitaka attempts to understand the procedures in terms of traditional Daoist beliefs.

THE JAPANESE DISCOVER FIREARMS

"There are two leaders among the traders, the one called Murashusa, and the other Christian Mota. In their hands they carried something two or three feet long, straight on the outside with a passage inside, and made of a heavy substance. The inner passage runs through it although it is closed at the end. At its side there is an aperture which is the passageway for fire. Its shape defies comparison with anything I know. To use it, fill it with powder and small lead pellets. Set up a small . . . target on a bank. Grip the object in your hand, compose your body, and closing one eye, apply fire to the aperture. Then the pellet hits the target squarely. The explosion is like lightning and the report like thunder. Bystanders must cover their ears. . . . This thing with one blow can smash a mountain of silver and a wall of iron. If one sought to do mischief in another man's domain and he was touched by it, he would lose his life instantly. Needless to say this is also true for the deer and stag that ravage the plants in the fields."

Lord Tokitaka saw it and thought it was the wonder of wonders. He did not know its name at first nor the details of its use. Then someone called it "iron-arms," although it was not known whether the Chinese called it so, or whether it was so called only on our island. Thus, one day, Tokitaka spoke to the two alien leaders through an interpreter: "Incapable though I am, I should like to learn about it." Whereupon, the chiefs answered, also through an interpreter: "If you wish to learn about it, we shall teach you its mysteries." Tokitaka then asked, "What is its secret?" The chief replied: "The secret is to put your mind aright and close one eye." Tokitaka said: "The ancient sages have often taught how to set one's mind aright, and I have learned something of it. If the mind is not set aright, there will be no logic for what we say or do. Thus, I understand what you say about setting our minds aright. However, will it not impair our vision for objects at a distance if we close an eye? Why should we close an eye?" To which the chiefs replied: "That is because concentration is important in everything. When one concentrates, a broad vision is not necessary. To close an eye is not to dim one's eyesight but rather to project one's concentration farther. You should know this." Delighted, Tokitaka said: "That corresponds to what Lao Tzu has said, 'Good sight means seeing what is very small.' "

That year the festival day of the Ninth Month fell on the day of the Metal and the Boar. Thus, one fine morning the weapon was filled with powder and lead pellets, a target was set up more than a hundred paces away, and fire was applied to the weapon. At first the people were astonished; then they became frightened. But in the end they all said in unison: "We should like to learn!" Disregarding the high price of the arms, Tokitaka purchased from the aliens two pieces of the firearms for his family treasure. As for the art of grinding, sifting, and mixing of the powder, Tokitaka let his retainer, Shinokawa Shoshiro, learn it. Tokitaka occupied himself, morning and night, and without rest in handling the arms. As a result, he was able to convert the misses of his early experiments into hits—a hundred hits in a hundred attempts.

missionary from trading activities, however, and merchants were permitted to continue their operations (see the box on p. 505).

The Jesuits protested the expulsion, and eventually Hideyoshi relented, permitting them to continue proselytizing so long as they were discreet. But he refused to repeal the edicts, and when the aggressive activities of newly arrived Spanish Franciscans aroused his ire, he ordered the execution of nine missionaries and a number of their Japanese converts. When the missionaries continued to interfere in local politics (some even tried to incite the daimyo in the southern islands against the shogunate government in Edo), Tokugawa Ieyasu completed the process by ordering the eviction of all missionaries in 1612. The persecution of Japanese Christians intensified, leading to an abortive revolt by Christian peasants on the island of Kyushu in 1637, which was bloodily suppressed.

At first, Japanese authorities hoped to maintain commercial relations with European countries even while suppressing the Western religion, but eventually they decided to prohibit foreign trade altogether and closed the two major foreign factories on the island of Hirado and at Nagasaki. The sole remaining opening to the West was at Deshima Island in Nagasaki harbor, where a small Dutch community was permitted to engage in limited trade with Japan (the Dutch, unlike the Portuguese and the Spanish, had not allowed missionary activities to interfere with their commercial interests). Dutch ships were permitted to dock at Nagasaki harbor only once a year and, after close inspection, were allowed to remain for two or three months. Conditions on the island of Deshima itself were

TOYOTOMI HIDEYOSHI EXPELS THE MISSIONARIES

When Christian missionaries in sixteenth-century Japan began to interfere in local politics and criticize traditional religious practices, Toyotomi Hideyoshi issued an edict calling for their expulsion. In this letter to the Portuguese viceroy in Asia, Hideyoshi explains his decision. Note his conviction that Buddhists, Confucianists, and followers of Shinto all believe in the same God and his criticism of Christianity for rejecting all other faiths.

TOYOTOMI HIDEYOSHI, LETTER TO THE VICEROY OF THE INDIES

Ours is the land of the Gods, and God is mind. Everything in nature comes into existence because of mind. Without God there can be no spirituality. Without God there can be no way. God rules in times of prosperity as in times of decline. God is positive and negative and unfathomable. Thus, God is the root and source of all existence. This God is spoken of by Buddhism in India, Confucianism in China, and Shinto in Japan. To know Shinto is to know Buddhism as well as Confucianism.

As long as man lives in this world, Humanity will be a basic principle. Were it not for Humanity and Righteousness, the sovereign would not be a sovereign, nor a minister of a state a minister. It is through the practice of Humanity and Righteousness that the foundations of our relationships between sovereign and minister, parent and child, and husband and wife are established. If you are interested in the profound philosophy of God and Buddha, request an explanation and it will be given to you. In your land one doctrine is taught to the exclusion of others, and you are not yet informed of the [Confucian] philosophy of Humanity and Righteousness. Thus there is no respect for God and Buddha and no distinction between sovereign and ministers. Through heresies you intend to destroy the righteous law. Hereafter, do not expound, in ignorance of right and wrong, unreasonable and wanton doctrines. A few years ago the so-called Fathers came to my country seeking to bewitch our men and women, both of the laity and clergy. At that time punishment was administered to them, and it will be repeated if they should return to our domain to propagate their faith. It will not matter what sect or denomination they represent—they shall be destroyed. It will then be too late to repent. If you entertain any desire of establishing amity with this land, the seas have been rid of the pirate menace, and merchants are permitted to come and go. Remember this.

THE PORTUGUESE ARRIVE AT NAGASAKI. Portuguese traders landed in Japan by accident in 1543. In a few years, they arrived regularly, taking part in a regional trade network between Japan, China, and Southeast Asia. In these panels done in black lacquer and gold leaf, we see a late-sixteenth-century Japanese interpretation of the first Portuguese landing at Nagasaki.

quite confining: the Dutch physician Engelbert Kaempfer complained that the Dutch lived in "almost perpetual imprisonment."[11] Nor were the Japanese free to engage in foreign trade. A small amount of commerce took place with China, but Japanese subjects of the shogunate were forbidden to leave the country on penalty of death.

The Tokugawa "Great Peace"

Once in power, the Tokugawa attempted to strengthen the system that had governed Japan for over three hundred years. They followed precedent in ruling through the *bakufu*, composed now of a coalition of daimyo, and a council of elders. But the system was more centralized than it had been previously. Now the shogunate government played a dual role. It set national policy on behalf of the emperor in Kyoto while simultaneously governing the shogun's own domain, which included about one-quarter of the national territory as well as the three great cities of Edo, Kyoto, and Osaka. As before, the state was divided into separate territories, called domains (*han*), which were ruled by a total of about 250 individual daimyo lords. The daimyo were themselves divided into two types: the *fudai* (inside) daimyo, who were mostly small daimyo directly subordinate to the shogunate, and the *tozama* (outside) daimyo, who were larger and more independent lords usually more distant from the center of shogunate power in Edo.

In theory, the daimyo were essentially autonomous, since they were able to support themselves from taxes on their lands (the shogunate received its own revenues from its extensive landholdings). In actuality, the shogunate was able to guarantee daimyo loyalties by compelling daimyo lords to maintain two residences, one in their own domains and the other at Edo, and to leave their families in Edo as hostages for the daimyo's good behavior. Keeping up two residences also placed the Japanese nobility in a difficult economic position. Some were able to defray the high costs by concentrating on cash crops such as sugar, fish, and forestry products, but most were rice producers, and their revenues remained roughly the same throughout the period. The daimyo were also able to protect their economic interests by depriving their samurai retainers of their proprietary rights over the land and transforming them into salaried officials. The fief thus became a stipend, and the personal relationship between the daimyo and his retainers gradually gave way to a bureaucratic authority.

The Tokugawa also tinkered with the social system by limiting the size of the samurai class and reclassifying samurai who supported themselves by tilling the land as commoners. In fact, with the long period of peace brought about by Tokugawa rule, the samurai gradually ceased to be a warrior class and were required to live in the castle towns. As a gesture to their glorious past, samurai were still permitted to wear their two swords, and a rigid separation was maintained between persons of samurai status and the nonaristocratic segment of the population. Jesuit missionary Francis Xavier observed that "on no account would a poverty-stricken gentleman marry with someone outside the gentry, even if he were given great sums to do so."[12]

SEEDS OF CAPITALISM

The long period of peace under the Tokugawa shogunate made possible a dramatic rise in commerce and manufacturing, especially in the growing cities of Edo, Kyoto, and Osaka. By the mid-eighteenth century, Edo, with a population of more than one million, was one of the largest cities in the world. The growth of trade and industry was stimulated by a rising standard of living—driven in part by technological advances in agriculture and an expansion of arable land—and the voracious appetites of the aristocrats for new products. The daimyo's need for income also contributed as many of them began to promote the sale of local goods from their domains, such as textiles, forestry products, sugar, and sake (a Japanese rice wine).

Most of this commercial expansion took place in the major cities and the castle towns, where the merchants and artisans lived along with the samurai, who were clustered in neighborhoods surrounding the daimyo's castle. Banking flourished and paper money became the normal medium of exchange in commercial transactions. Merchants formed guilds not only to control market conditions, but also to facilitate government control and the collection of taxes. Under the benign if somewhat contemptuous supervision of Japan's noble rulers, a Japanese merchant class gradually began to emerge from the shadows to play a significant role in the life of the Japanese nation. Some historians view the Tokugawa era as the first stage in the rise of an indigenous form of capitalism.

Eventually, the increased pace of industrial activity spread beyond the cities into rural areas. As in Great Britain, cotton was a major factor. Cotton had been introduced to China during the Song dynasty and had spread to Korea and Japan shortly thereafter. Traditionally, however, cotton cloth had been too expensive for the common people, who instead wore clothing made of hemp. Imports increased during the sixteenth century, however, when cotton cloth began to be used for uniforms, matchlock fuses, and sails. Eventually, technological advances reduced the cost, and specialized communities for producing cotton cloth began to appear in the countryside and were gradually transformed into towns. By the eighteenth century, cotton had firmly replaced hemp as the clothing of choice for most Japanese.

Not everyone benefited from the economic changes of the seventeenth and eighteenth centuries, however, notably the samurai, who were barred by tradition and prejudice from commercial activities. Although some profited from their transformation into a managerial class on the daimyo domains, most still relied on their revenues from

MAP 17.3 Tokugawa Japan

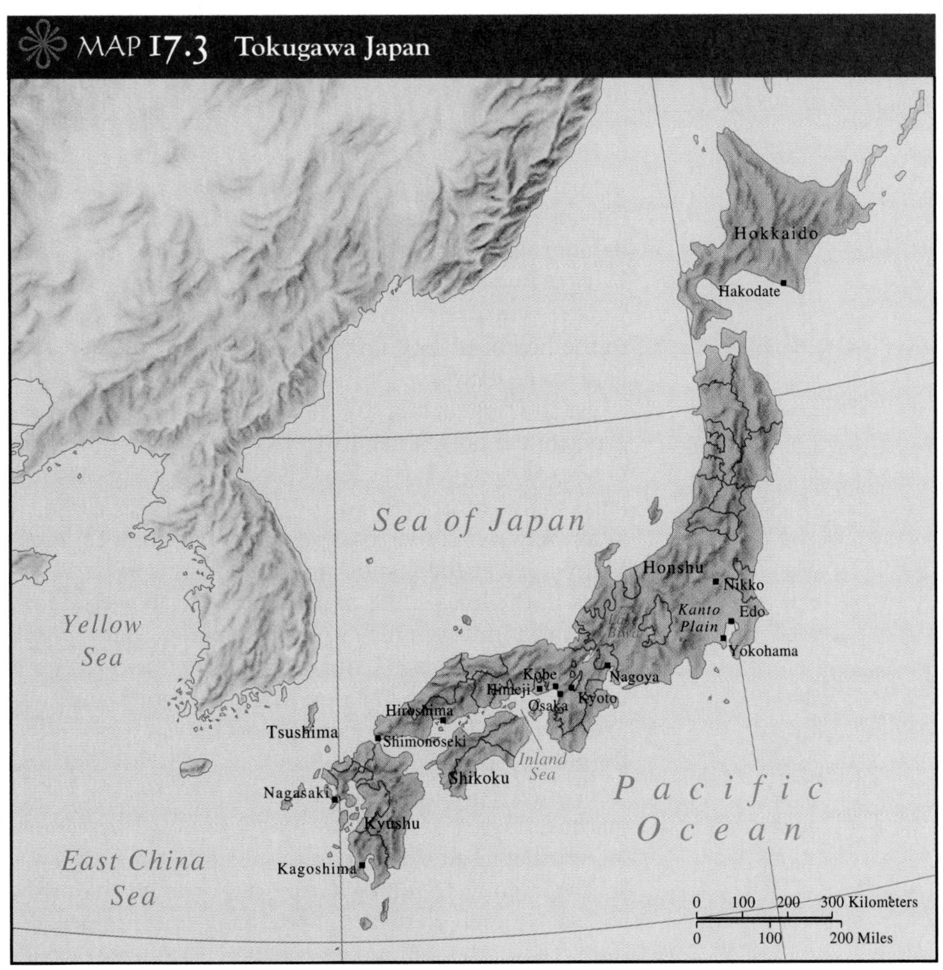

rice lands, which were often insufficient to cover their rising expenses; consequently, they fell heavily into debt. Others were released from servitude to their lord and became "masterless samurai." Occasionally, these unemployed warriors (known as *ronin*, or "wave men") revolted or plotted against the local authorities. In one episode, made famous in song and story as the "Forty-Seven Ronin," the masterless samurai of a local lord who had been forced to commit suicide by a shogunate official later assassinated the official in revenge. Although their act received wide popular acclaim, the *ronin* were later forced to take their own lives.

The effects of economic developments on the rural population during the Tokugawa era are harder to estimate. Some farm families benefited by exploiting the growing demand for cash crops. But not all prospered. Most peasants continued to rely on rice cultivation and were whipsawed between declining profits and rising costs and taxes (as daimyo expenses increased, land taxes often took up to 50 percent of the annual harvest). Many were forced to become tenants or to work as wage laborers on the farms of wealthy neighbors or in village industries. When rural conditions in some areas became desperate, peasant revolts erupted. According to one estimate, nearly seven thousand disturbances took place during the Tokugawa era. In general, though, the rural unrest during the Tokugawa era was probably motivated less by a decline in the standard of living than by local factors and a new sense of peasant assertiveness. Peasant disturbances became a more or less routine means of protesting against rising taxes and official corruption or of demanding "benevolence" from the manor lord in times of climatic disaster.

Some Japanese historians, influenced by a Marxist view of history, have interpreted such evidence as an indication that the Tokugawa economic system was highly exploitative, with feudal aristocrats oppressing powerless peasants. Recent scholars, however, have tended to adopt a more balanced view, maintaining that agriculture as well as manufacturing and commerce experienced extensive growth. Some point out that although the population doubled in the seventeenth century, a relatively low rate for the time period, so did the amount of cultivable land, while agricultural technology made significant advances.

CHRONOLOGY

JAPAN AND KOREA DURING THE EARLY MODERN ERA

First phonetic alphabet in Korea	Fifteenth century
Portuguese merchants arrive in Japan	1543
Francis Xavier arrives in Japan	1549
Rule of Oda Nobunaga	1568–1582
Seizure of Kyoto	1568
Rule of Toyotomi Hideyoshi	1582–1598
Edict prohibiting Christianity in Japan	1587
Invades Korea	1592
Death of Toyotomi Hideyoshi and withdrawal of army from Korea	1598
Rule of Tokugawa Ieyasu	1598–1616
Creation of Tokugawa shogunate	1603
Dutch granted permission to trade at Nagasaki	1609
Order evicting Christian missionaries	1612
Christian uprising suppressed	1637
Dutch post at Nagasaki transferred to Hirado	1641
Incident of forty-seven *ronin*	1702

The relatively low rate of population growth probably meant that Japanese peasants were spared the kind of land hunger that many of their counterparts in China faced. Recent evidence indicates that the primary reasons for the relatively low rate of population growth were late marriage, abortion, and infanticide. As Honda Toshiaki, a late-eighteenth-century demographer, described:

> Aware that if they have many children they will not have any property to leave them, [husbands and wives] confer and decide that rather than rear children who in later years will have great difficulty in making a decent living, it is better to take precautions before they are born and not add another mouth to feed. If they do have a child, they secretly destroy it, calling the process by the euphemism of "thinning out."[13]

Life in the Village

The changes that took place during the Tokugawa era had a major impact on the lives of ordinary Japanese. In some respects, the result was an increase in the power of the central government at the village level. The shogunate increasingly relied on Confucian maxims advocating obedience and hierarchy to enhance its authority with the general population. Decrees from the *bakufu* instructed the peasants on all aspects of their lives, including their eating habits and their behavior (see the box on p. 509). At the same time, the increased power of the government led to more autonomy from the local daimyo for the peasants. Villages now had more control over their local affairs and were responsible to the central government as much as to the nearby manor lord, although land taxes were still paid to the daimyo.

At the same time, the Tokugawa era saw the emergence of the nuclear family (*ie*) as the basic unit in Japanese society. In previous times, Japanese peasants had few legal rights. Most were too poor to keep their conjugal family unit intact or to pass property on to their children. Many lived at the manorial residence or worked as servants in the households of more affluent villagers. Now, with farm income on the rise, the nuclear family took on the same form as in China, although without the joint family concept. The Japanese system of inheritance was based on primogeniture. Family property was passed on to the eldest son, although younger sons often received land from their parents to set up their own families after marriage.

Another result of the changes under the Tokugawa was that women were somewhat more restricted than they had been previously. The rights of females were especially restricted in the samurai class, where Confucian values were highly influential. Male heads of households had broad authority over property, marriage, and divorce; wives were expected to obey their husbands on pain of death. Males often took concubines or homosexual partners, while females were expected to remain chaste. The male offspring of samurai parents studied the Confucian classics in schools established by the daimyo, while females were reared at home, where only the fortunate might receive a rudimentary training in Chinese characters. Some women, however, became accomplished poets and painters since, in aristocratic circles, female literacy was prized for enhancing the refinement, social graces, and moral virtue of the home. Under the Tokugawa, it was the obligation of the wife in elite families to reflect her husband's rank and status through a strict code of comportment and dress.

Women were similarly at a disadvantage among the common people. Marriages were arranged, and as in China, the new wife moved in with the family of her husband. A wife who did not meet the expectations of her spouse or his family was likely to be divorced. Still, gender relations were more egalitarian than among the nobility. Women were generally valued as childbearers and homemakers, and both sexes worked in the fields. Coeducational schools were established in villages and

FOLLOWING THE STRAIGHT AND NARROW IN TOKUGAWA JAPAN

Like the Qing dynasty in China, the Tokugawa shoguns attempted to keep their subjects in line with decrees that carefully prescribed all kinds of behavior. As this decree, which was circulated in all Japanese villages, shows, the bakufu *sought to be the moral instructor as well as the guardian and protector of the Japanese people. Compare and contrast this decree with Emperor Kangxi's Sacred Edict in the box earlier in this chapter.*

MAXIMS FOR PEASANT BEHAVIOR

1. Young people are forbidden to congregate in great numbers.
2. Entertainments unsuited to peasants, such as playing the samisen or reciting ballad dramas, are forbidden.
3. Staging sumo matches is forbidden for the next five years.
4. The edict on frugality issued by the *han* at the end of last year must be observed.
5. Social relations in the village must be conducted harmoniously.
6. If a person has to leave the village for business or pleasure, that person must return by ten at night.
7. Father and son are forbidden to stay overnight at another person's house. An exception is to be made if it is to nurse a sick person.
8. Corvée [obligatory labor] assigned by the *han* must be performed faithfully.
9. Children who practice filial piety must be rewarded.
10. One must never get drunk and cause trouble for others.
11. Peasants who farm especially diligently must be rewarded.
12. Peasants who neglect farm work and cultivate their paddies and upland fields in a slovenly and careless fashion must be punished.
13. The boundary lines of paddy and upland fields must not be changed arbitrarily.
14. Recognition must be accorded to peasants who contribute greatly to village political affairs.
15. Fights and quarrels are forbidden in the village.
16. The deteriorating customs and morals of the village must be rectified.
17. Peasants who are suffering from poverty must be identified and helped.
18. This village has a proud history compared to other villages, but in recent years bad times have come upon us. Everyone must rise at six in the morning, cut grass, and work hard to revitalize the village.
19. The punishments to be meted out to violators of the village code and gifts to be awarded the deserving are to be decided during the last assembly meeting of the year.

market towns, and about one-quarter of the students were female. Poor families, however, often put infant daughters to death or sold them into prostitution and the "floating world" of entertainment (see The Literature of the New Middle Class later in this chapter). During the late Tokugawa era, peasant women became more outspoken and active in social protests and in some cases played a major role in provoking demonstrations against government exactions or exploitative acts by landlords or merchants.

Such attitudes toward women operated within the context of the increasingly rigid stratification of Japanese society. Deeply conservative in their social policies, the Tokugawa rulers established strict legal distinctions between the four main classes in Japan (warriors, artisans, peasants, and merchants). Intermarriage between classes was forbidden in theory, although sometimes the prohibitions were ignored in practice. Below these classes were Japan's outcasts, the *eta*. Formerly, they were permitted to escape their status, at least in theory. The Tokugawa made their status hereditary and enacted severe discriminatory laws against them, regulating their place of residence, their dress, and even their hairstyles.

Tokugawa Culture

Under the Tokugawa, the tensions between the old society and the emerging new one were starkly reflected in the arena of culture. On the one hand, the classical culture, influenced by Confucian themes, Buddhist quietism, and the samurai warrior tradition, continued to flourish under the patronage of the shogunate. On the other, a vital new set of cultural values began to appear, especially in the cities. This innovative era witnessed the rise of popular literature written by and for the townspeople. With the development of woodblock printing in the early seventeenth century, literature became available to the common people, literacy levels rose, and lending libraries increased the accessibility of the printed word. In contrast to the previous mood of doom and gloom, the new prose was cheerful and even frivolous, its primary aim being to divert and amuse.

THE LITERATURE OF THE NEW MIDDLE CLASS

The best examples of this new urban fiction are the works of Saikaku (1642–1693), considered to be one of Japan's greatest novelists. Saikaku's greatest novel, *Five Women Who Loved Love,* relates the amorous exploits of five women of the merchant class. Based partly on real-life experiences, it broke from the Confucian ethic of wifely fidelity to her husband and portrayed women who were willing to die for love—and all but one eventually did. Despite the tragic circumstances, the tone of the novel is upbeat and sometimes comic, as the author's wry comments prevent the reader from becoming emotionally involved with the heroines' misfortunes. After all, they are experiencing a unique passionate love, and death is but a small price to pay for ecstasy.

THE FLOATING WORLD OF EDO. In eighteenth-century Japan, the self-confidence of the newly affluent bourgeoisie expressed itself in the woodblock print. Many prints portrayed "the floating world," as the pleasure district in Edo was called. Seen here are courtesans, storytellers, jesters, and various other entertainers. Like their counterparts in Europe, city-dwellers in Japan were beginning to create a new popular culture distinct from the elite culture of the nobility.

In addition to heterosexual novels for the merchant class, Saikaku wrote of homosexual liaisons among the samurai.

In the theater, the rise of *kabuki* threatened the long dominance of the *no* play, replacing the somewhat restrained and elegant thematic and stylistic approach of the classical drama with a new emphasis on violence, music, and dramatic gestures. Significantly, the new drama emerged not from the rarefied world of the court but from the new world of entertainment and amusement. Its very commercial success, however, led to difficulties with the government, which periodically attempted to restrict or even suppress it. Early *kabuki* was often performed by prostitutes and depicted the increasingly popular "floating world" of brothels, teahouses, and dance halls that began to proliferate in the growing cities. Shogunate officials feared that such activities could have a corrupting effect on the nation's morals and prohibited women from appearing on the stage; at the same time, they attempted to create a new professional class of male actors to impersonate female characters on stage. The decree had a mixed effect, however, because it encouraged homosexual activities, which had been popular among the samurai and in Buddhist monasteries since medieval times. Yet the use of male actors also promoted a greater emphasis on physical activities such as acrobatics and swordplay and furthered the evolution of *kabuki* into a mature dramatic art.

In contrast to the popular literature of the Tokugawa period, poetry persevered in its more serious tradition. Although linked verse, so popular in the fourteenth and fifteenth centuries, found a more lighthearted expression in the sixteenth century, the most exquisite poetry was produced in the seventeenth century by the greatest of all Japanese poets, Basho (1644–1694). He was concerned with the search for the meaning of existence and the poetic expression of his experience. Basho's genius lies in his sudden juxtaposition of a general or eternal condition with an immediate perception, an electrical spark that instantly reveals a moment of truth. With his love of Daoism and Zen Buddhism, Basho found answers to his quest for the meaning of life in nature, and his poems are grounded in seasonal imagery. The following are among his most famous poems:

The ancient pond
A frog leaps in
The sound of the water.

On the withered branch
A crow has alighted—
The end of autumn.

His last poem, dictated to a disciple only three days prior to his death, succinctly expressed his frustration with the unfinished business of life:

On a journey, ailing—
my dreams roam about
on a withered moor.

A JAPANESE CASTLE. In imitation of European castle architecture, the Japanese perfected a new type of fortress-palace in the early seventeenth century. Strategically placed high on a hilltop, constructed of heavy stone with tiny windows and fortified by numerous watchtowers and massive walls, these strongholds were impregnable to arrows and catapults. They served as a residence for the local daimyo, while the castle compound also housed his army and contained the seat of the local government. Himeji castle, shown here, is one of the most beautiful in Japan.

Like all great artists, Basho made his poems appear effortless and simple. He speaks directly to everyone, everywhere.

TOKUGAWA ART

Art also reflected the dynamism and changes in Japanese culture under the Tokugawa regime. The shogun's order that all daimyo and their families live every other year in Edo set off a burst of building as provincial rulers competed to erect the most magnificent mansion. Furthermore, the shoguns themselves constructed splendid castles adorned with sumptuous, almost ostentatious decor and furnishings. Lastly, the prosperity of the newly rising merchant class added fuel to the fire. Japanese paintings, architecture, textiles, and ceramics all flourished during this affluent era.

Court painters filled magnificent multipaneled screens with gold foil, which was also used to cover walls and even ceilings. This lavish use of gold foil mirrored the grandeur of the new Japanese rulers but also served a practical purpose: it reflected light in the dark castle rooms, where windows were kept small for defensive purposes. In contrast to the almost gaudy splendors of court painting, however, some Japanese artists of the late sixteenth century returned to the tradition of black ink wash. No longer copying the Chinese, these masterpieces expressed Japanese themes and techniques. In *Pine Forest* by Tohaku, a pair of six-panel screens depicting pine trees, 85 percent of the paper is left blank, suggesting mist and the quiet of an autumn dawn.

Although Japan was isolated from the Western world during much of the Tokugawa era, Japanese art was enriched by ideas from other cultures. Japanese pottery makers borrowed both techniques and designs from Korea to produce handsome ceramics. The passion for "Dutch learning" inspired Japanese to study Western medicine, astronomy, and languages and also led to experimentation with oil painting and Western ideas of perspective and the interplay of light and dark. Some painters depicted the "southern barbarians," with their strange ships and costumes, large noses, and plumed hats. Europeans desired Japanese lacquerware and metalwork, inlaid with ivory and mother-of-pearl, and especially the ceramics, which were now as highly prized as those of the Chinese.

Perhaps the most famous of all Japanese art of the Tokugawa era is the woodblock print. Genre painting, or representations of daily life, began in the sixteenth century and found its new mass-produced form in the eighteenth-century woodblock print. The now literate mercantile class was eager for illustrated texts of the amusing and bawdy tales that had circulated in oral tradition. At first, these prints were done in black and white, but later they included vibrant colors. The self-confidence of the age is dramatically captured in these prints, which represent a collective self-portrait of the late Tokugawa urban classes. Some prints depict entire city blocks filled with people, trades, and festivals, while others show the interiors of houses; thus, they provide us with excellent visual documentation of the times. Others portray the "floating world" of the entertainment quarter, with scenes of carefree revelers enjoying the pleasures of life.

One of the most renowned of the numerous block-print artists was Utamaro (1754–1806), who painted erotic and sardonic women in everyday poses, such as walking down the street, cooking, or drying their bodies after a bath. Hokusai (1760–1849) was famous for *Thirty-Six Views of Mount Fuji*, which created a new and bold interpretation of the Japanese landscape. Finally, Hiroshige (1797–1858) developed the genre of the travelogue print in his *Fifty-Three Stages of the Tokaido Highway*, which presented ordinary scenes of daily life, both in the country and in the cities, all enveloped in a lyrical, quiet mood.

Why did a new popular culture begin to appear in Tokugawa Japan, while traditional values continued to prevail in neighboring China? Certainly, one factor was the rapid growth of the cities as the main point of convergence for all the dynamic forces taking place in Japanese society. But other factors may have been at work as well. Despite the patent efforts of the Tokugawa rulers to promote traditional Confucian values, Confucian doctrine had historically occupied a relatively weak position in Japanese society. In China the scholar-gentry class served as the traditional defenders and propagators of traditional orthodoxy, but the samurai, who were steeped in warrior values and had little exposure to Confucian learning, did not play a similar role in Japan. Tokugawa policies also contributed. Whereas the scholar-gentry class in Qing China continued to reside in the villages, serving as members of the local council or as instructors in local schools, the samurai class in Japan was deliberately isolated by government fiat and class privilege from the remainder of the population. The result was an ideological and cultural vacuum that would eventually be filled by the growing population of merchants and artisans in the major cities.

Korea: The Hermit Kingdom

While Japan was gradually moving away from its agrarian origins, the Yi dynasty in Korea was attempting to pattern its own society on the Chinese model. The dynasty had been founded by the military commander Yi Song Gye in the late fourteenth century and immediately set out to establish close political and cultural relations with the Ming dynasty. From their new capital at Seoul, located on the Han River in the center of the peninsula, the Yi rulers accepted a tributary relationship with their powerful neighbor and engaged in the wholesale adoption of Chinese institutions and values. As in China, the civil service examinations tested candidates on their knowledge of the Confucian classics, and success was viewed as an essential step toward upward mobility.

There were differences, however. As in Japan, the dynasty continued to restrict entry into the bureaucracy to members of the aristocratic class, known in Korea as the *yangban* (or "two groups," the civilian and military). At the same time, the peasantry remained in virtually serflike conditions, working on government estates or on the manor holdings of the landed elite. A class of slaves (*chonmin*) labored on government plantations or served in certain occupations, such as butchers and entertainers, considered beneath the dignity of other groups in the population.

Eventually, Korean society began to show signs of independence from Chinese orthodoxy. In the fifteenth century, a phonetic alphabet for writing the Korean spoken language (*hangul*) was devised. Although it was initially held in contempt by the elites and used primarily as a teaching device, eventually it became the medium for private correspondence and the publishing of fictional stories for a popular audience. At the same time, changes were taking place in the economy, where rising agricultural production contributed to a population increase and the appearance of a small urban industrial and commercial sector, and in society, where the long domination of the *yangban* class began to weaken. As their numbers increased and their power and influence declined, some *yangban* became merchants or even moved into the ranks of the peasantry, thus further blurring the distinction between the aristocratic class and the common people.

In general, Korean rulers tried to keep the country isolated from the outside world, but they were not always successful. The Japanese invasion under Toyotomi Hideyoshi in the late sixteenth century had a disastrous impact on Korean society. A Manchu force invaded northern Korea in the 1630s and eventually compelled the Yi dynasty to grant allegiance to the new imperial government in Beijing. Korea was relatively untouched by the arrival of European merchants and missionaries, although information about Christianity was brought to the peninsula by Koreans returning from tribute missions to China, and a small Catholic community was established there in the late eighteenth century.

Conclusion

When Christopher Columbus sailed from southern Spain in his three ships in August of 1492, he was seeking a route to China and Japan. He did not find it, but others soon

SEOUL PALACE PAGODA. When the Yi dynasty came into power in the late fourteenth century, it established its capital at Seoul on the Han River. There it constructed a new palace. Korean public architecture was highly influenced by the Chinese classical model, as the multitiered pagoda on the palace grounds attests.

did. In 1514, Portuguese ships arrived on the coast of southern China. Thirty years later, a small contingent of Portuguese merchants became the first Europeans to set foot on the islands of Japan.

At first the new arrivals were welcomed, if only as curiosities. Eventually, several European nations established trade relations with China and Japan, and Christian missionaries of various religious orders were active in both countries and in Korea as well. But their success was short-lived. Europeans eventually began to appear as a detriment to law and order, and during the seventeenth century, the majority of the foreign merchants and missionaries were evicted from all three countries. From that time until the middle of the nineteenth century, China, Japan, and Korea were relatively little affected by events taking place beyond their borders.

For long, that fact has deluded many observers into the assumption that the societies of East Asia were essentially stagnant, characterized by agrarian institutions and values reminiscent of those of the feudal era in Europe. As we have seen, however, that picture is misleading, for all three countries were changing and by the early nineteenth century were quite different from what they had been three centuries earlier.

Ironically, these changes were especially marked in Tokugawa Japan, an allegedly "closed country," where traditional classes and institutions were under increasing strain, not only from the emergence of a new merchant class, but also from the centralizing tendencies of the powerful Tokugawa shogunate. Some historians have seen strong parallels between Tokugawa Japan and early modern Europe, which gave birth to centralized empires and a strong merchant class during the same period. The image of the monarchy is reflected in a song sung at the shrine of Toyotomi Hideyoshi in Kyoto:

Who's that
Holding over four hundred provinces
In the palm of his hand
And entertaining at a tea-party?
It's His Highness
So mighty, so impressive![14]

By the beginning of the nineteenth century, then, powerful tensions, reflecting a growing gap between ideal and reality, were at work in both Chinese and Japanese society. Under these conditions, both countries were soon forced to face a new challenge from the aggressive power of an industrializing Europe.

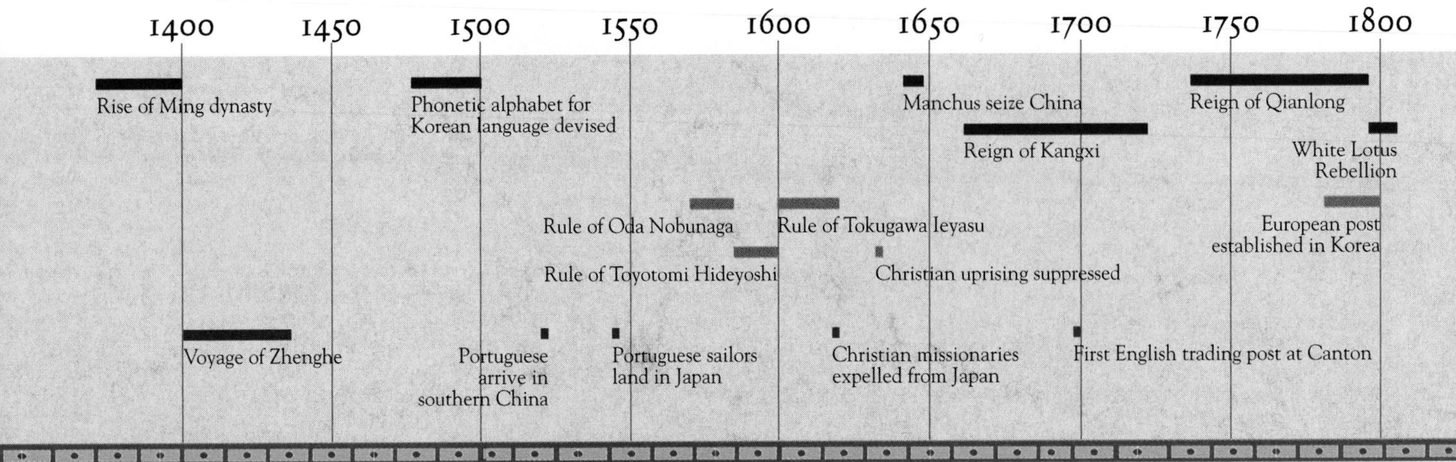

 Chapter Notes

1. From Jonathan D. Spence, *Emperor of China: Self-Portrait of K'ang Hsi* (New York, 1974), pp. 143–44.
2. Quoted in J. H. Parry, ed., *The European Reconnaissance: Selected Documents* (New York, 1968), p. 129.
3. Richard Strassberg, *The World of K'ang Shang-jen: A Man of Letters in Early Ch'ing China* (New York, 1983), p. 275.
4. Quoted in Frederick Wakeman, Jr., *The Great Enterprise* (Berkeley, Calif., 1985), p. 16.
5. Lynn Struve, *The Southern Ming, 1644–1662* (New Haven, Conn., 1984), p. 61.
6. Jonathan D. Spence, *The Search for Modern China* (New York, 1990), p. 123, citing J. L. Cranmer-Byng, *An Embassy to China: Lord MacArtney's Journal, 1793–1794* (London, 1912), p. 340.
7. Daniel J. Boorstin, *The Discoverers: A History of Man's Search to Know His World and Himself* (New York, 1983), p. 63.
8. Parry, *The European Reconnaissance*, citing C. R. Boxer, ed., *South China in the Sixteenth Century* (London, 1953), p. 265.
9. Chie Nakane and Sinzaburo Oishi, eds., *Tokugawa Japan* (Tokyo, 1990), p. 14.
10. Quoted in Jurgis Elisonas, "Christianity and the daimyo," in John Whitney Hall, ed., *The Cambridge History of Japan*, vol. 4 (Cambridge, 1991), p. 360.
11. Engelbert Kaempfer, *The History of Japan: Together with a Description of the Kingdom of Siam, 1690–1692*, vol. 2 (Glasgow, 1906), pp. 173–74.
12. Parry, *The European Reconnaissance*, p. 144.
13. Quoted in Donald Keene, *The Japanese Discovery of Europe, 1720–1830*, rev. ed. (Stanford, Calif., 1969), p. 114.
14. Quoted in Ryusaku Tsunda et al., *Sources of Japanese Tradition* (New York, 1964), p. 313.

Suggested Readings

For a general overview of this period in East Asian history, see J. K. Fairbank, E. O. Reischauer, and A. Craig, *East Asia: Tradition and Transformation* (Boston, 1973), and C. Shirokauer, *A Brief History of Chinese and Japanese Civilizations*, 2d ed. (San Diego, 1989). A more detailed treatment of specific issues can be found in volumes 8 and 9 of F. W. Mote and D. Twitchett, eds., *The Cambridge History of China* (Cambridge, 1976), and J. W. Hall, ed., *The Cambridge History of Japan*, vol. 4 (Cambridge, 1991).

The best documentary surveys are W. T. de Bary, *Sources of Chinese Tradition* (New York, 1964), and R. Tsunoda, W. T. de Bary, and D. Keene, *Sources of Japanese Tradition* (New York, 1958). Also, see F. Schurmann and O. Schell, *The China Reader*, vol. 1 (New York, 1967). Early documents on European activities can be found in J. H. Parry, *The European Reconnaissance: Selected Documents* (New York, 1968).

On the late Ming, see J. D. Spence, *The Search for Modern China* (New York, 1990), and L. Struve, *The Southern Ming, 1644–1662* (New Haven, Conn., 1984). On the rise of the Qing, see F. Wakeman, Jr., *The Great Enterprise: The Manchu Reconstruction of Imperial Order in Seventeenth Century China* (Berkeley, Calif., 1985). On Kangxi, see J. D. Spence, *Emperor of China: Self-Portrait of K'ang Hsi* (New York, 1974). Social issues are discussed in S. Naquin and E. Rawski, *Chinese Society in the Eighteenth Century* (New Haven, Conn., 1987). Also, see J. D. Spence and J. Wills, eds., *From Ming to Ch'ing* (New Haven, Conn., 1979). For a very interesting account of Jesuit missionary experiences in China, see L. J. Gallagher, ed. and trans., *China in the Sixteenth Century: The Journals of Matthew Ricci, 1583–1616* (New York, 1953). For brief biographies of Ming-Qing luminaries such as Wang Yangming, Zheng Chenggong, and the Emperor Qianlong, see J. E. Wills, Jr., *Mountains of Fame: Portraits in Chinese History* (Princeton, N.J., 1994).

The best surveys of Chinese literature are Liu Wu-chi, *An Introduction to Chinese Literature* (Bloomington, Ind., 1966); S. Owen, *An Anthology of Chinese Literature: Beginnings to 1911* (New York,

1996); and V. Mair, *The Columbia Anthology of Traditional Chinese Literature* (New York, 1994). For a concise and comprehensive introduction to the Chinese art of this period, see M. Sullivan, *The Arts of China*, 4th ed. (Berkeley, Calif., 1999); C. Clunas, *Art in China* (Oxford, 1997); and M. Tregear, *Chinese Art*, rev. ed. (London, 1997). For the best introduction to the painting of this era, see J. Cahill, *Chinese Painting* (New York, 1977), and Yang Xin et al., *Three Thousand Years of Chinese Paintings* (New Haven, Conn., 1997).

On Japan before the rise of the Tokugawa, see J. W. Hall, et al., eds., *Japan Before Tokugawa: Political Consolidation and Economic Growth* (Princeton, N.J., 1981), and G. Elison and B. L. Smith, eds., *Warlords, Artists, and Commoners: Japan in the Sixteenth Century* (Honolulu, 1981). See also M. E. Berry, *Hideyoshi* (Cambridge, Mass., 1982), the first biography of this fascinating figure in Japanese history. On the first Christian activities, see G. Elison, *Deus Destroyed: The Image of Christianity in Early Modern Japan* (Cambridge, Mass., 1973), and C. R. Boxer, *The Christian Century in Japan, 1549–1650* (Berkeley, Calif., 1951). Buddhism is dealt with in N. McMullin, *Buddhism and the State in Sixteenth Century Japan* (Princeton, N.J., 1984).

On the Tokugawa, see H. Bolitho, *Treasures Among Men: The Fudai Daimyo in Tokugawa Japan* (New Haven, Conn., 1974), and R. B. Toby, *State and Diplomacy in Early Modern Japan: Asia in the Development of the Tokugawa Bakufu* (Princeton, N.J., 1984). See also R. N. Bellah, *Tokugawa Religion: The Values of Pre-Industrial Japan* (New York, 1957). For a provocative interpretation of this period, see J. W. Dower, ed., *The Origins of the Meiji State: Selected Writings of E. H. Norman* (New York, 1975). See also C. I. Mulhern, ed., *Heroic with Grace: Legendary Women of Japan* (Armonk, N.Y., 1991). Three other recent studies are S. Vlastos, *Peasant Protests and Uprisings in Tokugawa Japan* (Berkeley, Calif., 1986); H. Ooms, *Tokugawa Ideology: Early Constructs, 1570–1680* (Princeton, N.J., 1985); and C. Nakane, ed., *Tokugawa Japan: The Social and Economic Antecedents of Modern Japan* (Tokyo, 1990).

For a brief introduction to women in the Ming and Qing dynasties as well as the Tokugawa era, see S. Hughes and B. Hughes, *Women in World History*, vol. 2 (Armonk, N.Y., 1997). To witness Chinese village life in 1670, consult the classic J. Spence, *The Death of Woman Wang* (New York, 1978). For women's literacy in seventeenth-century China, see J. Handlin, "Lu K'un's New Audience: The Influence of Women's Literacy on Sixteenth Century Thought," in *Women in Chinese Society*, eds. M. Wolf and R. Witke (Stanford, Calif., 1975), and D. Ko's, *Teachers of the Inner Chambers: Women and Culture in Seventeenth Century China* (Stanford, Calif., 1994). Most valuable is the collection of articles edited by G. L. Bernstein, *Recreating Japanese Women, 1600–1945* (Berkeley, Calif., 1991). For the role of peasant women in social protests, consult A. Walthall "Devoted Wives/Unruly Women: Invisible Presence in the History of Japanese Social Protest," in *Signs: Journal of Women in Culture and Society*, 1994, vol. 20, no. 1.

Of specific interest to Japanese literature of the Tokugawa era are D. Keene, *World Within Walls: Japanese Literature of the Pre-Modern Era, 1600–1867* (New York, 1976). Of special value for the college student are D. Keene's *Anthology of Japanese Literature* (New York, 1955), *The Pleasures of Japanese Literature* (New York, 1988), and *Japanese Literature: An Introduction for Western Readers* (London, 1953). For an introduction to Basho's life, poems, and criticism, consult the stimulating *Basho and His Interpreters: Selected Hokku with Commentary* (Stanford, Calif., 1991), by M. Ueda.

For the most comprehensive and accessible overview of Japanese art, see P. Mason, *Japanese Art* (New York, 1993). For a concise introduction to Japanese art of the Tokugawa era, see J. Stanley-Baker, *Japanese Art* (London, 1984). For magnificent photographs and stimulating interpretation, consult D. and V. Elisseeff, *Art of Japan* (New York, 1985), and J. E. Kidder, Jr., *The Art of Japan* (London, 1985).

For additional reading, go to InfoTrac College Edition, your online research library at http://web1.infotrac-college.com

Enter the search terms "Ming China" using Keywords.

Enter the search terms "China history" using Keywords.

Enter the search terms "Japan history" using Keywords.

Enter the search term "Tokugawa" using Keywords.

Enter the search term "Qing" using Keywords.

CHAPTER 18

Toward a New Heaven and a New Earth: An Intellectual Revolution in the West

CHAPTER OUTLINE

- THE SCIENTIFIC REVOLUTION
- THE ENLIGHTENMENT
- CULTURE AND SOCIETY IN AN AGE OF ENLIGHTENMENT
- RELIGION AND THE CHURCHES
- CONCLUSION

FOCUS QUESTIONS

- What did Copernicus, Kepler, Galileo, and Newton contribute to a new vision of the universe, and how did their vision differ from the Ptolemaic conception of the universe?
- Who were the leading figures of the Enlightenment, and what were their main contributions?
- What role did women play in the Scientific Revolution and the Enlightenment?
- How were the ideas of the Scientific Revolution and the Enlightenment disseminated, and what impact did they have on society?
- How did popular culture and popular religion differ from high culture and institutional religion in the eighteenth century?

In 1633, the Italian scientist Galileo was put on trial by the Catholic church for maintaining that the sun was the center of the universe and that the earth moves around the sun. Galileo, who was sixty-eight years old and in ill health, was kept waiting for two months before being tried and found guilty of heresy and disobedience. Completely shattered by the experience, he denounced his errors: "With a sincere heart and unfeigned faith I curse and detest the said errors and heresies contrary to the Holy Church, and I swear that I will nevermore in future say or assert anything that will give rise to a similar suspicion of me." Legend holds that when he left the trial room, Galileo muttered to himself: "And yet it does move!" Galileo was but one of the scientists of the seventeenth century who set the Western world on a new path known as the Scientific Revolution, which brought to Europeans a new way of viewing the universe and their place in it. In time, the Scientific Revolution would add to the European world's growing sense of power as the changes occurring in government, the economy, and military power increasingly enabled Europeans to dominate much of the rest of the world.

The Scientific Revolution affected only a small number of Europe's educated elite. But in the eighteenth century, this changed dramatically as a group of intellectuals known as the philosophes popularized the ideas of the Scientific Revolution and used them to undertake a dramatic reexamination of all aspects of life. The widespread impact of the philosophes' ideas on their society has caused historians ever since to call the eighteenth century in Europe the Age of Enlightenment.

For most of the philosophes, "enlightenment" included the rejection of traditional Christianity. The religious wars and intolerance of the sixteen and seventeenth centuries had created an environment in which intellectuals had become so disgusted with religious fanaticism that they were open to the new ideas of the Scientific Revolution. Whereas the great scientists of the seventeenth century believed that their work exalted God, the intellectuals of the eighteenth century read their conclusions a different way and increasingly turned their backs on their Christian heritage. Consequently, European intellectual life in the eighteenth century was marked by a revolutionary transition to the largely secular, rational, and materialistic perspective that in the nineteenth and twentieth centuries defined the modern Western mentality and dramatically affected much of the rest of the world as well.

The Scientific Revolution

In one sense, the Scientific Revolution was not a revolution. It was not characterized by the explosive change and rapid overthrow of traditional authority that we normally associate with the word *revolution*. The Scientific Revolution did overturn centuries of authority, but only in a gradual and piecemeal fashion.

Background to the Scientific Revolution

To say that the Scientific Revolution brought about a dissolution of the medieval worldview is not to say that the Middle Ages was a period of scientific ignorance. Many educated Europeans took an intense interest in the world around them because it was, after all, "God's handiwork" and therefore an appropriate subject for study. Many "natural philosophers," as medieval scientists were called, placed unquestioning reliance on a few ancient authorities, especially Aristotle and Galen, and preferred refined logical analysis to systematic observations of the natural world. A number of changes and advances in the fifteenth and sixteenth centuries may have played a major role in helping "natural philosophers" abandon their old views and develop new ones.

The Renaissance humanists mastered Greek as well as Latin and made available new works of Galen, Ptolemy, and Archimedes as well as Plato. These writings made it apparent that even the unquestioned authorities of the Middle Ages, Aristotle and Galen, had been contradicted by other thinkers. The desire to discover which school of thought was correct stimulated new scientific work that sometimes led to a complete rejection of the classical authorities.

Renaissance artists have also been credited with having an impact on scientific study. Their desire to imitate nature led them to rely on a close observation of nature. Their accurate renderings of rocks, plants, animals, and human anatomy established new standards for the study of natural phenomena. At the same time, the "scientific" study of the problems of perspective and correct anatomical proportions led to new insights. "No painter," one Renaissance intellectual declared, "can paint well without a thorough knowledge of geometry."[1]

Technical problems, such as calculating the tonnage of ships accurately, also stimulated scientific activity because they required careful observation and precise measurements. Then, too, the invention of new instruments and machines, such as the telescope and microscope, often made fresh scientific discoveries possible. Above all, the printing press played a crucial role in spreading innovative ideas quickly and easily.

Mathematics, which played such a fundamental role in the scientific achievements of the sixteenth and seventeenth centuries, was promoted in the Renaissance by the rediscovery of the works of ancient mathematicians and the influence of Plato, who had emphasized the importance of mathematics in explaining the universe. During the Renaissance, mathematics was not only applauded as the key to navigation, military science, and geography, but was also widely believed to be the key to

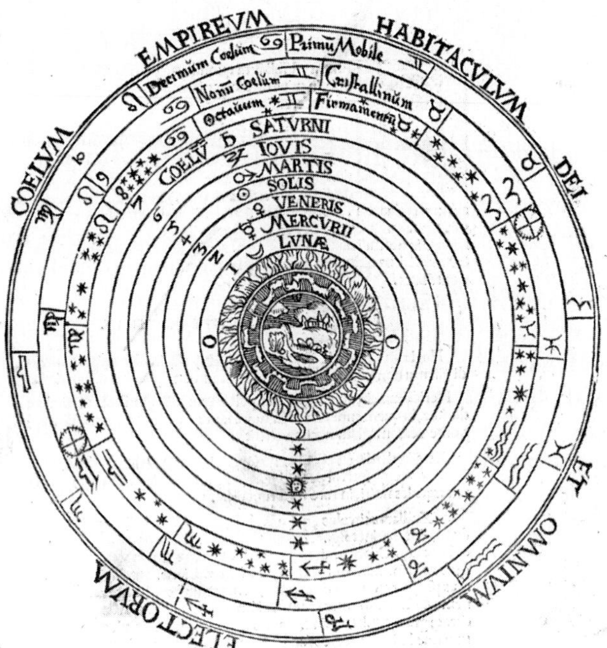

MEDIEVAL CONCEPTION OF THE UNIVERSE. As this sixteenth-century illustration shows, the medieval cosmological view placed the earth at the center of the universe, surrounded by a series of concentric spheres. The earth was imperfect and constantly changing, while the heavenly bodies that surrounded it were perfect and incorruptible. Beyond the tenth and final sphere was heaven, where God and all the saved souls were located.

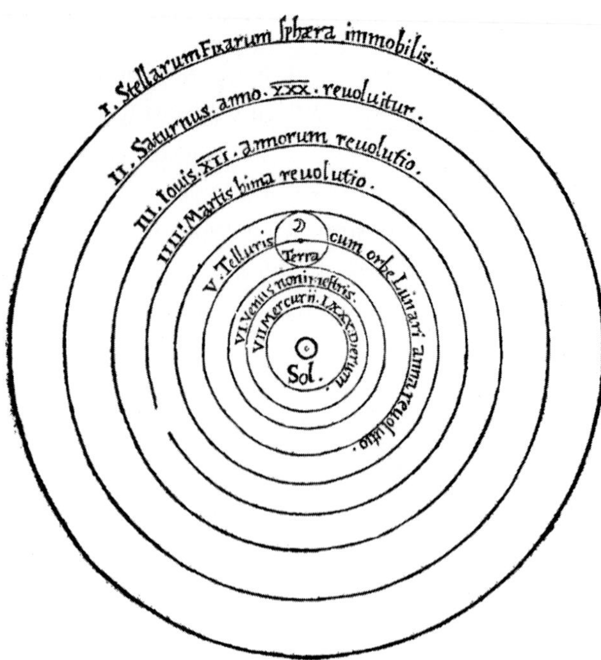

THE COPERNICAN SYSTEM. The Copernican system was presented in *On the Revolutions of the Heavenly Spheres*, published shortly before Copernicus's death. As shown in this illustration from the first edition of the book, Copernicus maintained that the sun was the center of the universe while the planets, including the earth, revolved around it. Moreover, the earth rotated daily on its axis.

understanding the nature of things. According to Leonardo da Vinci, God eternally geometrizes, so nature is inherently mathematical. Copernicus, Kepler, Galileo, and Newton were all great mathematicians who believed that the secrets of nature were written in the language of mathematics.

Another possible contributor to the origins of the Scientific Revolution was magic. Renaissance magic was the preserve of an intellectual elite from all of Europe. By the end of the sixteenth century, Hermetic magic had fused with alchemical thought to form a single intellectual framework. According to this tradition, the world was a living embodiment of divinity. Humans, who were also thought to have that spark of divinity within, could use magic, especially mathematical magic, to understand and dominate the world of nature or employ the powers of nature for beneficial purposes. Was it Hermeticism, then, that inaugurated the shift in consciousness that made the Scientific Revolution possible, since the desire to control and dominate the natural world was a crucial motivating force in the Scientific Revolution? Scholars debate the issue, but histories of the Scientific Revolution frequently overlook the fact that the great names we associate with the revolution in cosmology—Copernicus, Kepler, Galileo, and Newton—all had a serious interest in Hermetic ideas and the fields of astrology and alchemy. The mention of these names also reminds us of one final consideration in the origins of the Scientific Revolution: it largely resulted from the work of a handful of great intellectuals.

Toward a New Heaven: A Revolution in Astronomy

The philosophers of the Middle Ages had used the ideas of Aristotle, Claudius Ptolemy (the greatest astronomer of antiquity, who lived in the second century C.E.), and Christianity to construct the Ptolemaic or geocentric conception of the universe. In this conception, the universe was seen as a series of concentric spheres with a fixed or motionless earth at its center. Composed of material substance, the earth was imperfect and constantly changing. The spheres that surrounded the earth were made of a crystalline, transparent substance and moved in circular orbits around the earth. Circular movement, according to Aristotle, was the most "perfect" kind of motion and hence appropriate for the "perfect" heavenly bodies, which were thought to consist of a nonmaterial, incorruptible "quin-

ON THE REVOLUTIONS OF THE HEAVENLY SPHERES

Nicolaus Copernicus began a revolution in astronomy when he argued that the sun, not the earth, was at the center of the universe. Expecting controversy and scorn, Copernicus hesitated to publish the work in which he put forth his heliocentric theory. He finally relented, however, and managed to see a copy of it just before he died.

NICOLAUS COPERNICUS, *ON THE REVOLUTIONS OF THE HEAVENLY SPHERES*

For a long time, then, I reflected on this confusion in the astronomical traditions concerning the derivation of the motions of the universe's spheres. I began to be annoyed that the movements of the world machine, created for our sake by the best and most systematic Artisan of all, were not understood with greater certainty by the philosophers, who otherwise examined so precisely the most insignificant trifles of this world. For this reason I undertook the task of rereading the works of all the philosophers which I could obtain to learn whether anyone had ever proposed other motions of the universe's spheres than those expounded by the teachers of astronomy in the schools. And in fact first I found in Cicero that Hicetas supposed the earth to move. Later I also discovered in Plutarch that certain others were of this opinion. I have decided to set his words down here, so that they may be available to everybody:

> Some think that the earth remains at rest. But Philolaus the Pythagorean believes that, like the sun and moon, it revolves around the fire in an oblique circle. Heraclides of Pontus and Ecphantus the Pythagorean make the earth move, not in a progressive motion, but like a wheel in a rotation from the west to east about its own center.

Therefore, having obtained the opportunity from these sources, I too began to consider the mobility of the earth. And even though the idea seemed absurd, nevertheless I knew that others before me had been granted the freedom to imagine any circles whatever for the purpose of explaining the heavenly phenomena. Hence I thought that I too would be readily permitted to ascertain whether explanations sounder than those of my predecessors could be found for the revolution of the celestial spheres on the assumption of some motion of the earth.

Having thus assumed the motions which I ascribe to the earth later on in the volume, by long and intense study I finally found that if the motions of the other planets are correlated with the orbiting of the earth, and are computed for the revolution of each planet, not only do their phenomena follow therefrom but also the order and size of all the planets and spheres, and heaven itself is so linked together that in no portion of it can anything be shifted without disrupting the remaining parts and the universe as a whole. . . .

Hence I feel no shame in asserting that this whole region engirdled by the moon, and the center of the earth, traverse this grand circle amid the rest of the planets in an annual revolution around the sun. Near the sun is the center of the universe. Moreover, since the sun remains stationary, whatever appears as a motion of the sun is really due rather to the motion of the earth.

tessence." These heavenly bodies, pure orbs of light, were embedded in the moving, concentric spheres and in 1500 numbered ten. Working outward from the earth, the first eight spheres contained the moon, Mercury, Venus, the sun, Mars, Jupiter, Saturn, and the fixed stars. The ninth sphere imparted to the eighth sphere of the fixed stars its daily motion, while the tenth sphere was frequently described as the prime mover that moved itself and imparted motion to the other spheres. Beyond the tenth sphere was the Empyrean Heaven—the location of God and all the saved souls. This Christianized Ptolemaic universe, then, was a finite one. It had a fixed end in harmony with Christian thought and expectations. God and the saved souls were at one end of the universe, while humans were at the center. They had been given power over the earth, but their real purpose was to achieve salvation.

In May 1543, shortly before his death, Nicolaus Copernicus (1473–1543), who had studied mathematics and astronomy first at Cracow in his native Poland and later at the Italian universities of Bologna and Padua, published his famous book *On the Revolutions of the Heavenly Spheres*. Copernicus was a mathematician who felt that Ptolemy's geocentric system was too complicated and failed to accord with the observed motions of the heavenly bodies (see the box above). Copernicus hoped that his heliocentric or sun-centered conception would offer a more accurate explanation.

Copernicus argued that the universe consisted of eight spheres with the sun motionless at the center and the sphere of the fixed stars at rest in the eighth sphere. The planets revolved around the sun in the order of Mercury, Venus, the earth, Mars, Jupiter, and Saturn. The moon, however, revolved around the earth. Moreover, according to Copernicus, what appeared to be the movement of the sun and the fixed stars around the earth was really explained by the daily rotation of the earth on its axis and

THE STARRY MESSENGER

The Italian Galileo Galilei was the first European to use a telescope to make systematic observations of the heavens. His observations, as reported in The Starry Messenger *in 1610, stunned European intellectuals by revealing that the celestial bodies were not perfect and immutable, as had been believed, but were apparently composed of material substance similar to the earth. In this selection, Galileo describes how he devised a telescope and what he saw with it.*

GALILEO GALILEI, *THE STARRY MESSENGER*

About ten months ago a report reached my ears that a certain Fleming had constructed a spyglass by means of which visible objects, though very distant from the eye of the observer, were distinctly seen as if nearby. Of this truly remarkable effect several experiences were related, to which some persons gave credence while others denied them. A few days later the report was confirmed to me in a letter from a noble Frenchman at Paris, Jacques Badovere, which caused me to apply myself wholeheartedly to inquire into the means by which I might arrive at the invention of a similar instrument. This I did shortly afterwards, my basis being the theory of refraction. First I prepared a tube of lead, at the ends of which I fitted two glass lenses, both plane on one side while on the other side one was spherically convex and the other concave. Then placing my eye near the concave lens I perceived objects satisfactorily large and near, for they appeared three times closer and nine times larger than when seen with the naked eye alone. Next I constructed another one, more accurate, which represented objects as enlarged more than sixty times. Finally, sparing neither labor nor expense, I succeeded in constructing for myself so excellent an instrument that objects seen by means of it appeared nearly one thousand times larger and over thirty times closer than when regarded with our natural vision.

It would be superfluous to enumerate the number and importance of the advantages of such an instrument at sea as well as on land. But forsaking terrestrial observations, I turned to celestial ones, and first I saw the moon from as near at hand as if it were scarcely two terrestrial radii. After that I observed often with wondering delight both the planets and the fixed stars, and since I saw these latter to be very crowded, I began to seek (and eventually found) a method by which I might measure their distances apart. . . .

Now let us review the observations made during the past two months, once more inviting the attention of all who are eager for true philosophy to the first steps of such important contemplations. Let us speak first of that surface of the moon which faces us. For greater clarity I distinguish two parts of this surface, a lighter and a darker; the lighter part seems to surround and to pervade the whole hemisphere, while the darker part discolors the moon's surface like a kind of cloud, and makes it appear covered with spots. . . . From observation of these spots repeated many times I have been led to the opinion and conviction that the surface of the moon is not smooth, uniform, and precisely spherical as a great number of philosophers believe it (and the other heavenly bodies) to be, but is uneven, rough, and full of cavities and prominences, being not unlike the face of the earth, relieved by chains of mountains and deep valleys.

the journey of the earth around the sun each year. Copernicus, however, was basically conservative. He did not reject Aristotle's principle of the existence of heavenly spheres moving in circular orbits, and his system did not work considerably better than the Ptolemaic system.

The immediate response to Copernicus was muted—no revolution occurred overnight. Nevertheless, although most people were not yet ready to accept his theory, there were growing doubts about the Ptolemaic system. The next step in destroying the geocentric conception and supporting the Copernican system was taken by Johannes Kepler (1571–1630).

Kepler was a brilliant mathematician and astronomer who took a post as imperial mathematician to Emperor Rudolf II. Using the detailed astronomical data compiled by his predecessor, the astronomer Tycho Brahe, Kepler arrived at his laws of planetary motion that confirmed Copernicus's heliocentric theory. In his first law, however, he contradicted Copernicus by showing that the orbits of the planets around the sun were not circular but elliptical in shape with the sun at one focus of the ellipse rather than at the center.

Kepler's work effectively eliminated the idea of uniform circular motion as well as the idea of crystalline spheres revolving in circular orbits. The basic structure of the traditional Ptolemaic system had been destroyed, and people had been freed to think in new terms of the actual paths of planets revolving around the sun in elliptical orbits. By the end of Kepler's life, the Ptolemaic system was rapidly losing ground to the new ideas. Important questions remained unanswered, however. What were the planets made of? And how could motion in the universe be explained? It was an Italian scientist who achieved the next important breakthrough to a new cosmology by answering the first question.

Galileo Galilei (1564–1642) taught mathematics, first at Pisa and later at Padua, one of the most prestigious universities in Europe. Galileo was the first European to make systematic observations of the heavens by means of a telescope, thereby inaugurating a new age in astronomy. He had heard of a Flemish lens grinder who had created a "spyglass" that magnified objects seen at a distance and soon constructed his own after reading about it. Instead of peering at terrestrial objects, Galileo turned his telescope to the skies and made a remarkable series of discoveries: mountains on the moon, four moons revolving around Jupiter, the phases of Venus, and sunspots. Galileo's observations seemed to destroy yet another aspect of the geocentric conception in that the universe seemed to be composed of material substance similar to that of the earth rather than ethereal or perfect and unchanging substance.

Galileo's revelations, published in *The Starry Messenger* in 1610, stunned his contemporaries and probably did more to make Europeans aware of the new picture of the universe than did the mathematical theories of Copernicus and Kepler (see the box on p. 520). But even in the midst of his newfound acclaim, Galileo found himself increasingly suspect by the authorities of the Catholic church. The Roman Inquisition (or Holy Office) of the Catholic church condemned Copernicanism and ordered Galileo to abandon the Copernican thesis. The church attacked the Copernican system because it threatened not only Scripture, but also an entire conception of the universe. The heavens were no longer a spiritual world, but a world of matter. Humans were no longer at the center and God was no longer in a specific place. The new system raised such uncertainties that it seemed prudent simply to condemn it. In 1633, Galileo was found guilty of teaching the condemned Copernican system and was forced to recant his errors. Placed under house arrest on his estate near Florence, he spent the remaining eight years of his life studying mechanics, a field in which he made significant contributions.

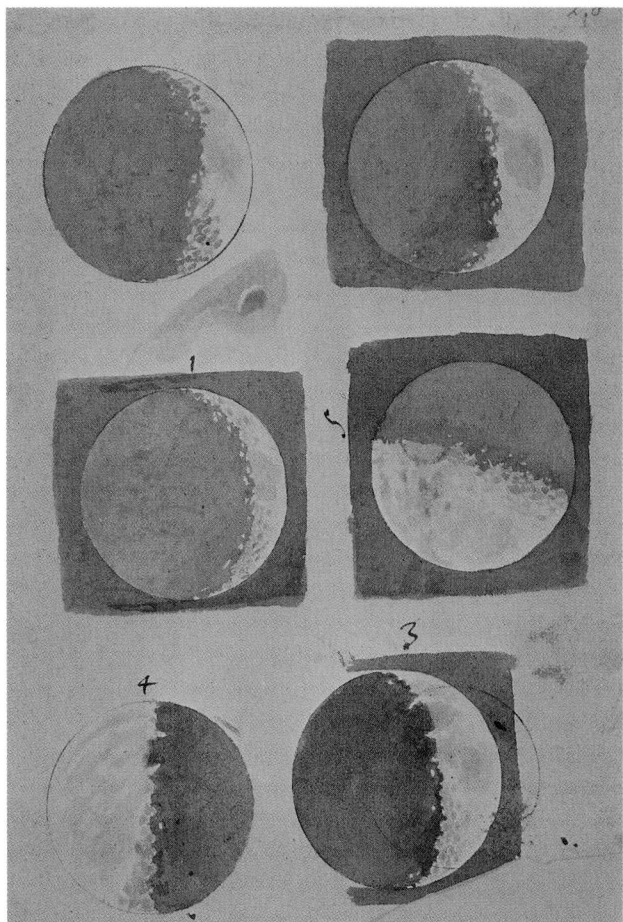

GALILEO'S SKETCH OF THE PHASES OF THE MOON. Galileo Galilei was the first European scientist to use a telescope in making systematic observations of the heavens. Galileo discovered mountains on the moon, sunspots, and the phases of Venus. Shown here are drawings of the moon from Galileo's notes for one of his books.

The condemnation of Galileo by the Inquisition seriously hampered further scientific work in Italy, which had been at the forefront of scientific innovation. Leadership in science now passed to the northern countries, especially England, France, and the Dutch Netherlands. By the 1630s and 1640s, no reasonable astronomer could overlook that Galileo's discoveries combined with Kepler's mathematical laws had made nonsense of the Ptolemaic-Aristotelian world system and clearly established the reasonableness of the Copernican model. Nevertheless, the problem of explaining motion in the universe and tying together the ideas of Copernicus, Galileo, and Kepler had not yet been solved. This would be the work of an Englishman who has long been considered the greatest genius of the Scientific Revolution.

Born in 1642, the young Isaac Newton showed little brilliance until he attended Cambridge University. In 1669, he accepted a chair of mathematics at the university. During an intense period of creativity from 1684 to 1686, he wrote his major work, *Mathematical Principles of Natural Philosophy*, known simply as the *Principia* by the first word of its Latin title. In this work, Newton set out the mathematical proofs demonstrating his universal law of gravitation. Newton's work was the culmination of the theories of Copernicus, Kepler, and Galileo. Although each had undermined some part of the Ptolemaic-Aristotelian cosmology, no one until Newton had pieced together a coherent synthesis for a new cosmology.

In the first book of the *Principia*, Newton defined the basic concepts of mechanics by elaborating the three laws of motion: the law of inertia, that every object continues in a state of rest or uniform motion in a straight line unless deflected by a force; that the rate of change of motion of an object is proportional to the force acting on it; and that to every action there is always an equal and opposite reaction. In Book Three, Newton applied his theories of mechanics to the problems of astronomy by demonstrating that these three laws of motion govern the planetary bodies as well as terrestrial objects. Integral to his whole argument was the use of the universal law of gravitation to explain why the planetary bodies did not go off in straight lines but continued in elliptical orbits about the sun. In mathematical terms, Newton explained that every object in the universe was attracted to every other object by a force called gravity.

The implications of Newton's universal law of gravitation were enormous, although it took another century before they were widely recognized. Newton had demonstrated that one universal law mathematically proved could explain all motion in the universe. The secrets of the natural world could be known by human investigations. At the same time, the Newtonian synthesis created a new cosmology in which the world was seen largely in mechanistic terms. The universe was one huge, regulated, and uniform machine that operated according to natural laws in absolute time, space, and motion. Although Newton believed that God was "everywhere present" and acted as the force that moved all bodies on the basis of the laws he had discovered, later generations dropped his spiritual assumptions. Newton's world-machine, conceived as operating absolutely in space, time, and motion, dominated the modern worldview until the twentieth century, when the Einsteinian revolution based on a concept of relativity superseded the Newtonian mechanistic concept.

CHRONOLOGY

IMPORTANT WORKS OF THE SCIENTIFIC REVOLUTION

Copernicus, *On the Revolutions of the Heavenly Spheres*	1543
Vesalius, *On the Fabric of the Human Body*	1543
Galileo, *The Starry Messenger*	1610
Harvey, *On the Motion of the Heart and Blood*	1628
Descartes, *Discourse on Method*	1637
Cavendish, *Grounds of Natural Philosophy*	1668
Newton, *Principia*	1687

The Breakthrough in Medicine

There was also a Scientific Revolution in medicine. Medicine in the Late Middle Ages was dominated by the teachings of the Greek physician Galen, who, like Ptolemy, had lived in the second century C.E. Galen had relied on animal, rather than human, dissection to arrive at a picture of human anatomy that was quite wrong in many instances. Physiology, the study of the functioning of the body, was also dominated by the ideas of Galen, including the belief that there were two separate blood systems: one controlled muscular activities and contained bright red blood moving upward and downward through the arteries; the other governed the digestive functions and contained dark red blood that ebbed and flowed in the veins.

Two major figures are associated with the changes in medicine in the sixteenth and seventeenth centuries: Andreas Vesalius and William Harvey. The new anatomy of the sixteenth century was the work of Andreas Vesalius (1514–1564), who studied medicine at Paris including the works of Galen. Especially important to him was a recently discovered text of Galen, *On Anatomical Procedures*, that led Vesalius to emphasize practical research as the principal avenue for understanding human anatomy. After receiving a doctorate in medicine at the University of Padua in 1536, he accepted a position there as professor of surgery. In 1543, he published his masterpiece, *On the Fabric of the Human Body*.

This book was based on his Paduan lectures, in which he deviated from traditional practice by personally dissecting a body to illustrate what he was discussing. Vesalius's anatomical treatise presented a careful examination of the individual organs and general structure of the human body. The book would not have been feasible without both the artistic advances of the Renaissance and the technical developments in the art of printing. Together, they made possible the creation of illustrations superior to any hitherto produced.

Vesalius's hands-on approach to teaching anatomy enabled him to overthrow some of Galen's most glaring errors. He did not hesitate, for example, to correct Galen's assertion that the great blood vessels originated at the liver because his own observations made it apparent that they came from the heart. Nevertheless, Vesalius still clung to a number of Galen's erroneous assertions, including the Greek physician's ideas on the ebb and flow of two kinds of blood in the veins and arteries. It was not until William Harvey's work on the circulation of the blood that this Galenic misperception was corrected.

William Harvey (1578–1657) attended Cambridge University and later Padua, where he received a doctorate of medicine in 1602. His reputation rests on his book *On the Motion of the Heart and Blood,* published in 1628. Although questions had been raised in the sixteenth century about Galen's physiological principles, no major break from his system had occurred. Harvey's work, which was based on meticulous observations and experiments, led him to demolish the ancient Greek's work. Harvey demonstrated that the heart and not the liver was the beginning point of the circulation of blood in the body, that the same blood flows in both veins and arteries, and, most importantly, that the blood makes a complete circuit as it passes through the body. Although Galen's ideas had received a severe blow, Harvey's work did not begin to achieve general recognition until the 1660s, when the capillaries, which explained how the body's blood passed from the arteries to the veins, were discovered. Harvey's theory of the circulation of the blood laid the foundation for modern physiology.

Women in the Origins of Modern Science

During the Middle Ages, except for members of religious orders, women who sought a life of learning were severely hampered by the traditional attitude that a woman's proper role was to be a daughter, wife, and mother. But in the late fourteenth and early fifteenth centuries, new opportunities for elite women emerged as enthusiasm for the new secular learning called humanism led Europe's privileged and learned men to encourage women to read and study classical and Christian texts. The ideal of a humanist education for some of the daughters of Europe's elite persisted into the seventeenth century.

In the same fashion as they were drawn to humanism, women were also attracted to the Scientific Revolution. Unlike females educated formally in humanist schools, women attracted to science had to obtain a largely informal education. European nobles had the leisure and resources that gave them easy access to the world of learning. This door was also open to noblewomen, who could participate in the informal scientific networks of their fathers and brothers. One of the most prominent female scientists of the seventeenth century, Margaret Cavendish (1623–1673), came from an aristocratic background. Cavendish was not a popularizer of science for women but a participant in the crucial scientific debates of her time. Despite her achievements, however, she was excluded from membership in the Royal Society (see The Spread of Scientific Knowledge later in this chapter), although she was once allowed to attend a meeting. She wrote a number of works on scientific matters, including *Observations upon Experimental Philosophy* and *Grounds of Natural Philosophy*. In these works she was especially critical of the growing belief that through science humans could master nature: "We have no power at all over natural causes and effects. . . . For man is but a small part, . . . his powers are but particular actions of Nature, and he cannot have a supreme and absolute power."[2]

MARGARET CAVENDISH. Shown in this portrait is Margaret Cavendish, the duchess of Newcastle. Her husband, who was thirty years older than she, encouraged her to pursue her literary interests. In addition to scientific works, she wrote plays, an autobiography, and a biography of her husband entitled *The Life of the Thrice Noble, High and Puissant Prince, William Cavendish, Duke, Marquess and Earl of Newcastle*. The autobiography and biography led one male literary critic to call her "a mad, conceited, and ridiculous woman."

As an aristocrat, the duchess of Cavendish was a good example of the women in France and England who worked in science. Women interested in science who lived in Germany came from a different background. There the tradition of female participation in crafts enabled some women to become involved in observational science, especially astronomy. Between 1650 and 1710, women constituted 14 percent of all German astronomers.

The most famous of the female astronomers in Germany was Maria Winkelmann (1670–1720). She was educated by her father and uncle and received advanced training in astronomy from a nearby self-taught astronomer. Her opportunity to be a practicing astronomer came when she married Gottfried Kirch, Germany's foremost astronomer. She became his assistant at the astronomical observatory operated in Berlin by the Academy of Science. She made some original contributions, including a hitherto undiscovered comet, as her husband related:

> Early in the morning (about 2:00 A.M.) the sky was clear and starry. Some nights before, I had observed a variable star, and my wife (as I slept) wanted to find and see it for herself. In so doing, she found a comet in the sky. At which time she woke me, and I found that it was indeed a comet . . . I was surprised that I had not seen it the night before.[3]

When her husband died in 1710, Winkelmann submitted herself as a candidate for a position as assistant astronomer, for which she was highly qualified. As a woman—with no university degree—she was denied the post by the Berlin Academy, which feared that it would establish a precedent by hiring a woman ("mouths would gape").

Winkelmann's difficulties with the Berlin Academy reflect the obstacles women faced in being accepted in scientific work, which was considered a male preserve.

Although no formal statutes excluded women from membership in the new scientific societies, no woman was invited to join either the Royal Society of England or the French Academy of Sciences until the twentieth century. All of these women scientists were exceptional women because a life devoted to any kind of scholarship was still viewed as at odds with the domestic duties women were expected to perform.

The nature and value of women had been the subject of an ongoing, centuries-long debate. Male opinions in the debate were largely a carryover from medieval times and were not favorable. Women were portrayed as inherently base, prone to vice, easily swayed, and "sexually insatiable." Hence, men needed to control them. Learned women were viewed as having overcome female liabilities to become like men. One man praised a woman scholar by remarking that her writings were so good that you "would hardly believe they were done by a woman at all."

In the seventeenth century, women joined this debate by arguing against the distorted images of women held by men. They argued that women also had rational minds and could grow from education. Further, since most women were pious, chaste, and temperate, there was no need for male authority over them. These female defenders of women emphasized education as the key to women's ability to move into the world. How, then, did the Scientific Revolution affect this debate over the nature of women? Since it was an era of intellectual revolution in which traditional authorities were being overthrown, we might expect significant change in men's views of women. But by and large, instead of becoming an instrument for liberation, science was used to find new support for the old, traditional views about a woman's true place in the scheme of things.

Overall the Scientific Revolution reaffirmed traditional ideas about women's nature. Male scientists used the new science to spread the view that women were inferior by nature, subordinate to men, and suited by nature to play a domestic role as nurturing mothers. The widespread distribution of books ensured the continuation of these ideas. Jean de La Bruyère, the seventeenth-century French moralist, was typical when he remarked that an educated woman was like a gun that was a collector's item, "which one shows to the curious, but which has no use at all, any more than a carousel horse."[4]

Toward a New Earth: Descartes, Rationalism, and a New View of Humankind

The fundamentally new conception of the universe contained in the cosmological revolution of the sixteenth and seventeenth centuries inevitably had an impact on the Western view of humankind. Nowhere is this more evident than in the work of René Descartes (1596–1650). Descartes began by reflecting the doubt and uncertainty that seemed pervasive in the confusion of the seventeenth century and ended with a philosophy that dominated Western thought until the twentieth century.

The starting point for Descartes's new system was doubt. As Descartes explained at the beginning of his most famous work, *Discourse on Method*, written in 1637, he decided to set aside all that he had learned and begin again. One fact seemed to Descartes beyond doubt—his own existence:

> But I immediately became aware that while I was thus disposed to think that all was false, it was absolutely necessary that I who thus thought should be something; and noting that this truth *I think, therefore I am*, was so steadfast and so assured that the suppositions of the skeptics, to whatever extreme they might all be carried, could not avail to shake it, I concluded that I might without scruple accept it as being the first principle of the philosophy I was seeking.[5]

With this emphasis on the mind, Descartes asserted that he would accept only those things that his reason said were true.

From his first postulate, Descartes deduced an additional principle, the separation of mind and matter. Descartes argued that since "the mind cannot be doubted but the body and material world can, the two must be radically different." From this came an absolute dualism between mind and matter, or what has also been called Cartesian dualism. Using mind or human reason, the path to certain knowledge, and its best instrument, mathematics, humans can understand the material world because it is pure mechanism, a machine that is governed by its own physical laws because it was created by God—the great geometrician.

Descartes's separation of mind and matter allowed scientists to view matter as dead or inert, as something that was totally separate from themselves and could be investigated independently by reason. The split between mind and body led Westerners to equate their identity with mind and reason rather than with the whole organism. Descartes has rightly been called the father of modern rationalism (see the box on p. 525). His books were placed on the papal Index of Forbidden Books and condemned by many Protestant theologians. The radical Cartesian split between mind and matter, and between mind and body, had devastating implications not only for traditional religious views of the universe, but for how Westerners viewed themselves; the perspective it provided would not be seriously questioned or challenged until the twentieth century.

Science and Religion in the Seventeenth Century

In Galileo's struggle with the Catholic church, we see the beginning of the conflict between science and religion that has marked the history of modern civilization. For centuries, theology had seemed to be the queen of the sciences. It was natural that the churches would continue to believe that religion was the final measure of everything. The emerging scientists, however, were discovering things about the nat-

THE FATHER OF MODERN RATIONALISM

René Descartes has long been viewed as the founder of modern rationalism and modern philosophy because he believed that human beings could understand the world—itself a mechanical system—by the same rational principles inherent in mathematical thinking. In his Discourse on Method, *he elaborated on his approach to discovering truth.*

RENÉ DESCARTES, *DISCOURSE ON METHOD*

In place of the numerous precepts which have gone to constitute logic, I came to believe that the four following rules would be found sufficient, always provided I took the firm and unswerving resolve never in a single instance to fail in observing them.

The first was to accept nothing as true which I did not evidently know to be such, that is to say, scrupulously to avoid precipitance and prejudice, and in the judgments I passed to include nothing additional to what had presented itself to my mind so clearly and so distinctly that I could have no occasion for doubting it.

The second, to divide each of the difficulties I examined into as many parts as may be required for its adequate solution.

The third, to arrange my thoughts in order, beginning with things the simplest and easiest to know, so that I may then ascend little by little, as it were step by step, to the knowledge of the more complex, and in doing so, to assign an order of thought even to those objects which are not of themselves in any such order of precedence.

And the last, in all cases to make enumerations so complete, and reviews so general, that I should be assured of omitting nothing.

Those long chains of reasonings, each step simple and easy, which geometers are wont to employ in arriving even at the most difficult of their demonstrations, have led me to surmise that all the things we human beings are competent to know are interconnected in the same manner, and that none are so remote as to be beyond our reach or so hidden that we cannot discover them—that is, provided we abstain from accepting as true what is not thus related, i.e., keep always to the order required for their deduction one from another. And I had no great difficulty in determining what the objects are with which I should begin, for that I already knew, namely, that it was with the simplest and easiest. Bearing in mind, too, that of all those who in time past have sought for truth in the sciences, the mathematicians alone have been able to find any demonstrations, that is to say, any reasons which are certain and evident, I had no doubt that it must have been by a procedure of this kind that they had obtained them.

ural world that were at odds with the teachings of religious leaders. These "natural philosophers" then tried to draw lines between the knowledge of religion and the knowledge of "natural philosophy" or nature. Many seventeenth-century intellectuals were both religious and scientific and believed that the split between science and religion would have tragic implications. Some believed that this split was largely unnecessary while others felt the need to combine God, humans, and a mechanistic universe into a new philosophical synthesis. Blaise Pascal illustrates how one European intellectual responded to the implications of the cosmological revolution of the seventeenth century.

Blaise Pascal (1623–1662) sought to keep science and religion united. Pascal had a brief but checkered career. He was an accomplished scientist and brilliant mathematician, who was at home with both the practical and the abstract; in the former area, he invented a calculating machine, while in the latter he devised a theory of chance or probability and worked on conic sections. After a profound mystical vision on the night of November 23, 1654, which assured him that God cared for the human soul, he devoted the rest of his life to religious matters. He planned to write an "Apology for the Christian Religion" but died before he could do so. He did leave a set of notes for the larger work, however, which in published form became known as *Pensées* or *The Thoughts*.

In *Pensées*, Pascal tried to convert rationalists to Christianity by appealing to both their reason and their emotions. Humans, he argued, were frail creatures, often deceived by their senses, misled by reason, and battered by their emotions. And yet they were beings whose very nature involved thinking: "Man is but a reed, the weakest in nature; but he is a thinking reed."[6]

Pascal was determined to show that the Christian religion was not contrary to reason: "If we violate the principles of reason, our religion will be absurd, and it will be laughed at." Christianity, he felt, was the only religion that recognized people's true state of being as both vulnerable and great. To a Christian, a human being was both fallen and at the same time God's special creation. But it was not necessary to emphasize one at the expense of the other—to view humans as only rational or only hopeless. Pascal even had an answer for skeptics in his famous wager. God is a reasonable bet; it is worthwhile to assume that God exists. If he does, then we win all; if he does not, we lose nothing.

Despite his own background as a scientist and mathematician, Pascal refused to rely on the scientist's world of order and rationality to attract people to God: "If we submit everything to reason, there will be no mystery and no supernatural element in our religion." In the new cosmology of the seventeenth century, "finite man," Pascal

DESCARTES WITH QUEEN CHRISTINA OF SWEDEN. René Descartes was one of the primary figures in the Scientific Revolution. Claiming to use reason as his sole guide to truth, Descartes posited a sharp distinction between mind and matter. He is shown here, standing to the right of Queen Christina of Sweden. The queen had a deep interest in philosophy and invited Descartes to her court.

believed, was lost in the new infinite world, a realization that frightened him: "The eternal silence of those infinite spaces strikes me with terror." The world of nature, then, could never reveal God: "Because they have failed to contemplate these infinities, men have rashly plunged into the examination of nature, as though they bore some proportion to her. . . . Their assumption is as infinite as their object." A Christian could only rely on a God who through Jesus cared for human beings. In the final analysis, after providing reasonable arguments for Christianity, Pascal came to rest on faith. Reason, he believed, could take people only so far: "The heart has its reasons of which the reason knows nothing." As a Christian, faith was the final step: "The heart feels God, not the reason. This is what constitutes faith: God experienced by the heart, not by the reason."[7]

In retrospect, it is obvious that Pascal failed to achieve his goal. Increasingly, the gap between science and traditional religion grew wider as Europe continued along its path of secularization. Of course, traditional religions were not eliminated, nor is there any evidence that churches had yet lost their numbers. That would happen later. Nevertheless, more and more of the intellectual, social, and political elites began to act on the basis of secular rather than religious assumptions.

The Spread of Scientific Knowledge

In the course of the seventeenth century, scientific learning and investigation began to increase dramatically. Major European universities established new chairs of science, especially in medicine. Royal and princely patronage of individual scientists became an international phenomenon. Of particular importance to the work of science were the creation of a scientific method and the emergence of new learned societies that enabled the new scientists to communicate their ideas to each other and to disseminate them to a wider, literate public.

In the course of the Scientific Revolution, attention was paid to the problem of establishing the proper means for examining and understanding the physical realm. This creation of a scientific method was crucial to the evolution of science in the modern world. Curiously enough, it was an Englishman with few scientific credentials who attempted to put forth a new method of acquiring knowledge that made an impact on English scientists in the seventeenth century and other European scientists in the eighteenth century. Francis Bacon (1561–1626), a lawyer and lord chancellor, rejected Copernicus and Kepler and misunderstood Galileo. And yet in his unfinished work *The Great Instauration* (*The Great Restoration*), he called for his contemporaries "to com-

LOUIS XIV AND COLBERT VISIT THE ACADEMY OF SCIENCES. In the seventeenth century, individual scientists received royal and princely patronage, and a number of learned societies were established. In France, Louis XIV, urged on by his minister Colbert, gave formal recognition to the French Academy in 1666. In this painting by Henri Testelin, Louis XIV is shown seated, surrounded by Colbert and members of the French Royal Academy of Sciences.

mence a total reconstruction of sciences, arts, and all human knowledge, raised upon the proper foundations." Bacon did not doubt humans' ability to know the natural world but believed that they had proceeded incorrectly: "The entire fabric of human reason which we employ in the inquisition of nature is badly put together and built up, and like some magnificent structure without foundation."

Bacon's new foundation—a correct scientific method—was to be built upon inductive principles. Rather than beginning with assumed first principles from which logical conclusions could be deduced, he urged scientists to proceed from the particular to the general. Carefully organized experiments and systematic, thorough observations would lead to the development of correct generalizations. Bacon was clear about what he believed his method could accomplish. His concern was more for practical than for pure science. He stated that "the true and lawful goal of the sciences is none other than this: that human life be endowed with new discoveries and power." He wanted science to contribute to the "mechanical arts" by creating devices that would benefit industry, agriculture, and trade. Bacon was prophetic when he said that "I am laboring to lay the foundation, not of any sect or doctrine, but of human utility and power." And how would this "human power" be used? To "conquer nature in action."[8] The control and domination of nature became a central proposition of modern science and the technology that accompanied it. Only in the twentieth and twenty-first centuries have some scientists wondered whether this assumption might not be at the heart of our present ecological crisis.

The first of the scientific societies appeared in Italy, but those of England and France were ultimately of more significance. The English Royal Society evolved out of informal gatherings of scientists at London and Oxford in the 1640s, although it did not receive a formal charter from King Charles II until 1662. The French Royal Academy of Sciences also arose out of informal scientific meetings, in Paris during the 1650s. In 1666, Louis XIV formally recognized the group. The French Academy received abundant state support and remained under government control; its members were appointed and paid salaries by the state. In contrast, the Royal Society of England received little government encouragement, and its fellows simply coopted new members.

Early on, both the English and French scientific societies formally emphasized the practical value of scientific research. The Royal Society appointed a committee to investigate technological improvements for industry, while the French Academy collected tools and machines. This concern with the practical benefits of science proved short-lived, however, as both societies came to focus their attention on theoretical work in mechanics and astronomy. The construction of observatories at Paris in 1667 and at Greenwich, England, in 1675 greatly facilitated research in astronomy by both groups. Although both the English and French societies made useful contributions to scientific knowledge in the second half of the seventeenth century, their true significance arose from their example that science should proceed along the lines of a cooperative venture.

The importance of science in the history of modern civilization is usually taken for granted. But how did science become such an integral part of Western culture in the seventeenth and early eighteenth centuries? Recent research has stressed that one cannot simply assert that people perceived that science was a rationally superior system. An important social factor, however, might help to explain the relatively rapid acceptance of the new science.

It has been argued that the literate mercantile and propertied elites of Europe were soon attracted to a new science that offered new ways to exploit resources for profit. Some of the early scientists made it easier for these groups to accept the new ideas when they showed how these ideas could be applied directly to specific industrial and technological needs. Galileo, for example, consciously sought an alliance between science and the material interests of the educated elite when he assured his listeners that the science of mechanics would be quite useful "when it becomes necessary to build bridges or other structures over water, something occurring mainly in affairs of great importance." At the same time, Galileo stressed that science was fit for the "minds of the wise" and not for "the shallow minds of the common people." This made science part of the high culture of Europe's wealthy elites at a time when that culture was being increasingly separated from the popular culture of the lower classes.

THE ENLIGHTENMENT

In 1784, the German philosopher Immanuel Kant defined the Enlightenment as "man's leaving his self-caused immaturity." Whereas earlier periods had been handicapped by the inability to "use one's intelligence without the guidance of another," Kant proclaimed as the motto of the Enlightenment: "Dare to Know!: Have the courage to use your own intelligence!" The eighteenth-century Enlightenment was a movement of intellectuals who dared to know. They were greatly impressed with the accomplishments of the Scientific Revolution, and when they used the word *reason*—one of their favorite words—they were advocating the application of the scientific method to the understanding of all life. All institutions and all systems of thought were subject to the rational, scientific way of thinking if people would only free themselves from the shackles of past, worthless traditions, especially religious ones. If Isaac Newton could discover the natural laws regulating the world of nature, then eighteenth-century intellectuals by using reason could find the laws that governed human society. This belief in turn led them to hope that they could make progress toward a better society than the one they had inherited. Reason, natural law, hope, progress—these were common words in the heady atmosphere of the eighteenth century.

The Paths to Enlightenment

The Enlightenment did not arrive full-blown in the eight-eenth century, but was the culmination of four intellectual developments that had begun in the seventeenth century: the popularization of science, skepticism about religion, the growth of travel literature, and the work of Isaac Newton and John Locke.

Although the intellectuals of the eighteenth century were much influenced by the scientific ideas of the seventeenth century, they did not always acquire this knowledge directly from the original sources. After all, Newton's *Principia* was not an easy book to read or comprehend. The spread of scientific ideas to ever widening circles of educated Europeans was accomplished not so much by the scientists themselves as by popularizers. Especially important as a direct link between the Scientific Revolution of the seventeenth century and the intellectuals of the eighteenth was Bernard de Fontenelle (1657–1757). In his *Plurality of Worlds*, he used the form of an intimate conversation between a lady aristocrat and her lover to present a detailed account of the new mechanistic universe. Scores of the educated elite of Europe learned the new cosmology in this lighthearted fashion.

Although religion had once again become the central focus of people's lives during the Reformation, it was perhaps inevitable that the dogmatic controversies, religious intolerance, and religious warfare engendered by it would open the door to the questioning of religious truths and values. The overthrow of medieval cosmology and the advent of scientific ideas and rational explanations in the seventeenth century likewise affected the belief of educated men and women in the traditional teachings of Christianity. Skepticism about religion and a growing secularization of thought were important factors in the emergence of the Enlightenment.

Skepticism about Christianity as well as about European culture itself was nourished by travel reports. In the course of the seventeenth century, traders, missionaries, physicians, and navigators began to publish an increasing number of travel books that gave accounts of many different cultures. By the end of the seventeenth century, this travel literature had begun to make an impact on the minds of educated Europeans. The discovery of highly developed civilizations with different customs such as the civilization of China forced Europeans to evaluate their own civilization relative to others. What had seemed to be practices grounded in reason now appeared to be matters of custom.

A final source of inspiration for the Enlightenment came primarily from two Englishmen, Isaac Newton and John Locke. Enchanted by the grand design of the Newtonian world-machine, the intellectuals of the Enlightenment were convinced that by following Newton's rules of reasoning they could discover the natural laws that governed politics, economics, justice, religion, and the arts. They regarded the world and everything in it as a giant machine.

John Locke's theory of knowledge made a great impact on eighteenth-century intellectuals. In his *Essay Concerning Human Understanding*, written in 1690, Locke denied Descartes's belief in innate ideas. Instead, argued Locke, every person was born with a *tabula rasa*, a blank mind:

> Let us then suppose the mind to be, as we say, white paper, void of all characters, without any ideas. How comes it to be furnished? Whence comes it by that vast store which the busy and boundless fancy of man has painted on it with an almost endless variety? Whence has it all the materials of reason and knowledge? To this I answer, in one word, from experience. . . . Our observation, employed either about external sensible objects or about the internal operations of our minds perceived and reflected on by ourselves, is that which supplies our understanding with all the materials of thinking.[9]

Our knowledge, then, is derived from our environment, not from heredity; from reason, not from faith. By denying innate ideas, Locke's philosophy implied that people were molded by their environment, by the experiences that they received through their senses from their surrounding world. By changing the environment and subjecting people to proper influences, they could be changed and a new society created. And how should the environment be changed? Newton had already paved the way by showing how reason enabled enlightened people to discover the natural laws to which all institutions should conform. No wonder the philosophes were enamored of Newton and Locke. Taken together, their ideas seemed to offer the hope of a "brave new world" built on reason.

The Philosophes and Their Ideas

The intellectuals of the Enlightenment were known by the French name of *philosophes*, although they were not all French and few were *philosophers* in the strict sense of the term. They were literary people, professors, journalists, statesmen, economists, political scientists, and, above all, social reformers. They came from both the nobility and the middle class, and a few even stemmed from lower-middle-class origins. Although it was a truly international and cosmopolitan movement, the Enlightenment also enhanced the dominant role being played by French culture; Paris was its recognized capital, and most of its leaders were French. The French philosophes, in turn, affected intellectuals elsewhere and created a movement that touched the entire Western world, including the British and Spanish colonies in America.

To the philosophes, the role of philosophy was to change the world, not just discuss it. As one writer said, the philosophe is one who "applies himself to the study of society with the purpose of making his kind better and happier." To the philosophes, rationalism did not mean the creation of a grandiose system of thought to explain all things. Reason was scientific method, and it meant an appeal to facts, to experience, to reasonableness. A spirit of rational criticism was to be applied to everything, including religion and politics. The philosophes aggressively pursued a secular view of life because their focus was not on an afterlife, but on this world and how it could be improved and enjoyed.

Although the philosophes constituted a kind of "family circle" bound together by common intellectual bonds, they often disagreed as well. Spanning almost an entire century, the Enlightenment evolved over time, with each succeeding generation becoming more radical as it built upon the contributions of its predecessors. A few people, however, dominated the landscape completely, and we might best begin our survey of the ideas of the philosophes by looking at the three French giants—Montesquieu, Voltaire, and Diderot.

Charles de Secondat, the baron de Montesquieu (1689–1755), came from the French nobility. His most famous work, *The Spirit of the Laws*, was published in 1748. This treatise was a comparative study of governments in which Montesquieu attempted to apply the scientific method to the social and political arena to ascertain the "natural laws" governing the social relationships of human beings. Montesquieu distinguished three basic kinds of governments: republics, suitable for small states and based on citizen involvement; monarchy, appropriate for middle-sized states and grounded in the ruling class's adherence to law; and despotism, apt for large empires and dependent on fear to inspire obedience. Montesquieu used England as an example of monarchy, and it was his praise and analysis of England's constitution that led to his most far-reaching and lasting contribution to political thought—the importance of checks and balances created by means of a separation of powers. He believed that England's system, with its separate executive, legislature, and judiciary that served to limit and control each other, provided the greatest freedom and security for a state. His work was translated into English two years after publication and was read by American philosophes, who incorporated its principles into the U.S. constitution.

The greatest figure of the Enlightenment was François-Marie Arouet, known simply as Voltaire (1694–1778). Son of a prosperous middle-class family from Paris, Voltaire

VOLTAIRE. François-Marie Arouet, better known as Voltaire, achieved his first success as a playwright. A philosophe, Voltaire was well known for his criticism of traditional religion and his support of religious toleration.

THE ATTACK ON RELIGIOUS INTOLERANCE

Although Voltaire's ideas on religion were in no way original, his lucid prose, biting satire, and clever wit caused his attacks to be widely read and all the more influential. These two selections present different sides of Voltaire's attack on religious intolerance. The first is from his straightforward treatise The Ignorant Philosopher, *while the second is from his only real literary masterpiece, the novel* Candide, *where he uses humor to make the same fundamental point about religious intolerance.*

VOLTAIRE, *THE IGNORANT PHILOSOPHER*

The contagion of fanaticism then still subsists. . . . The author of the Treatise upon Toleration has not mentioned the shocking executions wherein so many unhappy victims perished in the valleys of Piedmont. He has passed over in silence the massacre of six hundred inhabitants of Valtelina, men, women, and children, who were murdered by the Catholics in the month of September, 1620. I will not say it was with the consent and assistance of the archbishop of Milan, Charles Borome, who was made a saint. Some passionate writers have averred this fact, which I am very far from believing; but I say, there is scarce any city or borough in Europe where blood has not been spilt for religious quarrels; I say, that the human species has been perceptibly diminished because women and girls were massacred as well as men; I say, that Europe would have had a third larger population if there had been no theological disputes. In fine, I say, that so far from forgetting these abominable times, we should frequently take a view of them, to inspire an eternal horror for them; and that it is for our age to make reparation by toleration, for this long collection of crimes, which has taken place through the want of toleration, during sixteen barbarous centuries.

Let it not then be said, that there are no traces left of that shocking fanaticism, of the want of toleration; they are still everywhere to be met with, even in those countries that are esteemed the most humane. The Lutheran and Calvinist preachers, were they masters, would, perhaps, be as little inclined to pity, as obdurate, as insolent as they upbraid their antagonists with being.

VOLTAIRE, *CANDIDE*

At last he [Candide] approached a man who had just been addressing a big audience for a whole hour on the subject of charity. The orator peered at him and said:

"What is your business here? Do you support the Good Old Cause?"

"There is no effect without a cause," replied Candide modestly. "All things are necessarily connected and arranged for the best. It was my fate to be driven from Lady Cunégonde's presence and made to run the gauntlet, and now I have to beg my bread until I can earn it. Things could not have happened otherwise."

"Do you believe that the Pope is Antichrist, my friend?" said the minister.

"I have never heard anyone say so," replied Candide; "but whether he is or he isn't, I want some food."

"You don't deserve to eat," said the other. "Be off with you, you villain, you wretch! Don't come near me again or you'll suffer for it."

The minister's wife looked out of the window at that moment, and seeing a man who was not sure that the Pope was Antichrist, emptied over his head a chamber pot, which shows to what lengths ladies are driven by religious zeal.

received a classical education typical of Jesuit schools. Although he studied law, he wished to be a writer and achieved his first success as a playwright. Voltaire was a prolific author and wrote an almost endless stream of pamphlets, novels, plays, letters, philosophical essays, and histories. His writings brought him both fame and wealth.

Voltaire was especially well known for his criticism of traditional religion and his strong attachment to the ideal of religious toleration (see the box above). He lent his prestige and skills as a polemicist to fight cases of intolerance in France. In 1763, he penned his *Treatise on Toleration*, in which he argued that religious toleration had created no problems for England and Holland and reminded governments that "all men are brothers under God." As he grew older, Voltaire's denunciations became ever more strident. "Crush the infamous thing," he thundered repeatedly—the infamous thing being religious fanaticism, intolerance, and superstition.

Throughout his life, Voltaire championed not only religious tolerance, but also deism, a religious outlook shared by most other philosophes. Deism was built upon the Newtonian world-machine, which implied the existence of a mechanic (God) who had created the universe. To Voltaire and most other philosophes, God had no direct involvement in the world he had created and allowed it to run according to its own natural laws. Jesus might be a "good fellow," as Voltaire called him, but he was not divine as Christianity claimed. Deism proved to be a halfway house between belief in religion and disbelief and satisfied most philosophes. Voltaire feared atheism, however, feeling that it posed a threat to social stability among the masses.

DIDEROT QUESTIONS CHRISTIAN SEXUAL STANDARDS

Denis Diderot was one of the bolder thinkers of the Enlightement. He moved from outspoken criticism of the Christian religion to outright atheism. Although best remembered for the Encyclopedia, *he wrote many other works that he considered too advanced and withheld from publication. In his* Supplement to the Voyage of Bougainville, *he constructed a dialogue between Orou, a Tahitian, who symbolizes the wisdom of a philosophe, and a chaplain who defends Christian sexual mores. The dialogue gave Diderot the opportunity to criticize the practice of sexual chastity and monogamy.*

DENIS DIDEROT, *SUPPLEMENT TO THE VOYAGE OF BOUGAINVILLE*

[Orou:] "You are young and healthy [speaking to the chaplain] and you have just had a good supper. He who sleeps alone, sleeps badly; at night a man needs a woman at his side. Here is my wife and here are my daughters. Choose whichever one pleases you most, but if you would like to do me a favor, you will give your preference to my youngest girl, who has not yet had any children. . . ."

The chaplain replied that his religion, his holy orders, his moral standards, and his sense of decency all prevented him from accepting Orou's invitation.

Orou answered: "I don't know what this thing is that you call religion, but I can only have a low opinion of it because it forbids you to partake of an innocent pleasure to which Nature, the sovereign mistress of us all, invites everybody. It seems to prevent you from bringing one of your fellow creatures into the world, from doing a favor asked of by a father, a mother, and their children, from repaying the kindness of a host, and from enriching a nation by giving it an additional citizen. . . . Look at the distress you have caused to appear on the faces of these four women—they are afraid you have noticed some defect in them that arouses your distaste. . . ."

The Chaplain: "You don't understand—it's not that. They are all four of them equally beautiful. But there is my religion! My holy orders! . . . [God] spoke to our ancestors and gave them laws; he prescribed to them the way in which he wishes to be honored; he ordained that certain actions are good and others he forbade them to do as being evil."

Orou: "I see. And one of these evil actions which he has forbidden is that of a man who goes to bed with a woman or girl. But in that case, why did he make two sexes?"

The Chaplain: "In order that they might come together—but only when certain conditions are satisfied and only after certain initial ceremonies have been performed. By virtue of these ceremonies one man belongs to one woman and only to her; one woman belongs to one man and only to him."

Orou: "For their whole lives?"

The Chaplain: "For their whole lives. . . ."

Orou: "I find these strange precepts contrary to nature, and contrary to reason. . . . Furthermore, your laws seem to me to be contrary to the general order of things. For in truth is there anything so senseless as a precept that forbids us to heed the changing impulses that are inherent in our being, or commands that require a degree of constancy which is not possible, that violate the liberty of both male and female by chaining them perpetually to one another? . . . I don't know what your great workman [God] is, but I am very happy that he never spoke to our forefathers, and I hope that he never speaks to our children, for if he does, he may tell them the same foolishness, and they may be foolish enough to believe it."

Denis Diderot (1713–1784) was the son of a skilled artisan from eastern France. He received a Jesuit education and went on to the University of Paris to fulfill his father's hopes that he would be a lawyer or pursue a career in the church. Diderot did neither. Instead he became a freelance writer so that he could be free to study and read in many subjects and languages.

Diderot wrote numerous essays that reflected typical Enlightened interests. One of his favorite topics was Christianity, which he condemned as fanatical and unreasonable. As he grew older, his literary attacks on Christianity grew more vicious. Of all religions, he averred, Christianity was the worst, "the most absurd and the most atrocious in its dogma" (see the box above). This progression reflected his own transformation from deism to atheism, ending with a basic materialistic conception of life: "This world is only a mass of molecules."

Diderot's most famous contribution to the Enlightenment was the *Encyclopedia, or Classified Dictionary of the Sciences, Arts, and Trades*, a twenty-eight-volume compendium of knowledge that he edited and referred to as the "great work of his life." Its purpose, according to Diderot, was to "change the general way of thinking." It did precisely that, becoming a major weapon of the philosophes' crusade against the old French society. The contributors attacked religious superstition and advocated toleration as well as a program for social, legal, and political improvements that would lead to a society that was more cosmopolitan, more tolerant, more humane, and more reasonable. In later editions, the price of the *Encyclopedia* was drastically reduced, dramatically increasing its sales and making it available to doctors, clergy, teachers, lawyers, and even military officers, thus furthering the spread of the ideas of the Enlightenment.

TOWARD A NEW "SCIENCE OF MAN"

The Enlightenment belief that Newton's scientific methods could be used to discover the natural laws underlying all areas of human life led to the emergence in the eighteenth century of what the philosophes called a "science of man" or what we would call the social sciences. In a number of areas, such as economics, philosophes arrived at natural laws that they believed governed human actions. If these "natural laws" seem less than universal to us, it reminds us how much the philosophes were people of their times reacting to the conditions they faced. Nevertheless, their efforts laid the foundations for the modern social sciences.

The Physiocrats and Adam Smith have been viewed as the founders of the modern discipline of economics. The leader of the Physiocrats was François Quesnay (1694–1774), a highly successful French court physician. Quesnay and the Physiocrats claimed they would discover the natural economic laws that governed human society. Their major "natural law" of economics represented a repudiation of mercantilism, specifically, its emphasis on controlling the economy for the benefit of the state. Instead the Physiocrats stressed that the existence of the natural economic forces of supply and demand made it imperative that individuals be left free to pursue their own economic self-interest. All society would ultimately benefit from the actions of these individuals. Consequently, the Physiocrats argued that the state should in no way interrupt the free play of natural economic forces by imposing government regulations on the economy, but should leave it alone, a doctrine that subsequently became known by its French name, *laissez-faire* (to let alone).

The best statement of *laissez-faire* was made in 1776 by a Scottish philosopher, Adam Smith (1723–1790), in his famous work, *Inquiry into the Nature and Causes of the Wealth of Nations*, known simply as *The Wealth of Nations*. Like the Physiocrats, Smith believed that the state should not interfere in economic matters; indeed, he gave to government only three basic functions: it should protect society from invasion (army); defend individuals from injustice and oppression (police); and keep up certain public works, such as roads and canals that private individuals could not afford. Thus, in Smith's view the state should be a kind of "passive policeman" that remains out of the lives of individuals. In emphasizing the economic liberty of the individual, the Physiocrats and Adam Smith laid the foundation for what became known in the nineteenth century as economic liberalism.

THE LATER ENLIGHTENMENT

By the late 1760s, a new generation of philosophes who had grown up with the worldview of the Enlightenment began to move beyond their predecessors' beliefs. The most famous of these later philosophes was Jean-Jacques Rousseau (1712–1778). Almost entirely self-educated, he wandered about as a youth holding various jobs in France and Italy. Eventually, he made his way to Paris, where he became a friend of Diderot and was introduced into the circles of the philosophes. He never really liked the social life of the cities, however, and frequently withdrew into long periods of solitude.

CHRONOLOGY

WORKS OF THE PHILOSOPHES

Montesquieu, *The Spirit of the Laws*	1748
Diderot, *Encyclopedia*	1751–1765
Rousseau, *The Social Contract* and *Emile*	1762
Voltaire, *Treatise on Toleration*	1763
Smith, *The Wealth of Nations*	1776

Rousseau's political beliefs were presented in two major works. In his *Discourse on the Origins of the Inequality of Mankind*, Rousseau argued that people had adopted laws and governors in order to preserve their private property. In the process, they had become enslaved by government. In his celebrated treatise *The Social Contract*, published in 1762, Rousseau tried to harmonize individual liberty with governmental authority. The social contract was basically an agreement on the part of an entire society to be governed by its general will. If any individual wished to follow his own self-interest, then he should be compelled to abide by the general will. "This means nothing less than that he will be forced to be free," said Rousseau, because the general will represented a community's highest aspirations, that which was best for the entire community. Thus, liberty was achieved by being forced to follow what was best for each individual. To Rousseau, because everybody was responsible for framing the general will, the creation of laws could never be delegated to a parliamentary institution:

> Thus the people's deputies are not and could not be its representatives; they are merely its agents; and they cannot decide anything finally. Any law which the people has not ratified in person is void; it is not law at all. The English people believes itself to be free; it is gravely mistaken; it is free only during the election of Members of Parliament; as soon as the Members are elected, the people is enslaved; it is nothing.[10]

This is an extreme, idealistic statement, but it is the ultimate statement of participatory democracy.

Another influential treatise by Rousseau also appeared in 1762. Entitled *Emile*, it is one of the Enlightenment's most important works on education. Written in the form of a novel, the work was really a general treatise "on the education of the natural man." Rousseau's fundamental concern was that education should foster rather than

MAP 18.1 The Age of Enlightenment in Europe

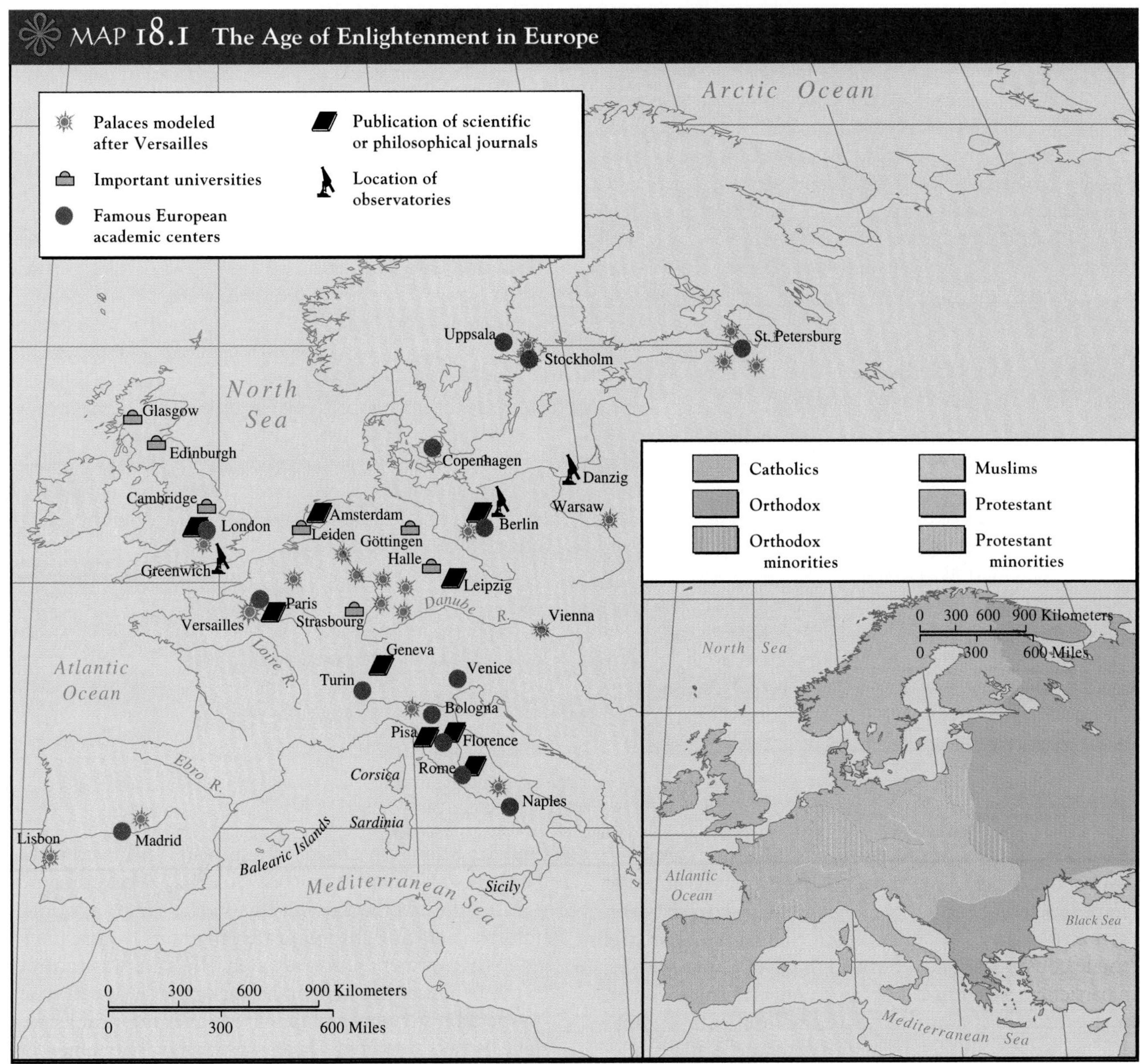

restrict children's natural instincts. Life's experiences had shown Rousseau the importance of the promptings of the heart, and what he sought was a balance between heart and mind, between sentiment and reason. This emphasis on heart and sentiment made him a precursor of the intellectual movement called Romanticism, which dominated Europe at the beginning of the nineteenth century.

But Rousseau did not necessarily practice what he preached. His own children were sent to foundling homes, where many children died at a young age. Rousseau also viewed women as "naturally" different from men: "to fulfill [a woman's] functions, an appropriate physical constitution is necessary to her . . . she needs a soft sedentary life to suckle her babies. How much care and tenderness does she need to hold her family together." In Rousseau's *Emile*, Sophie, who was Emile's intended wife, was educated for her role as wife and mother by learning obedience and the nurturing skills that would enable her to provide loving care for her husband and children. Not everyone in the eighteenth century agreed with Rousseau, however, making ideas of gender an important issue in the Enlightenment.

THE "WOMAN QUESTION" IN THE ENLIGHTENMENT

For centuries, men had dominated the debate about the nature and value of women. In general, many male intellectuals had argued that the base nature of women made them inferior to men and necessitated male domination

THE RIGHTS OF WOMEN

Mary Wollstonecraft responded to an unhappy childhood in a large family by seeking to lead an independent life. Few occupations were available for middle-class women in her day, but she survived by working as a teacher, chaperone, and governess to aristocratic children. All the while, she wrote and developed her ideas on the rights of women. This excerpt was taken from her Vindication of the Rights of Woman, *written in 1792. This work led to her reputation as the foremost British feminist thinker of the eighteenth century.*

MARY WOLLSTONECRAFT, *VINDICATION OF THE RIGHTS OF WOMAN*

It is a melancholy truth—yet such is the blessed effect of civilization—the most respectable women are the most oppressed; and, unless they have understandings far superior to the common run of understandings, taking in both sexes, they must, from being treated like contemptible beings, become contemptible. How many women thus waste life away the prey of discontent, who might have practiced as physicians, regulated a farm, managed a shop, and stood erect, supported by their own industry, instead of hanging their heads surcharged with the dew of sensibility, that consumes the beauty to which it at first gave luster. . . .

Proud of their weakness, however, [women] must always be protected, guarded from care, and all the rough toils that dignify the mind. If this be the fiat of fate, if they will make themselves insignificant and contemptible, sweetly to waste "life away," let them not expect to be valued when their beauty fades, for it is the fate of the fairest flowers to be admired and pulled to pieces by the careless hand that plucked them. In how many ways do I wish, from the purest benevolence, to impress this truth on my sex; yet I fear that they will not listen to a truth that dear-bought experience has brought home to many an agitated bosom, nor willingly resign the privileges of rank and sex for the privileges of humanity, to which those have no claim who do not discharge its duties. . . .

Would men but generously snap our chains, and be content with rational fellowship instead of slavish obedience, they would find us more observant daughters, more affectionate sisters, more faithful wives, and more reasonable mothers—in a word, better citizens. We should then love them with true affection, because we should learn to respect ourselves; and the peace of mind of a worthy man would not be interrupted by the idle vanity of his wife.

of women. In the seventeenth and eighteenth centuries, many male thinkers reinforced this view by arguing that it was based on "natural" biological differences between men and women. Like Rousseau, they argued that the female constitution made women mothers. Male writers, in particular, were critical of the attempts of some women in the Enlightenment to write on intellectual issues and insisted that women by nature were intellectually inferior to men. Nevertheless, some Enlightenment thinkers offered more positive views of women. Diderot, for example, maintained that men and women were not all that different, while Voltaire asserted that "women are capable of all that men are" in intellectual affairs.

It was women thinkers, however, who added new perspectives to the "woman question" by making specific suggestions for improving the condition of women. Mary Astell (1666–1731), daughter of a wealthy English coal merchant, argued in 1697 in *A Serious Proposal to the Ladies* that women needed to become better educated. Men, she believed, would resent her proposal, "but they must excuse me, if I be as partial to my own sex as they are to theirs, and think women as capable of learning as men are, and that it becomes them as well."[11]

The strongest statement for the rights of women in the eighteenth century was advanced by the English writer Mary Wollstonecraft (1759–1797), viewed by many as the founder of modern European feminism. In *Vindication of the Rights of Woman*, written in 1792, Wollstonecraft pointed out two contradictions in the views of women held by such Enlightenment thinkers as Rousseau. To argue that women must obey men, she said, was contrary to the beliefs of the same individuals that a system based on the arbitrary power of monarchs over their subjects or slave owners over their slaves was wrong. The subjection of women to men was equally wrong. In addition, she argued that the Enlightenment was based on an ideal of reason innate in all human beings. If women have reason, then they too are entitled to the same rights that men have. Women, Wollstonecraft declared, should have equal rights with men in education and in economic and political life as well (see the box above).

The Social Environment of the Philosophes

Of great importance to the Enlightenment was the spread of its ideas to the literate elite of European society. While the publication and sale of books and treatises were important to this process, equally important was the salon. Salons came into being in the seventeenth century but rose to new heights in the eighteenth. The salons were the elegant drawing rooms of the wealthy class's great urban

A LONDON COFFEEHOUSE. Coffeehouses first appeared in Venice and Constantinople but quickly spread throughout Europe by the beginning of the eighteenth century. In addition to drinking coffee, patrons of coffeehouses could read magazines and newspapers, exchange ideas, play chess, smoke, and even engage in business transactions. In this scene from a London coffeehouse of 1705, well-attired gentlemen make bids on commodities. Bidding went on until pins, which had been placed in lit candles, fell to the table. Thus, bidding stopped when patrons could "hear a pin drop."

houses where invited philosophes and guests gathered together and engaged in witty, sparkling conversations often centered on the new ideas of the philosophes. In France's rigid hierarchical society, the salons were important in bringing writers and artists together with aristocrats, government officials, and wealthy bourgeoisie.

In Paris, the cultural capital of Europe, women took the lead in bringing together groups of men and women to discuss the new ideas of the philosophes. At her fashionable home in the Rue St.-Honoré, Marie-Thérèse de Geoffrin (1699–1777), wife of a wealthy merchant, held sway over gatherings that became the talk of France and even Europe. Distinguished foreigners, including a future king of Sweden and a future king of Poland, competed to receive invitations. When Madame Geoffrin made a visit to Vienna, she was so well received that she exclaimed, "I am better known here than a couple of yards from my own house." Madame Geoffrin was an amiable but firm hostess who allowed wide-ranging discussions as long as they remained in good taste. When she found that artists and philosophers did not mix particularly well (the artists were high-strung and the philosophers talked too much), she set up separate meetings. Artists were only invited on Mondays; philosophers on Wednesdays. These gatherings were but one of many avenues for the spread of the ideas of the philosophes.

Other means of spreading Enlightenment ideas were also available. Coffeehouses, cafés, reading clubs, and public lending libraries created by the state were gathering places to exchange ideas. Learned societies spread to cities throughout Europe and America. At such gatherings as the Select Society of Edinburgh in Scotland and the American Philosophical Society in Philadelphia, lawyers, doctors, and local officials gathered to discuss Enlightened ideas. Secret societies were also formed. The most famous was the Freemasons, established in London in 1717, France and Italy in 1726, and Prussia in 1744. It was no secret that the Freemasons were sympathetic to the ideas of the philosophes.

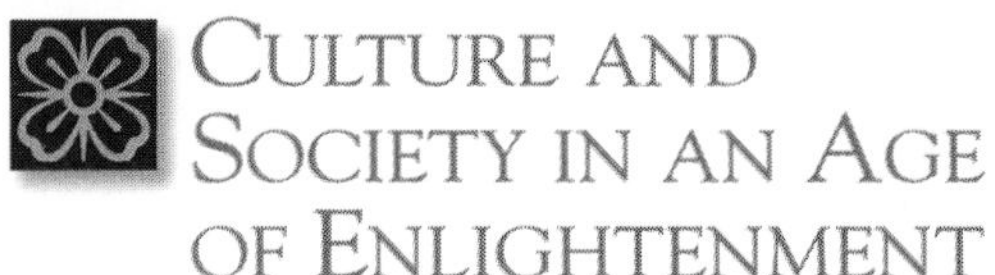

Culture and Society in an Age of Enlightenment

The intellectual adventure fostered by the philosophes was accompanied by both traditional practices and important changes in the eighteenth-century world of culture and daily life.

Innovations in Art, Music, and Literature

Although the Baroque and Neoclassical styles that had dominated the seventeenth century continued into the eighteenth century, by the 1730s, a new style of decoration and architecture known as Rococo had spread all over Europe. Though a French invention and enormously popular in Germany, Rococo became a truly international style.

Unlike the Baroque, which stressed majesty, power, and movement, Rococo emphasized grace and gentle action. Rococo rejected strict geometrical patterns and had a fondness for curves; it liked to follow the wandering lines of natural objects, such as seashells and flowers. It made much use of interlaced designs colored in gold with delicate contours and graceful curves. Highly secular, its lightness and charm spoke of the pursuit of pleasure, happiness, and love.

Some of Rococo's appeal is evident already in the painting of Antoine Watteau (1684–1721), whose lyrical views of aristocratic life—refined, sensual, civilized, with gentlemen and ladies in elegant dress—revealed a world of upper-class pleasure and joy. Underneath that exterior, however, was an element of sadness as the artist revealed the fragility and transitory nature of pleasure, love, and life.

The palace of Versailles had made an enormous impact on Europe. "Keeping up with the Bourbons" became important as the Austrian emperor, the Swedish king, German princes and prince-bishops, Italian princes, and even a Russian tsar built grandiose palaces. While imitating Versailles's size, they drew less upon its French classical

ANTOINE WATTEAU, *THE PILGRIMAGE TO CYTHERA.* Antoine Watteau was one of the most gifted painters in eighteenth-century France. His portrayal of aristocratic life reveals a world of elegance, wealth, and pleasure. In this painting, Watteau depicts a group of aristocratic pilgrims about to depart the island of Cythera, where they have paid homage to Venus, the goddess of love.

style than on the seventeenth-century Italian Baroque, as modified by a series of brilliant German and Austrian sculptor-architects. This Baroque-Rococo architectural style of the eighteenth century was conceived of as a total work of art in which building, sculptural figures, and wall and ceiling paintings were blended into a harmonious whole. This style was used in both palaces and ecclesiastical buildings, and often the same architects did both. This is evident in the work of one of the greatest architects of the eighteenth century, Balthasar Neumann (1687–1753).

Neumann's two masterpieces are the pilgrimage church of the Vierzehnheiligen (The Fourteen Saints) in southern Germany and the Bishop's Palace known as the Residenz, the residential palace of the Schönborn prince-bishop of Würzburg. Secular and spiritual become easily interchangeable as lavish and fanciful ornaments, light, bright colors, and an elaborate and rich detail greet visitors in both buildings.

The eighteenth century was one of the greatest in the history of European music. In the first half of the eighteenth century, two composers—Handel and Bach—stand out as musical geniuses. Johann Sebastian Bach (1685–1750) came from a family of musicians. Bach held the post of organist and music director at a number of small German courts before becoming director of church music at the church of St. Thomas in Leipzig in 1723. There Bach composed his Mass in B Minor, his St. Matthew Passion, and the cantatas and motets that have established his reputation as one of the greatest composers of all time. Above all, for Bach music was a means of worshiping God; in his own words, his task in life was to make "well-ordered music in the honor of God."

The other great musical giant of the early eighteenth century, George Frederick Handel (1685–1759) was, like Bach, born in Saxony in Germany and in the same year. Unlike Bach, however, he was profoundly secular in temperament. He began his career by writing operas in the Italian manner and thereafter remained faithful to the Italian Baroque style. In 1712, he moved to England and remained there the rest of his life. Although he found patrons at the English royal court, Handel wrote music for large public audiences and was not averse to writing huge, unusual-sounding pieces. The orchestra for his *Fireworks Music*, for example, was supposed to be accompanied by 101 cannons. Although he wrote much secular music, ironically the worldly Handel is probably best known for his religious music. He had no problem moving from Italian operas to religious oratorios when they proved to be in greater demand by his English public. An oratorio was an extended musical composition on a religious subject, usually taken from a biblical story. Handel's oratorio known as the *Messiah* has been called "one of those rare works that appeal immediately to everyone, and yet is indisputably a masterpiece of the highest order."[12]

Bach and Handel perfected the Baroque musical style with its monumental and elaborate musical structures. Two geniuses of the second half of the eighteenth century—Haydn and Mozart—were innovators who wrote music called Classical rather than Baroque. Their renown caused the musical center of Europe to shift from Italy to the Austrian Empire.

Franz Joseph Haydn (1732–1809) spent most of his adult life as musical director for the wealthy Hungarian princes, the Esterhazy brothers. Haydn was incredibly prolific, composing 104 symphonies in addition to string quartets, concerti, songs, oratorios, and masses. His visits to England in 1790 and 1794 introduced him to another world, where musicians wrote for public concerts rather than princely patrons. This "liberty," as he called it, induced him to write his two great oratorios *The Creation* and *The Seasons*, both of which were dedicated to the common people.

Wolfgang Amadeus Mozart (1756–1791) was truly a child prodigy: he gave his first harpsichord concert at six and wrote his first opera at twelve. He, too, sought a patron, but his discontent with the overly demanding archbishop of Salzburg forced him to move to Vienna, where his failure to achieve a permanent patron made his life miserable. Nevertheless, he wrote music prolifically and passionately: string quartets, sonatas, symphonies, concerti, and operas. *The Marriage of Figaro*, *The Magic Flute*, and *Don Giovanni* are three of the world's greatest operas. Mozart composed with an ease of melody and a blend of grace, precision, and emotion that arguably no one has ever excelled. Haydn remarked to Mozart's father that "your son is the greatest composer known to me either in person or by reputation."

The eighteenth century was also decisive in the development of the novel. The novel was not a completely new literary genre but grew out of the medieval romances and the picaresque stories of the sixteenth century. The English are credited with establishing the "modern novel as the chief vehicle" for fiction writing. With no established rules, the novel was open to much experimentation. It also proved especially attractive to women readers and women writers.

Henry Fielding (1707–1754) wrote novels about people without scruples who survived by their wits. His best work was *The History of Tom Jones, a Foundling*, a lengthy novel about the numerous adventures of a young scoundrel. Fielding presented scenes of English life from the hovels of London to the country houses of the English aristocracy. In a number of hilarious episodes, he described characters akin to real types in English society. Although he emphasized action rather than inner feeling, Fielding did his own moralizing by attacking the hypocrisy of his age.

VIERZEHNHEILIGEN, EXTERIOR VIEW. Balthasar Neumann, one of the most prominent architects of the eighteenth century, used the Baroque-Rococo style of architecture to design some of the most beautiful buildings of the century. Pictured here is the exterior of his pilgrimage church of the Vierzehnheiligen (The Fourteen Saints), located in southern Germany.

High Culture

Historians and cultural anthropologists have grown accustomed to distinguishing between a civilization's high and popular culture. By high culture is usually meant the literary and artistic culture of the educated and wealthy ruling classes; by popular culture is meant the written and unwritten culture of the masses, most of which is passed down orally. By the eighteenth century, European high culture consisted of a learned culture of theologians, scientists, philosophers, intellectuals, poets, and dramatists, for whom Latin remained a truly international language. Their work was supported by a wealthy and literate lay group, the most important of whom were the landed aristocracy and the wealthier upper classes in the cities. European high culture was noticeably cosmopolitan. In addition to Latin, French had become an international language of the cultural elites. This high culture of Europe's elite was institutionally expressed in the salons, universities, and academies.

Especially noticeable in the eighteenth century was the expansion of both publishing and the reading public. A recent study of French publishing, for example, reveals that the number of titles issued annually by French publishers rose from 300 titles in 1750 to about 1,600 in the 1780s. Although many of these titles were still geared for small groups of the educated elite, many were also directed to the new reading public of the middle classes, which included women and even urban artisans. The growth of publishing houses made it possible for authors to make money from their works and be less dependent on wealthy patrons.

An important aspect of the growth of publishing and reading in the eighteenth century was the development of magazines for the general public. Great Britain, an important center for the new magazines, saw 25 periodicals published in 1700, 103 in 1760, and 158 in 1780. Along with magazines came daily newspapers. The first was printed in London in 1702, but by 1780, thirty-seven other English towns had their own newspapers. Filled with news and special features, they were relatively cheap and were available free in coffeehouses.

Popular Culture

Popular culture refers to the often unwritten and unofficial culture passed down orally that was fundamental to the lives of most people. The distinguishing characteristic of popular culture is its collective and public nature. Group activity was especially common in the festival, a broad name used to cover a variety of celebrations: family festivals, such as weddings; community festivals in Catholic Europe that celebrated the feast day of the local patron saint; annual festivals, such as Christmas and Easter, which go back to medieval Christianity; and Carnival, the most spectacular form of festival, which was celebrated in the Mediterranean world of Spain, Italy, and France as well as in Germany and Austria. All of these festivals shared common characteristics. While having a spiritual function, they were celebrated in a secular fashion. They were special occasions on which people ate, drank, and celebrated to excess. In traditional societies, festival was a time of play because much of the rest of the year was a time of unrelieved work. As the poet Thomas Gray said of Carnival in Turin in 1739: "This Carnival lasts only from Christmas to Lent; one half of the remaining part of the year is passed in remembering the last, the other in expecting the future Carnival."[13]

"The example par excellence of the festival" was Carnival, which started in January and lasted until the beginning of Lent, traditionally the forty-day period of fasting and purification leading up to Easter. Carnival was a time of great indulgence, just the reverse of Lent, when people were expected to abstain from meat, sex, and most recreations. A heavy consumption of food, especially meat and other delicacies, and heavy drinking were the norm. Carnival was a time of intense sexual activity as well. Songs with double meanings could be sung publicly at this time of year, whereas otherwise they would be considered offensive to the community. A float of Florentine "key-makers," for example, sang this ditty to the ladies: "Our tools are fine, new and useful; We always carry them with us; They are good for anything; If you want to touch them, you can." Finally, Carnival was a time of aggression, a time to release pent-up feelings. Most often this took the form of verbal aggression because people could openly insult other people and were even allowed to criticize their social superiors and authorities. But other acts of violence were also permitted. People pelted each other with apples, eggs, flour, and pigs' bladders filled with water.

The same sense of community evident in festival was also present in the chief gathering places of the common people, the local taverns or cabarets. Taverns functioned as a regular gathering place for neighborhood men to talk, play games, conduct small business matters, and, of course, drink. In some countries, the favorite drinks of the poor, such as gin in England and vodka in Russia, proved devastating as poor people regularly drank themselves into oblivion. Gin was cheap; the classic sign in English taverns, "Drunk for a penny, dead drunk for two pence," was literally true. In England, the consumption of gin rose from two to five million gallons between 1714 and 1733 and only declined when complaints finally led to strict laws to restrict sales in the 1750s.

In the eighteenth century, the separation between elite and poor grew ever wider. In 1500, popular culture was for everyone; a second culture for the elite, it was the only culture for the rest of society. But between 1500 and 1800, the nobility, clergy, and bourgeoisie had abandoned popular culture to the lower classes. This was, of course, a gradual process, and in abandoning the popular festivals, the upper classes were also abandoning the popular worldview as well. The new scientific outlook had brought a new mental world for the upper classes, and they now viewed such things as witchcraft, faith healing, fortune-telling, and prophecy as the beliefs of "such as are of the weakest judgment and reason, as women, children, and ignorant and superstitious persons."

Crime and Punishment

By the eighteenth century, most European states had developed a hierarchy of courts to deal with civil and criminal cases. With the exception of England, they continued to use judicial torture as an important means of obtaining evidence before trial until almost the end of the century. Courts used the rack, thumbscrews, and other instruments to obtain confessions in criminal cases. Seventeenth-century legal reforms, however, led to the gradual demise of judicial torture. It persisted longer in France than in other European states but was finally abolished there in 1780.

Punishments for crimes were often cruel and even spectacular. Public spectacle was a basic part of traditional punishment because it was believed to deter potential offenders in an age when the state's police arm was too weak to assure the capture of criminals. Although nobles were executed by simple beheading, lower-class criminals condemned to death were tortured, broken on the wheel, or drawn and quartered (see the box on page 539). The death penalty was still commonly used in property as well as criminal cases. By 1800, the English listed over two hundred crimes that were subject to the death penalty. In addition to executions, European states resorted to forced labor in mines, forts, and navies. England also sent criminals as indentured servants to colonies in the New World and, after the American Revolution, to Australia.

Religion and the Churches

The music of Bach and the pilgrimage and monastic churches of southern Germany and Austria make us cognizant of a curious fact. While much of the great art and music of the time was religious, the thought of the time was antireligious as life became increasingly secularized and men of reason attacked the established churches. And yet most Europeans were still Christians. Except for gov-

THE PUNISHMENT OF CRIME

Torture and capital punishment remained common features of European judicial systems well into the eighteenth century. Public spectacles were especially gruesome, as this excerpt from the Nocturnal Spectator *of Restif de la Bretonne demonstrates.*

RESTIF DE LA BRETONNE, NOCTURNAL SPECTATOR: *THE BROKEN MAN*

I went home by way of rue Saint-Antoine and the Place de Grève. Three murderers had been broken on the wheel there, the day before. I had not expected to see any such spectacle, one that I had never dared to witness. But as I crossed the square I caught sight of a poor wretch, pale, half dead, wracked by the pains of the interrogation inflicted on him twenty hours earlier; he was stumbling down from the Hôtel de Ville supported by the executioner and the confessor. These two men, so completely different, inspired an inexpressible emotion in me! I watched the latter embrace a miserable man consumed by fever, filthy as the dungeons he came from, swarming with vermin! And I said to myself, "O Religion, here is your greatest glory!"

I saw a horrible sight, even though the torture had been mitigated. . . . The wretch had revealed his accomplices. He was garroted before he was put to the wheel. A winch set under the scaffold tightened a noose around the victim's neck and he was strangled; for a long while the confessor and the hangman felt his heart to see whether the artery still pulsed, and the hideous blows were dealt only after it beat no longer. . . . I left, with my hair standing on end in horror.

ernments, churches remained the most important institutions in people's lives. Even many of those most critical of the churches accepted that society could not function without religious faith.

In the eighteenth century, the established Catholic and Protestant churches were basically conservative institutions that upheld society's hierarchical structure, privileged classes, and traditions. Although churches experienced change because of new state policies, they did not sustain any dramatic internal changes. Whether in Catholic or Protestant countries, the parish church run by priest or pastor remained the center of religious practice. In addition to providing religious services, the parish church kept records of births, deaths, and marriages, provided charity for the poor, supervised whatever primary education there was, and cared for orphans.

Toleration and Religious Minorities

One of the chief battle cries of the philosophes had been a call for religious toleration. Out of political necessity, a certain level of tolerance of different creeds had occurred in the seventeenth century in such places as Germany after the Thirty Years' War and France after the divisive religious wars. But many rulers still found it difficult to accept. Louis XIV had turned back the clock in France at the end of the seventeenth century, insisting on religious uniformity and suppressing the rights of the Huguenots. Devout rulers continued to believe that there was only one path to salvation; it was the true duty of a ruler not to allow subjects to be condemned to hell by being heretics. Catholic minorities in Protestant countries and Protestant minorities in Catholic countries did not enjoy full civil or political rights. Persecution of heretics continued; the last burning of a heretic took place in 1781.

The Jews remained the despised religious minority of Europe. The largest population of Jews (known as the Ashkenazic Jews) lived in eastern Europe. Except in relatively tolerant Poland, Jews were restricted in their movements, forbidden to own land or hold many jobs, forced to pay burdensome special taxes, and also subject to periodic outbursts of popular wrath. The resulting pogroms in which Jewish communities were looted and massacred made Jewish existence precarious and dependent on the favor of their territorial rulers.

Another major group was the Sephardic Jews who had been expelled from Spain in the fifteenth century. Although many had migrated to Turkish lands, some of them had settled in cities—such as Amsterdam, Venice, London, and Frankfurt—where they were relatively free to participate in the banking and commercial activities that Jews had practiced since the Middle Ages. The highly successful ones came to provide valuable services to rulers, especially in central Europe, where they were known as the court Jews. But even these Jews were insecure because their religion set them apart from the Christian majority and served as a catalyst to social resentment.

Some Enlightenment thinkers in the eighteenth century favored a new acceptance of Jews. They argued that Jews and Muslims were all human and deserved the full rights of citizenship despite their religion. Many philosophes denounced persecution of the Jews but made no attempt to hide their hostility and ridiculed Jewish customs. Diderot, for example, said that the Jews had "all the defects peculiar to an ignorant and superstitious nation." Many Christians favored the assimilation of the Jews into the mainstream of society as the basic solution to the "Jewish problem," but only by the conversion of the Jews to Christianity. This, of course, was not acceptable to most Jews.

The Austrian emperor Joseph II (1780–1790) attempted to adopt a new policy toward the Jews, although it too was limited. It freed Jews from nuisance taxes and allowed them more freedom of movement and job opportunities, but they were still restricted from owning land and worshiping in public. At the same time, Joseph II encouraged Jews to learn German and work toward greater assimilation into Austrian society.

Popular Religion in the Eighteenth Century

Despite the rise of skepticism and the intellectuals' belief in deism and natural religion, it would appear that religious devotion remained strong in the eighteenth century. It is difficult to assess precisely the religiosity of Europe's Catholics. The Catholic parish church remained an important center of life for the entire community. How many people went to church regularly cannot be known exactly, but it has been established that 90 to 95 percent of Catholic populations did go to mass on Easter Sunday, one of the church's most special celebrations.

After the initial religious fervor that created Protestantism in the sixteenth century, Protestant churches in the seventeenth century had settled down into well-established patterns controlled by state authorities and served by a well-educated clergy. In time, these churches became bureaucratized and bereft of religious enthusiasm. In Germany and England, where rationalism and deism had become influential and moved some theologians to a more "rational" Christianity, the desire of ordinary Protestant churchgoers for greater depths of religious experience led to new and dynamic religious movements.

One of the most famous movements—Methodism—was the work of John Wesley (1703–1791). An ordained Anglican minister, John Wesley took religion very seriously, experienced a deep spiritual crisis, and underwent a mystical experience: "I felt I did trust in Christ alone for salvation; and an assurance was given me, that He had taken away my sins, even mine, and saved me from the law of sin and death. I felt my heart strangely warmed." To Wesley, "the gift of God's grace" assured him of salvation and led him to become a missionary to the English people, to bring the "glad tidings" of salvation to all people, despite opposition from the Anglican church, which criticized this emotional mysticism or religious enthusiasm as superstitious nonsense. To Wesley, all could be saved by experiencing God and opening the doors to his grace.

In taking the Gospel to the people, Wesley preached to the masses in open fields, appealing especially to the lower classes neglected by the socially elitist Anglican church. He tried, he said, "to lower religion to the level of the lowest people's capacities." Wesley's fiery preaching often provoked highly charged and even violent conversion experiences (see the box on p. 541). Afterward, converts were organized into so-called Methodist societies or chapels in which they could aid each other in doing the good works that Wesley considered a component of salvation. A Central Methodist Conference supervised new lay preachers from Methodist circles. Controlled by Wesley, it enabled him to dominate the evangelical movement he had created. Although Wesley sought to keep Methodism within the Anglican church, after his death it became a separate and independent sect. Methodism represents an important revival of Christianity and proved that the need for spiritual experience had not been expunged by the eighteenth-century search for reason.

JOHN WESLEY. In leading a deep spiritual revival in Britain, John Wesley founded a religious movement that came to be known as Methodism. He loved to preach to the masses, and this 1766 portrait by Nathaniel Hope shows him as he might have appeared before a crowd of people.

CONCLUSION

The Scientific Revolution represents a major turning point in modern civilization. In the Scientific Revolution, the Western world overthrew the medieval, Ptolemaic-Aristotelian worldview and arrived at a new conception of the universe: the sun at the center, the planets as material bodies revolving around the sun in elliptical orbits, and an infinite rather than a finite world. With the changes in the conception of "heaven" came changes in the conception of "earth." The work of Bacon and Descartes left Europeans with the separation of mind and matter and the belief that by using only reason they could, in fact, understand and dominate the world of nature. The development of a scientific method furthered the work

THE CONVERSION EXPERIENCE IN WESLEY'S METHODISM

After his own conversion experience, John Wesley traveled extensively to bring the "glad tidings" of Christ to other people. It has been estimated that he preached over 40,000 sermons, some of them to audiences numbering 20,000 listeners. Wesley gave his message wherever people gathered—in the streets, hospitals, private houses, and even pubs. In this selection from his journal, Wesley describes how emotional and even violent conversion experiences could be.

THE WORKS OF THE REVEREND JOHN WESLEY

Sunday, May 20 [1759], being with Mr. B—ll at Everton, I was much fatigued, and did not rise: but Mr. B. did, and observed several fainting and crying out, while Mr. Berridge was preaching: afterwards at Church, I heard many cry out, especially children, whose agonies were amazing: one of the eldest, a girl of ten or twelve years old, was full in my view, in violent contortions of body, and weeping aloud, I think incessantly, during the whole service. . . . The Church was equally crowded in the afternoon, the windows being filled within and without, and even the outside of the pulpit to the very top; so that Mr. B. seemed almost stifled by their breath; yet feeble and sickly as he is, he was continually strengthened, and his voice, for the most part, distinguishable, in the midst of all the outcries. I believe there were present three times more men than women, a great part of whom came from far; thirty of them having set out at two in the morning, from a place thirteen miles off. The text was, *Having a form of godliness, but denying the power thereof*. When the power of religion began to be spoken of, the presence of God really filled the place: and while poor sinners felt the sentence of death in their souls, what sounds of distress did I hear! The greatest number of them who cried or fell, were men: but some women, and several children, felt the power of the same almighty Spirit, and seemed just sinking into hell. This occasioned a mixture of several sounds; some shrieking, some roaring aloud. The most general was a loud breathing, like that of people half strangled and gasping for life: and indeed almost all the cries were like those of human creatures, dying in bitter anguish. Great numbers wept without any noise: others fell down as death: some sinking in silence; some with extreme noise and violent agitation. I stood on the pew-seat, as did a young man in the opposite pew, an able-bodied, fresh, healthy countryman: but in a moment, while he seemed to think of nothing less, down he dropped with a violence inconceivable. The adjoining pews seemed to shake with his fall: I heard afterwards the stamping of his feet; ready to break the boards, as he lay in strong convulsions, at the bottom of the pew. Among several that were struck down in the next pew, was a girl, who was as violently seized as he. . . . Among the children who felt the arrows of the Almighty, I saw a sturdy boy, about eight years old, who roared above his fellows, and seemed in his agony to struggle with the strength of a grown man. His face was as red as scarlet: and almost all on whom God laid his hand, turned either very red or almost black. . . .

The violent struggling of many in the above-mentioned churches, has broken several pews and benches. Yet it is common for people to remain unaffected there, and afterwards to drop down in their way home. Some have been found lying as dead on the road: others, in Mr. B.'s garden; not being able to walk from the Church to his house, though it is not two hundred yards.

of scientists, while the new scientific societies and learned journals spread their results. Although traditional churches stubbornly resisted the new ideas and a few intellectuals pointed to some inherent flaws, nothing was able to halt the replacement of the traditional ways of thinking by new ways of thinking that created a more fundamental break with the past than that represented by the breakup of Christian unity in the Reformation.

Highly influenced by the new worldview created by the Scientific Revolution, the philosophes of the eighteenth century hoped that they could create a new society by using reason to discover the natural laws that governed it. They believed that education could produce better human beings and a better human society. They attacked traditional religion as the enemy and developed the new "sciences of man" in economics, politics, and education. Together, the Scientific Revolution of the seventeenth century and the Enlightenment of the eighteenth century constituted an intellectual revolution that laid the foundations for a modern worldview based on rationalism and secularism.

An interesting question that arises is why the Scientific Revolution occurred in the West and not in China. In the Middle Ages, China had been the most technologically advanced civilization in the world. After 1500, that distinction passed to the West. Historians are not sure why. Some have compared the sense of order in Chinese society to the competitive spirit existing in Europe. Others have emphasized China's ideological viewpoint that favored living in harmony with nature rather than trying to dominate it. One historian has even suggested that China's civil service system drew the "best and the brightest" into government service rather than other occupations.

Whatever the reasons, this intellectual revolution contributed to the increased confidence of Western civilization as Europeans—with their strong governments, prosperous economies, and strengthened military forces—began to dominate other parts of the world, adding to a growing belief in the superiority of their civilization. And as we shall see in the next chapter, in the midst of intellectual revolution, economic, political, and social transformations of great importance were also taking shape that by the end of the eighteenth century were to lead to both political and industrial revolutions.

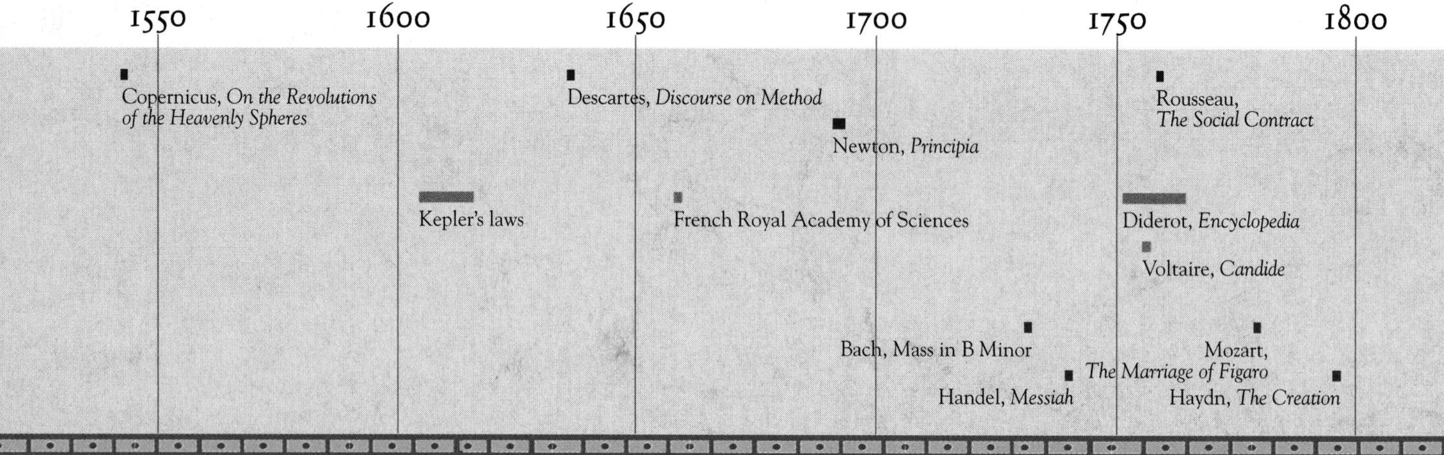

Chapter Notes

1. Quoted in Alan G. R. Smith, *Science and Society in the Sixteenth and Seventeenth Centuries* (London, 1972), p. 59.
2. Quoted in Londa Schiebinger, *The Mind Has No Sex? Women in the Origins of Modern Science* (Cambridge, Mass., 1989), pp. 52–53.
3. Ibid., p. 85.
4. Quoted in Phyllis Stock, *Better Than Rubies: A History of Women's Education* (New York, 1978), p. 16.
5. René Descartes, *Philosophical Writings*, ed. and trans. Norman K. Smith (New York, 1958), p. 118–19.
6. Blaise Pascal, *Pensées*, trans. J. M. Cohen (Harmondsworth, 1961), p. 100.
7. Ibid., pp. (in order of appearance) 31, 31, 52–53, 164, 165.
8. Francis Bacon, *The Great Instauration*, trans. Jerry Weinberger (Arlington Heights, Ill., 1989), pp. (in order of appearance) 2, 8, 2, 16, 21.
9. John Locke, *An Essay Concerning Human Understanding* (New York, 1964), pp. 89–90.
10. Jean-Jacques Rousseau, *The Social Contract*, trans. Maurice Cranston (Harmondsworth, 1968), p. 141.
11. Mary Astell, *A Serious Proposal to the Ladies*, in Moira Ferguson, ed., *First Feminists: British Women Writers, 1578–1799* (Bloomington, Ind., 1985), p. 190.
12. Kenneth Clark, *Civilisation* (New York, 1969), p. 231.
13. Quoted in Peter Burke, *Popular Culture in Early Modern Europe* (New York, 1978), p. 179.

Suggested Readings

Four general surveys of the entire Scientific Revolution are A. G. R. Smith, *Science and Society in the Sixteenth and Seventeenth Centuries* (London, 1972); J. R. Jacob, *The Scientific Revolution: Aspirations and Achievements, 1500–1700* (Atlantic Highlands, N. J., 1998);S. Shapin, *The Scientific Revolution* (Chicago, 1996); and J. Henry, *The Scientific Revolution and the Origins of Modern Science* (New York, 1997). Also of much value is A. G. Debus, *Man and Nature in the Renaissance* (Cambridge, 1978), which covers the period from the mid-fifteenth through the mid-seventeenth century. On the relationship of magic to the beginnings of the Scientific Revolution, see the pioneering works by F. Yates, *Giordano Bruno and the Hermetic Tradition* (New York, 1969), and *The Rosicrucian Enlightenment* (London, 1975).

On the important figures of the revolution in astronomy, see E. Rosen, *Copernicus and the Scientific Revolution* (New York, 1984); M. Sharratt, *Galileo: Decisive Innovator* (Oxford, 1994); S. Drake, *Galileo, Pioneer Scientist* (Toronto, 1990); M. Casper, *Johannes Kepler*, trans. C. D. Hellman (London, 1959), the standard biography;

and R. S. Westfall, *The Life of Isaac Newton* (New York, 1993). On Newton's relationship to alchemy, see M. White, *Isaac Newton: The Last Sorcerer* (Reading, Mass., 1997).

The standard biography of Vesalius is C. D. O'Malley, *Andreas Vesalius of Brussels, 1514–1564* (Berkeley, Calif., 1964). Harvey's work is discussed in G. Whitteridge, *William Harvey and the Circulation of the Blood* (London, 1971). The importance of Francis Bacon in the early development of science is underscored in P. Zagorin, *Francis Bacon* (Princeton, N.J., 1998). A good introduction to the work of Descartes can be found in G. Radis-Lewis, *Descartes: A Biography* (Ithaca, N.Y., 1998).

On the subject of women and early modern science, see the comprehensive and highly informative work by L. Schiebinger, *The Mind Has No Sex? Women in the Origins of Modern Science* (Cambridge, Mass., 1989). See also C. Merchant, *The Death of Nature: Women, Ecology, and the Scientific Revolution* (San Francisco, 1980). The social and political context for the triumph of science in the seventeenth and eighteenth centuries is examined in M. Jacobs, *The Cultural Meaning of the Scientific Revolution* (New York, 1988).

Two sound, comprehensive surveys of eighteenth-century Europe are I. Woloch, *Eighteenth-Century Europe* (New York, 1982), and M. S. Anderson, *Europe in the Eighteenth Century* (London, 1987).

Good introductions to the Enlightenment can be found in N. Hampson, *A Cultural History of the Enlightenment* (New York, 1968); U. Im Hof, *The Enlightenment* (Oxford, 1994); D. Goodman, *The Republic of Letters: A Cultural History of the French Enlightenment* (Ithaca, N.Y., 1994); and D. Outram, *The Enlightenment* (Cambridge, 1995). A more detailed synthesis can be found in the two volumes by P. Gay, *The Enlightenment: An Interpretation*, 2 vols. (New York, 1966–1969). For a short, popular survey on the French philosophes, see F. Artz, *The Enlightenment in France* (Kent, Oh., 1968). Studies on the major Enlightenment intellectuals include J. Sklar, *Montesquieu* (Oxford, 1987); H. T. Mason, *Voltaire: A Biography* (Baltimore, 1981); P. N. Furbank, *Diderot: A Critical Biography* (New York, 1992); and M. Cranston, *The Noble Savage: Jean-Jacques Rousseau* (New York, 1991). On women in the eighteenth century, see N. Z. Davis and A. Farge, eds., *A History of Women: Renaissance and Enlightenment Paradoxes* (Cambridge, Mass., 1993); C. Lougee, *Le Paradis des Femmes. Women, Salons, and Social Stratification* (Princeton, N.J., 1976); O. Hufton, *The Prospect Before Her: A History of Women in Western Europe, 1500–1800* (New York, 1998); and B. S. Anderson and J. P. Zinsser, *A History of Their Own*, vol. 2 (New York, 1988).

Two readable general surveys on the arts and literature are M. Levy, *Rococo to Revolution* (London, 1966), and H. Honour, *Neoclassicism* (Harmondsworth, 1968). Different facets of crime and punishment are examined in the important work by M. Foucault, *Discipline and Punish: The Birth of the Prison* (New York, 1977). Important studies on popular culture include P. Burke, *Popular Culture in Early Modern Europe* (New York, 1978), and R. Darnton, *The Great Cat Massacre and Other Episodes in French Cultural History* (New York, 1984).

A good introduction to the religious history of the eighteenth century can be found in G. R. Cragg, *The Church and the Age of Reason, 1648–1789* (London, 1966). On John Wesley, see H. Rack, *Reasonable Enthusiast: John Wesley and the Rise of Methodism* (New York, 1989).

For additional reading, go to InfoTrac College Edition, your online research library at http://web1.infotrac-college.com

Enter the search terms "Isaac Newton or Copernicus" using Keywords.

Enter the search term "Enlightenment" using the Subject Guide.

Enter the search term "Rousseau" using Keywords.

Enter the search terms "John Locke" using Keywords.

Enter the search terms "scientific revolution" using Keywords.

CHAPTER 19

Europe on the Eve of a New World Order

Chapter Outline

- ECONOMIC CHANGES AND THE PERSISTENCE OF A TRADITIONAL SOCIAL ORDER
- CHANGING PATTERNS OF WAR: GLOBAL CONFRONTATION
- COLONIAL EMPIRES AND REVOLUTION
- TOWARD A NEW POLITICAL ORDER
- CONCLUSION

Focus Questions

- What changes occurred in the European economy in the eighteenth century, and to what degree were these changes reflected in social patterns?
- How did Spain and Portugal administer their American colonies, and what were the main characteristics of Latin American society in the eighteenth century?
- What do historians mean by the term *enlightened absolutism*, and to what degree did eighteenth-century Prussia, Austria, and Russia exhibit its characteristics?
- What were the causes, the main events, and the results of the American Revolution and the French Revolution?
- What aspects of the French Revolution did Napoleon preserve, and which did he destroy?

Historians have often portrayed the eighteenth century as the final phase of Europe's old order before the violent upheaval and reordering of society associated with the French Revolution. The old order—still largely agrarian, dominated by kings and landed aristocrats—and grounded in privileges for nobles, clergy, towns, and provinces—seemed to continue a basic pattern that had prevailed in Europe since medieval times. Recent scholarship, however, has tended to undermine the idea of uniformity in the eighteenth century. Just as a new intellectual order based on rationalism and secularism was emerging in Europe from the intellectual revolution of the Scientific Revolution and the Enlightenment, demographic, economic, social, and political patterns were beginning to change in ways that reflect the emergence of a new modern order.

A key factor in the emergence of a new world order was the French Revolution. On the morning of July 14, 1789, a Parisian mob of some eight thousand men and women in search of weapons streamed toward the Bastille, a royal armory filled with arms and ammunition. The Bastille was also a state prison, and although it now held only seven prisoners, in the eyes of these angry Parisians, it was a glaring symbol of the government's despotic policies. It was defended by the Marquis de Launay and a small garrison of 114 men. The attack on the Bastille began in earnest in the early afternoon, and after three hours of fighting, de Launay and the garrison surrendered. Angered by the loss of ninety-eight of their members, the victors beat de Launay to death, cut off his head, and carried it aloft in triumph through the streets of Paris. When King Louis XVI was told the news of the fall of the Bastille by the Duc de La Rochefoucauld-Liancourt, he exclaimed, "Why, this is a revolt." "No, Sire," replied the duke. "It is a revolution."

The French Revolution has been portrayed as a major turning point in European political and social history, as a time when the institutions of the "old regime" were destroyed and a new order was created based on individual rights, representative institutions, and a concept of loyalty to the nation rather than the monarch. The revolutionary upheaval of the era, especially in France, did create new liberal and national political ideals, summarized in the French revolutionary slogan "Liberty, Equality, and Fraternity," that transformed France and then spread to other European countries and the rest of the world.

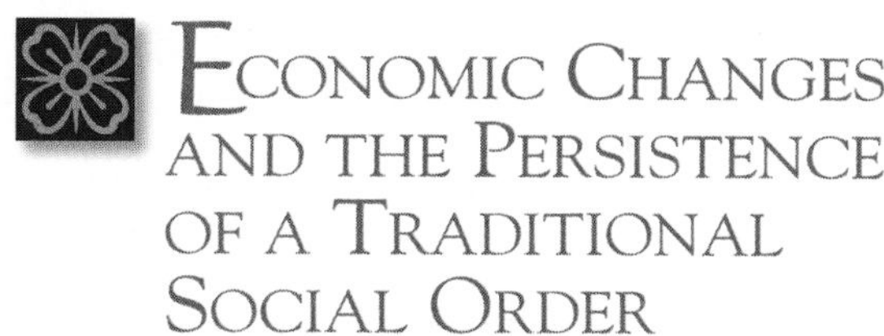

Economic Changes and the Persistence of a Traditional Social Order

The eighteenth century witnessed the beginning of economic changes in Europe that ultimately had a strong impact on the rest of the world. Rapid population growth, an agricultural revolution, the beginnings of an industrial revolution, and an increase in worldwide trade characterized the economic patterns of the eighteenth century.

Population, Food, and Industry

Europe's population began to grow around 1750 and continued a slow upward movement. The total European population was probably around 120 million in 1700, expanded to 140 million by 1750, and then grew to 190 million by 1790; thus, the growth rate in the second half of the century was more than double that of the first half. These increases occurred during the same period that several million Europeans were going abroad as colonists. A falling death rate was perhaps the most important cause of population growth. But why did the death rate decline? More plentiful food and better transportation of available food supplies led to some improvement in diet and relief from devastating famines. Also of great significance in lowering death rates was the disappearance of bubonic plague.

Food became more abundant due in part to improvements in agricultural practices and methods in the eighteenth century, especially in Britain, parts of France, and the Low Countries. The increases in food production can be attributed to four interrelated factors: more land under cultivation, increased yields per acre, healthier and more abundant livestock, and an improved climate. Climatologists believe that the "little ice age" of the seventeenth century declined in the eighteenth, especially evident in the moderate summers that provided more ideal growing conditions. Important to the increased yields was the spread of new vegetables, including two important American crops, the potato and maize (Indian corn). Although they were not grown in quantity until after 1700, they had been brought to Europe from America in the sixteenth century and were part of what some historians have called the Columbian exchange—a reciprocal exchange of plants and animals between Europe and America (see Map 19.1). The potato became a staple in Germany, the Low Countries, and especially Ireland, where repression by British landlords forced large numbers of poor peasants to survive on small plots of marginal land. The potato took relatively little effort to produce in large quantities. High in carbohydrates and calories, rich in vitamins A and C, it could be easily stored for winter use.

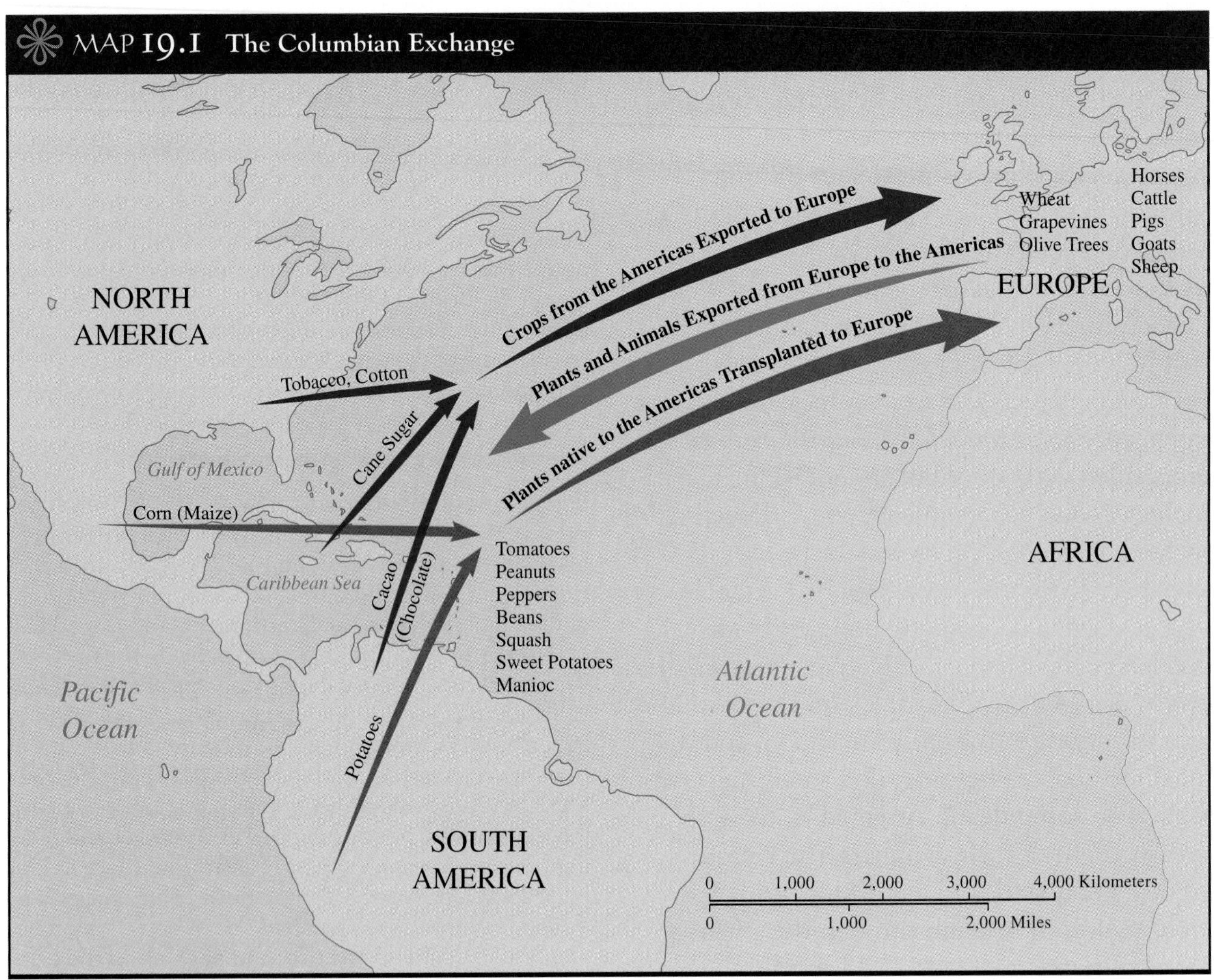

In the eighteenth century, it was primarily the British who adopted the new techniques that have been characterized as an agricultural revolution. This early modernization of British agriculture with its noticeable increase in productivity made possible the feeding of an expanding population about to enter a new world of industrialization and urbanization.

The most important product of European industry in the eighteenth century was textiles, most of which were still produced by traditional methods. In cities that were textile centers, master artisans used timeworn methods to produce finished goods in their guild workshops. But by the eighteenth century, textile production had begun to shift to the countryside in some parts of Europe. Textiles were produced in the countryside by the "putting-out" or "domestic" system in which a merchant-capitalist entrepreneur bought the raw materials, mostly wool and flax, and "put them out" to rural workers who spun the raw material into yarn and then wove it into cloth on simple looms. Capitalist entrepreneurs sold the finished products, made a profit, and used it to manufacture more. This system was also called "cottage industry," because spinners and weavers did their work on spinning wheels and looms in their own cottages. Cottage industry was truly a family enterprise because women and children could spin while men wove on the looms, enabling rural people to earn incomes that supplemented their pitiful wages as agricultural laborers. The cottage system with its traditional methods of manufacturing was established in many rural areas of Europe during the eighteenth century. But in the second half of the century, significant changes in industrial production began to occur that would lead to an industrial revolution (see Chapter 20).

Worldwide Trade

Although bankers and industrialists would come to dominate the nineteenth century economically, in the eighteenth century merchants and traders still reigned supreme. Intra-European trade still dominated total trade figures as wheat, timber, and naval stores from the Baltic, wines from France, wool and fruit from Spain, and silk from Italy were exchanged along with a host of other products. But the eighteenth century witnessed only a slight increase in this trade while overseas trade boomed. This increase in overseas trade has led some historians to speak of the emergence of a truly global economy in the eighteenth century.

To justify the term *global economy*, historians have usually pointed to the patterns of trade that interlocked Europe, Africa, the Far East, and the American continents. One such pattern involved the influx of gold and silver into Spain from its colonial American empire. Much of this gold and silver made its way to Britain, France, and the Netherlands in return for manufactured goods. British, Dutch, and French merchants in turn used their profits to buy tea, spices, silk, and cotton goods from China and India to sell in Europe. Another important source of trading activity came from the plantations of the Western Hemisphere. Plantations, extending from the southern colonies of North America through the West Indies and into Brazil, were worked by African slaves and produced tobacco, cotton, coffee, and sugar, all products in demand by Europeans. A third pattern of trade involved British merchant ships, which carried British manufactured goods to Africa, where they were traded for a cargo of slaves, which were then shipped to Virginia and paid for with tobacco, which in turn was shipped back to Britain, where it was processed and then sold in Germany for cash. Of all the goods traded in the eighteenth century, perhaps the most profitable and certainly the most infamous were African slaves (see Chapter 14).

Overseas trade created enormous prosperity for some European countries. By the beginning of the eighteenth century, Spain, Portugal, and the Dutch Republic, which had earlier monopolized overseas trade, found themselves increasingly overshadowed by France and Britain, which built enormously profitable colonial empires in the course of the eighteenth century. After 1763, however, when France lost the Seven Years' War and much of its overseas empire, Britain emerged as the world's strongest overseas trading nation, and London became the world's greatest port.

Society in the Eighteenth Century

Although dramatic economic changes were taking place in the eighteenth century, European society itself still clung to many of the social patterns established centuries earlier in the Middle Ages. The resulting tensions between

MAP 19.2 Global Trade Patterns of the European States in the Eighteenth Century

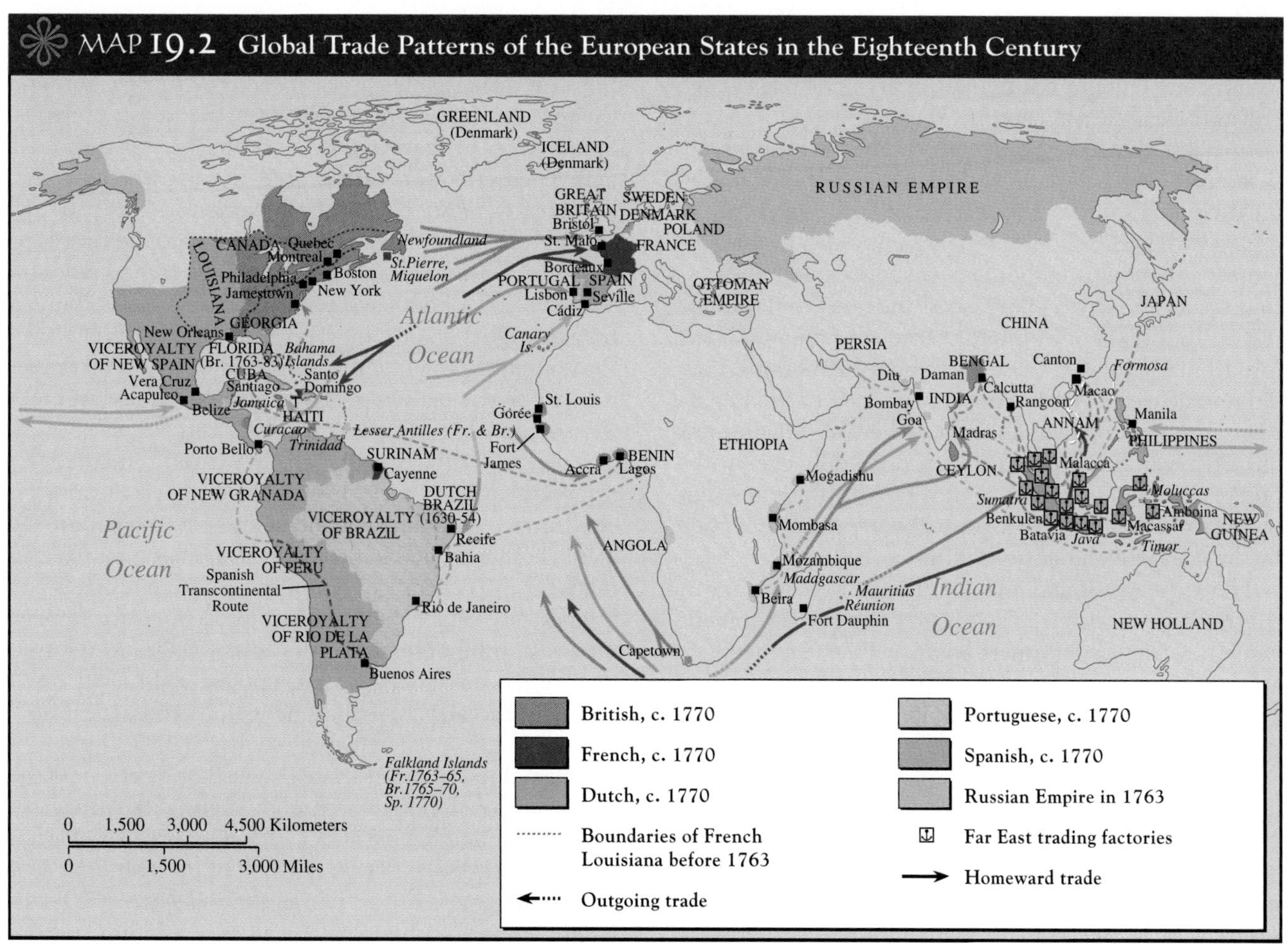

THE ARISTOCRATIC WAY OF LIFE. The eighteenth-century country house in Britain fulfilled the desire of aristocrats for both elegance and greater privacy. The painting above by Richard Wilson shows a typical English country house of the eighteenth century, surrounded by a simple and serene landscape. Thomas Gainsborough's *Conversation in the Park*, shown at right, captures the relaxed life of two aristocrats in the park of their country estate.

the new economic patterns and the old social institutions would contribute to the revolutionary upheavals at the end of the eighteenth century.

Social status in the eighteenth century was still largely determined not by wealth and economic standing but by the division into the traditional "orders" or "estates" determined by heredity. This divinely sanctioned division of society into traditional orders was supported by Christian teaching, which emphasized the need to fulfill the responsibilities of one's estate. Although Enlightenment intellectuals attacked these traditional distinctions, they did not die easily. In the Prussian law code of 1794, marriage between noble males and middle-class females was forbidden without a government dispensation. Even without government regulation, however, different social groups could be easily distinguished everywhere in Europe by the distinctive, traditional clothes they wore.

Nevertheless, some forces of change were at work in this traditional society. The ideas of the Enlightenment made headway as reformers argued that the concept of an unchanging social order based on privilege was hostile to the progress of society. Despite these ideas, however, it would take the revolutionary upheavals at the end of the eighteenth century before the old order would finally begin to disintegrate.

Since society was still mostly rural in the eighteenth century, the peasantry constituted the largest social group, making up as much as 85 percent of Europe's population. There were rather wide differences, however, between peasants from area to area. The most important distinction—at least legally—was between the free peasant and the serf. In Britain, northern Italy, the Low Countries, Spain, most of France, and some areas of western Germany, peasants were largely free. Legally free peasants, however, were not exempt from burdens. Many peasants owned little or no land. And peasants who did own land were not free from compulsory services. Peasants could still owe a variety of dues and fees. Local aristocrats claimed hunting rights on peasant land and had monopolies over the flour mills, community ovens, and wine and oil presses needed by the peasants. Hunting rights, dues, and fees were all deeply resented.

The local villages in which they dwelt remained the centers of peasants' social lives. Villages, especially in western Europe, maintained public order; provided poor relief, a village church, and sometimes a schoolmaster; collected taxes for the central government; maintained roads and bridges; and established common procedures for sowing, plowing, and harvesting crops. But villages were often dominated by richer peasants and proved highly resistant to innovations, such as new crops and agricultural practices.

The nobles, who constituted about 2 or 3 percent of the European population, played a dominating role in society. Being born a noble automatically guaranteed a place at the top of the social order with all of its attendant special privileges and rights. The legal privileges of the nobility included judgment by their peers, immunity from severe punishment, exemption from many forms of taxation, and rights of jurisdiction. Especially in central and eastern Europe, the rights of landlords over their serfs were overwhelming.

Nobles also played important roles in military and government affairs. Since medieval times, landed aristocrats had functioned as military officers. Although monarchs found it impossible to exclude commoners from the ranks of officers, the tradition remained that nobles made the most natural and hence the best officers. Moreover, the eighteenth-century nobility played a significant role in the administrative machinery of state. In some countries, such as Prussia, the entire bureaucracy reflected aristocratic values. Moreover, in most of Europe, the landholding nobility controlled much of the life of their local districts.

Townspeople were still a distinct minority of the total population except in the Dutch Republic, Britain, and parts of Italy. At the end of the eighteenth century, about one-sixth of the French population lived in towns of 2,000 or more. The biggest city in Europe was London, with its 1,000,000 inhabitants, while Paris numbered between 550,000 and 600,000. Altogether, at least twenty European cities in twelve countries had populations over 100,000, including Naples, Lisbon, Moscow, St. Petersburg, Vienna, Amsterdam, Berlin, Rome, and Madrid.

Although urban dwellers were vastly outnumbered by rural inhabitants, towns played an important role in Western culture. The contrasts between a large city with its education, culture, and material consumption and the surrounding, often poverty-stricken countryside were striking, as is evident in this British traveler's account of Russia's St. Petersburg in 1741:

> The country about Petersburg has full as wild and desert a look as any in the Indies; you need not go above 200 paces out of the town to find yourself in a wild wood of firs, and such a low, marshy, boggy country that you would think God when he created the rest of the world for the use of mankind had created this for an inaccessible retreat for all sorts of wild beasts.[1]

Peasants often resented the prosperity of towns and their exploitation of the countryside to serve urban interests. Palermo in Sicily used one-third of the island's food production while paying only one-tenth of the taxes. Towns lived off the countryside not by buying, but by using tithes, rents, and feudal dues to acquire peasant produce.

Many cities in western and even central Europe had a long tradition of patrician oligarchies that continued to control their communities by dominating town and city councils. Despite their domination, patricians constituted only a small minority of the urban population. Just below the patricians stood an upper crust of the middle classes: nonnoble officeholders, financiers and bankers, merchants, wealthy rentiers who lived off their investments, and important professionals, including lawyers. Another large urban group was the petty bourgeoisie or lower middle class made up of master artisans, shopkeepers, and small traders. Below them were the laborers or working classes. Much urban industry was still done in small guild workshops by masters, journeymen, and apprentices. Urban communities also had a large group of unskilled workers who served as servants, maids, and cooks at pitifully low wages.

Despite an end to the ravages of plague, eighteenth-century cities still experienced high death rates, especially among children, because of unsanitary living conditions, polluted water, and a lack of sewerage facilities. One observer compared the stench of Hamburg to an open sewer that could be smelled for miles around. Overcrowding also exacerbated urban problems as cities continued to grow from an influx of rural immigrants. But cities proved no paradise for them as unskilled workers found few employment opportunities. The result was a serious problem of poverty in the eighteenth century (see the box on p. 550).

Changing Patterns of War: Global Confrontation

The philosophes had denounced war as a foolish waste of life and resources in stupid quarrels of no value to humankind. Rulers, however, paid little attention to these comments and continued their costly struggles. By the eighteenth century, the European system of self-governing, individual states was grounded largely in the principle of self-interest. Because international relations were based on considerations of power, the eighteenth-century concept of a "balance of power" was predicated on how to counterbalance the power of one state by another to prevent any one power from dominating the others. This balance of power, however, did not imply a desire for peace. Large armies created to defend a state's security were often used for offensive purposes as well. As Frederick the Great of Prussia remarked: "The fundamental rule of governments is the principle of extending their territories." Nevertheless, the regular use of diplomacy served at times to lead to compromise.

The diplomacy of the eighteenth century still focused primarily on dynastic interests or the desire of ruling families to provide for their dependents and extend their dynastic holdings. But the eighteenth century also saw the emergence of the concept of "reason of state," on the basis of which rulers looked beyond dynastic interests to the long-term future of their states.

International rivalry and the continuing centralization of the European states were closely related. The need for taxes to support large armies and navies created its own imperative for more efficient and effective control of power in the hands of bureaucrats who could collect taxes and organize states for the task of winning

POVERTY IN FRANCE

Poverty was a highly visible problem in the eighteenth century. Unlike the British, who had a system of public-supported poor relief, the French responded to poverty with ad hoc policies when conditions became acute. This selection is taken from an intendant's report to the controller-general at Paris describing his suggestions for a program to relieve the grain shortages expected for the winter months.

M. DE LA BOURDONNAYE, INTENDANT OF BORDEAUX, TO THE CONTROLLER-GENERAL, SEPTEMBER 30, 1708

Having searched for the means of helping the people of Agen in this cruel situation and having conferred with His Eminence, the Bishop, it seems to us that three things are absolutely necessary if the people are not to starve during the winter.

Most of the inhabitants do not have seed to plant their fields. However, we decided that we would be going too far if we furnished it, because those who have seed would also apply [for more]. Moreover, we are persuaded that all the inhabitants will make strenuous efforts to find some seed, since they have every reason to expect prices to remain high next year. . . .

But this project will come to nothing if the collectors of the taille continue to be as strict in the exercise of their functions as they have been of late and continue to employ troops [to force collection]. Those inhabitants who have seed grain would sell it to be freed from an oppressive garrison, while those who must buy seed, since they had none left from their harvest and have scraped together a little money for this purchase, would prefer to give up that money [for taxes] when put under police constraint. To avoid this, I feel it is absolutely necessary that you order the receivers-general to reduce their operations during this winter, at least with respect to the poor. . . .

We are planning to import wheat for this region from Languedoc and Quercy, and we are confident that there will be enough. But there are two things to be feared: one is the greed of the merchants. When they see that general misery has put them in control of prices, they will raise them to the point where the calamity is almost as great as if there were no provisions at all. The other fear is that the artisans and the lowest classes, when they find themselves at the mercy of the merchants, will cause disorders and riots. As a protective measure, it would seem wise to establish two small storehouses. . . . Ten thousand ecus [30,000 livres] would be sufficient for each. . . .

A third point demanding our attention is the support of beggars among the poor, as well as of those who have no other resources than their wages. Since there will be very little work, these people will soon be reduced to starvation. We should establish public workshops to provide work as was done in 1693 and 1694. I should choose the most useful kind of work, located where there are the greatest number of poor. In this manner, we should rid ourselves of those who do not want to work and assure the others of a moderate subsistence. For these workshops, we would need about 40,000 livres, or altogether 100,000 livres. The receiver-general of the taille of Agen could advance this sum. The 60,000 livres for the storehouses he would get back very soon. I shall await your orders on all of the above.

MARGINAL COMMENTS BY THE CONTROLLER-GENERAL

Operations for the collection of the taille are to be suspended. The two storehouses are to be established; great care must be taken to put them to good use. The interest on the advances will be paid by the king. His Majesty has agreed to the establishment of the public workshops for the able-bodied poor and is willing to spend up to 40,000 livres on them this winter.

wars. At the same time, the development of large standing armies ensured that political disputes would periodically be resolved by armed conflict rather than diplomacy.

Between 1715 and 1740, however, it seemed that Europeans preferred peace. But in 1740, a major conflict erupted over the succession to the Austrian throne. After the death of the Habsburg emperor Charles VI (1711–1740), King Frederick II of Prussia (1740–1786) took advantage of the succession of a woman, Maria Theresa (1740–1780), to the throne of Austria by invading Austrian Silesia. The vulnerability of Maria Theresa encouraged France to enter the war against its traditional enemy Austria; in turn, Maria Theresa made an alliance with the British, who feared French hegemony over continental affairs. All too quickly, the Austrian succession had produced a worldwide conflagration. The war was fought not only in Europe, where Prussia seized Silesia, and France occupied the Austrian Netherlands, but in the East, where France took Madras in India from the British, and in North America, where the British captured the French fortress of Louisbourg at the entrance to the St. Lawrence River. By 1748, all parties were exhausted and agreed to stop. The peace treaty guaranteed the return of all occupied territories to their original owners except for Silesia. Prussia's refusal to return Silesia guaranteed another war, at least between the two hostile central European powers of Prussia and Austria.

The Seven Years' War (1756–1763): A Global War

Maria Theresa refused to accept the loss of Silesia and prepared for its return by rebuilding her army while working diplomatically to separate Prussia from its chief ally, France. In 1756, Austria achieved what was soon labeled a diplomatic revolution. French-Austrian rivalry had been a fact of European diplomacy since the late sixteenth century. But two new rivalries made this old one seem superfluous: Britain and France over colonial empires, and Austria and Prussia over Silesia. France now abandoned Prussia and allied with Austria. Russia, which saw Prussia as a major hindrance to Russian goals in central Europe, joined the new alliance. In turn, Great Britain allied with Prussia. This diplomatic revolution of 1756 now led to another worldwide war.

There were three major areas of conflict: Europe, India, and North America. Europe witnessed the clash of the two major alliances: the British and Prussians against the Austrians, Russians, and French. With his superb army and military prowess, Frederick the Great of Prussia was able for some time to defeat the Austrian, French, and Russian armies. Under attack from three different directions, however, Frederick's forces were gradually worn down and faced utter defeat until a new Russian tsar, Peter III (1762), withdrew Russian troops from the conflict and from the Prussian lands that the Russians had occupied. His withdrawal guaranteed a stalemate and led the parties to negotiate a peace. The European conflict ended in 1763. All occupied territories were returned, while Austria officially recognized Prussia's permanent control of Silesia.

The Anglo-French struggle in the rest of the world had more decisive results. Known as the Great War for Empire, it was fought in India and North America. The French had returned Madras to Britain after the War of the Austrian Succession, but jockeying for power continued as both the French and the British claimed the support of opposing native Indian princes. The British under Robert Clive (1725–1774) ultimately won out, not because they had better forces but because they were more persistent. By the Treaty of Paris in 1763, the French withdrew and left India to the British (see Chapter 16).

By far, the greatest conflicts of the Seven Years' War took place in North America. Both the French and British colonial empires in the New World consisted of large parts of the West Indies and the North American continent. In the former, the British held Barbados, Jamaica, and Bermuda, while the French possessed Saint Dominique, Martinique, and Guadeloupe. On these tropical islands,

MAP 19.3 The Seven Years' War

both the British and the French had developed plantation economies, worked by African slaves, which produced tobacco, cotton, coffee, and sugar.

On the North American continent, the French and British colonies were structured in different ways. French North America (Canada and Louisiana) was run autocratically as a vast trading area, valuable for the acquisition of fur, leather, fish, and timber. However, the inability of the French state to get its people to emigrate to these North American possessions left them thinly populated.

British North America had come to consist of thirteen colonies on the eastern coast of the present United States. They were well populated, containing about 1.5 million people by 1750, and were also prosperous. Supposedly run by the British Board of Trade, the Royal Council, and Parliament, these thirteen colonies had legislatures that tended to act independently. Merchants in such port cities as Boston, Philadelphia, New York, and Charleston resented and resisted regulation from the British government.

Both the North American and West Indian colonies of Britain and France were assigned roles in keeping with mercantilist theory. They provided raw materials for the mother country while buying the latter's manufactured goods. Navigation acts regulated what could be taken from and sold to the colonies. Theoretically, the system was supposed to provide a balance of trade favorable to the mother country.

British and French rivalry in North America led to two primary areas of contention. One consisted of the waterways of the Gulf of St. Lawrence, guarded by the fortress of Louisbourg and by forts near the Great Lakes and Lake Champlain that protected French Quebec and French traders. The other was the unsettled Ohio River valley. The French began to move down from the Great Lakes and up from their forts on the Mississippi to establish forts from the Appalachians to the Mississippi River. To British settlers in the thirteen colonies, French activity threatened to cut off this vast area from exploitation by the settlers. The French were able to gain the support of the Indians; as traders and not settlers, they were viewed by the natives with less hostility than the British.

Despite initial French successes, British fortunes were revived by the efforts of William Pitt the Elder, who was convinced that the destruction of the French colonial empire was a necessary prerequisite for the creation of Britain's own colonial empire. Pitt's policy focused on making a minimal effort in Europe while concentrating resources on the colonial war, especially through use of the British navy. Although the French troops outnumbered the British, the ability of the French to use their troops in the New World was contingent upon naval support. The defeat of French fleets in major naval battles in 1759 gave the British an advantage because the French could no longer easily reinforce their garrisons. A series of British victories soon followed. In 1759, British forces under General James Wolfe defeated the French under General Louis-Joseph Montcalm on the Plains of Abraham outside Quebec. Both generals died in the battle. The British went on to seize Montreal, the Great Lakes area, and the Ohio valley. The French were forced to make peace. By the Treaty of Paris, they ceded Canada and the lands east of the Mississippi to Britain. Their ally Spain transferred Spanish Florida to British control; in return, the French gave their Louisiana territory to the Spanish. By 1763, Great Britain had become the world's greatest colonial power.

European Armies and Warfare in the Eighteenth Century

The professional standing army, initiated in the seventeenth century, became a standard feature of eighteenth-century Europe. Especially noticeable was the increase in the size of armies, which paralleled the development of absolutist states. From 1740 to 1780, the French army grew from 190,000 to 300,000 men; the Prussian from 83,000 to 200,000; the Austrian from 108,000 to 282,000; and the Russian from 130,000 to 290,000.

The composition of these armies reflected the hierarchical structure of European society and the great chasm that separated the upper and lower classes. Officers were primarily from the landed aristocracy, which had for centuries regarded military activity as one of its major functions. Middle-class individuals were largely kept out of the higher ranks of the officer corps while being admitted to the middle ranks. Rank-and-file soldiers came mostly from the lower classes of society. Some states, such as Prussia and Russia, conscripted able-bodied peasants. But many

THE DEATH OF WOLFE. The great powers of Europe fought the Seven Years' War in Europe, India, and North America. Despite initial French successes in North America, the British went on to win the war. This painting by Benjamin West presents a heroic rendering of the death of General Wolfe, the British commander who defeated the French forces at the Battle of Quebec.

states realized that this was counterproductive because they could not afford to waste agricultural labor. For that reason, eighteenth-century armies were partially composed of foreign troops, many from Switzerland or the petty German states. Of the great powers, Britain alone had no regular standing army and relied on mercenaries, evident in its use of German troops in America. Most troops in European armies, especially the French and the Austrian, were natives who enlisted voluntarily for six-year terms. Some were not exactly volunteers; often vagabonds and the unemployed were pressed into service. Most, however, came from the lower classes—peasants and also artisans from the cities—who saw the military as an opportunity to escape from hard times or personal problems.

The maritime powers, such as Britain and the Dutch Republic, regarded navies as more important than armies. In the second half of the eighteenth century, the British possessed 174 warships manned by 80,000 sailors. Conditions on these ships were often poor. Diseases such as scurvy and yellow fever were rampant, and crews were frequently gang-pressed into duty.

Colonial Empires and Revolution

As we have seen, the colonial empires in the Western Hemisphere were an integral part of the European economy in the eighteenth century and became entangled in the conflicts of the European states. Despite these close ties with Europe, the colonies of Latin America and British North America were developing along lines that sometimes differed significantly from those of Europe.

The Society of Latin America

In the sixteenth century, Portugal came to dominate Brazil, while Spain established an enormous colonial empire in the New World that included Central America, most of South America, and parts of North America. Within the lands of Central and South America, a new civilization arose that we have come to call Latin America. It was a multiracial society. Iberian (Spanish and Portuguese) settlers who arrived in the Western Hemisphere were small in number compared to the native Indians; many of the newcomers, especially in the early decades of colonization, were males who not only used female natives for their sexual pleasure, but married them as well. Already by 1501, Spanish rulers had authorized intermarriage between Europeans and native American Indians. As a result, a new people—the mestizos—appeared. Europeans also used native Indians to do their work for them. So many Indians succumbed to European diseases (see Chapter 14), however, that another group of people was brought to Latin America—the Africans.

African slaves were first imported to the Western Hemisphere in 1502. Over a period of three centuries, possibly as many as eight million slaves were brought to Spanish and Portuguese America. In Brazil and the Caribbean, where the cultivation of cane sugar by the plantation system demanded much human labor, Africans constituted almost the entire labor force. Because plantation owners preferred males as field hands, two out of every three Africans were male. Although female slaves also worked in the fields, many were used as domestic servants, prostitutes, and mistresses. Over a period of time, Africans were also brought to the cities, where they worked as artisans, servants, small tradesmen, and miners. Although Africans made enormous contributions to the economic life of Spanish America and Portuguese Brazil, they were usually treated with contempt and badly abused. But in many ways—music, dance, folklore, diet, language, religion—African influence remained a permanent part of Latin American culture.

Africans also contributed to Latin America's multiracial character. Mulattoes—the offspring of Africans and whites—joined mestizos and descendants of whites, Africans, and native Indians to produce a unique society in Latin America (see the box on p. 554). Unlike Europe, and unlike British North America, which remained a largely white offshoot of Europe, Latin America developed a multiracial society with less rigid attitudes about race.

THE ECONOMIC FOUNDATIONS

After realizing that the Americas were not Asia, both the Portuguese and the Spanish sought ways to benefit economically from their discoveries. The search for precious metals became a major objective. The Spaniards were especially successful, finding supplies of gold in the Caribbean and New Granada (Colombia) and silver in Mexico and the viceroyalty of Peru. The silver mine of Potosí in Upper Peru (Bolivia) was one of the world's richest. Overall, mines in the viceroyalty of New Spain (largely Mexico) produced half of the precious metals found in the New World. Most of the gold and silver was sent to Europe, and little remained in the New World to benefit those whose labor had produced it.

Although the pursuit of gold and silver offered prospects of fantastic financial rewards, agriculture proved to be a more long-lasting and rewarding source of prosperity for Latin America. Early on, the Spanish had instituted the *encomienda* system, which enabled individual Spaniards to collect tribute from the natives and use them as laborers. Protests from Catholic missionaries, who were appalled at the mistreatment of Indians and the rapid decline in their numbers, forced the Spanish government to change its policy. Beginning in 1542, the monarchy abolished the *encomienda* and replaced it with the *repartimento*, a new system under which landowners were permitted to use Indian laborers only on a temporary basis and only with

CLASS AND CASTE IN COLONIAL LATIN AMERICA

The mixture of white Iberians, African slaves, and native Indians created a multiracial society in Latin America. Gradually, a caste system emerged in which individuals' social status was often determined by their racial background. These excerpts, which are taken from an account by two Spanish travelers, describe this complex class and caste system in the Caribbean port of Cartagena, Colombia, and Lima, Peru.

GEORGE JUAN AND ANTONIO DE ULLOA, *VOYAGE TO SOUTH AMERICA*

The inhabitants may be divided into different castes or tribes, who derive their origin from a coalition of Whites, Negroes, and Indians. Of each of these we shall treat particularly.

The Whites may be divided into two classes, the Europeans and Creoles, or Whites born in the country. The former are commonly called Peninsulars, but are not numerous; most of them either return into Spain after acquiring a competent fortune, or remove up into inland provinces in order to increase it. Those who are settled at Cartagena, carry on the whole trade of that place, and live in opulence; whilst the other inhabitants are indigent, and reduced to have recourse to mean and hard labor for subsistence. The families of the White Creoles compose the landed interest; some of them have large estates, and are highly respected, because their ancestors came into the country invested with honorable posts, bringing their families with them when they settled here. . . .

Among the other tribes which are derived from an intermarriage of the Whites with the Negroes, the first are the Mulattoes. Next to these the *Tercerones*, produced from a White and a Mulatto. . . . After these follow the *Quarterones*, proceeding from a White and a *Terceron*. The last are the *Quinterones*, who owe their origin to a White and a *Quarteron*. This is the last gradation, there being no visible difference between them and the Whites, either in color or features. . . . Every person is so jealous of the order of their tribe or caste, that if, through inadvertence, you call them by a degree lower than what they actually are, they are highly offended. . . . These castes, from the Mulattoes, . . . are the mechanics of the city; the Whites, whether Creoles or Peninsulars, disdaining such a mean occupation follow nothing below merchandise. . . .

The inhabitants of Lima are composed of whites, or Spaniards, Negroes, Indians, Mestizos, and other castes, proceeding from the mixture of all three.

The Spanish families are very numerous. . . . Among these are reckoned a third or fourth part of the most distinguished nobility of Peru. . . . All these families live in a manner becoming their rank, having estates equal to their generous dispositions, keeping a great number of slaves and other domestics, and those who affect making the greatest figure, have coaches, while others content themselves with chaises, which are here so common, that no family of any substance is without one. . . . The funds to support these expenses, which in other parts would ruin families, are their large estates and plantations, civil and military employments or commerce, which is here accounted no derogation to families of the greatest distinction; but by this commerce is not to be understood the buying and selling by retail or in shops, every one trading proportional to his character and substance. . . .

The Negroes, Mulattoes, and their descendants, form the greater number of the inhabitants; and of these are the greatest part of the mechanics. . . . The third, and last class of inhabitants are the Indians and Mestizos, but these are very small in proportion to the largeness of the city, and the multitudes of the second class. They are employed in agriculture, in making earthen ware, and bringing all kinds of provisions to market, domestic services being performed by Negroes and Mulattoes, either slaves or free, though generally by the former.

the permission of the royal officials, who, it was thought, would be more responsible for the welfare of the Indians.

By the seventeenth century, the decline in the number of Indians led to a new system in which the owners of large estates paid wages to their Indian agricultural workers. By making loans to the Indians that the Indians could not repay in their lifetimes because of their low wages, the large landowners created a class of peons—native peasants permanently dependent on the landowners.

This creation of an oppressed class of wage laborers reminds us of another noticeable feature of Latin American agriculture—the dominating role of the large landowners. Both Spanish and Portuguese landowners amassed immense estates, leaving the Indians to work either as peons on the estates or as poor farmers on marginal lands. This system of large landowners and dependent peasants has remained one of the persistent features of Latin American society. Haciendas (as the estates were called in Spanish America) and fazendas (in Portuguese Brazil) could reach enormous sizes. Some haciendas in Mexico, for example, included over a million acres. By the eighteenth century, both Spanish haciendas and Brazilian fazendas were producing primarily for sale abroad.

Trade was another avenue for the economic exploitation of the American colonies. Colonies, according to classic mercantilist theory, were intended to be sources of raw materials. The American colonies were certainly that for both Spain and Portugal, as gold, silver, sugar, tobacco, diamonds, animal hides, and a number of other natural products made their way to Europe. The decline of Spain and Portugal had led these two states to depend even more on resources from their colonies, and they imposed strict mercantilist rules on them to keep others out. Spain, in particular, closely regulated the trade of its American colonies. Only two Spanish ports, Cádiz and Seville, were permitted to trade with the American colonies. Each year two fleets sailed from these ports to Vera Cruz and Portobelo, the only officially recognized ports in Spanish America for the transshipment of Latin American goods in the New World. From these two ports, the products of the immense colonial empire were shipped to Spain.

The British and French, however, proved too powerful to be excluded from this lucrative Latin American market. The British cajoled the Portuguese into allowing them into their Brazilian trade. The French were the first to break into the Spanish Latin American market when the French Bourbons became kings of Spain. The British entered the Spanish American markets in 1713, when Britain was granted the privilege, known as the *asiento*, of transporting 4,500 slaves a year to Spanish Latin America.

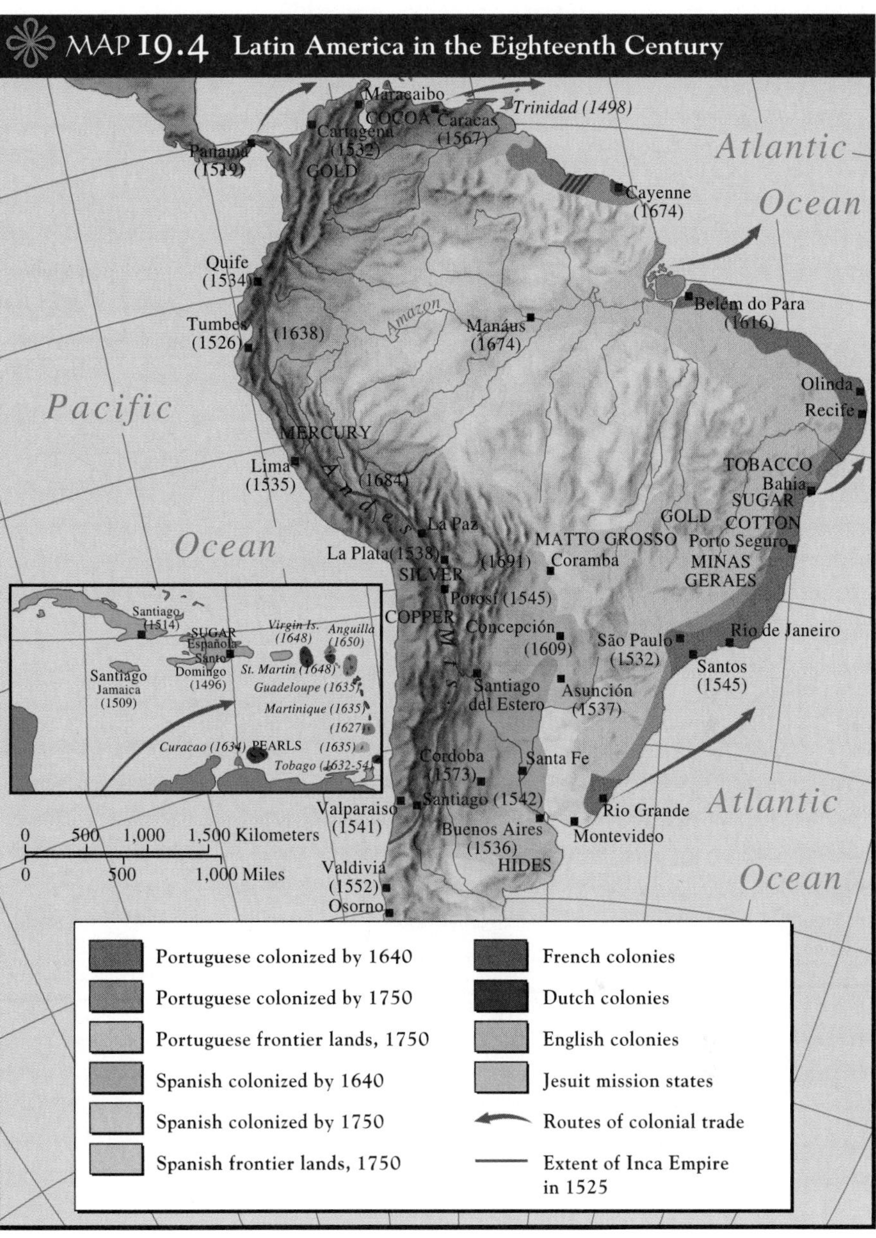

MAP 19.4 Latin America in the Eighteenth Century

In accordance with mercantilist theory, both Spain and Portugal tried to limit the role of their colonies to providing raw materials, while the mother countries supplied their colonists with manufactured goods. Decrees aimed at prohibiting manufacturing in the New World tended to be ignored, however. By the eighteenth century, Latin America was producing cotton cloth, pottery, shoes, and furniture for local markets.

THE STATE AND THE CHURCH IN COLONIAL LATIN AMERICA

Portuguese Brazil and Spanish America were colonial empires that lasted over three hundred years. The difficulties of communication and travel between the New World and Europe made it virtually impossible for the Spanish and Portuguese monarchs to maintain close regulation of their empires. Consequently, colonial officials in Latin America had much autonomy in implementing imperial policies, although the Iberians tried to keep the most important posts of colonial government in the hands of Europeans.

Beginning in the mid-sixteenth century, the Portuguese monarchy began to assert its control over Brazil by establishing the position of governor-general. The governor-general (later called a viceroy) developed a bureaucracy but had at best a loose control over the captains-general, who were responsible for governing the districts into which Brazil was divided. In the course of the eighteenth century, the Portuguese monarchy attempted to strengthen its control over Brazil by weakening the power of the captains-general and municipal governments. By 1800, the king and his viceroy were more powerful in Brazil than they had ever been.

THE MISSION

In 1609, two Jesuit priests embarked on a missionary calling with the Guarani Indians in eastern Paraguay. Eventually, the Jesuits established more than thirty missions in the region. Well organized and zealous, the Jesuits transformed their missions into profitable business activities. This description of a Jesuit mission in Paraguay was written by Félix de Azara, a Spanish soldier and scientist.

FÉLIX DE AZARA, *DESCRIPTION AND HISTORY OF PARAGUAY AND RIO DE LA PLATA*

Having spoken of the towns founded by the Jesuit fathers, and of the manner in which they were founded, I shall discuss the government which they established in them. . . . In each town resided two priests, a curate and a subcurate, who had certain assigned functions. The subcurate was charged with all the spiritual tasks, and the curate with every kind of temporal responsibility. . . .

The curate allowed no one to work for personal gain; he compelled everyone, without distinction of age or sex, to work for the community, and he himself saw to it that all were equally fed and dressed. For this purpose the curates placed in storehouses all the fruits of agriculture and the products of industry, selling in the Spanish towns their surplus of cotton, cloth, tobacco, vegetables, skins, and wood, transporting them in their own boats down the nearest rivers, and returning with implements and whatever else was required.

From the foregoing one may infer that the curate disposed of the surplus funds of the Indian towns, and that no Indian could aspire to own private property. This deprived them of any incentive to use reason or talent, since the most industrious, able, and worthy person had the same food, clothing, and pleasures as the most wicked, dull, and indolent. It also follows that although this form of government was well designed to enrich the communities it also caused the Indian to work at a languid pace, since the wealth of his community was of no concern to him.

It must be said that although the Jesuit fathers were supreme in all respects, they employed their authority with a mildness and a restraint that command admiration. They supplied everyone with abundant food and clothing. They compelled the men to work only half a day, and did not drive them to produce more. Even their labor was given a festive air, for they went in procession to the fields, to the sound of music . . . and the music did not cease until they had returned in the same way they had set out. They gave them many holidays, dances, and tournaments, dressing the actors and the members of the municipal councils in gold or silver tissue and the most costly European garments, but they permitted the women to act only as spectators.

They likewise forbade the women to sew; this occupation was restricted to the musicians, sacristans, and acolytes. But they made them spin cotton; and the cloth that the Indians wove, after satisfying their own needs, they sold together with the surplus cotton in the Spanish towns, as they did with the tobacco, vegetables, wood, and skins. The curate and his companion, or subcurate, had their own plain dwellings, and they never left them except to take the air in the great enclosed yard of their college. They never walked through the streets of the town or entered the house of any Indian or let themselves be seen by any woman—or indeed, by any man, except for those indispensable few through whom they issued their orders.

To rule his American empire, the king of Spain appointed a viceroy, the first of which was established for New Spain (Mexico) in 1535. Another viceroy was appointed for Peru in 1543. Not until the eighteenth century were two additional viceroyalties—New Granada and La Plata—added. Viceroyalties in turn were subdivided into smaller units administered by presidents and captains-general, who were theoretically subordinate to the viceroys. All of these major government positions were held by Spaniards. For creoles—American-born whites—the chief opportunity to hold a government post was the *cabildo* or city council.

In the eighteenth century, a new monarchical dynasty in Spain—the Bourbons—brought some noticeable changes to Spanish America. New royal officials called intendants were sent out to oversee financial and administrative affairs; they gave the monarchy more direct control of colonial Latin America—especially over finances. The Spanish Bourbon kings also liberalized economic policies by eliminating the old monopolistic trading practices.

From the beginning of their conquest of the New World, Iberian monarchs were determined to Christianize the native peoples. This policy meant that the Catholic church would play an important role in the New World, and one that added considerably to church power. It was also a role that facilitated the goals of the state. Conversion to Christianity meant conversion to European cultural patterns, and from the monarch's point of view, that meant a more stable empire. Church and state were closely interlinked in colonial Latin America.

Catholic missionaries—especially the Dominicans, Franciscans, and Jesuits—fanned out to different parts of the Spanish empire (see the box above). To facilitate their efforts, the missionaries brought Indians together into villages, where the natives could be converted, taught trades, and encouraged to grow crops. A German tourist in the eighteenth century commented, "The road leads through plantations of sugar, indigo, cotton, and coffee. The regularity which we observed in the construction of the villages reminded us that they all owe their origin to monks and missions. The streets are straight and parallel; they cross each other at right angles; and the church is erected in the great square situated in the center."[2] These missions enabled the missionaries to control the lives of the Indians and helped ensure that they would remain docile members of the empire. In such frontier districts as California and Texas, missions also served as military barriers to foreign encroachment.

The mass conversion of the Indians brought the organizational structures of Catholicism to the New World. By 1800, Spanish America possessed ten archbishoprics and thirty-eight bishoprics; Portuguese Brazil had one archbishopric and seven bishoprics. The Catholic church constructed hospitals and orphanages and accepted responsibility for educating native Americans. Monastic schools instructed Indian students in the basic rudiments of reading, writing, and arithmetic. Catholic clergy held most of the professorships at the University of Mexico, founded in 1551, as well as at the other twelve Spanish American universities. The Catholic church also provided outlets for women other than marriage. Nunneries were places of prayer and quiet contemplation, but women in religious orders, many of them of aristocratic background, often lived well and operated outside their establishments by running schools and hospitals. Indeed, one of these nuns, Sor Juana Inés de la Cruz (1651–1695), was one of seventeenth-century Latin America's best-known literary figures. She wrote poetry and prose and urged that women be educated.

The legacies bequeathed to the church by the rich enabled the Catholic church to build the magnificent cathedrals that adorn the cities of Latin America. Even today, their architectural splendor reminds us of the wealth and power that the Catholic church exercised in the Iberian colonial empires of the New World.

British North America

In the eighteenth century, Spanish power in the New World was increasingly challenged by the growing presence of the British. (The United Kingdom of Great Britain had come into existence in 1707 when the governments of England and Scotland were united; the term *British* came into use to refer to both English and Scots.) The eighteenth-century British political system was characterized by a sharing of power between king and Parliament, with Parliament gradually gaining the upper hand. The king chose ministers responsible to himself who set policy and guided Parliament; Parliament had the power to make laws, levy taxes, pass the budget, and indirectly influence the king's ministers. The eighteenth-century British Parliament was dominated by a landed aristocracy that historians usually divide into two groups: an upper aristocracy, or the peers who sat for life in the House of Lords, and the landed gentry, lesser nobles who were elected to the House of Commons. The two groups had much in common; both were landowners with similar economic interests, and they frequently intermarried. The deputies to the House of Commons were chosen from the boroughs and counties but not by popular voting and hardly in any equitable fashion. The number of persons eligible to vote in the boroughs varied wildly and was often quite small, enabling wealthy landed aristocrats to gain support by patronage and bribery. Although deputies from the counties were elected by holders of property worth at least forty shillings a year, members of the leading landed gentry families were elected over and over again.

SOR JUANA INÉS DE LA CRUZ. Nunneries in colonial Latin America gave women—especially upper-class women—some opportunity for intellectual activity. As a woman, Juana Inés de la Cruz was denied admission to the University of Mexico. Consequently, she entered a convent, where she wrote poetry and plays until her superiors forced her to focus on less worldly activities.

In 1714, a new dynasty—the Hanoverians—was established when the last Stuart ruler, Queen Anne (1702–1714), died without an heir. The crown was offered to the Protestant rulers of the German state of Hanover. Since the first Hanoverian king (George I) did not speak English and neither the first nor the second George had much familiarity with the British system, their chief ministers were allowed to handle Parliament. Robert Walpole served as prime minister from 1721 to 1742 and pursued a peaceful foreign policy to avoid new land taxes. But new forces were emerging in eighteenth-century Britain as growing trade and industry led an ever increasing middle class to favor expansion of trade and world empire. The exponents of empire found a spokesman in William Pitt the Elder, who became prime minister in 1757 and furthered imperial ambitions by acquiring Canada and India in the Seven Years' War.

THE AMERICAN REVOLUTION AND THE BIRTH OF A NEW NATION

At the end of the Seven Years' War in 1763, Great Britain had become the world's greatest colonial power. In North America, Britain now controlled Canada and the lands east of the Mississippi. After the war, British policy makers sought to obtain new revenues from the colonies to pay the expenses the British army incurred in defending the colonists. An attempt to levy new taxes by the Stamp Act in 1765 led to riots and the statute's quick repeal. The immediate crisis had ended, but the fundamental cause of the dispute had not been resolved.

In the course of the eighteenth century, significant differences had arisen between the American and British political worlds. Both peoples shared the same property requirement for voting—voters had to possess property that could be rented for at least forty shillings a year—but it resulted in a disparity in the number of voters in the two countries. In Britain fewer than one in five adult males had the right to vote. In the colonies, where a radically different economic structure led to an enormous group of independent farmers, the property requirement allowed over 50 percent of adult males to vote.

The Americans and British also had different ideas of empire. The British viewed their empire as a single entity with Parliament as the supreme authority throughout. Only Parliament could make laws for all the people in the empire, including the American colonists. The Americans, on the other hand, had their own representative assemblies; to them, neither king nor Parliament should interfere in their internal affairs. American colonists believed strongly that no tax could be levied without the consent of an assembly whose members actually represented the people.

THE DECLARATION OF INDEPENDENCE. John Trumbull's famous painting, *The Signing of the Declaration*, shows members of the committee responsible for the Declaration of Independence (from left to right, John Adams, Roger Sherman, Robert Livingston, Thomas Jefferson, and Benjamin Franklin) standing before John Hancock, president of the Second Continental Congress.

Crisis followed crisis in the 1770s. The colonies' desire to take collective action against what was perceived as Britain's repressive actions led to the First Continental Congress, which met at Philadelphia in September 1774. The more militant members refused to compromise and urged the colonists to "take up arms and organize militias." When a British army attempted to stop rebel mobilization in Massachusetts, fighting erupted at Lexington and Concord between colonists and redcoats (British soldiers) in April 1775.

Despite the outbreak of hostilities, the colonists did not rush headlong into rebellion and war. It was more than a year after Lexington and Concord before the decision was made to declare their independence from the British Empire. On July 4, 1776, the Second Continental Congress approved a Declaration of Independence written by Thomas Jefferson. A stirring political document, the Declaration of Independence affirmed the Enlightenment's natural rights of "life, liberty, and the pursuit of happiness" and declared the colonies to be "free and independent states absolved from all allegiance to the British crown." The war for American independence had formally begun.

The war against Great Britain was a great gamble. Britain was a strong European military power with enormous financial resources; by 1778, Britain had sent 50,000 regular British troops and 30,000 German mercenaries to America. The Second Continental Congress had authorized the formation of a Continental Army under George Washington as commander-in-chief. As a southerner, Washington added balance to an effort that up to now had been led by New Englanders. Nevertheless, compared to the British forces, the Continental Army consisted of undisciplined amateurs whose terms of service were usually very brief. The colonies also had militia units, but they likewise tended to be unreliable. Although 400,000 men served in the Continental Army and the militias during the course of the war, Washington never had more than 20,000 troops available for any single battle.

Of great importance to the colonies' cause was the support they received from foreign countries that were eager to gain revenge for their defeats in earlier wars at the hands of the British. The French were particularly generous in supplying arms and money to the rebels from the beginning of the war. French officers and soldiers also served in Washington's army. The defeat of the British at Saratoga in October 1777 finally led the French to grant diplomatic recognition to the American state. When Spain in 1779 and the Dutch Republic in 1780 entered the war against Great Britain, and Russia formed the League of Armed Neutrality in 1780 to protect neutral shipping from British attacks, the British were faced with war against much of Europe as well as the Americans. Despite having won most of the battles, the British were in danger of losing the war. When the army of General Cornwallis was forced to surrender to a combined American and French army and French fleet under Washington at Yorktown in 1781, the British decided to call it quits. After extensive negotiations, the Treaty of Paris was signed in 1783. It recognized the independence of the American colonies and surprisingly granted the Americans control of the western territory from the Appalachians to the Mississippi River.

Although the thirteen American colonies agreed to "hang together" to gain their independence from the British, a fear of concentrated power and concern for their own interests caused them to have little enthusiasm for establishing a united nation with a strong central government. The Articles of Confederation, ratified in 1781, did little to provide for a strong central government. A series of economic, political, and international problems soon led to a movement for a different form of national government. In the summer of 1787, fifty-five delegates met in a convention in Philadelphia that was authorized by the Confederation Congress "for the sole and express purpose of revising the Articles of Confederation." The convention's delegates—wealthy, politically experienced, well-educated, and nationalistically inclined—rejected revision and decided to devise a new constitution.

The proposed Constitution created a central government distinct from and superior to the governments of the individual states. The national government was given the power to levy taxes, raise a national army, regulate domestic and foreign trade, and create a national currency. Following Montesquieu's principle of a "separation of powers" to provide a system of "checks and balances," the central or federal government was divided into three branches, each with some power to check the functioning of the others. A president would serve as the chief executive with the power to execute laws, veto the legislature's acts, make judicial and executive appointments, supervise foreign affairs, and direct military forces. Legislative power was vested in the second branch of government, a bicameral legislature composed of a Senate elected by the state legislatures and a House of Representatives elected directly by the people. The federal judiciary, embodied in a Supreme Court and other courts "as deemed necessary" by Congress, provided the third branch of government. With judges nominated by the executive and approved by the legislative branch, the federal judiciary would enforce the Constitution as the "supreme law of the land."

The constitutional convention had stipulated that the new Constitution would have to be ratified by popularly chosen conventions in nine of the thirteen states before it would take effect. After fierce contests, the Federalists, who favored the new Constitution, won, although the margin of victory was quite slim. Important to their success had been a promise to add a Bill of Rights to the Constitution as the new government's first piece of business. Accordingly, in March of 1789, the new Congress enacted the first ten amendments to the Constitution, ever since known as the Bill of Rights. These guaranteed freedom of religion, speech, press, petition, and assembly, as well as the right to bear arms, the right to be protected against unreasonable searches and

MAP 19.5 North America, 1700–1803

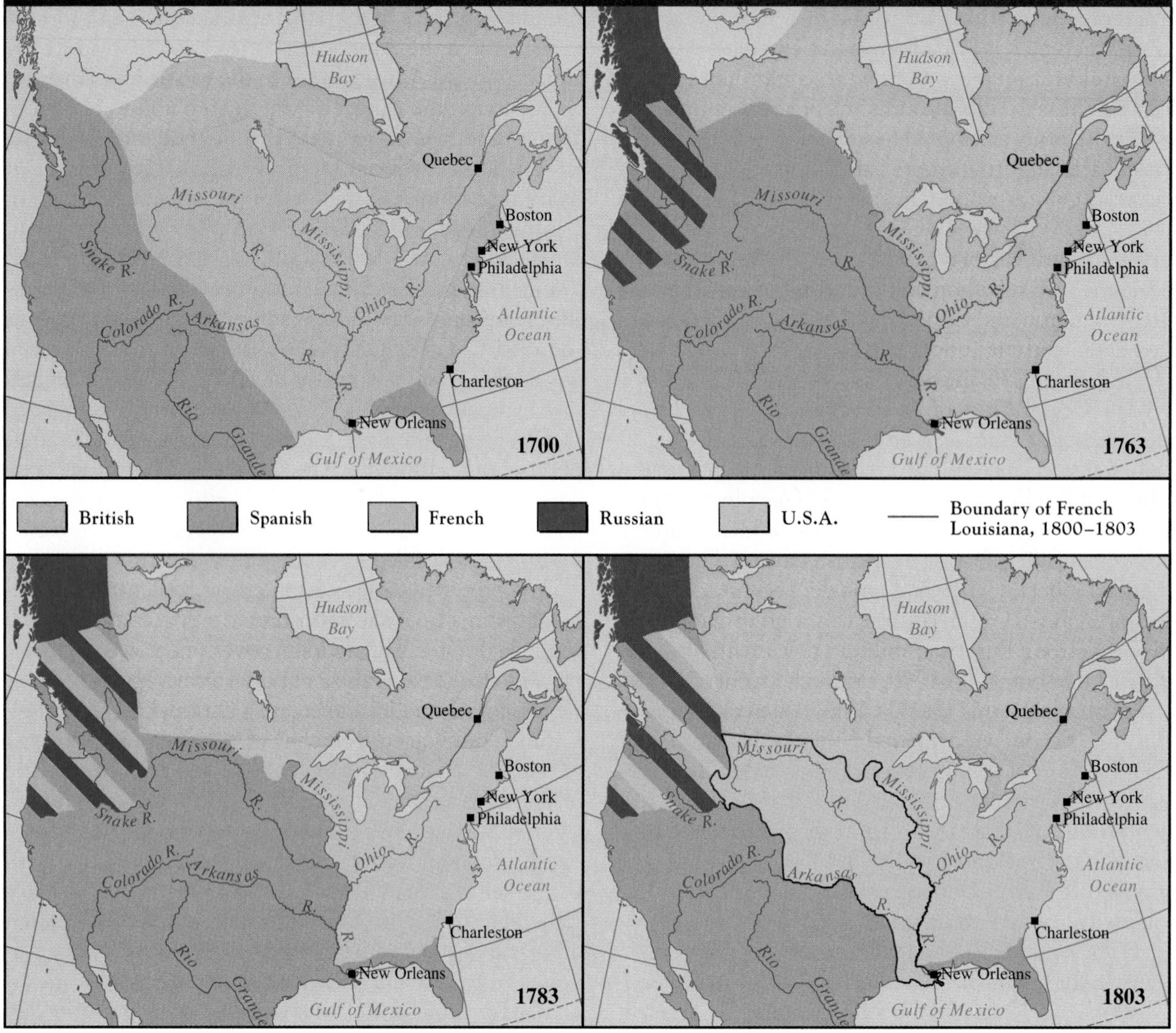

British | Spanish | French | Russian | U.S.A. | Boundary of French Louisiana, 1800–1803

arrests, trial by jury, due process of law, and the protection of property rights. Although many of these rights had their origins in English law, others were derived from the natural rights philosophy of the eighteenth-century philosophes and the American experience. Is it any wonder that many European intellectuals saw the American Revolution as the embodiment of the Enlightenment's political dreams?

Toward a New Political Order

The year 1789 witnessed two far-reaching events, the beginning of a new United States of America and the eruption of the French Revolution. Compared to the American Revolution, the French Revolution was more complex, more violent, and far more radical, with its attempt to reconstruct both a new political order and a new social order. But while the French were trying to create a new kind of state and a new kind of society, the rulers of other European states were attempting to come to terms with the ideas of the Enlightenment. Their failure helped ensure that the lessons of the French Revolution would find willing listeners elsewhere in Europe.

Background: Enlightened Absolutism in the Eighteenth Century

There is no doubt that Enlightenment thought had some impact on the political development of European states in the eighteenth century. Closely related to the Enlightenment idea of natural laws was the belief in natural rights, which were thought to be inalienable privileges that ought not to be withheld from any person. These natural rights included equality before the law, freedom of religious worship, freedom of speech and press, and the right to assemble, hold property, and pursue happiness. The American Declaration of Independence summarized the Enlightenment concept of natural rights in its opening paragraph: "We hold these truths to be self-evident, that all men are created equal; that they are endowed by their creator with certain unalienable rights; that among these are life, liberty and the pursuit of happiness."

But how were these natural rights to be established and preserved? In the opinion of many philosophes, most people needed the direction provided by an enlightened ruler. What, however, made rulers enlightened? They must allow religious toleration, freedom of speech and press, and the rights of private property. They must foster the arts, sciences, and education. Above all, they must not be arbitrary in their rule; they must obey the laws and enforce them fairly for all subjects. Only strong monarchs seemed capable of overcoming vested interests and effecting the reforms society needed. Reforms then should come from above—from the rulers—rather than from the people below. Distrustful of the masses, the philosophes believed that absolute rulers, swayed by enlightened principles, were the best hope of reforming their societies.

The extent to which rulers actually put these principles into practice has been much discussed. Many historians once assumed that a new type of monarchy emerged in the later eighteenth century, which they called "enlightened despotism" or "enlightened absolutism." Monarchs such as Frederick II of Prussia, Catherine the Great of Russia, and Joseph II of Austria supposedly followed the advice of the philosophes and ruled by enlightened principles, creating a path to modern nationhood. Recently, however, scholars have questioned the usefulness of the concept of "enlightened absolutism." We can best determine the extent to which it can be applied by examining the major "enlightened absolutists" of the later eighteenth century.

PRUSSIA: THE ARMY AND THE BUREAUCRACY

Two able Prussian kings in the eighteenth century, Frederick William I and Frederick II, further developed the two major institutions—the army and the bureaucracy—that were the backbone of Prussia. Frederick William I (1713–1740) promoted the evolution of Prussia's highly efficient civil bureaucracy by establishing the General Directory. Its supervision of military, police, economic, and financial affairs made it the chief administrative agent of the central government. Frederick William strove to maintain a highly efficient bureaucracy of civil service workers. It had its own code in which the supreme values were obedience, honor, and service to the king as the highest duty. As Frederick William asserted: "One must serve the king with life and limb, with goods and chattels, with honor and conscience, and surrender everything except salvation. The latter is reserved for God. But everything else must be mine."[3]

Frederick William's other major concern was the army. By the end of his reign, he had doubled its size. Though tenth in geographical size and thirteenth in population in Europe, Prussia had the fourth largest army, after France, Russia, and Austria. The nobility or landed aristocracy known as Junkers, who owned large estates with many serfs, were the officers in the Prussian army. They too had a strong sense of service to the king or state. Prussian nobles believed in duty, obedience, and sacrifice. At the same time, because of its size and reputation as one of the best armies in Europe, the Prussian army was the most important institution in the state.

Frederick the Great (1740–1786) was one of the best educated and most cultured monarchs in the eighteenth century. He was well versed in Enlightenment thought and even invited Voltaire to live at his court for several years. A believer in the king as the "first servant of the state," Frederick the Great became a conscientious ruler who made few innovations in administration. His diligence in overseeing its operation, however, made the Prussian bureaucracy famous for both efficiency and honesty.

For a time, Frederick seemed quite willing to follow the philosophes' recommendations for reform. He established a single code of laws for his territories that eliminated the use of torture except in treason and murder cases. He also granted a limited freedom of speech and press as well as complete religious toleration, no difficult task since he had no strong religious convictions anyway. Although Frederick was well aware of the philosophes' condemnation of serfdom, he was too dependent on the Prussian nobility to interfere with it or with the hierarchical structure of Prussian society. In fact, Frederick II was a social conservative who made Prussian society even more aristocratic than it had been before. Frederick reversed his father's policy of allowing commoners to have power in the civil service and reserved the higher positions in the bureaucracy for members of the nobility. The upper ranks of the bureaucracy came close to constituting a hereditary caste over time.

Like his predecessors, Frederick the Great took a great interest in military affairs and enlarged the Prussian army (to 200,000 men). Unlike his predecessors, he had no objection to using it. As we have seen, Frederick did not hesitate to take advantage of a succession crisis in the Habsburg monarchy to seize the Austrian province of Silesia for Prussia. This act led to Austria's bitter hostility toward Prussia and Frederick's engagement in two major wars, the War of the Austrian Succession and the Seven Years' War. Although the latter war left his country exhausted, Frederick succeeded in keeping Silesia. After the wars, the first partition of Poland with Austria and Russia in 1772 gave

MAP 19.6 Europe in 1763

him the Polish territory between Prussia and Brandenburg, which linked some of the scattered lands of Prussia. By the end of his reign, Prussia was recognized as a great European power.

THE AUSTRIAN EMPIRE OF THE HABSBURGS

The Austrian Empire had become one of the great European states by the beginning of the eighteenth century. The city of Vienna, center of the Habsburg monarchy, was filled with magnificent palaces and churches built in the Baroque style and became the music capital of Europe. And yet Austria—by its very nature as a sprawling empire composed of many different nationalities, languages, religions, and cultures—found it difficult to provide common laws and administrative centralization for its people. Although Empress Maria Theresa (1740–1780) managed to make administrative reforms that helped centralize the Austrian Empire, these reforms were done for practical reasons—to strengthen the power of the Habsburg state—and were accompanied by an enlargement and modernization of the armed forces. Maria Theresa remained staunchly conservative and was not open to the philosophes' calls for wider reform. But her successor was.

Joseph II (1780–1790) was determined to make changes; at the same time, he carried on his mother's chief goal of enhancing Habsburg power within the monarchy and Europe. Joseph II was an earnest man who believed in the need to sweep away anything standing in the path of reason. As Joseph expressed it: "I have made Philosophy the lawmaker of my empire; her logical applications are going to transform Austria."

Joseph's reform program was far-reaching. He abolished serfdom and tried to give the peasants hereditary rights to their holdings. A new penal code was instituted that abrogated the death penalty and established the principle of equality of all before the law. Joseph produced drastic religious reforms as well, including complete religious toleration and restrictions on the Catholic church. Altogether, Joseph II issued 6,000 decrees and 11,000 laws in his effort to transform Austria.

Joseph's reform program proved overwhelming for Austria, however. He alienated the nobility by freeing the serfs and alienated the church by his attacks on the monastic establishment. Even the serfs were unhappy, unable to

CHRONOLOGY

THE EUROPEAN STATES—ENLIGHTENED ABSOLUTISM IN THE EIGHTEENTH CENTURY

Prussia	
Frederick William I	1713–1740
Frederick II the Great	1740–1786
The Austrian Empire	
Maria Theresa	1740–1780
Joseph II	1780–1790
Russia	
Peter III	1762
Catherine II the Great	1762–1796
Pugachev's rebellion	1773–1775
Charter of the Nobility	1785
Poland	
First partition	1772
Second partition	1793
Third partition	1795

comprehend the drastic changes inherent in Joseph's policies. His attempt to rationalize the administration of the empire by imposing German as the official bureaucratic language alienated the non-German nationalities. As Joseph complained, there were not enough people for the kind of bureaucracy he needed. He realized his failure when he wrote his own epitaph for his gravestone: "Here lies Joseph II who was unfortunate in everything that he undertook." His successors undid many of his reform efforts.

RUSSIA UNDER CATHERINE THE GREAT

In Russia, Peter the Great was followed by a series of six weak successors who were made and unmade by the palace guard. After the last of these weak tsars, Peter III, was murdered by a faction of nobles, his German wife emerged as autocrat of all the Russias. Catherine II the Great (1762–1796) was an intelligent woman who was familiar with the works of the philosophes and seemed to favor enlightened reforms. She invited the French philosophe Diderot to Russia and, when he arrived, urged him to speak frankly "as man to man." He did, outlining a far-reaching program of political and financial reform. But Catherine was skeptical about impractical theories, which, she said, "would have turned everything in my kingdom upside down." She did consider the idea of a new law code that would recognize the principle of the equality of all people in the eyes of the law (see the box on p. 564). But in the end she did nothing, knowing that her success depended on the support of the Russian nobility. In 1785, she gave the nobles a Charter of Nobility that exempted them from taxes.

Catherine's policy of favoring the landed nobility led to even worse conditions for the Russian peasants and a rebellion. Led by an illiterate Cossack, Emelyan Pugachev, the rebellion spread across southern Russia. But the rebellion soon faltered, and Pugachev was captured, tortured, and executed. The rebellion collapsed completely, and Catherine responded by even greater measures against the peasantry. All rural reform was halted, and serfdom was expanded into newer parts of the empire.

Above all, Catherine proved a worthy successor to Peter the Great in her policies of territorial expansion westward (into Poland) and southward (to the Black Sea). Russia spread southward by defeating the Turks and gaining some land and the privilege of protecting Greek Orthodox Christians in the Ottoman Empire. Russian expansion westward occurred at the expense of neighboring Poland. In the three partitions of Poland, Russia gained about 50 percent of Polish territory.

CATHERINE THE GREAT. Autocrat of Russia, Catherine was an intelligent ruler who favored reform. She found it expedient, however, to retain much of the old system in order to keep the support of the landed nobility. This portrait by Dmitry Levitsky shows her in legislative regalia in the Temple of Justice in 1783.

THE PROPOSALS OF CATHERINE II FOR A NEW LAW CODE

Catherine II the Great of Russia appeared for a while to be an enlightened ruler. In 1767, she convened a legislative commission to prepare a new code of laws for Russia. In her famous Instruction, *she gave the delegates a detailed guide to the principles they should follow. Although the guidelines were obviously culled from the liberal ideas of the philosophes, the commission itself accomplished nothing, and Catherine's* Instruction *was soon forgotten.*

CATHERINE II, PROPOSALS FOR A NEW LAW CODE

13. What is the true End of Monarchy? Not to deprive People of their natural Liberty; but to correct their Actions, in order to attain the supreme good.
33. The Laws ought to be so framed, as to secure the Safety of every Citizen as much as possible.
34. The Equality of the Citizens consists in this; that they should all be subject to the same Laws.
38. A Man ought to form in his own Mind an exact and clear Idea of what Liberty is. Liberty is the Right of doing whatsoever the Laws allow: And if any one Citizen could do what the Law forbid, there would be no more Liberty; because others would have an equal Power of doing the same.
123. The Usage of Torture is contrary to all the Dictates of Nature and Reason; even Mankind itself cries out against it, and demands loudly the total Abolition of it.
180. That Law, therefore, is highly beneficial to the Community where it is established, which ordains that every Man shall be judged by his Peers and Equals. For when the Fate of a Citizen is in Question, all Prejudices arising from the Difference of Rank or Fortune should be stifled; because they ought to have no Influence between the Judges and the Parties accused.
194. No Man ought to be looked upon as guilty, before he has received his judicial Sentence; nor can the Laws deprive him of their Protection, before it is proved that he has forfeited all Right to it. What Right therefore can Power give to any to inflict Punishment upon a Citizen at a Time, when it is yet dubious, whether he is Innocent or guilty?

ENLIGHTENED ABSOLUTISM REVISITED

Of the three major rulers most closely associated traditionally with enlightened absolutism—Joseph II, Frederick II, and Catherine the Great—only Joseph II sought truly radical changes based on Enlightenment ideas. Both Frederick and Catherine liked to be cast as disciples of the Enlightenment, expressed interest in enlightened reforms, and even attempted some. But the policies of neither seemed seriously affected by Enlightenment thought. Necessities of state and maintenance of the existing system took precedence over reform. Indeed, many historians maintain that Joseph, Frederick, and Catherine were all primarily guided by a concern for the power and well-being of their states and that their policies were not all that different from those of their predecessors. In the final analysis, heightened state power was used to create armies and wage wars to gain more power. Nevertheless, in their desire to build stronger state systems, these rulers did pursue such enlightened measures as legal reform, religious toleration, and the extension of education because these served to create more satisfied subjects and strengthened the state in significant ways.

It would be foolish, however, to overlook the fact that the ability of enlightened rulers to make reforms was also limited by political and social realities. Everywhere in Europe the hereditary aristocracy was still the most powerful class in society. Enlightened reforms were often limited to those administrative and judicial reforms that did not seriously undermine the powerful interests of the European nobility. As the chief beneficiaries of a system based on traditional rights and privileges for their class, they were certainly not willing to support a political ideology that trumpeted the principle of equal rights for all. The first serious challenge to their supremacy would come in the French Revolution, which opened the door to a more modern world of politics.

The French Revolution Begins

Although we associate events like the French Revolution with sudden changes, the causes of such events involve long-range problems as well as immediate, precipitating forces. Hence the causes of the French Revolution must be found in a multifaceted examination of French society and its problems in the late eighteenth century.

BACKGROUND TO THE FRENCH REVOLUTION

The long-range or indirect causes of the French Revolution must first be sought in the condition of French society. Before the Revolution, France was a society grounded in the inequality of rights or the idea of privilege. Its population of 27 million was divided, as it had been since the Middle Ages, into three orders or estates.

The First Estate consisted of the clergy and numbered about 130,000 people, who owned approximately 10 percent of the land. Clergy were exempt from the *taille*, France's chief tax, although the church had agreed to pay a "voluntary" contribution every five years to the state. The clergy were also radically divided: the higher clergy, stemming from aristocratic families, shared the interests of the nobility, while the parish priests were often poor and from the class of commoners.

The Second Estate was the nobility, composed of 120,000 to 350,000 people, who nevertheless owned about 25 to 30 percent of the land. The nobility had continued to play an important and even crucial role in French society in the eighteenth century, holding many of the leading positions in the government, the military, the law courts, and the higher church offices. The French nobility was also divided. The nobility of the robe derived their status from officeholding, which had often opened the doors for commoners to receive noble status. These nobles now dominated the royal law courts and important administrative offices. The nobility of the sword claimed to be descended from the original medieval nobility. The nobles as a whole sought to expand their power at the expense of the monarchy—to defend liberty by resisting the arbitrary actions of the crown, as some nobles asserted—and to maintain their monopolistic control over positions in the military, church, and government. Moreover, the possession of privileges remained a hallmark of the nobility. Common to all nobles were tax exemptions, especially from the *taille*.

The Third Estate, or the commoners of society, constituted the overwhelming majority of the French population. They were divided by vast differences in occupation, level of education, and wealth. The peasants, who alone constituted 75 to 80 percent of the total population, were by far the largest segment of the Third Estate. They owned about 35 to 40 percent of the land, although their landholdings varied from area to area and over half had no or little land on which to survive. Serfdom no longer existed on any large scale in France, but French peasants still had obligations to their local landlords that they deeply resented. These "relics of feudalism," survivals from an earlier age, included the payment of fees for the use of village facilities, such as the flour mill, community oven, and winepress, as well as tithes to the clergy.

Another part of the Third Estate consisted of skilled artisans, shopkeepers, and other wage earners in the cities. Although the eighteenth century had been a period of rapid urban growth, 90 percent of French towns had fewer than 10,000 inhabitants, while only nine cities had more than 50,000. In the eighteenth century, consumer prices rose faster than wages, causing these urban groups to experience a noticeable decline in purchasing power. In Paris, for example, income lagged behind food prices and especially behind a 140 percent rise in rents for working people in skilled and unskilled trades. The economic discontent of this segment of the Third Estate and often simply their struggle to survive led them to play an important role in the Revolution, especially in the city of Paris.

About 8 percent of the population, or 2.3 million people, constituted the bourgeoisie or middle class, who owned about 20 to 25 percent of the land. This group included merchants, industrialists, and bankers, who controlled the resources of trade, manufacturing, and finance and benefited from the economic prosperity after 1730. The bourgeoisie also included professional people—lawyers, holders of public offices, doctors, and writers. Many members of the bourgeoisie sought security and status through the purchase of land. They had their own set of grievances because they were often excluded from the social and political privileges monopolized by the nobles. At the same time, remarkable similarities existed at the upper levels of society between the wealthier bourgeoisie and the nobility. It was still possible for wealthy middle-class individuals to enter the ranks of the nobility by obtaining public offices and entering the nobility of the robe. During the eighteenth century, 6,500 new noble families were created. Moreover, the new and critical ideas of the Enlightenment proved attractive to both aristocrats and bourgeoisie. Members of both groups shared a common world of liberal political thought. Both aristocratic and bourgeois elites, long accustomed to a new socioeconomic reality based on wealth and economic achievement, were increasingly frustrated by a monarchical system resting on privileges and an old and rigid social order based on the concept of estates. The opposition of these elites to the old order ultimately led them to take drastic action against the monarchical regime, although they soon split over the problem of how far to proceed in eliminating traditional privileges. In a real sense, the Revolution had its origins in political grievances.

The inability of the French monarchy to deal with new social realities and problems was exacerbated by specific problems in the 1780s. Although France had enjoyed fifty years of economic expansion, the French economy still experienced periodic crises. Bad harvests in 1787 and 1788 and the beginnings of a manufacturing depression resulted in food shortages, rising prices for food and other necessities, and unemployment in the cities. The number of poor, estimated by some at almost one-third of the population, reached crisis proportions on the eve of the Revolution.

The immediate cause of the French Revolution was the near collapse of government finances. French governmental expenditures continued to grow due to costly wars and royal extravagance. On the verge of a complete financial collapse, the government of Louis XVI (1774–1792) was finally forced to call a meeting of the Estates-General, the French parliamentary body, which had not met since 1614. The Estates-General consisted of representatives from the three orders of French society. In the elections for the Estates-General, the government had ruled that the Third Estate should get double representation (it did, after all, constitute 97 percent of the population). Consequently, while both the First Estate (the clergy) and the Second (the nobility) had about 300 delegates each, the commoners had almost 600 representatives. Two-thirds of the latter were people with legal training, while three-fourths were from towns of over 2,000 inhabitants, giving the Third Estate a particularly strong legal and urban representation. Most members of the Third Estate advocated a regular constitutional government that would abolish the fiscal privileges of the church and nobility as the major way to regenerate France.

FROM ESTATES-GENERAL TO A NATIONAL ASSEMBLY

The Estates-General opened at Versailles on May 5, 1789. It was troubled from the start with the problem of whether voting should be by order or by head (each delegate having one vote). Traditionally, each order would vote separately; each would have veto power over the other two, thus guaranteeing aristocratic control over reforms. But the Third Estate was opposed to this approach and pushed its demands for voting by head. Since it had double representation, with the assistance of liberal nobles and clerics, it could turn the three estates into a single-chamber legislature that would reform France in its own way. Most delegates still desired to make changes within a framework of respect for the authority of the king; revival or reform did not mean the overthrow of traditional institutions. But when the First Estate declared in favor of voting by order, the Third Estate felt compelled to respond in a significant fashion. On June 17, 1789, the Third Estate voted to constitute itself a "National Assembly" and decided to draw up a constitution. Three days later, on June 20, the deputies of the Third Estate arrived at their meeting place, only to find the doors locked; thereupon they moved to a nearby indoor tennis court and swore (hence, the Tennis Court Oath) that they would continue to meet until they had produced a French constitution. These actions

STORMING OF THE BASTILLE. Louis XVI planned to use force to dissolve the Estates-General, but a number of rural and urban uprisings by the common people prevented this action. The fall of the Bastille, pictured here in an anonymous painting, is perhaps the most famous of the urban risings.

of June 17 and June 20 constitute the first step in the French Revolution because the Third Estate had no legal right to act as the National Assembly. This revolution, largely the work of the lawyers of the Third Estate, was soon in jeopardy, however, as the king sided with the First Estate and threatened to dissolve the Estates-General. Louis XVI now prepared to use force.

The intervention of the common people, however, in a series of urban and rural uprisings in July and August of 1789 saved the Third Estate from the king's attempted counterrevolution. The most famous of the urban risings was the fall of the Bastille. Parisians organized a popular force and on July 14 attacked the Bastille, a royal armory. But the Bastille had also been a state prison, and though it now contained only seven prisoners, its fall quickly became a popular symbol of triumph over despotism. Paris was abandoned to the insurgents, and Louis XVI was soon informed that the royal troops were unreliable. Louis's acceptance of that reality signaled the collapse of royal authority; the king could no longer enforce his will. The fall of the Bastille had saved the National Assembly.

At the same time, independently of what was going on in Paris, popular revolutions broke out in numerous cities. The collapse of royal authority in the cities was paralleled by peasant revolutions in the countryside. Behind the popular uprisings was a growing resentment of the entire landholding system, with its fees and obligations. With the fall of the Bastille and the king's apparent capitulation to the demands of the Third Estate, the peasants decided to take matters into their own hands. From July 19 to August 3, peasant rebellions occurred throughout France. The agrarian revolts served as a backdrop to the Great Fear, a vast panic that spread like wildfire through France between July 20 and August 6. The fear of invasion by foreign troops, aided by a supposed aristocratic plot, encouraged the formation of citizens' militias and permanent committees. The greatest impact of the agrarian revolts and the Great Fear was on the National Assembly meeting in Versailles.

THE DESTRUCTION OF THE OLD REGIME

One of the first acts of the National Assembly was to destroy the relics of feudalism or aristocratic privileges. On the "night of 4 August" 1789, the National Assembly in an astonishing session voted to abolish landlords' feudal rights as well as the fiscal privileges of nobles, clergy, towns, and provinces. On August 26, the assembly provided the ideological foundation for its actions and an educational device for the nation by adopting the Declaration of the Rights of Man and the Citizen (see the box on p. 568). This charter of basic liberties began with a ringing affirmation of "the natural and imprescriptible rights of man" to "liberty, property, security and resistance to oppression." It went on to affirm the destruction of aristocratic privileges by proclaiming an end to exemptions from taxation, freedom and equal rights for all men, and access to public office based on talent. Freedom of speech and press were guaranteed, and arbitrary arrests were outlawed.

The declaration also raised another important issue. Did the ideal of equal rights for all men extend to women? Many deputies insisted that it did, at least in terms of civil liberties, provided that, as one said, "women do not aspire to exercise political rights and functions." Olympe de Gouges, a playwright and pamphleteer, refused to accept this exclusion of women from political rights. Echoing the words of the official declaration, she penned a Declaration of the Rights of Woman and the Female Citizen, in which she insisted that women should have all the same rights as men (see the box on p. 569). The National Assembly ignored her demands.

In the meantime, Louis XVI had remained inactive at Versailles. He did refuse to promulgate the decrees on the abolition of feudalism and the Declaration of Rights, but an unexpected turn of events soon forced the king to change his mind. On October 5, crowds of Parisian women, numbering in the thousands and described by one eyewitness as "detachments of women coming up from every direction, armed with broomsticks, lances, pitchforks, swords, pistols, and muskets," marched to Versailles and forced the king to accept the constitutional decrees. The crowd now insisted that the royal family return to Paris. On October 6, the king complied. As a goodwill gesture, he brought along wagonloads of flour from the palace stores, escorted by women armed with pikes singing, "We are bringing back the baker, the baker's wife, and the baker's boy" (the king, queen, and their son). The king was virtually a prisoner in Paris, and the National Assembly, now meeting in Paris, would also feel the influence of Parisian insurrectionary politics.

Because the Catholic church was viewed as an important pillar of the old order, reforms soon overtook it. Most of the lands of the church were confiscated to pay state debts, and the church was also secularized. In July 1790, a new Civil Constitution of the Clergy was put into effect. Both bishops and priests were to be elected by the people and paid by the state. All clergy were also required to swear an oath of allegiance to the Civil Constitution. Only 54 percent of the French parish clergy took the oath, while the majority of bishops refused. The Catholic church, still an important institution in the life of the French people, now became an enemy of the Revolution.

A NEW CONSTITUTION

By 1791, the National Assembly had finally completed a new constitution that established a limited, constitutional monarchy. There was still a monarch (now called king of the French), but he enjoyed few powers not subject to review by the new Legislative Assembly. The Legislative Assembly, in which sovereign power was vested, was to sit for two years and consist of 745 representatives chosen by

DECLARATION OF THE RIGHTS OF MAN AND THE CITIZEN

One of the important documents of the French Revolution, the Declaration of the Rights of Man and the Citizen was adopted in August 1789 by the National Assembly. The declaration affirmed that "men are born and remain free and equal in rights," that governments must protect these natural rights, and that political power is derived from the people.

DECLARATION OF THE RIGHTS OF MAN AND THE CITIZEN

The representatives of the French people, organized as a national assembly, considering that ignorance, neglect, and scorn of the rights of man are the sole causes of public misfortunes and of corruption of governments, have resolved to display in a solemn declaration the natural, inalienable, and sacred rights of man, so that this declaration, constantly in the presence of all members of society, will continually remind them of their rights and their duties. . . . Consequently, the National Assembly recognizes and declares, in the presence and under the auspices of the Supreme Being, the following rights of man and citizen:

1. Men are born and remain free and equal in rights; social distinctions can be established only for the common benefit.
2. The aim of every political association is the conservation of the natural and imprescriptible rights of man; these rights are liberty, property, security, and resistance to oppression.
3. The source of all sovereignty is located in essence in the nation; no body, no individual can exercise authority which does not emanate from it expressly.
4. Liberty consists in being able to do anything that does not harm another person. . . .
6. The law is the expression of the general will; all citizens have the right to concur personally or through their representatives in its formation; it must be the same for all, whether it protects or punishes. All citizens being equal in its eyes are equally admissible to all honors, positions, and public employments, according to their capabilities and without other distinctions than those of their virtues and talents.
7. No man can be accused, arrested, or detained except in cases determined by the law, and according to the forms which it has prescribed. . . .
10. No one may be disturbed because of his opinions, even religious, provided that their public demonstration does not disturb the public order established by law.
11. The free communication of thoughts and opinions is one of the most precious rights of man: every citizen can therefore freely speak, write, and print. . . .
12. The guaranteeing of the rights of man and citizen necessitates a public force; this force is therefore instituted for the advantage of all, and not for the private use of those to whom it is entrusted. . . .
14. Citizens have the right to determine for themselves or through their representatives the need for taxation of the public, to consent to it freely, to investigate its use, and to determine its rate, basis, collection, and duration.
15. Society has the right to demand an accounting of his administration from every public agent.
16. Any society in which guarantees of rights are not assured nor the separation of powers determined has no constitution.
17. Property being an inviolable and sacred right, no one may be deprived of it unless public necessity, legally determined, clearly requires such action, and then only on condition of a just and prior indemnity.

an indirect system of election that preserved power in the hands of the more affluent members of society. Only active citizens (those men over the age of twenty-five paying in taxes the equivalent of three days' unskilled labor) could vote for electors (those men paying taxes equal in value to ten days' labor). This relatively small group of 50,000 electors then chose the deputies. To qualify as a deputy, one had to pay taxes equal in value to fifty-four days' labor.

Thus, by 1791 a revolutionary consensus, largely the work of the wealthier bourgeoisie, had moved France to a drastic reordering of the old regime. By mid-1791, however, this consensus faced growing opposition from clerics opposed to the Civil Constitution of the Clergy, lower classes hurt by a rise in the cost of living, peasants angry that some dues still had not been abandoned, and political clubs like the Jacobins that offered more radical solutions to France's problems. In addition, by mid-1791, the government was still facing several financial difficulties due to massive tax evasion. Despite all of their problems, however, the bourgeois politicians in charge remained relatively unified on the basis of their trust in the king. But Louis XVI disastrously undercut them. Quite upset with the whole turn of revolutionary events, he sought to flee France in June 1791 and almost succeeded before being recognized, captured, and brought back to Paris. In this unsettled situation, with a discredited and seemingly dis-

DECLARATION OF THE RIGHTS OF WOMAN AND THE FEMALE CITIZEN

Olympe de Gouges (a pen name for Marie Gouze) was a butcher's daughter who wrote plays and pamphlets. She argued that the Declaration of the Rights of Man and the Citizen did not apply to women and composed her own Declaration of the Rights of Woman.

DECLARATION OF THE RIGHTS OF WOMAN AND THE FEMALE CITIZEN (1791)

Mothers, daughters, sisters and representatives of the nation demand to be constituted into a national assembly. Believing that ignorance, omission, or scorn for the rights of woman are the only causes of public misfortunes and of the corruption of governments, the women have resolved to set forth in a solemn declaration the natural, inalienable, and sacred rights of woman in order that this declaration, constantly exposed before all the members of the society, will ceaselessly remind them of their rights and duties. . . .

Consequently, the sex that is as superior in beauty as it is in courage during the sufferings of maternity recognizes and declares in the presence and under the auspices of the Supreme Being, the following Rights of Woman and of Female Citizens.

1. Woman is born free and lives equal to man in her rights. Social distinctions can be based only on the common utility.
2. The purpose of any political association is the conservation of the natural and imprescriptible rights of woman and man; these rights are liberty, property, security, and especially resistance to oppression.
3. The principle of all sovereignty rests essentially with the nation, which is nothing but the union of woman and man; no body and no individual can exercise any authority which does not come expressly from it [the nation].
4. Liberty and justice consist of restoring all that belongs to others; thus, the only limits on the exercise of the natural rights of woman are perpetual male tyranny; these limits are to be reformed by the laws of nature and reason. . . .
6. The law must be the expression of the general will; all female and male citizens must contribute either personally or through their representatives to its formation; it must be the same for all: male and female citizens, being equal in the eyes of the law, must be equally admitted to all honors, positions, and public employment according to their capacity and without other distinctions besides those of their virtues and talents.
7. No woman is an exception; she is accused, arrested, and detained in cases determined by law. . . .
10. No one is to be disquieted for his very basic opinions; woman has the right to mount the scaffold; she must equally have the right to mount the rostrum, provided that her demonstrations do not disturb the legally established public order.
11. The free communication of thoughts and opinions is one of the most precious rights of woman, since that liberty assured the recognition of children by their fathers. . . .
12. The guarantee of the rights of woman and the female citizen implies a major benefit; this guarantee must be instituted for the advantage of all, and not for the particular benefit of those to whom it is entrusted. . . .
14. Female and male citizens have the right to verify, either by themselves or through their representatives, the necessity of the public contribution. This can only apply to women if they are granted an equal share, not only of wealth, but also of public administration, and in the determination of the proportion, the base, the collection, and the duration of the tax.
15. The collectivity of women, joined for tax purposes to the aggregate of men, has the right to demand an accounting of his administration from any public agent.
16. No society has a constitution without the guarantee of rights and the separation of powers; the constitution is null if the majority of individuals comprising the nation have not cooperated in drafting it.
17. Property belongs to both sexes whether united or separate; for each it is an inviolable and sacred right; no one can be deprived of it, since it is the true patrimony of nature.

loyal monarch, the new Legislative Assembly held its first session in October 1791. France's relations with the rest of Europe soon led to Louis's downfall.

Meanwhile, some other European rulers had become concerned about the French example and feared that revolution would spread to their countries. On August 27, 1791, the monarchs of Austria and Prussia invited other European monarchs to use force to reestablish monarchical authority in France. Insulted by this threat, the Legislative Assembly declared war on Austria on April 20, 1792. The French fared badly in the initial fighting, and loud recriminations were soon heard in Paris. A frantic search for scapegoats began; as one observer noted, "Everywhere you hear the cry that the king is betraying us, the

CITIZENS ENLIST IN THE NEW FRENCH ARMY. To save the Republic from its foreign enemies, the National Convention created a new revolutionary army of unprecedented size. In this painting, citizens joyfully hasten to sign up at the recruitment tables set up in the streets. On this occasion, officials are distributing coins to those who have enrolled.

generals are betraying us, that nobody is to be trusted; . . . that Paris will be taken in six weeks by the Austrians . . . we are on a volcano ready to spout flames."[4] Defeats in war coupled with economic shortages in the spring reinvigorated popular groups that had been dormant since the previous summer and led to renewed political demonstrations, especially against the king. Radical Parisian political groups, declaring themselves an insurrectionary commune, organized a mob attack on the royal palace and Legislative Assembly in August 1792, took the king captive, and forced the Legislative Assembly to suspend the monarchy and call for a National Convention, chosen on the basis of universal male suffrage, to decide on the future form of government. The French Revolution was about to enter a more radical stage.

From Radical Revolution to Reaction

In September 1792, the newly elected National Convention began its sessions. Although it was called to draft a new constitution, it also acted as the sovereign ruling body of France. Socially, the composition of the National Convention was similar to that of its predecessors. Dominated by lawyers, professionals, and property owners, two-thirds of its deputies were under the age of forty-five, and almost all had had political experience as a result of the Revolution. Almost all were also intensely distrustful of the king and his activities. It was therefore no surprise that the convention's first major step on September 21 was to abolish the monarchy and establish a republic. At the beginning of 1793, the convention passed a decree condemning Louis XVI to death. On January 21, 1793, the king was executed and the destruction of the old regime was complete. There could be no turning back. But the execution of the king produced new challenges by creating new enemies for the Revolution both at home and abroad while strengthening those who were already its enemies.

Within Paris the local government known as the Commune, which drew a number of its leaders from the working classes, favored radical change and put constant pressure on the convention, pushing it to ever more radical positions. Moreover, the National Convention itself still did not rule all France. Peasants in western France as well as inhabitants of France's major provincial cities refused to accept its authority. Domestic turmoil was paralleled by a foreign crisis. By the beginning of 1793, after the king had been executed, most of Europe—an informal coalition of Austria, Prussia, Spain, Portugal, Britain, the Dutch Republic, and even Russia—was pitted against France, and by late spring some members of the anti-French coalition were poised for an invasion of France. If it succeeded, both the Revolution and the revolutionaries would be destroyed and the old regime reestablished.

To meet these crises, the convention gave broad powers to an executive committee of twelve known as the Committee of Public Safety, which came to be dominated by Maximilien Robespierre, the leader of the Jacobins. For a twelve-month period, from 1793 to 1794, virtually the same twelve members were reelected and gave the country the leadership it needed to weather the domestic and foreign crises of 1793.

To meet the foreign crisis and save the Republic from its foreign enemies, the Committee of Public Safety decreed a universal mobilization of the nation on August 23, 1793:

> Young men will fight, young men are called to conquer. Married men will forge arms, transport military baggage and guns and will prepare food supplies. Women, who at long last are to take their rightful place in the revolution and follow their true destiny, will forget their futile tasks: their delicate hands will work at making clothes for soldiers; they will make tents and they will extend their tender care to shelters where the defenders of the Patrie will receive the help that their wounds require. Children will make lint of old cloth. It is for them that we are fighting: children, those beings destined to gather all the fruits of the revolution, will raise their pure hands toward the skies. And old men, performing their missions again, as of yore, will be guided to the public squares of the cities, where they will kindle the courage of young warriors and preach the doctrines of hate for kings and the unity of the Republic.[5]

A VICTIM OF THE REIGN OF TERROR

The Reign of Terror created a repressive environment in which even quite innocent people could be accused of crimes against the Republic. As seen in this letter by Anne-Félicité Guinée, wife of a wig maker, merely insulting an official could lead to arrest and imprisonment.

LETTER OF ANNE-FÉLICITÉ GUINÉE

Citizen Anne-Félicité Guinée, twenty-four years old . . . informs you that she was arrested at the Place des Droits de l'Homme, where I had gone to get butter. I point out to you that for a long time I have had to feed the members in my household on bread and cheese and that, tired of complaints from my husband and my boys, I was compelled to go wait in line to get something to eat. For three days I had been going to the same market without being able to get anything, despite the fact that I had waited from 7 or 8 A.M. until 5 or 6 P.M. After the distribution of butter on the twenty-second, . . . a citizen came over to me and said that I was in a very delicate condition. To that I answered, "You can't be delicate and be on your legs for so long. I wouldn't have come if there were any other food." He replied that I needed to drink milk. I answered that I had men in my house who worked and that I couldn't nourish them with milk, that I was convinced that if he, the speaker, was sensitive to the difficulty of obtaining food, he would not vex me so, and that he was an imbecile and wanted to play despot, and no one had that right. Here, on the spot, I was arrested and brought to the guard house. I wanted to explain myself. I was silenced and dragged off to prison. . . . About 7 P.M., I was led to the Revolutionary Committee [of the section], where I was called a counterrevolutionary and was told I was asking for the guillotine because I told them I preferred death to being treated ignominiously the way he was treating me. . . . I was asked if I knew whom I had called a despot. I answered, "I didn't know him," and I was told that he was the commander of the post. I said that he was more [a commander] beneath his own roof than anyone, given that he was there to maintain order and not to provoke bad feelings. . . . I was told that I had done three times more than was needed to get the guillotine and that I would be explaining myself before the Revolutionary Tribunal. The next day, I was taken to the Revolutionary Committee, which, without waiting to hear me, had me taken to the Mairie, where I stayed for nine days without a bed or a chair with vermin and with women addicted to all sorts of crimes. . . .

On the ninth day I was transferred to the prison of La Force. . . . In the end I can give you only the very slightest idea of all the horrors that are committed in these terrible prisons. . . . I was thrown together not with women but with monsters who gloried in all their crimes and who gave themselves over to all the most horrible excesses. One day, two of them fought each other with knives. Day and night I lived in mortal fear. The food that was sent in to me was grabbed away immediately. That was my cruel situation for seventeen days. My whole body was swollen from . . . the poor treatment I had endured, . . . [Anne-Félicité Guinée was discharged provisionally after the authorities realized that she was pregnant.]

In less than a year, the French revolutionary government had raised an army of 650,000; by September 1794, it numbered 1,169,000. The Republic's army was the largest ever seen in European history. It now pushed the allies back across the Rhine and even conquered the Austrian Netherlands.

Historians have focused on the French revolutionary army as an important step in the creation of modern nationalism. Previously, wars had been fought between governments or ruling dynasties by relatively small armies of professional soldiers. Although innocent civilians had suffered in those struggles, all parties had considered them noncombatants, with no direct involvement in the conflicts. The new French army, however, was the creation of a "people's" government; its wars were now "people's" wars. The entire nation was to be involved in the war. But when dynastic wars became people's wars, warfare increased in ferocity and restraints disappeared. The wars of the French revolutionary era opened the door to the total war of the modern world.

To meet the domestic crisis, the National Convention and the Committee of Public Safety initiated the "Reign of Terror." Revolutionary courts were instituted to protect the revolutionary Republic from its internal enemies. In the course of nine months, 16,000 people were officially killed under the blade of the guillotine, the latter a revolutionary device for the quick and efficient separation of heads from bodies. But the true number of the Terror's victims was probably closer to 30,000. The bulk of the Terror's executions took place in cities and districts that had been in open rebellion against the authority of the National Convention. The Terror demonstrated no class prejudice. Estimates are that the nobles constituted 8 percent of its victims, the middle classes, 25, the clergy, 6, and the peasant and laboring classes, 60. To Robespierre and the Committee of Public Safety, this bloodletting was only a temporary expedient. Once the war and domestic emergency were over, "the republic of virtue" would follow, and the Declaration of the Rights of Man and the Citizen would be fully established (see the box above).

Military force in the form of revolutionary armies was used to bring recalcitrant cities and districts back under the control of the National Convention. The Committee of Public Safety decided to make an example of Lyons, which was France's second city after Paris and had defied the National Convention during a time when the Republic was in peril. By April 1794, 1,880 citizens of Lyons had been executed. When guillotining proved too slow, cannon fire was used to blow condemned men into open graves. A German observed:

> . . . whole ranges of houses, always the most handsome, burnt. The churches, convents, and all the dwellings of the former patricians were in ruins. When I came to the guillotine, the blood of those who had been executed a few hours beforehand was still running in the street. . . . I said to a group of sansculottes that it would be decent to clear away all this human blood. Why should it be cleared? one of them said to me. It's the blood of aristocrats and rebels. The dogs should lick it up.[6]

Along with the Terror, the Committee of Public Safety took other steps to control France. By spring 1793, they were sending "representatives on mission" as agents of the central government to all parts of the country to implement the laws dealing with the wartime emergency. The committee also attempted to provide some economic controls by establishing price limits on goods declared of first necessity, ranging from food and drink to fuel and clothing. The controls failed to work very well, however, because the government lacked the machinery to enforce them.

The National Convention also pursued a policy of dechristianization. A new calendar was instituted in which years were no longer numbered from the birth of Christ but from September 22, 1792, the first day of the French Republic. The new calendar also eliminated Sundays and church holidays. In Paris, the cathedral of Notre Dame was designated a Temple of Reason; in November 1793, a public ceremony dedicated to the worship of reason was held in the former cathedral in which patriotic maidens clad in white dresses paraded before a temple of reason where the high altar once stood.

By the summer of 1794, the French had been successful on the battlefield against their foreign foes. The military successes meant that there was now less need for the Terror. But the Terror continued because Robespierre, who had become a figure of power and authority, had become obsessed with purifying the body politic of all the corrupt. Many deputies in the National Convention began to fear that they were not safe while he was free to act. Forming an anti-Robespierre coalition in the National Convention, they soon gathered enough votes to condemn him. Robespierre was guillotined on July 28, 1794.

After the death of Robespierre, a reaction set in called the Thermidorean Reaction, named after the month of Thermidor on the new French calendar. The Terror came to a halt. The National Convention reduced the power of the Committee of Public Safety, closed the Jacobin club, and tried to provide better protection for its deputies against the Parisian mobs. Churches were allowed to reopen for public worship. Economic regulation was dropped in favor of *laissez-faire* policies, another clear indication that moderate forces were again gaining control of the Revolution. In addition, a new constitution was framed in August 1795 that reflected this more conservative republicanism or a desire for a stability that did not sacrifice the ideals of 1789. The constitution provided for five directors to act as the executive authority or Directory.

The period of the Revolution under the government of the Directory was an era of stagnation, corruption, and graft, a materialistic reaction to the sufferings and sacrifices that had been demanded in the Reign of Terror. Speculators made fortunes in property by taking advantage of the Republic's severe monetary problems. At the same time, the government of the Directory was faced with political enemies from both the left and the right of the political spectrum. On the right, royalists, who desired the restoration of the monarchy, continued their agitation. On the left, Jacobin hopes of power were revived by continuing economic problems. Battered by the left and right, unable to find a definitive solution to the country's economic problems, and still carrying on the wars left from the Committee of Public Safety, the Directory increasingly relied

WOMEN PATRIOTS. Women played a variety of roles in the events of the French Revolution. This picture shows a women's patriotic club discussing the decrees of the National Convention, an indication that some women became highly politicized by the upheavals of the revolution.

NAPOLEON AND PSYCHOLOGICAL WARFARE

In 1796, at the age of twenty-seven, Napoleon Bonaparte was given command of the French army in Italy, where he won a series of stunning victories. His use of speed, deception, and surprise to overwhelm his opponents is well known. In this selection from a proclamation to his troops in Italy, Napoleon also appears as a master of psychological warfare.

NAPOLEON BONAPARTE, PROCLAMATION TO FRENCH TROOPS IN ITALY (APRIL 26, 1796)

Soldiers:

In a fortnight you have won six victories, taken twenty-one standards [flags of military units], fifty-five pieces of artillery, several strong positions, and conquered the richest part of Piedmont [in northern Italy]; you have captured 15,000 prisoners and killed or wounded more than 10,000 men. . . . You have won battles without cannon, crossed rivers without bridges, made forced marches without shoes, camped without brandy and often without bread. Soldiers of liberty, only republican troops could have endured what you have endured. Soldiers, you have our thanks! The grateful Patrie [nation] will owe its prosperity to you. . . .

The two armies which but recently attacked you with audacity are fleeing before you in terror; the wicked men who laughed at your misery and rejoiced at the thought of the triumphs of your enemies are confounded and trembling.

But, soldiers, as yet you have done nothing compared with what remains to be done. . . . Undoubtedly the greatest obstacles have been overcome; but you still have battles to fight, cities to capture, rivers to cross. Is there one among you whose courage is abating? No. . . . All of you are consumed with a desire to extend the glory of the French people; all of you long to humiliate those arrogant kings who dare to contemplate placing us in fetters; all of you desire to dictate a glorious peace, one which will indemnify the Patrie for the immense sacrifices it has made; all of you wish to be able to say with pride as you return to your villages, "I was with the victorious army of Italy!"

on the military to maintain its power. This led to a coup d'etat in 1799 in which the successful and popular military general Napoleon Bonaparte was able to seize power.

The Age of Napoleon

Napoleon dominated both French and European history from 1799 to 1815. He was born in Corsica in 1769, only a few months after France had annexed the island. The son of a lawyer whose family stemmed from the Florentine nobility, the young Napoleon obtained a royal scholarship to study at a military school in France. When the revolution broke out in 1789, Napoleon was a lieutenant. The French Revolution and the European war that followed broadened his sights and presented him with new opportunities. Napoleon rose quickly through the ranks. In 1794, at the age of only twenty-five, he was promoted to the rank of brigadier general by the Committee of Public Safety. Two years later, he was made commander of the French army in Italy (see the box above), where he won a series of victories and dictated peace to the Austrians in 1797. He returned to France as a conquering hero. After a disastrous expedition to Egypt, Napoleon returned to Paris, where he participated in the coup d'etat that ultimately led to his virtual dictatorship of France. He was only thirty years old at the time.

With the coup d'etat of 1799, a new form of the Republic was proclaimed in which, as first consul, Napoleon directly controlled the entire executive authority of government. He had overwhelming influence over the legislature, appointed members of the administrative bureaucracy, controlled the army, and conducted foreign affairs. In 1802, Napoleon was made consul for life, and in 1804 he returned France to monarchy when he had himself crowned as Emperor Napoleon I. The revolutionary era that had begun with an attempt to limit arbitrary government had ended with a government far more autocratic than the monarchy of the old regime.

One of Napoleon's first domestic moves was to establish peace with the oldest and most implacable enemy of the Revolution, the Catholic church. In 1801, Napoleon arranged a Concordat with the pope that recognized Catholicism as the religion of a majority of the French people. Although the Catholic church was permitted to hold processions again and reopen the seminaries, the pope agreed not to raise the question of the church lands confiscated during the Revolution. As a result of the Concordat, the Catholic church was no longer an enemy of the French government. At the same time, the agreement reassured those who had acquired church lands during the Revolution that they would not be taken away, an assurance that obviously made the new owners supporters of the Napoleonic regime.

Napoleon's most famous domestic achievement was his codification of the laws. Before the Revolution, France did not have a single set of laws, but rather virtually three hundred different legal systems. During the Revolution, efforts were made to prepare a codification of the laws for the entire nation, but it remained for Napoleon to bring the work to completion in the famous Civil Code. This preserved most of the revolutionary gains by recognizing the principle of the equality of all citizens before the law, the

CHRONOLOGY

THE FRENCH REVOLUTION

	1789
Meeting of Estates-General	May 5
Formation of National Assembly	June 17
Tennis Court Oath	June 20
Fall of the Bastille	July 14
Great Fear	Summer
Abolition of feudalism	August 4
Declaration of the Rights of Man and the Citizen	August 26
March to Versailles; king's return to Paris	October 5–6
	1790
Civil Constitution of the Clergy	July 12
	1791
Flight of the king	June 20–21
	1792
France declares war on Austria	April 20
Attack on the royal palace	August 10
Abolition of monarchy	September 21
	1793
Execution of the king	January 21
Levy-in-mass	August 23
	1794
Execution of Robespierre	July 28
	1795
Constitution of 1795 is adopted—the Directory	August 22

right of the individual to choose his profession, religious toleration, and the abolition of serfdom and feudalism. Property rights continued to be carefully protected, while the interests of employers were safeguarded by outlawing trade unions and strikes. The Civil Code clearly reflected the revolutionary aspirations for a uniform legal system, legal equality, and protection of property and individuals.

At the same time, the Civil Code strictly curtailed the rights of some people. During the radical phase of the French Revolution, new laws had made divorce an easy process for both husbands and wives, restricted the rights of fathers over their children (they could no longer have their children put in prison arbitrarily), and allowed all children (including daughters) to inherit property equally. The Civil Code undid most of this legislation. The control of fathers over their families was restored. Divorce was still allowed but was made more difficult for women to obtain. A wife caught in adultery, for example, could be divorced by her husband and even imprisoned. A husband, however, could be accused of adultery only if he moved his mistress into his home. Women were now "less equal than men" in other ways as well. When they married, their property came under the control of their husbands. In lawsuits they were treated as minors, and their testimony was regarded as less reliable than that of men.

Napoleon also worked on rationalizing the bureaucratic structure of France by developing a powerful, centralized administrative machine. Administrative centralization required a bureaucracy of capable officials, and Napoleon worked hard to develop one. Early on, the regime showed its preference for experts and cared little whether that expertise had been acquired in royal or revolutionary bureaucracies. Promotion, whether in civil or military offices, was to be based not on rank or birth but only on demonstrated abilities. This was, of course, what many bourgeoisie had wanted before the Revolution. Napoleon, however, also created a new aristocracy based on merit in the state service. Napoleon created 3,263 nobles between 1808 and 1814; nearly 60 percent were military officers while the remainder came from the upper ranks of the civil service and other state and local officials. Socially, only 22 percent of Napoleon's aristocracy came from the nobility of the old regime; almost 60 percent were bourgeois in origin.

In his domestic policies, then, Napoleon both destroyed and preserved aspects of the Revolution. While equality was preserved in the law code and the opening of careers to talent, the creation of a new aristocracy, the strong protection accorded to property rights, and the use of conscription for the military demonstrate a loss of equality. Liberty had been replaced by an initially benevolent despotism that grew increasingly arbitrary. Napoleon shut down sixty of France's seventy-three newspapers and insisted that all manuscripts be subjected to government scrutiny before they were published. Even the mail was opened by government police. One prominent writer—Germaine de Staël—refused to accept Napoleon's growing despotism. Educated in Enlightenment ideas, Madame de Staël wrote novels and political works that denounced Napoleon's rule as tyrannical. Napoleon banned her books in France and exiled her to the German states, where she continued to write.

NAPOLEON'S EMPIRE AND THE EUROPEAN RESPONSE

When Napoleon became first consul in 1799, France was at war with a second European coalition, consisting of Russia, Great Britain, and Austria. Napoleon realized the need for a pause and achieved a peace treaty in 1802, which left France with new frontiers and a number of client territories

THE CORONATION OF NAPOLEON. In 1804, Napoleon restored monarchy to France when he had himself crowned as emperor. In the coronation scene painted by Jacques-Louis David, Napoleon is shown crowning the empress Josephine while the pope looks on. The painting shows Napoleon's mother seated in the box in the background, even though she was not at the ceremony.

from the North Sea to the Adriatic. But the peace did not last, and in 1803 war was renewed with Britain, which was soon joined by Austria, Russia, and Prussia in the Third Coalition. In a series of battles from 1805 to 1807, Napoleon's Grand Army defeated the continental members of the coalition, giving Napoleon the opportunity to create a new European order. The Grand Empire was composed of three major parts: the French empire, dependent states, and allied states. The French empire, the inner core of the Grand Empire, consisted of an enlarged France extending to the Rhine in the east and including the western half of Italy north of Rome. Dependent states were kingdoms under the rule of Napoleon's relatives; these came to include Spain, Holland, the kingdom of Italy, the Swiss Republic, the Grand Duchy of Warsaw, and the Confederation of the Rhine, the latter a union of all German states except Austria and Prussia. Allied states were those defeated by Napoleon and forced to join his struggle against Britain; they included Prussia, Austria, Russia, and Sweden.

Within his empire, Napoleon sought acceptance everywhere of certain revolutionary principles, including legal equality, religious toleration, and economic freedom. As he explained to his brother Jerome after he had made him king of the new German state of Westphalia:

> What the peoples of Germany desire most impatiently is that talented commoners should have the same right to your esteem and to public employments as the nobles, that any trace of serfdom and of an intermediate hierarchy between the sovereign and the lowest class of the people should be completely abolished. The benefits of the Code Napoléon, the publicity of judicial procedure, the creation of juries must be so many distinguishing marks of your monarchy. . . . What nation would wish to return under the arbitrary Prussian government once it had tasted the benefits of a wise and liberal administration? The peoples of Germany, the peoples of France, of Italy, of Spain all desire equality and liberal ideas. I have guided the affairs of Europe for many years now, and I have had occasion to convince myself that the buzzing of the privileged classes is contrary to the general opinion. Be a constitutional king.[7]

In the inner core and dependent states of his Grand Empire, Napoleon tried to destroy the old order. Nobility and clergy everywhere in these states lost their special privileges. He decreed equality of opportunity with offices open to talent, equality before the law, and religious toleration. This spread of French revolutionary principles was an important factor in the development of liberal traditions in these countries.

Like Hitler one hundred and thirty years later, Napoleon hoped that his Grand Empire would last for centuries; like Hitler's empire, it collapsed almost as rapidly as it had been formed. Two major reasons help to explain this: the survival of Great Britain and the force of nationalism. Britain's survival was primarily due to its sea power. As long as Britain ruled the waves, it was almost invulnerable to military attack. Although Napoleon contemplated an invasion of Britain and even collected ships for it, he could not overcome the British navy's decisive defeat of a combined French-Spanish fleet at Trafalgar in 1805. Napoleon then turned to his Continental System to defeat Britain. Put into effect between 1806 and 1808, it attempted to prevent British goods from reaching the European continent in order to weaken Britain economically and destroy its capacity to wage war. But the Continental System failed. Allied states resented the ever tightening French economic hegemony; some began to cheat and others to resist, thereby opening the door to collaboration with the British. New markets in the Levant and in Latin America also provided compensation for the British. Indeed, by 1809–1810, British overseas exports were at near-record highs.

A second important factor in the defeat of Napoleon was nationalism. This political creed had arisen during the French Revolution in the French people's emphasis on brotherhood (*fraternité*) and solidarity against other peoples. Nationalism involved the unique cultural identity

MAP 19.7 Napoleon's Grand Empire

CHRONOLOGY

THE AGE OF NAPOLEON, 1799–1815

Napoleon as first consul	1799–1804
Concordat with Catholic church	1801
Emperor Napoleon I	1804–1815
Continental System established	1806
Invasion of Russia	1812
War of liberation	1813–1814
Exile to Elba	1814
Battle of Waterloo; exile to St. Helena	1815
Death of Napoleon	1821

of a people based on common language, religion, and national symbols. The spirit of French nationalism had made possible the mass armies of the revolutionary and Napoleonic eras and had also opened the political process to new people who were not aristocrats. But by extending the principles of the French Revolution beyond France, Napoleon had inadvertently spread nationalism as well. The French aroused nationalism by making themselves hated oppressors, thus arousing the patriotism of others in opposition to French nationalism, and by showing the people of Europe what nationalism was and what a nation in arms could do. It was a lesson not lost on other peoples and rulers. A Spanish uprising against Napoleon's rule, aided by the British, kept a French force of 200,000 pinned down for years.

The beginning of Napoleon's downfall came in 1812 with the invasion of Russia. The latter's defection from the Continental System left Napoleon with little choice. Although aware of the risks in invading such a large country, he also knew that if the Russians were allowed to challenge the Continental System unopposed, others would soon follow suit. In June 1812, he led a Grand Army of over 600,000 men into Russia. Napoleon's hopes for victory depended on quickly meeting and defeating the Russian armies, but the Russian forces refused to give battle and retreated for hundreds of miles, torching their own villages and countryside to prevent Napoleon's army from finding food and forage. When the Russians did stop to fight at Borodino, Napoleon's forces won an indecisive and costly victory. When the remaining forces of the Grand Army arrived in Moscow, they found the city ablaze. Lacking food and supplies, Napoleon abandoned Moscow late in October and made the "Great Retreat" across Russia in terrible winter conditions. Only 40,000 out of the original army managed to arrive back in Poland in January 1813. This military disaster then led to a war of liberation all over Europe, culminating in Napoleon's defeat in April 1814.

The defeated emperor of the French was allowed to play ruler on the island of Elba, off the coast of Tuscany, while the Bourbon monarchy was restored to France in the person of Louis XVIII, brother of the executed king. But the new king had little support, and Napoleon, bored on the island of Elba, slipped back into France. The troops sent to capture him went over to his side, and Napoleon entered Paris in triumph on March 20, 1815. The powers who had defeated him pledged once more to fight this person they called the "Enemy and Disturber of the Tranquility of the World." Having decided to strike first at his enemies, Napoleon raised yet another army and moved to attack the nearest allied forces, stationed in Belgium. At Waterloo on June 18, Napoleon met a combined British and Prussian army under the Duke of Wellington and suffered a bloody defeat. This time the victorious allies exiled him to St. Helena, a small, forsaken island in the South Atlantic. Only Napoleon's memory would continue to haunt French political life.

CONCLUSION

Everywhere in Europe at the beginning of the eighteenth century, the old order remained strong. Nobles, clerics, towns, and provinces all had privileges. Everywhere in the eighteenth century, monarchs sought to enlarge their bureaucracies to raise taxes to support the new large standing armies that had originated in the seventeenth century. The existence of these armies guaranteed wars. The existence of five great powers, with two of them (France and Great Britain) in conflict in the East and the Western Hemisphere, initiated a new scale of global conflict; the Seven Years' War could legitimately be viewed as the first world war. Although the wars changed little on the European continent, British victories enabled Great Britain to emerge as the world's greatest naval and colonial power. Everywhere in Europe, increased demands for taxes to support these conflicts led to attacks on the privileged orders and a desire for change not met by the ruling monarchs. At the same time, sustained population growth and dramatic changes in finance, trade, and industry created tensions that undermined the traditional foundations of the old order. The inability of that old order to deal meaningfully with these changes led to a revolutionary outburst at the end of the eighteenth century that marked the beginning of the end for the old order.

The revolutionary era of the late eighteenth century witnessed a dramatic political transformation. Revolutionary upheavals, beginning in North America and continuing in France, produced movements for political liberty and equality. The documents created by these revolutions, the Declaration of Independence and the Declaration of the Rights of Man and the Citizen, embodied the fundamental ideas of the Enlightenment and created a liberal political agenda based on a belief in popular sovereignty—the people are the source of political power—and the principles of liberty and equality. Liberty, frequently limited in practice, meant, in theory, freedom from arbitrary power as well as the freedom to think, write, and worship as one chose. Equality meant equality in rights and the equality of opportunity based on talent rather than birth. In practice, equality remained limited; those who owned property had greater opportunities for voting and officeholding, while there was certainly no equality between men and women.

The French Revolution created a modern revolutionary concept. No one had foreseen or consciously planned the upheaval that began in 1789, but after 1789 "revolutionaries" knew that the proper use of mass uprisings could produce the overthrow of unwanted governments. For these people, the French Revolution became a symbol of hope; for those who feared such changes, it became a symbol of dread. The French Revolution became the classical political and social model for revolution. At the same time, the liberal and national political ideals created by the Revolution dominated the political landscape of the nineteenth and early twentieth centuries. A new era had begun, and the world would never be the same.

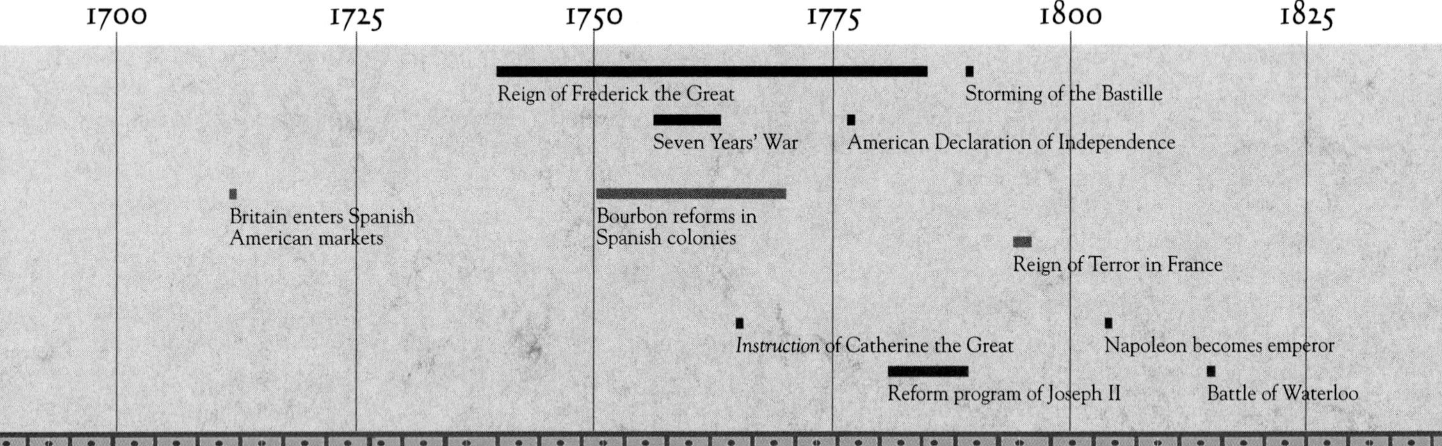

Chapter Notes

1. Igor Vinogradoff, "Russian Missions to London, 1711–1789: Further Extracts from the Cottrell Papers," *Oxford Slavonic Papers*, New Series (1982), 15:76.
2. Quoted in E. Bradford Burns, *Latin America: A Concise Interpretative History*, 4th ed. (Englewood Cliffs, N.J., 1986), p. 62.
3. Quoted in Reinhold A. Dorwart, *The Administrative Reforms of Frederick William I of Prussia* (Cambridge, Mass., 1953), p. 36.
4. Quoted in William Doyle, *The Oxford History of the French Revolution* (Oxford, 1989), p. 184.
5. Quoted in Leo Gershoy, *The Era of the French Revolution* (Princeton, N.J., 1957), p. 157.
6. Quoted in Doyle, *The Oxford History of the French Revolution*, p. 254.
7. Quoted in J. Christopher Herold, ed., *The Mind of Napoleon* (New York, 1955), pp. 74–75.

Suggested Readings

For a good introduction to the history of eighteenth-century Europe, see the relevant chapters in the general works by Woloch and Anderson listed in Chapter 18. See also G. Treasure, *The Making of Modern Europe, 1648–1780* (London, 1985), and O. Hufton, *Europe: Privilege and Protest, 1730–1789* (London, 1980). A good introduction to European population can be found in M. W. Flinn, *The European Demographic System, 1500–1820* (Brighton, 1981). A different perspective on economic history can be found in F. Braudel's *Capitalism and Material Life, 1400–1800* (New York, 1973). The subject of mercantile empires and worldwide trade is covered in J. H. Parry, *Trade and Dominion: European Overseas Empires in the Eighteenth Century* (London, 1971), and P. K. Liss, *Atlantic Empires: The Network of Trade and Revolution, 1713–1826* (Baltimore, Md., 1983). Eighteenth-century cottage industry and the beginnings of industrialization are examined in the early chapters of D. Landes, *The Unbound Prometheus: Technological Change and Industrial Development in Western Europe from 1750 to the Present* (New York, 1969).

On the European nobility, see J. Dewald, *The European Nobility 1400–1800* (Cambridge, 1996), and H. M. Scott, *The European Nobility in the Seventeenth and Eighteenth Centuries* (London, 1995). On European cities, see J. de Vries, *European Urbanization, 1500–1800* (Cambridge, Mass., 1984). There is no better work on the problem of poverty in the eighteenth century than O. Hufton, *The Poor of Eighteenth-Century France* (Oxford, 1974). The warfare of this period is examined in M. S. Anderson, *War and Society in Europe of the Old Regime, 1615–1789* (New York, 1988).

For a brief survey of Latin America, see E. B. Burns, *Latin America: A Concise Interpretative History*, 4th ed. (Englewood Cliffs, N.J., 1986). More detailed works on colonial Latin American history include S. J. Stein and B. H. Stein, *The Colonial Heritage of Latin America* (New York, 1970), and J. Lockhardt and S. B. Schwartz, *Early Latin America: A History of Colonial Spanish America and Brazil* (New York, 1983). A history of the revolutionary era in America can be found in R. Middlekauff, *The Glorious Cause: The American Revolution: 1763–1789* (New York, 1982), and C. Bonwick, *The American Revolution* (Charlottesville, Va., 1991). The importance of ideology is treated in G. Wood, *The Radicalism of the American Revolution* (New York, 1992). For an interesting comparative study, see the stimulating work by P. Higonnet, *Sister Republics: Origins of the French and American Revolutions* (Cambridge, Mass., 1988).

On enlightened absolutism, see H. M. Scott, ed., *Enlightened Absolutism: Reform and Reformers in Later Eighteenth-Century Europe* (Ann Arbor, Mich., 1990). Good biographies of some of Europe's monarchs include R. Asprey, *Frederick the Great: The Magnificent Enigma* (New York, 1986); I. De Madariaga, *Catherine the Great, A Short History* (New Haven, Conn., 1990); and T. C. W. Blanning, *Joseph II* (New York, 1994).

A well written, up-to-date introduction to the French Revolution can be found in W. Doyle, *The Oxford History of the French Revolution* (Oxford, 1989). For the entire revolutionary and Napoleonic eras, see O. Connelly, *The French Revolution and Napoleonic Era*, 2d ed. (Fort Worth, Tex., 1991), and D. M. G. Sutherland, *France 1789–1815: Revolution and Counter-Revolution* (London, 1985). Two brief works are A. Forrest, *The French Revolution* (Oxford, 1995), and J. M. Roberts, *The French Revolution*, 2d ed. (New York, 1997). A different approach to the French Revolution can be found in E. Kennedy, *A Cultural History of the French Revolution* (New Haven, Conn., 1989).

The origins of the French Revolution are examined in W. Doyle, *Origins of the French Revolution* (Oxford, 1988). On the early years of the Revolution, see T. Tackett, *Becoming a Revolutionary* (Princeton, N.J., 1996), and N. Hampson, *Prelude to Terror* (Oxford, 1988). Important works on the radical stage of the French Revolution include N. Hampson, *The Terror in the French Revolution* (London, 1981); R. R. Palmer, *Twelve Who Ruled* (Princeton, N.J., 1941); and R. Cobb, *The People's Armies* (London, 1987). The importance of the revolutionary wars in the radical stage of the Revolution is underscored in T. C. W. Blanning, *The French Revolutionary Wars, 1787–1802* (New York, 1996). On the Directory, see M. Lyons, *France Under the Directory* (Cambridge, 1975). On the Great Fear, there is the classic work by G. Lefebvre, *The Great Fear of 1789: Rural Panic in Revolutionary France* (London, 1973). On the role of women in revolutionary France, see O. Hufton, *Women and the Limits of Citizenship in the French Revolution* (Toronto, 1992), and J. Landes, *Women and the Public Sphere in the Age of the French Revolution* (Ithaca, N.Y., 1988). The best brief biography of Napoleon is F. Markham, *Napoleon* (New York, 1963). Also valuable are M. Lyons, *Napoleon Bonaparte and the Legacy of the French Revolution* (New York, 1994); G. J. Ellis, *Napoleon* (New York, 1997); and the recent massive biographies by F. J. McLynn, *Napoleon: A Biography* (London, 1997), and A. Schom, *Napoleon Bonaparte* (New York, 1997).

For additional reading, go to InfoTrac College Edition, your online research library at http://web1.infotrac-college.com

Enter the search terms "American Revolution" using Keywords.

Enter the search terms "French Revolution" using Keywords.

Enter the search term "Napoleon" using Keywords.

Enter the search terms "Napoleonic Wars" using Keywords.

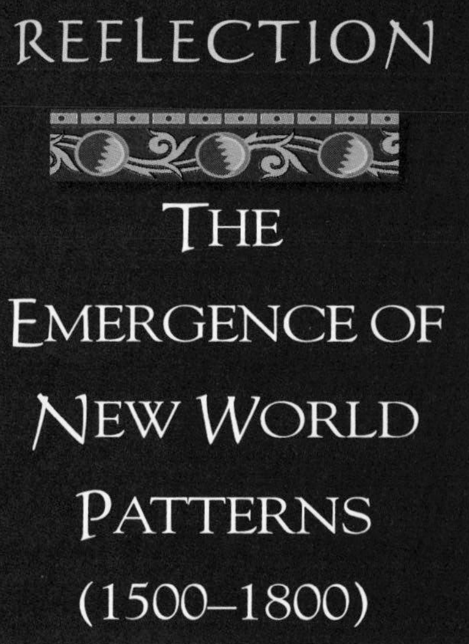

REFLECTION

THE EMERGENCE OF NEW WORLD PATTERNS (1500–1800)

Historians often refer to the period from the end of the fifteenth to the end of the eighteenth century as the early modern era. The phrase is not chosen lightly, for it was during these years that several factors were at work that created the conditions of our own time. It was during that era that maritime exploration opened the entire world to trade and colonization. It was then that centralized monarchies—and later nation-states—formed that led to the modern concept of statehood. It was then that an intellectual revolution laid the foundations for a modern worldview based on rationalism and secularism. And it was at the close of that era that technological advances began to lay the basis for the Industrial Revolution.

In a global perspective, perhaps the most noteworthy event of the period was the extension of the maritime trade network throughout the entire populated world. The primary instrument of that expansion, of course, was a resurgent Europe, which exploded onto the world scene with the initial explorations of the Portuguese and the Spanish at the end of the fifteenth century and then gradually came to dominate shipping on international trade routes during the next three centuries. The Chinese had inaugurated the process with their groundbreaking voyages to East Africa in the early fifteenth century but had inexplicably abandoned the effort shortly thereafter.

Some contemporary historians argue that it was this sudden burst of energy from Europe that created the first truly global economic system. According to Immanuel Wallerstein, one of the leading proponents of this theory, the age of exploration led to the creation of a new "world system" characterized by the emergence of global trade networks dominated by the rising force of European capitalism, which now began to scour the periphery of the system for access to markets and cheap raw materials.

Strictly speaking, it is true that only in the sixteenth century did trade patterns first encircle the earth. In the view of other contemporary historians, however, Wallerstein's view must be qualified. Some, for example, point to the Mongol expansion beginning in the thirteenth century, or even to the rise of the Arab empire in the Middle East a few centuries earlier, as signs of the creation of a global communications network enabling goods and ideas to travel from one end of the Eurasian supercontinent to the other.

Others take issue with the assertion that modern capitalism was the exclusive product of Europe during the fifteenth and sixteenth centuries and argue that its roots can be found in earlier centuries and in other environments. China during the Tang and the Song dynasties and the Arab empire under the Abbasid both displayed a vitality in the manufacturing and commercial sectors that compared favorably with that of Europe during the early modern era. Finally, some historians dispute the view of world system theorists that the year 1500 inaugurated an era of European dominance, pointing to the continuing vitality of many traditional Asian civilizations well into the nineteenth century. Only then, with the onset of the Industrial Revolution, would the global hegemony of the West become clearly established.

Whatever the truth of these debates, there are still many reasons for considering the end of the fifteenth century as a crucial date in world history. In the most basic sense, it marked the end of the long isolation of the Western Hemisphere from the rest of the inhabited world. In so doing, it led to the creation of the first truly global network of ideas and commodities, which would introduce plants, ideas, and (unfortunately) many new diseases to all humanity (see the box on p. 581). Second, the period gave birth to a stunning increase in trade and manufacturing that stimulated major economic changes not only in Europe but in other parts of the world as well. The world would never be the same again.

The period from 1500 to 1800, then, was an incubation period for the modern world and the launching pad for an era of Western domination that began in the nineteenth century. To understand why the West emerged as the leading force in the world at that time, it is necessary to understand what factors at work in Europe led to the scientific and industrial revolutions and why such factors were absent in other major civilizations around the globe.

Historians have identified the changes—in the form of improvements in navigation, shipbuilding, and weaponry—that took place in Europe in the early modern era as essential elements in the Age of Exploration. As we have seen, many of these technological advances were based on earlier discoveries that had taken place elsewhere—in China, India, and the Middle East—and had then been brought to Europe on Muslim ships or along the trade routes through Central Asia. Gunpowder, for example, had been invented in China, and eventually its mil-

THE COLUMBIAN EXCHANGE

In the Western world, the discovery of the Americas has traditionally been viewed essentially in a positive sense, as the first step in a process that expanded the global trade network and eventually led to the emergence of economic well-being and political democracy in societies throughout the world. That view has come under sharp attack from some observers, however, who claim that for the peoples of the New World, the primary legacy of the European conquest was not improved living standards but harsh colonial exploitation and the spread of pestilential diseases that decimated the local population. In recent years, the brunt of such criticism has been directed at Christopher Columbus, one of the chief initiators of the discovery and conquest of the Americas. Taking issue with the prevailing image of Columbus as a heroic figure in world history, critics view him as a symbol of Spanish colonial repression and a prime mover in the virtual extinction of the peoples and cultures of the New World.

There is no doubt that the record of the European conquistadors in the Western Hemisphere leaves much to be desired, and certainly the voyages of Columbus were not of universal benefit to his contemporaries or to the generations later to come. But to focus solely on the evils that were committed in the name of exploration and the propagation of Christianity distorts the historical realities of the era. The age of European expansion that began with Prince Henry the Navigator and Christopher Columbus was only the latest in a series of population movements that included the spread of nomadic peoples across Central Asia and the expansion of Islam from the Middle East after the death of the prophet Muhammad. In fact, the migration of peoples in search of survival and a better livelihood has been a central theme in the evolution of the human race since the dawn of prehistory.

MASSACRE OF THE INDIANS. This sixteenth-century engraving is an imaginative treatment of what was probably an all-too-common occurrence, as the Spanish attempted to enslave the American peoples and convert them to Christianity.

More importantly, it seems clear that the consequences of such population movements are too complex to be summed up in moral or ideological simplifications. The European expansion into the Americas, for example, not only brought the destruction of cultures and dangerous new diseases, but also initiated the exchange of plant and animal species that have ultimately been of widespread benefit to peoples living throughout the globe. The introduction of the horse, cow, and various grain crops vastly increased food productivity in the New World. The cultivation of corn, manioc, and the potato have had the same effect in Asia, Africa, and Europe. Whether Christopher Columbus was a hero or a villain is a matter of debate. That he and his contemporaries played a key role in the emergence of the modern world is a matter on which there can be no doubt.

itary uses came to the attention of the Ottomans, the Safavids, and the Mughals, as well as the Russian empire of Peter the Great, all of whom became dependent on the new military hardware. But it was the capacity and the desire of the Europeans to enhance their wealth and power by making practical use of the discoveries of others that was the significant factor in the equation. It was the firearms and artillery of European nations, in fact, that enabled them to dominate international sea lanes and create vast colonial empires in the New World.

But technological innovations by themselves cannot provide the final answer to the question of why at this time in history Europe suddenly became the engine for rapid global change. Another factor, certainly, was the change in the European worldview, the shift from a metaphysical to a materialist perspective and the growing inclination among European intellectuals to question first principles. Whereas in China, for example, the "investigation of things" had been put to the use of analyzing and confirming principles first established by Confucius during the Chinese "Golden Age," in early modern Europe, empirical scientists rejected received religious ideas, developed a new conception of the universe, and sought ways to improve material conditions around them.

But why were European thinkers more interested in practical applications for their discoveries than their counterparts elsewhere? One explanation, certainly, lies in the growing strength of the urban bourgeoisie in many areas of early modern Europe and the deliberate appeal that early scientists made to the literate mercantile elites of Europe when they showed how the new scientific ideas could be applied directly to specific technological needs. As we have seen, thriving commercial and manufacturing communities existed in the countries of East Asia, India, Central and East Africa, and the Middle East and were playing an increasingly important role in the life of their societies. But the European mercantile sector had begun to carve out an independent existence in the autonomous cities of southern and central Europe as early as the eleventh and twelfth centuries and by the eve of the early modern era suffered from few of the political and economic restrictions imposed on their counterparts elsewhere. By the sixteenth century, these affluent sectors of the community were enjoying increasing wealth and prosperity.

A final factor can be attributed to political changes that were beginning to take place in Europe during this period. The breakup of the world of Christendom, a consequence of the religious wars of the sixteenth and seventeenth centuries, helped to give birth to independent and relatively centralized monarchies in many areas of Europe. In the eighteenth century, the process of centralization that had characterized the growth of states since the Middle Ages continued as most European states enlarged their bureaucratic machinery and consolidated their governments in order to collect the revenues and amass the armies they needed to compete militarily with the other European states. In this highly competitive environment—evident in the wars of the century—political leaders desperately sought ways to enhance their wealth and power at the expense of rivals and grasped eagerly at whatever tools were available to guarantee their survival and prosperity. Where necessary and appropriate, they were more than willing to form alliances with the urban bourgeoisie to enhance state power and the prosperity of the people.

At the end of the eighteenth century, profound political upheavals led to additional political change and the emergence of a new political order. In discussing the upheavals of the late eighteenth century, it is appropriate to speak of a liberal movement to extend political rights and power to the bourgeoisie "possessing capital," namely, those besides the aristocracy who were literate and had become wealthy through capitalist enterprises in trade, industry, and finance. The years preceding and accompanying the French Revolution included attempts at reform and revolt in the North American colonies, Britain, the Dutch Republic, some Swiss cities, and the Austrian Netherlands. The success of the revolutionary upheavals in North America and France created a liberal political agenda based on principles of liberty and equality and a new sense of nationhood. The identity of citizens with their nation rather than their monarch created a new and powerful force—nationalism—that would lead to revolutionary movements throughout the world in the nineteenth and twentieth centuries.

Conditions in many areas of Asia and Africa were less conducive to these economic and political developments. In China, a centralized monarchy continued to rely on a prosperous agricultural sector as the economic foundation of the empire. Though Emperor Yongle briefly toyed with the idea of expanding China's commercial contacts with the outside world, his successor, urged on by domestic interests, reversed the process and unilaterally brought China's own Age of Exploration to an end. In Japan, power was centralized under the powerful Tokugawa shogunate, and the era of peace and stability that ensued saw an increase in manufacturing and commercial activity. But Japanese elites, after initially expressing interest in the outside world, abruptly shut the door on European trade and ideas in an effort to protect "the land of the gods" from external contamination.

In India and the Middle East, commerce and manufacturing had played a vital role in the life of societies since the emergence of the Indian Ocean trade network in the first centuries C.E. And while India was still a predominantly agricultural society, commerce was almost literally the life blood of many states in the Middle East, including the powerful Abbasid caliphate that had dominated the entire area during its apogee in the eighth and ninth centuries. But beginning in the eleventh century, the area had suffered through an extended period of political instability, marked by invasions by nomadic peoples from Central Asia. Although the Turks and the Mongols eventually formed their own states in the area and continued to promote trade with countries outside the region, the violence of the period and the local rulers' lack of experience in promoting maritime commerce had a severe depressing effect on urban manufacturing and commerce.

In the meantime, the countries of sub-Saharan Africa had their own problems. A number of trading states had begun to emerge in West Africa and along the eastern coast of the continent in the seventh and eighth centuries C.E., a process that was accelerated by Muslim penetration of the area in later centuries. But except for the eastern fringes, most parts of the continent still lacked the necessary infrastructure in terms of means of transportation, technology, and centralized states to compete aggressively for an active role in the regional trade passing through the area. For the most part, African states were suppliers rather than carriers of goods and remained too isolated from the main trade routes to benefit substantially from the technological and cultural diffusion that was taking place in many other areas of the world.

In the early modern era, then, Europe was best placed to take advantage of the technological innovations that

POPULATION EXPLOSION

Between 1700 and 1800, Europe, China, and to a lesser degree, India and the Ottoman Empire, experienced a dramatic growth in population. In Europe, for example, the population grew from 120 million people to almost 200 million by 1800; China, from less than 200 million to 300 million during the same period.

Four factors were important in causing this population explosion. First, better growing conditions, made possible by an improvement in climate, affected wide areas of the world and enabled people to produce more food. Summers in both China and Europe, for example, were warmer beginning in the early eighteenth century. Second, by the eighteenth century, people had begun to develop immunities to the epidemic diseases that had caused such widespread loss of life between 1500 and 1700. The spread of people by ship after 1500 had led to devastating epidemics. For example, the arrival of Europeans in Mexico led to smallpox, measles, and chicken pox among a native population that had no immunities to European diseases. In 1500, between 11 and 20 million people lived in the area of Mexico; by 1650, only 1.5 million remained. Gradually, however, people developed immunities to these diseases. By 1750, both epidemic diseases and plagues were no longer devastating in Europe, China, India, and the Middle East.

A third factor in population increase came from new food sources. As a result of the Columbian exchange (see the box on p. 581) American food crops—such as corn, potatoes, and sweet potatoes—were brought to other parts of the world, where they became important food sources: corn and potatoes were grown extensively in Africa and Europe, while sweet potatoes spread rapidly in southern China and West Africa. China, too, had imported a new species of rice from Southeast Asia that had a shorter harvest cycle than that of existing varieties. These new foods provided additional sources of nutrition that enabled more people to live for a longer time. At the same time, land development and canal building in the eighteenth century also enabled government authorities to move food supplies to areas threatened with crop failure and famine.

Finally, the use of new weapons based on gunpowder allowed states to control larger territories and ensure a new degree of order. The early rulers of the Qing dynasty, for example, pacified the Chinese empire and ensured a long period of peace and stability. Absolute monarchs achieved similar goals in a number of European states. Less violence led to fewer deaths at the same time that an increase in food supplies and a decrease in death from diseases were occurring, thus making possible in the eighteenth century the beginning of the world population explosion that persists to this day.

FESTIVAL OF THE YAM. The spread of a few major food crops made possible new sources of nutrition to feed more people. The importance of the yam to the Asante people of West Africa is evident in this celebration of a yam festival at harvest time in 1817.

had now become increasingly available throughout the Old World. It possessed the political stability, the capital, and what today might be called the "modernizing elite" that provided the spur to active efforts to take advantage of new conditions for their own benefit. Where other regions were still beset by internal obstacles or had deliberately "turned inward" to seek their destiny, Europe now turned outward to seek a new and dominant position in the world.

European expansion was not fueled solely by economic considerations, however. As had been the case with the rise of Islam in the seventh and eighth centuries, religion played a major role in motivating the European Age of Exploration in the early modern era. Although Christianity was by no means a new religion in the fifteenth century (as Islam had been at the moment of Arab expansion), the world of Christendom was in the midst of a major period of rivalry with the forces of Islam, a rivalry that was severely exacerbated by the conquest of the Byzantine Empire by the Ottoman Turks in the mid-fifteenth century.

Although the claims of Portuguese and Spanish adventurers that their activities were motivated primarily by a desire to bring the word of God to non-Christian peoples undoubtedly included a considerable measure of self-delusion and hypocrisy, there seems no reason to doubt that religious motives played a meaningful part in the European Age of Exploration. A perusal of the diaries of such famous explorers as Columbus, Vasco da Gama, and Francisco Pizarro attests to the sincerity and depth of their Christian beliefs. Religion undoubtedly provided a moral justification for some of the more heinous acts that were committed by Europeans in distant lands.

Religious motives were perhaps less evident in the activities of the non-Catholic powers that entered the competition beginning in the seventeenth century. English and Dutch merchants and officials were more inclined to be motivated purely by the pursuit of economic profit or by the prevailing "beggar thy neighbor" mercantile philosophy of the day. Eventually, however, the idea that trade benefits all participants provided a new moral justification, especially in the last quarter of the eighteenth century, when the free trade philosophy of Adam Smith became accepted wisdom in official and mercantile circles throughout much of Europe. The importance of free trade as a prerequisite for economic prosperity and political democracy became a common tenet of enlightened thinking in the colonial era in the nineteenth century and continues to be influential in our own day.

The fact that the early modern era was the incubation period for two of the most powerful forces that have dominated the nineteenth and twentieth centuries—the Industrial Revolution and the era of global imperialism—and that the explosive power of such forces originated in Europe, should not blind us to the facts that significant changes were taking place in other parts of the world as well and that many of these changes had relatively little to do with the situation in the West (see the box on p. 583). As we have seen, the impact of European expansion on the rest of the world was still limited up to the end of the eighteenth century. While European political authority was firmly established in a few key areas, such as the Spice Islands and Latin America, in most regions of Africa and Asia traditional societies remained relatively intact. And processes at work in these societies were often operating independently of events in Europe and would later give birth to forces that acted to limit or shape the Western impact.

One of these forces was the progressive emergence of centralized states, some of them built on the concept of ethnic unity. In Japan, the Tokugawa shogunate had asserted an unprecedented degree of political and cultural authority over a population traditionally ruled by decentralized forces reminiscent of the feudal era in medieval Europe. In India, a centralized empire had been created for the first time since the fall of the Mauryas

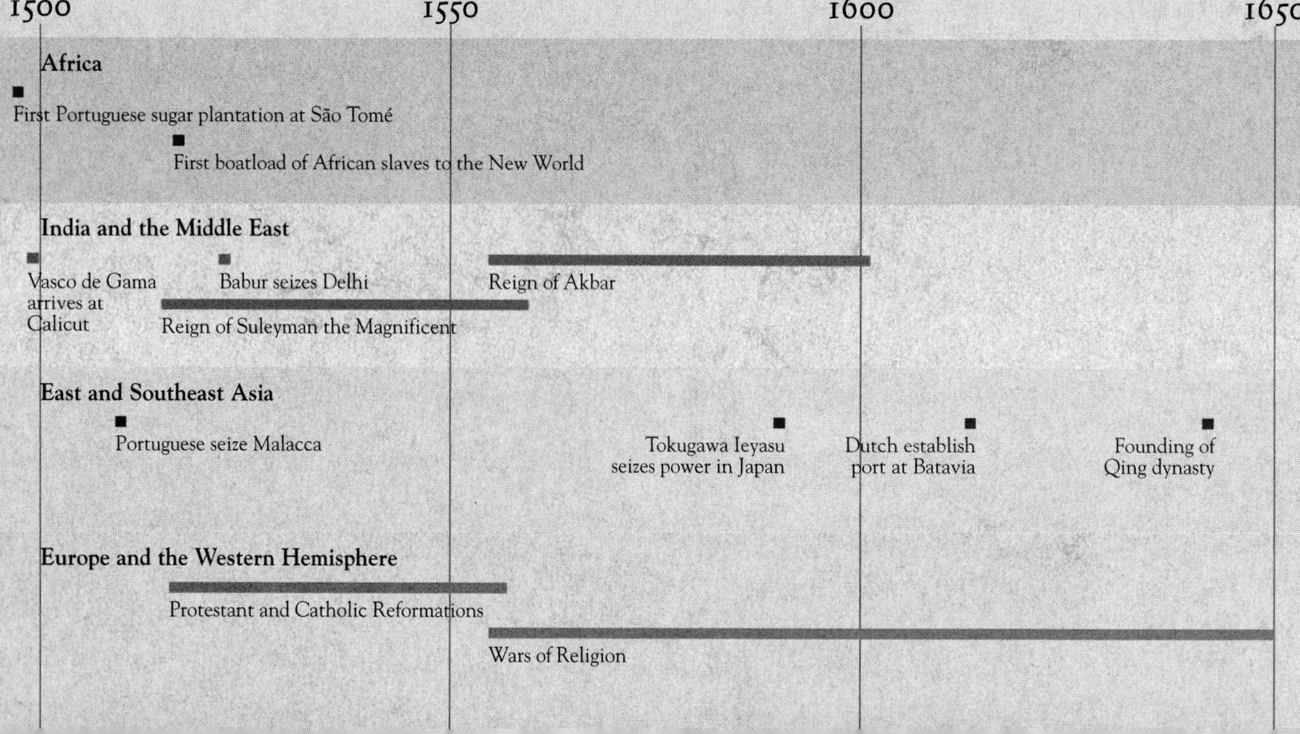

in the era of antiquity. In mainland Southeast Asia, organized states emerged in Burma, Thailand, and Vietnam that were broadly based on rising ethnic consciousness. This trend was somewhat less apparent in the Middle East, where the Ottoman Empire still laid claim to universal hegemony over the entire eastern Mediterranean and Mesopotamia, and in sub-Saharan Africa, where the forces of state building were still in an embryonic stage. But the concept of statehood was strengthening and laid the basis for the spread of nationalism in the twentieth century.

Within these centralized states, the steady growth of a commercial and manufacturing sector was beginning to create the conditions for a future industrial revolution. A number of Asian societies made technological advances during this period and witnessed the emergence of a more visible and articulate urban bourgeoisie. This process was especially evident in China and Japan, but it also occurred in India, the Middle East, and parts of North Africa. The restraints on industrial growth were political, social, and intellectual, not economic or technological.

For the moment, however, such forces were mere portents for the future, not signs of an imminent industrial revolution. At the beginning of the nineteenth century, the primary fact of life for most Asian and African societies was the expansionist power of an industrializing and ever more aggressive Europe. The power and ambition of the West provided an immediate challenge to the independence and destiny of societies throughout the rest of the world. The nature of that challenge will be the subject of our next section.

Suggested Readings

On different aspects of the global trade patterns of this era, see A. K. Smith, *Creating a World Economy: Merchant Capital, Capitalism, and World Trade, 1400–1825* (New York, 1991), and P. D. Curtin, *Cross-Cultural Trade in World History* (Cambridge, 1984). Important cultural exchanges of the period are examined in S. B. Schwartz, ed., *Implicit Understandings: Observing, Reporting, and Reflecting on the Encounters Between Europeans and Other Peoples in the Early Modern Era* (New York, 1994), and J. Thornton, *Africa and Africans in the Formation of the Atlantic World, 1400–1680* (Cambridge, 1992). On the Columbian Exchange, see the basic work by A. W. Crosby, *The Columbian Exchange: The Biological and Cultural Consequences of 1492* (Westport, Conn., 1972); N. D. Cook, *Born to Die. Disease and New World Conquest* (Cambridge, 1998); and W. H. McNeil, *The Global Connection: Conquerors, Catastrophes, and Community* (Princeton, N.J., 1992). For a broad perspective on the population explosion beginning in the eighteenth century, see M. Livi-Bacci, *A Concise History of World Population*, trans. C. Ipsen (Cambridge, Mass., 1992).

1650 1700 1750 1800

Dutch way station established at Cape of Good Hope

Founding of the Kingdom of Ashanti

Portuguese expelled from Mombasa

Collapse of Safavids

Battle of Plassey

Reign of Kangxi

Lord Macartney's mission to China

Development of absolutism—Reign of Louis XIV

Enlightened absolutism

American Revolution

French Revolution

MODERN PATTERNS OF WORLD HISTORY (1800–1945)

The period of world history from 1800 to 1945 was characterized, above all, by two major developments: the growth of industrialization and Western domination of the world. The two developments were, of course, directly interconnected. The Industrial Revolution became one of the major forces of change in the nineteenth century as it led Western civilization into the industrial era that has characterized the modern world. Beginning in Britain, it spread to the Continent and the Western Hemisphere in the course of the nineteenth century. At the same time, the Industrial Revolution created the technological means, including new weapons, by which the Western world achieved domination of much of the rest of the world by the end of the nineteenth century.

Europeans had begun to explore the world in the fifteenth century, but even as late as 1870, they had not yet completely penetrated North America, South America, and Australia. In Asia and Africa, with a few notable exceptions, the Western presence was limited to trading posts. Between 1870 and 1914, Western civilization expanded into the rest of the Americas and Australia, while the bulk of Africa and Asia was divided into European colonies or spheres of influence. Two major events explain this remarkable expansion: the migration of many Europeans to other parts of the world due to population growth and the revival of imperialism, which was made possible by the West's technological advancement. Beginning in the 1880s, European states began an intense scramble for overseas territory. This revival of imperialism—or the "new imperialism," as some have called it—led Europeans to carve up Asia and Africa.

The new imperialism had a dramatic effect on Africa and Asia as European powers competed for control of these two continents. Latin America was a major exception as it was able in the course of the nineteenth century to achieve political independence from its colonial rulers and embark on the building of new nations. Nevertheless, like the Ottoman Empire, Latin America still remained subject to commercial penetration by Western merchants. Another part of the world that escaped total domination by the West was East Asia, where China and Japan were able to maintain national independence during the height of the Western onslaught at the end of the nineteenth century.

Many Asian and African leaders resented Western attitudes of superiority and demanded human dignity for the indigenous people, but they nevertheless adopted the West's own ideologies for change. One of these—nationalism, with its emphasis on the right of people to have their own nations—was used to foster independence movements wherever native people suffered under foreign oppression. Colonial peoples soon learned the power of nationalism, and in the twentieth century, nationalism would become a powerful force in the rest of the world as nationalist revolutions moved through Asia, Africa, and the Middle East. Moreover, the exhaustive struggles of two world wars had destroyed the power of the European states, and the colonial powers no longer had the energy or wealth to maintain their colonial empires after World War II.

CHAPTER

20

THE BEGINNINGS OF MODERNIZATION: INDUSTRIALIZATION AND NATIONALISM, 1800–1870

CHAPTER OUTLINE

FOCUS QUESTIONS

- What were the basic features of the new industrial system created by the Industrial Revolution, and what effects did the new system have on urban life, social classes, family life, and standards of living?
- What were the major ideas associated with conservatism, liberalism, and nationalism, and what role did each ideology play in Europe and Latin America between 1800 and 1870?
- What were the causes of the revolutions of 1848, and why did these revolutions fail?
- What actions did Cavour and Bismarck take to bring about unification in Italy and Germany, respectively, and what role did war play in their efforts?
- What were the main characteristics of Romanticism and Realism?

In September 1814, hundreds of foreigners began to converge on Vienna, the capital city of the Austrian Empire. Many were members of European royalty—kings, archdukes, princes, and their wives—accompanied by their diplomatic advisers and scores of servants. Their congenial host was the Austrian emperor Francis I, who never tired of providing Vienna's guests with concerts, glittering balls, sumptuous feasts, and an endless array of hunting parties. One participant remembered, "Eating, fireworks, public illuminations. For eight or ten days, I haven't been able to work at all. What a life!" Of course, not every waking hour was spent in pleasure during this gathering of notables, known to history as the Congress of Vienna. These people were also representatives of all the states that had fought Napoleon, and their real business was to arrange a final peace settlement after almost a decade of war. On June 8, 1815, they finally completed their task.

The forces of upheaval unleashed during the French revolutionary and Napoleonic eras were temporarily quieted in 1815 as monarchs sought to restore stability by reestablishing much of the old order to a Europe ravaged by war. Kings and landed and bureaucratic elites regained their control over domestic governments, while internationally the forces of conservatism attempted to maintain the new status quo. But the Western world had been changed, and it would not readily go back to the old system. New ideologies of change, especially liberalism and nationalism, products of the revolutionary upheaval initiated in France, had become too powerful to be contained forever. Not content with the status quo, the forces of change called forth revolts and revolutions that periodically shook the West in the 1820s and 1830s and culminated in the widespread revolutions of 1848. Some of the revolutions and revolutionaries were successful; most were not. And yet within twenty-five years, many of the goals sought by the liberals and nationalists during the first half of the nineteenth century seemed to have been achieved. National unity became a reality in Italy and Germany, while many Western states developed constitutional-parliamentary features.

Reinforcing the forces unleashed by the French Revolution were the changes wrought by the Industrial Revolution. During the late eighteenth and early nineteenth centuries, another revolution—an industrial one—transformed the economic and social structure of Europe and created the industrial era that has characterized modern world history.

The Industrial Revolution and Its Impact

The period of the Industrial Revolution witnessed a quantum leap in industrial production. New sources of energy and power, especially coal and steam, replaced wind and water to create machines that dramatically decreased the use of human and animal labor and, at the same time, increased the level of productivity. New ways of organizing human labor were required, in turn, to maximize the benefits and profits from the new machines; accordingly, factories replaced shop and home workrooms. Farming very gradually lost its place as the largest employer of labor. During the Industrial Revolution, Europe experienced a shift from a traditional, labor-intensive economy based on agriculture and handicrafts to a more capital-intensive economy based on manufacturing by machines, specialized labor, and industrial factories.

Although the Industrial Revolution took decades to spread, it was truly revolutionary in that it fundamentally changed Europeans, their society, their relationship to other peoples, and the world itself. The development of large factories encouraged mass movements of people from the countryside to urban areas, where impersonal coexistence replaced the traditional intimacy of rural life. Higher levels of productivity led to a search for new sources of raw materials, new consumption patterns, and a revolution in transportation that allowed raw materials and finished products to be moved quickly around the world. The creation of a wealthy industrial middle class and a huge industrial working class (or proletariat) substantially transformed traditional social relationships. Finally, the Industrial Revolution fundamentally altered how people related to nature, ultimately producing an environmental crisis that in the twentieth century has finally been recognized as a danger to human existence itself.

The Industrial Revolution in Great Britain

The Industrial Revolution had its beginnings in Britain in the 1780s. A number of factors or conditions coalesced there to produce the first Industrial Revolution. The agricultural revolution of the eighteenth century led to a significant increase in food production. British agriculture could now feed more people at lower prices with less labor; even ordinary British families did not have to use most of their income to buy food, giving them the potential to purchase manufactured goods. At the same time, the rapid growth of population in the second half of the eighteenth century provided a pool of surplus labor for the new factories of the emerging British industry.

Britain had a ready supply of capital for investment in the new industrial machines and the factories that were needed to house them. In addition to profits from trade and cottage industry, Britain possessed an effective central bank and well-developed, flexible credit facilities. Many early factory owners were merchants and entrepreneurs who had profited from eighteenth-century cottage industry. But capital alone is only part of the story. Britain also had a fair number of individuals who were interested in making profits if the opportunity presented itself. The British were a people, as one historian has said, "fascinated by wealth and commerce, collectively and individually."

Britain was richly supplied with important mineral resources, such as coal and iron ore, needed in the manufacturing process. Britain was also a small country, and the relatively short distances made transportation facilities readily accessible. In addition to nature's provision of abundant rivers, from the mid-seventeenth century onward, both private and public investment poured into the construction of new roads, bridges, and canals. By 1780, roads, rivers, and canals linked the major industrial centers of the North, the Midlands, London, and the Atlantic coast.

Finally, a supply of markets gave British industrialists a ready outlet for their manufactured goods. British exports quadrupled between 1660 and 1760. In the course of its eighteenth-century wars and conquests, Great Britain had developed a vast colonial empire at the expense of its leading continental rivals, the Dutch Republic and France. Britain also possessed a well-developed merchant marine that was able to transport goods to any place in the world. A crucial factor in Britain's successful industrialization was the ability to produce cheaply those articles most in demand abroad. And the best markets abroad were not in Europe, where countries protected their own incipient industries, but in the Americas, Africa, and the Far East, where people wanted sturdy, inexpensive clothes rather than costly, highly finished luxury items. Britain's machine-produced textiles fulfilled that demand. Nor should we overlook the British domestic market. Britain had the highest standard of living in Europe and a rapidly growing population. It was the demand from both domestic and foreign markets and the inability of the old system to meet it that led entrepreneurs to seek and accept the new methods of manufacturing that a series of inventions provided. In so doing, these individuals produced the Industrial Revolution.

TECHNOLOGICAL CHANGES

The cottage system with its traditional methods of manufacturing had been established in many rural areas of Europe during the eighteenth century. But in the second half of the century, significant changes in industrial production began to occur, pushed along by the introduction of cotton, originally imported from India. The importation of raw cotton from slave plantations encouraged the production of cotton cloth in Europe, where a profitable market had developed for lightweight cotton clothes, which were less expensive than linens and woolens. But the traditional methods of the cottage industry proved incapable of keeping up with the growing demand, leading British cloth entrepreneurs to develop new methods and new machines. The flying shuttle sped up the process of weaving on a loom and enabled weavers to double their output. This, however, created shortages of yarn until James Hargreaves's spinning jenny, perfected by 1768, allowed spinners to produce yarn in greater quantities. Edmund Cartwright's power loom, invented in 1787, allowed the weaving of cloth to catch up with the spinning of yarn and presented new opportunities to entrepreneurs. It was much more efficient to bring workers to the machines and organize their labor collectively in factories located next to rivers and streams, the sources of power for many of these early machines. The concentration of labor in the new factories also brought the laborers and their families to live in the new towns that rapidly grew up around the factories.

The cotton industry was pushed to even greater heights of productivity by the invention of the steam engine, which played a major role in the Industrial Revolution. The steam engine revolutionized the production of cotton goods and caused the factory system to spread to other areas of production, thereby creating whole new industries. The steam engine secured the triumph of the Industrial Revolution.

In the 1760s, a Scottish engineer, James Watt (1736–1819), devised an engine powered by steam that could pump water from mines three times as quickly as previous engines. In 1782, Watt enlarged the possibilities of the steam engine when he developed a rotary engine that could turn a shaft and thus drive machinery. Steam power could now be applied to spinning and weaving cotton, and before long cotton mills using steam engines were multiplying across Britain. Because steam engines were fired by coal, they did not have to be located near rivers, giving entrepreneurs greater flexibility in choosing sites for their factories.

The new boost given to cotton textile production by technological changes was readily apparent. In 1760, Britain had imported 2.5 million pounds of raw cotton, which was farmed out to cottage industries. In 1787, the British imported 22 million pounds of cotton; most of it was spun on machines, some powered by water in large mills. By 1840, 366 million pounds of cotton—now Britain's most important product in value—were imported annually, much of it from the American South, where it was grown by slaves. By this time, most cotton industry employees worked in factories. The cheapest labor in India could not compete in quality or quantity with British workers. British cotton goods sold everywhere in the world.

The steam engine proved invaluable to Britain's Industrial Revolution. Unlike horses, the steam engine was a tireless source of power and depended for fuel on a substance—namely, coal—that seemed then to be available in unlimited quantities. The popular saying that "Steam is an Englishman" had real significance by 1850. The success of the steam engine increased the demand for coal and led to an expansion in coal production; between 1815 and 1850, the output of coal quadrupled. In turn, new processes using coal furthered the development of an iron industry.

The British iron industry was radically transformed during the Industrial Revolution. Britain had large resources of iron ore, but at the beginning of the eighteenth century, the basic process of producing iron had altered little since the Middle Ages and still depended heavily on charcoal. In the early eighteenth century, new methods of smelting iron ore to produce cast iron were devised based on the use of coke derived from coal. A better quality of iron was still not possible, however, until the 1780s, when Henry Cort developed a system called puddling in which coke was used to burn away impurities in pig iron and produce an iron of high quality. A boom then ensued in the British iron industry. In 1740, Britain produced 17,000 tons of iron; by the 1840s, over two million tons; and by 1852, almost three million tons, more than the rest of the world combined.

The high-quality wrought iron produced by the Cort process encouraged the growth of machinery in other industries, most noticeably in such new means of transportation as steamboats and railroads. In 1804, Richard Trevithick pioneered the first steam-powered locomotive on an industrial rail line in south Wales. It pulled ten tons of ore and seventy people at five miles per hour. Better locomotives soon followed. The engines built by George Stephenson and his son proved superior, and it was in their workshops in Newcastle upon Tyne that the locomotives for the first modern railways in Britain were built. George Stephenson's *Rocket* was used on the first public railway line, which opened in 1830, extending thirty-two miles from Liverpool to Manchester. *Rocket* sped along at sixteen miles per hour. Within twenty years, locomotives had reached fifty miles per hour, an incredible speed to contemporary passengers. During the same period, new companies were formed to build additional railroads as the infant industry proved to be not only technically but financially successful. In 1840, Britain had almost 2,000 miles of railroads; by 1850, 6,000 miles of railroad track crisscrossed much of the country.

The railroad was an important element in the success and maturing of the Industrial Revolution. The demands of railroads for coal and iron furthered the growth of those industries. Railway construction created new job opportunities, especially for farm laborers and peasants, who had long been accustomed to finding work outside their local villages. Perhaps most importantly, the cheaper and faster means of transportation provided by the railroads had a rippling effect on the industrial economy. Reductions in the price of goods created larger markets; increased sales meant more factories and more machinery, thereby reinforcing the self-sustaining aspect of the Industrial Revolution that marked a fundamental break with the traditional European economy. The great productivity of the Industrial Revolution enabled entrepreneurs to reinvest their profits in new capital equipment, further expanding the productive capacity of the economy. Continuous, even rapid, self-sustaining economic growth came to be seen as a fundamental characteristic of the new industrial economy.

RAILROAD LINE FROM LIVERPOOL TO MANCHESTER. The railroad line from Liverpool to Manchester, first opened in 1830, relied on steam locomotives. As is evident in this illustration, carrying passengers was the railroad's main business. First-class passengers rode in covered cars; second- and third-class passengers in open cars.

The railroad was the perfect symbol of this aspect of the Industrial Revolution. The ability to transport goods and people at dramatic speeds also provided visible confirmation of a new sense of power. When railway engineers pierced mountains with tunnels and spanned chasms with breathtaking bridges, contemporaries experienced a sense of power over nature not felt before in civilization.

THE INDUSTRIAL FACTORY

Another visible symbol of the Industrial Revolution was the factory, which became the chief means of organizing labor for the new machines. From its beginning, the factory system demanded a new type of discipline from its employees. Once factory owners purchased machinery, it had to be used constantly to enable them to profit from their investment. Workers were forced to work regular hours and in shifts to keep the machines producing at a steady pace for maximum output. This represented a massive adjustment for the first factory laborers.

Preindustrial workers were not accustomed to a "timed" format. Agricultural laborers had always kept irregular hours; hectic work at harvest time might be followed by periods of inactivity. Even in the burgeoning cottage industry of the eighteenth century, wool weavers and spinners who worked at home might fulfill their weekly quotas by working around the clock for two or three days and then proceed at a leisurely pace until the next week's demands forced another work spurt.

Factory owners, therefore, faced a formidable task. They had to create a system in which employees became accustomed to working regular, unvarying hours during which they performed a set number of tasks over and over again as efficiently as possible. One early industrialist said that his aim was "to make such machines of the men as cannot err." Such work, of course, tended to be repetitive and boring, and factory owners resorted to tough methods to accomplish their goals. Factory regulations were minute and detailed (see the box on p. 593). Adult workers were fined for a wide variety of minor infractions, such as being a few minutes late for work, and dismissed for more serious offenses, especially drunkenness. The latter was viewed as particularly offensive because it set a bad example for younger workers and also courted disaster in the midst of dangerous machinery. Employers found that dismissals and fines worked well for adult employees; in a time when great population growth had produced large masses of unskilled labor, dismissal meant disaster. Children were less likely to understand the implications of dismissal, so they were sometimes disciplined more directly—by beating. In one crucial sense, the efforts of the early industrialists proved successful. As the nineteenth century progressed, the second and third generations of workers came to view a regular working week as a natural way of life. It was, of course, an attitude that made possible Britain's incredible economic growth in that century.

By the mid-nineteenth century, Great Britain had become the world's first and richest industrial nation. Britain was the "workshop, banker, and trader of the world." It produced half of the world's coal and manufactured goods; in 1850, its cotton industry alone was equal in size to the industries of all other European countries combined. No doubt, Britain's certainty about its mission in the world in the nineteenth century was grounded in its incredible material success story.

The Spread of Industrialization

Beginning first in Great Britain, industrialization spread to the continental countries of Europe and the United States at different times and speeds during the nineteenth century. First to be industrialized on the Continent were Belgium, France, and the German states and in North America, the new nation of the United States. Not until after 1850 did the Industrial Revolution spread to the rest of Europe and other parts of the world.

Industrialization on the Continent faced numerous hurdles, and as it proceeded in earnest after 1815, it did so along lines that were somewhat different from Britain's. Lack of technical knowledge was a first major obstacle to industrialization. But the continental countries possessed an advantage here; they could simply borrow British techniques and practices. Gradually, however, the Continent achieved technological independence as local people learned all the skills they could from their British teachers. By the 1840s, a new generation of skilled mechanics from Belgium and France was spreading technological knowledge east and south. More importantly, continental countries, especially France and the German states, began to establish a wide range of technical schools to train engineers and mechanics.

That government played an important role in this regard brings us to a second difference between British and continental industrialization. Governments on much of the Continent were accustomed to playing a significant role in economic affairs. Furthering the development of industrialization was a logical extension of that attitude. Hence governments provided for the costs of technical education; awarded grants to inventors and foreign entrepreneurs; exempted foreign industrial equipment from import duties; and, in some places, even financed factories. Of equal if not greater importance in the long run, governments actively bore much of the cost of building roads and canals, deepening and widening river channels, and constructing railroads. By 1850, a network of iron rails had spread across Europe, although only Germany and Belgium had completed major parts of their systems by that time.

Like Belgium, France, and the German states, the United States experienced an industrial revolution and the urbanization that accompanied it during the first half of the nineteenth century. In 1800, society in the United

DISCIPLINE IN THE NEW FACTORIES

Workers in the new factories of the Industrial Revolution had been accustomed to a lifestyle free of overseers. Unlike the cottages, where workers spun thread and wove cloth in their own rhythm and time, the factories demanded a new, rigorous discipline geared to the requirements of the machines. This selection is taken from a set of rules for a factory in Berlin in 1844. They were typical of company rules everywhere the factory system had been established.

THE FOUNDRY AND ENGINEERING WORKS OF THE ROYAL OVERSEAS TRADING COMPANY, FACTORY RULES

In every large works, and in the coordination of any large number of workmen, good order and harmony must be looked upon as the fundamentals of success, and therefore the following rules shall be strictly observed.

1. The normal working day begins at all seasons at 6 A.M. precisely and ends, after the usual break of half an hour for breakfast, an hour for dinner, and half an hour for tea, at 7 P.M., and it shall be strictly observed. . . .
2. Workers arriving 2 minutes late shall lose half an hour's wages; whoever is more than 2 minutes late may not start work until after the next break, or at least shall lose his wages until then. Any disputes about the correct time shall be settled by the clock mounted above the gatekeeper's lodge. . . .
3. No workman, whether employed by time or piece, may leave before the end of the working day, without having first received permission from the overseer and having given his name to the gatekeeper. Omission of these two actions shall lead to a fine of ten silver groschen [pennies] payable to the sick fund.
4. Repeated irregular arrival at work shall lead to dismissal. This shall also apply to those who are found idling by an official or overseer, and refused to obey their order to resume work. . . .
6. No worker may leave his place of work otherwise than for reasons connected with his work.
7. All conversation with fellow-workers is prohibited; if any worker requires information about his work, he must turn to the overseer, or to the particular fellow-worker designated for the purpose.
8. Smoking in the workshops or in the yard is prohibited during working hours; anyone caught smoking shall be fined five silver groschen for the sick fund for every such offense. . . .
10. Natural functions must be performed at the appropriate places, and whoever is found soiling walls, fences, squares, etc., and similarly, whoever is found washing his face and hands in the workshop and not in the places assigned for the purpose, shall be fined five silver groschen for the sick fund. . . .
12. It goes without saying that all overseers and officials of the firm shall be obeyed without question, and shall be treated with due deference. Disobedience will be punished by dismissal.
13. Immediate dismissal shall also be the fate of anyone found drunk in any of the workshops. . . .
14. Every workman is obliged to report to his superiors any acts of dishonesty or embezzlement on the part of his fellow workmen. If he omits to do so, and it is shown after subsequent discovery of a misdemeanor that he knew about it at the time, he shall be liable to be taken to court as an accessory after the fact and the wage due to him shall be retained as punishment.

States was agrarian. There were no cities with a population over 100,000, and six out of every seven American workers were farmers. By 1860, the population of the United States had grown from 5 to 30 million people, larger than that of Great Britain. Almost half of these people lived west of the Appalachian Mountains. There were now thirty-four instead of sixteen states, and nine American cities had populations over 100,000. Only 50 percent of American workers were farmers.

The initial application of machinery to production was accomplished—as it had been in continental Europe—by borrowing from Great Britain. Soon, however, Americans began to equal or surpass British technical inventions. The Harpers Ferry arsenal, for example, built muskets with interchangeable parts. Because all the individual parts of a musket were identical (e.g., all triggers were the same), the final product could be put together quickly and easily; this enabled Americans to avoid the more costly system in which skilled craftspeople fitted together individual parts made separately. The so-called American system reduced costs and revolutionized production by saving labor, an important consideration in a society that had few skilled artisans.

Unlike Britain, the United States was a large country geographically. The lack of a good system of internal transportation seemed to limit American economic development by making the transport of goods prohibitively expensive. This was gradually remedied, however. Thousands of miles of roads and canals were built linking east and west. The steamboat facilitated transportation on the Great Lakes, Atlantic coastal waters, and rivers. It was especially important to the Mississippi River valley; by 1860, a thousand steamboats plied that river (see the box on p. 595). Most important of all in the development of an American transportation system was the railroad. It began with 100 miles in 1830, and by 1860 there were over 27,000 miles of railroad track covering the United States. This transportation revolution turned the United States into a single massive market for the manufactured goods of the Northeast, the early center of American industrialization.

Labor for the growing number of factories in this area came primarily from rural New England. The United States did not possess a large number of craftspeople, but it did have a rapidly expanding farm population; its size in the Northeast soon outstripped the available farmland. While some of this excess population, especially men, went west, others, mostly women, found work in the new textile and shoe factories of New England. Indeed, women made up more than 80 percent of the laboring force in the large textile factories. In Massachusetts mill towns, company boarding houses provided rooms for large numbers of young women who worked for several years before marriage. Outside Massachusetts, factory owners sought entire families including children to work in their mills; one mill owner ran this advertisement in a newspaper in Utica, New York: "Wanted: A few sober and industrious families of at least five children each, over the age of eight years, are wanted at the Cotton Factory in Whitestown. Widows with large families would do well to attend this notice." When a decline in rural births threatened to dry up this labor pool in the 1830s and 1840s, European immigrants, especially poor and unskilled Irish, English, Scottish, and Welsh, appeared in large numbers to replace American women and children in the factories.

By 1860, the United States was well on its way to being an industrial nation. In the Northeast, the most indus-

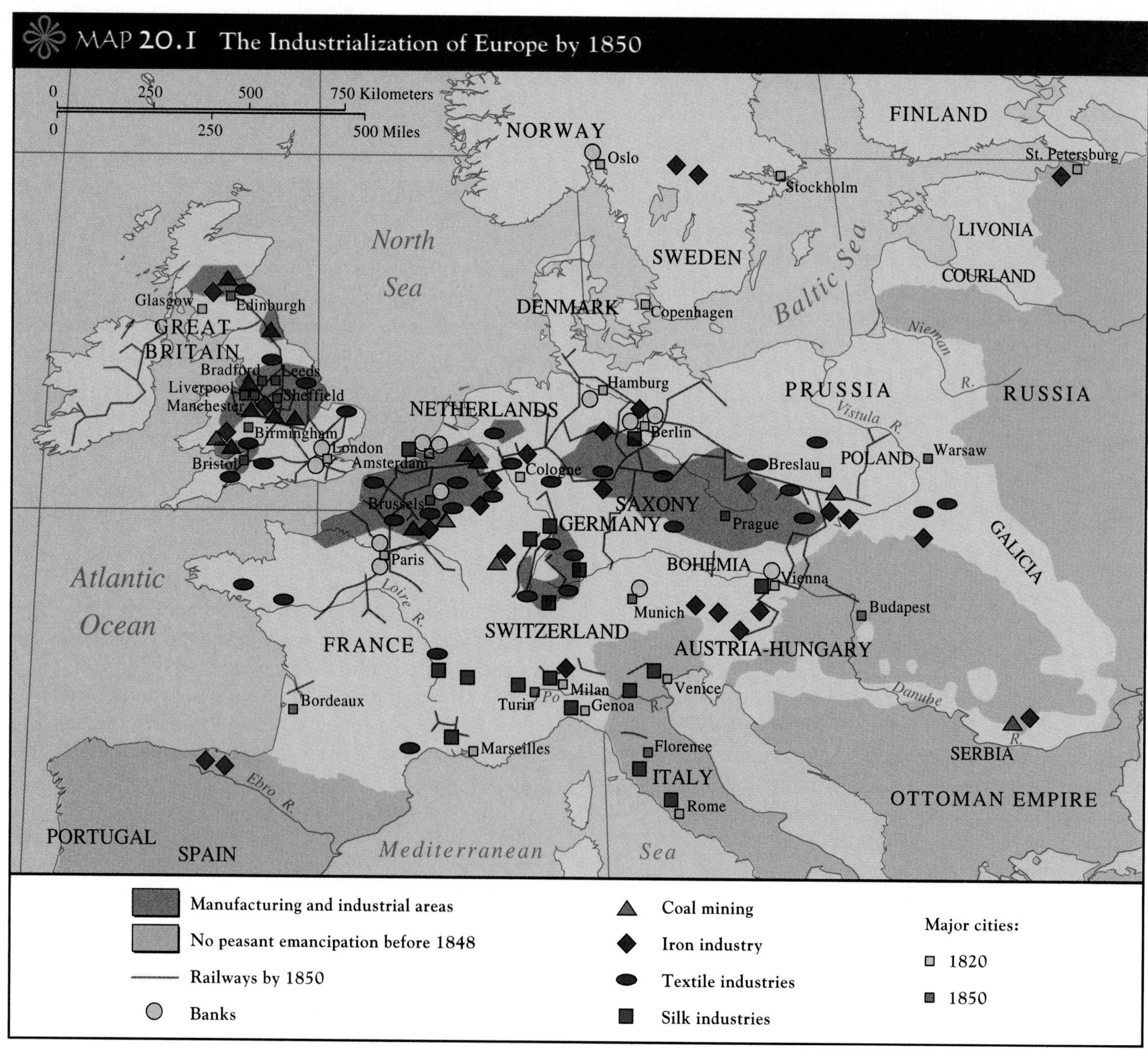

MAP 20.1 The Industrialization of Europe by 1850

S-T-E-A-M-BOAT A-COMIN'!

Steamboats and railroads were crucial elements in a transportation revolution that enabled industrialists to expand markets by shipping goods cheaply and efficiently. At the same time, these marvels of technology aroused a sense of power and excitement that was an important aspect of the triumph of industrialization. The American novelist Mark Twain captured this sense of excitement in this selection from Life on the Mississippi.

MARK TWAIN, *LIFE ON THE MISSISSIPPI*

After all these years I can picture that old time to myself now, just as it was then: the white town drowsing in the sunshine of a summer's morning; the streets empty, or pretty nearly so; one or two clerks sitting in front of the Water Street stores, with their splint-bottomed chairs tilted back against the wall, chins on breasts, hats slouched over their faces, asleep; . . . two or three lonely little freight piles scattered about the "levee"; a pile of "skids" on the slope of the stone-paved wharf, and the fragrant town drunkard asleep in the shadow of them; . . . the great Mississippi, the majestic, the magnificent Mississippi, rolling its mile-wide tide along, shining in the sun; the dense forest away on the other side; the "point" above the town, and the "point" below, bounding the river-glimpse and turning it into a sort of sea, and withal a very still and brilliant and lonely one. Presently a film of dark smoke appears above one of those remote "points"; instantly a Negro drayman, famous for his quick eye and prodigious voice, lifts up the cry, "S-t-e-a-m-boat a-comin'!" and the scene changes! The town drunkard stirs, the clerks wake up, a furious clatter of drays follows, every house and store pours out a human contribution, and all in a twinkling the dead town [Hannibal, Missouri] is alive and moving. Drays, carts, men, boys, all go hurrying from many quarters to a common center, the wharf. Assembled there, the people fasten their eyes upon the coming boat as upon a wonder they are seeing for the first time. And the boat *is* rather a handsome sight, too. She is long and sharp and trim and pretty; she has two tall, fancy-topped chimneys, with a gilded device of some kind swung between them; a fanciful pilot-house, all glass and "gingerbread," perched on top of the "texas" deck behind them; the paddle-boxes are gorgeous with a picture or with gilded rays above the boat's name; the boiler deck, the hurricane deck, and the texas deck are fenced and ornamented with clean white railings; there is a flag gallantly flying from the jack-staff; the furnace doors are open and the fires glaring bravely; the upper decks are black with passengers; the captain stands by the big bell, calm, imposing, the envy of all; great volumes of the blackest smoke are rolling and tumbling out of the chimneys—a husbanded grandeur created with a bit of pitch pine just before arriving at a town; the crew are grouped on the forecastle; the broad stage is run far out over the port bow, and an envied deck-hand stands picturesquely on the end of it with a coil of rope in his hand; the pent steam is screaming through the gauge-cocks; the captain lifts his hand, a bell rings, the wheels stop; then they turn back, churning the water to foam, and the steamer is at rest. Then such a scramble as there is to get aboard, and to get ashore, and to take in freight and to discharge freight, all at one and the same time; and such a yelling and cursing as the mates facilitate it all with! Ten minutes later the steamer is under way again, with no flag on the jack-staff and no black smoke issuing from the chimneys. After ten more minutes the town is dead again, and the town drunkard asleep by the skids once more.

trialized section of the country, per capita income was 40 percent higher than the national average. Diets, it has been argued, were better and more varied; machine-made clothing was more abundant. Nevertheless, despite a growing belief in a myth of social mobility based on equality of economic opportunity, the reality was that the richest 10 percent of the population in the cities held 70 to 80 percent of the wealth compared to 50 percent in 1800. Nevertheless, American historians generally argue that while the rich got richer, increased purchasing power at least prevented the poor from getting poorer.

Limiting the Spread of Industrialization to the Nonindustrialized World

Before 1870, the industrialization that had developed in western and central Europe and the United States did not extend in any significant way to the rest of the world. Even in eastern Europe, industrialization lagged far behind that of western and central Europe. Russia, for example, remained largely rural and agricultural with an autocratic regime that kept peasants in serfdom. There was not much of a middle class, and the tsarist regime, fearful of change, preferred to import industrial goods in return for the export of raw materials such as grain and timber. Russia would not have an Industrial Revolution until the end of the nineteenth century (see Chapter 21).

In other parts of the world where they had established control (see Chapter 22), newly industrialized European states pursued a deliberate policy of preventing the growth of mechanized industry. A good example is India. In the eighteenth century, India had become one of the world's greatest exporters of cotton cloth produced by hand labor. In the first half of the nineteenth century, much of India fell under the control of the British East India Company (see Chapter 22). With British control came inexpensive

British factory-produced textiles, and soon thousands of Indian spinners and hand loom weavers were unemployed. British policy encouraged Indians to export their raw materials while buying British-made goods. Although some limited forms of industrial factories for making textiles and jute (used in making rope) were opened in India in the 1850s, a lack of local capital and the advantages given to British imports limited the growth of new manufacturing operations. India, then, provides an excellent example of how some of the rapidly industrializing nations of Europe worked to deliberately thwart the spread of the Industrial Revolution to their colonial dominions.

The Social Impact of the Industrial Revolution

Eventually, the Industrial Revolution revolutionized the social life of Europe and the world. Although much of Europe remained bound by its traditional ways, already in the first half of the nineteenth century, the social impact of the Industrial Revolution was being felt, and future avenues of growth were becoming apparent. Vast changes in the numbers of people and where they lived were already dramatically evident.

POPULATION GROWTH AND URBANIZATION

Population increases had already begun in the eighteenth century, but they became dramatic in the nineteenth century. In 1750, the total European population stood at an estimated 140 million; by 1800, it had increased to 187 million, and by 1850, the population had almost doubled since 1750, to 266 million. The key to the rise in population was the decline in death rates evident throughout Europe. There was a drop in the number of deaths from famines, epidemics, and war. Major epidemic diseases in particular, such as plague and smallpox, declined noticeably. There was also a decline in the ordinary death rate as a general increase in the food supply, already evident in the agricultural revolution of Britain in the late eighteenth century, spread to more areas. More food enabled a greater number of people to be better fed and therefore more resistant to disease. Famine largely disappeared from western Europe, although there were dramatic exceptions in isolated areas where overpopulation magnified the already existing problem of rural poverty. In Ireland, famine produced the century's great catastrophe.

Irish peasants lived in mud hovels in desperate poverty. Cultivation of the potato, a nutritious and relatively easy food to grow that produced three times as much food per acre as grain, gave the peasants a basic staple that enabled them to survive and even expand in numbers. Between 1781 and 1845, the Irish population doubled from four to eight million. Probably half of this population depended on the potato for survival. In the summer of 1845, the potato crop in Ireland was struck by blight in the form of a fungus that turned the potatoes black. Between 1845 and 1851, the Great Famine decimated the Irish population. Over one million died of starvation and disease, while almost two million emigrated to the United States and Britain. Of all the European nations, only Ireland had a declining population in the nineteenth century.

The flight of so many Irish to America reminds us that the traditional safety valve for overpopulation has always been emigration. Between 1821 and 1850, the number of emigrants from Europe averaged about 110,000 a year. More often than emigrating, however, the rural masses sought a solution to their poverty by moving to towns and cities within their own countries to find work. It should not astonish us then that the first half of the nineteenth century was a period of rapid urbanization.

Cities and towns grew dramatically in the first half of the nineteenth century, a phenomenon related to industrialization. Cities had traditionally been centers for princely courts, government and military offices, churches, and commerce. By 1850, especially in Great Britain and Belgium, they were rapidly becoming places for manufacturing and industry. With the steam engine, entrepreneurs could locate their manufacturing plants in urban centers, where they had ready access to transportation facilities and unemployed people from the country looking for work.

In 1800, Great Britain had one major city, London, with a population of one million, and six cities with populations between 50,000 and 100,000. Fifty years later, London's population had swelled to 2,363,000, while there were nine cities over 100,000 and eighteen cities with populations between 50,000 and 100,000. When the populations of cities under 50,000 are added to these, we realize that over 50 percent of the British population lived in towns and cities by 1850. Urban populations also grew on the Continent, but less dramatically.

The dramatic growth of cities in the first half of the nineteenth century produced miserable living conditions for many of the inhabitants. Of course, this had been true for centuries in European cities, but the rapid urbanization associated with the Industrial Revolution intensified the problems in the first half of the nineteenth century and made these appalling living conditions all the more apparent. Wealthy, middle-class inhabitants, as usual, insulated themselves as best they could, often living in suburbs or the outer ring of the city, where they could have individual houses and gardens. In the inner ring of the city stood the small row houses, some with gardens, of the artisans and lower middle class. Finally, located in the center of most industrial towns were the row houses of the industrial workers. This report on working-class housing in the British city of Birmingham in 1843 gives an idea of the general conditions they faced:

> The courts [of working class row houses] are extremely numerous; . . . a very large portion of the poorer classes of the

> inhabitants reside in them. . . . The courts vary in the number of the houses which they contain, from four to twenty, and most of these houses are three stories high, and built, as it is termed, back to back. There is a wash-house, an ash-pit, and a privy at the end, or on one side of the court, and not unfrequently one or more pigsties and heaps of manure. Generally speaking, the privies in the old courts are in a most filthy condition. Many which we have inspected were in a state which renders it impossible for us to conceive how they could be used; they were without doors and overflowing with filth.

Rooms were not large and were frequently overcrowded, as this government report of 1838 revealed: "I entered several of the tenements. In one of them, on the ground floor, I found six persons occupying a very small room, two in bed, ill with fever. In the room above this were two more persons in one bed, ill with fever." Another report said: "There were 63 families where there were at least five persons to one bed; and there were some in which even six were packed in one bed, lying at the top and bottom—children and adults."[1]

Sanitary conditions in these towns were appalling. Due to the lack of municipal direction, sewers and open drains were common on city streets: "In the center of this street is a gutter, into which potato parings, the refuse of animal and vegetable matters of all kinds, the dirty water from the washing of clothes and of the houses, are all poured, and there they stagnate and putrefy."[2] Unable to deal with human excrement, cities in the new industrial era smelled horrible and were extraordinarily unhealthy. Towns and cities were fundamentally death traps. As deaths outnumbered births in most large cities in the first half of the nineteenth century, only a constant influx of people from the country kept them alive and growing.

To many of the well-to-do middle classes, this situation presented a clear danger to society. Were not these masses of workers, sunk in crime, disease, and immorality, a potential threat to their own well-being? Might not the masses be organized and used by unscrupulous demagogues to overthrow the established order? Some observers, however, wondered if the workers could be held responsible for their fate. One of the best of a new breed of urban reformers was Edwin Chadwick (1800–1890). Chadwick became obsessed with eliminating the poverty and squalor of the metropolitan areas. As secretary of the Poor Law Commission, he initiated a passionate search for detailed facts about the living conditions of the working classes. After three years of investigation, Chadwick summarized the results in his *Report on the Condition of the Labouring Population of Great Britain*, published in 1842. In it he concluded that "the various forms of epidemic, endemic, and other disease" were directly caused by the "atmospheric impurities produced by decomposing animal and vegetable substances, by damp and filth, and close overcrowded dwellings [prevailing] amongst the population in every part of the kingdom." Such conditions, he argued, could be

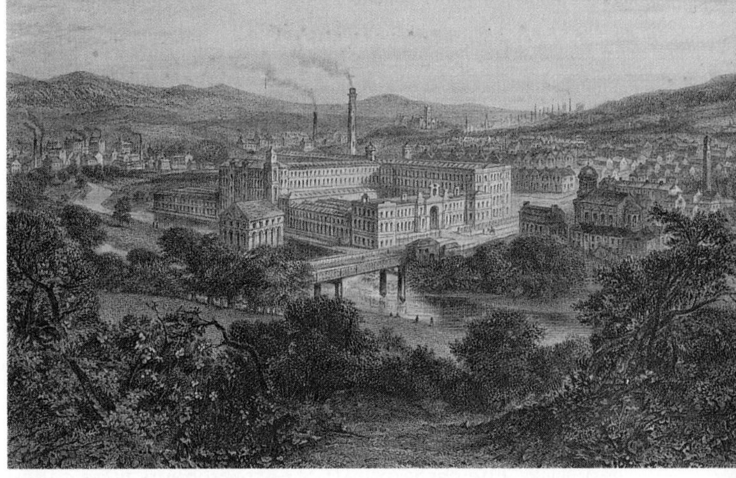

A NEW INDUSTRIAL TOWN. Cities and towns grew dramatically in Britain in the first half of the nineteenth century, largely as a result of industrialization. Pictured here is Saltaire, a model textile factory and town founded near Bradford by Titus Salt in 1851. To facilitate the transportation of goods, the town was built on the Leeds and Liverpool canals.

eliminated. As to the means: "The primary and most important measures, and at the same time the most practicable, and within the recognized province of public administration, are drainage, the removal of all refuse of habitations, streets, and roads, and the improvement of the supplies of water."[3] In other words, Chadwick was advocating a system of modern sanitary reforms including efficient sewers and a supply of piped water. Six years after his report and largely due to his efforts, Britain's first Public Health Act created a National Board of Health empowered to form local boards that would establish modern sanitary systems.

Fear of cholera convinced many middle-class citizens to support the public health reforms advocated by people like Chadwick. Outbreaks of this deadly disease ravaged Europe in the early 1830s and late 1840s and were especially rampant in overcrowded cities. As some city authorities and wealthier residents became convinced that filthy conditions helped to spread the disease, they began to support the call for new public health measures.

NEW SOCIAL CLASSES: THE INDUSTRIAL MIDDLE CLASS

The rise of industrial capitalism produced a new industrial middle-class group. The bourgeois or middle class was not new; it had existed since the emergence of cities in the Middle Ages. Originally, the bourgeois was a burgher or town dweller, whether active as a merchant, official, artisan, lawyer, or man of letters, who enjoyed a special set of rights from the charter of his town. As wealthy townspeople bought land, the original meaning of the word *bourgeois* became lost, and the term came to include people involved in commerce, industry, and banking as well as professionals, such as lawyers, teachers, and physicians, and government officials at varying levels. At the lower end of the economic scale were master craftspeople and shopkeepers.

Lest we make the industrial middle class too much of an abstraction, we need to look at who the new industrial entrepreneurs actually were. These were the people who constructed the factories, purchased the machines, and figured out where the markets were. Their qualities included resourcefulness, single-mindedness, resolution, initiative, vision, ambition, and often, of course, greed. As Jedediah Strutt, a cotton manufacturer said, "Getting of money . . . is the main business of the life of men." But this was not an easy task. The early industrial entrepreneurs were called upon to superintend an enormous array of functions that are handled today by teams of managers; they raised capital, determined markets, set company objectives, organized the factory and its labor, and trained supervisors who could act for them. The opportunities for making money were great, but the risks were also tremendous.

By 1850, in Britain at least, the kind of traditional entrepreneurship that had created the Industrial Revolution was declining and was being replaced by a new business aristocracy. This new generation of entrepreneurs stemmed from the professional and industrial middle classes, especially as sons inherited the successful businesses established by their fathers. Increasingly, the new industrial entrepreneurs—the bankers and owners of factories and mines—came to amass much wealth and play an important role alongside the traditional landed elites of their societies. The Industrial Revolution began at a time when the preindustrial agrarian world was still largely dominated by these landed elites. As the new bourgeoisie bought great estates and acquired social respectability, they also sought political power, and in the course of the nineteenth century, their wealthiest members would merge with those old elites.

NEW SOCIAL CLASSES: THE INDUSTRIAL WORKING CLASS

At the same time that the members of the industrial middle class sought to reduce the barriers between themselves and the landed elite, they were also trying to separate themselves from the laboring classes below them. The working class was actually a mixture of different groups in the first half of the nineteenth century. In the course of the nineteenth century, factory workers would form an industrial proletariat, but in the first half of that century, they by no means constituted a majority of the working class in any major city, even in Britain. According to the 1851 census in Britain, while there were 1.8 million agricultural laborers and 1 million domestic servants, there were only 811,000 workers in the cotton and woolen industries. Even one-third of these were still working in small workshops or in their own homes.

Industrial workers faced wretched working conditions. In the early decades of the Industrial Revolution "places of work," as early factories were called, were dreadful. Work hours ranged from twelve to sixteen hours a day, six days a week, with half an hour for lunch and dinner. There was no security of employment and no minimum wage. The worst conditions were in the cotton mills, where temperatures were especially debilitating. One report noted that "in the cotton-spinning work, these creatures are kept, fourteen hours in each day, locked up, summer and winter, in a heat of from eighty to eighty-four degrees." Mills were also dirty, dusty, and unhealthy:

> Not only is there not a breath of sweet air in these truly infernal scenes, but . . . there is the abominable and pernicious stink of the gas to assist in the murderous effects of the heat. In addition to the noxious effluvia of the gas, mixed with the steam, there are the dust, and what is called cotton-flyings or fuz, which the unfortunate creatures have to inhale; and . . . the notorious fact is that well constitutioned men are rendered old and past labour at forty years of age, and that children are rendered decrepit and deformed, and thousands upon thousands of them slaughtered by consumptions [lung diseases], before they arrive at the age of sixteen.[4]

Thus ran a report on working conditions in the cotton industry in 1824.

Conditions in the coal mines were also harsh. The introduction of steam power meant only that steam-powered engines mechanically lifted coal to the top. Inside the mines, men still bore the burden of digging the coal out, while horses, mules, women, and children hauled coal carts on rails to the lift. Dangerous conditions abounded in coal mines; cave-ins, explosions, and gas fumes (called

WOMEN IN THE MINES. Both women and children were often employed in the early factories and mines of the nineteenth century. As is evident in this illustration of a woman dragging a cart loaded with coal behind her, they often worked under very trying conditions.

CHILD LABOR: DISCIPLINE IN THE TEXTILE MILLS

Child labor was certainly not new, but in the early Industrial Revolution it was exploited more systematically. These selections are taken from the Report of Sadler's Committee, which was commissioned in 1832 to inquire into the condition of child factory workers.

HOW THEY KEPT THE CHILDREN AWAKE

It is a very frequent thing at Mr. Marshall's [at Shrewsbury] where the least children were employed (for there were plenty working at six years of age), for Mr. Horseman to start the mill earlier in the morning than he formerly did; and provided a child should be drowsy, the overlooker walks round the room with a stick in his hand, and he touches that child on the shoulder, and says, "Come here." In a corner of the room there is an iron cistern; it is filled with water; he takes this boy, and takes him up by the legs, and dips him over head in the cistern, and sends him to work for the remainder of the day. . . .

What means were taken to keep the children to their work?—Sometimes they would tap them over the head, or nip them over the nose, or give them a pinch of snuff, or throw water in their faces, or pull them off where they were, and job them about to keep them waking.

THE SADISTIC OVERLOOKER

Samuel Downe, age 29, factory worker living near Leeds; at the age of about ten began work at Mr. Marshall's mill at Shrewsbury, where the customary hours when work was brisk were generally 5 A.M. to 8 P.M., sometimes from 5:30 A.M. to 8 or 9:

What means were taken to keep the children awake and vigilant, especially at the termination of such a day's labour as you have described?—There was generally a blow or a box, or a tap with a strap, or sometimes the hand.

Have you yourself been strapped?—Yes, most severely, till I could not bear to sit upon a chair without having pillows, and through that I left. I was strapped both on my own legs, and then I was put upon a man's back, and then strapped and buckled with two straps to an iron pillar, and flogged, and all by one overlooker; after that he took a piece of tow, and twisted it in the shape of a cord, and put it in my mouth, and tied it behind my head.

He gagged you?—Yes; and then he ordered me to run round a part of the machinery where he was overlooker, and he stood at one end, and every time I came there he struck me with a stick, which I believe was an ash plant, and which he generally carried in his hand, and sometimes he hit me, and sometimes he did not; and one of the men in the room came and begged me off, and that he let me go, and not beat me any more, and consequently he did.

You have been beaten with extraordinary severity?—Yes, I was beaten so that I had not power to cry at all, or hardly speak at one time. What age were you at that time?—Between 10 and 11.

"bad air") were a way of life. The cramped conditions in the mines—tunnels often did not exceed three or four feet in height—and their constant dampness resulted in deformed bodies and ruined lungs.

Both children and women were employed in large numbers in early factories and mines. Children had been an important part of the family economy in preindustrial times, working in the fields or carding and spinning wool at home with the growth of cottage industry. In the Industrial Revolution, however, child labor was exploited more than ever and in a considerably more systematic fashion (see the box above). The owners of cotton factories appreciated certain features of child labor. Children had a particular delicate touch as spinners of cotton. Their smaller size made it easier for them to move under machines to gather loose cotton. Moreover, children were more easily broken to factory work. Above all, children represented a cheap supply of labor. In 1821, 49 percent of the British people were under twenty years of age. Hence children made up a particularly abundant supply of labor, and they were paid only about one-sixth or one-third of what a man was paid. In the cotton factories in 1838, children under eighteen made up 29 percent of the total workforce; children as young as seven worked twelve to fifteen hours per day six days a week in cotton mills.

By 1830, women and children made up two-thirds of the cotton industry's labor. As the number of children employed declined under the Factory Act of 1833, which established nine as the minimum work age, their places were taken by women, who came to dominate the labor forces of the early factories. Women made up 50 percent of the labor force in textile (cotton and woolen) factories before 1870. They were mostly unskilled labor and were paid half or less of what men received. Excessive working hours for women were outlawed in 1844, but only in textile factories and mines; not until 1867 were they outlawed in craft workshops.

The employment of children and women in large part represents a continuation of a preindustrial kinship pattern. Cottage industry had always involved the efforts of the entire family, and it seemed perfectly natural to continue this pattern. Men migrating from the countryside to industrial towns and cities took their wives and children with them into the factory or into the mines. Of 136 employees in Robert Peel's factory at Bury in 1801, 95 belonged to twenty-six families. The impetus for this family work often came from the family itself. The factory owner Jedediah Strutt was opposed to child labor under ten but was forced by parents to take children as young as seven.

The employment of large numbers of women in factories did not produce a significant transformation in female working patterns, as was once assumed. Studies of urban households in France and Britain, for example, have revealed that throughout the nineteenth century traditional types of female labor still predominated in the women's work world. In 1851, fully 40 percent of the female workforce in Britain consisted of domestic servants. In France, the largest group of female workers, 40 percent, worked in agriculture. In addition, only 20 percent of female workers labored in Britain's factories, only 10 percent in France. Regional and local studies have also indicated that most of these workers were single women. Few married women worked outside their homes.

The Factory Acts that limited the work hours of children and women also began to break up the traditional kinship pattern of work and led to a new pattern based on a separation of work and home. Men came to be expected to be responsible for the primary work obligations, while women assumed daily control of the family and performed low-paying jobs such as laundry work that could be done in the home. Domestic industry made it possible for women to continue their contributions to family survival.

EFFORTS AT CHANGE: EARLY SOCIALISM

In the first half of the nineteenth century, the pitiful conditions found in the slums, mines, and factories of the Industrial Revolution gave rise to a movement known as socialism. Early socialism was largely the product of intellectuals who believed in the equality of all people and wanted to replace competition with cooperation in industry. To later socialists, especially the followers of Karl Marx, such ideas were merely impractical dreams, and with contempt they labeled these theorists "utopian socialists." The term has lasted to this day.

Robert Owen, a British cotton manufacturer, was one such utopian socialist. He believed that humans would show their true natural goodness if they lived in a cooperative environment. At New Lanark in Scotland, he transformed a squalid factory town into a flourishing, healthy community. But when he tried to create such a cooperative community at New Harmony, Indiana, in the United States in the 1820s, fighting within the community eventually destroyed his dream.

With their plans for the reconstruction of society, utopian socialists attracted a number of women supporters, who believed that only a reordering of society would help women. One of Owen's disciples, a wealthy woman named Frances Wright, bought slaves in order to set up a model community at Nashoba, Tennessee. The community failed, but Wright continued to work for women's rights.

REACTION AND REVOLUTION: THE GROWTH OF NATIONALISM

After the defeat of Napoleon, European rulers moved to restore much of the old order. This was the goal of the great powers—Great Britain, Austria, Prussia, and Russia—when they met at the Congress of Vienna in September 1814 to arrange a final peace settlement. The leader of the congress was the Austrian foreign minister, Prince Klemens von Metternich (1773–1859), who claimed that he was guided at Vienna by the principle of legitimacy. To keep peace and stability in Europe, he said it was necessary to restore the legitimate monarchs, who would preserve traditional institutions. This had already been done in France by restoring the Bourbon monarchy.

In fact, however, the principle of legitimacy was largely ignored elsewhere. At the Congress of Vienna, the great powers all grabbed lands to add to their states. In doing so, they believed that they were forming a new balance of power that would keep any one country from dominating Europe. For example, to balance Russian gains, Prussia and Austria had been strengthened. According to Metternich, this arrangement had clearly avoided a great danger: "Prussia and Austria are completing their systems of defense; united, the two monarchies form an unconquerable barrier against the enterprises of any conquering prince who might perhaps once again occupy the throne of France or that of Russia."[5]

The peace arrangements of 1815 were but the beginning of a conservative reaction determined to contain the liberal and nationalist forces unleashed by the French Revolution. Metternich and his kind were representatives of the ideology known as conservatism. Most conservatives favored obedience to political authority, believed that organized religion was crucial to social order, hated revolutionary upheavals, and were unwilling to accept either the liberal demands for civil liberties and representative governments or the nationalistic aspirations generated by the French revolutionary era. The community took precedence over individual rights; society must be organized and ordered, and tradition remained the best guide for order. After 1815, the political philosophy of conservatism was supported by hereditary monarchs, government bureaucracies, land owning aristocracies, and revived churches, be they Protestant or Catholic. Although not unopposed, both internationally and domestically the conservative forces appeared dominant after 1815.

One method used by the great powers to maintain the new status quo they had constructed was the Concert of

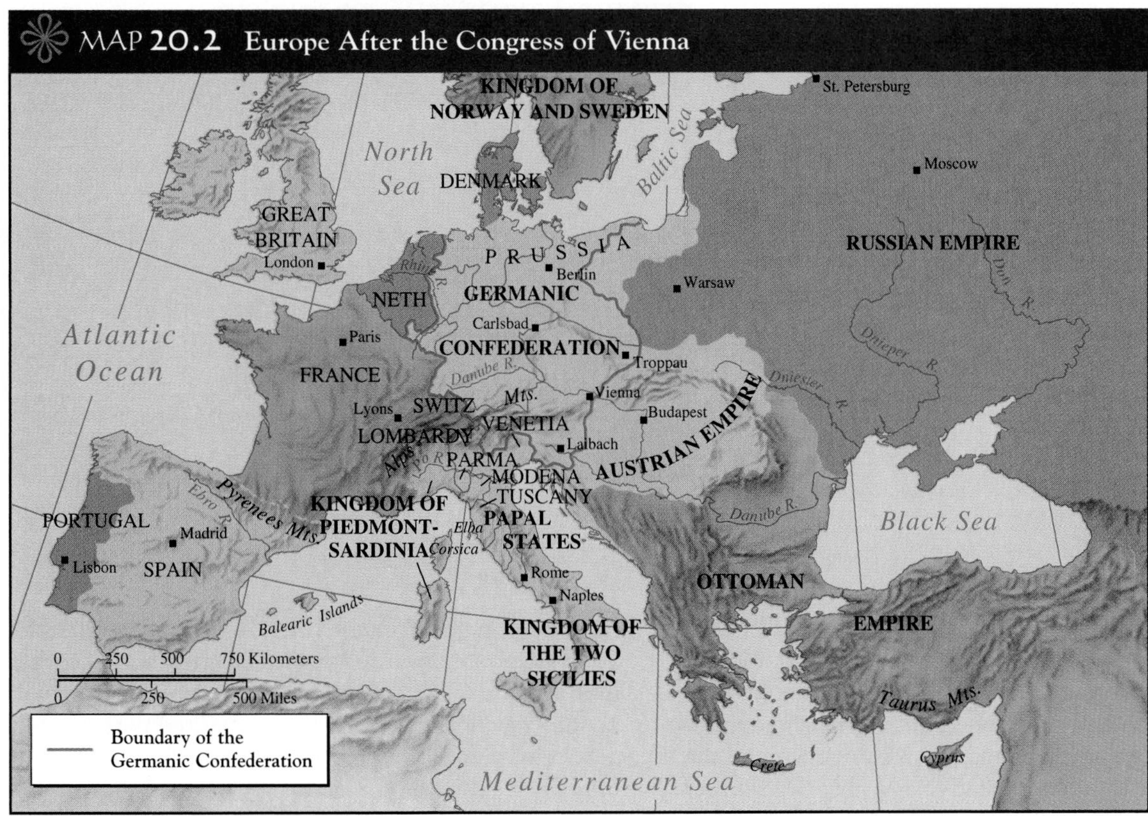

MAP 20.2 Europe After the Congress of Vienna

Europe, according to which Great Britain, Russia, Prussia, and Austria (and later France) agreed to meet periodically in conferences to discuss their common interests and examine measures that "will be judged most salutary for the repose and prosperity of peoples, and for the maintenance of peace in Europe." Eventually, the great powers adopted a principle of intervention, which meant that they claimed the right to use force to restore legitimate monarchs who had been toppled from their thrones by revolutions. Britain refused to agree to the principle, arguing that it had never been the intention of the great powers to interfere in the internal affairs of other states. Ignoring the British position, Austria, Prussia, Russia, and France used military intervention to defeat revolutionary movements in Spain and Italy and to restore legitimate (and conservative) monarchs to their thrones.

Revolutionary Outbursts

Between 1815 and 1830, the conservative domination of Europe evident in the Concert of Europe was also apparent in domestic affairs as conservative governments throughout Europe worked to maintain the old order. But powerful movements for change were also at work. These depended on ideas embodied in a series of political philosophies or ideologies—liberalism and nationalism—that came into their own in the first half of the nineteenth century. They continue to affect the entire world.

Liberalism owed much to the Enlightenment of the eighteenth century and the American and French Revolutions at the end of that century. In addition, liberalism became increasingly important as the Industrial Revolution progressed because the developing industrial middle class largely adopted it as its own. There were divergencies of opinion among people classified as liberals, but all began with a common denominator, a conviction that people should be as free from restraint as possible. This belief is evident in both economic and political liberalism.

Also called classical economics, economic liberalism was based on the primary tenet of *laissez-faire*, or the belief that the state should not interrupt the free play of natural economic forces, especially supply and demand. Government should not interfere with the economic liberty of the individual and should restrict itself to only three primary functions: defense of the country, police protection of individuals, and the construction and maintenance of public works too expensive for individuals to undertake. If individuals were allowed economic liberty, ultimately they would bring about the maximum good for the maximum number and benefit the general welfare of society.

Politically, liberals came to hold a common set of beliefs. Chief among them was the protection of civil liberties or the basic rights of all people, which included equality before the law, freedom of assembly, speech, and press, and freedom from arbitrary arrest. All of these freedoms should be guaranteed by a written document, such

THE 1830 REVOLUTION OF PARIS. In 1830, the forces of change began to undo the conservative domination of Europe. In France, the reactionary Charles X was overthrown. In this painting, students, former soldiers of the Empire, and middle-class citizens are seen joining the rebels who are marching on city hall to demand a republic. The forces of Charles X, seen firing from a building above, failed to halt the rebels.

as the American Bill of Rights or the French Declaration of the Rights of Man and the Citizen. In addition to religious toleration for all, most liberals advocated separation of church and state. The right of peaceful opposition to the government in and out of parliament and the making of laws by a representative assembly (legislature) elected by qualified voters constituted two other liberal demands. Many liberals believed, then, in a constitutional monarchy or constitutional state with limits on the powers of government to prevent despotism, and in written constitutions that would also help to guarantee these rights.

Many liberals also advocated ministerial responsibility or a system in which ministers of the king were responsible to the legislature rather than to the king, giving the legislative branch a check on the power of the executive. Liberals in the first half of the nineteenth century also believed in a limited suffrage. While all people were entitled to equal civil rights, they should not have equal political rights. The right to vote and hold office would be open only to men who met certain property qualifications. As a political philosophy, liberalism was tied to middle-class, and especially industrial middle-class, men who favored the extension of voting rights so that they could share power with the land owning classes. They had little desire to let the lower classes share that power. Liberals were not democrats.

Nationalism was an even more powerful ideology for change in the nineteenth century. Nationalism arose out of an awareness of being part of a community that has common institutions, traditions, language, and customs. This community is called a "nation," and the primary political loyalty of individuals would be to the nation rather than to a dynasty or a city-state or other political unit. Nationalism did not become a popular force for change until the French Revolution. From then on, nationalists came to believe that each nationality should have its own government. Thus, a divided people such as the Germans wanted national unity in a German nation-state with one central government. Subject peoples, such as the Hungarians, wanted national self-determination or the right to establish their own autonomy rather than be subject to a German minority in a multinational empire.

Nationalism threatened to upset the existing political order, both internationally and nationally, making nationalism fundamentally radical. A united Germany or united Italy would upset the balance of power established in 1815. By the same token, an independent Hungarian state would mean the breakup of the Austrian Empire. Because many European states were multinational, it is evident why conservatives tried so hard to repress the radical threat of nationalism.

At the same time, in the first half of the nineteenth century, nationalism found a strong ally in liberalism. Most liberals believed that freedom could only be realized by peoples who ruled themselves. Each people should have its own country; no state should try to dominate others. The alliance with liberalism also gave nationalism a cosmopolitan dimension. Many nationalists believed that once each people obtained its own state, all nations could be linked together into a broader community of all humanity.

Beginning in 1830, the forces of change began to break through the conservative domination of Europe, more successfully in some places than in others. In France, the attempt of the ultraroyalists under the Bourbon monarch Charles X (1824–1830) to restore the old regime as far as possible led to a revolt by liberals in 1830. After the overthrow of Charles, a limited constitutional monarchy was established under Louis-Philippe (1830–1848), soon called the bourgeois monarch because political support for his rule came from the upper middle class.

Supporters of liberalism played a primary role in the revolution in France, but nationalism was the crucial force in three other revolutionary outbursts in 1830. The Belgians, who had been annexed to the Dutch Republic in 1815 to create a larger state to act as a barrier to French aggression, rebelled against the Dutch and established an independent constitutional monarchy. The revolutionary scenarios in Poland and Italy were much less successful. Russian forces crushed the Poles' attempt to liberate themselves from foreign domination, while Austrian troops intervened in Italy to uphold reactionary governments in a number of Italian states.

THE REVOLUTIONS OF 1848

Despite the liberal and nationalist successes in France and Belgium, the conservative order continued to dominate much of Europe. But the forces of liberalism and nationalism continued to grow and gave rise to new groups of people who wanted change. In 1848, these forces of change erupted once more. As usual, revolution in France provided the spark for other countries, and soon most of central and southern Europe was ablaze with revolutionary fires. Tsar Nicholas I of Russia lamented to Queen Victoria in April 1848, "What remains standing in Europe? Great Britain and Russia."

In France, a severe industrial and agricultural depression beginning in 1846 brought untold hardship to the lower middle class, workers, and peasants. Scandals, graft, and corruption were rife, while the government's persistent refusal to extend the suffrage angered the disfranchised members of the middle class. As Louis-Philippe's government continued to refuse to make changes, opposition grew and finally overthrew the monarchy on February 24, 1848. A group of moderate and radical republicans established a provisional government and called for the election by universal manhood suffrage of a Constituent Assembly that would draw up a new constitution.

The provisional government also established national workshops to provide work for unemployed workers. The cost of the program became increasingly burdensome to the government. The result was a growing split between the moderate republicans, who had the support of most of France, and the radical republicans, whose main support came from the Parisian working class. From March to June, the number of unemployed enrolled in the national workshops rose from 6,100 to almost 120,000, emptying the treasury and frightening the moderates, who responded by closing the workshops on June 21. The workers refused to accept this decision and poured into the streets. Four days of bitter and bloody fighting by government forces crushed the working-class revolt. Thousands were killed, and 11,000 prisoners were deported to the French colony of Algeria in northern Africa.

The new constitution, ratified on November 4, 1848, established a republic (Second Republic) with a single legislature elected by universal male suffrage for three years and a president, also elected by universal male suffrage, for four years. In the elections for the presidency held in December 1848, Charles Louis Napoleon Bonaparte, the nephew of the famous French ruler, won a resounding victory. Within four years President Napoleon would become Emperor Napoleon.

News of the February revolution in Paris led to upheaval in central Europe as well (see the box on p. 604). The Vienna settlement in 1815 had recognized the existence of thirty-eight sovereign states (called the Germanic Confederation) in what had once been the Holy Roman Empire. Austria and Prussia were the two great powers, while the other states varied considerably in size. In 1848, revolutionary cries for change caused many German rulers to promise constitutions, a free press, jury trials, and other liberal reforms. In Prussia concessions were also made to appease the revolutionaries. King Frederick William IV (1840–1861) agreed to abolish censorship, establish a new constitution, and work for a united Germany. The latter promise had its counterpart throughout all the German states as governments allowed elections by universal male suffrage for deputies to an all-German parliament. Its purpose was to fulfill a liberal and nationalist dream—the preparation of a constitution for a new united Germany.

But the Frankfurt Assembly (as the all-German parliament was called) failed to achieve its goal. Although some members spoke of using force, they had no real means of compelling the German rulers to accept the constitution they had drawn up. The attempt of the German liberals at Frankfurt to create a German state had failed, and leadership for unification would now pass to the Prussian military monarchy.

The Austrian Empire also had its social, political, and nationalist grievances and needed only the news of the revolution in Paris to encourage it to erupt in flames in March 1848. The Austrian Empire was a multinational state, a collection of eleven different peoples including Germans, Czechs, Magyars (Hungarians), Slovaks, Romanians, Slovenes, Poles, Serbians, and Italians. Only the Habsburg emperor provided a common bond. The Germans, though only a quarter of the population, played a leading role in governing Austria. The Hungarians wanted their own legislature. In March, demonstrations in Budapest, Prague, and Vienna led to Metternich's dismissal. The arch-symbol of the conservative order fled abroad. In Vienna, revolutionary forces, carefully guided by the educated and propertied classes, took control of the capital and insisted that a constituent assembly be summoned to draw up a liberal constitution. Hungary's demands for its own legislature, a separate national army, and control over its foreign policy and budget were granted. In Bohemia, the Czechs began to clamor for their own government as well.

Although Austrian officials had made concessions to appease the revolutionaries, they awaited an opportunity

REVOLUTIONARY EXCITEMENT: CARL SCHURZ AND THE REVOLUTION OF 1848 IN GERMANY

The excitement with which German liberals and nationalists received the news of the February revolution in France and their own expectations for Germany are well captured in this selection from the Reminiscences *of Carl Schurz (1829–1906). Schurz made his way to the United States after the failure of the German revolution and eventually became a U.S. senator.*

CARL SCHURZ, *REMINISCENCES*

One morning, toward the end of February, 1848, I sat quietly in my attic-chamber, working hard at my tragedy of "Ulrich von Hutten" [sixteenth-century German humanist and knight], when suddenly a friend rushed breathlessly into the room, exclaiming: "What, you sitting here! Do you not know what has happened?"

"No; what?"

"The French have driven away Louis Philippe and proclaimed the republic."

I threw down my pen—and that was the end of "Ulrich von Hutten." I never touched the manuscript again. We tore down the stairs, into the street, to the market-square, the accustomed meeting-place for all the student societies after their midday dinner. Although it was still forenoon, the market was already crowded with young men talking excitedly. There was no shouting, no noise, only agitated conversation. What did we want there? This probably no one knew. But since the French had driven away Louis Philippe and proclaimed the republic, something of course must happen here, too. . . . We were dominated by a vague feeling as if a great outbreak of elemental forces had begun, as if an earthquake was impending of which we had felt the first shock, and we instinctively crowded together. . . .

The next morning there were the usual lectures to be attended. But how profitless! The voice of the professor sounded like a monotonous drone coming from far away. What he had to say did not seem to concern us. The pen that should have taken notes remained idle. At last we closed with a sigh the notebook and went away, impelled by a feeling that now we had something more important to do—to devote ourselves to the affairs of the fatherland. And this we did by seeking as quickly as possible again the company of our friends, in order to discuss what had happened and what was to come. In these conversations, excited as they were, certain ideas and catchwords worked themselves to the surface, which expressed more or less the feelings of the people. Now had arrived in Germany the day for the establishment of "German Unity," and the founding of a great, powerful national German Empire. In the first line the convocation of a national parliament. Then the demands for civil rights and liberties, free speech, free press, the right of free assembly, equality before the law, a freely elected representation of the people with legislative power, responsibility of ministers, self-government of the communes, the right of the people to carry arms, the formation of a civic guard with elective officers, and so on—in short, that which was called a "constitutional form of government on a broad democratic basis." Republican ideas were at first only sparingly expressed. But the word democracy was soon on all tongues, and many, too, thought it a matter of course that if the princes should try to withhold from the people the rights and liberties demanded, force would take the place of mere petition. Of course the regeneration of the fatherland must, if possible, be accomplished by peaceable means. . . . Like many of my friends, I was dominated by the feeling that at last the great opportunity had arrived for giving to the German people the liberty which was their birthright and to the German fatherland its unity and greatness, and that it was now the first duty of every German to do and to sacrifice everything for this sacred object.

to reestablish their firm control. Like the rulers of the German states, they were increasingly encouraged by the divisions between radical and moderate revolutionaries and played on the middle-class fear of a working-class social revolution. The counterrevolutionaries' first success came in June 1848 when Austrian military forces ruthlessly suppressed the Czech rebels in Prague. By the end of October, radical rebels had been crushed in Vienna, but it was only with the assistance of a Russian army of 140,000 men that the Hungarian revolution was finally crushed in 1849. The revolutions in the Austrian Empire had also failed. Autocratic government was restored; the emperor and propertied classes remained in control, while the numerous nationalities remained subject to the Austrian government.

The revolutions in Italy also failed. The Congress of Vienna had established nine states in Italy, including the kingdom of Piedmont in the north ruled by the house of Savoy; the kingdom of the Two Sicilies (Naples and Sicily); the Papal States; a handful of small duchies ruled by relatives of the Austrian emperor; and the important northern provinces of Lombardy and Venetia, which were now part of the Austrian Empire. Italy was largely under Austrian domination, while all the states had extremely reactionary governments eager to smother any liberal or nationalist sentiment. Attempts at change were ruthlessly crushed. But under the leadership of a new movement for Italian unity known as Young Italy, revolts against the foreigners were initially successful in 1848. By 1849, however, the Austrians had reestablished complete control over Lombardy and Venetia, and counterrevolutionary forces also prevailed elsewhere in Italy.

Throughout Europe in 1848, popular revolts had initiated revolutionary upheavals that had led to liberal constitutions and liberal governments. But the failure of the revolutionaries to stay united soon led to the reestablishment of authoritarian regimes. In other parts of the Western world—namely, the Western Hemisphere—nationalist revolutions would have more success.

Independence and the Development of the National State in Latin America

The force of nationalism also affected the Americas. In both North America and Latin America, nation building became a prominent process. The Spanish and Portuguese colonial empires in Latin America had been integrated into the traditional monarchical structure of Europe for centuries. When that structure was challenged, first by the ideas of the Enlightenment and then by the upheavals of the Napoleonic wars, Latin America, too, experienced change.

NATIONALISTIC REVOLTS IN LATIN AMERICA

By the end of the eighteenth century, the ideas of the enlightenment and the new political ideals stemming from the successful revolution in North America (see Chapters 18 and 19) were beginning to influence the creole elites (descendants of Europeans who became permanent inhabitants of Latin America). The principles of the equality of all people in the eyes of the law, free trade, and a free press proved very attractive. Sons of creoles, such as Simón Bolívar and José de San Martín, who became leaders of the independence movement, even went to European universities, where they imbibed the ideas of the Enlightenment. These Latin American elites, joined by a growing class of merchants, especially resented the domination of their trade by Spain and Portugal.

The creole elites soon began to use their new ideas to denounce the rule of the Iberian monarchs and the peninsulars (Spanish and Portuguese officials who resided temporarily in Latin America for political and economic gain). As Bolívar said in 1815, "the hatred that the peninsular has inspired in us is greater than the ocean that separates us." Bolívar reflected the growing nativism among the creole elites, who resented the peninsulars who dominated Latin America and drained the Americas of their wealth. At the beginning of the nineteenth century, Napoleon's continental wars provided the creoles with an opportunity for change. When Bonaparte toppled the monarchies of Spain and Portugal, the authority of the Spaniards and Portuguese in their colonial empires was severely weakened. Between 1807 and 1825, a series of revolts enabled most of Latin America to become independent.

An unusual revolution preceded the main independence movements. Saint Domingue—the western third of Hispaniola—was a French sugar colony. Led by Toussaint L'Ouverture (c. 1743–1803), a son of African slaves, over 100,000 black slaves rose in revolt and seized control of all of Hispaniola. An army sent by Napoleon captured L'Ouverture, but the French soldiers, weakened by disease, soon succumbed to the slave forces. On January 1, 1804, the western part of Hispaniola, now called Haiti, announced its freedom and became the first independent state in Latin America.

Beginning in 1810, Mexico, too, experienced a revolt, fueled initially by the desire of the creole elites to overthrow the rule of the peninsulars. The first real hero of Mexican independence was Miguel Hidalgo y Costilla, a parish priest in a small village about one hundred miles from Mexico City. Hidalgo had studied the French Revolution and roused the local Indians and mestizos to free themselves from the Spanish: "My children, this day comes to us as a new dispensation. Are you ready to receive it? Will you be free? Will you make the effort to recover from the hated Spaniards the lands stolen from your forefathers three hundred years ago?"[6] It was September 16, 1810, and a crowd of Indians and mestizos, armed with clubs, machetes, and a few guns quickly formed a mob army to attack the Spaniards. But Hidalgo was not a good organizer, and his forces were soon crushed. A military court sentenced Hidalgo to death, but his memory lived on. In fact, September 16, the first day of the uprising, is Mexico's Independence Day.

The participation of Indians and mestizos in Mexico's revolt against Spanish control frightened both creoles and peninsulars. Fearful of the masses, they cooperated in defeating the popular revolutionary forces. The conservative elites—both creoles and peninsulars—then decided to overthrow Spanish rule as a way of preserving their own power. They selected a creole military leader, Augustín de Iturbide, as their leader and the first emperor of Mexico in 1821.

Independence movements elsewhere in Latin America were the work of elites—primarily creoles—who overthrew Spanish rule and created new governments that they could dominate. The masses of people—Indians, blacks, mestizos, and mulattoes—gained little from the revolts. José de San Martín (1778–1850) of Argentina and Simón Bolívar (1783–1830) of Venezuela, leaders of the independence movement, were both members of the creole elite, and both were hailed as the Liberators of South America.

By 1810, the forces of San Martín had freed Argentina from Spanish authority. Simón Bolívar led the bitter struggle for independence in Venezuela and then went on to

JOSÉ DE SAN MARTÍN. José de San Martín of Argentina was one of the famous leaders of the Latin American independence movement. His forces liberated Argentina, Chile, and Peru from Spanish authority. In this painting by Theodore Géricault, San Martín is shown leading his troops at the Battle of Chacabuco in Chile.

liberate New Grenada (Colombia) and Ecuador. José de San Martín believed that the Spaniards must be removed from all of South America if any nation was to be free. In January 1817, he led his forces over the high Andes mountains, an amazing feat in itself. Two-thirds of their pack mules and horses died during the difficult journey. Many of the soldiers suffered from lack of oxygen and severe cold while crossing mountain passes that were more than two miles above sea level. The arrival of San Martín's forces in Chile completely surprised the Spaniards, whose forces were routed at the battle of Chacabuco on February 12, 1817. In 1821, San Martín moved on to Lima, Peru, the center of Spanish authority.

Convinced that he was unable to complete the liberation of Peru, San Martín welcomed the arrival of Bolívar and his forces. The Liberator of Venezuela took on the task of crushing the last significant Spanish army at Ayacucho on December 9, 1824. By then, Peru, Uruguay, Paraguay, Colombia, Venezuela, Argentina, Bolivia, and Chile had all become free states. In 1823, the Central American states became independent and in 1838–1839 divided into five republics (Guatemala, El Salvador, Honduras, Costa Rica, and Nicaragua). Earlier, in 1822, the prince regent of Brazil had declared Brazil's independence from Portugal.

In the early 1820s, only one major threat remained to the newly won independence of the Latin American states. Flushed by their success in crushing rebellions in Spain and Italy, the victorious continental powers favored the use of troops to restore Spanish control in Latin America. This time British opposition to intervention prevailed. Eager to gain access to an entire continent for investment and trade, the British proposed joint action with the United States against European interference in Latin America. Distrustful of British motives, President James Monroe acted alone in 1823, guaranteeing the independence of the new Latin American nations and warning against any further European intervention in the New World in the famous Monroe Doctrine. Actually more important to Latin American independence than American words was Britain's navy. All of the continental powers were reluctant to challenge British naval power, which stood between Latin America and any European invasion force.

THE DIFFICULTIES OF NATION BUILDING

The new Latin American nations, most of which began their existence as republics, faced a number of serious problems between 1830 and 1870. The wars for independence had themselves resulted in a staggering loss of population, property, and livestock. Despite the Monroe Doctrine, fear of European intervention persisted, and disputes often arose between the new nations over their precise boundaries. Poor transportation and communication systems fostered regionalism and made national unity difficult.

Severe struggles between church and state were common occurrences in the new nations. The Catholic church had enormous landholdings in Latin America and through its amassed wealth exercised great power. After independence, clerics often took positions in the new governments and wielded considerable influence. Throughout Latin America, a division arose between liberals, who wished to curtail the temporal powers of the church, and conservatives, who hoped to maintain all of the church's privileges and prerogatives. In Mexico, this division even led to civil war, the bloody War of Reform fought between 1858 and 1861, in which Catholic clergy and the military lined up against a liberal government.

The new nations of Latin America began with republican governments, but they had had no experience in ruling themselves. Soon after independence, strong leaders known as caudillos came into power. They ruled chiefly by military force and were usually supported by the landed elites. Many kept the new national states together. Sometimes they were also modernizers who built roads and canals, ports, and schools. Others were destructive, such as Antonio López y Santa Anna, who, in ruling Mexico from 1829 to 1855, misused state funds, halted reforms, created chaos, and helped lose one-third of Mexico's territory to the United States. Other caudillos were supported by the masses, became extremely popular, and served as an instrument for radical change. Juan Manuel de Rosas, for example, who led Argentina from 1829 to 1852, became very popular by favoring Argentine interests against foreigners. Rafael Carrera, who ruled Guatemala from 1839 to 1865, supported native Indian cultures and pursued a policy of land redistribution to aid the Indians. But he was disliked by the elites, who wanted to Europeanize the economy and Guatemalan culture, and his efforts were undone by his successor, Justo Rufino Barrios (1873–1885). A caudillo who was supported by the elites, Barrios pushed the economy to coffee production and forced the Indians to give up their lands and become wage laborers to serve the interests of large plantation owners.

Although political independence brought economic independence, old patterns were quickly reestablished. Instead of Spain and Portugal, Great Britain now dominated the Latin American economy. British merchants moved in in large numbers, while British investors poured in funds, especially into the mining industry. Old trade patterns soon reemerged. Because Latin America served as a source of raw materials and foodstuffs for the industrializing nations of Europe and the United States, exports—especially wheat, tobacco, wool, sugar, coffee, and hides—to the North Atlantic countries increased

MAP 20.3 Latin America in the First Half of the Nineteenth Century

A RADICAL CRITIQUE OF THE LAND PROBLEM IN MEXICO

The domination of Mexico by elites who owned large estates remained a serious problem throughout the nineteenth century. Conservatives, of course, favored the great estates as the foundation stones of their own political power, while even liberals shied away from any extremist attack on property rights. Nevertheless, there were some strong voices of protest, as this excerpt from a speech delivered in 1857 by Ponciano Arriaga demonstrates. Arriaga's appeal went unheeded; conservatives called him a "Communist."

PONCIANO ARRIAGA, SPEECH TO THE CONSTITUTIONAL CONVENTION OF 1856–1857

One of the most deeply rooted evils of our country—an evil that merits the close attention of legislators when they frame our fundamental law—is the monstrous division of landed property.

While a few individuals possess immense areas of uncultivated land that could support millions of people, the great majority of Mexicans languish in a terrible poverty and are denied property, homes, and work. . . .

There are Mexican landowners who occupy (if one can give that name to a purely imaginary act) an extent of land greater than the areas of some of our sovereign states, greater even than that of one of several European states.

In this vast area, much of which lies idle, deserted, abandoned, awaiting the arms and labor of men, live four or five million Mexicans who know no other industry than agriculture, yet are without land or the means to work it, and who cannot emigrate in the hope of bettering their fortunes. They must either vegetate in idleness, turn to banditry, or accept the yoke of a landed monopolist who subjects them to intolerable conditions of life. . . .

How can a hungry, naked, miserable people practice popular government? How can we proclaim the equal rights of men and leave the majority of the nation in conditions worse than those of helots or pariahs? How can we condemn slavery in words, while the lot of most of our fellow citizens is more grievous than that of the black slaves of Cuba or the United States? . . .

With some honorable exceptions, the rich landowners of Mexico, or the administrators who represent them, resemble the feudal lords of the Middle Ages. On his seignorial land, . . . the landowner makes and executes laws, administers justice and exercises civil power, imposes taxes and fines, has his own jails and irons, metes out punishments and tortures, monopolizes commerce, and forbids the conduct without his permission of any business but that of the estate. The judges or officials who exercise on the hacienda the powers attached to public authority are usually the master's servants or tenants, his retainers, incapable of enforcing any law but the will of the master.

An astounding variety of devices are employed to exploit the peons or tenants, to turn a profit from their sweat and labor. They are compelled to work without pay even on days traditionally set aside for rest. They must accept rotten seeds or sick animals whose cost is charged to their miserable wages. They must pay enormous parish fees that bear no relation to the scale of fees that the owner or majordomo has arranged beforehand with the parish priest. They must make all their purchases on the hacienda, using tokens or paper money that do not circulate elsewhere. At certain seasons of the year they are assigned articles of poor quality, whose price is set by the owner or majordomo, constituting a debt which they can never repay. They are forbidden to use pastures and woods, firewood and water, or even the wild fruit of the fields, save with the express permission of the master. In fine, they are subject to a completely unlimited and irresponsible power.

noticeably. At the same time, finished consumer goods, especially textiles, were imported in increasing quantities, causing a decline in industrial production in Latin America. The emphasis on exporting raw materials and importing finished products ensured the ongoing domination of the Latin American economy by foreigners.

A fundamental, underlying problem for all of the new Latin American nations was the persistent domination of society by the landed elites. Large estates remained an important aspect of Latin America's economic and social life (see the box above). After independence, the size of these estates even expanded. By 1848, the Sánchez Navarro family in Mexico owned seventeen haciendas comprising 16 million acres. Governments facilitated this process by selling off church lands, public domains, and the lands of Indian communities. In Argentina, five hundred people bought 21 million acres of public land. Estates were often so large that they could not be farmed efficiently. As one Latin American newspaper put it: "The huge fortunes have the unfortunate tendency to grow even larger, and their owners possess vast tracts of land, which lie fallow and abandoned. Their greed for land does not equal their ability to use it intelligently and actively."[7]

Land remained the basis of wealth, social prestige, and political power throughout the nineteenth century. The Latin American elites tended to identify with European standards of progress, which worked to their benefit, while the masses gained little. Landed elites ran governments,

FLORENCE NIGHTINGALE AND THE NURSING PROFESSION. By her efforts in the Crimean War, the British nurse Florence Nightingale helped to make nursing a modern profession for middle-class women. She is shown here supervising her hospital at Scutari. Her attention to strict hygiene greatly reduced the death rate for wounded British soldiers.

controlled courts, and maintained the system of debt peonage that provided large landowners with a supply of cheap labor. These landowners made enormous profits by concentrating on specialized crops for export, such as coffee, while the masses, left without land to grow basic food crops, lived in dire poverty.

Nationalism in the Balkans: The Ottoman Empire and the Eastern Question

The Ottoman Empire had long been in control of much of southeastern Europe (an area known as the Balkans). In the first half of the nineteenth century, a number of states in the Balkans sought to free themselves from the Ottomans. Serbia, for example, won its autonomy in 1817. As the Ottoman Empire began to decline and authority over its outlying territories in southeastern Europe waned, European governments began to take an active interest in its disintegration. The "Eastern Question," as it came to be called, troubled European diplomats throughout the nineteenth century. Russia's proximity to the Ottoman Empire and the religious bonds between the Russians and the Greek Orthodox Christians in Turkish-dominated southeastern Europe naturally gave Russia special opportunities to enlarge its sphere of influence. The Austrian Empire feared Russian ambitions and had its own interest in the apparent demise of the Ottoman Empire. France and Britain were interested in commercial opportunities and naval bases in the eastern Mediterranean.

In 1821, the Greeks revolted against their Turkish masters. Although subject to Muslim control for four hundred years, the Greeks had been allowed to maintain their language and their Greek Orthodox faith. A revival of Greek national sentiment at the beginning of the nineteenth century added to the growing desire for "the liberation of the fatherland from the terrible yoke of Turkish oppression." The Greek revolt was soon transformed into a noble cause by an outpouring of European sentiment for the Greeks' struggle. In 1827, a combined British and French fleet went to Greece and defeated a large Turkish fleet. A year later, Russia declared war on the Ottoman Empire and invaded its European provinces of Moldavia and Walachia. By the Treaty of Adrianople in 1829, which ended the Russian-Turkish War, the Russians received a protectorate over the two provinces. By the same treaty, the Turks agreed to allow Russia, France, and Britain to decide the fate of Greece. In 1830, the three powers declared Greece an independent kingdom, and two years later a new royal dynasty was established.

The Crimean War was yet another episode in the story of the Eastern Question. In 1853, war had erupted again between the Russians and Turks over Russian demands for the right to protect Christian shrines in Palestine, a privilege that had already been extended to the French. When the Turks refused, the Russians invaded Turkish Moldavia and Walachia. Failure to resolve the problem by negotiations led the Turks to declare war on Russia on October 4, 1853. In the following year, on March 28, Great Britain and France, fearful that the Russians would gain at the expense of the disintegrating Ottoman Empire, declared war on Russia.

The Crimean War was poorly planned and poorly fought. Britain and France decided on an attack on Russia's Crimean peninsula in the Black Sea. After a long siege and at a terrible cost in troops on both sides, the main Russian fortress of Sevastopol fell in September 1855, and the Russians soon sued for peace. By the Treaty of Paris, signed in March 1856, Russia was forced to give up Bessarabia at the mouth of the Danube and accept the neutrality of the Black Sea. In addition, the Danubian principalities of Moldavia and Walachia were placed under the protection of all the great powers.

The Crimean War proved costly to both sides. More than 250,000 soldiers died in the Crimean War, 60 percent of the deaths coming from disease (especially cholera). Even more would have died on the British side if it had not been for the efforts of Florence Nightingale (1820–1910). Her insistence on strict sanitary conditions saved many lives and helped to make nursing a profession of trained, middle-class women.

The Crimean War broke up long-standing European power relationships and effectively destroyed the Concert of Europe. Austria and Russia, the two chief powers maintaining the status quo in the first half of the nineteenth century, were now enemies because of Austria's unwillingness to support Russia in the war. Russia, defeated, humiliated, and weakened by the obvious failure of its armies, withdrew from European affairs for the next two decades. Great Britain, disillusioned by its role in the war, also pulled back from continental affairs. Austria, paying the price for its neutrality, was now without friends among the great powers. Not until the 1870s were new combinations formed to replace those that had disappeared, but in the meantime the European international situation remained fluid. Those willing to pursue the "politics of reality" found themselves presented with a situation filled with opportunity. It was this new international situation that made possible the unification of Italy and Germany.

National Unification and the National State

The revolutions of 1848 had failed, but within twenty-five years, many of the goals sought by liberals and nationalists during the first half of the nineteenth century were achieved. Italy and Germany became nations while many European states were led by constitutional monarchs.

The Unification of Italy

The breakdown of the Concert of Europe opened the way for the Italians and the Germans to establish national states. Their successful unifications transformed the power structure on the Continent. Well into the twentieth century, Europe and the world would still be dealing with the consequences.

In 1850, Austria was still the dominant power on the Italian peninsula. After the failure of the revolution of 1848–1849, a growing number of Italians now focused on the northern Italian state of Piedmont as their best hope to achieve unification of Italy. The royal house of Savoy ruled the kingdom of Piedmont, which also included the island of Sardinia. It appeared doubtful, however, that the little state could provide the leadership needed to unify Italy until King Victor Emmanuel II (1849–1878) named Count Camillo di Cavour (1810–1861) as his prime minister in 1852.

Cavour was a consummate politician with the ability to persuade others about the rightness of his own convictions. After becoming prime minister in 1852, he pursued a policy of economic expansion that increased government revenues and enabled him to pour money into equipping a large army. Cavour, however, had no illusions about Piedmont's military strength and was only too well aware that he could not challenge Austria directly. Consequently, he made an alliance with the French emperor Louis Napoleon and then provoked the Austrians into invading Piedmont in 1859. In the initial stages of fighting, the Austrians were defeated in two major battles by mostly French armies. A peace settlement gave the French Nice and

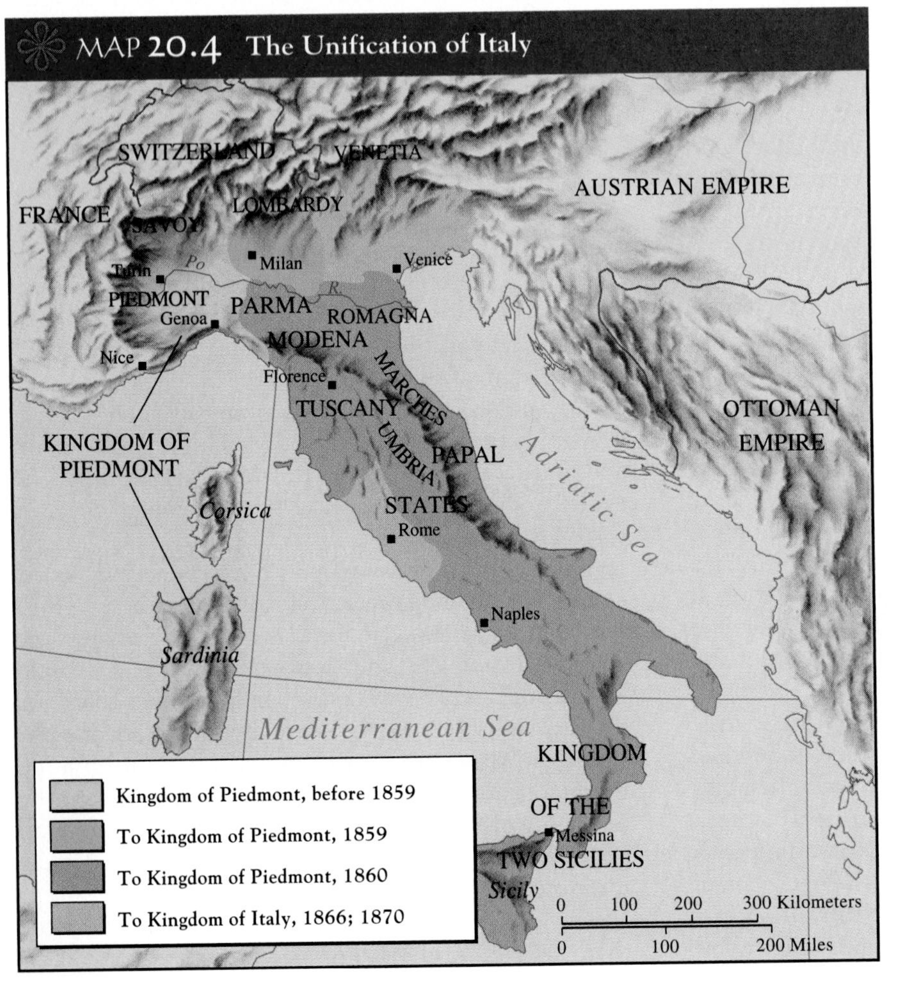

MAP 20.4 The Unification of Italy

GARIBALDI AND ROMANTIC NATIONALISM

Giuseppe Garibaldi was one of the more colorful figures involved in the unification of Italy. Accompanied by only a thousand of his famous "Red Shirts," the Italian soldier of fortune left Genoa on the night of May 5, 1860, for an invasion of the Kingdom of the Two Sicilies. The ragged band entered Palermo, the chief city on the island of Sicily, on May 31. This selection is taken from an account by a correspondent for The Times *of London, the Hungarian-born Nandor Eber.*

THE TIMES, JUNE 13, 1860

Palermo, May 31—Anyone in search of violent emotions cannot do better than set off at once for Palermo. However blasé he may be, or however milk-and-water his blood, I promise it will be stirred up. He will be carried away by the tide of popular feeling. . . .

In the afternoon Garibaldi made a tour of inspection round the town. I was there, but find it really impossible to give you a faint idea of the manner in which he was received everywhere. It was one of those triumphs which seem to be almost too much for a man. . . . The popular idol, Garibaldi, in his red flannel shirt, with a loose colored handkerchief round his neck, and his worn "wide-awake" [a soft-brimmed felt hat], was walking on foot among those cheering, laughing, crying, mad thousands; and all his few followers could do was to prevent him from being bodily carried off the ground. The people threw themselves forward to kiss his hands, or, at least, to touch the hem of his garment, as if it contained the panacea for all their past and perhaps coming suffering. Children were brought up, and mothers asked on their knees for his blessing; and all this while the object of this idolatry was calm and smiling as when in the deadliest fire, taking up the children and kissing them, trying to quiet the crowd, stopping at every moment to hear a long complaint of houses burned and property sacked by the retreating soldiers, giving good advice, comforting, and promising that all damages should be paid for. . . .

One might write volumes of horrors on the vandalism already committed, for every one of the hundred ruins has its story of brutality and inhumanity. . . . In these small houses a dense population is crowded together even in ordinary times. A shell falling on one, and crushing and burying the inmates, was sufficient to make people abandon the neighboring one and take refuge a little further on, shutting themselves up in the cellars. When the Royalists retired they set fire to those of the houses which had escaped the shells, and numbers were thus burned alive in their hiding places. . . .

If you can stand the exhalation, try and go inside the ruins, for it is only there that you will see what the thing means and you will not have to search long before you stumble over the remains of a human body, a leg sticking out here, an arm there, a black face staring at you a little further on. You are startled by a rustle. You look round and see half a dozen gorged rats scampering off in all directions, or you see a dog trying to make his escape over the ruins. . . . I only wonder that the sign of these scenes does not convert every man in the town into a tiger and every woman into a fury. But these people have been so long ground down and demoralized that their nature seems to have lost the power of reaction.

Savoy, which they had been promised for making the alliance, and awarded Lombardy to Cavour and the Piedmontese. Cavour's success caused nationalists in some northern Italian states (Parma, Modena, and Tuscany) to overthrow their governments and join their states to Piedmont.

Meanwhile, in southern Italy, a new leader of Italian unification had arisen. Giuseppe Garibaldi (1807–1882), a dedicated Italian patriot, raised an army of a thousand Red Shirts, as his volunteers were called because of their distinctive dress, and landed in Sicily, where a revolt had broken out against the Bourbon king of the Two Sicilies. By the end of July 1860, most of Sicily had been pacified under Garibaldi's control (see the box above). In August, Garibaldi and his forces crossed over to the mainland and began a victorious march up the Italian peninsula. Naples, and with it the Kingdom of the Two Sicilies, fell in early September. Ever the patriot, Garibaldi chose to turn over his conquests to Cavour's Piedmontese forces. On March 17, 1861, a new kingdom of Italy was proclaimed under a centralized government subordinated to the control of Piedmont and King Victor Emmanuel II (1861–1878) of the house of Savoy. Worn out by his efforts, Cavour died three months later.

Despite the proclamation of a new kingdom, the task of unification was not yet complete, as Venetia in the north was still held by Austria and Rome was under papal control, supported by French troops. To attack either one meant war with a major European state, which the Italian army was not prepared to handle. Instead, it was the Prussian army that indirectly completed the task of Italian unification. In the Austro-Prussian War of 1866, the new Italian state became an ally of Prussia. Although the Italian army was defeated by the Austrians, Prussia's victory left the Italians free to annex Venetia. In 1870, the Franco-Prussian War resulted in the withdrawal of French troops from Rome. The Italian army then annexed the city on September 20, 1870, and Rome became the new capital of the united Italian state.

The Unification of Germany

After the failure of the Frankfurt Assembly to achieve German unification in 1848–1849, German nationalists focused on Austria and Prussia as the only two states powerful enough to unify Germany. But Austria, a large multinational empire, feared the creation of a strong German state in central Europe, and more and more Germans began to look to Prussia for leadership in the cause of German unification.

In the 1860s, King William I (1861–1888) attempted to enlarge and strengthen the Prussian army. When the Prussian legislature refused to levy new taxes for the proposed military changes, William I appointed a new prime minister, Count Otto von Bismarck (1815–1898). Bismarck ignored the legislative opposition to the military reforms, arguing instead that "Germany does not look to Prussia's liberalism but to her power. . . . Not by speeches and majorities will the great questions of the day be decided—that was the mistake of 1848–1849—but by iron and blood."[8] Bismarck went ahead, collected the taxes, and reorganized the army anyway. From 1862 to 1866, Bismarck governed Prussia by simply ignoring parliament. In the meantime, opposition to his domestic policy determined Bismarck to engage in an active foreign policy, which led to war and German unification.

Because Bismarck succeeded in guiding Prussia's unification of Germany, it is often assumed that he had determined upon a course of action that led precisely to that goal. That is hardly the case. Bismarck was a consummate politician and opportunist. He was not a political gambler, but a moderate who waged war only when all other diplomatic alternatives had been exhausted and when he was reasonably sure that all the military and diplomatic advantages were on his side. Bismarck has often been portrayed as the ultimate realist, the foremost nineteenth-century practitioner of *realpolitik*—the "politics of reality." He was also quite open about his strong dislike of anyone who

MAP 20.5 The Unification of Germany

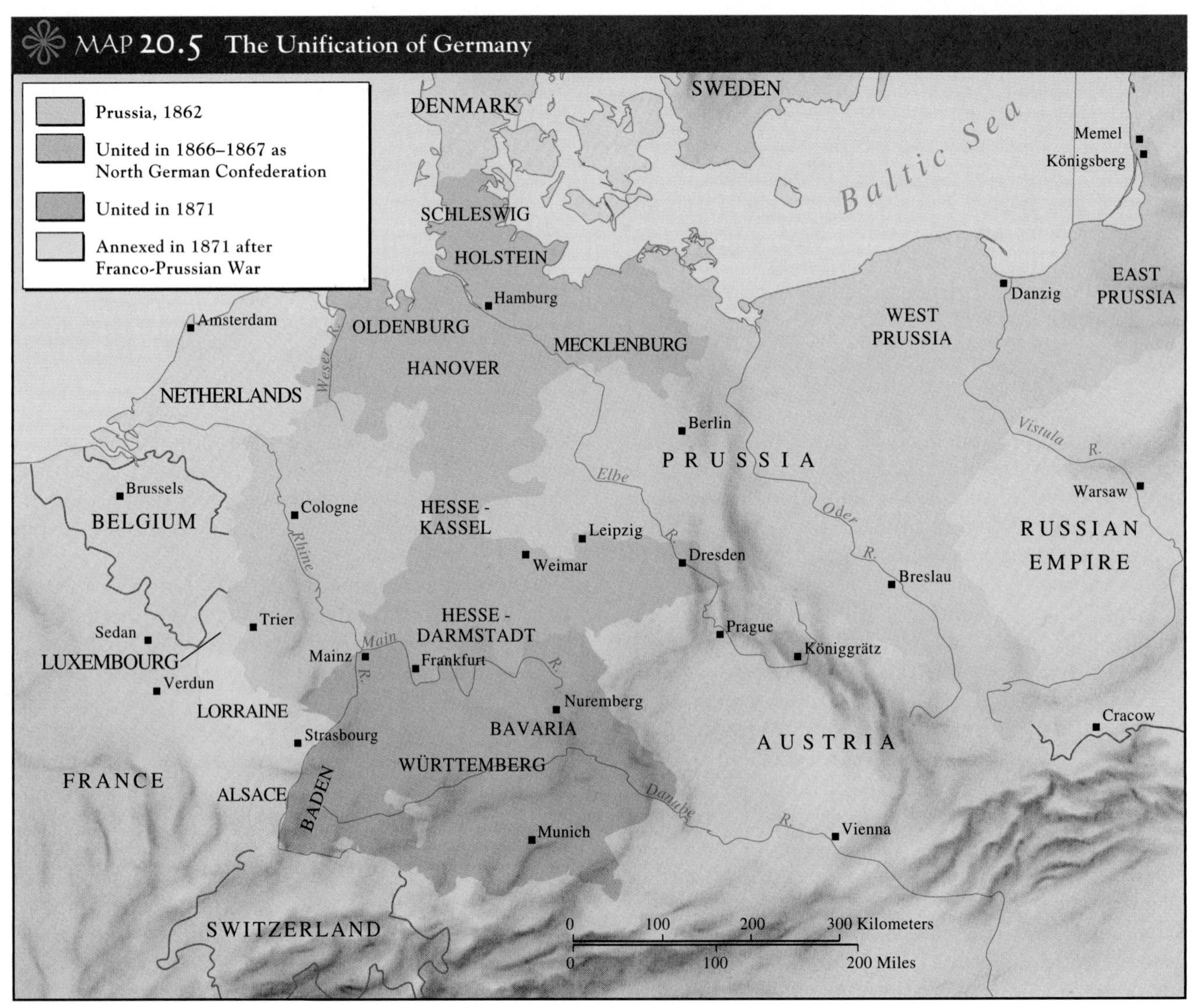

opposed him. He said one morning to his wife: "I could not sleep the whole night; I hated throughout the whole night."

Bismarck's first war was against Denmark and was fought over the duchies of Schleswig and Holstein. Bismarck persuaded the Austrians to join Prussia in declaring war on Denmark on February 1, 1864. The Danes were quickly defeated and surrendered Schleswig and Holstein to the victors. Austria and Prussia then agreed to divide the administration of the two duchies. But Bismarck used the joint administration of the two duchies to create friction with the Austrians and goad them into a war that began on June 14, 1866.

Many Europeans expected a quick Austrian victory, but they overlooked the effectiveness of the Prussian military reforms of the 1860s. The Prussian breech-loading needle gun had a much faster rate of fire than the Austrian muzzle loader, and a superior network of railroads enabled the Prussians to mass troops quickly. At Königgrätz (or Sadowa) on July 3, the Austrian army was decisively defeated. Austria was now excluded from German affairs, and the German states north of the Main River were organized into a North German Confederation controlled by Prussia.

Bismarck and William I had achieved a major goal by 1866. Prussia now dominated all of northern Germany, and Austria had been excluded from any significant role in German affairs. At the same time, unsettled business led to new international complications and further change. Bismarck realized that France would never be content with a strong German state to its east because of the potential threat to French security. At the same time, after a series of setbacks, Napoleon III, the French ruler, needed a diplomatic triumph to offset his serious domestic problems. The French were not happy with the turn of events in Germany and looked for opportunities to humiliate the Prussians.

In 1870, Prussia and France became embroiled in a dispute over the candidacy of a relative of the Prussian king for the throne of Spain. Bismarck manipulated the misunderstandings between the French and Prussians to goad the French into declaring war on Prussia on July 15, 1870. The French proved no match for the better led and organized Prussian forces. The south German states honored their military alliances with Prussia and joined the war effort against the French. The Prussian armies advanced into France, and at Sedan, on September 2, 1870, an entire French army and Napoleon III himself were captured. Paris finally capitulated on January 28, 1871, and an official peace treaty was signed in May. France had to pay an indemnity of five billion francs (about one billion dollars) and give up the provinces of Alsace and Lorraine to the new German state. The loss of Alsace-Lorraine rankled the French and left them burning for revenge.

Even before the war had ended, the south German states had agreed to enter the North German Confederation. On January 18, 1871, in the Hall of Mirrors in Louis XIV's palace at Versailles, William I was proclaimed kaiser or emperor of the Second German Empire (the first was the medieval Holy Roman Empire). German unity had been achieved by the Prussian monarchy and the Prussian army. In a real sense, Germany had been merged into Prussia, not Prussia into Germany. German liberals also rejoiced. They had dreamed of unity and freedom, but the achievement of unity now seemed much more important. One old liberal proclaimed:

THE UNIFICATION OF GERMANY. Under Prussian leadership, a new German empire was proclaimed on January 18, 1871, in the Hall of Mirrors in the palace at Versailles. King William of Prussia became Emperor William I of the Second German Empire. Otto von Bismarck, the man who had been so instrumental in creating the new German state, is shown here, resplendently attired in his white uniform, standing at the foot of the throne.

> I cannot shake off the impression of this hour. I am no devotee of Mars; I feel more attached to the goddess of beauty and the mother of graces than to the powerful god of war, but the trophies of war exercise a magic charm even upon the child of peace. One's view is involuntarily chained and one's spirit goes along with the boundless row of men who acclaim the god of the moment—success.[9]

The Prussian leadership of German unification meant that authoritarian, militaristic values would triumph over liberal, constitutional sentiments in the development of the new German state. With its industrial resources and military might, the new state had become the strongest power on the Continent. A new European balance of power was at hand.

Nationalism and Reform: The European National State in Mid-Century

While European affairs were dominated by the unification of Italy and Germany, other states in the Western world were also undergoing transformations. Unlike the nations on the Continent, Great Britain managed to avoid the revolutionary upheavals of the first half of the nineteenth century. In 1815, Britain was still governed by the aristocratic landowning classes, which dominated both houses of Parliament. But in 1832, to prevent revolutionary turmoil like that on the Continent, Parliament passed a Reform Bill that increased the numbers of male voters, primarily benefiting the upper middle class. By joining the industrial middle class to the landed interest in ruling Britain, Britain had no revolution in 1848.

In the 1850s and 1860s, the British liberal parliamentary system made both social and political reforms that enabled the country to remain stable. One of the reasons for Britain's stability was its continuing economic growth. After 1850, middle-class prosperity was at last coupled with some improvements for the working classes as well. Real wages for laborers increased over 25 percent between 1850 and 1870. The British feeling of national pride was well reflected in Queen Victoria, whose reign from 1837 to 1901 was the longest in English history. Victoria had nine children, and when she died at age eighty-one, thirty-seven great-grandchildren Her sense of duty and moral respectability reflected the attitudes of her age, which has ever since been known as the Victorian Age.

Meanwhile France in the aftermath of the revolution of 1848 had moved toward the restoration of monarchy. Even after his election as the president of the French Republic, many of his contemporaries dismissed Napoleon "the Small" as a nonentity whose success was due only to his name. But Louis Napoleon was a clever politician who was especially astute at understanding the popular forces of his day. Four years after his election as president, Louis Napoleon returned to the people to ask for the restoration of the empire. Ninety-seven percent responded affirmatively, and on December 2, 1852, Louis Napoleon assumed the title of Napoleon III (the first Napoleon had abdicated in favor of his son, Napoleon II, on April 6, 1814). The Second Empire had begun.

The government of Napoleon III was clearly authoritarian. As chief of state, Napoleon III controlled the armed forces, police, and civil service. Only he could introduce legislation and declare war. The Legislative Corps gave an appearance of representative government since its members were elected by universal male suffrage for six-year terms. But they could neither initiate legislation nor affect the budget.

The first five years of Napoleon III's reign were a spectacular success as he reaped the benefits of worldwide economic prosperity, although the government's policies also contributed to French economic renewal. Napoleon believed in using the resources of government to encourage the national economy and took many steps to expand industrial growth. Government subsidies were used to foster the rapid construction of railroads, harbors, roads, and canals. The major French railway lines were completed during Napoleon's reign, while industrial expansion was evident in the tripling of iron production. In the midst of this economic expansion, Napoleon III also undertook a vast reconstruction of the city of Paris. The medieval Paris of narrow streets and old city walls was destroyed and replaced by a modern Paris of broad boulevards, spacious buildings, circular plazas, public squares, an underground sewage system, a new public water supply, and gaslights.

In the 1860s, as opposition began to mount, Napoleon III liberalized his regime. He gave the Legislative Corps more say in affairs of state, including debate over the budget. In May 1870, in a plebiscite on whether to accept a new constitution that might have inaugurated a parliamentary regime, the French people gave Napoleon another resounding victory. This triumph was short-lived, however. Foreign policy failures led to growing criticism, and war with Prussia in 1870 turned out to be the death blow for Napoleon III's regime. Napoleon was ousted, and a republic proclaimed.

Although nationalism was a major force in nineteenth-century Europe, one of Europe's most powerful states—the Austrian Empire—was a multinational empire that managed to frustrate the desires of its ethnic groups for self-determination. After the Habsburg rulers had crushed the revolutions of 1848–1849, they restored centralized, autocratic government to the empire. But failure in war had severe internal consequences for Austria. The defeat at the hands of the Prussians in 1866 forced the Austrians to deal with the fiercely nationalistic Hungarians.

The result was the negotiated *Ausgleich*, or Compromise, of 1867, which created the dual monarchy of Austria-Hungary. Each part of the empire now had its own constitution, its own bicameral legislature, its own governmental machinery for domestic affairs, and its own capital (Vienna for Austria and Budapest for Hungary). Holding the two states together were a single monarch—Francis Joseph (1848–1916) was emperor of Austria and king of Hungary—and a common army, foreign policy, and system of finances. In domestic affairs, Hungary had become an independent nation. The *Ausgleich* did not, however, satisfy the other nationalities that made up the multinational Austro-Hungarian Empire. The dual monarchy simply enabled the German-speaking Austrians and Hungarian Magyars to dominate the minorities, especially the Slavs, in their respective states.

At the beginning of the nineteenth century, Russia was overwhelmingly rural, agricultural, and autocratic. The Russian tsar was still regarded as a divine-right monarch with unlimited power. The Russian imperial autocracy, based on soldiers, secret police, repression, and censorship, had withstood the revolutionary fervor of the first

CHRONOLOGY

DEVELOPMENTS IN EUROPE, 1800–1871

Great Britain	
Reform Act	1832
Queen Victoria	1837–1901
France	
Charles X	1824–1830
July Revolution	1830
Louis-Philippe	1830–1848
Abdication of Louis-Philippe; formation of provisional government	February 22–24, 1848
"June Days": Workers' revolt in Paris	1848 (June)
Establishment of Second Republic	1848 (November)
Election of Louis Napoleon as French president	1848 (December)
Emperor Napoleon III	1852–1870
Germany	
Germanic Confederation established	1815
Frederick William IV of Prussia	1840–1861
Revolution in Germany	1848
Frankfurt Assembly	1848–1849
Unification of Germany	
King William I of Prussia	1861–1888
The Danish War	1864
The Austro-Prussian War	1866
The Franco-Prussian War	1870–1871
German Empire is proclaimed	January 18, 1871
The Austrian Empire	
Revolt in Austrian Empire; Metternich dismissed	1848 (March)
Viennese rebels crushed	1848 (October)
Defeat of Hungarians with help of Russian troops	1849
Ausgleich: The dual monarchy	1867
Italy	
Revolutions in Italy	1848
Austria reestablishes control in Lombardy and Venetia	1849
Unification of Italy	
Victor Emmanuel II	1849–1878
Count Cavour becomes prime minister of Piedmont	1852
The Austrian War	1859
Garibaldi's invasion of the Two Sicilies	1860
Kingdom of Italy is proclaimed	March 17, 1861
Italy's annexation of Venetia	1866
Italy's annexation of Rome	1870
Russia	
Tsar Alexander II	1855–1881
Emancipation edict	March 3, 1861
The Ottoman Empire: The Eastern Question	
The Greek revolt	1821–1830
The Crimean War	1853–1856

half of the nineteenth century and even served as the "arsenal of autocracy" in crushing revolutions elsewhere in Europe. But the defeat at the hands of the British and French in the Crimean War in 1856 made it clear even to staunch conservatives that Russia was falling hopelessly behind the western European powers. Tsar Alexander II (1855–1881) turned his energies to a serious overhaul of the Russian system.

Serfdom was the most burdensome problem in tsarist Russia. The continuing subjugation of millions of peasants to the land and their landlords was an obviously corrupt and failing system. On March 3, 1861, Alexander issued his emancipation edict (see the box on p. 616). Peasants were now free to own property, marry as they chose, and bring suits in the law courts. But the system of land redistribution instituted after emancipation was not particularly favorable to them. The government provided land for the peasants by purchasing it from the landlords, but the landowners often chose to keep the best lands. The Russian peasants soon found that they had inadequate amounts of good arable land to support themselves, a situation worsened by the rapidly increasing peasant population in the second half of the nineteenth century.

Nor were the peasants completely free. The state compensated the landowners for the land given to the peasants, but the peasants, in turn, were expected to repay the state in long-term installments. To ensure that the payments were made, peasants were subjected to the

EMANCIPATION: SERFS AND SLAVES

Although overall their histories have been quite different, Russia and the United States shared a common feature in the 1860s. They were the only states in the Western world that still had large enslaved populations (the Russian serfs were virtually slaves). The leaders of both countries issued emancipation proclamations within two years of each other. The first excerpt is taken from the Imperial Decree of March 3, 1861, which freed the Russian serfs. The second excerpt is from Abraham Lincoln's Emancipation Proclamation, issued on January 1, 1863.

THE IMPERIAL DECREE, MARCH 3, 1861

By the grace of God, we, Alexander II, Emperor and Autocrat of all the Russias, King of Poland, Grand Duke of Finland, etc., to all our faithful subjects, make known:

Called by Divine Providence and by the sacred right of inheritance to the throne of our ancestors, we took a vow in our innermost heart to respond to the mission which is intrusted to us as to surround with our affection and our Imperial solicitude all our faithful subjects of every rank and of every condition, from the warrior, who nobly bears arms for the defense of the country, to the humble artisan devoted to the works of industry; from the official in the career of the high offices of the State to the laborer whose plough furrows the soil. . . .

We thus came to the conviction that the work of a serious improvement of the condition of the peasants was a sacred inheritance bequeathed to us by our ancestors, a mission which, in the course of events, Divine Providence called upon us to fulfill. . . .

In virtue of the new dispositions above mentioned, the peasants attached to the soil will be invested within a term fixed by the law with all the rights of free cultivators. . . .

At the same time, they are granted the right of purchasing their close, and, with the consent of the proprietors, they may acquire in full property the arable lands and other appurtenances which are allotted to them as a permanent holding. By the acquisition in full property of the quantity of land fixed, the peasants are free from their obligations toward the proprietors for land thus purchased, and they enter definitely into the condition of free peasants-landholders.

THE EMANCIPATION PROCLAMATION, JANUARY 1, 1863

Now therefore, I, Abraham Lincoln, President of the United States, by virtue of the power in me vested as Commander-in-Chief of the Army and Navy of the United States in time of actual armed rebellion against the authority and government of the United States, and as a fit and necessary war measure for suppressing such rebellion, do, on this 1st day of January, A.D. 1863, and in accordance with my purpose to do so, . . . order and designate as the States and parts of States wherein the people thereof, respectively, are this day in rebellion against the United States the following, to wit:

Arkansas, Texas, Louisiana, . . . Mississippi, Alabama, Florida, Georgia, South Carolina, North Carolina, and Virginia . . .

And by virtue of the power for the purpose aforesaid, I do order and declare that all persons held as slaves within said designated States and parts of States are, and henceforward shall be free; and that the Executive Government of the United States, including the military and naval authorities thereof, will recognize and maintain the freedom of said persons.

authority of their *mir* or village commune, which was collectively responsible for the land payments to the government. In a very real sense, then, the village commune, not the individual peasants, owned the land the peasants were purchasing. And since the village communes were responsible for the payments, they were reluctant to allow peasants to leave their land. Emancipation, then, led not to free, landowning peasants as in western Europe, but to unhappy, land-starved peasants who largely followed the old ways of agricultural production.

Alexander II attempted other reforms as well, including the election of local assemblies, which provided a moderate degree of self-government, and legal reforms that created a regular system of local and provincial courts. But even the autocratic tsar was unable to control the forces he unleashed by his reform program. Reformers wanted more and rapid change; conservatives opposed what they perceived as the tsar's attempts to undermine the basic institutions of Russian society. By 1870, Russia was witnessing increasing levels of dissatisfaction. When one group of radicals assassinated Alexander II in 1881, his son and successor, Alexander III, turned against reform and returned to the traditional methods of repression.

The Growth of the United States

The U.S. Constitution, ratified in 1789, committed the United States to two of the major forces of the first half of the nineteenth century, liberalism and nationalism. National unity did not come easily, however. Bitter conflict erupted between the Federalists and the Republicans over the power of the federal government in relation to that of the states. Led by Alexander Hamilton (1757–1804), the Federalists favored a financial program that would establish a strong central government. The Republicans, guided by Thomas Jefferson (1743–1826) and James Madison

(1751–1836), feared centralization and its consequences for popular liberties. These divisions were intensified by European rivalries as the Federalists were pro-British and the Republicans pro-French. The successful conclusion of the War of 1812 brought an end to the Federalists, who had opposed the war, while the surge of national feeling generated by the war served to heal the nation's divisions.

Another strong force for national unity came from the Supreme Court under the leadership of John Marshall (1755–1835), who was chief justice from 1801 to 1835. Marshall made the Supreme Court into an important national institution by asserting its right to overrule an act of Congress if the Court found it to be in violation of the Constitution. Under Marshall, the Supreme Court contributed further to establishing the supremacy of the national government by curbing the actions of state courts and legislatures.

The election of Andrew Jackson (1767–1845) as president in 1828 opened a new era in American politics. Jacksonian democracy introduced a mass democratic politics. The electorate was expanded by dropping traditional property qualifications; by the 1830s, suffrage had been extended to almost all adult white males. During the period from 1815 to 1850, the traditional liberal belief in the improvement of human beings was also given concrete expression. Americans developed detention schools for juvenile delinquents and new penal institutions, both motivated by the liberal belief that the right kind of environment would rehabilitate those in need of it.

By the mid-nineteenth century, however, American national unity was increasingly threatened by the issue of slavery. Like the North, the South had grown dramatically in population during the first half of the nineteenth century. But its development was quite different. Its cotton economy and social structure were based on the exploitation of enslaved black Africans and their descendants. The importance of cotton is evident from production figures. In 1810, the South produced a raw cotton crop of 178,000 bales, worth $10 million. By 1860, it was generating 4.5 million bales of cotton, with a value of $249 million. Ninety-three percent of southern cotton in 1850 was produced by a slave population that had grown dramatically in fifty years. Although new slave imports had been barred in 1808, there were four million African American slaves in the South by 1860, compared to one million in 1800. The cotton economy and plantation-based slavery were intimately related, and the attempt to maintain them in the course of the first half of the nineteenth century led the South to become increasingly defensive, monolithic, and isolated. At the same time, the growth of an abolitionist movement in the North challenged the southern order

MAP 20.6 The United States and Canada in the Nineteenth Century

CHRONOLOGY

DEVELOPMENTS IN THE WESTERN HEMISPHERE

Latin America	
Revolution in Haiti	1804
Revolution in Mexico	1810
Bolívar and San Martín free most of South America	1810–1824
Augustín de Iturbide becomes emperor of Mexico	1821
Brazil gains independence from Portugal	1822
Monroe Doctrine	1823
United States	
John Marshall as chief justice	1801–1835
Election of Andrew Jackson	1828
Election of Lincoln and secession of South Carolina	1860
Outbreak of Civil War	1861
Lincoln's Emancipation Proclamation	1863
Surrender of Lee	April 9, 1865
Canada	
Rebellions	1837–1838
Formation of United Provinces of Canada	1840
Dominion of Canada is established	1867

and created an "emotional chain reaction" that led to civil war.

As opinions over the issue of slavery grew more divided, compromise became less feasible. When Abraham Lincoln, the man who had said in a speech in Illinois in 1858 that "this government cannot endure permanently half slave and half free," was elected president in November 1860, the die was cast. Lincoln carried only 2 of the 1,109 counties in the South. On December 20, 1860, a South Carolina convention voted to repeal ratification of the Constitution of the United States. In February 1861, six more southern states did the same, and a rival nation—the Confederate States of America—was formed. In March, fighting erupted between North and South.

The American Civil War (1861–1865) was an extraordinarily bloody struggle. Over 600,000 soldiers died, either in battle or from deadly infectious diseases spawned by filthy camp conditions. Over a period of four years, the Union states mobilized their superior assets and gradually wore down the South. As the war dragged on, it had the effect of radicalizing public opinion in the North. What began as a war to save the Union became a war against slavery. On January 1, 1863, Lincoln's Emancipation Proclamation made the nation's slaves "forever free" (see the box on p. 616). The increasingly effective Union blockade of the South combined with a shortage of fighting men made the Confederate cause desperate by the end of 1864. The final push of Union troops under General Ulysses S. Grant forced General Robert E. Lee's army to surrender on April 9, 1865. Although the problems of reconstruction lay ahead, the Union victory confirmed that the United States would be "one nation, indivisible." National unity, not particularism, had prevailed in the United States.

The Emergence of a Canadian Nation

By the Treaty of Paris in 1763, Canada—or New France, as it was called—passed into the hands of the British. By 1800, most Canadians favored more autonomy, although the colonists disagreed on the form this autonomy should take. Upper Canada (now Ontario) was predominantly English-speaking, while Lower Canada (now Quebec) was dominated by French Canadians. Increased immigration to Canada after 1815 also fueled the desire for self-government. After two short rebellions against the government broke out in Upper and Lower Canada in 1837 and 1838, the British agreed to make some changes. In 1840, the British Parliament formally joined Upper and Lower Canada into the United Provinces of Canada. But Parliament failed to grant self-government, and Canada remained but a group of provinces with little sense of unity.

The head of Upper Canada's Conservative Party, John Macdonald, became an avid apostle for union and self-government. Fearful of American designs on Canada, the British government finally capitulated to Macdonald's campaign, and in 1867, Parliament passed the British North American Act, which established a Canadian nation—the Dominion of Canada—with its own constitution. John Macdonald became the first prime minister of the Dominion. Although Canada now possessed a parliamentary system and ruled itself as a national federation, provincial legislatures were given considerable latitude in local affairs, and foreign affairs still remained the preserve of the British government.

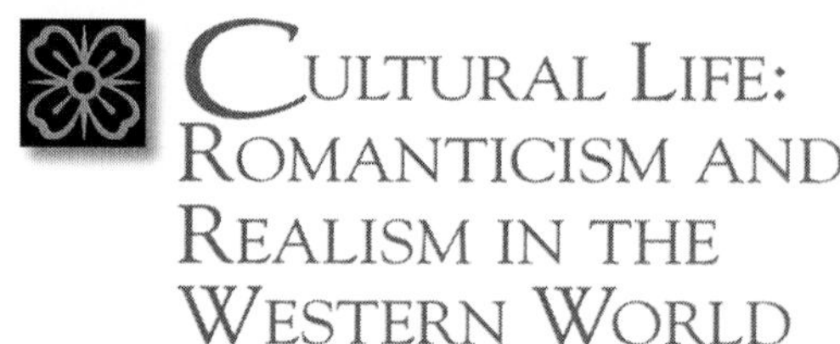

CULTURAL LIFE: ROMANTICISM AND REALISM IN THE WESTERN WORLD

At the end of the eighteenth century, a new intellectual movement known as Romanticism emerged to challenge the Enlightenment's preoccupation with reason in discovering truth. The Romantics tried to balance the use of reason by stressing the importance of feeling, emotion, and imagination as sources of knowing.

GOTHIC LITERATURE: EDGAR ALLAN POE

American writers and poets made significant contributions to the movement of Romanticism. Although Edgar Allan Poe (1809–1849) was influenced by the German Romantic school of mystery and horror, many literary historians give him the credit for pioneering the modern short story. This selection from the conclusion of "The Fall of the House of Usher" gives a feeling for the nature of so-called Gothic literature.

EDGAR ALLAN POE, "THE FALL OF THE HOUSE OF USHER"

No sooner had these syllables passed my lips, than—as if a shield of brass had indeed, at the moment, fallen heavily upon a floor of silver—I became aware of a distinct, hollow, metallic, and clangorous, yet apparently muffled, reverberation. Completely unnerved, I leaped to my feet; but the measured rocking movement of Usher was undisturbed. I rushed to the chair in which he sat. His eyes were bent fixedly before him, and throughout his whole countenance there reigned a stony rigidity. But, as I placed my hand upon his shoulder, there came a strong shudder over his whole person; a sickly smile quivered about his lips; and I saw that he spoke in a low, hurried, and gibbering murmur, as if unconscious of my presence. Bending closely over him, I at length drank in the hideous import of his words.

"Not hear it?—yes, I hear it, and *have* heard it. Long-long-long-many minutes, many hours, many days, have I heard it—yet I dared not—oh, pity me, miserable wretch that I am!—I dared not—I *dared* not speak! *We have put her living in the tomb!* Said I not that my senses were acute? I *now* tell you that I heard her first feeble movements in the hollow coffin. I heard them—many, many days ago—yet I dared not—*I dared not speak!* And now—to-night— . . . the rending of her coffin, and the grating of the iron hinges of her prison, and her struggles within the coppered archway of the vault! Oh whither shall I fly? Will she not be here anon? Is she not hurrying to upbraid me for my haste? Have I not heard her footstep on the stair? Do I not distinguish that heavy and horrible beating of her heart? MADMAN!"—here he sprang furiously to his feet, and shrieked out his syllables, as if in the effort he were giving up his soul—"MADMAN! I TELL YOU THAT SHE NOW STANDS WITHOUT THE DOOR!"

As if in the superhuman energy of his utterance there had been found the potency of a spell, the huge antique panels to which the speaker pointed threw slowly back, upon the instant, their ponderous and ebony jaws. It was the work of the rushing gust—but then without those doors there DID stand the lofty and enshrouded figure of the lady Madeline of Usher. There was blood upon her white robes, and the evidence of some bitter struggle upon every portion of her emaciated frame. For a moment she remained trembling and reeling to and fro upon the threshold, then, with a low moaning cry, fell heavily inward upon the person of her brother, and in her violent and now final death-agonies, bore him to the floor a corpse, and a victim to the terrors he had anticipated.

The Characteristics of Romanticism

Romantic writers emphasized emotion and sentiment and believed that these inner feelings were only understandable to the person experiencing them. An important model for Romantics was the tragic figure in *The Sorrows of Young Werther,* a novel by the great German writer Johann Wolfgang von Goethe (1749–1832), who later rejected Romanticism in favor of classicism. Werther was a Romantic figure who sought freedom in order to fulfill himself. Misunderstood and rejected by society, he continued to believe in his own worth through his inner feelings, but his deep love for a girl who did not love him finally led him to commit suicide. After Goethe's *The Sorrows of Young Werther,* numerous novels and plays appeared whose plots revolved around young maidens tragically carried off at an early age (twenty-three was most common) by disease (usually tuberculosis, at that time a protracted disease that was usually fatal) to the sorrows and sadness of their male lovers.

Another important characteristic of Romanticism was individualism or an interest in the unique traits of each person. The Romantics' desire to follow their inner drives led them to rebel against middle-class conventions. Long hair, beards, and outrageous clothes served to reinforce the individualism that young Romantics were trying to express.

Many Romantics also possessed a passionate interest in the past. This historical mindedness was furthered in many ways. In Germany, the Grimm brothers collected and published their nation's fairy tales. The revival of medieval Gothic architecture left European countrysides adorned with pseudo-medieval castles and cities bedecked with grandiose neo-Gothic cathedrals, city halls, parliamentary buildings, and even railway stations. Literature, too, reflected this historical consciousness. The novels of Walter Scott (1771–1832) became European best-sellers in the first half of the nineteenth century. *Ivanhoe,* in which Scott tried to evoke the clash between Saxon and Norman knights in medieval England, was one of his most popular works.

To the historical mindedness of the Romantics could be added an attraction to the bizarre and unusual. In an exaggerated form, this preoccupation gave rise to so-called Gothic literature (see the box above), chillingly evident in short stories of horror by the American Edgar

CASPAR DAVID FRIEDRICH, *MAN AND WOMAN GAZING AT THE MOON.* The German artist Caspar David Friedrich sought to express in painting his own mystical view of nature. "The divine is everywhere," he once wrote, "even in a grain of sand." In this painting, a couple is shown from the back gazing at the moon. They are overwhelmed by the powerful presence of nature and the immensity of the universe.

Allan Poe (1809–1849) and in *Frankenstein*, by Mary Shelley (1797–1851). Her novel was the story of a mad scientist who brings into being a humanlike monster who goes berserk. Some Romantics even sought the unusual in their own lives by pursuing extraordinary states of experience in dreams, nightmares, frenzies, and suicidal depression or by experimenting with cocaine, opium, and hashish to produce drug-induced, altered states of consciousness.

To the Romantics, poetry ranked above all other literary forms because it was regarded as the direct expression of one's soul. The Romantic poets were viewed as seers who could reveal the invisible world to others. Their incredible sense of drama made some of them the most colorful figures of their era, living intense but short lives. Percy Bysshe Shelley (1792–1822), expelled from school for advocating atheism, set out to reform the world. His *Prometheus Unbound*, completed in 1820, is a portrait of the revolt of human beings against the laws and customs that oppress them. He drowned in a storm in the Mediterranean. Lord Byron (1788–1824) dramatized himself as the melancholy Romantic hero that he had described in his own work, *Childe Harold's Pilgrimage*. He joined the movement for Greek independence and died in Greece fighting the Turks.

Romantic poetry gave full expression to one of the most important characteristics of Romanticism: love of nature, which is especially evident in the work of William Wordsworth (1770–1850), the foremost Romantic prophet of nature. His experience of nature was almost mystical as he claimed to receive "authentic tidings of invisible things":

One impulse from a vernal wood
May teach you more of man,
Of moral evil and of good,
Than all the sages can.[10]

To Wordsworth, nature contained a mysterious force that the poet could perceive and learn from. Nature served as a mirror into which humans could look to learn about themselves. Nature was, in fact, alive and sacred:

To every natural form, rock, fruits, or flower,
Even the loose stones that cover the highway,
I gave a moral life: I saw them feel,
Or link'd them to some feeling: the great mass
Lay bedded in a quickening soul, and all
That I beheld, respired with inward meaning.[11]

Other Romantics carried this worship of nature further into pantheism by identifying the great force in nature with God.

Romanticism was not only prevalent in Europe and the United States but also remained a dominant force in Latin American literary circles for much of the nineteenth century. Perhaps the best-known Romantic novel in Latin America was *María*, the work of the Colombian Jorge Isaacs. *María* was a Romantic, idealized account of hacienda life. Isaacs's portrayal of the beauties of nature and his account of individual suffering easily touched the emotions of his readers.

Like the literary arts, the visual arts were also deeply affected by Romanticism. Although they varied widely in what they produced, Romantic artists shared at least two fundamental characteristics. All artistic expression to them was a reflection of the artist's inner feelings; a painting should mirror the artist's vision of the world and be the instrument of his own imagination. Moreover, Romantic artists delib-erately rejected the principles of classicism. Beauty was not a timeless thing; its expression depended on one's own culture and one's age. The Romantics abadoned classical restraint for warmth, emotion, and movement.

The early life experiences of Caspar David Friedrich (1774–1840) left him with a lifelong preoccupation with

EUGÈNE DELACROIX, *THE DEATH OF SARDANAPALUS.* Delacroix's *The Death of Sardanapalus* was based on Lord Byron's verse account of the decadent Assyrian king's dramatic last moments. Beseiged by enemy troops and with little hope of survival, Sardanapalus orders that his harem women and prize horses go to their death with him. At the right, a guard stabs one of the women as the king looks on.

God and nature. Friedrich painted many landscapes but with an interest that transcended the mere presentation of natural details. His portrayals of mountains shrouded in mist, gnarled trees bathed in moonlight, and the stark ruins of monasteries surrounded by withered trees all conveyed a feeling of mystery and mysticism. For Friedrich, nature was a manifestation of divine life, as is evident in *Man and Woman Gazing at the Moon*. To Friedrich, the artistic process depended on the use of an unrestricted imagination that could only be achieved through inner vision.

Eugène Delacroix (1798–1863) was one of the most famous French exponents of the Romantic school of painting. Delacroix's paintings exhibited two primary characteristics, a fascination with the exotic and a passion for color. Both are visible in *The Death of Sardanapalus*. Significant for its use of light and its patches of interrelated color, this portrayal of the world of the last Assyrian king was criticized at the time for its brilliant color. In Delacroix, theatricality and movement combined with a daring use of color. Many of his works reflect his own belief that "a painting should be a feast to the eye."

To many Romantics, music was the most Romantic of the arts because it enabled the composer to probe deeply into human emotions. Music historians have called the eighteenth century an age of classicism and the nineteenth the era of Romanticism. One of the greatest composers of all time, Ludwig van Beethoven, served as a bridge between classicism and Romanticism.

Beethoven (1770–1827) was born in Bonn (Germany) but soon made his way to Vienna, then the musical capital of Europe, where he studied briefly under Mozart. Beginning in 1792, Vienna became his permanent residence. During his first major period of composing, from 1792 to 1802, his work was still largely within the classical framework of the eighteenth century, and his style differed little from that of Mozart and Haydn. But with his Third Symphony, the *Eroica*, originally intended for Napoleon, Beethoven broke through to the elements of Romanticism in his use of fierce rhythms to create dramatic struggle and uplifted resolutions. E. T. A. Hoffman, a contemporary composer and writer, said, "Beethoven's music opens the floodgates of fear, of terror, of horror, of pain, and arouses that longing for the eternal which is the essence of Romanticism. He is thus a pure Romantic composer."[12]

A New Age of Science

By the mid-nineteenth century, as theoretical discoveries in science led to an increased number of derived practical benefits, science came to have a greater and greater impact on European life. The Scientific Revolution of the sixteenth and seventeenth centuries had fundamentally transformed the Western worldview and initiated a modern, rational approach to the study of natural phenomena. Even in the eighteenth century, however, these intellectual developments had remained the preserve of an educated elite and resulted in few practical benefits. Moreover, the technical advances of the early Industrial Revolution had depended little on pure science and much more on the practical experiments of technologically oriented amateur inventors. Advances in industrial technology, however, fed an interest in basic scientific research, which, in turn, in the 1830s and afterward resulted in a rash of basic scientific discoveries that were soon transformed into technological improvements that affected everybody.

The development of the steam engine was important in encouraging scientists to work out its theoretical foundations, a preoccupation that led to thermodynamics, the science of the relationship between heat and mechanical energy. The laws of thermodynamics were at the core of nineteenth-century physics. In biology, the Frenchman Louis Pasteur postulated the germ theory of disease, which had enormous practical applications in the development of modern, scientific medical practices. In chemistry, the Russian Dmitri Mendeleyev in the 1860s classified all the material elements then known on the basis of their atomic weights and provided the systematic foundation for the periodic law. The Briton Michael Faraday discovered the phenomenon of electromagnetic induction and put together a primitive generator that laid the foundation for the use of electricity, although economically efficient generators were not built until the 1870s.

The steadily increasing and often dramatic material benefits generated by science and technology led Europeans to have a growing faith in the benefits of science. The popularity of scientific and technological achievement led to a widespread acceptance of the scientific method—based on observation, experiment, and logical analysis—as the only path to objective truth and objective reality. This, in turn, undermined the faith of many people in religious revelation and truth. It is no accident that the nineteenth century was an age of increasing secularization, particularly evident in the growth of materialism or the belief that everything mental, spiritual, or ideal was simply an outgrowth of physical forces. Truth was to be found in the concrete material existence of human beings, not as Romanticists imagined in revelations gained by feeling or intuitive flashes. The importance of materialism was strikingly evident in the most important scientific event of the nineteenth century, the development of the theory of organic evolution according to natural selection. On the theories of Charles Darwin could be built a picture of humans as material beings that were simply part of the natural world.

In 1859, Charles Darwin (1809–1882) published his celebrated book *On the Origin of Species by Means of Natural Selection*. The basic idea of this book was that all plants and animals had evolved over a long period of time from earlier and simpler forms of life, a principle known as organic evolution. Darwin was important in explaining how this natural process worked. In every species, he argued, "many more individuals of each species are born than can possibly survive." This results in a "struggle for existence." "As more individuals are produced than can possibly survive, there must in every case be a struggle for existence, either one individual with another of the same species, or with the individuals of distinct species, or with the physical conditions of life." Those who succeeded in this struggle for existence had adapted better to their environment, a process made possible by the appearance of "variants." Chance variations occurred in the process of inheritance, he thought, that enabled some organisms to be more adaptable to the environment than others, a process that Darwin called natural selection:

> Owing to this struggle [for existence], variations, however slight . . . , if they be in any degree profitable to the individuals of a species, in their infinitely complex relations to other organic beings and to their physical conditions of life, will tend to the preservation of such individuals, and will generally be inherited by the offspring.[13]

Those that were naturally selected for survival ("survival of the fit") survived. The unfit did not and became extinct. The fit who survived, in turn, propagated and passed on the variations that enabled them to survive until, from Darwin's point of view, a new separate species emerged.

In *On the Origin of Species*, Darwin discussed plant and animal species only. He was not concerned with humans themselves and only later applied his theory of natural selection to humans. In *The Descent of Man*, published in 1871, he argued for the animal origins of human beings: "man is the co-descendant with other mammals of a common progenitor." Humans were not an exception to the rule governing other species.

Although Darwin's ideas were eventually accepted, initially they were highly controversial. Some people claimed that Darwin's theory made human beings ordinary products of nature rather than unique beings. Others were disturbed by the implications of life as a struggle for survival, of "nature red in tooth and claw." Was there a place in the Darwinian world for moral values? For those who believed in a rational order in the world, Darwin's theory seemed to eliminate purpose and design from the universe. Gradually, however, Darwin's theory was accepted by scientists and other intellectuals. In the process of accepting Darwin's ideas, some people even tried to apply them to society, yet another example of science's increasing prestige.

Realism in Literature and Art

Closely related to the materialistic outlook was the belief that the world should be viewed realistically, an idea that was frequently expressed after 1850. The word *Realism* was first employed in 1850 to describe a new style of painting and soon spread to literature. The literary Realists of the mid-nineteenth century were distinguished by their deliberate rejection of Romanticism. The literary Realists wanted to deal with ordinary characters from actual life rather than Romantic heroes in exotic settings. They also sought to avoid exaggerated and emotional language by using close observation and precise description, an approach that led them to eschew poetry in favor of prose and the novel. Realists often combined their interest in everyday life with a searching examination of social questions.

The leading novelist of the 1850s and 1860s, the Frenchman Gustave Flaubert (1821–1880), perfected the Realist novel. His *Madame Bovary* (1857) was a straightforward description of barren and sordid provincial life in France. Emma Bovary, a woman of some vitality, is trapped in a marriage to a drab provincial doctor. Impelled by the images of romantic love she has read about in novels, she seeks the same thing for herself in adulterous love affairs. Unfulfilled, she is ultimately driven to suicide, unrepentant to the end for her lifestyle. Flaubert's hatred of bourgeois society was evident in his portrayal of middle-class hypocrisy and smugness.

GUSTAVE COURBET, *THE STONEBREAKERS.* Realism, largely developed by French painters, aimed at a lifelike portrayal of the daily activities of ordinary people. Gustave Courbet was the most famous of the Realist artists. As is evident in *The Stonebreakers*, he sought to portray things as they really appear. He shows an old road builder and his young assistant in their tattered clothes, engrossed in their dreary work of breaking stones to construct a road.

The British novelist Charles Dickens (1812–1870) achieved extraordinary success with his realistic novels focusing on the lower and middle classes in Britain's early industrial age. His descriptions of the urban poor and the brutalization of human life were vividly realistic.

Realism also made inroads into the Latin American literary scene by the second half of the nineteenth century. There, Realist novelists focused on the injustices of their society, evident in the work of Clorinda Matto de Turner (1852–1909). Her *Aves sin Nido* (*Birds Without a Nest*) was a brutal revelation of the pitiful living conditions of the Indians in Peru. She especially blamed the Catholic church for much of their misery.

In art, too, Realism became dominant after 1850, although Romanticism was by no means dead. Realist art demonstrated three major characteristics: a desire to depict the everyday life of ordinary people, whether peasants, workers, or prostitutes; an attempt at photographic realism; and an interest in the natural environment. The French became leaders in Realist painting.

Gustave Courbet (1819–1877) was the most famous artist of the Realist school. In fact, the word *Realism* was first coined in 1850 to describe one of his paintings. Courbet reveled in a realistic portrayal of everyday life. His subjects were factory workers, peasants, and the wives of saloon keepers. "I have never seen either angels or goddesses, so I am not interested in painting them," he exclaimed. One of his famous works, *The Stonebreakers*, painted in 1849, shows two roadworkers engaged in the deadening work of breaking stones to build a road. This representation of human misery was a scandal to those who objected to his "cult of ugliness." To Courbet, no subject was too ordinary, too harsh, or too ugly to interest him.

CONCLUSION

Between 1800 and 1870, the forces unleashed by two revolutions—the French Revolution and the Industrial Revolution—transformed much of the world and led to Western global dominance by the end of the nineteenth century. The Industrial Revolution seemed to prove to Europeans the underlying assumption of the Scientific Revolution of the seventeenth century—that human beings were capable of dominating nature. By rationally manipulating the material environment for human benefit, people could create new levels of material prosperity and produce machines not dreamed of in their wildest imaginings. Some of these new machines included weapons of war that enabled the Western world to devastate and control non-Western civilizations.

In 1815, a conservative order had been reestablished throughout Europe, and the great powers cooperated to try to ensure its durability. But the revolutionary waves in Latin America and Europe in the first half of the nineteenth century made it clear that the ideologies of liberalism and nationalism, unleashed by the French Revolution and now reinforced by the spread of the Industrial Revoltion, were still alive and active in the Western world. Between 1850 and 1871, the national state became the focus of people's loyalty. Wars, both foreign and civil, were fought to create unified nation-states, while both wars and changing political alignments served as catalysts for domestic reforms that made the nation-state the center of attention. In 1870, however, the political transformations stimulated by the force of nationalism were by no means complete. Significantly large minorities, especially in the polyglot empires controlled by the Austrians, Ottoman Turks, and Russians, had not achieved the goal of their own national states. Moreover, the nationalism that had triumphed by 1870 was no longer the nationalism that had been closely identified with liberalism. Liberal nationalists had believed that unified nation-states would preserve individual rights and lead to a greater community of peoples. But the new nationalism of the late nineteenth century, loud and chauvinistic, did not unify peoples, but divided them as the new national states became embroiled in bitter competition after 1870 and expanded abroad in a revived imperialism.

Many people, however, were hardly aware of nationalism's dangers in 1870. The spread of industrialization and the growing popularity of scientific and technological achievements were sources of optimism, not pessimism. After the revolutionary and military upheavals of the mid-century decades, many Westerners undoubtedly believed that they stood on the verge of a new age of progress.

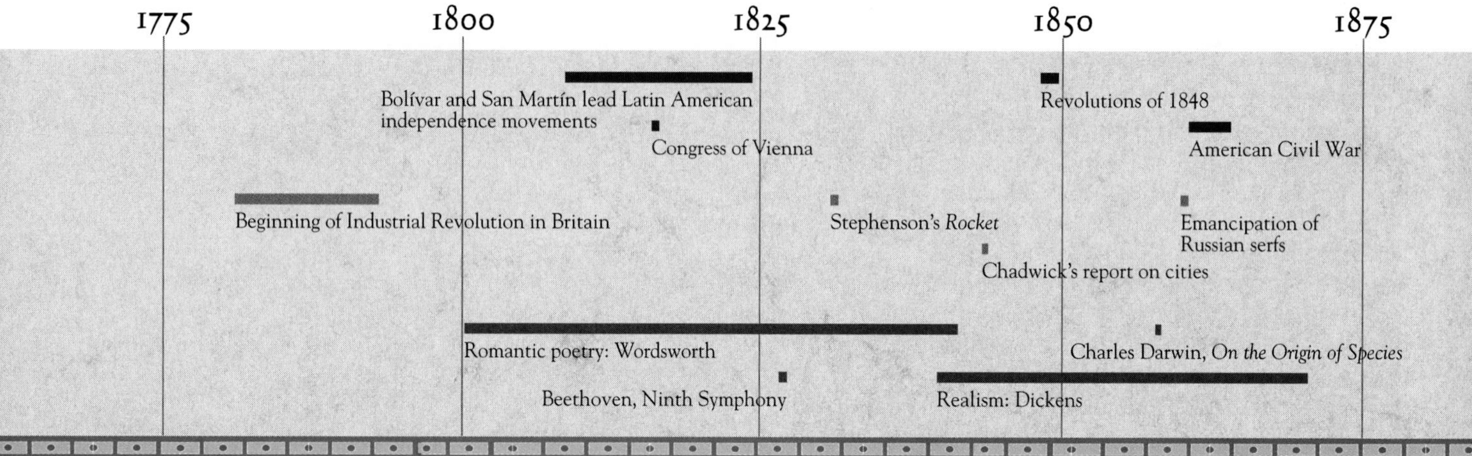

CHAPTER NOTES

1. Quotations can be found in E. Royston Pike, *Human Documents of the Industrial Revolution in Britain* (London, 1966), pp. (in order of quotations) 320, 314, 343.
2. Ibid., p. 315.
3. Ibid., pp. 343–44.
4. Ibid., pp. 60–61.
5. Quoted in M. S. Anderson, *The Ascendancy of Europe, 1815–1914*, 2d ed. (London, 1985), p. 1.
6. Quoted in Hubert Herring, *A History of Latin America* (New York, 1961), p. 255.
7. Quoted in E. Bradford Burns, *Latin America: A Concise Interpretative History*, 4th ed. (Englewood Cliffs, N.J., 1986), p. 116.
8. Louis L. Snyder, ed., *Documents of German History* (New Brunswick, N.J., 1958), p. 202.
9. Quoted in Otto Pflanze, *Bismarck and the Development of Germany: The Period of Unification, 1815–1871* (Princeton, N.J., 1963), p. 327.
10. William Wordsworth, "The Tables Turned," *Poems of Wordsworth*, ed. Matthew Arnold (London, 1963), p. 138.
11. William Wordsworth, *The Prelude* (Harmondsworth, 1971), p. 109.
12. Quoted in Siegbert Prawer, ed., *The Romantic Period in Germany* (London, 1970), p. 285.
13. Charles Darwin, *On the Origin of Species* (New York, 1872), 1:77, 79.

SUGGESTED READINGS

For a good, up-to-date survey of the entire nineteenth century, see R. Gildea, *Barricades and Borders, Europe 1800–1914*, 2d ed. (Oxford, 1996), in the Short Oxford History of the Modern World series. Also valuable is M. S. Anderson, *The Ascendancy of Europe, 1815–1914*, 2d ed. (London, 1985). The well-written work by D. Landes, *The Unbound Prometheus: Technological Change and Industrial Development in Western Europe from 1750 to the Present* (Cambridge, 1969), is still a good introduction to the Industrial Revolution. Also of value is D. Fisher, *The Industrial Revolution* (New York, 1992). There is a good collection of articles in M. Teich and R. Porter, eds., *The Industrial Revolution in National Context: Europe and the USA* (Cambridge, 1996). For a broader perspective, see P. Stearns, *The Industrial Revolution in World History* (Boulder, Colo., 1993). For an introduction to the Industrial Revolution in Britain, see P. Mathias, *The First Industrial Nation: An Economic History of Britain, 1700–1914*, 2d ed. (New York, 1983), and K. Morgan, *The Birth of Industrial Britain: Economic Change 1750–1850* (New York, 1999).

A general discussion of population growth in Europe can be found in T. McKeown, *The Modern Rise of Population* (London, 1976). For an examination of urban growth, see the work by A. R. Sutcliffe, *Toward the Planned City: Germany, Britain, the United States and France, 1780–1914* (Oxford, 1981). On the social impact of the Industrial Revolution, see P. Pilbeam, *The Middle Classes in Europe, 1789–1914* (Basingstoke, Great Britain, 1990); T. Koditschek, *Class Formation and Urban Industrial Society* (New York, 1990); and F. Crouzet, *The First Industrialists: The Problems of Origins* (Cambridge, 1985), on British entrepreneurs. G. Himmelfarb, *The Idea of Poverty: England in the Early Industrial Age* (New York, 1984) traces the concepts of poverty and poor from the mid-eighteenth century to the mid-nineteenth century. A classic work on female labor patterns is L. A. Tilly and J. W. Scott, *Women, Work, and Family* (New York, 1978). See also J. Lown, *Women and Industrialization: Gender at Work in Nineteenth-Century England* (Minneapolis, Minn., 1990).

A concise summary of the international events of the entire nineteenth century can be found in R. Bullen and F. R. Bridge, *The Great Powers and the European State System, 1815–1914* (London, 1980). For a survey of the period from 1814–1848, see M. Broers, *Europe After Napoleon: Revolution, Reaction, and Romanticism, 1814–1848* (New York, 1996). There are some useful books on individual countries that cover more than the subject of this chapter. These include R. Magraw, *France, 1815–1914: The Bourgeois Century* (London, 1983); D. Saunders, *Russia in the Age of Reaction and Reform, 1801–1881* (London, 1992); J. J. Sheehan, *German History, 1770–1866* (New York, 1989); N. McCord, *British History, 1815–1906* (New York, 1991); and C. A. Macartney, *The Habsburg Empire, 1790–1918* (London, 1971).

On the man whose conservative policies dominated this era, see the brief but good biography by A. Palmer, *Metternich* (New York, 1972). On the revolutions in Europe in 1830, see C. Church, *Europe in 1830: Revolution and Political Change* (Chapel Hill, N.C., 1983). The best introduction to the Revolutions of 1848 is J. Sperber, *The European Revolutions, 1848–1851* (New York, 1994).

For a comprehensive survey of Latin American history, see E. Williamson, *The Penguin History of Latin America* (London, 1992). On the revolts in Latin America, see J. Lynch, *The Spanish American Revolutions, 1808–1826* (New York, 1973). A good survey of nineteenth-century developments can be found in D. Bushnell and N. Macaulay, *The Emergence of Latin America in the Nineteenth Century* (Oxford, 1988). For a detailed account of the Ottoman Empire in the nineteenth century, see S. Shaw, *History of the Ottoman Empire and Modern Turkey*, vol. 2 (Cambridge, 1977).

The unification of Italy can be examined in the works of D. M. Smith, *Victor Emmanuel, Cavour and the Risorgimento* (London, 1971), and H. Hearder, *Cavour* (New York, 1994). The unification of Germany can be pursued first in two good biographies of Bismarck, E. Crankshaw, *Bismarck* (New York, 1981), and G. O. Kent, *Bismarck and His Times* (Carbondale, Ill., 1978). See also the brief study by B. Waller, *Bismarck*, 2d ed. (Oxford, 1997). For a good introduction to the French Second Empire, see A. Plessis, *The Rise and Fall of the Second Empire, 1852–1871*, trans. J. Mandelbaum (New York, 1985). Louis Napoleon's role can be examined in J. F. McMillan, *Napoleon III* (New York, 1991). On the emancipation of the Russian serfs, see D. Field, *The End of Serfdom: Nobility and Bureaucracy in Russia, 1855–1861* (Cambridge, 1976). The evolution of British political parties in mid-century is examined in H. J. Hanham, *Elections and Party Management: Politics in the Time of Disraeli and Gladstone*, 2d ed. (London, 1978). A good one-volume survey of the Civil War can be found in P. J. Parish, *The American Civil War* (New York, 1975). For a general history of Canada, see C. Brown, ed., *The Illustrated History of Canada* (Toronto, 1991).

For an introduction to the intellectual changes of the nineteenth century, see O. Chadwick, *The Secularization of the European Mind in the Nineteenth Century* (Cambridge, 1975). A beautifully illustrated introduction to Romanticism can be found in H. Honour, *Romanticism* (New York, 1979). On the ideas of the Romantics, see H. G. Schenk, *The Mind of the European Romantics* (Garden City, N.Y., 1969), and M. Cranston, *The Romantic Movement* (Oxford, 1994). For an introduction to the arts, see W. Vaughan, *Romanticism and Art* (New York, 1994). A detailed biography of Darwin can be found in J. Bowlby, *Charles Darwin, A Biography* (London, 1990). On Realism, J. Malpas, *Realism* (Cambridge, 1997) is a good introduction.

For additional reading, go to InfoTrac College Edition, your online research library at http://web1.infotrac-college.com

Enter the search terms "industrial revolution" using Keywords.

Enter the search term "Romanticism" using the Subject Guide.

Enter the search term "nationalism" using Keywords.

Enter the search terms "industrial development" using the Subject Guide.

CHAPTER

21

THE EMERGENCE OF MASS SOCIETY IN THE WESTERN WORLD

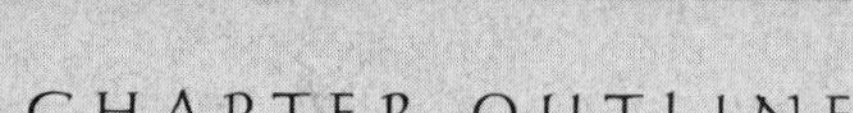

CHAPTER OUTLINE

- THE GROWTH OF INDUSTRIAL PROSPERITY
- THE EMERGENCE OF MASS SOCIETY
- THE NATIONAL STATE
- TOWARD THE MODERN CONSCIOUSNESS: INTELLECTUAL AND CULTURAL DEVELOPMENTS
- CONCLUSION

FOCUS QUESTIONS

- What was the Second Industrial Revolution, and what effects did it have on economic and social life?
- What were the main ideas of Karl Marx, and what role did they play in politics and the union movement in the late nineteenth and early twentieth centuries?
- What is meant by the term *mass society*, and what were its main characteristics?
- What general political trends were evident in the nations of western Europe in the late nineteenth and early twentieth centuries, and to what degree were those trends also apparent in the nations of Latin America, the United States, and the nations of central and eastern Europe?
- What intellectual and cultural developments in the late nineteenth and early twentieth centuries "opened the way to a modern consciousness," and how did this consciousness differ from earlier worldviews?

During the fifty years before 1914, the Western world witnessed a dynamic age of material prosperity. With new industries, new sources of energy, and new goods, a Second Industrial Revolution transformed the human environment and led people to believe that material progress meant human progress. Scientific and technological achievements, many naively believed, would improve humanity's condition and solve all human problems. The doctrine of progress became an article of great faith.

The new urban and industrial world created by the rapid economic changes of the nineteenth century led to the emergence of a mass society by the late nineteenth century. A mass society meant improvements for the lower classes, who benefited from the extension of voting rights, a better standard of living, and mass education. It also brought mass leisure. New work patterns established the "weekend" as a distinct time of recreation and fun, while new forms of mass transportation—railroads and streetcars—enabled even workers to make brief excursions to amusement parks. Coney Island was only eight miles from central New York City; Blackpool in England was a short train ride from nearby industrial towns. With their Ferris wheels and other daring rides that threw young men and women together, amusement parks offered a whole new world of entertainment. Thanks to the railroad, seaside resorts, once the preserve of the wealthy, also became accessible to more people for weekend visits, much to the disgust of one upper-class regular, who complained about the new "day-trippers": "They swarm upon the beach, wandering listlessly about with apparently no other aim than to get a mouthful of fresh air." Enterprising entrepreneurs in resorts like Blackpool welcomed the masses of new visitors, however, and built piers laden with food, drink, and entertainment to serve them.

The coming of mass society also created new roles for the governments of European nation-states, which now fostered national loyalty, created mass armies by conscription, and took more responsibility for public health and housing measures in their cities. By 1871, the national state had become the focus of Europeans' lives. Within many of these nation-states, the growth of the middle class had led to the triumph of liberal practices: constitutional governments, parliaments, and principles of equality. The period after 1871 also witnessed the growth of political democracy as the right to vote was extended to all adult males; women, though, would still have to fight for the same political rights. With political democracy came a new mass politics and a new mass press. Both would become regular features of the twentieth century.

The period between 1870 and 1914 was also a time of great tension as imperialist adventures, international rivalries, and cultural uncertainties disturbed the apparent calm. Europeans engaged in a great race for colonies that greatly intensified existing antagonisms among European states, while the creation of mass conscript armies and enormous military establishments served to further the tensions among the major powers. At the same time, despite the appearance of progress, Western philosophers, writers, and artists were creating modern cultural expressions that questioned traditional ideas and values and increasingly provoked a crisis of confidence. Before 1914, many intellectuals had a sense of unease about the direction society was headed, accompanied by a feeling of imminent catastrophe. They proved remarkably prophetic.

The Growth of Industrial Prosperity

At the heart of Europe's belief in progress between 1870 and 1914 was the stunning material growth produced by what historians have called the Second Industrial Revolution. The first Industrial Revolution had given rise to textiles, railroads, iron, and coal. In the second revolution, steel, chemicals, electricity, and petroleum led the way to new industrial frontiers.

New Products and New Patterns

The first major change in industrial development between 1870 and 1914 was the substitution of steel for iron. New methods for rolling and shaping steel made it useful in the construction of lighter, smaller, and faster machines and engines as well as for railways, shipbuilding, and armaments. In 1860, Great Britain, France, Germany, and Belgium produced 125,000 tons of steel; by 1913, the total was 32 million tons. By 1910, German steel production was double that of Great Britain, and both had been surpassed by the United States.

Electricity was a major new form of energy that proved to be of great value because it could be easily converted into other forms of energy—such as heat, light, and motion—and moved relatively effortlessly through space by means of transmitting wires. The first commercially practical generators of electrical current were not developed until the 1870s. By 1910, hydroelectric power stations and coal-fired steam-generating plants enabled entire districts to be tied into a single power distribution system that provided a common source of power for homes, shops, and industrial enterprises.

Electricity spawned a whole series of new products. The invention of the light bulb by the American Thomas Edison and the Briton Joseph Swan opened homes and cities to illumination by electric lights. A revolution in communications was fostered when Alexander Graham Bell invented the telephone in 1876 and Guglielmo Marconi sent the first radio waves across the Atlantic in 1901. Although most electricity was initially used for lighting, it was eventually put to use in transportation. By the 1880s, streetcars and subways had appeared in major European cities. Electricity also transformed the factory. Conveyor belts, cranes, machines, and machine tools could all be powered by electricity and located anywhere. Thanks to electricity, all countries could now enter the industrial age.

The development of the internal combustion engine had a similar effect. The processing of oil and gasoline made possible the widespread use of the internal combustion engine as a source of power in transportation. An oil-fired engine was made in 1897, and by 1902, the Hamburg-Amerika Line had switched from coal to oil on its new ocean liners. By the beginning of the twentieth century, some naval fleets had been converted to oil burners as well.

MAP 21.1 The Industrial Regions of Europe by 1914

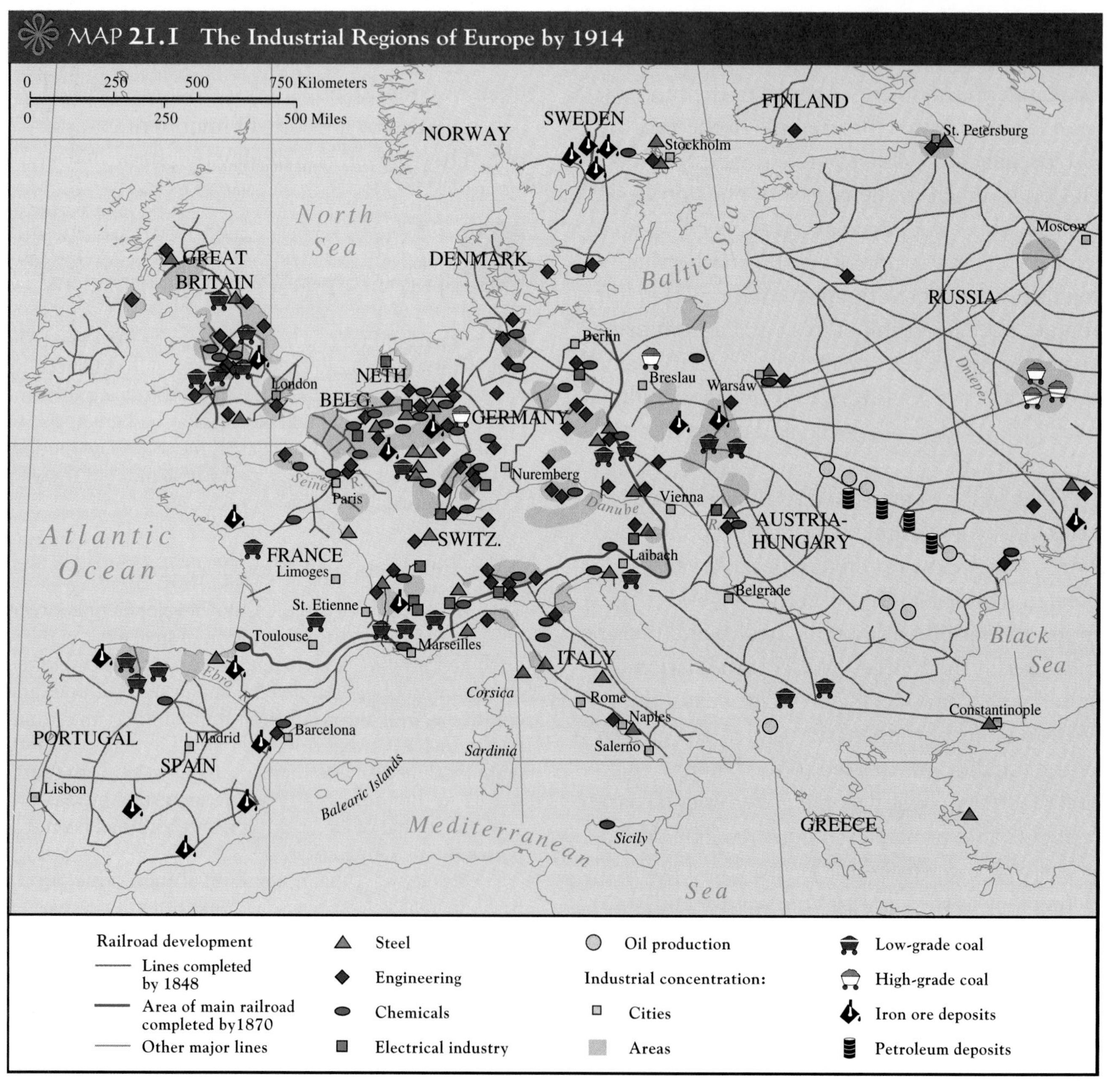

The internal combustion engine gave rise to the automobile and airplane. In 1900, world production stood at 9,000 cars; by 1906, Americans had overtaken the initial lead of the French. It was an American, Henry Ford, who revolutionized the car industry with the mass production of the Model T. By 1916, Ford's factories were producing 735,000 cars a year. In the meantime, air transportation had emerged with the zeppelin airship in 1900. In 1903, at Kitty Hawk, North Carolina, the Wright brothers made the first flight in a fixed-wing plane powered by a gasoline engine. It took World War I, however, to stimulate the aircraft industry, and it was not until 1919 that the first regular passenger air service was established.

The growth of industrial production depended on the development of markets for the sale of manufactured goods. After 1870, the best foreign markets were already heavily saturated, forcing Europeans to take a renewed look at their domestic markets. Between 1850 and 1900, real wages had increased in Britain by two-thirds and in Germany by one-third. A decline in the cost of food combined with lower prices for manufactured goods because of reduced transportation costs made it easier for Europeans to buy consumer products. Businesses soon perceived the value of using new techniques of mass marketing to sell the consumer goods made possible by the development of the steel and electrical industries. By bringing together a vast array of new products in one place, they created the department store (see the box on p. 630). The desire to own sewing machines, clocks, bicycles, and electric lights rapidly created a new consumer ethic that became a crucial part of the modern economy.

Meanwhile, increased competition for foreign markets and the growing importance of domestic demand led to a reaction against the free trade that had characterized much of the European economy between 1820 and 1870. To many industrial and political leaders, protective tariffs guaranteed domestic markets for the products of their own industries. By the 1870s, Europeans were returning to the practice of tariff protection. At the same time, cartels were being formed to decrease competition internally. In a cartel, independent enterprises worked together to control prices and fix production quotas, thereby restraining the kind of competition that led to reduced prices.

The formation of cartels was paralleled by a move toward ever larger manufacturing plants, especially in the iron and steel, machinery, heavy electrical equipment, and chemical industries. This growth in the size of industrial plants led to pressure for greater efficiency in factory production at the same time that competition led to demands for greater economy. The result was a desire to streamline or rationalize production as much as possible. The development of precision tools enabled manufacturers to produce interchangeable parts, which in turn led to the creation of the assembly line for production. First used in the United States for small arms and clocks, the assembly line had moved to Europe by 1850. In the last half of the nineteenth century, it was primarily used in manufacturing nonmilitary goods, such as sewing machines, typewriters, bicycles, and finally the automobile.

AN AGE OF PROGRESS. Between 1871 and 1914, a Second Industrial Revolution led many Europeans to believe that they were living in an age of progress when most human problems would be solved by scientific achievements. This illustration is taken from a special issue of *The Illustrated London News* celebrating the Diamond Jubilee of Queen Victoria in 1897. On the left are scenes from 1837, when Victoria came to the British throne; on the right are scenes from 1897. The vivid contrast underscored the magazine's conclusion: "The most striking . . . evidence of progress during the reign is the ever increasing speed which the discoveries of physical science have forced into everyday life. Steam and electricity have conquered time and space to a greater extent during the last sixty years than all the preceding six hundred years witnessed."

The emergence of protective tariffs and cartels was clearly a response to the growth of the multinational industrial system. Economic competition intensified the political rivalries of the age. The growth of the national state, which had seemed in the mid-nineteenth century

THE DEPARTMENT STORE AND THE BEGINNINGS OF MASS CONSUMERISM

Domestic markets were especially important for the sale of the goods being turned out by Europe's increasing number of industrial plants. New techniques of mass marketing arose to encourage the sale of the new consumer goods. The Parisians pioneered in the development of the department store, and this selection is taken from a contemporary's account of the growth of these stores in the French capital city.

E. LAVASSEUR, ON PARISIAN DEPARTMENT STORES, 1907

It was in the reign of Louis-Philippe that department stores for fashion goods and dresses, extending to material and other clothing, began to be distinguished. The type was already one of the notable developments of the Second Empire; it became one of the most important ones of the Third Republic. These stores have increased in number and several of them have become extremely large. Combining in their different departments all articles of clothing, toilet articles, furniture and many other ranges of goods, it is their special object so to combine all commodities as to attract and satisfy customers who will find conveniently together an assortment of a mass of articles corresponding to all their various needs. They attract customers by permanent display, by free entry into the shops, by periodic exhibitions, by special sales, by fixed prices, and by their ability to deliver the goods purchased to customers' homes, in Paris and to the provinces. Turning themselves into direct intermediaries between the producer and the consumer, even producing sometimes some of their articles in their own workshops, buying at lowest prices because of their large orders and because they are in a position to profit from bargains, working with large sums, and selling to most of their customers for cash only, they can transmit these benefits in lowered selling prices. They can even decide to sell at a loss, as an advertisement or to get rid of out-of-date fashions. Taking 5–6 per cent on 100 million brings them in more than 20 per cent would bring to a firm doing a turnover of 50,000 francs.

The success of these department stores is only possible thanks to the volume of their business, and this volume needs considerable capital and a very large turnover. Now capital, having become abundant, is freely combined nowadays in large enterprises, although French capital has the reputation of being more wary of the risks of industry than of State or railway securities. On the other hand, the large urban agglomerations, the ease with which goods can be transported by the railways, the diffusion of some comforts to strata below the middle classes, have all favored these developments.

As example we may cite some figures relating to these stores, since they were brought to the notice of the public in the *Revue des Deux-Mondes*. . . .

Le Louvre, dating to the time of the extension of the rue de Rivoli under the Second Empire, did in 1893 a business of 120 million at a profit of 6.4 per cent. *Le Bon-Marché*, which was a small shop when Mr. Boucicaut entered it in 1852, already did a business of 20 million at the end of the Empire. During the republic its new buildings were erected; Mme. Boucicaut turned it by her will into a kind of cooperative society, with shares and an ingenious organization; turnover reached 150 million in 1893, leaving a profit of 5 per cent. . . .

According to the tax records of 1891, these stores in Paris, numbering 12, employed 1,708 persons and were rated on their site values at 2,159,000 francs; the largest had then 542 employees. These same stores had, in 1901, 9,784 employees; one of them over 2,000 and another over 1,600; their site value has doubled (4,089,000 francs).

to be the answer to old problems, now seemed to be creating new ones.

Between 1870 and 1914, Germany replaced Great Britain as the industrial leader of Europe. Already in the 1890s, Germany's superiority was evident in new areas of manufacturing, such as organic chemicals and electrical equipment, and increasingly apparent in its ever greater share of worldwide trade. But the struggle for economic (and political) supremacy between Great Britain and Germany should not cause us to overlook the other great polarization of the age. By 1900, Europe was divided into two economic zones. Great Britain, Belgium, France, the Netherlands, Germany, the western part of the Austro-Hungarian Empire, and northern Italy constituted an advanced industrialized core that had a high standard of living, decent systems of transportation, and relatively healthy and educated peoples. Another part of Europe, the backward and little industrialized area to the south and east—consisting of southern Italy, most of Austria-Hungary, Spain, Portugal, the Balkan kingdoms, and Russia—was still largely agricultural and relegated by the industrial countries to the function of providing food and raw materials. The presence of Romanian oil, Greek olive oil, and Serbian pigs and prunes in western Europe served as reminders of an economic division of Europe that continued well into the twentieth century.

Toward a World Economy

The economic developments of the late nineteenth century, combined with the transportation revolution that saw the growth of marine transport and railroads, fostered a true world economy. By 1900, Europeans were receiving beef and wool from Argentina and Australia, coffee from Brazil, nitrates from Chile, iron ore from Algeria, and sugar from Java. European capital was also invested abroad to develop railways, mines, electrical power plants, and banks. High rates of return, such as 11.3 percent on Latin American banking shares that were floated in London, provided plenty of incentive for investors. Of course, foreign countries also provided markets for the surplus manufactured goods of Europe. With its capital, industries, and military might, Europe dominated the world economy by the beginning of the twentieth century.

Women and Work: New Job Opportunities

The Second Industrial Revolution had an enormous impact on the position of women in the labor market. During the course of the nineteenth century, considerable controversy erupted over a woman's "right to work." Working-class organizations tended to reinforce the underlying ideology of domesticity; women should remain at home to bear and nurture children and not be allowed in the industrial workforce. Working-class men argued that keeping women out of industrial work would ensure the moral and physical well-being of families. In reality, keeping women out of the industrial workforce simply made it easier to exploit them when they needed income to supplement their husbands' wages or to support their families when their husbands were unemployed. The desperate need to work at times forced women to do marginal work at home or labor as pieceworkers in sweatshops.

After 1870, however, new job opportunities for women became available. The development of larger industrial plants and the expansion of government services created a variety of service or white-collar jobs. The increased demand for white-collar workers at relatively low wages coupled with a shortage of male workers led employers to hire women. Big businesses and retail shops needed clerks, typists, secretaries, file clerks, and salesclerks. The expansion of government services created opportunities for women to be secretaries and telephone operators and to take jobs in health and social services. Compulsory education necessitated more teachers, while the development of modern hospital services opened the way for an increase in the number of nurses.

Many of the new white-collar jobs were by no means exciting. The work was routine and, except for teaching and nursing, required few skills beyond basic literacy. Although there was little hope for advancement, these jobs had distinct advantages for the daughters of the middle classes and especially the upward-aspiring working classes. For some middle-class women, the new jobs offered freedom from the domestic patterns expected of them. Moreover, because middle-class women did not receive an education comparable to that of men, they were limited in the careers they could pursue. Thus, they found it easier to fill the jobs at the lower end of middle-class occupations, such as teaching and civil service jobs, especially those in the post office. Most of the new white-collar jobs, however, were filled by working-class women who saw the job as an opportunity to escape from the physical labor of the lower-class world.

Organizing the Working Classes

The desire to improve their working and living conditions led many industrial workers to form socialist political parties and socialist labor unions. These emerged after 1870, but the theory that made them possible had already been developed by mid-century in the work of Karl Marx.

Marxism made its first appearance on the eve of the revolutions of 1848 with the publication of a short treatise entitled *The Communist Manifesto*, written by two Germans, Karl Marx (1818–1883) and Friedrich Engels (1820–1895). The work became one of the most influential political treatises in modern European history. At the same time, it contained the substance of the basic economic and political ideas that Marx elaborated on during the rest of his life.

What, then, was the basic picture of historical development that Marx and Engels offered in *The Communist Manifesto*? They began their treatise with the statement that "the history of all hitherto existing society is the history of class struggles." Throughout history, then, oppressor and oppressed have "stood in constant opposition to one another." In an earlier struggle, the feudal classes of the Middle Ages were forced to accede to the emerging middle class or bourgeoisie. As the bourgeoisie took control in turn, their ideas became the dominant views of the era, and government became their instrument. Marx and Engels declared: "The executive of the modern State is but a committee for managing the common affairs of the whole bourgeoisie."[1] In other words, the government of the state reflected and defended the interests of the industrial middle class and its allies.

Although bourgeois society had emerged victorious out of the ruins of feudal society, Marx and Engels insisted that it had not triumphed completely. Now once again the bourgeoisie were antagonists in an emerging class struggle, but this time they faced the proletariat, or the industrial working class. The struggle would be fierce; in fact, Marx and Engels predicted that the workers would eventually overthrow their bourgeois masters. After their victory, the proletariat would form a dictatorship to reorganize the means of production. Then, a classless society would emerge, and the state—itself an instrument of the bourgeoisie—would wither away because it no longer

THE CLASSLESS SOCIETY

In The Communist Manifesto, *Karl Marx and Friedrich Engels projected as the final end product of the struggle between the bourgeoisie and the proletariat the creation of a classless society. In this selection, they discuss the steps by which that classless society would be reached.*

KARL MARX AND FRIEDRICH ENGELS, *THE COMMUNIST MANIFESTO*

We have seen above, that the first step in the revolution by the working class, is to raise the proletariat to the position of ruling class. . . . The proletariat will use its political supremacy to wrest, by degrees, all capital from the bourgeoisie, to centralize all instruments of production in the hands of the State, i.e., of the proletariat organized as the ruling class; and to increase the total of productive forces as rapidly as possible.

Of course, in the beginning, this cannot be effected except by means of despotic inroads on the rights of property, and on the conditions of bourgeois production; by means of measures, therefore, which appear economically insufficient and untenable, but which, in the course of the movement, outstrip themselves, necessitate further inroads upon the old social order, and are unavoidable as a means of entirely revolutionizing the mode of production.

These measures will of course be different in different countries.

Nevertheless, in the most advanced countries, the following will be pretty generally applicable:

1. Abolition of property in land and application of all rents of land to public purposes.
2. A heavy progressive or graduated income tax.
3. Abolition of all right of inheritance. . . .
5. Centralization of credit in the hands of the State, by means of a national bank with State capital and an exclusive monopoly.
6. Centralization of the means of communication and transport in the hands of the State.
7. Extension of factories and instruments of production owned by the State. . . .
8. Equal liability of all to labor. Establishment of industrial armies, especially for agriculture.
9. Combination of agriculture with manufacturing industries; gradual abolition of the distinction between town and country, by a more equable distribution of the population over the country.
10. Free education for all children in public schools. Abolition of children's factory labor in its present form. . . .

When, in the course of development, class distinctions have disappeared, and all production has been concentrated in the whole nation, the public power will lose its political character. Political power, properly so called, is merely the organized power of one class for oppressing another. If the proletariat during its contest with the bourgeoisie is compelled, by the force of circumstances, to organize itself as a class, if, by means of a revolution, it makes itself the ruling class, and, as such, sweeps away by force the old conditions of production, then it will, along with these conditions, have swept away the conditions for the existence of class antagonisms and of classes generally, and will thereby have abolished its own supremacy as a class.

In place of the old bourgeois society, with its classes and class antagonisms, we shall have an association, in which the free development of each is the condition for the free development of all.

represented the interests of a particular class. Class struggles would then be over (see the box above).

After the failure of the revolutions of 1848, Marx went to Britain, where he spent the rest of his life in exile. Marx continued his writing on political economy, especially his famous work *Das Kapital* (*Capital*), but his preoccupation with organizing the working-class movement kept him from ever finishing *Capital*. In *The Communist Manifesto*, Marx had defined the communists as "the most advanced and resolute section of the working-class parties of every country." Their advantage was their ability to understand "the line of march, the conditions, and the ultimate general results of the proletarian movement." Marx saw his role in this light and participated enthusiastically in the activities of the International Working Men's Association. Formed in 1864 by British and French trade unionists, this "First International" served as an umbrella organization for working-class interests. Marx devoted much time to its activities. Internal dissension, however, soon damaged the organization, and it failed in 1872. A Second International was not formed until 1889, six years after Marx's death, but by that time the working-class movement had undergone a significant growth and transformation with the rise of socialist parties and trade unions, most of which were Marxist in orientation.

The growth of socialist parties after the demise of the First International was rapid and widespread. Most important was the formation of a socialist party in Germany. The German Social Democratic Party (SPD) emerged in 1875. Under the direction of its two Marxist leaders, Wilhelm Liebknecht and August Bebel, the SPD espoused revolutionary Marxist rhetoric while organizing itself as a mass

"PROLETARIANS OF THE WORLD, UNITE!" To improve their working and living conditions, many industrial workers, inspired by the ideas of Karl Marx, joined working-class or socialist parties. Pictured here is a socialist-sponsored poster that proclaims in German the closing words of *The Communist Manifesto:* "Proletarians of the World, Unite!"

political party to compete in elections for the Reichstag. Once in the Reichstag, SPD delegates worked to achieve legislation to improve the condition of the working class. As August Bebel explained, "Pure negation would not be accepted by the voters. The masses demand that something should be done for today irrespective of what will happen on the morrow."[2] Despite government efforts to destroy it, the SPD continued to grow. In 1890, it received 1.5 million votes and thirty-five seats in the Reichstag. When it received 4 million votes in the 1912 elections, it became the largest single party in Germany.

Socialist parties emerged in other European states, although not with the kind of success achieved by the German Social Democrats. As the socialist parties grew, agitation for an international organization that would strengthen their position against international capitalism intensified. In 1889, leaders of the various socialist parties formed the Second International. Significantly, while the First International had been formed by individuals and had been highly centralized, the Second International was created by representatives of national working-class parties and was organized as a loose association of national groups. Although the Second International took some coordinated actions—May Day (May 1), for example, was made an international labor day to be marked by strikes and mass labor demonstrations—differences often wreaked havoc at the congresses of the organization.

One divisive issue for international socialism was nationalism. Despite the belief of Karl Marx and Friedrich Engels that "the working men have no country," in truth, socialist parties varied from country to country and remained tied to national interests and issues. Nationalism proved to be a much more powerful force than socialism. Marxist parties also divided over the issue of revisionism. Some Marxists believed in a pure Marxism that accepted the imminent collapse of capitalism and the need for socialist ownership of the means of production. But others rejected the revolutionary approach and argued in a revisionist direction that the workers must continue to organize in mass political parties and even work together with the other progressive elements in a nation to gain reform. With the extension of the right to vote, workers were in a better position than ever to achieve their aims through democratic channels. Evolution by democratic means, rather than revolution, would achieve the desired goal of socialism.

Another force working for evolutionary rather than revolutionary socialism, and at the same time an expression of a nationalistically oriented socialism, was the development of trade unions. Attempts to organize the masses of unskilled and semiskilled workers in factory industries did not come in Great Britain until the last two decades of the nineteenth century, after unions had won the right to strike in the 1870s. Strikes proved necessary to achieve the goals of these workers. A walkout by female workers in the match industry in 1888 and another by dock workers in London the following year led to the establishment of trade unions for both groups. By 1900, there were two million workers in British trade unions, and by the outbreak of World War I, between three and four million workers, less than one-fifth of the total workforce, were collectively organized. By 1914, the German trade union movement with its three million members was the second largest in Europe, after Great Britain's.

THE EMERGENCE OF MASS SOCIETY

The new urban and industrial world created by the rapid economic and social changes of the nineteenth century has led historians to speak of the emergence of a mass

WORKING-CLASS HOUSING IN LONDON. Although urban workers experienced some improvements in the material conditions of their lives after 1871, working-class housing remained drab and depressing. This 1912 photograph of working-class housing in the East End of London shows rows of similar-looking buildings on treeless streets. Most often, these buildings had no gardens or green areas.

society by the late nineteenth century. For the lower classes, a mass society brought voting rights, an improved standard of living, and compulsory elementary education. However, mass society also made possible the development of organizations that manipulated and controlled the populations of the nation-states. Governments fostered national loyalty and created mass armies by conscription. A mass press swayed popular opinion by flamboyant journalistic practices. To understand this mass society, we need to examine some aspects of its structure.

The New Urban Environment

By far one of the most important consequences of industrialization and the population explosion of the nineteenth century was urbanization. In the course of the nineteenth century, urban inhabitants came to make up an ever increasing percentage of the European population. In 1800, they constituted 40 percent of the population in Britain, 25 percent in France and Germany, and only 10 percent in eastern Europe. By 1914, urban inhabitants had increased to 80 percent of the population in Britain, 45 percent in France, 60 percent in Germany, and 30 percent in eastern Europe. The size of cities also expanded dramatically, especially in industrialized countries. Between 1800 and 1900, London's population grew from 960,000 to 6.5 million and Berlin's from 172,000 to 2.7 million.

Urban populations grew faster than the general population primarily because of the vast migration from rural areas to cities. People were driven by sheer economic necessity—unemployment and physical want—from the countryside to the city. Urban centers offered something positive as well, usually mass employment in factories and later in service trades and professions. But cities also grew faster in the second half of the nineteenth century because health and the conditions of urban life were improving as reformers and city officials used new technology to improve the urban landscape.

In the 1840s, a number of urban reformers had pointed to filthy living conditions as the primary cause of epidemic diseases and urged sanitary reforms to correct the problem. Soon, legislative acts created boards of health that brought governmental action to bear on public health issues. Urban medical officers and building inspectors were authorized to inspect dwellings for public health hazards. New building regulations made it more difficult for private contractors to construct shoddy housing. The Public Health Act of 1875 in Britain, for example, prohibited the construction of new buildings without running water and an internal drainage system. For the first time in Western history, the role of municipal governments had been expanded to include detailed regulations for the improvement of the living conditions of urban dwellers.

Essential to the public health of the modern European city was the ability to bring clean water to it and to expel sewage from it. The need for potable freshwater was met by a system of dams and reservoirs that stored the water and aqueducts and tunnels that carried it from the countryside to the city and into individual dwellings. By the second half of the nineteenth century, regular private baths became accessible to many people as gas heaters in the 1860s and later electric heaters made hot baths possible. The treatment of sewage was also improved by laying mammoth underground pipes that carried raw sewage far from the city for disposal. In the late 1860s, a number of German cities began to construct sewer systems. Frankfurt began its program after a lengthy public campaign enlivened by the slogan "from the toilet to the river in half an hour."

Middle-class reformers who denounced the unsanitary living conditions of the working class also focused on their housing needs. Overcrowded, disease-ridden slums were viewed as dangerous not only to physical health, but to the political and moral health of the entire nation. V. A. Huber, the foremost early German housing reformer, wrote in 1861: "Certainly it would not be too much to say that

THE HOUSING VENTURE OF OCTAVIA HILL

Octavia Hill was a practical-minded British housing reformer who believed that workers and their families were entitled to happy homes. At the same time, she was convinced that the poor needed guidance and encouragement, not charity. In this selection, she describes her housing venture.

OCTAVIA HILL, HOMES OF THE LONDON POOR

About four years ago I was put in possession of three houses in one of the worst courts of Marylebone. Six other houses were bought subsequently. All were crowded with inmates.

The first thing to be done was to put them in decent tenantable order. The set last purchased was a row of cottages facing a bit of desolate ground, occupied with wretched, dilapidated cowsheds, manure heaps, old timber, and rubbish of every description. The houses were in a most deplorable condition—the plaster was dropping from the walls; on one staircase a pail was placed to catch the rain that fell through the roof. All the staircases were perfectly dark; the banisters were gone, having been burnt as firewood by tenants. The grates, with large holes in them, were falling forward into the rooms. The washhouse, full of lumber belonging to the landlord, was locked up; thus the inhabitants had to wash clothes, as well as to cook, eat and sleep in their small rooms. The dustbin, standing in the front part of the houses, was accessible to the whole neighbourhood, and boys often dragged from it quantities of unseemly objects and spread them over the court. The state of the drainage was in keeping with everything else. The pavement of the backyard was all broken up, and great puddles stood in it, so that the damp crept up the outer walls. . . .

As soon as I entered into possession, each family had an opportunity of doing better: those who would not pay, or who led clearly immoral lives, were ejected. The rooms they vacated were cleansed; the tenants who showed signs of improvement moved into them, and thus, in turn, an opportunity was obtained for having each room distempered and papered. The drains were put in order, a large slate cistern was fixed, the wash-house was cleared of its lumber, and thrown open on stated days to each tenant in turn. The roof, the plaster, the woodwork was repaired; the staircase walls were distempered; new grates were fixed; the layers of paper and rag (black with age) were torn from the windows, and glass was put in; out of 192 panes only eight were found unbroken. The yard and footpath were paved.

The rooms, as a rule, were re-let at the same prices at which they had been let before; but tenants with large families were counselled to take two rooms, and for these much less was charged than if let singly: this plan I continue to pursue. Incoming tenants are not allowed to take a decidedly insufficient quantity of room, and no subletting is permitted. . . .

The pecuniary result has been very satisfactory. Five per cent has been paid on all the capital invested. A fund for the repayment of capital is accumulating. A liberal allowance has been made for repairs. . . .

My tenants are mostly of a class far below that of mechanics. They are, indeed, of the very poor. And yet, although the gifts they have received have been next to nothing, none of the families who have passed under my care during the whole four years have continued in what is called "distress," except such as have been unwilling to exert themselves. Those who will not exert the necessary self-control cannot avail themselves of the means of livelihood held out to them. But, for those who are willing, some small assistance in the form of work has, from time to time, been provided—not much, but sufficient to keep them from want or despair.

the home is the communal embodiment of family life. Thus the purity of the dwelling is almost as important for the family as is the cleanliness of the body for the individual."[3] To Huber, good housing was a prerequisite for stable family life, and without stable family life one of the "stabilizing elements of society" would be dissolved, much to society's detriment.

Early efforts to attack the housing problem emphasized the middle-class, liberal belief in the power of private, or free, enterprise. Reformers such as Huber believed that the construction of model dwellings renting at a reasonable price would force other private landlords to elevate their housing standards. A fine example of this approach was the work of Octavia Hill (see the box above). With the financial assistance of a friend, she rehabilitated some old dwellings and constructed new ones to create housing for 3,500 tenants.

As the number and size of cities continued to mushroom, governments by the 1880s came to the conclusion—although reluctantly—that private enterprise could not solve the housing crisis. In 1890, a British Housing Act empowered local town councils to construct cheap housing for the working classes. London and Liverpool were the first communities to take advantage of their new powers. Similar activity had been set in motion in Germany by 1900. Everywhere, however, these lukewarm measures failed to do much to meet the real housing needs of the working classes. In housing, as in so many other areas of life in the late nineteenth and early twentieth centuries, the liberal principle that the government that governs least governs best had simply proved untrue. More and more, governments were stepping into areas of activity that they would have never touched earlier.

The Social Structure of Mass Society

At the top of European society stood a wealthy elite that made up 5 percent of the population while controlling between 30 and 40 percent of the wealth. In the course of the nineteenth century, landed aristocrats had joined with the most successful industrialists, bankers, and merchants (the wealthy upper-middle class) to form this new elite. Members of this elite, whether aristocratic or middle class in background, became leaders in the government and military. Marriage also served to unite the two groups. Daughters of business tycoons gained titles, while aristocratic heirs gained new sources of cash. When the American Consuelo Vanderbilt married the British duke of Marlborough, the new duchess brought $10 million to her husband.

The middle classes consisted of a variety of groups. Below the upper-middle class was a middle level that included such traditional groups as professionals in law, medicine, and the civil service as well as moderately well-to-do industrialists and merchants. The industrial expansion of the nineteenth century also added new groups to the middle-middle class. These included business managers and new professionals, such as the engineers, architects, accountants, and chemists who formed professional associations to symbolize their newfound importance. Beneath this solid and comfortable middle-middle class was a lower-middle class of small shopkeepers, traders, manufacturers, and prosperous peasants. Their chief preoccupation was the provision of goods and services for the classes above them.

Standing between the lower-middle class and the lower classes were new groups of white-collar workers who were the product of the Second Industrial Revolution. They were the traveling salespeople, bookkeepers, bank tellers, telephone operators, department store salespeople, and secretaries. Although largely propertyless and often paid little more than skilled laborers, these white-collar workers were often committed to middle-class ideals and optimistic about improving their status.

The moderately prosperous and successful middle classes shared a certain style of life, one whose values tended to dominate much of nineteenth-century society. The members of the middle class were especially active in preaching their worldview to their children and to the upper and lower classes of their society. This was especially evident in Victorian Britain, often considered a model of middle-class society. It was the European middle classes who accepted and promulgated the importance of progress and science. They believed in hard work, which they viewed as the primary human good, open to everyone and guaranteed to have positive results. They were also regular churchgoers, who believed in the good conduct associated with traditional Christian morality. The middle class was concerned with propriety, the right way of doing things, which gave rise to an incessant number of books aimed at the middle-class market with such titles as *The Habits of Good Society* or *Don't: A Manual of Mistakes and Improprieties More or Less Prevalent in Conduct and Speech.*

Below the middle classes on the social scale were the working classes of European society, who made up almost 80 percent of the European population. Many of the members of these classes were landholding peasants, farm laborers, and sharecroppers, especially in eastern Europe. The urban working class consisted of many different groups, including skilled artisans in such trades as cabinetmaking and printing and semiskilled laborers such as carpenters and many factory workers, who earned wages that were about two-thirds of those of highly skilled workers. At the bottom of the urban working class were the unskilled laborers. They were the largest group of workers and included day laborers and large numbers of domestic servants. One out of every seven employed persons in Great Britain in 1900 was a domestic servant. Most of them were women.

Urban workers did experience a real betterment in the material conditions of their lives after 1870. For one thing, urban improvements meant better living conditions. A rise in real wages, accompanied by a decline in many consumer costs, especially in the 1880s and 1890s, made it possible for workers to buy more than just food and housing. Workers' budgets now included money for more clothes and even leisure at the same time that strikes and labor agitation were winning ten-hour days and Saturday afternoons off. The combination of more income and more free time produced whole new patterns of mass leisure.

The "Woman Question": The Role of Women

The "woman question" was the term used to identify the debate over the role of women in society. In the nineteenth century, women remained legally inferior, economically dependent, and largely defined by family and household roles. Many women still aspired to the ideal of femininity popularized by writers and poets. Alfred Lord Tennyson's *The Princess* expressed it well:

> *Man for the field and woman for the hearth:*
> *Man for the sword and for the needle she:*
> *Man with the head and woman with the heart:*
> *Man to command and woman to obey;*
> *All else confusion.*

This traditional characterization of the sexes, based on gender-defined social roles, was virtually elevated to the status of universal male and female attributes in the nineteenth century, largely due to the impact of the Industrial Revolution on the family. As the chief family wage earners, men worked outside the home while women were left with the care of the family, for which they were paid nothing. Of course, the ideal did not always match reality, especially for the lower classes, where the need for supplemental income drove women to do "sweated" work.

A MIDDLE-CLASS FAMILY. Nineteenth-century middle-class moralists considered the family the fundamental pillar of a healthy society. The family was a crucial institution in middle-class life, and togetherness constituted one of the important ideals of the middle-class family. This painting by William P. Frith, entitled *Many Happy Returns of the Day,* shows a family birthday celebration for a little girl in which grandparents, parents, and children take part. The servant at the left holds the presents for the little girl.

MARRIAGE AND THE FAMILY

For most women, marriage was viewed as the only honorable and available career throughout most of the nineteenth century. While the middle class glorified the ideal of domesticity, for most women marriage was a matter of economic necessity. The lack of meaningful work and the lower wages paid to women for their work made it difficult for single women to earn a living. Most women chose to marry, which was reflected in the increase in marriage rates and a decline in illegitimacy rates over the course of the nineteenth century.

Birthrates also dropped significantly in the nineteenth century. The most significant development in the modern family was the decline in the number of offspring born to the average woman. The change was not necessarily due to new technology. Although the invention of vulcanized rubber in the 1840s made possible the production of condoms and diaphragms, they were not widely used as effective contraceptive devices until the era of World War I. Some historians maintain that the change in attitude that led parents to limit the number of offspring deliberately was more important than the method used. While some historians attribute increased birth control to more widespread use of coitus interruptus, or male withdrawal before ejaculation, others have emphasized female control of family size through abortion and even infanticide or abandonment. That a change in attitude occurred was apparent in the development of a movement to increase awareness of birth control methods. Europe's first birth control clinic, founded by Dr. Aletta Jacob, opened in Amsterdam in 1882.

The family was the central institution of middle-class life. Men provided the family income while women focused on household and child care. The use of domestic servants in many middle-class homes, made possible by an abundant supply of cheap labor, reduced the amount of time middle-class women had to spend on household work. At the same time, by reducing the number of children in the family, mothers could devote more time to child care and domestic leisure.

The middle-class family fostered an ideal of togetherness. The Victorians created the family Christmas with its yule log, Christmas tree, songs, and exchange of gifts. In the United States, Fourth of July celebrations changed from drunken revels to family picnics by the 1850s. The education of middle-class females in domestic crafts, singing, and piano playing prepared them for their function of providing a proper environment for home recreation.

Women in working-class families were more accustomed to hard work. Daughters in working-class families were expected to work until they married; even after marriage, they often did piecework at home to help support the family. For the children of the working classes, childhood was over by the age of nine or ten when they became apprentices or were employed in odd jobs.

Between 1890 and 1914, however, family patterns among the working class began to change. High-paying jobs in heavy industry and improvements in the standard of living made it possible for working-class families to depend on the income of husbands and the wages of grown children. By the early twentieth century, some working-class mothers could afford to stay at home, following the pattern of middle-class women. At the same time, new consumer products, such as sewing machines, clocks, bicycles, and cast-iron stoves, created a new mass consumer society whose focus was on higher levels of consumption.

These working-class families also followed the middle classes in limiting the size of their families. Children began to be viewed as dependents rather than wage earners as child labor laws and compulsory education took children out of the workforce and into schools. Improvements in public health as well as advances in medicine and a better diet resulted in a decline in infant mortality rates for the lower classes, especially noticeable in the cities after 1890, and made it easier for working-class families to choose to have fewer children. At the same time, strikes and labor agitation led to laws that reduced work hours to ten per day by 1900 and eliminated work on Saturday afternoons, which enabled working-class parents to devote more attention to their children and develop more emotional ties with them.

THE MOVEMENT FOR WOMEN'S RIGHTS

In the 1830s, a number of women in the United States and Europe, who worked together in several reform movements, became frustrated by the apparent prejudices against females. They sought improvements for women by focusing on family and marriage law because it was difficult for women to secure divorces and property laws gave husbands almost complete control over the property of their wives. These early efforts were not overly successful, however. For example, women did not gain the right to their own property until 1870 in Britain, 1900 in Germany, and 1907 in France.

Custody and property rights were only a beginning for the women's movement, however. Some middle- and upper-middle-class women gained access to higher education, while others sought entry into occupations dominated by men. The first to fall was teaching. As medical training was largely closed to women, they sought alternatives in the development of nursing. An upper-class nursing pioneer in Germany was Amalie Sieveking (1794–1859), who founded the Female Association for the Care of the Poor and Sick in Hamburg. As she explained: "To me, at least as important were the benefits which [work with the poor] seemed to promise for those of my sisters who would join me in such a work of charity. The higher interests of my sex were close to my heart."[4] Sieveking's work was followed by the more famous British nurse, Florence Nightingale, whose efforts during the Crimean War (1854–1856), combined with those of Clara Barton in the American Civil War (1861–1865), transformed nursing into a profession of trained, middle-class "women in white."

By the 1840s and 1850s, the movement for women's rights had entered the political arena with the call for equal political rights. Many feminists believed that the right to vote was the key to all other reforms to improve the position of women. Suffragists had one basic aim, the right of women to full citizenship in the nation-state.

The British women's movement was the most vocal and active in Europe, but divided over tactics. Moderates believed that women must demonstrate that they would use political power responsibly if they wanted Parliament to grant them the right to vote. Another group, however, favored a more radical approach. Emmeline Pankhurst (1858–1928) and her daughters, Christabel and Sylvia, founded the Women's Social and Political Union in 1903, which enrolled mostly middle- and upper-class women. Pankhurst's organization realized the value of the media and used unusual publicity stunts to call attention to its demands. Derisively labeled suffragettes by male politicians, its members pelted government officials with eggs, chained themselves to lampposts, smashed the windows of department stores on fashionable shopping streets, burned railroad cars, and went on hunger strikes in jail.

Before World War I, the demands for women's rights were being heard throughout Europe and the United States, although only in Norway and some American states did women actually receive the right to vote before 1914. It would take the dramatic upheaval of World War I before male-dominated governments capitulated on this basic issue.

Women reformers also took on issues besides suffrage. In many countries, women supported peace movements. Bertha von Suttner (1843–1914) became head of the Austrian Peace Society and protested against the growing arms race of the 1890s. Her novel *Lay Down Your Arms* became a best-seller and brought her the Nobel Peace Prize in 1905. Lower-class women also took up the cause of peace. A group of women workers marched in Vienna in 1911 and demanded: "We want an end to armaments, to the means of murder, and we want these millions to be spent on the needs of the people."

THE NEW WOMAN

Bertha von Suttner was but one example of the "new women" who were becoming more prominent at the turn of the century. These women defied tradition in regard to traditional feminine roles (see the box on p. 639). Although some of them supported political ideologies such as socialism that flew in the face of the ruling classes, others simply sought new freedom outside the household and new roles other than those of wives and mothers.

Maria Montessori (1870–1952) was another good example of the "new woman." Breaking with tradition, she attended medical school at the University of Rome. Although often isolated by her fellow (male) students, she persisted and in 1896 became the first Italian woman to receive a medical degree. Three years later she began a lecture tour in Italy on the subject of "The New Woman," whom she characterized as a woman who followed a rational, scientific perspective. In keeping with this ideal, Montessori put her medical background to work in a school for mentally retarded children. She devised new teaching materials that enabled these children to read and write and became convinced, as she later wrote, "that similar methods applied to normal students would develop or set free their personality in a marvelous and surprising way." Subsequently, she established a system of childhood education based on natural and spontaneous activities in which students learned at their own pace. By the 1930s, hundreds of Montessori schools had been established in Europe and the United States. As a professional woman and a woman who chose to have a child without being married, Montessori also embodied some of the freedoms of the "new woman."

Education in an Age of Mass Society

Mass education was a product of the "mass society" of the late nineteenth and early twentieth centuries. Being "educated" in the early nineteenth century meant attend-

ADVICE TO WOMEN: BE INDEPENDENT

Although a majority of women probably followed the nineteenth-century middle-class ideal of women as keepers of the household and nurturers of husband and children, an increasing number of women fought for the rights of women. This selection is taken from Act III of Henrik Ibsen's A Doll's House *(1879), in which the character Nora Helmer declares her independence from her husband's control over her life.*

HENRIK IBSEN: A *DOLL'S HOUSE*

NORA: *(Pause)* Does anything strike you as we sit here?
HELMER: What should strike me?
NORA: We've been married eight years; does it not strike you that this is the first time we two, you and I, man and wife, have talked together seriously?
HELMER: Seriously? What do you mean, *seriously*?
NORA: For eight whole years, and more—ever since the day we first met—we have never exchanged one serious word about serious things. . . .
HELMER: Why, my dearest Nora, what have you to do with serious things?
NORA: There we have it! You have never understood me. I've had great injustice done to me, Torvald; first by father, then by you.
HELMER: What! Your father and me? We, who have loved you more than all the world?
NORA *(Shaking her head)*: You have never loved me. You just found it amusing to think you were in love with me.
HELMER: Nora! What a thing to say!
NORA: Yes, it's true, Torvald. When I was living at home with father, he told me his opinions and mine were the same. If I had different opinions, I said nothing about them, because he would not have liked it. He used to call me his doll-child and played with me as I played with my dolls. Then I came to live in your house.
HELMER: What a way to speak of our marriage!
NORA *(Undisturbed)*: I mean that I passed from father's hands into yours. You arranged everything to your taste and I got the same tastes as you; or pretended to—I don't know which—both, perhaps; sometimes one, sometimes the other. When I look back on it now, I seem to have been living here like a beggar, on hand-outs. I lived by performing tricks for you, Torvald. But that was how you wanted it. You and father have done me a great wrong. It is your fault that my life has come to naught.
HELMER: Why, Nora, how unreasonable and ungrateful! Haven't you been happy here?
NORA: No, never. I thought I was, but I never was.
HELMER: Not—not happy! . . .
NORA: I must stand quite alone if I am ever to know myself and my surroundings; so I cannot stay with you.
HELMER: Nora! Nora!
NORA: I am going at once. I daresay [my friend] Christina will take me in for tonight.
HELMER: You are mad! I shall not allow it! I forbid it!
NORA: It's no use your forbidding me anything now. I shall take with me only what belongs to me; from you I will accept nothing, either now or later.
HELMER: This is madness!
NORA: Tomorrow I shall go home—I mean to what was my home. It will be easier for me to find a job there.
HELMER: Oh, in your blind inexperience—
NORA: I must try to gain experience, Torvald.
HELMER: Forsake your home, your husband, your children! And you don't consider what the world will say.
NORA: I can't pay attention to that. I only know that I must do it.
HELMER: This is monstrous! Can you forsake your holiest duties?
NORA: What do you consider my holiest duties?
HELMER: Need I tell you that? Your duties to your husband and children.
NORA: I have other duties equally sacred.
HELMER: Impossible! What do you mean?
NORA: My duties toward myself.
HELMER: Before all else you are a wife and a mother.
NORA: That I no longer believe. Before all else I believe I am a human being, just as much as you are—or at least that I should try to become one. I know that most people agree with you, Torvald, and that they say so in books. But I can no longer be satisfied with what most people say and what is in books. I must think things out for myself and try to get clear about them.

ing a secondary school or possibly even a university. Secondary schools mostly emphasized a classical education based on the study of Greek and Latin. Secondary and university education were primarily for the elite, the sons of government officials, nobles, or the wealthier middle class. After 1850, secondary education was expanded as more middle-class families sought employment in public service and the professions or entry into elite scientific and technical schools. Existing secondary schools also placed more emphasis on practical and scientific education by adding foreign languages and natural sciences to their curriculum.

In the decades after 1870, the functions of the state were extended to include the development of mass education in state-run systems. Between 1870 and 1914, most Western governments began to offer at least primary education to both boys and girls between the ages of six and

A WOMEN'S COLLEGE. Women were largely excluded from male-dominated universities before 1900. Consequently, the demand of women for higher education led to the establishment of women's colleges, most of which were primarily teacher-training schools. This photograph shows a group of women in an astronomy class at Vassar College in the United States in 1878. Maria Mitchell, a famous astronomer, was head of the department.

twelve. States also assumed responsibility for better training of teachers by establishing teacher-training schools.

By the beginning of the twentieth century, many European states, especially in northern and western Europe, had provided state-financed primary schools, salaried and trained teachers, and free, compulsory mass elementary education. Why did European states make this commitment to mass education? Liberals believed that education was important to personal and social improvement and in Catholic countries sought to supplant Catholic education with moral and civic training based on secular values. Even conservatives, however, were attracted to mass education as a means of improving the quality of military recruits and training people in social discipline. In 1875, a German military journal stated: "We in Germany consider education to be one of the principal ways of promoting the strength of the nation and above all military strength."[5]

Another incentive for mass education came from industrialization. In the early Industrial Revolution, unskilled labor was sufficient to meet factory needs, but the new firms of the Second Industrial Revolution demanded skilled labor. Both boys and girls with an elementary education had new possibilities of jobs beyond their villages or small towns, including white-collar jobs in railways, new metro stations, post offices, banking and shipping firms, teaching, and nursing. To industrialists, then, mass education furnished the trained workers they needed.

Nevertheless, the chief motive for mass education was political. For one thing, the increase in suffrage created the need for a more educated electorate. Even more important, however, mass compulsory education instilled patriotism and nationalized the masses, providing an opportunity for even greater national integration. As people lost their ties to local regions and even to religion, nationalism supplied a new faith. The use of a single national language created greater national unity than did loyalty to a ruler.

A nation's motives for universal elementary education largely determined what was taught in the elementary schools. Obviously, indoctrination in national values took on great importance. At the core of the academic curriculum were reading, writing, arithmetic, national history, especially geared to a patriotic view, geography, literature, and some singing and drawing. The education of boys and girls differed, however. Where possible, the sexes were separated. Girls did less math and no science but concentrated on such domestic skills as sewing, washing, ironing, and cooking, all prerequisites for providing a good home for husband and children. Boys were taught some practical skills, such as carpentry, and even some military drill. Most of the elementary schools also inculcated the middle-class virtues of hard work, thrift, sobriety, cleanliness, and respect for the family. For most students, elementary education led to apprenticeship and a job.

The development of compulsory elementary education created a demand for teachers, and most of them were female. In the United States, for example, females constituted two-thirds of all teachers by the 1880s. Many men viewed teaching children as an extension of women's "natural role" as nurturers of children. Moreover, females were paid lower salaries, in itself a considerable incentive for governments to encourage the establishment of teacher-training institutes for women. The first female colleges were really teacher-training schools. It was not until the beginning of the twentieth century that women were permitted to enter the male-dominated universities. In France, 3 percent of university students in 1902 were women; by 1914, their number had increased to 10 percent of the total.

The most immediate result of mass education was an increase in literacy. In Germany, Great Britain, France, and the Scandinavian countries, adult illiteracy was virtually eliminated by 1900. Where there was less schooling, the story is very different. Adult illiteracy rates were 79 percent in Serbia, 78 percent in Romania, and 79 percent in Russia. These were all countries where little had been invested in compulsory mass education.

With the dramatic increase in literacy after 1871 came the rise of mass newspapers, such as the *Evening News* (1881) and *Daily Mail* (1896) in London, which sold millions of copies a day. These newspapers were written in an easily understood style and tended to be extremely sensational. Unlike eighteenth-century newspapers, which were full of serious editorials and lengthy political analysis, these tabloids provided lurid details of crimes, jingoistic diatribes, gossip, and sports news. There were other forms of cheap literature as well. Specialty magazines, such as the *Family Herald* for the entire family, and women's magazines began in the 1860s. Pulp fiction for adults included the extremely popular westerns with their innumerable variations on conflicts between cowboys and Indians. Literature for the masses was but one feature of a new mass culture; another was the emergence of new forms of mass leisure.

Leisure in an Age of Mass Society

In the preindustrial centuries, play or leisure activities had been closely connected to work patterns based on the seasonal or daily cycles typical of agricultural and even artisanal life. The process of industrialization in the nineteenth century had an enormous impact on that traditional pattern. The factory imposed new work patterns that were determined by the rhythms of machines and clocks and removed work time completely from the family environment of farms and workshops. Work and leisure became opposites as leisure was viewed as what people did for fun after work. In fact, the new leisure hours created by the industrial system—evening hours after work, weekends, and later a week or two in the summer—largely determined the contours of the new mass leisure.

New technology also determined the forms of the new mass leisure. The new technology created novel experiences for leisure, such as the Ferris wheel at amusement parks, while the mechanized urban transportation systems of the 1880s meant that even the working classes were no longer dependent on neighborhood bars, but could make their way to athletic games, amusement parks, and dance halls. Likewise, railroads could take people to the beaches on weekends.

The upper and middle classes had created the first market for tourism, but as wages increased and workers were given paid vacations, tourism, too, became another form of mass leisure. Thomas Cook (1808–1892) was a British pioneer of mass tourism. Secretary to a British temperance group, Cook had accepted responsibility for organizing a railroad trip to temperance gatherings in 1841. This experience led him to offer trips on a regular basis after he found that he could make substantial profits by renting special trains, lowering prices, and increasing the number of passengers.

By the late nineteenth century, team sports had also developed into yet another important form of mass leisure. Unlike the old rural games, they were no longer chaotic and spontaneous activities, but became strictly organized with sets of rules and officials to enforce them. These rules were the products of organized athletic groups, such as the English Football Association (1863) and the American Bowling Congress (1895).

The new team sports rapidly became professionalized. In Britain, soccer had its Football Association in 1863 and rugby its Rugby Football Union in 1871. In the United States, the first National Association to recognize professional baseball players was formed in 1863. By 1900, the National League and American League had a monopoly over professional baseball. The development of urban transportation systems made possible the construction of stadiums where thousands could attend, making mass spectator sports into a big business.

The new forms of popular leisure were standardized amusements that drew mass audiences. Although some argued that they were important for improving people, in truth, they mostly served to provide entertainment and distract people from the realities of their work lives. The new mass leisure also represented a significant change from earlier forms of popular culture. Festivals and fairs had been based on an ethos of active community participation, whereas the new forms of mass leisure were standardized for largely passive mass audiences. Amusement parks and professional sports teams were, after all, big businesses organized to make profits.

The National State

Throughout much of the Western world by 1870, the national state had become the focus of people's loyalties and the arena for political activity. Only in Russia, eastern Europe, Austria-Hungary, and Ireland did national groups still struggle for independence.

Change and Tradition in Latin America

In the three decades after 1870, Latin America began to experience an era of prosperity with results that were by no means beneficial for all of its people. As industrialization progressed in Europe and the United States, those countries experienced an ever greater need for food and raw materials. Latin American nations provided these goods, and their increasing prosperity was based to a large extent on the export of one or two commodities from each region, such as wheat and beef from Argentina, coffee from Brazil, nitrates from Chile, coffee and bananas from Central America, and sugar and silver from Peru. Exports from Argentina doubled between 1873 and 1893; Mexican exports quadrupled between 1877 and 1900. These foodstuffs and raw materials were largely exchanged for finished goods—textiles, machines, and luxury products—from Europe and the United States. With economic growth came a boom in foreign investment. Between 1870 and 1913, British investments—mostly in railroads, mining, and public utilities—grew from £85 million to £757 million, which constituted two-thirds of all foreign investment in Latin America. As Latin Americans struggled to create more balanced economies after 1900, they concentrated on increasing industrialization, especially by building textile, food-processing, and construction material factories.

Nevertheless, the growth of the Latin American economy largely came from the export of raw materials, and economic modernization in Latin America simply added to the growing dependency of Latin America on the capitalist nations of the West. Modernization was basically a surface feature of Latin American society, where past patterns still largely prevailed. Rural elites dominated their estates and their rural workers. Although slavery was abolished by 1888, former slaves and their descendants were still at the bottom of society. The Indians remained poverty-stricken, debt servitude was still a way of life, and Latin America remained economically dependent on foreigners. Despite its economic growth, Latin America was still an underdeveloped region of the world.

The prosperity that resulted from the development of an export economy had both social and political repercussions. One result socially was the modernization of the elites, who grew determined to pursue their vision of modern progress. Large landowners increasingly sought ways to rationalize their production methods in order to make greater profits. As a result, cattle ranchers in Argentina and coffee barons in Brazil became more aggressive entrepreneurs.

Another result of the new prosperity was the growth in the middle sectors of Latin American society—lawyers, merchants, shopkeepers, businesspeople, schoolteachers, professors, bureaucrats, and military officers. These middle sectors, which made up only 5 to 10 percent of the population, depending on the country, were hardly large enough in numbers to constitute a true middle class. Nevertheless, after 1900, the middle sectors continued to expand. Regardless of the country, they shared some common characteristics. They lived in the cities, sought education and decent incomes, and increasingly saw the United States as the model to emulate, especially in regard to industrialization and education. The middle sectors in Latin America sought liberal reform, not revolution, and the elites found it relatively easy to co-opt them by extending them the right to vote.

As Latin American export economies boomed, the working class expanded, which in turn led to the growth of labor unions, especially after 1914. Radical unions often advocated the use of the general strike as an instrument for change. By and large, however, the governing elites succeeded in stifling the political influence of the working class by restricting their right to vote. The need for industrial labor also led Latin American countries to encourage European immigrants. Between 1880 and 1914, three million Europeans, primarily Italians and Spaniards, settled in Argentina. Over 100,000 Europeans, mostly Italian, Portuguese, and Spanish, arrived in Brazil each year between 1891 and 1900.

As in Europe and the United States, industrialization led to urbanization, evident in both the emergence of new cities and the rapid growth of old ones. Buenos Aires (the "Paris" of South America) had 750,000 inhabitants by 1900 and two million by 1914, which constituted a fourth of Argentina's population. By that time, urban dwellers made up 53 percent of Argentina's population overall. Brazil and Chile also witnessed a dramatic increase in the number of urban dwellers.

Political Change in Latin America

Latin America also experienced a political transformation after 1870. Large landowners began to take a more direct interest in national politics, sometimes expressed by a

EMILIANO ZAPATA. The inability of Francisco Madero to carry out far-reaching reforms led to a more radical upheaval in the Mexican countryside. Emiliano Zapata led a band of Indians in a revolt against the large landowners of southern Mexico and issued his own demands for land reform.

ZAPATA AND LAND REFORM

Emiliano Zapata was a sharecropper on a sugar plantation in Morelos, a mountainous state in southern Mexico. Using the slogan "Land and Liberty," Zapata formed a guerrilla band of Indians and led them in revolt against the haciendas of southern Mexico, burning the houses and sugar refineries. Convinced that the new president of Mexico, Francisco Madero, would not go far enough with land reform, Zapata issued his own plan, the Plan of Ayala, from which these excerpts are taken.

THE PLAN OF AYALA

The Liberating Plan of the sons of the State of Morelos, members of the insurgent army that demands the . . . reforms that it judges convenient and necessary for the welfare of the Mexican Nation.

We, the undersigned, constituted as a Revolutionary Junta, in order to maintain and obtain the fulfillment of the promises made by the revolution of November 20, 1910, solemnly proclaim in the face of the civilized world . . . , so that it may judge us, the principles that we have formulated in order to destroy the tyranny that oppresses us. . . .

1. Considering that the President of the Republic, Don Francisco I. Madero, has made a bloody mockery of Effective Suffrage by . . . entering into an infamous alliance with the . . . enemies of the Revolution that he proclaimed, in order to forge the chains of a new dictatorship more hateful and terrible than that of Porfirio Díaz. . . . For these reasons we declare the said Francisco I. Madero unfit to carry out the promises of the Revolution of which he was the author. . . .
4. The Revolutionary Junta of the State of Morelos formally proclaims to the Mexican people: That it endorses the Plan of San Luis Potosí [Madero's revolutionary plan] with the additions stated below for the benefit of the oppressed peoples, and that it will defend its principles until victory or death. . . .
6. As an additional part of the plan we proclaim, be it known: that the lands, woods, and waters usurped . . . through tyranny and venal justice henceforth belong to the towns or citizens who have corresponding titles to those properties, of which they were despoiled by the bad faith of our oppressors. They shall retain possession of the said properties at all costs, arms in hand. The usurpers who think they have a right to the said lands may state their claims before special tribunals to be established upon the triumph of the Revolution.
7. Since the immense majority of Mexican towns and citizens own nothing but the ground on which they stand and endure a miserable existence, denied the opportunity to improve their social condition or to devote themselves to industry or agriculture because a few individuals monopolize the lands, woods, and waters—for these reasons the great estates shall be expropriated, with indemnification to the owners of one-third of such monopolies, in order that the towns and citizens of Mexico may obtain colonies, town sites, and arable lands. Thus the welfare of the Mexican people shall be promoted in all respects.
8. The properties of those [landowners] who directly or indirectly oppose the present Plan shall be seized by the nation, and two thirds of their value shall be used for war indemnities and pensions for the widows and orphans of the soldiers who may perish in the struggle for this Plan.

direct involvement in governing. In Argentina and Chile, for example, landholding elites controlled the governments, and although they produced constitutions similar to those of the United States and Europe, they were careful to ensure their power by regulating voting rights.

In some countries, large landowners made use of dictators to maintain the interests of the ruling elite. Porfirio Díaz, who ruled Mexico from 1876 to 1910, established a conservative, centralized government with the support of the army, foreign capitalists, large landowners, and the Catholic church. All of them benefited from their alliance. But there were forces for change in Mexico that precipitated a true social revolution. The Mexican Revolution has long been considered a model for nationalistic revolutionary change.

Under Díaz's dictatorial regime, the real wages of the working class had declined. Moreover, 95 percent of the rural population owned no land, while about one thousand families owned almost all of Mexico. When a liberal landowner, Francisco Madero, forced Díaz from power, he opened the door to a wider revolution. Madero's ineffectiveness triggered a demand for agrarian reform led by Emiliano Zapata, who aroused the masses of landless peasants and began to seize the haciendas of the wealthy landholders (see the box above). Between 1910 and 1920, the revolution caused untold destruction to the Mexican economy. Finally, a new constitution in 1917 established a strong presidency, initiated land reform policies, established limits on foreign investors, and set an agenda for social welfare for workers. The revolution also led to an outpouring of nationalistic pride. Intellectuals and artists in particular sought to capture what was unique about Mexico with special emphasis on its Indian past. As the Mexican minister of education said, "Tired, disgusted of all this copied civilization, . . . we wish to cease being Europe's spiritual colonies."

By this time, a new power had begun to wield its influence over Latin America. At the beginning of the twentieth century, the United States, which had begun to emerge as a great world power, increasingly interfered in the affairs of its southern neighbors. As a result of the Spanish-American War (1898), Cuba became an American protectorate while Puerto Rico was annexed outright to the United States. American investments in Latin America soon followed; so too did American resolve to protect these investments. Between 1898 and 1934, U.S. military forces were sent to Cuba, Mexico, Guatemala, Honduras, Nicaragua, Panama, Colombia, Haiti, and the Dominican Republic to protect American interests. Some expeditions remained for many years; U.S. Marines were in Haiti from 1915 to 1934, while Nicaragua was occupied from 1909 to 1933. At the same time, the United States became the chief foreign investor in Latin America.

The Rise of the United States

Four years of bloody civil war had preserved American national unity. The old South had been destroyed; one-fifth of its adult white male population had been killed, and four million black slaves had been freed. For a while at least, a program of radical change in the South was attempted. Slavery was abolished by the Thirteenth Amendment to the U.S. Constitution in 1865, while the Fourteenth and Fifteenth Amendments extended citizenship to blacks and guaranteed them the right to vote. Radical Reconstruction in the early 1870s tried to create a new South based on the principle of the equality of black and white people, but the changes were soon largely undone. Militia organizations, such as the Ku Klux Klan, used violence to discourage blacks from voting. A new system of sharecropping made blacks once again economically dependent on white landowners. New state laws stripped blacks of their right to vote. By the end of the 1870s, supporters of white supremacy were back in power everywhere in the South.

Between 1860 and World War I, the United States made the shift from an agrarian to a mighty industrial nation. American heavy industry stood unchallenged in 1900. In that year, the Carnegie Steel Company alone produced more steel than Great Britain's entire steel industry. Industrialization also led to urbanization. While established cities, such as New York, Philadelphia, and Boston, grew even larger, other moderate-size cities, such as Pittsburgh, grew by leaps and bounds because of industrialization. Whereas 20 percent of Americans lived in cities in 1860, over 40 percent did in 1900.

By 1900, the United States had become the world's richest nation and greatest industrial power. Yet serious questions remained about the quality of American life. In 1890, the richest 9 percent of Americans owned an incredible 71 percent of all the wealth. Labor unrest over unsafe working conditions, strict work discipline, and periodic cycles of devastating unemployment led workers to organize. By the turn of the century, one national organization, the American Federation of Labor, emerged as labor's dominant voice. Its lack of real power, however, is reflected in its membership figures. In 1900, it constituted but 8.4 percent of the American industrial labor force.

During the so-called Progressive Era after 1900, the reform of many features of American life became a primary issue. At the state level, reforming governors sought to achieve clean government by introducing elements of direct democracy, such as direct primaries for selecting nominees for public office. State governments also enacted economic and social legislation, such as laws that governed hours, wages, and working conditions, especially for women and children. The realization that state laws were ineffective in dealing with nationwide problems, however, led to a progressive movement at the national level.

National progressivism was evident in the administrations of both Theodore Roosevelt and Woodrow Wilson. Under Roosevelt (1901–1909), the Meat Inspection Act and Pure Food and Drug Act provided for a limited degree of federal regulation of corrupt industrial practices. Roosevelt's expressed principle, "We draw the line against misconduct, not against wealth," guaranteed that public protection would have to be within limits tolerable to big corporations. Wilson (1913–1921) was responsible for the creation of a graduated federal income tax and a Federal Reserve System that permitted the federal government to have a role in important economic decisions formerly made by bankers. Like European states, the United States was moving slowly into policies that extended the functions of the state.

THE UNITED STATES AS A WORLD POWER

At the end of the nineteenth century, the United States began to expand abroad. The Samoan Islands in the Pacific became the first important American colony; the Hawaiian Islands were the next to fall. By 1887, American settlers had gained control of the sugar industry on the Hawaiian Islands. As more Americans settled in Hawaii, they sought to gain political power. When Queen Liliuokalani tried to strengthen the power of the monarchy in order to keep the islands for the native peoples, the American government sent United States Marines to "protect" American lives. The queen was deposed, and Hawaii was annexed by the United States in 1898.

The American defeat of Spain in the Spanish-American war in 1898 encouraged Americans to extend their empire by acquiring Cuba, Puerto Rico, Guam, and the Philippine Islands. Although the Filipinos hoped for independence, the Americans refused to grant it. As

President McKinley said, the United States had the duty "to educate the Filipinos and uplift and Christianize them," a remarkable statement in view of the fact that most of them had been Roman Catholics for centuries. It took three years and 60,000 troops to pacify the Philippines and establish American control. By the beginning of the twentieth century, the United States had become another Western imperialist power.

The Growth of Canada

Canada, too, faced problems of national unity between 1870 and 1914. At the beginning of 1870, the Dominion of Canada had only four provinces: Quebec, Ontario, Nova Scotia, and New Brunswick. With the addition of two more provinces in 1871—Manitoba and British Columbia—the Dominion of Canada now extended from the Atlantic Ocean to the Pacific. But real unity was difficult to achieve because of the distrust between the English-speaking and French-speaking peoples of Canada. Fortunately for Canada, Wilfred Laurier, who became the first French-Canadian prime minister in 1896, was able to reconcile Canada's two major groups and resolve the issue of separate schools for French-Canadians. Laurier's administration also witnessed increased industrialization and successfully encouraged immigrants from central and eastern Europe to help populate Canada's vast territories.

Europe

The domestic policies of the major European states focused on five major themes: the achievement of liberal practices (constitutions, parliaments, and individual liberties); the growth of political democracy through universal male suffrage; the organization of mass political parties as a result of a widened electorate; the rise of socialist, working-class parties; and the enactment of social welfare measures to meet the demands of the working classes. These developments varied in expression from place to place. In general, western European states (France and Britain) had the greatest success with the growth of parliamentary governments. Central European states (Germany, Austria-Hungary) had the trappings of parliamentary government, but authoritarian forces, especially powerful monarchies and conservative social groups, remained strong. In eastern Europe, especially Russia, the old system of autocracy was barely touched by the winds of change.

WESTERN EUROPE: THE GROWTH OF POLITICAL DEMOCRACY

By 1871, Great Britain had a functioning two-party parliamentary system. For fifty years, the Liberals and Conservatives alternated in power at regular intervals, although they also shared some common features. Both were dominated by a ruling class comprised of a coalition of aristocratic landowners frequently involved in industrial and financial activities and upper-middle-class businessmen. And both competed with each other in supporting legislation that expanded the right to vote. Reform Acts in 1867 and 1884 greatly expanded the number of adult males who could vote, and by the end of World War I, all males over twenty-one and women over thirty could vote. In 1911, parliamentary legislation curtailed the power of the House of Lords and instituted the payment of salaries to members of the House of Commons, which further democratized that institution by at least opening the door to people other than the wealthy. By the beginning of World War I, political democracy had become well entrenched and was soon accompanied by social welfare measures for the working class.

The growth of trade unions, which began to advocate more radical change of the economic system, and the emergence in 1900 of the Labour Party, which dedicated itself to workers' interests, caused the Liberals to favor new social legislation. The Liberals, who held the government from 1906 to 1914, perceived that they would have to initiate a program of social welfare or lose the support of the workers. Therefore, they abandoned the classical principles of *laissez-faire* and voted for a series of social reforms. The National Insurance Act of 1911 provided benefits for workers in case of sickness and unemployment, to be paid for by compulsory contributions from workers, employers, and the state. Additional legislation provided a small pension for those over seventy and compensation for those injured in accidents while at work. While the benefits of the program and tax increases were both modest, they were the first hesitant steps toward the future British welfare state.

In France, the confusion that ensued after the collapse of the Second Empire finally ended in 1875 when an improvised constitution established a republican form of government. This constitution established a bicameral legislature, with an upper house or Senate elected indirectly and a lower house or Chamber of Deputies chosen by universal male suffrage. The powers of the president, chosen by the legislature to be the executive of the government for seven years, were deliberately left vague. The premier (or prime minister) led the government, and he and his ministers were responsible not to the president, but to the Chamber of Deputies. The Constitution of 1875, intended only as a stopgap measure, solidified the republic—the Third Republic—which lasted sixty-five years. France failed, however, to develop a strong parliamentary system on the British two-party model because the existence of a dozen political parties forced the premier to depend on a coalition of parties to stay in power. The Third Republic was notorious for its changes of government. Between 1875 and 1914, there were no fewer than fifty cabinet changes; during the same

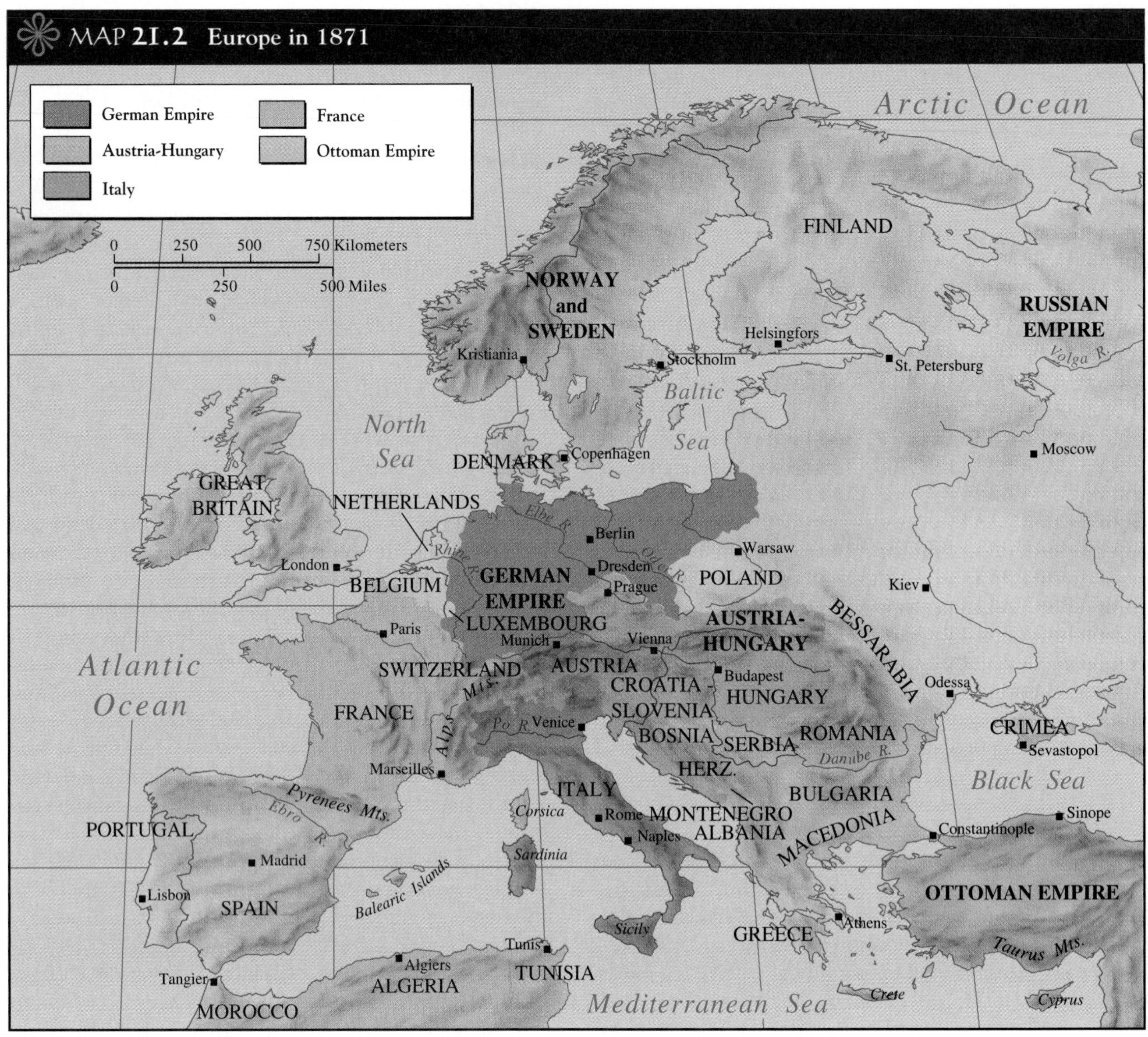

period, the British had eleven. Nevertheless, the government's moderation gradually encouraged more and more middle-class and peasant support, and by 1914, the Third Republic commanded the loyalty of most French people.

By 1870, Italy had emerged as a geographically united state with pretensions to great power status. Its internal weaknesses, however, gave that claim a particularly hollow ring. Sectional differences—a poverty-stricken south and an industrializing north—weakened any sense of community. Chronic turmoil between labor and industry undermined the social fabric. The Italian government was unable to deal effectively with these problems because of the extensive corruption among government officials and the lack of stability created by ever changing government coalitions. Even Italy's pretensions to great power status proved hollow when Italy became the first European power to lose to an African state, Ethiopia, a disgrace that later led to the costly (but successful) attempt to compensate by conquering Libya in 1911 and 1912.

CENTRAL AND EASTERN EUROPE: PERSISTENCE OF THE OLD ORDER

The constitution of the new imperial Germany begun by Bismarck in 1871 provided for a federal system with a bicameral legislature. The lower house of the German parliament, known as the Reichstag, was elected on the basis of universal male suffrage, but it did not have ministerial responsibility. Ministers of government, among whom the most important was the chancellor, were responsible not to the parliament, but to the emperor.

The emperor also commanded the armed forces and controlled foreign policy and internal administration. Although the creation of a parliament elected by universal male suffrage presented opportunities for the growth of a real political democracy, it failed to develop in Germany before World War I. Bismarck's high-handed tactics and the army's independence were two major reasons why it did not.

During the reign of Emperor William II (1888–1918), the new imperial Germany begun by Bismarck continued as an "authoritarian, conservative, military-bureaucratic power state." By the end of William's reign, Germany had become the strongest military and industrial power on the Continent. Over 50 percent of German workers had jobs in industry, while only 30 percent of the workforce was still in agriculture. Urban centers had mushroomed in number and size. These rapid changes in Wilhelmine Germany helped to produce a society torn between modernization and traditionalism. With the expansion of industry and cities came demands for more political participation and growing sentiment for reforms that would produce greater democratization. Conservative forces, especially the landowning nobility and representatives of heavy industry, two of the powerful ruling groups in Germany, tried to block it by supporting William II's activist foreign policy of finding Germany's "place in the sun." Expansionism, they believed, would divert people from demands for further democratization.

The tensions in German society created by the conflict between modernization and traditionalism were also manifested in a new, radicalized, right-wing politics. A number of nationalist pressure groups arose to support nationalistic goals. Antisocialist and antiliberal, such groups as the Pan-German League stressed strong German nationalism and advocated imperialism as a tool to overcome social divisions and unite all classes. They were also anti-Semitic and denounced Jews as the destroyers of national community.

After the creation of the dual monarchy of Austria-Hungary in 1867, the Austrian part received a constitution that theoretically recognized the equality of the nationalities and established a parliamentary system with the principle of ministerial responsibility. However, Emperor Francis Joseph (1848–1916) largely ignored ministerial responsibility by personally appointing and dismissing his ministers and ruling by decree when parliament was not in session.

The problem of the various nationalities remained a difficult one. The German minority that governed Austria felt increasingly threatened by the Czechs, Poles, and other Slavic groups within the empire. The granting of universal male suffrage in 1907 served only to exacerbate the problem when nationalities that had played no role in the government now agitated in the parliament for autonomy. This led prime ministers after 1900 to ignore the parliament and rely increasingly on imperial emergency decrees to govern. On the eve of World War I, the Austro-Hungarian Empire was as far away as ever from solving its minorities problem.

In Russia, the assassination of Alexander II in 1881 convinced his son and successor, Alexander III (1881–1894), that reform had been a mistake, and he quickly returned to the repressive measures of earlier tsars. Advocates of constitutional monarchy and social reform, along with revolutionary groups, were persecuted. Entire districts of Russia were placed under martial law if the government suspected the inhabitants of treason. When

CHRONOLOGY

THE NATIONAL STATE: 1870–1914

Great Britain	
Reform Act	1884
Formation of Labour Party	1900
Restriction of power of the House of Lords	1911
National Insurance Act	1911
France	
Surrender of French Provisional Government to Germany	1871 (Jan. 28)
Republican constitution (Third Republic)	1875
Germany	
Bismarck as chancellor	1871–1890
Emperor William II	1888–1918
Austria-Hungary	
Emperor Francis Joseph	1848–1916
Imperial Russia	
Tsar Alexander III	1881–1894
Tsar Nicholas II	1894–1917
First Congress of Social Democratic Party	1898
Russo-Japanese War	1904–1905
Revolution	1905
Latin America	
Rule of Porfirio Díaz in Mexico	1876–1910
Mexican Revolution begins	1910
United States	
Spanish-American War	1898
Theodore Roosevelt	1901–1909
Woodrow Wilson	1913–1921

Alexander III died, his weak son and successor, Nicholas II (1894–1917), began his rule with his father's conviction that the absolute power of the tsars should be preserved: "I shall maintain the principle of autocracy just as firmly and unflinchingly as did my unforgettable father."[6] But conditions were changing, especially with the growth of industrialization, and the tsar's approach was not realistic in view of the new circumstances he faced.

Although industrialization came late to Russia, it progressed rapidly after 1890, especially with the assistance of foreign investment capital. By 1900, Russia had become the fourth largest producer of steel, behind the United States, Germany, and Great Britain. At the same time, Russia was turning out half of the world's production of oil. With industrialization came factories, an industrial working class, and the development of socialist parties, although repression in Russia soon forced them to go underground and be revolutionary. The Marxist Social Democratic Party, for example, held its first congress in Minsk in 1898, but the arrest of its leaders caused the next one to be held in Brussels in 1903, attended by Russian émigrés. The Social Revolutionaries worked to overthrow the tsarist autocracy and establish peasant socialism. Having no other outlet for opposition to the regime, they advocated political terrorism and attempted to assassinate government officials and members of the ruling dynasty. The growing opposition to the tsarist regime finally exploded into revolution in 1905.

The defeat of the Russians by the Japanese in 1904–1905 encouraged antigovernment groups to rebel against the tsarist regime. Nicholas II granted civil liberties and agreed to create a Duma or legislative assembly elected directly by a broad franchise. But real constitutional monarchy proved short-lived. Already by 1907, the tsar had curtailed the power of the Duma and relied again on the army and bureaucracy to rule Russia.

International Rivalry and the Coming of War

Between 1871 and 1914, Europeans experienced a long period of peace. There were wars (including wars of conquest in the non-Western world) but none involved the great powers. There were, however, a series of crises that might easily have led to general war. Until 1890, Bismarck, the chancellor of Germany, exercised a restraining influence on Europeans. He realized that the emergence in 1871 of a unified Germany as the most powerful state on the Continent had upset the balance of power established at Vienna in 1815. Bismarck knew that Germany's success frightened Europeans. Fearful of a possible anti-German alliance between France and Russia and possibly even Austria, Bismarck made a defensive alliance with Austria in 1879. Both powers agreed to support each other in the event of an attack by Russia. In 1882, this German-Austrian alliance was enlarged with the entrance of Italy, angry with the French over conflicting colonial ambitions in North Africa. The Triple Alliance of 1882 committed the three powers to support the existing political and social order while providing a defensive alliance against France. At the same time, Bismarck maintained a separate treaty with Russia and tried to remain on good terms with Great Britain.

CHRONOLOGY

EUROPEAN DIPLOMACY: 1871–1914

Triple Alliance: Germany, Austria, and Italy	1882
Military alliance: Russia and France	1894
Entente Cordiale: France and Britain	1904
Triple Entente: France, Britain, and Russia	1907
First Balkan War	1912
Second Balkan War	1913

When Emperor William II cashiered Bismarck in 1890 and took over direction of Germany's foreign policy, he embarked on an activist foreign policy dedicated to enhancing German power by finding, as he put it, Germany's rightful "place in the sun." One of his changes in Bismarck's foreign policy was to drop the treaty with Russia, which he viewed as being at odds with Germany's alliance with Austria. The ending of the alliance achieved what Bismarck had feared: it brought France and Russia together. Republican France leapt at the chance to draw closer to tsarist Russia, and in 1894 the two powers concluded a military alliance. During the next ten years, German policies abroad caused the British to draw closer to France. By 1907, a loose confederation of Great Britain, France, and Russia—known as the Triple Entente—stood opposed to the Triple Alliance of Germany, Austria-Hungary, and Italy. Europe became divided into two opposing camps that became more and more inflexible and unwilling to compromise. When the members of the two alliances became involved in a new series of crises between 1908 and 1913 over the remnants of the Ottoman Empire in the Balkans, the stage was set for World War I.

The Ottoman Empire and Nationalism in the Balkans

Like the Austro-Hungarian Empire, the Ottoman Empire was severely troubled by the nationalist aspirations of its subject peoples, especially in the Balkans. Corruption and inefficiency had so weakened the Ottoman Empire that only the interference of the great European powers, who were fearful of each other's designs on the empire, kept it alive.

In the course of the nineteenth century, the Balkan provinces of the Ottoman Empire gradually gained their freedom, although the rivalry in the region between Austria and Russia complicated the process. Serbia had already received a large degree of autonomy in 1829, although it remained a province of the Ottoman Empire until 1878. Greece became an independent kingdom in 1830 after its successful revolt. By the Treaty of Adrianople in 1829, Russia received a protectorate over the principalities of Moldavia and Walachia but was forced to give them up after the Crimean War. In 1861, Moldavia and Walachia were merged into the state of Romania. Not until Russia's defeat of the Ottoman Empire in 1878, however, was Romania recognized as completely independent, as was Serbia at the same time. Although freed from Turkish rule, Montenegro was placed under an Austrian protectorate, while Bulgaria achieved autonomous status under Russian protection. The other Balkan territories of Bosnia and Herzegovina were placed under Austrian protection; Austria could occupy but not annex them. Despite these gains, by the end of the nineteenth century, the forces of Balkan nationalism were by no means stilled.

CRISES IN THE BALKANS, 1908–1913

The Bosnian Crisis of 1908–1909 began a chain of events that eventually spun out of control. Since 1878, Bosnia and Herzegovina had been under the protection of Austria, but in 1908 Austria took the drastic step of annexing these two Slavic-speaking territories. Serbia was outraged at this action because it dashed the Serbs' hopes of creating a large Serbian kingdom that would include most of the south Slavs. But this possibility was precisely why the Austrians had annexed Bosnia and Herzegovina. The creation of a large Serbia would be a threat to the unity of their empire with its large Slavic population. The Russians, as protectors of their fellow Slavs and also desiring to increase their own authority in the Balkans, supported the Serbs and opposed the Austrian action. Backed by the Russians, the Serbs prepared for war against Austria. At this point, William II intervened and demanded that the Russians accept Austria's annexation of Bosnia and Herzegovina or face war with Germany. Weakened from their defeat in the Russo-Japanese War in 1904–1905, the Russians were afraid to risk war and backed down. Humiliated, the Russians vowed revenge.

European attention returned to the Balkans in 1912 when Serbia, Bulgaria, Montenegro, and Greece organized a Balkan League and defeated the Turks in the First Balkan War. When the victorious allies were unable to agree on how to divide the conquered Turkish provinces of Macedonia and Albania, a second Balkan War erupted in 1913. Greece, Serbia, Romania, and the Ottoman Empire attacked and defeated Bulgaria. As a result, Bulgaria obtained only a small part of Macedonia, and most of the rest was divided between Serbia and Greece. Yet Serbia's aspirations remained unfulfilled. The two Balkan wars left the inhabitants embittered and created more tensions among the great powers.

MAP **21.3** **The Balkans in 1913**

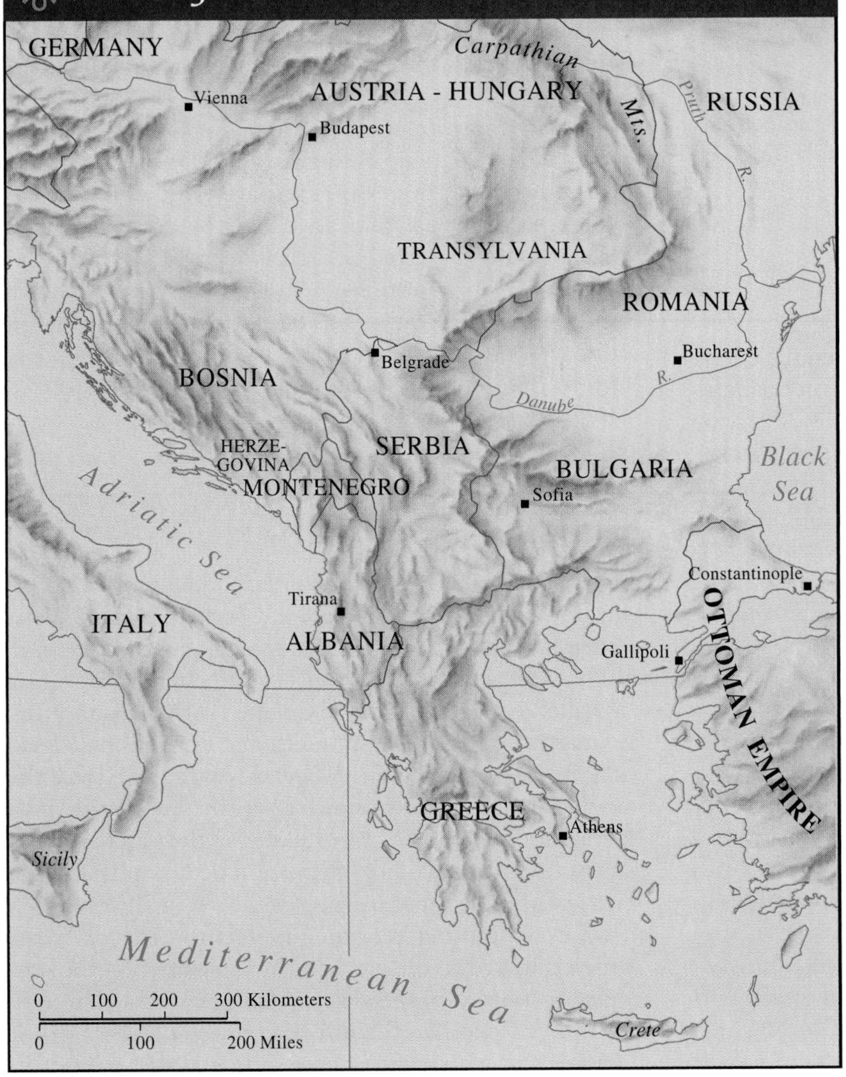

OTTOMAN ARMY IN RETREAT. In 1912, a coalition of Serbia, Bulgaria, Montenegro, and Greece defeated the Turks and took possession of the Ottoman provinces of Macedonia and Albania. This painting shows the Ottoman army in retreat, pursued by Bulgarian forces.

One of Serbia's major ambitions had been to acquire Albanian territory that would give it a port on the Adriatic. At the London Conference arranged by Austria at the end of the two Balkan wars, the Austrians had blocked Serbia's wishes by creating an independent Albania. The Germans, as Austrian allies, had supported this move. In their frustration, Serbian nationalists increasingly portrayed the Austrians as evil monsters who were keeping the Serbs from becoming a great nation. As Serbia's chief supporters, the Russians were also upset by the turn of events in the Balkans. A feeling had grown among Russian leaders that they could not back down again in the event of a confrontation with Austria or Germany in the Balkans. Moreover, as a result of the Balkan wars, both Russia and Austria expressed discontent that their supposed friends and allies, Great Britain and Germany, had not done enough to support them. This made the British and Germans more determined to support their allies in order to avoid endangering their alliances.

Austria-Hungary had achieved another of its aims, but it was left convinced that Serbia was a mortal threat to its empire and must at some point be crushed. Meanwhile, the French and Russian governments renewed their alliance and promised each other that they would not back down at the next crisis. Britain drew closer to France. By the beginning of 1914, two armed camps viewed each other with suspicion. The European "age of progress" was about to come to an inglorious and bloody end.

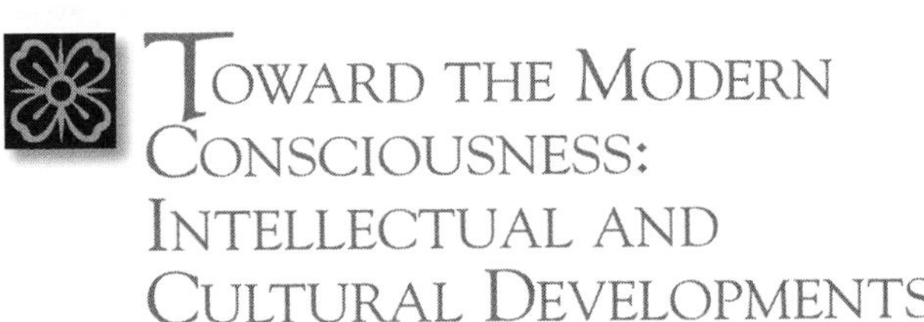

Toward the Modern Consciousness: Intellectual and Cultural Developments

Before 1914, most Westerners continued to believe in the values and ideals that had been generated by the impact of the Scientific Revolution and the Enlightenment. *Reason*, *science*, and *progress* were still important words in the European vocabulary. The ability of human beings to improve themselves and achieve a better society seemed to be well demonstrated by a rising standard of living, urban improvements, and mass education. Such products of modern technology as electric lights, phonographs, and automobiles reinforced the popular prestige of science and the belief in the ability of the human mind to understand the universe. Between 1870 and 1914, however, a dramatic transformation in the realm of ideas and culture challenged many of these assumptions. A new view of the physical universe, alternative views of human nature, and radically innovative forms of literary and artistic expression shattered old beliefs and opened the way to a modern consciousness. Although the real impact of many of these ideas was not felt until after World War I, they served to provoke a sense of confusion and anxiety before 1914 that would become even more pronounced after the war.

Developments in the Sciences: The Emergence of a New Physics

Science was one of the chief pillars underlying the optimistic and rationalistic view of the world that many Westerners shared in the nineteenth century. Supposedly based on hard facts and cold reason, science offered a certainty of belief in the orderliness of nature that was comforting to many people for whom traditional religious beliefs no longer had much meaning. Many naively believed that the application of already known scientific laws would give humanity a complete understanding of the physical world and an accurate picture of reality. The new physics dramatically altered that perspective.

Throughout much of the nineteenth century, Westerners adhered to the mechanical conception of the universe postulated by the classical physics of Isaac Newton. In this perspective, the universe was viewed as a giant machine in which time, space, and matter were objective realities that existed independently of those observing them. Matter was thought to be composed of indivisible and solid material bodies called atoms.

These views were first seriously questioned at the end of the nineteenth century. The French scientist Marie Curie (1867–1934) and her husband, Pierre (1859–1906), discovered that an element called radium gave off rays of radiation that apparently came from within the atom itself. Atoms were not simply hard, material bodies but small worlds containing such subatomic particles as electrons and protons, which behaved in seemingly random and inexplicable fashion. Inquiry into the disintegrative process within atoms became a central theme of the new physics.

Building on this work, in 1900 a Berlin physicist, Max Planck (1858–1947), rejected the belief that a heated body radiates energy in a steady stream but maintained instead that it did so discontinuously, in irregular packets of energy that he called "quanta." The quantum theory raised fundamental questions about the subatomic realm of the atom. By 1900, the old view of atoms as the basic building blocks of the material world was being seriously questioned, and the world of Newtonian physics was in trouble.

Albert Einstein (1879–1955), a German-born patent officer working in Switzerland, pushed these new theories into new terrain. In 1905, Einstein published a paper entitled "The Electro-dynamics of Moving Bodies" that contained his special theory of relativity. According to relativity theory, space and time are not absolute, but relative to the observer, and both are interwoven into what Einstein called a four-dimensional space-time continuum. Neither space nor time had an existence independent of human experience. As Einstein later explained simply to a journalist: "It was formerly believed that if all material things disappeared out of the universe, time and space would be left. According to the relativity theory, however, time and space disappear together with the things."[7] Moreover, matter and energy reflected the relativity of time and space. Einstein concluded that matter was nothing but another form of energy. His epochal formula $E = mc^2$—that the energy of each particle of matter is equivalent to its mass times the square of the velocity of light—was the key theory explaining the vast energies contained within the atom. It led to the atomic age.

Sigmund Freud and the Emergence of Psychoanalysis

At the end of the nineteenth and beginning of the twentieth century, the Viennese doctor Sigmund Freud (1856–1939) put forth a series of theories that undermined optimism about the rational nature of the human mind. Freud's thought, like the new physics, added to the uncertainties of the age. His major ideas were published in 1900 in his *Interpretation of Dreams,* which laid the basic foundation for what came to be known as psychoanalysis.

According to Freud, human behavior was strongly determined by the unconscious, by former experiences and inner drives of which people were largely oblivious. To explore the contents of the unconscious, Freud relied on both hypnosis and dreams, but the latter were dressed in an elaborate code that needed to be deciphered if the contents were to be properly understood.

But why did some experiences whose influence persisted in controlling an individual's life remain unconscious? According to Freud, this was repression (see the box on p. 652), a process by which unsettling experiences were blotted from conscious awareness but still continued to influence behavior because they had become part of the unconscious. To explain how repression worked, Freud elaborated an intricate theory of the inner life of human beings.

According to Freud, a human being's inner life was a battleground of three contending forces, the id, ego, and superego. The id was the center of unconscious drives and

MARIE CURIE. Marie Curie was born in Warsaw, Poland, but studied at the University of Paris, where she received degrees in both physics and mathematics. She was the first woman to win two Nobel Prizes, one in 1903 in physics and another in chemistry in 1911. She is shown here in her Paris laboratory in 1921.

FREUD AND THE CONCEPT OF REPRESSION

Freud's psychoanalytical theories resulted from his attempt to understand the world of the unconscious. This excerpt is taken from a lecture given in 1909 in which Freud describes how he arrived at his theory of the role of repression. Although Freud valued science and reason, his theories of the unconscious produced a new image of the human being as governed less by reason than by irrational forces.

SIGMUND FREUD, *FIVE LECTURES ON PSYCHOANALYSIS*

I did not abandon it [his technique of encouraging patients to reveal forgotten experiences], however, before the observations I made during my use of it afforded me decisive evidence. I found confirmation of the fact that the forgotten memories were not lost. They were in the patient's possession and were ready to emerge in association to what was still known by him; but there was some force that prevented them from becoming conscious and compelled them to remain unconscious. The existence of this force could be assumed with certainty, since one became aware of an effort corresponding to it if, in opposition to it, one tried to introduce the unconscious memories into the patient's consciousness. The force which was maintaining the pathological condition became apparent in the form of resistance on the part of the patient.

It was on this idea of resistance, then, that I based my view of the course of psychical events in hysteria. In order to effect a recovery, it had proved necessary to remove these resistances. Starting out from the mechanism of cure, it now became possible to construct quite definite ideas of the origin of the illness. The same forces which, in the form of resistance, were now offering opposition to the forgotten material's being made conscious, must formerly have brought about the forgetting and must have pushed the pathogenic experiences in question out of consciousness. I gave the name of "repression" to this hypothetical process, and I considered that it was proved by the undeniable existence of resistance.

The further question could then be raised as to what these forces were and what the determinants were of the repression in which we now recognized the pathogenic mechanism of hysteria. A comparative study of the pathogenic situations which we had come to know through the cathartic procedure made it possible to answer this question. All these experiences had involved the emergence of a wishful impulse which was in sharp contrast to the subject's other wishes and which proved incompatible with the ethical and aesthetic standards of his personality. There had been a short conflict, and the end of this internal struggle was that the idea which had appeared before consciousness as the vehicle of this irreconcilable wish fell a victim to repression, was pushed out of consciousness with all its attached memories, and was forgotten. Thus the incompatibility of the wish in question with the patient's ego was the motive for the repression; the subject's ethical and other standards were the repressing forces. An acceptance of the incompatible wishful impulse or a prolongation of the conflict would have produced a high degree of unpleasure; this unpleasure was avoided by means of repression, which was thus revealed as one of the devices serving to protect the mental personality.

was ruled by what Freud termed the pleasure principle. As creatures of desire, human beings directed their energy toward pleasure and away from pain. The id contained all kinds of lustful drives and desires, crude appetites and impulses, love and hates. The ego was the seat of reason and hence the coordinator of the inner life. It was governed by the reality principle. Although humans were dominated by the pleasure principle, a true pursuit of pleasure was not feasible. The reality principle meant that people rejected pleasure so that they might live together in society; reality thwarted the unlimited pursuit of pleasure. The superego was the locus of conscience and represented the inhibitions and moral values that society in general and parents in particular imposed on people. The superego served to force the ego to curb the unacceptable pressures of the id.

Thus, the conflict among the id, ego, and superego dominated the human being's inner life. The ego and superego exerted restraining influences on the unconscious id and repressed or kept out of consciousness what they wanted to. Repression began in childhood, and psychoanalysis was accomplished through a dialogue between psychotherapist and patient in which the therapist probed deeply into memory in order to retrace the chain of repression all the way back to its childhood origins. By making the conscious mind aware of the unconscious and its repressed contents, the patient's psychic conflict was resolved.

The Impact of Darwin: Social Darwinism and Racism

In the second half of the nineteenth century, scientific theories were sometimes wrongly applied to achieve other ends. The application of Darwin's principle of organic evolution to the social order came to be known as Social

Darwinism. The most popular exponent of Social Darwinism was the British philosopher Herbert Spencer (1820–1903). Using Darwin's terminology, Spencer argued that societies were organisms that evolved through time from a struggle with their environment. Progress came from "the struggle for survival," as the "fit"—the strong—advanced while the weak declined. Some prominent businessmen used Social Darwinism to explain their success in the competitive business world. The strong and fit, the able and energetic had risen to the top; the stupid and lazy had fallen by the wayside.

Darwin's ideas were also applied to human society in an even more radical way by rabid nationalists and racists. In their pursuit of national greatness, extreme nationalists often insisted that nations, too, were engaged in a "struggle for existence" in which only the fittest would survive. The German general Friedrich von Bernhardi argued in 1907 that

> War is a biological necessity of the first importance, a regulative element in the life of mankind which cannot be dispensed with, since without it an unhealthy development will follow, which excludes every advancement of the race, and therefore all real civilization. "War is the father of all things." The sages of antiquity long before Darwin recognized this.[8]

Numerous nationalist organizations preached the same doctrine as Bernhardi.

Although certainly not new to Western society, racism, too, was dramatically revived and strengthened by new biological arguments. Perhaps nowhere was the combination of extreme nationalism and racism more evident and more dangerous than in Germany, where racist nationalism was expressed in volkish thought. The concept of the *Volk* (nation, people, or race) had been an underlying idea in German history since the beginning of the nineteenth century. One of the chief propagandists for German volkish ideology at the turn of the century was Houston Stewart Chamberlain (1855–1927), an Englishman who became a German citizen. His book *The Foundations of the Nineteenth Century*, published in 1899, made a special impact on Germany. Modern Germans, according to Chamberlain, were the only pure successors of the Aryans, who were portrayed as the true and original creators of Western culture. The Aryan race, under German leadership, must be prepared to fight for Western civilization and save it from the destructive assaults of such lower races as Jews, Negroes, and Orientals. Increasingly, Jews were singled out by German volkish nationalists as the racial enemy who wanted to destroy the Aryan race.

ANTI-SEMITISM

Anti-Semitism was not new to European civilization. Since the Middle Ages, Jews had been portrayed as the murderers of Christ and subjected to mob violence; their rights had been restricted, and they had been physically separated from Christians in quarters known as ghettos.

In the nineteenth century, as a result of the ideals of the Enlightenment and the French Revolution, Jews were increasingly granted legal equality in many European countries. After the revolutions of 1848, emancipation became a fact of life for Jews throughout western and central Europe. For many Jews, emancipation enabled them to leave the ghetto and become assimilated as hundreds of thousands of Jews entered what had been the closed worlds of parliaments and universities. Many Jews became eminently successful as bankers, lawyers, scientists, scholars, journalists, and stage performers. In 1880, for example, Jews made up 10 percent of the population of the city of Vienna, Austria, but accounted for 39 percent of its medical students and 23 percent of its law students.

These achievements represent only one side of the picture, however. In Germany and Austria during the 1880s and 1890s, conservatives founded right-wing parties that used anti-Semitism to win the votes of traditional lower-middle-class groups, who felt threatened by the new economic forces of the times. These German anti-Semitic parties were based on race. To modern racial anti-Semites, one could not be both German and Jew. The worst treatment of Jews in the last two decades of the nineteenth century and the first decade of the twentieth occurred in eastern Europe, where 72 percent of the entire world Jewish population lived. Russian Jews were admitted to secondary schools and universities only under a quota system and were forced to live in certain regions of the country. Persecutions and pogroms were so widespread that hundreds of thousands of Jews decided to emigrate. Between 1881 and 1899, an average of 23,000 Jews left Russia each year. Many of them went to the United States, although some (probably about 25,000) moved to Palestine, which soon became the focus for a Jewish nationalist movement called Zionism.

The emancipation of the nineteenth century had presented vast opportunities to some Jews, but dilemmas to others. Did emancipation mean full assimilation, and did assimilation mean the disruption of traditional Jewish life? Many paid the price willingly, but others questioned its value and advocated a different answer, a return to Palestine. For many Jews, Palestine had long been the land of their dreams. During the nineteenth century, as nationalist ideas spread and Italians, Poles, Irish, Greeks, and others sought national emancipation, so too did the idea of national independence capture the imagination of some Jews. A key figure in the growth of political Zionism was Theodor Herzl (1860–1904). In 1896, he published a book called *The Jewish State* (see the box on p. 654), in which he straightforwardly advocated that "The Jews who wish it will have their state." Financial support for the development of *yishuvs* or settlements in Palestine came from

THE VOICE OF ZIONISM: THEODOR HERZL AND THE JEWISH STATE

The Austrian Jewish journalist Theodor Herzl wrote The Jewish State *in the summer of 1895 in Paris while he was covering the Dreyfus case for his Vienna newspaper. (Alfred Dreyfus, a French army officer who was also Jewish, was wrongly convicted of selling military secrets. Although he was later exonerated, the case revealed the depth of anti-Semitism in France.) In several weeks, during a period of feverish composition, he set about to analyze the fundamental causes of anti-Semitism and devise a solution to the "Jewish problem." In this selection, he discusses two of his major conclusions.*

THEODOR HERZL, *THE JEWISH STATE*

I do not intend to arouse sympathetic emotions on our behalf. That would be a foolish, futile, and undignified proceeding. I shall content myself with putting the following questions to the Jews: Is it true that, in countries where we live in perceptible numbers, the position of Jewish lawyers, doctors, technicians, teachers, and employees of all descriptions becomes daily more intolerable? True, that the Jewish middle classes are seriously threatened? True, that the passions of the mob are incited against our wealthy people? True, that our poor endure greater sufferings than any other proletariat?

I think that this external pressure makes itself felt everywhere. In our economically upper classes it causes discomfort, in our middle classes continual and grave anxieties, in our lower classes absolute despair.

Everything tends, in fact, to one and the same conclusion, which is clearly enunciated in that classic Berlin phrase: "Juden 'raus!" (Out with the Jews!)

I shall now put the Jewish Question in the curtest possible form: Are we to "get out" now? And if so, to what place?

Or, may we yet remain? And if so, how long?

Let us first settle the point of staying where we are. Can we hope for better days, can we possess our souls in patience, can we wait in pious resignation till the princes and peoples of this earth are more mercifully disposed toward us? I say that we cannot hope for a change in the current of feeling. And why not? . . . The nations in whose midst Jews live are all, either covertly or openly, Anti-Semitic. . . .

The whole plan is in its essence perfectly simple, as it must necessarily be if it is to come within the comprehension of all.

Let the sovereignty be granted us over a portion of the globe large enough to satisfy the rightful requirements of a nation; the rest we shall manage for ourselves.

The creation of a new State is neither ridiculous nor impossible. We have in our day witnessed the process in connection with nations which were not in the bulk of the middle class, but poorer, less educated, and consequently weaker than ourselves. The Governments of all countries scourged by Anti-Semitism will be keenly interested in assisting us to obtain the sovereignty we want. . . .

Palestine is our ever memorable historic home. The very name of Palestine would attract our people with a force of marvelous potency. Supposing his Majesty the Sultan were to give us Palestine, we could in return undertake to regulate the whole finances of Turkey. We should there form a portion of the rampart of Europe against Asia, an outpost of civilization as opposed to barbarism. We should as a neutral State remain in contact with all Europe, which would have to guarantee our existence. The sanctuaries of Christendom would be safeguarded by assigning to them an extraterritorial status such as is well known to the law of nations. We should form a guard of honor about these sanctuaries, answering for the fulfillment of this duty with our existence. This guard of honor would be the great symbol of the solution of the Jewish Question after eighteen centuries of Jewish suffering.

wealthy Jewish banking families, who wanted a refuge in Palestine for persecuted Jews, not a political Jewish state. Even settlements were difficult because Palestine was then part of the Ottoman Empire and Turkish authorities were opposed to Jewish immigration. Despite the problems, however, the First Zionist Congress, which met in Switzerland in 1897, proclaimed as its aim the creation of a "home in Palestine secured by public law" for the Jewish people. In 1900, 1,000 Jews migrated to Palestine. And although 3,000 Jews went annually to Palestine between 1904 and 1914, the Zionist dream remained just that on the eve of World War I.

The Attack on Christianity and the Response of the Churches

Science became one of the chief threats to all the Christian churches and even to religion itself in the nineteenth century. Darwin's theory of evolution, accepted by ever larger numbers of educated Europeans, seemed to contradict the doctrine of divine creation. Some Christian churches responded by rejecting modern ideas outright. Protestant fundamentalist sects were especially active in maintaining a literal interpretation of the Bible. By suppressing Darwin's books and forbidding the teaching of the evolutionary hypothesis, however, the churches often caused even larger numbers of educated people to reject established religions.

Other churches sought compromise, an approach especially evident in the Catholic church during the pontificate of Leo XIII (1878–1903). Pope Leo permitted the teaching of evolution as a hypothesis in Catholic schools and also responded to the challenges of modernization in the economic and social spheres. In his encyclical *De Rerum Novarum,* issued in 1891, he upheld the individual's right to private property but at the same time criticized "naked" capitalism for the poverty and degradation in which it had left the working classes. Much in socialism, he declared, was Christian in principle, but he condemned Marxian socialism for its materialistic and antireligious foundations. The pope recommended that Catholics form socialist parties and labor unions of their own.

The Culture of Modernity

The revolution in physics and psychology was paralleled by a revolution in literature and the arts. Before 1914, writers and artists were rebelling against the traditional literary and artistic styles that had dominated European cultural life since the Renaissance. The changes that they produced have since been called Modernism.

Throughout much of the late nineteenth century, literature was dominated by Naturalism. Naturalists accepted the material world as real and felt that literature should be realistic. By addressing social problems, writers could contribute to an objective understanding of the world. Although Naturalism was a continuation of Realism, it lacked the underlying note of liberal optimism about people and society that had still been prevalent in the 1850s. The Naturalists were pessimistic about Europe's future. They doubted the existence of free will and portrayed characters caught in the grip of forces beyond their control.

The novels of the French writer Émile Zola (1840–1902) provide a good example of Naturalism. Against a backdrop of the urban slums and coal fields of northern France, Zola showed how alcoholism and different environments affected people's lives. The materialistic science of his age had an important influence on Zola. He had read Darwin's *Origin of Species* and had been impressed by its emphasis on the struggle for survival and the importance of environment and heredity. These themes were central to his *Rougon-Macquart,* a twenty-volume series of novels on the "natural and social history of a family." Zola maintained that the artist must analyze and dissect life as a biologist would a living organism. He said, "I have simply done on living bodies the work of analysis which surgeons perform on corpses."

At the turn of the century, a new group of writers, known as the Symbolists, reacted against Realism. Primarily interested in writing poetry, the Symbolists believed that an objective knowledge of the world was impossible. The external world was not real but only a collection of symbols that reflected the true reality of the individual human mind. Art, they believed, should function for its own sake instead of serving, criticizing, or seeking to understand society. In the works of the Symbolist poets W. B. Yeats and Rainer Maria Rilke, poetry ceased to be part of popular culture because only through a knowledge of the poet's personal language could one hope to understand what the poet was saying (see the box on p. 656).

Since the Renaissance, the task of artists had been to represent reality as accurately as possible. By the late nineteenth century, however, artists were seeking new forms of expression. The period from 1870 to 1914 was one of the most fertile in the history of art and witnessed three major movements: Impressionism, Post-Impressionism, and abstract painting.

The preamble to modern painting can be found in Impressionism, a movement that originated in France in the 1870s when a group of artists rejected the studios and museums and went out into the countryside to paint nature directly. Camille Pissarro (1830–1903), one of Impressionism's founders, expressed what they sought:

> Precise drawing is dry and hampers the impression of the whole; it destroys all sensations. Do not define too closely the outlines of things; it is the brush stroke of the right value and color which should produce the drawing. . . . The eye should not be fixed on one point, but should take in everything, while observing the reflections which the colors produce on their surroundings. Work at the same time upon sky, water, branches, ground, keeping everything going on an equal basis and unceasingly rework until you have got it. . . . Don't proceed according to rules and principles, but paint what you observe and feel. Paint generously and unhesitatingly, for it is best not to lose the first impression.[9]

Above all, said Pissarro, "Don't be timid in front of nature: one must be bold, at the risk of being deceived, and making mistakes. One must have only one master—nature; she is the one always to be consulted."

An important Impressionist painter was Berthe Morisot (1841–1895), whose dedication to the new style of painting won her the disfavor of the traditional French academic artists. Morisot believed that women had a special vision, which was, as she said, "more delicate than that of men." Her special touch is evident in *Young Girl by the Window,* where she makes use of lighter colors and flowing brush strokes. Near the end of her life, she lamented the refusal of men to take her work seriously: "I don't think there has ever been a man who treated a woman as an equal, and that's all I would have asked, for I know I'm worth as much as they."[10]

By the 1880s, a new movement known as Post-Impressionism arose in France and soon spread to other European countries. Post-Impressionists sought to use both color and line to express inner feelings and produce a

SYMBOLIST POETRY: ART FOR ART'S SAKE

The Symbolist movement was an important foundation for Modernism. The Symbolists believed that the working of the mind was the proper study of literature. Arthur Rimbaud was one of Symbolism's leading practitioners in France. Although his verses seem to have little real meaning, they were not meant to describe the external world precisely, but to enchant the mind. Art was not meant for the masses, but only for "art's sake." Rimbaud wrote, "By the alchemy of the words, I noted the inexpressible. I fixed giddiness."

ARTHUR RIMBAUD, *THE DRUNKEN BOAT*

As I floated down impassable rivers,
I felt the boatmen no longer guiding me:
After them came redskins who with war cries
Nailed them naked to the painted poles.

I was oblivious to the crew,
I who bore Flemish wheat and English cotton.
When the racket was finished with my boatmen,
The waters let me drift my own free way.

In the tide's furious pounding,
I, the other winter, emptier than children's minds,
I sailed! And the unmoored peninsulas
Have not suffered more triumphant turmoils.

The tempest blessed my maritime watches.
Lighter than a cork I danced on the waves,
Those eternal rollers of victims,
Ten nights, without regretting the lantern-foolish eye!

Sweeter than the bite of sour apples to a child,
The green water seeped through my wooden hull,
Rinsed me of blue wine stains and vomit,
Broke apart grappling iron and rudder.

And then I bathed myself in the poetry
Of the star-sprayed milk-white sea,
Devouring the azure greens; where, pale
And ravished, a pensive drowned one sometimes floats;
Where, suddenly staining the blueness, frenzies
And slows rhythms in the blazing of day,
Stronger than alcohol, vaster than our lyres,
The russet bitterness of love ferments. . . .

I have dreamed of the green night bedazzled with snow,
A kiss climbing slowly to the eyes of the sea,
The flow of unforgettable sap,
And the yellow-blue waking of singing phosphorous!

Long months I have followed, like maddened cattle,
The surge assaulting the rocks
Without dreaming that the Virgin's luminous feet
Could force a muzzle on the panting ocean!

I have struck against the shares of incredible Floridas
Mixing panther-eyed flowers like human skins!
Rainbows stretched like bridle reins
Under the ocean's horizon, toward sea-green troops! . . .

personal statement of reality rather than an imitation of objects. Impressionist paintings had retained a sense of realism, but the Post-Impressionists shifted from objective reality to subjective reality and, in so doing, began to withdraw from the artist's traditional task of depicting the external world. Post-Impressionists were the real forerunners of modern art.

A famous Post-Impressionist was the tortured and tragic figure Vincent van Gogh (1853–1890). For van Gogh, art was a spiritual experience. He was especially interested in color and believed that it could act as its own form of lan-

BERTHE MORISOT, *YOUNG GIRL BY THE WINDOW.* Berthe Morisot came from a wealthy French family that settled in Paris when she was seven. The first female painter to join the Impressionists, she developed her own unique Impressionist style. Her gentle colors and strong use of pastels are especially evident in *Young Girl by the Window,* painted in 1878. Many of her paintings focus on women and domestic scenes.

VINCENT VAN GOGH, *THE STARRY NIGHT*. The Dutch painter Vincent van Gogh was a major figure among the Post-Impressionists. His originality and power of expression made a strong impact on his artistic successors. In *The Starry Night*, van Gogh's subjective vision was given full play as the dynamic swirling forms of the heavens above overwhelmed the village below. The heavens seem alive with a mysterious spiritual force.

guage. Van Gogh maintained that artists should paint what they feel. In his *The Starry Night*, he painted a sky alive with whirling stars that overwhelm the huddled buildings in the village below.

By the beginning of the twentieth century, the belief that the task of art was to represent "reality" had lost much of its meaning. By that time, the new psychology and the new physics had made it evident that many people were not sure what constituted reality anyway. Then, too, the growth of photography gave artists another reason to reject visual realism. First invented in the 1830s, photography became popular and widespread after George Eastman created the first Kodak camera for the mass market in 1888. What was the point of an artist doing what the camera did better? Unlike the camera, which could only mirror reality, artists could create reality. As in literature, so also in modern art, individual consciousness became the source of meaning. Between 1905 and 1914, this search for individual expression produced a great variety of painting schools that had their greatest impact after World War I.

By 1905, one of the most important figures in modern art was just beginning his career. Pablo Picasso (1881– 1973) was from Spain but settled in Paris in 1904.

PABLO PICASSO, *LES DEMOISELLES D'AVIGNON.* Pablo Picasso, a major pioneer and activist of modern art, experimented with a remarkable variety of modern styles. His *Les Demoiselles d'Avignon* was the first great example of Cubism, which one art historian has called "the first style of this century to break radically with the past." Geometric shapes replace traditional forms, forcing the viewer to recreate reality in his or her own mind.

Picasso was extremely flexible and painted in a remarkable variety of styles. He was instrumental in the development of a new style called Cubism that used geometric designs as visual stimuli to recreate reality in the viewer's mind. Picasso's 1907 work *Les Demoiselles d'Avignon* has been called the first Cubist painting.

The modern artist's flight from "visual reality" reached a high point in 1910 with the beginning of abstract painting. A Russian who worked in Germany, Vasily Kandinsky (1866–1944) was one of the founders of Abstract Expressionism. As is evident in his *Painting with White Border*, Kandinsky sought to avoid representation altogether. He believed that art should speak directly to the soul. To do so, it must avoid any reference to visual reality and concentrate on color.

Modernism in the arts revolutionized architecture and architectural practices. A new principle known as functionalism motivated this revolution. Functionalism meant that buildings, like the products of machines, should be "functional" or useful, fulfilling the purpose for which they were constructed. Art and engineering were to be unified, and all unnecessary ornamentation was to be stripped away.

The United States was a leader in these pioneering architectural designs. Unprecedented urban growth and the absence of restrictive architectural traditions allowed for new building methods, especially in the relatively "new city" of Chicago. The Chicago school of the 1890s, led by Louis H. Sullivan (1856–1924), used reinforced concrete, steel frames, and electric elevators to build skyscrapers virtually free of external ornamentation. One of Sullivan's most successful pupils was Frank Lloyd Wright (1869–1959), who

VASILY KANDINSKY, *COMPOSITION VIII, NO. 2 (PAINTING WITH WHITE BORDER).* One of the founders of Abstract Expressionism was the Russian Vasily Kandinsky, who sought to eliminate representation altogether by focusing on color and avoiding any resemblance to visual reality. In *Painting with White Border,* Kandinsky used color "to send light into the darkness of men's hearts." He believed that color, like music, could fulfill a spiritual goal of appealing directly to the human being.

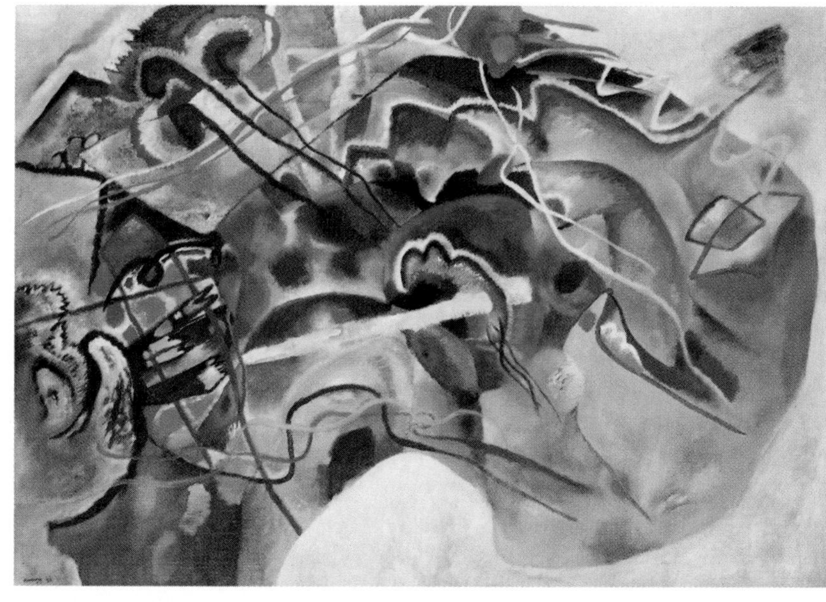

became known for innovative designs in domestic architecture. Wright's private houses, built chiefly for wealthy patrons, featured geometric structures with long lines, overhanging roofs, and severe planes of brick and stone. The interiors were open spaced and included cathedral ceilings and built-in furniture and lighting features. Wright pioneered the modern American house.

At the beginning of the twentieth century, developments in music paralleled those in painting. Expressionism in music was a Russian creation, the product of the composer Igor Stravinsky (1882–1971) and the Ballet Russe, the dancing company of Sergei Diaghilev (1872–1929). Together they revolutionized the world of music with Stravinsky's ballet *The Rite of Spring*. When it was performed in Paris in 1913, the savage and primitive sounds and beats of the music and dance caused a near riot from an audience outraged at its audacity.

CONCLUSION

Between 1870 and 1914, the national state began to expand its functions beyond all previous limits. Fearful of the growth of socialism and trade unions, governments attempted to appease the working masses by adopting such social insurance measures as protection against accident, illness, and old age. These social welfare measures were narrow in scope and limited in benefits before 1914. Moreover, they failed to halt the growth of socialism. Nevertheless, they signaled a new direction for state action to benefit the mass of its citizens.

This extension of state functions took place in an atmosphere of increased national loyalty. After 1870, nation-states increasingly sought to solidify the social order and win the active loyalty and support of their citizens by deliberately cultivating national feelings. Yet this policy contained potentially great dangers. Nations had discovered once again that imperialistic adventures and military successes could arouse nationalistic passions and smother domestic political unrest. But they also found—belatedly in 1914—that nationalistic feelings could also lead to intense international rivalries that made war almost inevitable.

What many Europeans liked to call their "age of progress" between 1870 and 1914 was also an era of anxiety. Frenzied imperialist expansion had created vast European empires and spheres of influence around the globe. This feverish competition for colonies, however, had markedly increased the existing antagonisms among the European states. At the same time, the Western treatment of native peoples as racial inferiors caused educated, non-Western elites in these colonies to initiate movements for national independence. Before these movements could be successful, however, the power that Europeans had achieved through their mass armies and technological superiority had to be weakened. The Europeans inadvertently accomplished this task for their colonial subjects by demolishing their own civilization on the battlegrounds of Europe in World War I and World War II.

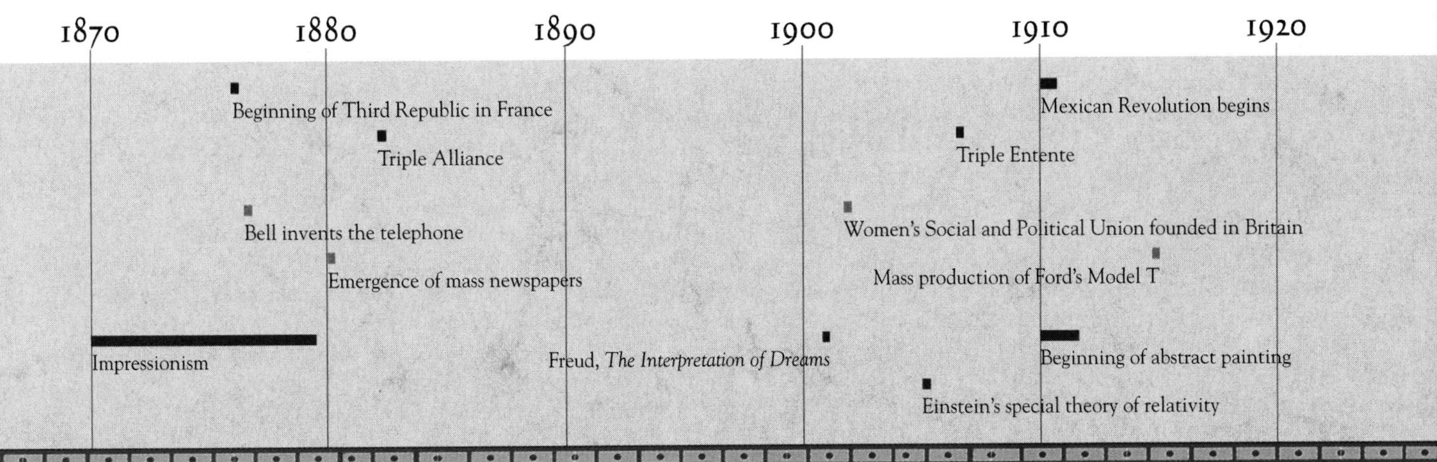

CHAPTER NOTES

1. Karl Marx and Friedrich Engels, *The Communist Manifesto* (Harmondsworth, 1967), pp. (in order of quotations) 79, 81, 102.
2. Quoted in W. L. Guttsman, *The German Social Democratic Party, 1875–1933* (London, 1981), p. 63.
3. Quoted in Nicholas Bullock and James Read, *The Movement for Housing Reform in Germany and France, 1840–1914* (Cambridge, 1985), p. 42.
4. Quoted in Catherine M. Prelinger, "Prelude to Consciousness: Amalie Sieveking and the Female Association for the Care of the Poor and the Sick," in John C. Fout, ed., *German Women in the Nineteenth Century: A Social History* (New York, 1984), p. 119.
5. Quoted in Robert Gildea, *Barricades and Borders: Europe, 1800–1914*, 2d ed. (Oxford, 1996), pp. 240–41.
6. Quoted in Shmuel Galai, *The Liberation Movement in Russia, 1900–1905* (Cambridge, 1973), p. 26.
7. Quoted in Arthur E. E. McKenzie, *The Major Achievements of Science* (New York, 1960), 1:310.
8. Friedrich von Bernhardi, *Germany and the Next War*, trans. Allen H. Powles (New York, 1914), pp. 18–19.
9. Quoted in John Rewald, *History of Impressionism* (New York, 1961), pp. 456–58.
10. Quoted in Anne Higonnet, *Berthe Morisot's Images of Women* (Cambridge, Mass., 1992), p. 19.

SUGGESTED READINGS

The subject of the Second Industrial Revolution is well covered in D. Landes, *The Unbound Prometheus*, cited in Chapter 20. For a fundamental survey of European industrialization, see A. S. Milward and S. B. Saul, *The Development of the Economies of Continental Europe, 1850–1914* (Cambridge, Mass., 1977). The impact of the new technology on European thought is imaginatively discussed in S. Kern, *The Culture of Time and Space, 1880–1918* (Cambridge, Mass., 1983).

On Marx, there is the standard work by D. McLellan, *Karl Marx: His Life and Thought* (New York, 1974). For an introduction to international socialism, see A. Lindemann, *A History of European Socialism* (New Haven, Conn., 1983), and L. Derfler, *Socialism Since Marx: A Century of the European Left* (New York, 1973). On the emergence of German social democracy, there is W. L. Guttsman, *The German Social Democratic Party, 1875–1933* (London, 1981).

For a good introduction to housing reform on the Continent, see N. Bullock and J. Read, *The Movement for Housing Reform in Germany and France, 1840–1914* (Cambridge, 1985). An interesting work on aristocratic life is D. Cannadine,*The Decline and Fall of the British Aristocracy* (New Haven, Conn., 1990). On the middle classes, see P. Pilbeam, *The Middle Classes in Europe, 1789–1914* (Basingstoke, 1990), and R. Magraw, *A History of the French Working Class* (Cambridge, Mass., 1992). On the working classes, see L. Berlanstein, *The Working People of Paris, 1871–1914* (Baltimore, 1984). There are good overviews of women's experiences in the nineteenth century in B. Smith, *Changing Lives: Women in European History Since 1700* (Lexington, Mass., 1989), and M. J. Boxer and J. H. Quataert, eds., *Connecting Spheres: Women in the Western World, 1500 to the Present* (Oxford, 1987). The world of women's work is examined in L. A. Tilly and J. W. Scott, *Women, Work, and Family* (New York, 1978). The rise of feminism is examined in J. Rendall, *The Origins of Modern Feminism: Women in Britain, France and the United States* (London, 1985). On the family and children, see M. Mitterauer and R. Sieder, *The European Family* (Chicago, 1982). On various aspects of education, see M. J. Maynes, *Schooling in Western Europe: A Social History* (Albany, N.Y., 1985), and J. S. Hurt, *Elementary Schooling and the Working Classes, 1860–1918* (London, 1979). A concise and well-presented survey of leisure patterns is G. Cross, *A Social History of Leisure Since 1600* (State College, Pa., 1989).

The domestic politics of the period can be examined in the general works listed in the bibliography for Chapter 20. There are also specialized works on aspects of each country's history. On Britain, see D. Read, *The Age of Urban Democracy: England, 1868–1914* (New York, 1994), and M. J. Wiener, *English Culture and the Decline of the Industrial Spirit, 1850–1980* (Cambridge, 1981). For a detailed examination of French history from 1871 to 1914, see J.-M. Mayeur and M. Reberioux, *The Third Republic from its Origins to the Great War, 1871–1914* (Cambridge, 1984). On Germany, see W. J. Mommsen, *Imperial Germany, 1867–1918* (New York, 1995), and V. R. Berghahn, *Imperial Germany, 1871– 1914* (Providence, R.I., 1995). On the nationalities problem in the Austro-Hungarian Empire, see R. Kann, *The Multinational Empire: Nationalism and National Reform in the Habsburg Monarchy, 1848–1918*, 2 vols. (New York, 1950). On aspects of Russian history, see H. Rogger, *Russia in the Age of Modernization and Revolution, 1881–1917* (London, 1983), and A. Ascher, *The Revolution of 1905: Russia in Disarray* (New York, 1988). On the United States, see D. Cashman, *America in the Gilded Age: From the Death of Lincoln to the Rise of Theodore Roosevelt* (New York, 1984), and J. W. Chambers, *The Tyranny of Change: America in the Progressive Era, 1900–1917* (New York, 1980). On Latin American economic developments, see B. Albert, *South America and the World Economy from Independence to 1930* (London, 1983). For a comprehensive examination of the Mexican Revolution, see A. Knight, *The Mexican Revolution*, 2 vols. (Cambridge, 1986). Two fundamental works on the diplomatic history of the period are W. L. Langer, *European Alliances and Alignments*, 2d ed. (New York, 1966), and *The Diplomacy of Imperialism*, 2d ed. (New York, 1965).

A well-regarded study of Freud is P. Gay, *Freud: A Life for Our Time* (New York, 1988). Also see R. Clark, *Freud: The Man and the Cause* (New York, 1980). The subject of modern anti-

Semitism is covered in J. Katz, *From Prejudice to Destruction* (Cambridge, Mass., 1980), and A. S. Lindemann, *Esau's Tears: Modern Anti-Semitism and the Rise of the Jews* (New York, 1997). European racism is analyzed in G. L. Mosse, *Toward the Final Solution* (New York, 1980). For a recent biography of Theodor Herzl, see J. Kornberg, *Theodor Herzl: From Assimilation to Zionism* (London, 1993). Very valuable on modern art are M. Powell-Jones, *Impressionism* (London, 1994); B. Denvir, *Post-Impressionism* (New York, 1992); and T. Parsons, *Post-Impressionism: The Rise of Modern Art* (London, 1992).

For additional reading, go to InfoTrac College Edition, your online research library at http://web1.infotrac-college.com

Enter the search terms "family nineteenth century" using Keywords.

Enter the search terms "industrial revolution" using Keywords.

Enter the search term "feminism" using the Subject Guide.

Enter the search terms "Charles Darwin" using Keywords.

Enter the search terms "Sigmund Freud" using Keywords.

CHAPTER

22

THE HIGH TIDE OF IMPERIALISM

CHAPTER OUTLINE

FOCUS QUESTIONS

- What were the causes of the new imperialism of the nineteenth century, and how did it differ from European expansion in earlier periods?
- What types of administrative systems did the various colonial powers establish for their colonies, and how did these systems reflect the general philosophy of colonialism?
- What economic policies were followed by the colonial powers, and who benefited from these policies?
- How did the subject peoples respond to colonialism, and what role did nationalism play in their response?
- What were the consequences of the new imperialism for the colonies and for the colonial powers?

In 1877, the young British empire builder Cecil Rhodes drew up his last will and testament. He bequeathed his fortune, achieved as a diamond magnate in South Africa, to two of his close friends and acquaintances. He also instructed them to use the inheritance to form a secret society with the aim of bringing about "the extension of British rule throughout the world, the perfecting of a system of emigration from the United Kingdom . . . especially the occupation of the whole continent of Africa, the Holy Land, the valley of the Euphrates, the Islands of Cyprus and Candia [Crete], the whole of South America. . . . The ultimate recovery of the United States as an integral part of the British Empire . . .

then finally the foundation of so great a power to hereafter render wars impossible and promote the best interests of humanity."[1]

Preposterous as such ideas appear to us today, they serve as a graphic reminder of the hubris that characterized the worldview of Rhodes and many of his contemporaries during the age of imperialism, as well as the complex union of moral concern and vaulting ambition that motivated their actions on the world stage.

Through their efforts, Western colonialism spread throughout much of the non-Western world during the nineteenth and early twentieth centuries. Spurred by the demands of the Industrial Revolution, a few powerful Western states—notably, Great Britain, France, Germany, Russia, and the United States—competed avariciously for consumer markets and raw materials for their expanding economies. By the end of the nineteenth century, virtually all of the traditional societies in Asia and Africa were under direct or indirect colonial rule. As the new century began, the Western imprint on Asian and African societies, for better or for worse, appeared to be a permanent feature of the political and cultural landscape.

The Spread of Colonial Rule

In the nineteenth century, a new phase of Western expansion into Asia and Africa began. Whereas European aims in the East before 1800 could be summed up in Vasco da Gama's famous phrase "Christians and spices," in the early nineteenth century a new relationship took shape, as European nations began to view Asian and African societies as sources of industrial raw materials and as markets for Western manufactured goods. No longer were Western gold and silver exchanged for cloves, pepper, tea, silk, and porcelain. Now the prodigious output of European factories was sent to Africa and Asia in return for oil, tin, rubber, and the other resources needed to fuel the Western industrial machine.

The reason for this change, of course, was the Industrial Revolution, which began in England in the late eighteenth century and spread to the Continent a few decades later. Now industrializing countries in the West needed vital raw materials that were not available at home as well as a reliable market for the goods produced in their factories. The latter factor became increasingly crucial as capitalist societies began to discover that their home markets could not always absorb domestic output. When consumer demand lagged, economic depression threatened.

As Western economic expansion into Asia and Africa gathered strength during the last quarter of the nineteenth century, it became fashionable to call the process imperialism. Although the term *imperialism* has many meanings, in this instance it referred to the efforts of capitalist states in the West to seize markets, cheap raw materials, and lucrative avenues for capital investment in the countries beyond Western civilization. In this interpretation, the primary motives behind the Western expansion were economic. The best-known promoter of this view was the British political economist John A. Hobson, who published a major analysis entitled *Imperialism: A Study* in 1902. In this influential book, Hobson maintained that modern imperialism was a direct consequence of the modern industrial economy.

As in the earlier phase of Western expansion, however, the issue was not simply an economic one. As Hobson himself conceded, economic concerns were inevitably tinged with political ones and with questions of national grandeur and moral purpose as well. In nineteenth-century Europe, economic wealth, national status, and political power went hand in hand with the possession of a colonial empire, at least in the minds of observers at the time. To nineteenth-century global strategists, colonies brought tangible benefits in the world of balance of power politics as well as economic profits, and many nations became involved in the pursuit of colonies as much to gain advantage over their rivals as to acquire territory for its own sake.

The relationship between colonialism and national survival was expressed directly in a speech by French politician Jules Ferry in 1885. A policy of "containment or abstinence," he warned, would set France on "the broad road to decadence" and initiate its decline into a "third-or-fourth-rate power." British imperialists agreed. To Cecil Rhodes, the most famous empire builder of his day, the extraction of material wealth from the colonies was only a secondary matter. "My ruling purpose," he remarked, "is the extension of the British Empire."[2] That British Empire, on which (as the saying went) "the sun never set," was the envy of its rivals and was viewed as the primary source of British global dominance during the latter half of the nineteenth century.

With the change in European motives for colonization came a corresponding shift in tactics. Earlier, when their economic interests were more limited, European states had generally been satisfied to deal with existing independent states rather than attempting to establish direct control over vast territories. There had been exceptions where state power at the local level was at the point of collapse (as in India), where European economic interests were especially intense (as in Latin America and the East Indies), or where there was no centralized authority (as in North America and the Philippines). But for the most part, the Western presence in Asia and Africa had been limited to controlling the regional trade network and establishing a few footholds where the foreigners could carry on trade and missionary activity.

After 1800, the demands of industrialization in Europe created a new set of dynamics. Maintaining access to industrial raw materials such as oil and rubber and setting up reliable markets for European manufactured products required more extensive control over colonial territories. As competition for colonies increased, the colonial powers sought to solidify their hold over their territories to protect them from attack by their rivals. During the last two decades of the nineteenth century, the quest for colonies became a scramble, as all the major European states, now joined by the United States and Japan, engaged in a global land grab. In many cases, economic interests were secondary to security concerns or the requirements of national prestige. In Africa, for example, the British engaged in a struggle with their rivals to protect their interests in the Suez Canal and the Red Sea. In Southeast Asia, the United States seized the Philippines from Spain at least partly to keep them out of the hands of the Japanese, and the French took over Indochina for fear that it would otherwise be occupied by Germany, Japan, or the United States.

By 1900, almost all the societies of Africa and Asia were either under full colonial rule or, as in the case of China and the Ottoman Empire, at a point of virtual collapse. Only a handful of states, such as Japan in East Asia, Thailand in Southeast Asia, Afghanistan and Iran in the Middle East, and mountainous Ethiopia in East Africa, managed to escape internal disintegration or subjection to colonial rule. For the most part, the exceptions were the result of good fortune rather than design. Thailand escaped subjugation primarily because officials in London and Paris found it more convenient to transform the country into a buffer state than to fight over it. Ethiopia and Afghanistan survived due to their remote location and mountainous terrain. Only Japan managed to avoid the common fate through a concerted strategy of political and economic reform.

"Opportunity in the Orient": The Colonial Takeover in Southeast Asia

In 1800, only two societies in Southeast Asia were under effective colonial rule: the Spanish Philippines and the Dutch East Indies. During the last half of the nineteenth

MAP 22.1 Colonial Southeast Asia

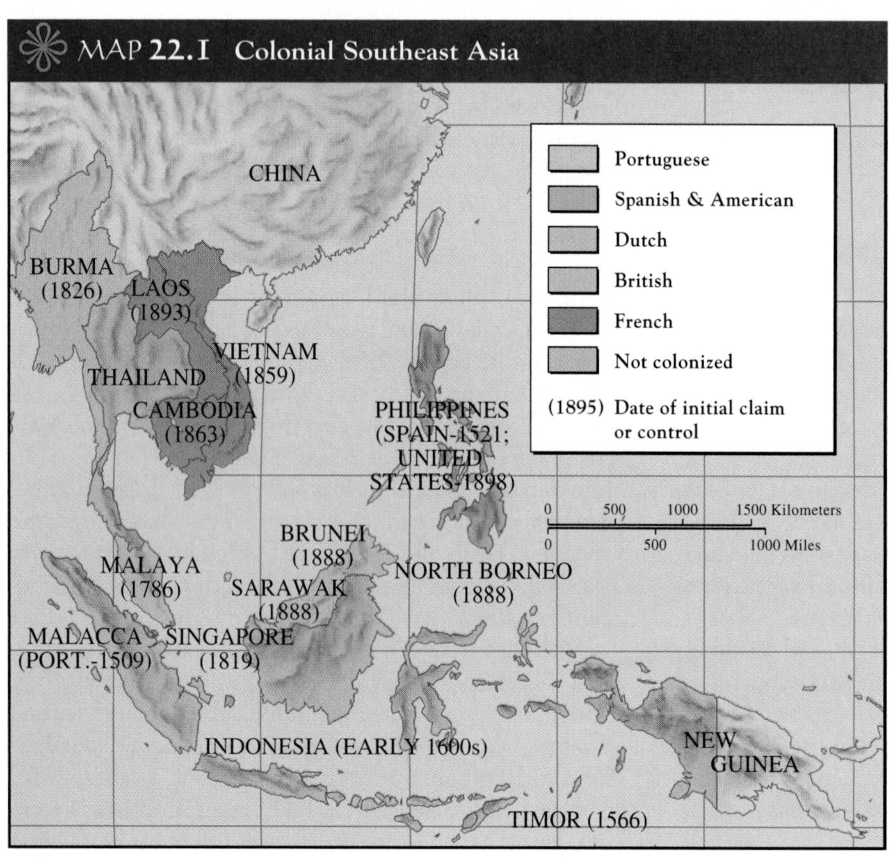

ROYAL PALACE AT BANGKOK. Few societies in Asia have been as adept at absorbing Western influence without destroying their own institutions and customs as the Thai. In some cases this talent has extended to the field of architecture. The illustration shown here depicts a late-nineteenth-century building on the grounds of the royal palace in Bangkok. Note the way in which the architect has attempted to synthesize Western classical techniques with the rooftop design and Buddhist stupas characteristic of traditional religious buildings in Thailand.

century, however, European interest in Southeast Asia increased rapidly, and by 1900 virtually the entire area was under colonial rule. The process began after the Napoleonic Wars, when the British, by agreement with the Dutch, abandoned their claims to territorial possessions in the East Indies in return for a free hand in the Malay peninsula. In 1819, the colonial administrator Stamford Raffles founded a new British colony on the island of Singapore at the tip of the peninsula. When the invention of steam power enabled merchant ships to save time and distance by passing through the Strait of Malacca rather than sailing with the westerlies across the southern Indian Ocean, Singapore became a major stopping point for traffic en route to and from China and other commercial centers in the region.

During the next few decades, the pace of European penetration into Southeast Asia accelerated, as the British established control over Burma, a move that aroused some anxiety in France. The French still maintained a clandestine missionary organization in Vietnam despite harsh persecution by the local authorities, who viewed Christianity as a threat to Confucian doctrine. In 1857, the French government decided to force the Vietnamese to accept French protection in order to prevent the British from obtaining a monopoly of trade in South China, which they sought to do from their new base in Burma. A naval attack launched a year later was not a total success, but the French eventually forced the Nguyen dynasty in Vietnam to cede territories in the Mekong River delta. A generation later, French rule was extended over the remainder of the country. By the end of the century, French seizure of neighboring Cambodia and Laos had led to the creation of the French-ruled Indochinese Union.

With the French conquest of Indochina, Thailand was the only remaining independent state on the Southeast Asian mainland. Under the astute leadership of two remarkable rulers, King Mongkut and his son, King Chulalongkorn, the Thai attempted to introduce Western learning and maintain relations with the major European powers without undermining internal stability or inviting an imperialist attack. In 1896, the British and the French agreed to preserve Thailand as an independent buffer zone between their possessions in Southeast Asia.

The final piece in the colonial edifice in Southeast Asia was put in place in 1898, when U.S. naval forces under Commodore George Dewey defeated the Spanish fleet in Manila Bay. President William McKinley agonized over the fate of the Philippines but ultimately decided that the moral thing to do was to turn the islands into an American colony to prevent them from falling into the hands of the Japanese. In fact, the Americans (like the Spanish before them) found the islands convenient as a jumping-off point for the China trade (see Chapter 23). The mixture of moral idealism and the desire for profit was reflected in a speech given in the Senate in January 1900 by Senator Albert Beveridge of Indiana:

> Mr. President, the times call for candor. The Philippines are ours forever, "territory belonging to the United States," as the Constitution calls them. And just beyond the Philippines are China's illimitable markets. We will not retreat from either. . . . We will not renounce our part in the mission of our race, trustee, under God, of the civilization of the world. And we will move forward to our work, not howling

> out regrets like slaves whipped to their burdens, but with gratitude for a task worthy of our strength, and thanksgiving to Almighty God that He has marked us as His chosen people, henceforth to lead in the regeneration of the world.[3]

Not all Filipinos agreed with Senator Beveridge's portrayal of the situation. Under the leadership of Emilio Aguinaldo, guerrilla forces fought bitterly against U.S. troops to establish their independence from both Spain and the United States. But America's first war against guerrilla forces in Asia was a success, and the bulk of the resistance collapsed in 1901. President McKinley had his stepping-stone to the rich markets of China.

Empire Building in Africa

Up to the beginning of the nineteenth century, the relatively limited nature of European economic interests in Africa had provided little temptation for the penetration of the interior or the political takeover of the coastal areas. The slave trade, the main source of European profit during the eighteenth century, could be carried on by using African rulers and merchants as intermediaries. Disease, political instability, the lack of transportation, and the generally unhealthy climate all deterred the Europeans from more extensive efforts in Africa.

THE GROWING EUROPEAN PRESENCE IN WEST AFRICA

As the new century dawned, the slave trade itself was in a state of decline. One reason was the growing sense of outrage among humanitarians in several European countries over the purchase, sale, and exploitation of human beings. Dutch merchants effectively ceased trafficking in slaves in 1795, and the Danes stopped in 1803. A few years later, the slave trade was declared illegal in both Great Britain and the United States. The British began to apply pressure on other nations to follow suit, and most did so after the end of the Napoleonic Wars in 1815, leaving only Portugal and Spain as practitioners of the trade south of the equator. In the meantime, the demand for slaves began to decline in the Western Hemisphere, and by the 1880s slavery had been abolished in all major countries of the world.

Economic as well as humanitarian interests contributed to the end of the slave trade. The cost of slaves had begun to rise after the middle of the eighteenth century, while the growth of the slave population reduced the need for additional labor on the plantations in the Americas. The British, with some reluctant assistance from France and the United States, added to the costs by actively using their navy to capture slave ships and free the occupants. When slavery was abolished in the United States in 1863 and in Cuba and Brazil seventeen years later, the slave trade across the Atlantic was effectively brought to an end.

As the slave trade in the Atlantic declined during the first half of the nineteenth century, European interest in what was sometimes called "legitimate trade" in natural resources increased. Exports of peanuts, timber, hides, and palm oil from West Africa increased substantially during the first decades of the century, while imports of textile goods and other manufactured products rose.

Stimulated by growing commercial interests in the area, European governments began to push for a more permanent presence along the coast. During the first decades of the nineteenth century, the British established settlements along the Gold Coast and in Sierra Leone, where they attempted to set up agricultural plantations for freed slaves who had returned from the Western Hemisphere or had been liberated by British ships while en route to the Americas. A similar haven for ex-slaves was developed with the assistance of the United States in Liberia. The French occupied the area around the Senegal River near Cape Verde, where they attempted to develop peanut plantations.

The growing European presence in West Africa led to the emergence of a new class of Afro-Europeans educated in Western culture and often employed by Europeans. Many became Christians and some studied in European or American universities. At the same time, the European presence inevitably led to increasing tensions with African governments in the area. British efforts to increase trade with Ashanti led to conflict in the 1820s, but British influence in the area intensified in later decades. Most African states, especially those with a fairly high degree of political integration, were able to maintain their independence from this creeping European encroachment, called "informal empire" by some historians, but the prospects for the future were ominous. When local groups attempted to organize to protect their interests, the British stepped in and annexed the coastal states as the British colony of Gold Coast in 1874. At about the same time, the British extended an informal protectorate over warring ethnic groups in the Niger delta.

IMPERIALIST SHADOW OVER THE NILE

A similar process was under way in the Nile valley. There had long been interest in shortening the trade route to the East by digging a canal across the low, swampy isthmus separating the Mediterranean from the Red Sea. The Turks had considered constructing a canal from Cairo to Suez in the sixteenth century, as had the French king Louis XIV a century later, but the French did nothing about it until the end of the eighteenth century. At that time, Napoleon planned a military takeover of Egypt to cement French power in the eastern Mediterranean and open a faster route to India.

Napoleon's plan proved abortive. French troops landed in Egypt in 1798 and destroyed the ramshackle Mamluk regime in Cairo, but the British counterattacked, destroying the French fleet and eventually forcing the French to evacuate in disorder. The British restored the Mamluks to power, but in 1805 Muhammad Ali, an Ottoman army officer of either Turkish or Albanian extraction, seized control.

During the next three decades, Muhammad Ali introduced a series of reforms to bring Egypt into the modern world. He modernized the army, set up a public educational system (supplementing the traditional religious education provided in Muslim schools), and sponsored the creation of a small industrial sector producing refined sugar, textiles, munitions, and even ships. Muhammad Ali also extended Egyptian authority southward into the Sudan and across the Sinai peninsula into Arabia, Syria, and northern Iraq and even briefly threatened to seize Istanbul itself. To prevent the possible collapse of the Ottoman Empire, the British and the French recognized Muhammad Ali as the hereditary pasha (later to be known as the *khedive*) of Egypt under the loose authority of the Ottoman government.

The growing economic importance of the Nile valley, along with the development of steam navigation, made the heretofore visionary plans for a Suez Canal more urgent. In 1854, the French entrepreneur Ferdinand de Lesseps signed a contract to begin construction of the canal, and it was completed in 1869. The project brought little immediate benefit to Egypt, however. The construction not only cost thousands of lives but left the Egyptian government deep in debt, forcing it to depend increasingly on foreign financial support. When an army revolt against growing foreign influence broke out in 1881, the British stepped in to protect their investment (they had bought Egypt's canal company shares in 1875) and establish an informal protectorate that would last until World War I.

Rising discontent in the Sudan added to Egypt's growing internal problems. In 1881, the Muslim cleric Muhammad Ahmad, known as the Mahdi (in Arabic, the "rightly guided one"), led a religious revolt that brought much of the upper Nile under his control. The famous British general Charles Gordon, who had earlier commanded Manchu armies fighting against the Taiping Rebellion in China (see Chapter 23), led a military force to Khartoum to restore Egyptian authority, but his besieged army was captured in 1885 by the Mahdi's troops, thirty-six hours before a British rescue mission reached Khartoum. Gordon himself died in the battle, which became one of the most dramatic news stories of the last quarter of the century.

The weakening of Turkish rule in the Nile valley had a parallel further to the west, where local viceroys in Tripoli, Tunis, and Algiers had begun to establish their autonomy. In 1830, the French, on the pretext of protecting European shipping in the Mediterranean from pirates, seized the area surrounding Algiers and integrated it into the French Empire. By the mid-1850s, more than 150,000 Europeans had settled in the fertile region adjacent to the coast. In 1881, the French imposed a protectorate on neighboring Tunisia. Only Tripoli and Cyrenaica (the Ottoman provinces that comprise modern Libya) remained under Turkish rule until the Italians took them in 1911–1912.

THE OPENING OF THE SUEZ CANAL. The Suez Canal, which connected the Mediterranean and the Red Seas for the first time, was constructed under the direction of the French promoter Ferdinand de Lesseps. Still in use today, the canal is Egypt's greatest revenue producer. This sketch shows the ceremonial passage of the first ships through the canal in 1869. Note the combination of sail and steam power which marked the transition to coal-powered ships in the mid-nineteenth century.

MAP 22.2 Africa in 1914

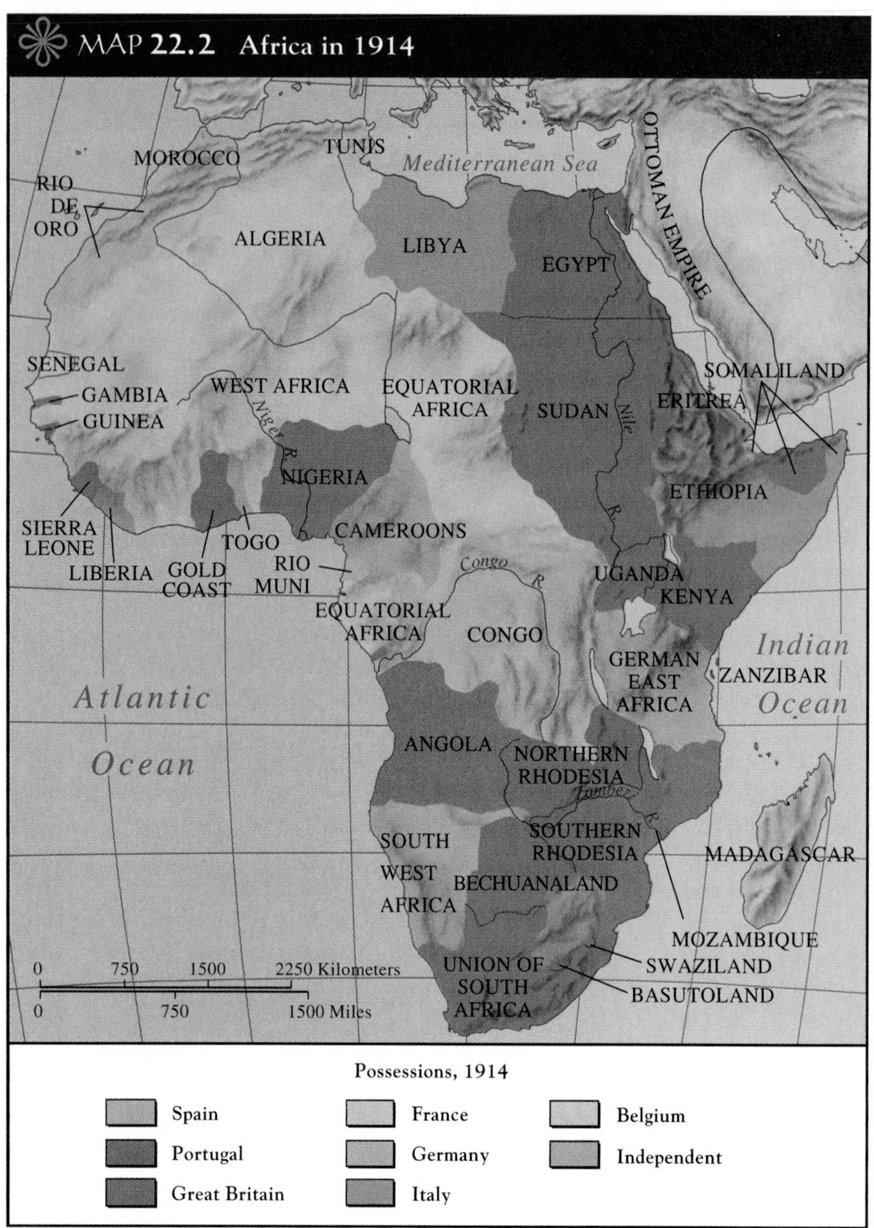

ARAB MERCHANTS AND EUROPEAN MISSIONARIES IN EAST AFRICA

As always, events in East Africa followed their own distinctive pattern of development. Whereas the Atlantic slave trade was in decline, demand for slaves was increasing on the other side of the continent due to the growth of plantation agriculture in the region and on the islands off the coast. The French introduced sugar to the island of Réunion early in the century, while clove plantations (the clove was first introduced from the Moluccas in the eighteenth century) were established under Omani Arab ownership on the island of Zanzibar. Zanzibar itself became the major shipping port along the entire east coast during the early nineteenth century, and the sultan of Oman, who had reasserted Arab suzerainty over the region in the aftermath of the collapse of Portuguese authority, established his capital at Zanzibar in 1840.

From Zanzibar, Arab merchants fanned out into the interior plateaus in search of slaves, ivory, and other local products. The competition for slaves spread as far as the Lake District and the lower Sudan, as traders from the north launched their own raids to obtain conscripts for the Egyptian army. The khedive sent General Charles Gordon to Uganda to stop the practice, but in the absence of alternative sources of income, local merchants could not easily be persuaded to give up a lucrative occupation.

The tenacity of the slave trade in East Africa—Zanzibar had now become the largest slave market in Africa—was undoubtedly a major reason for the rise of Western interest and Christian missionary activity in the region during the middle of the century. The most renowned mis-

A SLAVE RAID ON THE LUALABA RIVER. By the mid-nineteenth century, most European nations had prohibited the trade in African slaves, but slavery continued in East Africa under the sponsorship of the sultan of Zanzibar. In this sketch, slave traders massacre Africans in an 1871 slave raid on the Lualaba River, just west of Lake Tanganyika. Wrote David Livingstone of the occasion, "It gave me the impression of being in Hell."

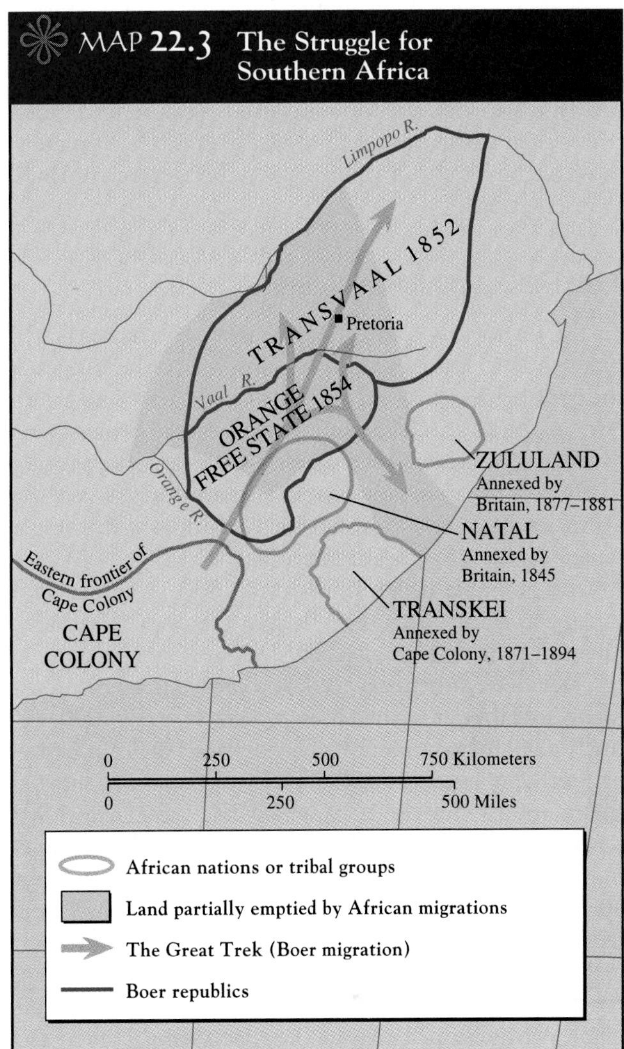

sionary was the Scottish doctor David Livingstone, who arrived in Africa in 1841. Because Livingstone spent much of his time exploring the interior of the continent, discovering Victoria Falls in the process, he was occasionally criticized for being more explorer than missionary. But Livingstone was convinced that it was his divinely appointed task to bring Christianity to the far reaches of the continent, and his passionate opposition to slavery did far more to win public support for the abolitionist cause than did the efforts of any other figure of his generation. Public outcries provoked the British to redouble their efforts to bring the slave trade in East Africa to an end, and in 1873 the slave market at Zanzibar was finally closed as the result of pressure from London. Shortly before, Livingstone had died of illness in central Africa, but some of his followers brought his body to the coast for burial. His legacy is still visible today in the form of an Anglican cathedral that was erected on the site of the slave market at Zanzibar.

BANTUS, BOERS, AND BRITISH IN THE SOUTH

Nowhere in Africa did the European presence grow more rapidly than in the south. During the eighteenth century, the Boers, the Afrikaans-speaking farmers who were descended from the original Dutch settlers of the Cape Colony, began to migrate eastward. After the British seized control of the cape from the Dutch during the Napoleonic Wars, the Boers' eastward migration intensified, culminating in the Great Trek of the mid-1830s. In part, the Boers' departure was provoked by the different attitude of the British to the native population. Slavery was abolished in the British Empire in 1834, and the British government was generally more sympathetic to the rights of the local African population than were the Afrikaners, many of whom believed white superiority was ordained by God and fled from British rule to control their own destiny. Eventually, the Boers formed their own independent republics—the Orange Free State and the South African Republic (usually called the Transvaal).

Although the Boer occupation of the eastern territory was initially facilitated by internecine warfare among the Bantu-speaking inhabitants of the region, the new settlers met some resistance. In the early nineteenth century, the Zulus, a Bantu people led by a talented ruler named Shaka, engaged in a series of wars with the Europeans that ended only when Shaka was overthrown. The local Khoisan people also sometimes reacted with violence when the Boers attempted to drive them off their grazing lands. One Dutch official complained that the Khoisan were driving settlers from their farms "for no other reason than because they saw that we were breaking up the best land and grass, where their cattle were accustomed to graze."[4] Ultimately, most of the blacks in the Boer republics were confined to reservations.

THE SCRAMBLE FOR AFRICA

At the beginning of the 1880s, most of Africa was still independent. European rule was limited to the fringes of the continent, such as Algeria, the Gold Coast, and South Africa. Other areas like Egypt, lower Nigeria, Senegal, and Mozambique were under various forms of loose protectorate. But the pace of European penetration was accelerating, and the constraints that had limited European rapaciousness were fast disappearing.

The scramble began in the mid-1880s, when several European states, including Belgium, France, Germany, Great Britain, and Portugal, engaged in what today would be called a feeding frenzy to seize a piece of African territory before the carcass had been picked clean. By 1900, virtually all of the continent had been placed under one form or another of European rule. The British had consolidated their authority over the Nile valley and seized additional territories in East Africa. The French retaliated by advancing eastward from Senegal into the central Sahara. They also occupied the island of Madagascar and other coastal territories in West and Central Africa. In between, the Germans claimed the hinterland opposite Zanzibar, as well as coastal strips in West and Southwest Africa north of the Cape, while King Leopold II of Belgium claimed the Congo. Eventually, Italy entered the contest and seized modern Libya and some of the Somali coast.

What had happened to spark the sudden imperialist hysteria that brought an end to African independence? Clearly, the level of trade between Europe and Africa was not sufficient to justify the risks and the expense of conquest. More important than economic interests were the intensified rivalries among the European states that led them to engage in imperialist takeovers out of fear that if they did not, another state might do so, leaving them at a disadvantage. As one British diplomatic official remarked, a protectorate at the mouth of the Niger River would be an "unwelcome burden," but a French protectorate there would be "fatal." In such circumstances, statesmen felt compelled to obtain colonies as a hedge against future actions by rivals. In the most famous example, the British solidified their control over the entire Nile valley to protect the Suez Canal.

Another consideration might be called the "missionary factor," as European missionary interests lobbied with their governments for colonial takeovers to facilitate their efforts to convert the African population to Christianity. The concept of social Darwinism and the "White Man's Burden" persuaded many that it was in the interests of the African people, as well as their conquerors, to be introduced more rapidly to the benefits of Western civilization (see box on p. 671). Even David Livingstone had become convinced that missionary work and economic development had to go hand in hand, pleading to his fellow Europeans to introduce the "three Cs" (Christianity, commerce, and civilization) to the continent. How much easier such a task would be if African peoples were under benevolent European rule!

A ZULU ENCAMPMENT IN SOUTHERN AFRICA. When white settlers moved beyond the original Cape Colony in search of good farmland, they encountered the Zulus, a Bantu-speaking people living in the lands northeast of the cape. Often the encounter was quite brutal on both sides. In this illustration from 1838, Boer leaders are entering a Zulu settlement to take part in a ceremony in their honor. Instead, they were executed by Zulu warriors.

THE WHITE MAN'S BURDEN

One of the justifications for European imperialism was the notion that the allegedly "more advanced" white peoples had the moral responsibility to raise ignorant native peoples to a higher level of civilization. Few captured this notion better than the British poet Rudyard Kipling (1865–1936) in his famous poem The White Man's Burden. *Though his appeal was addressed to the United States, the sentiments he expressed influenced all the imperialist powers.*

RUDYARD KIPLING, *THE WHITE MAN'S BURDEN*

Take up the White Man's burden—
Send forth the best ye breed—
Go bind your sons to exile
To serve your captives' need;
To wait in heavy harness,
On fluttered folk and wild—
Your new-caught sullen peoples,
Half-devil and half-child.

Take up the White Man's burden—
In patience to abide,
To veil the threat of terror
And check the show of pride;
By open speech and simple,
An hundred times made plain
To seek another's profit,
And work another's gain.

Take up the White Man's burden—
The savage wars of peace—
Fill full the mouth of Famine
And bid the sickness cease;
And when your goal is nearest
The end for others sought,
Watch Sloth and heathen Folly
Bring all your hopes to nought.

Take up the White Man's burden—
No tawdry rule of kings,
But toil of serf and sweeper—
The tale of common things.
The ports ye shall not enter,
The roads ye shall not tread,
Go mark them with your living,
And mark them with your dead!

Take up the White Man's burden—
And reap his old reward:
The blame of those ye better,
The hate of those ye guard—
The cry of hosts ye humour
(Ah, slowly!) toward the light:—
'Why brought ye us from bondage,
'Our loved Egyptian night?'

Take up the White Man's burden—
Ye dare not stoop to less—
Nor call too loud on Freedom
To cloak your weariness;
By all ye cry or whisper,
By all you leave or do,
The silent, sullen peoples
Shall weigh your Gods and you.

Take up the White Man's burden—
Have done with childish days—
The lightly proffered laurel,
The easy, ungrudged praise.
Comes now, to search your manhood
Through all the thankless years,
Cold-edged with dear-bought wisdom,
The judgment of your peers!

There were more prosaic reasons as well. Advances in Western technology and European superiority in firearms made it easier than ever for a small European force to defeat superior numbers. Furthermore, life expectancy for Europeans living in Africa had improved. With the discovery that quinine (extracted from the bark of the cinchona tree) could provide partial immunity from the ravages of malaria, the mortality rate for Europeans living in Africa dropped dramatically in the 1840s. By the end of the century, European residents in tropical Africa faced only slightly higher risks of death by disease than individuals living in Europe.

Under these circumstances, when King Leopold of Belgium used missionary activities as an excuse to claim vast territories in the Congo River basin (as "a small country, with a small people," he said, Belgium needed a colony to enhance its image),[5] he set off a desperate race to stake claims throughout sub-Saharan Africa. Leopold ended up with the territories south of the Congo River, while France occupied areas to the north (Leopold later bequeathed the Congo to Belgium on his death). Meanwhile, on the eastern side of the continent, Germany (through the activities of an ambitious missionary and with the agreement of the British, who needed German support against the French) annexed the colony of Tanganyika. To avert the possibility of violent clashes among the great powers, the German chancellor Otto von Bismarck convened a conference in Berlin in 1884 to set ground rules for future

CHRONOLOGY

IMPERIALISM IN AFRICA

Dutch abolish slave trade in Africa	1795
Napoleonic invasion of Egypt	1798
Slave trade declared illegal in Great Britain	1808
Boers' Great Trek in southern Africa	1830s
French seize Algeria	1830
Sultan of Oman establishes capital at Zanzibar	1840
David Livingstone arrives in Africa	1841
Slavery abolished in the United States	1863
Completion of Suez Canal	1869
Zanzibar slave market closed	1873
British establish Gold Coast colony	1874
British establish informal protectorate over Egypt	1881
Berlin Conference on Africa	1884
Charles Gordon killed at Khartoum	1885
Confrontation at Fashoda	1898
Boer War	1899–1902
Union of South Africa established	1910

annexations of African territory by European nations. Like the famous Open Door Notes fifteen years later (see Chapter 23), the conference combined high-minded resolutions with a hardheaded recognition of practical interests. The delegates called for liberty of commerce in the Congo and along the Niger River as well as for further efforts to end the slave trade. At the same time, the participants recognized the inevitability of the imperialist dynamic, agreeing only that future annexations of African territory should not be given international recognition until effective occupation had been demonstrated. No African delegates were present.

The Berlin Conference had been convened to avert war and reduce tensions among European nations competing for the spoils of Africa. It proved reasonably successful at achieving the first objective but less so at the second. During the next few years, African territories were annexed without provoking a major confrontation between the Western powers, but in the late 1890s, Britain and France reached the brink of conflict at Fashoda, a small town on the Nile River in the Sudan. The French had been advancing eastward across the Sahara with the transparent objective of controlling the regions around the upper Nile. In 1898, British and Egyptian troops seized the Sudan from successors of the Mahdi and then marched southward to head off the French. After a tense face-off at Fashoda, the French government backed down, and British authority over the area was secured. Except for the Mediterranean littoral and their small possessions of Djibouti and a portion of the Somali coast, the French were restricted to equatorial Africa.

Ironically, the only major clash between Europeans over Africa took place in southern Africa, where competition among the powers was almost nonexistent. The discovery of gold and diamonds in the Boer republic of the Transvaal was the source of the problem. Clashes between the Afrikaner population and foreign (mainly British) miners and developers led to an attempt by Cecil Rhodes, prime minister of the Cape Colony and a prominent entrepreneur in the area, to subvert the Transvaal and bring it under British rule. In 1899, the so-called Boer War broke out between Britain and the Transvaal, which was backed by its fellow republic, the Orange Free State. Guerrilla resistance by the Boers was fierce, but the vastly superior forces of the British were able to prevail by 1902. To compensate the defeated Afrikaner population for the loss of independence, the British government agreed that only whites would vote in the now essentially self-governing colony. The Boers were placated, but the brutalities committed during the war (the British introduced an institution later to be known as the concentration camp) created bitterness on both sides that continued to fester through future decades.

THE COLONIAL SYSTEM

Now that they were in control of most of the world, what did the colonial powers do with it? As we have seen, their primary objective was to exploit the natural resources of the subject areas and to open up markets for manufactured goods and capital investment from the mother country. In some cases, that goal could be realized in cooperation with local political elites, whose loyalty could be earned, or purchased, by economic rewards or by confirming them in their positions of authority and status in a new colonial setting. Sometimes, however, this policy of indirect rule was not feasible because local leaders refused to cooperate with their colonial masters or even actively resisted the foreign conquest. In such cases, the local elites were removed from power and replaced with a new set of officials recruited from the mother country.

In general, the societies most likely to actively resist colonial conquest were those with a long tradition of national cohesion and independence, such as China, Burma, and Vietnam in Asia and the African Muslim states in northern Nigeria and Morocco. In those areas, the colonial powers tended to dispense with local collaborators and govern directly. In parts of Africa, the Indian subcontinent, and the Malay peninsula, where the local authorities, for whatever reason, were willing to collaborate with the imperialist powers, indirect rule was more common.

The distinctions between direct and indirect rule were not merely academic and often had fateful consequences for the peoples involved. Where colonial powers encountered resistance and were forced to overthrow local political elites, they often adopted policies designed to eradicate the source of resistance and destroy the traditional culture. Such policies often had quite corrosive effects on the indigenous societies and provoked resentment and resistance that not only marked the colonial relationship but even affected relations after the restoration of national independence. The bitter struggles after World War II in Algeria, the Dutch East Indies, and Vietnam can be ascribed in part to that phenomenon.

The Philosophy of Colonialism

To justify their rule, the colonial powers appealed, in part, to the time-honored maxim of "might makes right." By the end of the nineteenth century, that attitude received pseudoscientific validity from the concept of social Darwinism, which maintained that only societies that moved aggressively to adapt to changing circumstances would survive and prosper in a world governed by the Darwinist law of "survival of the fittest."

Some people, however, were uncomfortable with such a brutal view of the law of nature and sought a moral justification that appeared to benefit the victim. Here again, as we have seen, the concept of social Darwinism pointed the way. By bringing the benefits of Western democracy, capitalism, and Christianity to the feudalistic and tradition-ridden societies of Africa and Asia, the colonial powers were enabling primitive peoples to adapt to the challenges of the modern world. Buttressed by such comforting theories, sensitive Western minds could ignore the brutal aspects of colonialism and persuade themselves that in the long run the results would be beneficial for both sides. Few were as adept at describing the "civilizing mission" of colonialism as the French administrator and twice governor-general of French Indochina Albert Sarraut. While admitting that colonialism was originally an "act of force" undertaken for commercial profit, he insisted that by redistributing the wealth of the earth, the colonial process would result in a better life for all:

> Is it just, is it legitimate that such [an uneven distribution of resources] should be indefinitely prolonged? . . . No! . . . Humanity is distributed throughout the globe. No race, no people has the right or power to isolate itself egotistically from the movements and necessities of universal life.[6]

SERVING THE WHITE RULER. Although European governments claimed to be carrying out the civilizing mission in Africa, all too often the local population was forced to labor in degrading conditions to serve the economic interests of the occupying power. Here African workers are depicted as they transport goods for a European merchant.

THE BLACK MAN'S BURDEN

The Western justification of imperialism that was based on a sense of moral responsibility, evident in Rudyard Kipling's poem, was often hypocritical. Edmund Morel, a British journalist who spent time in the Congo, pointed out the destructive effects of Western imperialism on native Africans in his book The Black Man's Burden.

EDMUND MOREL, *THE BLACK MAN'S BURDEN*

It is [the Africans] who carry the "Black man's burden." They have not withered away before the white man's occupation. Indeed . . . Africa has ultimately absorbed within itself every Caucasian and, for that matter, every Semitic invader, too. In hewing out for himself a fixed abode in Africa, the white man has massacred the African in heaps. The African has survived, and it is well for the white settlers that he has. . . .

What the partial occupation of his soil by the white man has failed to do; what the mapping out of European political "spheres of influence" has failed to do; what the Maxim [machine gun] and the rifle, the slave gang, labour in the bowels of the earth and the lash, have failed to do; what imported measles, smallpox, and syphilis have failed to do; whatever the overseas slave trade failed to do; the power of modern capitalistic exploitation, assisted by modern engines of destruction, may yet succeed in accomplishing.

For from the evils of the latter, scientifically applied and enforced, there is no escape for the African. Its destructive effects are not spasmodic; they are permanent. In its permanence resides its fatal consequences. It kills not the body merely, but the soul. It breaks the spirit. It attacks the African at every turn, from every point of vantage. It wrecks his polity, uproots him from the land, invades his family life, destroys his natural pursuits and occupations, claims his whole time, enslaves him in his own home.

In Africa, especially in tropical Africa, which a capitalistic imperialism threatens and has, in part, already devastated, man is incapable of reacting against unnatural conditions. In those regions man is engaged in a perpetual struggle against disease and an exhausting climate, which tells heavily upon childbearing; and there is no scientific machinery for saving the weaker members of the community. The African of the tropics is capable of tremendous physical labours. But he cannot accommodate himself to the European system of monotonous, uninterrupted labour, with its long and regular hours, involving, moreover, as it frequently does, severance from natural surroundings and nostalgia, the condition of melancholy resulting from separation from home, a malady to which the African is specially prone. Climatic conditions forbid it. When the system is forced upon him, the tropical African droops and dies.

Nor is violent physical opposition to abuse and injustice henceforth possible for the African in any part of Africa. His chances of effective resistance have been steadily dwindling with the increasing perfectibility in the killing power of modern armament.

Thus the African is really helpless against the material gods of the white man, as embodied in the trinity of imperialism, capitalistic exploitation, and militarism. . . .

To reduce all the varied and picturesque and stimulating episodes in savage life to a dull routine of endless toil for uncomprehended ends; to dislocate social ties and disrupt social institutions; to stifle nascent desires and crush mental development; to graft upon primitive passions the annihilating evils of scientific slavery, and the bestial imaginings of civilized man, unrestrained by convention or law; in fine, to kill the soul in a people—this is a crime which transcends physical murder.

But what about the possibility that historically and culturally the societies of Asia and Africa were fundamentally different from those of the West and could not, or would not, be persuaded to transform themselves along Western lines? Was the human condition universal, or were human beings so shaped by their history and geographical environment that their civilizations would inevitably remain distinct? In that case, a policy of cultural transformation could not be expected to succeed and could even lead to disaster.

In fact, colonial theorists never decided this issue one way or the other. The French, who were most inclined to philosophize about the problem, adopted the terms *assimilation* (which implied an effort to transform colonial societies in the Western image) and *association* (by which they meant collaboration with local elites, while leaving local traditions alone) to describe the two alternatives and then proceeded to vacillate between them. French policy in Indochina, for example, began as one of association but switched to assimilation under pressure from those who felt that colonial powers owed a debt to their subject peoples. But assimilation (which in any case was never accepted as feasible or desirable by many colonial officials) aroused resentment among the local population, many of whom opposed the destruction of their native traditions. In the end, the French abandoned the attempt to justify their presence and fell back on a policy of ruling by force of arms.

Other colonial powers had little interest in the issue. The British, whether out of a sense of pragmatism or of racial superiority, refused to entertain the possibility of assimilation and treated their subject peoples as culturally and racially distinct. In formulating a colonial policy for the Philippines, the United States adopted a policy of assimilation in theory but did not always put it into practice.

To many of the colonial peoples, such questions must have appeared academic, since the primary objectives of all the colonial states were economic exploitation and the retention of power (see the box on p. 674). Like the British soldier in Kipling's poem "On the Road to Mandalay," all too many Westerners living in the colonies believed that the Great Lord Buddha was nothing but a "bloomin' idol made of mud, what they call the great god Bud."

Colonialism in Action

In practice, colonialism in India, Southeast Asia, and Africa exhibited many similarities but also some differences. Some of these variations can be traced to political or social differences among the colonial powers themselves. The French, for example, often tried to impose a centralized administrative system on their colonies that mirrored the system in use in France, while the British sometimes attempted to transform local aristocrats into the equivalent of the landed gentry at home in Britain. Other differences stemmed from conditions in the colonies themselves and the colonizers' aspirations for them. For instance, the Western powers believed that their economic interests were far more limited in Africa than elsewhere and therefore treated their African colonies somewhat differently than those in India or Southeast Asia.

INDIA UNDER THE BRITISH RAJ

By the beginning of the nineteenth century, the once glorious empire of the Mughals had been reduced by British military power to a shadow of its former greatness. During the next few decades, the British sought to consolidate their control over the Indian subcontinent, expanding from their base areas along the coast into the interior. Some territories were taken over directly, first by the East India Company and later by the British crown; others were ruled indirectly through their local maharajas and rajas.

GATEWAY TO INDIA? Built in the Roman imperial style by the British to commemorate the visit to India of King George V and Queen Mary in 1911, the Gateway of India was erected at the water's edge in the harbor of Bombay, India's greatest port city. For thousands of British citizens arriving in India, the Gateway of India was the first view of their new home and a symbol of the power and majesty of the British raj. Only a few dozen yards away was the luxurious Taj Mahal Hotel. Constructed in the popular Anglo-Indian style, it was built to house European visitors upon their arrival to India.

INDIAN IN BLOOD, ENGLISH IN TASTE AND INTELLECT

Thomas Babington Macaulay (1800–1859) was named a member of the Supreme Council of India in the early 1830s. In that capacity he was responsible for drawing up a new educational policy for British subjects in the area. In his Minute on Education, *he considered the claims of English and various local languages to become the vehicle for educational training and decided in favor of the former. It is better, he argued, to teach Indian elites about Western civilization so as "to form a class who may be interpreters between us and the millions whom we govern; a class of persons, Indian in blood and color, but English in taste, in opinions, in morals, and in intellect." Later Macaulay became a prominent historian, while the debate over the relative benefits of English and the various Indian languages continues today.*

THOMAS BABINGTON MACAULAY, *MINUTE ON EDUCATION*

We have a fund to be employed as government shall direct for the intellectual improvement of the people of this country. The simple question is, what is the most useful way of employing it?

All parties seem to be agreed on one point, that the dialects commonly spoken among the natives of this part of India contain neither literary or scientific information, and are, moreover so poor and rude that, until they are enriched from some other quarter, it will not be easy to translate any valuable work into them. . . .

What, then, shall the language [of education] be? One half of the Committee maintain that it should be the English. The other half strongly recommend the Arabic and Sanskrit. The whole question seems to me to be, which language is the best worth knowing?

I have no knowledge of either Sanskrit or Arabic—but I have done what I could to form a correct estimate of their value. I have read translations of the most celebrated Arabic and Sanskrit works. I have conversed both here and at home with men distinguished by their proficiency in the Eastern tongues. I am quite ready to take the Oriental learning at the valuation of the Orientalists themselves. I have never found one among them who could deny that a single shelf of a good European library was worth the whole native literature of India and Arabia. . . .

It is, I believe, no exaggeration to say, that all the historical information which has been collected from all the books written in the Sanskrit language is less valuable than what may be found in the most paltry abridgments used at preparatory schools in England. In every branch of physical or moral philosophy the relative position of the two nations is nearly the same.

Not all of the effects of British rule were bad. British governance over the subcontinent brought order and stability to a society that had been rent by civil war. By the early nineteenth century, British control had been consolidated and led to a relatively honest and efficient government that in many respects operated to the benefit of the average Indian. One of the benefits of the period was the heightened attention given to education. Through the efforts of the British administrator and historian Thomas Babington Macaulay, a new school system was established to train the children of Indian elites, and the British civil service examination was introduced. Macaulay's attitude, however, was unashamedly Anglocentric (see the box above).

British rule also brought an end to some of the more inhumane aspects of Indian tradition. The practice of *sati* was outlawed, and widows were legally permitted to remarry. The British also attempted to put an end to the endemic brigandage (known as thuggee, which gave rise to the English word "thug") that had plagued travelers in India since time immemorial. Railroads, the telegraph, and the postal service were introduced to India shortly after they appeared in Great Britain itself. Work began on the main highway from Calcutta to Delhi in 1839, and the first rail network was opened in 1853. A new penal code based on the British model was adopted, and health and sanitation conditions were improved.

But the Indian people paid a high price for the peace and stability brought by the British raj (from the Indian *raja,* or prince). Perhaps the most flagrant cost was economic. While British entrepreneurs and a small percentage of the Indian population attached to the imperial system reaped financial benefits from British rule, it brought hardship to millions of others in both the cities and the rural areas. The introduction of British textiles put thousands of Bengali women out of work and severely damaged the local textile industry.

In rural areas, the British introduced the *zamindar* system (see Chapter 16) in the misguided expectation that it would both facilitate the collection of agricultural taxes and create a new landed gentry, who could, as in Britain itself, become the conservative foundation of imperial rule. But the local gentry took advantage of their new authority to increase taxes and force the less fortunate

MAP 22.4 India Under British Rule, 1805–1931

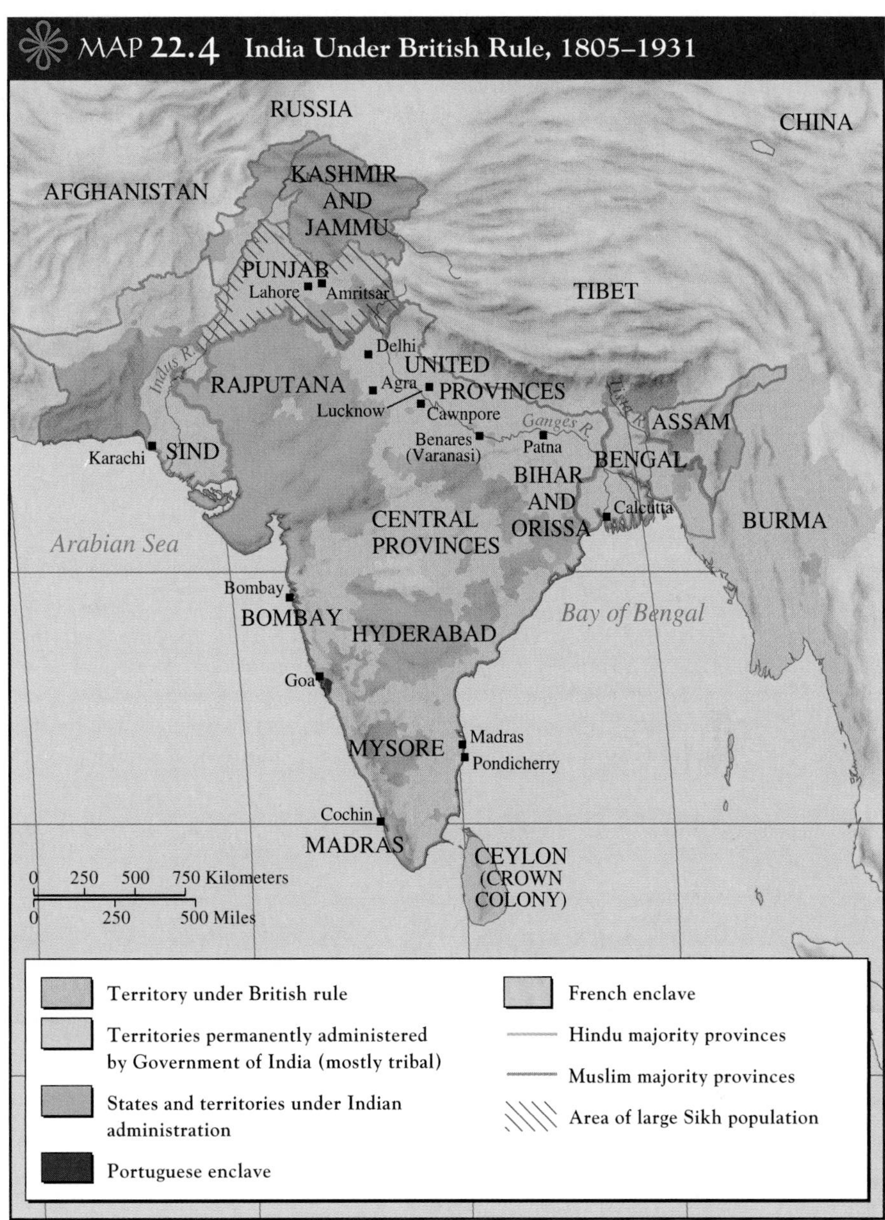

peasants to become tenants or lose their land entirely. When rural unrest threatened, the government passed legislation protecting farmers against eviction and unreasonable rent increases, but this measure had little effect outside the southern provinces, where it had originally been enacted.

British colonialism was also remiss in bringing the benefits of modern science and technology to India. Some limited forms of industrialization took place, notably in the manufacturing of textiles and jute (used in making rope). The first textile mill opened in 1856. Seventy years later, there were eighty mills in the city of Bombay alone. Nevertheless, the lack of local capital and the advantages given to British imports prevented the emergence of other vital new commercial and manufacturing operations.

Foreign rule also had a psychological effect on the Indian people. Although many British colonial officials sincerely tried to improve the lot of the people under their charge, British arrogance and contempt for native tradition cut deeply into the pride of many Indians, especially those of high caste, who were accustomed to a position of superior status in India. Educated Indians trained in the Anglo-Indian school system for a career in the civil service, as well as Eurasians born to mixed marriages, often imitated the behavior and dress of their rulers, speaking

English, eating Western food, and taking up European leisure activities, but many rightfully wondered where their true cultural loyalties lay. This cultural collision was poignantly described in the novel *A Passage to India* by the British writer E. M. Forster.

COLONIAL REGIMES IN SOUTHEAST ASIA

In Southeast Asia, economic profit was the immediate and primary aim of colonial enterprise. For that purpose, colonial powers tried wherever possible to work with local elites to facilitate the exploitation of natural resources. Indirect rule reduced the cost of training European administrators and had a less corrosive impact on the local culture. In the Dutch East Indies, for example, officials of the Dutch East India Company (VOC) entrusted local administration to the indigenous landed aristocracy, who maintained law and order and collected taxes in return for a payment from the VOC (see the box on p. 679). The British followed a similar practice in Malaya. While establishing direct rule over the crucial commercial centers of Singapore and Malacca, the British allowed local Muslim rulers to maintain princely power in the interior of the peninsula.

Indirect rule, however convenient and inexpensive, was not always feasible. In some instances, local resistance to the colonial conquest made such a policy impossible. In Burma, the staunch opposition of the monarchy and other traditionalist forces caused the British to abolish the monarchy and administer the country directly through their colonial government in India. In Indochina, the French used both direct and indirect means. They imposed

AN ENGLISH NABOB IN COLONIAL INDIA. When the British took over India in the late eighteenth and nineteenth centuries, many Indians began to imitate European customs for prestige or social advancement. Sometimes, however, the cultural influence went the other way. Here an English nabob, as European residents in the colonies were often called, apes the manner of an Indian aristocrat, complete with harem and hookah, the Indian water pipe. The paintings on the wall, however, are in the European style.

THE EFFECTS OF DUTCH COLONIALISM IN JAVA

E. Douwes Dekker was a Dutch colonial official who served in the East Indies for nearly twenty years. In 1860, he published a critique of the Dutch colonial system that had an impact in the Netherlands similar to that of Harriet Beecher Stowe's Uncle Tom's Cabin *in the United States. In the following excerpt from his book* Max Havelaar, or Coffee Auctions of the Dutch Trading Company, *Dekker described the system as it was applied on the island of Java, in the Indonesian archipelago.*

E. DOUWES DEKKER, *MAX HAVELAAR*

The Javanese is by nature a husbandman; the ground whereon he is born, which gives much for little labor, allures him to it, and, above all things, he devotes his whole heart and soul to the cultivating of his rice fields, in which he is very clever. He grows up in the midst of his sawahs [rice fields] . . . ; when still very young, he accompanies his father to the field, where he helps him in his labor with plow and spade, in constructing dams and drains to irrigate his fields; he counts his years by harvests; he estimates time by the color of the blades in his field; he is at home amongst the companions who cut paddy with him; he chooses his wife amongst the girls of the dessah [village], who every evening tread the rice with joyous songs. The possession of a few buffaloes for plowing is the ideal of his dreams. The cultivation of rice is in Java what the vintage is in the Rhine provinces and in the south of France. But there came foreigners from the West, who made themselves masters of the country. They wished to profit by the fertility of the soil, and ordered the native to devote a part of his time and labor to the cultivation of other things which should produce higher profits in the markets of Europe. To persuade the lower orders to do so, they had only to follow a very simple policy. The Javanese obeys his chiefs; to win the chiefs, it was only necessary to give them a part of the gain,—and success was complete.

To be convinced of the success of that policy we need only consider the immense quantity of Javanese products sold in Holland; and we shall also be convinced of its injustice, for, if anybody should ask if the husbandman himself gets a reward in proportion to that quantity, then I must give a negative answer. The Government compels him to cultivate certain products on his ground; it punishes him if he sells what he has produced to any purchaser but itself; and it fixes the price actually paid. The expenses of transport to Europe through a privileged trading company are high; the money paid to the chiefs for encouragement increases the prime cost; and because the entire trade *must* produce profit, that profit cannot be got in any other way than by paying the Javanese just enough to keep him from starving, which would lessen the producing power of the nation.

direct rule on the southern provinces in the Mekong delta but governed the north as a protectorate, with the emperor retaining titular authority from his palace in Huê. The French adopted a similar policy in Cambodia and Laos, where local rulers were left in charge with French advisers to counsel them.

Whatever method was used, colonial regimes in Southeast Asia, as elsewhere, were slow to create democratic institutions. The first legislative councils and assemblies were composed almost exclusively of European residents in the colony. The first representatives from the indigenous population were wealthy and conservative in their political views. When Southeast Asians complained, colonial officials gradually and reluctantly began to broaden the franchise. Albert Sarraut advised patience in awaiting the full benefits of colonial policy: "I will treat you like my younger brothers, but do not forget that I am the older brother. I will slowly give you the dignity of humanity."[7]

Colonial officials were also slow to adopt educational reforms. Although the introduction of Western education was one of the justifications of colonialism, colonial officials soon discovered that educating native elites could backfire. Often there were few jobs for highly trained lawyers, engineers, and architects in colonial societies, leading to the threat of an indigestible mass of unemployed intellectuals who would take out their frustrations on the colonial regime. Educational opportunities for the common people were even harder to come by. In French-controlled Vietnam, in 1917 only 3,000 of the 23,000 villages in the country had a public school. The French had opened a university in Hanoi, but it was immediately closed as a result of student demonstrations. As one French official noted in voicing his opposition to increasing the number of schools in Vietnam, educating the natives did not mean "one coolie less, but one rebel more."

Colonial powers were equally reluctant to take up the White Man's Burden in the area of economic development. As we have seen, their primary goals were to secure a source of cheap raw materials and to maintain markets for manufactured goods. Such objectives would be undermined by the emergence of advanced industrial economies. So colonial policy concentrated on the export of raw materials—teakwood from Burma, rubber and tin from Malaya, spices, tea and coffee, and palm oil from the East Indies, and sugar and copra from the Philippines.

A RUBBER TREE. Natural rubber was one of the most important cash crops in European colonies in Asia. Rubber trees, native to the Amazon River basin in Brazil, were eventually transplanted to Southeast Asia, where they became a major source of profit. Workers on the plantations received few benefits, however, for once the sap of the tree (known as latex and shown here) was extracted, the bulk of the refining process took place in Europe. Most of the laborers at the Malaysian rubber plantation where this photo was taken are immigrants or the sons of immigrants from India.

In some Southeast Asian colonial societies, a measure of industrial development did take place to meet the needs of the European population and local elites. Major manufacturing cities like Rangoon in lower Burma, Batavia on the island of Java, and Saigon in French Indochina grew rapidly. Although the local middle class benefited from the increased economic activity, most large industrial and commercial establishments were owned and managed by Europeans or, in some cases, by Indian or Chinese merchants. In Saigon, for example, even the production of *nuoc mam*, the traditional Vietnamese fish sauce, was under Chinese ownership. In most cities, foreigners controlled banking, major manufacturing activities, and the import-export trade. The natives were more apt to work in a family business, in factory or assembly plants, or as peddlers, day laborers, or rickshaw pullers—in other words, at less profitable and less capital-intensive businesses.

Despite the growth of an urban economy, the vast majority of people in the colonial societies continued to farm the land. Many continued to live by subsistence agriculture, but the colonial policy of emphasizing cash crops for export also led to the creation of a form of plantation agriculture in which peasants were recruited to work as wage laborers on rubber and tea plantations owned by Europeans. To maintain a competitive edge, the plantation owners kept the wages of their workers at a poverty level. Many plantation workers were "shanghaied" (the English term originated from the practice of recruiting laborers, often from the docks and streets of Shanghai, by unscrupulous means such as the use of force, alcohol, or drugs) to work on plantations, where conditions were often so inhumane that thousands died. High taxes, enacted by colonial governments to pay for administrative costs or improvements in the local infrastructure, were a heavy burden for poor peasants.

The situation was made even more difficult by the steady growth of the population. Peasants in Asia had always had large families on the assumption that a high proportion of their children would die in infancy. But improved sanitation and medical treatment resulted in lower rates of infant mortality and a staggering increase in population. The population of the island of Java, for example, increased from about a million in the precolonial era to about 40 million at the end of the nineteenth century. Under these conditions, the rural areas could no longer support the growing populations, and many young people fled to the cities to seek jobs in factories or shops. The migratory pattern gave rise to the squatter settlements in the suburbs of the major cities.

As in India, colonial rule did bring some benefits to Southeast Asia. It led to the beginnings of a modern economic infrastructure and to what is sometimes called a "modernizing elite" dedicated to the creation of an advanced industrialized society. The development of an export market helped to create an entrepreneurial class in rural areas. This happened, for example, on the outer islands of the Dutch East Indies (such as Borneo and Sumatra), where small growers of rubber trees, palm trees for oil, coffee, tea, and spices began to share in the profits of the colonial enterprise.

A balanced assessment of the colonial legacy in Southeast Asia must take into account that the early stages of industrialization are difficult in any society. Even in Western Europe, industrialization led to the creation of an impoverished and powerless proletariat, urban slums, and displaced peasants driven from the land. In much of Europe and Japan, however, the bulk of the population eventually enjoyed better material conditions as the profits from manufacturing and plantation agriculture were reinvested in the national economy and gave rise to increased consumer demand. In contrast, in Southeast Asia, most of the profits were repatriated to the colonial mother country, while displaced peasants fleeing to cities like Rangoon, Batavia, and Saigon found little opportunity for employment. Many were left with seasonal employment, with one foot on the farm and one in the factory. The old world was being destroyed, while the new had yet to be born.

COLONIALISM IN AFRICA

Colonialism had similar consequences in Africa, although with some changes in emphasis. As we have seen, European economic interests were more limited in Africa than elsewhere. Having seized the continent in what could almost be described as a fit of hysteria, the European powers had to decide what to do with it. With economic concerns relatively limited except for isolated areas like the gold mines in the Transvaal and copper deposits in the Belgian Congo, interest in Africa declined, and most European governments settled down to govern their new territories with the least effort and expense possible. In many cases, this meant a form of indirect rule similar to what the British used in the princely states in India. The British with their tradition of decentralized government at home were especially prone to adopt this approach.

In the minds of British administrators, the stated goal of indirect rule was to preserve African political traditions. The desire to limit cost and inconvenience was one reason for this approach, but it may also have been due to the conviction that Africans were inherently inferior to the white race and thus incapable of adopting European customs and institutions. In any event, indirect rule entailed relying to the greatest extent possible on existing political elites and institutions. Initially, in some areas the British simply asked a local ruler to formally accept British authority and to fly the Union Jack over official buildings. Sometimes it was the Africans who did the bidding, as in the case of the African leaders in the Cameroon who wrote to Queen Victoria:

> We *wish* to have your laws in our towns. We want to have every *fashion* altered; also we will do according to your Consul's *word*. Plenty wars here in our country. Plenty murder and plenty idol worshippers. Perhaps these *lines* of our writing will *look* to you as an *idle* tale.
>
> We have *spoken* to the English consul plenty times about having an English *government* here. We never have answer from you, so we wish to write you *ourselves*.[8]

CHRONOLOGY

IMPERIALISM IN ASIA

Stamford Raffles arrives in Singapore	1819
British attack lower Burma	1826
British rail network opened in northern India	1853
Sepoy Rebellion	1857
French attack Vietnam	1858
Indian National Congress established	1885
British and French agree to neutralize Thailand	1896
Commodore Dewey defeats Spanish fleet in Manila Bay	1898

Nigeria offers a typical example of British indirect rule. British officials maintained the central administration, but local authority was assigned to native chiefs, with British district officers serving as intermediaries with the central administration. Where a local aristocracy did not exist, the British assigned administrative responsibility to clan heads from communities in the vicinity. The local authorities were expected to maintain law and order and to collect taxes from the native population. As a general rule, indigenous customs were left undisturbed; a dual legal system was instituted that applied African laws to Africans and European laws to foreigners (see the box on p. 682).

One advantage of such an administrative system was that it did not severely disrupt local customs and institutions. Nevertheless, it had several undesirable consequences. In the first place, it was essentially a fraud, since all major decisions were made by the British administrators while the native authorities served primarily as the means of enforcing decisions. Moreover, indirect rule served to perpetuate the autocratic system often in use prior to colonial takeover. It was official policy to inculcate respect for authority in areas under British rule, and there was a natural tendency to view the local aristocracy as the African equivalent of the traditional British ruling class. Such a policy provided few opportunities for ambitious and talented young Africans from outside the traditional elite and thus sowed the seeds for class tensions after the restoration of independence in the twentieth century.

The situation was somewhat different in East Africa, especially in Kenya, which had a relatively large European population attracted by the temperate climate in the central highlands. The local government had encouraged white settlers to migrate to the area as a means of

A GUIDE FOR PEACE IN AFRICA: A BRITISH POINT OF VIEW

John Frederick Lugard (1858–1945) was the governor of British Nigeria prior to World War II. Earlier he had set forth the principles of indirect rule that became the foundation of British policy in Africa during the colonial era. In this short excerpt from his book The Dual Mandate in Tropical Africa, *Lord Lugard explained that effective policies could only be achieved if the British government and the native rulers established a cooperative arrangement, where each authority would govern within its own domain. The result, he argued, would be a careful balance between tradition and modernity that would maintain law and order and bring about evolutionary change in African society.*

JOHN FREDERICK LUGARD, *THE DUAL MANDATE IN TROPICAL AFRICA*

1. Native rulers are not permitted to raise and control armed forces, or to grant permission to carry arms. . . . No one with experience will deny the necessity of maintaining the strictest military discipline over armed forces or police in Africa if misuse of power is to be avoided, and they are not to become a menace and a terror to the native population and a danger in case of religious excitement—a discipline which an African ruler is incapable of appreciating or applying. . . .
2. The sole right to impose taxation in any form is reserved to the suzerain power. This fulfills the bilateral understanding that the peasantry . . . should be free of all other exactions whatsoever (including—unpaid labor), while a sufficient proportion of the tax is assigned to the native treasuries to meet the expenditure of the native administration. . . .
3. The right to legislate, is reserved. That this should remain in the hands of the central government . . . cannot be questioned. The native authority, however, exercises very considerable power in this regard. A native ruler, and the native courts, are empowered to enforce native law and custom, provided it is not repugnant to humanity, or in opposition to any ordinance.
4. The right to appropriate land on equitable terms for public purposes and for commercial requirements is vested in the governor. . . . In practice this does not interfere with the power of the native ruler (as the delegate of the governor) to assign lands to the natives under his rule, in accordance with native law and custom. . . .
5. To avoid friction and difficulties, it has been the recognized rule that the employees of the native administration should consist entirely of natives subject to the native authority. . . .
6. Finally, in the interests of good government, the right of confirming or otherwise the choice of the people of the successor to a chiefship, and of deposing any ruler for misrule or other adequate cause, is reserved to the governor.

promoting economic development and encouraging financial self-sufficiency. To attract Europeans, fertile farmlands in the central highlands were reserved for European settlement, while, as in South Africa, specified reserve lands were set aside for Africans. The presence of a substantial European minority (although, in fact, they represented only about 1 percent of the entire population) had an impact on Kenya's political development. The white settlers actively sought self-government and dominion status similar to that granted to such former British possessions as Canada and Australia. The British government, however, was not willing to run the risk of provoking racial tensions with the African majority and agreed only to establish separate government organs for the European and African populations.

The British used a different system in southern Africa, where there was a high percentage of European settlers. The situation was further complicated by the division between English-speaking and Afrikaner elements within the European population. In 1910, the British agreed to the creation of an independent Union of South Africa that combined the old Cape Colony and Natal with the Boer republics. The new union adopted a representative government, but only for the European population, while the African reserves of Basutoland (now Lesotho), Bechuanaland (now Botswana), and Swaziland were subordinated directly to the crown. The union was now free to manage its own domestic affairs and possessed considerable autonomy in foreign relations. Formal British rule was also extended to the remaining lands south of the Zambezi River, which were eventually divided into the territories of Northern and Southern Rhodesia. Southern Rhodesia attracted many British immigrants, and in 1922, after a popular referendum, it became a crown colony.

Most other European nations governed their African possessions through a form of direct rule. The prototype was the French system, which reflected the centralized administrative system introduced in France itself by Napoleon. As in the British colonies, at the top of the pyramid was a French official, usually known as a governor-general, who was appointed from Paris and governed with the aid of a bureaucracy in the capital city. At the provincial level, French commissioners were assigned to deal with local administrators, but the latter were required to be conversant in French and could be transferred to a new position at the needs of the central government.

Moreover, the French ideal was to assimilate their African subjects into French culture rather than preserving their native traditions. Africans were eligible to run for office and to serve in the French National Assembly, and a few were appointed to high positions in the colonial administration. Such policies reflected the relative absence of racist attitudes in French society, as well as the French conviction of the superiority of Gallic culture and their revolutionary belief in the universality of human nature.

After World War I, European colonial policy in Africa entered a new and more formal phase. The colonial administrative network was extended to a greater degree into outlying areas, where it was represented by a district official and defended by a small native army under European command. Greater attention was given to improving social services, including education, medicine and sanitation, and communications. The colonial system was now viewed more formally as a moral and social responsibility, a "sacred trust" to be maintained by the civilized countries until the Africans became capable of self-government. More emphasis was placed on economic development and on the exploitation of natural resources to provide the colonies with the means of achieving self-sufficiency. More Africans were now serving in colonial administrations, although relatively few were placed in positions of responsibility. On the other hand, race consciousness probably increased during this period. Segregated clubs, schools, and churches were established as more European officials brought their wives and began to raise families in the colonies.

At the same time, the establishment of European colonial rule often had the effect of reducing the rights and the status of women in Africa. African women had traditionally benefited from the prestige of matrilineal systems and were empowered by their traditional role as the primary agricultural producer in their community. Under colonialism, European settlers not only took the best land for themselves, but in introducing new agricultural techniques they tended to deal exclusively with males, encouraging the latter to develop lucrative cash crops, while women were restricted to traditional farming methods. Whereas African men applied chemical fertilizer to the fields, women used manure. While men began to use bicycles, and eventually trucks, to transport goods, women still carried their goods on their heads, a practice that continues today.

The Emergence of Anticolonialism

Thus far we have looked at the colonial experience primarily from the point of view of the colonial powers. Equally important is the way the subject peoples reacted to the experience. From the perspective of nearly half a century, it seems clear that their primary response was to turn to nationalism.

As we have seen, nationalism refers to a state of mind rising out of an awareness of being part of a community that possesses common institutions, traditions, language, and customs. Few nations in the world today meet such criteria. Most modern states contain a variety of ethnic, religious, and linguistic communities, each with its own sense of cultural and national identity. Should Canada, for example, which includes peoples of French, English and Native American heritage, be considered a nation? Another question is how nationalism differs from other forms of tribal, religious, or linguistic affiliation. Should every group that resists assimilation into a larger cultural unity be called nationalist?

Such questions complicate the study of nationalism even in Europe and North America and make agreement on a definition elusive. They create even greater dilemmas in discussing Asia and Africa, where most societies are deeply divided by ethnic, linguistic, and religious differences and the very term *nationalism* is a foreign phenomenon imported from the West (see the box on p. 684). Prior to the colonial era, most traditional societies in Africa and Asia were formed on the basis of religious beliefs, tribal loyalties, or devotion to hereditary monarchies. Although individuals in some countries may have identified themselves as members of a particular national group, others viewed themselves as subjects of a king, members of a tribe, or adherents to a particular religion.

The advent of European colonialism brought the consciousness of modern nationhood to many of the societies of Asia and Africa. The creation of European colonies with defined borders and a powerful central government led to the weakening of tribal and village ties and a significant reorientation in the individual's sense of political identity. The introduction of Western ideas of citizenship and representative government produced a new sense of participation in the affairs of government. At the same time, the appearance of a new elite class based not on hereditary privilege or religious sanction but on alleged racial or cultural superiority aroused a shared sense of resentment among the subject peoples who felt a common commitment to the creation of an independent society. By the first quarter of the twentieth century, political movements dedicated to the overthrow of colonial rule had arisen throughout much of the non-Western world.

A CRITIQUE OF INDIAN NATIONALISM

Rabindranath Tagore, one of India's greatest writers, was a prominent spokesman for the Indian people under colonial rule. Though indisputably a patriot, like many intellectuals he was torn between his commitment to his native land and his awareness of the benefits of Western civilization. In this passage from a book written at the height of World War I, he seeks to persuade his readers that the common destiny of all humanity is more important than that of an individual nation or people.

RABINDRANATH TAGORE, NATIONALISM IN INDIA

India has never had a real sense of nationalism. Even though from childhood I had been taught that idolatry of the nation is almost better than reverence for God and humanity, I believe I have outgrown that teaching, and it is my conviction that my countrymen will truly gain their India by fighting against the education which teaches them that a country is greater than the ideals of humanity. . . .

We must recognize that it is providential that the West has come to India. And yet someone must show the East to the West, and convince the West that the East has her contribution to make to the history of civilization. India is no beggar of the West. And yet even though the West may think she is, I am not for thrusting off Western civilization and becoming segregated in our independence. Let us have a deep association. If providence wants England to be the channel of that communication, of that deeper association, I am willing to accept it with all humility. I have great faith in human nature, and I think the West will find its true mission. I speak bitterly of Western civilization when I am conscious that it is betraying its trust and thwarting its own purpose. The West must not make herself a curse to the world by using her power for her own selfish needs, but by teaching the ignorant and helping the weak, she should save herself from the worst danger that the strong is liable to incur, by making the feeble acquire power enough to resist her intrusion. And also she must not make her materialism to be the final thing, but must realize that she is doing a service in freeing the spiritual being from the tyranny of matter. . . .

Once again I draw your attention to the difficulties India has had to encounter and her struggle to overcome them. Her problem was the problem of the world in miniature. India is too vast in its area and too diverse in its races. It is many countries packed in one geographical receptacle. It is just the opposite of what Europe truly is, namely, one country made into many. Thus, Europe in its culture and growth has had the advantage of the strength of the many as well as the strength of the one. India, on the contrary, being naturally many, yet adventitiously one, has all along suffered from the looseness of its diversity and the feebleness of its unity. A true unity is like a round globe, it rolls on, carrying its burden easily; but diversity is a many cornered thing which has to be dragged and pushed with all force. Be it said to the credit of India that this diversity was not her own creation; she has had to accept it as a fact from the beginning of her history.

Modern nationalism, then, was a product of colonialism and, in a sense, a reaction to it. But a sense of nationhood does not emerge full-blown in a given society. The rise of modern nationalism is a process that begins among a few members of the educated elite (most commonly among articulate professionals such as lawyers, teachers, journalists, and doctors) and then spreads only gradually to the mass of the population. Even after national independence has been realized, as we shall see, it is often questionable whether a mature sense of nationhood has been created.

Traditional Resistance: A Precursor to Nationalism

The beginnings of modern nationalism can be found in the initial resistance by the indigenous peoples to the colonial conquest. Although, strictly speaking, such resistance was not "nationalist," because it was essentially motivated by the desire to defend traditional institutions, it did reflect a primitive concept of nationhood in that it aimed at protecting the homeland from the invader; later patriotic groups have often hailed early resistance movements as the precursors of twentieth-century nationalist movements. Thus, traditional resistance to colonial conquest may logically be viewed as the first stage in the development of modern nationalism.

Such resistance took various forms. For the most part, it was led by the existing ruling class. In the Ashanti kingdom in Africa and in Burma and Vietnam in Southeast Asia, resistance to Western domination was initially directed by the imperial courts themselves. In some cases, traditionalists continued to oppose foreign conquest even after resistance had collapsed at the center. In Japan, conservatives led by nobles under Saigo Takamori launched an abortive movement to defeat the foreigners and restore Japan to its previous policy of isolation (see Chapter 23). In India, Tipu Sultan resisted the British in the Deccan after the collapse of the Mughal dynasty. Similarly, after the decrepit monarchy in Vietnam had bowed to French pressure, a number of civilian and military officials set up an organization called Can Vuong (literally "save the king") and continued their resistance without imperial sanction (see the box on p. 686).

The first stirrings of nationalism in India took place in the early nineteenth century with the search for a renewed sense of cultural identity. In 1828, Ram Mohan Roy, a brahmin from Bengal, founded the Brahmo Samaj (Society of Brahma). Roy probably had no intention of promoting Indian national independence but had established the new organization as a means of helping his fellow religionists defend the Hindu religion against verbal attacks by their British acquaintances. Roy was by no means a hidebound traditionalist. He opposed such practices as *sati* and recognized the benefit of introducing the best aspects of European culture into Indian society.

Sometimes traditional resistance to Western penetration went beyond elite circles. Most commonly, it appeared in the form of peasant revolts. Rural rebellions were not uncommon in traditional Asian societies as a means of expressing peasant discontent with high taxes, official corruption, rising rural debt, and famine in the countryside. Under colonialism, rural conditions often deteriorated, as population density increased and peasants were driven off the land to make way for plantation agriculture. Angry peasants then vented their frustration at the foreign invaders. For example, in Burma, the Buddhist monk Saya San led a peasant uprising against the British many years after they had completed their takeover. Similar forms of unrest occurred in various parts of India, where *zamindars* and rural villagers alike resisted government attempts to increase tax revenues. Yet another peasant uprising took place in Algeria in 1840.

Sometimes the resentment had a religious basis, as in the Sudan where the revolt led by the Mahdi had strong Islamic overtones, although it was initially provoked by Turkish misrule in Egypt. More significant than Roy's Brahmo Samaj in its impact on British policy was the famous Sepoy Rebellion of 1857 in India. The sepoys (derived from *sipahi*, a Turkish word meaning horseman or soldier) were native troops hired by the East India Company to protect British interests in the region. Unrest within Indian units of the colonial army had been common since early in the century, when it had been sparked by economic issues, religious sensitivities, or nascent anticolonial sentiment. Such attitudes intensified in the mid-1850s when the British instituted a new policy of shipping Indian troops abroad—a practice that exposed Hindus to pollution by foreigners. In 1857, tension erupted when the British adopted the new Enfield rifle for use by sepoy infantrymen. The new weapon was a muzzle loader that used paper cartridges covered with animal fat and lard; because the cartridge had to be bitten off, it broke

VIETNAMESE PRISONERS IN STOCKS. Whereas some Vietnamese took up Western ways, others resisted the foreign incursion but were vigorously suppressed by the French. In this photograph, Vietnamese prisoners who had plotted against the French are held in stocks in preparation for trial in 1907.

A CALL TO ARMS

In 1862, the Vietnamese imperial court at Huê ceded three provinces in southern Vietnam to the French. In outrage, many patriotic Vietnamese military officers and government officials appealed to their compatriots to rise up spontaneously and resist the foreigners. The following passage is from an anonymous document written in 1864.

AN APPEAL TO RESIST THE FRENCH

This is a general proclamation addressed to the scholars and the people.
Our country is about to undergo dangerous upheavals.
Certain persons are plotting treason.
Our people are now suffering through a period of anarchy and disorder. . . .
Nonetheless, even in times of confusion, there remain books that teach us how to overcome disorder.
Past generations can still be for us examples of right and wrong. . . .
Let us now consider our situation with the French today.
We are separated from them by thousands of mountains and seas.
By hundreds of differences in our daily customs.
Although they were very confident in their copper battleships surmounted by chimneys,
Although they had a large quantity of steel rifles and lead bullets,
These things did not prevent the loss of some of their best generals in these last years, when they attacked our frontier in hundreds of battles. . . .
Heaven will not leave our people enchained very long.
Heaven will not allow them [the French] the free enjoyment of their lives. . . .
You, officials of the country,
Do not let your resistance to the enemy be blunted by the peaceful stand of the court.
Do not take the lead from the three subjected provinces and leave hatred unavenged. . . .
Such a hostility, such a hatred, such an enmity; our heart will be quieted before we are avenged. . . .
Do not envy the scholars who now become provincial or district magistrates [in the French administration]. They are decay, garbage, filth, swine.
Do not imitate some who hire themselves out to the enemy. They are idiots, fools, lackeys, scoundrels.
At the beginning, you followed the way of righteousness. From beginning to end you ought to behave according to the moral obligations which bind you to your king.
Life has fame, death too has fame. Act in such a way that your life and your death will be a fragrant ointment to your families and to your country.

strictures against high-class Hindus eating animal products and Muslim prohibitions against eating pork. Protests among sepoy units in northern India turned into a full-scale mutiny, supported by risings in rural districts in various parts of the country. But the revolt lacked clear goals, while rivalries between Hindus and Muslims and discord among the leaders within each community prevented coordination of operations. Although Indian troops often fought bravely and outnumbered the British by 240,000 to 40,000, they were poorly organized, and the British forces (supplemented in many cases by sepoy troops) suppressed the rebellion.

Still, the revolt frightened the British and led to a number of major reforms. The proportion of native troops relative to those from Great Britain was reduced, and precedence was given to ethnic groups likely to be loyal to the British, such as the Sikhs of Punjab and the Gurkhas, an upland people from Nepal in the Himalaya Mountains. To avoid religious conflicts, ethnic groups were spread throughout the service rather than assigned to special units. The British also decided to suppress the final remnants of the hapless Mughal dynasty, which had supported the mutiny.

Like the Sepoy Rebellion, traditional resistance movements usually met with little success. Peasants armed with pikes and spears were no match for Western armies possessing the most terrifying weapons then known to human society. In a few cases, such as the revolt of the Mahdi at Khartoum, the natives were able to defeat the invaders temporarily. But such successes were rare, and the late nineteenth century witnessed the seemingly inexorable march of the Western powers, armed with the Gatling gun (the first rapid-fire weapon and the precursor of the modern machine gun), to mastery of the globe.

CONCLUSION

By the first quarter of the twentieth century, virtually all of Africa and a good part of South and Southeast Asia were under some form of colonial rule. With the advent of the age of imperialism, a global economy was finally established, and the domination of Western civilization over those of Africa and Asia appeared to be complete.

Defenders of colonialism argue that the system was a necessary if sometimes painful stage in the evolution of human societies. Although its immediate consequences were admittedly sometimes unfortunate, Western imperialism was ultimately beneficial to colonial powers and subjects alike, since it created the conditions for global economic development and the universal application of democratic institutions. Critics, however, charge that the Western colonial powers were driven by an insatiable lust for profits. They dismiss the Western civilizing mission as a fig leaf to cover naked greed and reject the notion that imperialism played a salutary role in hastening the adjustment of traditional societies to the demands of industrial civilization. In the blunt words of two Western critics of imperialism: "Why is Africa (or for that matter Latin America and much of Asia) so poor? . . . The answer is very brief: we have made it poor."[9]

Between these two irreconcilable views, where does the truth lie? This chapter has contended that neither extreme position is justified. The sources of imperialism lie not simply in the demands of industrial capitalism, but in the search for security, national greatness, and even such psychological factors as the spirit of discovery and the drive to excel. Though some regard the concept of the White Man's Burden as a hypocritical gesture to moral sensitivities, others see it as a meaningful reality justifying a lifelong commitment to the colonialist enterprise. Although the "civilizing urge" of missionaries and officials may have been tinged with self-interest, it was nevertheless often sincerely motivated.

Similarly, the consequences of colonialism have been more complex than either its defenders or its critics would have us believe. While the colonial peoples received little immediate benefit from the imposition of foreign rule, overall the imperialist era brought about a vast expansion of the international trade network and created at least the potential for societies throughout Africa and Asia to play an active and rewarding role in the new global economic arena. If, as the world historian William McNeill believes, the introduction of new technology through cross-cultural encounters is the driving force of change in world history, then Western imperialism, whatever its faults, served a useful purpose in opening the door to such change, much as the rise of the Arab empire and the Mongol invasions hastened the process of global economic development in an earlier time.

Still, the critics have a point. Although colonialism did introduce the peoples of Asia and Africa to new technology and the expanding economic marketplace, it was unnecessarily brutal in its application and all too often failed to realize the exalted claims and objectives of its promoters. Existing economic networks—often potentially valuable as a foundation for later economic development—were ruthlessly swept aside in the interests of providing markets for Western manufactured goods. Potential sources of native industrialization were nipped in the bud to avoid competition for factories in Amsterdam, London, Pittsburgh, or Manchester. Training in Western democratic ideals and practices was ignored out of fear that the recipients might use them as weapons against the ruling authorities.

The fundamental weakness of colonialism, then, was that it was ultimately based on the self-interests of the citizens of the colonial powers. Where those interests collided with the needs of the colonial peoples, those of the former always triumphed. Much the same might have been said about earlier periods in history, when Assyrians, Arabs, Mongols, and Chinese turned their conquests to their own profit. Where modern imperialism differed was in its tendency to cloak naked self-interest in the guise of a moral obligation. However sincerely the David Livingstones, Albert Sarrauts, and William McKinleys of the world were convinced of the rightness of their civilizing mission, the ultimate result was to deprive the colonial peoples of the right to make their own choices about their own destiny.

Did the system serve the interests of the colonial powers? On the face of it, the answer seems obvious: colonialism provided cheap raw materials and markets for Western manufactured goods, both essential to the effective operation of the capitalist system. But some recent observers have concluded that the possession of colonies was not always beneficial to those who possessed them. According to the French economic historian Jacques Marseille, for example, the cost of maintaining the French colonial empire, on balance, exceeded the economic benefits it provided, especially since the maintenance of a protected market in the colonies hindered the French effort to create an industrial sector capable of competing in the global marketplace. Such costs did not become fully apparent until after World War II, however, as we shall see in future chapters.

In one area of Asia, the spreading tide of imperialism did not result in the establishment of formal Western colonial control. In East Asia, the traditional societies of China and Japan were buffeted by the winds of Western expansionism during the nineteenth century but successfully resisted foreign conquest. In the next chapter, we will see how they managed to retain their independence while attempting to cope with the demands of a changing world.

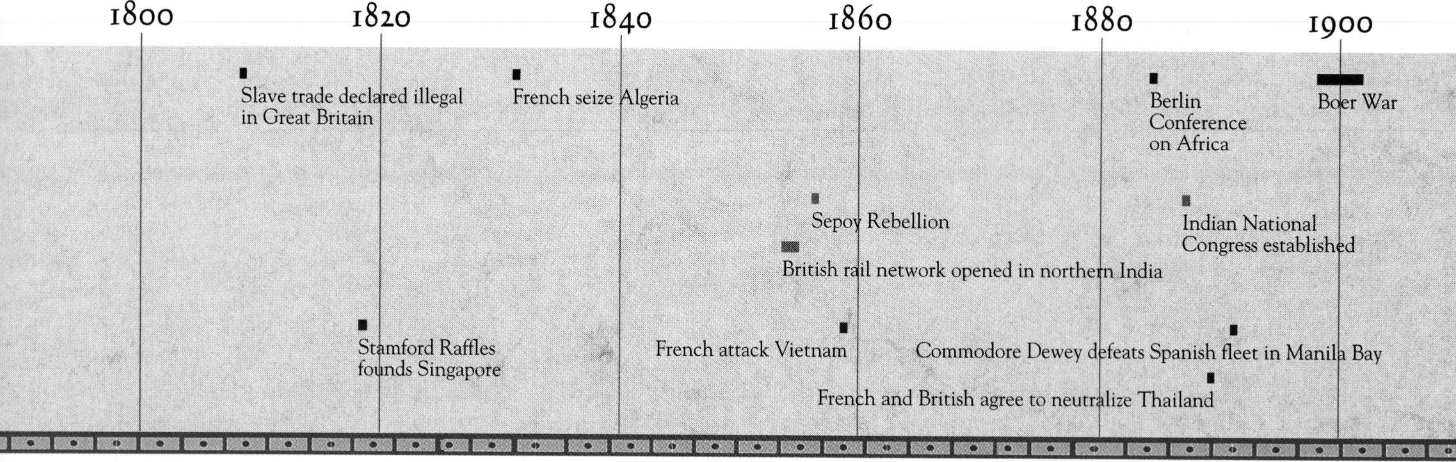

Chapter Notes

1. J. G. Lockhart and C. M. Wodehouse, *Rhodes* (1963), pp. 69–70, cited in Thomas Pakenham, *The Scramble for Africa* (New York, 1991), pp. 376–77.
2. Quoted in Henry Braunschwig, *French Colonialism, 1871–1914* (London, 1961), p. 80.
3. Quoted in Ruhl Bartlett, ed., *The Record of American Diplomacy: Documents and Readings in the History of American Foreign Relations* (New York, 1952), p. 385.
4. Quoted in John Iliffe, *Africans: The History of a Continent* (Cambridge, 1995), p. 124.
5. Pakenham, *The Scramble for Africa*, p. 13.
6. Quoted in Georges Garros, *Forceries Humaines* (Paris, 1926), p. 21.
7. Sarraut's comment is quoted in Louis Roubaud, *Vietnam: La Tragédie Indochinoise* (Paris, 1926), p. 80.
8. Quoted in Pakenham, *The Scramble for Africa*, p. 182, citing a letter to Queen Victoria, 7 Aug 1879.
9. Peter C. W. Gutkind and Immanuel Wallerstein, eds., *The Political Economy of Contemporary Africa* (Beverly Hills, 1976), p. 14, cited in Tony Smith, *The Pattern of Imperialism: The United States, Great Britain, and the Late-Industrial World Since 1815* (Cambridge, 1981), p. 81.

Suggested Readings

There are a number of good recent works on the subject of imperialism and colonialism. For example, see W. Baumgart, *Imperialism: The Idea and Reality of British and French Colonial Expansion, 1880–1914* (Oxford, 1982); M. Edwardes, *The West in Asia, 1850–1914* (New York, 1967); and H. M. Wright, ed., *The "New Imperialism": Analysis of Late Nineteenth Century Expansion* (New York, 1976). On technology, see D. R. Headrick, *The Tentacles of Progress: Technology Transfer in the Age of Imperialism, 1850–1940* (Oxford, 1988). For readings, see L. J. Snyder, *The Imperialism Reader* (New York, 1962).

On the imperialist age in Africa, above all see R. Robinson and J. Gallagher, *Africa and the Victorians: The Official Mind of Imperialism* (London, 1961). Also see B. Davidson, *Modern Africa: A Social and Political History* (London, 1989); T. Pakenham, *The Scramble for Africa* (New York, 1991); and his *The Boer War* (London, 1979). On southern Africa, see J. Guy, *The Destruction of the Zulu Kingdom* (London, 1979), and D. Nenoon and B. Nyeko, *Southern Africa Since 1800* (London, 1984). Also useful is R. O. Collins, ed., *Historical Problems of Imperial Africa* (Princeton, N.J., 1994).

For an overview of the British takeover and administration of India, see S. Wolpert, *A New History of India* (New York, 1989). C. A. Bayly, *Indian Society and the Making of the British Empire* (Cambridge, 1988) is a scholarly analysis of the impact of British conquest on the Indian economy. For a comparative approach, see R. Murphey, *The Outsiders: The Western Experience in China and India* (Ann Arbor, Mich., 1977).

General studies of the colonial period in Southeast Asia are rare because most authors focus on specific areas. For some stimulating essays on a variety of aspects of the topic, see *Continuity and Change in Southeast Asia: Collected Journal Articles of Harry J. Benda* (New Haven, Conn., 1972). The role of religion is examined in F. von der Mehden, *Religion and Nationalism in Southeast Asia* (Madison, Wis., 1963). On nationalist movements, see also R. Emerson's classic *From*

Empire to Nation (Boston, 1960). For a view of the region from the inside, see D. J. Steinberg, et al., eds., *In Search of Southeast Asia* (New York, 1986). On the French conquest of Indochina, see M. O. Osborne, *The French Presence in Cochin China and Cambodia* (Ithaca, 1969).

For an introduction to the effects of colonialism on women in Africa and Asia, see S. Hughes and B. Hughes, *Women in World History*, vol. 2 (Armonk, N.Y., 1997). Also consult the classic by E. Boserup, *Women's Role in Economic Development* (London, 1970), and see J. Taylor, *The Social World of Batavia* (Madison, Wis., 1983).

For additional reading, go to InfoTrac College Edition, your online research library at http://web1.infotrac-college.com

Enter the search term "imperialism" using the Subject Guide.

Enter the search terms "Boer War" using Keywords.

Enter the search term "nationalism" using Keywords.

CHAPTER

23

SHADOWS OVER THE PACIFIC: EAST ASIA UNDER CHALLENGE

CHAPTER OUTLINE

- THE DECLINE OF THE MANCHUS
- CHINESE SOCIETY IN TRANSITION
- A RICH COUNTRY AND A STRONG STATE: THE RISE OF MODERN JAPAN
- CONCLUSION

FOCUS QUESTIONS

- Why did the Qing dynasty decline and ultimately collapse, and what role did the Western powers play in this process?
- What role did Sun Yat-sen play in the collapse of the Qing dynasty, and what were his goals for China?
- How did China and Japan respond to Western pressures in the nineteenth century, and what implications did their different responses have for each nation's history?
- What political, economic, and social reforms were instituted by Meiji reformers in Japan?
- To what degree was the Meiji Restoration a "revolution," and to what degree did it succeed in transforming Japan?

The British emissary Lord Macartney had arrived in Beijing in 1793 with a caravan loaded with six hundred cases of gifts for the emperor. Flags and banners provided by the Chinese proclaimed in Chinese characters that the visitor was an "ambassador bearing tribute from the country of England." But the tribute was in vain, for Macartney's request for an increase in trade between the two countries was flatly rejected, and he left Beijing in October with nothing to show for his efforts. Not until half a century later would the Qing dynasty—at the point of a gun—agree to the British demand for an expansion of commercial ties.

Historians have often viewed the failure of the Macartney mission as a reflection of the disdain of Chinese rulers toward their counterparts in other countries and their serene confidence in the superiority of Chinese civilization in a world inhabited by barbarians, and of course it was. But in retrospect, it is clear that the Chinese concern was justified. At the beginning of the nineteenth century, China faced a growing challenge from the escalating power and ambitions of the West. Backed by European guns, European merchants and missionaries pressed insistently for the right to carry out their activities in China and the islands of Japan. Despite their initial reluctance, the Chinese and Japanese governments were eventually forced to open their doors to the foreigners, whose presence escalated rapidly during the final years of the century.

Unlike other Asian societies, both Japan and China were able to maintain their national independence against the Western onslaught. In other respects, however, the results in Japan and China were strikingly different. Japan responded quickly to the challenge by adopting Western institutions and customs and eventually becoming a significant competitor for the spoils of empire. In contrast, China grappled unsuccessfully with the problem, which eventually undermined the foundations of the Qing dynasty and brought it to an unceremonious conclusion. ❁

The Decline of the Manchus

In 1800, the Qing (Ch'ing) or Manchu dynasty appeared to be at the height of its power. China had experienced a long period of peace and prosperity under the rule of two great emperors, Kangxi and Qianlong. Its borders were secure, and its culture and intellectual achievements were the envy of the world. Its rulers, hidden behind the walls of the Forbidden City in Beijing, had every reason to describe their patrimony as the "Central Kingdom." But a little over a century later, humiliated and harassed by the black ships and big guns of the Western powers, the Qing dynasty, the last in a series that had endured for more than two thousand years, collapsed in the dust.

Historians once assumed that the primary reason for the rapid decline and fall of the Manchu dynasty was the intense pressure applied to a proud but somewhat complacent traditional society by the modern West. Now, however, most historians believe that internal changes played a role in the dynasty's collapse and point out that at least some of the problems suffered by the Manchus during the nineteenth century were self-inflicted.

Both explanations have some validity. Like so many of its predecessors, after an extended period of growth, the Qing dynasty began to suffer from the familiar dynastic ills of official corruption, peasant unrest, and incompetence at court. Such weaknesses were probably exacerbated by the rapid growth in population. The long era of peace and stability, the introduction of new crops from the Americas, and the cultivation of new, fast-ripening strains of rice enabled the Chinese population to double between 1550 and 1800. The population continued to grow, reaching the unprecedented level of 400 million by the end of the nineteenth century. Even without the irritating presence of the Western powers, the Manchus were probably destined to repeat the fate of their imperial predecessors. The ships, guns, and ideas of the foreigners simply highlighted the growing weakness of the Manchu dynasty and likely hastened its demise. In doing so, Western imperialism still exerted an indelible impact on the history of modern China—but as a contributing, not a causal, factor.

Opium and Rebellion

By 1800, Westerners had been in contact with China for more than two hundred years, but after an initial period of flourishing relations, Western traders had been limited to a small commercial outlet at Canton. This arrangement was not acceptable to the British, however. Not only did they chafe at being restricted to a tiny enclave, but the growing British appetite for Chinese tea created a severe balance-of-payments problem. The British tried negotiations, dispatching Lord Macartney to Beijing in 1793 and another mission, led by Lord Amherst, in 1816. But both missions foundered on the rock of protocol and managed only to worsen the already strained relations between the two countries. The British solution was opium. A product more addictive than tea, opium was grown in northeastern India and then shipped directly to China. Opium had been grown in southwestern China for several hundred years but had been used primarily for medicinal purposes. Now, as imports increased, popular demand for the product in southern China became insatiable despite an official prohibition on its use. Soon bullion was flowing out of the Chinese imperial treasury into the pockets of British merchants.

The Chinese became concerned and tried to negotiate. In 1839, Lin Zexu (Lin Tse-hsu; 1785–1850), a Chinese official appointed by the court to curtail the opium trade,

HAGGLING OVER THE PRICE OF TEA. An important item in the China trade of the eighteenth and early nineteenth centuries was tea, which had become extremely popular in Great Britain. This painting depicts the various stages of growing, processing, and marketing tea leaves. In the background, workers are removing tender young leaves from the bushes. In the foreground, British and Chinese merchants bargain over the price. After being dried, the leaves are packed into chests and loaded on vessels for shipment abroad.

appealed to Queen Victoria on both moral and practical grounds and threatened to prohibit the sale of rhubarb (widely used as a laxative in nineteenth-century Europe) to Great Britain if she did not respond (see the box on p. 693). But moral principles, then as now, paled before the lure of commercial profits, and the British continued to promote the opium trade, arguing that if the Chinese did not want the opium, they did not have to buy it. Lin Zexu attacked on three fronts, imposing penalties on smokers, arresting dealers, and seizing supplies from importers as they attempted to smuggle the drug into China. The last tactic caused his downfall. When he blockaded the foreign factory area in Canton to force traders to hand over their remaining chests of opium, the British government, claiming that it could not permit British subjects "to be exposed to insult and injustice," launched a naval expedition to punish the Manchus and force the court to open China to foreign trade.[1]

The Opium War (1839–1842) lasted for three years and demonstrated the superiority of British firepower and military tactics (including the use of a shallow-draft steamboat that effectively harassed Chinese coastal defenses). British warships destroyed Chinese coastal and river forts and seized the offshore island of Chusan, not far from the mouth of the Yangtze River. When a British fleet sailed virtually unopposed up the Yangtze to Nanjing and cut off the supply of "tribute grain" from southern to northern China, the Qing finally agreed to British terms. In the Treaty of Nanjing in 1842, the Chinese agreed to open five coastal ports to British trade, limit tariffs on imported British goods, grant extraterritorial rights to British citizens in China, and pay a substantial indemnity to cover the costs of the war. China also agreed to cede the island of Hong Kong (dismissed by a senior British official as a "barren rock") to Great Britain. Nothing was said in the treaty about the opium trade, which continued unabated until it was brought under control through Chinese government efforts in the early twentieth century.

THE OPIUM WAR. The Opium War, waged between China and Great Britain between 1839 and 1842, was China's first conflict with a European power. Lacking modern military technology, the Chinese suffered a humiliating defeat. In this painting, heavily armed British steamships destroy unwieldy Chinese junks along the Chinese coast. China's humiliation at sea was a legacy of its rulers' lack of interest in maritime matters since the middle of the fifteenth century when Chinese junks were among the most advanced sailing ships in the world.

A LETTER OF ADVICE TO THE QUEEN

Lin Zexu was the Chinese imperial commissioner in Canton at the time of the Opium War. Prior to the conflict, he attempted to use reason and the threat of retaliation to persuade the British to cease importing opium illegally into southern China. The following excerpt is from a letter that he wrote to Queen Victoria. In it, he appeals to her conscience while showing the condescension that the Chinese traditionally displayed to the rulers of other countries.

LIN ZEXU, LETTER TO QUEEN VICTORIA

The kings of your honorable country by a tradition handed down from generation to generation have always been noted for their politeness and submissiveness. . . . Privately we are delighted with the way in which the honorable rulers of your country deeply understand the grand principles and are grateful for the Celestial grace. . . . The profit from trade has been enjoyed by them continuously for two hundred years. This is the source from which your country has become known for its wealth.

But after a long period of commercial intercourse, there appear among the crowd of barbarians both good persons and bad, unevenly. Consequently there are those who smuggle opium to seduce the Chinese people and so cause the spread of the poison to all provinces. . . .

The wealth of China is used to profit the barbarians. That is to say, the great profit made by barbarians is all taken from the rightful share of China. By what right do they then in return use the poisonous drug to injure the Chinese people? . . . Let us ask, where is your conscience? I have heard that the smoking of opium is very strictly forbidden by your country; that is because the harm caused by opium is clearly understood. Since it is not permitted to do harm to your own country, then even less should you let it be passed on to the harm of other countries—how much less to China! Of all that China exports to foreign countries, there is not a single thing which is not beneficial to people. . . . Is there a single article from China which has done any harm to foreign countries? Take tea and rhubarb, for example; the foreign countries cannot get along for a single day without them. . . . On the other hand, articles coming from the outside to China can only be used as toys. We can take them or get along without them. Nevertheless our Celestial Court lets tea, silk, and other goods be shipped without limit and circulated everywhere without begrudging it in the slightest. This is for no other reason but to share the benefit with the people of the whole world. . . .

May you, O King, check your wicked and sift your vicious people before they come to China, in order to guarantee the peace of your nation, to show further the sincerity of your politeness and submissiveness, and to let the two countries enjoy together the blessings of peace. . . . After receiving this dispatch will you immediately give us a prompt reply regarding the details and circumstances of your cutting off the opium traffic. Be sure not to put this off.

Although the Opium War has traditionally been considered the beginning of modern Chinese history, it is unlikely that many Chinese at the time would have seen it that way. This was not the first time that a ruling dynasty had been forced to make concessions to foreigners, and the opening of five coastal ports to the British hardly constituted a serious threat to the security of the empire. Although a few concerned Chinese argued that the court should learn more about European civilization, others contended that China had nothing to learn from the barbarians and that borrowing foreign ways would undercut the purity of Confucian civilization (see the box on p. 694).

For the time being, the Manchus attempted to deal with the problem in the traditional way of playing the foreigners off against each other. Concessions granted to the British were offered to other Western nations, including the United States, and soon thriving foreign concession areas were operating in treaty ports along the southern Chinese coast from Canton to Shanghai.

In the meantime, the Qing court's failure to deal with pressing internal economic problems led to a major peasant revolt that shook the foundations of the empire. On the surface, the Taiping (T'ai p'ing) Rebellion owed something to the Western incursion; the leader of the uprising, Hong Xiuquan (Hung Hsiu-ch'uan), a failed examination candidate, was a Christian convert who viewed himself as a younger brother of Jesus and hoped to establish what he referred to as a "Heavenly Kingdom of Supreme Peace" in China. But there were many local causes as well. The rapid increase in population forced millions of peasants to eke out a living as sharecroppers or landless laborers. Official corruption and incompetence led to the whipsaw of increased taxes and a decline in government services; even the Grand Canal ceased to be dredged and silted up, hindering the shipment of grain. In 1853 the rebels seized the old Ming capital of Nanjing, but that proved to be the rebellion's high-water mark. Plagued by factionalism, the rebellion gradually lost momentum until it was finally suppressed in 1864.

One reason for the dynasty's failure to deal effectively with the internal unrest was its continuing difficulties with the Western imperialists. In 1856, the British and

EUROPE IN CHINESE EYES

Until the mid-nineteenth century, the Chinese expressed little interest in Europe and its people. In the aftermath of the Opium War, however, Chinese intellectuals gradually began to explore Western society and its underpinnings. In 1891, a Chinese named Wang Hsi-ch'i published a compilation of descriptions of foreign countries for the edification of his compatriots. The following excerpt from this volume provides a general description of Europe through the eyes of an anonymous Chinese writer. Note the author's assumption that civilization came to Europe from the Orient. The final paragraph pays tribute to European persistence in seeking scientific truth, perhaps an oblique swipe at the Chinese lack of interest in such matters.

A CHINESE DESCRIPTION OF EUROPE

Europe (*Ou-lo-pa*) is one of the five great continents. . . . Though it is smaller than the other four continents, its soil is fertile, its products are plentiful, it has many talented people and many famous places. For this reason, Europe's power in the present world is preeminent, and it has become a leading force in the five continents. Yet in ancient times its people hunted for a living, ate meat, and wore skins. Their customs were barbaric, and their spirit was wild and free. But during our own Shang period (2000 B.C.) Greece and other countries gradually came under the influence of the Orient. For the first time they began to till fields and manufacture products, build cities and dig lakes. . . . Before long, writing and civilization began to flourish. Thus they became beautiful like the countries of the East. . . .

Europe's people are all tall and white. Only those who live in the northeast where it is very cold are short, and dwarfish. They have big noses and deep eyes. . . . They have heavy beards that go up to their temples, or are wound around their jaws. . . . For their eating and drinking utensils they use gold, silver, and ceramics. When they eat they use knife and fork, and they do not use chopsticks. . . .

Now as to the way they build houses. On the outside they have no surrounding walls, and inside they have no courts. They do not pay much attention to the exact direction and position (geomancy), they do not have fixed standards; square or round, concave or convex—all depends on the discretion of the owner. Sometimes they have many-storied buildings that go up for five or six, or seven or eight floors. . . . Their foundations are deep and solid. Their walls are substantial and thick. . . . The upper classes use stone. The middle classes use brick. The lower classes use earth. . . .

Now for their machines. When they first invented them, they just relied on common sense. They tried this and rejected that, without ever finding out from anyone else how it ought to be done. However, they did some research and found people who investigated the fine points and propagated their usage. In this way they gradually developed all their machines such as steamships, steam trains, spinning machines, mining and canal-digging machines, and all machines for making weapons and gunpowder. Things improved day by day and helped enrich the nation and benefit the people. Day by day they became more prosperous and will keep on becoming so.

the French, still smarting from trade restrictions and limitations on their missionary activities, launched a new series of attacks against China and seized the capital of Beijing in 1860. As punishment, British troops destroyed the imperial summer palace just outside the city. In the ensuing Treaty of Tianjin (Tientsin), the Qing agreed to humiliating new concessions: the legalization of the opium trade, the opening of additional ports to foreign trade, and the cession of the peninsula of Kowloon (opposite the island of Hong Kong) to the British. Additional territories in the north were ceded to Russia.

The Climax of Imperialism in China

By the late 1870s, the old dynasty was well on the road to internal disintegration. In fending off the Taiping Rebellion, the Manchus had been compelled to rely for support on armed forces under regional command. After quelling the revolt, many of these regional commanders refused to disband their units and, with the support of the local gentry, continued to collect local taxes for their own use. The dreaded pattern of imperial breakdown, so familiar in Chinese history, was beginning to appear once again.

In its weakened state, the court finally began to listen to the appeals of reform-minded officials, who called for a new policy of "self-strengthening," in which Western technology would be adopted while Confucian principles and institutions were maintained intact. This policy, popularly known by its slogan "East for Essence, West for Practical Use," remained the guiding standard for Chinese foreign and domestic policy for nearly a quarter of a century. Some even called for reforms in education and in China's hallowed political institutions. Pointing to the power and prosperity of Great Britain, the journalist Wang Tao (Wang T'ao; 1828–1897) remarked: "The real strength of England . . . lies in the fact that there is a sympathetic understanding between the governing and the governed, a close relationship between the ruler and the people. . . . My observation is that the daily domestic political life of England actually embod-

MAP 23.1 Canton and Hong Kong

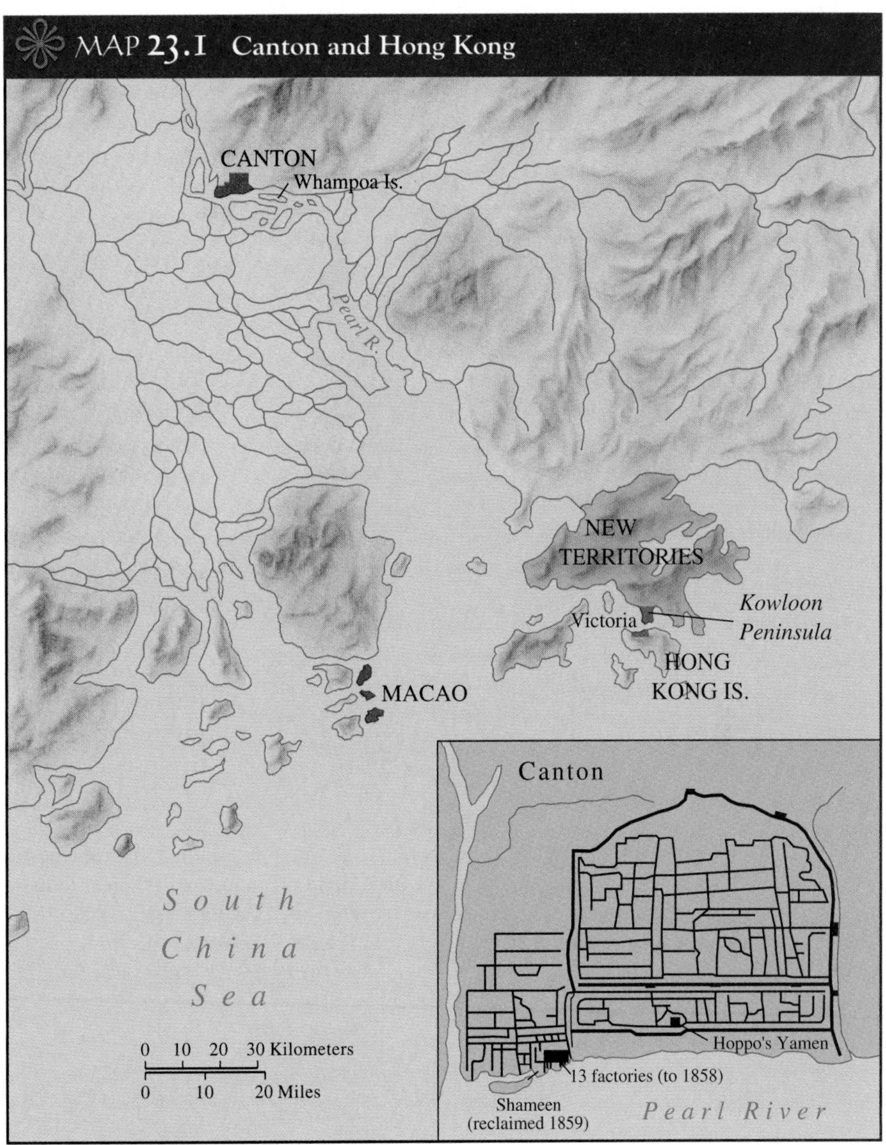

ies the traditional ideals of our ancient Golden Age."[2] Such democratic ideas were too radical for most reformers, however. One of the leading court officials of the day, Zhang Zhidong (Chang Chih-tung), countered:

> The doctrine of people's rights will bring us not a single benefit but a hundred evils. Are we going to establish a parliament? . . . Even supposing the confused and clamorous people are assembled in one house, for every one of them who is clear-sighted, there will be a hundred others whose vision is beclouded; they will converse at random and talk as if in a dream—what use will it be?[3]

For the time being, Zhang Zhidong's arguments won the day. During the last quarter of the century, the Manchus attempted to modernize their military establishment and build up an industrial base without disturbing the essential elements of traditional Chinese civilization. Railroads, weapons arsenals, and shipyards were built, but the value system remained essentially unchanged.

In the end, the results spoke for themselves. During the last two decades of the nineteenth century, the European penetration of China, both political and military, intensified. Rapacious imperialists began to bite off the outer edges of the Qing Empire. The Gobi Desert north of the Great Wall, Chinese Central Asia, and Tibet, all inhabited by non-Chinese peoples and never fully assimilated into the Chinese Empire, gradually were lost. In the north and northwest, the main beneficiary was Russia, which took advantage of the dynasty's weakness to force the cession of territories north of the Amur River in Siberia. In Tibet, competition between Russia and Great Britain prevented either power from seizing the territory outright, but at the same time enabled Tibetan authorities to revive local autonomy never recognized by the Chinese. In the

CHRONOLOGY

CHINA IN THE ERA OF IMPERIALISM

Lord Macartney's mission to China	1793
Opium War	1839–1842
Taiping rebels seize Nanjing	1853
Taiping Rebellion suppressed	1864
Cixi becomes regent for nephew Guangxu	1878
Sino-Japanese War	1894–1895
One Hundred Days Reform	1898
Open Door Notes	1899
Boxer Rebellion	1900
Commission to study constitution formed	1905
Deaths of Cixi and Guangxu	1908
Revolution in China	1911

south, British and French advances in mainland Southeast Asia removed Burma and Vietnam from their traditional vassal relationship to the Manchu court. Even more ominous were the foreign spheres of influence in the Chinese heartland, where local commanders were willing to sell exclusive commercial, railroad-building, or mining privileges.

The breakup of the Manchu dynasty accelerated during the last five years of the nineteenth century. In 1894, the Qing went to war with Japan over Japanese incursions into the Korean peninsula, which threatened China's long-held suzerainty over the area (see Joining the Imperialist Club later in this chapter). To the surprise of many observers, the Chinese were roundly defeated, confirming to some critics the devastating failure of the policy of self-strengthening by halfway measures. The disintegration of China accelerated in 1897, when Germany, a new entry in the race for spoils in East Asia, used the pretext of the murder of two German missionaries by Chinese rioters to demand the cession of territories in the Shandong (Shantung) peninsula. The approval of the demand by the imperial court set off a scramble for territory by other interested powers. Russia now demanded the Liaodong peninsula with its ice-free port at Port Arthur, and Great

THE EMPRESS DOWAGER'S NAVY. Historians have often interpreted the stone pavilion shown here as a symbol of the Qing dynasty's inability to comprehend the nature of the threat to its survival. At the command of Empress Dowager Cixi, funds meant to strengthen the Chinese navy against imperious Westerns at the end of the nineteenth century were used instead to construct this stone pleasure boat on the shore of a lake at the Summer Palace west of Beijing. Today the lake is a popular place for Chinese tourists.

Britain weighed in with a request for a coaling station in northern China.

The government responded to the foreign challenge with yet another effort at reform. In the spring of 1898, an outspoken advocate of reform, the progressive Confucian scholar Kang Youwei (K'ang Yu-wei), won the support of the young Emperor Guangxu (Kuang Hsu) for a comprehensive reform program patterned after recent measures in Japan. Without change, Kang argued, China would perish. During the next several weeks, the emperor issued edicts calling for major political, administrative, and educational reforms. Not surprisingly, Kang's proposals were opposed by many conservatives, who saw little advantage and much risk in copying the West. More important, the new program was opposed by the emperor's aunt, the Empress Dowager Cixi (Tz'u Hsi), the real power at court. Cixi had begun her political career as a concubine to an earlier emperor. After his death, she became a dominant force at court and in 1878 placed her infant nephew Guangxu on the throne. For two decades, she ruled in his name as regent. Cixi interpreted Guangxu's action as a British-supported effort to reduce her influence at court. With the aid of conservatives in the army, she arrested and executed several of the reformers and had the emperor incarcerated in the palace. Kang Youwei succeeded in fleeing abroad. With Cixi's palace coup, the so-called One Hundred Days of reform came to an end.

OPENING THE DOOR TO CHINA

During the next two years, foreign pressure on the dynasty intensified. With encouragement from the British, who hoped to avert a total collapse of the Manchu Empire, U.S. Secretary of State John Hay presented the other imperialist powers with a proposal to ensure equal economic access to the China market for all states. Hay also suggested that all powers join together to guarantee the territorial and administrative integrity of the Chinese Empire. Though probably motivated more by the United States's preference for open markets than by a benevolent wish to protect China, the Open Door policy did have the practical effect of reducing the imperialist hysteria over access to the China market. That hysteria, a product of decades of mythologizing among Western commercial interests about the "four hundred million" Chinese customers, had accelerated at the end of the century as fear of China's imminent collapse increased. The "gentlemen's

EMPRESS DOWAGER CIXI. Cixi was the most powerful figure in late nineteenth-century China. Originally a concubine at the imperial court, she later placed a nephew on the throne and dominated the political scene for a quarter of a century, until her death in 1908. Conservative in her views, she staunchly resisted her advisers' suggestions for changes to help China face the challenge posed by the West. Note the long fingernails, a symbol of the privileged class, in this photograph taken in her final years.

MAP 23.2 The Qing Empire in the Early Twentieth Century

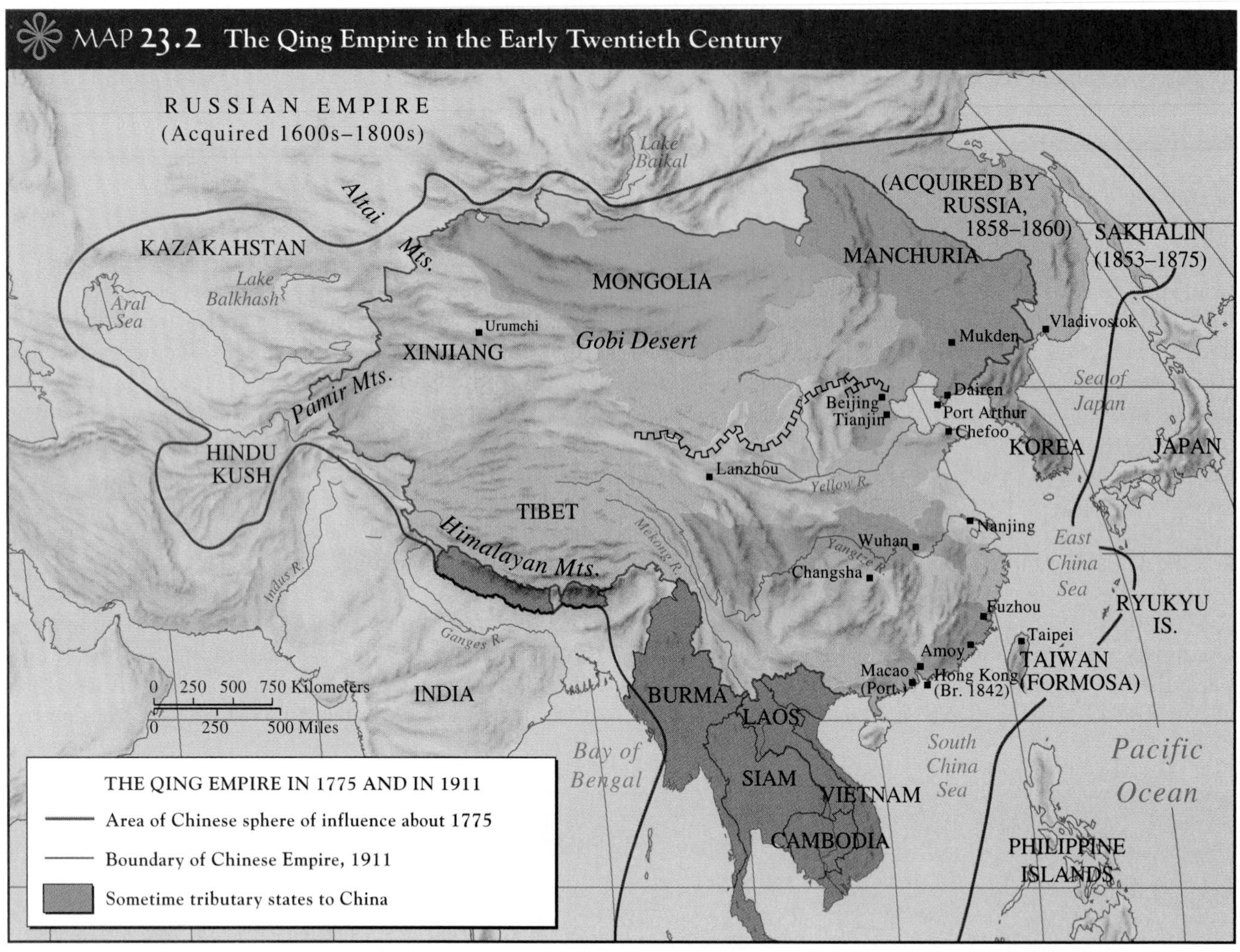

agreement" about the Open Door (it was not a treaty, but merely a pious and nonbinding expression of intent) served to deflate fears in Britain, France, Germany, and Russia that other powers would take advantage of China's weakness to dominate the China market.

In the long run, then, the Open Door was a positive step that brought a measure of sanity to imperialist behavior in East Asia. Unfortunately, it came too late to stop the domestic explosion known as the Boxer Rebellion. The Boxers, so-called because of the physical exercises they performed, were members of a secret society operating primarily in rural areas in northern China. Provoked by a damaging drought and high levels of unemployment caused in part by foreign economic activity (the introduction of railroads and steamships, for example, undercut the livelihood of barge workers on the rivers and canals), the Boxers attacked foreign residents and besieged the foreign legation quarter in Beijing until the foreigners were rescued by an international expeditionary force in the late summer of 1900. As punishment, the foreign troops destroyed a number of temples in the capital suburbs, while the Chinese government was compelled to pay a heavy indemnity to the foreign governments involved in suppressing the uprising.

The Collapse of the Old Order

During the next few years, the old dynasty tried desperately to reform itself. The empress dowager, who had long resisted change, now embraced a number of reforms. The venerable civil service examination system was replaced by a new educational system based on the Western model. In 1905, a commission was formed to study constitutional changes, and over the next few years, legislative assemblies were established at the provincial level, and elections for a national assembly were held in 1910.

Such moves helped to shore up the dynasty temporarily, but history shows that the most dangerous period for an authoritarian system is when it begins to reform itself, because change breeds instability and performance rarely matches rising expectations. Such was the case in China. The emerging new provincial elite, composed of merchants, professionals, and reform-minded gentry, soon became impatient with the slow pace of political change

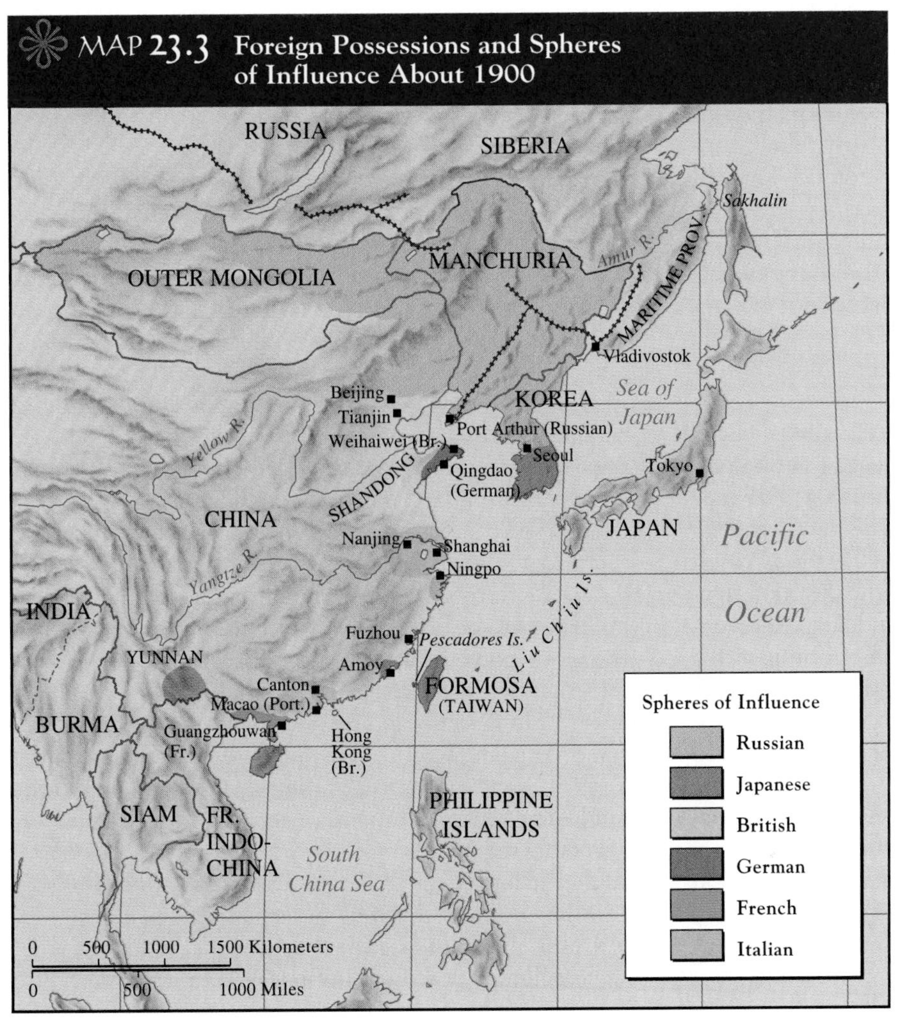

and were disillusioned to find that the new assemblies were intended to be primarily advisory rather than legislative. The government also alienated influential elements by financing railway development projects through foreign firms rather than local investors. The reforms also had little meaning for peasants, artisans, miners, and transportation workers, whose living conditions were being eroded by rising taxes and official venality. Rising rural unrest, as yet poorly organized and often centered on secret

JUSTICE OR MERCY: UNCLE SAM DECIDES. In the summer of 1900, Chinese rebels called Boxers besieged Western embassies in the imperial capital of Beijing. Western nations, including the United States, dispatched troops to northern China to rescue their compatriots. In this cartoon, which appeared in a contemporary American news magazine, China figuratively seeks pardon from a stern Uncle Sam. Washington participated in the international rescue operation but decided to apply the Chinese indemnity to create a scholarship fund for Chinese students to study in the United States.

societies such as the Boxers, was an ominous sign of deep-seated resentment to which the dynasty would not, or could not, respond.

To China's reformist elite, such signs of social discontent were a threat to be avoided. To its tiny revolutionary movement, they were a harbinger of promise. The first physical manifestations of future revolution appeared during the last decade of the nineteenth century with the formation of the Revive China Society by the young radical Sun Yat-sen (1866–1925). Born in a village south of Canton, Sun was educated in Hawaii and returned to China to practice medicine. Soon he turned his full attention to the ills of Chinese society.

At first, Sun's efforts yielded few positive results, but in a convention in Tokyo in 1905, he managed to unite radical groups from across China in a Revolutionary Alliance (Tongmenghui, or T'ung Meng Hui). The new organization's program was based on Sun's Three People's Principles of Nationalism (meaning primarily the destruction of Manchu rule over China), Democracy, and People's Livelihood. It called for a three-stage process beginning with a military takeover and ending with a constitutional democracy (see the box on p. 701). Although the new organization was small and relatively inexperienced, it benefited from the rising popular discontent.

In October 1911, Sun's followers launched an uprising in the industrial center of Wuhan, in central China. With Sun traveling in the United States, the insurrection lacked leadership, but the decrepit government's inability to react quickly encouraged political forces at the provincial level to take measures into their own hands. The dynasty was now in a state of virtual collapse: the dowager empress had died in 1908, one day after her nephew Guangxu; the throne was now occupied by China's "last emperor," the infant Henry Puyi (P'u Yi). Sun's party had neither the military strength nor the political base necessary to seize the initiative, however, and was forced to turn to a representative of the old order, General Yuan Shikai (Yuan Shih-k'ai). A prominent figure in military circles since the beginning of the century, Yuan had been placed in charge of the imperial forces sent to suppress the rebellion, but now he abandoned the Manchus and acted on his own behalf. In negotiations with representatives of Sun Yat-sen's party (Sun himself had arrived in China in January 1912), he agreed to serve as president of a new Chinese republic. The old dynasty and the age-old system that it had attempted to preserve were no more.

Although the dynasty was gone, Sun Yat-sen and his followers were unable to consolidate their gains. The program of the Revolutionary Alliance was based on Western liberal democratic principles aimed at the urban middle class. That class and program had provided the foundation for the capitalist democratic revolutions in western Europe and North America in the late eighteenth and nineteenth centuries, but the middle class in China was still too small to form the basis for a new political order. The vast majority of the Chinese people still lived on the land. Sun Yat-sen had hoped to win their support with a land reform program, but few peasants had participated in the 1911 revolution. In failing to create new institutions and values to provide a framework for a changing society, the events of 1911 were less a revolution than a collapse of the old order. Weakened by imperialism and its own internal weaknesses, the old dynasty had come to an abrupt end before new political and social forces were ready to fill the vacuum.

What China had experienced was part of a historical process that was bringing down traditional empires across the globe both in those regions threatened by Western imperialism and in Europe itself, where tsarist Russia, the Austro-Hungarian Empire, and the Ottoman Empire all came to an end within a few years after the collapse of the Qing. The circumstances of their demise were not all the same. The Austro-Hungarian Empire, for example, was dismembered by the victorious allies after World War I, while the fate of tsarist Russia was directly linked to that conflict. Still, all four regimes shared the responsibility for their common fate, in that they had failed to meet the challenges posed by the times. All had responded to

SUN YAT-SEN, FATHER OF MODERN CHINA. The son of a peasant in southern China, Sun Yat-sen rose to become a prominent revolutionary and the founder of the first Chinese republic. This photograph shows Sun as he assumed office as provisional president in January 1912. Shortly thereafter, he was forced to resign in favor of General Yuan Shikai, who moved the capital from Nanjing to Beijing.

A PROGRAM FOR A NEW CHINA

In 1905, Sun Yat-sen united a number of anti-Manchu groups into a single patriotic organization called the Revolutionary Alliance (Tongmenghui). The new organization eventually formed the of his Guomindang, or Nationalist Party. This excerpt is from the organization's manifesto, published in 1905 in Tokyo. Note that Sun believed that the Chinese people were not ready for democracy and required a period of tutelage to prepare them for the final era of constitutional political government. This was a formula that would be adopted by many other political leaders in Asia and Africa after World War II.

SUN YAT-SEN, MANIFESTO FOR THE TONGMENGHUI

By order of the Military Government, . . . the Commander-in-Chief of the Chinese National Army proclaims the purposes and platform of the Military Government to the people of the nation:

Therefore we proclaim to the world in utmost sincerity the outline of the present revolution and the fundamental plan for the future administration of the nation.

1. *Drive out the Tartars:* The Manchus of today were originally the eastern barbarians beyond the Great Wall. They frequently caused border troubles during the Ming dynasty; then when China was in a disturbed state they came inside Shanhaikuan, conquered China, and enslaved our Chinese people. . . . The extreme cruelties and tyrannies of the Manchu government have now reached their limit. With the righteous army poised against them, we will overthrow that government, and restore our sovereign rights.
2. *Restore China:* China is the China of the Chinese. The government of China should be in the hands of the Chinese. After driving out the Tartars we must restore our national state. . . .
3. *Establish the Republic:* Now our revolution is based on equality, in order to establish a republican government. All our people are equal and all enjoy political rights. . . .
4. *Equalize land ownership:* The good fortune of civilization is to be shared equally by all the people of the nation. We should improve our social and economic organization, and assess the value of all the land in the country. Its present price shall be received by the owner, but all increases in value resulting from reform and social improvements after the revolution shall belong to the state, to be shared by all the people, in order to create a socialist state, where each family within the empire can be well supported, each person satisfied, and no one fail to secure employment. . . .

The above four points will be carried out in three steps in due order. The first period is government by military law. When the righteous army has arisen, various places will join the cause. . . . Evils like the oppression of the government, the greed and graft of officials, . . . the cruelty of tortures and penalties, the tyranny of tax collections, the humiliation of the queue—shall all be exterminated together with the Manchu rule. Evils in social customs, such as the keeping of slaves, the cruelty of foot binding, the spread of the poison of opium, should also all be prohibited. . . .

The second period is that of government by a provisional constitution. When military law is lifted in each *hsien,* the Military Government shall return the right of self-government to the local people. . . .

The third period will be government under the constitution. Six years after the provisional constitution has been enforced a constitution shall be made. The military and administrative powers of the Military Government shall be annulled; the people shall elect the president, and elect the members of parliament to organize the parliament.

the forces of industrialization and popular participation in the political process with hesitation and reluctance, and their attempts at reform were too little and too late. All paid the supreme price for their folly.

CHINESE SOCIETY IN TRANSITION

The growing Western presence in China during the late nineteenth and early twentieth centuries obviously had a major impact on Chinese society; hence many historians have asserted that the arrival of the Europeans shook China out of centuries of slumber and launched it on the road to revolutionary change. In fact, when the European economic penetration began to accelerate in the mid-nineteenth century, Chinese society was already in a state of transition. The growth of industry and trade was particularly noticeable in the cities, where a national market for such commodities as oil, copper, salt, tea, and porcelain had developed. The foundation of an infrastructure more conducive to the rise of a money economy appeared to be in place. In the countryside, new crops introduced from abroad significantly increased food production and aided population growth.

The Chinese economy had never been more productive or complex.

Whether these changes by themselves would eventually have led to an industrial revolution and the rise of a capitalist society on the Western model in the absence of Western intervention is a question that historians cannot answer with assurance. Certainly, a number of obstacles would have made it difficult for China to embark on the Western path if it had wished to do so.

Although industrial production was on the rise, it was still based almost entirely on traditional methods of production. There was no uniform system of weights and measures, and the banking system was still primitive by European standards. The use of paper money, invented by the Chinese centuries earlier, had essentially been abandoned. The transportation system, which had been neglected since the end of the Yuan dynasty, was increasingly chaotic. There were few paved roads, and the Grand Canal, long the most efficient means of carrying goods from north to south, was silting up. As a result, merchants had to rely more and more on the coastal route, where they faced increasing competition from foreign shipping.

Although foreign concession areas in the coastal cities provided a conduit for the importation of Western technology and modern manufacturing methods, the Chinese borrowed less than they might have. Foreign manufacturing enterprises could not legally operate in China until the last decade of the nineteenth century, and their methods had little influence beyond the concession areas. Chinese efforts to imitate Western methods, notably in shipbuilding and weapons manufacture, were dominated by the government and often suffered from mismanagement.

Equally serious problems persisted in the countryside. The rapid increase in population had led to smaller plots and growing numbers of tenant farmers. Whether per capita consumption of food was on the decline is not clear from the available evidence, but apparently rice as a staple of the diet was increasingly being replaced by less nutritious foods. Some farmers benefited from switching to commercial agriculture to supply the markets of the growing coastal cities, but the shift entailed a sizable investment. Many farmers went so deeply into debt that they eventually lost their land. In the meantime, the traditional patron-client relationship was frayed, as landlords moved to the cities to take advantage of the glittering urban lifestyle.

Most important, perhaps, was that the Qing dynasty was still locked into a traditional mindset that discouraged commercial activities and prized the time-honored virtues of preindustrial agrarian society. China also lacked the European tradition of a vigorous and self-confident merchant class based in cities that were autonomous or even independent of the feudal political leader in the surrounding areas.

In any event, the advent of the imperialist era in the last half of the nineteenth century made such questions academic; imperialism created serious distortions in the local economy that resulted in massive changes in Chinese society during the twentieth century. Whether the Western intrusion was beneficial or harmful is debated to this day. The Western presence undoubtedly accelerated the development of the Chinese economy in some ways: the introduction of modern means of production, transport, and communications; the appearance of an export market; and the steady integration of the Chinese market into the nineteenth-century global economy. To many Westerners at the time, it was self-evident that such changes would ultimately benefit the Chinese people. Western civilization represented the most advanced stage of human development. By supplying (in the catch phrase of the day) "oil for the lamps of China," it was providing a backward society with an opportunity to move up a notch or two on the ladder of human evolution.

Not everyone agreed. The Russian Marxist Vladimir Lenin contended that Western imperialism actually hindered the process of structural change in preindustrial societies because it thwarted the rise of a local industrial and commercial sector in order to maintain colonies and semicolonies as a market for Western manufactured goods and a source of cheap labor and materials. Fellow Marxists in China such as Mao Zedong later took up Lenin's charge and asserted that if the West had not intervened, China would have found its own road to capitalism and thence to socialism and communism.

Many historians today would say that the answer was a little of both. By shaking China out of its traditional mindset, imperialism accelerated the process of change that had begun in the late Ming and early Qing periods and forced the Chinese to adopt new ways of thinking and acting. At the same time, China paid a heavy price in the destruction of its local industry, while many of the profits flowed abroad. Although the industrial revolution is a painful process whenever and wherever it occurs, the Chinese found the experience doubly painful because it was foisted on China from the outside.

Daily Life

At the beginning of the nineteenth century, daily life for most Chinese was not substantially different from what it had been for centuries. Most were farmers, living in millions of villages in rice fields and on hillsides throughout the countryside. Their lives were governed by the harvest cycle, village custom, and family ritual. Their roles in society were firmly fixed by the time-honored principles of Confucian social ethics. Male children, at least the more fortunate ones, were educated in the Confucian classics, while females remained in the home or in the fields. All children were expected to obey their parents, and wives to submit to their husbands.

A visitor to China a hundred years later would have seen a very different society, although it would have still been recognizably Chinese. The changes were most striking in the coastal cities, where the educated and affluent had been visibly affected by the growing Western cultural presence. Confucian social institutions and behavioral norms were declining rapidly in influence, while those of Europe and North America were on the ascendant. Changes were much less noticeable in the countryside, but even there the customary bonds had been dangerously frayed by the rapidly changing times.

Some of the change can be traced to the educational system. During the nineteenth century, the importance of a Confucian education steadily declined, as up to half of the degree holders had purchased their degrees. After 1906, when the government abolished the civil service examinations, a Confucian education ceased to be the key to a successful career, and Western-style education became more desirable. The old dynasty attempted to modernize by establishing an educational system on the Western model with universal education at the elementary level. Such plans had some effect in the cities, where public schools, missionary schools, and other private institutions educated a new generation of Chinese with little knowledge or respect for the past.

The status of women was also in transition. During the mid-Qing era, women were still expected to remain in the home. Their status as useless sex objects was painfully symbolized by the practice of foot binding, a custom that had probably originated among court entertainers in the Tang dynasty and later spread to the common people. By the mid-nineteenth century, more than half of all adult women probably had bound feet.

During the last half of the nineteenth century, signs of change began to appear. Women began to seek employment in factories—notably in cotton mills and in the silk industry, established in Shanghai in the 1890s. Some women were active in dissident activities, such as the Taiping rebellion (1850–1864) and the Boxer movement, and a few fought beside men in waging the 1911 revolution. Qiu Jin, a well-known female revolutionary, wrote a manifesto calling for women's liberation and then organized a revolt against the Manchu government, only to be captured and executed at the age of 32 in 1907.

By the end of the century, educational opportunities for women began to appear for the first time. Christian missionaries began to open girls' schools, mainly in the foreign concession areas. Although only a relatively small number of women were educated in these schools, they had a significant impact on Chinese society as progressive intellectuals began to argue that ignorant women produced ignorant children. In 1905, the court announced its intention to open public schools for girls, but few such schools ever materialized. Private schools for girls were established in some urban areas. The government also began to take steps to discourage the practice of foot binding, although initially with only minimal success.

A Rich Country and a Strong State: The Rise of Modern Japan

By the beginning of the nineteenth century, the Tokugawa shogunate had ruled the Japanese islands for two hundred years. It had revitalized the old governmental system, which had virtually disintegrated under its predecessors. It had driven out the foreign traders and missionaries and isolated the country from virtually all contacts with the outside world. The Tokugawa maintained formal relations only with Korea, although informal trading links with Dutch and Chinese merchants continued at Nagasaki. Isolation, however, did not mean stagnation. Although the vast majority of Japanese still depended on agriculture for their livelihood, a vigorous manufacturing and commercial sector had begun to emerge during the long period of peace and prosperity. As a result, Japanese society had begun to undergo deep-seated changes, and traditional class distinctions were becoming blurred. Eventually, these changes would end Tokugawa rule and destroy the traditional feudal system itself.

Some historians speculate that the Tokugawa system was beginning to come apart, just as the medieval order in Europe had begun to disintegrate at the beginning of the Renaissance. Factionalism and corruption plagued the central bureaucracy, while rural unrest, provoked by a series of poor harvests brought about by bad weather, swept the countryside. Farmers fled to the towns, where anger was already rising as a result of declining agricultural incomes and shrinking stipends for the samurai. Many of the samurai lashed out at the perceived incompetence and corruption of the government. In response, the *bakufu* became increasingly rigid, persecuting its critics and attempting to force fleeing peasants to return to their lands. The government also intensified its efforts to maintain the nation's isolation from the outside world, driving away foreign ships that were beginning to prowl along the Japanese coast in increasing numbers.

An End to Isolation

To the Western powers, the continued isolation of Japanese society was an affront and a challenge. Driven by the growing rivalry among themselves and convinced that the expansion of trade on a global basis would benefit all nations, Western nations began to approach Japan in the hope of opening up the hermit kingdom to foreign economic interests.

The first to succeed was the United States. American steamships crossing the northern Pacific needed a fueling station before going on to China and other ports in the area. In the summer of 1853, an American fleet of four warships under Commodore Matthew C. Perry arrived in Edo Bay (now Tokyo Bay) with a letter from President Millard Fillmore asking for the opening of foreign relations between the two countries (see the box on p. 705).

A few months later, Perry returned with an even larger fleet for an answer. In his absence, Japanese officials had debated the issue. Some argued that contacts with the West would be both politically and morally disadvantageous to Japan, while others pointed to U.S. military superiority and recommended concessions. For the shogunate in Edo, the big black guns of Perry's ships proved decisive, and Japan agreed to the Treaty of Kanagawa, which provided for the return of shipwrecked American sailors, the opening of two ports, and the establishment of a U.S. consulate on Japanese soil. In 1858, U.S. Consul Townsend Harris negotiated a more elaborate commercial treaty calling for the opening of several ports to U.S. trade and residence, the exchange of ministers, and the granting of extraterritorial privileges for U.S. residents in Japan.

COMMODORE PERRY ARRIVES IN JAPAN. In July 1853, U.S. Commodore Matthew Perry arrived in Tokyo Bay in command of a fleet of black ships. His goal was to open Japan to Western trade. In this painting by a Japanese artist, Perry is greeted by his Japanese host, both in full regalia. The U.S. fleet sits at anchor in the background.

Similar treaties were soon signed with several European nations.

The decision to open relations with the Western barbarians was highly unpopular in some quarters, particularly in regions distant from the shogunate headquarters in Edo. Resistance was especially strong in two of the key outside daimyo territories in the south, Satsuma and Choshu, both of which had strong military traditions. In 1863, the "Sat-Cho" alliance forced the hapless shogun to promise to end relations with the West. The shogun eventually reneged on the agreement, but the rebellious groups soon disclosed their own weakness. When Choshu troops fired on Western ships in the Strait of Shimonoseki, the Westerners fired back and destroyed the Choshu fortifications. The incident convinced the rebellious samurai of the need to strengthen their own military and intensified their unwillingness to give in to the West. Having strengthened their influence at the imperial court in Kyoto, they demanded the shogun's resignation and the restoration of the emperor's power. In January 1868 rebel armies attacked the shogunate's palace in Kyoto and proclaimed the restored authority of the emperor. After a few weeks resistance collapsed, and the venerable shogunate system was brought to an end.

The Meiji Restoration

Although the victory of the Sat-Cho faction had appeared on the surface to be a triumph of tradition over change, the new leaders soon realized that Japan must change to survive. Accordingly, they embarked on a policy of comprehensive reform that would lay the foundations of a modern industrial nation within a generation.

The symbol of the new era was the young emperor himself, who had taken the reign name Meiji (enlightened rule) on ascending the throne after the death of his father in 1867. Although the post-Tokugawa period was termed a "restoration," the Meiji ruler, who shared the modernist outlook of the Sat-Cho group, was controlled by the new leadership just as the shogunate had controlled his predecessors. In tacit recognition of the real source of political power, the new capital was located at Edo (now renamed Tokyo, or "Eastern Capital"), and the imperial court was moved to the shogun's palace in the center of the city.

THE TRANSFORMATION OF JAPANESE POLITICS

Once in power, the new leaders launched a comprehensive reform of Japanese political, social, economic, and cultural institutions and values. They moved first to abolish the remnants of the old order and strengthen executive power in their hands. To undercut the power of the daimyo, hereditary privileges were abolished in 1871, and the great lords lost title to their lands. As compensation, they were given government bonds and were named gov-

A LETTER TO THE SHOGUN

When U.S. Commodore Matthew Perry arrived in Tokyo Bay on his first visit to Japan, in July 1853, he carried a letter from the president of the United States, Millard Fillmore. The letter requested that trade relations between the two countries be established. The United States was already becoming a major participant in the race for the East Asian market. Little did the president know how momentous the occasion was, or with what eagerness the Japanese would eventually respond to the challenge.

A LETTER FROM THE PRESIDENT OF THE UNITED STATES

Millard Fillmore
President of the United States of America,
To His Imperial Majesty,
The Emperor of Japan.
Great and Good Friend!
I send you this public letter by Commodore Matthew C. Perry, an officer of the highest rank in the Navy of the United States, and commander of the squadron now visiting your Imperial Majesty's dominions.

I have directed Commodore Perry to assure your Imperial Majesty that I entertain the kindest feelings towards your Majesty's person and government; and that I have no other object in sending him to Japan, but to propose to your Imperial Majesty that the United States and Japan should live in friendship, and have commercial intercourse with each other. The constitution and laws of the United States forbid all interference with the religious or political concerns of other nations. I have particularly charged Commodore Perry to abstain from every act which could possibly disturb the tranquillity of your Imperial Majesty's dominions.

The United States of America reach from ocean to ocean, and our territory of Oregon and state of California lie directly opposite to the dominions of your Imperial Majesty. Our steamships can go from California to Japan in eighteen days. . . .

Japan is also a rich and fertile country, and produces many very valuable articles. . . . I am desirous that our two countries should trade with each other, for the benefit both of Japan and the United States.

We know that the ancient laws of your Imperial Majesty's government do not allow of foreign trade except with the Dutch. But as the state of the world changes, and new governments are formed, it seems to be wise from time to time to make new laws. . . . If your Imperial Majesty were so far to change the ancient laws as to allow a free trade between the two countries, it would be extremely beneficial to both. . . .

Many of our ships pass every year from California to China; and great numbers of our people pursue the whale fishery near the shores of Japan. It sometimes happens in stormy weather that one of our ships is wrecked on your Imperial Majesty's shores. In all such cases we ask and expect, that our unfortunate people should be treated with kindness, and that their property should be protected, till we can send a vessel and bring them away. . . .

May the Almighty have your Imperial Majesty in his great and holy keeping! . . .

Your Good Friend,
Millard Fillmore

ernors of the territories formerly under their control. The samurai, comprising about 8 percent of the total population, received a lump sum payment to replace their traditional stipends, but they were forbidden to wear the sword, the symbol of their hereditary status.

The Meiji modernizers also set out to create a modern political system on the Western model. In the Charter Oath of 1868, the new leaders promised to create a new deliberative assembly within the framework of continued imperial rule (see the box on p. 706). Although senior positions in the new government were given to the daimyo, the key posts were dominated by modernizing samurai, eventually to be known as the *genro*, or elder statesmen, from the Sat-Cho clique.

During the next two decades, the Meiji government undertook a systematic study of Western political systems. A constitutional commission under Prince Ito Hirobumi traveled to several Western countries, including Great Britain, Germany, Russia, and the United States, to study their political systems. As the process evolved, a number of factions appeared, each representing different political ideas. The most prominent were the Liberal Party and the Progressive Party. The Liberal Party favored political reform on the Western liberal democratic model with supreme authority vested in the parliament as the representative of the people. The Progressive Party called for the distribution of power between the legislative and executive branches, with a slight nod to the latter. There was also an imperial party, which advocated the retention of supreme authority exclusively in the hands of the emperor.

During the 1870s and 1880s, these factions competed for preeminence. In the end, the Progressives emerged victorious. The Meiji Constitution, which was adopted in 1890, was based on the Bismarckian model with authority vested in the executive branch; the imperialist faction was pacified by the statement that the constitution was

A PROGRAM FOR REFORM IN JAPAN

In the spring of 1868, the reformers drew up a program for transforming Japanese society along Western lines in the post-Tokugawa era. Though vague in its essentials, the Charter Oath is a good indication of the plans that were carried out during the Meiji Restoration. Compare this program with the Declaration of the Rights of Man drafted at the time of the French Revolution and discussed in Chapter 19.

THE CHARTER OATH OF EMPEROR MEIJI

By this oath we set up as our aim the establishment of the national weal on a broad basis and the framing of a constitution and laws.

1. Deliberative assemblies shall be widely established and all matters decided by public discussion.
2. All classes, high and low, shall unite in vigorously carrying out the administration of affairs of state.
3. The common people, no less than the civil and military officials, shall each be allowed to pursue his own calling so that there may be no discontent.
4. Evil customs of the past shall be broken off and everything based upon the just laws of Nature.
5. Knowledge shall be sought throughout the world so as to strengthen the foundations of imperial rule.

the gift of the emperor. Members of the cabinet were to be handpicked by the Meiji oligarchs. The upper house of parliament was to be appointed and have equal legislative powers with the lower house, called the Diet, whose members would be elected. The core ideology of the state was called the *kokutai* (national polity), which embodied (although in very imprecise form) the concept of the uniqueness of the Japanese system based on the supreme authority of the emperor.

The result was a system that was democratic in form but despotic in practice, modern in appearance but still traditional in that power remained in the hands of a ruling oligarchy. The system permitted the traditional ruling class to retain its influence and economic power while acquiescing in the emergence of new institutions and values.

EMPIRE MEIJI AND THE CHARTER OATH. In 1868, reformist elements overthrew the Tokugawa shogunate in an era of rapid modernization in Japanese society. Their intentions were announced in a Charter Oath of five articles promulgated in April 1868. In this contemporary print, the young emperor Meiji listens to the reading of the Charter Oath in his palace in Kyoto.

MEIJI ECONOMICS

With the end of the daimyo domains, the government needed to establish a new system of land ownership that would transform the mass of the rural population from indentured serfs into citizens. To do so, it enacted a land reform program that redefined the domain lands as the private property of the tillers, while compensating the previous owner with government bonds. One reason for the new policy was that the government needed operating revenues. At the time, public funds came mainly from the customs, which were limited by agreement with the foreign powers to 5 percent of the value of the product. To remedy the problem, the Meiji leaders added a new agriculture tax, which was set at an annual rate of 3 percent of the estimated value of the land. The new tax proved to be a lucrative and dependable source of income for the government, but it was quite onerous for the farmers, who previously had paid a fixed percentage of their harvest to the landowner. As a result, in bad years, many taxpaying peasants were unable to pay their taxes and were forced to sell their lands to wealthy neighbors. Eventually, the government reduced the tax to 2.5 percent of the land value. Still, by the end of the century, about 40 percent of all farmers were tenants.

With its budget needs secured, the government turned to the promotion of industry with the basic objective of guaranteeing Japan's survival against the challenge of Western imperialism. Building on the small but growing industrial economy that already existed under the Tokugawa, the Meiji reformers provided a massive stimulus to Japan's industrial revolution. The government provided financial subsidies to needy industries, training, foreign advisers, improved transport and communications, and a universal educational system emphasizing applied science. In contrast to China, Japan was able to achieve results with minimum reliance on foreign capital. Although the first railroad—built in 1872—was financed by a loan from Great Britain, future projects were all financed by local funds. The foreign currency holdings came largely from tea and silk, which were exported in significant quantities during the latter half of the nineteenth century.

During the late Meiji era, Japan's industrial sector began to grow. Besides tea and silk, other key industries were weaponry, shipbuilding, and sake (Japanese rice wine). From the start, the distinctive feature of the Meiji model was the intimate relationship between government and private business in terms of operations and regulations. Once an individual enterprise or industry was on its feet (or, sometimes, when it had ceased to make a profit), it was turned over entirely to private ownership, although the government often continued to play some role even after its direct involvement in management was terminated. One historian has explained the process:

> It [the Meiji government] pioneered many industrial fields and sponsored the development of others, attempting to cajole businessmen into new and risky kinds of endeavor, helping assemble the necessary capital, forcing weak companies to merge into stronger units, and providing private entrepreneurs with aid and privileges of a sort that would be corrupt favoritism today. All this was in keeping with Tokugawa traditions that business operated under the tolerance and patronage of government. Some of the political leaders even played a dual role in politics and business.[4]

From the workers' perspective, the Meiji reforms had a less attractive side. As we have seen, the new land tax provided the funds to subsidize the growth of the industrial sector, but it imposed severe hardships on the rural population, many of whom abandoned their farms and fled to the cities, where they provided an abundant source of cheap labor for Japanese industry. As in Europe during the early decades of the Industrial Revolution, workers toiled for long hours in the coal mines and textile mills, often under horrendous conditions. Reportedly, coal miners employed on a small island in the harbor of Nagasaki worked naked in temperatures up to 130 degrees Fahrenheit. When they tried to escape, they were shot.

BUILDING A MODERN SOCIAL STRUCTURE

By the late Tokugawa era, the rigidly hierarchical social order was showing signs of disintegration. Rich merchants were buying their way into the ranks of the samurai, and Japanese of all classes were beginning to abandon their rice fields and move into the growing cities. Nevertheless, community and hierarchy still formed the basis of Japanese society. The lives of all Japanese were determined by their membership in various social organizations—the family, the village, and their social class. Membership in a particular social class determined a person's occupation and social relationships with others. Women in particular were constrained by the "three obediences" imposed on their sex: child to father, wife to husband, and widow to son. Husbands could easily obtain a divorce, but wives could not (one regulation allegedly decreed that a husband could divorce his spouse if she drank too much tea or talked too much). Marriages were arranged, and the average age at marriage for females was sixteen years. Females did not share inheritance rights with males, and few received any education outside the family.

The Meiji reformers destroyed much of the traditional social system in Japan. With the abolition of hereditary rights in 1871, the legal restrictions of the past were brought to an end with a single stroke. Special privileges for the aristocracy were abolished, as were the legal restrictions on the *eta,* the traditional slave class (numbering about 400,000 in the 1870s). Another key focus of the reformers was the army. The Sat-Cho reformers had been struck by the weakness of the Japanese forces in clashes with Western powers and embarked on a major program to create a military force that could compete in the modern world. The old feudal army based on the traditional warrior class was abolished, and an imperial army based on universal conscription was formed in 1871. For many rural males, the army became a route of upward mobility.

Education also underwent major changes. The Meiji leaders recognized the need for universal education including technical subjects, and after a few years of experiment, they adopted the American model of a three-tiered system culminating in a series of universities and specialized institutes. In the meantime, they sent bright students to study abroad and brought foreign scholars to Japan to teach in the new schools, where much of the content was inspired by Western models. In another break with tradition, women for the first time were given an opportunity to get an education (see the box on p. 708).

Western influence was evident elsewhere as well. Western fashions became the rage in elite circles, and the ministers of the first Meiji government were known as the "dancing cabinet" because of their addiction to Western-style ballroom dancing. Young people, increasingly exposed to Western culture and values, began to imitate the clothing styles, eating habits, and social practices of their European and American counterparts. They even took up American sports as baseball was introduced.

The self-proclaimed transformation of Japan into a "modern society," however, by no means detached the country entirely from its traditional moorings. Although an educational order in 1872 increased the percentage of Japanese women exposed to public education, conservatives soon began to impose restrictions and bring about a return to more traditional social relationships. The importance of

IN THE BEGINNING, WE WERE THE SUN

One aspect of Western thought that the Meiji reformers did not seek to imitate was the idea of sexual equality. Although Japanese women sometimes tried to be "modern" like their male counterparts, Japanese society as a whole continued to treat women differently, as had been the case during the Tokugawa era. In 1911, a young woman named Hiratsuka Raicho founded a journal named Seito *(Blue Stockings) to promote the liberation of women in Japan. The goal of the new movement was to encourage women to develop their own latent talents, rather than to demand legal changes in Japanese society. The following document is the proclamation that was issued at the creation of the Seito Society. The comparison with the Declaration of the Rights of Women in 1791 (discussed in Chapter 19) is instructive.*

HIRATSUKA RAICHO, PROCLAMATION AT THE FOUNDING OF THE SEITO SOCIETY

Freedom and Liberation! Oftentimes we have heard the term "liberation of women." But what is it then? Are we not seriously misunderstanding the term freedom or liberation? Even if we call the problem the liberation of women, are there not many other issues involved? Assuming that women are freed from external oppression, liberated from constraint, given the so-called higher education, employed in various occupations, given franchise, and provided an opportunity to be independent from the protection of their parents and husbands, and to be freed from the little confinement of their homes, can all of these be called liberation of women? They may provide proper surroundings and opportunities to let us fulfill the true goal of liberation. Yet they remain merely the means, and do not represent our goal or ideals.

However, I am unlike many intellectuals in Japan who suggest that higher education is not necessary for women. Men and women are endowed by nature to have equal faculties. Therefore, it is odd to assume that one of the sexes requires education while the other does not. This may be tolerated in a given country and in a given age, but it is fundamentally a very unsound proposition.

I bemoan the facts that there is only one private college for women in Japan, and that there is no tolerance on man's part to permit entrance of women into many universities maintained for men. However, what benefit is there when the intellectual level of women becomes similar to that of men? Men seek knowledge in order to escape from their lack of wisdom and lack of enlightenment. They want to free themselves. . . . Yet multifarious thought can darken true wisdom, and lead men away from nature. . . .

Now, what is the true liberation which I am seeking? It is none other than to provide an opportunity for women to develop fully their hidden talents and hidden abilities. We must remove all the hindrances that stand in the way of women's development, whether they be external oppression or lack of knowledge. And above and beyond these factors, we must realize that we are the masters in possession of great talents, for we are the bodies which enshrine the great talents.

traditional values was underlined by the Imperial Rescript on Education in 1890 (see the box on p. 709). Displayed in every school and recited by the students, it stressed the Confucian virtues of filial piety, patriotism, and loyalty to the family and community. Traditional values were given a firm legal basis in the Constitution of 1890, which restricted the franchise to males and defined individual liberties as "subject to the limitations imposed by law," and by the Civil Code of 1898, which de-emphasized individual rights and essentially placed women within the context of their role in the family. In 1900, new police regulations prohibited women from joining political organizations or attending public meetings. Beginning in 1905, a group of independent-minded women petitioned the Japanese parliament to rescind this restriction, which was finally repealed in 1922.

In fact, women were now beginning to play a crucial role in their nation's effort to modernize. Urged by their parents to augment the family income, as well as by the government to fulfill their patriotic duty, young girls were sent en masse to work in textile mills. From 1894 to 1912, women represented sixty percent of the Japanese labor force. Thanks to them, by 1914 Japan was the world's leading exporter of silk and dominated cotton manufacturing. If it had not been for the export revenues earned from textile exports, Japan might not have been able to develop its heavy industry and military buildup so quickly and essentially without an infusion of foreign capital.

Joining the Imperialist Club

Traditionally, Japan had not been an expansionist country. As we have seen, except for sporadic forays against Korea, the Japanese had generally been satisfied to remain on their home islands and had even deliberately isolated themselves from their neighbors during the Tokugawa era. Now, however, the Japanese did not just imitate the domestic policies of their Western mentors; they also emulated the Western approach to foreign affairs. This is perhaps not surprising. The Japanese regarded themselves as particularly vulnerable in the world economic arena. Their territory was small, lacking in resources, and densely populated, and they had no natural outlet for expansion. To

THE RULES OF GOOD CITIZENSHIP IN MEIJI JAPAN

After seizing power from the Tokugawa shogunate in 1868, the new Japanese leaders turned their attention to the creation of a new political system that would bring the country into the modern world. After exploring various systems in use in the West, a constitutional commission decided to adopt the system used in imperial Germany because of its paternalistic character. To promote civic virtue and obedience among the citizenry, the government then drafted an imperial rescript that was to be taught to every schoolchild in the country. The rescript instructed all children to obey their sovereign and place the interests of the community and the state above their own personal desires.

IMPERIAL RESCRIPT ON EDUCATION OF 1890

Know ye, Our subjects:

Our Imperial Ancestors have founded Our Empire on a basis broad and everlasting, and have deeply and firmly implanted virtue. Our subjects ever united in loyalty and filial piety have from generation to generation illustrated the beauty thereof. This is the glory of the fundamental character of Our Empire, and herein also lies the source of Our education. Ye, Our subjects, be filial to your parents, affectionate to your brothers and sisters, as husbands and wives be harmonious, as friends true; bear yourselves in modesty and moderation; extend your benevolence to all; pursue learning and cultivate arts, and thereby develop intellectual faculties and perfect moral powers; furthermore, advance public good and promote common interests; always respect the Constitution and observe the laws; should emergency arise, offer yourselves to the State; and thus guard and maintain the prosperity of Our Imperial Throne coeval with heaven and earth. So shall ye not only be Our good and faithful subjects, but render illustrious the best traditions of your forefathers.

observant Japanese, the lessons of history were clear. Western nations had amassed wealth and power not only because of their democratic systems and high level of education, but also because of their colonies.

The Japanese began their program of territorial expansion close to home. In 1874, the Japanese claimed compensation from China for fifty-four sailors from the Ryukyu Islands who had been killed by aborigines on the island of Taiwan and sent a Japanese fleet to Taiwan to punish the perpetrators. When the Qing dynasty evaded responsibility for the incident while agreeing to pay an indemnity to Japan to cover the cost of the expedition, it weakened its claim to ownership of the island of Taiwan. Japan was then able to claim suzerainty over the Ryukyu Islands, long tributary to the Chinese Empire. Two years later, Japanese naval pressure forced Korea to open three ports to Japanese commerce.

During the early decades of the nineteenth century, Korea had followed Japan's example and attempted to isolate itself from outside contact except for periodic tribute missions to China. Christian missionaries, mostly Chinese or French, were vigorously persecuted. But Korea's problems were basically internal. In the early 1860s, a peasant revolt, inspired in part by the Taiping Rebellion in

THE GINZA IN DOWNTOWN TOKYO. This 1877 woodblock print shows the Ginza (a major commercial thoroughfare) in downtown Tokyo, with modern brick buildings, rickshaws, and a horse-drawn streetcar. The centerpiece and focus of public attention is a new electric streetlight.

China, caused considerable devastation before being crushed in 1864. In succeeding years, the Yi dynasty sought to strengthen the country by returning to traditional values and fending off outside intrusion, but rural poverty and official corruption remained rampant. A U.S. fleet, following the example of Commodore Perry in Japan, sought to open the country in 1871 but was driven off with considerable loss of life.

Korea's most persistent suitor, however, was Japan, which was determined to bring an end to Korea's dependency status with China and modernize it along Japanese lines. In 1876, the two countries signed an agreement opening three treaty ports to Japanese commerce in return for Japanese recognition of Korean independence. During the 1880s, Sino-Japanese rivalry over Korea intensified. China supported conservatives at the Korean court, while Japan promoted a more radical faction that was determined to break loose from lingering Chinese influence. When a new peasant rebellion broke out in Korea in 1894, China and Japan intervened on opposite sides. During the war, the Japanese navy destroyed the Chinese fleet and seized the Manchurian city of Port Arthur (see the box on p. 711). In the Treaty of Shimonoseki, the Manchus were forced to recognize the independence of Korea and cede Taiwan and the Liaodong peninsula with its strategic naval base at Port Arthur to Japan.

Shortly thereafter, under pressure from the European powers, the Japanese returned the Liaodong peninsula to China, but in the early twentieth century, they returned to the offensive. Rivalry with Russia over influence in Korea led to increasingly strained relations between the two countries. In 1904, Japan launched a surprise attack on the Russian naval base at Port Arthur, which Russia had taken from China in 1898. The Japanese armed forces were weaker, but Russia faced difficult logistical problems along its new Trans-Siberian Railway and severe political instability at home. In 1905, after Japanese warships sunk almost the entire Russian fleet off the coast of Korea, the Russians agreed to a humiliating peace, ceding the strategically located Liaodong peninsula back to Japan, as well as southern Sakhalin and the Kurile Islands. Russia also agreed to abandon its political and economic influence in Korea and southern Manchuria, which now came increasingly under Japanese control. The Japanese victory stunned the world, including the colonial peoples of Southeast Asia, who now began to realize that the white race was not necessarily invincible.

During the next few years, the Japanese consolidated their position in northeastern Asia, annexing Korea in 1908 as an integral part of Japan. When the Koreans protested the seizure, Japanese reprisals resulted in thousands of deaths. The United States was the first nation to recognize the annexation in return for Tokyo's declaration of respect for U.S. authority in the Philippines. In 1908, the United States recognized Japanese interests in the

CHRONOLOGY

JAPAN AND KOREA IN THE ERA OF IMPERIALISM

Commodore Perry arrives in Tokyo Bay	1853
Townsend Harris Treaty	1858
Fall of Tokugawa Shogunate	1868
U.S. fleet fails to open Korea	1871
Feudal titles abolished	1871
Imperial army formed	1871
Meiji Constitution adopted	1890
Imperial Rescript on Education	1890
Treaty of Shimonoseki awards Taiwan to Japan	1895
Russo-Japanese War	1904–1905
Korea annexed	1908

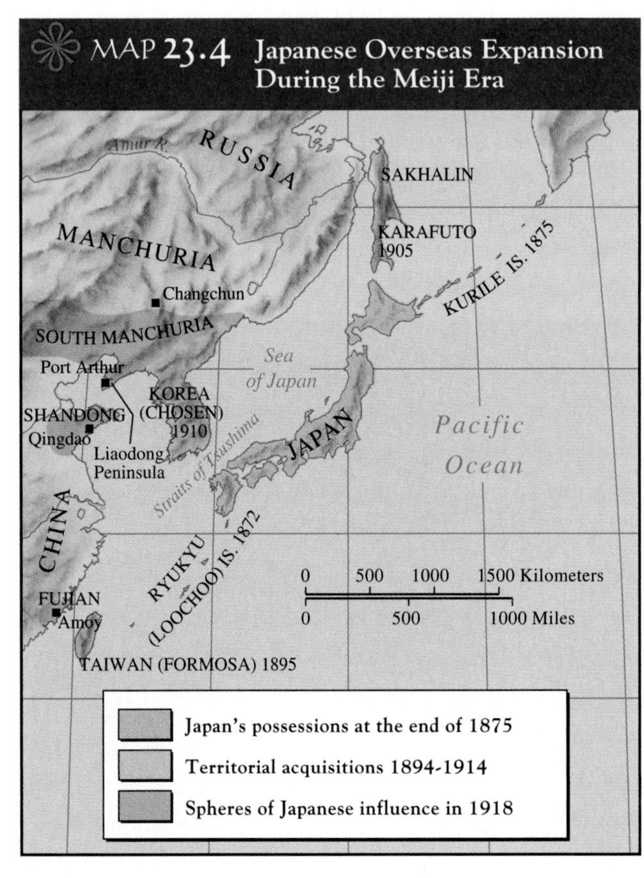

MAP 23.4 Japanese Overseas Expansion During the Meiji Era

TWO VIEWS OF THE WORLD

During the nineteenth century, China's hierarchical way of looking at the outside world came under severe challenge, not only from European countries avid for new territories in Asia, but also from the rising power of Japan, which accepted the Western view that a colonial empire was the key to national greatness. Japan's first objective was Korea, long a dependency of China, and in 1894 the competition between China and Japan in the peninsula led to war. The following declarations of war by the rulers of the two countries are revealing. Note the Chinese use of the derogatory term wojen (dwarf people) *in referring to Japan.*

DECLARATION OF WAR AGAINST CHINA

Korea is an independent state. She was first introduced into the family of nations by the advice and guidance of Japan. It has, however, been China's habit to designate Korea as her dependency, and both openly and secretly to interfere with her domestic affairs. At the time of the recent insurrection in Korea, China despatched troops thither, alleging that her purpose was to afford a succor to her dependent state. We, in virtue of the treaty concluded with Korea in 1882, and looking to possible emergencies, caused a military force to be sent to that country.

Wishing to procure for Korea freedom from the calamity of perpetual disturbance, and thereby to maintain the peace of the East in general, Japan invited China's cooperation for the accomplishment of the object. But China, advancing various pretexts, declined Japan's proposal. . . . Such conduct on the part of China is not only a direct injury to the rights and interests of this Empire, but also a menace to the permanent peace and tranquility of the Orient. . . . In this situation, . . . we find it impossible to avoid a formal declaration of war against China.

DECLARATION OF WAR AGAINST JAPAN

Korea has been our tributary for the past two hundred odd years. She has given us tribute all this time, which is a matter known to the world. For the past dozen years or so Korea has been troubled by repeated insurrections and we, in sympathy with our small tributary, have as repeatedly sent succor to her aid. . . . This year another rebellion was begun in Korea, and the King repeatedly asked again for aid from us to put down the rebellion. We then ordered Li Hung-chang to send troops to Korea; and they having barely reached Yashan the rebels immediately scattered. But the *Wojen,* without any cause whatever, suddenly sent their troops to Korea, and entered Seoul, the capital of Korea, reinforcing them constantly until they have exceeded ten thousand men. In the meantime the Japanese forced the Korean king to change his system of government, showing a disposition every way of bullying the Koreans. . . .

As Japan has violated the treaties and not observed international laws, and is now running rampant with her false and treacherous actions commencing hostilities herself, and laying herself open to condemnation by the various powers at large, we therefore desire to make it known to the world that we have always followed the paths of philanthropy and perfect justice throughout the whole complications, while the *Wojen,* on the other hand, have broken all the laws of nations and treaties which it passes our patience to bear with. Hence we commanded Li Hung-chang to give strict orders to our various armies to hasten with all speed to root the *Wojen* out of their lairs.

region in return for Japanese acceptance of the principles of the Open Door. But mutual suspicion between the two countries was growing, sparked in part by U.S. efforts to restrict immigration from all Asian countries. President Theodore Roosevelt, who mediated the Russo-Japanese War, had aroused the anger of many Japanese by turning down a Japanese demand for reparations from Russia. In turn, some Americans began to fear the rise of a "Yellow Peril" manifested by Japanese expansion in East Asia.

Japanese Culture in an Era of Transition

The wave of Western technology and ideas that entered Japan in the last half of the nineteenth century greatly altered the shape of traditional Japanese culture. Literature in particular was affected as European models eclipsed the repetitive and frivolous tales of the Tokugawa era. Dazzled by this "new" literature, Japanese authors began translating and imitating the imported models. Experimenting with Western verse, Japanese poets were at first influenced primarily by the British, but eventually adopted such French styles as Symbolism, Dadaism, and Surrealism, although some traditional poetry was still composed.

As the Japanese invited technicians, engineers, architects, and artists from Europe and the United States to teach their "modern" skills to a generation of eager students, the Meiji era became a time of massive consumption of Western artistic techniques and styles. Japanese architects and artists created huge buildings of steel and reinforced concrete adorned with Greek columns and cupolas, oil paintings reflecting the European concern with depth perception and shading, and bronze sculptures of secular subjects. All expressed the individual creator's emotional and aesthetic preferences.

Cultural exchange also went the other way, as Japanese arts and crafts, porcelains, textiles, fans, folding screens, and woodblock prints became the vogue in Europe and North America. Japanese art influenced Western painters such as Vincent van Gogh, Edgar Degas, and the American James Whistler, who experimented with flatter compositional perspectives and unusual poses. Japanese gardens, with their exquisite attention to the positioning of rocks and falling water, became especially popular in the United States.

After the initial period of mass absorption of Western art, a national reaction occurred at the end of the nineteenth century as many artists returned to pre-Meiji techniques. In 1889, the Tokyo School of Fine Arts (today the Tokyo National University of Fine Arts and Music) was founded to promote traditional Japanese art. Over the next several decades, Japanese art underwent a dynamic resurgence reflecting the nation's emergence as a prosperous and powerful state. While some Japanese artists attempted to synthesize native and foreign techniques, others returned to past artistic traditions for inspiration.

In architecture, Japan's split personality revealed itself most effectively in the Diet building. As the home of the new Japanese parliament, it was supposed to reflect both progress and the nation and culture of Japan. For half a century, conflicting views over the priority of these concepts delayed its construction. After a number of proposals were rejected, the government held a competition in 1919, but none of the designs won general approval. Finally, in 1936 the government decided on the final design, which followed neither traditional styles nor European architecture of the period.

A VIEW OF MOUNT FUJI. During the nineteenth century, the woodblock print continued to be one of the favored forms of illustration in Japan. A very successful example is the series Thirty-Six Views of Mount Fuji by Hokusai. Each view of the mountain differs in perspective, season, time of day, and general composition. Several portray Fujiyama in the background, while the foreground depicts everyday Japanese in various trades, as in this print of a fisher fighting the waves as he seeks to obtain his catch.

The Meiji Restoration: A Revolution from Above

Japan's transformation from a feudal, agrarian society to an industrializing, technologically advanced society in little more than half a century has frequently been described by outside observers (if not by the Japanese themselves) in almost miraculous terms. Some historians have questioned this characterization, pointing out that the achievements of the Meiji leaders were spotty. In *Japan's Emergence as a Modern State,* the Canadian historian E. H. Norman lamented that the Meiji Restoration was an "incomplete revolution" because it had not ended the economic and social inequities of feudal society or enabled the common people to participate fully in the governing process. Although the *genro* were enlightened in many respects, they were also despotic and elitist, and the distribution of wealth remained as unequal as it had been under the old system.[5]

These criticisms are persuasive, although they could also be applied to most other societies going through the early stage of industrialization. In any event, from an economic perspective, the Meiji Restoration was certainly one of the great success stories of modern times. Not only did the Meiji leaders put Japan firmly on the path to economic and political development; they also managed to remove the unequal treaty provisions that had been imposed at mid-century. Japanese achievements are especially impressive when compared with the difficulties experienced by China, which was not only unable to realize significant changes in its traditional society, but had not even reached a consensus on the need for doing so. Japan's achievements more closely resemble those of Europe, but whereas the West needed a century and a half to achieve a significant level of industrial development, the Japanese realized it in forty years.

One of the distinctive features of Japan's transition from a traditional to a modern society during the Meiji era was that it took place for the most part without violence or the kind of major social or political revolution that occurred in so many other countries. The Meiji Restoration, which began the process, has been called a "revolution from above," a comprehensive restructuring of Japanese society by its own ruling group.

Technically, of course, the Meiji Restoration was not a revolution, since it was not violent and did not result in the displacement of one ruling class by another. The existing elites undertook to carry out a series of major reforms that transformed society but left their own power intact. In the words of one historian, it was "a kind of amalgamation, in which the enterprising, adaptable, or lucky individuals of the old privileged classes [were] for most practical purposes tied up with those individuals of the old submerged classes, who, probably through the same gifts, were able to rise." In that respect, the Meiji Restoration resembles the American Revolution more than the French Revolution; it was a "conservative revolution" that resulted in gradual change rather than rapid and violent change.[6]

The differences between the Japanese response to the West and that of China and many other nations in the region have sparked considerable debate among students of comparative history, and a number of explanations have been offered. Some have argued that Japan's success was partly due to good fortune. Lacking abundant natural resources, it was exposed to less pressure from the West than many of its neighbors. That argument is problematical, however, and would probably not have been accepted by Japanese observers at the time. Nor does it explain why nations under considerably less pressure, such as Laos and Nepal, did not advance even more quickly. All in all, the "good luck" hypothesis is not very persuasive.

Some explanations have already been suggested in this book. Japan's unique geographical position in Asia was certainly a factor. China, a continental nation with a heterogeneous ethnic composition, was distinguished from its neighbors by its Confucian culture. By contrast, Japan was an island nation, ethnically and linguistically homogeneous, and had never been conquered. Unlike the Chinese or many other peoples in the region, the Japanese had little to fear from cultural change in terms of its effect on their national identity. If Confucian culture, with all its accoutrements, was what defined the Chinese gentleman, his Japanese counterpart, in the familiar image, could discard his sword and kimono and don a modern military uniform or a Western business suit and still feel comfortable in both worlds.

Whatever the case, as the historian W. G. Beasley has noted, the Meiji Restoration was possible because aristocratic and capitalist elements managed to work together in a common effort to bring about national wealth and power. The nature of the Japanese value system, with its emphasis on practicality and military achievement, may also have contributed. Finally, the Meiji also benefited from the fact that the pace of urbanization and commercial and industrial development had already begun to quicken under the Tokugawa. Japan, it was said, was ripe for change, and nothing could have been more suitable as an antidote for the collapsing old system than the Western emphasis on wealth and power. It was a classic example of challenge and response.

The final product was an amalgam of old and new, native and foreign, forming a new civilization that was still uniquely Japanese. There were some undesirable consequences, however. Because Meiji politics was essentially despotic, Japanese leaders were able to fuse key traditional elements such as the warrior ethic and the concept of feudal loyalty with the dynamics of modern industrial capitalism to create a state totally dedicated to the possession of material wealth and national power. This combination of *kokutai* and capitalism, which one scholar has described as a form of "Asian fascism," was highly effective but explosive in its international manifestation. Like modern Germany, which also entered the industrial age directly from feudalism, Japan eventually engaged in a policy of repression at home and expansion abroad in order to achieve its national objectives. In Japan, as in Germany, it took defeat in war to disconnect the drive for national development from the feudal ethic and bring about the transformation to a pluralistic society dedicated to living in peace and cooperation with its neighbors. Whether that transformation has been completed in Japan only the future will tell.

Conclusion

Few areas of the world resisted the Western incursion as stubbornly and effectively as East Asia. Although military, political, and economic pressure by the European powers was relatively intense during this era, two of the main states in the area were able to retain their independence, while the third—Korea—was temporarily absorbed by one of its larger neighbors. Why the Chinese and the Japanese were able to prevent a total political and military takeover by foreign powers is an interesting question. Certainly, a key reason was that both had a long history as well-defined states with a strong sense of national community and territorial cohesion. Although China had frequently been conquered, it had retained its sense of unique culture and identity. Geography, too, was in its favor. As a continental nation, China was able to survive partly because of its sheer size, while Japan possessed the advantage of an island location.

Even more striking, however, is the different way in which the two states attempted to deal with the challenge. While the Japanese chose to face the problem in a pragmatic manner, borrowing foreign ideas and institutions that appeared to be of value and at the same time not in conflict with traditional attitudes and customs, China agonized over the issue for half a century, while conservative elements fought a desperate battle to retain a maximum of the traditional heritage intact.

This chapter has discussed some of the possible reasons for those differences. In retrospect, it is difficult to avoid the conclusion that the Japanese approach was the more effective one. While the Meiji leaders were able to set in motion an orderly transition from a traditional to an advanced society, in China the old system collapsed in disorder, leaving chaotic conditions that were still not rectified a generation later. China would pay a heavy price for its failure to respond coherently to the challenge.

But the Japanese "revolution from above" was by no means an unalloyed success. Ambitious efforts by Japanese leaders to carve out a share in the spoils of empire led to escalating conflict with China as well as with rival Western powers, and in the early 1940s to global war. We will deal with that issue in Chapter 26. Meanwhile, in Europe, a combination of old rivalries and the effects of the Industrial Revolution were leading to a bitter regional conflict that eventually engulfed the entire world.

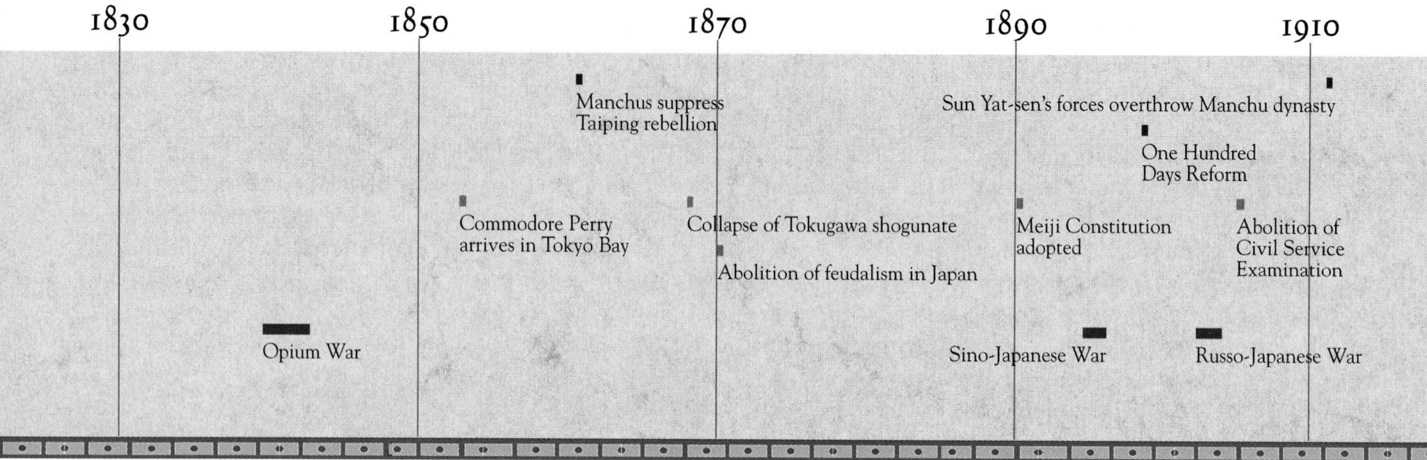

Chapter Notes

1. From Hosea Ballou Morse, *The International Relations of the Chinese Empire* (Shanghai and London, 1910–1918), 2:622, quoted in Jonathan D. Spence, *The Search for Modern China* (New York, 1990), p. 154.
2. Quoted in Ssu-yu Teng and John K. Fairbank, eds., *China's Response to the West: A Documentary Survey, 1839–1923* (New York, 1970), p. 140.
3. Ibid., p. 167.
4. John K. Fairbank, Albert M. Craig, and Edwin O. Reischauer, *East Asia: Tradition and Transformation* (Boston, 1973), p. 514.
5. Quoted in John W. Dower, ed., *The Origins of the Modern Japanese State: Selected Writings of E. H. Norman* (New York, 1975), p. 13.
6. Crane Brinton, *The Anatomy of Revolution* (New York, 1965), quoted in W. G. Beasley, *The Meiji Restoration* (Stanford, Calif., 1972), p. 423.

Suggested Readings

For a general overview of this period of East Asian history, see C. Schirokauer, *Modern China and Japan: A Brief History* (New York, 1982), and J. K. Fairbank, A. M. Craig, and E. O. Reischauer, *East Asia: Tradition and Transformation* (Boston, 1973). See also J. Spence's highly stimulating *The Search for Modern China* (New York, 1990); *The Cambridge History of China*, vols. 10–11 (Cambridge, 1978–1980), dealing with the Qing period; and *The Cambridge History of Japan*, vols. 5–6 (Cambridge, 1988).

On the Western intrusion into China during the nineteenth century, see the classic work by J. K. Fairbank, *Trade and Diplomacy on the China Coast* (Cambridge, 1953), and F. Wakeman, *Strangers at the Gate: Social Disorder in South China, 1839–1861* (Berkeley, Calif., 1966). On the Opium War, see A. Waley, *The Opium War Through Chinese Eyes* (London, 1958), and P. W. Fay, *The Opium War, 1840–1842* (Chapel Hill, N.C., 1975). On the Taiping Rebellion, see F. Michael and C. Chung-li, *The Taiping Rebellion: History and Documents*, 3 vols. (Seattle, 1966–1971), and J. D. Spence, *God's Chinese Son: The Taiping Heavenly Kingdom of Hong Xiuquan* (New York, 1996).

There are a number of important works on the final decades of the Chinese Empire. For a general overview, see F. Wakeman, Jr., *The Fall of Imperial China* (New York, 1975). For economic developments, see A. Feuerwerker's classic *China's Early Industrialization: Sheng Hsuan-huai and Mandarin Enterprise* (Cambridge, 1958).

China's response to the Western challenge is chronicled in S. Teng and J. K. Fairbank, eds., *China's Response to the West: A Documentary Survey, 1839–1923* (New York, 1970).

On the 1911 Revolution, see M. C. Wright, ed., *China in Revolution: The First Phase, 1900–1913* (New Haven, Conn., 1968). Sun Yat-sen's early career is explored in H. Z. Schiffren, *Sun Yat-sen and the Origins of the Chinese Revolution* (Berkeley, Calif., 1970). On the Boxer Rebellion, the definitive study is J. Esherick, *The Origins of the Boxer Uprising* (Berkeley, Calif., 1987).

For a recent survey of modern Japanese history, see J. Hunter, *The Emergence of Modern Japan: An Introductory History Since 1853* (London, 1989). For a provocative treatment in a comparative context, see A. M. Craig, ed., *Japan: A Comparative View* (Princeton, N.J., 1979). See also J. W. Dower, ed., *The Origins of the Modern Japanese State: Selected Writings of E. H. Norman* (New York, 1975).

The Meiji period is discussed in W. G. Beasley, *The Meiji Restoration* (Stanford, Calif., 1972). An earlier and more controversial view is E. H. Norman, *Japan's Emergence as a Modern State: Political and Economic Problems of the Meiji Period* (New York, 1940). See also C. Gluck, *Japan's Modern Myths: Ideology in the Late Meiji Period* (Princeton, N.J., 1985), C. Totman, *The Collapse of the Tokugawa Bakufu, 1862–1868* (Honolulu, 1980), and M. B. Janson, ed., *The Emergence of Meiji Japan* (Cambridge, 1995).

On the economy, see R. Smethurst, *Agricultural Development and Tenancy Disputes in Japan, 1870–1940* (Princeton, N.J., 1986), and G. C. Allen, *A Short Economic History of Japan, 1867–1937* (London, 1972). Social developments are examined in R. Dore, ed., *Aspects of Social Change in Modern Japan* (Princeton, N.J., 1967). The rise of the modern Japanese army is chronicled in R. F. Hackett, *Yamagata Aritomo and the Rise of Meiji Japan* (Cambridge, 1971). For the best introduction to Japanese art, consult P. Mason, *History of Japanese Art* (New York, 1993). See also J. S. Baker's concise *Japanese Art* (London, 1984).

On Japan's emergence as an imperialist power, see A. Iriye, *Pacific Estrangement: Japanese and American Expansion, 1897–1911* (Cambridge, 1972); M. R. Peattie and R. Myers, *The Japanese Colonial Empire, 1895–1945* (Princeton, N.J., 1984); and M. B. Jansen, *Japan and Its World: Two Centuries of Change* (Princeton, N.J., 1980).

For a brief introduction to the women of this era in China and Japan, see S. Hughes and B. Hughes, *Women in World History* (Armonk, N.Y., 1997). For a more detailed account, consult O. Kazuko, *Chinese Women in a Century of Revolution, 1850–1950*, ed. J. A. Fogel (Stanford, Calif., 1989), and O. Kazuko, *Japanese Women: New Feminist Perspectives on the Past, Present, and Future*, ed. K. Fujimura-Fanselow and A. Kameda (New York, 1995).

For additional reading, go to InfoTrac College Edition, your online research library at http://web1.infotrac-college.com

Enter the search terms "China history" using Keywords.

Enter the search term "Qing" using Keywords.

Enter the search terms "Sun Yat-sen" using Keywords.

Enter the search terms "Japan history" using Keywords.

Enter the search term "Meiji" using Keywords.

CHAPTER 24

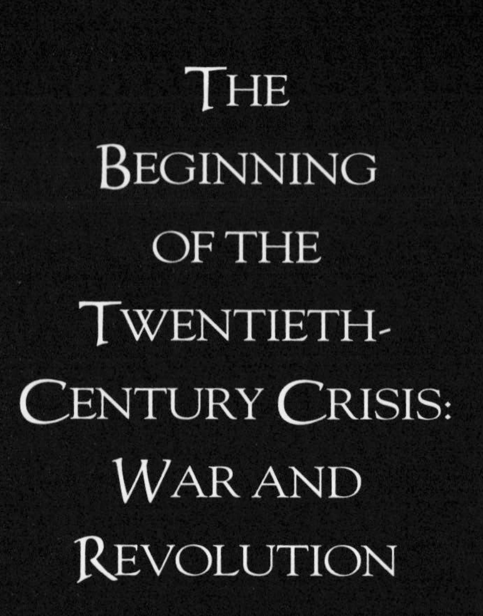

THE BEGINNING OF THE TWENTIETH-CENTURY CRISIS: WAR AND REVOLUTION

CHAPTER OUTLINE

- THE ROAD TO WORLD WAR I
- THE WAR
- WAR AND REVOLUTION
- THE FUTILE SEARCH FOR A NEW STABILITY IN EUROPE
- THE SEARCH FOR A NEW REALITY: CULTURAL AND INTELLECTUAL TRENDS
- CONCLUSION

FOCUS QUESTIONS

- What were the long-range and the immediate causes of World War I, and why did the course of the war turn out to be so different from what the belligerents had expected?
- How did World War I affect the belligerents' govermental and political institutions, economic affairs, and social life?
- What were the causes of the Russian Revolution of 1917, and why did the Bolsheviks prevail in the civil war and gain control of Russia?
- What were the objectives of the chief participants at the Paris Peace Conference of 1919, and how closely did the final settlement mirror their objectives?
- What crises did Europe and the United States face in the interwar years, and how did the cultural and intellectual trends of that period reflect those crises as well as the experience of World War I?

On July 1, 1916, British and French infantry forces attacked German defensive lines along a twenty-five-mile front near the Somme River in France. Each soldier carried almost seventy pounds of equipment, making it "impossible to move much quicker than a slow walk." German machine guns soon opened fire: "We were able to see our comrades move forward in an attempt to cross No-Man's-Land, only to be mown down like meadow grass," recalled one British soldier. "I felt sick at the sight of this carnage and remember weeping." In one day more than 21,000 British soldiers died. After six months of fighting, the British had advanced five miles; one million British, French, and German soldiers had been killed or wounded.

World War I (1914–1918) was the defining event of the twentieth century. It devastated the prewar economic, social, and political order of Europe while its uncertain outcome served to prepare the way for an even more destructive war. Overwhelmed by the scale of its battles, the extent of its casualties, and the effects of its impact on all facets of life, contemporaries referred to it simply as the "Great War."

The Great War was all the more disturbing to Europeans because it came after a period that many believed to have been an age of progress. There had been international crises before 1914, but somehow Europeans had managed to avoid serious and prolonged military confrontations. Material prosperity and a fervid belief in scientific and technological progress had convinced many people that the world stood on the verge of creating the utopia that humans had dreamed of for centuries. The historian Arnold Toynbee expressed what the pre–World War I era had meant to his generation:

> [it was expected] that life throughout the World would become more rational, more humane, and more democratic and that, slowly, but surely, political democracy would produce greater social justice. We had also expected that the progress of science and technology would make mankind richer, and that this increasing wealth would gradually spread from a minority to a majority. We had expected that all this would happen peacefully. In fact we thought that mankind's course was set for an earthly paradise.[1]

After 1918, it was no longer possible to maintain naive illusions about the progress of Western civilization. As World War I was followed by revolutionary upheavals, the mass murder machines of totalitarian regimes, and the destructiveness of World War II, it became all too apparent that instead of a utopia, Western civilization had become a nightmare. World War I and the revolutions it spawned can properly be seen as the first stage in the crisis of the twentieth century.

The Road to World War I

On June 28, 1914, the heir to the Austrian throne, the Archduke Francis Ferdinand, was assassinated in the Bosnian city of Sarajevo. Although this event precipitated the confrontation between Austria and Serbia that led to World War I, there were also long-range, underlying forces that were propelling Europeans toward armed conflict.

Nationalism and Internal Dissent

In the first half of the nineteenth century, liberals had maintained that the organization of European states along national lines would lead to a peaceful Europe based on a sense of international fraternity. They had been very wrong. The system of nation-states that had emerged in Europe in the last half of the nineteenth century led not to cooperation but to competition. Rivalries over colonial and commercial interests intensified during an era of frenzied imperialist expansion, while the division of Europe's great powers into two loose alliances (Germany, Austria, and Italy; and France, Great Britain, and Russia) only added to the tensions. The series of crises that tested these alliances in the 1900s and early 1910s had left European states with a dangerous lesson. Those governments that had exercised restraint in order to avoid war wound up being publicly humiliated, while those that went to the brink of war to maintain their national interests had often been praised for having preserved national honor. In either case, by 1914, the major European states had come to believe that their allies were important and that their security depended on supporting those allies, even when they took foolish risks.

Diplomacy based on brinkmanship was especially frightening in view of the nature of the European state system. Each nation-state regarded itself as sovereign, subject to no higher interest or authority. Each state was motivated by its own self-interest and success. Such attitudes made war an ever present possibility, particularly since most statesmen considered war an acceptable way to preserve the power of their national states.

The growth of nationalism in the nineteenth century had yet another serious consequence. Not all ethnic groups had achieved the goal of nationhood. Slavic minorities in the Balkans and the polyglot Habsburg empire, for example, still dreamed of creating their own national states. So did the Irish in the British Empire and the Poles in the Russian Empire.

National aspirations, however, were not the only source of internal strife at the beginning of the twentieth century. Socialist labor movements had grown more powerful and were increasingly inclined to use strikes, even violent ones, to achieve their goals. Some conservative leaders, alarmed at the increase in labor strife and class division, even feared that European nations were on the verge of revolution. Did these statesmen opt for war in 1914 because they believed that "prosecuting an active foreign policy," as some Austrian leaders expressed it, would smother "internal troubles"? Some historians have argued that the desire to suppress internal disorder may have encouraged some leaders to take the plunge into war in 1914.

Militarism

The growth of large mass armies after 1900 not only heightened the existing tensions in Europe, but made it inevitable that if war did come it would be highly destructive. Conscription had been established as a regular practice in most Western countries before 1914 (the United States and Britain were major exceptions). European military machines had doubled in size between 1890 and 1914. With its 1.3 million men, the Russian army had grown to be the largest, but the French and Germans were not far behind, with 900,000 each. The British, Italian, and Austrian armies numbered between 250,000 and 500,000 soldiers.

Militarism, however, involved more than just large armies. As armies grew, so too did the influence of military leaders, who drew up vast and complex plans for quickly mobilizing millions of men and enormous quantities of supplies in the event of war. Fearful that changing these plans would cause chaos in the armed forces, military leaders insisted that the plans could not be altered. In the crises during the summer of 1914, the generals' lack of flexibility forced European political leaders to make decisions for military instead of political reasons.

The Outbreak of War: The Summer of 1914

Militarism, nationalism, and the desire to stifle internal dissent may all have played a role in the coming of World War I, but the decisions made by European leaders in the

MAP 24.1 Europe in 1914

summer of 1914 directly precipitated the conflict. It was another crisis in the Balkans that forced this predicament upon European statesmen.

As we have seen, states in southeastern Europe had struggled to free themselves from Ottoman rule in the course of the nineteenth and early twentieth centuries. But the rivalry between Austria-Hungary and Russia for domination of these new states created serious tensions in the region. By 1914, Serbia, supported by Russia, was determined to create a large, independent Slavic state in the Balkans, while Austria, which had its own Slavic minorities to contend with, was equally set on preventing that possibility. Many Europeans perceived the inherent dangers in this combination of Serbian ambition bolstered by Russian hatred of Austria and Austrian conviction that Serbia's success would mean the end of its empire. The British ambassador to Vienna wrote in 1913:

> Serbia will some day set Europe by the ears, and bring about a universal war on the Continent. . . . I cannot tell you how exasperated people are getting here at the continual worry which that little country causes to Austria under encouragement from Russia. . . . It will be lucky if Europe succeeds in avoiding war as a result of the present crisis. The next time a Serbian crisis arises . . . , I feel sure that Austria-Hungary will refuse to admit of any Russian interference in the dispute and that she will proceed to settle her differences with her little neighbor by herself.[2]

It was against this backdrop of mutual distrust and hatred between Austria-Hungary and Russia, on the one hand, and Austria-Hungary and Serbia, on the other, that the events of the summer of 1914 were played out.

The assassination of the Austrian Archduke Francis Ferdinand and his wife, Sophia, on June 28, 1914, was carried out by a Bosnian activist who worked for the Black Hand, a Serbian terrorist organization dedicated to the creation of a pan-Slavic kingdom. Although the Austrian government did not know whether the Serbian government had been directly involved in the archduke's assassination, it saw an opportunity to "render Serbia innocuous once and for all by a display of force," as the Austrian foreign minister put it. Fearful of Russian intervention on Serbia's behalf, Austrian leaders sought the backing of their German allies. Emperor William II and his chancellor gave their assurance that Austria-Hungary could rely on Germany's "full support," even if "matters went to the length of a war between Austria-Hungary and Russia."

Strengthened by German support, Austrian leaders issued an ultimatum to Serbia on July 23 in which they made such extreme demands that Serbia had little choice but to reject some of them in order to preserve its sovereignty. Austria then declared war on Serbia on July 28. Still smarting from its humiliation in the Bosnian crisis of 1908, Russia was determined to support Serbia's cause. On July 28, Tsar Nicholas II ordered partial mobilization of the Russian army against Austria. At this point, the rigidity of the military war plans played havoc with diplomatic and political decisions. The Russian General Staff informed the tsar that their mobilization plans were based on a war against both Germany and Austria simultaneously. They could not execute partial mobilization without creating chaos in the army. Consequently, the Russian government ordered full mobilization of the Russian army on July 29, knowing that the Germans would consider this an act of war against them (see the box on p. 720). Germany responded to Russian mobilization with its own ultimatum that the Russians must halt their mobilization within twelve hours. When the Russians ignored it, Germany declared war on Russia on August 1.

At this stage of the conflict, German war plans determined whether or not France would become involved in the war. Under the guidance of General Alfred von Schlieffen, chief of staff from 1891 to 1905, the German General Staff had devised a military plan based on the assumption of a two-front war with France and Russia, because the two powers had formed a military alliance in 1894. The Schlieffen Plan called for a minimal troop deployment against Russia while most of the German army would make a rapid invasion of France before Russia could become effective in the east or before the British could cross the English Channel to help France. This meant invading France by advancing through neutral Belgium, with its level coastal plain on which the army could move faster than on the rougher terrain to the southeast. After the planned quick defeat of the French, the German army expected to redeploy to the east against Russia. Under the Schlieffen Plan, Germany could not mobilize its troops solely against Russia and therefore declared war on France on August 3 after it had issued an ultimatum to Belgium on August 2 demanding the right of German troops to pass through Belgian territory. On August 4, Great Britain declared war on Germany, officially over this violation of Belgian neutrality, but in fact over the British desire to maintain their world power. As one British diplomat argued, if Germany and Austria were to win the war, "what would be the position of a friendless England?" By August 4, all the great powers of Europe were at war.

The War

Before 1914, many political leaders had become convinced that war involved so many political and economic risks that it was not worth fighting. Others had believed that "rational" diplomats could control any situation and prevent the outbreak of war. At the beginning of August 1914, both of these prewar illusions were shattered, but the new illusions that replaced them soon proved to be equally foolish.

"YOU HAVE TO BEAR THE RESPONSIBIITY FOR WAR OR PEACE"

After Austria declared war on Serbia on July 28, 1914, Russian support of Serbia and German support of Austria threatened to escalate the conflict in the Balkans into a wider war. As we can see in these last-minute telegrams between the Russians and Germans, neither side was able to accept the other's line of reasoning.

COMMUNICATIONS BETWEEN BERLIN AND ST. PETERSBURG ON THE EVE OF WORLD WAR I

Emperor William II to Tsar Nicholas II, July 28, 10:45 P.M.

I have heard with the greatest anxiety of the impression which is caused by the action of Austria-Hungary against Servia [Serbia]. The inscrupulous agitation which has been going on for years in Servia has led to the revolting crime of which Archduke Franz Ferdinand has become a victim. The spirit which made the Servians murder their own King and his consort still dominates that country. Doubtless You will agree with me that both of us, You as well as I, and all other sovereigns, have a common interest to insist that all those who are responsible for this horrible murder shall suffer their deserved punishment. . . .

Your most sincere and devoted friend and cousin

(*Signed*) WILHELM

Tsar Nicholas II to Emperor William II, July 29, 1 P.M.

I am glad that you are back in Germany. In this serious moment I ask You earnestly to help me. An ignominious war has been declared against a weak country and in Russia the indignation which I full share is tremendous. I fear that very soon I shall be unable to resist the pressure exercised upon me and that I shall be forced to take measures which will lead to war. To prevent a calamity as a European war would be, I urge You in the name of our old friendship to do all in Your power to restrain Your ally from going too far.

(*Signed*) NICOLAS

Emperor William II to Tsar Nicholas II, July 29, 6:30 P.M.

I have received Your telegram and I share Your desire for the conservation of peace. However: I cannot—as I told You in my first telegram—consider the action of Austria-Hungary as an "ignominious war." Austria-Hungary knows from experience that the promises of Servia as long as they are merely on paper are entirely unreliable. . . . I believe that a direct understanding is possible and desirable between Your Government and Vienna, an understanding which—as I have already telegraphed You—my Government endeavors to aid with all possible effort. Naturally military measures by Russia, which might be construed as a menace by Austria-Hungary, would accelerate a calamity which both of us desire to avoid and would undermine my position as mediator which—upon Your appeal to my friendship and aid—I willingly accepted.

(*Signed*) WILHELM

Emperor William II to Tsar Nicholas II, July 30, 1 A.M.

My Ambassador has instructions to direct the attention of Your Government to the dangers and serious consequences of a mobilization. I have told You the same in my last telegram. Austria-Hungary has mobilized only against Servia, and only a part of her army. If Russia, as seems to be the case, according to Your advice and that of Your Government, mobilizes against Austria-Hungary, the part of the mediator with which You have entrusted me in such friendly manner and which I have accepted upon Your express desire, is threatened if not made impossible. The entire weight of decision now rests upon Your shoulders; You have to bear the responsibility for war or peace.

(*Signed*) WILHELM

German Chancellor to German Ambassador at St. Petersburg, July 31, URGENT

In spite of negotiations still pending and although we have up to this hour made no preparations for mobilization, Russia has mobilized her entire army and navy, hence also against us. On account of these Russian measures, we have been forced, for the safety of the country, to proclaim the threatening state of war, which does not yet imply mobilization. Mobilization, however, is bound to follow if Russia does not stop every measure of war against us and against Austria-Hungary within 12 hours, and notifies us definitely to this effect. Please to communicate this at once to M. Sazonoff and wire hour of communication.

1914–1915: Illusions and Stalemate

Europeans went to war in 1914 with remarkable enthusiasm (see the box on p. 722). Government propaganda had been successful in stirring up national antagonisms before the war. Now in August of 1914, the urgent pleas of governments for defense against aggressors fell on receptive ears in every belligerent nation. Most people seemed genuinely convinced that their nation's cause was just. A new set of illusions also fed the enthusiasm for war. In August 1914, almost everyone believed that the war would be over in a few weeks. People were reminded that all European wars since 1815 had, in fact, ended in a matter of weeks, conveniently overlooking the American Civil War (1861–1865), which was the "real prototype" for World War I. Both the soldiers who exuberantly boarded the trains for the war front in August 1914 and the jubilant citizens who bombarded them with flowers as they departed believed that the warriors would be home by Christmas.

German hopes for a quick end to the war rested upon a military gamble. The Schlieffen Plan had called for the German army to make a vast encircling movement through Belgium into northern France that would sweep around Paris and encircle most of the French army. But the German advance was halted only twenty miles from Paris at the First Battle of the Marne (September 6–10). The war quickly turned into a stalemate as neither the Germans nor the French could dislodge the other from the trenches they had begun to dig for shelter. Two lines of trenches soon extended from the English Channel to the frontiers of Switzerland. The Western Front had become bogged down in a trench warfare that kept both sides immobilized in virtually the same positions for four years.

THE EXCITEMENT OF WAR. World War I was greeted with incredible enthusiasm. Each of the major belligerents was convinced of the rightness of its cause. Everywhere in Europe, jubilant civilians sent their troops off to war with joyous fervor. Their belief that the soldiers would be home by Christmas proved to be a pathetic illusion.

In contrast to the west, the war in the east was marked by much more mobility, although the cost in lives was equally enormous. At the beginning of the war, the Russian army moved into eastern Germany but was decisively defeated at the Battles of Tannenberg on August 30 and the Masurian Lakes on September 15. The Russians were no longer a threat to German territory.

The Austrians, Germany's allies, fared less well initially. They had been defeated by the Russians in Galicia and thrown out of Serbia as well. To make matters worse, the Italians betrayed the Germans and Austrians and entered the war on the Allied side by attacking Austria in May 1915. By this time, the Germans had come to the aid of the Austrians. A German-Austrian army defeated and routed the Russian army in Galicia and pushed the Russians back three hundred miles into their own territory. Russian casualties stood at 2.5 million killed, captured, or wounded; the Russians had almost been knocked out of the war. Buoyed by their success, the Germans and Austrians, joined by the Bulgarians in September 1915, attacked and eliminated Serbia from the war.

1916–1917: The Great Slaughter

The successes in the east enabled the Germans to move back to the offensive in the west. The early trenches dug in 1914 had by now become elaborate systems of defense. Both lines of trenches were protected by barbed-wire entanglements three to five feet high and thirty yards wide, concrete machine-gun nests, and mortar batteries, supported further back by heavy artillery. Troops lived in holes in the ground, separated from each other by a "no-man's-land."

The unexpected development of trench warfare baffled military leaders, who had been trained to fight wars of movement and maneuver. The only plan generals could devise was to attempt a breakthrough by throwing masses of men against enemy lines that had first been battered by artillery barrages. Once the decisive breakthrough had been achieved, they thought, they could then return to the war of movement that they knew best. Periodically, the high command on either side would order an offensive that would begin with an artillery barrage to flatten the enemy's barbed wire and leave the enemy in a state of shock. After "softening up" the enemy in this fashion, a mass of soldiers would climb out of their trenches with fixed bayonets and hope to work their way toward the enemy trenches. The attacks rarely worked, as the machine gun put hordes of men advancing unprotected across open fields at a severe disadvantage. In 1916 and 1917, millions of young men were sacrificed in the search for the elusive breakthrough. In ten months at Verdun, 700,000 men lost their lives over a few miles of terrain.

THE EXCITEMENT OF WAR

The incredible outpouring of patriotic enthusiasm that greeted the declaration of war at the beginning of August 1914 demonstrated the power that nationalistic feeling had attained at the beginning of the twentieth century. Many Europeans seemingly believed that the war had given them a higher purpose, a renewed dedication to the greatness of their nation. This selection is taken from the autobiography of Stefan Zweig, an Austrian writer who captured well the orgiastic celebration of war in Vienna in 1914.

STEFAN ZWEIG, *THE WORLD OF YESTERDAY*

The next morning I was in Austria. In every station placards had been put up announcing general mobilization. The trains were filled with fresh recruits, banners were flying, music sounded, and in Vienna I found the entire city in a tumult. . . . There were parades in the street, flags, ribbons, and music burst forth everywhere; young recruits were marching triumphantly, their faces lighting up at the cheering. . . .

And to be truthful, I must acknowledge that there was a majestic, rapturous, and even seductive something in this first outbreak of the people from which one could escape only with difficulty. And in spite of all my hatred and aversion for war, I should not like to have missed the memory of those days. As never before, thousands and hundreds of thousands felt what they should have felt in peacetime, that they belonged together. A city of two million, a country of nearly fifty million, in that hour felt that they were participating in world history, in a moment which would never recur, and that each one was called upon to cast his infinitesimal self into the glowing mass, there to be purified of all selfishness. All differences of class, rank, and language were flooded over at that moment by the rushing feeling of fraternity. Strangers spoke to one another in the streets; people who had avoided each other for years shook hands; everywhere one saw excited faces. Each individual experienced an exaltation of his ego, he was no longer the isolated person of former times, he had been incorporated into the mass, he was part of the people, and his person, his hitherto unnoticed person, had been given meaning. . . .

What did the great mass know of war in 1914, after nearly half a century of peace? They did not know war, they had hardly given it a thought. It had become legendary, and distance had made it seem romantic and heroic. They still saw it in the perspective of their school readers and of paintings in museums; brilliant cavalry attacks in glittering uniforms, the fatal shot always straight through the heart, the entire campaign a resounding march of victory—"We'll be home at Christmas," the recruits shouted laughingly to their mothers in August of 1914. . . . A rapid excursion into the romantic, a wild, manly adventure—that is how the war of 1914 was painted in the imagination of the simple man, and the young people were honestly afraid that they might miss this most wonderful and exciting experience of their lives; that is why they hurried and thronged to the colors, and that is why they shouted and sang in the trains that carried them to the slaughter; wildly and feverishly the red wave of blood coursed through the veins of the entire nation.

Warfare in the trenches of the Western Front produced unimaginable horrors (see the box on p. 724). Battlefields were hellish landscapes of barbed wire, shell holes, mud, and injured and dying men. The introduction of poison gas in 1915 produced new forms of injuries, as one British writer described them:

> I wish those people who write so glibly about this being a holy war could see a case of mustard gas . . . could see the poor things burnt and blistered all over with great mustard-coloured suppurating blisters with blind eyes all sticky . . . and stuck together, and always fighting for breath, with voices a mere whisper, saying that their throats are closing and they know they will choke.[3]

Soldiers in the trenches also lived with the persistent presence of death. Since combat went on for months, soldiers had to carry on in the midst of countless bodies of dead men or the remains of men dismembered by artillery barrages. Many soldiers remembered the stench of decomposing bodies and the swarms of rats that grew fat in the trenches.

The Widening of the War

As another response to the stalemate on the Western Front, both sides looked for new allies who might provide a winning advantage. The Ottoman Empire had already come into the war on Germany's side in August 1914. Russia, Great Britain, and France declared war on the Ottoman Empire in November. Although the Allies attempted to open a Balkan front by landing forces at Gallipoli, southwest of Constantinople, in April 1915, the entry of Bulgaria into the war on the side of the Central Powers (as Germany, Austria-Hungary, and the Ottoman Empire were called) and a disastrous campaign at Gallipoli caused them to withdraw. The Italians, as we have seen, also entered the war on the Allied side after France and Britain promised to further their acquisition of Austrian territory. In the long run, however, Italian military incompetence forced the Allies to come to the assistance of Italy.

By 1917, the war that had originated in Europe had truly become a world conflict. In the Middle East, a British officer who came to be known as Lawrence of Arabia (1888–1935) incited Arab princes to revolt against their Ottoman overlords in 1917. In 1918, British forces from Egypt destroyed the rest of the Ottoman Empire in the Middle East. For their Middle East campaigns, the British mobilized forces from India, Australia, and New Zealand. The Allies also took advantage of Germany's preoccupations in Europe and lack of naval strength to seize German colonies in the rest of the world. Japan seized a number of German-held islands in the Pacific, while Australia took over German New Guinea.

Most important to the Allied cause was the entry of the United States into the war. At first, the United States tried to remain neutral in the Great War, but that became more difficult as the war dragged on. The immediate cause of American involvement grew out of the naval conflict between Germany and Great Britain. Britain used its superior naval power to maximum effect by imposing a naval blockade on Germany. Germany retaliated with a counterblockade enforced by the use of unrestricted submarine warfare. Strong American protests over the German sinking of passenger liners, especially the British ship *Lusitania* on May 7, 1915, where over a hundred Americans lost their lives, forced the German government to suspend unrestricted submarine warfare in September 1915 to avoid further antagonizing the Americans.

In January 1917, however, eager to break the deadlock in the war, the Germans decided on another military gamble by returning to unrestricted submarine warfare. German naval officers convinced Emperor William II that the use of unrestricted submarine warfare could starve the British into submission within five months, certainly before the Americans could act. The return to unrestricted submarine warfare brought the United States into the war on April 6, 1917. Although American troops did not arrive in Europe in large numbers until 1918, the entry of the United States into the war in 1917 gave the Allied powers a psychological boost when they needed it. The year 1917 was not a good year for them. Allied offensives on the Western Front were disastrously defeated. The Italian armies were smashed in October, and in November 1917 the Bolshevik Revolution in Russia (see The Russian Revolution later in this chapter) led to Russia's withdrawal from the war and left Germany free to concentrate entirely on the Western Front. The cause of the Central Powers looked favorable, although war weariness in the Ottoman Empire, Bulgaria, Austria-Hungary, and Germany was beginning to take its toll. The home front was rapidly becoming a cause for as much concern as the war front.

The Home Front: The Impact of Total War

The prolongation of World War I made it a total war that affected the lives of all citizens, however remote they might be from the battlefields. The need to organize masses of men and matériel for years of combat (Germany alone had 5.5 million men in active units in 1916) led

IMPACT OF THE MACHINE GUN. The development of trench warfare on the Western Front stymied military leaders, who had expected to fight a war based on movement and maneuver. Their efforts to effect a breakthrough by sending masses of men against enemy lines was the height of folly in view of the machine gun. Masses of men advancing across open land made magnificent targets.

THE HORRORS OF WAR. The slaughter of millions of men in the trenches of World War I created unimaginable horrors for the participants. For the sake of survival, many soldiers learned to harden themselves against the stench of decomposing bodies and the sight of bodies horribly dismembered by artillery barrages.

THE REALITY OF WAR: TRENCH WARFARE

The romantic illusion about the excitement and adventure of war that filled the minds of so many young men who marched off to battle quickly disintegrated after a short time in the trenches on the Western Front. This description of trench warfare is taken from the most famous novel that emerged from World War I, Erich Maria Remarque's All Quiet on the Western Front, *written in 1929. Remarque had fought in the trenches in France.*

ERICH MARIA REMARQUE, *ALL QUIET ON THE WESTERN FRONT*

We wake up in the middle of the night. The earth booms. Heavy fire is falling on us. We crouch into corners. We distinguish shells of every calibre.

Each man lays hold of his things and looks again every minute to reassure himself that they are still there. The dugout heaves, the night roars and flashes. We look at each other in the momentary flashes of light, and with pale faces and pressed lips shake our heads.

Every man is aware of the heavy shells tearing down the parapet, rooting up the embankment and demolishing the upper layers of concrete. . . . Already by morning a few of the recruits are green and vomiting. They are too inexperienced. . . .

The bombardment does not diminish. It is falling in the rear too. As far as one can see it spouts fountains of mud and iron. A wide belt is being raked.

The attack does not come, but the bombardment continues. Slowly we become mute. Hardly a man speaks. We cannot make ourselves understood.

Our trench is almost gone. At many places it is only eighteen inches high; it is broken by holes, and craters, and mountains of earth. A shell lands square in front of our post. At once it is dark. We are buried and must dig ourselves out. . . .

Towards morning, while it is still dark, there is some excitement. Through the entrance rushes in a swarm of fleeing rats that try to storm the walls. Torches light up the confusion. Everyone yells and curses and slaughters. The madness and despair of many hours unloads itself in this outburst. Faces are distorted, arms strike out, the beasts scream; we just stop in time to avoid attacking one another. . . .

Suddenly it howls and flashes terrifically, the dugout cracks in all its joints under a direct hit, fortunately only a light one that the concrete blocks are able to withstand. It rings metallically; the walls reel; rifles, helmets, earth, mud, and dust fly everywhere. Sulfur fumes pour in. . . . The recruit starts to rave again and two others follow suit. One jumps up and rushes out, we have trouble with the other two. I start after the one who escapes and wonder whether to shoot him in the leg—then it shrieks again; I fling myself down and when I stand up the wall of the trench is plastered with smoking splinters, lumps of flesh, and bits of uniform. I scramble back.

The first recruit seems actually to have gone insane. He butts his head against the wall like a goat. We must try tonight to take him to the rear. Meanwhile we bind him, but so that in case of attack he can be released.

Suddenly the nearer explosions cease. The shelling continues but it has lifted and falls behind us; our trench is free. We seize the hand grenades, pitch them out in front of the dugout, and jump after them. The bombardment has stopped and a heavy barrage now falls behind us. The attack has come.

No one would believe that in this howling waste there could still be men; but steel helmets now appear on all sides out of the trench, and fifty yards from us a machine gun is already in position and barking.

The wire entanglements are torn to pieces. Yet they offer some obstacle. We see the storm troops coming. Our artillery opens fire. Machine guns rattle, rifles crack. The charge works its way across. Haie and Kropp begin with the hand grenades. They throw as fast as they can; others pass them, the handles with the strings already pulled. Haie throws seventy-five yards, Kropp sixty; it has been measured; the distance is important. The enemy as they run cannot do much before they are within forty yards.

We recognize the distorted faces, the smooth helmets: they are French. They have already suffered heavily when they reach the remnants of the barbed-wire entanglements. A whole line has gone down before our machine guns; then we have a lot of stoppages and they come nearer.

I see one of them, his face upturned, fall into a wire cradle. His body collapses, his hands remain suspended as though he were praying. Then his body drops clean away and only his hands with the stumps of his arms, shot off, now hang in the wire.

to increased centralization of government powers, economic regimentation, and manipulation of public opinion to keep the war effort going.

Because the war was expected to be short, little thought had been given to economic problems and long-term wartime needs. Governments had to respond quickly, however, when the war machines failed to achieve their knockout blows and made ever greater demands for men and matériel. The extension of government power was a logical outgrowth of these needs. Most European countries had already devised some system of mass conscription or military draft. It was now carried to unprecedented heights as countries mobilized tens of millions of young men for that elusive breakthrough to victory. Even countries that

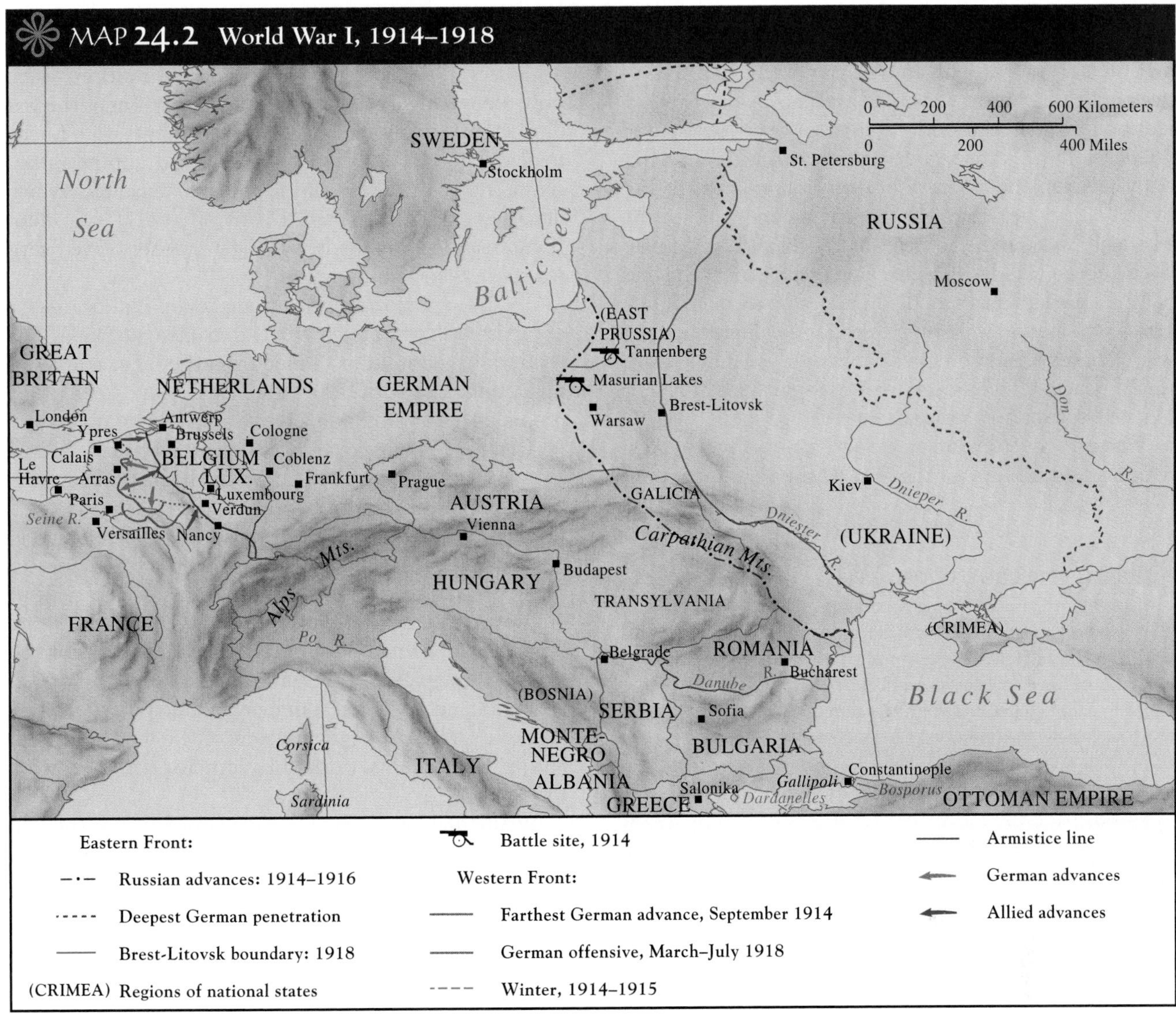

MAP 24.2 World War I, 1914–1918

continued to rely on volunteers (Great Britain had the largest volunteer army in modern history—one million men—in 1914 and 1915) were forced to resort to conscription, especially to ensure that skilled laborers did not enlist but remained in factories that were important to the production of munitions. In 1916, despite widespread resistance to this extension of government power, compulsory military service was introduced in Great Britain.

Throughout Europe, wartime governments expanded their powers over their economies. Free-market capitalistic systems were temporarily shelved as governments experimented with price, wage, and rent controls, the rationing of food supplies and materials, the regulation of imports and exports, and the nationalization of transportation systems and industries. Some governments even moved toward compulsory labor employment. In effect, in order to mobilize the entire resources of their nations for the war effort, European nations had moved toward planned economies directed by government agencies. Under total war mobilization, the distinction between soldiers at war and civilians at home was narrowed. In the view of political leaders, all citizens constituted a national army dedicated to victory. As the American president Woodrow Wilson expressed it, the men and women "who remain to till the soil and man the factories are no less a part of the army than the men beneath the battle flags."

As the Great War dragged on and both casualties and privations worsened, internal dissatisfaction replaced the patriotic enthusiasm that had marked the early stages of the conflict. By 1916, there were numerous signs that civilian morale was beginning to crack under the pressure of total war. War governments, however, fought back against the growing opposition to the war. Authoritarian regimes, such as those of Germany, Russia, and Austria-Hungary, had always relied on force to subdue their populations. Under the pressures of the war, however, even parliamentary regimes resorted to an expansion of police powers to stifle internal dissent. The British Parliament passed a Defence of the Realm Act (DORA) at the very beginning of the war that allowed the public authorities to arrest dissenters as traitors. The act was later extended to authorize public officials to censor newspapers by deleting objectionable material and even to suspend newspaper publication. In France, government authorities had initially been lenient about public opposition to the war. But by 1917, they began to fear that open opposition to the war might weaken the French will to fight. When Georges Clemenceau (1841–1929) became premier near the end of 1917, the lenient French policies came to an end, and basic civil liberties were suppressed for the duration of the war. When a former premier publicly advocated a negotiated peace, Clemenceau's government had him sentenced to prison for two years for treason.

Wartime governments made active use of propaganda to arouse enthusiasm for the war. At the beginning, public officials needed to do little to achieve this goal. The British and French, for example, exaggerated German atrocities in Belgium and found that their citizens were only too willing to believe these accounts. But as the war dragged on and morale sagged, governments were forced to devise new techniques for stimulating declining enthusiasm. In one British recruiting poster, for example, a small daughter asked her father, "Daddy, what did YOU do in the Great War?" while her younger brother played with toy soldiers and cannon.

BRITISH RECRUITING POSTER. As the conflict persisted month after month, governments resorted to active propaganda campaigns to generate enthusiasm for the war. In this British recruiting poster, the government tried to pressure men into volunteering for military service. By 1916, the British were forced to adopt compulsory military service.

Total war made a significant impact on European society, most visibly by bringing an end to unemployment. The withdrawal of millions of men from the labor market to fight, combined with the heightened demand for wartime products, led to jobs for everyone able to work.

World War I also created new roles for women. Because so many men went off to fight at the front, women were called on to take over jobs and responsibilities that had not been available to them before. Overall, the number of women employed in Britain who held new jobs or replaced men rose by 1,345,000. Women were also now employed in jobs that had been considered beyond the "capacity of women." These included such occupations as chimney sweeps, truck drivers, farm laborers, and, above all, factory workers in heavy industry (see the box on p. 727). Thirty-eight percent of the workers in the Krupp Armaments works in Germany in 1918 were women.

While male workers expressed concern that the employment of females at lower wages would depress their own wages, women began to demand equal pay legislation. A law passed by the French government in July 1915 established a minimum wage for women homeworkers in textiles, an industry that had grown dramatically because of the need for military uniforms. Later in 1917 the government decreed that men and women should receive equal rates for piecework. Despite the noticeable increase in women's wages that resulted from government regulations, women's industrial wages still were not equal to men's wages by the end of the war.

Even worse, women's place in the workforce was far from secure. Both men and women seemed to assume that many of the new jobs for women were only temporary, an expectation quite evident in the British poem "War Girls," written in 1916:

There's the girl who clips your ticket for the train,
And the girl who speeds the lift from floor to floor,
There's the girl who does a milk-round in the rain,
And the girl who calls for orders at your door.
Strong, sensible, and fit,
They're out to show their grit,
And tackle jobs with energy and knack.
No longer caged and penned up,
They're going to keep their end up
Till the khaki soldier boys come marching back.[4]

WOMEN IN THE FACTORIES

During World War I, women were called upon to assume new job responsibilities, including factory work. In this selection, Naomi Loughnan, a young, upper-middle-class woman, describes the experiences in a munitions plant that considerably broadened her perspective on life.

NAOMI LOUGHNAN, "MUNITION WORK"

We little thought when we first put on our overalls and caps and enlisted in the Munition Army how much more inspiring our life was to be than we had dared to hope. Though we munition workers sacrifice our ease, we gain a life worth living. Our long days are filled with interest, and with the zest of doing work for our country in the grand cause of Freedom. As we handle the weapons of war we are learning great lessons of life. In the busy, noisy workshops we come face to face with every kind of class, and each one of these classes has something to learn from the others. . . .

Engineering mankind is possessed of the unshakable opinion that no woman can have the mechanical sense. If one of us asks humbly why such and such an alteration is not made to prevent this or that drawback to a machine, she is told, with a superior smile, that a man has worked her machine before her for years, and that therefore if there were any improvement possible it would have been made. As long as we do exactly what we are told and do not attempt to use our brains, we give entire satisfaction, and are treated as nice, good children. Any swerving from the easy path prepared for us by our males arouses the most scathing contempt in their manly bosoms. . . . Women have, however, proved that their entry into the munition world has increased the output. Employers who forget things personal in their patriotic desire for large results are enthusiastic over the success of women in the shops. But their workmen have to be handled with the utmost tenderness and caution lest they should actually imagine it was being suggested that women could do their work equally well, given equal conditions of training—at least where muscle is not the driving force. . . .

The coming of the mixed classes of women into the factory is slowly but surely having an educative effect upon the men. "Language" is almost unconsciously becoming subdued. There are fiery exceptions, who make our hair stand up on end under our close-fitting caps, but a sharp rebuke or a look of horror will often straighten out the most savage. . . . It is grievous to hear the girls also swearing and using disgusting language. Shoulder to shoulder with the children of the slums, the upper classes are having their eyes opened at last to the awful conditions among which their sisters have dwelt. Foul language, immorality, and many other evils are but the natural outcome of overcrowding and bitter poverty. . . . Sometimes disgust will overcome us, but we are learning with painful clarity that the fault is not theirs whose actions disgust us, but must be placed to the discredit of those other classes who have allowed the continued existence of conditions which generate the things from which we shrink appalled.

At the end of the war, governments moved quickly to remove women from the jobs they had encouraged them to take earlier. By 1919, there were 650,000 unemployed women in Britain, while wages for women who were still employed were also lowered. The work benefits for women from World War I seemed to be short-lived as demobilized men returned to the job market.

Nevertheless, in some countries the role played by women in the wartime economies did have a positive impact on the women's movement for social and political emancipation. The most obvious gain was the right to vote that was given to women in Germany and Austria immediately after the war (in Britain already in January 1918). Contemporary media, however, tended to focus on the more noticeable, yet in some ways more superficial, social emancipation of upper- and middle-class women. In ever larger numbers, these young women took jobs, had their own apartments, and showed their new independence by smoking in public and wearing shorter dresses, cosmetics, and new hairstyles.

War and Revolution

By 1917, total war was creating serious domestic turmoil in all of the European belligerent states. Only one, however, experienced the kind of complete collapse that others were predicting might happen throughout Europe. Out of Russia's collapse came the Russian Revolution, whose impact would be widely felt in Europe and the world for decades to come.

The Russian Revolution

After the Revolution of 1905 had failed to bring any substantial changes to Russia, Tsar Nicholas II fell back on the army and bureaucracy as the basic props for his autocratic regime. But World War I magnified Russia's problems and put the tsarist government to a test that it could not meet. Russia was unprepared both militarily and technologically for the total war of World War I. Competent military leadership was lacking. Even worse, the tsar, alone of all European monarchs, insisted on taking personal charge of the armed forces despite his obvious lack of ability and training for such an awesome burden. Russian industry was unable to produce the weapons needed for the army. Ill-led and ill-armed, Russian armies suffered incredible losses. Between 1914 and 1916, two million soldiers were killed while another four to six million were wounded or captured. By 1917, the Russian will to fight had vanished.

The tsarist government was totally inadequate for the tasks that it faced in 1914. Even conservative aristocrats were appalled by the incompetent and inefficient bureaucracy that controlled the political and military system. In the meantime, Tsar Nicholas II was increasingly insulated from events by his German-born wife, Alexandra, a willful woman who had fallen under the influence of Rasputin, a Siberian peasant who belonged to a religious sect that indulged in sexual orgies. Rasputin's influence made him an important power behind the throne, and he did not hesitate to interfere in government affairs. As the leadership at the top stumbled its way through a series of military and economic disasters, the middle class, aristocrats, peasants, soldiers, and workers grew more and more disenchanted with the tsarist regime. Even conservative aristocrats who supported the monarchy felt the need to do something to reverse the deteriorating situation. For a start, they assassinated Rasputin in December 1916. By then it was too late to save the monarchy, and its fall came quickly.

At the beginning of March 1917, a series of strikes broke out in the capital city of Petrograd (formerly St. Petersburg). Here the actions of working-class women helped to change the course of Russian history. In February of 1917, the government had introduced bread rationing in the capital city after the price of bread had skyrocketed. Many of the women who stood in the lines waiting for bread were also factory workers who had put in twelve-hour days. The Russian government had become aware of the volatile situation in the capital from a police report:

> Mothers of families, exhausted by endless standing in line at stores, distraught over their half-starving and sick children, are today perhaps closer to revolution than [the liberal opposition leaders] and of course they are a great deal more dangerous because they are the combustible material for which only a single spark is needed to burst into flame.[5]

On March 8, about ten thousand Petrograd women marched through the city demanding "Peace and Bread" and "Down with Autocracy." Soon the women were joined by other workers, and together they called for a general strike that succeeded in shutting down all the factories in the city on March 10. Nicholas ordered the troops to disperse the crowds by shooting them if necessary, but soon significant numbers of the soldiers joined the demonstrators. The Duma or legislative body, which the tsar had tried to dissolve, met anyway and on March 12 established a Provisional Government that urged the tsar to abdicate. He did so on March 15.

THE WOMEN'S MARCH IN PETROGRAD. After the introduction of bread rationing in Petrograd, 10,000 women engaged in mass demonstrations and demanded "Peace and Bread" for the families of soldiers. This photograph shows the women marching through the streets of Petrograd on March 8, 1917.

The Provisional Government headed by Alexander Kerensky (1881–1970) decided to carry on the war to preserve Russia's honor—a major blunder because it satisfied neither the workers nor the peasants, who above all wanted an end to the war. The Provisional Government was also faced with another authority, the soviets, or councils of workers' and soldiers' deputies. The Petrograd soviet had been formed in March 1917; at the same time, soviets sprang up spontaneously in army units, factory towns, and rural areas. The soviets represented the more radical interests of the lower classes and were largely composed of socialists of various kinds. One group—the Bolsheviks—came to play a crucial role.

The Bolsheviks were a small faction of Marxist Social Democrats who had come under the leadership of Vladimir Ulianov, known to the world as V. I. Lenin (1870–1924). Arrested for his revolutionary activity, Lenin was shipped to Siberia. After his release, he chose to go into exile in Switzerland and eventually assumed the leadership of the Bolshevik wing of the Russian Social Democratic Party. Under Lenin's direction, the Bolsheviks became a party dedicated to violent revolution. He believed that only a violent revolution could destroy the capitalist system and that a "vanguard" of activists must form a small party of well-disciplined professional revolutionaries to accomplish the task. Between 1900 and 1917, Lenin spent most of his time in Switzerland. When the Provisional Government was formed in March 1917, he believed that an opportunity for the Bolsheviks to seize power had come. In April 1917, with the connivance of the German High Command, who hoped to create disorder in Russia, Lenin was shipped to Russia in a "sealed train" by way of Finland.

Lenin's arrival in Russia opened a new stage of the Russian Revolution. Lenin maintained that the soviets of soldiers, workers, and peasants were ready-made instruments of power. The Bolsheviks must work toward gaining control of these groups and then use them to overthrow the Provisional Government. At the same time, Bolshevik propaganda must seek mass support through promises geared to the needs of the people: an end to the war; redistribution of all land to the peasants; the transfer of factories and industries from capitalists to committees of workers; and the relegation of government power from the Provisional Government to the soviets. Three simple slogans summed up the Bolshevik program: "Peace, Land, Bread," "Worker Control of Production," and "All Power to the Soviets."

By the end of October, the Bolsheviks had achieved a slight majority in the Petrograd and Moscow soviets. The number of party members had also grown, from 50,000 to 240,000. With the close cooperation of Leon Trotsky (1877–1940), a fervid revolutionary, Lenin organized a Military Revolutionary Committee within the Petrograd soviet to plot the overthrow of the government. On the night of November 6–7, Bolshevik forces seized the Winter Palace, seat of the Provisional Government. The Provisional Government quickly collapsed with little bloodshed. This coup d'etat had been timed to coincide with a meeting in Petrograd of the all-Russian Congress of Soviets, representing local soviets from all over the country. Lenin nominally turned over the sovereignty of the Provisional Government to this Congress of Soviets. Real power, however, passed to a Council of People's Commissars, headed by Lenin (see the box on p. 730).

But the Bolsheviks, soon renamed the Communists, still had a long way to go. For one thing, Lenin had

LENIN ADDRESSES A CROWD. V. I. Lenin was the driving force behind the success of the Bolsheviks in seizing power in Russia and creating the Union of Soviet Socialist Republics. Here Lenin is seen addressing a rally in Moscow in 1917.

TEN DAYS THAT SHOOK THE WORLD: LENIN AND THE BOLSHEVIK SEIZURE OF POWER

John Reed was an American journalist who helped to found the American Communist Labor Party. Accused of sedition, he fled the United States and went to Russia. In Ten Days That Shook the World, *Reed left an impassioned eyewitness account of the Russian Revolution. It is apparent from his comments that Reed considered Lenin the indispensable hero of the Bolshevik success.*

JOHN REED, *TEN DAYS THAT SHOOK THE WORLD*

It was just 8:40 when a thundering wave of cheers announced the entrance of the presidium, with Lenin—great Lenin—among them. A short, stocky figure, with a big head set down in his shoulders, bald and bulging. Little eyes, a snubbish nose, wide, generous mouth, and heavy chin; clean-shaven now, but already beginning to bristle with the well-known beard of his past and future. Dressed in shabby clothes, his trousers much too long for him. Unimpressive, to be the idol of a mob, loved and revered as perhaps few leaders in history have been. A strange popular leader—a leader purely by virtue of intellect; colorless, humorless, uncompromising and detached; without picturesque idiosyncrasies—but with the power of explaining profound ideas in simple terms, of analyzing a concrete situation. And combined with shrewdness, the greatest intellectual audacity. . . .

Now Lenin, gripping the edge of the reading stand, letting his little winking eyes travel over the crowd as he stood there waiting, apparently oblivious to the long-rolling ovation, which lasted several minutes. When it finished, he said simply, "We shall now proceed to construct the Socialist order!" Again that overwhelming human roar.

"The first thing is the adoption of practical measures to realize peace. . . . We shall offer peace to the peoples of all the belligerent countries upon the basis of the Soviet terms—no annexations, no indemnities, and the right of self-determination of peoples. At the same time, according to our promise, we shall publish and repudiate the secret treaties. . . . The question of War and Peace is so clear that I think that I may, without preamble, read the project of a Proclamation to the Peoples of All the Belligerent Countries. . . ."

His great mouth, seeming to smile, opened wide as he spoke; his voice was hoarse—not unpleasantly so, but as if it had hardened that way after years and years of speaking—and went on monotonously, with the effect of being able to go forever. . . . For emphasis he bent forward slightly. No gestures. And before him, a thousand simple faces looking up in intent adoration.

[Reed then reproduces the full text of the Proclamation.]

When the grave thunder of applause had died away, Lenin spoke again: "We propose to the Congress to ratify this declaration. . . . This proposal of peace will meet with resistance on the part of the imperialist governments—we don't fool ourselves on that score. But we hope that revolution will soon break out in all the belligerent countries; that is why we address ourselves especially to the workers of France, England, and Germany. . . .

"The revolution of November 6th and 7th," he ended, "has opened the era of the Social Revolution. . . . The labor movement, in the name of peace and Socialism, shall win, and fulfill its destiny. . . ."

There was something quiet and powerful in all this, which stirred the souls of men. It was understandable why people believed when Lenin spoke.

promised peace, and that, he realized, was not an easy task because of the humiliating losses of Russian territory that it would entail. There was no real choice, however. On March 3, 1918, Lenin signed the Treaty of Brest-Litovsk with Germany and gave up eastern Poland, Ukraine, Finland, and the Baltic provinces. To his critics, Lenin argued that it made no difference because the spread of socialist revolution throughout Europe would make the treaty largely irrelevant. In any case, he had promised peace to the Russian people, but real peace did not come, for the country soon sank into civil war.

CIVIL WAR

There was great opposition to the new Bolshevik or Communist regime, not only from groups loyal to the tsar but also from bourgeois and aristocratic liberals and anti-Leninist socialists. In addition, thousands of Allied troops were eventually sent to different parts of Russia in the hope of bringing Russia back into the war.

Between 1918 and 1921, the Bolshevik (or Red) Army was forced to fight on many fronts. The first serious threat to the Bolsheviks came from Siberia, where a White (anti-Bolshevik) force attacked westward and advanced almost to the Volga River before being stopped. Attacks also came from the Ukrainians in the southeast and from the Baltic regions. In mid-1919, White forces swept through Ukraine and advanced almost to Moscow. At one point by late 1919, three separate White armies seemed to be closing in on the Bolsheviks but were eventually pushed back. By 1920, the major White forces had been defeated, and Ukraine retaken. The next year, the Communist regime regained control over the independent nationalist governments in the Caucasus: Georgia, Russian Armenia, and Azerbaijan.

How had Lenin and the Bolsheviks triumphed over what seemed at one time to be overwhelming forces? For one thing, the Red Army became a well-disciplined and formidable fighting force, largely due to the organizational genius of Leon Trotsky. As commissar of war, Trotsky reinstated the draft and insisted on rigid discipline; soldiers who deserted or refused to obey orders were summarily executed.

The disunity of the anti-Communist forces seriously weakened the efforts of the Whites. Political differences created distrust among the Whites and prevented them from cooperating effectively with each other. Some Whites insisted on restoring the tsarist regime, while others understood that only a more liberal democratic program had any chance of success. It was difficult enough to achieve military cooperation; political differences made it virtually impossible.

The Whites' inability to agree on a common goal was in sharp contrast to the Communists' single-minded sense of purpose. Inspired by their vision of a new socialist order, the Communists had the advantage of possessing the determination that comes from revolutionary fervor and revolutionary convictions.

The Communists also succeeded in translating their revolutionary faith into practical instruments of power. A policy of "war communism," for example, was used to ensure regular supplies for the Red Army. War communism included the nationalization of banks and most industries, the forcible requisition of grain from peasants, and the centralization of state administration under Bolshevik control. Another Bolshevik instrument was "revolutionary terror." Although the old tsarist secret police had been abolished, a new Red secret police—known as the Cheka—replaced it. The Red Terror instituted by the Cheka aimed at nothing less than the destruction of all those who opposed the new regime. The Red Terror added an element of fear to the Bolshevik regime.

Finally, the intervention of foreign armies enabled the Communists to appeal to the powerful force of Russian patriotism. Although the Allied powers had intervened initially in Russia to encourage the Russians to remain in the war, the end of the war on November 11, 1918, had made that purpose inconsequential. Nevertheless, Allied troops remained, and more were even sent as Allied countries did not hide their anti-Bolshevik feelings. At one point, over 100,000 foreign troops, mostly Japanese, British, American, and French, were stationed on Russian soil. These forces rarely engaged in pitched battles, however, nor did they pursue a common strategy, although they gave material assistance to anti-Bolshevik forces. This intervention by the Allies enabled the Communist government to appeal to patriotic Russians to fight the foreign invaders. Allied interference was never substantial enough to make a military difference in the civil war, but it did serve indirectly to help the Bolshevik cause.

CHRONOLOGY

THE RUSSIAN REVOLUTION

	1916
Murder of Rasputin	December
	1917
March of women in Petrograd	March 8
General strike in Petrograd	March 10
Establishment of Provisional Government	March 12
Tsar Nicholas II abdicates	March 15
Formation of Petrograd soviet	March
Lenin arrives in Russia	April 3
Bolsheviks gain majority in Petrograd soviet	October
Bolsheviks overthrow Provisional Government	November 6–7
	1918
Lenin disbands the Constituent Assembly	January
Treaty of Brest-Litovsk	March 3
Civil war	1918–1921

By 1921, the Communists had succeeded in retaining control of Russia. In the course of the civil war, the Bolshevik regime had also transformed Russia into a bureaucratically centralized state dominated by a single party. It was also a state that was largely hostile to the Allied powers that had sought to assist the Bolsheviks' enemies in the civil war. To most historians, the Russian Revolution is unthinkable without the total war of World War I, for only the collapse of Russia made it possible for a radical minority like the Bolsheviks to seize the reins of power. In turn, the Russian Revolution had an impact on the course of World War I.

The Last Year of the War

For Germany, the withdrawal of the Russians from the war in March 1918 offered renewed hope for a favorable end to the war. The victory over Russia persuaded Erich von Ludendorff (1865–1937), who guided German military operations, and most German leaders to make one final military gamble—a grand offensive in the west to break the military stalemate. The German attack was launched in March and lasted into July, but an Allied counterattack, supported by the arrival of 140,000 fresh American troops, defeated the Germans at the Second Battle of the Marne

CHRONOLOGY

WORLD WAR I

The Path to War	**1914**
Assassination of Archduke Francis Ferdinand	June 28
Austria's ultimatum to Serbia	July 23
Austria declares war on Serbia	July 28
Russia mobilizes	July 29
Germany's ultimatum to Russia	July 31
Germany declares war on Russia	August 1
Germany declares war on France	August 3
German troops invade Belgium	August 4
Great Britain declares war on Germany	August 4
The War	**1914**
Battle of Tannenberg	August 26–30
First Battle of the Marne	September 6–10
Battle of Masurian Lakes	September 15
Russia, Great Britain, and France declare war on Ottoman Empire	November
	1915
Battle of Gallipoli begins	April 25
Italy declares war on Austria-Hungary	May 23
Entry of Bulgaria into the war	September
	1916
Battle of Verdun	February 21–December 18
Battle of Jutland	May 31
	1917
Germany returns to unrestricted submarine warfare	January
United States enters the war	April 6
	1918
Last German offensive	March 21–July 18
Second Battle of the Marne	July 18
Allied counteroffensive	July 18–November 10
Armistice between Allies and Germany	November 11
	1919
Paris Peace Conference begins	January 18
Peace of Versailles	June 28

on July 18. Ludendorff's gamble had failed. With the arrival of two million more American troops on the Continent, Allied forces began to advance steadily toward Germany.

On September 29, 1918, General Ludendorff informed German leaders that the war was lost and demanded that the government sue for peace at once. When German officials discovered, however, that the Allies were unwilling to make peace with the autocratic imperial government, reforms were instituted to create a liberal government. But these constitutional reforms came too late for the exhausted and angry German people. On November 3, naval units in Kiel mutinied, and within days councils of workers and soldiers were forming throughout northern Germany and taking over the supervision of civilian and military administrations. William II capitulated to public pressure and abdicated on November 9, while the Socialists under Friedrich Ebert (1871–1925) announced the establishment of a republic. Two days later, on November 11, 1918, the new German government agreed to an armistice. The war was over.

The Peace Settlement

In January 1919, the delegations of twenty-seven victorious Allied nations gathered in Paris to conclude a final settlement of the Great War. Some delegates believed that this conference would avoid the mistakes made at Vienna in 1815 by aristocrats who rearranged the map of Europe to meet the selfish desires of the great powers. Harold Nicolson, one of the British delegates, expressed what he believed this conference would achieve instead: "We were journeying to Paris not merely to liquidate the war, but to found a New Order in Europe. We were preparing not Peace only, but Eternal Peace. There was about us the halo of some divine mission. . . . For we were bent on doing great, permanent, and noble things."[6]

National expectations, however, made Nicolson's quest for "eternal peace" a difficult one. Over the years, the reasons for fighting World War I had been transformed from selfish national interests to idealistic principles. No one expressed the latter better than Woodrow Wilson. The American president outlined "Fourteen Points" to the U.S.

THE VOICE OF PEACEMAKING: WOODROW WILSON

"We are fighting for the liberty, the self-government, and the undictated development of all peoples. . . ."

When the Allied powers met in Paris in January 1919, it soon became apparent that the victors had different opinions on the kind of peace they expected. These excerpts are from the speeches of Woodrow Wilson in which the American president presented his idealistic goals for a peace based on justice and reconciliation.

MAY 26, 1917

We are fighting for the liberty, the self-government, and the undictated development of all peoples, and every feature of the settlement that concludes this war must be conceived and executed for that purpose. Wrongs must first be righted and then adequate safeguards must be created to prevent their being committed again. . . .

No people must be forced under sovereignty under which it does not wish to live. No territory must change hands except for the purpose of securing those who inhabit it a fair chance of life and liberty. No indemnities must be insisted on except those that constitute payment for manifest wrongs done. No readjustments of power must be made except such as will tend to secure the future peace of the world and the future welfare and happiness of its peoples.

And then the free peoples of the world must draw together in some common covenant, some genuine and practical cooperation that will in effect combine their force to secure peace and justice in the dealings of nations with one another.

APRIL 6, 1918

We are ready, whenever the final reckoning is made, to be just to the German people, deal fairly with the German power, as with all others. There can be no difference between peoples in the final judgment, if it is indeed to be a righteous judgment. To propose anything but justice, even-handed and dispassionate justice, to Germany at any time, whatever the outcome of the war, would be to renounce and dishonor our own cause. For we ask nothing that we are not willing to accord.

JANUARY 3, 1919

Our task at Paris is to organize the friendship of the world, to see to it that all the moral forces that make for right and justice and liberty are united and are given a vital organization to which the peoples of the world will readily and gladly respond. In other words, our task is no less colossal than this, to set up a new international psychology, to have a new atmosphere.

Congress that he believed justified the enormous military struggle then being waged. Later, Wilson spelled out additional steps for a truly just and lasting peace. Wilson's proposals included "open covenants of peace, openly arrived at" instead of secret diplomacy; the reduction of national armaments to a "point consistent with domestic safety"; and the self-determination of people so that "all well-defined national aspirations shall be accorded the utmost satisfaction." Wilson characterized World War I as a people's war waged against "absolutism and militarism," two scourges of liberty that could only be eliminated by creating democratic governments and a "general association of nations" that would guarantee the "political independence and territorial integrity to great and small states alike" (see the box above). As the spokesman for a new world order based on democracy and international cooperation, Wilson was enthusiastically cheered by many Europeans when he arrived in Europe for the peace conference.

Wilson soon found, however, that other states at the Paris Peace Conference were guided by considerably more pragmatic motives. The secret treaties and agreements that had been made before the war could not be totally ignored, even if they did conflict with the principle of self-determination enunciated by Wilson. National interests also complicated the deliberations of the Paris Peace Conference. David Lloyd George (1863–1945), prime minister of Great Britain, had won a decisive electoral victory in December of 1918 on a platform of making the Germans pay for this dreadful war.

France's approach to peace was primarily determined by considerations of national security. To Georges Clemenceau, the feisty French premier who had led his country to victory, the French people had borne the brunt of German aggression. They deserved revenge and security against future German aggression. Clemenceau wanted a demilitarized Germany, vast German reparations to pay for the costs of the war, and a separate Rhineland as a buffer state between France and Germany, demands that Wilson viewed as vindictive and contrary to the principle of national self-determination.

Although twenty-seven nations were represented at the Paris Peace Conference, the most important decisions were made by Wilson, Clemenceau, and Lloyd George. Italy was considered one of the so-called Big Four powers but played a much less important role than the other three countries. Germany, of course, was not invited to attend, and Russia could not because of its civil war.

In view of the many conflicting demands at Versailles, it was inevitable that the Big Three would quarrel. Wilson was determined to create a League of Nations to prevent future wars. Clemenceau and Lloyd George were equally determined to punish Germany. In the end, only compromise made it possible to achieve a peace settlement. Wilson's wish that the creation of an international peacekeeping organization be the first order of business was granted, and already on January 25, 1919, the conference adopted the principle of a League of Nations. The details of its structure were left for later sessions, and Wilson willingly agreed to make compromises on territorial arrangements to guarantee the establishment of the league, believing that a functioning league could later rectify bad arrangements. Clemenceau also compromised to obtain some guarantees for French security. He renounced France's desire for a separate Rhineland and instead accepted a defensive alliance with Great Britain and the United States. Both states pledged to help France if it were attacked by Germany.

THE TREATY OF VERSAILLES

The final peace settlement of Paris consisted of five separate treaties with the defeated nations—Germany, Austria, Hungary, Bulgaria, and Turkey. The Treaty of Versailles with Germany, signed on June 28, 1919, was by far the most important one. The Germans considered it a harsh peace and were particularly unhappy with Article 231, the so-called War Guilt Clause, which declared Germany (and Austria) responsible for starting the war and ordered Germany to pay reparations for all the damage to which the Allied governments and their people were subjected as a result of the war "imposed upon them by the aggression of Germany and her allies."

THE BIG FOUR AT PARIS. Shown here are the Big Four at the Paris Peace Conference: David Lloyd George of Britain, Vittorio Orlando of Italy, Georges Clemenceau of France, and Woodrow Wilson of the United States. Although Italy was considered one of the Big Four powers, Britain, France, and the United States (the Big Three) made the major decisions at the peace conference.

The military and territorial provisions of the treaty also rankled the Germans, although they were by no means as harsh as the Germans claimed. Germany had to lower its army to 100,000 men, reduce its navy, and eliminate its air force. German territorial losses included the return of Alsace and Lorraine to France and sections of Prussia to the new Polish state. German land west and as far as thirty miles east of the Rhine was established as a demilitarized zone and stripped of all armaments or fortifications to serve as a barrier to any future German military moves westward against France. Outraged by the "dictated peace," the new German government complained but accepted the treaty.

THE OTHER PEACE TREATIES

The separate peace treaties made with the other Central Powers (Austria, Hungary, Bulgaria, and Turkey) extensively redrew the map of eastern Europe. Many of these changes merely ratified what the war had already accomplished. Both the German and Russian Empires lost considerable territory in eastern Europe, while the Austro-Hungarian Empire disappeared altogether. New nation-states emerged from the lands of these three empires: Finland, Latvia, Estonia, Lithuania, Poland, Czechoslovakia, Austria, and Hungary. Territorial rearrangements were also made in the Balkans. Romania acquired additional lands from Russia, Hungary, and Bulgaria. Serbia formed the nucleus of a new South Slav state, called Yugoslavia, which combined Serbs, Croats, and Slovenes. Although the Paris Peace Conference was supposedly guided by the principle of self-determination, the mixtures of peoples in eastern Europe made it impossible to draw boundaries along neat ethnic lines. Compromises had to be made, sometimes to satisfy the national interest of the victors. France, for example, had lost Russia as its major ally on Germany's eastern border and wanted to strengthen and expand Poland, Czechoslovakia, Yugoslavia, and Romania as much as possible so that those states could serve as barriers against Germany and Communist Russia. As a result of compromises, virtually every eastern European state was left with a minorities problem that could lead to future conflicts. Germans in Poland, Hungarians, Poles, and Germans in Czechoslovakia, and the combination of Serbs, Croats, Slovenes, Macedonians, and Albanians in Yugoslavia all became sources of later conflict. Moreover, the new map of eastern Europe was based on the temporary collapse of power in both Germany and Russia. As neither country accepted the new eastern frontiers, it seemed only a matter of time before a resurgent Germany or Russia would make changes.

Yet another centuries-old empire—the Ottoman Empire—was dismembered by the peace settlement after the war. To gain Arab support against the Turks during the war, the Western allies had promised to recognize the

MAP 24.3 Territorial Changes in Europe and the Middle East After World War I

independence of Arab states in the Middle Eastern lands of the Ottoman Empire. But the imperialist habits of Western nations died hard. After the war, France took control of Lebanon and Syria, while Britain received Iraq and Palestine. Officially, both acquisitions were called mandates. Because Woodrow Wilson had opposed the outright annexation of colonial territories by the Allies, the peace settlement had created a system of mandates whereby a nation officially administered a territory on behalf of the League of Nations. The system of mandates could not hide the fact that the principle of national self-determination at the Paris Peace Conference was largely for Europeans.

The peace settlement negotiated at Paris soon came under attack, not only by the defeated Central Powers, but by others who felt that the peacemakers had been short-sighted. The famous British economist John Maynard Keynes, for example, condemned the preoccupation with frontiers at the expense of economic issues that left Europe "inefficient, unemployed, disorganized."

Others, however, thought the peace settlement was the best that could be achieved under the circumstances. Self-determination, they believed, had served reasonably well as a central organizing principle, and the creation of the League of Nations, moreover, gave some hope that future conflicts could be resolved peacefully. And yet, within twenty years after the signing of the peace treaties, Europe was again engaged in war.

Some historians have suggested that perhaps the cause of the failure of the peace of 1919 was its lack of enforcement. To enforce the peace, the chief architects of the treaties needed to be actively involved, especially in assisting the new German state to develop a peaceful and democratic republic. The U.S. Senate failed, however, to ratify the Treaty of Versailles. As a result, the United States never even joined the League of Nations. In addition, the Senate also rejected Wilson's defensive alliance with Great Britain and France. Already by the end of 1919, the United States was limiting its involvement in European affairs.

This retreat had dire consequences. American withdrawal from the defensive alliance with Britain and France led Britain to withdraw as well. By removing itself from European affairs, the United States forced France to stand alone facing its old enemy. Frightened by this turn of events, the French decided to take strong actions against Germany, and that only made the Germans more resentful. By the end of 1919, it appeared that the peace treaties of 1919 were not going to bring peace.

THE FUTILE SEARCH FOR A NEW STABILITY IN EUROPE

Only twenty years after the Treaty of Versailles, the world was again at war. Yet, in the 1920s, many people continued to assume that Europe and the world were about to enter a new era of international peace, economic growth, and political democracy. In all of these areas, the optimistic hopes of the 1920s failed to be realized.

An Uncertain Peace: The Search for Security

The peace settlement at the end of World War I had tried to fulfill the nineteenth-century dream of nationalism by creating new boundaries and new states. From its inception, however, this peace settlement had left nations unhappy. Conflicts over disputed border regions between Germany and Poland, Poland and Lithuania, Poland and Czechoslovakia, Austria and Hungary, and Italy and Yugoslavia poisoned mutual relations in eastern Europe for years. Many Germans viewed the Peace of Versailles as a dictated peace and vowed to seek its revision.

The American president Woodrow Wilson had recognized that the peace treaties contained unwise provisions that could serve as new causes for conflicts and had placed many of his hopes for the future in the League of Nations. The league, however, was not particularly effective in maintaining the peace. The failure of the United States to join the league and the subsequent American retreat into isolationism undermined the effectiveness of the league from its beginning. Moreover, the league could use only economic sanctions to halt aggression. The French attempt to strengthen the league's effectiveness as an instrument of collective security by creating some kind of international army was rejected by nations that feared giving up any of their sovereignty to a larger international body.

The weakness of the League of Nations and the failure of both the United States and Great Britain to honor their defensive military alliances with France left France embittered and alone. France's search for security between 1919 and 1924 was founded primarily on a strict enforcement of the Treaty of Versailles. This tough policy toward Germany began with the issue of reparations, or the payments that the Germans were supposed to make to compensate for the "damage done to the civilian population of the Allied and Associated Powers and to their property," as the treaty asserted. In April 1921, the Allied Reparations Commission settled on a sum of 132 billion marks ($33 billion) for German reparations, payable in annual installments of 2.5 billion (gold) marks. Allied threats to occupy the Ruhr valley, Germany's chief industrial and mining center, led the new German republic to accept the reparations settlement and make its first payment in 1921. By the following year, however, faced with rising inflation, domestic turmoil, and lack of revenues due to low tax rates, the German government announced that it was unable to pay more. Outraged by what they considered to be Germany's violation of one aspect of the peace settlement, the French government sent troops to occupy the Ruhr valley. Since the Germans would not pay reparations, the French would collect reparations in kind by operating and using the Ruhr mines and factories.

Both Germany and France suffered from the French occupation of the Ruhr. The German government adopted a policy of passive resistance to French occupation that was largely financed by printing more paper money. This only intensified the inflationary pressures that had already begun in Germany by the end of the war. The German mark became worthless. Economic disaster fueled political upheavals as Communists staged uprisings in October and Adolf Hitler's band of Nazis attempted to seize power in Munich in 1923. All the nations, including France, were happy to cooperate with the American suggestion for a new conference of experts to reassess the reparations problem. By the time the conference did its work in 1924, both France and Germany were opting to pursue a more conciliatory approach toward each other.

The formation of liberal-socialist governments in both Great Britain and France opened the door to conciliatory approaches to Germany and the reparations problem. At the same time, a new German government led by Gustav Stresemann (1878–1929) ended the policy of passive resistance and committed Germany to carry out the provisions of the Versailles Treaty while seeking a new settlement of the reparations question.

In August 1924, an international commission produced a new plan for reparations. Named the Dawes Plan after the American banker who chaired the commission, it reduced reparations and stabilized Germany's payments on the basis of its ability to pay. The Dawes Plan also granted an initial $200 million loan for German recovery, which opened the door to heavy American investments in Europe, which helped create a new era of European prosperity between 1924 and 1929.

A new age of European diplomacy accompanied the new economic stability. A spirit of international cooperation was fostered by the foreign ministers of Germany and France, Gustav Stresemann and Aristide Briand (1862–1932), who concluded the Treaty of Locarno in 1925. This guaranteed Germany's new western borders with France and Belgium. Although Germany's new eastern borders with Poland were conspicuously absent from the agreement, the Locarno pact was viewed by many as the beginning of a new era of European peace. On the day after the pact was concluded, the headline in the *New York Times* ran "France and Germany Ban War Forever," while the London *Times* declared, "Peace at Last."[7]

Germany's entry into the League of Nations in March 1926 soon reinforced the new spirit of conciliation engendered at Locarno. Two years later, similar optimistic attitudes prevailed in the Kellogg-Briand pact, drafted by the American secretary of state Frank B. Kellogg and the French foreign minister Aristide Briand. Sixty-three nations signed this accord, in which they pledged "to renounce war as an instrument of national policy." Nothing was said, however, about what would be done if anyone violated the treaty.

The spirit of Locarno was based on little real substance. Germany lacked the military power to alter its western borders even if it wanted to. Pious promises to renounce war without mechanisms to enforce them were virtually worthless. And the issue of disarmament soon proved that even the spirit of Locarno could not bring nations to cut back on their weapons. The League of Nations Covenant had suggested the "reduction of national armaments to the lowest point consistent with national safety." Germany, of course, had been disarmed with the expectation that other states would do likewise. Numerous disarmament conferences, however, failed to achieve anything substantial as states proved unwilling to trust their security to anyone but their own military forces. When a World Disarmament Conference finally met in Geneva in 1932, the issue was already dead.

The Great Depression

After World War I, most European states hoped to return to the liberal ideal of a private-enterprise, market economy largely free of state intervention. But the war had vastly strengthened business cartels and labor unions, making some government regulation of these powerful organizations necessary. At the same time, reparations and war debts had severely damaged the postwar international economy, making the prosperity that did occur between 1924 and 1929 at best a fragile one and the dream of returning to the liberal ideal of a self-regulating market economy merely an illusion. What destroyed the concept altogether was the Great Depression.

Two factors played a major role in the coming of the Great Depression: a downturn in domestic economies and an international financial crisis created by the collapse of the American stock market in 1929. Already in the mid-1920s, prices for agricultural goods were beginning to decline rapidly due to overproduction of basic commodities such as wheat. In 1925, states in central and eastern Europe began to impose tariffs to close their markets to other countries' goods. An increase in the use of oil and hydroelectricity led to a slump in the coal industry even before 1929.

In addition to these domestic economic troubles, much of the European prosperity between 1924 and 1929 had been built upon American bank loans to Germany. Twenty-three billion marks had been invested in German municipal bonds and German industries since 1924. Already in 1928 and 1929, American investors had begun to pull money out of Germany in order to invest in the booming New York stock market. The crash of the American stock market in October 1929 led panicky American investors to withdraw even more of their funds from Germany and other European markets. The withdrawal of funds seriously weakened the banks of Germany and other central European states. The Credit-Anstalt, Vienna's most prestigious bank, collapsed on May 31, 1931. By that time, trade was slowing down, industrialists were cutting back production, and unemployment was increasing as the ripple effects of international bank failures had a devastating impact on domestic economies.

Economic depression was by no means a new phenomenon in European history. But the depth of the economic downturn after 1929 fully justifies the label Great Depression. During 1932, the worst year of the depression, one British worker in four was unemployed, while six million or 40 percent of the German labor force were out of work. Between 1929 and 1932, industrial production plummeted almost 50 percent in the United States and over 40 percent in Germany. The unemployed and homeless filled the streets of the cities throughout the advanced industrial countries (see the box on p. 738).

The economic crisis also had unexpected social repercussions. Women were often able to secure low-paying jobs as servants, housecleaners, or laundresses, while many men remained unemployed, either begging on the streets or remaining at home to do household tasks. This reversal of traditional gender roles caused resentment on the part of many unemployed men, opening them to the shrill cries of demagogues with simple solutions to the economic crisis. In addition, high unemployment rates among young males often led them to join gangs that gathered in parks or other public places, creating fear among local residents.

Governments seemed powerless to deal with the crisis. The classical liberal remedy for depression, a deflationary policy of balanced budgets, which involved cutting costs by lowering wages and raising tariffs to exclude other countries' goods from home markets, only served to worsen the economic crisis and create even greater mass discontent. This, in turn, led to serious political repercussions. Increased government activity in the economy was one reaction, even in countries like the United States that had a strong *laissez-faire* tradition. Another effect was a renewed interest in Marxist doctrines because Marx had predicted that capitalism would destroy itself through overproduction. Communism took on new popularity, especially with workers and intellectuals. Finally, the Great Depression increased the attractiveness of simplistic dictatorial solutions, especially from a new movement known

THE GREAT DEPRESSION: UNEMPLOYED AND HOMELESS IN GERMANY

In 1932, Germany had six million unemployed workers, many of them wandering aimlessly about the country, begging for food and seeking shelter in city lodging houses for the homeless. The Great Depression was an important factor in the rise to power of Adolf Hitler and the Nazis. This selection presents a description of the unemployed homeless in 1932.

HEINRICH HAUSER, "WITH GERMANY'S UNEMPLOYED"

An almost unbroken chain of homeless men extends the whole length of the great Hamburg-Berlin highway. . . . All the highways in Germany over which I have traveled this year presented the same aspect. . . .

Most of the hikers paid no attention to me. They walked separately or in small groups, with their eyes on the ground. And they had the queer, stumbling gait of barefooted people, for their shoes were slung over their shoulders. Some of them were guild members—carpenters . . . milkmen . . . and bricklayers . . . —but they were in a minority. Far more numerous were those whom one could assign to no special profession or craft—unskilled young people, for the most part, who had been unable to find a place for themselves in any city or town in Germany, and who had never had a job and never expected to have one. There was something else that had never been seen before—whole families that had piled all their goods into baby carriages and wheelbarrows that they were pushing along as they plodded forward in dumb despair. It was a whole nation on the march.

I saw them—and this was the strongest impression that the year 1932 left with me—I saw them, gathered into groups of fifty or a hundred men, attacking fields of potatoes. I saw them digging up the potatoes and throwing them into sacks while the farmer who owned the field watched them in despair and the local policeman looked on gloomily from the distance. I saw them staggering toward the lights of the city as night fell, with their sacks on their backs. What did it remind me of? Of the War, of the worst periods of starvation in 1917 and 1918, but even then people paid for the potatoes. . . .

I saw that the individual can know what is happening only by personal experience. I know what it is to be a tramp. I know what cold and hunger are. . . . But there are two things that I have only recently experienced—begging and spending the night in a municipal lodging house.

I entered the huge Berlin municipal lodging house in a northern quarter of the city. . . .

Distribution of spoons, distribution of enameled-ware bowls with the words "Property of the City of Berlin" written on their sides. Then the meal itself. A big kettle is carried in. Men with yellow smocks have brought it in, and men with yellow smocks ladle out the food. These men, too, are homeless and they have been expressly picked by the establishment and given free food and lodging and a little pocket money in exchange for their work about the house.

Where have I seen this kind of food distribution before? In a prison that I once helped to guard in the winter of 1919 during the German civil war. There was the same hunger then, the same trembling, anxious expectation of rations. Now the men are standing in a long row, dressed in their plain nightshirts that reach to the ground, and the noise of their shuffling feet is like the noise of big wild animals walking up and down the stone floor of their cages before feeding time. The men lean far over the kettle so that the warm steam from the food envelops them, and they hold out their bowls as if begging and whisper to the attendant, "Give me a real helping. Give me a little more." A piece of bread is handed out with every bowl.

My next recollection is sitting at table in another room on a crowded bench that is like a seat in a fourth-class railway carriage. Hundreds of hungry mouths make an enormous noise eating their food. The men sit bent over their food like animals who feel that someone is going to take it away from them. They hold their bowl with their left arm partway around it, so that nobody can take it away, and they also protect it with their other elbow and with their head and mouth, while they move the spoon as fast as they can between their mouth and the bowl.

as fascism. Everywhere, democracy seemed on the defensive in the 1930s.

The Democratic States

According to Woodrow Wilson, World War I had been fought to make the world safe for democracy. In 1919, there seemed to be some justification for his claim. Four major European states and a host of minor ones had functioning political democracies. In a number of states, universal male suffrage had even been replaced by universal suffrage as male politicians rewarded women for their contributions to World War I by granting them the right to vote (except in Italy, Switzerland, France, and Spain, where women had to wait until the end of World War II). In the 1920s, Europe seemed to be returning to the political trends of the prewar era—the broadening of parliamentary regimes and the fostering of individual liberties.

But it was not an easy process; four years of total war and four years of postwar turmoil made the desire for a "return to normalcy" a difficult and troublesome affair.

After World War I, Great Britain went through a period of painful readjustment and serious economic difficulties. During the war, Britain had lost many of the markets for its industrial products, especially to the United States and Japan. The postwar decline of such staple industries as coal, steel, and textiles led to a rise in unemployment, which reached the two million mark in 1921. But Britain soon rebounded and experienced an era of renewed prosperity between 1925 and 1929. This prosperity, however, was relatively superficial. British exports in the 1920s never compensated for the overseas investments lost during the war, and even in these so-called prosperous years, unemployment remained at a startling 10 percent level. Coal miners were especially affected by the decline of the antiquated and inefficient British coal mines, which also suffered from a world glut of coal.

By 1929, Britain was faced with the growing effects of the Great Depression. The Labour Party, which had now become the largest party in Britain, failed to solve the nation's economic problems and fell from power in 1931. A National Government, dominated by the Conservatives, claimed credit for bringing Britain out of the worst stages of the depression, primarily by using the traditional policies of balanced budgets and protective tariffs. British politicians largely ignored the new ideas of a Cambridge economist, John Maynard Keynes (1883–1946). In 1936, Keynes published his *General Theory of Employment, Interest, and Money*. Contrary to the traditional view that depressions should be left to work themselves out through the self-regulatory mechanisms of a free economy, Keynes argued that unemployment stemmed not from overproduction but from a decline in demand, and that demand could be increased by public works, financed, if necessary, through deficit spending to stimulate production. These policies, however, could only be accomplished by government intervention in the economy, and Britain's political leaders were unwilling to go that far in the 1930s.

After the defeat of Germany and the demobilization of the German army, France had become the strongest power on the European continent. Its biggest problem involved the reconstruction of the devastated areas of northern and eastern France. But neither the conservative National Bloc government nor a government coalition of leftist parties (the Cartel of the Left) seemed capable of solving France's financial problems between 1921 and 1926. The failure of the Cartel of the Left led to the return of the conservative Raymond Poincaré (1860–1934), whose government from 1926 to 1929 stabilized the French economy by a substantial increase in taxes during a period of relative prosperity.

France did not feel the effects of the depression as soon as other countries because of its more balanced economy. The French population was almost evenly divided between urban and agricultural pursuits, while a slight majority of French industrial plants were small enterprises. Consequently, France did not begin to feel the full effects of the Great Depression until 1932, but then economic instability soon had political repercussions. During a nineteen-month period in 1932 and 1933, six different cabinets were formed as France faced political chaos. Finally, in June 1936, fearful that rightists intended to seize power, a coalition of leftist parties—Communists, Socialists, and Radicals—formed a Popular Front government.

The Popular Front succeeded in initiating a program for workers that some have called the French New Deal. It included the right of collective bargaining, a forty-hour work week, two-week paid vacations, and minimum wages. The Popular Front's policies failed to solve the problems of the depression, however. Although the Popular Front

THE GREAT DEPRESSION: BREAD LINES IN PARIS. The Great Depression devastated the European economy and had serious political repercussions. Because of its more balanced economy, France did not feel the effects of the depression as quickly as other European countries. By 1931, however, even France was experiencing lines of unemployed people at free-food centers.

survived in name until 1938, it was for all intents and purposes dead before then. By 1938, the French were experiencing a serious decline of confidence in their political system that left them unprepared to deal with their aggressive Nazi enemy to the east.

After the Imperial Germany of William II had come to an end with Germany's defeat in World War I, a German democratic state known as the Weimar Republic had been established. From its beginnings, the Weimar Republic was plagued by a series of problems. The republic had no truly outstanding political leaders. Even its more able leaders, such as Friedrich Ebert, who served as president, and Gustav Stresemann, who had been both foreign minister and chancellor, died in the 1920s. When Ebert died in 1925, Paul von Hindenburg (1847–1934), the World War I military hero, was elected president. Hindenburg was a traditional military man, monarchist in sentiment, who at heart was not in favor of the republic. The young republic also suffered politically from attempted uprisings and attacks from both the left and the right.

The Weimar Republic also faced serious economic difficulties. Germany experienced runaway inflation in 1922 and 1923, with grave social effects. Widows, orphans, the retired elderly, army officers, teachers, civil servants, and others who lived on fixed incomes all watched their monthly stipends become worthless or their lifetime savings disappear. Their economic losses increasingly pushed the middle class to the rightist parties that were hostile to the republic. To make matters worse, after a period of prosperity from 1924 to 1929, Germany faced the Great Depression. Unemployment increased to 3 million in March 1930 and 4.38 million by December of the same year. The depression paved the way for social discontent, fear, and extremist parties. The political, economic, and social problems of the Weimar Republic help us to understand the environment in which Adolf Hitler and the Nazis were able to rise to power.

After Germany, no Western nation was more affected by the Great Depression than the United States. The full force of the depression had struck the United States by 1932. In that year industrial production fell to 50 percent of what it had been in 1929. By 1933, there were 15 million unemployed. Under these circumstances, the Democrat Franklin Delano Roosevelt (1882–1945) was able to win a landslide electoral victory in 1932. Following the example of the American experience during World War I, he and his advisers pursued a policy of active government intervention in the economy that came to be known as the New Deal.

Initially, the New Deal attempted to restore prosperity by creating the National Recovery Administration (NRA), which required government, labor, and industrial leaders to work out regulations for each industry. Declared unconstitutional by the Supreme Court in 1935, the NRA was soon superseded by other efforts collectively known as the Second New Deal. These included a stepped-up program of public works, such as the Works Progress Administration (WPA), established in 1935. This government organization employed between two and three million people who worked at building bridges, roads, post offices, and airports. The Roosevelt administration was also responsible for new social legislation that launched the American welfare state. In 1935, the Social Security Act created a system of old-age pensions and unemployment insurance. Moreover, the National Labor Relations Act of 1935 encouraged the rapid growth of labor unions.

No doubt, the New Deal provided some social reform measures that perhaps averted the possibility of social revolution in the United States. It did not, however, solve the unemployment problems of the Great Depression. In May 1937, during what was considered a period of full recovery, American unemployment still stood at 7 million. A recession the following year increased that number to 11 million. Only World War II and the subsequent growth of armaments industries brought American workers back to full employment.

Socialism in One Country: Soviet Russia

With their victory in the civil war in 1920, Soviet leaders could now turn to the challenging task of building the first socialist society in a world dominated by their capitalist enemies. But the civil war had taken an enormous toll of life. During the civil war, Lenin had pursued a policy of war communism, but once the war was over, peasants began to sabotage the program by hoarding food. Added to this problem was drought, which caused a great famine between 1920 and 1922 that claimed as many as five million lives. Industrial collapse paralleled the agricultural disaster. By 1921, industrial output was only 20 percent of its 1913 levels. Russia was exhausted. As Leon Trotsky said, "the collapse of the productive forces surpassed anything of the kind that history had ever seen. The country, and the government with it, were at the very edge of the abyss."[8]

In March 1921, Lenin pulled Russia back from the abyss by aborting war communism in favor of his New Economic Policy (NEP). Lenin's NEP was a modified version of the old capitalist system. Forced requisitioning of food from the peasants was halted, and peasants were now allowed to sell their produce openly. Retail stores as well as small industries that employed fewer than twenty employees could now operate under private ownership, although heavy industry, banking, utilities, and mines remained in the hands of the government. Already by 1922, a revived market and good harvest had brought an end to famine; Soviet agriculture climbed to 75 percent of its prewar level. Industry, especially state-owned heavy industry, fared less well and continued to stagnate. Only coal production had reached prewar levels by 1926. Overall, the NEP had saved Communist Russia from complete economic disaster even though Lenin and other leading Communists intended it to be only a temporary, tactical retreat from the goals of communism.

The new government also introduced a number of social changes. Alexandra Kollontai (1872–1952), who had become a supporter of revolutionary socialism while in exile in Switzerland, took the lead in pushing a Bolshevik program for women's rights and social welfare reforms. As Minister of Social Welfare, she tried to provide health care for women and children by establishing Palaces for the Protection of Maternity and Children. Between 1918 and 1920, the new regime issued a series of reforms that made marriage a civil act, legalized divorce, decreed the equality of men and women, and permitted abortions. Kollontai was also instrumental in establishing a Women's Bureau within the Communist Party known as Zhenotdel. This organization sent men and women to all parts of the Russian Empire to explain the new social order. Members of Zhenotdel were especially eager to help women with matters of divorce and women's rights. In the provinces in the East, Zhenotdel members were often brutally murdered by angry males who objected to any kind of liberation for their wives and daughters. Much to Kollontai's disappointment, many of these early Communist social reforms were also undone as the Communists came to face more pressing matters, including survival of the new regime.

Lenin's death in 1924 inaugurated a struggle for power among the seven members of the Politburo, the institution that had become the leading organ of the party. The Politburo was severely divided over the future direction of Soviet Russia. The Left, led by Leon Trotsky, wanted to end the NEP and launch Russia on the path of rapid industrialization, primarily at the expense of the peasantry. This same group wanted to carry the revolution on, believing that the survival of the Russian Revolution ultimately depended on the spread of communism abroad. Another group in the Politburo, called the Right, rejected the cause of world revolution and wanted to concentrate instead on constructing a socialist state in Russia. This group also favored a continuation of Lenin's NEP, because they believed that too rapid industrialization would harm the living standards of the Soviet peasantry.

These ideological divisions were underscored by an intense personal rivalry between Leon Trotsky and Joseph Stalin. In 1924, Trotsky held the post of commissar of war and was the leading spokesman for the Left in the Politburo. Joseph Stalin (1879–1953) was content to hold the dull bureaucratic job of party general secretary, while other Politburo members held party positions that enabled them to display their brilliant oratorical abilities. But Stalin was a good organizer (his fellow Bolsheviks called him "Comrade Card-Index"), and the other members of the Politburo soon found that the position of party secretary was really the most important in the party hierarchy. Stalin used his post as party general secretary to gain complete control of the Communist Party. Trotsky was expelled from the party in 1927. By 1929, Stalin had succeeded in eliminating the Old Bolsheviks of the revolutionary era from the Politburo and establishing a dictatorship so powerful that the Russian tsars of old would have been envious.

The Search for a New Reality: Cultural and Intellectual Trends

The mass destruction brought on by World War I precipitated a general disillusionment with Western civilization on the part of artists and intellectuals throughout Europe. Avant-garde art, which had sought to discover alternative techniques to portray reality, now gained broader acceptance, as Europeans began to come to grips with the anxieties of their time. Four years of devastating war left many Europeans with a profound sense of despair. To many people, World War I could only mean that something was dreadfully wrong with Western values. The experiences of World War I seemed to confirm the prewar avant-garde belief that human beings were really violent animals who were incapable of creating a sane and rational world. The Great Depression only added to the despair created by World War I.

Political and economic uncertainties were paralleled by social innovations. World War I had served to break down many traditional middle-class attitudes, especially toward sexuality. In the 1920s, women's physical appearance changed dramatically. Short skirts, short hair, the use of cosmetics that were once thought to be the preserve of prostitutes, and the new practice of suntanning gave women a new image. This change in physical appearance, which stressed more exposure of a woman's body, was also accompanied by frank discussions of sexual matters. In 1926, the Dutch physician Theodor van de Velde published *Ideal Marriage: Its Physiology and Technique*. Translated into a number of languages, it became an international best-seller. Van de Velde described female and male anatomy, discussed birth control techniques, and glorified sexual pleasure in marriage.

Nightmares and New Visions: Art

Uncertainty also pervaded the cultural and intellectual achievements of the interwar years. Postwar artistic trends were largely a working out of the implications of prewar developments. Abstract Expressionism, for example, became ever more popular as many pioneering artists of the early twentieth century matured between the two world wars. In addition, prewar fascination with the absurd and the unconscious contents of the mind seemed even more appropriate after the nightmare landscapes of World War I battlefronts. This gave rise to both the Dada movement and Surrealism.

Dadaism attempted to enshrine the purposelessness of life. Tristan Tzara (1896–1945), a Romanian-French poet and one of the founders of Dadaism, expressed the Dadaist contempt for the Western tradition in a lecture on Dada in 1922: "The acts of life have no beginning or end. Everything happens in a completely idiotic way. . . . Like everything in life, Dada is useless." Revolted by the insanity of life, the Dadaists tried to give it expression by creating anti-art. The 1918 Berlin Dada Manifesto maintained that "Dada is the international expression of our times, the great rebellion of artistic movements." In the hands of Hannah Höch (1889–1978), Dada became an instrument to comment on women's roles in the new mass culture. Höch was the only female member of the Berlin Dada Club, which featured the use of photomontage. Her work was part of the first Dada show in Berlin in 1920. In *Dada Dance*, she seemed to criticize the "new woman" by making fun of the way women were inclined to follow new fashion styles. In other works, however, she created positive images of the modern woman and expressed a keen interest in new freedoms for women.

HANNAH HÖCH, *CUT WITH THE KITCHEN KNIFE DADA THROUGH THE LAST WEIMAR BEER BELLY CULTURAL EPOCH OF GERMANY.* Hannah Höch, a prominent figure in the postwar Dada movement, used photomontage to create images that reflected on women's issues. In *Cut with the Kitchen Knife*, she combined pictures of German political leaders with sports stars, Dada artists, and scenes from urban life. One major theme emerged: the confrontation between the anti-Dada world of German political leaders and the Dada world of revolutionary ideals. Höch associated women with Dada and the new world.

Perhaps more important as an artistic movement was Surrealism, which sought a reality beyond the material, sensible world and found it in the world of the unconscious through the portrayal of fantasies, dreams, or nightmares. Employing logic to portray the illogical, the Surrealists created disturbing and evocative images. The Spaniard Salvador Dali (1904–1989) became the high priest of Surrealism and in his mature phase became a master of representational Surrealism. In *The Persistence of Memory*, Dali portrayed recognizable objects that have nevertheless been divorced from their normal context. By placing these objects into unrecognizable relationships, Dali created a disturbing world in which the irrational had become tangible.

The move to functionalism in modern architecture also became more widespread in the 1920s and 1930s. Especially important in the spread of functionalism was the Bauhaus school of art, architecture, and design, founded in 1919 at Weimar, Germany, by the Berlin architect Walter Gropius. The Bauhaus teaching staff was made up of architects, artists, and designers. They worked together to combine the study of fine arts (painting and sculpture) with the applied arts (printing, weaving, and furniture making). Gropius urged his followers to foster a new union of arts and crafts in order to create the buildings and objects of the future.

At the beginning of the twentieth century, a revolution had come to music with the work of Igor Stravinsky. But Stravinsky still wrote music in a definite key. In 1924, the Viennese composer Arnold Schönberg (1874–1951) wrote a piano suite in which he used a scale composed of twelve notes free of any tonal key. His atonal music was similar to abstract painting. Abstract painting arranged colors and lines without concrete images; atonal music organized sounds without any recognizable harmonies. Unlike modern art, however, modern music found little favor until after World War II.

The Search for the Unconscious

The interest in the unconscious, evident in Surrealism, was also apparent in the new literary techniques that emerged in the 1920s. One of its most apparent manifestations was in the "stream of consciousness" technique, in which the writer presented an interior monologue, or a report of the innermost thoughts of each character. One example of this genre was written by the Irish exile James Joyce (1882–1941). His *Ulysses*, published in 1922, told the story of one day in the life of ordinary people in Dublin by following the flow of their inner dialogue. Disconnected ramblings and veiled allusions pervade Joyce's work.

HESSE AND THE UNCONSCIOUS

The novels of Hermann Hesse made a strong impact on young people, first in Germany in the 1920s and then in the United States in the 1960s after they had been translated into English. Many of these young people shared Hesse's fascination with the unconscious and his dislike of modern industrial civilization. This excerpt from Demian spoke directly to many of them.

HERMANN HESSE, *DEMIAN*

The following spring I was to leave the preparatory school and enter a university. I was still undecided, however, as to where and what I was to study. I had grown a thin mustache, I was a full-grown man, and yet I was completely helpless and without a goal in life. Only one thing was certain: the voice within me, the dream image. I felt the duty to follow this voice blindly wherever it might lead me. But it was difficult and each day I rebelled against it anew. Perhaps I was mad, as I thought at moments; perhaps I was not like other men? But I was able to do the same things the others did; with a little effort and industry I could read Plato, was able to solve problems in trigonometry or follow a chemical analysis. There was only one thing I could not do: wrest the dark secret goal from myself and keep it before me as others did who knew exactly what they wanted to be—professors, lawyers, doctors, artists, however long this would take them and whatever difficulties and advantages this decision would bear in its wake. This I could not do. Perhaps I would become something similar, but how was I to know? Perhaps I would have to continue my search for years on end and would not become anything, and would not reach a goal. Perhaps I would reach this goal but it would turn out to be an evil, dangerous, horrible one?

I wanted only to try to live in accord with the promptings which came from my true self. Why was that so very difficult?

The German writer Hermann Hesse (1877–1962) dealt with the unconscious in a considerably different fashion. His novels reflected the influence of both Carl Jung's psychological theories and Eastern religions and focused among other things on the spiritual loneliness of modern human beings in a mechanized urban society. *Demian* was a psychoanalytic study of incest, whereas *Steppenwolf* mirrored the psychological confusion of modern existence. Hesse's novels made a large impact on German youth in the 1920s (see the box above). He won the Nobel Prize for literature in 1946.

For much of the Western world, the best way to find (or escape) reality was in the field of mass entertainment. The 1930s represented the heyday of the Hollywood studio system, which in the single year of 1937 turned out nearly 600 feature films. Supplementing the movies were cheap paperbacks and radio, which brought sports, soap operas, and popular music to the masses.

SALVADOR DALI, *THE PERSISTENCE OF MEMORY* (1931). Surrealism was another important artistic movement between the wars. Influenced by the theories of Freudian psychology, Surrealists sought to reveal the world of the unconscious, or the "greater reality" that they believed existed beyond the world of physical appearances. As is evident in this painting, Salvador Dali sought to portray the world of dreams by painting recognizable objects in unrecognizable relationships.

Mass forms of communication and entertainment were, of course, not new. But the increased size of audiences and the ability of radio and cinema, unlike the printed word, to provide an immediate mass experience did add new dimensions to mass culture. Favorite film actors and actresses became stars, whose lives then became subject to public adoration and scrutiny. Sensuous actresses such as Marlene Dietrich, whose appearance in the early sound film *The Blue Angel* catapulted her to fame, created new images of women's sexuality.

CONCLUSION

World War I shattered the liberal, rational society of late-nineteenth- and early-twentieth-century Europe. The incredible destruction and the death of almost 10 million people undermined the whole idea of progress. New propaganda techniques had manipulated entire populations into sustaining their involvement in a meaningless slaughter.

World War I was a total war and involved an unprecedented mobilization of resources and populations and increased government centralization of power over the lives of its citizens. Civil liberties, such as freedom of the press, speech, assembly, and movement, were circumscribed in the name of national security. World War I made the practice of strong central authority a way of life.

The turmoil wrought by World War I seemed to open the door to even greater insecurity. Revolutions in Russia and the Middle East dismembered old empires and created new states that gave rise to unexpected problems. Expectations that Europe and the world would return to normalcy were soon dashed by the failure to achieve a lasting peace, economic collapse, and the rise of authoritarian governments that not only restricted individual freedoms, but sought even greater control over the lives of their subjects in order to manipulate and guide them to achieve the goals of their totalitarian regimes.

Finally, World War I ended the age of European hegemony over world affairs. By demolishing their own civilization on the battlegrounds of Europe in World War I, Europeans inadvertently encouraged the subject peoples of their vast colonial empires to initiate movements for national independence. In the next chapter, we examine some of those movements.

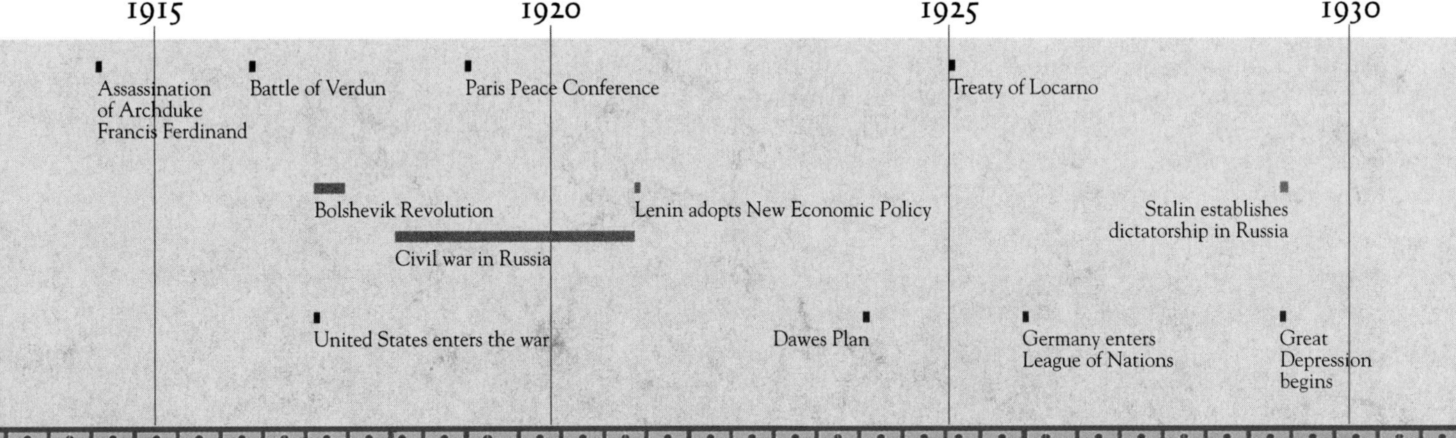

CHAPTER NOTES

1. Arnold Toynbee, *Surviving the Future* (New York, 1971), pp. 106–107.
2. Quoted in Joachim Remak, "1914—The Third Balkan War: Origins Reconsidered," *Journal of Modern History* 43 (1971): 364–65.
3. Quoted in J. M. Winter, *The Experience of World War I* (New York, 1989), p. 142.
4. Quoted in Catherine W. Reilly, ed., *Scars upon My Heart: Women's Poetry and Verse of the First World War* (London, 1981), p. 90.
5. Quoted in William M. Mandel, *Soviet Women* (Garden City, N.Y., 1975), p. 43.
6. Harold Nicolson, *Peacemaking, 1919* (Boston and New York, 1933), pp. 31–32.
7. Quoted in Robert Paxton, *Europe in the Twentieth Century*, 2d ed. (San Diego, 1985), p. 237.
8. Irving Howe, ed., *The Basic Writings of Trotsky* (London, 1963), p. 162.

SUGGESTED READINGS

The historical literature on the causes of World War I is enormous. A good starting point is the work by J. Joll, *The Origins of the First World War*, 2d ed. (London, 1992). The belief that Germany was primarily responsible for the war was argued vigorously by the German scholar F. Fischer in the following works: *Germany's Aims in the First World War* (New York, 1967), *World Power or Decline: The Controversy over Germany's Aims in World War I* (New York, 1974), and *War of Illusions: German Policies from 1911 to 1914* (New York, 1975). The role of each great power has been reassessed in a series of books on the causes of World War I. They include V. R. Berghahn, *Germany and the Approach of War in 1914* (London, 1973); Z. S. Steiner, *Britain and the Origins of the First World War* (New York, 1977); J. F. Keiger, *France and the Origins of the First World War* (New York, 1984); and D. C. B. Lieven, *Russia and the Origins of the First World War* (New York, 1984). On the role of militarism, see D. Hermann, *The Arming of Europe and the Making of the First World War* (New York, 1997).

There are two good recent accounts of World War I in M. Gilbert, *The First World War* (New York, 1994), and the lavishly illustrated book by J. M. Winter, *The Experience of World War I* (New York, 1989). See also the brief work by N. Heyman, *World War I* (Westport, Conn., 1997). There is an excellent collection of articles in H. Strachan, *The Oxford Illustrated History of the First World War* (New York, 1998). The nature of trench warfare is examined in T. Ashworth, *Trench Warfare, 1914–1918: The Live and Let-Live System* (London, 1980). On the morale of World War I soldiers, see J. Keegan, *The Face of Battle* (London, 1975). The war at sea is studied in R. Hough, *The Great War at Sea, 1914–18* (Oxford, 1983). In *The Great War and Modern Memory* (London, 1975), P. Fussell attempted to show how British writers described their war experiences. Although scholars do not always agree with her conclusions, B. Tuchman's *The Guns of August* (New York, 1962) is a magnificently written account of the opening days of the war. For an interesting perspective on World War I and the beginnings of the modern world, see M. Eksteins, *Rites of Spring: The Great War and the Birth of the Modern Age* (Boston, 1989).

On the role of women in World War I, see G. Braybon, *Women Workers in the First World War: The British Experience* (London, 1981); J. M. Winter and R. M. Wall, eds., *The Upheaval of War: Family, Work and Welfare in Europe, 1914–1918* (Cambridge, 1988); and G. Braybon and P. Summerfield, *Women's Experiences in Two World Wars* (London, 1987).

The role of war aims in shaping the peace settlement is examined in V. H. Rothwell, *British War Aims and Peace Diplomacy, 1914–1918* (Oxford, 1971), and D. R. Stevenson, *French War Aims Against Germany, 1914–1919* (New York, 1982).

A good introduction to the Russian Revolution can be found in S. Fitzpatrick, *The Russian Revolution, 1917–1932*, 2d ed. (New York, 1994). See also R. Pipes, *The Russian Revolution* (New York, 1990). On Lenin, see R. W. Clark, *Lenin* (New York, 1988), and the valuable work by A. B. Ulam, *The Bolsheviks* (New York, 1965). On social reforms, see W. Goldman, *Women, the State, and Revolution* (Cambridge, 1993). There is now a comprehensive study of the Russian civil war in W. B. Lincoln, *Red Victory: A History of the Russian Civil War* (New York, 1989).

World War I and the Russian Revolution are also well covered in two good general surveys, R. Paxton, *Europe in the Twentieth Century*, 2d ed. (San Diego, 1985), and A. Rudhart, *Twentieth Century Europe* (Englewood Cliffs, N.J., 1986).

For a general introduction to the interwar period, see R. J. Sontag, *A Broken World, 1919–39* (New York, 1971). On European security issues after the Peace of Paris, see S. Marks, *The Illusion of Peace: Europe's International Relations, 1918–1933* (New York, 1976). The Locarno agreements have been well examined in J. Jacobson, *Locarno Diplomacy* (Princeton, N.J., 1972). The best study on the problem of reparations is now M. Trachtenberg, *Reparations in World Politics* (New York, 1980), which paints a more positive view of French policies. The "return to normalcy" after the war is analyzed in C. S. Maier, *Recasting Bourgeois Europe: Stabilization in France, Germany, and Italy in the Decade After World War I* (Princeton, N.J., 1975). Also valuable is D. P. Silverman, *Reconstructing Europe After the Great War* (Cambridge, Mass., 1982). On the Great Depression, see C. P. Kindleberger, *The World in Depression, 1929–39*, rev. ed. (Berkeley, Calif., 1986). On Weimar Germany, see P. Bookbinder, *Weimar Germany* (New York, 1996), and R. Henig, *The Weimar Republic 1919–1933* (New York, 1998), a brief study.

INFOTRAC COLLEGE EDITION

For additional reading, go to InfoTrac College Edition, your online research library at http://web1.infotrac-college.com

Enter the search terms "World War, 1914–1918" using the Subject Guide.

Enter the search terms "Russia Revolution" using Keywords.

Enter the search term "Bolshevik" using Keywords.

Enter the search terms "Versailles Treaty" using Keywords.

Enter the search terms "Great Depression" using Keywords.

CHAPTER

25

NATIONALISM, REVOLUTION, AND DICTATORSHIP: AFRICA, ASIA, AND LATIN AMERICA FROM 1919 TO 1939

CHAPTER OUTLINE

- THE RISE OF NATIONALISM
- REVOLUTION IN CHINA
- JAPAN BETWEEN THE WARS
- NATIONALISM AND DICTATORSHIP IN LATIN AMERICA
- CONCLUSION

FOCUS QUESTIONS

- What developments contributed to the rise of nationalism after 1919, and what issues did the nationalists have to resolve as they struggled to build new nations?
- What forms did the independence movements in India and the Middle East take, and what problems did each movement face?
- What forms did modernization take in Turkey, Iran, and Japan in the interwar years?
- What problems did China face between 1919 and 1939, and what solutions did the Nationalists and the Communists propose to solve these problems?
- What problems did the nations of Latin America face in the interwar years, and how did they respond to these problems?

In the spring of 1913, the Bolshevik leader Vladimir Lenin wrote an article in the party newspaper *Pravda* on the awakening of Asia. "Was it so long ago," he asked his readers, "that China was considered typical of the lands that had been standing still for centuries? Today China is a land of seething political activity, the scene of a virile social movement and of a democratic upsurge." Similar conditions, he added, were spreading the democratic revolution to other parts of Asia—to Turkey, Persia, and China. Ferment was even on the rise in British India.[1]

A year later, the Great War erupted, and Lenin, like millions of others, turned his eyes to events in Europe. In February 1917, riots in the streets of Petrograd (the old St. Petersburg) marked the onset of the Russian Revolution. By the end of the year, the Bolsheviks were in power in Moscow. For the next few years, Lenin and his colleagues were preoccupied with consolidating their control over the vast territories of the old tsarist Russian Empire. But he had not forgotten his earlier prediction that the colonial world was on the verge of revolt. Now, with the infant Soviet state virtually surrounded by its capitalist enemies, Lenin argued that the oppressed masses of Asia and Africa were potential allies in the bitter struggle against the brutal yoke of world imperialism. For the next two decades, the leaders in Moscow periodically turned their attention to China and other parts of Asia in an effort to ride what they hoped would be a mounting wave of revolt against foreign domination.

The Rise of Nationalism

Although the West had emerged from World War I relatively intact, its political and social foundations and its self-confidence had been severely undermined. Within Europe, doubts about the future viability of Western civilization were widespread, especially among the intellectual elite. These doubts were quick to reach the attention of perceptive observers in Asia and Africa, and contributed to a rising tide of unrest against Western political domination throughout the colonial and semicolonial world. That unrest took a variety of forms but was most notably displayed in increasing worker activism, rural protest, and a rising sense of national fervor among anticolonialist intellectuals. In those areas of Asia, Africa, and Latin America where independent states had successfully resisted the Western onslaught, the discontent fostered by the war and later by the Great Depression led to a loss of confidence in democratic institutions and the rise of political dictatorships.

Modern Nationalism

The first stage of resistance to the West in Asia and Africa had met with humiliation and failure and must have confirmed many Westerners' conviction that colonial peoples lacked both the strength and the know-how to create modern states and govern their own destinies. In fact, the process was just beginning. The next phase—the rise of modern nationalism—began to take shape at the beginning of the twentieth century and was the product of the convergence of several factors. The primary source of anticolonialist sentiment was a new urban middle class of Westernized intellectuals. In many cases, these merchants, petty functionaries, clerks, students, and professionals had been educated in Western-style schools. A few had spent time in the West. Many spoke Western languages, wore Western clothes, and worked in occupations connected with the colonial regime. Some, like Mahatma Gandhi in India, José Rizal in the Philippines, and Kwame Nkrumah in the Gold Coast, even wrote in the languages of their colonial masters.

The results were paradoxical. On the one hand, this "new class" admired Western culture and sometimes harbored a deep sense of contempt for traditional ways. On the other hand, many strongly resented the foreigners and their arrogant contempt for colonial peoples. Though eager to introduce Western ideas and institutions into their own society, these intellectuals often resented the gap between ideal and reality, theory and practice, in colonial policy. Although Western political thought exalted democracy, equality, and individual freedom, democratic institutions were primitive or nonexistent in the colonies.

Equality in economic opportunity and social life was also noticeably lacking. Normally, the middle classes did not suffer in the same manner as impoverished peasants or menial workers on sugar or rubber plantations, but they, too, had complaints. They were usually relegated to menial jobs in the government or business and paid lower salaries than those of Europeans in similar occupations. The superiority of the Europeans was expressed in a variety of ways, including "whites only" clubs and the use of the familiar form of the language (normally used by adults to children) when addressing the natives.

Under these conditions, many of the new urban educated class were very ambivalent toward their colonial masters and the civilization that they represented. Out of this mixture of hopes and resentments emerged the first stirrings of modern nationalism in Asia and Africa. During the first quarter of the century, in colonial and semicolonial societies from the Suez Canal to the shores of the Pacific Ocean, educated native peoples began to organize political parties and movements seeking reforms or the end of foreign rule and the restoration of independence.

RELIGION AND NATIONALISM

At first, many of the leaders of these movements did not focus clearly on the idea of nationhood, but tried to defend native economic interests or religious beliefs. In Burma, for example, the first expression of modern nationalism came from students at the University of Rangoon, who protested against official persecution of the Buddhist religion and British lack of respect for local religious traditions. Calling themselves Thakin (a polite term in the Burmese language meaning "lord" or "master," thus emphasizing their demand for the right to rule themselves), they protested against British arrogance and failure to observe local customs in Buddhist temples (such as failing to remove their footwear). Only in the 1930s did the Thakins begin to focus specifically on national independence.

THE DILEMMA OF THE INTELLECTUAL

Sutan Sjahrir (1909–1966) was a prominent leader of the Indonesian nationalist movement who briefly served as prime minister of the Republic of Indonesia in the 1950s. Like many Western-educated Asian intellectuals, he was tortured by the realization that by education and outlook he was closer to his colonial masters than to his own people. He wrote the following passage in a letter to his wife in 1935 and later included it in his book Out of Exile.

SUTAN SJAHRIR, *OUT OF EXILE*

Am I perhaps estranged from my people? . . . Why are the things that contain beauty for them and arouse their gentler emotions only senseless and displeasing for me? In reality, the spiritual gap between my people and me is certainly no greater than that between an intellectual in Holland . . . and the undeveloped people of Holland. . . . The difference is rather . . . that the intellectual in Holland does not feel this gap because there is a portion—even a fairly large portion—of his own people on approximately the same intellectual level as himself. . . .

This is what we lack here. Not only is the number of intellectuals in this country smaller in proportion to the total population—in fact, very much smaller—but in addition, the few who are here do not constitute any single entity in spiritual outlook, or in any spiritual life or single culture whatsoever. . . . It is for them so much more difficult than for the intellectuals in Holland. In Holland they build—both consciously and unconsciously—on what is already there. . . . Even if they oppose it, they do so as a method of application or as a starting point.

In our country this is not the case. Here there has been no spiritual or cultural life, and no intellectual progress for centuries. There are the much-praised Eastern art forms but what are these except bare rudiments from a feudal culture that cannot possibly provide a dynamic fulcrum for people of the twentieth century? . . . Our spiritual needs are needs of the twentieth century; our problems and our views are of the twentieth century. Our inclination is no longer toward the mystical, but toward reality, clarity, and objectivity. . . .

We intellectuals here are much closer to Europe or America than we are to the Borobudur or Mahabharata or to the primitive Islamic culture of Java and Sumatra. . . .

So, it seems, the problem stands in principle. It is seldom put forth by us in this light, and instead most of us search unconsciously for a synthesis that will leave us internally tranquil. We want to have both Western science and Eastern philosophy, the Eastern "spirit," in the culture. But what is this Eastern spirit? It is, they say, the sense of the higher, of spirituality, of the eternal and religious, as opposed to the materialism of the West. I have heard this countless times, but it has never convinced me.

In the Dutch East Indies, the Sarekat Islam (Islamic Association) began as a self-help society among Muslim merchants to fight against domination of the local economy by Chinese interests. Eventually, activist elements began to realize that the source of the problem was not the Chinese merchants but the colonial presence, and in the 1920s, Sarekat Islam was transformed into a new organization—the Nationalist Party of Indonesia (PNI)—that focused on national independence. Like the Thakins in Burma, this party would eventually lead the country to independence after World War II.

INDEPENDENCE OR MODERNIZATION? THE NATIONALIST QUANDARY

Building a new nation, however, requires more than a shared sense of grievances against the foreign invader. A host of other issues also had to be resolved. Soon patriots throughout the colonial world were engaged in a lively and sometimes acrimonious debate over such questions as whether independence or modernization should be their primary objective. The answer depended in part on how the colonial regime was perceived. If it was viewed as a source of much-needed reforms in a traditional society, then a gradualist approach made sense. But if it was seen primarily as an impediment to change, then the first priority was to bring it to an end. The vast majority of patriotic individuals were convinced that to survive, their societies must adopt much of the Western way of life; yet many were equally determined that the local culture would not, and should not, become a carbon copy of the West. What was the national identity, after all, if it did not incorporate some elements from the traditional way of life?

Another reason for using traditional values was to provide ideological symbols that the common people could understand and would rally around. Though aware that they needed to enlist the mass of the population in the common struggle, most urban intellectuals had difficulty communicating with the teeming population in the countryside who did not understand such complicated and unfamiliar concepts as democracy and nationhood. As the Indonesian intellectual Sutan Sjahrir lamented, many Westernized intellectuals had more in common with their colonial rulers than with the native population in the rural villages (see the box above). As one French colonial official remarked in some surprise to a Vietnamese reformist, "Why, Monsieur, you are more French than I am!"

Gandhi and the Indian National Congress

Nowhere in the colonial world were these issues debated more vigorously than in India. Before the Sepoy Rebellion, Indian consciousness had focused primarily on the question of religious identity. But in the latter half of the nineteenth century, a stronger sense of national consciousness began to arise, provoked by the conservative policies and racial arrogance of the British colonial authorities.

The first Indian nationalists were almost invariably upper class and educated. Many of them were from urban areas such as Bombay, Madras, and Calcutta. Some were trained in law and were members of the civil service. At first, many tended to prefer reform to revolution and believed that India needed modernization before it could handle the problems of independence. An exponent of this view was Gopal Gokhale (1866–1915), a moderate nationalist who hoped that he could convince the British to bring about needed reforms in Indian society. Gokhale and other like-minded reformists did have some effect. In the 1880s, the government introduced a measure of self-government for the first time. All too often, however, such efforts were sabotaged by local British officials.

The slow pace of reform convinced many Indian nationalists that relying on British benevolence was futile. In 1885, a small group of Indians, with some British participation, met in Bombay to form the Indian National Congress (INC). They hoped to speak for all India, but most were high-caste English-trained Hindus. Like their reformist predecessors, members of the INC did not demand immediate independence and accepted the need for reforms to end traditional abuses like child marriage and *sati*. At the same time, they called for an Indian share in the governing process and more spending on economic development and less on military campaigns along the frontier. The British responded with a few concessions, but in general change was glacially slow. As impatient members of the INC became disillusioned, the radicals split off and formed the New Party, which called for the use of terrorism and violence to achieve national independence.

The INC also had difficulty reconciling religious differences within its ranks. The stated goal of the INC was to seek self-determination for all Indians regardless of class or religious affiliation, but many of its leaders were Hindu and inevitably reflected Hindu concerns. In the first decade of the twentieth century, a separate Muslim League was created to represent the interests of the millions of Muslims in Indian society.

In 1915, a young Hindu lawyer returned from South Africa to become active in the INC. He transformed the movement and galvanized India's struggle for independence and identity. Mohandas Gandhi was born in 1869 in Gujarat, in western India, the son of a government minister. In the late nineteenth century, he studied in London and became a lawyer. In 1893, he went to South Africa to work in a law firm serving Indian emigrés working as laborers there. He soon became aware of the racial prejudice and exploitation experienced by Indians living in the territory and tried to organize them to protect their interests.

On his return to India, Gandhi immediately became active in the independence movement. Using his experience in South Africa, he set up a movement based on nonviolent resistance (the Indian term was *satyagraha*, "hold fast to the truth") to try to force the British to improve the lot of the poor and grant independence to India. His goal was twofold: to convert the British to his views while simultaneously strengthening the unity and sense of self-respect of his compatriots. Gandhi was particularly concerned about the plight of the millions of untouchables, whom he called *harijans*, or "children of God." When the British attempted to suppress dissent, he called on his followers to refuse to obey British regulations. He began to manufacture his own clothes (Gandhi now dressed in a simple *dhoti* made of coarse homespun cotton) and adopted the spinning wheel as a symbol of Indian resistance to imports of British textiles.

Gandhi, now increasingly known as India's "Great Soul" (*Mahatma*), organized mass protests to achieve his

GANDHI AND NEHRU. Mahatma Gandhi (on the right), India's "Great Soul," became the emotional leader of India's struggle for independence from British colonial rule. Unlike many other nationalist leaders, Gandhi rejected the materialistic culture of the West and urged his followers to return to the native traditions of the Indian village. To illustrate his point, Gandhi dressed in the simple Indian *dhoti* rather than in the Western fashion favored by many of his colleagues. Along with Gandhi, Jawaharlal Nehru was a leading figure in the Indian struggle for independence. Unlike Gandhi, however, his goal was to transform India into a modern industrial society. After independence, he became the nation's prime minister until his death in 1964.

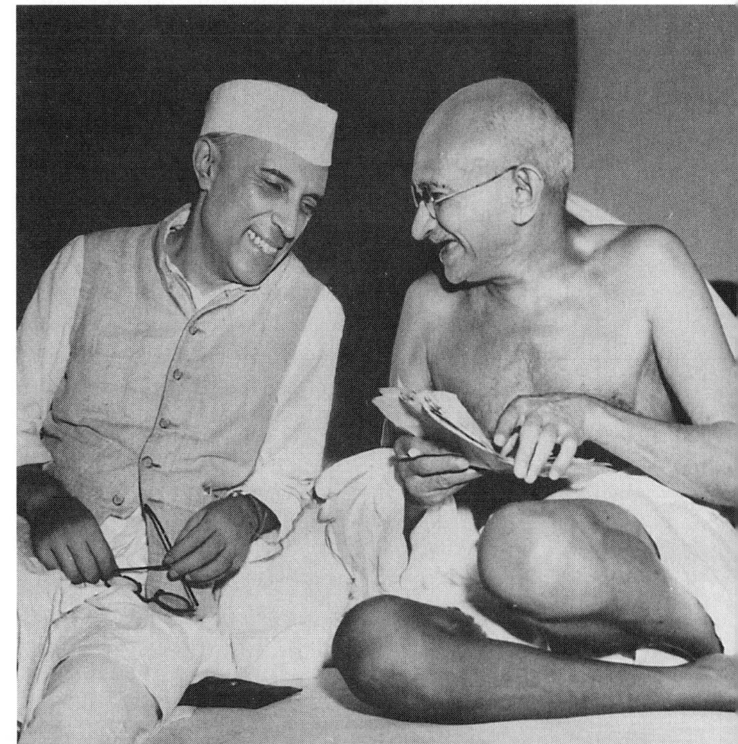

aims, but in 1919 they got out of hand and led to violence and British reprisals. British troops killed hundreds of unarmed protesters in the enclosed square in the city of Amritsar in northwestern India. When the protests spread, Gandhi was horrified at the violence and briefly retreated from active politics. Nevertheless, he was arrested for his role in the protests and spent several years in prison.

Gandhi combined his anticolonial activities with an appeal to the spiritual instincts of all Indians. Though he had been born and raised a Hindu, his universalist approach to the idea of God transcended individual religion, although it was shaped by the historical themes of Hindu belief. At a speech given in London in September 1931, he expressed his view of the nature of God as "an indefinable mysterious power that pervades everything . . . , an unseen power which makes itself felt and yet defies all proof."[2]

While Gandhi was in prison, the political situation continued to evolve. In 1921, the British passed the Government of India Act, transforming the heretofore advisory Legislative Council into a bicameral parliament, two-thirds of whose members would be elected. Similar bodies were created at the provincial level. In a stroke, 5 million Indians were enfranchised. But such reforms were no longer enough for many members of the INC, who wanted to push aggressively for full independence. The British exacerbated the situation by increasing the salt tax and prohibiting the Indian people from manufacturing or harvesting their own salt. Gandhi, now released from prison, returned to his earlier policy of civil disobedience by openly joining several dozen supporters in a 200-mile walk to the sea, where he picked up a lump of salt and urged Indians to ignore the law. Gandhi and many other members of the INC were arrested.

Indian women were active in the movement. Women comprised about 20,000, or nearly 10 percent of all those arrested and jailed for taking part in demonstrations during the interwar period. Women marched, picketed foreign shops, and promoted the spinning and wearing of homemade cloth. By the 1930s, women's associations were actively involved in promoting a number of reforms, including women's education, the introduction of birth control devices, an abolition of child marriage, and universal suffrage. In 1929, the Sarda Act raised the minimum age of marriage to 14 years of age.

In the 1930s, a new figure entered the movement in the person of Jawaharlal Nehru, son of an earlier INC leader. Educated in the law in Great Britain and a brahmin by birth, Nehru personified the new Anglo-Indian politician: secular, rational, upper class, and intellectual. In fact, he appeared to be everything that Gandhi was not. With his emergence, the independence movement embarked on two paths, religious and secular, native and Western, traditional and modern. The dual character of the INC leadership may well have strengthened the movement by bringing together the two primary impulses behind the desire for independence: elite nationalism and the primal force of Indian traditionalism. But it portended trouble for the nation's new leadership in defining India's future path in the contemporary world. In the meantime, Muslim discontent with Hindu dominance over the INC was increasing. In 1930, the Muslim League called for the creation of a separate Muslim state of Pakistan (meaning "the land of the pure") in the northwest (see the box on p. 751). As communal strife between Hindus and Muslims increased, many Indians came to realize with sorrow (and some British colonialists with satisfaction) that British rule was all that stood between peace and civil war.

The Nationalist Revolt in the Middle East

In the Middle East, as in Europe, World War I hastened the collapse of old empires. The Ottoman Empire, which had dominated the eastern Mediterranean since the seizure of Constantinople in 1453, had been growing steadily weaker since the end of the eighteenth century, troubled by rising governmental corruption, a decline in the effectiveness of the sultans, and the loss of considerable territory in the Balkans and southwestern Russia. In North Africa, Ottoman authority, tenuous at best, had disintegrated in the nineteenth century, enabling the French to seize Algeria and Tunisia and the British to establish a protectorate over the Nile River valley.

MUSTAPHA KEMAL AND THE MODERNIZATION OF TURKEY

Reformist elements in Istanbul, to be sure, had tried from time to time to resist the trend, but military defeats continued: Greece declared its independence, and Ottoman power declined steadily in the Middle East. A rising sense of nationality among Serbs, Armenians, and other minority peoples threatened the internal stability and cohesion of the empire. In the 1870s, a new generation of Ottoman reformers seized power in Istanbul and pushed through a constitution aimed at forming a legislative assembly that would represent all the peoples in the state. But the sultan they placed on the throne suspended the new charter and attempted to rule by traditional authoritarian means.

By the end of the nineteenth century, the defunct 1876 constitution had become a symbol of change for reformist elements, now grouped together under the common name Young Turks (undoubtedly borrowed from the Young Italy nationalist movement earlier in the century). They found support in the Ottoman army and administration and among Turks living in exile. In 1908, the Young Turks forced the sultan to restore the constitution, and he was removed from power the following year.

But the Young Turks had appeared at a moment of extreme fragility for the empire. Internal rebellions, com-

A CALL FOR A MUSLIM STATE

Mohammed Iqbal, a well-known Muslim poet in colonial India, was also a prominent advocate of the creation of a separate state for Muslims in South Asia. In this passage from an address he presented to the All-India Muslim League in December 1930, he explained the rationale for his proposal.

MOHAMMED IQBAL, SPEECH TO THE ALL-INDIA MUSLIM LEAGUE

It cannot be denied that Islam, regarded as an ethical ideal plus a certain kind of polity—by which expression I mean a social structure regulated by a legal system and animated by a specific ethical ideal—has been the chief formative factor in the life history of the Muslims of India. It has furnished those basic emotions and loyalties which gradually unify scattered individuals and groups and finally transform them into a well-defined people. Indeed it is no exaggeration to say that India is perhaps the only country in the world where Islam, as a people-building force, has worked at its best. In India, as elsewhere, the structure of Islam as a society is almost entirely due to the working of Islam as a culture inspired by a specific ethical ideal. What I mean to say is that Muslim society, with its remarkable homogeneity and inner unity, has grown to be what it is under the pressure of the laws and institutions associated with the culture of Islam.

Communalism in its higher aspect, then, is indispensable to the formation of a harmonious whole in a country like India. The units of Indian society are not territorial as in European countries. India is a continent of human groups belonging to different religions. Their behavior is not at all determined by a common race consciousness. Even the Hindus do not form a homogeneous group. The principle of European democracy cannot be applied to India without recognizing the fact of communal groups. The Muslim demand for the creation of a Muslim India within India is, therefore, perfectly justified.

The idea need not alarm the Hindus or the British. India is the greatest Muslim country in the world. The life of Islam, as a cultural force, in this country very largely depends on its centralization in a specified territory. This centralization of the most living portion of the Muslims of India, whose military and police service has, notwithstanding unfair treatment from the British, made the British rule possible in this country, will eventually solve the problem of India as well as of Asia. It will intensify their sense of responsibility and deepen their patriotic feeling. Thus possessing full opportunity of development within the body politic of India, the northwest India Muslims will prove the best defenders of India against a foreign invasion, be the invasion one of ideas or of bayonets. . . .

I therefore demand the formation of a consolidated Muslim State in the best interests of India and Islam. For India it means security and peace resulting from an internal balance of power; for Islam an opportunity to rid itself of the stamp that Arabian imperialism was forced to give it, to mobilize its law, its education, its culture, and to bring them into closer contact with its own original spirit and with the spirit of modern times.

bined with Austrian annexations of Ottoman territories in the Balkans, undermined support for the new government and provoked the army to step in. With most minorities from the old empire now removed from Istanbul's authority, many ethnic Turks began to embrace a new concept of a Turkish state based on all those of Turkish nationality.

The final blow to the old empire came in World War I, when the Ottoman government allied with Germany in the hope of driving the British from Egypt and restoring Ottoman rule over the Nile valley. In response, the British declared an official protectorate over Egypt and, aided by the efforts of the dashing if eccentric British adventurer T. E. Lawrence (popularly known as Lawrence of Arabia), sought to undermine Ottoman rule in the Arabian peninsula by encouraging Arab nationalists there. In 1916, the local governor of Mecca, encouraged by the British, declared Arabia independent from Ottoman rule, while British troops, advancing from Egypt, seized Palestine. In October 1918, having suffered more than 300,000 casualties during the war, the Ottoman Empire negotiated an armistice with the Allied powers.

During the next few years, the tottering empire began to fall apart, as the British and the French made plans to divide up Ottoman territories in the Middle East and the Greeks won Allied approval to seize the western parts of the Anatolian peninsula for their dream of re-creating the substance of the old Byzantine Empire. The impending collapse energized key elements in Turkey under the leadership of war hero Colonel Mustapha Kemal (1881–1938), who had commanded Turkish forces in their heroic defense of the Dardanelles against a British invasion during World War I. Now he resigned from the army and convoked a national congress that called for the creation of an elected government and the preservation of the remaining territories of the old empire in a new Republic of Turkey. Establishing his new capital at Ankara, Kemal's forces drove the Greeks from the Anatolian peninsula and persuaded the British to agree to a new treaty. In 1923, the last of the Ottoman sultans fled the country, which was now declared a Turkish republic. The Ottoman Empire had finally come to an end.

During the next few years, President Mustapha Kemal (now popularly known as Ataturk, or "father Turk") attempted to transform Turkey into a modern secular republic. The trappings of a democratic system were put in place, centered on an elected Grand National Assembly, but the president was relatively intolerant of opposition and harshly suppressed critics of his rule. Turkish nationalism was emphasized, and the Turkish language, now written in the Roman alphabet, was shorn of many of its Arabic elements. Popular education was emphasized, old aristocratic titles like pasha and bey were abolished, and all Turkish citizens were given family names in the European style.

MUSTAPHA KEMAL ATATURK. The war hero Mustapha Kemal took the initiative in creating a new Republic of Turkey. As president of the new republic, Ataturk (or "father Turk," as he came to be called) worked hard to transform Turkey into a modern secular state by modernizing the economy, adopting Western styles of dress, and breaking the powerful hold of Islamic traditions. Long regarded as a symbol of Turkey's emergence as a modern nation, he is now reviled by Muslim fundamentalists for his opposition to an Islamic state.

Ataturk also took steps to modernize the economy, overseeing the establishment of a light industrial sector producing textiles, glass, paper, and cement and instituting a five-year plan on the Soviet model to provide for state direction over the economy. Ataturk was no admirer of Soviet communism, however, and the Turkish economy can be better described as a form of state capitalism. He also encouraged the modernization of the agricultural sector through the establishment of training institutions and model farms, but such reforms had relatively little effect on the nation's predominantly conservative peasantry.

Perhaps the most significant aspect of Ataturk's reform program was his attempt to break the power of the Islamic religion and transform Turkey into a secular state. The caliphate was formally abolished in 1924 (see the box on p. 753), and the Shari'ya (Islamic law) was replaced by a revised version of the Swiss law code. The fez (the brimless cap worn by Turkish Muslims) was abolished as a form of headdress, and women were forbidden to wear the veil in the traditional Islamic custom. Women received the right to vote in 1934 and were legally guaranteed equal rights with men in all aspects of marriage and inheritance. Education and the professions were now open to citizens of both sexes, and some women even began to take part in politics. All citizens were given the right to convert to another religion at will. Finally, Ataturk attempted to break the waning power of the various religious orders of Islam, abolishing all monasteries and brotherhoods.

The legacy of Mustapha Kemal Ataturk was enormous. Although not all of his reforms were widely accepted in practice, especially by devout Muslims, the bulk of the changes that he introduced were retained after his death in 1938. In virtually every respect, the Turkish republic was the product of his determined efforts to create a modern Turkish nation.

MODERNIZATION IN IRAN

In the meantime, a similar process was under way in Persia. Under the Qajar dynasty (1794–1925), the country had not been very successful in resisting Russian advances in the Caucuses or resolving its domestic problems. To secure themselves from foreign influence, the shahs moved the capital from Tabriz to Tehran, in a mountainous area just south of the Caspian Sea. During the mid-nineteenth century, one modernizing shah attempted to introduce political and economic reforms but was impeded by resistance from tribal and religious—predominantly Shi'ite—forces. To buttress its rule, the dynasty turned increasingly to Russia and Great Britain to protect itself from its own people.

Eventually, the growing foreign presence led to the rise of a native Persian nationalist movement. Its efforts were largely directed against Russian advances in the northwest and the growing European influence in the small mod-

MUSTAPHA KEMAL'S CASE AGAINST THE CALIPHATE

As part of his plan to transform Turkey into a modern society, Mustapha Kemal Ataturk proposed to bring an end to the caliphate, which had been in the hands of Ottoman sultans since the formation of the empire. In the following passage from a speech to the National Assembly, he gives his reasons.

ATATURK'S SPEECH TO THE ASSEMBLY, OCTOBER 1924

I must call attention to the fact that Hodja Shukri Effendi [a pious Muslim who opposed Mustapha Kemal's religious policy] as well as the politicians who pushed forward his person and signature, had intended to substitute the sovereign bearing the title of Sultan or Padishah by a monarch with the title of Caliph. The only difference was that, instead of speaking of a monarch of this or that country or nation, they now spoke of a monarch whose authority extended over a population of three hundred million souls belonging to manifold nations and dwelling in different continents of the world. Into the hands of this great monarch, whose authority was to extend over the whole of Islam, they placed as the only power that of the Turkish people, that is to say, only from 10 to 15 millions of these three hundred million subjects. The monarch designated under the title of Caliph was to guide the affairs of these Muslim peoples and to secure the execution of the religious prescriptions which would best correspond to their worldly interests. He was to defend the rights of all Muslims and concentrate all the affairs of the Muslim world in his hands with effective authority.

The sovereign entitled Caliph was to maintain justice among the three hundred million Muslims on the terrestrial globe, to safeguard the rights of these peoples, to prevent any event that could encroach upon order and security, and confront every attack which the Muslims would be called upon to encounter from the side of other nations. It was to be part of his attributes to preserve by all means the welfare and spiritual development of Islam. . . .

If the Caliph and Caliphate, as they maintained, were to be invested with a dignity embracing the whole of Islam, ought they not to have realized in all justice that a crushing burden would be imposed on Turkey, on her existence; her entire resources and all her forces would be placed at the disposal of the Caliph? . . .

For centuries our nation was guided under the influence of these erroneous ideas. But what has been the result of it? Everywhere they have lost millions of men. "Do you know," I asked, "how many sons of Anatolia have perished in the scorching deserts of the Yemen? Do you know the losses we have suffered in holding Syria and Egypt and in maintaining our position in Africa? And do you see what has come out of it? Do you know?

"Those who favor the idea of placing the means at the disposal of the Caliph to brave the whole world and the power to administer the affairs of the whole of Islam must not appeal to the population of Anatolia alone but to the great Muslim agglomerations which are eight or ten times as rich in men.

"New Turkey, the people of New Turkey, have no reason to think of anything else but their own existence and their own welfare. She has nothing more to give away to others."

ern industrial sector, the profits from which left the country or disappeared into the hands of the dynasty's ruling elite. Supported actively by Shi'ite religious leaders, opposition to the regime rose steadily among both peasants and merchants in the cities, and in 1906 popular pressures forced the reigning shah to grant a constitution on the Western model. It was an eerie foretaste of the revolution of 1979.

As in the Ottoman Empire and Manchu China, however, the modernizers had moved too soon, before their power base was secure. With the support of the Russians and the British, the shah was able to retain control, while the two foreign powers began to divide the country into separate spheres of influence. One reason for the growing foreign presence in Persia was the discovery of oil reserves in the southern part of the country in 1908. Within a few years, oil exports increased rapidly, with the bulk of the profits going into the pockets of British investors.

In 1921, an officer in the Persian army by the name of Reza Khan (1878–1944) led a mutiny that seized power in Tehran. The new ruler's original intention had been to establish a republic, but resistance from traditional forces impeded his efforts, and in 1925 a new Pahlavi dynasty, with Reza Khan as shah, replaced the now defunct Qajar dynasty. During the next few years, Reza Khan attempted to follow the example of Mustapha Kemal Ataturk in Turkey, introducing a number of reforms to strengthen the central government, modernize the civilian and military bureaucracy, and establish a modern economic infrastructure.

Unlike Ataturk, Reza Khan did not attempt to destroy the power of Islamic beliefs, but he did encourage the establishment of a Western-style educational system and forbade women to wear the veil in public. To strengthen the sense of Persian nationalism and reduce the power of Islam, he attempted to popularize the symbols and beliefs of pre-Islamic times. Like his Qajar predecessors, however,

Reza Khan was hindered by strong foreign influence. When the Soviet Union and Great Britain decided to send troops into the country during World War II, he resigned in protest and died three years later.

THE RISE OF ARAB NATIONALISM AND THE PROBLEM OF PALESTINE

As we have seen, the Arab uprising during World War I helped bring about the demise of the Ottoman Empire. Actually, unrest against Ottoman rule had existed in the Arabian peninsula since the eighteenth century, when the Wahhabi revolt attempted to drive out the outside influences and cleanse Islam of corrupt practices that had developed in past centuries. The revolt was eventually suppressed, but Wahhabi influence persisted.

World War I offered an opportunity for the Arabs to throw off the shackles of Ottoman rule—but what would replace them? The Arabs were not a nation, but an idea, a loose collection of peoples who often do not see eye to eye on what constitutes their common sense of community. Disagreement over what constitutes an Arab has plagued generations of political leaders who have sought unsuccessfully to knit together the disparate peoples of the region into a single Arab nation.

When the Arab leaders in Mecca declared their independence from Ottoman rule in 1916, they had hoped for British support, but they were to be sorely disappointed. At the close of the war, the British and French agreed to create a number of mandates in the area under the general supervision of the League of Nations. Iraq and Jordan were assigned to the British; Syria and Lebanon (the two areas were separated so that Christian peoples in Lebanon could be placed under Christian administration) were given to the French.

The land of Palestine—once the home of the Jews but now inhabited primarily by Muslim Palestinians—became a separate mandate. According to the Balfour Declaration, issued by the British foreign secretary Lord Balfour in November 1917, Palestine was to be a national home for the Jews. The declaration was ambiguous on the legal status of the territory and promised that the decision would not undermine the rights of the non-Jewish peoples currently living in the area. But Arab nationalists were incensed. How could a national home for the Jewish people be established in a territory where 90 percent of the population was Muslim?

In the early 1920s, a leader of the Wahhabi movement, Ibn Saud (1880–1953), united Arab tribes in the northern part of the Arabian peninsula and drove out the remnants of Ottoman rule. Ibn Saud was a descendant of the family that had led the Wahhabi revolt in the eighteenth century. Devout and gifted, he won broad support among Arab tribal peoples and established the kingdom of Saudi Arabia throughout much of the peninsula in 1932.

At first his new kingdom, consisting essentially of the vast wastes of central Arabia, was desperately poor. Its financial resources were limited to the income from Muslim pilgrims visiting the holy sites in Mecca and Medina. But during the 1930s, American companies began

THE IMPACT OF OIL. Oil discoveries early in the twentieth century began to bring wealth to Persia. Shown here are workers developing the oil fields at Petroleum Springs, Dalaki, in Persia.

to explore for oil, and in 1938, Standard Oil made a successful strike at Dahran, on the Persian Gulf. Soon an Arabian-American oil conglomerate, popularly called Aramco, was established, and the isolated kingdom was suddenly inundated by Western oilmen and untold wealth.

In the meantime, Jewish settlers began to arrive in Palestine in response to the promises made in the Balfour Declaration. As tensions between the new arrivals and existing Muslim residents began to escalate during the 1930s, the British tried to restrict Jewish immigration into the territory and rejected the concept of a separate state. The stage was set for the conflicts that would take place in the region after World War II.

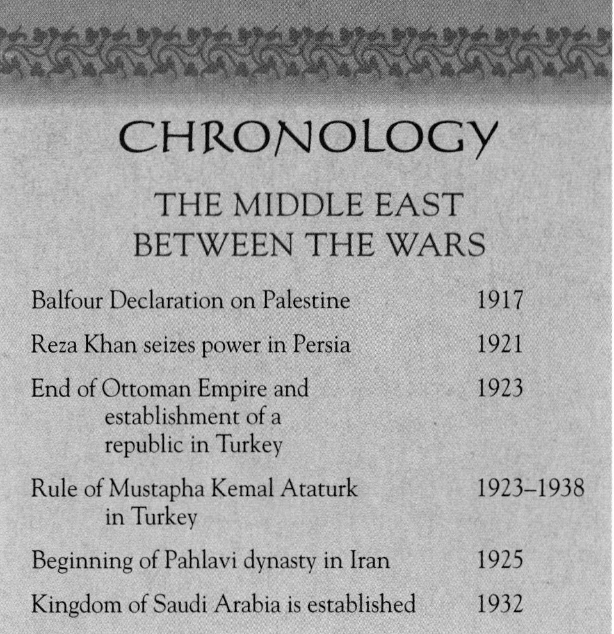

CHRONOLOGY

THE MIDDLE EAST BETWEEN THE WARS

Balfour Declaration on Palestine	1917
Reza Khan seizes power in Persia	1921
End of Ottoman Empire and establishment of a republic in Turkey	1923
Rule of Mustapha Kemal Ataturk in Turkey	1923–1938
Beginning of Pahlavi dynasty in Iran	1925
Kingdom of Saudi Arabia is established	1932

Nationalism and Revolution in Asia and Africa

Before the Russian Revolution, to most intellectuals in Asia and Africa, Westernization meant the capitalist democratic civilization of western Europe and the United States, not the doctrine of social revolution developed by Karl Marx. Until 1917, Marxism was regarded as a utopian idea rather than a concrete system of government. Moreover, to many intellectuals, Marxism appeared to have little relevance to conditions in Asia and Africa. Marxist doctrine, after all, declared that a communist society would arise only from the ashes of an advanced capitalism that had already passed through the stage of industrial revolution. From the perspective of Marxist historical analysis, most societies in Asia and Africa were still at the feudal stage of development; they lacked the economic conditions and political awareness to achieve a socialist revolution that would bring the working class to power. Finally, the Marxist view of nationalism and religion had little appeal to many patriotic intellectuals in the non-Western world. Marx believed that nationhood and religion were essentially false ideas that diverted the attention of the oppressed masses from the critical issues of class struggle and, in his phrase, the exploitation of one person by another. Instead, Marx stressed an "internationalist" outlook based on class consciousness and the eventual creation of a classless society with no artificial divisions based on culture, nation, or religion.

EUROPEAN JEWISH REFUGEES. European Jewish refugees emigrated to Palestine both before and after World War II. They had one goal: to build a new life in a Jewish homeland. Like the refugees aboard this ship, they all celebrated as they reached the safety of Palestine. The sign reads "Keep the gates open."

For these reasons, many patriotic non-Western intellectuals initially found Marxism to be both irrelevant and unappealing. That situation began to change after the Russian Revolution in 1917. The rise to power of Lenin's Bolsheviks demonstrated that a revolutionary party espousing Marxist principles could overturn a corrupt, outdated system and launch a new experiment dedicated to ending human inequality and achieving a paradise on earth. In 1920, Lenin proposed a new revolutionary strategy designed to relate Marxist doctrine and practice to non-Western societies. His reasons were not entirely altruistic. Soviet Russia, surrounded by capitalist powers, desperately needed allies in its struggle to survive in a hostile world. To Lenin, the anticolonial movements emerging in North Africa, Asia, and the Middle East after World War I were natural allies of the beleaguered new regime in Moscow. Lenin was convinced that only the ability of the imperialist powers to find markets, raw materials, and sources of capital investment in the non-Western world kept capitalism alive. If the tentacles of capitalist influence in Asia and Africa could be severed, then imperialism itself would ultimately weaken and collapse.

Establishing such an alliance was not easy, however. Most nationalist leaders in colonial countries belonged to the urban middle class, and many abhorred the idea of a comprehensive revolution to create a totally egalitarian society. In addition, many still adhered to traditional religious beliefs and were opposed to the atheistic principles of classical Marxism.

Since it was unrealistic to expect bourgeois nationalist support for social revolution, Lenin sought a compromise by which Communist parties could be organized among the working classes in the preindustrial societies of Asia and Africa. These parties would then forge informal alliances with existing middle-class parties to struggle against the common enemies of feudal reaction (the remnants of the traditional ruling class) and Western imperialism. Such an alliance, of course, could not be permanent because many bourgeois nationalists in Asia and Africa would reject an egalitarian, classless society. Once the imperialists had been overthrown, therefore, the Communist parties would turn against their erstwhile nationalist partners to seize power on their own and carry out the socialist revolution. Lenin thus proposed a two-stage revolution: an initial "national democratic" stage followed by a "proletarian socialist" stage.

Lenin's strategy became a major element in Soviet foreign policy in the 1920s. Soviet agents fanned out across the world to carry Marxism beyond the boundaries of industrial Europe. The primary instrument of this effort was the Communist International, or Comintern for short. Formed in 1919 at Lenin's prodding, the Comintern was a worldwide organization of Communist parties dedicated to the advancement of world revolution. At its headquarters in Moscow, agents from around the world were trained in the precepts of world communism and then sent back to their own countries to form Marxist parties and promote the cause of social revolution. By the end of the 1920s, almost every colonial or semicolonial society in Asia had a party based on Marxist principles. The Soviets had less success in the Middle East, where Marxist ideology appealed mainly to minorities such as Jews and Armenians in the cities, or in black Africa, where Soviet strategists in any case did not feel conditions were sufficiently advanced for the creation of Communist organizations.

According to Marxist doctrine, the rank and file of Communist parties should be urban factory workers alienated from capitalist society by inhuman working conditions. In practice, many of the leaders even in European Communist parties tended to be urban intellectuals or members of the lower middle class (in Marxist parlance, the "petty bourgeoisie"). That phenomenon was even more true in the non-Western world, where most early Marxists were rootless intellectuals. Some were probably drawn into the movement for patriotic reasons and saw Marxist doctrine as a new, more effective means of modernizing their societies and removing the colonial exploiters (see the box on p. 757). Others were attracted by the message of egalitarian communism and the utopian dream of a classless society. For those who had lost their faith in traditional religion, communism often served as a new secular ideology, dealing not with the hereafter but with the here and now or, indeed, with a remote future when the state would wither away and the "classless society" would replace the lost truth of traditional faiths.

Of course, the new doctrine's appeal was not the same in all non-Western societies. In Confucian societies such as China and Vietnam, where traditional belief systems had been badly discredited by their failure to counter the Western challenge, communism had an immediate impact and rapidly became a major factor in the anticolonial movement. In Buddhist and Muslim societies, where traditional religion remained strong and actually became a cohesive factor in the resistance movement, communism had less success. To maximize their appeal and minimize potential conflict with traditional ideas, Communist parties frequently attempted to adapt Marxist doctrine to indigenous values and institutions. In the Middle East, for example, the Ba'ath Party in Syria adopted a hybrid socialism combining Marxism with Arab nationalism. In Africa, radical intellectuals talked vaguely of a uniquely "African road to socialism."

The degree to which these parties were successful in establishing alliances with nationalist parties and building a solid base of support among the mass of the population also varied from place to place. In some instances, the Communists were briefly able to establish a cooper-

THE PATH OF LIBERATION

In 1919, the Vietnamese revolutionary Ho Chi Minh (1890–1969) was living in exile in France, where he first became acquainted with the new revolutionary experiment in Bolshevik Russia. He became a leader of the Vietnamese Communist movement. In the following passage, written in 1960, he reminisces about his reasons for becoming a Communist.

HO CHI MINH, "THE PATH WHICH LED ME TO LENINISM"

After World War I, I made my living in Paris, now as a retoucher at a photographer's, now as a painter of "Chinese antiquities" (made in France!). I would distribute leaflets denouncing the crimes committed by the French colonialists in Vietnam.

At that time, I supported the October Revolution only instinctively, not yet grasping all its historic importance. I loved and admired Lenin because he was a great patriot who liberated his compatriots; until then, I had read none of his books.

The reason for my joining the French Socialist Party was that these "ladies and gentlemen"—as I called my comrades at that moment—had shown their sympathy toward me, toward the struggle of the oppressed peoples. But I understood neither what was a party, a trade union, nor what was Socialism nor Communism.

Heated discussions were then taking place in the branches of the Socialist Party, about the question whether the Socialist Party should remain in the Second International, should a Second-and-a-Half International be founded, or should the Socialist Party join Lenin's Third International? I attended the meetings regularly, twice or three times a week, and attentively listened to the discussion. First, I could not understand thoroughly. Why were the discussions so heated? Either with the Second, Second-and-a-Half, or Third International, the revolution could be waged. What was the use of arguing then? As for the First International, what had become of it?

What I wanted most to know—and this precisely was not debated in the meetings—was: which International sides with the peoples of colonial countries?

I raised this question—the most important in my opinion—in a meeting. Some comrades answered: It is the Third, not the Second International. And a comrade gave me Lenin's "Thesis on the national and colonial questions," published by *l'Humanité*, to read.

There were political terms difficult to understand in this thesis. But by dint of reading it again and again, finally I could grasp the main part of it. What emotion, enthusiasm, clear-sightedness, and confidence it instilled in me! I was overjoyed to tears. Though sitting alone in my room, I shouted aloud as if addressing large crowds: "Dear martyrs, compatriots! This is what we need, this is the path to our liberation!"

After that, I had entire confidence in Lenin, in the Third International.

ative relationship with the bourgeois parties. The most famous example was the alliance between the Chinese Communist Party and Sun Yat-sen's Nationalist Party (discussed in the next section). In the Dutch East Indies, the Indonesian Communist Party (known as the PKI) allied with the middle-class nationalist group Sarekat Islam, but later broke loose in an effort to organize its own mass movement among the poor peasants. In French Indochina, Vietnamese Communists organized by the Moscow-trained revolutionary Ho Chi Minh sought at first to cooperate with bourgeois nationalist parties against the colonial regime, but these efforts were abandoned in 1928 when the Comintern, reacting to Chiang Kai-shek's betrayal of the alliance with the Chinese Communist Party, declared that Communist parties should restrict their recruiting efforts to the most revolutionary elements in society—notably, the urban intellectuals and the working class. Harassed by colonial authorities and saddled with strategic directions from Moscow that often had little relevance to local conditions, Communist parties in most colonial societies had little success in the 1930s and failed to build a secure base of support among the mass of the population.

REVOLUTION IN CHINA

Overall, revolutionary Marxism had its greatest impact in China, where a group of young radicals, including several faculty and staff members from Peking University, founded the Chinese Communist Party (CCP) in 1921. The rise of the CCP was a consequence of the failed revolution of 1911. When political forces are too weak or divided to consolidate their power during a period of instability, the military usually steps in to fill the vacuum. In China, Sun Yat-sen and his colleagues had accepted General Yuan Shikai as president of the new Chinese republic in 1911 because they lacked the military force to compete with his control over the army. Moreover, many feared, perhaps rightly, that if the revolt lapsed into chaos, the Western powers would intervene and the last shreds of Chinese sovereignty would be lost. But some had misgivings about Yuan's intentions. As one remarked in a letter to a friend, "We don't know whether he will be a George Washington or a Napoleon."

As it turned out, he was neither. Understanding little of the new ideas sweeping into China from the West, Yuan ruled in a traditional manner, reviving Confucian rituals and institutions and eventually trying to found a new imperial dynasty. Yuan's dictatorial inclinations rapidly led to clashes with Sun's party, now renamed the *Guomindang (Kuomintang)* or Nationalist Party. When Yuan dissolved the new parliament, the Nationalists launched a rebellion. When it failed, Sun Yat-sen fled to Japan.

Yuan was strong enough to brush off the challenge from the revolutionary forces, but not to turn back the clock of history. He died in 1916 (apparently of natural causes, although legend holds that his heart was broken by growing popular resistance to his imperial pretensions) and was succeeded by one of his military subordinates. For the next several years, China slipped into semi-anarchy, as the power of the central government disintegrated and military warlords seized power in the provinces.

MAP 25.1 The Northern Expedition

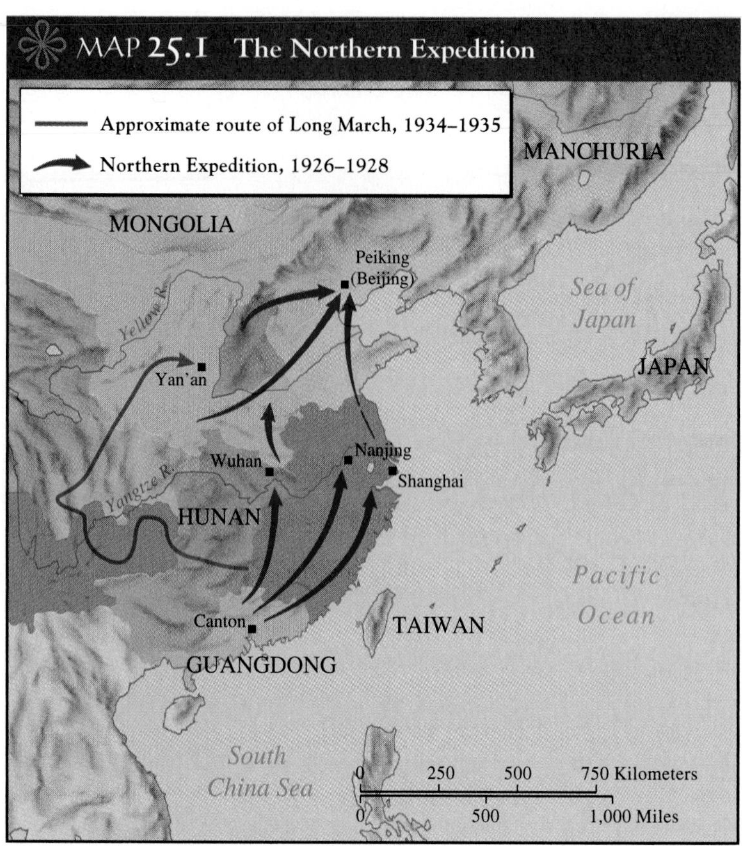

Mr. Science and Mr. Democracy: The New Culture Movement

Although the failure of the 1911 revolution was a clear sign that China was not yet ready for radical change, discontent with existing conditions continued to rise in various sectors of Chinese society. The most vocal protests came from radical intellectuals, who opposed Yuan Shikai's conservative rule but were now convinced that political change could not take place until the Chinese people were more familiar with trends in the outside world. Braving the displeasure of Yuan Shikai and his successors, progressive intellectuals at Peking University launched the New Culture Movement, aimed at abolishing the remnants of the old system and introducing Western values and institutions into China. Using the classrooms of China's most prestigious university as well as the pages of newly established progressive magazines and newspapers, the intellectuals introduced a bewildering mix of new ideas, from the philosophy of Friedrich Nietzsche and Bertrand Russell to the educational views of the American John Dewey and the feminist plays of Henrik Ibsen. As such ideas flooded into China, they stirred up a new generation of educated Chinese youth, who chanted "Down with Confucius and sons" and talked of a new era dominated by "Mr. Sai" (Mr. Science) and "Mr. De" (Mr. Democracy). No one was a greater defender of free thought and speech than the chancellor of Peking University, Cai Yuanpei (Ts'ai Yuan-p'ei):

> So far as theoretical ideas are concerned, I follow the principles of "freedom of thought" and an attitude of broad tolerance in accordance with the practice of universities the world over. . . . Regardless of what school of thought a person may adhere to, so long as that person's ideas are justified and conform to reason and have not been passed by through the process of natural selection, although there may be controversy, such ideas have a right to be presented.[3]

The problem was that appeals for American-style democracy and women's liberation had little relevance to Chinese peasants, most of whom were still illiterate and concerned above all with survival. Consequently, the New Culture Movement did not win widespread support outside the urban areas. It certainly earned the distrust of conservative military officers, one of whom threatened to lob artillery shells into Peking University to destroy the poisonous new ideas and their advocates.

Discontent among intellectuals, however, was soon joined by the rising chorus of public protest against Japan's efforts to expand its influence on the mainland. During the first decade of the twentieth century, Japan had taken advantage of the Qing's decline to extend its domination over Manchuria and Korea (see Chapter 23). In 1915, the Japanese government insisted that Yuan Shikai accept a series of "twenty-one demands" that would have given Japan a virtual protectorate over the Chinese government and economy. Yuan was able to fend off the most far-reaching Japanese demands by arousing popular outrage in China, but at the Paris Peace Conference four years later, Japan received Germany's sphere of influence in Shandong Province as a reward for its support of the Allied cause in World War I. On hearing that the Chinese government had accepted the decision, on May 4, 1919, patriotic students, supported by other sectors of the urban population, demonstrated in Beijing and other major cities of the country. Although this May Fourth Movement did not lead to the restoration of Shandong, it did alert a substantial part of the politically literate population to the threat to national survival and the incompetence of the warlord government.

By 1920, central authority had almost ceased to exist in China. Two competing political forces now began to emerge from the chaos. One was Sun Yat-sen's Nationalist Party. Driven from the political arena seven years earlier by Yuan Shikai, the party now reestablished itself on the mainland by making an alliance with the warlord ruler of Guangdong (Kwangtung) Province in South China. From Canton, Sun sought international assistance to carry out his national revolution. The other was the CCP. Following Lenin's strategy, Comintern agents soon advised the new party to link up with the more experienced Nationalists. Sun Yat-sen needed the expertise and the diplomatic support that the Soviet Union could provide, because his anti-imperialist rhetoric had alienated many Western powers; one English-language newspaper in the international concession in Shanghai remarked, "All his life, all his influence, are devoted to ideas which keep China in turmoil, and it is utterly undesirable that he should be allowed to prosecute those aims here."[4] In 1923, the two parties formed an alliance to oppose the warlords and drive the imperialist powers out of China.

For three years, with the assistance of a Comintern mission in Canton, the two parties submerged their mutual suspicions and mobilized and trained a revolutionary army to march north and seize control over China. The so-called Northern Expedition began in the summer of 1926. By the following spring, revolutionary forces were in control of all Chinese territory south of the Yangtze River, including the major river ports of Wuhan and Shanghai. But tensions between the two parties now surfaced. Sun Yat-sen had died of cancer in 1925 and was succeeded as head of the Nationalist Party by his military subordinate, Chiang Kai-shek. Chiang feigned support for the alliance with the Communists but actually planned to destroy them. In April 1927, he struck against the Communists and their supporters in Shanghai, killing thousands. After the massacre, most of the Communist leaders went into hiding in the city, where they attempted to revive the movement in its traditional base among the urban working class. Some party members, however, led by the young Communist organizer Mao Zedong (Mao Tse-Tung), fled to the hilly areas south of the Yangtze River.

Unlike most CCP leaders, Mao was convinced that the Chinese revolution must be based on the impoverished peasants in the countryside. The son of a prosperous peasant, Mao had helped organize a peasant movement in South China during the early 1920s, and then served as an agitator in rural villages in his native province of Hunan during the Northern Expedition in the fall of 1926. At that time, he wrote a famous report to the party

STUDENT DEMONSTRATIONS IN BEIJING. The massive popular demonstrations in Tiananmen Square in downtown Beijing in 1989 were not the first of their kind in China. On May 4, 1919, students gathered at the same spot to protest against the Japanese takeover of Shandong peninsula after World War I. The event triggered the famous May Fourth Movement, which highlighted the demand of progressive forces in China for political and social reforms.

A CALL FOR REVOLT

In the fall of 1926, Nationalist and Communist forces moved north from Canton on their Northern Expedition in an effort to defeat the warlords. The young Communist Mao Zedong accompanied revolutionary troops into his home province of Hunan, where he submitted a report to the CCP Central Committee calling for a massive peasant revolt against the ruling order. The report shows his confidence that peasants could play an active role in the Chinese revolution despite the skepticism of many of his colleagues.

MAO ZEDONG, "THE PEASANT MOVEMENT IN HUNAN"

During my recent visit to Hunan I made a firsthand investigation of conditions. . . . In a very short time, . . . several hundred million peasants will rise like a mighty storm, . . . a force so swift and violent that no power, however great, will be able to hold it back. They will smash all the trammels that bind them and rush forward along the road to liberation. They will sweep all the imperialists, warlords, corrupt officials, local tyrants, and evil gentry into their graves. Every revolutionary party and every revolutionary comrade will be put to the test, to be accepted or rejected as they decide. There are three alternatives. To march at their head and lead them? To trail behind them, gesticulating and criticizing? Or to stand in their way and oppose them? Every Chinese is free to choose, but events will force you to make the choice quickly.

The main targets of attack by the peasants are the local tyrants, the evil gentry and the lawless landlords, but in passing they also hit out against patriarchal ideas and institutions, against the corrupt officials in the cities and against bad practices and customs in the rural areas. . . . As a result, the privileges which the feudal landlords enjoyed for thousands of years are being shattered to pieces. . . . With the collapse of the power of the landlords, the peasant associations have now become the sole organs of authority, and the popular slogan "All power to the peasant associations" has become a reality.

The peasants' revolt disturbed the gentry's sweet dreams. When the news from the countryside reached the cities, it caused immediate uproar among the gentry. . . . From the middle social strata upwards to the Kuomintang right-wingers, there was not a single person who did not sum up the whole business in the phrase, "It's terrible!" . . . Even quite progressive people said, "Though terrible, it is inevitable in a revolution." In short, nobody could altogether deny the word "terrible." But . . . the fact is that the great peasant masses have risen to fulfill their historic mission. . . . What the peasants are doing is absolutely right; what they are doing is fine! "It's fine!" is the theory of the peasants and of all other revolutionaries. Every revolutionary comrade should know that the national revolution requires a great change in the countryside. The Revolution of 1911 did not bring about this change, hence its failure. This change is now taking place, and it is an important factor for the completion of the revolution. Every revolutionary comrade must support it, or he will be taking the stand of counterrevolution.

leadership suggesting that the CCP support peasant demands for a land revolution (see the box above). But his superiors refused, fearing that such radical policies would destroy the then existing alliance with the Nationalists.

The Nanjing Republic

In 1928, Chiang Kai-shek founded a new Chinese republic at Nanjing, and over the next three years, he managed to reunify China by a combination of military operations and inducements (known as "silver bullets") to various northern warlords to join his movement. He also attempted to put an end to the Communists, rooting them out of their urban base in Shanghai and their rural redoubt in the rugged hills of Jiangxi (Kiangsi) Province. He succeeded in the first task in 1931, when most party leaders were forced to flee Shanghai for Mao's base in southern China. Three years later, using their superior military strength, Chiang's troops surrounded the Communist base in Jiangxi, inducing Mao's young People's Liberation Army (PLA) to abandon its guerrilla lair and embark on the famous Long March, an arduous journey of thousands of miles on foot through mountains, marshes, and deserts to the small provincial town of Yan'an (Yenan) 200 miles north of the modern city of Xian in the dusty hills of northern China. Of the 90,000 who embarked on the journey in October 1934, only 10,000 arrived in Yan'an a year later. Contemporary observers must have thought that the Communist threat to the Nanjing regime had been averted forever.

Meanwhile, Chiang Kai-shek was trying to build a new nation. When the Nanjing republic was established in 1928, Chiang publicly declared his commitment to Sun Yat-sen's Three People's Principles. In a program announced in 1918, Sun had written about the all-important second stage of "political tutelage":

> China . . . needs a republic government just as a boy needs school. As a schoolboy must have good teachers and helpful friends, so the Chinese people, being for the first time

> under republican rule, must have a farsighted revolutionary government for their training. This calls for the period of political tutelage, which is a necessary transitional stage from monarchy to republicanism. Without this, disorder will be unavoidable.[5]

In keeping with Sun's program, Chiang announced a period of political indoctrination to prepare the Chinese people for a final stage of constitutional government. In the meantime, the Nationalists would use their dictatorial power to carry out a land reform program and modernize the urban industrial sector.

But it would take more than paper plans to create a new China. Years of neglect and civil war had severely frayed the political, economic, and social fabric of the nation. There were faint signs of an impending industrial revolution in the major urban centers, but most of the people in the countryside, drained by warlord exactions and civil strife, were still grindingly poor and overwhelmingly illiterate. A Westernized middle class had begun to emerge in the cities and formed much of the natural constituency of the Nanjing government. But this new Westernized elite, preoccupied with bourgeois values of individual advancement and material accumulation, had few links with the peasants in the countryside or the rickshaw drivers "running in this world of suffering," in the poignant words of a Chinese poet. In an expressive phrase, some critics dismissed Chiang Kai-shek and his chief followers as "banana Chinese"—yellow on the outside, white on the inside.

MAO ZEDONG AT YAN'AN. In 1934, Mao Zedong led his bedraggled forces on a famous "Long March" from southern China to a new location at Yan'an, in the hills just south of the Gobi Desert. Here Chairman Mao, next to Zhu De, one of his generals, poses for a photograph at his new headquarters. Note the thick padded jackets to keep out the cold.

Chiang Kai-shek was aware of the difficulty of introducing exotic foreign ideas into a society still culturally conservative. While building a modern industrial sector, he attempted to synthesize modern Western ideas with traditional Confucian values of hard work, obedience, and moral integrity. In the officially promoted New Life Movement, sponsored by his Wellesley-educated wife, Mei-ling Soong, Chiang sought to propagate traditional Confucian social ethics such as integrity, propriety, and righteousness, while rejecting what he considered the excessive individualism and material greed of Western capitalism.

Unfortunately for Chiang Kai-shek, Confucian ideas—at least in their institutional form—had been widely discredited by the failure of the traditional system to solve China's growing problems. With only a tenuous hold over the Chinese provinces (the Nanjing government had total control over only a handful of provinces in the Yangtze valley), a growing Japanese threat in the north, and a world suffering from the Great Depression, Chiang made little progress with his program. Lacking the political sensitivity of Sun Yat-sen and fearing Communist influence, Chiang repressed all opposition and censored free expression, thereby alienating many intellectuals and political moderates. Since the urban middle class and landed gentry were his natural political constituency, he shunned programs that would lead to a redistribution of wealth. A land reform program was enacted in 1930 but had little effect.

Chiang Kai-shek's government had little more success in promoting industrial development. During the decade of precarious peace following the Northern Expedition, industrial growth averaged only about 1 percent annually. Much of the national wealth was in the hands of the senior officials and close subordinates of the ruling elite. Military expenses consumed half the budget, and distressingly little was devoted to social and economic development.

The new government, then, had little success in dealing with China's deep-seated economic and social problems. The deadly combination of internal disintegration and foreign pressure now began to coincide with the virtual collapse of the global economic order during the Great Depression and the rise of militant political forces in Japan determined to extend Japanese influence and power in an unstable Asia. These forces and the turmoil they unleashed will be examined in the next chapter.

Down with Confucius and Sons: Economic, Social, and Cultural Change in Republican China

The transformation of the old order that had commenced at the end of the Qing era continued into the period of the early Chinese republic. The industrial sector continued to grow, albeit slowly. Although about 75 percent of all industrial production was still craft-produced in the early 1930s, mechanization was gradually beginning to replace manual labor in a number of traditional industries, notably in the manufacture of textile goods. Traditional Chinese exports, such as silk and tea, were hard-hit by the Great Depression, however, and manufacturing suffered a decline during the 1930s. It is difficult to gauge conditions in the countryside during the early republican era, but there is no doubt that farmers were often victimized by high taxes imposed by local warlords and the endemic political and social conflict.

Social changes followed shifts in the economy and the political culture. By 1915, the assault on the old system and values by educated youth was intense. The main focus of the attack was the Confucian concept of the family—in particular, filial piety and the subordination of women. Young people demanded the right to choose their own mates and their own careers. Women demanded rights and opportunities equal to those enjoyed by men. More broadly, progressives called for an end to the concept of duty to the community and praised the Western individualist ethos. The popular short story writer Lu Xun (Lu Hsun) criticized the Confucian concept of family as a "man-eating" system that degraded humanity. In a famous short story entitled "Diary of a Madman," the protagonist remarks:

> I remember when I was four or five years old, sitting in the cool of the hall, my brother told me that if a man's parents were ill, he should cut off a piece of his flesh and boil it for them if he wanted to be considered a good son. I have only just realized that I have been living all these years in a place where for four thousand years they have been eating human flesh.[6]

Such criticisms did have some beneficial results. During the early republic, the tyranny of the old family system began to decline, at least in urban areas, under the impact of economic changes and the urgings of the New Culture intellectuals. Women began to escape their cloistered existence and seek education and employment alongside their male contemporaries. Free choice in marriage and a more relaxed attitude toward sex became commonplace among affluent families in the cities, where the teenage children of Westernized elites aped the clothing, social habits, and even the musical tastes of their contemporaries in Europe and the United States.

But as a rule, the new individualism and women's rights did not penetrate to the villages. Here traditional attitudes and customs held sway. Arranged marriages continued to be the rule rather than the exception, and concubinage remained common. According to a survey taken in the 1930s, well over two-thirds of the marriages even among urban couples had been arranged by their parents (see the box on p. 763), while in one rural area, only 3 out of 170 villagers interviewed had even heard of the idea of "modern marriage." Even the tradition of binding the feet of female children continued despite efforts by the Nationalist government to eradicate the practice.

CHRONOLOGY
REVOLUTION IN CHINA

May Fourth Demonstrations	1919
Formation of Chinese Communist Party	1921
Northern Expedition	1926–1927
Chiang Kai-shek establishes the Nanjing Republic	1928
Long March	1934–1935

Nowhere was the struggle between traditional and modern more visible than in the field of culture. Beginning with the New Culture era, radical reformists criticized traditional culture as the symbol and instrument of feudal oppression that must be entirely eradicated before a new China could stand with dignity in the modern world. During the 1920s and 1930s, Western literature and art became highly popular, especially among the urban middle class. Traditional culture continued to prevail among more conservative elements, and some intellectuals argued for a new art that would synthesize the best of Chinese and foreign culture. But the most creative artists were interested in imitating foreign trends, while traditionalists were more concerned with preservation.

Literature in particular was influenced by foreign ideas, as Western genres like the novel and the short story attracted a growing audience. Although most Chinese novels written after World War I dealt with Chinese subjects, they reflected the Western tendency toward social realism and often dealt with the new Westernized middle class (Mao Dun's *Midnight,* for example, describes the changing mores of Shanghai's urban elites) or the disintegration of the traditional Confucian family (Ba Jin's famous novel *Family* is an example). Most of China's modern authors displayed a clear contempt for the past.

Japan Between the Wars

During the first two decades of the twentieth century, Japan made remarkable progress toward the creation of an advanced society on the Western model. The political sys-

AN ARRANGED MARRIAGE

Under Western influence, Chinese social customs changed dramatically for many urban elites in the interwar years. A vocal women's movement, inspired in part by translations of Henrik Ibsen's play A Doll's House, *campaigned aggressively for universal suffrage and an end to sexual discrimination. Some progressives called for free choice in marriage and divorce and even for free love. By the 1930s, the government had taken some steps to free women from patriarchal marriage constraints and realize sexual equality. But life was generally unaffected in the villages, where traditional patterns held sway. This often created severe tensions between older and younger generations, as this passage by the popular twentieth-century novelist Ba Jin shows.*

BA JIN, *FAMILY*

Brought up with loving care, after studying with a private tutor for a number of years, Chueh-hsin entered middle school. One of the school's best students, he graduated four years later at the top of his class. He was very interested in physics and chemistry and hoped to study abroad, in Germany. His mind was full of beautiful dreams. At that time he was the envy of his classmates.

In his fourth year at middle school, he lost his mother. His father later married again, this time to a younger woman who had been his mother's cousin. Chueh-hsin was aware of his loss, for he knew full well that nothing could replace the love of a mother. But her death left no irreparable wound in his heart; he was able to console himself with rosy dreams of his future. Moreover, he had someone who understood him and could comfort him—his pretty cousin Mei, "mei" for "plum blossom."

But then, one day, his dreams were shattered, cruelly and bitterly shattered. The evening he returned home carrying his diploma, the plaudits of his teachers and friends still ringing in his ears, his father called him into his room and said:

"Now that you've graduated, I want to arrange your marriage. Your grandfather is looking forward to having a great-grandson, and I, too, would like to be able to hold a grandson in my arms. You're old enough to be married; I won't feel easy until I fulfill my obligation to find you a wife. Although I didn't accumulate much money in my years away from home as an official, still I've put by enough for us to get along on. My health isn't what it used to be; I'm thinking of spending my time at home and having you help me run the household affairs. All the more reason you'll be needing a wife. I've already arranged a match with the Li family. The thirteenth of next month is a good day. We'll announce the engagement then. You can be married within the year. . . ."

Chueh-hsin did not utter a word of protest, nor did such a thought ever occur to him. He merely nodded to indicate his compliance with his father's wishes. But after he returned to his own room, and shut the door, he threw himself down on his bed, covered his head with the quilt and wept. He wept for his broken dreams.

He was deeply in love with Mei, but now his father had chosen another, a girl he had never seen, and said that he must marry within the year. What's more, his hopes of continuing his studies had burst like a bubble. It was a terrible shock to Chueh-hsin. His future was finished, his beautiful dreams shattered.

He cried his disappointment and bitterness. But the door was closed and Chueh-hsin's head was beneath the bedding. No one knew. He did not fight back, he never thought of resisting. He only bemoaned his fate. But he accepted it. He complied with his father's will without a trace of resentment. But in his heart he wept for himself, wept for the girl he adored—Mei, his "plum blossom."

tem based on the Meiji Constitution of 1890 began to evolve along Western pluralistic lines, and a multiparty system took shape, while the economic and social reforms launched during the Meiji era led to increasing prosperity and the development of a modern industrial and commercial sector. Optimists had reason to hope that Japan was on the road to becoming a full-fledged democracy.

Experiment in Democracy

During the first quarter of the twentieth century, the Japanese political system appeared to evolve significantly toward the Western democratic model. Political parties expanded their popular following and became increasingly competitive, and universal male suffrage was instituted in the 1920s. Individual pressure groups began to appear in Japanese society, along with an independent press and a bill of rights. The influence of the old ruling oligarchy, the *genro,* had not yet been significantly challenged, however, nor had that of its ideological foundation, the *kokutai.*

These fragile democratic institutions were able to survive throughout the 1920s (often called the era of Taisho democracy from the reign title of the ruling emperor). During that period, the military budget was reduced, and a suffrage bill enacted in 1925 granted the vote to all Japanese males, thus continuing the process of democratization begun earlier in the century. Women remained disenfranchised, but women's associations gained increasing visibility during the 1920s, and many women were active

IN SEARCH OF OLD JAPAN

Their confidence restored after victories over China and Russia, Japanese authors produced a host of superb works in the early twentieth century. Many authors blended Western psychology with Japanese sensibility in novels of yearning for old Japan. Here novelist Junichiro Tanizaki recalls the charm of an island as yet untouched and unpolluted by modernization.

JUNICHIRO TANIZAKI, *SOME PREFER NETTLES*

The island of Awaji showed not very large on the map, and its harbor very possibly consisted of but this one road. You go straight down, the inn manager had said, till you come out at the river, and the theater is in the flats beyond. The rows of houses therefore most probably ended at the river. This may have been the seat of some minor baron a century ago—even then it could hardly have been imposing enough to be called a castle town—and it had probably changed little since. A modern coating goes no farther than the large cities that are a country's arteries, and there are not many such cities anywhere. In an old country with a long tradition, China and Europe as well as Japan—any country, in fact, except a very new one like the United States—the smaller cities, left aside by the flow of civilization, retain the flavor of an earlier day until they are overtaken by catastrophe.

This little harbor, for instance: it had its electric wires and poles, its painted billboards, and here and there a display window, but one could ignore them and find on every side townsmen's houses that might have come from an illustration to a seventeenth-century novel. The earthen walls covered to the eaves with white plaster, the projecting lattice fronts with their solid, generous slats of wood, the heavy tiled roofs held down by round ridge-tiles, the shop signs—"Lacquer," "Soy," "Oil"—in fading letters on fine hardwood grounds, and inside, beyond earth-floored entrances, the shop names printed on dark-blue half-curtains—it was not the old man's remark this time but every detail brought back—how vividly!—the mood and air of old Japan. Kaname felt as if he were being drunk up into the scene, as if he were losing himself in the clean white walls and the brilliant blue sky. Those walls were a little like the sash around O-hisa's waist: their first luster had disappeared in long years under the fresh sea winds and rains, and bright though they were, their brightness was tempered by a certain reserve, a soft austerity.

Kaname felt a deep repose come over him. "These old houses are so dark you have no idea what's inside."

"Partly it's because the road is so bright." The old man had come up beside them. "The ground here seems almost white."

Kaname thought of the faces of the ancients in the dusk behind their shop curtains. Here on this street people with faces like theater dolls must have passed lives like stage lives. The world of the plays—of O-yumi, Jurobei of Awa, the pilgrim O-tsuru, and the rest—must have been just such a town as this. And wasn't O-hisa a part of it? Fifty years ago, a hundred years ago, a woman like her, dressed in the same kimono, was perhaps going down this same street in the spring sun, lunch in hand, on her way to the theater beyond the river. Or perhaps, behind one of these latticed fronts, she was playing "Snow" on her koto. O-hisa was a shade left behind by another age.

in the labor movement and in campaigning for various social reforms.

But the era was also marked by growing social turmoil, and two opposing forces within the system were gearing up to challenge the prevailing wisdom. On the left, a Marxist labor movement, which reflected the tensions within the working class and the increasing radicalism among the rural poor, began to take shape in the early 1920s in response to growing economic difficulties. Attempts to suppress labor disturbances led to further radicalization. On the right, ultranationalist groups called for a rejection of Western models of development and a more militant approach to realizing national objectives. In 1919, the radical nationalist Kita Ikki called for a military takeover and the establishment of a new system bearing strong resemblance to what would later be called National Socialism in Germany.

This cultural conflict between old and new, native and foreign, was reflected in literature. Japanese self-confidence had been somewhat restored after the victories over China and Russia, and this resurgence sparked a great age of creativity in the early twentieth century. Now more adept at handling European literary forms, Japanese writers blended Western psychology with Japanese sensibility in exquisite novels reeking with nostalgia for the old Japan. A well-known example is Junichiro Tanizaki's *Some Prefer Nettles*, published in 1928, which delicately juxtaposes the positive aspects of both traditional and modern Japan (see the box above). By the 1930s, however, military censorship increasingly inhibited free literary expression. Many authors continued to write privately, producing works that reflected the gloom of the era. This attitude is perhaps best exemplified by Shiga Naoya's *A Dark Night's Journey*, written during the early 1930s and capturing a sense of the approaching global catastrophe. It is regarded as the masterpiece of modern Japanese literature.

A Zaibatsu Economy

Japan also continued to make impressive progress in economic development. Spurred by rising domestic demand as well as continued government investment in the economy, the production of raw materials tripled between 1900 and 1930, while industrial production increased more than twelvefold. Much of the increase went into exports, and Western manufacturers began to complain about the rising competition from the Japanese.

As often happens, rapid industrialization was accompanied by some hardship and rising social tensions. In the Meiji model, various manufacturing processes were concentrated in a single enterprise, the so-called *zaibatsu*, or financial clique. Some of these firms were existing merchant companies, such as Mitsui and Sumitomo, that had the capital and the foresight to move into new areas of opportunity. Others were formed by enterprising samurai, who used their status and experience in management to good account in a new environment. Whatever their origins, these firms gradually developed, often with official encouragement, into large conglomerates that controlled a major segment of the Japanese economy. By 1937 the four largest *zaibatsu* (Mitsui, Mitsubishi, Sumitomo, and Yasuda) controlled 21 percent of the banking industry, 26 percent of mining, 35 percent of shipbuilding, 38 percent of commercial shipping, and more than 60 percent of paper manufacturing and insurance.

This concentration of power and wealth in a few major industrial combines created problems in Japanese society. In the first place, it resulted in the emergence of a dual economy: on the one hand, a modern industry characterized by up-to-date methods and massive government subsidies and on the other, a traditional manufacturing sector characterized by conservative methods and small-scale production techniques.

Concentration of wealth also led to growing economic inequalities. As we have seen, economic growth had been achieved at the expense of the peasants, many of whom fled to the cities to escape rural poverty. That labor surplus benefited the industrial sector, but the urban proletariat was still poorly paid and ill-housed. Rampant inflation in the price of rice led to food riots shortly after World War I. A rapid increase in population (the total population of the Japanese islands increased from an estimated 43 million in 1900 to 73 million in 1940) led to food shortages and the threat of rising unemployment. In the meantime, those left on the farm continued to suffer. As late as the beginning of World War II, an estimated one-half of all Japanese farmers were tenants.

Shidehara Diplomacy

A final problem for Japanese leaders in the post-Meiji era was the familiar colonial dilemma of finding sources of raw materials and foreign markets for the nation's manufactured goods. Until World War I, Japan had dealt with the problem by seizing territories such as Formosa, Korea, and southern Manchuria and transforming them into colonies or protectorates of the growing Japanese Empire. That policy had succeeded brilliantly, but it had also begun to arouse the concern and in some cases the hostility of the Western nations. China was also becoming apprehensive; as we have seen, Japanese demands for Shandong Province at the Paris Peace Conference in 1919 aroused massive protests in major Chinese cities.

The United States was especially concerned about Japanese aggressiveness. Although the United States had been less active than some European states in pursuing colonies in the Pacific, it had a strong interest in keeping the area open for U.S. commercial activities. In 1922, in Washington, D.C., the United States convened a major conference of nations with interests in the Pacific to discuss problems of regional security. The Washington Conference led to agreements on several issues, but the major accomplishment was a nine-power treaty recognizing the territorial integrity of China and the Open Door. The other participants induced Japan to accept these provisions by accepting its special position in Manchuria.

During the remainder of the 1920s, Japanese governments attempted to play by the rules laid down at the Washington Conference. Known as Shidehara diplomacy, after the foreign minister (and later prime minister) who attempted to carry it out, this policy sought to use diplomatic and economic means to realize Japanese interests in Asia. But this approach came under severe pressure as Japanese industrialists began to move into new areas, such as heavy industry, chemicals, mining, and the manufacturing of appliances and automobiles. Because such industries desperately needed resources not found in abundance locally, the Japanese government came under increasing pressure to find new sources abroad.

In the early 1930s, with the onset of the Great Depression and growing tensions in the international arena, nationalist forces rose to dominance in the government. The changes that occurred in the 1930s were not in the constitution or the institutional structure, which remained essentially intact, but in the composition and attitudes of the ruling group. Party leaders during the 1920s had attempted to realize Japanese aspirations within the existing global political and economic framework. The dominant elements in the government in the 1930s, a mixture of military officers and ultranationalist politicians, were convinced that the diplomacy of the 1920s had failed and advocated a more aggressive approach to protecting national interests in a brutal and competitive world.

Historians argue over whether Taisho democracy was merely a fragile period of comparative liberalization within a framework dominated by the Meiji vision of empire and *kokutai* or whether the militant nationalism of the 1930s was an aberration brought on by the depression, which caused the emerging Japanese democracy to wilt. Perhaps both contentions contain a little truth. A process of democratization was taking place in Japan during the first decades of the twentieth century, but without shaking the essential core of the Meiji concept of the state. When the "liberal" approach of the 1920s failed to solve the problems of the day, the shift toward a more aggressive approach was inevitable.

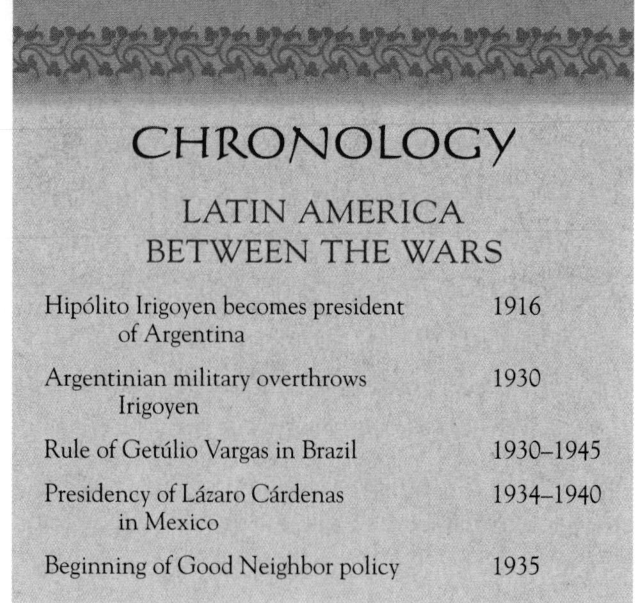

CHRONOLOGY

LATIN AMERICA BETWEEN THE WARS

Hipólito Irigoyen becomes president of Argentina	1916
Argentinian military overthrows Irigoyen	1930
Rule of Getúlio Vargas in Brazil	1930–1945
Presidency of Lázaro Cárdenas in Mexico	1934–1940
Beginning of Good Neighbor policy	1935

NATIONALISM AND DICTATORSHIP IN LATIN AMERICA

Although the nations of Latin America played little role in World War I, that conflict nevertheless exerted an impact on the region, and especially on its economy. By the end of the 1920s, the region was also strongly influenced by another event of global proportions—the Great Depression.

The Economy and the United States

At the beginning of the twentieth century, the economy of Latin America was based largely on the export of foodstuffs and raw materials. Some countries relied on exports of only one or two products. Argentina, for example, exported primarily beef and wheat; Chile, nitrates and copper; Brazil and the Caribbean nations, sugar; and the Central American states, bananas. A few reaped large profits from these exports, but for the majority of the population, the returns were meager.

World War I led to a decline in European investment in Latin America and a rise in the U.S. role in the local economies. By the late 1920s, the United States had replaced Great Britain as the foremost source of investment in Latin America. Unlike the British, however, U.S. investors invested directly in production enterprises, causing large segments of the area's export industries to fall into American hands. A number of Central American states, for example, were popularly labeled "banana republics" because of the power and influence of the U.S.–owned United Fruit Company. American firms also dominated the copper mining industry in Chile and Peru, as well as the oil industry in Mexico, Peru, and Bolivia.

Increasing economic power reinforced the traditionally high level of U.S. political influence in Latin America. This influence was especially evident in Central America and the Caribbean, regions that many Americans considered their backyard and thus vital to U.S. national security. The growing U.S. presence in the region provoked hostility and a growing national consciousness among Latin Americans who viewed the United States as an aggressive imperialist power. Some charged that Washington worked to keep ruthless dictators, such as Juan Vicente Gómez of Venezuela and Fulgencio Batista of Cuba, in power in order to preserve U.S. economic influence; sometimes, the United States even intervened militarily. In a bid to improve relations with Latin American countries, in 1935 President Franklin D. Roosevelt promulgated the Good Neighbor policy, which rejected the use of U.S. military force in the region. To underscore his sincerity, Roosevelt ordered the withdrawal of U.S. marines from the island nation of Haiti in 1936. For the first time in thirty years, there were no U.S. occupation troops in Latin America.

Because so many Latin American nations depended for their livelihood on the export of raw materials and food products, the Great Depression of the 1930s was a disaster for the region. The total value of Latin American exports in 1930 was almost 50 percent below the figure for the previous five years. Spurred by the decline in foreign revenues, Latin American governments began to encourage the development of new industries. In some cases—the steel industry in Chile and Brazil, the oil industry in Argentina and Mexico—government investment made up for the absence of local sources of capital.

The Move to Authoritarianism

During the late nineteenth century, most governments in Latin America had been increasingly dominated by landed or military elites, who controlled the mass of the population—mostly impoverished peasants—by the blatant use of military force. This trend toward authoritarianism

MAP 25.2 Latin America in the First Half of the Twentieth Century

increased during the 1930s, as domestic instability caused by the effects of the Great Depression led to the creation of military dictatorships throughout the region. This trend was especially evident in Argentina, Brazil, and Mexico—three countries that together possessed more than half of the land and wealth of Latin America.

The political domination of the country by an elite minority often had disastrous effects. The government of Argentina, controlled by landowners who had benefited from the export of beef and wheat, was slow to recognize the growing importance of establishing a local industrial base. In 1916, Hipólito Irigoyen (1852–1933), head of the Radical Party, was elected president on a program to improve conditions for the middle and lower classes. Little was achieved, however, as the party became increasingly corrupt and drew closer to the large landowners. In 1930, the army overthrew Irigoyen's government and reestablished the power of the landed class. But their efforts to return to the previous export economy and suppress the growing influence of labor unions failed, and in 1946 General Juan Perón—claiming the support of the *descamisados* ("shirtless ones")—seized sole power (see Chapter 29).

Brazil followed a similar path. In 1889, the army overthrew the Brazilian monarchy, installed by Portugal years before, and established a republic. But it was dominated by landed elites, many of whom had grown wealthy through their ownership of coffee plantations. By 1900, three-quarters of the world's coffee was grown in Brazil. As in Argentina, the ruling oligarchy ignored the importance of establishing an urban industrial base. When the Great Depression ravaged profits from coffee exports, a wealthy rancher, Getúlio Vargas (1883–1954), seized power and ruled the country as president from 1930 to 1945. At first, Vargas sought to appease workers by declaring an eight-hour day and a minimum wage, but, influenced by the apparent success of Fascist regimes in Europe, he ruled by increasingly autocratic means and relied on a police force that used torture to silence his opponents. His industrial policy was relatively enlightened, however, and by the end of World War II, Brazil had become Latin America's major industrial power. In 1945, the army, fearing that Vargas might prolong his power illegally after calling for new elections, forced him to resign.

Mexico, in the years after World War I, was not an authoritarian state, but neither was it democratic. The Mexican Revolution at the beginning of the twentieth century had been the first significant effort in Latin American history to overturn the system of large estates and improve the living standards of the masses (see Chapter 21). Out of the political revolution emerged a relatively stable political order. The revolution, however, was democratic in form only, as the official political party, known as the Institutional Revolutionary Party (PRI), controlled the levers of power throughout society. Every six years, PRI bosses chose the party's presidential candidate, who was then dutifully elected by the people.

The situation began to change with the election of Lázaro Cárdenas (1895–1970) as president in 1934. Cárdenas won wide popularity with the peasants by ordering the redistribution of 44 million acres of land controlled by landed elites. He also won popular support by adopting a stronger stand against the United States, seizing control over the oil industry, which had hitherto been dominated by major U.S. oil companies. Alluding to the Good Neighbor policy, President Roosevelt refused to intervene, and eventually Mexico agreed to compensate U.S. oil companies for their lost property. It then set up PEMEX, a state-run organization, to run the oil industry.

Latin American Culture

During the early twentieth century, modern European artistic and literary movements began to penetrate Latin America. In major cities, such as Buenos Aires and São Paulo, wealthy elites supported avant-garde trends, but other artists returned from abroad to adapt modern techniques to their native roots.

For many artists and writers, their work provided a means of promoting the emergence of a new national essence. An example was the Mexican muralist Diego Rivera (1886–1957). Rivera had studied in Europe, where he was influenced by fresco painting in Italy. After his return to Mexico, where the government provided financial support for the painting of murals on public buildings, he began to produce a monumental style of mural art that served two purposes: to illustrate the national past by portraying Aztec legends as well as Mexican festivals and folk customs, and also to promote a political message in favor of realizing the social goals of the Mexican Revolution. Rivera's murals can be found in such diverse locations as

GETÚLIO VARGAS. Shown here is Getúlio Vargas, a rancher and lawyer who turned to politics and became president of Brazil after a military coup in 1930. Vargas's New State imitated some of the features of Fascist Italy and Nazi Germany.

RIVERA'S MURAL ART. Diego Rivera was an important figure in the development of Mexico's mural art in the 1920s and 1930s. One of Rivera's goals—to portray Mexico's past and native traditions—is evident in this mural that conveys the complexity and variety of Aztec civilization. When the Spanish arrived, they were amazed at the variety of foods and merchandise for sale in the marketplace in Tenochtitlán (present-day Mexico City).

the Ministry of Education and the Social Security Hospital in Mexico City and the chapel of the Agricultural School at Chapingo.

CONCLUSION

The turmoil brought about by World War I not only resulted in the destruction of several of the major Western empires and a redrawing of the map of Europe; it also opened the door to political and social upheavals elsewhere in the world. In the Middle East, the decline and fall of the Ottoman Empire led to the creation of a new secular Republic of Turkey. A new state of Saudi Arabia emerged in the Arabian peninsula, while Palestine became a source of tension between newly arrived Jewish settlers and longtime Muslim Palestinians.

Other parts of Asia and Africa also witnessed the rise of movements for national independence. In Africa, these movements were led by native leaders educated in Europe or the United States. In India, Gandhi and his campaign of civil disobedience played a crucial role in his country's bid to be free of British rule. Communist movements also began to emerge in Asian societies, as radical elements sought new methods of bringing about the overthrow of Western imperialism. Japan continued to follow its own path to modernization, which, although successful from an economic point of view, took a menacing turn during the 1930s.

Between 1919 and 1939, China experienced a dramatic struggle to establish a modern nation. Two dynamic political organizations—the Nationalists and the Communists—competed for legitimacy as the rightful heirs of the old order. At first, they formed an alliance in an effort to defeat their common adversaries, but cooperation ultimately turned to conflict. The Nationalists under Chiang Kai-shek emerged supreme, but Chiang found it difficult to control the remnants of the warlord regime in China, while the Great Depression undermined his efforts to build an industrial nation.

During the interwar years, the nations of Latin America faced severe economic problems because of their dependence on exports. Increasing U.S. investments in Latin America contributed to growing hostility against the powerful neighbor to the north. The Great Depression forced the region to begin developing new industries, but it also led to the rise of authoritarian governments, some of them modeled after the Fascist regimes of Italy and Germany.

By demolishing the remnants of their old civilization on the battlefields of World War I, Europeans had inadvertently encouraged the subject peoples of their vast colonial empires to begin their own movements for national independence. The process was by no means completed in the two decades following the Treaty of Versailles, but the bonds of imperial rule had been severely strained. Once Europeans began to weaken themselves in the even more destructive conflict of World War II, the hopes of African and Asian peoples for national independence and freedom could at last be realized. It is to that devastating world conflict that we must now turn.

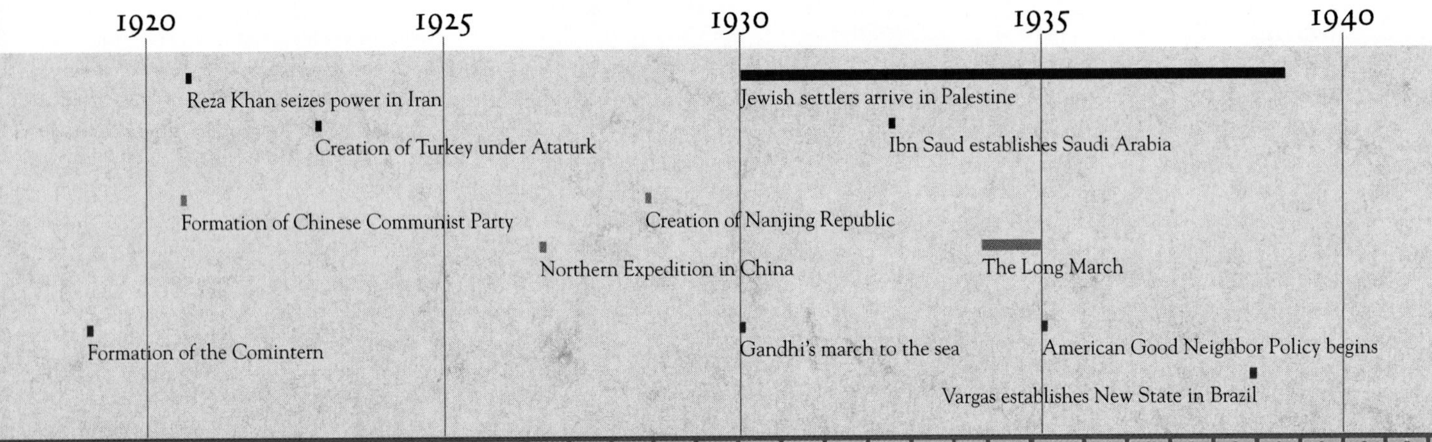

Chapter Notes

1. Vladimir I. Lenin, "The Awakening of Asia," in *The Awakening of Asia: Selected Essays* (New York, 1963–1968), p. 22.
2. Speech by Mahatma Gandhi, delivered in London in September 1931 during his visit for the first Roundtable Conference.
3. Ts'ai Yuan-p'ei, "Ta Lin Ch'in-nan Han," in *Ts'ai Yuan-p'ei Hsien-sheng Ch'uan-chi* [Collected Works of Mr. Ts'ai Yuan-p'ei] (Taipei, 1968), pp. 1057–1058.
4. Quoted in Nicholas Rowland Clifford, *Spoilt Children of Empire: Westerners in Shanghai and the Chinese Revolution of the 1920s* (Hanover, N.H., 1991), p. 93.
5. Quoted in William Theodore de Bary et al., eds., *Sources of Chinese Tradition* (New York, 1963), p. 783.
6. Lu Xun, "Diary of a Madman," in *Selected Works of Lu Hsun* (Peking, 1957), 1:20.

Suggested Readings

The classic study of nationalism in the non-Western world is R. Emerson, *From Empire to Nation* (Boston, 1960). Also see F. von der Mehden, *Religion and Nationalism in Southeast Asia* (Madison, Wis., 1963). For a recent approach, see B. Anderson, *Imagined Communities: Reflections on the Origin and Spread of Nationalism* (London, 1983). On nationalism in India, see S. Wolpert, *Congress and Indian Nationalism: The Pre-Independence Phase* (New York, 1988). Also see P. Chatterjee's interesting *The Nation and Its Fragments: Colonial and Postcolonial Histories* (Princeton, N.J., 1993).

There have been a number of studies of Mahatma Gandhi and his ideas. See, for example, J. M. Brown, *Gandhi: Prisoner of Hope* (New Haven, Conn., 1989), and the psychohistorical study by E. Erikson, *Gandhi's Truth: On the Origins of Militant Nonviolence* (New

York, 1969). Also see *All Men Are Brothers: The Life and Thought of Mahatma Gandhi as Told in His Own Words* (New York, 1960). For a study of Nehru, see S. Gopal, *Jawaharlal Nehru: A Biography*, vol. 1, *1889–1947* (Cambridge, 1976).

For a general survey of events in the Middle East in rhe interwar era, see H. M. Sachar, *The Emergence of the Middle East, 1914–1924* (New York, 1969). On modernization in Iran, see J. M. Upton, *The History of Modern Iran* (Cambridge, Mass., 1960). The role of Ataturk is examined in J. P. Balfour, *Ataturk: The Rebirth of a Nation* (London, 1964).

On the early republic in China, see L. Yu-sheng, *The Crisis of Chinese Consciousness: Radical Antitraditionalism in the May Fourth Era* (Madison, Wis., 1979). The rise of the Chinese Communist Party is discussed in B. Schwartz, *Chinese Communism and the Rise of Mao* (Cambridge, 1958), and A. Dirlik, *The Origins of Chinese Communism* (Oxford, 1989). There are a number of biographies of Mao Zedong. For a readable and informative version, see S. Schram, *Mao Tse-tung: A Political Biography* (Baltimore, 1966). Also see the same author's *The Political Thought of Mao Tse-Tung* (New York, 1966). For an inside account of the movement by a sympathetic Western journalist, see E. Snow's *Red Star Over China* (New York, 1938). The early Chiang Kai-shek period is dealt with persuasively in L. Eastman's *The Abortive Revolution: China Under Nationalist Rule, 1927–1937* (Cambridge, 1974).

For an overview of Latin American history in the 1920s and 1930s, see E. Williamson, *The Penguin History of Latin America* (Harmondsworth, 1992). On U.S.–Latin American relations, see the classic study by B. Wood, *The Making of the Good Neighbor Policy* (New York, 1960). On Argentina, Brazil, and Mexico, see D. Rock, *Argentina, 1516–1982* (London, 1986); E. B. Burns, *A History of Brazil*, 2d ed. (New York, 1980); and M. C. Meyer and W. L. Sherman, *The Course of Mexican History*, 3d ed. (New York, 1987). On Getúlio Vargas, see R. Bourne, *Getúlio Vargas of Brazil, 1883–1954: Sphinx of the Pampas* (London, 1974). On culture, see J. Franco, *The Modern Culture of Latin America: Society and the Artist* (Harmondsworth, 1970).

For a general introduction to the women's movement during this era, see S. Hughes and B. Hughes, *Women in World History*, vol. 2 (Armonk, N.Y., 1997). For a more comprehensive treatment, consult C. Johnson-Odim and M. Strobel, eds., *Restoring Women to History* (Bloomington, Ind., 1999). For collections of essays concerning African women, see C. Robertson and I. Berger, *Women and Class in Africa* (New York, 1986), and S. Stichter and J. I. Parparti, eds., *Patriarchy and Class: African Women in the Home and Workforce* (Boulder, Col., 1988). To follow the women's movement in India, see S. Tharu and K. Lalita, *Women Writing in India*, vol. 2 (New York, 1993). For Japan, see S. Sievers, *Flowers in Salt: The Beginnings of Feminist Consciousness in Modern Japan* (Stanford, Calif., 1983).

For additional reading, go to InfoTrac College Edition, your online research library at http://web1.infotrac-college.com

Enter the search term "Gandhi" using Keywords.

Enter the search terms "Mao Zedong" using the Subject Guide.

Enter the search terms "Chiang Kai-shek" using the Subject Guide.

Enter the search term "Ataturk" using Keywords.

CHAPTER

26

THE CRISIS DEEPENS: WORLD WAR II

CHAPTER OUTLINE

- THE RETREAT FROM DEMOCRACY: DICTATORIAL REGIMES
- THE PATH TO WAR
- THE COURSE OF WORLD WAR II
- THE NEW ORDER
- THE HOME FRONT
- THE AFTERMATH OF THE WAR: THE EMERGENCE OF THE COLD WAR
- CONCLUSION

FOCUS QUESTIONS

- What are the characteristics of totalitarian states, and to what degree were these characteristics present in Fascist Italy, Nazi Germany, and Stalinist Russia?
- What were the underlying causes of World War II, and what specific steps taken by Nazi Germany and Japan led to war?
- What were the main events of World War II in Europe and Asia, and what was the nature of the new orders that Germany and Japan attempted to establish in the territories they occupied?
- What were conditions like on the home front for the major belligerents in World War II?
- How did the Allies' visions of the postwar world differ, and how did these differences contribute to the emergence of the Cold War?

On February 3, 1933, only four days after he had been appointed chancellor of Germany, Adolf Hitler met secretly with Germany's leading generals. He revealed to them his desire to remove the "cancer of democracy," create a new authoritarian leadership, and forge a new domestic unity. All Germans would need to realize that "only a struggle can save us and that everything else must be subordinated to this idea." Youth especially must be trained and their wills strengthened "to fight with all means." Since Germany's living space was too small for its people, Hitler said, above all, Germany must rearm and prepare for "the conquest of new living space in the east and its ruthless Germanization." Even before he had consolidated his power, Adolf Hitler had a clear vision of his goals, and their implementation meant another war. World War II in Europe was clearly Hitler's war. Although other countries may have helped to make the war possible by not resisting Hitler's Germany earlier, it was Nazi Germany's actions that made World War II inevitable.

World War II was more than just Hitler's war, however. World War II consisted of two conflicts: one provoked by the ambitions of Germany in Europe, the other by the ambitions of Japan in Asia. By 1941, with the involvement of the United States in both wars, the two had merged into a single global conflict.

Although World War I had been described as a total war, World War II was even more so and was fought on a scale unheard of in history. Almost everyone in the warring countries was involved in one way or another: as soldiers; as workers in wartime industries; as ordinary citizens subject to invading armies, military occupation, or bombing raids; as refugees; or as victims of mass extermination. The world had never witnessed such widespread human-made death and destruction.

The Retreat from Democracy: Dictatorial Regimes

There was a close relationship between the rise of dictatorial regimes in the 1930s and the coming of World War II. The apparent triumph of liberal democracy in 1919 proved extremely short-lived. By 1939, only two major states in Europe, France and Great Britain, and a host of minor ones remained democratic. Italy and Germany had succumbed to the political movement called fascism, while Soviet Russia under Joseph Stalin moved toward a repressive totalitarian state. A host of other European states and Latin American countries as well adopted authoritarian structures of various kinds, while a militarist regime in Japan moved that country down the path of war.

The dictatorial regimes between the wars assumed both old and new forms. Dictatorship was by no means a new phenomenon, but the modern totalitarian state was. The totalitarian regimes, whose best examples can be found in Stalinist Russia and Nazi Germany, extended the functions and power of the central state far beyond what they had been in the past. The immediate origins of totalitarianism can be found in the total warfare of World War I when governments exercised controls over economic, political, and personal freedom in order to achieve victory.

The modern totalitarian state soon moved beyond the ideal of passive obedience expected in a traditional dictatorship or authoritarian monarchy. The new "total states" expected the active loyalty and commitment of their citizens to the regime's goals. They used modern mass propaganda techniques and high-speed communications to conquer the minds and hearts of their subjects. The total state aimed to control not only the economic, political, and social aspects of life, but the intellectual and cultural aspects as well. But that control also had a purpose: the active involvement of the masses in the achievement of the regime's goals, whether they be war, a socialist state, or a thousand-year Reich.

The modern totalitarian state was to be led by a single leader and single party. It ruthlessly rejected the liberal ideal of limited government power and constitutional guarantees of individual freedoms. Indeed, individual freedom was to be subordinated to the collective will of the masses, organized and determined for them by a leader or leaders. Modern technology also gave total states the ability to use unprecedented police powers to impose their wishes on their subjects.

Totalitarianism is an abstract term, and no state followed all its theoretical implications. The fascist states—Italy and Nazi Germany—as well as Stalin's Communist Russia have all been labeled totalitarian, although their regimes exhibited significant differences and met with varying degrees of success. Totalitarianism transcended traditional political labels. Fascism in Italy and Nazism in Germany grew out of extreme rightist preoccupations with nationalism and, in the case of Germany, with racism. Communism in Soviet Russia emerged out of Marxian socialism, a radical leftist program. Thus, totalitarianism could and did exist in what were perceived as extreme right-wing and extreme left-wing regimes. This fact helped bring about a new concept of the political spectrum in which the extremes were no longer seen as opposites on a linear scale, but came to be viewed as being similar to each other in at least some respects.

The Birth of Fascism

In the early 1920s, in the wake of economic turmoil, political disorder, and the general insecurity and fear stemming from World War I, Benito Mussolini burst upon the Italian scene with the first Fascist movement in Europe. Mussolini (1883–1945) began his political career as a socialist but was expelled from the socialist party after supporting Italy's entry into World War I, a position contrary to the socialist position of ardent neutrality. In 1919, Mussolini established a new political group, the *Fascio di Combattimento*, or League of Combat. It received little attention in the elections of 1919, but political stalemate in Italy's parliamentary system and strong nationalist sentiment saved Mussolini and the Fascists.

The new parliament elected in November 1919 quickly proved to be incapable of governing Italy, as the three major parties were unable to form an effective governmental coalition. Meanwhile the socialists, who had become the largest party, spoke theoretically of the need for revolution and alarmed conservatives, who quickly associated them with Bolsheviks or Communists. Thousands of industrial and agricultural strikes in 1919 and 1920 created a climate of class warfare and continual violence. In 1920 and 1921, bands of armed Fascists called *squadristi* were formed and turned loose to attack socialist offices and newspapers. Strikes by trade unionists and socialist workers and peasant leagues were broken up by force. Mussolini's Fascist movement began to gain support from middle-class industrialists fearful of working-class agitation and from large landowners, who objected to the agricultural strikes. Mussolini also perceived that Italians were angry over Italy's failure to receive more fruits of victory in the form of territorial acquisitions after World War I. By 1922, Mussolini's nationalist rhetoric and ability to play to middle-class fears of socialism, Communist revolution, and disorder were attracting even more adherents. On October 29, 1922, after Mussolini and the Fascists threatened to march on Rome if they were not given power, King Victor Emmanuel III (1900–1946) capitulated and made Mussolini prime minister of Italy.

By 1926, Mussolini had established the institutional framework for his Fascist dictatorship. Press laws gave the government the right to suspend any publications that fostered disrespect for the Catholic church, the monarchy, or the state. The prime minister was made "Head of Government," with the power to legislate by decree. A police law empowered the police to arrest and confine anybody for both nonpolitical and political crimes without due process of law. The government was given the power to dissolve political and cultural associations. In 1926, all anti-Fascist parties were outlawed. A secret police, known as the OVRA, was also established. By the end of 1926, Mussolini ruled Italy as *Il Duce*, the leader.

Mussolini conceived of the Fascist state as totalitarian: "Fascism is totalitarian, and the Fascist State, the synthesis and unity of all values, interprets, develops and gives strength to the whole life of the people."[1] He did try to create a totalitarian apparatus for police surveillance and for controlling mass communications, but this machinery was not all that effective. Police activities in Italy were never as repressive, efficient, or savage as those of Nazi Germany. Likewise, the Italian Fascists' attempt to exercise control over all forms of mass media, including newspapers, radio, and cinema, in order to use propaganda as an instrument to integrate the masses into the state failed to achieve its major goals. Most commonly, Fascist propaganda was disseminated by plastering simple slogans, such as "Mussolini is always right," on walls all over Italy.

Mussolini and the Fascists also attempted to mold Italians into a single-minded community by developing Fascist organizations. Because the secondary schools maintained considerable freedom from Fascist control, the regime relied more and more on the activities of Fascist youth organizations, known as the Young Fascists, to indoctrinate the young people of the nation in Fascist ideals. By 1939, about 6.8 million children, teenagers, and young adults of both sexes, or 66 percent of the population between eight and eighteen, were enrolled in some kind of Fascist youth group. Activities for these groups included Saturday afternoon marching drills and calisthenics, seaside and mountain summer camps, and youth contests. An underlying motif for all of these activities was the Fascist insistence on militarization. Beginning in the 1930s, all male groups were given some kind of premilitary exercises to develop discipline and provide training for war. Results were mixed. Italian teenagers, who liked neither military training nor routine discipline of any kind, simply refused to attend Fascist youth group meetings on a regular basis.

The Fascist organizations hoped to create a new Italian, who would be hardworking, physically fit, disciplined, intellectually sharp, and martially inclined. In practice, the Fascists largely reinforced traditional social attitudes in Italy, as is evident in their policies toward women. The Fascists portrayed the family as the pillar of the state and women as the basic foundation of the family. "Woman into the home" became the Fascist slogan. Women were to be homemakers and baby producers, "their natural and fundamental mission in life," according to Mussolini, who viewed population growth as an indicator of national strength. Employment outside the home was an impediment distracting from conception. "It forms an independence and consequent physical and moral habits contrary to childbearing."[2] A practical consideration also underlay the Fascist attitude toward women. Working women would compete with males for jobs in the depression economy of the 1930s. Eliminating women from the market reduced male unemployment figures.

Despite the instruments of repression, the use of propaganda, and the creation of numerous Fascist organizations, Mussolini never really achieved the degree of totalitarian control accomplished in Hitler's Germany or Stalin's Soviet Union. Mussolini and the Fascist Party never really destroyed the old power structure. Some institutions, including the armed forces and monarchy, were never absorbed into the Fascist state and mostly managed to maintain their independence. Mussolini had boasted that he would help workers and peasants, but instead he generally allied himself with the interests of

MUSSOLINI—THE IRON *DUCE*. One of Mussolini's favorite images of himself was that of the iron *Duce*—the strong leader who is always right. Consequently, he was often seen in military-style uniforms and military poses. This photograph shows Mussolini in one of his numerous uniforms with his Black Shirt bodyguards giving the Fascist salute.

industrialists and large landowners at the expense of the lower classes.

Even more indicative of Mussolini's compromise with the traditional institutions of Italy was his attempt to gain the support of the Catholic church. In the Lateran Accords of February 1929, Mussolini's regime recognized the sovereign independence of a small enclave of 109 acres within Rome, known as Vatican City, which had remained in the church's possession since the unification of Italy in 1870; in return, the papacy recognized the Italian state. The Lateran Accords also guaranteed the church a large grant of money and recognized Catholicism as the "sole religion of the state." In return, the Catholic church urged Italians to support the Fascist regime.

In all areas of Italian life under Mussolini and the Fascists, there was a noticeable dichotomy between Fascist ideals and practice. The Italian Fascists promised much but actually delivered considerably less, and they were soon overshadowed by a much more powerful Fascist movement to the north. Adolf Hitler was a great admirer of Benito Mussolini, but the German pupil soon proved to be far more adept in the use of power than his Italian teacher.

Hitler and Nazi Germany

In 1923, a small, south German rightist party known as the Nazis, led by an obscure Austrian rabble-rouser named Adolf Hitler, created a stir when it tried to seize power in southern Germany in conscious imitation of Mussolini's march on Rome in 1922. Although the attempt failed, Adolf Hitler and the Nazis achieved sudden national prominence. Within ten years, Hitler and the Nazis had taken over complete power.

Born on April 20, 1889, Adolf Hitler was the son of an Austrian customs official. He was a total failure in secondary school and eventually made his way to Vienna to become an artist. In Vienna, Hitler established the basic ideas of an ideology from which he never deviated for the rest of his life. At the core of Hitler's ideas was racism, especially his anti-Semitism. His hatred of the Jews lasted to the very end of his life. Hitler also became an extreme German nationalist who learned from the mass politics of Vienna how political parties could use propaganda and terror effectively. Finally, in his Viennese years, Hitler also came to a firm belief in the need for struggle, which he saw as the "granite foundation of the world."

HITLER'S RISE TO POWER, 1919–1933

At the end of World War I, after four years of service on the Western Front, Hitler went to Munich and decided to enter politics. Between 1919 and 1923, Hitler accomplished a great deal as a Munich politician. He joined the obscure German Workers' Party, one of a number of right-wing extreme nationalist parties in Munich. By the summer of 1921, he had assumed total control over the party, which he renamed the National Socialist German Workers' Party (NSDAP), or Nazi for short. His idea was that the party's name would distinguish the Nazis from the socialist parties while gaining support from both working-class and nationalist circles. Hitler worked assiduously to develop the party into a mass political movement with flags, party badges, uniforms, its own newspaper, and its own police force or party militia known as the SA, the *Sturmabteilung*, or Storm Troops. The SA was used to defend the party in meeting halls and break up the meetings of other parties. It added an element of force and terror to the growing Nazi movement. Hitler's own oratorical skills were largely responsible for attracting an increasing number of followers. By 1923, the party had grown from its early hundreds into a membership of 55,000 with 15,000 SA members.

Overconfident, Hitler staged an armed uprising against the government in Munich in November 1923. The Beer Hall Putsch was quickly crushed, and Hitler was sentenced to prison. During his brief stay in jail, he wrote *Mein Kampf*, an autobiographical account of his movement and its underlying ideology. Extreme German nationalism, virulent anti-Semitism, and vicious anti-communism are linked together by a Social Darwinian theory of struggle that stresses the right of superior nations to *Lebensraum* (living space) through expansion and the right of superior individuals to secure authoritarian leadership over the masses. What is perhaps most remarkable about *Mein Kampf* is its elaboration of a series of ideas that directed Hitler's actions once he took power. That others refused to take Hitler and his ideas seriously was one of his greatest advantages.

During his imprisonment, Hitler also came to the realization that the Nazis would have to come to power by constitutional means, not by overthrowing the Weimar Republic. This implied the formation of a mass political party that would actively compete for votes with the other political parties. After his release from prison, Hitler worked assiduously to build such a party. He reorganized the Nazi Party on a regional basis and expanded it to all parts of Germany. By 1929, the Nazi Party had a national party organization. It also grew from 27,000 members in 1925 to 178,000 by the end of 1929. Especially noticeable was the youthfulness of the regional, district, and branch leaders of the Nazi organization. Many were between the ages of twenty-five and thirty and were fiercely committed to Hitler because he gave them the kind of active politics they sought. Rather than democratic debate, they wanted brawls in beer halls, enthusiastic speeches, and comradeship in building a new Germany. One new, young Nazi member expressed his excitement about the party:

> For me this was the start of a completely new life. There was only one thing in the world for me and that was service in the movement. All my thoughts were centered on the movement. I could talk only politics. I was no longer aware of anything else. At the time I was a promising athlete; I was very keen on sport, and it was going to be my career. But I had to give this up too. My only interest was agitation and propaganda.[3]

Such youthful enthusiasm gave the Nazi movement the aura of a "young man's movement" and a sense of dynamism that the other parties could not match.

By 1932, the Nazi Party had 800,000 members and had become the largest party in the Reichstag. No doubt, Germany's economic difficulties were a crucial factor in the Nazi rise to power. Unemployment rose dramatically, from 4.35 million in 1931 to 6 million by the winter of 1932. The economic and psychological impact of the Great Depression made extremist parties more attractive. The Nazis were especially effective in developing modern electioneering techniques. In their election campaigns, party members pitched their themes to the needs and fears of different social groups. In working-class districts, for example, the Nazis attacked international high finance; in middle-class neighborhoods, they exploited fears of a Communist revolution and its threat to private property. At the same time that the Nazis made blatant appeals to class interests, they were denouncing conflicts of interest and maintaining that they stood above classes and parties. Hitler, in particular, claimed to stand above all differences and promised to create a new Germany free of class differences and party infighting. His appeal to national pride, national honor, and traditional militarism struck chords of emotion in his listeners.

Increasingly, the right-wing elites of Germany—the industrial magnates, landed aristocrats, military establishment, and higher bureaucrats—came to see Hitler as the man who had the mass support to establish a right-wing, authoritarian regime that would save Germany and their privileged positions from a Communist takeover. Under pressure, since the Nazi Party had the largest share of seats in the Reichstag, President Paul von Hindenburg agreed to allow Hitler to become chancellor (on January 30, 1933) and create a new government.

Within two months, Hitler had laid the foundations for the Nazis' complete control over Germany. On the day after a fire broke out in the Reichstag building (February 27), supposedly caused by the Communists, Hitler convinced President Hindenburg to issue a decree that gave the government emergency powers. It suspended all basic rights for the full duration of the emergency and thus enabled the Nazis to arrest and imprison anyone without redress. The crowning step in Hitler's "legal seizure" of power came on March 23, when the Reichstag passed the Enabling Act by a two-thirds vote. This legislation, which empowered the government to dispense with constitutional forms for four years while it issued laws that dealt with the country's problems, provided the legal basis for Hitler's subsequent acts. He no longer needed either the Reichstag or President Hindenburg. In effect, Hitler became a dictator appointed by the parliamentary body itself.

With their new source of power, the Nazis acted quickly to enforce *Gleichschaltung*, or the coordination of all institutions under Nazi control. The civil service was purged of Jews and democratic elements, concentration camps were established for opponents of the new regime, the autonomy of the federal states was eliminated, trade unions were dissolved, and all political parties except the Nazis were abolished. By the end of the summer of 1933, within seven months of being appointed chancellor, Hitler and the Nazis had established the foundations for a totalitarian state. When Hindenburg died on August 2, 1934, the office of Reich president was abolished, and Hitler became sole ruler of Germany. Public officials and soldiers were all required to take a personal oath of loyalty to Hitler as the "Führer of the German Reich and people."

THE NAZI STATE, 1933–1939

Having smashed the parliamentary state, Hitler now felt the real task was at hand: to develop the "total state." Hitler's aims had not been simply power for power's sake or a tyranny based on personal power. He had larger ideological goals. The development of an Aryan racial state that would dominate Europe and possibly the world for generations to come required a movement in which the German people would be actively involved, not passively cowed by force. Hitler stated:

> We must develop organizations in which an individual's entire life can take place. Then every activity and every need of every individual will be regulated by the collectivity represented by the party. There is no longer any arbitrary will; there are no longer any free realms in which the individual belongs to himself. . . . The time of personal happiness is over.[4]

The Nazis pursued the creation of this totalitarian state in a variety of ways.

Mass demonstrations and spectacles were employed to integrate the German nation into a collective fellowship and to mobilize it as an instrument for Hitler's policies (see the box on p. 778). These mass demonstrations, especially the Nuremberg party rallies that were held every

THE NAZI MASS SPECTACLE. Hitler and the Nazis made clever use of mass spectacles to rally the German people behind the Nazi regime. These mass demonstrations evoked intense enthusiasm, as is evident in this photograph of Hitler arriving at the Bückeberg near Hamelin for the Harvest Festival in 1937. Almost one million people were present for the celebration.

PROPAGANDA AND MASS MEETINGS IN NAZI GERMANY

Propaganda and mass rallies were two of the chief instruments that Hitler used to prepare the German people for the tasks he set before them. In the first selection, taken from Mein Kampf, *Hitler explains the psychological importance of mass meetings in creating support for a political movement. In the second excerpt, taken from his speech to a crowd at Nuremberg, he describes the kind of mystical bond he hoped to create through his mass rallies.*

ADOLF HITLER, *MEIN KAMPF*

The mass meeting is also necessary for the reason that in it the individual, who at first, while becoming a supporter of a young movement, feels lonely and easily succumbs to the fear of being alone, for the first time gets the picture of a larger community, which in most people has a strengthening, encouraging effect. . . . When from his little workshop or big factory, in which he feels very small, he steps for the first time into a mass meeting and has thousands and thousands of people of the same opinions around him, when, as a seeker, he is swept away by three or four thousand others into the mighty effect of suggestive intoxication and enthusiasm, when the visible success and agreement of thousands confirm to him the rightness of the new doctrine and for the first time arouse doubt in the truth of his previous conviction—then he himself has succumbed to the magic influence of what we designate as "mass suggestion." The will, the longing, and also the power of thousands are accumulated in every individual. The man who enters such a meeting doubting and wavering leaves it inwardly reinforced: he has become a link in the community.

ADOLF HITLER, SPEECH AT THE NUREMBERG PARTY RALLY, 1936

Do we not feel once again in this hour the miracle that brought us together? Once you heard the voice of a man, and it struck deep into your hearts; it awakened you, and you followed this voice. Year after year you went after it, though him who had spoken you never even saw. You heard only a voice, and you followed it. When we meet each other here, the wonder of our coming together fills us all. Not everyone of you sees me, and I do not see everyone of you. But I feel you, and you feel me. It is the belief in our people that has made us small men great, that has made us poor men rich, that has made brave and courageous men out of us wavering, spiritless, timid folk; this belief made us see our road when we were astray; it joined us together into one whole! . . . You come, that . . . you may, once in a while, gain the feeling that now we are together; we are with him and he with us, and we are now Germany!

September, combined the symbolism of a religious service with the merriment of a popular amusement. They had great appeal and usually evoked mass enthusiasm and excitement.

Some features of the state apparatus of Hitler's "total state" seem contradictory. One usually thinks of Nazi Germany as having an all-powerful government that maintained absolute control and order. In truth, Nazi Germany was the scene of almost constant personal and institutional conflict, which resulted in administrative chaos. In matters such as foreign policy, education, and economics, parallel government and party bureaucracies competed with each other over spheres of influence. Incessant struggle characterized relationships within the party, within the state, and between party and state. Some historians assume that Hitler's aversion to making decisions resulted in the chaos that subverted his own authority and made him a "weak dictator," while others maintain that Hitler deliberately created this institutional confusion. By fostering rivalry within the party and between party and state, he would be the ultimate decision maker and absolute ruler.

In the economic sphere, Hitler and the Nazis also established control. Although the regime pursued the use of public works projects and "pump-priming" grants to private construction firms to foster employment and end the depression, there is little doubt that rearmament contributed far more to solving the unemployment problem. Unemployment, which had stood at 6 million in 1932, dropped to 2.6 million in 1934 and less than 500,000 in 1937. The regime claimed full credit for solving Germany's economic woes, and this was an important factor in convincing many Germans to accept the new regime, despite its excesses.

For its enemies, the Nazi total state had its instruments of terror and repression. Especially important was the SS. Originally created as Hitler's personal bodyguard, the SS, under the direction of Heinrich Himmler (1900–1945), came to control all of the regular and secret police forces. Himmler and the SS functioned on the basis of two principles: terror and ideology. Terror included the instruments of repression and murder: the secret police, criminal police, concentration camps, and later the execution squads and death camps for the extermination of the Jews. For Himmler, the SS was a crusading order whose primary goal was to further the Aryan master race. SS members, who constituted a carefully chosen elite, were thoroughly indoctrinated in racial ideology.

Other institutions, such as the Catholic and Protestant churches, primary and secondary schools, and universities, were also brought under the control of the Nazi totalitarian state. Nazi professional organizations and leagues were formed for civil servants, teachers, women, farmers, doctors, and lawyers. Since the early indoctrination of youth would create the foundation for a strong totalitarian state for the future, youth organizations—the *Hitler Jugend* (Hitler Youth) and its female counterpart, the *Bund deutscher Mädel* (League of German Maidens)—were given special attention. The oath required of Hitler Youth members demonstrates the degree of dedication expected of youth in the Nazi state: "In the presence of this blood banner, which represents our Führer, I swear to devote all my energies and my strength to the savior of our country, Adolf Hitler. I am willing and ready to give up my life for him, so help me God."

The creation of the Nazi total state also had an impact on women. The Nazi attitude toward women was largely determined by ideological considerations. Women played a crucial role in the Aryan racial state as bearers of the children who would bring about the triumph of the Aryan race. To the Nazis, the differences between men and women were quite natural. Men were warriors and political leaders, while women were destined to be wives and mothers. By maintaining this clear distinction, each could best serve to "maintain the whole community."

Nazi ideas determined employment opportunities for women. The Nazis hoped to drive women out of certain areas of the labor market, including heavy industry or other jobs that might hinder women from bearing healthy children. Certain professions, including university teaching, medicine, and law, were also considered inappropriate for women, especially married women. Instead the Nazis encouraged women to pursue professional occupations that had direct practical application, such as social work and nursing. In addition to restrictive legislation against females, the Nazi regime pushed its campaign against working women with such poster slogans as "Get ahold of pots and pans and broom and you'll sooner find a groom!"

The Nazi total state was intended to be an Aryan racial state. From its beginning, the Nazi Party reflected the strong anti-Semitic beliefs of Adolf Hitler. Once in power, the Nazis translated anti-Semitic ideas into anti-Semitic policies. In September 1935, the Nazis announced new racial laws at the annual party rally in Nuremberg. These "Nuremberg laws" excluded German Jews from German citizenship and forbade marriages and extramarital relations between Jews and German citizens. The "Nuremberg laws" essentially separated Jews from the Germans politically, socially, and legally and were the natural extension of Hitler's stress upon the creation of a pure Aryan race.

Another, considerably more violent phase of anti-Jewish activity took place in 1938 and 1939. It was initiated on November 9–10, 1938, the infamous *Kristallnacht*, or night of shattered glass. The assassination of a third secretary in the German embassy in Paris became the occasion for a Nazi-led destructive rampage against the Jews in which synagogues were burned, 7,000 Jewish businesses were destroyed, and at least one hundred Jews were killed. Moreover, 20,000 Jewish males were rounded up and sent to concentration camps. *Kristallnacht* also led to further drastic steps. Jews were barred from all public buildings and prohibited from owning, managing, or working in any retail store. Finally, under the direction of the SS, Jews were encouraged to "emigrate from Germany." After the outbreak of World War II, the policy of emigration was replaced by a more gruesome one.

CHRONOLOGY

THE TOTALITARIAN STATES

Fascist Italy	
Creation of *Fascio di Combattimento*	1919
Squadristi violence	1920–1921
Mussolini is made prime minister	1922 (October 29)
Establishment of Fascist dictatorship	1925–1926
Lateran Accords with Catholic church	1929
Nazi Germany	
Hitler as Munich politician	1919–1923
Beer Hall Putsch	1923
Hitler is made chancellor	1933 (January 30)
Reichstag fire	1933 (February 27)
Enabling Act	1933 (March 23)
Hindenburg dies; Hitler as sole ruler	1934 (August 2)
Nuremberg laws	1935
Kristallnacht	1938 (November 9–10)
The Soviet Union	
First five-year plan begins	1928
Stalin's dictatorship is established	1929
Stalin's purge	1936–1938

The Stalinist Era in the Soviet Union

The Stalinist era marked the beginning of an economic, social, and political revolution in Russia that was more sweeping in its results than the revolutions of 1917. Joseph Stalin made a significant shift in economic policy in 1928 when he launched his first five-year plan. Its real goal was

THE FORMATION OF COLLECTIVE FARMS

Accompanying the rapid industrialization of the Soviet Union was the collectivization of agriculture, a feat that involved nothing less than transforming Russia's 26 million family farms into 250,000 collective farms (kolkhozes). This selection provides a firsthand account of how the process worked.

MAX BELOV, *THE HISTORY OF A COLLECTIVE FARM*

General collectivization in our village was brought about in the following manner: Two representatives of the [Communist] Party arrived in the village. All the inhabitants were summoned by the ringing of the church bell to a meeting at which the policy of general collectivization was announced. . . . The upshot was that although the meeting lasted two days, from the viewpoint of the Party representatives nothing was accomplished.

After this setback the Party representatives divided the village into two sections and worked each one separately. Two more officials were sent to reinforce the first two. A meeting of our section of the village was held in a stable which had previously belonged to a kulak. The meeting dragged on until dark. Suddenly someone threw a brick at the lamp, and in the dark the peasants began to beat the Party representatives, who jumped out the window and escaped from the village barely alive. The following day seven people were arrested. The militia was called in and stayed in the village until the peasants, realizing their helplessness, calmed down. . . .

By the end of 1930 there were two kolkhozes in our village. Though at first these collectives embraced at most only 70 percent of the peasant households, in the months that followed they gradually absorbed more and more of them.

In these kolkhozes the great bulk of the land was held and worked communally, but each peasant household owned a house of some sort, a small plot of ground and perhaps some livestock. All the members of the kolkhoz were required to work on the kolkhoz a certain number of days each month; the rest of the time they were allowed to work on their own holdings. They derived their income partly from what they grew on their garden strips and partly from their work in the kolkhoz.

When the harvest was over, and after the farm had met its obligations to the state and to various special funds (for insurance, seed, etc.) and had sold on the market whatever undesignated produce was left, the remaining produce and the farm's monetary income were divided among the kolkhoz members according to the number of "labor days" each one had contributed to the farm's work. . . . It was in 1930 that the kolkhoz members first received their portions out of the "communal kettle." After they had received their earnings, at the rate of 1 kilogram of grain and 55 kopecks per labor day, one of them remarked, "You will live, but you will be very, very thin."

In the spring of 1931 a tractor worked the fields of the kolkhoz for the first time. The tractor was "capable of plowing every kind of hard soil and virgin sod," as Party representatives told us at the meeting in celebration of its arrival. The peasants did not then know that these "steel horses" would carry away a good part of the harvest in return for their work. . . .

By late 1932 more than 80 percent of the peasant households . . . had been collectivized. . . . That year the peasants harvested a good crop and had hopes that the calculations would work out to their advantage and would help strengthen them economically. These hopes were in vain. The kolkhoz workers received only 200 grams of flour per labor day for the first half of the year; the remaining grain, including the seed fund, was taken by the government. The peasants were told that industrialization of the country, then in full swing, demanded grain and sacrifices from them.

---

nothing less than the transformation of Russia from an agricultural into an industrial country virtually overnight. Instead of consumer goods, the first five-year plan emphasized maximum production of capital goods and armaments and succeeded in quadrupling the production of heavy machinery and doubling oil production. Between 1928 and 1937, during the first two five-year plans, steel production increased from 4 to 18 million tons per year, while hard coal output went from 36 to 128 million tons. At the same time, new industrial cities, located near iron ore and coal deposits, sprang up overnight in the Urals and Siberia.

The social and political costs of industrialization were enormous. Little provision was made for absorbing the expanded labor force into the cities. While the industrial labor force increased by millions between 1932 and 1940, total investment in housing actually declined after 1929, with the result that millions of workers and their families lived in pitiful conditions. Real wages in industry also declined by 43 percent between 1928 and 1940, while strict laws limited workers' freedom of movement. To inspire and pacify the workers, government propaganda stressed the need for sacrifice to create the new socialist state.

Rapid industrialization was accompanied by an equally rapid collectivization of agriculture. Its goal was to eliminate private farms and push people into collective farms (see the box above). Strong resistance from peasants, who hoarded crops and killed livestock, only led Stalin to step up the program. By 1930, 10 million peasant households had been collectivized; by 1934, Russia's 26 million family farms had been collectivized into 250,000 units. This was done at tremendous cost, as the hoarding of food and the slaughter of livestock produced widespread famine. Stalin himself is supposed to have told Winston Churchill during World War II that 10 million peasants died in the artificially created famines of 1932 and 1933. The only concession Stalin made to the peasants was that each collective farm worker was allowed to have one tiny, privately owned garden plot.

Stalin's program of rapid industrialization entailed other costs as well. To achieve his goals, Stalin strengthened the Communist Party bureaucracy under his control. Those who resisted were sent into forced labor camps in Siberia. Stalin's desire for sole control of decision making also led to purges of the Old Bolsheviks (people who had joined the party before the 1917 revolution). Between 1936 and 1938, the most prominent Old Bolsheviks were put on trial and condemned to death. During this same time, Stalin undertook a purge of army officers, diplomats, union officials, party members, intellectuals, and numerous ordinary citizens. Estimates are that eight million Russians were arrested; millions were sent to Siberian forced labor camps, from which they never returned.

The Stalinist era also reversed much of the permissive social legislation of the early 1920s. Advocating complete equality of rights for women, the Communists had made divorce and abortion easy to obtain while also encouraging women to work outside the home and liberate themselves sexually. After Stalin came to power, the family was praised as a miniature collective in which parents were responsible for inculcating values of duty, discipline, and hard work. Abortion was outlawed, while divorced fathers who did not support their children were fined heavily. The new divorce law of June 1936 imposed fines for repeated divorces, and homosexuality was declared a criminal activity. The regime now praised motherhood and urged women to have large families as a patriotic duty. But by this time many Soviet women worked in factories and spent many additional hours in line waiting to purchase increasingly scarce consumer goods. There was no dramatic increase in the birthrate.

The Rise of Militarism in Japan

The rise of militarism in Japan resulted not from a seizure of power by a new political party, but from the growing influence of militant forces at the top of the political hierarchy. In the early 1930s, the growing confrontation with China in Manchuria, combined with the onset of the Great Depression, brought an end to the fragile stability of the immediate postwar years. The depression had a disastrous effect on Japan. The value of Japanese exports dropped by 50 percent from 1929 to 1931, and wages dropped nearly as much. Hardest hit were the farmers, as the price of rice and other staple food crops plummeted.

During the early 1930s, civilian cabinets managed to cope with the economic challenges presented by the depression. By abandoning the gold standard, Prime Minister Inukai Tsuyoshi was able to lower the price of Japanese goods on the world market, and exports climbed back to earlier levels. But the political parties were no longer

STALIN SIGNS A DEATH WARRANT. Terror played an important role in the totalitarian system established by Joseph Stalin. In this photograph, Stalin is shown signing what is supposedly a death warrant in 1933. As the terror increased in the late 1930s, Stalin signed such lists every day.

able to stem the growing influence of militant nationalist elements.

In May 1932, Inukai Tsuyoshi was assassinated by right-wing extremists. He was succeeded by a moderate, Admiral Saito Makoto, but extremist patriotic societies composed of ultranationalists began to terrorize opponents, assassinating businessmen and public figures identified with the Shidehara policy of conciliation toward the outside world. Some, like the publicist Kita Ikki, were convinced that the parliamentary system had been corrupted by materialism and Western values and should be replaced by a system that would return to traditional Japanese values and imperial authority. His message, "Asia for the Asians," had not won widespread support during the relatively prosperous 1920s but increased in popularity after the Great Depression, which convinced many Japanese that capitalism was unsuitable for Japan.

During the mid-1930s, the influence of the military and extreme nationalists over the government steadily increased. Minorities and left-wing elements were persecuted, and moderates were intimidated into silence. Terrorists tried for their part in assassination attempts portrayed themselves as selfless patriots and received light sentences. Japan continued to hold national elections, and moderate candidates continued to receive substantial popular support, but the cabinets were dominated by the military or advocates of Japanese expansionism. In February 1936, junior army officers led a coup, briefly occupying the Diet building and other key government installations in Tokyo and assassinating several members of the cabinet. The ringleaders were quickly tried and convicted of treason, but under conditions that further strengthened the influence of the military.

The Path to War

Only twenty years after the war to end war, the world plunged back into the nightmare of total war. The efforts at collective security in the 1920s—the League of Nations, the attempts at disarmament, the pacts and treaties—all proved meaningless in view of the growth of Nazi Germany and the rise of Japan.

The Path to War in Europe

World War II in Europe had its beginnings in the ideas of Adolf Hitler, who believed that only the Aryans were capable of building a great civilization. But to Hitler, the Germans (the leading group of Aryans) were threatened from the east by a large mass of inferior peoples, the Slavs, who had learned to use German weapons and technology. Germany needed more land to support a larger population and be a great power. Already in the 1920s, in the second volume of *Mein Kampf*, Hitler had indicated where a National Socialist regime would find this land: "And so we National Socialists . . . take up where we broke off six hundred years ago. We stop the endless German movement to the south and west, and turn our gaze toward the land in the east. . . . If we speak of soil in Europe today, we can primarily have in mind only Russia and her vassal border states."[5] Once Russia had been conquered, its land could be resettled by German peasants while the Slavic population could be used as slave labor to build the Aryan racial state that would dominate Europe for a thousand years. Hitler's conclusion was apparent: Germany must prepare for its inevitable war with the Soviet Union. Hitler's ideas were by no means secret. He had spelled them out in *Mein Kampf*, a book readily available to anyone who wished to read it.

When Hitler became chancellor on January 30, 1933, Germany's situation in Europe seemed weak. The Versailles treaty had created a demilitarized zone on Germany's western border that would allow the French to move into the heavily industrialized parts of Germany in the event of war. To Germany's east, the smaller states, such as Poland and Czechoslovakia, had defensive treaties with France. The Versailles treaty had also limited Germany's army to 100,000 troops with no air force and only a small navy.

Posing as the man of peace in his public speeches, Hitler emphasized that Germany wished only to revise the unfair provisions of Versailles by peaceful means and achieve Germany's rightful place among the European states. On March 9, 1935, he announced the creation of a new air force and, one week later, the introduction of a military draft that would expand Germany's army from 100,000 to 550,000 troops. Hitler's unilateral repudiation of the Versailles treaty brought a swift reaction, as France, Great Britain, and Italy condemned Germany's action and warned against future aggressive steps. But nothing concrete was done.

On March 7, 1936, buoyed by his conviction that the Western democracies had no intention of using force to maintain the Treaty of Versailles, Hitler sent German troops into the demilitarized Rhineland. According to the Versailles treaty, the French had the right to use force against any violation of the demilitarized Rhineland. But France would not act without British support, and the British viewed the occupation of German territory by German troops as reasonable action by a dissatisfied power. The London *Times* noted that the Germans were only "going into their own back garden."

Meanwhile, Hitler gained new allies. In October 1935, Benito Mussolini had committed Fascist Italy to imperial expansion by invading Ethiopia. Angered by French and British opposition to his invasion, Mussolini welcomed Hitler's support and began to draw closer to the German dictator he had once called a buffoon. The joint intervention of Germany and Italy on behalf of General Francisco Franco in the Spanish Civil War in 1936 also drew the two nations closer together. In October 1936, Mussolini and Hitler concluded an agreement that recognized their common political and economic interests, and one month later, Mussolini referred publicly to the new Rome-Berlin Axis. Also in November, Germany and Japan (the rising military power in the Far East) concluded the Anti-Comintern Pact and agreed to maintain a common front against communism.

By the end of 1936, Hitler and Nazi Germany had achieved a "diplomatic revolution" in Europe. The Treaty of Versailles had been virtually scrapped, and Germany was once more a "World Power," as Hitler proclaimed. Hitler was convinced that neither the French nor the British would provide much opposition to his plans and decided in 1938 to move on Austria. By threatening Austria with invasion, Hitler coerced the Austrian chancellor into putting Austrian Nazis in charge of the government. The new government promptly invited German troops to enter Austria and assist in maintaining law and order. One day later, on March 13, 1938, after his triumphal return to his native land, Hitler formally annexed Austria to Germany. Great Britain's ready acknowledgment of Hitler's action only increased the German dictator's contempt for Western weakness.

The annexation of Austria improved Germany's strategic position in central Europe and put Germany in position for Hitler's next objective—the destruction of Czechoslovakia. This goal might have seemed unrealistic since democratic Czechoslovakia was quite prepared to defend itself and was well supported by pacts with France and the Soviet Union. Hitler believed, however, that France and Britain would not use force to defend Czechoslovakia.

He was right again. On September 15, 1938, Hitler demanded the cession of the Sudetenland (an area in northwestern Czechoslovakia that was inhabited largely by ethnic Germans) to Germany and expressed his willingness to risk "world war" to achieve his objective. Instead of objecting, the British, French, Germans, and Italians—at a hastily arranged conference at Munich—reached an agreement that essentially met all of Hitler's demands. German troops were allowed to occupy the Sudetenland as the Czechs, abandoned by their Western allies, stood by helplessly. The Munich Conference was the high point of Western appeasement of Hitler. When Neville Chamberlain, the British prime minister, returned to England from Munich, he boasted that the Munich agreement meant "peace for our time." Hitler had promised Chamberlain that he had made his last demand. Like scores of German politicians before him, Chamberlain had believed Hitler's promises (see the box on p. 784).

In fact, Munich confirmed Hitler's perception that the Western democracies were weak and would not fight. Increasingly, Hitler was convinced of his own infallibility, and he had by no means been satisfied at Munich. In March 1939, Hitler occupied the Czech lands (Bohemia and Moravia) while the Slovaks, with his encouragement, declared their independence of the Czechs and became a puppet state (Slovakia) of Nazi Germany. On the evening of March 15, 1939, Hitler triumphantly declared in Prague that he would be known as the greatest German of them all.

At last, the Western states reacted vigorously to the Nazi threat. Hitler's naked aggression had made clear that

HITLER ENTERS THE SUDETENLAND. The Sudetenland was an area of Czechoslovakia inhabited by 3.5 million ethnic Germans. The Munich Conference allowed Germany to occupy the Sudetenland. This picture shows Hitler and his entourage arriving at Eger (now Cheb) in October 1938 to the cheers of an enthusiastic crowd.

THE MUNICH CONFERENCE

At the Munich Conference, the leaders of France and Great Britain capitulated to Hitler's demands on Czechoslovakia. While the British prime minister, Neville Chamberlain, defended his actions at Munich as necessary for peace, another British statesman, Winston Churchill, characterized the settlement at Munich as "a disaster of the first magnitude."

WINSTON CHURCHILL, SPEECH TO THE HOUSE OF COMMONS (OCTOBER 5, 1938)

I will begin by saying what everybody would like to ignore or forget but which must nevertheless be stated, namely, that we have sustained a total and unmitigated defeat, and that France has suffered even more than we have. . . . The utmost my right honorable Friend the Prime Minister . . . has been able to gain for Czechoslovakia and in the matters which were in dispute has been that the German dictator, instead of snatching his victuals from the table, has been content to have them served to him course by course. . . . And I will say this, that I believe the Czechs, left to themselves and told they were going to get no help from the Western Powers, would have been able to make better terms than they have got. . . .

We are in the presence of a disaster of the first magnitude which has befallen Great Britain and France. Do not let us blind ourselves to that. . . .

And do not suppose that this is the end. This is only the beginning of the reckoning. This is only the first sip, the first foretaste of a bitter cup which will be proffered to us year by year unless by a supreme recovery of moral health and martial vigor, we arise again and take our stand for freedom as in the olden time.

NEVILLE CHAMBERLAIN, SPEECH TO THE HOUSE OF COMMONS (OCTOBER 6, 1938)

That is my answer to those who say that we should have told Germany weeks ago that, if her army crossed the border of Czechoslovakia, we should be at war with her. We had no treaty obligations and no legal obligations to Czechoslovakia. . . . When we were convinced, as we became convinced, that nothing any longer would keep the Sudetenland within the Czechoslovakian State, we urged the Czech Government as strongly as we could to agree to the cession of territory, and to agree promptly. . . . It was a hard decision for anyone who loved his country to take, but to accuse us of having by that advice betrayed the Czechoslovakian State is simply preposterous. What we did was to save her from annihilation and give her a chance of new life as a new State, which involves the loss of territory and fortifications, but may perhaps enable her to enjoy in the future and develop a national existence under a neutrality and security comparable to that which we see in Switzerland today. Therefore, I think the Government deserve the approval of this House for their conduct of affairs in this recent crisis, which has saved Czechoslovakia from destruction and Europe from Armageddon.

his promises were utterly worthless. When he began to demand the return of Danzig (which had been made a free city by the Treaty of Versailles to serve as a seaport for Poland) to Germany, Britain recognized the danger and offered to protect Poland in the event of war. At the same time, both France and Britain realized that only the Soviet Union was powerful enough to help contain Nazi aggression and began political and military negotiations with Joseph Stalin and the Soviets. Their distrust of Soviet communism, however, made an alliance unlikely.

Meanwhile, Hitler pressed on in the belief that Britain and France would not really fight over Poland. To preclude an alliance between the western European states and the Soviet Union, which would create the danger of a two-front war, Hitler, ever the opportunist, negotiated his own nonaggression pact with Stalin and shocked the world with its announcement, on August 23, 1939. The treaty with the Soviet Union gave Hitler the freedom to attack Poland. He told his generals: "Now Poland is in the position in which I wanted her . . . I am only afraid that at the last moment some swine or other will yet submit to me a plan for mediation."[6] He need not have worried. On September 1, German forces invaded Poland; two days later, Britain and France declared war on Germany. Europe was again at war.

The Path to War in Asia

In September 1931, on the pretext that the Chinese had attacked a Japanese railway near Mukden (the "Mukden incident" had actually been carried out by Japanese saboteurs), Japanese military units seized Manchuria. Japanese officials in Tokyo were divided over the wisdom of the takeover, but the moderates were unable to control the army. Eventually, worldwide protests against the Japanese action led the League of Nations to send an investigative commission to Manchuria. When the commission issued a report condemning the seizure, Japan withdrew from the league. Over the next several years, the Japanese consolidated their hold on Manchuria, renaming it Manchukuo and placing it under the titular authority of the former Chinese emperor and now Japanese puppet Henry Pu Yi. Japan now began to expand into northern China.

Not all politicians in Tokyo agreed with this aggressive policy, but right-wing terrorists assassinated some of the key critics and intimidated others into silence. By the mid-1930s, militants connected with the government and the armed forces were effectively in control of Japanese politics. The United States refused to recognize the Japanese takeover of Manchuria but was unwilling to threaten the use of force. Instead the Americans attempted to appease Japan in the hope of encouraging Japanese moderates. As a senior U.S. diplomat with long experience in Asia warned in a memorandum to the president:

> Utter defeat of Japan would be no blessing to the Far East or to the world. It would merely create a new set of stresses, and substitute for Japan the USSR as the successor to Imperial Russia—as a contestant (and at least an equally unscrupulous and dangerous one) for the mastery of the East. Nobody except perhaps Russia would gain from our victory in such a war."[7]

For the moment, the prime victim of Japanese aggression was China. Chiang Kai-shek attempted to avoid a confrontation with Japan so that he could deal with the Communists, whom he considered the greater threat. When clashes between Chinese and Japanese troops broke out, he sought to appease the Japanese by granting them the authority to administer areas in northern China. But as Japan moved steadily southward, popular protests in Chinese cities against Japanese aggression intensified. In December 1936, Chiang was briefly kidnapped by military forces commanded by General Zhang Xueliang, who compelled him to end his military efforts against the Communists in Yan'an and form a new united front against the Japanese. After Chinese and Japanese forces clashed at Marco Polo Bridge, south of Beijing, in July 1937, China refused to apologize and hostilities spread.

Japan had not planned to declare war on China, but neither side would compromise, and the 1937 incident eventually turned into a major conflict. The Japanese advanced up the Yangtze valley and seized the Chinese capital of Nanjing in December, but Chiang Kai-shek refused to capitulate and moved his government upriver to Hankou. When the Japanese seized that city, he moved on to Chongqing, in remote Sichuan province. Japanese strategists had hoped to force Chiang to join a new Japanese-dominated New Order in East Asia, comprising Japan, Manchuria, and China. This was part of a larger plan to seize Soviet Siberia with its rich resources and create a new "Monroe Doctrine for Asia," in which Japan would guide its Asian neighbors on the path to development and prosperity (see the box on p. 786). After all, who better to instruct Asian societies on modernization than the one Asian country that had already achieved it?

During the late 1930s, Japan began to cooperate with Nazi Germany on the assumption that the two countries would ultimately launch a joint attack on the Soviet Union and divide up its resources between them. But when Germany surprised the world by signing a nonaggression pact with the Soviets in August 1939, Japanese strategists were compelled to reevaluate their long-term objectives. Japan was not strong enough to defeat the Soviet Union alone, as a small but bitter border war along

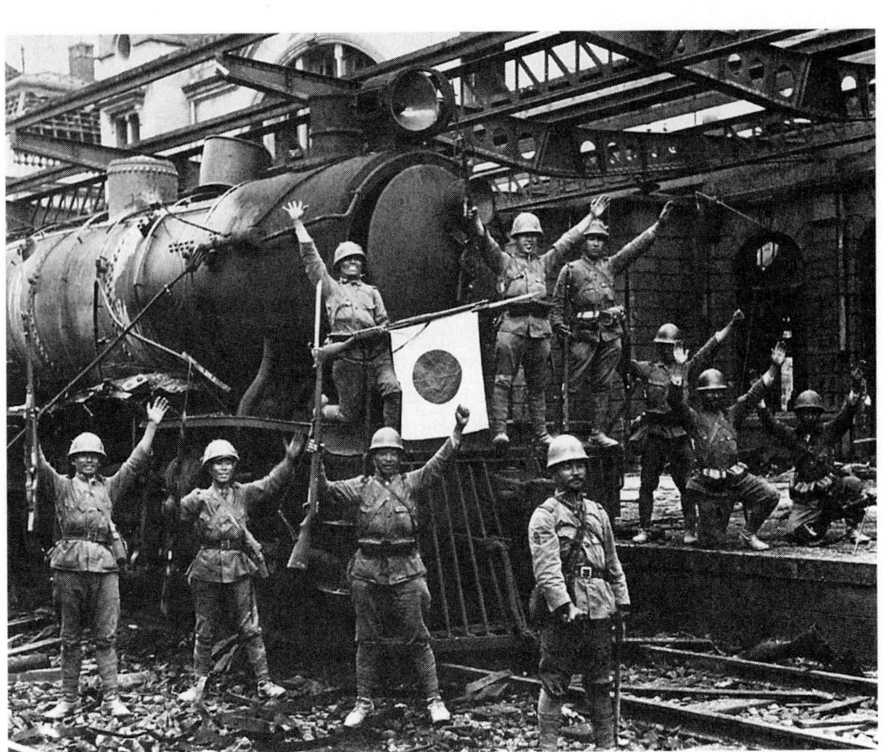

A JAPANESE VICTORY IN CHINA. After consolidating its authority over Manchuria, Japan began to expand into northern China. Direct hostilities between Japanese and Chinese forces began in 1937. By 1939, Japan had conquered most of eastern China. This photograph shows victorious Japanese soldiers amid the ruins of the railway station in Hankou, which became China's temporary capital after the fall of Nanjing.

JAPAN'S JUSTIFICATION FOR EXPANSION

Advocates of Japanese expansion justified their proposals by claiming both economic necessity and moral imperatives. Note the familiar combination of motives in this passage written by an extremist military leader in the late 1930s.

HASHIMOTO KINGORO, THE NEED FOR EMIGRATION AND EXPANSION

We have already said that there are only three ways left to Japan to escape from the pressure of surplus population. We are like a great crowd of people packed into a small and narrow room, and there are only three doors through which we might escape, namely emigration, advance into world markets, and expansion of territory. The first door, emigration, has been barred to us by the anti-Japanese immigration policies of other countries. The second door, advance into world markets, is being pushed shut by tariff barriers and the abrogation of commercial treaties. What should Japan do when two of the three doors have been closed against her?

It is quite natural that Japan should rush upon the last remaining door.

It may sound dangerous when we speak of territorial expansion, but the territorial expansion of which we speak does not in any sense of the word involve the occupation of the possessions of other countries, the planting of the Japanese flag thereon, and the declaration of their annexation to Japan. It is just that since the Powers have suppressed the circulation of Japanese materials and merchandise abroad, we are looking for some place overseas where Japanese capital, Japanese skills and Japanese labor can have free play, free from the oppression of the white race.

We would be satisfied with just this much. What moral right do the world powers who have themselves closed to us the two doors of emigration and advance into world markets have to criticize Japan's attempt to rush out of the third and last door?

If they do not approve of this, they should open the door which they have closed against us and permit the free movement overseas of Japanese emigrants and merchandise. . . .

At the time of the Manchurian incident, the entire world joined in criticism of Japan. They said that Japan was an untrustworthy nation. They said that she had recklessly brought cannon and machine guns into Manchuria, which was the territory of another country, flown airplanes over it, and finally occupied it. But the military action taken by Japan was not in the least a selfish one. Moreover, we do not recall ever having taken so much as an inch of territory belonging to another nation. The result of this incident was the establishment of the splendid new nation of Manchuria. The Powers are still discussing whether or not to recognize this new nation, but regardless of whether or not other nations recognize her, the Manchurian empire has already been established, and now, seven years after its creation, the empire is further consolidating its foundations with the aid of its friend, Japan.

And if it is still protested that our actions in Manchuria were excessively violent, we may wish to ask the white race just which country it was that sent warships and troops to India, South Africa, and Australia and slaughtered innocent natives, bound their hands and feet with iron chains, lashed their backs with iron whips, proclaimed these territories as their own, and still continues to hold them to this very day.

the Siberian frontier near Manchukuo had amply demonstrated. So the Japanese began to shift their eyes south to the vast resources of Southeast Asia—the oil of the Dutch East Indies, the rubber and tin of Malaya, and the rice of Burma and Indochina.

A move southward, of course, would risk war with the European colonial powers and the United States. Japan's attack on China in the summer of 1937 had already aroused strong criticism abroad, particularly from the United States, where President Franklin D. Roosevelt threatened to "quarantine" the aggressors after Japanese military units bombed an American naval ship operating in China. Public fear of involvement forced the president to draw back, but when Japan suddenly demanded the right to occupy airfields and exploit economic resources in French Indochina in the summer of 1940, the United States warned the Japanese that it would impose economic sanctions unless Japan withdrew from the area and returned to its borders of 1931.

The Japanese viewed the American threat of retaliation as an obstacle to their long-term objectives. Japan badly needed liquid fuel and scrap iron from the United States. Should they be cut off, Japan would have to find them elsewhere. The Japanese were thus caught in a vise. To obtain guaranteed access to natural resources that were necessary to fuel the Japanese military machine, Japan must risk being cut off from its current source of raw materials that would be needed in case of a conflict. After much debate, the Japanese decided to launch a surprise attack on American and European colonies in Southeast Asia in the hope of a quick victory that would evict the United States from the region.

CHRONOLOGY

THE PATH TO WAR, 1931–1939

Japan seizes Manchuria	September 1931
Hitler becomes chancellor	January 30, 1933
Hitler announces a German air force	March 9, 1935
Hitler announces military conscription	March 16, 1935
Mussolini invades Ethiopia	October 1935
Hitler occupies demilitarized Rhineland	March 7, 1936
Mussolini and Hitler intervene in Spanish Civil War	1936
Rome-Berlin Axis	October 1936
Anti-Comintern Pact (Japan and Germany)	November 1936
Japan invades China	1937
Germany annexes Austria	March 13, 1938
Munich Conference: Sudetenland goes to Germany	September 29, 1938
Germany occupies the rest of Czechoslovakia	March 1939
German-Soviet Nonaggression Pact	August 23, 1939
Germany invades Poland	September 1, 1939
Britain and France declare war on Germany	September 3, 1939

THE COURSE OF WORLD WAR II

Using *Blitzkrieg*, or "lightning war," Hitler stunned Europe with the speed and efficiency of the German attack. Armored columns or panzer divisions (a panzer division was a strike force of about three hundred tanks and accompanying forces and supplies) supported by airplanes broke quickly through Polish lines and encircled the bewildered Polish troops. Conventional infantry units then moved in to hold the newly conquered territory. Within four weeks, Poland had surrendered. On September 28, 1939, Germany and the Soviet Union officially divided Poland between them.

Europe at War

Although Hitler's hopes to avoid a war with the western European states were dashed when France and Britain declared war on September 3, he was confident that he could control the situation. After a winter of waiting (called the "phony war"), Hitler resumed the war on April 9, 1940, with another *Blitzkrieg,* against Denmark and Norway. One month later, on May 10, the Germans launched their attack on the Netherlands, Belgium, and France. The main assault through Luxembourg and the Ardennes forest was completely unexpected by the French and British forces. German panzer divisions broke through the weak French defensive positions there and raced across northern France, splitting the Allied armies and trapping French troops and the entire British army on the beaches of Dunkirk. Only by heroic efforts did the British succeed in a gigantic evacuation of 330,000 Allied (mostly British) troops. The French capitulated on June 22. German armies occupied about three-fifths of France, while the French hero of World War I, Marshal Henri Pétain (1856–1951), established an authoritarian regime (known as Vichy France) over the remainder. Germany was now in control of western and central Europe, but Britain had still not been defeated.

As Hitler realized, an amphibious invasion of Britain would only be possible if Germany gained control of the air. At the beginning of August 1940, the *Luftwaffe* (the German air force) launched a major offensive against British air and naval bases, harbors, communication centers, and war industries. The British fought back doggedly, supported by an effective radar system that gave them early warning of German attacks. Nevertheless, the British air force suffered critical losses by the end of August and was probably saved by Hitler's change in strategy. In September, in retaliation for a British attack on Berlin, Hitler ordered a shift from military targets to massive bombing of British cities to break British morale. The British rebuilt their air strength quickly and were soon inflicting major losses on *Luftwaffe* bombers. By the end of September, Germany had lost the Battle of Britain, and the invasion of Britain had to be postponed.

At this point, Hitler pursued the possibility of a Mediterranean strategy, which would involve capturing Egypt and the Suez Canal and closing the Mediterranean to British ships, thereby shutting off Britain's supply of oil. Hitler's commitment to the Mediterranean was never wholehearted, however. His initial plan was to let the Italians defeat the British in North Africa, but this strategy failed when the British routed the Italian army. Although Hitler then sent German troops to the North African theater of war, his primary concern lay elsewhere; he had already reached the decision to fulfill his lifetime obsession with the acquisition of territory in the east.

Although he had no desire for a two-front war, Hitler became convinced that Britain was remaining in the war only because it expected Soviet support. If the Soviet

Union were smashed, Britain's last hope would be eliminated. Moreover, Hitler had convinced himself that the Soviet Union, with what he regarded as its Jewish-Bolshevik leadership and a pitiful army, could be defeated quickly and decisively. Although the invasion of the Soviet Union was scheduled for spring 1941, the attack was delayed because of problems in the Balkans. Hitler had already obtained the political cooperation of Hungary, Bulgaria, and Romania, but Mussolini's disastrous invasion of Greece in October 1940 exposed Hitler's southern flank to British air bases in Greece. To secure his Balkan flank, German troops seized both Yugoslavia and Greece in April 1941. Now reassured, Hitler turned to the east and invaded the Soviet Union on June 22, 1941, in the belief that the Soviets could still be decisively defeated before winter set in.

The massive attack stretched out along an 1,800-mile front. German troops advanced rapidly, capturing two million Russian soldiers. By November, one German army group had swept through Ukraine, while a second was besieging Leningrad; a third approached within twenty-five miles of Moscow, the Russian capital. An early winter and unexpected Soviet resistance, however, brought a halt to the German advance. For the first time in the war, German armies had been stopped. A Soviet counterattack in December 1941 by a Soviet army supposedly exhausted by Nazi victories came as an ominous ending to the year for the Germans. By that time, another of Hitler's decisions—the declaration of war on the United States—probably made his defeat inevitable and turned another European conflict into a global war.

Japan at War

On December 7, 1941, Japanese carrier-based aircraft attacked the U.S. naval base at Pearl Harbor in the Hawaiian Islands. The same day, other units launched assaults on the Philippines and began advancing toward the British colony of Malaya. Shortly thereafter, Japanese forces invaded the Dutch East Indies and occupied a number of islands in the Pacific Ocean. In some cases, as on the Bataan peninsula and the island of Corregidor in the Philippines, resistance was fierce, but by the spring of 1942, almost all of Southeast Asia and much of the western Pacific had fallen into Japanese hands. Japan declared the creation of a Great East-Asia Co-Prosperity Sphere of the entire region under Japanese tutelage and announced its intention to liberate the colonies of Southeast Asia from Western rule. For the moment, however, Japan needed the resources of the region for its war machine and placed its conquests under its rule on a wartime basis.

Japanese leaders had hoped that their lightning strike at American bases would destroy the U.S. Pacific Fleet and persuade the Roosevelt administration to accept Japanese domination of the Pacific. The American people, in the eyes of Japanese leaders, had been made soft by material indulgence. But the Japanese had miscalculated. The attack on Pearl Harbor galvanized American opinion and won broad support for Roosevelt's war policy. The United States now joined with European nations and Nationalist China in a combined effort to defeat Japan and bring an end to its hegemony in the Pacific. Believing the American involvement in the Pacific would render the United States ineffective in the European theater of war, Hitler declared war on the United States four days after Pearl Harbor.

The Turning Point of the War, 1942–1943

The entry of the United States into the war created a coalition (the Grand Alliance) that ultimately defeated the Axis powers (Germany, Italy, and Japan). Nevertheless, the three major Allies—Britain, the United States,

GERMAN PANZER TROOPS IN RUSSIA. At first, the German attack on Russia was enormously successful, leading one German general to remark in his diary, "It is probably no overstatement to say that the Russian campaign has been won in the space of two weeks." This picture shows German panzer troops jumping from their armored troop carriers to attack Red Army snipers who had taken refuge in a farmhouse.

MAP 26.1 World War II in Europe and North Africa

and the Soviet Union—had to overcome mutual suspicions before they could operate as an effective alliance. Two factors aided that process. First, Hitler's declaration of war on the United States made it easier for the Americans to accept the British and Russian contention that the defeat of Germany should be the first priority of the United States. For that reason, the United States, under its Lend-Lease program (which had begun before U.S. entry into the war), sent large amounts of military aid, including $50 billion worth of trucks, planes, and other arms, to the British and Soviets. Also important to the alliance was the tacit agreement of the three chief Allies to stress military operations while ignoring political differences and larger strategic issues concerning any postwar settlement. At the beginning of 1943, the Allies agreed to fight until the Axis powers surrendered unconditionally. Although this principle of unconditional surrender prevented a repeat of the mistake of World War I, which was ended in 1918 with an armistice rather than a total victory, it likely discouraged dissident Germans and Japanese from overthrowing their governments in order to arrange a negotiated peace. At the same time, it did have the effect of cementing the Grand Alliance by making it nearly impossible for Hitler to divide his foes.

Defeat, however, was far from Hitler's mind at the beginning of 1942. As Japanese forces advanced into Southeast Asia and the Pacific after crippling the American naval fleet at Pearl Harbor, Hitler and his European allies continued the war in Europe against Britain and the Soviet Union. Until the fall of 1942, it appeared that the

Germans might still prevail on the battlefield. Reinforcements in North Africa enabled the Afrika Korps under General Erwin Rommel to break through the British defenses in Egypt and advance toward Alexandria. In the spring of 1942, a renewed German offensive in the Soviet Union led to the capture of the entire Crimea, causing Hitler to boast in August 1942:

> As the next step, we are going to advance south of the Caucasus and then help the rebels in Iran and Iraq against the English. Another thrust will be directed along the Caspian Sea toward Afghanistan and India. Then the English will run out of oil. In two years we'll be on the borders of India. Twenty to thirty elite German divisions will do. Then the British Empire will collapse.[8]

But this would be Hitler's last optimistic outburst. By the fall of 1942, the war had turned against the Germans.

In North Africa, British forces had stopped Rommel's troops at El Alamein in the summer of 1942 and then forced them back across the desert. In November 1942, British and American forces invaded French North Africa and forced the German and Italian troops to surrender in May 1943. On the Eastern Front, the turning point of the war occurred at Stalingrad. After the capture of the Crimea, Hitler's generals wanted him to concentrate on the Caucasus and its oil fields, but Hitler decided that Stalingrad, a major industrial center on the Volga, should be taken first. Between November 1942 and February 1943, German troops were stopped, then encircled, and finally forced to surrender on February 2, 1943 (see the box on p. 791). The entire German Sixth Army of 300,000 men was lost. By February 1943, German forces in Russia were back to their positions of June 1942. By the spring of 1943, long before Allied troops returned to the European continent,

MAP 26.2 World War II in Asia and the Pacific

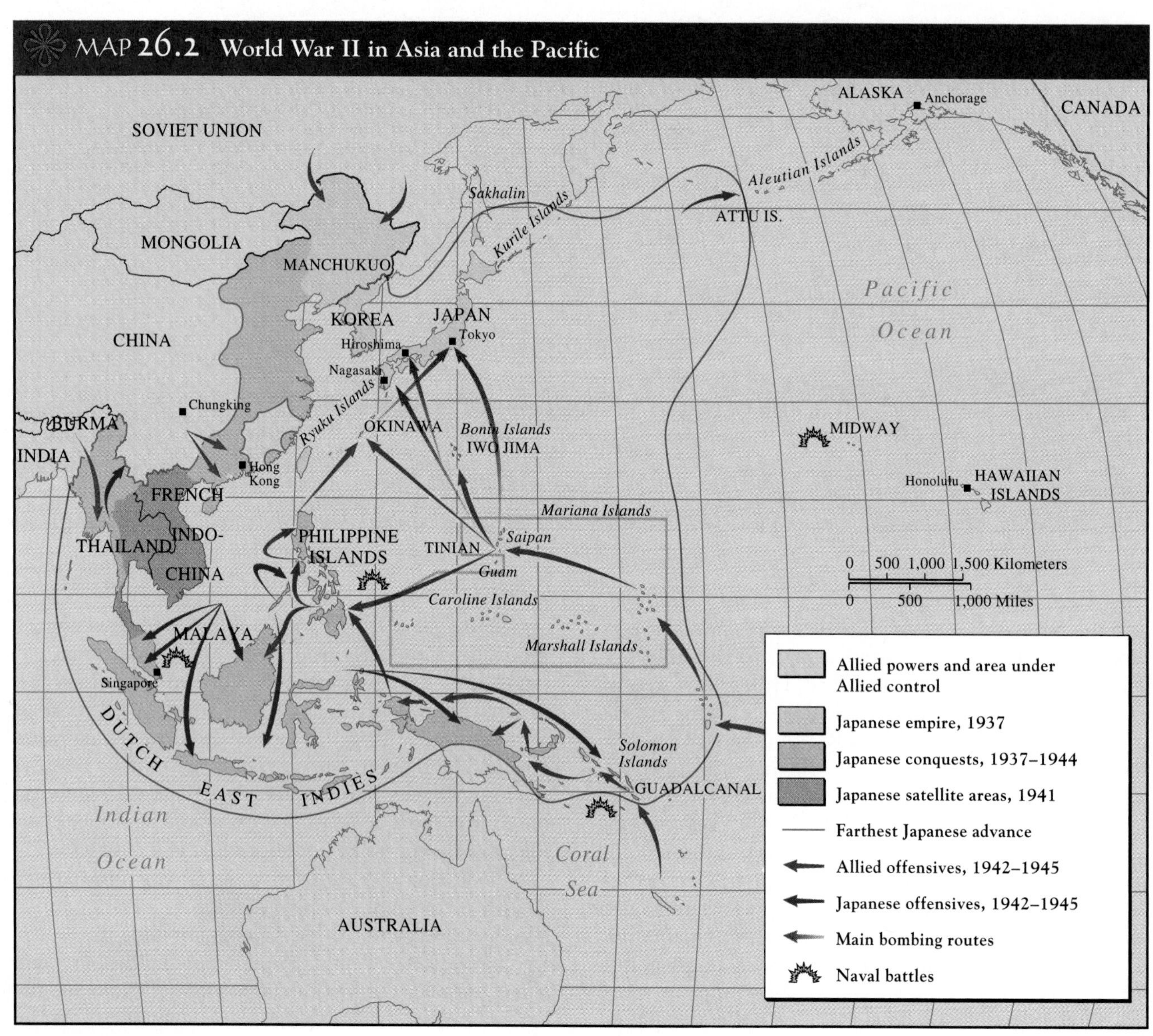

A GERMAN SOLDIER AT STALINGRAD

The Soviet victory at Stalingrad was a major turning point in World War II. This excerpt comes from the diary of a German soldier who fought and died in the Battle of Stalingrad. His dreams of victory and a return home with medals are soon dashed by the realities of Soviet resistance.

DIARY OF A GERMAN SOLDIER

Today, after we'd had a bath, the company commander told us that if our future operations are as successful, we'll soon reach the Volga, take Stalingrad, and then the war will inevitably soon be over. Perhaps we'll be home by Christmas.

July 29. The company commander says the Russian troops are completely broken, and cannot hold out any longer. To reach the Volga and take Stalingrad is not so difficult for us. The Führer knows where the Russians' weak point is. Victory is not far away. . . .

August 10. The Führer's orders were read out to us. He expects victory of us. We are all convinced that they can't stop us.

August 12. This morning outstanding soldiers were presented with decorations. . . . Will I really go back to Elsa without a decoration? I believe that for Stalingrad the Führer will decorate even me. . . .

September 4. We are being sent northward along the front toward Stalingrad. We marched all night and by dawn had reached Voroponovo Station. We can already see the smoking town. It's a happy thought that the end of the war is getting nearer. That's what everyone is saying. . . .

September 8. Two days of nonstop fighting. The Russians are defending themselves with insane stubbornness. Our regiment has lost many men. . . .

September 16. Our battalion, plus tanks, is attacking the [grain storage] elevator, from which smoke is pouring—the grain in it is burning; the Russians seem to have set light to it themselves. Barbarism. The battalion is suffering heavy losses. . . .

October 10. The Russians are so close to us that our planes cannot bomb them. We are preparing for a decisive attack. The Führer has ordered the whole of Stalingrad to be taken as rapidly as possible. . . .

October 22. Our regiment has failed to break into the factory. We have lost many men; every time you move you have to jump over bodies. . . .

November 10. A letter from Elsa today. Everyone expects us home for Christmas. In Germany everyone believes we already hold Stalingrad. How wrong they are. If they could only see what Stalingrad has done to our army. . . .

November 21. The Russians have gone over to the offensive along the whole front. Fierce fighting is going on. So, there it is—the Volga, victory, and soon home to our families! We shall obviously be seeing them next in the other world.

November 29. We are encircled. It was announced this morning that the Führer has said: "The army can trust me to do everything necessary to ensure supplies and rapidly break the encirclement."

December 3. We are on hunger rations and waiting for the rescue that the Führer promised. . . .

December 14. Everybody is racked with hunger. Frozen potatoes are the best meal, but to get them out of the ice-covered ground under fire from Russian bullets is not so easy. . . .

December 26. The horses have already been eaten. I would eat a cat; they say its meat is also tasty. The soldiers look like corpses or lunatics, looking for something to put in their mouths. They no longer take cover from Russian shells; they haven't the strength to walk, run away, and hide. A curse on this war!

even Hitler knew that the Germans would not defeat the Soviet Union.

The tide of battle in the Far East also turned dramatically in 1942. In the Battle of the Coral Sea on May 7–8, 1942, American naval forces stopped the Japanese advance and temporarily relieved Australia of the threat of invasion. On June 4, at the Battle of Midway Island, American carrier planes destroyed all four of the attacking Japanese aircraft carriers and established American naval superiority in the Pacific. By the fall of 1942, Allied forces were beginning to gather for offensive operations into southern China from Burma, through the Indonesian islands by a process of "island hopping" by troops commanded by the American general Douglas MacArthur, and across the Pacific with a combination of U.S. Army, Marine, and Navy attacks on Japanese-held islands. After a series of bitter engagements in the waters of the Solomon Islands from August to November 1942, Japanese fortunes began to fade.

The Last Years of the War

By the beginning of 1943, the tide of battle had turned against Germany, Italy, and Japan. After the Axis forces had surrendered in Tunisia on May 13, 1943, the Allies crossed the Mediterranean and carried the war to Italy. After taking Sicily, Allied troops began the invasion of mainland Italy in September. In the meantime, after the ouster and arrest of Benito Mussolini, a new Italian government offered to surrender to Allied forces. But Mussolini

CHRONOLOGY

THE COURSE OF WORLD WAR II

Germany and the Soviet Union divide Poland	September 28, 1939
Blitzkrieg against Denmark and Norway	April 1940
Blitzkrieg against Belgium, Netherlands, France	May 1940
France surrenders	June 22, 1940
Battle of Britain	Fall 1940
Nazi seizure of Yugoslavia and Greece	April 1941
Germany invades the Soviet Union	June 22, 1941
Japanese attack on Pearl Harbor	December 7, 1941
Battle of the Coral Sea	May 7–8, 1942
Battle of Midway Island	June 4, 1942
Allied invasion of North Africa	November 1942
German surrender at Stalingrad	February 2, 1943
Axis forces surrender in North Africa	May 1943
Battle of Kursk	July 5-12, 1943
Invasion of mainland Italy	September 1943
Allied invasion of France	June 6, 1944
Hitler commits suicide	April 30, 1945
Surrender of Germany	May 7, 1945
Atomic bomb dropped on Hiroshima	August 6, 1945
Japan surrenders	August 14, 1945

was liberated by the Germans in a daring raid and then set up as the head of a puppet German state in northern Italy while German troops moved in and occupied much of Italy. The new defensive lines established by the Germans in the hills south of Rome were so effective that the Allied advance up the Italian peninsula was a painstaking affair accompanied by heavy casualties. Rome did not fall to the Allies until June 4, 1944. By that time, the Italian war had assumed a secondary role anyway, as the Allies opened their long-awaited "second front" in western Europe.

Since the autumn of 1943, the Allies had been planning a cross-channel invasion of France from Britain. Under the direction of the American general Dwight D. Eisenhower (1890–1969), the Allies landed five assault divisions on the Normandy beaches on June 6, 1944, in history's greatest naval invasion. An initially indecisive German response enabled the Allied forces to establish a beachhead. Within three months, they had landed two million men and a half-million vehicles that pushed inland and broke through German defensive lines.

After the breakout, Allied troops moved south and east and liberated Paris by the end of August. By March 1945, they had crossed the Rhine River and advanced further into Germany. At the end of April 1945, Allied armies in northern Germany moved toward the Elbe River, where they finally linked up with the Soviets. The Soviets had come a long way since the Battle of Stalingrad in 1943. In the summer of 1943, Hitler gambled on taking the offensive by making use of newly developed heavy tanks. German forces were soundly defeated by the Soviets at the Battle of Kursk (July 5–12), the greatest tank battle of World War II. Soviet forces now began a relentless advance westward. The Soviets had reoccupied Ukraine by the end of 1943 and lifted the siege of Leningrad and moved into the Baltic states by the beginning of 1944. Advancing along a northern front, Soviet troops occupied Warsaw in January 1945 and entered Berlin in April. Meanwhile, Soviet troops along a southern front swept through Hungary, Romania, and Bulgaria.

In January 1945, Adolf Hitler had moved into a bunker fifty-five feet under Berlin to direct the final stages of the war. In his final political testament, Hitler, consistent to the end in his rabid anti-Semitism, blamed the Jews for the war: "Above all I charge the leaders of the nation and those under them to scrupulous observance of the laws of race and to merciless opposition to the universal poisoner of all peoples, international Jewry."[9] Hitler committed suicide on April 30, two days after Mussolini had been shot by partisan Italian forces. On May 7, German commanders surrendered. The war in Europe was over.

The war in Asia continued. Beginning in 1943, American forces had gone on the offensive and advanced their way, slowly at times, across the Pacific. American forces took an increasing toll of enemy resources, especially at sea and in the air. As Allied military power drew inexorably closer to the main Japanese islands in the first months of 1945, President Harry Truman, who had succeeded to the presidency on the death of Franklin Roosevelt in April, had an excruciatingly difficult decision to make. Should he use atomic weapons (at the time, only two bombs were available, and their effectiveness had not been demonstrated) to bring the war to an end without the necessity of an Allied invasion of the Japanese homeland? As the world knows, Truman answered that question in the affirmative. The first bomb was dropped on the city of Hiroshima on August 6. Truman then called on Japan to surrender or expect a "rain of ruin from the air." When the Japanese did not respond, a second bomb was dropped on Nagasaki. Japan surrendered unconditionally on

REFUGEES FLEE YOKOHAMA. American bombing attacks on Japanese cities began in earnest in November 1944. Built of flimsy materials, Japan's crowded cities were soon devastated by these air raids. This photograph shows a homeless family fleeing Yokohama, a shelter for refugees until American bombers devastated the city on May 29, 1945.

August 14. World War II, in which 17 million men died in battle and perhaps 18 million civilians perished as well (some estimate total losses at 50 million), was finally over.

THE NEW ORDER

The initial victories of the Germans and Japanese gave them the opportunity to create new orders in Europe and Asia. Although both countries presented positive images of these new orders for publicity purposes, in practice both followed policies of ruthless domination of their subject peoples.

The New Order in Europe

After the German victories in Europe, Nazi propagandists created glowing images of a new European order based on "equal chances" for all nations and an integrated economic community. This was not Hitler's conception of a European New Order. He saw the Europe he had conquered simply as subject to German domination. Only the Germans, he once said, "can really organize Europe."

The Nazi empire stretched across continental Europe from the English Channel in the west to the outskirts of Moscow in the east. In no way was this empire organized systematically or governed efficiently. Nazi-occupied Europe was largely organized in one of two ways. Some areas, such as western Poland, were directly annexed by Nazi Germany and made into German provinces. Most of occupied Europe was administered by German military or civilian officials in combination with varying degrees of indirect control from collaborationist regimes.

Racial considerations played an important role in how conquered peoples were treated. German civil administrations were established in Norway, Denmark, and the Netherlands because the Nazis considered their peoples to be Aryan or racially akin to the Germans and hence worthy of more lenient treatment. "Inferior" Latin peoples, such as the occupied French, were given military

HITLER'S PLANS FOR A NEW ORDER IN THE EAST

Hitler's nightly monologues to his postdinner guests, which were recorded by the Führer's private secretary, Martin Bormann, reveal much about the New Order he wished to create. On the evening of October 17, 1941, Hitler expressed his views on what the Germans would do with their newly conquered territories in the east.

HITLER'S SECRET CONVERSATIONS, OCTOBER 17, 1941

In comparison with the beauties accumulated in Central Germany, the new territories in the East seem to us like a desert. . . . This Russian desert, we shall populate it. . . . We'll take away its character of an Asiatic steppe; we'll Europeanize it. With this object, we have undertaken the construction of roads that will lead to the southernmost point of the Crimea and to the Caucasus. These roads will be studded along their whole length with German towns, and around these towns our colonists will settle.

As for the two or three million men whom we need to accomplish this task, we'll find them quicker than we think. They'll come from Germany, Scandinavia, the Western countries, and America. I shall no longer be here to see all that, but in twenty years the Ukraine will already be a home for twenty million inhabitants besides the natives. In three hundred years, the country will be one of the loveliest gardens in the world.

As for the natives, we'll have to screen them carefully. The Jew, that destroyer, we shall drive out. . . . We shan't settle in the Russian towns, and we'll let them fall to pieces without intervening. And, above all, no remorse on this subject! We're not going to play at children's nurses; we're absolutely without obligations as far as these people are concerned. To struggle against the hovels, chase away the fleas, provide German teachers, bring out newspapers—very little of that for us! We'll confine ourselves, perhaps, to setting up a radio transmitter, under our control. For the rest, let them know just enough to understand our highway signs, so that they won't get themselves run over by our vehicles. . . . There's only one duty: to Germanize this country by the immigration of Germans, and to look upon the natives as Redskins. If these people had defeated us, Heaven have mercy! But we don't hate them. That sentiment is unknown to us. We are guided only by reason. . . .

All those who have the feeling for Europe can join in our work.

In this business I shall go straight ahead, cold-bloodedly. What they may think about me, at this juncture, is to me a matter of complete indifference. I don't see why a German who eats a piece of bread should torment himself with the idea that the soil that produces this bread has been won by the sword.

administrations. By 1943, however, as Nazi losses continued to multiply, all the occupied territories of northern and western Europe were ruthlessly exploited for material goods and manpower for Germany's labor needs.

Because the conquered lands in the east contained the living space for German expansion and were populated in Nazi eyes by racially inferior Slavic peoples, Nazi administration there was considerably more ruthless. Hitler's racial ideology and his plans for an Aryan racial empire were so important to him that he and the Nazis began to implement their racial program soon after the conquest of Poland. Heinrich Himmler, a strong believer in Nazi racial ideology and the leader of the SS, was put in charge of German resettlement plans in the east. Himmler's task was to evacuate the inferior Slavic peoples and replace them with Germans, a policy first applied to the new German provinces created from the lands of western Poland. One million Poles were uprooted and dumped in southern Poland. Hundreds of thousands of ethnic Germans (descendants of Germans who had migrated years ago from Germany to different parts of southern and eastern Europe) were encouraged to colonize designated areas in Poland. By 1942, two million ethnic Germans had been settled in Poland.

The invasion of the Soviet Union inflated Nazi visions of German colonization in the east. Hitler spoke to his intimate circle of a colossal project of social engineering after the war, in which Poles, Ukrainians, and Russians would become slave labor while German peasants settled on the abandoned lands and Germanized them (see the box above). Nazis involved in this kind of planning were well aware of the human costs. Himmler told a gathering of SS officers that although the destruction of 30 million Slavs was a prerequisite for German plans in the east, "Whether nations live in prosperity or starve to death interests me only insofar as we need them as slaves for our culture. Otherwise it is of no interest."[10]

Labor shortages in Germany led to a policy of ruthless mobilization of foreign labor for Germany. After the invasion of the Soviet Union, the four million Russian prisoners of war captured by the Germans along with more than two million workers conscripted in France became a major source of heavy labor, but it was wasted by allowing more than three million of them to die from neglect. In 1942, a special office was created to recruit labor for German farms and industries. By the summer of 1944, seven million foreign workers were laboring in Germany and constituted 20 percent of Germany's labor force. At the same time, another seven million workers were supplying forced labor in their own countries on farms, in industries, and even in military camps. Forced labor, however, often proved counterproductive because it created economic chaos in occupied countries and disrupted industrial production that could have helped Germany. The brutal character of Germany's recruitment policies often led more and more people to resist the Nazi occupation forces.

The Holocaust

No aspect of the Nazi New Order was more terrifying than the deliberate attempt to exterminate the Jewish people of Europe. Racial struggle was a key element in Hitler's ideology and meant to him a clearly defined conflict of opposites: the Aryans, creators of human cultural development, against the Jews, parasites who were trying to destroy the Aryans. By the beginning of 1939, Nazi policy focused on promoting the "emigration" of German Jews from Germany. Once the war began in September 1939, the so-called Jewish problem took on new dimensions. For a while there was discussion of the Madagascar Plan, which aspired to the mass shipment of Jews to the African island of Madagascar. When war contingencies made this plan impractical, an even more drastic policy was conceived.

Heinrich Himmler and the SS organization closely shared Hitler's racial ideology. The SS was given responsibility for what the Nazis called their Final Solution to the Jewish problem, that is, the annihilation of the Jewish people. Reinhard Heydrich (1904–1942), head of the SS's Security Service, was given administrative responsibility for the Final Solution. After defeating Poland, Heydrich ordered the special strike forces (*Einsatzgruppen*) that he had created to round up all Polish Jews and concentrate them in ghettos established in a number of Polish cities.

In June 1941, the *Einsatzgruppen* were given new responsibilities as mobile killing units. These SS death squads followed the regular army's advance into the Soviet Union. Their job was to round up Jews in the villages and execute and bury them in mass graves, often giant pits dug by the victims themselves before they were shot. Such constant killing produced morale problems among the SS executioners. During a visit to Minsk in the Soviet Union, Himmler tried to build morale by pointing out that "he would not like it if Germans did such a thing gladly. But their conscience was in no way impaired, for they were soldiers who had to carry out every order unconditionally. He alone had responsibility before God and Hitler for everything that was happening, . . . and he was acting from a deep understanding of the necessity for this operation."[11]

Although it has been estimated that as many as one million Jews were killed by the *Einsatzgruppen*, this approach to solving the Jewish problem was soon perceived as inadequate. Instead, the Nazis opted for the systematic annihilation of the European Jewish population in specially built death camps. The plan was basically simple. Jews from countries occupied by Germany (or sympathetic to Germany) would be rounded up, packed like cattle into freight trains, and shipped to Poland, where six extermination centers were built for this purpose. The largest and most famous was Auschwitz-Birkenau. Medical technicians chose Zyklon B (the commercial name for hydrogen cyanide) as the most effective gas for quickly killing large numbers of people in gas chambers designed to look like "shower rooms" to facilitate the cooperation of the victims. After gassing, the corpses would be burned in specially built crematoria.

By the spring of 1942, the death camps were in operation. Although initial priority was given to the elimination of the ghettos in Poland, by the summer of 1942, Jews

THE HOLOCAUST: ACTIVITIES OF THE *EINSATZGRUPPEN*. The activities of the mobile killing units known as the *Einsatzgruppen* were the first stage in the mass killings of the Holocaust. This picture shows the execution of a Jew by a member of one of these SS killing squads. Onlookers include members of the German Army, the German Labor Service, and even Hitler Youth. When it became apparent that this method of killing was inefficient, it was replaced by the death camps.

THE HOLOCAUST: THE CAMP COMMANDANT AND THE CAMP VICTIMS

The systematic annihilation of millions of men, women, and children in extermination camps makes the Holocaust one of the most horrifying events in history. The first document is taken from an account by Rudolf Höss, commandant of the extermination camp at Auschwitz-Birkenau. In the second document, a French doctor explains what happened at one of the crematoria described by Höss.

COMMANDANT HÖSS DESCRIBES THE EQUIPMENT

The two large crematoria, Nos. I and II, were built during the winter of 1942–43. . . . They each . . . could cremate c. 2,000 corpses within twenty-four hours. . . . Crematoria I and II both had underground undressing and gassing rooms which could be completely ventilated. The corpses were brought up to the ovens on the floor above by lift. The gas chambers could hold c. 3,000 people.

The firm of Topf had calculated that the two smaller crematoria, III and IV, would each be able to cremate 1,500 corpses within twenty-four hours. However, owing to the wartime shortage of materials, the builders were obliged to economize, and so the undressing rooms and gassing rooms were built above ground and the ovens were of a less solid construction. But it soon became apparent that the flimsy construction of these two four-retort ovens was not up to the demands made on it. No. III ceased operating altogether after a short time and later was no longer used. No. IV had to be repeatedly shut down since after a short period in operation of 4–6 weeks, the ovens and chimneys had burnt out. The victims of the gassing were mainly burnt in pits behind crematorium IV.

The largest number of people gassed and cremated within twenty-four hours was somewhat over 9,000.

A FRENCH DOCTOR DESCRIBES THE VICTIMS

It is mid-day, when a long line of women, children, and old people enter the yard. The senior official in charge . . . climbs on a bench to tell them that they are going to have a bath and that afterward they will get a drink of hot coffee. They all undress in the yard. . . . The doors are opened and an indescribable jostling begins. The first people to enter the gas chamber begin to draw back. They sense the death which awaits them. The SS men put an end to this pushing and shoving with blows from their rifle butts beating the heads of the horrified women who are desperately hugging their children. The massive oak double doors are shut. For two endless minutes one can hear banging on the walls and screams which are no longer human. And then—not a sound. Five minutes later the doors are opened. The corpses, squashed together and distorted, fall out like a waterfall. . . . The bodies, which are still warm, pass through the hands of the hairdresser, who cuts their hair, and the dentist, who pulls out their gold teeth. . . . One more transport has just been processed through No. IV crematorium.

were also being shipped from France, Belgium, and Holland. Even as the Allies were making significant advances in 1944, Jews were being shipped from Greece and Hungary. These shipments depended on the cooperation of Germany's Transport Ministry, but despite desperate military needs, the Final Solution had priority in using railroad cars for the transportation of Jews to death camps.

A harrowing experience awaited the Jews when they arrived at one of the six death camps. Rudolf Höss, commandant at Auschwitz-Birkenau, described it:

> We had two SS doctors on duty at Auschwitz to examine the incoming transports of prisoners. The prisoners would be marched by one of the doctors, who would make spot decisions as they walked by. Those who were fit for work were sent into the camp. Others were sent immediately to the extermination plants. Children of tender years were invariably exterminated since by reason of their youth they were unable to work. . . . at Auschwitz we endeavored to fool the victims into thinking that they were to go through a delousing process. Of course, frequently they realized our true intentions and we sometimes had riots and difficulties due to that fact.[12]

About 30 percent of the arrivals at Auschwitz were sent to a labor camp, while the remainder went to the gas chambers (see the box above). After they had been gassed, the bodies were burned in the crematoria. The victims' goods and even their bodies were used for economic gain. Female hair was cut off, collected, and turned into mattresses or cloth. Some inmates were also subjected to cruel and painful "medical" experiments. The Germans killed between five and six million Jews, over three million of them in the death camps. Virtually 90 percent of the Jewish populations of Poland, the Baltic countries, and Germany were exterminated. Overall, the Holocaust was responsible for the death of nearly two out of every three European Jews.

The Nazis were also responsible for another Holocaust, the death by shooting, starvation, or overwork of at least another 9 to 10 million people. Because the Nazis also considered the Gypsies of Europe (like the Jews) a race containing alien blood, they were systematically rounded up for extermination. About 40 percent of Europe's one million Gypsies were killed in the death camps. The lead-

JAPAN'S PLAN FOR ASIA

The Japanese objective in World War II was to create a vast Great East-Asia Co-Prosperity Sphere to provide Japan with needed raw materials and a market for its exports. The fol-lowing passage is from a secret document produced by a high-level government committee in January 1942.

DRAFT PLAN FOR THE ESTABLISHMENT OF A GREAT EAST-ASIA CO-PROSPERITY SPHERE

The Plan. The Japanese empire is a manifestation of morality and its special characteristic is the propagation of the Imperial Way. It is necessary to foster the increased power of the empire, to cause East Asia to return to its original form of independence and co-prosperity by shaking off the yoke of Europe and America, and to let its countries and peoples develop their respective abilities in peaceful cooperation and secure livelihood.

The Form of East Asiatic Independence and Co-Prosperity. The states, their citizens, and resources, comprised in those areas pertaining to the Pacific, Central Asia, and the Indian Oceans formed into one general union are to be established as an autonomous zone of peaceful living and common prosperity on behalf of the peoples of the nations of East Asia. The area including Japan, Manchuria, North China, lower Yangtze River, and the Russian Maritime Province, forms the nucleus of the East Asiatic Union. The Japanese empire possesses a duty as the leader of the East Asiatic Union.

The above purpose presupposes the inevitable emancipation or independence of Eastern Siberia, China, Indo-China, the South Seas, Australia, and India. . . .

Outline of East Asiatic Administration. It is intended that the unification of Japan, Manchoukuo, and China in neighborly friendship be realized by the settlement of the Sino-Japanese problems through the crushing of hostile influences in the Chinese interior, and through the construction of a new China. . . . Aggressive American and British influences in East Asia shall be driven out of the area of Indo-China and the South Seas, and this area should be brought into our defense sphere. The war with Britain and America shall be prosecuted for that purpose. . . .

CHAPTER 3: POLITICAL CONSTRUCTION

Basic Plan. The realization of the great ideal of constructing Greater East Asia Co-Prosperity requires not only the complete prosecution of the current Greater East Asia War but also presupposes another great war in the future. . . .

The following are the basic principles for the political construction of East Asia. . . .

The desires of the peoples in the sphere for their independence shall be respected, and endeavors shall be made for their fulfillment, but proper and suitable forms of government shall be decided for them in consideration of military and economic requirements and of the historical, political, and cultural elements peculiar to each area.

It must also be noted that the independence of various peoples of East Asia should be based on the idea of constructing East Asia as "independent countries existing within the New Order of East Asia" and that this conception differs from an independence based on the idea of liberalism and national self-determination. . . .

Western individualism and materialism shall be rejected, and a moral worldview, the basic principle of whose morality shall be the Imperial Way, shall be established. The ultimate object to be achieved is not exploitation but co-prosperity and mutual help, not competitive conflict but mutual assistance and mild peace, not a formal view of equality but a view of order based on righteous classification, not an idea of rights but an idea of service, and not several worldviews but one unified worldview.

ing elements of the "subhuman" Slavic peoples—the clergy, intelligentsia, civil leaders, judges, and lawyers—were arrested and deliberately killed. Probably an additional four million Poles, Ukrainians, and Belorussians lost their lives as slave laborers for Nazi Germany, while at least three to four million Soviet prisoners of war were killed in captivity. The Nazis also singled out homosexuals for persecution, and thousands lost their lives in concentration camps.

The New Order in Asia

Once the takeover was completed, Japanese war policy in the occupied areas in Asia became essentially defensive, as Japan hoped to use its new possessions to meet its burgeoning needs for raw materials, such as tin, oil, and rubber, and also as an outlet for Japanese manufactured goods. To provide an organizational structure for the arrangement, Japanese leaders set up the Great East-Asia Co-Prosperity Sphere, a self-sufficient economic community designed to provide mutual benefits to the occupied areas and the home country (see the box above). A Ministry for Great East Asia, staffed by civilians, was established in Tokyo in October 1942 to handle arrangements between Japan and the conquered territories.

The Japanese conquest of Southeast Asia had been accomplished under the slogan "Asia for the Asiatics," and many Japanese probably sincerely believed that their government was bringing about the liberation of the Southeast Asian peoples from European colonial rule. Japanese officials in the occupied territories quickly made contact with anticolonialist elements and promised that independent governments would be established under Japa-nese tutelage. Such governments were eventually established in Burma, the Dutch East Indies, Vietnam, and the Philippines.

In fact, however, real power rested with the Japanese military authorities in each territory, and the local Japanese military command was directly subordinated to the Army General Staff in Tokyo. The economic resources of the colonies were exploited for the benefit of the Japanese war machine, while natives were recruited to serve in local military units or conscripted to work on public works projects. In some cases, the people living in the occupied areas were subjected to severe hardships. In Indochina, for example, forced requisitions of rice by the local Japanese authorities for shipment abroad created a food shortage that caused the starvation of over a million Vietnamese in 1944 and 1945.

The Japanese planned to implant a new moral and social order as well as a new political and economic order in the occupied areas. Occupation policy stressed traditional values such as obedience, community spirit, filial piety, and discipline that reflected the prevailing political and cultural bias in Japan, while supposedly Western values such as materialism, liberalism, and individualism were strongly discouraged. In order to promote the creation of this New Order, as it was called, occupation authorities gave particular support to local religious organizations but discouraged the formation of formal political parties.

At first, many Southeast Asian nationalists took Japanese promises at face value and agreed to cooperate with their new masters. In Burma, an independent government was established in 1943 and subsequently declared war on the Allies. But as the exploitative nature of Japanese occupation policies became increasingly clear, sentiment turned against the New Order. Japanese officials sometimes unwittingly provoked resentment by their arrogance and contempt for local customs. In the Dutch East Indies, for example, Indonesians were required to bow in the direction of Tokyo and recognize the divinity of the Japanese emperor, practices that were repugnant to Muslims. In Burma, Buddhist pagodas were sometimes used as military latrines.

Like German soldiers in occupied Europe, Japanese military forces often had little respect for the lives of their subject peoples. In their conquest of Nanjing, China, in 1937, Japanese soldiers had spent several days in killing, raping, and looting. Almost 800,000 Koreans were sent overseas, most of them as forced laborers, to Japan. Tens of thousands of Korean women were forced to be "comfort women" (prostitutes) for Japanese troops. In construction projects to help their war effort, the Japanese also made extensive use of labor forces composed of both prisoners of war and local peoples. In building the Burma-Thailand railway in 1943, for example, the Japanese used 61,000 Australian, British, and Dutch prisoners of war and almost 300,000 workers from Burma, Malaya, Thailand, and the Dutch East Indies. An inadequate diet and appalling work conditions in an unhealthy climate led to the deaths of 12,000 Allied prisoners of war and 90,000 native workers by the time the railway was completed.

Such Japanese behavior created a dilemma for many nationalists, who had no desire to see the return of the colonial powers. Some turned against the Japanese, while others lapsed into inactivity. Indonesian patriots tried to have it both ways, feigning support for Japan while attempting to sabotage the Japanese administration. In French Indochina, Ho Chi Minh's Indochinese Communist Party established contacts with American military units in southern China and agreed to provide information on Japanese troop movements and rescue downed American fliers in the area. In Malaya, where Japanese treatment of ethnic Chinese residents was especially harsh, many joined a guerrilla movement against the occupying forces. By the end of the war, little support remained in the region for the erstwhile "liberators."

THE HOME FRONT

World War II was even more of a total war than World War I. Fighting was much more widespread and covered most of the world. Economic mobilization was more extensive; so too was the mobilization of women. The number of civilians killed was far higher; almost 20 million were killed from bombing raids, mass extermination policies, and attacks by invading armies.

The Mobilization of Peoples: Four Examples

The home fronts of the major belligerents varied considerably, based on local circumstances. World War II had an enormous impact on the Soviet Union. Known to the Soviets as the Great Patriotic War, the German-Soviet war witnessed the greatest land battles in history as well as incredible ruthlessness. To Nazi Germany, it was a war of oppression and annihilation that called for merciless measures. Two out of every five persons killed in World War II were Soviet citizens.

The initial defeats of the Soviet Union led to drastic emergency mobilization measures that affected the civilian population. Leningrad, for example, experienced 900 days of siege, during which its inhabitants became so desperate for food that they ate dogs, cats, and mice. As the German army made its rapid advance into Soviet territory, the factories in the western part of the Soviet Union were dismantled and shipped to the interior—to the Urals, western Siberia, and the Volga region. Machines were placed on the bare ground, and walls went up around them as workers began their work.

This widespread military, industrial, and economic mobilization created yet another industrial revolution for the Soviet Union. Stalin labeled it a "battle of machines," and the Soviets won, producing 78,000 tanks and 98,000 artillery pieces. Fifty-five percent of Soviet national income went for war materials, compared to 15 percent in 1940. As a result of the emphasis on military goods, Soviet citizens experienced incredible shortages of both food and housing.

Soviet women played a major role in the war effort. Women and girls worked in industries, mines, and railroads. Overall, the number of women working in industry increased almost 60 percent. Soviet women were also expected to dig antitank ditches and work as air-raid wardens. In addition, the Soviet Union was the only country in World War II to use women as combatants. Soviet women functioned as snipers and also as aircrews in bomber squadrons. The female pilots who helped to defeat the Germans at Stalingrad were known as the "Night Witches."

The home front in the United States was quite different from those of its chief wartime allies, largely because the United States faced no threat of war in its own territory. Although the economy and labor force were slow to mobilize, eventually the United States became the arsenal of the Allied powers, producing the military equipment they needed. At the height of war production in 1943, the nation was constructing six ships a day and $6 billion worth of war-related goods a month.

The mobilization of the American economy produced social problems. The construction of new factories created boom towns where thousands came to work but then faced a shortage of houses, health facilities, and schools. The dramatic expansion of small towns into large cities often brought a breakdown in traditional social mores, especially evident in the increase in teenage prostitution. Economic mobilization also led to extensive movements of people, which in turn created new social tensions. Sixteen million men and women were enrolled in the military, while another 16 million, mostly wives and sweethearts of the servicemen or workers looking for jobs, also relocated. Over one million blacks migrated from the rural South to the industrial cities of the North and West, looking for jobs in industry. The presence of blacks in areas where they had not been present before led to racial tensions and sometimes even racial riots. In Detroit in June 1943, white mobs roamed the streets attacking blacks. Many of the one million blacks who enrolled in the military, only to be segregated in their own battle units, were angered by the way they were treated. Some became militant and prepared to fight for their civil rights.

Japanese Americans were treated even more shabbily. On the West Coast, 110,000 Japanese Americans, 65 percent of whom had been born in the United States, were removed to camps encircled by barbed wire and made to take loyalty oaths. Although public officials claimed this policy was necessary for security reasons, no similar treatment of German Americans or Italian Americans ever took place. The racism inherent in this treatment of Japanese Americans was evident when the California governor, Culbert Olson, said: "You know, when I look out at a group of Americans of German or Italian descent, I can tell whether they're loyal or not. I can tell how they think and even perhaps what they are thinking. But it is impossible for me to do this with inscrutable orientals, and particularly the Japanese."[13]

In August 1914, Germans had enthusiastically cheered their soldiers marching off to war. In September 1939, the streets were quiet. Many Germans were apathetic or, even worse for the Nazi regime, had a foreboding of disaster. Hitler was very aware of the importance of the home front. He believed that the collapse of the home front in World War I had caused Germany's defeat, and in his determination to avoid a repetition of that experience, he adopted economic policies that may indeed have cost Germany the war.

To maintain the morale of the home front during the first two years of the war, Hitler refused to cut the production of consumer goods or increase the production of armaments. *Blitzkrieg* allowed the Germans to win quick victories, after which they believed they could plunder the food and raw materials of the conquered countries to avoid diverting resources away from the civilian economy. After German defeats on the Russian front and the American entry into the war, the economic situation changed. Early in 1942, Hitler finally ordered a massive increase in armaments production and in the size of the army. Hitler's architect, Albert Speer, was made minister for armaments and munitions in 1942. By eliminating waste and rationalizing procedures, Speer was able to triple the production of armaments between 1942 and 1943 despite the intense Allied air raids. Speer's urgent plea for a total mobilization of resources for the war effort went unheeded, however. Hitler, fearful of civilian morale problems that would undermine the home front, refused any dramatic cuts in the production of consumer goods. A total mobilization of the economy was not implemented until 1944, when schools, theaters, and cafes were closed and Speer was finally permitted to use all remaining resources for the production of a few basic military items. By that time, it was in vain. Total war mobilization in July 1944 was too little too late to save Germany from defeat.

The war produced a reversal in Nazi attitudes toward women. Nazi resistance to female employment declined as the war progressed and more and more men were called up for military service. Nazi magazines now proclaimed: "We see the woman as the eternal mother of our people, but also as the working and fighting comrade of the man."[14] But the number of women working in industry, agriculture, commerce, and domestic service increased only slightly. The total number of employed women in September 1944 was 14.9 million compared to 14.6 in May 1939. Many women, especially those of the middle class, resisted regular employment, particularly in factories. Even the introduction of labor conscription for women in January 1943 failed to achieve much as women found ingenious ways to avoid the regulations.

In Japan, society was placed on a wartime footing even before the attack on Pearl Harbor. A conscription law was passed in 1938, and economic resources were placed under strict government control. Two years later, all political parties were merged into an Imperial Rule Assistance Association. Labor unions were dissolved, and education and culture were purged of all "corrupt" Western ideas in favor of traditional values emphasizing the divinity of the emperor and the higher spirituality of Japanese civilization. During the war, individual rights were severely curtailed, as the entire population was harnessed to the needs of the war effort. Traditional habits of obedience and hierarchy were emphasized to encourage citizens to sacrifice their resources, and sometimes their lives, for the national cause. The calls for sacrifice culminated in the final years of the war, when young Japanese were encouraged to volunteer en masse to serve as pilots in the suicide missions (known as kamikaze, or "divine wind") against American fighting ships.

Japan was extremely reluctant to mobilize women on behalf of the war effort. General Hideki Tojo, prime minister from 1941 to 1944, opposed female employment, arguing that "the weakening of the family system would be the weakening of the nation . . . we are able to do our duties only because we have wives and mothers at home."[15] Women should remain at home and fulfill their responsibilities by bearing more children. Female employment increased during the war, but only in areas, such as the textile industry and farming, where women traditionally had worked. Instead of using women to meet labor shortages, the Japanese government brought in Korean and Chinese laborers.

The Frontline Civilians: The Bombing of Cities

Bombing was used in World War II in a variety of ways: against nonhuman military targets, against enemy troops, and against civilian populations. The latter made World War II as devastating for civilians as for frontline soldiers. A small number of bombing raids in the last year of World War I had given rise to the argument, crystallized in 1930 by the Italian general Giulio Douhet, that the public outcry created by the bombing of civilian populations would be an effective way to coerce governments into making peace. Consequently, European air forces began to develop long-range bombers in the 1930s.

The first sustained use of civilian bombing contradicted Douhet's theory. Beginning in early September, the German *Luftwaffe* subjected London and many other British cities and towns to nightly air raids, making the Blitz (as the British called the German air raids) a national experience. Londoners took the first heavy blows and set the standard for the rest of the British population by keeping up their spirits. But London morale was helped by the fact that German raids were widely dispersed over a very large city. Smaller communities were more directly affected by the devastation. On November 14, 1940, for example, the *Luftwaffe* destroyed hundreds of shops and a hundred acres of the city center of Coventry. The destruction of smaller cities did produce morale problems as wild rumors of social collapse spread quickly in these communities. Nevertheless, morale was soon restored. War production in these areas, in any case, seems to have been little affected by the raids.

The British failed to learn from their own experience, however, and soon proceeded with the bombing of Germany. Prime Minister Winston Churchill (1874–1965) and his advisers believed that destroying German communities would break civilian morale and bring victory. Major bombing raids began in 1942 under the direction of Arthur Harris, the wartime leader of the British air force's Bomber Command, which was rearmed with four-engine heavy bombers capable of taking the war into the center of occupied Europe. On May 31, 1942, Cologne became the first German city to be subjected to an attack by a thousand bombers.

The entry of the Americans into the war produced a new bombing strategy. American planes flew daytime missions aimed at the precision bombing of transportation facilities and wartime industries, while the British Bomber Command continued nighttime saturation bombing of all German cities with populations over 100,000. Bombing raids added an element of terror to circumstances already made difficult by growing shortages of food, clothing, and fuel. Germans especially feared the incendiary bombs that created firestorms that swept destructive paths through the cities. Four raids on Hamburg in August 1943 produced temperatures of 1,800 degrees Fahrenheit, obliterated half the city's buildings, and killed 50,000 civilians. The ferocious bombing of Dresden for three days in 1945 (February 13–15) created a firestorm that may have killed as many as 100,000 inhabitants and refugees. Even some Allied leaders began to criticize what they saw as the unnecessary terror bombing of German cities.

Germany suffered enormously from the Allied bombing raids. Millions of buildings were destroyed, and possibly half a million civilians died from the raids. Nevertheless, it is highly unlikely that Allied bombing sapped the morale of the German people. Instead, Germans, whether pro-Nazi or anti-Nazi, fought on stubbornly, often driven simply by a desire to live. Nor did the bombing destroy Germany's industrial capacity. The Allied Strategic Bombing survey revealed that the production of war materials actually increased between 1942 and 1944. Even in 1944 and 1945, Allied raids cut German armaments production by only 7 percent. Nevertheless, the widespread destruction of transportation systems and fuel supplies made it extremely difficult for the new materials to reach the German military.

In Japan, the bombing of civilians reached a new level with the use of the first atomic bomb. Japan was especially vulnerable to air raids because its air force had been virtually destroyed in the course of the war, and its crowded cities were built of flimsy materials. Attacks on Japanese cities by the new American B-29 Superfortresses, the biggest bombers of the war, began in June 1944. By the summer of 1945, many of Japan's industries had been destroyed along with one-fourth of its dwellings. After the Japanese government decreed the mobilization of all people between the ages of thirteen and sixty into a People's Volunteer Corps, President Truman and his advisers feared that Japanese fanaticism might mean a million American casualties. This concern led them to drop the atomic bomb on Hiroshima (August 6) and Nagasaki (August 9). The destruction was incredible. Of 76,000 buildings near the hypocenter of the explosion in Hiroshima, 70,000 were flattened, while 140,000 of the city's 400,000 inhabitants died by the end of 1945. By the end of 1950, another 50,000 had perished from the effects of radiation. The dropping of the first atomic bomb introduced the world to the nuclear age.

HIROSHIMA. The most devastating destruction of civilians came near the end of World War II when the United States dropped atomic bombs on the Japanese cities of Hiroshima and Nagasaki. This panoramic view of Hiroshima after the bombing shows the incredible devastation produced by the atomic bomb.

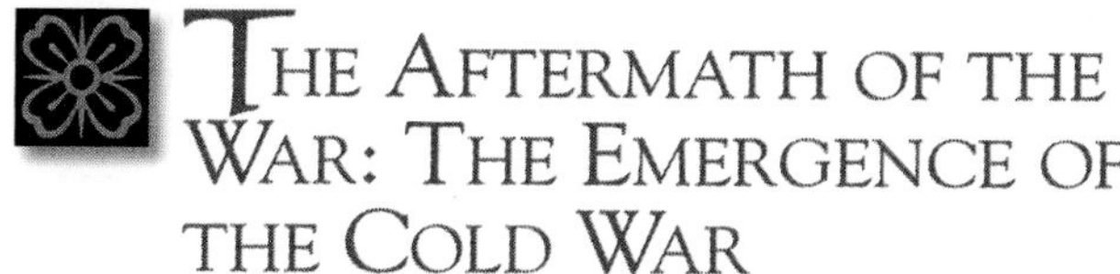

The Aftermath of the War: The Emergence of the Cold War

The total victory of the Allies in World War II was not followed by a real peace, but by the beginnings of a new conflict known as the Cold War, which dominated world politics until the end of the 1980s. The origins of the Cold War stemmed from the military, political, and ideological differences, especially between the Soviet Union and the United States, that became apparent at the Allied war conferences held in the last years of the war. Although Allied leaders were mostly preoccupied with how to end the war, they were also strongly motivated by differing, and often conflicting, visions of the postwar world.

The Conferences at Tehran, Yalta, and Potsdam

Stalin, Roosevelt, and Churchill, the leaders of the Big Three of the Grand Alliance, met at Tehran (the capital of Iran) in November 1943 to decide the future course of the war. Their major tactical decision concerned the final assault on Germany. Stalin and Roosevelt argued successfully for an American-British invasion of the Continent through France, which they scheduled for the spring of 1944. The acceptance of this plan had important consequences. It meant that Soviet and British-American forces would meet in defeated Germany along a north-south dividing line and that, most likely, Eastern Europe would be liberated by Soviet forces. The Allies also agreed to a partition of postwar Germany until denazification could take place.

By the time of the conference at Yalta in southern Russia in February 1945, the defeat of Germany was a foregone conclusion. The Western powers, which had earlier believed that the Soviets were in a weak position, were now faced with the reality of 11 million Red Army soldiers taking possession of Eastern and much of central Europe. Stalin was still operating under the notion of spheres of influence. He was deeply suspicious of the Western powers and desired a buffer to protect the Soviet Union from possible future Western aggression. At the same time, however, Stalin was eager to obtain economically important resources and strategic military positions. Roosevelt by this time was moving away from the notion of spheres of influence to the more Wilsonian ideal of self-determination. He called for "the end of the system of unilateral action, exclusive alliances, and spheres of influence." The Grand Alliance approved a "Declaration on Liberated Europe." This was a pledge to assist liberated Europe in the creation of "democratic institutions of their own choice." Liberated countries were to hold free elections to determine their political systems.

At Yalta, Roosevelt sought Soviet military help against Japan. The atomic bomb was not yet assured, and American military planners feared the possible loss of as many as one million men in amphibious assaults on the Japanese home islands. Roosevelt therefore agreed to Stalin's price for military assistance against Japan: possession of Sakhalin and the Kurile Islands, as well as two warm-water ports and railroad rights in Manchuria.

The creation of the United Nations was a major American concern at Yalta. Roosevelt hoped to ensure the participation of the Big Three powers in a postwar international organization before difficult issues divided them into hostile camps. After a number of compromises, both Churchill and Stalin accepted Roosevelt's plans for a United Nations organization and set the first meeting for San Francisco in April of 1945.

The issues of Germany and Eastern Europe were treated less decisively. The Big Three reaffirmed that Germany must surrender unconditionally and created four occupation zones. German reparations were set at $20 billion. A compromise was also worked out in regard to Poland. Stalin agreed to free elections in the future to determine a new government. But the issue of free elections in Eastern Europe caused a serious rift between the Soviets and the Americans. The principle was that Eastern European governments would be freely elected, but they were also supposed to be pro-Soviet. As Churchill expressed it: "The Poles will have their future in their own hands, with the single limitation that they must honestly follow in harmony with their allies, a policy friendly to Russia."[16] This attempt to reconcile two irreconcilable goals was doomed to failure, as soon became evident at the next conference of the Big Three powers.

THE VICTORIOUS ALLIED LEADERS AT YALTA. Even before World War II ended, the leaders of the Big Three of the Grand Alliance—Churchill, Roosevelt, and Stalin (shown from left to right)—met in wartime conferences to plan the final assault on Germany and negotiate the outlines of the postwar settlement. At the Yalta meeting (February 5–11, 1945), the three leaders concentrated on postwar issues. The American president, who died two months later, was already a worn-out man at Yalta.

Even before the conference at Potsdam took place in July 1945, Western relations with the Soviets were deteriorating rapidly. The Grand Alliance had been one of necessity in which ideological incompatibility had been subordinated to the pragmatic concerns of the war. The Allied powers' only common aim was the defeat of Nazism. Once this aim had all but been accomplished, the many differences that antagonized East-West relations came to the surface.

The Potsdam conference of July 1945 consequently began under a cloud of mistrust. Roosevelt had died on April 12 and had been succeeded as president by Harry Truman. During the conference, Truman received word that the atomic bomb had been successfully tested. Some historians have argued that this knowledge resulted in Truman's stiffened resolve against the Soviets. Whatever the reasons, there was a new coldness in the relations between the Soviets and Americans. At Potsdam, Truman demanded free elections throughout Eastern Europe. Stalin responded: "A freely elected government in any of these East European countries would be anti-Soviet, and that we cannot allow."[17] After a bitterly fought and devastating war, Stalin sought absolute military security. To him, it could only be gained by the presence of Communist states in Eastern Europe. Free elections might result in governments hostile to the Soviets. By the middle of 1945, only an invasion by Western forces could undo developments in Eastern Europe, and after the world's most destructive conflict had ended, few people favored such a policy.

As the war slowly receded into the past, the reality of conflicting ideologies had reappeared. Many in the West interpreted Soviet policy as part of a worldwide Communist conspiracy. The Soviets, on the other hand, viewed Western, especially American, policy as nothing less than global capitalist expansionism or, in Leninist terms, nothing less than economic imperialism. Vyacheslav Molotov, the Russian foreign minister, referred to the Americans as "insatiable imperialists" and "war-mongering groups of adventurers."[18] In March 1946, in a speech to an American audience, the former British prime minister Winston Churchill declared that "an iron curtain" had "descended across the continent," dividing Germany and Europe into two hostile camps. Stalin branded Churchill's speech a "call to war with the Soviet Union." Only months after the world's most devastating conflict had ended, the world seemed once again to be bitterly divided.

MAP 26.3 Territorial Changes in Europe After World War II

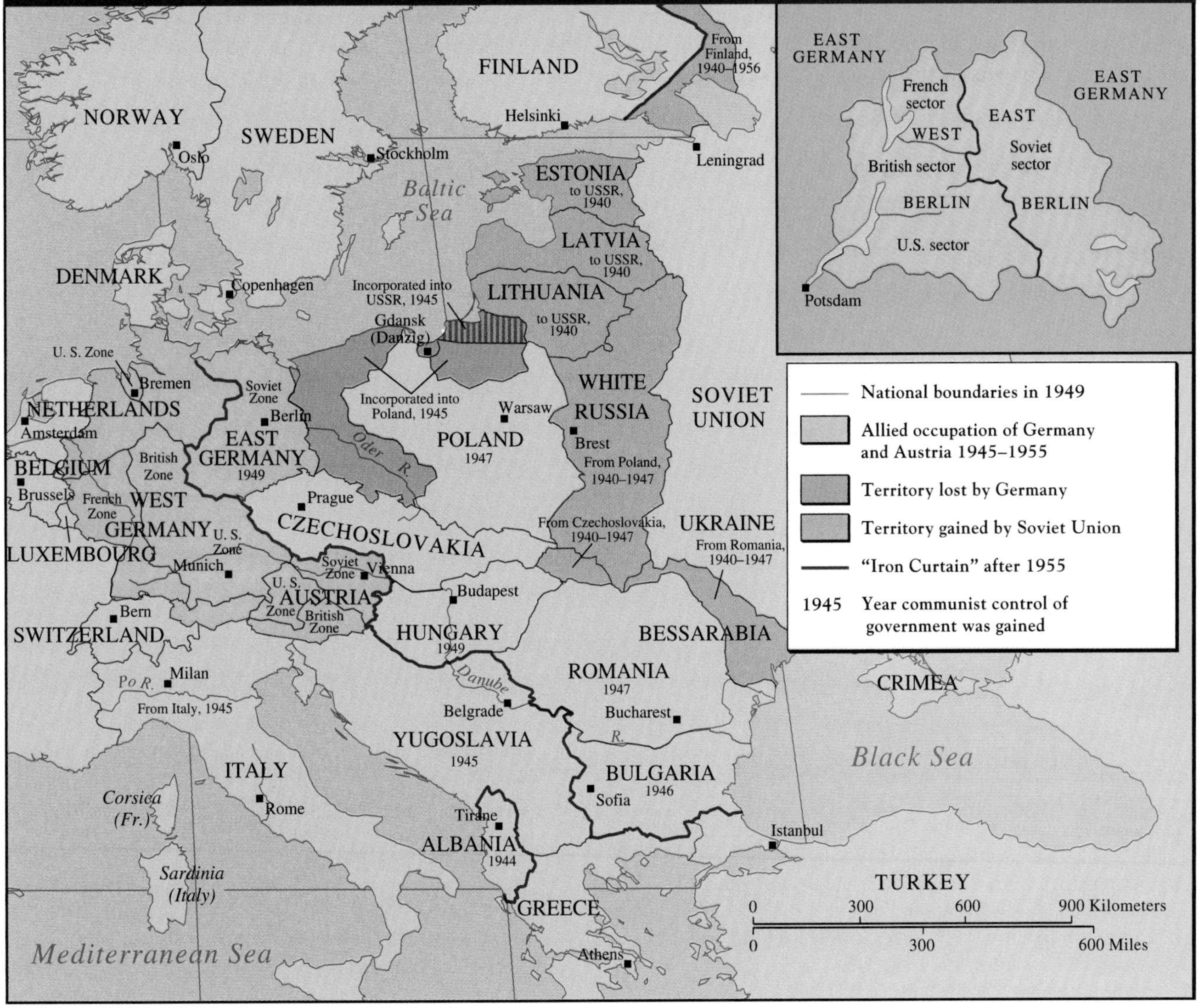

CONCLUSION

World War II was the most devastating total war in human history. Germany, Italy, and Japan had been utterly defeated. Perhaps as many as 40 million people—both soldiers and civilians—had been killed in only six years. In Asia and Europe, cities had been reduced to rubble, and millions of people faced starvation as once fertile lands stood neglected or wasted. Untold millions of people had become refugees.

What were the underlying causes of the war? Certainly, one direct cause of the conflict was the effort by two rising capitalist powers, Germany and Japan, to make up for their relatively late arrival on the scene to carve out their own global empires. Key elements in both countries had resented the agreements reached after the end of World War I that divided the world in a manner favorable to their rivals, and hoped to overturn them at the earliest opportunity. Neither Germany nor Japan possessed a strong tradition of political pluralism; to the contrary, in both countries the legacy of a feudal past marked by a strong military tradition still wielded strong influence over the political system and the mind-set of the entire population. It is no surprise that under the impact of the Great Depression, which had severe effects in both countries, fragile democratic institutions were soon overwhelmed by militant forces determined to enhance national wealth and power.

Whatever the causes of World War II, the consequences were soon to be evident. European hegemony over the world was at an end, and two new superpowers had emerged to take its place. Even before the last battles had been fought, the United States and the Soviet

Union had arrived at different visions of the postwar world. No sooner had the war ended than their differences created a new and potentially even more devastating conflict known as the Cold War. And even though Europeans seemed merely pawns in the struggle between the two superpowers, they managed to stage a remarkable recovery of their own civilization. In Asia, defeated Japan made a miraculous economic recovery, while an era of European domination finally came to an end.

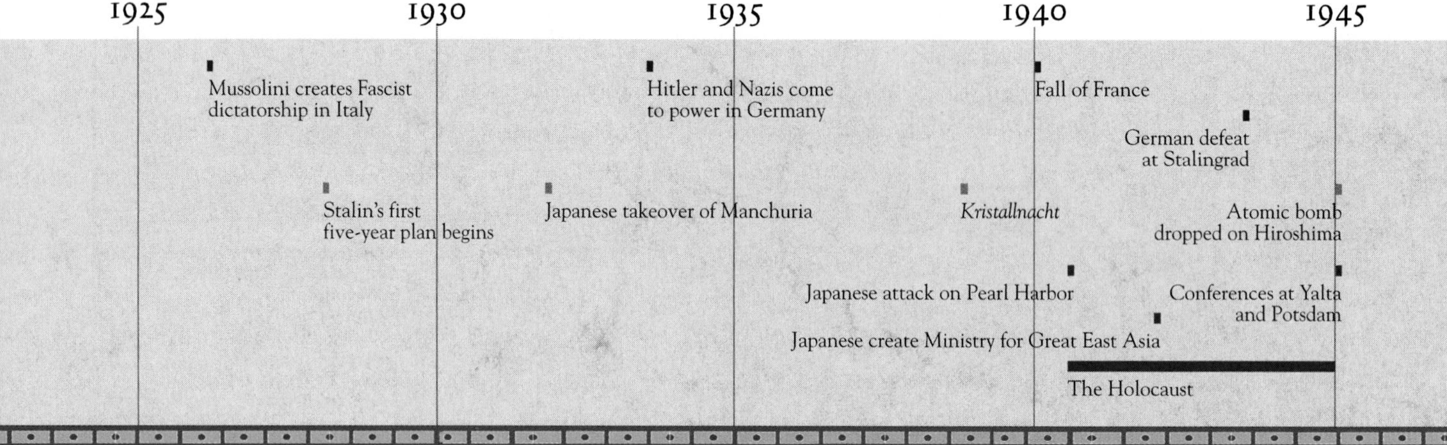

Chapter Notes

1. Benito Mussolini, "The Doctrine of Fascism," in Adrian Lyttleton, ed., *Italian Fascisms from Pareto to Gentile* (London, 1973), p. 42.
2. Quoted in Alexander De Grand, "Women Under Italian Fascism," *Historical Journal* 19 (1976): 958–59.
3. Quoted in Jeremy Noakes and Geoffrey Pridham, eds., *Nazism, 1919–1945* (Exeter, England 1983), 1:50–51.
4. Quoted in Joachim Fest, *Hitler,* trans. Richard and Clara Winston (New York, 1974), p. 418.
5. Adolf Hitler, *Mein Kampf,* trans. Ralph Manheim (Boston, 1971), p. 654.
6. *Documents on German Foreign Policy* (London, 1956), Series D, 7:204.
7. Memorandum by John Van Antwerp MacMurray, quoted in Arthur Waldron, *How the Peace Was Lost: The 1935 Memorandum* (Stanford, Calif., 1992), p. 5.
8. Albert Speer, *Spandau,* trans. Richard and Clara Winston (New York, 1976), p. 50.
9. *Nazi Conspiracy and Aggression* (Washington, D.C., 1946), 6:262.
10. International Military Tribunal, *Trial of the Major War Criminals* (Nuremberg, 1947–1949), 22:480.
11. Quoted in Raul Hilberg, *The Destruction of the European Jews,* rev. ed. (New York, 1985), 1:332–33.
12. *Nazi Conspiracy and Aggression,* 6:789.
13. Quoted in John Campbell, *The Experience of World War II* (New York, 1989), p. 170.
14. Quoted in Claudia Koonz, "Mothers in the Fatherland: Women in Nazi Germany," in Renate Bridenthal and Claudia Koonz, eds., *Becoming Visible: Women in European History* (Boston, 1977), p. 466.
15. Quoted in Campbell, *The Experience of World War II,* p. 143.
16. Quoted in Norman Graebner, *Cold War Diplomacy, 1945–1960* (Princeton, N.J., 1962), p. 117.
17. Quoted in ibid.
18. Quoted in Wilfried Loth, *The Division of the World, 1941–1955* (New York, 1988), p. 81.

Suggested Readings

For a general study of fascism, see S. G. Payne, *A History of Fascism* (Madison, Wis., 1996). The best biography of Mussolini is now D. Mack Smith, *Mussolini* (New York, 1982). Two brief but excellent surveys of Fascist Italy are A. Cassels, *Fascist Italy,* 2d ed. (Arlington Heights, Ill., 1985), and J. Whittam, *Fascist Italy* (New York, 1995).

Two brief but sound surveys of Nazi Germany are J. Spielvogel, *Hitler and Nazi Germany: A History,* 3d ed. (Englewood Cliffs, N.J., 1996), and J. Dülffer, *Nazi Germany 1933–1945* (New York, 1996). The best biographies of Hitler are A. Bullock, *Hitler: A Study in Tyranny* (New York, 1964); J. Fest, *Hitler,* trans. R. and C. Winston (New York, 1974); and the first volume of a massive new biography of Hitler, Ian Kershaw, *Hitler 1889–1936: Hubris* (New York, 1999). Two recent works that examine the enormous literature on Hitler are J. Lukacs, *The Hitler of History* (New York, 1997), and R. Rosenbaum, *Explaining Hitler* (New York, 1998). On the Nazi administration of the state, see M. Broszat, *The Hitler State: The Foundations and Development of the Internal Structure of the Third Reich* (New York, 1981). Basic studies of the SS include R. Koehl, *The Black Corps: The Structure and Power Struggles of the Nazi SS* (Madison, Wis., 1983), and H. Krausnick and M. Broszat, *Anatomy of the SS State* (London, 1970). On women, see C. Koonz, *Mothers in the Fatherland: Women, the Family, and Nazi Politics* (New York, 1987). The Hitler Youth is examined in H. W. Koch, *The Hitler Youth* (New York, 1976). On Nazi anti-Jewish policies between 1933 and 1939, see S. Friedländer, *Nazi Germany and the Jews*, vol. 1, *The Years of Persecution 1933–1939* (New York, 1997).

The collectivization of agriculture in the Soviet Union is examined in S. Fitzpatrick, *Stalin's Peasants: Resistance and Survival in the Russian Village After Collectivization* (New York, 1995). Industrialization is covered in H. Kuromiya, *Stalin's Industrial Revolution, Politics and Workers, 1928–1932* (New York, 1988). Stalin's purges are examined in R. Conquest, *The Great Terror: A Reassessment* (New York, 1990). On Stalin, see R. H. McNeal, *Stalin, Man and Ruler* (New York, 1988); R. Tucker, *Stalin in Power: The Revolution from Above, 1928–1941* (New York, 1990); and R. W. Thurston, *Life and Terror in Stalin's Russia, 1934–1941* (New Haven, Conn., 1996).

The basic study of Germany's foreign policy from 1933 to 1939 can be found in G. Weinberg, *The Foreign Policy of Hitler's Germany: Diplomatic Revolution in Europe, 1933–36* (Chicago, 1970), and *The Foreign Policy of Hitler's Germany: Starting World War II, 1937–1939* (Chicago, 1980). Japan's march to war is examined in A. Iriye, *The Origins of the Second World War in Asia and the Pacific* (London, 1987).

General works on World War II include M. K. Dziewanowski, *War at Any Price: World War II in Europe, 1939–1945*, 2d ed. (Englewood Cliffs, N.J., 1991); the comprehensive study by G. Weinberg, *A World at Arms: A Global History of World War II* (Cambridge, 1994); and J. Campbell, *The Experience of World War II* (New York, 1989). On Hitler as a military leader, see R. Lewin, *Hitler's Mistakes* (New York, 1986). On battles, see J. Keegan, *The Second World War* (New York, 1990).

The best studies of the Holocaust include R. Hilberg, *The Destruction of the European Jews*, rev. ed., 3 vols. (New York, 1985), and L. Yahil, *The Holocaust* (New York, 1990). For brief studies, see J. Fischel, *The Holocaust* (Westport, Conn., 1998), and R. S. Botwinick, *A History of the Holocaust* (Upper Saddle River, N.J., 1996). There is a good overview of the scholarship on the Holocaust in M. Marrus, *The Holocaust in History* (New York, 1987). On the problem of what the Allied countries knew about the Holocaust, see D. Wyman, *The Abandonment of the Jews: America and the Holocaust* (New York, 1984), and M. Gilbert, *Auschwitz and the Allies* (New York, 1981). Other Nazi atrocities are examined in B. Wytwycky, *The Other Holocaust* (Washington, D.C., 1980).

General studies on the impact of total war include J. Costello, *Love, Sex and War: Changing Values, 1939–1945* (London, 1985); P. Summerfield, *Women Workers in the Second World War: Production and Patriarchy in Conflict* (London, 1984); and M. R. Marrus, *The Unwanted: European Refugees in the Twentieth Century* (New York, 1985). On the home front in Germany, see E. R. Beck, *Under the Bombs: The German Home Front, 1942–1945* (Lexington, Ky., 1986), and M. Kitchen, *Nazi Germany at War* (New York, 1995). The Soviet Union during the war is examined in M. Harrison, *Soviet Planning in Peace and War, 1938–1945* (Cambridge, 1985). On the American home front, see the good collection of essays in K. P. O'Brien and L. H. Parsons, *The Home-Front War: World War II and American Society* (Westport, Conn., 1995). The Japanese home front is examined in T. R. H. Havens, *The Valley of Darkness: The Japanese People and World War Two* (New York, 1978).

On the destruction of Germany by bombing raids, see H. Rumpf, *The Bombing of Germany* (London, 1963). The German bombing of Britain is covered in T. Harrisson, *Living Through the Blitz* (London, 1985). On Hiroshima, see A. Chisholm, *Faces of Hiroshima* (London, 1985).

On the emergence of the Cold War, see W. Loth, *The Division of the World, 1941–1955* (New York, 1988). On the wartime summit conferences, see H. Feis, *Churchill, Roosevelt, Stalin: The War They Waged and the Peace They Sought*, 2d ed. (Princeton, N.J., 1967), and D. Clemens, *Yalta* (New York, 1970).

For additional reading, go to InfoTrac College Edition, your online research library at http://web1.infotrac-college.com

Enter the search terms "Weimar Republic" using Keywords.

Enter the search terms "Hitler or Nazi or Nazism" using Keywords.

Enter the search term "totalitarianism" using the Subject Guide.

Enter the search terms "World War, 1939–1945" using the Subject Guide.

Enter the search term "Holocaust" using the Subject Guide.

REFLECTION

MODERN PATTERNS OF WORLD HISTORY (1800–1945)

At the outset of Part IV, we remarked that two of the most significant developments during the nineteenth and early twentieth centuries were the Industrial Revolution and the onset of the era of imperialism. Of these two factors, the first was clearly the more important, for it created the conditions for the latter. It was, of course, the major industrial powers—Great Britain, France, and later Germany, Japan, and the United States—that took the lead in building large colonialist empires. Those European nations that did not achieve a high level of industrial advancement, such as Spain and Portugal, clearly declined in importance as colonial powers.

The advent of the industrial age had a number of lasting consequences for the world at large. On the one hand, the material wealth of those nations that successfully passed through the process increased significantly. In many cases, the creation of advanced industrial societies strengthened democratic institutions and led to a higher standard of living for the majority of the population. It also helped to reduce class barriers and bring about the emancipation of women from many of the legal and social restrictions that had characterized the previous era. The spread of technology and trade outside of Europe created the basis for a new international economic order based on the global exchange of goods.

On the other hand, as we have seen, not all the consequences of the Industrial Revolution were beneficial. In the industrializing societies themselves, rapid economic change often led to widening disparities in the distribution of wealth and, with the decline in pervasiveness of religious belief, a sense of rootlessness and alienation among much of the population. While some societies were able to manage these problems with some degree of success, others experienced a breakdown of social values and the rise of widespread political instability. In Imperial Russia, internal tensions became too much for the traditional landholding elites to handle, leading to social revolution and the rise of the Soviet state. In other cases, such as Germany, deep-seated ethnic and class antagonisms remained under the surface until conditions of economic depression led to the rise of militant fascist regimes.

Industrialization also had destabilizing consequences on the global scene. Rising economic competition among the industrial powers was a major contributor to heightened international rivalry over access to markets and resources and ultimately to global war. For many at the time, the dream of universal affluence that had been aroused by the age of industrialization had turned into a nightmare.

Of course, other forces were also at work during this period. A second development that had a major impact on the era was the rise of nationalism. Like the Industrial Revolution, the idea of nationalism originated in eighteenth-century Europe, where it was a product of the secularization of the age and the experiences of the French revolutionary and Napoleonic eras. Although the concept provided the basis for a new sense of community and the rise of the modern nation-state, it also gave birth to ethnic tensions and hatred that resulted in bitter disputes and civil strife in a number of countries and contributed to the competition among nations that eventually erupted into world war.

Finally, industrialization and the rise of national consciousness transformed the nature of war itself. New weapons of mass destruction created the potential for a new kind of warfare that reached beyond the battlefield into the very heartland of the enemy's territory, while the concept of nationalism transformed war from the sport of kings to a matter of national honor and commitment. Since the French Revolution, when the revolutionary government in Paris had mobilized the entire country by a levy-in-mass (mass conscription) to fight against the forces that opposed the Revolution, governments had relied on mass conscription to defend the national cause while their engines of destruction reached far into enemy territory to destroy the industrial base and undermine the will to fight. This trend was amply demonstrated in the two world wars of the twentieth century. Each was a product of antagonisms that had been unleashed by economic competition and growing national consciousness. Each resulted in a level of destruction that severely damaged the material foundations and eroded the popular spirit of the participants, the victors as well as the vanquished.

In the end, then, industrial power and the driving force of nationalism, the very factors that had created the conditions for European global dominance, contained the seeds for the decline of that dominance. These seeds germinated during the 1930s, when the Great Depression sharpened international competition and mutual antagonisms, and then sprouted in the ensuing conflict, which for the first time embraced the entire globe. By the time World War II came to an end, the once powerful countries

PATHS TO MODERNIZATION

Why some societies were able to embark on the road to industrialization and others were not has long been a matter of scholarly debate Some observers have found the answer in the cultural characteristics of individual societies, such as the Protestant work ethic in parts of Europe, or the tradition of social discipline and class hierarchy in Japan. Others have placed more emphasis on practical considerations, such as the lack of an urban market for agricultural goods in China (which reduced the landowners' incentives to introduce mechanized farming) or the absence of a foreign threat in Japan (which provided increased opportunities for local investment). To historian Peter Stearns, the availability of capital, natural resources, a network of trade relations, and navigable rivers all helped to stimulate industrial growth in nineteenth-century England.

Whatever the truth of such speculations, it is clear that there has been more than one road to industrialization. In his highly respected work on the subject entitled *Social Origins of Dictatorship and Democracy*, sociologist Barrington Moore found at least three paths to economic modernization: the bourgeois capitalist route followed in Great Britain, France, and the United States; the "revolution from above" approach adopted in Germany and Meiji Japan; and the Marxist-Leninist strategy used in the Soviet Union. The first approach, fostered by an independent urban mercantile class, led to the emergence of democratic societies on the capitalist model. The second, carried out by traditional elites in the absence of a strong independent bourgeois class, led ultimately to fascist and militarist regimes; the third, guided by a communist party in the almost total absence of an urban middle class, led to the creation of an advanced industrial society based on a totalitarian political system.

Which approach is the most effective? The bourgeois capitalist model appears to have had the most success in promoting economic growth based on the preservation of human rights, but often such results have been achieved at the cost of vast inequalities in the distribution of wealth within individual societies. Moreover, it is not clear that the bourgeois capitalist option is readily available to societies lacking a tradition of an independent urban middle class. For ambitious political leaders in such countries, fascism and communism provided alluring alternatives.

OLD CHINA, NEW CHINA. This illustration, used on a People's Republic of China calendar in 1960, was made by using traditional Chinese techniques of landscape painting. However, the drawing shows a modern industrial landscape instead of a tranquil pastoral scene. The three junks at the right are the only reminder of traditional China.

of Europe were exhausted, leaving the door ajar for the emergence of two new global superpowers, the United States and the Soviet Union, which dominated the postwar political scene. Although the new superpowers were both products of modern European civilization, they were physically and politically separate from it, and their intense competition, which marked the postwar period, threatened to transform the old map of Europe into a battleground for a new and even more destructive ideological conflict.

If in Europe the dominant fact of the era was the Industrial Revolution, in the rest of the world it was undoubtedly the sheer fact of Western imperialism. Between the end of the Napoleonic wars and the end of the nineteenth century, European powers, or their rivals in Japan and the United States, achieved political mastery over virtually the entire remainder of the world.

What was the overall economic effect of imperialism on the subject peoples? It seems clear from this narrative that for most of the population in colonial areas Western domination was rarely beneficial and often destructive. Although a limited number of merchants, large landowners, and traditional hereditary elites undoubtedly prospered under the umbrella of the expanding imperialist economic order, the majority of colonial peoples, urban and rural alike, probably suffered considerable hardship as a result of the policies adopted by their foreign rulers. The effects of the Industrial Revolution on the poor had been felt in Europe, too, but there the pain was eased somewhat by the fact that the industrial era had laid the foundations for future technological advances and material abundance. In the colonial territories, the importation of modern technology was limited, while most of the profits from manufacturing and commerce fled abroad. For too many, the White Man's Burden was shifted to the shoulders of the colonial peoples.

Some historians point out, however, that for all the inequities of the colonial system, there was a positive side to the experience as well. The expansion of markets and the beginnings of a modern transportation and communications network, while bringing few immediate benefits to the colonial peoples, offered considerable promise for future economic growth. At the same time, the introduction of new ways of looking at human freedom and the relationship between the individual and society set the stage for a reevaluation of such ideas after the restoration of independence following World War II.

Perhaps the Western concept that had the most immediate impact was that of nationalism. The concept of nationalism often served a useful role in many countries in Asia and Africa, where it provided colonial peoples with a sense of common purpose that later proved vital in knitting together the coherent elements in their societies to oppose colonial regimes and create the conditions for future independent states. At first such movements achieved relatively little success, but they began to gather momentum in the second quarter of the twentieth century, when full-fledged nationalist movements began to appear throughout the colonial world to lead their people in the struggle for independence.

Another idea that gained currency in colonial areas was that of democracy. As a rule, colonial regimes did not make a serious attempt to introduce democratic institutions to their subject populations; understandably, they feared that such institutions would inevitably undermine colonial authority. Nevertheless, Western notions of representative government and individual freedom had their advocates in India, Vietnam, China, and Japan well before the end of the nineteenth century. Later, countless Asians and Africans were exposed to such ideas in schools set up by the colonial regime or in the course of travel to Europe or the United States. Most of the nationalist parties founded in colonial territories espoused democratic principles and attempted to apply them when they took power after the restoration of independence.

Finally, the colonial experience offered new ways of looking at the relationship between men and women. Although colonial rule was by no means uniformly beneficial to the position of women in African and Asian societies, growing awareness of the struggle by women in the West to seek sexual equality offered their counterparts in the colonial territories a weapon to fight against the longstanding barriers of custom and legal discrimination.

As we shall see in later chapters, in many instances the initial promise represented by such ideas has proven to be tantalizingly illusory following the restoration of independence. For the most part, the experiment with democracy in postwar African and Asian societies was a brief one. Nationalism itself has proven to be a double-edged sword, as ethnic minorities have seized upon the idea as a means of liberating themselves from indigenous oppressors. But the continuing popularity of democratic ideals and the concept of nationalism throughout Africa and Asia has been a clear indication of the universal appeal of such concepts even after the dismantling of colonial regimes. The idea of the nation, composed of free, educated, and politically active citizens, was now widely accepted throughout much of the non-Western world.

How are we to draw up a final balance sheet on the era of Western imperialism? To its defenders, it was a necessary stage in the evolution of the human race, a flawed but essentially humanitarian effort to provide the backward peoples of Africa and Asia with a boost up the ladder of evolution. To its critics, it was a tragedy of major proportions. The insatiable drive of the advanced economic powers for access to raw materials and markets resulted in the widespread destruction of traditional cultures and created an exploitative environment that transformed the vast

IMPERIALISM AND THE GLOBAL ENVIRONMENT

Beginning in the 1870s, European states engaged in an intense scramble for overseas territory. This "New Imperialism" led Europeans to carve up Asia and Africa and create colonial empires. Within these empires, European states exercised complete political control over the indigenous societies and redrew political boundaries to meet their needs. In Africa, for example, in drawing the boundaries that separated one colony from another (boundaries that often became the boundaries of the modern countries of Africa), Europeans paid no attention to the political divisions of the tribes of Africa. Europeans often divided a tribe between two colonies, or made two tribes that were hostile to each other members of the same colony.

In a similar fashion, Europeans paid little or no heed to the economic needs of their colonial subjects, but refashioned the economies of their empires to meet their own needs in the new world market. In the process, Europeans often dramatically altered the global environment, a transformation that was made visible in a variety of ways. Westerners built railways and ports, erected telegraph lines, drilled for oil, and dug mines for gold, tin, iron ore, and copper. All of these projects transformed and often scarred the natural landscape.

Landscapes, however, were even more dramatically altered by Europe's demand for cash food crops. Throughout vast regions of Africa and Asia, tropical forests were felled to make way for plantations that cultivated crops that could be exported for sale. In Ceylon and India, the British cut down vast tropical forests to plant row upon row of tea bushes. The Dutch did the same in the East Indies, where they planted cinchona trees imported from Peru. Quinine, derived from the bark of the cinchona tree, dramatically reduced the death rate for malaria and made it possible for Europeans to live more securely in the tropical regions of Africa and Asia. In Southeast Asia, the French replaced extensive forests with sugar and coffee plantations. In Malaya, the British transformed tropical forests into plantation stands of rubber trees, the first of which they had smuggled into the area from Brazil. Native workers, who were usually paid pitiful wages by their European overseers, provided the labor for all of these vast plantations.

European states greatly profited from this transformed environment. In *Agriculture in the Tropics: An Elementary Treatise*, written in 1909, the British botanist John Christopher Willis expressed his thoughts on this European policy:

> Whether planting in the tropics will always continue to be under European management is another question, but the northern powers will not permit that the rich and as yet comparatively undeveloped countries of the tropics should be entirely wasted by being devoted merely to the supply of the food and clothing wants of their own people, when they can also supply the wants of the colder zones in so many indispensable products.

In Willis's eyes, the imperialist transformation of the environments of Asia and Africa to serve European needs was entirely justified.

PICKING TEA LEAVES IN CEYLON. Shown here in this 1900 photograph are women picking tea leaves for shipment abroad on a plantation in Ceylon (now Sri Lanka). The British cut down enormous stands of tropical forests in both Ceylon and India in order to grow tea bushes and satisfy the demand for tea back home.

majority of colonial peoples into a permanent underclass while restricting the benefits of modern technology to a privileged few. Sophisticated, age-old societies that should have been left to respond to the technological revolution in their own way were subjected to foreign rule and squeezed dry of precious national resources under the guise of the "civilizing mission."

In this debate, the critics surely have the best of the argument. All in all, the colonial experience was a brutal one, and its benefits accrued almost entirely to citizens of the ruling power. The argument that the Western societies had a "White Man's Burden" to civilize the world was all too often a hypocritical gesture to salve the guilty feelings of those who recognized imperialism for what it was—a savage act of rape.

But as with earlier periods of conquest and empire, not all the consequences were unfortunate ones. Because the ruling colonial powers did make a halfhearted gesture to introduce the technology and ideas that had accompanied the rise of modern Europe, they left behind a legacy that their subject peoples might hope to exploit once they had a chance to determine their own destinies. However slightly, the concept of the civilizing mission did have a mitigating effect on the enormity of the tragedy.

The final judgment on the age of European dominance, then, must be a mixed one. It was a time of unfulfilled expectations, of altruism and greed, of bright promise and tragic failure. The fact is, human beings had learned how to master some of the forces of nature before they had learned how to order relations among themselves or temper their own natures for the common good. The consequences were painful, for European and non-European peoples alike.

But although the experience was a painful one, human societies were able to survive it and to earn a second chance to make better use of the stunning promise of the industrial era. How they have fared in that effort will be the subject of the final section of this book.

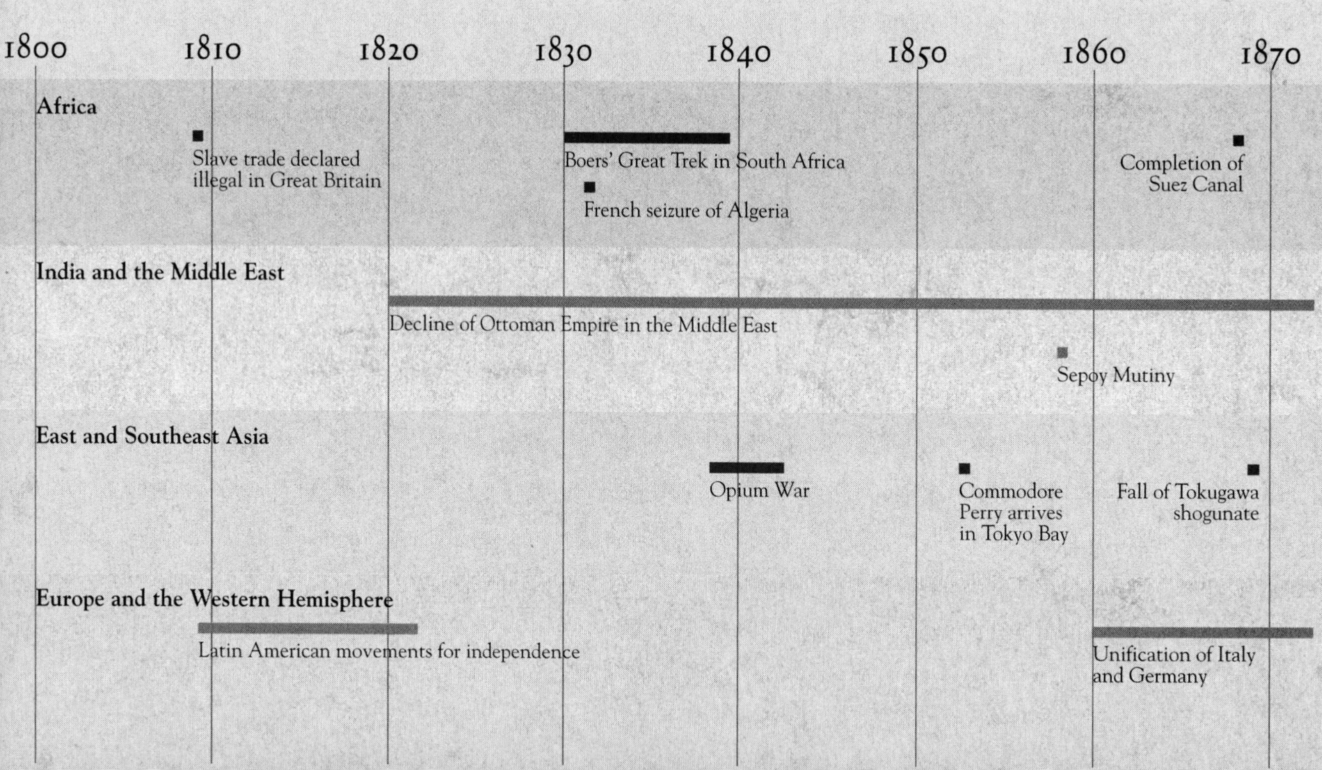

Suggested Readings

For different perspectives on imperialism, see W. Baumgart, *Imperialism: The Idea and Reality of British and French Colonial Expansion, 1880–1914* (New York, 1982), and D. R. Headrick, *The Tools of Empire, Technology and European Imperialism in the Nineteenth Century* (New York, 1981). Different paths to modernization are discussed in B. Moore, Jr., *Social Origins of Dictatorship and Democracy. Lord and Peasant in the Making of the Modern World* (Boston, 1966), and D. R. Headrick, *The Tentacles of Progress: Technology Transfer in the Age of Imperialism, 1850–1940* (New York, 1988). For background material on the role of the Industrial Revolution, see P. N. Stearns, *The Industrial Revolution in World History* (Boulder, Colo., 1993). On the impact of imperialism on the economy and environment of Africa and Asia, see C. Geertz, *Agricultural Involution: The Process of Ecological Change in Indonesia* (Berkeley, 1968); E. Wolf, *Europe and the People without History* (Berkeley, 1982); and R. P. Tucker and J. F. Richards, *Deforestation and the Nineteenth-Century World Economy* (Durham, N.C., 1983).

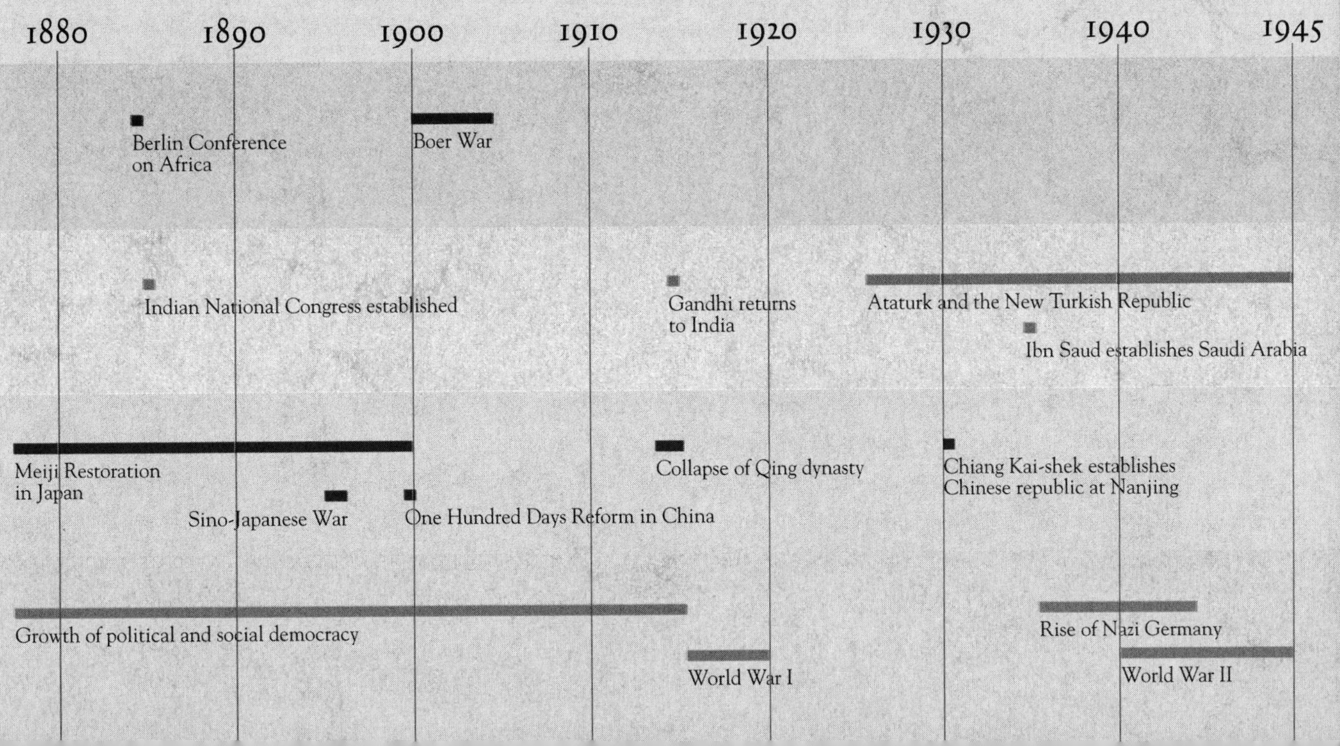

PART

Toward a Global Civilization? The World since 1945

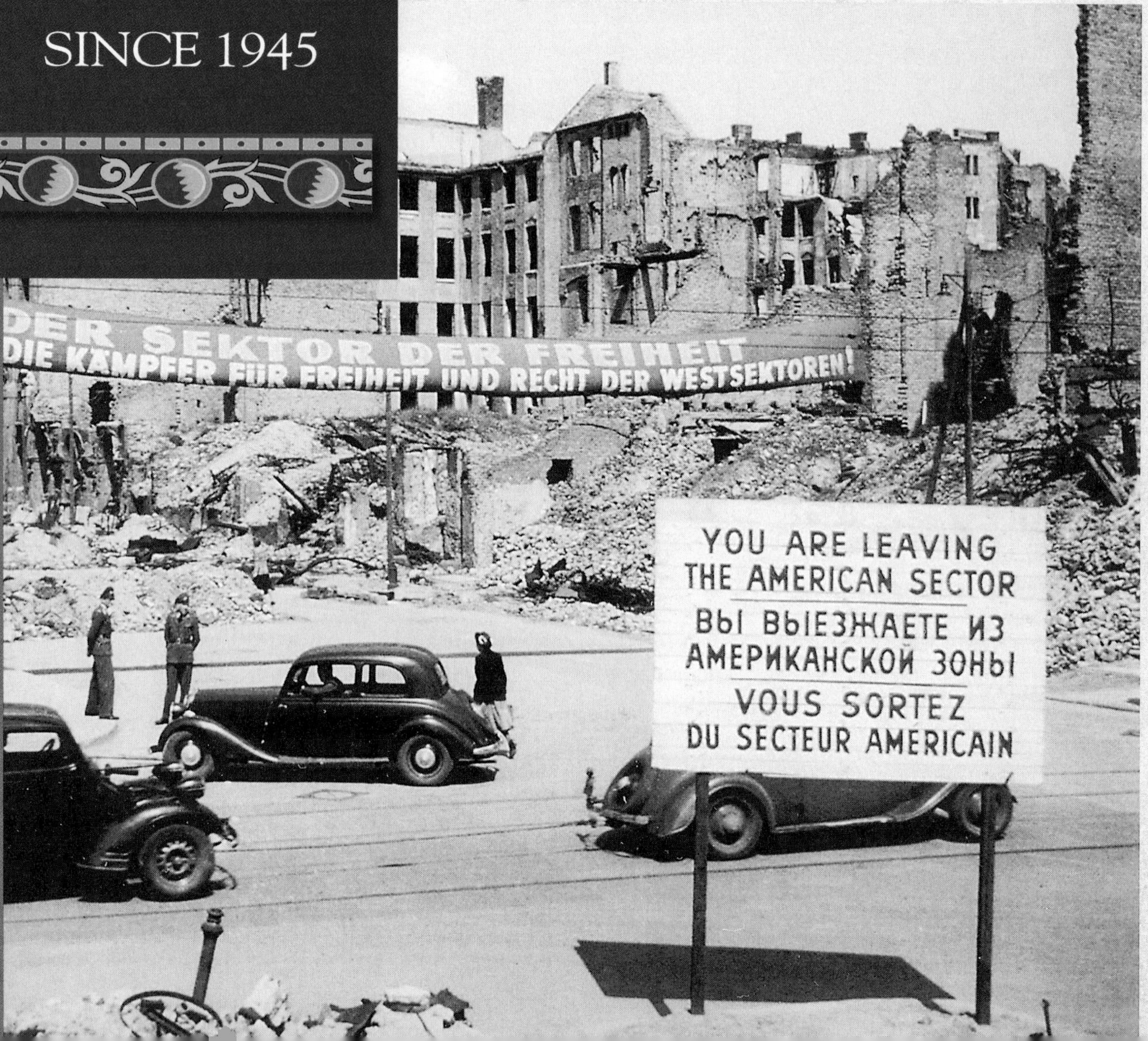

When President Franklin D. Roosevelt and British prime minister Winston Churchill met off the coast of Newfoundland in August 1941 to discuss their common objectives in a postwar world, they appeared to recognize that imperialist rivalry had been the crucial factor leading to the outbreak of the two world wars. The Atlantic Charter stated that the two countries hoped to realize equality of economic opportunity, abandonment of force, and friendly collaboration among the peoples of the world, as well as the right of nations to choose their own form of government.

In a number of respects, the wartime allies achieved their aims for the peace. The rapacious efforts of Germany and Japan to dominate the world were thwarted, and the intense rivalry that had characterized relations among the Western powers came to an end. Outside of Europe, the colonial system was gradually dismantled, and the peoples of Asia and Africa were granted self-determination in the form of independent states. But even before the final defeat of Japan, tension had begun to build in Europe between the Soviet Union and the Western powers. By the end of the 1940s, that tension had spread throughout the world, and the Cold War had begun.

In the meantime, the end of colonial empires did not bring to the peoples of Asia and Africa a new world of political stability, peaceful cooperation, and material prosperity. Economic difficulties, a product of their own inexperience and the continued Western domination of the global economy, led to internal factionalism, military rule, and sometimes regional conflict. Competition between the capitalist and socialist power blocs—led by the United States and the Soviet Union, respectively—compounded the problem. In the late 1980s, however, the Soviet empire began to come apart, and in December 1991, the Soviet Union itself became a memory, as onetime Soviet republics now split into independent states, bringing an end to the ideological Cold War. In the meantime, a number of nations in Asia have apparently entered the lists of the advanced industrial countries and have embarked on the road to political democracy. Half a century after the end of World War II, some of the dreams embodied in the Atlantic Charter appear to be reaching fruition.

But challenges remain, and many of them appear intimidating. The breakup of the Soviet empire has led to the emergence of squabbling nationalities throughout Eastern Europe, while in other parts of the world, including the Middle East, Africa, and Northern Ireland, age-old rivalries and ethnic and religious suspicions continue to create sources of potential bitter conflict. A global economic slowdown brought recession to the advanced nations and severe political and economic difficulties to many societies in the rest of the world. In the meantime, the effects of untrammeled industrial development are coming home to roost in the form of growing environmental pollution. Ethnic and religious differences, as well as continued intense competition for markets, are putting a severe strain on efforts to achieve global cooperation in solving the common problems of humanity.

CHAPTER

27

In the Grip of the Cold War: The Breakdown of the Yalta System

CHAPTER OUTLINE

- THE COLLAPSE OF THE GRAND ALLIANCE
- COLD WAR IN ASIA
- FROM CONFRONTATION TO COEXISTENCE
- AN ERA OF EQUIVALENCE
- CONCLUSION

FOCUS QUESTIONS

- Why were the United States and the Soviet Union suspicious of each other after World War II, and what events between 1945 and 1949 heightened the tensions between the two nations?
- How have historians answered the question of whether the United States or the Soviet Union bears the primary responsibility for the Cold War, and what evidence can be presented on each side of the issue?
- How and why did Mao Zedong and the Communists come to power in China, and what were the implications of their triumph for the Cold War?
- What were the major developments in the Cold War between 1950 and 1989?
- How and why did the Cold War change from a European confrontation to a conflict of global significance?

"Our meeting here in the Crimea has reaffirmed our common determination to maintain and strengthen in the peace to come that unity of purpose and of action which has made victory possible and certain for the United Nations in this war. We believe that this is a sacred obligation which our Governments owe to our peoples and to all the peoples of the world."[1]

With these ringing words, drafted at the Yalta Conference in February 1945, U.S. President Franklin D. Roosevelt, Soviet leader Joseph Stalin, and British prime minister Winston Churchill affirmed their common hope that the Grand Alliance that had been victorious in World War II could be sustained into the postwar era. Only through continuing and growing cooperation and understanding among the three Allies, the statement asserted, could a secure and lasting peace be realized that, in the words of the Atlantic Charter, would "afford assurance that all the men in all the lands may live out their lives in freedom from fear and want."

Roosevelt hoped that the decisions reached at Yalta would provide the basis for a stable peace in the postwar era. Allied occupation forces—American, British, and French in the West and Soviet in the East—were to bring about the end of Axis administration and the holding of free elections to create democratic governments throughout Europe. To foster mutual trust and an end to the suspicions that had marked relations between the capitalist world and the Soviet Union prior to the war, Roosevelt tried to reassure Stalin that Moscow's legitimate territorial aspirations and genuine security needs would be adequately met in a durable peace settlement.

However, this was not to be. Within months after the German surrender, the mutual trust among the Allies—if it had ever existed—rapidly disintegrated, and the dream of a stable peace was replaced by the specter of a nuclear holocaust. As the Cold War conflict between Moscow and Washington intensified, Europe was divided into two armed camps, while the two superpowers, glaring at each other across a deep ideological divide, held the survival of the entire world in their hands.

THE COLLAPSE OF THE GRAND ALLIANCE

The problem started in Europe. At the end of the war, Soviet military forces occupied all of Eastern Europe and the Balkans (except Greece, Albania, and Yugoslavia), while U.S. and other allied forces completed their occupation of the western part of the continent. Roosevelt had assumed that free elections administered by "democratic and peace-loving forces" would lead to democratic governments responsive to the local population. But it soon became clear that the Soviet Union and the United States interpreted the Yalta agreement differently. When Soviet occupation authorities began forming a new Polish government, Stalin refused to accept the Polish government-in-exile—headquartered in London during the war, it was composed primarily of landed aristocrats, who harbored a deep distrust of the Soviet Union—and instead created a government composed of Communists who had spent the war in Moscow. Roosevelt complained to Stalin but eventually agreed to a compromise whereby two members of the London government were included in a new Communist regime. A week later, Roosevelt was dead of a cerebral hemorrhage.

Similar developments took place in all of the states occupied by Soviet troops. Coalitions of all political parties (except fascist or right-wing parties) were formed to run the government, but within a year or two, the Communist parties in these coalitions had assumed the lion's share of power. The next step was the creation of one-party Communist governments. Between 1945 and 1947, Communist governments became firmly entrenched in East Germany, Bulgaria, Romania, Poland, and Hungary. In Czechoslovakia, with its strong tradition of democratic institutions, the Communists did not achieve their goals until 1948. After the elections of 1946, the Communist Party shared control of the government with the non-Communist parties. When it appeared that the latter might win new elections early in 1948, the Communists seized control of the government on February 25. All other parties were dissolved, and the Communist leader Klement Gottwald became the new president of Czechoslovakia.

Yugoslavia was a notable exception to the pattern of growing Soviet dominance in Eastern Europe. The Communist Party there had led resistance to the Nazis during the war and easily took over power when the war ended. Josip Broz, known as Tito (1892–1980), the leader of the Communist resistance movement, appeared to be a loyal Stalinist. After the war, however, he moved to establish an independent Communist state. Stalin hoped to take control of Yugoslavia, but Tito refused to capitulate to Stalin's demands and gained the support of the people (and some sympathy in the West) by portraying the struggle as one of Yugoslav national freedom. In 1958, the Yugoslav party congress asserted that Yugoslav Communists did not see themselves as deviating from communism, only from Stalinism. They considered their more decentralized system, in which workers managed themselves and local communes exercised some political power, closer to the Marxist-Leninist ideal.

To Stalin (who had once boasted "I will shake my little finger, and there will be no more Tito"), the creation of pliant pro-Soviet regimes throughout Eastern Europe may simply have represented his interpretation of the Yalta peace agreement and a reward for sacrifices suffered during the war, satisfying Moscow's aspirations for a buffer zone against the capitalist West. If the Soviet leader had any intention of promoting future Communist revolutions in Western Europe—and there is some indication that he did—such developments would have to await the appearance of a new capitalist crisis a decade or more into the future. As Stalin undoubtedly recalled, Lenin had always maintained that revolutions come in waves.

The Truman Doctrine and the Beginnings of Containment

To the United States, however, the Soviet takeover of Eastern Europe represented an ominous development that threatened Roosevelt's vision of a durable peace. Public suspicion of Soviet intentions grew rapidly, especially among the millions of Americans who still had relatives living in Eastern Europe. Winston Churchill was quick to put such fears into words. In a highly publicized speech at Fulton College in Fulton, Missouri, in March 1946, the former British prime minister declared that an "Iron Curtain" had "descended across the continent," dividing Germany and Europe itself into two hostile camps. Stalin responded by branding Churchill's speech a "call to war with the Soviet Union." But he need not have worried. Although public opinion in the United States placed increasing pressure on Roosevelt's successor, Harry S Truman (1884–1972), to devise an effective strategy to counter Soviet advances abroad, the American people were in no mood for another war.

A civil war in Greece created another potential arena for confrontation between the superpowers and an opportunity for the Truman administration to take a stand. Communist guerrilla forces supported by Tito's Yugoslavia had taken up arms against the pro-Western government in Athens. Great Britain had initially assumed primary responsibility for promoting postwar reconstruction in the eastern Mediterranean, but in 1947 continued economic problems caused the British to withdraw from the active role they had been playing in both Greece and Turkey. President Truman, alarmed by British weakness and the possibility of Soviet expansion into the eastern Mediterranean, responded with the Truman Doctrine (see the box on p. 817), which said in essence that the United States would provide money to countries that claimed they were threatened by communist expansion. If the Soviets were not stopped in Greece, the Truman argument ran, then the United States would have to face the spread of communism throughout the free world. As Dean Acheson, the U.S. secretary of state, explained, "Like apples in a barrel infected by disease, the corruption of Greece would infect Iran and all the East . . . likewise Africa . . . Italy . . . France. . . . Not since Rome and Carthage has there been such a polarization of power on this earth."[2]

The proclamation of the Truman Doctrine was followed in June 1947 by the European Recovery Program, better known as the Marshall Plan, which provided $13 billion for the economic recovery of war-torn Europe. Underlying the program was the belief that communist aggression fed off economic turmoil. General George C. Marshall noted in his commencement speech at Harvard, "Our policy is not directed against any country or doctrine but against hunger, poverty, desperation, and chaos."[3]

From the Soviet perspective, the Marshall Plan was nothing less than capitalist imperialism, a thinly veiled attempt to buy the support of the smaller European countries "in return for the relinquishing . . . of their economic

A CALL TO ARMS. In March 1946, former British prime minister Winston Churchill gave a speech before a college audience in Fulton, Missouri, that electrified the world. Soviet occupation of the countries of Eastern Europe, he declared, had divided the continent into two conflicting halves, separated by an "Iron Curtain." Churchill's speech has often been described as the opening salvo in the Cold War. In the photo at the left, Churchill, with President Harry S Truman behind him, prepares to give his address.

THE TRUMAN DOCTRINE

By 1947, the battle lines had been clearly drawn in the Cold War. This excerpt is taken from a speech by President Harry Truman to the U.S. Congress in which he justified his request for aid to Greece and Turkey. Truman expressed the urgent need to contain the expansion of communism. Compare this statement with that of Soviet leader Leonid Brezhnev cited later in this chapter.

TRUMAN'S SPEECH TO CONGRESS, MARCH 12, 1947

The peoples of a number of countries of the world have recently had totalitarian regimes forced upon them against their will. The Government of the United States has made frequent protests against coercion and intimidation, in violation of the Yalta agreement, in Poland, Rumania, and Bulgaria. I must also state that in a number of other countries there have been similar developments.

At the present moment in world history nearly every nation must choose between alternative ways of life. The choice is too often not a free one.

One way of life is based upon the will of the majority, and is distinguished by free institutions, representative government, free elections, guarantees of individual liberty, freedom of speech and religion, and freedom from political oppression.

The second way of life is based upon the will of a minority forcibly imposed upon the majority. It relies upon terror and oppression, a controlled press and radio, fixed elections, and the suppression of personal freedoms.

I believe that it must be the policy of the United States to support free peoples who are resisting attempted subjugation by armed minorities or by outside pressures.

I believe that we must assist free people to work out their own destinies in their own way.

I believe that our help should be primarily through economic and financial aid, which is essential to economic stability and orderly political processes. . . . I therefore ask the Congress for assistance to Greece and Turkey in the amount of $400,000,000.

and later also their political independence."[4] A Soviet spokesperson described the United States as the "main force in the imperialist camp," whose ultimate goal was "the strengthening of imperialism, preparation for a new imperialist war, a struggle against socialism and democracy, and the support of reactionary and antidemocratic, profascist regimes and movements." Though the Marshall Plan was open to the Soviet Union and its Eastern European satellite states, they refused to participate. The Soviets were in no position to compete financially with the United States, however, and could do little to counter the Marshall Plan.

Europe Divided

By 1947, the split in Europe between East and West had become a fact of life. At the end of World War II, the United States had favored a quick end to its commitments in Europe. But American fears of Soviet aims caused the United States to play an increasingly important role in European affairs. In an important article in *Foreign Affairs* in July 1947, George Kennan, a well-known U.S. diplomat with much knowledge of Soviet affairs, advocated a policy of containment against further aggressive Soviet moves. Kennan favored the "adroit and vigilant application of counter-force at a series of constantly shifting geographical and political points, corresponding to the shifts and maneuvers of Soviet policy." After the Soviet blockade of Berlin in 1948, containment of the Soviet Union became formal U.S. policy.

The fate of Germany had become a source of heated contention between East and West. Besides denazification and the partitioning of Germany (and Berlin) into four occupied zones, the Allied powers had agreed on little with regard to the conquered nation. Even denazification proceeded differently in the various zones of occupation. The Americans and British proceeded methodically—the British had tried 2 million cases by 1948—while the Soviets (and French) went after major criminals and allowed lesser officials to go free. The Soviet Union, hardest hit by the war, took reparations from Germany in the form of booty. The technology-starved Soviets dismantled and removed to Russia 380 factories from the western zones of Berlin before transferring their control to the Western powers. By the summer of 1946, 200 chemical, paper, and textile factories in the East German zone had likewise been shipped to the Soviet Union. At the same time, the German Communist Party was reestablished, under the control of Walter Ulbricht (1893–1973), and was soon in charge of the political reconstruction of the Soviet zone in eastern Germany.

Although the foreign ministers of the four occupying powers (the United States, the Soviet Union, Great Britain, and France) kept meeting in an attempt to arrive at a final peace treaty with Germany, they moved further and further apart. At the same time, the British, French, and Americans gradually began to merge their zones economically and, by February 1948, were making plans for the unification of these three western sections and the formal creation of a West German government. In an effort to secure all of Berlin and halt the creation of a West German government, the Soviet Union imposed a blockade of West Berlin that prevented all traffic from entering the city's western zones through Soviet-controlled territory in East Germany.

The Western powers were faced with a dilemma. Direct military confrontation seemed dangerous, and no one wished to risk World War III. Therefore, an attempt to break through the blockade with tanks and trucks was ruled out. The solution was to deliver supplies for the city's inhabitants by plane. At its peak, the Berlin Airlift flew 13,000 tons of supplies daily into Berlin. The Soviets, also not wanting war, did not interfere and finally lifted the blockade in May 1949. The blockade of Berlin had severely increased tensions between the United States and the Soviet Union and brought the separation of Germany into two states. The German Federal Republic (FRG) was formally created from the three Western zones in September 1949, and a month later, a separate German Democratic Republic (GDR) was established in East Germany. Berlin remained a divided city and the source of much contention between East and West.

The search for security in the new world of the Cold War also led to the formation of military alliances. The North Atlantic Treaty Organization (NATO) was formed in April 1949 when Belgium, Luxembourg, the Netherlands, France, Britain, Italy, Denmark, Norway, Portugal, and Iceland signed a treaty with the United States and Canada. All the powers agreed to provide mutual assistance if any one of them was attacked. A few years later, West Germany and Turkey joined NATO.

The Eastern European states soon followed suit. In 1949, they formed the Council for Mutual Economic Assistance (COMECON) for economic cooperation.

A CITY DIVIDED. In 1948, U.S. planes airlifted supplies into Berlin to break the blockade that Soviet troops had imposed to isolate the city. Shown here is "Checkpoint Charlie," located at the boundary between the U.S. and Soviet zones of Berlin, just as Soviet roadblocks are about to be removed. The banner at the entry to the Soviet sector reads: "The sector of freedom greets the fighters for freedom and right of the Western sector."

Then, in 1955, Albania, Bulgaria, Czechoslovakia, East Germany, Hungary, Poland, Romania, and the Soviet Union organized a formal military alliance, the Warsaw Pact. Once again, Europe was tragically divided into hostile alliance systems.

There has been considerable historical debate over who bears the most responsibility for starting the Cold War. In the 1950s, most scholars in the West assumed that the bulk of the blame must fall on the shoulders of Stalin, whose determination to impose Soviet rule on Eastern Europe snuffed out hopes for freedom and self-determination there and aroused justifiable fears of Communist expansion in the West. During the next decade, however, revisionist historians—influenced in part by aggressive U.S. policies in Southeast Asia—began to argue that the fault lay primarily in Washington, where Truman and his anti-Communist advisers abandoned the precepts of Yalta and sought to encircle the Soviet Union with a tier of pliant U.S. client states.

No doubt, both the United States and the Soviet Union took steps at the end of World War II that were unwise or might have been avoided. Both nations, however, were working within a framework conditioned by the past. Ultimately, the rivalry between the two superpowers stemmed from their different historical perspectives and their irreconcilable political ambitions. Intense competition for political and military supremacy had long been a regular feature of Western civilization. The United States

MAP 27.1 The New European Alliance Systems in the 1950s and 1960s

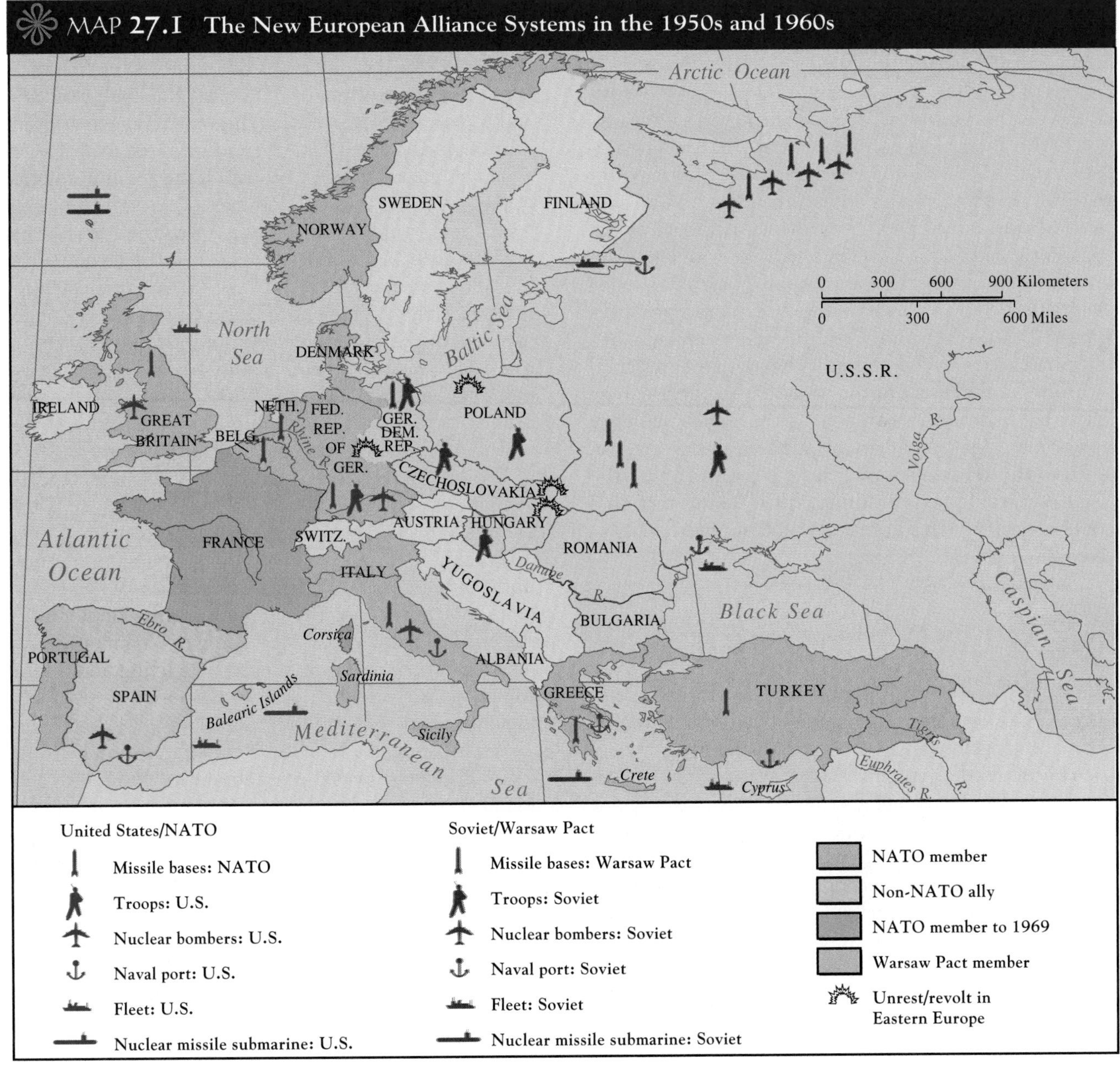

and the Soviet Union were the heirs of that European tradition of power politics, and it should not surprise us that two such different systems would seek to extend their way of life to the rest of the world. Because of its need to secure its western border, the Soviet Union was not prepared to give up the advantages it had gained in Eastern Europe from Germany's defeat. But neither were Western leaders prepared to accept without protest the establishment of a system of Soviet satellites that not only threatened the security of Western Europe but also deeply offended Western sensibilities because of its blatant disregard of the Western concept of human rights.

This does not necessarily mean that neither side bears primary responsibility for starting the Cold War. Some revisionist historians have claimed that the U.S. doctrine of containment was a provocative action that aroused Stalin's suspicions and drove Moscow into a position of hostility toward the West. This charge lacks credibility. As information from the Soviet archives and other sources has become available, it is increasingly clear that Stalin's suspicions of the West were rooted in his Marxist-Leninist worldview and long predated Washington's enunciation of the doctrine of containment. As his foreign minister Vyacheslav Molotov once remarked, Soviet policy was inherently aggressive in nature and would be triggered whenever the opportunity offered. Although Stalin apparently had no master plan to advance Soviet power into Western Europe, he was probably prepared to make every effort to do so once the next revolutionary wave appeared on the horizon. Western leaders were fully justified in reacting to this possibility by strengthening their own lines of defense. On the other hand, a case can be made that in deciding to respond to the Soviet challenge in a primarily military manner, Western leaders overreacted to the situation and virtually guaranteed that the Cold War would be transformed into an arms race that could conceivably result in a new and uniquely destructive war.

Cold War in Asia

The Cold War was somewhat slower to make its appearance in Asia. At Yalta, Stalin formally agreed to enter the Pacific War against Japan three months after the close of the conflict with Germany. As a reward for Soviet participation in the struggle against Japan, Roosevelt promised that Moscow would be granted "preeminent interests" in Manchuria (interests reminiscent of those possessed by imperial Russia prior to its defeat at the hands of Japan in 1904–1905) and the establishment of a Soviet naval base at Port Arthur. In return, Stalin promised to sign a treaty of alliance with the Republic of China, thus implicitly committing the Soviet Union not to provide the Chinese Communists with support in a possible future civil war. Although many observers would later question Stalin's sincerity in making such a commitment to the vocally anti-Communist Chiang Kai-shek, in Moscow the decision probably had a logic of its own. Stalin had no particular liking for the independent-minded Mao Zedong, and indeed did not anticipate a Communist victory in the eventuality of a civil war in China. Only an agreement with Chiang Kai-shek could provide the Soviet Union with a strategically vital economic and political presence in northern China.

Despite these commitments, the Allied agreements soon broke down, and East Asia was sucked into the vortex of the Cold War by the end of the 1940s. The root of the problem lay in the underlying weakness of the Chiang Kai-shek regime, which threatened to create a political vacuum in East Asia that both Moscow and Washington would be tempted to fill.

The Chinese Civil War

As World War II came to an end in the Pacific, relations between the government of Chiang Kai-shek in China and its powerful U.S. ally had become somewhat frayed. Although Roosevelt had hoped that republican China would be the keystone of his plan for peace and stability in Asia after the war, U.S. officials became disillusioned with the corruption of Chiang's government and his unwillingness to risk his forces against the Japanese (he hoped to save them for use against the Communists after the war in the Pacific ended), and China was no longer the focus of Washington's close attention as the war came to a close. Nevertheless, U.S. military and economic aid to China had been substantial, and at war's end the new Truman administration still hoped that it could rely on Chiang to support U.S. postwar goals in the region.

While Chiang Kai-shek wrestled with Japanese aggression and problems of national development, the Communists were building up their strength in northern China. To enlarge their political base, they carried out a "mass line" policy (from the masses, to the masses), reducing land rents and confiscating the lands of wealthy landlords. By the end of World War II, according to Communist estimates, 20 to 30 million Chinese were living under their administration, and their People's Liberation Army (PLA) included nearly one million troops.

As the war came to an end, world attention began to focus on the prospects for renewed civil strife in China. Members of a U.S. liaison team stationed in Yan'an were impressed by the performance of the Communists, and some recommended that the United States should support them or at least remain neutral in a possible conflict between Communists and Nationalists for control of China. The Truman administration, though skeptical of Chiang's ability to forge a strong and prosperous country, was increasingly concerned about the spread of communism in Europe and tried to find a peaceful solution through the formation of a coalition government of all parties in China.

The effort failed. By 1946, full-scale war between the Nationalist government, now reinstalled in Nanjing, and the Communists resumed. Now Chiang Kai-shek's errors came home to roost. In the countryside, millions of peasants, attracted to the Communists by promises of land and social justice, flocked to serve in Mao Zedong's PLA. In the cities, middle-class Chinese, who were normally hostile to communism, were alienated by Chiang's brutal suppression of all dissent and his government's inability to slow the ruinous rate of inflation or solve the economic problems it caused. With morale dropping in the cities, Chiang's troops began to defect to the Communists. Sometimes whole divisions, officers as well as ordinary soldiers, changed sides. By 1948, the PLA was advancing south out of Manchuria and had encircled Beijing. Communist troops took the old imperial capital, crossed the Yangtze the following spring, and occupied the commercial hub of Shanghai. During the next few months, Chiang's government and two million of his followers fled to Taiwan, which the Japanese had returned to Chinese control after World War II.

CHIANG KAI-SHEK AND MAO ZEDONG EXCHANGE A TOAST. After World War II, the United States sent General George C. Marshall to China in an effort to prevent civil war between Chiang Kai-shek's government and the Communists. Marshall's initial success was symbolized by this toast between Chiang and Mao. But suspicion ran too deep, and soon conflict ensued, leading to a Communist victory in 1949. Chiang Kai-shek's government retreated to the island of Taiwan.

The Truman administration reacted to the spread of Communist power in China with acute discomfort. Washington had no desire to see a Communist government on the mainland, but it had little confidence in Chiang Kai-shek's ability to realize Roosevelt's dream of a strong, united, and prosperous China. In December 1945, President Truman sent General George C. Marshall to China in a last-ditch effort to bring about a peaceful settlement, but anti-Communist elements in the Republic of China resisted U.S. efforts to create a coalition government with the Chinese Communist Party (CCP). During the next two years, the United States gave limited military support to Chiang's regime but refused to commit U.S. power to guarantee its survival. The administration's hands-off policy deeply angered many in Congress, who charged that the White House was "soft on communism" and declared further that Roosevelt had betrayed Chiang Kai-shek at Yalta by granting privileges in Manchuria to the Soviet Union. In their view, Soviet troops had hindered the dispatch of Chiang's forces to the area and provided the PLA with weapons to use against their rivals.

In later years, sources in both Moscow and Beijing suggested that the Soviet Union gave little assistance to the CCP in its struggle against the Nanjing regime. In fact, Stalin periodically advised Mao against undertaking the effort. Although Communist forces undoubtedly received some assistance from Soviet occupation troops in Manchuria, their victory ultimately stemmed from conditions inside China, not from the intervention of outside powers. So indeed argued the Truman administration in 1949, when it issued a White Paper that placed most of the blame for the debacle at the foot of Chiang Kai-shek's regime (see the box on p. 822).

Many Americans, however, did not agree. With the Communist victory, Asia became a theater of the Cold War and an integral element of American politics. During the spring of 1950, under pressure from Congress and public opinion to define U.S. interests in Asia, the Truman administration adopted a new national security policy that implied that the United States would take whatever steps were necessary to stem the further expansion of communism in the region.

The Korean War

Communist leaders in China, from their new capital of Beijing, hoped that their accession to power in 1949 would bring about an era of peace in the region and permit their new government to concentrate on domestic goals. But the desire for peace was tempered by their determination to erase a century of humiliation at the hands of imperialist powers and to restore the traditional outer frontiers of the empire. In addition to recovering territories that had been part of the Manchu Empire, such as Manchuria, Taiwan, and Tibet, the Chinese leaders also hoped to restore Chinese influence in former tributary areas such as Korea and Vietnam.

It soon became clear that these two goals were not always compatible. Negotiations with the Soviet Union led to Soviet recognition of Chinese sovereignty over Manchuria and Xinjiang (the desolate lands north of Tibet

IT'S NOT OUR FAULT

In 1949, with China about to fall under the control of the Communists, President Harry S Truman instructed the State Department to prepare a White Paper explaining why the U.S. policy of seeking to avoid a Communist victory in China had failed. The authors of the White Paper concluded that responsibility lay at the door of Nationalist Chinese leader Chiang Kai-shek and that there was nothing the United States could have reasonably done to alter the result. Most China observers today would accept that assessment, but it did little at the time to deflect criticism of the administration for selling out the interests of our ally in China.

U.S. STATE DEPARTMENT WHITE PAPER ON CHINA, 1949

When peace came the United States was confronted with three possible alternatives in China: (1) it could have pulled out lock, stock, and barrel; (2) it could have intervened militarily on a major scale to assist the Nationalists to destroy the Communists; (3) it could, while assisting the Nationalists to assert their authority over as much of China as possible, endeavor to avoid a civil war by working for a compromise between the two sides.

The first alternative would, and I believe American public opinion at the time so felt, have represented an abandonment of our international responsibilities and of our traditional policy of friendship for China before we had made a determined effort to be of assistance. The second alternative policy, while it may look attractive theoretically, in retrospect, was wholly impracticable. The Nationalists had been unable to destroy the Communists during the ten years before the war. Now after the war the Nationalists were, as indicated above, weakened, demoralized, and unpopular. They had quickly dissipated their popular support and prestige in the areas liberated from the Japanese by the conduct of their civil and military officials. The Communists on the other hand were much stronger than they had ever been and were in control of most of North China. Because of the ineffectiveness of the Nationalist forces, which was later to be tragically demonstrated, the Communists probably could have been dislodged only by American arms. It is obvious that the American people would not have sanctioned such a colossal commitment of our armies in 1945 or later. We therefore came to the third alternative policy whereunder we faced the facts of the situation and attempted to assist in working out a *modus vivendi* which would avert civil war but nevertheless preserve and even increase the influence of the National Government. . . .

The distrust of the leaders of both the Nationalist and Communist Parties for each other proved too deep-seated to permit final agreement, notwithstanding temporary truces and apparently promising negotiations. The Nationalists, furthermore, embarked in 1946 on an overambitious military campaign in the face of warnings by General Marshall that it not only would fail but would plunge China into economic chaos and eventually destroy the National Government. . . .

The unfortunate but inescapable fact is that the ominous result of the civil war in China was beyond the control of the government of the United States. Nothing that this country did or could have done within the reasonable limits of its capabilities could have changed that result; nothing that was left undone by this country has contributed to it. It was the product of internal Chinese forces, forces which this country tried to influence but could not. A decision was arrived at within China, if only a decision by default.

that were known as Chinese Turkestan because many of the peoples in the area were of Turkish origin), although the Soviets retained a measure of economic influence in both areas. Chinese troops occupied Tibet in 1950 and brought it under Chinese administration for the first time in more than a century. But in Korea and Taiwan, China's efforts to recreate the imperial buffer zone provoked new conflicts with foreign powers.

The problem of Taiwan was a consequence of the Cold War. As the civil war in China came to an end, the Truman administration appeared determined to avoid entanglement in China's internal affairs and indicated that it would not prevent a Communist takeover of the island, now occupied by Chiang Kai-shek's Republic of China. But as tensions between the United States and the new Chinese government escalated during the winter of 1949–1950, influential figures in the United States began to argue that Taiwan was crucial to U.S. defense strategy in the Pacific.

The outbreak of war in Korea also helped bring the Cold War to East Asia. After the Sino-Japanese War in 1894–1895, Korea, long a Chinese tributary, had fallen increasingly under the rival influences of Japan and Russia. After the Japanese defeated the Russians in 1905, Korea became an integral part of the Japanese Empire and remained so until 1945. The removal of Korea from Japanese control had been one of the stated objectives of the Allies in World War II, and on the eve of Japanese surrender in August 1945, the Soviet Union and the United States agreed to divide the country into two separate occupation zones at the 38th parallel. They originally planned to hold national elections after the restoration of peace to reunify Korea under an independent government. But as U.S.–Soviet relations deteriorated, two separate govern-

MAP 27.2 The Korean Peninsula

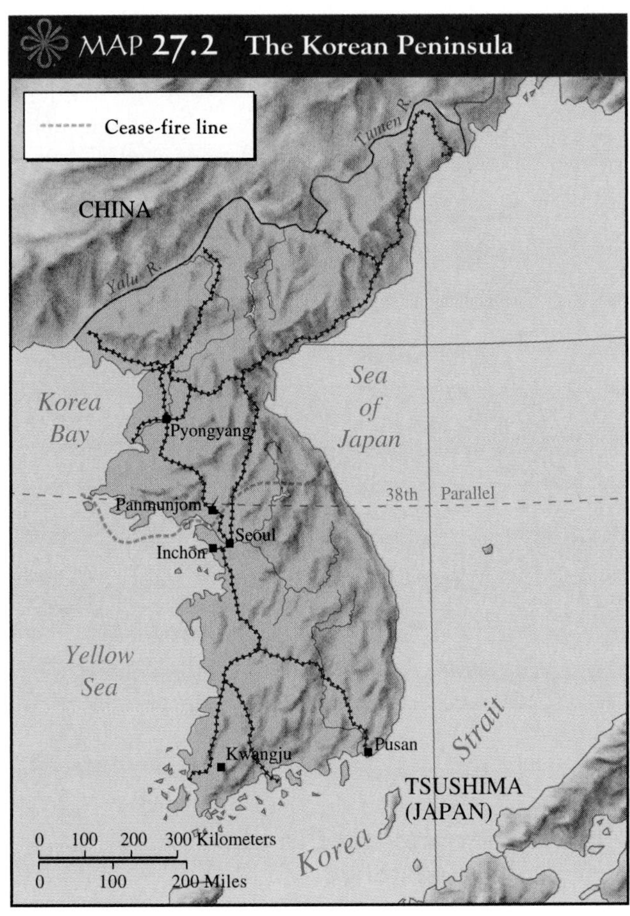

ments emerged in Korea, a Communist one in the north and an anti-Communist one in the south.

Tensions between the two governments ran high along the dividing line, and on June 25, 1950, with the apparent approval of Stalin, North Korean troops invaded the south. The Truman administration immediately ordered U.S. naval and air forces to support South Korea, and the United Nations Security Council passed a resolution calling on member nations to jointly resist the invasion. By September, United Nations (UN) forces under the command of U.S. General Douglas MacArthur marched northward across the 38th parallel with the aim of unifying Korea under a single, non-Communist government.

President Truman worried that by approaching the Chinese border at the Yalu River, the UN troops could trigger Chinese intervention, but was assured by MacArthur that China would not respond. In November, however, Chinese "volunteer" forces intervened in force on the side of North Korea and drove the UN troops southward in disarray. A static defense line was eventually established near the original dividing line at the 38th parallel, although the war continued.

To many Americans, the Chinese intervention in Korea was clear evidence that China intended to promote communism throughout Asia, and recent evidence suggests that Mao Zedong was convinced that a revolutionary wave was on the rise in Asia. In fact, however, China's decision to enter the war was probably motivated in large part by the fear that hostile U.S. forces might be stationed on the Chinese frontier and perhaps even launch an attack across the border. MacArthur intensified such fears by calling publicly for air attacks on Manchurian cities in preparation for an attack on Communist China. In any case, the outbreak of the Korean War was particularly unfortunate for China. Immediately after the invasion, President Truman dispatched the U.S. Seventh Fleet to the Taiwan Strait to prevent a possible Chinese invasion of Taiwan. Even more unfortunate, the invasion hardened Western attitudes against the new Chinese government and led to China's isolation from the major capitalist powers for two decades. As a result, China was cut off from all forms of economic and technological assistance and was forced to rely almost entirely on the Soviet Union, with which it had signed a pact of friendship and cooperation in early 1950.

Conflict in Indochina

During the mid-1950s, China sought to build contacts with the nonsocialist world. A cease-fire agreement brought the Korean War to an end in July 1953, and China signaled its desire to live in peaceful coexistence with other independent countries in the region. But a relatively minor conflict now began to intensify on Beijing's southern flank, in French Indochina. The struggle had begun after World War II, when Ho Chi Minh's Indochinese Communist Party, at the head of a multiparty nationalist alliance called the Vietminh Front, seized power in northern and central Vietnam after the surrender of imperial Japan. After abortive negotiations between Ho's government and the returning French, war broke out in December 1946. French forces occupied the cities and the densely populated lowlands, while the Vietminh took refuge in the mountains.

For three years, the Vietminh gradually increased in size and effectiveness. What had begun as an anticolonial struggle by Ho Chi Minh's Vietminh Front against the French after World War II became entangled in the Cold War in the early 1950s, when both the United States and the new Communist government in China began to intervene in the conflict to promote their own national security objectives. China began to provide military assistance to the Vietminh to protect its own borders from hostile forces. The Americans supported the French but pressured the French government to prepare for an eventual transition to non-Communist governments in Vietnam, Laos, and Cambodia.

At the Geneva Conference in 1954, with the French public tired of fighting the "dirty war" in Indochina, the French agreed to a peace settlement with Ho Chi Minh's Vietminh. Vietnam was temporarily divided into a northern Communist half (known as the Democratic Republic

HO CHI MINH PLANS AN ATTACK ON THE FRENCH. Unlike many peoples in Southeast Asia, the Vietnamese had to fight for their independence after World War II. That fight was led by the talented Communist leader Ho Chi Minh. In this photograph, Ho, assisted by his chief strategist Vo Nguyen Giap, plans an attack on French positions in Vietnam.

of Vietnam, or DRV) and a non-Communist southern half based in Saigon (eventually to be known as the Republic of Vietnam, or RVN). Elections were to be held in two years to create a unified government. Cambodia and Laos were both declared independent under neutral governments.

China had played an active role in bringing about the settlement and clearly hoped that it would reduce tensions in the area, but subsequent efforts to improve relations between China and the United States foundered on the issue of Taiwan. In the fall of 1954, the United States signed a mutual security treaty with the Republic of China guaranteeing U.S. military support in case of an invasion of Taiwan. When Beijing demanded U.S. withdrawal from Taiwan as the price for improved relations, diplomatic talks between the two countries collapsed.

From Confrontation to Coexistence

The decade of the 1950s opened with the world teetering on the edge of a nuclear holocaust. The Soviet Union had detonated its first nuclear device in 1949, and the two blocs—capitalist and socialist—viewed each other across an ideological divide that grew increasingly bitter with each passing year. Yet as the decade drew to a close, a measure of sanity crept into the Cold War, and the leaders of the major world powers began to seek ways to coexist in a peaceful and stable world.

Khrushchev and the Era of Peaceful Coexistence

The first clear sign of change occurred after Stalin's death in early 1953. His successor, Georgy Malenkov (1902–1988), openly hoped to improve relations with the Western powers in order to reduce defense expenditures and shift government spending to growing consumer needs. Nikita Khrushchev (1894–1971), who replaced Malenkov in 1955, continued his predecessor's efforts to reduce tensions with the West and improve the living standards of the Soviet people.

In an adroit public relations touch, Khrushchev publicized Moscow's appeal for a new policy of "peaceful coexistence" with the West. In 1955, he surprisingly agreed to negotiate an end to the postwar occupation of Austria by the victorious allies and allow the creation of a neutral country with strong cultural and economic ties with the West. He also called for a reduction in defense expenditures and reduced the size of the Soviet armed forces.

At first, Washington was suspicious of Khrushchev's motives, especially after the Soviet crackdown in Hungary in the fall of 1956 (see Chapter 28). A new crisis over Berlin added to the tension. The Soviet Union had launched its first intercontinental ballistic missile (ICBM) in August 1957, arousing U.S. fears of a missile gap between the United States and the Soviet Union. Khrushchev attempted to take advantage of the U.S. frenzy over missiles to solve the problem of West Berlin, which had remained a "Western island" of prosperity inside the relatively poverty-stricken state of East Ger-

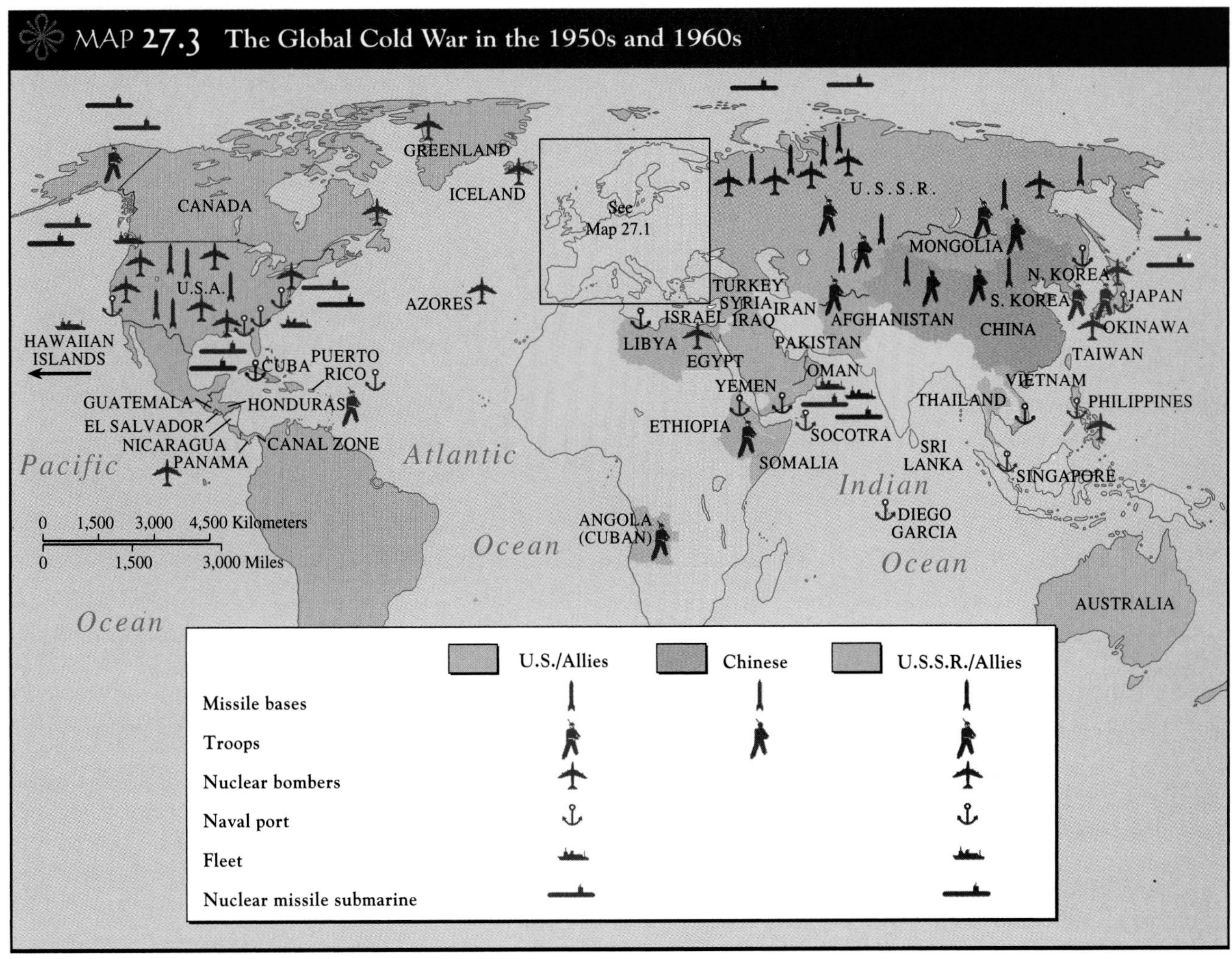

MAP 27.3 The Global Cold War in the 1950s and 1960s

many. Many East Germans sought to escape to West Germany by fleeing through West Berlin, a serious blot on the credibility of the GDR and a potential source of instability in East-West relations. In November 1958, Khrushchev announced that unless the West removed its forces from West Berlin within six months, he would turn over control of the access routes to the East Germans. Unwilling to accept an ultimatum that would have abandoned West Berlin to the Communists, President Dwight D. Eisenhower and the West stood firm, and Khrushchev eventually backed down.

Despite such periodic crises in East-West relations, there were tantalizing signs that an era of true peaceful coexistence between the two power blocs could be achieved. In the late 1950s, the United States and the Soviet Union initiated a cultural exchange program. While the Leningrad Ballet appeared at theaters in the United States, Benny Goodman and the film *West Side Story* played in Moscow. In 1958, Nikita Khrushchev visited the United States and had a brief but friendly encounter with President Eisenhower at the presidential retreat in northern Maryland.

Yet Khrushchev could rarely avoid the temptation to gain an advantage over the United States in the competition for influence throughout the world, and this resulted in an unstable relationship between the two superpowers. Moscow also took every opportunity to promote its interests in the Third World, as the countries of Asia, Africa, and Latin America were now popularly called. Unlike Stalin, Khrushchev viewed the dismantling of colonial regimes in the area as a potential advantage for the Soviet Union and sought especially to exploit the deep suspicions of the United States in Latin America. To improve Soviet influence in such areas, Khrushchev established alliances with key Third World leaders such as Sukarno in Indonesia, Gamel Abdul Nasser in Egypt, Jawaharlal Nehru in India, and Fidel Castro in Cuba. In January 1961, just as John F. Kennedy assumed the presidency, Khrushchev unnerved the new president at an informal summit meeting in Vienna by declaring that the Soviet Union would provide active support to national liberation movements throughout the world. There were rising fears in Washington of Soviet meddling in such sensitive trouble spots as Southeast Asia, Central Africa, and the Caribbean.

THE KITCHEN DEBATE. During the late 1950s, the United States and the Soviet Union sought to defuse Cold War tensions by encouraging cultural exchanges between the two countries. On one occasion, U.S. vice president Richard M. Nixon visited Moscow in conjunction with the arrival of an exhibit to introduce U.S. culture and society to the Soviet people. Here Nixon lectures Soviet party chief Nikita Khrushchev on the technology of the U.S. kitchen. To Nixon's left is future Soviet president Leonid Brezhnev.

The Cuban Missile Crisis and the Move Toward Détente

The Cold War confrontation between the United States and the Soviet Union reached frightening levels during the Cuban Missile Crisis. In 1959, a left-wing revolutionary named Fidel Castro (b. 1927) overthrew the Cuban dictator Fulgencio Batista and established a Soviet-supported totalitarian regime. After the utter failure of a U.S.–supported attempt (the "Bay of Pigs" incident) to overthrow Castro's regime in 1961, the Soviet Union decided to place nuclear missiles in Cuba in 1962. The United States was not prepared to allow nuclear weapons within such close striking distance of the American mainland, even though it had placed nuclear weapons in Turkey within easy range of the Soviet Union. Khrushchev was quick to point out that "your rockets are in Turkey. You are worried by Cuba . . . because it is 90 miles from the American coast. But Turkey is next to us."[5] When U.S. intelligence discovered that a Soviet fleet carrying missiles was heading to Cuba, President Kennedy decided to blockade Cuba and prevent the fleet from reaching its destination. This approach to the problem had the benefit of delaying confrontation and giving the two sides time to find a peaceful solution. Khrushchev agreed to turn back the fleet if Kennedy pledged not to invade Cuba. In a conciliatory letter to Kennedy, Khrushchev wrote:

> We and you ought not to pull on the ends of the rope in which you have tied the knot of war, because the more the two of us pull, the tighter that knot will be tied. And a moment may come when that knot will be tied too tight that even he who tied it will not have the strength to untie it. . . . Let us not only relax the forces pulling on the ends of the rope; let us take measures to untie that knot. We are ready for this.[6]

The intense feeling that the world might have been annihilated in a few days had a profound influence on both sides. A hot-line communications system between Moscow and Washington was installed in 1963 to expedite rapid communications between the two superpowers in time of crisis. In the same year, the two powers agreed to ban nuclear tests in the atmosphere, a step that at least served to lessen the tensions between the two nations.

The Sino-Soviet Dispute

Nikita Khrushchev had launched his slogan of peaceful coexistence as a means of improving relations with the capitalist powers; ironically, one result of the campaign was to undermine Moscow's ties with its close ally China. During Stalin's lifetime, Beijing had accepted the Soviet Union as the acknowledged leader of the socialist camp. After Stalin's death, however, relations began to deteriorate. Part of the reason may have been Mao Zedong's contention that he, as the most experienced Marxist leader, should now be acknowledged as the most authoritative voice within the socialist community. But another determining factor was that just as Soviet policies were moving toward moderation, China's were becoming more radical.

Several other issues were involved, including territorial disputes and China's unhappiness with limited Soviet economic assistance. But the key sources of disagreement involved ideology and the Cold War. Chinese leaders were convinced that the successes of the Soviet space program confirmed that the socialists were now technologically superior to the capitalists (the East wind, trumpeted the Chinese official press, had now triumphed over the West wind), and they urged Khrushchev to go on the offen-

A PLEA FOR PEACEFUL COEXISTENCE

The Soviet leader Vladimir Lenin had contended that war between the socialist and imperialist camps was inevitable because the imperialists would never give up without a fight. That assumption had probably guided the thoughts of Joseph Stalin, who told colleagues shortly after World War II that a new war would break out in fifteen to twenty years. But Stalin's successor, Nikita Khrushchev, feared that a new world conflict could result in a nuclear holocaust and contended that the two sides must learn to coexist, although peaceful competition would continue. In this speech given in Beijing in 1959, Khrushchev attempted to persuade the Chinese to accept his views. But Chinese leaders argued that the "imperialist nature" of the United States would never change and warned that they would not accept any peace agreement in which they had no part.

KHRUSHCHEV'S SPEECH TO THE CHINESE, 1959

Comrades! Socialism brings to the people peace—that greatest blessing. The greater the strength of the camp of socialism grows, the greater will be its possibilities for successfully defending the cause of peace on this earth. The forces of socialism are already so great that real possibilities are being created for excluding war as a means of solving international disputes. . . .

When I spoke with President Eisenhower—and I have just returned from the United States of America—I got the impression that the President of the U.S.A.—and not a few people support him—understands the need to relax international tension. . . .

There is only one way of preserving peace—that is the road of peaceful coexistence of states with different social systems. The question stands thus: either peaceful coexistence or war with its catastrophic consequences. Now, with the present relation of forces between socialism and capitalism being in favor of socialism, he who would continue the "cold war" is moving towards his own destruction. . . .

Already in the first years of the Soviet power the great Lenin defined the general line of our foreign policy as being directed towards the peaceful coexistence of states with different social systems. For a long time, the ruling circles of the Western Powers rejected these truly humane principles. Nevertheless the principles of peaceful coexistence made their way into the hearts of the vast majority of mankind. . . .

It is not at all because capitalism is still strong that the socialist countries speak out against war, and for peaceful coexistence. No, we have no need of war at all. If the people do not want it, even such a noble and progressive system as socialism cannot be imposed by force of arms. The socialist countries therefore, while carrying through a consistently peace-loving policy, concentrate their efforts on peaceful construction; they fire the hearts of men by the force of their example in building socialism, and thus lead them to follow in their footsteps. The question of when this or that country will take the path to socialism is decided by its own people. This, for us, is the holy of holies. . . .

sive to promote world revolution. Specifically, China wanted Soviet assistance in retaking Taiwan from Chiang Kai-shek. But Khrushchev was trying to improve relations with the West and rejected Chinese demands for support against Taiwan (see the box above).

By the end of the 1950s, the Soviet Union had begun to remove its advisers from China, and in 1961 the dispute broke into the open. Increasingly isolated, China voiced its hostility to what Mao described as the "urban industrialized countries" (which included the Soviet Union) and portrayed itself as the leader of the "rural underdeveloped countries" of Asia, Africa, and Latin America in a global struggle against imperialist oppression. In effect, China had applied Mao Zedong's famous concept of people's war in an international framework.

The Second Indochina War

China's radicalism was intensified in the early 1960s by the outbreak of renewed war in Indochina. The Eisenhower administration had opposed the peace settlement at Geneva in 1954, which divided Vietnam temporarily into two separate regroupment zones, specifically because the provision for future national elections opened up the possibility that the entire country would come under Communist rule. But Eisenhower had been unwilling to introduce U.S. military forces to continue the conflict without the full support of the British and the French, who preferred to seek a negotiated settlement. In the end, Washington promised not to break the provisions of the agreement but refused to commit itself to the results.

During the next several months, the United States began to provide aid to a new government in South Vietnam. Under the leadership of the anticommunist politician Ngo Dinh Diem, the South Vietnamese government began to root out dissidents. With the tacit approval of the United States, Diem refused to hold the national elections called for by the Geneva Accords. It was widely anticipated, even in Washington, that the Communists would win such elections. In 1959, Ho Chi Minh, despairing of the peaceful unification of the country under Communist rule, returned to a policy of revolutionary war in the south.

THE SAMPAN GIRL

Women played an active role in the insurgent movement in South Vietnam. Some were guerrilla fighters, others were spies, and still others served as transport workers carrying provisions to Viet Cong units in the field. In this poem by the young poet Giang Nam, a young woman transports guerrilla fighters across a river in her sampan. The poem promoted the cause of patriotism but also reminded readers of their loved ones back home.

GIANG NAM, "NIGHT CROSSING"

In the midst of the night, a sampan glides toward us.
Dark bamboos on the bank, swift current . . .
An oar shatters the star-studded firmament.
A bird wanders in the dark and disappears.
Silently the sampan glides between the palms
Whose crests are swept by a searchlight from the outpost.

Loaded rifles, all hands on alert,
We await the moment to dart across the river.

Tucking her black trousers up to her thigh
The boat-girl, smelling of grass and flowers, helps us
Unload our motley bundles.
In the dark, we imagine her red cheeks;
Holding her hand
We breathe her breath, sense her brisk gestures. . . .
A long burst has been fired from the outpost,
Red and white tracers thunder everywhere.
"Be quiet," she says, "don't be afraid,"
And the sampan swiftly
Darts toward the enemy, defying its bullets.
Silhouetted in the sky, what a dashing figure;
"Lie down," she whispers, "let me maneuver,
Don't be worried!" The boat moves ahead;
Emotion packs the night.
Our hearts are pinching; anger fills our eyes.
Bullets rain in the river.
In our hands, our rifles burn with anger.

In safe haven, the sampan is tied to a tree.
Slowly, we shake the girl's hand.
"Thank you," we say. . . . A smile lights
her face; "I belong to the youth corps,
And I only do my duty," she answers.
We press our march across the village.

Still thinking, still hearing
The light tread of her walk.

Valiant image, valiant girl
In future battles come with us.

By 1963, South Vietnam was on the verge of collapse. Diem's autocratic methods and inattention to severe economic inequality had alienated much of the population, and revolutionary forces, popularly known as the Viet Cong (Vietnamese Communists), expanded their influence throughout much of the country (see the box above). In the fall of 1963, with the approval of the Kennedy administration, senior military officers overthrew the Diem regime. But factionalism kept the new military leadership from reinvigorating the struggle against the insurgent forces, and the situation in South Vietnam grew worse. By early 1965, the Viet Cong, whose ranks were now swelled by military units infiltrating from North Vietnam, were on the verge of seizing control of the entire country. In March, President Lyndon Johnson decided to send U.S. combat troops to South Vietnam to prevent a total defeat for the anticommunist government in Saigon.

Chinese leaders observed the gradual escalation of the conflict in South Vietnam with mixed feelings. They were undoubtedly pleased to have a firm Communist ally—one that had in many ways followed the path of Mao Zedong—just beyond their southern frontier. Yet they were concerned that renewed bloodshed in South Vietnam might enmesh China in a new conflict with the United States. Nor did they welcome the specter of a powerful and ambitious united Vietnam, which might wish to extend its influence throughout mainland Southeast Asia, an area that Beijing considered its own backyard.

Chinese leaders therefore tiptoed delicately through the minefield of the Indochina conflict. As the war escalated in 1964 and 1965, Beijing publicly announced that the Chinese people fully supported their comrades seeking national liberation but privately assured Washington that China would not directly enter the conflict unless U.S. forces threatened its southern border. Beijing also refused to cooperate fully with Moscow in shipping Soviet goods to North Vietnam through Chinese territory (see the box on p. 830).

Despite its dismay at the lack of full support from China, the Communist government in North Vietnam responded to U.S. escalation by infiltrating more of its own regular force troops into the south, and by 1968 the war had reached a stalemate. The Communists were not strong enough to overthrow the government in Saigon, but President Lyndon Johnson was reluctant to engage in all-out war on North Vietnam for fear of provoking a global nuclear conflict. In the fall, after the Communist-led Tet

WAR IN THE RICE PADDIES. In the spring of 1965, Lyndon Johnson ordered U.S. combat troops to South Vietnam in a desperate bid to prevent a Communist victory in that beleaguered country. For the next seven years, American GIs fought against Viet Cong guerrillas and North Vietnamese regular forces until they were finally withdrawn as a result of the Paris Agreement reached in January 1973. Two years later, South Vietnam fell to a Communist offensive.

offensive aroused heightened antiwar protests in the United States, peace negotiations began in Paris.

Richard Nixon came into the White House in 1969 on a pledge to bring an honorable end to the Vietnam War. With U.S. public opinion sharply divided on the issue, he began to withdraw U.S. troops while continuing to hold peace talks in Paris. But the centerpiece of his strategy was to improve relations with China and thus undercut Chinese support for the North Vietnamese war effort. During the 1960s, relations between Moscow and Beijing had reached a point of extreme tension, and thousands of troops were stationed on both sides of their long common frontier. To intimidate their Communist rivals, Soviet sources hinted that they might launch a preemptive strike to destroy Chinese nuclear facilities in Xinjiang. Sensing an opportunity to split the two onetime allies, Nixon sent his emissary Henry Kissinger on a secret trip to China. Responding to assurances that the United States was determined to withdraw from Indochina and hoped to improve relations with the mainland regime, Chinese leaders invited President Nixon to visit China in early 1972 (see the box on p. 831).

Incensed at the apparent betrayal by their close allies, North Vietnamese leaders decided to seek a peaceful settlement of the war in the south. In January 1973, a peace treaty was signed in Paris calling for the removal of all U.S. forces from South Vietnam. In return, the Communists agreed to seek a political settlement of their differences with the Saigon regime. But negotiations between north and south over the political settlement soon broke down, and in early 1975, the Communists resumed the offensive. At the end of April, under a massive assault by North

A MANUAL FOR REVOLUTIONARIES

In the 1920s, Mao Zedong formulated his theory of people's war, which held that in preindustrial societies revolution could be more readily fomented in the countryside than in the cities. Forty years later, Lin Biao, Mao's colleague and the minister of defense, placed the concept in an international framework, arguing that the rural nations of the world (led, of course, by China) would defeat the industrialized "urban" nations (represented by the United States and the Soviet Union). This is an excerpt from the article in which Lin Biao presented his thesis. His message was also intended as a signal to North Vietnamese leaders not to escalate the conflict in South Vietnam to a point which might involve a direct confrontation with the United States.

LIN BIAO, "LONG LIVE THE VICTORY OF PEOPLE'S WAR"

Many countries and peoples in Asia, Africa, and Latin America are now being subjected to aggression and enslavement on a serious scale by the imperialists headed by the United States and their lackeys. The basic political and economic conditions in many of these countries have many similarities to those that prevailed in old China. As in China, the peasant question is extremely important in these regions. The peasants constitute the main force of the national-democratic revolution against the imperialists and their lackeys. In committing aggression against these countries, the imperialists usually begin by seizing the big cities and the main lines of communication. But they are unable to bring the vast countryside completely under their control. The countryside, and the countryside alone, can provide the broad areas in which the revolutionaries can maneuver freely. The countryside, and the countryside alone, can provide the revolutionary basis from which the revolutionaries can go forward to final victory. Precisely for this reason, Mao Tse-tung's theory of establishing revolutionary base areas in the rural districts and encircling the cities from the countryside is attracting more and more attention among the people in these regions.

Taking the entire globe, if North America and Western Europe can be called "the cities of the world," then Asia, Africa, and Latin America constitute "the rural areas of the world." Since World War II, the proletarian revolutionary movement has for various reasons been temporarily held back in the North American and West European capitalist countries, while the people's revolutionary movement in Asia, Africa, and Latin America has been growing vigorously. In a sense, the contemporary world revolution also presents a picture of the encirclement of cities by the rural areas. In the final analysis, the whole cause of world revolution hinges on the revolutionary struggles of the Asian, African, and Latin American peoples, who make up the overwhelming majority of the world's population. The socialist countries should regard it as their internationalist duty to support the people's revolutionary struggles in Asia, Africa, and Latin America. . . .

Ours is the epoch in which world capitalism and imperialism are heading for their doom and communism is marching to victory. Comrade Mao Tse-tung's theory of people's war is not only a product of the Chinese revolution, but has also the characteristic of our epoch. The new experience gained in the people's revolutionary struggles in various countries since World War II has provided continuous evidence that Mao Tse-tung's thought is a common asset of the revolutionary people of the whole world. This is the great international significance of the thought of Mao Tse-tung. . . .

A BRIDGE ACROSS THE COLD WAR DIVIDE. In January 1972, U.S. president Richard Nixon startled the world by visiting mainland China and beginning the long process of restoring normal relations between the two countries. Despite Nixon's reputation as a devout anti-Communist, the visit was a success, as the two sides agreed to put aside their most bitter differences in an effort to reduce tensions in Asia. Here Nixon and Chinese leader Mao Zedong exchange an historic handshake in Beijing.

NIXON PLAYS HIS CHINA CARD

In February 1972, President Richard Nixon visited mainland China, ending twenty years of U.S. unwillingness to recognize the existence of the Communist regime. In a joint communiqué issued in Shanghai at the close of the visit, the two nations agreed to set aside the question of Taiwan, which could not be resolved, and to seek common ground on other issues. In the communiqué, Nixon agreed that the Taiwan issue had to be resolved by the Chinese people themselves.

THE SHANGHAI COMMUNIQUÉ

The sides reviewed the long-standing serious disputes between China and the United States.

The Chinese side reaffirmed its position: The Taiwan question is the crucial question obstructing the normalization of relations between China and the United States; the Government of the People's Republic of China is the sole legal government of China; Taiwan is a province of China which has long been returned to the motherland; the liberation of Taiwan is China's internal affair in which no other country had the right to interfere; and all U.S. forces and military installations must be withdrawn from Taiwan. The Chinese government firmly opposes any activities which aim at the creation of "one China, one Taiwan," "one China, two governments," "two Chinas" and "independent Taiwan" or advocate that "the status of Taiwan remains to be determined."

The U.S. side declared: The United States acknowledges that all Chinese on either side of the Taiwan Strait maintain there is but one China and that Taiwan is a part of China. The United States Government does not challenge that position. It reaffirms its interest in a peaceful settlement of the Taiwan question by the Chinese themselves. With this prospect in mind, it affirms the ultimate objective of the withdrawal of all U.S. forces and military installations from Taiwan. In the meantime, it will progressively reduce its forces and military installations on Taiwan as the tension in the area diminishes.

Vietnamese military forces, the South Vietnamese government surrendered. A year later, the country was unified under Communist rule.

The Communist victory in Vietnam was a severe humiliation for the United States, but its strategic impact was limited because of the new relationship with China. During the next decade, Sino-American relations continued to improve. In 1979, diplomatic ties were established between the two countries under an arrangement whereby the United States renounced its mutual security treaty with the Republic of China in return for a pledge from China to seek reunification with Taiwan by peaceful means. By the end of the 1970s, China and the United States had forged a "strategic relationship" in which they would cooperate against the common threat of Soviet "hegemonism" (as China described Soviet policy) in Asia.

An Era of Equivalence

When the Johnson administration sent U.S. combat troops to South Vietnam in 1965, Washington's main concern was with Beijing, not Moscow. By the mid-1960s, U.S. officials viewed the Soviet Union as an essentially conservative power, more concerned with protecting its vast empire than with expanding its borders. In fact, U.S. policy makers periodically sought Soviet assistance in helping to bring about a peaceful settlement of the Vietnam War. So long as Khrushchev was in power, they found a receptive ear in Moscow. Khrushchev was firmly dedicated to promoting peaceful coexistence (at least on his terms) and sternly advised the North Vietnamese against a resumption of revolutionary war in South Vietnam.

After October 1964, when Khrushchev was replaced by a new leadership headed by party chief Leonid Brezhnev (1906–1982) and Prime Minister Alexei Kosygin (1904–1980), Soviet attitudes about Vietnam became more ambivalent. On the one hand, the new Soviet leaders had no desire to see the Vietnam conflict poison relations between the great powers. On the other hand, Moscow was anxious to demonstrate its support for the North Vietnamese to deflect Chinese charges that the Soviet Union had betrayed the interests of the oppressed peoples of the world. As a result, Soviet officials publicly voiced sympathy for the U.S. predicament in Vietnam but put no pressure on their allies to bring an end to the war. Indeed, the Soviet Union became Hanoi's main supplier of advanced military equipment in the final years of the war.

Still, under Brezhnev and Kosygin, the Soviet Union continued to pursue peaceful coexistence with the West and adopted a generally cautious posture in foreign affairs. By the early 1970s, a new age in Soviet-American relations had emerged, often referred to by the French term *détente*, meaning reduction of tensions between the Soviet Union and the United States. One appropriate symbol of the new relationship was the Antiballistic Missile (ABM) Treaty, often called SALT I (for Strategic Arms Limitation Talks), signed in 1972, in which the two nations agreed to limit their antiballistic missile systems.

Washington's objective in pursuing the treaty was to make it unlikely that either superpower could win a nuclear exchange by launching a preemptive strike against the other. U.S. officials believed that a policy of "equivalence," in which there was a roughly equal power balance on each side, was the best way to avoid a nuclear confrontation. Détente was pursued in other ways as well. When President Nixon took office in 1969, he sought to increase trade and cultural contacts with the Soviet Union. His purpose was to set up a series of "linkages" in U.S.–Soviet relations that would persuade Moscow of the economic and social benefits of maintaining good relations with the West.

A symbol of that new relationship was the Helsinki Agreement in 1975. Signed by the United States, Canada, and all European nations on both sides of the Iron Curtain, these accords recognized all borders in central and eastern Europe that had been established since the end of World War II, thereby formally acknowledging for the first time the Soviet sphere of influence in Eastern Europe. The Helsinki Agreement also committed the signatory powers to recognize and protect the human rights of their citizens, a clear effort by the Western states to improve the performance of the Soviet Union and its allies in that arena.

CHRONOLOGY

THE COLD WAR

Truman Doctrine	1947
Formation of NATO	1949
Soviet Union explodes first nuclear device	1949
Communists come to power in China	1949
Nationalist government retreats to Taiwan (Formosa)	1949
Korean War begins	June 26, 1950
Geneva Conference ends Indochina War	July 21, 1954
Warsaw Pact created	1955
Khrushchev calls for peaceful coexistence	1956
Sino-Soviet dispute breaks into the open	1961
Cuban Missile Crisis	1962
Salt Treaty signed	1972
Nixon's visit to China	1972
Fall of South Vietnam	1975
Soviet invasion of Afghanistan	1979

An End to Détente?

Protection of human rights became one of the major foreign policy goals of the next U.S. president, Jimmy Carter (b. 1924). Ironically, just at the point when U.S. involvement in Vietnam came to an end and relations with China began to improve, U.S.–Soviet relations began to sour, for several reasons. Some Americans had become increasingly concerned about aggressive new tendencies in Soviet foreign policy. The first indication came in Africa. Soviet influence was on the rise in Somalia, across the Red Sea in south Yemen, and later in Ethiopia. In Angola, once a colony of Portugal, an insurgent movement supported by Cuban troops came to power. Then, in 1979 Soviet troops were sent to neighboring Afghanistan to protect a newly installed Marxist regime faced with internal resistance from fundamentalist Muslims. Some observers suspected that the ultimate objective of the Soviet advance into hitherto neutral Afghanistan was to extend Soviet power into the oil fields of the Persian Gulf. To deter such a possibility, the White House promulgated the Carter Doctrine, which stated that the United States would use its military power, if necessary, to safeguard Western access to the oil reserves in the Middle East. In fact, sources in Moscow later disclosed that the Soviet advance had little to do with the oil of the Persian Gulf, but was an effort to increase Soviet influence in a region increasingly beset with Islamic fervor. Soviet officials feared that Islamic activism could spread to the Muslim populations in the Soviet republics in Central Asia and were confident that the United States was too distracted by the "Vietnam syndrome" (the public fear of U.S. involvement in another Vietnam-type conflict) to respond.

Another reason for the growing suspicion of the Soviet Union in the United States was that some U.S. defense analysts began to charge that the Soviet Union had rejected the policy of equivalence and was seeking strategic superiority in nuclear weapons. Accordingly, they argued for a substantial increase in U.S. defense spending. Such charges, combined with evidence of Soviet efforts in Africa and the Middle East and reports of the persecution of Jews and dissidents in the Soviet Union, helped to undermine public support for détente in the United States. These changing attitudes were reflected in the failure of the Carter administration to obtain congressional approval of a new arms limitation agreement (SALT II), signed with the Soviet Union in 1979.

Countering the Evil Empire

The early years of the administration of President Ronald Reagan (b. 1911) witnessed a return to the harsh rhetoric, if not all of the harsh practices, of the Cold War. President Reagan's anti-Communist credentials were well known. In a speech given shortly after his election in 1980, he referred to the Soviet Union as an "evil empire" and frequently voiced his suspicion of its motives in foreign affairs. In an effort to eliminate perceived Soviet advantages in strategic weaponry, the White House began a military buildup that stimulated a renewed arms race. In 1982, the Reagan administration introduced the nuclear-tipped cruise missile, whose ability to fly at low altitudes made it difficult to detect by enemy radar. Reagan also became an ardent exponent of the Strategic Defense Initiative (SDI), nicknamed "Star Wars." Its purposes were to create a space shield that could destroy incoming missiles and to force Moscow into an arms race that it could not hope to win.

The Reagan administration also adopted a more activist, if not confrontational, stance in the Third World. That attitude was most directly demonstrated in Central America, where the revolutionary Sandinista regime had been established in Nicaragua after the overthrow of the Somoza dictatorship in 1979. Charging that the Sandinista regime was supporting a guerrilla insurgency movement in nearby El Salvador, the Reagan administration began to provide material aid to the government in El Salvador, while simultaneously supporting an anticommunist guerrilla movement (called the Contras) in Nicaragua. Though the administration insisted that it was countering the spread of communism in the Western Hemisphere, its Central American policy aroused considerable controversy in Congress, where some charged that growing U.S. involvement could lead to a repeat of the nation's bitter experience in Vietnam.

The Reagan administration also took the offensive in other areas. By providing military support to the anti-Soviet insurgents in Afghanistan, the White House helped to maintain a Vietnam-like war in Afghanistan that would embed the Soviet Union in its own quagmire. Like the Vietnam War, the conflict in Afghanistan resulted in heavy casualties and demonstrated that the influence of a superpower was limited in the face of strong nationalist, guerrilla-type opposition.

CONCLUSION

At the end of World War II, a new conflict appeared in Europe, as the new superpowers, the United States and the Soviet Union, began to compete for political domination. This ideological division soon spread to the rest of the world, as the United States fought in Korea and Vietnam to prevent the spread of communism, promoted by the new Maoist government in China, while the Soviet Union used its influence to prop up pro-Soviet regimes in Asia, Africa, and Latin America.

Thus, what had begun as a confrontation across the great divide of the Iron Curtain in Europe eventually took on global significance. As a result, both Moscow and Washington became entangled in areas that, in themselves, had little importance in terms of real national security interests. To make matters worse, U.S. policy makers all too often applied the lessons of World War II (the so-called Munich syndrome, according to which efforts to appease an aggressor only encourage his appetite for conquest) to crisis points in the Third World, where conditions were not remotely comparable.

By the 1980s, however, there were tantalizing signs of a thaw in the Cold War. China and the United States, each hoping to gain leverage with Moscow, had agreed to establish diplomatic relations. Freed from its concerns over Beijing's open support of revolutions in the Third World, the United States decided to withdraw from South Vietnam, and the war there came to an end without involving the great powers in a dangerous confrontation. Although Washington and Moscow continued to compete for advantage all over the world, both sides gradually came to realize that the struggle for domination could best be carried out in the political and economic arena rather than on the battlefield.

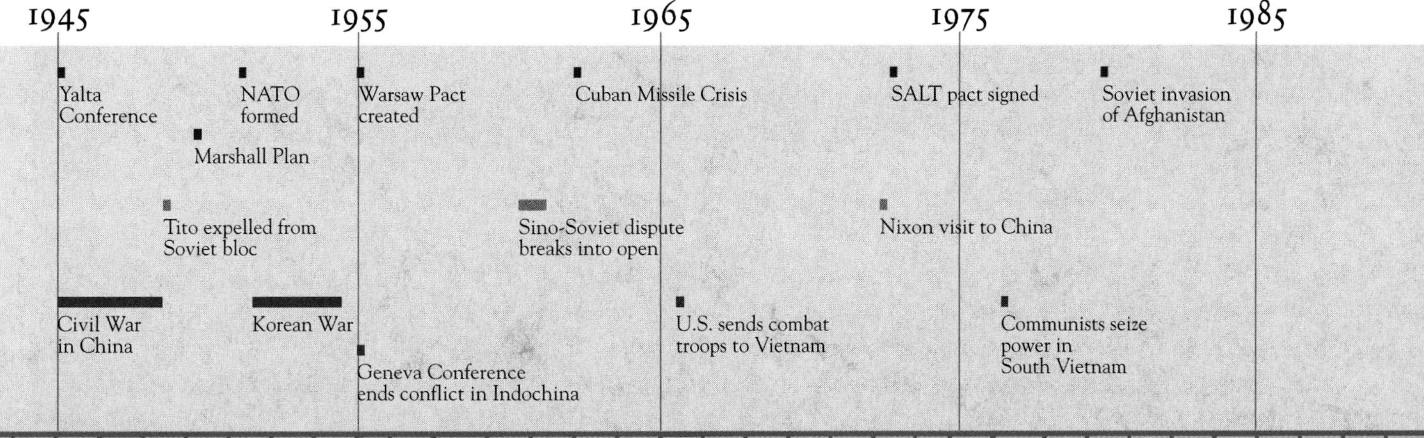

Chapter Notes

1. *Department of State Bulletin* 12 (February 11, 1945), pp. 213–16.
2. Quoted in Joseph M. Jones, *The Fifteen Weeks (February 21–June 5, 1947)*, 2d ed. (New York, 1964), pp. 140–41.
3. Quoted in Walter Laqueur, *Europe in Our Time* (New York, 1992), p. 111.
4. Quoted in Wilfried Loth, *The Division of the World, 1941–1955* (New York, 1988), pp. 160–61.
5. Quoted in Peter Lane, *Europe Since 1945: An Introduction* (Totowa, N.J., 1985), p. 248.
6. Quoted in Robert F. Kennedy, *Thirteen Days: A Memoir of the Cuban Missile Crisis* (New York, 1969), pp. 89–90.

Suggested Readings

There is a detailed literature on the Cold War. Two general accounts are R. B. Levering, *The Cold War, 1945–1972* (Arlington Heights, Ill., 1982), and B. A. Weisberger, *Cold War, Cold Peace: The United States and Russia Since 1945* (New York, 1984). There is a brief survey of the early Cold War in M. Dockrill, *The Cold War, 1945–1963* (Atlantic Highlands, N.J., 1988). The following works maintain that the Soviet Union was chiefly responsible for the Cold War: H. Feis, *From Trust to Terror: The Onset of the Cold War, 1945–1950* (New York, 1970), and A. Ulam, *The Rivals: America and Russia Since World War II* (New York, 1971). Revisionist studies on the Cold War have emphasized the responsibility of the United States for the Cold War, especially its global aspects. These works include J. and G. Kolko, *The Limits of Power: The World and United States Foreign Policy, 1945–1954* (New York, 1972); W. LaFeber, *America, Russia and the Cold War, 1945–1966*, 2d ed. (New York, 1972); and M. Sherwin, *A World Destroyed: The Atomic Bomb and the Grand Alliance* (New York, 1975). For a critique of the revisionist studies, see R. L. Maddox, *The New Left and the Origins of the Cold War* (Princeton, N.J., 1973). R. Garthoff, *Détente and Confrontation: American-Soviet Relations from Nixon to Reagan* (Washington, D.C., 1985) provides a detailed analysis of U.S.–Soviet relations in the 1970s and 1980s. See also F. Halliday, *The Making of the Second Cold War*, 2d ed. (New York, 1986).

There have been a number of recent studies of the early stages of the Cold War based on newly released documents. See, for example, O. A. Westad, *Cold War and Revolution: Soviet-American Rivalry and the Origins of the Chinese Civil War* (New York, 1993); D. A. Mayers, *Cracking the Monolith: U.S. Policy Against the Sino-Soviet Alliance, 1949–1955* (Baton Rouge, 1986); Chen Jian, *China's Road to the Korean War: The Making of the Sino-American Confrontation* (New York, 1994); and S. Goncharov, J. W. Lewis, and Xue Litai, *Uncertain Partners: Stalin, Mao, and the Korean War* (Stanford, Calif., 1993). The latter provides a fascinating view of the war from several perspectives.

On the end of the Cold War, see B. Denitch, *The End of the Cold War* (Minneapolis, Minn., 1990); W. G. Hyland, *The Cold War Is Over* (New York, 1990); and W. Laqueur, *Soviet Union 2000: Reform or Revolution?* (New York, 1990). For important studies of Soviet foreign policy, see A. B. Ulam, *Expansion and Coexistence: Soviet Foreign Policy, 1917–1973*, 2d ed. (New York, 1974), and *Dangerous Relations: The Soviet Union in World Politics, 1970–1982* (New York, 1983). The effects of the Cold War on Germany are examined in J. H. Backer, *The Decision to Divide Germany: American Foreign Policy in Transition* (Durham, N.C., 1978). On atomic diplomacy in the Cold War, see G. F. Herken, *The Winning Weapon: The Atomic Bomb in the Cold War, 1945–1950* (New York, 1981). For a good introduction to the arms race, see E. M. Bottome, *The Balance of Terror: A Guide to the Arms Race*, rev. ed. (Boston, 1986).

There are several surveys of Chinese foreign policy since the Communist rise to power. For the revolutionary period, see P. Van Ness, *Revolution and Chinese Foreign Policy* (Berkeley, Calif., 1971), and J. Gittings, *The World and China* (New York, 1974). For more recent developments, see R. G. Sutter, *Chinese Foreign Policy: Developments After Mao* (New York, 1986), and H. Harding, *Chinese Foreign Policy During the 1980s* (New Haven, Conn., 1984). On Sino-U.S. relations, see H. Harding, *A Fragile Relationship: The United States and China Since 1972* (Washington, D.C., 1992). On Chinese policy in Korea, see the classic by A. S. Whiting, *China Crosses the Yalu* (Stanford, Calif., 1960). On Sino-Vietnamese relations, see Ang Cheng Guan, *Vietnamese Communists' Relations with China and the Second Indochina Conflict* (Jefferson, N.C., 1997).

InfoTrac College Edition

For additional reading, go to InfoTrac College Edition, your online research library at http://web1.infotrac-college.com

Enter the search terms "Cold War" using the Subject Guide.

Enter the search terms "Soviet Union relations with the United States" using the Subject Guide.

Enter the search terms "Vietnamese conflict" using the Subject Guide.

Enter the search term "Gorbachev" using Keywords.

Enter the search terms "Korean War" using the Subject Guide.

CHAPTER

28

Brave New World: Communism

CHAPTER OUTLINE

- THE POSTWAR SOVIET UNION
- FERMENT IN EASTERN EUROPE
- CULTURE AND SOCIETY IN THE SOVIET BLOC
- THE DISINTEGRATION OF THE SOVIET EMPIRE
- THE EAST IS RED: CHINA UNDER COMMUNISM
- SERVE THE PEOPLE: CHINESE SOCIETY UNDER COMMUNISM
- THE LEGACY OF THE PAST: CONTINUITY AND CHANGE IN MODERN CHINA
- CHINA'S CHANGING CULTURE
- CONCLUSION

FOCUS QUESTIONS

- What were the chief characteristics of Soviet political, economic, and social life prior to Mikhail Gorbachev, and what reforms did he introduce?
- What were the main developments in Eastern Europe between 1945 and 1989, and what changes have occurred since 1989?
- What were Mao Zedong's goals for China, and what policies did he institute to try to achieve them?
- What have been the major political, economic, and social developments in China since Mao's death in 1976?
- Why has communism survived in China but not in Eastern Europe and Russia, and what impact has it had on Chinese life and culture?

According to Karl Marx, capitalism is a system that involves the exploitation of man by man; under socialism, it is the other way around. That wry joke was typical of popular humor in post-World War II Moscow, where the dreams of a future utopia had faded in the grim reality of life in the Soviet Union.

Grim though life in the Soviet Union might be, the Communist monopoly on power seemed secure, as did Moscow's hold over its client states in Eastern Europe. In fact, for three decades after the end of World War II, the Soviet

Empire appeared to be a permanent feature of the international landscape. But by the early 1980s, it became clear that there were cracks in the Kremlin wall. The Soviet economy was stagnant, the minority nationalities were restive, and Eastern European leaders were increasingly emboldened to test the waters of the global capitalist marketplace. In the United States, the newly elected president Ronald Reagan boldly predicted the imminent collapse of the "evil empire."

Although many observers questioned his remarks at the time, they soon appeared to be clairvoyant. Within a brief period between 1989 and 1991, the Soviet Union ceased to exist as a single nation, as Russia and other former Soviet republics declared their separate independence. At the same time, Communist regimes in Eastern Europe were toppled, and the long-standing division of postwar Europe came to an end. Although Communist parties survived the demise of the system and showed signs of renewed vigor in some countries in the region, their monopoly is gone, and they are only one of many parties competing for power.

The fate of communism in China has been quite different. Despite some turbulence, communism has survived in China, even as that nation takes giant strides toward becoming an economic superpower. Yet as China's leaders struggle to prepare for the twenty-first century, many of the essential principles of Marxist-Leninist dogma have been tacitly abandoned, while cynicism among the nation's youth is widespread. It remains an open question whether communism will continue to provide a usable framework for the challenges that lie ahead.

The Postwar Soviet Union

World War II had left the Soviet Union as one of the world's two superpowers and its leader, Joseph Stalin, at the height of his power. As a result of the war, Stalin and his Soviet colleagues were now in control of a vast empire that included Eastern Europe, much of the Balkans, and new territory gained from Japan in East Asia.

From Stalin to Khrushchev

World War II devastated the Soviet Union. Twenty million citizens lost their lives, and cities such as Kiev, Kharkov, and Leningrad suffered enormous physical destruction. As the lands that had been occupied by the German forces were liberated, the Soviet government turned its attention to restoring their economic structures. Nevertheless, in 1945, agricultural production was only 60 percent and steel output only 50 percent of prewar levels. The Soviet people faced incredibly difficult conditions: they worked longer hours; they ate less; they were ill-housed and poorly clothed.

In the immediate postwar years, the Soviet Union removed goods and materials from occupied Germany and extorted valuable raw materials from its satellite states in Eastern Europe. More important, however, to create a new industrial base, Stalin returned to the method he had used in the 1930s—the extraction of development capital from Soviet labor. Working hard for little pay and for precious few consumer goods, Soviet laborers were expected to produce goods for export with little in return for themselves. The incoming capital from abroad could then be used to purchase machinery and Western technology. The loss of millions of men in the war meant that much of this tremendous workload fell upon Soviet women, who performed almost 40 percent of the heavy manual labor.

Economic recovery in the Soviet Union was nothing less than spectacular. By 1947, Russian industrial production had attained 1939 levels; three years later, it had surpassed those levels by 40 percent. New power plants, canals, and giant factories were built, while new industrial enterprises and oil fields were established in Siberia and Soviet Central Asia. Stalin's new five-year plan, announced in 1946, reached its goals in less than five years.

Although Stalin's economic recovery policy was successful in promoting growth in heavy industry, primarily for the benefit of the military, consumer goods remained scarce. While the development of thermonuclear weapons, MIG fighters, and the first space satellite (*Sputnik*) in the 1950s elevated the Soviet state's reputation as a world power abroad, domestically the Soviet people were shortchanged. Heavy industry grew at a rate three times that of personal consumption. Moreover, the housing shortage was acute. A British military attaché in Moscow reported that "all houses, practically without exception, show lights from every window after dark. This seems to indicate that every room is both a living room by day and a bedroom by night. There is no place in overcrowded Moscow for the luxury of eating and sleeping in separate rooms."[1]

When World War II ended in 1945, Stalin had been in power for more than fifteen years. During that time, he had removed all opposition to his rule and emerged as the undisputed master of the Soviet Union. Political terror enforced by several hundred thousand secret police ensured that he would remain in power. By the late 1940s, there were an estimated 9 million people in Siberian concentration camps.

Increasingly distrustful of competitors, Stalin exercised sole authority and pitted his subordinates against each other. His morbid suspicions extended to even his closest colleagues. In 1948, Andrei Zhdanov, his presumed successor and head of the Leningrad party organization, died under mysterious circumstances, but presumably at Stalin's order. Within weeks, the Leningrad party organization was purged of several top leaders, many of whom were charged with traitorous connections with Western intelligence agencies. In succeeding years, Stalin directed his suspicion at other members of the inner circle, including Foreign Minister Vyacheslav Molotov. Known as "old stone butt" in the West for his stubborn defense of Soviet security interests, Molotov had been Stalin's loyal lieutenant since the early years of Stalin's rise to power. Now Stalin distrusted Molotov and had his Jewish wife placed in a Siberian concentration camp.

Stalin died in 1953 and, after some bitter infighting within the party leadership, was succeeded by Georgy Malenkov, a veteran administrator and ambitious member of the Politburo (the party's governing body). Malenkov came to power with a clear agenda. In foreign affairs, he hoped to promote an easing of Cold War tensions and improve relations with the Western powers. For Moscow's Eastern European allies, he advocated a "new course" in their mutual relations and a decline in Stalinist methods of rule. Inside the Soviet Union, he hoped to reduce defense expenditures and improve the standard of living. Such goals were laudable and probably had the support of the majority of the Russian people, but they did not necessarily appeal to key groups including the army, the party, the managerial elite, and the security services (known as the Committee on Government Security, or KGB). In 1953, Malenkov was removed from his position, and power shifted to his rival, the new party general secretary, Nikita Khrushchev.

During his struggle for power with Malenkov, Khrushchev had outmaneuvered him by calling for heightened defense expenditures and a continuing emphasis on heavy industry. Once in power, however, Khrushchev showed the political dexterity displayed by many an American politician and reversed his priorities. He now resumed the efforts of his predecessor to reduce tensions with the West and improve the standard of living of the Russian people. He moved vigorously to improve the performance of the Soviet economy and revitalize Soviet society. By nature, Khrushchev was a man of enormous energy as well as an innovator. In an attempt to release the stranglehold of the central bureaucracy over the national economy, he abolished dozens of government ministries and split up the party and government apparatus. Khrushchev also attempted to rejuvenate the stagnant agricultural sector, long the Achilles' heel of the Soviet economy. He attempted to spur production by increasing profit incentives and opened "virgin lands" in Soviet Kazakhstan to bring thousands of acres of new land under cultivation.

Like any innovator, Khrushchev had to overcome the inherently conservative instincts of the Soviet bureaucracy, as well as of the mass of the Soviet population. His plan to remove the "dead hand" of the state, however laudable in intent, alienated much of the Soviet official class, while his effort to split the party angered those who saw it as the central force in the Soviet system. Khrushchev's agricultural schemes inspired similar opposition. Although the

THE PORTALS OF DOOM. Perhaps the most feared location in the Soviet Union was Lyubyanka Prison, an ornate prerevolutionary building in the heart of Moscow. Taken over by the Bolsheviks after the 1917 revolution, it became the headquarters of the Soviet secret police, the Cheka, later to be known as the KGB. It was here that many Soviet citizens accused of "counterrevolutionary acts" were imprisoned and executed. The figure on the pedestal is that of Felix Dzerzhinsky, first director of Cheka. After the disintegration of the USSR, the statue was removed.

KHRUSHCHEV DENOUNCES STALIN

Three years after Stalin's death, the new Soviet premier, Nikita Khrushchev, addressed the Twentieth Congress of the Communist Party and denounced the former Soviet dictator for his crimes. This denunciation was the beginning of a policy of de-Stalinization.

KHRUSHCHEV ADDRESSES THE TWENTIETH PARTY CONGRESS, FEBRUARY 1956

Comrades, . . . quite a lot has been said about the cult of the individual and about its harmful consequences. . . . The cult of the person of Stalin . . . became at a certain specific stage the source of a whole series of exceedingly serious and grave perversions of Party principles, of Party democracy, of revolutionary legality.

Stalin absolutely did not tolerate collegiality in leadership and in work and . . . practiced brutal violence, not only toward everything which opposed him, but also toward that which seemed to his capricious and despotic character, contrary to his concepts.

Stalin abandoned the method of ideological struggle for that of administrative violence, mass repressions and terror. . . . Arbitrary behavior by one person encouraged and permitted arbitrariness in others. Mass arrests and deportations of many thousands of people, execution without trial and without normal investigation created conditions of insecurity, fear, and even desperation.

Stalin showed in a whole series of cases his intolerance, his brutality, and his abuse of power. . . . He often chose the path of repression and annihilation, not only against actual enemies, but also against individuals who had not committed any crimes against the Party and the Soviet government. . . .

Many Party, Soviet, and economic activists who were branded in 1937–8 as "enemies" were actually never enemies, spies, wreckers, and so on, but were always honest communists; they were only so stigmatized, and often, no longer able to bear barbaric tortures, they charged themselves (at the order of the investigative judges-falsifiers) with all kinds of grave and unlikely crimes.

This was the result of the abuse of power by Stalin, who began to use mass terror against the Party cadres. . . . Stalin put the Party and the NKVD up to the use of mass terror when the exploiting classes had been liquidated in our country and when there were no serious reasons for the use of extraordinary mass terror. The terror was directed . . . against the honest workers of the Party and the Soviet state. . . .

Stalin was a very distrustful man, sickly, suspicious. . . . Everywhere and in everything he saw "enemies," "two-facers," and "spies." Possessing unlimited power, he indulged in great willfulness and choked a person morally and physically. A situation was created where one could not express one's own will. When Stalin said that one or another would be arrested, it was necessary to accept on faith that he was an "enemy of the people." What proofs were offered? The confession of the arrested. . . . How is it possible that a person confesses to crimes that he had not committed? Only in one way—because of application of physical methods of pressuring him, tortures, bringing him to a state of unconsciousness, deprivation of his judgment, taking away of his human dignity.

Kazakhstan wheat lands would eventually demonstrate their importance, progress was slow, and his effort to persuade Russians to eat more corn (an idea he had apparently picked up during a visit to the United States) led to the mocking nickname of "Cornman." Disappointing in agricultural production, combined with high military spending, hurt the Soviet economy. The industrial growth rate, which had soared in the early 1950s, now declined dramatically, from 13 percent in 1953 to 7.5 percent in 1964.

Khrushchev was probably best known for his policy of de-Stalinization. Khrushchev had risen in the party hierarchy as a Stalin protégé, but he had been deeply disturbed by his mentor's excesses and, once in a position of authority, moved to excise the Stalinist legacy from Soviet society. The campaign began at the Twentieth National Congress of the Communist Party in February 1956, when Khrushchev gave a long secret speech criticizing some of Stalin's major shortcomings. The speech had apparently not been intended for public distribution, but it was quickly leaked to the Western press and created a sensation throughout the world (see the box above). During the next few years, Khrushchev encouraged more freedom for writers, artists, and composers, arguing that "readers should be given the chance to make their own judgments" about the acceptability of controversial literature and that "police measures shouldn't be used."[2] Under Khrushchev's instructions, thousands of prisoners were released from concentration camps.

Khrushchev's personality, however, did not endear him to higher Soviet officials, who frowned at his tendency to crack jokes and play the clown. Nor were the higher members of the party bureaucracy pleased when Khrushchev tried to curb their privileges. Foreign policy failures further damaged Khrushchev's reputation among his colleagues. His plan to place missiles in Cuba was the final straw (see Chapter 27). While he was away on vacation in 1964, a special meeting of the Soviet Politburo voted him out of office (because of "deteriorating health") and forced him into retirement. Although a group of leaders succeeded him, real power came into the hands of

Leonid Brezhnev (1906–1982), the "trusted" supporter of Khrushchev who had engineered his downfall.

The Brezhnev Years (1964–1982)

The overthrow of Nikita Khrushchev in October 1964 vividly demonstrated the challenges that would be encountered by any leader sufficiently bold to try to reform the Soviet system. In democratic countries, pressure on the government comes from various sources in society at large—the business community and labor unions, innumerable interest groups, and, of course, the general public. In the Soviet Union, pressure on government and party leaders originated from sources essentially operating inside the system—the government bureaucracy, the party apparatus, the KGB, and the armed forces.

Leonid Brezhnev, the new party chief, was undoubtedly aware of these realities of Soviet politics, and his long tenure in power was marked, above all, by the desire to avoid changes that might provoke instability, either at home or abroad. Brezhnev was himself a product of the Soviet system. He had entered the ranks of the party leadership under Stalin, and although he was not a particularly avid believer in party ideology—indeed, there were innumerable stories about his addiction to "bourgeois pleasures," including expensive country houses and fast cars (many of them gifts from foreign leaders)—he was no partisan of reform.

Still, Brezhnev sought stability in the domestic arena. He and his prime minister, Alexei Kosygin, undertook what might be described as a program of "de-Khrushchevization," returning the responsibility for long-term planning to the central ministries and reuniting the Communist Party apparatus. Despite some cautious attempts to stimulate the stagnant farm sector, there was no effort to revise the basic collective system. In the industrial sector, the regime launched a series of reforms designed to give factory managers (themselves employees of the state) more responsibility for setting prices, wages, and production quotas. These "Kosygin reforms" had little effect, however, because they were stubbornly resisted by the bureaucracy and were eventually adopted by relatively few enterprises in the vast state-owned industrial sector.

A CONTROLLED SOCIETY

Brezhnev also initiated a significant retreat from Khrushchev's policy of de-Stalinization. Criticism of the "Great Leader" had angered conservatives both within the party hierarchy and among the public at large, many of whom still revered Stalin as a hero and a defender of Russia against Nazi Germany. Many influential figures in the Kremlin feared that de-Stalinization could lead to internal instability and a decline in public trust in the legitimacy of party leadership—the hallowed "dictatorship of the proletariat." Early in Brezhnev's reign, Stalin's reputation began to revive. Although his alleged "shortcomings" were not totally ignored, he was now described in the official press as "an outstanding party leader" who had been primarily responsible for the successes achieved by the Soviet Union.

The regime also adopted a more restrictive policy toward dissidents in Soviet society. Critics of the Soviet system, such as the physicist Andrei Sakharov, were harassed and arrested or, like the famous writer Alexander Solzhenitsyn, forced to leave the country. There was also a qualified return to the anti-Semitic policies and attitudes that had marked the Stalin era. Such indications of renewed repression aroused concern in the West and were instrumental in the inclusion of a statement on human rights in the 1975 Helsinki Agreement (see Chapter 27).

Free expression was also restricted. The media were controlled by the state and presented only what the state wanted people to hear. The two major newspapers, *Pravda* (Truth) and *Izvestiya* (News), were the agents of the party and the government, respectively. Cynics joked that there was no news in *Pravda* and no truth in *Izvestiya*. According to Western journalists, airplane accidents in the Soviet Union were rarely publicized, on the grounds that they would raise questions about the quality of the Soviet airline industry. The government made strenuous efforts to prevent the Soviet people from exposure to harmful foreign ideas, especially modern art, literature, and contemporary Western rock music. When the Summer Olympic Games were held in Moscow in 1980, Soviet newspapers advised citizens to keep their children indoors to keep them from being polluted with "bourgeois" ideas passed on by foreign visitors.

For citizens of Western democracies, such a political atmosphere would seem highly oppressive, but for the Russian people, an emphasis on law and order was an accepted aspect of everyday life inherited from the tsarist period. Conformity was the rule in virtually every corner of Soviet society, from the educational system (characterized at all levels by rote memorization and political indoctrination), to child rearing (it was forbidden, for example, to be left-handed), and even to yearly vacations (most workers took their vacations at resorts run by their employer, where the daily schedule of activities was highly regimented). Young Americans studying in the Soviet Union reported that their Soviet friends were often shocked to hear U.S. citizens criticizing their own president, and to learn that they did not routinely carry identity cards.

A STAGNANT ECONOMY

Soviet leaders also failed to achieve their objective of revitalizing the national economy. Whereas growth rates during the early Khrushchev era had been impressive (prompting Khrushchev during one visit to the United States in the late 1950s to chortle "We will bury you"), during the Brezhnev years industrial growth declined to an annual rate of less than 4 percent in the early 1970s and less than 3 percent in the period from 1975 to 1980. Successes in the agricultural sector were equally meager. Grain production rose from less than 90 million tons in the early 1950s to nearly 200 million tons in the 1970s, but then stagnated at that level.

One of the primary problems with the Soviet economy was the absence of incentives. Salary structures offered little reward for hard labor and extraordinary achievement. Pay differentials operated a much narrower range than in most Western societies, and there was little danger of being dismissed. According to the Soviet Constitution, every Soviet citizen was guaranteed an opportunity to work.

There were, of course, some exceptions to this general rule. Athletic achievement was highly prized, and a gymnast of Olympic stature would receive great rewards in the form of prestige and lifestyle. Senior officials did not receive high salaries but were provided with countless perquisites, such as access to foreign goods, official automobiles with a chauffeur, and entry into prestigious institutions of higher learning for their children. For the elite, it was *blat* (influence) that most often differentiated them from the rest of the population. The average citizen, however, had little material incentive to produce beyond the minimum acceptable level. It is hardly surprising that overall per capita productivity was only about half that realized in most capitalist countries. At the same time, the rudeness of clerks and waiters became legendary.

The problem of incentives existed at the managerial level as well, where centralized planning discouraged initiative and innovation. Factory managers, for example, were assigned monthly and annual quotas by the Gosplan (the "state plan," drawn up by the central planning commission). Because state-owned factories faced little or no competition, managers did not care whether their products were competitive in terms of price and quality, so long as the quota was attained. One of the key complaints of Soviet citizens was the low quality of domestic consumer goods. Knowledgeable consumers quickly discovered that products manufactured at the end of the month were often of lower quality (because factory workers had to rush to meet their quotas) and attempted to avoid purchasing them.

Often, consumer goods were simply unavailable. Soviet citizens automatically got in line when they saw a queue forming in front of a store, because they never knew when something might be available again. When they reached the head of the line, most would purchase several of the same item in order to swap with their friends and neighbors. A popular joke at the time was that a Soviet inventor had

HOW TO SHOP IN MOSCOW. Because of the policy of state control over the Soviet economy, the availability of goods was a consequence not of market factors but of decisions made by government bureaucrats. As a result, needed goods were often in short supply. When Soviet citizens heard that a shipment of a particular product had arrived at a state store, they queued up to buy it. Here shoppers line up in front of a state-run store selling dinnerware in Moscow.

managed to produce an airplane that was cheap enough to be purchased by every citizen. Everyone was delighted because now when they heard that there was a sale of a particular item anywhere in the country, they would be able to fly in and buy it. This "queue psychology," of course, was a time-consuming process and inevitably served to reduce the per capita rate of productivity.

Soviet citizens often tried to overcome the shortcomings of the system by operating "on the left" (the black market). Private economic activities, of course, were illegal, but many workers took to moonlighting to augment their meager salaries. An employee in a state-run appliance store, for example, would promise to repair a customer's television set on his own time in return for a payment "under the table." Otherwise, servicing of the set might require several weeks. Knowledgeable observers estimated that as much as one-third of the entire Soviet economy operated outside the legal system.

THE MONSTER. Symbolic of the stunning failure of the Soviet system is this building in the Baltic port of Kaliningrad, once the German city of Königsberg. Twenty years in construction, "the monster," as it was dubbed by locals, was never occupied because of its serious structural flaws. The building was erected on the site of a sixteenth-century castle destroyed during a bombing raid in World War II. The site was then razed by Soviet bulldozers to wipe out all remnants of the past.

Another major obstacle to economic growth was inadequate technology. Except in the area of national defense, the overall level of Soviet technology was not comparable to that of the West or the advanced industrial societies of East Asia. Part of the problem, of course, stemmed from the issues already described. With no competition, factory managers had little incentive to improve the quality of their products. But another reason was the high priority assigned to defense. The military sector regularly received the most resources from the government and attracted the cream of the country's scientific talent.

PROBLEMS OF GERONTOCRACY

Such problems would be intimidating for any government; they were particularly so for the elderly generation of party leaders surrounding Leonid Brezhnev, many of whom were cautious to a fault. Though some undoubtedly recognized the need for reform and innovation, they were paralyzed by the fear of instability and change. The problem worsened during the late 1970s, when Brezhnev's health began to deteriorate.

Brezhnev died in November 1982 and was succeeded by Yuri Andropov (1914–1984), a party veteran and head of the Soviet secret services. During his brief tenure as party chief, Andropov was a vocal advocate of reform, but most of his initiatives were limited to the familiar nostrums of punishment for wrongdoers and moral exhortations to Soviet citizens to work harder. At the same time, material incentives were still officially discouraged and generally ineffective. Andropov had been ailing when he was selected to succeed Brezhnev as party chief, and when he died after only a few months in office, little had been done to change the system. He was succeeded, in turn, by a mediocre party stalwart, the elderly Konstantin Chernenko (1911–1985). With the Soviet system in crisis, Moscow seemed stuck in a time warp. As one concerned observer told an American journalist: "I had a sense of foreboding, like before a storm. That there was something brewing in people and there would be a time when they would say, 'That's it. We can't go on living like this. We can't. We need to redo everything.'"[3]

FERMENT IN EASTERN EUROPE

The key to Moscow's security along the western frontier of the Soviet Union was the string of satellite states that had been created in Eastern Europe in the aftermath of World War II. Once Communist power had been assured, a series of "little Stalins" put into power by Moscow instituted Soviet-type five-year plans that emphasized heavy industry rather than consumer goods, the collectivization of agriculture, and the nationalization of industry. They also appropriated the political tactics that Stalin had perfected in the Soviet Union, eliminating all non-Communist parties and establishing the classical institutions of repression—the secret police and military forces. Dissidents were tracked down and thrown into prison, and "national Communists" who resisted total subservience to the Soviet Union were charged with treason in mass show trials and executed.

Despite these repressive efforts, discontent became increasingly evident in several Eastern European countries. Hungary, Poland, and Romania harbored bitter memories of past Russian domination and suspected that Stalin, under the guise of proletarian internationalism, was seeking to revive the empire of the Romanovs. For the vast majority of peoples in Eastern Europe, the imposition of the so-called "people's democracies" (a term invented by Moscow to define a society in the early stage of socialist transition) resulted in economic hardship and severe threats to the most basic political liberties. The first indications of unrest appeared in East Berlin, where popular riots broke out against Communist rule in 1953. The riots eventually subsided, but the virus had spread to neighboring countries. In 1956 popular dissatisfaction erupted in Poland and Hungary.

In Poland, public demonstrations against an increase in food prices escalated into widespread protests against the regime's economic policies, restrictions on the freedom of Catholics to practice their religion, and the continued presence of Soviet troops (as called for by the Warsaw Pact) on Polish soil. In a desperate effort to defuse the unrest, the party leader stepped down and was replaced by Wladyslaw Gomulka (1905–1982), a popular figure who had previously been demoted for his "nationalist" tendencies. When Gomulka took steps to ease the crisis, Khrushchev flew to Warsaw to warn him against adopting policies that could undermine the political dominance of the party and weaken security links with the Soviet Union. Ultimately, Poland agreed to remain in the Warsaw Pact and to maintain the sanctity of party rule; in return, Gomulka was authorized to adopt domestic reforms, such as easing restrictions on religious practice and ending the policy of forced collectivization in rural areas.

MAP 28.1 The States of Eastern Europe and the Soviet Union

SOVIET REPRESSION IN EASTERN EUROPE: HUNGARY, 1956

Developments in Poland in 1956 inspired the Communist leaders of Hungary to begin to remove their country from Soviet control. But there were limits to Khrushchev's tolerance, and he sent Soviet troops to crush Hungary's movement for independence. The first selection is a statement by the Soviet government justifying its use of troops, while the second is the brief and tragic final statement from Imre Nagy, the Hungarian leader.

STATEMENT OF THE SOVIET GOVERNMENT, OCTOBER 30, 1956

The Soviet Government regards it as indispensable to make a statement in connection with the events in Hungary.

The course of the events has shown that the working people of Hungary, who have achieved great progress on the basis of their people's democratic order, correctly raise the question of the necessity of eliminating serious shortcomings in the field of economic building, the further raising of the material well-being of the population, and the struggle against bureaucratic excesses in the state apparatus.

However, this just and progressive movement of the working people was soon joined by forces of black reaction and counterrevolution, which are trying to take advantage of the discontent of part of the working people to undermine the foundations of the people's democratic order in Hungary and to restore the old landlord and capitalist order.

The Soviet Government and all the Soviet people deeply regret that the development of events in Hungary has led to bloodshed. On the request of the Hungarian People's Government, the Soviet Government consented to the entry into Budapest of the Soviet Army units to assist the Hungarian People's Army and the Hungarian authorities to establish order in the town.

THE LAST MESSAGE OF IMRE NAGY, NOVEMBER 4, 1956

This fight is the fight for freedom by the Hungarian people against the Russian intervention, and it is possible that I shall only be able to stay at my post for one or two hours. The whole world will see how the Russian armed forces, contrary to all treaties and conventions, are crushing the resistance of the Hungarian people. They will also see how they are kidnapping the Prime Minister of a country which is a Member of the United Nations, taking him from the capital, and therefore it cannot be doubted at all that this is the most brutal form of intervention. I should like in these last moments to ask the leaders of the revolution, if they can, to leave the country. I ask that all that I have said in my broadcast, and what we have agreed on with the revolutionary leaders during meetings in Parliament, should be put in a memorandum, and the leaders should turn to all the peoples of the world for help and explain that today it is Hungary and tomorrow, or the day after tomorrow, it will be the turn of other countries because the imperialism of Moscow does not know borders, and is only trying to play for time.

The developments in Poland sent shock waves throughout the region. The impact was strongest in neighboring Hungary, where the methods of the local "little Stalin," Matyas Rakosi, were so brutal that he had been summoned to Moscow for a lecture. In late October 1956, student-led popular riots broke out in the capital of Budapest and soon spread to other towns and villages throughout the country. Rakosi was forced to resign and was replaced by Imre Nagy (1896–1958), a "national Communist" who attempted to satisfy popular demands without arousing the anger of Moscow. Unlike Gomulka, however, Nagy was unable to contain the zeal of leading members of the protest movement, who sought major political reforms and the withdrawal of Hungary from the Warsaw Pact. On November 1, Nagy promised free elections, which, given the mood of the country, would probably have brought an end to Communist rule. After a brief moment of uncertainty, Moscow decided on firm action. Soviet troops, recently withdrawn at Nagy's request, returned to Budapest and installed a new government under the more pliant party leader Janos Kadar (1912–1989). While Kadar rescinded many of Nagy's measures, Nagy sought refuge in the Yugoslav Embassy. A few weeks later, he left the embassy under the promise of safety but was quickly arrested, convicted of treason, and executed (see the box above).

The dramatic events in Poland and Hungary graphically demonstrated the vulnerability of the Soviet satellite system in Eastern Europe, and many observers throughout the world anticipated that the United States would intervene on behalf of the freedom fighters in Hungary. After all, the Eisenhower administration had promised that it would "roll back" Communism, and radio broadcasts by the U.S.–sponsored Radio Liberty and Radio Free Europe had encouraged the peoples of Eastern Europe to rise up against Soviet domination. In reality, Washington was well aware that U.S. intervention could lead to nuclear war, and limited itself to protests against Soviet brutality in crushing the uprising.

The year of discontent was not without consequences, however. Soviet leaders now recognized that Moscow

THE BREZHNEV DOCTRINE

In the summer of 1968, when the new Communist Party leaders in Czechoslovakia were seriously considering proposals for reforming the totalitarian system there, the Warsaw Pact nations met under the leadership of Soviet party chief Leonid Brezhnev to assess the threat to the socialist camp. Shortly after, military forces of several Soviet bloc nations entered Czechoslovakia and imposed a new government subservient to Moscow. The move was justified by the spirit of "proletarian internationalism" and was widely viewed as a warning to China and other socialist states not to stray too far from Marxist-Leninist orthodoxy, as interpreted by the Soviet Union.

A LETTER TO CZECHOSLOVAKIA

To the Central Committee of the Communist Party of Czechoslovakia
Dear comrades!

On behalf of the Central Committees of the Communist and Workers' Parties of Bulgaria, Hungary, the German Democratic Republic, Poland, and the Soviet Union, we address ourselves to you with this letter, prompted by a feeling of sincere friendship based on the principles of Marxism-Leninism and proletarian internationalism and by the concern of our common affairs for strengthening the positions of socialism and the security of the socialist community of nations.

The development of events in your country evokes in us deep anxiety. It is our firm conviction that the offensive of the reactionary forces, backed by imperialists, against your Party and the foundations of the social system in the Czechoslovak Socialist Republic, threatens to push your country off the road of socialism and that consequently it jeopardizes the interests of the entire socialist system. . . .

We neither had nor have any intention of interfering in such affairs as are strictly the internal business of your Party and your state, nor of violating the principles of respect, independence, and equality in the relations among the Communist Parties and socialist countries. . . .

At the same time we cannot agree to have hostile forces push your country from the road of socialism and create a threat of severing Czechoslovakia from the socialist community. . . . This is the common cause of our countries, which have joined in the Warsaw Treaty to ensure independence, peace, and security in Europe, and to set up an insurmountable barrier against the intrigues of the imperialist forces, against aggression and revenge. . . . We shall never agree to have imperialism, using peaceful or nonpeaceful methods, making a gap from the inside or from the outside in the socialist system, and changing in imperialism's favor the correlation of forces in Europe. . . .

That is why we believe that a decisive rebuff of the anticommunist forces, and decisive efforts for the preservation of the socialist system in Czechoslovakia are not only your task but ours as well. . . .

We express the conviction that the Communist Party of Czechoslovakia, conscious of its responsibility, will take the necessary steps to block the path of reaction. In this struggle you can count on the solidarity and all-round assistance of the fraternal socialist countries.

Warsaw, July 15, 1968

could maintain control over its satellites in Eastern Europe only by granting them the leeway to adopt domestic policies appropriate to local conditions. Khrushchev had already embarked on this path in 1955, when he assured Josip Tito that there were "different roads to socialism." Eastern European Communist leaders now took Khrushchev at his word and adopted reform programs to make socialism more palatable to their subject populations. Even Janos Kadar, derisively labeled the "butcher of Budapest," managed to preserve many of Nagy's reforms to allow a measure of capitalist incentive and freedom of expression in Hungary.

Czechoslovakia did not share in the thaw of the mid-1950s and remained under the rule of Antonin Novotny (1904–1975), who had been placed in power by Stalin himself. By the late 1960s, however, Novotny's policies had led to widespread popular alienation, and in 1968, with the support of intellectuals and reformist party members, Alexander Dubcek was elected first secretary of the Communist Party. He immediately attempted to create what was popularly called "socialism with a human face," relaxing restrictions on freedom of speech and the press and the right to travel abroad. Economic reforms were announced, and party control over all aspects of society was reduced. A period of euphoria erupted that came to be known as the "Prague Spring."

It proved to be short-lived. Encouraged by Dubcek's actions, some called for more far-reaching reforms, including neutrality and withdrawal from the Soviet bloc. To forestall the spread of this "spring fever," the Soviet Red Army, supported by troops from other Warsaw Pact states, invaded Czechoslovakia in August 1968 and crushed the reform movement. Gustav Husak (b. 1913), a committed Stalinist, replaced Dubcek and restored the old order (see the box above).

Elsewhere in Eastern Europe, Stalinist policies continued to hold sway. The ruling Communist government in East Germany, led by Walter Ulbricht, consolidated its position in the early 1950s and became a faithful Soviet satellite. Industry was nationalized and agriculture collectivized. After the 1953 workers' revolt was crushed by Soviet tanks, a steady flight of East Germans to West Germany ensued, primarily through the city of Berlin. This exodus of mostly skilled laborers created economic problems and, in 1961, led the East German government to build the infamous Berlin Wall separating West from East Berlin, as well as equally fearsome barriers along the entire border with West Germany.

After building the Wall, East Germany succeeded in developing the strongest economy among the Soviet Union's Eastern European satellites. In 1971, Ulbricht was succeeded by Erich Honecker (b. 1912), a party hard-liner who was deeply committed to the ideological battle against détente. Propaganda increased, and the use of the Stasi, the secret police, became a hallmark of Honecker's virtual dictatorship. Honecker ruled unchallenged for the next eighteen years.

Culture and Society in the Soviet Bloc

In his occasional musings about the future communist utopia, Karl Marx had predicted that a new, classless society would replace the exploitative and hierarchical systems of feudalism and capitalism. Workers would engage in productive activities and share equally in the fruits of their labor. In their free time, they would help to produce a new, advanced culture, proletarian in character and egalitarian in content.

STALINIST HEROIC: AN EXAMPLE OF SOCIALIST REALISM. Under Stalin and his successors, art was assigned the task of indoctrinating the Soviet population on the public virtues, such as hard work, loyalty to the state, and patriotism. Grandiose statuary erected to commemorate the heroic efforts of the Red Army during World War II appeared in every Soviet city. Here is an example in Minsk, today the capital of Belarus. The current president of Belarus, Alexander Lukashenko, still proclaims his allegiance to the principles of communism.

Cultural Expression

The reality in the post–World War II Soviet Union and in Eastern Europe was somewhat different. Under Stalin, the Soviet cultural scene was a wasteland. Beginning in 1946, a series of government decrees made all forms of literary and scientific expression dependent on the state. All Soviet culture was expected to follow the party line. Historians, philosophers, and social scientists all grew accustomed to quoting Marx, Lenin, and, above all, Stalin as their chief authorities. Novels and plays, too, were supposed to portray Communist heroes and their efforts to create a better society. No criticism of existing social conditions was permitted. Even distinguished composers such as Dmitry Shostakovich were compelled to heed Stalin's criticisms, including his view that contemporary Western music was nothing but a "mishmash." Some areas of intellectual activity were virtually abolished; the science of genetics disappeared, and few movies were made during Stalin's final years.

Stalin's death brought a modest respite from cultural repression. Writers and artists banned during Stalin's years were again allowed to publish. Still, Soviet authorities, including Khrushchev, were reluctant to allow cultural freedom to move far beyond official Soviet ideology.

These restrictions, however, did not prevent the emergence of some significant Soviet literature, although authors paid a heavy price if they alienated the Soviet authorities. Boris Pasternak (1890–1960), who began his literary career as a poet, won the Nobel Prize in 1958 for his celebrated novel *Doctor Zhivago*, written between 1945 and 1956 and published in Italy in 1957. But the Soviet government condemned Pasternak's anti-Soviet tendencies, banned the novel, and would not allow him to accept the prize. The author had alienated the authorities by describing a society scarred by the excesses of Bolshevik revolutionary zeal.

Alexander Solzhenitsyn (b. 1918) created an even greater furor than Pasternak. Solzhenitsyn had spent eight years in forced-labor camps for criticizing Stalin, and his *One Day in the Life of Ivan Denisovich*, which won him the Nobel Prize in 1970, was an account of life in those camps (see the box on p. 847). Khrushchev allowed the book's publication as part of his de-Stalinization campaign. Later, Solzhenitsyn wrote *The Gulag Archipelago*, a detailed indictment of the whole system of Soviet oppression. Soviet authorities denounced Solzhenitsyn's efforts to inform the world of Soviet crimes against humanity and expelled him from the Soviet Union after he published *The Gulag Archipelago* abroad in 1973.

Exile abroad rather than imprisonment in forced-labor camps was perhaps a sign of modest progress. But even the limited freedom that had arisen during the Khrushchev

ONE DAY IN THE LIFE OF IVAN DENISOVICH

On November 20, 1962, a Soviet magazine published a work by Alexander Solzhenitsyn that created a literary and political furor. The short novel related one day in the life of its chief character, Ivan Denisovich, at a Siberian concentration camp, to which he had been sentenced at the end of World War II for supposedly spying for the Germans while a Soviet soldier. This excerpt narrates the daily journey from the prison camp to a work project through the 17 degrees-below-zero cold of Siberia. Many Soviets identified with Ivan as a symbol of the suffering they had endured under Stalin.

ALEXANDER SOLZHENITSYN, *ONE DAY IN THE LIFE OF IVAN DENISOVICH*

There were escort guards all over the place. They flung a semicircle around the column on its way to the power station, their machine guns sticking out and pointing right at your face. And there were guards with gray dogs. One dog bared its fangs as if laughing at the prisoners. The escorts all wore short sheepskins, except for half a dozen whose coats trailed the ground. The long sheepskins were interchangeable: they were worn by anyone whose turn had come to man the watchtowers.

And once again as they brought the squads together the escort recounted the entire power-station column by fives. . . .

Out beyond the camp boundary the intense cold, accompanied by a headwind, stung even Shukhov's face, which was used to every kind of unpleasantness. Realizing that he would have the wind in his face all the way to the power station, he decided to make use of his bit of rag. To meet the contingency of a headwind he, like many other prisoners, had got himself a cloth with a long tape on each end. The prisoners admitted that these helped a bit. Shukhov covered his face up to the eyes, brought the tapes around below his ears, and fastened the ends together at the back of his neck. Then he covered his nape with the flap of his hat and raised his coat collar. The next thing was to pull the front flap of the hat down into his brow. Thus in front only his eyes remained unprotected. He fixed his coat tightly at the waist with the rope. Now everything was in order except for his hands, which were already stiff with cold (his mittens were worthless). He rubbed them, he clapped them together, for he knew that in a moment he'd have to put them behind his back and keep them there for the entire march.

The chief of the escort guard recited the "morning prayer," which every prisoner was heartily sick of:

"Attention, prisoners. Marching orders must be strictly obeyed. Keep to your ranks. No hurrying, keep a steady pace. No talking. Keep your eyes fixed ahead and your hands behind your backs. A step to right or left is considered an attempt to escape and the escort has orders to shoot without warning. Leading guards, on the double."

The two guards in the lead of the escort must have set out along the road. The column heaved forward, shoulders swaying, and the escorts, some twenty paces to the right and left of the column, each man at a distance of ten paces from the next, machine guns held at the ready, set off too.

years was rejected after his fall from power. Cultural controls were reimposed, de-Stalinization was halted, and authors were again sent to labor camps for expressing outlawed ideas. These restrictive policies continued until the late 1980s, when Gorbachev's policy of *glasnost* (see p. 850) opened the doors to a new cultural freedom and new opportunities for expression.

In the Eastern European satellites, cultural freedom varied considerably from country to country. In Poland, intellectuals had access to Western publications as well as greater freedom to travel to the West. Hungarian and Yugoslav Communists, too, tolerated a certain level of intellectual activity that was not liked, but at least not prohibited. Elsewhere, intellectuals were forced to conform to the regime's demands. After the Soviet invasion of Czechoslovakia in 1968, Czech Communists pursued a policy of strict cultural control. This control did not stop a number of intellectuals from opposing the regime, however. Dissident writers and professionals, including the dramatist Václav Havel, later to be elected president of the Czech Republic, formed Charter 77 in January 1977 to protest human rights violations by the Communist regime. Although the regime struck back by prohibiting them from working in their professions, members of Charter 77 persisted and eventually founded Civic Forum, the political organization that guided the ouster of the Communist regime in the revolution of 1989.

The socialist camp also experienced the many facets of modern popular culture. By the early 1970s, there were 28 million television sets in the Soviet Union, although state authorities controlled the content of the programs that the Soviet people watched. Modern tourism, too, made inroads into the Communist world, as state-run industries provided vacation time and governments established resorts for workers on the Black Sea and Adriatic coasts. In Poland, the number of vacationers who used holiday retreats increased from 700,000 in 1960 to 2.8 million in 1972.

Spectator sports became a large industry and were also highly politicized as a result of Cold War divisions. "Each new victory," one party leader stated, "is a victory for the Soviet form of society and the socialist sport system; it provides irrefutable proof of the superiority of socialist culture over the decaying culture of the capitalist states."[4] Accordingly, the state provided money for the construction of gymnasiums and training camps and portrayed athletes as superheroes.

Social Changes in the Soviet Union and Eastern Europe

The imposition of Marxist systems in Eastern Europe had far-reaching social consequences. Most Eastern European countries made the change from peasant societies to modern, industrialized economies. In Bulgaria, for example, 80 percent of the labor force was engaged in agriculture in 1950, but only 20 percent was still working there in 1980. Although the Soviet Union and its Eastern European satellites never achieved the high standards of living of the West, they did experience some improvement. In 1960, the average real income of Polish peasants was four times higher than before World War II. Consumer goods also became more widespread. In East Germany, only 17 percent of families had television sets in 1960, but 75 percent had acquired them by 1972.

According to communist ideology, government control of industry and the elimination of private property were supposed to lead to a classless society. Although that ideal was never achieved, it did have important social consequences. For one thing, traditional ruling classes were stripped of their special status after 1945. The Potocki family in Poland, for example, which had owned 9 million acres of land before the war, lost all of its possessions, and family members were reduced to the ranks of common laborers.

The desire to create a classless society led to noticeable changes in education. In some countries, laws mandated quota systems based on class. In East Germany, for example, 50 percent of the students in secondary schools had to be children of workers and peasants. The sons of manual workers constituted 53 percent of university students in Yugoslavia in 1964 and 40 percent in East Germany, compared to only 15 percent in Italy and 5.3 percent in West Germany. Social mobility also increased. In Poland in 1961, 50 percent of white-collar workers came from blue-collar families. A significant number of judges, professors, and industrial managers stemmed from working-class backgrounds.

Education became crucial in preparing for new jobs in the communist system and led to higher enrollments in both secondary schools and universities. In Czechoslovakia, for example, the number of students in secondary schools tripled between 1945 and 1970, while the number of university students quadrupled between the 1930s and the 1960s. The type of education that students received also changed. In Hungary before World War II, 40 percent of students studied law, 9 percent engineering and technology, and 5 percent agriculture. In 1970, 35 percent were in engineering and technology, 9 percent in agriculture, and only 4 percent in law.

By the 1970s, the new managers of society, regardless of class background, realized the importance of higher education and used their power to gain special privileges for their children. By 1971, 60 percent of the children of white-collar workers attended university, and even though blue-collar families constituted 60 percent of the population, only 36 percent of their children attended institutions of higher learning. Even East Germany dropped its requirement that 50 percent of secondary students had to be the offspring of workers and peasants.

This shift in educational preferences demonstrates yet another aspect of the social structure in the communist world: the emergence of a new privileged class, made up of members of the Communist Party, state officials, high-ranking officers in the military and secret police, and a few special professional groups. The new elite not only possessed political power but also received special privileges, including the right to purchase high-quality goods in special stores (in Czechoslovakia, the elite could obtain organically grown produce not available to anyone else), paid vacations at special resorts, access to good housing and superior medical services, and advantages in education and jobs for their children. In 1980, in one Soviet province, 70 percent of Communist Party members came from the families of managers, technicians, and government and party bureaucrats.

Ideals of equality did not include women. Men dominated the leadership positions of the Communist parties. Women did have greater opportunities in the workforce and even in the professions, however. In the Soviet Union, women comprised 51 percent of the labor force in 1980; by the mid-1980s, they constituted 50 percent of the engineers, 80 percent of the doctors, and 75 percent of the teachers and teachers' aides. But many of these were low-paying jobs; most female doctors, for example, worked in primary care and were paid less than skilled machinists. The chief administrators in hospitals and schools were still men.

Moreover, although women were part of the workforce, they were never freed of their traditional roles in the home (see the box on p. 849). Most women confronted what came to be known as the "double shift." After working eight hours in their jobs, they came home to face the housework and care of the children. They might spend two hours a day in long lines at a number of stores waiting to buy food and clothes. Because of the housing situation, they were forced to use kitchens that were shared by a number of families.

Nearly three-quarters of a century after the Bolshevik Revolution, then, the Marxist dream of an advanced, egalitarian society was as far away as ever. Although in some respects conditions in the socialist camp were a distinct improvement over those before World War II, many problems and inequities were as intransigent as ever.

SOVIET WOMEN: "IT'S SO DIFFICULT TO BE A WOMAN HERE"

One of the major problems for Soviet women was the balancing of work and family roles, a problem noticeably ignored by authorities. This excerpt is taken from a series of interviews of thirteen women in Moscow conducted in the late 1970s by Swedish investigators. As is evident in this interview with Anna, a young wife and mother, these Soviet women took pride in their achievements but were also frustrated with their lives. At the same time, they maintained traditional views of women's roles.

MOSCOW WOMEN: INTERVIEW WITH ANNA

[Anna is twenty-one and married, has a three-month-old daughter, and lives with her husband and daughter in a one-room apartment with a balcony and a large bathroom. Anna works as a hairdresser; her husband is an unemployed writer.]

Are there other kinds of jobs dominated by women?
Of course! Preschool teachers are exclusively women. Also beauticians. But I guess that's about all. Here women work in every profession, from tractor drivers to engineers. But I think there ought to be more jobs specifically for women so that there are *some* differences. In this century women have to be equal to men. Now women wear pants, have short hair, and hold important jobs, just like men. There are almost no differences left. Except in the home.

Do women and men have the same goal in life?
Of course. Women want to get out of the house and have careers, just the same as men do. It gives women a lot of advantages, higher wages, and so on. In that sense we have the same goal, but socially I don't think so. The family is, after all, more important for a woman. A man can live without a family; all he needs is for a woman to come from time to time to clean for him and do his laundry. He sleeps with her if he feels like it. Of course, a woman can adopt this lifestyle, but I still think that most women want their own home, family, children. From time immemorial, women's instincts have been rooted in taking care of their families, tending to their husbands, sewing, washing—all the household chores. Men are supposed to provide for the family; women should keep the home fires burning. This is so deeply ingrained in women that there's no way of changing it.

Whose career do you think is the most important?
The man's, naturally. The family is often broken up because women don't follow their men when they move where they can get a job. That was the case of my in-laws. They don't live together any longer because my father-in-law worked for a long time as far away as Smolensk. He lived alone, without his family, and then, of course, it was only natural that things turned out the way they did. It's hard for a man to live without his family when he's used to being taken care of all the time. Of course there are men who can endure, who continue to be faithful, etc., but for most men it isn't easy. For that reason I think a woman ought to go where her husband does. . . .

That's the way it is. Women have certain obligations, men others. One has to understand that at an early age. Girls have to learn to take care of a household and help at home. Boys too, but not as much as girls. Boys ought to be with their fathers and learn how to do masculine chores. . . .

It's so difficult to be a woman here. With emancipation, we lead such abnormal, twisted lives, because women have to work the same as men do. As a result, women have very little time for themselves to work on their femininity.

The Disintegration of the Soviet Empire

On the death of Konstantin Chernenko in 1985, party leaders selected the talented and vigorous Soviet official Mikhail Gorbachev to succeed him. The new Soviet leader had shown early signs of promise. Born into a peasant family in 1931, Mikhail Gorbachev combined farmwork with school and received the Order of the Red Banner for his agricultural efforts. This award and his good school record enabled him to study law at the University of Moscow. After receiving his law degree in 1955, he returned to his native southern Russia, where he eventually became first secretary of the Communist Party in the city of Stavropol (he had joined the party in 1952) and then first secretary of the regional party committee. In 1978, Gorbachev was made a member of the party's Central Committee in Moscow. Two years later, he became a full member of the ruling Politburo and secretary of the Central Committee.

During the early 1980s, Gorbachev began to realize the enormity of Soviet problems and the crucial importance of massive reform in order to transform the system. During a visit to Canada in 1983, he discovered to his astonishment that Canadian farmers worked hard on their own initiative. "We'll never have this for fifty years," he reportedly remarked.[5] On his return to Moscow, he set in motion series of committees to evaluate the situation and recommend measures to improve the system.

The Gorbachev Era

With his election as party general secretary in 1985, Gorbachev seemed intent on taking earlier reforms to their logical conclusions. By the 1980s, Soviet economic problems were obvious. Rigid, centralized planning had led to mismanagement and stifled innovation. Although the Soviets still excelled in space exploration, they had fallen behind the West in high technology, especially in the development and production of computers for private and public use. Most noticeable to the Soviet people was the actual decline in the standard of living.

The cornerstone of Gorbachev's reform program was *perestroika*, or "restructuring." At first it meant only a reordering of economic policy, as Gorbachev called for the beginning of a market economy with limited free enterprise and some private property. Initial economic reforms were difficult to implement, however. Radicals demanded decisive measures; conservatives feared that rapid changes would be too painful. In his attempt to achieve compromise, Gorbachev often pursued partial liberalization, which satisfied neither faction and also failed to work, producing only more discontent.

Gorbachev soon perceived that in the Soviet system, the economic sphere was intimately tied to the social and political spheres. Any efforts to reform the economy without political or social reform would be doomed to failure. One of the most important instruments of *perestroika* was *glasnost*, or "openness." Soviet citizens and officials were encouraged to discuss openly the strengths and weaknesses of the Soviet Union. This policy could be seen in *Pravda*, the official newspaper of the Communist Party, where disasters such as the nuclear accident at Chernobyl in 1986 and collisions of ships in the Black Sea received increasing coverage. Soon this type of reporting was extended to include reports of official corruption, sloppy factory work, and protests against government policy. The arts also benefited from the new policy, as previously banned works were now published and motion pictures began to depict negative aspects of Soviet life. Music based on Western styles, such as jazz and rock, began to be performed openly.

Political reforms were equally revolutionary. In June 1987, the principle of two-candidate elections was introduced; previously, voters had been presented with only one candidate. Most dissidents, including Andrei Sakharov, who had spent years in internal exile, were released. At the Communist Party conference in 1988, Gorbachev called for the creation of a new Soviet parliament, the Congress of People's Deputies, whose members were to be chosen in competitive elections. It convened in 1989, the first such meeting in Russia since 1918. Because of its size, the Congress chose a Supreme Soviet of 450 members to deal with day-to-day activities. The revolutionary nature of Gorbachev's political reforms was evident in Sakharov's rise from dissident to elected member of the Congress of People's Deputies. As a leader of the dissident deputies, Sakharov called for an end to the Communist monopoly of power and, on December 11, 1989, the day he died, urged the creation of a new, non-Communist party. Early in 1990, Gorbachev legalized the formation of other political parties and struck out Article 6 of the Soviet Constitution, which guaranteed the "leading role" of the Communist Party. Hitherto, the position of first secretary of the party was the most important post in the Soviet Union, but as the Communist Party became less closely associated with the state, the powers of this office diminished. Gorbachev attempted to consolidate his power by creating a new state presidency, and in March 1990, became the Soviet Union's first president.

One of Gorbachev's most serious problems stemmed from the character of the Soviet Union. The Union of Soviet Socialist Republics was a truly multiethnic country, containing 92 nationalities and 112 recognized languages. Previously, the iron hand of the Communist Party, centered in Moscow, had kept a lid on the centuries-old ethnic tensions that had periodically erupted throughout the history of this region. As Gorbachev released this iron grip, tensions resurfaced, a by-product of *glasnost* that Gorbachev had not anticipated. Ethnic groups took advantage of the new openness to protest what they perceived to be ethnically motivated slights. As violence erupted, the Soviet army, in disarray since the Soviet intervention in Afghanistan in 1979, had difficulty controlling the situation. In some cases, independence movements and ethnic causes became linked, as in Azerbaijan, where the National Front became the spokesgroup for the Muslim Azerbaijanis in the conflict with Christian Armenians.

The period from 1988 to 1990 witnessed the emergence of nationalist movements throughout the republics of the Soviet Union. Often motivated by ethnic concerns, many of them called for sovereignty of the republics and independence from Russian-based rule centered in Moscow. Such movements sprang up first in Georgia in late 1988 and then in Latvia, Estonia, Moldavia, Uzbekistan, Azerbaijan, and most dramatically in Lithuania.

In December of 1989, the Communist Party of Lithuania declared itself independent of the Communist Party of the Soviet Union. A leading force in this independence movement was the nationalist Lithuanian Restructuring Movement, or "Popular Front for Perestroika," commonly known as *Sajudis*, led by Vytautas Landsbergis. Sajudis favored the radical policy of independence for Lithuania. Gorbachev made it clear that he supported self-determination but not secession, which he believed would be detrimental to the Soviet Union. Nevertheless, on March 11, 1990, the Lithuanian Supreme Council unilaterally declared Lithuania independent. Its formal name was now the Lithuanian Republic; the adjectives Soviet and Socialist had been dropped. On March 15, the Soviet Congress of People's Deputies, though recognizing a general right to secede from the Union of Soviet Socialist Republics, declared the Lithuanian declaration null and void; the Congress stated that proper procedures must be established and followed before secession would be acceptable.

During 1990 and 1991, Gorbachev struggled to deal with Lithuania and the other problems unleashed by his reforms. On the one hand, he tried to appease the conservative forces who complained about the growing disorder within the Soviet Union. On the other hand, he tried to accommodate the liberal forces, especially those in the Soviet republics, who increasingly favored a new kind of decentralized Soviet federation. Gorbachev especially labored to cooperate more closely with Boris Yeltsin, elected president of the Russian Republic in June 1991.

By 1991, the conservative leaders of the traditional Soviet institutions—the army, government, KGB, and military industries—had grown increasingly worried about the impending dissolution of the Soviet Union and its impact on their own fortunes. On August 19, 1991, a group of these discontented rightists arrested Gorbachev and attempted to seize power. Gorbachev's unwillingness to work with the conspirators and the brave resistance in Moscow of Yeltsin and thousands of Russians who had grown accustomed to their new liberties caused the coup to disintegrate rapidly. The actions of these right-wing plotters, however, served to accelerate the very process they had hoped to stop—namely, the disintegration of the Soviet Union.

Despite desperate pleas from Gorbachev, the Soviet republics soon opted for complete independence. Ukraine voted for independence on December 1, 1991. A week later, the leaders of Russia, Ukraine, and Belarus announced that the Soviet Union had "ceased to exist" and would be replaced by a Commonwealth of Independent States. Gorbachev resigned on December 25, 1991, and turned over his responsibilities as commander in chief to Boris Yeltsin, the president of Russia. By the end of 1991, one of the largest empires in world history had come to an end, and a new era had begun in its lands.

The New Russia: From Empire to Nation

Within Russia, a new power struggle soon ensued. Yeltsin was committed to introducing a free market economy as quickly as possible. In December 1991, the Congress of People's Deputies granted Yeltsin temporary power to rule

MAP 28.2 The States of Eastern Europe and the Former Soviet Union

BIG MAC MAKES A HIT. McDonald's restaurants have begun to appear all over Russia, as they have in most countries around the world. Although opposition to American-style fast-food restaurants is quite common in Russia, as it is elsewhere (see the box in Chapter 31), McDonald's is quite popular with the local population, not least because it is the only place to find good quality meat at an affordable price. To appease its critics, McDonald's attempts to purchase all of its ingredients locally and caters to local tastes. The sign here proclaims a "Big Mac Combo."

by decree. But the former Communist Party members and their allies in the Congress were opposed to many of Yeltsin's economic reforms and tried to place new limits on his powers. Yeltsin fought back. After winning a vote of confidence, both in himself and in his economic reforms, on April 25, 1993, Yeltsin pushed ahead with plans for a new Russian constitution that would abolish the Congress of People's Deputies, create a two-chamber parliament, and establish a strong presidency.

Nevertheless, the conflict between Yeltsin and the Congress continued and turned violent. On September 21, Yeltsin issued a decree dissolving the Congress of People's Deputies and scheduling new parliamentary elections for December. A hard-line parliamentary minority resisted and even took the offensive, urging supporters to take over government offices and the central television station. On October 4, Yeltsin responded by ordering military forces to storm the parliament building and arrest hard-line opponents. Yeltsin used his victory to consolidate his power; at the same time, he remained committed to holding new parliamentary elections on December 12.

During the mid-1990s, Yeltsin was able to maintain a precarious grip on power while seeking to implement reforms that would place Russia on a firm course toward a pluralistic political system and a market economy. But the new post-Communist Russia remains as fragile as ever. Burgeoning economic inequality and rampant corruption have aroused widespread criticism and shaken the confidence of the Russian people in the superiority of the capitalist system over that which existed under Communist rule. A nagging war in the Caucasus—where the people of Chechnya have resolutely sought national independence from Russia—has drained the government budget and exposed the decrepit state of the once vaunted Red Army. In presidential elections held in 1996, Yeltsin was reelected, but the rising popularity of a revived Communist Party and the growing strength of nationalist elements led by General Alexander Lebed, combined with Yeltsin's precarious health, raised serious questions about the future of the country. At the end of 1999, Yeltsin suddenly resigned his office and was replaced by Vladimir Putin, an ex-member of the KGB. Putin vowed to bring the breakaway state of Chechnya back under Russian authority, while adopting a more assertive role in international affairs.

Eastern Europe: From Soviet Satellites to Sovereign Nations

Stalin's postwar order had imposed Communist regimes throughout Eastern Europe. The process of sovietization seemed so complete that few people believed that the new order could be undone. But discontent with their Soviet-style regimes always simmered beneath the surface of these satellite states, and after Mikhail Gorbachev made it clear that his government would not intervene militarily, their Communist regimes fell quickly in the revolutions of 1989.

POLAND

As had been the case previously, the initial steps took place in Poland. Under Wladyslaw Gomulka, Poland had achieved a certain stability in the 1960s, but economic problems brought his ouster in 1971. His replacement, Edward Gierek, attempted to solve Poland's economic problems by borrowing heavily from the West. But in 1980, when he announced huge increases in food prices in an effort to pay off part of the Western debt, workers' protests erupted once again. This time, however, the revolutionary demands of the workers led directly to the rise of the independent labor movement called Solidarity. Led by Lech

CHRONOLOGY

THE SOVIET BLOC AND ITS DEMISE

Death of Joseph Stalin	1953
Rise of Nikita Khrushchev	1955
De-Stalinization speech	1956
Removal of Anti-Party Group	1957
Removal of Krushchev	1964
The Brezhnev Era	1964–1982
Rule of Andropov and Chernenko	1982–1985
Gorbachev comes to power in Soviet Union	1985
Collapse of Communist governments in Eastern Europe	1989
Disintegration of Soviet Union	1991
Presidency of Boris Yeltsin in Russia	1991–1999
Dayton Peace Accords on former Yugoslavia	1995
Vladimir Putin elected president of Russia	2000

Walesa (b. 1943), Solidarity represented 10 million of Poland's 35 million people. Almost instantly, Solidarity became a tremendous force for change and a threat to the government's monopoly of power. With the support of the workers, many intellectuals, and the Catholic church, Solidarity was able to win a series of concessions. The Polish government seemed powerless to stop the flow of concessions until December 1981, when it arrested Walesa and other Solidarity leaders, outlawed the union, and imposed military rule under General Wojciech Jaruzelski (b. 1923).

But martial rule did not solve Poland's serious economic problems. In 1988, new demonstrations broke out. After much maneuvering and negotiating with Solidarity, the Polish regime finally consented to free parliamentary elections—the first free elections in Eastern Europe in forty years—that led to even greater strength for Solidarity. Bowing to the inevitable, Jaruzelski's regime allowed the Solidarity-led coalition in the lower house of the new legislature to elect Tadeusz Mazowiecki, a leading member of Solidarity, as prime minister. The Communist monopoly of power in Poland had come to an end after forty-five years. In April 1990, it was decided that a new president would be freely elected by the populace by the end of the year, and in December, Lech Walesa was chosen as the new Polish president.

Poland's new path has not been an easy one. The existence of political parties has fragmented the political process and created the danger of parliamentary stalemate, while rapid free market reforms have created severe unemployment and popular discontent. At the same time, the effort of the powerful Catholic church to secure abortion law reform and religious education in the schools has raised new issues to divide the Polish people.

HUNGARY

In Hungary, too, the process of liberation from Communist rule had begun before 1989. Remaining in power for more than thirty years, the government of Janos Kadar tried to keep up with the changing mood by enacting the most far-reaching economic reforms in Eastern Europe. In the early 1980s, he legalized small private enterprises, such as shops, restaurants, and artisan shops. His economic reforms were called "Communism with a capitalist facelift." Hungary moved slowly away from its strict adherence to Soviet dominance and even established fairly friendly relations with the West. Multicandidate elections with at least two candidates per seat were held for the first time on June 8, 1985.

As the 1980s progressed, however, the economy sagged, and Kadar fell from power in 1988. By 1989, the Hungarian Communist government was aware of the growing dissatisfaction and began to undertake reforms. The more important new political parties united to form an opposition roundtable, whose negotiations with the Communists led to an agreement that Hungary would become a democratic republic. The Hungarian Communist Party changed its name to the Hungarian Socialist Party in order to have a greater chance of success in the new elections scheduled for March 15, 1990. The party came in fourth, however, winning only 8.5 percent of the vote, a clear repudiation of communism. The Democratic Forum, a right-of-center, highly patriotic party, won the election and formed a new coalition government, which committed Hungary to democratic government and a free-market economy.

CZECHOSLOVAKIA

Communist regimes in Poland and Hungary had attempted to make some political and economic reforms in the 1970s and 1980s, but this was not the case in Czechoslovakia. After Soviet troops crushed the reform movement in 1968, hard-line Czech Communists under Gustav Husak purged the party and followed a policy of massive repression to maintain their power. Only writers and other intellectuals provided any real opposition to the government. In January 1977, these dissident intellectuals formed Charter 77 as a vehicle for protest against violations of human rights. By the 1980s, Charter 77 members were also presenting their views on the country's economic and political problems, despite the government's harsh response to their movement.

Regardless of the atmosphere of repression, dissident movements continued to grow in the late 1980s. Government attempts to suppress mass demonstrations in Prague and other Czechoslovakian cities in 1988 and 1989 only led to more and larger demonstrations. By November 1989, crowds as large as 500,000, which included many students, were forming in Prague. A new opposition group, the Civic Forum, emerged and was officially recognized on November 17. The Czechoslovakian Federal Assembly now voted to delete the constitutional articles giving the Communists the leading role in politics. In December 1989, as demonstrations continued, the Communist government, lacking any real support, collapsed. President Husak resigned and at the end of December was replaced by Vaclav Havel, the dissident playwright who had been a leading figure in Charter 77 and had played an important role in bringing down the Communist government. In January 1990, Havel declared amnesty for some 30,000 political prisoners. He also set out on a goodwill tour to various Western countries in which he proved to be an eloquent spokesperson for Czech democracy and a new order in Europe.

The shift to non-Communist rule, however, was complicated by old problems, especially ethnic issues. Czechs and Slovaks disagreed over the makeup of the new state but were able to agree on a peaceful division of the country. On January 1, 1993, Czechoslovakia split into the Czech Republic and Slovakia.

THE REUNIFICATION OF GERMANY

In 1988, popular unrest in East Germany, fueled by the persistent economic slump of the 1980s (which affected most of Eastern Europe) as well as the ongoing oppressiveness of Honecker's regime, caused another mass exodus of East German refugees. Violent repression as well as Honecker's refusal to institute reforms only led to a larger exodus and mass demonstrations against the regime in the summer and fall of 1989. By the beginning of November 1989, the Communist government had fallen into complete disarray. Capitulating to popular pressure on November 9, it opened the entire border with the West. Hundreds of thousands of Germans swarmed across the borders, mostly to visit and return. The Berlin Wall, long the symbol of the Cold War, became the site of a massive celebration, and most of it was soon dismantled by joyful Germans from both sides of the border. By December, new political parties had emerged, and on March 18, 1990, in East Germany's first free elections ever, the Christian Democrats won almost 50 percent of the vote. The Christian Democrats supported rapid monetary unification followed shortly by political unification with West Germany. On July 1, 1990, the economies of West and East Germany were united, with the West German deutsche mark becoming the official currency of the two countries. Political reunification was achieved on October 3, 1990. What had seemed almost impossible at the beginning of 1989 had become a reality by the end of 1990. The country of East Germany had ceased to exist. Reunification, however, soon proved harder to bring about in practice than in principle (see Chapter 29).

The End of the Cold War

The dissolution of the Soviet satellite system in Eastern Europe, combined with the disintegration of the USSR itself, brought a dramatic end to the Cold War at the end of the 1980s. In fact, however, the thaw in relations between the two power blocs had begun with Gorbachev's accession to power in 1985. Gorbachev was willing to rethink many of the fundamental assumptions underlying Soviet foreign policy, and his "new thinking," as it was called, opened the door to a series of stunning changes. For one, Gorbachev initiated a plan for arms limitation that led in 1987 to an agreement with the United States to eliminate intermediate-range nuclear weapons (the INF Treaty). Both sides had incentives to dampen the expensive arms race. Gorbachev hoped to make extensive economic and internal reforms, while the United States had serious deficit problems. During the Reagan years, the United States had moved from being a creditor nation to being the world's biggest debtor nation. By 1990, both countries were becoming aware that their large military budgets were making it difficult for them to solve their serious social problems.

During 1989 and 1990, much of the Cold War's reason for being disappeared as the mostly peaceful revolutionary upheaval swept through Eastern Europe. Gorbachev's policy of allowing greater autonomy for the Communist regimes of Eastern Europe meant that the Soviet Union would no longer militarily support Communist governments faced with internal revolt. The unwillingness of the Soviet regime to use force to maintain the status quo, as it had in Hungary in 1956 and in Czechoslovakia in 1968, opened the door to the overthrow of the Communist regimes. The reunification of Germany on October 3, 1990, also destroyed one of the most prominent symbols of the Cold War era. The disintegration of the Soviet Union in 1991 brought an end to the global rivalry between two competing superpowers.

With the end of the Cold War, world leaders began to turn their attention to the construction of what U.S. president George Bush called the New World Order. Certainly both Moscow and Washington hoped to initiate a new era of peace and mutual cooperation. During the first administration of President Bill Clinton, the United States sought to engage Russia as well as its own NATO allies in an effort to resolve the numerous brushfire conflicts that began to arise in various parts of the world in the early 1990s.

Mikhail Gorbachev had already indicated his agreement with this sentiment in a 1992 speech at Westminster College in Fulton, Missouri—the same location where Winston Churchill had announced the opening of the Cold War nearly half a century before. Noting that the United States and the Soviet Union had missed a chance to build a peaceful relationship at the end of World War II, he warned that it would take a major effort to guarantee that the current favorable trends would not be reversed. One danger, he noted, was the rise of an "exaggerated nationalism," the product of centrifugal forces that had for half a century been frozen by the Cold War. Another was the growing inequality in the distribution of wealth between the rich nations and the poor nations.[6]

Yugoslavia: A Tragedy in the Making

Gorbachev's warning about the danger of "exaggerated nationalism" was probably a reference to the rise of nationalist sentiment among ethnic minorities in the Soviet Union that had led to the disintegration of the USSR in the early 1990s. But his comment could as easily have applied to the situation in Yugoslavia, where the fragile union forged by the Communist leader Joseph Tito after World War II came apart after his death.

From its beginning in 1919, Yugoslavia had been an artificial creation. After World War II, Tito had served as a cohesive force for the six republics and two autonomous provinces that constituted Yugoslavia. In the 1970s, Tito had become concerned that decentralization had gone too far in creating too much power at the local level and encouraging regionalism. As a result, he purged thousands of local Communist leaders who seemed more involved with local affairs than national concerns.

After Tito's death in 1980, no strong leader emerged, and his responsibilities passed to a collective state presidency and the presidium of the League of Communists of Yugoslavia (LCY). At the end of the 1980s, Yugoslavia was caught up in the reform movements sweeping through Eastern Europe. On January 10, 1990, the League of Communists called for an end to authoritarian socialism and proposed the creation of a pluralistic political system with freedom of speech and other civil liberties, free elections, an independent judiciary, and a mixed economy with equal status for private property. But division between Slovenes, who wanted a loose federation, and Serbians, who wanted to retain the centralized system, caused the collapse of the party congress, and hence the Communist Party. New parties quickly emerged. In multiparty elections held in the republics of Slovenia and Croatia in April and May of 1990 (the first multiparty elections in Yugoslavia in fifty-one years), the Communists fared poorly.

The Yugoslav political scene was complicated by the development of separatist movements that brought the disintegration of Yugoslavia in the 1990s. When new, non-Communist parties won elections in the republics of Slovenia, Croatia, Bosnia-Herzegovina, and Macedonia in 1990, they began to lobby for a new federal structure of Yugoslavia that would fulfill their separatist desires. Slobodan Milosevic, who had become the leader of the Serbian Communist Party in 1987 and had managed to stay in power by emphasizing his Serbian nationalism, rejected these efforts. He maintained that these republics could only be independent if new border arrangements were made to accommodate the Serb minorities in those republics who did not want to live outside the boundaries of a greater Serbian state. Serbs constituted 11.6 percent of Croatia's population and 32 percent of Bosnia-Herzegovina's population in 1981.

After negotiations among the six republics failed, Slovenia and Croatia declared their independence in June 1991. Milosevic's government sent the Yugoslavian army, which it controlled, into Slovenia, but without much success. In September 1991, it began a full assault against Croatia. Increasingly, the Yugoslavian army was the Serbian army, and Serbian irregular forces played an important role in military operations. Before a cease-fire was arranged, the Serbian forces had captured one-third of Croatia's territory in brutal and destructive fighting.

The recognition of Slovenia, Croatia, and Bosnia-Herzegovina by many European states and the United States early in 1992 did not stop the Serbs from turning their guns on Bosnia-Herzegovina. By mid-1993, Serbian forces had acquired 70 percent of Bosnian territory. The Serbian policy of "ethnic cleansing"—killing or forcibly removing Bosnian Muslims from their lands—revived memories of Nazi atrocities in World War II. Nevertheless, despite worldwide outrage, European governments failed to take a decisive and forceful stand against these Serbian activities, and by the spring of 1993, the Muslim population of Bosnia-Herzegovina was in desperate straits. As the fighting spread, European nations and the United States began to intervene to stop the bloodshed, and in the fall of 1995, a fragile cease-fire agreement was reached at a conference held in Dayton, Ohio. An international peacekeeping force was stationed in the area to maintain tranquillity and monitor the accords. Implementation has been difficult, however, as ethnic antagonisms continue to flare, notably in Kosovo, a part of Serbia inhabited primarily by Albanians, and a final solution seems as far away as ever.

The East Is Red: China Under Communism

In the fall of 1949, China was at peace for the first time in twelve years. The newly victorious Communist Party, under the leadership of its chairman, Mao Zedong, turned its attention to consolidating its power base and healing the wounds of war. Its long-term goal was to construct a socialist society, but its leaders realized that popular support for the revolution was based on the party's platform of honest government, land reform, social justice, and peace rather than on the utopian goal of a classless society. Accordingly, the new regime followed Soviet precedent in adopting a moderate program of political and economic recovery known as New Democracy.

New Democracy

With New Democracy—patterned after Lenin's New Economic Policy in Soviet Russia in the 1920s (see Chapter 24)—the new Chinese leadership tacitly recognized that time and extensive indoctrination would be needed to convince the Chinese people of the superiority of socialism. In the meantime, the party would rely on capitalist profit incentives to spur productivity. Manufacturing and commercial firms were permitted to remain under private ownership, although with stringent government regulations. To win the support of the poorer peasants, who made up the majority of the population, a land redistribution program was adopted, but the collectivization of agriculture was postponed.

In a number of key respects, New Democracy was a success. About two-thirds of the peasant households in the country received land and thus had reason to be grateful to the new regime. Spurred by official tolerance for capitalist activities and the end of internal conflict, the national economy began to rebound, although agricultural production still lagged behind both official targets and the growing population, which was increasing at an annual rate of more than 2 percent. But not all benefited. In the course of carrying out land redistribution, thousands if not millions of landlords and rich farmers lost their lands, their personal property, their freedom, and sometimes their lives. Many of those who died were tried and convicted of "crimes against the people" in people's tribunals set up under official sponsorship in towns and villages around the country. As Mao himself later conceded, many were innocent of any crime, but in the eyes of the party, their deaths were necessary to destroy the power of the landed gentry in the countryside (see the box on p. 857).

The Transition to Socialism

Originally, party leaders intended to follow the Leninist formula of delaying the building of a fully socialist society until China had a sufficient industrial base to permit the mechanization of agriculture. In 1953, they launched the nation's first five-year plan (patterned after similar Soviet plans), which called for substantial increases in industrial output. Lenin had believed that mechanization would induce Russian peasants to join collective farms, which, because of their greater size and efficiency, could better afford to purchase expensive farm machinery. But the difficulty of providing tractors and reapers for millions of rural villages eventually convinced Mao that it would take years, if not decades, for China's infant industrial base to meet the needs of a modernizing agricultural sector. He therefore decided to begin collectivization immediately, in the hope that collective farms would increase food production and release land, labor, and capital for the industrial sector. Accordingly, beginning in 1955, virtually all private farmland was collectivized (although peas-

THE GATE OF HEAVENLY PEACE. Located at the southern entrance to the imperial city in Beijing, the Gate of Heavenly Peace was the portal through which the Chinese emperor passed on his way out of the imperial palace. It was from this gate that Mao Zedong announced the founding of the new People's Republic of China on October 1, 1949. The square in front of the gate became the scene of mass demonstrations during the Great Proletarian Cultural Revolution.

LAND REFORM IN ACTION

One of the great achievements of the new Communist regime was the land reform program, which resulted in the distribution of farmland to almost two-thirds of the rural population in China. The program consequently won the gratitude of millions of Chinese. But it also had a dark side, as local land reform tribunals routinely convicted "wicked landlords" of crimes against the people and then put them to death. The following passage, written by a foreign observer, describes the process in one village.

REVOLUTION IN A CHINESE VILLAGE

T'ien-ming [a Party cadre] called all the active young cadres and the militiamen of Long Bow [village] together and announced to them the policy of the county government, which was to confront all enemy collaborators and their backers at public meetings, expose their crimes, and turn them over to the county authorities for punishment. He proposed that they start with Kuo Te-yu, the puppet village head. Having moved the group to anger with a description of Te-yu's crimes, T'ien-ming reviewed the painful life led by the poor peasants during the occupation and recalled how hard they had all worked and how as soon as they harvested all the grain the puppet officials, backed by army bayonets, took what they wanted, turned over huge quantities to the Japanese devils, forced the peasants to haul it away, and flogged those who refused.

As the silent crowd contracted toward the spot where the accused man stood, T'ien-ming stepped forward . . . "This is our chance. Remember how we were oppressed. The traitors seized our property. They beat us and kicked us. . . .

"Let us speak out the bitter memories. Let us see that the blood debt is repaid. . . ."

He paused for a moment. The peasants were listening to every word but gave no sign as to how they felt. . . .

"Come now, who has evidence against this man?"

Again there was silence.

Kuei-ts'ai, the new vice-chairman of the village, found it intolerable. He jumped up, struck Kuo Te-yu on the jaw with the back of his hand, "Tell the meeting how much you stole," he demanded.

The blow jarred the ragged crowd. It was as if an electric spark had tensed every muscle. Not in living memory had any peasant ever struck an official. . . .

The people in the square waited fascinated as if watching a play. They did not realize that in order for the plot to unfold they themselves had to mount the stage and speak out what was on their minds.

That evening T'ien-ming and Kuei-ts'ai called together the small groups of poor peasants from various parts of the village and sought to learn what it was that was really holding them back. *They soon found the root of the trouble was fear* of the old established political forces, and their military backers. The old reluctance to move against the power of the gentry, the fear of ultimate defeat and terrible reprisal that had been seared into the consciousness of so many generations lay like a cloud over the peasants' minds and hearts.

Emboldened by T'ien-ming's words, other peasants began to speak out. They recalled what Te-yu had done to them personally. Several vowed to speak up and accuse him the next morning. After the meeting broke up, the passage of time worked its own leaven. In many a hovel and tumbledown house talk continued well past midnight. Some people were so excited they did not sleep at all. . . .

On the following day the meeting was livelier by far. It began with a sharp argument as to who would make the first accusation, and T'ien-ming found it difficult to keep order. Before Te-yu had a chance to reply to any questions, a crowd of young men, among whom were several militiamen, surged forward ready to beat him.

ant families were allowed to retain small private plots) and most industry and commerce were nationalized.

Collectivization was achieved without provoking the massive peasant unrest that had taken place in the Soviet Union during the 1930s, perhaps because the Chinese government followed a policy of persuasion rather than compulsion (Mao Zedong remarked that Stalin had "drained the pond to catch the fish") and because the Communist land redistribution program had already earned the support of millions of rural Chinese. But the hoped-for production increases did not materialize, and in 1958, at Mao's insistent urging, party leaders approved a more radical program known as the Great Leap Forward. Existing rural collectives, normally the size of a traditional village, were combined into vast "people's communes," each containing more than 30,000 people. These communes were to be responsible for all administrative and economic tasks at the local level. The party's official slogan promised "Hard work for a few years, happiness for a thousand."[7]

Some party members were concerned that this ambitious program would threaten the government's rural base of support, but Mao argued that Chinese peasants were naturally revolutionary in spirit. The Chinese rural masses, he said, are

> first of all, poor, and secondly, blank. That may seem like a bad thing, but it is really a good thing. Poor people want

> change, want to do things, want revolution. A clean sheet of paper has no blotches, and so the newest and most beautiful words can be written on it, the newest and most beautiful pictures can be painted on it.[8]

Those words, of course, were *socialism* and *communism*.

The Great Leap Forward was a disaster. Administrative bottlenecks, bad weather, and peasant resistance to the new system (which, among other things, attempted to eliminate work incentives and destroy the traditional family as the basic unit of Chinese society) combined to drive food production downward, and over the next few years, as many as 15 million people may have died of starvation. Many peasants were reportedly reduced to eating the bark off trees and in some cases allowing infants to starve. In 1960, the experiment was essentially abandoned. Although the commune structure was retained, ownership and management were returned to the collective level. Mao was severely criticized by some of his more pragmatic colleagues (one remarked bitingly that "one cannot reach Heaven in a single step"), provoking him to complain that he had been relegated to the sidelines "like a Buddha on a shelf."

PUNISHING CHINESE ENEMIES DURING THE CULTURAL REVOLUTION. The Cultural Revolution, which began in 1966, was a massive effort by Mao Zedong and his radical supporters to eliminate rival elements within the Chinese Communist Party and the government. Accused of being "capitalist roaders," such individuals were subjected to public criticism and removed from their positions. Some were imprisoned or executed. Here, Red Guards parade a victim wearing a dunce cap through the streets of Beijing.

The Great Proletarian Cultural Revolution

But Mao was not yet ready to abandon either his power or his dream of a totally egalitarian society. In 1966, he returned to the attack, mobilizing discontented youth and disgruntled party members into revolutionary units known as Red Guards, who were urged to take to the streets to cleanse Chinese society—from local schools and factories to government ministries in Beijing—of impure elements who (in Mao's mind, at least) were guilty of "taking the capitalist road." Supported by his wife, Jiang Qing, and other radical party figures, Mao launched China on a new forced march toward communism.

The so-called Great Proletarian Cultural Revolution (literally, great revolution to create a proletarian culture) lasted for ten years, from 1966 to 1976. Some Western observers interpreted it as a simple power struggle between Mao Zedong and some of his key rivals such as Liu Shaoqi (Liu Shao-ch'i), Mao's designated successor, and Deng Xiaoping (Teng Hsiao-p'ing), the party's general secretary. Both were removed from their positions, and Liu later died, allegedly of torture, in a Chinese prison. But real policy disagreements were involved. Mao and his supporters feared that capitalist values and the remnants of "feudalist" Confucian ideas would undermine ideological fervor and betray the revolutionary cause. He was convinced that only an atmosphere of "uninterrupted revolution" could enable the Chinese to overcome the lethargy of the past and achieve the final stage of utopian communism. "I care not," he once wrote, "that the winds blow and the waves beat. It is better than standing idly in a courtyard."

His opponents argued for a more pragmatic strategy that gave priority to nation building over the ultimate communist goal of spiritual transformation. But with Mao's supporters now in power, the party carried out vast economic and educational reforms that virtually eliminated any remaining profit incentives, established a new school system that emphasized "Maozedong Thought," and stressed practical education at the elementary level at the expense of specialized training in science and the humanities in the universities. School learning was discouraged as a legacy of capitalism, and Mao's famous *Little Red Book* (a slim volume of Maoist aphorisms to encourage good behavior and revolutionary zeal) was hailed as the most important source of knowledge in all areas.

The radicals' efforts to destroy all vestiges of traditional society were reminiscent of the Reign of Terror in revolutionary France, when the Jacobins sought to destroy organized religion and even created a new revolutionary calendar. Red Guards rampaged through the country attempting to eradicate the "four olds" (old thought, old culture, old customs, and old habits). They destroyed temples and religious sculptures; they tore down street signs and replaced them with new ones carrying revolutionary names. At one point, the city of Shanghai even ordered that the significance of colors in stoplights be changed, so

MAP 28.3 The People's Republic of China

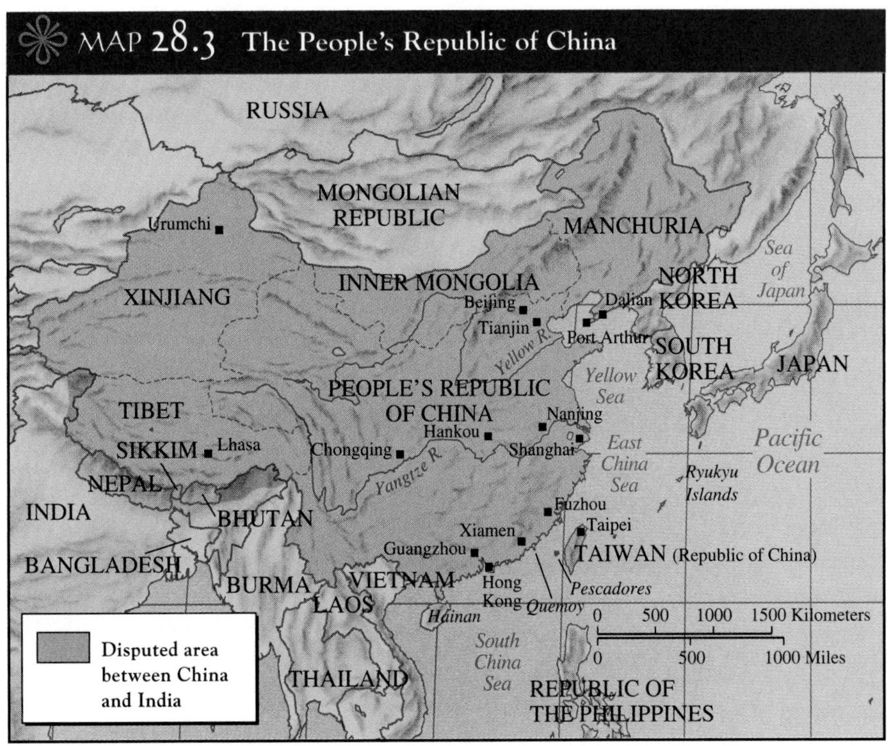

that red (the revolutionary color) would indicate that traffic could move.

But a mood of revolutionary ferment and enthusiasm is difficult to sustain. Key groups, including party bureaucrats, urban professionals, and many military officers, did not share Mao's belief in the benefits of "uninterrupted revolution" and constant turmoil. Many were alienated by the arbitrary actions of the Red Guards, who indiscriminately accused and brutalized their victims in a society where legal safeguards had almost entirely vanished (see the box on p. 860). Inevitably, the sense of anarchy and uncertainty caused popular support for the movement to erode, and when the end came with Mao's death in 1976, the vast majority of the population may well have welcomed its demise.

Personal accounts by young Chinese who took part in the Cultural Revolution show that their initial enthusiasm often turned to disillusionment. In *Son of the Revolution,* Liang Heng tells how at first he helped friends organize Red Guard groups:

> I thought it was a great idea. We would be following Chairman Mao just like the grown-ups, and Father would be proud of me. I suppose I too resented the teachers who had controlled and criticized me for so long, and I looked forward to a little revenge.[9]

Later, he had reason to repent. His sister ran off to join the local Red Guard group. Prior to her departure, she denounced her mother and the rest of her family as "rightists" and enemies of the revolution. Their home was regularly raided by Red Guards, and their father was severely beaten and tortured for having three neckties and "Western shirts." Books, paintings, and writings were piled in the center of the floor and burned before his eyes. On leaving, a few of the Red Guards helped themselves to his monthly salary and his transistor radio.

From Mao to Deng

In September 1976, Mao Zedong died at the age of eighty-three. After a short but bitter succession struggle, the pragmatists led by Deng Xiaoping seized power from the radicals and formally brought the Cultural Revolution to an end. Mao's widow, Jiang Qing, and three other radicals (derisively called the "gang of four" by their opponents) were placed on trial and sentenced to death or to long prison terms. The egalitarian policies of the previous decade were reversed, and a new program emphasizing economic modernization was introduced.

Under the leadership of Deng Xiaoping, who placed his supporters in key positions throughout the party and the government, attention focused on what were called the "four modernizations": industry, agriculture, technology, and national defense. Deng Xiaoping had been a leader of the faction that opposed Mao's program of rapid socialist transformation, and during the Cultural Revolution he had been forced to perform menial labor to "sincerely correct his errors." But Deng continued to espouse the pragmatic approach and reportedly once remarked, "Black cat, white cat, what does it matter so long as it catches the

MAKE REVOLUTION!

In 1966, Mao Zedong unleashed the power of revolution on China. Rebellious youth in the form of Red Guards rampaged through all levels of society, exposing anti-Maoist elements, suspected "capitalist roaders," and those identified with the previous ruling class. In this poignant excerpt, Nien Cheng, the widow of an official of Chiang Kai-shek's regime, describes a visit by Red Guards to her home during the height of the Cultural Revolution.

NIEN CHENG, *LIFE AND DEATH IN SHANGHAI*

Suddenly the doorbell began to ring incessantly. At the same time, there was furious pounding of many fists on my front gate, accompanied by the confused sound of hysterical voices shouting slogans. The cacophony told me that the time of waiting was over and that I must face the threat of the Red Guards and the destruction of my home. . . .

Outside, the sound of voices became louder. "Open the gate! Open the gate! Are you all dead? Whey don't you open the gate?" Someone was swearing and kicking the wooden gate. The horn of the truck was blasting too. . . .

I stood up to put the book on the shelf. A copy of the Constitution of the People's Republic caught my eye. Taking it in my hand and picking up the bunch of keys I had ready on my desk, I went downstairs.

At the same moment, the Red Guards pushed open the front door and entered the house. There were thirty or forty senior high school students, aged between fifteen and twenty, led by two men and one woman much older.

The leading Red Guard, a gangling youth with angry eyes, stepped forward and said to me, "We are the Red Guards. We have come to take revolutionary action against you!"

Though I knew it was futile, I held up the copy of the Constitution and said calmly, "It's against the Constitution of the People's Republic of China to enter a private house without a search warrant."

The young man snatched the document out of my hand and threw it on the floor. With his eyes blazing, he said, "The Constitution is abolished. It was a document written by the Revisionists within the Communist Party. We recognize only the teachings of our Great Leader Chairman Mao." . . .

Another young man used a stick to smash the mirror hanging over the blackwood chest facing the front door.

Mounting the stairs, I was astonished to see several Red Guards taking pieces of my porcelain collection out of their padded boxes. One young man had arranged a set of four Kangxi wine cups in a row on the floor and was stepping on them. I was just in time to hear the crunch of delicate porcelain under the sole of his shoe. The sound pierced my heart. Impulsively I leapt forward and caught his leg just as he raised his foot to crush the next cup. He toppled. We fell in a heap together. . . . The other Red Guards dropped what they were doing and gathered around us, shouting at me angrily for interfering in their revolutionary activities.

The young man whose revolutionary work of destruction I had interrupted said angrily, "You shut up! These things belong to the old culture. They are the useless toys of the feudal emperors and the modern capitalist class and have no significance to us, the proletarian class. They cannot be compared to cameras and binoculars, which are useful for our struggle in time of war. Our Great Leader Chairman Mao taught us, 'If we do not destroy, we cannot establish.' The old culture must be destroyed to make way for the new socialist culture."

mice?" Under the program of four modernizations, many of the restrictions against private activities and profit incentives were eliminated, and people were encouraged to work hard to benefit themselves and Chinese society. The familiar slogan "Serve the people" was replaced by a new one repugnant to the tenets of Maozedong Thought: "Create wealth for the people."

Crucial to the program's success was the government's ability to attract foreign technology and capital. For more than two decades, China had been isolated from technological advances taking place elsewhere in the world. Although China's leaders understandably prided themselves on their nation's capacity for "self-reliance," their isolationist policy had been exceedingly costly for the national economy. China's post-Mao leaders blamed the country's backwardness on the "ten lost years" of the Cultural Revolution, but the "lost years," at least in technological terms, extended back to 1949 and in some respects even before. Now, to make up for lost time, the government encouraged foreign investment and sent thousands of students and specialists abroad to study capitalist techniques.

By adopting this pragmatic approach in the years after 1976, China made great strides in ending its chronic problems of poverty and underdevelopment. Per capita income roughly doubled during the 1980s; housing, education, and sanitation improved; and both agricultural and industrial output skyrocketed.

But critics, both Chinese and foreign, complained that Deng Xiaoping's program had failed to achieve a "fifth modernization": that of democracy. Official sources denied such charges and spoke proudly of restoring "socialist legality" by doing away with the arbitrary punishments applied during the Cultural Revolution. Deng Xiaoping himself encouraged the Chinese people to speak out against earlier excesses. In the late 1970s, ordinary citizens pasted "big character posters" criticizing the abuses of the past on the so-called Democracy Wall near Tiananmen Square in downtown Beijing.

Yet it soon became clear that the new leaders would not tolerate any direct criticism of the Communist Party or of Marxist-Leninist ideology. Dissidents were suppressed, and some were sentenced to long prison terms. Among them was the well-known astrophysicist Fang Lizhi (Fang Li-chih), who spoke out publicly against official corruption and the continuing influence of Marxist-Leninist concepts in post-Mao China, telling an audience in Hong Kong that "China will not be able to modernize, if it does not break the shackles of Maoist and Stalinist-style socialism." Fang immediately felt the weight of official displeasure. He was refused permission to travel abroad, and articles that he submitted to official periodicals were rejected. Deng Xiaoping himself reportedly remarked, "We will not suppress people who hold differing political views from our own. But as for Fang Lizhi, he has been indulging in mud-slinging and spreading slander without any basis, and we should take legal action against him." Replied Fang, "I have never criticized any Chinese leader by name, nor accused any of them of illegal acts or immoral activities. But some perhaps feel guilty. If the cap fits, wear it."[10]

The problem began to intensify in the late 1980s, as more Chinese began to study abroad and more information about Western society reached educated individuals inside the country. Rising expectations aroused by the economic improvements of the early 1980s led to increasing pressure from students and other urban residents for better living conditions, relaxed restrictions on study abroad, and increased freedom to select employment after graduation.

Incident at Tiananmen Square

As long as economic conditions for the majority of Chinese were improving, other classes did not share the students' discontent, and the government was able to isolate them from other elements in society. But in the late 1980s, an overheated economy led to rising inflation and growing discontent among salaried workers, especially in the cities. At the same time, corruption, nepotism, and favored treatment for senior officials and party members were provoking increasing criticism. In May 1989, student protesters carried placards demanding Science and Democracy (reminiscent of the slogan of the May Fourth Movement, whose seventieth anniversary was celebrated in the spring of 1989), an end to official corruption, and the resignation of China's aging party leadership. These demands received widespread support from the urban population (although notably less in rural areas) and led to massive demonstrations in Tiananmen Square (see the box on p. 862).

The demonstrations divided the Chinese leaders. Reformist elements around party general secretary Zhao Ziyang were sympathetic to the protesters, but veteran leaders such as Deng Xiaoping saw the student demands for more democracy as a disguised call for an end to Communist Party rule. After some hesitation, the

GIVE ME LIBERTY—OR GIVE ME DEATH! The demonstrations that erupted in Tiananmen Square in the spring of 1989 spread rapidly to other parts of China, where students and other local citizens gave their vocal support to the popular movement in Beijing. Here, students from a high school march to the city of Guilin to display their own determination to take part in the reform of Chinese society. Their call to "give me liberty or give me death" (in Patrick Henry's famous phrase) echoes the determination expressed by many of their counterparts in Beijing.

STUDENTS APPEAL FOR DEMOCRACY

In the spring of 1989, thousands of students gathered in Tiananmen Square in downtown Beijing to provide moral support to their many compatriots who had gone on a hunger strike in an effort to compel the Chinese government to reduce the level of official corruption and enact democratic reforms, opening the political process to the Chinese people. The statement that follows was printed on flyers and distributed to participants and passersby on May 17, 1989, to explain the goals of the movement.

"WHY DO WE HAVE TO UNDERGO A HUNGER STRIKE?"

By 2:00 P.M. today, the hunger strike carried out by the petition group in Tiananmen Square has been under way for 96 hours. By this morning, more than 600 participants have fainted. When these democracy fighters were lifted into the ambulances, no one who was present was not moved to tears.

Our petition group now undergoing the hunger strike demands that at a minimum the government agree to the following two points:

1. To engage on a sincere and equal basis in a dialogue with the "higher education dialogue group." In addition, to broadcast the actual dialogue in its entirety. We absolutely refuse to agree to a partial broadcast, to empty gestures, or to fabrications that dupe the people.
2. To evaluate in a fair and realistic way the patriotic democratic movement. Discard the label of "trouble-making" and redress the reputation of the patriotic democratic movement.

It is our view that the request for a dialogue between the people's government and the people is not an unreasonable one. Our party always follows the principle of seeking truths from actual facts. It is therefore only natural that the evaluation of this patriotic democratic movement should be done in accordance with the principle of seeking truths from actual facts.

Our classmates who are going through the hunger strike are the good sons and daughters of the people! One by one, they have fallen. In the meantime, our "public servants" are completely unmoved. Please, let us ask where your conscience is.

government sent tanks and troops into Tiananmen Square to crush the demonstrators. Dissidents were arrested, and the regime once again began to stress ideological purity and socialist values. Although the crackdown provoked widespread criticism abroad, Chinese leaders insisted that economic reforms could only take place in conditions of party leadership and political stability.

Deng Xiaoping and other aging party leaders turned to the army to protect their base of power and suppress what they described as "counterrevolutionary elements." Deng was undoubtedly counting on the fact that many Chinese, particularly in rural areas, feared a recurrence of the disorder of the Cultural Revolution and craved economic prosperity more than political reform. In the months following the confrontation, the government issued new regulations requiring courses on Marxist-Leninist ideology in the schools, sought out dissidents within the intellectual community, and made it clear that while economic reforms would continue, the CCP's monopoly of power would not be allowed to decay. Harsh punishments were imposed on those accused of undermining the Communist system and supporting its enemies abroad.

Confucius Revived?

In the 1990s, the government began to nurture urban support by reducing the rate of inflation and guaranteeing the availability of consumer goods in great demand among the rising middle class. Under Deng Xiaoping's successor Jiang Zemin, who currently serves as both party chief and president of China, the government promotes rapid economic growth while cracking down harshly on political dissent. That policy has paid dividends in bringing about a perceptible decline in alienation among the population in the cities. Industrial production has been increasing rapidly, leading to predictions that China may become one of the economic superpowers in the twenty-first century. But problems in rural areas are on the increase. Farm income has lagged behind in recent years, and high taxes and official corruption have sparked rising resentment among the rural populace. In the meantime, food production has leveled off for a variety of reasons, promoting concerns from some observers that China will no longer be able to feed its growing population in the early years of the new century.

Partly out of fear that such changes could undermine the socialist system and the rule of the CCP, conservative leaders have attempted to curb Western influence and restore faith in Marxism-Leninism. Recently, in what may be a tacit recognition that Marxist exhortations are no longer an effective means of enforcing social discipline, the party has turned to Confucianism as an antidote. Ceremonies celebrating the birth of Confucius now receive official sanction, and the virtues promoted by the master, such as righteousness, propriety, and filial piety, are now widely cited as an antidote to the tide of antisocial behavior. A recent article in *People's Daily* asserted that the current spiritual crisis in contemporary Western culture stems from the incompatibility between science and the Christian religion. The solution, the author maintained, is Confucianism, "a nonreligious humanism that can provide the basis for morals and the value of life." Because a culture combining science and Confucianism is taking shape in East Asia today, "it will thrive particularly well in the next century and will replace modern and contemporary Western culture."[11]

In the short term, such efforts may have some success in slowing down the rush toward Westernization because many Chinese are understandably fearful of punishment and concerned for their careers. But one is inevitably reminded of Chiang Kai-shek's failed attempt in the 1930s to revive Confucian ethics as a standard of behavior for modern China—dead ideologies cannot be revived by decree.

Beijing's decision to emphasize traditional Confucian themes as a means of promoting broad popular support for its domestic policies is paralleled in the world arena, where it relies on the spirit of nationalism to achieve its goals. Today, China conducts an independent foreign policy and is playing an increasingly active role in the region. To some of its neighbors, including Japan, India, and post-Soviet Russia, China's new posture is cause for disquiet and gives rise to suspicions that it is once again preparing to assert its muscle as in the imperial era. A striking example of this new attitude took place as early as 1979, when Chinese forces briefly invaded Vietnam as punishment for the Vietnamese occupation of neighboring Cambodia. In the 1990s, China has aroused concern in the region by claiming sole ownership over the Spratly Islands in the South China Sea and over Diaoyu Island (also claimed by Japan) near Taiwan.

To Chinese leaders, however, such actions simply represent legitimate efforts to resume China's rightful role in the affairs of the region. After a century of humiliation at the hands of the Western powers and neighboring Japan, the nation, in Mao's famous words of 1949, "has stood up," and no one will be permitted to humiliate it again. For the moment, at least, a fervent sense of patriotism appears to be on the rise in China, a phenomenon that is actively promoted by the party as a means of holding the country together in uncertain times. Pride in the achievement of national sports teams is intense, and two young authors recently achieved wide acclaim with the publication of their book, *The China That Can Say No,* an obvious response to recent criticism of the country in the United States and Europe.

Whether the current leaders will be able by such artificial means to prevent further erosion of the party's power and prestige is unclear. Dissatisfaction with the CCP and alienation from the socialist system are running high in China, notably among the educated youth, the professionals, and the middle ranks of the bureaucracy. Although a disintegration of the authority of the Communist regime in China as in the Soviet Union cannot be predicted, the trend toward a greater popular role in the governing process will be difficult to reverse.

Serve the People: Chinese Society Under Communism

Enormous changes have taken place in Chinese society since the Communist rise to power in 1949. Yet beneath the surface are hints of the survival of elements of the old China. Despite all the efforts of Mao Zedong and his colleagues, the ideas of Confucius have still not been irrevocably discarded. China under communism remains a society that in many respects is in thrall to its past.

The Politics of the Mass Line

Nowhere is this uneasy balance between the old and the new more clearly demonstrated than in politics and government. In its broad outlines, the new political system followed the Soviet pattern. Yet from the start, the Communist leaders made it clear that the Chinese model would differ from the Soviet one in important respects. Whereas the Bolsheviks had severely distrusted nonrevolutionary elements in Russia and established a minority government based on the radical left, Mao Zedong and his colleagues were more confident that they possessed the basic support of the majority of the Chinese people. Under New Democracy, the party attempted to reach out to all progressive classes in the population to maintain the alliance that had brought it to power in the first place.

The primary link between the regime and the population was the system of "mass organizations," representing peasants, workers, women, religious groups, writers, and artists. The party had established these associations during the 1920s to mobilize support for the revolution. Now they served as a conduit between party and people, enabling the leaders to assess the attitude of the masses while at the same time seeking their support for the party's programs.

Initially, this "mass line" system worked fairly well. True, opposition to the regime was ruthlessly suppressed, but on the positive side, China finally had a government that appeared to be for the people. Although there was no pretense at Western-style democracy, and official corruption and bureaucratic mismanagement and arrogance had by no means been entirely eliminated, the new ruling class came preponderantly from workers and peasants and, at least by comparison with its predecessors, was willing to listen to the complaints and aspirations of its constituents.

But the failure of the Great Leap Forward betrayed a fundamental weakness in the policy of the mass line. While party leaders declared their willingness to listen to the concerns of the population, they were also determined to build a utopian society based on Marxist-Leninist principles. Popular acceptance of nationalization and collectivization during the mid-1950s indicates that the Chinese people were not entirely hostile to socialism, but when those programs were carried to an extreme during the Great Leap Forward, many, even within the party, resisted and forced the government to abandon the program.

The failure of the Great Leap Forward split the CCP and led to the revolutionary disturbances of the following decade. The Cultural Revolution can be seen above all as Mao's attempt to cleanse the system of its impurities and put Chinese society back on the straight road to egalitarian communism. As we have seen, the enthusiasms aroused by the Cultural Revolution did not last. As in the French Revolution, the efforts to achieve revolutionary purity eventually alienated all except the most radical elements in the country, and a period of reaction inevitably set in. In China, revolutionary fervor gave way to a new era in which belief in socialist ideals was replaced by a more practical desire for material benefits.

After Mao's death, the new Chinese leadership under Deng Xiaoping recognized the need to restore credibility to a system that was on the verge of breakdown. Deng's encouragement of the Democracy Wall in 1979 was an attempt to rebuild the links between the party and the masses. But like other Communist leaders, Deng soon discovered that once the people have been encouraged to criticize current conditions, it is difficult to prevent them from focusing on the linchpin of the entire Marxist-Leninist system: the dictatorship of the proletariat and the party's domination of power.

The regime attempted to suppress the criticism by closing down the Democracy Wall and providing new guidelines—called the "Four Cardinal Principles"—that prohibited criticism of the socialist system, the dictatorship of the proletariat, Marxist-Leninist-Maoist thought, and the final goal of communism. But the Tiananmen incident graphically demonstrated that the credibility of Marxist thought, and of the CCP itself, had been severely shaken, and in spite of the economic achievements that continued into the 1990s, party leaders had good reason to fear that their vaunted close relationship with the Chinese people had become a thing of the past. The fact is, the events of recent years have highlighted a serious dilemma facing China's aging leaders: How could they introduce Western technology and work habits without at the same time infecting the Chinese people with the virus of bourgeois individualism and the desire for personal profit and advancement? When the modernization program was first introduced in the late 1970s, conservative party officials warned that when the windows were opened, dust, flies, and all sorts of other bad things would come in. Deng Xiaoping sought to reassure them. In that case, he said, we will simply use our flyswatters. But would the flyswatters be enough? Or would the regime's effort to introduce Western technology while preserving the essence of Chinese socialism go the way of the nineteenth-century slogan "East for essence, West for practical use" (see Chapter 23)?

Economics in Command

After their rise to power in 1949, Communist leaders quickly determined that for the time being, economic considerations would be foremost in their set of priorities for continuing the Chinese Revolution. To highlight their new policy, they declared that in selecting revolutionary cadres, "expertise" (technical competence) would take precedence over "redness" (ideological commitment). That policy began to change in the late 1950s, when Mao decided that political considerations were more important than economic ones in building a socialist society. During the Cultural Revolution, the policy of "red" over "expert" reached its logical extreme, as anyone possessing professional skills was suspected of harboring counterrevolutionary tendencies.

After 1976, Deng Xiaoping and other party leaders were obviously hoping that rapid economic growth would satisfy the Chinese people and prevent them from demanding political reforms. The post-Mao leadership clearly placed economic performance over ideological purity. To stimulate the stagnant industrial sector, which had been under state control since the end of the New Democracy era, they reduced bureaucratic controls over state industries and allowed local managers to have more say over prices, salaries, and quality control. Productivity was encouraged by permitting bonuses for extra effort, a policy that had been discouraged during the Cultural Revolution. The regime also tolerated the emergence of a small private sector. Unemployed youth were encouraged to set up restaurants, bicycle or radio repair shops, and handicraft shops on their own initiative.

Finally, the regime opened up the country to foreign investment and technology. The Maoist policy of self-reliance was abandoned, and China openly sought the advice of foreign experts and the money of foreign capitalists. Special economic zones were established in urban centers near the coast (ironically, many were located in the old nineteenth-century treaty ports), where lucrative concessions were offered to encourage foreign firms to build factories. The tourist industry was encouraged, and students were sent abroad to study.

The new leaders especially stressed educational reform. The system adopted during the Cultural Revolution, emphasizing practical education and ideology at the expense of higher education and modern science, was rapidly abandoned (the *Little Red Book* itself was withdrawn from circulation and could no longer be found on bookshelves), and a new system based generally on the Western model was instituted. Admission to higher education was based on success in merit examinations, and courses on science and mathematics received high priority.

No economic reform program could succeed unless it included the countryside. Three decades of socialism had done little to increase food production or to lay the basis for a modern agricultural sector. China, with a population now numbering one billion, could still barely feed itself. Peasants had little incentive to work and few opportunities to increase production through mechanization, the use of fertilizer, or better irrigation.

Under Deng Xiaoping, agricultural policy made a rapid about-face. Under the new "rural responsibility system," adopted shortly after Deng had consolidated his authority, collectives leased land to peasant families, who paid a quota in the form of rent to the collective. Anything produced on the land above that payment could be sold on the private market or consumed. To soak up excess labor in the villages, the government encouraged the formation of so-called sideline industries, a modern equivalent of the traditional cottage industries in premodern China. Peasants raised fish or shrimp, made consumer goods, and even assembled living room furniture and appliances for sale to their newly affluent compatriots.

The reform program had a striking effect on rural production. Grain production increased rapidly, and farm income doubled during the 1980s. Yet it also created problems. In the first place, income at the village level became more unequal, as some enterprising farmers (known locally as "ten thousand dollar households") earned profits several times those realized by their less fortunate or industrious neighbors. When some farmers discovered that they could earn more by growing cash crops or other specialized commodities, they devoted less land to rice and other grain crops, thus threatening to reduce the supply of China's most crucial staple. Finally, the agricultural policy threatened to undermine the government's population control program, which party leaders viewed as crucial to the success of the four modernizations.

Since a misguided period in the mid-1950s when Mao Zedong had argued that more labor would result in higher productivity, China had been attempting to limit its population growth. By 1970, the government had launched a stringent family planning program—including education, incentives, and penalties for noncompliance—to persuade the Chinese people to limit themselves to one child per family. The program did have some success, and population growth was reduced drastically in the early 1980s. The rural responsibility system, however, undermined the program, because it encouraged farm families to pay the penalties for having additional children in the belief that their labor would increase family income and provide the parents with a form of social security for their old age.

Still, the overall effects of the modernization program were impressive. The standard of living improved for the majority of the population. Whereas a decade earlier the average Chinese had struggled to earn enough to buy a bicycle, radio, watch, or washing machine, by the late 1980s many were beginning to purchase videocassette recorders, refrigerators, and color television sets. The government popularized the idea that all Chinese would prosper, although not necessarily at the same speed. Earlier slogans such as "Serve the people" and "Uphold the banner of Marxist-Leninist-Maoist thought" were replaced by others that announced that "Time is money" and instructed citizens to "Create wealth for the people."

Yet the rapid growth of the economy created its own problems: inflationary pressures, greed, envy, increased corruption, and—most dangerous of all for the regime—rising expectations. Young people in particular resented restrictions on employment (most young people in China are still required to accept the jobs that are offered to them by the government or school officials) and opportunities to study abroad. Disillusionment ran high, especially in the cities, where high living by officials and rising prices for goods aroused widespread alienation and cynicism. Such attitudes undoubtedly contributed to the anger and frustration that burst out during the spring of 1989, when many workers, peasants, and functionaries joined the demonstrations against official corruption and one-party rule in Tiananmen Square.

The Legacy of the Past: Continuity and Change in Modern China

From the start, the Chinese Communist Party intended to bring an end to the Confucian legacy in modern China. At the root of Marxist-Leninist ideology is the idea of building a new citizen free from the prejudices, ignorance, and superstition of the "feudal" era and the capitalist desire for self-gratification. This new citizen would be characterized not only by a sense of racial and sexual equality, but also by the selfless desire to contribute his or her utmost for the good of all.

The new government wasted no time in keeping its promise. During the early 1950s, it took a number of steps to bring a definitive end to the old system in China. Women were permitted to vote and encouraged to become active in the political process. At the local level, an increasing number of women became active in the CCP and in collective organizations. In 1950, a new Marriage Law guaranteed women equal rights with men. Most important, perhaps, it permitted women for the first time to initiate divorce proceedings against their husbands. Within a year, nearly one million divorces had been granted.

The regime also undertook to destroy the influence of the traditional family system. To the Communists, loyalty to the family, a crucial element in the Confucian social order, undercut loyalty to the state and to the dictatorship of the proletariat.

At first, however, the new government moved carefully, to avoid alienating its supporters in the countryside unnecessarily. When collective farms were established in the mid-1950s, payment for hours worked in the form of ration coupons was made not to the individual, but to the family head. Because the payments went to the head of the family, the traditionally dominant position of the patriarch was maintained. When people's communes were established in the late 1950s, payments went to the individual.

During the political radicalism of the Great Leap Forward, children were encouraged to report to the authorities any comments by their parents that criticized the system. Such practices continued during the Cultural Revolution, when children were expected to report on their parents, students on their teachers, and employees on their superiors. Some have suggested that Mao deliberately encouraged such practices to bring an end to the traditional "politics of dependency." According to this theory, historically the famous "five relationships" forced individuals to swallow their anger and frustration and accept the hierarchical norms established by Confucian ethics (known in Chinese as "eat bitterness"). By encouraging the oppressed elements in society—the young, the female, and the poor—to voice their bitterness, Mao was helping to break the tradition of dependency. Such denunciations had been issued against landlords and other "local tyrants" in the land reform tribunals of the late 1940s and early 1950s. Later, during the Cultural Revolution, they were applied to other authority figures in Chinese society.

The post-Mao era brought a decisive shift away from revolutionary utopianism and a return to the pragmatic approach to nation building. For most people, it meant improved living conditions and a qualified return to family traditions (see the box on p. 867). For the first time, millions of Chinese saw the prospect of a house or an urban flat with a washing machine, television set, and indoor plumbing. Young people whose parents had given patriotic names such as Build the Country, Protect Mao Zedong, and Assist Korea began to choose more elegant and cosmopolitan names for their own children. Some names, such as Surplus Grain or Bring a Younger Brother, expressed hope for the future. One Western observer reported that he had encountered a young Chinese named Dian Shi, or Color Television. When asked for an explanation, the father replied that if he had not had to pay a fine for having an extra child, he would have bought a color television set with the money.

The new attitudes were also reflected in physical appearance. For a generation after the civil war, clothing had been restricted to the traditional baggy "Mao suit" in olive drab or dark blue, but by the 1980s young people craved such fashionable Western items as designer jeans, trendy sneakers, and sweat suits (or reasonable facsimiles). Cosmetic surgery to create a more buxom figure or a more Western facial look became increasingly common among affluent young women in the cities. Many had the epicanthic fold over their eyelids removed or their noses enlarged —a curious decision in view of the tradition of referring derogatorily to foreigners as "big noses."

Religious practices and beliefs also changed. As the government became more tolerant, some Chinese began returning to the traditional Buddhist faith, and Buddhist and Taoist temples were once again crowded with worshipers. Christianity became increasingly popular; like the "rice Christians" (persons who supposedly converted for

STUDENT FASHIONS: BEFORE AND AFTER DENG. The increasing affluence of Chinese society is evident in the changes in clothing styles since the end of the Cultural Revolution. The picture on the left shows student dress in the late 1970s. Two decades of modernization under Deng Xiaoping have led to more sophisticated styles, as the photo on the right attests. (One of the authors—William Duiker—is pictured on the left.)

MARRIAGE CHINESE STYLE

"What men can do, women can also do." So said Chairman Mao as he "liberated" and masculinized Chinese women to work alongside men. Women's individuality and sexuality were sacrificed for the collective good of his new socialist society. Marriage, which had traditionally been arranged by families for financial gain, was now dictated by duty to the state. The Western concept of romantic love did not enter into a Chinese marriage, as this interview of a schoolteacher by the reporter Zhang Xinxin in the mid-1980s illustrates. According to recent surveys, the same is true today.

ZHANG XINXIN, *CHINESE LIVES*

My husband and I never did any courting—honestly! We registered our marriage a week after we'd met. He was just out of the forces and a worker in a building outfit. They'd been given a foreign-aid assignment in Zambia, and he was selected. He wanted to get his private life fixed up before he went, and someone introduced us. Seeing how he looked really honest, I accepted him.

No, you can't say I didn't know anything about him. The person who introduced us told me he was a Party member who'd been an organization commissar. Any comrade who's good enough to be an organization cadre is politically reliable. Nothing special about our standing of living—it's what we've earned. He's still a worker, but we live all right, don't we?

He went off with the army as soon as we'd registered our marriage and been given the wedding certificates. He was away three years. We didn't have the wedding itself before he went because we hadn't got a room yet.

Those three years were a test for us. The main problem was that my family was against it. They thought I was still only a kid and I'd picked the wrong man. What did they have against him? His family was too poor. Of course I won in the end—we'd registered and got our wedding certificates. We were legally married whether we had the family ceremony or not.

We had our wedding after he came back in the winter of 1973. His leaders and mine all came to congratulate us and give us presents. The usual presents those days were busts of Chairman Mao. I was twenty-six and he was twenty-nine. We've never had a row.

I never really wanted to take the college entrance exams. Then in 1978 the school leadership got us all to put our names forward. They said they weren't going to hold us back: the more of us who passed, the better it would be for the school. So I put my name forward, crammed for six weeks, and passed. I already had two kids then. . . .

I reckoned the chance for study was too good to miss. And my husband was looking after the kids all by himself. I usually only came back once a fortnight. So I couldn't let him down.

My instructors urged me to take the exams for graduate school, but I didn't. I was already thirty-four, so what was the point of more study? There was another reason too. I didn't want an even wider gap between us: he hadn't even finished junior middle school when he joined the army.

It's bad if the gap's too wide. For example, there's a definite difference in our tastes in music and art, I have to admit that. But what really matters? Now we've set up this family we have to preserve it. Besides, look at all the sacrifices he had to make to see me through college. Men comrades all like a game of cards and that, but he was stuck with looking after the kids. He still doesn't get any time for himself—it's all work for him.

We've got a duty to each other. Our differences? The less said about them the better. We've always treated each other with the greatest respect.

Of course some people have made suggestions, but my advice to him is to respect himself and respect me. I'm not going to be like those men who ditch their wives when they go up in the world.

I'm the head of our school now. With this change in my status I've got to show even more responsibility for the family. Besides, I know how much he's done to get me where I am today. I've also got some duties in the municipal Women's Federation and Political Consultative Conference. No, I'm not being modest. I haven't done anything worth talking about, only my duty.

We've got to do a lot more educating people. There have been two cases of divorce in our school this year.

economic reasons) of the past, many viewed it as a symbol of success and cosmopolitanism.

Such changes have been much more prevalent among urban dwellers and China's still small middle class than among rural folk, who make up more than half the population. While prosperity has come to some parts of the countryside—notably in areas located near the major metropolitan centers—the vast majority of peasants have been only superficially affected by the events since Mao's death. In that sense, the yawning gap that has always separated town and country in China still remains.

As with all social changes, China's reintegration into the outside world has had a price. Arranged marriages, nepotism, and mistreatment of females (for example, many parents in rural areas reportedly have killed female infants in the hope of having a son) have come back, although such behavior likely had survived under the cloak of revolutionary purity for a generation. Materialistic attitudes

CHRONOLOGY

CHINA UNDER COMMUNIST RULE

New Democracy	1949–1955
The Era of Collectivization	1955–1958
The 100 Flowers Campaign	1956–1957
The Great Leap Forward	1958–1960
The Great Proletarian Cultural Revolution	1966–1976
Death of Mao Zedong	1976
The Era of Deng Xiaoping	1978–1997
The Tiananmen Square Incident	1989
Jiang Zemin appointed president of China	1993

are highly prevalent among young people, along with a corresponding cynicism about politics and the CCP. Expensive weddings are now increasingly common, and bribery and favoritism are all too frequent. Crime of all types, including an apparently growing incidence of prostitution and sex crimes against women, appears to be on the rise. To discourage sexual abuse, the government now seeks to provide free legal services for women living in rural areas.

CHINA'S CHANGING CULTURE

Like their contemporaries all over Asia, Chinese artists were strongly influenced by the revolutionary changes that were taking place in the art world of the West in the early twentieth century. In the decades following the 1911 revolution, Chinese artists began to experiment with Western styles, although the more extreme schools such as surrealism and abstract painting had little impact.

The rise to power of the communists in 1949 added a new dimension to the ongoing debate over the future of culture in China. The new leaders rejected the Western slogan of "Art for art's sake" and, like their Soviet counterparts, viewed culture as an important instrument of indoctrination. The standard would no longer be aesthetic quality or the personal preference of the artist, but "Art for life's safe," whereby culture would serve the interests of socialism.

At first, the new emphasis on socialist realism did not entirely extinguish the influence of traditional culture. Mao and his colleagues tolerated—and in some cases even encouraged—efforts by artists to synthesize traditional ideas with socialist concepts and Western techniques. During the Cultural Revolution, however, all forms of traditional culture came to be viewed as reactionary. Socialist realism became the only acceptable standard in literature, art, and music. All forms of traditional expression were forbidden.

Nowhere were the dilemmas of the new order more challenging than in literature. In the heady afterglow of the Communist victory, many progressive writers supported the new regime and enthusiastically embraced Mao's exhortation to create a new Chinese literature for the edification of the masses. But in the harsher climate of the late 1950s and 1960s, many writers were criticized by the party for their excessive individualism and admiration for Western culture. Such writers either toed the new line and suppressed their doubts or were jailed and silenced.

Characteristic of the changing cultural climate in China was the experience of author Ding Ling. Born in 1904 and educated in a school for women set up by leftist intellectuals during the hectic years after the May Fourth Movement, she began writing in her early twenties. At first she was strongly influenced by prevailing Western styles, but after her husband, a struggling young poet and a member of the CCP, was executed by Chiang Kai-shek's government in 1931, she became active in party activities and sublimated her talent to the revolutionary cause.

In the late 1930s, Ding Ling settled in Yan'an, where she became a leader in the party's women's and literary associations. She remained dedicated to revolution, but years of service to the party had not stifled her individuality, and in 1942 she wrote critically of the incompetence, arrogance, and hypocrisy of many party officials, as well as the treatment of women in areas under Communist authority. Such conduct raised eyebrows, but she was able to survive criticism and in 1948 wrote her most famous novel, *The Sun Shines over the Sangan River,* which described the land reform program in favorable terms. It was awarded the Stalin Prize three years later.

During the early 1950s, Ding Ling was one of the most prominent literary lights of the new China, but in the more ideological climate at the end of the decade, she was attacked for her individualism and her previous criticism of the party. Although temporarily rehabilitated, during the Cultural Revolution she was sentenced to hard labor on a commune in the far north and was only released in the late 1970s after Mao's death. Although crippled and in poor health, she began writing a biography of her mother that examined the role of women in twentieth-century China. She died in 1981. Ding Ling's story mirrors the fate of thousands of progressive Chinese intellectuals, who, despite their efforts, were not able to satisfy the constantly changing demands of a repressive regime.

After Mao's death, Chinese culture was once again released from the shackles of socialist realism. In painting, the new policies led to a revival of interest in both traditional and Western forms. A new generation of Chinese painters began to emerge in the 1980s. Although some continued the attempt to blend Eastern and Western styles, others imitated trends from abroad, experimenting with a wide range of previously prohibited art styles, including cubism and abstract expressionism.

In the late 1980s, two avant-garde art exhibits shocked the Chinese public and provoked the wrath of the party. An exhibition of nude paintings, the first ever held in China, attracted many viewers but reportedly offended many Chinese for reasons of modesty. The second was an exhibit presenting the works of various schools of modern and postmodern art. The event resulted in considerable commentary and some expressions of public hostility. After a Communist critic lambasted the works as promiscuous and ideologically reactionary, the government declared that henceforth it would regulate all art exhibits.

The limits of freedom of expression were most apparent in literature. During the early 1980s, party leaders encouraged Chinese writers to express their views on the mistakes of the past, and a new "literature of the wounded" began to describe the brutal and arbitrary character of the Cultural Revolution. One of the most prominent writers was Bai Hua, whose script for the film *Bitter Love* described the life of a young Chinese painter who joined the revolutionary movement during the 1940s but was destroyed during the Cultural Revolution when his work was condemned as counterrevolutionary. The film depicts the condemnation through a view of a street in Beijing "full of people waving the *Quotations of Chairman Mao*, all those devout and artless faces fired by a feverish fanaticism." Driven from his home for posting a portrait of a third-century B.C.E. defender of human freedom on a Beijing wall, the artist flees the city. At the end of the film, he dies in a snowy field, where his corpse and a semicircle made by his footprints form a giant question mark.

In criticizing the excesses of the Cultural Revolution, Bai Hua was only responding to Deng Xiaoping's appeal for intellectuals to speak out, but he was soon criticized for failing to point out the essentially beneficial role of the CCP in recent Chinese history, and his film was withdrawn from circulation in 1981. Bai Hua was compelled to recant his errors and to state that the great ideas of Mao Zedong on art and literature were "still of universal guiding significance today."[12]

As the attack on Bai Hua illustrates, many party leaders remained suspicious of the impact that "decadent" bourgeois culture could have on the socialist foundations of Chinese society, and the official press periodically warned that China should adopt only the "positive" aspects of Western culture (notably, its technology and its work ethic) and not the "negative" elements such as drug use, pornography, and hedonism. Conservatives were especially incensed by the tendency of many writers to dwell on the shortcomings of the socialist system and to come uncomfortably close to direct criticism of the role of the CCP (see the box on p. 870).

A STREET CALLIGRAPHER. During the Great Proletarian Cultural Revolution, all aspects of traditional culture were forbidden. Only items with revolutionary themes were permitted to be created or displayed. This elderly Chinese gentleman, a calligrapher by profession, had been prohibited from practicing his craft for two decades until the post-Mao era in the 1980s. He has now resumed his career at a roadside stand on a residential street in Beijing.

TROUBLE IN THE GARLIC FIELDS

Considered one of the masterpieces of recent Chinese literature, Mo Yan's The Garlic Ballads *(1988) describes with passion and intimacy the suffering of contemporary Chinese peasants in northern China. Based on real-life riots in northern China in the summer of 1987, the novel is a plea for social reform, as it exposes the greed, corruption, and inhumanity of the local government and the legacy of the feudal mentality. Oppressed and betrayed by their cadres, a group of garlic farmers are swept up into a riot against the local administrator. Mo Yan depicts the resilience and courage of Chinese peasants in the face of incredible hardship and violent oppression. In the closing pages of the novel, at the trial of the peasant rioters, a young military officer, speaking for the author and human decency, accuses the local judge of turning the court into a travesty of justice.*

MO YAN, *THE GARLIC BALLADS*

He turned to face the spectators, speaking with a passion that touched everyone who heard him. "Your Honors, ladies and gentlemen, the situation in our farming villages has changed drastically in the wake of the Party's Third Plenary Session of the Eleventh Central Committee, including those here in Paradise County. The peasants are much better off than they were during the Cultural Revolution. This is obvious to everyone. But the benefits they enjoyed as a result of rural economic reforms are gradually disappearing."

"Please don't stray too far from the subject," the presiding judge broke in.

"Thank you for reminding me, Your Honor: I'll get right to the point. In recent years the peasants have been called upon to shoulder ever heavier burdens: fees, taxes, fines, and inflated prices for just about everything they need. No wonder you hear them talk about plucking the wild goose's tail feathers as it flies by. Over the past couple of years these trends have gotten out of control, which is why, I believe, the Paradise County garlic incident should have come as no surprise."

The presiding judge glanced down at his wrist-watch.

"Not being able to sell their crops was the spark that ignited this explosive incident, but the root cause was the unenlightened policies of the Paradise County government!" the officer continued. "Before Liberation only about a dozen people were employed by the district government, and things worked fine. Now even a township government in charge of the affairs of a mere thirty thousand people employs more than sixty people! And when you add those in the communes it's nearly a hundred, seventy percent of whose salaries are paid by peasants through township fees and taxes. Put in the bluntest possible terms, they are feudal parasites on the body of society! So in my view, the slogans 'Down with corrupt officials!' and 'Down with bureaucrats!' comprise a progressive call for the awakening of the peasants. . . .

"What I want to say is this," the young officer continued. "The people have the right to overthrow any party or government that disregards their well-being. If an official assumes the role of public master rather than public servant, the people have the right to throw him out! . . . In point of fact, things have improved in the wake of the party rectification, and most of Paradise County's responsible party members are doing a fine job. But one rat turd can spoil a whole pot of porridge, and the unprincipled behavior of a single party member adversely affects the party's reputation and the government's prestige. The people aren't always fair and discerning, and can be forgiven if their dissatisfaction with a particular official carries over into their attitudes toward officials in general. But shouldn't that be a reminder to officials to act in such a way as to best represent the party and the government?

". . . If we endorse the proposition that all people are equal under the law, then we must demand that the Paradise County People's Procuratorate indict Paradise County administrator Zhong Weimin on charges of official misconduct! I have nothing more to say."

The young officer remained standing for a moment before wearily taking a seat behind the defense table. Thunderous applause erupted from the spectator section behind him.

One author whose writings fell under the harsh glare of official disapproval is Zhang Xinxin (b. 1953). Her controversial novellas and short stories, which explored Chinese women's alienation and spiritual malaise, were viewed by many as a negative portrayal of contemporary society, provoking the government in 1984 to prohibit her from publishing for a year. Determined and resourceful, Zhang turned to reportage. With a colleague, she interviewed 100 "ordinary" people to record their views on all aspects of everyday life.

CONCLUSION

For four decades after the end of World War II, the world's two superpowers competed for global hegemony. What began as a dispute on the future shape of Eastern Europe spread rapidly to Asia and ultimately penetrated virtually every part of the earth. The Cold War became the dominant feature on the international scene, and dominated the internal politics of many countries around the world as well.

By the early 1980s, some of the tension had gone out of the conflict, as it appeared that both Moscow and Washington had learned to tolerate the other's existence. Skeptical minds even suspected that both countries drew benefits from their mutual rivalry and saw it as an advantage in carrying on their relations with friends and allies. Few suspected that the Cold War, which had for long appeared to be a permanent feature of the political scene, was about to come to an end.

What brought about the collapse of the Soviet Empire? Some argue that the ambitious defense policies adopted by the Reagan administration forced Moscow into an arms race it could not afford, and thus ultimately led to a collapse of the Soviet economy. Others suggest that Soviet problems were more deep-rooted and would have led to the disintegration of the USSR even without outside stimulation. Both arguments have some validity, but the latter is surely closer to the mark. For years, if not decades, leaders in the Kremlin had disguised or ignored the massive inefficiencies of the Soviet system. In the years immediately preceding his ascent to power in the Politburo, the perceptive Mikhail Gorbachev had recognized the crucial importance of instituting radical reforms. At the time, he hoped that by doing so he could save the system. By then, however, it was too late. In the classic formulation of dictatorial regimes the world over, the most dangerous period is when leaders adopt reform measures to prevent collapse.

Why has Communism survived in China, albeit in a substantially altered form, when it collapsed in Eastern Europe and the Soviet Union? Although there may be many reasons, one of the primary factors is probably cultural. Although the doctrine of Marxism-Leninism originated in Europe, many of its main precepts, such as the primacy of the community over the individual and the denial of the concept of private property, run counter to the central trends in Western civilization. This inherent conflict is especially evident in the societies of Central Europe, which were strongly influenced by Enlightenment philosophy and the Industrial Revolution. These forces were weaker in the countries further to the east, but both had begun to penetrate tsarist Russia by the end of the nineteenth century.

By contrast, Marxism-Leninism found a more receptive climate in China and other countries in the region influenced by Confucian tradition. In its political culture, the Communist system exhibits many of the same characteristics as traditional Confucianism—a single truth, an elite governing class, and an emphasis on obedience to the community and its governing representatives—while feudal attitudes regarding female inferiority, loyalty to the family, and bureaucratic arrogance are hard to break. On the surface, China today bears a number of uncanny similarities to the China of the past.

Yet these similarities should not blind us to the real changes that are taking place in Chinese society today. Although the youthful protesters in Tiananmen Square are comparable in some respects to the reformist elements of the 1890s or the New Culture intellectuals of the early republic—two generations of reformers whose passionate strivings to create a modern China on the Western model helped to destroy the old system but failed to lay firm foundations for a new one—the China of today is fundamentally different from that of the late Qing or even the early republic. Literacy rates and the standard of living, on balance, are far higher; the pressures of outside powers are less threatening; and China has entered the opening stages of its own industrial and technological revolution. Where Sun Yat-sen, Chiang Kai-shek, and even Mao Zedong broke their lances on the rocks of centuries of tradition, poverty, and ignorance, China's present leaders rule a country much more aware of the world and its place in it.

REACH FOR THE SKY. This eighty-story television tower, erected in the new suburb of Pudong, is an example of Shanghai's dynamic effort to become one of the most modern cities in the world. Pudong, previously an uninhabited mudflat on the eastern shore of the Huangpu River, is now teeming with hotels, office buildings, and entertainment centers. But local citizens pay a heavy price for modernization in environmental pollution, which, as here, frequently hovers as a dense haze over the entire city.

Whether or not communism survives in China—or revives in some form in the lands of the former Soviet Union—the Cold War is not likely to return in its old form, and for that we can be thankful, because it not only kept the earth on the knife edge of a great power conflict but also distracted world leaders from turning their attention to the deeper problems that afflict all of humankind. Still, it is now clear that the end of the Cold War is not necessarily a harbinger of a new era of peace and prosperity. To the contrary, it is more likely to open a new stage of history that will be marked by increased global instability and severe challenges in the areas of environmental pollution, technological change, and population growth. These issues will be addressed in more detail in our final chapters.

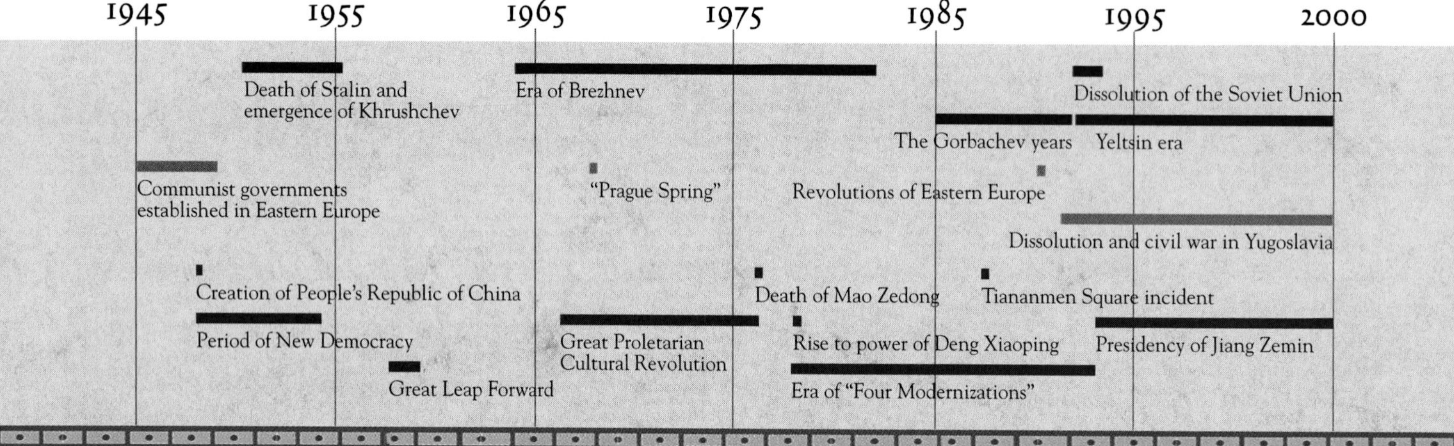

Chapter Notes

1. R. Hilton, *Military Attaché in Moscow* (London, 1949), p. 41.
2. Nikita Khrushchev, *Khrushchev Remembers*, trans. Strobe Talbott (Boston, 1970), p. 77.
3. Quoted in Hedrick Smith, *The New Russians* (New York, 1990) p. 30.
4. Quoted in Frank B. Tipton and Robert Aldrich, *An Economic and Social History of Europe from 1939 to the Present* (Baltimore, 1987), p. 193.
5. Hedrick Smith, *The New Russians*, p. 74.
6. *New York Times*, May 7, 1992.
7. Quoted in Stanley Karnow, *Mao and China: Inside China's Cultural Revolution* (New York, 1972), p. 95.
8. Quoted from an article by Mao Zedong in the June 1, 1958, issue of the journal *Red Flag*. See Stuart R. Schram, *The Political Thought of Mao Tse-tung* (New York, 1963), p. 253.
9. Liang Heng and Judith Shapiro, *Son of the Revolution* (New York, 1983).
10. Quoted in *Time*, March 13, 1989, pp. 10–11.
11. Quoted in Frank Ching, "Confucius, the New Saviour," in *Far Eastern Economic Review*, November 10, 1994, p. 37.
12. Quoted in Jonathan Spence, *Chinese Roundabout: Essays in History and Culture* (New York, 1992), p. 285.

Suggested Readings

For a general view of Soviet society, see D. K. Shipler, *Russia: Broken Idols, Solemn Dreams* (New York, 1983). On the Khrushchev years, see E. Crankshaw, *Khrushchev: A Career* (New York, 1966). For the final years of the Soviet era, see S. F. Cohen, *Rethinking the Soviet Experience* (Oxford and New York, 1985); R. J. Hill, *The Soviet Union: Politics, Economics, and Society*, 2d ed. (London, 1989); M. Lewin, *The Gorbachev Phenomenon* (Berkeley, Calif., 1988); G. Hosking, *The Awakening of the Soviet Union* (London, 1990); and S. White, *Gorbachev and After* (Cambridge, 1991). On economic conditions in post-Soviet Russia, see J. Blasi, M. Kroumova, and D. Kruse, *Kremlin Capitalism: The Privatization of the Russian Economy* (Ithaca, 1997).

For a general study of the Soviet satellites in Eastern Europe, see A. Brown and J. Gary, *Culture and Political Changes in Communist States* (London, 1977), and S. Fischer-Galati, *Eastern Europe in the 1980s* (London, 1981). The unique path of Yugoslavia is examined in L. J. Cohen and P. Warwick, *Political Cohesion in a Fragile Mosaic: The Yugoslav Experience* (Boulder, Colo., 1983). On

Romania, see L. S. Graham, *Rumania: A Developing Socialist State* (Boulder, Colo., 1978). On Hungary, see B. Kovrig, *The Hungarian People's Republic* (Baltimore, 1970). On East Germany, see C. B. Scharf, *Politics and Change in East Germany* (Boulder, Colo., 1984). Additional studies on the recent history of these countries include T. G. Ash, *The Polish Revolution: Solidarity* (New York, 1984); B. Kovrig, *Communism in Hungary from Kun to Kádár* (Stanford, Calif., 1979); T. G. Ash, *The Magic Lantern: The Revolution of '89 Witnessed in Warsaw, Budapest, Berlin and Prague* (New York, 1990); M. Shafir, *Romania: Politics, Economics and Society* (London, 1985); R. J. Crampton, *A Short History of Modern Bulgaria* (Cambridge, 1989); E. Biberaj, *Albania, A Socialist Maverick* (Boulder, Colo., 1990); and S. Ramet, *Nationalism and Federalism in Yugoslavia* (Bloomington, Ind., 1992).

A number of useful surveys deal with China after World War II. The most comprehensive treatment of the Communist period is M. Meisner, *Mao's China, and After: A History of the People's Republic* (New York, 1986). For shorter accounts of the period, see J. Grasso et al., *Modernization and Revolution in China* (Armonk, N.Y., 1991), and C. Dietrich, *People's China: A Brief History* (New York, 1986). For documents, see M. Selden, ed., *The People's Republic of China: A Documentary History of Revolutionary Change* (New York, 1978).

There are countless specialized studies on various aspects of the Communist period in China. For a detailed treatment of economic and political issues, see F. Schurmann, *Ideology and Organization in Communist China* (Berkeley, Calif., 1968). The Cultural Revolution is treated dramatically in S. Karnow, *Mao and China: Inside China's Cultural Revolution* (New York, 1972). For individual accounts of the impact of the revolution on people's lives, see the celebrated book by Nien Cheng, *Life and Death in Shanghai* (New York, 1986), and Liang Heng and J. Shapiro, *After the Revolution* (New York, 1986).

For the post-Mao period, see O. Schell, *To Get Rich Is Glorious* (New York, 1986), and the sequel, *Discoes and Democracy: China in the Throes of Reform* (New York, 1988). The 1989 demonstrations and their aftermath are chronicled in L. Feigon's eyewitness account, *China Rising: The Meaning of Tiananmen* (Chicago, 1990), and D. Morrison, *Massacre in Beijing* (New York, 1989). For commentary by Chinese dissidents, see Liu Binyan, *China's Crisis, China's Hope* (Cambridge, 1990), and Fang Lizhi, *Bringing Down the Great Wall: Writings on Science, Culture, and Democracy in China* (New York, 1991).

Several biographies of the Chinese party leaders are available. On Mao Zedong, see S. Schram, *Mao Tse-tung* (New York, 1966), and S. Uhalley, Jr., *Mao Tse-tung: A Critical Biography* (1977). For an interesting treatment of Mao's famous wife, a member of the gang of four, see R. Witke, *Comrade Chiang Ching* (Boston, 1972). On Deng Xiaoping, see R. Evans, *Deng Xiaoping and the Making of Modern China* (London, 1993).

On literature, see the interesting chapters on Ding Ling and her contemporaries in J. Spence, *The Gate of Heavenly Peace* (New York, 1981). To witness daily life in the mid-1980s, see Z. Xinxin and S. Ye, *Chinese Lives: An Oral History of Contemporary China* (New York, 1987). For a comprehensive introduction to twentieth-century Chinese literature, consult E. Widmer and D. Der-Wei Wang, eds., *From May Fourth to June Fourth: Fiction and Film in Twentieth-Century China* (Cambridge, Mass., 1993), and J. Lau and H. Goldblatt, *The Columbia Anthology of Modern Chinese Literature* (New York, 1995). An excellent survey of Chinese women writers is found in M. S. Duke, ed., *Modern Chinese Women Writers: Critical Appraisals* (Armonk, N.Y., 1989). For the most comprehensive analysis of twentieth-century Chinese art, consult M. Sullivan, *Arts and Artists of Twentieth-Century China* (Berkeley, Calif., 1996).

For a discussion of the women's movement in China during this period, see J. Stacey, *Patriarchy and Socialist Revolution in China* (Berkeley, Calif., 1983), and M. Wolf, *Revolution Postponed: Women in Contemporary China* (Stamford, Conn., 1985). To follow the first-hand account of a Chinese woman revolutionary, read Y. Daiyun and C. Wakeman, *To the Storm: The Oddyssey of a Revolutionary Chinese Woman* (Berkeley, Calif., 1985).

For additional reading, go to InfoTrac College Edition, your online research library at http://web1.infotrac-college.com

Enter the search terms "Mao Zedong" using the Subject Guide.

Enter the search term "Stalin" using Keywords.

Enter the search term "Khruschev" using Keywords.

Enter the search term "perestroika" using the Subject Guide.

Enter the search term "Gorbachev" using Keywords.

CHAPTER

29

EUROPE AND THE WESTERN HEMISPHERE SINCE 1945

CHAPTER OUTLINE

FOCUS QUESTIONS

- What problems have the nations of Western Europe faced since 1945, and what steps have they taken to try to solve these problems?
- What political, social, and economic changes have the United States and Canada experienced since 1945?
- What problems have the nations of Latin America faced since 1945, and what role has Marxist ideology played in their efforts to solve these problems?
- What major social developments have occurred in Western Europe and North America since 1945?
- What major cultural and intellectual developments have occurred in Western Europe and North America since 1945?

The end of World War II in Europe had been met with great joy. One visitor in Moscow reported: "I looked out of the window [at 2 A.M.]; almost everywhere there were lights in the windows—people were staying awake. Everyone embraced everyone else; someone sobbed aloud." But after the victory parades and celebrations, Europeans awoke to a devastating realization: their civilization was in ruins. Almost 40 million people (both soldiers and civilians) had been killed over the last six years. Massive air raids and artillery bombardments had reduced many of the great cities of Europe to heaps of rubble. An American general described Berlin: "Wherever we looked we saw desolation. It was like a city of the dead. Suffering and shock were visible in every face. Dead bodies still remained in canals and lakes and were being dug out from under bomb debris." Millions of Europeans faced starvation as grain harvests were only half of what they had been in 1939. Millions were also homeless. Untold millions of people had been uprooted by the war; now they became "displaced persons," trying to find food and then their way home.

Between 1945 and 1970, Europe not only recovered from the devastating effects of World War II, but also experienced an economic resurgence that seemed nothing less than miraculous to many people. Economic growth and virtually full employment continued so long that the first postwar recession, in 1973, came as a shock to Western Europe. Although economic growth resumed after the recession, Europeans faced a growing number of economic, social, and political problems in the 1980s and 1990s.

The most significant factor in the history of the Western world after 1945 was the emergence of the United States as the world's richest and most powerful nation. American prosperity reached new proportions in the two decades after World War II, but a series of economic and social problems—including racial division and staggering budget deficits—in the 1970s, 1980s, and early 1990s left the nation with an imposing array of difficulties that weakened its ability to function as the world's only superpower.

To the south of the United States lay the vast world of Latin America, with its own unique heritage. Although some Latin Americans in the nineteenth century had looked to the United States as a model for their own development, in the twentieth century, many attacked the United States for its military and economic domination of Central and South America. Some states, such as Cuba, even adopted a Marxian path to building a new society and broke completely with the United States. At the same time, many Latin American countries struggled with economic and political instability.

In the midst of the transformation from Cold War to post–Cold War realities, other changes also shaped a new Western world. New artistic and intellectual currents, the growth of science and technology, a religious revival, new threats from terrorists, the realization of environmental problems, the surge of a women's liberation movement—all of these spoke of a vibrant, ever changing, and yet challenging new world.

Western Europe: Recovery and Renewal

All the nations of Western Europe faced similar kinds of problems at the end of World War II. Above all, they needed to rebuild their economies and re-create their democratic institutions. Within a few years after the defeat of Germany and Italy, an incredible economic revival brought a renewed growth to European society.

Western Europe: The Triumph of Democracy

With the economic aid of the Marshall Plan, the countries of Western Europe recovered relatively rapidly from the devastation of World War II. Between 1947 and 1950, European countries received $9.4 billion to be used for new equipment and raw materials. Between the early 1950s and late 1970s, industrial production surpassed all previous records, and Western Europe experienced virtually full employment. Social welfare programs—in the form of affordable health care, housing, family allowances to provide a minimum level of material care for children, increases in sickness, accident, unemployment, and old age benefits, and educational opportunities—helped create the modern welfare state. Despite economic recessions in the mid-1970s and early 1980s, especially after the dramatic increase in the price of oil in 1973, the economies of the Western European states recovered in the course of the 1980s, although problems remained. France had a 10.6 unemployment rate in 1993; it reached 11.7 percent in 1995. Despite their economic woes, Western Europeans were full participants in the technological advances of the age and seemed quite capable of standing up to American and Japanese economic competition.

Politically, Western Europe became accustomed to democracy. Even Spain and Portugal, which had retained their prewar dictatorial regimes until the mid-1970s, established democratic systems in the late 1970s. Moderate political parties, especially the Christian Democrats in Italy and Germany, played a particularly important role in achieving Europe's economic restoration. Overall, moderate yet ideologically oriented socialist parties declined, though reformist mass parties only slightly left of center, such as the Labour Party in Britain and the Social Democrats in West Germany, largely continued to share power. Western European Communist Parties declined drastically. During the mid-1970s, a new variety of communism called Eurocommunism briefly emerged when Communist Parties tried to work within the democratic system as mass movements committed to better government. But by the 1980s, internal political developments in Western Europe and events within the Communist world itself had combined to undermine the Eurocommunist experiment.

FRANCE: FROM DE GAULLE TO NEW UNCERTAINTIES

The history of France for nearly a quarter century after the war was dominated by one man—Charles de Gaulle (1890–1970)—who possessed an unshakable faith that he had a historical mission to reestablish the greatness of the French nation. During the war, de Gaulle had assumed leadership of some resistance groups and played an important role in ensuring the establishment of a French provisional government after the war. The creation of the Fourth Republic, with a return to a parliamentary system that de Gaulle considered weak, led him to withdraw from politics. Eventually, he formed the French Popular Movement, a decidedly rightist organization. It blamed the parties for France's political mess and called for an even stronger presidency, a goal that de Gaulle finally achieved in 1958.

CHARLES DE GAULLE. As president, Charles de Gaulle sought to revive the greatness of the French nation. He is shown here dressed in his military uniform participating in a formal state ceremony.

The fragile political stability of the Fourth Republic had been badly shaken by the Algerian crisis. The French army had suffered defeat in Indochina in 1954 and was determined to resist Algerian demands for independence. But a strong antiwar movement among French intellectuals and church leaders led to bitter divisions that opened the door to the possibility of civil war. The panic-stricken leaders of the Fourth Republic offered to let de Gaulle take over the government and revise the constitution.

In 1958, de Gaulle immediately drafted a new constitution for the Fifth Republic, which greatly enhanced the power of the office of president, who now had the right to choose the prime minister, dissolve parliament, and supervise both defense and foreign policy. De Gaulle had always believed in strong leadership, and the new Fifth Republic was by no means a democratic system. As the new president, de Gaulle sought to return France to a position of great power. He believed that playing a pivotal role in the Cold War might enhance France's stature. For that reason, he pulled France out of the NATO high command. He increased French prestige among the less-developed countries by consenting to Algerian independence despite strenuous opposition from the army. With an eye toward achieving the status of a world power, de Gaulle invested heavily in the nuclear arms race. France exploded its first nuclear bomb in 1960. Despite his successes, de Gaulle did not really achieve his ambitious goals. Although his successors maintained that France was the "third nuclear power" after the United States and the Soviet Union, in truth France was too small for such global ambitions.

Although the cost of the nuclear program increased the defense budget, de Gaulle did not neglect the French economy. Economic decision making was centralized, a reflection of the overall centralization undertaken by the Gaullist government. Between 1958 and 1968, the French gross national product grew at an annual rate of 5.5 percent, faster than that of the United States. By the end of de Gaulle's era, France was a major industrial producer and exporter, particularly in automobiles and armaments. Nevertheless, problems remained. The expansion of traditional industries, such as coal, steel, and railroads, which had all been nationalized, led to large government deficits. The cost of living increased faster than in the rest of Europe.

Growing dissatisfaction with the inability of de Gaulle's government to deal with these problems soon led to more violent action. In May 1968, a series of student protests, followed by a general strike by the labor unions, shook the government. Although de Gaulle managed to restore order, the events of May 1968 had seriously undermined the French people's respect for their aloof and imperious

MAP 29.1 The New Europe

president. Tired and discouraged, de Gaulle resigned from office in April 1969 and died within a year.

The worsening of France's economic situation in the 1970s brought a shift to the left politically. By 1981, the Socialists had become the dominant party in the National Assembly, and the Socialist leader, François Mitterrand (1916–1995), was elected president. His first concern was with France's economic difficulties. In 1982, Mitterrand froze prices and wages in the hope of reducing the huge budget deficit and high inflation. Mitterrand also passed a number of liberal measures to aid workers: an increased minimum wage, expanded social benefits, a mandatory fifth week of paid vacation for salaried workers, a thirty-nine-hour work week, and higher taxes for the rich. Their victory had also convinced the Socialists that they could enact some of their more radical reforms. Consequently, the government nationalized the steel industry, major banks, the space and electronics industries, and important insurance firms.

The Socialist policies largely failed to work, however, and within three years, faced with declining support, the Mitterrand government returned some of the economy to private enterprise. Some economic improvements in the late 1980s enabled Mitterrand to win a second seven-year term in the 1988 presidential election. But France's economic decline continued. In 1993, French unemployment stood at 10.6 percent, and in the elections in March of that year, the Socialists won only 28 percent of the vote, while a coalition of conservative parties gained 80 percent of the seats in the National Assembly. The move to the right in France was strengthened when the conservative mayor of Paris, Jacques Chirac, was elected president in May 1995.

FROM WEST GERMANY TO GERMANY

As a result of the pressures of the Cold War, the unification of the three Western zones into the West German Federal Republic became a reality in 1949. Konrad

Adenauer (1876–1967), the leader of the Christian Democratic Union (CDU) who served as chancellor from 1949 to 1963, became the "founding hero" of the Federal Republic. Adenauer sought respect for Germany by cooperating with the United States and the other Western European nations. He was especially desirous of reconciliation with France—Germany's longtime enemy. The beginning of the Korean War in June of 1950 had unexpected repercussions for West Germany. The fear that South Korea might fall to the Communist forces of the north led many Germans and westerners to worry about the security of West Germany and led to calls for the rearmament of West Germany. Although many people, concerned about a revival of German militarism, condemned this proposal, Cold War tensions were decisive. West Germany rearmed in 1955 and became a member of NATO.

Adenauer's chancellorship was closely associated with the West German "economic miracle." It was largely guided by the minister of finance, Ludwig Erhard. Although West Germany had only 75 percent of the population and 52 percent of the territory of prewar Germany, by 1955 the West German gross national product exceeded that of prewar Germany. Real wages doubled between 1950 and 1965 even though work hours were cut by 20 percent. Unemployment fell from 8 percent in 1950 to 0.4 percent in 1965. In order to maintain its economic expansion, West Germany even imported hundreds of thousands of guest workers, primarily from Italy, Spain, Greece, Turkey, and Yugoslavia.

Throughout its postwar existence, West Germany was troubled by its Nazi past. The surviving major Nazi leaders had been tried and condemned as war criminals at the Nuremberg war crimes trials in 1945 and 1946. As part of the denazification of Germany, the victorious Allies continued to try lesser officials for war crimes, but these trials diminished as the Cold War produced a shift in attitudes. By 1950, German courts had begun to take over the war crimes trials, and the German legal machine persisted in prosecuting cases. Beginning in 1953, the West German government also began to make payments to Israel and to Holocaust survivors and their relatives in order to make some restitution for the crimes of the Nazi era. The German president Richard von Weizsäcker was especially eloquent in reminding Germans of their responsibility "for the unspeakable sorrow that occurred in the name of Germany."

After the Adenauer era, German voters moved politically from the center-right politics of the Christian Democrats to center-left politics, and in 1969 the Social Democrats became the leading party. By forming a ruling coalition with the small Free Democratic Party (FPD), the Social Democrats remained in power until 1982. The first Social Democratic chancellor was Willy Brandt (1913–1992). Brandt was especially successful with his "opening toward the east" (known as *Ostpolitik*), for which he received the Nobel Peace Prize in 1972. On March 19, 1971, Brandt met with Walter Ulbricht, the East German leader, and agreed to establish "good neighborly" relations with East Germany. This agreement led to greater cultural, personal, and economic contacts between West and East Germany. Despite this success, the discovery of an East German spy among Brandt's advisers caused his resignation in 1974.

His successor, Helmut Schmidt (b. 1918), was more of a technocrat than a reform-minded socialist and concentrated primarily on the economic problems largely brought about by high oil prices between 1973 and 1975. Schmidt was successful in eliminating a deficit of 10 billion marks in three years. In 1982, when the coalition of Schmidt's Social Democrats with the Free Democrats fell apart over the reduction of social welfare expenditures, the Free Democrats joined with the Christian Democratic Union of Helmut Kohl (b. 1930) to form a new government.

Helmut Kohl was a clever politician who benefited greatly from an economic boom in the mid-1980s. The 1989 revolution in East Germany led to the reunification of the two Germanies into a new Germany with 79 million people. Reunification, accomplished during Kohl's administration, brought rich political dividends to the Christian Democrats. In the first all-German federal election, Kohl's Christian Democrats won 44 percent of the vote, while their coalition partners—the Free Democrats—received 11 percent.

But the excitement over reunification soon dissipated as new problems arose. All too soon, the realization set in that the revitalization of eastern Germany would take far more money than was originally thought, and Kohl's government was soon forced to face the politically undesirable task of raising taxes substantially. Moreover, the virtual collapse of the economy in eastern Germany led to extremely high levels of unemployment and severe discontent. One response was a return to power for the Social Democrats as a result of elections in 1998. Another was an attack on foreigners (see the box on p. 879). For years, foreigners seeking asylum and illegal immigrants had found haven in Germany because of its extremely liberal immigration laws. In 1992, more than 440,000 immigrants came to Germany seeking asylum; 123,000 came from former Yugoslavia alone. Attacks against foreigners by right-wing extremists—especially young neo-Nazis—became an all-too-frequent part of German life.

THE DECLINE OF GREAT BRITAIN

The end of World War II left Britain with massive economic problems. In elections held immediately after the war, the Labour Party overwhelmingly defeated Winston Churchill's Conservative Party. The Labour Party had promised far-reaching reforms, particularly in the area of social welfare, and in a country with a tremendous shortage of consumer goods and housing, its platform was quite appealing. The new Labour government proceeded to

VIOLENCE AGAINST FOREIGNERS IN GERMANY

As the number of foreign guest workers and immigrants increased in Europe, violent attacks against them also escalated. Especially in the former East Germany, where unemployment rose dramatically after reunification, gangs of neo-Nazi youth have perpetrated violent attacks on foreigners. This document is taken from a German press account of an attack on guest workers from Vietnam and Mozambique who had originally been recruited by the East German government.

KNUD PRIES, "EAST GERMANS HAVE TO LEARN TOLERANCE"

The police headquarters in Dresden, the capital of Saxony, announced that "a political situation" had developed in the town of Hoyerswerda. Political leaders and the police needed to examine the problem and corresponding measures should be taken: "In the near future the residents of the asylum hostel will be moved."

The people of Hoyerswerda prefer to be more direct, referring to the problem of *Neger* (niggers) and *Fidschis* (a term for Asian foreigners). The loudmouths of the neo-fascist gangs make the message clear: "Niggers Go Home!"

It looks as if some Germans have had enough of bureaucratic officialese. What is more, they will soon make sure that no more foreign voices are heard in Hoyerswerda.

The municipality in northern Saxony has a population of just under 70,000, including 70 people from Mozambique and Vietnam who live in a hostel for foreigners and about 240 asylum seekers in a hostel at the other end of town.

The "political situation" was triggered by an attack by a neo-Nazi gang on Vietnamese traders selling their goods on the market square on 17 September. After being dispersed by the police, the Faschos carried out their first attack on the hostel for foreigners.

The attacks then turned into a regular evening "hunt" by a growing group of right-wing radicals, some of them minors, who presented their idea of a clean Germany by roaming the streets armed with truncheons, stones, steel balls, bottles, and Molotov cocktails. Seventeen people were injured, some seriously.

After the police stepped in on a larger scale the extremists moved across the town to the asylum hostel. To begin with, only the gang itself and onlookers were outside the building, but on the evening of 22 September members of the "Human Rights League" and about 100 members of "autonomous" groups turned up to help the foreigners who had sought refuge in the already heavily damaged block of flats.

A large police contingent, reinforced by men from Dresden and the Border Guard, prevented the situation from becoming even more critical. Two people were seriously injured. The mob was disbanded with the help of dogs, tear gas, and water cannons.

Thirty-two people were arrested, and blank cartridge guns, knives, slings and clubs were seized. On 23 September, a police spokesman announced that the situation was under control. It seems doubtful whether things will stay this way, since the pogroms have become an evening ritual. Politicians and officials are racking their brains about how to grapple with the current crisis and the basic problem. One thing is clear: without a massive intervention by the police the problem cannot even be contained. But what then?

Saxony's Interior Minister, Rudolf Krause, initially recommended that the hostels concerned should be "fenced in," but then admitted that this was "not the final solution." Providing the Defense Ministry approves, the "provisional solution" will be to move the foreigners to a barracks in Kamenz.

Even if this operation is completed without violence it would represent a shameful success for the right-wing radicals. Although the Africans and Asians still living in Hoyerswerda will have to leave at the end of November anyway, once the employment contracts drawn up in the former [East Germany] expire, they are unwilling to endure the terror that long. "Even if we're going anyway—they want all foreigners to go now," says the 29-year-old Martinho from Mozambique.

His impression is that the gangs of thugs are doing something for which others are grateful: "The neighbors are glad when the skinheads arrive."

Interior Minister Krause feels that the abuse of asylum laws, the social problems in East Germany and an historically rooted deficit explain this situation: "The problem is that we were unable in the past to practice the tolerance needed to accept alien cultures."

enact the reforms that created a modern welfare state. Clement Attlee (1883–1967), the new prime minister, was a pragmatic reformer and certainly not the leftist revolutionary that Churchill had warned against during the election campaign.

The establishment of the British welfare state began with the nationalization of the Bank of England, the coal and steel industries, public transportation, and public utilities, such as electricity and gas. In the area of social welfare, the government enacted the National Insurance Act and the National Health Service Act, both in 1946. The insurance act established a comprehensive social security program and nationalized medical insurance, thereby enabling the state to subsidize the unemployed, the sick, and the aged. The health act created a system of socialized medicine that forced doctors and dentists to work with state hospitals, although private practices could be maintained. This measure was especially costly for the state, but within a few years 90 percent of the medical profession was participating. The British welfare state became the norm for most European states after the war.

The cost of building a welfare state at home forced the British to reduce expenses abroad. This meant dismantling the British Empire and reducing military aid to such countries as Greece and Turkey. Not a belief in the morality of self-determination, but economic necessity brought an end to the British Empire.

Continuing economic problems, however, brought the Conservatives back into power from 1951 to 1964. Although they favored private enterprise, the Conservatives accepted the welfare state and even extended it. But the British economy was bedeviled by a long-term economic decline caused by a variety of factors. The demands of British trade unions for wages that rose faster than productivity were certainly a problem in the 1950s and 1960s. The unwillingness of the British to invest in modern industrial machinery and to adopt new methods also did not help. Underlying the immediate problems, however, was a deeper issue. As a result of World War II, Britain had lost much of its prewar revenues from abroad but was left with a burden of debt from its many international commitments. At the same time, with the rise of the United States and the Soviet Union, Britain's ability to play the role of a world power declined substantially.

MARGARET THATCHER. Great Britain's first female prime minister, Margaret Thatcher was a strong leader who dominated British politics in the 1980s. This picture of Thatcher was taken at the Chelsea Flower Show in May 1990. Six months later, a revolt within her own party caused her to resign as prime minister.

Between 1964 and 1979, Conservatives and Labour alternated in power. Both parties had to face seemingly intractable problems. Although separatist movements in Scotland and Wales were overcome, fighting between Catholics and Protestants in Northern Ireland was not so easily settled. Violence increased as the Irish Republican Army (IRA) staged a series of dramatic terrorist acts in response to the suspension of Northern Ireland's parliament in 1972 and the establishment of direct rule by London. The problems in Northern Ireland have not yet been solved, although recent efforts brokered by the U.S. president, Bill Clinton, carry some promise for long-term solutions. Nor was either party able to deal with Britain's ailing economy. Failure to modernize made British industry less and less competitive. Moreover, Britain was hampered by frequent labor strikes, many of them caused by conflicts between rival labor unions.

In 1979, after Britain's economic problems had seemed to worsen during five years under a Labour government, the Conservatives returned to power under Margaret Thatcher (b. 1925). She became the first female prime minister in British history (see the box on p. 881). Thatcher pledged to lower taxes, reduce government bureaucracy, limit social welfare, restrict union power, and end inflation. The "Iron Lady," as she was called, did break the power of the labor unions. Although she did not eliminate the basic components of the social welfare system, she did use austerity measures to control inflation. "Thatcherism," as her economic policy was termed, improved the British economic situation but at a price. The south of England, for example, prospered, but the old industrial areas of the Midlands and north declined and were beset by high unemployment, poverty, and even violence. Cutbacks in funding for education seriously undermined the quality of British schools, long regarded as among the world's finest.

In foreign policy, Thatcher, like Ronald Reagan in the United States, took a hard-line approach against communism. She oversaw a large military buildup aimed at replacing older technology and reestablishing Britain as a world policeman. In 1982, when Argentina attempted to take control of the Falkland Islands (one of Britain's few remaining colonial outposts) three hundred miles off its coast, the British successfully rebuked the Argentines.

Margaret Thatcher dominated British politics in the 1980s. The Labour Party, beset by divisions between moderate and radical wings, offered little effective opposition. Only in 1990 did Labour's fortunes seem to revive when Thatcher's government attempted to replace local property taxes with a flat-rate tax payable by every adult to his or her local authority. Many argued that this was nothing more than a poll tax that would enable the rich to pay the same rate as the poor. In 1990, after antitax riots broke out, Thatcher's once remarkable popularity fell to all-time lows. At the end of November, a revolt within her own party caused Thatcher to resign as prime minister. She was

MARGARET THATCHER: ENTERING A MAN'S WORLD

In 1979, Margaret Thatcher became the first woman to serve as Britain's prime minister. In this excerpt from her autobiography, Thatcher describes how she was interviewed by Conservative Party officials when they first considered her as a possible candidate for Parliament. Thatcher ran for Parliament for the first time in 1950; she lost but increased the Conservative vote total in the district by 50 percent over the previous election.

MARGARET THATCHER, *THE PATH TO POWER*

And, as always with me, there was politics. I immediately joined the Conservative Association and threw myself into the usual round of Party activities. In particular, I thoroughly enjoyed what was called the "'39–'45" discussion group, where Conservatives of the war generation met to exchange views and argue about the political topics of the day. . . . It was as a representative of the Oxford University Graduate Conservative Association (OUGCA) that I went to the Llandudno Conservative Party Conference in October 1948.

It had originally been intended that I should speak at the Conference, seconding an OUGCA motion deploring the abolition of university seats. At that time universities had separate representation in Parliament, and graduates had the right to vote in their universities as well as in the constituency where they lived. (I supported separate university representation, but not the principle that graduates should have more than one vote. . . .) It would have been my first Conference speech, but in the end the seconder chosen was a City man, because the City seats were also to be abolished.

My disappointment at this was, however, very quickly overcome and in a most unexpected way. After one of the debates, I found myself engaged in one of those speculative conversations which young people have about their future prospects. An Oxford friend, John Grant, said he supposed that one day I would like to be a Member of Parliament. "Well, yes," I replied, "but there's not much hope of that. The chances of my being selected are just nil at the moment." I might have added that with no private income of my own there was no way I could have afforded to be an MP on the salary then available. I had not even tried to get on the Party's list of approved candidates.

Later in the day, John Grant happened to be sitting next to the Chairman of the Dartford Conservative Association, John Miller. The Association was in search of a candidate. I learned afterwards that the conversation went something like this: "I understand that you're still looking for a candidate at Dartford?" . . .

"That's right. Any Suggestions?"

"Well, there's a young woman, Margaret Roberts, that you might look at. She's very good."

"Oh, but Dartford is a real industrial stronghold. I don't think a woman would do at all."

"Well, you know best of course. But why not just look at her?"

And they did. I was invited to have lunch with John Miller and his wife, Phee, and the Dartford Woman's Chairman, Mrs. Fletcher, on the Saturday on Llandudno Pier. Presumably, and in spite of any reservations about the suitability of a woman candidate for their seat, they liked what they saw. I certainly got on well with them. . . .

I did not hear from Dartford until December, when I was asked to attend an interview at Palace Chambers, Bridge Street. . . . Very few outside the political arena know just how nerve-racking such occasions are. The interviewee who is not nervous and tense is very likely to perform badly: for, as any chemist will tell you, the adrenaline needs to flow if one is to perform at one's best. . . .

I found myself short-listed, and was asked to go to Dartford itself for a further interview. . . . As one of five would-be candidates, I had to give a fifteen-minute speech and answer questions for a further ten minutes.

It was the questions which were more likely to cause me trouble. There was a good deal of suspicion of woman candidates, particularly in what was regarded as a tough industrial seat like Dartford. This was quite definitely a man's world into which not just angels feared to tread. . . .

The most reliable sign that a political occasion has gone well is that you have enjoyed it. I enjoyed that evening at Dartford, and the outcome justified my confidence. I was selected.

replaced by John Major (b. 1943), whose Conservative Party won a narrow victory in the general elections held in April 1992. His government, however, failed to capture the imagination of most Britons. In new elections on May 1, 1997, the Labour Party won a landslide victory. The new prime minister, Tony Blair (b. 1953), was a moderate whose youthful energy immediately instilled a new vigor on the political scene.

Western Europe: The Move Toward Unity

As we have seen, the divisions created by the Cold War led the nations of Western Europe to form the North Atlantic Treaty Organization (NATO) in 1949. But military unity was not the only kind of unity fostered in Europe after 1945. The destructiveness of two world wars caused many thoughtful Europeans to consider the need for some form of European unity. National feeling was still too powerful, however, for European nations to give up their political sovereignty. Consequently, the desire for unity was forced to focus primarily on the economic arena, not the political one.

In 1951, France, West Germany, the Benelux countries (Belgium, the Netherlands, and Luxembourg), and Italy formed the European Coal and Steel Community (ECSC). Its purpose was to create a common market for coal and steel products among the six nations by eliminating tariffs and other trade barriers. In 1957, the same six nations signed the Rome Treaty, which created the European Economic Community (EEC), also known as the Common Market. The EEC eliminated customs barriers for the six member nations and created a large free-trade area protected from the rest of the world by a common external tariff. By promoting free trade, the EEC also encouraged cooperation and standardization in many aspects of the six nations' economies. All the member nations benefited economically.

Europeans also moved toward further integration of their economies after 1970. The EEC expanded in 1973 when Great Britain, Ireland, and Denmark joined what its members now began to call the European Community (EC). By 1986, three additional members—Spain, Portugal, and Greece—had been added. The economic integration of the members of the EC led to cooperative efforts in international and political affairs as well.

Nevertheless, the EC was still primarily an economic union, not a political one. By 1992, the EC comprised 344 million people and constituted the world's largest single trading entity, transacting almost one-fourth of the world's commerce. In the 1980s and 1990s, the EC moved toward even greater economic integration. A

MAP 29.2 The Economic Division of Europe During the Cold War

CHRONOLOGY

WESTERN EUROPE

Welfare state emerges in Great Britain	1946
Konrad Adenauer becomes chancellor of West Germany	1949
Formation of European Coal and Steel Community	1951
West Germany joins NATO	1955
Formation of European Economic Community (Common Market)	1957
Charles de Gaulle assumes power in France	1958
Student protests in France	1968
Willy Brandt becomes chancellor of West Germany	1969
Common Market expands (European Community)	1973
Helmut Schmidt becomes chancellor of West Germany	1974
Margaret Thatcher becomes prime minister of Great Britain	1979
François Mitterrand becomes president of France	1981
Helmut Kohl becomes chancellor of West Germany	1982
European Community expands	1986
Reelection of Mitterrand	1988
First all-German federal election	1990
Treaty on European Union proposed	1991
Victory of Conservative Party under John Major	1992
Conservative victory in France	1993
Creation of European Union	1994
Labour Party victory in Great Britain	1997
Social Democratic victory in Germany	1998
Introduction of the euro	1999

Treaty on European Union (also called the Maastricht Treaty, after the city in the Netherlands where the agreement was reached) represented an attempt to create a true economic and monetary union of all EC members. The treaty did not go into effect until all members agreed on January 1, 1994, when the European Community became the European Union. One of its first goals was achieved in 1999 with the introduction of a common currency, called the "euro."

THE EMERGENCE OF THE WORLD'S SUPERPOWER: THE UNITED STATES

At the end of World War II, the United States emerged as one of the world's two superpowers. Reluctantly, the United States remained involved in European affairs and, as its Cold War confrontation with the Soviet Union intensified, directed much of its energy toward combating the spread of communism throughout the world. With the collapse of the Soviet Union at the beginning of the 1990s, the United States emerged as the world's foremost military power. And yet, its own domestic problems led some to question whether the designation of sole remaining superpower would have any lasting significance.

American Politics and Society Through the Vietnam Era

Between 1945 and 1970, Franklin Roosevelt's New Deal largely determined the parameters of American domestic politics. The New Deal gave rise to a distinct pattern that signified a basic transformation in American society. This pattern included a dramatic increase in the role and power of the federal government; the rise of organized labor as a significant force in the economy and politics; a commitment to the welfare state, albeit a restricted one (Americans did not have access to universal health care as most other industrialized peoples did); a grudging acceptance of minority problems; and a willingness to experiment with deficit spending as a means of spurring the economy. The New Deal in American politics was bolstered by the election of Democratic presidents—Harry Truman in 1948, John F. Kennedy in 1960, and Lyndon B. Johnson in 1964. Even the election of a Republican president, Dwight D. Eisenhower, in 1952 and 1956 did not significantly alter the fundamental direction of the New Deal. As Eisenhower stated in 1954, "Should any political party attempt to abolish Social Security and eliminate labor laws and farm programs, you would not hear of that party again in our political history."

No doubt, the economic boom after World War II fueled confidence in the American way of life. A shortage of consumer goods during the war left Americans with both surplus income and the desire to purchase these goods after the war. Then, too, the development of organized labor enabled more and more workers to get the wage increases that fueled the growth of the domestic market. Government expenditures also indirectly subsidized the American private economy. Especially after the Korean War began in 1950, outlays on defense provided money for scientific research in the universities and markets for weapons industries. After 1955, tax dollars built a massive system of interstate highways, while tax deductions for mortgages subsidized home owners. Between 1945 and 1973, real wages grew at an average of 3 percent a year, the most prolonged advance in American history.

The prosperity of the 1950s and 1960s also translated into significant social changes. Work patterns changed as more and more people in the labor force left the factories and fields and moved into white-collar occupations. In 1940, blue-collar workers made up 52 percent of the labor force; farmers and farm workers, 17 percent; and white-collar workers, 31 percent. By 1970, blue-collar workers constituted 50 percent; farmers and farm workers, 3 percent; and white-collar workers, 47 percent. Many of these white-collar workers now considered themselves middle class, and the growth of this middle class had other repercussions. From rural areas, small towns, and central cities, people moved to the suburbs. In 1940, 19 percent of the American population lived in suburbs, 49 percent in rural areas, and 32 percent in central cities. By 1970, those figures had changed to 38, 31, and 31 percent, respectively. The move to the suburbs also produced an imposing number of shopping malls and reinforced the American passion for the automobile, which provided the means of transport from suburban home to suburban mall and workplace.

A new prosperity was not the only characteristic of the early 1950s. Cold War confrontations abroad had repercussions at home. The takeover of China by Mao Zedong's Communist forces in 1949 and Communist North Korea's invasion of South Korea in 1950 led to a fear that Communists had infiltrated the United States. President Truman's attorney general warned that Communists "are everywhere—in factories, offices, butcher stores, on street corners, in private businesses. And each carries in himself the germ of death for society." The demagogic senator from Wisconsin, Joseph McCarthy, helped to intensify a massive "Red Scare" with his exposés of hundreds of supposed Communists in high government positions. McCarthy went too far when he attacked alleged "Communist conspirators" in the U.S. army and was censured by Congress in 1954. Very quickly, his anti-Communist crusade came to an end.

While the 1950s has been characterized (erroneously) as a tranquil age, the period between 1960 and 1973 was clearly a time of upheaval that brought to the fore some of the problems that had been glossed over in the 1950s. The 1960s began on a youthful and optimistic note. At age forty-three, John F. Kennedy (1917–1963) became the youngest elected president in the history of the United States, and the first born in the twentieth century. His own administration, cut short by an assassin's bullet on November 22, 1963, focused primarily on foreign affairs, although it inaugurated an extended period of increased economic growth. Kennedy's successor, Lyndon B. Johnson (1908–1973), who won a new term as president in a landslide in 1964, used his stunning mandate to pursue the growth of the welfare state first begun in the New Deal. Johnson's programs included health care for the elderly; a War on Poverty to be fought with food stamps and a Job Corps; a new Department of Housing and Urban Development to deal with the problems of the cities; and federal assistance for education.

Lyndon Johnson's other domestic passion was the acquisition of equal rights for African Americans. The civil rights movement had had its beginnings in 1954 when the U.S. Supreme Court took the dramatic step of striking down the practice of racially segregated public schools. According to Chief Justice Earl Warren, "separate educational facilities are inherently unequal." A year later, during a black boycott of segregated buses in Montgomery, Alabama, the eloquent Martin Luther King, Jr. (1929–1968) surfaced as the leader of a growing movement for racial equality.

By the early 1960s, a number of groups, including King's Southern Christian Leadership Conference (SCLC), were organizing demonstrations and sit-ins across the South to end racial segregation. In August 1963, King led a March on Washington for Jobs and Freedom. This march and King's impassioned plea for racial equality (see the box on p. 886) had an electrifying effect on the American people. By the end of 1963, 52 percent of the American people called civil rights the most significant national issue; only 4 percent had done so eight months earlier.

President Johnson took up the cause of civil rights. As a result of his initiative, Congress enacted a Civil Rights Act in 1964, which created the machinery to end segregation and discrimination in the workplace and all public accommodations. A Voting Rights Act the following year eliminated racial obstacles to voting in southern states. But laws alone could not guarantee a Great Society, and Johnson soon faced bitter social unrest, both from African Americans and from a burgeoning antiwar movement.

In the North and West, African Americans had had voting rights for many years, but local patterns of segregation resulted in considerably higher unemployment rates for blacks (and Hispanics) than for whites and left blacks segregated in huge urban ghettos. In these ghettos, calls for militant action of radical black nationalist leaders, such as Malcolm X of the Black Muslims, attracted more attention than the nonviolent appeals of Martin Luther King, Jr. Malcolm X's advice was straightforward: "If someone puts a hand on you, send him to the cemetery."

In the summer of 1965, race riots erupted in the Watts district of Los Angeles and resulted in thirty-four deaths and the destruction of more than one thousand buildings. Cleveland, San Francisco, Chicago, Newark, and Detroit likewise exploded in the summers of 1966 and 1967. After the assassination of Martin Luther King in

THE CIVIL RIGHTS MOVEMENT. In the early 1960s, Martin Luther King, Jr., and his Southern Christian Leadership Conference organized a variety of activities to pursue the goal of racial equality. He is shown here with his wife, Coretta (right), and Rosa Parks and Ralph Abernathy (far left) leading a march in 1965 against racial discrimination.

1968, more than one hundred cities experienced rioting, including Washington, D.C., the nation's capital. The combination of riots and extremist comments by radical black leaders led to a "white backlash" and a severe division of American society. In 1964, 34 percent of American whites agreed with the statement that blacks were asking for "too much"; by late 1966, that number had risen to 85 percent, a figure not lost on politicians eager to achieve political office.

Antiwar protests also divided the American people after President Johnson committed American troops to a costly war in Vietnam (see Chapter 28). The antiwar movement arose out of the Free Speech Movement that began in 1964 at the University of California at Berkeley as a protest against the impersonality and authoritarianism of the large university (the "multiversity"). As the war progressed and a military draft ensued, protests escalated. Teach-ins, sit-ins, and occupations of university buildings alternated with more radical demonstrations that increasingly led to violence. The killing of four students at Kent State University in 1970 by the Ohio National Guard caused a reaction, and the antiwar movement began to subside. By that time, however, antiwar demonstrations had helped to weaken the willingness of many Americans to continue the war. But the combination of antiwar demonstrations and ghetto riots in the cities also prepared many people for "law and order," an appeal used by Richard Nixon (1913–1994), the Republican presidential candidate in 1968. With Nixon's election in 1968, a shift to the right in American politics had begun.

The Shift Rightward: The American Domestic Scene (1973 to the Present)

That shift was only a partial one during the Nixon years. Nixon eventually ended American involvement in Vietnam, by gradually withdrawing American troops. Politically, he pursued a "southern strategy," carefully calculating that "law and order" issues and a slowdown in racial desegregation would appeal to southern whites. The South, which had once been a stronghold for the Democrats, began to form a new allegiance to the Republican Party. The Republican strategy, however, also gained support among white Democrats in northern cities, where court-mandated busing to achieve racial integration had produced a white backlash. But Nixon was less conservative on other social issues and, breaking with his own strong anti-Communist past, visited China in 1972 and opened the door toward the eventual diplomatic recognition of that state.

As president, Nixon was also paranoid about conspiracies and began to use illegal methods of gaining political intelligence about his political opponents. One of the president's advisers explained that their intention was to "use the available Federal machinery to screw our political enemies." "Anyone who opposes us, we'll destroy," said another aide. Nixon's zeal led to the infamous Watergate scandal—the attempted bugging of Democratic National Headquarters. Although Nixon repeatedly lied to the American public about his involvement in the affair, secret tapes of his own conversations in the White House

"I HAVE A DREAM"

In the spring of 1963, a bomb attack on a church that killed four children and the brutal fashion in which police handled black demonstrators brought the nation's attention to the policies of racial segregation in Birmingham, Alabama. A few months later, on August 28, 1963, Martin Luther King, Jr., led a march on Washington and gave an inspired speech that catalyzed the civil rights movement.

MARTIN LUTHER KING, JR., "I HAVE A DREAM"

I am happy to join with you today in what will go down in history as the greatest demonstration for freedom in the history of our nation.

Five score years ago, a great American, in whose symbolic shadow we stand today, signed the Emancipation Proclamation. This momentous decree came as a great beacon light of hope to millions of Negro slaves, who had been seared in the flames of withering injustice. It came as a joyous daybreak to end the long night of their captivity.

But one hundred years later, the Negro still is not free; one hundred years later, the life of the Negro is still sadly crippled by the manacles of segregation and the chains of discrimination; one hundred years later, the Negro lives on a lonely island of poverty in the midst of a vast ocean of material prosperity; one hundred years later, the Negro is still languished in the corners of American society and finds himself in exile in his own land. . . .

So we've come here today to dramatize a shameful condition. In a sense we've come to our nation's capital to cash a check. When the architects of our republic wrote the magnificent words of the Constitution and the Declaration of Independence, they were signing a promissory note to which every American was to fall heir. This note was the promise that all men, yes, black men as well as white men, would be guaranteed the unalienable rights of life, liberty, and the pursuit of happiness.

It is obvious today that America has defaulted on this promissory note in so far as her citizens of color are concerned. Instead of honoring this sacred obligation, America has given the Negro people a bad check, a check which has come back marked "insufficient funds." But we refuse to believe that the bank of justice is bankrupt. . . .

We have also come to this hallowed spot to remind America of the fierce urgency of now. This is no time to engage in the luxury of cooling off or to take the tranquilizing drug of gradualism. Now is the time to make real the promises of democracy; now is the time to rise from the dark and desolate valley of segregation to the sunlit path of racial justice; now is the time to lift our nation from the quicksands of racial injustice to the solid rock of brotherhood; now is the time to make justice a reality for all of God's children. It would be fatal for the nation to overlook the urgency of the moment. . . .

I say to you today, my friends, so even though we face the difficulties of today and tomorrow, I still have a dream. It is a dream deeply rooted in the American dream. I have a dream that one day this nation will rise up and live out the true meaning of its creed, "We hold these truths to be self-evident, that all men are created equal." I have a dream that one day on the red hills of Georgia, sons of former slaves and the sons of former slave owners will be able to sit down together at the table of brotherhood. . . . I have a dream that my four little children will one day live in a nation where they will not be judged by the color of their skin, but by the content of their character. . . .

This is our hope. This is the faith that I go back to the South with. With this faith we will be able to hew out of the mountain of despair a stone of hope. With this faith we will be able to transform the jangling discords of our nation into a beautiful symphony of brotherhood. With this faith we will be able to work together, to pray together, to struggle together, to go to jail together, to stand up for freedom together, knowing that we will be free one day. And this will be the day. This will be the day when all of God's children will be able to sing with new meaning, "My country 'tis of thee, sweet land of liberty, of thee I sing. Land where my father died, land of the pilgrims' pride, from every mountainside, let freedom ring." And if America is to be a great nation, this must become true. . . .

And when this happens, and when we allow freedom to ring, when we let it ring from every village and every hamlet, from every state and every city, we will be able to speed up that day when all of God's children, black men and white men, Jews and Gentiles, Protestants and Catholics, will be able to join hands and sing in the words of the old Negro spiritual: "Free at last. Free at last. Thank God Almighty, we are free at last."

revealed the truth. On August 9, 1974, Nixon resigned in disgrace, an act that saved him from almost certain impeachment and conviction.

After Watergate, American domestic politics focused on economic issues. Gerald Ford (b. 1913) became president when Nixon resigned, only to lose in the 1976 election to the former governor of Georgia, Jimmy Carter (b. 1924), who campaigned as an outsider against the Washington establishment. Both Ford and Carter faced severe economic problems. The period from 1973 to the mid-1980s was one of economic stagnation, which came to be known as stagflation—a combination of high inflation and high unemployment. In 1984, median family income was 6 percent below that of 1973.

In part, the economic downturn stemmed from a dramatic change in oil prices. Oil was considered a cheap and abundant source of energy in the 1950s, and Americans had grown dependent on its importation from the Middle East. By the late 1970s, 50 percent of the oil used in the United States came from the Middle East. But an oil embargo imposed by the Organization of Petroleum Exporting Countries (OPEC) as a result of the Arab-Israeli War in 1973 and OPEC's subsequent raising of prices led to a quadrupling of oil prices. As a result of additional price hikes, oil prices had increased twentyfold by the end of the 1970s, no doubt encouraging inflationary tendencies throughout the entire economy. Although the Carter administration produced a plan for reducing oil consumption at home while spurring domestic production, neither Congress nor the American people could be persuaded to follow what they regarded as drastic measures.

By 1980, the Carter administration was facing two devastating problems. High inflation and a noticeable decline in average weekly earnings were causing a perceptible drop in American living standards. At the same time, a crisis abroad had erupted when fifty-three Americans were taken and held hostage by the Iranian government of Ayatollah Khomeini. Although Carter had little control over the situation, his inability to gain the release of the American hostages led to perceptions at home that he was a weak president. His overwhelming loss to Ronald Reagan (b. 1911) in the election of 1980 brought forward the chief exponent of right-wing Republican policies and a new political order.

The Reagan Revolution, as it has been called, changed the direction of American policy on several fronts. Reversing decades of the expanding welfare state, Reagan cut spending on food stamps, school lunch programs, and job programs. At the same time, his administration fostered the largest peacetime military buildup in American history. Total federal spending rose from $631 billion in 1981 to over a trillion dollars by 1986. But instead of raising taxes to pay for the new expenditures, which far outweighed the budget cuts in social areas, Reagan convinced Congress to support supply-side economics. Massive tax cuts would supposedly stimulate rapid economic growth and produce new revenues. Much of the tax cut went to the wealthy. Between 1980 and 1986, the income of the lower 40 percent of the workforce fell 9 percent, while the income of the highest 20 percent rose by 5 percent.

Reagan's policies seemed to work in the short run, as the United States experienced an economic upturn that lasted until the end of the 1980s. But the spending policies of the Reagan administration also produced record government deficits, which loomed as an obstacle to long-term growth. In the 1970s, the total deficit was $420 billion; between 1981 and 1987, Reagan budget deficits were three times that amount. The inability of George Bush (b. 1924), Reagan's successor, to deal with the deficit problem or with the continuing economic downslide led to the election of a Democrat, Bill Clinton, in November 1992.

The new president was a southerner who claimed to be a new Democrat—one who favored fiscal responsibility and a more conservative social agenda—a clear indication that the rightward drift in American politics had not been ended by his victory. During his first term in office, Clinton reduced the budget deficit and signed a bill turning the welfare program back to the states, while pushing measures to strengthen the educational system and provide job opportunities for those Americans removed from the welfare rolls. By seizing the center of the American political agenda, Clinton was able to win reelection in 1996.

President Clinton's political fortunes were aided considerably by a lengthy economic revival. A steady reduction in the annual government budget deficit strengthened confidence in the performance of the national economy. Much of Clinton's second term, however, was overshadowed by charges of presidential misconduct stemming from the president's sexual affair with Monica Lewinsky, a White House intern. After a bitter

CHRONOLOGY

AMERICAN SOCIETY AND POLITICS

Presidency of Harry S Truman	1945–1953
Presidency of Dwight D. Eisenhower	1953–1961
Presidency of John F. Kennedy	1961–1963
Assassination of Kennedy	1963
Presidency of Lyndon B. Johnson	1963–1969
Martin Luther King's March on Washington	1963
Civil Rights Act	1964
Watts riot	1965
Assassination of Martin Luther King	1968
Presidency of Richard M. Nixon	1969–1974
Killing of students at Kent State	1970
Resignation of Nixon in Watergate scandal	1974
Presidency of Gerald Ford	1974–1977
Presidency of Jimmy Carter	1977–1981
Presidency of Ronald Reagan	1981–1989
Presidency of George Bush	1989–1993
Election of Bill Clinton	1992
Reelection of Bill Clinton	1996

partisan struggle, the U.S. Senate acquitted the president on two articles of impeachment brought by the House of Representatives.

The Development of Canada

Canada experienced many of the same developments as the United States in the postwar years. For twenty-five years after World War II, Canada realized extraordinary economic prosperity as it set out on a new path of industrial development. Canada had always had a strong export economy based on its abundant natural resources. Now it also developed electronic, aircraft, nuclear, and chemical engineering industries on a large scale. Much of the Canadian growth, however, was financed by capital from the United States, which resulted in American ownership of Canadian businesses. Though many Canadians welcomed the economic growth, others feared American economic domination of Canada and its resources.

A notable feature of Canada's postwar history has been its close relationship with the United States. In addition to fears of economic domination, Canadians have also worried about playing a subordinate role politically and militarily to the neighboring superpower. Canada agreed to join NATO in 1949 and even sent military contingents to fight in Korea the following year. But to avoid subordination to the United States or any other great power, Canada has consistently and actively supported the United Nations. Nevertheless, concerns about the United States have not kept Canada from maintaining a special relationship with its southern neighbor.

For three decades after 1945, the Liberal Party largely dominated Canadian politics and created Canada's welfare state by enacting a national social security system (the Canada Pension Plan) and a national health insurance program. The most prominent Liberal government was that of Pierre Trudeau (b. 1919), who came to power in 1968. Although French in background, Trudeau was dedicated to Canada's federal union, and in 1968 his government passed the Official Languages Act, which created a bilingual federal civil service and encouraged the growth of French culture and language in Canada. Although Trudeau's government vigorously pushed an industrialization program, high inflation and Trudeau's efforts to impose the will of the federal government on the powerful provincial governments alienated voters and weakened his government.

Economic recession in the early 1980s brought Brian Mulroney (b. 1939), leader of the Progressive Conservative Party, to power in 1984. Mulroney's government sought greater privatization of Canada's state-run corporations and negotiated a free trade agreement with the United States. Bitterly resented by many Canadians, the agreement cost Mulroney's government much of its popularity. In 1993, the ruling conservatives were drastically defeated. They won only two seats in the House of Commons, and the Liberal leader, Jean Chrétien, became prime minister.

The new Liberal government was also faced with an ongoing crisis over the French-speaking province of Quebec. In the late 1960s, the Parti Québécois, headed by René Lévesque, campaigned on a platform of Quebec's secession from the Canadian confederation. In 1970, the party won 24 percent of the popular vote in Quebec's provincial elections. To pursue their dream of separation, some underground separatist groups even used terrorist bombings and kidnapped two prominent government officials. In 1976, the Parti Québécois won Quebec's provincial elections and in 1980 called for a referendum that would enable the provincial government to negotiate Quebec's independence from the rest of Canada. Voters in Quebec narrowly rejected the plan in 1995, however, and debate over Quebec's status continues to divide Canada to this day.

Democracy, Dictatorship, and Development in Latin America Since 1945

As a result of the Great Depression of the 1930s, many Latin American countries experienced political instability that led to military coups and militaristic regimes (see Chapter 25). But the depression also helped to transform Latin America from a traditional to a modern economy. Since the nineteenth century, Latin Americans had exported raw materials, especially minerals and foodstuffs, while buying the manufactured goods of the industrialized countries. As a result of the Great Depression, exports were cut in half, and the revenues available to buy manufactured goods declined. In response, many Latin American countries encouraged the development of new industries to produce goods that were formerly imported.

By the 1960s, however, the policy of import substitution had begun to fail. Despite their gains, Latin American countries were still dependent on the United States, Europe, and now Japan for the advanced technology needed for modern industries. To make matters worse, the great poverty of Latin America limited the size of domestic markets, and many countries were unable to find markets abroad for their products. The failure of import-substituting industrialization led to instability and a new reliance on military regimes, especially to curb the demands of the new industrial middle class and working classes that had increased in size and power as a result of industrialization. Beginning in the 1960s, almost all economically advanced Latin American countries experienced some form of domestic strife and military despotism. In the 1960s, repressive military regimes in Chile, Brazil, and Argentina portrayed themselves as "antipolitical" as they abolished political parties and left few avenues for political opposition. These regimes often returned to export-import economies financed by foreigners while encouraging multinational companies to come into their countries. Because these companies were primarily interested in taking advantage of Latin America's raw materials and abundant supply of cheap labor, their presence only contributed to the ongoing dependency of Latin America on the industrially developed nations.

In the 1970s, Latin American regimes grew even more dependent on borrowing from abroad, especially from banks in Europe and the United States. Between 1970 and 1982, debt to foreigners increased from $27 billion to $315.3 billion. By 1982, a number of governments announced that they could no longer pay interest on their debts to foreign banks, and their economies began to crumble. Wages fell, and unemployment skyrocketed. Governments were forced to undertake fundamental reforms to qualify for additional loans and at the same time were encouraged to reevaluate the strategies they had used in their economic modernization. Many came to believe that the state sector had become too large and had overprotected domestic industries too long. The overly fast pace of industrialization had led to the decline of the rural economy as well, and many hoped that by improving agricultural production for home consumption, they could stem the flow of people from the countryside to the cities and at the same time strengthen the domestic market for Latin American industrial products.

In the 1980s, the debt crisis was paralleled by a movement toward democracy. In part, some military leaders were simply unwilling to deal with the monstrous debt problems. At the same time, many people realized that military power without popular consent was incapable of providing a strong state. Then, too, there was a swelling of popular support for basic rights and free and fair elections. The movement toward democracy was the most noticeable trend of the 1980s and early 1990s in Latin America. In the mid-1970s, only Colombia, Venezuela, and Costa Rica maintained democratic governments. In the mid-1980s, democratic regimes were everywhere except Cuba, some of the Central American states, Chile, and Paraguay. This revival of democracy proved fragile, however. In 1992, for example, President Alberto Fujimori (b. 1938) undermined democracy and returned Peru to an authoritarian system.

Latin America's economic problems were made worse by a dramatic growth in population. In 1950, Latin America and North America (the United States and Canada) had the same population—about 165 million people. By the mid-1980s, Latin America's population had exploded to 400 million, while that of North America was about 270 million. With the increase in population came a rapid rise in the number and size of cities. In 1930, only one Latin American city had more than one million people. By 1990, there were twenty-nine, including Mexico City with 16 million inhabitants and Buenos Aires with 8 million. Cities grew in large part because poverty-stricken peasants fled there to seek a better life. Rarely did they find it. Population growth far outstripped economic growth, leaving millions without jobs. The inability of the cities to cope with the needs of these people led to the growth of slums that became part of virtually every Latin American city.

The gap between the poor and the rich had always been enormous in Latin American history, and it remained so after 1945. Landholding and urban elites, largely descendants of the Europeans who had colonized Latin America centuries before, still owned huge estates and businesses. A small but growing middle class consisted of businesspeople and office and government workers. Peasants and the urban poor struggled just to survive. Nevertheless, the lower classes became more and more vocal. Peasants called for land reforms that would give them more land, while urban workers joined trade unions and demanded better wages and better working conditions.

The enormous gulf between rich and poor often undermined the stability of Latin American countries. So, too, did the international drug trade. Latin America's northern neighbor, the United States, was one of the world's largest consumers of drugs. Eighty percent of the cocaine and 90 percent of the marijuana used in the United States came from Latin America. Bolivia, Peru, and Colombia were especially big producers. For peasants in these countries, growing coca leaves and marijuana plants became an important part of their economic survival. In Colombia, drug traffickers became especially wealthy; they formed drug cartels that bribed and intimidated government officials and police officers into protecting their activities.

Other factors have also played important roles in the history of Latin America since 1945. Although most Latin American governments had separated church and state, by the beginning of the twentieth century, the Catholic church remained a potent social and cultural force. Eventually, the church pursued a middle way in Latin American society by advocating a moderate capitalist system that would respect workers' rights, institute land reform, and provide for the poor. This policy led to the formation of Christian Democratic Parties, which had some success in the 1960s and 1970s. In the 1960s, some Catholics took a more radical approach to change by advocating a theology of liberation. Influenced by Marxist ideas, they believed that Christians must fight to free the oppressed, even using violence if necessary. Some Catholic clergy recommended armed rebellions and even teamed up with Marxist guerrillas in rural areas. Other radical priests worked in factories alongside workers or carried on social work among the poor in the slums. Although liberation theology attracted much attention, it was by no means the ideology of the majority of Latin American Catholics and was rejected by the church hierarchy. Still, in the 1970s and 1980s, the Catholic church continued to play an important role as an advocate of human rights against authoritarian regimes.

In 1948, the states of the Western Hemisphere formed the Organization of American States (OAS), which was intended to eliminate unilateral action by one state in the internal or external affairs of any other state. Instead, the OAS encouraged regional cooperation and allowed for group action to maintain peace. It certainly did not end U.S. interference in Latin American affairs, however. As the Cold War intensified, U.S. policy makers grew anxious about the possibility of Communist regimes in Central America and the Caribbean and returned to a policy of unilateral action when they believed that Soviet agents were attempting to use local Communists or radical reformers to establish governments hostile to U.S. interests.

Especially after the success of Castro in Cuba (see the next section), the goal of preventing "another Cuba" largely determined U.S. policy toward Latin America until the end of the Cold War in the 1990s. In the 1960s, President Kennedy's Alliance for Progress encouraged social reform and economic development by providing private and public funds to elected governments whose reform programs were acceptable to the United States. But the Alliance failed to work, and after the Cubans began to export the Cuban Revolution by starting guerrilla wars in other Latin American countries, the United States responded by providing massive military aid to anti-Communist regimes, regardless of their nature. By 1979, 83,000 military personnel from twenty-one Latin American countries had received U.S.–assisted military training with special emphasis on antiguerrilla activity to fight social revolutionaries.

FIDEL CASTRO. On January 1, 1959, a band of revolutionaries led by Fidel Castro overthrew the authoritarian government of Fulgencio Batista. Castro is shown here in 1957 with some of his followers at a secret base near the Cuban coast.

The Threat of Marxist Revolutions

Until the 1960s, Marxism played little role in the politics of Latin America. The success of Fidel Castro in Cuba and his espousal of Marxism, however, opened the door for other Marxist movements that aimed to gain the support of peasants and industrial workers and bring radical change to Latin America.

THE CUBAN REVOLUTION

An authoritarian regime, headed by Fulgencio Batista (1901–1973) and closely tied economically to U.S. investors, had ruled Cuba since 1934. A strong opposition movement to Batista's government developed, led by Fidel Castro (b. 1926) and assisted by Ernesto "Ché" Guevara (1928–1967), an Argentinian who believed that revolutionary upheaval was necessary to change Latin America (see the box on p. 891). When their initial assaults brought little success, Castro's forces turned to guerrilla warfare. Batista's regime responded with such brutality that he alienated his own supporters. The dictator fled in December 1958, and Castro's revolutionaries seized Havana on January 1, 1959.

The new government proceeded cautiously, but relations with the United States quickly deteriorated. An agrarian reform law in May 1959 nationalized all landholdings over a thousand acres. A new level of antagonism emerged early in 1960 when the Soviet Union agreed to buy Cuban sugar and provide $100 million in credits. On March 17, 1960, President Eisenhower directed the Central Intelligence Agency (CIA) to "organize the training of Cuban exiles, mainly in Guatemala, against a possible future day when they might return to their homeland."[1] Arms from Eastern Europe began to arrive in Cuba, the United States cut its purchases of Cuban sugar, and the Cuban government nationalized U.S. companies and banks. In October 1960, the United States declared a trade embargo of Cuba, which drove Castro closer to the Soviet Union. In December 1960, Castro declared himself a Marxist.

On January 3, 1961, the United States broke diplomatic relations with Cuba. The new U.S. president, John F. Kennedy, supported a coup attempt against Castro's government, but the landing of 1,400 CIA-assisted Cubans in Cuba on April 17, 1961, turned into a total military disaster (the infamous Bay of Pigs). This fiasco encouraged the Soviets to place nuclear missiles in the country, an act that led to a showdown with the United States (see Chapter 27). As its part of the bargain to defuse the Missile Crisis, the United States agreed not to invade Cuba.

CASTRO'S REVOLUTIONARY IDEALS

On July 26, 1953, Castro and a small group of supporters launched an ill-fated attack on the Moncada Barracks in Santiago de Cuba. Castro was arrested and put on trial. This excerpt is taken from his defense speech, in which he discussed the goals of the revolutionaries.

FIDEL CASTRO, "HISTORY WILL ABSOLVE ME"

I stated that the second consideration on which we based our chances for success was one of social order because we were assured of the people's support. When we speak of the people we do not mean the comfortable ones, the conservative elements of the nation, who welcome any regime of oppression, any dictatorship, and despotism, prostrating themselves before the master of the moment until they grind their foreheads into the ground. When we speak of struggle, the people means the vast unredeemed masses, to whom all make promises and whom all deceive; we mean the people who yearn for a better, more dignified, and more just nation; who are moved by ancestral aspirations of justice, for they have suffered injustice and mockery, generation after generation; who long for great and wise changes in all aspects of their life; people, who, to attain these changes, are ready to give even the very last breath of their lives—when they believe in something or in someone, especially when they believe in themselves.

In the brief of this cause there must be recorded the five revolutionary laws that would have been proclaimed immediately after the capture of the Moncada barracks and would have been broadcast to the nation by radio. . . .

The First Revolutionary Law would have returned power to the people and proclaimed the Constitution of 1940 the supreme Law of the land, until such time as the people should decide to modify or change it. . . .

The Second Revolutionary Law would have granted property, not mortgageable and not transferable, to all planters, subplanters, lessees, partners, and squatters who hold parcels of five or less "caballerias" [tract of land, about 33 acres] of land, and the state would indemnify the former owners on the basis of the rental which they would have received for these parcels over a period of ten years.

The Third Revolutionary Law would have granted workers and employees the right to share 30 percent of the profits of all the large industrial, mercantile, and mining enterprises, including the sugar mills. . . .

The Fourth Revolutionary Law would have granted all planters the right to share 55 percent of the sugar production and a minimum quota of forty thousand "arrobas" [25 pounds] for all small planters who have been established for three or more years.

The Fifth Revolutionay Law would have ordered the confiscation of all holdings and ill-gotten gains of those who had committed frauds during previous regimes, as well as the holdings and ill-gotten gains of all their legatees and heirs. . . .

Furthermore, it was to be declared that the Cuban policy in the Americas would be one of close solidarity with the democratic people of this continent, and that those politically persecuted by bloody tyrants oppressing our sister nations would find generous asylum, brotherhood, and bread in [Cuba]. Not the persecution, hunger, and treason that they find today. Cuba should be the bulwark of liberty and not a shameful link in the chain of despotism.

But the Missile Crisis affected Cuba in another way as well. Castro realized that the Soviet Union had been unreliable. If revolutionary Cuba was to be secure, the Cubans would have to instigate social revolution in the rest of Latin America. Castro judged Bolivia, Haiti, Venezuela, Colombia, Paraguay, and a number of Central American states to be especially open to radical revolution. He believed that once guerrilla wars were launched, peasants would flock to the movement and overthrow the old regimes. Guevara began a guerrilla war in Bolivia but was caught and killed by the Bolivian army in the fall of 1967. The Cuban strategy had failed.

Nevertheless, within Cuba, Castro's socialist revolution proceeded, although with mixed results. The Cuban Revolution did secure some social gains for its people, especially in health care and education. The regime provided free medical services for all citizens, and the population's health improved noticeably. Illiteracy was wiped out by developing new schools and establishing teacher-training institutes that tripled the number of teachers within ten years. The theoretical equality of women in Marxist thought was put into practice in Cuba by new laws. One such law was the family code, which stated that husband and wife were equally responsible for the economic support of the family and household, as well as for child care. Such laws led to improvements but fell far short of creating full equality for women.

Eschewing the path of rapid industrialization, Castro encouraged agricultural diversification. Nevertheless, the Cuban economy continued to rely on the production and sale of sugar. Economic problems forced the Castro regime to depend on Soviet subsidies and the purchase of Cuban sugar by Soviet bloc countries. After the collapse of these Communist regimes in 1989, Cuba lost their support.

Although economic conditions in Cuba have steadily declined without the Soviet subsidies, Castro manages to remain in power.

CHILE'S MARXIST ADVENTURE

Another challenge to U.S. influence in Latin America came in 1970 when the Marxist Salvador Allende (1908–1973) was elected president of Chile and attempted to create a socialist society by constitutional means. Chile suffered from a number of economic problems. Wealth was concentrated in the hands of large landowners and a few large corporations. Inflation, foreign debts, and a decline in the mining industry (copper exports accounted for 80 percent of Chile's export income) caused untold difficulties. Right-wing control of the government failed to achieve any solutions, especially since foreign investments were allowed to expand. There was already growing resentment of U.S. corporations, especially Anaconda and Kennecott, which controlled the copper industry.

In the 1970 elections, a split in the moderate forces enabled Allende to become president of Chile as head of a coalition of Socialists, Communists, and Catholic radicals. A number of labor leaders, who represented the interests of the working classes, were given the ministries of labor, finance, public works, and interior in the new government. Allende increased the wages of industrial workers and began to move toward socialism by nationalizing the largest domestic and foreign-owned corporations. Nationalization of the copper industry—essentially without compensation for the owners—caused the Nixon administration to cut off all aid to Chile, creating serious problems for the Chilean economy. At the same time, the government offered only halfhearted resistance to radical workers who were beginning to take control of the landed estates.

SANDINISTA VICTORY IN NICARAGUA. After a series of military victories that overthrew the Somoza dictatorship, the Sandinista National Liberation Front established a new government in Nicaragua. Triumphant Sandinistas are seen here celebrating their victory.

In response, the upper and middle classes began to organize strikes against the government (with support from the American CIA). Allende attempted to stop the disorder by bringing three military officers into his cabinet. They succeeded in ending the strikes, but when Allende's coalition increased its vote in the congressional elections of March 1973, the Chilean army, under the direction of General Augusto Pinochet (b. 1915), decided on a coup d'état. In September 1973, Allende and thousands of his supporters were killed. Contrary to the expectations of many right-wing politicians, the military remained in power and set up a dictatorship. The regime moved quickly to outlaw all political parties, remove the congress, and restore many nationalized industries and landowners' estates to their original owners. The copper industry, however, remained in government hands. The regime's horrible abuse of human rights led to growing unrest against the government in the mid-1980s. In 1989, free elections produced a Christian Democratic president, Patricio Azócur, who advocated free-market economics.

NICARAGUA: FROM THE SOMOZAS TO THE SANDINISTAS

The United States had intervened in Nicaraguan domestic affairs in the early twentieth century, and U.S. marines even remained there for long periods of time. After the leader of the U.S.–supported National Guard, Anastasio Somoza, seized control of the government in 1937, his family remained in power for forty-three years. U.S. support for the Somoza military regime enabled the family to overcome any opponents while enriching themselves at the expense of the state.

Opposition to the regime finally arose from Marxist guerrilla forces known as the Sandinista National Liberation Front. By mid-1979, military victories by the Sandinistas left them in virtual control of the country. Inheriting a poverty-stricken nation, the Sandinistas organized a provisional government aligned with the Soviet Union. The Reagan and Bush administrations, believing that Central America faced the danger of another Communist state, financed Contra rebels in a guerrilla war against the Sandinista government. The Contra war and an American economic embargo damaged the Nicaraguan economy and undermined support for the Sandinistas. In 1990, they agreed to free elections and lost to a coalition headed by Violeta Barrios de Chamorro (b. 1929). Nevertheless, the Sandinistas remained the strongest single party in Nicaragua.

Nationalism and the Military: The Examples of Argentina and Brazil

The military became the power brokers of twentieth-century Latin America. Especially in the 1960s and 1970s, Latin American armies portrayed themselves as the guardians of national honor and orderly progress.

ARGENTINA

Juan Perón first rose to prominence as a member of the military regime that had seized power in Argentina in 1943. As labor secretary in the military government, he used his position to curry favor with the workers. But as Perón grew more popular, other army officers began to fear his power and arrested him. An uprising by workers forced the officers to back down, and in 1946, Perón was elected president.

To please his chief supporters—labor and the urban middle class—Perón pursued a policy of increased industrialization. At the same time, he sought to free Argentina from foreign investors. The government bought the railways, took over the banking, insurance, shipping, and communications industries, and assumed regulation of imports and exports. But Perón's regime was also authoritarian. His wife, Eva Perón, organized women's groups to support the government, while Perón created fascist gangs, modeled after Hitler's Brown Shirts, that used violence to overawe his opponents. But growing corruption in the Perón government and the alienation of more and more people by the regime's excesses encouraged the military to overthrow him in September 1955. Perón went into exile in Spain.

It had been easy for the military to seize power, but it was harder to rule, especially now that Argentina had a party of *Peronistas* clamoring for the return of the exiled leader. In the 1960s and 1970s, military and civilian governments (the latter closely watched by the military) alternated in power. When both failed to provide economic stability, military leaders decided to allow Perón to return. Reelected president in September 1973, Perón died one year later. In 1976, the military installed a new regime. Tolerating no opposition, the military leaders encouraged the "disappearance" of their opponents. Perhaps 30,000 people, including 6,000 leftists, were killed as a result.

But economic problems remained. To divert people's attention, the military regime invaded the Falkland Islands off the coast of Argentina in April 1982. Great Britain, which had controlled the islands since the nineteenth century, sent ships and troops to defend the islands. When the Argentine forces surrendered to the British in July, angry Argentinians denounced the military regime. The loss discredited the military and opened the door to civilian rule. In 1983, Raúl Alfonsín of the Radical Party was elected president and tried to restore democratic practices. In elections in 1989, the Peronist Carlos Saúl Menem (b. 1930) won. This peaceful transfer of power gave hope that Argentina was moving on a democratic path. Reelected in 1995, President Menem has pushed to control inflation and government spending.

BRAZIL

After the military put an end to the authoritarian regime of Getúlio Vargas in 1945, Brazil established a republic. Over the next two decades, various democratically elected presidents (including Vargas himself) struggled to solve Brazil's economic problems, especially its soaring inflation, but with little success. Finally, in the spring of 1964, the military decided to intervene and took over the government.

THE PERÓNS. Elected president of Argentina in 1946, Juan Perón soon established an authoritarian regime that nationalized some of Argentina's basic industries and organized fascist gangs to overwhelm its opponents. He is shown here with his wife, Eva, during the inauguration ceremonies initiating his second term as president, in 1952.

Unlike previous interventions by military leaders in politics, this time the armed forces remained in direct control of the country for twenty years. The military set course on a new economic direction, cutting back somewhat on state control of the economy and emphasizing market forces. Beginning in 1968, the new policies seemed to work, and Brazil experienced an "economic miracle" as it moved into self-sustaining economic growth, generally the hallmark of a modern economy. Economic growth also included the economic exploitation of the Amazon basin, which the regime opened to farming; some believe the corresponding destruction of the extensive Amazon rain forests, which is still going on, poses a threat to the ecological balance not only of Brazil but of the earth itself. Rapid economic growth had additional drawbacks. Ordinary Brazilians hardly benefited as the gulf between rich and poor, always wide, grew even wider. In 1960, the wealthiest 10 percent of Brazil's population received 40 percent of the nation's income; in 1980, they received 51 percent. Then, too, rapid development led to an inflation rate of 100 percent a year, while an enormous foreign debt added to the problems. By the early 1980s, the economic miracle was turning into an economic nightmare. Overwhelmed, the generals retreated and opened the door for a return to democracy in 1985.

The new democratic government faced herculean obstacles—a massive foreign debt, virtually runaway inflation, and the lack of any real social consensus. Presidential

MAP 29.3 Political Trends in Latin America in the 1960s and 1970s

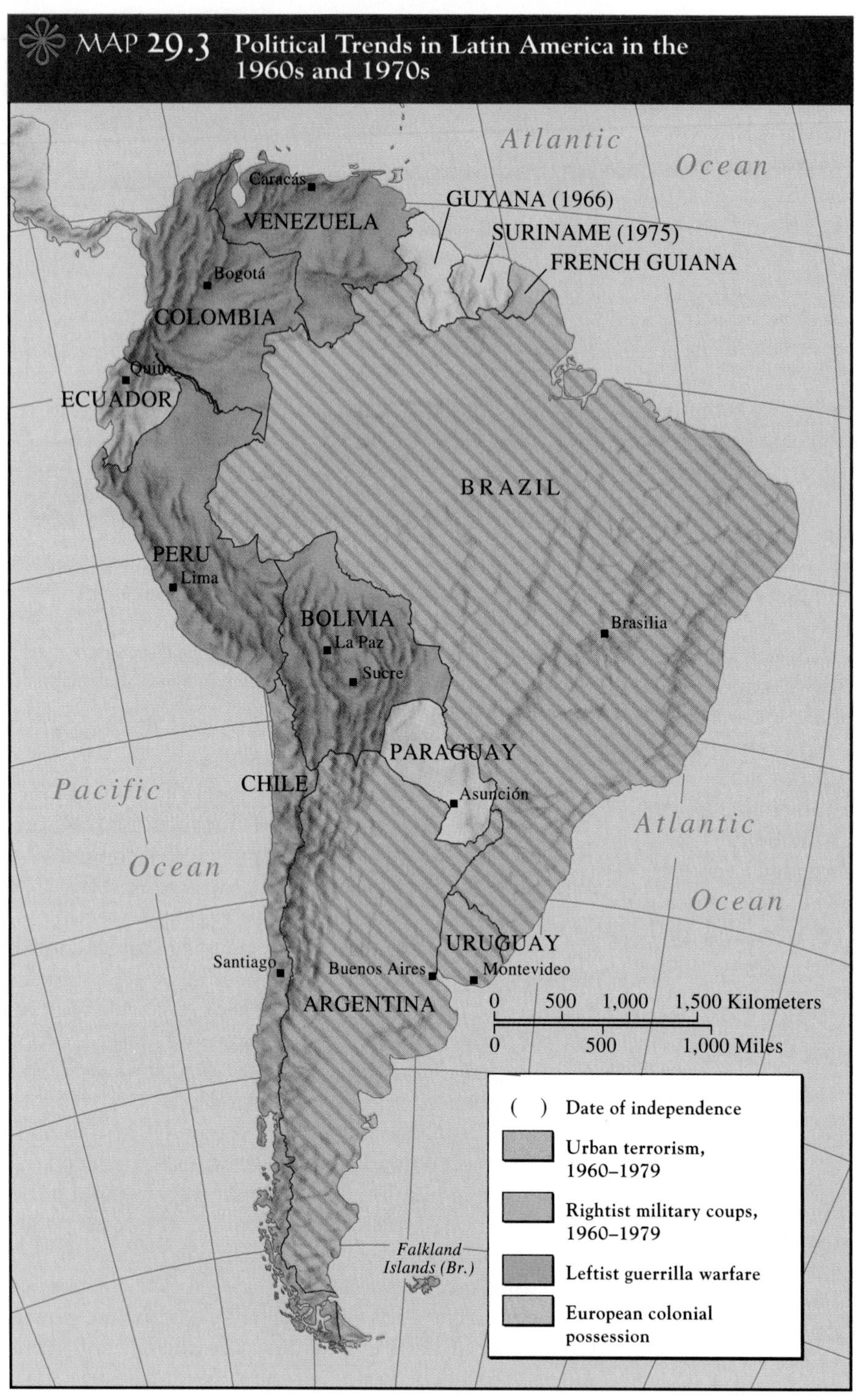

elections in 1990 brought a newcomer into office—Fernando Collor de Mello (b. 1949). He promised to end the inflation problem with a drastic reform program, based on squeezing money out of the economy by stringent controls on wages and prices, drastic reductions in public spendings, and cuts in the number of government employees. Collor de Mello's efforts were undermined by the corruption in his own administration, however, and he resigned from office at the end of 1992 after having been impeached. In new elections in 1994, Fernando Cardoso was elected president by an overwhelming majority of the popular vote.

The Mexican Way

During the 1950s and 1960s, Mexico's ruling party (the Institutional Revolutionary Party, or PRI) focused on a balanced industrial program. Fifteen years of steady economic growth combined with low inflation and real gains in wages

STUDENT REVOLT IN MEXICO

A growing conflict between government authorities and university students in Mexico came to a violent and bloody climax on October 2, 1968, when army troops killed and wounded large numbers of students in Mexico City. This excerpt is taken from an account of the events by the student National Strike Council.

NATIONAL STRIKE COUNCIL, EVENTS OF OCTOBER 2–3

After an hour and a half of a peaceful meeting attended by ten thousand people and witnessed by scores of domestic and foreign reporters, a helicopter gave the army the signal to attack by dropping flares into the crowd. Simultaneously, the plaza was surrounded and attacked by members of the army and all police forces, using weapons of every caliber, up to 9 mm.

The local papers have given the following information about the attack, confirmed by firsthand witnesses:

1. Numerous secret policemen had infiltrated the meeting in order to attack it from within, with orders to kill. They were known to each other by the use of a white handkerchief tied around their right hands. . . .
3. High caliber weaponry and expansion bullets were used. Seven hours after the massacre began, tanks cleaned up the residential buildings of Nonoalco-Tlaltelolco with short cannon blasts and machine-gun fire.
4. On the morning of October 3, the apartments of supposedly guilty individuals were still being searched, without a search warrant.
5. Doctors in the emergency wards of the city hospitals were under extreme pressure, being forced to forgo attention to the victims until they had been interrogated and placed under guard. Various interns who attended the demonstration for the purpose of giving medical aid had since disappeared.
6. The results of this brutal military operation include hundreds of dead (including women and children), thousands of wounded, an unwarranted search of all the apartments in the area, and thousands of violent arrests. Those arrested were taken to various illegal locations, such as Military Camp No. 1. It should be added that members of the National Strike Council who were captured were stripped and herded into a small archaeological excavation at Tlaltelolco, converted for the moment into a dungeon. Some of them were put up against a wall and shot.
7. Onesimo Mason, the general who directed the operation, praised the preparedness of his men, in contrast to the obvious lack of preparedness on the part of the students.

All this has occurred only ten days before the start of the Olympics. The repression is expected to become even greater after the Games, in view of the fact that national public opinion and the protest from the provinces are unified against a regime whose only interest lies in demonstrating its power to control.

Already individual liberties have been suspended, and restricted zones have been created where all vehicles are searched at gunpoint and personal identification is demanded. The Secretary of Defense declared that the friendly disposition of the regime will solve the conflict.

WE ARE NOT AGAINST THE OLYMPIC GAMES. WELCOME TO MEXICO.

for more and more people made those years appear to be a "golden age" in Mexico's economic development. But at the end of the 1960s, the true nature of Mexico's domination by one party became apparent with the student protest movement. On October 2, 1968, a demonstration of university students in Tlaltelolco Square in Mexico City was met by police forces, who opened fire and killed hundreds of students (see the box above). Leaders of the PRI became concerned about the need to change the system.

The next two presidents, Luis Echeverría (b. 1922) and José López Portillo (b. 1920), introduced political reforms. Rules for the registration of political parties were eased, making their growth more likely, and greater freedom of debate in the press and universities was allowed. But economic problems continued to trouble Mexico. In the late 1970s, vast new reserves of oil were discovered. As the sale of oil abroad increased dramatically, the government became even more dependent on oil revenues. When world oil prices dropped in the mid-1980s, Mexico was no longer able to make payments on its foreign debt, which had reached $80 billion in 1982. The government was forced to adopt new economic policies, including the increased sale of public-owned companies to private hands.

The debt crisis and rising unemployment left many people unhappy with the government, which was especially evident in the 1988 election. The PRI's choice for president was Carlos Salinas (b. 1948). Normally, he would have been expected to win in a landslide, but he received only 50.3 percent, a bare majority. The new president continued the economic liberalization of his predecessors and went even further by negotiating a free trade agreement with the United States and Canada, known as NAFTA (North American Free Trade Agreement). The success or failure of these economic policies will no doubt determine whether the PRI will

CHRONOLOGY

LATIN AMERICA

Presidency of Lázaro Cárdenas in Mexico	1934–1940
Vargas's New State in Brazil	1938–1945
Juan Perón becomes president of Argentina	1946
Creation of Organization of American States	1948
Perón goes into exile	1955
Castro's forces seize Cuba	1959
Bay of Pigs	1961
Cuban Missile Crisis	1962
Death of Ché Guevara in Bolivia	1967
Presidency of Luis Echeverría in Mexico	1970–1976
Overthrow of Salvador Allende in Chile	1973
Perón returns to power	1973
Presidency of José López Portillo in Mexico	1976–1982
Sandinistas establish provisional government	1979
Falklands War	1982
Election of Raúl Alfonsín in Argentina	1983
Election of Carlos Salinas in Mexico	1988
Resignation of Fernando Collor de Mello in Brazil	1992
Election of Fernando Cardoso in Brazil	1994
Reelection of Carlos Menem in Argentina	1995

continue to dominate Mexico politically. In 1995, a new challenge appeared when a group of rebels in the extreme south of Mexico led an armed revolt against the government.

Society and Culture in the Western World

Socially, culturally, and intellectually, the Western world during the last half of the twentieth century has been marked by much diversity. Although many trends represent a continuation of prewar modern developments, new directions in the last two decades have also led some to speak of a postmodern world.

The Emergence of a New Society

During the postwar era, Western society witnessed remarkably rapid change. Such products of new technologies as computers, television, jet planes, contraceptive devices, and new surgical techniques all dramatically and quickly altered the pace and nature of human life. The rapid changes in postwar society, fueled by scientific advances and rapid economic growth, led many to view it as a new society. Called a technocratic society by some and the consumer society by others, postwar Western society was characterized by a changing social structure and new movements for change.

The structure of European society was altered after 1945. Especially noticeable were the changes in the middle class. Such traditional middle-class groups as businesspeople and professionals in law, medicine, and the universities were greatly augmented by a new group of managers and technicians, as large companies and government agencies employed increasing numbers of white-collar supervisory and administrative personnel. Whether in Eastern or Western Europe, the new managers and experts were very much alike. Everywhere their positions depended on specialized knowledge acquired from some form of higher education. Everywhere they focused on the effective administration of their corporations. Since their positions usually depended on their skills, they took steps to ensure that their children would be similarly educated.

Changes also occurred among the traditional lower classes. Especially noticeable was the dramatic shift of people from rural to urban areas. The number of people in agriculture declined drastically; by the 1950s, the number of farmers throughout most of Europe had dropped by 50 percent. Nor did the size of the industrial working class expand. In West Germany, industrial workers made up 48 percent of the labor force throughout the 1950s and 1960s. Thereafter, the number of industrial workers began to dwindle as the number of white-collar service employees increased. At the same time, a substantial increase in their real wages enabled the working classes to aspire to the consumption patterns of the middle class, leading to what some observers have called the "consumer society." Buying on the installment plan, which was introduced in the 1930s, became widespread beginning in the 1950s and gave workers a chance to imitate the middle class by buying such products as televisions, washing machines, refrigerators, vacuum cleaners, and stereos. But the most visible symbol of mass consumerism was the automobile. Before World War II, cars were reserved mostly for the European upper classes. In 1948, there were 5 million cars in all of Europe, but by 1957, the number had tripled. By the 1960s, there were almost 45 million cars.

Rising incomes, combined with shorter working hours, created an even greater market for mass leisure activities. Between 1900 and 1980, the work week was reduced from sixty hours to a little more than forty hours, and the number of paid holidays increased. All aspects of popular culture—music, sports, media—became commercialized and offered opportunities for leisure activities including concerts, sporting events, and television viewing.

Another very visible symbol of mass leisure was the growth of mass tourism. Before World War II, most persons who traveled for pleasure were from the upper and middle classes. After the war, the combination of more vacation time, increased prosperity, and the flexibility provided by package tours with their lower rates and low-budget rooms enabled millions to expand their travel possibilities. By the mid-1960s, one hundred million tourists were crossing European boundaries each year.

Social change was also evident in new educational patterns and student revolts. Before World War II, higher education had largely remained the preserve of Europe's wealthier classes. After the war, European states began to foster greater equality of opportunity in higher education by eliminating fees, and universities experienced an influx of students from the middle and lower classes. Enrollments grew dramatically; in France, 4.5 percent of young people went to a university in 1950. By 1965, the figure had increased to 14.5 percent.

But there were problems. Overcrowded classrooms, professors who paid little attention to students, and administrators who acted in an authoritarian fashion aroused student resentment. In addition, despite changes in the curriculum, students often felt that the universities were not providing an education relevant to the modern age. This discontent led to an outburst of student revolts in the late 1960s. In part, these protests were an extension of the disruptions in American universities in the mid-1960s, which were often sparked by student opposition to the Vietnam War. Perhaps the most famous student revolt occurred in France in 1968. It erupted at the University of Nanterre outside Paris but soon spread to the Sorbonne, the main campus of the University of Paris. French students demanded a greater voice in the administration of the university, took over buildings, and then expanded the scale of their protests by inviting workers to support them.

STUDENT REVOLT IN PARIS, 1968. The discontent of university students exploded in the late 1960s in a series of student revolts. Perhaps best known was the movement in Paris in 1968. This photograph shows the barricades that students erected by overturning cars on a Parisian street on the morning of May 11 during the height of the revolt.

Half of France's workforce went on strike in May 1968. After the Gaullist government instituted a hefty wage hike, the workers returned to work, and the police repressed the remaining student protesters.

The student protest movement reached its high point in 1968, although scattered incidents lasted into the early 1970s. There were several reasons for the student radicalism. Some students were genuinely motivated by their desire to reform the university. Others were protesting the Vietnam War, which they viewed as a product of Western imperialism. They also attacked other aspects of Western society, such as its materialism, and expressed concern about becoming cogs in the large and impersonal bureaucratic jungles of the modern world. For many students, the calls for democratic decision making within the universities were a reflection of their deeper concerns about the direction of Western society. Although the student revolts fizzled out in the 1970s, the larger issues they raised were increasingly revived in the 1990s.

The Permissive Society

The "permissive society" was yet another term used by critics to describe the new society of postwar Europe. World War I had seen the first significant crack in the rigid code of manners and morals of the nineteenth century. Subsequently, the 1920s had witnessed experimentation with drugs, the appearance of hard-core pornography, and a new sexual freedom (police in Berlin, for example, issued cards that permitted female and male homosexual prostitutes to practice their trade). But these indications of a new attitude appeared mostly in major cities and touched only small numbers of people. After World War II, changes in manners and morals were far more extensive and far more noticeable.

Sweden took the lead in the propagation of the so-called sexual revolution of the 1960s, but the rest of Europe and the United States soon followed. Sex education in the schools and the decriminalization of homosexuality were but two aspects of Sweden's liberal legislation. The introduction of the birth control pill, which became widely available by the mid-1960s, gave people more freedom in sexual behavior. Meanwhile, sexually explicit movies, plays, and books broke new ground in the treatment of once hidden subjects. Cities like Amsterdam, which allowed open prostitution and the public sale of hard-core pornography, attracted thousands of curious tourists.

The new standards were evident in the breakdown of the traditional family. Divorce rates increased dramatically, especially in the 1960s, while the incidence of premarital and extramarital sexual experiences also rose substantially. A survey in the Netherlands in 1968 revealed that 78 percent of men and 86 percent of women had participated in extramarital sex.

The decade of the 1960s also saw the emergence of a drug culture. Marijuana was widely used among college and university students as the recreational drug of choice. For young people more interested in mind expansion into higher levels of consciousness, Timothy Leary, who had done psychedelic research at Harvard on the effects of LSD (lysergic acid diethylamide), became the high priest of hallucinogenic experiences.

New attitudes toward sex and the use of drugs were only two manifestations of a growing youth movement in the 1960s that questioned authority and fostered rebellion against the older generation. Spurred on by the Vietnam

THE "LOVE-IN." In the 1960s, a number of outdoor public festivals for young people combined music, drugs, and sex. Flamboyant dress, facial painting, free-form dancing, and drugs were vital ingredients in creating an atmosphere dedicated to "love and peace." Shown here is a "love-in" that was held on the grounds of an English country estate in the Summer of Love, 1967.

"THE TIMES THEY ARE A-CHANGIN'": THE MUSIC OF YOUTHFUL PROTEST

In the 1960s, the lyrics of rock music reflected the rebellious mood of many young people. Bob Dylan (b. 1941), a well-known recording artist, expressed the feelings of the younger generation. His song "The Times They Are a-Changin'," released in 1964, has been called an "anthem for the protest movement."

BOB DYLAN, "THE TIMES THEY ARE A-CHANGIN'"

Come gather 'round people
Wherever you roam
And admit that the waters
Around you have grown
And accept it that soon
You'll be drenched to the bone
If your time to you
Is worth savin'
Then you better start swimmin'
Or you'll sink like a stone
For the times they are a-changin'

Come writers and critics
Who prophesize with your pen
And keep your eyes wide
The chance won't come again
And don't speak too soon
For the wheel's still in spin
And there's no tellin' who
That it's namin'
For the loser now
Will be later to win
For the times they are a-changin'

Come senators, congressmen
Please heed the call
Don't stand in the doorway
Don't block up the hall
For he that gets hurt
Will be he who has stalled
There's a battle outside
And it is ragin'
It'll soon shake your windows
And rattle your walls
For the times they are a-changin'

Come mothers and fathers
Throughout the land
And don't criticize
What you can't understand
Your sons and your daughters
Are beyond your command
Your old road
Is rapidly agin'
Please get out of the new one
If you can't lend your hand
For the times they are a-changin'

The line it is drawn
The curse it is cast
The slow one now
Will later be fast
As the present now
Will later be past
The order is
Rapidly fadin'
And the first one now
Will later be last
For the times they are a-changin'

War and a growing political consciousness, the youth rebellion became a youth protest movement by the second half of the 1960s (see the box above).

New (and Old) Patterns: Women in the Postwar Western World

Despite their enormous contributions to the war effort, women at the end of World War II were removed from the workforce to provide jobs for the soldiers returning home. After the horrors of war, people seemed willing for a while to return to traditional family practices. Female participation in the workforce declined, and birthrates began to rise, creating a "baby boom." This increase in the birthrate, however, did not last, and birthrates—and thus the size of families—began to decline by the end of the 1950s. Largely responsible for this decline was the widespread practice of birth control. Invented in the nineteenth century, the condom was already in wide use, but the development in the 1960s of oral contraceptives, known as birth control pills, provided a reliable means of birth control that quickly spread to all Western countries.

No doubt, the trend toward smaller families contributed to the change in the character of women's employment in both Europe and the United States as women experienced considerably more years when they were not involved in rearing children. The most important development was the increased number of married women in the workforce. At the beginning of the twentieth century, even working-class wives tended to stay at home if they could afford to do so. In the postwar period, this was no longer the case. In the United States, for example, married women made up about 15 percent of the female labor force in 1900; by 1970, their number had increased to 62 percent. The percentage of married women in the female labor force in Sweden increased from 47 to 66 percent between 1963 and 1975.

But the increased number of women in the workforce did not change some old patterns. Working-class women in particular still earned salaries lower than those of men performing equivalent work. In the 1960s, women earned only 60 percent of men's wages in Britain, 50 percent in France, and 63 percent in West Germany. In addition, women still tended to enter traditionally female jobs. As one Swedish woman guidance counselor remarked in 1975: "Every girl now thinks in terms of a job. This is progress. They want children, but they don't pin their hopes on marriage. They don't intend to be housewives for some future husband. But there has been no change in their vocational choices."[2] Many European women also still faced the double burden of earning income on the one hand and raising a family and maintaining the household on the other. Such inequalities led increasing numbers of women to rebel.

WOMEN'S LIBERATION MOVEMENT. In the late 1960s, as women began once again to assert their rights, a revived women's liberation movement emerged. Feminists in the movement maintained that women themselves must alter the conditions of their lives. During this women's liberation rally, some women climbed the statue of Admiral Farragut in Washington, D.C., to exhibit their signs.

The participation of women in World Wars I and II helped them achieve one of the major aims of the nineteenth-century feminist movement—the right to vote. Already after World War I, many governments acknowledged the contributions of women to the war effort by granting them the right to vote. Sweden, Great Britain, Germany, Poland, Hungary, Austria, and Czechoslovakia did so in 1918, followed by the United States in 1920. Women in France and Italy did not obtain the right to vote until 1945. After World War II, European women tended to fall back into the traditional roles expected of them, and little was heard of feminist concerns. But by the late 1960s, women began to assert their rights again and speak as feminists. Along with the student upheavals of the late 1960s came renewed interest in feminism, or the women's liberation movement, as it was now called. Increasingly, women protested that the acquisition of political and legal equality had not brought true equality with men:

> We are economically oppressed: in jobs we do full work for half pay; in the home we do unpaid work full-time. We are commercially exploited by advertisement, television, and the press; legally we often have only the status of children. We are brought up to feel inadequate, educated to narrower horizons than men. This is our specific oppression as women. It is as women that we are, therefore, organizing.[3]

These were the words of a British Women's Liberation Workshop in 1969.

Of great importance to the emergence of the postwar women's liberation movement was the work of Simone de Beauvoir (1908–1986). Born into a Catholic middle-class family and educated at the Sorbonne in Paris, she supported herself as a teacher and later as a novelist and writer. She maintained a lifelong relationship (but not marriage) with the philosopher Jean-Paul Sartre. Her involvement in the existentialist movement—the leading intellectual movement of its time—led her to become active in political causes. De Beauvoir believed that she lived a "liberated" life for a twentieth-century European woman, but for all her freedom, she still came to perceive that as a woman she faced limits that men did not. In 1949, she published her highly influential work *The Second Sex,* in which she argued that as a result of male-dominated societies, women had been defined by their differences from men and consequently received second-class status (see the box on p. 901).

Another important influence in the growth of a women's movement in the 1960s came from Betty Friedan

THE VOICE OF THE WOMEN'S LIBERATION MOVEMENT

Simone de Beauvoir was an important figure in the emergence of the postwar women's liberation movement. This excerpt is taken from her influential book The Second Sex, *in which she argued that women have been forced into a position subordinate to men.*

SIMONE DE BEAUVOIR, *THE SECOND SEX*

Now, woman has always been man's dependent, if not his slave; the two sexes have never shared the world in equality. And even today woman is heavily handicapped, though her situation is beginning to change. Almost nowhere is her legal status the same as man's, and frequently it is much to her disadvantage. Even when her rights are legally recognized in the abstract, long-standing custom prevents their full expression in the mores. In the economic sphere men and women can almost be said to make up two castes; other things being equal, the former hold the better jobs, get higher wages, and have more opportunity for success than their new competitors. In industry and politics men have a great many more positions and they monopolize the most important posts. In addition to all this, they enjoy a traditional prestige that the education of children tends in every way to support, for the present enshrines the past—and in the past all history has been made by men. At the present time, when women are beginning to take part in the affairs of the world, it is still a world that belongs to men—they have no doubt of it at all and women have scarcely any. To decline to be the Other, to refuse to be a party to a deal—this would be for women to renounce all the advantages conferred upon them by their alliance with the superior caste. Man-the-sovereign will provide woman-the-liege with material protection and will undertake the moral justification of her existence; thus she can evade at once both economic risk and the metaphysical risk of a liberty in which ends and aims must be contrived without assistance. Indeed, along with the ethical urge of each individual to affirm his subjective existence, there is also the temptation to forgo liberty and become a thing. This is an inauspicious road, for he who takes it—passive, lost, ruined—becomes henceforth the creature of another's will, frustrated in his transcendence and deprived of every value. But it is an easy road; on it one avoids the strain involved in undertaking an authentic existence. When man makes of woman the *Other,* he may, then, expect her to manifest deep-seated tendencies toward complicity. Thus, woman may fail to lay claim to the status of subject because she lacks definite resources, because she feels the necessary bond that ties her to man regardless of reciprocity, and because she is often very well pleased with her role as the *Other*.

Now, what peculiarly signalizes the situation of woman is that she—a free and autonomous being like all human creatures—nevertheless finds herself living in a world where men compel her to assume the status of the Other.

(b. 1921). A journalist and the mother of three children, Friedan grew increasingly uneasy with her attempt to fulfill the traditional role of the "ideal housewife and mother." In 1963, she published *The Feminine Mystique*, in which she analyzed the problems of middle-class American women in the 1950s and argued that women were being denied equality with men. She wrote: "The problem that has no name—which is simply the fact that American women are kept from growing to their full human capacities—is taking a far greater toll on the physical and mental health of our country than any known disease."[4] *The Feminine Mystique* became a best-seller and propelled Friedan into a newfound celebrity.

TRANSFORMATION IN WOMEN'S LIVES

It is estimated that women need to average 2.1 children in order to ensure a natural replacement of a country's population. In many European countries, the population stopped growing in the 1960s, and the trend has continued since then. By the 1990s, birthrates were down drastically; among the nations of the European Union, the average number of children per woman of childbearing age was 1.4. Italy's rate—1.2—was the lowest in the world in 1997.

At the same time, the number of women in the workforce has continued to rise. In Britain, for example, the number of women in the labor force went from 32 percent to 44 percent between 1970 and 1990. Moreover, women have entered new employment areas. Greater access to universities and professional schools enabled women to take jobs in law, medicine, government, business, and education. In the Soviet Union, for example, about 70 percent of doctors and teachers were women. Nevertheless, economic inequality still often prevailed; women received lower wages than men for comparable work and received fewer opportunities for advancement to management positions.

Feminists in the women's liberation movement came to believe that women themselves must transform the fundamental conditions of their lives. They did so in a variety of ways after 1970. First, they formed numerous "consciousness-raising" groups to further awareness of women's issues. Women met together to share their personal experiences and become aware of the many ways that male dominance affected their lives. This "consciousness raising" helped many women to become activists.

Women sought and gained a measure of control over their own bodies by seeking to overturn legal restrictions on both contraception and abortion. In the 1960s and 1970s, hundreds of thousands of European women worked to repeal the laws that outlawed contraception and abortion and began to meet with success. A French law in 1968 permitted the sale of contraceptive devices, and in the 1970s French feminists worked to legalize abortion. In 1979, a new French law legalized abortion. Even in Catholic countries, where the church remained strongly opposed to abortion, legislation allowing contraception and abortion was passed in the 1970s and 1980s.

As more women became activists, they also became involved in new issues. In the 1980s and 1990s, women faculty in universities concentrated on developing new cultural attitudes through the new academic field of women's studies. Courses in women's studies, which stressed the role and contributions of women in history, mushroomed in both American and European colleges and universities.

Other women began to try to affect the political environment by allying with the antinuclear movement. In 1981, a group of women protested American nuclear missiles in Britain by chaining themselves to the fence of an American military base. Thousands more joined in creating a peace camp around the military compound. Enthusiasm ran high; one participant said: "I'll never forget that feeling; it'll live with me forever. . . . As we walked round, and we clasped hands . . . it was for women; it was for peace; it was for the world."[5]

Some women joined the ecological movement. As one German writer who was concerned with environmental issues said, it is women "who must give birth to children, willingly or unwillingly, in this polluted world of ours." Especially prominent was the number of women members in the Green Party in Germany (see The Environment and the Green Movements on the next page), which supported environmental issues and elected forty-two delegates to the West German parliament in 1987.

Women in the West have also reached out to work with women from the rest of the world in international conferences to change the conditions of their lives. Between 1975 and 1995, the United Nations held conferences in Mexico City, Copenhagen, Nairobi, and Beijing. These meetings made clear the differences between women from Western and non-Western countries. Whereas women from Western countries spoke about political, economic, cultural, and sexual rights, women from developing countries in Latin America, Africa, and Asia focused their attention on bringing an end to the violence, hunger, and disease that haunt their lives. Despite these differences, these meetings made it clear how women in both developed and developing nations were organizing to make people aware of women's issues.

The Growth of Terrorism

Acts of terror by those opposed to governments became a frightening aspect of modern Western society. Small bands of terrorists used assassination, indiscriminate killing of civilians, especially by bombing, the taking of hostages, and the hijacking of airplanes to draw attention to their demands or destabilize governments in the hope of achieving their political goals. Terrorist acts garnered considerable media attention. When Palestinian terrorists kidnapped and killed eleven Israeli athletes at the Munich Olympic games in 1972, hundreds of millions of people watched the drama unfold on television. Indeed, some observers believe that media exposure has been an important catalyst for some terrorist groups.

Motivations for terrorist acts varied considerably. Left- and right-wing terrorist groups flourished in the late 1970s and early 1980s. Left-wing groups, such as the Baader-Meinhof gang (also known as the Red Army Faction) in Germany and the Red Brigades in Italy, consisted chiefly of affluent middle-class young people who denounced the injustices of capitalism and supported acts of revolutionary terrorism in order to bring down the system. Right-wing terrorist groups, such as the New Order in Italy and the Charles Martel Club in France, used bombings to foment disorder and bring about authoritarian regimes. These groups received little or no public support, and authorities were able to crush them fairly quickly.

But terrorist acts also stemmed from militant nationalists who wished to create separatist states. Because they received considerable support from local populations sympathetic to their cause, these terrorist groups could maintain their activities over a long period of time. Most prominent was the Irish Republican Army (IRA), which resorted to vicious attacks against the ruling government and innocent civilians in Northern Ireland. Over a period of twenty years, IRA terrorists were responsible for the death of two thousand people in Northern Ireland; three-fourths of the victims were civilians.

Although left- and right-wing terrorist activities declined in Europe in the 1980s, international terrorism remained rather commonplace. Angered by the loss of their territory to Israel in 1967, some militant Palestinians responded with a policy of terrorist attacks against Israel's supporters. Palestinian terrorists operated throughout European countries, attacking both Europeans and American tourists; it was Palestinian terrorists who massacred vacationers at airports in Rome and Vienna in 1985. State-sponsored terrorism was often an integral part of international terrorism. Militant governments, especially in Iran, Libya, and Syria, assisted terrorist organizations that made attacks on Europeans and Americans. On December 21, 1988, Pan American flight 103 from

Frankfurt to New York exploded over Lockerbie, Scotland, killing all 259 passengers and crew members. A massive investigation finally revealed that the bomb responsible for the explosion had been planted by two Libyan terrorists who were connected to terrorist groups based in Iran and Syria.

Governments fought back by creating special antiterrorist units, which became extremely effective in responding to terrorist acts. In 1977, for example, the German special antiterrorist unit, known as GSG, rescued 91 hostages from a Lufthansa airplane that had been hijacked to Mogadishu in Somalia. Counterterrorism, or a calculated policy of direct retaliation against terrorists, also made states that sponsored terrorism more cautious. In 1986, the Reagan administration responded to the terrorist bombing of a West German disco club popular with American soldiers by launching an air attack on Libya, long suspected to be a major sponsor of terrorist organizations. Some observers attribute the overall decline in terrorist attacks in the late 1980s to the American action. In the 1990s, however, acts of terrorism continued to be a disturbing element in Western life.

Guest Workers and Immigrants

As the economies of the Western European countries revived in the 1950s and 1960s, a severe labor shortage forced them to rely on foreign workers. Thousands of Turks and eastern and southern Europeans came to Germany, North Africans to France, and people from the Caribbean, India, and Pakistan to Great Britain. Overall, there were probably 15 million guest workers in Europe in the 1980s. They constituted 17 percent of the labor force in Switzerland and 10 percent in Germany.

Although these workers were necessary for economic reasons, socially and politically their presence created problems for their host countries. Many foreign workers complained that they received lower wages and inferior social benefits. Moreover, their concentration in certain cities and even certain sections of those cities often created tensions with the local native populations. Foreign workers, many of them nonwhites, constituted almost one-fifth of the population in the German cities of Frankfurt, Munich, and Stuttgart. Having become settled in their new countries, many were unwilling to leave, even after the end of the postwar boom in the early 1970s led to mass unemployment. Moreover, as guest workers settled permanently in their host countries, additional family members migrated to join them. Although they had little success in getting guest workers already there to leave, some European countries passed legislation or took other measures to restrict new immigration.

In the 1980s, the problem of foreign workers was intensified by an influx of other refugees, especially to West Germany, which had liberal immigration laws that permitted people seeking asylum for political persecution to enter the country. During the 1970s and 1980s, West Germany absorbed over a million refugees from Eastern Europe and East Germany. In 1986 alone, two hundred thousand political refugees from Pakistan, Bangladesh, and Sri Lanka entered the country.

This great influx of foreigners, many of them nonwhite, strained not only the social services of European countries, but the patience of many native residents who opposed making their countries ethnically diverse. Antiforeign sentiment, especially in a time of growing unemployment, increased and was encouraged by new right-wing political parties that catered to people's complaints. Thus, the National Front in France, organized by Jean-Marie Le Pen, and the Republican Party in Germany, led by Franz Schönhuber, a former SS officer, advocated restricting all new immigration and limiting the assimilation of settled immigrants. Although these parties have had only limited success in elections so far, even that modest accomplishment has encouraged traditional conservative and even moderately conservative parties to adopt more nationalistic policies. Even more frightening, however, have been the organized campaigns of violence, especially against African and Asian immigrants, by radical, right-wing groups.

The Environment and the Green Movements

Beginning in the 1970s, environmentalism became a serious item on the European political agenda. By that time, serious ecological problems had become all too apparent. Air pollution, produced by nitrogen oxide and sulfur dioxide emissions from road vehicles, power plants, and industrial factories, was causing respiratory illnesses and having corrosive effects on buildings and monuments. Many rivers, lakes, and seas had become so polluted that they posed serious health risks. Dying forests and disappearing wildlife alarmed more and more people. The opening of Eastern Europe after the revolutions of 1989 brought to the world's attention the incredible environmental destruction of that region caused by unfettered industrial pollution.

Environmental concerns forced the major political parties in Europe to advocate new regulations for the protection of the environment. The Soviet nuclear power disaster at Chernobyl in 1986 made Europeans even more aware of potential environmental hazards, and 1987 was touted as the "year of the environment." Many European states also established government ministries to oversee environmental issues.

Growing ecological awareness also gave rise to Green movements and Green Parties that emerged throughout Europe in the 1970s. Some of these movements came from the antinuclear movement; others arose out of such causes as women's liberation and concerns for foreign workers. Most visible was the Green Party in Germany, which was officially organized in 1979 and, by 1987, had elected forty-two delegates to the West German parliament. Green Parties also competed successfully in Sweden, Austria, and Switzerland.

Although the Green movements and parties have played an important role in making people aware of ecological problems, they have by no means replaced the traditional political parties, as some political analysts in the mid-1980s forecast. For one thing, the coalitions that made up the Greens found it difficult to agree on all issues and tended to splinter into different cliques. Then, too, many of the founders of these movements, who often expressed a willingness to work with the traditional political parties, were ousted from their leadership positions by fundamentalists unwilling to compromise their principles in any way. Finally, traditional political parties have coopted the environmental issues of the Greens. By the 1990s, more and more European governments were beginning to sponsor projects to safeguard the environment and clean up the worst sources of pollution.

Recent Trends in Art and Literature

Modern art continued to prevail at exhibitions and museums. For the most part, the United States dominated the art world, much as it did the world of popular culture. American art, often vibrantly colored and filled with activity, reflected the energy and exuberance of the postwar United States. After 1945, New York City became the artistic center of the Western world. The Guggenheim Museum, the Museum of Modern Art, and the Whitney Museum of American art, together with New York's numerous art galleries, promoted modern art and helped determine artistic tastes not only in New York and the United States, but throughout much of the world.

Abstractionism, especially Abstract Expressionism, emerged as the artistic mainstream. American exuberance in Abstract Expressionism is evident in the enormous canvases of Jackson Pollock (1912–1956). In such works as *Lavender Mist* (1950), paint seems to explode, assaulting the viewer with emotion and movement. Pollock's swirling forms and seemingly chaotic patterns broke all conventions of form and structure. His drip paintings, with their total abstraction, were extremely influential with other artists, although the public was initially quite hostile to his work.

The early 1960s saw the emergence of Pop Art, which took images of popular culture and transformed them into works of fine art. Andy Warhol (1930–1987), who began as an advertising illustrator, was the most famous of the pop artists. Warhol adapted images from commercial art, such as the Campbell soup cans, and photographs of such celebrities as Marilyn Monroe. Derived from mass culture, these works were mass produced and deliberately "of the moment," expressing the fleeting whims of popular culture.

In the 1980s, styles emerged that some have referred to as Postmodern. Although as yet ill-defined, Postmodernism tends to move away from the futurism or "cutting edge" qualities of Modernism. Instead it favors "utilizing tradition," whether that includes more styles of painting or elevating traditional artisanship to the level of fine art. Weavers, potters, glassmakers, metalsmiths, and furniture makers gained respect as artists.

Of all the arts, architecture best reflects the extraordinary global economic expansion of the second half of the twentieth century, from the rapid postwar reconstruction of Japan and Europe, to the phenomenal prosperity of the West, to the newfound affluence of emerging Third World nations. No matter where one travels today, from Kuala Lumpur to Johannesburg, from Buenos Aires to Shanghai, the world's cities boast the identical monolithic rectangular skyscraper—the international symbol of modernization, money, and power.

The most significant new trend in postwar literature has been called the "Theater of the Absurd." This new

JACKSON POLLOCK DOES A PAINTING. One of the best-known practitioners of Abstract Expressionism, which remained at the center of the artistic mainstream after World War II, was the American Jackson Pollock, who achieved his ideal of total abstraction in his drip paintings. He is shown here at work in his Long Island studio. Pollock found it easier to cover his large canvases with exploding patterns of color when he put them on the floor.

convention in drama began in France in the 1950s, although its most famous proponent was the Irishman Samuel Beckett (1906–1990), who lived in France. In Beckett's *Waiting for Godot* (1952), it is readily apparent that the action on the stage is not realistic. Two men wait incessantly for the appearance of someone, with whom they may or may not have an appointment. No background information on the two men is provided. During the course of the play, nothing seems to be happening. The audience is never told if the action in front of them is real or unreal. Unlike traditional theater, suspense is maintained not by having the audience wonder, "what is going to happen next?" but by having them wonder simply, "what is happening now?"

The Theater of the Absurd reflected its time. The postwar period was a time of disillusionment with fixed ideological beliefs in politics or religion. The same disillusionment that inspired the existentialism of Albert Camus (1913–1960) and Jean-Paul Sartre (1905–1980), with its sense of the world's meaninglessness, underscored the bleak worldview of absurdist drama and literature. The beginning point of the existentialism of Sartre and Camus was the absence of God in the universe. While the death of God was tragic, it meant that humans had no preordained destiny and were utterly alone in the universe with no future and no hope. As Camus expressed it:

> A world that can be explained even with bad reasons is a familiar world. But, on the other hand, in a universe suddenly divested of illusions and lights, man feels an alien, a stranger. His exile is without remedy since he is deprived of the memory of a lost home or the hope of a promised land. This divorce between man and his life, the actor and his setting, is properly the feeling of absurdity.[6]

According to Camus, then, the world was absurd and without meaning; humans, too, are without meaning and purpose. Reduced to despair and depression, humans have but one ground of hope—themselves.

The New World of Science and Technology

Since the Scientific Revolution of the seventeenth century and the Industrial Revolution of the nineteenth century, science and technology have played increasingly important roles in world civilization. Many of the scientific and technological achievements since World War II have revolutionized people's lives. When American astronauts walked on the moon, millions watched the event on their televisions in the privacy of their living rooms.

Before World War II, theoretical science and technology were largely separated. Pure science was the domain of university professors, far removed from the practical technological matters of technicians and engineers. But during World War II, university scientists were recruited to work for their governments and develop new weapons and practical instruments of war. British physicists played a crucial role in the development of an improved radar system that helped to defeat the German air force in the Battle of Britain in 1940. The computer, too, was a wartime creation. The British mathematician Alan Turing designed a primitive computer to assist British intelligence in breaking the secret codes of German ciphering machines. The most famous product of wartime scientific research was the atomic bomb, created by a team of American and European scientists under the guidance of the physicist J. Robert Oppenheimer. Obviously, most wartime devices were created for destructive purposes, but computers and breakthrough technologies such as nuclear energy were soon adapted for peacetime uses.

The sponsorship of research by governments and the military during World War II led to a new scientific model. Science had become very complex, and only large organizations with teams of scientists, huge laboratories, and complicated equipment could undertake such large-scale projects. Such facilities were so expensive, however, that they could only be provided by governments and large corporations. Because of its postwar prosperity, the United States was able to lead in the development of the new science. In 1965, almost 75 percent of all scientific research funds in the United States came from the government. Unwilling to lag behind, especially in military development, the Soviet Union was also forced to provide large outlays for scientific and technological research and development. In fact, the defense establishments of the United States and the Soviet Union generated much of postwar scientific research. One-fourth of the trained scientists and engineers after 1945 were utilized in the creation of new weapons systems. Universities found their research agendas increasingly determined by government funding for military-related projects.

There was no more stunning example of how the new scientific establishment operated than the space race of the 1960s. The announcement by the Soviets in 1957 that they had sent the first space satellite—*Sputnik I*—into orbit around the earth caused the United States to launch a gigantic project to land a manned spacecraft on the moon within a decade. Massive government funds financed the scientific research and technological advances that attained this goal in 1969.

The postwar alliance of science and technology led to an accelerated rate of change that became a fact of life in Western society. One product of this alliance—the computer—may yet prove to be the most revolutionary of all the technological inventions of the twentieth century. Early computers, which used thousands of vacuum tubes to function, were large and took up considerable room space. The development of the transistor and then the silicon chip produced a revolutionary new approach to computers. With the invention in 1971 of the microprocessor, a machine that combines the equivalent of thousands of

SMALL IS BEAUTIFUL: THE LIMITS OF MODERN TECHNOLOGY

Although science and technology have produced an amazing array of achievements in the postwar world, some voices have been raised in criticism of their sometimes destructive aspects. In 1975, in his book Small Is Beautiful, *the British economist E. F. Schumacher examined the effects modern industrial technology has had on the earth's resources.*

E. F. SCHUMACHER, *SMALL IS BEAUTIFUL*

Is it not evident that our current methods of production are already eating into the very substance of industrial man? To many people this is not at all evident. Now that we have solved the problem of production, they say, have we ever had it so good? Are we not better fed, better clothed, and better housed than ever before—and better educated? Of course we are: most, but by no means all, of us: in the rich countries. But this is not what I mean by "substance." The substance of [humankind] cannot be measured by Gross National Product. Perhaps it cannot be measured at all, except for certain symptoms of loss. However, this is not the place to go into the statistics of these symptoms, such as crime, drug addiction, vandalism, mental breakdown, rebellion, and so forth. Statistics never prove anything.

I started by saying that one of the most fateful errors of our age is the belief that the problem of production has been solved. This illusion, I suggested, is mainly due to our inability to recognize that the modern industrial system, with all its intellectual sophistication, consumes the very basis on which it has been erected. To use the language of the economist, it lives on irreplaceable capital which it cheerfully treats as income. I specified three categories of such capital: fossil fuels, the tolerance margins of nature, and the human substance. Even if some readers should refuse to accept all three parts of my argument, I suggest that any one of them suffices to make my case.

And what is my case? Simply that our most important task is to get off our present collision course. And who is there to tackle such a task? I think every one of us. . . . To talk about the future is useful only if it leads to action *now*. And what can we do *now*, while we are still in the position of "never having had it so good"? To say the least . . . we must thoroughly understand the problem and begin to see the possibility of evolving a new lifestyle, with new methods of production and new patterns of consumption: a lifestyle designed for permanence. To give only three preliminary examples: in agriculture and horticulture, we can interest ourselves in the perfection of production methods which are biologically sound, build up soil fertility, and produce health, beauty, and permanence. Productivity will then look after itself. In industry, we can interest ourselves in the evolution of small-scale technology, relatively nonviolent technology, "technology with a human face," so that people have a chance to enjoy themselves while they are working, instead of working solely for their pay packet and hoping, usually forlornly, for enjoyment solely during their leisure time.

transistors on a single, tiny silicon chip, the road was open for the development of the personal computer. By the 1990s, the personal computer had become a regular fixture in businesses, schools, and homes. The Internet—the world's largest computer network—provides millions of people around the world with quick access to immense quantities of information, as well as rapid communication and commercial transactions. By 2000, an estimated 500 million people were using the Internet.

Despite the marvels produced by the alliance of science and technology, some people came to question the underlying assumption of this alliance—that scientific knowledge gave human beings the ability to manipulate the environment for their benefit. They maintained that some technological advances had far-reaching side effects damaging to the environment. The chemical fertilizers, for example, that were touted for producing larger crops wreaked havoc with the ecological balance of streams, rivers, and woodlands. *Small Is Beautiful*, written by the British economist E. F. Schumacher (1911–1977), was a fundamental critique of the dangers of the new science and technology (see the box above).

The Revival of Religion

Existentialism was one response to the despair generated by the apparent collapse of civilized values in the twentieth century. The revival of religion has been another. Ever since the Enlightenment of the eighteenth century, Christianity and religion had been on the defensive. But in the twentieth century, a number of religious thinkers and leaders attempted to bring new life to Christianity.

One expression of this religious revival was the attempt by such theologians as the Protestant Karl Barth (1886–1968) and the Catholic Karl Rahner (1904–1984) to infuse traditional Christian teachings with new life. In his numerous writings, Barth attempted to reinterpret the religious insights of the Reformation era for the modern world. To Barth, the sinful and hence imperfect nature of human beings meant that humans could know religious truth not through reason, but only through the grace of God. Karl Rahner attempted to revitalize traditional Catholic theology by incorporating aspects of modern thought. He was careful, however, to emphasize the continuity between ancient and modern interpretations of Catholic doctrine.

In the Catholic church, attempts at religious renewal also came from two charismatic popes—John XXIII and John Paul II. Pope John XXIII (1881–1963) reigned as pope for only a short time (1958–1963), but sparked a dramatic revival of Catholicism when he summoned the twenty-first ecumenical council of the Catholic church. Known as Vatican Council II, it liberalized a number of Catholic practices. The mass was henceforth to be celebrated in the vernacular languages rather than Latin. New avenues of communication with other Christian faiths were also opened for the first time since the Reformation.

John Paul II (b. 1920), who had been the archbishop of Cracow in Poland before his elevation to the papacy in 1978, was the first non-Italian to be elected pope since the sixteenth century. Although he alienated a number of people by reasserting traditional Catholic teaching on such issues as birth control, women in the priesthood, and clerical celibacy, John Paul's numerous travels around the world helped strengthen the Catholic church throughout the non-Western world. A strong believer in social justice, the charismatic John Paul II has been a powerful figure reminding Europeans of their spiritual heritage and the need to temper the pursuit of materialism with spiritual concerns.

The Explosion of Popular Culture

Popular culture in the twentieth century, especially since World War II, has played an important role in helping Western people define themselves. It also reflects the economic system that supports it, for this system manufactures, distributes, and sells the images that people consume as popular culture. Modern popular culture therefore is an integral part of the mass consumer society in which it has emerged, making it quite different from the folk culture of preceding centuries. Folk culture is something people make, while popular culture is something people buy.

POPULAR CULTURE AND THE AMERICANIZATION OF THE WORLD

The United States has been the most influential force in shaping popular culture in the West and, to a lesser degree, the entire world. Through movies, music, advertising, and television, the United States has spread its particular form of consumerism and the American Dream to millions around the world. Already in 1923 the New York *Morning Post* noted that "the film is to America what the flag was once to Britain. By its means Uncle Sam may hope some day . . . to Americanize the world."[7] In movies, television, and popular music, the impact of American popular culture on the Western world is apparent.

Motion pictures were the primary vehicle for the diffusion of American popular culture in the years immediately following the war and continued to dominate both European and American markets in the next decades. Although developed in the 1930s, television did not become readily available until the late 1940s. By 1954, there were 32 million sets in the United States, as television became the centerpiece of middle-class life. In the 1960s, as television spread around the world, American networks unloaded their products on Europe and developing countries at extraordinarily low prices. Only the establishment of quota systems prevented American television from completely inundating these countries.

The United States has also dominated popular music since the end of World War II. Jazz, blues, rhythm and blues, rap, and rock and roll have been by far the most popular music forms in the Western world—and much of the non-Western world—during this time. All of them originated in the United States, and all are rooted in African American musical innovations. These forms later spread to the rest of the world, inspiring local artists who then transformed the music in their own way.

In the postwar years, sports have become a major product of both popular culture and the leisure industry. The development of satellite television and various electronic breakthroughs helped make sports a global phenomenon. The Olympic Games could now be broadcast around the world from anyplace on earth. Sports became a cheap form of entertainment for consumers as fans did not have to leave their homes to enjoy athletic competitions. In fact, some sports organizations initially resisted television, fearing that it would hurt ticket sales. The tremendous revenues possible from television contracts overcame this hesitation, however. As sports television revenue escalated, many sports came to receive the bulk of their yearly revenue from television contracts.

Sports became big politics as well as big business. The politicization of sports has been one of the most significant trends in sports during the second half of the twentieth century. Football (soccer) remains the dominant world sport and more than ever has become a vehicle for nationalist sentiment and expression. The World Cup is the most watched event on television. Although the sport can be a positive outlet for national and local pride, all too often it has been marred by violence as nationalistic energies have overcome rational behavior.

CONCLUSION

Western Europe became a new community in the 1950s and 1960s as a remarkable economic recovery fostered a new optimism. Western European states became accustomed to political democracy, and with the development of the European Community, many of them began to move toward economic unity. But nagging economic problems, new ethnic divisions, resentment and violence toward immigrants, environmental degradation, and the inability to work together to stop a civil war in their own backyard have all indicated that what had been seen as a glorious new path for Europe in the 1950s and 1960s had become laden with pitfalls in the 1990s and the beginning of the new millennium.

In the Western Hemisphere, the two North American countries—the United States and Canada—built prosperous economies and relatively stable communities in the 1950s, but there too new problems, including ethnic, racial, and linguistic differences as well as economic difficulties, have dampened the optimism of the earlier decade. While some Latin American nations shared in the economic growth of the 1950s and 1960s, it was not matched by any real political stability. Only in the 1980s did democratic governments begin to replace oppressive military regimes with any consistency.

Western societies after 1945 were also participants in an era of rapidly changing international relationships. While Latin American countries struggled to find a new relationship with the colossus to the north, European states reluctantly let go of their colonial empires. Between 1947 and 1962, virtually every colony achieved independence and attained statehood. Although some colonial powers willingly relinquished their control, others, especially the French, had to be driven out by national wars of liberation. Decolonization was a difficult and even bitter process, but as we shall see in the next three chapters, it created a new world as the non-Western states ended the long-held ascendancy of the Western nations.

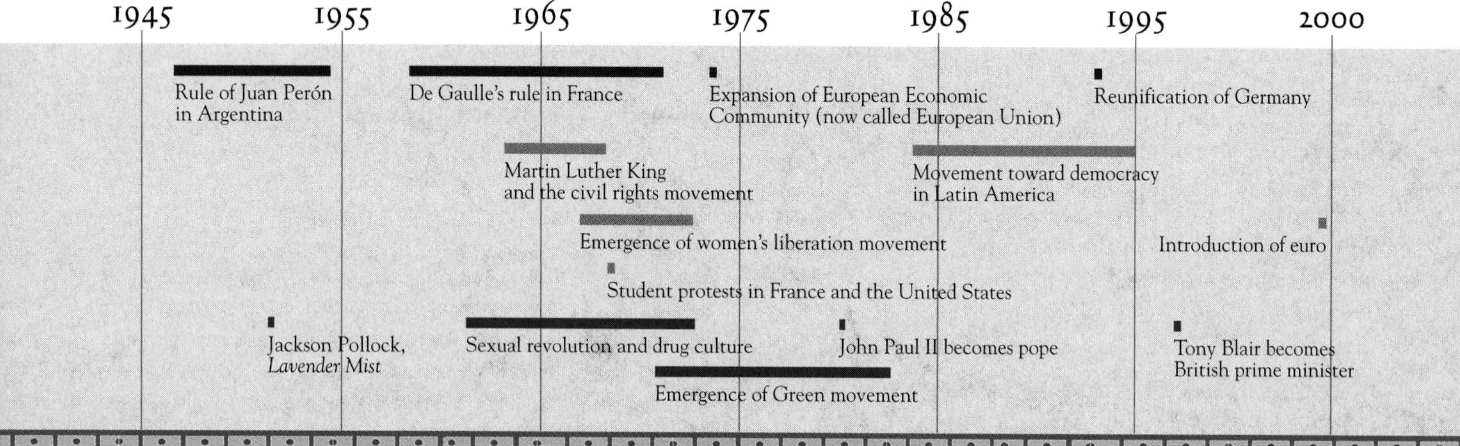

Chapter Notes

1. Dwight Eisenhower, *The White House Years: Waging Peace, 1956–1961* (Garden City, N.Y., 1965), p. 533.
2. Quoted in Hilda Scott, *Sweden's 'Right to Be Human'—Sex-Role Equality: The Goal and the Reality* (London, 1982), p. 125.
3. Quoted in Marsha Rowe et al., *Spare Rib Reader* (Harmondsworth, 1982), p. 574.
4. Betty Friedan, *The Feminine Mystique* (New York, 1963), p. 10.
5. Quoted in Renate Bridenthal, "Women in the New Europe," in Renate Bridenthal, Susan Mosher Stuard, and Merry E. Wiesner, eds., *Becoming Visible: Women in European History*, 3d ed. (Boston, 1998), pp. 564–65.
6. Quoted in Henry Grosshans, *The Search for Modern Europe* (Boston, 1970), p. 421.
7. Richard Maltby, ed., *Passing Parade: A History of Popular Culture in the Twentieth Century* (New York, 1989), p. 11.

Suggested Readings

For a general perspective on the events covered in this chapter, see T. E. Vadney, *The World Since 1945* (London, 1987). For a survey of postwar European history, see W. Laqueur, *Europe in Our Time* (New York, 1992). The rebuilding of postwar Europe is examined in A. S. Milward, *The Reconstruction of Western Europe, 1945–1951* (Berkeley, Calif., 1984), and M. Hogan, *The Marshall Plan: America, Britain, and the Reconstruction of Western Europe, 1947–1952* (New York, 1987). On the building of common institutions in Western Europe, see S. Henig, *The Uniting of Europe: From Discord to Concord* (London, 1997). For a survey of West Germany, see H. A. Turner, *Germany from Partition to Reunification* (New Haven, Conn., 1992). France under de Gaulle is examined in A. Shennan, *De Gaulle* (New York, 1993), and D. J. Mahoney, *De Gaulle: Statesmanship, Grandeur, and Modern Democracy* (Westport, Conn., 1996). On Britain, see K. O. Morgan, *The People's Peace: British History 1945–1990* (Oxford, 1992). On the recent history of these countries, see E. J. Evans, *Thatcher and Thatcherism* (New York, 1997); S. Baumann-Reynolds, *François Mitterrand* (Westport, Conn., 1995); and K. Jarausch, *The Rush to German Unity* (New York, 1994).

For a general survey of American history, see Stephan Thernstrom, *A History of the American People*, 2d ed. (San Diego, 1989). The Truman administration is covered in R. J. Donovan, *Tumultuous Years: The Presidency of Harry S Truman* (New York, 1977). On the Eisenhower years, see S. Ambrose, *Eisenhower: The President* (New York, 1984). D. J. Garrow, *Martin Luther King, Jr., and the Southern Christian Leadership Conference* (New York, 1986) discusses the emergence of the civil rights movement. On the postwar social transformations in America, see W. Nugent, *Structures of American Social History* (Bloomington, Ind., 1981). On the turbulent decade of the 1960s, see W. O'Neill, *Coming Apart: An Informal History of America in the 1960s* (Chicago, 1971). On Nixon and Watergate, see J. Anthony Lukas, *Nightmare: The Underside of the Nixon Years* (New York, 1976). Works on recent events include B. Glad, *Jimmy Carter: From Plains to the White House* (New York, 1980), and G. Wills, *Reagan's America: Innocents at Home* (New York, 1987). On recent Canadian history, see R. Bothwell, I. Drummond, and J. English, *Canada Since 1945* (Toronto, 1981).

For general surveys of Latin American history, see E. B. Burns, *Latin America: A Concise Interpretive Survey*, 4th ed. (Englewood Cliffs, N.J., 1986), and E. Williamson, *The Penguin History of Latin America* (London, 1992). The twentieth century is the focus of T. E. Skidmore and P. H. Smith, *Modern Latin America*, 3d ed. (New York, 1992). On the role of the military, see A. Rouquié, *The Military and the State in Latin America* (Berkeley, Calif., 1987). Recent United States–Latin American relations are examined in B. Wood, *The Dismantling of the Good Neighbor Policy* (Austin, Tex., 1985). Works on the countries examined in this chapter include L. A. Pérez, *Cuba: Between Reform and Revolution* (New York, 1988); B. Loveman, *Chile: The Legacy of Hispanic Capitalism*, 2d ed. (New York, 1988); J. A. Booth, *The End and the Beginning: The Nicaraguan Revolution* (Boulder, Colo., 1985); J. A. Page, *Perón: A Biography* (New York, 1983); D. Rock, *Argentina, 1516–1987: From Spanish Colonization to Alfonsín*, 2d ed. (Berkeley, Calif., 1987); E. B. Burns, *A History of Brazil*, 2d ed. (New York, 1980); R. DaMatta, *Carnivals, Rogues, and Heroes: An Interpretation of the Brazilian Dilemma* (Notre Dame, Ind., 1991); and M. C. Meyer and W. L. Sherman, *The Course of Mexican History*, 4th ed. (New York, 1991).

For a survey of contemporary Western society, see A. Sampson, *The New Europeans* (New York, 1968). The student revolts of the late 1960s are put into a broader context in D. Caute, *The Year of the Barricades: A Journey Through 1968* (New York, 1988). On the women's liberation movement, see D. Bouchier, *The Feminist Challenge: The Movement for Women's Liberation in Britain and the United States* (New York, 1983); D. Meyer, *Sex and Power: The Rise of Women in America, Russia, Sweden and Italy* (Middletown, Conn., 1987); T. Keefe, *Simone de Beauvoir* (New York, 1998); and C. Duchen, *Women's Rights and Women's Lives in France, 1944–1968* (New York, 1994). More general works that include much information on the contemporary period are B. G. Smith, *Changing Lives: Women in European History Since 1700* (Lexington, Mass., 1989), and F. Thebuad, ed., *A History of Women in the West, Vol. V: Toward a Cultural Identity in the Twentieth Century* (Cambridge, Mass., 1994). On terrorism, see W. Laqueur, *Terrorism*, 2d ed. (New York and London, 1988). The problems of guest workers and immigrants are examined in J. Miller, *Foreign Workers in Western Europe* (London, 1981). On the development of the Green parties, see M. O'Neill, *Green Parties and Political Change in Contemporary Europe* (Aldershot, 1997).

For a general view of postwar thought, see R. N. Stromberg, *European Intellectual History Since 1789*, 5th ed. (Englewood Cliffs, N.J., 1990). On contemporary art, see R. Lambert, *Cambridge Introduction to the History of Art: The Twentieth Century* (Cambridge, 1981), and the general work by B. Cole and A. Gealt, *Art of the Western World* (New York, 1989). A physicist's view of science is contained in J. Ziman, *The Force of Knowledge: The Scientific Dimension of Society* (Cambridge, 1976). The space race is examined in W. A. McDougall, *The Heavens and the Earth: A Political History of the Space Age* (New York, 1984). There is an excellent survey of twentieth-century popular culture in R. Maltby, ed., *Passing Parade: A History of Popular Culture in the Twentieth Century* (New York, 1989).

For additional reading, go to InfoTrac College Edition, your online research library at http://web1.infotrac-college.com

Enter the search terms "Single European Market" using the Subject Guide.

Enter the search terms "Europe Communism" using Keywords.

Enter the search terms "Green Parties" using Keywords.

Enter the search terms "Germany reunification" using Keywords.

Enter the search term "feminism" using the Subject Guide.

CHAPTER 30

CHALLENGES OF NATION BUILDING IN AFRICA AND THE MIDDLE EAST

CHAPTER OUTLINE

- UHURU: THE STRUGGLE FOR INDEPENDENCE
- THE ERA OF INDEPENDENCE
- CONTINUITY AND CHANGE IN MODERN AFRICAN SOCIETIES
- GATHERED AT THE BEACH
- CRESCENT OF CONFLICT
- POLITICS IN THE CONTEMPORARY MIDDLE EAST
- CONTEMPORARY LITERATURE AND ART IN THE MIDDLE EAST
- CONCLUSION

FOCUS QUESTIONS

- What impact did colonialism have on Africa and the Middle East, and how does its legacy continue to affect developments in these areas?
- What role has nationalism played in Africa and the Middle East since World War II, and how have other forces in each area exerted counteracting effects?
- How have dreams clashed with realities in the independent nations of Africa, and how have the resulting tensions affected African culture?
- How has the role of women changed in African and Middle Eastern society since 1945?
- What political and economic problems have Middle Eastern nations faced since 1945, and how have they attempted to solve these problems?

At the end of World War II, Africa had already been exposed to over half a century of colonial rule. Although many Europeans complacently assumed that colonialism was a necessary evil in the process of introducing civilization to the backward peoples of Africa and Asia, not all agreed. To some African intellectuals, the Western drive for economic profit and political hegemony was a plague that threatened ultimately to destroy civilization. It was the obligation of Africans to use their own humanistic and spiritual qualities to help save the human race. The Ghanaian official Michael Francis Dei-Anang agreed. In *Whither Bound Africa,* written in 1946, he scathingly unmasked the pretensions of Western superiority:

Forward! To What?
The Slums, where man is dumped upon man,
Where penury
And misery
Have made their hapless homes,
And all is dark and drear?
Forward! To what?
The factory
To grind hard hours
In an inhuman mill,
In one long ceaseless spell?

Forward! To what?
To the reeking round
Of medieval crimes,
Where the greedy hawks
of Aryan stock
Prey with bombs and guns
On men of lesser breed?
Forward to CIVILIZATION.[1]

To Africans like Dei-Anang, the new Africa that emerged from imperialist rule had a duty to seek new ways of resolving the problems of humanity.

In the three decades following the end of World War II, the peoples of Africa were gradually liberated from the formal trappings of European colonialism. The creation of independent states in Africa began in the late 1950s and proceeded gradually over the next thirty years, until the last colonial regimes were finally dismantled. But the transition to independence has not been an unalloyed success. The legacy of colonialism in the form of political inexperience and continued European economic domination has combined with overpopulation and climatic disasters to frustrate the new states' ability to achieve political stability and economic prosperity. At the same time, arbitrary boundaries imposed by the colonial powers and ethnic and religious divisions within the African countries have led to bitter conflicts, which have posed a severe obstacle to the dream of continental solidarity and cooperation in forging a common destiny. Today, the continent of Africa, although blessed with enormous potential, is one of the most volatile and conflict-ridden areas of the world. Michael Dei-Anang's dream has not yet been realized.

Uhuru: The Struggle for Independence

After World War II, Europeans reluctantly recognized that the end result of colonial rule in Africa would be African self-government, if not full independence. Accordingly, the African population would have to be trained to handle the responsibilities of representative government. In many cases, however, relatively little had been done to prepare the local population for self-rule. Early in the colonial era, during the late nineteenth century, African administrators had held influential positions in several British colonies, and one even served as governor of the Gold Coast. But with the formal institution of colonial rule, senior positions were reserved for the British, although local authority remained in the hands of native rulers.

After World War II, most British colonies introduced reforms that increased the representation of the local population. Members of legislative and executive councils were increasingly chosen through elections, and Africans came to constitute a majority of these bodies. Elected councils at the local level were introduced in the 1950s to reduce the power of the tribal chiefs and clan heads, who had controlled local government under indirect rule. An exception was South Africa, where European domination continued. In the Union of South Africa, the franchise was restricted to whites except in the former territory of the Cape Colony, where persons of mixed ancestry had enjoyed the right to vote since the mid-nineteenth century. Black Africans did win some limited electoral rights in Northern and Southern Rhodesia (now Zambia and Zimbabwe), although whites generally dominated the political scene.

A similar process of political liberalization was taking place in the French colonies. At first, as we have seen, the French tried to assimilate the African peoples into French culture. By the 1920s, however, racist beliefs in Western cultural superiority and the tenacity of traditional beliefs and practices among Africans had somewhat discredited this ideal. The French therefore substituted a more limited program of assimilating African elites into Western culture and using them as administrators at the local level as a link to the remainder of the population.

The Colonial Legacy

As in Asia, colonial rule had a mixed impact on the societies and peoples of Africa. The Western presence brought a number of short-term and long-term benefits to Africa, such as improved transportation and communication facilities, and in a few areas laid the foundation for a modern industrial and commercial sector. Improved sanitation and medical care in all probability increased life expectancy. The introduction of selective elements of Western political systems laid the basis for the gradual creation of democratic societies.

Yet the benefits of Westernization were distributed highly unequally, and the vast majority of Africans found their lives little improved, if at all. Only South Africa and French-held Algeria, for example, developed modern industrial sectors, extensive railroad networks, and modern communications systems. In both countries, European settlers were numerous, most investment capital for industrial ventures was European, and whites comprised almost the entire professional and managerial class. Members of the native population were generally restricted to unskilled or semiskilled jobs at wages less than one-fifth of those enjoyed by Europeans.

Many colonies concentrated on export crops—peanuts from Senegal and Gambia, cotton from Egypt and Uganda, coffee from Kenya, and palm oil and cocoa products from the Gold Coast. Here the benefits of development were somewhat more widespread. In some cases, the crops were grown on plantations, which were usually owned by Europeans. But plantation agriculture was not always suitable in Africa, and much farming was done by free or tenant farmers. In some areas, where land ownership was traditionally vested in the community, the land was owned and leased by the corporate village. The vast majority of the profits from the exports, however, accrued to Europeans or to merchants from other foreign countries, such as India and the Arab emirates. While a fortunate few benefited from the increase in exports, the vast majority of Africans continued to be subsistence farmers growing food for their own consumption. The gap was particularly wide in places like Kenya, where the best lands had been reserved for European settlers to make the colony self-sufficient. As in other parts of the world, the early stages of the Industrial Revolution were especially painful for the rural population, and ordinary subsistence farmers reaped few benefits from colonial rule.

The Rise of Nationalism

Political organizations for African rights did not arise until after World War I, and then only in a few areas, such as British-ruled Kenya and the Gold Coast. At first, organizations such as the National Congress of British West Africa (formed in 1919 in the Gold Coast) and Jomo Kenyatta's Kikuyu Central Association focused on improving living conditions in the colonies rather than on national independence. After World War II, however, following the example of independence movements elsewhere, these groups became organized political parties with independence as their objective. In the Gold Coast, Kwame Nkrumah (1909–1972) led the Convention People's Party, the first formal political party in black Africa. In the late 1940s, Jomo Kenyatta (1894–1978) founded the Kenya African National Union (KANU), which focused on economic issues but had an implied political agenda as well.

For the most part, these political activities were basically nonviolent and were led by Western-educated African intellectuals. Their constituents were primarily urban professionals, merchants, and members of labor unions. But the demand for independence was not entirely restricted to the cities. In Kenya, for example, the widely publicized Mau Mau movement among the Kikuyu people used terrorism as an essential element of its program to achieve *uhuru* (Swahili for "freedom") from the British. Although most of the violence was directed against other Africans—only about 100 Europeans were killed in the violence, compared with an estimated 1,700 Africans who lost their lives at the hands of the rebels—the specter of Mau Mau terrorism alarmed the European population and convinced the British government in 1959 to promise eventual independence.

A similar process was occurring in Egypt, which had been a protectorate of Great Britain (and under loose Turkish suzerainty until the breakup of the Ottoman Empire) since the 1880s. National consciousness had existed in Egypt since well before the colonial takeover, and members of the legislative council were calling for independence even before World War I. In 1918, a formal political party called the Wafd was formed to promote Egyptian independence. The intellectuals were opposed as much to the local palace government as to the British, however, and in 1952 an army coup overthrew King Farouk, the grandson of Khedive Ismail, and established an independent republic.

In areas such as South Africa and Algeria, where the political system was dominated by European settlers, the transition to independence was more complicated. In South Africa, political activity by local Africans began with the formation of the African National Congress (ANC) in 1912. Initially, the ANC was dominated by Western-oriented intellectuals and had little mass support. Its goal was to achieve economic and political reforms, including full equality for educated Africans, within the framework of the existing system. But the ANC's efforts met with little success, while conservative white parties managed to stiffen the segregation laws. In response, the ANC became increasingly radicalized, and by the 1950s, the prospects for a violent confrontation were growing.

In Algeria, resistance to French rule by Berbers and Arabs in rural areas had never ceased. After World War II, urban agitation intensified, leading to a widespread rebellion against colonial rule in the mid-1950s. At first, the French government tried to maintain its authority in Algeria, which was considered an integral part of metropolitan France. But when Charles de Gaulle became president in 1958, he reversed French policy, and Algeria became independent under President Ahmad Ben Bella

MAP 30.1 Modern Africa

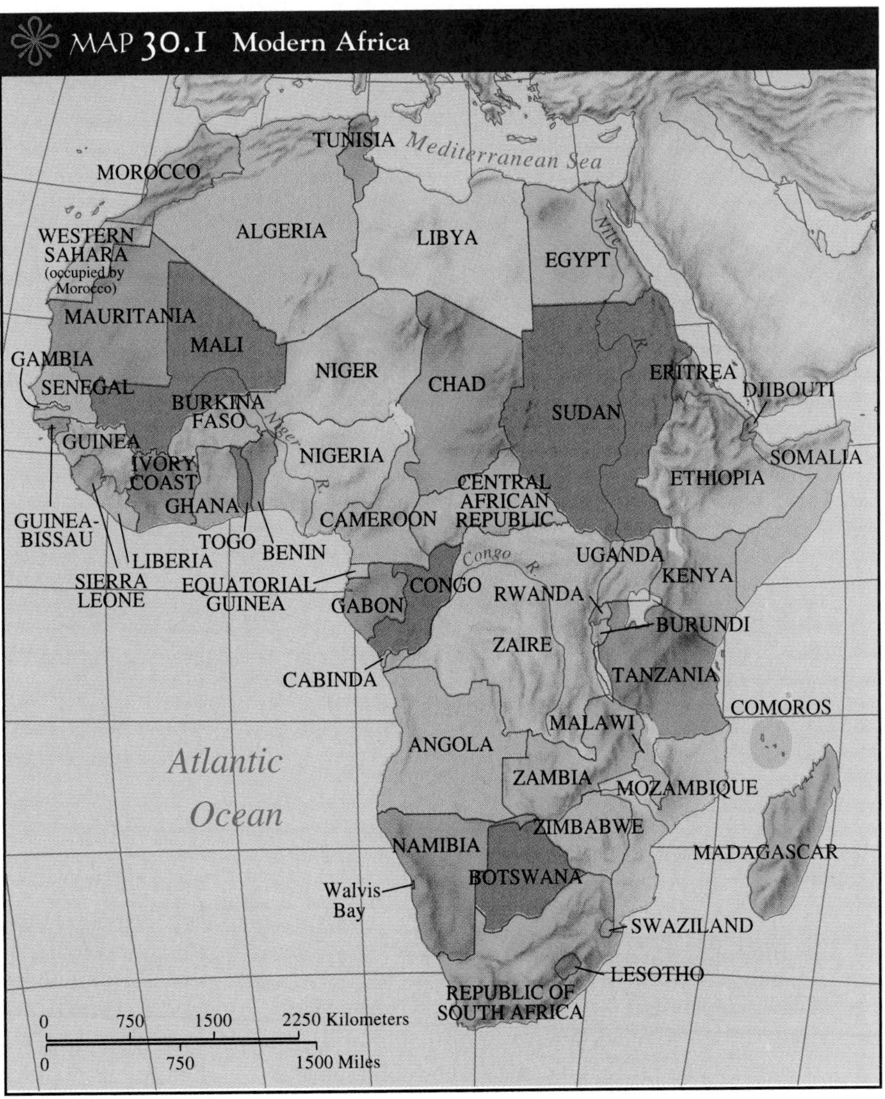

(b. 1918) in 1962. The armed struggle in Algeria hastened the transition to statehood in its neighbors as well. Tunisia won its independence in 1956 after some urban agitation and rural unrest, but retained close ties with Paris. The French attempted to suppress the nationalist movement in Morocco by sending Sultan Muhammad V into exile, but the effort failed, and in 1956 he returned as the ruler of the independent state of Morocco.

Most black African nations achieved their independence in the late 1950s and 1960s, beginning with the Gold Coast, now renamed Ghana, in 1957. Nigeria, the Belgian Congo (renamed Zaire), Kenya, Tanganyika (later, when joined with Zanzibar, renamed Tanzania), and several other countries soon followed. Most of the French colonies agreed to accept independence within the framework of de Gaulle's French Community. By the late 1960s, only parts of southern Africa and the Portuguese possessions of Mozambique and Angola remained under European rule.

Independence came later to Africa than to most of Asia. Several factors help explain the delay. For one thing, colonialism was established in Africa somewhat later than in most areas of Asia, and the inevitable reaction from the local population was consequently delayed. Furthermore, with the exception of a few areas in West Africa and along the Mediterranean, coherent states with a strong sense of cultural, ethnic, and linguistic unity did not exist in most of Africa. Most traditional states, such as Ashanti in West Africa, Songhai in the southern Sahara, and Bakongo in the Congo Basin, were collections of heterogeneous peoples with little sense of national or cultural identity. Even after colonies were established, the European powers often practiced a policy of "divide and rule," while the British encouraged political decentralization by retaining the authority of the traditional native chieftains. It is hardly surprising that when opposition to colonial rule emerged, unity was difficult to achieve.

TOWARD AFRICAN UNITY

In May 1963, the leaders of thirty-two African states met in Addis Ababa, the capital of Ethiopia, to discuss the creation of an organization that would represent the interests of all the newly independent countries of Africa. The result was the Organization of African Unity. An excerpt from its charter is presented here. Although the organization has by no means realized all of the aspirations of its founders, it provides a useful forum for the discussion and resolution of its members' common problems.

THE CHARTER OF THE ORGANIZATION OF AFRICAN UNITY

We, the Heads of African States and Governments assembled in the City of Addis Ababa, Ethiopia;
CONVINCED that it is the inalienable right of all people to control their own destiny;
CONSCIOUS of the fact that freedom, equality, justice, and dignity are essential objectives for the achievement of the legitimate aspirations of the African peoples;
CONSCIOUS of our responsibility to harness the natural and human resources of our continent for the total advancement of our peoples in spheres of human endeavor;
INSPIRED by a common determination to promote understanding among our peoples and cooperation among our States in response to the aspirations of our peoples for brotherhood and solidarity, in a larger unity transcending ethnic and national differences;
CONVINCED that, in order to translate this determination into a dynamic force in the cause of human progress, conditions for peace and security must be established and maintained;
DETERMINED to safeguard and consolidate the hard-won independence as well as the sovereignty and territorial integrity of our States, and to fight against neocolonialism in all its forms;
DEDICATED to the general progress of Africa; . . .
DESIROUS that all African States should henceforth unite so that the welfare and well-being of their peoples can be assured;
RESOLVED to reinforce the links between our states by establishing and strengthening common institutions;
HAVE agreed to the present Charter.

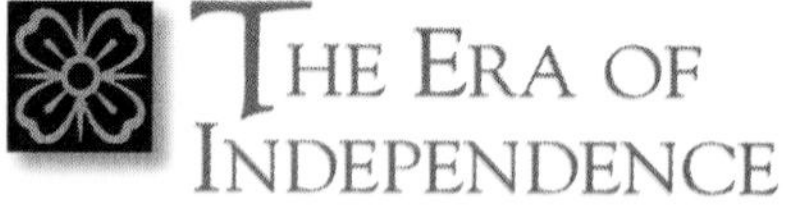

THE ERA OF INDEPENDENCE

The newly independent African states faced intimidating challenges. Like the new states in South and Southeast Asia, they had been profoundly affected by colonial rule. Yet the experience had been highly unsatisfactory in most respects. Although Western political institutions, values, and technology had been introduced, at least into the cities, the exposure to European civilization had been superficial at best for most Africans and tragic for many. At the outset of independence, most African societies were still primarily agrarian and traditional, and their modern sectors depended mainly on imports from the West.

Pan-Africanism and Nationalism: The Destiny of Africa

Like the leaders of the new states in South and Southeast Asia, most African leaders came from the urban middle class. They had studied in either Europe or the United States and spoke and read European languages. Although most were profoundly critical of colonial policies, they appeared to accept the relevance of the Western model to Africa and gave at least lip service to Western democratic values.

Their views on economics were somewhat more diverse. Some, like Jomo Kenyatta of Kenya and General Mobutu Sese Seko (1930–1998) of Zaire (previously the Belgian Congo), were advocates of Western-style capitalism. Others, like Julius Nyerere (b. 1922) of Tanzania, Kwame Nkrumah of Ghana, and Sékou Touré (1922–1984) of Guinea, preferred an "African form of socialism," which bore slight resemblance to the Marxist-Leninist socialism practiced in the Soviet Union. According to its advocates, it was descended from traditional communal practices in precolonial Africa.

Like the leaders of other developing countries, the new political leaders in Africa were highly nationalistic and generally accepted the colonial boundaries. But, as we have seen, these boundaries were artificial creations of the colonial powers. Virtually all of the new states included widely diverse ethnic, linguistic, and territorial groups. Zaire, for example, was composed of more than 200 different territorial groups speaking seventy-five different languages.

A number of leaders—including Nkrumah of Ghana, Touré of Guinea, and Kenyatta of Kenya—were enticed by the dream of pan-Africanism, a concept of continental unity that transcended national boundaries. Nkrumah in particular hoped that a pan-African union could be established that would unite all of the new countries of the continent in a broader community. His dream achieved concrete manifestation in the Organization of African Unity (OAU), which was founded in Addis Ababa in 1963 (see the box above).

Pan-Africanism originated among African intellectuals during the first half of the twentieth century. A basic element was the belief in negritude (blackness)—the conviction that there was a distinctive "African personality" that owed nothing to Western materialism and provided a common sense of destiny for all black African peoples. According to Aimé Césaire, a West Indian of African descent and a leading ideologist of the movement, whereas Western civilization prized rational thought and material achievement, African culture emphasized emotional expression and a common sense of humanity.

The concept of negritude was in part a natural defensive response to the social Darwinist concepts of Western racial superiority and African inferiority that were popular in Europe and the United States during the early years of the twentieth century. At the same time, it was stimulated by growing self-doubt among many European intellectuals after World War I, who feared that Western civilization was on a path of self-destruction.

Negritude had more appeal to Africans from French colonies than to those from British possessions. Yet it also found adherents in the British colonies, as well as in the United States and elsewhere in the Americas. African American intellectuals such as W. E. B. Dubois and the West Indian politician Marcus Garvey attempted to promote a "black renaissance" by popularizing the idea of a distinct African personality.

Dream and Reality: Political and Economic Conditions in Contemporary Africa

The program of the OAU called for an Africa based on freedom, equality, justice, and dignity, and on the unity, solidarity, and territorial integrity of African states. It did not take long for reality to set in. Vast disparities in education and income made it hard to establish democracy in much of Africa. Expectations that independence would lead to stable political structures based on "one person, one vote" were soon disappointed, as the initial phase of pluralistic governments gave way to a series of military regimes and one-party states. Between 1957 and 1982, more than seventy leaders of African countries were overthrown by violence, and in recent years, the pace has increased.

Hopes that independence would inaugurate an era of economic prosperity and equality were similarly dashed. Part of the problem could be (and was) ascribed to the lingering effects of colonialism. Most newly independent countries in Africa were dependent on the export of a single crop or natural resource. When prices fluctuated or dropped, these countries were at the mercy of the vagaries of the international market. In several cases, the resources were still controlled by foreigners, leading to the charge that colonialism had been succeeded by "neocolonialism," in which Western domination was maintained by economic rather than by political or military means. To make matters worse, most African states had to import technology and manufactured goods from the West, and the prices of those goods rose more rapidly than those of the export products.

The new states also contributed to their own problems. Scarce national resources were squandered on military equipment or expensive consumer goods rather than on building up their infrastructure to provide the foundation for an industrial economy. Corruption, a painful reality throughout the modern world, became almost a way of life in Africa, as bribery became necessary to obtain even the most basic services (see the box on p. 916).

Finally, population growth, which more than anything else has hindered economic growth in the new nations of Asia and Africa, became a serious problem and crippled efforts to create modern economies. By the mid-1980s, annual population growth averaged nearly 3 percent throughout Africa, the highest rate of any continent. Drought conditions and the inexorable spread of the Sahara (usually known as desertification, a condition caused partly by overcultivation of the land) have led to widespread hunger and starvation, first in West African countries such as Niger and Mali and then in Ethiopia, Somalia, and the Sudan.

In recent years, the spread of HIV and AIDS in Africa has reached epidemic proportions. According to one estimate, one-third of the entire population of sub-Saharan Africa is infected with the HIV virus, including a high percentage of the urban middle class. Some observers estimate that without measures to curtail the effects of the

MANIOC, FOOD FOR THE MILLIONS. Manioc, a tuber like the potato, was brought to Africa from the New World as a part of the Columbian exchange discussed in Part III. Although low in nutrient value, it can be cultivated in poor soil with little moisture, and is reportedly the staple food for nearly one-third of the population of sub-Saharan Africa. Manioc is also widely grown in tropical parts of Asia and is familiar to Westerners as the source of tapioca. In the illustration shown here, village women in Senegal rhythmically pound the manioc root to the chanting of those standing nearby.

STEALING THE NATION'S RICHES

After 1965, African novelists transferred their anger from the foreign oppressor to their own national leaders, deploring their greed, corruption, and inhumanity. One of the most pessimistic expressions of this betrayal of newly independent Africa is found in The Beautiful Ones Are Not Yet Born, *a novel published by the Ghanaian author Ayi Kwei Armah in 1968. The author decried the government of Kwame Nkrumah and was unimpressed with the rumors of a military coup, which, he predicted, would simply replace the present regime with a new despot and his entourage of "fat men."*

AYI KWEI ARMAH, *THE BEAUTIFUL ONES ARE NOT YET BORN*

The net had been made in the special Ghanaian way that allowed the really big corrupt people to pass through it. A net to catch only the small, dispensable fellows, trying in their anguished blindness to leap and to attain the gleam and the comfort the only way these things could be done. And the big ones floated free, like all the slogans. End bribery and corruption. Build Socialism. Equality. Shit. A man would just have to make up his mind that there was never going to be anything but despair, and there would be no way of escaping it. . . .

In the life of the nation itself, maybe nothing really new would happen. New men would take into their hands the power to steal the nation's riches and to use it for their own satisfaction. That, of course, was to be expected. New people would use the country's power to get rid of men and women who talked a language that did not flatter them. There would be nothing different in that. That would only be a continuation of the Ghanaian way of life. But here was the real change. The individual man of power now shivering, his head filled with the fear of the vengeance of those he had wronged. For him everything was going to change. And for those like him who had grown greasy and fat singing the praises of their chief, for those who had been getting themselves ready for the enjoyment of hoped-for favors, there would be long days of pain ahead. The flatterers with their new white Mercedes cars would have to find ways of burying old words. For those who had come directly against the old power, there would be much happiness. But for the nation itself there would only be a change of embezzlers and a change of the hunters and the hunted. A pitiful shrinking of the world from those days Teacher still looked back to, when the single mind was filled with the hopes of a whole people. A pitiful shrinking, to days when all the powerful could think of was to use the power of a whole people to fill their own paunches. Endless days, same days, stretching into the future with no end anywhere in sight.

disease, it will have a significant impact on several African countries by reducing population growth, which is presently predicted to increase throughout the continent by at least 300 million in the next fifteen years.

Poverty is endemic in Africa, particularly among the three-quarters of the population still living off the land. Urban areas have grown tremendously, but as in much of Asia, most are surrounded by massive squatter settlements of rural peoples who had fled to the cities in search of a better life. The expansion of the cities has overwhelmed fragile transportation and sanitation systems and led to rising pollution and perpetual traffic jams, while millions are forced to live without running water and electricity. Meanwhile, the fortunate few (all too often government officials on the take) live the high life and emulate the consumerism of the West (in a particularly expressive phrase, the rich in many East African countries are known as *wabenzi*, or Mercedes-Benz people).

In "Pedestrian, to Passing Benz-Man," the Kenyan poet Albert Ojuka voiced the popular discontent with economic inequality:

You man, lifted gently
out of the poverty and suffering
we so recently shared; I say—
why splash the muddy puddle on to
my bare legs, as if, still unsatisfied
with your seated opulence
you must sully the unwashed
with your diesel-smoke and mud-water
and force him to buy, beyond his means
a bar of soap from your shop?
a few years back we shared a master
today you have none, while I have
exchanged a parasite for something worse.
But maybe a few years is too long a time.[2]

It is a lament still voiced today.

THE SEARCH FOR SOLUTIONS

Concern over the dangers of economic inequality inspired a number of African leaders—including Nkrumah in Ghana, Nyerere in Tanzania, and Samora Michel of Mozambique—to restrict foreign investment and nationalize the major industries and utilities while promoting social ideals and values. Nyerere was the most consistent, promoting the ideals of socialism and self-reliance through his Arusha Declaration of 1967 (see the box on p. 918). Taking advantage of his powerful political influence, Nyerere placed limitations on income and established village collectives to avoid the corrosive effects of economic inequality and government corruption. Sympathetic foreign countries provided considerable economic aid to assist the experiment, and many observers noted that levels of corruption, political instability, and ethnic strife were lower in Tanzania than in many other African countries. Unfortunately, corruption has increased in recent years, while political elements on the island of Zanzibar, citing the stagnation brought by two decades of socialism, are agitating for autonomy or even total separation from the mainland. Tanzania also has poor soil, inadequate rainfall, and limited resources, all of which have contributed to its slow growth and continuing rural and urban poverty.

In 1985, Julius Nyerere voluntarily retired from the presidency. In his farewell speech, he confessed that he had failed to achieve many of his ambitious goals to create a socialist society in Africa. In particular, he admitted that his plan to collectivize the traditional private farm (*shamba*) had run into strong resistance from conservative peasants. "You can socialize what is not traditional," he remarked. "The *shamba* can't be socialized." But Nyerere insisted that many of his policies had succeeded in improving social and economic conditions, and he argued that the only real solution was to consolidate the multitude of small countries in the region into a larger East African Federation.[3]

The countries that opted for capitalism faced their own dilemmas. Neighboring Kenya, blessed with better soil in the highlands, a local tradition of aggressive commerce, and a residue of European settlers, welcomed foreign investment and profit incentives. The results have been mixed. Kenya has a strong current of indigenous African capitalism and a substantial middle class, mostly based in the capital, Nairobi. But landlessness, unemployment, and income inequities are high, even by African standards, and the rate of population growth—more than 4 percent annually—is one of the highest in the world. Eighty percent of the population remains rural, and 40 percent live below the poverty line. The result has been widespread unrest in a country formerly admired for its successful development.

Beginning in the mid-1970s, a few African nations decided to adopt Soviet-style Marxism-Leninism. In Angola and Ethiopia, Marxist parties followed the Soviet model and attempted to create fully socialist societies with the assistance of Soviet experts and Cuban troops and advisers. Economically, the results were disappointing, and both countries faced severe internal opposition. In Ethiopia, the revolt by Muslim tribal peoples in the province of Eritrea led to the fall of the Marxist leader Mengistu and his regime in 1990. A similar revolt erupted against the government in Angola, with the rebel group UNITA controlling much of the rural population and for a time threatening the capital city, Luanda.

CATCHING THE WIND. For centuries, seafarers in the Indian Ocean have used the triangular lateen sail as a means of catching the steady monsoon winds that blow alternatively from east and west in the winter and summer seasons. That type of rigging is still common for ships in the area, as this small craft in the waters off the East African island of Zanzibar demonstrates.

SOCIALISM IS NOT RACIALISM

At Arusha, Tanzania, in 1967, Julius Nyerere, the president of Tanzania, set forth the principles for building a socialist society. Nyerere made it clear that he was talking about an African style of socialism, which would put ownership of his country's wealth into the hands of the people rather than into the hands of foreign capitalists. Since then, Tanzania has taken a socialist approach to economic development. The results have been mixed: the country is not wealthy, but there are few extremes of rich and poor.

JULIUS NYERERE, THE ARUSHA DECLARATION

The Arusha Declaration and the actions relating to public ownership were all concerned with ensuring that we can build socialism in our country. The nationalization and the taking of a controlling interest in many firms were a necessary part of our determination to organize our society in such a way that our efforts benefit all our people and that there is no exploitation of one man by another.

Yet these actions do not in themselves create socialism. . . . The basis of socialism is a belief in the oneness of man and the common historical destiny of mankind. Its basis, in other words, is human equality.

Acceptance of this principle is absolutely fundamental to socialism. The justification of socialism is Man—not the State, not the flag. Socialism is not for the benefit of black men, nor brown men, nor white men, nor yellow men. The purpose of socialism is the service of man, regardless of color, size, shape, skill, ability, or anything else. . . .

Socialism has nothing to do with race, nor with country of origin. In fact any intelligent man, whether he is a socialist or not, realizes that there are socialists in capitalist countries—and from capitalist countries. Very often such socialists come to work in newly independent and avowedly socialist countries like Tanzania because they are frustrated in their capitalist homeland. . . .

Neither is it sensible for a socialist to talk as if all capitalists are devils. It is one thing to dislike the capitalist system and to try and frustrate people's capitalist desires. But it would be as stupid for us to assume that capitalists have horns as it is for people in Western Europe to assume that we in Tanzania have become devils.

In fact the leaders in the capitalist countries have now begun to realize that communists are human beings like themselves—that they are not devils. . . . It would be very absurd if we react to the stupidity they are growing out of and become equally stupid ourselves in the opposite direction! We have to recognize in our words and our actions that capitalists are human beings as much as socialists. They may be wrong; indeed by dedicating ourselves to socialism we are saying that they are. But our task is to make it impossible for capitalism to dominate us.

THE SEARCH FOR COMMUNITY

Finally, Africans have been disappointed that the dream of a united Africa has not been realized. No one skewered the pretensions of the apostles of negritude better than the Ugandan poet Taban Lo Liyong. In his poem "Negritude Is Crying over Spilt Milk," he observed:

Strange mules called Negritude
and African Personality
Overran the terrain
And kicked wisdom down
Or above our heads.

Politicians quite unaware
How low we are
On the ladder universal
Decided to halt the race
And embrace the niches sure
Where we were stuck for the moment.[4]

But while some criticize the tendency to pursue what Taban called the "vanishing exotica" of the past, most Africans feel a shared sense of continuing victimization at the hands of the West and are convinced that independence has not ended Western interference in and domination of African affairs. Many African leaders were angered when Western powers led by the United States conspired to overthrow the radical Congolese politician Patrice Lumumba in Zaire in the early 1960s. The episode reinforced their desire to form the OAU as a means of reducing Western influence. But aside from agreeing to adopt a neutral stance during the Cold War, African states have had difficulty achieving a united position on many issues, and their disagreements have left the region vulnerable to external influence and even led to conflict. During the late 1980s and early 1990s, border disputes festered in many areas of the continent and in some cases—as with Morocco and a rebel movement in the western Sahara, and between Kenya and Uganda—flared into outright war.

Even within many African nations, the concept of nationhood has been undermined by the renascent force of regionalism or tribalism. Nigeria, with the largest population on the continent, was rent by civil strife during the late 1960s, when dissident Ibo groups in the southeast attempted unsuccessfully to form an independent state of Biafra. Ethnic conflicts broke out among hostile territorial groups in Zimbabwe (the new name for Southern Rhodesia) and in several nations in Central Africa.

Another force undermining nationalism in Africa has been pan-Islamism. Its prime exponent in Africa was the Egyptian president Gamal Abdul Nasser. After Nasser's death in 1970, the torch of Islamic unity in Africa was carried by the Libyan president Muammar Qadhafi, whose ambitions to create a greater Muslim nation in the Sahara under his authority led to conflict with neighboring Chad. The Islamic resurgence also surfaced in Ethiopia, where Muslim tribespeople in Eritrea rebelled against the Marxist regime of Colonel Mengistu in Addis Ababa.

RECENT TRENDS

Not all the news in Africa has been bad. In recent years, popular demonstrations, fueled by stagnant economies, have led to the collapse of one-party regimes and the emergence of fragile democracies in several countries. Dictatorships were brought to an end in Ethiopia, Liberia, and Somalia, although in each case the fall of the regime was later followed by political instability or, in the latter two instances, by a bloody civil war. Perhaps the most notorious case was that of Idi Amin of Uganda. Colonel Amin led a coup against Prime Minister Milton Obote in 1971. After ruling by terror and brutal repression of dissident elements, he was finally deposed in 1979. In recent years, stability has returned to the country, which in May 1996 had its first presidential election in more than fifteen years. In Eritrea, a popular Islamic government is gradually rebuilding the country and planning for the creation of a parliamentary system.

Africa has also benefited from the end of the Cold War, as the superpowers have virtually ceased to compete for power and influence in Africa. When the Soviet Union withdrew its support from the Marxist government in Ethiopia, the United States allowed its right to maintain military bases in neighboring Somalia to lapse, resulting in the overthrow of the authoritarian government there. Unfortunately, clan rivalries led to such turbulence that many inhabitants were in imminent danger of starvation, and in the winter of 1992, U.S. military forces occupied the country in an effort to provide food to the starving population. Since the departure of foreign troops in 1993, the country has been divided into clan fiefdoms, while Islamic groups attempt to bring a return to law and order.

Perhaps Africa's greatest success story is in South Africa, where the white government—which long maintained a policy of racial segregation (apartheid) and restricted black sovereignty to a series of small "Bantustans" in relatively infertile areas of the country—finally accepted the inevitability of African involvement in the political process and the national economy. In 1990, the government of President F. W. de Klerk (b. 1936) released ANC leader Nelson Mandela (b. 1918) from prison, where he had been held since 1964. In 1993, the two leaders agreed to hold democratic national elections the following spring. In the meantime, ANC representatives agreed to take part in a transitional coalition government with de Klerk's National Party. Those elections resulted in a substantial majority for the ANC, and Mandela became president.

In May 1996, a new constitution was approved, calling for a multiracial state. The National Party immediately went into opposition, claiming that the new charter did not adequately provide for joint decision making by members of the coalition. The third group in the coalition government, the Zulu-based Inkatha Freedom Party, agreed to remain within the government, but rivalry between the ANC and Zulu elites intensified. Zulu chief Mangosuthu Buthelezi, drawing on the growing force of Zulu nationalism, has begun to invoke the memory of the great nineteenth-century Zulu ruler Shaka in a possible bid at future independence. Although many Zulus currently support the ANC, the future of a multiracial society in the Republic of South Africa remains in doubt. With all its problems, however, South Africa remains the wealthiest and most industrialized state on the continent. In 1999, a major step toward political stability was taken when Nelson Mandela stepped down from the presidency, to be replaced by his long-time disciple Thabo Mbeki.

If the situation in South Africa provides grounds for modest optimism, until recently the situation in Nigeria provided reason for serious concern. Africa's largest country in terms of population, and one of its wealthiest because of substantial oil reserves, Nigeria had for many years been in the grip of military rulers. During his rule, General Sani Abacha ruthlessly suppressed all opposition and in late 1995 ordered the execution of author Ken Saro-Wiwa despite widespread protests from human rights groups abroad. Saro-Wiwa had vocally criticized environmental damage caused by foreign interests in southern Nigeria, but the regime's major concern was his support for separatist activities in an area that had previously launched the Biafran insurrection in the late 1960s. After Abacha's death in 1998, however, his successor, General Abdulsalam Abubakr, called for national elections, which led to the creation of a civilian government under Olusegun of Obasanjo. Civilian leadership has not been a panacea for all of Nigeria's problems, however. In early 2000, religious riots between Christians and Muslims broke out in several northern cities as a result of the decision by provincial officials to apply Islamic law throughout their jurisdictions. President Obasanjo has attempted to defuse the unrest by calling for a delay in carrying out the decision, but the issue raises tensions between Christian peoples in the southern parts of the country and the primarily Islamic north.

Currently, the most tragic situation is in the central African states of Rwanda and Burundi, where a chronic conflict between the minority Tutsis and the Hutu majority has led to a bitter civil war, with thousands of refugees fleeing to neighboring Zaire. In a classic example of conflict between pastoral and farming peoples, the nomadic

CHRONOLOGY

MODERN AFRICA

Statehood for Ghana	1957
Algeria receives independence from France	1962
Formation of the Organization for African Unity	1963
Zimbabwe receives its independence	1980
Release of ANC chairman Nelson Mandela from prison	1990
United States sends troops to Somalia	1992
Nelson Mandela elected president of South Africa	1994
Civil War in Central Africa	1996–2000
Olusegun Obasanjo elected president of Nigeria	1999

Tutsis had long dominated the sedentary Hutu population. It was the attempt of the Bantu-speaking Hutus to bring an end to Tutsi domination that initiated the recent conflict, marked by massacres on both sides. In the meantime, the presence of large numbers of foreign troops and refugees intensified centrifugal forces inside Zaire, where General Mobutu Sese Seko had long ruled with an iron hand. In 1997, military forces led by Mobutu's longtime opponent Lauren Kabila managed to topple the general's corrupt government. Once in power, Kabila renamed the country the Democratic Republic of the Congo and promised a return to democratic practices. Outside observers, however, have charged that the rebels committed numerous atrocities en route to power, and that the new government is systematically suppressing political dissent.

It is clear that African societies have not yet begun to surmount the challenges they have faced since independence. Most African states are still poor and their populations illiterate. But as Tanzania's former president Julius Nyerere and the Nigerian author Wole Soyinka have pointed out, a significant part of the problem is related to the current inapplicability of the nation-state system to the African continent. Africans must find better ways to cooperate with each other and to protect and promote their own interests. A first step in that direction was taken in 1991, when the OAU agreed to establish a new African Economic Community (AEC). More recently, West African states have set up a peacekeeping force to monitor the fragile cease-fire in Liberia.

As Africa evolves, it is useful to remember that economic and political change is often an agonizingly slow and painful process. Introduced to industrialization and concepts of Western democracy only a century ago, African societies are still groping for ways to graft Western political institutions and economic practices onto a native structure still significantly influenced by traditional values and attitudes. As one African writer recently observed, it is easy to be cynical in Africa, because changes in political regimes have had little effect on people's livelihood. Still, he said, "let us welcome the wind of change. This, after all, is a continent of winds. The trick is to keep hope burning, like a candle protected from the wind."[5]

Continuity and Change in Modern African Societies

In general, the impact of the West has been greater on urban and educated Africans and more limited on their rural and illiterate compatriots. After all, the colonial presence was first and most firmly established in the cities. Many cities, including Dakar, Lagos, Johannesburg, Capetown, Brazzaville, and Nairobi, are direct products of the colonial experience. Most African cities today look like their counterparts elsewhere in the world. They have high-rise buildings, blocks of residential apartments, wide boulevards, neon lights, movie theaters, and traffic jams.

The educational system has been the primary means of introducing Western values and culture. In the precolonial era, formal schools did not really exist in Africa except for parochial schools in Christian Ethiopia and academies to train young males in Islamic doctrine and law in Muslim societies in North and West Africa. For the average African, education took place at the home or in the village courtyard and stressed socialization and vocational training. Traditional education in Africa was not necessarily inferior to that in Europe. Social values and customs were transmitted to the young by storytellers, often village elders, who could gain considerable prestige through their performance.

Europeans introduced modern Western education into Africa in the nineteenth century. At first, the schools concentrated on vocational training, with some instruction in European languages and Western civilization. Eventually, pressure from Africans led to the introduction of professional training, and the first institutes of higher learning were established in the early twentieth century.

With independence, African countries established their own state-run schools. The emphasis was on the primary level, but high schools and universities were established in major cities. The basic objectives have been to introduce vocational training and improve literacy rates. Unfortunately, both funding and trained teachers are scarce in most countries, and few rural areas have schools. As a result, illiteracy remains high, estimated at about 70 percent of the population across the continent. There has been a perceptible shift toward education in the vernacular languages. In West Africa, only about one in four adults is conversant in a Western language.

One interesting vehicle for popular education that emerged during the transition to independence in Nigeria was the Onitsha Market pamphlet. The pamphlets were "how-to" books advising readers on how to succeed in a rapidly changing Africa. They tended to be short, inexpensive, and humorous, with flashy covers to attract the potential buyer's attention. One, titled "The Nigerian Bachelor's Guide," sold 40,000 copies. Unfortunately, the Onitsha Market and the pamphlet tradition were destroyed during the Nigerian civil war of the late 1960s, but they undoubtedly played an important role during a crucial period in the country's history.

Outside the major cities, where about three-quarters of the continent's inhabitants live, Western influence has had less of an impact. Millions of people throughout Africa (as in Asia) live much as their ancestors did, in thatch huts without modern plumbing and electricity; they farm or hunt by traditional methods, practice time-honored family rituals, and believe in the traditional deities. Even here, however, change is taking place. Slavery has been eliminated, for the most part, although there have been persistent reports of raids by slave traders on defenseless villages in the southern Sudan. Economic need, though, has brought about massive migrations, as some leave to

UNDERNEATH THE BAOBAB TREE. For many peoples in Africa and Asia, the largest tree in each village has traditionally been considered to be the domain of the local village deity. Although the deity is expected to protect villagers from harm, children are warned to give a wide berth to the tree to avoid possible evil spirits lurking in the vicinity. This is obviously not the case here, where the two village elders gather with their grandchildren under the shade of a massive baobab tree near their homes in rural Kenya. The baobab, with its characteristically massive trunk, is native to tropical Africa and bears a gourdlike fruit.

BUILDING HIS DREAM HOUSE. In Africa, the houses of rural peoples are often constructed from a wooden frame, known as wattle, daubed with mud, and then covered with a thatch roof. Such houses are inexpensive to build and remain cool in the hot tropical climate. In this Kenyan village not far from the Indian Ocean, a young man is applying mud to the wall of his future house. Houses are built in a similar fashion throughout the continent, as well as in much of southern Asia.

work on plantations, others move to the cities, and still others flee to refugee camps to escape starvation.

African Women

One of the consequences of colonialism and independence has been a change in the relationship between men and women. In precolonial Africa, as in traditional societies in Asia, men and women had distinctly different roles. Women in sub-Saharan Africa, however, generally did not live under the severe legal and social disabilities that we have seen in such societies as China and India. Their role, it has been said, was "complementary rather than subordinate to that of men."[6]

Within the family, wives normally showed a degree of deference to their husbands, and polygamy was not uncommon. But because society was usually arranged on communal lines, property was often held in common, and production tasks were divided on a cooperative rather than hierarchical basis. The status of women tended to rise as they moved through the life cycle. Women became more important as they reared children; in old age, they often became eligible to serve in senior roles within the family, lineage, or village. In some societies, such as the Ashanti kingdom in West Africa, women such as the queen mother were eligible to hold senior political positions.

Sexual relationships changed profoundly during the colonial era, sometimes in ways that could justly be described as beneficial. Colonial governments attempted to bring an end to forced marriage, bodily mutilation such as clitoridectomy, and polygamy. Missionaries introduced women to Western education and encouraged them to organize themselves to defend their interests.

SALT OF THE EARTH. During the precolonial era, many West African societies were forced to import salt from Mediterranean countries in exchange for tropical products and gold. Today the people of Senegal satisfy their domestic needs by mining salt deposits contained in lakes like this one in the interior of the country. These lakes are the remnants of vast seas that covered the region of the Sahara in prehistoric times. Note that it is women who are doing much of the heavy labor, while men occupy the managerial positions.

But the new system had some unfavorable consequences as well. Like men, women now became a labor resource. As African males were taken from the villages to serve as forced labor on construction projects, the traditional division of labor was disrupted, and women were forced to play a more prominent role in the economy. At the same time, their role in the broader society was constricted. In British colonies, Victorian attitudes of sexual repression and female subordination led to restrictions on women's freedom, and the positions in government they had formerly held were closed to them.

Independence also had a significant impact on gender roles in African society. Almost without exception, the new governments established the principle of sexual equality and permitted women to vote and run for political office. Yet, as elsewhere, women continue to operate at a disability in a world dominated by males. Politics remains a male preserve, and although a few professions, such as teaching, child care, and clerical work, are dominated by women, most African women are employed in menial positions such as agricultural labor, factory work, and retail trade, or as domestics. Education is open to all at the elementary level, but women comprise less than 20 percent of students at the upper levels in most African societies today.

In rural areas, where traditional attitudes continue to exert a strong influence, individuals may still be subordinated to communalism. In some societies, clitoridectomy is still widely practiced. Polygamy is also not uncommon, and arranged marriages are still the rule rather than the exception. The dichotomy between rural and urban values can lead to acute tensions. Many African villagers regard the cities as the fount of evil, decadence, and corruption. Women in particular have suffered from the tension between the pull of the city and the village. As men are drawn to the cities in search of employment and excitement, their wives and girlfriends are left behind, both literally and figuratively, in the native village (see the box on p. 924).

Not surprisingly, women have made the greatest strides in the cities. Most urban women, like men, now marry on the basis of personal choice, although a significant minority are still willing to accept their parents' choice. After marriage, African women appear to occupy a more equal position than their counterparts in most Asian countries. Each marriage partner tends to maintain a separate income, and women often have the right to possess property separate from their husbands. While many wives still defer to their husbands in the traditional manner, others are like the woman in Abioseh Nicol's story "A Truly Married Woman," who, after years of living as a common-law wife with her husband, is finally able to provide the

MARKET DAY. In much of sub-Saharan Africa, women play a dominant role in the marketplace, merchandising their goods in the innumerable outdoor markets that proliferate like mushrooms in towns and villages throughout the continent. In this lively market in Banjul, the capital of Gambia, women are hawking their wares, from vegetables and fruit to textile goods and manufactured items of daily use. In their brightly-hued wraparound skirts and headwear, they make a colorful sight for the shopper.

price and finalize the marriage. After the wedding, she declares, "For twelve years I have got up every morning at five to make tea for you and breakfast. Now I am a truly married woman [and] you must treat me with a little more respect. You are now my husband and not a lover. Get up and make yourself a cup of tea."[7]

Within the cities, there is a growing feminist movement, but it is firmly based on conditions in the local environment. Many African women writers, for example, opt for a brand of African feminism much like that of Ama Ata Aidoo, a Ghanaian novelist, whose ultimate objective is to free African society as a whole, not just its female inhabitants. After receiving her education at a girls' school in the Gold Coast and attending Stanford University in the United States, she embarked on a writing career. Every African women and every man, she insists, "should be a feminist, especially if they believe that Africans should take charge of our land, its wealth, our lives, and the burden of our development. Because it is not possible to advocate independence for our continent without also believing that African women must have the best that the environment can offer."[8]

In a few cases, women are even going into politics. One example is Margaret Dongo of Zimbabwe, where a black African government under Robert Mugabe succeeded white rule in onetime Southern Rhodesia in 1980. Now an independent member of Zimbabwe's Parliament, she is labeled "the ant in the elephant's trunk" for her determined effort to root out corruption and bring about social and economic reforms. "We didn't fight to remove white skins," she remarks. "We fought discrimination against blacks in land distribution, education, employment. If we are being exploited again by our black leaders, then what did we fight for?"[9]

African Culture

Inevitably, the tension between traditional and modern, native and foreign, and individual and communal that has permeated contemporary African society has spilled over into culture. In general, in the visual arts and music, utility and ritual have given way to pleasure and decoration. In the process, Africans have been affected to a certain extent by foreign influences, but have retained their distinctive characteristics. Wood carving, metalwork, painting, and sculpture, for example, have preserved their traditional forms but are now increasingly adapted to serve the tourist industry and the export market.

Similar developments have taken place in music and dance. They retain their traditional popularity, but the earlier emphasis on religious ritual and the experience of the performer has been replaced to some degree by a new interest in the spectator. In the process, some of the social functions of traditional music and dance—to express grief or other emotions, to exorcise evil spirits, or to express community solidarity—have eroded, sometimes to the detriment of the society.

No area of African culture has been so strongly affected by political and social events as literature. Except for Muslim areas in North and East Africa, precolonial Africans

AN AFRICAN LAMENT

Like many other areas, Africa faces the challenge of adopting the technological civilization of the West while remaining true to its own cultural heritage. Often this challenge poses terrible personal dilemmas in terms of individual career choices and lifestyles. Few have expressed this dilemma more poignantly than the Ugandan writer p'Bitek Okot. In the following excerpts from two of his prose poems, Lawino laments that her husband is abandoning his African roots in a vain search for modernity. Ocol replies bitterly that African tradition is nothing but rotting buffalo and native villages in ruins.

SONG OF LAWINO

All I ask
Is that my husband should stop the insults,
My husband should refrain
From heaping abuses on my head.
Listen Ocol, my old friend,
The ways of your ancestors
Are good,
Their customs are solid
And not hollow
They are not thin, not easily breakable
They cannot be blown away
By the winds
Because their roots reach deep into the soil.

I do not understand
The ways of foreigners
But I do not despise their customs.
Why should you despise yours?
Listen, my husband,
You are the son of a Chief.
The pumpkin in the old homestead
Must not be uprooted!

SONG OF OCOL

Your song
Is rotting buffalo
Left behind by
Fleeing poachers, . . .

All the valley,
Make compost of the Pumpkins
And the other native vegetables,
The fence dividing
Family holdings
Will be torn down,
We will uproot
The trees demarcating
The land of clan from clan.

We will obliterate
Tribal boundaries
And throttle native tongues
To dumb death. . . .

Houseboy, Listen . . .
Help the woman
Pack her things,
Then sweep the house clean
And wash the floor,
I am off to Town
To fetch the painter.

did not have a written literature, although their tradition of oral storytelling served as a rich repository of history, custom, and folk culture. The first written literature in the vernacular or in European languages emerged during the nineteenth century in the form of novels, poetry, and drama.

Angry at the negative portrayal of Africa in Western literature, African authors initially wrote primarily for a European audience as a means of establishing black dignity and purpose. Embracing the ideals of negritude, many glorified the emotional and communal aspects of the traditional African experience.

Since 1965, however, the African novel has taken a dramatic turn, shifting its focus from the brutality of the foreign oppressor to the shortcomings of the new native leadership. After African nations gained independence, African politicians were portrayed as mimicking and even outdoing the injustices committed by their colonial predecessors. A prominent example of this genre is the work of the Kenyan Ngugi Wa Thiong'o (b. 1938). His first novel, *A Grain of Wheat*, takes place on the eve of *Uhuru*, or independence. Although it mocks local British society for its racism, snobbishness, and superficiality, its chief interest lies in its unsentimental and even unflattering portrayal of ordinary Kenyans in their daily struggle for survival.

Like most of his predecessors, Ngugi initially wrote in English, but he eventually decided to write in his native Kikuyu as a means of broadening his readership. For that reason, perhaps, in the late 1970s, he was placed under house arrest for writing subversive literature. From prison he secretly wrote *Devil on the Cross*, which urged his compatriots to overthrow the government of Daniel Arap Moi. Published in 1980, the book sold widely and was eventually read aloud by storytellers throughout Kenyan society. Fearing an attempt on his life, in recent years Ngugi has lived abroad.

Many of Ngugi's contemporaries have followed his lead and focused their frustration on the failure of the continent's new leadership to carry out the goals of independence. One of the most outstanding is the Nigerian Wole Soyinka (b. 1932). His novel *The Interpreters* (1965) lambasted the corruption and hypocrisy of Nigerian politics. Succeeding novels and plays have continued that tradition, resulting in a Nobel Prize for Literature in 1986. In 1994, however, Soyinka barely managed to escape arrest, and he now lives abroad. In a protest against the brutality of the Abacha regime in Nigeria, he published from exile a harsh exposé of the crisis. His book, *The Open Sore of a Continent*, placed the primary responsibility for failure not on Nigeria's long list of dictators, but on the very concept of the modern nation-state, which was introduced into Africa arbitrarily by Europeans. A nation, he contends, can only emerge from below, as the expression of the moral and political will of the local inhabitants, not be imposed artificially from above.

Among Africa's most prominent writers today, a number are women. Traditionally, African women were valued for their talents as storytellers, but writing was strongly discouraged by both traditional and colonial authorities on the grounds that women should occupy themselves with their domestic obligations. In recent years, however, a number of women have emerged as prominent writers of African fiction. Two examples are Buchi Emecheta (b. 1940) of Nigeria and Ama Ata Aidoo (b. 1942) of Ghana. Beginning with *Second Class Citizen* (1975), which chronicled the breakdown of her own marriage, Emecheta has published numerous works exploring the role of women in contemporary African society and decrying the practice of polygamy. In her own writings, Ama Ata Aidoo has focused on the identity of today's African women and the changing relations between men and women in society. In her recent novel *Changes: A Love Story* (1991), she chronicles the lives of three women, none presented as a victim, but all caught up in the struggle for survival and happiness.

One of the overriding concerns confronting African intellectuals since independence has been the problem of language. Unlike Asian societies, Africans have not inherited a long written tradition from the precolonial era. As a result, many intellectuals have written in the colonial language, a practice that sometimes results in guilt and anxiety. As we have seen, some have reacted by writing in their local languages to reach a native audience. The market for such work is limited, however, because of the high illiteracy rate, and also because novels written in African languages have no market abroad. Moreover, because of the deep financial crisis throughout the continent, there is little money for the publication of serious books. Many of Africa's libraries and universities are almost literally without books. It is little wonder that many African authors, to their discomfort, continue to write and publish in foreign languages.

Gathered at the Beach

Nowhere in the developing world is the dilemma of continuity and change more agonizing than in contemporary Africa. Mesmerized by the spectacle of Western affluence, yet repulsed by the bloody trail from slavery to World War II and the atomic bombs over Hiroshima and Nagasaki, African intellectuals have been torn between the dual images of Western materialism and African negritude.

What is the destiny of Africa? Some still yearn for the dreams embodied in the program of the OAU. Novelist Ngugi Wa Thiong'o calls for "an internationalization of all the democratic and social struggles for human equality, justice, peace, and progress."[10] Some African political leaders, however, have apparently discarded the democratic ideal and turned their attention to what is sometimes called the "East Asian model," based on the Confucian tenet of subordination of the individual to the community as the guiding principle of national development (see Chapter 32). Whether African political culture today is well placed to imitate the strategy adopted by the fast-growing nations of East Asia—who in any event are now encountering problems of their own—is questionable. Like all peoples, Africans must ultimately find their own solutions within the context of their own traditions, and not by seeking to imitate the example of others.

For the average African, of course, such intellectual dilemmas pale before the daily challenge of survival. But the fundamental gap between the traditional village and the modern metropolis is perhaps wider in Africa than anywhere else in the world and may well be harder to bridge. The solution is not yet visible.

In the meantime, writes Ghanaian author George Awoonor-Williams, all Africans are exiles:

The return is tedious
And the exiled souls gathered at the beach
Arguing and deciding their future
Should they return home
And face the fences the termites had eaten
And see the dunghill that has mounted their birthplace?
. . . The final strokes will land them on forgotten shores
They committed the impiety of self-deceit
Slashed, cut and wounded their souls
And left the mangled remainder in manacles.

The moon, the moon is our father's spirit
At the stars entrance the night revellers gather
To sell their chatter and inhuman sweat to the gateman
And shuffle their feet in agonies of birth.
Lost souls, lost souls, lost souls, that are
Still at the gate.[11]

CRESCENT OF CONFLICT

"We Muslims are of one family even though we live under different governments and in various regions."[12] So said the Ayatollah Ruholla Khomeini, the Islamic religious figure and leader of the 1979 revolution that overthrew the shah in Iran. The Ayatollah's remark was not just a pious wish by a religious mystic, but an accurate reflection of one crucial aspect of the political dynamics in the region.

If the concept of negritude represents an alternative to the system of nation-states in Africa, in the Middle East a similar role has been played by the forces of militant Islam. In both regions, a yearning for a sense of community beyond national borders tugs at the emotions and intellect of their inhabitants and counteracts the dynamic pull of nationalism that has provoked political turmoil and conflict in much of the rest of the world.

For the Middle East, the period between the two world wars was an era of transition. With the fall of the Ottoman and the Persian empires, new modernizing regimes emerged in Turkey and Iran, and a more traditionalist but fiercely independent government was established in Saudi Arabia. Elsewhere, European influence continued to be strong; the British and French had mandates in Syria, Lebanon, Jordan, and Palestine, and British influence persisted in Iraq, southern Arabia, and throughout the Nile valley. Pan-Arabism was on the rise, but it lacked focus and coherence.

During World War II, the region became the cockpit of European rivalries, as it had been during World War I. The region was more significant to the warring powers than previously because of the growing importance of oil and the Suez Canal's position as a vital sea route. For a brief period, the German Afrika Korps threatened to seize Egypt and the Suez Canal, but British troops defeated the German forces at El Alamein, west of Alexandria, in 1942. From that time until the end of the war, the entire region from the Mediterranean Sea eastward was under secure Allied occupation.

The Question of Palestine

As in other areas of Asia, the end of World War II led to the emergence of a number of independent states. Jordan, Lebanon, and Syria, all European mandates before the war, became independent. Egypt, Iran, and Iraq, though still under a degree of Western influence, became increasingly autonomous. Sympathy for the idea of Arab unity led to the formation of an Arab League in 1945, but different points of view among its members prevented it from achieving anything of substance.

The one issue on which all Arab states in the area could agree was the question of Palestine. As tensions between Jews and Arabs in that mandate intensified during the 1930s, the British reduced Jewish immigration into the area and firmly rejected proposals for independence. After World War II, the Zionists turned for support to the United States, and in March 1948, the Truman administration approved the concept of an independent Jewish state, even though only about one-third of the local population were Jews. In May, the new state of Israel was formally established.

To its Arab neighbors, the new state represented a betrayal of the interests of the Palestinian people, 90 percent of whom were Muslim, and a flagrant disregard for the conditions set out in the Balfour Declaration of 1917. Outraged at the lack of Western support for Muslim interests in the area, several Arab countries invaded the new Jewish state. The invasion did not succeed because of internal divisions among the Arabs, but both sides remained bitter, and the Arab states refused to recognize Israel.

The war had other lasting consequences as well, because it led to the exodus of thousands of Palestinian refugees into neighboring Muslim states. Jordan, which had become independent under its Hashemite ruler, was now flooded by the arrival of one million urban Palestinians in a country occupied by half a million Bedouins. To the north, the state of Lebanon had been created to provide the local Christian community with a country of their own, but the arrival of the Palestinian refugees upset the delicate balance between Christians and Muslims. In any event, the creation of Lebanon had angered the Syrians, who had lost it as well as other territories to Turkey as a result of European decisions before and after the war.

Nasser and Pan-Arabism

The dispute over Palestine placed Egypt in an uncomfortable position. Technically, Egypt was not an Arab state. King Farouk, who had acceded to power in 1936, had frequently declared support for the Arab cause, but the Egyptian people were not Bedouins and shared little of the culture of the peoples across the Red Sea. Nevertheless, Farouk committed Egyptian armies to the disastrous war against Israel.

In 1952, King Farouk, whose corrupt habits had severely eroded his early popularity, was overthrown by a military coup engineered by young military officers ostensibly under the leadership of Colonel Muhammad Nagib. The real force behind the scenes was Colonel Gamal Abdul Nasser (1918–1970), the son of a minor government functionary who, like many of his fellow officers, had been angered by the army's inadequate preparation for the war against Israel four years earlier. In 1953, the monarchy was replaced by a republic.

In 1954, Nasser seized power in his own right and immediately instituted a land reform program. He also adopted a policy of neutrality in foreign affairs and expressed sympathy for the Arab cause. The British presence had rankled many Egyptians for years, for even after

THE SUEZ CANAL BELONGS TO EGYPT!

The Suez Canal was built between 1854 and 1869, using mainly French capital and Egyptian labor, under the direction of the French promoter Ferdinand de Lesseps. It was managed by a Paris-based limited liability corporation, called the Suez Canal Company, under a ninety-nine-year lease. Over time, the canal came to symbolize colonial exploitation in the minds of many Egyptians. In this excerpt from a speech given in July 1956, President Nasser declared that it was time for the canal to be owned and managed by Egyptians. The decision led to a brief invasion by Great Britain and France, but under pressure the European powers backed down, and Nasser got his way.

NASSER'S SPEECH NATIONALIZING THE SUEZ CANAL COMPANY

The Suez Canal is an Egyptian canal built as a result of great sacrifices. The Suez Canal Company is an Egyptian company that was expropriated from Egypt by the British, who, since the canal was dug, have been obtaining the profits of the Company. . . . And yet the Suez Canal Company is an Egyptian limited liability company. The annual Canal revenue is 35 million Egyptian pounds. From this sum Egypt—which lost 120,000 workers in digging the Canal—takes one million pounds from the Company. . . .

It is a shame when the blood of peoples is sucked, and it is no shame that we should borrow for construction. We will not allow the past to be repeated again, but we will cancel the past by restoring our rights in the Suez Canal. . . . We will build the High Dam, and we will obtain our rights. We will build it as we wish, and we are determined to do so. The 35 million pounds which the Company collects each year will be collected by us. . . . When we build the High Dam, we will be building the dam of prestige, freedom, and dignity, and we will be putting an end to the dams of humiliation. . . .

Now that the rights have been restored to their people after one hundred years, we are achieving true liberation. The Suez Canal Company was a state within a state, depending on the conspiracies of imperialism and its supporters. The Canal was built for the sake of Egypt, but it was a source of exploitation. There is no shame in being poor, but it is a shame to suck blood. Today we restore these rights, and I declare in the name of the Egyptian people that we will protect these rights with our blood and soul. . . .

The people will stand united as one man to resist imperialist acts of treachery. . . . When we restore all our rights, we shall become stronger and our production will increase. At this moment, some of your brethren, the sons of Egypt, are now taking over the Egyptian Suez Canal Company and directing it. We have taken this decision to restore part of the glories of the past and to safeguard our national dignity and pride. May God bless you and guide you in the path of righteousness.

granting Egypt independence, Britain had retained control over the Suez Canal to protect its route to the Indian Ocean. In 1956, Nasser suddenly nationalized the Suez Canal Company, which had been under British and French administration. Seeing a threat to their route to the Indian Ocean, the British and the French launched a joint attack on Egypt to protect their investment. They were joined by Israel, whose leaders had grown exasperated at sporadic Arab commando raids on Israeli territory and now decided to strike back. But the Eisenhower administration in the United States, concerned that the attack smacked of a revival of colonialism, supported Nasser and brought about the withdrawal of foreign forces from Egypt and of Israeli troops from the Sinai Peninsula (see the box above).

Nasser now turned to pan-Arabism. Egypt had won approval from other states in the area for its successful eviction of the British and the French from the Suez Canal and for its sponsorship of efforts to replace Israel by an independent Palestinian state. In 1958, Egypt united with Syria in a new United Arab Republic (UAR). The union had been proposed by the Ba'ath Party, which advocated the unity of all Arab states in a new socialist society. In 1957, the Ba'ath Party assumed power in Syria and opened talks with Egypt on a union between the two countries, which took place in March 1958 following a plebiscite. Nasser was named president of the new state.

Egypt and Syria hoped that the union would eventually include all Arab states, but other Arab leaders, including young King Hussein of Jordan and the kings of Iraq and Saudi Arabia, were suspicious. The latter two in particular feared pan-Arabism on the reasonable assumption that they would be asked to share their vast oil revenues with the poorer states of the Middle East.

Nasser's concept of Arab socialism and his hopes for the union are more easily explained in terms of what he did not want than what he did. Nasser opposed existing relationships in which the world was dominated by two competing blocs while much of the wealth of the Middle East flowed into the treasuries of a handful of wealthy feudal states or, even worse, the pockets of foreign oil interests. In Nasser's view, through Arab unity, this wealth could be put to better use to improve the standard of living in the area. To achieve a more equitable division of the wealth of the region, natural resources and major industries would be nationalized; central planning would guarantee that

MAP 30.2 Israel and Its Neighbors

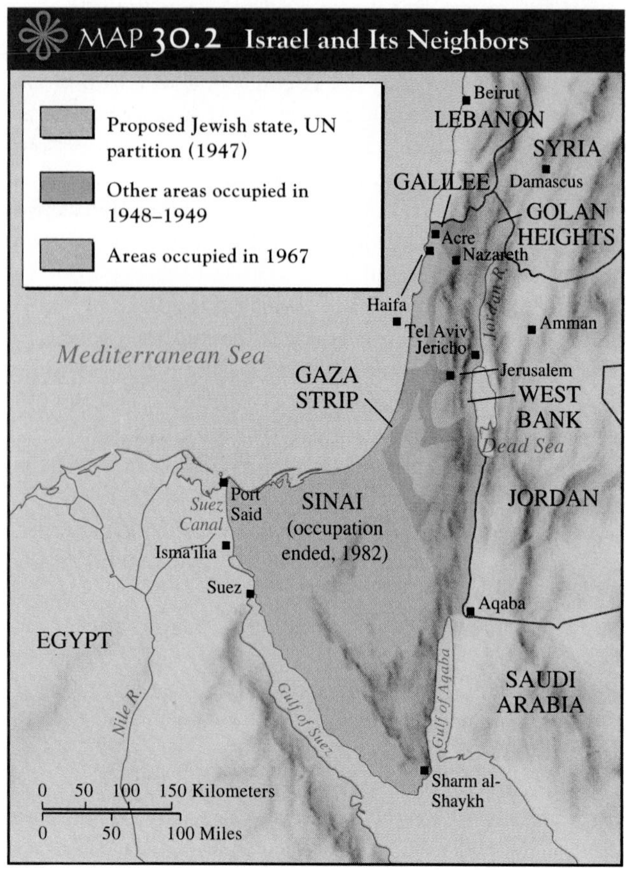

resources were exploited efficiently, but private enterprise would continue at the local level.

In the end, however, Nasser's determination to extend state control over the economy brought an end to the UAR. When the government announced the nationalization of a large number of industries and utilities in 1961, a military coup overthrew the Ba'ath leaders in Damascus, and the new authorities declared that Syria would end its relationship with Egypt.

The breakup of the UAR did not necessarily end Nasser's dream of pan-Arabism. In 1962, Algeria finally received its independence from France and, under its new president, Ahmad Ben Bella, established close relations with Egypt, as did a new republic in Yemen. During the mid-1960s, Egypt took the lead in promoting Arab unity against Israel. At a meeting of Arab leaders held in Jerusalem in 1964, the Palestine Liberation Organization (PLO) was set up under Egyptian sponsorship to represent the interests of the Palestinians. According to the charter of the PLO, only the Palestinian people (and thus not Jewish immigrants from abroad) had the right to form a state in the old British mandate. A guerrilla movement called al-Fatah, led by the dissident PLO figure Yasir Arafat (b. 1929), began to launch terrorist attacks on Israeli territory, prompting the Israeli government to raid PLO bases in Jordan in 1966.

The Arab-Israeli Dispute

Growing Arab hostility was a constant threat to the security of Israel. In the years after independence, Israeli leaders dedicated themselves to creating a Jewish homeland. Aided by reparations paid by the postwar German government of Chancellor Konrad Adenauer and private funds provided by Jews living abroad, notably in the United States, the government attempted to build a democratic and modern state that would be a magnet for Jews throughout the world and a symbol of Jewish achievement.

Ensuring the survival of the tiny state surrounded by antagonistic Arab neighbors was a considerable challenge, made more difficult by divisions within the Israeli population. Some were immigrants from Europe, while others came from the countries of Middle East. Some were secular and even socialist in their views, while others were politically conservative and stressed religious orthodoxy. There were also Christians as well as many Muslim Palestinians who had not fled to other countries. To balance these diverse interests, Israel established a parliament, called the Knesset, on the European model, with proportional representation based on the number of votes each party received in the general election. The parties were so numerous that none ever received a majority of votes, and all governments had to be formed from a coalition of several parties. As a result, moderate secular leaders such as longtime prime minister David Ben Gurion had to cater to more marginal parties composed of conservative religious groups.

During the late 1950s and 1960s, the dispute between Israel and other states in the Middle East intensified (see the box on p. 930). Essentially alone except for the sympathy of the United States and several Western European countries, Israel adopted a policy of determined resistance to and immediate retaliation against alleged PLO and Arab provocations. By the spring of 1967, relations between Israel and its Arab neighbors had deteriorated, as Nasser attempted to improve his standing in the Arab world by imposing a blockade against Israeli commerce through the Gulf of Aqaba.

Concerned that it might be isolated, and lacking firm support from Western powers (who had originally guaranteed Israel the freedom to use the Gulf of Aqaba), in June 1967, Israel suddenly launched air strikes against Egypt and several of its Arab neighbors. Israeli armies then broke the blockade at the head of the Gulf of Aqaba and occupied the Sinai Peninsula. Other Israeli forces attacked Jordanian territory on the West Bank of the Jordan River (Jordan's King Hussein had recently signed an alliance with Egypt and placed his army under Egyptian command), occupied the whole of Jerusalem, and seized Syrian military positions in the Golan Heights, along the Israeli-Syrian border.

Despite limited Soviet support for Egypt and Syria, in a brief, six-day war, Israel had mocked Nasser's pretensions of Arab unity and tripled the size of its territory, thus enhancing its precarious security. Yet the new Israel also aroused even more bitter hostility among the Arabs and included an additional million Palestinians inside its borders, most of them living on the West Bank.

During the next few years, the focus of the Arab-Israeli dispute shifted, as Arab states demanded the return of the occupied territories. Meanwhile, many Israelis argued that the new lands improved the security of the beleaguered state and should be retained. Concerned that the dispute might lead to a confrontation between the superpowers, the Nixon administration tried to achieve a peace settlement. The peace effort received a mild stimulus when Nasser died of a heart attack in September 1970 and was succeeded by his vice president, ex-general Anwar al-Sadat (1918–1981). Sadat soon showed himself to be more pragmatic than his predecessor, dropping the now irrelevant name United Arab Republic in favor of the Arab Republic of Egypt and replacing Nasser's socialist policies with a new strategy based on free enterprise and encouragement of Western investment. He also agreed to sign a peace treaty with Israel on condition that Israel retire to its pre-1967 frontiers. Concerned that other Arab countries would refuse to make peace and take advantage of its presumed weakness, Israel refused.

Rebuffed in his offer of peace, smarting from criticism of his moderate stand from other Arab leaders, and increasingly concerned over Israeli plans to build permanent Jewish settlements in the occupied territories, Sadat attempted once again to renew Arab unity through a new confrontation with Israel. On Yom Kippur (the Jewish Day of Atonement), an Israeli national holiday, Egyptian forces suddenly launched an air and artillery attack on Israeli positions in the Sinai just east of the Suez Canal. Syrian armies attacked Israeli positions in the Golan Heights. After early Arab successes, the Israelis managed to recoup

BONE OF CONTENTION. The Golan Heights, a range of mountains to the east of the Sea of Galilee in northern Israel, has become a major bone of contention between the state of Israel and its neighbor Syria. Israeli forces seized the area during the brief Arab-Israeli conflict in 1967 and continue to occupy it today. As the photo clearly shows, whoever controls the heights is in a position to dominate the Israeli lowlands below. The issue is but one example of the complexity of the Arab-Israeli dispute.

A PLEA FOR PEACE IN THE MIDDLE EAST

In an effort to end the Egyptian blockade of the Gulf of Aqaba against Israeli shipping, Israel joined Great Britain and France in attacking Egypt during the Suez Canal crisis in October 1956. Israel quickly captured the Sinai peninsula, but the United Nations condemned the attack and pressured Great Britain, France, and Israel to withdraw their troops. For four months Israel refused, demanding that the Arab states respect its right to use the Gulf of Aqaba. In March 1957, however, Golda Meir, Israel's foreign minister, announced that her government had agreed to withdraw from the Sinai and the Gaza Strip.

GOLDA MEIR ANNOUNCES AN ISRAELI WITHDRAWAL FROM SINAI

Interference, by armed force, with ships of Israeli flag exercising free and innocent passage in the Gulf of Aqaba and through the Straits of Tiran, will be viewed by Israel as an attack entitling it to exercise its inherent right of self-defense under article 51 of the United Nations Charter and to take all such measures as are necessary to ensure the free and innocent passage of its ships in the Gulf and in the Straits. We make this announcement in accordance with the accepted principles of international law under which all states have an inherent right to use their forces to protect their ships and their rights against interference by armed force. My government naturally hopes that this contingency will not occur. In a public address on 20 February 1957, President Eisenhower states: "We should not assume that, if Israel withdraws, Egypt will prevent Israel shipping from using the Suez Canal or the Gulf of Aqaba." This declaration has weighed heavily with my government in determining its action today. Israel is now prepared to withdraw its forces from the regions of the Gulf of Aqaba and the Straits of Tiran in the confidence that there will be continued freedom of navigation for international and Israeli shipping in the Gulf of Aqaba and through the Straits of Tiran. . . .

May I now add these few words to the states in the Middle East area and, more specifically, to the neighbors of Israel. We all come from an area which is a very ancient one. The hills and the valleys have been witnesses to many wars and many conflicts. But that is not the only thing which characterizes the part of the world from which we come. It is also a part of the world which is of an ancient culture. It is that part of the world which has given to humanity three great religions. It is also that part of the world which has given a code of ethics to all humanity. In our countries, in the entire region, all our peoples are anxious for and in need of a higher standard of living, of great programs of development and progress. Can we, from now on—all of us—turn a new leaf and, instead of fighting with each other, can we all, united, fight poverty and disease and illiteracy? Is it possible for us to put all our efforts and all our energy into one single purpose, the betterment and progress and development of all our lands and all our peoples? I can here pledge the government and the people of Israel to do their part in this united effort. There is no limit to what we are prepared to contribute so that all of us, together, can live to see a day of happiness for our peoples and can see again from that region a great contribution to peace and happiness for all humanity.

some of their losses on both fronts. As a superpower confrontation between the United States and the Soviet Union loomed, a cease-fire was finally reached.

In the next years, a fragile peace was maintained, marked by U.S. "shuttle diplomacy" (carried out by U.S. Secretary of State Henry Kissinger) and the rise to power in Israel of the militant Likud Party under Prime Minister Menachem Begin (1913–1992). The conflict now spread to Lebanon, where many Palestinians had found refuge and the PLO had set up its headquarters. Rising tension along the border was compounded by increasingly hostile disputes between Christians and Muslims over control of the capital, Beirut.

After his election as president in 1976, Jimmy Carter began to press for a compromise peace based on Israel's return of occupied Arab territories and Arab recognition of the state of Israel (an idea originally proposed by Henry Kissinger). By now, Sadat was anxious to reduce his military expenses and announced his willingness to visit Jerusalem to seek peace. The meeting took place in November 1977, with no concrete results, but Sadat persisted. In September 1978, he and Begin met with Carter at Camp David, the presidential retreat in Maryland. Israel agreed to withdraw from the Sinai but not from other occupied territories unless it was recognized by other Arab countries.

The promise of the Camp David agreement was not fulfilled. One reason was the assassination of Sadat by Islamic militants in October 1981. But there were deeper causes, including the continued unwillingness of many Arab governments to recognize Israel and the Israeli government's encouragement of Jewish settlements on the occupied West Bank.

During the early 1980s, the militance of the Palestinians increased, leading to rising unrest, popularly labeled the *intifada* (uprising) among PLO supporters living inside Israel. To control the situation, a new Israeli government under Prime Minister Itzhak Shamir invaded southern Lebanon to destroy PLO commando bases near the Israeli border. The invasion provoked international condemnation and further destabilized the perilous balance between Muslims and Christians in Lebanon. As the 1990s began, U.S.–sponsored peace talks opened between Israel and a number of its neighbors. The first major breakthrough came in 1993, when Israel and the PLO reached an agreement calling for Palestinian autonomy in selected areas of Israel in return for PLO recognition of the legitimacy of the Israeli state.

Progress in implementing the agreement, however, has been slow. Terrorist attacks by Palestinian militants have resulted in heavy casualties and shaken the confidence of many Jewish citizens that their security needs can be protected under the agreement. At the same time, Jewish residents of the West Bank have resisted the extension of Palestinian authority in the area. In November 1995, Prime Minister Yitzhak Rabin was assassinated by an Israeli opponent of the accords. National elections held a few months later led to the formation of a new government under Benjamin Netanyahu, which adopted a tougher stance in negotiations with the Palestinian Authority under Yasir Arafat. But when Netanyahu was replaced by a new Labour government under Prime Minister Ehud Barak, the latter promised to revitalize the peace process. Negotiations got underway with Syria over a peace settlement in Lebanon and the possible return of the Golan Heights to Syrian control, but so far without result.

A PALESTINIAN VILLAGE. After the creation of the state of Israel, many Palestinian Muslims left their homes there and created new settlements in the West Bank, an arid region east of Jerusalem that was part of the neighboring state of Jordan until its seizure by Israeli forces during the 1967 war. Since then, ownership over the area has been under dispute, and a number of Jewish settlements have been established there to create a permanent Israeli presence. Negotiations over ownership of the West Bank are a key prerequisite to any final settlement of the Arab-Israeli dispute. Shown here is a Palestinian settlement, with the mountains adjacent to the Red Sea in the background.

Revolution in Iran

The Arab-Israeli dispute also provoked an international oil crisis. In 1960, a number of oil-producing states formed the Organization of Petroleum Exporting Countries (OPEC) to gain control over oil prices, but the organization was not recognized by the foreign oil companies. During the 1973 Yom Kippur War, some OPEC nations announced significant increases in the price of oil to foreign countries. The price hikes were accompanied by an apparent oil shortage and created serious economic problems in the United States and Europe as well as in the Third World. They also proved to be a boon to oil-exporting countries, such as Libya, now under the leadership of the militantly anti-Western Colonel Muammar Qadhafi (b. 1942).

One of the key oil-exporting countries was Iran. Under the leadership of Shah Mohammad Reza Pahlavi (1919–1980), who had taken over from his father in 1941, Iran had become one of the richest countries in the Middle East. Although relations with the West had occasionally been fragile (especially after Prime Minister Mossadeq had briefly attempted to nationalize the oil industry in 1951), during the next twenty years Iran became a prime ally of the United States in the Middle East. With encouragement from the United States, which hoped that Iran could become a force for stability in the Persian Gulf, the shah attempted to carry through a series of social and economic reforms to transform the country into the most advanced in the region.

Statistical evidence suggests that his efforts were succeeding. Per capita income increased dramatically, literacy rates improved, a modern communications infrastructure took shape, and an affluent middle class emerged in the capital of Tehran. Under the surface, however, trouble was brewing. Despite an ambitious land reform program, many peasants were still landless, unemployment among intellectuals was dangerously high, and the urban middle class was squeezed by high inflation. Housing costs had skyrocketed, provoked in part by the massive influx of foreigners attracted by oil money.

Some of the unrest took the form of religious discontent, as millions of devout Muslims looked with distaste at a new Iranian civilization based on greed, sexual license, and material accumulation. Conservative *ulama* opposed rampant government corruption, the ostentation of the shah's court, and the extension of voting rights to women. Some opposition elements took to terrorism against wealthy Iranians or foreign residents in an attempt to provoke social and political disorder. In response, the shah's

CHRONOLOGY

THE MODERN MIDDLE EAST

Formation of the state of Israel	1948
Farouk overthrown in Egypt	1952
Egypt nationalizes the Suez Canal	1956
Formation of the United Arab Republic	1958
Founding of the Palestine Liberation Organization	1964
Six-day War between Israel and Arab states	1967
First oil crisis	1973
War between Israel, Egypt, and other Arab states	1973
Camp David accords	1978
Iranian Revolution	1979
Iran-Iraq War begins	1980
Israeli forces invade Lebanon	1982
Iraqi invasion of Kuwait	1990
Gulf War	1991
Agreement on Palestinian autonomy	1994
Assassination of Yitzhak Rabin	1995
Election of Benjamin Netanyahu as prime minister of Israel	1996
Peace talks between Israel and Syria begin	1999
Reformists win parliamentary majority in Iran	2000

U.S.–trained security police, the *Savak*, imprisoned and sometimes tortured thousands of dissidents.

Leading the opposition was the Ayatollah Ruholla Khomeini (1900–1989), an austere Shi'ite cleric who had been exiled to Iraq and then to France because of his outspoken opposition to the shah's regime. From Paris, Khomeini continued his attacks in print, on television, and in radio broadcasts. By the late 1970s, large numbers of Iranians—students, peasants, and townspeople—began to respond to Khomeini's diatribes against the "satanic regime," and demonstrations by his supporters were repressed with ferocity by the police. But workers' strikes (some of them in the oil fields, which reduced government revenue) grew in intensity. In January 1979, the shah appointed a moderate, Shapur Bakhtiar, as prime minister and then left the country for medical treatment.

Bakhtiar attempted to conciliate the rising opposition and permitted Khomeini to return to Iran, where he presided over a new Islamic Revolutionary Council and demanded the government's resignation. With rising public unrest and incipient revolt within the army, the government collapsed and was replaced by a hastily formed Islamic Republic. The new government, which was dominated by Shi'ite *ulama* under the guidance of Ayatollah Khomeini, immediately began to introduce and restore traditional Islamic law. A new reign of terror ensued, as supporters of the shah were rounded up and executed. Along the borders, ethnic groups such as the Kurds and the Azerbaijanis rose in rebellion.

Though much of the outside world focused on the U.S. Embassy in Tehran, where militants held a number of foreign hostages, the Iranian Revolution involved much more. In the eyes of the ayatollah and his followers, the United States was "the great Satan," the powerful protector of Israel, and the enemy of Muslim peoples everywhere. Furthermore, it was responsible for the corruption of Iranian society under the shah. Now Khomeini demanded that the shah be returned to Iran for trial and that the United States apologize for its acts against the Iranian people. In response, the Carter administration stopped buying Iranian oil and froze Iranian assets in the United States.

The effects of the disturbances in Iran quickly spread beyond its borders. Sunni militants briefly seized the holy places in Mecca and began to appeal to their brothers to launch similar revolutions in Islamic countries around the world, including far-off Malaysia and Indonesia. At the same time, the ethnic unrest among the Kurdish minorities along the border continued. In July 1980, the shah died of cancer in Cairo. Two months later, Iraq and Iran went to war (see the next section). With economic conditions in Iran rapidly deteriorating, the Islamic revolutionary government finally agreed to free the hostages in return for the release of Iranian assets in the United States. During the next few years, the intensity of the Iranian Revolution moderated slightly, and the government of President Hashemi Rafsanjani displayed a modest tolerance for a loosening of clerical control over freedom of expression and social activities. But rising criticism of rampant official corruption and a high rate of inflation sparked a new wave of government repression in the mid-1990s; newspapers were censored, the universities were purged of disloyal or "un-Islamic" elements, and religious militants raided private homes in search of blasphemous activities.

Crisis in the Gulf

Although much of the Iranians' anger was directed against the United States during the early phases of the revolution, Iran had equally hated enemies closer to home. To the north, the immense power of the Soviet Union, driven by atheistic communism, was viewed as a modern version of the Russian threat of previous centuries. To the west was a militant and hostile Iraq, now under the leadership of the ambitious Saddam Hussein (b. 1937). Problems from both directions appeared shortly after Khomeini's rise to power. Soviet military forces occupied Afghanistan to prop up a weak Marxist regime there. The following year, Iraqi forces suddenly attacked along the Iranian border.

Iraq and Iran had long had an uneasy relationship, fueled by religious differences (Iranian Islam is predominantly Shi'ite, while the ruling caste in Iraq is Sunni) and a perennial dispute over borderlands adjacent to the Persian Gulf, the vital waterway for the export of oil from both countries. Like several of its neighbors, Iraq had long dreamed of unifying the Arabs but had been hindered by internal factions and suspicion among its neighbors.

During the mid-1970s, Iran gave some support to a Kurdish rebellion in the mountains of Iraq. In 1975, the government of the shah agreed to stop aiding the rebels in return for territorial concessions at the head of the Gulf. Five years later, however, the Kurdish revolt had been suppressed, and President Saddam Hussein, who had assumed power in Baghdad in 1979, accused Iran of violating the territorial agreement and launched an attack on his neighbor. The war was a bloody one and lasted for nearly ten years. Poison gas was used against civilians, and children were employed to clear minefields. Finally, with both sides virtually exhausted, a cease-fire was arranged in the fall of 1988.

The bitter conflict with Iran had not slaked Saddam Hussein's appetite for territorial expansion. In early August 1990, Iraqi military forces suddenly moved across the border and occupied the small neighboring country of Kuwait at the head of the Gulf. The immediate pretext was the claim that Kuwait was pumping oil from fields inside Iraqi territory. Baghdad was also angry over the Kuwaiti government's demand for repayment of loans it had made to Iraq during the war with Iran. But the underlying reason was Iraq's contention that Kuwait was legally a part of Iraq. Kuwait had been part of the Ottoman Empire until the beginning of the twentieth century, when the local prince had agreed to place his patrimony under British protection. When Iraq became independent in 1932, it claimed the area on the grounds that the state of Kuwait had been created by British imperialism, but opposition from major Western powers and other countries in the region, who feared the consequences of a "greater Iraq," prevented an Iraqi takeover.

The Iraqi invasion of Kuwait in 1990 sparked an international outcry, and the United States amassed an international force that liberated the country and destroyed a substantial part of Iraq's armed forces. President George Bush had promised the American people that U.S. troops would not fight with one hand tied behind their backs (a clear reference to the Vietnam War), but the allied forces did not occupy Baghdad at the end of the war out of fear that doing so would cause a total breakup of the country, an eventuality that would operate to the benefit of Iran. The allies hoped instead that the Hussein regime would be ousted by an internal revolt. In the meantime, harsh economic sanctions were imposed on the Iraqi government as the condition for peace. The anticipated overthrow of Saddam Hussein did not materialize, however, and his tireless efforts to evade the conditions of the cease-fire continued to bedevil President Bill Clinton, who came into office in January 1993.

Recent statements by the newly elected president of Iran, Mohammed Khatemi, signal the tantalizing possibility that relations between the United States and Iran might begin to improve. Such a development could strengthen efforts to maintain a balance among competing states to prevent a single power from dominating the region. The struggle for political and economic dominance in the Middle East has been going on for centuries, however, and a lasting peace seems unlikely.

Politics in the Contemporary Middle East

Unlike the newly independent states of South and Southeast Asia, which generally attempted to set up Western-style governments (see Chapter 31), the Middle Eastern states that became independent after World War II exhibited a variety of forms of government.

In some cases, the traditional leaders survived into the postwar period—notably on the Arabian peninsula, where feudal rulers remain in power. The kings of Saudi Arabia, for example, continue to rule by traditional precepts and, citing the distinctive character of Muslim political institutions, have been reluctant to establish representative political institutions. As a general rule, these rulers maintain and even enforce the strict observance of traditional customs. Religious police in Saudi Arabia are responsible for enforcing the Muslim dress code, maintaining the prohibition against alcohol, and making sure offices close during the time for prayer. Reportedly, the government even forbade airing "The Muppet Show" on local television because its characters included a pig, which was considered offensive to Islamic strictures against eating pork.

In other societies, traditional authority has been replaced by charismatic one-party rule or military dictatorships. Nasser's regime in Egypt is a good example of a single-party state where the leader won political power by the force of his presence or personality. The Ayatollah Khomeini in Iran, Muammar Qadhafi in Libya, and Saddam Hussein in Iraq are other examples. Although their personal characteristics and images differ, they all have sought to take advantage of their personal appeal.

In other instances, charismatic rule has given way to modernizing bureaucratic regimes. Examples include the governments of Syria, Yemen, Turkey, and Egypt since

MAP 30.3 The Modern Middle East

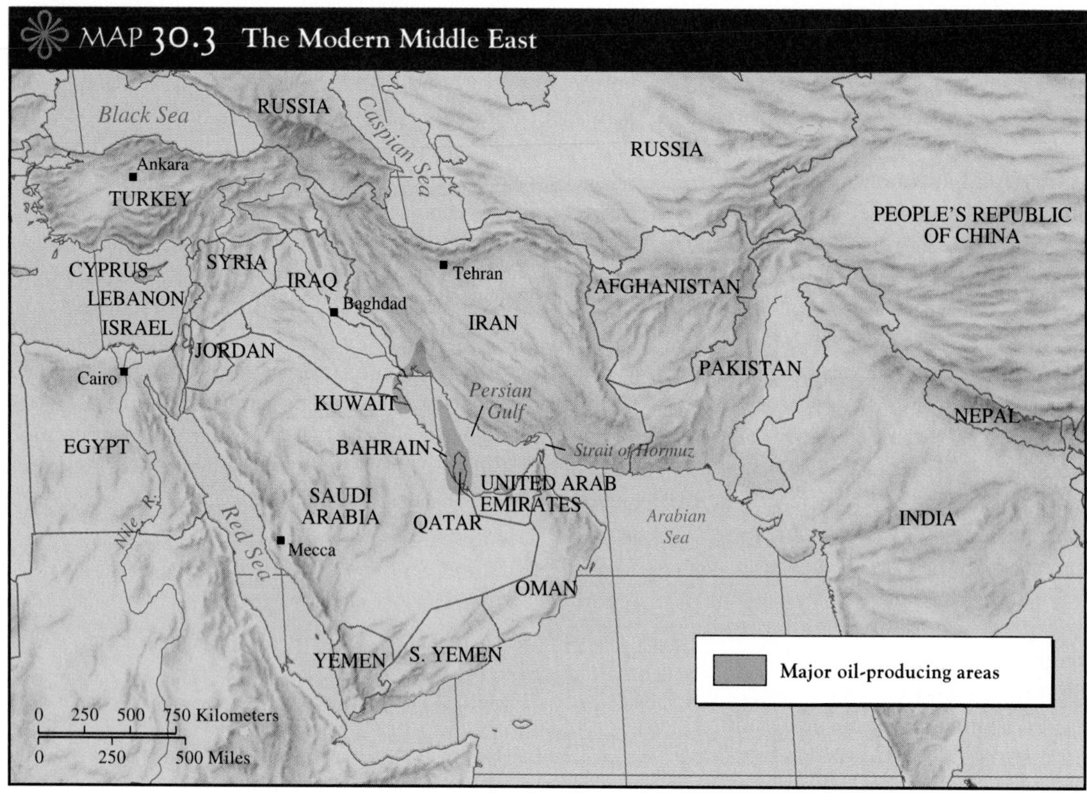

Nasser, where Anwar al-Sadat and his successor, Hosni Mubarak, have avoided dramatic personal appeal in favor of a regime focused on performance. Sometimes the authoritarian character of the regimes has been modified by some democratic tendencies, especially in Turkey, where free elections and the sharing of power have become more prevalent in recent years.

Only in Israel, however, are democratic institutions firmly established. The Israeli system suffers from the proliferation of minor parties, some of which are able to dictate policy because their support is essential to keeping a government in power. In recent years, divisions between religious conservatives and secular elements within the Jewish community have become increasingly sharp. Nevertheless, the government generally reflects the popular will, and power is transferred by peaceful and constitutional means.

The Economics of Oil

Few areas exhibit a greater disparity of individual and national wealth than the Middle East. While millions live in abject poverty, a fortunate few rank among the wealthiest people in the world. While the annual per capita income in Egypt is about $600 (in U.S. dollars), in the tiny states of Kuwait and United Arab Emirates, it is nearly $20,000. The primary reason for this disparity is oil. Unfortunately for most of the peoples of the region, oil reserves are distributed unevenly and all too often are located in areas where the population density is low. Egypt and Turkey, with more than 50 million inhabitants apiece, have almost no oil reserves. The combined population of Kuwait, the United Arab Emirates, and Saudi Arabia is well under 10 million people. This disparity in wealth inspired Nasser's quest for Arab unity (and perhaps Saddam Hussein's as well), but it has also posed a major obstacle to that unity.

The growing importance of petroleum has obviously been a boon to several of the states in the region, but it has been an unreliable one. Because of the violent fluctuations in the price of oil during the past thirty years, the income of oil-producing states has varied considerably. The spectacular increase in oil prices during the 1970s, when members of OPEC were able to raise the price of a barrel of oil from about $3 to $30, has not been sustained, forcing a number of oil-producing countries to scale back their economic development plans.

Not surprisingly, considering their different resources and political systems, the states of the Middle East have adopted diverse approaches to the problem of developing strong and stable economies. Some, like Nasser in Egypt and the leaders of the Ba'ath Party in Syria, attempted to create a form of Arab socialism, favoring a high level of government involvement in the economy to relieve the inequities of the free enterprise system. Others turned to the Western capitalist model to maximize growth, while using taxes or massive development projects to build a modern infrastructure, redistribute wealth, and maintain political stability and economic opportunity for all.

Whatever their approach, all the states have attempted to develop their economies in accordance with Islamic beliefs. Although the Koran has little to say about economics and can be variously interpreted as capitalist or socialist, it is clear in its opposition to charging interest and in its concern for the material welfare of the Muslim community, the *umma*. How these goals are to be achieved, however, is a matter of interpretation.

Socialist theories of economic development such as Nasser's were often suggested as a way to promote economic growth while meeting the requirements of Islamic doctrine. State intervention in the economic sector would bring about rapid development, while land redistribution and the nationalization or regulation of industry would minimize the harsh inequities of the marketplace. In general, however, the socialist approach has had little success, and most governments, including those of Egypt and Syria, have recently shifted to a more free enterprise approach while encouraging foreign investment to compensate for a lack of capital or technology.

Although the amount of arable land is relatively small, most countries in the Middle East rely to a certain degree on farming to supply food for their growing populations. Often, much of the fertile land was owned by wealthy absentee landlords, but land reform programs in several countries have attempted to alleviate this problem.

The most comprehensive, and probably the most successful, land reform program was instituted in Egypt, where Nasser and his successors managed to reassign nearly a quarter of all cultivable lands by limiting the amount a single individual could hold. Similar programs in Iran, Iraq, Libya, and Syria generally had less effect. After the 1979 revolution in Iran, many farmers seized lands forcibly from the landlords, creating questions of ownership that the revolutionary government has tried with minimal success to resolve.

Agricultural productivity throughout the region has been plagued by the lack of water. With populations growing at more than 2 percent annually on average in the Middle East (more than 3 percent in some countries), several governments have tried to increase the amount of water available for irrigation. Many attempts have been sabotaged by government ineptitude, political disagreements, and territorial conflicts, however. The best-known example is the Aswan Dam, which was built by Soviet engineers in the 1950s. The project was designed to control the flow of water throughout the Nile valley, but it has had a number of undesirable environmental consequences. Today, the dearth of water in the region is reaching crisis proportions.

Another way governments have attempted to deal with rapid population growth is to encourage emigration. Oil-producing states with small populations, such as Saudi Arabia and the United Arab Emirates, have imported labor from other countries in the region, mostly to work in the oil fields. By the mid-1980s, more than 40 percent of the population in those states was composed of foreign nationals, who often sent the bulk of their salaries back to their families in their home countries. The decline in oil revenues since the mid-1980s, however, has forced several governments to take measures to stabilize or reduce the migrant population. Since the Iraqi invasion, Kuwait, for example, has expelled all Palestinians and restricted migrant workers from other countries to three-year stays.

The economies of the Middle Eastern countries, then, are in a state of rapid flux. Political and military conflicts have exacerbated economic problems such as water use, which in turn have compounded political issues. For example, disputes between Israel and its neighbors over water rights and between Iraq and its neighbors over the exploitation of the Tigris and the Euphrates have caused serious tensions in recent years. In Saudi Arabia, declining oil revenues combined with the evidence of corruption among Saudi elites have aroused a deep sense of anger and support for radical politics among some segments of the populace.

The Islamic Revival

In recent years, many developments in the Middle East have been described in terms of a resurgence of traditional values and customs in response to Western influence. Indeed, some conservative religious forces in the area have consciously attempted to replace foreign culture and values with allegedly "pure" Islamic forms of belief and behavior.

But the Islamic revival is not a simple dichotomy between traditional and modern, native and foreign, or irrational and rational. In the first place, many Muslims in the Middle East believe that Islamic values and modern ways are not incompatible and may even be mutually reinforcing in some ways. Second, the resurgence of what are sometimes called "fundamentalist" Islamic groups may, in a Middle Eastern context, be a rational and practical response to destabilizing forces, such as corruption and hedonism, and self-destructive practices, such as drunkenness, prostitution, and the use of drugs. Finally, the reassertion of Islamic values can be a means of establishing cultural identity and fighting off the overwhelming impact of Western ideas.

Initially, many Muslim intellectuals responded to Western influence by trying to create a "modernized" set of Islamic beliefs and practices that would not clash with the demands of the twentieth century. This process took place to some degree in most Islamic societies, but it was especially prevalent in Turkey, Egypt, and Iran. Mustapha Kemal Ataturk embraced the strategy when he attempted to secularize the Islamic religion in the new Turkish republic. The Turkish model was followed by Shah Reza Khan and his son Mohammad Reza Pahlavi in Iran and then by Nasser in postwar Egypt, all of whom attempted to make use of Islamic values while asserting the primacy of other issues such as political and economic development. Religion, in effect, had become the handmaiden of political power, national identity, and economic prosperity.

For obvious reasons, these secularizing trends were particularly noticeable among the political, intellectual, and economic elites in urban areas. They had less influence in the countryside, among the poor, and among devout elements within the *ulama*. Many of the latter believed that Western secular trends in the cities had given birth to political and economic corruption, sexual promiscuity, hedonism, individualism, and the prevalence of alcohol, pornography, and drugs. Although such practices had long existed in the Middle East, they were now far more visible and socially acceptable.

This reaction intensified after World War I, when the Western presence increased. In 1928, devout Muslims in Egypt formed the Muslim Brotherhood as a means of promoting personal piety. Later the movement began to take a more activist approach, including eventually the use of terrorism by a radical minority. Despite Nasser's surface commitment to Islamic ideals and Arab unity, some Egyptians were fiercely opposed to his policies and regarded his vision of Arab socialism as a betrayal of Islamic principles. Nasser reacted harshly and executed a number of his leading opponents.

The movement to return to Islamic purity reached its zenith in Iran. It is not surprising that Iran took the lead in light of its long tradition of ideological purity within the Shi'ite sect as well as the uncompromisingly secular character of the shah's reforms in the postwar era. In revolutionary Iran, traditional Islamic beliefs are all-pervasive and extend into education, clothing styles, social practices, and the legal system. In recent years, for example, Iranian women have been heavily fined or even flogged for violating the Islamic dress code.

The cultural and social effects of the Iranian Revolution have been profound, as Iranian ideas have spread throughout the area. In Algeria, the political influence of fundamentalist Islamic groups has grown substantially and enabled them to win a stunning victory in the national elections in 1992. When the military stepped in to cancel the second round of elections and crack down on the militants, the latter responded with a campaign of terrorism against moderates that has claimed thousands of lives.

A similar trend has emerged in Egypt, where militant groups such as the Muslim Brotherhood have engaged in terrorism, including the assassination of Sadat and more recent attacks on foreign tourists, who are considered carriers of corrupt Western influence. In 1994, the prominent novelist Naguid Mahfouz was stabbed outside his home, apparently in response to earlier writings that were deemed blasphemous of Muslim belief.

Even in Turkey, generally considered the most secular of Islamic societies, a militant political group, known as the Islamic Welfare Party, took power in a coalition government formed in 1996. The new prime minister, Necmettin Erbakan, adopted a pro-Arab stance in foreign affairs and threatened to reduce the country's economic and political ties to Europe. Worried moderates voiced their concern that the secular legacy of Kemal Ataturk was being eroded, and eventually Erbakan agreed to resign under heavy pressure from the military. Rejected in its application for membership in the European Union and uncomfortable with the militancy of its Arab neighbors, Turkey has established a security relationship with Israel and seeks close ties with the United States. But religious and economic discontent lies just beneath the surface, and Ataturk's own legacy, known as "Kemalism," has come under close scrutiny by critics.

Throughout the Middle East, even governments and individuals who do not support efforts to return to pure Islamic principles have adjusted their behavior and beliefs in subtle ways. In Egypt, for example, the government now encourages television programs devoted to religion in preference to comedies and adventure shows imported from the West, and alcohol is discouraged or at least consumed more discreetly. On the other hand, criticism of strict government censorship is on the rise in Iran, and the recent election of a moderate majority in the Iranian parliament may undercut the domination of all aspects of social and cultural life by fundamentalist clerics.

The Role of Women

Nowhere have the fault lines between tradition and modernity within Muslim societies in the Middle East been so sharp as in the ongoing debate over the role of women. At the beginning of the twentieth century, women's place in Middle Eastern society had changed little since the death of the Prophet Muhammad. Women were secluded in their homes and had few legal, political, or social rights.

During the first decades of the twentieth century, advocates of modernist views began to contend that Islamic doctrine was not inherently opposed to women's rights. To modernists, Islamic traditions such as female seclusion, wearing the veil, and even polygamy were actually pre-Islamic folk traditions that had been tolerated in the early Islamic era and continued to be practiced in later centuries. Such views had considerable impact on a number of Middle Eastern societies, including Turkey and Iran. As we have seen, greater rights for women was a crucial element in the social revolution promoted by Kemal Ataturk in Turkey. In Iran, Shah Reza Khan and his son granted female suffrage and encouraged the education of women. In Egypt, a vocal feminist movement arose in educated women's circles in Cairo as early as the 1920s.

GOLDA MEIR. Golda Meir was one of the most beloved leaders of the new state of Israel. Born in Russia and raised in the United States, she became an ardent Zionist and immigrated to Palestine in the 1920s. An energetic pioneer with a dream and determination, Meir became Israel's fourth prime minister, in 1969, and led her nation through a period of tension in Arab-Israeli relations.

Modernist views had somewhat less effect in other Islamic states, such as Iraq, Jordan, Morocco, and Algeria, where traditional views of women continue to prevail in varying degrees. Particularly in rural areas, notions of women's liberation made little headway. Most conservative by far was Saudi Arabia, where women were not only segregated and expected to wear the veil in public, but were also restricted in education and forbidden to drive automobiles (see the box on p. 938).

Until recently, the general trend in urban areas of the Middle East was toward a greater role for women. With the exception of conservative religious communities, women in Israel have achieved substantial equality with men and are active in politics, the professions, and even the armed forces. Golda Meir (1898–1978), prime minister of Israel from 1969 to 1974, became an international symbol of the ability of women to be world leaders.

In 1999, a governmental edict declared that women would get the right to vote in Kuwait, while women have been granted an equal right to divorce in Egypt. On the other hand, there has been a notable shift toward a more traditional approach to gender roles in many Middle Eastern societies. The reactions were especially strong in Iran, where attacks by religious conservatives on the growing role of women contributed to the emotions underlying the Iranian Revolution of 1979. That revolution had repercussions in other Islamic societies. Women in secular countries such as Egypt, Turkey, and far-off Malaysia have begun to dress more modestly in public, while criticism of open sexuality in the media has become increasingly frequent.

Inside Iran, the revolution caused women to return to more traditional forms of behavior. They were instructed to wear the veil and to dress modestly in public. Films produced in postrevolutionary Iran expressed the new morality. They rarely featured women, and when they did, physical contact between men and women was prohibited. Still, Iranian women have many freedoms that they lacked before the twentieth century; for example, they can attend a university, receive military training, vote, practice birth control, and publish fiction. Recently, supporters of the moderate president Mohammed Khatemi have proposed that women be permitted to play a greater role in the political process.

GOSSIP AMONG THE PYRAMIDS. In modern Cairo, the suburbs of the city creep up to the very feet of the ancient pyramids of Giza. Just beyond the pyramid in the background lies the Sahara, a vast wasteland that stretches unbroken for three thousand miles to the Atlantic Ocean. In the foreground, seemingly oblivious to the majesty of the ancient empire of the pharaohs, local residents discuss the events of the day on their return from the markets.

Contemporary Literature and Art in the Middle East

As in other areas of Asia and Africa, the encounter with the West in the nineteenth and twentieth centuries stimulated a cultural renaissance in the Middle East. Muslim authors translated Western works into Arabic and Persian and began to experiment with new literary forms.

KEEPING THE CAMEL OUT OF THE TENT

"Almighty God created sexual desire in ten parts; then he gave nine parts to women and one to men." So pronounced Ali, Muhammad's son-in-law, as he explained why women are held morally responsible as the instigators of sexual intercourse. Consequently, over the centuries Islamic women have been secluded, veiled, and in many cases genitally mutilated in order to safeguard male virtue. Women are forbidden to look directly at, speak to, or touch a man prior to marriage. Even today, they are often sequestered at home or limited to strictly segregated areas away from all male contact. Women normally pray at home or in an enclosed antechamber of the mosque so their physical presence will not disturb men's spiritual concentration.

Especially limiting today are the laws governing women's behavior in Saudi Arabia. Schooling for girls has never been compulsory, because fathers believe that "educating women is like allowing the nose of the camel into the tent; eventually the beast will edge in and take up all the room inside." The country did not establish its first girls' school until 1956. The following description of Saudi women is from Nine Parts Desire: The Hidden World of Islamic Women, *by the journalist Geraldine Brooks.*

GERALDINE BROOKS, *NINE PARTS DESIRE*

Women were first admitted to university in Saudi Arabia in 1962, and all women's colleges remain strictly segregated. Lecture rooms come equipped with closed-circuit TVs and telephones, so women students can listen to a male professor and question him by phone, without having to contaminate themselves by being seen by him. When the first dozen women graduated from university in 1973, they were devastated to find that their names hadn't been printed on the commencement program. The old tradition, that it dishonors women to mention them, was depriving them of recognition they believed they'd earned. The women and their families protested, so a separate program was printed and a segregated graduation ceremony was held for the students' female relatives. . . .

But while the opening of women's universities widened access to higher learning for women, it also made the educational experience much shallower. Before 1962, many progressive Saudi families had sent their daughters abroad for education. They had returned to the kingdom not only with a degree but with experience of the outside world. . . . Now a whole generation of Saudi women have completed their education entirely within the country. . . .

Lack of opportunity for education abroad means that Saudi women are trapped in the confines of an education system that still lags men's. Subjects such as geology and petroleum engineering—tickets to influential jobs in Saudi Arabia's oil economy—remain closed to women. . . . Few women's colleges have their own libraries, and libraries shared with men's schools are either entirely off limits to women or open to them only one day per week. . . .

But women and men sit the same degree examinations. Professors quietly acknowledge the women's scores routinely outstrip the men's. "It's no surprise," said one woman professor. "Look at their lives. The boys have their cars, they can spend the evenings cruising the streets with their friends, sitting in cafés, buying black-market alcohol and drinking all night. What do the girls have? Four walls and their books. For them, education is everything."

Iran has produced one of the most prominent national literatures in the contemporary Middle East. Since World War II, Iranian literature has been hampered somewhat by political considerations, since it has been expected to serve first the Pahlavi monarchy and more recently the Islamic Republic. Nevertheless, Iranian writers are among the most prolific in the region and often write in prose, which has finally been accepted as the equal of poetry. Perhaps the most outstanding Iranian author of the twentieth century was the short story writer Sadeq Hedayat. Hedayat was obsessed with the frailty and absurdity of life and wrote with compassion about the problems of ordinary human beings. Frustrated and disillusioned at the government's suppression of individual liberties, he committed suicide in 1951. Like Japan's Mishima Yukio, Hedayat later became a cult figure among his country's youth.

Despite the male-oriented character of Iranian society, many of the new writers have been women. Since the revolution, the veil has become the central metaphor in Iranian women's writing. Those who favor the veil praise it as the last bastion of defense against Western cultural imperialism. Behind the veil, the Islamic woman can breathe freely, unpolluted by foreign exploitation and moral corruption. Other Iranian women, however, consider the veil a "mobile prison" or an oppressive anachronism from the Dark Ages. As one writer expressed it:

> As I pulled the chador [the veil] over me, I felt a heaviness descending over me. I was hidden and in hiding. There was nothing visible left of Sousan Azadi. I felt like an animal of the light suddenly trapped in a cave. I was just another faceless Moslem woman carrying a whole inner world hidden inside the chador.[13]

Whether or not they accept the veil, women writers are a vital part of contemporary Iranian literature.

Like Iran, Egypt in the twentieth century has experienced a flowering of literature accelerated by the establishment of the Egyptian republic in the early 1950s. The most illustrious contemporary Egyptian writer is Naguib Mahfouz, who won the Nobel Prize for Literature in 1988. His *Cairo Trilogy* (1952) chronicles three generations of a merchant family in Cairo during the tumultuous years between the world wars. Mahfouz is particularly adept at blending panoramic historical events with the intimate lives of ordinary human beings. Unlike many other modern writers, his message is essentially optimistic and reflects his hope that religion and science can work together for the overall betterment of humankind.

Although Israeli literature arises from a totally different tradition from that of its neighbors, it shares with them certain contemporary characteristics and a concern for ordinary human beings. As they identify with the aspirations of the new nation, many Israeli writers try to find a sense of order in the new reality, voicing terrors from the past and hopes for the future.

Some contemporary Israeli authors, however, have refused to serve as spokespersons for Zionism and are speaking out on sensitive national issues. The internationally renowned novelist Amos Oz, for example, has examined the problems inherent in the kibbutz, one of Israel's most hallowed institutions. A vocal supporter of peace with the Palestinians, Oz is a member of Peace Now and the author of a political tract titled *Israel, Palestine, and Peace*.

The novels of David Grossman, another Israeli author strongly committed to peace in the region, have been made into films, bringing him international attention. In his nonfiction work *The Yellow Wind*, he attempted to understand the feelings of the Palestinian people living in the occupied territories, presenting them empathetically as the reverse image of the Israelis, dreaming of their own homeland. Although he was criticized for such views by ultraconservative Jewish religious groups, Grossman wrote a sequel focusing on the many questions of identity, land, and language that Palestinians share with Israelis.

Like literature, the art of the modern Middle East has been profoundly influenced by its exposure to Western culture. At first artists tended to imitate Western models, but later they began to experiment with national styles, returning to earlier forms for inspiration. Some emulated the writers in returning to the village to depict peasants and shepherds, but others followed international trends and attempted to express the alienation and disillusionment that characterize so much of modern life.

Reflecting their hopes for the new nation, Israeli painters sought to bring to life the sentiments of pioneers arriving in a promised land. Many attempted to capture the longing for community expressed in the Israeli commune, or kibbutz. Others searched for the roots of Israeli culture in the history of the Jewish people or in the horrors of the Holocaust. The experience of the Holocaust has attracted particular attention from sculptors, who work in wood and metal as well as stone.

The popular music of the contemporary Middle East has also been strongly influenced by that of the modern West, but to different degrees in different countries. In Israel, many contemporary young rock stars voice lyrics as irreverent toward the traditions of their elders as do those of Europe and the United States. One idol of many Israeli young people, the rock star Aviv Ghefen, declares himself to be "a person of no values," and his music carries a shock value that attacks the country's political and social shibboleths with abandon. The rock music popular among Palestinians, on the other hand, makes greater use of Arab musical motifs and is closely tied to a political message. One recent recording, "The Song of the Engineer," lauds Yehia Ayash, a Palestinian accused of manufacturing many of the explosive devices used in recent terrorist attacks on Israeli citizens. The lyrics have their own shock value: "Spread the flame of revolution. Your explosive will wipe the enemy out, like a volcano, a torch, a banner." When one Palestinian rock leader from the Gaza Strip was asked why his group employed a musical style that originated in the West, he explained, "For us, this is a tool like any other. Young people in Gaza like our music, they listen to us, they buy our cassettes, and so they spread our message."

CONCLUSION

The Middle East, like the continent of Africa, is one of the most unstable regions in the world today. In part, this turbulence is due to the continued interference of outsiders attracted by the massive oil reserves under the parched wastes of the Arabian peninsula and in the vicinity of the Persian Gulf. Oil indeed is both a blessing and a curse to the peoples of the region.

Another factor contributing to the volatility of the Middle East is the tug-of-war between the sense of ethnic identity in the form of nationalism and the intense longing to be part of a broader Islamic community, a dream that dates back to the time of the Prophet Muhammad. The desire to create that community—a vision threatened by the presence of the alien state of Israel—inspired Gamal Abdul Nasser in the 1950s and the Ayatollah Khomeini in the 1970s and 1980s and probably motivates many of the actions of Saddam Hussein today.

A final reason for the turmoil currently affecting the Middle East is the intense debate over the role of religion in civil society. It has been customary in recent years for Western commentators to label Muslim efforts to return to a purer form of Islam as fanatical and extremist, reflecting a misguided attempt to reverse the course of history, and there is no doubt that many of the legal and social restrictions now being enforced in various Muslim countries in the Middle East appear excessively harsh and often repugnant to outside observers. But it is important to remember that Muslim societies are not alone in deploring the sense of moral decline that is now allegedly taking place in societies throughout the world. Nor are they alone in advocating a restoration of traditional religious values as a means of reversing the trend. Movements dedicated to such purposes are appearing in many other societies (including, among others, Israel and the United States) and can be viewed as an understandable reaction to the rapid and often bewildering changes that are now taking place in the contemporary world. Not infrequently, members of such groups turn to violence as a means of making their point. While the tensions between tradition and modernity appear to be strongest in the contemporary Middle East, then, they are hardly unique to that region. The consequences as yet cannot be foreseen.

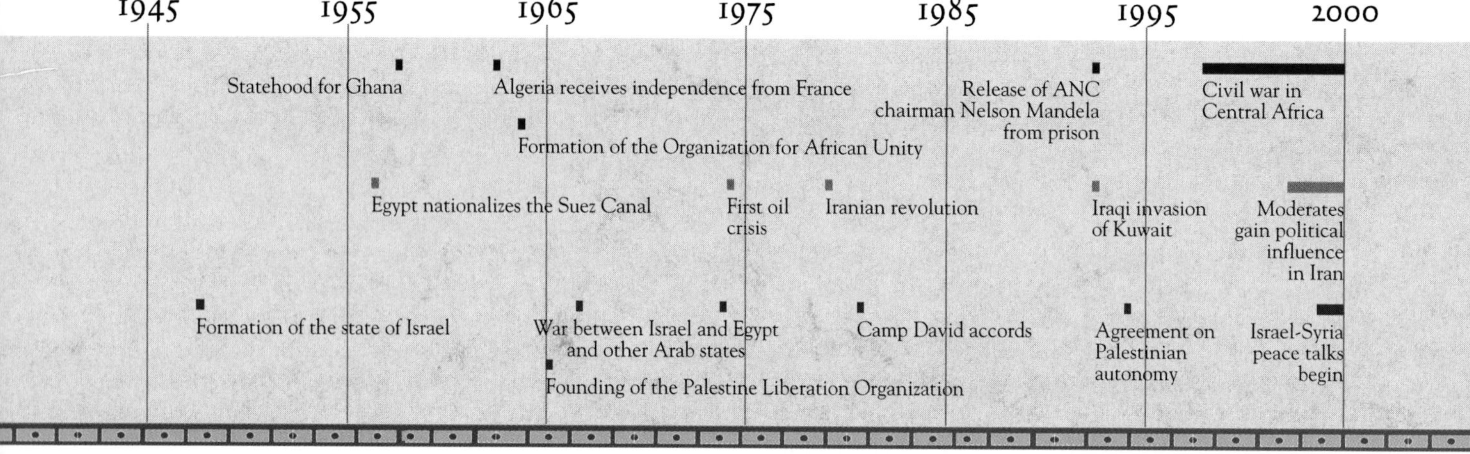

Chapter Notes

1. Quoted in G.-C. M. Mutiso, *Socio-Political Thought in African Literature* (New York, 1974), p. 117.
2. Albert Ojuka, "Pedestrian, to Passing Benz-Man," quoted in Adrian Roscoe, *Uhuru's Fire: African Literature East to South* (Cambridge, 1977), p. 103.
3. *New York Times,* September 1, 1996.
4. Taban Lo Liyong, "Student's Lament," quoted in Roscoe, *Uhuru's Fire,* pp. 120–21.
5. Dan Agbee, in *Newswatch* (Lagos), quoted in *World Press Review,* August 1991, p. 16.
6. Kenneth Little, *African Women in Towns: An Aspect of Africa's Social Revolution* (Cambridge, 1973), p. 6.
7. Abioseh Nicol, *A Truly Married Woman and Other Stories* (London, 1965), p. 12.
8. Ama Ata Aidoo, *No Sweetness Here* (New York, 1995), p. 136.
9. Quoted in the *New York Times,* May 13, 1996.
10. Ngugi Wa Thiong'o, *Decolonising the Mind: The Politics of Language in African Literature* (Portsmouth, N.H., 1986), p. 103.
11. George Awoonor-Williams, *Rediscovery and Other Poems* (Ibadan, 1964), quoted in Mutiso, pp. 81–82.
12. Quoted in Roy R. Andersen, Robert F. Seibert, and Jon G. Wagner, *Politics and Change in the Middle East: Sources of Conflict and Accommodation,* 4th ed. (Englewood Cliffs, N.J., 1982), p. 51.
13. Sousan Azadi, with Angela Ferrante, *Out of Iran* (London, 1987), p. 223, quoted in *Stories by Iranian Women Since the Revolution,* ed. S. Sullivan (Austin, Tex., 1991), p. 13.

Suggested Readings

For general surveys of contemporary African history, see R. Oliver and J. D. Fage, *A Short History of Africa* (Harmondsworth, 1986); R. Oliver, *The African Experience* (New York, 1992), which contains interesting essays on a variety of themes; and K. Shillington, *History of Africa* (New York, 1989), which takes a chronological and geographical approach and includes excellent maps and illustrations.

Two recent treatments are B. Davidson, *Africa in History: Themes and Outlines,* rev. ed. (New York, 1991), and P. Curtin et al., *African History* (London, 1995).

On nationalist movements, see P. Gifford and W. R. Louis, eds., *The Transfer of Power in Africa* (New Haven, Conn., 1982), and J. D. Hargreaves, *Decolonisation in Africa* (London, 1988). For an

African perspective, see K. Nkrumah, *Ghana* (London, 1959). For a poignant analysis of the hidden costs of nation building, see N. F. Mostert, *The Epic of South Africa's Creation and the Tragedy of the Xhosa People* (London, 1992).

For a survey of economic conditions in Africa, see *Sub-Saharan Africa: From Crisis to Sustainable Growth* (Washington, D.C., 1989), issued by the World Bank. Also see A. O'Connor, *The African City* (London, 1983), and J. Illiffe, *The African Poor* (Cambridge, 1983).

Political events in Africa are often examined on a regional basis. For an overview, see A. Mazrui and M. Tidy, *Nationalism and New States in Africa* (Portsmouth, N.H., 1984). See also S. A. Akintoye, *The Emergent African States* (London, 1976), and S. Decalo, *Coups and Army Rule in Africa* (New Haven, Conn., 1990).

For a country-by-country survey of African literature, see L. S. Klein, ed., *African Literatures in the Twentieth Century: A Guide* (New York, 1986). On art, see F. Willett, *African Art: An Introduction* (New York, 1985). Of the many short story collections showcasing different African authors, we recommend C. Achebe and C. L. Innes, eds., *The Heinemann Book of Contemporary Short Stories* (Portsmouth, N.H., 1992); C. H. Bruner, ed., *Unwinding Threads: Writing by Women in Africa* (Oxford, 1983); and C. H. Bruner, ed., *The Heinemann Book of African Women's Writing* (Oxford, 1993).

For interesting analyses of women's issues in the Africa of this time frame, see C. Robertson and I. Berger, eds., *Women and Class in Africa* (New York, 1986); S. B. Stichter and J. L. Parpart, eds., *Patriarchy and Class: African Women in the Home and the Workforce* (Boulder, Colo., 1988); and I. Berger and E. F. White, *Women in Sub-Saharan Africa* (Bloomington, Ind., 1999).

Good general surveys of the modern Middle East include A. Goldschmidt, Jr., *A Concise History of the Middle East* (Boulder, Colo., 1991), and G. E. Perry, *The Middle East: Fourteen Islamic Centuries* (Elizabeth City, N.J., 1992).

On Israel and the Palestinian question, see B. Reich, *Israel: Land of Tradition and Conflict* (Boulder, Colo., 1985), and C. C. O'Brien, *The Siege: The Saga of Israel and Zionism* (New York, 1986). On U.S.–Israeli relations, see S. Green, *Living by the Sword: America and Israel in the Middle East, 1968–1987* (London, 1988). Israeli politics are analyzed in D. Peretz, *The Government and Politics of Israel* (Boulder, Colo., 1983).

The issue of oil is examined in G. Luciani, *The Oil Companies and the Arab World* (New York, 1984), and P. Odell, *Oil and World Power* (New York, 1986). Also see M. H. Kerr and El Sayed Yassin, eds., *Rich and Poor States in the Middle East: Egypt and the New Arab Order* (Boulder, Colo., 1985). On Egypt, see A. Goldschmidt, Jr., *Modern Egypt: The Formation of a Nation-State* (Boulder, Colo., 1988).

On the Iranian Revolution, see S. Bakash, *The Reign of the Ayatollahs* (New York, 1984), and B. Rubin, *Iran Since the Revolution* (Boulder, Colo., 1985). On Ayatollah Khomeini's role and ideas, see H. Algar, *Islam and Revolution: The Writings and Declarations of Imam Khomeini* (Berkeley, Calif., 1981). The Iran-Iraq War is discussed in C. Davies, ed., *After the War: Iran, Iraq and the Arab Gulf* (Chichester, UK, 1990), and S. C. Pelletiere, *The Iran-Iraq War: Chaos in a Vacuum* (New York, 1992).

On the politics of the Middle East, see J. A. Bill and R. Springborg, *Politics in the Middle East* (London, 1990), and R. R. Anderson, R. F. Seibert, and J. G. Wagner, *Politics and Change in the Middle East: Sources of Conflict and Accommodation* (Englewood Cliffs, N.J., 1993). See also T. Ismael, *International Relations of the Contemporary Middle East* (Syracuse, 1986), and B. Reich, ed., *The Powers in the Middle East: The Ultimate Strategic Arena* (New York, 1987).

Two excellent surveys of women in Islam from pre-Islamic society to the present are L. Ahmed, *Women and Gender in Islam: Historical Roots of a Modern Debate* (New Haven, Conn., 1993), and G. Nashat and J. E. Tucker, *Women in the Middle East and North Africa* (Bloomington, Ind., 1999). Also consult the more detailed G. Nashat, ed., *Women and Revolution in Iran* (Boulder, Colo., 1983); M. Afkhami and E. Friedl, *In the Eye of the Storm: Women in Post-Revolutionary Iran* (Syracuse, N.Y., 1994); and W. Wiebke, *Women in Islam* (Princeton, N.J., 1995).

For a general anthology of Middle Eastern literature, see J. Kritzeck, *Modern Islamic Literature from 1800 to the Present* (New York, 1970). For a scholarly but accessible overview of Arabic literature, see M. M. Badawi, *A Short History of Modern Arab Literature* (Oxford, 1993). For Iranian literature, see M. Southgate, *Modern Persian Short Stories* (Washington, D.C., 1980), and S. Sullivan and F. Milani, *Stories by Iranian Women Since the Revolution* (Austin, Tex., 1991). For an accessible introduction to the life and work of Hedayat, see I. Bashiri, *The Fiction of Sadeq Hedayat* (Lexington, Ky., 1984). On Mahfouz, see M. N. Mikhail, *Studies in the Short Fiction of Mahfouz and Idris* (New York, 1992). See also T. S. Halman, *Contemporary Turkish Literature* (East Brunswick, N. J., 1982).

For additional reading, go to InfoTrac College Edition, your online research library at http://web1.infotrac-college.com

Enter the search terms "developing countries" using the Subject Guide.

Enter the search term "Africa" using the Subject Guide.

Enter the search terms "Nelson Mandela" using the Subject Guide.

Enter the search terms "Israel history" using Keywords.

Enter the search term "Palestine" using the Subject Guide.

CHAPTER 31

A House Divided: The Emergence of Independent States in South and Southeast Asia

CHAPTER OUTLINE

- THE END OF THE BRITISH RAJ
- INDEPENDENT INDIA
- THE LAND OF THE PURE: PAKISTAN SINCE INDEPENDENCE
- PROBLEMS OF POVERTY AND PLURALISM IN SOUTH ASIA
- INDIAN ART AND LITERATURE SINCE INDEPENDENCE
- GANDHI'S VISION
- THE DISMANTLING OF COLONIALISM IN SOUTHEAST ASIA
- THE ERA OF INDEPENDENT STATES
- DAILY LIFE: TOWN AND COUNTRY IN CONTEMPORARY SOUTHEAST ASIA
- CULTURAL TRENDS
- REGIONAL CONFLICT AND COOPERATION: THE RISE OF ASEAN
- CONCLUSION

FOCUS QUESTIONS

- How did Mahatma Gandhi's and Jawaharlal Nehru's goals for India differ, and what role have each leader's views played in shaping modern India?
- What problems has India faced since independence, and how have its leaders attempted to solve these problems?
- How have social and economic life, the position of women, and culture changed in India since independence, and to what extent do traditional patterns persist?
- What problems have the nations of Southeast Asia faced since 1945, and how have they attempted to solve these problems?
- How do the political, social, and economic developments in Southeast Asia since 1945 reflect an effort to adapt Western institutions and values to Southeast Asian traditions?

In a letter to his friend and colleague Jawaharlal Nehru in October 1945, the Indian spiritual leader Mahatma Gandhi argued passionately against Nehru's dream of building a modern industrialized society in India. "I believe," Gandhi said, "that if India, and through India the world, is to achieve real freedom, then sooner or later we shall have to go and live in the villages—in huts, not in palaces."[1] Truth and nonviolence, he insisted, could be found only in the simplicity of village life, not in modern industrialized cities patterned after those in the West. Nehru did not agree, and after independence in 1947, he set his country on the path of industrial revolution. As we shall see, Nehru's decision did not end the debate, which continues today, as Indians seek to reconcile their traditional values with the demands of modern life.

For more than a century, the resources of South and Southeast Asia were systematically plundered by the Western colonial powers. In the process, the region was linked ever more closely to the global capitalist economy. Yet, as in other areas of Asia and Africa, the experience brought only limited benefits to the local peoples, as little industrial development took place and the bulk of the profits went into the pockets of Western entrepreneurs.

Early in the twentieth century, nationalist forces began to seek reforms in colonial policy and the eventual overthrow of colonial power. But the peoples of South and Southeast Asia did not regain their national independence until after World War II. Finally, between 1945 and 1955, independent states emerged throughout the southern tier of Asia.

The leaders of these new nations were generally dedicated to building modern societies on the Western model. But escaping the legacy of the past was not easy. Most of the new states were weak and inexperienced and struggled with only limited success to develop advanced economies, establish stable political systems, and foster a sense of common identity among their diverse populations. Old animosities among the various ethnic groups reemerged and led to mutual suspicion and strife within the region. Half a century after independence, peace and prosperity are still more a dream than a reality for many peoples of the area.

The End of the British Raj

During the 1930s, the nationalist movement in India was severely shaken by factional disagreements between Hindus and Muslims within its own ranks. The outbreak of World War II interrupted these sectarian clashes and brought new problems. To the dismay of the leaders of the Indian National Congress, the British government committed India to the war without consulting its people or its elected leaders (the same thing had occurred during Would War I). At the news, a number of Congress legislators resigned, and Mohammed Ali Jinnah, leader of the Muslim League, demanded the creation of a separate state. Mahatma Gandhi started a new civil disobedience movement and demanded that the British "quit India." Jawaharlal Nehru was arrested. To dampen the protests, the British offered India dominion status after the war and the right of secession for individual states, but the offer was rejected by the Congress.

When the war ended in 1945, the British government offered a complicated union arrangement with divided powers and continued British presence, but Congress leaders were dubious. When clashes between Hindus and Muslims broke out in several cities, Jinnah called for "direct action," while British Prime Minister Clement Attlee announced that power would be transferred to "responsible Indian hands" by June 1948. To bring about the transfer of power, Lord Louis Mountbatten, a member of the British royal family, was appointed viceroy.

But the imminence of independence did not dampen communal strife. As riots escalated, Mountbatten reluctantly accepted the inevitability of partition, while the Congress and the Muslim League were reconciled to the division of Bengal and the Punjab, two provinces with Hindu and Muslim populations. Pakistan itself would be divided between the main area of Muslim habitation in the Indus River valley in the west and a separate territory in east Bengal 2,000 miles to the east. Among Congress leaders, Gandhi alone objected to the division of India. A Muslim woman criticized him for his opposition to partition, asking him, "If two brothers were living together in the same house and wanted to separate and live in two different houses, would you object?" "Ah," Gandhi replied, "if only we could separate as two brothers. But we will not. It will be an orgy of blood. We shall tear ourselves asunder in the womb of the mother who bears us."[2] But Gandhi was increasingly regarded as a figure of the past by many Indian leaders, and his views were ignored.

On July 15, 1947, the British declared that one month later, two independent nations—India and Pakistan—would be established. Mountbatten instructed the rulers in the princely states to choose which state they would join by August 15, but problems arose in predominantly Hindu Hyderabad, where the maharaja was a Muslim, and mountainous Kashmir, where a Hindu prince ruled over a Muslim population. Independence was declared on August 15, but the flight of millions of Hindus and Muslims across the borders in Bengal and the Punjab led to violence and the death of more than a million people. One of the casualties evoked widespread mourning. On January 30, 1948, a Hindu militant assassinated Gandhi as he was going to morning prayer. The assassin was apparently motivated by Gandhi's opposition to a Hindu India.

INDEPENDENT INDIA

With independence, the Indian National Congress, now renamed the Congress Party, moved from opposition to the responsibility of power. The prospect must have been intimidating. The vast majority of India's nearly 400 million people were poor and illiterate. The new nation encompassed a bewildering number of ethnic groups and fourteen major languages. Although Congress leaders spoke bravely of building a new nation, Indian society still bore many of the scars of past wars and divisions.

One advantage that India possessed was an intelligent, self-confident, and reasonably united leadership. In the crucible years of colonialism, the Congress Party had gained experience in government. Jawaharlal Nehru, the new prime minister, was respected and even revered by millions of Indians.

The government's first problem was to resolve the border disputes left over from the transition period. The rulers of Hyderabad and Kashmir had both followed their own preferences rather than the wishes of their subject populations. Nehru was determined to include both states within India. In 1948, Indian troops invaded Hyderabad and annexed the area. India was also able to seize most

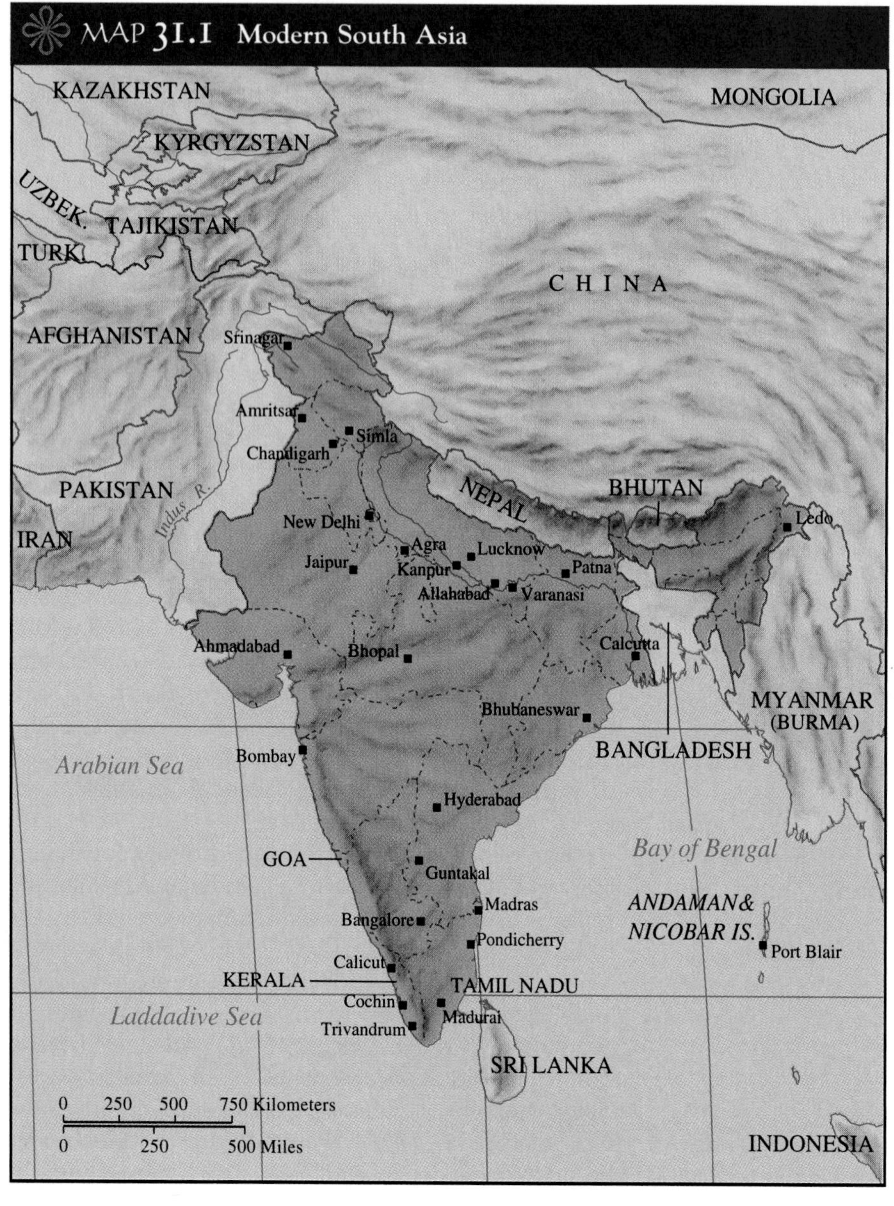

MAP 31.1 Modern South Asia

NEHRU'S PROGRAM FOR INDIA

Before World War II, Jawaharlal Nehru was a leading member of the Indian National Congress and an outspoken advocate of independence from British colonial rule. He rejected not only Western imperialism, but also the capitalist system that underlay the drive for empire. Nehru saw socialism as the answer for India but rejected the Soviet form in favor of a more moderate version that respected Western democratic principles and the concept of private property. The following excerpt is from a speech Nehru delivered to leading members of the Congress as its newly elected president in 1936.

NEHRU'S SOCIALIST CREED

I am convinced that the only key to the solution of the world's problems and of India's problems lies in socialism, and when I use this word I do so not in a vague humanitarian way but in the scientific economic sense. . . . I see no way of ending the poverty, the vast unemployment, the degradation and the subjection of the Indian people except through socialism. That involves vast and revolutionary changes in our political and social structure, the ending of vested interests in land and industry, as well as the feudal and autocratic Indian states system. That means the ending of private property, except in a restricted sense, and the replacement of the present profit system by a higher ideal of cooperative service. . . . In short, it means a new civilization, radically different from the present capitalist order. Some glimpse we can have of this new civilization in the territories of the U.S.S.R. Much has happened there which has pained me greatly and with which I disagree, but I look upon that great and fascinating unfolding of a new order and a new civilization as the most promising feature of our dismal age. If the future is full of hope it is largely because of Soviet Russia and what it has done, and I am convinced that, if some world catastrophe does not intervene, this new civilization will spread to other lands and put an end to the wars and conflicts which capitalism feeds. . . .

I work for Indian independence because the nationalist in me cannot tolerate an alien domination; I work for it even more because for me it is the inevitable step to social and economic change. I should like the Congress to become a socialist organization and to join hands with the other forces that in the world are working for the new civilization.

of Kashmir, but at the cost of incurring the hostility of Pakistan's new leaders. An intractable problem had been created that poisoned relations between the two countries for the next generation.

An Experiment in Democratic Socialism

India's new leaders had strong ideas on the future of Indian society. Nehru was an admirer of British political institutions, but had also been influenced by the Fabian socialist movement in England. With his dominating personality, he imposed his vision of an India with democratic political institutions but a moderately socialist economic structure and, in doing so, put a personal stamp on the country that would last long after his death (see the box above).

Under Nehru's leadership, the new Republic of India adopted a political system on the British model, with a figurehead president and a parliamentary form of government. A number of political parties operated legally, from the Indian Communist Party on the left to capitalist and religious parties on the right. But the Congress Party, with its enormous prestige and charismatic leadership, was dominant at both the central and the local levels. The Congress Party aspired to represent all Indians, from rich to poor, *brahmins* to *harijans* (untouchability was legally abolished by the new government), and Hindus to Muslims and other minority religious groups.

Economic policy was patterned roughly after the program of the British Labour Party, with adjustments for local circumstances. The state took over ownership of the major industries and resources, transportation, and utilities, while private enterprise was permitted at the local and retail levels. Farmland remained in private hands, but rural cooperatives were officially encouraged.

In other respects, Nehru was a devotee of Western materialism. He was fully convinced that to succeed, India must industrialize. In advocating industrialization, Nehru departed sharply from Gandhi. Gandhi believed firmly that materialism was morally corrupting and that only simplicity and nonviolence (as represented by the traditional Indian village and the symbolic spinning wheel) could save India, and the world itself, from self-destruction (see the box on p. 946). Nehru, however, had little fear of the corrupting consequences of material wealth and complained that Gandhi "just wants to spin and weave."

Accordingly, Nehru actively pursued industrialization, although he recognized that a more efficient agricultural sector was a prerequisite for success. Reflecting the strong anticolonial views of the Congress leadership, the Indian government also sought to avoid excessive dependence on foreign investment and technological assistance. All business enterprises were required by law to have majority Indian ownership.

Nehru's staunch sense of morality was also apparent in his foreign policy. Under his guidance, India adopted

GANDHI'S VISION FOR INDIA

Where Nehru saw socialism as the answer for India's ills, Gandhi found it in the traditional village. Where Nehru favored industrialization to achieve material affluence, Gandhi praised the simple virtues of manual labor. Gandhi wrote this letter to Nehru in October 1945. A little over two years later, Gandhi was dead of an assassin's bullet, and Nehru was about to become prime minister of an independent Republic of India.

A LETTER TO JAWAHARLAL NEHRU

I take first the sharp difference of opinion that has arisen between us. . . . I believe that if India, and through India the world, is to achieve real freedom, then sooner or later we shall have to go and live in the villages—in huts, not in palaces. Millions of people can never live in cities and palaces in comfort and peace. Nor can they do so by killing one another, that is, by resorting to violence and untruth. . . . We can have the vision of . . . truth and nonviolence only in the simplicity of the villages. That simplicity resides in the spinning wheel and what is implied by the spinning wheel. . . . The sum and substance of what I want to say is that the individual person should have control over the things that are necessary for the sustenance of life. If he cannot have such control the individual cannot survive. Ultimately, the world is made up only of individuals. If there were no drops there would be no ocean. . . .

You will not be able to understand me if you think that I am talking about the villages of today. My ideal village still exists only in my imagination. . . . In this village of my dreams the villager will not be dull—he will be all awareness. He will not live like an animal in filth and darkness. Men and women will live in freedom, prepared to face the whole world. There will be no plague, no cholera, and no smallpox. Nobody will be allowed to be idle or to wallow in luxury. Everyone will have to do body labor. Granting all this, I can still envisage a number of things that will have to be organized on a large scale. Perhaps there will even be railways and also post and telegraph offices. I do not know what things there will be or will not be. Nor am I bothered about it. If I can make sure of the essential thing, other things will follow in due course. But if I give up the essential thing, I give up everything.

I want that we two should understand each other fully. . . . We both live only for India's freedom, and will be happy to die too for that freedom. . . . Though I aspire to live up to 125 years rendering service, I am nevertheless an old man, while you are comparatively young. That is why I have said that you are my heir. It is only proper that I should at least understand my heir and my heir in turn should understand me. I shall then be at peace.

a neutral posture in the Cold War and sought to provide leadership to all newly independent nations in Asia, Africa, and Latin America. The primary themes of Indian foreign policy were anticolonialism and antiracism. India's neutrality put it at odds with the United States, which during the 1950s was trying to mobilize all nations against what it viewed as the menace of international communism.

Relations with Pakistan continued to be troubled. India refused to consider Pakistan's claim to Kashmir, even though the majority of the population there was Muslim. Tension between the two countries increased during the early 1960s, leading to war in 1965. India won a quick victory, and a cease-fire was signed in the Soviet city of Tashkent. Nevertheless, the sources of mutual hostility were not resolved, and when riots against the Pakistani government broke out in East Pakistan in 1971, India intervened on the side of East Pakistan, which declared its independence as the new nation of Bangladesh.

India also encountered difficulties with China. Nehru attempted to conciliate the Chinese government by supporting its demand for admission into the United Nations and recognizing Chinese sovereignty over the province of Tibet. But when China cracked down on Tibetan autonomy in the late 1950s, India was severely critical. Shortly after, Nehru became aware that China was constructing a road in an area of Tibet claimed by India. When India sent troops to the area in the late summer of 1962, Chinese forces crossed the border and drove them back. A cease-fire was reached, but the border dispute, a consequence of boundaries drawn by a British surveying team at the beginning of the century, was not resolved.

The Post-Nehru Era

Nehru's death in 1964 aroused widespread anxiety; many observers speculated that Indian democracy was dependent on the Nehru mystique. When his successor, the soft-spoken Congress Party veteran Lal Bahadur Shastri, died in 1966, Congress leaders selected Nehru's daughter, Indira Gandhi (no relation to Mahatma Gandhi), as the new prime minister. Gandhi was inexperienced in politics, and many thought the party bosses had chosen her because she would be easy to dominate, but she quickly showed the steely determination of her father.

In a number of respects, Gandhi followed in her father's footsteps, embracing democratic socialism and a policy of neutrality in foreign affairs. If anything, she was more activist than her father. Concerned that rural poverty had become chronic, she launched major programs, including nationalizing banks, providing loans to peasants on easy terms, building low-cost housing, and distributing land to the landless. As part of the land redistribution program, she attempted to lower the ceiling on landholdings to 100 acres per family. She also introduced electoral reforms to enfranchise the poor.

Gandhi was especially worried by India's growing population, which was increasing at an annual rate of more than 2 percent. To curb the rate of growth, she adopted a policy of enforced sterilization. This policy proved unpopular, however, and along with growing official corruption and Gandhi's authoritarian tactics and intolerance of opposition, led to her defeat in the general election of 1975, the first time the Congress Party had failed to win a majority at the national level since independence. Congress also lost control of a number of state governments, where regional and ethnic parties were gaining strength.

A minority government of procapitalist parties was formed under Prime Minister Morarji Desai, who attempted to reverse India's steady drift toward socialism. But India's first non-Congress government lacked the competence and experience to handle the country's enormous problems, and within two years Gandhi was back in power with an increased electoral mandate. She now faced a new challenge, however, in the rise of ethnic and religious strife. The most dangerous situation was in the Punjab, where militant Sikhs were demanding provincial autonomy or even independence from India. Gandhi did not shrink from a confrontation and attacked Sikh rebels hiding in their Golden Temple in the city of Amritsar. The incident aroused widespread anger among the Sikh community, and in 1984, Sikh members of Gandhi's personal bodyguard assassinated her.

By now, Congress politicians were convinced that the party could not remain in power without a member of the Nehru family at the helm. Gandhi's son Sanjay, the original heir apparent, had been killed in a plane crash. Now her elder son, Rajiv, a commercial airline pilot with little apparent interest in politics, was persuaded to replace his mother as prime minister. As a politician, Rajiv lacked the strong ideological and political convictions of his mother and grandfather and proceeded to allow a greater role for private enterprise. But his government was harshly criticized for cronyism, inefficiency, and corruption, as well as insensitivity to the poor. It steadily lost its political dominance over India, particularly at the local level.

In the late 1980s, India faced a new problem. The neighboring island of Sri Lanka (previously known as Ceylon) was torn by violence between the majority Sinhalese, who are Buddhist, and the Tamils, a racial and religious minority (most Tamils are Hindus) living primarily in the northern part of the island. The leading Tamil rebel organization, which called itself the Elam Tigers of Tamil Elam, sought support and sanctuary in the southern Indian province of Tamil Nadu, where the population was ethnically related. In an effort to reduce the violence, India sent troops to Sri Lanka to suppress the rebels. While campaigning for reelection in the spring of 1991, Rajiv Gandhi was assassinated, reportedly by a member of the Tiger organization. For almost the first time since independence, India faced the future without a member of the Nehru family as prime minister. Desperate, Congress leaders even considered conferring the premiership on Rajiv's Italian widow Sonia.

PORTRAIT OF INDIRA GANDHI. After Nehru's death in 1964, India's next great leader was his daughter Indira Gandhi, who became prime minister in 1966. Gandhi sought to realize her father's ideal of building an industrialized society, until her assassination by her own Sikh bodyguards in 1984.

In the years immediately following the assassination of Rajiv Gandhi, Congress remained the leading party, but the powerful hold it had once enjoyed over the Indian electorate was gone. Rising new parties, such as the militantly Hindu Bharata Janata Party (BJP), actively vied with Congress for control of the central and state governments. Growing political instability at the center was accompanied by rising ethnic tensions between Hindus and Muslims. In the city of Bombay, the militantly Hindu Shiv Sena (Army of Siva) Party bluntly rejected the Gandhian vision of ethnic and racial harmony and attacked Muslim and foreign interests in the country.

In national elections held in May 1996, the Congress Party was badly defeated, and Prime Minister Narasimha Rao resigned from office. But the BJP, which lacked a majority of seats in the new legislature, was unable to form a government, and in the end a coalition of left and center political groups was formed. Bickering within the coalition government was intense, however, while the Congress Party, with its own president, Narasimha Rao, under investigation for corruption, tried to get its own house in order. With the opposition divided, the BJP, under Prime Minister A. B. Vajpayee, came back in power and played on Hindu sensibilities to build its political base. Sonia Gandhi has taken over the leadership of the Congress Party to improve its own political fortunes.

The Land of the Pure: Pakistan Since Independence

In August 1947, the new nation of Pakistan declared its independence. Unlike its neighbor India, Pakistan was in all respects a new nation, based on religious conviction rather than historical or ethnic tradition. Comprising two separate territories 2,000 miles apart, Pakistan by its very nature was unique and distinctive. West Pakistan, including the basin of the Indus River and the West Punjab, was perennially short of water and was populated by dry crop farmers and peoples of the steppe. East Pakistan, comprising the eastern parts of the old Indian province of Bengal, was made up of the marshy deltas of the Ganges and Brahmaputra rivers. Densely populated with rice farmers, it was the home of the artistic and intellectual Bengalis.

The new state was a product of the Muslims' wish to have their own state, yet from the start, Pakistan's leaders made it clear that they did not intend to carry the logic of the Muslim League's demand for an Islamic state to extremes. Mohammed Ali Jinnah called for a state that would assure freedom of religion and equal treatment for all (see the box on p. 949). His vision of a democratic society based on equal treatment for all citizens was only partly realized, however. The bitter division between advocates of a state based on Islamic principles and supporters of a Western-style democracy resulted in a compromise. The Constitution of 1956 described Pakistan as an "Islamic Republic, under the sovereignty of Allah," where Muslims could live in accordance with "the Holy Qur'an and the Sunnah."

Even though Pakistan was an essentially Muslim society, its first years were marked by intense internal conflicts over linguistic, religious, and regional issues. Most dangerous was the growing division between east and west. Many in East Pakistan felt that the government, based in the west, ignored the needs of the eastern section of the country. In 1952, riots erupted in East Pakistan over the government's decision to adopt Urdu (a Muslim version of Hindi) as the national language of the entire country. Most East Pakistanis spoke Bengali, an unrelated language. In 1958, the civilian government was overthrown by a military coup by General Ayub Khan. His regime dissolved the constitution and set up a new system with a strong central government and a limited franchise of fewer than 100,000 voters. But the new military government was unable to curb the religious and ethnic tensions.

In elections for the National Assembly in 1970, supporters of autonomy led by Sheikh Mujibur Rahman won a majority in East Pakistan. The Pakistani People's Party, led by the populist Zulfikar Ali Bhutto, won a similar majority in the west, but the military government refused to step down and declared martial law. In March 1971, negotiations between representatives of east and west broke down, and East Pakistan declared its independence as the new nation of Bangladesh. Pakistani troops arrested Mujibur Rahman and attempted to restore central government authority in the capital of Dhaka, but rebel forces supported by India went on the offensive, and the government bowed to the inevitable. Sheikh Mujibur Rahman was released and soon became the first prime minister of the new nation of Bangladesh.

The breakup of the union between East and West Pakistan undermined the fragile authority of the military regime and led to its replacement by a civilian government under Zulfikar Ali Bhutto. But the religious tensions persisted, despite a new constitution that made a number of key concessions to conservative Muslims. In 1977, a new military government under General Zia Ul Ha'q came to power with a commitment to make Pakistan a truly Islamic state. Islamic law became the basis for social behavior as well as for the legal system. Laws governing the consumption of alcohol and the role of women were tightened in accordance with strict Muslim beliefs, and Zia promised a government that would conform to Islamic principles. But after Zia was killed in a plane crash, Pakistanis elected Benazir Bhutto, the daughter of Zulfikar Ali Bhutto and a supporter of secularism who had been educated in the United States. She too was removed from power by a military regime, in 1990, on charges of incompetence and corruption. Reelected in 1993, she attempted to crack down on opposition forces but was removed once again, by President Farooq Leghari, amidst widespread jubilation and

THE SOUL OF ISLAM

The poet Muhammad Iqbal was the prophet of Islam in the Indian subcontinent and a major voice in the struggle for a Muslim state of Pakistan. In the following passage from his poem "The Mysteries of Selflessness," Iqbal called on his fellow Muslims to transcend the narrow bonds of regionalism and nationalism and find a sense of unity in the community of Islam.

MUHAMMAD IQBAL, "THE MYSTERIES OF SELFLESSNESS"

A common aim shared by the multitude
Is unity which, when it is mature,
Forms the Community; the many live
Only by virtue of the single bond.
The Muslim's unity from natural faith
Derives, and this the Prophet taught us,
So that we lit a lantern on truth's way.

"MUSLIMS PROFESS NO FATHERLAND"

Our Essence is not bound to any place;
The vigor of our wine is not contained
In any bowl; Chinese and Indian
Alike the shard that constitutes our jar,
Turkish and Syrian alike the clay
Forming our body; neither is our heart
Of India, or Syria, or Rum,
Nor any fatherland do we profess
Except Islam.

"THE CONCEPT OF COUNTRY DIVIDES HUMANITY"

Now brotherhood has been so cut to shreds
That in the stead of community
The country has been given pride of place
In men's allegiance and constructive work;
The country is the darling of their hearts,
And wide humanity is whittled down
Into dismembered tribes. . . .
Vanished is humankind; there but abide
The disunited nations. Politics
Dethroned religion.

"THE MUSLIM COMMUNITY IS UNBOUNDED IN TIME"

When the burning brands
Of time's great revolution ring our mead,
Then Spring returns. The mighty power of Rome,
Conqueror and ruler of the world entire,
Sank into small account; the golden glass
Of the Sassanians was drowned in blood;
Broken the brilliant genius of Greece;
Egypt too failed in the great test of time,
Her bones lie buried neath the pyramids.
Yet still the voice of the muezzin rings
Throughout the earth, still the Community
Of World-Islam maintains its ancient forms.
Love is the universal law of life,
Mingling the fragmentary elements
Of a disordered world. Through our hearts' glow
Love lives, irradiated by the spark
There is no god but God.

renewed charges of official corruption. Her successor, Nawaz Sharif, soon came under fire for the same reason and in 1999 was ousted by the military, which promised to restore political stability and honest government.

PROBLEMS OF POVERTY AND PLURALISM IN SOUTH ASIA

The leaders of the new states that emerged in South Asia after World War II all hoped that with independence their peoples would enjoy prosperity, popular participation, and national unity. Although their approaches varied, all declared their intention to build modern states based on some adaptation of the Western model. They faced a number of problems distinctive to their part of the world, however. A century of British rule had changed the subcontinent in many ways, but some basic historical realities remained. The peoples of South Asia were still overwhelmingly poor and illiterate, while the sectarian, ethnic, and cultural divisions that had plagued Indian society for centuries had not dissipated. It was a daunting challenge for even the most self-confident of political leaders.

The Politics of Communalism

Like most leaders throughout Asia and Africa, South Asian leaders tried to broaden popular participation in government and establish democratic institutions and

CHRONOLOGY

SOUTH ASIA

India and Pakistan become independent	1947
Assassination of Mahatma Gandhi	January 1948
Sino-Indian border war	1962
Death of Jawaharlal Nehru	1964
Indo-Pakistani War	1965
Indira Gandhi elected prime minister	1966
Bangladesh declares its independence	1971
Assassination of Indira Gandhi	1984
Rajiv Gandhi assassinated	1991
Destruction of mosque at Ayodhya	1992
Benazir Bhutto removed from power in Pakistan	1997
Military coup overthrows civilian government in Pakistan	1999

values. Perhaps the most sincere effort was in India, where Nehru's government enacted a new constitution based on the British parliamentary model that called for social justice, liberty, equality of status and opportunity, and fraternity. All citizens were guaranteed protection from discrimination on the grounds of religious belief, race, caste, sex, or place of birth. The curse of untouchability was expressly forbidden (the constitution had been drafted under the direction of an untouchable, Bhimrao Ambedkar).

In theory, then, India became a full-fledged democracy on the Western model. In actuality, a number of distinctive characteristics may have made the system less than fully democratic (at least in the Western sense) but may also have enabled it to survive. As we have seen, India became in essence a one-party state. By leading the independence movement, the Congress Party had amassed massive public support, which enabled it to retain its preeminent position in Indian politics for three decades. The party benefited from Nehru's personal popularity and from his ability to position the party in the middle of the political spectrum, while rivals moved to the extremes. Congress also avoided being identified as a party exclusively for the Hindu majority by including prominent non-Hindus among its leaders and favoring measures to protect minority groups such as Sikhs and Muslims from discrimination.

Through such adept maneuvering, Nehru kept his party in power through three general elections, until his death in 1964; he also lost only one state election—to the Communists in the southern state of Kerala. But Nehru's success disguised the weakening of his party and the entire democratic political system that took place under his rule. Part of the problem was the familiar one of a party too long in power. Entering office with enthusiasm and high ideals, party officials became complacent and all too easily fell prey to the temptations of corruption and pork-barrel politics. Although the Congress Party sincerely sought to speak for all people, especially the poor and disadvantaged, many party deputies came from privileged backgrounds and had little in common with their constituents.

Another problem was communalism. Beneath the surface unity of the new republic lay age-old ethnic, linguistic, and religious divisions. Although the government was reasonably successful in avoiding internecine religious conflict, regional and linguistic tensions were more difficult to surmount. Because of India's vast size and complex history, no national language had ever emerged. Hindi, spoken mainly in the upper Ganges valley, was the most prevalent, but it was the native language of less than one-third of the population. During the colonial period, English had served as the official language of government, and many non-Hindi speakers suggested making it the official language of independent India. But English had its own difficulties. It was spoken only by the educated elite, and it represented an affront to national pride. Eventually, India recognized fourteen official tongues, making the parliament sometimes sound like the proverbial Tower of Babel.

These problems increased after Nehru's death in 1964. Under his successors, official corruption grew, and Congress began to look like a tired party that had forgotten its ideals. Only the limited appeal of its rivals and the magic of the Nehru name carried on by his daughter Indira Gandhi kept the party in power. But Gandhi was unable to prevent the progressive disintegration of the party's power base at the state level, where regional parties (such as in Tamil Nadu in the south) or ideological ones (such as the Communists in Bengal) won the allegiance of the local population by exploiting ethnic or social revolutionary themes.

During the 1980s, religious tensions began to intensify, not only among Sikhs in the northwest but also between Hindus and Muslims. As we have seen, Gandhi's uncompromising approach to Sikh separatism led to her assassination in 1987. Under her son and successor, Rajiv Gandhi, Hindu militants at Ayodhya, in northern India, demanded the destruction of a mosque built on the alleged site of King Rama's birthplace, where a Hindu temple had previously existed. In 1992, Hindu demonstrators destroyed the mosque and erected a temporary temple at the site, provoking widespread clashes between Hindus and Muslims throughout the country and shaking the Congress government of Narasimha Rao. In protest, rioters in neighboring Pakistan destroyed a number of Hindu shrines in that country.

During the mid-1990s, communal divisions continued to intensify. As we have seen, one element in the debate is ethnic and religious, as militant Hindu groups centered around the figure of Shiv Sena leader Balasaheb Thackeray, the self-styled "Hitler of Bombay," agitate for a state that caters to the interests and aspirations of the Hindu majority, now numbering more than 700 million people. During the parliamentary debate over the formation of a new government in May 1996, opposition figures criticized the BJP for its role in fomenting anti-Muslim riots during the incident at Ayodhya, as well as for its demand that all education throughout the country take place in Hindi.

In recent years, an equally serious source of tension in Indian politics has been the issue of caste. Inspired by political figures such as Phoolan Devi, low-caste Indians are beginning to use the political process to struggle against the restrictions limiting their activities in Indian society. Phoolan Devi, known as the "bandit queen," spent several years in jail on the charge of taking part in the murder of twenty men from a landowning caste in the early 1980s. Members of the caste had allegedly gang-raped her when she was an adolescent. Her campaign for office during the 1996 elections was the occasion of violent arguments between supporters and opponents.

One of Phoolan Devi's sponsors is Laloo Prasad Yadav, onetime chief minister of the state of Bihar, in the Ganges River valley. Yadav openly cites the memory of Mahatma Gandhi to promote the interests of the poor in his province. "I am fighting against evil," he remarked in an interview, "the evil of upper-caste domination of the backward and the downtrodden. And of course, the upper-caste people hate me. Now, they are thinking, he will be Prime Minister, and we will be slaves."[3]

Indian politics is thus assuming an increasingly class-based character, as members of the lower castes, representing more than 80 percent of the voting public, begin to demand affirmative action to relieve their disabilities and give them a more equal share in the national wealth. Officials at U.S. consulates in India have reportedly noticed an increase in applications for visas from members of the *brahmin* caste, who claim that they have "no future" in the new India.

The Economy

India's new leaders also realized the necessity of eliminating the social and economic inequality that had afflicted the subcontinent for centuries. Nehru's answer was socialism. Like many leaders of the Indian National Congress, he had been repelled by the excesses of European capitalism and impressed with the egalitarian principles of Marxism. He therefore instituted a series of five-year plans, which achieved some success. During the first decades of independence, India developed a relatively large and reasonably efficient industrial sector, centered on steel, vehicles, and textiles. Industrial production almost tripled between 1950 and 1965, and per capita income rose by 50 percent between 1950 and 1980, although it was still less than US$300.

By the 1970s, however, industrial growth had slowed. The lack of a modern, efficient infrastructure (transportation and communications, for example) was a problem, as was the rising price of oil, most of which had to be imported. Another problem was the relative weakness of the state-owned sector, which grew at an annual rate of only about 2 percent in the 1950s and 1960s, while the private sector averaged rates of more than 5 percent.

India's major economic weakness, however, was in agriculture. At independence, rural production techniques were still overwhelmingly primitive. Mechanization was almost unknown, fertilizer was rarely used, and most farms were small and uneconomical because of the Hindu tradition of dividing the land equally among all male children. As a result, the vast majority of the Indian people lived in conditions of abject poverty. Landless laborers outnumbered landowners by almost two to one.

The government attempted to relieve the problem by forcing a redistribution of land to the poor, limiting the size of landholdings, and encouraging farmers to form voluntary cooperatives. But all three programs ran into widespread opposition and apathy. Many landlords evaded restrictions on the maximum amount of land an individual could possess by distributing their land among family members. As a result, in many instances tenants were evicted from lands they had farmed for years. In one village, the sociologist Kusum Nair found 200 families who had been deprived of their tenancy rights and reduced to working as coolies. One villager explained:

> Not a single man in this village has or will benefit by the land reforms. The tenants were so convinced that even if they went to court or to the tribunal the case would be decided in favor of the landowner that they thought it wiser to negotiate and come to terms with the landowner. So they got as much cash as they could out of him and surrendered their tenancy.[4]

Another crucial problem India faced was overpopulation. Even before independence, drought, soil erosion, and primitive mechanization made it difficult for the country to support its population of nearly 400 million. In the 1950s and 1960s, the population increased at a rate of more than 2 percent annually. The annual rate of population growth increased from nine per thousand in the nineteenth century to more than twenty per thousand in the 1960s. Viewing children as a source of labor and security in their parents' old age, families were reluctant to limit the number of their children.

Beginning in the 1960s, the Indian government began to adopt stiff measures to curb population growth. Indira Gandhi instituted a program combining monetary rewards and compulsory sterilization. Males who had fathered too many children were sometimes forced to undergo a vasectomy. Popular resistance undermined the program, however, and the goals were scaled back in the 1970s. Despite such efforts, India has made little progress in holding down its burgeoning population, now estimated at more than 900 million. One factor is the decline in the death rate, especially the rate of infant mortality. Whereas life expectancy for the average Indian was less than thirty years in 1947, by the 1990s it had risen to nearly fifty.

The "Green Revolution" of the 1970s at least reduced the severity of the population problem. The introduction of new strains of rice and wheat that were more productive and more disease-resistant significantly increased grain production, from about 50 million tons per year in 1950 to 100 million in 1970. But the Green Revolution exacted its own cost in the form of increased rural inequality. Only the wealthy and more enterprising peasants were able to master the new techniques and purchase the necessary fertilizer, while poor peasants were often driven off the land. Millions fled to the cities, where they live in vast slums, working at menial jobs or even begging for a living. After the death of Indira Gandhi in 1984, her son Rajiv proved more receptive to foreign investment and a greater role for the private sector in the economy. Limitations on imports of consumer goods were loosened, and beggars were driven away from the downtown streets of major cities. The results were quickly apparent. In urban areas, the pace of manufacturing and commercial activity quickened, and a newly affluent middle class began to take on the characteristics of a consumer society. India began to export more manufactured goods, such as computer software, and produced more motor scooters than any other country in the world.

The pace of change has accelerated under Rajiv Gandhi's successors, who have continued to transfer state-run industries to private hands and rely on the free market for the allocation of resources. These policies have stimulated the growth of India's prosperous new middle class, now estimated at more than 100 million, or 11 percent of the entire population. Consumerism—reflected in Rajiv Gandhi's abandoning the traditional *dhoti* and sporting designer loafers and sunglasses—has soared, and the sale of television sets, automobiles, videocassette recorders, and telephones has increased dramatically in recent years. Equally important, Western imports are being replaced by new products manufactured in India with Indian brand names.

The trend toward privatization and the increase in foreign investment probably played a role in stimulating the growth of the industrial sector, estimated at more than 8 percent annually in 1994 and 1995. But the pull of Nehru's dream of a socialist society remains strong. State-owned enterprises still produce about one-half of all goods produced in the country, while high tariffs continue to stifle imports. There is a widespread fear of foreign influence over the economy, a fact eagerly played on by nationalist parties, who have brought about the cancellation of some contracts and forced some foreign firms to relocate. In one

INDIA'S HOPE, INDIA'S SORROW. In India, as in many other societies in southern Asia, overpopulation is a serious obstacle to economic development. The problem is particularly serious in large cities, where thousands of poor children are forced into begging or prostitution. Shown here are a few of the thousands of street children in the commercial hub of Bombay.

celebrated case, a combination of religious and environmental groups attempted unsuccessfully to prevent Kentucky Fried Chicken from establishing outlets in major Indian cities (see the box on p. 954).

As in the industrialized countries of the West, economic growth has been accompanied by environmental damage. Water and air pollution, as well as the leakage of chemicals in industrial zones, has led to illness and death for many people living in the vicinity, and a new environmental movement has emerged, taking its cue and its tactics from similar movements in Europe and the United States. Some critics, reflecting the traditional anti-imperialist attitude of Indian intellectuals, blame Western capitalist corporations for the problem, as in the highly publicized case of leakage from the foreign-owned chemical plant at Bhopal. Much of the problem, however, comes from state-owned factories erected with Soviet aid. But not all the environmental damage can be ascribed to industrialization. The river Ganges is so polluted by human overuse that it is risky for Hindu believers to bathe in it.[5]

Moreover, many Indians have not benefited from the new prosperity. The average annual income remains under $300 per person (in U.S. dollars), and nearly one-third of the population lives below the national poverty line. Millions continue to live in rural slums, such as the famous "City of Joy" in Calcutta, where thousands of families live in primitive shacks and lean-tos, sharing water and toilet facilities. And while a leisured class has begun to appear in the countryside, most farm families remain desperately poor. Despite the socialist rhetoric of India's leaders, the inequality of wealth in India is as pronounced as it is in capitalist nations like the United States. Indeed, India has been described as two nations: an educated urban India of 100 million people surrounded by over 800 million impoverished peasants in the countryside.

Caste, Class, and Gender

Drawing generalizations about the effect of these changes on the life of the average Indian is difficult because of the ethnic, religious, and caste differences among Indians. Furthermore, these differences are compounded by the vast gulf between town and country.

The Constitution of 1950 accepted the reality of caste distinctions but tried to eliminate their worst consequences. It guaranteed equal treatment and opportunity for all, regardless of caste, and prohibited discrimination based on untouchability. It set quotas to guarantee untouchables with access to government service and membership in legislative assemblies as well as admission to institutions of higher learning.

But prejudice is hard to eliminate. Untouchability persists, particularly in the villages, where *harijans*, now called *dalits*, still perform menial tasks and are often denied fundamental human rights. Mistreatment and exploitation by landlords or government officials have led to protests and even violence in the countryside and have become a major issue in national politics. In 1990, the prime minister, V. P. Singh, attempted to woo untouchables from their traditional support for the Congress Party by acceding to their demands for higher quotas for entrance into the bureaucracy and the universities. However, the measure led to widespread protests by members of higher castes, who claimed to be victims of reverse discrimination.

In general, urban Indians appear less conscious of caste distinctions. Material wealth rather than caste identity is increasingly beginning to define status. The days when

AN INDIAN VILLAGE. Nearly 80 percent of the Indian people still live in traditional rural villages such as the one shown here. Housing styles, village customs, and methods of farming have changed little since they were first described by Portuguese travelers in the sixteenth century. Note the thatched roofs and the mud-and-straw walls plastered with dung that have been used in constructing these houses. Few have running water or electricity.

SAY NO TO MCDONALD'S AND KFC!

One of the consequences of Rajiv Gandhi's decision to deregulate the Indian economy has been an increase in the presence of foreign corporations, including U.S. fast-food restaurant chains. Their arrival set off a storm of protest in India: from environmentalists concerned that raising grain for chickens is an inefficient use of land, from religious activists angry at the killing of animals for food, and from nationalists anxious to protect the domestic market from foreign competition. The author of this piece, which appeared in the Hindustan Times, *was Maneka Gandhi, a daughter-in-law of Indira Gandhi and a onetime minister of the environment who has emerged as a prominent rival of Congress Party president Sonia Gandhi.*

WHY INDIA DOESN'T NEED FAST FOOD

India's decision to allow Pepsi Foods Ltd. to open 60 restaurants in India—30 each of Pizza Hut and Kentucky Fried Chicken—marks the first entry of multinational, meat-based junk-food chains into India. If this is allowed to happen, at least a dozen other similar chains will very quickly arrive, including the infamous McDonald's.

The implications of allowing junk-food chains into India are quite stark. As the name denotes, the foods served at Kentucky Fried Chicken (KFC) are chicken-based and fried. This is the worst combination possible for the body and can create a host of health problems, including obesity, high cholesterol, heart ailments, and many kinds of cancer. Pizza Hut products are a combination of white flour, cheese, and meat—again, a combination likely to cause disease. . . .

Can our health systems take care of the fallout from these chicken restaurants? . . . Then there is the issue of the environmental impact of junk-food chains. Modern meat production involves misuse of crops, water, energy, and grazing areas. In addition, animal agriculture produces surprisingly large amounts of air and water pollution.

KFC and Pizza Hut insist that their chickens be fed corn and soybeans. Consider the diversion of grain for this purpose. As the outlets of KFC and Pizza Hut increase in number, the poultry industry will buy up more and more corn to feed the chickens, which means that the corn will quickly disappear from the villages, and its increased price will place it out of reach for the common man. Turning corn into junk chicken is like turning gold into mud. . . .

It is already shameful that, in a country plagued by famine and flood, we divert 37 percent of our arable land to growing animal fodder. Were all of that grain to be consumed directly by humans, it would nourish five times as many people as it does after being converted into meat, milk, and eggs. . . .

Of course, it is not just the KFC and Pizza Hut chains of Pepsi Foods Ltd. that will cause all of this damage. Once we open India up by allowing these chains, dozens more will be eagerly waiting to come in. Each city in America has an average of 5,000 junk-food restaurants [sic]. Is that what we want for India?

high-class Indians refused to eat in a restaurant unless assured that the cook was a *brahmin* are gone. Still, the legacy of tradition is difficult to shake. Color consciousness based on the age-old distinctions between upper-class Aryans and lower-class Dravidians remains strong. Class-conscious Hindus still express a distinct preference for light-skinned marital partners. Young Indians looking for a wife or husband sometimes place detailed advertisements in the newspapers. Among the attributes most often mentioned is a light skin.

In few societies was the life of women more restricted than in traditional India. Hindu favoritism toward men was compounded by the Muslim custom of *purdah* to create a society in which males were dominant in virtually all aspects of life. Females received no education and had no inheritance rights. They were restricted to the home and tied to their husbands for life. Widows were expected to shave their heads and engage in a life of religious meditation or even to immolate themselves on their husband's funeral pyre.

After independence, India's leaders sought to equalize treatment of the sexes. The constitution expressly forbade discrimination based on sex and called for equal pay for equal work. Laws prohibited child marriage, *sati*, and the payment of a dowry by the bride's family. Women were encouraged to attend school and enter the labor market.

Such laws, along with the dynamics of economic and social change, have had a major impact on the lives of many Indian women. Middle-class women in urban areas are much more likely to accept employment outside the home, and many hold managerial and professional positions. Before independence, a man's pride might have been offended if his wife were employed, but now the increasing demands of the consumer society lead many families to put their creature comforts first.

The sexual attitudes and practices of urban women have changed as well. While premarital sex is probably much less common than in most Western societies, it is becoming more frequent, and the mingling of the sexes in social situations is much more acceptable than in the past, even in high-class families. On the other hand, surveys suggest that many if not most young Indians still accept the idea of arranged marriages and will ultimately accede to their parents' wishes in the choice of a spouse.

BOLLYWOOD, THE HOLLYWOOD OF THE EAST. India produces more movies than any other country in the world, including the United States. The capital of the Indian film industry is Bombay, which is sometimes dubbed India's "Bollywood." Although billboards, such as this one, towering in downtown Bombay, tantalize viewers with larger than life promises of lasciviousness, the movies themselves adhere to strict moral codes. Indian movie stars have become national heroes, commanding enormous salaries and mass devotion and sometimes even political success.

In fact, Indian women, like some Western women, tend to play a modern role in their work and in the marketplace and a more submissive, traditional one at home. The dichotomy is especially apparent in a country like India, where the choice is not simply between the traditional and the modern, but the native and the foreign. An Indian woman is often expected to be a professional executive at work and a loving, dutiful wife and mother at home (see the box on p. 956).

Such attitudes are also reflected in the Indian movie industry, where aspiring actresses must often brave family disapproval to enter the entertainment world. Before World War II, female actors were routinely viewed as prostitutes or "loose women," and even now, such views are prevalent among conservative Indian families. Even Karisma Kapoor, one of India's current film stars and a member of the Kapoor clan, which has produced several generations of actors, had to defy her family's ban on the family women entering show business.

Nothing more strikingly indicates the changing role of women in South Asia than the fact that in recent years, three of the major countries in the area—India, Pakistan, and Sri Lanka—have had women as prime ministers. It is worthy of mention, however, that all three—Indira Gandhi, Benazir Bhutto, and Srimivao Bandaranaike—came from prominent political families and probably owed their initial success to a husband or a father who had served as a prime minister before them.

Like other aspects of life, the role of women has changed much less in rural areas. In the early 1960s, many villagers still practiced the institution of *purdah*. A woman who went about freely in society would get a bad reputation. Female children are still much less likely to receive an education. The overall literacy rate in India today is less than 40 percent, but it is undoubtedly much lower among women. Laws relating to dowry, child marriage, and inheritance are routinely ignored in the countryside. Dowry costs have escalated rapidly in recent years and often take the form of bargaining between the families of

YOUNG HINDU BRIDE IN GOLD BANGLES. Awaiting the marriage ceremony, a young bride sits with the female relatives of her family, at the Meenakshi Hindu Temple, one of the largest in southern India. Although child marriage is illegal, Indian girls are still married at a young age. With the marital union arranged by the parents, this young bride has perhaps never met the groom. Bedecked in gold jewelry and rich silks—part of her dowry—she nervously awaits the priest's blessing before she moves to her husband's home. There she will begin a life of servitude to her in-laws' family.

A CRITIQUE OF WESTERN FEMINISM

Organized efforts to protect the rights of women have been under way in India since the 1970s, when the Progressive Organization for Women (POW) instituted a campaign against sexual harassment and other forms of discrimination against women in Indian society. Like many of their counterparts in other parts of Asia and Africa, however, many activists for women's rights in India are critical of Western feminism, charging that it is irrelevant to their own realities. Although Indian feminists feel a bond with their sisters all over the world, they insist on resolving Indian problems with Indian solutions. The author of this editorial is Madhu Kishwar, founder and editor of a women's journal in New Delhi.

FINDING INDIAN SOLUTIONS TO WOMEN'S PROBLEMS

Western feminism, exported to India and many other Third World countries in recent decades, has brought with it serious problems.

As products of a more homogenized culture, most Western feminists assume women's aspirations the world over must be quite similar. Yet a person's idea of a good life and her aspirations are closely related to what is valued in her particular society. This applies to feminism itself. An offshoot of individualism and liberalism, it posits that each individual is responsible primarily to herself. . . .

In societies like India, most of us find it difficult to tune in to this extreme individualism. For instance, most Indian women are unwilling to assert rights in a way that estranges them not just from their family but also from their larger community. . . .

This isn't slavery to social opinion. Rather, many of us believe life is a poor thing if our own dear ones don't honor and celebrate our rights, if our freedom cuts us off from others. In our culture, both men and women are taught to value the interests of our families more than our self-interest. . . .

Cultural issues aside, my most fundamental reservation regarding feminism is that it has strengthened the tendency among India's Western-educated elites to adopt the statist authoritarian route to social reform. The characteristic feminist response to most social issues affecting women—in the workplace, in the media, in the home—is to demand more and more stringent laws. . . .

But dearly held and deeply cherished cultural norms cannot be changed simply by applying the instruments of state repression through legal punishment. Social reform is too complex and important a matter to be left to the police and courts. The best of laws will tend to fail if social opinion is contrary to them. Therefore, the statist route of using laws as a substitute for creating a new social consensus about women's rights tends to be counterproductive.

the bride and groom. All too often, families allow female children to die in the hope of later having a son. There have been a few highly publicized cases of *sati*, although undoubtedly more women die of mistreatment at the hands of their husband or of other members of his family. In a few instances, widows have been forcibly thrown on the funeral pyre by their in-laws.

Perhaps the most tragic aspect of continued sexual discrimination in India is the high mortality rate among girls. According to a recent UNICEF study, one-quarter of the female children born in India die before the age of fifteen as a result of neglect or even infanticide. Others are aborted before birth after gender-detection examinations.

INDIAN ART AND LITERATURE SINCE INDEPENDENCE

Recent decades have witnessed a prodigious outpouring of literature in India. Most works have been written in one of the Indian languages and have not been translated into a foreign tongue. Fortunately, however, many authors choose to write in English. Known as Indo-Anglian literature, such works are written primarily for the Indian elite or for foreign audiences. For that reason, some charge that Indo-Anglian literature lacks authenticity. Defenders respond that the English language is sufficiently flexible to express Indian idioms, style, and temperament.

Because of the vast quantity of works published (India is currently the third largest publisher of English-language books in the world), only a few of the most prominent fiction writers can be mentioned here. One of the most popular is R. K. Narayan (b. 1907). Born of a *brahmin* family in Madras, Narayan is a prolific writer who appeals to readers by his use of traditional themes and the vivid descriptions of his characters.

Born in New Delhi in 1937, Anita Desai was one of the first prominent female writers in contemporary India. Her writings focus on the struggle of Indian women of all classes and ages to achieve a degree of independence from the suffocating bondage imposed on them by traditional society. In her first novel, *Cry, the Peacock*, the heroine finally seeks liberation from the surrounding male-dominated society by murdering her husband, preferring freedom at any cost to remaining a captive of traditional society.

The best-known female writer in South Asia today is Taslima Nasrin of Bangladesh. She first became famous when she was sentenced to death for criticizing the Koran in one of her novels. Islam, she declared, obstructs human progress and women's equality. She now lives in exile in Europe.

Unquestionably the most controversial of modern writers in India today is Salman Rushdie (b. 1947). In *Midnight's Children*, published in 1980, the author linked his protagonist, born on the night of independence, to the history of modern India, its achievements and its frustrations. Like his contemporaries Günter Grass and Gabriel García Márquez, Rushdie used the technique of magical realism to jolt his audience into a recognition of the inhumanity of modern society and the need to develop a sense of moral concern for the fate of the Indian people, and for the world as a whole.

Rushdie's later novels have continued to attack such problems as religious intolerance, political tyranny, social injustice, and greed and corruption. His attack on Islamic fundamentalism in *The Satanic Verses* (1988) won plaudits from literary critics but provoked widespread criticism among Muslims, including a death sentence by the Ayatollah Khomeini in Iran. *The Moor's Last Sigh* (1995) turns its attention to the alleged excesses of Hindu nationalism and has been banned in India.

Indian art has also been affected by the colonial experience. Like Chinese and Japanese artists, Indian artists have agonized for more than a century over how best to paint with a modern yet indigenous mode of expression. During the colonial period, Indian art went in several directions at once. One school of painters favored sentimental renderings of traditional themes; another experimented with a colorful primitivism founded on folk art. Many Indian artists painted representational social art extolling the suffering and silent dignity of India's impoverished millions. After 1960, however, most Indian artists adopted abstract art as their medium. Surrealism in particular, with its emphasis on spontaneity and the unconscious, appeared closer to the Hindu tradition of favoring intuition over reason. Yet Indian artists are still struggling to find the ideal way to be both modern and Indian.

Gandhi's Vision

India, like other non-Western countries, is clearly changing. Traditional ways are giving way to modern ones, and often the result is a society that looks increasingly Western in form, if not in content. In India, as in a number of other Asian and African societies, the distinction between traditional and modern, or native and Westernized, sometimes appears to be a simple dichotomy between rural and urban areas. Downtown areas in the major cites are modern and Westernized in appearance, but the villages have changed little since precolonial days.

Yet it would be a mistake to draw simple comparisons between what is taking place in India and what is happening in other countries undergoing a similar transition. In India, traditional practices appear to be more resilient, and the result is often a synthesis rather than a frontal clash between conflicting institutions and values. Unlike China, India has not rejected its past but merely adjusted it to meet the needs of the present. Clothing styles in the streets, where the *sari* and *dhoti* continue to be popular, religious practices in the temples, and social relationships in the home all testify to the greater role of tradition in India than in China or many other societies in the region.

One disadvantage of the eclectic approach, which seeks to blend the old and the new rather than choosing one over the other, is that sometimes contrasting traditions and customs cannot be reconciled. Such was the lesson of the failed experiment of self-strengthening in late nineteenth-century China (see Chapter 23). In his book *India: A Wounded Civilization*, author V. S. Naipaul, a West Indian of Indian descent, charged that Mahatma Gandhi's legacy of glorifying poverty and the simple Indian village was a severe obstacle to Indian efforts to overcome the poverty, ignorance, and degradation of its past and build a prosperous modern society. Gandhi's vision of a spiritual India, Naipaul complained, was a balm for defeatism and an excuse for failure.

Certainly, India faces a difficult dilemma. Some of India's problems are undoubtedly a consequence of the colonial era, but the British cannot be blamed for all of the country's economic and social ills. To build a democratic, prosperous society, the Indian people must discard many of their traditional convictions and customs. Belief in karma and inherent caste distinctions are incompatible with the democratic belief in equality before the law. These traditional beliefs also undercut the work ethic and the assumption, basic to modern Western society, that hard work earns concrete rewards. Identification with class or caste undermines the modern sentiment of nationalism.

So long as Indians accept their fate as predetermined, they will find it difficult to change their environment and create a new society. Yet their traditional beliefs provide a measure of identity and solace often lacking in other societies, where such traditional spiritual underpinnings have eroded. Despite the difficulties the Indian people must surmount daily, they appear, at least on the surface, to be reasonably happy and content with their lot. Destroying India's traditional means of coping with a disagreeable reality without changing that reality would be cruel indeed. That, in a nutshell, is the dilemma India faces.

There is, of course, a final question that cannot be answered here. The vision of Mahatma Gandhi, maligned by some and treated with condescending amusement by others, was that materialism is ultimately a dead end. In light of contemporary concerns about the emptiness of life in the West and the self-destructiveness of material culture, can Mahatma's message be ignored?

NO ROOM IN PARADISE? The color and diversity of popular Hinduism are nowhere more fully displayed than on the gopuram, or gate tower, of the modern Hindu temple. The celestial figures shown here in rich profusion are located on the tower surmounting the entrance gate of a temple devoted to Siva in the southern Indian city of Madras. Depicting the various Hindu myths, each deity appeals to the needs and devotion of the believers. Often depicted as couples, these gods and goddesses represent the ideal physical and spiritual union, which is to be emulated by the faithful.

The Dismantling of Colonialism in Southeast Asia

First-time visitors to the Malaysian capital of Kuala Lumpur are astonished to observe on the skyline a pair of twin towers thrusting up above the surrounding buildings into the scudding monsoon clouds. The Petronas Towers, as they are known, rise 1,483 feet from ground level, leading to claims by Malaysian officials they are the world's tallest buildings, at least for the time being.

The new building is more than an architectural achievement; it is a deliberate statement announcing the emergence of Southeast Asia as a major player on the international scene and the aspirations of the state of Malaysia to be one of the world's advanced nations. It is probably no accident that the foundations were laid on the site of the Selangor Cricket Club, symbol of colonial hegemony in Southeast Asia. "These towers," commented one local official, "will do wonders for Asia's self-esteem and confidence, which I think is very important, and which I think at this moment are at the point of takeoff."[6]

Slightly more than a year after that remark, Malaysia and several of its neighbors were suddenly mired in a financial crisis that threatened to derail their rapid advance to economic affluence and severely undermined the "self-esteem" that the Petronas Towers were meant to symbolize. That ironic reality serves as a warning to the region's leaders that the road to industrialized status is often strewn with hidden obstacles. At the moment, the building serves as testament to the danger of hubris.

As we have seen, Japanese wartime occupation had a great impact on attitudes among the peoples of Southeast Asia. It demonstrated the vulnerability of colonial rule in the region and showed that an Asian power could defeat Europeans. The Allied governments themselves also contributed—sometimes unwittingly—to rising aspirations for independence by promising self-determination for all peoples at the end of the war. Although Winston Churchill later said that the Atlantic Charter did not apply to the colonial peoples, it would be difficult to put the genie back in the bottle again.

Some did not try. In July 1946, the United States lived up to the promise that it had made nearly ten years earlier and granted total independence to the Philippines.

The Americans insisted on maintaining a military presence on the islands, however, and U.S. citizens were able to retain economic and commercial interests in the new country, a decision that would later spur charges of neocolonialism.

The British were equally willing to bring an end to a century of imperialism in the region. As prime minister, Churchill had made it clear that he did not intend to preside over the dissolution of the British Empire. But his successor from the Labour Party, Clement Attlee, had different views. The Labour Party had long been critical of the British colonial legacy on both moral and economic grounds and, once in power, moved rapidly to grant independence to those colonies prepared to accept it. In 1948, the Union of Burma received its independence. Malaya's turn came in 1957, after a Communist guerrilla movement had been suppressed.

Other European nations were less willing to abandon their colonial possessions in Southeast Asia. The French and the Dutch both regarded their colonies in the region as economic necessities as well as symbols of national grandeur and refused to turn them over to nationalist movements at the end of the war. The Dutch returned to the East Indies and attempted to suppress a new Indonesian republic established by Sukarno, leader of the Indonesian Nationalist Party. But the United States, which feared a Communist victory in Indonesia, pressured the Dutch to grant independence to Sukarno and his non-Communist forces, and in 1950 the Dutch finally agreed to withdraw and recognize the new Republic of Indonesia.

The situation was somewhat different in Vietnam, where the Communists, led by the veteran Moscow-trained revolutionary Ho Chi Minh, seized power throughout most of Vietnam. In early September 1945, Ho Chi Minh was elected president of a new provisional republic in Hanoi, but the French refused to recognize the new government and reimposed their rule on the country. War broke out in December 1946. At the time it was only an anticolonial war, but it would soon become much more (see Chapter 27).

The Era of Independent States

The leaders of the newly independent states in Southeast Asia had been members of nationalist movements before the war. Although many of them had dedicated their lives to ending colonial rule, in general they admired Western political principles and institutions and hoped to apply them, subject to historical and cultural differences, in their own countries. New constitutions were patterned on Western democratic models, and multiparty political systems quickly sprang into operation.

The Search for Native Political Traditions: Guided Democracy

By the 1960s, most of these budding experiments in pluralist democracy had been abandoned or were under serious threat. Some had been replaced by military or one-party autocratic regimes. In Burma, a moderate government based on the British parliamentary system and dedicated to Buddhism and nonviolent Marxism had given way to a military government. In Thailand, too, where traditional kingship had been replaced by a constitutional monarchy, the military now ruled. In the Philippines, President Ferdinand Marcos discarded democratic restraints that had been widely abused by traditional landed elites, who manipulated the system for their own political and economic benefit, and established his own centralized control under a program called the "New Order." In South Vietnam, Ngo Dinh Diem and his successors paid lip service to the Western democratic model but ruled by authoritarian means.

Perhaps the most publicized example of a failed experiment in democracy was in Indonesia. When national independence was finally established in 1950, the new leaders drew up a constitution creating a parliamentary system under a titular presidency. Sukarno was elected as the first president. A spellbinding orator, Sukarno became widely popular and played a major role in creating a sense of national identity among the disparate peoples of the Indonesian archipelago (see the box on p. 960).

In the late 1950s, Sukarno, exasperated at the incessant maneuvering among conservative Muslims, Communists, and the army, dissolved the constitution and attempted to rule on his own through what he called "Guided Democracy." According to Sukarno, Guided Democracy was closer to Indonesian traditions and superior to the Western variety. The weakness of Western democracy was that it allowed the majority to dominate the minority, whereas Guided Democracy would reconcile different opinions and points of view in a government operated by consensus. Highly suspicious of the West, Sukarno nationalized foreign-owned enterprises and sought economic aid from China and the Soviet Union while relying for domestic support on the Indonesian Communist Party.

The main opposition to Sukarno came from the army and conservative Muslims, who resented his increasing reliance on the Communists. The Muslims were further upset by his refusal to consider a state based on Islamic principles. The combined opposition of the army and the orthodox Muslims proved too much for Sukarno to surmount. In 1965, military officers launched a coup d'etat that severely restricted his authority. The coup, whose origins are still widely debated, provoked a mass popular uprising, which resulted in the slaughter of several hundred thousand suspected Communists, many of whom were overseas Chinese, long distrusted by the Muslim

THE GOLDEN THROAT OF PRESIDENT SUKARNO

President Sukarno of Indonesia was a spellbinding speaker and a charismatic leader of his nation's struggle for independence. These two excerpts are from speeches in which Sukarno promoted two of his favorite projects: Indonesian nationalism and Guided Democracy. The force that would guide Indonesia, of course, was to be Sukarno himself.

SUKARNO ON NATIONALISM AND DEMOCRACY

Sukarno on Indonesian Greatness

What was Indonesia in 1945? What was our nation then? It was only two things, only two things. A flag and a song. That is all. (Pause, finger held up as afterthought.) But no, I have omitted the main ingredient. I have missed the most important thing of all. I have left out the burning fire of freedom and independence in the breast and heart of every Indonesian. That is the most important thing—this is the vital chord—the spirit of our people, the spirit and determination to be free. This was our nation in 1945—the spirit of our people!

And what are we today? We are a great nation. We are bigger than Poland. We are bigger than Turkey. We have more people than Australia, than Canada, we are bigger in area and have more people than Japan. In population now we are the fifth largest country in the world. In area, we are even bigger than the United States of America. The American Ambassador, who is here with us, admits this. Of course, he points out that we have a lot of water in between our thousands of islands. But I say to him—America has a lot of mountains and deserts, too!

Sukarno on Guided Democracy

Indonesia's democracy is not liberal democracy. Indonesian democracy is not the democracy of the world of Montaigne or Voltaire. Indonesia's democracy is not à la America, Indonesia's democracy is not the Soviet—NO! Indonesia's democracy is the democracy which is implanted in the breasts of the Indonesian people, and it is that which I have tried to dig up again, and have put forward as an offering to you. . . . If you, especially the undergraduates, are still clinging to and being borne along the democracy made in England, or democracy made in France, or democracy made in America, or democracy made in Russia, you will become a nation of copyists!

majority. In 1967, Sukarno was forced from office and was replaced by a military government under General Suharto. Sukarno died two years later.

The new government made no pretensions of reverting to democratic rule, but it did restore good relations with the West and sought foreign investment to repair the country's ravaged economy. But it also found it difficult to placate Muslim demands for an Islamic state. As in Pakistan, pressure for the strict application of Islamic law continued in Indonesia despite efforts by the government to repress it. In a few areas, including western Sumatra, militant Muslims took up arms against the state.

PORTRAIT OF SUKARNO. Sukarno was the leader of the anticolonialist movement in the Dutch East Indies. After independence was achieved in 1950, he served as the president of the new Republic of Indonesia. A charismatic speaker, Sukarno was initially highly popular, but the failure of many of his grandiose projects and his flirtation with the Indonesian Communist Party eventually led to his downfall, in 1965. His daughter, Megawati, was sworn in as vice president of the post-Suharto government, in 1999.

The Maoist Model: New Democracy in North Vietnam

The one country in Southeast Asia that explicitly rejected the Western model was the Democratic Republic of Vietnam, or North Vietnam. Its leaders under President Ho Chi Minh opted for the Stalinist pattern of national development, based on Communist Party rule and socialist forms of ownership. In 1958, probably stimulated to action by the success of collectivization policies in neighboring China, the government launched a three-year plan to lay the foundation for a socialist society in North Vietnam. Collective farms were established throughout the country, and all industry and commerce above the family level were nationalized. Two years later, the regime launched a five-year plan to carry out the first stage in building a highly industrialized socialist society, but by the mid-1960s the demands of the war in the south intervened, and the plan remained a dead letter.

Problems of National Development

As we have seen, by the end of the first decade of independence, it was apparent that Southeast Asia's progress toward capitalist democratic societies on the Western model would be more difficult than many had anticipated. Fragile experiments in Western-style democracy came to an end, ethnic and ideological tensions rose to the surface, and deep-rooted economic problems set back plans for rapid economic growth.

One problem was that independence had not brought material prosperity or ended economic inequality and the domination of the local economies by foreign interests. Most economies in the region were still characterized by tiny industrial sectors based on light industry and the processing of raw materials for export; they lacked technology, educational resources, capital investment, and leaders trained in developmental skills.

The presence of widespread ethnic, linguistic, cultural, and economic differences also made the transition difficult. In Malaya, for example, the majority Malays—most of whom were farmers—feared economic and political domination by the local Chinese minority, who were much more active and experienced in industry and commerce. In 1961, the Federation of Malaya, whose ruling party was dominated by Malays, integrated former British possessions on the island of Borneo into a new Union of Malaysia in a patent move to increase the non-Chinese proportion of the country's population. Similar reasons dictated the expulsion of the island of Singapore three years later. (Once a British Crown colony, Singapore—three-quarters of whose population were ethnic Chinese—had been attached to the new Federation of Malaya in 1959.) Yet periodic conflicts persisted as the Malaysian government attempted to guarantee the Malay peoples control over politics and a larger role in the economy. In 1969, tensions between Malays and Chinese erupted into violent confrontations on the streets of Malaysian cities.

In some cases, the tensions were economic or regional rather than ethnic. In Indonesia, for example, many urban intellectuals, supported by poor rice farmers on the inner islands of Java and southern Sumatra, advocated a socialist approach that would limit Western investment and equalize income among the Indonesian people. Prosperous planters and merchants on the outer island of Sumatra, on the other hand, preferred more free enterprise and a good relationship with the West, their primary market for exports. Such tensions contributed to the collapse of Indonesian democracy and the institution of Sukarno's experiment with Guided Democracy in 1959.

In addition, many Southeast Asians experienced lingering doubts about whether Western-style democracy and materialistic culture were even relevant to their region. They questioned whether Western secular institutions and values were appropriate in societies that traditionally ascribed a charismatic or semireligious character to their leaders (in Burma, for example, the ruler was viewed by his subjects as an incipient Buddha-to-be). Similar doubts were expressed about the introduction of capitalism into Southeast Asian societies.

Recent Trends Toward Democracy

In recent years, many Southeast Asian societies have shown signs of evolving toward more democratic forms. One example is the Philippines, where the dictatorial Marcos regime was overthrown by a massive public uprising in 1986 and replaced by a democratically elected government under President Corazon Aquino, the widow of a popular politician assassinated under mysterious circumstances a few years earlier. Although Aquino showed few political skills and was unable to resolve many of the country's chronic economic and social difficulties, her successor, Fidel Ramos, had somewhat more success, and the Philippines is exhibiting a few promising signs of entering a period of political stability. Here, too, however, ethnic tensions roil the waters, as Muslims in the southern island of Mindanao have mounted a terrorist campaign in their effort to obtain autonomy or independence.

In other areas, the results have been mixed. Although Malaysia is a practicing democracy, tensions persist between Malays and Chinese as well as between secular and orthodox Muslims. In neighboring Thailand, to prevent political unrest, the military has found it expedient to hold national elections for civilian governments, but the danger of a military takeover is never far beneath the surface. Meanwhile, widespread corruption has poisoned

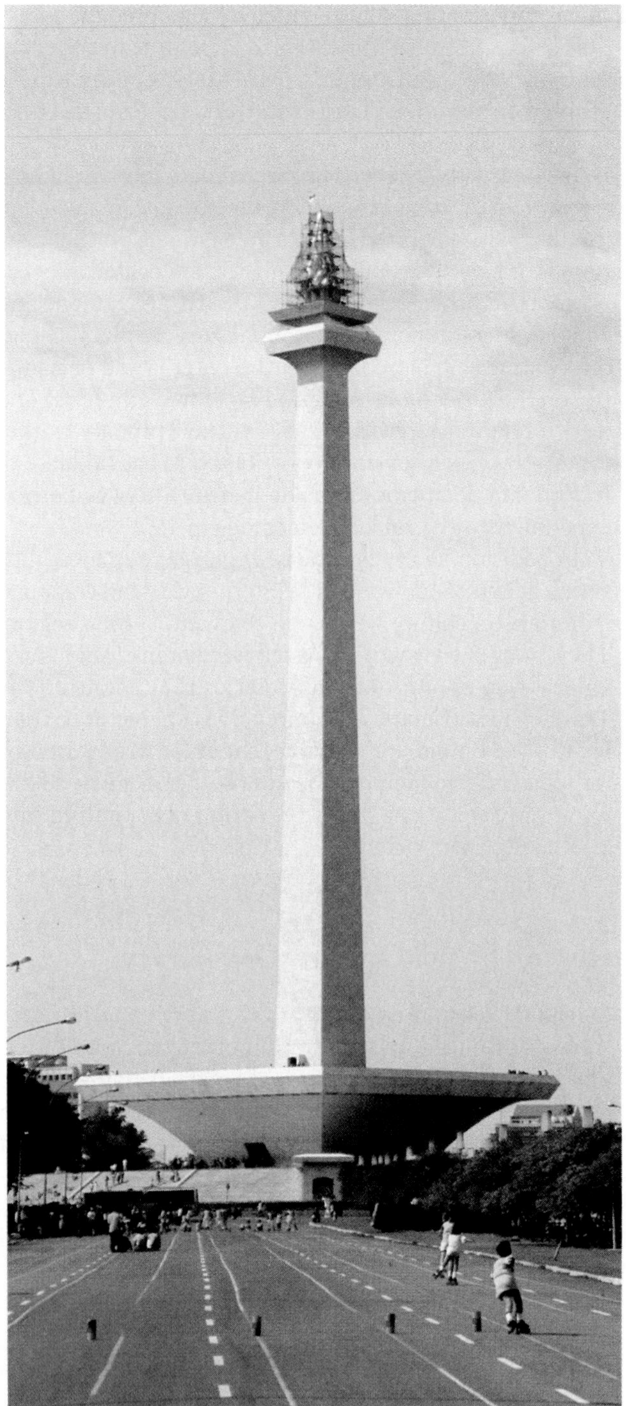

THE FREEDOM MONUMENT IN JAKARTA. President Sukarno ordered the erection of a massive monument to freedom (*Merdeka*) in downtown Jakarta. At the base of the obelisk is a museum portraying the key events in the Indonesian struggle for independence from the Dutch. Many Indonesians have criticized Sukarno for spending precious funds on a monument, while the country's many social and economic needs were neglected. Obviously unconcerned with such issues, these young Indonesian boys take advantage of the enormous square to practice their roller-blading.

the political system to such an extent that aspiring candidates purchase the votes not only of individuals, but of families and entire polling districts as well.

During the mid-1990s, tensions between authoritarian traditions and rising demands for democratic government were especially sharp in Indonesia. In the spring and summer of 1996, violent protests by students demanding increased freedoms and by Muslims demanding a larger role for Islam in society prompted Suharto's government to arrest many dissidents and warn against the possibility of the revival of the Communist Party. In elections held a few months later, Suharto and his party were reelected to power with relatively little difficulty, but popular anger at Suharto's family (many of whom reportedly used their position to amass considerable wealth) and the regime's close ties with wealthy businessmen of Chinese extraction exacerbated traditional suspicions between native Indonesians and the minority population and provoked demands for drastic political change.

In 1997, a financial crisis swept through the region, depressing economies and shaking political stability (see below). In Indonesia, where the impact of the crisis was especially sharp, Suharto was the first casualty. Forced to step down after a popular uprising in the spring of 1998, he was replaced by his deputy B. J. Habibie, who called for the establishment of a national assembly to select a new government based on popular aspirations. In the presidential vote, held the following year, the leading candidate was Sukarno's daughter, Megawati Sukarnoputri, whose popularity was undoubtedly inflated by her famous name. The assembly, however, selected the moderate Muslim leader Abdurrahman Wahid as Habibie's successor, with Megawati named his vice president. In the supercharged atmosphere provoked by recent events, the new government faces a severe challenge, especially in the eastern part of the archipelago, where religious tensions have erupted between Muslims and the Christian minority.

Even in Vietnam, where the Communist Party has long staked out its exclusive claim to power, the trend in recent years has been toward a greater popular role in the governing process. Elections for the unicameral parliament are more open than in the past, and local authorities lobby effectively in Hanoi for the interests of their constituents. The government remains suspicious of Western-style democracy, however, and represses any opposition to the Communist Party's guiding role over the state.

Only in Myanmar (formerly Burma), where the military has been in complete control since the early 1960s, have the forces of greater popular participation been virtually silenced. Even there, however, the power of the ruling regime of General Ne Win, known as SLORC, has been vocally challenged by Aung San Huu Kyi, the much-admired daughter of one of the heroes of the country's struggle for national liberation after World War II.

MAP 31.2 Modern Southeast Asia

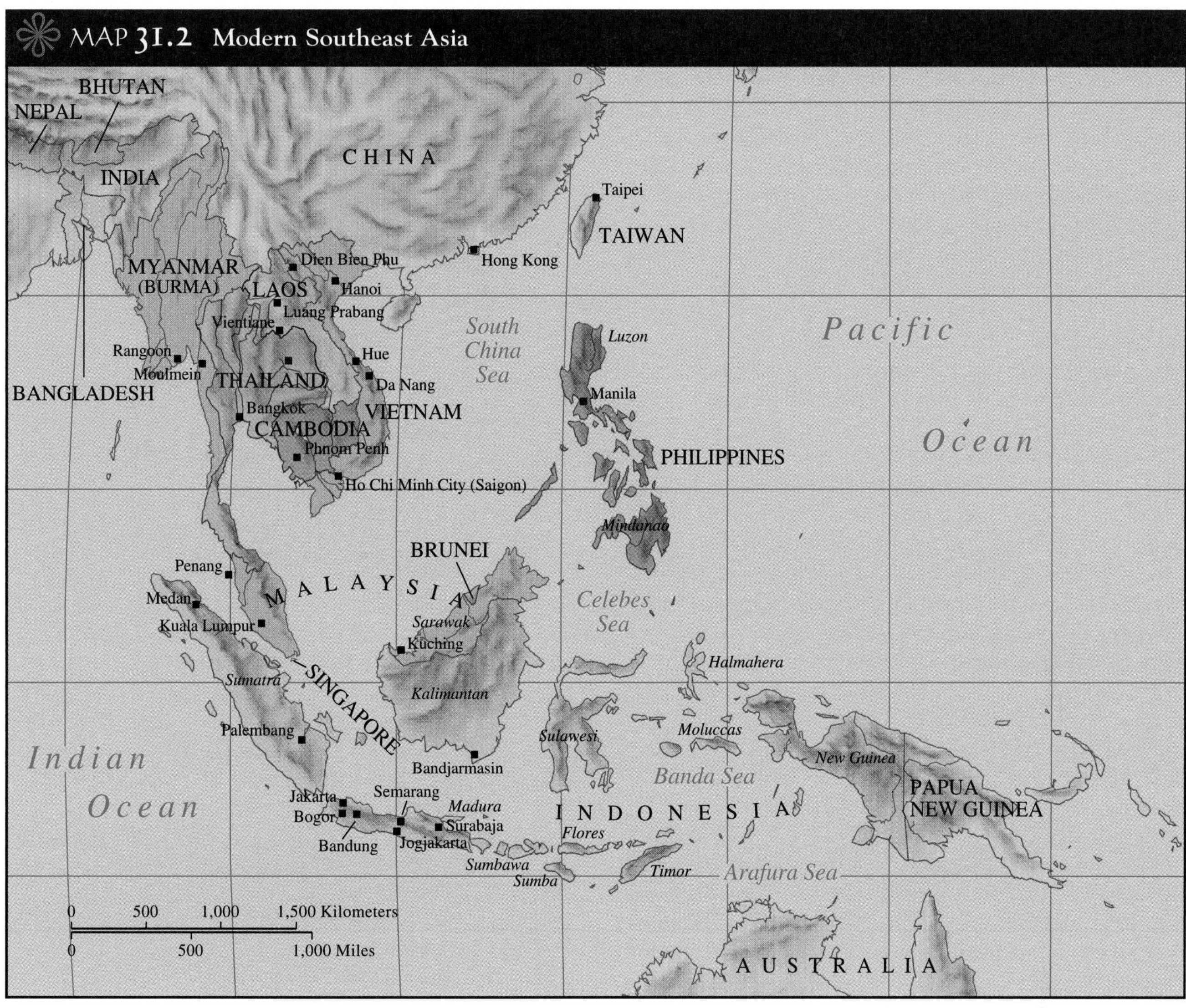

The trend toward more representative systems of government, however halting and imperfect, is due in part to increasing prosperity and the growth of an affluent and educated middle class. Although Indonesia, Myanmar, and the three Indochinese states are still overwhelmingly agrarian, Malaysia and Thailand have been undergoing relatively rapid economic development, and tiny Singapore, with its educated and industrious workforce, has become a leading exporter of manufactured goods and a major oil-refining center for oil-producing nations throughout the region.

In recent years, a number of manufacturing companies in the advanced countries have established factories in Indonesia and other states in the region. The practice has provoked criticism in the United States, where labor groups and human rights activists charge that workers in such factories—mostly young women—are underpaid and forced to labor in substandard conditions. It is true that daily wages are often less than US$2.50 and that fires and other accidents have taken the lives of workers in a few well-known cases. For many employees, however, these jobs represent opportunity. "Thanks to God, it's enough money for me," said one young women at a Nike factory in Serang. She claims to be able to save more than half her salary and send it back to her family. Her father is a schoolteacher.[7]

Despite the economic changes, the nations of the region still show a distinct preference for strong centralized leadership and the fostering of community spirit rather than Western individualism. Former prime minister Lee Kuan-yew, longtime leader of Singapore, for example, has rejected the Western liberal democratic and individualist model. He has persistently urged his people to follow the more communitarian Japanese model and to rely on their inherited Confucian traditions to foster community spirit, a work ethic, and high moral fiber. The authoritarianism inherent in Lee's interpretation of these values has aroused criticism in the West and even within Singapore itself. But for the most part, Singaporeans appear willing to accept the bargain as the necessary price for political stability and economic prosperity.

Lee Kuan-yew's cue has been taken up by other leaders in the region. In a recent book titled *The Asia That Can Say No,* coauthored with Shintaro Ishihara, Malaysian Prime Minister Mahathir Mohamad counsels his Asian readers to resist U.S. efforts to promote American values, warning them that the United States is trying to hold back economic growth in the region for its own benefit (see the box on p. 965).

In the late summer of 1997, the assumption of many observers that the rapid pace of economic development would continue into the indefinite future was suddenly shaken when a financial crisis swept through the region. The problem was triggered by a number of factors, including excessive government expenditures on ambitious devel-opment projects leading to growing budget deficits, irresponsible lending and investment practices by financial institutions, and an overvaluation of local currency relative to the U.S. dollar. One underlying cause of these problems was the prevalence of backroom deals between politicians and business leaders that temporarily enriched both groups at the cost of eventual economic dislocation.

As local currencies plummeted in value, the International Monetary Fund agreed to step in to provide assistance, but only on the condition that the governments concerned permit greater transparency in their economic systems and allow market forces to operate more freely, even at the price of bankruptcies and the loss of jobs. While there were signs that some political leaders recognized the serious nature of their problems and were willing to take steps to resolve them, the political cost of such changes remained uncertain. As the decade came to an end, it was also unclear whether the region's economic recovery was under way.

CHRONOLOGY

SOUTHEAST ASIA

August Revolution in Vietnam	1945
Philippines become independent	1946
Beginning of Franco-Vietminh War	December 1946
Burma becomes independent	1948
Recognition of the Republic of Indonesia	1950
Malaya becomes independent	1957
Beginning of Sukarno's Guided Democracy in Indonesia	1959
Military seizes power in Indonesia	1965
Foundation of ASEAN	1967
Fall of Saigon to North Vietnamese forces	1975
Vietnamese invade Cambodia	1978
Corazon Aquino elected president in the Philippines	1986
United Nations forces arrive in Cambodia	1991
Vietnam becomes a member of ASEAN	1996
Islamic and student protests in Indonesia	1996–1997
Suharto steps down as president of Indonesia	1998

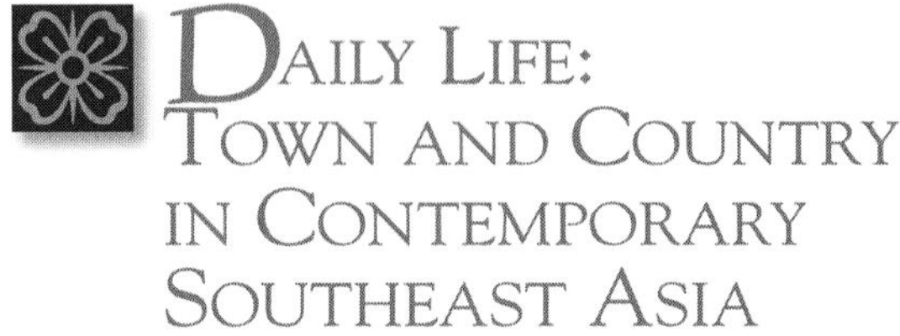

Daily Life: Town and Country in Contemporary Southeast Asia

Like much of the non-Western world, most Southeast Asian countries today can still be classified as dual societies. Their cities resemble those in the West, while the villages in the countryside often appear little changed from precolonial days.

No one who has traveled in contemporary Southeast Asia can fail to be affected by the difference between the peaceful rural scenes of palm trees and rice paddies and the congested and polluted atmosphere of the region's cities. In Bangkok, Manila, and Jakarta, broad boulevards lined with shiny white and silver skyscrapers alternate with muddy lanes passing through neighborhoods packed with wooden shacks topped by thatch or rusty tin roofs. Soft drink cans and coconut shells are scattered along the roadway, and there is a pervasive smell of urine, rotting fruit, and frying meat. Nevertheless, millions of Southeast Asians in recent decades have fled from the peaceful rice fields to the urban slums. Although most urban jobs are menial, the earnings are better than what they can get in their villages.

The urban migrants change not only their physical surroundings but their attitudes and values as well. Sometimes the move leads to a decline in traditional beliefs. Surveys suggest, for example, that belief in the existence of nature and ancestral spirits tends to decline among

WHOSE HUMAN RIGHTS?

In 1995, twenty years after the end of the Vietnam War, the United States and Vietnam finally agreed to exchange ambassadors. Yet many issues continue to cloud the relationship, including an accounting of U.S. soldiers missing in action during the conflict and U.S. concerns about Vietnamese violations of human rights. In this passage, vice foreign minister Tran Quang Co argues that developing countries like Vietnam should not be held to the same standard as the advanced countries of the West. His complaint echoes the feelings of many other Asians, who resent preaching on human rights from countries whose record during the colonial era was hardly unblemished.

TRAN QUANG CO, COMMENTS ON HUMAN RIGHTS

In the best of all worlds, human rights would become a field for cooperation rather than a battleground of confrontation. But for this to happen, it is important to keep in mind that such rights are a product of human evolution and as such evolve with time, being neither absolute nor immutable. It is therefore strange that some of those who advocate human rights as a cornerstone of international relations pay so little regard to differences in stages of socioeconomic development—and the ensuing differences in the perception of imperatives and the setting of national priorities. A starving country, for example, will be far more concerned with feeding its people . . . than [with] the forms and methods of democracy.

I hasten to add that my intention here is not to fall into the oversimplistic, quasi-mechanical argument that the higher the level of socioeconomic development, the higher too the level of human rights. All I wish to stress is that socioeconomic development provides objective conditions and possibilities for better implementation of human rights, both individual and collective.

The point is that human rights is an aggregate product that calls for a balanced, holistic approach. History shows that economic rights have always been as important as, if not more [important] than, civil and political rights. During the 1980s, we have had our own experience of this with the "boat people" problem. Facing hard economic conditions after decades of war, thousands of Vietnamese chose illegal immigration in hopes of finding a better material life abroad. But because of political motivation, some countries have interpreted this as an exodus of political refugees. It is blatantly clear that this is not at all the truth. Indeed, the success of our economic reform has halted this sad phenomenon.

It should also be clear that human rights cannot be summed up merely as individual rights. Human rights also encompass the collective rights of communities and nations to self-determination; the right to sovereign use of national natural resources, the right to development, the right to equality of status among nations.

To some in the developed North, these collective rights might appear somewhat abstract and remote. But to nations that have recently emerged from colonial bondage and are struggling to develop in an unfavorable and still unfair international environment, there is nothing remote about these aspirations at all. One is tempted to think sometimes that the reason affluent nations speak so little of self-determination, sovereignty, and equality is that in their everyday lives as rich and powerful nations they take these rights for granted. In other words, they call the shots.

More interesting still is that the same rights and rules so often invoked for judging relations between governments and their people are by no means followed when it comes to relations between states. If democracy is indeed a worthy goal for regulating relations within a society, for example, should it not also be followed among nations? It seems somehow strange to us that the heightened attention that certain quarters display over a few specific cases of what they consider to be human-rights violations in our country often goes together with a blithe indifference for the hundreds of thousands of Vietnamese whose human rights were abridged in many different ways during the war and from whose consequences they continue to suffer today.

To put it another way, we all need to remember that human rights will ever be a complex and sensitive issue, if only because by its nature it touches at the core of each society's scale of values and way of life. Certainly all states must strive to improve the human rights for their people, and they are accountable both to their own peoples and [to] the world community at large. What we find disquieting is the growing practice in bilateral dealings of pushing limited areas of concern without regard for our values, often going into details and aspects so specific that it raises the question of national sovereignty. At the international level, diversity no longer is hailed as a virtue.

the urban populations of Southeast Asia, although it has not disappeared.

In Thailand, for example, Buddhism has recently come under heavy pressure from the rising influence of materialism. Although temple schools still provide a ladder to upward mobility for thousands of rural youths whose families cannot afford the cost of public education, the behavior of Buddhist monks—many of whom chafe under the vows of chastity and fasting—has aroused deep concern among many observers. In one highly publicized recent case, a handsome young monk, whose popular appeal is reminiscent of the TV evangelists in the United States,

TRADITION AND MODERNITY IN MALAYSIA. Few countries in Southeast Asia have tried harder to achieve modernization without destroying their cultural heritage than Malaysia. In this photograph, modern skyscrapers tower over a mosque in the downtown section of the capital of Kuala Lumpur. The inner courtyard provides shelter from the heat of the tropical sun.

was involved in a sex scandal with some of his female followers. The case aroused a major controversy, in part because the church leadership had made use of his charismatic personality as a means of raising funds for Buddhist causes.

Nevertheless, Buddhist, Muslim, and even Confucian beliefs remain strong, even in cosmopolitan cities such as Bangkok, Jakarta, and Singapore. This preference for the traditional also shows up in lifestyle. Native dress—or, at least, an eclectic blend of Asian and Western dress—is still common. Traditional music, art, theater, and dance remain popular, although Western rock music has become fashionable among the young, and Indonesian filmmakers complain that Western films are beginning to dominate the market. Southeast Asian novels and short stories, although Western in form, still focus on local problems or political issues.

This Western veneer is less readily apparent among the less affluent urban dwellers. Yet their lifestyles are changing as well, stimulated by widespread access to television (including, in many countries, old American television programs like *Dallas*, *Kojak*, and *All in the Family*) and the rapid expansion of the educational system. Indeed, the spread of literacy is one of the most impressive aspects of the social changes taking place in Southeast Asia. The literacy rate is well above 80 percent in Singapore, Thailand, and the Philippines, and more than 75 percent even in such predominantly rural societies as Myanmar and Indonesia.

The increasing inroads made by Western culture have caused anxiety in some countries. In Malaysia, for example, fundamentalist Muslims criticize the prevalence of pornography, hedonism, drugs, and alcohol in Western culture and have tried to limit their presence in their own country. Signs stating "Dada means Death" (death to drugs) are a graphic illustration of what happens to drug pushers, whether native or foreign. The Malaysian government has attempted to limit the number of U.S. entertainment programs shown on local television stations and has replaced them with shows on traditional themes.

Neighboring countries have adopted similar measures. Pornography, long hair, and even chewing gum have been forbidden in Singapore. Even in easygoing Thailand, concern has been expressed that Christian missionaries have been undermining the Buddhist character of Thai society. A more immediate problem, however, is the rapid spread of HIV and AIDS, a consequence of the Thai government's tolerance of widespread prostitution as a means of encouraging tourism.

One of the most significant changes that has taken place in Southeast Asia in recent decades is in the role of women in society. In general, women in the region have historically faced fewer restrictions on their activities and enjoyed a higher status than women elsewhere in Asia. Nevertheless, they were not the equal of men in every respect. In Vietnam, Confucian precepts imported from China limited women's legal rights and occupational opportunities. In Buddhist and Muslim societies, women ranked lower on the social scale than men and generally did not play an active role in religious ritual. The advent of colonial rule brought some minor improvements in the status of women in Southeast Asia. With the opening of government-supported public schools, females for the first time began to be educated alongside males. And magazines for women were published in the major cities.

With independence, the trend toward liberating Southeast Asian women continued. Virtually all of the constitutions adopted by the newly independent states granted women full legal and political rights, including the right to work. In some respects, that promise has been fulfilled. In countries throughout the region, women have increased opportunities for education and have entered new careers previously reserved for men. Social restrictions on female behavior and activities have been substantially reduced, if not entirely eliminated. Women have become more active in politics, and in 1986, Corazon Aquino became the first woman to be elected president of a country in Southeast Asia. The wife of her predecessor, Imelda Marcos, was influential in Filipino politics in her own right, and Megawati Sukarnoputri is poised to play a major role in shaping the future of Indonesia.

Yet women are not truly equal to men in any country in Southeast Asia. Sometimes the distinction is simply a matter of custom. In Vietnam, women are legally equal to men, yet until recently no women had served on the Communist Party's ruling Politburo. In Thailand, Malaysia, and Indonesia, women rarely hold senior positions in government service or in the boardrooms of major corporations. Similar restrictions apply in Myanmar, although Aung San Huu Kyi is the leading figure in the democratic opposition movement.

Sometimes, too, women's rights have been undermined by a social or religious backlash. The revival of Islamic fundamentalism stemming from the Iranian Revolution has had an especially strong impact in Malaysia, where Malay women are expected to cover their bodies and wear the traditional Muslim headdress. Even in non-Muslim countries, women are still expected to behave demurely and exercise discretion in all contacts with the opposite sex. Yet the signs of change are everywhere. In predominantly Muslim Indonesia, talk radio programs provide advice to their listeners on how to gain greater sexual satisfaction from their marriage.

Cultural Trends

Culture is flourishing today in most countries in Southeast Asia, as writers, artists, and composers attempt to synthesize international styles and themes with local tradition and experience. The novel has become increasingly popular, as writers seek to find the best medium to encapsulate the dramatic changes that have taken place in the region in recent decades. Some of the best writers adopt a strong political orientation, as they take their stand on issues relevant to the lives of their compatriots.

The best-known writer in postwar Indonesia—at least to readers abroad—is Pramoedya Toer. Born in 1925 in eastern Java, he joined the Indonesian nationalist movement in his early twenties. Arrested in 1965 on the charge of being a Communist, he spent the next several years in prison. While incarcerated, he began writing his four-volume *Buru Quartet,* which recounts in fictional form the story of the struggle of the Indonesian people for freedom from colonial rule and the autocratic regimes of the independence period. He remains under house arrest in Java today, and his novels are forbidden to circulate in Indonesia. In an interview with a foreign journalist, he praised the Indonesian youth of today but called on them to avoid violence and to struggle for freedom by democratic means. "Without democracy," he contends, "all institutions that exercise power are nothing but mafia."[8]

As in Indonesia, novelists in contemporary Vietnam seek to play the dual role of writing good fiction and expressing the sometimes brutal realities of life in their country. Among the most talented of contemporary Vietnamese novelists is Duong Thu Huong (b. 1947). A member of the Vietnamese Communist Party who served on the front lines during the Sino-Vietnamese war in 1979, she later became outspoken in her criticism of the party's failure to carry out democratic reforms and was briefly imprisoned in 1991. Undaunted by official pressure, she has written several novels that express the horrors experienced by guerrilla fighters during the Vietnam War and the cruel injustices perpetrated by the regime in the cause of building socialism.

Tourism has had a tremendous but mixed impact on the revitalization of art and music throughout the region. In Vietnam, traditional drama and water puppetry have been revived at least in part to please tourists and earn precious foreign exchange. A similar process is under way in Indonesia, where woodworking, metalworking, and the textile industry have benefited from a large foreign presence. The island of Bali, however, demonstrates the risks involved in promoting tourism. Once the site of a unique and beautiful culture, parts of the island now reflect many of the more tawdry aspects of Western commercialism. Beyond the tourists, however, traditional culture in Bali, as elsewhere in Southeast Asia, still serves a purpose. On the island of Java, for example, traditional shadow puppet theater has been used by the government to promote its population control program, and in 1997 to assuage the fears of Indonesia farmers during a terrible drought.

Regional Conflict and Cooperation: The Rise of ASEAN

In addition to their continuing internal challenges, Southeast Asian states have been sporadically hampered by serious tensions among themselves. Some of these tensions were a consequence of historical rivalries and territorial disputes that had been submerged during the long era of colonial rule. Cambodia, for example, bickered with both of its neighbors, Thailand and Vietnam, over mutual frontiers drawn up originally by the French for their own convenience. A similar dispute erupted further to the south in the early 1960s, when Indonesian President Sukarno unleashed a policy of *konfrontasi* (confrontation) against the nearby government of Malaysia. Sukarno contended that the Malayan peninsula was populated by Malay peoples who had once been part of the traditional Indonesian empires and had only been separated from Indonesia as a result of colonial policies.

Sukarno's contention had some historical validity; the political separation of Malaysia from the Indonesian archipelago was in effect the result of a bargain between the British and the Dutch after the Napoleonic Wars. But it made little sense to the people of the resource-rich Malayan peninsula, who saw no advantage in the creation of a greater Indonesia dominated by the charismatic but demagogic Sukarno, who might be inclined to redistribute their wealth to the poorer Indonesian islands. In the end, Indonesia dropped its claim after Sukarno's fall from power in the mid-1960s (see the box on p. 969).

The territorial dispute between Cambodia and its neighbors was more difficult to resolve. During the Vietnam War, Cambodia's ruler, Norodom Sihanouk, sought close relations with China and North Vietnam at least partly because he feared that the United States would support claims by Thailand and South Vietnam for territories inside Cambodia.

The reunification of Vietnam under Communist rule in 1975 had an immediate impact on the region. By the end of the year, both Laos and Cambodia had Communist governments. In Cambodia, a brutal revolutionary regime under the leadership of the Khmer Rouge (Red Khmer) dictator Pol Pot carried out the massacre of more than one million Cambodians. But the Communist triumph in Indochina did not lead to the falling dominoes that many U.S. policy makers had feared. One reason was that the political and economic situation within the region had gradually stabilized during the 1960s and 1970s.

Another was that the Communist governments in China, Vietnam, and Cambodia immediately began to squabble among themselves. A key aspect of the problem was the lingering border dispute between Vietnam and Cambodia. The new Khmer Rouge regime in Phnom Penh claimed that vast territories in the Mekong Delta had been seized from Cambodia by the Vietnamese in previous centuries, and in the weeks following the end of the Vietnam War, Cambodia launched attacks across the common border to punctuate its demand. In response, Vietnamese forces invaded Cambodia in December 1978 and installed a new, pro-Hanoi regime in Phnom Penh.

The outbreak of war among the erstwhile Communist allies in the region aroused the concern of other countries in the neighborhood. In 1967, several non-Communist countries had established the Association of Southeast Asian Nations (ASEAN). Composed of Indonesia, Malaysia, Thailand, Singapore, and the Philippines, ASEAN at first concentrated on cooperative social and economic endeavors, but after the end of the Vietnam War, it began to seek a greater degree of political and military cohesion to resist further Communist encroachment in the region. After Vietnam invaded Cambodia in 1978, ASEAN cooperated with other states in supporting a loose coalition of non-Communist groups with the ultimate purpose of forcing the Vietnamese to withdraw. In 1991, the Vietnamese finally withdrew, and a new government was formed in Phnom Penh.

The emergence of ASEAN from its previous status as a weak collection of diverse states into a stronger organization involving military cooperation and a degree of political consensus among its members has helped to provide the nations of Southeast Asia with a more cohesive voice to represent their interests on the world stage. They will need it, for disagreements with Western countries over global economic issues and the rising power of China to the north will present major challenges to the region in coming years. Concern over China today is focused primarily on the dispute over ownership of the Spratly and Paracel Islands in the South China Sea. Most of the states in the region have staked claims to one or more of the islands, which are reportedly located over substantial oil reserves, but it is Beijing's insistence that both island groups are historically Chinese that has made a compromise settlement difficult. The admission of Vietnam into ASEAN

HOLOCAUST IN CAMBODIA. When the Khmer Rouge seized power in Cambodia in April 1975, they immediately emptied the capital of Phnom Penh and systematically began to eliminate opposition elements throughout the country. Thousands were tortured in the infamous Tuol Sleng prison and then marched out to the country-side, where they were massacred. Their bodies were thrown into massive pits. The succeeding government disinterred the remains, which are now displayed at an outdoor museum on the site.

AN INDONESIAN'S VIEW OF SUKARNO

In the early 1960s, Sukarno launched a campaign called konfrontasi (confrontation) to destroy the new nation of Malaysia and integrate the Malay peninsula into a Greater Indonesia. The campaign aroused suspicion throughout the region and was abandoned by his successor, General Suharto. In the following poem, an ordinary Indonesian, employed as a clerk in a hotel in Jakarta, expresses his opinion of Sukarno's grandiose plans.

"MY WIFE, THE FACELESS MEN, AND ME"

My wife crouches by the fire
Her fan flickering;
She is cooking a little fish for my dinner.
My wife is very beautiful—
Beneath her clothing she is like a goddess.
When we have eaten
She will lie beside me
And we will make love.

On the other side of the city,
At his desk,
A secretary of state is writing a speech
For his minister. Tomorrow it will be on the front page
Of every newspaper (by order);
Foreign correspondents will send it round the world;
It will be on the radio.

In his speech the minister will say,
"We, the People,
Will resist Imperialism to the last drop of Indonesian blood.
Ever onward, no retreat."
Tell me, please, who are these faceless men
Who speak for me,
Not knowing my name, calling me "The People,"
Spilling my blood for me?

Who will save me from them,
The statesmen,
The public officials, and security men?
Supposing I am the last Indonesian,
Lying with my wife
Who has a body like a goddess:
Do they think I will want to get up and resist Imperialism?
They should ask me first.

in 1996 should provide both Hanoi and its neighbors with greater leverage in dealing with their powerful neighbor to the north.

CONCLUSION

Today, the Western image of a Southeast Asia mired in the Vietnam conflict and the tensions of the Cold War has become a memory. In ASEAN the states in the region have created the framework for a regional organization that can serve their common political, economic, technological, and security interests. A few members of ASEAN are already on the road to advanced development. The remainder are showing signs of undergoing a similar process within the next generation. While ethnic and religious tensions continue to exist in most ASEAN states, there are promising signs of increasing political stability and pluralism throughout the region.

To be sure, there are continuing signs of trouble. The recent financial crisis has aroused serious political unrest in Indonesia and has the potential to create similar problems elsewhere. Myanmar remains isolated from trends in the region and appears mired in a state of chronic underdevelopment and brutal military rule. The three states of Indochina remain potentially unstable and have not yet been fully integrated into the region as a whole.

All things considered, however, the situation is more promising today than would have appeared possible a generation ago. The nations of Southeast Asia appear capable of coordinating their efforts to erase the internal divisions and conflicts that have brought so much tragedy to the peoples of the region for centuries. If the original purpose of the U.S. intervention in the Indochina conflict was to buy time for the other nations of the region to develop, the gamble may have paid off. Although the war in Vietnam was lost at considerable cost and bloodshed to the participants, the dire predictions in Washington of falling dominoes were not fulfilled, and some countries in the region appear ready to join the steadily growing ranks of developing nations.

To some observers, economic success in the region has come at a high price, in the form of political authoritarianism and a lack of attention to human rights. Indeed, proponents of the view that Asian values are different from those of the West should not be too complacent in their conviction that there is no correlation between economic prosperity and democracy. Still, a look at the historical record suggests that political pluralism is often a byproduct of economic advancement, and that political values and institutions evolve in response to changing societal conditions. In the end, the current growing pains in Southeast Asia may prove to be beneficial in their overall impact on societies in the region.

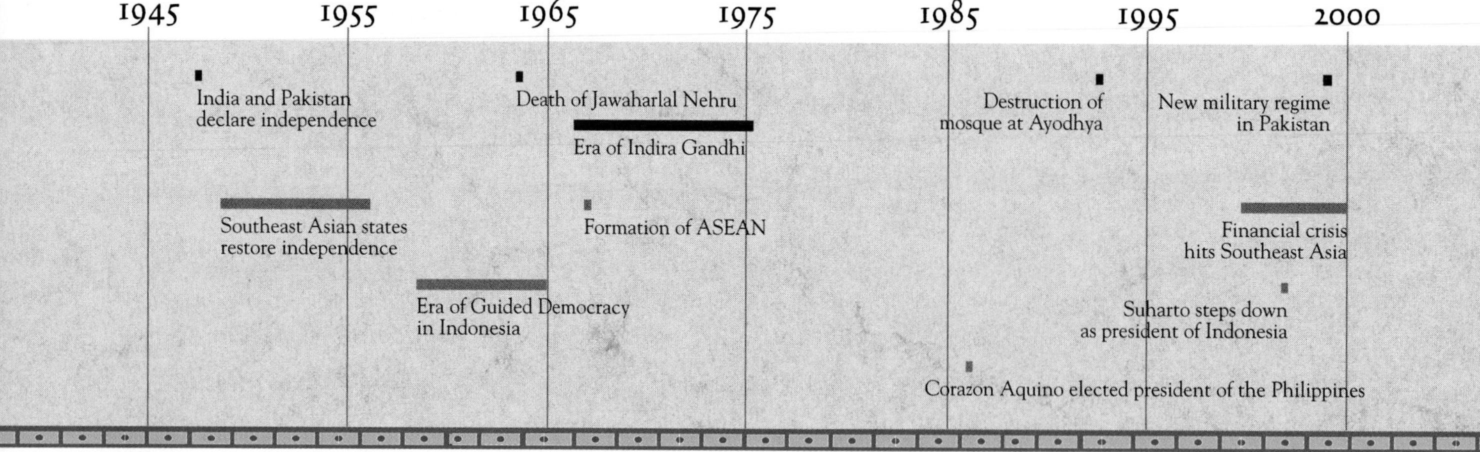

Chapter Notes

1. Martin Green, ed., *Gandhi in India: In His Own Words* (Hanover, N.H., 1987), p. 329.
2. Quoted in Larry Collins and Dominique Lapierre, *Freedom at Midnight* (New York, 1975), p. 252.
3. *New York Times*, April 26, 1996.
4. Kusum Nair, *Blossoms in the Dust: The Human Factor in Indian Development* (New York, 1961), p. 76.
5. *New York Times*, February 6, 1991.
6. Ibid., May 2, 1996.
7. Ibid., July 28, 1996.
8. *Far Eastern Economic Review*, October 10, 1996, p. 57.

Suggested Readings

For a recent survey of contemporary Indian history, see S. Wolpert, *A New History of India*, rev. ed. (New York, 1989). V. S. Naipaul, *India: A Wounded Civilization* (New York, 1977) is a provocative study of independent India from a friendly but sometimes critical perspective. Also see P. Brass, *The New Cambridge History of India: The Politics of Independence* (Cambridge, 1990); C. Baxter, *Bangladesh: From a Nation to a State* (Boulder, Colo., 1997); and S. Tharoor, *India: From Midnight to the Millennium* (New York, 1997).

On the period surrounding independence, see the dramatic account by L. Collins and D. Lapierre, *Freedom at Midnight* (New York, 1975). On Nehru's government, see D. Norman, ed., *Nehru: The First Sixty Years*, 2 vols. (London, 1965). For insight into Nehru's character, see S. Gandhi, ed., *Two Alone, Two Together: Letters Between Indira Gandhi and Jawaharlal Nehru, 1940–1964* (London, 1992).

The life and career of Indira Gandhi have been well chronicled. For two recent biographies, see T. Ali, *An Indian Dynasty: The Story of the Nehru-Gandhi Family* (New York, 1985), and K. Bhatia, *Indira: A Biography of Prime Minister Gandhi* (New York, 1974.)

Social issues are examined in a number of studies. For an overview, see K. Bhatia, *The Ordeal of Nationhood: A Social Study of India Since Independence, 1947–1970* (New York, 1971). See also J. M. Freeman, *Untouchable: An Indian Life History* (Stanford, Calif., 1979); R. G. Revankar, *The Indian Constitution: A Case Study of Backward Classes* (Rutherford, N.J., 1971); and W. and C. Wiser, *Behind Mud Walls, 1930–1960*, rev. ed. (New York, 1984). On Indian literature, see D. Ray and A. Singh, eds., *India: An Anthology of Contemporary Writing* (Athens, Ohio, 1983). See also S. Tharu and K. Lalita, eds., *Women Writing in India*, vol. 2 (New York, 1993). Novels mentioned in the text include A. Desai, *Cry, the Peacock* (New Delhi, 1980), and S. Rushdie, *Midnight's Children* (Harmondsworth, 1980).

There are a number of standard surveys of the history of modern Southeast Asia. Unfortunately, many of them are now out of date because of the changes that have taken place in the region since the end of the Vietnam War. For an introduction with a strong emphasis on recent events, see D. R. SarDesai, *Southeast Asia: Past and Present*, 2d ed. (Boulder, Colo., 1989). For a more scholarly approach, see D. J. Steinberg, ed., *In Search of Southeast Asia*, 2d ed. (New York, 1985).

The best way to approach modern Southeast Asia is through individual country studies. On Burma, see J. Silverstein, *Burmese Politics: The Dilemma of National Unity* (New Brunswick, N.J., 1980). On Thailand, see D. Wyatt, *Thailand* (New Haven, Conn., 1982). On the Philippines, the best overall survey is D. J. Steinberg, *The Philippines: A Singular and a Plural Place* (Boulder, Colo., 1994). On Malaya and Singapore, see K. von Vorys, *Democracy Without Consensus* (Princeton, N.J., 1975), and C. M. Turnbull, *A History of Singapore, 1819–1975* (Kuala Lumpur, 1977). For insight into the problem of racial tension in Malaysia, see M. bin Mohamad, *The Malay Dilemma* (Kuala Lumpur, 1970).

There is a rich selection of materials on modern Indonesia. On the Sukarno era, see J. Legge, *Sukarno* (New York, 1972), and H.

Jones, *Indonesia: The Possible Dream* (New York, 1971). On the Suharto era and its origins, see H. Crouch, *The Army in Indonesian Politics* (Ithaca, N.Y., 1978), and M. Vatikiotis, *Indonesian Politics Under Suharto* (London, 1993).

Most of the literature on Indochina in the last two decades has dealt with the Vietnam War and the related conflicts in Laos and Cambodia. For an excellent overall history, see S. Karnow, *Vietnam: A History* (New York, 1983), a companion volume for the PBS series on the war. F. Fitzgerald's *Fire in the Lake* (New York, 1970) won a Pulitzer Prize for its discussion of the reasons for the strength of the Viet Cong. On the brutal reign of the Khmer Rouge in Cambodia, see F. Ponchaud, *Cambodia Year Zero* (New York, 1977). On conditions in Vietnam since the end of the war, see R. Shaplen, *Bitter Victory* (New York, 1986), a study by a veteran journalist.

For an overview of women's issues in contemporary South and Southeast Asia, consult B. Ramusack and S. Sievers, *Women in Asia* (Bloomington, Ind., 1999). Articles that focus on the socioeconomic problems of women in India in the 1980s are found in M. Kishwar and R. Vanita, eds., *In Search of Answers: Indian Women's Voices from Manushi* (London, 1991). K. Bhasin, R. Menon, and N. S. Khan, eds., *Against All Odds: Essays on Women, Religion and Development from India and Pakistan* (New Delhi, 1994) presents fundamentalist conservatism among both Hindu and Muslim women since the mid-1980s. Of interest to Southeast Asian women's issues are W. Williams, *Javanese Lives: Women and Men in Modern Indonesian Society* (New Brunswick, N.J., 1991), and C. B. N. Chin, *In Service and Servitude: Foreign Female Domestic Workers and the Malaysian "Modernity" Project* (New York, 1998).

For additional reading, go to InfoTrac College Edition, your online research library at http://web1.infotrac-college.com

Enter the search terms "India history" using Keywords.

Enter the search terms "Pakistan history" using Keywords.

Enter the search term "Nehru" using Keywords.

Enter the search terms "Southeast Asia" using Keywords.

Enter the search term "Sukarno" using Keywords.

CHAPTER 32

TOWARD THE PACIFIC CENTURY? JAPAN AND THE LITTLE TIGERS

CHAPTER OUTLINE

- JAPAN: ASIAN GIANT
- THE JAPANESE MIRACLE: THE TRANSFORMATION OF SOCIETY IN MODERN JAPAN
- SOUTH KOREA: A PENINSULA DIVIDED
- TAIWAN: THE OTHER CHINA
- SINGAPORE AND HONG KONG: THE LITTLEST TIGERS
- ON THE MARGINS OF ASIA: POSTWAR AUSTRALIA AND NEW ZEALAND
- CONCLUSION

FOCUS QUESTIONS

- How did the Allied occupation after World War II change Japan's political and governmental structures, and what aspects remained unchanged?
- What changes have occurred in the Japanese economy since 1945?
- What are the major trends in Japanese society and culture since 1945?
- What are the major political and economic developments in South Korea, Taiwan, Singapore, and Hong Kong since 1945?
- What factors have contributed to the economic success achieved by Japan and the "little tigers" since 1945, and are any less beneficial effects associated with these factors?

In August of 1945, Japan was in ruins, its cities destroyed, its vast Asian empire in ashes, its land occupied by a foreign army. A decade earlier, Japanese leaders had proclaimed their national path to development as a model for other Asian nations to follow. During World War II, they had attempted to construct their vast Greater East Asia Co-Prosperity Sphere under Japanese tutelage. The result had been a bloody war and ultimate defeat.

Half a century later, Japan had emerged as the second greatest industrial power in the world, democratic in form and content and a source of stability throughout the region. Japan's achievement spawned a number of Asian imitators. Known as the "little tigers," the four industrializing societies of Taiwan, Hong Kong, Singapore, and South Korea achieved considerable success by following the path originally charted by Japan. Along with Japan, they became economic powerhouses and ranked among the world's top seventeen trading nations. Other nations in Asia and elsewhere took note and began to adopt the Japanese formula. It is no wonder that observers relentlessly heralded the coming of the "Pacific Century."

The impressive success of some countries in East and Southeast Asia prompted some commentators in the region to declare that the global balance of power had shifted away from Europe and the United States toward the lands of the Pacific. Some Western critics retorted that East Asia's achievements had taken place at great cost, as authoritarian governments in the region trampled on human rights and denied their citizens the freedoms that they required to fulfill their own destiny. Asian observers argued that freedom is not simply a matter of individuals' doing what they please but, in the words of the Singaporean diplomat Kishore Mahbubani, "can also result from greater social order and discipline."[1] Such views reflected not only the growing self-confidence of many societies in East and Southeast Asia, but also their growing inclination to defend Asian values and traditions against critics in the West.

Japan: Asian Giant

For five years after the end of the war in the Pacific, Japan was governed by an Allied administration under the command of U.S. General Douglas MacArthur. The occupation regime was dominated by the United States, although the country was technically administered by a new Japanese government. As commander of the occupation administration, MacArthur was responsible for demilitarizing Japanese society, destroying the Japanese war machine, trying Japanese civilian and military officials charged with war crimes, and laying the foundations of postwar Japanese society (see the box on p. 974).

But more than a written constitution was needed to demilitarize Japan and place it on a new course. Like the Meiji leaders in the late nineteenth century, occupation administrators wished to transform Japanese social institutions. The Meiji reforms, however, had been crafted to reflect native traditions and had set Japan on a path quite different from that of the modern West. Some Japanese observers believed that a fundamental reversal of trends begun with the Meiji Restoration would be needed before Japan would be ready to adopt the Western capitalist, democratic model.

One of the sturdy pillars of Japanese militarism had been the giant business cartels, known as *zaibatsu*. Allied policy was designed to break up the *zaibatsu* into smaller units in the belief that corporate concentration, in Japan as in the United States, not only hindered competition but was inherently undemocratic and conducive to political authoritarianism. Occupation planners also intended to promote the formation of independent labor unions, to lessen the power of the state over the economy, and

GENERAL MACARTHUR AND EMPEROR HIROHITO. After the end of World War II, U.S. General Douglas MacArthur was appointed supreme commander of the Allied powers. In that capacity, he directed U.S. policy during the occupation from 1945 to 1950. Here MacArthur stands side by side with Emperor Hirohito of Japan. Note the cultural and attitudinal differences of the two leaders expressed by their contrasting body language.

THE EMPEROR IS NOT DIVINE

At the close of World War II, the United States agreed that Japan could retain the emperor, but only on condition that he renounce his divinity. When the governments of Great Britain and the Soviet Union advocated that Hirohito be tried as a war criminal, General Douglas MacArthur, the supreme commander of Allied occupation forces in Japan, argued that the emperor had a greater grasp of democratic principles than most other Japanese and that his presence was vital to the success of Allied occupation policy. That recommendation was upheld. On New Year's Day, 1946, the emperor issued a rescript denying his divinity. To many Japanese of the era, however, he remained a divine figure.

HIROHITO, RESCRIPT ON DIVINITY

In greeting the New Year, we recall to mind that the Emperor Meiji proclaimed as the basis of our national policy the five clauses of the Charter at the beginning of the Meiji era. . . .

The proclamation is evident in its significance and high in its ideals. We wish to make this oath anew and restore the country to stand on its own feet again. We have to reaffirm the principles embodied in the Charter and proceed unflinchingly toward elimination of misguided practices of the past; and keeping in close touch with the desires of the people, we will construct a new Japan through thoroughly being pacific, the officials and the people alike obtaining rich culture and advancing the standard of living of the people.

The devastation of the war inflicted upon our cities, the miseries of the destitute, the stagnation of trade, shortage of food, and the great and growing number of the unemployed are indeed heart-rending, but if the nation is firmly united in its resolve to face the present ordeal and to see civilization consistently in peace, a bright future will undoubtedly be ours, not only for our country but for the whole of humanity.

Love of the family and love of country are especially strong in this country. With more of this devotion should we now work toward love of mankind.

We feel deeply concerned to note that consequent upon the protracted war ending in our defeat our people are liable to grow restless and to fall into the slough of despond. Radical tendencies in excess are gradually spreading and the sense of morality tends to lose its hold on the people with the result that there are signs of confusion of thoughts.

We stand by the people and we wish always to share with them in their moment of joys and sorrows. The ties between us and our people have always stood upon mutual trust and affection. They do not depend upon mere legends and myths. They are not predicated on the false conception that the Emperor is divine and that the Japanese people are superior to other races and fated to rule the world.

Our Government should make every effort to alleviate their trials and tribulations. At the same time, we trust that the people will rise to the occasion and will strive courageously for the solution of their outstanding difficulties and for the development of industry and culture. Acting upon a consciousness of solidarity and of mutual aid and broad tolerance in their civil life, they will prove themselves worthy of their best tradition. By their supreme endeavors in that direction they will be able to render their substantial contribution to the welfare and advancement of mankind.

The resolution for the year should be made at the beginning of the year. We expect our people to join us in all exertions looking to accomplishment of this great undertaking with an indomitable spirit.

to provide a mouthpiece for downtrodden Japanese workers. Economic inequality in rural areas was to be reduced by a comprehensive land reform program that would turn the land over to those who farmed it. Finally, the educational system was to be remodeled along American lines, so that it would turn out independent individuals rather than automatons subject to manipulation by the state.

The Allied program was an ambitious and even audacious plan to remake Japan society and has been justly praised for its clear-sighted vision and altruistic motives. Parts of the program, such as the constitution, the land reform program, and the educational system, succeeded brilliantly. But as other concerns began to intervene, changes or compromises were made that were not always successful. In particular, with the rise of Cold War sentiment in the United States in the late 1940s, the goal of decentralizing the Japanese economy gave way to the desire to make Japan a key partner in the effort to defend East Asia against international communism. Convinced of the need to promote economic recovery in Japan, U.S. policy makers began to show more tolerance for the *zaibatsu*. Concerned at growing radicalism within the new labor movement, U.S. occupation authorities placed less emphasis on the independence of the labor unions.

Cold War concerns also affected U.S. foreign relations with Japan. On September 8, 1951, the United States and other former belligerent nations signed a peace treaty restoring Japanese independence. In turn, Japan renounced any claim to such former colonies or territories as Taiwan (which had been returned to the Republic of China), Korea (which, after a period of joint Soviet and U.S. occupation, had become two independent states), and southern Sakhalin and the Kurile Islands (which had been ceded to the Soviet Union). The Soviet Union refused to sign the treaty on the grounds that the Soviet Union had not been permitted to play an active role in the occupation. On the same day, the Japanese and Americans signed a defensive alliance and agreed that the United States could maintain military bases on the Japanese islands. Japan was now formally independent, but in a new dependency relationship with the United States. A provision in the new constitution renounced war as an instrument of national policy and prohibited the raising of an army.

The Japanese Miracle: The Transformation of Society in Modern Japan

By the early 1950s, then, Japan had regained at least partial control over its own destiny. Although it was linked closely to the United States through the new security treaty and the new American-drafted constitution, Japan was now essentially free to move out on its own. As the world would soon discover, the Japanese adapted quickly to the new conditions. From a semifeudal society with autocratic leanings, Japan has progressed into one of the most stable and advanced democracies in the world today. It has risen from the ashes of total destruction in 1945 to become the second largest and in many ways the most advanced economy in the world.

Japan's achievements in the area of human services are especially noteworthy. Its record on health is impressive, even though it has one-third more people per doctor than the United States. Life expectancy is high, and the infant mortality rate is only 5 per 1,000, the lowest in the world. The literacy rate is almost 100 percent, and a significantly higher proportion of the population graduates from high school than in most advanced nations of the West. Crime rates are low (on an average day, according to a recent statistic, 4,584 crimes are committed in Japan, compared to 93,474 in the United States), and although Japan suffered badly from environmental pollution during the 1950s and 1960s, it has moved rapidly to improve its urban environments. Despite its near total lack of domestic sources of oil, Japan today is less dependent on oil imports than is the oil-rich United States.

Japan appears equally blessed in the area of foreign affairs. Under the umbrella of U.S. nuclear protection, Japan has been able to avoid conflicts with foreign countries and has adhered to its constitutional restriction of staying out of foreign wars, although, in agreement with the United States, it decided to establish a limited "self-defense force" to provide protection for the Japanese home islands. Though linked to the United States through the 1951 security treaty, Japan has carried out an increasingly independent foreign policy in recent years and has succeeded in maintaining amicable relations with virtually all nations. Its only serious dispute is with Russia, which has consistently refused Japan's request for the return of four islands in the Kurile chain, near the northern Japanese island of Hokkaido.

Japan's rapid emergence as an economic giant has often been described as the "Japanese miracle." Whether this description is justified (Japan's recent economic performance raises some doubts on that score), Japan has made a dramatic recovery from the war. Although the "miracle" is often described as beginning after the war as a result of the Allied reforms—a chronology that ascribes most of the credit to U.S. postwar policies—in fact, as we have seen, Japanese economic growth began much earlier, with the Meiji reforms, which helped to transform Japan from an autocratic society based on semifeudal institutions into an advanced capitalist democracy. The seeds of the Japanese miracle were sown in the Meiji period, or even in the late Tokugawa era, well over a century ago.

During the 1990s, the Japanese economy began to run into serious difficulties, raising the question as to whether the vaunted Japanese model was as appealing as many observers had earlier declared. The economic slowdown in turn was accompanied by growing problems in the social arena, including rising crime rates and an increase in unemployment, and a prospective breakdown in the political stability that marked the post-war era. As the new millennium dawns, Japan for the first time in half a century is experiencing a quiet crisis of self-confidence and an era of self-doubt.

Politics and Government

The Allied occupation administrators started with the conviction that Japanese expansionism was directly linked to the institutional and ideological foundations of the Meiji Constitution. Accordingly, they set out to change Japanese politics into something closer to the pluralistic model used in most Western nations. The concepts of universal suffrage, governmental accountability, and a balance of power among the executive, legislative, and judicial branches, which were embodied in the Constitution of 1947, held firm, and Japan became a stable and mature democratic society with a literate and politically active electorate and a government that actively seeks to meet the needs of its citizens.

Yet a number of characteristics of the postwar Japanese political system reflected the tenacity of the traditional political culture. Although Japan had a multiparty system with two major parties, the Liberal Democrats and the Socialists, in practice there was a "government party" and a permanent opposition—the Liberal Democrats were not voted out of office for thirty years. Many of the leading

MAP 32.1 Modern Japan

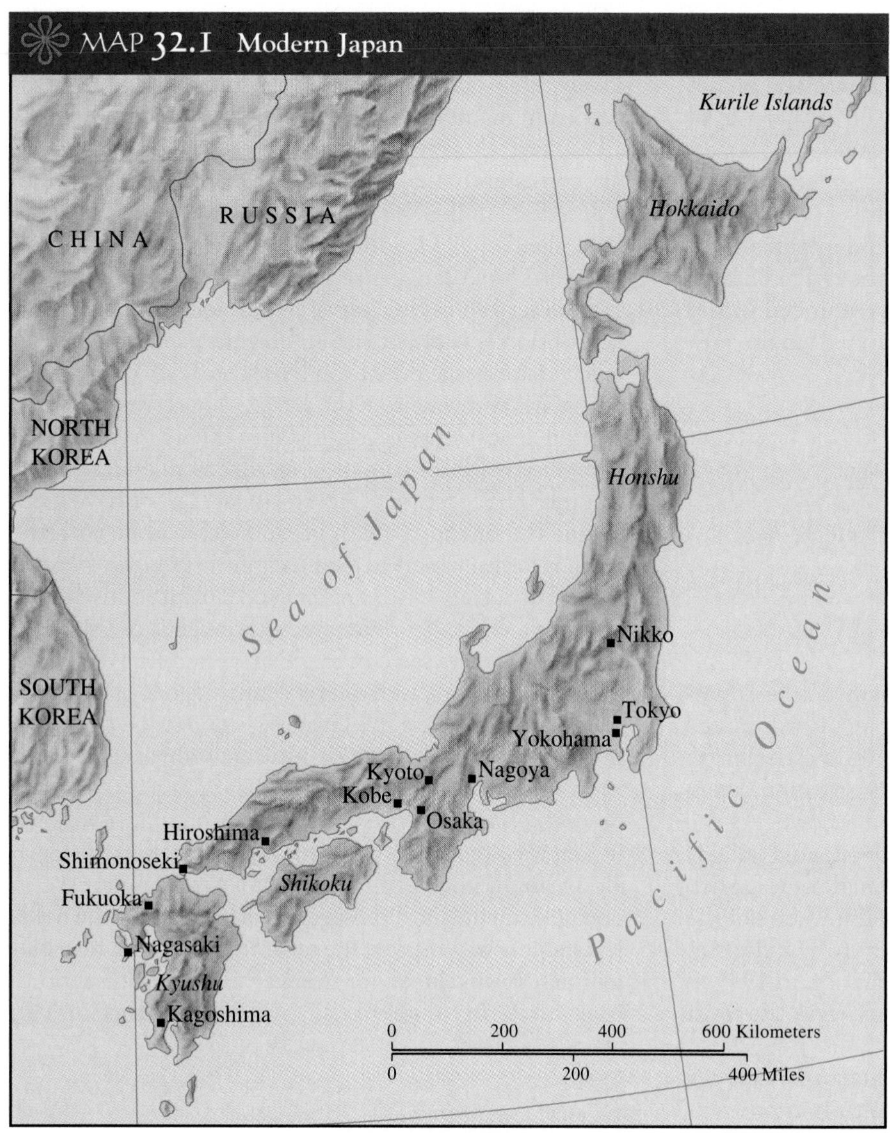

Liberal Democrats controlled factions on a patron-client basis, and decisions on key issues, such as who should assume the prime ministership, were decided by a modern equivalent of the *genro* oligarchs.

That tradition changed suddenly in 1993, when the "ruling" Liberal Democrats, shaken by persistent reports of corruption and "cronyism" between politicians and business interests, failed to win a majority of seats in parliamentary elections. Mirohiro Hosokawa, the leader of one of several newly created parties in the Japanese political spectrum, was elected prime minister. He promised to launch a number of reforms to clean up the political system. The new coalition government, however, quickly split into feuding factions, and in 1995 the Liberal Democratic Party returned to power under a new cabinet led by Prime Minister Ryutaro Hashimoto. Hashimoto promised to carry out a series of reforms to make the government more efficient and less prone to corruption. His successor as prime minister, Keizo Obuchi, sought to continue the process.

One of the problems has been that the current system continues the centralizing tendencies of the Meiji period. The central government plays an active and sometimes intrusive role in various aspects of the economy, mediating management-labor disputes, establishing price and wage policies, and subsidizing vital industries and enterprises producing goods for export. This government intervention in the economy has traditionally been widely accepted and was often cited as a key reason for the efficiency of Japanese industry and the emergence of the country as an industrial giant.

In recent years, however, government involvement in the economy has increasingly come under fire. Japanese business, which previously sought government protection from imports, now argues that deregulation is needed to enable Japanese firms to innovate to keep up with the competition. Such reforms, however, have been resisted by powerful government ministries in Tokyo, which are accustomed to playing an active role in national affairs.

Another problem in recent years has been corruption in government. A number of senior politicians, including two recent prime ministers, have been forced to resign because of serious questions about improper financial dealings with business associates. Political corruption was undoubtedly a major factor in the defeat of the Liberal Democrats 1993, and the issue continues to plague the political scene.

Last, but certainly not least, minorities such as the *eta* (now known as the Burakumin) and Korean residents in Japan continue to be subjected to legal and social discrimination. For years, official sources were reluctant to divulge growing evidence that thousands of Korean women were conscripted to serve as prostitutes (euphemistically, "comfort women") for Japanese soldiers during the war, and many Koreans living in Japan contend that such prejudicial attitudes continue to exist. Representatives of the "comfort women" have demanded both financial compensation and a formal letter of apology from the Japanese government for the treatment they received during the Pacific War. Negotiations over the issue are now under way.

The issue of Japan's behavior during World War II has been especially sensitive. An American political scientist teaching for a year at Kobe University reports that many of his students said they had learned about Pearl Harbor, the invasion of China, and the massacre of Chinese civilians in Nanjing "from my uncle, from my grandfather, from TV, from books, from family talk," but not from their classes. Several students told him that they knew of teachers who had been disciplined for teaching about the war. Asked why such things were not taught in school, they always answered, "Because the government, or the Education Ministry, does not want us to know."[2]

During the 1990s, critics at home and abroad charged that textbooks printed under the guidance of the Ministry of Education did not adequately discuss the atrocities committed by the Japanese government and armed forces during World War II. Other Asian governments were incensed at Tokyo's failure to accept responsibility for that behavior and demanded a formal apology. The government of Prime Minister Hashimoto responded with a statement that expressed remorse, but only in the context of the aggressive actions of all colonial powers during the imperialist era. In the view of many Japanese, the actions of their government during the Pacific War were a form of self-defense. A controversial new film, which appeared in 1998, played on that sentiment by portraying Hideki Tojo, the Japanese general who was hanged after World War II as a war criminal, as a patriotic figure. Although fear of the potential revival of Japanese militarism is still strong in the region, the United States has not shared this concern and has applauded a recent decision by Prime Minister Keizo Obuchi to enhance the role of Japanese self-defense forces in dealing with potential disturbances within the region. The issue has provoked vigorous debate in Japan, where some observers have argued that their country must begin to adopt a more assertive stance toward the United States and play a larger role in Asian affairs.

The Economy

Nowhere are the changes in postwar Japan so visible as in the economic sector, where Japan has developed into a major industrial and technological power in the space of a century, surpassing such advanced Western societies as Germany, France, and Great Britain. Here, indeed, is the Japanese miracle in its most concrete manifestation.

The process began a century ago in the single-minded determination of the Meiji modernizers to create a "rich country and strong state." Their initial motive was to guarantee Japan's survival against Western imperialism, but this defensive urge evolved into a desire to excel and, during the years before World War II, to dominate. That desire led to the war in the Pacific and, in the eyes of some, still contributes to Japan's problems with its trading partners in the world today.

As we have seen, the officials of the Allied occupation identified the Meiji economic system with centralized power and the rise of Japanese militarism. Accordingly, MacArthur's planners set out to break up the *zaibatsu* and decentralize Japanese industry and commerce. But with the rise of Cold War tensions, the policy was scaled back, and only the nineteen largest conglomerates were affected. In any event, the new antimonopoly law did not hinder the formation of looser ties between Japanese companies, and as a result, a new type of informal relationship, sometimes called the *keiretsu* or "interlocking arrangement," began to take shape. Through such arrangements among suppliers, wholesalers, retailers, and financial institutions, the *zaibatsu* system was reconstituted under a new name.

The occupation administration had more success with its program to reform the agricultural system. Half of the population still lived on farms, and half of all farmers were still tenants. Under a stringent land reform program in the late 1940s, all lands owned by absentee landlords and all cultivated landholdings over an established maximum were sold on easy credit terms to the tenants. The maximum size of an individual farm was set at 7.5 acres, while an additional 2.5 acres could be leased to tenants. The reform program created a strong class of yeoman farmers, and tenants declined to about 10 percent of the rural population.

During the past fifty years, Japan has re-created the stunning results of the Meiji era. At the end of the Allied occupation in 1950, the Japanese gross national product was about one-third that of Great Britain or France. Today, it is larger than both put together and well over half that of the United States. Japan is the greatest exporting nation in the world, and its per capita income equals or surpasses that of most advanced Western states.

By the mid-1980s, the economic challenge presented by Japan had begun to arouse increasing concern in both official and private circles in Europe and the United States. Explanations for Japan's success tended to fall into two major categories. Some pointed to cultural factors: The Japanese are naturally group-oriented and find it easy to cooperate with one another. Traditionally hardworking and frugal, they are more inclined to save than to consume, a trait that boosts the savings rate and labor productivity. The Japanese are family-oriented and therefore spend less on welfare for the elderly, who normally live with their children. Like all Confucian societies, the Japanese value education, and consequently the labor force is highly skilled. Finally, Japan is a homogeneous society, in which people share common values and respond in similar ways to the challenges of the modern world.

Others cited more practical reasons for Japanese success. Paradoxically, Japan benefited from the total destruction of its industrial base during World War II, because it did not face the problem of antiquated plants that plagued many industries in the United States. Under the terms of its constitution and the security treaty with the United States, Japan spent less than 1 percent of its gross national product on national defense, whereas the United States spent more than 5 percent. Labor productivity was high, not only because the Japanese are hard workers, but also because corporations rewarded innovation and maintained good management-labor relations. Consequently, employee mobility and the number of days lost to labor stoppages were minimized (on an average day, according to one estimate, 603 Japanese workers are on strike, compared to 11,956 Americans). Just as it did before World War II, the Japanese government promoted business interests rather than hindering them. Finally, some charge that Japan used unfair trade practices, subsidizing exports through the Ministry of International Trade and Industry (MITI), dumping goods at prices below cost to break into a foreign market, maintaining an artificially low standard of living at home to encourage exports, and unduly restricting imports from other countries.

A PACHINKO PARLOR. Pachinko, a game similar to the pinball played in the United States, is one of the favorite pastimes of many Japanese men. Since becoming a fad in the 1950s, it has been periodically criticized in the media as a useless activity that detracts from the legendary high productivity of the Japanese people. Yet it has retained its popularity, and pachinko parlors such as this one in Osaka can be found throughout the country.

The truth in this case is probably a little of both. Undoubtedly, Japan benefited from its privileged position beneath the U.S. nuclear umbrella as well as from its ability to operate in a free trade environment that provided both export markets and access to Western technology. The Japanese also took a number of practical steps to improve their competitive position in the world and the effectiveness of their economic system at home.

Yet many of these steps were possible precisely because of the cultural factors described here. The tradition of loyalty to the firm, for example, derives from the communal tradition in Japanese society. The concept of sacrificing one's personal interests to those of the state, though not necessarily rooted in the traditional period, was certainly fostered by the *genro* oligarchy during the Meiji era.

In recent years, the concern that Japan might overtake the United States and reduce it to a second-rank economic power has abated somewhat. One reason is the increasingly competitive position of U.S. firms in the global marketplace. Another is the economic downturn in the Japanese economy in the 1990s and the realization that Japan, too, is encountering some of the same problems that have afflicted the United States, as well as others that may be the result of factors unique to Japan. A rise in the value of the yen hurt exports and burst the bubble of investment by Japanese banks that had taken place under the umbrella of government protection. Lacking a domestic market equivalent in size to the United States, the Japanese economy slipped into a long-term recession.

These economic difficulties have placed heavy pressure on some of the vaunted features of the Japanese economy. The tradition of lifetime employment created a bloated white-collar workforce and has made downsizing difficult. Today, job security is on the decline as increasing numbers of workers are being laid off. Unfortunately, a disproportionate burden has fallen on women, who lack seniority and continue to suffer from various forms of discrimination in the workplace. A positive consequence is that job satisfaction is beginning to take precedence over job security in the minds of many Japanese workers, while salary is beginning to reflect performance more than time on the job.

A final factor is that slowly but inexorably the Japanese market is beginning to open up to international competition. Foreign automakers are winning a growing share of the domestic market, while the government—concerned at the prospect of growing food shortages—has committed itself to facilitating the importation of rice from abroad. This last move was especially sensitive, given the almost sacred role that rice farming holds in the Japanese mind-set.

KFC IN JAPAN. Although Japan has been widely criticized for its reluctance to import goods from other countries, the Japanese people display a strong interest in many aspects of Western culture. Items of American culture, including Mickey Mouse, fashionable sneakers, and Kentucky Fried Chicken, are especially prized. This outlet, complete with a statue of Colonel Sanders, is on a downtown street in Kobe.

A Society in Transition

During the occupation, Allied planners set out to change social characteristics that they believed had contributed to Japanese aggressiveness before and during World War II. The new educational system removed all references to filial piety, patriotism, and loyalty to the emperor while emphasizing the individualistic values of Western civilization. The new constitution and a revised civil code eliminated remaining legal restrictions on women's rights to obtain a divorce, hold a job, or change their domicile. Women were guaranteed the right to vote and were encouraged to enter politics.

Such efforts to remake Japanese behavior through legislation were only partially successful. During the past fifty years, Japan has unquestionably become a more individualistic and egalitarian society. Freedom of choice in marriage and occupation is taken for granted, and social mobility, though not so extensive as it is in the United States, has increased considerably beyond prewar levels.

At the same time, many of the distinctive characteristics of traditional Japanese society have persisted into the present day, although in somewhat altered form. The emphasis on loyalty to the group and community relationships, for example, is reflected in the strength of corporate loyalties in contemporary Japan. While competition among enterprises in a particular industry is often quite vigorous, social cohesiveness among both management and labor personnel is exceptionally strong within each individual corporation, although, as we have seen, the attitude has eroded somewhat in recent years.

One possible reason for this attitude may be the relatively egalitarian character of Japanese society in terms of income. According to recent statistics, a chief executive officer in Japan receives, on average, seventeen times the salary of the average worker, compared with eighty-five times in the United States. The disparity between wealth and poverty is also generally less in Japan than in most European countries and certainly less than in the United States. In 1992, the poorest 20 percent of the Japanese population possessed about 9 percent of the wealth, while the richest 20 percent owned 37 percent. In the United States, the poorest 20 percent possessed only 4 percent of the wealth, while the richest 20 percent owned 46 percent.[3]

Emphasis on the work ethic also remains strong. The tradition of hard work is taught at a young age within the educational system. The Japanese school year runs for 240 days a year, compared to 180 days in the United States, and work assignments outside class tend to be more extensive (according to one source, a Japanese high school student averages about five hours of homework per day). The results are impressive: the literacy rate in Japanese society is almost 100 percent, and Japanese schoolchildren consistently earn higher scores on achievement tests than children in other advanced countries. At the same time, this devotion to success has often been accompanied by bullying by teachers and what Americans might consider an oppressive sense of conformity (see the box on p. 980).

Some young Japanese find suicide the only escape from the pressures emanating from society, school, and family.

GROWING UP IN JAPAN

Japanese schoolchildren are exposed to a much more regimented environment than U.S. children experience. Most Japanese schoolchildren, for example, wear black-and-white uniforms to school. These regulations are examples of rules adopted by middle school systems in various parts of Japan. The Ministry of Education in Tokyo concluded that these regulations were excessive, but they are probably typical.

SCHOOL REGULATIONS: JAPANESE STYLE

1. Boys' hair should not touch the eyebrows, the ears, or the top of the collar.
2. No one should have a permanent wave, or dye his or her hair. Girls should not wear ribbons or accessories in their hair. Hair dryers should not be used.
3. School uniform skirts should be ____ centimeters above the ground, no more and no less (differs by school and region).
4. Keep your uniform clean and pressed at all times. Girls' middy blouses should have two buttons on the back collar. Boys' pant cuffs should be of the prescribed width. No more than 12 eyelets should be on shoes. The number of buttons on a shirt and tucks in a shirt are also prescribed.
5. Wear your school badge at all times. It should be positioned exactly.
6. Going to school in the morning, wear your book bag strap on the right shoulder; in the afternoon on the way home, wear it on the left shoulder. Your book case thickness, filled and unfilled, is also prescribed.
7. Girls should wear only regulation white underpants of 100% cotton.
8. When you raise your hand to be called on, your arm should extend forward and up at the angle prescribed in your handbook.
9. Your own route to and from school is marked in your student rule handbook; carefully observe which side of each street you are to use on the way to and from school.
10. After school you are to go directly home, unless your parent has written a note permitting you to go to another location. Permission will not be granted by the school unless this other location is a suitable one. You must not go to coffee shops. You must be home by ____ o'clock.
11. It is not permitted to drive or ride a motorcycle, or to have a license to drive one.
12. Before and after school, no matter where you are, you represent our school, so you should behave in ways we can all be proud of.

Ironically, once the student is accepted into college, the amount of work assigned tends to decrease, because graduates of the best universities are virtually guaranteed lucrative employment offers. Nevertheless, the early training instills an attitude of deference to group interests that persists throughout life. Some observers, however, believe such attitudes can have a detrimental effect on individual initiative. To give one example, the Japanese professional tennis player Kimiko Date played tennis with her right hand, at the insistence of her father, even though she was naturally left-handed. As a child she made no protest, she explains, "because I thought everybody played that way."[4]

The tension between the Japanese way and the foreign approach is especially noticeable in Japanese baseball, where major league teams frequently hire U.S. players. One American noted the case of Tatsunori Hara, one of the best Japanese players in the league. "He had so many different people telling him what to do," remarked Reggie Smith, a teammate, "it's a wonder he could still swing the bat. They turned him into a robot, instead of just letting him play naturally and expressing his natural talent." To Hara's Japanese coach, however, conformity brought teamwork, and teamwork in Japan is the road to success.[5]

By all accounts, independent thinking is on the increase in Japan. In some cases, it leads to antisocial behavior, such as crime or membership in a teenage gang. Usually it is expressed in more indirect ways, such as the recent fashion among young people of dyeing their hair brown (known in Japanese as "tea hair"). Because the practice is banned in many schools and generally frowned upon by the older generation (one police chief dumped a pitcher of beer on a student with brown hair whom he noticed in a bar), many young Japanese dye their hair as a gesture of independence. When seeking employment or getting married, however, they return their hair to its natural color.

One of the more tenacious legacies of the past in Japanese society is sexual inequality (see the box on p. 981). Although women are now legally protected against discrimination in employment, very few have reached senior levels in business, education, or politics, and, in the words of one Western scholar, they remain "acutely disadvantaged"—though ironically, in a recent survey of business executives in Japan, a majority declared that women were smarter than men. Women now comprise nearly 50 percent of the workforce, but most are in retail or service occupations, and their average salary is only about half that of men. The disparity extends even to literature.

AN ERA OF WOMEN

Although a considerable amount of serious scholarship on Japanese women has been written in the past few years, little has been translated into foreign languages. This is hardly surprising, since for every Japanese book translated into English, the Japanese publish thirty-five to forty titles from the United States and Europe in their own language. One recent collection of essays by Japanese women labels the current period "The Era of Women," thus implying that Japanese women are breaking out of their traditional feudal role and choosing new values and venues. In the introduction to the book, Kumiko Fujimura-Fanselow, a professor of education and women's studies at a leading Japanese university, provides an overview of the status of Japanese women today.

THE STATUS OF JAPANESE WOMEN

Recent advances in the area of politics, employment, education, and culture as well as marriage and family are cited in support of this notion of the era of women. . . . On the political front is the growing presence of female politicians, exemplified . . . by the appointment of Doi Takako as leader of Japan's largest opposition party, the Socialist Party, in 1986, as well as the successful election of a record high of twenty-two female candidates in the 1989 election for the House of Councilors of the National Diet. Women have increasingly become visible in local politics also. . . . A quick glance at educational statistics reveals a higher percentage of female as compared to male high school graduates entering colleges and universities. . . . The overwhelming majority of female college and university graduates, over 80 percent, are taking up employment and doing so in a wider range of fields than in the past. Better education and the availability of more job opportunities have increasingly made it possible for women to look upon marriage as an option rather than a prescribed lifestyle. . . .

Looking specifically at developments on the employment front, . . . the passage of the Equal Employment Opportunity Law (EEOL) in 1985 . . . opened up the previously all-male career track within Japanese companies to university-educated women, and . . . the Child Care Leave Law of 1991 . . . requires companies to grant unpaid leave to either parent until the child reaches the age of one. We see signs of women shedding traditional stereotypes and going into a variety of traditionally male occupations and professions. For example, in the years since the first female news co-announcer appeared on NHK (Japan's government-sponsored television network) in 1979, female newscasters have become a presence on nearly all news programs.

A dramatic development has been the advancement by married women, including those with children, into the labor force. Even in the cases of those who choose not to work outside the home, very few remain content to be housewives exclusively. Instead, they seek a life outside the home through a variety of activities, including study at privately run "culture centers," which offer courses in everything from foreign languages, literature, and law to traditional arts, handicrafts, cooking, and sports.

Japan has separate literary awards for men and women, and women are not considered capable of abstract or objective writing. Nevertheless, many contemporary women authors are daring to broach "male" subjects and are producing works of considerable merit. There is a feminist movement in Japan, but it has none of the vigor and mass support of its counterpart in the United States.

In the home, a Japanese woman has the primary responsibility for managing the family finances and raising the children. Japanese husbands carry little of the workload around the house, spending an average of nine minutes a day on housework, compared to twenty-six minutes for American husbands. At the same time, Japanese divorce rates are well below those of the United States, and only 1.4 million elderly Japanese (most of them undoubtedly women) live alone, compared to 8.6 million in the United States.

Japan's welfare system also differs profoundly from those of its Western counterparts. Applicants are required to seek assistance first from their own families, and the physically able are ineligible for government aid. As a result, less than 1 percent of the population receives welfare benefits, compared with more than 10 percent who receive some form of assistance in the United States. Outside observers interpret the difference as the product of several factors, including low levels of drug addiction and illegitimacy, as well as the importance in Japan of the work ethic and family responsibility.

Traditionally, it was the responsibility of the eldest child in a Japanese family to care for aging parents, but that system too is beginning to break down because of limited housing space and the growing tendency of working-age women to seek jobs in the marketplace. The proportion of Japanese over 65 years of age who live with their children has dropped from 80 percent in 1970 to just over 50 percent today. At the same time, public and private pension plans are under increasing financial pressure, partly because of a low birth rate and a graying population. Japan today has the highest proportion of people over 65—17 percent of the country's total population of 127 million—of any industrialized country in the world.

Whether the unique character of modern Japan will endure is unclear. Confidence in the Japanese "economic

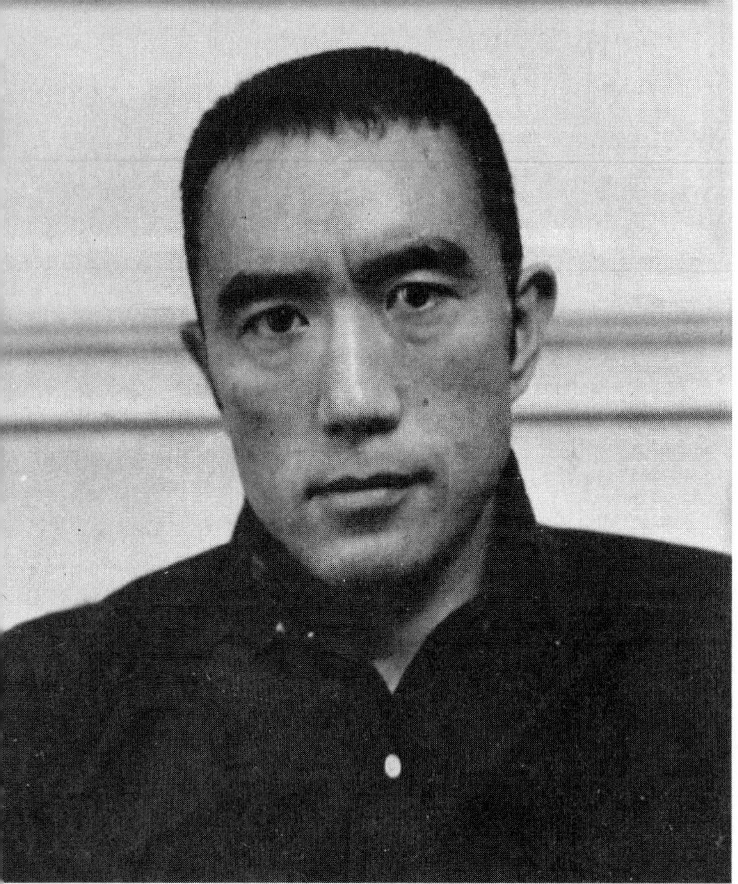

YUKIO MISHIMA. Postwar Japan gave rise to a "lost generation" of authors who, disillusioned and demoralized after the defeat, echoed the spiritual vacuum of the times. For some, the humiliation was compounded by what they perceived as the Americanization of Japan. This attitude is perhaps best exemplified by the writings of Yukio Mishima, who made it his crusade to restore the strengths of traditional Japan and stem the tide of U.S. "coca-colonization."

miracle" has been shaken because of the recent downturn, and there are indications of a growing tendency toward hedonism and individualism among Japanese youth. Older Japanese frequently complain that the younger generation lacks their sense of loyalty and willingness to sacrifice. There are also signs that the concept of loyalty to one's employer may be beginning to erode among Japanese youth. Some observers have predicted that with increasing affluence, Japan will become more like the industrialized societies in the West. Nevertheless, Japan is unlikely to evolve into a carbon copy of the United States. Not only is Japan a much more homogeneous society, but its small size and dearth of natural resources encourage a strong work ethic and a sense of togetherness that have long since begun to dissipate in American society.

Religion and Culture

When Japan was opened to the West in the nineteenth century, many Japanese became convinced of the superiority of foreign ideas and institutions and were especially interested in Western religion and culture. Although Christian converts were few, numbering less than 1 percent of the population, the influence of Christianity was out of proportion to the size of the community. Many intellectuals during the Meiji era were impressed by the emotional commitment shown by missionaries in Japan and viewed Christianity as a contemporary version of Confucianism.

Today, Japan includes almost 1.5 million Christians along with 93 million Buddhists and 111 million who follow Shintoism; these figures are large because they include the many Japanese who believe in both Buddhism and Shintoism. Shintoism has not been identified with reverence for the emperor and the state since the occupation period. As in the West, increasing urbanization has led to a decline in the practice of organized religion, although evangelical sects have proliferated in recent years. The largest and best-known sect is the Soka Gakkai, a lay Buddhist organization that has attracted millions of followers and formed its own political party, called the Komeito.

As we have seen, Western literature, art, and music also had a major impact on Japanese society. Western influence led to the rapid decline of traditional forms of drama and poetry and the growth in popularity of the prose novel. After the Japanese defeat in World War II, many of the writers who had been active before the war resurfaced, but now their writing reflected their demoralization. Many were attracted to existentialism, and some turned to hedonism and nihilism. For these disillusioned authors, defeat was compounded by fear of the Americanization of postwar Japan. One of the best examples of this attitude was the novelist Yukio Mishima, who led a crusade to stem the tide of what he described as America's "universal and uniform 'Coca-colonization'" of the world in general and Japan in particular.[6] Mishima's ritual suicide in 1970 was the subject of widespread speculation and transformed him into a cult figure.

One of Japan's most serious-minded contemporary authors is Kenzaburo Oe (b. 1935). His work, which was rewarded with a Nobel Prize for Literature in 1994, presents Japan's ongoing quest for modern identity and purpose (see the box on p. 983). His characters reflect the spiritual anguish precipitated by the collapse of the imperial Japanese tradition and the subsequent adoption of Western culture—a trend which, according to Oe, has culminated in unabashed materialism, cultural decline, and a moral void. Yet, unlike Mishima, Oe does not seek to reinstill the imperial traditions of the past, but rather to regain spiritual meaning by retrieving the sense of communality and innocence found in rural Japan. One of Oe's best-known novels is *A Personal Matter* (1964), in which he recounts in fictionalized form his own experience raising a brain-damaged son, leading him from despair to a final sense of transcendent humanism.

Since the 1970s, increasing affluence and a high literacy rate have contributed to a massive quantity of publications, ranging from popular potboilers to first-rate

THE AMBIGUITY OF BEING JAPANESE

Kenzaburo Oe is one of Japan's most prestigious contemporary authors. Admired for their riveting style and unbridled imagination, Oe's novels often portray anguished protagonists who appear paralyzed by despair. A key theme in his writings is Japan's post–World War II quest to restore its sense of identity and purpose. In his speech accepting the 1994 Nobel Prize for Literature, Oe spoke movingly of Japan's current position, caught between the ideologies of East and West. In this excerpt from the speech, note the author's pain in coming to terms with the recent history of his nation and the atrocities committed by Japanese soldiers during World War II.

KENZABURO OE, "JAPAN, THE AMBIGUOUS, AND MYSELF"

After a hundred and twenty years of modernization since the opening up of the country, contemporary Japan is split between two opposite poles of ambiguity. This ambiguity, which is so powerful and penetrating that it divides both the state and its people, and affects me as a writer like a deep-felt scar, is evident in various ways. The modernization of Japan was oriented toward learning from and imitating the West, yet the country is situated in Asia and has firmly maintained its traditional culture. The ambiguous orientation of Japan drove the country into the position of an invader in Asia, and resulted in its isolation from other Asian nations not only politically but also socially and culturally. And even in the West, to which its culture was supposedly quite open, it has long remained inscrutable or only partially understood.

In the history of modern Japanese literature, the writers most sincere in their awareness of a mission were the "postwar school" of writers who came onto the literary scene deeply wounded by the catastrophe of war yet full of hope for a rebirth. They tried with great pain to make up for the atrocities committed by Japanese military forces in Asia, as well as to bridge the profound gaps that existed not only between the developed nations of the West and Japan but also between African and Latin American countries and Japan. Only by doing so did they think that they could seek with some humility reconciliation with the rest of the world. It has always been my aspiration to cling to the very end of the line of that literary tradition inherited from those writers.

The present nation of Japan and its people cannot but be ambivalent. The Second World War came right in the middle of the process of modernization, a war that was brought about by the very aberration of that process itself. Defeat in this conflict fifty years ago created an opportunity for Japan, as the aggressor, to attempt a rebirth out of the great misery and suffering that the "postwar school" of writers depicted in their work. The moral props for a nation aspiring to this goal were the idea of democracy and the determination never to wage a war again—a resolve adopted not by innocent people but people stained by their own history of territorial invasion.

fiction. By 1975, Japan already produced twice as much fiction as the United States, a trend that has continued into the 1990s. Much of this new literature deals with the common concerns of all affluent industrialized nations, including the effects of urbanization, advanced technology, and mass consumption. One recent phenomenon is the so-called industrial novel, which seeks to lay bare the vicious infighting and pressure tactics that characterize Japanese business today. In the novel *Keiretsu*, author Ikko Shimizu describes the abortive efforts of the owner of Taisei Lighting, a headlight supplier, to cope with the pressure imposed by one of his main customers, the giant affiliate Tokyo Motors. Another popular genre is the "art-manga," or literary cartoon. Michio Hisauchi presents serious subjects, such as Japanese soldiers marooned after the war on an island in the South Pacific, in *Japan's Junglest Day*, a full-length novel in comic-book form, with cartoon characters posing philosophical questions.

Other aspects of Japanese culture have also been influenced by Western ideas, although without the intense preoccupation with synthesis that is evident in literature. Western art had begun to influence Japanese artists prior to the Meiji period, a process that accelerated in the late nineteenth and early twentieth centuries, when impressionists, cubists, and surrealists, among others, jockeyed for preeminence. Western music is highly popular in Japan, and scores of Japanese classical musicians have succeeded in the West. Even rap music has gained a foothold among Japanese youth, although without the association with sex, drugs, and violence that it has in the United States. Although some of the lyrics betray an attitude of modest revolt against the uptight world of Japanese society, most lack any such connotations. An example is the rap song "Street Life":

Now's the time to hip-hop,
Everybody's crazy about rap,
Hey, hey, you all, listen up,
Listen to my rap and cheer up.

As one singer remarked, "We've been very fortunate, and we don't want to bother our Moms and Dads. So we don't sing songs that would disturb parents."[7]

Many English words have entered the Japanese vocabulary, although with Japanese pronunciations. Corporate downsizing is known as *kosutu dau* (cost down). Teenagers have their own version of a separate adolescent language, known as *ko gyaro-go* (high school gal-talk), larded with English (or pseudo-English) phrases such as *esukeepu* ("escape," for cutting a class), *wonchu* (I want you), and *disu* (to diss, or show disrespect). Yet even as the Japanese enter the global marketplace, they retain ties to their own traditions. Businesspeople sometimes use traditional Daoist forms of physical and mental training to reduce the stress inherent in their jobs, while others retreat to a Zen monastery to learn to focus their willpower as a means of outwitting a competitor.

There are some signs that under the surface, the tension between traditional and modern is exacting a price. As novelists such as Yukio Mishima and Kenzaburo Oe feared, the growing focus on material possessions and the decline of traditional religious beliefs have left a spiritual void that cannot but undermine the sense of community and purpose that have motivated the country since the Meiji era. Some young people have reacted to the emptiness of their lives by joining religious cults such as Aum Shinri Kyo, which came to widespread world attention in 1995 when members of the organization, inspired by their leader, Asahara Shoko, carried out a poison gas attack on the Tokyo subway that killed several people. Such incidents serve as a warning that Japan is not immune to the social ills that currently plague many Western countries.

South Korea: A Peninsula Divided

While the world was focused on the economic miracle occurring on the Japanese islands, another miracle of sorts was taking place across the Sea of Japan on the Asian mainland. In 1953, the Korean peninsula was exhausted from three years of bitter fraternal war, a conflict that took the lives of an estimated four million Koreans on both sides of the 38th parallel and turned as much as one-quarter of the population into refugees. Although a cease-fire was signed at Panmunjom in July 1953, it was a fragile peace that left two heavily armed and mutually hostile countries facing each other suspiciously.

North of the truce line was the People's Republic of Korea (PRK), a police state under the dictatorial rule of the Communist leader Kim Il Sung (1912–1994). To the south was the Republic of Korea, under the equally autocratic President Syngman Rhee (1875–1965), a fierce anti-Communist who had led the resistance to the northern invasion and now placed his country under U.S. military protection. But U.S. troops could not protect Syngman Rhee from his own people, many of whom resented his reliance on the political power of the wealthy landlord class. After several years of harsh rule, marked by government corruption, fraudulent elections, and police brutality, demonstrations broke out in the capital city of Seoul in the spring of 1960 and forced him into retirement.

The Rhee era was followed by a brief period of multiparty democratic government, but in 1961, a coup d'état placed General Chung Hee Park (1917–1979) in power. The new regime promulgated a new constitution, and in 1963, Park was elected president of a civilian government. He set out to foster recovery of the economy from decades of foreign occupation and civil war. Adopting the nineteenth-century Japanese slogan "rich country and strong state," Park built up a strong military while relying on U.S. and later Japanese assistance to help build a strong manufacturing base in what had been a predominantly agricultural society (in 1961, about 40 percent of the gross national product came from agriculture). Because the private sector had been relatively weak under Japanese rule, the government played an active role in the process by instituting a series of five-year plans that targeted specific industries for development, promoted exports, and funded infrastructure development. Under a land reform program, large landowners were required to sell all their farmland above 7.4 acres to their tenants at low prices.

The program was a solid success. Benefiting from the Confucian principles of thrift, respect for education, and hard work (during the 1960s and 1970s, Korean workers spent an average of sixty hours a week at their jobs), as well as from Japanese capital and technology, Korea gradually emerged as a major industrial power in East Asia. The economic growth rate rose from less than 5 percent annually in the 1950s to an average of 9 percent under Chung Hee Park. The key areas selected for industrial development were chemicals, textiles, and shipbuilding. By the 1980s, Korea was moving aggressively into automobiles. The largest corporations—including Samsung, Daewoo, and Hyundai—were transformed into massive conglomerates called *chaebol,* the Korean equivalent of the *zaibatsu* of prewar Japan, although they were more recent in origin and were still under their original ownership. Taking advantage of relatively low wages and a stunningly high rate of saving, Korean businesses began to compete actively with the Japanese for export markets in Asia and throughout the world. Per capita income also increased dramatically, from less than $90 (in U.S. dollars) annually in 1960 to $1,560 (twice that of Communist North Korea) twenty years later.

But like many other countries in the region, South Korea was slow to develop democratic principles. Although his government functioned with the trappings of democracy, Park continued to rule by autocratic means and suppressed all forms of dissidence. Opposition began to develop under the leadership of the charismatic figure Kim Dae Jung. His power base was in the relatively impoverished rural districts in southwestern Korea, where the government's land reforms had had only minimal success in raising living standards.

MELDING PAST AND PRESENT IN SOUTH KOREA. South Korea has made a greater effort to preserve aspects of traditional culture than most of its neighbors in East Asia. Here an architect has tried to soften the impact of modernization by camouflaging a gas station in Seoul with a traditional Korean tile roof.

In 1979, Park was assassinated. Once again, a brief interregnum of democratic rule ensued, but in 1980, a new military government under General Chun Doo Hwan seized power. The new regime was as authoritarian as its predecessors, but opposition to autocratic rule had now spread to much of the urban population. Protest against government policies became increasingly frequent. In 1987, massive demonstrations drove government troops out of the southern city of Kwangju, but the troops returned in force and killed an estimated 2,000 demonstrators.

Under increasing pressure from the United States to moderate the oppressive character of his rule, Chun promised national elections in 1987 but then reversed his decision. Amid growing protests, the regime steadily lost credibility, and in 1989, elections were finally held. With the opposition candidates splitting the antigovernment vote, the government nominee,Roh Tae Woo, won the election with less than 40 percent of the vote.

The election results discouraged many Koreans, while the violent character of the student protests alienated many moderates. Nevertheless, new elections in 1992 brought Kim Young Sam to the presidency. Kim selected several women for his cabinet and promised to make Korea "a freer and more mature democracy." In the meantime, representatives of South Korea had made tentative contacts with the Communist regime in North Korea on possible steps toward eventual reunification of the peninsula.

During the mid-1990s, Kim Young Sam attempted to crack down on the rising influence of the giant *chaebols*, accused of giving massive bribes in return for favors from government officials. Ex-presidents Chun Doo Hwan and Roh Tae Woo were tried and convicted of using the office to enrich themselves and their families. But the problems of South Korea were more serious than the endemic problem of corruption. A growing trade deficit, combined with a declining growth rate, led to a rising incidence of unemployment and bankruptcy. Ironically, a second problem resulted from the economic collapse of Seoul's bitter rival, the PRK. Under the rule of Kim Il Sung's son Kim Jong Il, the North Korean economy was in a state of free fall, raising the specter of an outflow of refugees that could swamp neighboring countries. To relieve the immediate effects of a food shortage, the Communist government in Pyongyang relaxed its restrictions on private farming, while Seoul agreed to provide food aid to alleviate the famine.

In the fall of 1997, a sudden drop in the value of the Korean currency, the *won*, led to bank failures and a decision to seek assistance from the International Monetary Fund (IMF). In December, an angry electorate voted Kim Young Sam (whose administration was tarnished by reports of corruption) out of office and elected his rival, Kim Dae Jung, to the presidency. The new chief executive moved vigorously to attack the deep-seated problems that had led to the financial crisis, and economic conditions slowly began to improve.

TAIWAN: THE OTHER CHINA

South Korea was not the only rising industrial power trying to imitate the success of the Japanese in East Asia. To the south on the island of Taiwan, the Republic of China began to do the same.

After retreating to Taiwan following their defeat by the Communists, Chiang Kai-shek and his followers established a new capital at Taipei and set out to build a strong and prosperous nation based on Chinese traditions and the principles of Sun Yat-sen. The government, which continued to refer to itself as the Republic of China (ROC), contended that it remained the legitimate representative of the Chinese people and that it would eventually return in triumph to the mainland.

In some ways, the Nationalists had much more success on Taiwan than they had achieved on the mainland. In the relatively secure environment provided by a security treaty with the United States, signed in 1954, and the comforting presence of the U.S. Seventh Fleet in the Taiwan Strait, the ROC was able to concentrate on economic growth without worrying about a Communist invasion. The regime possessed a number of other advantages that it had not enjoyed in Nanjing. Fifty years of efficient Japanese rule had left behind a relatively modern economic infrastructure and an educated populace, although the island had absorbed considerable damage during World War II, and much of its agricultural produce had been exported to Japan at low prices. With only a small population to deal with (about 7 million in 1945), the ROC could make good use of foreign assistance and the efforts of its own energetic people to build a modern industrialized society.

The government moved rapidly to create a solid agricultural base. A land reform program led to the reduction of rents, while landholdings over 3 acres were purchased by the government and resold to the tenants at reasonable prices. As in Meiji Japan, the previous owners were compensated by government bonds. The results were gratifying: food production doubled over the next generation and began to make up a substantial proportion of exports.

In the meantime, the government strongly encouraged the development of local manufacturing and commerce. By the 1970s, along with Japan and South Korea, Taiwan was one of the most dynamic industrial economies in East Asia. The agricultural proportion of the gross national product declined from 36 percent in 1952 to only 9 percent thirty years later. At first, the industrial and commercial sector was composed of relatively small firms engaged in exporting textiles and food products, but the 1960s saw a shift to heavy industry, including shipbuilding, steel, petrochemicals, and machinery, and a growing emphasis on exports. The government played a major role in the process, targeting strategic industries for support and investing in infrastructure. At the same time, as in Japan, the government stressed the importance of private enterprise and encouraged foreign investment and a high rate of internal savings. During the 1960s and 1970s, industrial growth averaged well over 10 percent annually, while the value of exports reached nearly 50 percent of the gross national product. By the mid-1980s more than three-quarters of the population lived in urban areas.

CHRONOLOGY

JAPAN AND THE LITTLE TIGERS SINCE WORLD WAR II

End of World War II in the Pacific	August 1945
Chiang Kai-shek retreats to Taiwan	1949
End of U.S. occupation of Japan	1950
Beginning of Korean War	June 1950
Truce at Panmunjom ends Korean War	July 1953
United States–Republic of China security treaty	1954
Syngman Rhee overthrown in South Korea	1960
Rise to power of Chung Hee Park in South Korea	1961
Independence of Republic of Singapore	1965
Death of Chiang Kai-shek	1975
Chung Hee Park assassinated	1979
End of United States–Republic of China security treaty	1979
Students riot at Kwangju in South Korea	1987
First free general elections on Taiwan	1992
Election of Kim Young Sam as president in South Korea	1992
Return of Hong Kong to mainland control	1997
Financial crisis hits the region	1997
Chen Shuibian elected president of Taiwan	2000

In contrast to the People's Republic of China (PRC) on the mainland, the ROC actively maintained Chinese tradition, promoting respect for Confucius and the ethical principles of the past, such as hard work, frugality, and filial piety. Although there was some corruption in both the government and the private sector, income differentials between the wealthy and the poor were generally less than elsewhere in the region, and the overall standard of living increased substantially. Health and sanitation improved, literacy rates were quite high, and an active family-planning program reduced the rate of population growth. Nevertheless, the total population on the island increased to about 20 million in the mid-1980s.

In one respect, however, Chiang Kai-shek had not changed: increasing prosperity did not lead to the democratization of the political process. The Nationalists continued to rule by emergency decree and refused to permit the formation of opposition political parties on the ground that the danger of invasion from the mainland had not subsided. Propaganda material from the PRC was rigorously prohibited, and dissident activities (promoting either rapprochement with the mainland or the establishment of an independent Republic of Taiwan) were ruthlessly suppressed. Although representatives to the provincial government of the province of Taiwan were chosen in local elections, the central government (technically representing the entire population of China) was dominated by mainlanders who had fled to the island with Chiang Kai-shek in 1949.

Some friction developed between the mainlanders, who numbered about two million, and the native Taiwanese (mostly ethnic Chinese whose ancestors had emigrated to the island during the Qing Dynasty). Mainlanders tended to view the local population with a measure of condescension, and at least in the early years, intermarriage between members of the two groups was rare. By the 1980s, however, these fissures in Taiwanese society had begun to diminish; by that time, an ever higher proportion of the population had been born on the island and identified themselves as Taiwanese.

During the 1980s, the ROC slowly began to evolve toward a more representative form of government—a process that was facilitated by the death of Chiang Kai-shek in 1975. By the end of the 1980s, democratization was under way, including elections and the formation of legal opposition parties. A national election in 1992 resulted in a bare majority for the Nationalists over strong opposition from the Democratic Progressive Party (DPP).

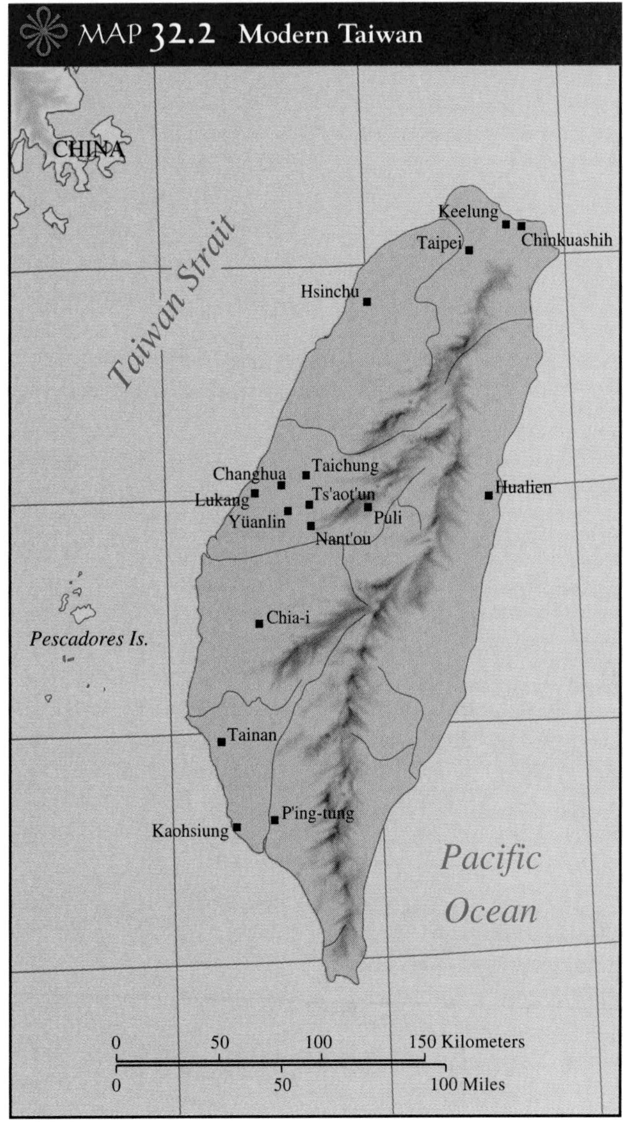

THE CHIANG KAI-SHEK MEMORIAL IN TAIPEI. While the Chinese government on the mainland attempted to destroy all vestiges of traditional culture, the Republic of China on Taiwan sought to preserve the cultural heritage as a link between past and present. This policy is graphically displayed in the mausoleum for Chiang Kai-shek in downtown Taipei, shown in this photograph. The mausoleum, with its massive entrance gate, not only glorifies the nation's leader, but recalls the grandeur of old China.

BEAUTIFUL ISLAND, BEAUTIFUL LITERATURE

In the period immediately following the end of the Chinese civil war, Taiwanese literature, fueled by the humiliation at the hands of the Communists, expressed a deep nostalgia for the mainland. By the 1960s, however, some Taiwanese authors had begun to turn to Western literature for models, while others found inspiration in the Taiwanese countryside. Known as the "nativists," the latter not only began to dominate the literary scene but also turned to politics. Some authors dared to criticize the repressive conditions under the Nationalist government and attempted to arouse the Taiwanese people's consciousness of their own cultural identity. One example is the novelist and short story writer Song Zelai (b. 1952). In this excerpt, Song attacks the inauthenticity of those Taiwanese writers who either ape Western authors or hark back to a distant Chinese imperial past.

SONG ZELAI ON TAIWANESE LITERATURE

More than once have I seen an intellectual of my generation. . . . Having chanced to hear about some Western writer in the bookstalls, or by word of mouth, he'd get some crazy idea that he'd penetrated the writer's soul, then look upon him as a kindred spirit and become his disciple. He'd swallow the author's words whole like a date, pit and all, without any critical or skeptical reflection. Then he'd publish an article brimming with high expectations and self-confidence, referring to himself as "Taiwan's Joyce" or "Taiwan's Lawrence," and patterning himself after the one or the other in every thought and gesture. How absurd! When it gets to the point of looking askance at all literature but that of their idol, these literati not only view Taiwan literature with disdain; they oppose the works of the ancient sages and philosophers in toto. In their insular and impoverished mental lives, there is no literary history and no writers, not even any living people; there is nothing at all but an exaggerated view of the "self."

There is another type of irresponsible writer who doesn't really understand or put into practice the essentials of Chinese culture, and who doesn't seek to understand China's present situation, either. His mind is totally wrapped up in the Tang-Song epoch. Ask him what it is in the Tang-Song epoch that so obsesses him, and he'll say something like "Along riverbanks of willow blow morning breezes under a waning moon." China is thus transformed into a fairy-tale princess for him to pursue. Perhaps he will boast that he is a rich young bravo, a footloose traveler who leaves a trail of flowers behind him. This sort of talk is sheer nonsense, first-class tommyrot. . . . In food and dress, he is as affluent as any man about town, yet he paints and composes poems in the Chinese style, proclaiming loudly that he is a descendant of the dragon, a son of China, and interminably shouting out its name in woe. Sometimes I wonder if he's still living in the same world as we are. . . .

My brothers, enough of your slogans; if your hearts are ill at ease, try going down to the fields with the peasants. If your spirit cannot tear itself away from the Tang-Song epoch, try going into business. If you are a captive of Joyce, please come out of the labyrinth and return to your parents' side. Then you will enjoy a fulfilling life and be able to see Taiwan, a beautiful island with a beautiful literature. Both you and your readers will be the beneficiaries.

As I have said repeatedly, I only hope that the people of this land will treasure instead of denigrate themselves. When we reach a happy medium between self-effacement and arrogance and are grateful for our happy lot, then may we count our blessings.

But political liberalization had its dangers; some leading Democratic Progressives began to agitate for an independent Republic of Taiwan, a possibility that aroused concern within the Nationalist government in Taipei and frenzied hostility in the PRC. When a presidential election in early 1996 aroused a political debate over the issue, Beijing responded by holding naval maneuvers in the Taiwan Strait. After his reelection, President Lee Teng-hui calmed the waters by making conciliatory remarks directed toward the mainland, although he continued to irritate mainland leaders with his remarks about maintaining a separate Taiwan. The election of DPP leader Chen Shui-bian as president in March 2000 angered Beijing, which threatened to invade Taiwan should the island continue to delay unification with the mainland.

Whether Taiwan will remain an independent state or be united with the mainland is impossible to predict. Certainly, the outcome depends in good measure on developments in the PRC. During his visit to China in 1972, President Richard Nixon said that this was a question for the Chinese people to decide (see Chapter 27). In 1979, President Jimmy Carter abrogated the mutual security treaty between the United States and the ROC that had been in force since 1954 and switched U.S. diplomatic recognition from the Republic of China to the PRC. But the United States continues to provide defensive military assistance to the Taiwanese armed forces and has made it clear that it supports self-determination for the people of Taiwan and that it expects the final resolution of the Chinese civil war to be by peaceful means. In the meantime, economic and cultural contacts between Taiwan and the mainland are steadily increasing. However, the Taiwanese have shown no inclination to accept the PRC's offer of "one country, two systems," under which the ROC would accept the PRC as the legitimate government of China in return for autonomous control over the affairs of Taiwan (see the box above).

SINGAPORE AND HONG KONG: THE LITTLEST TIGERS

The smallest, but by no means the least successful, of the little tigers are Singapore and Hong Kong. Both are essentially city-states, with large populations densely packed into small territories. Singapore, once a British Crown colony and briefly a part of the state of Malaysia, is now an independent state. Hong Kong was a British colony until it was returned to PRC control in 1997. In recent years, both have emerged as industrial powerhouses, with standards of living well above those of their neighbors.

The success of Singapore must be ascribed in good measure to the will and energy of its political leaders. When it became independent in August 1965, Singapore was in a state of transition. Its longtime position as an entrepôt for trade between the Indian Ocean and the South China Sea was declining in importance. With only 618 square miles of territory, much of it marshland and tropical jungle, Singapore had little to offer but the frugality and industriousness of its predominantly overseas Chinese population. But a recent history of political radicalism, fostered by the rise of influential labor unions, had frightened away foreign investors.

Within a decade, Singapore's role and reputation had dramatically changed. Under the leadership of Prime Minister Lee Kuan-yew (b. 1923), once the firebrand leader of the radical People's Action Party, the government encouraged the growth of an attractive business climate while engaging in massive public works projects to feed, house, and educate its two million citizens. The major components of success have been shipbuilding, oil refineries, tourism, electronics, and finance—the city-state has become the banking hub of the entire region.

Like the other little tigers, Singapore has relied on a combination of government planning, entrepreneurial spirit, export promotion, high productivity, and an exceptionally high rate of saving to achieve industrial growth rates of nearly 10 percent annually over the past two decades. Unlike some other industrializing countries in the region, Singapore has encouraged the presence of multinational corporations to provide much-needed capital and technological input. Population growth has been controlled by a stringent family-planning program, and literacy rates are among the highest in Asia.

As in the other little tigers, an authoritarian political system has guaranteed a stable environment for economic growth. Until his recent retirement, Lee Kuan-yew and his People's Action Party dominated Singaporean politics, and opposition elements were intimidated into silence or arrested. The prime minister openly declared that the Western model of pluralist democracy was not appropriate for Singapore and lauded the Meiji model of centralized development (see the box on p. 990). Confucian values of thrift, hard work, and obedience to authority have been promoted as the ideology of the state. The government has had a passion for cleanliness and at one time even undertook a campaign to persuade its citizens to flush the public urinals. In 1989, the local *Straits Times*, a mouthpiece of the government, published a photograph of a man walking sheepishly from a row of urinals. The caption read "Caught without a flush: Mr. Amar Mohamed leaving the Lucky Plaza [a local shopping center] toilet without flushing the urinal."[8]

But economic success is beginning to undermine the authoritarian foundations of the system, as a more

OLD AND NEW IN SINGAPORE. The city-state of Singapore is one of the most modern societies in all Asia and is sometimes referred to as the "showcase of tomorrow." Some Singaporeans regret that so much of the past has been destroyed in the process. In this photograph, skyscrapers tower above traditional sampans in the Singapore River; the buildings stand on the site where Stamford Raffles first landed on the island in 1819.

TO THOSE LIVING IN GLASS HOUSES

Kishore Mahbubani is permanent secretary in the Ministry of Foreign Affairs in Singapore. Previously, he served as his country's ambassador to the United Nations. In this article, adapted from a piece in the Washington Quarterly, *the author advises his audience to stop lecturing Asian societies on the issue of human rights and focus attention instead on problems in the United States. In his view, today the countries of the West have much to learn from their counterparts in East Asia. This viewpoint is shared by many other observers, political leaders, and foreign affairs specialists in the region.*

KISHORE MAHBUBANI, "GO EAST, YOUNG MAN"

For the last century or more, in the passage of ideas across the Pacific, the flow has fundamentally been one way. Poverty-stricken and backward Asian societies have looked to the United States for leadership. Not surprisingly, a deeply ingrained belief has settled in the American mind that the U.S. mission in East Asia is to teach, not to learn. The time may have come for this mind-set to change.

In a major reversal of a pattern lasting centuries, many Western societies, including the U.S., are doing some major things fundamentally wrong, while a growing number of East Asian societies are doing the same things right. The results are most evident in the economic sphere. In purchasing power parity terms, East Asia's gross domestic product is already larger than that of either the U.S. or European community. Such economic prosperity, contrary to American belief, results not just from free-market arrangements but also from the right social and political choices. Although many East Asian societies have assumed some of the trappings of the West, they have also kept major social and cultural elements intact—elements that may explain their growing global competitiveness.

In most Asian eyes, the evidence of real social decay in the U.S. is clear and palpable. Since 1960, the U.S. population has grown by 41%. In the same period, there has been a 560% increase in violent crimes, a 419% increase in illegitimate births, a 400% increase in divorce rates, a 300% increase in children living in single-parent homes, a more than 200% increase in teenage suicide rates, and a drop of almost 80 points in Scholastic Aptitude Test scores. A clear American paradox is that a society that places such a high premium on freedom has effectively reduced the physical freedom of most Americans, especially those who live in large cities. They live in heavily fortified homes, think twice before taking an evening stroll around their neighborhoods, and feel increasingly threatened by random violence when they are outside.

To any Asian, it is obvious that the breakdown of the family and social order in the U.S. owes itself to a mindless ideology that maintains that the freedom of a small number of individuals who are known to pose a threat to society (criminals, terrorists, street gang members, drug dealers) should not be constrained (for example, through detention without trial), even if to do so would enhance the freedom of the majority. In short, principle takes precedence over people's well-being. This belief is purely and simply a gross violation of common sense. But it is the logical end product of a society that worships the notion of freedom as religiously as Hindus worship their sacred cows. Both must be kept absolutely unfettered, even when they obviously create great social discomfort. . . .

My hope is that Americans will come to visit East Asia in greater numbers. When they do, they will come to realize that their society has swung much too much in one direction: liberating the individual while imprisoning society. The relatively strong and stable family and social institutions of East Asia will appear more appealing. And as Americans experience the freedom of walking on city streets in Asia, they may begin to understand that freedom can also result from greater social order and discipline. Perhaps the best advice to give to a young American is: "Go East, Young Man."

sophisticated citizenry begins to demand more political freedoms and an end to government paternalism. Lee Kuan-yew's successor, Goh Chok Tong, has promised a "kinder, gentler" Singapore, and political restrictions on individual behavior are gradually being relaxed. There is reason for optimism that a more pluralistic political system will gradually emerge.

The future of Hong Kong is not so clear-cut. As in Singapore, sensible government policies and the hard work of its people have enabled Hong Kong to thrive. At first, the prosperity of the colony depended on a plentiful supply of cheap labor. Inundated with refugees from the mainland during the 1950s and 1960s, the population of Hong Kong burgeoned to more than six million. Many of them were willing to work for starvation wages in sweatshops producing textiles, simple appliances, and toys for the export market. More recently, Hong Kong has benefited from increased tourism, manufacturing, and the growing economic prosperity of neighboring Guangdong Province, the most prosperous region of the PRC. In one respect, Hong Kong has differed from the other societies discussed in this chapter, in that it has relied on an unbridled free market system rather than active state intervention in the economy. At the same time, by allocating substantial funds for transportation, sanitation, education, and public housing, the government has created favorable conditions for economic development.

Unlike the other little tigers, Hong Kong remained under colonial rule until very recently. British authorities did little to foster democratic institutions or practices, and most residents of the colony cared more about economic survival than political freedoms. In 1983, in talks between representatives of Great Britain and the PRC, the Chinese leaders made it clear they were determined to have Hong Kong return to mainland authority in 1997, when the British ninety-nine-year lease over the New Territories, the foodbasket of the colony of Hong Kong, ran out. The British agreed, on condition that satisfactory arrangements could be made for the welfare of the population. The Chinese promised that for fifty years, the people of Hong Kong would live under a capitalist system and be essentially self-governing. Recent statements by Chinese leaders, however, have raised questions about the degree of autonomy Hong Kong will receive under Chinese rule, which began on July 1, 1997 (see the box on p. 992).

A JUNK IN HONG KONG HARBOR. Hong Kong, like Singapore, has become one of the most modern cities in the world. The island of Victoria, shown here in the background, groans under the weight of thousands of gleaming skyscrapers. Yet signs of the past still coexist with the present, as this picture of a traditional Chinese junk demonstrates.

On the Margins of Asia: Postwar Australia and New Zealand

From a geographic point of view, Australia and New Zealand are not part of Asia, and throughout their short history, both countries have identified themselves culturally and politically with the West rather than with their Asian neighbors. Their political institutions and values are derived from Europe, while in form and content their economies resemble those of the advanced countries of the world rather than the preindustrial societies of much of Southeast Asia. Both are currently members of the British Commonwealth and of the U.S.–led ANZUS alliance (Australia, New Zealand, and the United States), which serves to shield them from political turmoil elsewhere in the region.

Yet trends in recent years have been drawing both states, especially Australia, closer to Asia. In the first place, immigration from East and Southeast Asia has increased rapidly. More than one-half of current immigrants into Australia come from East Asia, and by early this century, about 7 percent of the population of about 18 million people will be of Asian descent. In New Zealand, residents of Asian descent represent only about 3 percent of the population of 3.5 million, but about 12 percent of the population are Maoris, Polynesian peoples who settled on the islands about 1,000 years ago. Second, trade relations with Asia are increasing rapidly. About 60 percent of Australia's export markets today are in East Asia, and the region is the source of about one-half of its imports. Asian trade with New Zealand is also on the increase.

At the same time, the links that bind both countries to Great Britain and the United States have been loosening. Ties with London became increasingly distant after Great Britain decided to join the European Community in the early 1970s. There are moves under way in Australia and New Zealand to withdraw from the British Commonwealth, although the outcome at this point appears far from certain. Security ties with the United States remain important, but many Australians opposed their government's decision to cooperate with Washington during the Vietnam War, and the government today is seeking to establish closer political and military ties with the ASEAN alliance. Further removed from Asia both physically and psychologically, New Zealand assigns less importance to its security treaty with the United States and has been vocally critical of U.S. nuclear policies in the region.

Whether Australia and New Zealand will ever become an integral part of the Asia-Pacific region is uncertain. Cultural differences stemming from the European origins of the majority of the population in both countries hinder mutual understanding on both sides of the divide, and many ASEAN leaders express reluctance to accept the two countries as full members of the alliance. But

RETURN TO THE MOTHERLAND

After lengthy negotiations, in December 1984 China and Great Britain agreed that on July 1, 1997, Hong Kong would return to Chinese sovereignty. Key sections of the agreement are included here. In succeeding years, authorities of the two countries held further negotiations. Some of the discussions raised questions in the minds of residents of Hong Kong as to whether their individual liberties would indeed be respected after the colony's return to China.

THE JOINT DECLARATION ON HONG KONG

The Hong Kong Special Administrative Region will be directly under the authority of the Central People's Government of the People's Republic of China. The Hong Kong Special Administrative Region will enjoy a high degree of autonomy, except in foreign and defense affairs, which are the responsibility of the Central People's Government.

The Hong Kong Special Administrative Region will be vested with executive, legislative, and independent judicial power, including that of final adjudication. The laws currently in force in Hong Kong will remain basically unchanged.

The Government of the Hong Kong Special Administrative Region will be composed of local inhabitants. The chief executive will be appointed by the Central People's Government on the basis of the results of elections or consultations to be held locally. Principal officials will be nominated by the chief executive of the Hong Kong Special Administrative Region for appointment by the Central People's Government. . . .

The current social and economic systems in Hong Kong will remain unchanged, and so will the lifestyle. Rights and freedoms, including those of the person, of speech, of the press, of assembly, of association, of travel, of movement, of correspondence, of strike, of choice of occupation, of academic research, and of religious belief will be ensured by law. . . . Private property, ownership of enterprises, legitimate right of inheritance, and foreign investment will be protected by law.

economic and geographic realities act as a powerful force, and should the Pacific region continue on its current course toward economic prosperity and political stability, the role of Australia and New Zealand will assume greater significance.

CONCLUSION

What explains the striking ability of Japan and the four little tigers to follow the Western example and transform themselves into export-oriented societies capable of competing with the advanced nations of Europe and the Western Hemisphere? Some point to the traditional character traits of Confucian societies, such as thrift, a work ethic, respect for education, and obedience to authority. In a recent poll of Asian executives, more than 80 percent expressed the belief that Asian values differ from those of the West, and most add that these values have contributed significantly to the region's recent success. Others place more emphasis on deliberate steps taken by government and economic leaders to meet the political, economic, and social challenges faced by their societies.

There seems no reason to doubt that cultural factors connected to East Asian social traditions have contributed to the economic success of these societies. Certainly, habits such as frugality, industriousness, and subordination of individual desires have all played a role in their governments' ability to concentrate on the collective interest. Political elites in these countries have been highly conscious of these factors and willing to use them for national purposes. Prime Minister Lee Kuan-yew of Singapore deliberately fostered the inculcation of such ideals among the citizens of his small nation and lamented the decline of Confucian values among the young.

The importance of specifically Confucian values, however, should not be overemphasized as a factor in what authors Roy Hofheinz and Kent E. Calder call the "Eastasia Edge." In the first place, until recently, mainland China did not share in the economic success of its neighbors despite a long tradition of espousing Confucian values. In fact, some historians in recent years have maintained that it was precisely those Confucian values that hindered China's early response to the challenge of the West.

Moreover, while such traits as frugality and hard work have undoubtedly played a significant role in the economic development of East Asian societies, they are not necessarily a direct product of the Confucian tradition. In Japan, for example, indigenous traditions have probably had a greater effect on behavior and attitudes than Confucian teachings, and in societies with a majority Chinese population, it is often precisely those groups least influenced by Confucian doctrine—such as merchant groups in southern China—that have participated most actively in the economic revolution of the late twentieth century. Thus, the determining factor is not so much Confucianism as the common emphasis on family values, self-sacrifice, and hard work that characterizes societies throughout the region.

THE AESTHETICS OF FOOD IN CHINA. In many countries of East Asia, the aesthetic presentation of food is as important as the taste. In this roadside stall in downtown Taipei, the vendor has attractively presented a variety of delectable foods for the prospective buyer. This spread illustrates how Asia has, over the millennia, tantalized the passerby with inexpensive and instant culinary delights.

As this and preceding chapters have shown, without active encouragement by political elites, such traditions cannot be effectively harnessed for the good of society as a whole. The creative talents of the Chinese people were not efficiently utilized under Mao Zedong or in the little tigers while they were under European or Japanese colonial rule (although Japanese colonialism did lead to the creation of an infrastructure more conducive to later development than was the case in European colonies). Only when a "modernizing elite" took charge and began to place a high priority on economic development were the stunning advances of recent decades achieved. Rural poverty was reduced if not eliminated by stringent land reform and population control programs. Profit incentives and foreign investment were encouraged, while the development of export markets received high priority.

There was, of course, another common factor in the successes achieved by Japan and its emulators. All the little tigers received substantial inputs of capital and technology from the advanced nations of the West—Taiwan and South Korea from the United States, and Hong Kong and Singapore from Britain. Japan relied to a greater degree on its own efforts but received a significant advantage by being placed under the U.S. security umbrella and guaranteed access to markets and sources of raw materials in a region dominated by U.S. naval power.

As in parts of Southeast Asia, economic advancement in the region has sometimes been achieved at the cost of political freedom and individual human rights. Until recently, government repression of opposition has been common throughout East Asia except in Japan. As many Western observers have pointed out, the rights of national minorities and women are often still limited in comparison with the advanced countries of the West. Until recently, for example, women in South Korea had no right to inheritance or the legal custody of their children in case of divorce. Some commentators within the region take vigorous exception to such criticism. In a recent article,

YOU CAN TAKE IT WITH YOU! While wealthy Chinese in traditional China buried clay models of personal possessions to accompany the departed to the next world, ordinary people burned paper effigies, which were transported to the afterlife by means of the rising smoke. This custom survives in many Chinese communities today, as this photograph taken in modern Singapore demonstrates. Some merchants make their living by manufacturing such popular paper objects as television sets, elegant furniture, and even Mercedes automobiles.

Singapore's minister of foreign affairs S. Jayakumar has argued that pluralistic political systems could be "very dangerous and destabilizing" in the heterogeneous societies that currently exist in the region. Moreover, he maintains that the central role of the government has been a key factor in the economic success achieved by many Asian countries in recent years.[9]

Recent developments such as the financial crisis that swept through the region in 1997 have somewhat tarnished the image of the "Asian miracle," and there is now widespread concern that some of the very factors that contributed to economic success in previous years are now making it difficult for governments in the region to develop increased openness and accountability in their financial systems. Still, it should be kept in mind that progress in political pluralism and human rights has not always been easy to achieve in Europe and North America, and even now frequently fails to match expectations. A rising standard of living, increased social mobility, and a changing regional environment brought about by the end of the Cold War should go far to enhance political freedoms and promote social justice in the countries bordering the western Pacific.

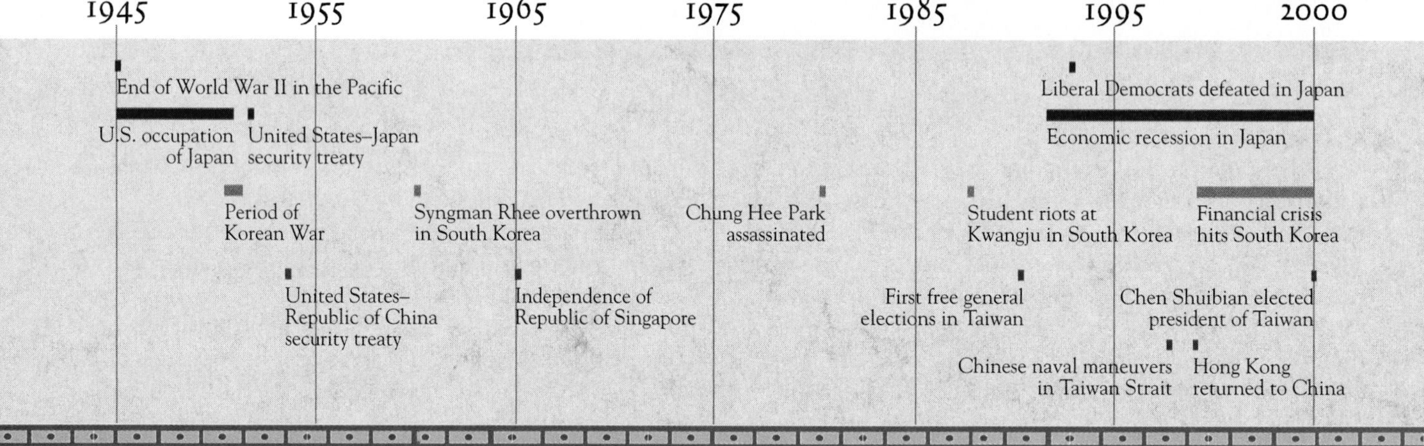

Chapter Notes

1. *Far Eastern Economic Review*, May 19, 1994, p. 32.
2. Bernard K. Gordon, "Japan's Universities," in *Far Eastern Economic Review*, January 14, 1993.
3. These figures are from Tom Heymann, *On an Average Day in Japan* (New York, 1992), pp. 152–56.
4. *New York Times*, November 19, 1996.
5. Robert Whiting, *You Gotta Have Wa* (New York, 1990), p. 69.
6. Yukio Mishima and Geoffrey Bownas, eds., *New Writing in Japan* (Harmondsworth, 1972), p. 16.
7. *New York Times*, January 29, 1996.
8. Stan Seser, "A Reporter at Large," *The New Yorker*, January 13, 1992, p. 44.
9. *Far Eastern Economic Review*, May 30, 1996.

Suggested Readings

The number of books in English on modern Japan has increased in virtually direct proportion to Japan's rise as a major industrial power. Though many deal with economic and financial issues and cater to the business world, increased attention is also being paid to political, social, and cultural issues. A number of standard treatments of the postwar period are available. Perhaps best known is J. K. Fairbank, E. O. Reischauer, and A. M. Craig, *East Asia: Tradition and Transformation* (Boston, 1976). For a more culture-oriented approach, see C. Schirokauer, *Modern China and Japan: A Brief History* (New York, 1982). For a more contem-porary view, see R. Buckley, *Japan Today* (Cambridge, 1985). P. Duus, ed., *The Cambridge History of Japan*, vol. 6 (Cambridge, 1988) contains a number of interesting scholarly articles on twentieth-century issues, although most of them deal with the prewar period. For a topical approach with strong emphasis on economic and social matters, J. E. Hunter, *The Emergence of Modern Japan: An Introductory History Since 1853* (London, 1989) is excellent.

Relatively little has been written on Japanese politics and government. A recent treatment is J. A. A. Stockwin, *Japan: Divided Politics in a Growth Economy* (London, 1982). For an extensive analysis of Japan's adjustment to the Allied occupation, see J. W. Dower, *Japan in the Wake of World War II* (New York, 1999). Political dissent and its consequences are dealt with in N. Fields, *In the Realm of the Dying Emperor* (New York, 1991).

Japanese social issues have often been examined from an economic perspective as foreign observers try to discover the reasons for the nation's economic success. C. Nakane, *Japanese Society* (Harmondsworth, 1979) provides a scholarly treatment, while R. J. Hendry, *Understanding Japanese Society* (Beckenham, 1987) is more accessible. For a more local treatment, see R. P. Dore, *Shinohata: A Portrait of a Japanese Village* (New York, 1978), and T. C. Bestor, *Neighborhood Tokyo* (Stanford, Calif., 1989). T. Heymann, *On an Average Day in Japan* (New York, 1992) provides an interesting statistical comparison of Japanese and American society. On the role of women in modern Japan, see D. Robins-Mowry, *The Hidden Sun: Women of Modern Japan* (Boulder, Colo., 1983), and N. Bornoff, *Pink Samurai: Love, Marriage and Sex in Contemporary Japan* (New York, 1991).

Books attempting to explain Japanese economic success have become a growth industry. The classic account is E. F. Vogel, *Japan as Number One: Lessons for America* (Cambridge, Mass., 1979). For a provocative response pointing to signs of Japanese weakness, see J. Woronoff, *Japan as—Anything but—Number One* (Armonk, N.Y., 1991). C. Johnson, *MITI and the Japanese Miracle* (Stanford, Calif., 1982) provides an excellent analysis of the role of government in promoting Japanese economic interests. For the costs of Japanese economic success on society, see R. J. Smith, *Kurusu: The Price of Progress in a Japanese Village* (Stanford, Calif., 1978), and I. P. Hall, *Cartels of the Mind: Japan's Intellectual Closed Shop* (New York, 1998). Y. Saisho, *Women Executives in Japan* (Tokyo, 1981) discusses women who are trying to find the key to economic success in Japanese business. An excellent recent study on women and work in Japan is Barbara Molony, "Japan's 1986 Equal Opportunity Law and the Changing Discourse on Gender," in *Signs*, No. 20. (1995), pp. 268–302. On Japanese literature after World War II, see the classic D. Keene, *Dawn to the West: Japanese Fiction in the Modern Era* (New York, 1984). Short story writing is chronicled in I. Morris, ed., *Modern Japanese Stories: An Anthology* (Rutland, Vt., 1962); Y. Mishima and G. Bownas, eds., *New Writing in Japan* (Harmondsworth, 1972); and A. Birnbaum, *Monkey Brain Sushi: New Tastes in Japanese Fiction* (Tokyo, 1991). On Japanese women authors, see N. M. Lippit and K. I. Selden, eds., *Stories by Contemporary Japanese Women Writers* (New York, 1982).

On the four little tigers and their economic development, see E. F. Vogel, *The Four Little Dragons: The Spread of Industrialization in East Asia* (Cambridge, Mass., 1991); J. W. Morley, ed., *Driven by Growth: Political Change in the Asia-Pacific Region* (Armonk, N.Y., 1992); and J. Woronoff, *Asia's Miracle Economies* (New York, 1986). For an interesting collection of articles on the role of Confucian ideology in promoting economic growth, see Hung-chao Tai, ed., *Confucianism and Economic Development* (Washington, D.C., 1989). For individual treatments of the little tigers, see Hak-kyu Sohn, *Authoritarianism and Opposition in South Korea* (London, 1989); D. F. Simon, *Taiwan: Beyond the Economic Miracle* (Armonk, N.Y., 1992); C. M. Turnbull, *A History of Singapore, 1819–1975* (Oxford, 1977); and K. Rafferty, *City on the Rocks: Hong Kong's Uncertain Future* (London, 1991).

For additional reading, go to InfoTrac College Edition, your online research library at http://web1.infotrac-college.com

Enter the search terms "Japan history" using Keywords.

Enter the search term "keiretsu" using Keywords.

Enter the search terms "Japan women" using Keywords.

Enter the search term "Korea" using the Subject Guide.

REFLECTION

TOWARD A GLOBAL CIVILIZATION? THE WORLD SINCE 1945

As World War II came to an end, the survivors of that bloody struggle could afford to face the future with at least a measure of cautious optimism. With the death of Adolf Hitler in his bunker in Berlin, there were reasons to hope that the bitter rivalry that had marked relations among the Western powers would finally be put to an end, and that the wartime alliance of the United States, Great Britain, and the Soviet Union could be maintained into the postwar era. In the meantime, the peoples of Asia and Africa saw the end of the war as a gratifying sign that the colonial system would soon come to an end and bring about a new era of political stability and economic development on a global scale.

With the perspective of over half a century, we can see that these hopes have been only partly realized. In the decades following the war, the capitalist nations managed to recover from the extended economic depression that had contributed to the start of World War II and advanced to a level of economic prosperity never before seen throughout world history. The bloody conflicts that had erupted among European nations during the first half of the twentieth century came to an end, and Germany and Japan were fully integrated into the world community.

At the same time, the prospects for a stable, peaceful world and an end to balance-of-power politics were hampered by the emergence of the grueling and sometimes tense ideological struggle between the socialist and capitalist camps, a competition headed by the only remaining great powers, the Soviet Union and the United States. While the two superpowers were able to avoid an open nuclear confrontation, the postwar world was divided into two heavily armed camps in a balance of terror that on one occasion—the Cuban Missile Crisis—brought the world briefly to the brink of nuclear holocaust.

Once again, Europe became divided into hostile camps, as the Cold War rivalry between the United States and the Soviet Union forced the European nations to become dependent on one or the other of the superpowers. The creation of two mutually antagonistic military alliances—NATO in 1949 and the Warsaw Pact in 1955—confirmed the new division of Europe, while a divided Germany—and a divided Berlin—remained its most visible symbols. Repeated crises over the status of Berlin only intensified the fears in both camps.

In the midst of this rivalry, the Western European states, with the assistance of the United States, made a remarkable economic recovery and reached new levels of prosperity. In Eastern Europe, Soviet domination, both politically and economically, seemed so complete that many doubted it could ever be undone. Soviet military intervention, as in Hungary in 1956 and Czechoslovakia in 1968, reminded the Soviet satellites of their real condition. But communism had always been a foreign ideology to many Eastern Europeans and had never developed deep roots. When a new Soviet leader—Mikhail Gorbachev—indicated that his government would no longer pursue military intervention, Eastern European states acted quickly at the end of the 1980s to establish their freedom and adopt new economic structures based on Western models. But although many Europeans rejoiced over the possibility of creating a new, undivided Europe, the ethnic hatreds and tensions that had plagued these nations before World War II reemerged and threatened to divide Europeans once again.

Outside the West, the peoples of Africa and Asia had their own reasons for optimism as World War II came to a close. In the Atlantic Charter, issued after a meeting near the coast of Newfoundland in August 1941, Franklin Roosevelt and Winston Churchill had set forth a joint declaration of their peace aims calling for the self-determination of all peoples and self-government and sovereign rights for all nations that had been deprived of them. Although Churchill later disavowed the assumption that he had meant these conditions to apply to colonial areas, Roosevelt on frequent occasions voiced his own intention to promote the end of colonial domination throughout the world.

In the end, that optimism was at least partly justified. Although some colonial powers were reluctant to divest themselves of their colonies, World War II had severely undermined the stability of the colonial order, and by the end of the 1940s, most colonies in Asia had received their independence. Africa followed a decade or two later. In a few instances—notably in Algeria, Indonesia, and Vietnam—the transition to independence was a violent one, but for the most part, it was realized by peaceful means.

Broadly speaking, the leaders of these newly liberated countries set forth three goals at the outset of independence. They wanted to throw off the shackles of Western economic domination and ensure material prosperity for all of their citizens. They wanted to introduce new political institutions that would enhance the right of self-determination of their peoples. And they wanted to develop a sense of common nationhood within the population and establish secure territorial boundaries. It was a measure of their optimism that the governments of most of the newly liberated countries opted to follow a capitalist or a moderately socialist path toward economic development. Only in a few cases—China and Vietnam were the most notable examples—did revolutionary leaders opt for the communist mode of development.

Regardless of the path they chose, however, most governments in Africa and Asia did not achieve their ambitious economic goals. Virtually all of them remained economically dependent on the advanced industrial nations or, in the case of those who chose to follow the socialist model of development, were forced to rely on the Soviet Union. Some faced severe problems of urban and rural poverty.

What had happened to tarnish the bright dream of economic affluence? During the late 1950s and early 1960s, one school of thought was dominant among scholars and government officials in the United States. Known as modernization theory, this school took the view that the problems faced by the newly independent countries were a consequence of the difficult transition from a traditional agrarian to a modern industrial society. Modernization theorists were convinced that the countries of Asia, Africa, and Latin America were destined to follow the path of the West toward the creation of modern industrial societies but would need time as well as substantial amounts of economic and technological assistance to complete the journey. In their view, it was the duty of the United States and other capitalist nations to provide such assistance while encouraging the leaders of these states to follow the path already adopted by the West. Some countries going through this difficult period were especially vulnerable to communist-led insurgent movements. In such cases, it was in the interests of the United States and its allies to intervene, with military power if necessary, to hasten the transition and put the country on the path of self-sustaining growth.

Beginning in the late 1960s, modernization theory began to come under attack from a new generation of younger scholars, many of whom had reached maturity during the Vietnam War and had growing doubts about the roots of the problem and the efficacy of the modernization approach. In their view, the responsibility for continued economic underdevelopment in the developing world lay not with the countries themselves, but with their continued domination by the ex-colonial powers. In this view, known as dependency theory, the countries of Asia, Africa, and Latin America were the victims of the international marketplace, which charged high prices for the manufactured goods of the West while dooming preindustrial countries to low prices for their own raw material exports. Efforts by such countries to build up their own industrial sectors and move into the stage of self-sustaining growth were hampered by foreign control—through European- and American-owned corporations —over many of their resources. To end this "neocolonial" relationship, the dependency theory advocates argued, developing societies should reduce their economic ties with the West and practice a policy of economic self-reliance, thereby taking control over their own destinies.

Both of these approaches, of course, were directly linked to the ideological divisions of the Cold War period and suffered from the weaknesses of their political bias. Although modernization theorists were certainly correct in pointing out some of the key factors that were involved in economic development and showing that in some instances traditional attitudes and practices were incompatible with economic change, they were too quick to see the Western developmental model as the only relevant one and ignored the fact that traditional customs and practices were not necessarily always incompatible with nation building. They also too readily identified economic development in the developing world with the interests of the United States and its allies and underestimated the degree to which Western economic policies and the presence of European or American corporations operated to the detriment of efforts to promote economic growth in Asia and Africa.

By the same token, the advocates of dependency theory alluded correctly to the unfair and often disadvantageous relationship that continued to exist between the ex-colonies and the industrialized nations of the world and the impact that this relationship had on the efforts of developing countries to overcome their economic difficulties. But they often explained away many of the mistakes made by the leaders of developing countries while assigning all of the blame for their plight to the evil and self-serving practices of the industrialized world. At the same time, the dependency theorists' recommendation for a policy of self-reliance was not only naive but sometimes disastrous.

In recent years, the differences between these two schools of thought have declined, as their advocates have attempted to respond to criticism of the perceived weaknesses in their theories. Although the two approaches still have some methodological and ideological differences, there is a growing consensus that there are different roads to development and that the international marketplace can have both beneficial and harmful effects. At the same time, a new school of developmental theory, known as the world systems approach, has attempted to place recent developments within the broad context of world history and the rise of capitalism in the West since the thirteenth century. According to world systems theory, the global economy that has emerged among previously autonomous states is now beginning to develop serious internal contradictions and may be in the process of transformation.

A second area of concern for the leaders of African and Asian countries after World War II was to create a new political culture responsive to the needs of their citizens. For the most part, they accepted the concept of democracy as the defining theme of that culture. Within a decade, however, democratic systems throughout the developing world were replaced by military dictatorships or one-party governments that redefined the concept of democracy to fit their own preferences. Some Western observers criticized the new leaders for their autocratic tendencies, while others attempted to explain that after traditional forms of authority were replaced, it would take time to lay the basis for pluralistic political systems. In the interval, a strong government party under the leadership of a single charismatic individual could mobilize the population to seek common goals. Whatever the case, it was clear that many political leaders and observers alike had underestimated the difficulties in building democratic political institutions in developing societies. Today, democratic institutions appear to be taking root in some countries in Africa and Asia, but future trends remain unclear.

The problem of establishing a common national identity has in some ways been the most daunting of all the challenges facing the new nations of Asia and Africa. Many of these new states were a composite of a wide variety of ethnic, religious, and linguistic groups who found it difficult to agree on common symbols of nationalism. Problems of establishing an official language and delineating territorial boundaries left over from the colonial era created difficulties in many countries. In some cases, these problems were exacerbated by political and economic change. The introduction of the concept of democracy sharpened the desire of individual groups to have a separate identity within a larger nation, while economic development often favored some at the expense of others. As the new century dawns, internal conflicts spawned by deep-rooted historical and ethnic hatreds are proliferating throughout the world, leading to a vast new movement of people across state boundaries equal to any that has occurred since the great population migrations of the thirteenth and fourteenth centuries.

The introduction of Western cultural values and customs has also had a destabilizing effect in many areas. Although such ideas are welcomed by some groups, they are firmly resisted by others. Where Western influence has the effect of undermining traditional customs and religious beliefs, it often provokes violent hostility and sparks tension and even conflict within individual societies. To some, Western customs and values represent the wave of the future and are welcomed as a sign of progress. To others, they are destructive of indigenous traditions and a barrier to the growth of a genuine national identity based on history and culture.

Among the most divisive of such issues is the role of women in society. In the West, the premise of full gender equality had become generally accepted, and remaining barriers tend to lie in the arena of custom rather than in that of law. In many societies in Asia, Africa, and Latin America, the idea that men and women have different roles to play continues to hold sway. Demands by women for equal treatment with men are thus met with suspicion and sometimes outright hostility on the part of those who maintain that woman's place is in the home, not the office or the marketplace.

From the 1950s to the 1970s, the political and economic difficulties experienced by many developing nations in Asia, Africa, and Latin America led to chronic instability in a number of countries and transformed the developing world into a major theater of Cold War confrontation. During the 1980s, however, a number of new factors entered the equation and shifted the focus away from ideological competition. China's shift to a more accommodating policy toward the West removed fears of more wars of national liberation supported by Beijing. At the same time, the Communist victory in Vietnam led not to falling dominoes throughout Southeast Asia but to a bitter war between the two erstwhile Communist allies, Vietnam and China. It was clear that in the post–Cold War era, national interests and historic rivalries often took precedence over ideological agreement.

In the meantime, the growing success of the "little tigers" and the poor economic performance of socialist regimes led a number of developing countries to reduce government regulations and adopt a free market approach to economic development. Still, the role of government leadership in hindering or promoting economic growth in many Asian and African countries should not be ignored. The situation in China is an obvious case in point. While Communist policies may have been beneficial in rectifying economic inequities and focusing attention on building up the infrastructure in the 1950s, the policies adopted during the Great Leap Forward and the Cultural Revolution had disastrous economic effects. Since the late 1970s, China has realized massive progress through a combination of centralized party leadership and economic policies emphasizing innovation and the interplay of free market forces. By some measures, China today has the third largest economy in the world.

Similarly, there have been tantalizing signs in recent years of a revival of interest in the democratic model in various parts of Asia, Africa, and Latin America. Free elections have been held recently in South Korea, Taiwan, and the Philippines, while similar developments have taken place in Nigeria, South Africa, and a number of other African countries. Nevertheless, it is clear that in many areas, democratic institutions are quite fragile, and experiments in democratic pluralism have failed in a number of areas. Many political leaders in Asia and Africa are convinced that Western traditions of individualism and unbridled freedom of the press can be destabilizing and destructive of other national objectives. A good case in point is China, where official tolerance of free expression led ultimately to the demonstrations in Tiananmen Square and the bloody crackdown that brought them to an end. Many still do not believe that democracy and economic development go hand in hand. During the 1990s, some Asian leaders like Malaysian prime minister Mahathir Mohamad have become openly critical of the Western tendency to place individual freedom over community responsibility and to lecture Asian countries about their record on human rights.

Nevertheless, social and political attitudes are changing rapidly in many Asian countries, as new economic circumstances have led to a more secular world view, a decline in traditional hierarchical relations, and a more open attitude toward sexual practices. In part, these changes have been a consequence of the influence of Western music, movies, and television. But they are also a product of the growth of an affluent middle class in many societies of Asia and Africa. This middle class is often strongly influenced by Western ways, and its sons and daughters ape the behavior, dress, and lifestyles of their counterparts in Europe and North America. When Reebok sneakers are worn and coveted in Lagos and Nairobi, Bombay and Islamabad, Beijing and Hanoi, it is clear that, for good or ill, the impact of modern Western civilization has been universalized.

Does this mean that the industrial nations of the West have triumphed and have remade the rest of the world in their own image? Some observers, like the U.S. scholar Francis Fukuyama, argue that capitalism and the Western concept of liberal democracy have vanquished all of their rivals and will ultimately be applied universally throughout the globe. In fact, however, it is much too early to reach such conclusions. It is true that virtually the entire world has now been transformed as the result of the Industrial Revolution that began in Western Europe at the end of the eighteenth century. Countries throughout the world today are not only linked to the economic marketplace put in place by the Western industrialized nations, but are also adopting political and social institutions and values originally introduced from Europe or the United States.

But such institutions have been severely modified to meet local conditions and traditions, and in East Asia today, some governments are effectively using such indigenous traditions as community spirit, the propensity to save, and government interventionism not only to imitate, but to surpass the performance of Western countries. It is no empty phrase to speak of the coming era as the Pacific Century, proving that capitalism is by no means a Western monopoly.

The financial crisis of the late 1990s is a useful reminder that the world economy today is highly vulnerable and increasingly dependent on the continued economic prosperity of the industrialized countries. A global economic turndown, or even the persistence of the economic stagnation of the early 1990s, could put a serious dent in the pace of economic development in many parts of the world. That in turn could lead to serious political instability and a crisis in the global economy.

Whatever happens to the current economic situation, it has clearly taken on a truly global character. In fact, today we live not only in a world economy, but in a world society, where an economic downturn in the United States can create stagnant conditions in Europe and Asia, where a revolution in Iran can cause a rise in the price of oil in the United States and a change in social behavior in Malaysia and Indonesia, and where the collapse of an empire in Russia can send shock waves as far as Hanoi and Havana, Cuba.

One consequence of this process of interdependence is a growing recognition of the common danger posed by environmental pollution (see the box on p. 1000). Some people in the West point to overpopulation in the developing countries and the high rate of destruction of the rain forest in developing areas such as Brazil and Malaysia. Observers from Asia or Africa are likely to retort that most of the damage is done by industrial pollution and that the advanced Western countries on a per capita basis use up much more than their share of world resources.

The fact that environmental damage is a common concern suggests the growing need for cooperation and coordination of efforts on a global scale. Such cooperation, however, has often been hindered by political, ethnic, and religious disputes. India, Pakistan, and Bangladesh have squabbled over the use of the waters of the Ganges and Indus Rivers, as have Israel and its neighbors over the scarce water resources of the Middle East. Pollution of the Rhine River by factories along its banks provokes angry disputes among European nations, while the United States and Canada have argued about the effects of acid rain on Canadian forests.

The collapse of the Soviet Union and its satellite system between 1989 and 1991 seemed to provide an enormous boost to the potential for international cooperation on global issues and led to optimistic predictions that the end of the Cold War would bring about what Francis Fukuyama called the "end of history," when political conflicts would be replaced by peaceful economic competition. So far, however, the collapse of the Soviet empire has had almost the opposite effect, as the disintegration of the Soviet Union has led to the emergence of several squabbling new nations and a general atmosphere of conflict and tension throughout much of Eastern Europe. The rise of nationalist sentiment among various ethnic and religious groups in Eastern Europe is, of course, a direct consequence of the collapse of a system that in its own way resembled the transitional empires of the Romanovs, the Habsburgs, and the Ottomans. But the phenomenon is worldwide and growing in importance, and can be seen as

ONE WORLD, ONE ENVIRONMENT

A crucial factor that is affecting the evolution of society and the global economy at the beginning of the twenty-first century is growing concern over the impact of industrialization on the earth's environment. There is nothing new about human beings causing damage to their natural surroundings, but never before has the danger of significant ecological damage been as extensive as during the past century. The effects of chemicals introduced into the atmosphere or into rivers, lakes, and oceans have increasingly threatened the health and well-being of all living species.

For many years, the main focus of environmental concern was in the developed countries of the West, where industrial effluents, automobile exhaust, and the use of artificial fertilizers and insecticides led to urban smog, extensive damage to crops and wildlife, and a major reduction of the ozone layer in the upper atmosphere. In recent years, the problem has spread elsewhere. China's headlong rush to industrialization has resulted in major ecological damage in that country. Industrial smog has created almost unlivable conditions in many cities in Asia, while hillsides denuded of their forests have caused severe problems of erosion and destruction of farmlands. Destruction of the rain forest is a growing problem in many parts of the world, notably in Brazil and in the Indonesian archipelago. With the forest cover throughout the earth rapidly disappearing, there is less plant life to perform the crucial process of reducing carbon dioxide levels in the atmosphere.

DESTRUCTION OF THE ENVIRONMENT. This stunted tree has been killed by acid rain, a combination of sulfuric and nitric acids mixed with moisture in the air. Entire forests of trees killed by acid rain are becoming common sights in Canada, the United States, and northern Europe.

One of the few beneficial consequences of such incidents has been a growing international consensus that environmental concerns have taken on a truly global character. Although the danger of global warming—allegedly caused by the release, as a result of industrialization, of hothouse gases into the atmosphere—has not yet been definitively proven, it has become a source of sufficient concern to bring about an international conference on the subject in Kyoto, Japan, in December 1997. If, as many scientists predict, worldwide temperatures should continue to increase, the rise in sea levels could pose a significant threat to low-lying islands and coastal areas throughout the world, while climatic change could lead to severe droughts or excessive rainfall in cultivated areas.

It is one thing to recognize a problem, however, and yet another to solve it. So far, cooperative efforts among nations to alleviate environmental problems have all too often been hindered by economic forces or by political, ethnic, and religious disputes. The 1997 conference on global warming, for example, was marked by bitter disagreement over the degree to which developing countries should share the burden of cleaning up the environment. As a result, it achieved few concrete results. The fact is, few nations have been willing to take unilateral action that might pose an obstacle to economic development plans or lead to a rise in unemployment. As President Bill Clinton remarked about a proposal to reduce the danger of global warming by raising energy prices, such a measure "either won't pass the Senate or it won't pass muster with the American people."

a natural consequence of the rising thirst for group identity in a vast and rapidly changing world. Shared culture is our defense against the impersonal world around us, a consequence of what the historian Theodore von Laue has aptly described as "global overload."

Even as the world becomes more global in culture and interdependent in its mutual relations, centrifugal forces are at work attempting to redefine the political, cultural, and ethnic ways in which it is divided. Such efforts are often disruptive and can sometimes work against measures to enhance our human destiny. But they also represent an integral part of human character and human history and cannot be suppressed in the relentless drive to create a world society. In his crusade against the "coca-colonization" of the world, Japanese novelist Yukio Mishima was expressing a fear that is shared today by mil-

FROM THE INDUSTRIAL TO THE TECHNOLOGICAL REVOLUTION

As many observers have noted, a key aspect of the world economy is that it is in the process of transition to what has been called a "postindustrial age," characterized by a system that is not only increasingly global in scope but also increasingly technology-intensive in character. Since World War II, a stunning array of technological changes—especially in transportation, communications, space exploration, medicine, and agriculture—have transformed the world in which we live. Technological changes have also raised new questions and concerns as well as unexpected results. Some scientists have questioned whether genetic engineering might result accidentally in new strains of deadly bacteria that cannot be controlled outside the laboratory. Some doctors have recently raised the alarm that the overuse of antibiotics has created supergerms, which are no longer subject to antibiotic treatment. The Technological Revolution has also led to the development of more advanced methods of destruction. Most frightening have been nuclear weapons. Although the end of the Cold War in the late 1980s reduced the chances of a major nuclear war, nuclear weapons continue to spread, making regional war even more of a likelihood.

The transition to a technology-intensive postindustrial world, which the futurologist Alvin Toffler has dubbed the Third Wave (the first two being the agricultural and industrial revolutions), has produced difficulties for people in many walks of life—for blue-collar workers, whose high wages price them out of the market as firms begin to move their factories abroad; for the poor and uneducated, who lack the technical skills to handle complex tasks in the contemporary economy; and even for some members of the middle class, who have been fired or forced into retirement as their employers seek to slim down to compete in the global marketplace.

It is now increasingly clear that the Technological Revolution, like the Industrial Revolution that preceded it, will entail enormous consequences and may ultimately give birth to a new era of social and political instability. The success of advanced capitalist states in the second half of the twentieth century has been built on a broad consensus on the importance of several propositions: (1) the importance of limiting income inequities in order to reduce the threat of political instability while maximizing domestic consumer demand; (2) the need for high levels of government investment in education, communications, and transportation as a means of meeting the challenges of continued economic growth and technological innovation; and (3) the desirability of cooperative efforts in the international arena as a means of maintaining open markets for the free exchange of goods.

ON THE ASSEMBLY LINE. Automation is sometimes cited as one of the key reasons for the vaunted efficiency of the Japanese industrial machine. Mechanical robots, as shown here, perform tasks in Japan that elsewhere are performed by human beings.

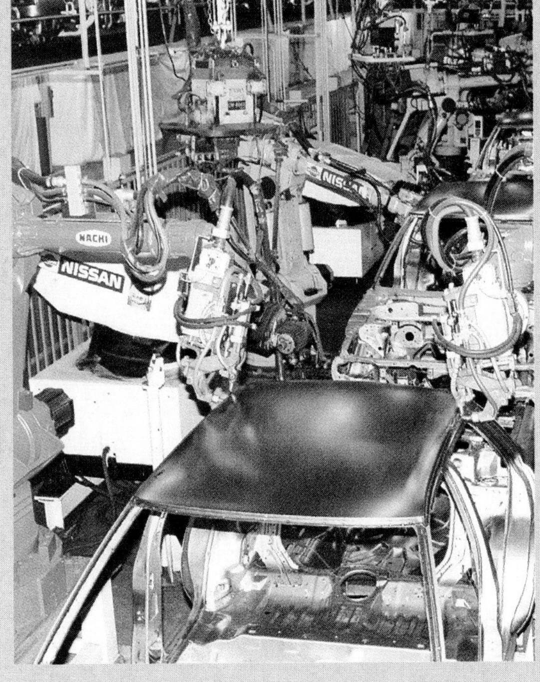

As the century nears an end, all of these assumptions are increasingly under attack, as citizens react with increasing hostility to the high tax rates needed to maintain the welfare state, refuse to support education, and oppose the formation of trading alliances to promote the free movement of goods and labor across national borders. The breakdown of the public consensus that brought modern capitalism to a pinnacle of achievement raises serious questions about the likelihood that the coming challenges of the Third Wave can be successfully met without a growing measure of political and social tension.

lions throughout the world, as Walt Disney, rock music, and McDonald's relentlessly erode the boundaries that separate one culture and people from another. What will result from this concern is as yet unclear. What is apparent is that the Technological Revolution is proceeding at a dizzying speed that can carry information, ideas, and images around the world in seconds (see the box above).

The ultimate effects of that revolution are as yet unclear, but it is already apparent that technological advances will have an enormous impact on human society in coming generations. Although many of these consequences may be welcome, others represent a serious challenge, as individuals raised on television, video games, and the computer find less and less time for human relationships or creative activities. To some, the only antidote to the sense of confusion and alienation afflicting contemporary life is to reject the scientific outlook, with its secularizing implications, and return to religious faith. Whether such an approach can succeed in the face of powerful forces for change set in motion by advances in scientific knowledge, however, remains uncertain. Others hope that a combination of scientific knowledge and spiritual revival can spark a renewal that will enable people to deal constructively with contemporary alienation and confusion.

In a recent book entitled *The Clash of Civilizations and the Remaking of the World Order,* the political scientist Samuel P. Huntington has suggested that the post–Cold War era, far from marking the "end of history" and the triumph of the Western idea, will be characterized by increased global fragmentation and a "clash of civilizations" based on ethnic, cultural, or religious distinctions. According to Huntington, cultural identity has replaced shared ideology as the dominant force in world affairs. As a result, he argues, the coming decades may see an emerging world dominated by disputing cultural blocs in East Asia, Western Europe and the United States, Eurasia, and the Middle East, with the societies in each region coalescing around common cultural features against perceived threats from rival forces elsewhere around the globe. The dream of a universal order dominated by Western values, he concludes, is a fantasy.

In the confusing conditions at the end of the twentieth century, Huntington's thesis may serve as a corrective to

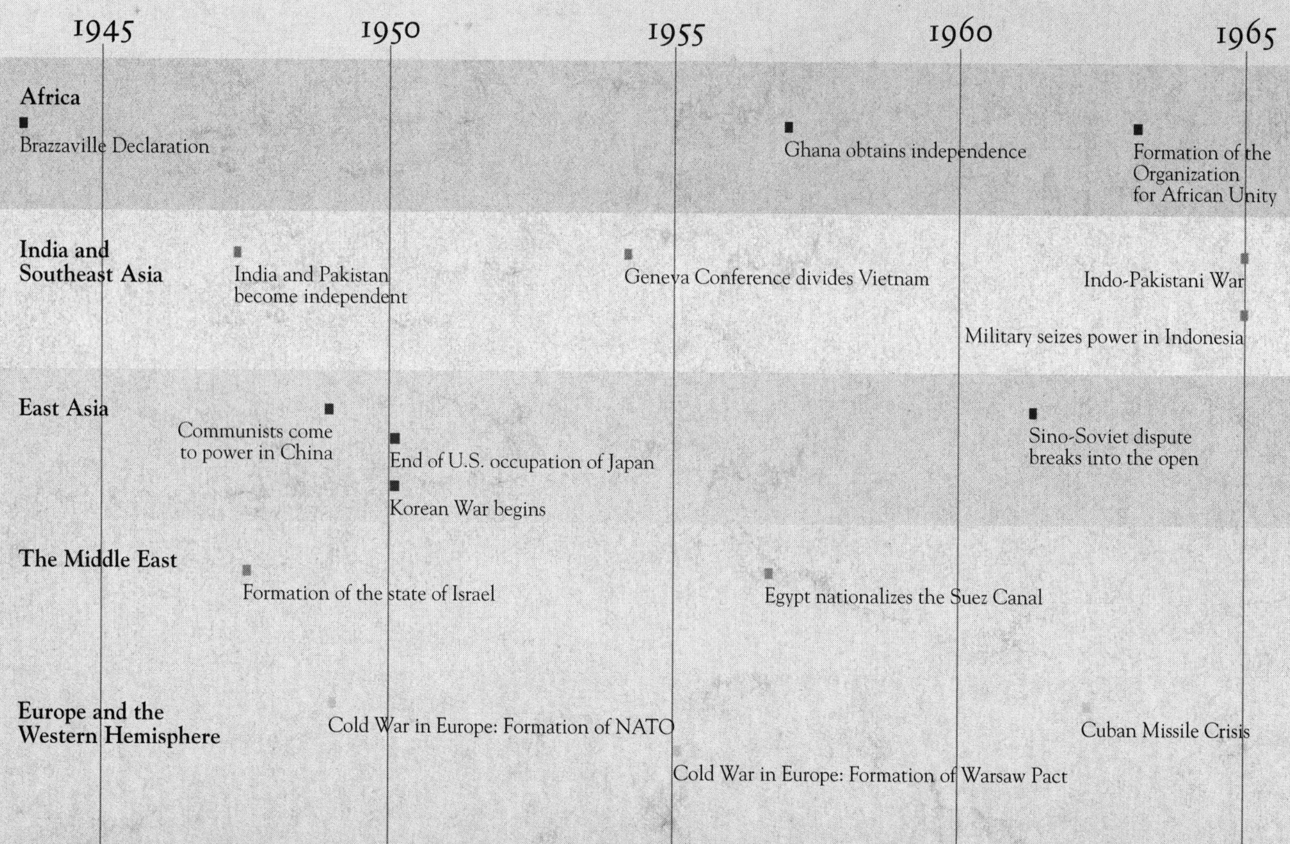

the tendency of many observers in Europe and the United States to see Western civilization as the zenith and final resting place of human achievement. But in dividing the world into competing cultural blocs, he has seriously underestimated the centrifugal forces that exist within each region, as well as the transformative effect of the Industrial Revolution and the emerging global informational network. There are already initial signs that as the common dangers posed by environmental damage, overpopulation, and scarcity of resources become even more apparent, societies around the world will find ample reason to turn their attention from cultural differences to the demands of global interdependence. As the world faces a new century, its greatest challenge may be to reconcile the drive for individual and group identity with the common needs of the human community.

Suggested Readings

For a general view of world history since 1945, see J. A. S. Grenville, *A History of the World in the Twentieth Century* (Cambridge, Mass., 1994), and T. E. Vadney, *World since 1945: A Complete History of Global Change from 1945 to the Present*, 3d ed. (New York, 1998). On different facets of environmental issues, see J. L. Simon, *Population Matters: People, Resources, Environment and Immigration* (New Brunswick, N. J., 1990); M. Feshbach and A. Friendly, *Ecocide in the U.S.S.R.: Health and Nature Under Siege* (New York, 1992); S. Hecht and A. Cockburn, *The Fate of the Forest: Developers, Destroyers, and Defenders of the Amazon* (New York, 1989); and B. L. Turner II et al, eds., *The Earth as Transformed by Human Action: Global and Regional Changes in the Biosphere over the Past 300 Years* (New York, 1990). For speculations on the future, see P. Kennedy, *Preparing for the 21st Century* (New York, 1993); A. and H. Toffler, *Creating a New Civilization: The Politics of the Third Wave* (Atlanta, 1995); S. P. Huntington, *The Clash of Civilizations and the Remaking of the World Order* (New York, 1996); and F. Fukuyama, *The Great Disruption: Human Nature and the Reconstitution of Social Order* (New York, 1999).

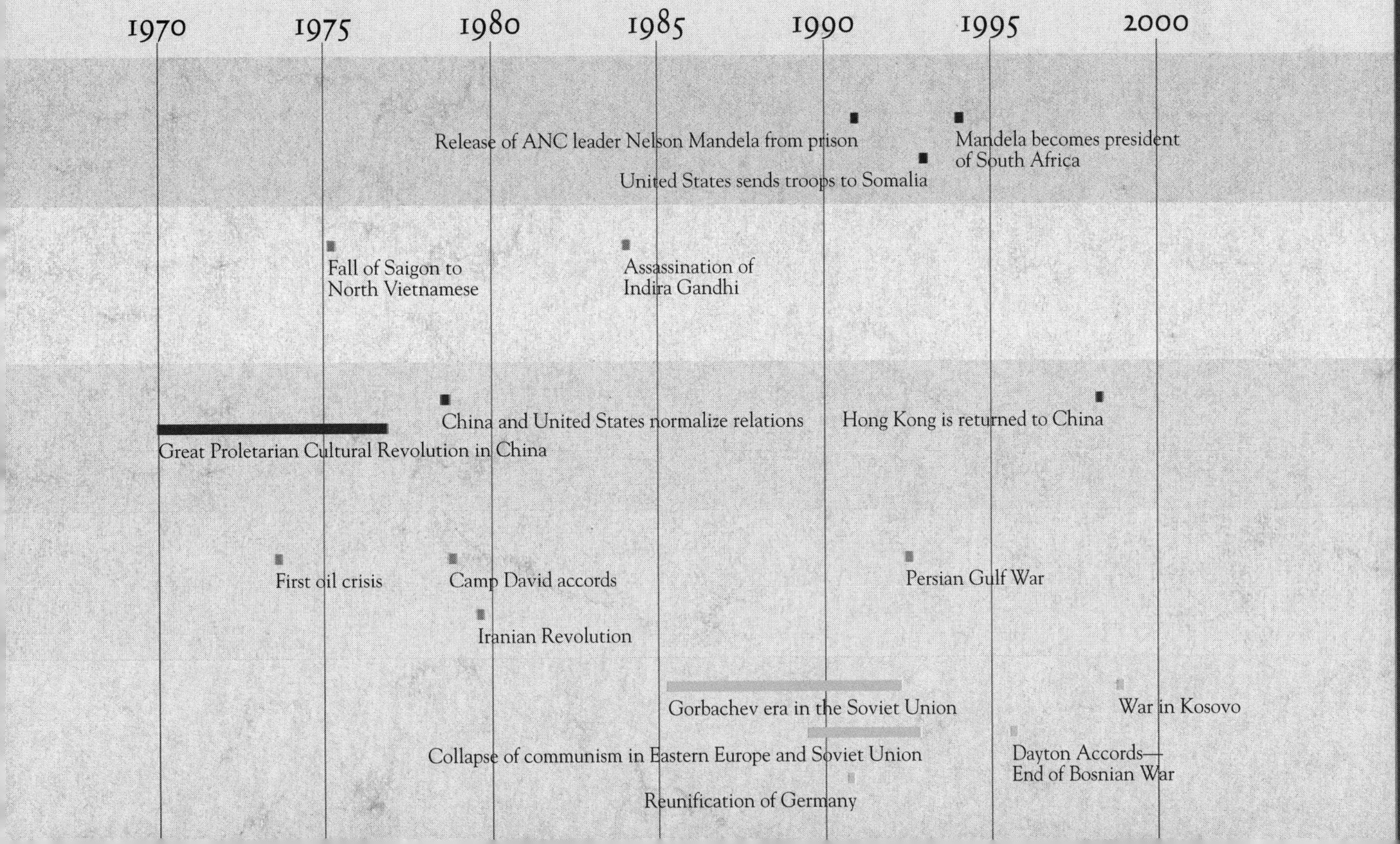

1970 1975 1980 1985 1990 1995 2000

Release of ANC leader Nelson Mandela from prison

Mandela becomes president of South Africa

United States sends troops to Somalia

Fall of Saigon to North Vietnamese

Assassination of Indira Gandhi

China and United States normalize relations

Hong Kong is returned to China

Great Proletarian Cultural Revolution in China

First oil crisis

Camp David accords

Persian Gulf War

Iranian Revolution

Gorbachev era in the Soviet Union

War in Kosovo

Collapse of communism in Eastern Europe and Soviet Union

Dayton Accords— End of Bosnian War

Reunification of Germany

GLOSSARY

absolutism a form of government where the sovereign power or ultimate authority rested in the hands of a monarch who claimed to rule by divine right and was therefore responsible only to God.

Agricultural (Neolithic) Revolution the shift from hunting animals and gathering plants for sustenance to producing food by systematic agriculture that occurred gradually between 10,000 and 4000 B.C. (the Neolithic or "New Stone" Age).

agricultural revolution the application of new agricultural techniques that allowed for a large increase in productivity in the eighteenth century.

anarchism a political theory that holds that all governments and existing social institutions are unnecessary and advocates a society based on voluntary cooperation.

ANC the African National Congress. Founded in 1912, it was the beginning of political activity by South African blacks. Banned by politically dominant European whites in 1960, it was not officially "unbanned" until 1990. It is now the official majority party of the South African government.

Anelects the body of writing containing conversations between Confucius and his disciples which preserves his worldly wisdom and pragmatic philosophies.

anti-Semitism hostility toward or discrimination against Jews.

appeasement the policy, followed by the European nations in the 1930s, of accepting Hitler's annexation of Austria and Czechoslovakia in the belief that meeting his demands would assure peace and stability.

Arianism a Christian heresy that taught that Jesus was inferior to God. Though condemned by the Council of Nicaea in 325, Arianism was adopted by many of the Germanic peoples who entered the Roman Empire over the next centuries.

aristocracy a class of hereditary nobility in medieval Europe; a warrior class who shared a distinctive lifestyle based on the institution of knighthood, although there were social divisions within the group based on extremes of wealth.

Arthasastra an early Indian political treatise that sets forth many fundamental aspects of the relationship of rulers and their subjects. It has been compared to Machiavelli's well-known book, *The Prince*, and has provided principles upon which many aspects of social organization have developed in the region.

ASEAN the Association for the Southest Asian Nations formed in 1967 to promote the properity and political stability of its member nations. Currently Brunei, Indonesia, Laos, Malaysia, Myanmar, the Philippines, Singapore, Thailand, and Vietnam are members. Other countries in the region participate as "observer" members.

Ausgleich the "Compromise" of 1867 that created the dual monarchy of Austria-Hungary. Austria and Hungary each had its own capital, constitution, and legislative assembly, but were united under one monarch.

authoritarian state a state that has a dictatorial government and some other trappings of a totalitarian state, but does not demand that the masses be actively involved in the regime's goals as totalitarian states do.

auxiliaries troops enlisted from the subject peoples of the Roman Empire to supplement the regular legions composed of Roman citizens.

balance of power a distribution of power among several states such that no single nation can dominate or interfere with the interests of another.

benefice in the Christian church, a position, such as a bishopric, that consisted of both a sacred office and the right of the holder to the annual revenues from the position.

bicameral legislature a legislature with two houses.

Black Death the outbreak of plague (mostly bubonic) in the mid-fourteenth century that killed from 25 to 50 percent of Europe's population.

Blitzkrieg "lightning war." A war conducted with great speed and force, as in Germany's advance at the beginning of World War II.

Bolsheviks a small faction of the Russian Social Democratic Party who were led by Lenin and dedicated to violent revolution; seized power in Russia in 1917 and were subsequently renamed the Communists.

boyars the Russian nobility.

Brezhnev Doctrine the doctrine, enunciated by Leonid Brezhnev, that the Soviet Union had a right to intervene if socialism was threatened in another socialist state; used to justify the use of Soviet troops in Czechoslovakia in 1968.

caliph the secular leader of the Islamic community.

capital material wealth used or available for use in the production of more wealth.

caste system a system of rigid social hierarchcy in which all members of that society are assigned by birth to specific "ranks," and inherit specific roles and privileges.

cartel a combination of independent commercial enterprises that work together to control prices and limit competition.

Cartesian dualism Descartes's principle of the separation of mind and matter (and mind and body) that enabled scientists to view matter as something separate from themselves that could be investigated by reason.

chaebol a South Korean business structure similar to the Japanese keiretsu.

chansons de geste a form of vernacular literature in the High Middle Ages that consisted of heroic epics focusing on the deeds of warriors.

chivalry the ideal of civilized behavior that emerged among the nobility in the eleventh and twelfth centuries under the influence of the church; a code of ethics knights were expected to uphold.

Christian (northern) humanism an intellectual movement in northern Europe in the late fifteenth and early sixteenth centuries that combined the interest in the classics of the Italian Renaissance with an interest in the sources of early Christianity, including the New Testament and the writings of the church fathers.

civic humanism an intellectual movement of the Italian Renaissance that saw Cicero, who was both an intellectual and a statesman, as the ideal and held that humanists should be involved in government and use their rhetorical training in the service of the state.

civil rights the basic rights of citizens including equality before the law, freedom of speech and press, and freedom from arbitrary arrest.

Cold War the ideological conflict between the Soviet Union and the United States after World War II.

collective farms large farms created in the Soviet Union by Stalin by combining many small holdings into one large farm worked by the peasants under government supervision.

collective security the use of an international army raised by an association of nations to deter aggression and keep the peace.

coloni free tenant farmers who worked as sharecroppers on the large estates of the Roman Empire (singular: *colonus*).

common law law common to the entire kingdom of England; imposed by the king's courts beginning in the twelfth century to replace the customary law used in county and feudal courts that varied from place to place.

commune in medieval Europe, an association of townspeople bound together by a sworn oath for the purpose of obtaining basic liberties from the lord of the territory in which the town was located; also, the self-governing town after receiving its liberties.

conciliarism a movement in fourteenth- and fifteenth-century Europe that held that final authority in spiritual matters resided with a general church council, not the pope; emerged in response to the Avignon papacy and the Great Schism and used to justify the summoning of the Council of Constance (1414–1418).

condottieri leaders of bands of mercenary soldiers in Renaissance Italy who sold their services to the highest bidder.

conquistadors "conquerors." Leaders in the Spanish conquests in the Americas, especially Mexico and Peru, in the sixteenth century.

conscription a military draft.

conservatism an ideology based on tradition and social stability that favored the maintenance of established institutions, organized religion, and obedience to authority and resisted change, especially abrupt change.

consuls the chief executive officers of the Roman Republic. Two were chosen annually to administer the government and lead the army in battle.

consumer society a term applied to Western society after World War II as the working classes adopted the consumption patterns of the middle class and installment plans, credit cards, and easy credit made consumer goods such as appliances and automobiles widely available.

Continental System Napoleon's effort to bar British goods from the Continent in the hope of weakening Britain's economy and destroying its capacity to wage war.

cosmopolitanism the quality of being sophisticated and having wide international experience.

cottage industry a system of textile manufacturing in which spinners and weavers worked at home in their cottages using raw materials supplied to them by capitalist entrepreneurs.

cultural relativism the belief that no culture is superior to another because culture is a matter of custom, not reason, and derives its meaning from the group holding it.

cuneiform "wedge-shaped." A system of writing developed by the Sumerians that consisted of wedge-shaped impressions made by a reed stylus on clay tablets.

daimyo prominent Japanese families who provided allegiance to the local shogun in exchange for protection; similar to vassals in Europe.

decolonization the process of becoming free of colonial status and achieving statehood; occurred in most of the world's colonies between 1947 and 1962.

deism belief in God as the creator of the universe who, after setting it in motion, ceased to have any direct involvement in it and allowed it to run according to its own natural laws.

demesne the part of a manor retained under the direct control of the lord and worked by the serfs as part of their labor services.

depression a very severe, protracted economic downturn with high levels of unemployment.

destalinization the policy of denouncing and undoing the most repressive aspects of Stalin's regime; begun by Nikita Khrushchev in 1956.

détente the relaxation of tension between the Soviet Union and the United States that occurred in the 1970s.

dialectic logic, one of the seven liberal arts that made up the medieval curriculum. In Marxist thought, the process by which all change occurs through the clash of antagonistic elements.

Diaspora the scattering of Jews throughout the ancient world after the Babylonian captivity in the sixth century B.C.

dictator in the Roman Republic, an official granted unlimited power to run the state for a short period of time, usually six months, during an emergency.

diocese the area under the jurisdiction of a Christian bishop; based originally on Roman administrative districts.

direct representation a system of choosing delegates to a representative assembly in which citizens vote directly for the delegates who will represent them.

divination the practice of seeking to foretell future events by interpreting divine signs, which could appear in various forms, such as in entrails of animals, in patterns in smoke, or in dreams.

divine-right monarchy a monarchy based on the belief that monarchs receive their power directly from God and are responsible to no one except God.

domino theory the belief that if the Communists succeeded in Vietnam, other countries in Southeast and East Asia would also fall (like dominoes) to communism; a justification for the U.S. intervention in Vietnam.

dualism the belief that the universe is dominated by two opposing forces, one good and the other evil.

dynastic state a state where the maintenance and expansion of the interests of the ruling family is the primary consideration.

economic imperialism the process in which banks and corporations from developed nations invest in underdeveloped regions and establish a major presence there in the hope of making high profits; not necessarily the same as colonial expansion in that businesses invest where they can make a profit, which may not be in their own nation's colonies.

empiricism the practice of relying on observation and experiment.

enclosure movement in the eighteenth century, the fencing in of the old open fields, combining many small holdings into larger units that could be farmed more efficiently.

encyclical a letter from the pope to all the bishops of the Roman Catholic church.

enlightened absolutism an absolute monarchy where the ruler follows the principles of the Enlightenment by introducing reforms for the improvement of society, allowing freedom of speech and the press, permitting religious toleration, expanding education, and ruling in accordance with the laws.

Enlightenment an eighteenth-century intellectual movement, led by the philosophes, that stressed the application of reason and the scientific method to all aspects of life.

entrepreneur one who organizes, operates, and assumes the risk in a business venture in the expectation of making a profit.

Epicureanism a philosophy founded by Epicurus in the fourth century B.C. that taught that happiness (freedom from emotional turmoil) could be achieved through the pursuit of pleasure (intellectual rather than sensual pleasure).

equestrians a group of extremely wealthy men in the late Roman Republic who were effectively barred from high office, but sought political power commensurate with their wealth; called equestrians because many had gotten their start as cavalry officers (*equites*).

ethnic cleansing the policy of killing or forcibly removing people of another ethnic group; used by the Serbs against Bosnian Muslims in the 1990s.

eucharist a Christian sacrament in which consecrated bread and wine are consumed in celebration of Jesus' Last Supper; also called the Lord's Supper or communion.

evolutionary socialism a socialist doctrine espoused by Eduard Bernstein who argued that socialists should stress cooperation and evolution to attain power by democratic means rather than by conflict and revolution.

fascism an ideology or movement that exalts the nation above the individual and calls for a centralized government with a dictatorial leader, economic and social regimentation, and forcible suppression of opposition; in particular, the ideology of Mussolini's Fascist regime in Italy.

feminism the belief in the social, political, and economic equality of the sexes; also, organized activity to advance women's rights.

fief a landed estate granted to a vassal in exchange for military services.

Final Solution the physical extermination of the Jewish people by the Nazis during World War II.

folk culture the traditional arts and crafts, literature, music, and other customs of the people; something that people make, as opposed to modern popular culture, which is something people buy.

free trade the unrestricted international exchange of goods with low or no tariffs.

general strike a strike by all or most workers in an economy; espoused by Georges Sorel as the heroic action that could be used to inspire the workers to destroy capitalist society.

gentry well-to-do English landowners below the level of the nobility; played an important role in the English Civil War of the seventeenth century.

geocentric theory the idea that the earth is at the center of the universe and that the sun and other celestial objects revolve around the earth.

glasnost "openness." Mikhail Gorbachev's policy of encouraging Soviet citizens to openly discuss the strengths and weaknesses of the Soviet Union.

good emperors the five emperors who ruled from 96 to 180 (Nerva, Trajan, Hadrian, Antoninus Pius, and Marcus Aurelius), a period of peace and prosperity for the Roman Empire.

Great Schism the crisis in the late medieval church when there were first two and then three popes; ended by the Council of Constance (1414–1418).

guest workers foreign workers working temporarily in European countries.

guild an association of people with common interests and concerns, especially people working in the same craft. In medieval Europe, guilds came to control much of the production process and to restrict entry into various trades.

gymnasium in classical Greece, a place for athletics; in the Hellenistic Age, a secondary school with a curriculum centered on music, physical exercise, and literature.

heliocentric theory the idea that the sun (not the earth) is at the center of the universe.

Hellenistic literally, "to imitate the Greeks"; the era after the death of Alexander the Great when Greek culture spread into the Near East and blended with the culture of that region.

helots serfs in ancient Sparta, who were permanently bound to the land that they worked for their Spartan masters.

heresy the holding of religious doctrines different from the official teachings of the church.

Hermeticism an intellectual movement beginning in the fifteenth century that taught that divinity is embodied in all aspects of nature; included works on alchemy and magic as well as theology and philosophy. The tradition continued into the seventeenth century and influenced many of the leading figures of the Scientific Revolution.

hetairai highly sophisticated courtesans in ancient Athens who offered intellectual and musical entertainment as well as sex.

hieroglyphics a highly pictorial system of writing most often associated with ancient Egypt. Also used (with different "pictographs") by other ancient peoples such as the Mayans.

high culture the literary and artistic culture of the educated and wealthy ruling classes.

Holocaust the mass slaughter of European Jews by the Nazis during World War II.

hoplites heavily armed infantry soldiers used in ancient Greece in a phalanx formation.

Huguenots French Calvinists.

humanism an intellectual movement in Renaissance Italy based upon the study of the Greek and Roman classics.

iconoclasm an eighth-century Byzantine movement against the use of icons (pictures of sacred figures), which was condemned as idolatry.

ideology a political philosophy such as conservatism or liberalism.

imperium "the right to command." In the Roman Republic, the chief executive officers (consuls and praetors) possessed the *imperium*; a military commander was an *imperator.* In the Roman Empire, the title *imperator,* or emperor, came to be used for the ruler.

indirect representation a system of choosing delegates to a representative assembly in which citizens do not choose the delegates directly but instead vote for electors who choose the delegates.

individualism emphasis on and interest in the unique traits of each person.

indulgence the remission of part or all of the temporal punishment in purgatory due to sin; granted for charitable contributions and other good deeds. Indulgences became a regular practice of the Christian church in the High Middle Ages, and their abuse was instrumental in sparking Luther's reform movement in the sixteenth century.

infanticide the practice of killing infants.

inflation a sustained rise in the price level.

intendants royal officials in seventeenth-century France who were sent into the provinces to execute the orders of the central government.

intervention, principle of the idea, after the Congress of Vienna, that the great powers of Europe had the right to send armies into countries experiencing revolution to restore legitimate monarchs to their thrones.

isolationism a foreign policy in which a nation refrains from making alliances or engaging actively in international affairs.

jihad "striving in the way of the Lord." In Islam, the practice of conducting raids against neighboring peoples, which was an expansion of the Arab tradition of tribal raids against their persecutors.

joint-stock company a company or association that raises capital by selling shares to individuals who receive dividends on their investment while a board of directors runs the company.

joint-stock investment bank a bank created by selling shares of stock to investors. Such banks potentially have access to much more capital than do private banks owned by one or a few individuals.

justification of faith the primary doctrine of the Protestant Reformation; taught that humans are saved not through good works, but by the grace of God, bestowed freely through the sacrifice of Jesus.

keiretsu a type of powerful industrial or financial conglomerate that emerged in post-World War II Japan following the abolition of zaibatsu.

laissez-faire "to let alone." An economic doctrine that holds that an economy is best served when the government does not interfere but allows the economy to self-regulate according to the forces of supply and demand.

latifundia large landed estates in the Roman Empire (singular: *latifundium*).

lay investiture the practice in which a layperson chose a bishop and invested him with the symbols of both his temporal office and his spiritual office; led to the Investiture Controversy, which was ended by compromise in the Concordat of Worms in 1122.

Lebensraum "living space." The doctrine, adopted by Hitler, that a nation's power depends on the amount of land it occupies; thus, a nation must expand to be strong.

legitimacy, principle of the idea that after the Napoleonic wars peace could best be reestablished in Europe by restoring legitimate monarchs who would preserve traditional institutions; guided Metternich at the Congress of Vienna.

Leninism Lenin's revision of Marxism that held that Russia need not experience a bourgeois revolution before it could move toward socialism.

liberal arts the seven areas of study that formed the basis of education in medieval and early modern Europe. Following Boethius and other late Roman authors, they consisted of grammar, rhetoric, and dialectic or logic (the *trivium*) and arithmetic, geometry, astronomy, and music (the *quadrivium*).

liberalism an ideology based on the belief that people should be as free from restraint as possible. Economic liberalism is the idea that the government should not interfere in the workings of the economy. Political liberalism is the idea that there should be restraints on the exercise of power so that people can enjoy basic civil rights in a constitutional state with a representative assembly.

limited liability the principle that shareholders in a joint-stock corporation can be held responsible for the corporation's debts only up to the amount they have invested.

limited (constitutional) monarchy a system of government in which the monarch is limited by a representative assembly and by the duty to rule in accordance with the laws of the land.

mandates a system established after World War I whereby a nation officially administered a territory (mandate) on behalf of the League of Nations. Thus, France administered Lebanon and Syria as mandates, and Britain administered Iraq and Palestine.

manor an agricultural estate operated by a lord and worked by peasants who performed labor services and paid various rents and fees to the lord in exchange for protection and sustenance.

Marshall Plan the European Recovery Program, under which the United States provided financial aid to European countries to help them rebuild after World War II.

Marxism the political, economic, and social theories of Karl Marx, which included the idea that history is the story of class struggle and that ultimately the proletariat will overthrow the bourgeoisie and establish a dictatorship en route to a classless society.

mass education a state-run educational system, usually free and compulsory, that aims to ensure that all children in society have at least a basic education.

mass leisure forms of leisure that appeal to large numbers of people in a society including the working classes; emerged at the end of the nineteenth century to provide workers with amusements after work and on weekends; used during the twentieth century by totalitarian states to control their populations.

mass politics a political order characterized by mass political parties and universal male and (eventually) female suffrage.

mass society a society in which the concerns of the majority—the lower classes—play a prominent role; characterized by extension of voting rights, an improved standard of living for the lower classes, and mass education.

materialism the belief that everything mental, spiritual, or ideal is an outgrowth of physical forces and that truth is found in concrete material existence, not through feeling or intuition.

Meiji Restoration the period during the late 19th and early 20th century in which fundamental economic and cultural changes occured in Japan, tranforming it from a fuedal and agrarian society to an industrial and technological society.

mercantilism an economic theory that held that a nation's prosperity depended on its supply of gold and silver and that the total volume of trade is unchangeable; therefore, advocated that the government play an active role in the economy by encouraging exports and discouraging imports, especially through the use of tariffs.

Mesolithic Age the period from 10,000 to 7000 B.C., characterized by a gradual transition from a food-gathering/hunting economy to a food-producing economy.

metics resident foreigners in ancient Athens; not permitted full rights of citizenship but did receive the protection of the laws.

militarism a policy of aggressive military preparedness; in particular, the large armies based on mass conscription and complex, inflexible plans for mobilization that most European nations had before World War I.

ministerial responsibility a tenet of nineteenth-century liberalism that held that ministers of the monarch should be responsible to the legislative assembly rather than to the monarch.

Modernism the new artistic and literary styles that emerged in the decades before 1914 as artists rebelled against traditional efforts to portray reality as accurately as possible (leading to Impressionism and Cubism) and writers explored new forms.

monotheistic/monotheism having only one god; the doctrine or belief that there is only one god.

mutual deterrence the belief that nuclear war could best be prevented if both the United States and the Soviet Union had sufficient nuclear weapons so that even if one nation launched a preemptive first strike, the other could respond and devastate the attacker.

mystery religions religions that involve initiation into secret rites that promise intense emotional involvement with spiritual forces and a greater chance of individual immortality.

nationalism a sense of national consciousness based on awareness of being part of a community—a "nation"—that has common institutions, traditions, language, and customs and that becomes the focus of the individual's primary political loyalty.

nationalities problem the dilemma faced by the Austro-Hungarian Empire in trying to unite a wide variety of ethnic groups including, among others, Austrians, Hungarians, Poles, Croats, Czechs, Serbs, Slovaks, and Slovenes in an era when nationalism and calls for self-determination were coming to the fore.

nationalization the process of converting a business or industry from private ownership to government control and ownership.

nation in arms the people's army raised by universal mobilization to repel the foreign enemies of the French Revolution.

nation-state a form of political organization in which a relatively homogeneous people inhabits a sovereign state, as opposed to a state containing people of several nationalities.

NATO the North Atlantic Treaty Organization; a military alliance formed in 1949 in which the signatories (Belgium, Canada, Denmark, France, Great Britain, Iceland, Italy, Luxembourg, the Netherlands, Norway, Portugal, and the United States) agreed to provide mutual assistance if any one of them was attacked; later expanded to include other nations, including former members of the Warsaw Pact—Poland, the Czech Republic and Hungary.

natural laws a body of laws or specific principles held to be derived from nature and binding upon all human society even in the absence of positive laws.

natural rights certain inalienable rights to which all people are entitled; include the right to life, liberty, and property, freedom of speech and religion, and equality before the law.

natural selection Darwin's idea that organisms that are most adaptable to their environment survive and pass on the variations that enabled them to survive, while other, less adaptable organisms become extinct; "survival of the fittest."

Nazi New Order the Nazis' plan for their conquered territories; included the extermination of Jews and others considered inferior, ruthless exploitation of resources, German colonization in the east, and the use of Poles, Russians, and Ukrainians as slave labor.

negritude a philosophy shared among African blacks that there exists a distinctive "African personality" that owes nothing to Western values and provides a common sense of purpose and destiny for black Africans.

Neoplatonism a revival of Platonic philosophy. In the third century A.D., a revival associated with Plotinus; in the Italian Renaissance, a revival associated with Marsilio Ficino who attempted to synthesize Christianity and Platonism.

New Economic Policy a modified version of the old capitalist system introduced in the Soviet Union by Lenin in 1921 to revive the economy after the ravages of the civil war and war communism.

new imperialism the revival of imperialism after 1880 in which European nations established colonies throughout much of Asia and Africa.

new monarchies the governments of France, England, and Spain at the end of the fifteenth century, where the rulers were successful in reestablishing or extending centralized royal authority, suppressing the nobility, controlling the church, and insisting upon the loyalty of all peoples living in their territories.

nobiles "nobles." The small group of families from both patrician and plebeian origins who produced most of the men who were elected to office in the late Roman Republic.

nominalism a school of thought in medieval Europe that, following Aristotle, held that only individual objects are real and that universals are only names created by humans.

nuclear family a family group consisting only of father, mother, and children.

old regime/old order the political and social system of France in the eighteenth century before the Revolution.

oligarchy rule by a few.

optimates "best men." Aristocratic leaders in the late Roman Republic who generally came from senatorial families and wished to retain their oligarchical privileges.

orders/estates the traditional tripartite division of European society based on heredity and quality rather than wealth or economic standing, first established in the Middle Ages and continuing into the eighteenth century; traditionally consisted of those who pray (the clergy), those who fight (the nobility), and those who work (all the rest).

organic evolution Darwin's principle that all plants and animals have evolved over a long period of time from earlier and simpler forms of life.

Paleolithic Age the period of human history when humans used simple stone tools (c. 2,500,000–10,000 B.C.).

pan-Africanism the concept of African continental unity and solidarity in which the common interests of African countries transcend regional boundries.

pantheism a doctrine that equates God with the universe and all that is in it.

paterfamilias the dominant male in a Roman family whose powers over his wife and children were theoretically unlimited, though they were sometimes circumvented in practice.

patriarchal/patriarchy a society in which the father is supreme in the clan or family; more generally, a society dominated by men.

patriarchal family a family in which the husband/father dominates his wife and children.

patricians great landowners who became the ruling class in the Roman Republic.

patronage the practice of awarding titles and making appointments to government and other positions to gain political support.

Pax Romana "Roman peace." A term used to refer to the stability and prosperity that Roman rule brought to the Mediterranean world and much of western Europe during the first and second centuries A.D.

Pentateuch the first five books of the Hebrew Bible (Genesis, Exodus, Leviticus, Numbers, and Deuteronomy).

perestroika "restructuring." A term applied to Mikhail Gorbachev's economic, political, and social reforms in the Soviet Union.

permissive society a term applied to Western society after World War II to reflect the new sexual freedom and the emergence of a drug culture.

Petrine supremacy the doctrine that the bishop of Rome—the pope—as the successor of Saint Peter (traditionally considered the first bishop of Rome) should hold a preeminent position in the church.

phalanx a rectangular formation of tightly massed infantry soldiers.

philosophes intellectuals of the eighteenth-century Enlightenment who believed in applying a spirit of rational criticism to all things, including religion and politics, and who focused on improving and enjoying this world, rather than on the afterlife.

plebeians the class of Roman citizens who included nonpatrician landowners, craftspeople, merchants, and small farmers in the Roman Republic. Their struggle for equal rights with the patricians dominated much of the Republic's history.

pluralism the practice in which one person holds several church offices simultaneously; a problem of the late medieval church.

pogroms organized massacres of Jews.

polis an ancient Greek city-state encompassing both an urban area and its surrounding countryside; a small but autonomous political unit where all major political and social activities were carried out in a central location.

political democracy a form of government characterized by universal suffrage and mass political parties.

politiques a group who emerged during the French Wars of Religion in the sixteenth century; placed politics above religion and believed that no religious truth was worth the ravages of civil war.

polytheistic/polytheism having many gods; belief in or the worship of more than one god.

popular culture as opposed to high culture, the unofficial, written and unwritten culture of the masses, much of which was passed down orally; centers on public and group activities such as festivals. In the twentieth century, refers to the entertainment, recreation, and pleasures that people purchase as part of mass consumer society.

populares "favoring the people." Aristocratic leaders in the late Roman Republic who tended to use the people's assemblies in an effort to break the stranglehold of the *nobiles* on political offices.

popular sovereignty the doctrine that government is created by and subject to the will of the people, who are the source of all political power.

praetorian guard the military unit that served as the personal bodyguard of the Roman emperors.

predestination the belief, associated with Calvinism, that God, as a consequence of his foreknowledge of all events, has predetermined those who will be saved (the elect) and those who will be damned.

price revolution the dramatic rise in prices (inflation) that occurred throughout Europe in the sixteenth and early seventeenth centuries.

primogeniture an inheritance practice in which the eldest son receives all or the largest share of the parents' estate.

principate the form of government established by Augustus for the Roman Empire; continued the constitutional forms of the Republic and consisted of the *princeps* ("first citizen") and the senate, although the *princeps* was clearly the dominant partner.

proletariat the industrial working class. In Marxism, the class who will ultimately overthrow the bourgeoisie.

Puritans English Protestants inspired by Calvinist theology who wished to remove all traces of Catholicism from the Church of England.

querelles des femmes "arguments about women." A centuries-old debate about the nature of women that continued during the Scientific Revolution as those who argued for the inferiority of women found additional support in the new anatomy and medicine.

rationalism a system of thought based on the belief that human reason and experience are the chief sources of knowledge.

realism in medieval Europe, the school of thought that, following Plato, held that the individual objects we perceive are not real but merely manifestations of universal ideas existing in the mind of God. In the nineteenth century, a school of painting that emphasized the everyday life of ordinary people, depicted with photographic realism.

Realpolitik "politics of reality." Politics based on practical concerns rather than theory or ethics.

real wages/income/prices wages/income/prices that have been adjusted for inflation.

reason of state the principle that a nation should act on the basis of its long-term interests and not merely to further the dynastic interests of its ruling family.

relativity theory Einstein's theory that holds, among other things, that (1) space and time are not absolute but are relative to the observer and interwoven into a four-dimensional space-time continuum and (2) matter is a form of energy ($E = mc^2$).

relics the bones of Christian saints or objects intimately associated with saints that were considered worthy of veneration.

Renaissance the "rebirth" of classical culture that occurred in Italy between c. 1350 and c. 1550; also, the earlier revivals of classical culture that occurred under Charlemagne and in the twelfth century.

rentier a person who lives on income from property and is not personally involved in its operation.

reparations payments made by a defeated nation after a war to compensate another nation for damage sustained as a result of the war; required from Germany after World War I.

revisionism a socialist doctrine that rejected Marx's emphasis on class struggle and revolution and argued instead that workers should work through political parties to bring about gradual change.

revolution a fundamental change in the political and social organization of a state.

revolutionary socialism the socialist doctrine espoused by Georges Sorel who held that violent action was the only way to achieve the goals of socialism.

rhetoric the art of persuasive speaking; in the Middle Ages, one of the seven liberal arts.

sacraments rites considered imperative for a Christian's salvation. By the thirteenth century consisted of the eucharist or Lord's Supper, baptism, marriage, penance, extreme unction, holy orders, and confirmation of children; Protestant reformers of the sixteenth century generally recognized only two—baptism and communion (the Lord's Supper).

salons gatherings of philosophes and other notables to discuss the ideas of the Enlightenment; so-called from the elegant drawing rooms (salons) where they met.

samurai literally "retainer"; similar to European knights. Usually in service to a particular shogun, these warriors lived by a strict code of ethics and duty.

sans-culottes the common people who did not wear the fine clothes of the upper classes (sans-culottes means "without breeches") and played an important role in the radical phase of the French Revolution.

sati the Hindu ritual requiring a wife to throw herself upon her her deceased husband's funeral pyre.

satrap/satrapy a governor with both civil and military duties in the ancient Persian Empire, which was divided into satrapies, or provinces, each administered by a satrap.

scholasticism the philosophical and theological system of the medieval schools, which emphasized rigorous analysis of contradictory authorities; often used to try to reconcile faith and reason.

scientific method a method of seeking knowledge through inductive principles; uses experiments and observations to develop generalizations.

Scientific Revolution the transition from the medieval worldview to a largely secular, rational, and materialistic perspective; began in the seventeenth century and was popularized in the eighteenth.

secularization the process of becoming more concerned with material, worldly, temporal things and less with spiritual and religious things.

self-determination the doctrine that the people of a given territory or a particular nationality should have the right to determine their own government and political future.

senate/senators the leading council of the Roman Republic; composed of about 300 men (senators) who served for life and dominated much of the political life of the Republic.

serf a peasant who is bound to the land and obliged to provide labor services and pay various rents and fees to the lord; considered unfree but not a slave because serfs could not be bought and sold.

shogunate system the system of government in Japan in which the emporor exercised only titular authority while the shogun (regional military dictators) exercised actual political power.

skepticism a doubtful or questioning attitude, especially about religion.

Social Darwinism the application of Darwin's principle of organic evolution to the social order; led to the belief that progress comes from the struggle for survival as the fittest advance and the weak decline.

socialism an ideology that calls for collective or government ownership of the means of production and the distribution of goods.

social security/social insurance government programs that provide social welfare measures such as old age pensions and sickness, accident, and disability insurance.

Socratic method a form of teaching that uses a question-and-answer format to enable students to reach conclusions by using their own reasoning.

Sophists wandering scholars and professional teachers in ancient Greece who stressed the importance of rhetoric and tended toward skepticism and relativism.

soviets councils of workers' and soldiers' deputies formed throughout Russia in 1917; played an important role in the Bolshevik Revolution.

sphere of influence a territory or region over which an outside nation exercises political or economic influence.

Stoicism a philosophy founded by Zeno in the fourth century B.C. that taught that happiness could be obtained by accepting one's lot and living in harmony with the will of God, thereby achieving inner peace.

subinfeudation the practice in which a lord's greatest vassals subdivided their fiefs and had vassals of their own, and those vassals, in turn, subdivided their fiefs and so on down to simple knights whose fiefs were too small to subdivide.

suffrage the right to vote.

suffragists those who advocate the extension of the right to vote (suffrage), especially to women.

surplus value in Marxism, the difference between a product's real value and the wages of the worker who produced the product.

syncretism the combining of different forms of belief or practice, as, for example, when two gods are regarded as different forms of the same underlying divine force and are fused together.

tariffs duties (taxes) imposed on imported goods; usually imposed both to raise revenue and to discourage imports and protect domestic industries.

tetrarchy rule by four; the system of government established by Diocletian (284–305) in which the Roman Empire was divided into two parts, each ruled by an "Augustus" assisted by a "Caesar."

theocracy a government ruled by a divine authority.

three-field system in medieval agriculture, the practice of dividing the arable land into three fields so that one could lie fallow while the others were planted in winter grains and spring crops.

tithe a tenth of one's harvest or income; paid by medieval peasants to the village church.

Tongmenghui the political organization—"Revolutionary Alliance"—formed by Sun Yat-sen in 1905 which united various revolutionary factions and ultimately toppled the Manchu dynasty.

Torah the body of law in Hebrew Scripture, contained in the Pentateuch (the first five books of the Hebrew Bible).

totalitarian state a state characterized by government control over all aspects of economic, social, political, cultural, and intellectual life, the subordination of the individual to the state, and insistence that the masses be actively involved in the regime's goals.

total war warfare in which all of a nation's resources, including civilians at home as well as soldiers in the field, are mobilized for the war effort.

trade union an association of workers in the same trade, formed to help members secure better wages, benefits, and working conditions.

transubstantiation a doctrine of the Roman Catholic church that teaches that during the eucharist the substance of the bread and wine is miraculously transformed into the body and blood of Jesus.

trench warfare warfare in which the opposing forces attack and counterattack from a relatively permanent system of trenches protected by barbed wire; characteristic of World War I.

trivium* and *quadrivium together formed the seven liberal arts that were the basis of medieval and early modern education. Grammar, rhetoric, and dialectic or logic made up the *trivium;* arithmetic, geometry, astronomy, and music made up the *quadrivium*.

Truman Doctrine the doctrine, enunciated by Harry Truman in 1947, that the United States would provide economic aid to countries that said they were threatened by Communist expansion.

tyrant/tyranny in an ancient Greek *polis* (or an Italian city-state during the Renaissance), a ruler who came to power in an unconstitutional way and ruled without being subject to the law.

uncertainty principle a principle in quantum mechanics, posited by Heisenberg, that holds that one cannot determine the path of an electron because the very act of observing the electron would affect its location.

unconditional surrender complete, unqualified surrender of a belligerent nation.

utopian socialists intellectuals and theorists in the early nineteenth century who favored equality in social and economic conditions and wished to replace private property and competition with collective ownership and cooperation; deemed impractical and "utopian" by later socialists.

vassal a person granted a fief, or landed estate, in exchange for providing military services to the lord and fulfilling certain other obligations such as appearing at the lord's court when summoned and making a payment on the knighting of the lord's eldest son.

vernacular the everyday language of a region, as distinguished from a language used for special purposes. For example, in medieval Paris, French was the vernacular, but Latin was used for academic writing and for classes at the University of Paris.

volkish thought the belief that German culture is superior and that the German people have a universal mission to save Western civilization from inferior races.

war communism Lenin's policy of nationalizing industrial and other facilities and requisitioning the peasants' produce during the civil war in Russia.

War Guilt Clause the clause in the Treaty of Versailles that declared that Germany (and Austria) were responsible for starting World War I and ordered Germany to pay reparations for the damage the Allies had suffered as a result of the war.

Warsaw Pact a military alliance, formed in 1955, in which Albania, Bulgaria, Czechoslovakia, East Germany, Hungary, Poland, Romania, and the Soviet Union agreed to provide mutual assistance. Dissolved in 1991, some former members joined NATO.

welfare state a social/political system in which the government assumes the primary responsibility for the social welfare of its citizens by providing such things as social security, unemployment benefits, and health care.

wergeld "money for a man." In early Germanic law, a person's value in monetary terms, which was paid by a wrongdoer to the family of the person who had been injured or killed.

world-machine Newton's conception of the universe as one huge, regulated, and uniform machine that operated according to natural laws in absolute time, space, and motion.

zaibatsu powerful business cartels formed in Japan during the Meiji era and outlawed following World War II.

ziggurat a massive stepped tower upon which a temple dedicated to the chief god or goddess of a Sumerian city was built.

Zionism an international movement that called for the establishment of a Jewish state or a refuge for Jews in Palestine.

Zoroastrianism a religion founded by the Persian Zoroaster in the seventh century B.C.; characterized by worship of a supreme god Ahuramazda who represents the good against the evil spirit, identified as Ahriman.

Pronunciation Guide

Abbasid AB-uh-sid *or* a-BA-sid
Adenauer, Konrad AD-n'our-er
Aeschylus ESS-kuh-lus
Afrikaners a-fri-KAH-ners
Agincourt AJ-in-kor
Ahuramazda ah-HOOR-ah-MAHZ-duh
Akhenaton ah-kuh-NAH-tun
Akkadian a-KAY-dee-un
Albigensian al-bi-GEN-see-un
Albuquerque, Afonso de AL-buh-kur-kee, ah-FON-soh d'
Allah AH-luh *or* AL-uh
al-Ma'mun al-MAH-moon
al-Rahman, Abd al-RAH-mun, abd
Amenhotep ah-mun-HOE-tep
Andropov, Yuri an-DROP-ov, YOOR-ee
Antigonid an-TIG-oh-nid
apella a-PELL-uh
Aquinas, Thomas uh-KWIGH-nus
aratrum a-RA-trum
Archimedes are-kuh-MEE-deez
Argonautica ARE-guh-NOT-i-kuh
Aristotle ar-i-STAH-tul
Arsinoë ar-SIN-oh-ee
Arthasastra ar-tuh-SAHS-tra
Ashkenazic ash-kuh-NAH-zic
Ashurnasirpal ah-shoor-NAH-suh-pul
asiento a-SEE-en-toh
assignat as-seen-YAH *or* AS-sig-nat
Assyrians uh-SEER-ee-uns
Attalid AT-a-lid
audiencias ah-DEE-en-CEE-ahs
Augustine AW-gus-STEEN
Auschwitz-Birkenau OUSH-vitz-BUR-kuh-now
Ausgleich OUS-glike
Avicenna av-i-SEN-uh
Avignon ah-veen-YONE
Axum OX-oom
Bach, Johann Sebastian BAHK, yoh-HAHN suh-BASS-chen
Barbarossa bar-buh-ROH-suh
Bastille ba-STEEL
Beauvoir, Simone de boh-VWAH, see-MOAN duh
Bebel, August BAY-bul
Beguines bi-GEENS
Belisarius bell-i-SAR-ee-us
benefice BEN-uh-fiss
Bernini, Gian Lorenzo bur-NEE-nee, JAHN loh-RENT-soh
Bhagavadgita bog-ah-vahd-GEE-ta
Blitzkrieg BLITZ-kreeg
Boccaccio, Giovanni boh-KAH-chee-oh, joe-VAHN-nee
Boer BOHR
Boleyn, Anne BUH-lin
Bólívar, Simón BOH-luh-VAR, see-MOAN
Bologna buh-LOHN-yuh
Boticelli, Sandro BOT-i-CHELL-ee, SAHN-droh
Boulanger, Georges boo-lahn-ZHAY, ZHORZH
Bracciolini, Poggio braht-choh-LEE-nee, POD-joh
Brahe, Tycho BRAH, TIE-koh
Bramante, Donato brah-MAHN-tee, doe-NAY-toe
Brandt, Willy BRAHNT, VIL-ee
Brétigny bray-tee-NYEE
Brezhnev, Leonid BREZH-nef, lyi-on-YEET
Briand, Aristide bree-AHN, a-ree-STEED
Brunelleschi, Filippo BROO-nuh-LES-kee, fee-LEEP-poe
Brüning, Heinrich BROO-ning, HINE-rik
Bulganin, Nilolai bul-GAN-in, nyik-uh-LYE
Bund deutscher Mädel BUNT DOICHer MAIR-del
Burschenschaften BOOR-shen-shaft-un
Buthelezi, Mangosuthu boo-teh-LAY-zee, man-go-SOO-tu
Calais ka-LAY
caliph/caliphate KAY-lif/KAY-li-FATE
Cambyses kam-BY-seez
Camus, Albert kuh-MOO, al-BEAR
Canaanites KAY-nuh-nites
Cao Cao tsau tsau
Capet/Capetian ka-PAY *or* KAY-put/kuh-PEE-shun
Caraffa, Gian Pietro kah-RAH-fuh, JAHN PYEE-troh
carbonari kar-buh-NAH-ree
Carolingian kar-oh-LIN-jun
carruca ca-ruh-kuh
Carthage/Carthaginian KAR-thij/KAR-thuh-JIN-ee-un
Castlereagh, Viscount KAS-ul-RAY
Catharism KA-tha-ri-zem
Catullus ka-TULL-us
Cavendish, Margaret KAV-un-dish
Cavour, Camillo di ka-VOOR, kah-MIL-oh
Cèzanne, Paul say-ZAN
Chaeronea ker-oh-NEE-uh
Chaldean kal-DEE-un
chanson de geste shahn-SAWN duh ZHEST
Charlemagne SHAR-luh-mane
Chernenko, Konstantin cher-NYEN-koh, kon-stun-TEEN
Chiang Kai-Shek CHANG KIGH-shek
Chrétien de Troyes KRAY-tee-ahn duh TRWAH
Cicero SIS-uh-roh

ciompi CHOM-pee
Cistercians si-STIR-shuns
Cixi TSE-she
Cleisthenes KLISE-thuh-neez
Clemenceau, Georges klem-un-SOH, ZHORZH
Clovis KLOH-vis
colonus kuh-LOH-nus
Columbanus kol-um-BAHN-us
comitia centuriata kuh-MISH-ee-uh sen-TYOO-ree-ah-tuh
concilium plebis con-CIL-ee-um PLE-bis
Concordat of Worms kon-KOR-dat of WURMZ *or* VAWRMZ
condottieri kon-dah-TEE-AIR-ee
consul KON-sul
conversos kon-VAIR-sohs
Copernicus, Nicolaus koh-PURR-nuh-kus, nee-koh-LAH-us
Corinth KOR-inth
corregidores kor-REG-uh-DOR-ays
Cortés, Hernán kor-TEZ, er-NAHN
Courbet, Gustave koor-BAY, guh-STAWV
Crassus KRASS-us
Crécy kray-SEE
Crédit Mobilier kred-EE mohb-eel-YAY
d'Este, Isabella ES-tay
d'Holbach, Paul awl-BAHK
Daimyo die-AIM-yo
Dao De Jing dow duh JING
Darius duh-RYE-us
dauphin DAW-fin
de Gaulle, Charles duh GOLL, SHARL
Debussy, Claude de-BYOO-see, KLODE
Decameron di-KAM-uh-run
Delacroix, Eugène del-uh-KWAW, yoo-ZHAHN
Deng Xiaoping DUNG shee-ow-ping
Descartes, René day-KART, ruh-NAY
Dias, Bartholomeu DEE-us, bar-too-loo-MAY
Diaspora die-AS-pur-uh
Diderot, Denis DEE-duh-roh, duh-NEE
Diem, Ngo Dinh dzee-EM, NGOH Den
Diocletian die-uh-KLEE-shun
Domitian doh-MISH-un
Dorians DOR-ee-uns
Douhet, Giulio doo-EE, JOOL-yoh
Duma DOO-muh
Dürer, Albrecht DOO-er, AWL-brekt
ecclesia eh-KLEE-zee-uh
encomienda en-koh-mee-EN-dah
Engels, Friedrich ENG-ulz, FREE-drik
Entente Cordiale ahn-TAHNT kor-DYALL
Epaminondas i-PAM-uh-NAHN-dus
ephor EF-or
Epicurus/Epicureanism EP-i-KYOOR-us/EP-i-kyoo-REE-uh-ni-zem
Erasmus, Desiderius i-RAZZ-mus, des-i-DIR-ee-us
eremitical air-uh-MITT-i-cul
Erhard, Ludwig AIR-hart
Etruscan i-TRUSS-kuhn
Euripides yoo-RIP-i-deez
exchequer EX-chek-ur
Fa Xian fa SHIEN
fasces FASS-eez
Fascio di Combattimento FASH-ee-oh di com-BATT-ee-men-toh
Fatimid FAT-i-mid
Ficino, Marsilio fee-CHEE-noh, mar-SIL-ee-oh
Flaubert, Gustave floh-BEAR, guh-STAWV
Fleury, Cardinal floe-REE
Fontainebleau FAWN-tin-BLOW
Fontenelle, Bernard de fawnt-NELL, BER-nar duh
Frequens FREE-kwens
Friedan, Betty fri-DAN
Frimaire free-MARE
Fronde FROND
Führerprinzip FYOOR-ur-PRIN-tseep
gabelle gah-BELL
Garibaldi, Giuseppe gar-uh-BAWL-dee, joo-ZEP-pay
Gaugamela gaw-guh-MEE-luh
Gentileschi, Artemisia jen-tul-ESS-kee, are-tee-MISS-ee-uh
gerousia juh-ROO-see-uh
Gierek, Edward GYER-ek
Gilgamesh GILL-guh-mesh
glasnost GLAZ-nohst
Gleichschaltung GLIKE-shalt-ung
Gomulka, Wladyslaw goh-MOOL-kuh, vla-DIS-lawf
gonfaloniere gon-fa-loh-NEE-ree
Gorbachev, Mikhail GOR-buh-chof, meek-HALE
grandi GRAHN-dee
Gropius, Walter GROH-pee-us, VAHL-ter
Grossdeutsch gross-DOICH
Habsburg HAPS-burg
Hadrian HAY-dree-un
Hagia Sophia HAG-ee-uh soh-FEE-uh
hajj HAJ
Hammurabi ham-uh-RAH-bee
Hannibal HAN-uh-bul
Harappan har-RAP-an
Hatshepsut hat-SHEP-soot
Haussmann, Baron HOUS-mun
Havel, Vaclav HAH-vuhl, VAHT-slaf
Haydn, Franz Joseph HIDE-n, FRAHNTS
hegemon HEJ-uh-mon
Hellenistic hell-uh-NIS-tik
helots HELL-uts
hermandades er-mahn-DAHDH-ays
Herodotus hi-ROD-oh-tus
Herzen, Alexander HER-tsun

Herzl, Theodor HERT-sul, TAY-oh-dor
Heydrich, Reinhard HIGH-drik, RINE-hart
hieroglyph HIGH-ur-oh-glif
Hildegard of Bingen HILL-duh-gard of BING-en
Hitler Jugend JOO-gunt
Ho Chi Minh HOE CHEE MIN
Höch, Hannah HOKH
Hohenstaufen HOE-un-SHTAU-fun
Hohenzollern HOE-un-ZAHL-lurn
hoplites HOP-lites
Horace HOR-us
Huguenots HYOO-guh-nots
Husak, Gustav HOO-sahk, guh-STAHV
Ibn Sina ib-en SEE-nuh
Ieyasu, Tokugawa ee-eye-AY-soo, toe-koo-GAH-wah
Ignatius of Loyola ig-NAY-shus of loi-OH-luh
Il Duce eel DOO-chay
imperator im-puh-RAH-tor
imperium im-PIER-ee-um
intendant in-TEN-duhnt
Isis EYE-sis
Issus ISS-us
ius gentium YOOS GEN-tee-um
Jacobin JAK-uh-bin
Jacquerie zhah-KREE
Jagiello yah-GYELL-oh
Jahn, Friedrich Ludwig YAHN, FREE-drik
Jaruzelski, Wojciech yahr-uh-ZEL-skee, VOI-chek
Jaurés, Jean zhaw-RESS, ZHAHN
Jiang Qing JIANG CHING
jihad ji-HAHD
Jinnah, Mohammed Ali JEE-nah, moe-HA-mud a-LEE
Judaea joo-DEE-uh
Judas Maccabaeus JOO-dus mak-uh-BEE-us
Junkers YOONG-kers
Justinian juh-STIN-ee-un
Juvenal JOO-vuh-nul
Ka'aba stone KAH-BAH
Kadar, Janos KAY-dahr, YAHN-us
Kadinsky, Vasily kan-DIN-skee, vus-YEEL-yee
Kangxi KANG-she
Keiretsu business arrangement kai-RET-su
Kerensky, Alexander kuh-REN-skee
Keynes, John Maynard KAYNZ
Khan, Khubilai KHAN, KOO-bil-eye
Khmer Rouge ka-MEHR roozh
Khoisan KOY-SAN
Khrushchev, Nikita KROOSH-chef, nuh-KEE-tuh
Kleindeutsch kline-DOICH
Koguryo ko-GOOR-yo
Kohl, Helmut KOLE, HELL-mut
koiné koi-NAY
Kollantai, Alexandra kawl-un-TIE
kouros KOO-raws
Kraft durch Freude CRAFT durch FROI-duh
Kristallnacht KRIS-tal-NAHCHT
Kshatriya kuh-SHOT-ria
Kuchuk-Kainarji koo-CHOOK-kigh-NAR-jee
kulaks koo-LAKS
kulturkampf kool-TOOR-kahmf
laissez-faire les-ay-FAIR
Lamarck, Jean-Baptiste luh-MAHRK, ZHAHN-buh-TEEST
Lao Tzu LAUW DZU
latifundia lat-uh-FUN-dee-uh
Latium LAY-shee-um
Lebensraum LAY-benz-roum
Lee Kuan-yew LEE KWAN YEW
Lespinasse, Julie de les-peen-AHS
Lévesque, René luh-VEK, ruh-NAY
Leyster, Judith LE-ster
Liebenfels, Lanz von LEE-bun-felz, LAHNZ
Liebknecht LEEP-knekt
Liszt, Franz LIST, FRAHNZ
Livy LIV-ee
Luddites LUD-ites
Ludendorff, Erich LOOD-un-dorf
Luftwaffe LUFT-vaf-uh
Machiavelli, Niccolò mak-ee-uh-VELL-ee, nee-koh-LOH
Magyars MAG-yars
Mahabharata MA-HA-bah-rah-tah
Maistre, Joseph de MES-truh
Majapahit mah-ja-PAH-heet
Malleus Maleficarum mall-EE-us mal-uh-FIK-ar-um
Manetho MAN-uh-THOH
Mao Zedong mau zee-DONG
Marie Antoinette muh-REE an-twuh-NET
Marius MAR-ee-us
Mazarin maz-uh-RAN
Mbecki, Thabo mu-BEK-ee, TYE-bo
Meiji MAY-jee
Mein Kampf mine KAHMF
Menander me-NAN-der
Mendeleyev, Dmitri men-duh-LAY-ef, di-MEE-tri
Meroë mer-OH-ee
Mesopotamia mess-oh-poh-TAME-ee-uh
Metternich, Klemens von MET-er-nik, KLAY-mens
Michelangelo my-kell-AN-juh-loh
Mieszko MYESH-koh
Millet, Jean-François mi-LAY, ZHAHN-FRAN-swah
missi dominici MISS-ee doe-MIN-ee-chee
Moche MO-chay
Moctezuma mahk-tuh-ZOO-muh
Moldavia mahl-DAY-vee-uh
Molière, Jean-Baptiste mole-YAIR, ZHAHN-buh-TEEST

Monet, Claude moh-NAY, KLODE
Montefeltro, Federigo da mahn-tuh-FELL-troh, fay-day-REE-goh dah
Montesquieu MONT-ess-skyoo
Montessori, Maria mon-ti-SOR-ee
Morisot, Berthe mor-ee-ZOH, BERT
Muawiyah moo-AH-wee-yah
Mughal MOO-gahl
Muhammad moe-HA-mud
Muslim MUZ-lum
Mutsuhito moo-tsoo-HEE-toe
Mycenaean my-suh-NEE-un
Nagy, Imry NAHJD, IM-re
Nebuchadnezzar neb-uh-kad-NWZZ-ar
Nehru, Jawaharlal NAY-roo, jah-WAH-har-lahl
Nero NEE-roh
Neumann, Balthasar NOI-mahn, BAHL-tah-zar
Nevsky, Alexander NEW-skee
Ngo Dinh Diem NGOH din dee-EM
Ngugi Wa Thiong'o en-GU-ji WA THIE-ong-oh
Nietzsche, Friedrich NEE-chuh, FREE-drik
Nimwegen NIM-vay-gun
Ninhursaga nin-HUR-sah-guh
Nkrumah, Kwame en-KRU-may, KWA-may
Novotny, Antonin noh-VOT-nee, AN-ton-yeen
Nyerere, Julius nyay-RARE-ee
Nystadt nee-STAHD
Octavian ok-TAY-vee-un
optimates opp-tuh-MAH-tays
Osiris oh-SIGH-ris
Ovid OV-id
Pahlavi dynasty pah-LAH-vee
Palenque pah-LENG-kay
Paleologus pay-lee-OHL-uh-gus
papal curia PAY-pul KOOR-ee-uh
Parlement par-luh-MAHN
Pascal, Blaise pass-KAL, BLEZ
paterfamilias pay-ter-fuh-MILL-ee-us
Pentateuch PEN-tuh-tuke
Pepin PEP-in
perestroika pair-ess-TROY-kuh
Pergamum PURR-guh-mum
Pericles PER-i-kleez
perioeci per-ee-EE-sie
Pétain, Henri pay-TAN, AHN-ree
Petrarch PE-trark
philosophe fee-luh-ZAWF
Phoenicians fi-NISH-uns
Picasso, Pablo pi-KAW-soh
Pisistratus pi-SIS-truh-tus
Pissaro, Camille pi-SARR-oh, kah-MEEYL
Pizarro, Francesco pi-ZARR-oh, frahn-CHASE-koh
Planck, Max PLAHNK
Plantagenet plan-TA-juh-net
Plato PLAY-toe
Poincaré, Raymond pwan-kah-RAY, re-MOAN
polis POE-lis
politiques puh-lee-TEEKS
Polybius poe-LIB-ee-us
Pompey POM-pee
pontifex maximus PON-ti-feks MAK-suh-mus
populares POP-yoo-lar-ays
populo grasso POP-uh-loh GRAH-soh
Poussin, Nicholas poo-SAN, NEE-kaw-lah
Praecepter Germaniae PREE-sep-ter ger-MAN-ee-eye
praetor PREE-ter
princeps PRIN-seps
procurator PROK-yuh-ray-ter
Ptolemy/Ptolemaic TOL-uh-mee/TOL-uh-MAY-ik
Punic PYOO-nik
Pyrrhus/Pyrrhic PIR-us/PIR-ik
Qin Shi Huangdi chin SHE hwang-DEE
Qing dynasty CHING
quaestors KWES-ters
Quetzelcoatl ket-SAHL-koh-AHT-ul
Quipu KEE-poo
Quran kuh-RAN
Racine, Jean-Baptiste ra-SEEN, ZHAHN-buh-TEEST
Rameses RAM-i-seez
Raphael RAFF-ee-ul
Rasputin rass-PYOO-tin
Realpolitik ray-AHL-poe-li-teek
Reichsrat RIKES-raht
Rembrandt van Rijn REM-brant vahn RINE
Ricci, Matteo REECH-ee, mah-TAY-oh
Richelieu RISH-uh-loo
Rilke, Rainer Maria RILL-kuh, RYE-ner
risorgimento ree-SOR-jee-men-toe
Robespierre, Maximilien ROHBZ-pee-air, mak-SEE-meel-yahn
Rococo ro-KOH-koh
Rousseau, Jean-Jacques roo-SOH ZHAHN-ZHAHK
Sacrosancta sak-roh-SANK-tuh
Sakharov, Andrei SAH-kuh-rof, ahn-DRAY
Saladin SAL-uh-din
Sallust SALL-ust
Samnites SAM-nites
Sartre, Jean-Paul SAR-truh, ZHAHN-PAUL
satrap/satrapy SAY-trap/SAY-truh-pee
Satyricon SAY-tir-ee-kon
Schleswig-Holstein SCHLES-vig-HOLE-stine
Schmidt, Helmut SHMIT, HELL-mut
Schönberg, Arnold SHURN-burg, ARR-nawlt
Schutzmannschaft SHOOTS-mun-shaft
Scipio Aemilianus SI-pee-oh i-mill-ee-AY-nus
Scipio Africanus SI-pee-oh af-ri-KAY-nus

scriptoria skrip-TOR-ee-uh
Sejm SAME
Seleucus/Seleucid si-LOO-kus/si-LOO-sid
Seljuk Turks SELL-juke
Seneca SEN-i-kuh
Sephardic suh-FAR-dik
Septimius Severus sep-TIM-ee-us se-VIR-us
Sforza SFORT-zuh
Shi'ite SHE-ite
Shotoku Taishi show-TOE-koo tie-ISH-ee
Siddhartha Gautama sid-AR-tha guh-TAW-mah
Sieveking, Amalie SEEVE-king
signoria seen-YOOR-ee-uh
Socrates SOK-ruh-teez
Solon SOH-lun
Solzhenitsyn, Alexander SOLE-zhuh-NEET-sin
Sophocles SOF-uh-kleez
Spartacus SPAR-tuh-kus
Speer, Albert SHPIER
squadristi sqah-DREES-tee
Srivijaya sree-vee-JAH-ya
Stoicism STOH-i-siz-um
Stravinsky, Igor struh-VIN-skee, EE-gor
Stresemann, Gustav SHTRAY-zuh-mahn, GUS-tahf
Suleyman I the Magnificent soo-lee-MAHN
Sumerian soo-MER-ee-un
Suttner, Bertha von ZOOT-ner
Taafe, Edward von TAH-fuh
Tacitus TASS-i-tus
taille TAH-yuh *or* TIE
Tang Taizong TANG TYE-zawng
Tanzania tan-zah-NEE-ah
Tenochtitlán tay-NAWCH-teet-LAHN
Teotihuacán TAY-oh-tee-WAH-kahn
Tertullian tur-TULL-yun
Theocritus thee-OCK-ri-tus
Thermidor ter-mee-DOR
Thermopylae thur-MOP-uh-lee
Thucydides thoo-SID-uh-deez
Thutmosis thoot-MOH-sus
Tiberius tie-BIR-ee-us
Tito TEE-toh
Tlaxcala tlah-SKAHL-uh
Torah TOR-uh
Tordesillas tor-duh-SEE-yus
Trajan TRAY-jun
Trevithick, Richard TREV-uh-thik
Tyche TIE-kee
Uighur yu-EE-gur
Ulbricht, Walter UL-brikt, VAHL-ter
Umayyads oo-MY-ads
Unam Sanctam OON-ahm SANK-tahm
universitas yoo-ni-VER-si-tahs
Valois VAL-wah
van Eyck, Jan van IKE
van Gogh, Vincent van GOE
Vega, Lope de VAY-guh, LOH-pay day
Venetia vuh-NEE-shee-uh
Vesalius, Andreas vi-SAY-lee-us, ahn-DRAY-us
Vespucci, Amerigo ves-POO-chee, ahm-ay-REE-goe
Vierzenheiligen feer-tsun-HILE-i-gun
Virchow, Rudolf FEER-koh, roo-DOLF
Virgil VUR-jul
Volkschulen FOLK-shool-un
Voltaire vole-TAIR
von Bora, Katherina BOR-uh
Walesa, Lech va-WENZ-uh, LEK
Wallachia wah-lay-KEE-uh
Watteau, Antoine wah-TOE, AHN-twahn
Weizsäcker, Richard von VITS-zek-er, RIK-art
wergeld wur-GELD
Winkelmann, Maria VING-kul-mun
Xavier, Francis ZAY-vee-ur
Xerxes ZURK-seez
Xhosa KOH-suh
Xinjiang shin-JI-ang
Xiongnu (Hsiung-nu) she-ONG-noo
Yahweh YAH-wah
Yeats, William Butler YATES
Yeltsin, Boris YELT-sun
Yi Song-gye YEE sohn-GEE
yishuv YISH-uv
zemstvos ZEMPST-voh
Zeno ZEE-noh
Zhang Xueliang JANG shwee-lee-ONG
Zhou JOE
Zhu Yuanzhang jew whan-JANG
ziggurat ZIG-guh-rat
Zimbabwe zim-BAH-bway
Zola, Emile ZOH-luh, ay-MEEL
zollverein TSOL-fuh-rine
Zoroaster ZOR-oh-as-ter

Document Credits

Continued from page xix

THE DAOIST ANSWER TO CONFUCIANISM 75

Reprinted with the permission of Macmillan College Publishing Company from *The Way of Lao Tzu (Tao-Te Ching)*, by Wing-Tsit Chan, trans. Copyright © 1963 by Macmillan College Publishing Company, Inc.

THE ART OF WAR 76

From *Sun Tzu: The Art of War*, Ralph D. Sawyer (Boulder: Westview Press, 1994), pp. 177–179.

MEMORANDUM ON THE BURNING OF BOOKS 79

Excerpt from *Sources of Chinese Tradition*, by William Theodore De Bary. Copyright © 1960 by Columbia University Press, New York. Reprinted with permission of the publisher.

LOVE SPURNED IN ANCIENT CHINA 90

From *A History of Chinese Literature*, by Herbert A. Giles (New York: Grove Press 1923), pp. 15–16.

CHAPTER 4

HOMER'S IDEAL OF EXCELLENCE 99

From *The Iliad*, by Homer, translated by E. V. Rieu (Penguin Classics, 1950) copyright © the Estate of R. V. Rieu, 1950. Reproduced by permission of Penguin Books, Ltd.

THE LYCURGAN REFORMS 103

From *Herodotus, The Lives of the Noble Grecians and Romans*, translated by John Dryden, New York: Modern Library. Reprinted with permission of Random House, Inc.

ATHENIAN DEMOCRACY: THE FUNERAL ORATION OF PERICLES 107

From *The History of the Peloponnesian War*, by Thucydides, translated by Rex Warner (Penguin Classics, 1954) copyright © Rex Warner, 1954. Reproduced by permission of Penguin Books Ltd.

ATHENIAN COMEDY: SEX AS AN ANTIWAR INSTRUMENT 110

Excerpt from "Lysistrata" in *Aristophanes: Four Comedies*, copyright 1954 by Harcourt Brace & Company and renewed 1982 by Cornelia Fitts, Daniel H. Fitts and Deborah W. Fitts, reprinted by permission of Harcourt, Brace & Company.

HOUSEHOLD MANAGEMENT AND THE ROLE OF THE ATHENIAN WIFE 115

From *Xenophon: Memorabilia and Oeconomicus*, by E. C. Marchant, copyright 1923 by the Loeb Classical Library. Used with permission of Harvard University Press.

THE DESTRUCTION OF THE PERSIAN PALACE AT PERSEPOLIS 117

Arrian, The Life of Alexander the Great: From *The Life of Alexander the Great by Arrian*, translated by Aubrey de Sélincourt (Penguin Classics, 1958) copyright © Aubrey de Sélincourt, 1958. Reproduced by permission of Penguin Books Ltd. Diodorus of Sicily, *Library of History*: Reprinted by permission of the publishers and the Loeb Classical Library from *Library of History*, Diodorus Siculus, trans. by Bradford Welles, Cambridge, Mass.: Harvard University Press, 1963.

A NEW AUTONOMY FOR WOMEN 120

From Roger S. Bagnall and Peter Derow, *Greek Historical Documents: The Hellenistic Period* (Chico, California: The Scholars Press for the Society of Biblical Literature, 1981), pp. 202, 235.

THE STOIC IDEAL OF HARMONY WITH GOD 123

Reprinted with permission of the publisher from *Hellenistic Philosophy*, A. A. Long. Copyright © 1986 by A. A. Long, Berkeley, California: University of California Press.

CHAPTER 5

CINCINNATUS SAVES ROME: A ROMAN MORALITY TALE 131

From *The Early History of Rome by Livy* translated by Aubrey de Sélincourt (Penguin Classics, 1960) copyright © the Estate of Aubrey de Sélincourt, 1960. Reproduced by permission of Penguin Books, Ltd.

THE DESTRUCTION OF CARTHAGE 135

Reprinted by permission of the publishers and the Loeb Classical Library from *Appian: Roman History*, vol. I, trans. by Horace White, Cambridge, Mass.: Harvard University Press, 1912.

THE ASSASSINATION OF JULIUS CAESAR 139

From *Plutarch: The Lives of the Noble Grecians and Romans*, trans. by John Dryden and rev. by Arthur Clough. Reprinted with permission of the Modern Library, Random House.

OVID AND THE ART OF LOVE 145

From *The Love Books of Ovid*, by J. Lewis May, copyright © 1930 by Rarity Press.

CATO THE ELDER ON WOMEN 147

Reprinted by permission of the publishers and the Loeb Classical Library from *Livy: History of Rome*, Book 34, vol. II–IV, trans. by Evan T. Sage, Cambridge, Mass.: Harvard University Press, 1935.

THE ROMAN FEAR OF SLAVES 149

Tacitus, The Annals of Imperial Rome: From *The Annals of Imperial Rome*, by Tacitus, translated by Michael Grant (Penguin Classics, Second revised edition 1971) copyright © Michael Grant, Productions Ltd., 1956, 1959, 1971. Reproduced by permission of Penguin Books, Ltd. Pliny the Younger to Acilius: From *The Letters of the Younger Pliny*, translated by Betty Radice (Penguin Classics, 1963) copyright © Betty Radice, 1963. Reproduced by permission of Penguin Books Ltd.

THE PUBLIC BATHS OF THE ROMAN EMPIRE 150

Excerpt from *Roman Civilization*, Vol. II by Napthali Lewis and Meyer Reinhold. Copyright © 1955 Columbia University Press, New York. Reprinted with permission of the publisher.

CHRISTIAN IDEALS: THE SERMON ON THE MOUNT 153

Reprinted from the Holy Bible, New International Version.

CHAPTER 6

THE CREATION OF THE WORLD: A MAYAN VIEW 173

From *Popul-Vuh: The Sacred Book of the Ancient Quiché Maya*, translated by Adrián Recinos. Copyright © 1950 by the University of Oklahoma Press.

A SAMPLE OF MAYAN WRITING 174

From Michael Coe, et al., *Atlas of Ancient America* (New York: Facts on File, 1986).

MARKETS AND MERCHANDISE IN AZTEC MEXICO 178

From *The Conquest of New Spain*, by Bernal Diaz. Copyright © 1975. (Harmondsworth: Penguin), pp. 232–233.

AZTEC RELIGION THROUGH SPANISH EYES 180

Excerpt from Diego Duran, *The Aztecs: The History of the Indies of New Spain*, Doris Heyden and Fernando Horcasitas, trans. (New York: Orion Press, 1964), pp. 120–121.

A DESCRIPTION OF TENOCHTITLAN 181

From *The Conquest of New Spain*, by Bernal Diaz. Copyright © 1975. (Harmondsworth: Penguin), pp. 234–235.

MOCTEZUMA'S GREETING TO HERNAN CORTES 182

From *Letters from Mexico*, by Hernan Cortes, Anthony Pagden, trans. Copyright © 1986 by Yale University Press. Used with permission.

VIRGINS WITH RED CHEEKS 186

From *Letter to a King* by Guaman Poma de Ayala. Translated and edited by Christopher Dilke. Published by E. P. Dutton, New York, 1978.

AN INCAN AIDE-MEMOIRE 187

Reprinted from *Royal Commentaries of the Incas and General History of Peru, Part One*, by Garcilaso de la Vega, translated by Harold V. Livermore. Copyright © 1966. By permission of the University of Texas Press.

CHAPTER 7

THE KORAN AND THE SPREAD OF THE MUSLIM FAITH 196

From *The Koran*, translated by N J Dawood (Penguin Classics, Fifth revised edition 1990) copyright © N J Dawood, 1956, 1959, 1966, 1968, 1974, 1990. Reproduced by permission of Penguin Books Ltd.

A PILGRIMAGE TO MECCA 197

Excerpt from *The Travels of Ibn Jubayr*, J. R. C. Broadhurst, trans. (London: Jonathan Cape, Ltd., 1952). Used with permission of the estate of J. R. C. Broadhurst and Jonathan Cape, Publishers.

THE MURDER OF JA'FAR AL-BARMAKI 201

Excerpt from *The Meadows of Gold: The Abbasids*, by Mas'udi (London: Kegan Paul International, 1989), pp. 115–117.

THE CRUSADES IN MUSLIM EYES 203

Excerpt from *An Arab-Syrian Gentleman and Warrior in the Period of the Crusades*, Philip K. Hitti. Copyright 1929 by Philip K. Hitti.

A CONSUMER'S GUIDE TO THE IDEAL SLAVE 204

Excerpt from *A Mirror for Princes*, by Kai kaus Ibn Iskandar, translated by Reuben Levy (London, The Cresset Press, Ltd., 1951).

DRAW THEIR VEILS OVER THEIR BOSOMS 206

From *Women in World History*, Volume One, edited by Sarah Shaver Hughes and Brady Hughes, copyright 1965. Reprinted with the permission of the publisher, M. E. Sharpe.

LOVE FOR A CAMEL 207

Excerpt from *The Seven Odes*, translated by A. J. Arberry, copyright by George Allen & Unwin, Ltd.

BE THANKFUL FOR SMALL FAVORS 208

Reprinted by permission of The Putnam Publishing Group from *The Gulistan or Rose Garden of Sa'di*, by Edward Rehatsek. Copyright © 1964 by George Allen & Unwin Ltd.; Renewed © 1992 by George Allen & Unwin Ltd.

THE PASSIONS OF A SUFI MYSTIC 209

From *Persian Literature*, Ehsan Yarshatar, ed. 1988, © Columbia University Press, New York. Reprinted with permission of the publisher.

CHAPTER 8

THE CONQUEST OF KUSH 220

From *The Dawn of African History*, Roland Oliver, ed. (New York: Oxford University Press, 1968), p. 26.

BEYOND THE PILLARS OF HERCULES 223

Excerpt from *Beyond the Pillars of Hercules: The Classical World Seen Through the Eyes of Its Discoverers*, Rhys Carpenter (London: Tandem, 1966), p. 26.

THE COAST OF ZANJ 226

From G. S. P. Freeman-Grenville, *The East African Coast: Select Documents*, copyright © 1962 by Oxford University Press. Used with permission.

A DESCRIPTION OF A GHANAIAN CAPITAL 229

Adapted from translation quoted in J. S. Trimingham, *A History of Islam and West Africa*, copyright 1970 by Oxford University Press, p. 55.

WOMEN AND ISLAM IN NORTH AFRICA 233

From *The History and Description of Africa*, by Leo Africanus (New York: Burt Franklin), pp. 158–159. Used with permission of Ayer Company Publishers.

A CHINESE VIEW OF AFRICA 236

Excerpt from *Chau Ju-kua: His Work on the Chinese and Arab Trade in the Twelfth and Thirteenth Centuries*, entitled Chu-fan-chi, Friedrich Hirth and W. W. Rockhill, eds., copyright © 1966 by Paragon Reprint.

A WEST AFRICAN ORAL TRADITION 239

From *The Epic of Son-Jura: A West African Tradition*, text by Fa-Digi Sisòkò, notes, translation, and new introduction by John William Johnson (Bloomington: Indiana University Press, 1992), pp. 91–92.

CHAPTER 9

THE GOOD LIFE IN MEDIEVAL INDIA 242

"Fu-kwo-ki," in Hiuen Tsang, *Si-Yu Ki: Buddhist Records of the Western World*, translated by Samuel Beal (London: Routledge and Kegan Paul). Used with permission.

THE EDUCATION OF A BRAHMIN 245

"Fu-kwo-ki," in Hiuen Tsang, *Si-Yu Ki: Buddhist Records of the Western World*, translated by Samuel Beal (London: Routledge and Kegan Paul), pp. 79–80. Used with permission.

THE ISLAMIC CONQUEST OF INDIA 249

Excerpt from *A History of India: From the Earliest Times to the Present Day*, by Michael Edwardes (London: Thames and Hudson, 1961), p. 108. Reprinted with permission.

THE PRACTICE OF SATI 250

Excerpt from *The Book of Duarte Barbosa* (Nedeln, Liechtenstein: The Haklvy Society, 1967), II, p. 19.

UNTOUCHABLES IN SOUTH INDIA 251

Excerpt from *The Book of Duarte Barbosa* (Nedeln, Liechtenstein: The Haklvy Society, 1967), I, p. 215.

AN INDIAN LOVE POEM 256

Excerpt from *The Wonder That Was India*, by A. L. Basham (London: Sidgwick & Jackson, 1964), pp. 286–288.

THE KINGDOM OF ANGKOR 257

Excerpt from *Chau Ju-kua: His Work on the Chinese and Arab Trade in the Twelfth and Thirteenth Centuries*, entitled Chu-fan-chi, Friedrich Hirth and W. W. Rockhill, eds., copyright © 1966 by Paragon Reprint.

CHAPTER 10

A DAOIST CRITIQUE OF CONFUCIANISM 269

From *Chinese Civilization and Bureaucracy*, by Etienne Balasz. Copyright © 1964 by Yale University Press. Used with permission.

THE GOOD LIFE IN THE HIGH TANG 271

From *Perspectives on the T'ang*, by Arthur F. Wright and Denis Twitchett. Copyright © 1973 by Yale University Press. Used with permission.

THE SAINTLY MISS WU 278

From *The Inner Quarters: Marriage and the Lives of Chinese Women in the Sung Period*, Patricia Ebrey (Berkeley: University of California Press, 1993), pp. 197–198.

A LETTER TO THE POPE 280

From Prawdin, Michael, *The Mongol Empire: Its Rise and Legacy* (Free Press, 1961), pp. 280–281.

HOW KHUBILAI KHAN CHOOSES HIS CONSORTS 282

Excerpt from *The Travels of Marco Polo* (New York, Basic Books), pp. 121–122.

THE WAY OF THE GREAT BUDDHA 284

Excerpt from *Sources of Chinese Tradition*, by William Theodore De Bary. Copyright © 1960 by Columbia University Press, New York. Reprinted with permission of the publisher.

A CONFUCIAN WEDDING CEREMONY 285

Excerpted from *Confucianism and Family Rituals in Imperial China: A Social History of Writing About Rites*, "A Welcoming In Person," translated and edited by P. B. Ebrey. Copyright © Princeton University Press, 1991.

TWO TANG POETS 287

Reprinted from China's Imperial Past by Charles O. Hucker with the permission of the publishers, Stanford University Press. © 1975 by the Board of Trustees of the Leland Stanford Junior University.

A BATTLE TO THE DEATH 289

From *An Introduction to Chinese Literature*, by Liu Wu-chi. Copyright © 1966 by Indiana University Press. Used with permission of the publisher.

CHAPTER 11

THE EASTERN EXPEDITION OF EMPEROR JIMMU 296

Excerpt from *Sources of Japanese History*, David Lu, ed. (New York: McGraw-Hill, 1974), I, p. 7.

THE SEVENTEEN-ARTICLE CONSTITUTION 298

Excerpt from *Sources of Japanese History*, David Lu, ed. (New York: McGraw-Hill, 1974), I, p. 7.

JAPAN'S WARRIOR CLASS 300

Excerpt from *Sources of Japanese Tradition*, by William Theodore De Bary. Copyright © 1958 by Columbia University Press, New York. Reprinted with permission of the publisher.

LIFE IN THE LAND OF WA 303

Excerpt from *Sources of Japanese History*, David Lu, ed. (New York: McGraw-Hill, 1974), I, p. 7.

A SAMPLE OF LINKED VERSE 306

Excerpt from *The Cambridge History of Japan*, Vol. III, edited by Koza Yamamura, excerpt from "A Sample of Linked Verse" by H. Paul Varley, from p. 480. Copyright © 1990. Reprinted with the permission of Cambridge University Press.

THE SEDUCTION OF THE AKASHI LADY 307

From *The Tale of Genji*, by Muraski Shikibu, trans., E. Seidensticker. Copyright © 1976 by Edward G. Seidensticker. Reprinted by permission of Alfred A. Knopf, Inc.

THE FLOWER GARDEN SCRIPTURE 312

From *Sourcebook of Korean Civilization*, Vol. I, Peter H. Lee (ed.), (New York, 1993), pp. 200–201.

THE CHINESE CONQUEST OF VIETNAM 313

Excerpt from *Birth of Vietnam*, Keith W. Taylor. Copyright © 1983 The Regents of the University of California. Used with the permission of the publisher, University of California Press.

CHAPTER 12

GERMANIC CUSTOMARY LAW: THE ORDEAL 321

From *Translations and Reprints from the Original Sources of European History*, Series I, Vol. 4, No. 4, by A. C. Howland, copyright 1898 by Department of History, University of Pennsylvania Press.

THE ACHIEVEMENTS OF CHARLEMAGNE 323

From Einhard, *The Life of Charlemagne*, translated by S. E. Turner, pp. 50–54. Copyright © 1960 by The University of Michigan. Translated from the Monumenta Germaine. Used with permission.

MURDER IN THE CATHEDRAL 325

From *The Letters of John of Salisbury*, Vol. II, W. J. Millar and C. N. L. Brooke, eds. (Oxford: Oxford at the Clarendon Press), 1979. Reprinted with permission of Oxford University Press.

A MUSLIM'S DESCRIPTION OF THE RUS 334

From *The Vikings*, by Johannes Brønsted, translated by Kalle Skov (Penguin Books 1965) copyright © the Estate of Johannes Brønsted, 1960, 1965. Reproduced by permission of Penguin Books Ltd.

THE MEDIEVAL CITY 339

From *English Historical Documents III*, H. Rothwell, ed., 1975. Reprinted with permission of Methuen & Co. Ltd. and Eyre & Spottiswood as publishers.

A MIRACLE OF SAINT BERNARD 342

From R. H. C. Davis, *A History of Medieval Europe*, 2nd ed. (London: Longman Group) 1988, pp. 265–266. Reprinted by permission of Addison Wesley Longman Ltd.

A WESTERN VIEW OF THE BYZANTINE EMPIRE 350

From *Works of Liudprand of Cremona*, F. A. Wright, Copyright © 1930 by Routledge and Kegan Paul. Reprinted with permission of the publisher.

TREATMENT OF THE JEWS 353

From *The Jews of Angevin England*, Joseph Jacobs (London: David Nutt, 1893), p. 45.

CHAPTER 13

A MEDIEVAL HOLOCAUST: THE CREMATION OF THE STRASBOURG JEWS 360

Excerpt from *The Jew in the Medieval World*, by Jacob Marcus. Copyright © 1972 by Atheneum. Reprinted with permission of the Hebrew Union College Press.

A REVOLT OF FRENCH PEASANTS 361

From *Chronicles*, by Froissart, translated by Geoffrey Brereton (Penguin Classics, 1968) copyright © Geoffrey Brereton, 1968. Reproduced by permission of Penguin Books Ltd.

THE TRIAL OF JOAN OF ARC 364

From *The Trial of Joan of Arc*, translated by W. P. Barret, copyright 1932 by Gotham House, Inc.

THE LETTERS OF ISABELLA D'ESTE 370

From *The Bed and the Throne: The Life of Isabella d'Este*, George R. Marek. Copyright © 1976 by George R. Marek. Reprinted by permission of HarperCollins Publishers, Inc.

BONIFACE VIII'S DEFENSE OF PAPAL SUPREMACY 372

Extract taken from *Select Historical Documents of the Middle Ages*, by Ernest F. Henderson. Copyright © 1892 by George Bell & Sons.

MARRIAGE NEGOTIATIONS 377

Excerpt from *The Society of Renaissance Florence*, edited by Gene Brucker. Copyright © 1971 by Gene Brucker. Reprinted by permission of HarperCollins Publishers, Inc.

PICO DELLA MIRANDOLA AND THE DIGNITY OF MAN 380

From Ernst Cassirer, Paul Kristeller, and John Randall, Jr., *The Renaissance Philosophy of Man*. Copyright © 1948 by The University of Chicago Press. Reprinted with permission of the publisher.

DANTE'S VISION OF HELL 381

From Dante Alighieri, *The Divine Comedy*, translated by John Ciardi. Translation copyright 1954, 1957, 1959, 1960, 1961, 1965, 1967, 1970 by the Ciardi Family Publishing Trust. Reprinted by permission of W. W. Norton & Company, Inc.

CHAPTER 14

THE PORTUGUESE CONQUEST OF MALACCA 403

From *The World of Southeast Asia: Selected Historical Readings*, Harry J. Benda and John A. Larkin, eds. Copyright © 1967 by Harper & Row, Publishers. Used with permission of the author.

LAS CASAS AND THE SPANISH TREATMENT OF THE AMERICAN NATIVES 407

From *The Tears of the Indians*, Bartolome de Las Casas. Copyright © 1970 by The John Lilburne Company Publishers.

AN AZTEC'S LAMENT 408

Miguel Leon-Portilla (ed.), *Broken Spears: The Aztec Account of the Conquest of Mexico* (Boston: Beacon Press, 1992), p. 149.

KING OF SONGHAI 412

From *The Epic of Askia Mohammed*, by Thomas Hale, Indiana University Press, 1996, pp. 22–26.

A SLAVE MARKET IN AFRICA 415

From *The Great Travelers*, vol. I, Milton Rugoff, ed. Copyright © 1960 by Simon & Schuster. Used by permission of Milton Rugoff.

AN EXCHANGE OF ROYAL CORRESPONDENCE 419

From *The World of Southeast Asia: Selected Historical Readings*, Harry J. Benda and John A. Larkin, eds. Copyright © 1967 by Harper & Row, Publishers. Used with permission of the author.

THE TIMELY END OF SULTAN ZAINAL-'ABIDIN 421

From *The World of Southeast Asia: Selected Historical Readings*, Harry J. Benda and John A. Larkin, eds. Copyright © 1967 by Harper & Row, Publishers. Used with permission of the author.

CHAPTER 15

LUTHER AND THE NINETY-FIVE THESES 429

Copyright © 1970 by E. G. Rupp and Benjamin Drewery. From *Martin Luther*, by E. G. Rupp and Benjamin Drewery. Reprinted with permission of St. Martin's Press, Incorporated.

A REFORMATION DEBATE: THE MARBURG COLLOQUY 432

From *Great Debates of the Reformation* by Donald J. Ziegler, editor. Copyright © 1969 by Random House, Inc. Reprinted by permission of Random House, Inc.

A PROTESTANT WOMAN 435

Excerpt from *Not in God's Image: Women in History from the Greeks to the Victorians* by Julia O'Faolain and Lauro Martines. Copyright © 1973 by Julia O'Faolain and Lauro Martines. Reprinted by permission of HarperCollins Publishers, Inc.

A WITCHCRAFT TRIAL IN FRANCE 442

From *Witchcraft in Europe, 1100–1700: A Documentary History* by Alan Kors and Edward Peters (Philadelphia: University of Pennsylvania Press, 1972), pp. 266–275. Used with permission of the publisher.

PETER THE GREAT DEALS WITH A REBELLION 449

From James Harvey Robinson, *Readings in European History* (Lexington, Mass.: Ginn & Co.), 1934. Reprinted with permission of Silver, Burdett & Ginn Inc.

THE BILL OF RIGHTS 452

From *The Statutes: Revised Edition* (London: Eyre and Spottiswoode, 1871), Vol. 2, pp. 10–12.

WILLIAM SHAKESPEARE: IN PRAISE OF ENGLAND 457

Excerpt from "Richard II" in *Shakespeare, The Complete Works* by G. B. Harrison, copyright © 1968 by Harcourt Brace & Company and renewed 1980 by G. B. Harrison, reprinted by permission of the publisher.

CHAPTER 16

THE FALL OF CONSTANTINOPLE 464

From William H. McNeill and M. R. Waldham, *The Islamic World*, copyright © 1973 by The University of Chicago Press. Used with permission.

A PORTRAIT OF SULEYMAN THE MAGNIFICENT 465

From William H. McNeill and M. R. Waldham, *The Islamic World*, copyright © 1973 by The University of Chicago Press. Used with permission.

A TURKISH DISCOURSE ON COFFEE 468

From *The Balance of Truth* by Katib Chelebi, translated by G. L. Lewis, copyright 1927.

THE RELIGIOUS ZEAL OF SHAH ABBAS THE GREAT 472

From Eskander Beg Monshi in *History of Shah Abbas the Great*, Vol. II by Roger M. Savory by Westview Press, 1978.

THE MUGHAL CONQUEST OF NORTHERN INDIA 476

From *The Memoirs of Zehir-ed-Din Muhammed Baber*, translated by John Leyden and William Erskine (London: Longman and Cadell, 1826). Reprinted with permission.

AN ELEPHANT FIGHT FOR THE KING'S ENTERTAINMENT 478

Excerpt from *Travels in the Mogul Empire, A.D. 1656–1668* by Francois Bernier (Delhi: S. Chand & Co., 1968).

THE USES OF THE COCONUT 480

From "The Uses of the Coconut" by Duarte Barbosa from *The European Reconnaissance: Selected Documents* by John H. Parry. Copyright © 1968 by John H. Parry. Reprinted by permission of HarperCollins Publishers, Inc.

CHAPTER 17

THE ART OF PRINTING 492

From *China in the Sixteenth Century*, by Matthew Ricci, translated by Louis J. Gallagher. Copyright © 1942 and renewed 1970 by Louis J. Gallagher, S. J. Reprinted by permission of Random House, Inc.

A CONFUCIAN SIXTEEN COMMANDMENTS 494

From *Popular Culture in Late Imperial China* by David Johnson et al. Copyright © 1985 The Regents of the University of California. Used with permission.

THE TRIBUTE SYSTEM IN ACTION 497

Reprinted by permission of the publishers from *China's Response to the West: A Documentary Survey, 1839–1923*, by Ssu-yu Teng and John K. Fairbank. Cambridge, Mass.: Harvard University Press. Copyright © 1954 by the President and Fellows of Harvard College, © renewed 1982 by Ssu-yu Teng and John K. Fairbank.

THE ART OF USING CHOPSTICKS 500

From Liu Wu-chi, *An Introduction to Chinese Literature*, Chi-Chan, trans. Copyright © 1966 by Indiana University Press. Used with permission.

A PRESENT FOR LORD TOKITAKA 504

From *Sources of Japanese Tradition* by William De Bary. Copyright © 1958 by Columbia University Press, New York. Reprinted with permission of the publisher.

TOYOTOMI HIDEYOSHI EXPELS THE MISSIONARIES 505

From *Sources of Japanese Tradition* by William De Bary. Copyright © 1958 by Columbia University Press, New York. Reprinted with permission of the publisher.

FOLLOWING THE STRAIGHT AND NARROW IN TOKUGAWA JAPAN 509

From Chi Nakane and Oishi Shinsabura, *Tokugawa Japan: The Social and Economic Antecedents of Modern Japan*, (Japan: University of Tokyo, 1990), pp. 51–52. Translated by Conrad Totman. Copyright 1992 by Columbia University Press.

CHAPTER 18

ON THE REVOLUTIONS OF THE HEAVENLY SPHERES 519

From Copernicus, Nicholas, *On the Revolutions*. Edited by Jerzey Dobrzycki. Translated by Edward Rosen. The Johns Hopkins University Press, Baltimore/London, 1992.

THE STARRY MESSENGER 520

From *Discoveries and Opinions of Galileo*, Stillman Drake, ed., trans. Copyright © 1957 by Doubleday and Co. Reprinted with permission of the publisher.

THE FATHER OF MODERN RATIONALISM 525

From Descartes, *Philosophical Writings*, translated by Norman Kemp Smith, copyright © 1958 by Macmillan Education. Reprinted with permission of the publisher, Macmillan, London, & Basingstoke.

THE ATTACK ON RELIGIOUS INTOLERANCE 530

Reprinted with the permission of Macmillan College Publishing Company from *From Absolutism to Revolution: 1648–1848*, 2/e by Herbert Rowen. Copyright © 1968 by Macmillan College Publishing Company, Inc.

DIDEROT QUESTIONS CHRISTIAN SEXUAL STANDARDS 531

From Denis Diderot, *Rameau's Nephew and Other Works*, Jacques Barzun and Ralph Bowen, trans. Copyright © 1956 by Jacques Barzun and Ralph Bowen. Reprinted with permission of Doubleday and Co., a division of Bantam, Doubleday, Dell Publishing Group, Inc.

THE RIGHTS OF WOMEN 534

From *First Feminists: British Women Writers, 1578–1799* by Moira Ferguson. Copyright © 1985. Reprinted with permission of Indiana University Press.

THE PUNISHMENT OF CRIME 539

Excerpt from *European Society in the Eighteenth Century* by Robert and Elborg Forster. Copyright © 1969 by Robert and Elborg Forster. Reprinted by permission of HarperCollins Publishers Inc.

THE CONVERSION EXPERIENCE IN WESLEY'S METHODISM 541

Excerpt from *European Society in the Eighteenth Century* by Robert and Elborg Forster. Copyright © 1969 by Robert and Elborg Forster. Reprinted by permission of HarperCollins Publishers Inc.

CHAPTER 19

POVERTY IN FRANCE 550

Excerpt from *European Society in the Eighteenth Century* by Robert and Elborg Forster. Copyright © 1969 by Robert and Elborg Forster. Reprinted by permission of HarperCollins Publishers Inc.

CLASS AND CASTE IN COLONIAL LATIN AMERICA 554

Excerpt from *Latin American Civilization* by Benjamin Keen, ed. (Boston: Houghton Mifflin, 1974), vol. I, pp. 223–224.

THE MISSION 556

Excerpt from *Latin American Civilization* by Benjamin Keen, ed. (Boston: Houghton Mifflin, 1974), vol. I, pp. 223–224.

THE PROPOSALS OF CATHERINE II FOR A NEW LAW CODE 564

Excerpt from *Documents of Catherine the Great* by W. F. Reddaway, copyright © 1931. Reprinted with the permission of Cambridge University Press.

DECLARATION OF THE RIGHTS OF MAN AND THE CITIZEN 568

Excerpt from *The French Revolution* edited by Paul H. Beik. Copyright © 1971 by Paul Beik. Reprinted by permission of HarperCollins Publishers, Inc.

DECLARATION OF THE RIGHTS OF WOMAN AND THE FEMALE CITIZEN 569

From *Women in Revolutionary Paris, 1789–1795* by Darlene Gay Levy, Harriet Branson Applewhite, and Mary Durham Johnson. Copyright © 1979 by the Board of Trustees of the University of Illinois. Used with permission of the publisher.

A VICTIM OF THE REIGN OF TERROR 571

From *Women in Revolutionary Paris, 1789–1795* by Darleen Gay Levy, Harriet Branson Applewhite, and Mary Durham Johnson. Copyright © 1979 by University of Illinois Press. Used with permission of the publisher.

NAPOLEON AND PSYCHOLOGICAL WARFARE 573

Reprinted with the permission of Macmillan College Publishing Company from *A Documentary Survey of the French Revolution* by John Hall Stewart, ed. Copyright © 1951 by Macmillan College Publishing Company, renewed 1979 by John Hall Stewart.

CHAPTER 20

DISCIPLINE IN THE NEW FACTORIES 593

Copyright © 1968 by S. Pollard and C. Holmes. From *Documents of European Economic History* by Sidney Pollard and Colin Holmes. Reprinted with permission of St. Martin's Press, Incorporated.

S-T-E-A-M-B-O-A-T A-COMIN'! 595

From *Life on the Mississippi* by Mark Twain. Copyright © 1911 by Harper & Brothers. Reprinted with permission of HarperCollins Publishers, Inc.

CHILD LABOR: DISCIPLINE IN THE TEXTILE MILLS 599

Extract taken from *Human Documents of the Industrial Revolution* by E. Royston Pike, reproduced by kind permission of Unwin Hyman, Ltd. Copyright © 1966.

REVOLUTIONARY EXCITEMENT: CARL SCHURZ AND THE REVOLUTION OF 1848 IN GERMANY 604

From *The Reminiscences of Carl Schurz* by Carl Schurz (New York: The McClure Co., 1907), vol. I, pp. 112–113.

A RADICAL CRITIQUE OF THE LAND PROBLEM IN MEXICO 608

Excerpt from *Latin American Civilization* by Benjamin Keen, ed. (Boston: Houghton Mifflin, 1974), vol. 2, pp. 270–272.

GARIBALDI AND ROMANTIC NATIONALISM 611

From *The Times of London*, June 13, 1860.

EMANCIPATION: SERFS AND SLAVES 616

From *Annual Register* (New York: Longmans, Green, 1861), p. 207. From *U.S. Statutes at Large* (Washington, D.C., Government Printing Office, 1875), vol. 12, pp. 1268–1269.

GOTHIC LITERATURE: EDGAR ALLAN POE 619

From *Selected Prose and Poetry*, Edgar Allan Poe, copyright © 1950 by Holt, Rinehart, and Winston, Inc.

CHAPTER 21

THE DEPARTMENT STORE AND THE BEGINNINGS OF MASS CONSUMERISM 630

Copyright © 1968 by S. Pollard and C. Holmes. From *Documents of European Economic History*, by Sidney Pollard and Colin Holmes. Reprinted with permission of St. Martin's Press, Incorporated.

THE CLASSLESS SOCIETY 632

From *The Communist Manifesto* by Karl Marx and Friedrich Engels.

THE HOUSING VENTURE OF OCTAVIA HILL 635

Extract taken from *Human Documents of the Victorian Age* by E. Royston Pike, copyright © 1967 by Frederick A. Praeger. Reproduced by kind permission of Unwin Hyman, Ltd.

ADVICE TO WOMEN: BE INDEPENDENT 639

From *Roots of Western Civilization* by Wesley D. Camp. Copyright © 1983 by John Wiley & Sons. Reproduced with permission of McGraw-Hill, Inc.

ZAPATA AND LAND REFORM 643

Excerpt from *Latin American Civilization* by Benjamin Keen, ed. (Boston: Houghton Mifflin, 1974), vol. 2, pp. 188–189.

FREUD AND THE CONCEPT OF REPRESSION 652

Reprinted from *Five Lectures on Psychoanalysis* by Sigmund Freud. Translated and edited by James Strachey, by permission of W.W. Norton & Company, Inc. Copyright 1909, 1910 by Sigmund Freud. Copyright © 1961 by James Strachey. Copyright renewed 1989. Used with permission of Sigmund Freud Copyrights, the Institute of Psycho-Analysis and the Hogarth Press.

THE VOICE OF ZIONISM: THEODOR HERZL AND THE JEWISH STATE 654

From Theodor Herzl, *The Jewish State*, 3rd ed. Sylvie d'Anigdor, trans., copyright © 1936. Reprinted with permission of The Central Zionist Organization.

SYMBOLIST POETRY: ART FOR ART'S SAKE 656

"The Drunken Boat" by Arthur Rimbaud from *Realism, Naturalism, Symbolism: Mode of Thought and Expression in Europe* by Roland N. Stromberg. English translation copyright © 1968 by Roland Stromberg. Reprinted by permission of HarperCollins Publishers.

CHAPTER 22

THE WHITE MAN'S BURDEN 671

From *Verse* by Rudyard Kipling. Copyright © 1920 by Doubleday, a division of Bantam, Doubleday, Dell Publishing Group, Inc. Used with permission of the publisher.

THE BLACK MAN'S BURDEN 674

From Louis L. Snyder, ed., *The Imperialism Reader* (Princeton: Van Nostrand, 1962).

INDIAN IN BLOOD, ENGLISH IN TASTE AND INTELLECT 676

From Michael Edwards, *A History of India: From the Earliest Times to the Present Day* (London: Thames and Hudson, 1961), pp. 261–265.

THE EFFECTS OF DUTCH COLONIALISM IN JAVA 679

From *The World of Southeast Asia: Selected Historical Readings*, Harry J. Benda and John A. Larkin, eds. Copyright © 1967 by Harper & Row, Publishers. Used with permission of the author.

A GUIDE FOR PEACE IN AFRICA: A BRITISH POINT OF VIEW 682

From John Frederick Lugard, *The Dual Mandate in Tropical Africa* (London, 1965), quoted in Robert O. Collins, ed., *Historical Problems of Imperial Africa* (Marcus Wiener Publishers Inc., 1994), pp. 114–116.

A CRITIQUE OF INDIAN NATIONALISM 684

From *Nationalism* by Rabindranath Tagore (New York: Macmillan, 1917). Used with permission of the publisher.

A CALL TO ARMS 686

From *The Vietnamese Response to Foreign Intervention*, Truong Buu Lam, ed. (New Haven: Yale University Press, Monograph Series no. 11, Southeast Asian Studies, 1967), pp. 76–78.

CHAPTER 23

A LETTER OF ADVICE TO THE QUEEN 693

Reprinted by permission of the publishers from *China's Response to the West: A Documentary Survey, 1839–1923*, by Ssu-yu Teng and John K. Fairbank. Cambridge, Mass.: Harvard University Press. Copyright © 1954 by the President and Fellows of Harvard College, © renewed 1982 by Ssu-yu Teng and John K. Fairbank.

EUROPE IN CHINESE EYES 694

From *Wang Hsi-ch'i, Hsiao-fang hu-chai yu-ti ts'ung-ch'ao*, tr. Franz Schurmann, in Franz Schurmann and Orville Schell (eds.) *The China Reader: Imperial China* (New York: Vintage, 1967), arranged by Alfred Knopf, pp. 122–126.

A PROGRAM FOR A NEW CHINA 701

Excerpt from *Sources of Chinese Tradition* by William Theodore De Bary. Copyright © 1960 by Columbia University Press, New York. Reprinted with permission of the publisher.

A LETTER TO THE SHOGUN 705

Excerpt from *Commodore Perry in Japan*, Robert L. Reynolds (New York: Harper & Row, 1963), p. 68.

A PROGRAM FOR REFORM IN JAPAN 706

Excerpt from *Sources of Japanese Tradition* by William De Bary. Copyright © 1958 by Columbia University Press, New York. Reprinted with permission of the publisher.

IN THE BEGINNING: WE WERE THE SUN 708

From John David Lu, *Sources of Japanese Tradition* (New York: McGraw-Hill, 1974), vol. II, pp. 118–119, from *Chuo Koren*, November 1965. pp. 354–357.

THE RULES OF GOOD CITIZENSHIP IN MEIJI JAPAN 709

From Ryusaku Tsunoda et al., *Sources of Japanese Tradition* (New York: Columbia Univeristy Press, 1958), vol. 2, p. 139.

TWO VIEWS OF THE WORLD 711

From MacNair, *Modern Chinese History*, pp. 530–534, quoted in Franz Schurmann and Orville Schell, eds., *The China Reader: Imperial China* (New York: Vintage, 1967), pp. 251–259.

CHAPTER 24

"YOU HAVE TO BEAR THE RESPONSIBILITY FOR WAR OR PEACE" 720

From *The Western World: From 1700*, Vol. II, by W. E. Adams, R. B. Barlow, G. R. Kleinfeld, and R. D. Smith (Dodd, Mead, and Co., 1968), pp. 421–442.

THE EXCITEMENT OF WAR 722

From *The World of Yesterday* by Stefan Zweig, translated by Helmut Ripperger. Translation copyright 1943 by the Viking Press, Inc. Used by permission of Viking Penguin, a division of Penguin Books USA Inc.

THE REALITY OF WAR: TRENCH WARFARE 724

All Quiet on the Western Front by Erich Maria Remarque. "Im Westen Nichts Neues," copyright 1928 by Ullstein A.G.; copyright renewed © 1956 by Erich Maria Remarque. "All Quiet on the Western Front," copyright 1929, 1930 by Little, Brown and Company; Copyright renewed © 1957, 1958 by Erich Maria Remarque. All Rights Reserved.

WOMEN IN THE FACTORIES 727

From "Munition Work," by Naomi Loughnan in Gilbert Stone, ed., *Women War Workers* (London: George Harrap and Company, 1917), pp. 25, 35–38.

TEN DAYS THAT SHOOK THE WORLD: LENIN AND THE BOLSHEVIK SEIZURE OF POWER 730

From *Ten Days That Shook the World* by John Reed. Copyright © by John Reed. Reprinted with permission of the publisher.

THE VOICE OF PEACEMAKING: WOODROW WILSON 733

Excerpts from *The Public Papers of Woodrow Wilson: War and Peace*, edited by Ray Stannard Baker. Copyright 1925, 1953 by Edith Bolling Wilson. Reprinted by permission of HarperCollins Publishers, Inc.

THE GREAT DEPRESSION: UNEMPLOYED AND HOMELESS IN GERMANY 738

From *Living Age*, Vol. 344, no. 4398 (March 1933), pp. 27–31, 34–38.

HESSE AND THE UNCONSCIOUS 743

From *Demian*, by Hermann Hesse. (New York: Bantam Books, 1966), p. 30.

CHAPTER 25

THE DILEMMA OF THE INTELLECTUAL 748

From *The World of Southeast Asia: Selected Historical Readings*, Harry J. Benda and John A. Larkin, eds. Copyright © 1967 by Harper & Row, Publishers. Used with permission of the author.

A CALL FOR A MUSLIM STATE 751

Excerpt from *Sources of Indian Tradition*, Stephen Hay, ed. Copyright © 1988 by Columbia University Press, New York. Reprinted with permission of the publisher.

MUSTAPHA KEMAL'S CASE AGAINST THE CALIPHATE 753

From *Ataturk's Speech to the Assembly*, pp. 432–433. A speech delivered by Ghazi Mustapha Kemal, President of the Turkish Republic, October 1927.

THE PATH OF LIBERATION 757

From *Vietnam: History, Documents, and Opinions on a Major World Crisis*, Marvin Gentleman, ed. (New York: Fawcett Publications, 1965), pp. 30–32.

A CALL FOR REVOLT 760

From *Selected Works of Mao Tse-Tung* (London: Lawrence and Wishart, Ltd., 1954) , Vol. 1, pp. 21–23.

AN ARRANGED MARRIAGE 763

Excerpt from "Family" by Ba Jin. Copyright © 1964 Foreign Languages Press, 24 Baiwanzhuang Rd., Beijing 10037, P.R. China. Used with permission.

IN SEARCH OF OLD JAPAN 764

Excerpt from *Some Prefer Nettles*, Junichiro Tanazaki (New York: Medallion Books, 1960), pp. 96–98.

CHAPTER 26

PROPAGANDA AND MASS MEETINGS IN NAZI GERMANY 778

Excerpt from *Mein Kampf* by Adolf Hitler, translated by Ralph Manheim. Copyright 1943, © renewed 1971 by Houghton Mifflin Co. Reprinted by permission of Houghton Mifflin Company. All rights reserved. From Norman Baynes, ed., *The Speeches of Adolf Hitler* (New York: Oxford University Press, 1942), 1:206–207.

THE FORMATION OF COLLECTIVE FARMS 780

From Sidney Harcave, *Readings in Russian History* (New York: Thomas Crowell and Co., 1962), pp. 208–210.

THE MUNICH CONFERENCE 784

From *Parliamentary Debates, House of Commons* (London: His Majesty's Stationery Office, 1938), vol. 339, pp 361–369. From Neville Chamberlain, *In Search of Peace* (New York: Putnam, 1939), pp. 215, 217.

JAPAN'S JUSTIFICATION FOR EXPANSION 786

From *Sources of Japanese Tradition* by William Theodore De Bary. Copyright © 1958 by Columbia University Press, New York. Reprinted with the permission of the publisher.

A GERMAN SOLDIER AT STALINGRAD 791

From Vasili Chuikov, *The Battle of Stalingrad* (Grafton Books).

HITLER'S PLANS FOR A NEW ORDER IN THE EAST 794

From *Hitler's Conversations*, Hugh Trevor Roper, copyright © 1953 by New American Library, published by Octagon Books, A Div. of Hippocrene Books, Inc. Used with permission.

THE HOLOCAUST: THE CAMP COMMANDANT AND THE CAMP VICTIMS 796

From *Commandant of Auschwitz: The Autobiography of Rudolph Hoess*, Cleveland World Publishing Company. From *Nazism: A History in Documents & Eyewitness Accounts*, Vol. II by J. Noakes and G. Pridham. Copyright © 1988 by Department of History and Archaeology, University of Exeter. Reprinted by permission of Pantheon Books, A Division of Random House, Inc.

JAPAN'S PLAN FOR ASIA 797

From *Sources of Japanese Tradition* by William De Bary. Copyright © 1958 by Columbia University Press, New York. Reprinted with permission of the publisher.

CHAPTER 27

THE TRUMAN DOCTRINE 817

U.S. Congress, *Congressional Record*, 80th Congress, 1st Session (Washington, D.C.: U. S. Government Printing Office, 1947), Vol. 93, p. 1981.

IT'S NOT OUR FAULT 822

From *United States Relations with China* (Washington, D.C., Dept. of State, 1949), pp. iii–xvi.

A PLEA FOR PEACEFUL COEXISTENCE 827

From G. F. Hudson et al., eds., *The Sino-Soviet Dispute* (New York: Frederick Praeger, 1961), pp. 61–63, cited in Peking Review, No. 40, 1959.

THE SAMPAN GIRL 828

From *We the Vietnamese* by Francois Scully, ed. (New York: Praeger Publications, 1967), pp. 252–253.

A MANUAL FOR REVOLUTIONARIES 830

From *Nationalism and Communism*, Norman Grabner, ed. Copyright © 1977 by D. C. Heath and Company. Used with permission.

NIXON PLAYS HIS CHINA CARD 831

From *The Shanghai Communiqué* (New York Times, February 28, 1972). Copyright © 1972 by The New York Times Company. Reprinted by permission.

CHAPTER 28

KHRUSHCHEV DENOUNCES STALIN 839

From *Congressional Record*, 84th Congress, 2d Session, Vol. 102, Part 7, pp. 9389–9402 (June 4, 1956).

SOVIET REPRESSION IN EASTERN EUROPE: HUNGARY, 1956 844

From *Department of State Bulletin*, Nov. 12, 1956, pp. 746–747.

THE BREZHNEV DOCTRINE 845

From *Moscow News*, Supplement to No. 30 (917), 1968, pp. 3–6.

ONE DAY IN THE LIFE OF IVAN DENISOVICH 847

From *One Day in the Life of Ivan Denisovich* by Alexander Solzhenitsyn, translated by Ralph Parker, Translation copyright © 1963 by E. P. Dutton and Victor Gollancz, Ltd. Copyright renewed © 1991 by Penguin USA and Victor Gollancz, Ltd. Used by permission of Dutton Signet, a division of Penguin Books USA Inc.

SOVIET WOMEN: "IT'S SO DIFFICULT TO BE A WOMAN HERE" 849

From *Moscow Women* by Carola Hansson and Karin Liden. Text copyright © 1983 by Random House, Inc. Reprinted by permission of Pantheon Books, a division of Random House, Inc.

LAND REFORM IN ACTION 857

From Richard Solomon, *Mao's Revolution and the Chinese Political Culture*, pages 198–199. Copyright © 1971 Center for Chinese Studies, University of Michigan. Used with permission of the University of California Press.

MAKE REVOLUTION! 860

From *Life and Death in Shanghai* by Nien Cheng (New York: Penguin, 1986).

STUDENTS APPEAL FOR DEMOCRACY 862

From a flyer in the archives of William J. Duiker.

MARRIAGE CHINESE STYLE 867

From *Chinese Lives: An Oral History of Contemporary China*, edited by W. J. F. Jenner and Delia Davin (New York: Pantheon Books, 1987), pp. 71–73.

TROUBLE IN THE GARLIC FIELDS 870

From *The Garlic Ballads* by Yan Mo, translated by Howard Goldblatt, Translation copyright © 1995 by Howard Goldblatt. Used by permission of Penguin, a division of Penguin Books USA Inc., Penguin Books, New York, 1995, pp. 268–271.

CHAPTER 29

VIOLENCE AGAINST FOREIGNERS IN GERMANY 879

From "East Germans Have Yet to Learn Tolerance" by Knud Pries, in *The German Tribune*, October 6, 1991. Copyright Suddeutsche Zeitung. Used with permission.

MARGARET THATCHER: ENTERING A MAN'S WORLD 881

From *The Path to Power* by Margaret Thatcher. (New York: HarperCollins Publishers, 1995), pp. 62–65.

"I HAVE A DREAM" 886

Reprinted by permission of Joan Daves, copyright 1963, Martin Luther King, Jr.

CASTRO'S REVOLUTIONARY IDEALS 891

Excerpt from *Latin American Civilization* by Benjamin Keen, ed. (Boston: Houghton Mifflin, 1974), pp. 369–373.

STUDENT REVOLT IN MEXICO 895

Excerpt from *Latin American Civilization* by Benjamin Keen, ed. (Boston: Houghton Mifflin, 1974), pp. 226–227.

"THE TIMES THEY ARE A-CHANGIN'": THE MUSIC OF YOUTHFUL PROTEST 899

From *Bob Dylan, Lyrics 1962–1985* (New York: Alfred A. Knopf, 1992), p. 91. Rights controlled by Special Rider Music, Cooper Station, New York, NY.

THE VOICE OF THE WOMEN'S LIBERATION MOVEMENT 901

From *The Second Sex* by Simone De Beauvoir, trans., H M Parshley. Copyright 1952 and renewed 1980 by Alfred A. Knopf, Inc. Reprinted by permission of the publisher.

SMALL IS BEAUTIFUL: THE LIMITS OF MODERN TECHNOLOGY 906

Excerpt from *Small Is Beautiful: Economics as if People Mattered* by E. F. Schumacher. Copyright © 1973 by E. F. Schumacher. Reprinted by permission of HarperCollins Publishers Inc.

CHAPTER 30

TOWARD AFRICAN UNITY 914

From *Organizing African Unity* by J. Woronoff, pp. 642–649. Copyright © 1980 by Scarecrow Press, Inc. Used with permission of the publisher.

STEALING THE NATION'S RICHES 916

From *The Beautyful Ones Are Not Yet Born* by Ayi Kwei Armah (Heinemann, 1989).

SOCIALISM IS NOT RACIALISM 918

From Julius Nyerere, "The Arusha Declaration" in *Freedomways* (magazine) (Dar es Salaam: Second Quarter, 1970), pp. 124–127.

AN AFRICAN LAMENT 924

From *Okot p'Bitek, I Do Not Know the Dances of White People* (Nairobi: East African Publishing House, 1974), pp. 48, 204–205.

THE SUEZ CANAL BELONGS TO EGYPT! 927

From a speech nationalizing the Suez Canal, Gamal Abdul Nasser, in *The Egyptian Gazette* (July 27, 1956), p. 5.

A PLEA FOR PEACE IN THE MIDDLE EAST 930

From *The United Nations: Official Records of the Eleventh Session of the General Assembly*, 666th Plenary Meeting, New York, 1 March 1957 (A/PV.666), II, 1275f.

KEEPING THE CAMEL OUT OF THE TENT 938

From *Nine Parts of Desire: The Hidden World of Islamic Women*, by Geraldine Brooks (Doubleday, 1996).

CHAPTER 31

NEHRU'S PROGRAM FOR INDIA 945

From *Sources of Indian Tradition* by William Theodore De Bary. Copyright © 1988 by Columbia University Press, New York. Reprinted with permission of the publisher.

GANDHI'S VISION FOR INDIA 946

Excerpt from Gandhi "Letter to Jawaharlal Nehru," pp. 328–331 from *Gandhi in India: In His Own Words*, Martin Green, ed. Copyright © 1987 by Navajivan Trust, reprinted with permission of University Press of New England.

THE SOUL OF ISLAM 949

From *Sources of Indian Tradition* by William Theodore de Bary. Copyright © 1988 by Columbia University Press, New York. Reprinted with permission of the publisher.

SAY NO TO MCDONALD'S! 954

From *World Press Review* (September 1995), p. 47.

A CRITIQUE OF WESTERN FEMINISM 956

From *Far Eastern Economic Review* (May 16, 1996), p. 30.

THE GOLDEN THROAT OF PRESIDENT SUKARNO 960

From Howard Jones, *Indonesia: The Possible Dream* (New York: Harcourt Brace Jovanovich, Hoover Institute, 1971), pp. 223, 237.

WHOSE HUMAN RIGHTS? 965

From *Far Eastern Economic Review* (August 4, 1994), p. 17.

AN INDONESIAN'S VIEW OF SUKARNO 969

From *Five Journeys from Jakarta*, Maslyn Williams (New York: William Morrow, 1966), pp. 116–117.

CHAPTER 32

THE EMPEROR IS NOT DIVINE 974

John David Lu, *Sources of Japanese Tradition* (New York: McGraw-Hill, 1974), vol. II, pp. 190–191, from *New York Times*, January 1, 1946.

GROWING UP IN JAPAN 980

From *The Material Child: Coming of Age in Japan and America* (New York: Free Press, 1993). Used with permission of Merry White.

AN ERA OF WOMEN 981

From *Japanese Women: New Feminist Perspectives on the Past, Present, and Future*, Kumiko Fujimura-Fanselow et al., ed. (New York: The Feminist Press at The City Univeristy of New York, 1995), pp. xvii–xviii.

THE AMBIGUITY OF BEING JAPANESE 983

From *Japan, the Ambiguous, and Myself* by Kenzaburo Oe (Tokyo: Kodansha International, 1995), pp. 117–119.

BEAUTIFUL ISLAND, BEAUTIFUL LITERATURE 988

From *Modern Chinese Writers: Self-Portrayals*, Helmut Martin et al., ed. (New York: M. E. Sharpe, 1992), pp. 235–236.

TO THOSE LIVING IN GLASS HOUSES 990

From *Far Eastern Economic Review* (May 19, 1994), p. 32.

RETURN TO THE MOTHERLAND 992

From Kevin Rafferty, *City on the Rocks* (New York: Penguin, 1989 and 1991).

Map Credits

The authors wish to acknowledge their use of the following books as reference in preparing the maps listed here:

Map 2.2 Geoffrey Barraclough, ed., *Times Atlas of World History*, (Maplewood, N.J.: Hammond Inc., 1978), p. 65.

Map 3.2 Geoffrey Barraclough, ed., *Times Atlas of World History*, (Maplewood, N.J.: Hammond Inc., 1978), p. 63.

Map 3.3 Conrad Schirokauer, *A Brief History of Chinese and Japanese Civilizations*, 2d ed. (San Diego: Harcourt Brace Jovanovich, 1989), p. 52.

Map 3.4 Hammond Past Worlds: *The Times Atlas of Archeology*, (Maplewood, N.J.: Hammond Inc. 1988), pp. 190–191.

Maps 6.1 & 6.2 Geoffrey Barraclough, ed., *Times Atlas of World History*, (Maplewood, N.J.: Hammond Inc., 1978), p. 47.

Map 6.4 Michael Coe, Dean Snow and Elizabeth Benson, *Atlas of Ancient America* (New York: Facts on File, 1988), p. 144.

Map 6.5 Phillipa Fernandez-Arnesto, *Atlas of World Exlporation*, (New York: Harper Collins, 1991), p. 35.

Map 7.3 Geoffrey Barraclough, ed., *Times Atlas of World History*, (Maplewood, N.J.: Hammond Inc., 1978), pp. 134–135.

Map 7.4 Geoffrey Barraclough, ed., *Times Atlas of World History*, (Maplewood, N.J.: Hammond Inc., 1978), p. 135.

Map 8.1 Geoffrey Barraclough, ed., *Times Atlas of World History*, (Maplewood, N.J.: Hammond Inc., 1978), pp. 44–45.

Map 8.4 Geoffrey Barraclough, ed., *Times Atlas of World History*, (Maplewood, N.J.: Hammond Inc., 1978), pp. 136–137.

Map 9.1 Michael Edwardes, *A History of India* (London: Thames and Hudson, 1961), p. 79.

Map 10.1 John K. Fairbank, Edwin O. Reischauer, and Albert M. Craig, *East Asia: Tradition and Transformation* (Boston: Houghton Mifflin, 1973), p. 103.

Map 10.2 Albert Hermann, *An Historical Atlas of China* (Chicago: Aidine, 1966), p. 13.

Map 11.1 John K. Fairbank, Edwin O. Reischauer, and Albert M. Craig, *East Asia: Tradition and Transformation* (Boston: Houghton Mifflin, 1973), p. 363.

Map 14.1 Geoffrey Barraclough, ed., *Times Atlas of World History*, (Maplewood, N. J.: Hammond, Inc. 1978), p. 160.

Map 16.3 Geoffrey Barraclough, ed., *Times Atlas of World History*, (Maplewood, N. J.: Hammond, Inc. 1978), p. 173.

Map 17.1 Jonathan Spence, *The Search for Modern China*, (New York: W. W. Norton, 1990), p. 19.

Map 17.2 Conrad Schirokauer, *A Brief History of Chinese and Japanese Civilizations, 2d ed.*, (San Diego: Harcourt Brace Jovanovich, 1989), p. 330.

Map 17.3 John K. Fairbank, Edwin O. Reischauer, and Albert M. Craig, *East Asia: Tradition and Tranformation*, (Boston: Houghton Mifflin, 1973), pp. 402–403.

Map 18.1 *Atlas of World History*, (New York: Harper & Row Publishers, 1987), p. 187.

Map 22.4 Geoffrey Barraclough, ed., *Times Atlas of World History*, (Maplewood, N. J.: Hammond, Inc. 1978), p. 235.

Map 23.1 John K. Fairbank, Edwin O. Reischauer, and Albert M. Craig, *East Asia: Tradition and Tranformation*, (Boston: Houghton Mifflin, 1973), p. 451.

Map 23.4 Geoffrey Barraclough, ed., *Times Atlas of World History*, (Maplewood, N. J.: Hammond, Inc. 1978), p. 243.

Photo Credits

COVER

Collection Musée Guimet, Paris, Photo © Michael Holford, London

PART I OPENING

xxxii Werner Forman Archive, British Library/Art Resource, NY

CHAPTER 1

2 © British Museum, London, reproduced by Courtesy of the Trustees of the British Museum **5** Francois Ducasse/Photo Researchers, Inc. **7** Courtesy of the Arthur M. Sackler Gallery, Smithsonian Institution, Washington, DC. **10** © British Museum, London, reproduced by Courtesy of the Trustees of the British Museum **11** Babylonian, *Stele of Hammurabi*, Musée du Louvre, © Photo R.M.N. **14** Musée du Louvre, © Photo R.M.N.—Herve Lewandowski **18** *Pair Statue of King Mycerinus and His Queen*; From Giza, Dynasty IV, 2599–1571 B.C.E. Slate Schist, 54 1/2 in. Harvard MFA Expedition. Courtesy, Museum of Fine Arts, Boston **19** © Will & Deni McIntyre/Photo Researchers, Inc. **22** © Brian Blake/Photo Researchers, Inc. **23** © Adam Woolfitt/Robert Harding Picture Library **26** © British Museum, London, reproduced by Courtesy of the Trustees of the British Museum **31** © British Museum, London, reproduced by Courtesy of the Trustees of the British Museum **34** *Archers of the Persian Guard*, Musée du Louvre, © Photo R.M.N.

CHAPTER 2

38 Robert Harding Picture Library **41** Borromeo/Art Resource, NY **42** Scala/Art Resource, NY **43** © Royal Smeets Offset, Weert **50** Courtesy of the British Library, Oriental and India Office Collection **51** © Royal Smeets Offset, Weert **57** Borromeo/Art Resource, NY **58 top/bottom** Robert Harding Picture Library **60 left** Borromeo/Art Resource, NY **60 right** © Royal Smeets Offset, Weert

CHAPTER 3

64 Courtesy of William J. Duiker **68** Werner Forman Archive, British Library/Art Resource, NY **70** Courtesy of William J. Duiker **78** Robert Harding Picture Library **80** Courtesy of William J. Duiker **82** Courtesy of William J. Duiker **83** Robert Harding Picture Library **84** Courtesy of William J. Duiker **86** © Michael Holford, London **87** Robert Harding Picture Library **88** Robert Harding Picture Library **89** O. Louis Mazzatenta/National Geographic Society Image Collection

CHAPTER 4

95 Leonard von Matt/Photo Researchers, Inc. **96** Robert Harding Picture Library **98** © Michael Holford, London **100** Scala/Art Resource, NY **105** © G. Dagli Orti, PARIS **105 inset** Courtesy of William M. Murray **111 bottom** © Michael Holford, London **111 top** Art Resource, NY **112** Scala/Art Resource, NY **114** The Metropolitan Museum of Art, Fletcher Fund, 1931(31.11.10) **116** *Bust of Alexander*, Musée du Louvre, © Photo R.M.N. **121** The Metropolitan Museum of Art, Fletcher Fund, 1920 (20.2.21) **122** The Metropolitan Museum of Art, Rogers Fund, 1909 (09.39) **124** Leonard von Matt/Photo Researchers, Inc.

CHAPTER 5

128 Leonard von Matt/Photo Researchers, Inc. **130** Art Resource, NY **133** British Museum, Photo © Michael Holford, London **138** Scala/Art Resource, NY **140** Photo Vatican Museums **143** Photo © Eberhard Thiem, Lotos-Film,Kaufbeuren, Germany **144** Leonard von Matt/Photo Researchers, Inc. **146** © Thomas S. England/Photo Researchers, Inc. **147** The Metropolitan Museum of Art/Rogers Fund, 1903 (03.14.5) **151** Scala/Art Resource, NY **154** Scala/Art Resource, NY **161** Fitzwilliam Museum, University of Cambridge **162** © British Museum, London, reproduced by Courtesy of the Trustees of the British Museum **166** Bibliotheque Nationale, Paris 01 Atlas Catalan RcC 2102

PART II OPENING

166 Bibliotheque Nationale, Paris 01 Atlas Catalan RcC 2102

CHAPTER 6

168 Richard A Cooke III/Stone **172** Richard A Cooke III/Stone **174 top** From *Atlas of Ancient America* by Michael Coe, Dean Snow and Elizabeth Benson/Andromeda Oxford Limited, Oxford, England **174 bottom** Detail-Mural Room 2, Bonampak, Chiapas, Mexico. © Pres. and fellows of Harvard College, 1988, All rights reserved. Peabody Museum, Harvard, Photography by Hillel Burger **175 top** Lee Boltin Picture Library **175 bottom** Courtesy of William J. Duiker **179** Courtesy of William J. Duiker **181** Lee Boltin Picture Library **184** Courtesy of William J. Duiker **185** Robert Harding Picture Library **186** Courtesy of William J. Duiker **189** Courtesy of William J. Duiker

CHAPTER 7

192 Courtesy of William J. Duiker **193** Robert Harding Picture Library **195** E.U.L.M.S. 20, fol.25r, reproduced by permission of the Edinburgh University Library **196** Courtesy of William J. Duiker **204** Courtesy of William J. Duiker **210** Courtesy of William J. Duiker **211 left** Fred J. Maroon/Photo Researchers, Inc. **211 right** Scala/Art Resource, NY **212 top** Courtesy of William J. Duiker **212 bottom** Courtesy of William J. Duiker **213** Courtesy of William J. Duiker

CHAPTER 8

216 Robert Harding Picture Library **219** Robert Harding Picture Library **220** Werner Forman/Art Resource, NY **225** Courtesy of William J. Duiker **227** Courtesy of William J. Duiker **229** Bibliotheque Nationale, Paris 01 Atlas Catalan RcC 2102 **230** 10095 i3; drawing by Caillie of Timbuktu; reproduced by permission of the British Library **231** Corbis **234** © Michael Holford, London **235 bottom** Werner Forman /Art Resource, NY **235 top** Werner Forman/British Museum/Art Resource, NY **236** Angela Fisher/Robert Estall Photographs

CHAPTER 9

240 Courtesy of William J. Duiker **244** Courtesy of William J. Duiker **248** Courtesy of William J. Duiker **252** S. Fiore/Explorer **253** Courtesy of William J. Duiker **254** Courtesy of William J. Duiker **255** Marcello Berntinetti/Photo Researchers, Inc.

258 Courtesy of Sharon Littlefield **260** Courtesy of William J. Duiker **261** Courtesy of Sharon Littlefield **262** Courtesy of William J. Duiker **263** Courtesy of William J. Duiker

CHAPTER 10

266 Courtesy of William J. Duiker **268** Bibliotheque Nationale, Paris, *Pelliot Chinois* 4518 (39) RcB4296 **272** Courtesy of William J. Duiker **275** Courtesy of Yvonne V. Duiker **276** Courtesy of William J. Duiker **277** *Spring Festival on the River*; Detail, The Metropolitan Museum of Art, Fletcher Fund, 1947, The A.W. Bahr Collection, (47.18.1) **283** Courtesy of William J. Duiker **286** Courtesy of the Board of Trustees of the Victoria and Albert Museum **288** Courtesy of William J. Duiker **290** National Palace Museum, Taipei, Taiwan, Republic of China **291** Courtesy of the Tokyo National Museum

CHAPTER 11

294 Courtesy of William J. Duiker **297** Courtesy of William J. Duiker, **301 top** © Michael Holford, London **301 bottom** Detail—troops fighting as palace burns, scroll w/depictions of the night attack on the Sanjo Palace, from the *Illustrated scrolls of the events of the Heiji Period* second half of the thirteenth c., Unknown, Japanese, Kamakura Period, hand scroll; ink and colors on paper, Fenollosa-Weld Collection, Courtesy of the Museum of Fine Arts, Boston **302** Courtesy of the Tokyo National Museum **308 left** Courtesy of the Freer Gallery of Art, Smithsonian Institution, Washington, D.C. #49.21 **308 right** Robert Harding Picture Library **309** Courtesy of William J. Duiker **310 top** Courtesy of Matthew Kroenig **310 bottom** Courtesy of the Korean Cultural Service Library **311** Courtesy of William J. Duiker **314** Courtesy of William J. Duiker **315** Courtesy of William J. Duiker

CHAPTER 12

318 Scala/Art Resource, NY **320** Bibliotheque Nationale, Paris, Ms. Nouv. Acq. Fr. 1098 **325** The Granger Collection **326** The Pierpont Morgan Library/Art Resource, New York, M.736, f.9v **328** Bibliotheque Nationale, Paris **336** E.T. Archive, London, from the collections of the British Library, Psalter, Calendar, c 1250–1260 **338** Bibliotheque Nationale, Paris **341** © Bibliotheque royale Albert ler (Ms IV 119, fol.72 verso) **344** Staatliche Museen, Berlin, Photo © Bildarchiv Preussischer Kulturbesitz, Berlin **345** © G. Dagli Orti **346** © Sylvain Grandadam/Photo Researchers, Inc. **348** Scala/Art Resource, NY **349** © Erich Lessing/Art Resource, NY

CHAPTER 13

356 Photo Vatican Museums **359** © Bibliotheque royale Albert ler, Bruxelles (Ms. 13076–77, f. 12v) **360** Bibliotheque Nationale, Paris **365** Giraudon/Art Resource, NY **369, left** Scala/Art Resource, NY **369, right** Scala/Art Resource, NY **374** Photo Vatican Museums **376** Private Collection/The Bridgeman Art Library **382** British Library, London, folio 290, Harley ms. 4431 **383** Scala/Art Resource, NY **384 top** Scala/Art Resource, NY **384 bottom** Erich Lessing/Art Resource, NY **385** Photo Vatican Museums **386 left** Reproduced by Courtesy of the Trustees; The National Gallery, London **386 right** Alinari/Art Resource, NY **391** Bibliotheque Nationale, Paris Paris Arabe 5847, FOL 138, RcC1230 **392** Leiden, University Library, BPL 20, f.60r **396** Collection Musée Guimet, Paris, Photo © Michael Holford, London

PART III OPENING

396 Collection Musée Guimet, Paris, Photo © Michael Holford, London

CHAPTER 14

398 Courtesy of William J. Duiker **401** Jomard, *Les Monuments de la Geographie*: Paris, 1862, Photo courtesy of the New York Public Library, Map Division, Stor, Lenox and Tilden Foundations **402** Courtesy of William J. Duiker **404** North Wind Picture Archives **406** North Wind Picture Archives **408** Courtesy of William J. Duiker **409** Courtesy of William J. Duiker **410** Courtesy of William J. Duiker **411** Courtesy of William J. Duiker **414** Historical Society of Pennsylvania **418** Courtesy of William J. Duiker **422** Courtesy of William J. Duiker **423** Courtesy of William J. Duiker

CHAPTER 15

426 The National Galleries of Scotland, by permission of Earl of Rosebery **430** Staliche Museen Preussicher Kulturbesitz, Kupferstichkabinett, Berlin (West), Photo: Jorg P. Anders **431** Alte Pinakothek, Munich **433** Bibliotheque Publique et Universitaire, Geneva **436** Scala/Art Resource, NY **440** Kunsthishorisches Museum, Vienna **445** Hyacinthe Rigaud, *Louise XIV*, Musée du Louvre, © Photo R.M.N. **446** Giraudon/Art Resource, NY **448** Russian School, *Czar Peter the Great*, Rijksmuseum, Amsterdam **450** The National Galleries of Scotland, by permission of Earl of Rosebery **454** Laocoon, *El Greco*, National Gallery of Art, Washington, Samuel H. Kress Collection **455 left** Peter Paul Reubens, *The Landing of Marie de Medicis at Marseilles*, Musée du Louvre, © Photo R.M.N. **455 right** Alinari/Art Resource, NY **456** Nicholas Poussin, *Landscape with the Burial of a Phocian*, Musée du Louvre, © Photo R.M.N.

CHAPTER 16

460 George Holton/Photo Researchers, Inc. **462** MS Fr.9087,f.207, Bibliotheque Nationale, Paris; photo © Sonia Halliday Photographs **467** Courtesy of the Topkapi Sarayi Musezi, Istanbul **470** Giraudon/Art Resource, NY **473 top** George Holton/Photo Researchers, Inc. **473 bottom** Reza-ye Abbasi, *Two Lovers*, 1630, The Metropolitan Museum of Art, Francis M. Weld Fund 1950(50.164) **477** Courtesy of the Board of Trustees of the Victoria and Albert Museum **479** Courtesy of William J. Duiker **482** SEF/Art Resource, NY **483** Stone **484** Werner Forman/Art Resource, NY

CHAPTER 17

488 Courtesy of William J. Duiker **490** Courtesy of William J. Duiker **496** © British Museum, London, reproduced by Courtesy of the Trustees of the British Museum **501 bottom** Dean Conger/National Geographic Image Collection **501 top** Courtesy of William J. Duiker **502** Werner Forman/Art Resource, NY **503** Courtesy of William J. Duiker **505** Collection Musée Guimet, Paris, Photo © Michael Holford, London **510** Torii Kiyotada, Japanese,act.c.1720–1750, *Naka-no-cho Street of the Yoshiwara*, wood block print, c. 1740, Clarence Buckingham Collection, 1939.2152, Photograph © 1993, The Art Institute of Chicago **511** Courtesy of William J. Duiker **513** Courtesy of William J. Duiker

CHAPTER 18

516 Dumesnil, *Queen Christina of Sweden with Descartes*, Musée du Louvre, © Photo R.M.N. **521 left** Courtesy of the Lilly Library, Indiana University, Bloomington, Indiana **521 right** Courtesy of the Lilly Library, Indiana University, Bloomington, Indiana **522** Bibliotheca Nazionale Centrale, Firenze **523** Corbis **526** Dumesnil, *Queen Christina of Sweden with Descartes*, Musée du Louvre, © Photo R.M.N. **527** Giraudon/Art Resource, NY **529** Mary Evans Picture Library **535** © Michael Holford, London **536** Antoine Watteau, *The Pilgrimage to Cythera*, Musée du Louvre, © Photo R.M.N. **537** Courtesy of James R. Spencer **540** Nathaniel Hone, *John Wesley*, ca. 1766, by Courtesy of the National Portrait Gallery, London

CHAPTER 19

544 Anonymous, *Fall of the Bastille*, (Detail) Musée National des Chateau de Versailles, © Photo R.M.N. **548 right** Erich Lessing/Art Resource, NY **548 left** *Wilton House, East View Showing the Old Entrance* by Richard Wilson (1714–82) Collection of the Earl of Pembroke, WIlton House, Wilts., UK/Bridgeman Art Library, London/New York **552** Benjamin West, *The Death of General Wolfe*, Transfer from the Canadian War Memorial, 1921, Gift of the second Duke of Westminster **557** The Granger Collection, NY **558** John Trumbull, *The Declaration of Independence, 4 July 1776*, Yale University Art Gallery, Trumbull Collection **563** Scala/Art Resource, NY **566** Anonymous, *Fall of the Bastille*, (Detail) Musée National des Chateau de Versailles, © Photo R.M.N. **570** Giraudon/Art Resource, NY **572** Giraudon/Art Resource, NY **575** Louis David, *Sacre de l-empereur* (detail), Musée du Louvre, © Photo R.M.N. **581** Fotomas Archive **583** ET Archive **586** Werner Forman Archive/C. D. Wertheim Collection/Art Resource, New York

PART IV OPENING

586 Werner Forman Archive/C. D. Wertheim Collection/Art Resource, New York

CHAPTER 20

588 Photo Bulloz **591** Mansell/Time Inc. **597** © Ann Ronan at Image Select **598** Corbis **602** Lecomte, *Battle in the rue de Rohan*, 1830, Giraudon/Art Resource, NY **606** © G. Dagli Orti **609** Wellcome Institute Library, London **613** *Proclamation of the German Empire at Versailles*, 1871, Anton von Werner, Photo © Bildarchiv Preussischer Kulturbesitz, Berlin **620** Casper David Friedrich, *Man and Woman Gazing at the Moon*, Nationalgalerie SMPK Berlin, Photo: Jorg P. Anders, © Bildarchive Preussischer Kulturbesitz, Berlin **621** Erich Lessing/Art Resource, NY **623** Gustave Courbet, *The Stonebreakers*, Gemaldegalerie Neue Meister, Staatliche Kunstsammlungen Dresden; Photo by Reinhold, Leipzig-Molkau

CHAPTER 21

626 Tate Gallery/Art Resource, NY **629** The Fotomas Index **633** Verein fur Geschichte der Arbeiterbewegung, Vienna **634** Corbis **637** William Powell Frith, *Many Happy Returns of the Day*, Harrogate Museums and Art Gallery/Bridgeman Art Library, London **640** Courtesy, Vassar College Library **642** Brown Brothers **650** E.T. Archive, London **651** AP/Wide World Photos **656** Erich Lessing/Art Resource, NY **657** Vincent van Gogh, *The Starry Night*, (1889), Collection, The Museum of Modern Art, New York; Acquired through the Lillie P. Bliss Bequest **658, top** Pablo Picasso, *Les Demoiselles d'Avignon*, Paris, (Begun May reworked July 1907) Collection, the Museum of Modern Art, New York, Acquired through the Lillie P. Bliss Bequest/© 2000 Estate of Pablo Picasso/Artist's Rights Society (ARS), New York. **658, bottom** Vasily Kandinsky, *Composition VIII, No. 2* (Painting with White Border), May 1913, Collection, the Solomon R. Guggenheim Museum, N.Y. Photograph David Heald, © The Solomon Guggenheim Foundation, New York, (37.245) © 2000 Artist's Rights Society (ARS), New York/ADAGP, Paris

CHAPTER 22

662 Bildarchiv Preussischer Kulturbesitz, Berlin **665** Courtesy of William J. Duiker **667** Bildarchiv Preussischer Kulturbesitz, Berlin **669** Aberdeen University Library **670** The Granger Collection **673** Mary Evans Picture Library **675** Courtesy of William J. Duiker **678** Courtesy of the British Library, Oriental and India Office Collections **680** Courtesy of William J. Duiker **685** Sipahioglu/Liaison Agency

CHAPTER 23

690 National Maritime Museum, London **692 top** Peabody Essex Museum, Salem, MA, photo © Mark Sexton **692 bottom** National Maritime Museum, London **696** Courtesy of William J. Duiker **697** 49.21 *Empress Dowager* 255 Courtesy of the Freer Gallery of Art, Smithsonian Institution, Washington, D.C. **699** Leslie's Weekly, 10/14/1900 **700** CameraPress/Globe Photos **704** Courtesy of the United States Naval Academy Museum **706** Scala/Art Resource, NY **709** Scala/Art Resource, NY **712** Christie's Images, New York/Superstock

CHAPTER 24

716 Librarie Larouse, Paris **721** Librairie Larouse, Paris **723 right** Roger-Viollet/Liaison Agency **723 left** Bilderdienst Suddeutscher Verlag, Munich **726** E.T. Archive, London **728** Sovfoto **729** Brown Brothers **734** Hulton Getty/Liaison Agency **739** Roger-Viollet/Liaison Agency **742** Erich Lessing/Art Resource, NY, Hoech, Hannah, *Cut With the Kitchen Knife*, Photomontage. 1919. © 2000 Artist's Rights Society (ARS), New York/VG Bild-Kunst, Bonn **743** Salvador Dali, *The Persistence of Memory*, 1931, Oil on canvas, 9 1/2 x 13", Collection the Museum of Modern Art, New York, Given Anonymously, © 2000 Foundation Gala-Salvadore Dali/VEGAP/Artist Right's Society (ARS), New York

CHAPTER 25

746 Schalkwijk/Art Resource, NY **749** AP/Wide World Photos **752** © Culver Pictures, Inc. **754** Hulton Getty/Liaison Agency **755** Corbis **759** YMCA of the USA Archives, University of Minnesota Libraries **761** © Earl Leaf/Rapho/Liaison Agency **768** Hulton Getty/Liaison Agency **769** Schalkwijk/Art Resource, NY

CHAPTER 26

772 Hugo Jaeger, Life Magazine, © Time, Inc. **775** AP/Wide World Photos **777** Hugo Jaeger, Life Magazine, © Time, Inc. **781** © David King Collection, London **783** Hugo Jaeger, Life Magazine, © Time, Inc. **785** Paul Dorsey, Life Magazine, © 1938 Time Inc **788** Hulton Getty/Liaison Agency **793** © Mainichi Shimbun, Tokyo **795** YIVO Institute for Jewish Research, courtesy of the USHMM Photo Archives **801** J.R. Eyerman, Life Magazine, © Time, Inc. **802** E.T. Archives, London **807** People's Republic of China Calendar Illustration, circa 1960. Artist unknown, courtesy of William J. Duiker **809** Archive Photos/Popperfoto **812** Hulton Getty/Liaison Agency

PART V OPENING

812 Jack Wiles, Life Magazine © 1945 Time, Inc.

CHAPTER 27

814 © Black Star **816** Corbis **818** Hulton Getty/Liaison Agency **821** Jack Wiles, Life Magazine © 1945 Time, Inc. **824** © Black Star **826** AP/Wide World **829** AP/Wide World Photos **830** AP/Wide World Photos

CHAPTER 28

836 Courtesy of William J. Duiker **838** Courtesy of William J. Duiker **841** Courtesy of William J. Duiker **842** Courtesy of William J. Duiker **846** Courtesy of William J. Duiker **852** Courtesy of William J. Duiker **856** Courtesy of William J. Duiker **858** AP/Wide World Photos **861** Courtesy of William J. Duiker **866** Courtesy of William J. Duiker **869** Courtesy of William J. Duiker **871** Courtesy of William J. Duiker

CHAPTER 29

874 Corbis **876** Pierre Boulat-Cosmos/Woodfin Camp & Associates **880** © Mark Stewart/Camera Press, London **885** © Bob Adelman/Magnum Photos **890** Corbis **892** Corbis **893** Corbis **897** © C.Raimond-Dityvon/Viva,/Woodfin Camp & Associates **898** Popperfoto/Archive **900** AP/Wide World Photos **905** Hans Namuth/Photo Researchers Inc.

CHAPTER 30

910 Courtesy of William J. Duiker **915** Courtesy of William J. Duiker **917** Courtesy of William J. Duiker **921 bottom** Courtesy of William J. Duiker **921 top** Courtesy of William J. Duiker **922** Courtesy of William J. Duiker **923** Courtesy of William J. Duiker **929** Courtesy of William J. Duiker **931** Courtesy of William J. Duiker **937 bottom** Courtesy of William J. Duiker **937 top** Corbis

CHAPTER 31

942 © John Elk/Stock Boston **947** Corbis **952** Courtesy of William J. Duiker **953** Courtesy of William J. Duiker **955 top** Courtesy of William J. Duiker **955 bottom** Courtesy of William J. Duiker **958** Courtesy of William J. Duiker **960** AP/Wide World Photos **962** Courtesy of William J. Duiker **966** © John Elk/Stock Boston **968** Courtesy of William J. Duiker

CHAPTER 32

972 Courtesy of William J. Duiker **973** Corbis **978** Courtesy of William J. Duiker **979** Courtesy of William J. Duiker **982** Corbis **985** Courtesy of William J. Duiker **987** Courtesy of William J. Duiker **989** Courtesy of William J. Duiker **991** Courtesy of William J. Duiker **993 bottom** Courtesy of William J. Duiker **993 top** Courtesy of William J. Duiker **1000** Judyth Platt, Ecoscene/Corbis **1001** Reuters/Susumu Takahashi/Archive Photos

INDEX

A

C

D

E

F

G

H

I

L

N

O

P

S

U

X